LIABILITIES	January 1, 1983	January 2, 1982
Current Liabilities		
Current portion of long-term debt	$ 41,577	$ 3,281
Current portion of obligations under capital leases	4,355	4,193
Accounts payable	608,385	589,100
Accrued expenses:		
Salaries and wages	128,988	122,704
Taxes, other than income taxes	78,586	69,310
Other	120,823	79,542
Accrued income taxes	20,078	13,966
Total current liabilities	1,002,792	882,096
Other Liabilities		
Long-term debt:		
Short-term borrowings to be refinanced	75,755	
Senior debt	462,662	372,816
Convertible subordinated debt		50,000
Obligations under capital leases	146,788	134,523
Deferred federal income taxes	148,699	135,253
Employees' benefit fund	21,810	23,131
Total other liabilities	855,714	715,723
Total Liabilities	1,858,506	1,597,819
SHAREOWNERS' EQUITY		
Convertible preferred capital stock,		
Cumulative, voting, par $100		
Authorized: 5,000,000 shares		
Issued: 1982—500,000, 9% Series B shares		
1981—500,000, 9% Series B shares	50,000	50,000
Common capital stock, par $1, at stated value		
Authorized: 50,000,000 shares		
Issued: 1982—30,634,966 shares		
1981—28,280,429 shares	164,778	100,083
Accumulated earnings	763,199	673,740
	977,977	823,823
Common stock in treasury, at cost		
1982—2,635,824 shares		
1981— 287,873 shares	(98,749)	(4,509)
Net unrealized loss on marketable equity securities	(8,175)	(11,843)
Total Shareowners' Equity	871,053	807,471
Total Liabilities and Shareowners' Equity	$ 2,729,559	$ 2,405,290

Source: Kroger Company, *Financial Report,* 1982.

Qualified Opinion
by:
A. LIM
林

Intermediate Accounting

Jan R. Williams
The University of Tennessee

Keith G. Stanga
The University of Tennessee

William W. Holder
University of Southern California

HARCOURT BRACE JOVANOVICH, PUBLISHERS

San Diego   New York   Chicago   Washington, D.C.   Atlanta
London   Sydney   Toronto

To Our Families

Elaine, Jennifer, and Julie Williams
Josie, Ben, and Brian Stanga
Carolyn and Mark Holder
and Marc Carlson

Material from Uniform CPA Examination Questions and Unofficial Answers, copyright © 1957 through 1982 by the American Institute of Certified Public Accountants, Inc., is adapted with permission.

Material from the Certificate in Management Accounting Examinations, copyright © 1972 through 1981 by the National Association of Accountants, is adapted with permission.

ISBN: 0-15-541514-X
Library of Congress Catalog Card Number: 83-82766
Printed in the United States of America

PREFACE

The subject of *Intermediate Accounting* is primarily financial reporting for corporate enterprises. Financial reporting practices of U.S. corporations involve a complicated but interesting array of principles and procedures that have emerged over several decades. Most procedures can be explained by a few broad accounting principles; some can only be justified by their having been used for many years.

In this book we have attempted to strike a balance between a detailed explanation of accounting procedures and a discussion of the theoretical foundation of those procedures. Serious accounting students must understand both theory and practice in order to enter the accounting profession and meet the challenges facing them in the future. We have also attempted to strike a balance between current generally accepted accounting principles and alternatives to these principles. Again, the serious student must understand alternatives to current practice in order to understand accounting as it exists and as it may evolve.

Organization of the Text

The text is organized into six major sections:

1. Theoretical Foundation for Financial Reporting (Chapters 1–4)
2. Tools of Accounting (Chapters 5–6)
3. Asset Accounting (Chapters 7–13)
4. Liability and Stockholders' Equity Accounting (Chapters 14–17)
5. Additional Financial Reporting Issues (Chapters 18–24)
6. Financial Reporting by Publicly Held Companies (Chapters 25–27)

In the first section, Theoretical Foundation for Financial Reporting, we prepare the student for the remainder of the text by providing the conceptual background necessary to understand generally accepted accounting principles and alternatives to those principles. Chapter 1 discusses the environment of corporate financial reporting. Chapter 2 presents the current conceptual framework of corporate financial reporting. This chapter is important because it explains the accounting principles for many specific procedures currently used to prepare financial statements. These principles are emphasized in Chapter 2, then highlighted throughout the text as they relate to the discussion of specific reporting practices. Chapter 3 introduces the student to the nature and measurement of the elements of financial statements, stressing alternatives to current practice in a way that is understandable at this early point in the student's study of financial accounting. Chapter 4 reviews the four basic financial statements at the level of understanding that the student should have when entering intermediate accounting. By discussing all of the financial statements in a single chapter, we can stress an important feature of financial statements—*articulation*.

The second section of the text, Tools of Accounting, covers two major topics. Chapter 5 reviews the accounting cycle, and Chapter 6 explains compound interest concepts in depth. Both tools are used frequently throughout the text.

The third section, Asset Accounting, includes seven chapters (Chapters 7–13) which deal with the major asset categories typically found on corporate balance sheets: cash, receivables, inventories, investments, plant assets, and intangible assets. Throughout these chapters, material that students have studied in introductory accounting courses is reviewed and new, more advanced topics are discussed. Care has been taken to thoroughly explain new material, and extensive use has been made of examples and illustrations to enhance student understanding.

The fourth section, Liability and Stockholders' Equity Accounting, encompasses four chapters. Chapter 14 addresses current and contingent liabilities. Chapter 15 discusses long-term debt. Chapters 16 and 17 cover a variety of topics related to stockholders' equity. The purpose of this section is to make students aware of the alternative methods of corporate financing and the many accounting practices that underlie the liability and stockholders' equity sections of corporate balance sheets.

The fifth section, Additional Financial Reporting Issues, covers many advanced topics that are essentially new to accounting students. It includes chapters on financial reporting of income taxes (Chapter 18), accounting for changes and error correction (Chapter 19), revenue measurement and income presentation (Chapter 20), accounting for leases and pensions (Chapters 21 and 22), reporting funds-flow information and changes in financial position (Chapter 23), and financial-statement disclosure and analysis (Chapter 24). These chapters require students to recall and apply material from earlier chapters. They also require students to integrate subjects studied earlier and to understand their new, more advanced applications.

The final section of the text includes three chapters that present financial reporting requirements which, at the present time, apply only to publicly held companies. Chapter 25 introduces the concept of reporting responsibilities of publicly held companies and the current deliberations about accounting standards overload. This chapter also introduces interim reporting and segment reporting. Chapter 26 describes the complexities of earnings per share presentations, with emphasis on companies with complex capital structures. Finally, Chapter 27 discusses constant dollar and current cost disclosures, approaches designed to communicate information about the impact of changing prices on a company's financial position and results of operations.

End-Of-Chapter Material

Questions, cases, exercises, and problems appear at the end of each chapter. They offer a variety of opportunities for students to continue the learning process by applying concepts presented in the text.

Questions are typically short-discussion type and emphasize the major points of the chapter. Some questions are multiple-choice.

Cases are generally more extended discussion questions, often involving in-depth consideration of the issues emerging from topics covered in the chapter. Sometimes the cases require the student to make and support decisions based on logical reasoning and a knowledge of current accounting principles. Cases enable students to develop written communication skills in a context similar to what they may encounter in the accounting profession.

Exercises typically involve computations and usually focus on a major point.

Problems require computations and, often, discussion. Problems usually require the student to relate major points discussed in the text.

Where appropriate, questions, cases, exercises, and problems have been adapted from CPA and CMA examinations.

Features

A brief review of *Intermediate Accounting* reveals many features that will help students understand the text. Each chapter begins with objectives that preview the chapter and ends with key points that highlight the most important subjects in the chapter.

The basic accounting principles discussed in Chapter 2 are highlighted in the margin throughout the text. This feature is designed to clearly demonstrate how important accounting principles, such as revenue realization, matching, historical cost, and consistency, are applied in practice.

Throughout the text, short readings are provided to expand the student's understanding of accounting principles and the issues and controversies surrounding those principles. Most readings are taken from business periodicals and provide insight into the importance of corporate financial reporting to investors and creditors.

At appropriate points in the text, diagrams and flowcharts follow discussions and examples in order to summarize complex procedures, such as accounting for current and noncurrent marketable equity securities, accounting for leases, and preparing earnings-per-share figures for companies with complex capital structures.

End-of-chapter appendixes are designed to present specialized subjects, complex topics, and less frequently used accounting methods.

Throughout the text, excerpts from published financial statements of major U.S. corporations illustrate how various accounting principles are applied. These excerpts are usually preceded by a brief description of the company to familiarize the student with the nature of the reporting enterprise.

The annual report and basic financial statements of one major U.S. corporation, Kroger Company, are reproduced in their entirety and are cited throughout the text. The annual report is presented as an appendix, and three financial statements are printed on the inside front and back covers (endpapers).

Supplements

A variety of supplements have been prepared for use with this text. The following supplements are available as instructional aids *for students:* (1) student study guide (prepared by James M. Reeve); (2) two practice sets—one devoted to the accounting cycle, to be used in conjunction with Chapter 5; the other encompassing the entire text, to be used at or near the end of the text (prepared by Thomas J. Beirne, Jr.); (3) ruled working papers for all problems in the text; and (4) a professional examination manual (prepared by Sharon M. Lightner).

The following supplements are available *for instructors:* (1) solutions manual for all end-of-chapter material (prepared by the authors); (2) instructor's manual, which includes checklist of key figures in the text and solutions to the practice sets (prepared by Jan R. Williams); (3) overhead projector transparencies for all text problems; (4) test book (prepared by Jan R. Williams, Keith G. Stanga, and Thomas A. Gavin); (5) computerized format of the test book; and (6) checklist of key figures in the text available *free* in quantity.

Acknowledgments

Many people have contributed to the writing, review, revision, and publication of *Intermediate Accounting*. The authors recognize the important contributions of these people and deeply appreciate their involvement in the successful completion of this project.

Several times during the writing of this book, we requested reviews of the quality and organization of our manuscript. We gratefully acknowledge the valuable comments made by the following reviewers: Durwood L. Alkire, University of Washington; Edna M. Andrews, California State University, Long Beach; Thomas E. Balke, The University of Nebraska, Lincoln; Robert G. Bowman, University of Oregon; Bruce Budge, University of Montana; Lucian G. Conway, Jr., Baylor University; Louis S. Corsini, Boston College; David W. Harvey, Tulane University; Loyd C. Heath, University of Washington; Bertrand Horwitz, State University of New York, Binghamton; Richard Kochanek, University of Connecticut; Joyce C. Lambert, The University of Nebraska, Lincoln; Sharon Lightner, San Diego State University; Charles Neyhart, Oregon State University; Arnold J. Pahler, San Jose State University; James M. Reeve, The University of Tennessee, Knoxville; Ronald N. Savey, Western Washington University; J. David Spiceland, Memphis State University; Lynn Stephens, Eastern Washington University; Frederic M. Stiner, Jr., University of Delaware; Donald L. Tang, Portland State University; Richard L. Townsend, The University of Tennessee, Knoxville; Edwin D. Waters, Tennessee Tech University; David P. Weiner, University of San Francisco; and Albert W. Wright, California State University, Northridge.

Steven A. Dowling, former senior editor at Harcourt Brace Jovanovich, was instrumental in bringing the authors together, helping us determine the structure and content of the text, and advancing the manuscript to near-completion. We are especially grateful to Steve for his contribution. He was a great encouragement to us and continues to be an interested, contributing friend.

William A. Knowles assumed Steve Dowling's position and immediately began to work with us in completing the manuscript. He has helped us in a number of important ways and has encouraged us in the final stages of this project.

The staff of Harcourt Brace Jovanovich has been supportive and cooperative in all aspects of this project. Johanna Schmid, manuscript editor, has shown insight and enthusiasm far beyond that expected by the authors. Her personal interest in and coordination of our work and her extreme sensitivity to the importance of accuracy and precision have greatly enhanced the quality of this book.

Mary Kitzmiller has also been very helpful as a manuscript editor and has assisted in coordinating our work on the text and the solutions manual. Her input and enthusiasm for the project have been important ingredients. Bill Teague, production editor, has carefully guided edited manuscript into printed pages and has been sensitive to important details concerning the placement of material in the text. We also wish to thank Nancy Shehorn, who designed the book and its supplements, and Pat Braus, who served as production manager of the project.

We are extremely grateful to the many students who assisted us in checking and class testing our material. In addition, during the last year of manuscript preparation, four students at The University of Tennessee, Knoxville, were engaged to read the manuscript and verify solutions prepared by the authors to end-of-chapter material. We owe a great deal to Sandra Crowell, Cindy Ingrum, David Mautz, and Patrick Min.

James M. Reeve (The University of Tennessee, Knoxville), Thomas J. Beirne (California State University, Sacramento), and Thomas A. Gavin (The University of Tennessee, Chattanooga) have played a special role in the completion of *Intermediate Accounting* and the accompanying supplements.

James Reeve reviewed the manuscript in its early stages and assisted in the final revision of several chapters and in the preparation of end-of-chapter material for those chapters. Jim is also the author of the student study guide. However, his contribution has extended far beyond the study guide and text chapters. He has been and remains a valued consultant.

Thomas Beirne's contribution centers on the two practice sets which accompany the text. We appreciate Tom's efforts and think that these practice sets go far in our attempt to help students understand intermediate accounting. Tom has been extremely cooperative in working with us to coordinate the practice sets and the text.

Thomas Gavin assisted us in preparing several chapters of the test book. We gratefully acknowledge Tom's conscientious approach to his work and his keen interest in this project.

We want to thank several persons who provided clerical assistance. Louise Lacey, Michelle Joiner, Frieda Bedelle, Kimberly Atchley, Candance Wages, Jeanne McDonald, Patricia Flynn, Patricia Hunley, and Brenda Henderson were particularly helpful.

Throughout the text, we cite authoritative accounting literature published by the American Institute of Certified Public Accountants (AICPA) and the Financial Accounting Standards Board. We are grateful for the work done by these organizations. We also acknowledge and thank the AICPA and the Institute of Management Accounting of the National Association of Accountants for allowing us to adapt material from past CPA and CMA examinations.

Our text includes many financial reporting examples taken from the published financial statements of U.S. corporations. We have also included a number of articles from business publications. We appreciate the willingness of these organizations for us to use this material, which greatly enriches the technical content of the text.

Finally, we wish to acknowledge the contributions of our families during the five years required to complete this book. Perhaps their greatest contribution has been their patience and understanding during the many hours we were unable to be with them because we were working on the book. We recognize and appreciate their support and feel that much of this text belongs to them.

Jan R. Williams

Keith G. Stanga

William W. Holder

CONTENTS

Preface iii

Part 1 Theoretical Foundation for Financial Reporting   1

1 THE FINANCIAL ACCOUNTING ENVIRONMENT   2

Accounting as an Information System   3
Preparers and Auditors of Financial Statements   7
Generally Accepted Accounting Principles   10
Development of Generally Accepted Accounting Principles   11
Sources of Generally Accepted Accounting Principles   20
Future Development of Generally Accepted Accounting Principles   21
Concluding Remarks   25
Key Points   27
Questions   28
Cases   29

2 FINANCIAL ACCOUNTING THEORY   31

A Model   35
Objectives of Financial Reporting   35
Qualitative Characteristics of Accounting Information   37
Assumptions   39
Concepts and Elements   41
Broad Principles   43
Detailed Principles   50
Modifying Conventions   51
Concluding Remarks   55
Key Points   55
Questions   56
Cases   56
Exercises   61

3 NATURE AND MEASUREMENT OF THE ELEMENTS OF FINANCIAL STATEMENTS   65

Measurement in Accounting   66
The Measuring Unit   67
Assets   69
Liabilities   74

Owners' Equity   78
Income   79
Financial Forecasts   91
Concluding Remarks   96
Key Points   99
Questions   100
Cases   100
Problems   104

4 BASIC FINANCIAL STATEMENTS   107

Characteristics of Basic Financial Statements   108
Income Statement   108
Statement of Retained Earnings   116
Statement of Stockholders' Equity   119
Balance Sheet   120
Statement of Changes in Financial Position   129
Relationship Between Basic Financial Statements   130
Other Financial Statement Topics   132
Concluding Remarks   136
Key Points   136
Questions   137
Cases   138
Exercises   142
Problems   146

Part **2** **Tools of Accounting**   **155**

5 THE ACCOUNTING CYCLE   156

Steps in the Accounting Cycle   157
Key Points   177
Appendix A: The Worksheet   177
Appendix B: Special Journals   181
Questions   185
Cases   186
Exercises   186
Problems   192

6 COMPOUND INTEREST CONCEPTS   201

Simple Versus Compound Interest   202
Basic Concepts   204
Lump Sum Problems   205
Annuity Problems   211
Concluding Remarks   224
Key Points   225
Questions   226
Cases   226
Exercises   227
Problems   228

Part 3 Asset Accounting 241

7 CASH AND RECEIVABLES 242

Cash 243
Receivables 255
Concluding Remarks 276
Key Points 277
Questions 277
Cases 278
Exercises 279
Problems 284

8 INVENTORIES: BASIC VALUATION METHODS 292

Inventories 293
Nature of the Inventory Valuation Problem 296
Determination of Inventory Quantities 296
Determination of Inventory Valuation at Cost 298
Inventory Valuation at the Lower of Cost or Market (LCM) 312
Inventory Valuation Above Cost 317
Effects of Inventory Errors on Financial Statements 318
Conceptual Considerations 319
Key Points 323
Appendix A: The Base Stock Method 324
Questions 325
Cases 325
Exercises 327
Problems 333

9 INVENTORIES: ADDITIONAL VALUATION METHODS 342

LIFO Application Methods 343
Retail Inventory Method 350
Gross Margin Method 360
Key Points 363
Questions 364
Cases 365
Exercises 366
Problems 369

10 ACCOUNTING AND REPORTING FOR INVESTMENTS AND FUNDS 375

Temporary Investments 376
Noncurrent Investments 391
Funds 415
Concluding Remarks 416
Key Points 416
Questions 417
Cases 417
Exercises 420
Problems 424

11 PROPERTY, PLANT, AND EQUIPMENT: ACQUISITION AND DISPOSAL   433

Classification of Plant and Intangible Assets   434
Definitions and Basic Accounting Principles   435
Application of the Cost Principle to Specific Items of Property, Plant, and Equipment   437
Problems of Establishing Historical Cost   440
Postacquisition Expenditures   450
Disposal of Plant Assets   458
Acquisitions and Disposals by Exchange   460
Departures from Historical Cost   466
Financial-Statement Disclosure   469
Key Points   471
Questions   471
Cases   472
Exercises   474
Problems   477

12 PROPERTY, PLANT, AND EQUIPMENT: DEPRECIATION, DEPLETION, AND SPECIAL PROBLEMS   485

Revenue-Expense Association   486
The Depreciation Process   486
Depreciation Estimation Methods: Individual Assets   489
Selecting an Appropriate Depreciation Method   497
Fractional-Year Problems   498
Group-Depreciation Systems   500
Natural Resources and Depletion   506
The Allocation Problem   509
Financial-Statement Presentation   511
Changes in Estimates and Corrections of Errors   515
Key Points   516
Appendix A: Alternative Depreciation Methods   516
Appendix B: Casualty Insurance   519
Questions   522
Cases   523
Exercises   525
Problems   530

13 INTANGIBLE ASSETS   540

Defining Intangible Assets   541
Accounting Standards for Intangible Assets   541
Separately Identifiable Intangible Assets   547
Intangible Assets Not Separately Identifiable: Goodwill   552
Special Problem Areas   564
Concluding Remarks   572
Key Points   574
Questions   575
Cases   576
Exercises   578
Problems   582

Part 4 Liability and Stockholders' Equity Accounting   591

14 CURRENT AND CONTINGENT LIABILITIES   592

Characteristics of Liabilities   593
Current Liabilities   593
Contingent Liabilities   609
Key Points   618
Questions   618
Cases   619
Exercises   621
Problems   624

15 LONG-TERM DEBT   630

The Nature and Characteristics of Debt   631
Accounting for Bonds Payable   633
Long-Term Debt Accounting Problems   646
Concluding Remarks   651
Key Points   652
Appendix A: Troubled-Debt Restructurings   652
Appendix B: Accounting Problems of Serial Bonds   661
Questions   664
Cases   665
Exercises   668
Problems   671

16 STOCKHOLDERS' EQUITY: CORPORATE FORMATION AND CONTRIBUTED CAPITAL   675

The Corporate Environment   676
Stockholders' Rights and Types of Stockholders' Equity   679
Accounting for Capital Stock   685
Treasury Stock   691
Retirement of Stock   696
Property and Treasury Stock Donations   698
Concluding Remarks   699
Key Points   701
Questions   701
Cases   702
Exercises   702
Problems   705

17 STOCKHOLDERS' EQUITY: OPERATIONS, EARNINGS, DIVIDENDS, AND OTHER ISSUES   711

Retained Earnings   712
Capital Stock and Employee Compensation   732
Stock Warrants and Convertible Securities   740
Miscellaneous Stockholders' Equity Considerations   742
Concluding Remarks   746
Key Points   747
Questions   747
Cases   748

Exercises   749
Problems   753

Part 5 Additional Financial Reporting Issues   761

18 FINANCIAL REPORTING OF INCOME TAXES   762

Introduction to Income Tax Reporting   763
Intraperiod Income Tax Allocation   764
Interperiod Income Tax Allocation   769
Operating-Loss Carrybacks and Carryforwards   788
Investment Tax Credit   797
Financial-Statement Disclosure of Income Taxes   803
Concluding Remarks   806
Key Points   806
Appendix A: Examples of Timing Differences   807
Appendix B: Impact of Economic Recovery Act of 1981 on Interperiod Income Tax
  Allocation   809
Questions   810
Cases   811
Exercises   812
Problems   817

19 ACCOUNTING CHANGES AND CORRECTIONS OF ERRORS   823

Accounting Changes and Corrections of Errors: A Conceptual Analysis   824
Reporting Alternatives for Accounting Changes   826
Changes in Accounting Principle: The General Rule   830
Changes in Accounting Estimate   837
Changes and Events Requiring Retroactive Restatement   839
Concluding Remarks   847
Key Points   848
Appendix A: Error Analysis   849
Questions   853
Cases   854
Exercises   856
Problems   860

20 REVENUE MEASUREMENT AND INCOME PRESENTATION   869

Complexities in Income Determination   870
Revenue Recognition: A Conceptual Analysis   870
Special Revenue-Recognition Problems   873
Income Presentation   884
Concluding Remarks   897
Key Points   899
Appendix A: Special Revenue-Recognition Practices   899
Questions   903
Cases   904
Exercises   907
Problems   911

21 ACCOUNTING FOR LEASES   919

Reasons for Leasing   920
Important Leasing Terms   922
Lease Classification   925
Financial Accounting and Reporting—Lessees   930
Financial Accounting and Reporting—Lessors   941
Special Leasing Situations   950
Concluding Remarks   953
Key Points   953
Appendix A: Leveraged Leases   954
Appendix B: Other Special Leasing Issues   955
Questions   957
Cases   958
Exercises   960
Problems   962

22 ACCOUNTING FOR PENSIONS   968

The Evolution and Significance of Pension Plans   969
The Nature of Pension Plans   969
Basic Concepts of Pension Accounting   972
Financial Accounting and Reporting for Pension Obligations   977
Miscellaneous Pension Accounting Issues   986
Disclosure of Pension Plans in Financial Statements   995
The Future of Pension Accounting   997
Concluding Remarks   998
Key Points   999
Appendix A: Financial Accounting and Reporting for Defined Benefit Pension Plans   999
Appendix B: Supporting Calculations for Exhibit 22-7   1002
Questions   1004
Cases   1004
Exercises   1006
Problems   1009

23 REPORTING FUNDS-FLOW INFORMATION AND CHANGES IN
        FINANCIAL POSITION   1013

Need for Funds-Flow Information   1014
Role of the Statement of Changes in Financial Position   1014
Reporting Funds-Flow Information   1019
Reporting All Changes in Financial Position   1022
Sources and Uses of Funds   1024
Preparing the Statement of Changes in Financial Position: Working Capital and Cash
  Definitions of Funds   1026
Comprehensive Illustration: Working Capital Definition of Funds   1032
Comprehensive Illustration: Cash Definition of Funds   1044
Additional Statement Presentation Considerations   1051
Concluding Remarks   1054
Key Points   1057
Appendix A: T-Account Approach to Transactions Analysis   1058
Questions   1060

Cases   1061
Exercises   1064
Problems   1068

24   FINANCIAL-STATEMENT DISCLOSURE AND ANALYSIS   1081

Need for Financial-Statement Disclosures   1082
The Role of Disclosure in Communicating Financial Information   1082
Analysis of Financial Statements   1098
Concluding Remarks   1119
Key Points   1119
Appendix A: Example Disclosure Checklist   1120
Questions   1122
Cases   1123
Exercises   1128
Problems   1132

Part **6**   **Financial Reporting by Publicly Held Companies**   **1139**

25   PUBLICLY HELD COMPANIES: SELECTED FINANCIAL
         REPORTING TOPICS   1140

The Standards Overload Problem   1141
Interim Reporting   1147
Segment Reporting   1155
Concluding Remarks   1164
Key Points   1165
Appendix A: Reporting to the Securities and Exchange Commission   1165
Questions   1168
Cases   1169
Exercises   1172
Problems   1175

26   PUBLICLY HELD COMPANIES: EARNINGS PER SHARE   1181

Basic Earnings-Per-Share Concepts   1182
EPS Computations for Simple Capital Structures   1187
EPS Computations for Complex Capital Structures   1191
Example EPS Computations   1205
Concluding Remarks   1210
Key Points   1211
Appendix A: Additional EPS Considerations   1211
Questions   1215
Cases   1216
Exercises   1218
Problems   1221

27   PUBLICLY HELD COMPANIES: FINANCIAL REPORTING AND
         CHANGING PRICES   1229

Nature and Measurement of Price Changes   1230
Four Bases of Accounting   1232
Authoritative Pronouncement on Accounting for Changing Prices   1235
Constant Dollar Accounting   1235

Current Value Accounting   1245
Current Cost/Constant Dollar Accounting   1254
Statement of Financial Accounting Standards No. 33   1258
Concluding Remarks   1269
Key Points   1270
Questions   1270
Cases   1271
Exercises   1273
Problems   1277

AUTHORITATIVE ACCOUNTING PRONOUNCEMENTS   1284

APPENDIX   1291

INDEX   1318

Theoretical Foundation for Financial Reporting

1

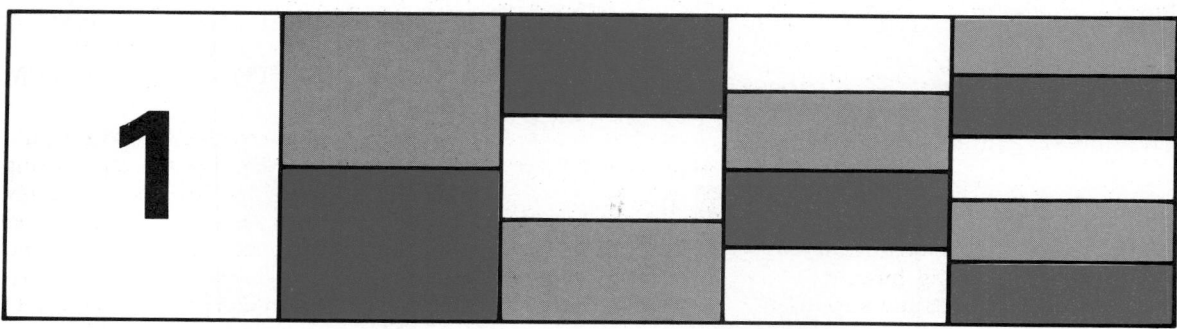

THE FINANCIAL ACCOUNTING ENVIRONMENT

Objectives

To introduce and discuss financial accounting.

To distinguish clearly between preparers, auditors, and users of financial statements.

To introduce the concept of generally accepted accounting principles.

To explain how generally accepted accounting principles have been developed.

To indicate the major sources of generally accepted accounting principles.

To discuss some major issues that are likely to affect the development of generally accepted accounting principles.

ACCOUNTING AS AN INFORMATION SYSTEM

Accounting is an activity designed to **identify, measure,** and **communicate** information about **economic entities** that is intended to be **useful** in making **economic decisions.**[1] An accountant's primary task is therefore to supply information that will help users, such as stockholders, bankers, and managers, to make better decisions. These decisions largely determine how scarce resources are allocated within and among business enterprises. Accounting information helps our society determine what goods and services to produce, as well as how and for whom to produce them. We should not be surprised to find, then, that accounting is an exciting, often controversial discipline.

Accounting is closely related to several fields of study, including economics, finance, psychology, sociology, communications theory, and political science. By applying psychological principles, for example, accountants learn how people process accounting information and how that information affects their decisions.

Internal and External Users

A distinction often is made between internal and external users of accounting information. The primary **internal users** are managers, who need accounting information to assist them in basic planning and control. Because of their authority within their companies, managers are usually able to obtain the internal information they need. When providing information to managers, accountants are not constrained by generally accepted accounting principles, which are principles that have substantial authoritative support. Instead, they prepare whatever information management believes is most useful, such as financial statements for external users as well as many other kinds of information. The branch of accounting that is concerned with providing information for internal users is called **managerial, or management, accounting.** Managerial accounting is the subject of other textbooks and courses.

External users of accounting information are those outside the business enterprise who have or contemplate having a direct or an indirect interest in the enterprise. They include present and potential owners (stockholders), lenders, suppliers, employees, and customers, as well as financial analysts, stock exchanges, regulatory authorities, and the general public. Compared with management, external users generally have much less authority to request information about a business enterprise. When preparing information for external users, accountants follow generally accepted accounting principles, which are presently established by the Financial Accounting Standards Board. The use of such principles enhances the confidence and understanding of users and helps them to make more meaningful comparisons between companies.

Financial accounting is the branch of accounting that is concerned with measuring and reporting the financial position of a business enterprise as well as the changes that occur in financial position. The main output of the financial accounting process is a set of basic, general purpose financial statements. As we discuss and illustrate in Chapter 4, the basic financial statements are the balance sheet, the income statement, the statement of changes in financial position, and the statement of retained earnings or statement of stockholders' equity. Financial accounting information is designed primarily to meet the needs of external users. This textbook deals with financial accounting. In this chapter we discuss the environment of financial accounting.

---

[1]This definition is based on *A Statement of Basic Accounting Theory* (Evanston, Ill.: American Accounting Association, 1966), p. 1, and on *APB Statement No. 4,* "Basic Concepts and Accounting Principles Underlying Financial Statements of Business Enterprises," 1970, par. 40.

Basic Needs of External Users

Although there are many types of external users, financial accounting has traditionally focused on meeting the needs of present and potential owners, such as preferred and common stock investors, and creditors, such as bankers and bondholders. Owners and creditors are the most obvious external groups that use financial statements. Moreover, information that is useful to investors and creditors is likely to be useful to other external users as well.

Fundamentally, investors and creditors want to know how much cash they will receive in return and when they will receive it. Stockholders, for example, typically make decisions **to buy, sell, or hold equity investments.** Before they invest cash in exchange for shares of stock, they seek information that will help them to assess the amounts, timing, and uncertainties of expected cash flows in the form of dividends and appreciated market prices. Similarly, commercial bank loan officers make decisions **to extend or not extend loans.** When making these decisions, bankers want information that will help them to assess their chances of receiving cash via interest and repayment of principal.[2]

Investment and credit decisions basically involve a comparison of expected cash outflows with expected cash inflows. In most cases, the outflows are known, based on, for example, the market price of the stock on the date of purchase or the amount of the loan requested. But the investor or creditor usually must **predict the amount of cash inflows** and **assess the risk that those inflows will be less than expected.** What an investor or creditor would really like, then, is a knowledge of the future. However, no one, not even an accountant, can supply such knowledge directly.

The expected cash flows to investors and creditors are related to the expected cash flows to the enterprise to which they have committed their funds. More precisely: "The prospects [of investors and creditors] for those cash receipts are affected by an enterprise's ability to generate enough cash to meet its obligations when due and its other cash operating needs, to reinvest in operations, and to pay cash dividends and may also be affected by perceptions of investors and creditors generally about that ability, which affect market prices of the enterprise's securities."[3]

In order for an enterprise to generate favorable cash flows over the long run, it must operate profitably and remain solvent. Thus, **profitability** and **solvency** are two basic factors that investors and creditors try to evaluate based on the information presented in financial statements. Profitability refers to the ability of an enterprise to generate earnings. Solvency refers to its ability to pay its debts when they come due. A company may be highly profitable yet be on the verge of bankruptcy because of a shortage of liquid assets such as cash and accounts receivable. Investors and creditors must therefore evaluate both aspects of a business enterprise.[4] Furthermore, in order for a business to operate profitably and remain solvent, it must be **managed effectively.** Thus, an important use of financial statements is to evaluate management's performance.

To summarize, investors and creditors provide cash, and they want to know how much cash they will receive in return and when they will receive it. To help resolve these questions, they use financial statements to:

---

[2]*FASB Statement of Financial Accounting Concepts No. 1,* "Objectives of Financial Reporting by Business Enterprises," 1978, par. 25.

[3]*FASB Statement of Financial Accounting Concepts No. 1,* par. 37.

[4]Loyd C. Heath and Paul Rosenfield, "Solvency: The Forgotten Half of Financial Reporting," *Journal of Accountancy* (January 1979), pp. 48–54. These authors point out that before about 1930, solvency was the primary concern in financial reporting. Since that time, however, financial reporting has shifted away from this emphasis, and it now focuses on issues related to profitability evaluation. The authors believe that the accounting profession should give more attention than it now gives to providing information that is useful in evaluating solvency.

1. Make predictions.
2. Assess risk.
3. Evaluate profitability.
4. Evaluate solvency.
5. Evaluate management's performance.

These uses are interrelated.

General Purpose Financial Statements

Even when we narrow the list of external users to owners and creditors, we find that these users make different kinds of decisions under a variety of circumstances. Bankers, for example, make short-term, intermediate-term, and long-term loans to many different types of customers. As a result, their needs for certain items of accounting information may vary. Moreover, users differ in their abilities to read, analyze, and understand accounting information. At one extreme we may find an unsophisticated stockholder who has virtually no understanding of accounting information. At the other extreme we may encounter a Chartered Financial Analyst, a person who has met rigorous education, experience, and examination requirements, and who renders professional advice on investment matters.

Clearly, the existence of diverse users poses a problem for accountants. Should accountants prepare many sets of financial statements, each of which is "tailor-made" to meet the needs of a particular user? Or should accountants prepare a single, general purpose set of financial statements that is designed to reasonably satisfy the needs of most users? At the present time, financial accounting emphasizes general purpose statements because: (1) accountants believe that many users need similar information; and (2) general purpose statements are more favorable from a benefit/cost standpoint. As a general rule, **the benefits of information (including financial accounting information) should exceed the costs of providing and using it.** In general purpose financial statements, accountants strive to present information that is "comprehensible to those who have a reasonable understanding of business and economic activities and are willing to study the information with reasonable diligence."[5]

Financial Statements and Financial Reporting

The main output of the financial accounting process today is a set of basic, general purpose **financial statements.** These statements are:

1. A **balance sheet,** which summarizes an enterprise's financial position at a particular point in time.
2. An **income statement,** which summarizes an enterprise's income and the components of income over a period of time.
3. A **statement of changes in financial position,** which summarizes an enterprise's financing and investing activities over a period of time.
4. A **statement of retained earnings,** which describes the changes in an enterprise's retained earnings during a period, or a **statement of stockholders' equity,** which describes the changes in retained earnings as well as in other accounts that compose stockholders' equity.

You may have seen actual examples of these financial statements in annual reports to shareholders. Companies also present them in other disclosure media such as registration statements and annual reports filed with the Securities and Exchange Commission. This textbook focuses on general purpose financial statements including their related notes (footnotes), which are an integral part of the financial statements. To assist you in becoming

---

[5]*FASB Statement of Financial Accounting Concepts No. 1,* par. 34.

familiar with financial statements, we have reproduced a set of actual financial statements of Kroger Company on the endpapers (inside the front and back covers) of this textbook. Take a few minutes to look over these financial statements now. We shall refer to the statements again at various times throughout the book. As an additional learning aid, the Appendix to the book contains most of the material presented in a recent annual report of Kroger Company.

The output of the financial accounting process is not confined to the information reported in financial statements. **Financial reporting** is a broad term that encompasses not only financial statements but also other means of communicating information that relates directly or indirectly to the financial accounting process. Corporate managers may communicate financial accounting information outside of the financial statements because they are required to do so by rule or custom or because they simply want to do so voluntarily.[6] Annual reports to shareholders, for example, include not only financial statements but also other types of financial accounting information such as financial highlights and a multi-year summary of important financial figures. These reports also include various kinds of **nonfinancial** information such as a description of major products and a listing of corporate officers and directors.[7]

Financial reporting provides a major portion, but not all, of the information needed by external users for making investment, credit, and similar decisions. Professional financial analysts, for example, usually gather and evaluate economic information, such as gross national product and interest rate figures provided by the government, and industry information, such as weekly and monthly production figures provided for many industries, before they analyze information about individual companies. Also, many analysts obtain information by talking with representatives of corporate management.

Characteristics and Limitations of Financial Statements

The financial statements that accountants currently prepare have several characteristics and limitations. Some of the more important of these are briefly described below:[8]

1. **Financial nature.** The information shown in financial statements is primarily financial in nature. It is generally expressed in **units of money** regardless of changes in money's purchasing power.
2. **Business entities.** The information pertains to individual business entities (which may be a group of related companies) rather than to industries or to the entire economy.
3. **Estimates and judgment.** The information reflects estimates and judgment and is therefore inexact.
4. **Historical report.** The information reflects the financial effects of transactions and events that have already occurred. Financial statements do not contain future projections.
5. **General purpose.** The information is designed to reasonably meet the needs of many diverse users, particularly present and potential owners and creditors.
6. **Interrelatedness.** Financial statements are interrelated because measuring financial position is related to measuring changes in financial position. Thus we say that financial statements **articulate** with one another.

---

[6]*FASB Statement of Financial Accounting Concepts No. 1,* par. 7.

[7]To summarize certain key terms, **financial accounting** is the branch of accounting concerned with measuring and reporting the financial position of a business enterprise as well as the changes that occur in financial position. **Financial statements** (i.e., balance sheet, income statement, statement of changes in financial position, and statement of retained earnings or statement of stockholders' equity) represent the main output of the financial accounting process. **Financial reporting** is a broad term that encompasses financial statements as well as other means of communicating information that relates directly or indirectly to the financial accounting process.

[8]*APB Statement No. 4,* par. 35, and *FASB Statement of Financial Accounting Concepts No. 1,* pars. 17–23.

7. **Summarization and classification.** The information is summarized and classified in a manner designed to help meet users' needs.
8. **Several measurement bases.** Financial statements reflect several measurement or valuation bases (e.g., accounts receivable are reported at net realizable value, plant assets are usually reported at their original cost less accumulated depreciation).
9. **A single source.** Financial statements are only one source of the information needed by investors and creditors.
10. **Cost.** Financial statements involve a cost to provide and use. They can be justified only if the benefits they provide exceed the costs.

Objectives of Financial Reporting

The objectives of financial reporting are:[9]

1. To provide information useful in **investment, credit, and similar decisions.**
2. To provide information useful in **assessing cash flow prospects.**
3. To provide information about **enterprise resources, claims to those resources, and changes in them.**

Notice that the first objective is the most general, while the next two are progressively more specific. Moreover, the third objective flows logically from the second, which in turn flows logically from the first. We explain these objectives more fully in the next chapter.

PREPARERS AND AUDITORS OF FINANCIAL STATEMENTS

Financial statements pertain to an entity such as a corporation. The management of that entity has the primary responsibility for preparing and disseminating its financial statements. Financial statements therefore contain **assertions** or **representations made by management,** such as sales, net income, and total assets.

Management's role in the financial reporting process has evolved over many years and is related to the fact that the corporation is the dominant medium for pooling productive resources in our economy. As corporations have grown in size, the separation between those who own the company (stockholders) and those who control it (managers) has widened. As a result, owners have demanded a periodic accounting from those to whom they have entrusted economic resources.

Many critics have charged that management has too much responsibility in the financial reporting process. They claim that since financial statements are reports *on* management's performance, management should have less responsibility for determining their contents. Despite the critics' views, the traditional position of the accounting profession has been that managers, because they are highly familiar with company objectives and operations, are best suited to present pertinent information about the company to external parties.

To summarize, management has certain important **accountability** responsibilities to external parties. In discharging these responsibilities, management typically obtains the services of internal and external accountants.

Internal Accountants

Management hires **internal accountants** (commonly called **industrial accountants** or **management accountants**) to work as employees within the company. Internal accoun-

---

[9]*FASB Statement of Financial Accounting Concepts No. 1,* pars. 34, 37, and 40. For an excellent critical review of these objectives, see Nicholas Dopuch and Shyam Sunder, "FASB's Statements on Objectives and Elements of Financial Accounting: A Review," *Accounting Review* (January 1980), pp. 1–21. Dopuch and Sunder (p. 8) believe that these objectives "are unlikely to help resolve major accounting issues or to set standards of financial reporting as the FASB had expected."

tants perform many services, depending on the size and complexity of the enterprise for which they work. Perhaps the most distinguishing service of internal accountants is to produce and analyze many kinds of information designed to help management make better planning and control decisions. Should a company buy some new material-handling equipment? What is the optimal quantity of inventory for a company to order? When should a company place an order for inventory? These are only a few of the questions that internal accountants can help to answer.

In addition to providing management with important information, internal accountants design and implement accounting systems. In larger companies, internal accountants may serve on an **internal audit staff** that seeks to ensure that the company safeguards its assets, produces reliable accounting information, operates efficiently, and adheres to management's policies.

Although internal accountants can perform many diverse services, the most important services that relate to financial accounting are **collecting data** and **preparing the financial statements.** Internal accountants must therefore understand and apply the accounting principles we discuss throughout this text.

Some internal accountants have earned the **Certificate in Management Accounting (CMA).** The CMA is the professional designation for management accountants. As you might expect, not all internal accountants have earned the CMA. Moreover, not all persons who have CMAs are internal accountants. Many people with CMAs work in public accounting, colleges and universities, government, and elsewhere. In addition to meeting certain other requirements, a person wishing to earn a CMA must pass a rigorous examination that consists of the following parts:

1. Economics and business finance.
2. Organization and behavior, including ethical considerations.
3. Public reporting standards, auditing, and taxes.
4. Periodic reporting for internal and external purposes.
5. Decision analysis, including modeling and information systems.

Several assignment problems in this textbook have been adapted from recent CMA examinations.

External Accountants

Although most managers and internal accountants are both competent and honest, it is necessary that an independent outside party attest to the fairness of management's financial statements so that users will have more confidence in them. This is the major role of **external** or **public accountants.**

Certified Public Accountant (CPA) is the major professional designation of those who practice public accounting. Not all public accountants are CPAs; not all CPAs practice public accounting. To become a CPA, a person must satisfy certain education and experience requirements and pass a rigorous, uniform examination that the American Institute of Certified Public Accountants prepares and grades. The examination consists of four parts:

1. Accounting practice
2. Accounting theory
3. Auditing
4. Business law

The assignment material in this textbook contains many problems that we have adapted from CPA examinations.

Although CPA firms provide such services as tax advice and management advisory services, their primary service is **auditing** (often called the **attest function**). In an audit, CPAs serve management as independent contractors, but they have a primary responsibility to external users of financial statements. Basically, an **audit** consists of an examination of a company's financial statements followed by the issuance of a report which expresses the auditor's opinion about whether the financial statements have been presented fairly in accordance with generally accepted accounting principles. The **audit report** lends credibility to management's financial statements so that users can be more confident that the statements accurately represent what they purport to represent. In other words, an audit adds reliability to financial statements.

The most common type of audit report is one in which the auditor expresses an **unqualified opinion.** The issuance of an unqualified opinion means that the auditor believes that the financial statements have been presented fairly in accordance with generally accepted accounting principles. The example shown in Exhibit 1–1 illustrates the wording of a typical audit report in which an unqualified opinion is given. In the first paragraph, called the **scope paragraph,** the auditor explains what was done. The second paragraph, called the **opinion paragraph,** presents the auditor's opinion on the financial statements.

Auditors may also render qualified opinions, adverse opinions, and disclaimers. A **qualified opinion** is given when the auditor feels that the overall financial statements are fairly presented "except for" certain items (which the auditor discloses) or "subject to" the outcome of some uncertainty (which the auditor discloses). An **adverse opinion** means that the auditor feels the financial statements have not been presented fairly in accordance with generally accepted accounting principles. Finally, a **disclaimer of opinion** means that the auditor has not been able to evaluate the fairness of the financial statements and, as a result, expresses no opinion on them.

EXHIBIT 1–1
Unqualified Audit Report

Report of Certified Public Accountants

ARTHUR YOUNG

ARTHUR YOUNG & COMPANY
520 BROAD STREET
NEWARK, NEW JERSEY 07102

The Board of Directors and Stockholders
General Instrument Corporation

We have examined the accompanying consolidated balance sheets of General Instrument Corporation and subsidiaries at February 28, 1982 and 1981 and the related consolidated statements of income, stockholders' equity and changes in financial position for each of the three fiscal years in the period ended February 28, 1982. Our examinations were made in accordance with generally accepted auditing standards and, accordingly, included such tests of the accounting records and such other auditing procedures as we considered necessary in the circumstances.

In our opinion, the statements mentioned above present fairly the consolidated financial position of General Instrument Corporation and subsidiaries at February 28, 1982 and 1981 and the consolidated results of operations and changes in financial position for each of the three fiscal years in the period ended February 28, 1982, in conformity with generally accepted accounting principles applied on a consistent basis during the period.

Arthur Young and Company

April 5, 1982

SOURCE: General Instrument Corporation, 1982 Annual Report.

Publicly owned companies and thousands of nonpublicly owned companies usually issue audited financial statements once each year. The Securities and Exchange Commission and the stock exchanges require that the annual financial statements of companies subject to their jurisdiction be audited by independent CPAs. Bankers often require a company's audited statements before making loans. Even when no one requires audited statements, managers often obtain audits and issue the audited statements.

Auditors must be **competent** and **independent** of the management of any company whose financial statements they audit. To be competent, auditors must have a working knowledge of generally accepted auditing standards, which govern how an audit should be conducted and are covered in auditing textbooks, as well as generally accepted accounting principles, many of which we cover in this textbook. To be independent, auditors must be honest and must not have any financial or family interest in the company they are auditing. Auditors must be independent in fact and in appearance. Users of financial statements simply will not attribute much importance to the auditor's opinion unless they perceive that the auditor is independent of the company being audited.

Exhibit 1–2 provides an overview of the major parties who are directly involved in the financial reporting process. These parties include preparers, auditors, and users of financial statements.

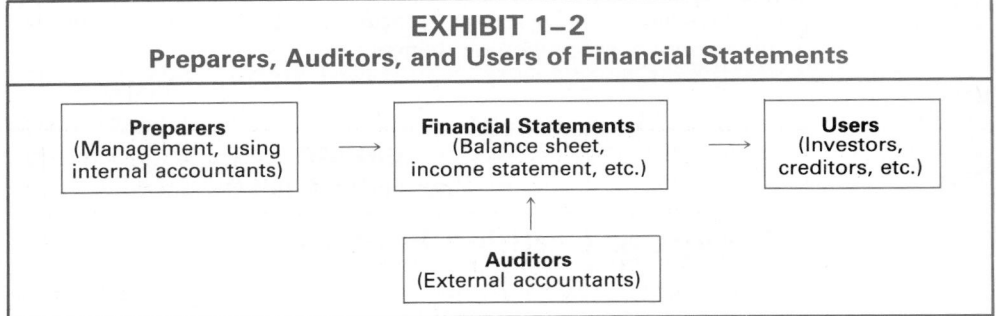

EXHIBIT 1–2
Preparers, Auditors, and Users of Financial Statements

Preparers
(Management, using internal accountants) →

Financial Statements
(Balance sheet, income statement, etc.) →

Users
(Investors, creditors, etc.)

Auditors
(External accountants)

GENERALLY ACCEPTED ACCOUNTING PRINCIPLES

Basically, accounting principles are guidelines to use when gathering and communicating accounting information.[10] Imagine the situation that could exist if companies were free to choose whatever accounting principles they preferred. One company, for example, might report its inventory at historical cost (the cost actually incurred to purchase or produce the inventory), while others might use replacement costs, current selling prices, or other measurements. Or one company might publish only an income statement while another might report only a balance sheet. Such a situation could seriously reduce the ability of users to make valid comparisons between companies.

To help overcome this problem, the accounting profession has given some accounting principles the special status of being **generally accepted accounting principles** (commonly called **GAAP**). Generally accepted accounting principles are those that have **substantial authoritative support.**[11] Specifically, they represent "the consensus at any time as to which economic resources and obligations should be recorded as assets and liabilities, which changes in them should be recorded, when these changes should be recorded, how

---

[10]Accounting principles have also been called standards, concepts, procedures, rules, and practices.
[11]AICPA Special Bulletin, *Disclosure of Departures from Opinions of Accounting Principles Board* (October 1964), par. 3.

the recorded assets and liabilities and changes in them should be measured, what information should be disclosed and how it should be disclosed, and which financial statements should be prepared."[12] Internal and external accountants must have a thorough knowledge of generally accepted accounting principles in order to prepare and attest to financial statements. Moreover, users should be familiar with these principles so that they can understand the nature and limitations of the information presented in financial statements.

In some ways, generally accepted accounting principles are similar to laws (i.e., laws within our legal system, not laws of science) in that companies ordinarily must use such principles when they prepare financial statements for external users. Like laws, generally accepted accounting principles are formulated *by people,* often in an atmosphere in which considerable *political pressures* exist. Thus, instead of having been discovered in nature, generally accepted accounting principles "have developed on the basis of experience, reason, custom, usage, and, to a significant extent, practical necessity."[13] These principles should and do *change* as conditions warrant change. Furthermore, they are often *controversial,* as are laws that govern draft registration, drinking, gambling, and many other areas. Just as laws should be judged in relation to how effective they are in contributing to the achievement of society's goals, generally accepted accounting principles should be evaluated on the basis of how much they contribute to the **objectives of financial accounting.** Unlike laws, however, generally accepted accounting principles in the United States have largely been determined within the **private sector** rather than the public sector (i.e., the government sector) of our economy.

DEVELOPMENT OF GENERALLY ACCEPTED ACCOUNTING PRINCIPLES

Although accounting has a long and interesting history, most of the progress made in the development of generally accepted accounting principles (standards) in the United States occurred during and after the 1930s. This progress was spurred by such factors as the growth during the early part of this century of the corporate form of business organization, with its separation of ownership from management; the introduction of income taxation in 1913, which made accounting records necessary for tax purposes; the intense criticism of corporate reporting practices in the financial press during the early part of this century; the stock market crash of 1929 and the depression which followed it; and the passage in 1933–1934 of federal legislation designed to help ensure that investors have adequate information on which to base their investment decisions.

Understanding generally accepted accounting principles requires a knowledge of the various organizations that have influenced their development. Primary among these are the American Institute of Certified Public Accountants, the Financial Accounting Standards Board, and the Securities and Exchange Commission. Materials published by these and other organizations often are helpful to students taking intermediate accounting and more advanced courses in financial accounting.

American Institute of Certified Public Accountants

The **American Institute of Certified Public Accountants (AICPA)** is the national professional organization of CPAs. In addition to many other useful publications, the AICPA publishes a monthly journal, called *The Journal of Accountancy,* that deals primarily with issues that are of concern to practicing accountants.

Committee on Accounting Procedure

The AICPA's first major involvement in developing accounting principles occurred in 1938 when it established the **Committee on Accounting Procedure (CAP).** The CAP was

---

[12]*APB Statement No. 4,* par. 27.
[13]*APB Statement No. 4,* par. 139.

composed of 21 volunteer members, most of whom were practicing accountants and all of whom were AICPA members. The CAP's purpose was to further the development of accounting principles, primarily by reducing the number of alternatives available in practice for use in accounting for a given type of transaction or item.

The CAP issued pronouncements called **Accounting Research Bulletins (ARBs).** These pronouncements summarized the committee's views concerning the proper accounting treatment for various types of transactions and items. ARBs were designed primarily to help practicing accountants resolve a variety of specific problems. They covered such specific topics as declining-balance depreciation and long-term construction-type contracts.

The assenting votes of two-thirds of the CAP's members were required to issue an ARB, and from 1939 to 1959, the CAP issued 51 ARBs. In 1953, the first 42 ARBs were revised and reissued as *Accounting Research Bulletin No. 43.* The committee published eight more ARBs before it was dissolved in 1959. Those ARBs which have not been superseded by professional pronouncements are still important sources of generally accepted accounting principles.

ARBs were primarily **advisory** in nature. Although accountants generally followed the principles recommended in the ARBs, they were not required to do so. The AICPA could only encourage its members to observe the ARBs since it lacked the authority to require compliance. Ultimately, the authority of the ARBs was based on their general acceptance within the financial community.

The CAP authorized the publication of **Accounting Terminology Bulletins.** These bulletins were developed by a Committee on Terminology, which was usually comprised of a few members of the CAP. As the name implies, the purpose of Accounting Terminology Bulletins was to explain and improve accounting terminology. The first eight bulletins were reissued in 1953 as *Accounting Terminology Bulletin No. 1.* Three more bulletins were later published.

Even though the ARBs helped to improve the quality of accounting practice, the CAP was criticized for several reasons. The primary criticism was the committee's failure to develop a coherent framework of objectives and broad principles within which to resolve specific accounting problems. Instead, the CAP followed a more expedient "piecemeal" approach, trying to resolve immediate problems on a case-by-case basis. A result was that the ARBs were sometimes inconsistent with one another. Other major criticisms were that the CAP permitted too many alternative accounting principles to exist, did not move quickly enough, and did not support conclusions with research results.

Accounting Principles Board

In 1959 the AICPA replaced the CAP with a new committee charged with the responsibility of developing accounting principles. This committee, called the **Accounting Principles Board (APB),** consisted of 18–21 volunteer members who were accountants drawn from public practice, industry, colleges and universities, and government. The APB issued pronouncements called **Opinions.** These opinions presented the board's views concerning proper accounting in various specific areas such as income taxes, earnings per share, and intangible assets. Issuance of an opinion required a two-thirds vote of the APB's members. From 1959 to 1973 the board issued 31 opinions. Although the APB was replaced in 1973 by the Financial Accounting Standards Board, opinions that have not been superseded are still important sources of generally accepted accounting principles.

In addition to the 31 opinions, the APB issued four **Statements.** These statements did not have the same status as opinions. The APB felt that its statements contained recommendations rather than requirements. In 1970 the APB issued *Statement No. 4,* entitled "Basic Concepts and Accounting Principles Underlying Financial Statements of Business Enterprises." In this statement, the board identified the broad fundamentals of financial accounting as they were reflected by accounting practice at that time. *Statement No. 4* is a milestone in the accounting profession's search for a coherent theoretical framework, and we cite it frequently in this textbook.

APB Opinions often dealt with complex issues. Thus, the AICPA published a series of **Accounting Interpretations** (of APB Opinions) that were designed primarily to guide practitioners in applying various opinions. Interpretations were not, however, formal pronouncements of the APB.

During the early years of the APB's existence, the AICPA could not require practitioners to comply with APB Opinions. In October 1964, however, the AICPA's governing council adopted a recommendation that AICPA members "should see to it that departures from Opinions of the Accounting Principles Board (as well as effective Accounting Research Bulletins issued by the former Committee on Accounting Procedure) are disclosed, either in footnotes to financial statements or in the audit reports of members in their capacity as independent auditors."[14] In 1972 this recommendation was incorporated in **Rule 203** of the AICPA Code of Professional Ethics. This rule prohibits an AICPA member from expressing an opinion that financial statements conform with generally accepted accounting principles if the statements contain a material departure from an accounting principle established by the Financial Accounting Standards Board (as well as accounting principles established by effective ARBs and APB Opinions), unless the member can demonstrate clearly that, because of unusual circumstances, following such a principle would result in misleading financial statements.[15]

In 1978 the AICPA included **Rule 204** in the Code of Ethics. This rule requires AICPA members to justify departures from Financial Accounting Standards Board standards that relate to the disclosure of information outside of the published financial statements, such as supplementary financial statements adjusted for the effects of inflation.[16] *Rules 203* and *204* are very important because they effectively require that AICPA members either comply with authoritative accounting pronouncements or assume the risk of having to defend why they did not do so. Generally, few accountants want to assume such a risk.

When the AICPA established the APB, it also created a separate Accounting Research Division (within the AICPA). Unlike the CAP, an important feature of the APB was the emphasis placed on research. When it established the APB, the AICPA expected that the board's opinions would be influenced by the results of logical and thorough **Accounting Research Studies** conducted for the Research Division by competent investigators. These studies were designed as a basis for identification and discussion of accounting problems, but their conclusions were those of the authors and did not represent the official position of the AICPA. Fifteen Accounting Research Studies ultimately were published.

The Accounting Research Studies did not have as much impact on the APB's conclusions as most accountants had hoped for when the Research Division was organized. For example, two of the earliest studies were expected to identify a set of basic postulates (assumptions) and broad principles that would serve as a logical foundation for the APB's Opinions.[17] After these studies were published, the APB in 1962 merely acknowledged that they were valuable contributions to accounting thought. But the board did not accept the studies because it believed that they were too radically different from the generally accepted accounting principles in existence at that time.

Although the APB made significant progress in the development of generally accepted

---

[14]AICPA Special Bulletin, *Disclosure of Departures from Opinions of Accounting Principles Board,* par. 1.

[15]*AICPA Professional Standards—Volume 2* (Chicago: Commerce Clearing House), ET Sec. 203.01.

[16]*AICPA Professional Standards—Volume 2,* ET Sec. 204.01.

[17]These studies are: *Accounting Research Study No. 1,* "The Basic Postulates of Accounting" (New York: AICPA, 1961) by Maurice Moonitz, and *Accounting Research Study No. 3,* "A Tentative Set of Broad Accounting Principles for Business Enterprises" (New York: AICPA, 1962) by Robert T. Sprouse and Maurice Moonitz.

accounting principles, it was criticized for most of the same reasons that the CAP had been criticized earlier. Critics also charged that the views of large public accounting firms and the AICPA had, and were *seen* to have, too much influence on the APB's decisions. Some charged, for example, that public accountants on the board were hard-pressed to criticize poor accounting principles that their own clients were using.

In response to these criticisms, the AICPA appointed a seven-person committee, chaired by Francis M. Wheat, to study the process of establishing accounting principles and to make recommendations for improving that process. The Wheat Committee issued its report in March 1972, and this report led to the establishment of the Financial Accounting Standards Board.

Financial Accounting Standards Board

Since July 1973, the **Financial Accounting Standards Board (FASB)** has been the official private sector body charged with the responsibility of establishing and improving generally accepted accounting principles in the United States.[18] At its outset the board decided that ARBs and APB opinions should remain in force until superseded by an FASB pronouncement.

Like the CAP and the APB, the FASB formulates accounting principles in a committee context. However, the FASB now has several important characteristics that make it different from its predecessors:

1. The FASB consists of only **seven members.** It has considerably fewer members than either of its predecessors, which tends to reduce the time needed to respond to emerging problems.
2. All FASB members are **fully remunerated** and **serve full time.** Whereas the members of the predecessor committees were part-time volunteers who continued to hold their positions elsewhere, FASB members must sever their ties with former employers before they serve on the board. This feature reduces the possibility of actual or apparent conflicts of interests.
3. FASB members are **not required to be CPAs.** In contrast, members of the predecessor committees were AICPA members and therefore were CPAs. This FASB characteristic reduces the likelihood that FASB pronouncements will reflect only the views of preparers and auditors of financial statements.
4. An affirmative **vote of four of the seven FASB members is needed** to approve a pronouncement. The need for only a simple majority contrasts with the two-thirds vote that the predecessor committees required. The FASB's voting rules enable the board to deal with reducing the number of undesirable compromises that often are necessary to get a two-thirds vote.
5. The FASB is an **independent body.** It is not part of the AICPA, as were its predecessors. This feature reduces the chances that FASB pronouncements will reflect, and be seen to reflect, only the views of the AICPA.

The FASB issues three types of pronouncements:

1. **Statements of Financial Accounting Standards (SFASs).** These establish new or amend existing generally accepted accounting principles.
2. **Interpretations.** These clarify, explain, or elaborate on SFASs, APB Opinions, or ARBs. Interpretations are themselves a part of generally accepted accounting principles.
3. **Statements of Financial Accounting Concepts (SFACs).** These set forth objectives and concepts that the FASB uses as the basis for establishing and improving generally accepted accounting principles. SFACs do not establish generally accepted accounting principles.

---

[18]The Wheat Committee recommended use of the term "standards" instead of "principles" because of confusion over the meaning of "accounting principles." In this textbook we use the terms "principles" and "standards" interchangeably.

In addition, the FASB's staff issues **Technical Bulletins** that are designed to provide timely advice concerning how to apply existing standards to specific problems.

The FASB tries to involve in its standard-setting process everyone who is interested in financial reporting and wants to participate. These people include preparers, auditors, users, and others. FASB members may therefore have backgrounds in financial analysis, industry, government, and academia, as well as in public accounting. FASB meetings are open to the public, and the board keeps a public record. The board's due process system of formulating an SFAS typically involves the following major steps, which are illustrated in Exhibit 1–3:[19]

1. The board **identifies an accounting problem** (such as accounting for leases or pension plans) and places the problem on its agenda.
2. The board appoints a task force of technical experts which **conducts extensive research** on the problem.
3. The board **issues a Discussion Memorandum,** which summarizes the major issues and possible solutions and serves as the basis for public comment.

_____
[19]The FASB follows similar steps when issuing Interpretations and SFACs.

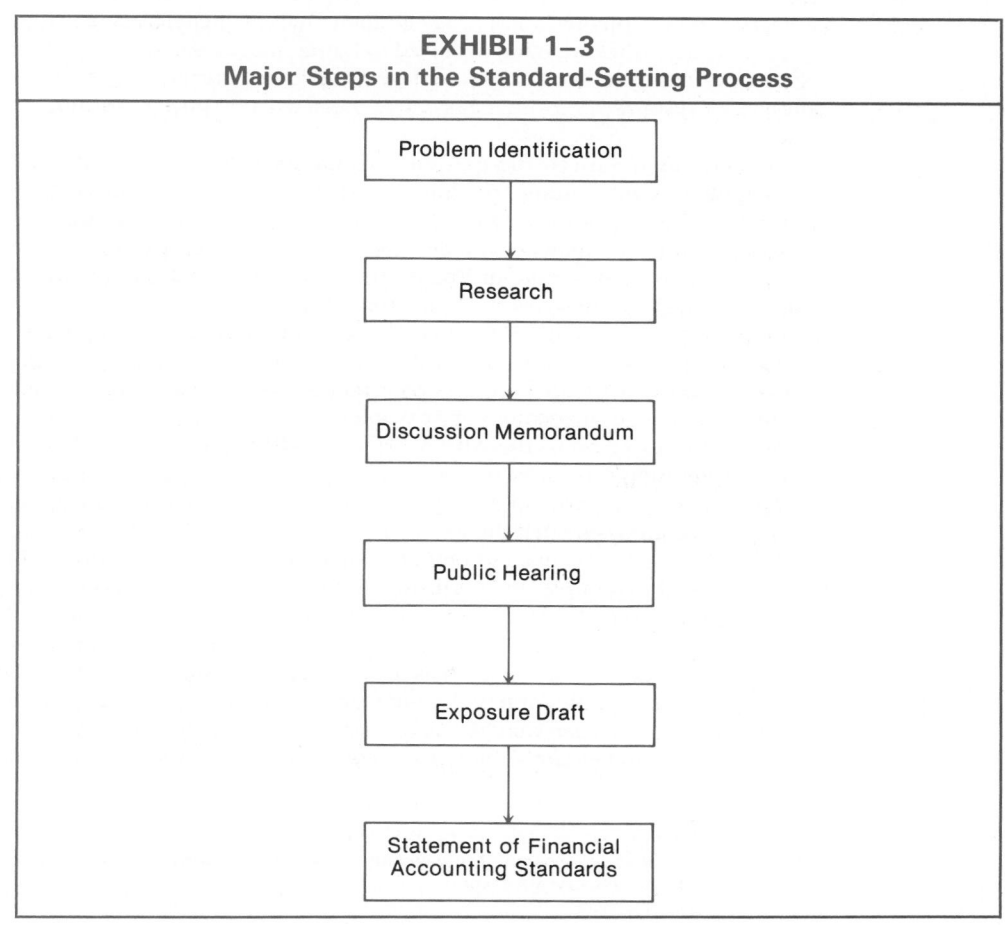

EXHIBIT 1–3
Major Steps in the Standard-Setting Process

Problem Identification

↓

Research

↓

Discussion Memorandum

↓

Public Hearing

↓

Exposure Draft

↓

Statement of Financial Accounting Standards

4. The board **conducts a public hearing** at which it invites interested parties to present their views.
5. The board **issues an Exposure Draft,** which is a *proposed* SFAS that is distributed for public comment.
6. The board **issues an SFAS** after it has analyzed public responses to the exposure draft.

The **Financial Accounting Foundation** is the independent entity whose board of trustees oversees the basic structure of the standard-setting process. In addition, the trustees appoint members to the FASB and to the FASB's advisory council. They also secure private contributions to fund the FASB's operations. The trustees are appointed by a panel of representatives from several national organizations whose members have a knowledge of and an interest in corporate financial reporting.[20]

The **Financial Accounting Standards Advisory Council** is a group of varying size that helps the FASB to set priorities and to establish ad hoc task forces. Moreover, the advisory council reacts to proposed FASB pronouncements and assists the board in other ways. Often the FASB appoints a task force to help the board resolve a specific problem. Members of the advisory council frequently serve on these task forces. The FASB is also assisted by full-time research and administrative staffs.

Thus far, the FASB has set accounting standards using a case-by-case approach similar to that of its predecessors. But one of the initial tasks undertaken by the FASB was a **Conceptual Framework Project.** The purpose of this project is to develop an authoritative, coherent structure of objectives and broad fundamentals of financial accounting. The FASB calls it a "constitution" that hopefully will lead to better, more consistent standards. Certain phases of this project have been completed, and the board currently is spending a considerable amount of resources on other phases. We discuss this project in more detail later in the chapter.

As you might expect, the existence of the FASB has changed the AICPA's role in the development of accounting principles. Currently, the AICPA has an **Accounting Standards Executive Committee (AcSEC).** This committee issues **Statements of Position (SOPs)** that are intended to influence the development of accounting principles in specialized areas not covered by FASB pronouncements. Currently, the FASB is in the process of developing statements that may designate as standards many of the specialized accounting and reporting principles contained in the SOPs. In fact, the FASB has already issued a few statements based on certain SOPs. Until the FASB's project is complete, the specialized accounting principles contained in the SOPs are considered preferable accounting principles only for purposes of justifying a change in accounting principles.

In addition to AcSEC, the AICPA has an **Auditing Standards Board (ASB).** The ASB develops auditing standards and enforces the application of professional ethics.

Since accounting principles help to determine how resources are allocated in our economy, it is not surprising that the FASB, like its predecessor committees, often has had to deal with political pressures in addition to having to decide what is theoretically sound accounting. In 1979, for example, the Securities and Exchange Commission, acting under pressure from Congress and the Department of Energy, in effect forced the FASB to change the accounting principles it had developed for oil and gas producing companies. Why did the SEC take this action? One major reason was that many smaller producers claimed that the FASB's principles would force these companies to report lower earnings, thereby making it harder for them to raise capital. According to these smaller producers, this in turn would adversely affect the nation's ability to discover oil and gas. Clearly, the ability of the FASB to

---

[20]These organizations include the American Accounting Association, American Institute of Certified Public Accountants, National Association of Accountants, Financial Executives Institute, Financial Analysts Federation, and Securities Industry Association.

survive as a private-sector, standard-setting body will depend to a large extent on how effectively it handles the many conflicting political pressures that are brought on it.

Securities and Exchange Commission

The level of stock prices in the United States declined dramatically between 1929 and 1933. This occurrence brought considerable public pressure for better disclosure of corporate information. In the midst of this pressure and of a severe depression, Congress enacted legislation that has had a tremendous influence on corporate financial reporting. Basically, Congress passed the **Securities Act of 1933** to improve the disclosures made by companies when they sell a *new* issue of securities to the public. Then it passed the **Securities Exchange Act of 1934** to improve the periodic disclosures made by companies whose shares are publicly traded. The 1934 Act created the **Securities and Exchange Commission (SEC)** as a public sector organization to enforce both of these so-called disclosure statutes.

The SEC does not protect investors from sustaining losses. Instead, its basic purpose is to ensure that companies provide investors with adequate information on which to base their investment decisions. Accordingly, companies that are subject to the SEC's jurisdiction must report to the SEC a substantial quantity of information on a variety of different forms.[21] This information is available for public use. The most important corporate reports required by the SEC are the:

1. **Registration statement.**   This is a detailed report required under the 1933 Act when a company makes a public offering of its securities. It includes such information as the nature of the company's business, a description of the securities being registered, and audited financial statements.
2. **10-K report.**   This is a detailed report that companies file annually under the 1934 Act. It includes a description of various corporate activities as well as audited financial statements. Companies usually disclose considerably more information in their 10-K reports than they disclose in their annual reports to shareholders.
3. **10-Q report.**   This is a quarterly report filed under the 1934 Act. It is much less detailed than the 10-K. In addition to a description of various activities, the 10-Q report includes financial information that has been reviewed but not audited by an independent CPA.
4. **8-K report.**   This report, required under the 1934 Act, explains a material event (such as a major acquisition or a lawsuit) that investors want to know about. An 8-K report usually must be filed within 15 days after a material event has occurred.

These reports evidence the SEC's concern that companies disclose relevant financial and nonfinancial information on a timely basis. The SEC also is concerned about the costs that companies must incur to comply with the various disclosure requirements. Recently the SEC designed a new **integrated disclosure system** that allows companies to avoid having to file duplicate copies of certain information that already has been made publicly available.

The primary sources of the SEC's financial information requirements are:

1. **Regulation S-X.**   This is the original source which prescribes the form and content of financial statements filed with the SEC. It is revised frequently.
2. **Accounting Series Releases (ASRs).**   These are pronouncements which modify the SEC's financial information requirements.
3. **Staff Accounting Bulletins (SABs).**   These are interpretations and practices followed by

---

[21]In essence, the 1933 Act applies to a company when it makes a public offering of its securities. The 1934 Act applies mainly to companies whose securities are traded on a national securities exchange and to "over-the-counter" companies that have at least $3,000,000 in assets and at least 500 stockholders.

the SEC's staff in administrating the commission's disclosure requirements. SABs are not official rules or interpretations of the SEC itself.

4. **Financial Reporting Releases (FRRs).** These pronouncements were first issued in 1982 and are intended to replace ASRs. The first FRR is a codification of portions of ASRs that were relevant when it was issued.

5. **Accounting and Auditing Enforcement Releases (AAERs).** These pronouncements began in 1982 and deal with enforcement-related matters.

Since its inception, the SEC has had **broad legal authority to establish accounting and reporting standards.** To date, the Commission has largely delegated this authority to private sector organizations (the CAP, APB, and FASB). But the SEC can in effect veto the standards set by these organizations, and it has done so occasionally.[22] How can the SEC effectively veto a standard set by the FASB? The SEC can simply refuse to force companies to apply the standard in reports filed with the Commission. *Remember:* the SEC has statutory authority to prescribe accounting and reporting standards for companies under its jurisdiction.

Generally, the SEC and each of the private sector, standard-setting organizations have cooperated with one another. In *ASR No. 150,* the SEC indicated that it looked to the FASB to provide leadership in establishing and improving accounting principles. The SEC nevertheless has considerable influence on the development of accounting principles. The main ways that the SEC has exerted its influence are by responding to planned and existing pronouncements of the FASB and of its predecessors and by strongly encouraging these organizations to resolve emerging accounting problems.

During the 1970s, the SEC began to play a more active role in the process of developing accounting principles. An understanding of the significance of the SEC's role is extremely important in the study of financial accounting.

Other Influences on Accounting Principles

The AICPA, FASB, and SEC are the organizations that have had the most influence in shaping generally accepted accounting principles as they exist today. However, certain other organizations as well as the income tax law have had an important impact.[23]

Income Tax Law

The **income tax law,** as enacted by Congress, administered by the Internal Revenue Service, and interpreted by the courts, has influenced the development and the implementation of accounting principles. For example, many smaller businesses maintain accounting records primarily for income tax purposes. Moreover, in order to avoid having to maintain one set of books for financial accounting purposes and a different set for tax purposes, many companies tend to use financial accounting principles that will reduce and postpone their income tax payments. Suppose, for example, that a company formed in 1980 plans to use an accelerated depreciation method for tax purposes but has no strong theoretical reason to favor the use of any particular depreciation method for financial reporting purposes. The company may well decide to use the accelerated method for financial reporting purposes (as well as for tax purposes) in order to avoid the need for two sets of depreciation records.

---

[22]In 1972 an APB member likened the SEC to top management and the APB to lower-level management. See Charles T. Horngren, "Accounting Principles: Public or Private Sector?" *Journal of Accountancy* (May 1972), pp. 37–41.

[23]Some students who have taken cost accounting may notice that we have not included the **Cost Accounting Standards Board (CASB)** in the following discussion. The CASB was a federal agency created by Congress in 1970. It was a public sector body charged with developing cost accounting standards for use by most businesses with government contracts in excess of $100,000. The CASB was abolished in 1980. Overall, it had a very limited impact on financial accounting.

Finally, the tax law states that if a company uses the last-in, first-out (LIFO) inventory method for tax purposes, it must also use LIFO for financial reporting purposes. We explain this conformity requirement in Chapter 8.

Although tax law has played a role in shaping generally accepted accounting principles, an important point to remember is that **the principles that a company should use for tax purposes are not necessarily the same as those it should use for financial accounting purposes.** Tax accounting focuses on the measurement of taxable income using principles established by tax laws. In contrast, a primary focus of financial accounting is the measurement of accounting income using generally accepted accounting principles. The objectives of the tax law are to raise money for the operation of the government and to achieve certain social goals. In contrast, the primary objective of generally accepted accounting principles is to provide useful information to investors, creditors, and other users. Since the objectives of tax accounting and financial accounting differ, we find that the principles of tax accounting frequently differ from those of financial accounting.

This textbook deals with financial accounting principles. In Chapter 18, we examine several financial accounting issues that relate directly to the existence of corporate income taxes.

Interestingly, many accountants feel that income tax law often has played a major role in the "nondevelopment" of generally accepted accounting principles. For example, the use of current value accounting in a company's primary financial statements is not now a generally accepted accounting principle. One reason why the opponents of such accounting have rejected it is their fear that it will "create new kinds of income" that the government will want to tax.

American Accounting Association

The **American Accounting Association (AAA)** is dominated by accounting educators, although many practicing accountants are active members. In addition to fostering improvements in accounting education and research, the AAA has contributed to the development of accounting principles, especially in the area of financial accounting theory.

From 1936 to the present, various AAA committees have published six major statements that deal with various aspects of accounting theory. In addition, several supplementary statements have been issued. AAA committees have traditionally followed a broader, more conceptual approach to the development of accounting principles than either the FASB or its predecessors. Publications of the AAA often concentrate on what accounting *should be* rather than on what accounting *is now.*

Unlike the FASB, the AAA is not an organization designed to promulgate accounting principles that practitioners must observe. The AAA has therefore not been highly concerned about whether the work of its committees receives immediate acceptance in practice. AAA works often affect practice in indirect ways several years after they are published. For example, many of the major aspects of *A Statement of Basic Accounting Theory* (published by the AAA in 1966) are reflected in *APB Statement No. 4* (published by the AICPA in 1970). Moreover, many AAA publications apparently are having an impact on the FASB's Conceptual Framework Project.

Included among many AAA publications is a quarterly journal, called *The Accounting Review,* which contains articles that present the results of basic and applied accounting research.

The AAA is actively involved in the work of the FASB. For example, an AAA representative serves on the panel that selects the trustees of the Financial Accounting Foundation, and an AAA committee reacts to FASB pronouncements.

Financial Executives Institute

The **Financial Executives Institute (FEI)** primarily comprises financial executives, such as controllers and treasurers, from large corporations. Members of this organization are an important subset of *preparers* of financial statements. Views expressed by FEI members have played a significant role in the development of generally accepted accounting principles.

The FEI publishes a monthly journal called *Financial Executive,* and it has sponsored several important research studies in financial accounting. Like the AAA, the FEI has been actively involved in the work of the FASB.

National Association of Accountants

The **National Association of Accountants (NAA)** consists largely of industrial accountants. Traditionally, the NAA has focused its attention on cost and managerial accounting. In recent years, however, it has increased its role in the development of financial accounting standards.

The NAA publishes a monthly journal called *Management Accounting.* In addition, it has published several important research studies in financial accounting, and it administers the CMA program. Like the AAA and the FEI, the NAA has been actively involved in the FASB's work.

Financial Analysts Federation

The **Financial Analysts Federation (FAF),** a national organization of financial analysts, is one of the most knowledgeable and influential groups that *use* accounting information. A **financial analyst** is a person who analyzes information and renders professional advice on investment matters. Many analysts have earned the designation **Chartered Financial Analyst (CFA).** A CFA is an individual who has met certain education and experience requirements and who has passed a rigorous examination on such subjects as accounting, economics, financial analysis, portfolio management, and ethics.

The FAF publishes the bimonthly *Financial Analysts Journal.* The organization maintains a strong interest in corporate financial reporting, and it plays an active role in the work of the FASB. Financial analysts frequently have served as respondents or subjects in behavioral studies on the uses of accounting information.

Robert Morris Associates

Robert Morris Associates (RMA) is a national organization of bank loan and credit officers. As *users* of accounting information, commercial bank loan officers have influenced the development of generally accepted accounting principles. Much of this influence occurred around the beginning of this century, when bankers were the dominant external users of accounting information. Like financial analysts, bank loan officers often serve as respondents or subjects in accounting research studies. RMA publishes a monthly journal called *The Journal of Commercial Bank Lending.*

SOURCES OF GENERALLY ACCEPTED ACCOUNTING PRINCIPLES

As stated earlier, generally accepted accounting principles are those that have substantial authoritative support. The accounting profession has never published a complete, official list of such principles. Furthermore, because the profession has not defined precisely what is meant by the phrase "substantial authoritative support," the boundary that separates generally accepted accounting principles from others is sometimes hazy. In practice, therefore, determining whether an accounting principle is generally accepted sometimes requires judgment. Accountants and auditors must be familiar with the sources of generally accepted accounting principles so that they can derive answers to difficult measurement and disclosure questions.

The most authoritative sources of generally accepted accounting principles are FASB Statements of Financial Accounting Standards and Interpretations, along with Accounting Research Bulletins and APB Opinions that are currently in force. These sources contain accounting principles as contemplated in *Rules 203* and *204* that we discussed earlier.[24] Other common sources of generally accepted accounting principles are:

1. Certain other publications of the FASB and its predecessors (such as APB statements).
2. Accounting Interpretations, Statements of Position, Industry Audit Guides, and Industry Accounting Guides published by the AICPA.
3. Publications of the SEC such as Accounting Series Releases.
4. Current accounting practice as reflected in a compilation such as *Accounting Trends and Techniques,* published annually by the AICPA.
5. Current accounting textbooks and articles.

The isolated appearance of an accounting principle, either in practice or in a textbook, does not necessarily mean that the principle is generally accepted. However, substantial use of a principle or substantial agreement among authors that its use is appropriate do lend support to a claim that the principle has general acceptance.

FUTURE DEVELOPMENT OF GENERALLY ACCEPTED ACCOUNTING PRINCIPLES

Although considerable progress has been made in the development of generally accepted accounting principles, much more work remains to be done. Some of the major issues that are likely to affect the nature and extent of progress in this area are briefly discussed below.

Conceptual Framework Issue

A project that may ultimately have the greatest overall impact on the accounting standard-setting process is the FASB's Conceptual Framework Project. As stated earlier, this project seeks to develop an authoritative, coherent structure of objectives and broad fundamentals of financial accounting. This structure will be the basis for developing new financial accounting standards and eliminating inconsistencies that exist in current standards. The structure should provide the FASB with a strong foundation that it can rely on to help resolve difficult accounting questions. The FASB also intends that the structure will help everyone who has an interest in financial accounting to better understand the nature and limitations of financial accounting information.

To give you a more concrete idea of what the FASB means by a conceptual framework, here are some of the topics that are comprised in the Conceptual Framework Project:

1. Objectives of financial reporting by business enterprises.
2. Qualitative characteristics of accounting information.
3. Elements of financial statements of business enterprises (e.g., assets, liabilities, revenues).
4. Objectives of financial reporting by nonbusiness organizations.
5. Reporting earnings.
6. Financial statements and other means of financial reporting.
7. Accounting recognition criteria for elements.
8. Funds flows, liquidity, and financial flexibility.

The development of an authoritative conceptual framework takes a lot of time. No easy solutions are apparent. In the long run, the FASB's success as a policy-making organization will probably depend heavily on the success of the Conceptual Framework Project. Yet, a conceptual framework is unlikely to be a panacea. Certain factors will limit the usefulness of a conceptual framework: (1) the accounting policy-making process entails complex social

---

[24]*AICPA Professional Standards—Volume 2,* ET Sec. 203.01 and 204.01.

choices; (2) the conceptual framework may not be interpreted uniformly by all FASB members at a given time; and (3) the FASB membership will continue to change over time, thereby possibly altering the board's interpretation of the conceptual framework.[25]

Economic Impact Issue

Accounting principles affect the allocation of scarce resources in our society because they determine the content of financial statements which investors, creditors, and others use to make many important decisions. Perhaps less obvious but also very important is the fact that a manager's behavior, as reflected in various operating and financial decisions, often is influenced by the manager's knowledge of the information that accounting principles require. Corporate directors often use financial accounting information to help determine management's compensation. In a recent compensation contract, for example, the chairman and chief executive of International Harvester received a $1.8 million loan and was told the loan would be forgiven if within a seven-year period he raised the company's profitability to that of the average of six competitors: Caterpillar, Deere, Ford, General Motors, Paccar, and Massey-Ferguson.[26]

A former chief accountant of the SEC has aptly stated that "the way you keep score determines at least in part the way you play the game."[27] Under current generally accepted accounting principles, for example, a company is not required to include all types of leases among its liabilities. Many people believe that if the FASB required companies to include all leases among their liabilities, the number of leasing transactions in which companies engage would be reduced. Because of the actions of preparers and users of financial statements, accounting principles have an important *economic impact* on our society. Simply put, they help to determine who gets how much wealth.

In recent years, accounting principles have been directly linked to such issues as bank lending policies, the merger movement, gross national product, national energy policy, and tax policy designed to encourage business investment. This fact has raised questions about whether and to what extent the FASB should be concerned with the economic impact of the standards that it sets. When the FASB established standards for oil and gas producing companies, to use a recent example that we mentioned earlier, should the FASB have been concerned only with trying to do what it considered correct according to accounting theory, or should it also have been concerned with doing what some energy producers claimed was best for the nation's energy program?

During the 1970s, the economic impact issue began to play an increasingly more important role in the standard-setting process of both the APB and the FASB.[28] An awareness of this role is important to an understanding of some of the generally accepted accounting principles that exist today.

In the future, the FASB is likely to be guided in its decisions primarily by the accounting theory that the board adopts in its Conceptual Framework Project. However, the board will also consider the economic impact of its decisions by assessing the economic benefits and costs that its decisions are likely to produce. Doing this will not, of course, be easy.

Public Versus Private Sector Issue

As noted earlier, private sector organizations have played the dominant role in shaping the development of generally accepted accounting principles in the United States. Nevertheless,

---

[25]See Charles T. Horngren, "Uses and Limitations of a Conceptual Framework," *Journal of Accountancy* (April 1981), pp. 86, 88, 90, 92, 94–95.
[26]Carol J. Loomis, "Archie McCardell's Absolution," *Fortune* (December 15, 1980), p. 90.
[27]"Why Everybody's Jumping on the Accountants These Days," *Forbes* (March 15, 1977), p. 39.
[28]See Stephen A. Zeff, "The Rise of 'Economic Consequences,' " *Journal of Accountancy* (December 1978), pp. 56–63.

the SEC has the legal authority to prescribe accounting principles, and Congress can effectively tell the SEC what to do. Will Congress ever decide that accounting principles should be formulated in the public sector?

In the past, Congress has chosen to exert relatively little direct influence on the standard-setting process. The most notable exceptions to this policy have been in the areas of LIFO inventory pricing, accounting for the investment tax credit, and accounting for oil and gas producing companies.

In 1976, however, a report issued by a House of Representatives subcommittee chaired by John E. Moss criticized the lack of uniformity in generally accepted accounting principles. Later that year, a Senate subcommittee chaired by Lee Metcalf issued a staff study which recommended, among other things, that the federal government should establish financial accounting standards for publicly owned corporations. The same Senate subcommittee issued a report in 1977 that was much less critical of the accounting profession and the standard-setting process. The accounting profession has responded to these Congressional criticisms in many ways, and for the time being, it appears that Congress does not have a strong interest in creating a federal board to establish financial accounting standards. Nevertheless, the work of the Congressional subcommittees has shown that some elected officials are not pleased with the progress that private sector organizations have made in developing accounting standards.

Most accountants and other business people feel strongly that standard setting should remain in the private sector. In fact, a survey of the preferences of 1,329 preparers, auditors, and users of financial reports "showed a clear preference for financial accounting reporting standards to be set within the private sector, by a body similar in composition to the current FASB."[29] The reasons for favoring the private sector determination of GAAP appear to be based on such important factors as objectivity, prestige and acceptability, expertise, competence, and image. Expertise is probably the most important of these factors.[30]

In the final analysis, whether or not accounting standard setting remains in the private sector will likely depend on how successful the FASB is in satisfying the various groups who are interested in its decisions, including Congress.

Uniformity Versus Flexibility Issue

People can usually think of several ways to account for a given type of transaction. Take depreciation for example. Generally accepted accounting principles support the concept that depreciation is a cost allocation process. But even though most accountants may agree with this concept, several depreciation methods are currently used. These methods include straight-line, double-declining balance, sum-of-the-years'-digits, and others. The depreciation method that a company uses will influence the amount of its net income and other financial-statement variables. This fact and the fact that people use financial statements to make *comparisons* between companies are the basis for one of the accounting profession's oldest debates—uniformity versus flexibility of accounting principles.

Proponents of uniformity have argued that company managers have too many accounting options available to them. They believe that these options create confusion and reduce the ability of financial statement users to make meaningful comparisons. On the other side, proponents of flexibility believe that some alternatives should be allowed. These people feel that some flexibility is needed because each company is complex and unique.

Uniformity and flexibility lie on a continuum, and most accountants dislike both extremes. Strict uniformity would probably result in a "cookbook" prescribing everything from the detailed procedures for gathering data to the precise format to use when preparing

---

[29]Joshua Ronen and Michael Schiff, "The Setting of Financial Accounting Standards—Private or Public?" *Journal of Accountancy* (March 1978), p. 69.
[30]Ronen and Schiff, pp. 69–70.

financial statements. At the opposite extreme, unlimited flexibility would make it difficult for users to make comparisons and would undermine the integrity of the financial reporting process. The critical issue, therefore, is where on the uniformity/flexibility continuum the accounting profession should be.

One of the major tasks of the FASB and its predecessors has been to eliminate undesirable accounting alternatives. In doing this today, accountants tend to emphasize the goal of **achieving comparability** rather than either uniformity or flexibility. A requirement for financial statements to be comparable is that any differences between the financial statements of different companies should reflect basic differences between the companies themselves and not merely differences between the accounting principles that they use. Achieving comparability requires: "(1) identifying and describing the circumstances that justify or require the use of a particular accounting practice or method, [and] (2) eliminating the use of alternative practices under these circumstances."[31] Accomplishing this goal has not been and will not be easy. History reveals that when the accounting profession's critics feel that it has fallen short of achieving comparability, cries for more uniformity tend to become louder. An important determinant of the FASB's success will be the extent to which it contributes to comparability through an acceptable resolution of the uniformity/flexibility debate.

Market Efficiency Issue

An issue with important implications for the uniformity/flexibility debate and for other accounting matters is that of market efficiency. Basically, an **efficient market** is one in which stock prices behave as if they fully reflect publicly available information, including that reported in general purpose financial statements. Although the evidence is not yet conclusive, a large body of empirical literature in accounting and finance suggests that the stock market is highly efficient.

An efficient market reacts to financial statements in a sophisticated manner. It is not fooled when two companies use different accounting methods. Instead, it looks beyond the reported numbers and recognizes that the numbers were generated by different methods. A high degree of market efficiency implies that the market is strongly influenced by the decisions of people who have considerable knowledge of accounting and business. In other words, an efficient market tends to be dominated by sophisticated rather than naive users of financial statements.

An important implication of an efficient market for accounting is that many financial reporting issues can be resolved by a relatively simple strategy of **adequate disclosure.**[32] Consider the various depreciation methods that we discussed earlier. Those who believe that the market is highly efficient would argue that the reporting of several depreciation figures, each computed according to one of the widely used methods, involves only a small cost. Therefore, a company should use one method in its financial statements but disclose in the footnotes what depreciation would be under the other methods. Users, who are presumed to be highly sophisticated, can then adjust the statements to reflect the other methods if they want to do so.

Efficient-market research has not been fully accepted by all accounting authorities. The research pertains to the market as a whole and not to the behavior of individual investors. Moreover, it says nothing about the information needs of financial statement users, such as bankers, whose decisions do not directly involve publicly traded stocks. Nevertheless, the efficient-markets issue is an emerging one that may have an important effect on the course of standard setting in the United States.

---

[31]*APB Statement No. 4,* par. 102.
[32]See William H. Beaver, "What Should Be the FASB's Objectives?" *Journal of Accountancy* (August 1973), pp. 49–56.

Big GAAP/Little GAAP Issue

General purpose financial statements must conform with generally accepted accounting principles. These principles apply to any business regardless of its size or ownership characteristics. But consider a small, closely held business such as a family-owned jewelry shop or a "mom and pop" grocery store. Do those who use the financial statements of these kinds of businesses (primarily owners and bankers) really need the same types of information as those who use the financial statements of such companies as Texaco, U.S. Steel, and Procter & Gamble? Many people say no. And as a result, some have argued that one set of generally accepted accounting principles (which they would call "big GAAP") should apply to larger and/or publicly held companies, while a somewhat different set ("little GAAP") should apply to smaller and/or closely held companies.

Proponents of the big GAAP/little GAAP view believe that general purpose financial statements of smaller companies often are unnecessarily costly because they include information that users really do not want. Proponents also feel that the cost of presenting all this information effectively precludes smaller companies from presenting information that is not required by GAAP but that users would find more useful. As a result, they feel that present accounting standards tend to discriminate against smaller businesses.[33]

The accounting profession has never defined precisely what constitutes a large or a small company. Accountants conveniently use the catchy term "big GAAP/little GAAP" to refer to the broad question of whether differential accounting principles should exist for different types of companies, whether based on size or ownership characteristics, or both.

The number and complexity of pronouncements issued by the APB and the FASB have increased the importance of the big GAAP/little GAAP issue. The FASB is very concerned about this issue and has taken steps to reduce the financial reporting burden of smaller companies. In April 1978, for example, the FASB declared that nonpublic enterprises no longer are required to report earnings per share and segment information. In the following year, the board made its inflation-accounting requirements applicable only to very large companies. The big GAAP/little GAAP controversy is likely to continue to influence the standard-setting process in the future. We discuss the big GAAP/little GAAP issue again in Chapter 25.

CONCLUDING REMARKS

Accounting seeks to identify, measure, and communicate information about economic entities that is intended to be useful in making economic decisions. Financial accounting is the branch of accounting that provides information about the financial position of a business enterprise and the changes that occur therein. Its primary focus is meeting the needs of external users such as stockholders and bankers. As you study the remaining chapters, you should continually question whether the accounting principles presented really aid the decision-making processes of external users.

General purpose financial statements constitute the main output of financial accounting. Accountants prepare these statements in accordance with generally accepted accounting principles, which are largely determined within the private sector of our economy. Because these principles constantly change, the study of accounting is a lifelong process.

In the following chapters, we examine the hows, whys, and so whats of intermediate accounting. The next chapter focuses on why and deals with the basic theory of general purpose financial statements.

---

[33]See "Report of the Committee on Generally Accepted Accounting Principles for Smaller and/or Closely Held Businesses," *Journal of Accountancy* (October 1976), pp. 116–120.

THE WORLD ACCORDING TO GAAP

NO ONE SAID it was easy for General Motors or IBM to remain always in compliance with the voluminous Generally Accepted Accounting Principles. But what the accounting profession is beginning to realize is that it's even rougher for small businessmen to live with GAAP. "When the FASB develops standards, they're probably developed with larger companies in mind," says Harvey Moskowitz, Seidman & Seidman's national director of accounting. "Sometimes the standards they develop are too costly and complicated for smaller businesses."

Stanley Scott, chairman of the American Institute of Certified Public Accountant's new Special Committee to Study Accounting Standards Overload, agrees. "There's a strong feeling that a lot of the standards emanating from the standards setters do not really have an applicability to small or privately held companies," he says.

Small businessmen also agree:

● Privately held Dierckx Equipment Corp. (annual sales: $25 million) does a lot of leasing as part of its equipment business. GAAP requires that those leases be capitalized, and that has placed Dierckx in the middle of a catch-22 with the banks. If it doesn't capitalize its leases, it's not in compliance with GAAP, and the bank may not like that. If it does capitalize leases, its leverage ratio looks a lot worse, and the banks may not like that. Not only does this GAAP requirement endanger Dierckx' credit rating, but the cost of complying with that *one* requirement is $7,500 annually. Says Financial Vice President Ray Romano: "It's just a paper entry. It's immaterial. But it adds a lot of bookkeeping time. Our auditors must spend at least three days just going through the lease transactions, and without that requirement that wouldn't be necessary."

●New Brunswick Scientific Co., Inc. (annual sales: $16 million) has two accountants and a small bookkeeping staff. Keeping up with the slew of GAAP requirements has become a significant time problem. Controller Steve Rothstein finds GAAP burdensome and costly. "It's impossible to keep up with it all," he says.

● AW Computer Systems, Inc. (annual sales: $3 million) has a staff of 22 people. Before it went public last year, an accountant used to come in once or twice a year and a bookkeeper handled the ledger. Now it spends $70,000 annually for public report-

ing. The annual report has 12 footnotes covering 7 full pages. Says Controller Brad Smith: "It's a terrible burden. There's an awful lot of disclosure and I'm not really too sure that it's all that informative to the readers of the statements. What's going on here?"

Now some accounting firms are exploring the possibility of creating a sort of "little GAAP" for small companies. That might disturb statement users like bankers and investors, but there need be no significant information loss if little GAAP were intelligently designed, the firms argue.

This may be easier said than done, however. Take the obvious task of defining "small," for instance. The logical source for such a definition, the FASB, doesn't have one. Inflation might make any dollar cutoff meaningless in a short time, it feels. A split between publicly held and privately owned companies wouldn't do the trick either. After all, some private companies are huge and some public ones are tiny.

Then there is the thorny question of which disclosure requirements to drop. Although most accounting firms agree that some disclosure requirements are too severe for small businesses, they differ widely as to which ones are painful enough to alter. When it comes to measurement principles—the rules for reporting that affect the bottom-line performance of a company—the disagreements are strong. Says Seidman's Moskowitz: "Only chaos could result from using different measurement principles for small and large companies, because users would be thoroughly confused. It would certainly raise credibility questions about the financial statements."

Proponents of alternate measurement standards for small companies claim that such confusion could be avoided if the alternative principles were sanctioned by the standards setters and limited to a well-defined group. "There are some of us in the profession that feel we should at least take a good look at whether we can develop alternative measurement principles," says Charles Chazen, a partner at Laventhol & Horwath. "Not all clients are quite the size of GM."

Certainly for clients smaller than GM, many principles seem nearly useless. Take, for example, FASB Statement 13, Accounting for Leases, issued in 1976. Capitalizing a lease changes the net income of a company, but to small companies with few leased items that don't normally need the accounting manpower to do the test procedure, FASB 13 is an unnecessary complication. Says New Brunswick Scientific Controller Rothstein: "Things like lease capitalization are impossible for a small firm to administer with a small staff. It's putting a tremendous strain on us just to keep current with the regulations."

"On one hand, if I leave his figures in and take exception to GAAP in a footnote, he gets all upset and says, 'What do you mean I'm not reporting correctly?'" says Terry Most, a partner at Most & Horowitz, a small Madison Avenue firm whose largest client has annual sales of $15 million. "But if I make all the changes, he won't even recognize his own numbers. I'd have to spend a few hours explaining and a few hours to do all the new calculations. We might have just doubled his accounting fee."

That doesn't sit well with the small-business owner who only uses his statements as part of the formality to get a loan from the bank. The bank doesn't necessarily care to see GAAP statements—in many cases, it would be satisfied with a representative alternative—but pressure within the industry and GAAP's "golden rule" reputation can make the bank balk when it's not applied.

Some other FASB statements that often come into question include compensated absences and capitalization of interest costs which many practitioners feel are accounted for generally anyway. Says Most: "An expense is an expense and I accrue it. But if you go to a small businessman and tell him that his bookkeeper has to track compensated absences, he says, 'the hell with you.'"

What's more, there have been many complaints that auditing procedures as a whole have also been designed for larger companies that have a fairly extensive segregation of accounting duties. The AICPA is aware of the problem and is looking at ways to fix it. Says Dan Guy, director of auditing research: "You can't apply a large-client audit approach in a small-business setting. It doesn't work." Still, that large-client approach *is* applied in many cases—whether it works well or not.

Although these difficulties have been an issue for several years, until now the AICPA and FASB have been addressing them at a glacial pace. Finally, last year, the AICPA offered two categories of membership, one for public company practitioners and one for private ones. A step. The FASB also admitted that it just isn't necessary for private companies to report earnings per share. Another step. And supplemental current value accounting is only required for the top 1,500 or so public companies. Progress.

"We're trying to understand the problems and their underlying causes better," says Glen Hildebrand, the FASB's assistant director of research and technical activities, "but we've reached no conclusions." Clearly, the AICPA and FASB are going to have to reach some conclusions soon. Says Laventhol & Horwath partner Edward O'Grady: "It would be unrealistic for both of those bodies to ignore it. It's going to happen because it's got to."

SOURCE: Jay Gissen, "The World According to GAAP," *Forbes,* June 8, 1981, pp. 148–149. Reprinted by permission of *Forbes* Magazine, © Forbes Inc., 1981.

KEY POINTS

1. Accounting seeks to identify, measure, and communicate information about economic entities that is intended to be useful in making economic decisions.

2. Financial accounting is the branch of accounting that is concerned with measuring and reporting the financial position of a business enterprise and the changes that occur in financial position. Financial accounting information is designed primarily to meet the needs of external users.

3. External users of financial statements include present and potential owners, lenders, suppliers, employees, and customers, in addition to financial analysts, stock exchanges, regulatory agencies, and the general public.

4. Investors and creditors use financial statements to make predictions, assess risk, and evaluate profitability, solvency, and management's performance.

5. The basic financial statements are the balance sheet, income statement, statement of changes in financial position, and statement of retained earnings or statement of stockholders' equity.

6. The management of an entity has the primary responsibility for preparing its financial statements. Managers in turn hire internal accountants to collect

data and prepare the statements.

7. Public (external) accountants examine financial statements and express an opinion about whether the statements have been prepared in accordance with generally accepted accounting principles.

8. Auditors must be competent and independent from the companies they audit.

9. Generally accepted accounting principles are those principles that have substantial authoritative support.

10. The organizations that have had the most influence in developing generally accepted accounting principles are the Committee on Accounting Procedure, the Accounting Principles Board, the Financial Accounting Standards Board, and the Securities and Exchange Commission.

11. Certain other organizations and the income tax law have also affected the development of generally accepted accounting principles.

12. Experience, reason, custom, usage, and practical necessity are important factors in developing generally accepted accounting principles.

13. FASB Statements of Financial Accounting Standards and Interpretations, APB Opinions, and Accounting Research Bulletins are the most authoritative sources of generally accepted accounting principles.

14. Several important issues are likely to affect the development of generally accepted accounting principles. These include the outcome of the FASB's Conceptual Framework Project, the economic impact issue, the public versus private sector issue, the uniformity versus flexibility issue, the market efficiency issue, and the big GAAP/little GAAP issue.

QUESTIONS

1-1 Distinguish between internal and external users of accounting information.

1-2 What is financial accounting?

1-3 What is meant by the term "general purpose financial statements"? Why does the accounting profession emphasize general purpose statements instead of single purpose statements?

1-4 Give three examples of accounting applications that illustrate the following point: "Financial statements are not usually as precise as they appear to be."

1-5 Identify five sources that investors and creditors commonly use to obtain information about specific companies.

1-6 Distinguish between financial statements and financial reporting.

1-7 Briefly explain the role of corporate management in the financial reporting process.

1-8 Briefly explain the professional designations of CMA and CPA.

1-9 What is an audit?

1-10 The following terms relate to audit reports. Briefly explain each one.
   [a] Unqualified opinion
   [b] Qualified opinion
   [c] Adverse opinion
   [d] Disclaimer of opinion

1-11 What is meant by the term "generally accepted accounting principles"?

1-12 Distinguish among the following types of pronouncements:
   [a] Accounting Research Bulletins
   [b] APB Opinions
   [c] Statements of Financial Accounting Standards
   [d] Statements of Financial Accounting Concepts
   [e] FASB Interpretations

1-13 Briefly explain *Rule 203* of the AICPA Code of Professional Ethics. What is the significance of this rule?

1-14 What are the major differences between the FASB and its predecessor standard-setting bodies (the CAP and APB)?

1-15 What major steps does the FASB usually follow when formulating a Statement of Financial Accounting Standards?

1-16 Briefly explain the Securities Act of 1933 and the Securities Exchange Act of 1934.

1-17 What is the SEC's fundamental purpose?

1-18 What is the SEC's role in establishing accounting standards?

1-19 Why do the principles of income tax law often differ from those of financial accounting?

1-20 Of what significance are financial analysts and commercial bank loan officers to the accounting profession?

1-21 What are the major sources of GAAP?

1-22 What is the FASB's Conceptual Framework Project?

1-23 Briefly explain how accounting principles affect the manner in which our society allocates its scarce resources.

1-24 Briefly explain the uniformity versus flexibility debate in financial accounting.

1-25 Do generally accepted accounting principles apply only to larger companies? Explain.

CASES

C1-1 Financial statements are an important means of communicating economic information to interested parties. Over the years financial statements have received the attention of the accounting profession, the business community, the government, and the general public at various times and in various degrees.

Instructions

[a] Discuss the responsibilities of management for the entity's financial statements.

[b] Does management prepare financial statements in order to reflect past performance of the business entity or to help predict its future performance? Discuss briefly.

[c] Briefly describe how financial statements can be used by investors in making investment decisions.

(CMA adapted)

C1-2 At the completion of the Darby Department Store audit, the president asks about the meaning of the phrase "in conformity with generally accepted accounting principles" that appears in your audit report on the management's financial statements. He observes that the meaning of the phrase must include more than what he thinks of as "principles."

Instructions

[a] Explain the meaning of the term "accounting principles" as used in the audit report. (Do *not* discuss in this part the significance of "generally accepted.")

[b] The president wants to know how you determine whether or not an accounting principle is generally accepted. Discuss the sources of evidence for determining whether an accounting principle has substantial authoritative support.

[c] The president believes that diversity in accounting practice always will exist among independent entities despite continual improvements in comparability. Develop arguments that *support* his belief.

(AICPA adapted)

C1-3 Some accountants have said that the development and acceptance of generally accepted accounting principles (i.e., standard setting) is being politicized. Some use the term "politicization" in a narrow sense to mean influence by governmental agencies, particularly the SEC, on the development of generally accepted accounting principles. Others use the term more broadly to mean the compromising that takes place in bodies responsible for developing generally accepted accounting principles because of the influence and pressure of interested groups (e.g., SEC, AAA, NAA, businesses through their various organizations, financial analysts, bankers, and lawyers).

Instructions

[a] The CAP of the AICPA was established in the middle to late 1930s and functioned until 1959, when it was replaced by the APB. In 1973 the FASB was formed and the APB dissolved. Explain how these groups were formed, their methods of operation, and the reasons for the demise of the CAP and the APB. Indicate whether these events show increasing politicization (in the broad sense) of accounting standard setting. Cite specific developments to support your answer.

[b] What arguments can be raised to support the "politicization" of accounting standard setting?

[c] What arguments can be raised against the "politicization" of accounting standard setting?

(CMA adapted)

C1-4 The development of accounting theory and practice has been influenced directly and indirectly by many organizations and institutions. Two of the most important are the FASB and the SEC.

Instructions

[a] What official role does the SEC have in the development of financial accounting theory and practice?

[b] What is the relationship between the FASB and SEC with respect to the development and establishment of financial accounting theory and practices?

(CMA adapted)

C1-5 An AICPA news release dated July 20, 1972, states that the FASB "will become the established authority for setting accounting principles under which corporations report to the shareholders and others."

Instructions

[a] No mention is made of the SEC in the press release. What role does the SEC play in setting accounting principles?

[b] Describe the process used by the FASB to arrive at its decisions concerning SFASs.

(CMA adapted)

C1–6 One of your friends is a law school student who recently decided to take an introductory course in financial accounting. After his first day of class, he tells you: "I'm having some trouble understanding what financial accounting is all about. In law school, I learned how to calculate income according to tax laws. Why aren't the tax laws used to calculate income in financial accounting?"

Instructions

[a] Answer your friend's question.

[b] Discuss the significance of income tax law in the development of generally accepted accounting principles.

C1–7 In 1975 the FASB issued *SFAS No. 7,* "Accounting and Reporting by Development Stage Enterprises." This pronouncement states that "an enterprise shall be considered to be in the development stage if it is devoting substantially all of its efforts to establishing a new business and either of the following conditions exists:

[a] Planned principal operations have not commenced.

[b] Planned principal operations have commenced but there has been no significant revenue therefrom" (par. 8).

In essence *SFAS No. 7* concluded that development-stage companies must use the same accounting principles as established companies. But when the Exposure Draft that preceded *SFAS No. 7* was issued, "some respondents to the Exposure Draft expressed concern that requiring development stage enterprises to present the same basic financial statements and to apply the same generally accepted accounting princi-

ples as established operating enterprises might make it difficult, if not impossible, for development stage enterprises to obtain capital" (par. 48).

Instructions

Identify and explain the broad issue that underlies the concern expressed by the respondents to the Exposure Draft that preceded *SFAS No. 7.*

C1–8 At an open meeting in July 1981, it was stated that the SEC "intends to apply the efficient market theory . . . to public offerings by widely-followed companies to take advantage of periodic reports filed under the Securities Exchange Act prior to a new registration statement." (From "The Week in Review," Deloitte Haskins & Sells, July 31, 1981, p. 1.)

Instructions

[a] What is an efficient market?

[b] Briefly indicate how you think the SEC could apply the efficient market theory "to take advantage of periodic reports filed under the Securities Exchange Act prior to a new registration statement."

C1–9 In an open letter to the FASB, Alexander Grant & Company, a large, international CPA firm, stated "we are genuinely concerned that you are not reacting to a serious problem. A recent exchange of correspondence between the AICPA and the FASB makes it clear to us that the present FASB does not intend to consider relief from onerous accounting and disclosure requirements for the thousands of smaller and/or closely-held businesses across this country" (*Wall Street Journal,* October 25, 1977, p. 24).

Instructions

[a] Take the position that the accounting profession should have one set of generally accepted accounting principles that apply to all companies, regardless of size or ownership characteristics. Develop arguments that support your position.

[b] Take the position that the accounting profession should have one set of generally accepted accounting principles for larger and/or publicly held companies and a somewhat different set for smaller and/or closely held companies. Develop arguments that support your position.

2

FINANCIAL ACCOUNTING THEORY

Objective

To describe financial accounting theory as currently applied. The theory consists of:

1. Objectives
2. Qualitative characteristics
3. Assumptions
4. Concepts and elements
5. Broad principles
6. Detailed principles
7. Modifying conventions

One author defines accounting theory as "logical reasoning in the form of a set of broad principles that (1) provide a general frame of reference by which accounting practice can be evaluated and (2) guide the development of new practices and procedures."[1] This chapter provides an overview of descriptive financial accounting theory as it pertains to general-purpose external reporting by business enterprises. Note carefully the following words in the preceding sentence:

1. **Overview.** In this chapter we introduce the most important components of financial accounting theory. Entire textbooks have been devoted to explaining these and other components in more depth.
2. **Descriptive.** Descriptive theory seeks to describe theory as it is currently applied. In contrast, normative theory attempts to prescribe how theory ought to be. This chapter is primarily descriptive.
3. **Financial accounting theory.** We present a logical framework that helps to explain why financial accounting is applied the way it is today.
4. **General-purpose external reporting.** The chapter focuses on a theoretical structure for general-purpose (rather than single or limited purpose), external (rather than internal) reporting.

A knowledge of accounting theory should help you to understand and apply generally accepted accounting principles (GAAP) as well as changes in those principles. Because accounting problems often appear to be routine, accountants sometimes bog down in the mechanics of problem solving and lose sight of the theory they seek to apply. For this reason, you should study this chapter carefully. Later, as you study other chapters, reread the appropriate sections of this chapter. Always strive for a conceptual understanding of the solutions to accounting problems. Sound conceptual understanding can help you to solve most accounting problems, whether you encounter them in a textbook, on an examination, or in the business world.

---

[1] Eldon S. Hendricksen, *Accounting Theory,* 3rd ed. (Homewood, Ill.: Irwin, 1977), p. 1.

CONDITIONS NECESSARY FOR DEVELOPING A CONCEPTUAL FRAMEWORK

I WISH TO DESCRIBE, at least partially, three conditions that I think are necessary for the FASB to develop a useful conceptual framework for financial accounting and reporting. The first condition relates to the concepts themselves. The others relate to the environment in which the conceptual framework is being developed.

Concepts rooted in the real world

Concepts, to be useful, must involve limits, and the first condition for a useful conceptual framework is probably the most fundamental limit needed by concepts that are to underlie financial statements: The concepts themselves must be rooted in the real world. That condition flows from the utilitarian and representational nature of financial accounting and financial statements. Just as lines of various shapes and sizes in a road map represent different kinds of

highways and roads, rivers and political boundaries, so also various descriptions and amounts in financial statements represent cash in bank, buildings, wages due, sales, use of labor, earthquake damage to property and a host of other things owned or owed by particular business enterprises as well as events and circumstances that affect them or their values. The items in financial statements are quantitative representations of economic things and events in the real world relating to and affecting actual business enterprises.

The usefulness of quantitative representations lies in the accuracy of their representation—in their essential agreement with the things or events represented. Representations in financial statements are intended to be utilitarian. They are supposed to be useful in the same way that the lines in a road map help a traveler reach a destination. Utilitarian representations contrast with aesthetic representations, which do not necessarily require accuracy. An artist may change the number or location of eyes, ears, arms, legs and the like and may use colors in any way desired—for example, green nose or purple hair—and still describe a painting as representing a person. . . . However, a cartographer cannot add roads and bridges where none exist, or remove some that do exist, to enhance the aesthetic impact of a map without spoiling the uefulness of the representation. It may then be nice artwork, but it is no longer a road map. Similarly, accountants cannot add imaginary things and events to financial statements, or remove things and events that do exist, without spoling the usefulness of the representation.

Changing attitudes: time and patience
The habits and modes of thought that I have described have developed over many years, and I have no illusions that they will be changed easily or quickly. That brings me to the next condition for a successful conceptual framework: We need to change some attitudes and modes of thought, and that will take a long time and require a lot of patience. . . .

All of us resist change. It takes time to get used to new ideas or procedures. Moreover, our society has created institutional factors that put tremendous pressure on people to show certain kinds of results, including certain kinds of accounting results. Thus, I do not find it surprising that folks—including management, accountants and even financial analysts—are prone to defend the status quo, which they find known and comfortable, and resist change, which they find uncertain and unsettling.

The preceding paragraph is meant as a preface to some observations about the inevitability of change, the inevitability of resistance to change and the contribution of a conceptual framework. First, I think the handwriting is already on the wall for the present model (which is often mislabeled "historical cost accounting") because, among other things, it can't cope with everyday complications, such as changing prices and fluctuating foreign exchange rates. Those kinds of problems magnify the faults of the existing model's particular mixture of historical costs, current costs, current exit values, net realizable values and present values in a way that all can see them, although our propensity to defend the status quo leads us to seek explanations for those faults other than in the existing model and to seek solutions that patch it up.

The board and the concepts
The last condition of a conceptual framework that I wish to mention is that the board and its staff must take the concepts seriously if they expect others to do so. It goes without saying that the board and its staff must use the concepts and be seen to use them. The board's example of how to use the concepts will do more to enhance their stature and make them operational than any number of admonitions.

Even more significant, perhaps, is that the board's example not abuse the concepts. Nothing will undercut the concepts quicker and more fatally than for the board to change them merely because they result in unpopular answers. I do not mean that concepts should not be changed, but if they are to mean anything, they should be changed only for causes such as changing environmental conditions and discoveries of errors in reasoning, not merely because they produce answers we don't like.

SOURCE: Reed K. Storey, "Conditions Necessary for Developing a Conceptual Framework," *Journal of Accountancy,* June 1981, pp. 84, 86, 88, 90, 92–94, and 95. Copyright © 1981 by the American Institute of Certified Public Accountants, Inc.

The accounting profession today does not have a single, comprehensive, generally accepted framework of accounting theory. As we pointed out in Chapter 1, however, the Financial Accounting Standards Board (FASB) currently is developing a conceptual framework that it hopes will be eventually accepted in the financial community. Recognize, therefore, that accounting is a relatively young and dynamic discipline for which a theoretical structure is still being developed. The theoretical framework presented in this chapter is based on several sources and represents descriptive financial accounting theory today.[2]

[2]The framework that we present draws heavily from the works published to date by the FASB in its Conceptual Framework Project and from *APB Statement No. 4,* "Basic Concepts and Accounting Principles Underlying Financial Statements of Business Enterprises," 1970.

EXHIBIT 2–1
Financial Accounting Theory: A Model

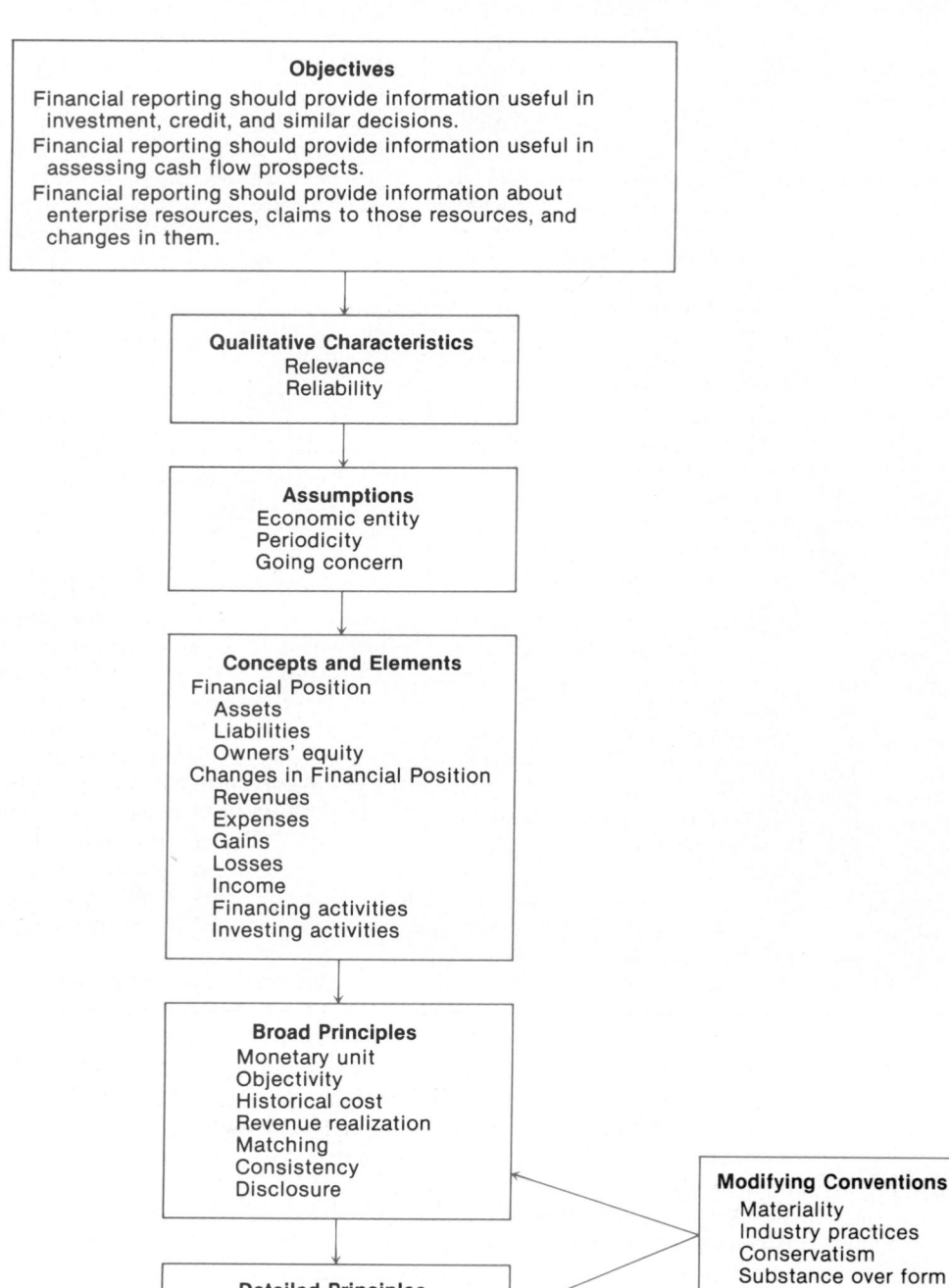

A MODEL

Exhibit 2–1 presents the theoretical components discussed in this chapter. These components are **objectives, qualitative characteristics, assumptions, concepts and elements, broad principles, detailed principles,** and **modifying conventions.**[3] In general, a move from the top to the bottom of the exhibit represents a move from the general to the specific. While objectives are very general, detailed principles are quite specific. Accountants traditionally have had less difficulty agreeing on the more general components of the model than on the more specific ones. Most accountants agree, for example, that an important accounting objective should be to provide useful information. On the other hand, less agreement is likely about which principles the accounting profession should adopt to achieve the objective of providing useful information.

When studying the model of financial accounting theory, remember that the components are not all independent of one another. Many important **interrelationships** exist that are too complex to identify meaningfully in one model. Furthermore, it is important to understand that accounting principles have not always developed on the basis of explicit objectives. As we pointed out in Chapter 1, generally accepted accounting principles "have developed on the basis of experience, reason, custom, usage, and, to a significant extent, practical necessity."[4] For this reason some accountants think that certain principles are inconsistent with certain objectives. These components may therefore change as a result of further development of the FASB's conceptual framework. Despite these limitations of the model, we believe that it provides a useful framework in which to study financial accounting.

OBJECTIVES OF FINANCIAL REPORTING

Before 1970 there was no general agreement among accountants concerning the objectives of financial accounting. Some accountants, for example, believed that the primary objective of financial accounting was to report on management's stewardship (i.e., what management did with the resources entrusted to them), while others maintained that the main objective was to communicate useful information. During the 1970s the accounting profession spent considerable time and effort developing a set of objectives for financial accounting. In 1973 the American Institute of Certified Public Accountants (AICPA) published a major study called "Objectives of Financial Statements." This study, commonly called the *Trueblood Report,* set forth several objectives but concluded that "the basic objective of financial statements is to provide information useful for making economic decisions."[5] In 1978 the FASB issued *Statement of Financial Accounting Concepts No. 1,* entitled "Objectives of Financial Reporting by Business Enterprises."[6] This FASB pronouncement was greatly influenced by the *Trueblood Report.*

The objectives outlined in *SFAC No. 1* stem largely from the important needs of external users, who lack the authority to require the information that they want about a given enterprise. Furthermore, the objectives are affected by the economic, legal, political, and social environment in the United States, and as a result, they may change over time. Finally, the objectives are affected by the characteristics and limitations of the information that financial reporting traditionally has provided.

---

[3]The labels attached to certain components of the model vary somewhat in practice. Principles, for example, are sometimes called standards, concepts, procedures, rules, and practices.

[4]*APB Statement No. 4,* par. 139.

[5]*Report of the Study Group on the Objectives of Financial Statements,*"Objectives of Financial Statements" (New York: AICPA, 1973), p. 61.

[6]*FASB Statement of Financial Accounting Concepts No. 1,* "Objectives of Financial Reporting by Business Enterprises," 1978.

SFAC No. 1 has identified three major objectives of financial reporting, which includes financial statements. These objectives are summarized in Exhibit 2–1 and discussed below. Note that the first objective is the most general, while the next two are progressively narrower in scope.

Objectives

Financial reporting should provide information useful in investment, credit, and similar decisions.

Financial reporting should provide information useful in assessing cash flow prospects.

Financial reporting should provide information about enterprise resources, claims to those resources, and changes in them.

Useful Information

The initial objective states that "financial reporting should provide information that is useful to present and potential investors and creditors and other users in making rational investment, credit, and similar decisions. The information should be comprehensible to those who have a reasonable understanding of business and economic activities and are willing to study the information with reasonable diligence."[7] This objective underscores the fact that financial reporting is not an end in itself. Instead, the *output* of the financial accounting process should serve as useful *input* for the making of rational investment, credit, and similar decisions in our society.

Traditionally, anyone proposing usefulness as an accounting objective has had to respond to the important questions, useful to whom? And for what purpose? In stating its initial objective, the FASB's responses to these questions were quite broad. As a result, the scope of financial reporting is not confined to one, or even a few, user groups. Instead, financial reporting attempts to serve many diverse users. These users, however, are expected to have a reasonable understanding of business affairs and be willing to spend reasonable amounts of time and effort analyzing accounting information. Accountants should always try to produce reports that are understandable to these kinds of users. Naive users of accounting information should consider taking steps to improve their understanding of business matters. Alternatively, they should rely on professional advisors.

Cash Flow Prospects

Rational investment, credit, and similar decisions are made after careful consideration of such factors as expected cost, risk, and return. As we pointed out in Chapter 1, investors and creditors invest and lend cash, and they want to know how much cash they will receive in return and when they will receive it. Information that helps to resolve these uncertainties is surely regarded as useful.

Accordingly, the second objective is that "financial reporting should provide information to help present and potential investors and creditors and other users in assessing the amounts, timing, and uncertainty of prospective cash receipts from dividends or interest and the proceeds from the sale, redemption, or maturity of securities or loans. Since investors' and creditors' cash flows are related to enterprise cash flows, financial reporting should provide information to help investors, creditors, and others assess the amounts, timing, and

---

[7]*FASB Statement of Financial Accounting Concepts No. 1,* p. viii.

uncertainty of prospective net cash inflows to the related enterprise."[8] Note that this objective differentiates between cash flows to investors and creditors and cash flows to a given enterprise to which they have committed funds. Naturally, investors and creditors want to assess their own chances of receiving cash via dividends, interest, and otherwise. These chances, however, depend on the expected cash flows to the enterprise. If the enterprise is successful in generating favorable cash flows, the probability of investors and creditors receiving favorable cash flows is increased.

Enterprise Resources, Claims, and Changes

What information is helpful to investors, creditors, and other users in assessing prospective cash receipts from a business enterprise? *SFAC No. 1* responds to this question with the third major objective of financial reporting. This objective holds that "financial reporting should provide information about the economic resources of an enterprise, the claims to those resources (obligations of the enterprise to transfer resources to other entities and owners' equity), and the effects of transactions, events, and circumstances that change its resources and claims to those resources."[9]

Some of the most significant transactions and events that change a firm's resources and the claims to those resources are used to measure financial performance. The FASB stated that "the primary focus of financial reporting is information about an enterprise's performance provided by measures of earnings and its components."[10] Thus, investors and creditors may use past measures of earnings to help predict future earnings and, indirectly, to help predict their chances of receiving cash from a given enterprise.

The FASB believes that applying **accrual accounting** results in performance measures that are better than those of cash basis accounting. However, the board has emphasized that "accrual accounting provides measures of earnings rather than evaluations of management's performance, estimates of 'earning power,' predictions of earnings, assessments of risk, or confirmations or rejections of predictions or assessments. Investors, creditors, and other users of the information do their own evaluating, estimating, predicting, assessing, confirming, or rejecting."[11] Thus, accountants provide useful historical measurements, but they cannot accurately predict the future and they surely do not make decisions for external information users.

While the primary focus of financial reporting is earnings, information about financial position as well as significant changes in financial position (besides earnings) is important when assessing an enterprise's cash flow prospects. Moreover, since management knows more about a firm than do outsiders, the usefulness of information often can be enhanced by management's explanation of the financial impact of certain transactions, events, and circumstances.

QUALITATIVE CHARACTERISTICS OF ACCOUNTING INFORMATION

Given that the basic objective of external financial reporting is to provide information that is useful to people making rational economic decisions, a logical question is: What qualitative characteristics determine the usefulness of accounting information? Many studies have addressed this issue and have generally produced similar results.

The FASB believes that **relevance** and **reliability** are the two most fundamental quali-

---

[8]*FASB Statement of Financial Accounting Concepts No. 1,* p. viii.
[9]*FASB Statement of Financial Accounting Concepts No. 1,* p. viii.
[10]*FASB Statement of Financial Accounting Concepts No. 1,* par. 43.
[11]*FASB Statement of Financial Accounting Concepts No. 1,* par. 48.

Qualitative Characteristics
Relevance
Reliability

tative characteristics of useful accounting information.[12] Relevance means "the capacity of information to make a difference in a decision by helping users to form predictions about the outcome of past, present, and future events or to confirm or correct prior expectations."[13] For example, when stockholders decide to buy, sell, or hold equity investments, earnings-per-share information is generally regarded as highly relevant. In contrast, the serial numbers of plant assets, although highly reliable, are irrelevant to the decisions made by financial statement users.

The major characteristics of relevant information are the following:[14]

1. **Predictive value.**   Information has predictive value when it can help users to increase the likelihood of correctly forecasting the outcome of events. For example, if the accounting measure "cash provided by operations" proves valuable in predicting loan default, it is said to have predictive value.
2. **Feedback value.**   Information has feedback value when it enables users to confirm or correct expectations. A net income measure, for example, has feedback value if it can help stockholders to confirm or revise their expectations about a company's ability to generate earnings.
3. **Timeliness.**   Information is timely when it is available to a decision maker before decisions are made. For example, one of the most important attributes of quarterly financial information is its timeliness.

To be relevant, information must have predictive value *or* feedback value or both, and it must be timely.

Reliability is "the quality of information that assures that information is reasonably free from error and bias and faithfully represents what it purports to represent."[15] In other words, users can trust that reliable measurements will accurately represent the reality that the measurements claim to represent. For example, most people consider the amount of cash that a company has in its bank account to be highly reliable information. However, information about a company's projected earnings per share fifty years from now is not usually regarded as reliable.

Reliable information has three major characteristics:[16]

1. **Verifiability.**   Information is considered verifiable when, through consensus among accountants, it represents what it purports to represent or the method of measurement has been used without error or bias. The amount of a company's cash on hand, for example, usually is highly verifiable because accountants can simply count it.
2. **Neutrality.**   Information is neutral when it is free of bias toward a desired result or behavior. Accounting information would not be neutral, for example, if it systematically produced results that favored one group of users, such as bankers, over another such as labor organizations.
3. **Representational faithfulness.**   Information is representationally faithful when a measure

---

[12]*FASB Statement of Financial Accounting Concepts No. 2,* "Qualitative Characteristics of Accounting Information," 1980, p. x.
[13]*FASB Statement of Financial Accounting Concepts No. 2,* p. xvi.
[14]*FASB Statement of Financial Accounting Concepts No. 2,* pp. xv–xvi.
[15]*FASB Statement of Financial Accounting Concepts No. 2,* p. xvi.
[16]*FASB Statement of Financial Accounting Concepts No. 2,* p. xvi.

or description agrees with the phenomenon that it purports to represent. A measure of a company's accounts receivable, for example, would have a low degree of representational faithfulness if it included a material amount of accounts that are uncollectible.

To be reliable, information must have all three characteristics described above.

Many accountants have argued that relevance and reliability may require important trade-offs. That is, to increase the relevance of accounting information, accountants may have to sacrifice some reliability, and vice versa. For example, generally accepted accounting principles call for reporting plant assets in the balance sheet using the historical cost principle. It is possible, however, that the current cost of plant assets is a more relevant, yet less reliable, measure than the historical cost of these assets. If so, the question then becomes: Which measure of plant assets, historical cost or current cost, results in information that is most useful? One of the great challenges of the accounting profession is to achieve an optimal balance between relevance and reliability to ensure that accounting information will be as useful as possible. As one might expect, arriving at this balance requires considerable research and is likely to generate many interesting debates in the financial community.

Even when information is both relevant and reliable, and therefore useful, it should not always be reported. Useful information is worth reporting only when **the benefits to be derived from the information exceed the costs associated with it.** Thus, the overriding criterion by which all accounting choices (such as the choice between historical cost and current cost) must be judged is that "the better choice is the one that, subject to considerations of cost, produces from among the available alternatives information that is most useful for decision making."[17] Evaluating the benefits and costs of information is very subjective and requires considerable judgment.

ASSUMPTIONS

To provide information that is both relevant and reliable, and therefore useful, accountants begin by making certain **assumptions.** These assumptions, often called **postulates,** generally relate to things that are taken for granted. By starting with basic assumptions, other components in the theoretical framework may be logically derived.

Economic Entity Assumption

Applying the principles of accounting requires the identification of specific units of economic activity. Each unit serves as a focal point to guide the accountant's recording and reporting functions. Accordingly, accountants make the **economic entity assumption,** which says that **economic activities can be meaningfully associated with specific entities or units of accountability.** Typical examples of an economic entity are a person (such as a candidate for public office), a sole proprietorship, a partnership, and a corporation. The entity assumed may be somewhat narrow in scope, such as a division of a diversified company, or quite broad, as when consolidated financial statements are prepared for a

Assumptions
Economic entity
Periodicity
Going concern

---

[17]*FASB Statement of Financial Accounting Concepts No. 2,* p. ix.

group of corporations having common ownership. In any case, the name of the entity should appear at the top of the financial statements.

The economic entity assumption requires a careful separation of the financial affairs of a business (the entity) from the affairs of its owners and other businesses. For example, when a building contractor purchases lumber for an addition to his personal residence, this cost should not be included in the financial affairs of his building company.

Accountants sometimes ignore certain legal considerations when complying with the economic entity assumption. For example, the accounting records of a partnership must be kept separate and distinct from the records of the individual partners, even though the partners may be personally liable for partnership debts if liquidation occurs. Similarly, although a parent corporation and one or more subsidiaries constitute separate *legal* entities, accountants often prepare consolidated financial reports depicting the companies as a single *economic* entity.

Periodicity Assumption

The most reliable method of calculating a new firm's income is to wait until the firm is finally liquidated. At that time, lifetime income can be measured as the amount of resources paid by the firm to the owners over the amount paid in by the owners. Of course, measuring income only when a firm is terminated is not a practical way of satisfying the needs of financial statement users. Indeed, for information to be relevant and thereby have an impact on important decisions, it must be disseminated in a timely manner.

The need for timely dissemination of information has led accountants to make **the periodicity assumption: the economic activities of a firm can be meaningfully related to arbitrary time periods that are shorter than the firm's life.** In practice, annual, quarterly, and monthly time periods are commonly used. An annual period may be a calendar year, ending December 31, or a fiscal year, the end of which often coincides with the lowest point in a firm's business activities.

It is important to understand that the economic activities of a typical business are complex and continuous. When a manufacturing firm buys a new machine, for example, the machine will likely last for several accounting periods. During these periods the machine will be used—with raw materials, labor, and other machines—to produce a product that may be sold at some future date for a price that is now uncertain. Given this interaction and uncertainty, no one can precisely determine the benefits of the machine to the firm. Therefore, depreciation expense under accrual accounting cannot be precisely determined for a period shorter than the life of the machine. As this example shows, financial reporting for any brief period requires estimates and professional judgment. As a result, the accountant's measurements are often tentative. In general, as the time period becomes shorter, it becomes increasingly difficult to make meaningful estimates, and the reliability of accounting information is reduced.

Going-Concern (Continuity) Assumption

The **going-concern assumption** holds that **in the absence of evidence to the contrary, accountants assume that entity operations will continue for a reasonable period of time; that is, the entity will not be liquidated in the near future.** There is no assumption that the entity will exist permanently but simply that it will last at least long enough to fulfill its plans and commitments. This assumption is supported by the fact that most businesses expect to operate for extended periods of time. This expectation is fostered by our relatively stable economic, political, and social environment, in which laws and customs afford certain rights and protections.

The going-concern assumption helps to provide a rationale for several important aspects of accounting. It permits assets to be defined as probable future economic benefits to a firm. Moreover, it supports the historical cost system of measurement, which is based on the premise that historical accounting infomation can be used to help predict interesting events. If, for example, the firm were expected to liquidate in the immediate future, assets would be better stated at their net realizable values. The going-concern assumption also supports such interperiod allocation procedures as depreciation, amortization, and interperiod tax allocation. It would not make sense, for example, to depreciate a new machine over ten years if the company that owned it was expected to fold next year. Finally, the going-concern assumption serves as a basis for conventional balance sheet classification. Why list certain liabilities as long term, for example, if the firm is expected to go out of business within six months?

The accountant should periodically reevaluate the logic of assuming a going concern for any given enterprise. Perhaps management would like to liquidate in the near future, or perhaps a long period of substantial losses will soon result in a forced liquidation. When evidence indicates that liquidation is imminent, the going-concern assumption should be abandoned in favor of the quitting-concern (i.e., liquidation) assumption, under which assets should be measured at their net realizable values and the priority rights of creditors should be reported. Accounting for companies under the quitting-concern assumption is covered in advanced accounting courses.

CONCEPTS AND ELEMENTS

The economic entity, periodicity, and going-concern assumptions support certain basic **concepts** and **elements.** The concepts are financial position and changes in financial position. The elements that compose financial position are assets, liabilities, and owners' equity; these elements appear on an entity's balance sheet. The major elements that explain the changes in an entity's financial position are revenues, expenses, gains, losses, income, financ-

---

Concepts and Elements
Financial Position
    Assets
    Liabilities
    Owners' equity
Changes in Financial Position
    Revenues
    Expenses
    Gains
    Losses
    Income
    Financing activities
    Investing activities

---

ing activities, and investing activities. Revenues, expenses, gains, losses, and income appear on an entity's income statement, while financing and investing activities are summarized on its statement of changes in financial position. The relationship of concepts and elements is illustrated in Exhibit 2–2.

Financial Position

The **financial position** of an entity is determined by its economic resources and the claims against those resources **at a particular point in time.**[18] Financial position primarily consists of:

---

[18]The definitions of assets, liabilities, owners' equity, revenues, expenses, gains, and losses are based on *FASB Statement of Financial Accounting Concepts No. 3,* "Elements of Financial Statements of Business Enterprises," 1980.

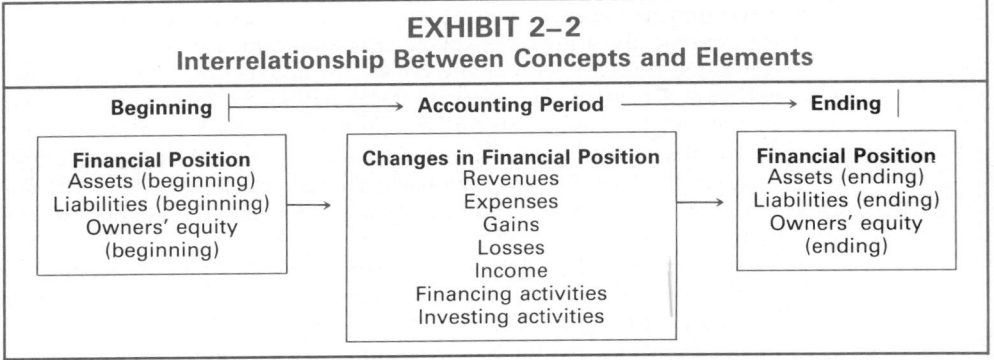

EXHIBIT 2–2
Interrelationship Between Concepts and Elements

1. **Assets,** or the probable future economic benefits obtained or controlled by an entity as a result of past transactions or events. Examples are cash, merchandise inventory, and land.
2. **Liabilities,** or the probable future sacrifices of economic benefits arising from present obligations of an entity to transfer assets or provide services to other entities in the future as a result of past transactions or events. Examples are accounts payable, bonds payable, and unearned revenues.
3. **Owners' equity,** which is the residual interest in the assets of an entity that remains after deducting its liabilities. Examples of owners' equity are common stock, paid-in capital in excess of par value, and retained earnings.

Changes in Financial Position

Changes in financial position are the result of certain events that occur **during a period of time.** The key elements that account for changes in financial position are:

1. **Revenues,** that is, inflows or other enhancements of assets of an entity or settlements of its liabilities (or both) during a period, based on production and delivery of goods, provision of services, and other activities that constitute the entity's major operations. Examples are sales revenue, interest revenue, and rent revenue.
2. **Expenses,** which include outflows or other use of assets or incurrences of liabilities (or both) during a period as a result of delivering or producing goods, rendering services, or carrying out other activities that constitute the entity's major operations. Examples are cost of goods sold, salaries expense, and advertising expense.
3. **Gains,** or increases in owners' equity (net assets) from peripheral or incidental transactions of an entity and from all other transactions and events affecting the entity during a period, except those that result from revenues or investments by owners. Examples are a gain on the sale of plant assets and a gain on the early retirement of long-term debt.
4. **Losses,** or decreases in owners' equity (net assets) from peripheral or incidental transactions of an entity and from all other transactions and events affecting the entity during a period, except those that result from expenses or distributions to owners. Examples are losses on the sale of investments and on litigation.
5. **Income,** which results from adding all revenues and gains for a period and subtracting all expenses and losses for the period.
6. **Financing activities,** or events that produce inflows of funds during a period.[19] Examples are the sale of bonds and the sale of common stock.

---

[19]The term **funds** is usually defined as either working capital (i.e., current assets minus current liabilities) or cash.

7. **Investing activities,** or events that result in outflows of funds during a period. Examples are the purchase of plant assets and the retirement of long-term debt.

Take a few minutes now to examine the Kroger Company financial statements reprinted on the endpapers of this book. Observe that these statements reflect an application of the concepts and elements discussed above.

The elements described above are fairly broad. Although we have defined the term "assets," for example, we have not yet stated what attribute of assets (e.g., historical cost or current value) should be reported on the balance sheet. In order to give the elements a more concrete and practical focus, we must consider broad and detailed principles as well as modifying conventions.

BROAD PRINCIPLES

To implement the concepts and elements, accountants apply certain generally accepted principles. Broad principles are those that have a pervasive impact on the form and content of financial statements. These principles relate to the basic accounting functions of measurement and disclosure.

Monetary Unit Principle

Quantification generally makes information more useful. It may be helpful to know, for example, that a firm generated net income during a particular period, but it would be more helpful to know *how much*. Quantification decreases uncertainty about the firm's performance.

In order to quantify financial position and the changes in it, a measuring unit is necessary. It serves as a common denominator that permits variables (inventories, cost of goods sold, and so on) to be related to one another. It also permits the aggregation of diverse items using basic arithmetic operations (addition, subtraction, and so on). In a barter economy, any valuable resource (for example, cows) could be used as a measuring unit. In a more advanced economy, such as that of the United States, money is a widely accepted medium of exchange. It is a convenient, customary, and understandable way of expressing wealth as well as changes in wealth. The **monetary unit principle** maintains that **accountants should measure in units of money,** that is, **number of dollars,** or **nominal dollars.**

Money measures command over goods and services, just as the mile measures distance and the pound measures weight. Unfortunately, as a measuring unit, money has a major drawback. Most measuring units remain stable over time, but the ability of money to command goods and services (its **general purchasing power,** or **GPP**) usually changes. During a period of inflation (a rise in the overall level of prices), the GPP of money declines. Conversely, during a period of deflation (a decline in the overall level of prices), the GPP of money rises. Clearly, the economic problem of inflation has persisted in the United States for many years. This phenomenon has resulted in financial statements that reflect dollars of mixed, rather than uniform, purchasing power. A dollar invested in plant assets thirty years

---

Broad Principles
Monetary unit
Objectivity
Historical cost
Revenue realization
Matching
Consistency
Disclosure

ago, for example, may be combined in financial statements with a dollar that resulted from sales made yesterday. Many observers feel that this tends to distort interperiod as well as intercompany comparisons and thereby reduces the usefulness of financial statements.

To help make financial statements more useful, some people have proposed that accountants stop measuring in nominal dollars and begin measuring in **constant dollars,** that is, dollars that have uniform, rather than mixed, purchasing power. These proposals usually call for companies to issue **constant dollar financial statements,** a topic that we explain in Chapter 27. Current generally accepted accounting principles do not require companies to publish constant dollar financial statements, although they do require certain large companies to report as supplementary information selected items of information prepared on a constant dollar basis. The prevailing thought in the financial community is that, given the imprecise nature as well as the costs of preparing and interpreting constant dollar financial statements, the distortive effects of inflation are not now sufficiently material to require a modification of the monetary unit principle. For this reason, we emphasize the monetary unit principle throughout the text.

Objectivity Principle

As stated earlier, reliability is an important quality of useful accounting information. To help ensure that users can confidently depend on accounting information, the **objectivity principle** maintains that, **to the extent possible, accounting measurements should be based on verifiable evidence.** Such evidence enables an accountant to generate measures similar to those that other competent accountants would develop under the same circumstances. In other words, verifiable evidence helps to ensure that different accountants, working independently to solve the same measurement problem, reach similar conclusions. Information based on verifiable evidence is not significantly distorted by personal biases, and the possibility of serious measurement errors is reduced.

Because of the need for verifiable evidence to support accounting measurements, financial accounting is based primarily on the results of **arm's-length exchange transactions,** which are transactions between unrelated parties in which the parties behave in their own best economic interests. For example, although revenue is theoretically generated during a product's planning and production phases, accountants usually wait until a sale is made to record revenue. At the time of sale, an arm's-length exchange transaction occurs, which results in certain verifiable evidence, such as the sales invoice, that is used to document the amount of revenue generated.

The quality of verifiable evidence varies considerably. On the one hand, the evidence in support of such items as cash and marketable securities is usually quite strong. On the other hand, the evidence supporting such items as bad-debts expense and depreciation expense is much weaker, and as a result, accountants must make many estimates. Since estimates are always subject to measurement errors, financial statements are never completely objective and verifiable.

The existence of verifiable measurements facilitates the auditing function of independent CPAs. As we indicated in Chapter 1, a major part of the auditor's job is to examine the evidence for the assertions that management makes in its financial statements. When the evidence is adequate, the CPA may render an unqualified opinion on the financial statements. This opinion lends credibility to the financial statements and increases the confidence of users.

Historical Cost Principle

The **historical cost principle,** one of the most fundamental and controversial components of accounting theory, holds that **historical cost (acquisition or original cost) is usually the best measurement in accounting for goods and services acquired by an enter-**

prise. Historical cost (often referred to simply as "cost") is a measure of the actual cost (the cash equivalent price) of acquiring an economic resource and putting it to use. In the case of purchasing a new machine, for example, cost would include the net invoice price as well as transportation, set-up, and break-in charges.

According to the historical cost principle, nonmonetary assets (those assets, such as inventories and plant assets, that cannot be expressed in terms of a fixed or predetermined number of dollars to be received by the reporting entity) are recorded initially at cost and reported in later balance sheets in terms of unexpired or unallocated cost. For example, land acquired twenty years ago for $50,000 would be reported on today's balance sheet at its historical cost even though it may now be worth $200,000. Moreover, because liabilities and owners' equity represent equities in a firm's assets, these items are also affected by the historical cost principle. Additionally, expenses and losses are measured and reported on the basis of expired historical costs.

Historical cost, of course, is only one of several measurement bases that could be used in accounting. In recent years many critics have attacked the historical cost principle. These critics argue that, given the magnitude of past inflation in this country, historical cost figures lack relevance and may even mislead certain users of financial information. They believe that the FASB should require some form of current value accounting, under which an asset reported on an ending balance sheet would be measured in terms of its current cost (the price that would currently have to be paid to acquire the asset), its current selling price (the price that could be currently received by selling the asset), or the present discounted value of the expected future net cash inflows that the asset would generate for the enterprise. Of course, if an asset account balance were increased to reflect a currect value measurement, some account would have to be credited. This account might be a special "revenue" account or perhaps an owners' equity account. Clearly, current value accounting represents a departure from the historical cost principle; we explore this topic in more depth in the next chapter.

In light of the various forms of current value accounting, why do accountants continue to emphasize historical costs? Perhaps the most significant reason is that historical costs can be determined with greater precision than any of the alternative bases of measurement. Based on completed (as opposed to hypothetical) transactions, historical costs are a matter of record. As a result, they can be verified and are therefore perceived as more reliable than the alternatives. To illustrate, the historical cost of an oil refinery can be determined by inspecting documented evidence. In contrast, determining the current cost of the refinery would be very subjective and could lead to serious disputes among company managers, accountants, engineers, appraisers, and others.

A second major reason in support of historical costs is that if current value accounting were adopted, a firm's assets and liabilities would have to be revalued each time financial statements were prepared (annually, quarterly, or perhaps even monthly). Certainly, this procedure would be expensive and time consuming, and there is reasonable doubt that the benefits of the resulting information would exceed the costs of providing and using it.

Another reason in support of historical cost is that government agencies, such as the Internal Revenue Service, require that historical cost measurements be used in reports, such as tax returns, filed with them. These legal requirements have caused the historical cost system of measurement to be firmly established in the business community.

Proper determination of historical cost is not always easy. It often requires estimates, allocations, and the application of judgment. For example, what is the historical cost of a new machine acquired in exchange for an old machine plus a two-year, noninterest-bearing promissory note? We answer this question, as well as many similar ones, in later chapters.

It is worth noting that the historical cost principle is closely related to both the objectivity principle and the revenue realization principle. That is, historical costs are widely regarded as relatively objective measurements, and accountants normally ignore increases in the value of a recorded asset until the increase has been validated by an arm's-length exchange transaction (sale).

Unfortunately, many people confuse the historical cost principle with the monetary unit principle. The monetary unit principle tells us that accountants measure in units of money, but it does not tell us *what* accountants measure in units of money. The historical cost principle tells us what accountants measure (i.e., they measure historical costs as opposed to, say, current values). We explain this fundamental distinction more fully in Chapter 3.

Revenue Realization Principle

Companies engage in many different kinds of earning activities. Generally, these activities include planning, investing cash in productive assets, selling products or services to customers, collecting cash from customers, and providing warranty services. Collectively, a firm's earning activities constitute its earning process, and companies engage in this process with the goal of ultimately receiving more cash (hopefully much more) than they invested in productive assets. Because the goal of the earning process is to receive cash, it is logical for accountants to construct their measure of revenue based on past cash receipts or claims to future cash receipts that result from earning activities during an accounting period.

From a conceptual point of view, a firm generates revenue *continuously* during all phases of its earning process. In theory, therefore, accountants should initially measure revenue when a new product is planned. Later, additional revenue should be measured when the product is produced, when it is sold, and when cash is finally collected. As might be expected, measuring revenue during the early stages of an earning process is difficult because of the tremendous uncertainty about the amount of cash that the firm will ultimately receive.

Consequently, despite the theory that revenue is earned continuously, the accounting profession has had to resolve the following practical question: When can revenue be measured with sufficient objectivity (the objectivity principle) to enter it in the accounting records? The profession's answer to this question is found in the **revenue realization principle.** This principle states that **revenue should be recognized (recorded) when (1) the earning process is complete or virtually complete, and (2) an exchange transaction has taken place.**[20] When these two conditions are met, most of the uncertainty about the existence and amount of revenue has been resolved. As a result, revenue can be measured with sufficient reliability.

The two conditions for revenue realization are normally satisfied when a product is sold (when title passes from the seller to the buyer). Thus, an asset such as inventory should generally be carried at cost (the historical cost principle) until an increase in its value is verified by a sale transaction. At the time of sale, most of the significant earning activities have been completed, and objective evidence provided by an exchange transaction supports the existence and amount of revenue to be recorded. Furthermore, expenses incurred to produce the revenue are either known or can be estimated with reasonable accuracy. Therefore, the accountant can apply the matching principle to measure periodic income.

The revenue realization principle also governs the recognition of revenue from sources other than product sales. For instance, revenue generated by providing services is recorded when the services have been rendered and are billable. Furthermore, revenue, such as rent revenue and interest revenue, generated by allowing others to use enterprise resources is usually recorded as time passes or as the resources are used.[21]

Because the revenue realization principle requires an exchange transaction, accountants measure revenue in terms of the fair market value of the consideration received in the

---

[20]*APB Statement No. 4,* par. 150
[21]*APB Statement No. 4,* par 151.

exchange transaction or the fair market value of the consideration given up, whichever is more clearly determinable. Moreover, the requirement that the earning process be complete or virtually complete implies that any amount received in advance of providing goods or services must be recorded as a liability, such as unearned subscriptions revenue, until it is earned.

Although the revenue realization principle normally requires accountants to measure revenue only when a sale occurs, certain departures from this principle are acceptable, according to GAAP, under prescribed circumstances. The accounting profession justifies these departures because of the many different kinds of transactions in which companies engage. Contractors, for example, often engage in construction projects, such as office buildings and dams, that span several accounting periods. Rather than waiting until a contract is completed to measure revenue, contractors may choose to recognize revenue *during production* using the percentage-of-completion method. This method may be used when there is a definite contract price and when reasonable estimates can be made of progress toward project completion. As another example, revenue is sometimes recorded *at the completion of production,* before a sale has occurred. This procedure is appropriate for products, such as certain metals and agricultural commodities, for which a guaranteed market exists in which the firm can sell all that it has produced at a definite price. Finally, the recognition of revenue is sometimes delayed beyond the time of sale to the time *when cash is collected.* This occurs when significant uncertainty exists about the value of the assets received in the sale or the amount of additional expenses that will be incurred in connection with the sale. Under these circumstances, which occasionally pertain to certain kinds of installment sales, either the installment sales method or the cost recovery method may be appropriate for recognizing revenue. Further discussion of the revenue realization principle and its exceptions appears in Chapter 20.

Matching Principle

Today, the income statement is generally regarded as the most important financial statement, and net income is one of the most significant numbers that accountants compute. In measuring periodic income, accountants usually apply the revenue realization principle first to determine when revenue should be recognized. Then, after revenue for a period has been independently determined, they turn to the matching principle to determine when expenses should be recognized. The **matching principle** dictates that **costs should be recognized as expenses when the goods or services represented by the costs contribute to revenue.** In other words, accountants should attempt to associate (match) the revenues of a given accounting period with all expenses that were incurred to generate those revenues.

From a conceptual point of view, the matching principle implies that the accountant should analyze historical costs to determine the extent to which the goods and services represented by these costs have contributed to revenues during the accounting period. Costs that have contributed to revenues should be reported as expenses, and costs that are expected to contribute in the future should be reported as assets. This approach is called **direct matching,** but from a practical standpoint, it can be applied only to certain kinds of costs. For instance, a manufacturing company's costs of direct materials and direct labor can be reasonably identified with the firm's product (inventory). When the product is sold, sales revenue is recognized. Accordingly, since the direct materials and direct labor costs contributed directly to the sales revenue, those costs constitute expenses and should be reflected in the cost of goods sold. As another example, the costs of sales commissions can be directly related to the sales transactions that give rise to the commissions. When sales revenue is recognized, the costs of related commissions should be expensed. Direct matching therefore involves associating expenses with revenues on the basis of a presumed cause-and-effect relationship.

Unfortunately, for most types of costs it is virtually impossible to accurately determine the extent to which the goods or services that are represented by the costs contribute to revenues. For example, when Sears Roebuck & Company purchases a new computer for use in its accounting system, who can precisely determine the pattern of the computer's contribution to revenues? Or when Anheuser Busch incurs advertising costs, who can accurately assess the pattern of future benefits to the company? Because of the lack of answers to these and many similar questions, direct matching is often impractical, and accountants must use **indirect matching.** With this approach, which involves estimates, the accountant initially tries to match revenues with expenses based on a systematic and rational allocation of historical costs, such as depreciation expense or amortization expense. At times, however, the accountant cannot make a systematic and rational allocation, either because of the uncertainty of future revenues or the difficulty of associating certain costs with future revenues in a reliable manner. Under these circumstances, costs are reported as expenses in the period in which they are incurred. Some examples of costs that fall in this category are advertising and research and development. Note that accounting for these kinds of costs reflects the modifying convention of conservatism (discussed later in the chapter), the accountant's general guide for dealing with uncertain situations.

The revenue realization principle and the matching principle are the essence of the accrual basis of accounting. Under cash basis accounting, revenue is recorded only when received in cash, and expenses are recorded only when paid in cash. In contrast, accrual basis accounting requires recognition of revenue when earned (according to the revenue realization principle) and recognition of expenses when incurred (according to the matching principle). Differences between cash basis and accrual basis accounting are explained more fully in Chapter 3. To fully implement the accrual basis, the accountant must make certain adjusting entries at the end of every accounting period, as we explain in Chapter 5. These entries are necessary because of the accountant's desire to observe the principles of revenue realization and matching.

A final important point is that in conventional accounting, income measurement is closely related to asset and liability measurement. Thus, the balance sheet and the income statement are said to be "fundamentally related." Notice, for example, that measuring depreciation expense, in compliance with the matching principle, directly affects the reported measurement of the asset that is being depreciated. The term **articulation** refers to the fundamental relationship among all financial statements prepared according to GAAP.

Consistency Principle

To formulate rational investment, credit, and similar decisions, users of accounting information typically make comparisons. Specifically, they compare circumstances of different companies **(intercompany comparisons)** and circumstances of a single company over time **(interperiod comparisons).** As a result, accounting information is regarded as more useful when it can help financial statement users make better comparisons.

Alternative generally accepted accounting principles exist in many areas of accounting. For example, in accounting for depreciation, a company may choose among the double-declining balance method, the sum-of-the-years'-digits method, the straight-line method, and others. Because a company may choose among these alternatives, intercompany comparisons based on financial statements may sometimes be distorted. Nevertheless, these alternatives exist because different companies face substantially different circumstances. The accounting profession recognizes that the validity of intercompany comparisons is enhanced when differences between the financial statements of different companies result from basic differences between the companies themselves or from the nature of their transactions and not merely from differences in accounting principles.[22] For this reason, the

---

[22]*APB Statement No. 4,* par. 101.

FASB and its predecessor committees have sought to eliminate alternative accounting principles that cannot reasonably be justified on the basis of differences in factual circumstances. In the past, for example, some companies capitalized research and development (R&D) costs, while others expensed R&D costs when incurred. The FASB stated that capitalizing most kinds of R&D costs could not be justified, and in 1974 the board issued *Statement of Financial Accounting Standards No. 2,* which basically requires companies to expense R&D costs when incurred. A major aim of this pronouncement was to enable financial statement users to make better comparisons between firms engaged in R&D activities.

The accounting profession is also highly concerned with interperiod comparisons. Users of accounting information make interperiod comparisons in order to discern important trends. Knowing past trends, users can presumably make more accurate predictions about their prospects of receiving cash from an enterprise. To improve the interperiod comparability of accounting information, accountants observe the **consistency principle,** which holds that **accountants must measure and disclose information about an entity in the same manner from one accounting period to the next.** In other words, once a company adopts a certain set of accounting principles, it must observe those principles consistently over time. A company cannot use the double-declining balance method of computing depreciation in 1985, the sum-of-the-years'-digits method in 1986, the straight-line method in 1987, and so forth. Further, a company cannot use the first-in, first-out (FIFO) method of inventory cost determination in 1985; the last-in, first-out (LIFO) method in 1986; and the average cost method in 1987. It should be noted, however, that the consistency principle does not require a company to measure and disclose all information in the same manner in a single accounting period. For example, the consistency principle does not prohibit a company from using the FIFO method for one part of its inventories and the average cost method for another part.

The consistency principle also does not prohibit a firm from changing from one accounting principle to another if it has a good reason for doing so. *Accounting Principles Board Opinion No. 20* stated that "the presumption that an entity should not change an accounting principle may be overcome only if the enterprise justifies the use of an alternative acceptable accounting principle on the basis that it is preferable."[23] The accounting profession has not yet defined precisely what it means by the term "preferable." When a company changes from one accounting principle to another, it must clearly disclose the nature of, reason for, and dollar effects of the change. We cover the topic of accounting changes in Chapter 19.

The consistency principle is very important to independent auditors. One of the generally accepted auditing standards of the AICPA requires that "the [auditor's] report shall state whether [generally accepted accounting] principles have been consistently observed in the current period in relation to the preceding period."[24] Accordingly, a standard part of the independent auditor's report reads as follows:

> *In our opinion, the financial statements . . . present fairly the financial position of X Company as of December 31, 1985, and the results of its operations and the changes in its financial position for the year then ended, in conformity with generally accepted accounting principles* applied on a basis consistent with that of the preceding year.[25] *[Emphasis added.]*

Disclosure Principle

The disclosure principle (often called adequate, fair, or full disclosure) is one of the most significant and far reaching components of accounting theory. In fact, the disclosure prin-

---

[23]*APB Opinion No. 20,* "Accounting Changes," 1971, par. 16.
[24]*AICPA Professional Standards—Volume 1* (Chicago: Commerce Clearing House), AU Sec. 420.01.
[25]*AICPA Professional Standards—Volume 1,* AU Sec. 509.07.

ciple formed the basis for the securities legislation that was enacted in the United States in 1933 and 1934. In recognition of the prime importance of adequate disclosure, one of the generally accepted auditing standards of the AICPA holds that "informative disclosures in the financial statements are to be regarded as reasonably adequate unless otherwise stated in the [auditor's] report."[26]

Consistent with the accountant's aim of providing useful information, the **disclosure principle** calls for **revealing information that will be useful in the decision-making processes of reasonably informed users.** To determine an appropriate level of disclosure for a given company, an accountant must apply generally accepted accounting principles to the circumstances involved. This requires considerable professional judgment.

When disclosing information, the accountant must be an effective communicator. The information must be sufficiently relevant and reliable, and it must be disseminated in a timely manner. Moreover, a delicate balance must be achieved between completeness and understandability. Although accountants want to issue complete financial reports, the understandability of the reports is impaired by excessive details. Do external users really want to know the 5,000 individual customer balances that may exist in the accounts receivable subsidiary ledger? Certainly not. If accountants did not carefully summarize the mass of detail that could potentially be disclosed, financial statement users would be overwhelmed by information, and the quality of their decisions would surely diminish.

The disclosure principle requires that appropriate terminology be used in financial reports. Further, it implies that important information of an unfavorable nature should not be hidden by the use of crafty language, small type, and other means.

Several methods of disclosure are commonly used to achieve effective communication. The most important information is generally disclosed in the **body of the financial statements.** For example, publicly held companies are required to disclose earnings-per-share information on the face of their income statements. **Notes** (footnotes) are an integral part of the financial statements and may effectively be used to disclose such facts as accounting policies, contractual restrictions, and certain details about leases. In addition, accountants use **schedules** to disclose such items as inventory (i.e., raw materials, work-in-process, and finished goods), operating expenses, and changes in the components of working capital. At times, **supplementary statements,** such as financial statements adjusted for the effects of inflation, constitute an effective method of disclosure.

Attempting to comply with the disclosure principle raises many interesting questions. For example, suppose that you are the independent auditor for a paper company. During the course of examining the evidence for the financial statements, you discover that the company has violated an environmental protection statute. If the violation is discovered, the company could be sued and possibly lose millions of dollars. How would you apply the disclosure principle under these circumstances? Clearly, adequate disclosure will continue to be a challenge to the practicing accountant in the years ahead.

DETAILED PRINCIPLES

Accountants use **detailed principles** to apply the broad principles. Detailed principles are highly specific, and more than one level of detailed principles may exist in a given area of accounting. Accountants often use the terms "procedures" and "methods" when referring to detailed principles. With plant assets, for example, accountants implement matching (a broad principle) by using depreciation (a detailed principle), which is computed by one of several methods (an even more detailed principle). Like broad principles, detailed principles relate to the basic accounting functions of measurement and disclosure.

Detailed principles are far too numerous to list and explain in this chapter. For this

---

[26]*AICPA Professional Standards—Volume 1,* AU Sec. 430.01.

reason they are covered in other chapters of this text and in other financial accounting courses. Accounting Research Bulletins (ARBs), APB Opinions, and FASB Statements of Financial Accounting Standards (SFASs) contain many detailed accounting principles.

MODIFYING CONVENTIONS

To be useful, accounting theory must be applied in the business world by individual accountants, each of whom must use informed judgment to resolve many difficult questions. In an effort to help accountants resolve these questions practically and consistently, the accounting profession has adopted conventions (or customs) that modify basic accounting theory. To a large extent, accountants apply these **modifying conventions** by using generally accepted rules of broad and detailed accounting principles; modifying conventions are therefore technically a part of generally accepted accounting principles. They are usually

> **Modifying Conventions**
> Materiality
> Industry practices
> Conservatism
> Substance over form

called modifying conventions, rather than accounting principles, because they cause the accountant to modify the "theoretically ideal" treatment of certain economic things and events. In other words, they enable the accountant in some cases to depart from a rigid interpretation of broad and detailed accounting principles. Modifying conventions, therefore, may be viewed as exceptions to accounting principles. These exceptions are justified on the grounds that accounting theory:

1. Must yield information for which the benefits exceed the costs.
2. Must be applied in complex business enterprises among which facts and circumstances may differ substantially.
3. Must be applied under conditions of uncertainty.
4. Should focus on the economic substance of business transactions.

Materiality

All FASB Statements of Financial Accounting Standards contain the following appendage: "The provisions of this Statement need not be applied to immaterial items." While all transactions must be recorded and their effects ultimately reflected in the financial statements, the requirements of sound theory may be modified somewhat when dealing with immaterial items. For example, current generally accepted accounting principles require that extraordinary items (if material) be presented in a separate section of the income statement. This disclosure principle presumably results in useful information because a knowledge of extraordinary items should assist financial statement users to evaluate enterprise performance and to make important predictions. An important practical question that the accountant must frequently answer is: How large must an extraordinary item be to become material and thereby require separate disclosure in the income statement? Clearly, a $100 tornado loss sustained by a multimillion dollar company would not require separate disclosure, but would likely be combined with other items in the body of the income statement. Cluttering the financial statements with trivial details would be a disservice to statement users and may in some cases make the financial statements misleading. **Materiality,** therefore, refers to "the magnitude of an omission or misstatement of accounting information that, in the light of surrounding circumstances, makes it probable that **the**

judgment of a reasonable person relying on the information would have been changed or influenced by the omission or misstatement."[27] [Emphasis added.]

The basic test that accountants use when making materiality decisions is whether knowledge of a particular item of information would likely affect a decision made by an informed user of financial statements. The materiality evaluation is complicated by the lack of information about the specific ways in which accounting information influences investment, credit, and similar decisions.

Materiality decisions may involve quantitative as well as qualitative considerations. Quantitative considerations refer to such factors as the effect of the item on the company's earnings trend or the relationship between the item and key financial variables such as assets, liabilities, owners' equity, revenues, expenses, and net income. Qualitative considerations center around the basic nature of the item. Does the item result in a contractual violation? Does the item represent an illegal transaction such as a bribe paid to a foreign official? Does the item represent an insider transaction such as an interest-free loan made to the company president? Affirmative answers to these and similar questions may indicate that the item in question should be disclosed regardless of the dollar magnitudes immediately involved.

Materiality is one of the most complex, pervasive, and elusive components of accounting theory. Making materiality decisions requires considerable judgment. Because of differences in circumstances, an item that is judged material for one company may not necessarily be judged material for another one. To the dismay of some accountants, the accounting profession has not developed a comprehensive set of criteria to aid the practicing accountant in making materiality judgments. A relatively small number of materiality guidelines are contained in authoritative accounting pronouncements about certain areas (e.g., earnings per share and segment reporting). The FASB's current position, however, is that "no general standards of materiality can be formulated to take into account all the considerations that enter into an experienced human judgment."[28]

Industry Practices

Generally accepted accounting principles are intended for use in general purpose external financial reporting by business enterprises. Accountants must therefore apply broad as well as detailed accounting principles to many different kinds of companies. In applying these principles, accountants have found that certain industries (groups of similar companies) have peculiar characteristics that sometimes warrant a modification of accounting principles. The term **industry practices** pertains to **modifications of accounting principles necessitated by the unusual characteristics of some industries.** Because these modifications presumably enhance the usefulness of accounting information, they have become generally accepted within the accounting profession and are therefore a part of GAAP.

For example, most manufacturing companies produce inventory within a relatively short period of time, and the selling price is determined only when a sale occurs. Thus, the revenue realization principle normally requires the recognition of revenue at the time of sale. Companies in the construction industry, however, routinely engage in construction projects that take several years to complete. Further, these companies typically sign a contract at the start of each project, ensuring them a certain contract price. In light of these peculiar circumstances, generally accepted accounting principles permit a modification of the revenue realization principle. Specifically, as discussed earlier in the chapter, companies that engage in long-term construction projects may recognize revenue (and income) during production using the percentage-of-completion method.

---

[27] *FASB Statement of Financial Accounting Concepts No. 2,* p. xv.
[28] *FASB Statement of Financial Accounting Concepts No. 2,* p. xiii.

As another example, the investment company industry consists of firms that sell their own shares of capital stock to the public and invest most of the proceeds in the securities of other entities. Thus, investment securities comprise most of the assets of a typical investment company. Given the importance of these securities and the fact that accountants can usually determine the market value of the securities in a sufficiently reliable manner, generally accepted accounting principles call for reporting the investment securities of investment companies on a market value basis. Notice that this industry practice represents a clear departure from the historical cost principle. Additionally, it constitutes an exception to the revenue realization principle because the statement of operations (income statement) for an investment company includes unrealized increases and decreases (i.e., not verified by actual sales) in the value of investment securities held.

Industry practices cause many accounting principles to be modified. In fact, these practices have a significant impact on the published financial statements of such companies as banks, savings and loan associations, finance companies, life insurance companies, and public utilities. Knowledgeable preparers and users of external accounting information should be aware of the nature of industry practices, including their role in the framework of generally accepted accounting principles. AICPA Industry Accounting and Audit Guides are excellent authoritative sources of information about industry practices.

Conservatism

As stated earlier, accountants attempt to generate reliable measurements. Often these measurements must be made in the presence of significant uncertainties. How long will a company benefit from research and development costs? Will a company successfully defend itself in an ongoing lawsuit involving product safety? What assumption should be made about the way inventory costs flow through a business? Given the difficult nature of such questions that must be adequately resolved when measuring financial position and the changes in it, accountants cannot possibly prepare precise financial statements.

When accountants attempt to resolve measurement uncertainties, they recognize that corporate managers tend to be confident and optimistic (sometimes too optimistic) about their companies. Moreover, many managers desire to maximize their reported earnings each period. From the pragmatic standpoint of avoiding unfavorable legal exposure, it is less risky for the accountant to understate than to overstate net income and net assets. These factors cause most accountants to adopt a cautious attitude toward the inherent risks and uncertainties of the measurement process. This attitude is reflected in the modifying convention of conservatism.

The **conservatism** convention holds that **when alternative solutions to an accounting problem can be reasonably supported, an accountant should favor the solution that least favorably affects net income and net assets of the current period.** Thus, conservatism is a practical and prudent, yet an imprecise, response to the problem of measurement risk. Implicit in the conservatism convention is the belief that, when faced with significant uncertainties, the accountant should observe the following moderating tendencies:

1. Measure revenues and gains lower rather than higher and later rather than earlier.
2. Measure expenses and losses higher rather than lower and earlier rather than later.
3. Measure net income lower rather than higher.
4. Measure assets lower rather than higher.
5. Measure liabilities higher rather than lower.
6. Measure owners' equity lower rather than higher.

Ideally, the accountant's measurements should be accurate, neither overstated nor understated. Conservatism is not a license to deliberately understate net income and net assets. If a firm having cash of $100,000 reports only $25,000, this is not conservatism but simply inaccurate reporting.

Companies are not required to select the most conservative accounting treatment available in every situation. Thus, conservatism is not a basic accounting principle. Instead, because it often results in the modification of a basic principle, it is more appropriately viewed as a modifying convention. For example, the common practice of immediately expensing the costs of major advertising programs is a modification of the matching principle, owing to the uncertainty associated with the existence and timing of future benefits.

Many examples of conservatism are found in accounting practice. These include the lower of cost or market rule for valuing inventories and marketable securities; accelerated depreciation and LIFO; recording goodwill only when purchased in an arm's-length transaction; amortizing organization costs over a relatively brief period even though the life of the firm is benefited; recognizing accrued net losses (but not gains) on firm purchase commitments for inventory; recording a loss contingency if a loss will probably occur but not recording a gain contingency until the gain occurs; and immediately expensing most R & D and advertising costs even though future periods will likely be benefited.

Many users of financial statements support the conservatism convention. Bankers, for example, have long favored the lower of cost or market rule for inventory valuation. Moreover, most financial analysts evaluate enterprise performance on the basis not only of the quantity but also the quality of reported earnings. An important factor when assessing quality of earnings is the extent to which a firm uses conservative accounting policies. All other things being equal, many analysts tend to look more favorably on a company that adopts conservative accounting policies. Such companies are sometimes said to have "conservative accounting personalities."

Substance over Form

Financial accounting is concerned with the legal as well as the economic effects of accountable events. But **when an apparent conflict exists between the economic substance and the legal form of a business transaction, accountants tend to emphasize economic substance.** To illustrate, computing earnings per share of common stock would appear to involve little more than dividing net income for a period by the average number of common shares outstanding. Certain securities, however, such as bonds that are convertible into common stock, may in substance be equivalent to common stock even though they are not common stock in legal form. *APB Opinion No. 15* therefore requires accountants to include these types of securities in earnings-per-share calculations under certain circumstances. By modifying the way in which accountants had computed earnings-per-share numbers, the APB attempted to put economic substance over legal form.

As another example, accountants sometimes encounter long-term notes that have no stated interest rates. Legally, then, these notes do not bear interest. Nevertheless, the accounting profession recognizes the economic reality that money has a time value, and as a result, the notes that companies typically issue contain interest even though the interest may not be explicitly stated. Accordingly, even though a long-term note may have no stated interest rate, *APB Opinion No. 21* requires accountants to impute (estimate and record) interest under certain circumstances.

As a final example of putting substance over form, current accounting principles require a lessee to report certain kinds of leases as assets and liabilities even though the lessee does not actually own the leased property. In substance, these leases convey to lessees certain rights that are almost identical to the rights held by companies that purchase rather than lease their property.

CONCLUDING REMARKS

We cannot overemphasize the importance of developing a sound conceptual understanding of financial accounting. You should apply this understanding when solving the problems in this book. A procedural approach to solving problems, emphasizing mechanics and memorization, should be avoided. Accounting problems that appear in textbooks, on examinations, and in the business world often are complex and may vary in an endless number of ways. To solve these problems, accountants must have a solid base of theoretical knowledge. In the following chapters, we explain in more detail how theory applies to specific accounting issues. Throughout these chapters we highlight in the margin the key elements of accounting theory explained in Chapter 2.

The model presented in this chapter explains most, but not all, of financial accounting as accountants apply it today. In Chapter 1, we explained that since accounting principles help to determine how scarce resources are allocated in our economy, the FASB and its predecessor committees often have had to deal with political pressures in addition to deciding what is theoretically sound accounting. We believe that some accounting principles exist primarily because of political pressures, not because they are consistent with the model. The existence of these principles, however, does not mean that the model is worthless. Instead, it simply reflects the reality that accounting is a pragmatic discipline concerned with producing information that ultimately affects the welfare of people. At appropriate places throughout the text, we point out accounting principles that do not appear to exist primarily because of the model.

One indication of the importance of conceptual knowledge to beginning CPAs is the fact that one of the four sections of the Uniform Certified Public Accountant Examination deals exclusively with accounting theory. Many of the cases at the end of this chapter have been adapted from the theory section of past examinations.

In the next chapter we explore certain aspects of descriptive accounting theory in greater depth. We also introduce some proposals that, if adopted, would change the basic information that accountants currently report.

KEY POINTS

1. Financial reporting should (1) provide information useful in investment, credit, and similar decisions; (2) provide information useful in assessing cash flow prospects; and (3) provide information about enterprise resources, claims to those resources, and changes in them.

2. Relevance and reliability are the two primary qualities of useful accounting information.

3. Financial accounting theory is based on three major assumptions or postulates: (1) economic entity; (2) periodicity; and (3) going concern.

4. The assumptions listed above support basic concepts and elements. The first basic concept is financial position, and its elements are assets, liabilities, and owners' equity. The second basic concept is changes in financial position, and its elements are revenues, expenses, gains, losses, income, financing activities, and investing activities.

5. Accountants apply certain generally accepted principles in order to implement the concepts and elements. Broad principles have a pervasive impact on the form and content of financial statements. The broad principles of financial accounting are: (1) monetary unit; (2) objectivity; (3) historical cost; (4) revenue realization; (5) matching; (6) consistency; and (7) disclosure.

6. Detailed principles are the highly specific ones that accountants use to apply the broad principles in practice. Detailed principles are numerous and are covered in later chapters of this text and in other courses.

7. Modifying conventions may be viewed as exceptions to accounting principles. These conventions are: (1) materiality; (2) industry practices; (3) conservatism; and (4) substance over form.

2–1   What is accounting theory?

2–2   What are the objectives of financial reporting? How are these objectives interrelated?

2–3   Why are explicitly stated objectives considered important in the development of a structure of accounting theory?

2–4   In general, how much knowledge does the accounting profession expect of the users of financial statements? Why is it important for the accounting profession to state, at least in general terms, how much knowledge it expects users to have?

2–5   Briefly explain the qualities of relevance and reliability. How do these qualities relate to the basic accounting objective of providing useful information?

2–6   Explain the significance of the contention that relevance and reliability require important trade-offs.

2–7   Should the FASB require companies to report all information that users of financial statements regard as useful? Justify your answer.

2–8   Briefly explain each of the following accounting assumptions: (1) economic entity; (2) periodicity; and (3) going concern.

2–9   Define the concept of financial position and each of the elements that compose financial position.

2–10 Define the concept of changes in financial position and each of the elements that represent changes in financial position.

2–11 Briefly explain the monetary unit principle. Why is this principle criticized during periods of rapid inflation?

2–12 Briefly explain the objectivity principle. How is this principle related to the accounting quality of reliability?

2–13 Briefly explain the historical cost principle. Why has the accounting profession traditionally preferred historical costs over current costs for financial reporting purposes?

2–14 Briefly explain the revenue realization princi-

ple. When are the two conditions for revenue realization normally satisfied? At what times, other than at the time of sale, might it be appropriate under generally accepted accounting principles for a company to recognize revenue?

2–15 Briefly explain the matching principle. Distinguish between direct matching and indirect matching.

2–16 Distinguish between cash basis and accrual basis accounting.

2–17 Briefly explain the consistency principle. Why is this principle important to the users of financial statements?

2–18 Does the existence of the consistency principle mean that:

[a] A company must use the same depreciation method in a given year to account for all of its depreciable assets?

[b] All companies in the steel industry must use the same inventory cost determination method, such as FIFO or LIFO?

[c] A company can never change from one generally accepted accounting principle to another?

2–19 Briefly explain the disclosure principle. In general, how does an accountant determine an appropriate amount of disclosure for a given company?

2–20 Briefly explain the modifying convention of materiality. Why is materiality regarded as one of the most pervasive aspects of accounting theory?

2–21 Briefly explain the term "industry practices." Cite three industries in which industry practices have an important effect on the information reported in corporate financial statements.

2–22 Briefly explain the modifying convention of conservatism. What do financial analysts mean when they say that certain companies have "conservative accounting personalities"?

2–23 Briefly explain the modifying convention of substance over form.

C2–1 A company may occasionally change from one accounting principle to another. For example, it may change from the LIFO method of inventory pricing to the FIFO method and from the double-declining balance method of depreciation to the straight-line

method. *APB Opinion No. 20* (par. 17) states that "the nature of and justification for a change in accounting principle and its effect on income should be disclosed in the financial statements of the period in which the change is made." In the context of the theoretical model presented in Chapter 2, this requirement of *Opinion No. 20* is an example of a *detailed principle*.

Instructions

Explain how the detailed principle referred to above logically relates to the objectives of financial reporting.

C2–2 The FASB has been working on a conceptual framework for financial accounting and reporting. The FASB has issued SFACs to set forth objectives and fundamentals that will be the basis for developing financial accounting and reporting standards. The objectives identify the goals and purposes of financial reporting. The fundamentals are the concepts that guide the selection of transactions, events, and circumstances to be accounted for, their recognition and measurement, and the means of summarizing and communicating them to interested parties.

The purpose of *SFAC No. 2*, "Qualitative Characteristics of Accounting Information," is to examine the characteristics that make accounting information useful and that should be sought when accounting choices are made.

Instructions

[a] Identify and discuss the benefits that can be expected from the FASB's conceptual framework study.
[b] Briefly discuss the most important qualities of useful accounting information as identified in *SFAC No. 2*.

(CMA adapted)

C2–3 According to *SFAC No. 1*, a major objective of financial reporting is to provide information that helps stockholders, bankers, and others to assess their chances of receiving *cash* from a given enterprise. Nevertheless, the accounting profession believes that income statements prepared under the *accrual basis* of accounting are more useful than either *cash basis income statements* or *statements of cash receipts and disbursements*.

Instructions

[a] Distinguish clearly between the cash basis and the accrual basis of accounting.
[b] Distinguish clearly between (1) an accrual basis income statement, (2) a cash basis income statement, and (3) a statement of cash receipts and disbursements.
[c] Explain why an accrual basis income statement

should be useful to stockholders, bankers, and other users when assessing their chances of receiving cash from a given enterprise.

C2–4 Economic entity often is considered the most fundamental and pervasive accounting assumption.

Instructions

[a] Explain economic entity.
[b] Explain why economic entity is fundamental to accounting.
[c] For each of the following, indicate whether the accounting economic entity assumption is applicable. Discuss and give illustrations.
   [1] A unit created by or under law.
   [2] The product-line segment of an enterprise.
   [3] A combination of legal units or product-line segments.
   [4] All of the activities of an owner or a group of owners.
   [5] An industry.
   [6] The economy of the United States.

(AICPA adapted)

C2–5 The general manager of the Cumberland Manufacturing Company received an income statement from his controller. The statement covered the calendar year 1985. "Joe," he said to the controller, "this statement indicates that a net income of two million dollars was earned last year. You know the value of the company is not that much more than it was this time last year."

"You're probably right," replied the controller. "You see, there are factors in accounting which sometimes keep reported operating results from reflecting the change in the value of the company."

Instructions

Prepare a detailed explanation of the accounting conventions to which the *controller* referred. Include justification, to the extent possible, for the accounting methods generally used.

(AICPA adapted)

C2–6 Section 446 of the 1954 Internal Revenue Code states: "Taxable income shall be computed under the method of accounting on . . . which the taxpayer regularly computes his income in keeping his books"; the method employed shall "clearly reflect income." Among the permissible methods are: "(1) the cash receipts and disbursements method" and "(2) an accrual method."

Instructions

Generally accepted accounting principles normally require the use of accrual accounting to "fairly present" income. If the cash receipts and disbursements method of accounting will "clearly reflect" taxable income, why does this method not usually also "fairly present" income?

(AICPA adapted)

C2–7 The earning of revenue by a business enterprise is recognized for accounting purposes when the transaction is recorded. In some situations, revenue is recognized approximately as it is earned in the economic sense. In other situations, however, accountants have developed guidelines for recognizing revenue by other criteria, such as at the point of sale.

Instructions

Ignoring income taxes:
[a] Explain and justify why revenue is often recognized as earned at the time of sale.
[b] Explain in what situations it would be appropriate to recognize revenue as the productive activity takes place.
[c] At what times, other than those included in [a] and [b] above, may it be appropriate to recognize revenue? Explain.

(AICPA adapted)

C2–8 Revenue is usually recognized at the point of sale. Under special circumstances, however, bases other than the point of sale are used for the timing of revenue recognition.

Instructions

[a] Why is the point of sale usually used as the basis for the timing of revenue recognition?
[b] Disregarding the special circumstances when bases other than the point of sale are used, discuss the merits of each of the following objections to the sales basis of revenue recognition:
   [1] It is too conservative because revenue is earned throughout the entire production process.
   [2] It is not conservative enough because accounts receivable do not represent disposable funds, sales returns and allowances may be made, and collection and bad debt expenses may be incurred in a later period.
[c] Revenue may also be recognized (1) during production and (2) when cash is received. Give an example of the circumstances in which each of the two

bases of timing revenue recognition is properly used. Discuss the accounting merits of its use in lieu of the sales basis.

(AICPA adapted)

C2–9 After the presentation of your report on the examination of the financial statements to the board of directors of the Savage Publishing Company, one of the new directors says he is surprised the income statement assumes that an equal proportion of the revenue is earned with the publication of every issue of the company's magazine. He feels that the "crucial event" in the process of earning revenue in the magazine business is the cash sale of the subscription. He does not understand why—other than for the smoothing of income—most of the revenue cannot be "realized" in the period of the sale.

Instructions

Discuss the propriety of timing the recognition of revenue in the Savage Publishing Company's accounts with
[a] The cash sale of the magazine subscription.
[b] The publication of the magazine every month.
[c] Both events, by recognizing a portion of the revenue with cash sale of the magazine subscription and a portion of the revenue with the publication of the magazine every month.

(AICPA adapted)

C2–10 On May 5, 1984, Sterling Corporation signed a contract with Stony Associates under which Stony agreed (1) to construct an office building on land owned by Sterling, (2) to accept responsibility for procuring financing for the project and finding tenants, and (3) to manage the property for 50 years. The annual profit from the project, after debt service, was to be divided equally between Sterling Corporation and Stony Associates. Stony was to accept its share of future profits as full payment for its services in construction, obtaining finances and tenants, and management of the project.

By April 30, 1985, the project was nearly completed and tenants had signed leases to occupy 90% of the available space at annual rentals totaling $2,600,000. It is estimated that, after operating expenses and debt service, the annual profit will amount to $850,000. Stony Associates believes that the economic benefit derived from the contract should be reflected on its financial statements for the fiscal year ended April 30, 1985. Management has directed that revenue be accrued in an amount equal to the commercial value of the services Stony rendered during the year, that this amount be carried in contracts receivable, and that all related expenditures be charged against the revenue.

Instructions

[a] Explain the main difference between the economic concept of business income as reflected by Stony's management, and the measurement of income under generally accepted accounting principles.
[b] Discuss the factors to be considered in determining when revenue has been realized for the measurement of periodic income.
[c] Does Stony's management's measurement of revenue and expense for the year agree with generally accepted accounting principles? Support your opinion by citing the factors to be considered for asset measurement and revenue and expense recognition.

(AICPA adapted)

C2–11 Bonanza Trading Stamps, Inc., was formed early this year to sell trading stamps throughout the Southwest to retailers who distribute the stamps gratuitously to their customers. Books for accumulating the stamps and catalogs illustrating the merchandise for which the stamps may be exchanged are given free to retailers for distribution to stamp recipients. Centers with inventories of merchandise premiums have been established to redeem stamps. Retailers may not return unused stamps to Bonanza.

The following schedule expresses Bonanza's expectations of a "normal month's activity," defined as the level of operations expected when expansion of activities ceases or tapers off to a stable rate. The company expects this level to be attained in the third year, when stamp sales will average $2,000,000 a month.

Month	Actual Stamp Sales	Merchandise Premium Purchases	Stamp Redemptions
6th	30%	40%	10%
12th	60	60	45
18th	80	80	70
24th	90	90	80
30th	100	100	95

Bonanza plans to adopt an annual closing date at the end of each 12-month period.

Instructions

[a] Discuss the factors to be considered in determining when revenue should be recognized in measuring

the income of a business enterprise.
[b] Discuss the accounting alternatives that should be considered by Bonanza Trading for the recognition of its revenues and related expenses.
[c] For each accounting alternative discussed in [b], provide a balance sheet account and indicate how each should be classified.

(AICPA adapted)

C2–12 An accountant must be familiar with the concepts involved in determining earnings of a business entity. The amount of earnings reported for a business entity generally depends on the proper recognition of revenue and expense for a given time period. In some situations, costs are recognized as expenses at the time of product sale; in other situations, guidelines have been developed for recognizing costs as expenses or losses by other criteria.

Instructions

[a] Explain the rationale for recognizing costs as expenses at the time of product sale.
[b] Explain the rationale for appropriately treating costs as expenses of a period instead of assigning the costs to an asset.
[c] Under what circumstances would it be appropriate to treat a cost as an asset instead of as an expense? Explain.
[d] Some expenses are assigned to specific accounting periods on the basis of systematic and rational allocation of asset cost. Explain the rationale for recognizing expenses on the basis of systematic and rational allocation of asset cost.
[e] Under what conditions would it be appropriate to treat a cost as a loss?

(AICPA adapted)

C2–13 You have been asked to deliver your auditor's report to the board of directors of Sebal Manufacturing Corporation and to answer questions about the financial statements. While reading the statements, one director asks: "What are the precise meanings of the terms 'cost', 'expense', and 'loss'? These terms sometimes seem to identify similar items and other times seem to identify dissimilar items."

Instructions

[a] Explain the meanings of these terms and their use in financial reporting under generally accepted accounting principles. Also discuss the distinguishing characteristics of the terms and their similarities and interrelationships.

[b] Classify each of the following items as a cost, expense, loss, or other category and explain how the classification of each item may change:

[1] Cost of goods sold.
[2] Bad debts expense.
[3] Depreciation expense for plant machinery.
[4] Organization costs.
[5] Spoiled goods.

[c] The terms "period cost" and "product cost" are sometimes used to describe certain items in financial statements. Define these terms and distinguish between them. To what types of items does each apply?

(AICPA adapted)

C2-14 Kwik-Bild Corporation sells and erects "shell houses." These are frame structures that are completely finished on the outside but are unfinished on the inside except for flooring, partition studding, and ceiling joists. Shell houses are sold chiefly to customers who are handy with tools and who have time to do the interior wiring, plumbing, wall completion and finishing, and other work necessary to make the shell houses livable dwellings.

Kwik-Bild buys shell houses from a manufacturer in unassembled packages consisting of all lumber, roofing, doors, windows, and similar materials. Before building in a new area, Kwik-Bild buys or leases land for its local warehouse, field office, and display houses. Display houses are erected at a total cost of from $3,000 to $7,000, including the cost of the unassembled packages. The chief element of cost is the unassembled packages; erection is a short, low-cost operation. Old models are torn down or altered every three to seven years. Sample houses have little salvage value because dismantling and moving costs amount to nearly as much as the cost of an unassembled package.

Instructions

[a] A choice must be made between (1) expensing the costs of display houses in the period in which the expenditure is made and (2) spreading the costs over more than one period. Discuss the advantages of each method.

[b] Should Kwik-Bild amortize the cost of display houses on the basis of (1) the passage of time or (2) the number of shell houses sold? Explain.

(AICPA adapted)

C2-15 The general ledger of Enter-tane, Inc., a corporation engaged in the development and production of television programs for commercial sponsorship, contains the following accounts before amortization at the end of the current year:

Account	Balance (Debit)
Sealing Wax & Kings	$51,000
The Messenger	36,000
The Desperado	17,500
Shin Bone	8,000
Studio Rearrangement	5,000

An examination of contracts and records reveals the following:

[1] The first two accounts listed above represent the total cost of completed programs that were televised during the accounting period just ended. Under the terms of an existing contract, Sealing Wax & Kings will be rerun during the next accounting period, at a fee equal to 50% of the fee for the first program televised. The contract for the first run produced $300,000 of revenue. The contract with the sponsor of The Messenger provides that he may, at his option, rerun the program during the next season at a fee of 75% of the fee for the first program televised.

[2] The balance in The Desperado account is the cost of a new program which has just been completed and is being considered by several companies for commercial sponsorship.

[3] The balance in the Shin Bone account represents the cost of a partially completed program for a projected series that has been abandoned.

[4] The balance of the Studio Rearrangement account consists of payments made to a firm of engineers which prepared a report on using studio space and equipment more efficiently.

Instructions

[a] State the general principles of accounting that apply to the first four accounts.

[b] Describe how you would report each of the first four accounts in the financial statements of Enter-tane, Inc.

[c] In what way, if at all, does the Studio Rearrangement account differ from the first four?

(AICPA adapted)

C2-16 Toole Tool Company is a large manufacturing concern that uses the FIFO method of inventory cost determination. The other major companies in Toole's industry use the LIFO method. At a recent stockholders' meeting, one of Toole's shareholders made the following statement:

"I'm having a lot of trouble comparing the performance of our company with that of others in the industry because we are the only company that uses FIFO. It seems to me that because of the *consistency principle* of accounting, we should be using LIFO so that our financial results will be consistent with those of our major competitors."

Instructions

Explain the consistency principle and evaluate the stockholder's statement.

C2–17 Assume that you are the independent auditor of a successful brewing company that has spent approximately 5% of each sales dollar on advertising during each of the past 10 years. The company charges all advertising costs to expense in the period in which the costs are incurred, and in past years, it has separately disclosed the amount of advertising expense in its income statment.

This year management has decided to save money by curtailing its advertising, and advertising expense for the year amounts to only 0.5% of sales. When examining the annual financial statements and the footnotes, you find no mention of advertising expense for the period. Upon asking management about the omission, you are told: "We have not disclosed advertising expense separately in our income statement because the amount clearly is immaterial. We don't want to clutter our financial statements, and thereby confuse our stockholders, by disclosing every minor detail concerning our operations. We have therefore included advertising in the 'other expenses' category of our income statement."

Instructions

[a] Evaluate management's contention that this year's advertising expense is immaterial.
[b] What disclosure relating to the company's advertising do you recommend for this year? Defend your answer from the standpoint of accounting theory.

EXERCISES

E2–1 Listed below are the assumptions, broad principles, and modifying conventions discussed in Chapter 2:
[a] Economic entity assumption
[b] Periodicity assumption
[c] Going-concern assumption
[d] Monetary unit principle
[e] Objectivity principle
[f] Historical cost principle
[g] Revenue realization principle
[h] Matching principle
[i] Consistency principle
[j] Disclosure principle
[k] Materiality
[l] Industry practices
[m] Conservatism
[n] Substance over form

Instructions

Select the letter corresponding to the assumption, broad principle, or modifying convention that best justifies the accounting practice described in each statement. *Do not use any letter more than once.*
[1] A company charges its sales commissions costs to expense.
[2] A company reports land at its acquisition cost even though the current cost is much higher.

[3] A company reports its financial statements in dollars that do not have the same purchasing power.
[4] The balance sheet of a small retail store does not include the owner's personal assets (home, car, etc.).
[5] A large company decides to expense all costs that are less than $25.
[6] A company reports all important details about its stockholders' equity.
[7] A company decides to use an accelerated depreciation method because it has no reason to prefer one depreciation method to another.
[8] A company uses the same accounting principles from one year to the next.
[9] Meatpacking companies report their inventories at net realizable value (estimated selling price less costs to complete and sell) because it is too difficult for them to determine historical cost.
[10] A company records transactions primarily based on arm's-length exchanges.

E2–2 Refer to the list presented in E2–1.

Instructions

Select the letter corresponding to the assumption, broad principle, or modifying convention that best justifies the accounting practice described in each statement below. *Do not use any letter more than once.*

[1] The lower of cost or market rule is used to value inventories.

[2] Financial reporting occurs at definite time intervals rather than only when business activity is at a low point.

[3] Convertible bonds (bonds that the owner can convert to common stock) are sometimes treated like common stock when computing earnings per share.

[4] Rent received in advance represents a liability until it is earned.

[5] Companies do not normally report the priority rights that creditors would have if the company were to liquidate.

[6] The income statement of the AB Partnership excludes personal expenses incurred by partners A and B.

[7] Petty cash is not usually listed separately on a company's balance sheet.

[8] Financial statements are reported in nominal dollars.

[9] A company should report all major accounting policies that it uses.

[10] Investment companies value their investments in common stock based on current market value.

E2–3 Refer to the list presented in E2–1.

Instructions

Select the letter corresponding to the assumption, broad principle, or modifying convention that best supports each of the following statements. *Do not use any letter more than once.*

[1] Investors and creditors ordinarily invest in or lend to enterprises that they expect to continue in operation.

[2] Many users of financial statements prefer accounting principles that tend to state a company's net income on the "low side" rather than the "high side."

[3] Users can depend on financial statements with greater confidence when they feel that the statements are not significantly distorted by the personal biases of the accountants who prepared them.

[4] User decisions would not likely be affected if a company expensed rather than capitalized a $10 wastebasket that it expected to last for five years.

[5] Many users are skeptical about the reliability of current value measurements.

[6] Users expect to know certain details about a company's long-term debt.

[7] Many users believe that companies should measure revenues only at the time of sale.

[8] Investors and creditors expect companies to report at definite time intervals.

[9] Many knowledgeable users of financial statements believe that because money has a time value, accountants should estimate and record interest on long-term notes that have no stated interest rates.

[10] Users generally expect companies to apply the same accounting principles over time.

E2–4 Refer to the list presented in E2–1.

Instructions

Select the letter corresponding to the assumption, broad principle, or modifying convention that is most clearly *violated* by the accounting practice described in each statement below. *Do not use any letter more than once.*

[1] A company prepares its financial statements in constant end-of-year dollars.

[2] A company reports its patents at their current market value.

[3] A company guesses the amount of its depreciation expense each year.

[4] A company records revenue as it produces its product.

[5] A company charges an asset account whenever it is in doubt about whether a certain cost should be capitalized or expensed.

[6] A company fails to report major details about its pension plan.

[7] A large company lists as a separate current liability a $1 credit balance that appears in a customer's account.

[8] A company owned by Myron Hall reports the cost of Hall's personal automobile on its balance sheet.

[9] A company changes from the sum-of-the-years'-digits method to the straight-line method of depreciating its plant assets.

[10] A company fails to record amortization of its intangible assets.

E2–5 Select the one best answer in each of the following items.

[1] The principle of objectivity includes the concept of

    [a] Summarization.

    [b] Classification.

    [c] Conservatism.

    [d] Verifiability.

[2] Financial statements that are expressed assuming a stable monetary unit are

[a] Constant dollar financial statements.

[b] Historical dollar financial statements.

[c] Current value financial statements.

[d] Fair value financial statements.

[3] The valuation of a promise to receive cash in the future at present value on the financial statements of a business entity is valid because of the accounting concept of

[a] Entity.

[b] Materiality.

[c] Going concern.

[d] Neutrality.

[4] The information provided by financial reporting pertains to

[a] Individual business enterprises, rather than to industries or an economy as a whole or to members of society as consumers.

[b] Individual business enterprises and industries, rather than to an economy as a whole or to members of society as consumers.

[c] Individual business enterprises and an economy as a whole, rather than to industries or to members of society as consumers.

[d] Individual business enterprises, industries, and an economy as a whole, rather than to members of society as consumers.

[5] When bad-debt expense is estimated on the basis of the percentage of past actual losses from bad debts to past net credit sales, and this percentage is adjusted for anticipated conditions, the accounting concept of

[a] Matching is being followed.

[b] Matching is *not* being followed.

[c] Substance over form is being followed.

[d] Going concern is *not* being followed.

[6] What is the underlying concept that supports the immediate recognition of a loss?

[a] Matching.

[b] Consistency.

[c] Judgment.

[d] Conservatism.

(AICPA adapted)

E2–6 Select the one best answer in each of the following items.

[1] The computation of earnings per share in accordance with generally accepted accounting principles may involve the consideration of securities deemed common stock equivalents. Common stock equivalents are an example of

[a] Form over substance.

[b] Substance over form.

[c] Form over accounting principle.

[d] Substance over accounting principle.

[2] Accounting changes are often made and the monetary impact is reflected in the financial statements of a company even though, in theory, this may be a violation of the accounting concept of

[a] Materiality.

[b] Consistency.

[c] Conservatism.

[d] Objectivity.

[3] During the lifetime of an entity, accountants produce financial statements at arbitrary points in time in accordance with what basic accounting concept?

[a] Objectivity.

[b] Periodicity.

[c] Conservatism.

[d] Matching.

[4] The broad principle of objectivity is complied with when an accounting transaction occurs that

[a] Involves an arm's-length transaction between two independent interests.

[b] Furthers the objectives of the company.

[c] Is promptly recorded in a fixed amount of dollars.

[d] Allocates revenues or expense items in a rational and systematic manner.

[5] Generally, revenues should be recognized when

[a] Management decides it is appropriate to do so.

[b] The product is available for sale to the ultimate consumer.

[c] An exchange has taken place and the earnings process is virtually complete.

[d] An order for a definite amount of merchandise has been received for shipment FOB destination.

[6] Continuation of an accounting entity in the absence of evidence to the contrary is an example of the basic concept of

[a] Accounting entity.

[b] Consistency.

[c] Going concern.

[d] Substance over form.

(AICPA adapted)

E2–7 Miner Company purchased a used delivery truck from Ball Company on July 1, 1985. Ball had acquired the truck new on July 1, 1984, for $25,000 and had taken $5,000 of depreciation for the fiscal year ending June 30, 1985. To acquire the truck, Miner issued to Ball 1,000 shares of Miner's $10 par value common stock. The stock was traded on a national stock exchange, and on July 1, 1985, it had a fair market value of $23 per share. A reputable local mechanic estimated that the truck was worth $21,500 cash on July 1, 1985. Miner had offered Ball this amount, but Ball refused. Immediately after Miner purchased the truck, Jones Company offered to buy it from Miner for $24,000 cash.

Instructions

[a] Record the appropriate journal entry on the books of Miner Company on July 1, 1985.
[b] Explain the rationale for your answer to [a].

Bryson Company recorded the following events as indicated during the current accounting period:
[1] The company purchased equipment on sale for $8,000 cash. The equipment would have cost Bryson $10,000 if it had not been on sale.

Equipment	10,000	
Cash		8,000
Revenue		2,000

[2] The company recorded depreciation on its plant assets. The dollar amount was correctly computed according to the straight-line method.

Retained Earnings	25,000	
Accumulated Depreciation		25,000

[3] An appraisal indicated that land acquired for $32,000 at the end of the previous accounting period was worth $40,000 at the end of the current period.

Land	8,000	
Gain from Holding Land		8,000

[4] Because the inflation rate during the current accounting period was 10%, the company reasoned that $50,000 of liabilities held throughout the period could now be paid using "cheaper" dollars.

Liabilities	5,000	
Purchasing Power Gain		5,000

[5] The company purchased a pencil sharpener that was expected to last five years.

Miscellaneous Expense	5	
Cash		5

[6] The company gave its president a new swimming pool for his personal use at home.

Plant Assets	20,000	
Cash		20,000

[7] A three-month loan was made on the last day of the accounting period to the company president.

Accounts Receivable	30,000	
Cash		30,000

Instructions

[a] From the standpoint of the theoretical model presented in the chapter, comment on the appropriateness of the manner in which Bryson Company has recorded each of the above events.
[b] Record the journal entries, if any, that Bryson should have made for each of the above events.

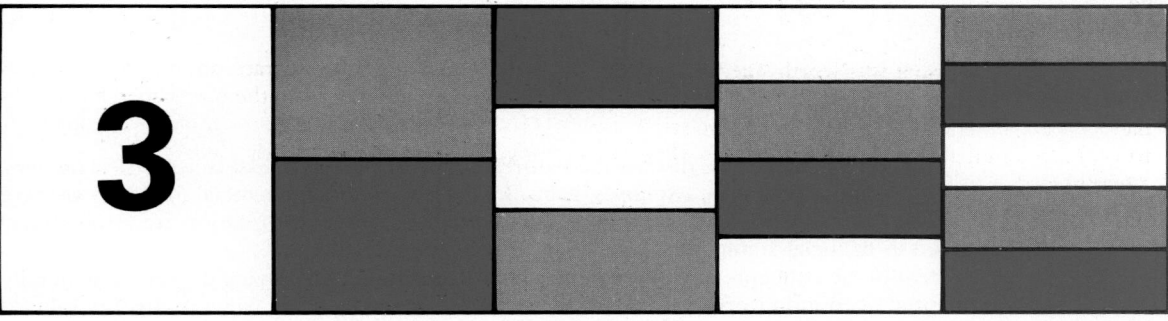

3

NATURE AND MEASUREMENT OF THE ELEMENTS OF FINANCIAL STATEMENTS

Objectives

To introduce the measuring units that may be used in financial statements.

To discuss the nature and measurement of assets, liabilities, and owners' equity.

To discuss the nature, measurement, and components of net income.

To discuss the usefulness of accounting net income.

To present the arguments favoring and opposing the publication of financial forecasts.

In this chapter we discuss the nature and measurement of assets, liabilities, owners' equity, revenues, expenses, gains, losses, and income. Financial forecasts also are discussed so that you may contrast them with the information traditionally reported in financial statements.

Most of the concepts discussed in this chapter are applied to varying degrees in generally accepted accounting principles (GAAP). Other concepts may be viewed as proposals for changing GAAP. If adopted by the accounting profession, these proposals would alter the present scope of accounting information.

This chapter provides a conceptual foundation that will enable you to better understand the strengths and limitations of conventional financial statements (i.e., statements prepared today in accordance with GAAP). The specific content of these statements is covered in Chapter 4. The conceptual foundation will also help you to understand some of the more serious proposals that have been made for changing conventional financial statements. We explain and illustrate these proposals more extensively in other chapters, particularly Chapter 27.

MEASUREMENT IN ACCOUNTING

Accounting has often been described as a measurement and disclosure discipline. The reason is that accountants measure the various elements of a company's financial statements, such as assets, liabilities, and revenues, and disclose the results of their measurements to users in order to help them make better decisions. The information that accountants choose to measure and disclose should be useful, which means that it should be both relevant and reliable.

The term **measurement** refers to the assignment of numbers to objects, such as inventories and plant assets, and events, such as purchases and sales. Measurement allows us to use numbers to conveniently relate certain objects and events to others. If, for example, we are told that one box weighs 100 pounds and another weighs 200 pounds, we know how heavy the second box is relative to the first without ever having seen or lifted either box. In accounting, the term **valuation** is frequently used to convey the same meaning as measurement. Accountants often say, for example, that a company's inventories are valued (measured) at a certain amount on the balance sheet.

The elements of financial statements are the subject matter of financial accounting and are the things accountants seek to measure. Users need measurements of assets, liabilities, and other elements in order to make rational investment, credit, and similar decisions. But before we can measure these elements, we must select a measuring unit and a financial attribute to measure.

To illustrate, assume that a company owns some land that we want to measure for financial reporting purposes. The measuring unit could be constant dollars that measure purchasing power as of the balance sheet date, or it could be nominal dollars that reflect the dollar's purchasing power at the time the land was acquired. The monetary unit principle requires the use of nominal dollars in conventional financial statements. The land has several financial attributes, such as how much it actually cost, how much it would cost to replace, and how much it could be sold for. Which one of these financial attributes should we measure? Although historical cost is the financial attribute required in conventional financial statements, other attributes could result in more useful information. Determining which measuring unit and which financial attribute would provide the most useful information are two major challenges that the accounting profession has faced for many years. We explore these issues more fully in later sections of this chapter and in Chapter 27.

Monetary Unit

THE MEASURING UNIT

Financial statements are expressed in money, which measures command over goods and services in the economy. If the general level of prices of goods and services remained constant over time, money would not be a controversial measuring unit to use in financial statements. Under these circumstances, money received or paid ten years ago could be compared meaningfully with money received or paid today, because both sums would represent the same amount of purchasing power or command over goods and services.

In reality, the general level of prices in the economy usually changes over time. An increase in the general price level means that money's command over goods and services has decreased; this is called **inflation.** Similarly, a decrease in the general price level, known as **deflation,** means that money's command over goods and services has increased. In the United States as well as in most other countries, inflation has existed for many years and is regarded by many people as simply a way of life. Between 1970 and 1980, for example, inflation in the United States was more than 100%. The existence of persistent inflation has caused accountants to actively debate the pros and cons of the two different types of measuring units that have been suggested for use in financial statements. These measuring units are called **nominal dollars** and **constant dollars.**

A nominal dollar is one that has not been adjusted for inflation (or deflation); a constant dollar is one that has been adjusted. Dollars are adjusted for inflation or deflation by using a **general price-level index,** which is a measure that reveals how much the average price of a given group of goods and services has changed over time. General price-level indexes show the changes that have occurred over time in the overall level of prices in the economy. A general price-level index should be distinguished from a **specific price index** which is a measure that reveals changes over time in the price of some relatively specific good or service, such as televisions or hospital care. The price of a specific good or service does not necessarily change at the same rate or even in the same direction as do prices in general. In a given year, for example, the inflation rate, which refers to prices in general, might be 10%, while the price of pocket calculators (a specific good) actually falls by 15%.

The most important general price-level indexes are the **Consumer Price Index for All Urban Consumers** and the **Gross National Product Implicit Price Deflator Index.** The federal government derives each index by monitoring the changes over time that occur in the prices of a variety of goods and services that form a "market basket." Each index has its own market basket, or predetermined group of goods and services. When constructing an index, a base period is selected and assigned an index number of 100. All other periods are then assigned index numbers that relate to the base. If prices in general rose by 10% in the period immediately following the base, for example, this period would be assigned an index number of 110.

To illustrate the nominal dollar and constant dollar measuring units, suppose that a company acquired land for $10,000 at the beginning of the current year, when the general price-level index was 100. At the end of the year, the general price-level index was 110, which means that the inflation rate during the year was 10%. In an ending balance sheet prepared in accordance with GAAP, we would report the land at $10,000. This amount is simply the historical cost of the land measured in nominal dollars. On the other hand, if we wanted to measure the historical cost of the same land using year-end constant dollars, the land would be measured at $11,000 ($10,000 × 110/100). Observe in this example that we measured the *historical cost* of the land in two ways; we did *not* measure the current market value of the land. Using the nominal dollar measuring unit, we measured the historical cost at $10,000. Measured in constant dollars, the historical cost is $11,000. We derived different amounts simply because we used different measuring units. Because of inflation, we would need $11,000 at the end of the year to have the same purchasing power as $10,000 at the beginning.

As another example of nominal versus constant dollar measurement, suppose that a company buys a product costing $200 at the beginning of the year, when the general price-level index is 110, and sells the product for $220 at the end of the year, when the general price-level index is 121. How much income did the company earn as a result of these events?

Measured in nominal dollars, as required under GAAP, the income is $20, as shown below:

Sales (measured when the general price-level index was 121)	$220
Less: Cost of product sold (measured when the general price-level index was 110)	200
Nominal-dollar income	$ 20

Observe that the conventional nominal-dollar income of $20 is the result of matching a revenue ($220) and an expense ($200) that are measured in dollars having different amounts of purchasing power. In contrast, the income measured in year-end constant dollars is zero, as shown below:

Sales (measured when the general price-level index was 121)	$220
Less: Cost of product sold (measured when the general price-level index was 121: $200 × 121/110 = $220)	$220
Constant-dollar income	$–0–

Under the nominal dollar approach, the company's income is $20 because the sale allowed the company to recover a larger *number of dollars* than was originally spent to buy the product. In contrast, under the constant dollar approach, income is zero because the sale merely allowed the company to recover the same *amount of purchasing power* that was originally invested in the product.

As a final example contrasting the nominal dollar and constant dollar measuring units, suppose that at the beginning of the current year you invested $1,000 in a savings account that will pay 6% interest on the last day of the year. Ignoring income taxes and assuming that the current annual inflation rate is 12%, how much income will you earn from your savings account during the year? The nominal-dollar income, which ignores inflation, would simply equal the interest of $60 ($1,000 × 6%) to be paid at year-end. This amount suggests that you will be economically better off by $60 at the end of the year. But because of inflation, you were actually better off with $1,000 at the beginning of the year than you will be with $1,060 at year-end. The constant-dollar income for the period would reflect this reality by recognizing a loss of purchasing power as a result of holding cash during a period of inflation. On a constant dollar basis you would actually have a *loss* of $60 for the year, computed as follows:

Interest revenue ($1,000 × .06)	$ 60
Less: Purchasing power loss from holding cash [($1,000 × 1.12) − $1,000]	120
Constant-dollar loss	$(60)

Purchasing power gains and losses exist when the measuring unit is constant dollars, but not when the measuring unit is nominal dollars. These gains and losses occur as a result of holding monetary assets (cash or claims to a fixed number of dollars of cash) or monetary liabilities (obligations to pay a fixed number of dollars of cash) during periods of inflation or deflation. During a period of inflation, a company gains purchasing power by being in debt because the debt can be paid with dollars having less purchasing power. On the other hand, a company loses purchasing power by holding monetary assets, such as cash, accounts receivable, and notes receivable, during a period of inflation because the assets lose some of their potential for buying goods and services. The opposite results occur in periods of deflation. Purchasing power gains and losses are not presently reported in conventional financial statements because the measuring unit is the nominal dollar.

The desirability of using constant dollars as the measuring unit in financial statements has been one of the most widely discussed topics in financial accounting for several decades. Proponents claim that constant dollar measurements would be useful to users of financial statements by revealing the impact of inflation on business enterprises. Opponents argue that constant dollar measurements are imprecise and costly and that inflation rates in the United States have not been sufficiently high to warrant a departure from nominal dollar accounting. At the present time, conventional financial statements are prepared using nominal dollars, and we emphasize the use of nominal dollars in this textbook. As you read the remaining chapters, however, remember the distinction between nominal dollars and constant dollars and that the use of nominal dollars creates certain distortions in financial statements. You will understand financial statements much better if you are aware of their strengths as well as their limitations. In Chapter 27 we explain constant dollar accounting in greater depth. We also discuss the Financial Accounting Standards Board (FASB) *Statement of Financial Accounting Standards No. 33,* which requires large corporations to report selected constant dollar measurements as supplementary information to their basic nominal dollar financial statements.[1]

Now that we have explored the question of what measuring unit should be used in financial statements, we shall discuss the nature and measurement of the major elements of financial statements.

ASSETS

Nature of Assets

In Chapter 2 we define assets as probable future economic benefits obtained or controlled by an entity as a result of past transactions or events.[2] As this definition implies, assets have three essential characteristics:

1. Assets embody probable future economic benefits.
2. The economic benefits of assets must accrue to a particular entity.
3. Assets are the result of transactions or events that have already occurred.

Note carefully that these characteristics pertain to *all* assets, such as cash, accounts receivable, merchandise inventory, land, and machinery. Note also that historical cost is *not* an essential characteristic of assets. Some assets, such as the land a city donates to attract a company to the area, may be acquired without cost.

The most important characteristic of an asset is the probable future economic benefits. These benefits usually result in net cash inflows to a company. A company may obtain the future economic benefits of an asset by exchanging the asset for something else of value or by using the asset. Two of a tire manufacturer's assets, for example, are the inventory of tires

---

[1]*FASB Statement of Financial Accounting Standards No. 33,* "Financial Reporting and Changing Prices," 1979.

[2]*FASB Statement of Financial Accounting Concepts No. 3,* "Elements of Financial Statements of Business Enterprises," 1980, par. 19. The discussion of the nature of assets relies heavily on *SFAC No. 3.*

and the machinery used to make tires. The manufacturer usually derives benefits by exchanging the tire inventory for cash or claims to cash and by using the machinery to manufacture tires that can later be sold.

Because the economic benefits of an asset are received in the future, accountants sometimes are uncertain about whether a particular item constitutes an asset. Cash is obviously an asset because it can buy goods and services. Uncollectible accounts receivable are clearly not assets because of the absence of future benefits. But what about a new advertising program that a U.S. automobile manufacturer implements to convince consumers that they should buy American products? When the manufacturer spends money for the advertising, the company hopes to derive future benefits. To an objective observer, however, the future benefits may be too uncertain to acknowledge an asset.

To qualify as an asset, the economic benefits of an item must be controlled by a particular entity. Public highways and public parks are therefore not considered assets of a particular company. Although the company may regularly use the highways to transport goods and the parks to have employee picnics, the company does not have the right to regulate the use of the highways and parks by others. On the other hand, private roads and parks that a company has built on its own land are considered assets because the company can regulate access by others.

In accounting we define assets as probable future economic benefits rather than as physical objects. A subtle but important point is that the "bundle" of benefits, and not the physical object itself, is the essence of an asset. A building, for example, is a physical structure that may provide many benefits such as office space and residual value after the building has been used. These benefits constitute the asset. At times, two or more entities may share the benefits that a building or other asset provides. In a building that is leased, for example, one party may have the right to use the property while another has the right to receive periodic rents and to realize the residual value of the property when the lease expires. In this case, the building provides economic benefits to both parties to the lease.

Assets result from past transactions or events of a particular entity. A ten-year-old machine therefore becomes an asset to a particular company on the date the company acquires it, not when the machine was manufactured. Similarly, a machine that a company plans to acquire next year will not be an asset to the company until the acquisition occurs.

Measurement of Assets

Historical Cost

Assets have several financial attributes that can be measured. As discussed in Chapter 2, conventional accounting emphasizes the historical cost attribute. That is why financial statements today are frequently referred to as historical cost financial statements. But as we saw in the previous section, historical cost is not an essential characteristic of an asset. Furthermore, historical cost is not the only attribute that accountants measure. Indeed, the asset measurements reported in financial statements today reflect a mixture of financial attributes.

A company operates in both an input market and an output market, and exchange prices exist in both markets. The financial attributes that may be used for asset measurement fall into two general categories that correspond to these markets, as shown below:[3]

Market	Asset Measurement Category	Financial Attribute
Input	Input values	Historical cost
		Current cost

---

[3]The discussion of financial attributes of assets relies heavily on *FASB Discussion Memorandum,* "Conceptual Framework for Financial Accounting and Reporting: Elements of Financial Statements and Their Measurement," 1976, pars. 402–437.

Output	Output values	Current exit value in orderly liquidation
		Expected exit value in due course of business
		Present value of expected cash flows

Fundamentally, an **input market** is one in which a company acquires goods and services from suppliers, employees, and others. An **input value** refers to a measure of the amount a company has to give up to acquire the goods and services. In contrast, an **output market** is one in which a company sells its products to customers. An **output value** refers to a measure of the amount a company will receive in exchange for its product.

As we discuss each of the financial attributes in the following sections, keep the following points in mind:

1. Each attribute pertains to an existing asset.
2. Each attribute pertains to an actual transaction (one that has actually occurred), an expected transaction (one that is expected to occur), *or* a hypothetical transaction (one that would occur if certain circumstances existed).
3. Each attribute pertains to the past, the present, *or* the future.
4. Each attribute is used in practice for measuring certain kinds of assets under current GAAP.
5. Asset valuations (and income measurements) may differ significantly depending on which financial attribute is used. Under certain circumstances, the measurement of two or more financial attributes of a given asset may result in the same dollar amounts. Nevertheless, each attribute differs conceptually from the others.

Historical Cost

As we discussed in Chapter 2, the historical or acquisition cost of an asset is the amount of the cash or cash-equivalent payment actually made to acquire the asset. Historical cost is therefore an input value based on an actual past transaction. In conventional financial statements, historical cost is generally used to measure such assets as inventories; property, plant, and equipment; and intangible assets.

Historical costs are based on arm's-length exchange transactions that have actually occurred and can be verified by invoices, canceled checks, and other source documents. The historical cost of an asset equals the market value of the asset at the time the company acquired it. Changes in an asset's market value that occur after acquisition generally are ignored until the company sells the asset.

Proponents of historical cost measurement emphasize that historical costs are objective and reliable. Opponents argue that historical costs lack relevance because they fail to reflect current market values after a company acquires an asset.

Current Cost

The current cost of an asset is the amount of cash or cash-equivalent payment that a company would have to make today to acquire the same asset. Like historical cost, current cost is an input value, but unlike historical cost, current cost is based on a hypothetical present transaction. Suppose, for example, that a company owns land that it acquired a year ago for $20,000 (a historical cost). If the company would have to pay $25,000 for the land today, the land has a current cost of $25,000 to the company. Assuming that no inflation occurred during the year, the company has earned a $5,000 **holding gain** simply by holding the land during a time when its market value increased. Holding gains are *not* separately recognized under generally accepted accounting principles, which, as we have stated, are based primarily on the use of historical costs. However, applying the lower of cost or market rule when measuring inventories sometimes results in current cost measurements that appear in conventional financial statements. We explain this rule in detail in Chapter 8.

Various methods can be used to determine the current costs of a company's assets. The current cost of a raw material may be determined by examining the prices listed in the supplier's current catalog. It is often possible to determine the current cost of certain equipment used in operations by applying specific price indexes which measure changes in the price of the equipment over time. Appraisals may be effectively used to determine the current cost of such assets as land and specialized machinery. As we discuss and illustrate in Chapter 27, *FASB Statement of Financial Accounting Standards No. 33* requires certain large companies to report selected current cost measurements as supplementary information to their conventional financial statements. The major items required by *SFAS No. 33* are inventories, cost of goods sold, plant assets, and depreciation. In essence, *SFAS No. 33* is a large-scale experiment that focuses on the preparation and use of current cost and constant dollar measurements.

Proponents argue that the use of current cost measurements in financial statements would help users to make more accurate predictions of future cash flows and more meaningful evaluations of a company's financial position and performance. Critics, on the other hand, contend that current cost measurements are generally too subjective and unreliable to be useful in making investment and credit decisions.

Current Exit Value in Orderly Liquidation

The current exit value of an asset is the amount of cash the asset could be sold for in an orderly liquidation. In other words, the current exit value of a machine tells us how much cash a company could receive if it were to sell the machine (not the entire business, only the machine) in an orderly manner as opposed to a forced sale. Current exit value is an output value based on a hypothetical present transaction and is used in practice today to measure the securities held by investment companies and certain other entities.

Recall that when an asset is measured at historical cost, changes in the asset's market value are generally ignored until the time of sale. In contrast, when an asset is measured at current exit value, changes in the asset's current exit value are recognized in both the asset valuation and income. Assume, for example, that a company buys an inventory item on December 31, 1984, for $100. Assume further that the current exit value of the item on that date is $140, and the company actually sells the item for $150 on March 3, 1985. Under the historical cost approach, the company would report the asset at $100 at the end of 1984 and would report income of $50 ($150 − $100) in 1985, when the asset is sold. The current exit value approach, in contrast, would require the company to report the asset at $140 at the end of 1984 and to report income of $40 ($140 − $100) during 1984 and $10 ($150 − $140) during 1985.

Proponents argue that current exit values are relevant because they reveal the cash receipts a company can command at the present time. On the other hand critics maintain that companies acquire many assets for use rather than sale and that current exit value measurements of most assets are unreliable. Critics further argue that some intangible assets, work-in-process inventory, and specialized plant assets, such as an oil refinery in a foreign country that has an unstable government, have no current exit values.

Expected Exit Value in Due Course of Business

The expected exit value of an asset, often called **net realizable value,** is the amount of cash or cash-equivalent value that a company expects to receive for the asset in the ordinary course of business, minus the costs of completing and selling the asset. Suppose, for example, that a company owns some partially completed inventory that could be sold as is for $6,000. Completing and selling the goods, which the company plans to do, will cost approximately $500, and the company estimates that the completed goods can be sold for $8,000. Under these circumstances, the goods have a current exit value of $6,000. The expected exit value of the goods in due course of business, however, is $7,500 ($8,000 − $500). Expected exit value is therefore an output value based on an expected future transaction. Changes that occur over time in an asset's expected exit value are recognized in both the asset valuation and income. In practice, expected exit values are used to measure accounts receivable and, under certain circumstances, to measure inventories.

An asset's expected exit value is relevant to users because it indicates the net amount of cash the company expects to receive for the asset in the future. Expected exit values, however, are generally subject to the same criticisms as current exit values.

Present Value of Expected Cash Flows

An economic fact universally accepted by rational business people is that money has a time value, commonly called **interest.** Suppose that your neighbor (whom you trust) offers to give you in exchange for cash a written and signed IOU for $112 payable to you one year from now. How much cash would you be willing to pay for the IOU today assuming you want to earn 12% interest on your investment? Clearly you should not pay $112 because you would not earn any interest. The answer of course is $100 ($112 ÷ 1.12). We would say, then, that your neighbor's IOU has a **present value** (that is, a value at the present time) as an asset to you of $100. To determine the present value we **discounted** the amount you would receive at the end of the year ($112) using a 12% discount rate.

Here's the point of the preceding exercise. Ultimately, the value of an asset to a company depends on the asset's ability to generate net cash inflows (cash inflows − cash outflows = net cash inflows) for the company in the future. Inventory, for example, has value because of the net cash inflows that generally result from the future sale. Equipment used in the manufacturing process has value because it is used to produce products that can later be sold to generate cash. The present value of an asset is the discounted amount of the net cash inflows that the asset is expected to generate. Present value, then, is an output value based on expected future transactions.

To determine the present value of an asset, we must discount all the net cash inflows that an asset is expected to generate. This process requires an estimate of (1) the **amount** of net cash inflows that an asset will generate, (2) the **timing** of those cash flows, and (3) the **discount rate.** Changes that occur over time in an asset's present value are recognized in valuing the asset and in determining income. At this point in your study, you should concentrate on *why* present value is an important financial attribute of assets. Computing present values is not difficult and is explained in Chapter 6.

From the standpoint of relevance, present value is widely regarded as the best of the various asset valuation concepts. Assets are essentially expected future economic benefits, and present values tell us how much those benefits are currently worth to the company. The benefits are expressed as the net cash inflows that the company expects the asset to generate in the future. Little doubt exists that investors, creditors, and other users of financial statements would like to know the present values of a company's assets. The problem is that accountants cannot measure present values in a reliable manner for most types of assets. Consider a machine used in the manufacturing process, for example. The machine is likely used with other machines, materials, and labor services to produce a product that the company hopes to sell in the future for some amount of cash. But who knows whether the product will actually sell, how much cash it will sell for, and when the company will receive the cash from the sale? Who knows how much cash is attributable to the machine we are trying to measure, exclusive of the other factors (e.g., materials, labor services, advertising) that are important in producing and selling the product? And what discount rate should we use to compute the present value? The difficulty of answering these kinds of questions is what makes the present value approach impractical for most types of assets. However, the present value approach is used in GAAP today for measuring certain long-term receivables under *Accounting Principles Board Opinion No. 21.*[4] The amount and timing of cash

---

[4] *APB Opinion No. 21,* "Interest on Receivables and Payables," 1971.

receipts for long-term receivables can usually be estimated with reasonable accuracy, and the discount rate used in practice is one that is reasonable at the time the receivable was created.

Summary

Exhibit 3–1 summarizes the financial attributes we have discussed. Although each attribute is used under GAAP for measuring certain types of assets, the historical cost attribute is presently emphasized. Proponents of historical cost tend to emphasize the reliability of the measurement, while proponents of each alternative to historical cost tend to emphasize the relevance of the measurement to users of a company's financial statements. Recall that relevance and reliability are the most important determinants of the usefulness of information. Assuming that relevance and reliability require important trade-offs, an important question facing the accounting profession is which financial attribute is in fact the most useful for decision making. Is it really the historical cost attribute, or is it some other one?

Historical Cost

LIABILITIES

Nature of Liabilities

In Chapter 2 we define liabilities as probable future sacrifices of economic benefits arising from present obligations of an entity to transfer assets or provide services to other entities in the future as a result of past transactions or events.[5] A liability has three essential characteristics:

1. It embodies a probable future sacrifice of economic benefits.
2. It obligates a particular entity to transfer assets or provide services in the future.
3. It is the result of a transaction or event that has already occurred.

The essential characteristics of a liability are similar to those of an asset, except that an asset entitles an entity to *receive* economic benefits, whereas a liability obligates the entity to *pay* economic benefits. Most liabilities, such as accounts payable, are settled by paying cash, but some, such as the liability for magazine subscriptions paid in advance by customers, require settlement in the form of services or assets other than cash. For a liability to exist, it is not necessary to know either the exact amount of the liability or the specific identity of the parties to whom the entity is obligated. For example, companies report liabilities under product warranties in their financial statements without knowing the identity of the customers whose products will become defective and require servicing. The dollar amounts are estimated based on past experience.

The most significant characteristic of a liability is the duty or requirement to sacrifice economic benefits in the future, either by expending assets or providing services. Liabilities may be payable on demand, on certain maturity dates, or when certain specific events occur. Because a liability entails a probable future sacrifice, uncertainty often exists about whether a particular item qualifies as a liability. For example, accounts payable, interest payable, and wages payable are clearly liabilities because they represent probable future sacrifices. On the other hand, determining that an entity will probably lose a lawsuit and therefore have to pay damages is much more difficult and requires considerable judgment.

Most liabilities, such as bonds payable, are evidenced by contracts or other agreements and by the fact that the entity incurring the liability usually receives proceeds (cash, other assets, or services). However, contracts and the receipt of proceeds are not essential characteristics of a liability. Some liabilities, such as income taxes and lawsuit settlements, are the

---

[5]*FASB Statement of Financial Accounting Concepts No. 3,* par. 28. The discussion of the nature of liabilities relies heavily on *SFAC No. 3.*

	EXHIBIT 3–1		
	Financial Attributes of Assets		
Financial Attribute	Description	Transaction	Time
Input Values			
Historical cost	Amount of cash or cash-equivalent payment actually made to acquire the asset.	Actual	Past
Current cost	Amount of cash or cash-equivalent payment that a company would have to make today to acquire the same asset.	Hypothetical	Present
Output Values			
Current exit value in orderly liquidation	Amount of cash the asset could be sold for in an orderly liquidation.	Hypothetical	Present
Expected exit value in due course of business	Amount of cash or cash-equivalent value that a company expects to receive for the asset in the ordinary course of business, minus the costs of completing and selling the asset.	Expected	Future
Present value of expected cash flows	Amount of discounted net cash inflows that the asset is expected to generate.	Expected	Future

result of governmental or legal actions and do not involve proceeds to the entity. Other liabilities, such as donations to charity, are the result of discretionary actions by an entity's management and the entity does not receive proceeds.

A liability does not have to be legally enforceable, although most liabilities, such as notes payable, are. A liability may exist simply because an entity is bound by custom or tradition to provide money, goods, or services in the future. A liability for year-end bonuses, for example, may exist because a company has always paid such amounts even without a contractual requirement to do so.

Probable future sacrifices alone do not constitute a liability. For a liability to exist, a particular entity must be obligated to transfer assets or provide services to other entities in the future as a result of past transactions or events. A company that has sold all of its inventory has no liability to pay for new inventory until acquired from another entity. Similarly, the amount shown in the next year's budget for labor services is not a liability until the company has received the services.

Measurement of Liabilities

The five financial attributes discussed earlier for assets also pertain to liabilities.[6] But relative to asset measurement, liability measurement has received much less attention in the accounting literature. The measurement of a liability in practice is often the result of measuring the other side of the transaction that created the liability. When a company acquires an inventory item for $100 on credit, for example, the asset is measured at $100 in accor-

---

[6]The discussion of financial attributes of liabilities relies heavily on *FASB Discussion Memorandum,* "Conceptual Framework for Financial Accounting and Reporting: Elements of Financial Statements and Their Measurement," 1976, pars. 534–576.

dance with the historical cost principle; the liability is also measured at $100, which is the amount the company expects to spend to liquidate the liability.

Liabilities enable companies to delay payment until a later time. The cost of delaying payment is interest, or the time value of money. Whether interest is explicitly stated or not, it is always inherent in liabilities. Two important issues in liability measurement therefore are (1) whether the interest should be separately recognized, and (2) what rate should be used to recognize the interest.

Each of the following financial attributes pertains to a liability that presently exists. Although each attribute is conceptually different from the others, the measurement of two or more financial attributes of a given liability may result in the same dollar amount under certain circumstances. Measurements of liabilities and income may differ considerably depending on which financial attribute is used.

Present Value of Expected Cash Flows

Conceptually, a liability should be measured on a present-value basis, and many liabilities are measured this way in current practice. The present value of a liability is the discounted amount of the net cash outflows that are expected to be necessary to liquidate the liability. Suppose, for example, that a company has a debt of $1,000 that is payable one year from today. Assuming that an interest rate of 12% is appropriate for the company, the present value of the liability today is $892.86 ($1,000 ÷ 1.12).[7] The $107.14 difference between $1,000 and $892.86 is the interest charge that the company will incur by being indebted during the coming year. Under the present-value approach, the interest would be separately recognized and accounted for.

Present-value measurements reflect the time value of money and are required in current practice when measuring certain long-term payables under *APB Opinion No. 21.* In practice, accountants apply the present value approach throughout the time a liability exists by using a discount rate equal to the market rate of interest at the time the liability was initially incurred. This discount rate is called the **historical market rate.** Very often the historical market rate is simply the interest rate stated in the loan agreement.

Expected Exit Value in Due Course of Business

The expected exit value of a liability is the amount of cash or cash-equivalent value that the company expects to pay to eliminate the liability in the ordinary course of business. The amount of the cash or cash-equivalent payment is not discounted to a present value. Assume, for example, that a company acquires some merchandise on credit. The goods cost $5,000, and the company agrees to pay this amount in 60 days. The expected exit value of the liability is $5,000.

Expected exit values show how much cash the company expects to spend to liquidate a liability, but they ignore the time value of money completely. In the example above, the interest on the $5,000 liability for 60 days is not separately considered. To illustrate this point more dramatically, assume that a company currently sells at par value $100,000, 12%, 20-year bonds that the company expects to retire at maturity. The expected exit value of the bonds today would be $340,000 [$100,000 maturity value + $240,000 ($100,000 × .12 × 20) interest]. Recording the bond liability at $340,000 fails to reflect the economic reality that interest of $240,000 will be incurred during the 20-year life of the bonds. Under current GAAP the company would measure the bond liability at $100,000, an amount equal to the present value of the interest and principal payments required to liquidate the bonds.

Expected exit values are used under GAAP for measuring many liabilities. For example, accounts payable to suppliers are usually measured at expected exit values. The interest is ignored on the ground that the credit period is usually relatively brief and therefore the

---

[7]Computing present values is discussed more fully in Chapter 6.

interest is immaterial. As another example, liabilities for product warranties are usually measured at their expected exit value. In this case, the interest is ignored because the amount and timing of payment are too uncertain to permit a meaningful estimate of the interest.

Historical Proceeds

The historical proceeds of a liability is the amount of the cash or cash-equivalent proceeds actually received when the liability was incurred. To illustrate, assume that a company receives $18,000 from customers for magazine subscriptions paid in advance for three years. The company now is obligated to provide the magazines for the next three years, and it would measure the liability for unearned subscriptions revenue at $18,000, the amount of the cash proceeds received.

Historical proceeds is generally used under GAAP to measure liabilities for products or services that a company has agreed to provide to customers in the future. The time value of money is generally ignored for these types of liabilities because it is considered too impractical to measure.

Current Proceeds

The current proceeds of a liability is the amount of cash or cash-equivalent value that a company would receive today by incurring the same liability. The amount of this measurement changes in response to changes in the level of interest rates in the market and to changes in the perceived risk of the company that has the liability. As market interest rates rise, the amount of the current proceeds of a given liability tend to decrease; similarly, as market interest rates fall, the current proceeds tend to increase.

To illustrate, suppose that on January 1, 1985, a company issues a $10,000, 10%, two-year note payable with interest of $1,000 ($10,000 × 10%) payable at the end of each year. On that date the market rate of interest is 10%, and the company receives proceeds of $10,000, because the present value of the note (including the interest) at the market rate of interest is $10,000. On December 31, 1985, the company pays $1,000 of interest for the year 1985, the current market rate of interest is 12%, and the company's risk level is unchanged from the beginning of the year. Under these circumstances, the current proceeds of the note will be $9,821.43 on December 31, 1985. This amount equals the $10,000 face amount plus $1,000 of interest due at the end of 1986, divided by 1.12 ($11,000 ÷ 1.12 = $9,821.43). We are saying, then, that *if* the company were to issue on December 31, 1985, a $10,000, 10% note with one year remaining to maturity, the company would obtain proceeds of $9,821.43. The reason that the current proceeds are less than $10,000 is because the current market rate of interest (12%) exceeds the interest rate stated in the note (10%). A lender who invested $9,821.43 in the note at the end of 1985 would earn 12% interest (the current market rate) during 1986 [$9,821.43 + ($9,821.43 × 12%) = $11,000]. Notice that $9,821.43 is simply the present value of the note computed using the current market rate of interest (12%) at the end of 1985.

We emphasize that the note payable in the example above would be reported at $10,000 (not $9,821.43) in conventional financial statements prepared at the end of 1985. This is so because $10,000 is the present value of the note at the end of 1985 computed using the market rate of interest that prevailed when the note was originally issued ($11,000 ÷ 1.10 = $10,000).

Under the current proceeds approach to liability measurement, the time value of money is measured using a current rather than historical interest rate. Some people believe that the use of current proceeds would enhance the usefulness of financial statements for making predictions of cash flows and evaluations of management. But current proceeds represents a departure from historical cost accounting and is not used for measuring liabilities under GAAP.

Current Exit Value in Orderly Liquidation

The current exit value of a liability is the amount of cash a company would have to pay currently to eliminate the liability in an orderly manner. Assume, for example, that a company has $100,000 of bonds payable outstanding and that each of the 100 bonds was originally sold at par value of $1,000. Assume further that market interest rates have fallen since the bonds were issued and that each of the 100 bonds now has a market price of $1,050. Under these circumstances the current exit value of the bonds is $105,000 ($1,050 × 100) because this is the amount the company would have to pay currently to retire the bonds by purchasing them in the market.

When a liability requires specified cash payments, such as the bond liability in the example above, the current exit value and current proceeds will usually be the same amount. Nevertheless, current exit value and current proceeds differ conceptually. Current exit value refers to how much a company would have to *pay* to eliminate the liability; current proceeds refers to how much a company would *receive* by incurring the liability. Some people argue that current exit values would be relevant to users when assessing the ability of an entity to adapt to a changing environment. The counterargument is that most companies do not intend to eliminate all of their liabilities currently. Like current proceeds, current exit value measurements represent a departure from historical cost accounting and are not used when measuring liabilities in financial statements prepared in accordance with GAAP.

Summary

The various financial attributes of liabilities are summarized in Exhibit 3–2.

OWNERS' EQUITY

Nature of Owners' Equity

Owners' equity is "the residual interest in the assets of an entity that remains after deducting its liabilities."[8] In other words, owners' equity equals net assets, which are assets minus liabilities.

Like liabilities, owners' equity represents an interest in the assets of an entity. But liabilities and owners' equity differ in several important aspects:

1. Liabilities represent the interest of creditors in the assets of an entity; owners' equity represents the interest of owners.
2. Liabilities rank ahead of owners' equity when an entity's assets are distributed. A company may not pay dividends to owners until it has made the required interest and principal payments to creditors. Moreover, when a company is liquidated, liabilities must be paid before distributions can be made to owners.
3. The amount of liability payments is usually more certain than is the amount of payments to owners. Oral or written agreements, such as bond contracts, usually specify how much cash a company must pay to liquidate its liabilities. The amount of dividend payments to owners, however, is usually determined at the discretion of a company's board of directors.
4. The timing of liability payments is usually more certain than the timing of payments to owners. Many liabilities have specific maturity dates; owners' equity does not mature.

Owners' equity represents the interest of parties who stand to lose the largest amount if an entity is unsuccessful and gain the largest amount if it is successful. Owners are the primary beneficiaries of an entity's net income, but they also must bear its losses. Owners' equity is originally created when owners invest cash or other assets in an entity. Subse-

---

[8]*FASB Statement of Financial Accounting Concepts No. 3,* par. 43. The discussion of the nature of owners' equity relies heavily on *SFAC No. 3.*

EXHIBIT 3–2			
Financial Attributes of Liabilities			
Financial Attribute	**Description**	**Transaction**	**Time**
Present value of expected cash flows	Amount of discounted net cash outflows that are expected to be necessary to liquidate the liability.	Expected	Future
Expected exit value in due course of business	Amount of cash or cash-equivalent value that a company expects to pay to eliminate the liability in the ordinary course of business.	Expected	Future
Historical proceeds	Amount of cash or cash-equivalent proceeds actually received when the liability was incurred.	Actual	Past
Current proceeds	Amount of cash or cash-equivalent value that a company would receive today by incurring the same liability.	Hypothetical	Present
Current exit value in orderly liquidation	Amount of cash that a company would have to pay currently to eliminate the liability in an orderly manner.	Hypothetical	Present

quently, the interest of owners may be increased by additional investments and net income, and it may be decreased by distributions to owners (dividends) and net losses.

Owners' equity provides an important frame of reference when measuring a company's net income. In the absence of additional investments by owners or distributions to them during a period, net income for the period will equal the increase in owners' equity that occurred during the period.

Measurement of Owners' Equity

As indicated earlier, owners' equity is a residual figure derived by deducting liabilities from assets. The measurement of owners' equity is therefore not an independent process. Instead, it depends on the valuations assigned to the individual assets and liabilities. Suppose that a company had only one asset, an account receivable with an expected exit value of $10,000 and no liabilities. Under these circumstances, owners' equity would simply reflect the expected exit value measurement of $10,000 ($10,000 − $0). As we have seen, however, companies actually use a mixture of financial attributes (historical costs, expected exit values, present values, etc.) when measuring their individual assets and liabilities. Owners' equity therefore reflects a mixture of financial attributes. For this reason and because many assets and liabilities are simply too difficult to measure and report at all, owners' equity does not reveal the current market value of the company to its owners.

INCOME

In the following sections we discuss the nature, measurement, and usefulness of net income. Many of the concepts we review are controversial. Accountants are still attempting to determine the nature of net income. Is net income simply revenues minus expenses? If so, how do we define revenues and expenses? Is the present system of accrual accounting preferable to cash accounting? Are accounting earnings useful for decision making, and if so, what are their limitations? These are some of the questions discussed in the following sections.

Nature of Net Income

The famous economist J. R. Hicks defined an individual's income as the maximum amount the person could consume in a period and still be as well off at the end of the period as he was at the beginning.[9] This definition can be adapted to a business enterprise: the **net income** of a business is the increase in the net assets (owners' equity) of the firm, assuming no new capital contributions by the owners or dividend distributions by the business.[10] More specifically, to determine the net income of the enterprise, we must compare the beginning and ending owners' equity, as adjusted for new stockholder investments and dividend distributions. To illustrate, a company with net assets of $20,000 at the beginning of the year and $25,000 at the end of the year has realized a net income of $5,000. If, however, the company received $8,000 in new capital investment from the owners and distributed $3,000 in dividends, the net income was $0 [$25,000 − ($20,000 + $8,000 − $3,000)].

Important to the understanding of net income is the distinction between a return *of* capital and a return *on* capital. Stockholders make investments in business enterprises to earn a return *on* capital, or an amount in excess of their original investment. A return *of* capital is simply an erosion of the capital invested in the firm. Earnings result only after the capital used from the beginning of the period is maintained. This concept is known as **capital maintenance.** In the Hicksian sense, the same level of "well-offness" must be maintained before earnings are acknowledged. Revenues must be applied to the recovery of the resources used in the business before any of the revenues can be considered earnings. An important concept to recognize is that the capital used in the business does not have to be physically replaced with the exact type of resources consumed. Capital maintenance is a measurement concept, not a statement of how managers should reinvest resources.

To illustrate the concept of capital maintenance, consider a retail store with all its capital invested in an inventory of 800 stereophonic records costing $5 each. If the retailer sells 600 records at $7 each, the total return is $4,200 (600 × $7). Therefore, at the end of the period, the retailer has 200 records and $4,200. To determine net income, we must deduct from $4,200 an amount that represents the capital invested in the 600 records that were sold. One way of doing this is to deduct $3,000 (600 × $5) from the $4,200 as a return *of* capital and then consider the remaining $1,200 (600 × $2) as a return *on* capital (i.e., net income). The retailer need not actually replace the 600 records that were sold. Our objective in deducting $3,000 is merely to measure the capital consumed by the sale of 600 records so that we can determine net income.[11]

Lifetime Net Income

The most definitive measure of net income can be made when a company is liquidated. At that time, the **lifetime net income** of the firm can be determined with certainty. After liquidation, the lifetime net income (or loss) equals the difference between the cash invested at the beginning of business and the cash left after assets are liquidated and liabilities are satisfied (assuming no further contributions or borrowings by owners and the

[9]J. R. Hicks, *Value and Capital* (Oxford: Clarendon Press, 1946), p. 172.
[10]Robert T. Sprouse and Maurice Moonitz, *Accounting Research Study No. 3,* "A Tentative Set of Broad Accounting Principles for Business Enterprises" (New York: AICPA, 1962), p. 54.
[11]Central to the concept of capital maintenance is the accountant's assessment of "well-offness." The accountant's definition of capital has a direct bearing on what is considered as net income. It is beyond the scope of this text to discuss the various concepts of capital. A lucid discussion can be found in Keith Shwayder, "The Capital Maintenance Rule and the Net Asset Valuation Rule," *Accounting Review* (April 1969), pp. 304–316.

LIFETIME NET INCOME

ACCOUNTING METHODS are not as difficult as some would have us believe. A restaurant owner from the old country kept his accounts payable in a cigar box, accounts due on a spindle and cash in his register.

"I don't see how you can run our business this way," chided his son, an accountant. "How do you know what your profits are?"

"Well, son," the father replied, "when I got off the boat, I had nothing but the pants I was wearing. Today your brother is a doctor, your sister is an art teacher and you are an accountant. Your mother and I have a nice car, a city house and a country home. We have a good business and everything is paid for. So, you add all that together, subtract the pants, and there's your profit!"

SOURCE: *Life,* First Baptist Church, Tulsa, Oklahoma, vol. 2, no. 11, August 12, 1982.

---

retention of all earnings by the business). Over the life of the enterprise, total revenues equal all cash receipts from operations, and total expenses equal all cash disbursements to operations. Lifetime net income therefore equals lifetime cash receipts minus lifetime cash disbursements, or total net cash inflows from operations during the life of the business.

Periodic Net Income

Although the lifetime net income of an enterprise corresponds with its net cash flows from operations, this situation does not help the investor or creditor to make *timely* decisions. Investors and creditors are not interested in knowing the net income of a firm after final disposition of assets. Instead, they need periodic disclosures of operating performance in order to assess current investments and loans or to evaluate future capital commitments.

One function of the accountant is to provide statements of periodic earnings. This presents a challenge because, in contrast to lifetime earnings, periodic earnings do not necessarily reflect cash flows for the period. Cash flows for all expenses and revenues are realized sometime during the life of the enterprise, but not necessarily in corresponding periods. At the time income is recognized, there may be some uncertainty about cash outcome, as in the case of uncollectible accounts receivable. The accountant attempts to reconcile the recognition of revenues and expenses with the actual cash flows of past, present, and future periods. This reconciliation requires the recognition of certain assets and liabilities, as shown in Exhibit 3–3.[12]

The upper left cell of Exhibit 3–3 illustrates the situation in which cash inflow precedes the recognition of revenue. Consider, for example, a business that rents space in return for a fee received in advance. When the fee is collected, there is no revenue, only the liability of providing rental space. Revenue is recognized only as rental space is provided. Likewise, the lower left cell of Exhibit 3–3 represents the case of cash outflow preceding the recognition of an expense. This occurs when a business advances cash in exchange for future services, as in the case of prepaid insurance. The prepaid insurance represents the right to future protection that is amortized as an expense only as the protection is received.

The upper right cell of the exhibit illustrates transactions in which cash inflow follows revenue recognition. An obvious example is accounts receivable from credit sales, which are collected in cash after the revenue has been recognized. The lower right cell concerns transactions in which cash outflow follows expense recognition. Frequently, at the end of a reporting period, an enterprise has received employee services for which it has not yet paid.

---

[12]These assets and liabilities are commonly called "accruals" and "deferrals." A more detailed discussion of these types of assets and liabilities is provided in Chapter 5.

EXHIBIT 3-3
Reconciliation Between Cash Flow and
Revenue/Expense Recognition

	Cash Precedes Recognition	Cash Follows Recognition
Revenues	**Liability** Example: Unearned Rent	**Asset** Example: Accounts Receivable
Expenses	**Asset** Example: Prepaid Insurance	**Liability** Example: Accrued Wages Payable

The labor represents a liability to the firm that will later be compensated by actual cash payment.

In each of the above cases, revenue and expense recognition for the period do not exactly correspond to cash flows. Although cash flows are reconciled with revenues and expenses over the lifetime of a company, it is unreasonable to postpone income measurement until business is terminated. Instead, methods must be used to measure periodic net income.

The Measurement of Periodic Net Income

The measurement of periodic net income depends on the valuation of assets and liabilities, because the net income for the period is the change in the net assets for the period, assuming no new capital contributions or dividends. At a very simple level, a cash basis system could be used to determine periodic income. In the next section we compare cash basis accounting and traditional accrual basis accounting.

Cash Basis Accounting Versus Accrual Basis Accounting

Cash basis accounting defines revenues as cash inflows from earning activities, such as the sale of goods and services, and expenses as cash outflows in earning activities, such as payments to suppliers and employees. Frequently, cash inflows and outflows occur in different periods than the related accomplishments and efforts. For example, the purchase of machinery results in an immediate cash outflow but provides useful service over a period of years. **Accrual basis accounting** allows for such cases by recording the results of significant operating events when they occur rather than when cash is received or paid. Under accrual basis accounting, revenues are recognized when earned, regardless of when cash is received, and expenses are recognized when incurred, regardless of when cash is paid.

Because investors and creditors are interested in cash flows (see Chapter 2), wouldn't a simple cash basis income statement be preferable to an accrual basis statement? Most accountants think not. A cash basis system usually fails to provide valuable information about the earning capability of the firm. In addition, cash receipts and disbursements for successive periods are generally unrelated and can produce misleading trends. The following example illustrates these points.

Consider a college student who started a business, the Nimble Fingers Typing Service. The following events occurred during the first three months of the academic year.

September

Rented a typewriter for $25 on account.
Purchased paper for $30 on account.

Placed an advertisement in the campus newspaper
for $40 on account.
Typed several projects and charged customers a total
fee of $200 on account.

October

Collected $200 in fees from customers.

November

Remitted payments to paper supplier, campus newspaper,
and office equipment lessor.

Under cash accounting the income statement and balance sheet would appear as shown in Exhibit 3–4. Close examination of these financial statements reveals some difficulties of cash basis accounting. If we attempted to evaluate the performance of Nimble Fingers based on the monthly cash flow figures, our conclusions would change from month to month. For September we might conclude that the business accomplished nothing, because the financial statements contain all zeros. We know, however, this is not the case. Nimble Fingers provided typing services throughout September.

October appears much more promising with a large increase in net income. At this point we might conclude that the business is proving successful. This, however, is misleading, because we know, as early as the end of September, that of the $200 cash inflow reported in October, only $105 represents a return *on* invested capital, while the remaining $95 is a return *of* capital. This information is known, but the reporting is delayed under cash basis accounting.

For November the income statement reports a net loss of $95. This turn of events leaves the outside observer frustrated, unable to determine what might happen in December. Taking the three months together, the total net income is $105 ($0 + $200 − $95), which is accurate. What is not meaningful is the time period in which the $105 was disclosed. Under cash basis accounting we must wait for the final cash payment in November before we have an accurate picture of the events for the first three months. The criticism is that this information was known with reasonable certainty as early as the end of September, but recognition was delayed until actual cash changed hands.

Accrual accounting alleviates these problems by recording net income when it was *earned* rather than when cash was collected or paid. Exhibit 3–5 presents the Nimble Fingers financial statements under accrual accounting. The information disclosed in September under accrual accounting differs markedly from that under cash accounting. Net income is disclosed in the period in which effort is applied to the typing business, and accomplishments accrue as the jobs are completed. All net income is disclosed in September, because the main activities of the business were completed in this month. After September, all that remains are the incidental activities of collecting customer accounts and satisfying creditor obligations. The income statement reflects this by attributing zero earnings to October and November. The balance sheet includes Accounts Receivable and Accounts Payable among the assets and liabilities in order to reconcile cash flow with revenue and expense recognition (Exhibit 3–3).

In comparing cash basis and accrual basis accounting, we find that under both methods the net income for a period is equal to the change in the net assets, and the lifetime net income is $105. The major difference between the two methods is the assignment of income to periods. Under accrual accounting, revenues and expenses are recorded at the earliest appearance of objective evidence. This frequently precedes cash flow. As a result, accrual

---

EXHIBIT 3–4
Financial Statements for Nimble Fingers
Under Cash Basis Accounting

Income Statement
(month ending)

	September	October	November
Revenues	$-0-	$200	-0-
Expenses	-0-	-0-	$ 95
Net income (Loss)	$-0-	$200	$(95)

Balance Sheet
(last day of the month)

	September	October	November
Total assets (Cash)	$-0-	$200	$105
Owner's capital	$-0-	$200	$105

---

accounting assigns income to the period in which it is earned, which is often a more timely measurement than that of cash basis accounting.

Measuring Income Under Accrual Accounting

There are several methods of measuring income under accrual accounting. These methods relate to the financial attributes used in measuring assets and liabilities, as discussed earlier in the chapter. Accrual basis income may be measured under historical cost, current cost, current exit value, expected exit value, and present value methods.

To illustrate the various methods of measuring income under accrual accounting, consider the wholesaler Horizon Sales, Inc. Horizon Sales has only one asset—an inventory of

---

EXHIBIT 3–5
Financial Statements for Nimble Fingers
Under Accrual Basis Accounting

Income Statement
(month ending)

	September	October	November
Revenues	$200	$-0-	$-0-
Expenses	95	-0-	-0-
Net income	$105	$-0-	$-0-

Balance Sheet
(last day of the month)

	September	October	November
Cash	-0-	$200	$105
Accounts receivable	$200	-0-	-0-
Total assets	$200	$200	$105
Accounts payable	$ 95	$ 95	-0-
Owner's capital	105	105	$105
Total liabilities and owner's capital	$200	$200	$105

fur coats purchased on January 1, 1984. Information about the fur coats is given as follows.

January 1, 1984

Fur coats are purchased at a cost of $100,000.

December 31, 1984

Current cost to replace the fur coats is $125,000.
Amount of cash that could be received in orderly
liquidation (current exit value) of the fur
coats is $133,000.
Amount of cash expected to be received for the fur
coats after selling costs (expected exit value)
is $135,000.

December 31, 1985

Fur coat inventory is sold for $144,000 on account.

January 1, 1986

$144,000 is collected from customers.

Historical Cost. If the inventory of fur coats is measured under historical cost, recognition of income is delayed until the actual sale. This is consistent with the revenue realization principle, which requires that income be recorded when the earnings process is substantially complete and an exchange transaction has occurred. Objective evidence, such as a bona fide transaction (sale), is usually necessary to determine when the earnings process has been completed. Therefore, earnings of $44,000 ($144,000 − $100,000) would be recorded for Horizon Sales in 1985.

| Revenue Realization |

Current Cost. Although the concept of historical cost is consistent with GAAP, it is helpful to understand the alternatives to conventional accounting methods. Under the current cost method, on December 31, 1984, Horizon Sales would write up the inventory to current cost ($125,000). The $25,000 difference between the beginning and ending balance of the inventory is called a holding gain (or holding loss if the ending balance was less than the beginning balance). The holding gain would be reported on the 1984 income statement. In 1985 the $19,000 difference between the selling price ($144,000) and the current cost valuation of the inventory on December 31, 1984 ($125,000) would be included in income.[13]

Current Exit Value. If we assume that the fur coats are reported at their current exit value, the holding gain for 1984 would be $33,000. This is the increase in the exit value of the inventory from the beginning to the end of the period ($133,000 − $100,000 = $33,000). Horizon's 1985 current exit value income on the sale of the fur coats would be $11,000 ($144,000 − $133,000).

Expected Exit Value. As discussed previously in the chapter, current exit value and expected exit value are likely to result in two different valuations of the same item because

[13]If the current cost valuation of the inventory remained unchanged from December 31, 1984, to December 31, 1985, all of the $19,000 would be considered "current operating profit." If, however, the current cost valuation of the inventory changed during 1985, the $19,000 would be separated into two parts, current operating profit and holding gain. As an example, if the current cost valuation of the inventory was $134,000 on December 31, 1985, then $10,000 ($144,000 − $134,000) would be current operating profit and $9,000 ($134,000 − $125,000) would be a holding gain. We discuss this more fully in Chapter 27.

EXHIBIT 3–6
Net Income of Horizon Sales for 1984 and 1985
Under Five Asset Valuation Methods

| | Reported Earnings | | |
Method	1984	1985	Total
Historical cost	–0–	$44,000	$44,000
Current cost	$25,000	19,000	44,000
Current exit value	33,000	11,000	44,000
Expected exit value	35,000	9,000	44,000
Present value of expected cash flows	20,000	24,000	44,000

of the different assumptions used in each method. In the example of Horizon Sales, the holding gain for 1984 would be $35,000 ($135,000 − $100,000), while the expected exit value income recognized in 1985 would be $9,000 ($144,000 − $135,000).

Present Value of Expected Cash Flows.   To illustrate the measurement of earnings under present value, we must first assume that at the time the fur coats were purchased on January 1, 1984, it was *known* that $144,000 cash would be received for their sale two years later. This is, of course, an unrealistic assumption in the case of an inventory of fur coats.[14] As a result, we illustrate present value income measurement for Horizon Sales, bearing in mind the limitations of this approach to applications involving assets and liabilities with uncertain future cash flows.

Horizon Sales invested $100,000 in an asset (fur coats) that will be worth $144,000 in two years. The *annual* rate of growth necessary to increase the inventory from its present value of $100,000 to the future value of $144,000 is 20%.[15] For 1984 the investment in the inventory is assumed to grow by 20%, or $20,000 ($100,000 × .20). Therefore, the inventory has a value of $120,000 on December 31, 1984. The $20,000, or the difference between the beginning and ending inventory valuation, is the income earned and reported in 1984. For 1985 the investment has a beginning value of $120,000. A 20% annual return on this amount yields $24,000 ($120,000 × .20) and increases the value of the inventory to $144,000. This is not a coincidence. The annual rate of return is determined so that the inventory balance increases to the selling amount of $144,000. The income earned in 1985 would be $24,000, and the increase in the inventory balance would reflect the 20% rate of return.

Summary.   The net income of Horizon Sales under all five methods is summarized in Exhibit 3–6. Clearly, the total income on the sale of the fur coats is $44,000. The question is how to assign the $44,000 return on investment to the two periods. Under GAAP (historical cost), the $44,000 is reported in 1985, the year of the sale. Under the four alternatives to historical cost, at least part of the $44,000 is reported in 1984. This points to one of the frequent criticisms of historical cost, namely, the delay in recognizing income. Critics suggest that alternatives are generally more timely in the recognition of income and are therefore more relevant to users of financial statements in their attempts to predict future cash flows.

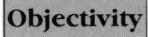

Supporters of historical cost counter that the alternatives lack objectivity and also generate income numbers that are less likely to result in cash flows. For example, if the fur coats

---

[14]The assumption of perfect foreknowledge is not so unreasonable in the case of assets and liabilities resulting in fixed cash flows. Examples include notes receivable and payable, which are contracts for certain cash flows in the future. In these cases a present value approach is generally accepted.
[15]The annual rate of return can be determined with the aid of present value interest tables. Use of these tables is discussed in Chapter 6.

were sold for $100,000 on December 31, 1985, the current cost and exit value (current and expected) methods would recognize income in 1984 and a loss in 1985. Supporters of the present system argue that the reporting of income in 1984 could have harmed users, because that income failed to materialize. The uncertainty of eventual cash realization was too great and resulted in the reversal in 1985 of income recognized in 1984.

Components of Net Income

Net income is composed of revenues, expenses, gains, and losses. Each component can be defined according to the asset/liability view or the revenue/expense view. According to the **asset/liability view,** the components of net income are defined by reference to definitions of assets and liabilities. Under the **revenue/expense view,** the components of net income are defined without reference to definitions of assets and liabilities. Both views are used in practice, but the FASB currently favors the asset/liability view, as implied in the following definitions, which we presented in Chapter 2:

1. **Revenues.**   Inflows or other enhancements of assets of an entity or settlements of its liabilities (or both) during a period, based on production and delivery of goods, provision of services, and other activities that constitute the entity's major operations. Examples are sales revenue, interest revenue, and rent revenue.
2. **Expenses.**   Outflows or other use of assets or incurrences of liabilities (or both) during a period as a result of delivering or producing goods, rendering services, or carrying out other activities that constitute the entity's ongoing major or central operations. Examples are cost of goods sold, salaries expense, and advertising expense.
3. **Gains.**   Increases in owners' equity (net assets) from peripheral or incidental transactions of an entity and from all other transactions and events affecting the entity during a period, except those that result from revenues or investments by owners. Examples are a gain on the sale of plant assets and a gain on the early retirement of long-term debt.
4. **Losses.**   Decreases in owners' equity (net assets) from peripheral or incidental transactions of an entity and from all other transactions and events affecting the entity during a period, except those that result from expenses or distributions to owners. Examples are losses on the sale of investments and on litigation.

Notice the references in the above definitions to assets, liabilities, and owners' equity (net assets). The components of net income are *not* defined independently of definitions of assets and liabilities. In a sense, the definitions of assets and liabilities are the anchor, or reference point, for the definitions of revenues, expenses, gains, and losses. The FASB calls this the asset/liability view.

According to the alternative conceptual approach—the revenue/expense view—revenues, expenses, gains, and losses are defined without direct reference to definitions of assets and liabilities. Proponents of this view do not agree about the correct definition of the components of income, but they generally view revenues as a measure of the operating accomplishments of the enterprise in a particular period and expenses as the efforts necessary to generate the revenues for the period. Fundamental to this position is the principle of matching expenses with revenues. Under the revenue/expense view, how we define assets and liabilities is secondary to how we define revenues and expenses. Assets and liabilities are essentially the debits and credits that remain after revenues and expenses are properly matched on the income statement.

| Matching |

Both the asset/liability view and the revenue/expense view are compatible with financial statements that *articulate* with one another. Articulated financial statements, which are the kind that accountants produce under GAAP, are fundamentally related or tied to one another.

The major issue in the asset/liability and revenue/expense controversy is whether definitions of assets and liabilities or revenues and expenses should take precedence. This is far from a trivial concern. Many critics of the revenue/expense view believe that the matching principle lacks objectivity. Furthermore, they believe the income statement may be open to recognition of revenues and expenses that are not changes in enterprise assets or liabilities. It is suggested that such revenues and expenses are meaningless to understanding the change in wealth of a business. Under the revenue/expense view, the balance sheet can become a "dumping ground" for nonresources and nonobligations because of vague definitions of revenues and expenses. Supporters of the asset/liability view impose an objective limit on what will be considered as admissible revenues, expenses, gains, and losses. Only transactions that increase or decrease the assets or liabilities of an enterprise can be considered revenues or expenses.

As indicated earlier, current practice reflects a combination of both views. There is a significant overlap in the disclosure results under both views, which makes the distinction between them difficult to observe in practice. The FASB has decided to emphasize one view in order to guide future accounting policy decisions. Because the FASB has supported the asset/liability view, we have embraced this view throughout the conceptual discussion in this chapter.

Usefulness of Accounting Net Income

In the mid-1960s many critics of financial reporting argued that the net income number was meaningless. They based their opposition on continued adherence to historical cost, which they thought misrepresented reality. In addition, skeptics denounced the diversity of acceptable accounting methods (e.g., LIFO versus FIFO in inventory costing) for determining earnings. They suggested that managers could disclose net income in various ways according to GAAP because of the lack of uniform measurement principles. Indeed, one author showed how identical firms could produce an earnings per share of either $.80 or $1.79, depending on the choice of accounting principles.[16] Critics asserted that such ambiguity reduced the credibility of accounting income numbers as a source of information to statement users. One financial analyst described the situation this way:

| Matching |

> The accountant defines it [earnings] as what he gets when he matches costs against revenues, making any necessary allocations of costs to prior periods; or as the change in the equity account over the period. These costs are not economic definitions of earnings but merely descriptions of the motions the accountant goes through to arrive at the earnings number.[17]

Fortunately, subsequent research on the usefulness of net income disclosures allayed many of these concerns. One such study investigated whether knowledge of the next year's net income would be sufficient to earn superior returns in the price of a company's stock.[18] Obviously, if such advance knowledge could not be used in profitable investment strategy, it would be of little value. Results of this study indicated that if just the direction of change in the next year's net income were known for a number of companies, investment decisions could be made that would consistently produce better-than-average returns. This suggests that disclosure of net income has value for investors.

Although strong evidence indicates that the net income number is useful for investor decision making, it says nothing about the timeliness of net income disclosures. Such information could have already reached investors in other forms. Investors could use alternative

---

[16]The illustration was provided by Leonard Spacek, "Business Success Requires an Understanding of Unsolved Problems of Accounting and Financial Reporting," in J. Lories and R. Brealey (Eds.), *Modern Developments in Investment Management* (New York: Praeger, 1972), pp. 630–644.

[17]Jack Treynor, "The Trouble with Earnings," *Financial Analysts Journal* (September 1972), p. 41.

[18]Ray Ball and Phillip Brown, "An Empirical Investigation of Accounting Income Numbers," *Journal of Accounting Research* (Autumn 1968), pp. 159–178.

EXHIBIT 3–7
Preliminary Earnings Announcement

INT'L BUSINESS MACHINES (N)

Quar Mar 31:	1983	a1982
Revenues ...	$8,287,000,000	$7,066,000,000
Net income	976,000,000	789,000,000
Avg shares	603,600,000	593,200,000
Shr earns:		
Net income ..	1.62	1.33
a-Restated.		

SOURCE: *Wall Street Journal,* April 15, 1983, p. 36.

---

sources of information, such as investment advisory services and government reports, to estimate the current earnings of a company.

A study was conducted to test the timeliness of net income disclosures.[19] This study investigated whether present and potential investors reacted to the initial disclosure of the accounting net income number. Initial disclosure of a corporation's quarterly or annual earnings precedes the dissemination of quarterly or annual reports to shareholders. Major stock exchanges require listed companies to release earnings announcements to the press and wire services as soon as the information becomes available. Most U.S. corporations release earnings data publicly via the Dow-Jones News Service (the Broad Tape), which is a financial-news wire service. The earnings release is then printed in *The Wall Street Journal* the next business day. Exhibit 3–7 shows a typical quarterly earnings release as printed in *The Wall Street Journal.* If information in the preliminary earnings release had already reached investors, we would not expect investors to react to the net income disclosure. The study found that the volume of trading increases dramatically in the week the net income disclosure is released publicly, compared to the rest of the year. This finding strongly supports the timeliness of net income disclosure.

Evidence strongly supports the proposition that accounting net income is both useful and timely to investors in their buying and selling decisions. However, the question remains: Why do investors perceive the net income number as relevant information? The significance of net income as a source of information can be viewed in two interrelated ways. In one sense, net income is a measure of *past* performance; in another sense, it is an indicator of *future* cash flows. These uses are discussed in the following sections.

Net Income as a Measure of Past Performance

A business enterprise begins operations by obtaining financing from the equity owners, and possibly from creditors. The cash received from the financing activity is converted into labor, raw materials, plant, equipment, and other inputs of production. The goal of the organization is to convert these inputs to an output (product) whose value is greater than the sum of the inputs. This is accomplished by adding time, form, and place utility to the inputs. For example, grapes from the Rhine Valley can be pressed into wine; the bottled wine is then aged for several years, after which it may be shipped to The Plaza in New York. The inputs, including vineyard, winepress, storage area, and shipping, combine to produce a fine table wine that can be sold for an amount greater than the sum of the input costs. This is accomplished by adding time (the aging process), form (grapes to wine), and place (West Germany to New York) to the product. This process can be characterized as the **earnings process** of the firm.

---

[19]William Beaver, "The Information Content of Annual Earnings Announcements," *Journal of Accounting Research* (Supplement 1968), pp. 87–92.

The earnings process and financing activities of a firm become interrelated through time. Each firm must compete with other firms for investment dollars. The amount and cost of funds that a firm can obtain is a function of its earnings performance relative to other companies. Earnings tells owners and creditors how efficiently management converts inputs to outputs. Firms that have been very successful, as demonstrated by past earnings activities, enjoy a competitive advantage in the financing markets. In contrast, firms that have not experienced the same level of success may find their sources of capital diminished or unavailable. The result can be the final liquidation of an inefficient firm.

The earnings of an enterprise can also be viewed as a "report card" of management's performance. Did management responsibly utilize the resources entrusted to them? If the answer is no, the stockholders have two choices: they can replace existing management with new management, or they can sell their interest in the firm. It should be noted, however, that the evaluation of management performance can be very difficult. In many instances, evaluating management efficiency solely on the basis of net income is insufficient. Assume, for example, the latest year-to-year net income results of a company show a 10% decrease. From this information alone, we might conclude that past performance is rather poor. However, if we know that during the same period the net income of all firms in the economy decreased by an average of 30%, we might conclude that our company performed rather well. An informed user of financial statements should also recognize that many events affecting a company's performance, such as floods and earthquakes, are outside the control of management.

Net Income as a Predictor of Cash Flows

Net income not only helps investors and creditors to evaluate the past performance of a firm, but also helps them to predict the cash returns they will receive. For stockholders, the value of shares relates to future dividends. For example, the price of a share is generally higher when stockholders expect to receive larger dividends, all else equal. As a result, shareholders want information that helps them predict future dividends. Net income disclosures may be useful in this regard, because future dividends depend on future earnings.

As a first step in predicting cash flow, present earnings should be separated into a transitory component and a permanent component.[20] The **transitory component** of net income is that part which investors do not expect again in the near future. Transitory income can result from unusual or incidental activities of limited duration or in unconventional markets. For example, a publishing company purchases a downtown parking lot as the site of a future office building. Until construction begins, the company operates the parking lot and collects parking fees. The parking fees are income of limited duration (until construction begins), are incidental to the main function of the company (publishing), and are therefore not expected to continue. Transitory income (or loss) can also result from unusual events. Examples include a casualty loss from an earthquake, an expropriation of plant assets by a foreign country, and a loss due to a strike by employees.

The **permanent component** of net income is the part that investors expect to continue. Permanent income results from the primary functions of the enterprise. In the case of the publishing company, permanent income is generated from producing and marketing books. Permanent income is affected by changes in the demand for books, the price of the books, and the cost of making the books.

As you might expect, investors are much more interested in permanent earnings, because only permanent earnings are useful in predicting income. Transitory earnings are not expected to affect future income. Because accounting policy makers, such as the FASB, understand the importance of distinguishing between the two components of net income, various types of transitory earnings must presently be identified. In Chapter 4 we discuss in

---

[20]A more detailed discussion of these two components of earnings and reporting considerations can be found in *FASB Discussion Memorandum,* "Reporting Earnings" (Stamford, Conn.: FASB, 1979).

greater detail the reporting requirements for several of these nonrecurring events. Unfortunately, the financial reporting requirements for net income do not permit these two types of earnings to be clearly distinguished from one another.

The needs of creditors are similar to those of investors. Whereas investors are concerned with the ability of the firm to pay dividends, creditors are interested in the ability of the firm to make interest and principal payments on loans. Both investors and creditors are forward-looking in this regard. As a result, creditors also focus on the permanent component of net income in assessing the future earnings capability of the firm. Future earnings protect interest payments, because interest is paid to creditors before dividends are distributed to stockholders.

As the needs of investors and creditors are satisfied, so too are the needs of other users. Major customers, for example, are interested in the long-term viability of the enterprise, especially if there are major warranty contracts or if major support is necessary for the product line (as in the case of computer equipment). Employees are concerned with the future prospects of the firm as they evaluate employment security and compensation. In both cases, the permanent net income can help predict income.

In summary, a firm's earnings have been shown to be useful in the investment decision. Net income is useful because it reflects past performance and can be used to indicate future performance. Net income can tell financial statement users where the firm has been and, to a more limited degree, where it is going.

FINANCIAL FORECASTS

As stated in the previous section, financial statement users want information about the ability of a business to generate income. Some observers have suggested that enterprises could provide this information directly to financial statement users in the form of published financial forecasts. A **financial forecast** is an estimate, or a range of estimates, of future financial results, such as revenues, net income, and earnings per share. Financial forecasts are *not* required by GAAP at this time, but companies may disclose them voluntarily.

The construction of a financial forecast requires certain assumptions about the future state of the overall economy and the interaction of the firm with the economy. The accuracy of the forecasts is directly related to the accuracy of the assumptions used in making the forecasts. As a result, some people have advocated the publication of a range of forecasts during a given period. In this way, financial statement users would be aware of management's range of expectations, from pessimistic to optimistic, and could then select a scenario consistent with their own expectations.

Exhibit 3–8 illustrates the financial forecasts and explanations of Days Inns of America, Inc., in their financial statements of September 30, 1982. Days Inns is a fast-growing motel chain in the eastern and southwestern United States. Days Inns provides a five-year forecast, along with management's explanation of assumptions and limitations of the forecast. Management also attempts to give the statement user an idea of the sensitivity of the income projections to changes in critical assumptions.

In 1973 the Securities and Exchange Commission (SEC) reversed its long-standing opposition to public disclosure of financial forecasts by issuing guidelines for voluntary disclosures to be filed with the Commission. Since that time there has been a great deal of controversy about mandated public disclosure of financial forecasts. Various surveys have found widespread dissatisfaction with the concept of published financial forecasts.[21] Moreover, very few companies publish financial projections.[22] In the rest of this section we briefly discuss the arguments favoring and opposing public disclosure of financial forecasts.

---

[21]See, for example, *Public Accounting in Transition: A Survey by Opinion Research Corporation* (Chicago: Arthur Andersen & Co., 1974), pp. 106, 107.
[22]Moustafa H. Abdelsamad and Glenn H. Gilbreath, "Publications of Earnings Forecasts: A Report of Financial Executives' Opinions," *Managerial Planning* (January 1978), pp. 26–30.

EXHIBIT 3–8
Days Inns of America, Inc.
Financial Forecasts and Explanations

Days Inns of America, Inc.
CONSOLIDATED STATEMENTS OF FORECASTED INCOME AND STOCKHOLDERS' EQUITY

For the year ending September 30,	1983	1984	1985	1986	1987
NET REVENUE:					
Lodging	$143,556,000	$167,702,000	$200,116,000	$245,444,000	$303,658,000
Food, gasoline and novelties	63,800,000	71,692,000	82,066,000	94,406,000	109,332,000
Franchise fees	8,233,000	8,686,000	9,164,000	9,668,000	10,199,000
Rental income	2,231,000	2,348,000	2,471,000	2,600,000	2,735,000
Other income	5,811,000	7,445,000	9,634,000	10,351,000	11,626,000
	223,631,000	257,873,000	303,451,000	362,469,000	437,550,000
COSTS AND EXPENSES:					
Cost of food, gasoline and novelties	37,767,000	41,769,000	46,705,000	52,219,000	58,587,000
Selling, general, administrative and operating expenses	131,707,000	153,715,000	182,309,000	219,721,000	266,674,000
Depreciation and amortization	17,819,000	19,369,000	22,076,000	25,776,000	30,803,000
Interest expense, net of interest income	26,182,000	30,857,000	37,642,000	47,031,000	60,104,000
	213,475,000	245,710,000	288,732,000	344,747,000	416,168,000
Income before provision for income taxes	10,156,000	12,163,000	14,719,000	17,722,000	21,382,000
Provision for income taxes	3,859,000	4,622,000	5,593,000	6,734,000	8,125,000
Net income	$ 6,297,000	$ 7,541,000	$ 9,126,000	$ 10,988,000	$ 13,257,000
Stockholders' equity	$ 46,444,000	$ 53,985,000	$ 63,111,000	$ 74,099,000	$ 87,356,000
Occupancy	68.0%	68.5%	69.0%	69.5%	70.0%
Average room rate	$29.75	$31.75	$33.75	$36.25	$38.85
Number of company motel openings	8	12	16	20	24
Number of franchise motel openings	0	5	5	5	5
Number of motels disfranchised	5	4	3	3	3
Total rooms at year end (operating and under construction)	45,300	47,600	50,700	54,600	59,100

Days Inns of America, Inc.
COMMENTS ON FORECASTED RESULTS OF OPERATIONS 1983–1987

Policy On Forecasting

Since the Company began making earnings forecasts in 1977, there has been extensive dialogue on the subject in the business community. It is in the interest of the readers of the Company's financial statements to have insight into Management's perspective of the Company's business outlook. While historical results are readily available and amply discussed in financial reports, the probability for continuation, or for changes, in these trends is a most influential factor in reaching investment decisions.

It is important to understand what is meant by a "forecast." The forecast issued each year is the best appraisal of the Company's anticipated results. This appraisal is based on Management's interpretation of the overall business climate and willingness to support new projects and take risks, as well as the perception of operations personnel.

This financial forecast is based upon Management's assumptions concerning future events and circumstances. The assumptions discussed herein are those which Management believes are significant to the forecast or are key factors upon which the financial results of the Company depend. Some assumptions inevitably will not materialize and unanticipated events and circumstances may occur subsequent to September 30, 1982. Therefore, the actual results achieved during the forecast periods will vary from the forecasts, and the variations may be material.

Days Inns of America, Inc. will pursue an aggressive program during the next five years. The forecasts include the development of eighty properties, approximately 14,000 rooms, emphasizing metropolitan locations near suburban shopping centers, office parks, commercial areas, airports, historical areas and civic centers. Both existing and new properties will experience inflationary increases in revenues and expenses. It is also expected that volume increases will occur in room occupancy and food and novelty sales.

Assumptions Made By Management In Preparation Of These Forecasts

Lodging revenues are based upon (a) an average occupancy of 68.0% in 1983 increasing to 70.0% in 1987, (b) an average room rate of $29.75 in 1983 increasing about 7% each year through 1987, and (c) the addition of eight to twenty-four properties each year from 1983 through 1987. It is estimated that a variance from the projected occupancy of 1%, with no variance in the average room rate, would result in a change in income before income taxes of approximately 14%, and that a variance in the average room rate of 1%, with no variance in occupancy, would result in a change in income before income taxes of approximately 13%.

Food sales, forecasted on the basis of covers per available room, will increase for room additions and an inflation rate of 5–7%. Gasoline revenues will increase due to inflation of 7% per year. Novelty sales per rented room will increase for inflation but decrease in volume as new properties are opened with smaller novelty shops. The cost of goods sold for food, gasoline and novelties will remain constant at 33%, 92% and 65%, respectively.

Initial franchise fees are based on openings each year, plus charges for conversions of other motels, ownership transfers and site inspections. Recurring franchise fees are forecasted using (a) an increase in total available rooms for motel openings, net of disfranchised properties, (b) an occupancy rate approximating Company operated units and (c) an average room rate slightly lower than Company operated units.

Rental and other income includes revenue from leased motels, based on agreements in effect as of September 30, 1982, membership fees and conventions related to September Days Club, commissions and miscellaneous income. No attempt has been made to forecast the impact of property sales.

For the five-year period, selling, general, administrative and operating expenses are forecasted to increase approximately 100%. Inflation will impact various costs from 5%–10% annually. In addition the Company has forecast continuing improvement and enhancement of its internal financial, accounting, reporting and management information systems. The operating costs of new properties will account for the remaining increase.

Estimates of depreciation are based on estimated lives for various classes of assets using the straight-line method of depreciation. Increases in expense are due to the addition of new properties and replacements and improvements at existing properties. Expenditures for new properties are forecasted at $475,000,000 during the next five years.

Interest expense is based on loans in effect at September 30, 1982, plus assumed financing at rates of 12½%–14% per annum on the new properties. All other interest is based on a constant level of debt. Interest income is projected to increase due to higher cash reserves.

Provisions for income taxes are calculated using the applicable tax rates, less investment tax credits from qualifying capital expenditures and estimated targeted jobs tax credits available to the Company.

Forecasted stockholders' equity assumes that the only changes arise from operations. No attempt has been made to forecast dividends for 1983 through 1987.

The accounting policies used in the forecasts are consistent with those applied in the financial statements for 1982 and should be read in conjunction with the consolidated financial statements and accompanying notes for the years ended September 30, 1982 and 1981.

SOURCE: Days Inns of America, Inc., 1982 Annual Report.

Benefits of Public Disclosure

Investors and creditors could benefit from financial forecasts by learning about management's plans and expectations. Relative to the outside investor, management generally knows more about the firm and at least as much about the impact of the external environment. Therefore, it is frequently argued that publication of financial forecasts would provide useful information about the performance capability of the firm. Forecasts may also benefit outside investors who have access to corporate forecasts.

Managers could also benefit by the publication of financial forecasts. Once financial projections are issued, managers' reputations are at stake and there is strong incentive to achieve projected figures. Moreover, preparing forecasts for publication forces managers to plan for the future. Such planning may enable managers to take advantage of opportunities and avoid mistakes in judgment. Kenneth Niemann, chief financial officer of Days Inns, started providing financial forecasts for his company in 1977. Before this time Days Inns did very little business planning, according to Niemann. Now, he says, the company must plan: "If we know our forecasts are out there in print, we are extra committed to following them through. We hold a lot of feet to the fire because of them."[23]

Costs of Public Disclosure

The publication of financial projections has some serious limitations. A major concern is the possible misinterpretation of the forecasts by financial statement users. Because many investors are untrained in the interpretation of financial forecasts, they are likely to be unaware of the uncertainty of forecasts. Statement users may also have difficulty interpreting the variety of assumptions underlying the projection. Moreover, across various firms, different forecast assumptions would lead to difficulty in comparing forecasts.

Another possible source of misinterpretation is management's tendency to bias forecasts. Managers may present overly optimistic projections in order to place the firm in the most favorable light. Such forecasts may help the firm obtain bank loans or may raise the stock price, but they may also harm unwary investors as the actual operating results emerge. Likewise, managers may decide to play it safe by presenting overly conservative forecasts. Managers can protect themselves by issuing forecasts that are nearly certain to be attained. If the projection is exceeded, all the better. Unfortunately, the outside investor may be misled into selling the stock or avoiding its initial purchase, only to find that the company was more prosperous than anticipated.

This limitation can be mitigated by having an independent auditor examine the reasonableness of the assumptions made by management. Exhibit 3–9 is a report by Price Waterhouse on the financial forecasts of Days Inns. The auditor's report states that an examination of the underlying assumptions was made and that they were found reasonable. However, because assumptions can prove faulty, the report is not a guarantee of future performance.

Management has long opposed the publication of financial forecasts because of the possible disclosure of sensitive information, such as major marketing, product, or investment strategies. Competitors could develop counter-strategies to block the firm from realizing its goals. This, of course, would not be beneficial to the forecasting company or its shareholders.

Another serious limitation of financial forecasts is the potential exposure to legal liability. What happens if actual results deviate sharply from projections? Was management deceptive? How can one tell? Holding management responsible for inaccurate forecasts is questionable when there has been an honest attempt to plan properly, make full disclosure, and manage the company as efficiently as possible. For example, the airlines could not have predicted the effect of the 1973 oil embargo on their operating costs. To hold the airlines responsible for inaccurate projections under these circumstances would be inequitable.

Some observers argue further that managers should not engage in the investment function by making financial forecasts. These critics suggest that financial forecasting is largely the domain of investors, who either reap the rewards of accurate forecasting or incur the penalty of inaccurate forecasting. Harvey Kapnick of Arthur Andersen & Co. states that "predictions of the future must be the responsibility of the investor. This is the essence of risk taking, and predicting and interpreting the future is the primary function in investment evaluation. No one can take to insure [through lawsuits] the results of future events."[24]

---

[23]"The Unexpected Benefit of Forecasting," *Forbes* (October 26, 1981), p. 189.
[24]"Forecasting Earnings," *Forbes* (December 1, 1972), p. 37.

EXHIBIT 3–9
Auditor's Report on a Financial Forecast Published by
Days Inns of America, Inc.

To the Board of Directors
and Stockholders of
Days Inns of America, Inc.

The Consolidated Statements of Forecasted Income and Stockholders' Equity of Days Inns of America, Inc., for each of the five years ending September 30, 1987, including the assumptions made by Management in preparation of these forecasts, are Management's estimate of the most probable results of operations for the forecast periods. Accordingly, the forecasts reflect Management's judgment based on present circumstances of the most likely set of conditions and its most likely course of action.

We have made a review of such financial forecasts in accordance with applicable guidelines of the American Institute of Certified Public Accountants for a review of a financial forecast. Our review included procedures to evaluate the assumptions made by Management in the preparation and pre-sentation of the forecasts. We have no responsibility to update the report for events and circumstances occurring after the date of this report. The summarized historical financial information presented with the forecasts for comparative purposes is taken from the financial statements of the Company for the year ended September 30, 1982, which we examined and reported on under this same date.

Based on our review, we believe that the accompanying financial forecasts are presented in conformity with applicable guidelines established by the American Institute of Certified Public Accountants for presentation of a financial forecast. We believe that the underlying assumptions provide a reasonable basis for Management's forecasts. However, some assumptions inevitably will not materialize and unanticipated events and circumstances may occur; therefore, the actual results achieved during the forecast periods will vary from the forecasts, and the variations may be material.

Price Waterhouse

Atlanta, Georgia
November 19, 1982

SOURCE: Days Inns of America, Inc., 1982 Annual Report.

Summary

The issue of mandated disclosure of financial forecasts will be controversial for some time. The SEC and the FASB have been emphasizing disclosures that have a future orientation. In contrast, most managers have opposed the concept for most of the reasons listed above. One survey indicated that 90% of the managers questioned believed the costs of publicly disclosed financial projections outweighed the benefits.[25] At this time it is difficult to predict the outcome of this controversy.

CONCLUDING REMARKS

Financial accounting is constantly changing to achieve greater relevance and reliability. It is a mistake to believe that an understanding of the present system of accounting will be sufficient for future use. The educational process of the professional accountant is continuous. A degree program in business should be thought of as a foundation from which to build and adapt skills to changing circumstances.

This chapter was written with these thoughts in mind. We have presented a conceptual

---

[25]Abdelsamad and Gilbreath, p. 28.

MAKING COMPANY FORECASTS MORE ACCEPTABLE

ALTHOUGH THE Securities & Exchange Commission began to promote the notion of having companies include forecasts of future sales and earnings in their financial reports eight years ago, the hoped-for flood of new data has been more like a trickle. A handful of companies now regularly make such projections in annual reports to shareholders, but there has not been enough experience with the controversial information to gauge whether it will be a bane or blessing.

Even though the SEC added a "safe-harbor" provision last year to help shield those who prepare and review forecasts from potential lawsuits when reasonable "good-faith" estimates go awry, overall guidelines have been fuzzy at best. Most corporations and public accounting firms have been reluctant to become involved.

A bit of that cloud now is being lifted. This month the American Institute of Certified Public Accountants (AICPA) plans to issue detailed guidelines for outside auditors that want to work with forecasts. And that paves the way for the more aggressive CPA firms to market a new service to clients by adding the assurance of an auditor's name to the forecast.

Accountants do not foresee an immediate surge of regular annual forecasts in shareholder reports, but they do expect that future sales, earnings, and cash-flow estimates will become increasingly common in registration statements for new securities issues, especially for developing companies that are coming to the public market for the first time. In the tax shelter area, most investors now first look to the financial and tax projections, with which CPAs often are associated, as the essence of the entire deal.

Accountants also see a growing demand for cash-flow projections to accompany loan applications, particularly for smaller, privately held companies. And among not-for-profit and governmental institutions, five-year, 10-year, or even 20-year revenue forecasts could become an accepted part of new bond issues for hospitals, bridge and tunnel authorities, and similar organizations.

"It's strictly a cost-benefit decision," asserts Robert K. Elliott, partner at Peat, Marwick, Mitchell & Co. and chairman of the AICPA's special task force that drew up the new forecasting guidelines. The cost of a forecast has to be weighed against the possible benefits; reducing some of the uncertainty about future sales, earnings, or revenues could result in a lower cost of capital, he explains.

Dangers. Both proponents and critics of financial forecasts readily admit that forecasting has its dangers—especially to the public. At worst, uncontrolled estimates may be overly optimistic and amount to little more than stock touting. Some fear that company managements, saddled with projections for the year ahead, will be tempted to take short-run actions to make those predictions come true, to the detriment of the corporation's welfare.

But Peat Marwick's Elliott insists that there is even more opportunity for problems with the present system, under which earnings estimates are developed by securities analysts who spend much of their time trying to get some hint or confirmation of profit prospects from top company management. "It's informal, no one knows the assumptions," Elliott complains. "There is no disclosure, no accountability, and there is uneven dissemination of the data."

The SEC used much the same reasoning when it decided to reverse its long-standing policy that prohibited forecasts in public financial documents. In fact, during the mid-1970s, the commission even proposed rules that in effect would have required companies to issue press releases whenever profit projections were discussed with analysts. Both corporations and analysts immediately complained of overkill, arguing that such a rule would make companies unwilling to talk with analysts at all. As a result, the SEC backed away and substituted its present voluntary forecasting policy with "safe-harbor" provisions.

Dialogue. Many of the companies that have tried their hand at forecasting remain positive about the move. "There's no doubt in my mind that our forecasting program has helped us as a medium-size company to build a following," concludes Donald E. Bindler, vice-president of communications at Allen Group Inc. "It has enabled us to have a serious dialogue with the better analysts," he adds. "You get beyond the cat-and-mouse game of trying to ferret out earnings numbers."

Allen once had a policy of refusing to discuss earnings estimates with analysts. In 1972 it saw the price of its stock run up, largely on the basis of one analyst's overly rosy profit projection, only to see it tumble some months later when those earnings results were not achieved. As a result, since 1973 the company has made its own public forecasts for the year ahead, normally in March in a separate report to shareholders when the annual report is mailed. Allen has been reasonably accurate, except in 1976, when gyrations in the citizens-band radio market forced the company to revise its forecast twice. Bindler concedes that 1980 will be one of the "miss" years. "The recession has been worse than we forecast," he says.

Ever since Baldor Electric Co. went public in 1976, it has been making two-year forecasts of sales and earnings in its annual report. Roland S. Boreham Jr., Baldor's president, is impatient with the SEC's voluntary approach, even though he thinks it is a move in the right direction. The SEC should require companies to make forecasts completely and consistently public, Boreham argues, or prohibit forecasts altogether. "This half-way stuff is for the birds," he grumbles. "If you do it, you've got to do it all the time, even when it hurts."

For the past three years, Masco Corp. has included a five-year cash flow and sales forecast in its annual report. John C. Nicholls Jr., Masco's treasurer, contends that the company's 23-year record of increasing earnings makes the forecasts credible. But he admits to some reservations about short-term projections. "I don't agree with specific yearly forecasts," Nicholls says. "That would be a little tough, and it would be a disaster for companies that haven't had the record we have."

Caught by inflation. Forecasts also are beginning to appear on a somewhat limited basis in prospectuses for new securities issues. Last month, Huth-nance Drilling Co. included a forecast, reviewed by an outside auditor, when it went public with a new limited partnership venture. And when Best Products Co. marketed an offering of 825,000 new common shares a year ago, the "red herring" contained a predicted range of sales and earnings for the end of the fiscal year, some nine months ahead. "We had some concern about forecasting in a prospectus," recalls Harry B. Underwood II, vice-president and treasurer. But because the company had been forecasting in its two most recent annual reports, "we felt we needed to continue to do this." Although Best's forecasts have not been too far off the mark, the company is concerned about the problem of making forecasts in an inflationary climate. As a result, Best omitted the forecasts in its new annual report now being mailed to investors.

Fuqua Industries Inc. can well appreciate that dilemma. With considerable fanfare it projected sales and earnings in its annual reports for 1972 and 1973, when it was convinced that the SEC eventually was going to require forecasts. But it dropped the practice when 1974 earnings, which were projected at $2.75 per share, came in at $1.07. Chairman J. B. Fuqua blames the recession, rising interest costs, and a switch to LIFO (last-in, first-out) accounting for the gap.

"We don't have any plans to do it again unless there are very clear guidelines that apply to all companies and until I think we have a more stable economy," Fuqua concludes. Under present conditions, Fuqua contends, "if you forecast two or three years or even 12 months, it's almost worthless; you can't determine what interest rates will be three months from now."

SOURCE: "Making Company Forecasts More Acceptable," *Business Week*, October 27, 1980, pp. 145–146. Reprinted by special permission, © 1980 by McGraw-Hill, Inc.

discussion of the nature and measurement of the elements of financial statements. Throughout this discussion we have presented alternatives to the present accounting model in order to acquaint you with not only what is presently accepted but also what may be generally accepted in the future. An understanding of this chapter should broaden your concepts in accounting and should therefore allow you to accommodate more contemporary accounting ideas. Moreover, this conceptual material should enhance your understanding of present generally accepted accounting principles. Current practice employs, to varying degrees, many of the ideas and valuation methods discussed in this chapter.

In Chapter 27 we use in more practical applications many of the concepts discussed in this chapter. In Chapter 4 we extend our presentation of generally accepted accounting principles for external reporting with an overview of the major financial statements.

1. Measurement refers to the assignment of numbers to objects and events. To measure the elements of financial statements, we must select a measuring unit and a financial attribute to measure.

2. The measuring units that have been suggested for use in financial statements are nominal dollars and constant dollars. A nominal dollar has not been adjusted for inflation or deflation; a constant dollar has been adjusted. Conventional financial statements use nominal dollars.

3. A general price-level index indicates changes over time in the overall level of prices in the economy. A specific price index indicates changes over time in the price of a specific good or service.

4. Purchasing power gains and losses are reported when financial statements are presented in constant dollars. These gains and losses result from holding monetary assets or liabilities during periods of inflation or deflation.

5. Assets are probable future economic benefits that accrue to an entity as a result of past transactions or events.

6. Financial attributes of assets include historical cost, current cost, current exit value in orderly liquidation, expected exit value in due course of business, and present value of expected cash flows. Conventional financial statements reflect a mixture of these attributes, although historical cost is emphasized.

7. Liabilities are probable future sacrifices of economic benefits that obligate an entity to transfer assets or perform services in the future as a result of past transactions or events.

8. Important issues in liability measurement are (1) whether the interest inherent in a liability should be recognized separately, and (2) what interest rate should be used to recognize the interest.

9. Financial attributes of liabilities include present value of expected cash flows, expected exit value in due course of business, historical proceeds, current proceeds, and current exit value in orderly liquidation. Conceptually, a liability should be measured on a present value basis; many liabilities are measured this way under GAAP.

10. Owners' equity equals net assets, which are assets minus liabilities. Owners' equity is not measured as an independent element of financial statements. Instead, its valuation depends on the valuations assigned to the individual assets and liabilities.

11. Net income is a measure of the change in net assets of an enterprise for a period of time, assuming no new capital contributions by the owners or dividend distributions by the business.

12. Net income should be recognized only after the capital used from the beginning of the period is maintained.

13. Lifetime net income is the total income of an enterprise from inception to termination. Lifetime revenues of an enterprise equal the total cash received from operations, and lifetime expenses equal the total cash disbursed to operations.

14. Periodic net income is the change in the wealth of a business over a short period of time, generally one year.

15. Accrual basis accounting is generally preferred over cash basis accounting, because earnings disclosures are more timely and less subject to meaningless fluctuations.

16. Net income measurement under accrual accounting depends on the valuation concepts used to measure assets and liabilities. Unlike lifetime net income, periodic net income is affected by the valuation concepts employed.

17. Net income is composed of revenues, expenses, gains, and losses. Each component can be defined by the asset/liability or the revenue/expense view. According to the asset/liability view, the components of net income are defined by direct reference to definitions of assets and liabilities. Under the revenue/expense view, the components of net income are defined without reference to definitions of assets and liabilities. Both concepts are used in practice, but the FASB supports the asset/liability view.

18. Strong evidence supports both the usefulness and timeliness of accounting net income.

19. Accounting net income can be used to evaluate past performance and predict future earnings.

20. Financial forecasts are published predictions of future financial results. Presently, there is a great deal of controversy about requiring the publication of financial forecasts. Many believe the benefits of increased information for financial statement users are outweighed by the costs of misinterpretation, biased forecasts, competitive disadvantages, and potential legal liability.

3–1   What does the term "measurement" mean? Why is measurement important in accounting?

3–2   What is the difference between nominal dollars and constant dollars? Which one of these measuring units does GAAP require? Why?

3–3   What is the difference between a general price-level index and a specific price index?

3–4   What are purchasing power gains and losses? Are they reported in conventional financial statements? Explain why or why not.

3–5   Identify three essential characteristics of assets and give ten examples of assets under GAAP.

3–6   Identify and define the financial attributes that may be used when measuring assets.

3–7   Identify three essential characteristics of liabilities and give ten examples of liabilities under GAAP.

3–8   Identify and define the financial attributes that may be used when measuring liabilities.

3–9   What does the term "owners' equity" mean? How does owners' equity differ from liabilities? Give five examples of items classified as owners' equity under GAAP.

3–10 How is owners' equity measured in conventional financial statements?

3–11 Provide a conceptual definition of net income.

3–12 Explain the term "capital maintenance." Why is this concept important in determining income for a period?

3–13 What is the lifetime net income of a business entity? What are some distinguishing characteristics of lifetime net income? How does lifetime net income differ from periodic net income?

3–14 Define cash basis accounting. What are some disadvantages of this system?

3–15 Define accrual basis accounting. How can this system produce different periodic net income numbers for the same periods?

3–16 What are the advantages and disadvantages of using historical cost to determine income?

3–17 What are the components of net income? How are they similar?

3–18 How does the revenue/expense view differ from the asset/liability view?

3–19 Is accounting net income a useful number? What are the uses of the accounting net income disclosure?

3–20 What is a financial forecast? What are some of its advantages and disadvantages?

C3–1   Matt Craft invested $150,000 in a parcel of land on January 1, 1985. He sold the land for $160,000 on December 31, 1985. The Consumer Price Index for All Urban Consumers was 100 on January 1, 1985, and 110 on December 31, 1985.

Instructions

[a] Compute the gain or loss on the sale in accordance with GAAP. Ignore income taxes.
[b] Compute the gain or loss on the sale in constant end-of-1985 dollars. Ignore income taxes.
[c] Based only on the information presented above, was Matt Craft better or worse off at the end of 1985 than at the beginning? Explain your answer.
[d] In your opinion, should financial statements continue to emphasize the nominal dollar measuring unit, or should they emphasize the constant dollar measuring unit? Present arguments that support your position.

C3–2   At the beginning of 1985, Robin Clark purchased 1,000 shares of Max Company's common stock for $50 per share. During 1985 the general price level *declined* by 10%. At the end of 1985 Robin Clark sold the 1,000 shares for $48 per share.

Instructions

[a] Compute the gain or loss on the sale in accordance with GAAP. Ignore income taxes.
[b] Compute the gain or loss on the sale in constant end-of-1985 dollars. Ignore income taxes.
[c] Based only on the information presented above, was Robin Clark better or worse off at the end of 1985 than at the beginning? Explain your answer.
[d] Did Robin Clark have a purchasing power gain during 1985? Did she have a purchasing power loss during 1985? Explain your answers.

C3–3   On January 1, 1985, Martin, Inc., sold merchandise to Sanders, Inc. for $80,000 on account. Inflation was 10% during 1985, and as of December 31, 1985, Martin had not received the $80,000 payment due from Sanders.

Instructions

[a] Calculate the amount of purchasing power gain or loss for Martin and for Sanders.
[b] Explain why each company had a purchasing power gain or loss.
[c] Are purchasing power gains and losses reported in conventional financial statements? Why or why not?

C3–4 You have been asked to determine whether each of the following items is an asset of Hicks Company.
[1]   One hundred shares of General Electric Company's common stock that Hicks has purchased.
[2]   A county-owned road constructed on land owned by Hicks.
[3]   An order placed by Hicks for merchandise that the supplier has in a warehouse and will ship in 10 days.
[4]   A patent, owned by Hicks, to produce a drug that has been linked to cancer and banned by the Food and Drug Administration.
[5]   Ten $1,000, 12%, 20-year bonds of Ford Motor Company that Hicks has purchased.
[6]   The excellent credit reputation that Hicks has earned in the business community.
[7]   A note receivable from a debtor who has been declared bankrupt and will not pay the amount owed to Hicks.
[8]   A franchise that Hicks has acquired to market a successful product in three states.
[9]   An order received from a customer for merchandise that Hicks will ship in five days.
[10] A machine that Hicks has purchased and received from a manufacturer.
[11] Merchandise owned by Wilbur Company that Hicks is holding on consignment. (Hicks is the consignee or selling agent and will try to sell the goods for Wilbur.)
[12] A noncancelable lease that gives Hicks the right to use a machine owned by Jones Company for five years, which is the estimated economic life of the machine.
[13] Cash received from a customer who has placed a prepaid order for merchandise to be shipped by Hicks in 30 days.
[14] A privately owned park that Hicks has built on its own land and that often is used by the city for sporting events.
[15] A parcel of land that has been given to Hicks by the county.

Instructions

Indicate whether each of the above items is an asset of Hicks Company, according to GAAP. Briefly explain the reason for each decision.

C3–5 Valuation of assets is an important topic in accounting theory. Suggested valuation methods include the following:
[1]   Historical cost (past purchase prices).
[2]   Historical cost adjusted to reflect general price-level changes.
[3]   Discounted cash flow (future exchange prices).
[4]   Market price (current selling prices).
[5]   Replacement cost (current purchase prices).

Instructions

[a] Why is the valuation of assets a significant issue?
[b] Explain the basic theory of each valuation method cited above. Do not discuss advantages and disadvantages of each method.

(AICPA adapted)

C3–6 Financial statements are tools for communicating quantifiable economic information to readers who use them in making management and investment decisions. To fulfill this function, accounting data should be quantifiable and relevant to the kinds of decisions made. They should be verifiable and free from personal bias. Many people believe that for some purposes current cost is a more useful measure than historical cost and recommend that statements be prepared showing both historical and current costs.

Instructions

[a] Discuss the ways in which historical costs and current costs conform to the standards of verifiability and freedom from bias.
[b] Briefly describe how the current cost of the following assets might be determined:
    [1]   Inventory
    [2]   Investments in marketable securities
    [3]   Equipment and machinery
    [4]   Natural resources
    [5]   Goodwill

(AICPA adapted)

C3–7 You have been asked to determine whether each of the following items is a liability of Rubin Company on December 31, 1985.

[1] The cash outlay expected to be made on January 7, 1986, to purchase equipment on that date.

[2] The amount expected to be needed to provide warranty services to customers for products sold before the end of 1985.

[3] The expected cash outlay for employee wages that will be earned during 1986.

[4] The obligation to provide future issues of a monthly newsletter for which subscriptions were prepaid during 1985.

[5] The obligation to provide merchandise to a customer who submitted a prepaid order on December 10, 1985.

[6] The obligation to fill orders expected to be made by regular customers during 1986.

[7] An obligation to distribute shares of Rubin's own common stock to Rubin's stockholders as a result of a 10% stock dividend declared on December 15, 1985, and distributable on January 10, 1986.

[8] The obligation that may be required to settle a lawsuit against Rubin Company that is pending on December 31, 1985. Rubin's attorneys expect to win the case.

[9] The obligation to retire at maturity $100,000, 12%, 10-year bonds issued at par value on December 31, 1985. (Interest on the bonds is to be paid annually, beginning on December 31, 1986.)

[10] The obligation to pay $120,000 interest ($100,000 × 12% × 10 years) on the bonds in [9] above.

[11] The burden associated with having earned a poor credit reputation during 1985.

[12] The obligation to provide office space to a tenant who paid six months of rent in advance on December 31, 1985.

Instructions

Indicate whether each of the above items is a liability, according to GAAP, of Rubin Company on December 31, 1985. Briefly explain the reason for each decision.

C3–8 On January 1, 1985, Rox Company borrowed $50,000 cash from Planter Company by signing a $50,000, 12%, two-year promissory note calling for interest of $6,000 ($50,000 × 12% = $6,000) to be paid at the end of 1985 and 1986. On that date the market rate of interest for similar notes was 12%.

On December 31, 1985, Rox paid the $6,000 inter-est for 1985. At that time the market rate of interest for notes similar to the one issued by Rox was 14%.

As the controller for Rox, you are trying to determine the amount the company should report for the note payable on December 31, 1985, in a balance sheet prepared in accordance with GAAP. You are considering the following alternatives:

[1] Report the note payable at $56,000. This amount equals the face amount of the note plus the interest that must be paid at the end of 1986 ($50,000 + $6,000 = $56,000).

[2] Report the note payable at $49,122.81. This amount equals the amount in [1] above, discounted for one year at the current market interest rate of 14% ($56,000 ÷ 1.14 = $49,122.81).

[3] Report the note payable at $50,000. This amount equals the amount in [1] above, discounted for one year at the market interest rate of 12% that was in effect when the note was issued ($56,000 ÷ 1.12 = $50,000).

Instructions

Which of the above alternatives should you select? Explain your answer.

C3–9 James Decker, an accountant employed by Rolfe Company, has asked for your help in deciding whether each of the items listed below should be reported in Rolfe Company's balance sheet as a liability or as stockholders' equity:

[1] An issue of subordinated income bonds that mature in 10 years. The bonds provide for interest at an annual rate of 12%, to be paid only in those years during which the company's income is sufficient to cover the interest.

[2] An issue of preferred stock that Rolfe is required to redeem on specified future dates. The stock confers no voting rights and has a stated cumulative dividend rate of 12%.

[3] An issue of preferred stock that Rolfe has an option to redeem at any time. The stock confers no voting rights and has a stated cumulative dividend rate of 13%.

Instructions

[a] Explain how the substance over form modifying convention relates to the reporting problem indicated above.

[b] Indicate whether each item listed above should be classified as a liability or as stockholders' equity. Explain your answers.

C3–10 On December 31, 1985, Janus Corporation reported total assets of $8,000,000, total liabilities of $2,000,000, and total stockholders' equity of $6,000,000. The stockholders' equity consisted of common stock of $1,000,000 and retained earnings of $5,000,000. Janus had 100,000 shares of $10 par value common stock outstanding on December 31, 1985, and the market price per share on that date was $55.

Instructions

[a] Explain how stockholders' equity is measured in conventional accounting.

[b] Explain why the reported stockholders' equity of $6,000,000 does not equal the ending market price per share multiplied by the shares outstanding ($55 × 100,000 = $5,500,000).

C3–11 Agran Foundation is a not-for-profit organization dedicated to the support of the arts in the surrounding communities. The foundation is quite large and has investments in real estate, stocks and bonds, and mortgages, as well as unpaid pledges from supporters. The real estate investments have outstanding mortgages against them. The foundation has been operating its accounting system on a cash basis since its inception in 1956. The trustees have embarked on a program to increase the activities of the foundation, including an aggressive annual fund-raising campaign.

The trustees have decided that the foundation's accounting records should be audited annually and have engaged a CPA firm to conduct the first audit. One of the auditors recommends that the foundation convert its accounting system to an accrual basis from the cash basis. The auditor has stated that accrual accounting is used in profit-making companies but has not been used extensively in many governmental or not-for-profit organizations. The auditor believes that accrual accounting has many advantages over cash accounting and would be very useful for Agran Foundation.

Instructions

[a] Describe how the foundation's statement of financial position and statement of receipts and disbursements prepared on an accrual basis would differ from those prepared on a cash basis.

[b] Identify and briefly explain the advantages accrual accounting provides to profit-making companies that would also be applicable to Agran Foundation.

[c] Explain how the trustees' ability to evaluate the performance of the foundation's executive director would be improved if the foundation used financial statements prepared on the accrual basis rather than the cash basis method of accounting.

(CMA adapted)

C3–12 Alan Ardmore bought a four-bedroom home on January 1, 1984, for $95,000 cash. After this purchase Ardmore had only $15,000 cash left in his noninterest-bearing checking account. On December 31, 1984, Ardmore could sell his house for $120,000 cash. At that time he could engage in one of the following independent transactions:

[1] Sell the house and buy a similar four-bedroom home in the same town for $120,000.

[2] Sell the house and buy a similar four-bedroom home in another region of the country for $95,000.

[3] Sell the house and buy a similar four-bedroom home in another region of the country for $135,000.

[4] Sell the house and buy a six-bedroom home in the same town for $135,000.

[5] Not sell the house.

Instructions

[a] Determine the 1984 income (gain) Ardmore would record for each of the five independent situations above, according to GAAP. Assume no transaction costs or taxes. Also assume that Ardmore is indifferent about regional location.

[b] How well does GAAP capture the economic substance of each transaction above?

C3–13 The following definitions of assets and liabilities are given in *Accounting Terminology Bulletin No. 1* (New York: AICPA, 1953), pars. 26 and 27:

Asset—something represented by a debit balance that is or would be properly carried forward upon a closing of books of account according to the rules or principles of accounting.

Liability—something represented by a credit balance that is or would be properly carried forward upon a closing of books of account according to the rules or principles of accounting.

Instructions

Are the above definitions consistent with the asset/liability or the revenue/expense view? What deficiencies can you identify in the above definitions?

C3–14 Recent proposals by investors and others have suggested that corporations include financial forecasts in their annual reports. It has been further suggested that the CPA attest to those forecasts.

Instructions

[a] What arguments are advanced to support the publication of such forecasts?
[b] What arguments are advanced to oppose the publication of such forecasts?

(CMA adapted)

C3–15 Holt Electronics is a new company in the high-growth electronics field. It produces a unique electronic test package for the defense industry. Holt Electronics, which has been run very successfully as a private company for two years, will be making its first public offering of common stock within the next month. Naturally, the company wants to obtain the highest price possible for the new offering. The treasurer of the company, H. Bigsly, has suggested that the publication of a three-year earnings forecast may enhance the offering price of the new shares.

Instructions

What factors must Bigsly consider in the construction of the earnings forecast? What shortcomings in the public disclosure of financial forecasts should Bigsly be aware of?

C3–16 Hotel management must make many assumptions in constructing financial forecasts. Listed below are some variables management may have to consider

in making a financial forecast.
[1] Gasoline prices
[2] Aging population
[3] Financing costs
[4] Characteristics of automobiles
[5] Land values
[6] General economic conditions

Refer to Exhibit 3–8, which presents the financial forecasts of Days Inns of America. The following is some background information about Days Inns from the annual report.

Days Inns serves a broad and growing market—the value-conscious traveler. We offer quality lodging at prices substantially below our competition by eliminating costly amenities, such as expensive lobbies, convention space and lounges, while at the same time maintaining the conveniences that customers want. The resulting cost savings are passed along to our guests. In addition to our urban properties, we also provide our guests traveling the interstate highway system the convenience of one-stop service for lodging, food, novelties and gasoline.

Instructions

Explain how each of the above variables may be interpreted by the managers of Days Inns of America in constructing a financial forecast.

PROBLEMS

P3–1 During the last four months of the academic year, the yearbook committee of Mountain State University produced and distributed the university's yearbook. The yearbook was published in April at a cost of $15 a copy. The selling price was $22.00 each. If ordered in advance, the yearbook sold for $18.00. The committee estimated that 9,000 yearbooks would be sold for the 1984–1985 academic year.

In February the yearbook committee authorized the payment of $1,500, which was the amount left from last year's yearbook sales, to the local newspaper, the campus newspaper, and a local radio station for advertising to be provided in March. In March advance payments for 5,000 yearbooks were received. The printing of 9,000 yearbooks was completed in April and paid for on April 30. The difference between the cash on hand and the printing costs was made up by a short-term loan. In May all advance orders were filled and 3,500 more yearbooks were sold on a cash basis. The short-term loan of April was paid off in May, including an interest charge of $500. The unsold year-

books were considered worthless and were therefore destroyed.

Instructions

[a] Prepare both cash basis and accrual basis income statements and balance sheets for February, March, April, and May. (The difference between assets and liabilities is termed "fund balance," because the yearbook operation has no owners.)
[b] What is the total income from the yearbook sales for this academic year under each method?
[c] From this problem, what is an obvious limitation of a cash-based system?

P3–2 Albert Foss Sales Company, an automobile dealership, started business on January 1, 1984, with $39,000 in cash. Albert Foss decided to "wait out" the current model year and start purchasing inventory when the 1985 models became available. As a result the Foss dealership purchased four new 1985 model automobiles on September 1, 1984. The cost of the new models were as follows:

Model	Cost
1985 Astra	$ 8,000
1985 Blaze	9,000
1985 Cortez Deluxe	10,000
1985 Dynasty Wagon	12,000

On November 1, the dealership sold the Astra for $9,400. On December 30, the manufacturer increased the wholesale price on the 1985 models by 10%. Foss believed he could sell the Blaze, Cortez, and Dynasty for $11,100, $12,800, and $15,700, respectively, on December 31. The salesmen's commissions were equal to 5% of the sales price. During calendar year 1985 the Blaze was sold to a customer for $11,300 and the Cortez for $13,100. Foss still held the 1985 Dynasty Wagon on the lot as of October 1, 1985. He discounted the vehicle and finally sold it for $13,300 on October 15. On December 31, 1985, Albert Foss Sales Company ceased operations.

Instructions

[a] Determine the net income for Albert Foss Sales Company for calendar years 1984 and 1985, assuming the automobile inventory is valued under (1) historical cost, (2) current cost, and (3) current exit value.
[b] What is the lifetime net income of the Foss dealership under each of the valuation methods above?
[c] Which pattern of income flows do you believe is most fair and reasonable?

P3-3 On January 1, 1984, K. F. Knudson Beer Company began business with a $440,000 cash investment from the Knudson family. The company did not intend to brew beer from raw materials but to use a newly developed aging process on beer purchased wholesale from other producers. After two years of aging by this special process, a top-quality premium beer was to result. One beer distributor was so impressed with the aging process that a contract was made for 10,000 barrels at a price of $60 a barrel, to be delivered and paid for on December 31, 1985.

On January 1, 1984, Knudson purchased 10,000 barrels of freshly brewed beer at $20 a barrel in order to start the aging process, which cost $1 per barrel per month. On December 31, 1984, the wholesale price of beer aged one year was $38 a barrel. The company estimated they could sell their beer for $45 a barrel after only one year of aging. On December 31, 1985, the aging process was completed and the beer was delivered to the distributor.

Instructions

[a] Prepare balance sheets for December 31, 1984, for Knudson Beer Company under the following four valuation methods: (1) historical cost, (2) current cost, (3) current exit value, and (4) expected exit value.
[b] What is the reported net income for 1984 and 1985 under each valuation method?
[c] Which pattern of income flows do you believe is most fair and reasonable?

P3-4 Transylvania State University's 1984–1985 basketball season began on December 1, 1984, and will end on March 31, 1985. The TSU basketball arena (fully depreciated) holds 15,000 fans. The *number of home dates* per month are as follows: December, 7; January, 5; February, 5; and March, 5.

Five thousand seats per game are reserved for the TSU students at an admission price of $5 per student per game. The remaining seats are sold to alumni and other fans on a season ticket basis. A season ticket costs $308. Season ticket orders are mailed on November 30. Season ticket holders have the choice of paying the $308 as a lump sum by December 6 (the first home date) or using a payment plan of $77 per month with the first payment due by December 7. Forty percent of the season ticket holders choose the payment plan.

The university also operates the concession stands in the arena. The concession stands cost $3,000 per game and generate $8,000 in cash revenues per game. All concession items are purchased COD seven days before a home date. There is no ending inventory of concession stand items on December 31.

The major cost to the university in managing the arena is the utility bill for heat and lighting. The university receives the utility bill on the fifth of each month for the previous month's usage. The arena uses no heat or lighting in the off season. Monthly usage during the basketball season is $240,000. Arena workers receive wages on a per game basis and are paid on the day following a home date. The payroll cost for a home date is $12,000. In addition, the university insures the arena at a cost of $24,000 per year. The insurance is paid in advance each December 1. The arena had $3,000 cash left from the preceding basketball season.

On December 31, 1984, after a particularly exciting game in which TSU upset their conference rival, the president of the university asks you to prepare financial statements for December. The president noticed that the arena was sold out for each of the home dates in December and, as a result, wants to know how much cash the arena operation is generating.

Instructions

[a] Prepare for the president an income statement for December and a balance sheet on December 31, 1984, under a cash basis assumption. Develop an alternative set of statements under an accrual approach. (Identify the difference between assets and liabilities as "fund balance" rather than owners' equity, because a university does not have shareholders.)

[b] Assuming the arena is used only for basketball, what will the arena operation earn for the period from December 1, 1984, to November 30, 1985?

[c] Show the president the shortcomings of cash basis financial statements in evaluating the arena's operating performance for December.

4

BASIC FINANCIAL STATEMENTS

Objectives

To describe the major characteristics of basic financial statements.

To discuss and illustrate most major components of the income statement.

To discuss and illustrate the statement of retained earnings and the statement of stockholders' equity.

To discuss and illustrate the balance sheet, including the major classifications commonly used.

To provide a general introduction to the statement of changes in financial position.

To provide a general introduction to certain other topics related to basic financial statements.

CHARACTERISTICS OF BASIC FINANCIAL STATEMENTS

What was the net income of Exxon last year? Was this figure large or small in relation to the company's sales and to its stockholders' equity? What was the relationship last year between IBM's dividends and earnings? What proportion of General Motors' assets at the end of last year did the company finance through debt? In what ways did General Electric use its financial resources last year? These are a few of the many questions that investors, creditors, and other users seek to answer based on information presented in the companies' financial statements.

The primary objective of financial statements is to provide information that is useful to users in making rational decisions. The basic financial statements are the **balance sheet,** the **income statement,** the **statement of changes in financial position,** and the **statement of retained earnings** (or **statement of stockholders' equity**). Companies usually present basic financial statements in their annual reports to shareholders and in other disclosure media. The balance sheet summarizes the financial position of an enterprise **at a particular point in time.** The other basic statements summarize various changes in financial position that have occurred **during a period of time.**

Basic financial statements have several important characteristics:

1. They are only a **subset,** although an important subset, of the information needed by users for making rational investment, lending, and similar decisions.
2. They are primarily **historical** in nature.
3. They **summarize** information.
4. They reflect many **estimates.**
5. They are **general-purpose** reports designed to serve the needs of many different users.
6. They **articulate** with one another (i.e., they are **interrelated**).

In this chapter we review the form and content of the basic financial statements. In subsequent chapters we discuss aspects of these statements in greater detail and thereby develop the statements more fully.

This chapter presents the statements in the order in which accountants typically prepare them (i.e., income statement; statement of retained earnings, or statement of stockholders' equity; balance sheet; and statement of changes in financial position). To emphasize the interrelatedness of basic financial statements, the chapter illustrates a set of statements prepared for the Sunrise Corporation.[1]

INCOME STATEMENT

The **income statement** is generally regarded as the most important financial statement. Two major ways that investors, creditors, and others use income statements are:

1. **To predict cash flows.** Users of financial statements typically invest or lend cash, and they want to know *how much* cash they will receive in return and *when* they will receive it. Knowledge of a company's past income and its components helps users to predict more accurately the company's income and to better assess their own chances of receiving various amounts of cash from the company.

---

[1]A complete set of financial statements of Kroger Company is presented in the appendix and inside the front and back covers of this book.

The authors recommend *Accounting Trends and Techniques* for additional examples of disclosures made in financial statements. This annual publication of the American Institute of Certified Public Accountants is based on a survey of the annual reports to shareholders of 600 companies.

2. **To evaluate management's performance.** Users regard the income statement as an important indication of management's success. Stockholders typically want to reward good managers and replace poor ones.

From a societal standpoint, measurements reported on the income statement help to ensure that we put our scarce resources to their best uses. If a company produces and distributes its products successfully, it should earn income. Moreover, a record of profitable operations should help the company to raise capital and other resources. Generally, resources should flow into companies that have unusually high incomes and out of those that sustain losses.

Elements of the Income Statement

| Revenue Realization |
| Matching |
| Historical Cost |

Accountants traditionally have measured a company's income by focusing on transactions that caused changes in the company's assets and liabilities during a period of time. These transactions include revenues, expenses, gains, and losses. As you might expect, accountants disagree about the best way to measure these components of a company's income. For example, we could measure expenses using current costs, opportunity costs, or historical costs. Traditionally, accountants have relied primarily on historical costs. Income measurement in conventional accounting involves primarily the **revenue realization, matching,** and **historical cost** principles, as discussed in Chapter 2.

The fundamental elements of the income statement and their relationships to net income are demonstrated in the following equation:

$$\text{Revenues} - \text{Expenses} + \text{Gains} - \text{Losses} = \text{Net income}$$

A review of several definitions presented in Chapter 2 is appropriate at this point:[2]

1. **Revenues.** Inflows or other enhancements of assets of an entity or settlements of its liabilities (or both) during a period, based on production and delivery of goods, provision of services, and other activities that constitute the entity's major operations.
2. **Expenses.** Outflows or other use of assets or incurrences of liabilities (or both) during a period as a result of delivering or producing goods, rendering services, or carrying out other activities that constitute the entity's major operations.
3. **Costs.** Sacrifices incurred in acquiring resources. We include the term "cost" here so that you can differentiate it from the term "expense." Costs do not enter into the calculation of net income until they expire. An **expense** in conventional accounting is an **expired cost** (more precisely, an **expired historical cost**). In contrast, a **cost that has not yet expired** is reported as an **asset.**
4. **Gains and losses.** **Gains** are increases in owners' equity (net assets) from peripheral or incidental transactions of an entity and from all other transactions and events affecting the entity during a period, except those resulting from revenues or investments by owners. **Losses** are decreases in owners' equity (net assets) from peripheral or incidental transactions of an entity and from all other events affecting the entity during a period, except those that result from expenses or distributions to owners. Unlike revenues and expenses, which are measured and reported at **gross amounts,** gains and losses are measured and reported at **net amounts.** For example, if a company paid $70,000 for land and later sold the land for $100,000, the company would report a $30,000 gain. This gain equals the gross selling price of $100,000, net of the land's cost of $70,000. In practice, gains are sometimes classified broadly as revenues; losses are sometimes classified broadly as expenses.

---

[2]These definitions are based largely on *FASB Statement of Financial Accounting Concepts No. 3,* "Elements of Financial Statements of Business Enterprises," 1980, pars. 63, 65, 67, and 68.

5. Net income. The net result of adding revenues and gains for a period and deducting expenses and losses for the period. Terms such as **earnings** and **profit** often are used as synonyms for **income.**

Several items that may appear on an income statement are somewhat peculiar and should be explained further at this time. These items include extraordinary gains and losses, unusual or infrequently occurring gains and losses, gains and losses resulting from the disposal of business segments, and the cumulative effect of a change in accounting principles.

Extraordinary Gains and Losses

Suppose that a company sustains a loss from an earthquake. Clearly, this kind of loss is rare. Do you believe that users of financial statements could make more accurate predictions and more meaningful evaluations of management's performance if they knew about unusual and nonrecurring gains and losses? Most accountants would answer yes. As a result, generally accepted accounting principles (GAAP) require companies to report material extraordinary gains and losses in a special section of their income statements.

Materiality

To be considered an extraordinary gain or loss, an event or transaction must meet *both* of the following criteria:[3]

1. **Unusual nature.**   The underlying event or transaction should be highly unusual and clearly unrelated to, or only incidentally related to, the ordinary activities of the entity, considering the environment in which the entity operates.
2. **Infrequent occurrence.**   The underlying event or transaction should not reasonably be expected to recur in the foreseeable future, considering the environment in which the entity operates.

Note carefully that to be considered extraordinary, an item must be both unusual and nonrecurring.[4] The term **extraordinary item** therefore has a technical meaning in accounting that differs somewhat from the everyday connotation of items that are simply unusual or peculiar. Furthermore, applying the criteria requires the accountant to consider the specific **characteristics of the company** as well as the **environment in which it operates.** For example, an accountant would be more likely to judge a loss from a hurricane as extraordinary if it were sustained by a company located in Iowa rather than by one located on the Louisiana Gulf Coast.[5]

Accountants must use *judgment* when applying the above criteria. In so doing, they should recognize that the criteria are very restrictive and are rarely satisfied in practice.[6] In many cases an event or transaction will meet both criteria only if it is the direct result of a **major casualty** (such as an earthquake), an **expropriation** (takeover of property by a government), or a **prohibition** under a newly enacted law. To help clarify the restrictive nature of the criteria, the Accounting Principles Board (APB) indicated that the following gains and losses would *not* be reported as extraordinary unless they were the direct result of a major casualty, expropriation, or prohibition:[7]

---

[3]*APB Opinion No. 30,* "Reporting the Results of Operations," 1973, par. 20.

[4]As is true of most rules, there are exceptions to the criteria for extraordinary items. In most circumstances the tax benefits of operating-loss carryforwards are classified as extraordinary items regardless of the criteria in *APB Opinion No. 30.* Similarly, the FASB in *Statement of Financial Accounting Standards No. 4* stated that gains and losses from extinguishment of debt should be classified as extraordinary. We explain these exceptions in Chapters 15 and 18.

[5]Note that we are referring to a loss in excess of insurance proceeds or a loss not covered at all by insurance.

[6]*Accounting Trends and Techniques,* 36th ed. (New York: AICPA, 1982), p. 284, reveals that only 57 extraordinary items were reported in the 600 annual reports examined. Of the 57 items, 33 were *exceptions* to the criteria for extraordinary items set forth in *APB Opinion No. 30* (see footnote 4).

[7]*APB Opinion No. 30,* par. 23.

1. Write-downs or write-offs of receivables, inventories, equipment leased to others, or intangible assets.
2. Gains or losses from foreign currency transactions and translation of foreign currency financial statements.
3. Gains or losses on disposal of a segment of a business.
4. Other gains or losses from sale or abandonment of property, plant, or equipment used in the business.
5. Effects of a strike, including those against competitors and major suppliers.
6. Adjustments of accruals on long-term contracts.

Below are some examples of events or transactions that meet both criteria and should therefore be judged extraordinary:

1. A large portion of a tobacco manufacturer's crops are destroyed by a hailstorm. Severe damage from hailstorms in the locality where the manufacturer grows tobacco is rare.
2. A food canner destroys a large quantity of inventory because of a government ban on canned goods containing cyclamates. Government prohibitions of this kind rarely occur.
3. An earthquake destroys an oil refinery owned by a large multinational oil company. Earthquakes rarely occur in the area where the oil refinery is located.

In contrast, here are some examples of events or transactions that should *not* be judged extraordinary since they do not meet both criteria for extraordinary items:

1. A citrus grower's Florida crop is damaged by frost. Frost damage is normally experienced every three or four years. In this case the criterion of infrequent occurrence is not met.
2. A company which operates a chain of warehouses sells the excess land surrounding one of its warehouses. When the company buys property to establish a new warehouse, it usually buys more land than it will use for the warehouse because it expects the land to appreciate in value. In the past five years, there have been two instances in which the company sold such excess land. Here the criterion of infrequent occurrence has not been met.
3. A large diversified company sells a block of shares from its portfolio of securities, which it has acquired for investment purposes. This is the first sale from its portfolio. The criterion of unusual nature has not been met in this case because the company owns several securities.
4. A textile manufacturer with only one plant moves to another location. It has not relocated a plant in twenty years and has no plans to do so in the foreseeable future. Here the criterion of unusual nature has not been met because, in general, moving from one location to another is a common business occurrence.[8]

Unusual or Infrequently Occurring Items

An accountant sometimes encounters a gain or loss that is unusual in nature *or* occurs infrequently, *but not both.* Such a gain or loss is therefore *not* extraordinary. In addition to the above four examples of items not qualifying as extraordinary, other examples of unusual or infrequently occurring items are gains or losses from the sale of plant assets, losses from inventory write-offs, and losses due to a strike. According to *APB Opinion No. 30,* these gains and losses should be reported as separate items in the income statement if they are

| Materiality |

material. They should *not,* however, be reported as extraordinary items or in any way which implies that they are extraordinary in nature.

In practice, the distinction between extraordinary items and unusual or infrequently occurring items is sometimes hazy, and accountants must therefore use judgment to cor-

---

[8]Most of the examples above were taken from *Accounting Interpretations of APB Opinion No. 30,* "Reporting the Results of Operations" (New York: AICPA, 1973).

rectly classify certain events or transactions. Accountants should be aware that, because the income statement reports management's performance, many managers tend to favor the reporting of gains as nonextraordinary and losses as extraordinary. This tendency should not influence the accountant's judgment about whether a particular event or transaction is extraordinary.

Disposal of a Business Segment

The term **segment of a business** refers to "a component of an entity whose activities represent a separate major line of business or class of customer. A segment may be in the form of a subsidiary, a division, or a department, . . . provided that its assets, results of operations, and activities can be clearly distinguished, physically and operationally and for financial reporting purposes, from the other assets, results of operations, and activities of the entity."[9] A company may **dispose** of a segment of its business. For example, a company that has a furniture division and a clothing division may sell its clothing division.

Gains and losses from disposal of a business segment are *not* extraordinary items. Instead, they must be reported in a special income statement category called **discontinued operations.** The reporting requirements for discontinued operations are complex; we discuss and illustrate them in detail in Chapter 20.

Changes in Accounting Principles

A company may occasionally change from one generally accepted accounting principle to another. For example, it may change from the first-in, first-out (FIFO) to the last-in, first-out

---

[9]*APB Opinion No. 30,* par. 13.

A HIGH-LEVEL CONFLICT OF INTEREST

AIRLINE PILOTS are, of course, among the most highly paid professionals in the U.S.—the captain of a 747 can make $100,000 nowadays—and like other high-income people they tend to own securities. Frequently, they own stock in the airlines that employ them; indeed, most of the carriers have stock-purchase plans that encourage pilots to load up heavily. The plans are supposed to give the pilots a special incentive to help the company boost earnings.

Until quite recently, we assumed that these arrangements were all very logical. However, we're suddenly not so sure. A couple of news items have led us to wonder if there mightn't be just a tiny problem about pilots who want to boost their airlines' earnings.

One of the items was a report on the Continental Airlines annual meeting. It developed at the meeting that the company had earned $1.59 a share in the first quarter this year—up from a mere $.06 in the comparable 1977 quarter. The great bulk of this gain was attributable to the crash of a Continental DC-10 at Los Angeles International Airport in March. The company collected $33 million in insurance on the aircraft, a figure that was substantially above its depreciated value before the crash. The difference was taken into income.

The other item concerned the loss of that National Airlines 727 in the waters off Pensacola in May. Once again, the crash resulted in a gain to the airline—in this case of about $.18 a share.

In case you're wondering, there was nothing fishy about the accounting in either case. It is natural for airlines to insure their equipment at replacement value, not book, and this means that there will almost always be a large gain on the insurance. The accounting rules specified by both the Securities and Exchange Commission and the Civil Aeronautics Board *require* this gain to be taken into income.

We assume, of course, that there are limits to the average pilot's dedication to earnings. Still, they do tend to be organization men. Why can't they invest in real estate?

(LIFO) method of inventory cost determination, or from the sum-of-the-years'-digits method to the straight-line method of computing depreciation. Such changes are called **changes in accounting principles,** and they are permitted under generally accepted accounting principles if the company can establish that the new principle is preferable to the old.

Changes in accounting principles are *not* extraordinary items. Instead, *most* changes in accounting principles are reported in a special income statement category called the **cumulative effect of a change in accounting principles.**[10] Financial reporting requirements for changes in accounting principles are complex; we discuss and illustrate these requirements in detail in Chapters 19 and 20.

Income Statement Format

The form and content of the income statement have been greatly affected by recent professional pronouncements relating to such issues as intraperiod income tax allocation, accounting changes, discontinued operations, extraordinary items, and earnings per share. These issues often are complex and require careful study before the implications of income statement reporting can be fully understood. For this reason, we review in this section the fundamental aspects of the income statement format. In Chapter 20 we consider some additional reporting complexities of the income statement.

The accounting profession has not adopted a uniform format for the entire income statement. Instead, it permits some flexibility, and this enables the practicing accountant to structure an income statement that best fits the circumstances of the reporting entity. Accountants traditionally have presented the income statement in either a multiple-step or a single-step form.

Multiple-Step Form

A **multiple-step** income statement presents subtotals for gross margin and operating income before showing net income. Net income is therefore derived in intermediate steps. To illustrate we present a multiple-step income statement for the Sunrise Corporation in Exhibit 4–1. In practice, many details shown in this example may be condensed or may be reported in footnotes or parenthetically in the statement. For example, the income statement may begin with net sales if the accountant thinks that the balances in the revenue contra accounts are immaterial. Moreover, the accountant may report in the income statement only the totals for cost of goods sold, selling expenses, and general and administrative expenses. The details may then be presented in separate schedules in the footnotes.

As Exhibit 4–1 suggests, a multiple-step format calls for deducting cost of goods sold from net sales to measure **gross margin on sales** (often called **gross profit on sales**). Gross margin is an intermediate measure of profitability that indicates the difference between the selling prices and costs of products sold during the accounting period.

To the extent possible, **operating expenses** usually are divided into two categories: selling expenses and general and administrative expenses. **Selling expenses** relate to the sale of the company's products; **general and administrative expenses** relate to the general operations of the business.

Income from operations (also called **operating income**) is an intermediate income measure that indicates how profitable the company has been as a result of its primary business activities. **Other revenues** and **other expenses** are related to the secondary activities of the company; these two sections often are combined. Note in the exhibit that Sunrise Corporation correctly reported an unusual item (loss on sale of long-term investments) as "other expense." As stated earlier, items that are unusual or nonrecurring (but not both) must not be reported in the same manner as extraordinary items.

Income before taxes and extraordinary item is an intermediate measure of income

---

[10]*APB Opinion No. 20,* "Accounting Changes," 1971, par. 20.

that would simply be called "income before taxes" if Sunrise Corporation did not have an extraordinary item. **Income tax** is the final expense deducted. The amount is determined by multiplying the income before taxes and extraordinary item by the income tax rate, which we assume is 40%.[11] The amount therefore includes the income tax effect of all income statement items that appear before it. Income tax expense should always be shown separately, not combined with any other expenses.

---

[11]So that we can concentrate on the basic form and content of financial statements without being diverted by income tax calculations, we assume a tax rate of 40% for the financial statements presented in this chapter.

EXHIBIT 4–1
Multiple-Step Income Statement

Sunrise Corporation
INCOME STATEMENT
For the Year Ended December 31, 1985

Sales revenue			
Sales			$579,500
Less: Sales returns and allowances		$ 18,200	
Sales discounts		11,300	29,500
Net sales			550,000
Cost of goods sold			
Merchandise inventory, January 1, 1985		40,000	
Purchases	$340,000		
Less: Purchase returns and allowances	(20,000)		
Purchase discounts	(6,800)		
Add: Transportation-in	11,800		
Net purchases		325,000	
Cost of goods available for sale		365,000	
Less: Merchandise inventory, December 31, 1985		(35,000)	
Cost of goods sold			330,000
Gross margin on sales			220,000
Operating expenses			
Selling expenses			
Sales salaries	48,000		
Advertising	12,000		
Transportation-out	7,300		
Depreciation of delivery equipment	3,000		
Other selling expenses	2,700	73,000	
General and administrative expenses			
Office salaries	27,100		
Utilities	9,900		
Supplies	7,700		
Insurance	5,800		
Depreciation of building	2,500		
Depreciation of office equipment	2,000		
Amortization	3,200		
Bad debts	4,500		
Other general and administrative expenses	1,800	64,500	
Total operating expenses			137,500

Income from operations		82,500
Other revenues		
Interest	2,100	
Dividends	5,200	
Rent	7,200	
Gain on sale of equipment	6,500	21,000
		103,500
Other expenses		
Interest	14,400	
Unusual item—loss on sale of long-term		
investments	5,100	19,500
Income before taxes and extraordinary		
item		84,000
Income tax expense		33,600
Income before extraordinary item		50,400
Extraordinary item—gain from		
expropriation of land, less applicable		
income tax expense of $16,000		24,000
Net income		$ 74,400
Per share of common stock		
Income before extraordinary item		$2.32
Extraordinary gain (net of tax)		1.20
Net income		$3.52

Note to Students: Generally accepted accounting principles require special income statement categories for discontinued operations and the cumulative effect of a change in accounting principles. In Chapter 20 we discuss and illustrate these categories. We also present a comprehensive income statement that includes these categories.

Income before extraordinary item indicates how profitable the company was without considering the effects of the extraordinary item. Since extraordinary items are unusual *and* nonrecurring, many financial statement users rely heavily on the income before extraordinary item when they make predictions and evaluate management's performance.

The **extraordinary item** is presented next, as required by generally accepted accounting principles. In the exhibit, Sunrise Corporation reported an extraordinary *gain* because the proceeds received from a government expropriation of land exceeded the land's cost. An extraordinary gain or loss is always reported in a special income statement section. Further, the generally accepted accounting principle of **intraperiod tax allocation,** which is discussed in detail in Chapter 18, requires that the gross amount of an extraordinary gain be reduced by the amount of **income tax expense** associated with the gain. Similarly, it requires that the gross amount of an extraordinary loss be reduced by the amount of the **income tax reduction** associated with the loss. Extraordinary gains and losses are therefore always reported **net** of their income tax effects, or on a **net of tax basis.** Note in the exhibit that if the extraordinary gain had not been reported on a net of tax basis, the reported income tax expense (associated with income before taxes and extraordinary item) would have been $49,600 ($33,600 + $16,000). Income before extraordinary item would then have been reported as only $34,400 ($84,000 − $49,600). This erroneous figure could cause some users to evaluate the company in a misleading (and in this case, less favorable) light.

Net income includes the effects of all revenues, expenses, gains, and losses. The beneficiaries of net income are the stockholders, both preferred and common.

Earnings per share of common stock is a widely used financial measurement that appears below net income.[12] The beneficiaries of this measurement are *common* stockholders. In the simplest case, an accountant calculates earnings per share by dividing net income by the weighted average number of common shares outstanding during the period. In our illustration, Sunrise Corporation had preferred stock outstanding (see Exhibit 4–6). We therefore subtracted preferred dividends from net income when calculating earnings per share of common stock. Note that because Sunrise Corporation had an extraordinary item, it reported *three* per-share numbers. These three are: (1) income before extraordinary item; (2) extraordinary gain (net of tax); and (3) net income. Companies report these numbers separately in order to help users of financial statements make better predictions and more meaningful evaluations of management's performance. Calculating and reporting earnings per share can be extremely complex; we discuss and illustrate these complexities in Chapter 26.

Single-Step Form

In the **single-step** income statement, the accountant deducts total expenses from total revenues in a single step to measure net income. No separate disclosure is made of gross margin or operating income. Most companies that prepare single-step income statements deduct income tax as a separate, last item.[13] We illustrate such a statement for the Sunrise Corporation in Exhibit 4–2. Note that we have presented a somewhat condensed, single-step income statement. Such condensation is not an essential feature of the single-step form. Indeed, **condensed income statements** may be presented in either a multiple-step or a single-step format. The typical annual report to shareholders contains a condensed income statement. As you can see by comparing Exhibits 4–1 and 4–2, extraordinary items must always be reported in a special income statement category, whether a multiple-step or a single-step format is used.

Multiple-Step Versus Single-Step Form

Many preparers and users of financial statements prefer the multiple-step form because it highlights gross margin and operating income. On the other hand, many prefer the single-step form because it often is easier to understand and does not suggest a priority of expenses. In other words, the format does not imply that a company must recover its cost-of-goods-sold expense before it can recover any other expenses. In reality, of course, a company must generate enough revenues to cover all of its expenses if it is to have net income. Proponents of the single-step form also point out that several terms often used in a multiple-step statement (especially "income from operations") have not been clearly defined by the accounting profession. A recent survey of the annual reports to shareholders of 600 companies indicated that in 1981, 333 companies used the single-step form while 267 companies used the multiple-step form.[14]

STATEMENT OF RETAINED EARNINGS

The **statement of retained earnings** describes the changes in a company's retained earnings during a period and relates the income statement to the balance sheet. The retained earnings statement usually is fairly simple and may consist of three sections: (1) **prior**

---

[12]Nonpublic enterprises are not required under generally accepted accounting principles to report earnings per share. Unless stated otherwise, you should assume in all end-of-chapter assignments that earnings per share is required.
[13]*Accounting Trends and Techniques,* 1982, p. 218.
[14]*Accounting Trends and Techniques,* 1982, p. 218.

EXHIBIT 4–2
Single-Step Income Statement

Sunrise Corporation
INCOME STATEMENT
For the Year Ended December 31, 1985

Revenues		
Net sales		$550,000
Other revenues		21,000
Total revenues		571,000
Expenses		
Cost of goods sold	$330,000	
Selling expenses	73,000	
General and administrative expenses	64,500	
Interest	14,400	
Unusual item—loss on sale of long-term investments	5,100	
Total expenses		487,000
Income before taxes and extraordinary item		84,000
Income tax expense		33,600
Income before extraordinary item		50,400
Extraordinary item—gain from expropriation of land, less applicable income tax expense of $16,000		24,000
Net income		$ 74,400
Per share of common stock		
Income before extraordinary item		$2.32
Extraordinary gain (net of tax)		1.20
Net income		$3.52

Note to Students: Generally accepted accounting principles require special income statement categories for discontinued operations and the cumulative effect of a change in accounting principles. In Chapter 20 we discuss and illustrate these categories. We also present a comprehensive income statement that includes these categories.

---

period adjustments; (2) **net income;** and (3) **dividends declared.** Thus, investors, creditors, and other users of financial statements can analyze the statement to determine whether any prior period adjustments exist and what relationship exists between a company's net income and its dividends.

A statement of retained earnings for the Sunrise Corporation is shown in Exhibit 4–3.

Prior Period Adjustments

Prior period adjustments are charged or credited directly to retained earnings. These items therefore do not appear on the income statement of the period in which they occur.

In 1977 the Financial Accounting Standards Board (FASB) issued *Statement of Financial Accounting Standards No. 16,* which greatly reduced the number of items that a company could report as prior period adjustments. In this pronouncement the FASB stated that:

> *Items of profit and loss related to the following shall be accounted for and reported as prior period adjustments and excluded from the determination of net income for the current period:*

EXHIBIT 4–3
Sunrise Corporation
STATEMENT OF RETAINED EARNINGS
For the Year Ended December 31, 1985

Retained earnings, January 1, 1985, as previously reported		$ 45,600
Less: Prior period adjustment—correction of depreciation understatement in 1984 due to error, less applicable income tax effect of $2,000		3,000
Retained earnings, January 1, 1985, as restated		42,600
Add: Net income		74,400
Subtotal		117,000
Less: Dividends declared on preferred stock ($.80 per share)	$ 4,000	
Dividends declared on common stock ($.60 per share)	12,000	16,000
Retained earnings, December 31, 1985		$101,000

---

1. Correction of an error in the financial statements of a prior period and
2. Adjustments that result from realization of income tax benefits of pre-acquisition operating loss carryforwards of purchased subsidiaries.[15]

A **correction of an error** that was made in the financial statements of a **prior period** is accounted for in the **current period** as a prior period adjustment.[16] The error may have resulted from mathematical mistakes, errors in selecting or applying accounting principles, or oversight or misuse of facts when the company prepared its erroneous financial statements.[17] Examples of errors are an overstatement of merchandise inventory at the end of the preceding period because of an inaccurate physical count, and an understatement of previously reported depreciation because of an error in computation. A change from an accounting principle that is not generally accepted to one that is generally accepted is considered to be a correction of an error.

In practice, prior period adjustments due to errors are rare. In its 1979 annual report, Itel Corporation (a San Francisco–based company) reported a very large prior period adjustment of $25,700,000. The company indicated in the notes to its financial statements that it learned of certain charges recorded in 1979 which apparently should have been recorded in 1978. The effect of the error was to reduce the 1978 reported net income from $47,200,000 to $21,500,000. As this example shows, prior period adjustments due to errors can have a significant effect on a company's financial statements.

An accountant must carefully distinguish a *correction of an error* from a *change in an accounting estimate*. A change in an accounting estimate is a consequence of the need for accountants to make many estimates. Changes in these estimates often result from new

---

[15]*FASB Statement of Financial Accounting Standards No. 16*, "Prior Period Adjustments," 1977, par. 11. This pronouncement did not affect the manner of reporting accounting changes required or permitted by an FASB Statement or Interpretation, or an APB Opinion. We discuss the reporting of accounting changes in Chapter 19, where we see that adjustments to the opening balance of a company's retained earnings need not be confined to prior period adjustments.

[16]Moreover, when comparative statements are reported, erroneous amounts previously reported should be corrected.

[17]*APB Opinion No. 20*, par. 13.

information or subsequent developments that improve the accountant's judgment. Examples include changes in estimates of uncollectible accounts receivable and changes in the estimated service lives or salvage values of plant assets. Changes in accounting estimates are *not* prior period adjustments. The effects of these changes should be accounted for in the period of change if the change affects that period only, or in the period of change and future periods if the change affects both.[18] We explain corrections of errors and changes in accounting estimates in detail in Chapter 19.

The second type of prior period adjustment—adjustments that result from realization of income tax benefits of preacquisition operating loss carryforwards of purchased subsidiaries—is beyond the scope of this text. Coverage of this topic is appropriate in advanced accounting courses.

As shown in Exhibit 4–3, a prior period adjustment is added to or deducted from the previously reported opening balance of retained earnings to derive a **restated (revised) opening balance.** Furthermore, a prior period adjustment is reported **net of its related income tax effect,** like that for extraordinary items. As we discuss in Chapter 18, the principle of intraperiod tax allocation requires that prior period adjustments be reported on a net of tax basis.

Net Income and Dividends

The **net income** figure on the statement of retained earnings is taken directly from the income statement. When a company sustains a **net loss** during a period, the loss is deducted on the retained earnings statement.

Dividends declared during the period are deducted on the retained earnings statement and dividends per share ordinarily are disclosed. Dividends declared may be in the form of cash, other assets, or the company's own stock. Further, they may relate to both preferred and common stock. Note carefully that dividends declared are deducted on the statement since the declaration represents a reduction in retained earnings. Sometimes a company declares a dividend in one period but does not pay or distribute it until the next. As a result, dividends declared during a period may include an amount paid or distributed during the period and an amount that will be paid or distributed in the next period.

Combined Statement of Income and Retained Earnings

Many companies issue a **combined statement of income and retained earnings,** similar to the one shown for the Sunrise Corporation in Exhibit 4–4.

Some accountants favor a combined statement of income and retained earnings because it integrates important and related information. Other accountants object to the combined statement because they believe it may be too complicated for many users and because it deemphasizes net income by not placing this item at the bottom of the combined statement.

STATEMENT OF STOCKHOLDERS' EQUITY

Sometimes a company has changes during a period not only in its retained earnings account but also in other accounts that comprise stockholders' equity. These changes occur as the company sells additional stock, buys and sells treasury stock, or engages in other kinds of capital stock transactions. Such changes must be disclosed in a separate statement, in the basic statements, or in the notes to the financial statements. Changes in the number of shares outstanding should also be disclosed.[19]

---

[18]*APB Opinion No. 20,* par. 31.
[19]*APB Opinion No. 12,* "Omnibus Opinion—1967," 1967, par. 10.

EXHIBIT 4–4

Sunrise Corporation
COMBINED STATEMENT OF INCOME AND RETAINED EARNINGS
For the Year Ended December 31, 1985

Net income*		$ 74,400
Add: Retained earnings, January 1, 1985, as previously reported	$45,600	
Less: Prior period adjustment—correction of depreciation understatement in 1984 due to error, less applicable income tax effect of $2,000	3,000	
Retained earnings, January 1, 1985, as restated		42,600
Subtotal		117,000
Less: Dividends declared on preferred stock ($.80 per share)	4,000	
Dividends declared on common stock ($.60 per share)	12,000	16,000
Retained earnings, December 31, 1985		$101,000
Per share of common stock**		
Income before extraordinary item		$2.32
Extraordinary gain (net of tax)		1.20
Net income		$3.52

*The items shown in Exhibits 4–1 or 4–2 would appear above net income.
**Alternatively, earnings per share may be presented parenthetically in the body of the combined statement of income and retained earnings.

Many companies report all of these changes in a separate **statement of stockholders' equity.** In effect, this statement combines the retained earnings statement with one that shows changes in all the other components of stockholders' equity. As a result, a company that reports a statement of stockholders' equity need not report a separate retained earnings statement. A statement of stockholders' equity for the Sunrise Corporation appears in Exhibit 4–5.

BALANCE SHEET

The **balance sheet** (sometimes called the **statement of financial position**) shows the financial position of an enterprise at a particular point in time. Investors, creditors, and other users of financial statements analyze an enterprise's balance sheet to evaluate such factors as **liquidity** (how close the assets are to cash realization) and **capital structure** (what amount of assets has been financed by creditors and what amount by owners). Ideally, these evaluations should assist users in making their predictions and evaluating management.

At one time the balance sheet was generally regarded as the most important financial statement, but, as stated earlier, most users now regard the income statement as paramount. Nevertheless, the balance sheet may be regaining some of the attention that it once had. For example, a recent article stated that: "Investors, including the biggest bank trust departments, still look at earnings before they buy a security, but today the deal must also make sense in terms of a company's current ratio, debt/equity ratio, and return on investments. Corporations with balance sheets that cannot pass muster will find themselves closed out of the marketplace."[20]

---

[20]"Focus on Balance Sheet," *Business Week* (June 7, 1976), p. 52.

Elements of the Balance Sheet

Fundamentally, the balance sheet consists of three major elements, presented in the equation below:

$$\text{Assets} = \text{Liabilities} + \text{Owners' equity}$$

In Chapter 2, we defined these elements as follows:[21]

1. **Assets.**   Probable future economic benefits obtained or controlled by an entity as a result of past transactions or events.
2. **Liabilities.**   Probable future sacrifices of economic benefits arising from present obligations of an entity to transfer assets or provide services to other entities in the future as a result of past transactions or events.
3. **Owners' equity.**   The residual interest in the assets of an entity that remains after deducting its liabilities.

Balance Sheet Classifications

Generally accepted accounting principles require a company to report its assets, liabilities, and owners' equity in several classifications or categories designed to aid users in analyzing

---

[21]The definitions are based on *FASB Statement of Financial Accounting Concepts No. 3*, pars. 19, 28, and 43.

EXHIBIT 4–5

Sunrise Corporation
STATEMENT OF STOCKHOLDERS' EQUITY
For the Year Ended December 31, 1985

	Preferred Stock	Common Stock	Additional Paid-In Capital	Retained Earnings	Total
Balance, January 1, 1985, as previously reported	$50,000	$ 60,000	$25,000	$ 45,600	$180,600
Less: Prior period adjustment—correction of depreciation understatement in 1984 due to error, less applicable income tax effect of $2,000				(3,000)	(3,000)
Balance, January 1, 1984, as restated	50,000	60,000	25,000	42,600	177,600
Add: Net income				74,400	74,400
Less: Dividends declared on preferred stock ($.80 per share)				(4,000)	(4,000)
Dividends declared on common stock ($.60 per share)				(12,000)	(12,000)
Add: Common stock issued on January 2, 1985 (8,000 shares)		40,000	15,000		55,000
Balance, December 31, 1985	$50,000	$100,000	$40,000	$101,000	$291,000

the company's financial position. Although some flexibility is permitted in selecting and naming balance sheet categories and in grouping specific items into them, the following categories (in the order shown) are representative of those found in practice:

Assets
    Current assets
    Investments and funds   ⎫
    Property, plant, and equipment ⎬ Noncurrent assets
    Intangible assets   ⎭
    Other assets

Liabilities
    Current liabilities
    Long-term liabilities

EXHIBIT 4–6
Sunrise Corporation
BALANCE SHEET
December 31, 1985

Assets

Current Assets			
Cash		$22,500	
Marketable securities (at cost; market value $42,400)		40,000	
Accounts receivable	$ 55,000		
Less: Allowance for doubtful accounts	4,500	50,500	
Notes receivable		26,000	
Merchandise inventory (at lower of average cost or market)		35,000	
Prepaid expenses			
Supplies	5,350		
Insurance	4,650	10,000	
Total current assets			$184,000
Investments and Funds			
Investment in Case Company common stock (at cost; market value $46,400)		41,800	
Land held for future plant site		55,000	
Plant expansion fund		48,700	
Total investments and funds			145,500
Property, Plant, and Equipment			
Land		22,000	
Building	100,000		
Less: Accumulated depreciation	30,000	70,000	
Equipment	80,000		
Less: Accumulated depreciation	20,000	60,000	
Total property, plant, and equipment			152,000
Intangible Assets			
Goodwill			38,500
Other Assets			
Bond issue costs			8,000
Total assets			$528,000

Owners' Equity
Paid-in capital
Capital stock
Preferred stock
Common stock
Additional paid-in capital
Retained earnings

The balance sheet of the Sunrise Corporation appears in Exhibit 4-6. The exhibit shows the **account form** of balance sheet. In this form the liabilities and owners' equity are listed on the right-hand side of the assets. Two other acceptable formats are the **report form** and the **financial position form.** The report form shows the liabilities and owners' equity directly below the assets. The financial position form shows current liabilities deducted from current assets to determine working capital. Noncurrent assets are then added to working capital and noncurrent liabilities are deducted to arrive at owners' equity.[22]

---

[22]*Accounting Trends and Techniques,* 1982, p. 105, indicates that in 1981, 55% of the 600 companies surveyed used the account form, 44% used the report form, and only 1% used the financial position form.

Liabilities and Stockholders' Equity

Current Liabilities			
Accounts payable		$ 44,400	
Notes payable		12,000	
Interest payable		4,200	
Salaries payable		6,400	
Dividends payable		4,000	
Income tax payable		10,000	
Advances from customers		7,200	
Unearned rent revenue		4,800	
Total current liabilities			$ 93,000
Long-Term Liabilities			
Bonds payable (10%, due December 31, 1995)		150,000	
Less: Unamortized discount		6,000	144,000
Total liabilities			237,000
Stockholders' Equity			
Paid-in capital			
Capital stock			
Preferred stock ($10 par, 8%, cumulative and nonparticipating, 10,000 shares authorized, 5,000 shares issued and outstanding)	$ 50,000		
Common stock ($5 par, 25,000 shares authorized, 20,000 shares issued and outstanding)	100,000	150,000	
Additional paid-in capital		40,000	
Total paid-in capital			190,000
Retained earnings			101,000
Total stockholders' equity			291,000
Total liabilities and stockholders' equity			$528,000

We discuss each balance sheet classification below. Our discussion of each classification includes a brief indication of how some of the major items reported in it are valued on the balance sheet. You will see that although balance sheets are based largely on historical costs, they actually reflect several valuation methods. Many of the remaining chapters in this book are organized within a balance sheet framework. In these chapters we explain in detail the nature and valuation of individual assets, liabilities, and owners' equity.

Assets

Current Assets.   Current assets are cash and other assets which are reasonably expected to be realized in cash or sold or consumed during the normal operating cycle of the business or within one year from the balance sheet date, whichever is *longer*.[23] An **operating cycle** for a given enterprise is the average time that it takes for the enterprise to spend cash for inventory, sell the inventory in exchange for a receivable, and collect the receivable in cash. The cycle thus progresses from cash, through inventories and receivables, back to cash. We illustrate this process in Exhibit 4–7.

Most companies have operating cycles that are less than one year. Some companies, however, such as those involved in distilling, tobacco, and lumber operations, have operating cycles longer than one year. A balance sheet of one of these companies may therefore contain current assets, such as inventory, for which cash realization is not expected within the next year.

Current assets are usually listed in the order of their liquidity. The most common types of current assets are cash, short-term investments, receivables, inventories, and prepaid expenses.

Cash (on hand and on deposit) is included among current assets only if it is available for current operations. Any cash that has been restricted for purposes other than current operations should be reported in the investments and funds section of the balance sheet. Cash is reported on the balance sheet at its face amount.

Short-term investments are those that are readily marketable and that management *intends* to convert into cash within the next year or operating cycle, whichever is longer. Often they consist entirely of marketable securities such as stocks or bonds. These securities are normally reported at the lower of their cost or market value.

Receivables, such as accounts receivable and notes receivable, represent claims to cash and are ordinarily reported at the amount that the company expects to collect. Accounts receivable typically compose the largest dollar value of receivables. An estimated allowance for doubtful accounts should be deducted from the gross amount of accounts receivable so that the accounts are properly reported at their **net realizable value** (estimated amount collectible).

Inventory in a merchandising company normally consists only of merchandise that is ready for sale to customers. On the other hand, the inventories of a manufacturing concern may consist of factory supplies, raw materials, work (goods) in process, and finished goods. Inventories are usually reported at the lower of cost or market value.

Prepaid expenses consist of such items as insurance, rent, advertising, taxes, and operating supplies. These items are not current assets in the sense that they will be converted into cash but rather in the sense that if they had not been paid for in advance, they would require the use of current assets during the next year or operating cycle. A prepaid expense is reported at the amount of its unexpired or unconsumed cost.

In practice, the distinction between current and noncurrent assets is sometimes hazy and is based in part on judgment, custom, and materiality. For example, a company that has a three-month operating cycle may report a two-year prepaid insurance policy as a current asset because the amount involved is immaterial. As another example, companies do not

Materiality

---

[23]*Accounting Research Bulletin No. 43,* "Restatement and Revision of Accounting Research Bulletins," 1953, Ch. 3, Sec. A, par. 4.

EXHIBIT 4–7
Operating Cycle

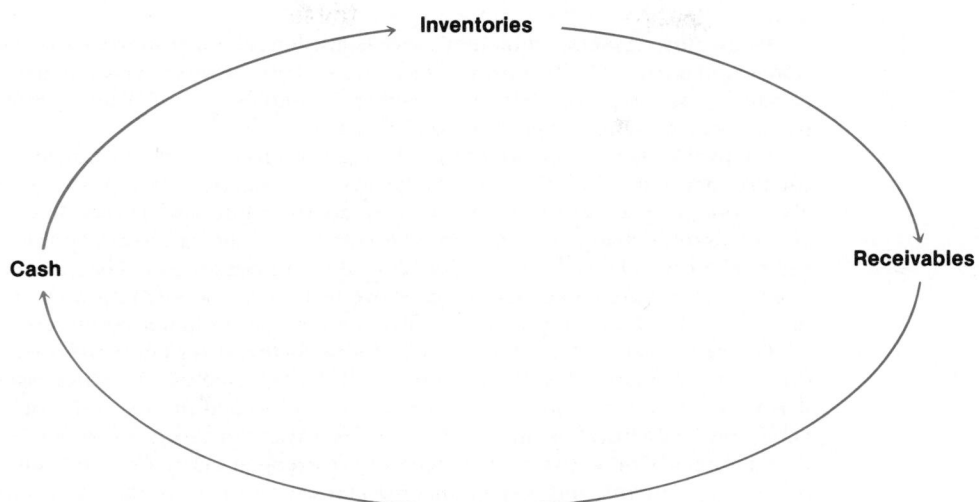

customarily report the following year's depreciation as a current asset, although a portion of plant assets will be consumed in the next year's operations.

Investments and Funds.   This category is used to report various types of investments and fund balances that management *intends* to hold for a period longer than the normal operating cycle or one year, whichever is longer, and that are *not* used in the business operations. Assets reported here need not be readily marketable. This category often is called **long-term investments,** or simply, **investments.**

Assets commonly included in this category are:

1. Long-term investments in securities of other companies, such as stocks, bonds, and notes.
2. Investments in plant assets that are not currently used in operations, such as land held for a future plant site or for speculation.
3. Special fund balances accumulated for a particular purpose, such as future plant expansion or bond retirement.
4. Cash surrender value of life insurance policies.

The valuation basis used for assets in this category depends on the type of asset. For example, a special fund balance is normally reported at the amount accumulated in the fund, while an investment in bonds is usually reported at face value plus unamortized premium (or face value minus unamortized discount). Long-term equity investments may be valued using the cost, lower of cost or market, or equity method, depending on whether the investment is readily marketable and on the extent of ownership interest held. We discuss the valuation of investments and funds more fully in Chapter 10.

Property, Plant, and Equipment.   This section of the balance sheet is used to report assets that are tangible (have physical substance) and long-lived, and that are used in the business operations. **Plant assets** is a shorter title that accountants often use when referring to property, plant, and equipment. Examples of plant assets are business sites (the land on which the business is located), buildings, equipment, machinery, furniture, fixtures, tools, containers, and natural resources. Accountants ordinarily record depreciation or depletion on all plant assets except land.

Plant assets are reported on the balance sheet at their historical cost less any accumulated depreciation or depletion. Accountants often use the term **book value** (or **net book value**) to refer to the difference between cost and accumulated depreciation or depletion.

Intangible Assets.   Intangible assets are long-lived resources that lack physical substance and are used in the business operations. These assets have value because they convey certain rights and privileges to the business. Examples include patents, copyrights, goodwill, trademarks, franchises, and organization costs.

Intangible assets often are quite valuable to a given enterprise. An accountant, however, usually cannot measure this value with sufficient objectivity to report it in the balance sheet. Therefore, the accountant initially records an intangible asset at cost, based on a completed, arm's-length exchange transaction. The cost is then allocated in a systematic manner over the periods benefited through a process called **amortization.** The balance sheet valuation assigned to an intangible asset is therefore its cost less amortization taken to date. Companies generally do not report accumulated amortization in a separate contra account.

Other Assets.   This category includes assets that do not fit conveniently into one of the other four categories. Ideally, accountants should seldom use the other assets category since it is very general and since most assets can be classified in one of the other, more specific categories. Nevertheless, in practice, a wide variety of assets are reported as other assets.

Examples of other assets are machinery rearrangement costs, bond issue costs, long-term rental prepayments, and prepaid income taxes resulting from the application of interperiod tax allocation (a concept we explain in Chapter 18). The valuation reported is usually the unallocated cost. Accountants sometimes use the term **deferred charges** (meaning simply **delayed debits**) to describe certain assets in this category. In essence, a deferred charge is simply a long-term prepayment of an expense. Many accountants oppose the use of this term since, technically speaking, buildings, patents, and many similar assets classified elsewhere are also deferred charges.

Liabilities

Current Liabilities.   Current liabilities are "obligations whose liquidation is reasonably expected to require the use of existing resources properly classifiable as current assets or the creation of other current liabilities."[24] Notice that the definition of current liabilities is closely related to that of current assets.

Current liabilities include the following:[25]

1. Payables for items which have entered the operating cycle or which relate directly to the operating cycle, such as accounts payable, wages payable, commissions payable, and income taxes payable.
2. Collections received in advance of delivering goods or performing services, such as advances from customers for merchandise ordered or cash received for advance ticket sales.
3. Other obligations that will be liquidated through the use of current assets or the creation of other current liabilities within the next year or operating cycle, whichever is longer. Examples include short-term notes payable resulting from the purchase of equipment and the currently maturing portion of long-term debt.

Not all short-term obligations require the use of current assets or the creation of other current liabilities during the next year or operating cycle. For example, a bond issue that matures during the next year may be paid using cash accumulated in a sinking fund (clas-

---

[24]*Accounting Research Bulletin No. 43,* Ch. 3, Sec. A, par. 7.
[25]*Accounting Research Bulletin No. 43,* Ch. 3, Sec. A, par. 7.

sified in the investments and funds category), or a short-term note payable may be refinanced on a long-term basis. These obligations should be reported as long-term rather than as current liabilities.

Current liabilities are normally listed in the order of their liquidation dates and are usually reported at the amount to be paid.

Working capital (sometimes called **net working capital**) is the difference between total current assets and total current liabilities. Working capital is an approximate measure of the net amount of a company's relatively liquid resources, and many creditors believe that it constitutes a margin of safety for paying short-term debts.[26] Companies without adequate working capital may be more likely than others to have liquidity problems.

Because of the emphasis placed by many users of financial statements on working capital and on the size of a company's **current ratio** (current assets *divided by* current liabilities), corporate managers have at times wanted to incorrectly report certain noncurrent assets as current and certain current liabilities as long-term. Accountants and auditors must be careful to detect and request that management correct these errors before the financial statements are issued.

Long-Term Liabilities. Long-term liabilities are obligations that will *not* require the use of current assets or the creation of other current liabilities within the next year or operating cycle, whichever is longer. In other words, this category comprises all liabilities other than those properly classified as current. Examples of liabilities that are ordinarily classified as long-term are bonds payable, long-term notes payable, deferred income taxes resulting from the application of interperiod tax allocation (discussed in Chapter 18), long-term obligations under warranty contracts, obligations under capital leases, and pension obligations. Conceptually, a long-term liability should be measured on the date incurred at an amount equal to the present value of the payments expected to be made in the future.

When bonds payable are reported, any premium associated with the bonds should be added to the face or maturity value; similarly, any discount should be subtracted. An obligation classified as long-term sometimes requires the use of current assets or the creation of other current liabilities within the next year or operating cycle, whichever is longer. Such an obligation, along with any related premium or discount, should be reclassified as a current liability. An example is a five-year note payable that matures within the next year and will be paid using cash that is classified as a current asset.

Some companies use a **deferred credits** category to report certain long-term obligations, such as deferred income taxes and collections received in advance of performing services on a long-term basis. Deferred credits are simply delayed credits which will increase reported income in future periods.

Owners' Equity

Owners' equity is a measure of the owners' interests in the assets of a business. In traditional accounting, the accountant measures individual assets and liabilities directly. Owners' equity is simply a residual, indirect measurement whose value depends on the values assigned to assets and liabilities.

The three primary forms of business organization are sole proprietorships, partnerships, and corporations. In proprietorships and partnerships, owners' equity is usually summarized in a single capital account for each owner. The balance in a capital account summarizes the owner's investments and withdrawals as well as the owner's share of past net incomes and losses. The balance sheet of a proprietorship or partnership generally does not distinguish between amounts paid into the firm by owners and reinvested earnings, because state laws

---

[26]For an interesting discussion of the limitations of the working capital concept, see Philip Fess, "The Working Capital Concept," *Accounting Review* (April 1966), pp. 266–270.

usually do not restrict the amount of withdrawals that a proprietor or partner can make. Creditors of proprietorships and partnerships are usually more interested in the personal financial conditions of the owners since, in the event of liquidation, owners may be held personally liable for business debts.

Corporations report owners' equity (usually called **stockholders'** or **shareholders' equity**) in two major categories: **paid-in capital** (often called **contributed** or **invested capital**) and **retained earnings.** The use of these categories results in a stockholders' equity that is classified approximately according to *sources* of capital.

Historically, legal considerations have played a large role in the reporting of stockholders' equity. Since creditors usually cannot hold corporate stockholders personally liable for company debts, state laws provide that corporations cannot distribute assets to stockholders if so doing would reduce owners' equity below a minimum amount known as **legal** or **stated capital.** The legal capital of a given company depends on the laws of the state in which it is organized.

Paid-In Capital.   This category is used to report amounts that stockholders have paid into the company in exchange for shares of stock. It may be divided further into capital stock and additional paid-in capital.

Capital stock includes both preferred and common stock. Here companies report the par or stated value per share multiplied by the number of shares issued. The total amount received is reported for stock that has no par or stated value. If a company has both preferred and common stock outstanding, it should report each type separately.

Additional paid-in capital generally represents amounts received in excess of the par or stated value of shares sold. These amounts are usually called paid-in (or contributed) capital in excess of par (or stated) value. Additional paid-in capital may be presented as a single amount, but if several material sources of additional paid-in capital exist, a breakdown by source may be helpful to financial statement users.

| Materiality |

Retained Earnings.   Retained earnings, which represent a company's accumulated earnings less its dividends, are added to total paid-in capital when determining total stockholders' equity. A negative (debit) balance in retained earnings, called a **deficit,** occurs when a company's losses and dividends have exceeded its earnings. An accountant should simply deduct a deficit from total paid-in capital to arrive at total stockholders' equity.

The retained earnings category is sometimes divided into **appropriated** and **unappropriated** components. Companies may appropriate (or restrict) retained earnings for legal, contractual, or discretionary reasons. An appropriation of retained earnings means that the amount appropriated is not available as a basis for declaring dividends during the time of appropriation. Companies usually disclose appropriations of retained earnings in the notes to their financial statements. Occasionally, however, a company may make a formal journal entry for the amount appropriated. This entry involves a debit to retained earnings and a credit to retained earnings appropriated for the designated purpose, such as future plant expansion. These kinds of entries ultimately produce balances in appropriated retained earnings accounts, such as Retained Earnings Appropriated for Future Plant Expansion or Retained Earnings Restricted by the Purchase of Treasury Stock. These accounts and their balances are reported as appropriated retained earnings.

When a company has created accounts for retained earnings appropriations, it reports the amount of its unappropriated retained earnings separate from the amounts appropriated. Unappropriated retained earnings are simply those available as a basis for declaring dividends.[27]

Companies sometimes purchase and hold shares of their own stock which they previously sold to investors. These shares constitute **treasury stock.** A company may acquire treasury stock for several reasons. For example, it may want to use the stock to satisfy

---

[27]A decision to declare dividends is, of course, influenced by many factors other than retained earnings.

employee stock option contracts or to effect a merger. Treasury stock is *not* an asset but rather a reduction in stockholders' equity. The vast majority of companies account for treasury stock at cost by debiting a treasury stock account for the cost of the shares purchased. The company later deducts the amount in the treasury stock account as the final account in the stockholders' equity section. Some companies account for treasury stock at par value; under this method treasury stock is deducted in the capital stock subcategory of stockholders' equity. We explain the methods of accounting for and reporting treasury stock in Chapter 16.

STATEMENT OF CHANGES IN FINANCIAL POSITION

In 1971 the APB issued *Opinion No. 19,* which expanded the set of basic financial statements to include the statement of changes in financial position. The objectives of this statement are: (1) to summarize a company's financing and investing activities during a period of time; and (2) to complete the company's disclosure of changes in its financial position during the period.[28] **Financing activities,** such as the sale of bonds or capital stock, are those that result in **inflows** of funds; they therefore constitute **sources of funds. Investing activities,** such as the purchase of plant assets, are those that result in **outflows** of funds; these activities represent **uses of funds.** A statement of changes in financial position helps to explain *why* a company's financial position, as reported in its balance sheet, has changed from the beginning to the end of a period. Thus, the statement helps users to answer such questions as: How was the growth in company assets financed during the period? Why has working capital decreased during the period despite huge reported earnings? Why are dividend payments not higher?

With respect to the statement of changes in financial position, **funds** are usually defined as either **working capital** or **cash.** We emphasize the working capital definition in the following discussion because the vast majority of companies use it.[29]

Regardless of which definition of funds a company uses, the statement of changes in financial position should be based on a broad concept called the **all financial resources concept.** Under this concept the statement prepared according to the working capital definition of funds will disclose the financing and investing aspects of all significant transactions that affect financial position during a period, whether or not these transactions directly affect working capital. For example, if a company issues common stock in exchange for land, the company should report both a source (issuance of common stock) and a use (acquisition of land) of working capital, even though the transaction does not actually produce an inflow or an outflow of working capital. Under the all financial resources concept, this transaction is reported *as if* it affects working capital, because a failure to do so would result in the omission of significant financing and investing activities from the statement of changes in financial position. Other examples of transactions that would appear as both sources and uses of working capital, even though they do not directly affect working capital, include conversions of long-term debt or preferred stock to common stock and exchanges of one noncurrent asset for another.

Assuming that we use a working capital definition of funds, the major categories in the statement of changes in financial position are **sources of working capital** and **uses of working capital.** The major sources of working capital typically are: (1) operations; (2) sale of noncurrent assets; (3) issuance of long-term debt; and (4) issuance of capital stock. The major uses usually are: (1) acquisition of noncurrent assets; (2) retirement of long-term debt; (3) reacquisition of capital stock; and (4) cash dividend declarations. In addition to the

---

[28]*APB Opinion No. 19,* "Reporting Changes in Financial Position," 1971, par. 4.
[29]*Accounting Trends and Techniques,* 1982, p. 344, indicates that in 1981, 78% of the 600 companies surveyed used the working capital definition.

sources and uses categories, the statement of changes in financial position may have a separate category for financing and investing activities that do not directly affect working capital, such as the issuance of common stock in exchange for land.

The statement of changes in financial position for the Sunrise Corporation is presented in Exhibit 4–8. Preparation of such a statement requires comparative balance sheets as well as information that explains changes in the account balances during the period. We have not included all this information in the chapter, because at this point you should concentrate on the basic form and content of the statement as well as on the general types of information that it conveys. In Chapter 23 we discuss the statement more fully and explain how to prepare it.

As Exhibit 4–8 shows, the statement should begin with working capital provided by operations. This measure should be prominently disclosed, because users of financial statements generally are interested in evaluating the ability of a company to generate working capital through its operations. When reporting working capital provided by operations, most companies begin with net income and add (or deduct) items recognized in determining net income that did not use (or provide) working capital. For example, depreciation expense is added to net income because, although depreciation is an appropriate deduction when measuring net income, it does not use working capital. An alternative and more direct approach to reporting working capital provided by operations is to begin with revenues that provided working capital and deduct expenses that used working capital. The amount of working capital provided by operations is, of course, the same regardless of which approach a company uses to report it.

As Exhibit 4–8 also shows, extraordinary items are excluded from the calculation of working capital provided by operations. The working capital provided by the extraordinary item (i.e., the proceeds from expropriation of land) is reported as a separate source and listed immediately below "working capital provided by operations, exclusive of extraordinary items." Beyond this point, some flexibility is permitted in arranging the contents of the statement. The statement must, however, disclose all important changes in financial position that occurred during the period.

Observe in Exhibit 4–8 that we have included in the statement a separate section called "financing and investing activities not directly affecting working capital." In this section we see that Sunrise Corporation issued common stock to acquire land. Remember that under the all financial resources concept, accountants regard this transaction as substantially equivalent to the company's having sold common stock for cash and then used the cash to buy land. Many companies would therefore report the "issuance of common stock for land" among the sources of working capital and the "acquisition of land by issuance of common stock" among the uses of working capital. Although this method of reporting is acceptable under generally accepted accounting principles, we have reported both items in a special category to emphasize that the items do not actually produce an inflow or an outflow of working capital. In practice, companies use several acceptable methods to report the statement of changes in financial position, as we explain in Chapter 23.

A **schedule of working capital changes** should accompany a statement of changes in financial position. This schedule shows the change that occurred in each working capital account during the period, and it therefore provides a detailed analysis of the increase or decrease in working capital that is reported on the statement of changes in financial position ($30,000 in the case of Sunrise Corporation).

RELATIONSHIP BETWEEN BASIC FINANCIAL STATEMENTS

As we have stated earlier, the basic financial statements **articulate** with one another. Their relationship is summarized in simplified terms in Exhibit 4–9.

EXHIBIT 4–8

Sunrise Corporation
STATEMENT OF CHANGES IN FINANCIAL POSITION
For the Year Ended December 31, 1985

Sources of Working Capital
Operations

Income before extraordinary item	$ 50,400	
Add (Deduct): Items not affecting working capital		
Depreciation expense	7,500	
Amortization	3,200	
Loss on sale of long-term investments	5,100	
Gain on sale of equipment	(6,500)	
Working capital provided by operations, exclusive of extraordinary items		$ 59,700
Other sources		
Proceeds from expropriation of land	60,000	
Sale of long-term investments	10,900	
Sale of equipment	16,400	87,300
Total sources of working capital		147,000

Uses of Working Capital

Deposit made in plant expansion fund	7,000	
Payment of long-term note	110,000	
Total uses of working capital		117,000
Subtotal		30,000

Financing and Investing Activities Not Directly Affecting Working Capital

Issuance of common stock for land		55,000
Acquisition of land by issuance of common stock		(55,000)
Increase in working capital		$ 30,000

Schedule of Working Capital Changes

Working Capital Account	Jan. 1, 1985	Dec. 31, 1985	Working Capital Increase (Decrease)
Current Assets			
Cash	$ 17,000	$ 22,500	$ 5,500
Marketable securities	42,000	40,000	(2,000)
Accounts receivable (net)	41,000	50,500	9,500
Notes receivable	16,000	26,000	10,000
Merchandise inventory	40,000	35,000	(5,000)
Prepaid expenses	8,000	10,000	2,000
Total current assets	164,000	184,000	
Current Liabilities			
Accounts payable	53,800	44,400	9,400
Notes payable	14,000	12,000	2,000
Interest payable	4,700	4,200	500
Salaries payable	7,900	6,400	1,500
Dividends payable	3,000	4,000	(1,000)
Income tax payable	7,000	10,000	(3,000)
Advances from customers	9,000	7,200	1,800
Unearned rent revenue	3,600	4,800	(1,200)
Total current liabilities	103,000	93,000	
Working capital	$ 61,000	$ 91,000	$30,000

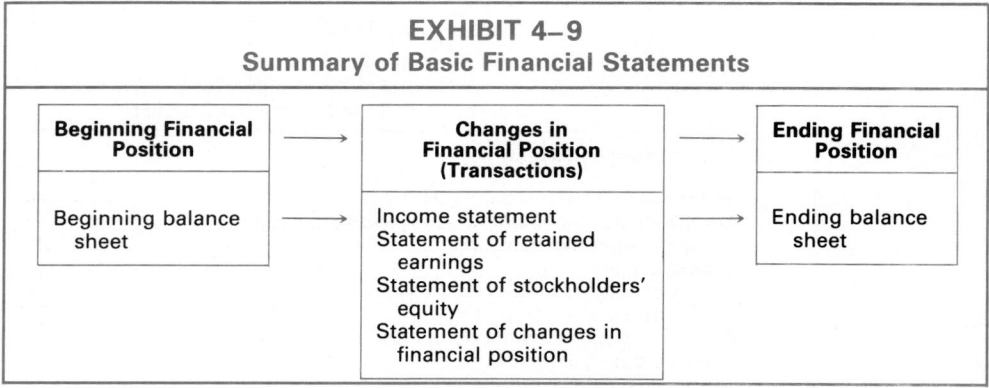

A company's financial position at a particular moment in time is shown on the balance sheet. The other basic financial statements summarize various types of changes in financial position that have occurred during a period of time. The income statement explains the changes in financial position that are the result of earnings activities. The statement of retained earnings (or statement of stockholders' equity) explains certain changes in the equity component of financial position. Finally, the statement of changes in financial position summarizes all important financing and investing activities during a period.

The income statement reports the revenues, expenses, gains, losses, and net income for a period. The net income explains a part of the change in retained earnings that is shown on the statement of retained earnings (or statement of stockholders' equity). The statement of changes in financial position summarizes not only the income earned during the period but also the other financing and investing activities that have occurred. The income statement, statement of retained earnings (or statement of stockholders' equity), and statement of changes in financial position are tied together by the beginning and ending balance sheets. All of the basic financial statements articulate with one another because of the double-entry system of accounting and because revenues, expenses, gains, losses, financing activities, and investing activities represent flows associated with the economic resources and obligations presented on the balance sheet.

OTHER FINANCIAL STATEMENT TOPICS

Disclosure

The **disclosure principle** requires an accountant to report information that might affect the decisions made by reasonably informed users of financial statements. To comply with this principle, an accountant usually must report in financial statements considerably more information than we have illustrated thus far in the chapter. Moreover, all of this information must be effectively communicated. In the remaining sections of this chapter, we shall discuss several other topics pertaining to basic financial statements.

To assist you in understanding the kinds of information that companies actually report, we have included a set of financial statements of Kroger Company on the endpapers of this book. Take a few minutes to look over these statements now and refer to them frequently as you study the remaining chapters. Although the statements contain material that you have not yet encountered, you will understand them much better after you have studied this book.

Notes to Financial Statements

As illustrated earlier, financial statements are summaries that consist of very few words and dollar amounts. **Notes to financial statements** (often called **footnotes**) are used to report information that does not fit in the body of the statements without reducing the understandability of the statements. **Notes are an integral part of the financial statements and therefore must be prepared and read carefully.** The notes often require several pages of an annual financial report.

The major types of information commonly disclosed in notes are:

1. Information on **accounting policies.** As discussed below, a company must disclose the major accounting policies that it uses in preparing its financial statements.
2. Information on **subsequent events.** As discussed below, companies are required to disclose certain types of events that occur between the date shown on the balance sheet and the date on which the financial statements are issued.
3. Information on **contingencies.** Companies often disclose certain contingencies, which are events, such as pending lawsuits, involving uncertainty about possible gain or loss that will be resolved in the future. We discuss accounting for contingencies in Chapter 14.
4. Information on major **contracts, commitments, and restrictions.** Important details about leases and pension plans, for example, usually are reported in the notes.
5. Information that **amplifies data** presented in the body of the statements. For example, a company may provide a schedule that separates its inventories into raw materials, work in process, and finished goods.

In general, notes to financial statements should be concise, complete, and easily understood by a reader who has a reasonable understanding of business affairs and is willing to spend reasonable amounts of time and effort studying the financial statements. The precise nature of disclosures required in notes is too detailed to cover in this chapter. We discuss these disclosures more fully at appropriate places in most of the remaining chapters.

Summary of Accounting Policies

Knowledgeable users of financial statements recognize that the numbers reported in a company's financial statements depend on the accounting policies that the company uses to generate them. As a result, when analyzing a company's financial statements, users typically want answers to questions such as: What inventory cost determination method (such as FIFO, LIFO, or average cost) does the company use? What depreciation method (such as double-declining balance, sum-of-the-years'-digits, or straight-line) does the company use?

To ensure that users have the information needed to answer these kinds of questions, *APB Opinion No. 22* requires a company to disclose the accounting policies that it uses. The term **accounting policies** refers to the specific principles and methods that a company has adopted for preparing its financial statements. The accounting policies that a company discloses should be those that: (1) involve a selection from existing acceptable alternatives; (2) are peculiar to the reporting company's industry; or (3) are unusual or innovative applications of generally accepted accounting principles.[30]

A company should preferably disclose its accounting policies in a separate **summary of significant accounting policies.** This summary should precede the notes to the financial statements or appear as the first note.[31]

Subsequent Events

Financial statements seldom are issued on the date shown on the balance sheet. Instead, a period of time usually elapses during which the accountants and auditors complete their work on the statements. During this period, many important things can occur that have a material effect on the financial statements being prepared.

Materiality

---

[30]*APB Opinion No. 22,* "Disclosure of Accounting Policies," 1972, par. 12.
[31]*APB Opinion No. 22,* par. 15.

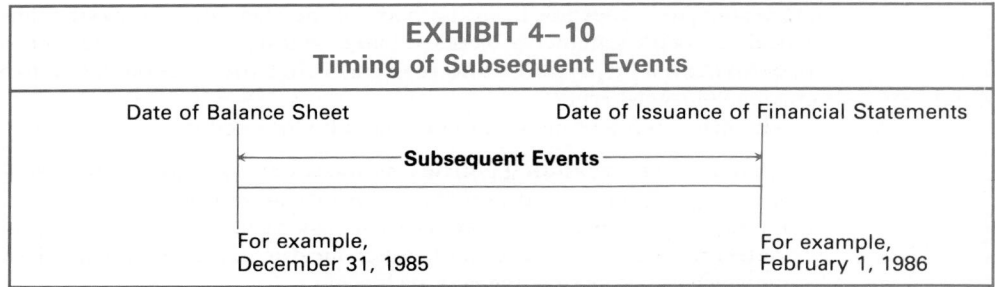

EXHIBIT 4–10
Timing of Subsequent Events

Date of Balance Sheet ———————————— Date of Issuance of Financial Statements

————————— Subsequent Events —————————

For example,
December 31, 1985

For example,
February 1, 1986

Subsequent events are events that occur between the date shown on the balance sheet and the date on which the financial statements are issued, as shown in Exhibit 4-10.

There are two types of subsequent events. The first type consists of events that provide additional evidence about **conditions that existed on the balance sheet date** and that affect the estimates used in preparing the financial statements. The appropriate accounting for this type of subsequent event is to adjust the account balances reported in the financial statements in order to reflect the new information. For example, the bankruptcy of a major customer ten days after the balance sheet date usually reflects a condition (namely, the poor financial health of the customer) that existed on the balance sheet date, and the estimate of bad debts may therefore need to be revised upward to reflect the new information.

The second type of subsequent event is one that provides evidence about **conditions that arose after the balance sheet date.** Events of this type do not result in adjustments of the account balances of the previous period. They may, however, require disclosure in order to prevent the financial statements from being misleading. Examples of subsequent events that require disclosure are the purchase of a business, the loss of inventories or plant assets due to a casualty, and the sale of a bond or capital stock issue.[32]

Obviously, a subsequent event also affects the financial statements of the period in which the event occurs. A more thorough treatment of subsequent events usually appears in auditing texts.

Comparative Financial Statements

The financial statements illustrated in this chapter were prepared for one period only. In practice, **comparative financial statements** are ordinarily presented for two or more periods, as shown in the financial statements on the endpapers of this book. Such statements are more useful than single-period statements because they reveal important trends. When comparative financial statements are presented, all elements reported in the current period's statements should be comparable to those reported for the prior period(s). Any exceptions must be clearly explained.

Rounding of Amounts

The dollar amounts reported in financial statements are usually rounded. For example, a recent survey of the annual reports of 600 companies found that 89 rounded to the nearest dollar, 414 rounded to the nearest thousand dollars, and 97 rounded to the nearest million dollars.[33] Rounding is justified because of materiality and the many estimates in financial statements. Failure to round may imply a degree of precision that simply does not exist in financial statements.

Materiality

---

[32]*Statement on Auditing Standards No. 1,* "Codification of Auditing Standards and Procedures" (New York: AICPA, 1973), Sec. 560, par. .06.
[33]*Accounting Trends and Techniques,* 1982, p. 36.

Disclosure Methods

Accountants use several methods of disclosure. Generally, the most important information is reported in the **body of the financial statements.** In addition to the account titles and amounts, certain **parenthetical disclosures** may be made in the body of the statements. For example, the market value of marketable securities may be shown in parentheses if it is greater than cost. Or a related asset and liability, such as inventory pledged as collateral on a note payable, may be cross-referenced by a parenthetical remark made beside each respective account title.

Notes to the financial statements are used to report details that simply do not fit conveniently in the body of the statements. In addition, accountants often use **schedules** (presented alone or as part of the notes) to report such information as major inventory categories and operating expense details. The use of such schedules is particularly appropriate when a company prepares condensed financial statements. At certain times, accountants may use **supplementary statements** effectively. Such statements may be used, for example, to present financial statements that have been adjusted for inflation.

Amount of Disclosure

An elusive problem that the accountant faces when preparing financial statements is deciding on an appropriate **amount (extent) of disclosure.** Accountants want to prepare financial statements that are reasonably complete, yet understandable. Clearly, to achieve understandability, an accountant must summarize many details. The question is: To what extent can the accountant summarize and still present statements that are sufficiently complete and therefore in compliance with the disclosure principle?

Disclosure

Materiality

Deciding on an appropriate amount of disclosure in a given case depends on such related factors as the objectives of the statements, generally accepted accounting principles, the circumstances involved, the modifying convention of materiality, and professional judgment. Statements prepared for bankers, for example, often are fairly detailed in order to satisfy the bankers' needs. Those prepared for publication in annual reports to shareholders often are highly condensed.

As a general principle, the **offsetting** of assets and liabilities in the balance sheet is improper except when a specific legal right of offset exists. For example, cash in a bond sinking fund should not be offset against the bond liability, even though the company intends to use the cash to pay the bonds.

As another general principle, material **related-party transactions** should be disclosed. Examples are loans made by the company to its management or to a subsidiary.

Terminology

The language of accounting is technical, consisting of some words whose meanings differ from their everyday connotations. Because accountants must be effective communicators when preparing financial statements, they must select words and phrases that the average user can understand.

There is no requirement that the financial statements contain the same account titles that appear in the general ledger. For example, "accounts receivable" in the general ledger is sometimes reported on the balance sheet as "amounts due from customers."

The accounting profession has been very concerned with improving the terminology used in financial statements. *Accounting Terminology Bulletin No. 1,* for example, noted that accountants have used the term "reserve" to describe asset contra accounts, liability accounts, retained earnings appropriations, and loss accounts. To help avoid confusion of users, the bulletin recommended that the use of "reserve" be limited to retained earnings appropriations. The bulletin further recommended that accountants stop using the term "surplus" because it may mislead users by connoting an amount in excess of that needed.

Accountants should use such terms as "paid-in capital" or "contributed capital" instead of "paid-in surplus" or "capital surplus." Likewise, the use of "retained earnings" is preferable to "earned surplus."[34] In 1971 *APB Opinion No. 19* recommended the title "Statement of Changes in Financial Position" instead of the older title, "Funds Statement."[35]

One reason that we mention the terminology recommendations above is that the terms *not* recommended are still sometimes encountered in practice. You should therefore be aware of them. We emphasize the use of modern, preferred terminology throughout the text. Remember that financial statements will not be useful if they do not communicate effectively.

Auditor's Report

As explained in Chapter 1, financial statements often are accompanied by an independent auditor's report. Financial statements contain the representations of management. The functions of an independent auditor are to **examine the statements** and **express an opinion** on them. The auditor's opinion lends credibility to management's representations, and this enables users to have greater confidence in the statements.

CONCLUDING REMARKS

Financial statements are the culmination of an accountant's work. They constitute the *output* of the accounting information system and serve as *input* for investment, credit, and similar decisions that help to determine how resources are allocated in our society.

Financial statements are summaries that are primarily historical. They are interrelated and general purpose, and they reflect many estimates. Underlying the information reported in financial statements are many important measurement and disclosure principles that we discuss throughout the text.

All financial statements bear the name of the reporting entity, the title of the statement, and the date or period of time covered. The balance sheet presents financial position at a particular point in time; the other basic statements present various changes in financial position during a period of time.

The financial statements discussed in this chapter are currently reported under generally accepted accounting principles. To help ensure that companies provide financial statements regularly, accountants follow certain steps during an accounting period. These steps, collectively called the **accounting cycle,** are presented in the next chapter.

---

[34]*Accounting Terminology Bulletin No. 1,* "Review and Résumé," 1953, pars. 57–70.
[35]*APB Opinion No. 19,* par. 8.

KEY POINTS

1. The basic financial statements are the balance sheet, the income statement, the statement of changes in financial position, and the statement of retained earnings (or statement of stockholders' equity).

2. Basic financial statements have several important characteristics:
   a. They are only a subset of the information needed by users for making rational investment, lending, and similar decisions.
   b. They are primarily historical in nature.
   c. They summarize information.
   d. They reflect many estimates.
   e. They are general-purpose reports designed to serve the needs of many different users.
   f. They articulate with one another.

3. Extraordinary gains and losses result from events or transactions that are unusual in nature *and* not expected to recur in the foreseeable future.

4. A multiple-step income statement presents subtotals for gross margin and operating income; a single-step income statement does not.

5. Prior period adjustments, such as the correction of

an error made in the financial statements of a prior period, should be charged or credited directly to retained earnings.

6. The major balance sheet categories are:
   a. Assets
      Current assets
      Investments and funds
      Property, plant, and equipment
      Intangible assets
      Other assets
   b. Liabilities
      Current liabilities
      Long-term liabilities
   c. Owners' equity

Paid-in capital
   Capital stock
      Preferred stock
      Common stock
   Additional paid-in capital
   Retained earnings

7. The statement of changes in financial position is always based on the all financial resources concept and is usually based on a working capital definition of funds.

8. Notes (footnotes) are an integral part of the basic financial statements.

9. The role of an independent auditor is to examine financial statements and express an opinion on them.

QUESTIONS

4–1 What are the basic financial statements?

4–2 What are some important characteristics of the basic financial statements?

4–3 What are the criteria used to determine whether a gain or loss is extraordinary?

4–4 Why does the accounting profession require that extraordinary gains and losses be presented in a special section of the income statement?

4–5 Make up three examples of extraordinary items. (Do not use the examples presented in the chapter.)

4–6 May gains and losses from disposal of a business segment and from changes in accounting principles be included in the extraordinary items category? Explain your answer.

4–7 Distinguish clearly between a multiple-step and a single-step income statement.

4–8 What are the advantages of using a multiple-step format for presenting the income statement? What are the advantages of using a single-step format?

4–9 What does the term "prior period adjustments" mean? How should prior period adjustments be reported in the financial statements?

4–10 Suppose that in 1985 a company changes its estimate of the *total* useful life of its 12-year-old building from 30 years to 40 years. For accounting purposes, what kind of an event is this, and how should the event be accounted for?

4–11 Define the term "current assets" and cite five examples of current assets.

4–12 Why are special fund balances and the cash surrender value of life insurance not usually reported among the current assets?

4–13 Define the term "current liabilities" and cite five examples of current liabilities.

4–14 Define the terms "working capital" and "current ratio."

4–15 Explain the various categories that may be used in the stockholders' equity section of the balance sheet.

4–16 What is treasury stock? Is treasury stock an asset? Explain your answer.

4–17 Identify the major sources and uses of working capital typically found in the statement of changes in financial position.

4–18 What does the all financial resources concept imply about the statement of changes in financial position? In your answer assume a working capital definition of funds.

4–19 Why are the notes to the financial statements important to users?

4–20 Define the term "subsequent events." Indicate the two types (i.e., categories) of subsequent events and the appropriate accounting treatment for each type in the financial statements of the period preceding the subsequent event.

4–21 What factors should affect an accountant's decision about how detailed a given set of financial statements should be?

4–22 Why is terminology considered an important aspect of accounting?

4–23 What are the roles of management and the independent auditor in relation to a set of financial statements?

C4–1 As an audit partner for Harmon & Jones, CPAs, you are responsible for many clients. The events listed below occurred during 1985 and have come to your attention:

[1]   Ajax Company changed from the average cost method to the FIFO method of inventory cost determination.

[2]   Cutler Company sustained a loss when it sold its computer division. Cutler had been manufacturing computers and household appliances in separate divisions since 1973.

[3]   Big Apple Company lost some uninsured equipment because of an earthquake. This is the first earthquake to occur in the area where the equipment was located, and geologists believe that the area will not experience earthquakes in the future.

[4]   It was discovered that Parker Company's bookkeeper forgot to deduct salvage value when computing straight-line depreciation for each of the two preceding years.

[5]   Wright Corporation wrote off some plant assets because of obsolescence.

[6]   Because of an expropriation, Miller Company lost all of its inventory held in a Middle Eastern country.

[7]   Jameson Enterprises determined that certain depreciable assets would probably have useful lives 10 years longer than projected when the assets were purchased.

[8]   Cox Children's Wear destroyed a large portion of its inventory because of a government ban on the sale of clothing made of a flameproof fabric that causes skin irritations.

[9]   Woodson, Inc., discovered that the ending inventory for the previous year had been misstated because of a counting error.

[10] Bridgeport Company lost some inventory because of a flood. Floods occur every three to five years in the area where the inventory was lost.

[11] Shure, Inc., lost all of its perishable inventory because the company's employees went on strike.

[12] International Business Enterprises had a gain from foreign currency transactions.

[13] Kinney Corporation realized a gain from an insurance settlement. The settlement pertained to the company's South American plant, which was expropriated in 1985.

[14] Nunley Company sustained a loss from selling some of the common stock in the company's investment portfolio.

[15] Based on recent collection experience, Lucus, Inc., changed the percentage used to estimate bad-debts expense. The percentage was changed from 1% to 1.5% of net sales.

Instructions

Indicate which of the above events should be reported as extraordinary items. If an event should not be reported as an extraordinary item, indicate the appropriate financial statement category in which the event should be reported. Assume a multiple-step format for the income statement and that all events are material.

C4–2 The new bookkeeper at Bradford Company prepared the annual income statement shown below. The company uses a calendar-year accounting period.

Bradford Company
INCOME STATEMENT
December 31, 1985

Revenues		
Sales revenue		$643,495
Interest revenue		7,980
Gain on sale of land		16,845
Revenue earned in 1984 but incorrectly omitted		
from 1984 income statement		31,890
Total		700,210
Expenses		
Cost of goods sold	$263,500	
Sales returns and allowances	21,150	
Operating expenses	106,380	
Unusual loss from obsolescence of equipment	18,600	

Extraordinary loss of inventory caused by flood	45,470	
Dividends declared	20,000	
Total		475,100
Net income		$225,110

Instructions

Indicate the deficiencies in the above income statement. In your answer assume that (1) Bradford Company wants a detailed, multiple-step income statement, (2) the company's income tax rate is 40%, and (3) the amounts shown have been correctly determined.

C4–3 As an audit partner with the CPA firm of Holland & Holland, you have been asked to comment on the following balance sheet prepared by an accountant at Massey Company, one of your clients.

Massey Company
BALANCE SHEET
For the Year Ended December 31, 1985

Assets

Current Assets

Cash		$ 18,655	
Cash surrender value of life insurance		51,785	
Bond sinking fund		208,000	
Investment in 80% of Borg Company's common stock (at cost; market value $217,857)		180,000	
Merchandise inventory		45,600	
Total current assets			$ 504,040

Intangible Assets

Accounts receivable	$ 36,000		
Less: Reserve for doubtful accounts	1,500	34,500	
Interest receivable		3,700	
Bond issue costs		11,800	
Discount on bonds payable		8,000	
Prepaid insurance		12,000	
Patents		29,600	
Total intangible assets			99,600

Investments and Funds

Note receivable (12%; due September 1, 1986)		75,000	
Treasury stock (at cost)		38,000	
Total investments and funds			113,000

Property, Plant, and Equipment

Land held for long-term speculation		130,000	
Building in process of construction (intended for Massey Company's future use)		300,360	
Building in use	250,000		
Less: Reserve for depreciation	105,000	145,000	

Furniture and fixtures in use	115,000	
Less: Accumulated depletion	20,000	95,000
Total property, plant, and equipment		670,360
Total assets		$1,387,000

Liabilities and Stockholders' Equity

Long-Term Liabilities

Bonds payable (10%, due July 1, 1998)	$500,000	
Note payable (13%, due August 1, 1986)	100,000	
Advances from customers on goods that Massey Company will ship in 1986	40,000	
Total long-term liabilities		$ 640,000

Current Liabilities

Accounts payable	23,000	
Interest payable	10,500	
Reserve for income taxes due in 1986	12,600	
Total current liabilities		46,100
Total liabilities		686,100

Stockholders' Equity

Preferred and common stock	150,000	
Paid-in surplus on common stock	200,000	
Earned surplus	350,900	
Total stockholders' equity		700,900
Total liabilities and stockholders' equity		$1,387,000

Instructions

Indicate the deficiencies in the above balance sheet.

C4–4 The following is the complete set of financial statements prepared by Ober Corporation:

Ober Corporation
STATEMENT OF EARNINGS AND
RETAINED EARNINGS
For the Fiscal Year Ended August 31, 1985

Sales		$3,500,000
Less returns and allowances		35,000
Net sales		3,465,000
Less cost of goods sold		1,039,000
Gross margin		2,426,000
Less:		
Selling expenses	$1,000,000	
General administrative expenses	1,079,000	2,079,000
Operating earnings		347,000

Add other revenue:

Purchase discounts	10,000	
Gain on increased value of investments in real estate	300,000	
Correction of error in last year's statement	90,000	400,000
Ordinary earnings		747,000
Add extraordinary item—gain on sale of fixed asset		53,000
Earnings before income tax		800,000
Less income tax expense		380,000
Net earnings		420,000
Add beginning retained earnings		3,258,000
		3,678,000
Less:		
Dividends (12% stock dividend declared but not yet issued)		120,000
Contingent liability [Note 2]		808,000
Ending unappropriated retained earnings		$2,750,000

Ober Corporation
STATEMENT OF FINANCIAL POSITION
August 31, 1985

Assets

Current Assets

Cash	$ 80,000	
Accounts receivable, net	110,000	
Inventory	130,000	
Total current assets		$ 320,000

Other Assets

Land and building, net	4,160,000	
Investments in real estate (current value)	1,508,000	
Goodwill [Note 1]	250,000	
Discount on bonds payable	42,000	
Total other assets		5,960,000
Total assets		$6,280,000

Liabilities and Stockholders' Equity

Current Liabilities

Accounts payable	$ 140,000	
Income taxes payable	320,000	
Stock dividend payable	120,000	
Total current liabilities		$ 580,000

Other Liabilities

Due to Grant, Inc. [Note 2]	808,000	
Bonds payable (including portion due within one year)	1,000,000	
Total other liabilities		1,808,000
Total liabilities		2,388,000

142   4/ BASIC FINANCIAL STATEMENTS

Stockholders' Equity

Common stock	1,000,000	
Paid-in capital in excess of par	142,000	
Unappropriated retained earnings	2,750,000	
Total stockholders' equity		3,892,000
Total liabilities and stockholders' equity		$6,280,000

Notes to the Financial Statements

[1] As required by federal income tax laws, goodwill is not amortized. The goodwill was "acquired" in 1982.
[2] The amount due to Grant, Inc., depends on the outcome of a lawsuit which is currently pending. The amount of loss, if any, is not expected to exceed $808,000.

Instructions

Identify and explain the deficiencies in the presentation of Ober's financial statements. There are *no* arithmetical errors in the statements. Organize your answer as follows:
[a] Deficiencies in the statement of earnings and retained earnings.
[b] Deficiencies in the statement of financial position.
[c] General comments.
  If an item appears on both statements, identify the deficiencies for each statement separately.

(AICPA adapted)

EXERCISES

E4-1 The following information pertains to Jumbo, Inc., for the 1985 accounting period:

Transportation-out	$ 9,500
Purchases	150,000
Sales returns	11,200
Inventory, Dec. 31	30,800
Purchase allowances	2,300
Sales	310,000
Inventory, Jan. 1	25,000
Transportation-in	7,100
Sales discounts	5,200
Purchase returns	6,000
Purchase discounts	3,000
Advertising	28,000
Sales allowances	3,600

Instructions

[a] Prepare the cost of goods sold section of Jumbo, Inc.'s income statement for 1985.
[b] Compute the gross margin for 1985.
[c] Indicate how the accounts not used in [a] and [b] should be classified in the income statement for 1985.

E4-2 The following information pertains to the 1985 accounting period of Cullen Company:

Cost of goods sold	$150,000
Dividend revenue	6,000
General and administrative expenses	21,000
Interest expense	5,000

Interest revenue	9,000
Net sales	270,000
Selling expenses	29,000
Income tax rate	40%
Number of common shares outstanding	10,000

Instructions

[a] Prepare a multiple-step income statement for 1985.
[b] Prepare a single-step income statement for 1985.

E4-3 Ajax Company has been manufacturing and selling computers, household appliances, and medical supplies since 1973. The following events occurred during the company's 1985 accounting period:
[1] The company adopted the FIFO method of inventory cost determination. Prior to 1985, the company used the average cost method.
[2] The company sold its computer division.
[3] The company lost one of its plants because of an earthquake.
[4] The company lost its inventory held in a Middle Eastern country because of a government expropriation.
[5] The company sold its household appliance division.
[6] The company adopted the straight-line method of accounting for all depreciable assets. Prior to 1985, the company used the double-declining balance method.

Instructions

Assume that each of the above events is material and qualifies for reporting in one of the following income statement sections: (1) discontinued operations; (2) extraordinary items; and (3) cumulative effect of a change in accounting principles. In what section should each of the above events be reported?

E4–4 At the beginning of its 1985 calendar-year accounting period, Wall, Inc., had retained earnings of $103,000. During 1985 the company earned a net income of $51,000 and declared cash dividends of $10,000 on its common stock. None of these dividends had been paid as of year-end. In addition, the company discovered that because of a mathematical error, depreciation expense had been overstated by $10,000 in 1984.

The company's income tax rate was 40% in 1984 and 1985. The company had 5,000 shares of common stock outstanding throughout 1985.

Instructions

Prepare a statement of retained earnings for Wall for 1985.

E4–5 The following information pertains to the 1985 calendar-year accounting period of King Corporation:

Number of common shares outstanding throughout the year	10,000
Cost of goods sold	$151,200
Dividends declared	50,000
Loss from earthquake (extraordinary item)	20,000
General and administrative expenses	41,000
Loss due to write-off of worthless equipment (unusual item)	17,000
Net sales	378,000
Selling expenses	48,800

Additional Information

King Corporation reported retained earnings of $187,000 on December 31, 1984. During 1985 the company discovered that because of a material counting error, ending inventory for 1984 had been overstated by $16,000. The company's income tax rate was 40% in 1984 and 1985.

Instructions

Prepare a combined statement of income and retained earnings for King Corporation for 1985. Use the single-step format.

E4–6 The following information pertains to Grower Company on December 31 of the current year:

Equipment	$120,000
Accumulated depreciation—equipment	20,000
Accounts receivable	27,000
Prepaid insurance	3,000
Short-term notes payable	12,000
Cash	10,000
Bonds payable maturing in 20 years	100,000
Total assets	238,000
Land	50,000
Accounts payable	40,000
Allowance for doubtful accounts	2,000
Merchandise inventory	34,000
Short-term investments	16,000
Wages payable	4,000
Total liabilities	161,000
Premium on bonds payable	5,000

Instructions

Compute the amount of Grower Company's working capital on December 31. Show all of your work clearly.

E4–7 Listed below are some of the account balances of Quality Oil Company on December 31, 1985, the end of the company's annual accounting period:

Land held for future building site	$ 72,000
Oil deposit	900,000
Term bonds payable (10%, due June 30, 1996)	400,000
Accumulated depreciation—equipment	180,000
Building	250,000
Land on which building is located	35,000
Notes payable (12%, due Apr. 30, 1990)	50,000
Equipment	360,000
Accumulated depletion of oil deposit	150,000
Notes payable (10%, due August 31, 1986)	30,000
Accumulated depreciation—building	75,000
Serial bonds payable (11%, due July 31, 1993 to July 31, 1998, inclusive)	300,000
Unamortized discount on term bonds payable	8,000
Accumulated depreciation—furniture and fixtures	20,000
Bond issue costs	5,000
Furniture and fixtures	50,000

Instructions

[a] Prepare the property, plant, and equipment and long-term liabilities section of Quality Oil Company's balance sheet on December 31, 1985.
[b] Indicate how Quality Oil Company should classify

any accounts that you did not use in [a].

E4–8 The following information pertains to Red Rider Company on December 31 of the current year: [1] The company has preferred and common stock outstanding. The preferred stock is $5 par value, 10%, cumulative and nonparticipating. A total of 20,000 shares were authorized, of which 10,000 shares are issued and outstanding on December 31. Red Rider sold its preferred stock for $6 per share. [2] The common stock has a $1 par value. A total of 50,000 shares were authorized, of which 40,000 shares are issued and outstanding on December 31. Red Rider sold its common stock for $10 per share. [3] The company has retained earnings of $1,030,000, of which $160,000 have been appropriated for plant expansion.

Instructions

Prepare the stockholders' equity section of Red Rider Company's balance sheet on December 31.

E4–9 The following list of accounts and balances pertains to Miller Company on December 31, 1985, the end of the company's annual accounting period:

Accounts payable	$ 14,000
Accounts receivable	37,000
Accumulated depreciation—furniture and fixtures	10,000
Advances from customers (pertaining to goods that Miller Company will supply in 1986)	6,000
Allowance for doubtful accounts	1,800
Bond sinking fund	75,000
Bonds payable (14%, due Jan. 1, 1998)	150,000
Cash	12,000

Common stock ($1 par, 50,000 shares authorized, 30,000 shares issued and outstanding)	30,000
Franchise	86,000
Furniture and fixtures	70,000
Merchandise inventory	48,400
Paid-in capital in excess of par value	60,000
Premium on bonds payable	4,000
Prepaid rent (pertains to the first quarter of 1986)	8,400
Retained earnings	?

Instructions

Prepare a balance sheet in good form for Miller Company on December 31, 1985.

E4–10 The following *independent* cases pertain to a 1985 calendar-year accounting period:

	Case A	Case B	Case C	Case D
Revenues	$100,000	$200,000	?	?
Expenses	?	?	$ 50,000	$ 70,000
Net income	40,000	?	60,000	?
Retained earnings, Jan. 1	?	300,000	180,000	120,000
Dividends declared	50,000	70,000	?	30,000
Retained earnings, Dec. 31	120,000	310,000	?	?
Current assets, Dec. 31	?	60,000	100,000	?
Noncurrent assets, Dec. 31	420,000	?	580,000	300,000
Total assets, Dec. 31	500,000	?	?	410,000
Current liabilities, Dec. 31	?	30,000	?	20,000
Noncurrent liabilities, Dec. 31	270,000	?	170,000	?
Total liabilities, Dec. 31	?	140,000	?	?
Paid-in capital, Dec. 31	?	520,000	210,000	100,000
Total stockholders' equity, Dec. 31	200,000	?	410,000	210,000

Instructions

Determine the missing amounts.

E4–11 Listed below are several categories that may be used in a multiple-step income statement and a balance sheet:

[a] Net sales
[b] Cost of goods sold
[c] Operating expenses
[d] Other revenues
[e] Other expenses
[f] Extraordinary items
[g] Current assets
[h] Investments and funds
[i] Property, plant, and equipment
[j] Intangible assets
[k] Other assets
[l] Current liabilities
[m] Long-term liabilities

[n] Capital stock
[o] Additional paid-in capital
[p] Retained earnings

Instructions

Use the letters above to indicate where each of the following items should usually be classified.
[1]   Cash.
[2]   Purchase returns.
[3]   Patents.
[4]   Buildings.
[5]   Interest expense.
[6]   Accounts payable.
[7]   Common stock.
[8]   Bonds payable (due in 20 years).
[9]   Advertising.
[10] Investment in subsidiary company.
[11] Timber stand.
[12] Dividend revenue.
[13] Sales discounts.
[14] Paid-in capital in excess of par value.
[15] Loss of property in Kansas due to a hurricane.
[16] Write-off of inventories due to obsolescence.
[17] Transportation-out.
[18] Goodwill.
[19] Accumulated depreciation.
[20] Accounts receivable.

E4–12 Refer to the list of categories ([a] through [p]) in E4–11.

Instructions

Use the appropriate letters to indicate where each of the following items should usually be classified.
[1]   Bond sinking fund.
[2]   Allowance for doubtful accounts.
[3]   Common stock dividend distributable.
[4]   Merchandise inventory (ending).
[5]   Note receivable (due in three months).
[6]   Reserve for plant expansion.
[7]   Wages payable.
[8]   Premium on bonds that are payable in 10 years.
[9]   Transportation-in.
[10] Bond issue costs.
[11] Preferred stock.
[12] Common stock subscriptions receivable.
[13] Organization costs.
[14] Interest payable.
[15] Sales returns and allowances.
[16] Depreciation expense.
[17] Note payable (due in five years).
[18] Oil deposit.
[19] Copyrights.

[20] Accumulated depletion.

E4–13 Refer to the list of categories ([a] through [p]) in E4–11.

Instructions

Use the appropriate letters to indicate where each of the following items should usually be classified.
[1]   Small tools used in the business.
[2]   Merchandise inventory (beginning).
[3]   Gain from foreign exchange transactions.
[4]   Building site.
[5]   Pension obligations.
[6]   Investment in 100 shares of Exxon's common stock that will likely be sold in three months.
[7]   Prepaid insurance.
[8]   Taxes payable.
[9]   Common stock subscribed.
[10] Equipment used in the business.
[11] Salaries.
[12] Building.
[13] Flood loss in an area that floods every two to three years.
[14] Purchases.
[15] Pension fund.
[16] Reserve for bond sinking fund.
[17] Cash surrender value of life insurance.
[18] Franchise.
[19] Premium on preferred stock.
[20] Discount on bonds payable (bonds are payable in 13 years).

E4–14 Refer to the list of categories ([a] through [p]) in E4–11.

Instructions

Use the appropriate letters to indicate where each of the following items should usually be classified. If an item should not be reported on either an income statement or a balance sheet, indicate where the item should be reported.
[1]   Bad-debts expense.
[2]   Dividends payable.
[3]   Treasury stock.
[4]   Correction of an error made last year when computing depreciation expense.
[5]   Raw materials.
[6]   Building that is being constructed for the company's own use.
[7]   Purchase allowances.
[8]   Unearned rent revenue (will be earned in the first quarter of the next accounting period).
[9]   Returnable containers used in the business.

[10] Machinery rearrangement costs.

[11] Bonds payable (due in six months; payment will be made from current assets).

[12] Equipment held for sale (was previously used in the business).

[13] Dividends declared.

[14] Appropriation for contingencies.

[15] Land held for future plant site.

[16] Deficit.

[17] Loss on sale of land.

[18] Trademarks.

[19] Work-in-process.

[20] Unusual and nonrecurring loss of inventories because of expropriation by a foreign government.

E4–15 The following information pertains to Browning Company during 1985:

Net income	$125,000
Depreciation expense	30,000
Issuance of 20-year bonds payable	200,000
Issuance of common stock	100,000
Acquisition of land	165,000
Declaration of cash dividends	220,000

Instructions

Prepare a statement of changes in financial position (working capital definition of funds) for 1985. Do not prepare a schedule of working capital changes.

E4–16 Ferris Company's accounting period ends on December 31, and the company issues its financial statements on the following February 1. Below are some events that occurred during *1986:*

Jan. 4 Sale of common stock.

7 Write-off of an account receivable because customer was formally declared bankrupt on January 7. The bankruptcy litigation was in process on December 31, 1985.

11 Loss of a material portion of inventories because of a sudden flood.

18 Purchase of a competing business.

22 Write-off of an account receivable because the customer's business was destroyed by an earthquake on January 22.

28 Purchase of additional inventory.

Instructions

Indicate the appropriate treatment for each of the above events in Ferris Company's financial statements for *1985.* Assume that each event is material.

PROBLEMS

P4–1 The following list of items pertains to the 1985 calendar-year accounting period of Weimer, Inc.:

Advertising expense	$ 19,000
Gain on sale of investments	15,200
Interest expense	7,500
Interest revenue	8,900
Loss of inventory due to flood (considered unusual and nonrecurring)	21,000
Loss on write-off of plant assets due to obsolescence	21,800
Merchandise inventory, Dec. 31	51,000
Merchandise inventory, Jan. 1	62,000
Miscellaneous general and administrative expenses	7,800
Miscellaneous selling expenses	12,000
Office salaries expense	47,500
Office supplies expense	8,100
Purchases	455,000
Purchase discounts	8,700
Purchase returns and allowances	31,000
Sales	781,000
Sales discounts	15,200
Sales returns and allowances	22,800
Sales salaries expense	52,000
Transportation-in	13,700
Utilities expense	10,400

Weimer, Inc., had 10,000 shares of common stock outstanding throughout 1985. The company's income tax rate is 40%.

Instructions

[a] Prepare a detailed, multiple-step income statement for 1985.

[b] Prepare a condensed, single-step income statement for 1985.

[c] Which of the two forms of income statements do you prefer? Explain your answer.

P4–2 The accountant for Kearns Company has just handed you the income statement and retained earnings statement that appear below:

Kearns Company
INCOME STATEMENT
As of December 31, 1985

Revenues
Net sales		$628,000
Extraordinary gain from expropriation of property by a foreign government		50,000
Correction of understatement of 1984 ending inventory due to error		30,000
Rent revenue		11,800
Dividend revenue		7,200
Total revenues		727,000

Expenses
Cost of goods sold	$345,000	
Selling expenses	109,600	
General and administrative expenses	84,200	
Interest expense	12,200	
Total expenses		551,000
Net income		$176,000

Kearns Company
STATEMENT OF RETAINED EARNINGS
As of December 31, 1985

Retained earnings, Jan. 1		$789,000
Add: Net income		176,000
		965,000
Less: Extraordinary loss of plant assets due to earthquake	$60,000	
Unusual loss on sale of long-term investments	23,000	
Dividends declared	37,000	120,000
Retained earnings, Dec. 31		$845,000

Additional Information

[1] You have determined that the account balances in the above statements are correct. The statements, however, are not presented according to generally accepted accounting principles (GAAP).

[2] The company had 10,000 shares of common stock outstanding throughout 1985.

[3] The company's income tax rate was 40% in 1984 and 1985.

[4] The company uses a calendar-year accounting period.

Instructions

[a] Prepare a condensed, multiple-step income statement for 1985 that complies with GAAP.

[b] Prepare a condensed, single-step income statement for 1985 that complies with GAAP.

[c] Prepare a statement of retained earnings for 1985 that complies with GAAP.

[d] From the standpoint of user decision making, why should extraordinary gains and losses be presented in a special section of the income statement?

P4–3 The bookkeeper for Bryan Company recently prepared the following statement of retained earnings:

Bryan Company
STATEMENT OF RETAINED EARNINGS
December 31, 1985

Retained earnings, Jan. 1, 1985		$683,478
Add: Net income for 1985	$93,477	
Gain on sale of land	65,420	
Gain from settlement of litigation that began in 1984	25,000	
Gain from foreign currency transaction	6,134	190,031
		873,509
Less: Dividends declared during 1985	10,000	
Loss of inventory caused by a government prohibition judged to be unusual and nonrecurring	30,000	
Recognition of salaries expense incurred in 1984 but erroneously not recognized in the 1984 income statement	19,500	
Loss from write-off of equipment leased to others	12,119	71,619
Retained earnings, Dec. 31, 1985		$801,890

Instructions

[a] Prepare a corrected statement of retained earnings for 1985. Assume an income tax rate of 40% and 10,000 shares of common stock outstanding throughout 1985. (*Note:* The additions and deductions in the statement shown above are *before* income taxes, except for net income.)

[b] Indicate specifically where Bryan Company should report any items that do not belong on the statement of retained earnings.

P4–4 The following information pertains to the 1985 calendar-year accounting period of Apple Corporation:

Cost of goods sold	$228,636
Dividend revenue	7,590
Dividends declared	80,000
Gain on sale of investments (not considered unusual or nonrecurring for this company)	89,340
General and administrative expenses	69,587
Interest expense	12,650
Loss from expropriation of properties (considered unusual and nonrecurring)	48,000
Loss from settlement of litigation that began in 1984 (not considered unusual or nonrecurring for this company)	35,000
Loss of warehouse due to hurricane (considered unusual but recurring for this company)	42,150
Net sales	471,590
Selling expenses	63,473
Write-off of inventory due to obsolescence (considered unusual but recurring for this company)	17,024

Additional Information

Apple Corporation reported retained earnings of $273,000 on its balance sheet dated December 31, 1984. During 1985 it was discovered that $60,000 of revenue earned in 1984 had not been reported on the 1984 income statement. The company had 5,000 shares of common stock outstanding throughout 1985.

Instructions

[a] Prepare a combined statement of income and retained earnings for 1985. Use the multiple-step format and assume an income tax rate of 40%.

[b] Do you favor a combined statement of income and retained earnings over separate statements of income and retained earnings? Explain your answer.

P4–5 Hinton Company reported the following amounts in the stockholders' equity section of its balance sheet dated December 31, 1984:

Preferred stock ($100 par value; 1,000 shares)	$100,000
Common stock ($25 par value; 10,000 shares)	250,000
Additional paid-in capital	400,000
Retained earnings	237,460

On January 3, 1985, the company sold 2,000 additional shares of common stock for $60 per share. During 1985 it was discovered that $25,000 of revenue earned in 1984 had not been reported on the 1984 income statement.

Hinton Company reported a net income for 1985 of $55,000. The company declared cash dividends of $2,500 on the preferred stock and $7,500 on the common stock at the end of *each* of the four quarters of 1985. Dividends are paid in cash 30 days after being declared.

Instructions

Prepare a statement of stockholders' equity for the year ended December 31, 1985. Assume an income tax rate of 40%.

P4–6 The following accounts and balances pertain to Hayes Corporation on December 31, 1985:

Accounts payable	$ 26,300
Accounts receivable	38,900
Accumulated depletion	165,300
Accumulated depreciation	70,000
Additional paid-in capital	369,000
Advances from customers (advances pertain to goods that Hayes Corporation will supply in 1986)	6,000
Advances to suppliers (advances pertain to goods that suppliers will provide in 1986)	7,100
Allowance for doubtful accounts	2,600
Appropriation for plant expansion	50,000
Bond issue costs	21,300

Bond sinking fund	195,700
Bonds payable (10%, due July 1, 1996)	500,000
Building	210,000
Cash	10,600
Cash surrender value of life insurance	12,300
Common stock ($1 par, 50,000 shares authorized, 40,000 shares issued and outstanding)	40,000
Common stock subscribed (1,000 shares)	1,000
Franchise	21,840
Interest payable	3,000
Investment in bonds—long term (at cost; market value $72,000)	65,000
Land	54,000
Land held for future plant site	128,000
Marketable securities—short term (at cost which approximates market value)	18,570
Merchandise inventory (at lower of FIFO cost or market)	41,430
Note payable (12%, due April 1, 1989)	20,000
Oil deposit	568,300
Organization costs	10,560
Prepaid insurance	4,300
Salaries payable	6,700
Stock subscriptions receivable (due in 3 months)	10,000
Unamortized discount on bonds payable	11,000
Unappropriated retained earnings	169,000

Instructions

Prepare a balance sheet in good form.

P4–7 The following information pertains to Whitney Enterprises on December 31, 1985:

Patents	$163,100
Supplies	8,400
Common stock ($10 par, 20,000 shares authorized, 10,000 shares issued and outstanding)	100,000
Cash	52,590
Land	160,200
Machinery rearrangement costs	48,300
Unappropriated retained earnings	?
Serial 12% debenture bonds, $50,000 installments due annually from June 1, 1986 through June 1, 1995	500,000
Cash surrender value of life insurance	11,400
Trademarks	39,900
Appropriation for contingencies	80,000
Advances from customers (advances pertain to goods that Whitney Enterprises will provide in 1986)	15,875

Allowance for doubtful accounts	3,300
Plant expansion fund	203,100
Accounts payable	31,000
Accumulated depreciation—building	45,000
Investment in land (held for long-term speculative purposes)	196,500
Machinery and equipment	290,800
Unearned rent revenue (Whitney Enterprises will earn this revenue during the first quarter of 1986)	6,125
Paid-in capital in excess of par value	400,000
Accumulated depreciation of machinery and equipment	30,000
Building	250,000
Accounts receivable	73,410

Long-term investment in common stock (at cost; market value $98,700)	87,000
Note receivable (due on May 15, 1986)	21,000
Marketable securities (at cost; market value $44,430)	37,000
Notes payable (due in 1986)	40,000
Merchandise inventory (at lower of FIFO cost or market)	58,600

Instructions

Prepare a balance sheet in good form. Compute the missing amount of unappropriated retained earnings.

P4–8 The bookkeeper for Nix Corporation has prepared the following balance sheet:

Nix Corporation
BALANCE SHEET
For 1985

Debits

Current Debits

Cash	$ 22,870	
Cash surrender value of life insurance	20,000	
Building fund	112,000	
Accounts receivable	58,760	
Merchandise inventory	61,010	
Unamortized discount on bonds payable	12,000	
Total current debits		$ 286,640

Noncurrent Debits

Marketable securities	20,300	
Advances to suppliers	7,500	
Prepaid rent	8,400	
Land held for future plant site	80,000	
Land	125,000	
Building	215,000	
Machinery and equipment	396,000	
Mineral deposit	327,000	
Goodwill	75,700	
Patents	41,300	
Machinery rearrangement costs	51,000	
Total noncurrent debits		1,347,200
Total debits		$1,633,840

Credits

Current Credits

Allowance for doubtful accounts	$ 4,340	
Accounts payable	41,500	
Interest payable	8,000	
Income tax payable	22,500	
Pension obligations	119,000	
Total current credits		$ 195,340

Noncurrent Credits

Accumulated depreciation of building	58,000	
Accumulated depreciation of machinery and equipment	66,000	
Accumulated depletion of mineral deposit	70,000	
Note payable	20,000	
Advances from customers	6,000	
Bonds payable	500,000	
Preferred stock	100,000	
Common stock	45,000	
Additional paid-in capital	384,140	
Retained earnings	189,360	
Total noncurrent credits		1,438,500
Total credits		$1,633,840

Additional Information

[1] You have determined that although the *dollar amounts* reported are correct, the balance sheet is not in accordance with GAAP.

[2] Merchandise inventory is reported at the lower of average cost or market value.

[3] The marketable securities, which had a market value of $32,600 on December 31, 1985, are reported at cost. Management plans to sell the securities in 1986.

[4] The advances to suppliers pertain to goods that will be provided during 1986.

[5] The prepaid rent applies to the first quarter of 1986.

[6] The pension obligations will be paid after 1993.

[7] The note payable is due on May 1, 1986.

[8] The advances from customers pertain to goods that Nix Corporation will provide in 1986.

[9] The bonds payable pay interest of 10% and are due on June 30, 1997.

[10] Relevant details about the preferred and common stock are as follows:

Preferred stock—$10 par value, 8%, cumulative and nonparticipating, 20,000 shares authorized, 10,000 shares issued and outstanding.

Common stock—$1 par value, 50,000 shares authorized, 45,000 shares issued and outstanding.

Instructions

Prepare a balance sheet in good form.

P4–9 The bookkeeper for Fisher Company prepared the following balance sheet on December 31, 1985:

Fisher Company
BALANCE SHEET
December 31, 1985

Assets

Current assets		$ 570,525
Investments and funds		28,520
Property, plant, and equipment		793,600
Intangible assets		80,355
Other assets		138,000
Total assets		$1,611,000

Liabilities and Stockholders' Equity

Current liabilities	$144,000	
Long-term liabilities	562,000	
Total liabilities		$ 706,000
Stockholders' equity		905,000
Total liabilities and stockholders' equity		$1,611,000

Upon inquiry you learn the following additional facts:

[1] Current assets include cash, $95,000; merchandise inventory (at lower of FIFO cost or market), $75,125; note receivable (13%, due June 1, 1988), $100,000; investment in subsidiary (held for control), $215,000; and plant expansion fund, $85,400.

[2] Investments and funds include prepaid insurance (applicable to the first six months of 1986), $12,000; and bond issue costs, $16,520.

[3] Property, plant, and equipment includes land, $237,000; land held for future plant site, $146,600; building, $375,000 less accumulated depreciation, $45,000; and furniture and fixtures, $114,600 less accumulated depreciation, $34,600.

[4] Intangible assets include accounts receivable of $63,000 less an allowance for doubtful accounts of $4,125; and organization costs, $21,480.

[5] Other assets consist of goodwill, $138,000.

[6] Current liabilities include accounts payable, $35,595; interest payable, $8,405; and a note payable (12%, due May 1, 1988), $100,000.

[7] Long-term liabilities include serial 10% debenture bonds, $500,000 ($50,000 installments are payable annually from April 1, 1986 through April 1, 1995); advances from customers (advances pertain to goods that Fisher Company will ship in 1986) $12,000; and retained earnings appropriated for bond retirement, $50,000.

[8] Stockholders' equity consists of common stock ($1 par, 50,000 shares authorized, 40,000 shares issued and outstanding), $40,000; additional paid-in capital, $430,000; and unappropriated retained earnings, $435,000.

Instructions

Prepare a balance sheet in good form.

P4–10 The information shown below was obtained from the accounting records of Hopwood Company on December 31, 1985, the end of the company's annual accounting period. The account balances shown have been updated through December 31.

Accounts payable	$ 49,400
Accounts receivable	68,000
Accumulated depletion	65,000
Accumulated depreciation	70,000
Additional paid-in capital	236,000
Advances from customers (advances pertain to goods that Hopwood Company will ship in 1986)	21,400
Allowance for doubtful accounts	3,000
Bond issue costs	16,000
Bond sinking fund	115,000
Bonds payable (10%, due June 1, 1998)	400,000
Building	275,000
Cash	32,110
Cash surrender value of life insurance	31,600
Common stock ($10 par, 20,000 shares authorized, 10,000 shares issued and outstanding throughout 1985)	100,000
Cost of goods sold	503,140
Dividend revenue	8,390
Dividends declared	100,000

Gain from expropriation of property by a foreign government (considered unusual and nonrecurring)	100,000
General and administrative expenses	253,430
Goodwill	53,100
Interest expense	50,000
Interest payable	12,500
Investment in common stock—long term (at cost; market value $72,000)	67,000
Land	145,000
Land held for future plant site	90,000
Loss of plant assets due to flood (considered unusual and nonrecurring)	70,000
Loss on sale of long-term investments (considered unusual but not nonrecurring)	10,000
Marketable securities—short term (at cost which approximates market value)	21,890
Merchandise inventory (at lower of FIFO cost or market)	73,500
Mineral deposit	236,400
Net sales	1,257,850
Note payable (12%, due May 1, 1989)	100,000
Patents	12,900
Prepaid insurance	8,500
Rent revenue	12,500
Salaries payable	19,700
Selling expenses	287,170
Unamortized discount on bonds payable	11,000

Additional Information

Hopwood Company had retained earnings of $157,000 on January 1, 1985. The company's income tax rate is 40%.

Instructions

[a] Prepare an income statement (multiple-step format) for the year ended December 31, 1985.

[b] Prepare a statement of retained earnings for the year ended December 31, 1985.

[c] Prepare a balance sheet as of December 31, 1985.

P4–11 Listed below are the account balances of Waltrip Company on December 31, 1985, the end of the company's annual accounting period. The account balances have been updated through December 31.

Additional paid-in capital	$ 361,600
Net sales	1,568,750
Dividends declared	200,000
Cash	118,000
Land	114,000
Franchise	68,300
Note receivable (14%, due July 30, 1990)	50,000
Accounts payable	53,700
Bond issue costs	13,000
Common stock ($10 par, 25,000 shares authorized, 10,000 shares issued and outstanding throughout 1985)	100,000
Note payable (12%, due July 1, 1991)	200,000
Other revenue	45,250
Supplies	12,300
Plant expansion fund	115,000
Accumulated depreciation—furniture and fixtures	37,000
Organization costs	21,700
Serial 10% debenture bonds ($50,000 installments are due annually from June 1, 1986 through June 1, 1993)	400,000
Loss of inventory due to earthquake (considered unusual and nonrecurring)	100,000
Land held for future plant site	90,000
Merchandise inventory (at lower of average cost or market)	87,400
Furniture and fixtures	123,000
Advances from customers (advances pertain to goods that Waltrip Company will ship in 1986)	25,300
Cost of goods sold	657,500
Loss from write-off of plant assets due to obsolescence (considered unusual but not nonrecurring)	22,000
Investment in subsidiary (held for control)	179,000
Building	375,000
Interest expense	60,000
General and administrative expenses	296,400
Accounts receivable	75,000
Selling expenses	214,100
Allowance for doubtful accounts	3,700
Interest payable	10,000
Accumulated depreciation of building	75,000

Additional Information

Waltrip Company reported retained earnings of $193,000 on its balance sheet dated December 31, 1984. On July 14, 1985, it was discovered that $40,000 of revenue earned during 1984 had been incorrectly omitted from the 1984 income statement. The company's income tax rate was 40% in 1984 and 1985.

Instructions

[a] Prepare an income statement (single-step format) for the year ended December 31, 1985.
[b] Prepare a statement of retained earnings for the year ended December 31, 1985.
[c] Prepare a balance sheet as of December 31, 1985.

P4–12 The following events pertain to the 1985 calendar-year accounting period of Tiger Company:
[1] Earned net income of $263,851. The company had no extraordinary items, and $50,000 of depreciation was deducted when measuring net income.
[2] Issued long-term bonds for cash of $400,000.
[3] Issued common stock for cash of $250,000.
[4] Purchased a building for cash of $230,800.
[5] Paid a long-term note payable using cash of $500,000.
[6] Purchased stock for cash of $103,051.
[7] Declared cash dividends of $150,000.
[8] Issued preferred stock in exchange for land costing $100,000.

The following information is available concerning the company's working capital accounts:

	Balances	
	Jan. 1, 1985	Dec. 31, 1985
Accounts payable	$53,000	$64,000
Accounts receivable (net)	45,000	55,000
Cash	56,000	26,000
Dividends payable	39,000	30,000
Interest payable	12,000	8,000
Merchandise inventory	36,000	31,000
Prepaid expenses	17,000	20,000

Instructions

Prepare a statement of changes in financial position and a schedule of working capital changes for 1985. Use the working capital definition of funds.

Tools of Accounting

2

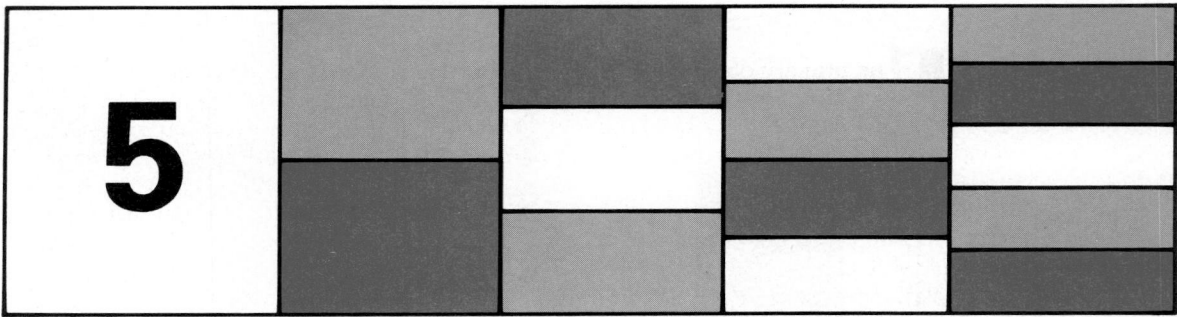

THE ACCOUNTING CYCLE

Objective

To discuss and illustrate the steps in the accounting cycle. These steps are the following:

1. Identify transactions.
2. Analyze transactions.
3. Record transactions in journals.
4. Post to ledger accounts.
5. Prepare an unadjusted trial balance.
6. Prepare adjusting entries.
7. Prepare an adjusted trial balance.
8. Prepare financial statements.
9. Prepare closing entries.
10. Prepare a post-closing trial balance (optional).
11. Prepare reversing entries (optional).

The primary objective of financial reporting is to provide information useful in making investment, lending, and similar decisions. To provide this information, accountants follow a sequence of steps during an enterprise's accounting period, which is usually one year. This sequence is called the **accounting cycle** or the **accounting process.**

In this chapter we review the steps in the accounting cycle. Most students have been introduced to these steps in previous courses. However, a thorough review of the accounting cycle will help you solidify the base of knowledge required to understand the remaining material in this text.

The widespread use of electronic computers has had a profound impact on business data processing in recent years. In this chapter, however, we emphasize manual processing methods often used by smaller businesses. Emphasizing a manual system enables us to illustrate the accounting cycle in the simplest, most understandable manner. Fundamentally, the chapter covers the basic accounting functions of recording and summarizing business data. Accountants apply these basic functions regardless of whether a company processes information manually, mechanically, or electronically.

STEPS IN THE ACCOUNTING CYCLE

Step 1. Identify Transactions

The initial step in the accounting cycle is transaction identification. Accountants must systematically identify all transactions so that they can be properly recorded. Broadly defined, a

Objectivity

transaction is an event that (1) changes a firm's financial position *and* (2) can be measured with sufficient objectivity. For example, a cash purchase of supplies is a transaction which changes a firm's financial position by increasing one asset (supplies) and decreasing another (cash). In contrast, employing a new office manager is not presently considered a transaction under generally accepted accounting principles (GAAP). A major reason why hiring activities are not considered accountable events is that the impact on the firm's financial position is too uncertain to measure with sufficient objectivity.

Transactions may be external or internal in nature. **External transactions** are those that involve outside parties. Examples include sales, purchases, and loans. **Internal transactions** are those confined to the accounting entity itself. Examples are depreciation, amortization, and conversion of production costs into inventory.

A firm's accounting system should be designed to identify pertinent information about every transaction. When a transaction occurs, a **source document,** often called a **business paper,** is prepared to evidence the transaction. For external transactions, for example, a sales invoice is a source document that supports a sale transaction, a check supports a payment transaction, and a promissory note supports a loan. Depreciation schedules, amortization schedules, and inventory schedules are common examples of source documents for internal transactions. Since entries in accounting records are based on information in the source documents, these documents must be carefully designed, prepared, and controlled. To be reasonably sure that the information reported in financial statements is accurate, an accountant should be able to trace financial statement numbers to the source documents. This tracing process is an important aspect of the auditing function. The term **audit trail** refers to the evidence that links the balances shown in the financial statements with the thousands of transactions that are summarized in those balances.

Step 2. Analyze Transactions

After identifying transactions, the accountant analyzes them to determine their impact on financial position as represented by the basic equation Assets = Liabilities + Owners' Equity. This analysis occurs within the **double-entry system** of accounting. Under this system, which was first described in the fifteenth century by an Italian mathematician named

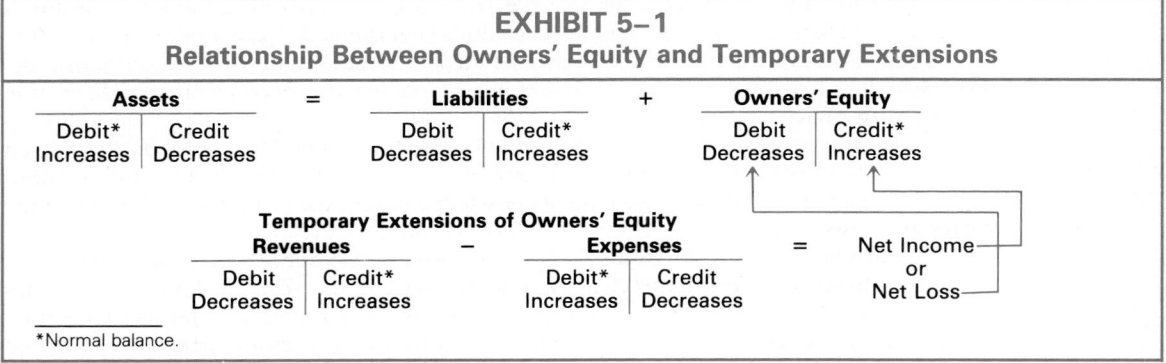

EXHIBIT 5-1
Relationship Between Owners' Equity and Temporary Extensions

Paciolo, the accountant makes entries in which debits equal credits for every transaction. These entries are made in records called **accounts;** every transaction affects at least two accounts.

There are several forms of accounts. The simplest form, illustrated below, is called a **T account** because it resembles the letter T.

Account Title	
Debits	Credits
(left side)	(right side)

Companies actually use account forms that are more detailed than the T account. Nevertheless, the T account is a convenient and widely used instructional device. We therefore use it throughout the text.

The term **debit** (sometimes called **charge**) refers to the left-hand side of an account; **credit** refers to the right-hand side. When the debit and credit sides of an account are each totaled and the smaller sum is subtracted from the larger, the difference is called the **balance** of the account. Every account has a **normal balance,** which is simply the balance that one would ordinarily find in the account. The normal balance may be either debit or credit, depending on the type of account.

Proper analysis of a transaction requires an understanding of the major types of accounts and the manner in which debit and credit entries affect each.[1] This information is summarized below:

Type (Category) of Account	Balance Increased by	Balance Decreased by	Normal Balance
Asset	Debit	Credit	Debit
Liability	Credit	Debit	Credit
Owners' equity	Credit	Debit	Credit
Revenue	Credit	Debit	Credit
Expense	Debit	Credit	Debit

Note that debits and credits affect asset and expense accounts in one way and liability, owners' equity, and revenue accounts in the opposite way. Also note that the normal balance in an account coincides with what is done to increase the balance in the account. For example, we increase the balance in an asset account with a debit; the normal balance in an asset account is therefore debit.

---

[1] Other types of accounts will be discussed at appropriate places in the text.

Remember that any transaction affects financial position as represented by the basic equation Assets = Liabilities + Owners' Equity. Revenue and expense accounts are also reflected in this equation because they are **temporary extensions of owners' equity,** as shown in Exhibit 5–1. Companies conveniently use these temporary accounts to determine net income. With these accounts they measure revenue and expense activities in many individual accounts and thereby avoid excessive detail in the owners' equity account. At the end of the accounting period, the balances in the revenue and expense accounts are transferred to the owners' equity account via the closing process explained later in the chapter.[2]

Step 3.   Record Transactions in Journals

After the information shown on source documents has been gathered and analyzed, it is entered in chronological order in a journal. Thus, a **journal** is a chronological record of transactions. The process of recording transactions in a journal is called **journalizing.** Because this marks the first time that transactions are recorded in the debit-and-credit framework, a journal is often called a **book of original entry.**

General Journal

The most fundamental journal is the **general journal,** often called simply the **journal.** A general journal entry consists of the transaction date, the accounts and amounts to be debited (Dr.), the accounts and amounts to be credited (Cr.), and an explanation of the transaction. A **simple journal entry** consists of one debit and one credit. A **compound journal entry** consists of two or more debits or two or more credits. To illustrate, consider the following two transactions of Brookshire Corporation during October 1985:

Oct. 1   Sold merchandise to Johnson Company for $1,200 on account.

4   Purchased machinery from Roberts Tool Company for $10,000. Paid $2,000 cash and signed a 90-day, 12% promissory note for the remainder of the purchase price.

These transactions would be entered in Brookshire's general journal as follows:

General Journal Page J7

Date		Description	Post. Ref.	Dr.	Cr.
1985 Oct.	1	Accounts Receivable	111	1,200	
		Sales	401		1,200
		Sold merchandise to Johnson Company on account.			
	4	Machinery	161	10,000	
		Cash	101		2,000
		Notes Payable	211		8,000
		Purchased machinery from Roberts Tool Company. Paid $2,000 cash and signed a 90-day, 12% promissory note.			

[2]Gain accounts (e.g., Gain on Sale of Land) function in the same way as revenue accounts; loss accounts (e.g., Loss of Building Caused by Fire) function in the same way as expense accounts.

As shown above, it is customary to list the account to be debited before listing the account to be credited. The account credited is also indented to distinguish it clearly from the account debited. The posting reference column contains the identification numbers of the individual ledger accounts to which each part of every journal entry has been posted. These numbers are inserted in the column when posting occurs; they permit cross-referencing between the general journal and the ledger accounts. Also, account numbers in the posting reference column verify that journal entries have been posted.

Special Journals

Although all transactions *could* be recorded in a general journal, a business usually has several **special journals** in addition to a general journal in order to facilitate the efficient recording of large numbers of similar transactions. Common types of special journals and the nature of the transactions recorded in each type are listed below:

Type of Special Journal	Nature of Transactions Recorded
Sales journal	Sales of merchandise on credit
Cash receipts journal	Receipts of cash from any source
Purchases journal	Purchases of merchandise on credit[3]
Cash payments journal	Payments of cash for any purpose

The number, purpose, and format of special journals vary considerably. Each business must decide on its special journals based on its needs. The topic of special journals is covered in more depth in Appendix B.

When a company uses special journals, it uses the general journal to record all transactions that do not fit the special journals. The general journal, then, is an integral part of an accounting system whether or not special journals are used. For this reason and because the general journal offers a convenient instructional format, we use it throughout the text to illustrate the application of various accounting concepts and principles.

Step 4.   Post to Ledger Accounts

General Ledger

After transactions have been journalized, the next step is to transfer the information to accounts in the general ledger. This transfer process is called **posting.** Posting may occur at various times during an accounting period, and it involves reorganizing information from a chronological system to a system of individual accounts. When we post, we bring all like items (e.g., all cash items) together in one place. To illustrate, the journal entries shown earlier for Brookshire Corporation are posted to the general ledger T accounts below:

	Cash	**Acct. No. 101**
		Oct. 4 J7 2,000

	Accounts Receivable	**Acct. No. 111**
Oct. 1 J7 1,200		

	Machinery	**Acct. No. 161**
Oct. 4 J7 10,000		

---

[3]Sometimes a purchases journal is expanded to record *all credit purchases,* including merchandise, equipment, and supplies.

Notes Payable	Acct. No. 211
	Oct. 4 J7 8,000

Sales	Acct. No. 401
	Oct. 1 J7 1,200

As shown above, the accountant must post each part of every general journal entry. The posting process consists of (1) transferring the date and amount to the appropriate side (debit or credit) of the ledger account, (2) inserting the journal page number as a posting reference in the ledger account, and (3) inserting the ledger account number in the posting reference column of the general journal.

The **general ledger,** often called simply the **ledger,** consists of many accounts. Each account is a record of information about a particular asset, such as Cash and Accounts Receivable; liability, such as Accounts Payable and Notes Payable; owners' equity, such as Common Stock and Retained Earnings; revenue, such as Sales and Service Fees Earned; and expense, such as Salaries and Advertising. Based on the scope of its operations and the extent of detail desired for reporting purposes, each business determines the exact nature of its accounts. The **chart of accounts** is a listing of a firm's general ledger accounts. The accounts are usually numbered to permit easy identification and cross-referencing with the journals. Each asset account, for example, might be assigned a code number between 101 and 199, each liability account might be assigned a code number between 201 and 299, and so forth.

In a computer-based accounting system, the general ledger information is stored on a machine-sensible device such as magnetic tape or disc. In a manual system, the general ledger is often a bound collection of pages. Each page represents an account. Typically, the first group of pages represents the asset accounts, followed by those of the liability, owners' equity, revenue, and expense accounts, in that order.

Certain ledger accounts are called real accounts, whereas others are known as nominal accounts. **Real** (or **permanent**) **accounts** remain open. These include asset, liability, and owners' equity accounts. Real accounts measure stocks of things, such as resources or debts, that exist at a certain point in time. **Nominal** (or **temporary**) **accounts** are closed at the end of every accounting period. These include revenue and expense accounts. Nominal accounts measure flows, such as sales or cost of goods sold, that occur over time. During an accounting period, certain accounts contain both real and nominal components; these are called **mixed accounts.** At the end of the period, adjusting entries separate mixed accounts into their real and nominal components. For example, before adjusting entries, the Supplies account usually has both consumed (nominal) and unconsumed (real) portions. An adjusting entry places the consumed portion in a nominal account (Supplies Expense) and allows the unconsumed portion to remain in a real account (Supplies). After the accountant makes adjusting entries, all accounts in the ledger are either real or nominal.

The general ledger ordinarily includes certain adjunct and contra accounts. An **adjunct account** is one whose balance is added to the balance in the account to which it relates. For example, Transportation-In is an adjunct account to Purchases, and Premium on Bonds Payable is an adjunct account to Bonds Payable. A **contra** (or **offset**) **account** is one whose balance is subtracted from the balance in the account to which it relates. For instance, Sales Discounts is a contra account to Sales, and Allowance for Doubtful Accounts is a contra account to Accounts Receivable. Adjunct and contra accounts are closed at the end of an accounting period only if the accounts they relate to are also closed.

Subsidiary Ledgers

In addition to a general ledger, most businesses have one or more **subsidiary ledgers.** The purpose of a subsidiary ledger is to store the details of certain general ledger accounts. For example, a company may have thousands of credit customers. While it is certainly necessary to know the total amount that these customers owe the company, it is also essential to know the name and address of each customer and how much each one owes. This information facilitates the billing process and is useful when the company makes credit-granting decisions. Rather than have a separate Accounts Receivable for each customer in the general ledger, firms usually create an Accounts Receivable subsidiary ledger. This ledger is often in the form of a tray of alphabetized cards, each card representing a customer's account. The Accounts Receivable account in the general ledger then becomes a **control (or main) account** that is supported by many detailed accounts in the subsidiary ledger.

When a subsidiary ledger exists, posting must appear in both the control account and the appropriate subsidiary ledger accounts. The control account is debited for the total debits and credited for the total credits made to the subsidiary ledger accounts. After all accounts have been posted, the balance in the control account should equal the total of the individual account balances in the subsidiary ledger. To assure this equality, the accountant periodically reconciles each control account with its subsidiary ledger accounts.

Why use subsidiary ledgers? One important reason that a company uses them is to reduce the number of accounts in its general ledger. With fewer accounts it is easier to avoid errors and to find them when they occur. Subsidiary ledgers also facilitate the division of labor in an accounting department. Individuals with limited education or experience can often be assigned responsibility for one or more subsidiary ledgers. Work on the various ledgers can thereby proceed simultaneously.

A subsidiary ledger may be created to support any general ledger account. Subsidiary ledgers are often set up for Cash (when a company has several bank accounts), Accounts Receivable, Merchandise Inventory (when a company uses a perpetual inventory system), Plant Assets, Accounts Payable, Capital Stock, Selling Expenses, and Administrative Expenses.

Step 5.   Prepare an Unadjusted Trial Balance

A **trial balance** is a list of general ledger accounts and their debit or credit balances. It summarizes, usually on one sheet of paper, information that appears in a company's general ledger. The accountant prepares a trial balance at the end of every accounting period, before making the adjusting entries. Because the account balances do not yet reflect adjustments, the trial balance prepared at this time is often called an **unadjusted trial balance.**

A trial balance serves two main purposes:

1. It provides evidence that total debits in a company's general ledger equal total credits.
2. It provides information that helps the accountant to formulate adjusting entries.

The trial balance is a control device that helps to eliminate accounting errors. When total debits in a company's general ledger do not equal total credits, the trial balance is said to be **out of balance.** This condition alerts the accountant that one or more errors have been made. The accountant of course must find and correct these errors before preparing financial statements. On the other hand, a trial balance which is **in balance** does not necessarily signify the absence of errors. For example, the trial balance does not indicate the failure to record a transaction or the recording of a transaction in the wrong accounts. To summarize, a trial balance which is in balance is a necessary but not a sufficient condition for controlling accounting errors.

The unadjusted trial balance for Eagle Company at December 31, 1985, is illustrated below. Information pertaining to this company, which uses a calendar-year accounting period, will be used to help explain the subsequent steps in the accounting cycle.

Eagle Company
UNADJUSTED TRIAL BALANCE
December 31, 1985

Account	Dr.	Cr.
Cash	$ 21,079	
Accounts receivable	60,000	
Allowance for doubtful accounts		$ 500
Note receivable	10,000	
Merchandise inventory	57,606	
Prepaid insurance	1,200	
Land	40,000	
Building	100,000	
Accumulated depreciation—building		10,000
Office equipment	120,000	
Accumulated depreciation—office equipment		24,000
Accounts payable		38,405
Unearned rent revenue		4,800
Long-term note payable		72,000
Common stock, $5 par		50,000
Paid-in capital in excess of par value		65,000
Retained earnings		34,215
Sales		523,000
Purchases	187,000	
Purchase returns		2,000
Purchase allowances		2,500
Purchase discounts		3,600
Transportation-in	7,250	
Sales salaries expense	78,000	
Advertising expense	24,000	
Transportation-out	6,000	
Miscellaneous selling expenses	5,141	
Officers' salaries expense	76,000	
Professional services	23,000	
Utilities expense	8,244	
Miscellaneous administrative expenses	5,500	
Totals	$830,020	$830,020

Step 6.   Prepare Adjusting Entries

Revenue Realization

Matching

Under the **cash basis of accounting,** revenue is recorded only when received in cash, and expenses are recorded only when paid in cash. In contrast, the **accrual basis of accounting** requires recognition of revenue when it is earned according to the revenue realization principle and recognition of expenses when they are incurred according to the matching principle. Under accrual basis accounting, the cash inflows typically associated with a given period's revenues may occur in past, present, or future periods. Similarly, the cash outflows typically associated with a given period's expenses may occur in past, present, or future periods. Thus, the primary difference between cash basis and accrual basis accounting is the timing of the recognition of revenues and expenses.

Current generally accepted accounting principles require accrual basis accounting, because this system generates measures of performance and financial position that are superior to those of cash basis accounting. To help implement the accrual basis of accounting, the accountant makes certain **adjusting entries** (often called **adjustments**) at the end of every accounting period. Adjusting entries are initially recorded in the general journal, then posted to the appropriate general ledger accounts. If an entry requires an account that is not in the general ledger, the accountant simply creates (opens) a new account.

WHAT TO DO WHEN A TRIAL BALANCE IS OUT OF BALANCE

WHEN THE DEBIT and credit columns of a trial balance are unequal, an accountant should first determine the exact amount of the difference. Sometimes this amount is a clue to the nature of the error.

If the difference between the debit and credit totals is evenly divisible by **9**, an error due to a transposition or a slide may have occurred. A **transposition** means that the digits of a number have been reversed. For example, if the number $860 is incorrectly written as $680, a transposition error of $180 ($860 − $680) exists. This error is evenly divisible by 9 ($180 ÷ 9 = $20). A **slide** means that an error has been made in recording a decimal point. For example, if the number $2,080 is incorrectly written as $208, a slide in the decimal point has occurred. Observe once again that the error of $1,872 ($2,080 − $208) can be divided evenly by 9 ($1,872 ÷ 9 = $208).

If the trial balance is out of balance by an amount equally divisible by **2**, a debit may have been entered as a credit, or vice versa. If, for example, the trial balance debit total is $96,482 and the credit total is $96,042, the difference of $440 may indicate that a credit of $220 ($440 ÷ 2 = $220) was incorrectly posted as a debit. Alternatively, the difference may indicate that only the debit half of an entry for $440 was recorded.

An error that frequently occurs when using a calculator to obtain the total of a trial balance column is depressing a numerical key above or below the one desired. For example, the amount $459 may be incorrectly entered in the calculator as $456 or as $159. Such an error will cause the trial balance to be out of balance by an amount equally divisible by 3 ($459 − $456 = $3; $459 − $159 = $300).

The hints described above are frequently helpful when a trial balance reflects only a single error. If several errors exist, however, an accountant should systematically retrace the journalizing, posting, and trial balance preparation steps of the accounting cycle, in reverse order. Of course, a habit of rechecking all computations as we move through the accounting cycle helps to avoid errors in the first place.

Purpose of Adjusting Entries

Revenue Realization

Matching

The purpose of adjusting entries is to permit accurate measurement of earnings and financial position on the accrual basis. Adjusting entries are based on two accounting principles: **revenue realization** and **matching** (see Chapter 2). Every adjusting entry allocates revenues or expenses between current and future periods. Moreover, every adjusting entry affects both a balance sheet account (asset or liability) and an income statement account (revenue or expense).[4]

Accumulating Adjusting Data

An external event such as a purchase or sale signals the accountant to record the transaction. At the end of the accounting period, however, no external events signal the accountant to record adjusting entries. How then does the accountant determine the nature and amounts of adjusting entries to record? Basically, the accountant carefully considers each account in the trial balance and examines certain source documents. Accounts that have mixed bal-

---

[4]Certain **correcting entries** and **reclassification entries** are sometimes made during the adjustment process. For example, a correcting entry might be made to charge to Advertising Expense an amount that was mistakenly charged to Research and Development Expense during the year. A reclassification entry might be made to reclassify to current liability status the portion of long-term debt that will mature within the next year. As these examples suggest, a correcting or reclassification entry often affects only nominal accounts or only real accounts.

ances (i.e., mixed accounts) must be separated into real and nominal components. In addition, certain information not reflected on the trial balance must be entered in the accounting records. For example, the presence of Prepaid Insurance on the trial balance causes the accountant to inquire whether any insurance has expired and therefore should be charged to expense. This inquiry normally involves a review of the company's insurance policies. A Notes Receivable account usually leads the accountant to review the notes to determine whether any interest has been earned. Interest earned should be entered in a revenue account. Since many adjusting entries are somewhat repetitive from one accounting period to the next, accountants can often gain insight into the nature and amounts of this period's adjusting entries by examining the ones that were made at the end of the preceding period.

Classification of Adjusting Entries

We shall classify adjusting entries using the following three categories:

1. Accruals
2. Deferrals
3. Special items

Accruals. Accruals are adjusting entries that normally have *one* of the following characteristics:

1. A revenue is recognized before the related cash receipt, *or*
2. An expense is recognized before the related cash payment.

Accruals are appropriate for revenues and related assets and for expenses and related liabilities that increase or accumulate gradually during the accounting period. Rather than recording these items weekly, daily, or even more frequently, the accountant records them by making adjusting entries at the end of the accounting period.

As an example of **accrued revenues** (accrued assets), on July 1, 1985, Eagle Company acquired a $10,000, one-year, 12% note receivable, with interest payable at maturity. This note represents money loaned by the company and is reflected on its trial balance. The revenue realization principle holds, in part, that revenue generated by allowing others to use enterprise assets, such as money, should be recorded as time passes. Accordingly, the company should make the following adjusting entry on December 31, 1985, the end of the company's annual accounting period:

> | Revenue |
> | Realization |

Dec. 31	Interest Receivable	600	
	Interest Revenue		600
	To accrue interest for 6 months on note receivable. Accrued interest is computed as follows:		
	$10,000 × .12 × 6/12 = $600		

> | Revenue |
> | Realization |

The adjusting entry assigns the $600 of interest revenue to 1985, the period in which the revenue was earned according to the revenue realization principle. The cash receipt associated with the interest will occur in the next accounting period, specifically on June 30, 1986. Note that the adjusting entry affects both a balance sheet account (Interest Receivable) and an income statement account (Interest Revenue). This journal entry, like all others, must be posted to the general ledger accounts affected.

As an example of **accrued expenses** (accrued liabilities), on October 1, 1985, Eagle

Company issued a $72,000, 10-year, 10% note payable with interest payable annually on September 30. September 30, 1986, is therefore the first date that interest will be paid. Nevertheless, the money borrowed has been used during the last three months of 1985. Accordingly, the cost of that money (interest) must be reported as an expense in 1985 to comply with the matching principle. The accountant should make the following adjusting entry:

Matching

Dec. 31	Interest Expense	1,800	
	Interest Payable		1,800
	To accrue interest for		
	3 months on note payable.		
	Accrued interest is computed		
	as follows:		
	$72,000 \times .10 \times 3/12 = \$1,800$		

The adjusting entry assigns the $1,800 of interest expense to the current accounting period (1985), the period in which the expense was incurred. The cash payment associated with the accrued interest will occur on September 30 of the next accounting period. Notice that the adjusting entry affects both a balance sheet account (Interest Payable) and an income statement account (Interest Expense).

Eagle Company must make one other major accrual, that of income tax expense. This is usually the final adjusting entry, because the amount depends on the size of a company's pretax income. We shall therefore make this entry later in the chapter, after we have calculated Eagle's 1985 income before taxes.

Deferrals. Deferrals are adjusting entries required to separate mixed accounts into their real and nominal components. A deferral-type adjusting entry typically has *one* of the following characteristics:

1. A revenue is recognized after the related cash receipt, *or*
2. An expense is recognized after the related cash payment (or incurrence of a liability).

In Exhibit 5–2 we compare accruals with deferrals.

Adjusting entries to reflect **deferred (unearned) revenues** are necessary for mixed accounts in which a portion of the balance represents revenue that has been earned currently and a portion represents revenue that will be earned in one or more future accounting periods. For example, Eagle Company's trial balance shows Unearned Rent Revenue of $4,800. The lease contract shows that the $4,800 represents one year's rent received in advance on an office in the company's building. When the amount was received on September 1, 1985, Cash was debited and Unearned Rent Revenue (a liability account) was credited.

Revenue Realization

The revenue realization principle holds, in part, that revenue generated by allowing others to use an enterprise asset, such as an office, is earned as time passes. Accordingly, on December 31, 1985, the following adjusting entry is required to reflect the fact that one-third of the $4,800 has been earned:

Dec. 31	Unearned Rent Revenue	1,600	
	Rent Revenue		1,600
	To record revenue earned		
	on office rented, computed		
	as follows:		
	$4,800 \times 4/12 = \$1,600$		

EXHIBIT 5-2
Comparison of Accruals and Deferrals

Accrued Revenue	Revenue recognition ———————————————— Cash receipt →
	Time

Accrued Revenue

Revenue recognition ——————————————————————— Cash receipt →
Time

Deferred (Unearned) Revenue

Cash receipt ———————————————————— Revenue recognition →
Time

Accrued Expense

Expense recognition ——————————————————— Cash payment →
Time

Deferred (Prepaid) Expense

Cash payment (or incurrence of liability) ——————— Expense recognition →
Time

As usual, the adjusting entry affects a balance sheet account (Unearned Rent Revenue) and an income statement account (Rent Revenue). After the entry has been posted, the Unearned Rent Revenue account has a $3,200 credit balance ($4,800 − $1,600 = $3,200). This balance is a liability, because it represents the company's obligation to provide the rented asset (i.e., the office) during the first eight months of the next accounting period.

Some companies follow the practice of crediting a revenue account whenever revenues are collected in advance of being earned. *If* Eagle had observed this practice, it would have debited Cash and credited Rent Revenue for $4,800 on September 1, 1985. Then on December 31, 1985, the adjusting entry would require a debit to Rent Revenue to reduce it and a credit to the liability account Unearned Rent Revenue for $3,200. The amounts reported on the 1985 financial statements would be the same as before, because the economic circumstances have not changed. Rent Revenue for 1985 would therefore still be $1,600 and Unearned Rent Revenue at December 31, 1985, would still be $3,200.

Adjusting entries to reflect **deferred (prepaid) expenses** are necessary for mixed accounts in which a portion of the balance represents an expense that has been incurred currently and a portion represents an expense that will be incurred in one or more future accounting periods. For example, Eagle Company's trial balance shows Prepaid Insurance of $1,200. The insurance policy shows that this amount represents the cost of fire protection for one year, paid in advance on April 1, 1985. When the original amount was paid, the company debited Prepaid Insurance and credited Cash.

Matching

The matching principle requires that costs be recognized as expenses when the goods or services represented by the costs contribute to revenue. During 1985, three-fourths of the insurance protection has presumably contributed to revenue. The expired portion of the insurance cost must therefore be entered in an expense account. The following adjusting entry is required:

```
Dec. 31   Insurance Expense              900
               Prepaid Insurance                   900
               To record expired portion
               of insurance, computed
               as follows:
               $1,200 × 9/12 = $900
```

Notice once again that the adjusting entry affects a balance sheet account (Prepaid Insurance) and an income statement account (Insurance Expense). After posting, the Prepaid Insurance account has a $300 debit balance. This balance represents an asset, specifically, the right to receive fire insurance protection during the first three months of the next accounting period.

Some companies follow the practice of debiting an expense account for short-term prepayments. *If* Eagle had observed this practice, it would have debited Insurance Expense and credited Cash for $1,200 on April 1, 1985. On December 31, 1985, the adjusting entry would require a debit to Prepaid Insurance and a credit to Insurance Expense for $300. The amounts reported on the 1985 financial statements would be the same as before; Insurance Expense for 1985 would still be $900, and Prepaid Insurance at December 31, 1985, would still be $300.

Matching

The matching principle further requires that Eagle Company record depreciation on its building and office equipment. These assets have contributed to revenues throughout 1985; accordingly, a portion of their cost must be allocated to 1985 expense. Eagle uses the straight-line method to depreciate the building and office equipment over 50 and 10 years, respectively. Furthermore, the company expects each asset to have no salvage value.[5] The adjusting entry appears below:

Dec. 31	Depreciation Expense—Building	2,000	
	Depreciation Expense—Office Equipment	12,000	
	Accumulated Depreciation—		
	Building		2,000
	Accumulated Depreciation—Office		
	Equipment		12,000
	To record depreciation, computed as follows:		

$$\text{Building} \quad \frac{\$100,000 - 0}{50 \text{ years}} = \$2,000$$

$$\text{Office Equipment} \quad \frac{\$120,000 - 0}{10 \text{ years}} = \$12,000$$

Note that a compound entry was made to record depreciation. Two simple entries would also have been appropriate. Once again, the adjusting entry affects a balance sheet account (Accumulated Depreciation) and an income statement account (Depreciation Expense). The credits are made to accumulated depreciation accounts rather than directly to the asset accounts. Accumulated Depreciation is a contra account that permits the balance sheet to show both the cost and the accumulated depreciation of the major types of plant assets. Both pieces of information are generally considered relevant and are required disclosures according to *Accounting Principles Board Opinion No. 12.*[6] The cost of an asset minus its accumulated depreciation is often called the asset's **book value** (or **net book value**).

When a company incurs costs that will likely benefit several accounting periods, such as the cost of buildings and equipment, the normal procedure is to debit an asset account instead of an expense account. Therefore, adjusting entries to record long-term cost allocations, such as depreciation, are usually similar to the one illustrated above.

Special Items.   These are adjusting entries that do not fit neatly into the accrual and deferral categories and are therefore classified separately. Common examples include the

---

[5]Under the straight-line method, we compute depreciation using the following formula:

$$\text{Annual depreciation} = \frac{\text{Cost} - \text{Salvage value}}{\text{Years of service life}}$$

[6]*APB Opinion No. 12,* "Omnibus Opinion—1967," 1967, par. 5.

adjusting entries for bad debts expense and for cost of goods sold in a company that uses the periodic inventory system.

Companies that sell on credit do not usually expect to collect all of their accounts receivable. Therefore, some portion of credit sales made during a period and some portion of accounts receivable at the end of the period will likely never be collected in cash. To reflect these expectations, companies having credit sales make an adjusting entry to record **estimated bad debts.**

Procedures for estimating bad debts expense are covered in Chapter 7. For the time being, assume that all of Eagle Company's sales are on credit and that the company expects that 0.5% of its sales will never be collected. The company makes the following adjusting entry:

Dec. 31	Bad Debts Expense	2,615	
	Allowance for Doubtful Accounts		2,615
	To record estimated bad		
	debts, computed as follows:		
	$523,000 × .005 = $2,615		

The adjusting entry assigns Bad Debts Expense of $2,615 to the current accounting period, where it is matched on the income statement with the revenue from credit sales. Credit sales give rise to the uncollectibles. Bad debts expense is regarded as a cost of making credit sales, and recording it helps implement the matching principle. The credit in the above entry is made to the Allowance for Doubtful Accounts. We do not credit Accounts Receivable because we do not yet know which specific accounts will become uncollectible. The Allowance for Doubtful Accounts is a contra account to Accounts Receivable; we therefore subtract it from Accounts Receivable on the balance sheet. Accounts Receivable minus the Allowance for Doubtful Accounts is often called the **net realizable value** of accounts receivable. The net realizable value of Eagle's accounts receivable at December 31, 1985, is $56,885 [$60,000 − ($500 + $2,615)]. The $500 amount is the balance in the Allowance for Doubtful Accounts before adjustments are made.

> **Matching**

An outflow of resources is associated with most expenses. This outflow may occur in past, present, or future periods. In regard to bad debts, however, no such outflow occurs. Instead, there is simply a reduction in the inflow of cash expected. Thus, Bad Debts Expense is somewhat peculiar, and some accountants think it should be treated as a revenue contra account (perhaps called Sales Uncollectible) rather than an expense. We have treated the adjusting entry for bad debts as a special item because of its peculiar nature.

Another special item is the **adjustment for Cost of Goods Sold.** A company using the periodic inventory system debits Purchases whenever it makes a merchandise purchase. Furthermore, the recording of a sale does not involve entries in either Cost of Goods Sold or Merchandise Inventory accounts. As a result, the Merchandise Inventory balance shown on the ending trial balance is the balance that was on hand at the *beginning* of the accounting period.[7]

The objectives of the Cost of Goods Sold adjustment are therefore threefold:

1. To enter the ending inventory balance in the Merchandise Inventory account and remove the beginning inventory balance. The ending balance can then be presented on the ending balance sheet.
2. To close all of the accounts included in the calculation of net purchases. These accounts

---

[7]Throughout this chapter we assume that a periodic inventory system is used. In Chapter 8 we review in detail the differences between periodic and perpetual systems.

include Purchases, Purchase Returns, Purchase Allowances, Purchase Discounts, and Transportation-In.

3. To enter the Cost of Goods Sold Expense in the accounting records. One computes cost of goods sold using the following formula:

Cost of Goods Sold = Beginning Inventory
+ Purchases
− Purchase Returns
− Purchase Allowances
− Purchase Discounts
+ Transportation-In
− Ending Inventory

To illustrate, Eagle Company's physical inventory count at the end of 1985 shows merchandise costing $43,756. The adjusting entry for Cost of Goods Sold appears below:

Dec. 31	Merchandise Inventory (Dec. 31)	43,756	
	Purchase Returns	2,000	
	Purchase Allowances	2,500	
	Purchase Discounts	3,600	
	Cost of Goods Sold	200,000	
	Merchandise Inventory (Jan. 1)		57,606
	Purchases		187,000
	Transportation-In		7,250
	(To record cost of goods sold and ending inventory.)		

The adjusting entry accomplishes the three objectives described above. Actually, the entry is nothing more than the implementation of the basic cost of goods sold formula in general journal form. After the entry is posted, the Cost of Goods Sold account will have a $200,000 debit balance. Since Cost of Goods Sold is a nominal account, it must be closed during the closing process.

The adjusting entry for the Cost of Goods Sold is part adjusting and part closing. Some accountants prefer to treat it as a closing entry. Because it is peculiar, we have classified it as a special item.

Step 7.   Prepare an Adjusted Trial Balance

After journalizing and posting the adjusting entries, the accountant prepares a second trial balance. This is called an **adjusted trial balance** because the account balances listed reflect the company's adjusting entries. An adjusted trial balance serves three major purposes:

1. It provides evidence that, after the adjusting entries have been made, total debits in a company's general ledger equals total credits. It thus helps to control errors made during the adjustment process.
2. It enables the accountant to calculate income before taxes so that the adjusting entry for Income Tax Expense can be made.
3. It provides a convenient listing of account balances used to prepare the financial statements.

The adjusted trial balance of Eagle Company appears on the opposite page.

Note that the columns are subtotaled and an informal calculation of income before taxes is made. This calculation may be made on an adding machine and need not be shown in detail on the adjusted trial balance. Income before taxes is the difference between the income statement accounts with credit balances and the income statement accounts with debit balances. For Eagle Company, this difference is $80,000.

Eagle Company
ADJUSTED TRIAL BALANCE
December 31, 1985

Account	Dr.	Cr.
Cash	$ 21,079	
Accounts receivable	60,000	
Allowance for doubtful accounts		$ 3,115
Note receivable	10,000	
Interest receivable	600	
Merchandise inventory	43,756	
Prepaid insurance	300	
Land	40,000	
Building	100,000	
Accumulated depreciation—building		12,000
Office equipment	120,000	
Accumulated depreciation—office equipment		36,000
Accounts payable		38,405
Interest payable		1,800
Unearned rent revenue		3,200
Long-term note payable		72,000
Common stock, $5 par		50,000
Paid-in capital in excess of par value		65,000
Retained earnings		34,215
Sales		523,000
Interest revenue		600
Rent revenue		1,600
Cost of goods sold	200,000	
Sales salaries expense	78,000	
Advertising expense	24,000	
Transportation-out	6,000	
Miscellaneous selling expenses	5,141	
Officers' salaries expense	76,000	
Professional services	23,000	
Utilities expense	8,244	
Interest expense	1,800	
Insurance expense	900	
Depreciation expense—building	2,000	
Depreciation expense—office equipment	12,000	
Bad debts expense	2,615	
Miscellaneous administrative expenses	5,500	
Subtotal	840,935	840,935
Income tax expense	38,400	
Income tax payable		38,400
Total	$879,335	$879,335

Income before taxes =
$523,000 + 600 + 1,600 − 200,000 − 78,000 − 24,000 − 6,000 − 5,141 − 76,000 − 23,000 − 8,244 − 1,800 − 900 − 2,000 − 12,000 − 2,615 − 5,500 = $80,000

Income tax expense = $80,000 × .48 = $38,400

Income Tax Expense is typically a major expense. Unlike most other expenses, it can be computed only after calculating income before taxes. Eagle Company's income tax rate is 48%.[8] The company therefore records the accrual of its Income Tax Expense as follows:

Dec. 31	Income Tax Expense	38,400	
	Income Tax Payable		38,400
	(To accrue income tax		
	expense at a rate of 48%.)		

As usual, this adjusting entry is journalized and posted to the general ledger accounts affected. These accounts are listed near the bottom of the adjusted trial balance, after which the columns are totaled.

Step 8. Prepare Financial Statements

Using the information on the adjusted trial balance, the accountant prepares the formal **financial statements.**[9] These statements summarize many important things and events. They are the output of the accounting information system and serve as input for many investment, credit, and similar decisions. Preparing the statements is therefore a crucial step in the accounting cycle.

The accountant ordinarily prepares financial statements in the following order: (1) income statement, (2) statement of retained earnings, (3) balance sheet, and (4) statement of changes in financial position. These are the basic financial statements explained in Chapter 4. Preparing the statement of changes in financial position requires more information than appears on the adjusted trial balance. In Chapter 23 we discuss and illustrate how to prepare the statement of changes in financial position. The income statement, statement of retained earnings, and balance sheet for Eagle Company appear in Exhibit 5–3. We present

---

[8]In this chapter we review the accounting cycle without being diverted by the mechanics of calculating income taxes. We therefore assume that a tax rate of 48% applies to all income and that no differences exist between the company's pretax-accounting income and its taxable income. In Chapter 18, we discuss and illustrate how to account for income taxes under more complex circumstances.

[9]Financial statements may also be prepared using a worksheet, as discussed in Appendix A. A **worksheet** is used to accumulate and organize the information required to prepare financial statements.

EXHIBIT 5–3
Preparation of Financial Statements

Eagle Company
INCOME STATEMENT
For the Year Ended December 31, 1985

Sales revenue			
Sales			$523,000
Cost of goods sold			
Merchandise inventory, Jan. 1, 1985		$ 57,606	
Purchases	$187,000		
Less: Purchase returns	2,000		
Purchase allowances	2,500		
Purchase discounts	3,600		
Add: Transportation-in	7,250		
Net purchases		186,150	
Cost of goods available for sale		243,756	
Merchandise inventory, Dec. 31, 1985		43,756	
Cost of goods sold			200,000
Gross margin on sales			323,000

Operating expenses			
Selling expenses			
Sales salaries	78,000		
Advertising	24,000		
Transportation-out	6,000		
Miscellaneous	5,141	113,141	
Administrative expenses			
Officers' salaries	76,000		
Professional services	23,000		
Utilities	8,244		
Insurance	900		
Depreciation of building	2,000		
Depreciation of office equipment	12,000		
Bad Debts	2,615		
Miscellaneous	5,500	130,259	
Total operating expenses			243,400
Income from operations			79,600
Other revenues			
Interest		600	
Rent		1,600	2,200
			81,800
Other expense			
Interest			1,800
Income before taxes			80,000
Income tax expense ($80,000 × .48)			38,400
Net income			$ 41,600
Earnings per share ($41,600 ÷ 10,000 shares outstanding)			$4.16

Eagle Company
STATEMENT OF RETAINED EARNINGS*
For the Year Ended December 31, 1985

Retained earnings, Jan. 1, 1985	$34,215
Add: Net income	41,600**
Retained earnings, Dec. 31, 1985	$75,815

*Eagle Company declared no dividends during 1985. If dividends had been declared, they would be subtracted on the retained earnings statement, as discussed and illustrated in Chapter 4.
**This number was obtained from the income statement.

Eagle Company
BALANCE SHEET
December 31, 1985

Assets

Current Assets		
Cash		$ 21,079
Accounts receivable	$ 60,000	
Less: Allowance for doubtful accounts	3,115	56,885
Note receivable		10,000
Interest receivable		600
Merchandise inventory		43,756
Prepaid insurance		300
Total current assets		$132,620

Plant Assets

Land		40,000	
Building	100,000		
Less: Accumulated depreciation	12,000	88,000	
Office equipment	120,000		
Less: Accumulated depreciation	36,000	84,000	
Total plant assets			212,000
Total assets			$344,620

Liabilities and Stockholders' Equity

Current Liabilities

Accounts payable	$ 38,405	
Interest payable	1,800	
Income tax payable	38,400	
Unearned rent revenue	3,200	
Total current liabilities		$ 81,805

Long-Term Liabilities

Notes payable		72,000
Total liabilities		153,805

Stockholders' Equity

Paid-in capital			
Common stock, $5 par,			
10,000 shares issued			
and outstanding	$ 50,000		
Paid-in capital in excess of par value	65,000		
Total paid-in capital		115,000	
Retained earnings		75,815*	
Total stockholders' equity			190,815
Total liabilities and stockholders' equity			$344,620

*This number was obtained from the statement of retained earnings.

Materiality

these statements for illustrative purposes; most accountants would probably combine several items shown on the statements, based on materiality considerations.

Step 9. Prepare Closing Entries

After preparing the financial statements, the accountant prepares **closing entries.** These entries are made at the end of the accounting period. They are first recorded in the general journal, then posted to the appropriate ledger accounts.

The accountant closes *only* the nominal accounts. Furthermore, *all* nominal accounts are closed. To **close an account** means to reduce its balance to zero. Closing nominal accounts is logical, because they measure activities or flows that have occurred *during a given period of time.* At the end of the period, nominal accounts have served their purpose. Their balances must therefore be reduced to zero so that the accounts can be used to measure activities in the *next* accounting period. The measurement of any activity, whether it is sales or the 100-meter dash, logically begins at zero.

Because nominal accounts are temporary extensions of owners' equity (see Exhibit 5–1), their balances may be transferred directly to an owners' equity account (Retained Earnings in the case of a corporation) during closing. However, most accountants transfer revenue and expense balances to a clearing account called **Income Summary** (or **Revenue and Expense Summary**). This account merely summarizes the net income or loss for the period, and its balance is closed (i.e., reduced to zero and transferred) to owners' equity.[10] Closing entries are formulated based on the nominal account balances shown on the adjusted trial balance. The closing entries for Eagle Company are presented below:

Dec. 31	Sales	523,000	
	Interest Revenue	600	
	Rent Revenue	1,600	
	Income Summary		525,200
	(To close revenue accounts.)		
Dec. 31	Income Summary	483,600	
	Cost of Goods Sold		200,000
	Sales Salaries Expense		78,000
	Advertising Expense		24,000
	Transportation-Out		6,000
	Miscellaneous Selling Expenses		5,141
	Officers' Salaries Expense		76,000
	Professional Services		23,000
	Utilities Expense		8,244
	Interest Expense		1,800
	Insurance Expense		900
	Depreciation Expense—Building		2,000
	Depreciation Expense—Office Equipment		12,000
	Bad Debts Expense		2,615
	Miscellaneous Administrative Expenses		5,500
	Income Tax Expense		38,400
	(To close expense accounts.)		
Dec. 31	Income Summary	41,600	
	Retained Earnings		41,600
	(To close the Income Summary account.)		

Although compound entries were used to illustrate the closing process, it would also have been appropriate to use a series of simple entries. Note carefully that after closing entries are posted, zero balances will exist in each revenue account, each expense account, and the Income Summary clearing account. Furthermore, the ending balance in the Retained Earnings account is $75,815 ($34,215 + $41,600). Through no coincidence, this is the same figure reported for Retained Earnings on Eagle's balance sheet dated December 31, 1985.

---

[10]Some corporations record the declaration of a dividend by debiting a **Dividends Declared** account, while others charge Retained Earnings directly. Dividends Declared is a nominal account and is presented on the statement of retained earnings. It normally has a debit balance and is closed directly to Retained Earnings at the end of the accounting period in the following manner:

Dec. 31	Retained Earnings	XXX	
	Dividends Declared		XXX
	(To close the Dividends Declared account.)		

In sole proprietorships and partnerships, **Drawing** accounts are used instead of Dividends Declared. Drawing accounts are closed directly to Owners' Capital at the end of the accounting period.

Step 10.   Prepare Post-Closing Trial Balance (Optional)

After journalizing and posting the closing entries, the accountant usually prepares a **post-closing trial balance.** This is simply a listing of general ledger accounts and their balances after the closing entries have been made. The post-closing trial balance therefore consists entirely of real accounts. Its purpose is to provide evidence that equal debits and credits exist in the general ledger after closing. Thus, it helps to insure that the closing process has been performed correctly. The post-closing trial balance is not a required step in the accounting cycle, because its purpose is solely error detection.

Step 11.   Prepare Reversing Entries (Optional)

The final step in the accounting cycle is to journalize and post **reversing entries.** These entries bear the first date of the new accounting period. They are called reversing entries because they are the reverse or opposite of certain adjusting entries made at the end of the preceding period. Reversing entries do not mean that the adjusting entries reversed were unnecessary or inaccurate.

The sole purpose of reversing entries is to *simplify* the subsequent recording of certain kinds of recurring transactions. Since their only purpose is simplification, reversing entries are optional. To illustrate, recall that on December 31, 1985, Eagle Company had outstanding a $72,000, 10-year, 10% note payable with interest payable annually on September 30. In Exhibit 5–4, we summarize selected accounting entries pertaining to the note under alternative assumptions about reversing entries.

Under either assumption the interest expense recorded for the first nine months of 1986 is $5,400. Therefore, either assumption results in the same amounts on the 1986 financial statements. Making the reversing entry on January 1, however, eliminates the need to allocate the September 30 interest payment between the amount currently expensed and the amount previously accrued. This may seem like a trivial simplification for Eagle Company with its single note payable. However, some companies have many notes payable. Moreover,

---

EXHIBIT 5–4
Effect of Reversing Entries

Event	Accrued Interest Expense Is Reversed		Accrued Interest Expense Is Not Reversed	

Dec. 31, 1985
Adjusting entry to accrue
interest expense
	Interest Expense 1,800
	    Interest Payable
		1,800	Interest Expense 1,800
			    Interest Payable
				1,800

Dec. 31, 1985
Closing entry applicable to
accrued interest
expense
	Income Summary 1,800
	    Interest Expense
		1,800	Income Summary 1,800
			    Interest Expense
				1,800

Jan. 1, 1986 Reversing entry	Interest Payable 1,800 Interest Expense	1,800	No entry	

Sept. 30, 1986
Payment of Interest
	Interest Expense 7,200
	    Cash
		7,200	Interest Expense 5,400
			Interest Payable 1,800
			    Cash
				7,200

the recording of interest payments is often assigned to a clerical employee who may have had little more than high school bookkeeping courses. Under these circumstances, a qualified accountant may well decide to make reversing entries to simplify the recording of interest payments by the clerical employee. At the end of the period, the accountant can then analyze each note payable and formulate the appropriate adjusting entry for accrued interest.

The following types (i.e., categories) of adjusting entries *may* be reversed: (1) adjusting entries to record accruals (either revenues or expenses), and (2) adjusting entries to record deferrals when the original amount to which the adjusting entry pertains was recorded in a nominal account. A company may choose to reverse any number of adjusting entries as long as the entries fall into one of the two categories discussed above. Since reversing entries are optional, companies should not make them unless the benefits exceed the costs.

KEY POINTS

1. A transaction is an event that changes a company's financial position and can be measured with sufficient objectivity.

2. Source documents serve as evidence that transactions have occurred.

3. The term "debit" refers to the left-hand side of an account, while "credit" refers to the right-hand side.

4. A journal is a chronological record of transactions. A company should always have a general journal and may have one or more special journals.

5. Posting involves transferring information from journals to accounts in a ledger. A company should always maintain a general ledger and may have one or more subsidiary ledgers.

6. The unadjusted trial balance provides evidence that total debits in a company's general ledger equal total credits. It also provides information that helps the accountant to formulate adjusting entries.

7. Adjusting entries permit accurate measurement of earnings and financial position on the accrual basis.

8. Adjusting entries are based on the revenue realization and matching principles.

9. An adjusted trial balance provides a convenient listing of account balances that may be used to prepare the financial statements.

10. The accountant usually prepares financial statements in the following order:
  a. Income statement.
  b. Statement of retained earnings.
  c. Balance sheet.
  d. Statement of changes in financial position.

11. Closing entries transfer nominal account balances to owners' equity. After closing, all nominal accounts should have zero balances.

12. A post-closing trial balance consists entirely of real accounts.

13. Accountants use reversing entries to simplify the subsequent recording of certain kinds of recurring transactions, such as interest payments.

APPENDIX A THE WORKSHEET

USING A WORKSHEET TO PREPARE ANNUAL STATEMENTS

A **worksheet** is a multicolumn sheet of paper that the accountant often uses to accumulate and organize the information required to prepare financial statements. Worksheets facilitate the preparation of financial statements by (1) providing a place where adjusting entries can be made informally before they are journalized and posted, (2) providing an orderly means whereby each account can be classified according to the financial statement in which it will appear, and (3) providing a

balancing mechanism that helps to uncover accounting errors. Worksheets are never published, because they are not formal financial statements.

In practice, many different worksheet formats exist. The format used in any given case depends on individual or company preferences.

A twelve-column worksheet for Eagle Company is shown in Exhibit 5–5. This worksheet includes the same basic data used earlier in the chapter. Eagle Com-

EXHIBIT 5-5

Eagle Company
WORKSHEET
For the Year Ended December 31, 1985

Accounts	Unadjusted Trial Balance Dr.	Cr.	Adjustments Dr.	Cr.	Adjusted Trial Balance Dr.	Cr.	Income Statement Dr.	Cr.	Retained Earnings Dr.	Cr.	Balance Sheet Dr.	Cr.
Cash	21,079				21,079						21,079	
Accounts receivable	60,000				60,000						60,000	
Allowance for doubtful accounts		500		(f) 2,615		3,115						3,115
Note receivable	10,000				10,000						10,000	
Merchandise inventory, Jan. 1, 1985	57,606			(g) 57,606								
Prepaid insurance	1,200			(d) 900	300						300	
Land	40,000				40,000						40,000	
Building	100,000				100,000						100,000	
Accumulated depreciation—building		10,000		(e) 2,000		12,000						12,000
Office equipment	120,000				120,000						120,000	
Accumulated depreciation—office equipment		24,000		(e) 12,000		36,000						36,000
Accounts payable		38,405				38,405						38,405
Unearned rent revenue		4,800	(c) 1,600			3,200						3,200
Long-term note payable		72,000				72,000						72,000
Common stock		50,000				50,000						50,000
Paid-in capital in excess of par value		65,000				65,000						65,000
Retained earnings, Jan. 1, 1985		34,215				34,215				34,215		
Sales		523,000				523,000		523,000				
Purchases	187,000			(g) 187,000								
Purchase returns		2,000	(g) 2,000									
Purchase allowances		2,500	(g) 2,500									
Purchase discounts		3,600	(g) 3,600									

Worksheet (for the year ended December 31, 1985)

Account	Trial Balance Dr	Adjustments Dr	Adjustments Cr	Adjusted Trial Balance Dr	Adjusted Trial Balance Cr	Income Statement Dr	Income Statement Cr	Balance Sheet Dr	Balance Sheet Cr
Transportation-in	7,250		(g) 7,250						
Sales salaries expense	78,000			78,000		78,000			
Advertising expense	24,000			24,000		24,000			
Transportation-out	6,000			6,000		6,000			
Miscellaneous selling expenses	5,141			5,141		5,141			
Officers' salaries expense	76,000			76,000		76,000			
Professional services	23,000			23,000		23,000			
Utilities expense	8,244			8,244		8,244			
Miscellaneous administrative expenses	5,500			5,500		5,500			
	830,020	830,020							
Interest receivable		(a) 600		600				600	
Interest revenue			(a) 600		600		600		
Interest expense		(b) 1,800		1,800		1,800			
Interest payable			(b) 1,800		1,800				1,800
Rent revenue			(c) 1,600		1,600		1,600		
Insurance expense		(d) 900		900		900			
Depreciation expense—building		(e) 12,000		12,000		12,000			
Depreciation expense—office equipment		(e) 2,000		2,000		2,000			
Bad-debts expense		(f) 2,615		2,615		2,615			
Merchandise inventory, Dec. 31, 1985		(g) 43,756		43,756				43,756	
Cost of goods sold		(g) 200,000		200,000		200,000			
		273,371	273,371	840,935	840,935	445,200	525,200		
Income tax expense		(h) 38,400		38,400		38,400			
Income tax payable			(h) 38,400		38,400				38,400
		311,771	311,771	879,335	879,335				
Net income						41,600			41,600
						525,200	525,200		
Retained earnings, Dec. 31, 1985								75,815	75,815
								75,815	75,815
								395,735	395,735

pany's worksheet consists of six pairs of amount columns. Sometimes accountants reduce the worksheet's size by eliminating the adjusted trial balance columns or by combining the retained earnings and balance sheet columns. The financial statement balances, of course, are not affected by worksheet size. Eagle Company's worksheet has no columns for the statement of changes in financial position. Preparing this statement may require a separate worksheet, which we explain in Chapter 23.

The steps required to prepare the worksheet are described below.

1. Enter the unadjusted trial balance by using the first pair of amount columns and determine that the columns balance.

2. Enter all adjusting entries, except income taxes, in the adjustments columns. Then subtotal these columns to determine that they balance. The adjusting entries are identified by small letters (a–g) and are presented in the order in which they are discussed in the chapter. Note that when an adjustment requires an account that is not listed in the unadjusted trial balance, a new account is listed below the unadjusted trial balance totals. When a worksheet is used, the adjusting entries are usually made informally in the adjustments columns *before* they are journalized and posted. In this way errors can often be found and corrected before entering the formal accounting records.

3. Determine the adjusted account balances by combining the unadjusted trial balance amounts with the adjustments amounts. Extend the adjusted balances in the adjusted trial balance columns. Then subtotal these columns and determine that they balance.

4. Extend each debit account balance in the adjusted trial balance to the debit column of the financial statement in which the balance will appear. Similarly, extend each credit account balance to the credit column of the financial statement in which the balance will appear.

5. Subtotal the income statement columns. The difference between the columns is the *pretax* income or loss for the period. For Eagle Company the difference is $80,000 ($525,200 − $445,200), and it represents pretax income.

6. Compute the Income Tax Expense by applying the appropriate income tax rate to the pretax income. The Income Tax Expense for Eagle Company is $80,000 × .48 = $38,400.

7. Enter the income tax accrual in the adjustments columns. Then extend the Income Tax Expense balance to the debit column of the adjusted trial balance and of the income statement. Extend the Income Tax Payable balance to the credit column of the adjusted trial balance and of the balance sheet. Totals may now be derived for the adjustments columns and for the adjusted trial balance columns.

8. Enter net income in the income statement debit column to balance the two income statement columns. The balancing figure is also entered in the Retained Earnings credit column.

9. Subtotal the Retained Earnings columns and enter the balance, which is ending retained earnings, in the Retained Earnings debit column and the balance sheet credit column.

10. Total the balance sheet columns and determine that they balance.

Eagle Company's financial statements may now be prepared directly from the worksheet. These statements would be identical to those illustrated in the chapter. After the statements are prepared, the adjusting entries are journalized and posted on the basis of information shown in the adjustments columns of the worksheet. To complete the accounting cycle, the accountant would close the nominal accounts as illustrated in the chapter. Finally, the accountant *may* prepare a post-closing trial balance as well as reversing entries.

USING A WORKSHEET TO PREPARE INTERIM STATEMENTS

Most companies formally prepare adjusting and closing entries only at the end of each fiscal year. Nevertheless, companies typically desire interim (e.g., monthly or quarterly) financial statements in addition to annual statements. A worksheet similar to the one for Eagle Company is often used to help prepare interim statements. At the end of each interim period, the accountant enters the necessary adjustments on the worksheet and does not formally record them in journals or ledgers. Adjustments shown on the year-end worksheet then pertain to the entire year; these amounts are journalized and posted to the accounts in the general ledger.

Since the balance sheet represents financial position at a point in time, the accountant obtains information about assets and equities directly from the balance sheet columns of an interim worksheet. On the other hand, revenue and expense amounts that appear on an interim worksheet are cumulative since the beginning of the fiscal year. Therefore, to determine revenues and expenses associated with a particular interim period, the accountant must subtract revenues and expenses attributable to previous interim periods from the corresponding amounts shown on the worksheet. To illustrate, assume that a company closes its books each December 31. To prepare an income statement for March, the accountant must subtract the revenues and expenses for January and February from the corresponding amounts shown on the March 31 worksheet. Similarly, to prepare an income statement for the second quarter, the accountant must subtract the revenues and expenses for the first quarter from the corresponding amounts shown on the June 30 worksheet. Like the income statement, the retained earnings statement pertains to a certain period of time. It therefore is typically prepared in the manner of the income statement.

APPENDIX B SPECIAL JOURNALS

Throughout this book we use a general journal format to illustrate the initial recording of transactions. Using this format deemphasizes certain procedural details and enables us to illustrate more clearly how to apply basic accounting concepts and principles. In practice, most businesses have several special journals in addition to a general journal. Special journals typically process most of a company's transactions. The purpose of this appendix is to review some of the more commonly encountered types of special journals.

A **special journal** is used to initially record a single type of transaction that often recurs. A company may create a special journal to handle virtually any kind of routine transaction. When a company uses special journals, it still needs a general journal to record transactions that do not fit the intended purpose of one of its special journals. Typically, adjusting entries, correcting entries, closing entries, reversing entries (if used), and entries for transactions that occur infrequently, such as the sale of common stock in exchange for land, are recorded in the general journal.

What advantages does a business gain by using special journals? First of all, special journals save time in journalizing and posting transactions. When journalizing, there is no need to rewrite account titles; when posting, transaction *totals* rather than individual amounts may be transferred to general ledger accounts. By simplifying the journalizing and posting requirements for routine transactions, special journals tend to reduce the number of errors made. Moreover, errors are easier to pinpoint once they have occurred.

Another important reason that companies use special journals is to permit a division of labor within the accounting department. Instead of several people attempting to use the general journal simultaneously, certain individuals can assume responsibility for one or more special journals. This often enables the company to better use the services of persons with limited education or experience in bookkeeping or accounting. Such separation of duties also strengthens the company's internal control system.

There are many types and formats of special journals, and each business must determine what it needs based on the nature of its transactions. The types and formats presented below are for illustrative purposes only.

SALES JOURNAL

The sales journal is used to record all *credit* sales of merchandise. It is therefore a chronological listing of a company's credit sales. For a company that makes five thousand credit sales a month, use of a sales journal relieves the company of (1) recording five thousand general journal entries debiting Accounts Receivable and crediting Sales, and (2) posting these entries individually to the general ledger. A sales invoice or sales ticket typically initiates an entry in a sales journal.

An abbreviated sales journal of Star-Bright, Inc., is presented in Exhibit 5–6. Special journals are normally arranged in columns. Star-Bright's sales journal contains five columns. We assume in the illustration that the company's credit terms are 2/10, n/30.[11] If credit

---

[11]In other words, a customer who pays within 10 days after the invoice date may deduct 2% from the invoice price; a customer who does not pay within the 10-day discount period must pay the gross invoice amount within 30 days after the invoice date.

EXHIBIT 5–6
Sales Journal

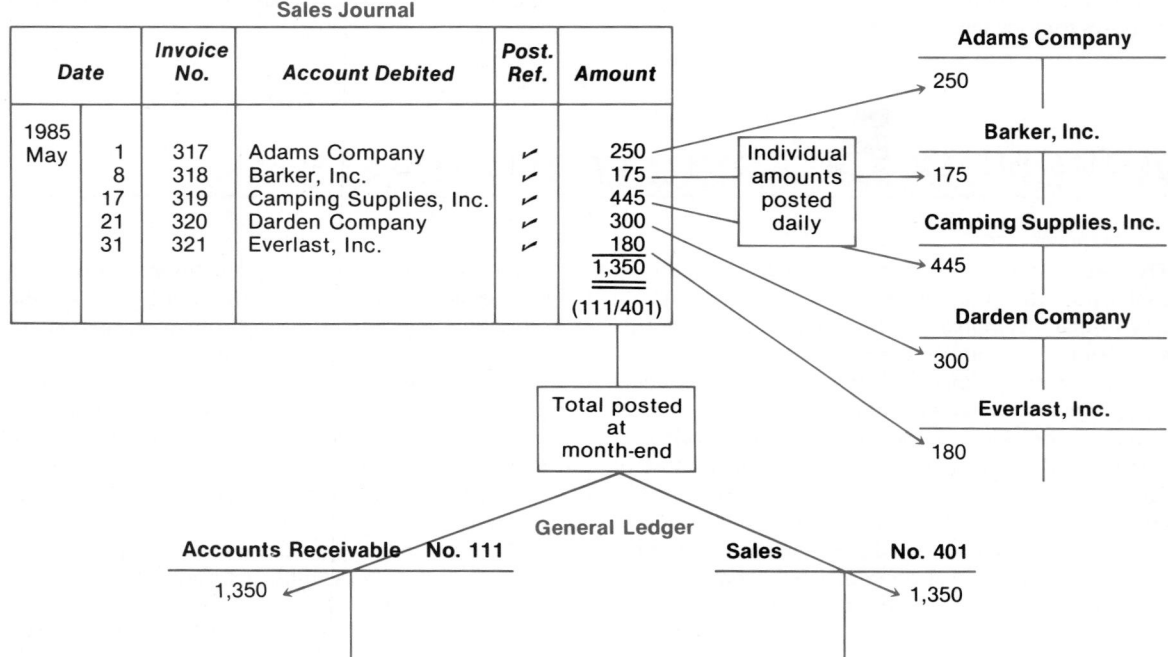

terms varied by customer, a journal column could easily be added to record the terms of each sale.

The process of posting from a sales journal is depicted by the arrows. Individual amounts in the sales journal are posted daily as debits to the appropriate accounts in the accounts receivable subsidiary ledger. Daily posting helps provide the company with up-to-date credit records, and it facilitates the billing process. The check marks in the posting reference column indicate that individual accounts have been posted. At the end of each month, the amount column *total* is posted in the general ledger as a debit to the Accounts Receivable control account and a credit to Sales. The notation (111/401) at the bottom of the amount column indicates that general ledger accounts bearing these numbers have been posted. Note that if each sale were recorded in the general journal instead of the sales journal, each debit and credit would have to be separately posted to the general ledger. This would be time-consuming and expensive. As the sales journal illustrates, posting any journal involves making equal debits and credits in the general ledger. Moreover, the sum of the debits (or credits) posted to subsidiary ledger accounts should equal the amount posted as a debit (or credit) to the related control account.

CASH RECEIPTS JOURNAL

The cash receipts journal is used to record all cash receipts, including those resulting from cash sales. Star-Bright's cash receipts journal, illustrated in Exhibit 5–7, consists of nine columns. Five of these columns are used to record amounts. The following posting features of the cash receipts journal are noteworthy:

1. Column *totals* for cash, sales discounts, and sales are posted at the end of each month. Individual

EXHIBIT 5-7
Cash Receipts Journal

Cash Receipts Journal

Date		Account Credited	Explanation	Post. Ref.	Cash Debit	Sales Discounts Debit	Accounts Receivable Credit	Sales Credit	Sundry Accounts Credit
1985 May	3	Sales	Cash sales		500			500	
	11	Adams Company	Payment in full	✓	245	5	250		
	14	Notes Payable	90-day, 10% loan from City National Bank	211	2,000				2,000
	27	Barker, Inc.	Payment in full	✓	175		175		
	31	Darden Company	Payment in full	✓	294	6	300		
					3,214	11	725	500	2,000
					(101)	(402)	(111)	(401)	(X)

Total debits = $3,225   Total credits = $3,225

amounts in these columns are not posted. The account numbers posted are inserted parenthetically at the bottom of these columns to indicate that posting has occurred.

2. The term "sundry accounts" means various individual accounts. Therefore, sundry accounts are posted *individually*. Their total is not posted. The account number 211 in the posting reference column indicates that the notes payable account has been posted. The (X) notation at the bottom of the sundry accounts column signifies that the column

total is not posted.

3. Amounts in the accounts receivable column are posted *individually and in total*. Individual amounts, referenced by the check marks, are posted daily as credits to the customer accounts in the accounts receivable subsidiary ledger. The column total is posted at the end of the month as a credit to the Accounts Receivable control account in the general ledger. The notation (111) at the bottom of the column indicates that the column total has been posted.

EXHIBIT 5-8
Purchases Journal

Purchases Journal

Date		Account Credited	Invoice Date	Terms	Post. Ref.	Amount
1985 May	1	Modern Supply Company	Apr. 29	2/10, n/30	✓	200
	16	Dresser, Inc.	May 15	2/10, n/60	✓	550
	18	Office Products Distributors	May 16	n/30	✓	450
	24	Ebenezer, Inc.	May 23	1/10, n/30	✓	196
	31	Wilson Manufacturing Company	May 29	2/10, n/30	✓	254
						1,650
						(501/201)

EXHIBIT 5–9
Cash Payments Journal

Date	Check No.	Account Debited	Explanation	Post. Ref.	Cash Credit	Purchase Discounts Credit	Accounts Payable Debit	Purchases Debit	Sundry Accounts Debit
1985 May 2	477	Purchases	Cash purchases		300			300	
8	478	Modern Supply Company	Payment in full	✓	196	4	200		
12	479	Prepaid Insurance	Fire insurance policy	131	450				450
25	480	Dresser, Inc.	Payment in full	✓	539	11	550		
31	481	Advertising	WACK Radio Station	517	250				250
					1,735	15	750	300	700
					(101)	(502)	(201)	(501)	(X)

Total credits = $1,750

Total debits = $1,750

PURCHASES JOURNAL

Some companies use a purchases journal to record *all credit purchases;* others use it to record only *credit purchases of merchandise.* A purchase invoice normally initiates each entry in a purchases journal. Star-Bright's purchases journal, illustrated in Exhibit 5–8, consists of six columns; its purpose is confined to recording credit acquisitions of merchandise. If the company wanted to record all credit acquisitions in its purchases journal, it would have to add columns to record items such as supplies and equipment.

Individual amounts in the purchases journal are posted daily as credits to the appropriate accounts in the accounts payable subsidiary ledger. The check marks in the posting reference column indicate that individual accounts have been posted. The column *total* is posted in the general ledger at the end of each month as a debit to the Purchases account and a credit to the Accounts Payable control account. The notation (501/201) at the bottom of the amount column indicates that the monthly posting has occurred.

CASH PAYMENTS JOURNAL

The cash payments journal is used to record all cash payments, including those resulting from cash purchases. Star-Bright's cash payments journal, illustrated in Exhibit 5–9, consists of ten columns; five of these are amount columns. Significant posting features in the cash payments journal are described below:

1. Column *totals* for cash, purchase discounts, and purchases are posted at the end of each month. Individual amounts in these columns are not posted. The account numbers posted are inserted parenthetically at the bottom of these columns to indicate that posting has occurred.
2. Amounts in the sundry accounts column are posted *individually.* The total of these amounts is not posted. The account numbers 131 and 517 in the posting reference column indicate postings made to the Prepaid Insurance and Advertising Expense accounts, respectively. The (X) notation at the bottom of the sundry accounts column signifies that the column total is not posted.
3. Amounts in the accounts payable column are posted *individually and in total.* Individual amounts, referenced by the check marks, are posted daily as debits to the supplier accounts in the accounts payable subsidiary ledger. The column total is posted at the end of the month as a debit to the Accounts Payable control account in

the general ledger. The (201) notation at the bottom of the column indicates that the column total has been posted.

OTHER SPECIAL JOURNALS

To avoid repetition, we have confined our illustrations of special journals to four common types. It is important to remember, however, that companies may use other types.

For example, many companies use a voucher system to help control cash payments. With this system, a voucher is prepared for each transaction that requires a cash payment. A **voucher** is a business paper containing detailed information about a liability and its payment. Each voucher is recorded in a journal called a **voucher register.** This journal is similar to an expanded purchases journal and thus takes the place of the purchases journal. Checks are drawn only in payment of approved vouchers. A journal called the **check register,** which is merely a modified cash payments journal, replaces the cash payments journal in a voucher system.

A **payroll register** is a widely used journal for recording payroll information. A **sales returns and allowances journal** and a **purchases returns and allowances journal** are often used by companies that have many such transactions.

QUESTIONS

5–1 Describe the purpose of the accounting cycle and list in sequence the steps involved.

5–2 Describe the nature of source documents and list five examples.

5–3 State whether the normal balance in each of the following accounts is debit or credit:
[a] Prepaid Insurance
[b] Wages Expense
[c] Sales
[d] Accounts Payable
[e] Gain on Sale of Land
[f] Accumulated Depreciation
[g] Discount on Bonds Payable
[h] Common Stock
[i] Dividends
[j] Loss on Sale of Investments
[k] Sales Returns

5–4 Indicate whether a debit increases or decreases the balance in each of the following types of accounts:
[a] Revenue
[b] Liability
[c] Expense
[d] Asset
[e] Owners' Equity

5–5 What is a journal? Why might a company want to use several special journals?

5–6 Give an example of a general journal entry to record each of the following:
[a] An increase in an asset and an increase in a liability.
[b] A decrease in a liability and a decrease in an asset.
[c] An increase in an expense and a decrease in an asset.
[d] An increase in an asset and an increase in a revenue.
[e] An increase in an asset and an increase in owners' equity.

5–7 What is a general ledger? Why is posting to general ledger accounts necessary?

5–8 Distinguish between real, nominal, and mixed accounts.

5–9 What is a subsidiary ledger and a control account? Why might a company want to use several subsidiary ledgers?

5–10 What are the major purposes of an unadjusted trial balance? Does an unadjusted trial balance prove that no errors have been made during an accounting period?

5–11 Distinguish between the cash basis and the accrual basis of accounting.

5–12 What are adjusting entries? Why are they needed?

5–13 A company recently made an adjusting entry to record depreciation and one to record accrued interest on notes receivable. Briefly explain how each entry relates to an accounting principle.

5–14 Briefly describe how a practicing accountant accumulates the information needed to prepare adjusting entries.

5–15 Distinguish between accruals and deferrals.

5–16 Give two examples of adjusting entries that are based on the revenue realization principle. Give two examples that are based on the matching principle.

5–17 Give an example that illustrates two ways in which an adjusting entry applicable to Prepaid Rent might be recorded.

5–18 Give an example that illustrates two ways in which an adjusting entry applicable to Unearned Subscriptions Revenue might be recorded.

5–19 What are the purposes of the Cost of Goods Sold adjustment assuming the use of a periodic inventory system?

5–20 What are the major purposes of an adjusted trial balance?

5–21 Why is the income tax adjustment usually the final adjusting entry prepared?

5–22 Why are the following statements usually prepared in the sequence indicated?
[a] Income statement
[b] Statement of retained earnings
[c] Balance sheet

5–23 What are closing entries? Why are they needed?

5–24 What types of accounts appear on a post-closing trial balance?

5–25 What are reversing entries? Why are these entries often desirable?

5–26 What is a worksheet? How does a worksheet facilitate the preparation of financial statements?

CASES

C5–1 Generally accepted accounting principles require the use of accruals and deferrals in the determination of income.

Instructions

[a] How does accrual accounting affect the determination of income? Include in your discussion what constitutes an accrual and a deferral, and give appropriate examples of each.
[b] Compare accrual accounting and cash accounting.

(AICPA adapted)

C5–2 Firms prepare annual financial statements for internal management and for distribution to outside parties. In addition, many firms prepare some type of summary reports or statements quarterly, monthly, and weekly for both internal use and external distribution. The frequency of reporting may affect the preparation cost and the objectivity of the reports or statements.

Instructions

[a] Explain why the accounting period appropriate for internal and external reporting for most firms is one year.
[b] Explain in general terms why summary reports or statements are prepared for reporting periods less than one year. Give an example why (1) internal management and (2) an outside party may want reports or statements which cover a shorter period.
[c] Adjustments to the accounting records are made when summary reports or statements are prepared annually, quarterly, or monthly.
   [1] Explain why these adjustments are needed.
   [2] Cite specific examples of adjustments that would have to be made to the accounting records.
[d] How is the objectivity of financial information in summary reports or statements affected when more frequent reports are prepared?

(CMA adapted)

EXERCISES

E5–1   A list of accounts appears below:
[1]   Cash.
[2]   Common Stock.
[3]   Accounts Payable.
[4]   Salaries Expense.
[5]   Sales.
[6]   Dividends.
[7]   Accumulated Depreciation.
[8]   Unearned Subscriptions Revenue.
[9]   Dividends Payable.
[10] Discount on Bonds Payable.
[11] Paid-In Capital in Excess of Par Value.
[12] Allowance for Doubtful Accounts.
[13] Treasury Stock.
[14] Goodwill.
[15] Retained Earnings.
[16] Retained Earnings Appropriated for Plant Expansion.
[17] Interest Earned.
[18] Advertising.
[19] Prepaid Insurance.
[20] Investment in Bonds.

Instructions

State whether the balance in each account is increased by a debit or a credit.

E5–2 During July, Holmes Company engaged in the transactions listed below. The company uses a periodic inventory system.

July 1 Purchased on account merchandise costing $20,000.
  1 Paid $800 of freight charges in connection with merchandise referred to above.
  6 Purchased land for $10,000.
  10 Sold merchandise for cash of $5,000.
  14 Borrowed $8,000 by signing a 90-day, 10% note.
  16 Sold 1,000 shares of $10 par value common stock for $15,000.
  19 Sold merchandise on account for $7,000.
  23 Sold land that was purchased on July 6. The cash selling price was $11,000.
  27 Received a $1,000, 90-day, 12% note from a customer on account.
  31 Paid July salaries of $4,000.

Instructions

Record the above transactions in general journal form.

E5–3 MARYCO, Inc., recorded the following journal entries during its first month of operations:

Aug.	1	Cash	8,000	
		Common Stock		8,000
	3	Prepaid Rent	1,200	
		Cash		1,200
	4	Equipment	5,000	
		Cash		5,000
	11	Purchases	4,000	
		Accounts Payable		4,000
	13	Accounts Receivable	6,000	
		Sales		6,000
	24	Cash	2,000	
		Accounts Receivable		2,000
	27	Accounts Payable	1,000	
		Cash		1,000
	31	Salaries Expense	1,400	
		Advertising Expense	200	
		Utilities Expense	100	
		Cash		1,700

Instructions

[a] Set up a general ledger and post each journal entry to appropriate T accounts.
[b] Prepare an unadjusted trial balance on August 31.

E5–4 A trial balance for Will Hurt, M.D., at the end of his first month in practice is presented below:

Will Hurt, M.D.
TRIAL BALANCE
October 31, 1985

Account	Dr.	Cr.
Cash	$ 9,560	
Supplies	11,730	
Prepaid rent	6,800	
Equipment	58,000	
Accounts payable		$ 9,640
Will Hurt, capital		75,000
Revenues from patients		5,450
Salaries expense	1,300	
Utilities expense	400	
Miscellaneous office expenses	300	
Will Hurt, drawing	2,000	
	$90,090	$90,090

Additional Information

Upon examining Hurt's books, you discover the following:
[1] Cash of $50 received from a patient had been recorded as $500. (Hurt renders services on a cash basis only.)
[2] A $964 purchase of supplies on account had been recorded as $694.
[3] A $2,000 purchase of equipment had been charged to prepaid rent.
[4] A $677 payment on account had been recorded as $767.

Instructions

[a] Journalize the necessary correcting entries on October 31. (Do not record adjusting entries.)
[b] Prepare a corrected trial balance.

E5–5 The following information pertains to Carr Company:
[1] On November 1, 1985, the company received a $5,000, 90-day, 10% note from a customer.
[2] Accrued wages as of December 31, 1985, amount to $1,236.
[3] On September 1, 1985, the company received $2,400 for rent paid in advance for six months on a warehouse that Carr Company leases to Moore Company. Carr Company credited a nominal account.
[4] On October 1, 1985, the company paid $1,800 for

a one-year fire insurance policy and debited a nominal account.

[5] The company computes $11,000 of depreciation for 1985.

[6] The company estimates $2,235 of bad debts for 1985.

Instructions

[a] Prepare the necessary adjusting journal entries on December 31, 1985, the end of the company's annual accounting period.

[b] Assuming that Carr Company wants to make reversals, prepare the reversing entries that are appropriate on January 1, 1986.

E5–6   Joe Yu owns the Yu Hair Styling Center. A trial balance for the business at the end of its first year of operations appears below:

Yu Hair Styling Center
TRIAL BALANCE
December 31, 1985

Account	Dr.	Cr.
Cash	$13,000	
Supplies	14,000	
Prepaid rent	12,000	
Equipment	25,000	
Accounts payable		$ 3,000
Note payable		20,000
Joe Yu, capital		7,000
Styling revenues		56,500
Advertising expense	7,000	
Salaries expense	13,000	
Utilities expense	2,500	
	$86,500	$86,500

Additional information

[1] A physical count reveals that supplies costing $4,000 are on hand at year-end.

[2] Rent on the shop was paid in advance for two years on January 1, 1985.

[3] The equipment was acquired on January 1, 1985. It has an estimated useful life of 10 years and no expected salvage value. Yu elects to use the straight-line depreciation method.

[4] The note payable relates to a one-year, 15% loan obtained from First National Bank on April 1, 1985.

[5] Salaries earned by employees but unpaid to them at year-end amount of $1,000.

Instructions

Using the trial balance and the additional information

presented above, prepare the necessary adjusting entries in general journal form at December 31, 1985.

E5–7   The account balances for Garrett Company on December 31, 1985, are shown below. Each account has a normal balance.

Account	Balance
Transportation-out	$ 12,000
Merchandise inventory, Dec. 31	47,000
Purchase discounts	3,000
Sales returns	11,000
Transportation-in	8,000
Sales discounts	7,000
Merchandise inventory, Jan. 1	40,000
Purchase returns	6,000
Sales allowances	9,000
Purchase allowances	4,000
Purchases	210,000
Sales	357,000

Instructions

[a] Prepare a schedule showing the computation of cost of goods sold for 1985.

[b] Calculate the amount of gross margin for 1985.

E5–8   The adjusted trial balance of Garner Company on December 31, 1985, appears below:

Account	Dr.	Cr.
Cash	$ 22,000	
Accounts receivable	50,000	
Allowance for doubtful accounts		$ 3,000
Note receivable (short-term)	10,000	
Merchandise inventory	20,000	
Prepaid rent (for one year)	6,000	
Equipment	100,000	
Accumulated depreciation		15,000
Accounts payable		23,000
Salaries payable		2,000
Income tax payable		22,000
Common stock ($10 par value; 6,000 shares)		60,000
Paid-in capital in excess of par value		40,000
Retained earnings		50,000
Sales		195,000
Interest revenue		1,000
Cost of goods sold	80,000	
Salaries expense	20,000	
Rent expense	6,000	

Advertising expense	17,000	
Depreciation expense	10,000	
Bad-debts expense	3,000	
Miscellaneous expense	5,000	
Income tax expense	22,000	
Dividends	40,000	
	$411,000	$411,000

Instructions

Prepare an income statement, a statement of retained earnings, and a balance sheet for 1985.

E5–9   Refer to the information presented for Garner Company in E5–8.

Instructions

[a] Journalize the closing entries on December 31, 1985.
[b] Prepare a post-closing trial balance.

E5–10 Listed below are the adjusted account balances of Craig Company on December 31, 1985. Each account has a normal balance.

Account	Balance
Accounts payable	$ 25,000
Accounts receivable	30,000
Accumulated depreciation—equipment	20,000
Advertising expense	8,000
Allowance for doubtful accounts	1,000
Bad-debts expense	1,000
Cash	8,000
Common stock	40,000
Cost of goods sold	105,000
Depreciation expense—equipment	10,000
Equipment	100,000
Income tax expense	16,000
Interest expense	6,000
Interest payable	3,000
Merchandise inventory	50,000
Note payable	30,000
Prepaid rent	4,000
Rent expense	12,000
Retained earnings	53,000
Salaries expense	20,000
Sales	208,000
Sales returns	3,000
Transportation-out	5,000
Utilities expense	2,000

Instructions

Prepare closing entries in general journal form at December 31, 1985.

E5–11 Ten adjusting entries are presented below:

[1]	Rent Revenue	7,000	
	Unearned Rent Revenue		7,000
[2]	Interest Receivable	2,000	
	Interest Revenue		2,000
[3]	Depreciation Expense	10,000	
	Accumulated Depreciation		10,000
[4]	Unearned Advertising Revenues	4,000	
	Advertising Revenues		4,000
[5]	Bad Debts Expense	1,000	
	Allowance for Doubtful Accounts		1,000
[6]	Salaries Expense	3,000	
	Salaries Payable		3,000
[7]	Supplies	2,500	
	Supplies Expense		2,500
[8]	Insurance Expense	3,500	
	Prepaid Insurance		3,500
[9]	Utilities Expense	500	
	Utilities Payable		500
[10]	Merchandise Inventory, Dec. 31	6,000	
	Cost of Goods Sold	30,000	
	Merchandise Inventory, Jan. 1		5,000
	Purchases		31,000

Instructions

List the numbers of the adjusting entries that a company may appropriately reverse.

E5–12 Owenby Publishing Company made the following adjusting entries on December 31, 1985:

[1]	Rent Receivable	1,000	
	Rent Revenue		1,000
[2]	Insurance Expense	700	
	Prepaid Insurance		700
[3]	Property Tax Expense	1,500	
	Property Tax Payable		1,500
[4]	Subscriptions Revenue	2,400	
	Unearned Subscriptions Revenue		2,400
[5]	Supplies Expense	850	
	Supplies		850
[6]	Amortization Expense	1,700	
	Copyrights		1,700
[7]	Bad Debts Expense	650	
	Allowance for Doubtful Accounts		650
[8]	Advertising Revenue	1,100	
	Unearned Advertising Revenue		1,100

Instructions

Assuming that the company wants to make reversals, prepare all reversing journal entries that are appropriate on January 1, 1986.

E5–13 On November 1, 1984, Briar Company issued at par value $100,000 of 20-year, 12% bonds with interest payable semiannually on April 30 and October 31. The company uses a calendar-year accounting period.

Instructions

Record all appropriate journal entries using a table similar to the one shown below.

	Assumption	
Event	Briar Company makes reversing entries for accrued interest.	Briar Company does not make reversing entries for accrued interest.
12/31/84 adjusting entry to record accrued interest		
12/31/84 entry to close accrued interest		
1/1/85 reversing entry applicable to accrued interest		
4/30/85 entry to record payment of interest		
10/31/85 entry to record payment of interest		

E5–14 A recent comparative balance sheet of Raymond Company revealed the following information:

	Balance	
Explanation	12/31/84	12/31/85
Interest receivable	$100	$300
Consulting fees receivable	800	200
Prepaid insurance	500	800
Supplies	400	100
Salaries payable	500	900
Utilities payable	300	100
Unearned subscriptions revenue	800	900
Unearned advertising revenue	600	400

Selected information about the company's 1985 cash receipts and disbursements appears below:

Explanation	Cash Receipts	Cash Disbursements
Interest	$1,800	
Consulting fees	3,000	
Insurance		$2,500
Supplies		1,200
Salaries		3,400
Utilities		1,000
Subscriptions	4,000	
Advertising	3,500	

Instructions

Compute each of the following income statement amounts for 1985 under the accrual basis of accounting: (1) interest revenue, (2) consulting fees earned, (3) insurance expense, (4) supplies expense, (5) salaries expense, (6) utilities expense, (7) subscriptions revenue, and (8) advertising revenue.

E5–15 (Appendix B) Beckner Company uses the following journals: sales, sales returns and allowances, purchases, purchases returns and allowances, cash receipts, cash payments, and general. The following events occurred during December:
[1]   Paid accounts payable.
[2]   Purchased merchandise on account.
[3]   Collected cash from customers on account.
[4]   Made credit sales.
[5]   Issued common stock for legal services received.
[6]   Paid December rent.
[7]   Returned defective merchandise to suppliers and received credit.
[8]   Borrowed money from bank.
[9]   Purchased merchandise for cash.
[10] Received defective merchandise from customers

and granted credit.

[11] Discovered that a cash purchase of equipment in October had inadvertently been charged to the Land account at that time.

[12] Received payments made by customers on account.

[13] Made cash sales.

[14] Computed annual depreciation.

Instructions

Indicate the journal in which the company should record each of the above events.

E5–16 (Appendix B) Presented below are several transactions of Sharp Company that occurred during December 1985. The company uses a periodic inventory system and a calendar-year accounting period.

Dec. 1 Purchased merchandise on account from Prince Company. The cost was $210.

4 Sold merchandise to Larry Gordon for $205 cash.

5 Paid Engle Company $320 on account.

8 Borrowed $10,000 from City & County Bank and signed one-year, 12% note.

12 Sold merchandise on account for $1,200 to Hoffmann, Inc.

13 Signed a two-year, 13% note for $20,000 in exchange for land purchased from Windsor Corporation.

17 Received $175 on account from Payne Company.

20 The company discovered that a $5,000 purchase of equipment on November 14, 1985, had inadvertently been entered in the Land account.

22 Purchased merchandise from Moore Company for $340 cash.

30 Paid a utility bill of $235 for services received in December.

31 Estimated depreciation for the year at $3,500.

31 Determined that $400 of prepaid insurance had expired during 1985.

Instructions

[a] Record the above transactions in general journal form.

[b] Assume that Sharp Company uses the following journals: sales, cash receipts, purchases, cash payments, and general. Indicate where the company should record each of the above transactions.

E5–17 (Appendix B)   Perlen Company began operations on May 1 and transacted the following credit sales during May:

Date	Customer	Invoice No.	Amount
May 1	Macy Company	101	$325
8	Gresham, Inc.	102	140
16	Epling Enterprises	103	675
21	Davis Company	104	460
31	Cathey, Inc.	105	200

Instructions

[a] Set up a sales journal and record each of the above transactions.

[b] Post the journal entries to appropriate general and subsidiary ledger accounts.

E5–18 (Appendix A)   Presented below is the unadjusted trial balance of Curlee Consultants, Inc., on December 31, 1985, the end of the company's annual accounting period:

Account	Dr.	Cr.
Cash	$ 16,000	
Note receivable	5,000	
Prepaid rent	12,000	
Equipment	100,000	
Accumulated depreciation		$ 20,000
Accounts payable		7,000
Common stock		30,000
Retained earnings		15,000
Consulting revenues		175,000
Salaries expense	90,000	
Travel expense	10,000	
Utilities expense	6,000	
Dividends	8,000	
	$247,000	$247,000

Additional Information

This information is available on December 31:

[1] Accrued interest on note receivable is $250.

[2] Seventy-five percent of the prepaid rent shown above has expired.

[3] Depreciation expense for 1985 is $12,000.

[4] The December utility bill of $550 has not been paid or recorded.

[5] The income tax rate is 40%.

Instructions

Prepare a twelve-column worksheet (as shown in Appendix A).

P5–1 Pannell Retail Company started business on June 1. The company uses a periodic inventory system and records purchases of merchandise at gross amounts. The following transactions occurred during June:

June 1 Issued 1,000 shares of $10 par value common stock for $50,000.

2 Borrowed $10,000 by signing a one-year, 10% note.

3 Purchased the following for cash:

	Cost
Land	$10,000
Building	30,000
Equipment	5,000
Total	$45,000

4 Purchased a three-year fire insurance policy for $3,600. (Debit an asset account.)

5 Purchased office supplies for $4,000. (Debit an asset account.)

6 Received merchandise and an invoice dated June 5 from Black, Inc., for $6,000. Credit terms are 2/10, n/30.

6 Paid freight of $300 on merchandise received from Black, Inc.

8 Sold merchandise on credit to McKeever Company, for $10,000. Terms are n/30.

10 Purchased merchandise from Nee, Inc., for cash of $4,000.

12 Returned $600 of defective merchandise to Nee, Inc., and received a cash refund.

14 Sold merchandise for cash of $5,000.

15 Paid Black, Inc., the amount of the June 5 invoice, less the discount.

17 Received merchandise returned by McKeever Company. Granted credit of $1,000.

20 Received one-year's rent of $4,800 in advance on a small office. (Credit a liability account.)

23 Received merchandise and an invoice dated June 21 from Small, Inc., for $7,500. Credit terms are 1/10, n/60.

25 Sold merchandise on credit to James Company for $3,000. Terms are n/30.

29 Received payment in full from McKeever Company. (See June 8 and June 17 transactions.)

30 Paid the following June expenses:

Salaries	$1,900
Advertising	600
Utilities	500
Total	$3,000

Instructions

[a] Record each of the June transactions in a general journal.

[b] Post each journal entry to appropriate general ledger accounts.

[c] Prepare an unadjusted trial balance on June 30.

P5–2 Presented below is an unadjusted trial balance for Thomas Company on November 30:

Thomas Company
UNADJUSTED TRIAL BALANCE
November 30

Account	Dr.	Cr.
Cash	$ 14,000	
Accounts receivable	21,000	
Allowance for doubtful accounts		$ 1,000
Notes receivable	7,000	
Merchandise inventory, Jan. 1	15,000	
Prepaid insurance	3,000	
Prepaid rent	8,000	
Investment in Ace Company stock	20,000	
Equipment	60,000	
Accumulated depreciation		10,000
Accounts payable		11,000
Note payable		5,000
Common stock		40,000
Retained earnings		61,000
Sales		110,000
Sales returns	4,000	
Purchases	55,000	
Purchase returns		2,000
Purchase discounts		1,000
Transportation-in	5,000	
Salaries expense	20,000	
Advertising expense	6,000	
Utilities expense	3,000	
Interest expense	–0–	
	$241,000	$241,000

Additional Information

The following transactions occurred during December:

Dec. 1 Sold the investment in Ace Company stock for $12,000.

3 Received a $2,000, 90-day, 13% note from a customer on account.

4 Purchased merchandise for cash of $2,500.

6 Paid the $5,000 note listed above. The note, which matured on Dec. 6, was for 120 days at 12% interest.

7 Paid $8,000 of accounts payable. Cash discounts of 2% were taken.

8 Returned $400 of defective merchandise purchased on Dec. 4 and received a cash refund.

9 Collected $13,000 from customers on account.

11 Wrote off uncollectible accounts receivable of $800.

13 Purchased merchandise on account for $3,000. Terms are n/30.

13 Paid freight of $200 on merchandise purchased.

16 Received merchandise returned by a customer. Granted credit of $700.

18 Sold merchandise on account for $6,000.

22 Made cash sales of $5,000.

23 Purchased a one-year insurance policy for $3,600.

28 Purchased $10,000 of equipment for use in the business. Paid $2,000 cash and signed an $8,000, one-year, 12% note.

31 Paid the following expenses:

Salaries	$1,800
Advertising	600
Utilities	300
Total	$2,700

Instructions

[a] Record each of the December transactions in a general journal. (Do not record adjusting entries.)
[b] Set up general ledger accounts and enter the opening balances for December. Post each journal entry to appropriate accounts.
[c] Prepare an unadjusted trial balance on December 31.

P5-3 The Geological Consulting Company began operations on December 1, 1985. The following transactions occurred during the first month:

Dec. 1 Sold 400 shares of $100 par value common stock for $40,000 cash.

1 Purchased equipment for $30,000 cash.

(The equipment has an estimated useful life of 10 years and no expected salvage value. The company plans to use straight-line depreciation.)

1 Purchased a one-year insurance policy for $2,400. (The company records all prepaid amounts in *real*, i.e., balance sheet, accounts.)

1 Paid $4,800 office rent in advance for one year.

2 Purchased on account supplies costing $8,000.

10 Received $2,000 from a client for services rendered.

16 Borrowed $5,000 from City Bank and signed a 90-day, 12% note.

30 Paid half of the amount owed for the purchase of supplies on December 2.

31 Billed clients $4,000 for services rendered during December.

31 Paid $500 for advertisements run in the local newspaper during December.

31 Paid the utility bill for $180 for December.

31 Paid December salaries of $1,800.

Instructions

[a] Record the December transactions in general journal form.
[b] Post the journal entries to general ledger T accounts.
[c] Prepare an unadjusted trial balance at December 31.
[d] Journalize and post all necessary adjusting entries. (A count reveals that supplies costing $7,000 are on hand December 31. The income tax rate is 40%.)
[e] Prepare an adjusted trial balance.
[f] Prepare an income statement, a statement of retained earnings, and a balance sheet for December.
[g] Journalize and post closing entries.
[h] Prepare a post-closing trial balance.

P5-4 Presented below is the post-closing trial balance of Kyle Corporation on December 31, 1984:

Kyle Corporation
POST-CLOSING TRIAL BALANCE
December 31, 1984

Account	Dr.	Cr.
Cash	$ 12,000	
Accounts receivable	18,000	
Allowance for doubtful accounts		$ 900
Merchandise inventory	23,000	

Prepaid rent	24,000	
Equipment	50,000	
Accumulated depreciation		10,000
Accounts payable		21,000
Income tax payable		11,000
Common stock		40,000
Retained earnings		44,100
	$127,000	$127,000

Following is a summary of transactions that occurred during 1985:

[1] Purchased merchandise on account for $85,000. (The company uses a periodic inventory system.)

[2] Paid transportation charges of $4,600 on merchandise purchased.

[3] Sold merchandise as follows:

On account	$145,000
For cash	51,600
Total	$196,600

[4] Collected $136,000 of accounts receivable.

[5] Wrote off uncollectible accounts of $850.

[6] Paid the income tax liability that was reported on December 31, 1984.

[7] Paid $78,000 on accounts payable.

[8] Paid the following expenses:

Salaries	$21,000
Advertising	12,000
Utilities	8,000
Telephone and telegraph	4,400
Total	$45,400

[9] Declared dividends of $20,000. The company will pay the dividends early in 1986.

Additional Information

This information is available on December 31, 1985:

[1] The company estimates that 1% of credit sales made during 1985 will never be collected.

[2] A physical count reveals that merchandise costing $19,000 is on hand at year-end.

[3] One-half of the prepaid rent as of December 31, 1984, expired during 1985.

[4] The equipment has an estimated useful life of 10 years and no expected salvage value. The company uses straight-line depreciation.

[5] The income tax rate for 1985 is 40%.

Instructions

[a] Set up general ledger T accounts for the post-closing trial balance accounts and for the following accounts: Dividends Payable, Sales, Cost of Goods Sold, Purchases, Transportation-In, Salaries Expense, Advertising Expense, Utilities Expense, Telephone and Telegraph, Bad Debts Expense, Rent Expense, Depreciation Expense, Income Tax Expense, Dividends, and Income Summary. Enter the opening balances for 1985 in the ledger T accounts.

[b] Journalize the 1985 transactions in the order in which they are presented above. Use the number at the left of each transaction to indicate the date.

[c] Post the journal entries to the general ledger T accounts.

[d] Prepare an unadjusted trial balance.

[e] Journalize and post adjusting entries.

[f] Prepare an adjusted trial balance.

[g] Prepare an income statement, a statement of retained earnings, and a balance sheet.

[h] Journalize and post closing entries.

[i] Prepare a post-closing trial balance.

P5–5 Midtown Newspaper Company recorded the following transactions during its 1985 calendar-year accounting period:

Apr. 1   Received $18,000 from customers for subscriptions paid in advance for one year.

May 1   Paid $2,400 for a one-year fire insurance policy.

Sept. 1   Received $9,000 from a tenant paying rent in advance for six months.

Nov. 1   Paid $6,000 to a local radio station for advertising time. The station agreed to broadcast two ads each month for 12 months, beginning in November.

Instructions

[a] Journalize the above transactions assuming that the company enters in *real* (balance sheet) accounts the amounts that are received or paid in advance.

[b] Under the assumption stated in [a], journalize the necessary adjustments on December 31, 1985.

[c] Assuming that the company uses reversing entries, journalize the reversals that are appropriate for the adjusting entries in [b].

[d] Journalize the above transactions asuming that the company enters in *nominal* (income statement) accounts the amounts that are received or paid in advance.

[e] Under the assumption stated in [d], journalize the necessary adjustments on December 31, 1985.

[f] Assuming that the company uses reversing entries, journalize the reversals that are appropriate for the adjusting entries in [e].

P5-6 The following information pertains to Larry's Laundry Service on June 30, 1985, the end of the company's fiscal year:

[1] On March 1, 1985, the company purchased a three-year fire insurance policy for $3,600. A *real* (balance sheet) account was debited.

[2] The company's estimate of bad debts for the fiscal year is $1,500.

[3] On October 1, 1984, the company received $3,000 for rent received in advance for one year for storage space that it leases to Hill Company. A nominal account was credited.

[4] The company's estimate of depreciation for the year is $10,000.

[5] On April 1, 1985, the company paid $600 to the local newspaper for advertising space and debited a nominal account. The newspaper agreed to publish four ads each month for one year, beginning in April.

[6] On May 31, 1985, the company borrowed $5,000 from Citizens' Bank and signed a 120-day, 12% note.

[7] Employees have earned wages of $780 that the company has not paid or recorded as of June 30, 1985.

[8] On December 1, 1984, the company purchased at par value ten $1,000, 15%, 20-year bonds of Tenco, Inc. The bonds pay interest semiannually on May 31 and November 30.

[9] On March 1, 1985, the company received $6,000 from customers for diaper service that the company will provide for one year, beginning on that date. A *real* (balance sheet) account was credited.

[10] Property taxes owed and unrecorded as of June 30 total $1,450.

Instructions

[a] Prepare adjusting entries in general journal form at June 30, 1985.

[b] Assuming that the company wants to make reversing entries, identify the adjusting entries that it may appropriately reverse.

P5-7 Presented below is the trial balance of Marvin's Merchandising Mart at December 31, 1985, the end of the company's annual accounting period:

Account	Dr.	Cr.
Cash	$ 24,500	
Accounts receivable	25,000	
Allowance for doubtful accounts		150
Merchandise inventory, Jan. 1	53,000	

	Dr.	Cr.
Investment in DEBTCO, Inc., bonds	30,000	
Land	47,000	
Building	200,000	
Accumulated depreciation—building		$ 22,500
Equipment	80,000	
Accumulated depreciation—equipment		24,000
Accounts payable		19,000
Note payable		50,000
Common stock		100,000
Retained earnings, Jan. 1		174,528
Sales		452,000
Interest revenue		2,700
Rent revenue		9,000
Purchases	280,380	
Purchase returns and allowances		11,180
Transportation-in	10,000	
Salaries expense	86,200	
Rent expense	21,000	
Utilities expense	7,678	
	$864,908	$864,908

Additional Information

[1] Ninety percent of 1985 sales were made on credit. The company estimates that 0.5% of credit sales will never be collected.

[2] A physical count reveals that merchandising costing $61,000 is on hand at year-end.

[3] On March 17, 1984, the company purchased thirty $1,000, 12%, 20-year bonds of DEBTCO, Inc. The bonds pay interest semiannually on March 31 and September 30.

[4] The company computes annual depreciation as follows:

Building	2.5% of cost
Equipment	5% of cost

[5] The note payable relates to a 90-day, 10% loan obtained from Last National Bank on October 20, 1985.

[6] The company has rented a portion of its building to Robin's Retail Store since July 1, 1983. The rent is $6,000 per year, payable by Robin's in advance each July 1.

[7] As of December 31, employees had earned salaries of $2,300 that the company had not paid or recorded.

[8] The company has rented a warehouse from the Safe Storage Company since October 1, 1984. The rent is $12,000 per year, payable by Marvin's in advance each October 1.

[9]   The utility bill for December 1985 is $547. As of December 31, this amount had not been paid or recorded.

[10] The company has determined that income taxes for the year are $27,856. This amount will be paid in 1986.

Instructions

[a] Prepare the adjusting entries in general journal form on December 31, 1985.

[b] Identify the broad accounting principle that underlies each adjusting entry. (*Hint:* Review the principles discussed in Chapter 2.)

[c] Assuming that Marvin's wants to make reversing entries, identify the adjusting entries that the company may appropriately reverse.

P5–8   Presented below is the trial balance of Wishart Corporation at December 31, 1985, the end of the company's annual accounting period:

Wishart Corporation
TRIAL BALANCE
December 31, 1985

Account	Dr.	Cr.
Cash	$ 12,925	
Accounts receivable	24,000	
Allowance for doubtful accounts		$ 300
Note receivable	4,000	
Merchandise inventory, Jan. 1	10,000	
Supplies	1,300	
Prepaid insurance	3,000	
Land	70,000	
Building	60,000	
Accumulated depreciation—building		6,000
Equipment	20,000	
Accumulated depreciation—equipment		4,000
Goodwill	9,375	
Accounts payable		8,600
Unearned rent revenue		7,200
Bonds payable (20-year, 10%)		100,000
Common stock		50,000
Paid-in capital in excess of par value		10,000
Retained earnings, Jan. 1		15,000
Sales		200,000
Purchases	95,000	
Purchase returns		3,000
Transportation-in	8,000	

Salaries expense	30,000	
Travel expense	7,000	
Advertising expense	16,000	
Transportation-out	10,000	
Telephone expense	5,000	
Utilities expense	11,000	
Interest expense	7,500	
	$404,100	$404,100

Additional Information

[1]   The company makes all its sales on credit. It estimates that 1% of sales made during 1985 will never be collected.

[2]   The note receivable is a 90-day, 12% note taken from a customer on December 1, 1985.

[3]   A physical inventory indicates that merchandise costing $30,000 is on hand December 31, 1985.

[4]   A count reveals that supplies costing $450 are on hand December 31, 1985.

[5]   The prepaid insurance account pertains to a three-year fire policy purchased on July 1, 1984, for $3600.

[6]   The following information concerns the building and equipment:

	Estimated Useful Life in Years	Estimated Salvage Value	Depreciation Method
Building	40	None	Straight line
Equipment	20	None	Straight line

[7]   The company recorded $10,000 of goodwill when it acquired a competing firm on October 1, 1983. Wishart Corporation uses the straight-line method of amortizing goodwill.

[8]   On July 1, 1985, the company leased a portion of its building to Candor Company and received a check for $7,200 for one year's rent paid in advance.

[9]   The company issued the bonds payable at par value on October 1, 1982. The bonds pay interest semiannually on March 31 and September 30.

[10] Salaries earned but unpaid to employees as of year-end totaled $2,100.

[11] On December 17, 1985, the company paid $1,400 for advertising time on a local television show that will be broadcast on January 12, 1986.

[12] A utility bill of $1,100 for December 1985 has been received but not yet recorded or paid.

[13] Property taxes that accrued during 1985 amounted to $3,100.

[14] The company determines that income tax expense for 1985 is $8,700. This amount will be paid in 1986.

Instructions

[a] Prepare adjusting entries in general journal form at December 31, 1985.

[b] Identify the broad accounting principle that underlies each adjusting entry. (*Hint:* Review the principles discussed in Chapter 2.)

[c] Identify adjusting entries that Wishart Corporation may appropriately reverse, assuming that the company wants to make reversing entries.

P5–9 Presented below are trial balances of Weaver Company at December 31, 1985:

| | | | Trial Balance | | |
| Account | Unadjusted | | | Adjusted | |
	Dr.	Cr.		Dr.	Cr.
Cash	$ 14,000			$ 14,000	
Accounts receivable	22,000			22,000	
Allowance for doubtful accounts	56				$ 2,000
Note receivable	10,000			10,000	
Interest receivable				1,000	
Supplies	6,000			3,209	
Merchandise inventory, Jan. 1	20,000				
Merchandise inventory, Dec. 31				25,000	
Prepaid rent	18,000			6,000	
Equipment	120,000			120,000	
Accumulated depreciation— equipment		$ 30,000			40,000
Accounts payable		12,000			12,000
Salaries payable					1,000
Income tax payable					16,000
Common stock		40,000			40,000
Retained earnings		67,265			67,265
Sales		205,631			205,631
Interest revenue					1,000
Cost of goods sold				102,840	
Purchases	107,840				
Salaries expense	29,000			30,000	
Miscellaneous expenses	8,000			8,000	
Supplies expense				2,791	
Rent expense				12,000	
Depreciation expense				10,000	
Bad-debts expense				2,056	
Income tax expense				16,000	
	$354,896	$354,896		$384,896	$384,896

Instructions

Based on the above information, *reconstruct* the adjusting journal entries that Weaver Company made on December 31, 1985.

P5–10 At the end of 1985, ABC Company failed to record the adjusting entries indicated below:

[1] Depreciation of plant assets.

[2] Accrued interest on note receivable.

[3] Earned portion on one year's rent that had been received by ABC in advance on July 1, 1985, and recorded in a liability account.

[4] Accrued wages owed to employees.

[5] Estimate of bad debts.

[6] Unexpired portion of a one-year fire insurance policy that ABC paid for on September 1, 1985, and charged to a nominal account.

Instructions

Prepare a table similar to the one shown below and indicate the effect of each error on the 1985 financial statement elements shown. Use the following code in marking your answers: O = overstated, U = understated, and NE = no effect. Assume that each error is independent of the others.

Error	Total Revenues	Total Expenses	Net Income	Total Assets	Total Liabilities	Total Stockholders' Equity
Example: Failed to record accrued interest on note payable.	**NE**	**U**	**O**	**NE**	**U**	**O**
[1]						
[2]						
[3]						
[4]						
[5]						
[6]						

P5–11 (Appendix B) Tressler Company uses the following journals: purchases, sales, cash receipts, cash payments, and general. The company uses a periodic inventory system and makes all credit sales subject to terms of 2/10, n/30. The following transactions occurred during February:

Feb. 1 Borrowed $10,000 from First National Bank and signed a 90-day, 10% note.

3 Purchased merchandise from Wright Company for cash of $1,000. Issued check no. 816.

4 Received merchandise and an invoice dated February 2 from Finch Company for $2,000. Terms are 2/10, n/30.

8 Sold merchandise on credit to Miller, Inc., for $3,000. Issued invoice no. 982.

12 Issued check no. 817 to Finch Company in payment of February 2 invoice, less the discount.

14 Purchased equipment for use in the business by issuing a $7,000, one-year, 12% note.

18 Received a check from Miller, Inc., in payment of February 8 invoice, less the discount.

20 Issued 500 shares of $1 par value common stock for legal services received during February. The fair value of the legal services is $2,500.

22 Sold merchandise to Meehan Company for cash of $1,500.

24 Received merchandise and an invoice dated February 23 from Snider, Inc., for $3,600. Terms are 1/10, n/30.

26 Sold merchandise on credit to Keeling Company for $4,800. Issued invoice no. 983.

28 Paid the February utility bill of $400. Issued check no. 818.

Instructions

Record each of the February transactions in the appropriate journal.

P5–12 (Appendix B) Maloy Company began operations on May 1, 1985. The company uses a periodic inventory system. All credit sales are subject to terms of 2/10, n/30. The following transactions occurred during May:

May 1 Issued 10,000 shares of $5 par value common stock for $50,000.

2 Issued 1,000 shares of $5 par value common stock for land valued at $5,000.

3 Purchased a building for $30,000. Check no.

101 was issued.

5 Received merchandise and an invoice dated May 2 from Brown Company for $2,000. Terms are 1/15, n/30.

7 Sold merchandise on credit to Albert Company for $3,000. Invoice no. 1001 was issued.

9 Purchased merchandise from Dantley Company for cash of $1,500. Check no. 102 was issued.

11 Sold merchandise on credit to Hadler Company for $2,500. Invoice no. 1002 was issued.

12 Received merchandise and an invoice dated May 10 from Gatlin Company for $4,000. Terms are 2/10, n/60.

13 Sold merchandise to Finger Company for cash of $5,500.

15 Issued check no. 103 for $1,980 to Brown Company in payment of May 2 invoice, less the discount.

16 Received a check for $2,940 from Albert Company in payment of May 7 invoice, less the discount.

18 Received a check for $2,450 from Hadler Company in payment of May 11 invoice, less the discount.

19 Issued check no. 104 for $3,920 to Gatlin Company in payment of May 10 invoice, less the discount.

24 Received merchandise and an invoice dated May 23 from Early Company for $1,000. Terms are 2/10, n/30.

25 Sold merchandise on credit to Canton Company for $6,000. Invoice no. 1003 was issued.

28 Received merchandise and an invoice dated May 26 from Ison Company for $1,800. Terms are 3/15, n/30.

31 Sold merchandise on credit to Jasper Company for $2,800. Invoice no. 1004 was issued.

Instructions

[a] Record the transactions for May using the following journals (as shown in Appendix B): sales, purchases, cash receipts, cash payments, and general.

[b] Post the appropriate amounts in a general ledger and in accounts receivable and accounts payable subsidiary ledgers. Systematically number all accounts and use posting references.

[c] Prepare a trial balance on May 31.

[d] Reconcile the subsidiary ledgers with the appropriate control accounts.

P5–13 (Appendix A)   Henson Company has adopted a calendar-year accounting period. The company's unadjusted trial balance on December 31, 1985, appears below:

Account	Dr.	Cr.
Cash	$ 26,775	
Accounts receivable	30,000	
Allowance for doubtful accounts		225
Merchandise inventory, Jan. 1	42,000	
Investment in bonds (long-term)	20,000	
Land	52,000	
Building	100,000	
Accumulated depreciation—building		$ 25,000
Equipment	50,000	
Accumulated depreciation—equipment		15,000
Accounts payable		42,000
Common stock ($10 par value, 10,000 shares)		100,000
Retained earnings, Jan. 1		109,500
Sales		475,000
Interest revenue		1,500
Rent revenue		12,000
Purchases	305,000	
Purchase returns		12,000
Salaries expense	88,000	
Advertising expense	22,000	
Utilities expense	6,000	
Supplies expense	30,000	
Dividends	20,000	
	$792,000	$792,000

Additional Information

This information is available on December 31:

[1] The company estimates that bad debts expense for 1985 is $3,500.

[2] The December 31, 1985, merchandise inventory is $50,000.

[3] Unrecorded interest of $500 has accrued on the investment in bonds.

[4] The company estimates depreciation for 1985 as follows:

Building	$2,500
Equipment	$5,000

[5] One-fourth of the rent revenue shown above has *not* been earned as of December 31.
[6] Employees have earned salaries of $4,000 that the company has not paid or recorded.
[7] The cost of supplies on hand December 31 is $12,000.
[8] The income tax rate is 40%.

Instructions

[a] Enter the unadjusted trial balance on a twelve-column worksheet (as shown in Appendix A).
[b] Enter the adjusting entries on the worksheet.
[c] Complete the worksheet.
[d] Prepare an income statement, a statement of retained earnings, and a balance sheet.
[e] Record the adjusting and closing entries in the general journal.

P5–14 (Appendix A)   Presented below is the unadjusted trial balance of Graham, Inc. on December 31, 1985, the end of the company's annual accounting period:

Account	Dr.	Cr.
Cash	$ 14,500	
Accounts receivable	18,000	
Allowance for doubtful accounts		$ 300
Notes receivable (due in six months)	10,000	
Merchandise inventory, Jan. 1	23,000	
Prepaid insurance	4,800	
Land	40,000	
Building	50,000	
Accumulated depreciation—building		30,000
Equipment	20,000	
Accumulated depreciation— equipment		12,000
Accounts payable		11,000
Dividends payable		8,000
Unearned rent revenue		6,000
Common stock ($5 par value, 10,000 shares)		50,000
Retained earnings, Jan. 1		22,000
Sales		225,000
Purchases	123,000	
Transportation-in	7,000	
Salaries expense	34,000	
Advertising expense	8,000	
Utilities expense	4,000	
Dividends	8,000	
	$364,300	$364,300

Additional Information

This information is available on December 31:
[1] Accrued interest on notes receivable totals $500.
[2] Employees have earned salaries of $1,500 that the company has not paid or recorded.
[3] One-half of the unearned rent revenue shown above was earned during 1985.
[4] Three-fourths of the prepaid insurance shown above expired during 1985.
[5] Depreciation for 1985 is as follows:

Building	$2,000
Equipment	$4,000

[6] Bad-debts expense for 1985 is $900.
[7] The inventory on hand December 31 has a cost of $27,000.
[8] The income tax rate is 40%.

Instructions

[a] Enter the unadjusted trial balance on a twelve-column worksheet (as shown in Appendix A).
[b] Enter the adjusting entries on the worksheet.
[c] Complete the worksheet.
[d] Prepare an income statement, a statement of retained earnings, and a balance sheet.
[e] Record the adjusting and closing entries in the general journal.

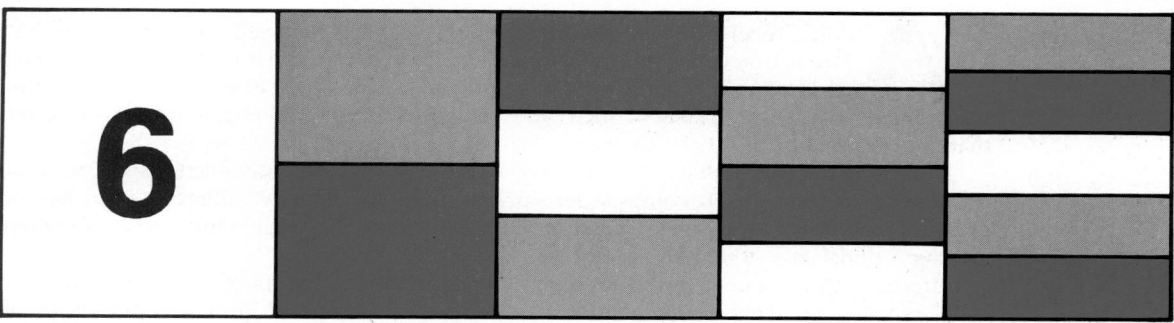

6

COMPOUND INTEREST CONCEPTS

Objectives

To discuss and illustrate the fundamentals of compound interest.

To distinguish clearly between simple and compound interest.

To apply compound interest concepts in deriving solutions to accounting problems.

To discuss and illustrate how to solve each of the following types of compound interest problems:

1. Amount and present value of a lump sum.
2. Amount and present value of an ordinary annuity.
3. Amount and present value of an annuity due.
4. Amount and present value of a deferred annuity.

A dollar received today is worth more than a dollar received one year from today. This is true even if we ignore inflation, because the dollar received today can be invested to earn a return. Thus, we could place $1.00 in a 6% savings account today and have $1.06 at the end of one year. Having $1.06 one year hence is obviously better than receiving only $1.00 at that time.

Money has been regarded as a valuable resource ever since scientists first discovered that it doesn't grow on trees. It comes as no surprise, then, that money cannot be used free of charge. Money has a time value, commonly called **interest,** that people must consider when making rational investment and credit decisions.

Interest is the cost of using money over time. From the standpoint of a borrower, interest is the excess money that is paid over the amount that was borrowed. From a lender's point of view, interest is the excess money that is received over the amount that was loaned. Because the value of money changes over time, cash inflows and outflows that occur at different points in time are not directly comparable. For this reason, they should not be lumped together for comparative purposes; instead, they should be compared as of a common point in time. We may choose to compare cash flows as of some future time. Usually, however, we compare cash flows as of the present time, because the present is the time within which we live and think.

To illustrate, assume that you have just decided to sell your wristwatch. Allen offers you $100, payable immediately, while Baker offers $103, to be paid in one year. Assuming that you can earn a 6% return on your money, which offer should you accept? Clearly, if we compare the alternatives as of one year hence, we find that Allen's offer is worth $106 ($100 × 1.06) to you, whereas Baker's offer is worth only $103. Making the comparison as of the present time, we find that Allen's offer is worth $100 while Baker's offer is worth less ($103 ÷ 1.06 = $97.17). In either case, we conclude that Allen's offer should be accepted. The important point to note is that, because money has a time value, we could not meaningfully compare the two offers until we determined the value of each offer as of a common point in time.

In this chapter we explain and illustrate the fundamentals of compound interest. In other words, we are concerned in this chapter with the time value of money. This topic has so many applications in business that it often is covered in several college courses, such as accounting, business finance, investments, economics, and mathematics. As a result, you may have been exposed to the concepts in this chapter in other courses. Readers of this textbook must acquire a working knowledge of compound interest concepts in order to understand many of the topics covered in subsequent chapters. Examples of these topics are accounting for certain notes receivable and notes payable under *Accounting Principles Board Opinion No. 21,* accounting for bonds as investments and liabilities, accounting for leases under *Financial Accounting Standards Board Statement No. 13,* accounting for pension plans under *APB Opinion No. 8,* accounting for sinking funds, and accounting for installment contracts. That money has a time value is clearly recognized in *APB Opinion No. 21,* a pronouncement that frequently requires accountants to estimate and record interest even though a long-term note may contain no stated interest rate.

In this chapter we are not concerned with changes in general purchasing power of money over time (inflation or deflation). We will compare various sums of money without regard to the ability of those sums to buy goods and services. Assuming a 6% interest rate, for example, the question of whether $1.00 today can buy more or fewer goods and services than can $1.06 one year hence is beyond the scope of this chapter.

SIMPLE VERSUS COMPOUND INTEREST

Interest is earned over a period of time. Therefore, a stated interest rate relates to a particular time period. Because interest is normally stated as an **annual percentage rate,** such as

8%, 10%, or 12%, we assume throughout the text that a stated interest rate is a rate *per year*, unless indicated otherwise.

There are two types of interest: simple and compound. **Simple interest** means that interest is earned only on the principal sum of money invested. The formula for simple interest is:

$$i = prt$$

where i = simple interest

p = principal sum of money

r = interest rate per unit of time

t = time expressed in units that correspond to the rate

If $1,500 is borrowed at 8% for one year, the simple interest is $1,500 × .08 × 1 = $120. If the same amount is borrowed for only six months, simple interest is $1,500 × .08 × ⁶⁄₁₂ = $60. Note that r and t must correspond with one another. If r is an annual rate, t must be expressed in years; if r is a monthly rate, t must be expressed in months; and so forth.

Simple interest is used in many short-term (less than one year) business transactions. Recall, for example, that we assumed simple interest in Chapter 5 when we illustrated adjusting entries for the accrual of interest on notes receivable and notes payable.

Compound interest means that interest is earned on the principal sum of money invested *and* on the interest accumulated. In other words, the principal earns interest and the accumulated interest earns interest. To illustrate, assume that $1,500 is invested for three years at 8%. A comparison of simple versus compound interest on this investment follows:

Simple Interest
$i = prt$ = $1,500 × .08 × 3 = $360 Accumulated amount at the end of three years is: $1,500 + $360 = $1,860

Compound Interest					
(A)	(B)	(C)	(D)	(E)	(F)
Year	Principal	Rate	Time	Compound Interest	Accumulated Amount (B + E)
1	$1,500.00 ×	.08 ×	1 =	$120.00	$1,620.00
2	1,620.00 ×	.08 ×	1 =	129.60	1,749.60
3	1,749.60 ×	.08 ×	1 =	139.97	1,889.57
			Total	$389.57	

Notice that with compound interest, the accumulated amount at the end of each year becomes the new principal sum on which interest is earned during the next year. Notice further that $29.57 ($389.57 − $360.00 or $1,889.57 − $1,860.00) of additional interest resulted from compound interest. This is the interest on prior interest accumulations, which can be verified as follows:

Year	Prior Interest Accumulation		Rate		Time		Interest on Prior Interest Accumulation
1	–0–*	×	.08	×	1	=	–0–
2	$120.00**	×	.08	×	1	=	$ 9.60
3	249.60†	×	.08	×	1	=	19.97
						Total	$29.57

*No interest was accumulated prior to Year 1.
**This is the $120.00 interest for Year 1.
†This is the $120.00 interest for Year 1 plus the $129.60 interest for Year 2.

Compound interest is used in most long-term (beyond one year) business transactions, and it is the primary focus of this chapter. Recall that interest is typically stated as an annual percentage rate. However, when compound interest is assumed, interest may be compounded (calculated and added to principal) for periods of less than one year. For example, interest may be compounded semiannually, quarterly, monthly, daily, or even continuously.[1] To avoid repetition, we make the customary assumption throughout the text that a stated annual interest rate is compounded annually, unless indicated otherwise.

BASIC CONCEPTS

The fundamental concepts underlying all compound interest problems are as follows:

1. **Present value (PV).** As the name implies, present value usually refers to a value at the present time (today). In a more general sense it can refer to a value at the beginning of any time span that is of concern.
2. **Future value (FV).** This usually refers to a value at some time in the future. More generally, future value can refer to a value at the end of any time period that is of concern.
3. **Interest rate (i).** This refers to a rate that corresponds to the length of each compounding period. This rate is computed by dividing the annual interest rate by the number of times a year interest is compounded. For example, if interest is stated at 8%, compounded annually (once per year), the interest rate is 8% per annual period (8% ÷ 1). If interest is stated at 8%, compounded semiannually (twice per year), the interest rate is 4% per semiannual period (8% ÷ 2). And if interest is stated at 8%, compounded quarterly (four times per year), the interest rate is 2% per quarterly period (8% ÷ 4).[2]
4. **Time periods (n).** This refers to the number of compounding periods. It may be computed by multiplying the number of years involved by the number of compounding periods in each

---

[1]Continuous compounding is accomplished using logarithms.

[2]The interest rate (i) is called a **stated**, or **nominal**, rate. Furthermore, the term **frequency of compounding** (usually denoted by the letter m) refers to the number of times a year interest is compounded.

It is worthwhile to note that whenever m is greater than 1, the effective or true rate of interest (r) on an investment is greater than the stated annual rate. The **effective rate** is the rate that, when compounded annually, generates the same annual interest as the stated annual rate does when compounded m times per year. The effective rate may be calculated using the following formula:

$$r = (1 + i)^m - 1$$

For example, if the stated annual rate is 8% compounded quarterly, the effective annual rate is:

$$\begin{aligned} r &= (1 + i)^m - 1 \\ &= (1 + .02)^4 - 1 \\ &= (1.02)^4 - 1 \\ &= 1.08243 - 1 \\ &= .08243 \\ &= 8.243\% \end{aligned}$$

year. For example, interest for three years, compounded semiannually, involves 6 (3 × 2) compounding periods. Likewise, interest for three years, compounded quarterly, involves 12 (3 × 4) compounding periods.

Using these four fundamental concepts, we can solve compound interest problems that occur in business.

Quite often, sketching the known components of a compound interest problem in the form of a **time diagram** aids in understanding the problem and in finding a solution. The four basic compound interest concepts, discussed above, are depicted in the following time diagram:

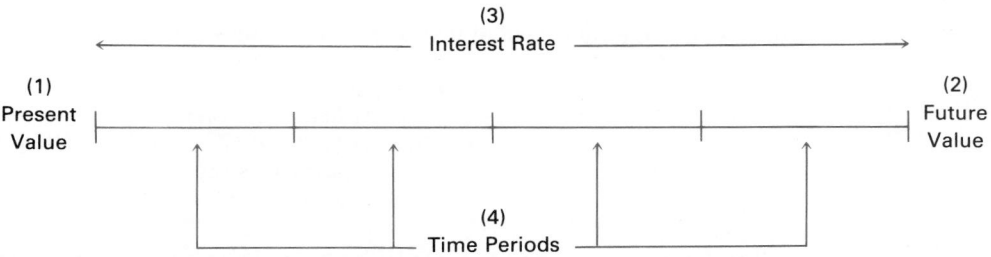

LUMP SUM PROBLEMS

Lump sum problems involve a single sum of money and generally fall into one of the following two categories:

1. Problems that focus on the future value of a lump sum of money that is left on deposit for a certain number of periods at a certain interest rate per period.
2. Problems that focus on the present value of a lump sum of money that is discounted for a certain number of periods at a certain interest rate per period.

Amount (Future Value) of a Lump Sum

In everyday conversation, the term "amount" refers to any amount, past, present, or future. In discussions of compound interest, amount refers only to a future value. The amount of a lump sum is therefore the future value to which the sum will accumulate if left on deposit for a certain number of periods at a certain interest rate per period. For example, in the earlier discussion of simple and compound interest, $1,889.57 (a future value) is the amount to which $1,500 (a lump sum of money) will accumulate if left on deposit for three years at 8% compounded annually. The solution is illustrated in the time diagram in Exhibit 6–1. Note in Exhibit 6–1 that the arrow points to the right, the direction of the future value.

The period-by-period approach used earlier to calculate future value ($1,889.57) is somewhat cumbersome, and it would be even more so in a problem involving more than

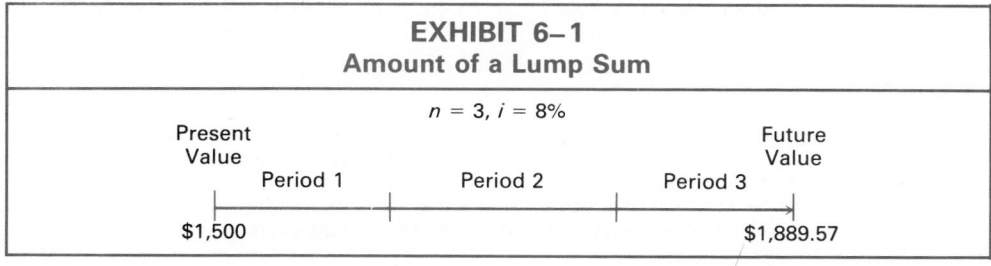

EXHIBIT 6–1
Amount of a Lump Sum

three periods. To simplify the calculations required to solve such a problem, the following formula is often applied:

$$FV = PV (1 + i)^n$$

where FV = future value of a lump sum

PV = present value (principal sum) of a lump sum

i = interest rate per compounding period

n = number of compounding periods

Applying this formula, we find that $1,889.57 is indeed the future value:

$$
\begin{aligned}
FV &= PV (1 + i)^n \\
&= \$1,500 (1 + .08)^3 \\
&= \$1,500 (1.08)^3 \\
&= \$1,500 (1.25971) \\
&= \$1,889.57
\end{aligned}
$$

The formula $FV = PV (1 + i)^n$ is the basic compound interest formula. Note that it consists of four variables: $FV, PV, i,$ and n. If we know the values of any three, we can solve for the fourth using algebra.

Focus your attention for a moment on the $(1 + i)^n$ part of the basic compound interest formula. Because of the frequent need to apply compound interest concepts in the business world, tables have been published that provide solutions for $(1 + i)^n$ for many combinations of i and n. We shall refer to each of these solutions as a **future value factor (fvf)**. Table 6–1 at the end of this chapter contains future value factors for most of the commonly encountered i and n values.[3] It can be used to save time in solving problems that involve the amount of a lump sum.

Table 6–1 is entitled "Amount of 1" because it gives the amounts (future values) to which 1 (such as one dollar, one peso, or one mark) will accumulate if left on deposit for n periods at i compound interest. If we know the amount to which 1 will accumulate, we can find the amount to which any lump sum will accumulate by simply multiplying the lump sum by the amount to which 1 will accumulate. Note that the table consists of rows of compounding periods (n) and columns of interest rates (i). A future value factor is located at the intersection of each row and column.[4] For example, the future value factor of $n = 5$ and $i = 10\%$ is 1.61051. To illustrate the process of finding a table factor, Exhibit 6–2 presents a portion of Table 6–1 with the factor circled for $n = 5$ and $i = 10\%$ (1.61051).

To really understand the solutions to compound interest problems, you should remember how Table 6–1 was constructed—that is, by solving $(1 + i)^n$ for different combinations of i and n values. With this knowledge, you should not be surprised to find that future value factors increase with each increase in i or n.

Since we know that $FV = PV (1 + i)^n$ and $(1 + i)^n = fvf$, we can now state:

$$FV = PV \cdot fvf_{\overline{n}|i} \tag{6–1}$$

---

[3]Table 6–1, as well as the other tables at the end of the chapter, are partial. In practice, more comprehensive tables are widely available. Of course, any compound interest table can be extended by using the formula on which the table is based.

[4]Notice that each table factor is rounded to five decimal places. In practice, tables rounded to ten places are often used when dealing with extremely large numbers in order to minimize the effects of rounding.

EXHIBIT 6–2
Finding the Future Value Factor of $n = 5$, $i = 10\%$
Using Table 6–1 (Amount of 1)

Number of Periods (n)	Interest Rate (i)		
	8%	**10%**	**12%**
1	1.08000	1.10000	1.12000
2	1.16640	1.21000	1.25440
3	1.25971	1.33100	1.40493
4	1.36049	1.46410	1.57352
5	1.46933	(1.61051)	1.76234
6	1.58687	1.77156	1.97382

---

where FV = future value of a lump sum

PV = present value (principal sum) of a lump sum

$fvf_{\overline{n}|i}$ = future value factor (from Table 6–1) for the relevant n and i

The expression $fvf_{\overline{n}|i}$ is read as "*fvf* sub n at i" or "*fvf* angle n at i." When setting up an equation to solve a compound interest problem, it is helpful to put in the values for n and i. This helps to ensure that you will locate and use the correct table factor.

Recall that we have determined, using both a period-by-period approach and a formula approach, that $1,889.57 is the future value of $1,500 deposited for 3 years at 8% compounded annually. Now we can use Equation 6–1 and Table 6–1 to implement a third approach to solving the problem. This approach is the easiest of all, because some of the calculations have already been performed, and the results appear in Table 6–1. First, note in Table 6–1 that the *fvf* for $n = 3$ and $i = 8\%$ is 1.25971. Now we can say:

$$FV = PV \cdot fvf_{\overline{n}|i}$$
$$= \$1,500 \cdot fvf_{\overline{3}|8\%}$$
$$= \$1,500 \,(1.25971)$$
$$= \$1,889.57$$

Because of the wide availability of compound interest tables and the computational ease and time savings they offer, we emphasize a table-based solution to the problems in this chapter.

Accounting Examples

Problem 1.   At the beginning of Year 1, Florida Electric Coil Company deposited $50,000 in a special building fund that earns 8% interest compounded quarterly. How much cash will be in the fund at the end of Year 10?

Solution 1.   In this problem we know the present value ($50,000), the interest rate per period (8% ÷ 4 = 2%), and the number of periods (4 × 10 = 40). We are asked to solve for the future value, which we can do conveniently with Equation 6–1 and Table 6–1:

$$FV = PV \cdot fvf_{\overline{n}|i}$$
$$= \$50,000 \cdot fvf_{\overline{40}|2\%}$$
$$= \$50,000 \,(2.20804)$$
$$= \$110,402$$

Problem 2. To keep things relatively simple, let's just modify the information in Problem 1. Assume that Florida Electric Coil Company wants to accumulate $110,402 for the purchase of a new building. If at the beginning of Year 1 the company deposited $50,000 in a special building fund that earns 8% interest compounded quarterly, how many years will it take for the fund to accumulate to $110,402?

Solution 2. We know the present value ($50,000), the future value ($110,402), and the interest rate per period (8% ÷ 4 = 2%). We are asked to solve for the number of years, which we can easily do using Equation 6–1 and Table 6–1. Since $FV = PV \cdot fvf_{\overline{n}|i}$, we can divide both sides of the equation by PV and find:

$$fvf_{\overline{n}|i} = \frac{FV}{PV}$$

$$fvf_{\overline{n}|2\%} = \frac{\$110,402}{\$50,000}$$

$$= 2.20804$$

Now that we know the future value factor and the interest rate per period, we simply run our finger down the 2% column of Table 6–1 until we find 2.20804. Since 2.20804 is found at $n = 40$, we conclude that it will take *10 years* (40 quarterly interest periods ÷ 4) to accumulate $110,402. If we had not found the number 2.20804 in the 2% column of Table 6–1, we could have approximated our answer using linear interpolation, a procedure explained later in the chapter.

Problem 3. Suppose that the problem were phrased this way. Florida Electric Coil Company wants to accumulate $110,402 for the purchase of a new building. If at the beginning of Year 1 the company deposited $50,000 in a special building fund in which interest is compounded quarterly, what annual rate of interest is required for the $50,000 deposit to accumulate to $110,402 at the end of Year 10?

Solution 3. We follow the same approach taken in Problem 2, except that we look for the future value factor of 2.20804 in Table 6–1 along the row in which $n = 40$ (10 years × 4 compounding periods per year). Because 2.20804 is in the 2% column, we conclude that the required annual rate of interest is 8% (2% × 4).

Present Value of a Lump Sum

Determining the present value of a lump sum is the inverse of determining the amount of a lump sum. Instead of moving forward in time using the process of accumulation to determine a future value, we move backward in time using a process called **discounting** to determine a present value. For example, suppose that we want to know the present value of $1,889.57 to be received or paid in three years discounted at 8% compounded annually. We could determine the answer by preparing a decumulation table similar to the compound interest accumulation table presented earlier in the chapter. Instead of going forward in time, we would go backward, and instead of multiplying each year's principal by 1.08, we would multiply by 1/1.08 (which is the same as dividing by 1.08), as shown on page 209.

The time diagram shown in Exhibit 6–3 illustrates the solution to the problem. The arrow in the diagram points to the left, which is the direction of the present value.

That $1,500 is the present value (the decumulated amount at the beginning of Year 1) is no surprise, because this problem was used earlier to explain the amount of a lump sum. Preparing decumulation tables is tedious and time consuming. Fortunately, there are easier ways to solve the problem.

Remember that the basic compound interest formula states that $FV = PV(1 + i)^n$. If we divide both sides of this equation by $(1 + i)^n$, we get:

$$PV = \frac{FV}{(1 + i)^n}$$

Compound Discount					
(A)	(B)	(C)	(D)	(E)	(F)
Year	Principal	Discount Rate	Time	Decumulated Amount	Compound Discount (B − E)
3	$1,889.57 ×	$\frac{1}{1.08}$ ×	1 =	$1,749.60	$139.97
2	1,749.60 ×	$\frac{1}{1.08}$ ×	1 =	1,620.00	129.60
1	1,620.00 ×	$\frac{1}{1.08}$ ×	1 =	1,500.00	120.00
				Total	$389.57

We can now apply this formula to the problem and determine that $1,500 is indeed the present value:

$$PV = \frac{FV}{(1 + i)^n}$$
$$= \frac{\$1,889.57}{(1.08)^3}$$
$$= \frac{\$1,889.57}{1.25971}$$
$$= \$1,500$$

We can easily rewrite the above formula as follows:

$$PV = FV \cdot \frac{1}{(1 + i)^n}$$

The $1/(1 + i)^n$ part of the equation is simply the reciprocal (the inverse) of the formula used to calculate the amount of 1. Tables are widely available that provide solutions for $1/(1 + i)^n$ for combinations of i and n. We shall refer to each of these solutions as a **present value factor** (*pvf*). A present value factor is simply the reciprocal of the future value factor for a given i and n. Table 6–2 at the end of the chapter contains present value factors for many i and n combinations. Given the formula used to construct the table, you should not be surprised that present value factors decrease with an increase in n or i. Note that the table is

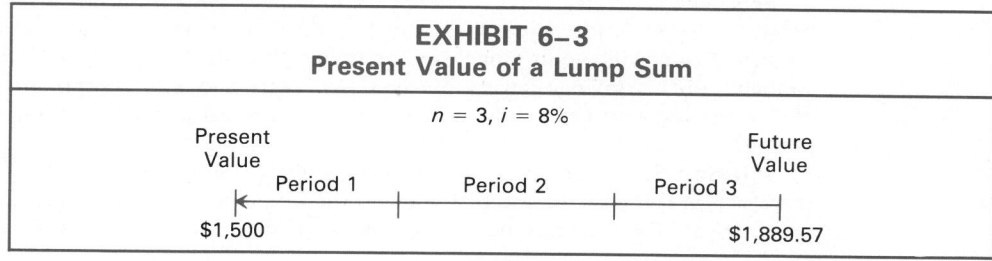

EXHIBIT 6–3
Present Value of a Lump Sum

$n = 3, i = 8\%$

Present Value

Period 1   Period 2   Period 3

Future Value

$1,500 $1,889.57

entitled "Present Value of 1." If we know the present value of 1 for a certain i and n, we can easily compute the present value of any lump sum by multiplying the lump sum by the present value of 1.

Since we know that $PV = FV \cdot 1/(1 + i)^n$ and $1/(1 + i)^n = pvf$, we can now state:

$$PV = FV \cdot pvf_{\overline{n}|\,i} \tag{6--2}$$

where PV = present value (principal sum) of
        a lump sum

FV = future value of a lump sum

$pvf_{\overline{n}|\,i}$ = present value factor (from Table
        6--2) for the relevant n and i

Equation 6--2 saves time in solving problems for the present value of a lump sum. To illustrate its application to the example problem, we first find in Table 6--2 that the pvf for $n = 3$ and $i = 8\%$ is .79383. Now we can say:

$$
\begin{aligned}
PV &= FV \cdot pvf_{\overline{n}|\,i} \\
&= \$1,889.57 \cdot pvf_{\overline{3}|\,8\%} \\
&= \$1,889.57\,(.79383) \\
&= \$1,500
\end{aligned}
$$

Accounting Examples

Problem 4.   What is the value at the beginning of Year 1 of a noninterest-bearing note that has a maturity value of $10,000 at the end of Year 4? Assume that the market rate of interest for similar notes is 8% compounded annually.

Solution 4.   In this problem we know the future value (the $10,000 maturity value), the interest rate per period (8%), and the number of periods (4). We are asked to solve for the present value, which we can conveniently do using Equation 6--2 and Table 6--2:

$$
\begin{aligned}
PV &= FV \cdot pvf_{\overline{n}|\,i} \\
&= \$10,000 \cdot pvf_{\overline{4}|\,8\%} \\
&= \$10,000\,(.73503) \\
&= \$7,350.30
\end{aligned}
$$

In other words, $7,350.30 is the sum that a person would pay today to receive $10,000 at the end of four years, assuming 8% interest compounded annually. That the note could only be sold at a discount ($10,000 − $7,350.30 = $2,649.70) appears reasonable since the note has no stated interest and similar notes yield 8%.

As in the examples concerning the amount of a lump sum, we could alter the information in Problem 4 to illustrate solutions for other variables. However, this exercise seems unnecessary since the point should now be clear. That is, we are dealing with one basic equation of four variables. When three of the variables are known, solving for the one unknown is not difficult. So let's use the next example to introduce something new.

Problem 5.   You are a practicing CPA and one of your clients, I. M. Rich, tells you that he wants to put aside some money to buy his son an $8,000 automobile when his son graduates from college in four years. Assuming that Mr. Rich will earn 6%, compounded annually, on his savings during the first two years and 8%, compounded semiannually, during the last two years, how much should he deposit at the beginning of the four-year period?

Solution 5.   Once again we are seeking the present value of a lump sum ($8,000). However, in this case the interest rate and the frequency of compounding change after the second year. We therefore need to break down the problem into two components. First, compute the present value, *as of the beginning of the third year*, of $8,000 to be received at the end of four semiannual periods discounted at 4% per period. (Remember that the 8% interest is compounded semiannually during the last two years.) Second, compute the present value, *as of the beginning of the first year*, of the value calculated in the first step when discounted for 2 years at 6%. Thus, we have:

$$\text{Step 1.} \quad PV = FV \cdot pvf_{\overline{n}|i}$$
$$= \$8,000 \cdot pvf_{\overline{4}|4\%}$$
$$= \$8,000\,(.85480)$$
$$= \$6,838.40$$

The value $6,838.40 is the present value as of the beginning of the *third year*. To determine the present value as of the beginning of the *first year*, we must perform Step 2.

$$\text{Step 2.} \quad PV = FV \cdot pvf_{\overline{n}|i}$$
$$= \$6,838.40 \cdot pvf_{\overline{2}|6\%}$$
$$= \$6,838.40\,(.89000)$$
$$= \$6,086.18$$

Mr. Rich should therefore deposit $6,086.18 so that he will have the $8,000 required to purchase the automobile at the end of the four-year period.

An important point to remember from this example is that whenever a compound interest problem appears complex, try to solve the problem by dividing it into its components.

ANNUITY PROBLEMS

An **annuity** is a series of equal receipts or payments, called **rents,** that occur at uniform intervals at a constant interest rate.[5] This book assumes a standard annuity in which interest is compounded once at the end of each interval. Annuities commonly occur at annual, semiannual, quarterly, or monthly intervals. Lease payments, sinking fund payments, mortgage payments, and retirement payments are only a few examples of annuities that accountants encounter every day.

Annuities may be classified as ordinary annuities or annuities due.[6] The difference between the two lies solely in the timing of the rents. With an **ordinary annuity,** the rents occur at the *end* of each period. With an **annuity due,** the rents occur at the *beginning* of each period. In both kinds of annuities *one* rent occurs during each period, either at the beginning (annuity due) or at the end (ordinary annuity). For this reason the symbol n in annuity problems refers to either the number of compounding periods or the number of rents.

As in the lump sum problems discussed earlier, annuities involve present and future value concepts. Whereas earlier discussions dealt with the present and future values of a single lump sum, the following sections concern the present and future values of multiple sums, each of which is equal in size.

Amount (Future Value) of an Ordinary Annuity

As shown earlier, a lump sum of $1,500 left on deposit for three years at 8% will accumulate to $1,889.57. Now we seek to answer this kind of question: What is the amount (future

---

[5]Note that the term **rents** refers to a series of equal receipts or payments of any kind. In compound interest discussions, use of this term is not confined to its everyday connotation of payments on a leased asset.
[6]Ordinary annuities are sometimes called annuities in arrears, while annuities due are sometimes called annuities in advance.

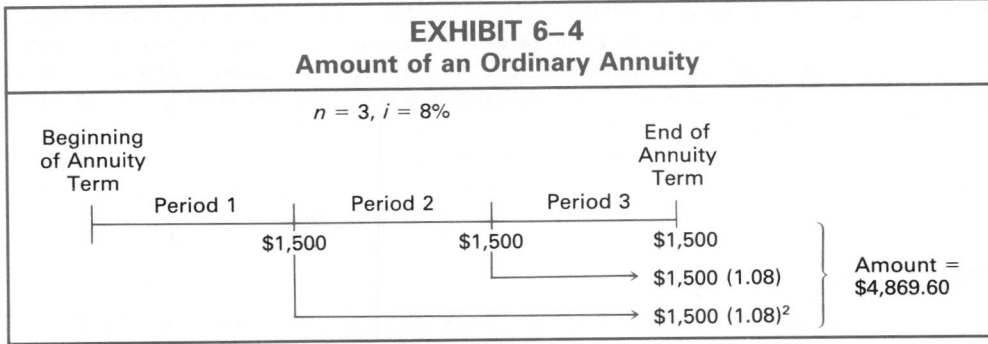

EXHIBIT 6–4
Amount of an Ordinary Annuity

$n = 3$, $i = 8\%$

value) at the end of three years of three periodic rents of $1,500 each that occur at the end of each year at 8% compounded annually? The question involves the amount of an ordinary annuity, as the time diagram shows in Exhibit 6–4.

As the diagram suggests, computing the amount of an ordinary annuity involves nothing more than computing the total amount of a series of lump sums.[7] Algebraically, we have:

3rd Rent		2nd Rent		1st Rent		Amount of the Ordinary Annuity
$1,500	+	$1,500 (1.08)	+	$1,500 (1.08)^2	=	$4,869.60

Note that although the annuity encompasses three periods, only two rents earn interest. The first rent earns interest during periods two and three; the second rent earns interest during period three only. The third rent earns no interest, because it occurs at the end of the three-year span. In an amount of an ordinary annuity of n rents, only $n - 1$ rents will earn interest, because the last rent occurs at the end of the annuity term and no interest period exists for that rent.

Of course, the $1,500 rent in the preceding equation could be factored out:

$$\$1,500 \ (1 + 1.08 + 1.08^2) = \$4,869.60$$
$$\$1,500 \ (1 + 1.08 + 1.1664) = \$4,869.60$$
$$\$1,500 \ (3.24640) = \$4,869.60$$

Turn to Table 6–3 at the end of the chapter and locate the factor for $n = 3$, $i = 8\%$. You will see that it is 3.24640, the number by which we multiplied $1,500 in the last equation. Note that Table 6–3 is entitled "Amount of an Ordinary Annuity of 1" and that it contains factors for many combinations of n and i. We shall refer to each of these factors as an **amount of an ordinary annuity factor (aoaf).** Each factor could have been determined by the approach used above for $n = 3$ and $i = 8\%$, but the following formula was applied to save time in generating each factor:

$$aoaf_{\overline{n}|\,i} = \frac{(1 + i)^n - 1}{i}$$

---

[7]You may find it helpful to verify this statement by applying Equation 6–1 and Table 6–1 to each of the $1,500 rents. This would give the following results:

1st rent	$1,500	(1.16640) =	$1,749.60
2nd rent	1,500	(1.08000) =	1,620.00
3rd rent	1,500	(1.00000) =	1,500.00
		Total	$4,869.60

Each table factor, then, is based on an equation that incorporates values for both n and i.

Using Table 6–3, we can find the amount to which an ordinary annuity of any size rent will accumulate. All we have to do is multiply the size of each rent by the amount to which an ordinary annuity of 1 will accumulate. Expressed algebraically, we have:

$$AOA = R \cdot aoaf_{\overline{n}|i} \qquad\qquad (6\text{–}3)$$

where AOA = amount (future value) of an ordinary annuity of n rents at i interest rate

R = size of each periodic rent

$aoaf_{\overline{n}|i}$ = amount of an ordinary annuity of 1 factor (from Table 6–3) for the relevant n and i

Notice that Equation 6–3 contains four variables (AOA, R, n, and i) and if we know the values of any three, we can solve for the fourth using algebra.

Accounting Examples

Problem 6. On January 1, 1985, Control Systems Corporation creates a sinking fund to accumulate cash that will be needed to retire a $1,000,000 issue of bonds payable that matures in 10 years. Accordingly, the company decides to make 20 semiannual payments of $30,000 each into a sinking fund. The first payment will be made on June 30, 1985, and the fund is expected to earn interest at 10% compounded semiannually. How much cash will be in the fund at the end of 10 years?

Solution 6. The problem clearly involves an annuity, because periodic payments (rents) of $30,000 each will be placed in a sinking fund. Furthermore, it is an ordinary annuity, because the initial rent occurs at the end of the first semiannual period. Since the payments are made semiannually, we know that $n = 10 \times 2 = 20$ and $i = 10\% \div 2 = 5\%$. Our problem then is to determine the amount of an ordinary annuity of 20 rents of $30,000 each at 5% interest. Using Equation 6–3 and Table 6–3, we have:

$$
\begin{aligned}
AOA &= R \cdot aoaf_{\overline{n}|i} \\
&= \$30{,}000 \cdot aoaf_{\overline{20}|\,5\%} \\
&= \$30{,}000\,(33.06595) \\
&= \$991{,}978.50
\end{aligned}
$$

Unfortunately, the amount in the sinking fund at the end of 10 years will be $8,021.50 ($1,000,000 − $991,978.50) less than the company needs to retire the bonds.

Problem 7. Referring to the information in Problem 6, how much would the Control Systems Corporation have to deposit at the end of each semiannual period to accumulate $1,000,000 in the sinking fund at the end of 10 years?

Solution 7. In Problem 6, semiannual deposits of $30,000 left the company $8,021.50 short of its goal of $1,000,000. Thus, logic dictates that the company will have to deposit somewhat more than $30,000 each period. To find the exact size of each deposit, we refer to Equation 6–3, which states that $AOA = R \cdot aoaf_{\overline{n}|i}$. Dividing both sides of the equation by $aoaf_{\overline{n}|i}$ and substituting the values of the known variables, we have:

$$
\begin{aligned}
R &= \frac{AOA}{aoaf_{\overline{n}|i}} \\
&= \frac{\$1{,}000{,}000}{aoaf_{\overline{20}|\,5\%}} \\
&= \frac{\$1{,}000{,}000}{33.06595} \\
&= \$30{,}242.59
\end{aligned}
$$

Control Systems Corporation must therefore deposit $30,242.59 at the end of each semi-annual period to accumulate $1,000,000 at the end of 10 years.

Problem 8. You are a local CPA and one of your clients, Tom Mack, hands you a cigar and tells you that his wife has just given birth to a baby girl. After you have extended your congratulations, Tom tells you that he wants to accumulate a $10,000 cash gift for his daughter. He plans to do this by depositing $300 at yearly intervals beginning one year from now. The periodic deposits will be placed in a 6% savings account. When Tom accumulates the $10,000 he desires, how old will his daughter be?

Solution 8. We know that this problem involves an ordinary annuity, because the periodic deposits of $300 begin one year from now. Furthermore, we know the desired future amount ($10,000), the size of the periodic rents ($300), and the interest rate per period (6%). The unknown that we seek is the number of periods, which we can determine by rewriting Equation 6–3 and using Table 6–3. Equation 6–3 states that $AOA = R \cdot aoaf_{\overline{n}|i}$. Dividing both sides of the equation by R and substituting the known values, we have:

$$aoaf_{\overline{n}|i} = \frac{AOA}{R}$$

$$aoaf_{\overline{n}|6\%} = \frac{\$10,000}{\$300}$$

$$= 33.33333$$

We now search the 6% column of Table 6–3 for the factor 33.33333. We won't find it, but we can determine that it would lie between 30.90565 (the factor for $n = 18$) and 33.75999 (the factor for $n = 19$). Since it is closer to the factor for $n = 19$, we conclude that it will take almost 19 years for Tom Mack to accumulate $10,000. In other words, Tom's daughter will be almost 19 years old when she receives the $10,000 gift from her father.

A closer approximation may be achieved by using linear interpolation. In general, when a factor is computed but does not appear in the pertinent compound interest table, interpolation may be used to find a reasonable approximation of the unknown number of periods (n) or interest rate (i).[8] The smaller the range of interpolation, the smaller the error will be. Interpolation is based on the principle of proportion, as the following format suggests:

	When n is:	The corresponding $aoaf$ is:		
	18	30.90565		
1 { x { ?		33.33333	} 2.42768	} 2.85434
	19	33.75999		

We can set up the following proportion:

$$\frac{x}{1} = \frac{2.42768}{2.85434}$$

Solving for x, we find that it equals .85. Since x is the distance between 18 and n, we conclude that $n = 18 + .85 = 18.85$. Tom's daughter, then, will be approximately 18.85 years old when she receives her gift. Any time you want to interpolate, you may do so by setting up a proportion similar to the one illustrated above.

Problem 9. Referring to the information in Problem 8, what interest rate would Tom

---

[8]An exact answer may be determined using logarithms.

Mack have to earn on his investment so that he could give his daughter the $10,000 present on her eighteenth birthday?

Solution 9.   Logic dictates that since it would take approximately 18.85 years to accumulate $10,000 at 6% interest, Tom will have to earn more than 6% to accumulate the same amount in less time. Once again, dividing both sides of Equation 6–3 by R, we have:

$$aoaf_{\overline{n}|i} = \frac{AOA}{R}$$

Therefore, $aoaf_{\overline{18}|i} = \$10{,}000/\$300 = 33.33333$. Looking across the eighteenth row of Table 6–3, we determine that 33.33333 would lie between 30.90565 (the factor for $i = 6\%$) and 37.45024 (the factor for $i = 8\%$). Approximating the answer through interpolation, we have:

		When i is:	The corresponding $aoaf$ is:		
2%	x	6%	30.90565	2.42768	6.54459
		?	33.33333		
		8%	37.45024		

Setting up a proportion, we have:

$$\frac{x}{2\%} = \frac{2.42768}{6.54459}$$

Solving for x, we find that it equals .74%. Since x is the distance between 6% and i, we conclude that $i = 6\% + .74\% = 6.74\%$. Tom Mack would therefore have to earn approximately 6.74% interest if he wanted to give his daughter $10,000 on her eighteenth birthday.

Amount (Future Value) of an Annuity Due

Earlier we stated that an annuity due is one in which the rents occur at the *beginning* of each period. Further, we saw that $4,869.60 is the amount of an *ordinary* annuity of three annual rents of $1,500 each at 8%. Now we are concerned with this kind of question: What is the amount at the end of three years of three annual rents of $1,500 each that occur at the *beginning* of each year at 8% compounded annually? The time diagram in Exhibit 6–5 illustrates the solution.

As the diagram suggests, an annuity due begins with a rent and ends one period *after* the last rent. Thus, if we took the amount of an ordinary annuity of three $1,500 rents at 8% and left all the money on deposit at 8% for one additional period, we would have the amount of an annuity due of three $1,500 rents at 8%. For any given values of n and i, the amount of an annuity due is greater than the amount of an ordinary annuity by the interest on the latter amount for one period. Stated differently, the amount of an annuity due for given values of n and i is equal to the amount of an ordinary annuity of $(n + 1)$ rents at i interest rate, *minus* one rent (the final rent).

In an amount of an annuity due of n rents, all of the n rents earn interest. Note carefully in Exhibit 6–5 that the third rent earns interest for one period, the second rent earns interest for two periods, and the first rent earns interest for three periods. Algebraically, we have:

$$\$1{,}500\,(1.08) + \$1{,}500\,(1.08)^2 + \$1{,}500\,(1.08)^3 = \$5{,}259.17$$

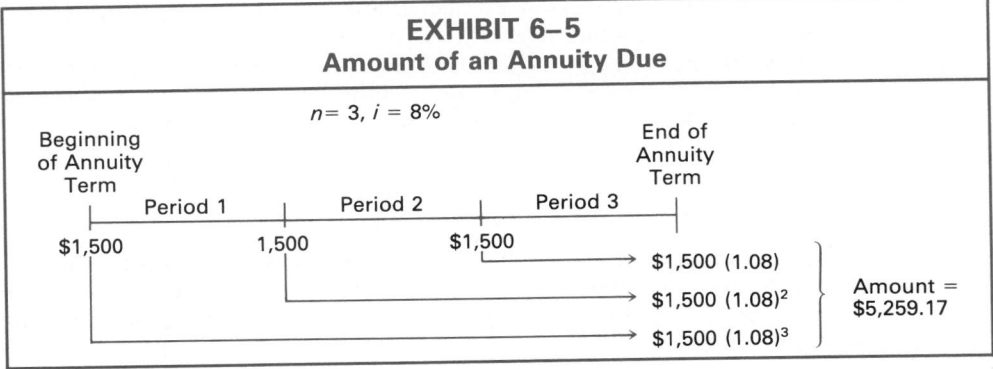

EXHIBIT 6–5
Amount of an Annuity Due

Factoring out the $1,500 rent, we have:

$$\$1,500 \, (1.08 + 1.08^2 + 1.08^3) = \$5,259.17$$
$$\$1,500 \, (1.08 + 1.1664 + 1.25971) = \$5,259.17$$
$$\$1,500 \, (3.50611) = \$5,259.17$$

In the last equation, 3.50611 is simply a factor for computing the amount of an annuity due (*aadf*) where $n = 3$ and $i = 8\%$. We could construct a table of these factors and call it "Amount of an Annuity Due of 1." However, the relationship between the amount of an ordinary annuity and the amount of an annuity due is so straightforward that a separate table is unnecessary. We can use the "Amount of an Ordinary Annuity of 1" table (Table 6–3) to determine an *aadf* simply by finding the factor for $(n + 1)$ periods and *i*, and subtracting 1 from the factor we find. Stated algebraically,

$$aadf_{\overline{n}|\,i} = aoaf_{\overline{n+1}|\,i} - 1$$

To illustrate, let's use Table 6–3 to calculate $aadf_{\overline{3}|\,8\%}$. We simply look up the table factor for $n + 1 = 4$ periods and $i = 8\%$, and we find 4.50611. Subtracting 1 from this, we get 3.50611. Now that we know how to derive an *aadf* using Table 6–3, we can state:

$$AAD = R \cdot aadf_{\overline{n}|\,i} \qquad \qquad (6\text{–}3A)$$

where AAD = amount of an annuity due of *n*
　　　　　　rents at *i* interest rate

　　　R = size of each periodic rent

　$aadf_{\overline{n}|\,i}$ = amount of an annuity due of 1 factor
　　　　　　(from Table 6–3, *as adjusted*) for the
　　　　　　relevant *n* and *i*

Since the values of *n* and *i* determine the value of $aadf_{\overline{n}|\,i}$, Equation 6–3A consists of four variables: *AAD, R, n,* and *i*. Remember that if we know the values of any three, we can solve for the fourth using algebra.

Accounting Example

Problem 10.   Warren Wilson, a local dentist, has decided to create a fund for his retirement in 35 years. He deposits $3,000 today in a special 8% account at the People's Bank, and he plans to make periodic deposits of $3,000 each at annual intervals over the next 34 years. How much cash will be in Wilson's retirement fund when he retires?

Solution 10. Since the initial rent occurs at the beginning of the first year, we are dealing with an annuity due. Specifically, we are asked to calculate the amount (a future value) of an annuity due of 35 rents of $3,000 at 8%. Using Equation 6–3A and Table 6–3, as adjusted, we have:

$$
\begin{aligned}
AAD &= R \cdot aadf_{\overline{n}|i} \\
&= \$3,000 \cdot aadf_{\overline{35}|8\%} \\
&= \$3,000\,(aoaf_{\overline{35+1}|8\%} - 1) \\
&= \$3,000\,(187.10215 - 1) \\
&= \$3,000\,(186.10215) \\
&= \$558,306.45
\end{aligned}
$$

Present Value of an Ordinary Annuity

We have seen that the amount of an ordinary annuity of three annual rents of $1,500 each at 8% is $4,869.60. Accountants often must solve problems that are the inverse of this one, for example: What is the present value of an ordinary annuity of three annual rents of $1,500 each discounted at 8%? The time diagram in Exhibit 6–6 illustrates the solution.

Note carefully that the initial rent occurs at the end of the first time period, consistent with our definition of an ordinary annuity. When the present value of an ordinary annuity of n rents is computed, each rent is discounted.

As shown in Exhibit 6–6 we can compute the present value of an ordinary annuity by computing the present value of each rent and summing the results. Algebraically, we have:

1st Rent		2nd Rent		3rd Rent		Present Value of the Ordinary Annuity
$1,500 $(\frac{1}{1.08})$	+	$1,500 $(\frac{1}{1.08})^2$	+	$1,500 $(\frac{1}{1.08})^3$	=	$3,865.65

Factoring out the $1,500 rent, we have:

$$
\$1,500\left[\left(\frac{1}{1.08}\right) + \left(\frac{1}{1.08}\right)^2 + \left(\frac{1}{1.08}\right)^3\right] = \$3,865.65
$$

$$
\$1,500\,(.92593 + .85734 + .79383) = \$3,865.65
$$

$$
\$1,500\,(2.57710) = \$3,865.65
$$

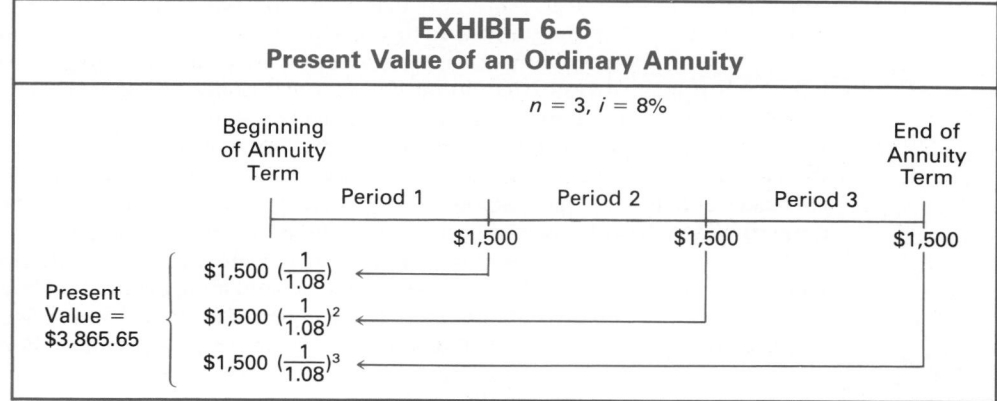

EXHIBIT 6–6
Present Value of an Ordinary Annuity

Turn to Table 6–4 at the end of the chapter and locate the table factor for $n = 3, i = 8\%$. Through no coincidence, you will find that it is 2.57710, the number we multiplied by $1,500 in the last equation. Table 6–4 is titled "Present Value of an Ordinary Annuity of 1." It contains many factors, each of which we shall call a **present value of an ordinary annuity factor (*pvoaf*)**. Although each *pvoaf* could have been calculated by the approach illustrated above for $n = 3$ and $i = 8\%$, the following formula was used to save time:

$$pvoaf_{\overline{n}|\,i} = \frac{1 - \dfrac{1}{(1 + i)^n}}{i}$$

As the title indicates, Table 6–4 includes present value factors assuming an ordinary annuity of 1. For given n and i values, we can easily calculate the present value of an ordinary annuity of any size rent. We simply multiply the size of each rent by the present value of an ordinary annuity of 1. We can state this algebraically as follows:

$$PVOA = R \cdot pvoaf_{\overline{n}|\,i} \qquad\qquad (6\text{–}4)$$

$$\text{where} \quad PVOA = \text{present value of an ordinary annuity of } n \text{ rents at } i \text{ interest rate}$$

$$R = \text{size of each periodic rent}$$

$$pvoaf_{\overline{n}|\,i} = \text{present value of an ordinary annuity of 1 factor (from Table 6–4) for the relevant } n \text{ and } i$$

Once again we note four variables ($PVOA$, R, n, and i), any three of which must be known to solve for the fourth.

Accounting Example

Problem 11. On January 1, 1985, Allied Steel Company issues $5,000,000 of 8%, 20-year term bonds that pay interest semiannually each June 30 and December 31. How much cash will the bonds sell for if, on January 1, 1985, the market rate of interest for bonds similar to those of Allied Steel Company is 10%?

Solution 11. Note that Allied's bonds have a **coupon interest rate** (often called **nominal rate** or **stated rate**) of 8%. This is simply the annual rate of interest stated in the bond contract. This rate is used to compute the amount of cash that will be paid as interest to bondholders each year. Note also that when the bonds are sold, the **market rate of interest** (often called the **yield rate** or the **effective rate**) for similar bonds is 10%. Intuitively, what do you think must happen to entice bond investors to purchase Allied's 8% bonds when these investors could purchase similar bonds and earn 10%?

Of course, the bonds must sell for a price that is less than their par or face value. In other words, the bonds will sell **at a discount.** The discount will be the amount necessary to bring the yield rate on Allied's bonds up to 10%, the rate that prevails in the marketplace. Logic also dictates that when the coupon rate is greater than the market rate, the bonds will sell **at a premium.** When the two rates are equal, the bonds will sell **at par.**

Now that we have used intuition, let's formulate a more precise solution to the problem. First, recognize that since the bonds pay interest semiannually, they include $20 \times 2 = 40$ periods ($n = 40$), and the stated interest rate per period is $8\% \div 2 = 4\%$. Second, recognize that in addition to paying the $5,000,000 maturity value (a lump sum) to bondholders in 20 years, Allied must also pay $200,000 (4% × $5,000,000) interest at the end of each semi annual period for 20 years. The interest payments constitute an ordinary annuity. Finally, recognize that to compute the present value of the bonds (the price bondholders would be willing to pay on January 1, 1985), we must discount the maturity value and the interest annuity using the market rate of interest per period, so $i = 10\% \div 2 = 5\%$. Now we can determine the present value of Allied's bonds using the following two steps:

Step 1. Compute the present value of the lump sum maturity value of $5,000,000 for $n = 40$ and $i = 5\%$. (Use Equation 6–2 and Table 6–2.)

$$PV = FV \cdot pvf_{\overline{n}|i}$$
$$= 5,000,000 \cdot pvf_{\overline{40}|5\%}$$
$$= \$5,000,000 (.14205)$$
$$= \$710,250$$

Step 2. Compute the present value of the ordinary interest annuity of $200,000 for $n = 40$ and $i = 5\%$. (Use Equation 6–4 and Table 6–4.)

$$PVOA = R \cdot pvoaf_{\overline{n}|i}$$
$$= \$200,000 \cdot pvoaf_{\overline{40}|5\%}$$
$$= \$200,000 (17.15909)$$
$$= \$3,431,818$$

Summing the results of Steps 1 and 2, we get $710,250 + $3,431,818 = $4,142,068, which is the present value of the bonds. Thus, if bondholders pay $4,142,068 for Allied's bonds, they will earn 10%, compounded semiannually, on their investment. Note that our intuition was correct; the bonds sell at a discount of $857,932 ($5,000,000 − $4,142,068). This discount is nothing more than extra interest that Allied must pay on its bonds. To help implement the matching principle, this discount must be amortized over the life of the bond issue. We discuss discount (and premium) amortization more fully in Chapter 15.

| Matching |

The bond pricing problem illustrates that with a seemingly complex problem, it is often helpful to divide it into its components. As the problem suggests, we sometimes need more than one equation and table. Nevertheless, the same basic compound interest concepts are applicable.

Present Value of an Annuity Due

Recall that an annuity due is one in which the rents occur at the beginning of each time period. In the previous section we saw that $3,865.65 is the present value of an ordinary annuity of three rents of $1,500 each discounted at 8%. Now we will simply change the timing of the $1,500 rents and ask this question: What is the present value of three annual rents of $1,500 each that occur at the *beginning* of each year (an annuity due) discounted at 8%? Once again a time diagram (Exhibit 6–7) helps us to visualize the solution. Note that the initial rent is not discounted, because it occurs at the beginning of the three-year span. In general, when the present value of an annuity due of n rents is computed, only $(n - 1)$ rents will be discounted.

As shown in Exhibit 6–7, an annuity due begins with a rent and ends one period *after* the last rent. Therefore, if we computed the present value of an annuity due of three $1,500 rents at 8% and then *discounted* all the money at 8% for one more period, we would have the present value of an ordinary annuity of three $1,500 rents at 8%. Similarly, if we com-

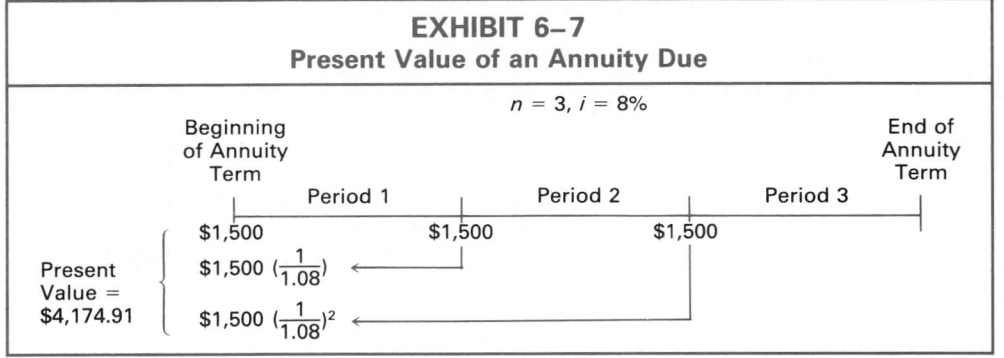

EXHIBIT 6-7
Present Value of an Annuity Due

puted the present value of an ordinary annuity of three $1,500 rents at 8% and then *compounded* all the money at 8% for one period into the future, we would have the present value of an annuity due of three rents of $1,500 at 8%. The relationship, then, between the present value of an ordinary annuity and the present value of an annuity due is straightforward. For any given values of n and i, the present value of an annuity due will be greater than the present value of an ordinary annuity by the interest on the latter amount for one period. Stated somewhat differently, the present value of an annuity due for any given values of n and i will be equal to the present value of an ordinary annuity of $(n - 1)$ rents at i interest rate, *plus* one rent (the initial rent).

As Exhibit 6–7 suggests, we could compute the present value of an annuity due by computing the present value of each rent and summing the results. Expressed algebraically, we have:

$$\$1,500 + \$1,500 \left(\frac{1}{1.08}\right) + \$1,500 \left(\frac{1}{1.08}\right)^2 = \$4,174.91$$

Factoring out the $1,500 rent, we have:

$$\$1,500 \left[1 + \frac{1}{1.08} + \left(\frac{1}{1.08}\right)^2\right] = \$4,174.91$$
$$\$1,500 \left(1 + .92593 + .85734\right) = \$4,174.91$$
$$\$1,500 \left(2.78327\right) = \$4,174.91$$

The 2.78327 component in the last equation is simply a factor for computing the present value of an annuity due (*pvadf*) where $n = 3$ and $i = 8\%$. A complete table of these factors would be called a "Present Value of an Annuity Due of 1" table. We have not constructed such a table because we already have Table 6–4 and we know that a relatively simple relationship exists between the present value of an ordinary annuity and the present value of an annuity due. Thus, we can use Table 6–4 to determine a *pvadf* simply by finding the factor for $(n - 1)$ periods and i, and adding 1 to the factor. Stated algebraically,

$$pvadf_{\overline{n}|\,i} = pvoaf_{\overline{n-1}|\,i} + 1.$$

To illustrate, let's use Table 6–4 to calculate $pvadf_{\overline{3}|\,8\%}$. Looking at the table, we find that the factor for $n - 1 = 2$ periods and $i = 8\%$ is 1.78326. Adding 1 to this number, we get 2.78326.

Now that we know how to use Table 6–4 to calculate a *pvadf,* we can state:

$$PVAD = R \cdot pvadf_{\overline{n}|i} \qquad\qquad\qquad (6\text{–}4A)$$

where $PVAD$ = present value of an annuity due
of *n* rents at *i* interest rate

R = size of each periodic rent

$pvadf_{\overline{n}|i}$ = present value of an annuity due
of 1 factor (from Table 6–4, *as
adjusted*) for the relevant *n* and *i*

The four variables that make up Equation 6–4A are *PVAD, R, n,* and *i.* As usual, if we know the values of any three, we can solve for the fourth.

Accounting Examples

Problem 12.   On July 1, 1985, Rockwell Drilling Company signed a 12-year, noncancelable lease with Equipment Leasing Corporation. The lease gave Rockwell the right to use certain drilling equipment that had a 12-year estimated useful life and no salvage value. In exchange for this right, Rockwell agreed to make 12 annual lease payments of $15,000 each, beginning on July 1, 1985. Assuming a relevant interest rate of 10%, what is the present value of the lease on July 1, 1985?

Solution 12.   Since the initial lease payment occurs at the beginning of the first interval, we know that the lease payments represent an annuity due. To determine the present value of the lease, we compute the present value of an annuity due of 12 rents ($n = 12$) of $15,000 each at $i = 10\%$. Using Equation 6–4A and Table 6–4, we have:

$$
\begin{aligned}
PVAD &= R \cdot pvadf_{\overline{n}|i} \\
&= \$15,000 \cdot pvadf_{\overline{12}|10\%} \\
&= \$15,000 \,(pvoaf_{\overline{12-1}|10\%} + 1) \\
&= \$15,000 \,(6.49506 + 1) \\
&= \$15,000 \,(7.49506) \\
&= \$112,425.90
\end{aligned}
$$

Observe in this problem that the *timing* of the lease payments has an important impact on the present value of the lease. **In general, the timing of cash inflows and outflows has an important impact on the valuation of assets and liabilities and on the measurement of revenues and expenses in accounting.**

Problem 13.   Jane Thomas retired today after 40 years of loyal service to the Stork Candy Company. She has accumulated $187,298.32 in her retirement account, and she wants to withdraw $20,000 annually, beginning today, for as long as her retirement money lasts. Assuming that all money in Jane's account earns 10% interest, how many $20,000 annual withdrawals can she make?

Solution 13.   In this problem we know that $187,298.32 is the present value of an annuity due of *n* rents of $20,000 each at $i = 10\%$. Dividing both sides of Equation 6–4A by *R,* we have:

$$\frac{PVAD}{R} = pvadf_{\overline{n}|i}$$

$$\text{or } pvadf_{\overline{n}|i} = \frac{PVAD}{R}$$

Substituting the known values for *PVAD, R,* and *i,* we have:

$$pvadf_{\overline{n}|\,10\%} = \frac{\$187{,}298.32}{\$20{,}000}$$

$$pvadf_{\overline{n}|\,10\%} = 9.36492$$

Of course, we should not look for 9.36492 in Table 6–4, because we have seen that this table assumes an ordinary annuity. However, remember that $pvadf_{\overline{n}|\,i} = pvoaf_{\overline{n-1}|\,i} + 1$. Subtracting 1 from both sides of this equation, we have:

$$pvadf_{\overline{n}|\,i} - 1 = pvoaf_{\overline{n-1}|\,i}$$

Substituting the known values, we have:

$$9.36492 - 1 = pvoaf_{\overline{n-1}|\,10\%}$$
$$\text{or} \quad pvoaf_{\overline{n-1}|\,10\%} = 8.36492$$

Now we can go to Table 6–4 and look down the 10% column until we find 8.36492. We find it in the row in which $n = 19$; since 19 is the *pvoaf* for $(n - 1)$ rents, we conclude that Jane Thomas can make *20 withdrawals* $(19 + 1 = 20)$ from her retirement account. If we had not found 8.36492, we could have interpolated to approximate n.

Deferred Annuities

A deferred annuity is one in which the initial rent occurs two or more periods in the future. In other words, the initial rent does not occur at either the beginning or the end of the first time period but at some later date. For computational convenience, it is customary to treat all deferred annuities as deferred ordinary annuities instead of deferred annuities due. For this reason we shall omit the adjective "ordinary" when referring to deferred annuities.

The **deferral period** is the length of time between the present and the *beginning* of the first period in which a rent occurs. Remember, therefore, that the deferral period ends one period *before* the initial rent occurs. Thus, if an annuity begins to produce rents at the end of six periods, we say that it is deferred five periods. Similarly, an annuity which is deferred for nine periods will produce its first rent at the end of ten periods.

The time diagram in Exhibit 6–8 illustrates an annuity of three annual rents of $1,500 at 8%, deferred four years.

The deferral period does not affect the calculation of an amount (future value). Since there is nothing on deposit to accumulate interest during the deferral period, the amount of a deferred annuity is the same as the amount of an annuity that is not deferred, assuming that the two annuities have the same values for n, i, and R. In the example cited above, the amount would be $4,869.60, the same figure computed in the earlier discussion of the

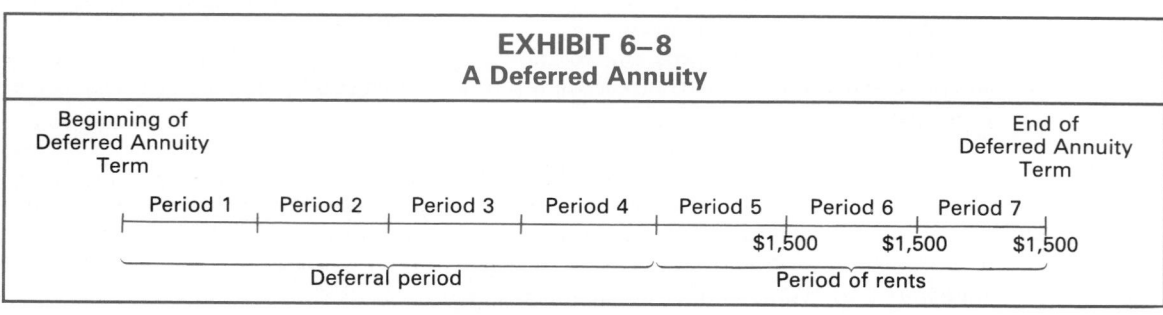

EXHIBIT 6–8
A Deferred Annuity

amount of an ordinary annuity.

On the other hand, assuming that the two annuities have the same values for n, i, and R, the present value of a deferred annuity is less than the present value of an annuity which is not deferred. The reason is that when we compute a present value, we must discount through the deferral period.

The easiest way to compute the present value of a deferred annuity is to find the *pvoaf* for the *total* number of periods involved, that is, the number of periods that the annuity is deferred (k) plus the number of periods in which rents occur (n). Then subtract the *pvoaf* associated with the ordinary annuity that is nonexistent during the deferral period. The resulting factor is then multiplied by the size of the periodic rent. Algebraically, we have the following:

$$PVDA = R \cdot (pvoaf_{\overline{k+n}|i} - pvoaf_{\overline{k}|i}) \tag{6-5}$$

where $PVDA$ = present value of an ordinary annuity
of n rents at i interest rate, *deferred*
k periods

R = size of each periodic rent

$pvoaf_{\overline{k+n}|i}$ = present value of an ordinary
annuity factor for the *total* number
of periods involved

$pvoaf_{\overline{k}|i}$ = present value of an ordinary
annuity factor for the number of
periods in which no rents occur

If we want to know the present value of an annuity of three annual rents of \$1,500 at 8% deferred four years, we would proceed as follows:

$$\begin{aligned} PVDA &= R \cdot (pvoaf_{\overline{7}|8\%} - pvoaf_{\overline{4}|8\%}) \\ &= \$1,500\,(5.20637 - 3.31213) \\ &= \$1,500\,(1.89424) \\ &= \$2,841.36 \end{aligned}$$

Another way to compute the present value of a deferred annuity is to first compute the present value of the annuity at the beginning of the first period in which a rent occurs (using Equation 6–4 and Table 6–4) and then discount this lump sum to the present (using Equation 6–2 and Table 6–2). Following this approach, we find that the present value of the annuity at the beginning of Period 5 is \$3,865.65 (\$1,500 × 2.57710). Discounting this lump sum to the present, we find that it equals \$2,841.37 (\$3,865.65 × .73503). The \$.01 discrepancy (\$2,841.37 − \$2,841.36) between answers is the result of rounding.

Accounting Example

Problem 14.   Sam Sharpe purchases a \$50,000 annuity contract that promises a return of 8% compounded annually. The contract provides that Sam shall receive 15 equal annual payments, the first of which is due 10 years from now. How much will each annual payment be?

Solution 14.   Since the annuity begins to produce rents at the end of 10 years, we say that it is deferred 9 years. Therefore, in this problem we know that \$50,000 is the present value of an ordinary annuity of 15 annual rents at 8%, deferred 9 years. We are asked to solve for the size of the periodic rent. Dividing both sides of Equation 6–5 by $(pvoaf_{\overline{k+n}|i} - pvoaf_{\overline{k}|i})$, we have:

$$R = \frac{PVDA}{(pvoaf_{\overline{k+n}|i} - pvoaf_{\overline{k}|i})}$$

$$= \frac{\$50,000}{(pvoaf_{\overline{24}|8\%} - pvoaf_{\overline{9}|8\%})}$$

$$= \frac{\$50,000}{10.52876 - 6.24689}$$

$$= \frac{\$50,000}{4.28187}$$

$$= \$11,667.14$$

CONCLUDING REMARKS

When solving a compound interest problem, it is extremely important to first read the problem very carefully. Try to determine what type of problem you are being asked to solve. Distinguishing between lump sum problems and annuity problems is fairly easy, because periodic rents of equal size clearly indicate an annuity problem.

On the other hand, the authors have found that learning to distinguish between the following types of *annuity problems* is often difficult:

1. Amount of an ordinary annuity.
2. Amount of an annuity due.
3. Present value of an ordinary annuity.
4. Present value of an annuity due.

When solving an annuity problem that seems difficult, draw a time diagram and remember the following points:

1. An annuity problem involves a value that represents a single sum of money. This value may occur either before or after the rents. If the value (which may be the unknown variable) occurs *after* the rents, the value is an *amount* (future value). Consequently, we have an amount of an annuity problem. To determine whether the annuity is ordinary or due, note the timing of the *final rent.* If the final rent occurs *at the same time* as the value, we have an amount of an *ordinary* annuity problem (see Exhibit 6–4). If the final rent occurs *one period before* the value, we have an amount of an annuity *due* problem (see Exhibit 6–5).
2. If the value (which may be the unknown variable) in the problem occurs *before* the rents, the value is a *present value.* Consequently, we have a present value of an annuity problem. To determine whether the annuity is ordinary or due, observe the timing of the *first rent.* If the first rent occurs *one period after* the value, we have a present value of an *ordinary* annuity problem (see Exhibit 6–6). If the first rent occurs *at the same time* as the present value, we have a present value of an annuity *due* problem (see Exhibit 6–7).

A deferred annuity is not difficult to recognize, because the first rent occurs two or more periods after the beginning of the annuity term (see Exhibit 6–8).

After you have determined the type of problem you are dealing with, you may solve it using the appropriate equation(s) and table(s). The major equations presented in the chapter are summarized in Exhibit 6–9.

Finally, try to form the habit of examining your answers to compound interest problems from a common-sense perspective. We know, for example, that the present value of $1,000 discounted for 2 years at 8% could not possibly be $8,573.40. The actual present value is only $857.34. As this example shows, misplacing a decimal can greatly affect the solution to a compound interest problem.

In the remaining chapters of this textbook, you will be asked to apply many of the tools discussed in this chapter and the previous chapter on the accounting cycle. The next chapter, which covers cash and receivables, is the first of a series of seven chapters that explain

---

EXHIBIT 6–9
Summary of Compound Interest Equations

Equation Number	Equation	Appropriate Table
6–1	$FV = PV \cdot fvf_{\overline{n}|i}$	6–1
6–2	$PV = FV \cdot pvf_{\overline{n}|i}$	6–2
6–3	$AOA = R \cdot aoaf_{\overline{n}|i}$	6–3
6–3A	$AAD = R \cdot aadf_{\overline{n}|i}$	6–3 (adjusted)
6–4	$PVOA = R \cdot pvoaf_{\overline{n}|i}$	6–4
6–4A	$PVAD = R \cdot pvadf_{\overline{n}|i}$	6–4 (adjusted)
6–5	$PVDA = R \cdot (pvoaf_{\overline{x+n}|i} - pvoaf_{\overline{x}|i})$	6–4

---

asset accounting. As we move into our study of various types of assets, you will see the application of these tools.

_____ **KEY POINTS**

1. Simple interest means that interest is earned only on the principal sum of money invested; compound interest means that interest is earned not only on the principal but also on the interest accumulated.

2. Four fundamental concepts underlie all compound interest problems:
   a. present value (PV)
   b. future value (FV)
   c. interest rate (i)
   d. time periods (n)

3. In a compound interest problem, the values of i and n should reflect the number of times a year that interest is compounded.

4. An amount of a lump sum problem focuses on the future value to which a lump sum of money will accumulate if left on deposit for a certain number of periods at a certain interest rate per period.

5. A present value of a lump sum problem focuses on the present value of a lump sum of money that is discounted for a certain number of periods at a certain interest rate per period.

6. An annuity is a series of equal receipts or payments, called rents, that occur at uniform time intervals at a constant interest rate. In an ordinary annuity, the rents occur at the end of each time period; in an annuity due, the rents occur at the beginning of each

---

EXHIBIT 6–10
Characteristics of Annuity Problems

Type of Annuity Problem	Focus	Rents
Amount of an ordinary annuity	A future value	End of each period. Final rent occurs at same time as future value.
Amount of an annuity due	A future value	Beginning of each period. Final rent occurs one period before future value.
Present value of an ordinary annuity	A present value	End of each period. Initial rent occurs one period after the present value.
Present value of an annuity due	A present value	Beginning of each period. Initial rent occurs at same time as present value.

time period. Present value and future value concepts apply to annuities, just as these concepts apply to lump sum problems.

7. Important characteristics of the major types of annuity problems are summarized in Exhibit 6–10.

8. A deferred annuity is one in which the initial rent occurs two or more periods in the future. A deferral period does not affect the calculation of an amount, but it does affect the calculation of a present value.

9. When solving a compound interest problem, you should read the problem carefully to determine the type of problem you are dealing with, solve the problem using the appropriate equations and tables, and make sure your answer seems reasonable.

10. A complex problem can usually be solved by dividing it into its components.

QUESTIONS

6–1 Explain what is meant by the time value of money.

6–2 Distinguish between simple and compound interest.

6–3 Distinguish between the amount of a lump sum and the present value of a lump sum.

6–4 What is an annuity?

6–5 Distinguish between an ordinary annuity and an annuity due.

6–6 Distinguish between the amount of an ordinary annuity and the amount of an annuity due.

6–7 Distinguish between the present value of an ordinary annuity and the present value of an annuity due.

6–8 What is a deferred annuity?

6–9 Explain how the factors in each of the following tables were calculated:
  [a] Table 6–1
  [b] Table 6–2
  [c] Table 6–3
  [d] Table 6–4

6–10 Explain how an Amount of 1 table could be converted to a Present Value of 1 table.

6–11 Explain how an Amount of an Ordinary Annuity of 1 table could be converted to an Amount of an Annuity Due of 1 table.

6–12 Explain how a Present Value of an Ordinary Annuity of 1 table could be converted to a Present Value of an Annuity Due of 1 table.

6–13 Indicate the number of compounding periods (n) and the interest rate per period (i) for each of the following:
  [a] Three years, 12% compounded annually.
  [b] Three years, 12% compounded semiannually.
  [c] Three years, 12% compounded quarterly.
  [d] Three years, 12% compounded monthly.

6–14 Assuming that $n = 15$ and $i = 10\%$, what is:
  [a] The amount of 1?
  [b] The present value of 1?
  [c] The amount of an ordinary annuity of 1?
  [d] The amount of an annuity due of 1?
  [e] The present value of an ordinary annuity of 1?
  [f] The present value of an annuity due of 1?

CASES

C6–1 In Chapter 2 we stated that the historical cost of an asset equals the cash equivalent price of acquiring the asset and putting it to its intended use. Suppose that on July 1, 1985, Stern Corporation buys 100 shares of common stock of Wate Company as an investment in exchange for a three-year note. The note has a face amount of $14,049.29 and no stated interest rate. Wate Company is a small, closely held enterprise, and the market value of its common stock is not readily determinable. On July 1, 1985, the market rate of interest for notes similar to the one issued by Stern is 12%.

Instructions

[a] Explain how Stern should determine the historical cost of its investment in Wate Company.
[b] Justify your answer to [a] from the standpoint of accounting theory.

C6–2 On December 31, 1985, Western Galleries, Inc., sold a unique painting to Green Company in exchange for a five-year note receivable. The note had a face amount of $161,051 and no stated interest rate. The market rate of interest for similar notes on December 31, 1985, was 10%. The painting could not be appraised in a reliable manner.

Instructions

Explain how Western Galleries should determine the amount of revenue to recognize on the sale for the period ending December 31, 1985.

EXERCISES

E6–1 To what amount will $7,500 accumulate if it is deposited for five years at 10%, assuming:
[a] Simple interest?
[b] Interest compounded annually?
[c] Interest compounded semiannually?
[d] Interest compounded quarterly?

E6–2 Assuming an interest rate of 12%, compounded quarterly, how many years will it take for a deposit of $1,800 to accumulate to $2,888.48?

E6–3 What annual interest rate, when compounded annually, would cause an initial deposit of $6,600 to accumulate to $25,063.50 in 14 years?

E6–4 Assuming in each case that interest is compounded annually, what is the present value of each of the following:
[a] $25,000 due in 9 years discounted at 10%?
[b] $30,000 due in 16 years discounted at 8%?
[c] $35,000 due in 3 years discounted at 6% *and* $43,000 due in 7 years discounted at 8%?

E6–5 Compute the amount of each of the following at the end of three years:
[a] $2,000 deposited at the end of each year for three years at 4%, compounded annually.
[b] $3,000 deposited at the end of each quarter for three years at 10%, compounded quarterly.
[c] $4,000 deposited at the end of each month for three years at 12%, compounded monthly.

E6–6 Assuming an interest rate of 6%, compounded semiannually, how much cash must a person deposit at the end of each semiannual period in order to accumulate $25,000 at the end of 12 years?

E6–7 As of today, Roger Stanback has accumulated $182,764.85 in a retirement account that pays 8% interest compounded annually. He accumulated this sum by depositing $2,500 at the end of each year that he worked in the furniture business. The last deposit was made today. How many deposits did Roger make?

E6–8 Mary Jones has $9,433.42 today as a result of having deposited $750 at the end of each year for the last 10 years. Assuming annual compounding, what interest rate did Mary earn on her periodic deposits?

E6–9 Compute the amount of the following periodic deposits at the end of three years:
[a] $15,000 deposited at the beginning of each year at 8% compounded annually.
[b] $1,250 deposited at the beginning of each month at 12% compounded monthly.
[c] $3,500 deposited at the beginning of each quarter at 10% compounded quarterly.

E6–10 Assuming an interest rate of 8% compounded annually, what equal amounts of cash must a person deposit at the beginning of each year for 18 years in order to accumulate $30,000 at the end of 18 years?

E6–11 When Hank Riley's son was born, Hank deposited $250 in a special savings account that pays interest at 8% compounded annually. Later, Hank deposited $250 on each of his son's birthdays. How old is Hank's son if today is his son's birthday and, just *before* Hank makes his current deposit, the amount accumulated in the account is $7,331.07?

E6–12 Ken Rogers deposited $1,000 in an investment account at the beginning of each year for the last five years. Assuming that interest is compounded annually and that Ken has accumulated $6,715.61 in his account as of today, what stated interest rate did he earn?

E6–13 Compute the value today of:
[a] $60,000 to be received at the end of each year for the next 6 years at 4% compounded annually.
[b] $40,000 to be received at the end of each semiannual period for the next 10 years at 8% compounded semiannually.
[c] $20,000 to be received at the end of each quarter for the next 8 years at 10% compounded quarterly.

E6–14 Today Joe Johnson deposited $10,000 in a savings account that pays 6% interest compounded semiannually. Assuming that Joe wants to liquidate the balance in his account by making equal withdrawals at the end of each semiannual period for four years, how large will each withdrawal be?

E6-15 Norma Washburn has $54,138 in a savings account that pays 6% interest compounded annually. How many annual withdrawals of $5,000 each can she make from the account, assuming that she makes the first withdrawal one year from now?

E6-16 An automobile with a cash price of $6,473.70 is purchased for $1,500 down and payments of $2,000 at the end of each year for three years. Assuming annual compounding, what is the stated interest rate in this transaction?

E6-17 What is the present value of each of the following:
[a] $18,000 to be paid at the beginning of each year for 12 years? Assume an interest rate of 6% compounded annually.
[b] $27,000 to be paid at the beginning of each quarter for 10 years? Assume an interest rate of 10% compounded quarterly.
[c] $3,000 to be paid at the beginning of each month for 3 years? Assume an interest rate of 12% compounded monthly.

E6-18 Mary Sue Goldman wants to use all the money in her $15,000 savings account to pay for her college education, which begins today. The account pays 8% interest compounded annually. What constant amount of cash can she withdraw at the beginning of each of her four years in college?

E6-19 Joe Washington currently owes a debt of $2,188.43. The debt accrues interest at 10% compounded annually on the unpaid balance. How many annual payments of $800 each will Joe have to make to liquidate the debt and interest, assuming that the first payment is made today?

E6-20 Alice Robinson purchased a new television set that had a cash price of $526.59. She made an $80 down payment and paid the balance in $80 installments at the end of each year for seven years. What is the stated annual interest rate?

E6-21 Assume that it is now the beginning of Year 1. Answer each of the following questions, assuming an interest rate of 8% compounded annually.
[a] What is the amount at the end of Year 10 of ten annual deposits of $5,000 each, the first of which is made at the end of Year 1?
[b] What is the amount at the end of Year 20 of ten annual deposits of $5,000 each, the first of which is made at the end of Year 11?
[c] As of the beginning of Year 11, what is the present value of ten annual receipts of $5,000 each, the first of which is received at the end of Year 11?
[d] As of the beginning of Year 1, what is the present value of ten annual receipts of $5,000 each, the first of which is received at the end of Year 11?
[e] Why are the correct answers to [a] and [b] the same?
[f] Why are the correct answers to [c] and [d] different?

PROBLEMS

P6-1 First Savings and Loan Association, whose slogan is "our interest is more interesting," currently pays interest at a rate of 8%, compounded quarterly. Second Savings and Loan Association, whose slogan is "our interest interests more," pays 10% compounded annually. If you have $5,000 that you want to deposit for five years, what would be the total additional interest that you could earn by depositing the money in Second Savings and Loan rather than First Savings and Loan?

P6-2 Chemstone Mineral Company deposited $5,000 with each of four investment companies. The terms of each investment are as follows:

Investment Company	Annual Rate	Compounded	Investment Term in Years
A	12%	Annually	8
B	10%	Quarterly	6
C	10%	Semiannually	4
D	8%	Quarterly	2

What will be the balance in each investment account at its maturity?

P6-3 Margaret Stanton was informed by the attorney managing her deceased uncle's estate that the following deposits would be made in her new savings account at the end of each of the following years:

Year	Deposit
1982	$2,000
1983	3,000
1984	4,000
1985	5,000

The account pays 8% interest compounded annually.

Instructions

[a] Assuming that Margaret makes no additional deposits or withdrawals, what will be the balance in her savings account at the end of 1985, immediately after the last deposit?

[b] What would be the balance in the savings account at the end of 1985 if, instead of the deposits shown above, a deposit of $3,500 was made at the end of each year?

[c] Explain the similarities and differences in the techniques you used to solve [a] and [b].

P6–4 Mike Blass has admired for many years a refurbished Model T automobile owned by his neighbor. Thus, Blass quickly accepted his neighbor's recent offer to sell the car. Which of the following two payment options offered by the neighbor should Blass take?

[1] $9,500 cash payable immediately.

[2] $11,000 cash payable in one lump sum after two years.

Blass knows that he can earn 8%, compounded annually, on his money.

P6–5 Your neighbor has a $5,000 noninterest-bearing note receivable that matures at the end of three years. You recently inherited $25,000, and you know that you could earn 10%, compounded annually, on investments that are similar in risk to your neighbor's note. Your goal is to maximize your income.

Instructions

[a] What is the maximum amount of cash that you would be willing to pay today for your neighbor's note?

[b] What is the maximum amount of cash that you would be willing to pay today if the $5,000 note paid you interest of 3% at the end of each year? (*Hint:* You will receive $5,000 × 3% = $150 at the end of Years 1, 2, and 3 and the $5,000 maturity value at the end of Year 3.)

P6–6 On February 1, 1983, Highland Tool Company leased equipment from Munson Manufacturing Corpo-ration. The lease term is three years, which equals the estimated economic life of the equipment. The lease requires Highland to make 36 monthly rental payments of $7,000 each, with the first payment due on February 1, 1983.

Instructions

[a] Assuming a relevant interest rate of 12% compounded monthly, what is the value of the lease to Highland Tool Company on February 1, 1983?

[b] Answer [a], assuming that the first of the 36 monthly rental payments is made on March 1, 1983.

P6–7 Angus Shepard, a local veterinarian, opens a tax-deferred retirement account that pays 8% interest compounded annually. He plans to deposit $1,500 at the beginning of each year for 25 years, with the initial deposit made today.

Instructions

[a] How much cash will Angus have in his account when he retires at the end of 25 years?

[b] How much of the sum that you calculated in [a] is interest?

[c] What equal-size deposits would Angus have to make at the beginning of each year to accumulate $200,000 at the end of 25 years?

P6–8 Doris Kearns retired from State University today with $128,392.20 in a retirement account that pays 8% interest compounded annually.

Instructions

[a] How many $15,000 annual withdrawals can Doris make from her account if she makes the first withdrawal one year from now?

[b] What equal amount should she withdraw at the end of each year if she wants to make the final withdrawal 20 years from today?

[c] What equal amount should she withdraw annually if she wants to make a total of 15 withdrawals, with the initial withdrawal made today?

[d] What equal amount should she withdraw annually if she wants to make a total of 15 withdrawals, with the initial withdrawal made 5 years from now?

P6–9 Keap Trucking Company purchased a new truck from Black Motor Company in exchange for a three-year, noninterest-bearing promissory note with a maturity value of $80,000. The market rate of interest for similar notes is 10% compounded annually.

Instructions

[a] What is the historical cost of the truck to Keap Trucking Company?

[b] Answer [a], assuming that the $80,000 note paid interest of 2% at the end of each year for three years. (*Hint*: The note pays interest of $80,000 × 2% = $1,600 to the holder at the end of each of the three years, and it pays the maturity value of $80,000 at the end of the third year.)

P6–10 Harry Foster buys a new home costing $60,205.56. He makes a $10,000 down payment and gets a 10-year mortgage loan for the balance. The mortgage bears interest at 10%, compounded quarterly, and calls for equal payments at the end of each 3-month interval.

Instructions

[a] How much will each quarterly payment be?

[b] What is the total sum of cash that Harry will spend on the down payment and the loan?

[c] What is the total amount of interest that Harry will pay on the loan?

[d] What is the total amount of interest that Harry could save if he could get the required loan at 8% compounded quarterly?

P6–11 Thompson Tire and Rubber Company will need $8,000,000 at the end of 20 years to retire a maturing issue of term bonds. To accumulate the desired sum, the company deposits $215,000 at the end of each year in a sinking fund that pays 6% interest compounded annually.

Instructions

[a] Will the fund at the end of 20 years be sufficient to retire the bonds?

[b] If your answer to [a] is no, what equal amount of cash would the company have to deposit at the end of each of the 20 years to accumulate the desired sum?

P6–12 Devore Hardware Company wants to purchase a new warehouse in 3 years. The company expects the warehouse to cost $135,000 at that time. To accumulate this amount, the company plans to make 12 quarterly deposits of $9,000 each in a special account that pays 10% interest compounded quarterly. The first deposit is made today.

Instructions

[a] Will the amount in the fund at the end of three years be sufficient to purchase the warehouse?

[b] If your answer to [a] is no, what equal amount of cash would the company have to deposit at the beginning of each quarter to accumulate $135,000 at the end of three years?

P6–13 Determine the stated annual interest rate in each of the following independent cases (assume annual compounding in each case):

[a] A deposit of $650 accumulates to $925.15 in 9 years.

[b] A person lends $75,131 today in exchange for $100,000 to be received at the end of 3 years.

[c] Periodic deposits of $1,200 made at the end of each year accumulate to $25,218.08 at the end of 14 years.

[d] Periodic deposits of $2,800 made at the beginning of each year accumulate to $57,075.97 at the end of 11 years.

[e] An annuity contract purchased for $53,373.90 promises to pay $5,000 at the end of each year for the next 25 years.

[f] A person borrows $50,000 in exchange for a written promise to pay $4,821.78 at the beginning of each year for 30 years, with the first payment due now.

P6–14 On April 1, 1983, International Farm Equipment Corporation issues 10%, 20-year bonds payable with a total par value of $80,000. Interest is payable semiannually on September 30 and March 31.

Instructions

[a] How much will the bonds sell for if, on April 1, 1983, the market rate of interest for similar bonds is:

    [1] 8%?

    [2] 10%?

    [3] 12%?

[b] Make the journal entry for International Farm Equipment Corporation to record the bond issuance under each of the three assumptions in [a].

P6–15 Shamrock Incorporated, maker of fine china and crystal, has projected substantial growth in sales over the next 10 years. To ensure that sufficient funds are available for capital expansion, Shamrock plans to deposit $75,000 in a building fund at the end of each year for the next 5 years.

Instructions

[a] What will be the balance in the fund at the end of the fifth year if interest is earned at 8% compounded annually?

[b] How many years would it take for the fund to accumulate $348,075 if interest is earned at 10% compounded annually?

[c] What interest rate, compounded annually, would be necessary to accumulate $414,422 by the end of the fifth year?

P6–16 Determine the number of *years* involved in each of the following independent situations:

[a] A deposit of $1,800 accumulates to $4,572.63 at 6% compounded annually.

[b] A person lends $33,778.25 today in exchange for $50,000 to be received in the future, which includes interest at 8% compounded semiannually.

[c] Deposits of $300 at the end of each quarter accumulate to $11,115.36 at the end of the final quarter. The interest rate is 8% compounded quarterly.

[d] Deposits of $600 at the beginning of each year accumulate to $14,787.25 at the end of the final year. The interest rate is 4% compounded annually.

[e] A person deposits $1,635.14 today in a savings account that pays interest at 8% compounded quarterly. The account is liquidated by withdrawals of $100 at the end of each quarter, with the initial withdrawal made at the end of the first quarter.

[f] A person deposits $1,777.37 today in a savings account that pays interest at 6% compounded annually. The account is liquidated by annual withdrawals of $200, with the initial withdrawal made today.

P6–17 On January 1, 1983, Helen Wilson buys new furniture costing $5,000. To pay for it, she signs a promissory note calling for equal payments at the end of each month for three years. The note bears interest at 12% compounded monthly.

Instructions

[a] How much will each monthly payment be?

[b] Helen is a calendar-year taxpayer, and she knows that interest is deductible for federal income tax purposes. How much interest will Helen pay on the furniture loan in each of the following years:

    [1] 1983?
    [2] 1984?
    [3] 1985?

P6–18 Jim Watson is thinking about buying a log cabin kit from Leisure Homes, Inc., for $15,000 cash. The best alternative use of Jim's money is an investment account that pays 8% interest compounded annually. Jim expects that it would take him two years working part-time to complete the exterior of the cabin and an additional year to finish the interior. If Jim decides to buy the kit, he will leave his present part-time job of making Christmas ornaments from pine cones. As a result, he will lose $2,000 cash income at the end of each of the three years that he worked on the cabin.

The cabin would be constructed on a lake in a retirement community. Jim expects that the annual rent for the first five years after completion would be $2,400 and for the second five years would be $3,600. Rental payments would be due at the beginning of each year. Jim expects that he would sell the cabin for $20,000 after renting it for 10 years.

Instructions

Using appropriate compound interest concepts, determine whether the log cabin is a sound economic investment for Jim Watson. Ignore income taxes.

TABLE 6–1
Amount of 1

$$fvf_{\overline{n}|i} = (1 + i)^n$$

Periods (n)	1%	2%	2.5%	3%	4%	5%
1	1.01000	1.02000	1.02500	1.03000	1.04000	1.05000
2	1.02010	1.04040	1.05062	1.06090	1.08160	1.10250
3	1.03030	1.06121	1.07689	1.09273	1.12486	1.15762
4	1.04060	1.08243	1.10381	1.12551	1.16986	1.21551
5	1.05101	1.10408	1.13141	1.15927	1.21665	1.27628
6	1.06152	1.12616	1.15969	1.19405	1.26532	1.34010
7	1.07214	1.14869	1.18869	1.22987	1.31593	1.40710
8	1.08286	1.17166	1.21840	1.26677	1.36857	1.47746
9	1.09369	1.19509	1.24886	1.30477	1.42331	1.55133
10	1.10462	1.21899	1.28008	1.34392	1.48024	1.62889
11	1.11567	1.24337	1.31209	1.38423	1.53945	1.71034
12	1.12683	1.26824	1.34489	1.42576	1.60103	1.79586
13	1.13809	1.29361	1.37851	1.46853	1.66507	1.88565
14	1.14947	1.31948	1.41297	1.51259	1.73168	1.97993
15	1.16097	1.34587	1.44830	1.55797	1.80094	2.07893
16	1.17258	1.37279	1.48451	1.60471	1.87298	2.18287
17	1.18430	1.40024	1.52162	1.65285	1.94790	2.29202
18	1.19615	1.42825	1.55966	1.70243	2.02582	2.40662
19	1.20811	1.45681	1.59865	1.75351	2.10685	2.52695
20	1.22019	1.48595	1.63862	1.80611	2.19112	2.65330
21	1.23239	1.51567	1.67958	1.86029	2.27877	2.78596
22	1.24472	1.54598	1.72157	1.91610	2.36992	2.92526
23	1.25716	1.57690	1.76461	1.97359	2.46472	3.07152
24	1.26973	1.60844	1.80873	2.03279	2.56330	3.22510
25	1.28243	1.64061	1.85394	2.09378	2.66584	3.38635
26	1.29526	1.67342	1.90029	2.15659	2.77247	3.55567
27	1.30821	1.70689	1.94780	2.22129	2.88337	3.73346
28	1.32129	1.74102	1.99650	2.28793	2.99870	3.92013
29	1.33450	1.77584	2.04641	2.35657	3.11865	4.11614
30	1.34785	1.81136	2.09757	2.42726	3.24340	4.32194
31	1.36133	1.84759	2.15001	2.50008	3.37313	4.53804
32	1.37494	1.88454	2.20376	2.57508	3.50806	4.76494
33	1.38869	1.92223	2.25885	2.65234	3.64838	5.00319
34	1.40258	1.96068	2.31532	2.73191	3.79432	5.25335
35	1.41660	1.99989	2.37321	2.81386	3.94609	5.51602
36	1.43077	2.03989	2.43254	2.89828	4.10393	5.79182
37	1.44508	2.08069	2.49335	2.98523	4.26809	6.08141
38	1.45953	2.12230	2.55568	3.07478	4.43881	6.38548
39	1.47412	2.16474	2.61957	3.16703	4.61637	6.70475
40	1.48886	2.20804	2.68506	3.26204	4.80102	7.03999

TABLE 6–1   AMOUNT OF 1

233

TABLE 6–1
Amount of 1

6%	8%	10%	12%	16%	20%	24%	Periods (n)
1.06000	1.08000	1.10000	1.12000	1.16000	1.20000	1.24000	1
1.12360	1.16640	1.21000	1.25440	1.34560	1.44000	1.53760	2
1.19102	1.25971	1.33100	1.40493	1.56090	1.72800	1.90662	3
1.26248	1.36049	1.46410	1.57352	1.81064	2.07360	2.36421	4
1.33823	1.46933	1.61051	1.76234	2.10034	2.48832	2.93163	5
1.41852	1.58687	1.77156	1.97382	2.43640	2.98598	3.63522	6
1.50363	1.71382	1.94872	2.21068	2.82622	3.58318	4.50767	7
1.59385	1.85093	2.14359	2.47596	3.27841	4.29982	5.58951	8
1.68948	1.99900	2.35795	2.77308	3.80296	5.15978	6.93099	9
1.79085	2.15892	2.59374	3.10585	4.41144	6.19174	8.59443	10
1.89830	2.33164	2.85312	3.47855	5.11726	7.43008	10.65709	11
2.01220	2.51817	3.13843	3.89598	5.93603	8.91610	13.21479	12
2.13293	2.71962	3.45227	4.36349	6.88579	10.69932	16.38634	13
2.26090	2.93719	3.79750	4.88711	7.98752	12.83918	20.31906	14
2.39656	3.17217	4.17725	5.47357	9.26552	15.40702	25.19563	15
2.54035	3.42594	4.59497	6.13039	10.74800	18.48843	31.24259	16
2.69277	3.70002	5.05447	6.86604	12.46768	22.18611	38.74081	17
2.85434	3.99602	5.55992	7.68997	14.46251	26.62333	48.03860	18
3.02560	4.31570	6.11591	8.61276	16.77652	31.94800	59.56786	19
3.20714	4.66096	6.72750	9.64629	19.46076	38.33760	73.86415	20
3.39956	5.03383	7.40025	10.80385	22.57448	46.00512	91.59155	21
3.60354	5.43654	8.14027	12.10031	26.18640	55.20614	113.57352	22
3.81975	5.87146	8.95430	13.55235	30.37622	66.24737	140.83116	23
4.04893	6.34118	9.84973	15.17863	35.23642	79.49685	174.63064	24
4.29187	6.84848	10.83471	17.00006	40.87424	95.39622	216.54199	25
4.54938	7.39635	11.91818	19.04007	47.41412	114.47546	268.51207	26
4.82235	7.98806	13.10999	21.32488	55.00038	137.37055	332.95497	27
5.11169	8.62711	14.42099	23.88387	63.80044	164.84466	412.86416	28
5.41839	9.31727	15.86309	26.74993	74.00851	197.81359	511.95156	29
5.74349	10.06266	17.44940	29.95992	85.84988	237.37631	634.81993	30
6.08810	10.86767	19.19434	33.55511	99.58586	284.85158	787.17672	31
6.45339	11.73708	21.11378	37.58173	115.51959	341.82189	976.09913	32
6.84059	12.67605	23.22515	42.09153	134.00273	410.18627	1210.36292	33
7.25103	13.69013	25.54767	47.14252	155.44317	492.22352	1500.85002	34
7.68609	14.78534	28.10244	52.79962	180.31407	590.66823	1861.05403	35
8.14725	15.96817	30.91268	59.13557	209.16432	708.80187	2307.70699	36
8.63609	17.24563	34.00395	66.23184	242.63062	850.56225	2861.55667	37
9.15425	18.62528	37.40434	74.17966	281.45151	1020.67470	3548.33027	38
9.70351	20.11530	41.14478	83.08122	326.48376	1224.80964	4399.92954	39
10.28572	21.72452	45.25926	93.05097	378.72116	1469.77157	5455.91262	40

TABLE 6–2
Present Value of 1

$$pvf_{\overline{n}|i} = \frac{1}{(1 + i)^n}$$

Periods

(n)	1%	2%	2.5%	3%	4%	5%
1	.99010	.98039	.97561	.97087	.96154	.95238
2	.98030	.96117	.95181	.94260	.92456	.90703
3	.97059	.94232	.92860	.91514	.88900	.86384
4	.96098	.92385	.90595	.88849	.85480	.82270
5	.95147	.90573	.88385	.86261	.82193	.78353
6	.94205	.88797	.86230	.83748	.79031	.74622
7	.93272	.87056	.84127	.81309	.75992	.71068
8	.92348	.85349	.82075	.78941	.73069	.67684
9	.91434	.83676	.80073	.76642	.70259	.64461
10	.90529	.82035	.78120	.74409	.67556	.61391
11	.89632	.80426	.76214	.72242	.64958	.58468
12	.88745	.78849	.74356	.70138	.62460	.55684
13	.87866	.77303	.72542	.68095	.60057	.53032
14	.86996	.75788	.70773	.66112	.57748	.50507
15	.86135	.74301	.69047	.64186	.55526	.48102
16	.85282	.72845	.67362	.62317	.53391	.45811
17	.84438	.71416	.65720	.60502	.51337	.43630
18	.83602	.70016	.64117	.58739	.49363	.41552
19	.82774	.68643	.62553	.57029	.47464	.39573
20	.81954	.67297	.61027	.55368	.45639	.37689
21	.81143	.65978	.59539	.53755	.43883	.35894
22	.80340	.64684	.58086	.52189	.42196	.34185
23	.79544	.63416	.56670	.50669	.40573	.32557
24	.78757	.62172	.55288	.49193	.39012	.31007
25	.77977	.60953	.53939	.47761	.37512	.29530
26	.77205	.59758	.52623	.46369	.36069	.28124
27	.76440	.58586	.51340	.45019	.34682	.26785
28	.75684	.57437	.50088	.43708	.33348	.25509
29	.74934	.56311	.48866	.42435	.32065	.24295
30	.74192	.55207	.47674	.41199	.30832	.23138
31	.73458	.54125	.46511	.39999	.29646	.22036
32	.72730	.53063	.45377	.38834	.28506	.20987
33	.72010	.52023	.44270	.37703	.27409	.19987
34	.71297	.51003	.43191	.36604	.26355	.19035
35	.70591	.50003	.42137	.35538	.25342	.18129
36	.69892	.49022	.41109	.34503	.24367	.17266
37	.69200	.48061	.40107	.33498	.23430	.16444
38	.68515	.47119	.39128	.32523	.22529	.15661
39	.67837	.46195	.38174	.31575	.21662	.14915
40	.67165	.45289	.37243	.30656	.20829	.14205

TABLE 6–2 PRESENT VALUE OF 1   235

TABLE 6–2
Present Value of 1

6%	8%	10%	12%	16%	20%	24%	Periods (n)
.94340	.92593	.90909	.89286	.86207	.83333	.80645	1
.89000	.85734	.82645	.79719	.74316	.69444	.65036	2
.83962	.79383	.75131	.71178	.64066	.57870	.52449	3
.79209	.73503	.68301	.63552	.55229	.48225	.42297	4
.74726	.68058	.62092	.56743	.47611	.40188	.34111	5
.70496	.63017	.56447	.50663	.41044	.33490	.27509	6
.66506	.58349	.51316	.45235	.35383	.27908	.22184	7
.62741	.54027	.46651	.40388	.30503	.23257	.17891	8
.59190	.50025	.42410	.36061	.26295	.19381	.14428	9
.55839	.46319	.38554	.32197	.22668	.16151	.11635	10
.52679	.42888	.35049	.28748	.19542	.13459	.09383	11
.49697	.39711	.31863	.25668	.16846	.11216	.07567	12
.46884	.36770	.28966	.22917	.14523	.09346	.06103	13
.44230	.34046	.26333	.20462	.12520	.07789	.04921	14
.41727	.31524	.23939	.18270	.10793	.06491	.03969	15
.39365	.29189	.21763	.16312	.09304	.05409	.03201	16
.37136	.27027	.19784	.14564	.08021	.04507	.02581	17
.35034	.25025	.17986	.13004	.06914	.03756	.02082	18
.33051	.23171	.16351	.11611	.05961	.03130	.01679	19
.31180	.21455	.14864	.10367	.05139	.02608	.01354	20
.29416	.19866	.13513	.09256	.04430	.02174	.01092	21
.27751	.18394	.12285	.08264	.03819	.01811	.00880	22
.26180	.17032	.11168	.07379	.03292	.01509	.00710	23
.24698	.15770	.10153	.06588	.02838	.01258	.00573	24
.23300	.14602	.09230	.05882	.02447	.01048	.00462	25
.21981	.13520	.08391	.05252	.02109	.00874	.00372	26
.20737	.12519	.07628	.04689	.01818	.00728	.00300	27
.19563	.11591	.06934	.04187	.01567	.00607	.00242	28
.18456	.10733	.06304	.03738	.01351	.00506	.00195	29
.17411	.09938	.05731	.03338	.01165	.00421	.00158	30
.16425	.09202	.05210	.02980	.01004	.00351	.00127	31
.15496	.08520	.04736	.02661	.00866	.00293	.00102	32
.14619	.07889	.04306	.02376	.00746	.00244	.00083	33
.13791	.07305	.03914	.02121	.00643	.00203	.00067	34
.13011	.06763	.03558	.01894	.00555	.00169	.00054	35
.12274	.06262	.03235	.01691	.00478	.00141	.00043	36
.11579	.05799	.02941	.01510	.00412	.00118	.00035	37
.10924	.05369	.02673	.01348	.00355	.00098	.00028	38
.10306	.04971	.02430	.01204	.00306	.00082	.00023	39
.09722	.04603	.02209	.01075	.00264	.00068	.00018	40

TABLE 6–3
Amount of an Ordinary Annuity of 1

$$aoaf_{\overline{n}|i} = \frac{(1 + i)^n - 1}{i}$$

Periods

(n)	1%	2%	2.5%	3%	4%	5%
1	1.00000	1.00000	1.00000	1.00000	1.00000	1.00000
2	2.01000	2.02000	2.02500	2.03000	2.04000	2.05000
3	3.03010	3.06040	3.07562	3.09090	3.12160	3.15250
4	4.06040	4.12161	4.15252	4.18363	4.24646	4.31012
5	5.10101	5.20404	5.25633	5.30914	5.41632	5.52563
6	6.15202	6.30812	6.38774	6.46841	6.63298	6.80191
7	7.21354	7.43428	7.54743	7.66246	7.89829	8.14201
8	8.28567	8.58297	8.73612	8.89234	9.21423	9.54911
9	9.36853	9.75463	9.95452	10.15911	10.58280	11.02656
10	10.46221	10.94972	11.20338	11.46388	12.00611	12.57789
11	11.56683	12.16872	12.48347	12.80780	13.48635	14.20679
12	12.68250	13.41209	13.79555	14.19203	15.02581	15.91713
13	13.80933	14.68033	15.14044	15.61779	16.62684	17.71298
14	14.94742	15.97394	16.51895	17.08632	18.29191	19.59863
15	16.09690	17.29342	17.93193	18.59891	20.02359	21.57856
16	17.25786	18.63929	19.38022	20.15688	21.82453	23.65749
17	18.43044	20.01207	20.86473	21.76159	23.69751	25.84037
18	19.61475	21.41231	22.38635	23.41444	25.64541	28.13238
19	20.81090	22.84056	23.94601	25.11687	27.67123	30.53900
20	22.01900	24.29737	25.54466	26.87037	29.77808	33.06595
21	23.23919	25.78332	27.18327	28.67649	31.96920	35.71925
22	24.47159	27.29898	28.86286	30.53678	34.24797	38.50521
23	25.71630	28.84496	30.58443	32.45288	36.61789	41.43048
24	26.97346	30.42186	32.34904	34.42647	39.08260	44.50200
25	28.24320	32.03030	34.15776	36.45926	41.64591	47.72710
26	29.52563	33.67091	36.01171	38.55304	44.31174	51.11345
27	30.82089	35.34432	37.91200	40.70963	47.08421	54.66913
28	32.12910	37.05121	39.85980	42.93092	49.96758	58.40258
29	33.45039	38.79223	41.85630	45.21885	52.96629	62.32271
30	34.78489	40.56808	43.90270	47.57542	56.08494	66.43885
31	36.13274	42.37944	46.00027	50.00268	59.32834	70.76079
32	37.49407	44.22703	48.15028	52.50276	62.70147	75.29883
33	38.86901	46.11157	50.35403	55.07784	66.20953	80.06377
34	40.25770	48.03380	52.61289	57.73018	69.85791	85.06696
35	41.66028	49.99448	54.92821	60.46208	73.65222	90.32031
36	43.07688	51.99437	57.30141	63.27594	77.59831	95.83632
37	44.50765	54.03425	59.73395	66.17422	81.70225	101.62814
38	45.95272	56.11494	62.22730	69.15945	85.97034	107.70955
39	47.41225	58.23724	64.78298	72.23423	90.40915	114.09502
40	48.88637	60.40198	67.40255	75.40126	95.02552	120.79977

TABLE 6–3 AMOUNT OF AN ORDINARY ANNUITY OF 1   237

TABLE 6–3
Amount of an Ordinary Annuity of 1

6%	8%	10%	12%	16%	20%	24%	Periods (n)
1.00000	1.00000	1.00000	1.00000	1.00000	1.00000	1.00000	1
2.06000	2.08000	2.10000	2.12000	2.16000	2.20000	2.24000	2
3.18360	3.24640	3.31000	3.37440	3.50560	3.64000	3.77760	3
4.37462	4.50611	4.64100	4.77933	5.06650	5.36800	5.68422	4
5.63709	5.86660	6.10510	6.35285	6.87714	7.44160	8.04844	5
6.97532	7.33593	7.71561	8.11519	8.97748	9.92992	10.98006	6
8.39384	8.92280	9.48717	10.08901	11.41387	12.91590	14.61528	7
9.89747	10.63663	11.43589	12.29969	14.24009	16.49908	19.12294	8
11.49132	12.48756	13.57948	14.77566	17.51851	20.79890	24.71245	9
13.18079	14.48656	15.93742	17.54874	21.32147	25.95868	31.64344	10
14.97164	16.64549	18.53117	20.65458	25.73290	32.15042	40.23787	11
16.86994	18.97713	21.38428	24.13313	30.85017	39.58050	50.89495	12
18.88214	21.49530	24.52271	28.02911	36.78620	48.49660	64.10974	13
21.01507	24.21492	27.97498	32.39260	43.67199	59.19592	80.49608	14
23.27597	27.15211	31.77248	37.27971	51.65951	72.03511	100.81514	15
25.67253	30.32428	35.94973	42.75328	60.92503	87.44213	126.01077	16
28.21288	33.75023	40.54470	48.88367	71.67303	105.93056	157.25336	17
30.90565	37.45024	45.59917	55.74971	84.14072	128.11667	195.99416	18
33.75999	41.44626	51.15909	63.43968	98.60323	154.74000	244.03276	19
36.78559	45.76196	57.27500	72.05244	115.37975	186.68800	303.60062	20
39.99273	50.42292	64.00250	81.69874	134.84051	225.02560	377.46477	21
43.39229	55.45676	71.40275	92.50258	157.41499	271.03072	469.05632	22
46.99583	60.89330	79.54302	104.60289	183.60138	326.23686	582.62984	23
50.81558	66.76476	88.49733	118.15524	213.97761	392.48424	723.46100	24
54.86451	73.10594	98.34706	133.33387	249.21402	471.98108	898.09164	25
59.15638	79.95442	109.18177	150.33393	290.08827	567.37730	1114.63363	26
63.70577	87.35077	121.09994	159.37401	337.50239	681.85276	1383.14570	27
68.52811	95.33883	134.20994	190.69889	392.50277	819.22331	1716.10067	28
73.63980	103.96594	148.63093	214.58275	456.30322	984.06797	2128.96483	29
79.05819	113.28321	164.49402	241.33268	530.31173	1181.88157	2640.91639	30
84.80168	123.34587	181.94342	271.29261	616.16161	1419.25788	3275.73632	31
90.88978	134.21354	201.13777	304.84772	715.74746	1704.10946	4062.91304	32
97.34316	145.95062	222.25154	342.42945	831.26706	2045.93135	5039.01217	33
104.18375	158.62667	245.47670	384.52098	965.26979	2456.11762	6249.37509	34
111.43478	172.31680	271.02437	431.66350	1120.71295	2948.34115	7750.22511	35
119.12087	187.10215	299.12681	484.46312	1301.02703	3539.00937	9611.27913	36
127.26812	203.07032	330.03949	543.59869	1510.19135	4247.81125	11918.98612	37
135.90421	220.31595	364.04343	609.83053	1752.82197	5098.37350	14780.54279	38
145.05846	238.94122	401.44778	684.01020	2034.27348	6119.04820	18328.87306	39
154.76197	259.05652	442.59256	767.09142	2360.75724	7343.85784	22728.80260	40

TABLE 6-4
Present Value of an Ordinary Annuity of 1

$$pvoaf_{\overline{n}|i} = \frac{1 - \dfrac{1}{(1 + i)^n}}{i}$$

Periods (n)	1%	2%	2.5%	3%	4%	5%
1	0.99010	0.98039	0.97561	0.97087	0.96154	0.95238
2	1.97040	1.94156	1.92742	1.91347	1.88609	1.85941
3	2.94099	2.88388	2.85602	2.82861	2.77509	2.72325
4	3.90197	3.80773	3.76197	3.71710	3.62990	3.54595
5	4.85343	4.71346	4.64583	4.57971	4.45182	4.32948
6	5.79548	5.60143	5.50813	5.41719	5.24214	5.07569
7	6.72819	6.47199	6.34939	6.23028	6.00205	5.78637
8	7.65168	7.32548	7.17014	7.01969	6.73274	6.46321
9	8.56602	8.16224	7.97087	7.78611	7.43533	7.10782
10	9.47130	8.98259	8.75206	8.53020	8.11090	7.72173
11	10.36763	9.78685	9.51421	9.25262	8.76048	8.30641
12	11.25508	10.57534	10.25776	9.95400	9.38507	8.86325
13	12.13374	11.34837	10.98318	10.63496	9.98565	9.39357
14	13.00370	12.10625	11.69091	11.29607	10.56312	9.89864
15	13.86505	12.84926	12.38138	11.93794	11.11839	10.37966
16	14.71787	13.57771	13.05500	12.56110	11.65230	10.83777
17	15.56225	14.29187	13.71220	13.16612	12.16567	11.27407
18	16.39827	14.99203	14.35336	13.75351	12.65930	11.68959
19	17.22601	15.67846	14.97889	14.32380	13.13394	12.08532
20	18.04555	16.35143	15.58916	14.87747	13.59033	12.46221
21	18.85698	17.01121	16.18455	15.41502	14.02916	12.82115
22	19.66038	17.65805	16.76541	15.93692	14.45112	13.16300
23	20.45582	18.29220	17.33211	16.44361	14.85684	13.48857
24	21.24339	18.91393	17.88499	16.93554	15.24696	13.79864
25	22.02316	19.52346	18.42438	17.41315	15.62208	14.09394
26	22.79520	20.12104	18.95061	17.87684	15.98277	14.37519
27	23.55961	20.70690	19.46401	18.32703	16.32959	14.64303
28	24.31644	21.28127	19.96489	18.76411	16.66306	14.89813
29	25.06579	21.84438	20.45355	19.18845	16.98371	15.14107
30	25.80771	22.39646	20.93029	19.60044	17.29203	15.37245
31	26.54229	22.93770	21.39541	20.00043	17.58849	15.59281
32	27.26959	23.46833	21.84918	20.38877	17.87355	15.80268
33	27.98969	23.98856	22.29188	20.76579	18.14765	16.00255
34	28.70267	24.49859	22.72379	21.13184	18.41120	16.19290
35	29.40858	24.99862	23.14516	21.48722	18.66461	16.37419
36	30.10751	25.48884	23.55625	21.83225	18.90828	16.54685
37	30.79951	25.96945	23.95732	22.16724	19.14258	16.71129
38	31.48466	26.44064	24.34860	22.49246	19.36786	16.86789
39	32.16303	26.90259	24.73034	22.80822	19.58448	17.01704
40	32.83469	27.35548	25.10278	23.11477	19.79277	17.15909

TABLE 6–4   PRESENT VALUE OF AN ORDINARY ANNUITY OF 1   239

TABLE 6–4
Present Value of an Ordinary Annuity of 1

6%	8%	10%	12%	16%	20%	24%	Periods (n)
0.94340	0.92593	0.90909	0.89286	0.86207	0.83333	0.80645	1
1.83339	1.78326	1.73554	1.69005	1.60523	1.52778	1.45682	2
2.67301	2.57710	2.48685	2.40183	2.24589	2.10648	1.98130	3
3.46511	3.31213	3.16987	3.03735	2.79818	2.58873	2.40428	4
4.21236	3.99271	3.79079	3.60478	3.27429	2.99061	2.74538	5
4.91732	4.62288	4.35526	4.11141	3.68474	3.32551	3.02047	6
5.58238	5.20637	4.86842	4.56376	4.03857	3.60459	3.24232	7
6.20979	5.74664	5.33493	4.96764	4.34359	3.83716	3.42122	8
6.80169	6.24689	5.75902	5.32825	4.60654	4.03097	3.56550	9
7.36009	6.71008	6.14457	5.65022	4.83323	4.19247	3.68186	10
7.88687	7.13896	6.49506	5.93770	5.02864	4.32706	3.77569	11
8.38384	7.53608	6.81369	6.19437	5.19711	4.43922	3.85136	12
8.85268	7.90378	7.10336	6.42355	5.34233	4.53268	3.91239	13
9.29498	8.24424	7.36669	6.62817	5.46753	4.61057	3.96160	14
9.71225	8.55948	7.60608	6.81086	5.57546	4.67547	4.00129	15
10.10590	8.85137	7.82371	6.97399	5.66850	4.72956	4.03330	16
10.47726	9.12164	8.02155	7.11963	5.74870	4.77463	4.05911	17
10.82760	9.37189	8.20141	7.24967	5.81785	4.81219	4.07993	18
11.15812	9.60360	8.36492	7.36578	5.87746	4.84350	4.09672	19
11.46992	9.81815	8.51356	7.46944	5.92884	4.86958	4.11026	20
11.76408	10.01680	8.64869	7.56200	5.97314	4.89132	4.12117	21
12.04158	10.20074	8.77154	7.64465	6.01133	4.90943	4.12998	22
12.30338	10.37106	8.88322	7.71843	6.04425	4.92453	4.13708	23
12.55036	10.52876	8.98474	7.78432	6.07263	4.93710	4.14281	24
12.78336	10.67478	9.07704	7.84314	6.09709	4.94759	4.14742	25
13.00317	10.80998	9.16095	7.89566	6.11818	4.95632	4.15115	26
13.21053	10.93516	9.23722	7.94255	6.13636	4.96360	4.15415	27
13.40616	11.05108	9.30657	7.98442	6.15204	4.96967	4.15657	28
13.59072	11.15841	9.36961	8.02181	6.16555	4.97472	4.15853	29
13.76483	11.25778	9.42691	8.05518	6.17720	4.97894	4.16010	30
13.92909	11.34980	9.47901	8.08499	6.18724	4.98245	4.16137	31
14.08404	11.43500	9.52638	8.11159	6.19590	4.98537	4.16240	32
14.23023	11.51389	9.56943	8.13535	6.20336	4.98781	4.16322	33
14.36814	11.58693	9.60857	8.15656	6.20979	4.98984	4.16389	34
14.49825	11.65457	9.64416	8.17550	6.21534	4.99154	4.16443	35
14.62099	11.71719	9.67651	8.19241	6.22012	4.99295	4.16486	36
14.73678	11.77518	9.70592	8.20751	6.22424	4.99412	4.16521	37
14.84602	11.82887	9.73265	8.22099	6.22779	4.99510	4.16549	38
14.94907	11.87858	9.75696	8.23303	6.23086	4.99592	4.16572	39
15.04630	11.92461	9.77905	8.24378	6.23350	4.99660	4.16590	40

Asset 3 Accounting

7

CASH AND RECEIVABLES

Objectives

To discuss and illustrate the financial accounting and reporting requirements for cash and receivables classified as current assets.

To explain the accounting for a petty cash fund.

To discuss and illustrate the preparation of a bank reconciliation and a proof of cash.

To explain the accounting for credit sales.

To discuss and illustrate the accounting for uncollectible accounts receivable.

To explain certain financing methods under which companies use their accounts receivable to generate cash.

To discuss and illustrate the accounting for notes receivable.

I n Part 1 of this book, we discussed the theoretical basis for financial reporting, and in Part 2 we presented the tools that accountants use every day. In Part 3, which begins with this chapter, our focus shifts to asset accounting. Each of the seven chapters in Part 3 discusses important measurement and disclosure principles that relate to certain assets, and each is related to the theoretical framework presented in Chapter 2. Recall that in Chapter 2 we defined assets as probable future economic benefits obtained or controlled by a particular entity as a result of past transactions or events. The Kroger Company balance sheet printed on the endpapers of this book shows several of the assets discussed in Part 3.

This chapter focuses on cash and receivables classified as current assets. Cash and receivables classified as noncurrent assets are discussed in Chapter 10. Recall that in Chapter 3 we discussed the nature of asset valuation. Generally, the valuation of cash and short-term receivables is less complex and controversial than the valuation of most other assets.

The assets described in this chapter are highly liquid (i.e., cash or close to cash realization) and are therefore important in an assessment of a company's overall liquidity. A recent study provided evidence that users of financial statements are becoming more concerned about liquidity evaluations. This study found that: "While security analysts used to be concerned primarily with earnings per share, they are now devoting increased attention to the balance sheet and cash flow. Liquidity analysis plays a significant part in security analysts' evaluation of companies."[1] Liquidity analysis has been particularly important during recent periods of high interest rates because of the difficulty many companies have had in generating enough cash to pay interest.

CASH

Composition of Cash

Cash is the standard medium of exchange in business transactions. It includes currency, coins, checks, bank drafts, money orders, and demand deposits (checking accounts). Savings accounts are also usually considered cash, because banks generally do not enforce their legal right to demand a notice before the depositor makes a withdrawal. As a result, savings account balances are usually available for immediate expenditure.

Most companies maintain several general ledger accounts for cash in order to provide management with adequate details concerning cash balances. For example, a company might establish:

1. A **petty cash** account for currency and coins (called a petty cash fund) used to make small disbursements.
2. A **cash on hand** account for undeposited cash receipts.
3. A separate **cash in bank** account for each checking account maintained.

External users of financial statements generally are interested in the total amount of cash that a company has and in the relationship between this amount and other financial statement amounts. That is why companies typically combine the amounts shown in the various cash accounts and report only a single total as "cash" on the balance sheet.

The valuation of cash is not highly controversial. Cash is simply reported at its **face amount.** The classification of cash as current or noncurrent depends on management's intended use of the cash. In order to be classified as a current asset, cash must be available for use in current operations. Because it is highly liquid, cash is usually listed first among the

---

[1]Morton Backer and Martin L. Gosman, *Financial Reporting and Business Liquidity* (New York: National Association of Accountants, 1978), p. 251.

SEEN A $500 BILL LATELY?

INFLATION OR NOT, The United States Treasury still has no intention of printing anything larger than a $100 bill.

Since the end of World War II, the C-note, adorned with a picture of Benjamin Franklin on the front and Independence Hall in Philadelphia on the back, has been the largest denomination of paper currency issued in the U.S. In the past, the government has printed $500, $1000, $5000, $10,000 and even $100,000 bills—and, with prices skyrocketing as they have in recent years, some people have wondered whether the bigger bucks might be coming back.

Don't count on it, says Peter Daly, former chief of the Office of Planning and Policy Development for the Bureau of Engraving and Printing in Washington, D.C.

"In the old days," says Peter Daly, "the larger values of currency were used principally for interbank transfers, business payments, etc. With the advent of electronics, the larger notes fell into disuse, so in 1945 we stopped printing them.

"Cash in this country is used principally as a convenience—half of all cash transactions are still under $1. Once they get beyond items costing $15 to $20, people tend to move away from cash to credit cards and checks."

Daly says $4 billion in new currency is printed every year, 60 percent of which consists of $1 bills. The $2 bill is still doing badly. "We were hopeful of abating the strong demand for $1 bills," Daly explains, "but it hasn't worked out that way." Similarly, the $1 Susan B. Anthony coin continues to languish. "They aren't making them at the mint anymore," says Daly, adding a bit wistfully: "They have a large inventory on hand."

One sign of soaring inflation is the growing number of $100 bills in circulation. In 1971, they represented 25 percent of the total value of currency in use; today, the figure is up to 41 percent. As of last August, $52 billion worth of $100 bills was in circulation.

Incidentally, just because the Treasury isn't making anything larger than a century note these days doesn't mean that larger denominations no longer exist. On the contrary, they're still around and, what's more, are legal tender. Mostly they're in the hands of dealers and collectors.

Just in case you haven't seen one in a while, the $500 bill has a picture of William McKinley; the $1000 bill, Grover Cleveland; the $5000 bill, James Madison; the $10,000 bill, Salmon P. Chase; the $100,000, Woodrow Wilson.

What should you do if somebody offers you such a bill?

"I'd examine it carefully," says Mr. Daly, "but it's OK to take—that is, if you aren't afraid to carry it around these days."

SOURCE: Herbert Kupferberg, "Seen a $500 Bill Lately?" *Parade*, April 11, 1982, p. 18. Reprinted by permission of Parade Publications, Inc.

current assets. A material amount of cash that has been restricted or designated for some current purpose, such as the payment of current bond interest, should be reported separately among the current assets. On the other hand, cash that is not available for current purposes, such as cash accumulated in a sinking fund to retire the principal amount of long-term bonds, should be reported in the investments and funds category and not in current assets.

Several noteworthy considerations in accounting for cash are described below.

1. **Certificates of deposit (CDs)** should normally be included in short-term investments instead of cash, because banks usually impose substantial interest penalties that discourage CD-holders from making withdrawals before the CDs mature.
2. **Postdated checks, NSF checks** (not sufficient funds checks, those that cannot be covered by funds in the debtor's bank account), and **IOUs** should be reported as receivables rather than cash.
3. **Expense advances,** such as advances for employee travel, and **postage stamps** should be reported as prepaid expenses, not cash.

4. A **bank overdraft,** which occurs when a depositor has written checks for a sum greater than that in the depositor's bank account, should be reported as a current liability, except when the depositor has sufficient funds in another account with the *same bank* to cover the account which is overdrawn. Under these circumstances, which may arise when a company maintains a regular operating account and a payroll account with the same bank, the bank will transfer funds to the overdrawn account if the depositor fails to do so. As a result, the depositor may appropriately offset the overdraft against the cash balance and report the net amount of cash among the current assets.

5. **Undelivered checks,** as of the balance sheet date, should be considered part of a debtor's cash. Technically, checks drawn by a company should not be deducted from the company's cash balance until they have been mailed or otherwise delivered. As a result, liabilities that the checks are intended to liquidate still exist and should be reported as current payables.

6. **Compensating balances** are minimum amounts that a company agrees to maintain in a bank checking account as partial consideration for a loan or line of credit. Users of financial statements generally want information about a company's compensating balances, because these balances limit the amount of cash that a company can spend in everyday operations. Moreover, compensating balances increase a company's effective interest cost if they are higher than the checking account balances that the company would normally maintain. For these reasons a company should disclose information about compensating balances in the notes to its financial statements. An example of such a note is as follows: "During 1982 informal arrangements were maintained with a number of banks which generally required the Company to maintain compensating cash balances of 8% of the loan commitments plus 8% of the average daily outstanding debt balances. At December 31, 1982, the cash balance includes $9.5 million of such compensating balances."

Management of Cash

Companies need cash to buy goods and services, to pay off debts, and to make distributions to owners. Because of its critical importance to the health of any business, cash must be managed effectively. As the chief executive of Firestone Tire & Rubber Company recently stated: "Cash becomes the final determinant in the way you run a company."[2] Effective cash management involves striking a delicate balance between *risk* and *profitability.* On the one hand, managers try to avoid having too little cash on hand in order to minimize the company's risk of insolvency. On the other hand, they try to avoid excessive cash balances because uninvested cash does not contribute to the company's profits.

Effective cash management requires careful **planning** and **control.** The major aspect of **cash planning** is the **cash budget,** which is an internal statement of projected cash inflows, outflows, and balances. Among other things, the cash budget enables managers to prepare in advance for such activities as the raising of additional cash through borrowing and the investing of idle cash in productive assets. Cash planning is usually covered in managerial accounting and in financial management courses.

Cash control is an important part of a firm's **internal control system.** Internal control has been defined as: "The plan of organization and all of the coordinate methods and measures adopted within a business to safeguard its assets, check the accuracy and reliability of its accounting data, promote operational efficiency, and encourage adherence to prescribed managerial policies."[3] Internal control includes **accounting controls,** which relate to the safeguarding of assets and the reliability of financial records, and **administrative controls,** which relate to operational efficiency and adherence to managerial policies. Accountants should have a general awareness of administrative controls, including statistical analyses, time and motion studies, performance reports, employee training programs, and quality

---

[2]Thomas O'Hanlon, "Less Means More at Firestone," *Fortune* (October 20, 1980), p. 116.
[3]*AICPA Professional Standards—Volume 1* (Chicago: Commerce Clearing House), AU Sec. 320.09.

controls.[4] In addition, accountants should have a thorough understanding of accounting controls. Several important **principles of internal accounting control** are listed below:

1. Company personnel should be competent and honest, and they should be given specific responsibilities.
2. The responsibility for a series of related events, such as receiving merchandise and paying for it, should be divided between two or more persons.
3. The accounting function should be separated from the custodianship of company assets.
4. Adequate accounting records should be kept at all times.
5. Certain clerical personnel should be rotated among various jobs.
6. Assets should be protected by insurance and by physical safeguards.
7. An internal audit staff should be maintained if management believes the benefits of such a staff exceed the costs.

The maintenance of an adequate system of internal accounting control for all assets is important, but it is particularly important for cash. Cash appeals to virtually everyone and is relatively easy to steal if not properly safeguarded. If one person, for example, receives and records a company's cash, that person can easily pocket some of the receipts and fail to record them. The specific features of internal accounting controls over cash vary from company to company. Generally, however, these controls are designed to ensure that:

1. Responsibilities are divided between those employees who account for cash and those who have custody of it.
2. All cash receipts are recorded as soon as received and that they are deposited immediately and intact in the bank.
3. All disbursements are made for authorized purposes.
4. All disbursements, except for small ones made from petty cash, are made by check.

Specific accounting controls for cash are usually covered in more depth in auditing courses. Two important control measures designed to help safeguard a company's cash— the maintenance of a petty cash fund and the periodic reconciliation of the bank statement—are discussed below.

Petty Cash

As a general rule, a business enterprise should make all payments by check. But most businesses find it inconvenient or impossible to write checks for such small items as taxi fares, newspaper delivery charges, postage, express charges, and minor supplies. A company usually makes expenditures for these kinds of items using currency and coins from a **petty cash fund,** often called an **imprest cash fund.** An imprest fund is one that is established for a fixed amount. Such a fund allows a company to effectively control small amounts of cash in a fairly simple manner.

The following discussion explains how a petty cash fund works.

1. A responsible employee is appointed **petty cashier.** A check is drawn payable to petty cash. It is then cashed, and the petty cashier places the money in the petty cash fund (which is often kept in a locked box). The check which establishes the fund is usually for an amount ($300, for example) that the company estimates will last from two to four weeks. The journal entry required is:

Petty Cash	300	
Cash		300

---

[4]*AICPA Professional Standards—Volume 1,* AU Sec. 320.10.

2. As time passes, the petty cashier disburses money from the fund. To evidence each disbursement, the petty cashier places in the fund a prenumbered receipt, signed by the person who received cash. At all times, therefore, the amount of petty cash on hand and the amounts shown on the signed receipts should equal the original amount of the fund ($300 in our example). The company does *not* make journal entries when petty cash is disbursed.

3. When the amount of cash in the fund is low, the petty cashier submits the signed receipts and requests reimbursement from the general cashier for an amount that will increase the cash in the fund to the original amount. At this time, the receipts are canceled so that no one can use them again. In addition, the company records increases in those expenses (or other accounts) that are documented by the receipts.

To continue our example, assume that after three weeks only $25 remain in the petty cash fund. An analysis of the signed receipts shows that petty cash has been disbursed as follows:

Postage	$ 45
Office supplies	102
Transportation-in	125
Total	$272

Since the fund contains only $25, the general cashier must write a check for $275 ($300 − $25) in order to restore the fund to its original amount ($300). After the check is written, the company makes the following journal entry:

Postage Expense	45	
Office Supplies Expense	102	
Transportation-In	125	
Cash Short and Over	3	
Cash		275

The check is then cashed and the money is placed in the petty cash fund.

Cash Short and Over is a nominal account that is debited for cash shortages and credited for overages. Such shortages and overages usually result from errors in making change or failure to obtain receipts for exceptionally small amounts. A debit balance in the Cash Short and Over account at the end of a period should be reported as a miscellaneous 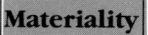 expense and a credit balance as a miscellaneous revenue. However, a material cash shortage resulting from a cause such as theft should be charged to a receivable account if the company expects to recover the amount of the shortage. If recovery is not expected, the company should charge a loss account.

Observe in the example that the company debited the Petty Cash account when the fund was established and made no other entries in this account. At the end of an accounting period, therefore, the petty cash fund should ordinarily be replenished. This ensures that all expenses paid with petty cash are recorded and that the petty cash on hand corresponds with the amount shown in the Petty Cash account. If for some reason the fund is not replenished at the end of an accounting period, the company should still debit the appropriate expense accounts, but it should credit the Petty Cash account directly. Over time the pattern of petty cash disbursements may suggest that the original amount of the petty cash fund is either too low or too high. If this occurs, the amount of petty cash and the balance shown in the Petty Cash account should be increased or decreased as appropriate.

Cash in Bank

The cash that a business has on hand may include petty cash funds, change funds (funds used to make change with customers), and undeposited receipts. As stated earlier, a business normally keeps most of its cash in one or more checking accounts. The use of a checking account gives a company a **double record** of its cash transactions, the company's own record plus that provided by the bank. The bank's record is summarized on a **bank statement** which the bank mails, usually at the end of every month, to each of its depositors.

An accountant verifies the cash that a company has on hand simply by counting it. In contrast, because the cash in a checking account cannot be conveniently counted, accountants verify it by preparing a bank reconciliation.

Bank Reconciliation

When a company receives a bank statement, the company's accountant should immediately prepare a **bank reconciliation.** This is simply a schedule that explains any differences between a company's book balance of cash in a particular bank account and the bank statement balance. A bank reconciliation helps to identify errors made by the depositor or by the bank in recording cash transactions. It also helps in making journal entries to update the depositor's accounting records.

On a depositor's books (accounting records), the cash balance in a bank account is an asset. On the bank's books, however, the cash in the depositor's account is a liability. Because the depositor and the bank do not simultaneously record all transactions that affect the depositor's account, and because either party can make mistakes, the asset balance on the depositor's books usually does not equal the liability balance on the bank statement. Many factors may explain why the two balances differ. Some of the more common ones are:

1. **Deposits in transit.**   These are additions to cash in the bank that the depositor has recorded but that do not appear on the bank statement. For example, on the last day of the month, the depositor may place the day's cash receipts in the bank's night depository. Since the bank will record the receipts on the next business day, the receipts should appear on the next month's bank statement.

2. **Outstanding checks.**   These are checks that the depositor has issued and recorded but that have not yet cleared the bank. Outstanding checks have therefore not yet been deducted on the bank statement.

3. **Bank collections.**   Promissory notes are often made payable at the payee's bank. The bank may therefore collect a note for the depositor and credit the proceeds to the depositor's account. Such collections made near the end of a month may appear on the bank statement but not yet appear on the depositor's books because the depositor is not yet aware of the collection.

4. **Bank charges.**   The bank often makes various charges that are not yet recorded on the depositor's books. Examples of such charges are those for bank services, checkbooks, NSF checks, and repayment of depositor loans.

5. **Bank errors.**   Occasionally, the bank makes an error that affects the depositor's account. For example, the bank might erroneously charge one company's check to another company's checking account. The depositor should instruct the bank to correct such errors.

6. **Depositor errors.**   Sometimes an error is made in the depositor's accounting records (commonly called a **book error**). For example, the depositor may have written a check for one amount but recorded the check at a different amount. The depositor should correct the accounting records when a book error is discovered.

An accountant may prepare a bank reconciliation by reconciling from the bank statement balance to the book balance, or vice versa. Accountants prefer, however, to reconcile from both of these balances to the **correct cash balance.** Such a reconciliation is relatively easy to understand, it shows in one place the information needed for making journal entries, and it indicates the correct cash balance that a company can spend from its checking account (the balance after all errors are corrected and all outstanding items clear the bank). A

EXHIBIT 7–1
Bank Reconciliation Form

Balance per bank statement		$XXX
Add: Deposits in transit	$XX	
Bank errors that understate the balance per bank statement		
(e.g., the bank charges someone else's check to the		
depositor's account)	XX	XX
		XXX
Deduct: Outstanding checks	XX	
Bank errors that overstate the balance per bank statement		
(e.g., the bank charges one of the depositor's checks to		
someone else's account)	XX	XX
Correct cash balance		$XXX
Balance per books		$XXX
Add: Deposits credited by the bank but not yet recorded by the		
depositor (e.g., collection of a promissory note)	$XX	
Book errors that understate the balance per books (e.g., the		
depositor writes a check for $10 but deducts $100 on the		
books)	XX	XX
		XXX
Deduct: Bank charges not yet recorded by the depositor (e.g., bank		
service charges and NSF checks)	XX	
Book errors that overstate the balance per books (e.g., the		
depositor writes a check for $100 but deducts $10 on the		
books)	XX	XX
Correct cash balance		$XXX

convenient form for this type of bank reconciliation is shown in Exhibit 7–1.

Observe that the bank reconciliation is divided into two sections: "balance per bank statement," and "balance per books." The logic of the additions and deductions in each section is not difficult to understand. Both sections end with the same "correct cash balance." This is the amount of cash that the depositor can spend from the checking account and the amount that should appear on the depositor's balance sheet.

In most cases, the depositor must make journal entries after the reconciliation is completed. These entries are necessary to update the depositor's accounting records and are based on the items added or deducted in the "balance per books" section. Additions and deductions in the other section either have already been recorded by the depositor or represent errors that the bank must correct.

To illustrate, assume that Todd Company keeps all of its cash in a checking account. An examination of the company's accounting records and its bank statement for the month ended May 31, 1985, revealed the following information:

1. The cash balance shown as of May 31 on the bank statement was $17,631.
2. The cash balance shown as of May 31 on the company's books was $15,214.
3. A deposit of $1,500 mailed to the bank on May 31 did not appear on the bank statement.
4. On May 30 the bank collected a note receivable for Todd Company and credited the proceeds of $2,100 to the company's account. The proceeds included $100 of interest, all of which the company earned during 1985. Todd Company has not yet recorded the collection.
5. Outstanding checks as of May 31 were as follows:

No. 902	$ 132
No. 922	870
No. 923	1,645

6. The company discovered that check no. 916, written in May for $527 in payment of an account payable, had been incorrectly recorded as $257.
7. The bank returned a check for $548 that the company had deposited on May 29. The check was drawn by James Roberts, a customer who did not have sufficient funds in his bank account to cover the check.
8. The bank statement showed a $12 service charge for May.

The bank reconciliation for Todd Company is shown in Exhibit 7–2. As stated earlier, the journal entries to update the depositor's accounting records should be based on the items added or deducted in the "balance per books" section. The journal entries required after completion of Todd Company's reconciliation are:

Cash	2,100	
Notes Receivable		2,000
Interest Revenue		100
(To record collection of note		
and interest by bank.)		
Miscellaneous Expense	12	
Cash		12
(To record bank service charge.)		
Accounts Receivable	548	
Cash		548
(To record NSF check.)		
Accounts Payable	270	
Cash		270
(To correct error made in		
recording check no. 916.)		

The entries shown above may be combined into a single compound entry. When the entries are posted, Todd Company's cash account will show a balance of $16,484, the correct amount as shown on the bank reconciliation.

An accountant should reconcile the monthly bank statement for each checking account that a company maintains. If a company has more than one checking account, the amount of cash to report on a balance sheet will be the sum of the correct cash balances shown on the bank reconciliations and any cash that the depositor has on hand.

Proof of Cash

Auditors frequently prepare an expanded version of the bank reconciliation illustrated in the previous section. This expanded version is known as a **four-column bank reconciliation,** or simply a **proof of cash.**

A proof of cash includes four reconciliations:

1. A reconciliation of the bank statement and book balances of cash at the end of the *previous month.*
2. A reconciliation of the cash receipts (deposits) shown on the bank statement with those shown on the books for the *current month.*
3. A reconciliation of the cash payments shown on the bank statement with those shown on the books for the *current month.*

```
┌─────────────────────────────────────────────────────────────────────────┐
│                            EXHIBIT 7–2                                   │
│                            Todd Company                                  │
│                         BANK RECONCILIATION                             │
│                            May 31, 1985                                  │
├─────────────────────────────────────────────────────────────────────────┤
```

Balance per bank statement		$17,631
Add: Deposit in transit		1,500
		19,131
Deduct: Outstanding checks		
No. 902	$ 132	
No. 922	870	
No. 923	1,645	2,647
Correct cash balance		$16,484
Balance per books		$15,214
Add: Note and interest collected by bank		2,100
		17,314
Deduct: Bank service charge	$ 12	
NSF check received from James Roberts	548	
Error made in recording check no. 916 ($527 − $257)	270	830
Correct cash balance		$16,484

4. A reconciliation of the bank statement and book balances of cash at the end of the *current month.*

The proof of cash is a stronger control measure than the single-column bank reconciliation. Auditors frequently prepare a proof of cash when a company is found to have weak internal control over cash. Because it provides a reconciliation of cash transactions as well as cash balances, the proof of cash makes it easier to pinpoint errors made by the company or the bank. This feature is particularly important when a company has made cash transfers from one bank account to another during the month. If a transfer is shown as a payment from one account but is not shown as a receipt by the other, an accountant or auditor would want to know why.

To illustrate the proof of cash, we shall use the information presented in the previous section for Todd Company for the month ended May 31, 1985. In addition, assume that the following facts pertain to the company during June 1985:

1. The cash receipts (deposits) shown on the June bank statement were $78,839. These receipts included the deposit of $1,500 that was in transit on May 31.
2. The cash receipts shown on the company's books during June were $79,864.
3. The cash payments shown on the June bank statement were $76,188. These payments included the checks of $2,647 that were outstanding on May 31.
4. The cash payments shown on the company's books during June were $77,261.
5. The cash balance shown as of June 30 on the bank statement was $20,282.
6. The cash balance shown as of June 30 on the company's books was $17,817.
7. A deposit of $3,600 mailed to the bank on June 30 did not appear on the June bank statement.
8. On June 30 the bank collected a note receivable for Todd Company and credited the proceeds of $3,175 to the company's account. The proceeds included $175 of interest, all of which the company earned during 1985. Todd Company has not yet recorded the collection.

9. Outstanding checks as of June 30 totaled $2,910.
10. The bank statement showed a $20 service charge for June.

The proof of cash for Todd Company appears in Exhibit 7–3. The form is divided into two sections, like the form in Exhibit 7–1. In the "per bank statement" section, we reconcile from four amounts shown on the bank statement to the correct (true) amounts. In the "per books" section, we reconcile from four amounts shown on the company's books to the same correct amounts that are determined in the "per bank statement" section.

The first column of the proof of cash is simply the single-column bank reconciliation prepared at the end of May (see Exhibit 7–2); the fourth column is a single-column reconciliation for June. The second column reconciles the June receipts, and the third column reconciles the June payments.

To prepare a proof of cash, we may begin by completing the top line in each section. We do this simply by copying the necessary information from the bank statement and the company's books. Next, we copy in the first column the information shown in the fourth column of the proof of cash prepared for the *previous* month. We then prepare in the fourth column a single-column reconciliation for the *current* month. Finally, each reconciling item in one of the two outside columns must be added or deducted in one of the two inside columns.

A logical analysis of each reconciling item should enable you to determine whether to add or deduct the item. For example:

1. The May 31 deposit in transit of $1,500 is deducted from the June receipts shown on the bank statement. Because this amount is a *May* receipt that is shown as a receipt on the *June* bank statement, we must deduct it in order to derive the *correct amount* of June receipts.

EXHIBIT 7–3
Todd Company
PROOF OF CASH
For June 1985

	May 31 Balance	June Receipts	June Payments	June 30 Balance
Per bank statement	$17,631	$78,839	$76,188	$20,282
Deposits in transit				
May 31	1,500	(1,500)		
June 30		3,600		3,600
Outstanding checks				
May 31	(2,647)		(2,647)	
June 30			2,910	(2,910)
Correct amounts	$16,484	$80,939	$76,451	$20,972
Per books	$15,214	$79,864	$77,261	$17,817
Note and interest				
collected by bank				
May	2,100	(2,100)		
June		3,175		3,175
Bank service charge				
May	(12)		(12)	
June			20	(20)
NSF check	(548)		(548)	
Error made in recording				
check no. 916	(270)		(270)	
Correct amounts	$16,484	$80,939	$76,451	$20,972

2. The outstanding checks of $2,910 on June 30 are added to the June payments shown on the bank statement. Because these checks are June payments that simply have not cleared the bank as of June 30, we must add them in order to derive the *correct amount* of June payments.

3. The note and interest collected by the bank in June ($3,175) are added to the June receipts shown on the company's books. Because this amount is a June receipt not yet shown on the company's books, we must add it in order to derive the *correct amount* of June receipts.

4. The bank service charge of $12 for May is deducted from the June payments shown on the company's books. Because this amount is a *May* payment (i.e., the bank charged the company's checking account in May) that the company recorded as a payment in *June*, we must deduct it in order to derive the *correct amount* of June payments.

Remember that a company must usually prepare journal entries based on the information shown on its bank reconciliations. Our illustration assumes that Todd Company prepares such entries near the beginning of the month that follows each reconciliation. In practice, many companies do this because they do not receive their bank statements in the mail on the last day of each month. When a company wants to prepare accurate financial statements (e.g., at year-end), the company should record its journal entries as transactions of the month to which the bank reconciliation pertains.

CASHING IN

POLAROID STOCK has been a real dog for investors ever since it hit its all-time high of $149.50 ten years ago. It has never begun to recover, and lately it has been trading at around $19 a share. However, a close look at the company's balance sheet for the end of 1981 reveals that Polaroid has $10.10 a share, or more than half the market price of its stock, in cash on hand. Polaroid's working capital—its current assets (including cash) minus its current liabilities—comes to $22.81 a share.

Thus, $19 spent on a share of Polaroid will buy you the equivalent of $3 more in cash and assets that can be converted into cash than you're paying for. And that's not counting another $10.13 worth of plant and other fixed investment.

Polaroid is just one stock in a fascinating new study, "Cash, Cash, Cash . . . Anyone?," published by Oppenheimer & Company. Oppenheimer vice-presidents Norman Weinger and E. Michael Metz have screened all publicly traded stocks to assemble a list of 74 companies that are sitting on massive hoards of cash or are otherwise highly liquid and therefore make potentially appealing investments.

At a time when slumping sales, plunging profits, and high borrowing costs have left many businesses severely strapped for cash, a number of firms are in the catbird seat. "An accelerating frequency of liquidity problems is drawing greater attention to the condition of balance sheets," the report explains. "The companies in this screening have particularly strong cash positions that, in addition to aiding survival in this difficult period, also enable management to take advantage of sharply depressed prices to make acquisitions or to shrink capitalizations. Simultaneously, entrepreneurs looking for leveraged buyouts or other opportunities may find companies with large cash positions particularly attractive targets." In other words, the companies can expand without borrowing, can buy assets that are currently underpriced, and make excellent takeover possibilities.

To look only at a company's cash on hand can be misleading. A company might be hoarding cash even as it teeters on the brink of bankruptcy. Or it might be selling off properties to accumulate cash because it expects large operating losses. The Oppenheimer analysis applies a number of criteria to winnow out such businesses, leaving on the list companies that are likely to appeal as takeover targets or that can use their cash and assets to make acquisitions and improve operations.

To qualify for the list, a company must have had cash as of its most recent reporting equal to at least 35 percent of the market price of its stock as of May 5, 1982. Its working capital must exceed 75 percent of the stock's price. And the shares must be trading at less than the company's book value, or what the company would be worth if it were liquidated and its debts were paid off. Companies that have large amounts of debt and are highly leveraged are eliminated. Total long-term debt must be less than 80 percent of a company's book value. Finally, only firms whose total outstanding stock is worth more than $10 million are included. Smaller businesses can be hard to trade.

The Oppenheimer approach is really nothing new. It reflects the emphasis on the strength of a company's balance sheet that lies at the core of Graham and Dodd's *Security Analysis,* the classic text on the subject. Most stock pickers today focus on a company's earnings potential, both for the current year and for the more distant future. However, projecting earnings is particularly difficult in a period like the present. Witness the wholesale revisions of earnings forecasts that have been taking place.

"No one can forecast earnings right now, and you can't buy a stock based on your expectation of 1982 earnings," says Metz. "You can buy on a forecast of survivability, and on the basis of values on the balance sheet. This uncertainty is likely to create unusual inefficiencies in the market, for who can really say what a company is worth just based on earnings? On a balance-sheet basis, the companies we have come up with are definitely undervalued."

It's possible that a company on the Oppenheimer list will decide to buy shares of its own stock to reduce market capitalization. Or management might decide to "go private" and buy up all outstanding shares. Either action could bring shareholders big profits.

An undervalued, cash-rich stock is not automatically assured of a price rise. Undervalued stocks can stay that way a long time, until their true worth is recognized by investors. That may take years. And Oppenheimer cautions that its list does not represent stock picks—investment decisions must be made on a close analysis of what problems may lurk behind what appears to be a healthy balance sheet. The investor is therefore advised to use the list as a starting point, and to seek other information and analyses in order to reach sound investment decisions.

The same caveat holds for the dozen names on the accompanying chart, which were culled from the report. These companies do not necessarily have the largest proportions of cash or working capital on Oppenheimer's list, but they all have interesting investment potential and a high degree of liquidity.

☐ Bassett Furniture Industries, with cash representing 40.7 percent of its market price, is one of the country's leading home-furniture manufacturers, and appears ready for a strong earnings advance when the recovery comes.

☐ Bayuk Cigars, which is being liquidated, has more than twice its market price in cash—the highest ratio on the list. Warren Buffett, head of Berkshire Hathaway and one of the country's most astute investors, recently bought 5.7 percent of Bayuk.

☐ Bendix, one of the best-known companies mentioned, recently bought 7.2 percent of RCA. There has been talk that Bendix chairman William Agee wants to turn his company into an investment conglomerate like Teledyne, buying a 20 percent interest in each of a number of companies. Its strong cash position makes this a possibility.

☐ Firestone Tire & Rubber, another strong company, recently held discussions about buying RCA's Hertz car-rental unit. Firestone withdrew, but the company clearly has the capability to make some major acquisition that could markedly increase its profit potential.

☐ Playboy Enterprises' problems have been well publicized, and some readers may be surprised to see it on this list. But since the company has sold off most of its hotel operations it is highly liquid. There has been speculation that Playboy may go private, buying all its own shares.

☐ Olla Industries, a handbag manufacturer, may also go private.

☐ Sybron Corporation is drastically restructuring its operations and getting rid of marginal units to increase its profitability.

☐ National Presto, a manufacturer of kitchen appliances; Chelsea Industries, a mini-conglomerate; Jewelcor, a jewelry retailer; and Jonathan Logan, a major clothing manufacturer, are all attractive companies laden with cash and could turn out to be takeover candidates.

☐ Polaroid, as the Oppenheimer report notes, "represents an unusual investment opportunity in that companies of such technological capability rarely sell at so conservative a relationship to balance sheet values."

Company	Stock Price per Share (May 5, 1982)	Cash as a Percentage of Price	Working Capital as a Percentage of Price
TWELVE THAT ARE LOADED			
Bassett Furniture	24.38	40.70	76.04
Bayuk Cigars	5.75	218.87	182.90
Bendix	54.63	54.29	99.11
Chelsea Industries	10.00	79.61	220.28
Firestone Tire & Rubber	10.63	56.19	103.36
Jewelcor	4.38	40.30	218.68
Jonathan Logan	15.00	63.61	159.84
National Presto Industries	34.50	65.04	96.29
Olla Industries	13.13	88.28	124.08
Playboy Enterprises	8.38	36.40	90.86
Polaroid	19.38	52.12	117.74
Sybron Corp.	19.38	41.56	104.15

SOURCE: Oppenheimer & Company.

SOURCE: Jack Egan, "Cashing In," *New York*, May 31, 1982, pp. 12, 14. Copyright © 1983 by News Group Publications, Inc. Reprinted with the permission of *New York* magazine.

As with the single-column bank reconciliation, preparation of a proof of cash usually indicates that a company has to make journal entries to update its accounting records. The entries necessary for Todd Company are suggested by the information shown in the "per books" section of the proof of cash. They are:

Cash	3,175	
Notes Receivable		3,000
Interest Revenue		175
(To record collection of note and		
interest by bank.)		
Miscellaneous Expense	20	
Cash		20
(To record bank service charge.)		

RECEIVABLES

Receivables are claims held against others for money, goods, or services. They generally result in an inflow of cash. An enterprise should classify a receivable as a *current asset* only if collection of the receivable is expected within the next year or operating cycle, whichever is longer. Other receivables should be reported in the investments and funds category or in other assets, as we discuss and illustrate in Chapter 10.

Because of the operating cycle concept, current assets include "installment or deferred accounts and notes receivable if they conform generally to normal trade practices and terms within the business."[5] These receivables are often collectible over periods that are longer than one year after the balance sheet date. Accounting for installment receivables is discussed in Chapter 20.

Proper accounting for a receivable requires an assessment of the **amount, timing,** and **uncertainty** associated with its collection. In theory, an accountant should initially value (measure) a receivable at an amount equal to the present value of the cash that the enterprise expects to collect. Such a valuation reflects the economic reality that money has a time value; an enterprise therefore earns **interest** by waiting to collect money. The amount of interest is the difference between a receivable's maturity value and its present value. In practice, accountants often ignore interest for short-term receivables, because they regard the amount as immaterial.

Materiality

Receivables may be classified as **trade receivables** or **nontrade receivables.** Generally, these categories should be reported separately on the balance sheet. **Trade receivables** result from sales of goods or services to customers. They usually compose most of the total dollar value of a company's receivables. All other receivables are **nontrade.** Examples of nontrade receivables are:

1. Receivables from officers or employees.
2. Advances to subsidiaries.
3. Various types of deposits made with other parties.
4. Claims against insurance companies.
5. Receivables arising from stock subscriptions.
6. Dividends receivable (from other companies).
7. Interest receivable.

A receivable may be represented by an open account (a nonwritten promise to pay) or by a note (a written promise to pay). These two types of receivables, called **accounts receivable** and **notes receivable,** respectively, should be reported separately on the balance sheet. They are discussed below.

Accounts Receivable

In a broad sense, the term "accounts receivable" includes all receivables not evidenced by written promises to pay. But accountants normally use the term in a more restrictive sense to refer only to open accounts that have resulted from selling goods or services on credit. Because accounts receivable are very important assets to many companies, they must be managed effectively. Such management involves a trade-off between the revenues generated by credit sales and the costs associated with carrying the resulting accounts receivable.

Generally accepted accounting principles (GAAP) require companies to report accounts receivable at **net realizable value.** This is the amount that the company expects to collect, and it equals the face amount of the receivables less an amount that is estimated to be uncollectible. Because of materiality, accountants generally ignore the interest inherent in the face amount of accounts receivable.

Materiality

Recording Credit Sales

Revenue Realization

Recording accounts receivable is closely related to the revenue realization principle (discussed in Chapter 2). That is, a seller should record a receivable that arises from a sale of goods on the date that the sale occurs. This is also the time at which the seller recognizes revenue. Under most circumstances the sales revenue and the related receivable should be

---

[5]*Accounting Research Bulletin No. 43,* "Restatement and Revision of Accounting Research Bulletins," 1953, Ch. 3, Sec. A, par. 4.

recorded at the precise moment that title passes from the seller to the buyer. For practical reasons, however, accounts receivable and related sales revenue are usually recorded when the seller ships the goods.

Trade Discounts. A trade discount is an amount that a seller deducts from a list price to determine the invoice price of goods sold. List prices are quoted in the seller's catalogs or price lists, while trade discounts usually appear in a separate schedule. A trade discount, then, is merely a convenient device that manufacturers and wholesalers often use to price their goods. The use of trade discounts enables a company to revise its prices periodically without having to reprint its catalogs and to set different prices for different types of customers and for different quantities sold.

Neither sellers nor purchasers should record trade discounts in their accounts. To illustrate, assume that All Star Wholesalers sells 100 footballs to Retail Sports, Inc., for the list price of $30 each, less a trade discount of 40%. The invoice price is therefore $18 ($30 − $12) per football and the total invoice price is $1,800 ($18 × 100). Here is how All Star Wholesalers should record the transaction:

Accounts Receivable	1800	
Sales		1800

Many sellers express trade discounts in a series such as 40/20/10. The use of multiple trade discounts allows the seller to conveniently vary the selling price based on such factors as the type of customer or the quantity purchased. If the terms are 40/20/10, a customer may receive a trade discount of (1) 40%; (2) 40% and 20%; *or* (3) 40%, 20%, and 10% depending on the circumstances. Suppose, for example, that MCA, Inc., sells Model 21 television sets for the list price of $100 each, less the following discounts:

40%	If 50 or fewer sets are purchased.
40% and 20%	If more than 50 but fewer than 100 sets are purchased.
40%, 20%, and 10%	If 100 or more sets are purchased.

Assuming that customers Aim, Bar, and Cam purchase 30, 60, and 200 television sets, respectively, Exhibit 7–4 shows how MCA, Inc., would determine the invoice price for each customer.

Cash Discounts. Companies frequently offer cash discounts to their credit customers. A **cash discount** is a reduction from an invoice price that is offered to buyers to encourage prompt payment. Companies use trade discounts to establish an invoice price and cash

---

EXHIBIT 7–4
Trade Discount

Customer	Quantity Purchased	Applicable Trade Discount	Invoice Price Per Unit	Total Invoice Price
Aim	30	40%	$100 − ($100 × 40%) = $60	$60 × 30 units = $1,800
Bar	60	40% and 20%	$100 − ($100 × 40%) = $60 $60 − ($60 × 20%) = $48	$48 × 60 units = $2,880
Cam	200	40%, 20%, and 10%	$100 − ($100 × 40%) = $60 $60 − ($60 × 20%) = $48 $48 − ($48 × 10%) = $43.20	$43.20 × 200 units = $8,640

discounts to reduce the invoice price. From the seller's point of view, a cash discount is called a **sales discount;** from the purchaser's point of view, a cash discount is called a **purchase discount.** A cash discount is usually expressed in terms such as 2/10, n/30; or 2/10, EOM (end of month). Terms of 2/10, n/30 means that the buyer may deduct 2% from the invoice price if payment is made within 10 days after the invoice date. A buyer who does not pay within the 10-day discount period must pay the gross invoice amount within 30 days after the invoice date.

Purchasers generally take cash discounts offered to them because it is usually to their advantage to do so. Suppose, for example, that Sim Company sells goods to Burt Company for an invoice price of $1,000, terms 2/10, n/30. Burt Company can liquidate its debt by paying $980 within 10 days after the invoice date. In effect, $980 is the **cash price** of the goods. Instead of paying the $980 by the tenth day, Burt Company may choose to pay a $20 premium in order to keep the $980 for an additional 20 days (30 days − 10 days). This choice will result in an interest rate of 2.04% ($20 ÷ 980) for 20 days. This is equivalent to an effective *annual* rate of 36.7% (2.04% × 360/20). Clearly, most companies try to avoid such a high interest cost.

In theory, an account receivable and the related sales revenue should be measured net of any cash discounts allowable. This is consistent with the **net method** of recording credit sales. In Exhibit 7−5, we compare the net method with the **gross method** of recording credit sales. The net method correctly states the receivable at its realizable value on the date of sale, and correctly states the amount of revenue earned on that date. Under the net method, we record the receivable and the related revenue at an amount that equals the **cash equivalent price** on the date of sale. Remember that sellers offer cash discounts to encourage buyers to pay promptly. A buyer who fails to take a cash discount has in effect decided to engage in a deferred payment transaction. The buyer therefore incurs an interest cost, and the seller earns interest revenue. The interest that the seller earns is reflected in the Sales Discounts Not Taken account. The seller should report the balance in this account on the income statement as financial revenue.

EXHIBIT 7−5
Net and Gross Methods of Recording Credit Sales

Transaction	Net Method		Gross Method		
July 1					

Jam Company sells merchandise for $100, terms 2/10, n/30.	Accounts Receivable
	  Sales
		98
		98
			Accounts Receivable
			  Sales
				100	100

Alternative Assumption No. 1					
July 10					

Jam Company receives payment that buyer made within the discount period.	Cash
	  Accounts Receivable
		98
		98
			Cash
			Sales Discounts
			  Accounts Receivable
				98
				2
					100

Alternative Assumption No. 2					
July 30					

Jam Company receives payment that buyer made after the discount period.	Cash
	  Accounts Receivable
	  Sales Discounts Not
	    Taken
		100
		98
		
		2
			Cash
			  Accounts Receivable
				100	100

In practice, most companies record credit sales using the gross method. Under this method a company records credit sales at gross amounts. When the seller later receives the buyer's payment, the seller records any cash discounts taken in a Sales Discounts account. The seller later deducts the balance in this account from sales to arrive at net sales. Although the gross method tends to result in an overstatement of accounts receivable and sales revenue, it is practical and convenient, and it enables a company to make a year-end adjusting entry to estimate sales discounts and thereby eliminate material errors from financial statements.

Accounting for Uncollectible Accounts

Companies sell on credit, rather than only for cash, to increase total sales and thereby increase profits. But a company that sells on credit assumes the risk that some customers will not pay their accounts. When a customer's account becomes uncollectible, the company has sustained a **bad-debt loss.** These losses are simply one of the costs of doing business on credit. Accounting for bad-debt losses would be fairly easy if they occurred in the same period as the sale. In reality, bad-debt losses often occur in subsequent periods.

One method of accounting for uncollectible accounts, called the **direct write-off method,** involves debiting Bad Debts Expense and crediting Accounts Receivable in the period in which the company finally determines that the accounts are uncollectible.[6] This method is simple and is based on actual rather than estimated bad-debt losses. The problem, however, is that the direct write-off method usually violates the matching principle. The reason is that the bad-debts expense is often recognized in a later accounting period than the one in which the related sales revenue was recognized. The result is a mismatching of sales revenue and bad-debts expense. In addition, the direct write-off method leads to the reporting of accounts receivable at an amount greater than their net realizable value (i.e., at an amount greater than the company expects to collect).

> Matching

Use of the direct write-off method may be appropriate if a company's bad-debt losses are immaterial or if a company is unable to reasonably estimate its losses from uncollectible receivables.[7] Generally, however, the inability to estimate bad-debt losses suggests that collectibility is so uncertain that the company should defer the recognition of revenue beyond the time of sale. We discuss this point more fully in Chapter 20. Since bad-debt losses usually are material, and since most companies can reasonably estimate their bad-debt losses, based on their own collection experience or that of other similar companies, use of the direct write-off method is discouraged.

> Materiality

Companies that can estimate their uncollectibles use the **allowance method** to account for them.[8] Under this method, a company estimates the total amount of its uncollectible accounts at the end of every accounting period. As we discuss later in the chapter, this estimate may be based on credit sales or on accounts receivable. The company records the estimate in a year-end **adjusting entry** similar to the one shown below (the $5,200 amount is assumed):

Bad Debts Expense	5,200	
Allowance for Doubtful Accounts		5,200

---

[6]An entry debiting Accounts Receivable and crediting Bad Debts Expense would be made if an account that had been written off was later recovered in the *same* accounting period. If a recovery occurred in a *subsequent* accounting period, Accounts Receivable would be debited and Bad Debts Recovered (a revenue account) would be credited. An entry debiting Cash and crediting Accounts Receivable would be made to record the actual collection.

[7]*FASB Statement of Financial Accounting Standards No. 5,* "Accounting for Contingencies," 1975, par. 23.

[8]For income tax purposes, a company may use either the direct write-off method or the allowance method. Companies generally prefer the allowance method because it tends to postpone tax payments.

The balance in Bad Debts Expense usually appears as an operating expense on the income statement where the expense is matched with sales revenue.[9] The Allowance for Doubtful Accounts (also called the Allowance for Uncollectible Accounts and the Allowance for Bad Debts) is a contra account to Accounts Receivable. The allowance is therefore deducted from Accounts Receivable on the balance sheet to estimate the net realizable value of the receivables. The use of an allowance account relieves a company of the necessity of crediting individual customer accounts each time it estimates bad debts. Obviously, when a company estimates bad debts and makes an adjusting entry, it does not yet know which accounts will become uncollectible.

The allowance method tends to overcome the matching and asset valuation problems inherent in the direct write-off method. That is why accountants prefer the allowance method, even though it is based on estimated figures.

Accountants usually consult with a company's credit department personnel to estimate the amount of bad debts. As indicated earlier, the company's collection experience and that of similar companies are usually the most important factors in determining the estimate. These factors should be evaluated in the context of current and projected circumstances that may affect the company's future collection experience. Assessing the collectibility of accounts receivable is a challenging task, particularly in the difficult economic situation that many companies and cities have faced in recent years. When estimating bad debts under the allowance method, accountants may use either an income statement approach or a balance sheet approach.

Income Statement Approach. Under this approach to the allowance method, an accountant first determines the average percentage relationship between a company's *credit sales* and its actual bad-debt losses. This percentage is then multiplied by credit sales for the current year to estimate bad-debts expense.

Matching

The income statement approach is so called because it emphasizes the Bad Debts Expense account rather than the Allowance for Doubtful Accounts. With the income statement approach, credit sales (an income statement number) is multiplied by a percentage to estimate the amount of bad-debts expense (another income statement number) as accurately as possible. This approach emphasizes the matching principle because the bad-debts estimate is based directly on the related sales revenue. We shall illustrate the two approaches to the allowance method by using the information in Exhibit 7–6, which pertains to Downes Company, an enterprise that uses a calendar-year accounting period.

---

[9]Because uncollectibles are *expected* when a company makes credit sales, a strong argument can be made that uncollectibles should not be included in revenue. Therefore, the estimated amount of a company's bad debts should be treated as a revenue offset (similar to Sales Returns) rather than an expense. Following this approach, a company should debit Sales—Uncollectibles instead of Bad Debts Expense when it estimates bad debts. The balance in Sales—Uncollectibles would later appear as a deduction from sales on the income statement.

In practice, companies usually debit Bad Debts Expense. The rationale is that even if a receivable proves uncollectible, it existed on the date of sale and revenue was generated for the full amount of the sale.

EXHIBIT 7–6
Downes Company
Facts to Illustrate Allowance Method

Credit sales made during 1985	$210,000
Accounts receivable, 12/31/85	50,000
Allowance for doubtful accounts, 12/31/85, before adjustment	400 (credit balance)

To illustrate the income statement approach, let us further assume that in previous years, actual bad-debt losses each year have averaged 1% of credit sales and that the company expects this percentage to continue in the future. Here is the adjusting entry that the company should make on December 31, 1985:

Bad Debts Expense	2,100	
Allowance for Doubtful Accounts		2,100
($210,000 × .01 = $2,100)		

Observe that we made the above entry *without considering* the previous balance ($400 credit) in the Allowance for Doubtful Accounts. The reason is that under the income statement approach, we focus on Bad Debts Expense, not on the Allowance account. After the above entry is posted, Bad Debts Expense will have a balance of $2,100, and the balance in the Allowance account will be $2,500 ($400 + $2,100).

In another variation of the income statement approach, bad-debts expense is based on a percentage of total sales (cash and credit) rather than only credit sales. The use of a percentage based on credit sales is logical, because bad debts arise only from credit sales. Nevertheless, the use of total sales is acceptable since it would produce reasonable results if a company's mix of cash and credit sales is fairly stable over time.

Balance Sheet Approach. The primary objective of this approach to the allowance method is to report accounts receivable on the balance sheet at net realizable value (and so the name *balance sheet* approach). To accomplish this objective, the balance sheet approach focuses on establishing a **desired balance** in the Allowance for Doubtful Accounts. The desired balance equals the estimated amount of uncollectible accounts receivable. This is the amount that, when subtracted from Accounts Receivable, will reduce the receivables to their net realizable value.

1. Percentage of Accounts Receivable. A simple way to implement the balance sheet approach is to multiply the year-end Accounts Receivable balance by a percentage that the company estimates from experience will be uncollectible. The product is the desired balance in the Allowance account. The adjusting entry to estimate bad debts is then recorded for the amount that is necessary to produce the desired balance.

To illustrate, assume the facts that were presented in Exhibit 7–6 for Downes Company. Now, however, assume that instead of using the income statement approach, the company elects to use the balance sheet approach and that it estimates that approximately 4% of the accounts receivable balance on December 31, 1985, will be uncollectible. The company should make the following adjusting entry on December 31, 1985:

Bad Debts Expense	1,600	
Allowance for Doubtful Accounts		1,600

Notice carefully that the above entry reflects the amount necessary to produce the desired balance in the Allowance account. The computation is shown below:

Desired balance in Allowance account	$2,000
($50,000 × .04)	
Less: Credit balance in Allowance	
account before adjustment	400
Amount of adjusting entry	$1,600

After the above entry is posted, Bad Debts Expense will have a balance of $1,600; the balance in the Allowance account will be $2,000 ($400 + $1,600).

The Allowance account sometimes has a *debit* balance before adjustment. As we discuss and illustrate later in the chapter, a company writes off uncollectible accounts by debiting the Allowance account and crediting Accounts Receivable. A debit balance in the Allowance account therefore occurs when a company has written off a greater amount of accounts receivable than it had previously estimated as uncollectible. A debit balance in the Allowance account before adjustment would simply be *added* to the desired balance in order to determine the amount of the adjusting entry. For example, if Downes Company had a $400 *debit* balance (instead of a $400 *credit* balance) in its Allowance account before adjustment, the company would make the adjusting entry on December 31, 1985, for $2,400 ($2,000 + $400).

2. Aging of Accounts Receivable.   A more accurate way to implement the balance sheet approach is to determine the desired balance in the Allowance account by aging the accounts receivable. Here the accountant groups a company's individual accounts receivable into categories based on how long they have been outstanding. This schedule is called an **aging of accounts receivable.** Next, the total amount in each category is multiplied by an estimated uncollectible percentage. The accountant then adds the products to derive a total amount that is estimated to be uncollectible. Since this total is the desired amount in the Allowance account, the adjusting entry to estimate bad debts should be recorded for the amount necessary to produce the desired balance.

The percentages referred to above are based on a company's collection experience and on the advice of its credit department personnel. Higher percentages are usually associated with the higher-age categories since, generally, the longer that an account has been outstanding, the less likely it is to be collected.

To illustrate, refer again to Exhibit 7–6. In addition, assume that Downes Company now elects to estimate its bad debts using the aging form of the balance sheet approach and that it prepares the information shown in Exhibits 7–7 and 7–8. The company should make the following adjusting entry on December 31, 1985:

| Bad Debts Expense | 1,969 | |
| Allowance for Doubtful Accounts | | 1,969 |

Note once again that the above entry is for the amount necessary to produce the desired balance in the allowance account. The computation is shown below:

Desired balance in Allowance account (total		
estimated amount uncollectible shown in		
Exhibit 7–8)		$2,369
Less: Credit balance in Allowance account		
before adjustment		400
Amount of adjusting entry		$1,969

After the above entry is posted, Bad Debts Expense will have a balance of $1,969, and the Allowance balance will be $2,369 ($400 + $1,969). If the Allowance account had a $400 *debit* balance (instead of a $400 *credit* balance) before adjustment, the adjusting entry would have been for $2,769 ($400 + $2,369).

Summary and Evaluation of Approaches.   To summarize, there are two basic approaches to the allowance method of accounting for uncollectible accounts. Each approach has two forms or variations, as shown below:

1. Income statement approach
   a. Percentage of credit sales
   b. Percentage of total sales

EXHIBIT 7–7

Downes Company
AGING OF ACCOUNTS RECEIVABLE
December 31, 1985

Customer	Accounts Receivable Balance 12/31/85	Time Outstanding				
		Under 30 Days	30–60 Days	61–120 Days	121–180 Days	Over 180 Days
Adams Company	$ 1,200	$ 900	$ 300			
Blunt & Company	600			$ 600		
Carver Enterprises	750	600	150			
Dandridge, Inc.	350					$ 350
Zimmerman Company	500				$500	
Total	$50,000	$39,300	$5,600	$3,400	$600	$1,100

EXHIBIT 7–8

Downes Company
ESTIMATED AMOUNT UNCOLLECTIBLE BASED ON AGING ANALYSIS
December 31, 1985

Time Outstanding	Amount	Estimated Percentage Uncollectible	Estimated Amount Uncollectible
Under 30 days	$39,300	1%	$ 393
30–60 days	5,600	6%	336
61–120 days	3,400	25%	850
121–180 days	600	40%	240
Over 180 days	1,100	50%	550
Total	$50,000		$2,369

2. Balance sheet approach
   a. Percentage of accounts receivable
   b. Aging of accounts receivable

Matching

A company may use any form of the allowance method to estimate its bad debts since all are acceptable under GAAP. The income statement approach emphasizes the matching principle, while the balance sheet approach emphasizes the reporting of accounts receivable at their net realizable value. Notice that both approaches demonstrate that financial statements *articulate* with one another. Under the income statement approach, what we do to benefit the income statement directly affects the balance sheet; under the balance sheet approach, what we do to benefit the balance sheet directly affects the income statement. Because modern financial reporting emphasizes the income statement over the balance sheet, many accountants favor the income statement approach.

Remember that all variations of the allowance method are based on *estimates.* A company's actual bad-debt losses will therefore equal its estimates only by chance. Under the income statement approach, the percentage of credit sales usually produces the most accurate results, because bad-debt losses relate only to credit sales. Under the balance sheet approach, an aging of accounts receivable generally produces the most accurate results.

Over time, a company's collection experience may indicate that its estimates of bad debts were too high or too low, and the company's Allowance balance before year-end adjustment thus contains an excessive credit or debit balance. When this occurs, the company should change the percentage that it uses to estimate bad debts. Such a change is an example of a **change in an accounting estimate,** and as we discussed briefly in Chapter 4 and will discuss in more depth in Chapter 19, the change should be accounted for in current and future periods. In other words, the company should begin using a revised percentage to estimate its bad debts, but should not make a prior period adjustment.

Writing Off Uncollectible Accounts. When all reasonable attempts to collect an account have failed, a company's credit manager should authorize the accounting department to write off the account as uncollectible. Assume that the following balances were taken from the accounting records of Ace Enterprises:

Accounts receivable	$100,000	(Debit)
Allowance for doubtful accounts	1,700	(Credit)

If the company's credit manager decides that an account of $500 from W. Grant is uncollectible, the following entry should be made:

Allowance for Doubtful Accounts	500	
Accounts Receivable		500

The accountant would post the above entry to the appropriate general and subsidiary ledger accounts. After posting, the Accounts Receivable balance will be $99,500 ($100,000 − $500), and the Allowance balance will be $1,200 ($1,700 − $500). Notice that although the write-off reduces Accounts Receivable and the Allowance account, it has no effect on the net realizable value of the receivables. Before the write-off, the net realizable value was $98,300 ($100,000 − $1,700); after the write-off, it is still $98,300 ($99,500 − $1,200).

Collection of Accounts Written Off. Occasionally, a company collects all or part of an account that it wrote off as uncollectible. When this occurs, the company should first reverse, to the extent of the recovery, the entry that it made to write off the account. Then the company should record the collection in the usual manner. To illustrate, refer to the information presented in the previous section for Ace Enterprises and assume that Ace later collects the account of $500 from W. Grant. Ace should record the following entries:

Accounts Receivable	500	
Allowance for Doubtful Accounts		500
(To reinstate W. Grant's account.)		
Cash	500	
Accounts Receivable		500
(To record the collection.)		

Notice that there are two entries rather than only a single entry debiting Cash and crediting the Allowance account. Making two entries is preferable since this permits Ace Enterprises to accumulate in its accounts receivable subsidiary ledger a complete record of its credit experience with W. Grant.

Other Applications of the Allowance Method

Our discussion of the allowance method has thus far been confined to its use in accounting for uncollectible accounts. We have seen that through the use of estimates, the allowance method enables a company to better match expenses and revenues and to report receivables at their net realizable value. The same logic applies to the use of the allowance method in

Matching

accounting for other items that affect the cash realization of accounts receivable. For example, a company may use the allowance method to account for:

1. Sales discounts that customers will probably take (assuming that the company records accounts receivable at gross amounts).
2. Anticipated sales returns and allowances.
3. Anticipated collection costs (e.g., attorney's fees) that the company will incur when trying to collect accounts receivable.
4. Anticipated freight costs that customers will be allowed to deduct from their remittances because of the company's shipping terms.

To illustrate, assume that Allen Beam & Company determines from experience that the actual cost of collecting its accounts receivable averages 1% of the year-end accounts receivable balance. If the current year-end accounts receivable balance is $100,000, the company should make the following adjusting entry:

Collection Expense	1,000	
Allowance for Collection Expense		1,000
($100,000 × .01 = $1,000)		

Collection Expense would then be reported as an operating expense on the income statement, and the Allowance for Collection Expense would be deducted from Accounts Receivable on the balance sheet. In a subsequent period, the company would charge actual collection costs to the Allowance account, and would credit Cash or other appropriate accounts.

Adjusting entries similar to the one shown above are appropriate to record estimated sales discounts, sales returns and allowances, and freight costs. In each case, a contra-revenue account (e.g., Sales Discounts) or an expense account (e.g., Transportation-Out) is debited and the appropriate Allowance account is credited. The effect of these entries is to reduce current net income and lower the net realizable value of accounts receivable reported on the balance sheet. For example, American Brands, Inc., makers of such diverse products as Jergens lotion, Titleist golf balls, and Jim Beam bourbon, uses the allowance method to account for sales discounts, uncollectible accounts, and sales returns. In its 1982 Annual Report, the company provided the following information about its accounts receivable:

	December 31	
(In thousands)	*1982*	*1981*
Accounts receivable, customers, less allowances for discounts, doubtful accounts and returns, 1982, $17,927; 1981, $16,462	$560,687	$642,565

Materiality

Despite the theoretical merits of applying the allowance method to items other than uncollectible accounts, most companies do not do so. Instead of estimating these items in advance, companies usually account for them when they actually occur. This approach, which is required for income tax purposes, is justified under GAAP because of immateriality and because the amounts involved often do not fluctuate significantly from year to year.

Use of an Allowance Account When a Right of Return Exists

Many companies allow customers to return defective merchandise. Some companies, such as those in the newspaper, perishable food, and book publishing industries, typically give their customers the right to return merchandise under certain circumstances, even when the merchandise is not defective. These circumstances may include customer dissatisfaction with the product or an inability of the customer to resell the product to others.

When customers have the right to return products, the seller should recognize revenue at the time of sale only if *all* of the following conditions are met:

1. The seller's price to the buyer is substantially fixed or determinable at the date of sale.
2. The buyer has paid the seller, or the buyer is obligated to pay the seller and the obligation is not contingent on resale of the product.
3. The buyer's obligation to the seller would not be changed in the event of theft or physical destruction or damage of the product.
4. The buyer acquiring the product for resale has economic substance apart from that provided by the seller.
5. The seller does not have significant obligations for future performance to directly bring about resale of the product by the buyer.
6. The amount of future returns can be reasonably estimated.[10]

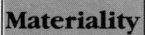

Further discussion of these conditions appears in Chapter 20. The sixth condition stated above is particularly important for our purposes. In effect, the condition requires that if sales returns are material, companies that sell products with a right of return must use the allowance method of accounting for sales returns to properly recognize revenue at the time of sale.

To illustrate, assume that Averill Company gives customers the right to return products. Recent experience indicates that customers will return approximately 20% of the merchandise Averill Company has sold and that the company can later resell the merchandise for approximately 60% of the original sales price. During the current year, Averill Company made sales of $100,000. Here is the adjusting entry the company should make at year-end, assuming a perpetual inventory system:

Sales Returns	20,000	
Inventory-Estimated Returns	12,000	
Allowance for Sales Returns		20,000
Cost of Goods Sold		12,000

The Inventory-Estimated Returns account is a current asset and reveals the net realizable value of inventory that is expected to be returned ($100,000 \times 20\% \times 60\% = \$12,000$). The Allowance for Sales Returns is deducted from Accounts Receivable on the balance sheet. The effect of the above entry is to reduce gross margin and current assets by $8,000.

Suppose now that during the first month of the next accounting period, a customer returns merchandise that had an original sales price of $1,000. Assuming that the customer has not paid for the goods, Averill Company should make the following entry:

Inventory-Returned Goods	600	
Allowance for Sales Returns	1,000	
Inventory-Estimated Returns		600
Accounts Receivable		1,000

Use of Accounts Receivable to Generate Cash

Instead of waiting until customers pay their accounts, companies often want the cash immediately. This is usually accomplished by **pledging, assigning,** or **factoring** the accounts. Below we explain these alternatives and the appropriate accounting under each.

---

[10]*FASB Statement of Financial Accounting Standards No. 48,* "Revenue Recognition When Right of Return Exists," 1981, par. 6.

Pledging Accounts Receivable. Companies sometimes obtain loans by pledging their accounts receivable as collateral. In a pledging arrangement, the borrower agrees to collect its accounts receivable and to use the proceeds to repay the lender. The borrower records the loan and related interest in the usual manner, and the loan balance is reduced as the borrower remits its collections. If the borrower defaults, the lender can recover the amount owed by selling the accounts pledged.

If a company has pledged some or all of its accounts receivable, the company should disclose the amount pledged, either parenthetically or in a note to its financial statements.

Assigning Accounts Receivable. An assignment of accounts receivable is a more formal type of pledging arrangement. In an assignment, a borrower (called the **assignor**) transfers its rights in some or all of its accounts receivable to a lender (called the **assignee**) in exchange for a loan. The money received from collecting the accounts is later used to pay off the loan.

An assignment is evidenced by a **financing agreement** and a **promissory note,** both of which are signed by the assignor. The financing agreement may indicate that the assignment is on either a **nonnotification** or a **notification** basis. When accounts are assigned on a nonnotification basis, as is usually the case, customers are not informed that their accounts have been assigned. As a result, they continue to make payments to the assignor, who in turn forwards them to the assignee. When accounts are assigned on a notification basis, customers are notified to make their payments directly to the assignee.

The assignor retains ownership of the accounts assigned. As a result, the assignor assumes the risk that accounts receivable will not be realized for their full face amount because of such factors as sales discounts, sales returns and allowances, and bad-debt losses.

Before entering into an assignment, the assignee (usually a bank or a finance company) analyzes the borrower's accounts receivable. The assignee generally refuses to lend money secured by accounts believed to be too risky. Furthermore, the assignee usually lends only a certain percentage (often between 60% and 90%) of the face amount of the accounts that it is willing to lend against. This helps to insulate the assignee from collection losses that the assignor might sustain. As additional protection the assignee frequently requires the assignor to substitute new accounts for ones that become past due or uncollectible. Naturally, the assignee charges **interest** for the loans that it makes. In addition, the assignee usually requires a **service charge** for processing the assignment.

From an accounting standpoint, an assignor should report assigned accounts receivable separate from any unassigned accounts. Moreover, the note payable to the assignee should be reported on the balance sheet as a deduction from the assigned accounts. The difference, called "equity in assigned accounts receivable," should be added to the other amounts reported in the current assets section. Here we see an unusual case in which the offsetting of a liability against an asset is correct according to GAAP. The reason is that the assignor has contractually committed the proceeds from collecting the assigned accounts to pay off the loan.

To illustrate, assume that on December 31, 1984, Smith Company assigns $100,000 of accounts receivable to Citibank under a nonnotification arrangement. Citibank advances $80,000 less a service charge of $1,600, and Smith Company signs a promissory note that provides for interest of 1% per month on the unpaid loan balance. Smith Company should make the following entries on December 31:

Assigned Accounts Receivable	100,000	
Accounts Receivable		100,000
Cash	78,400	
Service Charge Expense	1,600	
Notes Payable		80,000

The first entry transfers the assigned accounts to a specific account. The second entry records the receipt of cash on the loan. The current asset section of Smith Company's balance sheet on December 31, 1984, would show the following:

Current Assets

Assigned accounts receivable	$100,000	
Less: Notes payable	80,000	
Equity in assigned accounts receivable		$20,000

To continue the illustration, a series of 1985 transactions and the corresponding journal entries appear below:

1. From January 1 to January 31, Smith Company collected assigned accounts of $60,000, less sales discounts of $700 and sales returns and allowances of $1,300.

Cash	58,000	
Sales Discounts	700	
Sales Returns and Allowances	1,300	
Assigned Accounts Receivable		60,000

2. On January 31, Smith Company remitted the January collections to Citibank.

Notes Payable	57,200	
Interest Expense ($80,000 × .01)	800	
Cash		58,000

3. From February 1 to February 28, Smith Company collected $29,000 of assigned accounts and wrote off as uncollectible $3,000 of assigned accounts.

Cash	29,000	
Allowance for Doubtful Accounts	3,000	
Assigned Accounts Receivable		32,000

4. On February 28, Smith Company paid off the remaining loan balance and transferred the remaining balance in Assigned Accounts Receivable to Accounts Receivable.

Notes Payable ($80,000 − $57,200)	22,800	
Interest Expense ($22,800 × .01)	228	
Cash		23,028
Accounts Receivable	8,000	
Assigned Accounts Receivable		8,000
($100,000 − $60,000 − $32,000)		

The example shown above provides a general view of accounting for assigned accounts receivable. In practice, the accounting requirements depend in part on the financing agreement. A general description of this agreement should be disclosed in the footnotes to the assignor's financial statements.

Factoring of Accounts Receivable.   In a factoring arrangement, a company (the **seller**) sells its accounts receivable to a financial institution, called a **factor.** In most cases the factor is a bank or a finance company. Factoring differs from an assignment in that the seller actually transfers ownership of its accounts receivable to the factor. Although accounts may be factored **with recourse** (the factor may hold the seller liable if debtors do

FACTORING—A FINANCING ALTERNATIVE FOR CLIENTS

UNTIL RECENTLY, most accountants apart from those working in the textile industry saw factoring only as a last resort for their clients' credit needs—a sort of pawnshop approach to borrowing where businesses paid exorbitant rates for the use of money. Instead, many accountants would usually recommend borrowing the needed cash from a bank or other sources of credit.

Today many of these same accountants may enthusiastically recommend the services of a factor. Factoring has become a source of strength—rather than a sign of weakness—for many businesses. Factoring, in fact, is a way of life in the textile, apparel, carpet and furniture industries. In the last 20 years, it has also expanded into housewares, marine products, paints, hardware, plastics, metal products, toys and sporting goods.

Factoring has become a $28 billion business in this country, and some experts see annual factoring volume doubling in the next four or five years. It appears that the only reason factoring hasn't caught on with other industries is the apparent lack of familiarity with what factoring is all about. . . . In general, the kinds of businesses that might want to align themselves with a factor are manufacturers, converters, assemblers and other concerns which fabricate materials and finish products. Factoring also is used by concerns whose chief activity is in the distribution of manufactured articles at the wholesale level such as jobbers, importers, etc. Factoring is not yet available to businesses that sell to the ultimate consumer. However, there is a close parallel between factoring on the commercial level and the use of credit cards, such as VISA, Master Card and American Express, on the consumer level.

Mechanics of factoring

A factoring arrangement is accomplished through a written contract between the factor and the client. The contract contains a provision permitting either party to terminate the arrangement at any time on 60 days prior written notice.

The typical factoring contract uses informal language and is usually cast in the form of a letter of exchange which confirms the agreement. The factor undertakes to purchase all of the client's accounts receivable and to assume the risks of loss resulting from a customer's nonpayment because of financial inability.

Here is how conventional factoring works:

1 The client signs a contract in which he agrees to factor all of his sales.

2 As orders are obtained, the client submits customers' names, dollar amounts and terms of credit approval.

3 As shipments are made, the client bills his customers in the usual manner; however, each invoice carries a printed notice requesting that payment be made to the factor.

4 As invoices are issued, the client sends copies along with an assignment to the factor. The factor credits the client with the value of each invoice.

5 The client may draw cash against these invoices or leave a credit balance until funds are needed.

6 The client maintains just one account on his books—with the factor. The factor takes full responsibility for handling the client's accounts receivable and for collecting them. The only recourse to the client is if the goods are claimed to be defective or if some dispute arises concerning shipment.

7 For his records the client receives a monthly accounting of all financial transactions.

Choosing a factor

Before entering into an agreement with a factor, a business should make sure that its line of business is one with which the factor has had previous experience and that the factor makes a careful analysis of the company's customer lists and credit requirements. In addition, the potential client should remember that factoring is different from any other financial relationship.

As a start, a glance through the yellow pages of most major city telephone directories under "Factors" will usually turn up a number of possibilities. Many of these factors have set up special management service departments to aid industries new to factoring. Another source of aid to potential factoring clients is the National Commercial Finance Conference, Inc., located in New York City.

SOURCE: Edmond C. Boullianne, "Factoring—A Financing Alternative for Clients," *Journal of Accountancy,* December 1980, pp. 22, 24, 26, 27, and 28. Copyright © 1980 by the American Institute of Certified Public Accountants, Inc.

not pay), accounts are usually factored **without recourse** (the factor bears the risk that debtors will not pay). Moreover, accounts are usually factored on a notification basis.

The details of a factoring arrangement vary considerably and should be spelled out in a factoring contract. A typical factoring arrangement is continuous. The factor maintains a credit department that performs all functions related to the seller's accounts receivable. In addition to deciding to whom the seller may extend credit, the factor assumes responsibility for billing and collecting, and for bad-debt losses. The seller ships merchandise to approved customers and immediately sells the receivables to the factor. Thus, the advantage of factoring to a seller are immediate cash and relief from the burden of carrying accounts receivable. Factoring arrangements are common in the textile, apparel, carpet, and furniture industries.

When accounts are factored, the factor charges a **factoring fee** for its services of credit approval, billing, collecting, and assuming bad-debt losses. This fee is usually 1% to 3% of the net amount of the receivables factored. The factor then credits the seller's account for the net amount of the receivables factored less the factoring fee. The factor may also withhold some predetermined amount (usually about 10% of the net amount of receivables factored) to protect itself against sales returns and allowances. At this time, the seller may draw money from its account, and the factor charges interest for any cash that it advances to the seller before the average due date of the receivables.

To illustrate, assume that on September 1, 1985, Riley Company factors $20,000 of accounts receivable (terms n/30) with First Finance Corporation. First Finance charges a factoring fee of 2% of the amount of receivables factored. In addition, it charges interest of 1% per month on all amounts withdrawn before the end of the average collection period of the receivables (which in this example is 30 days). Finally, First Finance withholds 10% of the amount of receivables factored to cover sales returns and allowances. Assuming that Riley Company withdraws the maximum amount of cash available on September 1, the journal entry on Riley's books would be:

Cash	17,424	
Receivable from Factor ($20,000 × .10)	2,000	
Factoring Expense ($20,000 × .02)	400	
Interest Expense ($17,600* × .01)	176	
Accounts Receivable		20,000

*$20,000 − $2,000 − $400 = $17,600.

Riley Company would classify the Receivable from Factor as a current asset. This account would later be credited when sales returns and allowances occur and when the factor remits the ending balance in Riley's account.

The appropriate accounting practices for a factoring arrangement depend on the specific agreement. If a company has entered into a factoring agreement, the company should briefly describe the agreement in the notes to its financial statements.

Notes Receivable

A **promissory note,** often called simply a **note,** is a written promise to pay a certain sum of money at a designated time. The note is signed by the **maker** and is usually made payable to the order of a specified **payee,** who in turn may endorse the note and thereby sell (discount) it to a subsequent holder. From a payee's viewpoint, a note represents a **receivable** and therefore an asset. Generally, notes receivable are more desirable than accounts receivable for the following reasons:

1. Notes are often easier to collect because they represent written claims. Thus, their use may reduce a company's bad-debt losses.
2. Notes can usually be converted into cash by discounting them with a bank or other lender, and

this process (which we explain in a subsequent section) is usually quicker and cheaper than assigning or factoring accounts receivable.

3. Notes receivable usually bear a specified rate of interest, while accounts receivable do not.

Companies often acquire notes receivable in exchange for merchandise when customers need credit for a period longer than usual for open accounts. Occasionally, companies acquire notes in exchange for account receivable claims against customers who simply need additional time to pay their accounts. Notes receivable may also result from the sale of other assets and from lending money.

Valuation of Notes Receivable

As indicated earlier in the chapter, notes receivable should be valued initially at an amount equal to the present value of the cash that the company expects to collect. This approach is theoretically sound because it recognizes the time value of money.

If a company can reasonably estimate the amount of its uncollectible notes receivable, the company should establish an allowance for such notes in a manner similar to that used for accounts receivable. Companies that acquire many notes as a result of selling merchandise can usually estimate their uncollectibles with reasonable accuracy.

Because money has a time value, all commercial notes contain interest. Nevertheless, notes are commonly classified as either **interest-bearing** or **noninterest-bearing.** Interest-bearing notes specifically state a certain interest rate; noninterest-bearing notes do not. In a noninterest-bearing note, the interest is simply included in the face amount of the note and is not explicitly stated.

Interest-Bearing Notes Receivable.   Because interest-bearing notes receivable specifically state a certain interest rate, the present value of the note at the time of issuance equals its face amount, assuming that the interest rate is reasonable. Consequently, such notes are initially recorded at their face amount (which equals their present value). Interest revenue is then recognized on the accrual basis as time passes.

To illustrate, let us assume that on October 1, 1984, Sun Company, which uses a calendar-year accounting period, sells merchandise having a sales price of $1,000 to Bin Company in exchange for a one-year, *interest-bearing* note. The note has a face amount of $1,000 and a stated interest rate of 12% (equal to the going market rate for similar notes) payable at maturity. Sun Company would account for the note as shown in Exhibit 7–9.

Noninterest-Bearing Notes Receivable.   The present value of a noninterest-bearing note receivable is less than its face amount. The reason is that the face amount includes interest even though no interest is specifically stated. Although it is theoretically correct to account for this interest, many companies fail to do so.

To illustrate, let us assume that on October 1, 1984, Sun Company (referred to in the previous section) sells merchandise having a sales price of $1,000 to Bur Company in exchange for a one-year, *noninterest-bearing* note. The note has a face amount of $1,120, and the going market rate for similar notes is 12%. The note therefore has a present value of $1,000, an amount that equals the sales price of the merchandise as well as the face amount of the note ($1,120) divided by 1.12. Sun Company would account for the note using one of the alternative methods shown in Exhibit 7–10.

Under Method 1, the note is initially recorded at its present value of $1,000. This is done by debiting Notes Receivable for the face amount ($1,120) and crediting Discount on Notes Receivable for the total amount of interest that the note contains ($120). Notice that the interest equals 12% of the sales price of $1,000 for one year. The balance in the Discount account is deducted from Notes Receivable on the balance sheet. Consequently, if Sun Company prepared a balance sheet on October 1, the company would report a net amount of $1,000, which equals the present value of the note on that date.

Observe that the present value of the Bur Company note ($1,000) is the same as the present value of the Bin Company note recorded in the previous section. The reason is that

<table>
<tr><td colspan="2" align="center">**EXHIBIT 7–9**
Accounting for Interest-Bearing Notes Receivable</td></tr>
<tr><td align="center">Transaction</td><td align="center">Entry</td></tr>
</table>

EXHIBIT 7–9
Accounting for Interest-Bearing Notes Receivable

Transaction	Entry		
Oct. 1, 1984 Sun Company sells merchandise having a sales price of $1,000 to Bin Company in exchange for a one-year *interest-bearing* note. The note has a face amount of $1,000 and a stated interest rate of 12% (equal to the going market rate for similar notes) payable at maturity.	Notes Receivable Sales	1,000	1,000
Dec. 31, 1984 Sun Company computes accrued interest for three months ($1,000 × .12 × ³⁄₁₂ = $30).	Interest Receivable Interest Revenue	30	30
Sept. 30, 1985 Sun Company collects principal and interest at maturity.*	Cash Note Receivable Interest Receivable Interest Revenue	1,120	1,000 30 90

*The illustration assumes that Sun Company does not make reversing entries.

these are similar one-year notes with maturity values of $1,120. Under Method 1, as shown in Exhibit 7–10, $30 of interest revenue is recorded in 1984 and $90 in 1985. These are the same amounts recorded for the Bin Company note in Exhibit 7–9. Method 1 is theoretically correct because it reflects the economic reality that money has a time value. Method 1 puts substance (i.e., the economic fact that the note contains interest) over form (i.e., the fact that the note has no stated interest rate). Notes receivable, sales, and interest revenue are all correctly reported under Method 1.

Substance over Form

In practice, many companies use Method 2 to record short-term, noninterest-bearing, trade notes receivable. Using this method, these companies initially record such notes at their face amounts, not at their present values. The use of Method 2 leads to several misstatements in the financial statements. In the example shown, sales, net income, assets, and stockholders' equity would each be overstated in 1984, while interest revenue would be understated. In 1985, interest revenue and net income would be understated.

Accounting Principles Board Opinion No. 21, which we explain in Chapter 10, requires companies under certain circumstances to impute (estimate and record) interest in transactions involving receivables and payables for which there is either no stated interest or an unreasonable amount of stated interest. Applying the principles set forth in this pronouncement would produce the results shown under Method 1. However, *APB Opinion No. 21* states that it is not intended to apply to "receivables and payables arising from transactions with customers or suppliers in the normal course of business which are due in customary trade terms not exceeding approximately one year."[11] Consequently, many companies use Method 2 to account for these types of notes receivable. Because the receivables are short-term, an argument can be made that the amount of interest often is not material. In addition, net income may not be significantly distorted if the receivables occur fairly evenly over time.

Materiality

---

[11]*APB Opinion No. 21,* "Interest on Receivables and Payables," 1971, par. 3.

Discounting Notes Receivable

Most notes are **negotiable,** which means that a payee may transfer its rights to collect a note to a subsequent holder. On the maturity date, the holder collects the amount of the note's maturity value from the maker.

When a note is negotiable, therefore, the payee may obtain cash before the maturity date by **discounting** (selling) the note at a bank or other entity. To discount the note, the payee endorses it. In rare cases the endorsement is made **without recourse,** which means that the endorser avoids future liability on the note. Usually, however, banks require that endorsements be made **with recourse,** which means that the endorser agrees to pay the holder if the maker does not. Consequently, endorsers typically remain **contingently liable** on notes receivable that they have discounted.

Contingent liabilities, discussed more fully in Chapter 14, are obligations that must be paid if certain conditions occur. For example, if the maker of a note fails to pay the holder on the maturity date, an endorser (with recourse) must pay. Users of financial statements want to know about a company's contingent obligations. Consequently, the Financial Accounting Standards Board *(FASB),* in its *Statement of Financial Accounting Standards No. 5,* requires companies to disclose contingent liabilities that relate to notes receivable discounted, even if there is only a remote chance that the company will actually have to pay.[12]

---

[12]*FASB Statement of Financial Accounting Standards No. 5,* par. 12.

EXHIBIT 7–10
Accounting for Noninterest-Bearing Notes Receivable

Transaction	Method 1: Record at Present Value (theoretically correct)			Method 2: Record at Face Amount (theoretically incorrect)		
Oct. 1, 1984 Sun Company sells merchandise having a sales price of $1,000 to Bur Company in exchange for a one-year, *noninterest-bearing* note. The note has a face amount of $1,120 and the going market rate for similar notes is 12%.	Notes Receivable Sales Discount on Notes Receivable*	1,120	1,000 120	Notes Receivable Sales	1,120	1,120
Dec. 31, 1984 Sun Company computes accrued interest for three months ($1,000 × .12 × 3/12 = $30).	Discount on Notes Receivable Interest Revenue	30	30	No entry		
Sept. 30, 1985 Sun Company collects principal and interest at maturity.**	Cash Discount on Notes Receivable Notes Receivable Interest Revenue	1,120 90	1,120 90	Cash Notes Receivable	1,120	1,120

*Some firms prefer *not* to use a Discount account. These firms would debit Notes Receivable for $1,000 on October 1 and for $30 on December 31. They would then credit Notes Receivable for $1,030 on September 30, 1985. This approach is an acceptable variation of Method 1 because it produces essentially the same results.
**The illustration assumes that Sun Company does not make reversing entries.

When a company discounts a note at a bank, the company receives cash **proceeds.** These proceeds, which the bank calculates, are equal to the **maturity value** of the note less the bank's **discount.** To calculate the discount, the bank multiplies the **maturity value** of the note by the bank's **discount rate** (the interest rate that the bank charges for discounting the note) and by the **remaining time to maturity.** These calculations are illustrated in the following example.

Suppose that on March 1, 1985, Blue Inc. receives a $10,000, 90-day, 10% note from a customer on account. Thirty days later, on March 31, 1985, Blue Inc. discounts the note with recourse at Park National Bank. The bank's discount rate is 12%, and Blue Inc. receives proceeds of $10,045, computed as follows:

Face amount of note	$10,000
Interest to maturity ($10,000 × .10 × 90/360)	250
Maturity value of note[13]	10,250
Bank discount ($10,250 × .12 × 60/360)	205
Proceeds	$10,045

Blue Inc. accounts for the above transactions using one of the two approaches shown in Exhibit 7–11. Because most makers pay their notes at maturity, the **footnote approach** is easier to apply. Under this approach, Notes Receivable is credited when a note is discounted, and the contingent liability is disclosed in a footnote such as: "The company is contingently liable for $10,250 on a note receivable discounted at the bank. It does not expect the maker of the note to default." The company, of course, stops making this disclosure when it is no longer contingently liable on the note. Instead of using a footnote, the company may disclose essentially the same information parenthetically on the balance sheet.

Some accountants prefer the **contra account approach,** under which Notes Receivable Discounted is credited when a company discounts a note. Notes Receivable Discounted is a contra account to Notes Receivable and is deducted from Notes Receivable in the current assets section of the balance sheet in order to disclose the contingent liability. The contra account approach requires slightly more bookkeeping than the footnote approach. Moreover, it fails to disclose the full amount of the contingent liability. Notice in the example that the contingent liability is actually $10,250 (principal + interest). The Notes Receivable Discounted account, however, shows only the face amount of $10,000.

Observe that Interest Revenue is credited for $45 on March 31. Actually, Blue Inc. has earned $83.33 ($10,000 × .10 × 30/360 = $83.33) as a result of holding the note for thirty days. This suggests that on March 31, Blue Inc. should record $83.33 as interest revenue and debit a loss account (or Interest Expense) for $38.33 ($83.33 − $45 = $38.33), as shown below:

Cash	10,045.00	
Loss from Discounting Notes Receivable	38.33	
Notes Receivable (or Notes Receivable		
Discounted)		10,000.00
Interest Revenue		83.33

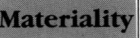

Although this approach is logical, companies rarely use it because of materiality considerations.

When a note has been discounted, the bank will try to collect the maturity value from the maker on the maturity date. If the maker defaults, the bank must promptly notify the endorser. Therefore, the endorser who has not heard from the bank within a few days after the

---

[13]Remember that the maturity value equals the face amount of a noninterest-bearing note.

EXHIBIT 7–11
Accounting for Notes Receivable Discounted

Transaction	Footnote Approach			Contra Account Approach		
Mar. 1, 1985 Blue Inc. receives a $10,000, 90-day, 10% note from a customer on account.	Notes Receivable Accounts Receivable	10,000	10,000	Notes Receivable Accounts Receivable	10,000	10,000
Mar. 31, 1985 Blue Inc. discounts the note (with recourse) at Park National Bank at a discount rate of 12%.	Cash Notes Receivable Interest Revenue	10,045	10,000 45	Cash Notes Receivable Discounted Interest Revenue	10,045	10,000 45
Alternative Assumption No. 1						
May 30, 1985 The customer pays Park National Bank.	No entry			Notes Receivable Discounted Notes Receivable	10,000	10,000
Alternative Assumption No. 2						
May 30, 1985 The customer dishonors the note and the bank charges Blue Inc. with the maturity value plus a protest fee of $25.	Dishonored Notes Receivable Cash	10,275	10,275	Dishonored Notes Receivable Cash	10,275	10,275
				Notes Receivable Discounted Notes Receivable	10,000	10,000

maturity date may generally assume that the maker has paid the note and thereby ended the endorser's contingent liability. If, on the other hand, the maker does not pay the bank, we say that the note has been **dishonored.** In this case, the bank promptly notifies the endorser and holds the endorser liable for the full maturity value plus any **protest fee** (any reasonable cost that the bank incurs in protesting the note). The endorser pays the bank and then has a claim against the maker for the full amount paid. Because the endorser pays the note, the endorser no longer has a contingent liability to the bank.

To illustrate the accounting entries involved, assume that on the maturity date, May 30, 1985, the customer pays Park National Bank the amount owed, thereby ending Blue Inc.'s contingent liability. As shown in Exhibit 7–11, Blue Inc. would not make an entry under the footnote approach but would under the contra account approach. In practice, the entry required under the contra account approach would likely be made a few days after the maturity date, because a company that is contingently liable on a note does not usually know on the maturity date that the maker has paid.

Assume now that instead of paying the note on May 30, 1985, the customer dishonored it and the bank charged Blue Inc. with the maturity value plus a protest fee of $25. Under these circumstances, Blue Inc. should make the appropriate entry or entries shown in Exhibit 7–11.

Dishonored Notes Receivable is a special note receivable account and should be reported separately from Notes Receivable on the balance sheet. This account should be used for all dishonored notes receivable, whether or not they have been discounted. Blue Inc. will earn interest on the amount in this account at the rate allowed by law. The Dishonored Notes Receivable account should be credited if Blue Inc. collects from the maker. If the company cannot collect the dishonored note, it should write off the amount uncollectible to an Allowance for Uncollectible Notes account, assuming that it uses such an account for its notes receivable.

Balance Sheet Presentation of Receivables

As stated earlier, an enterprise should classify a receivable as a current asset only if collection is expected within the next year or operating cycle, whichever is longer. Within the current assets category, trade receivables should be reported separately from nontrade receivables. Moreover, a company should report separately those receivables that reflect **related-party transactions,** such as loans made by the company to officers or to affiliated companies. Accounts and notes receivable should be segregated when the amount of each is

Materiality material. Exhibit 7–12 shows a receivables disclosure that Strawbridge & Clothier made in its 1982 Annual Report. Strawbridge & Clothier operates 29 retail stores that sell general merchandise in Pennsylvania, New Jersey, and Delaware.

CONCLUDING REMARKS

Cash is the standard medium of exchange in business transactions, and receivables are claims held against others which generally result in a future inflow of cash. To be classified as a current asset, cash must be available for use in current operations. Similarly, receivables are properly classified as current assets only when they are collectible within the next year or operating cycle, whichever is longer.

Cash and receivables are two examples of monetary assets because they are fixed or determinable in terms of the number of dollars on hand or to be received, regardless of how prices change. For this reason, the valuation of cash and receivables is less controversial than the valuation of nonmonetary assets. In the next two chapters we focus on accounting for inventory. Inventory is a current asset that is nonmonetary in nature and is considerably more challenging to value than either cash or receivables.

EXHIBIT 7–12
Strawbridge & Clothier
Receivables Disclosure

	January 29 1983	January 30 1982
Accounts receivable:		
Customers:		
Flexible charge accounts	76,956,599	68,816,633
Deferred payment accounts	22,684,067	20,700,995
Regular charge accounts	5,785,400	5,939,451
Suppliers and sundry	3,490,247	3,807,537
	108,916,313	99,264,616
Allowance for doubtful accounts	(3,250,000)	(3,250,000)
	105,666,313	96,014,616

SOURCE: Strawbridge & Clothier, 1982 Annual Report.

1. Cash may include currency, coins, checks, bank drafts, money orders, checking accounts, and savings accounts.

2. On a balance sheet, cash is valued at face amount and classified as a current asset only if the cash is available for use in current operations.

3. A petty cash fund is typically used to disburse relatively small amounts of currency and coins for such items as taxi fares, postage, and minor supplies.

4. A bank reconciliation is a schedule that explains any differences between a company's book balance of cash in a particular bank account and the bank statement balance.

5. A proof of cash is an expanded, four-column reconciliation that is a stronger control measure than the single-column bank reconciliation.

6. The preparation of either a bank reconciliation or a proof of cash usually indicates that a company has to make certain adjusting entries to update its accounting records.

7. Receivables are claims held against others for money, goods, or services.

8. A receivable should be valued initially at an amount equal to the present value of the cash that the company expects to collect. A receivable should be classified as a current asset only if collection is expected within the next year or operating cycle, whichever is longer.

9. From the standpoint of accounting theory, the net method of recording credit sales is better than the gross method. But most companies use the gross method because of convenience and materiality.

10. The allowance method, rather than the direct write-off method, should be used when accounting for uncollectible accounts. The direct write-off method usually violates the matching principle; the allowance method does not.

11. The allowance method requires that bad debts be estimated by an income statement approach or a balance sheet approach.

12. The income statement approach emphasizes the matching principle and requires that the adjusting entry for bad debts be made without considering the previous balance in the Allowance for Doubtful Accounts.

13. The balance sheet approach emphasizes the reporting of accounts receivable at net realizable value and requires that the previous balance in the Allowance for Doubtful Accounts be considered in recording the adjusting entry for bad debts.

14. In addition to its use in accounting for uncollectible accounts, the allowance method can be used in accounting for other items that affect the cash realization of accounts receivable (e.g., sales discounts).

15. Many companies use accounts receivable to generate cash immediately by pledging, assigning, or factoring the accounts. Each method of accounts receivable financing has important financial statement implications.

16. Although some notes have no stated interest rates, all commercial notes contain interest, because money has a time value.

17. To be theoretically correct, we should always account for the interest component of a note receivable, whether or not the interest is explicitly stated. In practice, many companies do not separately account for the interest component of short-term, noninterest-bearing, trade notes receivable because of materiality.

18. A company may use either a footnote approach or a contra account approach to accounting for notes receivable discounted.

7–1   What are the normal components of cash?

7–2   What are the guidelines for the valuation and classification of cash on the balance sheet?

7–3   How should a company report each of the following items?

    [a] Bank overdrafts.
    [b] Certificates of deposit.
    [c] NSF checks received from customers.

    [d] Expense advances made to employees.
    [e] Postdated checks received from customers.
    [f] Postage stamps.
    [g] IOUs received from employees.

7–4   What do accountants mean by the term "internal control"?

7–5   Why should a company divide the responsibility for a series of related transactions between two or more persons?

7–6   What is the purpose of a petty cash fund?

7–7   Explain the nature of a Cash Short and Over account.

7–8   What is a bank reconciliation? What purposes does it serve?

7–9   What is a proof of cash? What purposes does it serve?

7–10   What does the term "receivables" mean? How should receivables be classified on the balance sheet?

7–11   How should short-term receivables be valued on the balance sheet?

7–12   What is the difference between a trade discount and a cash discount?

7–13   Explain the distinction between the net method and the gross method of recording credit sales. Which method do companies generally use? Why?

7–14   Briefly compare the direct write-off method and the allowance method of accounting for uncollectible accounts.

7–15   Assume that a company uses the allowance method of accounting for uncollectible accounts. What is the major argument in favor of using the income statement approach? What is the major argument in favor of using the balance sheet approach?

7–16   Why does the Allowance for Doubtful Accounts sometimes have a debit balance?

7–17   What is the theoretical argument for using the allowance method to account for expected sales returns and allowances? (Assume that the expected amount is material.)

7–18   Briefly describe and defend the balance sheet reporting of assigned accounts receivable by an assignor.

7–19   Why is it theoretically correct to account for interest when accounting for a noninterest-bearing note receivable?

7–20   What is the fundamental difference between the two approaches to accounting for notes receivable discounted?

CASES

C7–1   Asset measurement involves the valuation or pricing of the future service of an asset. Receivables are assets that represent future claims to fixed amounts of monies.

Instructions

Discuss how asset measurement applies to receivables (short-term and long-term).

(AICPA adapted)

C7–2   When a company has a policy of extending credit on sales, it is reasonable to expect some accounts to be uncollectible. A company must therefore recognize bad-debt expense. Two basic methods of recognizing bad-debt expense are: (1) the direct write-off method, and (2) the allowance method.

Instructions

[a]   Describe both the direct write-off method and the allowance method of recognizing bad-debt expense.
[b]   Explain why one of the above methods is preferable to the other and why the other method is not usually in accordance with generally accepted accounting principles.

(AICPA adapted)

C7–3   One of your corporate clients operates a full-line department store that dominates its market area, is easily accessible to public and private transportation, has adequate parking facilities, and is near a large, permanent military base. The president of the company seeks your advice on a proposal he received.

A local bank in which your client has an account recently affiliated with a popular national credit card plan and has invited your client to participate. Under the plan, affiliated banks mail credit card applications to persons in the community who have good credit ratings, regardless of whether they are bank customers. If the recipient wishes to receive a credit card, he completes, signs, and returns the application and installment credit agreement. Card holders may charge merchandise or services at any participating establishment throughout the nation.

The bank guarantees payment to all participating merchants on invoices that have been properly completed, signed, and validated with the impression of credit cards that have not expired or been reported stolen or otherwise canceled. Local merchants, including your client, may turn in all card-validated sales tickets or invoices to their affiliated local bank at any time and receive immediate credits to their checking accounts of 96.5% of the face value of the invoices. If card users pay the bank in full within 30 days for amounts billed, the bank levies no added charges against them. If they elect to make their payments under a deferred payment plan, the bank adds a service charge with an effective annual interest rate of 18% on unpaid balances. Only the local affiliated banks and the franchiser of the credit card plan share in these revenues.

The 18% service charge approximates what your client has been billing customers who pay their accounts over an extended period on a schedule similar to that of the credit card plan. Participation in the plan does not prevent your client from continuing its credit business.

Instructions

[a] What are (1) the positive and (2) the negative financial factors and accounting factors that your client should consider in deciding whether to participate in the credit card plan? Explain.

[b] If your client participates in the plan, which income statement and balance sheet accounts may change materially as the plan becomes fully operative? (Such factors as market position, sales mix, prices, and markup are expected to remain about the same as in the past.) Explain.

(AICPA adapted)

EXERCISES

E7–1 The controller of Westside Women's Wear is trying to determine the total amount to report as *cash* on a balance sheet dated December 31. The following items are under consideration:

[1] NSF checks received during December from customers on account and returned by the bank with the December bank statement.

[2] Currency and coins in a change fund (used for making change with customers) on December 31.

[3] Certificates of deposit held on December 31.

[4] Checks that the company has drawn payable to suppliers. Checks have been recorded but not mailed as of December 31.

[5] Postage stamps on hand December 31.

[6] Correct cash balance on December 31 in special checking account used for writing payroll checks.

[7] Petty cash on hand December 31.

[8] A check received from a customer and dated January 5 of the following year.

[9] IOUs from company personnel.

[10] Correct cash balance on December 31 in Chemical Bank general checking account.

Instructions

[a] Identify the items that the controller should report as cash on the December 31 balance sheet.

[b] Indicate the proper balance sheet reporting for items that the company should not include as cash.

E7–2 The following information pertains to Lite Brewing Company on December 31:

Correct cash balance in general checking account with First Bank	$ 2,846
Overdraft in special checking account with Second Bank (Lite does not have another account with Second Bank.)	290
Cash accumulated in a special fund that will be used for plant expansion in five years	15,187
Cash surrender value of life insurance	3,265
Cash travel advances in the hands of company salespersons	860
Currency and coins in a petty cash fund (The company has not replenished the fund to the imprest amount of $200.)	31

Instructions

[a] Calculate the total amount that the company should report as *cash* in the current assets section of the balance sheet dated December 31.

[b] Indicate the proper balance sheet reporting of items that you omitted in [a].

E7–3 On April 1, Toups Insurance Agency established an imprest petty cash fund for $200 by writing a check on City National Bank. On April 23 the fund contained the following:

Currency and coins	$37
Receipts for office supplies expense	87
Receipts for postage expense	56
Receipts for advertising expense	18

On April 23 the agency wrote a check to increase the fund to the imprest amount.

Instructions

Prepare the necessary journal entries to record the

petty cash transactions during April.

E7–4   The following information pertains to Block Drug Company as of November 30:

Bank statement balance	$3,658
Bank service charge for November (not previously recorded on Block's books)	8
Checks outstanding	215
Interest on bank balance credited by bank during November (not previously recorded on Block's books)	21
Deposit in transit	490

Instructions

Based on the above information, compute the general ledger cash balance on November 30 *before* adjustments.

E7–5   The following information pertains to Holiday, Inc., as of September 30:

Cash balance per general ledger	$2,500
Cash balance per bank statement	2,705
Checks outstanding	325
Bank service charge shown on September bank statement	10
Error made by Holiday, Inc., in recording a check that cleared the bank in September (check was drawn in September for $135 but recorded at $185)	50
Deposit in transit	160

Instructions

Prepare a September bank reconciliation for Holiday.

E7–6   The bookkeeper for Minton Lock Company recently prepared the following bank reconciliation.

Minton Lock Company
BANK RECONCILIATION
September 30

Balance per bank statement			$12,642
Add: Deposit in transit		$870	
Checkbook printing charge		21	
Error made in recording check no. 1782 (issued in September to acquire equipment)		160	
NSF check from a customer returned with the bank statement		500	1,551
			14,193
Deduct: Outstanding checks			
No. 1763	$235		
No. 1795	168		
No. 1796	45	448	
Note collected by bank (includes $50 interest)		950	1,398
Balance per books			$12,795

Instructions

[a] What amount should Minton report as *cash* on the balance sheet dated September 30? Assume that the company has $580 cash on hand on September 30.

[b] Prepare the necessary compound journal entry.

E7–7   Akron Corporation keeps all its cash in a checking account. An examination of the company's accounting records and bank statement for the month ended June 30 revealed the following information:

[1] The cash balances as of June 30 are:

Bank statement balance	$8,469
Book balance	8,324

[2] A deposit of $750 that was placed in the bank's night depository on June 30 does not appear on the bank statement.

[3] The bank statement shows that on June 30, the bank collected a note for Akron and credited the proceeds of $935 to the company's account. The proceeds included $35 interest, all of which Akron earned during the current accounting period. Akron has not yet recorded the collection.

[4] Checks outstanding on June 30 are:

No. 151	$150
No. 157	48
No. 166	72

[5] Akron discovered that check no. 159, written in June for $183 in payment of an account payable, had been recorded in the company's records as $138.

[6] Included with the June bank statement was an NSF check for $250 that Akron had received from Winston Company on account on June 26. Akron has not yet recorded the returned check.

[7] The bank statement shows a $15 service charge for June.

Instructions

[a] Prepare a June 30 bank reconciliation for Akron.
[b] Prepare the necessary journal entries.
[c] Post the journal entries to Akron's cash account and determine the adjusted cash balance.

E7–8 The following information pertains to the cash of Tom's Candy Company:

[1]

	July 31	August 31
Balance shown on bank statement	$2,738	$2,696
Balance shown in general ledger before reconciling the bank account	2,578	2,500
Outstanding checks	863	1,015
Deposit in transit	685	1,245

[2]

	For August
Deposits shown on bank statement	$5,588
Charges shown on bank statement	5,630
Cash receipts shown on company's books	5,398
Cash payments shown on company's books	5,476

[3] The bank service charge was $18 in July (recorded by the company during August) and $24 in August (not yet recorded by the company).

[4] Included with the August bank statement was a check for $500 that had been received on August 25 from a customer on account. The returned check, marked "NSF" by the bank, has not yet been recorded on the company's books.

[5] During August the bank collected $750 of bond interest for Tom's Candy Company and credited the proceeds to the company's account. The company earned the interest during the current accounting period but has not yet recorded it.

[6] During August the company issued a check for $696 for equipment. The check, which cleared the bank during August, was incorrectly recorded by the company for $896.

Instructions

Prepare a proof of cash for August.

E7–9 Green, Inc., engaged in the following transactions during August:

Aug. 1   Sold merchandise to K Company for $10,000; terms 2/10, n/30.

   2   Sold merchandise to M Company for $15,000; terms 2/10, n/30.

   11   Received payment from M Company for the August 2 sale.

   30   Received payment from K Company for the August 1 sale.

Instructions

Prepare general journal entries for the above transactions on Green's books, using:
[a] The *net method* of recording credit sales.
[b] The *gross method* of recording credit sales.

E7–10 The following data pertain to two companies that have calendar-year accounting periods:

1985 Credit Sales	Accounts Receivable Dec. 31, 1985	Allowance for Doubtful Accounts Dec. 31, 1985 Before Adjustment
Apple Company $200,000	$25,000	$250 credit balance
Pear Company 500,000	60,000	450 debit balance

Instructions

Journalize the necessary adjusting entry on December 31, 1985, based on the following independent assumptions:

[a] For Apple Company, assuming the company estimates that 1% of credit sales are uncollectible.

[b] For Apple Company, assuming the company estimates that 6% of the accounts receivable balance on December 31, 1985, will be uncollectible.

[c] For Pear Company, assuming the company estimates that 0.5% of credit sales are uncollectible.

[d] For Pear Company, assuming the company estimates that 5% of the accounts receivable balance on December 31, 1985, will be uncollectible.

E7–11 The following information pertains to Robinson Enterprises.

[1] Sales made during 1985:

Cash	$ 90,000
Credit	310,000
Total	$400,000

[2] Accounts Receivable classified by age on December 31, 1985:

Age of Accounts	Accounts Receivable Balance
Under 30 days	$40,000
30–60 days	20,000
61–120 days	10,000
Over 120 days	5,000
Total	$75,000

[3] The Allowance for Doubtful Accounts had a $300 credit balance before adjustment on December 31, 1985.

Instructions

Prepare the adjusting entry on December 31, 1985, to record estimated bad debts under each of the following:

[a] The income statement approach, assuming that the uncollectible rate is 1% of *credit* sales.

[b] The income statement approach, assuming that the uncollectible rate is 0.75% of *total* sales.

[c] The balance sheet approach, assuming that the uncollectible rate is 5% of gross accounts receivable.

[d] The balance sheet approach, assuming that the following uncollectible percentages are appropriate: under 30 days, 1%; 30–60 days, 3%; 61–120 days, 10%; over 120 days, 30%.

E7–12 An aging of Melton Company's accounts receivable on December 31, 1985, reveals the following information:

Time Outstanding	Amount of Accounts Receivable
Under 30 days	$ 80,000
30–60 days	16,000
61–120 days	12,000
121–180 days	8,000
Over 180 days	4,000
Total	$120,000

Based on past experience, the company believes that the following uncollectible percentages are appropriate: under 30 days, 1.5%; 30–60 days, 3%; 61–120 days, 15%; 121–180 days, 40%; over 180 days, 60%.

Instructions

Using the aging of accounts receivable variation of the balance sheet approach, prepare the adjusting entry on December 31, 1985 to record estimated bad debts, assuming that the balance in the Allowance for Doubtful Accounts *before adjustment* is:

[a] $670 credit

[b] $410 debit

E7–13 Ingram, Inc., reported the following information on its balance sheet dated December 31, 1984:

Accounts receivable	$53,800
Less: Allowance for doubtful accounts	2,400
	$51,400

The following events occurred during 1985:

[1] Made credit sales of $210,000 and cash sales of $56,000.

[2] Collected $201,800 from customers on account.

[3] Wrote off $3,100 of accounts considered to be uncollectible.

[4] Collected $400 from customers whose accounts had been written off as uncollectible.

[5] Estimated that 5% of the accounts receivable balance at year-end would prove to be uncollectible.

Instructions

Prepare journal entries to record the above events.

E7–14 Rapp Company uses the allowance method to account for its sales returns. Based on past experience, Rapp estimates that customers will return approximately 10% of the goods that the company sold. The company also estimates that it can resell goods returned by customers for approximately 70% of the original selling price. Rapp's sales during the current accounting period were $200,000. The company uses a perpetual inventory system.

Instructions

[a] Prepare an adjusting journal entry to record estimated sales returns for the current accounting period.

[b] Prepare a journal entry to record the return in the next accounting period of goods that Rapp sold for $5,000. Assume that customers have not paid for the goods.

E7–15 On July 1, 1985, Wheeler Company assigned $50,000 of accounts receivable to its bank on a non-notification basis. On that date the bank advanced $40,000, less a service charge of 1% of the total accounts assigned, and Wheeler signed a $40,000 note bearing interest of 1% per month on the unpaid loan balance at the beginning of the month.

During July Wheeler collected $33,000 on assigned accounts. The company remitted this amount to the bank on July 31.

During August the company collected the remaining balance of assigned accounts. On August 31 the company paid off the remaining loan balance.

Instructions

Record the above events in general journal form.

E7–16 On October 1, 1985, Fine Furniture Company factored $60,000 of accounts receivable with Fast

Finance Company on a notification basis. Fast Finance charged a factoring fee of 3% of the amount factored and interest of 1.5% per month on all amounts withdrawn before the end of the 30-day average collection period of the receivables. To cover sales returns and allowances, Fast Finance withheld 5% of the amount of receivables factored.

Instructions

Prepare the necessary journal entry for Fine Furniture on October 1, 1985, assuming that the company received the maximum amount of cash available from Fast Finance.

E7–17 On September 30, Alex Company engaged in the following transactions:

[1] Obtained a $10,000, 30-day, 12% loan from First National Bank. The company pledged $10,000 of accounts receivable as security for the loan.

[2] Assigned $30,000 of accounts receivable on a non-notification basis to Commerce Bank. The bank advanced $21,000, less a service charge of $420, and Alex signed a $21,000 note calling for interest of 1% per month on the unpaid loan balance.

[3] Factored $50,000 of accounts receivable on a notification basis with Quick Finance Company. Quick Finance charged a factoring fee of 2% of the amount factored and interest of 1.5% per month on all amounts withdrawn before the end of the 30-day average collection period of the receivables. Quick Finance withheld 10% of the amount of receivables factored and advanced to Alex the maximum amount of cash available to the company on September 30.

Instructions

Journalize each of the above transactions on September 30.

E7–18 On November 1, 1984, Barney Manufacturing Company sold land in exchange for a $40,000, 12%, 90-day promissory note. The 12% interest rate was the going market rate for similar notes. Barney had paid $24,000 to acquire the land in 1978. When the note matured, Barney collected principal and interest.

Instructions

Prepare all journal entries (including an adjusting entry) required to record the above events on Barney's books in 1984 and 1985. Assume that Barney uses a calendar-year accounting period and does not make reversing entries.

E7–19 On October 1, 1984, Profitt's, Inc., sold merchandise having a sales price of $5,000 and received a one-year promissory note with a face amount of $5,500. The note had no stated interest rate, although the market rate for similar notes was 10%. When the note matured, Profitt's collected the face amount. Profitt's, Inc., uses a calendar-year accounting period and does not make reversing entries.

Instructions

[a] Prepare all journal entries (including an adjusting entry) required to record the above events on Profitt's books, assuming that the company records the note at present value.

[b] Prepare all journal entries required to record the above events on Profitt's books, assuming that the company records the note at face amount.

[c] From a theoretical standpoint, is it better for Profitt's to record the note at present value or at face amount? Explain your answer.

E7–20 Sealy Company has the following three notes receivable:

Note	Date of Note	Face Amount	Interest Rate	Time of Note
A	April 1, 1985	$10,000	8%	90-day
B	May 1, 1985	20,000	9%	90-day
C	May 16, 1985	30,000	10%	60-day

Instructions

For each note, calculate the proceeds that Sealy would receive by discounting the note on May 31, 1985, at a rate of 12%.

PROBLEMS

P7–1   The following events pertain to Kern's Supply House:

July 1   Established an imprest petty cash fund for $300 by writing a check on Anderson County Bank.

12   Wrote a check to replenish the fund. The fund contained:

Currency and coins	$ 26
Receipts for transportation-in	203
Receipts for postage expense	66

20   Wrote a check to replenish the fund and to increase the imprest amount to $400. The fund contained:

Currency and coins	$ 21
Receipts for transportation-in	187
Receipts for postage expense	60
Receipts for charitable contributions	35

Instructions

Prepare the necessary journal entries to record the petty cash transactions during July.

P7–2   Wilson Company keeps all its cash in a checking account. Presented below are the company's bank reconciliation prepared at the end of May, the general ledger account for cash, and a summary of the company's bank statement for June:

Wilson Company
BANK RECONCILIATION
May 31

Balance per bank statement	$6,250
Add: Deposits in transit	225
	6,475
Deduct: Outstanding checks	418
Correct cash balance	$6,057

Balance per books	$6,072
Deduct: Bank service charge	15
Correct cash balance	$6,057

Cash

Balance, June 1	6,057	June disbursements	25,679
June receipts	26,182		

Summary of Wilson Company's Bank Statement for June

Balance, June 1	$ 6,250
Deposits shown for June	25,692
Note and interest collected during June	1,575
Checks that cleared during June	(25,707)
June service charge	(17)
Balance, June 30	7,793

Additional Information

[1] During June, Wilson incorrectly recorded two checks. Check no. 507 was drawn for $233 but recorded as $323; check no. 521 was drawn for $180 but recorded as $18. Both checks were issued in payment of accounts payable and cleared the bank in June.

[2] During June the bank erroneously charged a $210 check of Williams Company to Wilson Company's account.

[3] Of the $1,575 note and interest collected by the bank during June, $75 represents interest, all of which Wilson earned during 1985. The company has not yet recorded the collection.

Instructions

[a] Prepare a June 30 bank reconciliation.

[b] Prepare journal entries to bring Wilson Company's accounting records up to date.

[c] What amount should Wilson report as *cash* on the balance sheet dated June 30?

P7-3 Schwinn Company uses a calendar-year accounting period. The following information is available about the company's cash.

Schwinn Company
BANK RECONCILIATION
April 30

Balance per bank statement		$4,642
Add: Deposit in transit		610
		5,252
Deduct: Outstanding checks		
No. 606	$177	
No. 607	248	425
Correct cash balance		$4,827
Balance per books		$4,839
Deduct: Bank service charge		12
Correct cash balance		$4,827

Park National Bank
General Account: Schwinn Company

Date	Debits		Credits	Balance
4–30				4,642
5–01			610	5,252
5–02	177			5,075
5–04	248	755	1,552	5,624
5–05	437			5,187
5–09	489		3,621	8,319
5–12	705		1,986	9,600
5–20	930			8,670
5–22	423			8,247
5–26			2,549	10,796
5–29	255 NSF			10,541
5–30	20 DM	5,798		4,723
5–31	14 SC		1,290 CM	5,999
Total debits $10,251			**Total credits $11,608**	

Legend: DM: Debit memo   NSF: Not sufficient funds check
CM: Credit memo   SC: Service charge

Information Taken from Schwinn Company

Cash Receipts Journal			Cash Payments Journal	
Date	**Cash Debit**	**Date**	**Check No.**	**Cash Credit**
5–03	1,552	5–01	608	755
5–08	3,621	5–03	609	473
5–12	1,986	5–06	610	489
5–25	2,549	5–11	611	705
5–31	875	5–16	612	930
	10,583	5–21	613	243
		5–27	614	511
		5–29	615	5,798
		5–30	616	346
		5–31	617	566
				10,816

Schwinn Company's Cash Account Taken from General Ledger

Cash

Balance, April 30	4,839	Cash Payments		
Cash Receipts		Journal, May 31	10,816	
Journal, May 31	10,583			

Additional Information

[1] During May a collection charge of $20 that was applicable to Shinn Company was erroneously deducted by the bank from Schwinn Company's account.

[2] The credit memo shown on the bank statement relates to a note that the bank collected on Schwinn's behalf. The note had a face value of $1,200 and Schwinn earned interest of $90 during the current accounting period. The company has not yet recorded the collection.

[3] Schwinn failed to record the bank service charge for April (see April reconciliation).

[4] The NSF check shown on the bank statement had been received during May from a customer on account. The return of the check has not yet been recorded by Schwinn.

[5] Schwinn made two errors in recording cash payments during May:

Check No.	Actual Amount of Check	Amount Recorded
609	$437	$473
613	423	243

Check no. 609 was for delivery expense; check no. 613 was issued to purchase equipment.

Instructions

[a] Prepare a bank reconciliation dated May 31.
[b] Prepare the necessary journal entries.

P7–4   Refer to the information given for Schwinn Company in P7–3.

Instructions

[a] Prepare a proof of cash for May.
[b] Prepare the necessary journal entries.

P7–5   The accounting period of Winn Company ends on December 31. The following information is available about the company's cash.

Winn Company
BANK RECONCILIATION
October 31

Balance per bank statement		$17,705
Add: Deposit in transit		1,790
		19,495
Deduct: Outstanding checks		
No. 773	$4,563	
No. 774	2,118	6,681
Correct cash balance		$12,814
Balance per books		$11,234
Add: Note collected by bank		
Principal	1,500	
Interest earned during current accounting period	100	1,600
		12,834
Deduct: Bank service charge		20
Correct cash balance		$12,814

Information Taken from Winn Company

Cash Receipts Journal			Cash Payments Journal	
Date	**Cash Debit**	**Date**	**Check No.**	**Cash Credit**
11–03	5,967	11–01	775	4,567
11–06	3,410	11–04	776	963
11–11	1,037	11–05	777	2,515
11–23	4,255	11–10	778	3,264
11–30	3,600	11–17	779	3,325
	18,269	11–22	780	694
		11–27	781	619
		11–28	782	760
		11–29	783	3,000
		11–30	784	1,868
				21,575

```
┌──────────────────────────────────────────────────────────────────────┐
│                        City National Bank                              │
│                 General Account: Winn Company                          │
│                                                                        │
│  Date           Debits              Credits      Balance               │
│  10-31                                            17,705               │
│  11-01                               1,790        19,495               │
│  11-02       4,563                                14,932               │
│  11-04       2,118        4,567      5,967        14,214               │
│  11-05        963                                 13,251               │
│  11-06                               3,410        16,661               │
│  11-07       2,515                                14,146               │
│  11-11                               1,037        15,183               │
│  11-13       2,264                                12,919               │
│  11-18       3,325                                 9,594               │
│  11-24        964                    4,255        12,885               │
│  11-28        619                    750 CM       13,016               │
│  11-29       3,000        35 DM      500 CM       10,481               │
│  11-30       665 NSF      22 SC                    9,794               │
│                                                                        │
│            Total debits  $25,620   Total credits  $17,709             │
│                                                                        │
│  Legend:  DM: Debit memo      NSF: Not sufficient funds check         │
│           CM: Credit memo     SC: Service charge                       │
└──────────────────────────────────────────────────────────────────────┘
```

Winn Company's Cash Account
Taken from General Ledger

Cash

Balance, Oct. 31	11,234	Cash Payments	
Cash Receipts		Journal, Nov. 30	21,575
Journal, Nov. 30	18,269		

Additional Information

[1] After preparing the October 31 reconciliation, Winn failed to record the necessary journal entries.

[2] The NSF check had been received during November from a customer on account. Winn has not yet recorded the return of the check.

[3] The credit memos shown on the bank statement pertain to $750 of bond interest that Winn earned during 1985 and that the bank collected on the company's behalf (collection not yet recorded on Winn's books) and a $500 collection made for Wyld Company that the bank erroneously credited to Winn's account.

[4] The $35 debit memo shown on the bank statement pertains to the rental of a safe deposit box during November.

[5] Winn made two errors in recording cash payments during November:

Check No.	Actual Amount of Check	Amount Recorded
778	$2,264	$3,264
780	964	694

Check no. 778 was issued to purchase equipment; check no. 780 was for advertising expense.

Instructions

[a] Prepare a bank reconciliation dated November 30.
[b] Prepare the necessary journal entries.

P7-6 Refer to the information given for Winn Company in P7-5.

Instructions

[a] Prepare a proof of cash for November.
[b] Prepare the necessary journal entries.

P7-7 Abbott, Inc., began operations in 1985. During the year the company sold merchandise with a gross invoice price of $100,000. All sales were subject to credit terms of 3/10, n/60. Of the total sales of $100,000, the company received payments for 50% within the discount period and 30% after the discount period had expired. The company had not collected the other 20% as of year-end.

Instructions

[a] Prepare general journal entries to record the above transactions using: (1) the *net method* of recording credit sales, and (2) the *gross method* of recording credit sales.
[b] What financial statement balances would Abbott report on December 31, 1985, for sales, sales discounts

not taken, sales discounts, and accounts receivable under (1) the net method, and (2) the gross method?

[c] Which of the above methods of recording credit sales is theoretically superior? Why?

P7–8 Prescott Stores, Ltd., reported the following information on its balance sheet dated December 31, 1984:

Accounts receivable	$138,000
Less: Allowance for doubtful accounts	7,000
	$131,000

The company engaged in the following transactions during 1985:

[1] Made cash sales of $320,000 and credit sales of $670,000.

[2] Collected $650,800 from customers on account.

[3] Wrote off $7,200 of accounts considered to be uncollectible.

[4] Collected $600 from customers whose accounts had been written off as uncollectible.

Instructions

[a] Prepare journal entries to record the above transactions.

[b] Journalize the adjusting entry to record estimated bad debts at the end of 1985 under each of the following *independent* assumptions:

[1] The company estimates that 1.1% of *credit* sales are uncollectible.

[2] The company estimates that 0.7% of *total* sales are uncollectible.

[3] The company estimates that 5% of the accounts receivable balance at the end of 1985 will be uncollectible.

[4] The company estimates that 75% of the year-end balance of accounts receivable has an uncollectible percentage of 3%; the remaining 25% has an uncollectible percentage of 10%.

[c] Assume that the company estimates its bad debts on the basis of assumption [b-1].

[1] Show how accounts receivable would be presented on the balance sheet prepared at the end of 1985.

[2] What is the dollar effect of the year-end bad-debt adjustment on the before-tax income for 1985?

[3] What is the dollar effect of the year-end bad-debt adjustment on the working capital (current assets minus current liabilities) reported at the end of 1985?

P7–9 Jackson Corporation operates in an industry which has a high rate of bad debts. On December 31, 1985, before any year-end adjustments, Jackson's Accounts Receivable balance was $500,000 and its Allowance for Doubtful Accounts balance was $25,000. The year-end balance reported in the statement of financial position for the Allowance for Doubtful Accounts will be based on the aging schedule shown below.

Time Outstanding	Amount of Accounts Receivable	Probability of Collection
Under 15 days	$300,000	.98
16–30 days	100,000	.90
31–45 days	50,000	.80
46–60 days	30,000	.70
61–75 days	10,000	.60
Over 75 days	10,000	.00

Instructions

[a] What is the appropriate balance for the Allowance for Doubtful Accounts on December 31, 1985?

[b] Show how Accounts Receivable would be presented on the balance sheet on December 31, 1985.

[c] What is the dollar effect of the year-end bad-debt adjustment on the before-tax income for 1985?

(CMA adapted)

P7–10 Hopkins Company has been in business for five years, but its financial statements have never been audited. Engaged to perform an audit for 1985, you find that the company's balance sheet has no allowance for doubtful accounts. Bad debts have simply been expensed as written-off and recoveries credited to income as collected. The company's policy is to write off at December 31 of each year those accounts on which no collections have been received for three months. The installment contracts are for two years.

Upon your recommendation, the company agrees to revise its accounts for 1985 to reflect the allowance method of accounting for bad debts. The estimate of bad debts is to be based on a percentage of sales that is derived from the experience of prior years.

Statistics for the past five years are as follows:

Year	Charge Sales	Accounts Written Off and Year of Sale			Recoveries and Year of Sale
1981	$100,000	(1981) $ 550			
1982	250,000	(1981) 1,500	(1982) $1,000		(1981) $100
1983	300,000	(1981) 500	(1982) 4,000	(1983) $1,300	(1982) 400
1984	325,000	(1982) 1,200	(1983) 4,500	(1984) 1,500	(1983) 500
1985	275,000	(1983) 2,700	(1984) 5,000	(1985) 1,400	(1984) 600

Accounts receivable at December 31, 1985, were as follows:

1984 sales	$ 15,000
1985 sales	135,000
	$150,000

Instructions

Prepare the adjusting journal entry or entries with appropriate explanations to set up the Allowance for Doubtful Accounts. Support each item with organized computations. Ignore income tax implications.

(AICPA adapted)

P7–11 The following information pertains to Magic Carpet Enterprises:

June 1 Assigned $40,000 of accounts receivable to County Bank on a nonnotification basis. The bank advanced $32,000, less a service charge of $800. Magic Carpet signed a $32,000 promissory note bearing interest of 1% per month on the unpaid loan balance.

28 Collected assigned accounts of $25,000, less sales returns and allowances of $750.

29 Sold goods on account for $45,000.

30 Remitted the June 28 collection to County Bank.

30 Factored $40,000 of accounts receivable with Sun Bank on a notification basis. Sun Bank charged a factoring fee of 3% of the amount factored and interest of 1½% per month on all amounts withdrawn before the end of the 30-day average collection period of the receivables. Sun Bank withheld 10% of the amount of receivables factored to cover sales returns and allowances. Magic

Carpet withdrew the maximum amount of cash available on June 30.

Instructions

[a] Journalize the above events on Magic Carpet's books.
[b] Illustrate how Magic Carpet should report the receivables that pertain to the assignment and factoring arrangements on a balance sheet dated June 30.
[c] Why are the financial reporting requirements for an assignment considered somewhat unusual?

P7–12 The following events pertain to Donnes Company:

May 1 Donnes receives a $20,000, 90-day, 10% note in satisfaction of Mark Company's account receivable of $20,000.

31 Donnes discounts the note with recourse at Clark Bank. The discount rate is 12%.

July 30 Mark Company pays Clark Bank the total amount owed on the note.

Instructions

[a] Prepare journal entries to record the above events on Donnes' books using each of the following approaches to accounting for notes receivable discounted:
   [1] Footnote approach.
   [2] Contra account approach.
[b] Assume that instead of paying the note on July 30, Mark Company dishonors it. Clark Bank charges Donnes with the maturity value and a $20 protest fee. Journalize the entry or entries required for Donnes on July 30 under the:
   [1] Footnote approach.
   [2] Contra account approach.

[c] What is the fundamental difference between these two approaches to accounting for notes receivable discounted?

P7-13 The following events pertain to Lane Company:

Dec. 1, 1984   Lane Company sells merchandise to Hart Company. The merchandise has a selling price of $10,000, and Lane receives a one-year promissory note that has a face amount of $11,000 and no stated interest rate. The market rate for similar notes is 10%.

Dec. 16, 1984   Lane sells land to Warner Company in exchange for a $90,000, 10%, 90-day promissory note. The 10% interest rate equals the going market rate for similar notes. The cost of the land to Lane is $60,000.

Jan. 30, 1985   Lane discounts the Warner note with recourse at Highland Bank. The discount rate is 12%.

Mar. 16, 1985   Warner pays Highland Bank the full amount owed.

Nov. 30, 1985   Hart pays Lane the full amount owed.

Lane Company uses a calendar-year accounting period and does not make reversing entries. The company records notes receivable at present value on the date received, and it uses the footnote approach to accounting for notes receivable discounted.

Instructions

[a] Prepare journal entries (including adjusting entries) to record the above events on Lane's books.
[b] Assume that the Hart and Warner notes are dishonored when they mature. Highland Bank charges Lane with the maturity value of the Warner note and a $30 protest fee. Journalize the entry or entries required for Lane on March 16, 1985, and November 30, 1985.

P7-14 You are examining Brown Corporation's financial statements for the year ended December 31, 1985. Your analysis of the 1985 entries in the Trade Notes Receivable account was as follows.

Brown Corporation
ANALYSIS OF TRADE NOTES RECEIVABLE
For the Year Ended December 31, 1985

Date		Folio	Trade Notes Receivable Debit	Credit
Jan. 1	Balance forward		$118,000	
Feb. 28	Received $25,000 6% note due 10/29/85 from Daley, whose trade account was past due.	MEMO		
28	Discounted Daley note at 6%.	CR		$ 24,960
Mar. 29	Received noninterest-bearing demand note from Edge, the Corporation's treasurer, for a loan.	CD	6,200	
Aug. 30	Received principal and interest due from Allen and, in accordance with agreement, two principal payments in advance.	CR		34,200
Sept. 4	Paid protest fee on note dishonored by Charnes.	CD	5	
Nov. 1	Received check dated 2/1/86 in settlement of Bailey note. The check was included in cash on hand 12/31/85.	CR		8,120
4	Paid protest fee and maturity value of Daley note to bank. Note discounted 2/28/85 was dishonored.	CD	26,031	

Dec. 27	Accepted furniture and fixtures with a fair market value of $24,000 in full settlement from Daley.	GJ		24,000
31	Received check dated 1/3/86 from Edge in payment of 3/29/85 note. (The check was included in petty cash until 1/2/86, when it was returned to Edge in exchange for a new demand note of the same amount.)	CR		6,200
31	Received principal and interest on Charnes note.	CR		42,437
31	Accrued interest on Allen note.	GJ	1,200	
	Totals		$151,436	$139,917

The following information is available:

[1] Balances at January 1, 1985, were a debit of $1,400 in the Accrued Interest Receivable account and a credit of $400 in the Unearned Interest Income account. The $118,000 debit balance in the Trade Notes Receivable account consisted of the following three notes:

Allen note dated 8/31/81, payable in annual installments of $10,000 principal plus accrued interest at 6% each Aug. 31	$70,000
Bailey note discounted to Braun at 6% on 11/1/84, due 11/1/85	8,000
Charnes note for $40,000 plus 6% interest dated 12/31/84, due on 9/1/85	40,000

[2] No entries were made during 1985 to the Accrued Interest Receivable account or the Unearned Interest Income account, and only one entry for a credit of $1,200 on December 31 appeared in the Interest Income account.

[3] All notes were from trade customers unless otherwise indicated.

[4] Debits and credits offsetting Trade Notes Receivable debit and credit entries were correctly recorded unless the facts indicate otherwise.

[5] Brown Corporation uses the contra account approach when accounting for notes receivable discounted. The company also follows the practice of debiting Trade Accounts Receivable instead of Dishon-

ored Notes Receivable when a customer's note is dishonored.

Instructions

Prepare a worksheet to adjust each entry to correct or properly reclassify it, if necessary. Enter your adjustments in the proper columns to correspond with the date of each entry. Do not combine related entries for different dates. Your completed worksheet will provide the basis for one compound journal entry to correct all entries to Trade Notes Receivable and related accounts for 1985. Formal journal entries are not required. In addition to the information shown in the above analysis, the following headings are suggested:

Adjustment or Reclassification Required

Trade Notes Receivable	Trade Accounts Receivable	Interest Income	Other Accounts		
			Account Title	Amount	
Debit (Credit)	Debit (Credit)	Debit (Credit)	Account Title	Debit	Credit

(AICPA adapted)

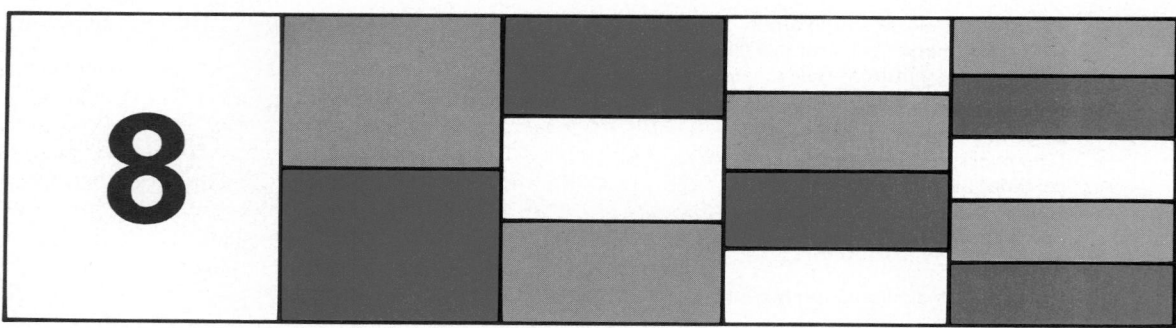

INVENTORIES: BASIC VALUATION METHODS

Objectives

To discuss and illustrate the financial accounting and reporting requirements for inventories.

To explain the methods used to determine inventory quantities on hand.

To explain the nature of costs that should be included in inventory.

To discuss and illustrate various inventory cost flow methods.

To discuss and illustrate the valuation of inventory at the lower of cost or market value.

To indicate exceptional cases under generally accepted accounting principles of inventory valuation above cost.

To indicate effects of inventory errors on financial statements.

To explain conceptual considerations in accounting for inventories.

I**nventories** are goods that are held for sale in the ordinary course of business, as well as goods that are in production or that will soon be used in production. A **service business,** such as a firm of attorneys, normally has no inventories. In contrast, inventories are one of the most important assets of **merchandising businesses** (either wholesale or retail) and **manufacturing businesses.** Merchandising and manufacturing companies typically derive most of their revenues from sales of inventories. Moreover, cost of goods sold is usually the largest expense of such companies. It is not surprising, then, that the managers of merchandising and manufacturing companies often devote substantial resources to inventory planning and control. Furthermore, users of financial statements regard inventory information as extremely important when they make investment, lending, and similar decisions.

In this chapter and the next, we shall discuss the accounting valuation of inventories. Inventories are physical resources, and our primary concern is how accountants obtain a financial representation of such resources for external reporting purposes. Most of our discussion focuses on **inventory valuation methods,** often called **inventory pricing methods,** that companies use to prepare their external financial statements in accordance with generally accepted accounting principles (GAAP). In this chapter we present an overview of basic valuation methods; in Chapter 9 we shall introduce several additional methods.

Acquisition of Inventories

A merchandising company buys inventory in a finished condition and later resells it. In contrast, a manufacturing company produces its inventory. In doing so, a manufacturing company incurs the following types of **manufacturing** (or **production**) **costs:**

1. **Direct materials.**   Raw materials costs that can be traced directly and practically to units of the firm's product. In the case of a manufacturer of wooden desks, for example, the cost of the wood is a direct materials cost.
2. **Direct labor.**   Labor costs that can be traced directly and practically to units of the firm's product. In the case of the desk manufacturer, the labor costs of the employees who assemble the desks are direct labor costs.
3. **Manufacturing overhead.**   All manufacturing costs, other than direct materials and direct labor, necessary to construct the company's product. For the desk manufacturer, examples are the costs of factory maintenance, the depreciation of factory equipment, and the glue used on certain parts of each desk.

Classification of Inventories

A merchandising company has one class of inventory, commonly called **merchandise** (or **merchandise inventory**). A manufacturing company, however, may have the following four categories of inventory:

1. **Raw materials.**   Goods that can be traced directly to units of the firm's product. An example is the desk manufacturer's inventory of wood.
2. **Factory supplies.**   Goods that can be traced only indirectly to units of the firm's product. An example is the desk manufacturer's supply of glue. Generally, it is not practical to trace glue to specific desks. The cost of factory supplies used is an element of overhead that is commonly called **indirect materials.**
3. **Work (goods) in process.**   Goods that are partially completed. Goods in process have been assigned appropriate manufacturing costs and will remain in production until completed.
4. **Finished goods.**   Products that are completed and ready for sale. Finished goods have been assigned their full share of manufacturing costs.

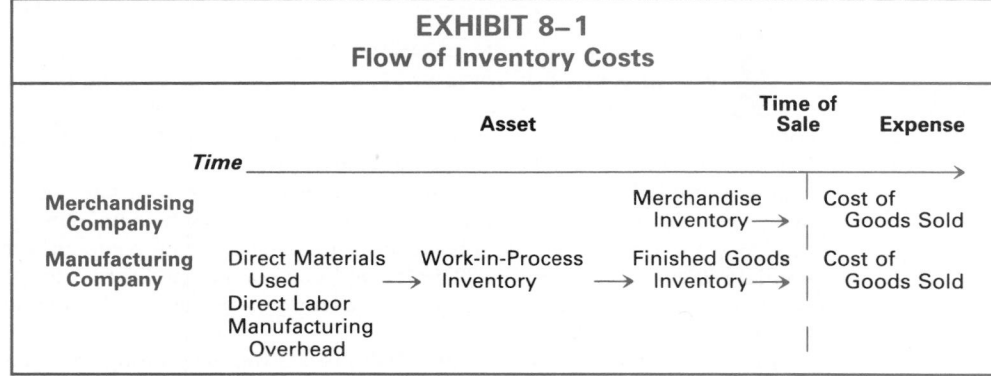

EXHIBIT 8–1
Flow of Inventory Costs

Flow of Inventory Costs

Exhibit 8–1 compares the typical flow of inventory costs in a merchandising company with that in a manufacturing concern. Note that inventory costs are initially accounted for as assets. In other words, a company's inventory is first measured at cost, in accordance with the historical cost principle. To implement the matching principle, the costs are expensed in the period when the inventory is sold. In this way the revenue generated by the sale of inventory can be related to the costs incurred to purchase or produce it.

A merchandising company and a manufacturing company calculate cost of goods sold in somewhat different ways. In the comparison shown in Exhibit 8–2, we assume a periodic inventory system.

Note in Exhibit 8–2 that a merchandising company adds the cost of its net purchases to the cost of its beginning inventory to derive the cost of goods available for sale. Because a manufacturing company *produces* (rather than *purchases*) its finished goods inventory, it adds the cost of goods manufactured. We discussed the calculation of net purchases in Chapter 5. The computation of the cost of goods manufactured by Parker Company is shown in Exhibit 8–3 (dollar amounts assumed). The schedule of cost of goods manufactured is generally used for internal purposes only and seldom appears in published financial statements.

Observe in Exhibit 8–3 that to calculate cost of goods manufactured, we add the total manufacturing costs incurred during the period to the beginning work-in-process inventory. The total ($257,000) tells us the amount of manufacturing costs that we must account for

Historical Cost
Matching

EXHIBIT 8–2
Calculation of Cost of Goods Sold

Merchandising Company	Manufacturing Company
Beginning Merchandise Inventory	Beginning Finished Goods Inventory
+ Net Purchases	+ Cost of Goods Manufactured
= Cost of Goods Available for Sale	= Cost of Goods Available for Sale
− Ending Merchandise Inventory	− Ending Finished Goods Inventory
= Cost of Goods Sold	= Cost of Goods Sold

```
                            EXHIBIT 8–3
                           Parker Company
                SCHEDULE OF COST OF GOODS MANUFACTURED
                   For the Year Ended December 31, 1985
```

Direct materials used		
Raw materials inventory, Jan. 1, 1985	$ 23,000	
Add: Net purchases of raw materials	157,000	
Cost of raw materials available for use	180,000	
Less: Raw materials inventory, Dec. 31, 1985	25,000	$155,000
Direct labor		47,000
Manufacturing overhead		
Indirect labor	12,000	
Indirect materials	3,000	
Factory utilities	5,000	
Depreciation of factory building	3,500	
Depreciation of factory equipment	6,000	
Taxes on factory properties	7,000	
Miscellaneous factory expenses	1,500	38,000
Total manufacturing costs incurred during 1985		240,000
Add: Work-in-process inventory, Jan. 1, 1985		17,000
Total manufacturing costs to account for		257,000
Less: Work-in-process inventory, Dec. 31, 1985		15,000
Cost of goods manufactured		$242,000

during the period. From this total we subtract the cost of the ending work-in-process inventory (the partially completed goods on hand at the end of the period) in order to derive the cost of goods manufactured during the period. As we noted in Exhibit 8–2, the cost of goods manufactured is included in the calculation of a manufacturing company's cost of goods sold.

As our discussion thus far suggests, a manufacturing company accounts for inventories somewhat differently from a merchandising company. For example, many manufacturing companies use **direct costing** (also called **variable costing**) for internal reporting purposes, because this method enables managers to better plan and control their company's operations. Under direct costing, the accountant classifies all manufacturing costs as either variable or fixed. Variable manufacturing costs are those that vary in total in direct proportion to changes in production volume. They include direct materials, direct labor, and variable overhead. Fixed manufacturing costs, in contrast, are those that remain constant in total as production volume changes over a relevant range of production. Fixed manufacturing costs are confined to such overhead costs as property taxes and depreciation. Under the direct costing method, the accountant records as inventory costs only the variable manufacturing costs. Fixed overhead costs are expensed in the period in which they are incurred, because it is assumed that a company incurs these costs primarily to allow production to occur.

Direct costing contrasts with **absorption costing,** in which fixed overhead costs are treated as a part of the cost of inventory. Proponents of absorption costing point out that both variable and fixed overhead costs are normally necessary to produce specific goods. As a result, both types of costs should be inventoried. Generally accepted accounting principles require the use of absorption costing for external reporting purposes, because most accountants believe that fixed overhead is an important component of the historical cost of inventory that is manufactured.

Historical Cost

Many manufacturing companies use standard costs to account for their inventories. Primarily a management tool, **standard costing** requires a company to accumulate inventory costs using amounts that *should be* incurred to manufacture the inventory rather than actual costs incurred. The use of standard costing allows a company to detect variances between what it should cost to produce a product and what it actually costs. Standard costs are acceptable for external reporting under GAAP, however, if they reasonably approximate actual costs determined using a recognized cost flow method. Peculiarities in accounting for inventories of manufacturing companies, such as direct costing and standard costing, are covered more extensively in cost and managerial accounting courses.

NATURE OF THE INVENTORY VALUATION PROBLEM

Inventory accounting problems would be relatively simple if a company instantaneously sold all the inventory that it purchased or produced. Of course, this situation rarely occurs. Instead, there is normally a lag between the time goods are purchased or produced and the time they are sold. As a result, most companies have an inventory of unsold goods on hand at the end of the accounting period, and accountants must then resolve the question of how to allocate the cost of goods available for sale between (1) the goods on hand (ending inventory) and (2) the goods sold.

The accountant may determine cost of goods sold **residually,** that is, by subtracting the cost of the ending inventory from the cost of goods available for sale. To do this, the accountant must value the ending inventory directly, which means resolving the following important questions:

1. What is the physical quantity of goods on hand?
2. What is the accounting valuation of those goods?

We shall analyze these questions in the remaining sections of the chapter.

DETERMINATION OF INVENTORY QUANTITIES

The method for determining the physical quantity of goods on hand differs depending on whether a company uses a periodic or a perpetual inventory system. Regardless of which system a company uses, the accountant must understand the general principles used to determine which goods properly belong in inventory and which goods do not.

Periodic Versus Perpetual Inventory System

Under a **periodic inventory system,** inventory quantities are *not* maintained on a day-to-day basis in the accounting records. Instead, at the end of each accounting period, the quantity of unsold goods is determined by a physical count. The accountant then determines the inventory's cost by using one of the generally accepted inventory cost flow methods discussed later in the chapter. The inventory cost thus derived is subtracted from the cost of goods available for sale to determine the cost of goods sold. In a periodic system, therefore, cost of goods sold is a residual figure that includes the cost of goods actually sold as well as the cost of those lost by theft, spoilage, and similar causes. Although a periodic system is not ideal for inventory planning and control, it is relatively inexpensive and is often appropriate for products that turn over rapidly and have low unit costs, such as groceries and hardware.

In contrast with a periodic system, a **perpetual inventory system** requires the accountant to maintain continuous records of the quantity of inventory on hand. Under a perpetual system, an account may be established for each product; these accounts are kept in an **inventory subsidiary ledger.** The account for each product shows increases and decreases, as well as the balance on hand. In a complete perpetual system, the subsidiary ledger accounts are maintained in cost dollars as well as in units. Consequently, the balance in the merchandise inventory control account in the general ledger should agree with the total of the individual account balances in the subsidiary ledger.

In a perpetual system it is still desirable to physically count the inventory at least once each year, but the count need not occur at year-end. The purpose of the count is to test the accuracy of the perpetual records. An actual count frequently reveals differences between the records and the physical units on hand. These differences may exist for several reasons, including theft, evaporation, and inaccurate recording. Whenever a careful count indicates differences, the accounting records should be appropriately adjusted. If, for example, the accounting records show inventory on hand costing $10,000 but the physical count indicates only $9,885, the following entry is necessary:

Inventory Shortage	115	
Merchandise Inventory		115
(To record inventory shortage. $10,000 − $9,885 = $115.)		

Materiality

The inventory shortage is a loss account that, if material in amount, should be reported separately in the income statement. Many companies simply report inventory shortages as part of cost of goods sold. This practice is justified on the ground that some shortages may be considered a normal cost in the selling process.

Although the perpetual system is more costly than the periodic system to implement, it facilitates better inventory planning and control. In the past, perpetual records were used primarily for low-volume, high-cost items such as jewelry, fur coats, and automobiles. In recent years, however, the widespread use of electronic computers has enabled companies to maintain perpetual records for a greater variety of inventory items. With computers, companies can conveniently store and retrieve large amounts of data in a cost-effective manner. Many companies account for part of their inventories on a periodic basis and the remainder on a perpetual basis.

In a periodic inventory system, merchandise purchases are debited to the Purchases account. Throughout the accounting period, therefore, the Merchandise Inventory account contains only the balance that was on hand at the beginning of the period. At the end of the period, the accountant makes an adjusting entry to record the ending inventory as well as the cost of goods sold for the entire period, as we discussed and illustrated in Chapter 5. In contrast, under a perpetual system, the Merchandise Inventory and Cost of Goods Sold accounts are continually maintained. Merchandise purchases are therefore charged directly to an Inventory account. Moreover, an entry to record a sale is accompanied by an entry that reduces the Inventory account and recognizes an increase in Cost of Goods Sold. At the end of the accounting period, an adjusting entry is not required, because the Inventory account reflects the balance on hand and the Cost of Goods Sold account reflects the expense incurred during the entire period. The proper accounting for selected merchandise transactions under periodic and perpetual inventory systems is shown in Exhibit 8–4.

Goods to Include in Inventory

The general rule for determining what items to include in inventory is that goods belong to the entity that has legal title, regardless of where the goods are located. Consequently, when title to goods passes from seller to buyer, the seller should record a sale and exclude the goods from inventory. The buyer in turn should record a purchase and include the goods in inventory.

The Uniform Commercial Code provides that title to goods may pass at any time expressly agreed to by buyer and seller. When the time of title passage is not expressly agreed on, the buyer takes title when goods exist and are identified to the contract, and the seller has completed performance in regard to delivering the goods. If goods are shipped **FOB (free on board) shipping point,** title passes to the buyer when the seller delivers the goods to the carrier. Title to goods shipped **FOB destination** passes when the goods arrive

---

EXHIBIT 8–4
Accounting Under Periodic and Perpetual Inventory Systems

Transaction	Periodic Inventory System		Perpetual Inventory System		
Purchase merchandise costing $4,000 on account	Purchases Accounts Payable	4,000 4,000	Merchandise Inventory Accounts Payable	4,000 4,000	
Pay freight of $45 on purchase	Transportation-In Cash	45 45	Merchandise Inventory Cash	45 45	
Return defective merchandise costing $250	Accounts Payable Purchase Returns	250 250	Accounts Payable Merchandise Inventory	250 250	
Sell goods costing $3,000 on account for $6,000	Accounts Receivable Sales	6,000 6,000	Accounts Receivable Sales	6,000 6,000	
			Cost of Goods Sold Merchandise Inventory	3,000 3,000	

---

at their ultimate destination. If the buyer agrees to pick up the goods at the seller's place of business, title passes when the seller has completed the goods and identified them to the contract.

Application of the legal title rule may pose problems when a company owns goods that are located elsewhere or when it holds goods that belong to someone else. We discuss these problems in the following sections.

Goods in Transit

Materiality

During an accounting period, the accountant normally records purchases when goods are received and sales when goods are shipped, regardless of the precise moment at which title passes. This procedure is expedient, and because title usually passes in the same period, no material misstatements occur in the financial statements.

On the other hand, the accountant should carefully analyze the invoice terms of goods that are in transit at the end of an accounting period to determine who has legal title. The analysis should encompass goods purchased as well as goods sold. Goods shipped FOB shipping point belong to the buyer; those shipped FOB destination belong to the seller. When analyzing goods in transit, the accountant should examine invoices for several days before and after the end of the accounting period in order to ensure a proper cutoff at year-end.

Consigned Goods

A **consignment** is a method of marketing goods in which the owner (the **consignor**) transfers physical possession of certain goods to an agent (the **consignee**) who sells the goods on the owner's behalf. Goods on consignment should be included in the consignor's inventory and excluded from the consignee's inventory. Similarly, goods in the hands of others for sale, storage, processing, or other reasons should be included in the inventory of the party holding title. We explain accounting for consignments in Chapter 20.

DETERMINATION OF INVENTORY VALUATION AT COST

Historical Cost

In accordance with the historical cost principle, the quantity of inventory on hand should be valued initially at its cost. Two questions must be answered when determining an inventory cost valuation:

1. What costs should be included in inventory?
2. What method should be used to associate inventory costs with the physical units on hand?

Costs to Include in Inventory

An important inventory valuation issue that the accountant must resolve is differentiating between product costs and period costs. **Product costs** "attach to" the inventory. These costs are initially capitalized and are regarded as assets (i.e., inventory). When the inventory is later sold, the product costs expire and are therefore charged to expense (cost of goods sold). In contrast, **period costs** are expensed in the period in which they are incurred. In other words, period costs are not inventoried, because their relationship to the product (inventory) is generally considered too difficult to trace. Selling expenses, general and administrative expenses, and income tax expense are examples of period costs.

Product costs are incurred, either directly or indirectly, to purchase or produce inventory as well as to bring the inventory to a condition and location for sale. These costs include direct materials, direct labor, and overhead. They also include the invoice cost of purchased merchandise as well as the costs of inbound transportation, insurance, inspection, handling, warehousing, and purchasing.

The specific content of product costs varies somewhat between companies. Many companies use only the invoice cost plus the cost of inbound transportation to value inventories of purchased goods. Other costs that should in theory be inventoried (such as insurance, handling, and purchasing costs) are treated as period costs. This treatment is justified on the ground that it is often impossible to meaningfully allocate certain indirect costs to inventory. The treatment is considered acceptable if a company applies it *consistently* over time (in accordance with the consistency principle) either to a certain portion or to all of its inventories.

> **Consis-tency**

Generally accepted accounting principles do not permit a company to capitalize the interest cost associated with inventories that are routinely manufactured or otherwise produced in large quantities on a repetitive basis. On the other hand, interest cost should be capitalized if it is a material part of the cost of acquiring inventory items that are constructed as discrete projects, such as ships.[1] For these items, interest cost represents an important component of historical cost. Companies should also capitalize interest as part of the historical cost of acquiring certain plant assets. We explain interest capitalization more fully in Chapter 11.

> **Materiality**
> **Historical Cost**

Invoice Cost

The largest component of product cost for purchased inventory is the invoice cost itself. In determining the invoice cost, **trade discounts** must be subtracted from the list price and not entered in the accounting records.[2] Theory and practice usually differ about whether the invoice cost component of product cost should also exclude **cash discounts**.[3]

In theory, the cost of purchases (and of inventory) should be measured net of cash discounts allowable. This is known as the **net method** of recording purchases; it is compared with the **gross method** in Exhibit 8–5. The cost measured under the net method

[1] *FASB Statement of Financial Accounting Standards No. 34,* "Capitalization of Interest Cost," 1979.

[2] A **trade discount** is a reduction from a catalog list price granted by manufacturers and wholesalers of certain products. The use of trade discounts enables a company (1) to revise its prices periodically without having to reprint its catalogs, and (2) to set different prices for different types of customers.

[3] A **cash discount** is a reduction from the amount of an invoice that is offered for early payment of cash. The purpose of a cash discount is to encourage early payment. A cash discount is usually expressed in terms such as "2/10, n/30." These terms mean that the purchaser may deduct 2% from the amount of the invoice if payment is made within 10 days of the invoice date. A purchaser who fails to pay within 10 days must pay the entire invoice amount within 30 days of the invoice date. As we explained in Chapter 7, the effective annual interest cost associated with not paying within 10 days is 36.7%. It is usually advantageous for a company to take all available cash discounts, even if the company must borrow money to do so.

EXHIBIT 8–5
Net and Gross Methods of Recording Purchases

Transaction	Net Method			Gross Method		
July 1 ABC Company purchases merchandise for $100, terms 2/10, n/30.	Purchases* Accounts Payable	98	98	Purchases* Accounts Payable	100	100
Alternative Assumption No. 1						
July 10 ABC Company pays within the discount period.	Accounts Payable Cash	98	98	Accounts Payable Purchase Discounts Cash	100	2 98
Alternative Assumption No. 2						
July 30 ABC Company pays after the discount period.	Accounts Payable Discounts Lost (or Interest Expense) Cash	98 2	100	Accounts Payable Cash	100	100

*Assuming a periodic inventory system.

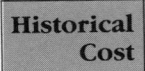

represents the cash-equivalent price on the date of purchase and therefore the correct historical cost. Cash discounts are granted to encourage early payment. Any discount not taken represents the cost of engaging in a deferred payment transaction. Accordingly, this cost should be shown as a financing expense on the income statement.

In practice, most companies record purchases (and inventory) at gross invoice amounts. Cash discounts taken are recorded in a Purchase Discounts account at the time of payment. The balance in this account is deducted from purchases when measuring cost of goods sold.[4] This procedure is theoretically deficient in two major respects. First, it technically violates the matching principle, because discounts are recorded only when cash is paid rather than when the purchases that give rise to the discounts are made. Second, the procedure does not allocate discounts taken between goods sold and those on hand. This tends to understate cost of goods sold and overstate net income and ending inventory. Despite its theoretical shortcomings, the gross method is supported on the practical grounds that (1) it is more convenient than the net method from a bookkeeping standpoint, and (2) if applied consistently over time, it usually produces no material errors in the financial statements.

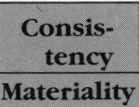

Transportation Costs

If practical, the costs of inbound transportation should be allocated to specific units of inventory purchased. This procedure, which is facilitated by the use of a perpetual inventory system, permits transportation charges to be appropriately reflected in cost of goods sold as well as in ending inventory. Transportation costs are inventoried because they are an important part of the cost of acquiring goods. In the purchase of coal, for example, rail transportation costs constitute a substantial portion of inventoriable costs.

In a periodic inventory system, inbound transportation charges are usually accumulated in a nominal account entitled Transportation-In or Freight-In. Theoretically, the balance in this account at the end of an accounting period should be allocated in a reasonable manner

---

[4]Some companies treat purchase discounts as financial revenue similar to interest. This treatment lacks theoretical support. A purchaser of goods who pays for them within the discount period has not thereby made a loan to the seller. Since no loan has been made, no financial revenue has been realized.

**Conserva-
tism**
Materiality
**Consis-
tency**

between cost of goods sold and ending inventory. Instead of implementing this approach, firms often use the more expedient alternative of including all transportation-in costs in the calculation of net purchases. Although the expedient approach tends to overstate cost of goods sold and understate net income and ending inventory, it is often supported on the grounds of conservatism, materiality, and consistency of application.

Inventory Cost Flow Methods

Inventory costs flow into a business and are treated as assets when goods are purchased or manufactured; they flow out and are charged to expense when goods are sold. The difference between the cost inflows and the cost outflows represents the cost of the inventory on hand.

If inventory unit cost prices remained constant over time, the process of inventory cost determination would be relatively simple. That is, it would simply involve multiplying the quantity of each inventory item on hand by its constant unit cost and summing the results. In reality, of course, unit costs usually fluctuate. With inflation, they tend to rise over time. The reality of fluctuating unit costs underscores the critical importance of the various inventory cost flow methods. When reflecting on these methods, keep the following points in mind:

**Historical
Cost**

1. Each method leads to a determination of inventory and cost of goods sold based on the historical cost principle.
2. A company can use one method to account for a certain portion of its inventories (such as raw materials) and other methods to account for different portions (such as finished goods).
3. The method(s) adopted should be used consistently over time and should be disclosed in the financial statements.

**Consis-
tency**
Disclosure

Specific Identification Method

The **specific identification method** requires a company to maintain detailed records which permit the accountant to identify individually the actual unit costs of (1) inventory items on hand and (2) inventory items sold. Each item of inventory, then, is identified in some way (e.g., a code on a sales tag) with its actual unit cost. When an item is sold, the difference between its selling price and its actual cost represents the gross margin.

At first glance this method usually seems appealing. For one thing, the flow of inventory costs corresponds with the physical flow of goods. In addition, the method may be used with either a periodic or a perpetual inventory system.

Despite its intuitive appeal, the specific identification method has certain theoretical and practical shortcomings. On the theoretical side, the method is often criticized because it may permit income manipulation by management. Suppose, for example, that a company has two identical gold watches that sell for $500 each. Because of recent fluctuations in gold prices, one watch cost $250 and the other $350. If a customer asks to purchase one of the watches, management can earn a gross profit of either $250 or $150 simply by choosing which watch to sell. On the practical side, the detailed record keeping requirements usually limit the applicability of the specific identification method to inventories that consist of relatively expensive, slow-moving items such as automobiles, farm equipment, art objects, fur coats, jewelry, and long-term construction projects.

Cost Flow Methods Based on Assumptions

Since it is usually not feasible to specifically identify inventory unit costs, most companies make an **assumption** about the way inventory costs flow through the business. The major cost flow assumptions available under GAAP and the method of implementing each are shown on the next page. A seldom-used method, known as **base stock,** is discussed in the Appendix to this chapter.

Cost Flow Assumption	Cost Flow Method
1. Cost flow is in the same order in which costs were incurred.	1. First-in, first-out (FIFO).
2. Cost flow is an average of the costs incurred.	2. Average cost.
3. Cost flow is in the reverse order in which costs were incurred.	3. Last-in, first-out (LIFO).

A 1982 survey of the annual reports to shareholders of 600 companies found a total of 1,072 disclosures of inventory cost flow methods. Some companies obviously use more than one method. The use of FIFO, LIFO, and average cost was reported by 371, 408, and 241 companies, respectively.[5]

In reflecting on the FIFO, average cost, and LIFO methods, bear in mind that each method reflects an **assumed cost flow pattern.** Any method may be used **regardless of the way goods physically flow through the business.** For example, goods may (and usually do) physically flow in the FIFO manner, yet LIFO may be used as the cost flow method.

Jackson Company is a merchandising concern that, for accounting purposes, identifies its inventory items using a combination of numbers and letters. The following inventory data for the company's Product 19-C for 1985 will be used to illustrate the application of the FIFO, average cost, and LIFO methods.

Date	Product 19-C	Number of Units	Unit Cost	Total Cost
Jan. 1	Inventory on hand	300	$5	$ 1,500
Mar. 21	Purchase	900	6	5,400
Aug. 19	Purchase	600	7	4,200
Nov. 3	Purchase	200	8	1,600
	Available for sale	2,000		$12,700

We will assume that 800 units of Product 19-C were sold on May 27 and another 800 units were sold on October 9. A physical count on December 31, 1985, indicates that 400 units of Product 19-C are on hand.

First-In, First-Out (FIFO) Method.   The FIFO method is based on the assumption that inventory costs should be matched with sales revenue in the same order in which the costs were incurred. The most recent costs incurred are therefore used in determining the cost of inventory on hand. Assuming a periodic system, the cost of the 400 units of Product 19-C is determined as follows:

Most recent costs (Nov. 3 purchase)	200 units @ $8	$1,600
Next most recent costs (Aug. 19 purchase)	200 units @ $7	$1,400
Inventory, Dec. 31, 1985	400	$3,000

Recall that cost of goods sold is a residual figure determined by subtracting the cost of the ending inventory from the cost of goods available for sale. For Product 19-C, cost of goods sold under FIFO is $9,700 ($12,700 − $3,000). Note that under the FIFO method, cost of goods sold consists of the earliest costs incurred [(300 units @ $5) + (900 units @ $6) + (400 units @ $7) = $9,700].

The FIFO method produces the same financial statement cost figures regardless of

[5]*Accounting Trends and Techniques,* 36th ed. (New York: AICPA, 1982), p. 118.

EXHIBIT 8–6
Perpetual Inventory—FIFO Method

	Purchased			Sold			Balance		
Date	Number of Units	Unit Cost	Total Cost	Number of Units	Unit Cost	Total Cost	Number of Units	Unit Cost	Total Cost
Jan. 1							300	$5	$1,500
Mar. 21	900	$6	$5,400				300	5	1,500
							900	6	5,400
May 27				300	$5	$1,500			
				500	6	3,000	400	6	2,400
Aug. 19	600	7	4,200				400	6	2,400
							600	7	4,200
Oct. 9				400	6	2,400			
				400	7	2,800	200	7	1,400
Nov. 3	200	8	1,600				200	7	1,400
							200	8	1,600

Ending inventory = $3,000

Cost of goods sold $9,700

whether a company uses a periodic or a perpetual system. For example, if the Jackson Company maintained perpetual records for Product 19-C, the company would use a form similar to the one shown in Exhibit 8–6. Observe in the exhibit that the cost of the ending inventory and the cost of goods sold are still $3,000 and $9,700, respectively.

The FIFO method has been supported on the ground that its assumed cost flow pattern corresponds closely to the physical flow of goods in most businesses. Therefore, when goods physically move in the first-in, first-out manner, the FIFO method approximates specific identification. Unlike specific identification, however, FIFO gives management little opportunity to manipulate income.

In terms of financial statement impact, the use of FIFO produces an ending inventory cost based on the most recent acquisition prices. This cost frequently approximates current replacement cost, a fact often cited in support of FIFO. On the other hand, since the balance sheet and income statement *articulate* with one another, the use of FIFO produces a cost of goods sold figure that is based on the earliest costs incurred. These costs often depart considerably from current replacement costs. The failure of FIFO to match current costs with current revenues on the income statement is perhaps the most frequently cited shortcoming of this method.

Matching

Average Cost Method. The average cost method is based on the assumption that a weighted average of all inventory costs should be used to measure inventory cost flow. This average is computed by dividing the total cost of goods available for sale by the total number of units available for sale. Assuming a periodic system, the cost of the 400 units of Product 19-C is determined as follows:

Weighted average unit cost $12,700 ÷ 2,000 = $6.35
Inventory, Dec. 31, 1985 400 units @ $6.35 = $2,540

Cost of goods sold is therefore $10,160 ($12,700 − $2,540). We can verify this by multiplying the 1600 units sold by $6.35 (1600 × $6.35 = $10,160). Note that a *weighted average*, rather than a *simple average*, unit cost figure should be used. A weighted average reflects the number of units acquired at each price; a simple average [($5 + $6 + $7 + $8) ÷ 4 = $6.50] does not.

When used with a perpetual inventory system, the average cost method is called the **moving average method.** Under this method, a new weighted average unit cost must be **computed after every purchase;** the average is therefore said to "move." The moving average method for Product 19-C is illustrated in Exhibit 8–7.

Observe carefully that a new weighted average unit cost is computed after each purchase. This is done by dividing the total cost of goods available for sale (immediately after the purchase) by the total number of units available for sale (immediately after the purchase). For example, the weighted average unit cost after the first purchase (March 21) is computed as follows:

Jan. 1	Inventory	300 units @ $5	$1,500
Mar. 21	Purchase	900 units @ $6	$5,400
	Available for sale immediately after Mar. 21 purchase	1,200 units	$6,900

Weighted average unit cost $6,900 ÷ 1,200 = $5.75

The same procedure is used to determine the weighted average unit cost after the August 19 purchase and the November 3 purchase.

Under the average cost method, the cost of the ending inventory usually differs depending on whether a company uses a periodic or a perpetual inventory system. It follows that when ending inventories differ, cost of goods sold figures also differ. These differences are shown below for Product 19-C.

Average Cost Method	Ending Inventory	+	Cost of Goods Sold	=	Cost of Goods Available for Sale
Periodic system	$2,540		$10,160		$12,700
Perpetual system	2,900		9,800		12,700

The average cost method is supported on the basis that it generally produces figures for

---

EXHIBIT 8–7
Perpetual Inventory—Moving Average Method

	Purchased			Sold			Balance			
Date	Number of Units	Unit Cost	Total Cost	Number of Units	Unit Cost	Total Cost	Number of Units	Unit Cost	Total Cost	
Jan. 1							300	$5.00	$1,500	
Mar. 21	900	$6	$5,400				1,200	5.75*	6,900	
May 27				800	$5.75	$4,600	400	5.75	2,300	
Aug. 19	600	7	4,200				1,000	6.50*	6,500	
Oct. 9				800	6.50	5,200	200	6.50	1,300	
Nov. 3	200	8	1,600			_____	400	7.25*	2,900	} Ending inventory = $2,900

Cost of goods sold $9,800

*Weighted average unit cost is computed after each purchase.

both ending inventory and cost of goods sold that lie between those produced under the FIFO and LIFO methods. The method is essentially a compromise solution to the complex question of how we should assume that inventory costs flow through a business. Furthermore, the method is relatively easy to apply, and it affords management little opportunity to manipulate income.

On the other hand, the weighted average method is not as accurate as FIFO in approximating the current cost of the ending inventory, nor is it as accurate as LIFO in approximating the current cost of goods sold. Furthermore, average cost corresponds with the physical flow of goods only when goods available for sale are sold in essentially a random pattern, which may occur with inventories of liquid products such as chemicals and petroleum.

Last-In, First-Out (LIFO) Method. The LIFO method assumes that inventory costs should be matched with sales revenue in the reverse order in which the costs were incurred (the opposite of FIFO). Inventory is therefore valued at the earliest costs incurred. Referring to the Jackson Company data and assuming a *periodic* system, we determine the LIFO cost of the ending inventory of 400 units of Product 19-C as follows:

Earliest costs (Jan. 1 inventory)	300 units @ $5	$1,500
Next earliest costs (Mar. 21 purchase)	100 units @ $6	$ 600
Inventory, Dec. 31, 1985	400	$2,100

Observe that the ending inventory of 400 units is divided into *two layers* (300 units @ $5 and 100 units @ $6). Cost of goods sold for 1985 is $10,600 ($12,700 − $2,100) and consists of the most recent costs incurred [(200 units @ $8) + (600 units @ $7) + (800 units @ $6) = $10,600].

The application of LIFO using a *perpetual* system, for Product 19-C is shown in Exhibit 8–8. Under the perpetual system, units sold are costed at the time of sale. Since LIFO is therefore applied currently throughout the period rather than only at the period's end, LIFO results usually differ between a periodic and a perpetual system. These differences are shown below for Product 19-C.

LIFO Method	Ending Inventory	+	Cost of Goods Sold	=	Cost of Goods Available for Sale
Periodic system	$2,100		$10,600		$12,700
Perpetual system	2,600		10,100		12,700

Observe that for Product 19-C, cost of goods sold is higher under the periodic than the perpetual system. This occurred because of the timing of the purchases and sales and because the unit cost prices of Product 19-C rose steadily during 1985. In our example, the cost of goods sold differences relate to the sale on October 9. Under the perpetual system, the October 9 sale was costed using the most recent cost prices at that time [(600 units @ $7) + (100 units @ $6) + (100 units @ $5) = $5,300]. Under the periodic system, the October 9 sale was costed using the most recent cost prices as of the end of the year [(200 units @ $8) + (600 units @ $7) = $5,800]. As we shall discuss shortly, many companies that experience rising inventory costs use LIFO for tax purposes, because it tends to produce a higher cost of goods sold and therefore less income taxes. The tax law states that companies using LIFO for tax purposes must also use it for financial reporting purposes. Consequently, if a company uses LIFO with a perpetual system, the company often restates its cost of goods sold and inventory at year-end to conform with the results that would have occurred under a periodic system. This restatement is done for income tax and external financial reporting purposes.

EXHIBIT 8–8
Perpetual Inventory—LIFO Method

	Purchased			Sold			Balance			
Date	Number of Units	Unit Cost	Total Cost	Number of Units	Unit Cost	Total Cost	Number of Units	Unit Cost	Total Cost	
Jan. 1							300	$5	$1,500	
Mar. 21	900	$6	$5,400				300	5	1,500	
							900	6	5,400	
May 27				800	$6	$ 4,800	300	5	1,500	
							100	6	600	
Aug. 19	600	7	4,200				300	5	1,500	
							100	6	600	
							600	7	4,200	
Oct. 9				600	7	4,200				
				100	6	600				
				100	5	500	200	5	1,000	
Nov. 3	200	8	1,600				200	5	1,000	⎫ Ending
					_____		200	8	1,600	⎬ inventory =
										⎭ $2,600

Cost of goods sold $10,100

Most companies that use LIFO for income tax and financial reporting purposes maintain their inventory records throughout the year using a different cost flow method, such as FIFO or average cost. This is ordinarily done to facilitate the internal reporting preferences of management. At year-end the accountant uses a LIFO Allowance account to adjust the results to a LIFO basis. This account frequently is called a LIFO reserve, although many accountants do not like the term "reserve." Notice on the endpapers of this textbook that Kroger Company uses a LIFO reserve account.

To illustrate, assume that in 1985 a company adopts the LIFO method for financial reporting purposes. In the past, the company used the FIFO method, and the company plans to continue to maintain its inventory records on a FIFO basis for internal reporting purposes. If the ending inventory for 1985 is $56,000 on a FIFO basis and $50,000 on a LIFO basis, the following year-end entry would be appropriate:

Cost of Goods Sold	6,000	
Allowance to Reduce Inventory		
Cost to LIFO Basis		6,000

The balance in the Allowance account would be deducted from the inventory of $56,000 on the balance sheet.

Applying LIFO to each of a company's products, as we have done for Jackson Company's Product 19-C, is called the **specific goods method** of applying LIFO. This method requires that LIFO be applied to *each product* in a company's inventory. In the next chapter, we present three additional methods of applying LIFO.

1. Major Arguments for LIFO.   LIFO is perhaps the most controversial inventory cost flow method. Nevertheless, certain theoretical and economic arguments support its use. From a theoretical standpoint, the use of LIFO is often said to produce a better matching of

Matching

cost of goods sold expense (measured using recent cost prices) with sales revenue (measured using recent selling prices). As a result, it is often claimed that LIFO produces a better measure of net income than either FIFO or average cost. When inventory costs are rising, as they generally have done during most of this century, net income normally includes a component called **inventory profits.** These profits equal the difference between the current replacement cost of sales and the cost of sales determined using a generally accepted cost flow method. Inventory profits are illusory, however, because they generally must be used to replace depleted inventories at higher costs. The LIFO method greatly reduces inventory profits, thereby causing net income to more accurately reflect an amount that can be distributed to stockholders and still enable the company to replace its inventories. Many financial analysts consider the use of LIFO as a favorable factor when they evaluate the **quality of a company's earnings.** It should be noted that during periods of rising prices, LIFO tends to produce net income and inventory measurements that reflect conservatism.[6]

> **Conservatism**

LIFO is often supported on the economic ground that, during periods of rising prices, its use tends to lower taxable income and thereby postpone income tax payments. These taxes are postponed until the time, if ever, that inventory unit costs or physical quantities decline. Federal income tax law permits a company to compute taxable income using LIFO only if the company also uses LIFO for financial reporting purposes. This is known as the **LIFO conformity requirement,** and as the name implies, this requirement pertains only to LIFO. Although Congress believed that the conformity requirement was fair and reasonable when LIFO was initially allowed for tax purposes in 1938, many people today feel strongly that the requirement adversely affects GAAP and should be eliminated. With the major exception of LIFO, a company does not have to use the same methods for financial reporting purposes as it uses for income taxes purposes, or vice versa.

The LIFO conformity requirement has deterred some companies from adopting LIFO. Nevertheless, persistently high inflation rates in the United States have made LIFO one of the most popular accounting methods in the past several years. Hoover Ball & Bearing, for example, changed from FIFO to LIFO in 1974 (a year of high inflation during which many companies switched to LIFO), and in so doing, the company saved $3.3 million in income taxes.[7] One author has estimated that the use of LIFO has permitted General Electric Company to save approximately $1 billion of income taxes during a twenty-five year period ending in 1979.[8] Tax savings such as these enhance a company's availability of cash. This increased cash flow is in effect an interest-free loan of indefinite and perhaps permanent duration. It reduces borrowing requirements and thereby tends to lower interest costs, which in turn contributes even further toward improving a company's cash flow.

2. Major Arguments Against LIFO. Despite the theoretical and economic advantages of LIFO, the method has been attacked for several reasons. The major arguments against LIFO are summarized below.

1. LIFO inventories are often valued using outdated cost prices. Some say that LIFO-valued inventories are "unrealistic" because they fail to reflect current costs. When inventory valuations are unrealistic, related measurements such as working capital, the current ratio, and inventory turnover are also distorted.
2. The LIFO cost flow assumption is usually opposite to the physical flow of goods. Only a few types of inventories, such as coal or gravel, physically flow in a LIFO manner.

---

[6]Not all companies have experienced a rising trend of inventory costs over time. Some companies in the electronics industry, for example, have actually experienced declining costs. For these companies, using FIFO is considered more conservative than using LIFO.

[7]"FIFO to LIFO: More and More Companies are Making the Switch," *Barron's* (October 21, 1974), p. 5.

[8]S. Thomas Moser, "LIFO: Inflation Lifeline," *Management Focus* (March–April 1981), p. 24.

NO FREE LIFO

EVERYBODY KNOWS that LIFO inventory accounting helps minimize the effect of inflation on an income statement by using the most recent inventory cost. The latest additions to inventory (last in), with the highest costs, are counted as being the first shipped (first out). This eliminates the lag effect of the more traditional first-in, first-out method in which oldest costs are matched first against most recent prices, thus inflating earnings continuously until prices stop rising.

But there is a price for having a more realistic income statement à la LIFO: an increasingly *less* realistic balance sheet. It works like this: Usually, when a company switches from FIFO to LIFO, its existing stock of raw materials, work in progress and finished goods stay on the books at costs prevalent at the time of the switch, which is generally much less than their current value. The difference between that ever older stock of goods with its frozen values and current market values is the "LIFO cushion." That cushion can grow in periods of rising prices as inventory grows—the difference between this year's larger stock of goods and last year's then becomes another layer of the cushion. But the cushion doesn't show on the balance sheet, thus stockholers' equity is understated.

When a company pares inventory and cuts into the cushion, it gets a major and misleading shot in the arm from matching frozen older costs against current prices. That's what a number of oil companies have been doing since last year. But until that happens the LIFO cushion is not transferred to stockholders' equity.

Just how distorted those equity figures can be for a company with a lot of capital tied up in inventory was underscored recently in a survey of the chemical industry done by Norman Weinger of Oppenheimer & Co., the brokerage house. Weinger calculated that Union Carbide's net worth was understated by about 18% just because of its aging LIFO cushion.

Obviously that throws off return-on-equity calculations considerably. In Union Carbide's case, for example, ROE looked like a respectable 12.3% last year. But it falls to a mediocre 10% once it is adjusted for the undervalued LIFO cushion.

Other yardsticks are distorted, too. Inventory turnover is a traditional measure of efficiency. Last year, for example, Monsanto's inventory turnover looked like a nifty (by chemical industry standards) 6. But add back the LIFO reserve and the figure comes out a sluggish 4. Now compare that with similar adjustments at Carbide, 4 to 2, and Grace, 4.8 to 4.2.

The LIFO news is not all bad, of course. A big LIFO cushion can be a very pleasant surprise for stockholders. According to Weinger, many steel companies' LIFO cushions equal or exceed the companies total stock market value. National Steel's LIFO cushion at the end of 1981 totaled $742 million—towering over its recent market value of $322 million.

What happens now that inflation is slowing down? To the extent that it continues to slow, the LIFO cushions will cease growing; but they'll still be there—unless real deflation sets in. But here's another complication: This year, with so many companies cutting inventories, a good part of those cushions are helping to pad earnings, making them look better than they are. That's the fascinating thing about accounting: The more you strive to make it reflect the real world, the more complex it becomes.

SOURCE: Richard Greene, "No Free LIFO," *Forbes,* December 6, 1982, pp. 168, 171. Reprinted by permission of *Forbes* Magazine. © Forbes Inc., 1982.

Matching

3. When a liquidation of LIFO inventory layers occurs, outdated costs tend to be matched with sales revenue, thereby reducing the matching benefits that LIFO generally produces. Matching outdated costs with current revenues is said to produce an "unrealistic" measure of net income. Frequently, the liquidation of LIFO layers is involuntary, as when a strike disrupts production or a supplier fails to deliver goods on a timely basis at the end of an accounting period. During 1980, Goodyear Tire and Rubber Company liquidated some of its LIFO inventory quantities, and the result was an increase in net income of $22,310,000. This amount equals 9.7% of the company's reported net income for 1980.

4. The use of LIFO permits income manipulation, such as by making end-of-period purchases designed to preserve existing inventory layers. At times these purchases may not even be in the best economic interests of the company.

5. LIFO generally results in a greater administrative burden than either FIFO or average cost. As stated earlier, most companies that use LIFO for external reporting maintain their records on some other basis (such as FIFO) for internal reporting. Moreover, because LIFO involves many complex tax regulations, its use for tax purposes may cause the Internal Revenue Service (IRS) to take a closer look at a firm's inventory accounting system to determine whether all the tax requirements have been met. A LIFO election can be invalidated because of a technicality.

6. The variations in methods of applying LIFO as well as the fact that most LIFO users have adopted it at different times tend to distort intercompany comparisons, even those made between two LIFO companies in the same industry.

7. During periods of rising inventory costs, the use of LIFO for tax purposes, coupled with the conformity requirement, creates a paradox. That is, it postpones taxes and thereby makes the firm better off economically, yet it lowers reported net income and thereby makes the firm appear worse than it would under FIFO or average cost. One study has found that many companies "have voluntarily paid tens of millions of dollars in additional income taxes by continuing to use FIFO rather than switching to LIFO."[9] Many managers are reluctant to adopt LIFO out of fear that the reduced reported earnings will cause investors to penalize the market price of their company's stock. Empirical research has suggested, however, that this fear may be unjustified, because changes to LIFO do not appear to result in unfavorable market reactions.[10] A retired chairman of General Electric Company has speculated that some managers may not want to use LIFO because "most top executive contracts are tied to reported earnings."[11]

Comparison of Results Between FIFO, Average Cost, and LIFO. Exhibit 8–9 summarizes the financial statement impact of the FIFO, average cost, and LIFO methods of Product 19-C of Jackson Company for 1985. We do not show the results under the specific

---

[9]Gary C. Biddle, "Accounting Methods and Management Decisions: The Case of Inventory Costing and Inventory Policy," *Journal of Accounting Research* (Supplement 1980), p. 273.

[10]See, for example, Shyam Sunder, "Stock Price and Risk Related to Accounting Changes in Inventory Valuation," *Accounting Review* (April 1975), pp. 305–315. It is also worth noting that the LIFO conformity requirement does *not* prohibit the disclosure of supplemental non-LIFO income information. This supplemental information, such as the amount of net income that would have been reported if the FIFO method had been used, cannot be presented on the face of the financial statements.

[11]Quotation made by Reginald H. Jones, reprinted in *Journal of Accountancy* (July 1981), p. 28.

EXHIBIT 8–9
Comparison of Results Under FIFO, Average Cost, and LIFO

	FIFO		Average Cost		LIFO	
	Periodic System	Perpetual System	Periodic System	Perpetual System	Periodic System	Perpetual System
Cost of goods available for sale	$12,700	$12,700	$12,700	$12,700	$12,700	$12,700
Cost of ending inventory (Dec. 31)	3,000	3,000	2,540	2,900	2,100	2,600
Cost of goods sold	$ 9,700	$ 9,700	$10,160	$ 9,800	$10,600	$10,100

identification method, because they depend on which units were actually sold and which are on hand.

As Exhibit 8-9 suggests, certain key financial statement variables for Jackson Company differ depending on which cost flow method the company adopts. These variables include inventory, total current assets, working capital, cost of goods sold, gross margin, and net income. The fact that the various cost flow methods produce different financial statement **Disclosure** effects underscores the importance of each company disclosing the method(s) that it uses.

Since the unit cost of Product 19-C rose steadily during 1985, FIFO produces the lowest cost of goods sold figure, while LIFO used with a periodic system produces the highest. The nature of the differences produced under the various cost flow methods depends primarily on the direction and magnitude of unit cost movements as well as on the length of time that a company has used LIFO.

Kroger Company, a large retailer of food and drug products, whose financial statements are reproduced on the endpapers and in the Appendix, can be used to illustrate the impact of the FIFO and LIFO methods. Kroger Company uses LIFO to value most of its inventories, and for 1982, the company reported net income of $143.8 million. If the company had used FIFO during 1982, the reported net income would have been $153.8 million, an increase of 6.95%.

Selection of a Cost Flow Method

We have just seen that the various inventory cost flow methods can lead to substantially different financial statement results. We also know that accountants seek to produce information that enables users to make meaningful intercompany comparisons. To help ensure the propriety of these comparisons, differences between the financial statements of different companies should result from basic differences between the companies themselves or from the nature of their transactions and not merely from differences in accounting principles.[12] Given these facts, why does GAAP permit companies to choose among several inventory cost flow methods?

The basic reason is that circumstances may differ substantially between companies. Accountants generally believe that a company should have some leeway in selecting a cost flow method that is most appropriate in light of the circumstances the company faces. The accounting profession has therefore tended to favor *some flexibility,* rather than *strict uniformity,* when formulating accounting principles. Nevertheless, two of the great challenges of the Financial Accounting Standards Board (FASB) and its predecessor committees have been (1) to identify the circumstances that warrant the use of a particular accounting principle and (2) to eliminate alternative principles that are not justified by differences in circumstances.

Given the alternatives currently available under GAAP, what basic criterion should a corporate manager use in selecting an inventory cost flow method? *Accounting Research Bulletin No. 43* states that "the major objective in selecting a method should be to choose the one which, under the circumstances, most clearly reflects periodic income."[13] The phrases "under the circumstances" and "most clearly reflects periodic income" have not been well defined. As a result, they often convey significantly different meanings to different people. The absence of more concrete criteria for selecting a cost flow assumption has increased the importance of judgment. In reality many companies appear to select a method based largely on factors such as tax minimization, steady growth in reported earnings, and so forth. Thus, it seems fair to say that financial statements today often reflect certain differences that are unrelated to basic differences between companies or their transactions.

---

[12]*APB Statement No. 4,* "Basic Concepts and Accounting Principles Underlying Financial Statements of Business Enterprises," 1970, par. 101.
[13]*Accounting Research Bulletin No. 43,* "Restatement and Revision of Accounting Research Bulletins," Ch. 4, Stmt. 4.

INVENTORY METHODS USED BY SELECTED COMPANIES

Company	Inventory Method(s)
Sears, Roebuck and Co.	LIFO
General Instrument Corporation	FIFO
Goodyear Tire & Rubber Company	LIFO—domestic inventories Average cost—other inventories
Aluminum Company of America	LIFO—domestic inventories Average cost—other inventories
The Gillette Company	Standard cost, which approximates FIFO
Gulf + Western Industries, Inc.	FIFO, Average cost
Levi Strauss & Co.	Average cost
Anheuser-Busch Companies, Inc.	LIFO
Litton Industries, Inc.	FIFO—raw materials Average cost—work-in-process and finished goods
General Motors Corporation	LIFO—domestic inventories FIFO or Average cost—other inventories
Shell Oil Company	LIFO—oils and chemicals Average cost—materials and supplies
Kellogg Company	Average cost
The Quaker Oats Company	FIFO—direct to consumer segment and international toys LIFO—domestic chemicals, toys, and packaging materials Average cost—other inventories
Harcourt Brace Jovanovich, Inc.	FIFO
Bristol-Myers Company	Average cost

SOURCE: 1982 Annual Reports.

The author of *Accounting Research Study No. 13* concluded that:

> *Specific identification of costs and, if that is not practicable, the FIFO cost flow assumption represent approaches to inventory cost determination which are sound in principle. . . . Enterprises using any cost flow assumption other than specific identification or FIFO should be required to disclose (1) the effect on net income for the period and on the balance sheet inventory amounts of the method used as compared with FIFO and (2) related tax effects.*[14]

These conclusions have not been adopted by the FASB.

---

[14]Horace G. Barden, *Accounting Research Study No. 13*, "The Accounting Basis of Inventories" (New York: AICPA, 1973), pp. 12–13.

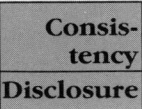

Consistency Disclosure

When a company adopts a cost flow method for a certain portion or for all of its inventories, the company should use the method consistently over time. As stated earlier, the accountant should disclose the method(s) in the financial statements. When a company changes from one inventory cost flow method to another, the accountant should disclose the nature of the change, the justification for the change, and the dollar effects of the change on income. We shall explain accounting changes in detail in Chapter 19.

INVENTORY VALUATION AT THE LOWER OF COST OR MARKET (LCM)

Historical Cost

The accountant initially values inventory items by multiplying quantities on hand by unit costs derived under a cost flow method (specific identification, FIFO, etc.). The resulting valuation is at total cost and is therefore consistent with the historical cost principle that GAAP usually requires. In the area of inventory accounting, however, GAAP requires a departure from the historical cost principle when the utility of inventory has declined below cost. This departure is known as the **lower of cost or market rule,** or simply the **LCM rule.**[15]

The LCM rule is stated as follows in *Accounting Research Bulletin No. 43:*

> *A departure from the cost basis of pricing the inventory is required when the utility of the goods is no longer as great as its cost. Where there is evidence that the utility of goods, in their disposal in the ordinary course of business, will be less than cost, whether due to physical deterioration, obsolescence, changes in price levels, or other causes, the difference should be recognized as a loss of the current period. This is generally accomplished by stating such goods at a lower level commonly designated as* market.[16]

A company purchases or manufactures inventory for ultimate sale. The term **utility of goods** thus refers to the ability of the goods to generate revenue via sale. Utility is a very subjective concept, and **market** is used simply as a practical means of measuring it. Therefore, if the market measure of goods on hand at the end of the current period has declined below cost, the accountant should report the difference as a loss of the period in which the decline occurred.

Meaning of Market

What does **market** mean? *Accounting Research Bulletin No. 43* states:

> *As used in the phrase* lower of cost or market *the term market means current replacement cost (by purchase or by reproduction, as the case may be) except that:*
>
> *(1) Market should not exceed the net realizable value (i.e., estimated selling price in the ordinary course of business less reasonably predictable costs of completion and disposal); and*
>
> *(2) Market should not be less than net realizable value reduced by an allowance for an approximately normal profit margin.*[17]

---

[15]A company cannot use LCM with LIFO for federal income tax purposes. Generally accepted accounting principles, however, do not prohibit a company from using LCM with LIFO for financial reporting purposes. Other differences exist between the way in which a company applies LCM for income tax versus financial reporting purposes. Readers interested in the details of how to apply LCM for income tax purposes should consult appropriate tax references.

[16]*Accounting Research Bulletin No. 43,* Ch. 4, Stmt. 5.

[17]*Accounting Research Bulletin No. 43,* Ch. 4, Stmt. 6.

As a general guide, therefore, market means **current replacement cost** on the balance sheet date. In the case of purchased inventories, this cost includes not only the purchase price that would have to be paid for the quantities usually purchased, but also incidental acquisition costs such as freight and handling. For manufactured inventories, replacement cost is based on current materials prices, prevailing labor rates, and current overhead costs. Note that replacement cost is an **input** (or **entry**) **value,** because it represents an amount that would have to be paid to acquire inventory.

The purpose of using replacement cost to represent market (and therefore utility) is that declines in replacement cost are often associated with declines in selling prices. Selling prices, however, may be influenced by factors other than replacement costs. *Bulletin No. 43* therefore states that in applying the LCM rule, "judgment must always be exercised and no loss should be recognized unless the evidence indicates clearly that a loss has been sustained."[18] To assist the practicing accountant in determining whether or not a loss has been sustained, the bulletin specifies an upper and a lower limit within which market must fall. Each limit is an **output** (or **exit**) **value,** because each is based directly on expected selling prices that the firm will receive for the goods being valued.

The upper limit on market, commonly called the **ceiling,** is **net realizable value.** The lower limit, commonly called the **floor,** is **net realizable value reduced by an allowance for an approximately normal profit margin.** These concepts are illustrated below for one unit of Inventory Item Q.

Estimated selling price in the ordinary course of business	$10
− Reasonably predictable costs of completion and disposal	1
= Net realizable value (ceiling)	9
− Allowance for an approximately normal profit margin (30% of selling price)	3
= Net realizable value less an allowance for an approximately normal profit margin (floor)	$ 6

When applying the LCM rule, **replacement cost is used as market only when it falls between the ceiling and the floor.** On the other hand, **if replacement cost is greater than the ceiling, the ceiling is used as market.** The use of a ceiling is defended on the ground that if inventory were reported at more than its net realizable value, the amount reported would exceed the inventory's utility. This would result in a loss when the inventory is sold. If **replacement cost is less than the floor, the floor is used as market.** Limiting market to the floor is defended on the basis that writing down inventory items below the floor understates the inventory's utility and thereby permits the recognition of an abnormally high profit when the inventory is sold.

From a practical standpoint, the LCM rule requires (1) selecting as market the middle amount from among the ceiling, replacement cost, and floor, and (2) selecting the lower of cost or market to use for inventory valuation purposes. This is illustrated in Exhibit 8–10 for four inventory items. The assumed dollar amounts are on a *per unit basis.*

Observe in Exhibit 8–10 that for each item, market is the middle value selected from among the ceiling, replacement cost, and floor. After we have determined market, we compare it with cost. The lower of cost or market is then entered in the LCM column. Unit amounts in the LCM column are the correct ones to use for inventory valuation purposes. Note that these amounts represent the cost for Item A, the ceiling for Item B, the replace-

---

[18]*Accounting Research Bulletin No. 43,* Ch. 4, par. 9.

EXHIBIT 8–10
The LCM Rule

Inventory Item			Market Determinants			
	Ceiling[1]	Replacement Cost[2]	Floor[3]	Market[4]	Cost[5]	LCM[6]
A	$7	$6	$5	$6	$3	$3
B	7	8	5	7	9	7
C	7	6	5	6	8	6
D	7	4	5	5	8	5

[1]Net realizable value (the estimated selling price less reasonably predictable costs of completion and disposal).
[2]The current replacement cost as of the balance sheet date.
[3]Net realizable value less a normal profit margin.
[4]The middle amount selected from among the ceiling, replacement cost, and floor.
[5]Determined using a cost flow method (specific identification, FIFO, etc.).
[6]Lower of cost or market (the lower amount selected from the cost and market). This amount is used for inventory valuation purposes on the balance sheet.

---

ment cost for Item C, and the floor for Item D.[19]

The LCM rule applies to goods that a company will sell in the ordinary course of business. At times a company may own damaged, deteriorated, or obsolete goods that it cannot sell in the usual manner. These goods may have been damaged by fire or other unusual causes. Such goods should be carried in a separate account and, for accounting purposes, should be valued below cost, at their estimated selling prices less disposal costs. The accounting principles that should be used for inventory received in a trade-in are discussed in Chapter 11; accounting for repossessed inventory is presented in Chapter 20.

Methods of Applying the LCM Rule

In the preceding example we assumed that the LCM rule was applied to each item in inventory. Actually, a company may choose to apply the rule to (1) each inventory item, (2) major categories of items, or (3) the inventory as a whole. According to *Bulletin No. 43,* the application method selected should be the one that most clearly reflects periodic income. Moreover, the method should be applied consistently over time. Most companies use the individual item method.[20] Regardless of what method is used, the quantity of each item should initially be multiplied by (1) unit costs to derive aggregate cost, and (2) unit market values to derive aggregate market.[21] This is shown in Exhibit 8–11, in which we assume the same inventory items (A, B, C, and D) as in Exhibit 8–10. For simplicity, we assume that 1,000 units of each item are on hand.

Observe in Exhibit 8–11 that the final inventory valuation is $21,000, $23,000, or $24,000, depending on how the LCM rule is applied. In certain cases the results under the different methods may be equal. If the results are not equal, applying LCM to individual

Consistency

---

[19]Lindbeck and Rogow have reported a concise decision rule to select the correct LCM inventory valuation price from among the cost, ceiling, replacement cost, and floor amounts. Their rule is: "Use *cost,* if the cost price is lowest; otherwise, use the *next-to-lowest* price." Rudolph S. Lindbeck and Robert B. Rogow, "A Straightforward Decision Rule for Selecting Lower-of-Cost or Market Price: A Contraction," *Accounting Review* (July 1975), p. 617.
[20]Lower of cost or market must be applied to each inventory item for federal income tax purposes.
[21]Multiplying by unit costs overcomes the problem of having to compare more than one unit cost with a single unit market value. Under the FIFO method, for example, more than one unit cost may exist for certain inventory items.

EXHIBIT 8–11
Methods of Applying the LCM Rule

	Number of Units	Unit Cost	Unit Market	Aggregate Cost	Aggregate Market	LCM Applied to (1) Individual Items	(2) Major Categories	(3) Inventory as a Whole
Category I								
Item A	1,000	$3	$6	$ 3,000	$ 6,000	$ 3,000		
Item B	1,000	9	7	9,000	7,000	7,000		
Subtotal				12,000	13,000		$12,000	
Category II								
Item C	1,000	8	6	8,000	6,000	6,000		
Item D	1,000	8	5	8,000	5,000	5,000		
Subtotal				16,000	11,000		11,000	
Total				$28,000	$24,000			$24,000
Inventory valuation						$21,000	$23,000	$24,000

items produces the lowest inventory valuation; applying it to the inventory as a whole produces the highest.

Once an inventory item has been written down to a value below cost, that value is regarded as its "new cost" for purposes of subsequent accounting. If the market value of an item that has been written down subsequently increases, the increase is *not* reflected in the accounts until a sale occurs.

Recording LCM in the Accounts

When application of the LCM rule indicates that inventory should be reported at market, how should the accountant record this in the accounts? Ideally, a loss account should be debited and a valuation allowance account (an inventory *contra* account) should be credited. To illustrate, let's assume the following facts for Bradley Company:

Inventory, Jan. 1, 1985, at cost	$ 50,000
Purchases during 1985	200,000
Inventory, Dec. 31, 1985	
At cost	40,000
At market	33,000

If the company uses the periodic inventory system, the cost of goods sold adjusting entry would appear as shown below.

Dec. 31	Inventory, Dec. 31	40,000	
	Loss on Reduction of Inventory Cost to Market	7,000	
	Cost of Goods Sold	210,000	
	Inventory, Jan. 1		50,000
	Allowance to Reduce Inventory Cost to Market		7,000
	Purchases		200,000

On the other hand, the following adjusting entry would be made if the company uses a perpetual system.

Dec. 31	Loss on Reduction of Inventory Cost		
	to Market	7,000	
	Allowance to Reduce Inventory		
	Cost to Market		7,000

Under either system, cost of goods sold would be reported at $210,000 and the loss of $7,000 would be shown in the body of the income statement (*not* as an extraordinary item). A clear distinction is therefore made between an *expense* associated with *goods sold* and a *loss* associated with holding *goods on hand.* Separating the expense from the loss is conceptually correct since the two amounts are caused by different factors. Moreover, a separate reporting of the two amounts may help financial statement users to make more accurate predictions of future cash flows.

The Allowance account is deducted from inventory on the balance sheet, as shown below.

Inventory, at cost	$40,000	
Less: Allowance to reduce inventory		
cost to market	7,000	$33,000

Disclosure

Use of the Allowance account facilitates the disclosure of the ending inventory at both cost ($40,000) and market ($33,000).

At the end of the *next* accounting period, the Allowance account should be closed to the Beginning Inventory if a periodic system is used or to Cost of Goods Sold if a perpetual system is used. This avoids overstatement of the beginning inventory and cost of goods sold. If the market value of the ending inventory is below cost, the difference should again be entered in the Loss and the Allowance account.

Materiality

In practice, a number of acceptable variations of the above procedure are encountered. Conceptually, these variations are less desirable than the procedure described above. They may be supported, however, on the grounds of materiality and practicality. For example, the LCM rule is sometimes applied in the accounts by:

1. Debiting Cost of Goods Sold (instead of the Loss account) and crediting the Allowance account.
2. Debiting the Loss account and crediting the Inventory account (instead of the Allowance account).
3. Debiting Cost of Goods Sold (instead of the Loss account) and crediting the Inventory account (instead of the Allowance account).

It should also be noted that when an Allowance account is used, some accountants leave it open and merely adjust it upward or downward at year-end so that it agrees with the difference between cost and market. An increase in the Allowance account requires the recognition of a loss. A decrease requires the recognition of a recovery of loss, sometimes called a gain. The balance in the Allowance account is never reduced below zero. In other words, a debit balance should never exist in the Allowance account, because it would cause the carrying value of the inventory to be above cost.

Pros and Cons of LCM

The LCM rule is an example of the conservatism modifying convention. It permits accountants to modify the historical cost principle to recognize a loss on inventory, even though evidence of the loss does not result from a sale. The rule has a long history in accounting. Its early use was supported as a means of achieving balance sheet conservatism at a time when creditors were the primary users of external financial statements and the balance sheet was regarded as the most important financial statement. Modern financial reporting emphasizes the income statement, and the LCM rule is now supported on the basis that it produces a conservative income measure in the current period.

Many users of financial statements support the LCM rule because they think it reduces their risk of making poor decisions. In an empirical study involving in-depth interviews of important financial statement users, Backer found that "all but one of the 74 bankers interviewed favored the lower of cost or market rule. . . . The security analysts also overwhelmingly supported the rule. Only four of these 72 analysts interviewed opposed the rule."[22]

Despite the alleged benefits of the LCM rule, it has long been one of the most controversial elements of GAAP. Critics have leveled many arguments against it. Some of the major objections are listed below.

1. The rule requires a write-down to market when cost exceeds market, but it does not permit a write-up to market when market exceeds cost. Some accountants consider this inconsistent and illogical.
2. The rule permits the use of four different inventory measures. Some inventory items may therefore be valued at cost, while others are valued using ceiling, replacement cost, and floor amounts. The existence of these different valuation bases may inhibit the ability of statement users to make valid intercompany and interperiod comparisons.
3. Different methods may be used to apply the LCM rule (i.e., to individual items, major categories, or the inventory as a whole) and to record it in the accounts. As a result, intercompany comparisons may be distorted.
4. Determining a "normal profit" in order to establish a floor is difficult and very subjective. These profits vary between inventory items and over time as selling prices and cost prices change.
5. Valuing an inventory item at the floor in order to prevent an abnormally high profit on its sale may be closer to income manipulation than to income measurement. The function of management is to earn a profit, while the accountant's function is to measure and report it.
6. The LCM rule may produce conservative results in the first year of its use. However, when the lower inventory costs are charged to cost of goods sold in a subsequent period, net income tends to be greater and therefore unconservative.
7. The rule is often complicated to apply. Furthermore, there is reasonable room to suspect that many preparers and users of financial statements may not adequately understand it.[23]

INVENTORY VALUATION ABOVE COST

Thus far we have discussed the valuation of inventory at cost and at the lower of cost or market. In Chapter 3, we discussed several alternatives to conventional historical cost measurement. These include current cost (replacement cost), current exit value in orderly liquidation, expected exit value in due course of business (net realizable value), and present value of expected cash flows. Many critics of historical cost accounting believe that accounting information would be more useful if inventories were consistently measured using any of the alternatives to conventional historical cost. Some accountants, for example, believe that inventories should be measured and reported at current cost, regardless of whether the current cost measurement is above or below historical cost. Although many theoretical arguments lend support to the valuation of inventory at amounts greater than historical cost, such valuation is permissible under GAAP only in certain exceptional cases.

For example, construction companies often engage in projects that take several years to complete. These projects include office buildings, ships, and dams. Instead of waiting until

---

[22]Morton Backer, *Financial Reporting for Security Investment and Credit Decisions* (New York: National Association of Accountants, 1970), p. 102.
[23]Barden, p. 104.

the end of a project to recognize income, these companies may, under GAAP, choose to recognize income *during production* using the percentage of completion method. Under this method, an inventory account called "Construction in Progress" consists of **historical costs incurred plus income recognized to date.** The reporting of inventory in this manner is considered appropriate for these companies, given the unusual nature of the construction business. We further explain and illustrate the percentage of completion method in Chapter 20.

The reporting of inventory at **net realizable value,** even though such value may be above cost, is permitted under GAAP in certain exceptional cases. Precious metals that have a fixed monetary value and no substantial marketing costs may be reported at net realizable value. Similarly, certain agricultural and mineral products, units of which are interchangeable, can be sold immediately at quoted market prices, and are difficult to cost appropriately, may be reported at net realizable value.[24] In addition, it is customary for companies within certain industries to report inventories at net realizable value, because it is virtually impossible for them to determine costs with sufficient objectivity. A meat packing company, for example, buys its raw material "on the hoof" and divides it into many cuts, such as ribs and chuck. Since any allocation of the cost of the animal to the resulting cuts would be purely arbitrary, these companies value their inventories of cuts at net realizable value.[25]

When a company values its inventory above cost, the company is considered to have earned income before the time of sale. Clearly, this is an exceptional treatment, given the revenue realization principle. Financial statements of companies that value inventories above cost should disclose the valuation basis used.

| Industry Practices |
| Revenue Realization |

EFFECTS OF INVENTORY ERRORS ON FINANCIAL STATEMENTS

Inventory errors often occur because of mechanical errors in counting, pricing, or extending inventory amounts. Inventory errors may also arise because certain goods have been either incorrectly included or incorrectly excluded when the inventory was taken. We may better appreciate the importance of accurately accounting for inventories by focusing on the impact of certain inventory errors on financial statements. Several common types of errors made in accounting for merchandise and the effects of each are summarized below.

1. The company's accountant **incorrectly includes** in the ending inventory the cost of certain goods that do not belong to the company.
   a. If the credit purchase of the goods has *not* been recorded, the effects will be an overstatement of ending inventory, an understatement of cost of goods sold, and an overstatement of net income and ending retained earnings.
   b. If the credit purchase of the goods has been recorded, then *two* errors will have occurred (i.e., incorrectly including the goods in inventory *and* incorrectly recording the purchase). The effects will be an overstatement of ending inventory and of accounts payable. Cost of goods sold, net income, and ending retained earnings, however, will be correctly stated, since both purchases and ending inventory are overstated by the same amounts and therefore offset one another in the calculation of cost of goods sold and net income.
2. The company's accountant **incorrectly excludes** from ending inventory the cost of certain goods that belong to the company.
   a. If the credit purchase of the goods has been recorded, the effects will be an understatement of ending inventory, an overstatement of cost of goods sold, and an understatement of net income and ending retained earnings.

---

[24]*Accounting Research Bulletin No. 43,* Ch. 4, par 16.
[25]*Accounting Research Bulletin No. 43,* Ch. 1A, par 1.

b. If the credit purchase of the goods has *not* been recorded, then *two* errors will have occurred (i.e., incorrectly excluding the goods from inventory *and* incorrectly failing to record the purchase). The effects will be an understatement of ending inventory and of accounts payable. Cost of goods sold, net income, and ending retained earnings, however, will be correctly stated, since both purchases and ending inventory are understated by the same amounts and therefore offset one another in the calculation of cost of goods sold and net income.

The types of inventory errors discussed above relate to purchase transactions. Similar errors may arise in relation to sales transactions. For example, the cost of certain goods that have actually been sold may erroneously be included in the ending inventory.

The various types of inventory errors just discussed affected the current accounting period. Recognize, however, that an error in the ending inventory of the current period has the opposite effect in the next period, since the ending inventory of one period is the beginning inventory of the next. If the error is not corrected in the second period, it will offset the error made in the first period.

Correcting an inventory error requires a logical analysis of the error's effects on the financial statements. The appropriate correction depends in part on when the error is detected. An error in the ending inventory of one period that is discovered near the end of the next, for example, requires a prior period adjustment. We shall discuss the overall topic of error correction in greater depth in Chapter 19.

CONCEPTUAL CONSIDERATIONS

Throughout this text we stress the importance of understanding the relationship between the individual topics covered and the theoretical model presented in Chapter 2. The following elements of the model are especially pertinent in the area of inventory accounting.

Historical Cost

1. **Historical cost principle.** The primary basis of accounting for inventories is historical cost. Remember that determining historical cost is not as easy as it may appear. Resolving important issues such as what costs should be inventoried and what cost flow method should be used is a real challenge to the practicing accountant.

Revenue Realization

2. **Revenue realization principle.** When an increase in the value of inventory is verified by a sale, revenue is usually recorded. Only in certain exceptional cases may accountants properly value inventory above cost and therefore recognize revenue before the time of sale.

Matching

3. **Matching principle.** The cost of the inventory sold must be charged to expense in the period in which the sale occurs. By so doing, the sales revenue is matched with the cost of the goods sold to produce the revenue.

Consistency

4. **Consistency principle.** A company should account for its inventories using the same methods over time. This principle is particularly important in inventory accounting, because several alternative accounting methods exist.

Disclosure

5. **Disclosure principle.** The following disclosure guidelines should be observed when reporting inventories on the balance sheet and in the related notes:
   a. Report inventories in the current assets section.
   b. Disclose separately each major class of inventory, such as raw materials, work-in-process, finished goods, factory supplies, and goods on consignment. Remember to include in inventory only those goods for which the company (i.e., the accounting entity) has legal title on the balance sheet date.
   c. List inventories in order of their liquidity.
   d. Disclose parenthetically, in a footnote, or in a summary of significant accounting policies, the inventory cost flow method used (FIFO, average cost, etc.) as well as basis used in

---

EXHIBIT 8–12
Example Inventory Disclosures

EXAMPLE NO. 1:   CBS INC.

CONSOLIDATED
BALANCE SHEETS

CBS Inc. and subsidiaries (note 16)   (Dollars in thousands)

ASSETS

	1982	December 31 1981	1980
Current assets:			
Cash and equivalents:			
Cash and cash items	$ 12,643	$ 1,745	$ 79,927
Short-term marketable securities, at cost plus accrued interest (approximates market)	15,292	26,275	22,776
	27,935	28,020	102,703
Notes and accounts receivable, less allowances for doubtful accounts, returns and discounts: 1982, $153,663; 1981, $166,567; 1980, $166,225	733,521	713,331	720,176
Inventories (note 8).....................................	306,955	306,845	315,691
Program rights and feature film productions	381,413	340,277	277,530
Prepaid expenses and other..........................	172,084	111,393	99,538
Total current assets	**1,621,908**	**1,499,866**	**1,515,638**

NOTES TO CONSOLIDATED
FINANCIAL STATEMENTS

1. Statement of Significant Accounting Policies

Inventories. Inventories are stated at the lower of cost (principally based on average cost) or market value.

8. Inventories

Inventories are summarized as follows:

	1982	December 31 1981	1980
		(Dollars in thousands)	
Finished goods	$193,864	$192,285	$193,780
Work in process	43,517	39,600	37,511
Raw materials	64,413	69,291	81,274
Supplies	5,161	5,669	3,126
	$306,955	$306,845	$315,691

SOURCE: CBS Inc., 1982 Annual Report.

EXAMPLE NO. 2:   NATIONAL DISTILLERS AND CHEMICAL CORPORATION

NATIONAL DISTILLERS AND CHEMICAL CORPORATION AND SUBSIDIARY COMPANIES

CONSOLIDATED BALANCE SHEET

(dollar amounts in millions)

	December 31	
	1982	1981
Assets		
Current assets		
Cash	$ 26.6	$ 54.1
Short-term investments and marketable securities (Note 9)	114.5	82.6
Receivables — less allowance for doubtful accounts of $2.5 — 1982; $3.2 — 1981	243.3	266.0
Inventories (Note 10)	412.2	432.9
Prepaid expenses and other assets	20.1	20.9
Total current assets	816.7	856.5

NATIONAL DISTILLERS AND CHEMICAL CORPORATION AND SUBSIDIARY COMPANIES

NOTES TO CONSOLIDATED FINANCIAL STATEMENTS

(dollar amounts in millions except for per share data)

Note 1—Summary of Accounting Policies

Inventories

Inventories are valued at the lower of cost or market. Cost is determined for the various categories of inventory using the first-in, first-out; last-in, first-out; or average cost method as deemed appropriate. Whiskey in storage for aging over a number of years is included in current assets in accordance with the general practice in the distilling industry.

Note 10—Inventories

	December 31	
	1982	1981
Finished goods	$140.4	$151.1
Work in process	24.9	28.3
Raw materials and supplies	69.1	90.1
Bulk whiskey, other spirits and wines	177.8	163.4
	$412.2	$432.9

Inventory costs of $128.9 million at December 31, 1982 and $140.1 million at December 31, 1981 were determined under the last-in, first-out (LIFO) method. The remaining inventory costs were determined under either the first-in, first-out or average cost methods. If inventories valued under the LIFO method had been determined under the first-in, first-out or average cost methods, total inventory value would have been increased by approximately $137 million at December 31, 1982 and $147 million at December 31, 1981.

At December 31, 1982 inventories accounted for under the LIFO method are stated at $7 million in excess of the amount used for federal income tax purposes.

SOURCE: National Distillers and Chemical Corporation, 1982 Annual Report.

EXAMPLE NO. 3:   THE TIMES MIRROR COMPANY

The Times Mirror Company and Subsidiaries

Consolidated Balance Sheets

Assets	(In thousands of dollars) December 31	1982	1981
Current Assets	Cash	$ 21,212	$ 25,165
	Marketable securities	2,425	8,519
	Accounts receivable, less allowances for doubtful accounts and returns (1982 − $41,551, 1981 − $40,178)	343,527	309,684
	Inventories	160,948	164,628
	Prepaid expenses	43,495	47, 555
	Total current assets	571,607	555,551

Notes to Consolidated Financial Statements

Note A
Summary of Significant Accounting Policies

Inventories
Inventories are carried at the lower of cost or market and are determined under the first-in, first-out method for books and certain finished products, and under the last-in, first-out method for newsprint, paper, lumber, logs and certain other inventories (see Note E).

Note E
Inventories

Inventories consist of the following:

(In thousands of dollars)	1982	1981	1980
Newsprint and paper	$ 60,668	$ 46,342	$ 29,521
Books and other finished products	46,620	53,754	60,965
Lumber, veneer and plywood	3,127	2,489	4,215
Work-in-process	16,890	19,469	15,563
Raw materials and logs	33,643	42,574	42,835
	$160,948	$164,628	$153,099

The total inventories would have been higher by $19,750,000 in 1982, $28,309,000 in 1981, and $17,412,000 in 1980 had the first-in, first-out method (which approximates current cost) been used exclusively.

SOURCE: The Times Mirror Company, 1982 Annual Report.

pricing the inventory (cost or LCM). Also disclose any methods used that are peculiar to the firm's industry.

e. If the company has made a change in its inventory accounting principles, disclose the nature of and justification for the change. The effect of the change on income should also be disclosed. We explain and illustrate accounting changes in Chapter 19.

f. Subtract the amount in an inventory allowance account (such as the Allowance to Reduce Inventory Cost to Market) from the amount in the Inventory account to derive the net amount. Report all three amounts on the balance sheet or in the related notes.

g. Do *not* offset the cost of inventories pledged as collateral against the loan liability. These inventories are properly reported as assets. However, the nature of the pledge agreement should be disclosed.

h. Do *not* include in inventories advance payments made to suppliers for goods that the company has ordered but title to which has not been received as of the balance sheet date. These advances should be reported after inventories in an account called "Advances to Suppliers."

Exhibit 8–12 shows the inventory disclosures made by three large companies in recent annual reports to shareholders. CBS Inc. is a well-known company with its original base in the broadcasting business. National Distillers and Chemical Corporation is a large company that makes industrial chemicals, whiskey, and brass products. The Times Mirror Company publishes newspapers, books, and magazines. The company also produces newsprint and forest products.

Industry Practices

6. **Industry practices.** This modifying convention sometimes requires the reporting of inventories at amounts above cost. Companies in the meat packing industry, for example, typically value their inventories of cuts at net realizable value.

Conservatism

7. **Conservatism.** This modifying convention is reflected in the LCM rule. Under this rule a departure from the historical cost principle is required when the utility of inventory has declined below cost.

KEY POINTS

1. Inventories are goods that are held for sale in the ordinary course of business, as well as goods that are in production or that will soon be used in production.

2. To value an inventory for financial reporting purposes, an accountant must determine (1) the physical quantity of goods on hand and (2) the accounting valuation that should be associated with those goods.

3. Inventory quantities are maintained on a day-to-day basis in a perpetual inventory system, but not in a periodic system.

4. Inventory items should be included in the inventory of the entity that has legal title. Goods in transit at the end of an accounting period that were shipped FOB shipping point belong to the buyer; those shipped FOB destination belong to the seller. Consigned goods belong to the consignor.

5. To determine the cost of an inventory, an accountant must determine (1) what costs to include in inventory and (2) what method to use in associating inventory costs with the physical units on hand.

6. Product costs are inventoried; period costs are charged to expense in the period in which they are incurred.

7. Trade discounts are deducted when determining product costs. In theory, cash discounts should also be deducted, but in practice, most companies account for inventory at gross invoice amounts (i.e., without deducting cash discounts).

8. Inventory cost flow methods include specific identification, FIFO, average cost, and LIFO. Each method leads to a valuation of inventory and cost of goods sold based on historical cost.

9. The specific identification method requires that the actual unit costs of goods on hand and goods sold be identified individually. In contrast, the FIFO, average cost, and LIFO methods reflect assumed cost flow patterns.

10. Many companies have elected to use LIFO for income tax purposes. A company that uses LIFO for tax purposes must also use it for financial reporting purposes. The LIFO method is an important exception to the general principle that a company does not have to use the same methods for financial reporting purposes that it uses for income tax purposes.

11. A company should select the inventory cost flow method that most clearly reflects its periodic income; once selected, the method should be used consistently over time and disclosed in the financial statements.

12. Inventory should ordinarily be reported on a balance sheet at the lower of cost or market value. In essence, the term "market" refers to the middle value selected from among the ceiling, replacement cost, and floor amounts.

13. The lower of cost or market rule may be applied to each inventory item, to major categories of items, or to the inventory as a whole.

14. The lower of cost or market rule is an exception to the historical cost principle that is justified on the basis of conservatism.

15. The valuation of inventory at an amount greater than historical cost is permissible under GAAP only in certain exceptional cases.

16. Inventory errors can cause several important misstatements to occur in the financial statements.

17. The following elements of accounting theory are especially important in the area of inventory accounting: historical cost, revenue realization, matching, consistency, disclosure, industry practices, and conservatism.

APPENDIX A THE BASE STOCK METHOD

The **base stock method** of inventory valuation was somewhat popular during the nineteenth century and the early part of the twentieth century, but it is seldom used today. The method is based on the assumption that certain companies, such as chemical manufacturers, must maintain a minimum quantity of inventory, called the base stock, to carry on normal business operations. The base stock represents a permanent commitment of corporate resources; it is therefore somewhat similar to a plant asset, although it is reported as inventory among the current assets. Goods are currently purchased or produced in order to meet current sales requirements. Any difference between the actual stock of goods in ending inventory and the base stock is viewed as a temporary condition.

To implement the method, we begin by determining the base quantity of goods and the base cost per unit. The base quantity is the *minimum* needed to

maintain normal operations. The base cost per unit is a long-run "normal" cost, usually the *lowest* cost experienced by the company. We then value the quantity of goods in the base stock using the base cost per unit. If the actual quantity of goods on hand at the end of a period exceeds the base quantity, we view the excess as a temporary increment. We value the temporary increment at current costs, determined by applying the LIFO, average cost, or FIFO cost flow assumptions. If the actual quantity is less than the base, we regard the decrease as temporary and subtract it at current cost from the base. We illustrate the application of these procedures in Exhibit 8–13.

The main advantage of the base stock method is that it tends to produce a matching of current costs against current revenues, thereby tending to eliminate inventory profits. The base stock method has several major shortcom-

Matching

EXHIBIT 8–13
Base Stock Method

	Jan. 1, 1983	Dec. 31, 1983	Dec. 31, 1984	Dec. 31, 1985
Base cost per unit	$2.00	$2.00	$2.00	$2.00
Current cost per unit	$2.00	$3.00	$2.50	$2.75
Actual quantity on hand	1,000 units	1,100 units	900 units	1,200 units
Base quantity	1,000 units	1,000 units	1,000 units	1,000 units
Increase (or decrease) in actual quantity compared with base quantity	–0–	100 units	(100) units	200 units
Inventory Valuation				
Base quantity × base cost per unit (1,000 units @ $2.00)	$2,000	$2,000	$2,000	$2,000
Add: Increase in actual quantity over base quantity × current cost per unit (Dec. 31, 1983: 100 units @ $3.00) (Dec. 31, 1985: 200 units @ $2.75)		300		550
Deduct: Decrease in actual quantity below base quantity × current cost per unit (Dec. 31, 1984: 100 units @ $2.50)			(250)	
Inventory valuation under base stock method	$2,000	$2,300	$1,750	$2,550

ings, however, that limit its usefulness. These are listed below.

1. Determining the base quantity and the base cost per unit is extremely subjective and therefore may violate the objectivity principle.

Objectivity

2. Inventory is valued at an arbitrarily low amount that may bear no relation to current costs. This ultra-conservative valuation may stretch the conservatism modifying convention too far.

Conservatism

3. Since the base stock is assumed to represent a permanent commitment of corporate resources, classifying inventory as a current asset appears to violate the definition of current assets.

The base stock method is similar to LIFO in terms of financial statement impact. Unlike LIFO, however, the base stock method is not acceptable for federal income tax purposes. The method has limited support as a generally accepted accounting principle, although it is seldom used. The authors believe that the shortcomings of this method outweigh its advantages. We therefore do not recommend the method for use in accounting practice.

QUESTIONS

8–1   What are the major differences between trading and manufacturing companies regarding the classification of inventories and the calculation of cost of goods sold? Why do these differences exist?

8–2   The primary basis of accounting for inventories under GAAP is historical cost. Identify three inventory valuation methods that are alternatives to historical cost and briefly explain why these methods are not generally accepted today.

8–3   What is a periodic inventory system? What is a perpetual system? What factors should a company manager consider when deciding which system the company should use?

8–4   What general rule determines which goods properly belong in a company's inventory? How does the accountant apply this general rule to goods in transit on the balance sheet date and to consigned goods?

8–5   Distinguish between product costs and period costs.

8–6   Why is the net method of recording purchases theoretically superior to the gross method?

8–7   What are the major arguments for and against the specific identification method of inventory cost determination?

8–8   What are the major arguments for and against the FIFO method of inventory cost determination?

8–9   What are the major arguments for and against the average cost method of inventory cost determination?

8–10   What are the major arguments for and against the LIFO method of inventory cost determination?

8–11   What basic problem does the existence within GAAP of several inventory cost flow methods create for external users of financial statements? How does the accounting profession justify these alternative methods?

8–12   What basic criterion should a company manager use in selecting an inventory cost flow method? Why is this criterion difficult to apply?

8–13   What are the major arguments for and against the LCM rule in accounting for inventories?

8–14   What does the term "market" mean in the context of the LCM rule?

8–15   What is the rationale for ceiling and floor limits on market under the LCM rule?

8–16   Under what circumstances, if any, is it appropriate under GAAP to value inventories at amounts greater than historical cost?

8–17   Relate inventory accounting to the historical cost principle, revenue realization principle, and matching principle.

8–18   Why is the consistency principle especially important in accounting for inventories?

8–19   Relate inventory accounting to the conservatism modifying convention.

8–20 (Appendix A)   What are the major arguments for and against the base stock method of inventory cost determination?

CASES

C8–1 Ron Hansen, president of Carter, Inc., recently read an article which claimed that at least 100 of the country's largest 500 companies were either adopting or considering adopting the last-in, first-out (LIFO) method for valuing inventories. The article stated that the firms were switching to LIFO to (1) neutralize the effect of inflation in their financial statements, (2) eliminate inventory profits, and (3) reduce income taxes. Hansen wonders if the switch would benefit his company.

Carter currently uses the first-in, first-out (FIFO) method of inventory valuation in its periodic inventory system. The company has a high inventory turnover rate, and inventories represent a significant proportion of the assets.

In discussing this trend toward LIFO inventory with business friends, Hansen has been told that the LIFO system is more costly to operate and will provide little benefit to companies with high turnover. Hansen intends to use the inventory method that is best for the company in the long run and not to select a method just because it is the current fad.

Instructions

[a] Explain to Mr. Hansen what "inventory profits" are

and how the LIFO method of inventory valuation could reduce them.

[b] Explain to Mr. Hansen the conditions that must exist for Carter to receive tax benefits from the LIFO method.

(CMA adapted)

C8–2 Inventory may be computed under one of various cost flow assumptions, such as FIFO and LIFO. In the past, some companies changed from FIFO to LIFO for computing some or all of their inventory.

Instructions

[a] Ignoring income tax, what effect does a change from FIFO to LIFO have on net earnings and working capital? Explain.

[b] Explain the difference between the FIFO and the LIFO assumption of earnings and operating cycle.

(AICPA adapted)

C8–3 Elof Company is considering changing its inventory valuation method from FIFO to LIFO because of the potential tax savings. However, the management wishes to consider all of the effects on the company, including its reported performance, before making the final decision.

The inventory account, currently valued on the FIFO basis, consists of 1,000,000 units at $7 per unit on January 1, 1985. There are 1,000,000 shares of common stock outstanding as of January 1, 1985, and the cash balance is $400,000.

The company has made the following forecasts for the period 1985–1987.

	1985	1986	1987
Unit sales (in millions of units)	1.1	1.0	1.3
Sales price per unit	$10	$10	$12
Unit purchases (in millions of units)	1.0	1.1	1.2
Purchase price per unit	$7	$8	$9
Annual depreciation (in thousands of dollars)	$300	$300	$300
Cash dividends per share	$.15	$.15	$.15
Cash payments for additions to and replacement of plant and equipment (in thousands of dollars)	$350	$350	$350
Income tax rate	40%	40%	40%
Operating expense (exclusive of depreciation) as a percent of sales	15%	15%	15%
Common shares outstanding (in millions)	1	1	1

Instructions

[a] Prepare a schedule which illustrates and compares the following data for Elof Company under the FIFO and the LIFO inventory method for 1985–1987. Assume the company would begin LIFO at the beginning of 1985.

  [1] Year-end inventory balances.
  [2] Annual net income after taxes.
  [3] Earnings per share.
  [4] Cash balance.

Assume all sales are collected in the year of sale and all

purchases, operating expenses, and taxes are paid during the year incurred.

[b] Using the data above, your answer to [a], and any additional issues you believe need to be considered, prepare a report which recommends whether or not Elof Company should change to the LIFO inventory method. Support your conclusions with appropriate arguments.

(CMA adapted)

C8–4 Wein, Inc., employs the lower of cost or market (LCM) rule in valuing its ending inventory. The company has divided its products into two basic groups, with two grades in each group. The LCM rule has always been applied to each group of products. The following schedule presents the relevant inventory data as of December 31, 1985.

| | Group A | | Group B | |
	Grade 1	Grade 2	Grade 3	Grade 4
Number of units on hand (000 omitted)	50	100	100	200
Selling price per unit	$30	$ 40	$ 35	$ 20
Selling price less selling expenses per unit	24	36	30	16
Selling price less selling expenses and normal profit per unit	18	28	23	12
Replacement cost per unit at Dec. 31, 1985	20	25	26	17
Cost per unit	19	29	27	15

Instructions

[a] Explain in detail how to apply the LCM rule to inventories.

[b] Calculate the value of inventory as of December 31, 1985, by applying the LCM rule to each group of products.

(CMA adapted)

EXERCISES

E8–1 Listed below are selected accounts and their balances that appeared on the *unadjusted* trial balance of Boone, Inc., at April 30, 1985, the end of the company's annual fiscal period. Each account has a normal balance.

Sales returns	$ 10,000
Merchandise inventory	40,000
Transportation-out	14,000
Purchase returns	5,000
Sales	260,000
Advertising	15,000
Transportation-in	8,000
Purchases	135,000
Sales discounts	4,000
Sales commissions	12,000
Officers' salaries	40,000

A physical count on April 30 indicates that merchandise costing $28,000 is on hand.

Instructions

[a] Prepare the adjusting journal entry to record cost of goods sold on Boone's books at April 30, 1985.

[b] What account(s) in [a] will Boone have to close when it prepares closing entries on April 30, 1985?

[c] Indicate where the accounts you did *not* include in [a] should appear in Boone's financial statements.

[d] Prepare a schedule of cost of goods sold for Boone, Inc., for the year ending April 30, 1985.

[e] Calculate the amount of gross margin.

E8–2 Information pertaining to Rolf Manufacturing Corporation for the year ended December 31, 1985, appears below.

Indirect labor	$ 32,000
Salesmen's salaries	42,000
Raw materials inventory, Dec. 31	53,000
Depreciation of factory properties	30,000
Work-in-process, Jan. 1	40,000
Direct labor	110,000
Factory utilities	10,000
Finished goods, Dec. 31	88,000
Work-in-process, Dec. 31	33,000
Advertising expense	25,000
Raw materials inventory, Jan. 1	60,000
Indirect materials	7,000
Purchases of raw materials	400,000
Property taxes on factory	18,000
Finished goods, Jan. 1	68,000
Returned purchases of raw materials	10,000
Net sales	835,000
Miscellaneous factory expenses	4,000

Instructions

[a] Prepare in good form a schedule of cost of goods manufactured for the year ended December 31, 1985.
[b] Calculate the cost of goods sold.
[c] Calculate the amount of gross margin.

E8–3 The following information pertains to Charger Manufacturing Company during its first year of business.

Sales	10,000 units
Production	12,000 units
Cost per unit produced	
Direct materials	$1.00
Direct labor	3.00
Variable overhead	2.50
Fixed overhead	1.50

Instructions

Calculate the cost of the company's year-end inventory, assuming (1) absorption costing and (2) direct costing.

E8–4 Baby Love, Inc., is a wholesaler of infant car seats. At the beginning of 1985, the company's inventory consisted of 900 car seats priced at $10 each. During 1985 the following events occurred:
[1] Purchased 8,000 car seats on account at $10 each, terms n/30.
[2] Returned 500 defective car seats to supplier and received credit.
[3] Paid for 6,000 of the car seats purchased in [1].
[4] Sold 7,900 car seats on account for $16 each, terms n/30.
[5] Received 200 car seats returned by a customer and gave credit. The goods were in excellent condition and were therefore returned to regular inventory.
[6] Received cash for 6,800 of the car seats sold in item [4].
[7] Physical count at year-end revealed 600 units on hand.

Instructions

[a] Prepare journal entries (including adjusting entries) to record the above events on Baby Love's books, assuming that the company uses (1) a periodic system and (2) a perpetual system.
[b] What is the amount of the company's cost of goods sold for 1985 under (1) the periodic system and (2) the perpetual system? Explain any difference you find between the two numbers.

E8–5 Do-Right Company had the following purchase and sale transactions near the end of 1985:

No.	Transaction	Terms	Date Merchandise Shipped by Seller	Date Merchandise Received by Buyer
1	Purchase	FOB shipping point	12/31/85	1/5/86
2	Purchase	FOB destination	12/31/85	1/5/86
3	Sale	FOB shipping point	12/31/85	1/5/86
4	Sale	FOB destination	12/31/85	1/5/86

Instructions

For each transaction, indicate whether Do-Right Company should include the merchandise in its inventory at December 31, 1985. Assume that all dollar amounts are material. Explain your answer in each case.

E8–6 As the independent CPA for Yorkshire Corporation, state whether the goods in each of the following 1985 events should be included in Yorkshire's inventory for the fiscal year ending June 30, 1985. Explain your answer in each case.

[1]   Certain raw materials owned by Yorkshire were at Rollins Company for processing on June 30.

[2]   An order, accompanied by cash payment for the total sales price, was received on June 29 for goods that Yorkshire shipped on July 2.

[3]   Yorkshire made advance payments of $3,000 to suppliers for goods ordered but not shipped as of June 30.

[4]   On June 30 Yorkshire shipped goods FOB destination to Burbank Corporation, which received the goods on July 5.

[5]   On June 29 Willowbend Company shipped goods FOB shipping point to Yorkshire. Yorkshire received the goods on July 2.

[6]   Finished goods pledged as collateral for a 90-day loan from City & County Bank were on hand June 30.

[7]   Yorkshire had certain goods on hand for which it was acting as a selling agent for Swingline Company.

[8]   On June 26 Highlark, Inc., shipped goods FOB destination to Yorkshire. Yorkshire received the invoice on June 30 and the goods on July 2.

[9]   On June 29 H. B. Springer Company shipped goods FOB shipping point to Yorkshire. Yorkshire received the invoice and the goods on July 2.

[10] On June 30 Yorkshire sent goods to a consignee and prepaid the freight charges. The consignee received the goods on July 5.

E8–7   During an annual audit at December 31, 1985, you find the following transactions:

[1] Merchandise costing $1,822 was received on January 3, 1986, and the related purchase invoice recorded January 5. The invoice showed the shipment was made on December 29, 1985, FOB destination.

[2] Merchandise costing $625 was received on December 28, 1985, and the invoice was not recorded. You located it in the hands of the purchasing agent; it was marked "on consignment."

[3] A packing case containing a product costing $816 was not included in the physical inventory because it was marked "hold for shipping instructions." Your investigation revealed that the customer's order was dated December 18, 1985, but that the case was shipped and the customer billed on January 10, 1986. The product was a stock item of your client.

[4] Merchandise received on January 6, 1986, costing $720 was entered in the purchase register on January 7, 1986. The invoice showed shipment was made FOB

supplier's warehouse on December 31, 1985. Since it was not on hand December 31, it was not included in inventory.

[5] A special machine, made to order, was finished and in the shipping room on December 31, 1985. The customer was billed on that date and the machine excluded from inventory although it was shipped on January 4, 1986.

Instructions

Assume that the amount is material in each case. State whether the merchandise should be included in the client's inventory, and give the reason for your decision.

(AICPA adapted)

E8–8   JS Company, which uses a periodic inventory system, had the following merchandise transactions during December 1985:

Dec. 1   Purchased merchandise from YU Company for $1,000, terms 2/10, n/30.

    2   Purchased merchandise from ME Company for $2,000, terms 3/10, n/30.

   11   Paid ME Company for Dec. 2 purchase.

   30   Paid YU Company for Dec. 1 purchase.

Instructions

[a] Prepare the general journal entries to record the above transactions on the books of JS Company using (1) the *net method* of recording purchases and (2) the *gross method* of recording purchases.

[b] Discuss the accounting logic of the net method and the gross method of recording purchases.

E8–9   Pigskin, Inc., is a wholesaler of footballs. The following information pertains to the company's inventory during July 1985:

Balance, July 1	2,000 units @ $10
Purchase, July 12	2,000 units @ $12
Purchase, July 26	2,000 units @ $14
Balance, July 31	2,500 units

Instructions

Assuming that Pigskin uses a periodic inventory system, calculate each of the following amounts for July 1985:

[a] Ending inventory under FIFO.

[b] Cost of goods sold under LIFO.

[c] Ending inventory under LIFO.

[d] Cost of goods sold under FIFO.

E8-10 Bee Gee Company sells honey. The following information is available from the company's inventory records for 1985:

	Jars	Cost per Jar
Inventory, Jan. 1	200	$1.00
Purchases		
Jan. 23	300	1.50
Feb. 18	600	2.00
Mar. 2	500	2.50
Mar. 19	400	3.00

During the first quarter of 1985, the company sold 1,400 jars at $6 each. The company uses a periodic system. A physical inventory on March 31 reveals 600 jars on hand.

Instructions

Prepare a schedule in the form shown below and compute the missing values. Show all supporting computations.

	1st Quarter, 1985			
	Inventory Mar. 31, 1985	Sales	Cost of Goods Sold	Gross Margin
LIFO	$	$	$	$
FIFO				
Average cost				

E8-11 Cameco, Inc., uses Raw Material X in its production process. The following changes occurred in Cameco's inventory of Raw Material X during August 1985:

Aug. 1	Balance on hand	100 units @ $27
6	Purchased	300 units @ $25
14	Purchased	600 units @ $28
25	Purchased	400 units @ $21
Aug. 9	Issued to production	200 units @ ?
28	Issued to production	800 units @ ?

Instructions

[a] Assuming that Cameco maintains complete *perpetual* records for Raw Material X, compute the cost of the inventory at August 31 and the cost of materials issued to production during August using the (1) FIFO, (2) average cost, and (3) LIFO methods. (Round unit cost calculation to three places.)
[b] Assuming that Cameco uses a *periodic* system to account for Raw Material X, compute the cost of the inventory at August 31 and the cost of materials issued to production during August using the (1) FIFO, (2)

average cost, and (3) LIFO methods. (Round unit cost calculations to three places.)

E8-12 Streater Company began operations on January 1, 1982, and adopted the LIFO method of inventory pricing. The following additional facts pertain to the company:

Year	Reported Net Income	Ending Inventory Under LIFO	Ending Inventory That the Company Would Have Reported Under FIFO
1982	$30,000	$10,000	$15,000
1983	36,000	12,000	20,000
1984	45,000	18,000	11,000
1985	60,000	23,000	20,000

The company's income tax expense has consistently been 40% of income before taxes.

Instructions

Calculate the amount of net income the company would have reported for 1982, 1983, 1984, and 1985 under the FIFO method.

E8-13 For each of the following *independent* cases, determine the correct unit value for inventory valuation under the LCM rule:

Case	Historical Cost	Cost to Replace	Ceiling	Floor
A	$52	$48	$60	$50
B	78	75	86	72
C	39	37	48	40
D	80	82	79	71
E	21	24	27	22
F	18	17	20	16
G	60	61	59	50
H	89	84	97	88

E8-14 Cagle, Inc., compiled the following inventory information on November 30, 1985, the end of the company's fiscal year:

	Quantity	Unit Cost	Unit Market
Category A			
Product 1	400	$20	$18
Product 2	500	28	32
Category B			
Product 3	700	17	19
Product 4	600	18	14

Category C

Product 5	400	35	39
Product 6	300	31	28

Instructions

Compute Cagle's inventory valuation at November 30, assuming that the company applies the LCM rule to (1) each product, (2) major categories of products, and (3) the inventory as a whole.

E8–15 The following information pertains to O. J., Inc., at December 31, 1985:

Inventory, Jan. 1	$ 75,000
Purchases during 1985	325,000
Inventory, Dec. 31	
Cost	60,000
Market	48,000

Before 1985, application of the LCM rule never produced a need to write down the company's inventory to an amount below cost.

Instructions

Prepare the necessary *adjusting* journal entries to record cost of goods sold and to reflect the application of the LCM rule under each of the following assumptions:

[a] The company uses a *periodic* inventory system and applies the LCM rule using a loss account and a valuation allowance account.

[b] The company uses a *periodic* inventory system and applies the LCM rule using neither a loss account nor a valuation allowance account.

[c] The company uses a *perpetual* inventory system and applies the LCM rule using a loss account and a valuation allowance account.

[d] The company uses a *perpetual* inventory system and applies the LCM rule using neither a loss account nor a valuation allowance account.

E8–16 AMESSCO, Inc., began operations on January 1, 1984. The following data pertain to the company's first two years in business:

	Reported Amount	Correct Amount
Inventory		
Dec. 31, 1984	$ 20,000	$40,000
Dec. 31, 1985	35,000	35,000
Net Income		
For 1984	60,000	?
For 1985	66,000	?

Retained earnings

Dec. 31, 1984	60,000	?
Dec. 31, 1985	126,000	?

During 1984 and 1985 the company's income tax expense rate was 40%, and the company declared no dividends.

Instructions

Compute the correct amount for each of the following variables:
[a] Net income for 1984.
[b] Net income for 1985.
[c] Retained earnings, December 31, 1984.
[d] Retained earnings, December 31, 1985.

E8–17 Viking Company uses a periodic inventory system and sells its merchandise for 100% above cost. The following events occurred near the end of the first year of operations (Year 1):

[1] The company failed to record the credit purchase of goods to which it received legal title during Year 1. Although the goods had not been sold by year-end, the company did not include them in its ending inventory.

[2] The company failed to record the credit sales of goods to which it surrendered legal title during Year 1. The company included the goods in its ending inventory.

[3] The company included certain goods to which it had not yet received legal title in its ending inventory. The company did not record a purchase of these goods.

[4] The company recorded a credit purchase of goods to which it received legal title during Year 1. Although the goods had not been sold by year-end, the company did not include them in its ending inventory.

[5] The company recorded a credit purchase of goods to which it did not receive legal title during Year 1. These goods were included in the company's ending inventory.

[6] The company recorded a credit sale of goods to which it had not surrendered legal title as of the end of Year 1. These goods were excluded from the company's ending inventory.

Instructions

Set up a matrix like the one shown below. At the intersection of each row and column, indicate the effect of the event on the financial-statement variable at the end of Year 1, using the following code: O = Overstated, U = Understated, NE = No Effect. Treat each event independently. (*Note:* You should have 36 answers in the completed matrix.)

Event No.	Total Revenues	Total Expenses	Net Income	Total Assets	Total Liabilities	Total Stockholders' Equity
1						
2						
3						
4						
5						
6						

E8–18 The following data were taken from the financial statements of Prentiss, Inc., a calendar-year merchandising corporation:

[1] Balance sheet data:

	Dec. 31, 1984	Dec. 31, 1985
Trade accounts receivable, net	$ 84,000	$ 78,000
Inventory	150,000	140,000
Accounts payable, merchandise (credit)	(95,000)	(98,000)

[2] Total sales were $1,200,000 for 1985 and $1,100,000 for 1984. Cash sales were 20% of total sales each year.

[3] Cost of goods sold was $840,000 for 1985.

[4] Variable general and administrative (G&A) expenses for 1985 were $120,000. They have varied in proportion to sales; 50% have been paid in the year incurred and 50% the following year. Unpaid G&A expenses are *not* included in accounts payable above.

[5] Fixed G&A expenses, including $35,000 depreciation and $5,000 bad-debt expense, totaled $100,000 each year. Eighty percent of fixed G&A expenses involving cash were paid in the year incurred and 20% the following year. Each year there was a $5,000 bad-debt estimate and a $5,000 write-off. Unpaid G&A expenses are *not* included in accounts payable above.

Instructions

[a] Compute the amount of cash collected during 1985 resulting from total sales in 1984 and 1985.

[b] Compute the amount of cash disbursed during 1985 for purchases of merchandise.

[c] Compute the amount of cash disbursed during

1985 for variable and fixed general and administrative expenses.

(AICPA adapted)

E8–19 The controller of Robinson Company is discussing a comment you made in the course of presenting your audit report.

". . . and frankly," Mr. Fisher continued, "I agree that we, too, are responsible for finding ways to produce more relevant financial statements which are as reliable as the ones we now produce.

"For example, suppose the Company acquired a finished item for inventory for $40 when the general price-level index was 110. And, later, the item was sold for $75 when the general price-level index was 121 and the current replacement cost was $54. We could calculate a 'holding gain.' "

Instructions

[a] Explain to what extent and how current replacement costs already are used in generally accepted accounting principles to value inventories.

[b] Compute the amount of the holding gain in Mr. Fisher's example.

[c] Why is the use of current replacement cost for *both* inventories and cost of goods sold preferred by some accounting authorities to the generally accepted use of FIFO or LIFO?

[d] Why do some authorities believe that the present market resale (exit or output) price is a conceptual improvement on current replacement (entry or input) cost for inventory measurement?

(AICPA adapted)

E8–20 (Appendix A) On January 1, 1985, McDonald Company adopted the base stock method of accounting for its inventory of Raw Material A. On that date the inventory consisted of 5,000 units at $10 each; these figures are the base quantity and the base cost per unit, respectively. The company uses a periodic inventory system, and it prices increases and decreases in the base stock on a FIFO basis.

The company engaged in the following transactions involving the inventory of Raw Material A during the first quarter of 1985:

Jan.	8	Purchased	6,000 units @ $12
	21	Purchased	1,000 units @ $14
	28	Issued to production	5,000 units

Feb.	4	Purchased	7,000 units @ $16
	21	Issued to production	10,000 units
Mar.	3	Purchased	8,000 units @ $17
	18	Issued to production	6,000 units

Physical counts revealed 7,000 units of Raw Material A in inventory on January 31, 4,000 units on February 28, and 6,000 units on March 31.

Instructions

Calculate the cost of the ending inventory of Raw Material A at January 31, February 28, and March 31, 1985.

PROBLEMS

P8–1 Longview Stores, Inc., uses a periodic inventory system and a fiscal year ending September 30. On September 30, 1984, the company correctly reported inventory on hand costing $15,000. During the fiscal year ending September 30, 1985, the company recorded purchases of $39,000. A physical count on September 30, 1985, revealed that goods costing $18,000 were on hand. The following material events occurred between September 23 and October 7, 1985:

[1] Goods costing $1,500 that Longview was holding as a consignee were included in the physical count.

[2] An invoice for goods costing $2,300 was received and entered as a credit purchase on September 29. The goods arrived on October 2. The supplier shipped the goods FOB destination on September 27.

[3] An invoice for goods costing $1,800 was received and entered as a credit purchase on October 3. The goods arrived on that date and were in satisfactory condition. The invoice indicates that the supplier shipped the goods FOB shipping point on September 29.

[4] Goods that Longview specially purchased from an overseas supplier for ultimate sale to Capital Enterprises, Inc., were included in the physical count. A contract between Longview and Capital pertaining to the goods states that "title passes when buyer approves the goods." A representative from Capital Enterprises inspected and approved the goods in Longview's warehouse on September 28. Longview shipped the goods and recorded a sale on October 4. The goods cost $2,500 and were sold on credit for $3,600.

[5] Goods costing $900 and housed in a special storeroom were inadvertently overlooked when the physical count was taken.

[6] An invoice for goods costing $3,100 was received and entered as a credit purchase on September 28. The supplier shipped the goods FOB shipping point on September 26. The receiving report indicates that Longview received the goods on October 1.

Instructions

[a] Make all necessary correcting entries in general journal form for the fiscal year ending September 30, 1985. Assume that the adjusting entry for cost of goods sold has not been made and that the books for the year have not been closed.

[b] Compute the correct inventory amount for Longview's balance sheet dated September 30, 1985.

[c] Make the adjusting journal entry to record the cost of goods sold for the fiscal year ending September 30, 1985.

P8–2 Met Company of New York City uses a periodic inventory system and a fiscal year ending June 30. The company makes all its merchandise purchases and sales on credit. The following information is available from the company's inventory records:

Beginning inventory, July 1, 1984	$19,000
Purchases, July 1, 1984–June 30, 1985	80,000
Purchase returns, July 1, 1984–June 30, 1985	2,000
Ending inventory, June 30, 1985 (per physical count)	12,000

The following events occurred near the end of the fiscal year that ended on June 30, 1985:

[1] Goods costing $2,000 received on June 27 were recorded as a purchase twice.

[2] Goods shipped by rail from New York to a Los Angeles customer were recorded as a sale on June 30. The goods cost $1,800; the selling price was $3,000.

The goods were shipped on June 30, FOB Los Angeles. Met Company did not include these goods in its physical inventory.

[3] Goods costing $2,500 received on June 29 were recorded as a purchase on July 2.

[4] Goods costing $4,000 were recorded as a purchase on July 5. A Seattle supplier shipped the goods to New York by rail, FOB Seattle, on June 30.

[5] Goods costing $5,000 held by Yankee Company on consignment were not counted. Met Company recorded a sale of $8,000 when it shipped the goods to Yankee on June 23.

[6] Goods costing $3,800 were received on June 18 and returned for credit on June 20 because they were not satisfactory. Met Company did not record these events.

Instructions

[a] Make all necessary correcting entries in general journal form for the fiscal year ending June 30, 1985. Assume that the adjusting entry for the cost of goods sold has not been made and that the books for the year have not been closed.

[b] Compute the correct inventory amount for Met Company's balance sheet dated June 30, 1985.

[c] Make the adjusting journal entry to record the cost of goods sold for the fiscal year ending June 30, 1985.

P8-3 Ace, Inc., began operations in 1985. The company maintains complete perpetual records for its merchandise inventory. During 1985 Ace purchased merchandise having a gross invoice cost of $100,000. All purchases were made under the terms 2/10, n/30. Ace paid freight charges of $5,000 for the merchandise.

During the year, Ace paid for 80% of the merchandise within the discount period; it paid for the other 20% after the discount period had expired. The company sold 70% of the merchandise it acquired for cash of $120,000; the other 30% remains in inventory at year-end.

Instructions

[a] Prepare the general journal entries to record the above transactions on Ace's books using (1) the *net method* of recording purchases and (2) the *gross method* of recording purchases.

[b] What financial statement balances would Ace report at December 31, 1985, for sales, cost of goods sold, gross margin, discounts lost (or interest expense), and ending inventory under (1) the *net method* and (2) the *gross method?*

[c] Which method of recording purchases (net method or gross method) is generally regarded as theoretically superior? Why?

P8-4 The following information pertains to Model T calculators of IBU Corporation for the month of June, 1985:

Date	Calculators	Units	Unit Cost	Unit Selling Price
June 1	Beginning inventory	1,000	$52	
7	Purchase	3,000	50	
12	Sale	2,000		$100
17	Purchase	6,000	45	
22	Purchase	2,000	43	
28	Sale	7,000		100
30	Ending inventory	3,000		

Instructions

[a] Assuming that the company uses a *periodic* inventory system, calculate the cost of the ending inventory and the cost of goods sold using (1) the FIFO method, (2) the average cost method, and (3) the LIFO method. (Round unit cost calculations to three places.)

[b] Assuming that the company uses a *perpetual* inventory system, calculate the cost of the ending inventory *and* the cost of goods sold using (1) the FIFO method, (2) the average cost method, and (3) the LIFO method. (Round unit cost calculations to three places.)

[c] Calculate the amount of gross margin in [a-1, 2, 3] and [b-1, 2, 3].

[d] Assume that the inflation rate (i.e., the increase in the overall level of prices in the economy) was 1% during June 1985. Use your answer to [c] to logically evaluate the claim that the use of LIFO produces lower earnings during inflationary periods.

P8-5 The following inventory information pertains to Sleepy-Boy recliners of Case Furniture Company for the year ended December 31, 1985:

Date	Recliners	Units	Unit Cost	Total Cost
Jan. 1	Inventory on hand	200	$150	$ 30,000
Apr. 3	Purchase	300	175	52,500
Sept. 28	Purchase	400	200	80,000
	Available for sale	900		$162,500

The company sold 400 recliners on June 25 and 300 on December 10. A physical count on December 31 indicates that 200 recliners are on hand.

Instructions

[a] Assuming that the company uses a *periodic* inventory system, calculate the cost of the ending inventory *and* the cost of goods sold using (1) the FIFO method, (2) the average cost method, and (3) the LIFO method. (Round unit cost calculations to three places.)

[b] Assuming that the company uses a *perpetual* inventory system, calculate the cost of the ending inventory *and* the cost of goods sold using (1) the FIFO method, (2) the average cost method, and (3) the LIFO method. (Round unit cost calculations to three places.)

P8–6 Topanga Manufacturing Company manufactures two products: Mult and Tran. On December 31, 1984, Topanga used the FIFO inventory method. On January 1, 1985, Topanga changed to the LIFO method. The cumulative effect of this change is not determinable and, as a result, the ending inventury of 1984 under FIFO is also the beginning inventory for 1985 under LIFO. Any layers added during 1985 should be costed by reference to the first acquisitions of 1985, and any layers liquidated during 1985 should be considered a permanent liquidation.

The following information was available from Topanga's inventory records for the last two years:

	Mult		Tran	
	Units	**Unit Cost**	**Units**	**Unit Cost**
1984 Purchases				
Jan. 7	5,000	$4.00	22,000	$2.00
Apr. 16	12,000	4.50		
Nov. 8	17,000	5.00	18,500	2.50
Dec. 13	10,000	6.00		
1985 Purchases				
Feb. 11	3,000	7.00	23,000	3.00
May 20	8,000	7.50		
Oct. 15	20,000	8.00		
Dec. 23			15,500	3.50
Units on Hand				
Dec. 31, 1984	15,000		14,500	
Dec. 31, 1985	16,000		13,000	

Instructions

Compute the effect of the change from the FIFO to the LIFO inventory method on income before income taxes for the year ended December 31, 1985.

(AICPA adapted)

P8–7 The controller of the Investor Corporation, a retail company, made three different schedules of gross margin for the first quarter ended September 30, 1985. These schedules appear below.

	Sales ($10 per unit)	Cost of Goods Sold	Gross Margin
Schedule A	$280,000	$118,550	$161,450
Schedule B	280,000	116,900	163,100
Schedule C	280,000	115,750	164,250

The computation of cost of goods sold in each schedule is based on the following data.

	Units	Cost per Unit	Total Cost
Beginning inventory, July 1	10,000	$4.00	$40,000
Purchase, July 25	8,000	4.20	33,600
Purchase, Aug. 15	5,000	4.13	20,650
Purchase, Sept. 5	7,000	4.30	30,100
Purchase, Sept. 25	12,000	4.25	51,000

The president of the corporation cannot understand how three different gross margins can be computed from the same set of data. As controller, you have explained that the three schedules are based on three different assumptions concerning the flow of inventory costs: FIFO, LIFO, and weighted average. Schedules A, B, and C were not necessarily prepared in this sequence of cost flow assumptions.

Instructions

Prepare three separate schedules computing cost of goods sold and supporting schedules. Show the composition of the ending inventory under each of the three cost flow assumptions.

(AICPA adapted)

P8–8 Windjammer Company manufactures four products and prices its inventory using the lower of average cost or market value. The company maintains a normal profit margin rate of 20% of selling price. Windjammer's accountant gathered the following information, all on a per unit basis, at December 31, 1985:

Product	Historical Cost	Current Replacement Cost	Estimated Selling Price	Estimated Cost to Dispose
A	$18	$22	$30	$ 3
B	28	24	40	6
C	50	48	70	10
D	80	82	90	12

Instructions

[a] Prepare a schedule to determine the correct unit values for the inventory valuation of each product under the LCM rule. ·

[b] Explain the rationale for the use of selling prices when applying the LCM rule.

P8–9   Selected items of merchandise information for eight independent cases (A through H) appear below. In each case the normal profit margin rate is 30% of selling price.

Instructions

Set up a table similar to the one shown below and compute the missing values.

Case	Estimated Selling Price	Estimated Cost to Dispose	Ceiling	Allowance for Normal Profit Margin	Floor	Replacement Cost	Market	Historical Cost	LCM
A	$60		$50			$52		$51	
B		$5		$15		28		33	
C			18	6			$16		$15
D	30	4						20	18
E	10		9			7		8	
F		6		12		35			32
G			69	24		72		70	
H	70	9				37		42	

P8–10 The following inventory information pertains to Benjamin Enterprises at December 31, 1985:

		Per Unit			
	Quantity	Original Cost	Cost to Replace	Net Realizable Value	Floor
Office products					
Product A	500	$25	$21	$27	$23
Product B	300	31	33	36	30
Home products					
Product C	600	14	18	19	13
Product D	800	21	22	20	15

Instructions

[a] Determine the inventory valuation at December 31, 1985, assuming that the company applies the LCM rule to (1) each product, (2) major categories of products, and (3) the inventory as a whole.

[b] The accountant for Benjamin Enterprises is trying to determine which one of the three amounts in [a] he should use in the company's published financial statements. What major factors should the accountant consider?

P8–11 Condensed income statements for Electric Light Company for 1980–1985 appear below.

| | Year Ending December 31 | | | | | |
	1980	*1981*	*1982*	*1983*	*1984*	*1985*
Net sales	$125,000	$132,000	$141,000	$156,000	$163,000	$176,000
Cost of goods sold	75,000	80,000	85,000	94,000	98,000	106,000
Gross margin	50,000	52,000	56,000	62,000	65,000	70,000
Selling and administrative expenses	30,000	31,000	34,000	39,000	41,000	45,000
Pretax income	20,000	21,000	22,000	23,000	24,000	25,000
Income taxes (40%)	8,000	8,400	8,800	9,200	9,600	10,000
Net income	$ 12,000	$ 12,600	$ 13,200	$ 13,800	$ 14,400	$ 15,000

The above statements were prepared without knowledge of the inventory errors shown below.

Date	Inventory
Dec. 31, 1979	Correctly stated
Dec. 31, 1980	Understated $5,000
Dec. 31, 1981	Overstated $8,000
Dec. 31, 1982	Understated $6,000
Dec. 31, 1983	Correctly stated
Dec. 31, 1984	Overstated $12,000
Dec. 31, 1985	Overstated $3,000

Instructions

[a] Using the condensed format shown above, prepare corrected income statements for Electric Light Company for 1980–1985.

[b] Describe the overall impact that the correction of the inventory errors in [a] has on the company's earnings trend.

P8–12 You have been asked to review the records and prepare corrected financial statements for Graber Corporation. The books of account are in agreement with the following balance sheet:

Graber Corporation
BALANCE SHEET
December 31, 1985

Assets

Cash	$ 5,000
Accounts receivable	10,000
Notes receivable	3,000
Inventory	25,000
	$43,000

Liabilities and Capital

Accounts payable	$ 2,000
Notes payable	4,000
Capital stock	10,000
Retained earnings	27,000
	$43,000

A review of Graber's books indicates that the following errors and omissions had *not* been corrected during the applicable years:

Dec. 31	Inventory Overvalued	Inventory Undervalued	Prepaid Expense	Unearned Revenue	Accrued Expense	Accrued Revenue
1982	—	$6,000	$900	—	$200	—
1983	$7,000	—	700	$400	75	$125
1984	8,000	—	500	—	100	—
1985	—	9,000	600	300	50	150

According to the books, profits are $7,500 in 1983, $6,500 in 1984, and $5,500 in 1985. No dividends were declared during these years and no adjustments were made to retained earnings.

Instructions

Prepare a worksheet to develop the correct profits for 1983, 1984, and 1985 and the adjusted balance sheet accounts as of December 31, 1985. (Ignore possible income tax effects.)

(AICPA adapted)

P8–13 You have been engaged to audit Y Company for the year ended December 31, 1985. Y Company, a wholesale chemical business, makes all sales at 25% over cost.

Shown below are portions of the client's sales and purchases accounts for the calendar year 1985.

Sales

Date	Reference	Amount	Date	Reference	Amount
12/31	Closing entry	699,860	Balance forward		658,320
			12/27	SI#965	5,195
			12/28	SI#966	19,270
			12/28	SI#967	1,302
			12/31	SI#969	5,841
			12/31	SI#970	7,922
			12/31	SI#971	2,010
		699,860			699,860

Purchases

Date	Reference	Amount	Date	Reference	Amount
Balance forward		360,300	12/31	Closing entry	385,346
12/28	RR#1059	3,100			
12/30	RR#1061	8,965			
12/31	RR#1062	4,861			
12/31	RR#1063	8,120			
		385,346			385,346

RR = Receiving report.
SI = Sales invoice.

You observed the physical inventory of goods in the warehouse on December 31, 1985, and were satisfied that it was properly taken. When you conducted a sales and purchases cutoff test (to determine that these transactions are recorded in the proper period), you found that at December 31, 1985, the last receiving report which had been used was no. 1063 and that no shipments had been made on any sales invoices with numbers larger than no. 968. You also obtained the following additional information:

[1] Included in the physical inventory were chemicals which had been purchased and received on receiving report no. 1060 but for which an invoice was not received until 1986. The cost was $2,183.

[2] In the warehouse at December 31, 1985, were goods which had been sold and paid for by the customer but which were not shipped until 1986. They were all sold on sales invoice no. 965 and were not inventoried.

[3] On the evening of December 31, 1985, there were two cars on Y Company siding:

[a] Car #AR38162 was unloaded on January 2, 1986, and received on receiving report no. 1063. The freight was paid by the vendor.

[b] Car #BAE74123 was loaded and sealed on December 31, 1985, and was switched off the company's siding on January 2, 1986. The sales price was $12,700 and the freight was paid by the customer. This order was sold on sales invoice no. 968.

[4] Two cars of chemicals enroute to Z Pulp and Paper Company were temporarily stranded on December 31, 1985, on a railroad siding. They were sold on sales invoice no. 966 and the terms were FOB destination.

[5] A truckload of material enroute to Y Company on December 31, 1985, was received on receiving report no. 1064. The material was shipped FOB destination and freight of $75 was paid by Y Company. However, the freight was deducted from the purchase price of $975.

[6] Chemicals exposed to rain in transit and deemed unsalable were included in the physical inventory. Their invoice cost was $1,250 and freight charges of $350 had been paid on the chemicals.

Instructions

[a] Compute the adjustments which should be made to the client's physical inventory at December 31, 1985.

[b] Prepare the adjusting entries required as of December 31, 1985.

(AICPA adapted)

P8–14 Renken Company cans two food commodities which it stores at various warehouses. The company uses a perpetual inventory system under which the finished goods inventory is charged with production and credited for sales at standard cost. The detail of the finished goods inventory is maintained on punched cards by the tabulating department in units and dollars for the various warehouses.

The accounting department receives copies of daily production reports and sales invoices. Units are then extended at standard cost and a summary of the day's activity is posted to the Finished Goods Inventory general ledger control account. Next the sales invoices and production reports are sent to the tabulating department for processing. Every month the control account and detailed tab records are reconciled and adjustments recorded. The last reconciliation and adjustments were made at November 30, 1985.

Your CPA firm observed the taking of the physical inventory at all locations on December 31, 1985. The inventory count began at 4:00 p.m. and was completed at 8:00 p.m. The company's figure for the physical inventory is $331,400. The general ledger control account balance at December 31 was $373,900, and the final "tab run" of the inventory punched cards showed a total of $392,300.

Unit cost data for the company's two products are as follows:

Product	Standard Cost
A	$2
B	3

A review of December transactions disclosed the following:

[1] Sales invoice no. 1301, Dec. 2, was priced at standard cost for $11,700 but was listed on the accounting department's daily summary at $11,200.

[2] A production report for $23,900, Dec. 15, was processed twice in error by the tabulating department.

[3] Sales invoice no. 1423, Dec. 9, for 1,200 units of product A, was priced at a standard cost of $1.50 per unit by the accounting department. The tabulating department corrected the error but did not notify the accounting department of the error.

[4] A shipment of 3,400 units of Product A was invoiced by the billing department as 3,000 units on sales invoice no. 1504, Dec. 27. The error was discovered by your review of transactions.

[5] On December 27 the Memphis warehouse notified the tabulating department to remove 2,200 unsalable units of Product A from the finished goods inventory, which it did without receiving a special invoice from the accounting department. The accounting department received a copy of the Memphis warehouse noti-

fication on December 29 and prepared a special invoice which was processed in the normal manner. The units were not included in the physical inventory.

[6] A report for the production on January 3 of 2,500 units of Product B was processed for the Omaha plant as of December 31.

[7] A shipment of 300 units of Product B was made from the Portland warehouse to Ken's Markets, Inc., at 8:30 p.m. on December 31 as an emergency service. The sales invoice was processed as of December 31. The client prefers to treat the transaction as a sale in 1985.

[8] The working papers of the auditor observing the physical count at the Chicago warehouse revealed that 700 units of Product B were omitted from the client's physical count. The client concurred that the units were omitted in error.

[9] A sales invoice for 600 units of Product A shipped from the Newark warehouse was mislaid and was not processed until January 5. The units involved were shipped on December 30.

[10] The physical inventory of the St. Louis warehouse excluded 350 units of Product A marked "reserved." Investigation revealed that this merchandise was being stored as a convenience for Steve's Markets, Inc., a customer. This merchandise, which has not been recorded as a sale, is billed as it is shipped.

[11] A shipment of 10,000 units of Product B was made on December 27 from the Newark warehouse to the Chicago warehouse. The shipment arrived on January 6 but had been excluded from the physical inventories.

Instructions

Prepare a worksheet to reconcile the balances for the physical inventory, Finished Goods Inventory general ledger control account, and tabulating department's detail of finished goods inventory ("tab run"). Use the format shown below.

	Physical Inventory	General Ledger Control Account	Tabulating Department's Detail of Inventory
Balance per client	$331,400	$373,900	$392,300

(AICPA adapted)

P8–15 You are engaged in an audit of Wayne Manufacturing Company for the year ended December 31, 1985. To reduce the workload at year-end, the company took its annual physical inventory under your

observation on November 30, 1985. The company's Inventory account, which includes raw material and work-in-process, is on a perpetual basis and the FIFO method of pricing is used. There is no finished goods inventory. The company's physical inventory revealed that the book inventory of $60,570 was understated by $3,000. To avoid distorting the interim financial statements, the company decided not to adjust the book inventory, except for obsolete inventory items, until year-end.

Your audit revealed the following information about the November 30 inventory:

[1] Pricing tests showed that the physical inventory was overpriced by $2,200.

[2] Footing and extension errors resulted in a $150 understatement of the physical inventory.

[3] Direct labor included in the physical inventory amounted to $10,000. Overhead was included at the rate of 200% of direct labor. You determined that the amount of direct labor was correct and the overhead rate was proper.

[4] The physical inventory included obsolete materials recorded at $250. During December these obsolete materials were removed from the inventory account and charged to Cost of Sales.

Your audit also disclosed the following information about the December 31 inventory:

[1] Total debits to certain accounts during December are listed below:

Purchases	$24,700
Direct labor	12,100
Manufacturing overhead	25,200
Cost of sales	68,600

[2] The cost of sales of $68,600 included direct labor of $13,800.

[3] Normal scrap loss on established product lines is negligible. However, a special order started and completed during December had excessive scrap loss of $800 which was charged to Manufacturing Overhead.

Instructions

[a] Compute the correct amount of the physical inventory at November 30, 1985.

[b] Without prejudice to your solution to [a], assume that the correct amount of the physical inventory at November 30, 1985, was $57,700. Compute the amount of the inventory at December 31, 1985.

(AICPA adapted)

P8–16 The president of Rab Company, your client, asks for your assistance because he believes that a former employee has stolen a large quantity of finished goods. The employee, a production manager, who disappeared on May 1, 1985, had access to all production and inventory records. The president needs the information to file a claim with the insurance company.

The Rab Company manufactures two types of kitchen chairs, "All Steel" and "Open Seat." The legs and frames of the chairs are made of ⅞" metal tubing which is purchased in both random mill lengths and precut 72" lengths. Each chair has four 24" legs. The All Steel chair frame is made from a 72" length of tubing; the Open Seat chair frame requires a 36" length of tubing. The scrap loss in cutting random mill lengths has averaged 3%. Other fabrication losses are negligible.

Under your observation a physical inventory is taken promptly and by applying cutoff techniques, you determine the following physical inventory on May 1, 1985. Other chair components are not subject to verification. Your working papers for the 1984 audit show the following inventory quantities on December 31, 1984:

	May 1, 1985	Dec. 31, 1984
Raw materials		
72" lengths of tubing	8,500	13,500
Random mill lengths	34,800 feet	9,800 feet
Work-in-process		
Individual legs	9,700	2,900
All Steel chair frames	800	1,300
Open Seat chair frames	100	300
Finished goods		
All Steel chairs	5,500	10,700
Open Seat chairs	1,300	900

Metal tubing purchases during 1985 amounted to 202,000 pieces of 72" lengths and 125,000 feet of random mill lengths. The company shipped 100,000 chairs to customers during 1985. Of this number, 10,000 were Open Seat chairs selling for $3.75 each. The All Steel chair sells for $5 each. Your work papers show that Rab Company has generally added 25% to its manufacturing cost to arrive at selling prices.

Instructions

For insurance claim purposes, compute the dollar loss sustained by Rab Company. Assume that the types of chairs missing were in the same ratio as the sales.

(AICPA adapted)

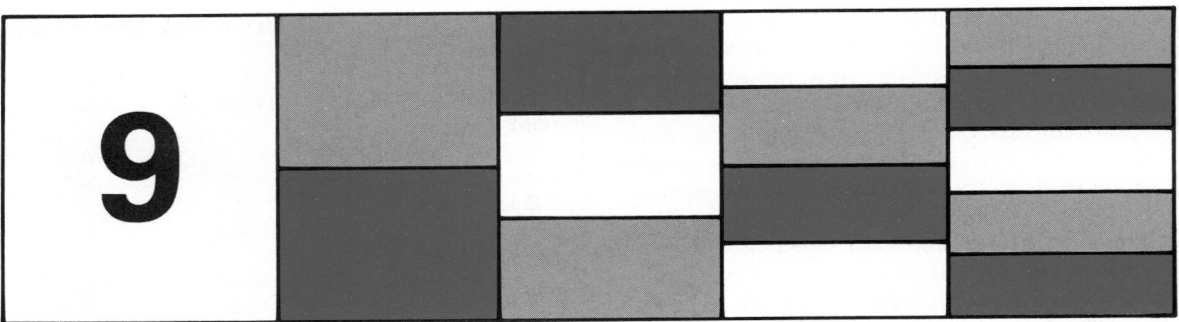

INVENTORIES: ADDITIONAL VALUATION METHODS

Objective

To discuss and illustrate each of the following methods of inventory valuation:

1. The specific goods pooling method of applying the last-in, first-out (LIFO) concept.
2. The dollar-value LIFO method.
3. The conventional retail method.
4. The retail LIFO method.
5. The gross margin method.

The previous chapter provided an overview of basic inventory valuation methods. The objective of this chapter is to explain and illustrate several additional methods of inventory valuation. These methods are the specific goods pooling method of applying the last-in, first-out (LIFO) concept, the dollar-value LIFO method, the conventional retail method, the retail LIFO method, and the gross margin method. Some of these methods may initially appear to be more complex than they really are. Although the methods may initially seem complex, one reason that companies use them is to simplify the enormous clerical tasks that accounting for inventory can produce.

LIFO APPLICATION METHODS

In Chapter 8 we discussed the **specific goods method** of applying LIFO. According to this method, LIFO is applied to each product in a company's inventory. Although the specific goods method is conceptually simple, its practical application is usually confined to inventories of only a small variety of products. When a company has many kinds of products, use of the specific goods method can create a large clerical burden. A company that handles hundreds of different goods, for example, usually wants a more efficient method of applying the basic LIFO concept. In this chapter we present three commonly used methods of applying LIFO: (1) the specific goods pooling method; (2) the dollar-value LIFO method; and (3) the retail LIFO method. Each method is acceptable for income tax purposes and for financial reporting purposes in accordance with generally accepted accounting principles (GAAP). Most LIFO companies use the same method of applying LIFO for financial reporting purposes as they use for income tax purposes. We present the first two methods below; the third is presented in a later section on the retail method. Throughout our discussion we shall focus primarily on the general concepts that underlie these methods. In practice, many detailed rules and regulations of the income tax law pertain to the use of LIFO. An accountant who wants to apply the LIFO method must thoroughly understand these rules and regulations and their implications.

Specific Goods Pooling Method

Under this method the inventory is divided into **pools,** each of which must consist of **substantially identical goods.** Each **pool,** rather than each product, then becomes the basis for applying LIFO. When a pool is established, its units are assigned a weighted average of all costs in the pool. The quantity of goods in the pool then forms the original, or base, LIFO layer. If the *total number of units in the pool* at the end of a period exceeds the number at the beginning, the increase is considered a new LIFO inventory layer. The new layer is costed using the weighted average unit cost of purchases of pooled items during the period. In contrast, if the *total number of units in the pool* at the end of a period is less than the number at the beginning, the decrease is removed from previously established inventory layers and charged to cost of goods sold in a last-in, first-out sequence. Thus, the last layer added is assumed to be the first to be sold.

To illustrate the specific goods pooling method and compare it with the specific goods method, consider the data of Cameron Corporation on page 344. Given these data, use of the *specific goods method* of applying LIFO (as discussed in Chapter 8) produces the ending inventory amounts shown in Exhibit 9–1. Note carefully that the specific goods method requires us to apply LIFO to each product (A and B) in the inventory. Each year we must sum the LIFO ending inventory costs of each product to get the total LIFO cost of the inventory.

In contrast, assuming that Products A and B constitute a *pool,* use of the *specific goods pooling method* of applying LIFO yields the results shown in Exhibit 9–2.

Observe that the results differ between the two methods of applying LIFO. Under the specific goods pooling method, the initial inventory (on December 31, 1983) consists of

| | Product A | | Product B | |
	Number of Units	Unit Cost	Number of Units	Unit Cost
Inventory, Dec. 31, 1983	300	$5	100	$4
Purchases during 1984:	400	6	200	5
	200	7	400	6
Available for sale during 1984	900		700	
Sales during 1984	500		400	
Inventory, Dec. 31, 1984	400		300	
Purchases during 1985:	200	7	400	6
	400	8	200	7
Available for sale during 1985	1,000		900	
Sales during 1985	900		700	
Inventory, Dec. 31, 1985	100		200	

400 total units (300 units of Product A + 100 units of Product B). We have assigned these units a weighted average of all costs in the pool, thereby constructing a base layer of 400 total units at $4.75 each. At the end of 1984, a total of 700 units are in the pool (400 units of Product A + 300 units of Product B). The increase of *300 total units* (700 total units − 400 total units) from the *beginning inventory* is costed at the weighted average unit cost of purchases made during 1984. We now have two LIFO layers, the base plus the layer added in 1984. The inventory at the end of 1985 declined to 300 total units (100 units of Product A + 200 units of Product B). As a result, the entire 1984 layer and part of the base layer is charged to cost of goods sold. The December 31, 1985, inventory therefore consists of only the remaining portion of the base layer.

Our illustration of how to apply the specific goods pooling method with LIFO was, of course, simplified. A company with hundreds of inventory items would likely have several pools, each of which would contain many items that are substantially identical. Such a company could realize substantial clerical savings by using the pooling method. When more than one pool exists, the LIFO costs of each pool are summed to obtain the LIFO cost of the entire inventory.

Dollar-Value LIFO Method

Under the specific goods method and the specific goods pooling method, LIFO is applied on the basis of changes in the *quantity of physical units* in the inventory. The former method

---

EXHIBIT 9–1
LIFO—Specific Goods Method

Inventory	Product A	+	Product B	=	Total LIFO Cost
Dec. 31, 1983	300 units @ $5 = $1,500	+	100 units @ $4 = $ 400	=	$1,900
Dec. 31, 1984	300 units @ $5 = $1,500		100 units @ $4 = $ 400		
	100 units @ 6 = 600		200 units @ 5 = 1,000		
	$2,100	+	$1,400	=	$3,500
Dec. 31, 1985	100 units @ $5 = $ 500		100 units @ $4 = $ 400		
			100 units @ 5 = 500		
	$ 500	+	$ 900	=	$1,400

	EXHIBIT 9–2		
	LIFO—Specific Goods Pooling Method		
	Specific Goods Pool		
	(Products A and B)		
Inventory	Number of Units	Unit Cost	Total LIFO Cost
Dec. 31, 1983	400	$4.75*	$1,900 (base layer)
Dec. 31, 1984	400	4.75	$1,900 (base layer)
	300	6.00**	1,800 (1984 layer)
	700		$3,700
Dec. 31, 1985	300	4.75	$1,425 (remaining base layer)

*(300 units @ $5 + 100 units @ $4) ÷ 400 units = $4.75.
**(400 units @ $6 + 200 units @ $7 + 200 units @ $5 + 400 units @ $6) ÷ 1,200 units = $6.00.

focuses on changes in the quantity of each product, while the latter focuses on changes in the quantity of goods in designated pools. The dollar-value LIFO method is also applied to goods in **designated pools.** However, it is applied on the basis of **inventory changes measured in cost dollars, not in physical units.**

In 1938, LIFO was initially accepted as a tax method designed to allow companies to charge to expense the higher costs associated with the most recent inventory acquisitions. Dollar-value LIFO was developed during the 1940s as a way to allow companies whose products have style or design changes, such as clothing and automobiles, to obtain the tax benefits of LIFO. If these companies were required to apply LIFO on the basis of specific physical units in inventory, old inventory costs would be expensed whenever the number of physical units of a product declined because of style or design changes. In essence, the dollar-value LIFO method helps companies save taxes by giving them a greater opportunity to preserve old inventory costs while charging the more recent (and presumably higher) costs to expense. This opportunity to preserve old inventory costs exists because dollar-value LIFO is applied on the basis of dollars invested in broadly defined pools of goods. It is not applied to specific physical units of inventory.

A complicating factor when applying dollar-value LIFO is that the cost dollar is seldom a stable device with which to measure inventory changes. Since the ability of a dollar to acquire inventory usually changes over time, we cannot accurately measure inventory changes simply by comparing cost dollars incurred in different time periods. For this reason the dollar-value method requires us to measure all inventory changes in **cost dollars of the same year,** commonly called the **base year.** The term "base-year cost" refers to the total cost, determined as of the *beginning* of the period in which a company adopts the dollar-value LIFO method, of all inventory items in a designated pool. Inland Steel Company, for example, adopted the dollar-value LIFO method in 1950. The company therefore determines its base-year inventory costs as of January 1, 1950.

The accountant uses a year-end **conversion factor** to convert **cost dollars of the current year** to **cost dollars of the base year.** This factor measures changes in the level of inventory cost prices that have occurred since the base period. It is computed as follows:

$$\text{Conversion factor} = \frac{\text{Current year-end specific price index}}{\text{Base-year specific price index}}$$

Note that the conversion factor is derived by using a *specific* price index. A specific rather than a general price index is used because the direction and magnitude of changes in a company's inventory cost prices may differ from those of the overall level of prices in the economy.

Ideally, a company should construct its own **internal index** at the end of each year using the **double extension method.** Under this method we multiply the actual quantity of each inventory item on hand at year-end by its current-year unit cost. Next, we multiply the actual quantity of each item by its base-year unit cost. We now have two columns of extensions, which explains the name "double extension method." We then total the extensions and divide the total current-year cost by the total base-year cost to derive the current year-end specific price index. We illustrate these procedures in Exhibit 9–3 for a simplified inventory of only three items.

Many companies have numerous inventory items and find it impractical to double-extend their entire inventory in the manner shown in Exhibit 9–3. For these companies a year-end specific price index may be developed by using only a representative **sample** of inventory items. If sampling is not practical, a company may rely on a published (external) price index if the company can show that the index is a suitable measure of the change in cost prices of the specific goods that it actually purchases or produces.

Over time the dollar-value LIFO method may produce several inventory layers, each of which is expressed in *cost dollars rather than physical units.* Therefore, because of changes in the mix of physical units in the inventory, the dollar-value LIFO cost of the ending inventory may exceed that of the beginning inventory even though the total number of physical units in the inventory has declined during the period. The accounting records must permit us to associate each layer with the conversion factor in existence when the layer was constructed.

To implement the dollar-value LIFO method, the accountant must measure in *base-year costs* both the beginning and the ending inventories of the current period. If the ending inventory exceeds the beginning inventory when each is measured in base-year costs, an inventory increment (measured in base-year costs) has occurred. Since the increment occurred in the current year, we price it at current-year costs. To do this, we multiply the

EXHIBIT 9–3
Double Extension Method

Item	Actual Quantity at Year-end	Unit Cost		Total Cost	
		Current Year	*Base Year*	*Current Year*	*Base Year*
A	1,000	$16	$15	$16,000	$15,000
B	2,500	11	10	27,500	25,000
C	500	25	20	12,500	10,000
				$56,000	$50,000

Year-end specific price index = $56,000 ÷ $50,000 = 112%.

Year-end conversion factor = $\frac{112}{100}$ = 1.12.[1]

---

[1]Observe that the base is 100 ($50,000 ÷ $50,000 = 100%, or 1.00) when a company develops its own internal index. When the base is 100, the year-end conversion factor is the same as the year-end specific price index (112% = 1.12). If the base is not 100, as is often the case when a company relies on an *external* price index, the year-end conversion factor will differ from the year-end specific price index.

increment by the current-year conversion factor to obtain a new LIFO inventory layer.[2] We then add this layer to those in existence at the beginning of the current period to get the ending dollar-value LIFO inventory amount.

Conversely, if the ending inventory is less than the beginning inventory when each is measured in base-year costs, a reduction in inventory has occurred in the current period. This reduction requires that we charge previously established LIFO layers to cost of goods sold in a last-in, first-out sequence at amounts that reflect the cost prices in existence when the layers were constructed.

Three major reasons explain why many companies use the dollar-value LIFO method. First, the method greatly eases the clerical burden of applying LIFO to specific goods. Second, since the method maintains inventory layers in cost dollars instead of physical units, it gives a company some room to change the composition of inventory without expensing old (and presumably lower) inventory costs. Finally, the dollar-value LIFO method permits considerable flexibility when grouping inventory items into pools. Under the specific goods pooling method, goods in each pool must be substantially identical. Under dollar-value LIFO, pooled goods must only be *similar*. Thus, dollar-value LIFO enables a company to pool many more items than does the specific goods pooling method. The more items that a company pools, the more room there is for increases in the quantity of certain goods to offset decreases in the quantity of others. As a result, dollar-value LIFO helps to preserve old inventory costs, thereby helping a company to realize more of the tax benefits that it usually seeks from using LIFO.

To illustrate the pooling concepts that may be applied under LIFO, assume that Brian Enterprises sells ten different models of *each* of the following product lines: sofas, chairs, lamps, tents, exercise bicycles, and canoes. Under the specific goods method of applying LIFO, pools would not exist and the company would therefore apply LIFO to each of its sixty different products ($10 \times 6 = 60$). Under the specific goods pooling method, the company would likely apply LIFO to six pools: sofas, chairs, lamps, tents, exercise bicycles, and canoes. Finally, under dollar-value LIFO, the company would likely apply LIFO to only two pools: home furniture (sofas, chairs, and lamps) and sporting goods (tents, exercise bicycles, and canoes).

It is possible to include the entire inventory in a single pool under the dollar-value LIFO method. Most companies have several pools, however. A company that has more than one pool must apply the dollar-value method to each pool. The ending dollar-value inventory amounts determined in the various pools are summed to get the overall ending inventory at LIFO cost.

Application Procedures

The following five steps summarize the procedures used to apply the dollar-value LIFO method to a designated pool of goods:

Step 1. Price the ending inventory at the current-year cost. A good measure of this cost is obtained by multiplying the physical quantities on hand by the actual unit costs of the goods most recently purchased or produced.

Step 2. Obtain an appropriate year-end conversion factor (as explained earlier in the chapter) which measures the change in inventory *cost prices* that has occurred since the base period.

---

[2]Remember that we derive the current-year's conversion factor by dividing the current *year-end* specific price index by the base-year specific price index. Use of the year-end (rather than beginning-of-year) index to derive the conversion factor that we use to price inventory increments may imply that we are using the FIFO (rather than the LIFO) method. Nevertheless, the year-end index is the one that companies use under the dollar-value *LIFO* method.

Step 3. Restate the ending inventory from current-year cost (as determined in Step 1) to base-year cost by dividing the results in Step 1 by the year-end conversion factor obtained in Step 2.

Step 4. From the ending inventory priced at base-year cost (as determined in Step 3), subtract *the inventory on hand at the beginning of the current period, also priced at base-year cost.*

Step 5. Compute the cost of the ending dollar-value LIFO inventory as follows:

1. If the difference in Step 4 is zero, inventory is unchanged. Thus, the ending dollar-value LIFO inventory valuation is the same as the beginning valuation.

2. If the difference in Step 4 is positive, inventory has increased. Price the increase by multiplying the difference obtained in Step 4 by the year-end conversion factor obtained in Step 2. Then add the result to the beginning dollar-value LIFO inventory valuation to get the correct ending valuation at LIFO cost.

3. If the difference in Step 4 is negative, inventory has decreased. Subtract the decrease from the most recently acquired layer(s) at base-year cost in a last-in, first-out sequence. The correct dollar-value LIFO ending inventory valuation will be the remaining layers multiplied by their respective conversion factors.

Application of the five steps summarized above will produce the correct dollar-value LIFO ending inventory amount. One may then determine cost of goods sold residually by subtracting the ending inventory amount from the cost of goods available for sale.

An Illustration

To illustrate the procedures for deriving an ending dollar-value LIFO inventory, let's assume that a company adopts the dollar-value LIFO method on January 1, 1982. The company's inventory priced at current costs on that date was $10,000, and the specific price index derived internally was 100. This inventory is subsequently regarded as the base LIFO layer from which changes may occur. The current-year cost of the ending inventory, as well as the year-end conversion factor for December 31, 1982, and for each of the succeeding three years, are given below.

December 31	Ending Inventory at Current-Year Cost*	Year-End Conversion Factor**
1982	$12,480	1.20
1983	16,950	1.50
1984	14,420	1.40
1985	14,040	1.30

---

*Obtained by multiplying the physical quantities on hand by the actual unit costs of the goods most recently acquired.
**Obtained by dividing the current-year cost of the entire ending inventory by the total base-year cost of the same ending inventory items. In other words, each year-end conversion factor was derived by applying the double extension method, as illustrated in Exhibit 9–3.

We use this basic information in Exhibit 9–4 to illustrate how to compute the ending dollar-value LIFO inventory amounts. We have keyed the illustration to the five steps presented earlier.

Observe carefully the following major points:

1. On December 31, 1982, the application of Step 4 shows an inventory increase of $400 expressed in *base-year costs.* In Step 5 we price this increase using the conversion factor from Step 2 (1.20). The inventory therefore consists of *two layers,* the base plus the 1982 layer, for a total LIFO cost of $10,480.

2. On December 31, 1983, applying Step 4 indicates an inventory increase of $900 expressed in *base-year costs.* Once again, we price the increase using the conversion factor from Step 2

EXHIBIT 9–4
Dollar-Value LIFO

December 31	Ending Inventory at Current-Year Cost (Step 1)		Year-End Conversion Factor (Step 2)		Ending Inventory at Base-Year Cost (Step 3)	Ending Minus Beginning Inventory, Both at Base-Year Cost (Step 4)	Cost of Ending Dollar-Value LIFO Inventory (Step 5)
1982	$12,480	÷	1.20	=	$10,400	$10,400 − $10,000 = $ 400	$10,000 × 1.00 = $10,000 (base layer) 400 × 1.20 = 480 (1982 layer) $10,480*
1983	16,950	÷	1.50	=	11,300	11,300 − 10,400 = 900	$10,000 × 1.00 = $10,000 (base layer) 400 × 1.20 = 480 (1982 layer) 900 × 1.50 = 1,350 (1983 layer) $11,830*
1984	14,420	÷	1.40	=	10,300	10,300 − 11,300 = (1,000)	$10,000 × 1.00 = $10,000 (base layer) 300 × 1.20 = 360 (remaining 1982 layer) $10,360*
1985	14,040	÷	1.30	=	10,800	10,800 − 10,300 = 500	$10,000 × 1.00 = $10,000 (base layer) 300 × 1.20 = 360 (remaining 1982 layer) 500 × 1.30 = 650 (1985 layer) $11,010*

*This is the correct amount to report on the ending balance sheet and to subtract from the cost of goods available for sale to measure the cost of goods sold for the year.

(1.50). The inventory now consists of *three layers,* the base plus the 1982 and 1983 layers, for a total LIFO cost of $11,830.

3. On December 31, 1984, the application of Step 4 shows an inventory *decrease* of $1,000 expressed in *base-year costs.* When a decrease occurs, we must remove it from the existing LIFO inventory layers in a last-in, first-out sequence. In other words we assume that the last layer(s) in is the first to go out. Any layer removed is charged to cost of goods sold at an amount equal to the base-year cost of the layer multiplied by the conversion factor in existence when the layer was created. Expressed in base-year costs, the $1,000 decrease eliminates all of the 1983 layer ($900) and $100 of the 1982 layer. Had the inventory decrease been larger, it could have eliminated the entire 1982 layer and some or all of the base. An inventory layer, once eliminated, cannot subsequently be reconstructed. The inventory at the end of 1984 consists of *two layers,* the base plus three-fourths of the 1982 layer, for a total LIFO cost of $10,360. Note that we do not construct a 1984 layer, because the inventory that year does not increase.

4. On December 31, 1985, applying Step 4 indicates an inventory increase of $500 expressed in *base-year costs.* As usual, we price the increase using the year-end conversion factor (1.30) derived in Step 2. The inventory now consists of *three layers:* the base, the remaining 1982 layer, and the new 1985 layer. Adding these layers produces a total LIFO cost of $11,010. Note that the entire 1983 layer and one-fourth of the 1982 layer are *not* reflected in the 1985 ending inventory; they were eliminated in 1984 and are therefore never added back.

At first glance the dollar-value LIFO method usually appears formidable. In practice, however, many companies find that it is a convenient way to apply LIFO to a large, complex inventory. The financial statement numbers it produces are ordinarily somewhat different from those produced by the specific goods method of applying LIFO. Nevertheless, dollar-value LIFO has many practical advantages, and the numbers that it produces are acceptable for financial reporting and income tax purposes. It is important to understand clearly that dollar-value LIFO is a widely used method of applying the historical cost principle to inventories. Although a specific price index is used to implement the method, dollar-value LIFO is a method of determining an inventory's historical cost, not its current value.

Historical Cost

RETAIL INVENTORY METHOD

The **retail inventory method** is a reversed markup procedure of inventory pricing used by many retail businesses, such as department stores. The main advantage of the method is that it produces accounting information and facilitates inventory control at less cost than other methods that could be used in retail concerns. Ending inventory and cost of goods sold figures derived under the retail method are acceptable for financial reporting and income tax purposes.

When applying the retail method, the accountant records the beginning inventory, purchases, and sales in the accounts in the usual manner under a periodic inventory system. Moreover, supplementary records are kept of certain additional information. This information includes the beginning inventory and net purchases, each stated at **retail** (i.e., **selling**) **prices.** The accumulation of supplementary records at retail prices is facilitated by the fact that retail concerns usually price their merchandise for sale soon after its acquisition. The accountant divides the **cost** of goods available for sale during a period by the **retail value** of the same goods to produce a cost-to-retail percentage that is commonly called the **cost percentage.** This percentage reflects the relationship between cost and retail that prevails in the *current* period. Sales for the period are then deducted from the retail value of goods available for sale to derive an ending inventory valued at *retail prices.* The accountant multiplies the ending inventory at retail by the cost percentage to derive an *estimate* of the *cost* of the ending inventory to use for balance sheet reporting purposes. Cost of goods sold

Historical Cost

may then be computed in the usual manner for a periodic system. Alternatively, cost of goods sold may be computed by multiplying the sales for the period by the cost percentage. The following simplified example illustrates the essence of the retail method.

	At Cost	At Retail
Beginning inventory	$ 9,800	$ 14,000
Net purchases	65,200	86,000
Goods available for sale	$75,000	100,000
Cost percentage		
($75,000 ÷ $100,000 = 75%)		
Deduct:		
Sales		80,000
Ending inventory		
At retail		$ 20,000
At cost ($20,000 × 75%)	$15,000	
Cost of goods sold		
($9,800 + $65,200 − $15,000 = $60,000, *or*		
$80,000 × 75% = $60,000)	$60,000	

Observe in the example that the retail method enables us to calculate the cost of the ending inventory without knowing how many physical units are actually on hand. Nevertheless, a company using the retail method **must count its physical inventory at least once each year** for good internal control. Goods counted are extended at retail prices and compared with the inventory at retail value derived under the retail method. Differences may occur for several reasons, including theft, breakage, inaccurate records, and an inaccurate physical count. Assuming that the physical count has been performed correctly, the accounting records should be adjusted to agree with it.

The main uses of the retail method are listed below:

1. The retail method enables a company to estimate its inventory at any time without a physical count, because both cost and retail figures are always available. These estimates are used for annual as well as interim reporting purposes.
2. Even when the inventory is counted, the retail method enables a company to take its physical inventory at marked selling prices, thereby expediting the work of personnel since they do not have to refer to purchase invoices.
3. The retail method provides results that are useful when determining insurance coverage and settlements.

The major limitation of the retail method is that the cost percentage is merely an average of all goods reflected in its calculation. The average yields accurate results if the same relationship between cost and selling price exists for all goods or if the mix of goods in ending inventory is the same as that in the goods available for sale. Since some departure from these conditions usually occurs, the retail method produces accounting values of ending inventory and cost of goods sold that are only *approximations.* When the relationship between cost and selling price varies substantially between departments, the accountant should apply the retail method separately to each department. Doing this will improve the accuracy of the method. Ending inventory costs computed in each department are summed to derive the cost for the entire inventory.

A company using the retail method does not have to apply the method to its entire inventory. For example, a large department store may use the retail method when accounting for certain types of merchandise, such as men's clothing, and the specific identification method when accounting for others, such as expensive jewelry.

When applying the retail inventory method, we add the cost of inbound transportation when computing net purchases under the cost column, but not under the retail column. Inbound transportation costs are a part of the cost of goods purchased during a period, but not a part of the sales value of those goods. Moreover, sales returns and allowances should be deducted from sales under the retail column, because sales returns and allowances reduce the sales value of goods sold during a period. On the other hand, sales discounts should not be deducted from sales, because goods available for sale at retail as well as sales are ordinarily measured at gross amounts.

Retail Method Terminology

The example presented above was simplified so that we could introduce the rationale, uses, and limitations of the retail method. To properly handle the complexities encountered in practice, the accountant must understand the meaning of the following important terms used by retailers:

1. **Original retail price**—the price at which merchandise is first marked for sale to customers. This price includes an initial markup equal to the difference between the original retail price and the cost.
2. **Additional markup**—amount added to the original retail price.
3. **Markup cancellation**—cancellation, either in part or in total, of an additional markup. A markup cancellation does not reduce the selling price below the original retail price.
4. **Net markup**—amount of additional markups less markup cancellations.
5. **Markdown**—amount subtracted from the original retail price.
6. **Markdown cancellation**—cancellation, either in part or in total, of a markdown. A markdown cancellation does not increase the selling price above the original retail price.
7. **Net markdown**—amount of markdowns less markdown cancellations.

To illustrate the application of these terms, assume that a retail concern purchases a new line of summer dresses for $60 each and immediately prices each dress for sale at $100. The *original retail price* is therefore $100. This price, which actually includes an *initial markup* of $40, is now an important point of reference when labeling future changes in selling price. If, in response to great demand for the dresses, the company raises the selling price to $110, we have an *additional markup* of $10. If the price is later lowered from $110 to $106, we have a *markup cancellation* of $4. The *net markup* is now $6. Suppose that near the end of the summer the company lowers its selling price from $106 to $90. This action represents a *markup cancellation* of $6 and a *markdown* of $10. If the company later raises the price from $90 to $92, we have a *markdown cancellation* of $2. The *net markdown* is now $8.

Conventional Retail Method

The existence of additional markups, markup cancellations, markdowns, and markdown cancellations introduces new complexities in the application of the retail method. First, a company's accounting system must permit an accurate accumulation of each of these items in supplementary records. Second, since these items represent adjustments to the original retail price, they must be included in a logical manner in the basic retail inventory procedures that we illustrated earlier.

The **conventional retail method,** the one most commonly used by retailers, requires (1) including net markups when calculating the cost percentage and (2) subtracting net markdowns along with sales when measuring the ending inventory at retail. These procedures are illustrated in the following example:

	At Cost	At Retail
Beginning inventory		$10,000	$ 13,000
Net purchases		47,600	64,000
Additional markups	$ 7,000		
Less: Markup cancellations	4,000		
Net markups			3,000
Goods available for sale		$57,600	80,000
Cost percentage ($57,600 ÷ $80,000 = 72%)			
Deduct:			
Sales			(56,000)
Markdowns	12,000		
Less: Markdown cancellations	8,000		
Net markdowns			(4,000)
Ending inventory			
At retail			$ 20,000
At lower of cost or market ($20,000 × 72%)		$14,400	

The conventional retail method produces an ending inventory valuation that approximates the *lower of cost or market.* Observe in our example that the lower of cost or market valuation is $14,400. *If* we had ignored net markups as well as net markdowns when computing our cost percentage, the cost percentage would have been 74.8% ($57,600 ÷ $77,000). Note that the $77,000 amount equals the retail value of the beginning inventory ($13,000) plus the retail value of the net purchases ($64,000). Ending inventory at cost would then have been $14,960 ($20,000 × 74.8%). *If,* on the other hand, we had included net markups *and* net markdowns when calculating our cost percentage, the cost percentage would have been 75.8% ($57,600 ÷ $76,000). Note that the $76,000 amount equals the retail value of the beginning inventory ($13,000) plus the retail value of the net purchases ($64,000) plus the net markups ($3,000) minus the net markdowns ($4,000). Ending inventory at cost would then have been $15,160 ($20,000 × 75.8%). As these numbers illustrate, the conventional retail method produces the lowest ending inventory valuation when compared with alternative methods of handling net markups and net markdowns.

Are the results under the conventional retail method simply the most conservative, or do they really approximate those achieved by applying the lower of cost or market rule? Let's take a simplified example. Suppose that a company began operations near the end of a year and bought only a single item of merchandise that it was unable to sell. The item cost $100 and was originally priced to sell for $200. The retail price was subsequently raised to $250 (an additional markup of $50). Later the price was lowered to $125 (a markup cancellation of $50 and a markdown of $75). The following illustration shows how to value the ending inventory item using the conventional retail method:

	At Cost	At Retail
Beginning inventory		–0–	–0–
Net purchases		$100.00	$200
Additional markup	$50		
Less: Markup cancellation	50		
Net markup			–0–
Goods available for sale		100.00	200

Cost percentage ($100 ÷ $200 = 50%)		
Deduct:		
Sales		(–0–)
Markdown	75	
Less: Markdown cancellation	–0–	
Net markdown		(75)
Ending inventory		
At retail		$125
At lower of cost or market		
($125 × 50%)		$ 62.50

Conservatism

The lower of cost or market valuation produced by the conventional retail method represents an approximation of the inventory's net realizable value less an allowance for a normal profit margin (i.e., the floor). In our example, the inventory item which cost $100 was originally priced at $200 to allow a 50% profit margin based on selling price. The sales price of the item was finally reduced to $125. This price indicates that the item's **utility** (its ability to produce future revenue) has declined. Observing the lower of cost or market rule requires that we recognize the decline in the current period, the one in which it occurred. This reflects the conservatism modifying convention. Accordingly, the conventional retail method produces an ending inventory valuation of $62.50, an amount clearly below the historical cost of $100. Note that the lower of cost or market valuation of $62.50 represents the estimated selling price ($125) less an allowance for a normal profit margin of 50% of selling price ($125 × 50% = $62.50).

We emphasize that the conventional retail method only *approximates* an ending inventory valuation at lower of cost or market. The method does *not* measure "market" by comparing ceiling, replacement cost, and floor values. Moreover, accountants apply the method to many inventory items, not simply to a single unit. An averaging effect therefore occurs. The conventional retail method is also limited because it assumes that markdowns apply only to goods sold during a period. This assumption is justified on the ground that goods marked down are more likely than not to have been sold during the period. In reality, however, some of the goods marked down may still be in ending inventory.

Retail LIFO Method

Matching

Many companies adapt the retail method to reflect the LIFO cost flow assumption. This adaptation is called the **retail LIFO method.** Use of this method enables retailers to secure the matching benefits and tax advantages that LIFO usually produces while, at the same time, reducing substantially the clerical burden of applying LIFO.

Compared with the conventional retail method, the retail LIFO method requires two important changes in the manner of calculating the periodic **cost percentage.**

1. The beginning inventory is *excluded* from the calculation. Under retail LIFO the sole purpose of the cost percentage is to price any new LIFO layer that might be added in the current period. Thus, the beginning inventory is excluded to ensure that the resulting cost percentage reflects cost and retail prices of the current period only.
2. Net markups as well as net markdowns are *included* in the calculation. The rationale for including both is that LIFO is a method of arriving at *cost,* not lower of cost or market.

To illustrate the changes described above, assume that the following information pertains to Lite Company for the current year:

	At Cost	At Retail
Inventory, Jan. 1 (base LIFO layer)	$ 19,500	$ 30,000
Net purchases	140,000	208,000
Net markups		7,000
Net markdowns		15,000
Sales		190,000

If we now make the simplifying assumption that the level of specific retail prices remained *constant* during the year, here is how Lite Company would determine the cost percentage and the LIFO cost of the ending inventory.

	At Cost	At Retail
Net purchases	$140,000	$ 208,000
Net markups		7,000
Net markdowns		(15,000)
Subtotal	$140,000	200,000
Cost percentage ($140,000 ÷ $200,000 = 70%)		
Beginning inventory at retail		30,000
Goods available for sale at retail		230,000
Deduct: Sales		(190,000)
Ending inventory at retail		$ 40,000
Ending inventory at retail		$ 40,000
Less: Beginning inventory at retail		30,000
Inventory increase at retail		$ 10,000
Ending inventory at LIFO cost		
Beginning inventory	$ 19,500	
Add: Inventory increase		
($10,000 × 70%)	7,000	
Ending inventory	$ 26,500	

Note in the example that the beginning inventory was excluded and the net markups and net markdowns were included in the calculation of the cost percentage (70%). The cost percentage was then used to convert the inventory *increase* that occurred during the year from a retail measure ($10,000) to a cost measure ($7,000). The cost of the inventory increase was then added to the cost of the beginning inventory to derive the cost of the ending LIFO inventory ($26,500).

The above example is very simplified; in reality, the retail dollar (like the cost dollar) is rarely a stable device for measuring inventory changes. Indeed, the level of specific retail prices usually fluctuates over time. For this reason the retail LIFO method requires us to measure all inventory changes in **retail dollars of the base year.** The term "base year" refers to the *beginning* of the year in which a company adopts the retail LIFO method. In the remaining discussion of the retail LIFO method, we shall make the realistic assumption that the level of specific retail prices changes over time.

The retail LIFO method is very similar to the dollar-value LIFO method discussed earlier in the chapter. In fact, the retail LIFO method is sometimes called the **dollar-value retail LIFO method.** Like dollar-value LIFO, retail LIFO is applied to **designated pools** of similar goods. In addition, retail LIFO is applied on the basis of **inventory changes measured in dollars as opposed to physical units.** In contrast with dollar-value LIFO, however, retail LIFO measures inventory changes in *retail dollars* rather than in cost dollars.

As with the dollar-value LIFO method, retail LIFO requires that we use a conversion factor. Again, we compute this factor by dividing a specific price index for the current year by a specific price index for the base year. However, since the retail method requires a conversion of *retail dollars,* the price index used must measure the change in the level of *retail prices* that has occurred since the base year.

For income tax and financial reporting purposes, department stores ordinarily use the Department Store Inventory Price Indexes published semiannually by the Bureau of Labor Statistics (BLS). BLS index numbers measure changes in the level of retail prices of goods in twenty department groups. Examples include infant's wear, men's clothing, housewares, and major appliances. The accountant simply selects the index numbers that are appropriate given the nature of the inventory pool to which retail LIFO is applied. If the BLS indexes are not appropriate for a given retail concern, the company may construct its own *internal* price index.

Over time the retail LIFO method may produce several inventory layers. Each layer is expressed in *retail dollars rather than in physical units.* The accounting records must permit us to associate each layer with (1) the year-end conversion factor in existence when the layer was created and (2) the cost percentage for the year the layer was created.

To implement the retail LIFO method, the accountant must measure in *base-year retail prices* both the beginning and the ending inventories of the current period. If the ending inventory exceeds the beginning inventory when each is measured in base-year retail prices, an inventory increment (measured in base-year retail prices) has occurred. Since the increment occurred in the current year, we should price it at current-year costs. To convert the increment from *base-year retail* prices to *current-year cost* prices, we must multiply it by (1) the current year-end conversion factor (this converts the increment from *base-year* retail prices to *current-year* retail prices) and (2) the current-year's cost percentage (this converts the increment from current-year *retail* prices to current-year *cost* prices). The inventory increment so priced forms a layer which is added to those in existence at the beginning of the current period to determine the ending retail LIFO inventory cost.

On the other hand, if the ending inventory is less than the beginning inventory when each is measured at base-year retail prices, a reduction in inventory has occurred. This reduction requires us to charge previously established LIFO layers to cost of goods sold in a last-in, first-out sequence at amounts that reflect the cost prices in existence when the layers were constructed.

Application Procedures

The five steps summarized below are used to apply the retail LIFO method to a designated pool of goods. Note that these steps closely parallel those used to apply the dollar-value LIFO method.

Step 1. Determine the current-year cost percentage and the ending inventory at retail. As we stated earlier, be sure to (1) exclude the beginning inventory and (2) include net markups and net markdowns when calculating the cost percentage.[3]

Step 2. Obtain an appropriate year-end conversion factor which measures the overall change in inventory *retail prices* that has occurred since the base period. We compute the conversion factor as follows:

$$\text{Conversion factor} = \frac{\text{Current year-end specific price index}}{\text{Base-year specific price index}}$$

Step 3. Restate the ending inventory at current-year retail prices (as determined in Step 1)

---

[3]Actually, calculating the cost percentage is required only when a LIFO layer is added in the current period. Nevertheless, we have included it as a part of Step 1 since it is relatively easy to derive in the process of calculating the ending inventory at retail.

to base-year retail prices by dividing the results in Step 1 by the year-end conversion factor obtained in Step 2.

Step 4. From the ending inventory priced at base-year retail prices (as determined in Step 3), subtract *the inventory on hand at the beginning of the current period, also priced at base-year retail prices.*

Step 5. Compute the cost of the ending retail LIFO inventory as follows:

1. If the difference in Step 4 equals zero, inventory is unchanged. Consequently, the ending retail LIFO inventory valuation is the same as the beginning valuation.

2. If the difference in Step 4 is positive, inventory has increased. Price the increase at current-year *cost* by multiplying the difference in Step 4 by (1) the year-end conversion factor obtained in Step 2 *and* (2) the current-year cost percentage obtained in Step 1. Then add the result to the beginning retail LIFO inventory valuation to get the correct ending valuation at LIFO cost.

3. If the difference in Step 4 is negative, inventory has decreased. Subtract the decrease from the most recently acquired layer(s) at base-year retail prices in a last-in, first-out manner. The correct retail LIFO ending inventory valuation will then be the remaining layers multiplied by (1) their respective conversion factors *and* (2) their respective cost percentages.

An Illustration

Let's assume that a retail concern adopts the retail LIFO method on January 1, 1982. On that date the company's inventory at retail prices is $20,000 and its cost percentage is 70%. Furthermore, an appropriate specific retail price index obtained externally is 125. The cost of the inventory on January 1, 1982, is therefore $14,000 ($20,000 × 1.00 × 70%).[4] This inventory layer is regarded in future years as the base. Additional information for 1982, 1983, 1984, and 1985 appears in Exhibit 9–5.

The dollar amounts shown in Exhibit 9–5 for net purchases, net markups, net markdowns, beginning inventory at retail, and sales are obtained from the company's general ledger and supplementary records. Using this information, we *calculated* each year's cost percentage and ending inventory at retail, thereby complying with Step 1 of the basic retail LIFO procedures. Step 2 requires us to obtain an appropriate year-end conversion factor. We computed these factors using the specific price index numbers shown near the bottom of Exhibit 9–5. The index numbers themselves are obtained from an appropriate external source.

Using the information shown in our example, we illustrate in Exhibit 9–6 how to compute each year's ending retail LIFO inventory valuation.

The following points are particularly noteworthy:

1. On December 31, 1982, applying Step 4 reveals an inventory increase of $800 expressed in *base-year retail prices.* In Step 5 we price this increase at *current-year cost* by multiplying it by the year-end conversion factor (1.20) obtained in Step 2 *and* by the current-year cost percentage obtained in Step 1 (72%). The inventory therefore consists of *two layers,* the base plus the 1982 layer, for a total retail LIFO cost of $14,691.

2. On December 31, 1983, applying Step 4 indicates an inventory increase of $2,000 expressed in *base-year retail prices.* Once again, we price the increase at *current-year cost* by multiplying it by the year-end conversion factor from Step 2 (1.40) *and* by the current-year cost percentage from Step 1 (75%). The inventory now consists of *three layers,* the base plus the 1982 and 1983 layers, for a total retail LIFO cost of $16,791.

3. On December 31, 1984, applying Step 4 shows an inventory *decrease* of $2,400 expressed in *base-year retail prices.* When a decrease occurs, we must remove it from the existing LIFO

---

[4]125/125 = 1.00.

EXHIBIT 9–5
Information to Illustrate Retail LIFO Method

	1982		1983		1984		1985	
	At Cost	At Retail	At Cost	At Retail	At Cost	At Retail	At Cost	At Retail
Net purchases	$108,000	$155,000	$120,000	$164,000	$113,150	$159,000	$133,200	$187,000
Net markups		6,000		10,000		4,000		12,000
Net markdowns		(11,000)		(14,000)		(8,000)		(19,000)
Subtotal	$108,000	150,000	$120,000	160,000	$113,150	155,000	$133,200	180,000
Cost percentage								
1982 ($108,000 ÷ $150,000 = 72%)								
1983 (120,000 ÷ 160,000 = 75%)								
1984 (113,150 ÷ 155,000 = 73%)								
1985 (133,200 ÷ 180,000 = 74%)								
Beginning inventory at retail		20,000		24,960		31,920		31,008
Goods available for sale at retail		170,000		184,960		186,920		211,008
Deduct: Sales		145,040		153,040		155,912		181,904
Ending inventory at retail		$ 24,960		$ 31,920		$ 31,008		$ 29,104
Year-end specific retail price index obtained externally		150		175		190		170
Conversion factor		150/125 = 1.20		175/125 = 1.40		190/125 = 1.52		170/125 = 1.36

EXHIBIT 9–6
Retail LIFO

December 31	Current-Year Cost Percentage (Step 1)	Ending Inventory at Current-Year Retail Prices (Step 1)		Year-End Conversion Factor (Step 2)		Ending Inventory at Base-Year Retail Prices (Step 3)	Ending Minus Beginning Inventory, Both at Base-Year Retail Prices (Step 4)	Cost of Ending Retail LIFO Inventory (Step 5)
1982	72%	$24,960	÷	1.20	=	$20,800	$20,800 − $20,000 = $ 800	$20,000 × 1.00 × 70% = $14,000 (base layer) 800 × 1.20 × 72% = 691 (1982 layer) $20,800 $14,691*
1983	75%	31,920	÷	1.40	=	22,800	22,800 − 20,800 = 2,000	$20,000 × 1.00 × 70% = $14,000 (base layer) 800 × 1.20 × 72% = 691 (1982 layer) 2,000 × 1.40 × 75% = 2,100 (1983 layer) $22,800 $16,791*
1984	73%	31,008	÷	1.52	=	20,400	20,400 − 22,800 = (2,400)	$20,000 × 1.00 × 70% = $14,000 (base layer) 400 × 1.20 × 72% = 346 (remaining 1982 layer) $20,400 $14,346*
1985	74%	29,104	÷	1.36	=	21,400	21,400 − 20,400 = 1,000	$20,000 × 1.00 × 70% = $14,000 (base layer) 400 × 1.20 × 72% = 346 (remaining 1982 layer) 1,000 × 1.36 × 74% = 1,006 (1985 layer) $21,400 $15,352*

*This is the correct amount to report on the ending balance sheet and to subtract from the cost of goods available for sale to measure the cost of goods sold for the year.

inventory layers in a last-in, first-out sequence. In other words, we assume that the last layer(s) in is the first to go out. Any layer removed is charged to cost of goods sold at an amount equal to the base-year retail value of the layer multiplied by the conversion factor and by the cost percentage in existence when the layer was created. Expressed in base-year retail prices, the $2,400 decrease eliminates all of the 1983 layer ($2,000) and one-half ($400) of the 1982 layer. Had the inventory decrease been larger, it could have eliminated the entire 1982 layer and some or all of the base. Once eliminated, an inventory layer cannot later be reconstructed. The 1984 ending inventory consists of *two layers,* the base plus one-half of the 1982 layer, for a total retail LIFO cost of $14,346. We do not construct a 1984 layer, because the inventory that year does not increase.

4. On December 31, 1985, applying Step 4 shows an inventory increase of $1,000 expressed in *base-year retail prices.* We therefore price the increase by multiplying it by the year-end conversion factor (from Step 2) *and* by the current-year cost percentage (from Step 1). The inventory now consists of *three layers:* the base, the remaining 1982 layer, and the new 1985 layer. Summing these layers produces a total retail LIFO cost of $15,352. Observe that the entire 1983 layer and one-half of the 1982 layer are *not* reflected in the 1985 ending inventory; they were eliminated forever in 1984.

Because of the high rates of inflation in recent years, many companies have adopted the LIFO method. In 1974, for example, the inflation rate exceeded 10%, and many companies adopted LIFO in that year. Many retailers find that the retail LIFO method is a practical means of realizing LIFO's costing benefits. Although the method appears complex, its use can produce substantial clerical savings. The apparent complexity of the method is greatly reduced when we focus on its similarity to the dollar-value LIFO method. This similarity can be seen more clearly by observing the parallel form of Exhibits 9–4 and 9–6.

GROSS MARGIN METHOD

Historical Cost

The **gross margin method** (often called the **gross profit method**) is widely used to obtain the **estimated cost** of an ending inventory. The method requires adding the beginning inventory at cost to the net purchases at cost to produce the cost of goods available for sale during the period. Net sales for the period are then multiplied by a gross margin on sales percentage; the result is subtracted from net sales to produce an estimated cost of goods sold figure. This figure is then subtracted from the cost of goods available for sale to produce an estimate of the cost of the ending inventory. Below we illustrate how to apply these procedures.

Beginning inventory (measured at cost)		$ 30,000
Net purchases (measured at cost)		150,000
Cost of goods available for sale		180,000
Deduct:		
Net sales (measured at selling prices)	$200,000	
Less: Estimated gross margin		
($200,000 × 20%)	40,000	
Estimated cost of goods sold		160,000
Estimated cost of ending inventory		$ 20,000

Dollar amounts for the beginning inventory, net purchases, and net sales are taken directly from the company's accounting records. The estimated gross margin on sales percentage (20% in this example) is a *historical* rate (not a current rate such as the one we use under the retail method) that reflects recent past experience. Typically, it is an average of the percentage applicable to the past few years.

Notice the similarity between the procedures used in applying the gross margin method

THEORETICAL DEVELOPMENT OF LIFO—RETAIL

WHEN LIFO WAS approved by Congress in 1938, only a handful of industries were permitted to use it. Retailers weren't among them. In 1939, Congress allowed anyone to use Lifo. However, retailers, who were also concerned with cyclical profits, found that they had a problem, even in 1939.* Since they didn't deal in homogeneous inventories, the retailers would be forced to apply the Lifo concept to many small classes of goods called *pools*. This would involve voluminous record keeping. Furthermore, because of the vagueness in the law defining what qualifies as a Lifo pool, the retailers weren't sure how similar the goods in a pool had to be. Stringent interpretations of pools by agents in the field made matters even worse.

Furthermore, the original intent of Lifo proponents was obviously to exclude retailers. Peloubet, an early supporter of Lifo, wrote: "Obviously any trade or industry where one type of material is completely disposed of, is not replaced, and another different type is substituted is not suited to the use of the LIFO method. . . . Responsible writers on LIFO do not generally advocate the indiscriminate extension of the method to all types of trade and industry. . . . LIFO is not applicable to merchandising businesses."**

Carman G. Blough, one of the three people who helped draft the 1939 revenue act, had this to say about the universal application of Lifo: "Everyone who has given any consideration to the question of costing inventories recognizes that there are certain types of businesses to which the last-in, first-out method of figuring costs is not at all appropriate. . . . the ordinary retail store, the usual manufacturing business, etc., would not qualify."†

Obviously, the early proponents of Lifo didn't envision a Lifo—retail. Early Lifo was envisioned as a flow assumption applicable only to homogeneous inventory.

A solution to the retailers' problems was devised by Thomas McAnly. Instead of viewing inventories as pools of homogeneous goods, he considered an inventory, even of heterogeneous goods, as one basic inventory measured in dollars rather than in units. McAnly's method is similar to the retail inventory system, which dispenses with the pricing of individual units of inventory and instead multiplies departmental retail values by the markup percentages. Similarly, Lifo—retail dispenses with individual units and instead considers only layers of departmental inventory. Each layer of inventory is restated into the base-year price at which it was acquired. The rise in the value of the base inventory is removed from the inventory and charged to cost of goods sold.

---

*Malcolm P. McNair and Anita C. Hersum, *The Retail Inventory Method and LIFO* (New York: McGraw-Hill, 1952), pp. 144–145.

**Maurice Peloubet, "Last-in, First-out Once More: A Discussion of Certain Points Raised by Professor Paton," JofA, June 40, pp. 447–448; idem., *Valuation of Normal Stocks at Fixed Prices*, p. 571.

†Carman G. Blough, "Applicability of the 'Last-in, First-out' Method to Different Types of Industry," *Papers on Auditing Procedure and Other Accounting Subjects* (New York: AIA, 1939), pp. 78 and 80.

SOURCE: Harry Zvi Davis, "History of Lifo," *Journal of Accountancy,* May 1983, pp. 106, 108. Copyright © 1983 by the American Institute of Certified Public Accountants, Inc. Reprinted from *Accounting Historians Journal,* vol. 9, no. 1, Spring 1982.

---

and those used in calculating cost of goods sold in a periodic inventory system. In both calculations, we begin by deriving the cost of goods available for sale. Under the gross margin method, we then subtract the estimated cost of goods sold to obtain the estimated cost of the ending inventory. Under the periodic system, we subtract the cost of the ending inventory from the cost of goods available for sale to derive the cost of goods sold.

Gross Margin on Sales Percentage

Under the gross margin method, we use a **gross margin on sales percentage** when reducing net sales to an estimated cost basis. Gross margin percentages are usually derived and expressed in relation to selling prices. To illustrate, if a soccer ball costs $8 and sells for $10, the gross margin is $2. The gross margin percentage based on selling price is therefore 20% ($2 ÷ $10 = .20 = 20%). The remaining 80% ($8 ÷ $10 = .80 = 80%) is called the cost of goods sold percentage. The gross margin on sales percentage and the cost of goods sold percentage always sum to 100%.

At times, a gross margin percentage may be based on cost prices instead of selling prices. Using the same basic data shown above for the soccer ball, the gross margin percentage based on cost is 25% ($2 ÷ $8 = .25 = 25%). When we are given a gross margin on cost percentage, we should first convert it to a gross margin on sales percentage in order to correctly apply the gross margin method. The following widely used formulas enable us to convert a gross margin on cost percentage to a gross margin on sales percentage, and vice versa:

$$\text{Gross margin on sales percentage} = \frac{\text{Gross margin on cost percentage}}{100\% + \text{Gross margin on cost percentage}}$$

$$\text{Gross margin on cost percentage} = \frac{\text{Gross margin on sales percentage}}{100\% - \text{Gross margin on sales percentage}}$$

Obviously, only the first formula is required to find an unknown gross margin on sales percentage. Accountants nevertheless should be familiar with both types of conversions. The following examples illustrate how to apply the formulas:

Gross Margin on Sales Percentage		Gross Margin on Cost Percentage
20% (given)	→	$\frac{20\%}{100\% - 20\%} = 25\%$
25% (given)	→	$\frac{25\%}{100\% - 25\%} = 33\frac{1}{3}\%$
$\frac{50\%}{100\% + 50\%} = 33\frac{1}{3}\%$	←	50% (given)
$\frac{100\%}{100\% + 100\%} = 50\%$	←	100% (given)

Because cost prices are less than selling prices, each gross margin on cost percentage is greater than the related percentage based on sales. The gross margin on sales percentage is often called the **markup on sales;** similarly, the gross margin on cost percentage frequently is called the **markup on cost.**

Uses of the Gross Margin Method

Remember that we use an average *historical* (as opposed to a current) gross margin on sales percentage to implement the gross margin method. A major assumption underlying the method is that this percentage reasonably approximates the rate of gross margin in the current period. Since the rate of gross margin in the current period usually differs to some extent from the average historical rate, the gross margin method yields only an *estimate* of the cost of the ending inventory. This estimate generally approximates the results under whatever inventory cost flow method the company uses (FIFO, average cost, and so forth). An exception to this statement may occur when a company using LIFO liquidates layers consisting of outdated costs. In this case the ending inventory estimate under the gross margin method may depart considerably from the actual LIFO cost; we must therefore use caution when interpreting the results produced by the gross margin method.

The estimates produced by the gross margin method are generally considered too imprecise for use in annual financial statements prepared according to GAAP. Nevertheless, many companies use the method when preparing their internal as well as external interim reports (i.e., monthly or quarterly reports). Companies that use the gross margin method in their external interim reports and companies that use other methods than those used for annual reporting purposes "should disclose the method used at the interim date and any significant adjustments that result from reconciliations with the annual physical inventory."[5]

Accountants often use the gross margin method to estimate the cost of an inventory lost by fire or other casualty. The information needed to apply the method may be taken directly from the accounting records. If the records have been lost, the accountant can sometimes construct estimates of the needed information using prior years' financial statements, microfilm copies of bank records showing details of receipts and disbursements, and contact with

Historical Cost

suppliers and customers. When inventory has been lost, a company may apply the gross margin method to help determine an insurance settlement. We must remember, however, that the method produces an estimate of the *historical cost* of the inventory lost. Insurance coverage and settlements are often based on *replacement costs.* Thus, the results produced by the gross margin method may have to be adjusted to an estimated current replacement cost basis.

Auditors often use the gross margin method as a rough test of the validity of an inventory's cost determined under either a periodic or a perpetual system. If a material difference exists between the ending inventory cost determined using the gross margin method and that determined under the company's accounting system, the auditor should inquire concerning the reasons for the difference. This inquiry may simply reveal that the gross margin on sales percentage used in the gross margin method does not properly reflect current conditions. On the other hand, the inquiry may reveal errors made when determining cost within the company's accounting system.

Gross Margin Method Applied to Classes of Goods

Gross margin percentages sometimes vary considerably between different classes of goods within a single company. When such variation occurs, the use of a single, company-wide gross margin percentage assumes that goods in the various classes are sold in the same mix each period. This assumption is, of course, seldom valid. As a result, we should apply the gross margin method separately to each class of goods, thereby enhancing the method's accuracy. We can then sum the ending inventory costs determined for each class to produce an overall cost for the company's inventory.

---

[5]*APB Opinion No. 28,* "Interim Financial Reporting," 1973, par. 14a.

KEY POINTS

1. The specific goods pooling method, the dollar-value LIFO method, and the retail LIFO method help to simplify the clerical tasks associated with applying LIFO in practice.

2. The specific goods pooling method is a way of applying LIFO on the basis of changes in the total number of units in a pool of substantially identical goods.

3. The dollar-value LIFO method is a way of applying LIFO on the basis of changes in base-year cost dollars associated with a pool of similar goods. Under this method, LIFO layers are expressed in cost dollars rather than in physical units.

4. The dollar-value LIFO method gives companies considerable flexibility when grouping their inventory items into pools. The result is that dollar-value LIFO

helps to preserve old inventory costs while charging the most recent costs to expense (i.e., cost of goods sold).

5. Applying dollar-value LIFO requires the use of a specific price index that measures changes in the level of a company's inventory cost prices over time.

6. The retail inventory method is a reversed markup procedure of inventory pricing used by many retail businesses such as department stores.

7. The conventional retail method requires that we include net markups when calculating the cost percentage and subtract net markdowns along with sales when measuring the ending inventory at retail. The method produces an ending inventory valuation that approximates the lower of cost or market.

8. The retail LIFO method is an adaptation of the retail method used by many retailers to reflect the LIFO cost flow assumption. Under this method, we apply LIFO on the basis of changes in base-year retail dollars associated with a pool of similar goods. LIFO layers are expressed in retail dollars rather than in physical units; retail LIFO is therefore very similar to dollar-value LIFO.

9. When calculating the periodic cost percentage under the retail LIFO method, the beginning inventory is excluded, while net markups and net markdowns are included.

10. Applying retail LIFO requires the use of a specific price index that measures changes in the level of a company's retail prices over time.

11. The gross margin method is used to estimate the cost of an inventory. The method relies on the use of a historical gross margin on sales percentage. Although the estimate produced by this method is generally considered too imprecise for use in annual financial statements, the method is frequently used for interim reporting purposes, for estimating the cost of an inventory lost by fire or other casualty, and for testing the reasonableness of an inventory cost derived in some other manner.

12. When we are given a gross margin on cost percentage, we should first convert it to a gross margin on sales percentage in order to correctly apply the gross margin method.

QUESTIONS

9–1   What is the basic difference between the specific goods method of applying LIFO and the specific goods pooling method?

9–2   How is the existence of an incremental LIFO inventory layer determined under the specific goods pooling method? How is it determined under the dollar-value LIFO method?

9–3   Why is it considered appropriate to use a specific price index rather than a general price-level index when implementing the dollar-value LIFO or the retail LIFO method?

9–4   Explain the double extension method of constructing an internal price index.

9–5   Briefly describe the operation of the dollar-value LIFO method.

9–6   Assume that the total number of physical units in a dollar-value LIFO pool has declined from the beginning to the end of a period. Is it possible under this condition for the dollar-value LIFO cost of the ending inventory to exceed that of the beginning inventory? Why?

9–7   Assuming that a company has decided to use LIFO, what are the major advantages of the dollar-value method?

9–8   Briefly describe the general operation of the retail inventory method.

9–9   What are the major uses of the retail method?

9–10 What major assumption about the composition of the ending inventory is inherent in the retail method?

9–11 What is the meaning of each of the following terms?
  [a] Original retail price
  [b] Additional markup
  [c] Markup cancellation
  [d] Net markup
  [e] Markdown
  [f] Markdown cancellation
  [g] Net markdown

9–12 Explain why the conventional retail method produces an ending inventory valuation that approximates the lower of cost or market.

9–13 Explain the major differences between the conventional retail method and the retail LIFO method with regard to the manner in which the periodic cost percentage is calculated. Why do these differences exist?

9–14 Briefly describe the operation of the retail LIFO method.

9–15 Briefly describe the operation of the gross margin method.

9–16 Distinguish between a markup on cost and a markup on sales price.

9–17 Should we use a gross margin on cost percentage or a gross margin on sales percentage when applying the gross margin method? Why?

9–18 What are the major uses of the gross margin method?

C9–1 In January 1985 Apex Company began using the dollar-value LIFO method of determining inventory cost for income tax and financial reporting purposes.

Instructions

[a] Explain why inventories should be included (1) in a statement of financial position and (2) in the computation of net income.

[b] The *Internal Revenue Code* allows some accountable events to be reported differently for income tax purposes and financial accounting purposes, while other accountable events must be reported the same for both. Discuss why it might be desirable to report some accountable events differently.

[c] Discuss the ways and conditions under which the FIFO and LIFO inventory costing methods produce different inventory valuations. Do not discuss procedures for computing inventory cost.

[d] The LIFO inventory specific goods method and the dollar-value LIFO inventory costing method will produce different valuations if the composition of the inventory base changes. Explain why this is true.

[e] Describe the similarities and differences of the dollar-value LIFO inventory method used by Apex and the base stock inventory method. (The base stock method is discussed in the Appendix to Chapter 8.)

(AICPA adapted)

C9–2 Lowman Paint Company, your client, manufactures paint. The company's president, Mr. Lowman, has

decided to open a retail store to sell Lowman paint as well as wallpaper and other supplies that would be purchased from other suppliers. He has asked you for information about the retail method of pricing inventories at the retail store.

Instructions

Prepare a report to the president explaining the retail method of pricing inventories. Your report should include the following points:

[a] Description and accounting features of the method.

[b] Conditions that may distort the results under the method.

[c] Advantages of using the method when compared to cost methods of inventory pricing.

[d] Accounting theory underlying the treatment of net markdowns and net markups under the method.

(AICPA adapted)

C9–3 The owner of Erik's Retail Hardware computes income on a cash basis. At the end of each year, he takes a physical inventory and computes the cost of all merchandise on hand. To this he adds the ending balance of accounts receivable, because he considers this a part of inventory on the cash basis. Using this logic he deducts from this total the ending balance of accounts payable for merchandise and arrives at what he calls inventory (net).

The following information has been taken from Erik's cash basis income statements:

	1985	1984	1983
Cash received	$173,000	$164,000	$150,000
Cost of goods sold			
Inventory (net), Jan. 1	8,000	11,000	3,000
Total purchases	109,000	102,000	95,000
Goods available for sale	117,000	113,000	98,000
Inventory (net), Dec. 31	1,000	8,000	11,000
Cost of goods sold	116,000	105,000	87,000
Gross margin	$ 57,000	$ 59,000	$ 63,000

The following additional information is available:

	1985	1984	1983
Cash sales	$151,000	$147,000	$141,000
Credit sales	24,000	18,000	14,000

Accounts receivable, Dec. 31	8,000	6,000	5,000
Accounts payable for merchandise, Dec. 31	33,000	20,000	13,000

Instructions

[a] Without reference to the above, discuss the various cash basis concepts of revenue and income and indicate the conceptual merits of each.
[b] Is the gross margin for Erik's Retail Hardware being computed on a cash basis? Evaluate and explain the approach used with illustrative computations of the cash basis gross margin for 1984.
[c] Explain why the gross margin for Erik's Retail Hardware shows a decrease while sales and cash receipts are increasing.

(AICPA adapted)

EXERCISES

E9–1 Ryan Company uses the specific goods pooling method of applying LIFO. The following data pertain to Inventory Pool No. 1, which consists of two homogeneous products:

Inventory Pool No. 1

	Product X		Product Y	
	Number of Units	Unit Cost	Number of Units	Unit Cost
Inventory, Jan. 1, 1985 (base)	400	$5	800	$ 8
Purchases in 1985	1,500	6	1,000	10
	2,000	7	3,000	12
Sales in 1985	2,900		4,100	

Instructions

Calculate the cost of the December 31, 1985, inventory for Pool No. 1 using the specific goods pooling method of applying LIFO.

E9–2 Bianco Corporation applies the dollar-value LIFO method to each of the eight pools into which it has divided its inventory. The following information pertains to Pool No. 1:

	Year-End Quantity		Current-Year Unit Cost		Base-Year
Product	1984	1985	1984	1985	Unit Cost
A	1,000	900	$21	$22	$20
B	1,700	1,800	12	13	10
C	2,100	1,800	31	33	30

Instructions

Compute the year-end specific price index for Pool No. 1 for 1984 and 1985 using the double extension method. (The base-year specific price index is 100.)

E9–3 On January 1, 1983, Cooke, Inc., adopted the dollar-value LIFO method. The company's inventory priced at current costs on that date was $50,000. Additional inventory data are as follows:

Date	Inventory at Year-End Prices	Price Index*
Dec. 31, 1983	$58,300	106
Dec. 31, 1984	59,890	113
Dec. 31, 1985	64,260	119

*Price index at Jan. 1, 1983 = 100.

Instructions

Compute the cost of the company's inventory at December 31, 1983, 1984, and 1985, using the dollar-value LIFO method.

E9–4 Butterworth Company adopted the dollar-value LIFO method on January 1, 1985. The company's inventory priced at current costs on that date was $100,000. During 1985 the company purchased merchandise costing $500,000. The inventory on December 31, 1985, measured by reference to the actual unit costs of the goods most recently purchased, was $132,000. The specific price index for the company's inventory was 100 on January 1, 1985, and 110 on December 31, 1985.

Instructions

[a] Compute the cost of the inventory at December 31, 1985, using the dollar-value LIFO method.
[b] Compute the cost of goods sold for 1985 under the dollar-value LIFO method.

E9–5 The following information was taken from the accounting records of Reed Department Store for the current year:

	Cost	Retail
Beginning inventory	$15,000	$20,000
Net purchases	65,000	75,000
Net markups		5,000
Net markdowns		6,000
Sales		80,000

Instructions

Calculate the ending inventory using the conventional retail method.

E9–6 The information shown below was taken from the financial records of Hardy Hardware Store:

Inventory, Jan. 1, 1985	
At cost	$ 6,000
At retail	10,000
Purchases during 1985	
At cost	37,540
At retail	67,000
Purchase returns during 1985	
At cost	1,140
At retail	2,000
Additional markups during 1985, at retail	6,000
Markdowns during 1985, at retail	8,000
Markup cancellations during 1985, at retail	1,000
Markdown cancellations during 1985, at retail	3,000
Transportation-in during 1985, at cost	1,600
Sales during 1985, at retail	60,000

Instructions

Calculate the inventory valuation at December 31, 1985, using the conventional retail method.

E9–7 Red Department Store uses the retail inventory method. Information relating to the computation of the inventory at December 31, 1985, is as follows:

	Cost	Retail
Inventory at Jan. 1, 1985	$ 32,000	$ 80,000
Sales		600,000
Purchases	270,000	590,000
Freight-in	7,600	
Additional markups		60,000
Markup cancellations		10,000
Markdowns		25,000
Markdown cancellations		5,000
Estimated normal shrinkage, 2% of sales		

Instructions

Prepare a schedule to calculate the estimated ending inventory at the lower of cost or market at December 31, 1985, using the retail inventory method. Show supporting computations in good form.

(AICPA adapted)

E9–8 The following data pertain to Trivett Shoe Company for 1985:

	Cost	Retail
Inventory, Jan. 1	$15,000	$25,000
Net purchases	30,000	65,000
Net markups		10,000
Net markdowns		15,000
Sales		53,640

Instructions

Calculate the estimated ending inventory on the basis of lower of cost or market using the retail method.

E9–9 Using the data presented in E9–8, calculate the cost of the ending inventory using the retail LIFO method. Assume that the inventory on January 1, 1985, is the base LIFO layer and that the retail price index increased by 12% during 1985.

E9–10 The following data pertain to Fulton Supply Company for the current year:

	Cost	Retail
Inventory, Jan. 1 (base LIFO layer)	$18,250	$ 25,000
Sales		92,000
Net markups		7,000
Net markdowns		10,000
Net purchases	75,000	103,000

Instructions

Calculate the cost of the ending inventory at December 31 using the retail LIFO method. Assume no change in the level of retail prices during the year.

E9-11 Using the data presented in E9-10 and assuming that the retail price index increased by 10% during the year, calculate the cost of the ending inventory at December 31 using the retail LIFO method.

E9-12 Jericho Variety Store uses the retail LIFO inventory method. Information relating to the computation of the inventory at December 31, 1985, is shown below.

	Cost	Retail
Inventory, Jan. 1, 1985 (base)	$ 29,000	$ 45,000
Purchases	120,000	172,000
Freight-in	20,000	
Sales		190,000
Net markups		40,000
Net markdowns		12,000

Instructions

Assuming that there was no change in the price index during the year, compute the inventory at December 31, 1985, using the retail LIFO inventory method.

(AICPA adapted)

E9-13 Prepare a table similar to the one shown below and fill in the missing amount for each case.

Case	Gross Margin on Sales Percentage	Gross Margin on Cost Percentage
1	40%	
2		150%
3	25%	
4		20%
5	75%	
6		60%

E9-14 On May 8, 1985, a fire destroyed the entire uninsured merchandise inventory of Gray Company. You obtained the following data:

Inventory, Jan. 1, 1985	$12,000
Purchases, Jan. 1 through May 8	69,000
Sales, Jan. 1 through May 8	80,000
Gross margin on sales percentage	20%

Instructions

Calculate the estimated fire loss to report in Gray Company's income statement for 1985.

E9-15 Partridge Company uses the gross margin method to estimate its inventories for interim reporting purposes. The following data pertain to the company:

Inventory, Jan. 1, 1985	$ 30,000
Purchases, Jan. 1 through Mar. 31, 1985	110,000
Sales, Jan. 1 through Mar. 31, 1985	120,000
Markup on cost	25%

Instructions

Calculate the estimated cost of the inventory at the end of the first quarter of 1985.

E9-16 You are the independent auditor for Miller's Department Store. Tomorrow is the last day of the current fiscal year. The store will be closed and you will observe the taking of the physical inventory to accurately determine its cost.

Miller's accounting records as of the end of today provide the following data that pertain to the current fiscal year: sales, $446,000; sales returns, $20,000; beginning inventory, $50,000; purchases, $194,000; purchase returns, $4,000; transportation-in, $10,000.

The average rate of gross margin on sales during the last three years is 50%.

Instructions

Calculate an estimate of the cost of the ending inventory.

E9-17 The following data were obtained from the accounting records of Watson, Inc.:

Inventory, July 1	$ 12,000
Purchases	
July	60,000
August	70,000
September	79,600
Sales	
July	70,000
August	82,000
September	110,000

The company's markup on cost has averaged 25% during the past few years.

Instructions

Estimate the ending inventory costs for July, August, and September for monthly reporting purposes.

P9–1 The following information pertains to Vincent Company:

	Product S		Product T	
	Number of Units	Unit Cost	Number of Units	Unit Cost
Inventory, Jan. 1, 1984	200	$2	300	$3
Purchases				
1984	300	3	600	4
	500	4	600	5
1985	900	5	600	7
	700	6	300	8
Sales				
1984	600		1,300	
1985	1,900		800	

Instructions

[a] Calculate each of the following amounts using the specific goods method of applying LIFO to each product:

[1] Total cost of inventory at December 31, 1984.

[2] Total cost of goods sold for 1984.

[3] Total cost of inventory at December 31, 1985.

[4] Total cost of goods sold for 1985.

[b] Assuming that Products S and T constitute a single pool and are the only products that the company sells, calculate each amount in [a] using the specific goods pooling method of applying LIFO. The inventory on January 1, 1984, is the base.

P9–2 Rider Company adopted the dollar-value LIFO inventory method on January 1, 1982. The company's inventory on that date was $10,000, which is considered the base LIFO layer. Additional data about the company appear below.

Year	Purchases	December 31 Inventory at Current-Year Prices	Price Index*
1982	$62,000	$13,200	110
1983	68,000	18,150	121
1984	71,000	14,630	133
1985	82,000	20,300	145

*Price index at Jan. 1, 1982 = 100.

Instructions

[a] Compute the cost of the inventory at December 31, 1982, 1983, 1984, and 1985, using the dollar-value LIFO method.

[b] Compute the cost of goods sold for 1982, 1983, 1984, and 1985, under the dollar-value LIFO method.

P9–3 Jason Enterprises sells Products A, B, and C. On January 1, 1983, the company adopted the dollar-value LIFO method. The company's inventory priced at current costs on that date was $200,000. Other data about the company's inventory appear below.

	Quantity			Current-Year Unit Cost		
Dec. 31	A	B	C	A	B	C
1983	1,000	500	100	$110	$220	$330
1984	1,020	510	102	121	242	363
1985	350	250	50	140	260	380

Instructions

Compute the ending inventories for 1983, 1984, and 1985 using the dollar-value LIFO method. The base-year unit costs are $100, $200, and $300 for Products A, B, and C, respectively.

P9–4 Dumic, Inc., uses the FIFO inventory method for internal reporting purposes. On January 1, 1982, the company adopted the dollar-value LIFO method for income tax and external reporting purposes. The company's inventory priced at current costs on that date was $20,000. When applying the dollar-value LIFO method, the company relies on an appropriate external price index. Additional data appear below.

Date	Inventory Priced at Current-Year Cost	External Price Index
Dec. 31, 1982	$22,800	132.0
Dec. 31, 1983	31,680	145.2
Dec. 31, 1984	34,650	181.5
Dec. 31, 1985	51,480	217.8

Instructions

[a] Assuming the external price index was 110 on January 1, 1982, compute the cost of the inventory at December 31, 1982, 1983, 1984, and 1985, using dollar-value LIFO.

[b] Explain why a price index is needed to implement the dollar-value LIFO method.

P9–5 The following information pertains to King Incorporated for the fiscal year ended June 30, 1985:

	Cost	Retail
Inventory, July 1, 1984	$12,600	$20,000
Purchases	46,160	80,500
Purchase returns	1,860	3,000
Purchase allowances	900	1,500
Transportation-in	4,000	
Additional markups		8,000
Markdowns		13,000
Markup cancellations		4,000
Markdown cancellations		8,000
Gross sales		80,000
Sales returns		2,000
Employee discounts granted		1,000
Normal breakage		2,000

Instructions

Calculate the June 30, 1985, inventory at lower of cost or market using the conventional retail method.

P9–6 White Store applies the conventional retail method to each of its three departments in order to estimate its monthly inventories for internal reporting purposes. The following information for January 1985 is available from the company's accounting records:

Purchase returns	
At cost	2,100
At retail	2,800
Additional markups	2,500
Markup cancellations	265
Markdowns (net)	800
Normal spoilage and breakage	4,500
Sales	135,730

Instructions

[a] Using the conventional retail method, prepare a schedule computing the estimated lower of cost or market inventory on October 31, 1985.

[b] A department store using the conventional retail inventory method estimates the cost of its ending inventory at $29,000. An accurate physical count reveals only $22,000 of inventory at lower of cost or market. List the factors that may have caused the difference between the computed inventory and the physical count.

(AICPA adapted)

P9–8 The information below pertains to Coors, Inc., which adopted the retail LIFO method Jan. 1, 1982:

	Department					
	Men's Clothing		**Women's Clothing**		**Infants' Wear**	
	Cost	*Retail*	*Cost*	*Retail*	*Cost*	*Retail*
Beginning inventory	$1,003	$1,700	$2,040	$ 4,000	$1,176	$2,800
Net purchases	3,797	6,000	5,960	11,500	3,624	8,800
Net markups		300		500		400
Net markdowns		700		900		500
Sales		6,000		11,300		7,000

Instructions

Calculate the estimated January 31 inventory for White Store by applying the conventional retail method to each department separately and summing the results.

P9–7 Grand Department Store, Inc., uses the retail inventory method to estimate ending inventory for its monthly financial statements. The following data pertain to a single department for October 1985.

Inventory, Oct. 1	
At cost	$ 20,000
At retail	30,000
Purchases (exclusive of freight and returns)	
At cost	100,151
At retail	146,495
Freight-in	5,100

Date	Inventory at Retail Prices	Cost Percentage	Retail Price Index
Jan. 1, 1982	$100,000	50%	100
Dec. 31, 1982	123,200	51%	110
Dec. 31, 1983	150,040	55%	124
Dec. 31, 1984	133,280	54%	136
Dec. 31, 1985	166,750	56%	145

Instructions

[a] Calculate the cost of the inventory at December 31, 1982, 1983, 1984, and 1985, using the retail LIFO method.

[b] Explain why a retail price index is needed to implement the retail LIFO method, assuming that the level of retail prices changes over time.

P9–9 I. M. Swift & Company adopted the retail LIFO method on January 1, 1983. On that date the company's inventory at retail prices was $50,000, its cost percentage was 45%, and a suitable retail price index was 100. Additional information for 1983, 1984, and 1985, appears below.

	1983	1984	1985
Beginning inventory at retail	$ 50,000	$ 61,040	$ 64,660
Net purchases			
At cost	86,000	101,200	112,800
At retail	205,000	233,000	247,000
Net markups at retail	10,000	7,000	9,000
Net markdowns at retail	15,000	20,000	16,000
Sales at retail	188,960	216,380	226,360
Year-end retail price index	109	122	135

Instructions

[a] Calculate the cost of ending inventory for 1983, 1984, and 1985, using the retail LIFO method.
[b] Calculate the cost of goods sold for 1983, 1984, and 1985, under the retail LIFO method.

P9–10 Under your guidance Little Corner Sporting Goods Store installed the retail method of accounting for its merchandise inventory as of January 1, 1985. When you prepared the store's financial statements on June 30, 1985, the following data were available:

	Cost	Selling Price
Inventory, Jan. 1	$26,900	$ 40,000
Markdowns		10,500
Additional markups		19,500
Markdown cancellations		6,500
Markup cancellations		4,500
Purchases	86,200	111,800
Sales		122,000
Purchase returns and allowances	1,500	1,800
Sales returns and allowances		6,000

Instructions

[a] Prepare a schedule to compute the store's June 30, 1985, inventory under the retail LIFO method. Assume that the level of retail prices remained constant from January 1 through June 30.
[b] Without prejudice to your solution to [a], assume that you computed the June 30, 1985, inventory to be $44,100 at retail and the cost percentage to be 80%.

The level of retail prices has increased from 100 at January 1 to 105 at June 30. Prepare a schedule to compute the June 30, 1985, inventory under the retail LIFO method.

(AICPA adapted)

P9–11 Blank Corporation, which uses the conventional retail inventory method, wishes to change to the retail LIFO method beginning with the accounting year ending December 31, 1985. Amounts indicated by the firm's accounting records are as follows:

	Cost	Retail
Inventory, Jan. 1, 1985	$ 5,210	$ 15,000
Net purchases in 1985	47,250	100,000
Net markups in 1985		7,000
Net markdowns in 1985		2,000
Sales in 1985		95,000

Assume that all net markups and net markdowns apply to 1985 purchases and that it is appropriate to treat the entire inventory as a single department. Also assume that the level of specific retail prices remained constant in 1985.

Instructions

Compute the inventory valuation at December 31, 1985, using:
[a] The conventional retail method.
[b] The retail LIFO method, effecting the change in method as of January 1, 1985.

(AICPA adapted)

P9–12 Lopez Department Store converted from the conventional retail method to the retail LIFO method on January 1, 1984. In your examination of the financial statements for the year ended December 31, 1985, management asks that you give a summary of certain computations of inventory costs for the past 3 years.

The following information is available.

[1] The inventory at January 1, 1983, had a retail value of $45,000 and a cost of $27,500, based on the conventional retail method.

[2] Transactions during 1983 were as follows:

	Cost	Retail
Gross purchases	$282,000	$490,000
Purchase returns	6,500	10,000
Purchase discounts	5,000	
Gross sales		492,000
Sales returns		5,000
Employee discounts		3,000
Freight-in	26,500	
Net markups		25,000
Net markdowns		10,000

[3] The retail value of the December 31, 1984, inventory was $56,100; the cost percentage for 1984 under the retail LIFO method was 62%; and the retail price index was 102% of the January 1, 1984, price level.

[4] The retail value of the December 31, 1985, inventory was $48,300; the cost percentage for 1985 under the retail LIFO method was 61%; and the retail price index was 105% of the January 1, 1984, price level.

Instructions

[a] Prepare a schedule showing the computation of the cost of inventory on hand at December 31, 1983, based on the conventional retail method.

[b] Prepare a schedule showing the computation of the cost of inventory on hand at December 31, 1983, based on the retail LIFO method. Lopez Department Store does not consider beginning inventories in computing its retail LIFO cost percentage. Assume that the retail value of the December 31, 1983, inventory was $50,000.

[c] Without prejudice to your solution to [b], assume that you computed the December 31, 1983, inventory (retail value $50,000) under the retail LIFO method at a cost of $28,000. Prepare a schedule showing the computations of the cost of the store's 1984 and 1985 year-end inventories under the retail LIFO method.

(AICPA adapted)

P9–13 A major portion of Steeler Company's inventory was stolen on the night of August 16, 1985. A physical count the next day revealed that goods costing $14,000 were still on hand. Your examination of the company's accounting records reveals the following:

Inventory, Jan. 1, 1985	$ 20,000
Transactions, Jan. 1 through Aug. 16, 1985	
Purchases	83,000
Purchase returns	2,500
Transportation-in	5,400
Sales	141,500
Sales returns	5,000

The company began operations early in 1984, and its income statement for that year appears below.

Steeler Company
INCOME STATEMENT
For the Year Ended December 31, 1984

Net sales		$195,000
Cost of goods sold		117,000
Gross margin on sales		78,000
Operating expenses		
Selling expenses	$11,000	
Administrative expenses	17,000	
Total		28,000
Income before income taxes		50,000
Income tax expense		20,000
Net income		$ 30,000

Instructions

Calculate an estimate of the cost of the inventory that was stolen.

P9–14 On the night of September 30, 1985, a fire destroyed most of the merchandise inventory of Bargain Mart, Inc. All goods were completely destroyed except for (1) partially damaged goods that normally sell for $10,000 and that had an estimated net realizable value of $3,000 after the fire, and (2) undamaged goods that normally sell for $8,000.

The following data are available from the company's accounting records, which were locked in a fireproof safe:

Inventory, Jan. 1, 1985	$ 40,000
Net purchases, Jan. 1 through Sept. 30, 1985	423,750
Net sales, Jan. 1 through Sept. 30, 1985	525,000

Condensed income statement information for the past three years appears below.

	1984	1983	1982
Net sales	$500,000	$300,000	$100,000
Cost of goods sold	384,000	220,000	71,000
Gross margin	116,000	80,000	29,000
Operating expenses	25,000	20,000	9,000
Income before income taxes	91,000	60,000	20,000
Income tax expense	36,400	24,000	8,000
Net income	$ 54,600	$ 36,000	$ 12,000

The company estimates that the rate of gross margin on sales in 1985 is equal to the weighted average rate for the past three years.

Instructions

Estimate the amount of the fire loss, assuming that Bargain Mart carries no insurance on its inventory.

P9–15 On April 15, 1985, fire damaged the office and warehouse of King Wholesale Corporation. The only accounting record saved was the general ledger, from which the following trial balance was prepared.

King Wholesale Corporation
TRIAL BALANCE
March 31, 1985

Cash	$ 7,000	
Accounts receivable	27,000	
Inventory, Dec. 31, 1984	50,000	
Land	24,000	
Building and equipment	120,000	
Accumulated depreciation		$ 27,200
Other assets	3,600	
Accounts payable		23,700
Accrued liabilities		7,200
Capital stock		100,000
Retained earnings		47,700
Sales		90,400
Purchases	42,000	
Other expenses	22,600	
	$296,200	$296,200

The following additional information has been gathered:

[1] The fiscal year of the corporation ends on December 31.

[2] An examination of the April bank statement and canceled checks revealed that checks written April 1– 15 totaled $11,600: $5,700 for accounts payable as of March 31; $2,000 for April merchandise shipments; and $3,900 for other expenses. Deposits during the same period amounted to $10,650, which consisted of receipts on account from customers, with the exception of a $450 refund from a vendor for merchandise returned in April.

[3] Correspondence with suppliers revealed unrecorded obligations at April 15 of $8,500 for April merchandise shipments, including $1,300 for shipments in transit on that date.

[4] Customers acknowledged indebtedness of $26,400 at April 15, 1985. It was also estimated that customers owe another $5,000 that will never be acknowledged or recovered. Of the acknowledged indebtedness, $600 will probably be uncollectible.

[5] The companies insuring the inventory agreed that the corporation's fire loss claim should be based on the assumption that the overall margin on sales percentage for the past two years was in effect during the current year. The corporation's audited financial statements disclosed the following:

	Year Ended December 31	
	1984	1983
Net sales	$400,000	$300,000
Net purchases	226,000	174,000
Beginning inventory	45,000	35,000
Ending inventory	50,000	45,000

[6] Inventory with a cost of $6,500 was salvaged and sold for $3,000. The balance of the inventory was a total loss.

Instructions

Prepare a schedule computing the amount of the inventory fire loss. The supporting schedule of the computation of the gross margin on sales percentage should be in good form.

(AICPA adapted)

P9–16 Borow Corporation is an importer and wholesaler. Its merchandise is purchased from a number of suppliers and is warehoused by Borow until it is sold to customers.

In conducting the audit for the year ended June 30, 1985, the company's CPA determined that the internal control system was good. Accordingly, the physical inventory was observed at an interim date, May 31, 1985, instead of at year-end.

The following information was obtained from the general ledger:

Inventory, July 1, 1984	$ 87,500
Physical inventory, May 31, 1985	95,000
Sales for 11 months ended May 31, 1985	840,000
Sales for year ended June 30, 1985	950,000
Purchases for 11 months ended May 31, 1985 (before audit adjustments)	675,000
Purchases for year ended June 30, 1985 (before audit adjustments)	790,000

The CPA's audit disclosed the following information:

Shipments received in May and included in the physical inventory but recorded as June purchases	$7,500
Shipments received in unsalable condition and excluded from physical inventory (Credit memos had not been received nor had chargebacks to vendors been recorded.)	
Total at May 31, 1985	1,000
Total at June 30, 1985 (including the May unrecorded chargebacks)	1,500
Deposit made with vendor and charged to purchases in April 1985 (Product was shipped in July 1985.)	2,000
Deposit made with vendor and charged to purchases in May 1985 (Product was shipped, FOB destination, on May 29, 1985, and was included in May 31, 1985, physical inventory as goods in transit.)	5,500

Instructions

In audit engagements in which interim physical inventories are observed, a frequently used auditing procedure is to test the reasonableness of the year-end inventory by the gross margin method. Prepare in good form the following schedules:

[a] Computation of the gross margin on sales percentage for the 11 months ended May 31, 1985.

[b] Computation by the gross margin method of cost of goods sold during June 1985.

[c] Computation by the gross margin method of the June 30, 1985, inventory.

(AICPA adapted)

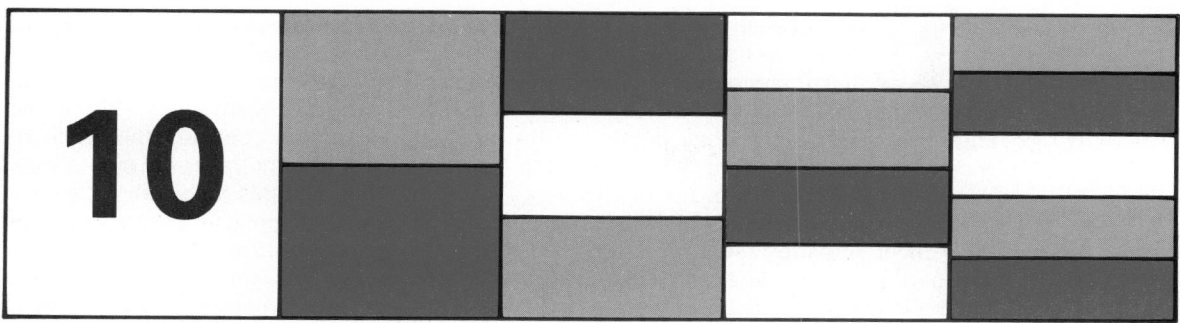

ACCOUNTING AND REPORTING FOR INVESTMENTS AND FUNDS

Objectives

To discuss many of the major reasons that businesses invest in the securities of other companies.

To develop the concepts and theories underlying financial accounting and reporting for various types of investments.

To define the classifications for various types of investments for financial accounting and reporting purposes.

To describe acceptable accounting practices for the acquisition, holding, and disposal of a variety of investments.

To illustrate the preparation of necessary financial-statement disclosures for many investing activities and circumstances.

Enterprises invest moneys in income-producing securities for a variety of reasons, including: (1) earning a return on otherwise temporarily idle cash; (2) accumulating resources to retire long-term bonds; and (3) acquiring the stock of another enterprise to gain influence, control, or some other business advantage. When one enterprise acquires the stock, bonds, or other securities of another company, the pertinent accounting issues concern the classification (current or noncurrent), measurement (valuation basis and cost flow), and disclosure of the accounting methods followed.

This chapter discusses the financial accounting and reporting implications of a variety of investment activities and circumstances. The first major section of the chapter considers accounting concepts and practices for short-term or temporary investments. The next major section discusses the issues associated with accounting for long-term or noncurrent investments. Both sections consider investments in both debt and equity securities. The final major section reviews accounting and reporting for several types of funds that a company may create and maintain.

As we begin our study of current and noncurrent investments, turn to Kroger Company's balance sheet on the inside front cover of your text. Notice that temporary cash investments are combined with cash as the first current asset presented. Also, notice among noncurrent assets a major category entitled "investments," which includes marketable investment securities and other investments. The fact that Kroger Company includes some investments with cash and others among the noncurrent assets implies that these represent distinctly different types of assets. We shall see many different types as we progress through Chapter 10.

TEMPORARY INVESTMENTS

This section deals with accounting measurement and disclosure problems of various investments considered to be current assets. You will recall that **current assets** are defined as cash and other assets that can reasonably be expected to be sold, used up, or converted to cash within one year or one operating cycle, whichever is *longer.*[1]

Cash or investments that may mature or be sold in the near future may be restricted or designated by management for some noncurrent purpose. Even though the asset is highly liquid, it should be classified as noncurrent on the basis of management intent. For example, if a company acquires a short-term treasury bill of the U.S. government to earn a return on otherwise temporarily idle cash, the investment is considered **current.** If the same treasury bill is acquired to provide a fund for the retirement of bonds payable that mature in several years, however, then the investment is considered **noncurrent.** Cash and investments should also be considered noncurrent when held: (1) to acquire or construct a noncurrent asset; (2) to acquire influence or control over another business; or (3) to achieve some other continuing business advantage. Thus, it is the objective of the investment—as well as the nature of the security held—that must be considered in classifying the item.

Conceptually, we may view the operating cycle of a business as the time and activity required for resources to be productively applied, a product manufactured and sold or service rendered, and cash finally collected (as illustrated in Exhibit 10–1). If there are several operating cycles each year, then a one-year period should be used as the basis for classifying current assets. If the period of time represented by an operating cycle is greater than one year, however, the longer operating cycle is used for purposes of classifying current assets. For example, operating cycles exceed one year in the lumber, tobacco, and distillery businesses. Enterprises that have no clear operating cycle should adopt a one-year period for purposes of distinguishing between current and noncurrent assets.

---

[1]*Accounting Research Bulletin No. 43,* "Restatement and Revision of Accounting Research Bulletins," 1953, Ch. 3, par. 4.

EXHIBIT 10–1
Operating Cycle of a Business

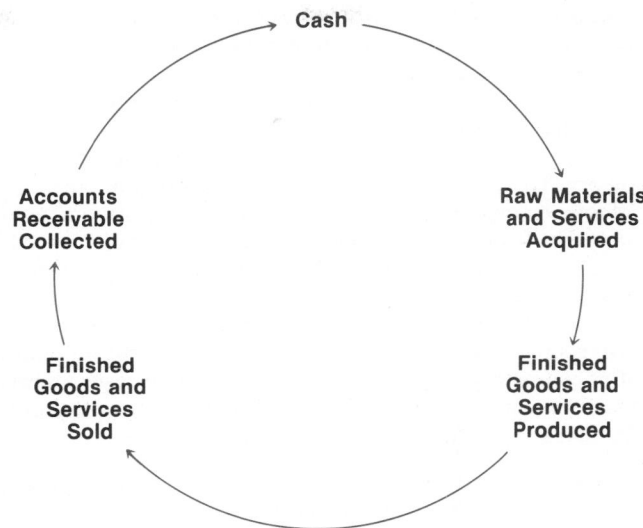

Therefore, investments classified as current assets should represent securities acquired with temporarily idle cash. The investment is also expected to be liquidated within a year or operating cycle, whichever is longer. Temporarily excess cash may be invested in either debt or equity securities. The following paragraphs consider accounting and reporting practices for temporary investments in equity securities.

Temporary Investments in Equity Securities

The *Financial Accounting Standards Board* (FASB), in its *Statement of Financial Accounting Standards No. 12,* addresses many financial accounting and reporting issues for **marketable equity securities.**[2] A **marketable security** is a security for which sales prices or bid and ask prices are available from a national securities exchange or in the over-the-counter market. When the sale of stock is restricted by a governmental or contractual requirement, the stock is considered nonmarketable unless the restriction can be removed within one year.[3]

An **equity security** is any instrument representing an ownership interest or the right to acquire or dispose of ownership shares in an enterprise at a fixed or determinable price. Thus, the term includes warrants, common and preferred stock, and certain other ownership instruments. The term does not include preferred stock that must be redeemed or is redeemable at the discretion of the investor. For example, if a share of stock can be presented to the issuing corporation and redeemed for cash, an investor should not consider the share an equity security. Rather, such an item is considered a debt of the issuing corporation and a receivable of the investor. Furthermore, equity securities do not include

---

[2]*FASB Statement of Financial Accounting Standards No. 12,* "Accounting for Certain Marketable Securities," 1975.
[3]*FASB Statement of Financial Accounting Standards No. 12,* par. 7.

treasury stock or convertible bonds. In essence, the term relates to outstanding stock and other instruments not subject to a maturity or call date.[4]

Valuation of Marketable Equity Securities

All marketable equity securities owned by an investing company should be recorded at their original cost (or fair market value if donated) and divided into two separate portfolios: current and noncurrent. Subsequent to acquisition, each portfolio should be reported in the financial statements at the lower of cost or market. For purposes of applying the lower of cost or market rule, each portfolio should be valued at the lower of *aggregate* cost or market as of the balance sheet date.

Conserva-
tism

Remember that conservatism is one of the modifying conventions of financial accounting theory. The role of conservatism is to ensure that business risks and uncertainties are given adequate consideration in the financial statements and generally requires the recognition of apparent losses and the deferral of all gains until realized.

Accountants value all assets that are to be sold or otherwise converted directly into cash at an amount not exceeding the net realizable value of the asset. Marketable equity securities are valued at the lower of cost or market as are items of inventory. Accounts receivable are also reported at net realizable value, which is the amount of cash expected to be collected after estimating uncollectable accounts. In the case of marketable equity securities, the FASB merely requires a conservative valuation basis consistent with other assets that are held for exchange or collection.

An Illustration of Accounting for Current Marketable Equity Securities

To illustrate, assume that Stable Company acquires 50 shares of Ace Enterprise's common stock at $25 per share as a temporary investment. The following entry should be made to record the stock purchase:

Current Marketable Equity Securities	1,250	
Cash		1,250
($25 × 50 shares = $1,250)		

The asset title Current Marketable Equity Securities is used in this entry. Other appropriate titles frequently used are Temporary Investments and Short-Term Investments. In addition to the Ace stock, Stable also holds several other equity securities as temporary investments. Exhibit 10–2 illustrates the determination of the lower of aggregate cost and aggregate market value for the entire current portfolio of marketable equity securities held by Stable Company at December 31, 1983.

Application of the lower of aggregate cost or market rule indicates that the carrying amount of this current portfolio should be $2,580, the aggregate market value of the portfolio. The difference between the aggregate cost and market value is accounted for as a valuation allowance, and a loss is recognized in the income of the period.

Unrealized Losses.   We recognize the decline in aggregate market value below cost of a current portfolio of securities even if we expect the decline to be short term. Thus, even *unrealized* losses are recognized on temporary investments in marketable equity securities. The FASB defines an **unrealized loss** as a temporary decline in the market value of a security below its cost. Realized losses result from sales of securities at amounts less than cost and permanent declines in the market value of securities below cost.

We measure unrealized gains and losses as the difference between the aggregate market value and the aggregate cost of the marketable equity security portfolio at the balance sheet date. The following entry reflects this determination for Stable Company.

---

[4]*FASB Statement of Financial Accounting Standards No. 12,* par. 7.

EXHIBIT 10–2
Lower of Aggregate Cost or Market Valuation—Current Portfolio
December 31, 1983

Security	(1) Number of Shares	(2) Cost per Share	(3) Market Price per Share	(4) (Col. 1 × Col. 2) Total Cost	(5) (Col. 1 × Col. 3) Total Market Value
Ace Enterprise, common stock	50	$25	$27	$1,250	$1,350
Stress Company, preferred stock	100	15	12	1,500	1,200
Stress Company, warrants	30	2	1	60	30
Aggregate totals				$2,810	$2,580

Dec. 31, 1983	Unrealized Loss on Valuation of Current Marketable Equity Securities	230	
	Allowance to Reduce Current Marketable Equity Securities to Lower of Cost or Market		230
	($2,810 − $2,580 = $230)		

The second account (Allowance to Reduce Current Marketable Equity Securities to Lower of Cost or Market) is a contra asset, or valuation allowance, to the marketable equity securities account. The valuation allowance is subtracted from the aggregate cost of marketable equity securities to arrive at a lower of cost or market valuation of the current equity portfolio. Whenever the valuation allowance account has a positive (credit) balance, the current portfolio will be valued at market. In contrast, if the valuation allowance account has a zero balance, the current equity portfolio will be valued at cost. The valuation allowance cannot have a negative (debit) balance, because the securities cannot be carried in the accounts in excess of their cost.

In the 1983 balance sheet, Stable Company will include current marketable equity securities, less the valuation allowance, among the current assets:

Current Marketable Equity Securities	$2,810
Less: Allowance to reduce current marketable equity securities to lower of cost or market	230
	$2,580

Unrealized Loss Recoveries. If the market value of the portfolio rises in subsequent years, losses already recognized may be partially or fully recovered. Losses that are recovered in future years because of increases in market value are reflected in the financial statements in the period of the recovery. Loss *recoveries* are recognized only to the extent of previously recognized losses. Stated differently, we never recognize increases in the aggregate market value of the security portfolio above its original cost. To illustrate, Exhibit 10–3 reflects the December 31, 1984, current marketable equity security portfolio of Stable Company.

EXHIBIT 10–3
Lower of Aggregate Cost or Market Valuation—Current Portfolio
December 31, 1984

Security	(1) Number of Shares	(2) Cost per Share	(3) Market Price per Share	(4) (Col. 1 × Col. 2) Total Cost	(5) (Col. 1 × Col. 3) Total Market Value
Ace Enterprise, common stock	50	$25	$32	$1,250	$1,600
Stress Company, preferred stock	100	15	12	1,500	1,200
Stress Company, warrants	30	2	1	60	30
Aggregate totals				$2,810	$2,830

The entry to record the change in aggregate market value of the current marketable equity security portfolio during 1984 is:

Dec. 31, 1984	Allowance to Reduce Current Marketable Equity Securities to Lower of Cost or Market	230	
	Unrealized Loss Recovery on Valuation of Current Marketable Equity Securities		230
	(To remove valuation allowance for market recoveries.)		

As you can see, even though the market recovery is so large that it causes the aggregate market value of the entire portfolio to exceed its aggregate cost, the portfolio is written up only to its original cost. Therefore, the unrealized loss recovery (gain) to be recognized in the income statement is limited to the previously recognized losses. Stated another way, the maximum amount of an unrealized loss recovery that may be recognized is limited to the amount of the valuation allowance. If the increase in the market value of the portfolio only partially recovers previously recognized losses, then the portfolio is valued at market value, and an unrealized loss recovery for the partial recovery is recognized in the income of the period.

As an example, *if* the total market value of Stable's current marketable equity security portfolio was $2,790 (instead of $2,830), the valuation allowance account should contain a $20 ($2,810 − $2,790) balance. Since the valuation allowance account has a balance of $230 from the previous period, a journal entry to reduce the valuation allowance by $210 would be necessary:

Dec. 31, 1984	Allowance to Reduce Current Marketable Equity Securities to Lower of Cost or Market	210	
	Unrealized Loss Recovery on Valuation of Current Marketable Equity Securities		210

Indeed, the valuation allowance account always has a credit or zero balance; the allowance can never represent a debit balance, because securities are not written up to an amount greater than their original cost.

Notice that the credit to the unrealized loss recovery account is not the same as a credit to the unrealized loss account. The unrealized loss of the previous period is a nominal account that has been closed to Retained Earnings. Therefore, an increase in market prices that recovers previously recognized unrealized losses should not be accounted for by credits to the unrealized loss account. To do so would result in the reporting of a "negative loss" on the income statement. Such an accounting is unattractive from an informational perspective. Creating a separate account, such as Unrealized Loss Recovery, that is added within the income statement is more meaningful.

Realized Gains and Losses.   A company may also incur realized gains or losses. *FASB Statement No. 12* defines a **realized gain** or **loss** as the difference between the net proceeds from the sale of a marketable equity security and its cost.[5] Other circumstances giving rise to realized losses will be discussed later in this chapter.

When a company disposes of a current marketable equity security by sale or otherwise, accountants generally recognize a realized gain or loss to the extent of the difference between the original cost of the security and the proceeds received from its disposition. The valuation allowance account attaches to the whole portfolio of current marketable equity securities, and not to individual equity securities within the portfolio. As a result, the valuation allowance is not adjusted in any way when various individual securities are sold. The purpose for this procedural approach is to ease the record-keeping burden. Current marketable equity securities are, by their very nature, acquired and disposed of with great regularity. Attaching the valuation allowance to each equity security would add a great burden to the accounting system. A corporation frequently invests in many different marketable equity securities and has a high trading volume. Thus, the method of adjusting the valuation allowance on the complete portfolio at the end of the reporting period is more economical than maintaining subsidiary valuation allowance records for each security.

To illustrate a sale, assume that Stable Company sells all its Ace common stock for $20 a share early in 1985. The following entry is necessary to record the sale:

Jan. 15, 1985	Cash	1,000	
	Realized Loss on Disposal of		
	Marketable Equity Securities	250	
	Current Marketable		
	Equity Securities		1,250
	($20 × 50 shares = $1,000)		

This entry does not affect the valuation allowance in any way, because accountants adjust the balance in the valuation allowance only at each balance sheet date. Therefore, if the sale of Ace common stock was the only activity during 1985 related to current marketable equity securities and if the market value of the remaining securities remained constant, then the situation at the end of 1985 would be as illustrated in Exhibit 10–4.

Because the aggregate cost of the portfolio exceeds the aggregate market value, a $330 entry is necessary to adjust the valuation allowance ($1,560 − $1,230 = $330). The difference between the aggregate cost and aggregate market value at the balance sheet date represents what the balance in the valuation allowance account should be. If the valuation allowance contains a balance from the previous year, then an entry is made for the amount of the difference between the current balance of the valuation allowance and the amount that the valuation allowance should contain. In the Stable illustration, the aggregate market value exceeded the aggregate cost of the current marketable equity securities portfolio at Decem-

---

[5]*FASB Statement of Financial Accounting Standards No. 12,* par. 7.

EXHIBIT 10–4
Lower of Aggregate Cost or Market Valuation—Current Portfolio
December 31, 1985

Security	(1) Number of Shares	(2) Cost per Share	(3) Market Price per Share	(4) (Col. 1 × Col. 2) Total Cost	(5) (Col. 1 × Col. 3) Total Market Value
Stress Company, preferred stock	100	$15	$12	$1,500	$1,200
Stress Company, warrants	30	2	1	60	30
Aggregate totals				$1,560	$1,230

---

ber 31, 1984, and the valuation allowance account was completely eliminated at that date. Therefore, it is necessary to prepare the following entry for the full $330 excess of aggregate cost over aggregate market value at December 31, 1985:

Dec. 31, 1985	Unrealized Loss on Valuation of Current Marketable Equity Securities	330	
	Allowance to Reduce Current Marketable Equity Securities to Lower of Cost or Market		330

This entry is necessary even though there has been *no* change in either the cost or market values of the securities remaining in the portfolio following the sale of the Ace common stock. An unrealized loss (due merely to the absence of the Ace stock at December 31, 1985) is reported in the 1985 income statement.

By requiring this treatment, the FASB places a heavy emphasis on distinguishing between realized gains or losses and unrealized gains or losses. A company may recognize an *unrealized* loss in one period if the market value of a security declines below cost and a *realized* loss in the following period if the security is sold for less than its cost. In these circumstances, an unrealized loss recovery may also be recognized in the period of disposal. To illustrate, assume that Ervin Company buys a single share of Remote, Inc., stock for $10 as a temporary investment on January 10, 1984. Assume further that the market value of the Remote stock declines to $8 at December 31, 1984, and that this investment was the only one made by Ervin. The following entries will record the acquisition of the stock and recognize the unrealized loss:

Jan. 10, 1984	Current Marketable Equity Security	10	
	Cash		10
Dec. 31, 1984	Unrealized Loss on Valuation of Current Marketable Equity Security	2	
	Allowance to Reduce Current Marketable Equity Security to Lower of Cost or Market		2

If we now assume that Ervin Company sells the share of Remote stock on February 4, 1985, for $8 and makes no further acquisitions of marketable equity securities during 1985, the following entries are necessary.

Feb. 4, 1985	Realized Loss on Disposal of Marketable			
	Equity Security		2	
	Cash		8	
	Current Marketable Equity Security			10
	(To report sale of security at loss of $2.)			
Dec. 31, 1985	Allowance to Reduce Current Marketable			
	Equity Security to Lower of Cost or Market		2	
	Unrealized Loss Recovery on			
	Valuation of Current Marketable			
	Equity Security			2
	(To remove valuation allowance account.)			

This unusual result of recognizing an unrealized loss in one year and a realized loss recovery in the next occurs because the FASB places a high degree of significance on distinguishing between realized and unrealized losses. If the December 31, 1985, adjusting entry had been omitted, then the $2 loss would have been recognized twice, once as unrealized at the end of 1984 and then again as realized in February 1985. Only the December 31, 1985, adjusting entry eliminates this undesirable effect. The combined income statement effect for 1984 and 1985 properly reflects a $2 loss. In practice, such results are generally not directly observed, because corporations hold many different securities in their portfolios. The impact on the valuation allowance of transactions such as those illustrated above is combined with the market value changes of all securities in the portfolio and not recognized separately. Nevertheless, reported results of operations are directly affected in the manner described.

Disclosure

Financial Statement Disclosures. The financial statement disclosures required for current marketable equity securities include:[6]

1. Aggregate cost and market values.
2. As of date of the latest balance sheet, **gross unrealized gains** and **gross unrealized losses.** (Both terms are defined below.)
3. For each period for which an income statement is presented, the net realized gain or loss included in net income and the basis of cost computation (e.g., specific identification, weighted average).

Gross unrealized gains and losses are merely the total gains and total losses that, when combined, represent the net unrealized gain or loss for the aggregate portfolio. In the example for Stable Company, presented in Exhibit 10–2, the gross unrealized gains and losses are determined as follows:

Security	Cost	Market	Gain(Loss)
Stress Company,			
preferred	$1,500	$1,200	$(300)
Stress Company,			
warrants	60	30	(30)
Gross unrealized losses			(330)
Ace Enterprise, common	1,250	1,350	100
Net unrealized losses			$(230)

Gross losses and gross gains are usually disclosed in a footnote to the financial statements along with the other required information.

---

[6]*FASB Statement of Financial Accounting Standards No. 12,* par. 12.

Furthermore, if a company engages in several transactions that involve the same class of security, assumptions concerning the cost flow of the securities may be necessary. In this regard, marketable securities may be viewed in a fashion similar to items of inventory. Because most securities are serially numbered, many companies apply specific identification procedures. Other methods of cost identification, such as first-in, first-out or weighted average, are also commonly encountered. Income tax consequences may also influence the selection of the cost-flow assumptions to be used. An illustration of proper disclosure is demonstrated by PNC Financial Corp, a multi-bank holding company, in Exhibit 10–5. Notice in 1982 that the company's portfolio includes corporate stocks with a carrying value of $87 million and a market value of $111.1 million. The explanation of the gross unrealized gains and losses presented at the bottom of the exhibit accounts for only part of the market value of the corporate stocks, because securities other than marketable equity securities are included among the corporate stock investments.

A Learning Tool

The learning summary in Exhibit 10–6 displays the significant accounting practices involved in accounting for current marketable equity securities. Although the preceding

---

EXHIBIT 10–5
PNC Financial Corp
Illustration of *FASB Statement No. 12* Disclosure

Investment Securities

The carrying and approximate market values of investment securities are as follows:

December 31	1982		1981	
	Carrying Value	Market Value	Carrying Value	Market Value
	(in millions)			
U.S. Treasury	$ 791.9	$ 806.9	$ 639.0	$ 634.0
U.S. Government agencies and corporations	590.7	556.5	714.6	587.4
State and municipal	321.4	265.0	373.8	238.4
Corporate stocks	87.0	111.1	71.7	89.7
Other	13.0	13.0	7.2	7.2
Total....................	$1,804.0	$1,752.5	$1,806.3	$1,556.7

The following table presents data related to the marketable equity securities included in corporate stocks:

December 31	1982	1981
	(in thousands)	
Gross unrealized gains....................................	$24,532	$15,982
Gross unrealized losses	(1,417)	(165)
Aggregate cost	70,262	53,194
Aggregate market value...................................	$93,377	$69,011
Net realized gains	$ 254	$ 2,470

SOURCE: PNC Financial Corp, 1982 Annual Report.

section discusses and illustrates practices, the flowchart provides a useful summary and review tool to ensure your complete understanding of accounting for current marketable equity securities.

EXHIBIT 10–6
Current Marketable Equity Securities Portfolio

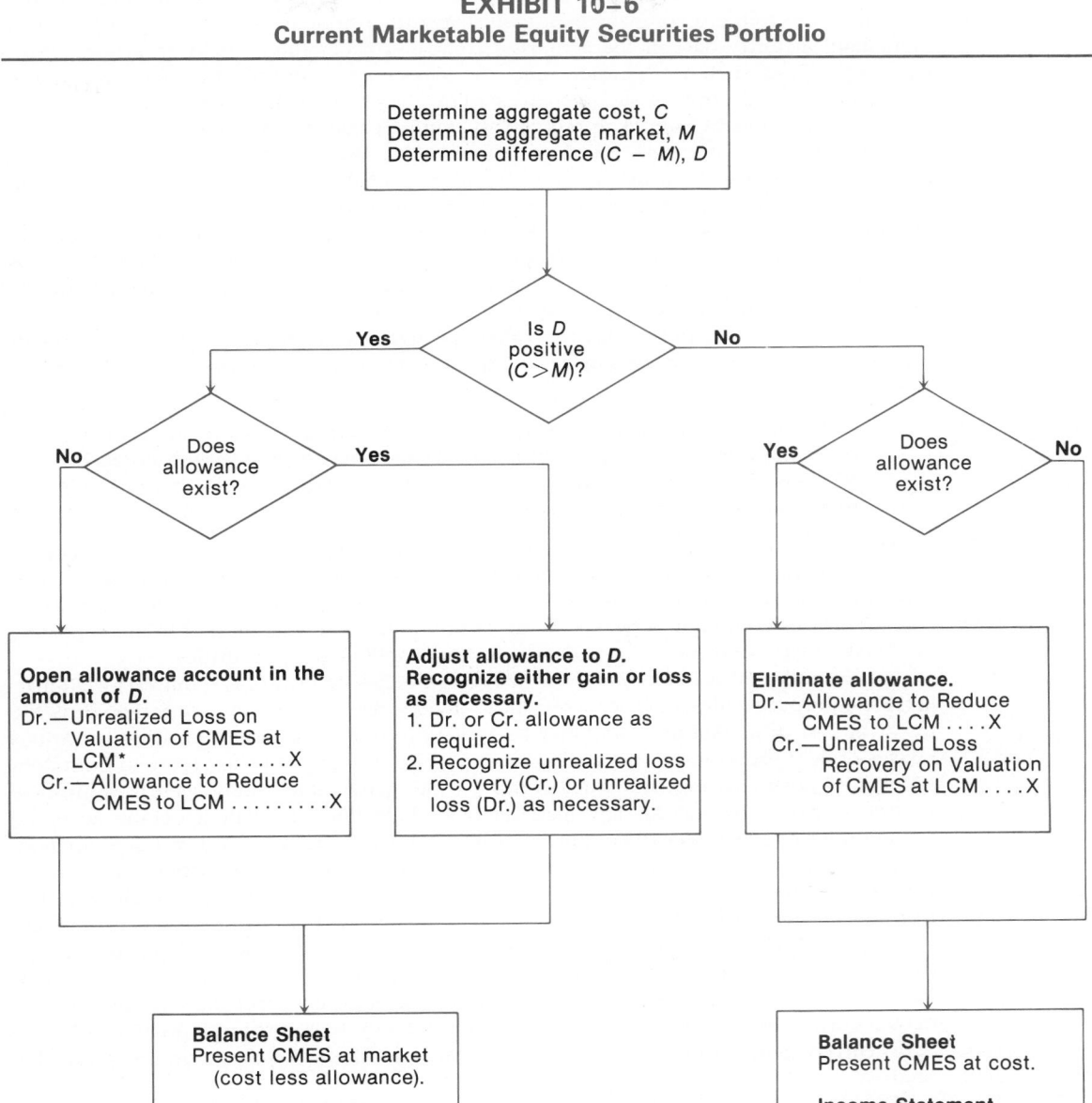

*CMES = current marketable equity securities; LCM = lower of cost or market.

Temporary Investments in Debt Securities

Companies also frequently invest in or acquire **debt securities** for relatively short periods of time. If a debt security is *not marketable,* a current maturity date is generally necessary for classifying the investment as a current asset. The maturity date of a *marketable* debt instrument, however, does not necessarily indicate whether or not the item is considered current. For example, a company may acquire a note or bond of another company with an immediate maturity date. If the acquiring company places the security in a noncurrent investment fund, such as a pension fund, the investment is classified as noncurrent. The noncurrent classification of such an investment possessing a short-term maturity date is based on management's intent to reinvest the funds at maturity for some noncurrent purpose. In contrast, if a company invests temporarily idle cash in marketable bonds that have a distant maturity date with the intention to dispose of the investment quickly, a current classification is appropriate. Management intent is therefore an important consideration in classifying investments in both debt and equity securities. Of course, the expressed intent of corporate management should be supported by logic and corroborative evidence, such as the purposes of the investment, the history of similar activities, a ready market for the security, and events subsequent to the balance sheet date.

While *SFAS No. 12* applies only to marketable *equity* securities, financial accounting for *debt* securities reflects many similarities. In fact, *Accounting Research Bulletin No. 43* states:

> *In the case of marketable securities where market value is less than cost by a substantial amount and it is evident that the decline in market value is not due to a mere temporary condition, the amount to be included as a current asset should not exceed the market value.*[7]

Therefore, market valuation is required for current marketable debt securities whenever the investment has suffered a permanent decline in market value. In such a case, a loss should be reported on the income statement in the period of the investment write-down. Outside of this condition, however, some of the latitude in accounting for and reporting marketable debt securities is not allowed for marketable equity securities.

For example, valuation at the lower of *aggregate* cost or market is required for all marketable equity securities, but such a specification does not exist for debt securities. Thus, the lower of cost or market provision may be applied to individual debt securities, to various classes of debt securities, to the aggregate debt portfolio, or to the aggregate of both debt and equity portfolios together. Furthermore, while marketable equity securities must be written down to market for any material market declines, current generally accepted accounting principles (GAAP) require that debt securities be written down only for nontemporary declines. Little guidance is available to help accountants distinguish between temporary and permanent declines. Although accountants may write down debt securities treated as current assets for temporary market declines, such a practice is not mandatory. Finally, *ARB No. 43* does not consider whether or not loss recoveries taking place in later periods may be recognized. Since the practice is not prohibited and, in fact, is required for current marketable equity securities, accountants may logically apply the same practices to debt securities as are applied to current marketable equity securities. Exhibit 10—7 compares current generally accepted accounting principles for each type of current marketable security.

The exhibit shows that the accounting practices specified by the two documents *permit* differences rather than prescribe them. That is, no differences are explicitly established by either of the two statements. Rather, *ARB No. 43* is merely silent about three of the account-

---

[7]*Accounting Research Bulletin No. 43,* Ch. 3, par. 9.

EXHIBIT 10–7
Accounting for Short-Term Investments

Issue	Marketable Equity Securities (*SFAS No. 12*)	Marketable Debt Securities (*ARB No. 43*)
Valuation basis	Lower of *aggregate* cost or market.	Cost or lower of cost or market. Aggregation level not specified.
Criteria for loss recognition	All material market declines required to be recognized. Unrealized losses must be recognized in income.	Permanent market declines required to be recognized. Temporary market declines may be recognized. Losses must be recognized in income.
Loss recoveries	All material market recoveries to be recognized to the extent of previously recognized unrealized losses.	Loss recoveries not required to be recognized.

---

ing issues addressed by *SFAS No. 12*. As a result of these factors, practice varies somewhat in this area; however, logic and consistency support treating current marketable equity and debt securities in a similar fashion. This means that all current marketable securities would be treated in accordance with the more precise requirements of *SFAS No. 12*. The authors support this position.

The following illustration demonstrates acceptable accounting practices for short-term investments in debt securities. Assume Stable Company acquires a bond of Timeless Corporation on March 1, 1985. The bond is dated January 1, 1985, pays interest semiannually at a stated rate of 12%, matures in 1992, and was acquired by Stable for $1,020 (102) plus accrued interest.

The acquisition or issue price of a bond is frequently stated as a percentage of face value. In this case, the bond was acquired at an amount 2% greater than the face amount of the bond or at "102." Furthermore, certain transaction costs, such as broker fees, are frequently incurred in the acquisition of bonds and are considered part of the cost of the bonds. In this simplified example no costs are considered except the direct cost of the bond and related accrued interest. Stable company would make the following journal entry:

Mar. 1, 1985	Short-Term Debt Investment	1,020	
	Interest Receivable	20	
	Cash		1,040
	(To record acquisition of Timeless Corporation bond.)		

The total cash investment is computed as follows:

$$\$1,000 \times 102\% = \$1,020 \text{ Bond price}$$
$$\$1,000 \times 12\% \times 2/12 = \underline{20} \text{ Accrued interest}$$

Total cash
investment $\underline{\$1,040}$

The debit of $20 to Interest Receivable could also have been recorded as a charge to Interest Revenue. In that case, when the semiannual interest is received, the entire cash received ($1,000 \times 12\% \times \frac{1}{2} = \$60$) would be credited directly to the Interest Revenue account. Resuming the example in which Interest Receivable was charged, we find that the following entry is necessary on July 1, 1985, to record receipt of the interest payment:

July 1, 1985	Cash	60	
	Interest Revenue		40
	Interest Receivable		20
	(To record semiannual interest payment. $1,000 \times 12\% \times \frac{1}{2} = \$60$, $\frac{1}{3}$ of which had previously been recorded as receivable.)		

Note that none of the premium ($\$1,020 - \$1,000 = \$20$) is amortized. If we assume that Stable was intending to make a short-term investment, we can also assume that the bond will not be held until maturity. Accountants do not usually amortize premium or discount on temporary investments; rather, any difference between the acquisition cost of a security and the proceeds from its sale is reflected as a gain or loss on the disposal of the security. This treatment is consistent with the overall objectives of short-term investments; that is, a temporary productive application of otherwise idle resources.

Finally, if Stable Company sells the bond on November 1, 1985, at 97 plus accrued interest, the following entry is necessary:

Nov. 1, 1985	Cash	1,010	
	Realized Loss on Sale of Bond	50	
	Short-Term Debt Investment		1,020
	Interest Revenue		40
	(To record sale of bond at 97, plus accrued interest for four months. $1,000 \times 12\% \times \frac{4}{12} = \$40$.)		

The cash received is the sum of $970 ($1,000 \times 97\% $) plus $40 interest accrued from July 1 ($1,000 \times 12\% \times \frac{4}{12}$). Since the bond cost $1,020 and was sold for $970, a loss of $50 is recognized. The loss can be determined by ignoring the interest and subtracting the price for which the bond was sold from the acquisition price ($1,020 - $970 = $50 loss). Again note the absence of any premium amortization during the holding period.

Special Problems

Many types of unusual or unique investment instruments are available to companies, and we shall consider several at this time. A commonly encountered situation involves accounting for **stock warrants** and **stock rights.** Stock warrants and stock rights are generally considered temporary marketable investments because they have limited lives. Both security types satisfy the definition of "equity" securities contained in *SFAS No. 12* and are therefore included in the current portfolio for lower of cost or market determination. Stock warrants and stock rights can be acquired in isolation or in conjunction with ownership of other securities. For rights and warrants obtained in conjunction with other security investments, the classification of the "other securities" should not be used solely to determine the classification of the stock right or warrant. Conceivably, a corporation that purchases a long-term bond investment with detachable warrants could classify the bond investment as non-current and the warrants as temporary.

In the paragraphs that follow we discuss accounting for warrants that are acquired when other securities are acquired and rights acquired under the preemptive right of stockholders when the issuing corporation expands its outstanding stock. We close this section with a discussion of accounting for the receipt of shares of stock from stock dividends and stock splits issued by companies whose stock is held as an investment. Stock warrants and rights, as well as stock dividends and splits, are discussed in greater depth from the viewpoint of the issuing company in Chapters 16 and 17 on stockholders' equity.

Warrants, Rights, Stock Dividends, and Splits

1. Stock Warrants. Stock warrants (sometimes called stock-purchase warrants) convey to the holder the ability to buy a given number of shares of stock at a stated price for a specified period of time. Warrants are often issued when a company sells bonds or stock to make the securities being issued more attractive.

When an investor acquires a stock warrant along with another security such as a bond or share of preferred stock, accountants must allocate the total price paid between the two securities. They normally accomplish this by using the relative market values of the two securities as indicated in the following formula:

$$\begin{matrix} \text{Allocated cost} \\ \text{of stock} \\ \text{warrants} \end{matrix} = \frac{\text{Fair market value of warrants}}{\left(\begin{matrix}\text{Fair market}\\\text{value of}\\\text{warrants}\end{matrix}\right) + \left(\begin{matrix}\text{Fair market}\\\text{value of}\\\text{other security}\end{matrix}\right)} \times \begin{matrix}\text{Total cost}\\\text{of}\\\text{investment}\end{matrix}$$

For example, assume that Stable Company purchases ten $1,000 bonds for $1,050 each and receives with every bond 10 warrants, each of which may be used to acquire one additional share of common stock. Immediately after the securities are acquired, separate markets arise for the warrants and the bonds. The fair market value of each bond is $1,025, while the fair market value of each warrant is $5. The following calculation is necessary to allocate the total cost:

$$\begin{aligned}\text{Cost of warrants} &= \frac{\$5 \times 100 \text{ warrants}}{(\$5 \times 100 \text{ warrants}) + (\$1,025 \times 10 \text{ bonds})} \\ &\quad \times (\$1,050 \times 10 \text{ bonds}) \\ &= \$488.37\end{aligned}$$

The following entry records the acquisition of the two securities:

Stock-Purchase Warrants	488	
Investment in Bonds	10,012	
Cash		10,500
(To record acquisition of bonds with stock-purchase warrants.)		

Each warrant has an allocated cost of $4.88 ($488 ÷ 100). Since the life of most warrants is limited, they must be exercised or sold, or else they become worthless. If the warrants expire without being sold or exercised, a loss is recognized to the extent of the allocated cost of the warrants.

To illustrate the accounting for stock warrants subsequent to purchase, assume that the bond investor exercises half of the warrants (50 warrants). Further assume that the investor can exercise each warrant at $50. The journal entry would be:

Marketable Equity Securities	2,744	
Stock-Purchase Warrants ($4.88 × 50)		244
Cash ($50 × 50)		2,500
(To exercise 50 stock-purchase warrants.)		

The market price of the stock when the warrants are exercised had no impact on the cost of the stock acquired. If the remaining warrants are sold for $5.50 each, a gain should be recognized as follows:

Cash (50 × $5.50)	275	
Stock-Purchase Warrants		244
Gain on Sale of Warrants		31
(To record the sale of the remaining warrants.)		

Warrants that expire unexercised or unsold are eliminated from the accounting records by recognizing a loss equal to the allocated cost of the expired warrants. To illustrate, assume that the investor allowed the 50 warrants that were not exercised in the previous example to expire rather than sell them. A loss is recognized as follows:

Loss on Expiration of Stock-Purchase Warrants	244	
Stock-Purchase Warrants		244
(To record expiration of warrants.)		

2. Stock Rights. A stock right is a document frequently distributed by a corporation to employees or shareholders on a pro rata basis. Rights allow current shareholders to maintain their proportionate interest in the corporation pursuant to a new stock issue by exercising the rights and acquiring additional stock. A stockholder may choose instead to sell the rights on the open market.

When stock rights are received, the accountant for the investor allocates the cost of the original stock investment between (1) the original investment and (2) the rights just received. This allocation should be based on the relative fair market values of the rights and the stock at the time the rights are received. When separate stock rights are issued, a market price will exist for them as well as for the related stock. Therefore, the following formula should be used to determine the amount to be assigned to the rights:

$$\begin{array}{c} \text{Allocated} \\ \text{cost of} \\ \text{rights} \end{array} = \frac{\text{Fair market value of rights}}{\left(\begin{array}{c}\text{Fair market}\\\text{value of}\\\text{rights}\end{array}\right) + \left(\begin{array}{c}\text{Fair market}\\\text{value of}\\\text{stock}\end{array}\right)} \times \begin{array}{c}\text{Total}\\\text{cost of}\\\text{investment}\end{array}$$

For example, assume that Stable Company acquires 10 shares of Cypress Company's common stock for $50 per share and later receives a stock right for each share of stock held. If the market value of the rights is $5 per right and the value of the stock is $60 per share at the time the rights are received, the following calculation is necessary:

$$\text{Allocated cost of rights} = \frac{\$50}{\$50 + \$600} \times \$500 = \$38.46$$

A journal entry is then made to reflect the allocation of cost to the new investment:

Investment in Stock Rights	38	
Investment in Common Stock		38
(To record receipt of stock rights.)		

If the rights are sold, a gain or loss is recognized if the proceeds from the sale differ from the allocated cost. If the rights are exercised and new shares are acquired, the cost of the new shares is calculated as the allocated cost of the rights plus the additional amount paid for the shares. If the rights expire and become worthless, then the Investment in Stock Rights account is eliminated with a loss recognized equal to the allocated cost. The loss represents the dilution of the ownership interest experienced by the investor because of nonexercise of the rights. The journal entries to account for the disposition of stock rights are essentially the same as those for stock-purchase warrants presented in the previous section.

3. Stock Dividends and Stock Splits.   Occasionally a company may receive a dividend from its investments that consists of additional shares of stock of the investee company. A similar situation exists when a **stock split** occurs and the investor receives additional shares of stock from the investee.

In such cases, the recipient (investor) of the additional stock makes no accounting entry. Rather, a memorandum is written to indicate that the original investment cost must now be allocated over the greater number of shares.

To illustrate, assume that Stable Company holds 200 shares of Hill Company's common stock that were purchased for $11,000 ($55 a share) when Hill declares a 10% stock dividend. Stable will receive an additional 20 shares (200 × 10%) of Hill stock. Subsequent to the dividend, Stable holds 220 shares of stock at a cost of $11,000, or $50 per share. If 50 shares are now sold for $60 per share, the following entry is appropriate:

Cash	3,000	
Investment in Common Stock		2,500
Realized Gain on Sale of Stock		500
(To record sale of 50 shares		
of Hill Company's common stock.		
50 × $60 = $3,000.)		

The remaining 170 shares of Hill stock are carried on Stable's books at $8,500 ($11,000 − $2,500), or $50 per share.

If Hill Company had issued a stock split rather than a stock dividend, essentially the same procedure would be followed. However, the increase in shares would have been much greater than 10%; for example, it could have been 100% or 200%.

NONCURRENT INVESTMENTS

As previously noted, companies frequently invest in the securities of different enterprises for purposes other than the temporary investment of idle cash. In such circumstances, these investments are excluded from current assets and reported as noncurrent investments in the investing company's balance sheet.

In addition to the reasons mentioned earlier, such as the retirement of debt or the ability to control another enterprise, a company may make long-term investments in another business for other reasons. For example, a company that desires to expand operations to a new product line or geographic area may presently lack adequate liquid resources. The company may discover, however, that it can capitalize on such opportunities immediately by investing in other enterprises that are already involved in those activities. In such cases, the company may have other investment objectives as well, and accountants should understand completely the nature and purpose of the investment in order to provide the appropriate accounting and reporting treatment.

Noncurrent Investments in Debt Securities

A company may acquire the debt securities of other businesses as long-term investments for such reasons as (1) accumulating liquid resources for some noncurrent purpose, and (2) earning an acceptable rate of return on those liquid resources during the accumulation process.

These objectives contrast with the purposes of making short-term investments in debt securities; that is, to invest temporarily excess cash for a short period of time. Because of these differing investment objectives, accounting practices for noncurrent debt investments differ from those appropriate for current debt investments.

When a company acquires the debt securities of another company as a noncurrent investment, the acquisition price frequently differs from the maturity value of the debt instrument. The rate of interest stated on a bond may become unrealistic as a result of changing economic conditions in money markets as well as changes in the risk class of the company issuing the bond. In such cases, buyers may be willing to pay more or less for the bond than its stated or face value. If this occurs, the difference between the cash paid to acquire a security and the face value of the security is viewed as an adjustment of the security's stated rate of interest. *Accounting Principles Board Opinion No. 21* deals with this particular phenomenon and many other areas of financial accounting.[8] However, since this is the first chapter that contains material that is directly related to the provisions of *APB Opinion No. 21,* this chapter will discuss those provisions. Other assets and liabilities that are subject to the requirements of *Opinion No. 21* are discussed fully in later chapters.

Present-Value Applications

APB Opinion No. 21 establishes accounting practices for bonds, notes, and other similar receivables and payables; it was issued to deal with an increased use of notes that departed from normal borrowing and lending practices. Such transactions are normally made to achieve economic benefit other than those produced by the stated rate of interest and the face or maturity value of the note. Types of notes that are involved in such transactions include: (1) noninterest-bearing notes; (2) notes containing stated interest rates that vary from appropriate prevailing market rates; and (3) other notes used in ways that are inconsistent with general lending practices.

In general, investments in bonds and notes receivable are recorded at the fair market value of the consideration given for the note. When notes are issued or acquired solely for cash, the value of the note is presumed to be the amount of cash received or paid. If a note is exchanged for noncash consideration, the fair market value of the noncash consideration is presumed to represent the present value of the note. If the fair market value of the noncash consideration is not determinable, however, we must then select an appropriate interest rate and compute the present value of the note by using techniques described in Chapter 6. In such cases the interest rate to be used in valuing the transaction can be affected by several considerations, such as the credit standing of the issuer, any restrictive covenants in the note, tax consequences, and collateral. Of course, prevailing rates of interest for similar notes of issuers with similar credit ratings also help in the selection of an appropriate interest rate for determining the present value of a specific note. In essence, the objective in selecting an interest rate is to approximate the rate that would have been incurred in an arm's-length transaction involving cash lending or borrowing.

Substance over Form

In some circumstances, a stated rate of interest on a note may not represent the rate that would exist in an arms'-length transaction. For example, the existence of related parties and related-party transactions may indicate that the stated rate of interest is not reasonable. In such situations, stated or unstated rights and privileges may alter the effective (or actual) rate of interest. If a right to abnormal purchase or sales discounts is granted as part of the consideration for a loan, the difference between the present value of the note receivable and the cash loaned is properly regarded as discount or premium on the note. Since premium or discount is treated as an element of interest, the effective rate of interest implicit in such notes will differ from the stated rate.

Accounting for Premium and Discount

Any **premium** or **discount** recognized in conjunction with a note is treated as a direct

---

[8]*APB Opinion No. 21,* "Interest on Receivables and Payables," 1971.

increase (premium) or reduction (discount) in the carrying amount of the note. That is, the note is originally presented in the balance sheet at its present value, the market value of the note when it is acquired. The related premium or discount is then amortized as an adjustment to interest revenue over the life of the note by using the effective rate of interest implicit in the note.[9] The effective rate of interest in a note is represented by the discount rate that equates the proceeds of the note with the two future cash flows (interest payments and maturity amount) obtainable from the note. We apply the effective rate of interest in a note to the carrying value of the note at the beginning of each period to determine annual interest. In this manner a constant rate of interest is recognized over the life of the note. The difference between the total interest revenue, determined by applying the effective rate of interest in the note to the carrying amount of the note, and the cash received in a period represents the amount of premium or discount to be amortized. Of course, this is consistent with the amortization practices discussed in Chapter 6.

The straight-line method of amortizing premium or discount is not acceptable unless the results of applying that method are not materially different from the **effective interest** method (also called the **compound interest method** or simply the **interest method**).

A Comprehensive Example

The following example illustrates the provisions of *APB Opinion No. 21* as applied to noncurrent investments in debt securities. Later chapters illustrate applications in related circumstances.

Assume that Stable Company acquires ten $1,000 bonds of the Leverage Company on January 1, 1984, as a long-term investment at 89.2 (i.e., at 89.2% of the face amount). The bonds mature in five years and bear a stated rate of interest of 9% payable annually on December 31. The following entry would record the acquisition of the bonds:

Jan. 1, 1984	Investment in Bonds	10,000	
	Discount on Bond Investment		1,080
	Cash		8,920

The computations are as follows:

$1,000 × 10 = $10,000 Face amount
$1,000 × 10 × 89.2% = (8,920) Cash paid
$ 1,080 Discount

The determination of the interest rate (12%) implicit in this transaction requires trial and error, because it represents a present-value problem involving both an annuity and a single amount. To illustrate, note that when Stable bought the Leverage bonds, rights to two cash flows were acquired:

1. Interest payments of $900 (9% × $1,000 × 10) per year for five years.
2. The maturity value of $10,000 at the end of five years.

Since the Stable Company is willing to pay only $8,920 for both of these rights, there is some interest rate (r) that will equate both future cash flows (interest and principal) with the investment price or present value (PV) of $8,920. The equation may be expressed as follows:

PV of both types of future cash flows for n years at r rate = PV of investment

or

---

[9]*APB Opinion No. 21,* par. 15.

PV of the interest payment annuity for five years at r rate
+ PV of the maturity value in five years at r rate = PV of total investment

In the case of Stable Company, the equation would become:

$900 yearly for five years at r + $10,000 in five years at r = $8,920

Since both the present values of an annuity (series of payments) and an amount (single payment) are involved, it is necessary to "guess" at the effective rate and use the present-value tables contained in Chapter 6. Since the bonds were acquired at a discount, the effective rate is logically greater than the stated rate of 9%.

Try 12%:

$$(\$900 \times 3.60478^{[10]}) + (\$10,000 \times .56743^{[11]}) \approx \$8,920$$
$$\$3,244 + \$5,674 \approx \$8,920$$
$$\$8,918 \approx \$8,920$$

The effective interest rate of 12% approximately equates both of the future cash flows with the present value of the investment and is therefore the effective rate of interest in the investment. If a higher or lower rate had been selected originally, then the computation would have failed to equate the two numbers, thereby requiring the testing of different rates until the equation was satisfied.

At the end of the year, the 9% interest payment is received and a portion of the discount on the bonds is amortized:

Dec. 31, 1984	Cash	900	
	Interest Revenue		900
	(9% × $10,000 = $900 interest)		
Dec. 31, 1984	Discount on Bond Investment	170	
	Interest Revenue		170
	(To record amortization of discount.		
	$8,920 × 12% = $1,070;		
	$1,070 − $900 = $170.)		

During the first year of the investment, 12% is earned on the carrying amount of the investment at the beginning of the period. Since the carrying amount of the investment during the year is $8,920, then $1,070 ($8,920.00 × 12%) total interest revenue is earned. Since $900 ($10,000 × 9%) is received in cash, the difference of $170 ($1,070 − $900) represents the amount of discount to be amortized. Exhibit 10–8 presents an amortization table developed for Stable Company as an aid to accounting for this investment.

At the end of the second year the effective interest rate (12%) is applied to whatever the investment's carrying amount was at the beginning of the *second* period. Since $170 of discount was amortized at the end of the first year, the carrying amount of the investment changed by that amount as demonstrated below:

Investment in Bonds

Balance, Dec. 31, 1984	10,000

---

[10] 3.60478 is the present value of 5 rents of $1 at 12%. See Table 6–4.
[11] .56743 is the present value of a single $1 due five years from now at 12%. See Table 6–2.

EXHIBIT 10–8
Amortization Table for Investment in Bonds at Discount

Date	Explanation	(1) (12% carrying value [Col. 6]) Total Interest Revenue	(2) (9% × $10,000) Cash Received	(3) (Col. 1 − Col. 2) Discount To Be Amortized	(4) Face Amount of Bonds	(5) (Reduced by Col. 3) Remaining Discount	(6) (Col. 4 − Col. 5) Carrying Amount
Jan. 1, 1984	Acquisition of bonds	—	—	—	$10,000	$1,080	$ 8,920
Dec. 31, 1984	Recognition of interest	$1,070	$900	$170	10,000	910	9,090
Dec. 31, 1985	Recognition of interest	1,091	900	191	10,000	719	9,281
Dec. 31, 1986	Recognition of interest	1,114	900	214	10,000	505	9,495
Dec. 31, 1987	Recognition of interest	1,139	900	239	10,000	266	9,734
Dec. 31, 1988	Recognition of interest	1,166*	900	266	10,000	—	10,000

*Minor rounding adjustment in 1988 figures to eliminate remaining discount.

Discount on Bonds

		1,080	Balance, Jan. 1, 1984
Amortization, Dec. 31, 1984	170		
		910	Balance, Jan. 1, 1985

Investment in Bonds	$10,000
Discount at Jan. 1, 1985	910
Carrying amount at Jan. 1, 1985	$ 9,090

Therefore, the carrying amount of the investment is $9,090 at the beginning of the second year. By multiplying the carrying value of the note by the effective interest rate (12%), we compute the total interest revenue for the second year to be $1,091. Again, since $900 of this amount is received in cash, the difference of $191 ($1,091 − $900) represents the amount of discount to be amortized as additional interest revenue. This process continues each year until all of the discount has been amortized and the bonds mature. Since all of the discount is amortized, no gain or loss is recognized at the maturity of the bonds as reflected in Exhibit 10–8. The carrying value of the investment at the maturity date (December 31, 1988) is $10,000.

If the straight-line method of amortization had been used in this example, the amount of amortization would be $216 ($1,080/5) per year. As in the effective interest method, the carrying amount of the bond investment would increase to $10,000, except the increase would accumulate in equal increments of $216. Compared to the effective interest method, the straight-line method is conceptually inferior. The interest revenue would be overstated in the earlier years and understated in the latter years for a bond purchased at a discount. The opposite pattern would hold for bonds purchased at a premium. As a result, the straight-line amortization method is not generally acceptable unless the periodic difference between the straight-line and effective interest methods is immaterial.

Materiality

How would these procedures differ if the bonds had been acquired at a price greater than par value rather than less? The effective interest rate would be less than the stated rate. This rate is applied to the carrying amount of the investment to determine interest revenue for the period, which would be an amount less than the cash received. The difference between the interest revenue and the cash received is amortized as a *reduction* in the carrying amount of the investment. As in the case of an investment acquired at a discount, the straight-line method of amortization is appropriate only if it renders amounts that do not vary materially from those obtained from the effective interest method.

To illustrate, assume that Stable Company acquired the $10,000 par value bonds at $10,400, which results in an approximate effective interest rate of 8%. The journal entries to record the acquisition of the bonds on January 1, 1984, and to recognize interest revenue at December 31, 1984, are as follows:

Jan. 1, 1984	Investment in Bonds	10,000	
	Premium on Bond Investment	400	
	Cash		10,400
Dec. 31, 1984	Cash	900	
	Interest Revenue ($10,400 × 8%)		832
	Premium on Bond Investment		68

The December 31, 1984, entry reduces the Premium on Bond Investment to $332 ($400 − $68), and interest revenue for 1985 is computed as $827 ($10,332 × 8%). If straight-line amortization were applied, annual amortization of the premium would be $80 ($400/5 years).

In both the discount and premium examples illustrated above we have debited the Investment in Bonds account for the par value of the bonds and used a separate Discount (or Premium) on Bond Investment account for the difference between the acquisition price of the investment and the par value of the bonds. The Investment in Bonds account and the Discount (or Premium) on Investment account are usually combined for presentation in the balance sheet and may be combined in the company's records as well. If the investment is carried in a single investment account rather than in separate accounts as illustrated here, amortization of any discount or premium is made directly to the Investment account.

If the bonds are sold before their maturity date, a gain or loss may arise. Because any premium or discount recognized at the acquisition of the bond has been subject to amortization since acquisition, the amount of gain or loss depends in part on the remaining unamortized premium or discount. Returning to the previous discount example, assume that Stable sells the Leverage bonds on June 30, 1985, for $10,200 plus accrued interest. The following entries would be necessary:

June 30, 1985	Interest Receivable	450	
	Interest Revenue		450
	(To accrue interest receivable.		
	$10,000 × 9% × ½ = $450.)		
June 30, 1985	Discount on Bond Investment	95	
	Interest Revenue		95
	(To amortize discount on bonds for the period		
	Jan. 1, 1985 through June 30, 1985.)		

Calculations for the discount are as follows:

$9,090 × 12% × ½	= $ 545
Less: Amount to be received in cash	(450)
Discount to be amortized	$ 95

A third entry would also be required:

June 30, 1985	Cash	10,650	
	Discount on Bond Investment	815	
	Gain on Sale of Bonds		1,015
	Investment in Bonds		10,000
	Interest Receivable		450

(To record receipt of cash, $10,200 + $450 = $10,650; elimination of remaining discount, $910 − $95 = $815; elimination of investment in bonds; and recognition of gain.)

In this illustration we have assumed that the entire investment in the bonds held by Stable Company was sold. If only part of the bonds had been sold, the entries to record interest receivable, amortization of discount, and the sale would be made for only that part of the investment that was sold. For example, if 4 of the 10 bonds had been sold, only $180 of interest revenue would be recognized ($450 × 40%); only $38 of bond discount amortization would be recognized ($95 × 40%); and a gain of only $406 would be recognized ($1,015 × 40%).

Accounting for noncurrent investments in debt securities is the same regardless of the level of the investment; however, accounting for noncurrent investments in equity securities may differ substantially, depending on the level of investment. We examine these phenomena closely in the following portion of this chapter.

Noncurrent Investments in Equity Securities

If one company acquires the equity securities of another firm as a noncurrent investment, we must classify the investment as one of the following types:

1. **Passive.** The investment is consummated in order to earn a return (dividends and/or long-term capital increment). Securities may be voting or nonvoting. Securities are reported at the lower of cost or market.
2. **Significant influence.** The investment is consummated in order to affect the operating or financial policies of the investee and to earn a return. Securities must convey voting rights to the investor to establish influence. Securities are reported by using the equity method in which investee earnings (net income) are accrued by the investor and dividends reduce the investment carrying amount.
3. **Control.** The investment is consummated to obtain the ability to mandate operating or financial policies of a subsidiary and to earn a return. Securities must convey voting rights to permit control. The financial statements of the investee are normally consolidated with those of the investor, because in substance only a single "economic" entity exists.

Substance over Form

An accountant's determination of whether an investment is passive or designed to obtain significant influence or control of the investee is based primarily on the magnitude of the investment. Different accounting and reporting practices are appropriate for each type of equity investment. Exhibit 10–9 displays the nature and objective of each type of investment and describes the general reporting practice for each. The next three subsections of this chapter consider the conceptual differences and appropriate accounting practices for each of the three types of equity investments.

EXHIBIT 10–9
Summary of Investments in Equity Securities

Issue	Level of Investment		
Ownership of voting stock	Less than 20%	20%–50%	More than 50%
Character of investment	Passive	Significant influence	Control
General reporting practice	Lower of cost or market	Equity method	Consolidation
Primary relevant literature	*SFAS No. 12; ARB No. 43, Ch. 3*	*APB Opinion No. 18.*	*ARB No. 51; APB Opinion Nos. 16 and 17.*

Passive Equity Investments

Our previous discussion of marketable equity securities revealed that *SFAS No. 12* specifies accounting and reporting practices for both current and noncurrent portfolios of marketable equity securities. At this point we shall consider financial accounting and reporting standards for noncurrent portfolios of marketable equity securities.

Revenue Realization

The noncurrent portfolio, like the current portfolio, should be valued at the lower of aggregate cost or market at each balance sheet date. Several accounting practices specified for noncurrent marketable equity securities, however, differ from those employed for the current portfolio. Foremost among the differences is the practice of recognizing only *realized* gains and losses in the income statement. Although the carrying amount of the noncurrent marketable equity securities portfolio is reduced from aggregate cost to a lower aggregate market for all market declines, only *permanent* aggregate market declines are recognized in the income of the period. Aggregate market declines that are *temporary,* while requiring recognition in the asset valuation allowance, do not result in losses reported in the income statement.[12] Rather, we report a temporary aggregate market decline below aggregate cost as a direct reduction of stockholders' equity, thereby avoiding the recognition of a loss in the income statement. The practice of not recording in the income statement the losses on noncurrent marketable equity securities that result from temporary market declines is different from the treatment accorded the current marketable equity securities portfolio. Although it may appear somewhat unusual, the practice is supported theoretically; that is, temporary market declines do not cause a company to sustain losses on long-term investments, because such securities are held for an extended period of time and later market recoveries are expected to prevent the realization of the reportable loss.

A temporary market decline in the value of a security is much more likely to cause a company to sustain a loss if the security is to be held for only a short period of time. Therefore, such temporary declines are recognized in income if the investment is current; however, only permanent market declines are recognized in income for noncurrent investments in marketable equity securities. To illustrate, assume that Stable Company acquires the portfolio of noncurrent marketable equity securities indicated in Exhibit 10–10 during 1984.

---
[12]*FASB Statement of Financial Accounting Standards No. 12,* par. 11.

If we assume that the total market decline is considered to be due to temporary market conditions, the following entry will be necessary at December 31, 1984, to value these noncurrent marketable equity securities (NCMES):

Dec. 31, 1984	Net Unrealized Loss on NCMES	110,000	
	Valuation Allowance to		
	Reduce NCMES to Lower		
	of Aggregate Cost or		
	Market		110,000
	($650,000 − $540,000 = $110,000)		

The noncurrent investments and stockholders' equity sections of the Stable Company balance sheet reflect the results of the above entry in the following manner:

Noncurrent investment	
Noncurrent marketable equity	
securities carried at market on	
December 31, 1984	$540,000
Stockholders' equity	
Net unrealized loss on noncurrent	
marketable equity securities	$(110,000)

Disclosure The negative stockholders' equity account is typically presented as one of the last stockholders' equity items in the balance sheet, immediately before or after retained earnings. Footnote disclosure of the amount of the valuation allowance and other required information, which is similar to that required for the current portfolio presented earlier, should accompany the financial statements.

Since the loss is unrealized and relates to a noncurrent marketable equity security portfolio, net income is not affected. Any subsequent reductions in the valuation allowance arising from an increase in the market value of the long-term portfolio is recorded as a reduction in the Net Unrealized Loss on NCMES (stockholders' equity) account. The reduction in the Net Unrealized Loss on NCMES account can never exceed the balance of the

---

EXHIBIT 10–10
Lower of Aggregate Cost or Market Valuation—Noncurrent Portfolio
December 31, 1984

Security	(1) Number of Shares	(2) Cost per Share	(3) Market Price per Share	(4) (Col. 1 × Col. 2) Total Cost	(5) (Col. 1 × Col. 3) Total Market Value
Volunteer Corporation, common	10,000	$ 30	$ 20	$300,000	$200,000
Crossville Company, common	2,000	50	95	100,000	190,000
Sunshine Corporation, common	1,000	250	150	250,000	150,000
Aggregate totals				$650,000	$540,000

account, and therefore a lower of cost or market valuation is ensured. Since the Net Unrealized Loss on NCMES account is part of the stockholders' equity, and thus a real account, direct credits can be made to the account for subsequent market recoveries.

Continuing the example of Stable Company from Exhibit 10–10, assume that one year later the company holds the same securities, but now they have an aggregate market value of $615,000. The entry to record the $75,000 market value recovery ($615,000 − $540,000) would be as follows:

| Dec. 31, 1985 | Valuation Allowance to Reduce NCMES to Lower of Aggregate Cost or Market | 75,000 | |
| | Net Unrealized Loss on NCMES | | 75,000 |

How would this entry have differed if the market had risen to $660,000? The market value would then *exceed* cost, and both the valuation allowance account and the Net Unrealized Loss on NCMES account would have to be totally eliminated. The same entry as above would be made, except the amounts would be $110,000. Notice that any increase in market value beyond the original cost is not recorded.

As mentioned previously, the FASB distinguishes between realized and unrealized losses by stating that only realized losses on noncurrent marketable equity securities should be recognized in income. The FASB gives three conditions under which losses on noncurrent investments must be treated as realized losses and recognized in income in the year of the loss: (1) sale or disposal of the security (discussed earlier); (2) transfer of the security to the current marketable equity security classification, or vice versa; or (3) a permanent decline in the market value of an individual security below its cost.[13]

Conditions one and three provide convincing evidence that a permanent loss has been sustained by the investing company, and, therefore, income statement recognition of the loss is necessary. Transfers of securities between the current and noncurrent portfolios (condition two) may also give rise to a realized loss on the income statement. The purpose of this condition is to prevent managers from "dressing up" the income statement via classification changes between current and noncurrent investments in equity securities. In the absence of condition two, a manager could transfer a security with a large unrealized loss position to the noncurrent portfolio. This would effectively shift the recognition of the unrealized loss from the income statement to the stockholders' equity section and, hence, arbitrarily improve net income. Condition two reduces the incentive for this type of behavior by requiring a loss position to be recognized on the income statement upon portfolio reclassification of a security.

A realized gain or loss resulting from the sale of a security is handled as the sale of any other asset: A debit is made to Cash for the amount received, the investment account is reduced (credited) by the cost of the security, and a realized gain or loss is recognized for the difference between the two. As is the case with the current portfolio of marketable equity securities discussed earlier, the valuation allowance is not adjusted at the time of the sale of the security. Also, with the noncurrent portfolio the Unrealized Loss on NCMES account in stockholders' equity is not adjusted at the time of sale. Both the valuation allowance and the Unrealized Loss on NCMES accounts are adjusted at the end of the accounting period, and the fact that securities were sold during the period may affect the amount of the adjustment to these accounts.

To illustrate changing to the current classification, assume that Stable Company changes its investment intent regarding the Sunshine stock on January 30, 1985, when the stock has a market value of $195 per share. The entry to recognize the realized loss and to reclassify the stock as a current asset is as follows:

Jan. 30, 1985	Current Marketable Equity Securities	195,000	
	Realized Loss on Valuation of		
	Marketable Equity Securities	55,000	
	Noncurrent Marketable		
	Equity Securities		250,000

The recognition of a permanent decline in an individual security in the noncurrent portfolio of marketable equity securities is relatively straightforward. The difference between the cost and the lower market value of the security is debited to a realized loss account and credited to the investment account. The valuation allowance is unaffected by this procedure. In subsequent aggregate cost and market comparisons made to determine the lower of the two, the revised (lower) cost figure is used rather than the original (higher) cost figure.

Changes in the value of marketable equity securities taking place after the balance sheet date should not be reflected in the financial statements, even if such a decline is considered permanent. For example, if the market value of a portfolio declines subsequent to the balance sheet date, the amount of the decline should not be recorded as an increase in the valuation allowance. However, when changes in the market value of securities take place after the balance sheet date, the following considerations apply:[14]

1. For marketable equity securities for which a change in carrying amount is included in stockholders' equity (rather than in net income), in judging whether a decline is other than temporary, a gain or loss realized on subsequent disposition or changes in market prices occurring after the date of the financial statements shall be taken into consideration along with other factors.

2. A recovery in market value after the balance sheet date tends to indicate that a portion or all of the decline at the balance sheet date was temporary. Such recovery should be considered when estimating the amount of decline as of the balance sheet date judged to be permanent.

Thus, we use information becoming available after the date of the balance sheet to guide financial reporting for the year just ended. The amount of gain or loss to be realized, however, is measured by the market value of the securities at the balance sheet date.

When cash dividends are received on passive investments in marketable equity securities, revenue is recognized in the amount of the dividend. For example, if Stable Company receives a dividend of $3,000 from Volunteer Corporation, the following entry is needed:

Cash	3,000	
Dividend Revenue		3,000
(To record receipt of cash dividend.)		

Occasionally, an investee company declares a dividend that exceeds its existing retained earnings. In such cases the recipient company recognizes the receipt of a liquidating dividend and, instead of recognizing dividend revenue, records a recovery of a portion of the original investment. Liquidating dividends are fairly common in mining and petroleum operations. To illustrate, assume that Stable Company receives a $1,000 liquidating dividend from Volunteer Corporation. The following entry should be made:

---

[14]*FASB Interpretation No. 11*, "Changes in Market Value After the Balance Sheet Date," 1976, pars. 3–4.

Cash	1,000	
Noncurrent Marketable		
Equity Securities		1,000
(To record receipt of liquidating dividend.)		

Passive investments in *nonmarketable* equity securities, such as stock of a closely held corporation, should be carried at cost unless there is clear evidence of an impairment in carrying value. Since no market value exists, such investments are not considered current except in unusual circumstances such as an imminent sale. We apply the general criteria for recognizing any loss contingency to investments in nonmarketable securities. Chapter 14, which deals with a wide variety of contingent losses, discusses these issues further.

A Learning Tool

The learning summary flowchart in Exhibit 10–11 describes accounting and reporting practices for noncurrent marketable equity securities. These same principles apply for marketable equity securities in unclassified balance sheets. The flowchart provides a useful review tool and condenses the preceding illustrations and explanations to facilitate a comprehensive understanding of financial accounting and reporting for noncurrent marketable equity securities.

Equity Investments Representing Significant Influence

Different accounting practices are required if the level of a long-term investment in voting marketable equity securities reaches a point at which **significant influence** is exercised by the investor over the operating and financial policies of the investee. The ability to significantly influence an investee company provides evidence that the earnings of the investee have direct implications for the investor. Indeed, the actions of the investor may lead to increased (or depressed) levels of the investee's earnings. For example, an investor may influence an investee to adopt new technologies (leading to increased profitability) that the investee would not have been able or willing to adopt without the equity investment.

The range of business activities and purposes for which significant influence investments are made is broad. If an investor exercises significant influence over an investee, then the investor should accrue a portion of the income earned by the investee during that period. The amount of investee income to be reported as an increase in the investment account and as income to the investor is based on the level of the equity investment in the investee.

The **equity method** of accounting for significant influence investments is a sound accounting principle, because the carrying amount of the investment is directly affected by the results of the investee's operations. In this fashion, application of the equity method represents a type of "automatic valuation" accounting. An investment in the voting stock of a company represents, in substance, an investment in the net assets of that company. Changes in the investee's net assets that result from earnings or dividend payments require immediate accounting for the changes in the investment account of the investor.

Revenue Realization

In essence, the equity method of accounting is an example of accrual accounting. The investor company recognizes its share of the investee earnings on the income statement in the period earned. The income is later realized either via dividend distributions by the investee or via later disposition of the investment by the investor. The undistributed earnings (earnings retained after dividends are distributed) of the investee represent an increase in the net assets of the investee. A profitable investee company should experience a rise in the market value of its outstanding equity as the net assets increase from undistributed earnings. Therefore, the cash flow that an investor could realize from the disposition of the investment is simply the realization of previously recognized income.

Obviously the "automatic valuation" represented by the equity method is simply a surrogate for measuring the investment at current value. Indeed, if the current value of the investee equity shares were the accepted method of valuation, the equity method would be

EXHIBIT 10–11
Noncurrent and Unclassified Marketable
Equity Securities Portfolio

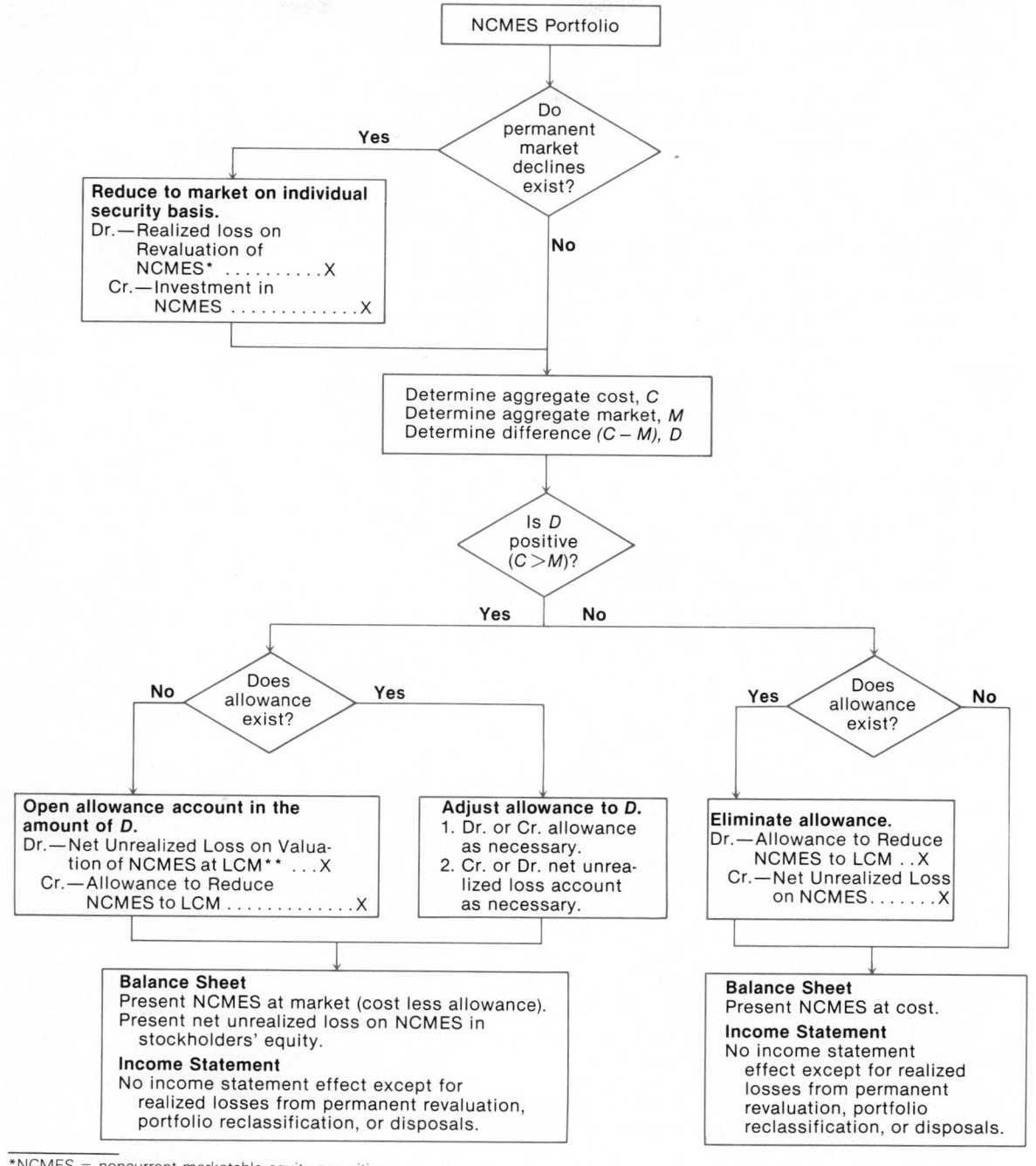

*NCMES = noncurrent marketable equity securities.
**LCM = lower of cost or market.

EQUITY EARNINGS

MANAGEMENTS ONCE AGAIN have found a way to get more smoke out of their earnings chimneys even though there isn't much fire in their stoves. The smoke—smoke screen might be a better term—comes from what accountants call equity earnings. Equity earnings are profits earned by another company but carried on your P&L statement as well as on the other company's.

To oversimplify, it works like this: Suppose you own 100 shares of General Motors. In 1979 GM earned $10.04 a share and paid out $5.30 in dividends. As a shareholder you received $530. But you wanted to make your income statement look good and you decided to report your entire share of GM profits. So, you reported income of $1,004 instead of just $530. The extra $474 was "equity earnings." For you, it was not real income, even though it was being reinvested to work for you over the long term.

Sensibly, you wouldn't count on that extra $474, but a lot of companies that own stock in other companies report equity earnings as though they were income to them. The accountants mandate that they do so, provided their shareholdings equal or exceed 20% of the other companies' stock. You'll find equity earnings on a separate line in many corporate P&L statements. Although they are listed separately, they are taken directly to the famous bottom line. (Dividends, of course, are another matter; they are cash actually received and are counted as investment income. Equity earnings, by contrast, are only a bookkeeping fiction, consisting of the difference between earnings and dividends.)

The prime mover in this smoke-and-fire business was Dr. Henry E. Singleton, chairman of Teledyne. Shortly after the unorthodox Singleton personally took over management of his insurance subsidiary's stock portfolio, he flouted convention by concentrating his investments in a few stocks. His auditors advised him of the accounting consequences of Teledyne's owning more than 20% of the equity of Brockway Glass, Curtiss-Wright, Litton Industries and Reichhold Chemicals. The auditors insisted Teledyne must report on a separate line its proportionate share in these four companies' earnings in Teledyne's operating report. Mind you, the accountants didn't tell Singleton he *could* do this;

they said he *must*.

Singleton did not (and still does not) like consolidating any of TDY's earnings from investments because he does not consider equity earnings to be real earnings. He did not like the fact that including equity earnings would unrealistically inflate Teledyne's reported earnings. Still he surrendered to avoid confrontation with his auditors.

The percentage would have been higher—and so would Teledyne's reported earnings—if Singleton hadn't held back his holdings of Walter Kidde and National Can to under 20%. By doing so he avoided having to consolidate his equity holdings in these companies, too. If Singleton bought a mere $16 million more of Walter Kidde and National Can, Teledyne's equity earnings would then jump another $20 million annually, since the magic 20% ownership mark would have been surpassed.

The game that Singleton is playing reluctantly, others have begun to play eagerly. Borg-Warner CEO James F. Beré is swapping a division of his company to Hughes Tool for Hughes stock, raising Borg's Hughes holdings from 16% to over 20%. The swap will permit Borg to take in over $11 million of Hughes' 1980 earnings into Borg's total profits. Borg's 1980 earnings, which would otherwise have dipped from 1979, will now hold up or even increase, and the stock temporarily jumped 8%. But what has really changed? The reality is, a division has been shifted from one company to another. More smoke out of the chimney, with less operating fire.

Borg is hardly alone. Some companies have made a practice of triple-counting earnings by applying equity accounting principles. The case of Kennecott to Curtiss-Wright to Teledyne is a prime example. Curtiss-Wright owns 14% of Kennecott but consolidates 14% of earnings even though it is below the 20% mark. Thus Teledyne, which owns 32% of C-W, must consolidate the Kennecott equity earnings, too.

Have the accountants, once again, in attempting to clarify matters, ended by confusing them? . . . Does the inclusion of equity earnings mislead investors into capitalizing earnings that are not real? Smoke, after all, is not the same thing as fire.

SOURCE: Maria Latorraca and Stephen Gilbarg, "Equity Earnings," *Forbes,* March 31, 1980, pp. 100 –102. Reprinted by permission of *Forbes* Magazine. © Forbes, Inc., 1980.

superfluous. Alternatively, if the equity method of accounting were *not* required for investors holding significant influence, income would be recognized when dividends were received or when the investment was sold. In the latter case, if the investment was sold for a price greater than original cost, the gain would be both recognized and realized in the period of disposition. This approach would have the undesirable effect of delaying the recognition of income until the investment was sold and then recognizing in a single period the lump sum gain (or loss). In contrast, the equity method provides users of financial statements a more timely recognition of earned income from equity investments.

The ability to exercise significant influence may be evident in several ways. For example, representation on the investee's board of directors, material intercompany transactions, technological dependency of the investee, and other relationships may indicate an ability to exercise significant influence. Because of the difficulties in determining whether an investor exercises significant influence over the investee, *APB Opinion No. 18* established a threshold level of investment to guide practice.[15] It states that a direct or indirect investment of 20% or more in the *voting* stock of an investee indicates, in the absence of contrary evidence, that an investor has the ability to exercise significant influence over an investee.[16] The opinion thus establishes a presumption of significant influence arising at investment levels of 20% or more. The presumption may be rebutted, however, if evidence is available to support alternative practices. Recently, for example, several companies have applied the equity method of accounting to holdings of investee voting stock as small as 5% to 10%, contending that even such small investments create significant influence if the rest of the investee's stock is widely held.

Another important observation is also appropriate at this point. *APB Opinion No. 18* does not absolutely require application of the equity method if 20% or more of the voting stock of an investee is held. *FASB Interpretation No. 35* provides valuable guidance as to what types of evidence may overcome the presumption of significant influence arising at investment levels of 20% of the voting stock. Specifically, it provides five examples of evidence which tend to rebut the presumption of significant influence:

> *Opposition by the investee, such as litigation or complaints to governmental regulatory authorities, challenges the investor's ability to exercise significant influences.*

> *The investor and investee sign an agreement under which the investor surrenders significant rights as a shareholder.*

> *Majority ownership of the investee is concentrated among a small group of shareholders who operate the investee without regard to the views of the investor.*

> *The investor needs or wants more financial information to apply the equity method than is available to the investee's other shareholders (for example, the investor wants quarterly financial information from an investee that publicly reports only annually), tries to obtain that information, and fails.*

> *The investor tries and fails to obtain representation on the investee's board of directors.*[17]

Finally, although the test for significant influence is based on voting stock, the equity method is applied only to investments in common stock, whether or not it is voting stock. Thus, the

---

[15]*APB Opinion No. 18,* "The Equity Method of Accounting for Investments in Common Stock," 1971.
[16]*APB Opinion No. 18,* par. 17.
[17]*FASB Interpretation No. 35,* "Criteria for Applying the Equity Method of Accounting for Investments in Common Stock: An Interpretation of APB Opinion No. 18," 1981, par. 4.

investment level used to assess the existence of significant influence may differ from the investment level used in accounting for the investment.

A Basic Example of the Equity Method. An investor applying the equity method bases the recognition of income and a direct increase in the investment account on the share of the investee's income represented by the investment. The amount of income recognized is based on the proportion of investee's common stock held by the investor. Under the equity method, the receipt of dividends is treated as a reduction of the carrying amount of the investor's investment account. In essence, the receipt of dividends represents a conversion of the investment to cash from equity in the investee's assets. Equity investments may thus be recovered in cash through the receipt of dividends as well as through the direct sale of the securities.

The following example illustrates accounting practices appropriate for the equity method. Assume that Stable Company acquires a 25% interest in the voting stock of Tiny Company on January 1, 1985. Also assume that Tiny Company has only one class of common stock, all of which is voting, and that both companies report on a calendar-year basis. If Stable paid $500,000 for the investment, and Tiny reports a net income of $100,000 for 1985 and pays a $20,000 dividend in December 1985, the following entries are necessary:

Jan. 1, 1985	Investment in Equity Securities	500,000	
	Cash		500,000
	(To record acquisition of 25% voting interest in Tiny Company.)		
Dec. 31, 1985	Investment in Equity Securities	25,000	
	Equity in Investee Income		25,000
	(To record equity in investee net income. $100,000 \times 25\% =$ $25,000.)		
Dec. 31, 1985	Cash	5,000	
	Investment in Equity Securities		5,000
	(To record receipt of dividend. $20,000 \times 25\% = \$5,000.)$		

Excerpts from the 1985 balance sheet and income statement of Stable Company would appear as follows:

Stable Company
PARTIAL BALANCE SHEET
December 31, 1985

Noncurrent assets
Investment in equity securities $520,000
($500,000 + $25,000 − $5,000 = $520,000)

Stable Company
PARTIAL INCOME STATEMENT
For the Year Ended December 31, 1985

Other revenue
Equity in investee income $25,000

The favorable impact of the investee's earnings are, thus, immediately reflected in the investor's financial statements. The dividends received by the investor are treated as a partial recovery or liquidation of the investment. Financial reporting for investments accounted for under the equity method contain many additional significant issues, and the following paragraphs discuss several of these.

Intercompany Eliminations.   If material transactions occur between the investor and investee, such **intercompany transactions** should be eliminated when financial statements are prepared. Intercompany transactions usually represent selling and purchasing or lending and borrowing activities between the two companies. The effects of payables and receivables between investor and investee companies are eliminated on the investor's books by removing the specific payable or receivable and a like amount in the investment account.

If a company sells products to (or buys products from) another company in which an investment in voting stock is held and the equity method of accounting is employed, an unrealized revenue (or expense) arises and must be eliminated for financial reporting purposes. To illustrate, assume that Stable Company sells some of its inventory with a carrying value of $90,000 to Tiny Company for $100,000. Each company makes the following entry on its separate books.

Stable Company				Tiny Company		
Cash	100,000			Purchases	100,000	
Sales		100,000		Cash		100,000
Cost of						
Goods Sold	90,000					
Inventory		90,000				

Under the equity method the two entities are viewed as closely related and, to the extent of the equity investment, the gross profit of $10,000 on the sale and the increased carrying amount of $10,000 of the inventory are not deemed to be realized until the inventory is sold by Tiny Company to an external customer. Therefore, if the inventory remains unsold by Tiny at year-end, the following working paper "entry" is necessary to eliminate the unrealized profit:

Equity in Investee Income	2,500	
Investment in Equity Securities		2,500
($10,000 × 25% = $2,500 portion of total profit not realized)		

We eliminate only 25% of the profit and related asset amount because Stable Company owns only 25% of the voting stock of Tiny Company. This procedure should be followed whether the intercompany transaction is **downstream** (sale by investor to investee) or **upstream** (sale by investee to investor).

When the goods are sold to an outsider by Tiny Company, then the revenue is realized and should be recognized. Many more complex issues relating to the elimination of intercompany transactions are discussed in greater depth in subsequent accounting courses.

Revenue Realization

The Existence of Positive and Negative Differential.   Another issue arises in applying the equity method if the investor pays more or less for an investment than the book value of the underlying assets. For example, if the earning potential of the investee is abnormally high, the current value of the investee's net assets as represented by the market value of the investee's stock is frequently greater than the carrying amount on the investee's books. Regardless of the cause of a difference between the cost of an equity investment and the book value of the underlying assets, however, the investor is affected by that difference only during the economic life of the related assets.

If an excess amount is paid to acquire an equity interest in specifically identifiable undervalued assets, the difference is amortized over the individual lives of those assets. For example, assume that the book value of the net assets of Tiny Company is $1,960,000 and that Stable Company acquires a 25% ownership interest in Tiny Company for a cost of $500,000. A 25% ownership in Tiny's net assets, however, equals only $490,000 ($1,960,000 × 25%); therefore, Stable Company paid $10,000 more for the investment than is represented by the book value. If the management of Stable Company concludes that this differential represents an excess of the current value over the book value of Tiny Company's plant assets, which have a 20-year life, the following entry to amortize this differential is necessary at the end of each year.

Equity in Investee Income	500	
Investment in Equity Securities		500
($10,000 ÷ 20 years = $500)		

In practice, accountants frequently find it difficult to determine which specific assets are overvalued or undervalued and how much of the difference relates to general excess earning capacity. If the differential relates to excess earning capacity, rather than to specific assets, the excess is considered **goodwill**. *APB Opinion No. 17* specifies that amounts recorded for goodwill must be amortized over a period not to exceed 40 years.[18] Accountants frequently attribute all of the difference between the cost of an equity-method investment and the book value of the underlying net assets to goodwill because information about the value of specific assets is difficult to obtain. Furthermore, differences caused by this simplifying assumption are normally not material. Therefore, in most situations any excess of cost over the book value of the underlying assets is amortized as goodwill over a period no greater than 40 years. For example, in Stable Company's acquisition of Tiny Company—resulting in a $10,000 difference between cost and book value—if the $10,000 is interpreted as goodwill with a 10-year life, $1,000 would be amortized against the Equity in Investee Income account each year. Any negative differential (excess of carrying value over investment cost) is usually amortized in a similar fashion; however, the amortization results in increases, rather than decreases, in Equity in Investee Income and Investment in Equity Securities.

Materiality

Investee Operating Losses.   Another significant accounting issue arises if an investee company incurs operating losses to such an extent that application of the equity method reduces the investor's investment account to zero or to a credit balance. To illustrate, assume that Tiny Company incurs a $24,000 loss; then Stable Company should prepare the following entry:

Equity in Investee Loss	6,000	
Investment in Equity Securities		6,000
($24,000 × 25% = $6,000)		

This entry is appropriate unless it brings the investment account to a credit balance. In such circumstances, accountants consider several factors. Specifically, investors ordinarily discontinue applying the equity method if the investment account reaches zero, unless the investor: (1) has guaranteed the indebtedness of the investee or (2) is otherwise committed to provide financial support. For example, if the stock of the investee was acquired *from* the investee at less than par, then the investor may be obligated (in the event of investee dissolution) to contribute amounts that would make the investment equal to the par value of the stock. In such cases the Investment account may properly contain a credit balance and be reported as a liability to the extent of any contingent liability.

If the investee subsequently reports net income, the investor should resume applying the

---

[18]*APB Opinion No. 17,* "Intangible Assets," 1970, par. 29

equity method only after its share of the net income equals the share of net losses that were not recognized during the period the equity method was suspended. Of course, accountants maintain detailed workpapers to ensure proper application of the equity method in unusual circumstances.

Changing Investment Levels. Another issue related to the equity method involves changing investment levels and the related accounting and reporting treatments. We shall initially consider *increasing* levels of investments.

1. Changes *to* the Equity Method. When an investment first qualifies for using the equity method because of increasing investment levels, the investor should *retroactively* apply the equity method. In such cases, the investor company must calculate what the amount of the investment account would have been at the beginning of the current year if the equity method had been employed throughout the entire ownership period by using the percentages of ownership in effect during those periods. The resulting amount that would have been in the investment account is then compared with the balance actually in the investment account and an entry is made to adjust the investment account and Retained Earnings at the beginning of the year.

To illustrate, assume that Stable Company acquires a 10% interest in the voting stock of Balky Corporation for $100,000 on January 1, 1984. The following entry records the acquisition:

Jan. 1, 1984	Investment in Equity Securities	100,000	
	Cash		100,000

Since the level of investment is relatively small, the lower of cost or market method of accounting is applied to this investment. Therefore, if Balky Corporation earns net income of $400,000 during 1984 and pays $50,000 in dividends, Stable Company makes the following entry at the end of 1984.

Dec. 31, 1984	Cash	5,000	
	Dividend Revenue		5,000
	($50,000 × 10% = $5,000)		

Stable Company does not record any equity in the reported earnings of Balky Corporation, because the investment is not being accounted for on the equity method. Now assume, however, that Stable Company acquires an additional 20% interest in the voting stock of Balky Corporation for $250,000 on February 1, 1985. The following entry records this acquisition:

Feb. 1, 1985	Investment in Equity Securities	250,000	
	Cash		250,000

The management of Stable Company concludes that the investment should now be accounted for by using the equity method, because the total investment level equals 30% and significant influence will now be exercised over the affairs of Balky Corporation. In order to retroactively apply the equity method, Stable Company's share of the net income of Balky Corporation for 1984 must be computed and recorded:

Feb. 1, 1985	Investment in Equity Securities	40,000	
	Retained Earnings		40,000
	($400,000 × 10% = $40,000)		

Retained Earnings rather than a revenue account is credited, because the income was earned by Balky Corporation and reported in a previous year. The dividends received during 1984 must also be recorded differently under the equity method:

Feb. 1, 1985	Retained Earnings	5,000	
	Investment in Equity		
	Securities		5,000

The debit is made to Retained Earnings rather than the Dividend Revenue account that was originally credited, because the Dividend Revenue account has been closed to Retained Earnings. Of course, the two previous entries may be combined into a single entry of $35,000 to record the retroactive application of the equity method.[19]

The balance of the investment account is computed as follows:

Jan. 1, 1984	Original investment	$100,000
Feb. 1, 1985	Subsequent investment	250,000
1984	Share of Balky Corporation income	40,000
1984	Dividend of Balky Corporation received	(5,000)
	Balance on Feb. 1, 1985	$385,000

Retroactive adjustments would also need to accommodate any amortization of the excess of investment cost over the carrying value of the underlying net assets.

2. Changes *from* the Equity Method. If the level of investment falls below that necessary to continue applying the equity method, the investor changes to the lower of cost or market accounting method at that time. When the investment level is reduced, the investor simply discontinues applying the equity method and adopts the appropriate new method. The investment account is not adjusted retroactively as a result of the lower level of investment; therefore, no retroactive or catch-up adjustments are made. The balance accumulated under the equity method simply becomes "cost" for future accounting and reporting purposes.

If dividends received in periods following the reduction of the investment level exceed the investor's new (smaller) percentage of earnings for those periods, the excess is treated as a reduction of the investment account, because the excess relates to previous earnings which were accrued under the equity method.

To illustrate, assume Stable Company reduces an ownership interest in Minor Company from 30% to 10% on January 1, 1983. Exhibit 10–12 displays Stable's share of the net income and dividend distributions of Minor Company for the years 1983–1985. In the first two years the accumulated earnings since the reduction of Stable's ownership in Minor Company exceed dividends distributed. Thus, dividends received by Stable can be recorded by debiting Cash and crediting Dividend Revenue for $10,000 and $20,000 in 1983 and 1984, respectively. In 1985 the dividends distributed to Stable Company exceed the percentage of Stable's share of Minor's accumulated earnings. As a result, the investment account is reduced by the following journal entry to record the 1985 dividend:

Cash	35,000	
Investment in Equity Securities		5,000
Dividend Revenue		30,000
(To record dividend in excess of earnings' share.)		

---

[19]In this example we are not considering income tax implications of using the equity method. This complicating factor is discussed briefly in Chapter 18.

| | | | EXHIBIT 10–12 | | |

EXHIBIT 10–12
Income Recognized by Stable Company in
Minor Company Investment

Year	Earnings (Stable's Portion)	Cash Dividends (Stable's Portion)	Accumulated Excess of Earnings over Dividends	Stable Company Dividend Revenue
1983	$25,000	$10,000	$ 15,000	$10,000
1984	15,000	20,000	(5,000)	20,000
			10,000	
1985	20,000	35,000	(15,000)	30,000
	$60,000	$65,000	$ (5,000)	

Disclosure

Equity-Method Disclosures. *APB Opinion No. 18* requires the following disclosures for investments in common stock when such investments are significant to the financial position and results of operations of the investor:[20]

1. Name of each investee.
2. Percentage of ownership of common stock.
3. Accounting policies with respect to the investment. (In cases where 20% or more of the voting stock is held and the equity method is not used or where less than 20% of the voting stock is held and the equity method is used, the following should be disclosed: name of the investee and the reason(s) for departure from the 20% guideline.)
4. Difference between investor's carrying value and the underlying equity in net assets, and the accounting treatment for this difference.
5. Aggregate value, based on quoted market price, of the investment in common stock of each identified investee which is not a subsidiary.
6. Summarized financial information of investees (either individually or combined).
7. Material effects of the possible exercise of options or warrants, possible conversions, etc.

Exhibit 10–13 provides a comprehensive illustration of proper disclosure techniques for equity investments representing significant influence. The illustration is from the Gulf and Western Industries (a major conglomerate) 1982 Annual Report. As can be seen, Gulf and Western holds a greater than 20% ownership in a variety of concerns, including a captive finance company (First Capital), a publisher (Esquire, Inc.), a textiles manufacturer (J. P. Stevens), and an automotive supplier (Libbey-Owens-Ford). The disclosure also includes summarized financial information of the investees as required by *APB Opinion No. 18*.

Equity Investments Representing Control of Investee

If a company acquires an investment in the voting stock of an investee that exceeds 50%, the investor is presumed to be capable of **controlling** the investee's operating and financial policies. The investor is then called the **parent** and the investee is called the **subsidiary.** In such circumstances accountants usually prepare **consolidated financial statements** for both entities rather than separate financial statements for each. This practice is based on the position that the two separate legal entities represent only one *economic* entity as a result of the majority investment. Therefore, financial reporting reflects the economic reality—not the mere legal form of organization—by consolidating the financial statements of both companies. Accounting and reporting practices underlying consolidated financial statements, while similar to the equity method, are discussed at length in advanced accounting

Substance over Form

---

[20]*APB Opinion No. 18,* par. 20.

EXHIBIT 10–13
Gulf and Western Industries
Equity Method Disclosures

Note D—Investment in Affiliated Companies and Other Corporate Securities

Investment in affiliated companies and other corporate securities at July 31, 1982 includes $654,191,000 ($627,907,000 at July 31, 1981) applicable to the Company's ownership of all of the outstanding capital stock of Associates First Capital Corporation (First Capital). Also included in this caption are net payables to First Capital of approximately $208,000,000 at July 31, 1982 ($207,000,000 at July 31, 1981). The Company's investment in First Capital is $141,513,000 greater than the underlying equity in the net assets of such company. This difference, which arose prior to November 1, 1970, is not being amortized because, in the opinion of management, it is considered to have a continuing value. The Company received dividends of $28,300,000, $21,500,000 and $19,800,000 from First Capital in fiscal 1982, 1981 and 1980, respectively. The condensed financial statements of First Capital are presented below.

	(000 omitted)	
July 31	**1982**	**1981**
Assets		
Cash	$ 50,455	$ 64,195
Marketable securities	285,122	266,138
Net finance and other receivables	4,622,220	4,600,553
Other assets	543,540	387,017
	$5,501,337	$5,317,903
Liabilities and Stockholder's Equity		
Notes payable, current maturities of debt and other liabilities	$2,663,369	$2,640,789
Reserve for insurance claims and benefits	131,426	148,139
Long-term debt	2,193,864	2,042,581
Stockholder's Equity	512,678	486,394
	$5,501,337	$5,317,903

	(000 omitted)		
Year Ended July 31	**1982**	**1981**	**1980**
Revenues			
Finance charges	$ 945,221	$ 858,048	$711,675
Insurance premiums	90,695	103,128	97,095
Investment and other income	55,900	62,085	38,514
	$1,091,816	$1,023,261	$847,284
Expenses and Other			
Operating expenses	$ 303,584	$ 295,951	$255,321
Interest expense	566,043	516,404	399,994
Provision for losses on finance receivables	85,068	74,439	61,499
Insurance benefits paid or provided	36,808	46,857	43,368
Other expense (income)		16,618	(2,294)
Provision for income taxes	34,332	30,526	34,214
	$1,025,835	$ 980,795	$792,102
Net Earnings	$ 65,981	$ 42,466	$ 55,182

In addition, the Company owns voting stock of certain publicly-held companies, the investments in which are accounted for by the equity method (investees). The companies and the approximate percentage of ownership at the indicated dates are as follows:

July 31	**1982**	**1981**	**1980**
Amfac, Inc.[1]	24%	23%	23%
Esquire, Inc.	27	28	28

The General Tire & Rubber Company	25	21	9[2]
Libbey-Owens-Ford Company	26	16[2]	3[2]
Mohasco Corporation	23	20	–0–
Munsingwear, Inc.	35	28	5[2]
J. P. Stevens & Co., Inc.	20	9[2]	–0–

[1]Held by the Company's unconsolidated financial services operations.
[2]Included in marketable securities in 1981 or 1980; not accounted for by the equity method.

The above companies operate primarily in the United States and produce a variety of products for, and provide services to, a number of markets including aerospace and defense, agricultural, apparel, automotive, communications, engineering and construction, fluid power and fluid systems, food processing, glass, home furnishings, hotels and resorts, leisure activities, plastic and textiles.

The investments in investees at July 31, 1982 were $470,125,000 ($274,850,000 at July 31, 1981), including $115,876,000 ($112,375,000 at July 31, 1981) held by the Company's unconsolidated financial services subsidiary. The Company received dividends of $20,200,000, $10,200,000 and $3,700,000 from investees in the years ended July 31, 1982, 1981 and 1980, respectively. Investments in investees were approximately $264,141,000 less at July 31, 1982 ($173,500,000 at July 31, 1981) than the underlying equity in the net assets of such investees. In accordance with generally accepted accounting principles, these differences have been related to the assets of the investees and are being amortized over a period which approximates the remaining useful life of the investees' property, plant and equipment. The aggregate market value of investments in investees, at July 31, 1982 was $346,374,000 ($256,500,000 at July 31, 1981). Based upon annual and interim filings with the Securities and Exchange Commission, the condensed combined financial statements of the seven investees held at July 31, 1982 are presented below:

	(000 omitted)		
	1982	1981	1980
Current assets	$2,949,412	$3,170,248	
Property, plant and equipment and other assets	2,717,901	2,600,980	
Current liabilities	1,366,869	1,440,647	
Long-term debt and other long-term liabilities	1,528,580	1,545,115	
Net sales and other revenues	8,258,884	8,178,562	$7,792,088
Gross profit	1,736,859	1,723,937	1,636,226
Income from continuing operations before extraordinary items	82,703	242,958	149,724
Net income	124,599	176,947	163,085

Equity in earnings of unconsolidated affiliates includes:

	(000 omitted)		
Year ended July 31	1982	1981	1980
Financial services operations:			
First Capital	$100,313	$ 89,610	$ 87,102
Other affiliates		17,018	23,596
Eliminations			(1,591)
	$100,313	$106,628	$109,107
Other affiliates	76,896	44,672	5,499
Eliminations[1]	(45,682)	(41,857)	(30,176)
	$131,527	$109,443	$ 84,430

[1]Elimination of intercompany interest income earned by the financial services operations on intercompany indebtedness of the Company.

Included in consolidated retained earnings at July 31, 1982 is $314,000,000 of undistributed earnings of First Capital and affiliates accounted for by the equity method.

SOURCE: Gulf and Western Industries, 1982 Annual Report.

texts[21] and are discussed here only briefly.

Consolidating the financial statements of two or more corporations involves aggregating the adjusted trial balances of each company after eliminating the residual effects of all intercompany transactions. Such transactions may involve buying and selling, lending and borrowing, and investing activities. Furthermore, *consolidated net income* generally remains the same whether the investor applies the equity method to the investee or fully consolidates the investee into a complete set of consolidated financial statements. The difference between the equity method and the **consolidation method** is, thus, one of the degree of detail disclosed and not one of earnings measurement. Under the equity method, only a single asset account and revenue account are presented in the investor's financial statements which represent the investment in the investee. Hence, the equity method is frequently called a **single-line consolidation.** The consolidation method requires adding the specific individual asset, liability, revenue, and expense accounts of the subsidiary to those of the parent for financial reporting purposes. Any **minority interest**—outstanding stock held by individuals or entities other than the parent company—is usually included as part of the stockholders' equity of the consolidated entity.

Cash Surrender Value of Life Insurance

Frequently a corporation will insure the lives of top executives and name the corporation as the beneficiary. Such insurance arrangements are established with what are called **key man insurance policies.** The purpose of key man insurance is to compensate the corporation for the loss of services arising from the untimely death of a top executive. A common form of key man insurance used to meet these objectives is called **ordinary life insurance.** Ordinary life insurance policies have the unique feature of accumulating **cash surrender values** in addition to providing life insurance coverage. The cash surrender value of an ordinary life insurance policy is a form of investment. At any time, the corporation can borrow the accumulated cash value from the insurance company at a favorable interest rate or terminate the policy and receive the cash surrender value outright.

When the corporation pays an annual premium towards life insurance, part of the premium is recognized as Insurance Expense. The remaining portion reflects a buildup of cash surrender value and should, therefore, be recognized as an increase in an investment asset. The amount of the annual premium reflecting an increase in the cash surrender value is frequently specified by the insurance contract. The insurance contract will frequently include a schedule of cash surrender values listed by the number of years the policy has been in effect. On the financial statements of the company the cash surrender value should be disclosed as a noncurrent asset, because corporations do not usually intend to terminate insurance policies within the operating cycle.

To illustrate the accounting for cash surrender values, assume Falcon Sporting Goods Company establishes a key man insurance policy, naming the company as beneficiary. The insurance contract calls for insurance coverage of $200,000 on the life of Falcon's chief executive officer (CEO) in return for premiums of $3,500 per year. The cash surrender value schedule indicates the cash value increases for the first three years as follows:

End of Coverage Year	Cash Surrender Value
1	–0–
2	$ 500
3	1,025

---

[21]For an excellent discussion of financial accounting and reporting for various business combinations, see Arnold J. Pahler and Joseph E. Mori, *Advanced Accounting: Concepts and Practice* (New York: Harcourt Brace Jovanovich, 1981).

Because the first year's premium does not result in an increased cash surrender value, the entire $3,500 premium is debited to Insurance Expense when paid. The journal entries to record the second and third years' premiums would be:

Insurance Expense	3,000	
Cash Surrender Value of Life Insurance	500	
Cash		3,500
Insurance Expense	2,975	
Cash Surrender Value of Life Insurance	525	
Cash		3,500

Notice that the increase in the cash surrender value is debited to an investment account, Cash Surrender Value of Life Insurance, and the remainder of the $3,500 premium is debited to Insurance Expense.

If Falcon's CEO died at the end of the second year of coverage, the following journal entry would be necessary to record the receipt of the death benefit:

Cash	200,000	
Cash Surrender Value of Life Insurance		1,025
Gain from Life Insurance Settlement		198,975

A corporation may also establish life insurance coverage for the benefit of employees and their named beneficiaries. Since this type of insurance is for the benefit of the employee, not the company, all of the premium is considered a form of compensation expense. Any accumulation of cash surrender value belongs to the employee and should not therefore be identified as a company asset.

FUNDS

Business enterprises establish special funds for a variety of purposes, including bond or other debt redemption, future plant expansion, and pension commitments. When such funds are established, usually as a result of contractual clauses or at the direction of a company's board of directors, several significant accounting and reporting issues arise.

Fund assets may be held and managed by corporate personnel, or fund resources may be transferred to a **fiscal agent** or **trustee,** such as a bank, for administration. Although many long-term special funds are created in compliance with such things as contractual provisions, bond indentures, or covenants in debt instruments or pension plans, others are the result of internal management decisions.

To illustrate, assume that Stable Company management decides to create a bond-retirement fund in the amount of $10,000; then the following entry would be necessary:

Bond-Retirement Fund Cash	10,000	
Cash		10,000
(To establish bond-retirement fund.)		

If the Stable Company management decides to acquire treasury bills so that the fund will earn interest, the investment is recorded at cost:

Bond-Retirement Fund Investment	10,000	
Bond-Retirement Fund Cash		10,000
(To record acquisition of treasury bills by bond-retirement fund.)		

Subsequent accounting for investments made by such a fund follow the principles previously described and depend on the nature, extent, and investment objectives of the fund. Dividends and interest earned on fund investments are debited to the Bond-Retirement Fund Investment account.

When fund assets are transferred to a fiscal agent, the fund assets and related liabilities may be excluded from the financial statements. Liabilities are excluded only to the extent that the company's obligations have been discharged. Pension-fund assets and liabilities are frequently accounted for in this manner. Bond sinking funds and related bonds payable are normally reported in corporate financial statements, however, even if sinking-fund assets have been transferred to a fiscal agent.

Usually, the individual assets of a fund are aggregated for purposes of financial reporting. Although a fund may consist of a variety of assets, such as cash and investments in several types of securities, all these assets normally are aggregated into a single account for balance sheet presentation.

A fund is usually created by an original contribution and augmented by additional contributions and the earnings of the fund itself. If a company desires to accumulate a certain amount in the fund by some specific date, it will need estimates of the earning power of the assets in the fund in order to ascertain the specific amount of the contributions. The company may then use present-value techniques to determine the future contribution necessary to accumulate the desired amount. The accountant should track the performance of the fund in terms of earnings and contributions to ascertain whether the fund is accumulating resources at the level anticipated in the original present-value calculation. If fund assets earn at a level higher than anticipated, the remaining contributions may be reduced. Conversely, if the fund performs more poorly than planned, the company must increase its contributions to meet its goals for the fund. The techniques incident to evaluating the earnings performance of a fund involve the compound interest concepts discussed in Chapter 6. You are encouraged to consult that material in applying present-value techniques such as these.

CONCLUDING REMARKS

This chapter has considered a variety of financial accounting and reporting problems for several types of investments. Many practice problems are evident in this area, and their resolutions have represented a continuous process over a long period. Furthermore, as new business forms or investment opportunities are created, other accounting and reporting problems may continue to emerge. Therefore, the practices described in this chapter should be viewed as applicable not only to the specific transactions discussed, but as desirable procedures in other circumstances as well.

KEY POINTS

1. Companies invest in a variety of securities for many business reasons.

2. Investments in voting equity securities must be classified as either passive, significant influence, or control in nature.

3. All marketable securities representing passive investments should be valued at the lower of cost or market for financial reporting purposes.

4. Classification of securities between current and noncurrent categories involves assessing management intent, marketability and maturity dates of the security,

and other corroborative evidence.

5. Unrealized losses and unrealized loss recoveries on the current marketable equity securities portfolio are recognized in the income statement of the period of the change.

6. Unrealized losses on noncurrent marketable equity securities portfolios are recognized as a direct reduction of stockholders' equity rather than in the income statement for the period of the decline.

7. Investments in voting stock representing significant influence are accounted for by using the equity method.

8. A proportionate amount of the investee's net income is accrued by an investor using the equity method, whereas dividends are reported as reductions of the Investment account.

9. Investment of more than 50% in the voting stock of an investee results in control of the investee by the investor, and consolidated financial statements are generally appropriate.

10. Business enterprises frequently establish funds for a variety of reasons, such as meeting bond maturities or pension commitments and expanding plant operations.

11. Extensive financial-statement disclosures are required for material investments.

QUESTIONS

10–1 What methods of cost identification are most commonly used for securities which have been sold? Which are acceptable for income tax purposes?

10–2 In accounting for temporary investments in bonds, how should one treat discounts or premiums for financial reporting purposes?

10–3 Distinguish between temporary and noncurrent investments. Is it possible for purchases of a specific company's stock to be a current investment for one company and a long-term investment for another? Why?

10–4 Explain the difference in the cost and equity methods of accounting for a long-term investment in common stock.

10–5 How should the excess of investment cost over the proportionate share of the investee's book value at the date of acquisition be recognized in the investor's balance sheet? Discuss the implications of this excess for the income statement.

10–6 How is a stock dividend that is received by an investor company recognized?

10–7 Give three circumstances under which an investment that is accounted for by the cost method will be written down.

10–8 What is the proper accounting procedure for an investment that has previously been reported under the cost method and is now accounted for under the equity method?

10–9 What are "current assets" as the term is used to classify amounts on a balance sheet?

10–10 With regard to marketable equity securities, when should realized gains be recognized?

10–11 With marketable equity securities, in what circumstances should realized losses be recognized?

10–12 *APB Opinion No. 18* specifies that a direct or indirect investment of 20% or more of the voting stock of an investee company leads to a *presumption* that, in the absence of evidence to the contrary, an investor has an ability to exercise significant influence over an investee. What are some examples of "contrary evidence" that might tend to refute this presumption?

10–13 What is a stock right? What three events can transpire after receiving a stock right? How are they accounted for?

10–14 In accounting for long-term investments in bonds, what is the nature of premiums and discounts? What are the accounting procedures for discounts and premiums?

10–15 What is the proper accounting treatment for an equity investment that was previously reported under the equity method but for which the cost method is now appropriate?

10–16 How are investee operating losses accounted for under the equity method?

10–17 Distinguish between the accounting for temporary investments in marketable equity securities and noncurrent investments in marketable equity securities when the investor owns less than 20% of the investee's stock.

10–18 What is the cash surrender value of a life insurance policy? How should the cash surrender value be disclosed on the balance sheet?

10–19 What is a fund? What are the significant issues related to accounting for a fund?

CASES

C10–1 One of your audit clients is a closely held corporation, Clean Clothes Coin Laundries, Inc. Since large amounts of cash are generated by Clean Clothes, the company has invested in other businesses from time to time.

One of the investments is in another closely held company, Waterbed Sleep Shops, Inc. Since Clean Clothes owns 30% of the voting stock of Waterbed, the equity method of accounting has been applied by Clean Clothes. A bitter dispute arose last year between

Clean Clothes and the other three Waterbed share-holders. Now, the other three shareholders totally ignore the efforts of Clean Clothes to influence the conduct of Waterbed's operation. Clean Clothes, nevertheless, intends to retain the 30% investment in Waterbed even though one of the other investors has offered to buy the voting stock.

Instructions

[a] Should Clean Clothes discontinue the use of the equity method?

[b] Assuming Clean Clothes decides it is proper to discontinue applying the equity method of accounting for the Waterbed investment, describe the procedure for discontinuing the equity method.

[c] Assuming the equity method is discontinued, describe the proper accounting and financial reporting practices that should be applied to the investment account in subsequent accounting periods. Include a discussion of balance sheet classification and valuation.

C10–2 The temporary marketable equity security portfolio of Daisy Food Company read as follows on December 31, 1984:

	Cost	Market
Thayer Company	$16,000	$14,000
Webber, Inc.	21,000	20,000
Lincoln Company	32,000	25,000
Totals	$69,000	$59,000

On December 31, 1984, Daisy established a lower of cost or market (LCM) valuation for the marketable equity securities (MES) by the following adjusting journal entry:

Dec. 31, 1984

Unrealized Loss on Valuation of Current MES	10,000	
Allowance to Reduce Current MES to Lower of Cost or Market		10,000

(To adjust MES to LCM valuation.)

Prior to this journal entry the allowance account had a zero balance.

On January 2, 1985, Daisy sold all its holdings in Lincoln Company for a market price of $25,000. The following journal entry was made to record the sale:

Jan. 2, 1985

Cash	25,000	
Loss on Sale of Current MES	7,000	
Current MES		32,000

(To record sale of Lincoln Company investment.)

The controller of Daisy Foods is confused by the January 2, 1985, journal entry and suggests that the company has double counted the loss on the Lincoln Company sale. He believes that the loss has been counted once as an unrealized loss on December 31, 1984, and again as realized on January 2, 1985. The controller further suggests that the following journal entry would alleviate the double counting:

Jan. 2, 1985

Cash	25,000	
Allowance to Reduce Current MES to Lower of Cost or Market	7,000	
Current MES		32,000

Instructions

[a] Respond to the controller's observation. Do you agree or disagree?

[b] Do you agree with the controller's alternative journal entry? Why?

C10–3 Apple Publishing Company purchased $1,000,000 of face amount, 5%, six-year bonds at 71.22 on January 1, 1982. Calendar year 1985 was a poor year for Apple because of declining revenues and tighter operating margins. The company had an operating income of only $100,000 on revenues of $2,000,000 (or 5%). The treasurer of the company decided to remedy the situation by selling the $1,000,000 face amount, 5% bonds on December 31, 1985, at 90 and recognizing a gain for that period. The following calculation was used to determine the gain on the sale:

Proceeds	$900,000
Carrying value	712,200
Gain	$187,800

As a result of this transaction, Apple Publishing Company recognized a total net income of $287,800, or 14.4% of sales. The treasurer was very pleased. The company was now above the industry-wide profitability average for 1985, the stockholders would be satisfied, and the treasurer's year-end bonus, which is based on a percentage of reported net income, would be almost three times as great as his bonus would have been before the transaction. As the treasurer's assistant, you are not comfortable with his remedy. Therefore, you confront the treasurer and tell him, "I have good news, and I have bad news."

Instructions

[a] What is the "good news"?
[b] What is the "bad news"?

C10–4 The following is a reprint from the *Forbes* "Numbers Game" column. The article is critical of the use of the equity method.

Instructions

Read the article carefully. Do you agree with the conclusions of this article? Why? How would you respond to the allegations presented in this article?

EQUITY ACCOUNTING ISN'T EQUITABLE

UNDER A 1971 ACCOUNTING Principles Board [APB] ruling, if company A owns between 20% and 50% of company B, A is required to report a portion of B's earnings—equal to A's percentage of ownership. Nevertheless, B continues to show 100% of its earnings. It's called equity accounting [see reprint of "Equity Earnings" earlier in this chapter].

There's nothing equitable about equity accounting, It is grossly misleading.

The crux of the problem lies in how you define "earnings." Most investors think of earnings as the money a company has to spend—the dollars left over after all the obligations are taken care of. But that's not how the accountants define it: "Earnings are simply not synonymous with cash or working capital," explains Michael J. Walters, a partner with Peat, Marwick, Mitchell & Co., a big-eight accounting firm. So, earnings aren't necessarily dollars you can spend. They are dollars that can contribute to assets.

Fair enough, but this use of equity accounting brings in alleged earnings, not corresponding revenues. So it can throw off all the common measures of success: profit margin, return on equity, even price/earnings multiples.

Take a modest example of the resulting confusion: Giant Bendix Corp. ($3.8 billion revenues) has a 21% interest in ASARCO, a metals producer. Bendix adds on to its income statement some $25.5 million from ASARCO, driving up its earnings to $163 million. This deflates Bendix' current P/E from 8.2 to 6.9, inflates its profit margin from 3.6% to 4.2% and blows up its return on equity from 15% to a more impressive 18%.

Mark this, however: When ASARCO was losing money, Bendix carefully kept its interest below 20%. But it became apparent that ASARCO was going to make money. So in 1978 Bendix signed an

antitakeover agreement with ASARCO—an increasingly common move—then picked up more stock and started to pick up earnings.

Bendix is not doing anything shady. It is simply complying with generally accepted accounting principles (GAAP).

What is happening here is an exercise in *reductio ad absurdum.* Start with a shaky premise and extend the logic further and further until it becomes ridiculous. Before 1971, earnings were generally brought in only when a firm achieved a 51% interest—clear control—in a second company. At that point the two balance sheets were consolidated entirely, with minority interests in earnings subtracted out. This is still the method that is used for companies with more than 50% ownership.

Now that *seems* logical. You run a company, you get the earnings. But that isn't entirely true. Even at 51% you can't simply take those earnings. However, since the statements were totally consolidated, the earnings ratios still have meaning.

But companies liked the idea of being able to report those earnings and wanted to carry it a step further and bring in earnings from minority investments. After all, they said, you can have control over the use of much of a firm's income with less than 51% of its stock. You can elect directors, and those directors mean influence over dividend policy and most other major decisions. That influence, they argued, should give them the right to show a portion of the resulting income on their own income statements. The Accounting Principles Board was compliant, and all that remained was to pick a percentage at which significant influence would be presumed.

Somewhat arbitrarily, the APB set forth 20% as the point at which you could *presume* control. Earnings could be brought in with a smaller investment if you could *prove* control. So now Saul Stein-

EXERCISES

E10–1 Great Plains Oil Company had the following securities in its current marketable equity securities portfolio on December 31, 1984:

	Cost	Market
Horton Company	$ 25,000	$ 28,000
Austin Company	50,000	47,000
Myrna Company	30,000	25,000
Lawton, Inc.	15,000	4,000
Total	$120,000	$104,000

All the securities were purchased during December 1984. The following events, which were relative to the marketable equity securities, took place during 1985:

Mar. 15 Lawton, Inc., filed for protection under the federal bankruptcy laws. The market value of Great Plains' holdings in Lawton stock fell to $500. Lawton's situation was apparently permanent.

June 5 One thousand shares of Orbit Electronics were purchased at $28 per share. The Orbit shares were a temporary investment. The brokerage commission on this purchase was $140.

July 17 Half of the Austin Company holdings were sold for $31,000 net of commissions.

Nov. 10 Great Plains Oil Company decided to begin developing a controlling interest in Myrna Company, and the Myrna shares were transferred to a noncurrent equity investment status. The Myrna stock had a market value of $29,000 on the transfer date.

On December 31, 1985, the market value of Great Plains' holdings in marketable equity securities appeared as follows:

	Market Value
Horton Company	$19,000
Austin Company	30,000
Orbit Electronics	24,000
Lawton, Inc.	400
Myrna Company	30,000

Instructions

[a] Provide the appropriate journal entries relating to the marketable securities. (Beginning with the December 31, 1984, adjusting entry, list the entries in chronological order.)

[b] What information relative to temporary investments in marketable equity securities should be disclosed?

E10–2 During 1984, Richfield Mining Company made several transactions in short-term marketable debt instruments. Richfield uses the lower of cost or market method, applied on an aggregate basis, for valuation of temporary debt investments.

Jan. 31 Richfield purchased $10,000 face amount, 11% bonds at 103 plus accrued interest. Interest is payable on July 1 and January 1.

Feb. 28 Richfield purchased $20,000 face value, 10% bonds at 97 plus accrued interest. Interest is payable on July 1 and January 1.

July 1 Interest on both bond investments is received.

Aug. 31 Richfield sold half of the 11% bonds at 95 plus accrued interest.

Oct.   1 Richfield sold half of the 10% bonds at 101 plus accrued interest.

Dec. 31 Interest is accrued.

31 The market prices of the bonds are:

11% bonds	102
10% bonds	95

Instructions

Provide the appropriate journal entries for the above transactions.

E10–3 Nifty Thrifty Supermarkets have invested in marketable equity securities for long-term funding purposes. On February 15, 1984, Nifty Thrifty made the following purchases:

	Market Price (net of commissions)
900 shares General Electric	$99
500 shares Ford Motor	42
300 shares Alcoa	33

During 1984 the following transactions were made:

June 30 Nifty Thrifty received dividends of $3,700 on the three investments.

Aug.   1 150 shares of Ford Motor were sold for $45 per share. Commissions on the transaction were $120.

Sept. 15 200 shares of General Electric were sold for $98 per share. Commissions on the transaction were $180.

Nov. 11 The remaining General Electric shares were transferred to a temporary investment status when the GE stock was trading for $94 per share.

On December 31, 1984, the market values of Nifty Thrifty's holdings were as follows:

General Electric	$90
Ford Motor	41
Alcoa	30

On December 31, 1985, the market values of Nifty Thrifty's holdings were as follows:

General Electric	$85
Ford Motor	43
Alcoa	29

Instructions

[a] Provide the appropriate journal entries for Nifty Thrifty's transactions and adjustments.

[b] In the balance sheet and income statement, what reporting distinctions are made in accounting for *temporary* versus *noncurrent* investment portfolios? Outline your answer by utilizing the December 31, 1984, information on Nifty Thrifty Supermarkets.

E10–4 At the beginning of 1984, Red River Company held in its current investments account the following:

[1] $150,000 face amount, 8% bonds purchased at a cost of $137,000.

[2] 1,200 shares of $50 par value, 12% preferred stock purchased at a cost of $66,000.

Interest on the bonds is payable on March 31 and September 30, and the preferred dividend is paid quarterly on a calendar-year basis. On October 31, 1984, half the bonds were sold for $77,000 (including accrued interest) and 500 shares of stock were sold for $24,000.

Instructions

Prepare the necessary journal entries for 1984. (Assume all dividends declared were received by December 31, 1984.)

E10–5 Banard Corporation purchased $20,000 face value, 10-year, zero coupon bonds (bonds with a zero nominal interest rate) for 38.55 on January 1, 1984, for long-term funding purposes. On the same date Banard purchased $30,000 face value, 5-year, 12% bonds that were priced to yield 8%, with interest payable annually on December 31. Banard utilizes the effective interest method of amortization and carries the investment and related discount and premium in a single account.

Instructions

[a] Provide the necessary journal entries to record the purchase of the bond investments.

[b] Provide the necessary journal entries related to the interest on the bond investments for December 31, 1984.

[c] Why are bond investments sometimes purchased at prices that differ from the face value?

E10–6 The following is a partial effective interest amortization table for a bond investment due in eight years:

Date	Interest Revenue	Cash Received	Amortization	Present (Carrying) Value
Jan. 1, 1984				$11,000
July 1, 1984	$440	$600	$160	?
Jan. 1, 1985				

Instructions

[a] Is the effective rate less than or greater than the nominal rate?
[b] Is the carrying value less than or greater than the face value?
[c] What is the nominal rate?
[d] What is the effective rate?
[e] What is the carrying value on July 1, 1984?
[f] What is the face amount of bond investment?
[g] What will be the sum of the amortization column for the eight years?
[h] At the end of eight years, what will be the final carrying value?

E10–7 On September 1, 1984, George Company purchased $300,000 face value, 8% bonds, which would mature in eight years. The bonds were purchased as a long-term investment at a price to yield 12% compounded semiannually. Interest is payable on August 31 and February 28.

Instructions

[a] Using the appropriate present-value table, compute the purchase price of the bonds and prepare the journal entry to record their purchase in a single account.
[b] Prepare the December 31, 1984, adjusting entry.
[c] Prepare the February 28, 1985, journal entry.

E10–8 On January 1, 1984, Carmel Company purchased as a noncurrent investment a 20% interest in Maverick Corporation for $150,000. Maverick had outstanding 60,000 shares of common stock during 1984. Maverick's book value per share was $10 on the date of Carmel's purchase. Maverick earned $85,000 during 1984, and the market value of Maverick stock was $11 per share on December 31, 1984.

Instructions

For each of the following *independent* situations compute Maverick Corporation's book value per share and Carmel Company's investment carrying amount per share at the end of 1984.
[a] Carmel Company accounts for the investment under the cost method, and Maverick declares a $.50 per share cash dividend.
[b] Carmel Company accounts for the investment under the cost method, and Maverick declares a 10% stock dividend and a $.40 per share cash dividend.
[c] Carmel Company accounts for the investment under the equity method, and Maverick declares a $.50 per share cash dividend. Any excess of investment cost over book value is assigned to undervalued assets with average remaining lives of five years.

E10–9 On January 1, 1984, Giant Company purchased 20% of Green Company's outstanding common stock for $1,000,000 when the underlying book value of the company was $4,500,000. Forty percent of the excess is attributable to assets with a remaining life of 10 years, and the remainder to unrecorded goodwill to be amortized over 40 years. Green Company reported net income of $260,000 in 1984 and declared dividends of $.75 per share on all 200,000 outstanding shares.

Instructions

Prepare Giant's journal entries, relative to the Green investment, that should be recorded on December 31, 1984.

E10–10 On January 1, 1981, Kids Stuff Toy Company purchased a 40% influential interest in Clothes for Tots, Inc., for $110,000. The subsequent earnings and dividend distributions of Clothes for Tots were as follows:

Year	Net Income	Dividends
1981	$ 50,000	$60,000
1982	(160,000)	40,000
1983	(150,000)	10,000
1984	20,000	–0–
1985	140,000	10,000

Instructions

For each of the five years determine Kid Stuff's reported income (loss) from the investment in Clothes for Tots. Determine the balance of the investment account at the end of 1985.

E10–11 Redbank Manufacturing Company established a sinking fund on January 1, 1984, for the retirement to a bond issue. The following transactions occurred:

Jan.	1, 1984	Established a sinking fund with $260,000 cash.
Jan.	18	Purchased marketable equity securities for $200,000.
July	15	Paid fund expenses of $15,000.
Sept.	9	Sold marketable equity securities having an original cost of $60,000 for $53,000.
Dec.	20	Received dividends on marketable equity securities of $12,000.
Feb.	12, 1985	Purchased certificate of deposit for $100,000.
Dec.	31	Interest and dividends of $22,000 were received.
Dec.	31	Sold all securities in the fund for $310,000 and retired an outstanding bond issue of $300,000. The remaining fund balance was transferred back to the corporate Cash account.

Instructions

Provide the appropriate journal entries for the above transactions.

E10–12 On March 1, 1982, Lakewood Properties, Inc., insured its president with a $500,000 face value life insurance policy with Lakewood as the beneficiary. Premiums of $2,000 per year are payable on each March 1, beginning in 1982. The cash surrender value of the policy was listed as follows:

Feb. 28, 1983	$ 500
Feb. 28, 1984	$1,050

The president of Lakewood died on February 28, 1984.

Instructions

Provide the appropriate journal entries relative to the insurance policy for 1982 through 1984. Assume Lakewood uses the calendar year for financial reporting purposes.

E10–13 Rainy Day Company owns 1,200 shares of stock purchased for $75 per share. One right is

received for each share of stock outstanding; the market values of the stock and rights at the issuance date of the rights are $90 and $4, respectively. Two rights are required to purchase one share of stock at $80.

Rainy Day exercises 500 rights one month later. Rainy Day sells 400 rights at $5.50 per right toward the end of the year. Rainy Day allows the remaining rights to expire.

Instructions

[a] Provide the appropriate journal entry for:
    [1] The receipt of the rights.
    [2] The exercise of 500 rights.
    [3] The sale of 400 rights.
    [4] The expiration of the remaining rights.
[b] Is the investment account credited for the receipt of stock rights? Why? Could the receipt of the stock rights be recorded as a memorandum entry similar to that for stock dividends? Why?

E10–14 On January 1, 1984, Holland Shipbuilders, Inc., purchased a 35% interest in Vernon Iron Works at $20 per share. As a result, Holland was able to appoint two members of the board of directors. The balance sheet of Vernon Iron Works appeared as follows on January 1, 1984:

Vernon Iron Works
BALANCE SHEET
January 1, 1984

Assets

Current assets		$ 20,000
Land		40,000
Fixed assets	$160,000	
Accumulated depreciation	(50,000)	110,000
Total assets		$170,000

Liabilities and Owners' Equity

Current liabilities	$ 15,000
Long-term liabilities	75,000
Common stock (no par; 6,000 shares authorized, issued, and outstanding)	50,000
Retained earnings	30,000
Total liabilities and owners' equity	$170,000

Vernon Company had a net income of $25,000 and declared dividends of $10,000 during 1984. The depreciable assets of Vernon are undervalued by $30,000. The average remaining life of the depreciable assets is 6 years. Holland Shipbuilders amortize goodwill over a 40-year period.

Instructions

[a] Provide Holland's journal entry to record the acquisition of 35% of Vernon Iron Works.

[b] Provide the journal entry to record Holland's share in the income and dividends of Vernon Iron Works.

[c] Provide the journal entry to amortize the excess of investment cost over equity.

E10–15 Northeastern Gas Company purchased a 30% (20,000 shares) interest in the Lone Star Pipeline Company for $360,000 on January 2, 1982. Northeastern utilized the equity method to account for this investment. Significant changes in the investment account resulted from the following factors:

Year	Equity in Lone Star Net Income	Dividends Received from Lone Star	Excess of Cost over Equity Amortization
1982	$30,000	$15,000	$1,500
1983	50,000	20,000	1,500

On January 2, 1984, Northeastern sold 15,000 shares of Lone Star for $350,000. Lone Star earned income (loss) of $100,000 and $(10,000) in 1984 and 1985, respectively. Northeastern received dividends from Lone Star of $5,000 and $6,000 for 1984 and 1985, respectively.

Instructions

[a] Provide the appropriate journal entries on the books of Northeastern Gas Company for transactions related to the Lone Star investment for the years 1984 and 1985.

[b] What general accounting principles are related to accounting for changes to and from the equity method of accounting?

E10–16 On January 1, 1984, Overland Railroad Company established significant influence over K&K Railroad by acquiring 60,000 shares of common stock, a 30% interest, for $570,000. The book value of K&K was $1,300,000 on January 1, 1984. Since this purchase K&K earned income and paid dividends as follows:

Year	Net Income	Dividends
1984	$180,000	$100,000
1985	310,000	140,000

The market value per share on K&K common stock on December 31, 1984 and 1985, was $8 and $9, respectively. The Overland Railroad incorrectly accounted for this investment as if significant influence had not been established.

Instructions

[a] As a result of incorrectly applying accounting principles, the financial statements of the Overland Railroad Company are incorrect. At December 31, 1984 and 1985, were the following accounts overstated, understated, or correct? If incorrect, by what amount? Show supporting computations. Assume that any excess of cost over book value is amortized over 30 years.

[1] Net Investment in K&K Railroad.

[2] Net Income.

[b] If the K&K investment were sold on January 1, 1986, would a greater gain be reported under the incorrect approach or the equity method? Which method better assigns income to periods? Discuss your reasoning.

PROBLEMS

P10–1 Synthetic Fuels Company has invested its idle cash in temporary marketable equity securities. Synthetic Fuels uses the FIFO method of assigning cost to security investments. On January 31, 1983, the following investment was made:

	Market Price per Share (net of commissions)
500 shares of Westinghouse	$ 47
1,000 shares of IBM	100
700 shares of McDonalds	70

On March 31, 1983, IBM issued a 20% stock dividend. Cash dividends of $9,000 were declared and paid by the three investments.

On September 7, 1983, Synthetic Fuels Company invested additional idle cash in the following temporary investments:

	Market Price per Share (net of commissions)
200 shares of Westinghouse	$51
400 shares of IBM	86

On December 20, 1983, Synthetic Fuels sold 1,100 shares of IBM for $90 per share.

The market values per share of Synthetic Fuels' temporary investment holdings on December 31, 1983, were:

Westinghouse	$48
IBM	88
McDonalds	55

On February 28, 1984, Synthetic Fuels Company sold 300 shares of Westinghouse at $45 per share. Dividends of $6,000 were earned by Synthetic Fuels on March 31, 1984. The Company purchased 200 additional shares of IBM at $85 per share on August 31, 1984.

The market values of Synthetic Fuels' temporary investment holdings on December 31, 1984, were:

Westinghouse	$49
IBM	83
McDonalds	65

On December 31, 1985, the market values for the Synthetic Fuels' holdings were:

Westinghouse	$48
IBM	87
McDonalds	75

Instructions

Provide the appropriate journal entries for the transactions and adjustments from January 31, 1983, to December 31, 1985.

P10–2 Himmel Brewery engaged in the following transactions during 1985.

Jan. 6   Purchase of 500 shares of Kodak Company common stock at $87 per share. Brokerage commissions were $390. The Kodak stock is to be held for long-term funding purposes.

May 27   Kodak issued a 10% stock dividend, followed by cash dividend of $2.50 per share.

Aug. 1   Himmel Brewery received one stock right from Kodak for every share of Kodak common held. Four stock rights entitled the owner to purchase one share of Kodak common at $50 per share. Each right had a market value of $11, while Kodak common was trading ex-rights (without rights) at $80 per share. The stock rights expire on August 1, 1986.

Sept. 10   Himmel sold 200 rights for $12.50 per right.

Sept. 30   300 stock rights were exercised for the acquisition of Kodak common.

Dec. 31   The market value for Kodak stock rights was $16.50 per right. Kodak common closed at $70 per share.

Instructions

Provide the appropriate journal entries and year-end adjustments for the Himmel transactions.

P10–3   Delta Power Company used idle cash to invest in current marketable equity securities (CMES). The following table summarizes relevant information related to the CMES portfolio for the years 1983–1985.

				Market Price per Share		
	Date Purchased	Shares Purchased	Purchase Price	12/31/83	12/31/84	12/31/85
Sears	1/15/83	700	$45	$44	$46	$47
Exxon	3/1/83	400	47	50	45	49
Citicorp	9/21/83	1,000	56	50	51	53
U.S. Steel	2/2/84	500	31	29	25	30

Marketable Equity Securities

In 1984 Delta sold 200 shares of Sears for $28 per share and 400 shares of Citicorp for $52 per share.

Instructions

Provide all the appropriate journal entries relating to the current marketable equity securities portfolio for 1983, 1984, and 1985.

P10–4 Hybrid Engineering, Inc., decided to invest in bonds to achieve long-term funding objectives. On January 2, 1983, Hybrid purchased $100,000 face amount, 6% bonds due in 3 years. The bonds were priced to yield an effective interest rate of 10%. Interest is payable semiannually on June 30 and December 31. Hybrid Engineering utilizes the effective interest method of amortization and adjusts the carrying value of the bonds on interest payment dates. On June 30, 1984, Hybrid sold half the bond investment at 98.

Instructions

[a] Provide the appropriate journal entry for the acquisition of the bond investment on January 2, 1983.
[b] Provide the appropriate journal entries related to the bond investment through December 31, 1985. Construct a table similar to Exhibit 10–8 to determine the proper amortization, adjusted for the June 30, 1984, sale.

P10–5 On June 1, 1984, Warner, Inc., purchased as a long-term investment 800 of the $1,000 face value, 8% bonds of Universal Corporation for $738,300. The bonds were purchased to yield 10% interest. Interest is payable semiannually on December 1 and June 1. The bonds mature on June 1, 1989. Warner uses the effective interest method of amortization. On November 1, 1985, Warner sold the bonds for $785,000. This amount includes the appropriate accrued interest.

Instructions

[a] Prepare a schedule of interest revenue and bond discount amortization for the original bond investment from June 1, 1984, to June 1, 1989.
[b] Prepare a schedule showing the income or loss before income taxes from the bond investment that Warner should record for the years ended December 31, 1984 and 1985. Show supporting computations in good form.

(AICPA adapted)

P10–6 On May 1, 1984, Boston Bean Company purchased for long-term funding purposes $20,000 face amount, 12% bonds, due in three years, at 105.076. The bonds pay interest on May 1 and November 1. Boston Bean utilizes the effective interest method of amortization on interest dates and at calendar year-end. Boston Bean sold $5,000 face amount bonds for 101.5 plus accrued interest on August 1, 1985.

Instructions

[a] Provide the appropriate journal entries for the bond investment from the date of original purchase through December 31, 1985. Construct an effective interest amortization table to support your journal entries based on the $20,000 investment without regard to the August 1, 1985, sale.
[b] Might a rational business person ever purchase bonds with a $20,000 face value for an amount greater than this? Why?

P10–7 For purposes of redeeming a bond issue, Wall Company has established a sinking fund. The following transactions relate to this fund for 1985:

Jan.	1	Dividends of $6,000 received on West Company stock held in the fund.
Jan.	12	Expenses of $325 paid by the fund.
Feb.	23	Annual company contribution of $75,000 transferred to the fund.
Apr.	1	Purchased at par, $120,000 of 8% bonds plus accrued interest. Interest payable June 30 and December 31.
May	31	Sold bonds purchased on April 1 at 102 plus accrued interest.
Aug.	15	Sold $450,000 of sinking-fund assets for $435,000.
Nov.	27	Received dividends of $8,000 on Wood Company stock.
Dec.	19	Sold remaining fund assets for 105% of carrying value for $680,400.
Dec.	23	Fund cash now totals $1,234,670, of which $1,200,000 is used to retire bond issue.
Dec.	31	Remaining fund cash returned to the general Cash account.

Instructions

Prepare journal entries for the above transactions.

P10–8 On June 30, 1983, Basket Company purchased 30% of the outstanding common voting stock of Jack Company for $1,300,000. At that time, the net assets of Jack Company amounted to $4,000,000. The level of investment is sufficient to provide Basket significant influence over the activities of Jack. Any difference between the purchase price and the underlying book value of Jack Company's net assets is due to the following:

[1] Land is undervalued by $25,000.

[2] Depreciable assets with a 10-year remaining life are worth $30,000 more than the book value.

[3] Goodwill is determined to exist for any balance. Goodwill is estimated to have a useful life of 40 years from the date of the stock purchase described above.

The following relates to Basket Company:

Year	Net Income	Dividends Declared and Paid on December 31
1983	$100,000	$25,000
1984	120,000	40,000
1985	80,000	–0–

Instructions

[a] Prepare all necessary journal entries for the transactions described above on the books of Basket Company through 1985.

[b] Compute the investment account balance on December 31, 1983, 1984, and 1985.

P10–9 On January 1, 1983, Madison Electric Company purchased 5,000 shares of outstanding stock of Parker Supply Company for $20,000. The investment was made to establish a long-term position in Parker Supply Company. Parker's balance sheet appeared as follows on January 1, 1983.

Parker Supply Company
BALANCE SHEET
January 1, 1983

Assets

Current assets	$ 50,000
Land	60,000
Fixed assets	120,000
Less: Accumulated depreciation	(30,000)
Total assets	$200,000

Liabilities and Owners' Equity

Current liabilities	$ 30,000
Long-term liabilities	40,000
Common stock (no par, 100,000 shares authorized, issued, and outstanding)	70,000
Retained earnings	60,000
Total liabilities and owners' equity	$200,000

Parker's earnings, dividends, and per share market value were as follows:

Year	Net Income	Dividends	Per Share Market Value
1983	$20,000	$ 5,000	$3.50
1984	26,000	10,000	5.00
1985	38,000	20,000	7.50

On January 1, 1985, Madison Electric purchased an additional 20,000 shares of Parker stock at an average per share cost of $4. Parker Supply Company did not issue additional common stock during 1983–1985. Any excess of acquisition cost over underlying equity is applied first to fixed assets, which had an average remaining life of 10 years on January 1, 1983. Any additional excess of cost over book value is then applied to goodwill and will be amortized over 40 years. Parker's fixed assets were undervalued by $30,000 on January 1, 1983, and January 1, 1985.

Instructions

[a] Provide all journal entries for Madison Electric from January 1, 1983, to December 31, 1985, relative to Madison's investment in Parker Supply. Provide necessary supporting schedules for your journal entries.

[b] Identify the items and dollar amounts that will appear in Madison's balance sheets and income statements at December 31, 1983, 1984, and 1985 relative to the Parker investment.

P10–10 On January 1, 1984, Jeffries, Inc., paid $700,000 for 10,000 shares of Wolf Company's voting common stock, which gave Jeffries a 10% interest in Wolf. At that date the net assets of Wolf totaled $6,000,000. The fair values of all Wolf's identifiable assets and liabilities were equal to their book values. Jeffries does not have the ability to exercise significant influence over the operating and financial policies of Wolf. Jeffries received dividends of $.90 per share from Wolf on October 1, 1984. Wolf reported net income of $400,000 for the year ended December 31, 1984.

On July 1, 1985, Jeffries paid $2,300,000 for 30,000 additional shares of Wolf Company's voting common stock, which represented a 30% investment in Wolf. The fair values of all Wolf's identifiable assets net of liabilities were equal to their book values of $6,500,000. As a result of this transaction, Jeffries has the ability to exercise significant influence over the operating and financial policies of Wolf. Jeffries received dividends of $1.10 per share from Wolf on April 1, 1985, and $1.35 per share on October 1, 1985. Wolf reported net income of $500,000 for the year ended December 31, 1985, and $200,000 for the six months ended December 31, 1985. Jeffries amortizes goodwill over a 40-year period.

Instructions

[a] Prepare a schedule showing the income or loss before income taxes for the year ended December 31, 1984, that Jeffries should report from its investment in Wolf in its income statement issued in March 1985.

[b] During March 1986 Jeffries issued comparative financial statements for 1984 and 1985. Prepare schedules showing the income or loss before income taxes for the years ended December 31, 1984 and 1985, that Jeffries should report from its investment in Wolf. Show supporting computations in good form.

(AICPA adapted)

P10–11 The following asset side of the balance sheet was provided by the Xavier Corporation on December 31, 1984.

Xavier Corporation
December 31, 1984

Assets

Cash	$ 20,000
Temporary marketable equity securities (market: $16,000)	22,000
Inventory	30,000
Current assets	72,000
Noncurrent investment in 8%, 10-year bonds (at face value; cost: $87,711)	100,000
Noncurrent marketable equity securities (at market; cost: $62,000)	75,000
Fixed assets	100,000
Less: Accumulated depreciation	(25,000)
Total assets	$322,000

The long-term investment in bonds was purchased on January 1, 1984. The difference between cost and face value was recognized on the 1984 income statement as an unrealized gain on the acquisition date. The interest on the bonds is payable annually on January 1. The noncurrent marketable equity securities include a 30% interest in the Dayton Music Company. This investment (with a $45,000 market value on December 31, 1984) was purchased on January 2, 1984, for $40,000 and represents a significant influence. Dayton had net income of $50,000 and dividends of $20,000 in 1984. Xavier reported 1984 net income of $45,000. The books for Xavier Corporation have not been closed for 1984. Assume that all items are material.

Instructions

[a] Provide correcting and adjusting journal entries for Xavier Corporation in light of the information given.

[b] What is Xavier's correct net income for 1984? Show your computations.

[c] Recast the asset side of the December 31, 1984, balance sheet for Xavier Corporation according to generally accepted accounting principles.

P10–12 The following correct balance sheet was provided by Waller, Inc., on December 31, 1984:

Waller, Inc.
BALANCE SHEET
December 31, 1984

Assets

Current marketable equity securities	$ 12,000	
Less: Allowance to reduce CMES to LCM	(1,500)	$ 10,500.00
Other current assets		40,000.00
Total current assets		50,500.00
Investment in bonds		94,793.25
Noncurrent investment in marketable equity securities	75,000	
Less: Allowance to reduce NCMES to LCM	(25,000)	50,000.00
Investment in Baxter Company (accounted for by the equity method)*		75,000.00
Land		74,500.00
Total assets		$344,793.25

Liabilities and Owners' Equity

Current liabilities	$ 35,000.00
Bonds payable (issued at face value)	100,000.00
Common stock (no par, 40,000 shares authorized, issued, and outstanding)	100,000.00
Unrealized loss on NCMES	(25,000.00)
Retained earnings	134,793.25
Total liabilities and owners' equity	$344,793.25

*The investment in Baxter Company is a 25% interest and represents significant influence.

The market values of the various investments held by Waller, Inc., on December 31, 1985, were:

Current marketable equity securities	$ 11,000
Noncurrent marketable equity securities	45,000
Investment in bonds	100,000
Investment in Baxter Company	70,000

Waller did not have any significant financing or investing transactions during 1985. The bond investment was a $80,000 face amount, 10-year, 12% bond purchased on December 31, 1980. Interest is received annually on December 31. Waller uses the effective interest method of amortization. Baxter Company reported income for 1985 of $100,000 and declared dividends of $80,000. The operating income of Waller, Inc., for 1985 was $15,000. Current liabilities on December 31, 1985, were $35,000. Assume no taxes.

Instructions

Prepare the December 31, 1985, balance sheet for Waller, Inc. Provide a supporting schedule to derive the balances for retained earnings and other current assets.

P10–13 Sterling, Inc., a domestic corporation having a fiscal year ending June 30, purchased common stock in several other domestic corporations. As of June 30, 1985, the balance in Sterling's Investments account was $870,600, the total cost of stock purchased less the cost of stock sold. Sterling wishes to restate the Investments account to reflect the provisions of *APB Opinion No. 18*, "The Equity Method of Accounting for Investments in Common Stock."

Data concerning the investments follow:

		Turner, Inc.	Grotex, Inc.	Scott, Inc.
Shares of common stock outstanding		3,000	32,000	100,000
Shares purchased by Sterling	(a)	300	8,000	30,000
	(b)	810		
Date of purchase	(a)	July 1, 1982	June 30, 1983	June 30, 1984
	(b)	July 1, 1984		
Cost of shares purchased	(a)	$ 49,400	$ 46,000	$ 670,000
	(b)	$ 142,000		
Balance sheet at date indicated:				
Assets		*July 1, 1984*	*June 30, 1983*	*June 30, 1984*
Current assets		$ 362,000	$ 39,600	$ 994,500
Fixed assets, net of depreciation		1,638,000	716,400	3,300,000
Patent, net of amortization				148,500
		$2,000,000	$756,000	$4,443,000
Liabilities and Capital		*July 1, 1984*	*June 30, 1983*	*June 30, 1984*
Liabilities		$1,500,000	$572,000	$2,494,500
Common stock		260,000	80,000	1,400,000
Retained earnings		240,000	104,000	548,500
		$2,000,000	$756,000	$4,443,000
Changes in common stock since July 1, 1982		None	None	None
Average remaining life of fixed assets at date of balance sheet (above)		12 years	9 years	22 years
Analysis of retained earnings				
Balance, July 1, 1982		$234,000		
Net income, July 1, 1982 to June 30, 1983		53,400		
Dividend paid—April 1, 1983		(51,000)		
Balance, June 30, 1983		236,400	$104,000	
Net income (loss), July 1, 1983 to June 30, 1984		55,600	(2,000)	
Dividend paid—April 1, 1984		(52,000)		
Balance, June 30, 1984		240,000	102,000	$548,500
Net income, July 1, 1984 to June 30, 1985		25,000	18,000	330,000
Dividends paid—				
December 28, 1984				(150,000)
June 1, 1985			(5,600)	
Balance, June 30, 1985		$265,000	$114,400	$728,500

Additional Information

Sterling's first purchase of Turner's stock was made because of the high rate of return expected on the investment. All later purchases of stock have been made to gain substantial influence over the operations of the various companies.

In December 1984, changing market conditions caused Sterling to reevaluate its relation to Grotex. On December 31, 1984, Sterling sold 6,400 shares of Grotex for $54,400.

For Turner and Grotex, the fair values of the net assets did not differ materially from the book values as shown in the above balance sheets. For Scott, fair values exceeded book values only with respect to the

patent, which had a fair value of $300,000 and a remaining life of 15 years as of June 30, 1984.

At June 30, 1985, Sterling's inventory included $48,600 of items purchased from Scott during May and June at a 20% markup over Scott's cost.

Instructions

Prepare a workpaper to restate Sterling's Investments account as of June 30, 1985, and its investment revenue by year for the three years then ended. Transactions should be listed in chronological order and supporting computations should be in good form. *Ignore income taxes.* Amortization of goodwill, if any, is to be over a 40-year period. Use the following columnar headings for your workpaper:

		Investments			Investment Revenue, Year Ended June 30			Other Accounts	
		Turner	Grotex	Scott	1983	1984	1985	Amount	
Date	Description	Dr. (Cr.)	Dr. (Cr.)	Dr. (Cr.)	Cr. (Dr.)	Cr. (Dr.)	Cr. (Dr.)	Dr. (Cr.)	Name

(AICPA adapted)

P10–14 During your examination of the financial statements of Craig Corporation for the year ended December 31, 1985, you found a new account, Investments. Your examination revealed that during 1985 Craig began a program of investments, and all investment-related transactions were entered in this account. Your analysis of this account for 1985 follows:

Craig Corporation
ANALYSIS OF INVESTMENTS
For the Year Ended December 31, 1985

Date 1985		Debit	Credit
(a)			
Ace Tool Company Common Stock			
Mar. 15	Purchased 1,000 shares at $25 per share.	$ 25,000	
June 28	Received 50 shares of Bymore Sales Company common stock as a dividend on Ace Tool Company common stock (memorandum entry in general ledger).		
Sept. 30	Sold 50 shares of Bymore Sales Company common stock at $14 per share.		$ 700
Oct. 31	Awarded 500 shares of Ace Tool Company common stock to selected members of Craig's management as an incentive award and accounted for as employee compensation.		12,500
(b)			
Mascot, Inc., Common and Preferred Stock			
Mar. 15	Purchased 600 units of common and preferred stock at $36 per unit.		

	Each unit consists of one share of preferred and two shares of common stock.	21,600	
Apr. 30	Sold 300 shares of common stock at $13 per share.		3,900
June 28	Received 900 common stock rights. Each right entitles the holder to purchase one share of common stock for $12 (memorandum entry in general ledger).		
Sept. 30	Exercised 450 common stock rights to acquire 450 shares of common stock at $12 per share.	5,400	
30	Sold remaining 450 common stock rights at $4 per right.		1,800

(c)

Standard Service, Inc., Common Stock

Mar. 15	Purchased 10,000 shares at $17 per share.	170,000	
Oct. 31	Received dividend of $.75 per share.		7,500

(d)

Azuma Mines, Inc., Convertible Bonds
(Due September 30, 1994, with Interest at
7% Payable March 31 and September 30)

Apr. 30	Purchased forty $1,000 bonds at 100 plus accrued interest.	40,233	
Sept. 30	Received interest due.		1,400
30	Converted ten bonds into 200 shares of Azuma Mines common stock.		10,000
30	Received 200 shares of common stock on conversion of bonds.	10,000	
Oct. 31	Sold the remaining thirty bonds at 102 plus interest for one month. The interest was credited to interest revenue.		30,600

(e)

Kevin Instruments, Inc., Common Stock

Mar. 15	Purchased 4,000 shares at $28 per share.	112,000	
Apr. 30	Purchased 2,000 shares at $30 per share.	60,000	
June 28	Received dividend of $.40 per share.		2,400

(f)

Other Investment

Oct. 31	Reacquired 1,600 shares of its own (Craig) outstanding common stock at $14 per share with the intention of retiring them.	22,400	

Additional Information

[1] The fair market values for each security as of the 1985 date of each transaction follow:

Security	March 15	April 30	June 28	September 30	October 31
Ace Tool Company Common Stock	25				42
Bymore Sales Company Common Stock			8	14	
Mascot, Inc., Preferred Stock	20				
Mascot, Inc., Common Stock	10	13	15*	16	
Mascot, Inc., Common Stock Rights			3	4	
Standard Service, Inc., Common Stock	17				
Azuma Mines, Inc., Bonds		100		100	102
Azuma Mines, Inc., Common Stock				65	
Kevin Instruments, Inc., Common Stock	28	30			
Craig Corporation, Common Stock					14

*Ex-rights

[2] Assume that in accordance with Craig's practice, no gain was recognized on conversion of the Azuma convertible bonds into Azuma common stock.

[3] Standard Service, Inc., has only one class of stock authorized, and there were 30,000 shares of its common stock outstanding throughout 1985. Craig's cost of its investment in Standard was *not* materially different from its equity in the recorded values of Standard's net assets; recorded values were *not* materially different from fair values (individually or collectively). Standard's net income from the date of acquisition of Craig's investment to December 31, 1985, was $336,000. There were *no* intercompany transactions requiring elimination.

[4] Kevin Instruments, Inc., has only one class of stock authorized, and there were 40,000 shares of its common stock outstanding throughout 1985. Craig's cost of its investment in Kevin was *not* materially different from its equity in the recorded values of Kevin's net assets; recorded values were *not* materially different from fair values (individually or collectively). Kevin's net income from the date of acquisition of Craig's investment to December 31, 1985, was $120,000.

There were no intercompany transactions requiring elimination.

[5] All other investments of Craig are widely held, and Craig's percentage of ownership in each is nominal (5% or less).

[6] At December 31, 1985, Craig Corporation had 98,400 shares of its $10 par value common stock outstanding. The balance in the Premium on Common Stock account was $100,000.

Instructions

Prepare necessary adjusting journal entries classified by each of the securities analyzed in (a) through (f) to properly adjust the Investments account. Identify each security by type (preferred stock, common stock, rights, etc.) as well as by company. Schedules supporting calculations should be in good form and either included as part of the journal entry explanation or properly cross-referenced to the appropriate journal entry. Ignore brokers' fees and transfer and income taxes.

(AICPA adapted)

11

PROPERTY, PLANT, AND EQUIPMENT: ACQUISITION AND DISPOSAL

Objectives

To describe the roles of tangible and intangible assets in the revenue-producing process.

To discuss the basic accounting principles that underlie accounting for tangible and intangible assets.

To apply the historical cost principle to specific plant assets.

To discuss problems encountered in applying the historical cost principle to plant assets.

To discuss the proper accounting treatment of plant-asset expenditures that are incurred after the initial acquisition of the related assets.

To discuss transactions that result in the disposal of plant assets, including their sale, abandonment, destruction, or exchange for other plant assets.

CLASSIFICATION OF PLANT AND INTANGIBLE ASSETS

Although assets are used in the production or distribution of goods or services in virtually all businesses, they vary in nature from enterprise to enterprise because of the differences in the business activities of the enterprises. These assets include both tangible properties, such as equipment and buildings, and intangible assets, such as patents and franchise rights. **Tangible assets** are often called **property, plant, and equipment** or simply **plant assets** or **fixed assets. Assets lacking physical substance** are typically referred to as **intangible assets.**

All plant and intangible assets have two basic characteristics in common:

1. **They are acquired as operating assets.** Plant and intangible assets are acquired for use in the production or distribution of goods or services. They are *not* acquired primarily for purposes of resale, even though they may later be sold.
2. **They are relatively long-lived.** Plant and intangible assets are expected to have relatively long lives in terms of their contribution to the production and distribution of goods and services. In most cases, therefore, the cost of these assets is allocated as an expense over their productive lives.

Despite these similarities characteristics of *specific* plant and intangible assets vary considerably. For example, although most are readily transferable between enterprises, others cannot be separated from the original enterprise. Furthermore, some are natural resources while others are man-made properties. Numerous classifications of plant and intangible assets are available. For purposes of discussion in this text, we use the classification as shown at the top of page 435.

STATEMENT CLASSIFICATION

[AN] IMPORTANT BALANCE sheet classification divides all properties into "fixed" and "current assets." . . . What constitutes a fixed asset, a current asset? Four points of difference (not all applicable to every case) may be noted. First may be mentioned normal length of life within the business. A fixed asset is one that normally will remain an economic factor within the particular business for at least two or more accounting periods (assuming the period to be one year), such as a piece of durable equipment, a fireproof building. . . . A second consideration is liquidity. . . . A fixed asset is one which may or will with difficulty, or only in a roundabout fashion, be liquidated. . . . Third, a current asset is one which passes rapidly into the expense division, while a fixed asset is transferred to expense account over perhaps many accounting periods. Finally, a typical fixed asset, such as a machine unit, is used in its entirety to furnish a series of similar services. The business man in buying the machine acquires, essentially, a bundle of services. . . . The fixed asset is not used up bit by bit, each of essentially the same significance. Instead the whole item is used more or less continuously until its efficiency is so impaired that it is no longer economical to repair it and continue it in operation.

SOURCE: William A. Paton, *Accounting Theory* (Houston: Scholars Book, 1973), pp. 214–215.

Asset Classification	Example Assets	Allocation of Cost
Tangible Plant Assets		
Property, plant, and equipment subject to depreciation	Buildings Equipment Furniture Fixtures	Depreciation
Property not subject to depreciation	Land	—
Natural resources subject to depletion	Oil and gas reserves Mineral deposits	Depletion
Intangible Assets		
Separately identifiable	Patents Copyrights Trademarks Franchises Leaseholds	Amortization
Not separately identifiable	Goodwill	Amortization

Chapters 11, 12, and 13 deal with accounting for plant and intangible assets. If you turn to the balance sheet inside the front cover of your book, you will see "Property, Plant, and Equipment" listed as an asset category in the balance sheet of Kroger Company. These assets represent significant investments in tangible assets that are used in the day-to-day operations of the company. We discuss land, buildings and land improvements, and equipment, as well as other plant assets, in Chapters 11 and 12. The leased assets included in the Kroger balance sheet are discussed in Chapter 21 of this text. The single intangible asset in the Kroger balance sheet, "Excess of cost of investments in consolidated subsidiaries over equities in net assets," is included in our discussion of intangible assets in Chapter 13. You may also want to turn to the inside back cover of your text and notice the expense category, "Depreciation and Amortization," in the Kroger income statement and observe the reference to plant assets in the company's statement of changes in financial position.

The first part of Chapter 11 presents general concepts of accounting for all plant and intangible assets. We then turn our attention to specific issues concerning the acquisition and disposal of various types of plant assets. Chapter 12 introduces the depreciation and depletion of plant assets and includes several special accounting problems. In Chapter 13 the accounting principles discussed in Chapters 11 and 12 are applied to intangible assets, and several problems associated with accounting for assets that lack physical substance are identified and discussed. Because a detailed discussion of depreciation is included in Chapter 12, Chapter 11 uses only *straight-line* depreciation.

DEFINITIONS AND BASIC ACCOUNTING PRINCIPLES

Plant assets are acquired primarily for use in the production and distribution of goods and services, are expected to be used over a relatively long period, and have tangible physical properties. Although plant assets are apparent through their physical qualities, their value lies in their **service potential** (i.e. in the positive contribution that an asset is capable of making to the revenue-producing process in which the enterprise is engaged). Service potential can also exist in an intangible asset; in such cases, the service potential manifests itself in the form of rights and privileges that accrue to the holder of the asset.

Several principles that underlie accounting for all plant and intangible assets are discussed in the following paragraphs. Application of the principles to specific assets, problems encountered in applying the principles, and specified exceptions to the general principles are discussed throughout this and subsequent chapters.

Historical Cost

Principle 1. Plant and intangible assets are initially recorded at historical cost.

Plant and intangible assets are *initially* recorded at **historical cost,** which is the cash price or the cash-equivalent value of consideration given other than cash. The cash or cash-equivalent price represents the bargained value of the asset at the time of acquisition. From the viewpoint of the acquirer, the cash or cash-equivalent price represents the future value of the service potential expected from the asset.

Nevertheless, the principle of historical cost that is used in accounting for plant and intangible assets is broader than simply the cash or cash-equivalent price. All costs related to the acquisition and preparation of the asset for its intended use are considered part of the asset's cost. In addition, subsequent costs to extend the useful life of the asset (beyond that originally expected) or to increase either the quantity or quality of service rendered by the asset are considered part of the cost of the asset.

The principle of historical cost, as applied to plant and intangible assets, is best described as a **full-cost concept,** because it includes expenditures related to the acquisition of the asset and the continuing enhancement of the service potential of the asset.

Matching

Principle 2. The cost of plant and intangible assets is allocated as depreciation, depletion, or amortization in a systematic and rational manner to achieve a matching of expenses and revenues during the useful life of the asset.

As plant and intangible assets are used in the production of revenue, their *future* service potential declines. Since these assets are established in the accounts at historical cost, this decline in service potential is measured by treating a portion of that historical cost as an expense in the periods that benefit from the use of the asset. From the accountant's perspective, **depreciation** is the process of allocating the cost of property, plant, and equipment as an expense to those periods during which the asset contributes to the revenue-producing process. The terms **depletion** and **amortization** are used to describe this allocation process for **natural resources** and **intangible assets,** respectively. Deprecia-

NATURE OF DEPRECIATION

DESTRUCTION IS THE LAW of nature. Fixed capital, using the term here in its economic rather than its accounting sense, despite its name, is not exempt from this law. Even so-called permanent improvements, such as buildings are all subject to the ravages of time, which Alfred Marshall aptly defines as "the complex of destructive agencies." All machinery is on an irresistible march to the junk heap, and its progress, while it may be delayed, cannot be prevented by repairs.

This obvious economic fact is of momentous import to accounting. . . . It implies that, in valuing all fixed assets, account must be taken of the lapse of time, and even in the case of machinery giving no evidence either of use or misuse, the mere fact that it is a year nearer its inevitable goal is an item of which technical account must be taken.

In the language of accounting this inevitable decline in value is called depreciation.

SOURCE: Henry Rand Hatfield, *Accounting: Its Principles and Problems* (Houston: Scholars Book, 1971), p. 130.

tion, depletion, and amortization are, thus, important parts of the matching process when plant and intangible assets are used in the revenue-producing process.

Although expenditures for plant and intangible assets are typically made when the assets are initially acquired, the cost is allocated as an expense over the useful life of the assets; only *part* of the cost is charged as an expense in the period of acquisition. This procedure is part of the process of matching the revenues and the expenses of producing those revenues in the determination of net income.

Matching

Methods to determine depreciation expense must be **systematic** and **rational.** To be systematic, a method must be able to calculate the periodic depreciation charge in advance or on the basis of the activity level during a particular period. To be rational the method must identify the association between the amount of depreciation expense recognized and the decline in the service potential of the asset during the period. Chapter 12 covers in detail a number of systematic methods that are widely practiced. However, specific circumstances must be considered in evaluating the rational feature of a particular method.

Principle 3. **The establishment of cost and the subsequent allocation of that cost is necessarily based on many estimates and assumptions about the use of the plant or intangible asset.**

Estimates and assumptions are an important part of accounting for plant and intangible assets. If cash transactions are not used in acquiring the assets and if costs related to acquisition are incurred, judgments must be made in determining the historical cost. Cost allocation methods (i.e., depreciation, depletion, and amortization) require an estimate of useful life in terms of calendar time, service time, or productive output. Finally, an estimate of residual (or salvage) value is required in applying the various cost allocation methods that are used in practice.

An additional judgment must estimate the pattern of the decline in the service potential of a plant or intangible asset. Since the allocation method must be rational, it should reflect—to the extent possible—the estimated decline in the service potential of the asset on a periodic basis over its estimated useful life.

Principle 4. **The unallocated cost of a plant or intangible asset, called "book value," is *not* intended to approximate the current value of the asset.**

Matching

As indicated in Principle 2, the process for allocating the cost for plant and intangible assets to those periods that benefit from their use must match the expenses and revenues in determining net income. The historical cost of the asset, less accumulated depreciation, depletion, or amortization, is called **book value.** We can define book value best in terms of the process followed in its calculation: the historical cost reduced by the accumulated depreciation, depletion, or amortization recognized to date. Alternatively, book value can be defined as the *un*allocated portion of the historical cost of the asset.

However, we cannot *expect* the book value to equal the current market value of the asset. After an asset is acquired its market value may remain constant, decline, or increase. If the market value declines, it may or may not equal the book value. The term "book value" may be a misnomer, because it seems to imply that the number measures the current worth of the asset. Although "unallocated cost" is more descriptive of the number, "book value" is widely used in practice.

APPLICATION OF THE COST PRINCIPLE TO SPECIFIC ITEMS OF PROPERTY, PLANT, AND EQUIPMENT

Assets identified as property, plant, and equipment—or simply plant assets—should be established in appropriate accounts at cost. The full cost includes expenditures necessary to acquire the assets and to prepare them for their intended use. The following paragraphs develop and apply the full-cost concept to specific types of plant assets.

Land

The cost of land includes a variety of expenditures related to the acquisition of the land and its preparation for use as intended by the acquiring enterprise. The following list includes some of the major expenditures that should be capitalized as the cost of land:

1. The original bargained acquisition price.
2. Commissions related to acquisition.
3. Legal fees related to acquisition.
4. Cost of surveys.
5. Cost of an option to buy the acquired land.
6. Cost of removing unwanted buildings from the land, less any proceeds from salvage.
7. Unpaid taxes (to date of acquisition) assumed by the purchaser.
8. Cost of permanent improvements (e.g., landscaping) and improvements maintained and replaced by the government (e.g., street lights and sewers).

Costs associated with land that is *not* acquired should not be included in the Land account. For example, costs of surveying and options to purchase land that is ultimately *not* acquired should be expensed as incurred, despite their similarity to costs that are capitalized when land is acquired.

Expenditures for land improvements that have limited lives should be capitalized in accounts other than the Land account and depreciated over their estimated useful lives. Examples of these assets are private driveways, sidewalks, fences, parking lots, and easements or rights-of-way of limited duration.

Land and other plant assets that are held for speculative or other investment purposes should be classified as investments rather than as property, plant, and equipment. Taxes and other expenditures required to maintain these assets should be capitalized as part of the cost of the assets if they are not producing revenue while they are considered an investment. If the assets produce revenue (e.g., through rental) these expenditures should be treated as expenses and matched against the revenue that the investments generate.

Land is generally considered to have an unlimited life and is not expected to decline in service potential as it is used. Thus, land is usually carried at the original cost figure and not depreciated over the periods during which it is used in the operations of the enterprise.

Matching

Buildings

The cost of a building includes all necessary expenditures to acquire or construct and prepare the building for its intended use. The following lists include some major expenditures that should be capitalized as part of the cost of buildings:

If acquired by purchase:

1. The original bargained purchase price of the building.
2. Cost of renovation necessary to prepare the building for its intended use.
3. Cost of building permits related to renovation.
4. Unpaid taxes (to date of acquisition) assumed by the purchaser.

If acquired by construction:

1. Cost of constructing new building, including material, labor, and overhead.[1]
2. Cost of excavating land in preparation for construction.
3. Cost of plans, blueprints, specifications, and estimates related to construction.
4. Cost of building permits.
5. Architectural and engineering fees.

---

[1] The subject of overhead as part of the cost of internally constructed plant assets is covered in a later section of this chapter.

The cost of a building that is acquired but *immediately* removed to prepare the land for construction of a new building should be treated as part of the cost of the *land* rather than as part of the cost of the new building. As we indicated earlier, the cost of *removal* is also treated as part of the land costs. Also the cost of removing an existing building that the new purchaser actually used for a time should be treated as an adjustment to the gain or loss on the disposal of the old building rather than as part of the cost of the newly constructed building.

Care must be taken in distinguishing between building costs and the cost of other assets, such as removable fixtures. The latter represent separate assets that should be recorded in appropriate asset accounts and depreciated over their expected useful lives. This holds even if they were acquired with the building and used in a manner closely related to it.

Machinery, Equipment, Furniture, and Fixtures

Machinery, equipment, furniture, and fixtures are various types of property, plant, and equipment that are used by enterprises in the production and distribution of goods and services. The following list includes some of the costs that should be capitalized in the appropriate asset account:

1. The original bargained acquisition price.
2. Freight, insurance, handling, storage, and other costs related to acquiring the asset.
3. Costs of installation, including preparing the site for the asset, assembling the asset, and installing it.
4. Costs of trial runs and other tests required before the asset can be put into full operation.
5. Costs of reconditioning equipment acquired in a used state.

Making the proper distinction in the accounting records between the types of property, plant, and equipment is important because the life of an asset and the method of depreciation may vary among the various asset categories.

Natural Resources

Natural resources (e.g., timber, coal, and oil) represent tangible assets that are recorded at cost when they are acquired. These costs are then allocated, usually on a production basis, as depletion to the periods benefiting from the use of the natural resources, as we explain in Chapter 12.

The cost of natural resources includes the original purchase price plus exploration and development costs related to the location and extraction of the resources.[2] Other plant assets, separate from the natural resource, are frequently acquired for use in the development and production of natural resources. Buildings and equipment are examples of assets that are typically used in the successful exploitation of natural resources. These assets are established in separate accounts and depreciated over the shorter of (1) their expected useful lives or (2) the expected useful life of the related natural resource.

Other Plant Assets

Types of property, plant, and equipment are as numerous as types of enterprises. Each enterprise must acquire those plant assets required to succeed in the business activities of that enterprise. In addition to those plant assets that are common to many enterprises—land, buildings, machinery, equipment, furniture, fixtures, and natural resources—a wide variety of assets are used by some enterprises. Several of these are discussed in the following paragraphs.

---

[2]Unique problems associated with accounting for exploration costs in the oil and gas industry are covered in Chapter 13.

Returnable containers are used in certain types of businesses to transfer products between the enterprise and its customers. Such containers may represent a significant asset, particularly when a large number are in circulation at any particular time. In some cases the customer makes no deposit; the container is simply returned by the customer or picked up by the enterprise after it has been used. In these cases the enterprise typically uses an inventory method whereby the asset cost is increased as units are acquired and reduced as a periodic count reveals the number of units that are no longer in use. The reduction may be due to normal wear and tear, breakage, or other causes. When customers place deposits that will be returned when the containers are returned, the amounts on deposit represent a liability of the enterprise. This liability is often called **deposits from customers.** Return-

Matching

able containers that are not returned by customers within a reasonable period should be treated as sales at the deposit amount. To complete the matching process, the cost of unreturned containers should then be charged to Expense.

Miscellaneous tools and other small items of equipment are another type of plant asset, despite their relatively low unit cost. The practical limitations of capitalization and depreciation and the large number of relatively inexpensive assets result in the typical treatment

Materiality

of the cost of such items as expenses when incurred—or later on an inventory basis similar to that for returnable containers. Materiality is an important consideration in these situations, and a departure from the strict application of the matching principle may be justified if expensing small assets or using an inventory approach does not have a significant impact on the financial statements.

In a manufacturing process various tools and other devices are used to mold, stamp, cut, and shape other materials. Such devices, commonly called patterns and dies, should be capitalized in appropriate asset accounts and depreciated over their estimated useful lives. If such devices are useful only in a particular job rather than in a continuous manufacturing process, they should be charged to cost for that particular job.

PROBLEMS OF ESTABLISHING HISTORICAL COST

The concept of full cost, whereby plant assets are established at the cost of acquisition and preparation for intended use, is more easily stated than applied. Numerous problems are encountered in attempting to apply this general concept in specific situations. Judgment is required in assessing which expenditures should be classified as part of the cost of assets and which costs should be treated in other ways.

This section discusses several frequently encountered problems: cash discounts; deferred-payment plans; internally constructed assets; capitalization of interest; acquisition by issuing securities; basket purchases; and installation, preparation, and start-up costs. Although these problems and their resolution can generally be applied to a wide range of plant assets, they are illustrated here in the context of *specific* plant assets.

Cash Discounts

The bargained purchase price of a plant asset is the cash paid or the cash-equivalent price. If cash discounts are available for early payment, the question arises about whether cost should include or exclude the cash discount. A related question is whether the amount of the recorded cost should depend on whether or not the cash discount is taken.

Theoretically, the cash-equivalent price should equal the original price *minus* any cash discount available, whether or not the discount is taken, because the net amount is the price at which the asset could be acquired in a cash transaction. If the discount is not taken, a **discount lost** should be recorded and treated as an expense in the current period.

As an illustration, assume that Tinker Company acquired equipment with a list price of $88,000 with terms 2/10, n/30. The asset should be recorded at the net amount of $86,240 [$88,000 − (.02 × $88,000)]:

Equipment	86,240	
Accounts Payable		86,240

If payment is made within the 10-day period, the $86,240 payment of Accounts Payable is recorded. If payment is made *after* the 10-day period, however, the following entry is appropriate:

Accounts Payable	86,240	
Discount Lost	1,760	
Cash		88,000

Materiality

Recording the asset at the **net amount** is preferable, because this represents the cash equivalent price. However, some accountants record the asset at the total price paid ($88,000 in the above example) even if the discount is not taken. The basis for this treatment is that the total price was the actual amount paid; in some particular circumstances it may not even be appropriate for management to take the discount. Again, materiality may be an important consideration in these decisions, because relatively small discounts may not have a significant impact on the financial statements.

Deferred-Payment Plans

Plant assets may be acquired on a long-term financing plan whereby periodic payments are made or a single payment is made at some future date. An asset acquired in this manner should be recorded at the current cash-equivalent price and any interest included in the financing plan recognized as expense in the appropriate period(s). The objective of this practice is to distinguish properly between the portion of payments that represents the historical cost of the asset acquired and that portion representing interest charges for the credit received. Failure to make this distinction results in a misstatement of the related asset, the depreciation, and the interest expense.

Historical Cost

If interest is not stated in a deferred-payment contract, if the stated interest is not reasonable in view of current market conditions, or if the face amount of the obligation differs from the current selling price for the same or equivalent asset, interest may need to be *imputed.* The amount of the obligation is assumed to include two elements: the **acquisition price** of the asset and **interest charges.** The obligation is recorded at the asset's estimated fair value and the difference between the face amount of the obligation and the estimated fair value of the asset at the date of acquisition is recognized as interest over the life of the obligation. The asset and related obligation should be recorded at an amount equal to (1) the fair value of the asset being acquired, (2) the market value of the obligation, or (3) the present value of the obligation determined by present-value techniques that use an estimated interest rate. The most objectively determinable of the first two measures should generally be used. In some cases, however, these amounts are not available and the value of the asset and related obligation must be estimated by the third method. If either of the first two methods are used to record the transaction, the difference between the **face value of the note** and the **recorded amount of the asset** must be used to compute a rate upon which the recognition of interest will be based. If the third method is used, the borrower's (i.e., the purchaser's) incremental borrowing rate should be used as a basis for computing the recorded amount of the asset, the obligation, and the subsequent recognition of interest. This process is a *specific* application of the general process of imputing interest required by *Accounting Principles Board Opinion No. 21* that we discussed in Chapter 10.

Exhibit 11–1 summarizes the processes used in accounting for deferred-payment acquisitions, and two independent examples illustrate the process of imputing interest on such acquisitions.

To illustrate the process of imputing interest, we shall assume that Greeneville Produc-

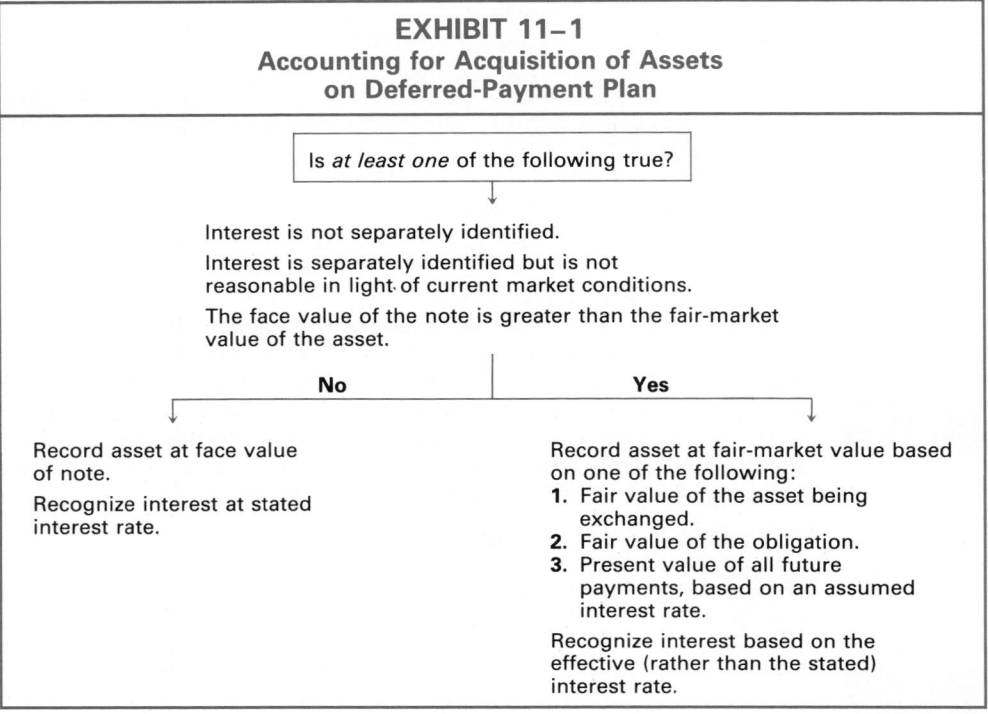

EXHIBIT 11-1
Accounting for Acquisition of Assets
on Deferred-Payment Plan

tion Company acquired a used machine by issuing a $150,000 noninterest-bearing note. The transaction took place on December 31, 1983, and payment is due on December 31, 1986. Neither the market value of the note nor the fair value of the property are determinable. Recently, however, Greeneville Production paid 12% interest on similar transactions.

Since no stated interest rate exists and market values of the note and the asset are unknown, the portion of the note representing interest must be separated by using the 12% interest rate. Using the present-value factor from Table 6-2, we can determine the face value as follows:

$$\text{Present value of note} = \left[\begin{matrix} \text{Face} \\ \text{value} \end{matrix} \cdot pvf_{\overline{n}|\,i} \right]$$
$$= [\,\$150,000\,] \cdot [\,pvf_{\overline{3}|\,12\%}\,]$$
$$= (\,\$150,000\,)\,(.71178)$$
$$= \$106,767$$

The machinery is recorded at $106,767 and the note payable, net of a discount to reduce the face value of $150,000 to its present value, is recorded at the same amount. This is preferably done by using a Discount account as follows:

Machinery	106,767	
Discount on Notes Payable	43,233	
Notes Payable		150,000

The discount of $43,233 is then recognized as interest over the life of the note according to the following schedule:

Date	Interest Computation	Carrying Value of Obligation
		$ 106,767
Dec. 31, 1984		
Interest recognition	(12% × $106,767 = $12,812)	12,812
		119,579
Dec. 31, 1985		
Interest recognition	(12% × $119,579 = $14,349)	14,349
		133,928
Dec. 31, 1986		
Interest recognition	($150,000 − $133,928 = $16,072)	16,072
		150,000
Payment of note		(150,000)
		–0–

Interest at December 31, 1986, can also be determined by applying the 12% rate to the carrying value of the obligation, as was done in 1984 and 1985: 12% × $133,928 = $16,071. The $1 difference from the amount in the preceding schedule is due to a rounding difference caused by stating the amounts in whole dollars. A convenient way to get around this rounding problem is simply to adjust for the difference between the face value and carrying value of the note in the last year, as we did in the schedule.

An entry is made to recognize the interest at December 31 of each intervening year, as follows:

	1984	1985	1986
Interest Expense	12,812	14,349	16,072
Discount on Notes Payable	12,812	14,349	16,072

As each entry recognizing interest is made, the carrying value of the note is increased—as indicated in the schedule. The final payment at December 31, 1986, is made by a debit to the Notes Payable account and a credit to the Cash account for $150,000. The cost of the asset for purposes of depreciation and financial-statement presentation is $106,767.

Plant acquisitions resulting in *multiple* payments may also require interest imputations. We illustrate this process with the case of Blacksburg Manufacturing Company, which—we shall assume—acquired a machine by issuing three $50,000 noninterest-bearing notes, payable one, two, and three years from the transaction date of December 31, 1983. Neither the market value of the notes nor the fair value of the asset is determinable. In recent similar transactions, however, Blacksburg Manufacturing paid 12% interest.

As in the previous case, no interest rate is stated and the market values of the notes and asset are not determinable. The portion of the notes representing interest must be separated by using the appropriate present-value factor from Table 6–4, as follows:

Face value of notes (representing both principal and interest)	$ 150,000
Present value of notes [$50,000] · [$pvoaf_{\overline{3}|\,12\%}$] ($50,000) · (2.40183) =	(120,092)
Amount of imputed interest	$ 29,908

The purchase of the asset and the related obligation are then recorded as follows:

Machinery	120,092	
Discount on Notes Payable	29,908	
Notes Payable		150,000

The portion of each $50,000 payment that represents interest is separated and recognized periodically over the life of the notes according to the following schedule:

Date	Interest Computation	Carrying Value of Obligation
		$120,092
Dec. 31, 1984		
Interest recognition	12% × $120,092 = $14,411	14,411
Payment		(50,000)
		84,503
Dec. 31, 1985		
Interest recognition	12% × $84,503 = $10,140	10,140
Payment		(50,000)
		44,643
Dec. 31, 1986		
Interest recognition	12% × $44,643 = $5,357	5,357
Payment		(50,000)
		–0–

An entry is made to record the periodic payment and to recognize interest at December 31 of each intervening year, as follows:

	1984	1985	1986
Notes Payable	50,000	50,000	50,000
Cash	50,000	50,000	50,000
Interest Expense	14,411	10,140	5,357
Discount on Notes Payable	14,411	10,140	5,357

This series of entries results in the complete elimination of the obligation of $120,092 recognized at the date of acquisition and the proper recognition of interest for the intervening accounting periods. The cost of the asset for purposes of depreciation and financial statement presentation is $120,092.

Historical Cost

Imputing interest for a plant-asset acquisition is required in order to distinguish between the historical cost of the plant asset and interest expense. This, in turn, results in a proper statement of the asset in the balance sheet and interest and depreciation expense in the income statement. Failure to impute interest in those situations described in Exhibit 11–1 results in improper figures for these important financial-statement items.

Internally Constructed Assets

In certain circumstances companies construct their own plant assets rather than acquire them from other enterprises. For some companies this is done on a relatively constant basis and is an expected part of business operations; for others this is done only occasionally. Reasons for constructing assets internally vary from situation to situation. Several frequently cited reasons for constructing assets rather than acquiring them externally are:

1. To acquire needed productive services at prices lower than those from external sources.
2. To make use of facilities and personnel that would otherwise be idle in slack periods.
3. To produce specialized assets that might not otherwise be available.
4. To ensure the privacy of information concerning future production plans.

Historical Cost

The principle of historical cost applies to plant assets that are either developed internally or acquired from external sources. However, measuring the cost of internally constructed assets poses some unusual problems. Costs of producing inventory are generally identified in terms of material, labor, and overhead costs. This classification also provides the basis for determining the cost of plant assets that are constructed internally.

Accountants generally agree that materials and direct labor should be included in the cost of an internally constructed asset since they represent both tangible material and payment to employees involved in the production of the asset. Overhead costs are more controversial, however, because they are indirect costs of production that do not attach directly to any specific product or any specific constructed asset.

Several positions exist concerning inclusion of manufacturing overhead in the cost of internally constructed assets. One position holds that the costs of such assets should not include any overhead charge because of the indirect nature of overhead and the inability to associate overhead charges with the particular asset being constructed. The basis of this assumption is that overhead costs are the same whether or not assets (other than inventory) are being constructed. However, the exclusion of overhead does not appear viable if overhead costs increase as a result of constructing plant assets internally. A second position, thus, requires only the *incremental* overhead to be included as a part of the cost of the internally constructed asset. While intuitively logical, isolating the increase in overhead costs that can be specifically identified with the activity of constructing the plant asset internally is difficult.

The concept of full cost supports a third position concerning the amount of overhead, if any, to be capitalized as part of the cost of a plant asset that is constructed internally. This position holds that the asset should be charged overhead on the same basis as inventory that is also being produced. For example, if overhead is charged to the manufacture of inventory at $1.50 per hour of direct labor, the same allocation procedure is used to charge overhead to the plant asset; thus, the cost of the asset includes $1.50 of overhead per hour of direct labor. While this method is widely used in practice, it is difficult to justify if production below capacity is a major reason for constructing the asset internally. Absorbing the cost of idle capacity in the cost of the internally constructed asset relieves current income and inventory of charges that would otherwise have been made to them and results in a higher cost of the constructed asset. This process increases income of the current and near-future years (by reducing costs of sales and inventory) and reduces income of distant-future years (by increasing depreciation charges).

Authoritative accounting pronouncements do not resolve the controversy of the amount of overhead, if any, that should be included in the cost of internally constructed plant assets. Proper accounting is, thus, a matter of professional judgment in applying the concept of full cost. The authors believe that the full-cost concept should be generally followed and that the total cost of internally developed assets should include material, labor, and overhead prorated in the same manner as for inventory being manufactured. A logical exception to this general policy would arise if the company were operating below capacity and constructing a plant asset internally in order to utilize more efficiently its employees and facilities. In such a case, if it is *practical* to determine the incremental overhead, only the incremental overhead associated *specifically* with the manufacture of the asset should be included in the cost of the asset.

What amount should be capitalized as the cost of an internally constructed asset when the internal costs total more than the price at which the asset could have been purchased externally? Accountants generally agree that the *maximum* amount at which the asset should be established is its *market value*. Any costs beyond that amount represent inefficiencies of internal construction and should not be included in the cost of the asset. Future periods should not be burdened by the greater depreciation charges that would result from the capitalization of those costs. Any costs beyond the external market price of the internally constructed asset should be treated as expenses in the period in which they are incurred.

Capitalization of Interest

Historical Cost

Our earlier discussion of deferred payment for plant assets emphasizes the importance of distinguishing between expenditures that represent payments for interest on money borrowed and expenditures that are made to acquire the productive services of various types of assets. Controversy has surrounded the determination of historical costs of assets, however, when interest costs are incurred specifically for the acquisition and preparation of assets for their intended use and if they will presumably benefit future periods.

Historically most enterprises have treated all interest as an expense when incurred. The **capitalization of interest** as part of the historical cost of assets has been a common practice among public utilities, however, because customers are charged regulated rates based on costs incurred and designed to provide stockholders of the utilities with a fair rate of return on their investments. When interest costs are incurred to construct utility facilities, interest is capitalized as part of the cost of those facilities so that the costs being depreciated are representative of the costs incurred. Therefore, utility rates on the new facilities are based on higher asset-acquisition costs, and future utility users in those areas will pay rates that cover the interest costs required to finance the facilities that produce the services they consume.

Historical Cost

The practice of capitalizing interest has not been limited to public utilities. An increasing number of other enterprises have adopted a policy of capitalizing interest in certain circumstances. Standards of accounting and reporting in this area were subsequently established by the Financial Accounting Standards Board (FASB) in its *Statement of Financial Accounting Standards No. 34.*[3] This pronouncement requires the capitalization of interest by all enterprises in certain circumstances on the premise that the historical cost of acquiring an asset includes all costs necessary to bring the asset to the condition and location required for its intended use.

Materiality

Interest should be capitalized as part of the cost of acquiring an asset if an **extended period** is required to prepare the asset for its intended use and **significant expenditures** related to the asset take place during that period. The objectives of capitalizing interest in such cases are (1) to obtain an asset cost that more closely reflects the enterprise's total investment in the asset and (2) to reflect an expense in future periods that more closely charges the cost of services provided by the asset. Interest should be capitalized *only* if the amounts are material and the benefits of capitalization exceed the costs of accumulating the required information. Within those constraints, capitalization of interest is appropriate in situations such as the following:

1. Assets constructed by the enterprise for its own use.
2. Assets constructed for an enterprise by another enterprise if the acquiring enterprise makes deposits or progress payments.
3. Land under development for a particular use.
4. Assets intended for sale or lease that are constructed as discrete projects.

Common characteristics of these assets are (1) they are *not yet* being used in earning activities and (2) they are undergoing preparation for use in earning activities in the *future.* If the production of an asset is complete, if the asset is not being changed in some way, or if obsolescence, excess capacity, or need of repair prevents an asset from being used in earning activities, the asset does not qualify for the capitalization of interest. Also, interest is not capitalized on inventories that are routinely manufactured or otherwise produced in large quantities on a repetitive basis.

Theoretically, capitalized interest is the interest that was actually incurred during a period but that *could have been avoided* if expenditures related to the qualifying asset had not been made. Interest is based on the average accumulated expenditures for the asset during the period.

---

[3]*FASB Statement of Financial Accounting Standards No. 34,* "Capitalization of Interest Cost," 1979.

If specific borrowings are associated with a specific asset for which interest is being capitalized, the interest rates on those borrowings are used. If this direct association cannot be made, a **weighted average interest rate** on all borrowings of the company is used to determine the amount of interest to be capitalized. Since the interest to be capitalized is based on actual outstanding debt, the amount capitalized cannot exceed the interest incurred during the period. Interest capitalization begins when the initial expenditure related to the development of the asset is made and continues as long as the asset is undergoing active development. Interest capitalization ends when the asset is ready for its intended use, whether or not it is placed in use at that time.

To illustrate the process of interest capitalization, we shall assume that High Ridge Company is constructing a warehouse for use in its own operations. Costs of material, labor, and overhead of $150,000 have been identified and charged to the asset account. Initial expenditures in early January 1984 were $70,000. In early May of that year $50,000 more was invested; in early September, an additional $30,000. On January 2, 1984, the company arranged for a 12%, $100,000 line of credit to partially finance the construction. In January the company drew $70,000 on this line of credit; an additional $30,000 was borrowed in May. The company has a substantial amount of additional debt outstanding at an average interest rate of 10%.

The cost of the asset is determined as follows:

January–April, 1984		
Material, labor, and overhead	$70,000	
Interest: $70,000 \times 12\% \times \frac{1}{3}$ year	2,800	$ 72,800
May–August, 1984		
Material, labor, and overhead	50,000	
Interest: $100,000 \times 12\% \times \frac{1}{3}$ year	4,000	
$\underline{20,000} \times 10\% \times \frac{1}{3}$ year	667	54,667
$120,000		
September–December, 1984		
Material, labor, and overhead	30,000	
Interest: $100,000 \times 12\% \times \frac{1}{3}$ year	4,000	
$\underline{50,000} \times 10\% \times \frac{1}{3}$ year	1,667	35,667
$150,000		
Total asset cost		$163,134

If we assume that interest on the $100,000 debt incurred specifically for this asset is charged directly to the asset account as incurred and that other interest is allocated from interest expense previously recognized, the entry to record the capitalization of interest is as follows:

Warehouse	13,134	
Cash (or Interest Payable)		10,800
Interest Expense		2,334

In reality, several entries totaling the amounts in the above entry may be made at different points in time. The $10,800 interest on debt incurred specifically for this asset ($2,800 + $4,000 + $4,000) would be charged to the asset as it was paid or accrued. The transfer of interest previously recognized as an expense is most likely made when the asset is complete or at the end of the accounting period if the asset is still in process. This is necessary in order to state properly the asset cost and the interest expense for the period.

When the $13,134 interest is combined with the $150,000 of material, labor, and overhead costs that are capitalized as part of the cost of the asset, the total asset cost is $163,134

($150,000 + $13,134). This amount is the basis for financial-statement presentation and depreciation calculation.

In this case the investment in the asset for which interest is being capitalized is greater than the debt directly related to that project. In addition, High Ridge has other debt outstanding that provides the basis for the capitalization of interest on the additional investment of $50,000 ($150,000 investment, less $100,000 of directly related debt). If the company had no debt beyond the $100,000 directly related to the asset under construction, no additional interest could be capitalized, because the amount of capitalized interest is limited to the amount of interest actually incurred during the construction period.

When a company has capitalized a part of interest incurred during an accounting period in accordance with *FASB Statement No. 34* (see footnote 3), special disclosure must be made in notes to the financial statements. Exhibit 11–2 presents an example of this disclosure from the 1982 financial statements of Oneida Ltd., a diversified company serving consumer, industrial, and foreign markets in several product lines: tableware, cookware, industrial wire and cable, and jewelry.

Acquisition by Issuing Securities

Plant assets may be acquired by issuing securities (e.g., stock certificates) rather than paying cash or transferring other assets to the seller. In such transactions accountants record the equivalent amount of cash that would have been transferred in a comparable cash transaction. Several problems may obscure the determination of the cash-equivalent amount. Market values of either the securities or the asset(s) exchanged may not be readily available. On the other hand, although a "market value" of the securities may be readily determinable from a market quotation, such value may be based on a level of market activity substantially different from the number of shares involved in the acquisition. In such situations, the market price may not indicate the value of the shares if the number issued in the acquisition is included in the transactions determining the market price.

Objectivity

When securities are issued in exchange for assets, the market value of the shares issued should normally be used as the basis for recording both the assets acquired and the stock issued. When the market value of the property exchanged is more objectively determinable than the market value of the stock, the value of the property should be used as the basis for recording the transaction. If the market value of the stock is based on a level of market activity so far below the number of shares included in the transaction that the current market value is not appropriate, the estimated valuation of the property exchanged or an estimate of the value of the stock apart from the original market value should be made by the officers of the issuing corporation. This value is used in recording the transaction. Generally, neither the **par** (or **stated**) **value** nor the current book value of the stock is an appropriate base for recording transactions in which securities are exchanged for plant assets.

EXHIBIT 11–2
Oneida Ltd.
Capitalization of Interest Disclosure

11. Capitalized Interest

Effective January 27, 1980, the Company adopted the provisions of Financial Accounting Standard No. 34—Capitalization of Interest Cost. Accordingly, interest which relates to the cost of acquiring certain fixed assets as defined in the statement is capitalized. For the year ended January 30, 1982, the Company incurred $8,853,577 in interest costs of which $515,857 has been capitalized. For the year ended January 31, 1981, the Company did not capitalize interest cost due to the insignificance of the amount.

SOURCE: Oneida, Ltd., 1982 Annual Report.

For an illustration, assume that Lighter Company purchases land from another enterprise by issuing 10,000 shares of its $25 par value stock. The market price of the stock is $30 at the time of the transaction. The 10,000 shares do not represent a substantial number of shares in relation to the volume of stock activity in the market. The purchase of the land is recorded by the following entry:

Land	300,000	
Common Stock (10,000 × $25)		250,000
Additional Paid-In Capital		50,000
[10,000 × ($30 − $25)]		

Basket Purchases

Historical Cost

Basket purchase is a term that refers to the acquisition of several assets for a single price. The primary accounting problem arising from the basket (lump-sum) purchase is the apportionment of the total price paid to the individual assets acquired. Sometimes several assets can be purchased in a single transaction for less than the individual assets could be acquired separately. In such cases the allocation of the total price paid for the group of assets to the individual assets is based on the relative values of the individual assets acquired. In accordance with the historical cost principle, the total cost recorded must not exceed the total price paid, even if the total appraised value exceeds that amount. The individual asset values that are assigned for purposes of allocation may be based on current market prices, appraisal values, the present values of expected future benefits, or other appropriate estimations.

To illustrate this process, we will assume that Robertson Company acquires several assets in a single transaction from a competitor who is going out of business. The total purchase price is $855,000. The acquired assets and their individually estimated values, based on current market prices and independent appraisals, are as follows:

Inventory	$100,000
Building	500,000
Land	150,000
Fixtures	200,000

The allocation of the $855,000 cost to the individual assets is based on the relative estimated value of the individual assets, as follows:

Asset	Appraisal Value	Cost Allocation	
Inventory	$100,000	(100/950) $855,000 =	$ 90,000
Building	500,000	(500/950) $855,000 =	450,000
Land	150,000	(150/950) $855,000 =	135,000
Fixtures	200,000	(200/950) $855,000 =	180,000
	$950,000		$855,000

Alternatively, a percentage of cost to total appraisal value may be computed as follows: $855,000/$950,000 = 90%. This percentage is then applied to the estimated value of each asset to determine the portion of the total cost allocated to that asset. For example, Land would be allocated $135,000, as follows: $150,000 × 90% = $135,000.

The entry to record the basket purchase in this example is as follows:

Inventory	90,000	
Building	450,000	
Land	135,000	
Fixtures	180,000	
Cash		855,000

Although the Robertson illustration deals with a basket purchase of several different classes of assets, the same process applies to the allocation of the cost of several items of the same type to individual items. For example, several inventory items or several pieces of machinery may be purchased for a single price. The cost of each individual inventory or machinery item is determined by allocating the cost of all items on the basis of the relative value of the individual items.

Installation, Preparation, and Start-up Costs

Under the full-cost concept plant assets are established at the cost of acquisition, including expenditures necessary to bring the assets to the appropriate location and to prepare them for their intended use. Prior to placing an asset into operation, substantial outlays for transportation, installation, remodeling, and reconditioning may be required to advance the asset to the point of becoming a positive factor in the generation of revenue.

A significant period of time may lapse between the purchase of the asset and the placement of the asset into service. This is particularly true in the case of buildings undergoing extensive renovation. Costs related to the asset incurred during this period (e.g., insurance, taxes, and supervisory salaries) are capitalized as part of the cost of the asset. For some assets, such as machinery, trial runs and other tests may be necessary before the asset can be put into full service. These tests may require supplies, materials, and other assets. Such costs are also part of the cost of acquiring the asset and preparing it for its intended use.

Matching

Depreciation is not recognized on assets until they are placed into service, even if they were acquired at some previous date. No depreciation is recognized during a period of remodeling or renovation between the time the asset is acquired and placed into service. These concepts are consistent with the matching principle; recognition of depreciation is deferred until the asset becomes a part of the revenue-producing process.

POSTACQUISITION EXPENDITURES

After plant assets are acquired and placed into service, additional costs may be related to the continued use of the assets. An important distinction is that of capital and revenue expenditures. **Capital expenditures** are those expected to benefit *future* periods and, thus, are recorded as assets and depreciated over those periods. **Revenue expenditures** are normal, recurring expenditures designed to sustain the usefulness of the asset through the *current* accounting period and, thus, are charged to expense as incurred.

As a practical matter the distinction between capital and revenue expenditures is frequently a difficult one. In distinguishing between the two, accountants commonly identify capital expenditures as those expenditures expected to allow the related asset to render greater future benefits to the enterprise.

Accordingly, capital expenditures are *expected* to have one or both of the following positive impacts on future operations:

1. The *quantity* of services received from the asset will be increased. This may take the form of a longer useful life or more units of output.
2. The *quality* of the services from the asset will be increased.

If neither of these conditions is met, the expenditure is apparently designed to maintain the present level and quality of services rendered by the asset. These expenditures are appropriately designated as revenue expenditures and charged to expense as incurred.

Materiality

A common practice to distinguish between capital and revenue expenditures is to establish a dollar amount that represents a materiality threshold. Expenditures that are less than the designated amount are treated as expenses when incurred, even if they are beneficial to future periods. The designated level for this distinction varies with the size of the enterprise.

For example, a small company might expense all expenditures below $100, and a large company might follow the same practice for expenditures of less than $10,000. While this practice is *justifiable* only on grounds of materiality, it also eliminates the practical problem of depreciating a large number of small assets.

Expenditures related to plant assets incurred after the original acquisition are classified in four categories: (1) additions, (2) replacements and betterments, (3) rearrangement and relocation, and (4) repair and maintenance. The following discussion of this type of expenditure in terms of the four categories will help you to distinguish between capital and revenue expenditures and to identify the period over which the capital expenditures should be allocated.

Additions

Additions represent major expenditures that, by definition, are capital in nature because they increase the service potential of the related asset. Additions to buildings are common when the size of the asset can be increased by adding a new wing or an additional level to the existing facility.

Two major problems exist in relation to additions. First, the period over which the expenditure is to be depreciated must be determined. If the estimated useful life of the addition is independent of the asset to which it relates, the addition is treated as a *separate* asset and depreciated over its estimated useful life, regardless of the life of the original asset. This is common practice when structures are built as components and the addition would continue to exist even if the original structure were removed. In many cases, however, the addition is not independent of the original structure, and the period of depreciation for the addition must be determined in relation to the original structure. In such cases the cost of the addition is depreciated over the shorter of the estimated life of the addition or the remaining life of the original asset.

The second accounting problem associated with an addition is the identification of the costs that are appropriately capitalized. Adding to a facility frequently requires alteration of the original structure. For example, the addition of a wing to a building may involve changes in the original structure, such as removing walls or rerouting plumbing and electrical systems. If the original unit was constructed with a plan to expand, costs related to the original asset incurred when the addition takes place are appropriately capitalized as part of the cost of the addition. On the other hand, costs incurred that *could have been avoided* if appropriate planning had taken place at an earlier date should be expensed rather than carried forward as part of the addition. Distinguishing between such costs is difficult, and great care should be taken to ensure proper classification.

Replacements and Betterments

Replacements and betterments represent the substitution of a new part of an asset for an existing part. For example, the base of a machine may be replaced with a new base, or the roof of a building may be replaced with a new roof.

If the new part of the asset is similar in nature to the part being eliminated, the substitution is called a **replacement.** If the new part represents an improvement in quality over the part being eliminated, the substitution is called a **betterment.** For example, if an existing roof on a warehouse is replaced with a new but similar roof, the expenditure is a replacement. On the other hand, if the new roof is constructed of improved materials, it is a betterment.

An important consideration in determining the appropriate accounting treatment of replacements and betterments is whether the original part of the existing asset is separately identifiable. If separate identification is possible, the new expenditure should be substituted for the portion of the book value being replaced or improved. This is possible when the components of the asset have been separately identified and depreciated.

To illustrate this process, we can assume that Sir Walter Company acquires a building at a cost of $250,000. Separate identification of the cost components indicates that $30,000 of the cost relates to the roof of the building. The building is being depreciated over a 25-year life by the straight-line method, with an estimated salvage value of $20,000. The roof, however, is being depreciated over a 10-year life by the straight-line method, with no estimated salvage value. After nine years the roof is replaced at a cost of $50,000. The replacement is expected to last for the remaining years of the original estimate of the building's life.

The replacement is substituted in the accounts as follows:

Building (new roof)	50,000	
Accumulated Depreciation	27,000	
(90% × $30,000)		
Loss on Replacement of Roof	3,000	
Building (old roof)		30,000
Cash		50,000

The cost of the building, other than that allocated to the roof, should continue to be depreciated over the remaining unchanged useful life. The roof is depreciated at $3,125 per year ($50,000/16) over the remaining 16 years of the life of the building.

Conceptually, this substitution approach is logical in accounting for replacements and betterments. The separate identification of elements of an asset, however, is frequently not possible, due to the lack of separate records of the components of the asset or the integrated nature of the asset. Also, the parts of an asset changed by replacements and betterments during remodeling or renovation are generally difficult to separate in the manner we have described.

If separate identification is not possible or practical, the cost of replacements and betterments should be treated as an increase in the book value of the asset, thereby increasing the basis for depreciation over the remaining life of the asset. If the replacement or betterment is designed primarily to enhance the quality of the service potential of the asset, the cost should be charged to the asset account and an appropriate increase in depreciation expense should be recognized in future years. Although the book value of the replaced or improved portion remains in the appropriate asset account and the Accumulated Depreciation account (due to its inseparability from the remainder of the asset), presumably the replacement or betterment takes place at a time when the original expenditure is nearing the point of being fully depreciated and when the book value is a relatively small amount.

If the replacement is designed primarily to extend the length of the service life of the asset rather than to enhance the quality of the service rendered, the book value should be increased by charging Accumulated Depreciation. The accountant then depreciates the revised book value, less any salvage value, over the revised useful life.

For an illustration, we can assume that Cookeville Corporation replaces the electrical system in its building at a cost of $100,000. The building originally cost $800,000 and had $425,000 accumulated depreciation at the time of the replacement. The company has no record of the separate components of the building. Prior to the replacement the asset had a remaining life of 10 years with an expected $50,000 residual value.

If the replacement is made in order to enhance the quality of service potential in the future, the replacement should be accounted for as follows:

Building	100,000	
Cash		100,000

This entry increases the book value to $475,000, computed as follows:

Original cost of building	$ 800,000
Accumulated depreciation	(425,000)
	375,000
Cost of replacement of electrical system	100,000
	$ 475,000

Depreciation thereafter is recognized at $42,500 per year [($475,000 − $50,000) ÷ 10 years].

If the replacement is made in order to extend the useful life, the replacement is accounted for as follows:

Accumulated Depreciation—Building	100,000	
Cash		100,000

This entry also increases the book value to $475,000, computed as follows:

Original cost of building		$800,000
Accumulated depreciation prior to replacement	$ 425,000	
Cost of replacement of electrical system	(100,000)	
		325,000
		$475,000

If we further assume that the replacement adds seven years to the current estimated service period of 10 years and that the estimated residual value is unchanged, the depreciation thereafter is recognized at $25,000 per year [($475,000 − $50,000) ÷ 17].

The distinction between charging the asset account or the accumulated depreciation with the cost of the replacement is one of classification, because the impact on book value is identical. Capitalization by debiting the asset (i.e., the Building account) provides recognition of the increased value of the asset to the enterprise in terms of future service potential. Alternatively, capitalization by charging Accumulated Depreciation recognizes that costs extending the asset's life are a recovery of past depreciation charges.

Rearrangements and Relocations

Materiality

Matching

Rearrangements and **relocations** frequently occur to facilitate future operations. If the costs of such activities are material and can be separated from recurring operating expenses, they should be capitalized and recognized as expenses over the periods expected to benefit in accordance with the matching principle. Alternatively, if the costs are *not* material, if they are *inseparable* from recurring operating expenses, or if the future benefits in terms of increased efficiency are *questionable,* they should be expensed in the period in which they are incurred.

The unamortized portion of costs of previously capitalized rearrangement and relocation costs is sometimes presented as an intangible asset, but it is more appropriately described as a **deferred charge** (i.e., an unamortized balance awaiting amortization). Deferred charges are usually presented in the balance sheet as a part of an "other-asset" category. Chapter 13 discusses this balance sheet category in more detail.

Repair and Maintenance

Repair and **maintenance** expenditures are necessary to maintain the current operating capabilities of plant assets. Such expenditures range from custodial care and recurring minor

AT&T's $2.6 BILLION PASSALONG

BY CHANGING ITS accounting practices, AT&T will be adding an estimated $2 billion-plus to its annual cash flow by 1984, saving hundreds of millions in interest expense and sending the telephone installation fee through the roof.

Here's the story: Around four years ago AT&T appealed to the Federal Communications Commission to allow it to expense its station connections—the wires that connect your telephone to the outside wall. Ma Bell has pithily dubbed these cables Account 232. AT&T argued that these wires have a relatively short real life, since there is so much changing of homes in this country. When a new occupant moves into an old home, he immediately wants a new phone line in the bedroom and another phone line moved from one side of the kitchen to the other. So the phone company claimed that it no longer made sense to continue depreciating these wires over eight years.

At the beginning of this year, the FCC decided to go along with Bell and allow it to stop capitalizing and start expensing the station connections. In some states, that will be accomplished through the so-called flash-cut system, in which they will start expensing immediately. In most states the new system will be phased in over four years. In many cases—regardless of which system is used—expensing will be retroactive to last Jan. 1. It has been estimated that Bell will be expensing about $2.6 billion worth of the stuff by 1984.

As for the "imbedded equipment"—the station connections that are already in place—AT&T will write down its $10 billion capital cost over the next ten years.

Who is going to pay for the "expensing"? Under the old system, the excess cost of installation was paid for by all telephone users; it was built into the rate base. So now the telephone company is going to rate commissions and is asking to be allowed to recover the full cost of installation from the customer who is having the equipment installed. In effect, you will be buying that piece of wire from AT&T instead of renting it. How much will the new tab be? In Illinois, for example, the rates for telephone installation will probably go up from $36 to $109, according to William Springer, Illinois Bell's chief financial officer.

Naturally, if the phone company gets all the rate relief it is requesting, there will be absolutely no

repairs on buildings to periodic inspection and servicing of machinery and equipment. Repair and maintenance expenditures are treated as expenses when incurred since they are designed to ensure continued and dependable service of the asset.

Distinguishing between repair or maintenance expenditures and those expenditures that should be capitalized may be difficult in some circumstances. Major repairs that take on the characteristics of replacements and betterments in terms of the expected future use of the asset are capitalized if the impact on future income is judged to be material.

Materiality

The treatment of repair and maintenance as expenses when incurred is based on the assumption that such expenses are evenly distributed over time and that individual expenditures are relatively small. Expenditures made in one period that provide for the use of the asset in a subsequent period are presumably small and/or are offset by similar expenditures incurred during the subsequent period. If financial statements are prepared on a monthly or quarterly basis, the assumptions of immateriality and even distribution over time may be less appropriate. In these cases repair and maintenance expense may be accrued on an estimated basis by establishing an Allowance account, with actual expenditures charged to that allowance when made.

For an illustration of the accrual of repair and maintenance, assume that Georgia Instruments Company incurs substantial amounts of repair and maintenance related to its equipment. Because of the size of the expenditures, their relative infrequency, and the need to prepare monthly financial statements, the company recognizes the estimated annual cost of $120,000 for 1984 on a monthly basis. Actual costs incurred during January, February, and effect on earnings—billions will be going out in expensing and coming back in higher rates. But that's a big if. Public utility commissions are not known for their sympathy for giant corporations, and are less known for their speed. There's a real danger that regulatory lag will leave AT&T holding the bag for a fair amount of its expensed station equipment, as it waits for the commissions to make up their minds.

Brad Peery, an analyst with Paine Webber Mitchell Hutchins, figures that lag could cost AT&T from 20 to 25 cents a share next year, with at least some possibility of going as high as 40 cents.

But the risk is worth it. Eventually, Bell will get the rates it wants. In the meantime, the company will start saving the huge amounts of cash it has been spending to carry capitalized installations. Says Illinois Bell's Springer, "That's where the principal advantage comes in. To the extent that we can save 16% carrying charges, it will be a big help."

What does the consumer get out of all this? Well, according to Carl Horn, assistant vice president for state regulations at AT&T, "He gets to choose who installs the wire," And who is competing for that service now? Horn: "You could call up your local electrician and say, 'Would you run the inside wire for me?' I have a fireman who washes my windows and I can't stand to wash windows. And that fireman is very good at doing a lot of things around the house and he may also do it. . . ."

Presumably, the consumer will also get actual dollar savings in the long run, equivalent to the amount AT&T will save on its borrowings if the phone company passes those savings along. But in the past, when the FCC has tried to figure out exactly where the dollars in the Bell System go, it has been thoroughly befuddled. So, a savings in one place has absolutely no guarantee of winding up in a consumer's pocket.

But this move is far more significant than an adjustment on a few million consumers' bills. It's a sign that AT&T is drastically changing its corporate strategy. No longer is the rate base all-important. For years, AT&T has capitalized every wire, every screw, every bit of electronic gear, in order to get its capital base as high as possible—and rush to the regulators for rate increases based on that.

But now Ma Bell is waking up to the fact that while future dollars are nice, cash flow is what really counts. It's pleasant to see an influx of dollars stretching far into the horizon, but when you have to finance those dollars at 16% interest rates it's a luxury not even Ma Bell can afford.

SOURCE: Richard Greene, "AT&T's $2.6 Billion Passalong," *Forbes,* October 26, 1981, p. 44. Reprinted by permission of *Forbes* Magazine. © Forbes Inc., 1981.

March 1984 are $500, $18,500, and $1,200, respectively.

Entries to recognize the expenses and related expenditures are as follows:

January

Various dates	Allowance for Repair and Maintenance	500	
	Cash (or other asset, liability, or expense account, as appropriate)		500
31	Repair and Maintenance Expense ($120,000/12)	10,000	
	Allowance for Repair and Maintenance		10,000

February

Various dates	Allowance for Repair and Maintenance	18,500	
	Cash (or appropriate account)		18,500
28	Repair and Maintenance Expense	10,000	
	Allowance for Repair and Maintenance		10,000

March

Various dates	Allowance for Repair and Maintenance	1,200	
	Cash (or appropriate account)		1,200
31	Repair and Maintenance Expense	10,000	
	Allowance for Repair and Maintenance		10,000

This method results in equal repair and maintenance expense of $10,000 each month, even though expenditures vary considerably from period to period. A question arises, however, as to the nature of the balance in the Allowance for Repair and Maintenance account at the end of a reporting period. For Georgia Instruments Company this amount is as follows:

		Balance in Allowance Account
January	Expense recognized	$(10,000)
	Costs charged to allowance	500
	Balance in allowance at January 31	(9,500)
February	Expense recognized	(10,000)
	Costs charged to allowance	18,500
	Balance in allowance at February 28	(1,000)
March	Expense recognized	(10,000)
	Costs charged to allowance	1,200
	Balance in allowance at March 31	$ (9,800)

Diversity in practice exists in the treatment of the Allowance account in balance sheets prepared at the end of each month. The nature of the item, as well as the process giving rise to it, points toward treating the allowance in the same way that accumulated depreciation is treated (i.e., as a deduction in determining the book value of the related asset). The alternative interpretation of the allowance (which treats the allowance as a liability) is difficult to justify, because expenditure in the future depends on future events. Also, the notion that the enterprise has a liability to itself for repair and maintenance on its assets is difficult to support. A related question concerns the treatment of any balance in the Allowance account at the end of the annual reporting period. If the estimated accrual method is used to spread the expense over the interim periods of the year, the estimated amount should be continually evaluated and an adjustment should be made in the final month or quarter so that the Allowance account is eliminated at year-end.

The nature of a credit balance that results from the estimation of repair and maintenance expense raises an interesting point: debit or credit balances in accounts can result from the recognition of revenues and expenses that do not fit logically into any of the traditional balance sheet categories. In this case, the desire to recognize repair and maintenance expense as the related assets are used (rather than when cash is paid) may leave us with a difficult credit-balance account to place in the balance sheet. Although some accountants disagree, this account is properly treated like accumulated depreciation (i.e., as a reduction in the book value of the asset) at the end of interim accounting periods. As indicated in the previous paragraph, an adjustment should be made in the final interim period of the year so that no balance remains on the balance sheet at the end of the annual accounting period.

Matching
Consistency

A great deal of judgment is required in accounting for plant-asset-related expenditures that are made subsequent to original acquisition. The overriding objective is to match properly the cost of the expiration of the service potential with the revenue generated by that effort. Consistency in application is also important, because inconsistent treatment of these expenditures may materially affect the financial position and the results of operation. Accounting policies should reflect the most logical and realistic assumptions available.

Accounting for the various types of capital and revenue expenditures discussed in this section are summarized in Exhibit 11–3. In some cases, companies present their accounting policies concerning repairs, maintenance, and other postacquisition expenditures in notes to the financial statements. Exhibit 11–4 includes the disclosure from the 1982 financial statements of Meredith Corporation, a company dealing in broadcasting, publishing, and related services. The statement of accounting policy includes a reference to various post-acquisition expenditures, such as repairs, maintenance, replacements, and betterments.

	EXHIBIT 11–3	
	Summary of Accounting for Postacquisition Expenditures	
Type of Expenditure	**Circumstances**	**Accounting Treatment**
Additions	Useful life is *independent* of original asset.	Capitalize expenditure in separate account and depreciate over the estimated useful life.
	Useful life is *limited* to remaining life of original asset.	Capitalize expenditure as part of the original asset and increase the depreciation recognized over the remaining useful life.
Replacement and Betterment	*Separate* identification of portion of asset substituted is possible.	Capitalize expenditure to asset account and depreciate over shorter of the estimated useful life of (1) the replacement/betterment or (2) the original asset. Cost of and accumulated depreciation on portion of asset being replaced are removed, and gain or loss is recognized.
	Separate identification of portion of asset substituted is *not* possible; service *potential* of asset is improved.	Charge expenditure to asset account and depreciate over the shorter of the estimated life of (1) the replacement/betterment or (2) the original asset.
	Separate identification of portion substituted is *not* possible; service *life* of asset is extended.	Charge expenditure to Accumulated Depreciation and depreciate book value over revised estimated life.
Rearrangement and Relocation	Costs are *identifiable* and *material* in amount; changes are expected to produce *discernible* future benefits.	Capitalize expenditure and amortize over the period expected to benefit.
	Costs are *not* separately identifiable nor material in amount; future benefits are *not* discernible.	Treat expenditure as expense when incurred.
Repair and Maintenance	Incurrence of costs is *evenly* distributed over the annual period.	Treat expenditures as expenses when incurred.
	Incurrence of costs is *not* evenly distributed over the annual period.	Accrue periodic expense on an estimated basis and charge actual expenditures to Allowance. (No allowance should be carried forward from one annual period to the next.)

EXHIBIT 11-4
Meredith Corporation
Plant Asset Disclosure

Excerpt from Summary of Significant Accounting Policies

Property, Plant and Equipment

Depreciation expense is provided primarily on the straight-line method over the estimated useful lives of the assets. Expenditures for maintenance, repairs and minor replacements are charged to operations, and expenditures for major replacements and betterments are added to the property, plant and equipment accounts. The cost and accumulated depreciation of property, plant and equipment retired or sold are eliminated from the property accounts at the time of retirement or sale and the resulting gain or loss is recorded in income.

3. Property, Plant and Equipment

A comparative summary of property, plant and equipment follows:

	1982	1981	1980
	(in thousands)		
Land and land improvements	$ 5,337	$ 5,308	$ 5,150
Buildings and improvements	47,446	42,315	35,068
Machinery and equipment	98,601	92,427	86,791
Leasehold improvements	1,814	1,726	1,486
Construction in progress	536	3,125	4,238
	153,734	144,901	132,733
Less accumulated depreciation	63,315	57,801	56,711
	$ 90,419	$ 87,100	$ 76,022
Depreciation expense for the year	$ 10,601	$ 9,408	$ 9,778

For each classification of property, plant and equipment, depreciable life is as follows:

	Depreciable Life
Buildings and improvements	5 to 45 years
Machinery and equipment	5 to 20 years
Furniture and fixtures	5 to 15 years
Leasehold improvements	4 to 10 years

SOURCE: Meredith Corporation, 1982 Annual Report.

DISPOSALS OF PLANT ASSETS

Plant assets are disposed of for a variety of reasons and in a variety of ways. They may be **sold;** or they may be **abandoned** or **converted involuntarily,** as in the case of loss by fire, flood, or other natural disaster. (They can also be **exchanged;** however, a separate section of this chapter is devoted to exchange transactions.) Regardless of the cause of the disposal of the asset, two basic steps are followed in accounting for the disposal. First, depreciation is recognized to the date of the disposal. This is necessary in order to reflect properly the cost of operations for that portion of the year in which the asset is used. Second, the cost and accumulated depreciation of the asset are eliminated from the accounts, any proceeds received are recognized, and a gain or loss on the disposal is recognized.

For an illustration, assume that Gatlin Corporation has a building that it acquired in January 1978 at a total cost of $510,000. The building has been depreciated by the straight-line method using a 20-year life with an estimated residual value of $60,000. On June 30, 1984, the building is **sold** for $425,000.

Depreciation must be brought up to date prior to recording the sale itself. To account for the half-year depreciation in 1984, the following entry should be made:

Depreciation Expense	11,250	
[½ × ($510,000 − $60,000)/20]		
Accumulated Depreciation		11,250

This brings accumulated depreciation on the asset up to $146,250, determined as follows:

Depreciation, 1978–1983
[($510,000 − $60,000)/20 years] (6 years) $135,000

Depreciation, partial year 1984
[($510,000 − $60,000)/20 years](½ year)   <u>11,250</u>
                                            <u>$146,250</u>

Many companies defer recording the depreciation of $11,250 until the end of the year, when depreciation on all plant assets is recognized. Regardless of when the entry is made, the accumulated depreciation used in recording the sale of the asset is $146,250.

The entry for the sale of the asset is then recorded as follows:

Cash	425,000	
Accumulated Depreciation—Building	146,250	
Building		510,000
Gain on Sale of Building		61,250

The gain is measured by subtracting the book value from the proceeds of the sale:

$$\text{Gain} = \$425,000 - (\$510,000 - \$146,250) = \$61,250$$

At certain times assets are **abandoned** without selling or otherwise disposing of them. The process of recording a disposal by abandonment is the same as that illustrated above except that no proceeds are received. In this case the loss equals the book value of the asset after depreciation is updated to the date of abandonment.

Sometimes assets are disposed of by **involuntary conversion,** in which the enterprise loses an asset due to factors other than its own choice. Examples are loss by fire, flood, or other disaster. The accounting procedures parallel those for abandonment if *no* insurance proceeds are received; if insurance proceeds *are* received, the accounting procedures are much like those for the sale of plant assets.[4]

Materiality

Gains and losses on the disposal of plant assets are ordinarily not considered to be extraordinary items in the income statement. Depending on the extent of detail presented in the income statement, such items may be separately disclosed, however. If a gain or loss of this type is material in amount and is judged to be either unusual in nature or infrequent in occurrence, separate disclosure should be made. An exception to the general statement that such gains and losses are not extraordinary items is found in the case of involuntary conversions. *Accounting Principles Board Opinion No. 30* states that in rare instances an event or transaction may occur that clearly meets the criteria of **unusual in nature** and **infrequent in occurrence** and that results in the disposal of a plant asset.[5] (An example of such an event is the destruction of a plant asset by an earthquake.) Therefore, it is important to consider the underlying cause of a write-down or write-off of a plant asset in judging whether it should be presented as an **extraordinary** item or not. While such write-downs or write-offs are ordinarily not presented as extraordinary items, they may be considered such if they are the result of a major casualty *and* are clearly unusual in nature and infrequent in occurrence.

---

[4]Property insurance, including the computation of amounts to be received on insurance policies that include coinsurance requirements, is covered in Chapter 12. In Chapter 11, any situation involving insurance proceeds states the amount to be received from the insurance recovery.
[5]*APB Opinion No. 30,* "Reporting the Results of Operations," 1973, par. 23.

ACQUISITIONS AND DISPOSALS BY EXCHANGE

A business enterprise can participate in an **exchange** transaction whereby it simultaneously acquires an asset and disposes of another asset—neither of which is cash. For example, an enterprise may exchange land that it owns for land held by another enterprise. Also, used machinery may be exchanged for other used machinery. These transactions may include either the *receipt* or *payment* of cash to adjust for the perceived difference in the value of the assets exchanged. Transactions like this are called **nonmonetary transactions.** The Accounting Principles Board (APB) established the proper accounting for nonmonetary transactions in *Opinion No. 29.*[6]

An understanding of the accounting for transactions in which plant assets are exchanged requires an understanding of several terms, including the following:

1. **Monetary assets and liabilities.**   Assets and liabilities whose amounts are fixed in terms of units of currency by contract or otherwise. Examples are cash and short- and long-term receivables and payables in cash.
2. **Nonmonetary assets and liabilities.**   Assets and liabilities other than monetary ones. Examples are inventories, investments in stock, and tangible and intangible productive assets.
3. **Exchange.**   A reciprocal transfer between an enterprise and another entity that results in the enterprise's acquiring assets or services or satisfying liabilities by surrendering other assets or services or incurring other obligations.

Monetary assets and liabilities represent fixed claims on dollars, regardless of changes in prices. The claims of nonmonetary assets and liabilities are not fixed in this way. In the typical nonmonetary transaction a nonmonetary asset is exchanged for another nonmonetary asset. In some nonmonetary transactions a relatively small amount of cash may be involved. This small amount of cash in what is otherwise an exchange of nonmonetary assets is called **boot.**

Concepts Underlying Exchange Transactions

The general principle governing the recording of a nonmonetary exchange is to record the acquired asset at the **fair value** of the assets involved in the exchange. Accordingly, the fair value of the surrendered asset is used as a measure of the historical cost of the acquired asset, and a gain or loss may be recognized on the exchange. However, if the fair value of the asset received is more clearly evident than the fair value of the asset surrendered, the former amount is used. Fair value of a nonmonetary asset may be established in a number of ways: estimated realizable value in cash transactions of similar assets, quoted market prices, independent appraisals, and other available evidence.

Modification of this fair value concept is required in several circumstances, including instances in which fair value is not determinable or the transaction does not result in the completion of an earning process.

In some circumstances the fair value of assets surrendered or received cannot be determined within reasonably objective limits. In these cases the acquired asset is recorded at the book value of the surrendered asset. No gain or loss on the exchange is recorded, because the new asset is simply substituted for the old asset in the accounts.

Two types of transactions are not considered to result in the completion of an earning process:

1. An exchange of a product or property held for sale in the ordinary course of business for a product or property to be sold in the same line of business to

---

[6]*APB Opinion No. 29,* "Accounting for Nonmonetary Transactions," 1973.

facilitate sales to customers other than parties to the exchange.

2. An exchange of a productive asset not held for sale in the ordinary course of business for a similar productive asset or an equivalent interest in the same or similar productive asset.[7]

In the first case inventory is exchanged for inventory. A subsequent exchange in which the inventory is sold to the ultimate customer must take place before the earning process is considered to be complete. In the second case productive assets are exchanged for similar productive assets of the same general type performing essentially the same function. The earning process is not considered to be complete until these assets are used in the production of goods or services that are sold. These transactions are sometimes referred to as **swaps** of inventory or similar productive assets.

Assets acquired in swaps are generally recorded at the book value of the assets surrendered, and no gain is recognized as a result of the exchange if no boot is involved or if boot is paid in an essentially nonmonetary transaction. On the other hand, if boot is received in a transaction in which a gain is apparent (i.e., the fair value received exceeds the book value surrendered), the recipient of the boot has realized a gain to the extent that the cash received exceeds a pro rata share of the book value of the surrendered asset. This gain and the acquired asset should be recorded at a pro rata share of the book value of the surrendered asset. This process requires that the transaction be divided into parts: that portion representing a sale and that portion representing a trade. An example in the following section illustrates this method.

In certain circumstances the fair value inherent in a swap of inventory or plant assets may indicate that a loss would be recorded if the fair value (rather than the book value) were the basis for recording the entire transaction. In such cases the fair value is used and the loss is recognized in accordance with the modifying convention of conservatism. Methods of accounting for assets acquired through nonmonetary exchanges are summarized in Exhibit 11–5.

In summary, recording nonmonetary transactions represents an interesting application of the accounting principles of revenue realization and historical cost and of the modifying convention of conservatism. Transactions are generally recorded on the basis of fair value, which is consistent with both the revenue-realization and historical cost principles if the transaction represents the completion of an earning process. If the earning process is not complete, however, the acquired asset is recorded at the book value of the surrendered asset unless a loss is apparent; in that case, the loss is recorded in accordance with the modifying convention of conservatism. In a nonmonetary transaction that does not complete the earning process and in which a gain is apparent, the revenue-realization principle requires that a gain be recognized to the extent that boot received exceeds a proportionate share of the book value of the asset surrendered.

| Conserva-tism |

| Revenue Realization |
| Historical Cost |
| Conserva-tism |

Illustrations of Nonmonetary Transactions

This section analyzes a number of transactions, each of which illustrates a different concept in recording nonmonetary transactions. In each independent case Albertson Manufacturing Company is trading equipment. The following information is common to all cases:

Cost of equipment being traded	$100,000
Accumulated depreciation to date of trade	40,000
Book value of equipment traded	$ 60,000

---

[7]APB Opinion No. 29, par. 21.

EXHIBIT 11–5
Recording Bases of Assets Acquired in Nonmonetary Exchanges

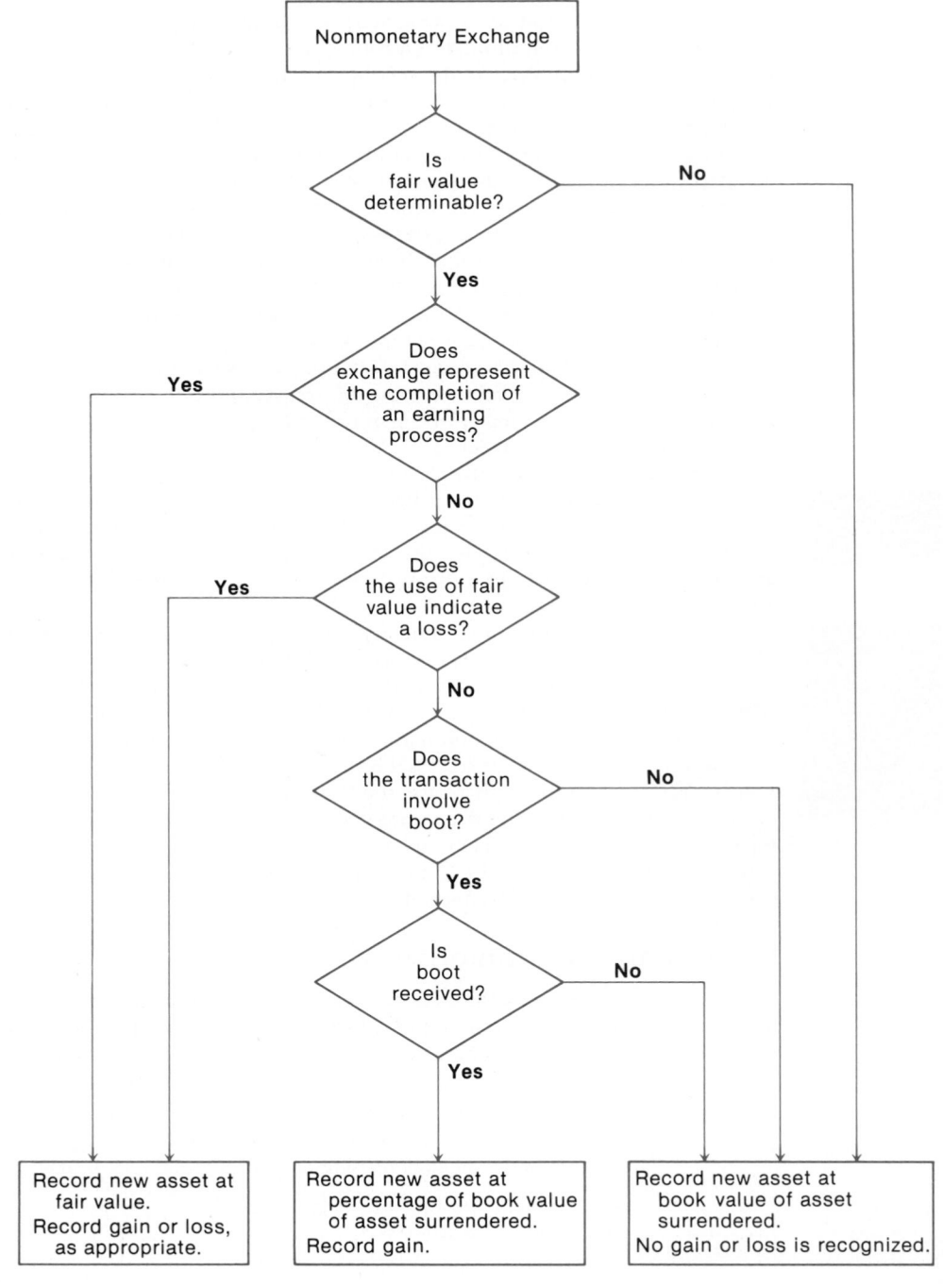

To facilitate a summary of the different cases (see Exhibit 11–6), the examples are numbered 1 through 6.

Example 1

Albertson Manufacturing Company trades the equipment for several trucks. The value of the equipment is not determinable, but the trucks have a total estimated market value of $75,000. No cash is involved in the transaction.

This transaction is a nonmonetary exchange that represents the **completion** of an earning process, because the assets exchanged are not similar in nature. Since the fair value of the equipment is not determinable, the fair value of the trucks received should be used as the value inherent in the transaction. The assets acquired are recorded at fair value, and any resulting gain or loss is recorded, as indicated in the following entry:

Trucks	75,000	
Accumulated Depreciation—Equipment	40,000	
Equipment		100,000
Gain on Exchange of Assets		15,000

If boot had been either received or paid, cash would have been either debited or credited as part of the entry.

Example 2

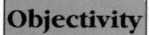

Albertson Manufacturing Company trades the equipment for office furniture. The value of neither the equipment nor the office furniture can be determined objectively.

This transaction must be recorded on the basis of the book value of the assets surrendered, because the fair value being exchanged cannot be determined. No gain or loss is recognized. The following entry is appropriate:

Office Furniture	60,000	
Accumulated Depreciation—Equipment	40,000	
Equipment		100,000

Example 3

Albertson Manufacturing Company exchanges the equipment, which has an appraised value of $50,000, and pays an additional $15,000 in exchange for similar equipment for which a value cannot be readily determined.

This transaction does not represent the completion of an earning process, because similar assets are exchanged. While such transactions would normally be recorded on the basis of the book value of the assets surrendered, any loss indicated must be recorded. In this case a loss is indicated, and it is determined as follows:

Book value surrendered		
Equipment	$60,000	
Cash	15,000	$75,000
Fair value inherent in transaction		
Fair value of equipment surrendered	50,000	
Cash paid	15,000	65,000
Loss indicated		$10,000

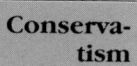

Since a loss is indicated, conservatism prevails and the assets acquired are recorded at fair value and the loss recognized, as follows:

Equipment (new)	65,000	
Loss on Exchange of Equipment	10,000	
Accumulated Depreciation—Equipment	40,000	
Equipment (old)		100,000
Cash		15,000

Example 4

Albertson Manufacturing Company trades the equipment, valued at $67,000 for other similar equipment for which no fair value is determinable. A gain is apparent in the transaction, and it is computed as follows:

Fair value inherent in transaction	
Fair value of asset surrendered	$67,000
Book value of asset surrendered	
Equipment	60,000
Gain indicated	$ 7,000

However, the gain is not recorded, because the earning process has not been completed. The transaction is recorded as follows:

Equipment (new)	60,000	
Accumulated Depreciation—Equipment	40,000	
Equipment (old)		100,000

Example 5

Albertson Manufacturing Company exchanges the equipment (valued at $65,000) and $15,000 cash for similar equipment for which a market value cannot readily be determined.

This transaction does not represent the completion of an earning process, because similar items of equipment are being exchanged. A gain is indicated, however, because the fair value inherent in the transaction exceeds the book values surrendered:

Fair value inherent in transaction		
Fair value of equipment surrendered	$65,000	
Cash	15,000	$80,000
Book value surrendered		
Equipment	60,000	
Cash	15,000	75,000
Gain indicated		$ 5,000

The gain is not recorded, and the equipment acquired is recorded at the book value of the equipment surrendered plus the $15,000 cash paid:

Equipment (new)	75,000	
Accumulated Depreciation—Equipment	40,000	
Equipment (old)		100,000
Cash		15,000

Example 6

Albertson Manufacturing Company trades the equipment for similar productive equipment valued at $70,000. In addition, Albertson receives $10,000 in cash.

Although this is a nonmonetary exchange that does not represent the completion of an earning process, the receipt of boot in a gain situation requires recognition of a gain to the extent that the cash received exceeds an appropriate portion of the book value surrendered. The gain inherent in the transaction is computed as follows:

Fair value inherent in transaction		
Cash received	$10,000	
Fair value of equipment received	70,000	$80,000
Book value surrendered		
Equipment		60,000
Gain indicated		$20,000

The portion of the transaction that represents a sale is determined by dividing the cash received by the total fair value inherent in the transaction:

$$\text{Sale \%} = \frac{\$10,000}{\$80,000} = 12.5\%$$

The book value of the equipment surrendered must be separated into the portion sold (12.5%) and the portion traded (100% − 12.5% = 87.5%):

Book value sold: $60,000 × 12.5% =	$ 7,500
Book value traded: $60,000 × 87.5% =	52,500
	$60,000

The gain recognized in the transaction is measured as follows:

Cash received	$10,000
Book value sold	(7,500)
Gain recognized	$ 2,500

The $2,500 can also be computed by multiplying the total gain on the transaction by the percentage of the transaction representing a sale:

$$\$20,000 \times 12.5\% = \$2,500.$$

The acquired equipment is recorded at the book value of that portion of the assets surrendered that is considered to have been traded ($60,000 × 87.5% or $52,500):

Equipment (new)	52,500	
Accumulated Depreciation—Equipment	40,000	
Cash	10,000	
Equipment (old)		100,000
Gain on Exchange of Equipment		2,500

This series of examples illustrates the various situations involved in accounting for non-monetary exchanges. Exhibit 11–6 reveals six combinations of circumstances during an exchange transaction that may lead to recording an acquired asset at either the fair value inherent in the transaction or at the book value (or a figure based on the book value) of the surrendered asset.

Historical Cost

These methods reveal the influence of the historical cost principle and the modifying

Conserva-
tism

convention of conservatism. The nonrecognition of gains in transactions that do not complete the earning process is designed to prevent artificial write-ups of assets and the recording of gains in value from holding assets that result from meaningless transactions in which similar assets are exchanged. One word of caution is in order: The use of fair value in recording exchanges of unlike assets is *not a departure* from historical cost. Rather, it is an *application* of that principle, because the historical cost in a noncash transaction (or part-cash transaction) is the fair value of the consideration given up to acquire that asset. If the fair value of the asset received is more clearly determinable, however, we use it as a substitute measure of historical cost.

DEPARTURES FROM HISTORICAL COST

Historical
Cost

The concept of historical cost as the basis for accounting for property, plant, and equipment is well established in accounting practice and is supported by authoritative pronouncements. As is the case with most accounting principles, however, exceptions exist to the general practice of recording and depreciating assets at cost. Although departures from historical cost are not frequent, this section discusses several situations representing departures from the general concepts developed earlier in this chapter.

EXHIBIT 11-6
Summary of Example Transactions

Example	Is Fair Value Determinable?	Is Earning Process Complete?	Is Gain or Loss Indicated?	Is Boot Received or Paid?	Resulting Accounting Treatment
1	Yes	Yes	Gain	No	Asset recorded at fair value on the assumption that a sale has been completed.
2	No	Yes	No	No	Asset recorded at book value due to unavailability of fair value.
3	Yes	No	Loss	Paid	Asset recorded at fair value in order to recognize loss and avoid recording asset in excess of fair value.
4	Yes	No	Gain	No	Asset recorded at book value on the assumption that earning process is not complete.
5	Yes	No	Gain	Paid	Asset recorded at book value (plus cash) on the assumption that earning process is not complete.
6	Yes	No	Gain	Received	Asset recorded at percentage of book value on the assumption that earning process is not complete. Gain is recognized on portion of transaction representing a sale.

Donated Assets

Enterprises may receive assets by donation. A common situation arises when land is donated to an enterprise by a city as an inducement to locate a facility in the city. The advantages that accrue to the city in the future result from increased property-tax revenues, increased levels of employment, improved reputation, and other positive aspects of an increased level of business activity in the city.

Historical Cost

Strict application of the historical cost principle in such cases would result in recording the asset acquired at a zero cost or at an amount equal to the relatively minor costs incidental to the acceptance of the land, such as the cost of transferring title. Accounting for donated assets at a zero cost, however, is not generally thought to represent the substance of the transaction in terms of the fair value of the donated asset received by the enterprise.

Accounting for **nonreciprocal transfers,** which are transfers of assets or services in one direction, either to or from the enterprise, is also discussed in *APB Opinion No. 29,* which concludes that the receipt of an asset in a nonreciprocal transfer should be based on the fair value of the asset received.[8] The APB relied heavily on the modifying convention of substance over form in reaching this conclusion.

Substance over Form

To illustrate the receipt of a donated asset, we assume that Newman Company receives land appraised at $75,000 as an inducement to locate a manufacturing facility in the city of Williamsville. The receipt of the land and the related contribution by the city is recorded with the following entry:

Land	75,000	
Donated Capital—Plant Site		75,000

Costs incurred relative to the transfer that *would have been incurred* had the asset been purchased are also charged to the asset account. Any other costs are treated as expenses in the current period. The Donated Capital account becomes a part of the stockholders' equity of the enterprise that receives the donated asset.

Permanent Impairment in Value

The price that an enterprise pays for a plant asset is based on estimates of future use, of future demand for products and services, and of other considerations of future events. When circumstances dramatically change, plant assets may experience a **permanent impairment in value.**

A permanent impairment in value may occur when the demand for products or services significantly declines when assets become obsolete or inadequate for their intended purpose, or when various other circumstances change. Depreciation (allocating cost to the periods benefiting from the use of the asset) is designed to facilitate the determination of net income via the matching process. Although depreciation accounting is not designed as a method of asset valuation, generally assets are not carried at amounts exceeding their value. We have already seen this practice in the rule of applying the lower of cost or market value to inventory and marketable securities.

Matching

In the case of plant assets this general rule translates into the practice of not carrying assets in the accounts or in the balance sheet at amounts exceeding the value of the assets to the enterprise. In some cases this means that the value of the assets in terms of their future use has been reduced from that originally expected, even though the assets will continue to be used. In other cases, it means that the assets have become valueless for their original

---

[8]*APB Opinion No. 29,* par. 18.

purpose and are worth only their salvage value.

If a permanent impairment in value has occurred, the book value of the asset is reduced by crediting the accumulated depreciation and recognizing a loss. If the asset is to continue in use, future depreciation charges may require adjustment to account for revised estimates of useful life, salvage value, and other factors.

To illustrate, we shall assume that Pride Toy Company acquired machinery in 1981 for use in producing a line of toys. The asset cost $100,000 and had an expected $20,000 residual value at the end of an expected eight-year life. At the end of 1983 the machinery had a book value of $70,000, computed as follows:

Asset cost in 1981	$100,000
Accumulated depreciation at December 31, 1983 [($100,000 − $20,000)/8](3 years)	30,000
Book value at December 31, 1983	$ 70,000

Because of changes in consumer demand, management determines in early 1984 that the asset is worth substantially less than originally expected. Specifically, it is determined that the book value should be reduced to $25,000; the remaining life, to two years; and the salvage value, to $1,000.

The entry to record this impairment in value is as follows:

Loss—Obsolescence of Machinery ($70,000 − $25,000)	45,000	
Accumulated Depreciation—Machinery		45,000

Depreciation recognized in 1984 and 1985 will be $12,000 [($25,000 − $1,000)/2 years]. If material, the loss of $45,000 should be separately disclosed in the income statement on the basis that it is not a typical transaction that reflects business operations. However, this type of loss should *not* be treated as extraordinary.

If the book value of an asset is being reduced to the salvage value and no future use of the asset is expected, an entry similar to the one in the previous paragraph is made for the amount that leaves the estimated residual value as the book value. No further depreciation is recognized on the asset after it has been retired from active service.

Quasi Reorganization

A **quasi reorganization** is a specialized situation in which assets are reduced from their book values to lower estimates of future value. To this extent, the quasi reorganization is similar to a permenent impairment in value.

The quasi reorganization, however, is different in that it involves a simultaneous reduction in the book values of several assets. It represents a general decline in the value of the enterprise rather than the decline in usefulness of one asset or a few specific assets. The quasi reorganization involves adjustments to several stockholders' equity accounts, including Retained Earnings, as part of the process by which the book values of assets are reduced. This subject and the specialized circumstances in which the quasi reorganization process is appropriate are considered in Chapter 17.

Discovery Value

The value of property may increase significantly if a hidden quality is discovered subsequent to acquisition. An example is the discovery of a valuable natural resource on land subsequent to acquisition. Since the existence of the resource was unknown at the time the land was acquired, the original cost would not reflect the value exchanged.

The accounting treatment of assets discovered subsequent to acquisition varies considerably, ranging from nonrecognition to the complete recognition of the estimated value of the discovered assets. Accountants are generally hesitant to record increases in asset values that have not been verified by transactions with other enterprises. Thus, the most common treatment of discovery value appears to be nonrecognition. This is consistent with the APB's conclusion:

> The Board is of the opinion that property, plant and equipment should not be written up by an entity to reflect appraisal, market or current values which are above cost to the entity.... Whenever appreciation has been recorded on the books, income should be charged with depreciation computed on the written up amounts.[9]

Some increases in value were recorded prior to this APB pronouncement. In addition, some accountants believe that the discovery of assets that existed but were unknown at the time of acquisition is different from the appreciation in asset value that results from changing market conditions, changes in consumer tastes, or other factors occurring after acquisition. Therefore, an accountant may occasionally encounter an increase in the recorded basis of a plant asset that represents the recording of discovery value. As indicated in *APB Opinion No. 6* (see footnote 9), depreciation (or depletion) of the asset should reflect the increased cost basis of the asset. Accountants generally agree that when such asset write-ups are appropriate, the credit side of the entry should be to the stockholders' equity rather than to a revenue or gain account.

To illustrate, we shall assume that Royal Mining Company acquired land for $200,000 in 1983. In 1985 mineral deposits in the estimated amount of 75,000 tons and appraised at $4.25 per ton (net of anticipated extraction costs) were discovered on the land. Management estimates that the land will be worth its original cost of $200,000 after the exploitation of the mineral deposits. The entries to record the above events are as follows, assuming that 15,700 tons were extracted and sold in 1985:

1983	Land	200,000	
	Cash		200,000
1985	Land—Mineral Deposits Discovered	318,750	
	Unrealized Capital Increment—		
	Discovery of Mineral Deposits		318,750
	(75,000 × $4.25 = $318,750)		
	Depletion Expense	66,725	
	Land—Mineral Deposits Discovered		66,725
	[(15,700/75,000) × $318,750 = $66,725]		

The capital account, Unrealized Capital Increment—Discovery of Mineral Deposits, is presented as part of the stockholders' equity section in the balance sheet.

FINANCIAL-STATEMENT DISCLOSURE

At the end of Chapter 12, after completing our study of plant assets and depreciation, we look at the general disclosure requirements for property, plant, and equipment. At that point we also review the **financial-statement disclosure** of property, plant, and equipment and related depreciation of a large U.S. corporation.

Many companies provide detailed descriptions of plant assets as of the financial-

---

[9]*APB Opinion No. 6,* "Omnibus Opinion," 1965, par. 17

statement date and acquisitions and dispositions of assets during the related accounting period. An example of this type of disclosure is found in the June 30, 1981, financial statements of Arcata, a company that operates in three lines of business: printing, forest products, and molded containers. This disclosure is presented in Exhibit 11–7.

EXHIBIT 11–7
Arcata
Plant Asset Disclosure

Property and Equipment

Printing conducts its operations from ten major printing facilities in the Publications and Book Groups and three major manufacturing plants in the Printed Products Group. Molded Container pulp or foam plastic products are produced at eight major U.S. manufacturing plants and four major European facilities. All of these facilities are regarded as adequate in size and design for present operations.

The Forest Products Group owned approximately 77,500 acres of timberland in northern California at June 30, 1981, of which 10,500 were acquired as exchange property for the 1968 Park taking, 38,000 acres were purchased in the past several years and 29,000 acres were added in the July 1979 acquisition of Arcata Lumber. The Forest Products Group now owns an estimated 877 million board feet of merchantable timber (approximately 34% old growth redwood, 19% second growth redwood, 47% whitewood). To augment its supply of merchantable timber, while young second growth redwood matures and becomes merchantable, the Group is acquiring additional second growth redwood and whitewood supplies through outright purchase or through timber harvesting contracts. At June 30, 1981 cutting rights were held on approximately 46 million board feet of market timber under contracts ranging up to 4 years. The Forest Products Group's operations are subject to intensive State and Federal regulations dealing with timber harvesting, milling and reforestation activities and their impact on the environment.

Capital additions in 1981 totalled $39.5 million, including $1.2 million for 900 acres of timberlands, $6.6 million for land and buildings and $31.7 million for machinery and equipment. The value assigned to Arcata Lumber properties in July 1979 totalled $75.8 million, including $64 million for timber and timberlands, $2.3 million for land and buildings and $9.5 million for machinery and equipment. Other capital additions in 1980 were $60.4 million, including $.8 million for 400 acres of timberlands, $7.6 million for land and buildings and $52 million for machinery and equipment. The value assigned to the Molded Container Group property and equipment at its November 1978 acquisition totalled

$101.4 million, including $35.2 million for land and buildings and $66.2 million for machinery and equipment. Other capital additions in 1979 were $55.3 million, including $5.7 million for 2,000 acres of predominantly Douglas fir timberlands, $14.9 million for land and buildings and $34.7 million for machinery and equipment. Capital additions (excluding additions due to the acquisitions of Arcata Lumber and the Molded Container Group) and depreciation and depletion by industry segment for the past three years were as follows:

(Thousands)	1981	1980	1979
Additions to property and equipment:			
Printing	$23,036	$33,770	$37,122
Forest Products	3,668	7,990	6,851
Molded Containers	12,328	16,652	8,711
Other	334	1,764	2,490
Corporate	180	216	102
TOTAL	$39,546	$60,392	$55,276
Depreciation:			
Printing	$15,700	$14,267	$13,245
Forest Products	2,591	2,296	804
Molded Containers	9,526	8,404	4,275
Other	683	1,411	1,459
Corporate	264	223	275
	28,764	26,601	20,058
Depletion—Forest Products	2,828	3,136	240
TOTAL	$31,592	$29,737	$20,298

Most of the major plants and facilities used by the Corporation are owned. Several major facilities occupied under capital-type leases have been capitalized. Total rental expense was $7 million in 1981, $7.1 million in 1980, and $4.3 million in 1979. Rental commitments at June 30, 1981 were due as follows (in millions): 1982—$2.3; 1983—$2.1; 1984—$1.6; 1985—$1.3; 1986—$1.3; 1987–1991—$4; 1992–1996—$2.2.

SOURCE: Arcata, 1981 Annual Report.

1. Property, plant, and equipment and intangible assets are long-lived assets that are acquired for use in the production and distribution of goods and services.

2. Several basic accounting principles are important in understanding proper accounting for plant and intangible assets. Most notable of these are the historical cost and matching principles.

3. Many unique problems are encountered in attempting to apply the historical cost principle to specific types of plant assets, such as land, buildings, machinery, equipment, furniture, fixtures, and natural resources.

4. General problems of establishing historical cost include the treatment of:
   a. Cash discounts.
   b. Deferred-payment plans.
   c. Internally constructed plant assets.
   d. Capitalization of interest.
   e. Acquisition by issuing securities.
   f. Basket purchases.
   g. Installation, preparation, and start-up costs.

5. An important distinction in accounting for postacquisition expenditures is to separate capital expenditures from revenue expenditures. Capital expenditures are amortized over their estimated useful lives, whereas revenue expenditures are charged to expense as incurred.

6. Disposals of plant assets may result from sales, abandonments, involuntary conversions, or exchanges. Disposals may result in gains or losses, which are presented as part of net income.

7. Nonmonetary exchanges are typically accounted for in terms of the fair value inherent in the exchange transaction. Certain exceptions to this general policy are followed, however, if fair value is not determinable or if the exchange does not represent the completion of an earning process.

8. In certain specialized situations, a departure may be made from the historical cost principle in accounting for plant assets. These exceptions are found in the cases of donated assets, permanent impairments in value, quasi reorganizations, and discovery value.

11–1 Identify the two basic characteristics of all plant and intangible assets.

11–2 Distinguish between plant and intangible assets and identify several types of each.

11–3 Identify four principles that underlie accounting for plant and intangible assets under generally accepted accounting principles.

11–4 What is meant by the "full-cost" interpretation of historical cost, as applied to plant assets?

11–5 In determining the full cost of land, what expenditures in addition to the bargained acquisition price might be included?

11–6 Why is it generally desirable for land improvements to be capitalized in a separate account from the Land account?

11–7 How should land which is held for investment or speculative purposes be classified in the balance sheet?

11–8 For items of machinery, equipment, furniture, and fixtures, what expenditures may be included in the cost figure in addition to the original acquisition price?

11–9 What is the preferred treatment of cash discounts in determining the cost of plant assets?

11–10 In what circumstances may it be necessary to *impute* interest included in the payments in a deferred-payment plan for plant assets? What is the purpose of this imputation?

11–11 What distortions will exist in the financial statements of the buyer of a plant asset if interest is not imputed in an installment contract for which interest should have been imputed?

11–12 As a general rule, a careful distinction is maintained between interest and the cost of plant assets. In certain circumstances, however, it is appropriate to capitalize interest. What are these circumstances?

11–13 When a plant asset is acquired by issuing capital stock, what is the appropriate basis for recording the asset acquired?

11–14 If several assets are acquired in a single transaction at one price, how is the historical cost of the individual assets acquired determined?

11–15 Enterprises may produce their own plant assets for use in future operations. Determining the cost of such assets is complicated by the fact that production activities of plant assets may be mixed with production activities of inventory items. Describe how the cost of internally developed assets should be determined, including an identification of specific costs to be included.

11–16 Distinguish between capital expenditures and revenue expenditures, citing several examples of each.

11–17 Distinguish between the accounting treatment of the following three types of betterments:

[a] Substitution of part of an asset when separate cost identification is possible.

[b] Substitution of part of an asset when separate cost identification is not possible and the advantage of the expenditure is improved quality of future services.

[c] Substitution of part of an asset when separate cost identification is not possible and the advantage of the expenditure is an extension of the useful life of the asset.

11–18 Under what circumstances should the allowance method of recognizing repair and maintenance expense be used as an alternative to recognizing them as costs are incurred? What is the purpose of the allowance method?

11–19 Assets acquired in exchange transactions for other assets may be recorded in one of several ways, depending on the circumstances of the exchange. Identify the circumstances in which each of the following bases are appropriate for recording an asset acquired in a nonmonetary exchange:

[a] Fair value inherent in the exchange.

[b] Book value of asset(s) surrendered.

[c] A percentage of the book value of asset(s) surrendered.

11–20 Dekovan Equipment Company acquired a three-acre site for the construction of a new branch plant. Which of the following costs (or groups of costs) should not be charged to the Land account of the company?

[a] Title examination fees, recording fees, and surveying fees.

[b] Costs of grading, clearing, and draining the property.

[c] Costs of removing the old, unwanted building from the land.

[d] Property taxes accruing during the period of plant construction.

(AICPA adapted)

11–21 Good Deal Company received $20,000 in cash and a used computer with a fair value of $180,000 from Harvest Corporation for Good Deal's existing computer having a fair value of $200,000 and an undepreciated cost of $160,000 recorded on its books. Which answer shows, respectively, how much gain Good Deal should recognize on this exchange and at what amount Good Deal should record the acquired computer?

[a] Zero and $140,000

[b] $4,000 and $144,000

[c] $20,000 and $160,000

[d] $40,000 and $180,000

(AICPA adapted)

11–22 Kelly Company exchanged inventory items that cost $8,000 and normally sold for $12,000 for a new delivery truck with a list price of $13,000. At which figure should the delivery truck be recorded on Kelly's books?

[a] $8,000

[b] $8,667

[c] $12,000

[d] $13,000

(AICPA adapted)

CASES

C11–1 Five years ago, JK Manufacturing, Inc., began producing "probos," a new type of instrument it hoped to sell to doctors, dentists, and hospitals. The demand for probos far exceeded initial expectations, and the company was unable to produce enough probos to meet the demand.

The company was manufacturing its product on equipment which it built at the start of its operations. To meet the demand more efficient equipment was needed. The company decided to design and build the equipment, since that currently available on the market was unsuitable.

In 1984 a section of the plant was devoted to development of the new equipment and a special staff was hired. Within six months a machine was developed at a cost of $170,000 that successfully increased production and reduced labor costs substantially. Sparked by the success, the company built three more machines of the same type at a cost of $80,000 each.

Instructions

[a] In addition to satisfying a need that outsiders cannot meet within the desired time, why might a firm construct plant assets for its own use?
[b] In general, what costs should be capitalized for a self-constructed plant asset?
[c] Discuss the propriety of including in the capitalized cost of self-constructed assets:
   [1] The increase in overhead caused by the self-construction of plant assets.
   [2] A proportionate share of overhead on the same basis as that applied to goods manufactured for sale.
[d] Discuss the proper accounting treatment of the $90,000 difference by which the cost of the first machine exceeded the cost of the subsequent machines.

(AICPA adapted)

C11-2 Business enterprises may dispose of plant assets and acquire other plant assets in the same transaction. Exchanges such as these are identified as "nonmonetary."

Instructions

[a] Define the following terms as they relate to transactions such as those described above:
   [1] Exchange
   [2] Monetary asset and liability
   [3] Nonmonetary asset and liability
   [4] Boot
[b] Under what combinations of circumstances will assets acquired in nonmonetary exchanges be recorded at the following amounts?
   [1] Book value of the assets surrendered.
   [2] Fair value inherent in the exchange.
   [3] A percentage of the book value of the assets surrendered.
[c] Describe the accounting concepts which are apparent in the procedures outlined in [b].

C11-3 One of the frequently cited virtues of historical cost as a method of measuring assets for financial-statement purposes is its objectivity in comparison with other measurement techniques. While historical cost is generally more objective, in certain situations significant assumptions, allocations, and estimates may

be necessary to establish the historical cost of plant assets.

Instructions

Identify several assumptions, allocations, and estimates that may be required in determining historical cost. Explain the circumstances in which the assumption, allocation, or estimate must be made.

C11-4 The distinction between revenue expenditures and capital expenditures is significant in accounting for costs related to plant assets.

Instructions

With respect to this important area:
[a] Distinguish between revenue expenditures and capital expenditures and discuss the importance of this distinction for the determination of income.
[b] Distinguish between an expansion or addition and a replacement or betterment. Describe the proper accounting treatment of both.
[c] What is the rationale for the capitalization of relocation and rearrangement costs?
[d] What basic criterion should be used to distinguish between costs which should be capitalized and repair and maintenance costs which should be expensed as incurred?

C11-5 The controller of the Dearborn Division of Brooks, Inc., asked a staff member to review the Repair and Maintenance Expense account for 1984 to determine if all of the charges are appropriate. The staff member has identified the following ten transactions for further scrutiny. All of these transactions are considered material in amount.

Date	Amount	Description
Jan. 3	$10,000	Service contract on office equipment.
Mar. 7	10,000	Initial design fee for proposed extension of office building.
Apr. 12	18,500	New condenser for central air conditioning unit located on the roof of office building.
Apr. 20	7,000	Purchase of two executive chairs and desks.
May 12	40,850	Purchase of storm windows and screens and their installation on all office windows.

May 18	38,450	Sealing of roof leaks in production plant.
June 19	28,740	Replacement of large door to production area.
July 3	11,740	Installation of automatic door-opening system on the above door to speed opening.
Sept. 14	38,500	Overhead crane for the assembly department to speed up production.

Oct. 18	11,000	Replacement of broken gear on machine in the machining department.

Instructions

For each of the above transactions, indicate whether the Repair and Maintenance Expense account is properly charged, and if not, indicate the appropriate account to which the transaction should be charged. Explain your reasoning in each case.

(CMA adapted)

EXERCISES

E11–1 Ash Down Company acquired land and a building for $275,000 on October 15, 1984. The land was appraised at $125,000 and the building at $175,000. Unpaid property taxes assumed by Ash Down were $12,000, 40% allocated to the land and 60% to the building. Additional costs incurred were:
[1] Building renovation, $37,500.
[2] Option on alternative land and building which were not acquired, $1,200.
[3] Cost of survey, $125.

Instructions

Determine the cost of the building and the land, identifying the individual elements of cost included in each asset.

E11–2 Ranger corporation recently acquired several items of property, plant, and equipment. The transactions are described as follows:

June 17	Purchased land appraised at $100,000 and machinery appraised at $50,000 for a total of $142,000.
July 7	Purchased a building by paying $175,000 in cash and issuing 100,000 shares of the company's $5 par value common stock. The stock sold for $6 on the transaction date.
Aug. 27	Received a parcel of land from the City of Rockford as an inducement to locate a plant in the city. No payment was required. The land was appraised at $62,500.
Sept. 7	Acquired furniture and fixtures by issuing a $75,000, two-year, noninterest-bearing note. In similar transactions the company has been required to pay 12% interest.

Instructions

Prepare the journal entry appropriate in each case to record the acquisition of property, plant, and equipment.

E11–3 Barger Company acquired land on June 1, 1984, for $125,000, on which a new building will be constructed. Plans call for the construction of the new facility immediately. Costs related to the acquisition include:
[1] A commission of 2% of the price for the location of the land and the negotiation of the acquisition price.
[2] $1,000 for legal fees related to the transfer of the title of the land and other matters.
[3] $200 for a survey pursuant to the closing of the transaction.
[4] $2,500 for options acquired at an earlier date: $1,500 for the land acquired, and $1,000 for an alternative parcel of land which was seriously considered but not acquired.
[5] $15,000 for removal of an existing building. $2,750 was received from the salvage of materials.
[6] $2,400 for 1983 property taxes which were delinquent on June 1, 1984. Taxes for 1984 are expected to be $3,000 and will be paid by Barger before December 31, 1984.

Instructions

Determine the historical cost of the land as it should be presented in the company's balance sheet on December 31, 1984.

E11–4 Robbins Company acquired several fixtures for its new building, including display cases, shelves, and hanging racks on which to display merchandise. The invoice price of the fixtures was $70,000. The company received 2% cash discount by paying within the discount period. Freight and insurance during shipment totaled $278. Costs of assembling and installing the fixtures were $560. While installing a display case, a new employee carelessly dropped and broke a glass top. This top was replaced at a cost of $175.

Instructions

Determine the total cost of the fixtures, identifying the individual elements making up the total.

E11–5 On January 2, 1985, Carolina Manufacturing Company acquired used equipment by issuing to the seller a two-year, noninterest-bearing note for $200,000. It is apparent that the value of the equipment is less than $200,000, but a specific amount cannot be determined. In other recent borrowings, Carolina has paid 10% interest.

On January 7 the company installed the equipment. Estimated costs of installation were $1,500 for labor and $600 for materials, both of which are included in the manufacturing accounts. On January 10 the company paid $650 for freight and insurance charges during shipment.

Instructions

Prepare general journal entries for the above transactions and for adjustments required on December 31, 1985. Provide supporting computations. The company plans to depreciate the asset over ten years, with the salvage value being approximately equal to the costs of removal. Straight-line depreciation should be used. Interest is recognized by the effective interest method.

E11–6 Scheiner Company acquired the following plant assets during 1984:

Equipment. Acquired at an invoice price of $50,000, subject to a 1% cash discount which was not taken. Costs of freight and insurance during shipment were $285. The equipment is expected to have a five-year life and a salvage value of 10% of the invoice price.

Land. Acquired by issuing 10,000 shares of $5 par value common stock when the market price of the stock was $11. The stock issued was treasury stock which had been acquired at an earlier date at $8 per share.

Machinery. Acquired at a cost of $19,500. Installation costs were $725. Trial runs and other testing cost $675. These expenses have been included in the Manufacturing Overhead account. The machinery is expected to be useful for ten years, at the end of which it will have a $900 salvage value.

Instructions

Prepare all general journal entries necessary to record the acquisition and depreciation of the assets for 1984. Straight-line depreciation should be used with a full year taken in 1984.

E11–7 Felix Production Company decided to construct its own equipment rather than acquire similar assets from other companies. It believed that the assets could be built for less cost than they could be bought. Material and labor costs were determined to be $160,000 and $220,000, respectively. Overhead is normally charged to production at the rate of 85% of the direct labor cost. The actual increment in overhead resulting from the construction was determined to be $160,000.

Instructions

Assuming the company is operating at full capacity and must curtail production operations to construct the equipment, determine the appropriate amounts to be capitalized as the cost of the equipment. Justify your treatment of overhead costs.

E11–8 On December 1, 1984, Bennett Company acquired a new delivery truck in exchange for a truck that had been acquired in 1983. The new truck was acquired because the old truck was inadequate for the company's needs. The old truck was purchased for $7,000; it had a $5,500 book value and an estimated market value of $6,000 at the time of the exchange. To complete the transaction, Bennett paid $2,000 cash for the new truck, which had a list price of $9,000.

Instructions

[a] Prepare the general journal entry to record the acquisition of the new delivery truck.
[b] Explain your reason for the amount that you used in [a].

E11–9 Minor Baseball Company had a player contract with Doe that was recorded in the accounting records at $145,000. Better Baseball Company had a player contract with Smith that was recorded in its accounting records at $140,000. Minor traded Doe to Better for Smith by exchanging each player's contract. The fair value of each contract was $150,000.

Instructions

[a] Explain the proper recording of the exchange on the books of Minor Baseball Company.
[b] Explain the proper recording of the exchange on the books of Better Baseball Company.

(AICPA adapted)

E11−10 Sonic Company replaced a portion of its building for $700,000. Immediately before the replacement, the Building and Accumulated Depreciation accounts were as follows:

Building	$ 3,500,000
Accumulated depreciation	(2,250,000)
	$ 1,250,000

Instructions

Prepare the general journal entry to record the $700,000 expenditure in each of the following *independent* cases:
[a] Separate identification of the portion of the building being replaced is not possible. The replacement was designed to improve the service potential of the total facility for the remainder of its original expected useful life.
[b] It is determined that the portion of the building being replaced accounts for $1,000,000 and $675,000 of the Building and Accumulated Depreciation accounts, respectively.
[c] Separate identification of the portion of the building being replaced is not possible. The primary purpose of the expenditure is to lengthen the life of the building from that originally estimated.

E11−11 Capital Company performed the following transactions involving plant assets during 1985:
[1] A building expansion costing $179,000 was completed. The expansion is expected to provide service for 20 years, even though the original building will be useful for only ten more years.
[2] The base of a machine was replaced for $7,000. The portion of the original cost allocated to the base was $5,000, and the cost of the asset was 40% depreciated at the time of the replacement. The old base was sold for $500. The new base is expected to serve the machine to the end of its useful life.
[3] A number of improvements were made in a building for $62,500. The cost of items replaced could not be determined. The improvements were made to ensure the original estimated useful life of the building.
[4] The reorganization required to move into the new addition cost $12,000. It is believed that the rearrangement will prove beneficial to the company for at least five years.
[5] Servicing of machinery on a regular basis resulted in expenditures of $5,800.

Instructions

[a] Prepare the general journal entry to record each transaction.
[b] Describe the appropriate period of depreciation or amortization of any items capitalized in each entry.

E11−12 Stereo Company invested heavily in equipment that was needed to produce a new line of stereophonic equipment. On January 1, 1985, the cost and accumulated depreciation balances on the equipment were as follows:

Equipment	$ 4,250,000
Accumulated depreciation	(1,700,000)
	$ 2,550,000

Due to changes in consumer tastes and unexpected advances in electronics, the company now believes that the future service potential of the equipment is greatly reduced and the useful life is much shorter than originally estimated. Specifically, the company believes the future service potential of the asset is limited to $1,000,000 and the future life extends only through 1986.

Instructions

Determine the amounts which should be presented in the company's balance sheet and income statement relative to the equipment at December 31, 1985.

E11−13 Job Shoe Company carried out a number of transactions involving the acquisition of several assets. All expenditures were recorded in the following single asset account, identified as Fixed Assets:

Fixed Assets

Acquisition price of land and building	$125,000
Options taken out on several pieces of property	2,000
List price of machinery purchased	37,500
Freight on machinery purchased	851
Repair to machinery resulting from damage during shipment	176
Removal of old machinery	565
Driveways and sidewalks	9,250
Building remodeling	12,600
Utilities paid since acquisition of building	1,200
	$189,142

Based on property tax assessments, which are believed to fairly represent the relative values involved, the building is worth twice as much as the land. The machinery was subject to a 2% cash discount, which was taken and credited to Purchases Discounts. Of the two options, $750 related to the building and land purchased and $1,250 related to those not purchased. The old machinery was sold at book value.

Instructions

Prepare the general journal entry or entries to correct the Fixed Asset account. Provide supporting calculations for the amounts capitalized in individual plant asset accounts. All expenditures were made in the current year and the books have not been closed.

E11–14 Holmes Corporation has a building with a book value of $85,000 on October 31, 1984, the end of the company's fiscal year.

Building	$180,000
Accumulated depreciation	(95,000)
	$ 85,000

Depreciation is computed by the straight-line method at $1,250 per month.

Instructions

Prepare the general journal entry or entries to record the disposal of the building under each of the following *independent* situations:
[a] The building is sold on June 30, 1985, for $100,000.
[b] The company incurs costs of $5,500 to improve the building in preparation for its sale. The building is sold on August 31, 1985, for $90,000.
[c] The building is destroyed by fire on March 31, 1985. Proceeds from insurance total $57,800.

E11–15 Waco Company entered into a contract with Dallas Company to construct a building for Waco. The contract called for work to begin on June 1, 1984, and for Waco to make an initial payment of $100,000 at

that time. Another $50,000 was to be paid by Waco at the end of each three-month period until May 31, 1985, when the building was to be completed, transferred to Waco, and placed into service.

All aspects of the contract were completed on schedule. Waco Company made the payments from existing working capital and did not incur any additional debt for the specific purpose of financing the construction of the building. Throughout the construction period, however, Waco had $750,000 of debt outstanding at an average interest rate of 11%.

Instructions

[a] Determine the appropriate cost of the building on the books of Waco Company.
[b] Explain the rationale for the various components of cost in [a].

E11–16 Multi-Sonic Corporation has a machine which it plans to eliminate. The machine has the following cost and accumulated depreciation at the time of the anticipated transaction:

Machinery	$ 75,000
Accumulated depreciation	(62,500)
	$ 12,500

Instructions

Prepare the general journal entry to record the disposal in each of the following *independent* cases:
[a] The machine, which has an appraisal value of $17,000, is traded for a patent with an unknown value.
[b] The machine, which has an appraisal value of $5,000, is traded for a similar machine with an indeterminate value. In addition, cash of $25,000 is paid.
[c] The machine is sold for $18,750 cash.
[d] The machine is traded, along with $7,500 cash, for a similar machine with an appraisal value of $28,000.
[e] The machine is traded for a similar machine with a value of $15,000. In addition, $5,000 cash is received.

PROBLEMS

P11–1 The determination of historical cost may be complicated by a number of factors related to the transaction in which the asset is acquired. Katie Company has been involved in a number of transactions in which plant assets have been acquired.

Instructions

In each of the following *independent* situations, determine the historical cost of the plant assets to Katie Company:
[a] Land and building are acquired by Katie for

$525,000. The building is destroyed at a cost of $25,000 to make way for a new facility which is to be constructed in the future. Proceeds of $5,000 were received from salvaged materials from the old building.

[b] Land and building are acquired by Katie for $525,000 and are appraised at $200,000 and $350,000, respectively. Plans call for the renovation of the building, after which it will be used in future operations.

[c] Land is acquired by Katie at a cost of $105,000. An option had been taken out earlier for $5,000 which guaranteed the $105,000 purchase price for 90 days. Another option for $5,000 was negotiated on an alternative land site which was not acquired. Legal costs related to the transaction were $450.

[d] Land was purchased by Katie by issuing 1,000 shares of common stock. The stock has a market value of $17.50 per share and a par value of $12. No independent appraisal has been made on the land.

[e] Equipment was purchased by Katie by issuing a $45,000, three-year, noninterest-bearing note. The purchaser's borrowing rate is estimated to be 12%, based on other recent borrowing. Transportation and installation costs incurred by the purchase totaled $1,260.

[f] Equipment was acquired by Katie at an invoice price of $85,000. A 1% cash discount was taken by payment within the 10-day period required under the terms of the agreement. Damage to the asset during shipment required a $125 payment by the purchaser. The costs of installation were $2,250. Insurance on the equipment for one year ($350) was paid.

[g] Katie exchanged items of specialized equipment with another company; $10,000 cash was paid by Katie. The book value of the equipment surrendered was $95,000 and the estimated market value was $125,000.

[h] Upon the advice of a management consulting firm, Katie reorganized its production facilities. Costs of $15,750 were incurred for rearrangement activities. At the same time, equipment costing $35,000 was acquired, on which an available 2% cash discount was not taken due to an oversight by the bookkeeper. The equipment which was being replaced was sold at a price which resulted in a $1,000 loss.

P11–2 Joplin Manufacturing Company recently acquired land and a building in a single transaction.

Instructions

Prepare the journal entry to record the acquired assets in each of the following *independent* situations:

[a] Cash of $275,000 is paid. The land is appraised at $250,000 and an existing building, which will be destroyed to make room for a new one, is appraised at $50,000.

[b] Cash of $275,000 is paid. The land is appraised at $175,000 and an existing building, which will be retained and used, is appraised at $125,000.

[c] Cash of $275,000 is paid. In addition, $10,500 is received from the salvage of an existing building which was destroyed to make room for a new one. The land was appraised at $250,000 and the old building at $35,000.

[d] A $375,000 noninterest-bearing note that requires a single payment at the end of three years is given for the land. No appraisal on the land is available. Joplin Manufacturing Company has recently borrowed money at 10%.

[e] Cash of $500,000 is paid. The land was appraised at $250,000; other assets were appraised as follows:

Equipment	$100,000
Fixtures	100,000
Patent	85,000

P11–3 [1] The Maddox Corporation acquired land, buildings, and equipment from a bankrupt company for $90,000. At the time of acquisition, Maddox paid $6,000 to have the assets appraised. The appraisal disclosed the following values:

Land	$60,000
Buildings	40,000
Equipment	20,000

What cost should be assigned to the land, buildings, and equipment, respectively?

[a] $30,000, $30,000, and $30,000.
[b] $32,000, $32,000, and $32,000.
[c] $45,000, $30,000, and $15,000.
[d] $48,000, $32,000, and $16,000.

[2] Sherman Company purchased a new machine on May 1, 1975, for $25,000. At the time of acquisition, the machine had an estimated life of ten years and an estimated salvage value of $1,000. The company recorded monthly depreciation using the straight-line method. On March 1, 1984, the machine was sold for $800. What should be the loss recognized for the sale of the machine?

[a] $0
[b] $2,000
[c] $3,000
[d] $3,400

[3] Williamson Company exchanged 100 shares of treasury stock ($50 par value common stock) for some land to be used in its business. The treasury stock had cost $60 per share, and on the exchange date it had a fair market value of $65 per share. Williamson received $1,200 for scrap when an existing building was immediately removed from this land. Based on these facts, at what amount should this land be capitalized?

    [a] $3,800
    [b] $4,800
    [c] $5,300
    [d] $6,500

[4] On February 1, 1984, Reflection Corporation purchased land as a factory site for $50,000. An old building on the property was demolished, and construction of a new building was completed on November 1, 1984. Costs incurred during this period are listed below:

Demolition of old building	$ 4,000
Architect's fees	10,000
Legal fees for title investigation and purchase contract	2,000
Construction costs	500,000

(Salvaged materials resulting from demolition were sold for $1,000.)

Reflection should record the cost of the land and new building, respectively, as:

    [a] $52,000 and $513,000
    [b] $53,000 and $512,000
    [c] $53,000 and $510,000
    [d] $55,000 and $510,000

[5] On January 1, 1984, Kent Corporation purchased a machine for $50,000. Kent paid shipping expenses of $500 as well as installation costs of $1,200. The machine was estimated to have a useful life of 10 years and an estimated salvage value of $3,000. In January 1985, additions costing $3,600 were made in order to comply with pollution control ordinances. These additions did not prolong the life of the machine or have any salvage value. Using the straight-line method, the depreciation expense for Kent in 1985 is:

    [a] $4,870
    [b] $5,170
    [c] $5,270
    [d] $5,570

[6] On August 1, 1984, Bameo Corporation purchased a new machine on a deferred-payment basis. A down payment of $1,000 was made, and four monthly installments of $2,500 each are to be made beginning on September 1, 1984. The cash-equivalent price of the machine was $9,500. Bameo incurred and paid installation costs of $300. The amount to be capitalized as the cost of the machine is:

    [a] $9,500
    [b] $9,800
    [c] $11,000
    [d] $11,300

(AICPA adapted)

P11–4 Entertainment, Inc., acquired several items of property, plant, and equipment during 1984, its first year of operation:

Jan. 2   The city of Nashburg donated land to the company as an inducement to locate facilities in the city. The land was appraised at $215,000 and resulted in no cash payment by the company.

Jan. 15   Issued 50,000 shares of $50 par value common stock and paid $500,000 cash for assets appraised as follows:

Building	$1,700,000
Land	850,000
Machinery	150,000
Inventory	450,000

At the time of the transaction the common stock was selling for $51 per share.

Feb. 1   Acquired machinery on account for $120,000, terms 2/10, n/30. Payment was made on Feb. 28.

July 17   Machinery priced at $25,000 was acquired by issuing a 90-day, 12% note. The note was paid at maturity.

Aug. 1   Machinery was purchased by issuing a noninterest-bearing note for $85,000, payable at the end of two years. In similar transactions the company has paid an interest rate of 10%.

Instructions

Prepare the journal entries necessary to record the acquisitions of property, plant, and equipment indicated above. Also, prepare any additional entries which would be required during 1984 as a result of the information given. (Do not prepare adjusting entries to recognize depreciation at the end of 1984.)

P11–5 Jacksonville Manufacturing Company recently acquired a building and the surrounding land. The company's accountant established a Land and Building account and has made the following entries:

1984		Land and Building Account
Jan. 3	Acquisition price	$425,000
3	Prepayment of insurance on building (2 years)	10,500
Feb. 1	Payment of property taxes ($2,400 delinquent for 1983; $3,600 for 1984)	6,000
Mar. 7	Renovation costs on building	42,500
Apr. 1	Cost of open house to familiarize the public with new facility opened that day	2,000
		486,000
Dec. 31	Depreciation for 1984, computed as straight-line method with 20-year life	(24,300)
		$461,700

The company's accountant has shown the $461,700 Land and Building account in the balance sheet and the $24,300 as Depreciation Expense in the income statement. As a staff member of the independent CPA firm responsible for auditing the financial statements of the company, you must propose any adjustments you consider necessary. Your investigation reveals the following:

[1] Upon acquisition, the land was independently appraised at $115,000 and the building at $325,000.

[2] Company policy calls for depreciation by the straight-line method, computed monthly.

[3] The building is expected to have a residual value of 10% of its cost basis at the end of its 20-year life. The building was placed in service on April 1, 1984.

[4] Property taxes are allocated 74% to the building and 26% to the land.

Instructions

Prepare any adjusting entry or entries which you think are necessary. Provide computations which you would present to your supervisor to support your position. (All amounts may be rounded to the nearest dollar.)

P11–6 Two independent companies, Beam and Wall, are in the home building business. Each owned a tract of land ready for development, but each company preferred to build on the other's land. Accordingly, they agreed to exchange their land. An appraiser was hired, and from his report and the companies' records, the following information was obtained:

	Beam's Land	Wall's Land
Cost and book value	$ 80,000	$50,000
Fair value based on appraisal	100,000	90,000

The land was exchanged, and based on the difference in appraised fair values, Wall paid $10,000 cash to Beam.

Instructions

[a] Prepare the general journal entry for Wall Company's records. Briefly explain the amount you have recorded.

[b] Prepare the general journal entry for Beam Company's records. Briefly explain the amount you have recorded.

(AICPA adapted)

P11–7 Honey's Health Spa plans to dispose of certain gymnastics equipment in one of several ways. The equipment originally cost $200,000, and depreciation recognized to date is $70,000. A recent appraisal indicates that the equipment is worth approximately $150,000 on the used equipment market. Honey's owner seeks your advice about the impact that various alternative methods of disposal would have on the company's financial statements.

Instructions

Prepare the general journal entry or entries for the following *independent* alternative methods of disposal. Following each entry, comment on the impact the alternative would have on the income statement for the year in which the transaction took place.

[a] Honey trades the equipment for a vacant lot whose current value is not known.

[b] Honey trades the equipment for similar equipment valued at $175,000 and pays $25,000 in the exchange.

[c] Honey trades the equipment for similar equipment valued at $140,000 and receives $10,000 cash.

[d] Honey sells the equipment for $150,000. The proceeds are combined with an additional $50,000 cash and a $100,000, five-year, 10% note to purchase new equipment. (The 10% interest rate on the note appears fair.)

[e] Honey trades the equipment for similar equipment also valued at $150,000. No cash is included in the transaction.

P11–8 Kohler Company uses the allowance method

of accounting for equipment repair and maintenance expenditures. A monthly amount of $1,200 is recognized as an expense and credited to the allowance on a quarterly basis. Expenditures for repairs and maintenance are charged to this allowance. Any existing balance in the allowance is adjusted to zero through the expense at the end of the company's fiscal year, March 31. Depreciation on equipment is computed at 2% of the gross asset balance at the end of each quarter. Account balances on April 1, 1984, are as follows:

Equipment	$125,000
Accumulated depreciation	(57,200)
	$ 67,800

Kohler Company engaged in the following transactions involving equipment from April 1, 1984, through March 31, 1985:

Apr. 15	Repair costs	$ 550
May 17	Equipment acquisition	5,275
July 28	Repair costs	3,620
Oct. 19	Repair costs	5,200
Dec. 1	Equipment acquisition	10,900
Feb. 14	Repair costs	4,990

Instructions

[a] Determine the amounts to be included in the company's balance sheet based on the equipment accounts at the end of each quarter from April 1, 1984, through March 31, 1985. Compute all amounts to the nearest dollar.

[b] What amount of repair and maintenance expense will appear in the annual income statement on March 31, 1985?

[c] Briefly explain the rationale for the allowance method of accounting for repairs and maintenance in this situation, as opposed to simply recognizing repair and maintenance expenditures as expenses when they are incurred.

P11-9 Bookston, Inc., needs additional machines to meet the growing demand for its product. The Machine Supply Company offers to provide the machines under any one of the options listed below (each option gives Bookston exactly the same machines and gives Machine Supply approximately the same net present-value cash equivalent at 8%):

Option A—Cash purchase $100,000.
Option B—Installment purchase requiring 15 equal payments of $11,700.

Option C—10-year lease with right to purchase for $1,000, annual lease payments of $14,800.
Option D—15-year rental contract at $11,300 per year.

The expected economic life of these machines is 15 years. The estimated salvage value is $10,000.

Instructions

[a] Based on current generally accepted accounting principles, state how the machines and the obligations will appear on the balance sheet, if at all, of Bookston, Inc., for each option. Use the following format. If the option should not appear in the statement, write "not shown."

	Assets		Liabilities	
	Account Name	*Amount*	*Account Name*	*Amount*
Option A				
Option B				
Option C				
Option D				

[b] If you treat one or more of the options differently, explain why.

(CMA adapted)

P11-10 H. Jones Company presented the following items of property, plant, and equipment in its balance sheet on December 31, 1983, the end of the fiscal year:

Property, Plant, and Equipment		
Equipment	$ 126,250	
Accumulated depreciation	(32,500)	$ 93,750
Buildings	751,000	
Accumulated depreciation	(251,500)	499,500
Land		162,720

During 1984 the company engaged in the following transactions involving property, plant, and equipment:

Jan. 1   The first progress payment ($10,000) on the office building was made. (See Aug. 1 transaction.)

   2   Bonds in the face amount of $200,000 were sold at par value. Annual interest of 12% is to be paid semiannually on June 30 and Dec. 31. The company plans to use the proceeds

to purchase several property, plant, and equipment items in the near future.

Feb. 1   A piece of equipment with a list price of $35,250 was acquired. A 2% cash discount was received by paying on Feb. 8, within the 10-day discount period.

28   The second progress payment ($20,000) on the office building was made.

April 30   The third progress payment ($20,000) on the office building was made.

May 1   A second piece of equipment was acquired in a trade for a similar asset which the company had acquired several years before. The newly acquired asset had a market value of $15,750. The asset surrendered had a book value of $8,250 (cost $19,500; accumulated depreciation $11,250). H. Jones paid $10,000 cash.

June 30   The fourth progress payment ($20,000) on the office building was made.

July 1   Land was acquired by issuing a $55,000, two-year noninterest-bearing note. The note calls for two payments of $27,500, one and two years after the date of the note. A recent appraisal of the land indicates an estimated value of $46,475.

Aug. 1   A small office building was completed and placed in service. The building had been constructed by another company between Jan. 1 and Aug. 1. H. Jones made the final payment of $10,000 on Aug. 1.

Instructions

[a] Prepare all journal entries for the preceding transactions and any additional necessary entries.

[b] Prepare any adjusting entries required on December 31, 1984. Depreciation is computed at 10% of the ending account balance for equipment and 4% of the ending account balance for buildings, approximating straight-line depreciation with 10- and 25-year lives for equipment and buildings, respectively.

[c] Prepare the presentation of property, plant, and equipment to be included in the December 31, 1984, balance sheet.

P11–11 Normal Furniture Company included the following items in its Building asset account on December 31, 1985:

Jan. 1	Contract price of building	$ 975,000
1	Premium for insurance policy on building	12,000

15	Book value of existing building which was replaced	85,000
15	Materials salvaged upon demolition of existing building	(9,500)
July 15	Display fixtures used in building	27,500
Dec. 31	Implicit interest on investment in building, Jan. 1–Dec. 31	98,000
		$1,188,000

An analysis of the company's records reveals the following:

[1] A loss of $17,800 was recognized on the demolition of the old building. This amount represents the cost of having the building removed. The book value of the old building ($85,000) was charged to the new building. Proceeds from salvaged material from the old building reduced the cost of the new building by $9,500.

[2] The building was placed in use immediately upon acquisition in early 1985.

[3] The insurance premium paid on January 1, 1985, covers the policy on the building for a two-year period.

[4] The display fixtures of $27,500 are considered separately. The company expects to use these fixtures for varying lengths of time, all of which are less than the expected life of the building itself.

[5] The company incurred interest of $98,000 on a loan directly related to the acquisition of the building.

[6] Costs of $37,500 were charged to Repair and Maintenance Expense during the period. These costs represent painting and other finishing work which were not part of the original contract under which the building was constructed. This work was completed in early 1985 as soon as the building was accepted from the contractor.

Instructions

Prepare general journal entries necessary to correct the Building account on December 31, 1985. Provide an explanation for each entry. The books have not been closed for 1985.

P11–12 Holiday End Company owns Asset A, a used asset for which no current market value is readily determinable. Asset A cost $125,000 several years ago, and has a book value of $65,000 on June 30, 1984. The company is considering alternative opportunities to dispose of Asset A in an exchange transaction which would result in the acquisition of another similar asset.

Instructions

For each of the following independent cases, prepare the general journal entry necessary to record the exchange of Asset A for the appropriate alternative asset. For each alternative, briefly explain the amount at which the asset is capitalized.

	Asset B	Asset C	Asset D	Asset E	Asset F
Original cost	$145,000	$90,000	$100,000	$ 165,000	$110,000
Accumulated depreciation	(75,000)	–0–	(25,000)	(100,000)	(10,000)
Book value	$ 70,000	$90,000	$ 75,000	$ 65,000	$100,000
Current market value	*	$90,000	$ 50,000	$ 90,000	$100,000
Cash paid by (received by) Holiday End	–0–	$20,000	$ (10,000)	$ (10,000)	$ 45,000

*Unable to determine.

P11–13 Faultless Company had several transactions during 1983 and 1984 concerning plant assets. Several of these transactions are described below, followed by the entry or entries made by the company's accountant.

Equipment. Several used items were acquired on February 1, 1983, by issuing a $100,000 noninterest-bearing note. The note is due one year from the date of issuance. No market value of the note or the equipment is available. Faultless Company's most recent borrowing rate was 8%.

Feb. 1, 1983	Equipment	100,000	
	Notes Payable		100,000
Dec. 31, 1983	Depreciation Expense	10,000	
	Accumulated Depreciation—Equipment		10,000

Buildings. A building was acquired on June 1, 1983, by issuing 100,000 shares of the company's $5 par value common stock. The common stock is not widely traded, therefore no market price is available. The building was appraised on the transaction date at $650,000.

June 1, 1983	Building	500,000	
	Common Stock		500,000
Dec. 31, 1983	Depreciation Expense	20,000	
	Accumulated Depreciation—Building		20,000

Inventory/Fixtures. Inventory and display fixtures were acquired for $125,000 cash on April 1,

1984, from a competitor who was liquidating his business. The estimated value of the inventory was $85,000 and the value of the fixtures was $55,000.

Apr. 1, 1984	Inventory	85,000	
	Display Fixtures	55,000	
	Cash		125,000
	Gain on Acquisition of Inventory		
	and Fixtures		15,000

Land.   Land was donated to the company by the city of Waltersville in September 1984 as an inducement to build a facility there. Plans call for construction at an undetermined future date. The land was appraised at $24,500. No entry was made.

Machinery.   Machinery was acquired in an exchange for similar equipment on October 12, 1983. The assets surrendered had originally cost $52,500, had $16,000 accumulated depreciation, and were appraised at $45,000 on the date of the exchange. Faultless received machinery valued at $40,000 and $5,000 in cash in the transaction.

Oct. 12, 1983	Machinery	40,000	
	Cash	5,000	
	Accumulated Depreciation—Machinery	16,000	
	Machinery		52,500
	Gain on Exchange of Machinery		8,500
Dec. 31, 1983	Depreciation Expense	4,000	
	Accumulated Depreciation—Machinery		4,000

Additional Information

Faultless Company uses straight-line depreciation, applied to all assets as follows:
[1] A full year's depreciation taken in the year of acquisition and no depreciation taken in the year of disposal.
[2] Estimated life: 25 years for buildings; 10 years on all other assets. (No salvage values are assumed.)

Instructions

For each of the items of property, plant, and equipment above:
[a] Describe the error(s) made in recording the assets and related depreciation, if any.
[b] Prepare journal entries to correct the accounts and to properly record depreciation for 1984. The books for 1984 have not been adjusted or closed.

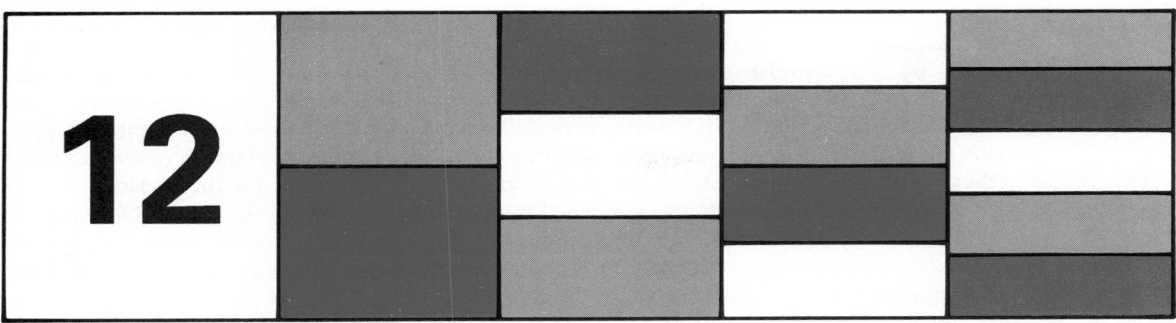

12

PROPERTY, PLANT, AND EQUIPMENT: DEPRECIATION, DEPLETION, AND SPECIAL PROBLEMS

Objectives

To describe the depreciation process as a necessary part of the matching principle in accounting for property, plant, and equipment.

To describe and illustrate several depreciation methods that are applied to individual assets, including both methods based on time and those based on activity level.

To describe and illustrate several group-depreciation methods that are applied to numerous assets as a group rather than to individual assets.

To discuss accounting for natural resources and the related amortization of historical cost through the depletion process.

To illustrate typical presentations of plant assets and related disclosures of depreciation in the primary financial statements and related notes.

To introduce the accounting treatment of changes in estimates and corrections of errors affecting plant assets.

Matching

The **matching principle** is a term used to identify the method by which accountants determine net income. This process involves the recognition of revenues associated with business activities during a certain period and the further identification of expenses related to the generation of those revenues. The difference between these revenues and expenses is the **net income** of the enterprise for that period.

Three principles explain the rationale for including an expenditure (or part of an expenditure) as an expense in the matching process for a particular time period. The principles are (1) associating cause and effect, (2) systematic and rational allocation, and (3) immediate recognition.[1]

Associating cause and effect refers to the fact that some expenditures have a direct association with specific revenues and, thus, are included in determining net income for the period in which those revenues are received. For example, certain manufacturing costs, such as direct materials and direct labor, are directly related to items of inventory produced and are included in income when those items are sold.

Systematic and rational allocation refers to those costs that do not have a direct cause-and-effect relationship on the generation of revenue but that are recognized as expenses in an attempt to allocate costs in a systematic and rational manner among several accounting periods in which benefits are provided. An expenditure that is made in one period but provides benefits to several accounting periods, such as the cost of a plant asset, provides an example of the need for interperiod allocations in the determination of income.

Immediate recognition refers to those costs that are included in the determination of income because expenditures of the current period (or those carried forward from previous periods) have no discernible future benefits. The recognition of numerous operating expenses, such as research and development, and the expensing of items that do not result in increased revenues, such as the write-off of obsolete equipment, provide examples of the immediate recognition of costs in the determination of income.

THE DEPRECIATION PROCESS

Accounting for property, plant, and equipment when they enter the productive processes of the enterprise is best described by systematic and rational allocation. We have seen in Chapter 11 that plant assets are acquired with the intent of being used in the production or distribution of other goods or services and are expected to be useful over a relatively long period. With the exception of land, plant assets are believed to possess valuable, but limited, economic usefulness to the enterprise holding the rights to the service potential of the assets.

Depreciation Defined

Historical Cost

Plant assets are recorded at historical cost, and that cost is allocated to the periods benefiting from the use of the assets on the basis of several estimates concerning the use of the assets. In theory, the accountant prefers to allocate the cost of property, plant, and equipment in a manner that is proportionate to the contribution that the assets make to the generation of revenue each period. In other words, the greater the contribution to revenue for a particular accounting period, the more depreciation expense should be charged for a given asset. However, because of the uncertainties concerning the precise pattern in which a given asset contributes to revenue, accountants estimate periodic depreciation by methods that include simplifying assumptions and that are both systematic and rational.

---

[1] *APB Statement No. 4,* "Basic Concepts and Accounting Principles Underlying Financial Statements of Business Enterprises," 1970, pars. 156–160.

Cost allocation via depreciation does not measure the value of an asset; it is intended to recognize a portion of the cost of the asset as an expense each period in determining net income. Accordingly, **depreciation** is defined as the process of allocating the cost of property, plant, and equipment as an expense in a systematic and rational manner to those periods expected to benefit from the use of the asset.

A common misconception is that the depreciation process provides a cash fund that is available for the replacement of the asset at the end of its useful life. However, depreciation is a process of cost allocation intended primarily to determine net income during those accounting periods in which the asset is used as part of the revenue-producing process. When **periodic depreciation** is recognized, cash is not affected. The company may set aside cash in a special fund for the replacement of depreciable assets at the end of their useful lives, but this would be done in addition to the recognition of depreciation expense for purposes of determining income. Incidentally, setting aside cash to replace plant assets is not a common practice among business enterprises.

The depreciation process and the impact of this process on income determination are illustrated in Exhibit 12–1, in which the acquisition of the plant asset requires a significant cash outlay in the period of acquisition ($100,000 for the asset in 1984). This expenditure is *not* included as an expense in determining income in the year of the expenditure, however, because it represents the cost of a service potential to be realized over several accounting periods. Accordingly, the $100,000 expenditure of 1984 is allocated to periods from 1984 through 1987 in a systematic and rational manner.

If the cash expenditure of $100,000 had been treated as an expense entirely in the year of acquisition, significant distortions in income would take place; for example, in 1984 a net *loss* of $65,000 would be shown. Assuming we have the figures for the next three years, we see that the loss would be followed by net *incomes* in 1985, 1986, and 1987 of $45,000, $50,000, and $44,000, respectively. These variations would result from the failure to match costs and revenues in each accounting period, and the figures would not reflect the essence of the economic activity underlying the income. Depreciation is an important part of deter-

| Matching |

mining net income for each accounting period through the application of the matching principle.

The assumption that the economic usefulness or service potential of plant assets declines over time is supported by the realities of the process of producing and distributing goods and services. Declining service potential is caused by changes in both the asset and the environment in which the asset is used.

The changes in property, plant, and equipment that support the notion of declining service potential result from routine wear and tear, deterioration, and other effects of con-

---

EXHIBIT 12–1
Depreciation as a Factor in Determining Income

	1984	1985	1986	1987
Revenue (given)	$100,000	$115,000	$125,000	$120,000
Expenses				
Depreciation*	25,000	25,000	25,000	25,000
Other (given)	65,000	70,000	75,000	76,000
	90,000	95,000	100,000	101,000
Net income	$ 10,000	$ 20,000	$ 25,000	$ 19,000
Cash expenditure for plant asset	$100,000	—	—	—

*Depreciation is determined by the straight-line method, four-year life, no salvage value.

stant use in normal business operations. Over time these **physical factors** result in a decline in the future service potential of the assets and provide support for the concept of allocating the acquisition cost of assets as an expense. Due to the finite service potential of most plant assets, use of the assets in one period results in a decline in the service potential available for use in future periods.

Changes in the environment in which property, plant, and equipment are used, sometimes referred to as **functional factors,** also influence the amount of future service potential present in an asset at a given time. Business expansion and growth may render a plant asset unsuitable for future use. At that time the asset is **inadequate for the intended purpose,** although it may still be quite suitable for its original purpose. For example, adequate buildings acquired at the inception of a business may become limited in their future service potential when unexpected growth requires larger facilities for efficient operation.

Supercession, on the other hand, results when an enterprise acquires improved assets that are capable of providing the same service as present plant assets at an increased level of efficiency or at a significantly reduced cost. **Obsolescence** is a broad term referring to the decline in future service potential that is due to the functional factors relating to the environment in which the enterprise operates rather than to a decrease in the physical utility of the asset. Functional factors include inadequacy, supercession, and various other changes that affect the asset's potential to provide future service.

Estimates Required in the Depreciation Process

Historical Cost

The depreciation process requires several estimates concerning property, plant, and equipment. Determining historical cost involves estimates, assumptions, and allocations, many of which are described in Chapter 11. These include the treatment of acquisition-related costs, the capitalization of interest costs, the treatment of overhead for internally constructed assets, and many other estimates, assumptions, and allocations. Nevertheless, the historical cost of plant assets is better described as an actual or computed figure than an estimate. However, other figures necessary to apply the depreciation process (i.e., the useful life and salvage value of the asset) are clearly estimates of future events.

Allocating the cost of an asset over future periods requires an estimate of its **useful life,** which may be expressed in **time** (e.g., months or years), **productive output** (e.g., units produced), or **service quantities** (e.g., machine hours operated or miles driven). The logical basis for estimating useful life varies from asset to asset. Accountants attempt to identify the measure of useful life that is most closely associated with the decline in the service potential of the asset to the enterprise. Time is usually the measure used for buildings, furniture, and fixtures. The useful life of machinery that turns out identifiable units of a product may be appropriately stated in terms of a variable measuring productive output. In still other cases service capacity (stated in terms of some physical quantity used or consumed) may be appropriate; for example, miles driven may provide the best estimate of the useful life of a vehicle. Regardless of the nature of the depreciable asset, however, an estimate of the useful life must be made in order to identify the period over which the asset will be depreciated. This life may be identified by a number of titles, all of which have common meanings: service life, economic life, estimated useful life, and other similar terms.

In all widely used methods of depreciation the amount ultimately depreciated is the difference between the historical cost of the asset and the estimated salvage value expected to accrue to the asset holder at the end of the useful life. Thus, the residual value of the asset when it is no longer useful to the enterprise must be estimated. In some methods this estimate must be made initially, when the depreciation schedule is established. In other cases this estimate can be deferred to a later point in the life of the asset.

The amount expected to be available at the end of the service life is identified by a variety of terms, all of which have common meanings: residual value, salvage value, and other similar terms. Any anticipated costs of preparing the asset for disposal at the end of its expected useful life should be treated as a reduction in the residual value for purposes of determining depreciation.

The estimates of useful life and salvage value should be based on the expected usefulness of the asset to the present owner, even though the asset may have a longer useful life for its next owner.

Regardless of the depreciation method selected, depreciation is recorded at the end of each accounting period by an adjusting entry in which Depreciation Expense is debited and Accumulated Depreciation is credited, as discussed in Chapter 5. The depreciation expense then becomes a component of income determination for that period and represents an application of the matching principle. The increase in accumulated depreciation further reduces the book value of the asset.

Matching

DEPRECIATION ESTIMATION METHODS: INDIVIDUAL ASSETS

A number of methods have been developed to apply the general concept of depreciation to property, plant, and equipment. To determine the amount of depreciation expense that should enter into the determination of income, these methods combine the historical cost, the estimated useful life, and the estimated residual value of the asset with certain assumptions about the pattern of decline in the service potential of the asset.

This section discusses several methods for determining periodic depreciation for individual assets. These methods may be classified as those based on time and those based on activity level.

Depreciation Methods Based on Time
1. Straight line
2. Accelerated
   a. Sum-of-the-years'-digits
   b. Declining balance

Depreciation Methods Based on Activity Level
1. Productive output
2. Service quantity

Three additional methods are discussed briefly in Appendix A of this chapter: the method of fixed percentage on book value; the annuity method; and the sinking-fund method. Although these methods are not widely practiced, they represent some systematic and rational alternatives.

Periodic depreciation expense that is determined by any of the methods based on time can be computed in advance and will be the same regardless of the level of activity during the period. Depreciation that is determined by any method based on activity level results in the determination of a constant depreciation charge per unit of activity. Depreciation expense for any single period is then computed at the end of that period and is based on the activity level achieved during the period.

To illustrate the depreciation methods in this section, the following asset is assumed:

Asset 147

Cost	$12,000
Estimated salvage value	$2,000
Estimated life	
In years	5
In units of output	25,000
In service hours	60,000

It would be unusual to have a depreciable asset for which the useful life could be stated equally well in terms of years, units of output, and service hours. The example here includes all three to facilitate the illustration of the methods. As we discuss each method we indicate the circumstances most appropriate for applying the individual method. All methods would usually not apply to the same asset.

Straight-Line Method

The **straight-line method** of depreciation is a relatively simple method and results in the same amount of depreciation expense for each full year in the life of the asset. The depreciation charge is based on the **passage of time** rather than the level of productive activity.

Periodic depreciation under the straight-line method is computed as follows (D = depreciation):

$$D = \frac{(\text{Cost}) - (\text{Salvage value})}{\text{Number of years in asset life}}$$

Depreciation for the first year (D_1) for Asset 147 is, thus, computed as follows:

$$D_1 = \frac{\$12,000 - \$2,000}{5}$$
$$= \$2,000$$

Due to the straightforward nature of the calculation, the absence of complicating assumptions, and the ease of understanding, the straight-line method is widely used in practice. The method is conceptually appropriate if the decline in service potential relates primarily to the passage of time rather than to the level of activity and if the decline is thought to be approximately the same amount each period. The straight-line method may also provide a reasonable basis for depreciation when the level of activity is important but the use of the asset is relatively constant from period to period.

Applying the straight-line method to the five-year life of Asset 147, we arrive at the schedule in Exhibit 12-2.

The resulting book value at the end of the fifth year is the $2,000 salvage value originally used to determine the total depreciation to be charged ($10,000). The book value at the end of each year is the amount presented as an asset in the enterprise's balance sheet. The financial-statement disclosure requirements for plant assets are covered in a later section of this chapter.

EXHIBIT 12–2
Depreciation Schedule for Asset 147
Straight-Line Method

End of Year	Depreciation Entry: Dr.: Depreciation Expense Cr.: Accumulated Depreciation	Balance: Accumulated Depreciation	Book Value
—	—	—	$12,000
1	$2,000	$ 2,000	10,000
2	2,000	4,000	8,000
3	2,000	6,000	6,000
4	2,000	8,000	4,000
5	2,000	10,000	2,000

Accelerated Methods

Accelerated depreciation methods, sometimes referred to as **reducing-charge methods,** are designed to incorporate into income determination a greater amount of depreciation in the early years of an asset's life and a smaller amount in the later years. Of the several variations of accelerated depreciation, the most widely used are the declining-balance method and the sum-of-the-years'-digits method. Both are presented in this section. Even though the amount of depreciation varies from year to year with accelerated methods, depreciation is still based on the passage of time; it is computed in advance and is based on estimates of useful life and salvage value.

Accelerated depreciation methods emerged out of income tax law, which allowed companies to take more depreciation in the early years in the asset's life than in later years. As we discuss later in this section, the use of accelerated depreciation for income tax purposes does not necessitate its use for financial reporting purposes. However, accelerated depreciation may be conceptually sound if the declining pattern of expense recognition is consistent with the actual contribution the asset makes to the revenue-generating process.

Accelerated depreciation methods are conceptually attractive when the asset is believed to provide superior performance (i.e., operate with greater efficiency) in the early years of its life. Further support for accelerated depreciation is found in the expected pattern of repair and maintenance. If repair and maintenance costs are expected to increase during the life of the asset, the declining depreciation charged coupled with the increasing repair and maintenance charges will result in a pattern of periodic expense that relates more closely to the decline in service potential than would the results of some other depreciation method. The potential for obsolescence is also cited as a reason for using accelerated depreciation: The large charges to income in the early years of the asset's life reduce the book value early and reduce the probability that a significant write-off will have to be made later because of a permanent impairment in value due to obsolescence.

Sum-of-the-Years'-Digits Method

The **sum-of-the-years'-digits method** is applied by computing a fraction, the denominator of which equals the **life of the asset in years plus all digits between that number and zero.** The numerator of the fraction represents the **specific number of the year** in the useful life of the asset, but the number is applied in **descending order** throughout the life of the asset; for example, if the useful life is 10 years, the number 10 would be used to determine D_1, the number 9 would be used to determine D_2, etc. This fraction is then multiplied by **depreciable cost** (i.e., the cost minus salvage value). Thus, depreciation is computed:

$$D = \left(\frac{\text{Current year digit}}{\text{Sum-of-the-years'-digits}} \right) \times (\text{Cost} - \text{Salvage value})$$

Applying these concepts to Asset 147, we find that the denominator (the sum-of-the-years'-digits, $5 + 4 + 3 + 2 + 1$) equals 15. Depreciation is determined for each year by multiplying the appropriate fraction by the depreciable amount. Remember that the numerator is selected in *reverse (descending)* order; therefore, the computations would be:

$$
\begin{aligned}
D_1 &= {}^5\!/_{15} \times (\$12{,}000 - \$2{,}000) = \$\ 3{,}333 \\
D_2 &= {}^4\!/_{15} \times (\$12{,}000 - \$2{,}000) = \ \ \ 2{,}667 \\
D_3 &= {}^3\!/_{15} \times (\$12{,}000 - \$2{,}000) = \ \ \ 2{,}000 \\
D_4 &= {}^2\!/_{15} \times (\$12{,}000 - \$2{,}000) = \ \ \ 1{,}333 \\
D_5 &= {}^1\!/_{15} \times (\$12{,}000 - \$2{,}000) = \ \underline{\ \ \ 667} \\
&\qquad\qquad\qquad\qquad\qquad\qquad\quad \underline{\$10{,}000}
\end{aligned}
$$

These computations result in a schedule for Asset 147 as illustrated in Exhibit 12–3.

As in the case of straight-line depreciation, the book value of $2,000 at the end of the five years is equal to the salvage value anticipated at the beginning of the asset's life.

For assets with relatively long lives, determining the sum of the digits as computed above may be burdensome. In these cases the denominator in the fraction may be determined as follows (n = years in asset's life; SYD = sum-of-the-years'-digits):

$$SYD = n \left(\frac{n + 1}{2} \right)$$

For example, for an asset with a 35-year life, the sum of the digits is computed as follows:

$$SYD = 35 \left(\frac{35 + 1}{2} \right)$$
$$= 630$$

Depreciation is then determined at the rate of 35/630 for the first year, 34/630 for the second year, etc.

Declining-Balance Method

The **declining-balance method** is a second type of accelerated depreciation in which the charge in early years exceeds that of later years. In the sum-of-the-years'-digits method a declining fraction is multiplied by a constant base. In the declining-balance method the opposite is true: a **constant percentage** is multiplied by a **declining base.**

In the declining-balance method a percentage is based on some multiple of the straight-line rate. The most common application of this method is the **double-declining balance,** wherein the percentage is twice the straight-line rate. This fixed percentage is then applied to the declining book value of the asset, giving a depreciation figure that declines throughout the life of the asset. **The book value, however, should never be reduced below the estimated salvage value.**

The double-declining balance rate is computed as twice the straight-line rate, as follows (DDB = double-declining balance):

$$DDB\% = \left(\frac{100\%}{\text{Life in years}} \right) \times (2)$$

For Asset 147 this rate is 40%:

$$DDB\% = \left(\frac{100\%}{5} \right) \times (2)$$
$$= 40\%$$

Applying 40% to the declining book value of Asset 147 and ignoring salvage value until the book value is reduced to salvage value, we compute the depreciation for each year in the asset's life as follows:

EXHIBIT 12–3
Depreciation Schedule for Asset 147
Sum-of-the-Years'-Digits Method

End of Year	Depreciation Entry: Dr.: Depreciation Expense Cr.: Accumulated Depreciation	Balance: Accumulated Depreciation	Book Value
—	—	—	$12,000
1	$3,333	$ 3,333	8,667
2	2,667	6,000	6,000
3	2,000	8,000	4,000
4	1,333	9,333	2,667
5	667	10,000	2,000

$$D_1 = 40\% (\$12,000) = \$4,800$$
$$D_2 = 40\% (\$12,000 - \$4,800) = \$2,880$$
$$D_3 = 40\% [\$12,000 - (\$4,800 + \$2,880)] = \$1,728$$
$$D_4 = \$10,000 - (\$4,800 + \$2,880 + \$1,728) = \$592$$

Depreciation at 40% of the book value cannot be taken in Year 4 because this would reduce book value below the $2,000 salvage value expected. For the same reason no depreciation can be taken in Year 5.

Exhibit 12–4 shows a schedule for Asset 147 that results from applying the double-declining balance method.

Accelerated depreciation is an area in which the determination of a company's federal income tax liability has had a significant impact on financial reporting practices. The popularity of the double-declining balance method in past years has resulted, at least in part, from the fact that for many assets the maximum depreciation that could be deducted in computing the income tax liability was an amount equal to twice the straight-line rate in the first year, without regard to salvage value. Because this maximum has not applied to all assets, however, variations of the declining-balance method are found in practice. For example, maximum depreciation on used assets, acquired before 1954, and certain other assets is 1½ times the straight-line amount. Accordingly, the declining-balance method at 150% of the straight-line rate is used in some circumstances. The mechanics of applying the declining-balance method are the same regardless of the multiple of the straight-line rate used.

EXHIBIT 12–4
Depreciation Schedule for Asset 147
Double-Declining Balance Method

End of Year	Depreciation Entry: Dr.: Depreciation Expense Cr.: Accumulated Depreciation	Balance: Accumulated Depreciation	Book Value
—	—	—	$12,000
1	$4,800	$ 4,800	7,200
2	2,880	7,680	4,320
3	1,728	9,408	2,592
4	592	10,000	2,000
5	–0–	10,000	2,000

The use of a multiple of less than two, however, results in a less dramatic acceleration of depreciation in the early years of the asset's life.

As we again relate in Chapter 18, which deals with accounting for income taxes in financial reporting, companies may use different accounting methods for financial reporting and for income tax purposes. Regardless of this option many small companies use their tax depreciation method for their financial statements to avoid keeping two sets of depreciation records. The objective of selecting a depreciation method for financial reporting purposes is to match properly the revenues and expenses. The inability to associate directly the decline in service potential of plant assets with revenues produced by those assets, however, precludes precise measurements of the amount of cost to treat as depreciation each period. Thus, methods designed primarily for income tax purposes frequently become a part of financial reporting on the basis that the tax methods are consistent with the general principle of matching.

Matching

In 1981 the income tax law was changed to incorporate a new method of determining the portion of the cost of assets that could be deducted in determining a company's income tax liability. This system, the **Accelerated Cost Recovery System (ACRS),** permits accelerated recovery of the cost of assets over periods that are generally shorter than the estimated useful lives of those assets. In the opinion of the authors, the amounts determined under this system are generally not appropriate for financial reporting purposes, primarily because they are not based on the estimated useful lives of the assets. A primary motivation for the use of accelerated depreciation was to align figures for financial reporting with those for income tax depreciation. As companies move to the ACRS for income tax purposes, we expect them to use accelerated depreciation less frequently and the straight-line method more frequently for financial reporting, because straight-line depreciation presents a more favorable net income in the early years of the asset's life. Since assets acquired before the ACRS came into effect will continue to be depreciated for tax purposes under previous depreciation methods, this transition will be lengthy. Chapter 18 discusses the ACRS in greater detail and considers more carefully the differences between (1) the way the cost of plant assets is recognized in reporting both financial position and the results of operations in financial statements, and (2) the way the cost is recognized in preparing tax returns.

Productive-Output Method

The **productive-output** (or **units-of-output**) **method** uses the output of plant assets as a basis for recognizing periodic depreciation. The rationale for this method is that some assets are capable of producing a determinable number of units of productive output and that depreciation should be recognized in relation to the portion of the output that occurs in each accounting period.

A cost factor per unit of output is first calculated. This factor is then applied to the actual output for the period to determine the depreciation charge. Depreciation expense cannot be determined in advance, because it is dependent on the level of output during the period. The depreciation computation on the productive-output method is generalized as follows:

$$D = \left(\frac{\text{Cost} - \text{Salvage value}}{\text{Life in units of output}} \right) \times \left(\begin{array}{c} \text{Units of output} \\ \text{for period} \end{array} \right)$$

The first element in the computation may be stated as depreciation rate per unit of output. Applying this concept to Asset 147 results in a cost per unit of $.40, as follows:

$$\text{Estimated cost per unit of output} = \frac{\$12,000 - \$2,000}{25,000 \text{ units}}$$

$$= \$.40$$

We shall assume that units are produced in Years 1–5 in the following pattern: 4,000, 9,000, 8,000, 2,000, and 2,000. Depreciation may then be computed for each year by applying the $.40 cost per unit to the units of output:

$$D_1 = \$.40 \times 4,000 = \$1,600$$
$$D_2 = \$.40 \times 9,000 = \$3,600$$
$$D_3 = \$.40 \times 8,000 = \$3,200$$
$$D_4 = \$.40 \times 2,000 = \quad\$800$$
$$D_5 = \$.40 \times 2,000 = \quad\$800$$

Exhibit 12–5 shows the schedule that results for Asset 147 when the units-of-output method is applied to the five years in the asset's life. As in the other methods, the book value at the end of five years equals the expected salvage value of $2,000, because the total amount that has been recognized as depreciation expense is $10,000.

The productive-output method is suitable only if the asset provides a separate, identifiable unit of product. This is the case, for example, with equipment used to manufacture items of inventory. The productivity of many plant assets, such as buildings and fixtures, however, cannot be measured in terms of a unit of output. In such cases, the productive-output method is *not* appropriate. For those assets whose contribution to operations can best be measured in terms of units of productive output, this method is particularly suitable if the decline in service potential is thought to be more closely tied to the production of units than to the passage of time. If an asset is used very little in a period, depreciation by the units-of-output method will be small; if the level of activity is high, depreciation will be high. If obsolescence or additional factors other than physical output are considered important in determining the pattern of decline in the asset's service potential from period to period, the productive-output method is *not* suitable.

Service-Quantity Method

The productivity of some assets is best measured in terms of service quantity; for example, we state the productivity of certain machinery in terms of operating hours and the produc-

---

EXHIBIT 12–5
Depreciation Schedule for Asset 147
Productive-Output Method

End of Year	Depreciation Entry: Dr.: Depreciation Expense Cr.: Accumulated Depreciation	Balance: Accumulated Depreciation	Book Value
—	—	—	$12,000
1	$1,600	$ 1,600	10,400
2	3,600	5,200	6,800
3	3,200	8,400	3,600
4	800	9,200	2,800
5	800	10,000	2,000

tivity of vehicles in terms of miles. While the mechanics of applying the service-quantity method are similar to those of the productive-output method, the concepts underlying the methods are somewhat different.

Under the **service-quantity method** the contribution to operations is stated in terms of **productive-input factors** rather than output of the production process. Accordingly, depreciation recognized in the determination of income in any period is dependent on the quantity of the productive-input factor consumed in the use of the asset during that period. The amount of the productive input is limited, and the depreciable amount (cost less salvage value) is recognized as an expense on the basis of the expiration of this limited quantity of productive inputs.

Depreciation under the service-quantity method is generalized as follows:

$$D = \left(\frac{\text{Cost} - \text{Salvage value}}{\substack{\text{Total quantity of} \\ \text{productive} \\ \text{service}}} \right) \times \left(\substack{\text{Productive} \\ \text{service for} \\ \text{period}} \right)$$

As in the case of the productive-output method, the first factor may be stated as a depreciation rate per unit of productive service. For Asset 147 the appropriate service quantity is 60,000 service hours, resulting in a cost per hour of $.1667:

$$\frac{\text{Estimated cost per unit}}{\text{of productive service}} = \frac{\$12,000 - \$2,000}{60,000 \text{ hours}}$$

$$= \$.1667$$

The asset is used during Years 1–5 in the following service hours: 14,000, 15,000, 20,000, 4,000, and 7,000. Depreciation is computed for each year as follows:

$$D_1 = \$.1667 \times 14,000 = \$2,334$$
$$D_2 = \$.1667 \times 15,000 = \$2,501$$
$$D_3 = \$.1667 \times 20,000 = \$3,334$$
$$D_4 = \$.1667 \times 4,000 = \$667$$
$$D_5 = \$.1667 \times 7,000 = \$1,164$$

A $3 rounding adjustment is made in the D_5 computation.

The schedule for Asset 147 that results when we apply the service-quantity method to the five years in the asset's life is illustrated in Exhibit 12–6.

The amount of depreciation recognized each year varies from the previous year, depending on the level of use of the asset during the period. If we conclude that the decline in service potential relates closely to the physical use of the asset, the service-quantity method is appropriate. In particular, if the use of the asset varies considerably from period to period, this method more realistically reflects the decline in service potential through depreciation expense than does a method that recognizes depreciation based on the passage of time and that disregards the level of activity. If the decline in the service potential relates more closely to the passage of time or obsolescence, however, the straight-line or an accelerated method is more suitable than the service-quantity method, even though the contribution of the asset may be stated in terms of service quantities.

In our discussion of depreciation methods based on time, we computed annual depreciation for each year without regard to the actual use of the asset. In discussing depreciation methods based on activity level, we assumed activity levels that coincided precisely with our original estimates of output or input variables. Chapter 11 states that plant assets may be disposed of prior to the end of their estimated useful lives. In these cases, any gain or loss on

EXHIBIT 12–6
Depreciation Schedule for Asset 147
Service-Quantity Method

End of Year	Depreciation Entry: Dr.: Depreciation Expense Cr.: Accumulated Depreciation	Balance: Accumulated Depreciation	Book Value
—	—	—	$12,000
1	$2,334	$ 2,334	9,666
2	2,501	4,835	7,165
3	3,334	8,169	3,831
4	667	8,836	3,164
5	1,164	10,000	2,000

the disposal is determined by comparing the proceeds received in the disposal with the book value of the asset, regardless of the depreciation method that was used.

What is the proper accounting treatment when fully depreciated assets continue to be used by an enterprise? Obviously, the estimate of useful life in terms of either time or activity level proved to be inaccurate, even if it was based on the best information available at the time. The cost and accumulated depreciation of fully depreciated assets should remain in the accounts as long as the assets are actively used, even though these figures effectively cancel each other out in the determination of book value. The use of fully depreciated plant assets in the revenue-producing process presents a theoretical problem, because no portion of the cost of these assets is included among expenses for the period. This violates the matching **Matching** principle. If fully depreciated assets make significant contributions to revenue, this fact should be disclosed in the financial statements. This is usually not a major problem, because fully depreciated assets still in use are usually not an important part of total assets.

SELECTING AN APPROPRIATE DEPRECIATION METHOD

How does a company select the depreciation method it will use for plant assets? We have discussed several concepts that should be considered in this decision: physical use, expected obsolescence, the expected pattern of decline in usefulness, the periodic contribution of the asset to the revenue-producing process, and others. Many times these considerations are difficult, if not impossible, to quantify, and they sometimes offset each other, resulting in some uncertainty about the most appropriate method in a given set of circumstances. The authoritative literature gives only general guidance in answering this question when it states that the depreciation method should be both systematic and rational.

Many times *practical,* rather than conceptual, considerations govern the selection of a depreciation method. For example, the simplicity of the straight-line method offers some explanation for its frequent use in accounting practice. In many cases companies adopt accelerated depreciation for income tax purposes and straight-line depreciation for financial reporting. This offers the advantage of deferring income tax payments without depressing the net income reported in the financial statements in the very early years of the related assets' lives. This combination is particularly popular among rapidly expanding companies that are investing additional amounts in plant assets on a continuous basis. In other cases, however, simplicity influences the choice, and a company will use either accelerated depreciation or straight-line depreciation for both income tax reporting and financial reporting to avoid the cost and inconvenience of retaining two sets of depreciation records. In many cases depreciation methods used in the past are carried forward and applied to new assets without any real consideration of the appropriateness of those methods. In some cases depreciation methods used by other companies with which the enterprise may be compared may influence the methods of depreciation used for particular classes of assets.

Consistency is an important accounting principle when considering the depreciation of plant assets. Once a depreciation method is selected for a particular asset or class of assets, the method should be used consistently from period to period so that the net incomes of successive accounting periods are comparable.

In summary, it is difficult to generalize exactly how companies determine the depreciation methods they use. Conceptual as well as practical considerations are important, and consistency over time must also be considered.

Consis- tency

FRACTIONAL-YEAR PROBLEMS

In all of the previous examples, we have assumed that the **depreciation year** and the **financial reporting period** are the same. That is, Asset 147 was acquired at the beginning of a financial reporting period and a full year's depreciation was taken in that year.

Plant assets are not always acquired at the beginning of an enterprise's fiscal period. Likewise, assets are not always disposed of at the end of the period. The problem of accounting for depreciation for assets acquired and disposed of at various times during the year is frequently encountered in applying all of the individual asset-depreciation methods that were discussed in the previous section. The computation of depreciation expense is different, however, only for those methods in which depreciation is based on the passage of time. Depreciation for partial years under the activity-based methods is computed in the same way as for full years of use, because the expense is based on productive output or service quantity rather than the passage of time.

Numerous policies may be adopted in applying depreciation methods in reporting periods when assets have been held only part of the period. This situation potentially occurs twice in the life of every asset: once in the period the asset is acquired and once in the period of disposal of the asset. Only if acquisition and disposal transactions occur on or very close to the first and last days of the financial reporting period are the problems of depreciation for partial years avoided.

To illustrate several problems and alternative approaches to depreciation for partial years, the example of Asset 286 is used.

Asset 286

Cost	$100,000
Estimated salvage value	None
Estimated life in years	4
Date of acquisition	Aug. 10, 1982
Financial reporting period	Jan. 1–Dec. 31

A fractional-year problem exists because the four years in the asset's life do not correspond precisely to four financial reporting years. We can depict this problem as follows:

```
                              1  2  3  4  5
Financial reporting years: /--/--/--/--/--/
                              :  :  :  :  :
Depreciation years:          /--/--/--/--/
```

The first depreciation year begins during the first financial reporting year and ends during the second financial reporting year. This sequence continues throughout the life of Asset

286, with the financial reporting periods following a January-through-December pattern and the depreciation years following an August-to-August pattern.

A number of policies may be adopted for the fractional-year problem that exists in the first and last years in the asset's life. Several of these are applied to Asset 286 in Exhibit 12-7 which uses the straight-line method of depreciation.

Several observations are possible concerning these approaches to the fractional-year problem. Policy 1 is used widely in practice and results in the most precise recognition of depreciation in terms of time. Since the depreciation computation incorporates numerous

---

EXHIBIT 12-7
Alternative Approaches to
Fractional-Year Problem for Asset 286
Straight-Line Method

Fractional-Year Policy	Depreciation Recognized in Financial-Reporting Periods				
	1	2	3	4	5
1. Recognize depreciation to nearest full month.	10,417*	25,000**	25,000	25,000	14,583†
2. Recognize depreciation to nearest full year.	–0–	25,000	25,000	25,000	25,000
3. Recognize depreciation to nearest half year.	12,500‡	25,000	25,000	25,000	12,500
4. Recognize one-half year's depreciation in period of acquisition and one-half in period of disposal.	12,500	25,000	25,000	25,000	12,500
5. Recognize full-year depreciation in period of acquisition and none in period of disposal.	25,000	25,000	25,000	25,000	–0–
6. Recognize no depreciation in period of acquisition and full year in period of disposal.	–0–	25,000	25,000	25,000	25,000

*5/12 (100,000/4)
**(100,000/4)
†7/12 (100,000/4)
‡(25,000 × ½)

assumptions and estimates, computations based on period of time shorter than one month are rarely made. In the case of Asset 286, five months (August–December) of depreciation are recognized in the first financial reporting period, because the asset was acquired in the first half of August. Seven months of depreciation remain to be recognized in the fifth financial reporting period. Under Policy 2 no depreciation is taken in the first year, because the enterprise acquired the asset in the last half of the year. If the asset had been acquired in the first half, a full year's depreciation would have been taken in the first year and none in the last year. In Policy 3 depreciation is recognized to the nearest half year. Thus, if the asset is acquired in the period of January–March, a full year's depreciation is taken in the first year. If the asset is acquired in the period April–September, a half-year's depreciation is taken; and if the asset is acquired in the period October–December, no depreciation is taken. In Policies 1, 2, and 3 the date of the acquisition of the asset influences the amount of depreciation recognized in the first and last years.

Policies 4, 5, and 6 differ from Policies 1, 2, and 3 in that assets are treated the same, regardless of when they are acquired. In Policy 4 a half-year's depreciation is taken in the first year and the same in the last year. In Policy 5 a full year's depreciation is taken in the first year and none in the last year. In Policy 6 no depreciation is taken in the first year and a full year's depreciation is taken in the last year. Policies 5 and 6 resolve the fractional-year problem by requiring the depreciation year and the financial reporting year to coincide.

Applying Policies 1, 3, and 4 in situations in which an accelerated depreciation method is used differs only because the amount of depreciation varies each year. The depreciation for each depreciation year must be allocated to financial reporting periods in a manner consistent with the particular policy being followed. The remaining policies are applied for accelerated methods in the same way as for the straight-line method.

Consis-tency

The key to applying fractional-year policies is practicality, logic, and consistency. If numerous assets are acquired and disposed of frequently and during various times of the year, all of the policies in Exhibit 12–7 are suitable for coping with the fractional-year problem. However, the policy selected must be applied consistently. Infrequent acquisitions and disposals of major assets that individually have a material impact on financial position and results of operations should be depreciated under an appropriate depreciation method to the nearest full month.

GROUP-DEPRECIATION SYSTEMS

The depreciation methods discussed earlier are designed to apply the concept of depreciation to specific individual assets. In some cases, however, it is impractical or even impossible to apply one of the generally accepted depreciation methods to individual assets or to individual components of a complex asset. Several systems are available to compute depreciation for groups of assets that are treated as a single asset for purposes of determining periodic depreciation expense.

Of the many variations of group-depreciation systems, the following are included in this section: inventory system, retirement and replacement systems, and groups and composite-life systems.

Inventory System

The **inventory system** of determining periodic depreciation of plant assets parallels closely the determination of cost of goods sold in a periodic merchandise-inventory system. As assets are acquired, an asset account is debited. At the end of the financial reporting period, an inventory count is made of the items on hand. The difference between the asset balance and the cost of the items on hand, possibly adjusted to an amount below cost to reflect wear and tear, represents the depreciation charge for the period.

The inventory system is appropriate if a large number of items with a small unit cost are

WRONG NUMBERS

IN THE ROW over the breakup of American Telephone & Telegraph, there has been a lot of talk about defending the public from rocketing local telephone bills. But all the while another group of ordinary people—AT&T's stockholders—may be getting mugged in the confusion. Billions of dollars may be at stake.

The problem centers on what AT&T calls customer premises equipment—telephones and switchboards in customers' homes and offices. These are currently owned by local Bell companies, but, along with Bell Laboratories and Bell Long Lines, they will remain with AT&T after the local companies are spun off.

The transfer means customer premises equipment, unlike local customer service, will be out from under regulation. Fine, except for one thing: Much of the stuff is badly underdepreciated, perhaps by as much as $6 billion. After the breakup, AT&T may have lost forever the chance to recover billions of dollars of depreciation it should already have charged to telephone users. Why? Listen to Steven Chrust, telecommunications analyst at Sanford C. Bernstein: "Under the new deal, AT&T will bill customers for the lease of the equipment. But much of it is out-of-date and AT&T cannot charge too much without people switching to newer, cheaper equipment from other suppliers."

According to Harry Edelson at the First Boston Corp., AT&T's best course would be to make an immediate writedown to market values when it emerges as an unregulated company. While that would cut AT&T earnings in half in its first year after deregulation, analysts like Edelson think Wall Street would quickly forget its initial disappointment.

"If they wrote off the underdepreciation immediately, it would all be over in a day," says Edelson. "The damage to the stock price would be minimal and, although the asset value per share would be reduced, this hardly affects how the market sees an unregulated company."

An immediate writeoff would also probably bring tax benefits that could actually boost AT&T's cash flow by billions in its first year of freedom. This is because the writeoff could be charged to operating expenses and thus would reduce taxable income. But AT&T is far more likely to write off the underdepreciation piecemeal over several years as individual bits of obsolete equipment are scrapped. This would produce a steady drag on earnings for perhaps five to ten years. AT&T Chairman Charles Brown told FORBES: "If the older equipment must be replaced and is underdepreciated, we would have to write off the difference. But you know we are not going to go around replacing the telephones." Meaning: We'll take the writeoffs only as fast as the customers throw out the old equipment.

Brown dismisses suggestions that there will be a massive writeoff. "We are in no danger of suddenly taking a big loss of $5 billion, whatever somebody wants to dream up," he says.

How has AT&T landed itself with the the problem? For years it suited everyone—regulators and stockholders—to understate depreciation. That way, telephone rates were kept down for the short term. Meanwhile AT&T was happy because the profits it was allowed were calculated as a percentage of net qualifying assets (the "rate base"), so the slower the depreciation the more handsome reported profits.

It was a strategy designed to maximize reported profits rather than to maximize cash flow. Analysts also believe that thousands of central switching offices now owned by the local companies, but which will be retained by AT&T, are even more overvalued. But here there is no problem for earnings because these assets will remain within the regulatory net. AT&T will get its money back through telephone bills in years to come.

Less clear is what will happen with the Bell companies' so-called inside wire account. This is in the books as an asset totalling $11 billion and it represents the cost of installing the wiring needed in customers' homes and offices to connect them to the local telephone system. Most of the account is capitalized labor costs. As with underdepreciation, the rationale was simply to put off until tomorrow an item that would otherwise have had to be expensed today—a concession to militant rate commissions and consumers. Even before the breakup decision, AT&T was planning to phase out the account over the next decade, adding to costs and the pressure for higher telephone bills.

Industry observers say that AT&T may be forced to take part, at least, of the account, thus relieving some of the pressure on local telephone rates. Several regulators have been breathing fire about the account, saying that as you need inside wiring to make long distance calls, it should not be expensed solely to local telephone rates.

One of the loudest critics of the breakup agreement is Neil Swift, staff director of the New York State Department of Public Service. He insists that inside wiring should be a deregulated function, and should go with AT&T in its entirety. Then AT&T would have to recover what it could from telephone users in the face of competition from other installers and from do-it-yourself enthusiasts.

Swift suggests, however, that AT&T might make up the shortfall by tacking some of the costs on to the long distance service, which it will retain. At any rate, these capitalized costs will be a bone of contention for a long time to come.

According to Brown, only those local company assets specifically mentioned in the decree are being retained by AT&T—everything else including inside wiring goes to the local operating companies.

"This whole thing is not our idea, it is an idea of the Justice Department," Brown says of the wire's fate.

So far so good. But the deal still awaits ratification by Judge Harold Greene of the U.S. District Court in Washington. Given AT&T's incredibly complex accounting, there is plenty of scope for accountants, lawyers and regulators to continue arguing. And there are clearly a lot of pitfalls for stockholders.

SOURCE: Eamonn Fingleton, "Wrong Numbers," *Forbes,* March 1, 1982, pp. 41–42. Reprinted by permission of *Forbes* Magazine. © Forbes Inc., 1982.

---

used in the productive process and if the application of a depreciation method to individual assets is impractical. Examples are machine tools, hand tools, and patterns used in the manufacturing process. The inventory method results in a reasonable approximation of the depreciation amount that would have resulted from depreciating the assets on an individual basis.

To illustrate, we assume that Tennyson Manufacturing Company uses a large number of small hand tools in its manufacturing process. Rather than compute depreciation individually on these relatively inexpensive tools, the company uses the inventory method of depreciating them. The asset account reflects the following activity in it during 1984:

Small Tools Account

Balance, January 1, 1984	$12,750
Acquisitions	
March 5, 1984	1,300
August 29, 1984	5,420
October 7, 1984	3,500
	$22,970

An inventory of hand tools at December 31, 1984 reveals that hand tools costing $17,250 are on hand. Management determines that these assets should be reduced by 20% due to wear and tear on them to date. Depreciation expense to be recognized in 1985 is determined as follows:

Balance in Small Tools account	$22,970
Value of ending inventory	
$17,250 − .20($17,250)	13,800
Depreciation for 1985	$ 9,170

The entry to recognize depreciation is:

Depreciation Expense	9,170	
Hand Tools		9,170

No accumulated depreciation account is maintained, and Depreciation Expense is debited periodically for the reduction in the asset account necessary to bring it to the appropriate balance.

Cash may be received when assets are sold. In the entry debiting Cash, the asset account is credited. This effectively reduces the difference between the ending balance in the asset account and the value of the inventory of tools on hand, thus reducing the depreciation recognized.

For example, for the Tennyson case we will assume that the beginning balance and acquisitions are the same as previously stated but, in addition, that $1,500 was received from the sale of used hand tools at December 31, 1984. The following general journal entries would be required:

Cash	1,500	
Hand Tools		1,500
Depreciation Expense	7,670	
Hand Tools		7,670

The $1,500 from the cash sale is credited directly into the asset account (Hand Tools), reducing the balance from $22,970 to $21,470. Depreciation is then computed as $7,670 ($21,470 − $13,800).

Retirement and Replacement Systems

The retirement and replacement systems may be used in much the same situations as the inventory system. They are suitable depreciation systems if a large number of similar items are employed by the enterprise and the items are being replaced on a relatively constant schedule. Under both systems, no depreciation is recognized until items are replaced.

The retirement and replacement systems are used primarily by public utilities, which have large numbers of virtually identical items that are constantly being installed and retired: utility poles, utility lines, accessories used in utility lines, railroad ties, and telephone receivers.

Under the **retirement system** the cost of retired items is debited to Depreciation Expense at the time of retirement, and the asset account is reduced by the same amount. The cost of the new items that replace the existing ones is debited to the asset account, and the process continues. No identification of depreciation by individual unit is kept, no accumulated depreciation account is maintained, and no depreciation is taken until units are replaced.

Assume that Lonzo Utility Company uses the retirement system to determine depreciation on a large number of utility poles located throughout the city of Lonzo. The balance in the Utility Pole account is $250,000 at the beginning of 1984. During the year poles originally costing $72,500 are replaced with new poles costing $97,000. In addition, new poles that are installed in a new service area cost $19,600. The following entries are necessary to recognize these events:

Depreciation Expense	72,500	
Utility Poles		72,500
Utility Poles	97,000	
Cash		97,000
Utility Poles	19,600	
Cash		19,600

Any cash received from the salvage of the poles being replaced is treated as a reduction in the $72,500 depreciation expense.

The **replacement system** is similar to the retirement system in terms of the circumstances in which it is appropriate. Under the replacement system, however, the cost of replacing the assets—not the cost of the original assets—is treated as the periodic depreciation. In applying the replacement system to the Lonzo Utility situation, we need to record the following entries:

Depreciation Expense	97,000	
Cash		97,000
Utility Poles	19,600	
Cash		19,600

The original cost of the utility poles is left in the asset account and the cost of replacement ($97,000) is the depreciation amount recognized. Normally the asset account would be affected only if new poles were acquired for purposes other than replacement of existing poles (such as those for $19,600 in the Lonzo case).

As is the case with the retirement system, in the replacement system no identification or depreciation by individual unit is kept, no accumulated depreciation account is maintained, and depreciation expense is not recognized until existing units are replaced. Also, any cash received from the salvage of individual units is treated as a reduction of depreciation expense.

A criticism of both the retirement and the replacement system is that they do not present the allocation of historical cost as an expense during the period of time when the assets are being used to produce revenue. The reasonableness of either system as an approximation of the allocation of cost depends on the constancy of retirement and replacement over time on a continuous basis. If this continuous retirement and replacement of a large number of similar assets does not apply, these systems should not be used.

Historical Cost

The retirement system is a type of first-in, first-out (FIFO) cost determination, since the oldest costs are charged to expense and the most recent costs are maintained in the asset account. In the case of Lonzo Utility Company, the 1984 depreciation expense is $72,500 (made up of the oldest costs), and the balance sheet asset is $294,100 ($250,000 − $72,500 + $97,000 + $19,600), which includes the more recent costs of replacement. On the other hand, the replacement system is a form of last-in, first-out (LIFO) since the most recent costs are charged as an expense and the older costs are retained in the asset account. In the case of Lonzo Utility Company, the 1984 depreciation expense is $97,000 (made up of the most recent costs), and the balance sheet asset is $269,600 ($250,000 + $19,600), including the original cost of those items that have now been replaced.

Group and Composite Systems

In some cases individual assets are combined and depreciated at an average depreciation rate for the assets included. When assets are combined in this manner because of their similarity (e.g., a fleet of vehicles), the depreciation system is called a **group system.** Dissimilar assets may be combined for depreciation purposes if they are used in operations as an integrated unit (e.g., components of an integrated manufacturing assembly). In such cases the depreciation system is called a **composite system.**

The group and composite systems differ from the other methods of multiple-asset depreciation that we discussed earlier in that an Accumulated Depreciation account is kept for the **group of assets** involved. However, the accumulated depreciation does not relate to any particular asset within the group. The mechanics of applying the group and composite systems are outlined in the following steps:

1. The cost of individual assets that comprise the group are debited to a single asset account.
2. An average depreciation rate is determined by stating the total of the annual depreciation of

			EXHIBIT 12–8			
			Digital-Watch Production Assembly			
Component	Historical Cost	Estimated Salvage Value	Depreciable Amount	Estimated Useful Life in Years	Depreciation per Year	
L	$ 27,000	$ 3,000	$ 24,000	8	$ 3,000	
M	19,000	4,000	15,000	10	1,500	
N	5,000	-0-	5,000	5	1,000	
O	62,000	2,000	60,000	12	5,000	
P	12,000	2,000	10,000	8	1,250	
	$125,000	$11,000	$114,000		$11,750	

the individual assets as a percentage of a total cost of the assets included in the group.

3. Depreciation on the group of assets is charged to the Depreciation Expense account and credited to the Accumulated Depreciation account in an amount equal to the percentage computed in Step 2 multiplied by the cost of the assets.

4. The removal of an individual asset from the group is recorded as a debit to the Accumulated Depreciation account and a credit to the asset account in an amount equal to the cost of the individual asset removed. No gain or loss is recognized. Any proceeds received on the asset removal are debited to Cash and serve to reduce the amount that would otherwise be charged to Accumulated Depreciation.

To illustrate, we shall assume that Time Manufacturing Company has a number of small production processes that operate simultaneously to produce several consumer products. The composite depreciation system is used for the assets employed in each process. Information concerning the components of the integrated production assembly for digital watches is presented in Exhibit 12–8.

The five components have been debited to a single asset account, Digital-Watch Production Assembly. We compute the depreciation per year on each component by using the straight-line method. The average depreciation rate is 9.4%, determined by dividing the total depreciation per year of $11,750 by the historical cost of the assets, $125,000. The composite life is 9.7 years ($114,000/$11,750). This indicates that the group of assets will be fully depreciated in approximately 10 years if the 9.4% depreciation rate is applied to the historical cost annually.

A single depreciation entry is made each year for the group of assets, as follows:

Depreciation Expense	11,750	
Accumulated Depreciation—Digital-		
Watch Production Assembly		11,750

The disposal of a component of the group of assets is recorded by charging the Accumulated Depreciation account. No gain or loss is recognized, because the accumulated depreciation cannot be associated with any particular asset or component of the group. For example, if Component P is sold for $1,000 after five years of service, the following entry is made:

Cash	1,000	
Accumulated Depreciation—Digital-		
Watch Production Assembly	11,000	
Digital-Watch Production Assembly		12,000

When the components of a composite asset significantly change, the depreciation rate is revised to reflect the changed relationship between the depreciation per year and the historical cost of the components.

The major advantage of the group and composite method is the clerical cost savings that result from maintaining a single asset account and a single Accumulated Depreciation account for a large number of individual assets. In summary, these assets may either be similar in nature (group method) or comprise a single integrated group of assets (composite method). A major problem in the case of the composite method is the application of a single depreciation rate, based on a weighted average life, to diverse components whose lives may vary considerably. This variance is illustrated in the Time Manufacturing example, in which the estimated lives of the components range from 5 to 12 years, but the same rate of depreciation is applied to all components. This problem does not arise in the group method, because the basis for combining the assets is their similarity; therefore, the life of each asset is similar to that of the other assets in the group.

Another problem with both the group method and the composite method is that no gain or loss is recorded on the disposal of individual assets within the group, because the cost of the individual asset, minus any proceeds from disposal, is charged to the Accumulated Depreciation account. Inaccurate estimates of useful lives and individual assets that are not productive may go unnoticed more easily under the group and composite methods than they would if the assets were depreciated on an individual basis.

NATURAL RESOURCES AND DEPLETION

Business operations frequently use **natural resources,** sometimes referred to as **wasting assets.** Examples of natural resources include coal, oil, ore, precious metals (e.g., silver, gold), and timber. Natural resources are characterized by their removal and consumption and, thus, the loss of physical characteristics. The replacement of natural resources comes about only by the process of nature and is not subject to human production. **Depletion** is the term used to describe the accounting procedure by which the cost of natural resources is allocated to expense as they contribute to the revenue-producing processes of the enterprise.

| Historical |
| Cost |
| Matching |

Accounting for natural resources parallels closely accounting for property, plant, and equipment. The historical cost of the natural resource is based on the sacrifice made to acquire the asset. The allocation of this cost over the quantities of the natural resource used to produce revenue (i.e., depletion) is typically computed on a unit basis, Much like the units-of-output method of depreciation. This allocation matches revenues with expenses in the determination of periodic income. The book value of the natural resource at any time is that portion of the cost that has not been charged to income. Book value does not necessarily represent the current market value of the natural resource, because the book value is only a portion of the original cost of the asset. The similarity between plant assets and natural resources is further emphasized by the fact that they are usually presented together in the balance sheet, with separate disclosure by major categories.

The **depletion rate,** an estimate of the cost per unit of the natural resource, is based on the historical cost of the natural resource, reduced by any expected residual value after the natural resource has been fully exploited. The depletion rate is then applied to the number of units of the natural resource withdrawn during the period.

To illustrate the depletion process, we shall assume that Digger Company acquired the rights to mineral deposits for $2,250,000. Management expected 500,000 tons of the mineral to be economically removed and sold. If, during 1984, 65,000 tons are removed and sold, the depletion rate and depletion charge for 1984 would be computed as follows:

$$\text{Depletion rate per ton} = \frac{\$2,250,000}{500,000 \text{ tons}} = \$4.50 \text{ per ton}$$

$$\text{Cost of mineral removed in 1984} = (\$4.50 \times 65{,}000 \text{ tons})$$
$$= \$292{,}500$$

Depletion is recognized by the following general journal entry:

Depletion Expense	292,500	
Accumulated Depletion		292,500

The natural resource and related depletion are presented in the balance sheet as follows:

Mineral deposits	$2,250,000	
Less: Accumulated depletion	(292,500)	$1,957,500

The depletion expense for the period ($292,500) is presented as a cost of production in the income statement.

If some portion of the natural resource is not sold and thus remains in inventory, that portion of the depletion will be included in the inventory cost and not charged to income as a cost in the period of production. For example, in the Digger case, if 15,000 of the 65,000 tons extracted in 1984 remained in inventory at the end of the year, depletion expense and the cost of the depletable resource held in inventory would be as follows:

Depletion expense =	50,000 tons × $4.50 =	$225,000	
Inventory	= 15,000 tons × $4.50 =	67,500	
	65,000	$292,500	

Although this process appears relatively straightforward and analogous to the depreciation process presented earlier in this chapter, several unique aspects of natural resources are frequently encountered, including the following:

1. The costs of exploration, development, and restoration.
2. The discovery of natural resources subsequent to acquisition.
3. Unique tax aspects of natural resources.
4. The distribution of liquidating dividends.

These aspects of accounting for natural resources are discussed individually in the following paragraphs.

Exploration, Development, and Restoration Costs

The cost of natural resources may include a variety of expenditures after the initial acquisition of the property or rights to explore on another's property. In some cases the initial acquisition cost is the outright purchase of the property containing (or believed to contain) the natural resource. In other cases the initial acquisition price represents only the right to explore for natural resources on the property of another enterprise or individual.

Exploration costs are frequently incurred in attempts to locate physically the reserves of the natural resource that can be economically extracted. Sometimes these costs result in the location of reserves that can be economically exploited, and at other times, in the failure to locate reserves that can be economically exploited. This difference has led to two accounting methods for exploration costs. Under the **successful-efforts method** only those exploration costs that can be associated with the discovery of producible reserves are considered to be a part of the depletion base of the natural resource; costs not associated with the discovery of producible reserves are expensed as incurred on the basis that they fail to represent the cost of future expected benefits. The alternative, the **full-cost method,** assumes that all exploration costs are necessary expenditures to discover the location of producible reserves and thus are a part of the cost of those producible reserves. Although both methods are used in practice, a great deal of controversy has surrounded the use of the two methods in the oil and gas industry. We discuss this controversy in greater depth in Chapter 13.

Development costs are expenditures that are necessary to exploit reserves of natural resources that have been located through successful exploration activities. Development costs may include tangible assets, such as special machinery and equipment, tunnels, shafts, and wells. Development costs in the form of tangible assets should be separately classified in appropriate asset accounts and depreciated over their estimated useful lives in accordance with normal depreciation policies. If these assets are limited in their usefulness to the development of a specific natural resource project, however, they should be depreciated over the life of that project by the same method used for the particular natural resource.

The property containing a natural resource may be sold after extraction activities are complete. The amount expected to be derived from such sale represents the salvage or residual value and reduces the depletion base. To prepare the property for sale, however, **restoration costs** may be necessary to return the property to its natural state. Restoration costs reduce the net amount expected to be received in the form of a salvage value and therefore increase the depletion base.

To illustrate, we shall assume that at a cost of $1,750,000 Jefferson Mines acquires property believed to contain valuable mineral deposits. The company incurs $500,000 in exploration costs and an additional $1,550,000 in tangible developmental costs before successful extraction of the mineral can take place. Geological estimates indicate that 8,000,000 tons of the mineral is a reasonable estimate of the amount that can be economically extracted. Jefferson Mines expects to sell the property for $500,000 after exploitation. However, restoration costs of $150,000 will be required to prepare the property for sale. The depletion base and depletion rate per ton are computed as follows:

Initial acquisition price		$1,750,000
Exploration costs		500,000
Development costs		1,550,000
		3,800,000
Less: Estimated residual value	$ 500,000	
Restoration costs	(150,000)	(350,000)
Depletion base		$3,450,000
Depletion rate per ton		
($3,450,000/8,000,000 tons)		$.43125

Discovery Subsequent to Acquisition

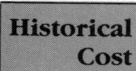

Natural resource reserves may be discovered on previously acquired property. In this case the historical cost of the property does not include a price paid for the natural resource, because that resource was not known to exist at the time of purchase. As we mention in Chapter 11, diversity in practice in recording discovery value ranges from the full recognition of the discovered amount to not recording the amount at all. In terms of including a reasonable depletion charge in the determination of income in future years, substantial support exists for the capitalization of discovery value and its inclusion in the depletion base on which the periodic depletion charge is computed.

Tax Aspects of Natural Resources

Under certain provisions of the Internal Revenue Code, the amount of depletion that can be deducted in determining a company's income tax liability may be computed as a percentage of **gross income,** which is essentially what we refer to as **revenue** in financial reporting. This method of computing depletion is called **percentage depletion,** and the percentage of gross income that may be deducted for tax purposes varies from 5% to 22%, depending on the particular natural resource. If the gross income is large, the percentage depletion may exceed the depletion based on the allocation of historical cost in any one period or in total over the life of the asset. Tax law allows this deduction in excess of the historical cost of the depletable asset as an incentive for companies to take the risk of exploring for necessary natural resources.

Historical Cost Matching

Despite this unique approach for determining depletion for income tax purposes, the historical cost approach is used in applying the matching principle for financial reporting purposes. Recent changes in the Internal Revenue Code, which have limited considerably the applicability of percentage depletion, have reduced the differences in accounting for depletion between income tax reporting and financial-statement reporting.

Distribution of Liquidating Dividends

In some cases the major business activity of a company centers around the exploitation of natural resources, and no plans exist for the replacement of the resource upon exhaustion. A common practice is to distribute dividends to stockholders in amounts up to the total of the retained earnings plus accumulated depletion. To the extent that dividends exceed the amount of retained earnings, however, distributions represent **liquidating dividends** or a **return of stockholders' investments** to them rather than a return on their investments. Care must be taken to account for the distribution of any liquidating dividend and to disclose to stockholders the portion of their dividends representing liquidations of their investments.

To illustrate, we shall assume that Nature Company has a retained earnings balance of $1,200,000 at December 31, 1984. Accumulated depletion on natural resources totals $1,000,000. Cash dividends of $2,000,000 are declared. Shares of common stock outstanding total 1,000,000. The entry to record the dividend is as follows, assuming additional paid-in capital of at least $800,000 exists:

Retained Earnings (or Dividends Declared)	1,200,000	
Additional Paid-In Capital	800,000	
Dividends Payable		2,000,000

Care must be taken to indicate to stockholders that the $2.00 dividend per share represents a $1.20-per-share return on the investment and an $.80-per-share liquidating dividend.

THE ALLOCATION PROBLEM

Matching

This chapter has made frequent references to the fact that depreciation and depletion are cost allocation processes. They are an integral part of the matching process that assigns the costs of an enterprise's nonmonetary inputs, such as inventories and plant assets, to accounting periods for purposes of determining net income. The costs that have not yet been assigned to an accounting period are maintained as assets in anticipation of future assignment as expenses. In a sense we are attempting to match the various **inputs** into an enterprise's revenue-producing process with the **outputs** of that process, namely its revenues.

As Arthur L. Thomas has indicated, however, the outputs of a process are the result of not only a number of inputs but the *interaction* of those inputs:

> *The allocation problem has several dimensions, some of which are subtle. But one is easily described: to match costs with revenues, we must know what the contributions of the firm's individual inputs are. Unfortunately, . . . there is no way to know this.*

Seeing why this is so requires introducing a final concept, interaction. Inputs to a process interact whenever they generate an output different from the total of what they would yield separately. For instance, labor and equipment interact whenever people and machines working together produce more goods than the total of what people could make with their bare hands and machines could make untended. As this example suggests, interaction is extremely common. Almost all of a firm's inputs interact with each other—their failure to do so would ordinarily signal their uselessness.

Surprising as it may seem, it can be proved that whenever inputs interact, calculations of how much total revenue or cash flow has been contributed by any individual input are as meaningless as, say, calculations of the proportion of a worker's services due to any one internal organ: heart, liver or lungs. Thus, despite all textbooks and American Institute of CPAs or FASB releases to the contrary—despite what you have been trained to believe—our attempts to match costs with revenues must almost always fail.[2]

Does this interaction mean that the allocation of asset costs is futile and that we should not attempt to match costs with revenues? Thomas further suggests that wherever possible the Financial Accounting Standards Board (FASB) should develop accounting standards that do not rely on arbitrary allocation. Two primary allocation-free alternatives to conventional financial reporting exist: current value accounting and reporting of fund flows based on cash and near-cash assets. Where allocations cannot be eliminated in financial reporting, allocations should be kept simple. Complex cost allocation methods should be avoided, and care should be taken not to extend allocation methods to additional areas of financial reporting wherever possible.[3]

---

[2]Arthur L. Thomas, "The FASB and the Allocation Fallacy," *Journal of Accountancy* (November 1975), p. 66.
[3]Thomas, p. 68.

AN EXAMPLE OF THE ALLOCATION PROBLEM

A PROSPECTOR MANUFACTURES sourdough bread by a three-stage process:

1 He makes leaven by mixing flour, sugar and water in a crock, then keeps it in a warm place for about a week (until it bubbles).

2 He makes bread by transferring all but a cup of leaven to a large pot, where he mixes it with soda and additional flour, sugar and water, kneads it slightly and then lets it rise. He digs a shallow pit, fills it with coals from his camp fire, covers the pot, places it in the pit, buries it in hot coals and keeps it there until the bread is baked.

3 He replenishes the leaven (for the next baking) by adding enough flour and water to restore the crock to its original level.

Water, airborne yeasts and wood are free goods here. We accountants would be concerned with the following inputs to this process: flour, sugar, soda, labor, the crock, the pot and a shovel. Finally, part of the flour and sugar leaven for one loaf becomes included in the leaven for the next. The output of each baking is one loaf of bread.

Although its manufacture is simple, the moment we try to calculate the contributions of any individual input to this output we face a dilemma. Each input (except, perhaps, the soda and the shovel) is essential. Therefore, we could plausibly assign all of the output to any individual input. For example, we could assign all of the output to the flour, reasoning that were flour withheld from the process there would be no bread. Yet we could equally well assign all of the output to the pot, since without it the loaf would have been incinerated.

Having assigned all output to any one input,

we've implicitly assigned zero to each other input. But if either all or zero is appropriate for each input, any intermediate allocation will be equally appropriate—say, half the loaf to the flour and a sixth each to the pot, labor and the crock.

I'm unable to prove which of the infinitely many possible ways of allocating the loaf is correct. Therefore, I can't specify the individual contributions of the inputs; instead, all I'm entitled to say is that they generate the loaf jointly. Research shows that other writers on economics and accounting— even efficient-markets investigators—are equally unable to solve this problem. Perhaps the reader can. But until someone does, any contributions calculated for these inputs must be incorrigible [incapable of being corrected or improved]:

1 One can't verify them, because any other calculation is just as good.

2 One can't refute them, because their calculation is just as good as any other.

Therefore, any attempts at matching based on these contributions (say, depreciation of the pot or calculation of a value for the ending leaven inventory) will also be incorrigible. But the sourdough process is so much simpler than the productive processes of business enterprises, that *matching must necessarily be incorrigible for them, too*—unless, again, the reader can show how complications ease the calculations. To generalize, when a company tries to match costs with revenues there's no way either to refute or to verify the results. Instead, all possible ways of matching will be just as good—or bad—as each other.

If it's any consolation, I don't like this conclusion either, and have spent years trying to disprove it. Nor should you accept it without further inquiry. But I urge you at least to suspend disbelief in it (and in what follows) until you've read the detailed research, cited earlier, that backs it up.

And please notice that the difficulty here isn't one of being unable to allocate—there might be some way of getting around that problem. Instead, we're drowned in possible allocations, with no defensible way to choose among them. To be sure, since we must prepare reports, we eventually do pick one set of figures or another. Long before completing our training, we became accustomed to do this with few (if any) pangs. First, we narrow the possibilities by looking to generally accepted accounting principles and then select one of the survivors according to industry custom, apparent advantage to the company, apparent appropriateness of the method to the firm's circumstances or some other plausible rationale. But how can the incorrigible results be useful to decision makers?

Unless you (or someone) can suggest ways in which calculations that can neither be verified nor refuted assist decisions, our allocations of the costs of depreciable assets, inventories, labor and other inputs are irrelevant to investor needs. Indeed, although it's painful to say this, they are mere rituals—solemn nonsense—and our beliefs in them are fallacies. This should trouble all of us, because practitioners spend much time conducting such rituals, and theorists much time elaborating on such fallacies.

The Accounting Principles Board was well aware of this, but, underrating its severity, was satisfied to claim that exact measurements are seldom possible and that allocation often requires informed judgment. With all due respect, acknowledging that few allocations are exact is like replying, "Few animals are ever completely healthy," in response to the statement, "Sir, your cow is dead."

SOURCE: Adapted from Arthur L. Thomas, "The FASB and the Allocation Fallacy," *Journal of Accountancy,* November 1975, pp. 65–68. Copyright © 1975 by the American Institute of Certified Public Accountants, Inc.

FINANCIAL-STATEMENT PRESENTATION

Property, plant, and equipment have a significant impact on the financial position of business enterprises. For many enterprises the investment in property, plant, and equipment exceeds that of any other asset category. The method of depreciation used may also influence both the financial position and the results of operations of the reporting enterprise.

The Accounting Principles Board (APB) identified four specific disclosures related to property, plant, and equipment to be included in the financial statements or in related notes:[4]

---

[4]*APB Opinion No. 12,* "Omnibus Opinions," 1967, pars. 4–5.

1. Depreciation expense for the period.
2. Balances of major classes of depreciable assets, by nature or function, at the balance sheet date.
3. Accumulated depreciation, either by major classes of depreciable assets or in total, at the balance sheet date.
4. A general description in the method or methods used in computing depreciation with respect to major classes of depreciable assets.

Due to differences in assets of various enterprises and the flexibility allowed in the placement of the previously mentioned disclosures, information concerning property, plant, and equipment and depreciation is presented in numerous ways in financial statements. Exhibit 12–9 includes the presentation of property, plant, and equipment for United Foods, Inc. from their 1982 financial statements. United Foods processes and markets frozen vegetables. The United Foods presentation includes a single item in the balance sheet, Property and Equipment, that does not provide any detail concerning specific types of assets. The summary of accounting policies includes a section on depreciation in which the method of depreciation is described. Note 2 to the financial statements provides the detailed balances of land, buildings, and equipment. Throughout this disclosure, references are made to capitalized leases and the amortization of those leases. Chapter 21 treats that subject in detail.

EXHIBIT 12–9
United Foods, Inc.
Disclosure of Plant Assets

Balance Sheet Excerpt

	February 28,	
	1982	**1981**
Property and Equipment, less accumulated depreciation and amortization	$24,666,813	$20,895,304

Excerpt from Summary of Accounting Policies

Property, Equipment, Depreciation and Amortization

Property and equipment, other than capital leases, are stated at cost. Capital leases are capitalized based on the lower of the present value of future minimum lease obligations or the fair market value of the asset leased. Expenditures for additions, renewals and betterments are capitalized; expenditures for maintenance and repairs are charged to expense as incurred. Upon retirement or disposal of assets, the cost and accumulated depreciation or amortization are eliminated from the accounts and the resulting gain or loss is included in determining the results of operations.

Depreciation on property and equipment, other than capital leases, acquired prior to January 1, 1981, is computed principally on the straight-line method for financial reporting purposes and accelerated methods for income tax reporting purposes. Depreciation on property and equipment acquired after December 31, 1980, is computed in accordance with the provisions of the Accelerated Cost Recovery System for income tax purposes. Amortization of capital leases is computed on the straight-line method for both financial reporting and income tax purposes. Depreciation and amortization for financial reporting purposes are computed over the following estimated useful lives:

	Years
Buildings	15–60
Equipment	3–12
Capital leases	Term of lease

Property and equipment, held for disposal, represents non-operating properties carried at the lower of cost less accumulated depreciation or estimated realizable value.

Note to the Financial Statements

Note 2—Property and Equipment

Major classes of property and equipment consist of the following:

	February 28,	
	1982	**1981**
Land	$ 1,941,549	$ 1,096,509
Buildings	20,305,571	17,707,384
Equipment	27,014,198	21,779,206
	49,261,318	40,583,099
Less accumulated depreciation and amortization	24,594,505	19,687,795
Net property and equipment	$24,666,813	$20,895,304

Property and equipment used in the Company's operations or that is held for disposal includes the following amounts for leases which have been capitalized:

	February 28,	
	1982	**1981**
Land	$ 459,481	$ 459,481
Buildings	10,238,303	10,149,629
Equipment	3,444,813	3,999,254
	14,142,597	14,608,364
Less accumulated amortization	5,095,181	5,051,609
Totals	$ 9,047,416	$ 9,556,755

Substantially all of the property and equipment was pledged to collateralize first mortgage notes and other indebtedness (see Notes 4 and 10).

During the year ended February 28, 1981, the Company ceased operations in certain food processing plants and cold storage warehouses and transferred the $3,984,043 net book value of these facilities to property and equipment, held for disposal. Subsequently, in fiscal 1982, the Company placed certain of these facilities back into operation for use in its frozen vegetable and public cold storage operations. Accordingly, the net book value of $3,465,123 has been reclassified to property and equipment.

SOURCE: United Foods, Inc., 1982 Annual Report.

Asset categories that are closely related are frequently combined to avoid unnecessary detail in the balance sheet. For example, land may be combined with land improvements or other assets closely related to land. Buildings may be combined with improvements, equipment, or other assets closely related to buildings.

In recent years straight-line depreciation has been the most widely used method in financial reporting. *Accounting Trends and Techniques* indicates than in a study of six hundred companies during 1978–1981, 72%–74% were using straight-line depreciation and 20%–22% were using an accelerated depreciation method.[5] Other methods were used less frequently, and some companies used one method for one class of assets and another method for another class of assets. Thus, the number of depreciation methods exceeds the number of companies reporting. For example, in 1981 the 600 companies reporting used straight-line depreciation in 565 instances, accelerated depreciation in 150 instances, and units of production in 52 instances, a total of 767. Declining-balance depreciation is the most widely used acceleration method.[6]

---

[5]*Accounting Trends and Techniques* (New York: AICPA, 1982), p. 249.
[6]*Accounting Trends and Techniques*, p. 249.

CHANGES IN ESTIMATES AND CORRECTIONS OF ERRORS

Companies often have to change estimates incorporated in depreciation methods. They may also have to correct errors in past historical cost and depreciation amounts.

Changes in Estimates

Matching

Historical Cost

As we have seen in applying the concepts of depreciation and depletion, matching revenues and expenses requires several estimates. Determination of the asset's historical cost may also involve some estimates, assumptions, and allocations. Furthermore, estimates of useful life—in terms of either time or service quantities—must be made, as well as estimates of the residual value of the asset.

These estimates are made when the asset is placed into service, and they are based on information available at that time. As conditions change, however, estimates of useful lives may need to be either lengthened or shortened. Likewise, estimates of salvage value may also require revision either upward or downward. Management has a responsibility to continuously monitor its operations and to periodically reevaluate the estimates used in recognizing depreciation and depletion.

A change in estimated life or salvage value is not a correction of an error if the estimates were originally made in good faith and were based on the best information available at the time. The changes simply verify the fact that as time passes and more information becomes available, more accurate estimates are possible.

Changes in estimates of useful lives and salvage values should be treated on a **prospective basis,** according to *APB Opinion No. 20.*[7] This means that the effect of the change is allocated to the current period (i.e., the period in which the change is made) and future periods. No recognition is made of the depreciation or depletion that would have been recognized in the past if new estimates had been in effect.

To illustrate the change in depreciation estimates, we shall assume that Rodriguez Company acquired machinery in early 1981 for $275,000. The machinery was expected to have a five-year life and a salvage value of $25,000. Depreciation recognized in 1981, 1982, and 1983 was based on these estimates. In 1984, management determines that the machine can be used five more years (including 1984), at the end of which it will have an approximate $5,000 salvage value.

Depreciation for 1984 and the remaining years in the asset's life is $24,000:

Cost	$275,000
Depreciation, 1981–1983	
[($275,000 − $25,000)/5 years] × 3 years	(150,000)
Book value at beginning of 1984	125,000
Expected salvage value, end of 1988	(5,000)
Depreciation base, 1984–1988	$120,000
Depreciation expense, 1984–1988	
($120,000/5 years)	$ 24,000

The book value ($125,000) at the time of the change in estimate is used as the cost figure in the revised depreciation computation, and the depreciation method is applied as usual. At the end of 1988 the book value of the asset will be $5,000, the expected salvage value:

$$\$275,000 - [(\$50,000 \times 3 \text{ years}) + (\$24,000 \times 5 \text{ years})] = \$5,000$$

The same basic process is followed with other depreciation methods if either the useful life or the salvage value is changed.

---

[7]*APB Opinion No. 20,* "Accounting Changes," 1971, par. 31.

Corrections of Errors

Corrections of past errors in recording assets, depreciation, and depletion are treated as **prior-period adjustments** in accordance with *FASB Statement of Financial Accounting Standards No. 16.*[8] The impact of these errors on the financial statements of the period in which they are discovered is reflected by adjustments in the appropriate accounts of the current period before the financial statements are prepared. Errors involving property, plant, and equipment frequently result from the expensing of asset costs that should have been capitalized and from the incorrect application of depreciation methods.

We illustrate the correction of plant-asset and depreciation errors by assuming that Lett Singer Corporation acquired equipment in 1982 that was expected to be used for 10 years. The asset cost $150,000 and was expected to have a $10,000 salvage value at the end of its 10-year life. During the 1985 audit it was discovered that the equipment had been incorrectly expensed in 1982. Correct depreciation policy would have called for the use of the straight-line method of depreciation with a half-year depreciation taken in the first and last years of the asset's life.

Ignoring any income tax effects of the error, we can make the following analysis to determine the appropriate corrections to the accounts and the proper depreciation expense for 1985:

Cost of equipment		$150,000
Depreciation expense		
1982: [($150,000 − $10,000)/10]½ = $ 7,000		
1983: [($150,000 − $10,000)/10] = $14,000		
1984: [($150,000 − $10,000)/10] = $14,000	(35,000)	
Book value at beginning of 1985	115,000	
Depreciation expense		
1985: [($150,000 − $10,000)/10]	(14,000)	
Book value at end of 1985	$101,000	

The entry required to correct the failure to record the asset and related depreciation properly in previous years is as follows:

Equipment	150,000	
Accumulated Depreciation		35,000
Retained Earnings		
(or Prior Period Adjustment)		115,000

The credit to retained earnings represents the net effect of the $150,000 understatement of income resulting from the expensing of the asset in 1982, less the $35,000 overstatement to income in 1982, 1983, and 1984 resulting from the failure to record depreciation ($7,000 + $14,000 + $14,000).[9] The entry to record depreciation for 1985 is made as if the asset and related depreciation had been properly recorded in the past:

Depreciation Expense	14,000	
Accumulated Depreciation		14,000

---

[8]*FASB Statement of Financial Accounting Standards No. 16,* "Prior Period Adjustments," 1977, par. 11.
[9]The income tax consequences of the correction are not considered in this illustration. As we have seen in Chapter 4, the correction should be presented in the financial statements on a net-of-tax basis. The subject of corrections of errors, including the income tax implications, is covered more extensively in Chapters 18 and 19 of this text.

The prior period adjustment is presented on the statement of retained earnings as a restatement of the beginning balance, as discussed in Chapter 4. In the Lett Singer case the adjustment of the beginning retained earnings of 1985 would be $115,000, the amount credited to retained earnings in the entry above.

The location of errors and the analysis required to determine the impact of errors on the financial statements may be quite complicated, particularly if comparative financial statements are presented. Companies may also change accounting methods (e.g., depreciation method), a subject not covered at this point. Accounting changes and correction of errors are covered more extensively in Chapter 19.

KEY POINTS

1. Depreciation is the process of allocating the cost of property, plant, and equipment as an expense in a systematic and rational manner to those periods expected to benefit from the use of the asset.

2. Depreciation is a necessary part of applying the matching principle to long-lived assets that are used in the production of revenue.

3. Several accounting methods are used to allocate the historical cost of individual plant assets to the periods that benefit from the use of those assets. Those methods can be divided into methods based on time and those based on activity level.

4. Special accounting policies must be adopted to handle situations in which plant assets are used for less than a complete accounting period. Consistency is an important accounting principle in handling this special accounting problem.

5. Group-depreciation systems are sometimes used to solve the problem of depreciating large numbers of small assets and assets that are combined and depreciated as a composite asset.

6. Natural resources are a special type of property, plant, and equipment. The allocation of the historical cost of natural resources is called depletion and is similar to depreciation of other plant assets.

7. Authoritative accounting pronouncements require several specific items of information to be disclosed in the financial statements concerning plant assets. These include the balances in major classes of depreciable assets, accumulated depreciation, depreciation expense, and a general description of the depreciation methods used.

8. Changes in estimates required to recognize depreciation and depletion are handled on a prospective basis and, therefore, recognized in the period of the change and in future periods.

9. Corrections of errors in accounting for plant assets, depreciation, and depletion are treated as prior period adjustments. Previously issued financial statements are restated, and retained earnings are corrected for the past errors.

APPENDIX A ALTERNATIVE DEPRECIATION METHODS

Several alternatives to the widely used depreciation methods presented in Chapter 12 are available. While these methods are not as widely used in practice, they do represent alternatives that meet the criteria of being both systematic and rational. Three of these alternatives are presented here: the fixed percentage on book-value method, the annuity method, and the sinking-fund method.

To illustrate these methods, Asset 147 is again used. For your convenience, we repeat the necessary infor-

mation as follows:

Asset 147

Cost	$12,000
Estimated salvage value	$2,000
Estimated life in years	5

An assumed interest rate of 10% is used for the annuity and sinking-fund methods.

FIXED PERCENTAGE ON BOOK-VALUE METHOD

The **fixed percentage on book-value method** works much like the declining-balance method, except the method of computing the rate used to depreciate the asset is different. Under this method the annual depreciation rate is determined as follows:

$$\text{Fixed percentage rate} = 1 - \sqrt[n]{\frac{\text{Salvage value}}{\text{Cost}}}$$

In the calculation, n equals the life of the asset in years. If no expected salvage value exists for the asset, some nominal amount must be used so that a rate can be computed. The computed rate is applied annually to the declining book value of the asset, leaving an unamortized cost at the end of the life of the asset exactly equal to the estimated salvage value.

Applying these concepts to Asset 147, we compute the depreciation rate, which equals 30.12%:

$$\text{Fixed percentage rate, Asset 147} = 1 - \sqrt[5]{\frac{2,000}{12,000}}$$
$$= 30.12\%$$

Depreciation expense for Years 1 through 5 are then computed as follows:

$D_1 = 30.12\%\ (\$12,000) = \$3,614$
$D_2 = 30.12\%\ (\$12,000 - \$3,614) = \$2,526$
$D_3 = 30.12\%\ [\$12,000 - (\$3,614 + \$2,526)] = \$1,765$
$D_4 = 30.12\%\ [\$12,000 - (\$3,614 + \$2,526 + \$1,765)] = \$1,233$
$D_5 = 30.12\%\ [\$12,000 - (\$3,614 + \$2,526 + \$1,765 + \$1,233)] = \$862$

The fixed percentage on book-value method is not widely used for several reasons: First, as you can see in the example, the method involves a complex computation of the depreciation rate. Second, prior to 1981 companies preferred to use the double-declining balance method for income tax purposes because it provided the maximum amount of depreciation that could be deducted in determining the company's income tax liability. Since the results of the double-declining balance method and the fixed percentage on book-value method are similar, the former was more widely used. Also, unusually low salvage values relative to the assets'

costs result in very large fixed percentage rates and extreme acceleration of depreciation expenses.

ANNUITY METHOD

The **annuity method** of depreciation is based on the assumption that in acquiring property, plant, and equipment, an enterprise makes an investment much like an annuity (i.e., an investment yielding a fixed return for a stated period of time). Periodic returns on the investment are separated into two elements: a return of the principal amount and an interest revenue on the investment. Throughout the life of the asset, the interest revenue diminishes as the return of the principal reduces the investment.

Under the annuity method, periodic depreciation is computed by using the equation stated below, where PV is equal to the present value of 1 at the assumed rate for the estimated life of the asset and $PVOA$ is equal to the present value of an ordinary annuity of 1 at the assumed rate for the estimated life of the asset:

$$D = \frac{\text{Cost} - (\text{Salvage value} \times PV)}{PVOA}$$

Applying this equation to Asset 147 at an assumed 10% interest rate, we determine depreciation as $2,838:

$$D_1 = \frac{\$12,000 - (\$2,000 \times .62092)}{3.79079}$$
$$= \$2,838$$

Depreciation is recognized at the constant amount of $2,838 each year. Interest revenue is recognized each year in an amount equal to the book value of the asset times the appropriate interest rate, and Accumulated Depreciation is credited for the difference between the depreciation expense ($2,838) and the interest revenue. Since interest revenue declines each year, the credit to Accumulated Depreciation increases each year.

The application of these concepts to Asset 147 is illustrated in Exhibit 12–10.

The primary limitation with the annuity method, in addition to judgment involved in selecting an appropriate interest rate, is that total depreciation expense recognized over the life of the asset exceeds the cost of the asset by the amount of the interest revenue recognized. In the case of Asset 147 this relationship is as follows:

Total depreciation expense recognized
($2,838 × 5 years) $14,190
Total interest revenue recognized
($1,200 + $1,036 + $856 + $658
+ $440)   (4,190)
Cost less estimated salvage value of
Asset 147 $10,000

Also, the net effect on income is an *increasing* charge, since depreciation expense is constant while interest revenue declines over time. These problems of the amount and pattern of depreciation recognition raise questions as to the appropriateness of the method under current generally accepted accounting principles.

SINKING-FUND METHOD

The **sinking-fund method** is a variation of the annuity method, wherein interest revenue and depreciation expense are not recognized as separate elements in the determination of income during the life of the asset. The computations under the sinking-fund method are the same as those for the annuity method.

Applying the sinking-fund method to Asset 147, we find that the depreciation expense is the difference between the $2,838 depreciation cost and the interest revenue each year. This is the same as the credit to the accumulated depreciation column of Exhibit 12–10 and is not recomputed here.

The concept of establishing a sinking fund to provide for the replacement of property, plant, and equipment is rarely applied in practice. However, the existence of the fund is not a prerequisite to the use of the depreciation method derived from this concept. If a fund is established, cash is provided in an amount equal to the cost of the asset, less the estimated salvage value at the end of the asset's life. For an asset with a relatively long life in a period of rising prices, it is unlikely that the amount would be sufficient to replace the asset.

The sinking-fund method poses some of the same questions as does the annuity method, for example, in regard to an increasing depreciation charge during the life of the asset and the appropriate interest rate for applying the method.

EXHIBIT 12–10
Depreciation Schedule for Asset 147
Annuity Method

End of Year	Depreciation Entry			Balance: Accumulated Depreciation	Book Value
	Dr.: Depreciation Expense	Cr.: Interest Revenue	Cr.: Accumulated Depreciation		
—	—	—	—	—	$12,000
1	$2,838	$1,200	$ 1,638	$ 1,638	10,362
2	2,838	1,036	1,802	3,440	8,560
3	2,838	856	1,982	5,422	6,578
4	2,838	658	2,180	7,602	4,398
5	2,838	440	2,398	10,000	2,000

Computations:
Interest revenue is the book value of the asset multiplied by the interest rate.

Example—Year 1: $12,000 × 10% = $1,200
         Year 2: ($12,000 − $1,638) × 10% = $1,036

The credit to Accumulated Depreciation is the difference between the Depreciation Expense and the Interest Revenue.

Example—Year 1: $2,838 − $1,200 = $1,638
         Year 2: $2,838 − $1,036 = $1,802

APPENDIX **B** CASUALTY INSURANCE

To reduce the risk of financial loss due to casualties (e.g., from fires, thefts, floods, or accidents), business enterprises commonly acquire **casualty insurance.** The purpose of this insurance is to shift to an insurance company the burden of a potential loss from such unexpected occurrences. The **face value** of the insurance policy is the largest amount that the insurance company may be required to pay if a loss occurs. Payments made to the insurance company are called **premiums** and are paid in advance of the period of insurance coverage. Thus, payments initially represent prepaid expenses when they are made. Since premiums are typically lower when insurance contracts provide for coverage over longer periods of time (i.e., more than one year) and payment for the entire period may be made in advance, the current portion of the prepayments appears in the balance sheet as a current asset and the remainder as a noncurrent asset (i.e., other asset or deferred charge).

We are accustomed to thinking in terms of historical cost or book value of property, plant, and equipment. For insurance purposes, however, the relevant dollar measurement of these assets is **fair market value.** The amount recoverable from an insurance company is the lesser of the loss based on fair market value or the face value of the insurance policy, unless the policy includes a coinsurance clause, which is discussed in the next section. The recorded basis of the asset—the historical cost or book value—is *not* the basis for determining the insurance reimbursement and is used only to determine the book gain or loss resulting from the asset loss and related insurance reimbursement.

Common complexities in accounting for casualty insurance are coinsurance and coverage by multiple insurance policies. These topics are discussed in the following sections, after which the accounting process for recording an insured casualty loss is illustrated.

COINSURANCE

Casualty insurance policies frequently contain **coinsurance requirements** to encourage companies to insure assets at amounts based on their fair market values. Companies realize that many casualties result in only partial destruction of plant assets. In the absence of coinsurance requirements, companies are sometimes inclined to insure assets at substantially less than their fair market values, because they would receive full reimbursement for any losses up to the face amounts of the insurance policies.

The coinsurance requirement is stated as a percentage of fair market value of the insured asset and requires the property to be insured to at least the percentage indicated or the insured must share in any loss that occurs. For example, if an asset with a fair market value of $100,000 is insured under a policy including an 80% coinsurance requirement, the asset must be insured for at least $80,000 ($100,000 × 80%) to collect the full amount of any loss from the insurance company. The amount paid, however, will not exceed the face value of the insurance policy in any case.

The amount recoverable under a coinsurance situation is computed by multiplying the loss incurred (based on fair market value at the time of the casualty) by the percentage of face value of the policy to the coinsurance requirement in dollars. The amount actually reimbursed is the smallest of three amounts: the amount recoverable under the coinsurance requirements, the amount of the loss, or the face value of the policy. These relationships are presented in the following diagram:

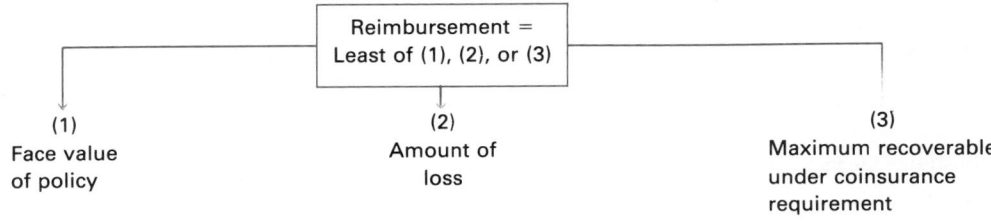

To illustrate, we assume that Stevens Company has insurance for several of its assets under separate insurance policies containing coinsurance requirements. These policies are described below, including losses incurred from casualties on each asset:

	Asset A	Asset B	Asset C
Fair market value of asset	$200,000	$250,000	$300,000
Face value of policy	$180,000	$150,000	$250,000
Coinsurance requirement	90%	70%	80%
Amount of loss from casualty (based on fair market value)	$150,000	$120,000	$290,000

For Asset A, the coinsurance requirement is met since the $180,000 face value of the policy is exactly equal to the coinsurance requirement ($200,000 × 90%). Thus, the computation of the amount recoverable under the coinsurance requirement is not necessary and the insurance company will pay $150,000, the smaller of the face value of the policy ($180,000) or the amount of the loss ($150,000).

For Asset B the coinsurance requirement is not met since the $150,000 face value of the policy is less than the coinsurance requirement of $175,000 ($250,000 × 70%). The maximum amount recoverable is computed as follows:

$$\frac{\$150,000}{\$250,000 \times 70\%} \times \$120,000 = \$102,857$$

Since the policy will pay the least of the face value of the policy ($150,000), the amount of the loss ($120,000), or the amount recoverable under the coinsurance requirement ($102,857), only $102,857 will be recovered. The insured party will share in any loss, with the insurance company paying 85.7% of the loss ($102,857/$120,000) and the insured paying 14.3% of the loss [($120,000 − $102,857)/$120,000]. The maximum amount that the insurance company would pay under *any* circumstances is the $150,000 face value of the policy.

For Asset C the coinsurance requirement is met, because the $250,000 face value of the policy is greater than the coinsurance requirement of $240,000 ($300,000 × 80%). Thus, the computation of the amount recoverable is not necessary and the insurance company will pay the $250,000 face value of the policy since it is less than the $290,000 loss. The case of Asset C illustrates the fact that the full amount of the loss will

not necessarily be paid by the insurance company, even if a coinsurance requirement is met, because the amount reimbursed is limited to the face value of the policy. If the loss exceeds the face value of the policy, the insured party must cover the excess.

COVERAGE BY MULTIPLE INSURANCE POLICIES

If more than one insurance policy covers the same property, the amount reimbursable under each policy is determined in essentially the same way as described in the previous section. Each policy will pay the *least* of the following: (1) the face value of the policy; (2) an allocated portion of the loss; or (3) the maximum recoverable under a coinsurance requirement.

The allocated portion of the loss is based on the face value of the policies. For example, if a company has a $100,000 policy on a piece of property and another policy of $50,000 on the same property, the first policy would be allocated two-thirds ($100,000/ $150,000) of any loss and the second policy would be allocated one-third ($50,000/$150,000) of the loss. The maximum recoverable under a coinsurance requirement is computed as illustrated in the previous section, with the face value of the individual policy used in the numerator of the computation.

ACCOUNTING FOR CASUALTIES

The following steps summarize the process of accounting for a casualty:

1. Depreciation expense is recognized to the date of the casualty; other adjustments, such as the expiration of prepaid insurance, are made.
2. A Casualty account is established to serve as a clearing account for amounts relative to the casualty.
3. The Casualty account is debited and credited for appropriate amounts, as follows:
   Debits: Book value of the asset(s) destroyed or damaged.

Adjustments to prepaid insurance resulting from the reduction in insurance coverage for the remainder of the period for which premiums have been paid.

Other costs incidental to the settlement.

Credits: Amounts recoverable from insurance companies.

Amounts recoverable from the salvage of damaged assets.

4. The Casualty account is closed into the Income Summary as a single amount representing the net loss or gain on the casualty and related insurance settlement.

Since the amounts relative to the casualty and related insurance settlement become available over an extended period of time, the Casualty account is used temporarily to house the various components as they become available. A debit balance in the account represents a loss, and a credit balance represents a gain. The latter results when insurance is based on the fair market value of assets and the final settlement from the insurance company exceeds the book value of the lost asset(s) and other costs related to the settlement.

Amounts recoverable from the insurance company are classified as current assets when collection is anticipated in the near future. The loss or gain resulting from the closing of the Casualty account is presented as an extraordinary item in the income statement if it is both unusual in nature and infrequent in occurrence. If the item is not considered infrequent in occurrence, and thus not an extraordinary item, it should be presented as a separate item in the income statement on the grounds that it is unusual in nature.

To illustrate the process of recording a casualty, we shall assume that Murray Manufacturing Company, a calendar-year corporation, has a building that was damaged by fire on May 1, 1984. Specific information on the building and the fire loss are as follows:

Cost of building	$450,000	
Accumulated depreciation through December 31, 1983	125,000	$325,000
Fair value of building at May 1, 1984		$700,000
Face value of insurance policy		$500,000
Amount of fire loss (based on fair value)		$350,000
Coinsurance requirement		80%
Prepaid insurance at January 1, 1984		$1,800

Depreciation expense is computed on a monthly basis at an annual rate of $45,000. The prepaid insurance at January 1 represents the premium for the calendar year 1984 that was paid in advance in late 1983. The insurance policy continues in effect after the loss for the remainder of 1984 in an amount adjusted forward for the payment for the fire loss.

The building is determined to have been a 50% loss, based on the relationship of the fire loss to the fair value of the building ($350,000/$700,000). The following general journal entries are required to record the casualty if we assume that depreciation expense is computed to the nearest full month.

To Adjust Accounts to the Date of the Fire Loss

Depreciation Expense	15,000	
Accumulated Depreciation		15,000
[4 months × ($45,000/12) = $15,000]		
Insurance Expense	600	
Prepaid Insurance		600
(4/12 × $1,800 = $600)		

To Close Accounts to Casualty Account

Casualty ($225,000 − $70,000)	155,000	
Accumulated Depreciation	70,000	
[½ ($125,000 + $15,000)]		
Building (½ × $450,000)		225,000
Casualty	750	
Prepaid Insurance		750
[($312,500/$500,000) × $1,200 = $750]		

| Receivable from Insurance Company | 312,500 | |
| Casualty | | 312,500 |

$$\left[\frac{\$500,000}{\$700,000 \times 80\%} \times \$350,000 = \$312,500 \right]$$

To Close Casualty to Income Summary

Casualty	156,750	
Income Summary		156,750
($155,000 + $750 − $312,500)		

The entry for $750 to reduce prepaid insurance and adjust the Casualty account is necessary because the insurance in effect after the payment of $312,500 is reduced to $187,500 ($500,000 − $312,500). The Casualty is charged with a pro-rata share of the premium related to the remainder of the year. The balance in the Prepaid Insurance account is $450 ($1,200 − $750), representing the premium related to insurance coverage of $187,500 for the remainder of 1984.

In this situation, the Casualty account had a credit balance, indicating that the company had a gain rather than a loss. This was true because the company had insured its property in terms of its replacement cost, not the amortized historical cost that is included in the balance sheet as an asset. When this gain is presented in the income statement, it should be described as "proceeds from insurance in excess of book value of building destroyed by fire" or another appropriate title.

QUESTIONS

12–1 What is the primary theoretical justification for recognizing the cost of property, plant, and equipment as an expense over their estimated useful lives?

12–2 Identify the specific elements in the definition of the term "depreciation."

12–3 Under the matching principle, what distortion in income would take place if plant assets were written off as expenses when they were acquired rather than during their estimated useful lives through depreciation?

12–4 Distinguish between "physical" and "functional" factors as they relate to the decline in usefulness of property, plant, and equipment.

12–5 Identify the specific estimates that are required in applying the widely used methods of depreciation.

12–6 What is the primary justification for the use of the straight-line method of depreciation?

12–7 What are primary justifications for the use of accelerated depreciation methods?

12–8 For an asset with a relatively long life, computing the denominator base for the sum-of-the-years'-digits depreciation method can be burdensome if done by adding the digits from zero to the number of years in the asset's life. Apply the shortcut method of determining the denominator for an asset with an estimated useful life of 18 years.

12–9 The double-declining balance depreciation rate can be computed by dividing the dollar amount of straight-line depreciation by the cost less the estimated salvage value of the asset and then doubling the resulting rate. How can the same rate be computed without using dollar amounts of depreciation?

12–10 What has been the primary impetus behind the use of accelerated depreciation methods?

12–11 What justification exists for the use of depreciation methods based on productive output or service quantities?

12–12 Under all depreciation methods, the book value of a plant asset declines through the life of the asset. What does this declining book value represent?

12–13 When a plant asset is acquired at a time other than the beginning or ending of a year, how should depreciation be handled for the first and last financial reporting periods during which the asset is used?

12–14 What is the basic justification for group depreciation systems in which numerous assets are depreciated as a single asset?

12–15 Describe the amount that represents the debit to depreciation expense in each of the following group-depreciation methods:

[a] Inventory system
[b] Retirement system
[c] Replacement system
[d] Group and composite systems

12–16 What is depletion and how is it different from or similar to depreciation?

12–17 What is a change in an accounting estimate and how should such changes be treated in the financial statements of the period of change?

12–18 If an accountant determines in 1985 that a depreciable asset with a 10-year life was incorrectly treated as an expense in 1982, what accounting treatment is appropriate in 1985 and future years?

12–19 (Appendix B) What is coinsurance and how does it affect the amount that a company will receive from the insurer in the event of a loss?

12–20 (Appendix A) Which of the following depreciation methods does *not* result in decreasing charges?

[a] Double-declining balance.
[b] Fixed percentage on book value.
[c] Sinking fund.
[d] Sum-of-the-years'-digits.

12–21 Property, plant, and equipment are conventionally presented in the balance sheet at which of the following amounts?

[a] Replacement cost less accumulated depreciation.
[b] Historical cost less salvage value.
[c] Original cost adjusted for general price-level changes.
[d] Acquisition cost less depreciated portion thereof.

(AICPA adapted)

12–22 As generally used in accounting, which statement(s) applies (apply) to depreciation?

[a] It is a process of asset valuation for balance sheet purposes.
[b] It applies only to long-lived intangible assets.
[c] It is used to indicate a decline in market value of a long-lived asset.
[d] It is an accounting process that allocates long-lived asset cost to accounting periods.

(AICPA adapted)

12–23 Which of the following statements is the assumption on which straight-line depreciation is based?

[a] The operating efficiency of the asset decreases in later years.
[b] Service value declines as a function of time rather than use.
[c] Service value declines as a function of obsolescence rather than time.
[d] Physical wear and tear are more important than economic obsolescence.

(AICPA adapted)

12–24 A graph is set up with "depreciation expense" on the vertical axis and the years listed along the horizontal axis. Assuming linear relationships, how would the graphs for straight-line and sum-of-the-years'-digits depreciation, respectively, be drawn?

[a] Vertically and sloping down to the right.
[b] Vertically and sloping up to the right.
[c] Horizontally and sloping down to the right.
[d] Horizontally and sloping up to the right.

(AICPA adapted)

CASES

C12–1 Depreciation continues to be one of the most controversial, difficult, and important problem areas in accounting.

Instructions

[a] [1] Explain the conventional concept of depreciation accounting.
     [2] Discuss its conceptual merit with respect to (a) the value of the asset, (b) the charge(s) to expense, and (c) the discretion of management in selecting the method.
[b] [1] Explain the factors that should be considered when using depreciation to determine how the value of a newly acquired computer system should be assigned to expense for financial reporting purposes. Income tax considerations should be ignored.
     [2] What depreciation methods might be used for the computer system?

(AICPA adapted)

C12–2 Conco Corporation sells and erects "shell houses." These are frame structures that are completely finished on the outside but are unfinished on the inside except for flooring, partition studding, and ceiling joists. Shell houses are sold chiefly to customers who are handy with tools and who have time to do the interior wiring, plumbing, wall finishing, and other work necessary to complete the houses.

Conco buys shell houses from a manufacturer in unassembled packages consisting of all lumber, roofing, doors, windows, and similar materials. Upon commencing operations in a new area, Conco buys or leases land for its local warehouse, field office, and display houses. Sample display houses are erected for $3,000 to $7,000. The unassembled packages constitute the majority of the expense; erection is a short, low-cost operation. Sample models are torn down or altered every three to seven years. Sample display houses have little salvage value because dismantling and moving costs amount to nearly as much as the cost of an unassembled package.

Instructions

[a] A choice must be made between (1) expensing the costs of sample display houses in the period in which the expenditure is made and (2) spreading the costs over more than one period. Discuss the advantages of each method.
[b] Would it be preferable to amortize the cost of display houses on the basis of (1) the passage of time or (2) the number of shell houses sold? Explain.

(AICPA adapted)

C12–3 Mano Company manufactures electrical appliances, most of which are used in homes. Company engineers have designed a new type of blender which, through the use of a few attachments, will perform more functions than any blender currently on the market. Demand for the new blender can be projected with reasonable probability. In order to make the blenders, Mano needs a special machine which is not available from outside sources. The company has decided to make such a machine in its own plant.

Instructions

[a] Mano's plant may be operating at capacity or below capacity. Compare and contrast the problems in determining the cost to be assigned to the machine at these different levels of operations.
[b] [1] Discuss the effect of projected demand in units for the new blender (which may be steady, decreasing, or increasing) on the determination of a depreciation method for the machine.
[2] What other factors should be considered in determining the depreciation method? Ignore income tax considerations.

(AICPA adapted)

C12–4 The following questions concern accounting for property, plant, and equipment.
[a] Define depreciation.
[b] Widely used depreciation methods can be categorized into three basic types: straight-line, accelerated, and activity-based (service quantity and units of output). Describe the situations in which each type is most appropriate.
[c] Identify the basic principles used in accounting for property, plant, and equipment. Indicate how each concept may affect specific accounting procedures.

C12–5 Len's Manufacturing Company was organized January 1, 1983. During 1983 it has used in its reports to management the straight-line method of depreciating its plant assets.

On November 8 you meet with Len's officers to discuss the depreciation method to be used for income tax and stockholder reporting. Len's president has suggested a new method, which he feels is more suitable than the straight-line method for the period of rapid expansion of production and capacity that he foresees. Below, the proposed method is applied to a fixed asset with an original cost of $32,000, an estimated useful life of five years, and an estimated salvage value of $2,000.

The president favors the new method because he has heard that
[1] It will increase the funds recovered during the years near the end of the assets' useful lives, when maintenance and replacement disbursements will be high.
[2] It will result in increased write-offs in later years and thereby reduce taxes.

Year	Years of Life Used	Fraction Rate	Depreciation Expense	Accumulated Depreciation at Year-End	Book Value at Year-End
1	1	1/15	$ 2,000	$ 2,000	$30,000
2	2	2/15	4,000	6,000	26,000
3	3	3/15	6,000	12,000	20,000
4	4	4/15	8,000	20,000	12,000
5	5	5/15	10,000	30,000	2,000

Instructions

[a] What is the purpose of accounting for depreciation?

[b] Is the president's proposal within the scope of generally accepted accounting principles? Discuss the circumstances under which the method would be reasonable and those under which it would not be reasonable.

[c] The president asks your advice:

[1] Do depreciation charges recover or create funds? Explain.

[2] Assume that the IRS will accept the proposed depreciation method in this particular case. If the method were used for stockholder and tax reporting purposes, how would it affect the availability of funds generated by operations?

(AICPA adapted)

EXERCISES

E12–1 Raleigh Company has acquired a new machine costing $125,000. The machine is expected to have a $25,000 residual value at the end of its six-year life. Management estimates that the machine will provide 12,500 hours of productive service.

Instructions

Determine the first full year's depreciation, to the nearest dollar, under each of the following methods. The machine was used 2,100 hours during the year.
[a] Straight line
[b] Sum-of-the-years'-digits
[c] Double-declining balance
[d] Service hours

E12–2 The Newberry News acquired a delivery truck to distribute newspapers throughout the city of Newberry. The truck cost $9,800 and is expected to last approximately four years, during which it will be driven approximately 60,000 miles. The estimated salvage value of the truck is $1,300. The truck was driven 14,620 and 17,810 miles in its first two years.

Instructions

Determine annual depreciation for the first two years of the truck's life using each of the following methods:
[a] Straight line
[b] Service miles
[c] Sum-of-the-years'-digits
[d] Double-declining balance

E12–3 In January 1985, Action Corporation entered into a contract to acquire a new machine for its factory. The machine, which had a cash purchase price of $150,000, was paid for as follows:

Down payment	$ 15,000
Notes payable in ten equal monthly installments	120,000

500 shares of Action common stock with an agreed value of $50 per share	25,000
Total	$160,000

Action paid an additional $4,000 for installation. The machine has an estimated useful life of ten years and an estimated salvage value of $5,000.

Instructions

Determine the depreciation expense that Action should recognize for 1985 using each of the following methods:
[a] Straight line
[b] Sum-of-the-years'-digits
[c] Double-declining balance
[d] Units of output, if expected total output of the machine is 100,000 units and 12,250 units are produced in 1985.

(AICPA adapted)

E12–4 Miller Merchandising Company acquired equipment for $500,000 on April 8, 1983. The asset is expected to have a four-year life, and a salvage value of $60,000. Straight-line depreciation is to be used.

Instructions

[a] Compute depreciation to be recognized in 1983, 1984, 1985, 1986, and 1987 under each of the following *independent* fractional year policies:

[1] Depreciation recognized to nearest full month.

[2] Depreciation recognized to nearest full year.

[3] Half-year depreciation taken in the year of acquisition and in the year of disposal.

[4] Full-year depreciation taken in the year of acquisition and no depreciation taken in the year of disposal.

[b] If the asset had been acquired on November 26, 1983, instead of April 8, under which policies would

depreciation in 1983 and 1987 be different from that computed in [a]? Why?

E12–5 On January 1, 1984, Dan Company purchased a new machine for $4,000,000. The machine has an estimated useful life of eight years and an estimated salvage value of $400,000. Depreciation was computed using the sum-of-the-years'-digits method.

Instructions

[a] What amount should be shown on Dan's balance sheet on December 31, 1985, net of accumulated depreciation, for this machine?
[b] Assume the asset was acquired on August 11, 1984, rather than January 1. Compute the book value of the machine on December 31, 1984, and 1985, under each of the following *independent* fractional year policies:

[1] A half-year's depreciation taken in the years of acquisition and disposal.
[2] Depreciation computed to the nearest full month.

(AICPA adapted)

E12–6 The Building account of Tullahoma Taxi Company includes the following items on December 31, 1984:

Building

Contract price	175,000	Gain on sale of	
Options	7,000	old building	17,500
Repair and maintenance	12,000		

The building was acquired in early 1984 and all entries have been made since the acquisition. The options include $5,000 on the building acquired and $2,000 on a building which was not acquired. Repair and maintenance costs relate to routine activities occurring after the occupation of the building.

Instructions

[a] Prepare the entry (or entries) needed to correct the Building account on December 31, 1984, before the books are closed.
[b] Determine depreciation expense for 1984 using each of the following methods, assuming a 20-year life and $60,000 salvage value. A half-year depreciation is taken in the year of acquisition and the year of disposal.

[1] Straight line
[2] Sum-of-the-years'-digits
[3] Double-declining balance

E12–7 Samson Manufacturing Company, a calendar-year company, purchased a machine for $65,000 on January 1, 1983. On that day Samson incurred the following additional costs:

Loss on sale of old machinery	$1,000
Freight-in	500
Installation	2,000
Testing before regular operation	300

The estimated salvage value of the machine was $5,000. Samson estimated that the machine would have a useful life of 20 years, with depreciation being computed on the straight-line method. In January 1985 accessories costing $3,600 were added to the machine to reduce its operating costs. The accessories neither prolonged the machine's life nor provided salvage value.

Instructions

[a] Compute depreciation expense for 1983.
[b] Compute depreciation expense for 1985.

(AICPA adapted)

E12–8 On January 1, 1982, Kent Corporation purchased a machine for $50,000. Kent paid shipping expenses of $500 as well as installation costs of $1,200. The machine was estimated to have a useful life of ten years and a salvage value of $3,000. In January 1983, additions costing $3,600 were made in order to comply with pollution control ordinances. These additions neither prolonged the life of the machine nor provided salvage value.

Instructions

Prepare a schedule showing the components of book value for the machine at the end of years 1982 through 1985 under the straight-line method of depreciation.

(AICPA adapted)

E12–9 Carter Company acquired a used machine in an exchange for a similar machine from Darter Company. Just before the exchange, the book values of the respective assets were as follows:

	Cost	Accumulated Depreciation	Book Value
Carter Company	$55,000	$25,000	$30,000
Darter Company	47,500	22,500	25,000

Instructions

Prepare the journal entries to record the exchange and the first year's depreciation expense on the books of both companies in the following *independent* situations:

[a] No market value of either asset is available. The Carter Company uses straight-line depreciation with an eight-year life for the asset acquired. The Darter Company uses double-declining balance depreciation with a 10-year life for the asset acquired. No salvage value is expected from either asset.

[b] The asset relinquished by Carter Company is valued at $22,000. No value can be determined for the asset relinquished by Darter Company. The Carter Company uses straight-line depreciation with an eight-year life and a $2,000 salvage value on the asset acquired. The Darter Company uses sum-of-the-years'-digits depreciation with a six-year life and no salvage value on the asset acquired.

E12–10 Proctor Machine Company uses the inventory system to account for numerous small tools used by employees. Under this system depreciation is based on an inventory of tools on hand at the end of the year. Expenditures are charged to a Tools account throughout the year. The balance in the Tools account at the beginning of 1983 was $35,000. The following activity concerning small tools took place during 1983:

Acquisitions (at cost)	
Mar. 5	$17,200
Aug. 22	5,100
Sale of used tools (at salvage value)	
Dec. 1	4,600

The inventory of tools at the end of the year revealed that tools costing $28,800 were on hand and in use.

Instructions

[a] Prepare all general journal entries for activities related to small tools during 1983.

[b] Prepare the balance sheet and income statement for small tools for 1983.

E12–11 Des Moines Railroad Corporation has a balance in its Railroad Ties account of $1,790,000 on January 1, 1984. This balance represents a large number of items, each of which has a small dollar value. The company is continually replacing the ties as tracks are inspected and replaced. During 1984 the company installed new ties in three different geographical areas, as follows:

Date of Job Completion	Cost of New Ties Installed	Cost of Old Ties Replaced	Proceeds from Sale of Old Ties
Feb. 5	$265,000	$192,000	$17,000
May 17	350,000	—	—
Oct. 19	160,000	93,000	5,000

Instructions

[a] Prepare all journal entries for the above transactions using the following inventory methods:
  [1] Retirement method
  [2] Replacement method
[b] Prepare the balance sheet and income statement using both of the above methods for the year ended December 31, 1984.

E12–12 A schedule of machinery owned by Barker Manufacturing Company for its Assembly M is presented below:

	Total Cost	Estimated Salvage Value	Estimated Life in Years
Component M1	$440,000	$40,000	10
Component M2	280,000	20,000	5
Component M3	175,000	—	4

Barker computes depreciation by the straight-line method.

Instructions

[a] Compute the composite life of the machines (in years) and the average depreciation rate for the machines (as a percentage).
[b] Prepare the general journal entry to record depreciation on the machines as a group for one year.

E12–13 On January 2, 1983, Decker Company exchanged a business automobile for a new automobile.

The original cost of the old automobile was $7,000. It had an undepreciated cost of $3,200 and a market value of $4,000 at the time of the exchange. Decker paid an additional $4,400 cash for the new automobile, which had a list price of $8,600.

The accountant for Decker Company recorded the automobile at its list price of $8,600 on January 2, 1983. He recorded depreciation on the basis of miles driven, assuming a total of 50,000 miles with 12,200 miles driven in 1983. However, he failed to consider the $700 expected residual value after the 50,000-mile life.

Instructions

[a] At what amount should the new automobile have been recorded by Decker? Why?

[b] Assume that the accountant's errors are found in 1984 before depreciation has been recognized. Prepare the journal entries necessary to correct the accounts and to recognize depreciation for 1984 (14,700 miles were driven in 1984).

E12–14 Thornton Company acquired a used truck for $9,250 to be used in its delivery service. The following expenditures were made upon acquisition:

New tires	$350
Body repair and paint	175
Installation of special shelves	525
One-year insurance premium	450

It is expected that the truck will be of service for four years and will be driven a total of 50,000 miles. A $1,000 residual value is expected.

Instructions

[a] Determine the cost of the truck for financial accounting purposes.

[b] Determine the depreciation expense for the first and second years using each of the following methods:

[1] Straight line

[2] Service quantity—miles (The truck was driven 9,860 and 13,750 miles in the first and second years, respectively.)

E12–15 Challenge Corporation purchased machinery in early January of 1983 that has been depreciated by the straight-line method during 1983 and 1984. The machinery cost $78,200 and has an estimated salvage value of $8,000 at the end of its five-year life.

In 1985 Challenge reevaluated its plant assets and determined that this machinery would be useful for another seven years, including 1985. There will be no salvage value, however, at the end of this period.

Instructions

[a] What amount of depreciation was recorded in 1983 and in 1984?

[b] When the change in estimated useful life is made in 1985, what entry, if any, should be made to account for the difference between depreciation taken in previous years and that which will be taken in future years?

[c] Prepare the general journal entry to record depreciation expense for 1985.

E12–16 Flood Corporation purchased a machine on January 1, 1980, for $150,000. Upon acquisition, the machine had an estimated useful life of ten years with no salvage value. The machine is being depreciated on a straight-line basis. On January 1, 1985, as a result of Flood's experience with the machine, it was decided that the machine had an estimated useful life of 15 years from the date of purchase. This change in useful life is to be reflected in 1985 and future years.

Instructions

[a] Prepare the general journal entry to record depreciation for 1985.

[b] Independent of your answer to [a], assume that on January 1, 1985, Flood Corporation determines that it can extend the asset's life 10 years beyond that date only by investing an additional $15,000 in the asset. The company anticipates a residual value at the end of the revised life of $5,000. Prepare the journal entries required in 1985, including the recognition of depreciation for the year.

(AICPA adapted)

E12–17 In 1982 Florida Production Company bought a piece of machinery the cost of which was erroneously charged to Depreciation Expense in 1982. The company depreciates this class of assets by the double-declining balance method. One-half year's depreciation is taken in the year of acquisition and in the year of disposal. This particular machine cost $88,000 and is expected to have an $8,000 residual value at the end of eight years, at which time the company plans to dispose of the asset.

The error indicated above was discovered in 1984 as a result of the periodic evaluation of the estimated useful lives of all plant assets.

Instructions

Prepare the general journal entries to correct the accounts and to properly record Depreciation Expense for 1984.

E12–18 Gunther Company acquired a tract of land containing an extractable natural resource. The purchase contract requires Gunther to restore the land to a condition suitable for recreation after it has extracted the natural resource. Geological surveys estimate recoverable reserves of 4,000,000 tons and a land value of $1,000,000 after restoration. Relevant cost information follows:

Land	$9,000,000
Estimated restoration costs	1,200,000

Instructions

[a] What is the depletion charge per ton of the recoverable reserves?
[b] If the company extracts 550,000 tons in the first year and sells 510,000 tons, determine the following amounts:
   [1] Depletion expense.
   [2] Inventory cost of the recovered natural resource.

(AICPA adapted)

E12–19 Odell Corporation quarries limestone at two locations, crushes it, and sells it to be used in road building. The Internal Revenue Code provides for 5% depletion on such limestone. Quarry No. 1 is leased, and Odell is paying a royalty of $.01 per ton of limestone quarried. Quarry No. 2 is owned, Odell having paid $100,000 for the site; the Company estimates that the property can be sold for $30,000 after production ceases. Other data follow:

	Quarry No. 1	Quarry No. 2
Estimated total reserves (tons)	30,000,000	100,000,000
Tons quarried through Dec. 31, 1982	2,000,000	40,000,000
Tons quarried, 1983	800,000	1,380,000
Sales, 1983	$600,000	$1,000,000

Instructions

[a] 1983 depletion of Quarry No. 1 for financial reporting purposes is
   [1] $3,000
   [2] $8,000
   [3] $30,000
   [4] $29,600
   [5] None of the above
[b] 1983 depletion of Quarry No. 2 for financial reporting purposes is
   [1] $0
   [2] $1,380
   [3] $966
   [4] $50,000
   [5] None of the above
[c] Assume the same information except that a new engineering study performed early in 1983 indicated that as of January 1, 1983, 75,000,000 tons of limestone were available in Quarry No. 2. Depletion of Quarry No. 2 in 1983 for financial reporting purposes is
   [1] $772.80
   [2] $840
   [3] $0
   [4] $50,000
   [5] None of the above

(AICPA adapted)

E12–20 (Appendix B) Information about four independent cases concerning casualty insurance on equipment is presented below:

	Case A	Case B	Case C	Case D
Fair market value of equipment at date of fire	$75,000	$100,000	$120,000	$150,000
Amount of fire loss	65,000	80,000	70,000	120,000
Face value of insurance policy	50,000	90,000	75,000	110,000
Coinsurance requirement	None	80%	90%	70%

Instructions

[a] For each case, determine the amount which would be recoverable from the insurance company.

[b] Prepare the general journal entry to record the fire loss and insurance recovery for Case B. Assume that the equipment destroyed had originally cost $150,000 and had accumulated depreciation of $82,500. No adjustment to Prepaid Insurance is required.

PROBLEMS

P12-1 Concord Company acquired machinery for $575,000 in early January 1983. The machinery has an estimated life of five years, during which it is expected to produce 1,000,000 units of output. The machine has an estimated salvage value of $35,000.

Instructions

[a] Determine depreciation expense for the first two years of the asset's life using each of the following methods. The asset was used to produce 254,000 units in 1983 and 187,200 units in 1984.
 [1] Straight line
 [2] Sum-of-the-years'-digits
 [3] Productive output
 [4] Double-declining balance
[b] Prepare the balance sheet presentation of the machine for the December 31, 1984, financial statements under each of the methods in [a].

P12-2 Dexter, Inc., acquired heavy machinery at a cost of $125,000. In addition to the purchase price, $5,000 was paid for delivery of the machinery and $2,000 was paid for training of company personnel to operate the equipment. The machinery was expected to provide 8,000 machine hours of service for approximately five years, after which the machine can be sold for approximately $17,000. Actual machine operating hours during the first five years are as follows: 1,700, 2,200, 2,400, 1,600, and 500.

Instructions

Compute depreciation for each of the five years using the following depreciation methods:
[a] Straight line
[b] Service quantity—machine hours
[c] Sum-of-the-years'-digits
[d] Double-declining balance

P12-3   Arnold Production Company was involved in a series of transactions involving plant assets during 1983, its first year of operations. These transactions are summarized as follows:

Jan. 10 Machinery was acquired for $10,250 on account, terms 2/10, n/30.

  12   Freight-in of $250 on machinery acquired on Jan. 10 was paid. The machine was immediately put into service.

  18   The account related to the machinery acquired on Jan. 10 was paid.

Mar. 19 Inventory, fixtures, a building, and land were acquired for a single price of $520,000. The assets were appraised as follows:

Inventory	$150,000
Fixtures	70,000
Building	250,000
Land	100,000

May 1   Renovation costs of $50,000 on the building acquired on Mar. 19 were paid, and the fixtures, building, and land placed into service.

Nov. 1   A truck was acquired and immediately placed into service. The truck had a list price of $9,000 and was purchased by issuing an $8,200, 12%, two-year note. The 12% interest rate was typical for this type of transaction and is payable annually. The truck was driven 2,750 miles in 1983.

Dec. 5   A second machine was acquired, similar to that acquired on Jan. 10. (Both machines will be used.) The machine was acquired on account for $10,700, terms 2/10, n/30. Payment was not made until 1984.

  31   The executive group of Arnold Production Company decided that the following policies should be used to determine the periodic depreciation on plant assets:

Asset	Life	Salvage	Method	Fractional-Year Policy
Machinery	8 yrs.	None	Double-declining balance	Nearest full month
Fixtures	12 yrs.	$10,000	Sum-of-the-years'-digits	Half-year in years of acquisition and disposal
Building	25 yrs.	$60,000	Straight line	Half-year in years of acquisition and disposal
Truck	50,000 miles	$800	Service quantity—miles	None

Instructions

[a] Prepare general journal entries to record the transactions described above.
[b] Prepare all adjusting entries.
[c] Prepare the property, plant, and equipment section of the balance sheet for Arnold Production Company on December 31, 1983.
[d] Briefly describe the meaning of the book values you included in [c]. Explain their relationship to the current market value of the assets.

P12–4 Items [1] and [2] are based on the following information:

On July 1, 1984, Miller Mining, a calendar-year corporation, purchased the rights to a copper mine. Of the total purchase price, $2,800,000 was appropriately allocated to the copper. Estimated reserves of copper were 800,000 tons. Miller expects to extract and sell 10,000 tons of copper per month. Production began immediately. The selling price is $25 per ton. Miller uses percentage depletion (15%) for tax purposes. To aid production, Miller also purchased some new equipment on July 1, 1984. The equipment cost $76,000 and had an estimated useful life of eight years. However, after all the copper is removed from this mine, the equipment will be sold for an estimated $4,000.

[1] If sales and production meet expectations, what is Miller's depletion expense on this mine for financial accounting purposes for calendar year 1984?
   [a] $105,000
   [b] $210,000
   [c] $225,000
   [d] $420,000

[2] If sales and production meet expectations, what is Miller's depreciation expense on the new equipment for accounting purposes for calendar year 1984?
   [a] $4,500
   [b] $5,400
   [c] $9,000
   [d] $10,800

[3] Apex Company purchased a tooling machine in 1975 for $30,000. The machine was being depreciated by the straight-line method over an estimated useful life of twenty years, with no salvage value.

At the beginning of 1985, when the machine had been in use for ten years, the company paid $5,000 for an overhaul. As a result, the company estimated that the useful life of the machine would be extended five years.

What should be the depreciation expense recorded for the above machine in 1985?
   [a] $1,000
   [b] $1,333
   [c] $1,500
   [d] $1,833

[4] On July 1, 1984, Gusto Corporation purchased equipment for $22,000. The equipment has an estimated salvage value of $3,000 and is being depreciated by the double-declining balance method of depreciation over an estimated life of eight years. For the six months ended December 31, 1984, Gusto recorded one-half year's depreciation.

What should be the charge for depreciation (to the nearest dollar) of this equipment for the year ended December 31, 1985?
   [a] $4,158
   [b] $4,750
   [c] $4,813
   [d] $5,500

[5] A schedule of machinery owned by Lester Manufacturing Company is presented below:

	Total Cost	Estimated Salvage Value	Estimated Useful Life in Years
Machine A	$550,000	$50,000	20
Machine B	200,000	20,000	15
Machine C	40,000	—	5

Lester computes depreciation by the straight-line

method. Based on the information presented, the composite life of these assets (in years) should be:

[a] 13.3
[b] 16.0
[c] 18.0
[d] 19.8

[6] On January 2, 1982, Mogul Company acquired factory equipment with an estimated useful life of ten years and an estimated salvage value of $5,000. The depreciation applicable to this equipment was $24,000 for 1984, under the sum-of-the-years'-digits method. What was the acquisition cost of the equipment?

[a] $165,000
[b] $170,000
[c] $24,000
[d] $245,000

(AICPA adapted)

P12–5 Eagle Tool Company produces tools which are sold to a variety of manufacturing companies for use in their production operations. Many items of machinery are used to produce these tools. Presented below are the Machinery account and the related Depreciation account of Eagle Tool Company on January 1, 1984, the beginning of the company's fiscal year:

Machinery	$725,400
Accumulated depreciation	(276,100)
	$449,300

The company uses the straight-line method of depreciation. The machinery is expected to have a ten-year life and no salvage value. A half-year's deprecia-

Feb. 1   A machine acquired in 1982 for $10,500 was sold for $5,250.

15   New machinery costing $15,750 was acquired to replace the machine sold Feb. 1.

Mar. 25   Repair and maintenance costs of $5,500 were incurred.

Nov. 7   A machine costing $25,500, acquired in 1981, was traded for a similar machine. The acquired machine had a fair market value of $30,000. Eagle paid $10,000 as a part of the exchange.

11   Repair and maintenance costs of $6,215 were incurred.

Dec. 5   A machine acquired in 1981 for $7,250 was sold for $3,000.

10   New machinery costing $9,550 was acquired.

31   Depreciation for all machinery for 1984 was recorded.

Instructions

[a] Prepare general journal entries for all machine-related transactions for 1984, including the recognition of depreciation for the year. Provide supporting computations for your entries.

[b] Determine the balances in the Machinery and Accumulated Depreciation accounts for the December 31, 1984, balance sheet.

P12–6 Miller-Guy Company takes a full year's depreciation in the year of acquisition and no depreciation in the year of disposal for all long-lived assets.

At the beginning of 1985 the company had five assets, described below:

	Asset V	Asset W	Asset X	Asset Y	Asset Z
Historical cost	$75,000	$105,000	$27,800	$70,000	$100,000
Year of acquisition	1982	1985	1980	1981	1985
Depreciation method	Straight line	Double-declining balance	Units of production	Straight line	Sum-of-the-years'-digits
Estimated life	10 yrs.	5 yrs.	100,000 units	7 yrs.	5 yrs.
Estimated salvage value	None	$5,000	$3,800	None	$20,000

tion is taken in the years of acquisition and disposal. Depreciation is recorded on December 31 of each year.

The following transactions involving machinery took place during 1984:

Additional information about four of the assets has been collected to facilitate making the appropriate journal entries at the end of 1985.

Asset V—Management has determined that the asset will be useful for 15 years rather than the 10 years originally estimated. No salvage value is expected at the end of the asset's life.

Asset X—During 1985, $10,000 was spent to improve the asset, adding 50,000 units of output to its total expected capacity. Before 1985, 65,000 units had been produced; during 1985 the asset produced 20,000 units. The estimated salvage value remained unchanged as a result of the improvement in 1985. The improvement was recorded as a debit to accumulated depreciation.

Asset Y—During 1985 Asset Y was sold for $25,000. The bookkeeper recorded the sale as follows:

Depreciation Expense	10,000	
Cash	25,000	
Asset Y		35,000

Asset Z—Asset Z was acquired in late 1985 to replace Asset Y, which was sold.

Instructions

Prepare general journal entries for each asset on December 31, 1985, the end of Miller-Guy Company's reporting period, to correct any errors made during the year and to properly record depreciation for the year. Present computations to support your entries.

P12–7 You have been assigned to help audit Faultless Company for 1983. Part of your responsibility is to evaluate the accounting procedures used to record plant assets and depreciation during 1981 and 1982, the first two years of the company's existence. No audit was made during those years.

The company applies the straight-line method of depreciation to buildings and the double-declining balance method to equipment. A full year's depreciation is taken in the year of acquisition and none is taken in the year of disposal. Balances in these accounts at the end of 1983 (before 1983 depreciation has been recognized) are as follows:

	Building (10-year life)	Equipment (5-year life)
Cost	$425,000	$160,000
Accumulated depreciation	(80,000)	(102,400)
	$345,000	$ 57,600

Your analysis of the company's records reveals the following:

Buildings. The building was acquired before the beginning of operations on January 1, 1981, for $425,000. Of this amount, $75,000 was allocable to the land on which the building is situated. Transaction costs were an additional $25,000. Another $152,000 in renovation costs were incurred before the building was placed in service. The transaction and renovation costs were charged to expense when incurred. The building was originally expected to have a residual value of $25,000, which appears to have been a reasonable estimate at that time. Recent changes in economic conditions during 1983 indicate that the building will likely be disposable at $100,000 at the end of its 10-year life.

Equipment. No salvage value was expected from the equipment at the end of its five-year life. It now (1983) appears that the equipment will be worth $40,000 at the end of that period. It is also determined that machinery acquired during 1983 for $40,000 was incorrectly recorded as repair and maintenance expense. This mistake has not been corrected.

Instructions

For the Building and Equipment accounts separately, prepare all general journal entries necessary to correct the accounts and to properly record depreciation for 1983. Present supporting computations with your entries.

P12–8 Don's Fashions acquired the assets of a competitor in order to establish a branch of Don's main store. Don's Fashions paid $500,000 in cash and issued 10,000 shares of common stock which had a $25 par value and a $30 market value at the date of issuance. The market value is based on active trading of the stock in quantities far in excess of the 10,000 shares exchanged in the acquisition. An appraisal of the assets, used by Don's to negotiate the purchase price, reveals the following values on the transaction date:

Inventory	$200,000
Accounts receivable	100,000
Display fixtures	100,000
Building	300,000
Land	100,000
	$800,000

An inexperienced bookkeeper for Don's Fashions recorded the acquisition as follows:

Inventory	200,000	
Accounts Receivable	100,000	
Fixed Assets	450,000	
Cash		500,000
Common Stock		250,000
(10,000 shares @ $25)		

A further analysis of the Fixed Asset account reveals that the same bookkeeper entered the following items in the account during 1985:

Debit Entries

May 1 Acquisition price	$450,000	
May 1 Insurance on building and fixtures (May 1, 1985, to April 30, 1986)	10,000	$460,000

Credit Entries

May 1 Proceeds from the sale of unneeded display fixtures	17,500	
Dec. 31 Depreciation for 1985	22,125	(39,625)
Balance, December 31, 1985		$420,375

A computation accompanying the depreciation figure for 1985 is as follows: ($460,000 − $17,500)/20 years = $22,125. It is determined that the unneeded display fixtures which were sold represent 10% of the fixtures acquired from the competitor on May 1.

It is learned that Don's Fashions depreciates fixtures over a 10-year life by the sum-of-the-years'-digits method and assumes a salvage value of 10% of the cost. The building is subject to straight-line depreciation over a 20-year life. The building will have an estimated $50,000 residual value at the end of the 20 years. All depreciation is computed to the nearest full month. This information was apparently ignored by the bookkeeper.

Instructions

[a] Prepare general journal entries to correct the accounts on December 31, 1985, assuming the books have not been closed. For each entry, explain to the bookkeeper why the entry is necessary and what error(s) were made in the original recording of the item.

[b] Prepare the balance sheet for property, plant, and equipment on December 31, 1985.

[c] Determine the appropriate depreciation expense amounts for the display fixtures and building for 1986.

P12–9 Arrow Mine Corporation acquired property in 1983 which is believed to include valuable mineral deposits. The cost of the property was $900,000. Geological estimates indicate that approximately 12,000,000 tons of the mineral may be economically extracted. It is further estimated that the property can be sold for $250,000 to be used for commercial development following mineral extraction. For $80,000, Arrow expects to restore the land to a condition appropriate for resale.

After initial acquisition, the following costs were incurred:

Exploration costs—$250,000 (related to expected producible mineral reserves).

Development costs—$325,000 (related to development of tunnels and shafts in the ground); $460,000 (related to specialized production equipment).

Instructions

[a] Prepare general journal entries necessary to record the above transactions, beginning with the initial acquisition and including depletion and depreciation for 1983 using the following additional information:

[1] 2,650,000 tons of the mineral are extracted and sold during 1983.

[2] The specialized production equipment will be useful in ongoing production operations, and is expected to have an eight-year life and a $35,000 salvage value. Double-declining balance depreciation is to be used, with a full year's depreciation taken in 1983.

[b] How would your entries in [a] differ if the specialized production equipment was acquired exclusively for use in the extraction of the mineral for this project? (The $35,000 salvage value is still a reasonable estimate.)

P12–10 Brock Mining Company went into business in January 1983 to mine and sell a mineral. Assets were acquired as follows:

Asset	Cost	Estimated Useful Life	Residual Value
Land and mineral deposit	$1,000,000(a)	10,000,000 tons	$200,000(b)
Mine building	75,000	life of mine	5,000
Equipment	650,000	8 years	65,000

(a) Additional costs

Exploration costs (related to minerals discovered)	$ 88,000
Development costs	110,000

(b) Restoration costs (estimated cost of preparing
land for sale at $200,000) | 75,000

Depreciation policies of the company are as follows:
Mineral deposits—tons extracted basis
Mine building—same basis as mineral deposits
Equipment—double-declining balance

Operating data for 1983 and 1984 are as follows:

	1983	1984
Tons of mineral extracted	1,500,000	2,500,000
Tons of mineral sold at $4 per ton	1,200,000	2,000,000
Costs of mineral extraction, exclusive of depreciation and depletion (labor, maintenance, etc.)	$1,175,000	$2,260,000
Selling and administrative costs	$985,000	$1,660,000

Inventory of extracted minerals is carried on the first-in, first-out basis. The cost basis for inventory produced during a given period is computed at the average production cost for that period.

Brock Mining Company had 400,000 shares of common stock outstanding in 1983 and 1984.

Instructions

Prepare comparative income statements for 1983 and 1984, providing computations to support your entries. The company's year-end is December 31.

P12–11 Morris Manufacturing Company uses the composite depreciation method for its Production Assembly L35. The individual components in the assembly and their estimated residual values and estimated lives are presented below:

Component	Cost	Estimated Salvage Value	Estimated Useful Life in Years
L35-1	$125,000	$25,000	5
L35-2	36,000	1,000	7
L35-3	117,000	17,000	10
L35-4	42,000	–0–	6
L35-5	19,500	1,500	6
L35-6	211,250	11,250	8
L35-7	82,600	1,600	9

Instructions

[a] Determine the composite life of Assembly L35 and the annual depreciation rate.

[b] Prepare the adjusting entry to record depreciation for the first year of the assembly's life. Depreciation is recorded to the nearest hundred dollars.

[c] During the second year of the asset's life, Component L35-2 is determined to be incompatible with the other components and is sold for $20,000. Record the disposal of Component L35-2.

[d] Component L35-2 is replaced with a new component costing $50,000 and having an estimated nine-year life and a $500 salvage value. Record this replacement and depreciation for the second year.

[e] Disregard the information in [d]. Management determines that Component L35-2 must be replaced with a highly specialized piece of equipment, now in the

experimental stage. This component costs $100,000, is expected to be useful for only two years, and will have no salvage value. Record the replacement and depreciation for the second year.

P12–12 Rogers Products is considering the use of a group depreciation method for Asset X. The company has many units of Asset X in use at all times and is constantly replacing the units, each of which has a relatively low price.

Statistics about Asset X for 1983 have been estimated as follows:

	Units
Beginning balance	100,000
Additions	78,000
Retirements	(62,000)
Ending balance	116,000

Asset X is replaced on a FIFO basis. The beginning balance in Asset X is $250,000, indicating a $2.50 unit cost. Additions were made at a $2.60 unit cost during 1983. Retirements were salvaged for $5,000.

Instructions

[a] Prepare the general journal entries to record additions, retirements, and depreciation for the year using each of the following group depreciation methods:
[1] Inventory system
[2] Replacement system
[3] Retirement system
[b] Determine the depreciation expense and the asset balance to be presented in the 1983 financial statements under each depreciation method in [a].

P12–13 (Appendix B) P12–13 contains two *independent* parts.

Part 1. Brothers Company has several assets under separate insurance policies which contain coinsurance requirements. Descriptions of these policies and insurable losses sustained on each asset are as follows:

	Asset W	Asset X	Asset Y
Fair market value of asset	$35,000	$25,000	$40,000
Face value of policy	$30,000	$22,500	$25,000
Coinsurance requirement	80%	90%	85%
Amount of casualty loss	$25,000	$25,000	$20,000

Instructions

Determine the amount to be reimbursed by the insurance company for Assets W, X, and Y.

Part 2. Sisters Company has two insurance policies on its building. Policy 1 has a face value of $500,000; Policy 2 has a face value of $300,000. The estimated value of the building is $1,000,000. A loss of $750,000 was recently sustained when a fire destroyed a major portion of the building.

Instructions

Determine the amount to be received from each policy in the following independent cases:
[a] The policies contain no coinsurance requirements.
[b] Both policies have 90% coinsurance requirements.
[c] Policy 1 has a 90% coinsurance requirement and Policy 2 has a 70% coinsurance requirement.

P12–14 Johnson Corporation, a manufacturer of steel products, began operations on October 1, 1982. The accounting department started the fixed-asset and depreciation schedule presented on page 537.

Additional Information

You have been asked to assist in completing this schedule. In addition to ascertaining that the data recorded are correct, you have obtained the following information from the company's records and personnel:

Depreciation is computed from the first of the month of acquisition to the first of the month of disposition.

Land A and Building A were acquired from another corporation. Johnson paid $812,500 for the land and building together. At the time of acquisition, the land had an appraised value of $72,000 and the building had an appraised value of $828,000.

Land B was acquired on October 2, 1982, in exchange for 3,000 newly issued shares of Johnson's common stock. At the date of acquisition, the stock had a par value of $5 per share and a fair value of $25 per share. During October 1982, Johnson paid $10,400 to demolish an existing building on this land so it could construct a new building.

Construction of Building B on the newly acquired land began on October 1, 1983. By September 30, 1984, Johnson had paid $210,000 of the estimated total construction costs of $300,000. Estimated date of completion and occupancy is July 1985.

Johnson Corporation
FIXED ASSET AND DEPRECIATION SCHEDULE
For Fiscal Years Ended September 30, 1983, and 1984

Asset	Acquisition Date	Cost	Salvage	Depreciation Method	Estimated Useful Life in Years	Depreciation Expense Year Ended September 30, 1983	1984
Land A	Oct. 1, 1982	$ (1)	N/A*	N/A	N/A	N/A	N/A
Building A	Oct. 1, 1982	(2)	$47,500	straight line	(3)	$14,000	$ (4)
Land B	Oct. 2, 1982	(5)	N/A	N/A	N/A	N/A	N/A
Building B	under construction	210,000 to date	—	straight line	thirty	—	(6)
Donated equipment	Oct. 2, 1982	(7)	2,000	150% declining-balance	ten	(8)	(9)
Machinery A	Oct. 2, 1982	(10)	5,500	sum-of-years'-digits	ten	(11)	(12)
Machinery B	Oct. 1, 1983	(13)	—	straight line	fifteen	—	(14)

*N/A = Not applicable.

Certain equipment was donated to the corporation by a local university. An independent appraisal of the equipment donated placed the fair value at $16,000 and the salvage value at $2,000.

Machinery A's total cost of $110,000 included installation expense of $550 and normal repairs and maintenance of $11,000. Salvage value is estimated as $5,500. Machinery A was sold on February 1, 1984.

On October 1, 1983, Machinery B was acquired with a down payment of $4,000 and the remaining payments to be made in ten annual installments of $4,000 each beginning October 1, 1984. The prevailing interest rate was 8%. The following data were abstracted from present-value tables:

Present value of $1 at 8%

10 years	.463
11 years	.429
15 years	.315

Present value of ordinary annuity of $1 at 8%

10 years	6.710
11 years	7.139
15 years	8.559

Instructions

Number your answer sheet from 1 to 14. For each numbered item on the schedule above, supply the correct amount to the nearest dollar, next to the corresponding number on your answer sheet. Present supporting computations.

(AICPA adapted)

P12–15 (Appendix A) MCP Corporation bought a new asset on January 1, 1985. MCP plans to put the asset into service immediately. The following information is available:

Cost	$100,000
Expected salvage value	$5,000
Estimated life in years	15
Current corporate interest rate	12%

Instructions

[a] Calculate the depreciation for the first two years of the asset's life using each of the following methods:
  [1] Fixed percentage on book-value method. (The fifteenth root of 5,000/100,000 is .8189637.)
  [2] Annuity method. (Show both the depreciation expense and accumulated depreciation amounts.)
  [3] Sinking-fund method.
[b] Explain how an expected salvage value of zero would affect the depreciation calculations using the fixed percentage on book-value method.

P12–16 StyCo, Inc., manufactures a variety of medical instruments and supplies. The company uses the calendar year for reporting purposes. Information regarding StyCo's assets as of December 31, 1983, before any year-end adjustments, is given below.

Short- and Long-term Investments. StyCo invests excess funds in short-term marketable securities. The company also has long-term investments in the common stock of other companies. StyCo's holdings of common stock represent less than 5% ownership in those companies. Details are shown below.

Date of Note	Maturity Date	Face Amount	Annual Interest Rate
Apr. 1, 1983	Mar. 31, 1984	$150,000	8%
July 1, 1983	June 30, 1984	275,000	8%
Jan. 1, 1982	Dec. 31, 1986	450,000	9%
		$875,000	

Information on StyCo's Holdings of Common Stocks

Investments	Acquisition Date	Purchase Price	Market Values Dec. 31, 1982	Market Values Dec. 31, 1983
Short-term				
PWR, Inc.	Mar. 1, 1983	$ 130,000	—	$ 123,000
Tyra Company	Aug. 15, 1983	80,000	—	75,500
Marank Company	Nov. 20, 1983	50,000	—	51,500
Total short-term investments		260,000	—	250,000
Long-term				
Grabill Corporation	July 1, 1982	117,000	$112,000	113,000
Mikott, Inc.	Mar. 1, 1981	242,000	260,000	252,000
Stanor Company	Dec. 15, 1980	165,000	168,000	170,000
Clarmit, Inc.	Aug. 22, 1979	286,000	272,000	260,000
Total long-term investments		810,000	812,000	795,000
Total investments		$1,070,000	$812,000	$1,045,000

None of the declines in market prices are considered permanent. Dividends which have been declared but have not been received as of December 31, 1983, total $10,300.

Accounts Receivable. The outstanding accounts receivable as of December 31, 1983, total $304,000. The allowance for uncollectible accounts had a credit balance of $16,800 on December 31, 1982. A total of $6,400 in uncollectible accounts was written off during 1983. An aging of the accounts receivable on December 31, 1983, shows a total of $12,400 of the accounts receivable will be uncollectible.

Notes Receivable. StyCo holds two notes from trade customers which are due in 1984. In addition, StyCo holds a note which resulted from the sale of some of its manufacturing equipment. This note is not due until 1986. Interest is due on the anniversary date of the note and has not been accrued as of December 31, 1983. Details are given below, with the two trade notes listed first.

Inventories. Inventories are valued at the lower of cost or market value. Cost is determined by the FIFO method. StyCo's physical count of inventory reflects that merchandise with a cost of $2,500,000 and market value of $3,200,000 was on hand on December 31, 1983. In addition to this inventory, StyCo had merchandise still out on consignment. The cost of this merchandise was $240,000, the handling and shipping charges to get the merchandise to the consignee totaled $8,000, and the market value was $300,000.

Property, Plant, and Equipment. StyCo states all property at cost. The property and related account balances before the current year's depreciation expense are shown below. The depreciation expense for 1983 is $125,000 for the building and $150,000 for the equipment and furniture.

	Cost	Accumulated Depreciation (before adjustment)
Land	$1,450,000	—
Buildings	3,600,000	$1,425,000
Equipment and furniture	1,750,000	785,000
	$6,800,000	$2,210,000

Included in the amount for land is $250,000 for a parcel of land acquired on December 28, 1983, as a potential building site. As part of the contract to acquire the land, StyCo also had to pay $20,000 in delinquent property taxes; this amount was recorded as an expense.

Additional Information

Cash. The total in the various bank accounts and imprest petty cash funds amounts to $165,000.

Insurance. StyCo has purchased insurance to protect its assets and operations. The policies which will be in effect during 1984 are shown below:

Policy No.	Date of Policy	Premium Amount	Coverage in Years
JNA-XY5782	July 1, 1981	$18,000	3
DOME-NX85472	Apr. 1, 1982	30,000	3
FMC-BD287X	Oct. 1, 1983	8,000	1

Patent. StyCo acquired patent rights on January 2, 1983, for $75,000. At that time, management estimated that the patent would provide economic benefits to the company for the next five years.

Instructions

[a] Prepare a classified asset section of the statement of financial position for StyCo, Inc., on December 31, 1983, as it should appear in StyCo's annual report to its shareholders.

[b] Describe the information pertaining to StyCo's assets which would have to be disclosed in the notes to the 1983 financial statements in StyCo's annual report to its shareholders.

(CMA adapted)

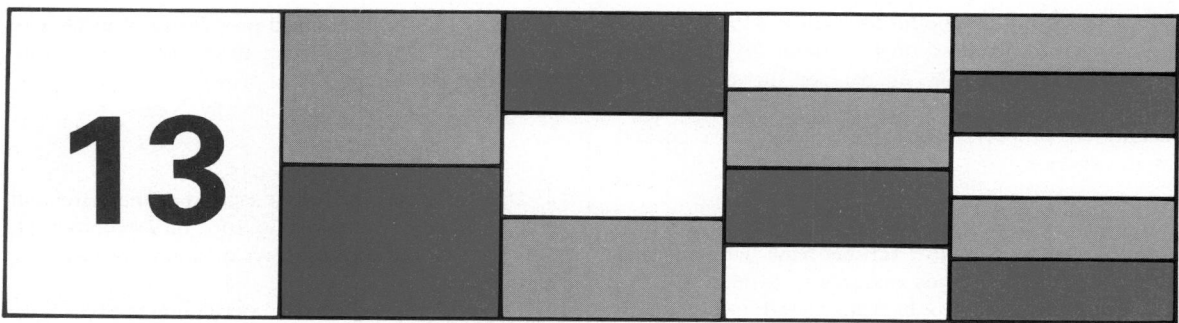

INTANGIBLE ASSETS

Objectives

To distinguish between intangible assets and property, plant, and equipment and to explain how intangible assets may contribute to the revenue-producing process.

To distinguish between separately identifiable intangible assets and goodwill, an intangible asset relating to the enterprise as a whole.

To apply basic accounting principles, such as matching and historical cost, in accounting for intangible assets.

To illustrate the preparation of the financial-statement items and accompanying disclosures for intangible assets.

To explain the intangible asset "goodwill," including how it arises, how to estimate its value, and how to determine its cost.

To discuss the accounting problems associated with several special areas of accounting that involve intangible assets.

DEFINING INTANGIBLE ASSETS

Intangible assets are factors in the production or distribution of goods or services that generate revenue. Most intangible assets have relatively long lives and are subject to amortization over several periods subsequent to their acquisition. They are distinctly similar in some respects to property, plant, and equipment. However, the distinguishing feature of intangibles is their **lack of physical characteristics.** Additionally, the uncertainty of the amount and timing of future benefits is generally thought to be greater with intangible assets than with other long-lived assets. The value of an intangible asset accrues primarily from the rights or privileges that the intangible provides the owner.

The balance sheet category of "intangible assets" refers to assets lacking physical substance that convey rights and privileges used in the production or distribution of goods and services over a relatively long period of time. However, the absence of physical existence alone does not qualify an asset to be presented as an "intangible." Assets that lack physical existence are also found in several balance sheet categories other than intangibles. For example, receivables, short-term investments, and prepaid expenses are presented as current assets; noncurrent receivables and investments are classified as investments and funds; and long-term prepayments are presented as other assets or deferred charges. Thus, in addition to the lack of physical existence, assets classified as intangible must be used in the production or distribution of other goods or services and must have relatively long lives, making them subject to amortization.

Intangible assets are frequently divided into those that are separately identifiable and those that lack specific identification. Examples of **separately identifiable intangible assets** are patents, copyrights, franchises, licensing agreements, trade names, trademarks, and organization costs. Intangible assets lacking specific identification are inherent in a continuing business and relate to an enterprise as a whole. While the name given such assets varies from entity to entity, a common name for this type of intangible asset is **goodwill,** the term used in this chapter.

Despite the fact that intangible assets lacking specific identification, such as goodwill, vary considerably in nature from separately identifiable intangibles, such as patents, specific standards that guide the accounting for *all* intangibles have been developed by the accounting profession. The most significant of these standards are in *Accounting Principles Board Opinion No. 17,* which provides the basis for much of the material in this chapter.[1]

ACCOUNTING STANDARDS FOR INTANGIBLE ASSETS

> **Historical Cost**
>
> **Matching**

Generally accepted standards of accounting for intangible assets have been established to apply the basic principles of historical cost and matching of revenues and expenses. In much the same way as with property, plant, and equipment, intangible assets are recorded initially at historical cost, determined as the fair value of the asset at the time of acquisition. This cost is subsequently amortized over those periods in which the assets are used as factors in the production or distribution of goods and services. Accounting for intangible assets is described below in terms of acquisition, amortization, disposal, and financial-statement presentation.

Acquisition of Intangible Assets

An intangible asset is recorded at cost, which may generally be described as the sacrifice in assets or the incurrence of liabilities necessary to acquire the asset. Intangible assets may be acquired from other enterprises, in which case cost is normally the fair value of consideration given in the exchange transaction. In unusual circumstances the value of the intangible

---

[1]*APB Opinion No. 17,* "Accounting for Intangible Assets," 1970.

asset received may be more readily determinable than the fair value of the consideration given, and in such cases the former should be used to record the cost of the intangible asset received.

Intangible assets may also be acquired as part of a group of assets or as part of the acquisition of an entire enterprise. Separately identifiable assets and liabilities, including intangible assets, acquired in such transactions are assigned part of the total cost of the group of assets or enterprise acquired. This assignment is normally based on the fair value of individual assets. The cost of an intangible asset not specifically identifiable that is acquired in this manner is measured by the difference between the total cost of the group of assets the enterprise acquired and the cost assigned to the other assets, including the separately identifiable intangible assets. This process is developed in greater depth in a subsequent section of this chapter.

Some intangible assets are developed internally. Costs of developing, maintaining, or restoring intangible assets that can be separately identified and have determinate lives are capitalized in appropriate intangible-asset accounts. Similar costs that do not relate to separately identifiable, intangible assets, that have indeterminate lives, or that are inherent in a continuing business should not be capitalized as intangible assets.

We must take care in distinguishing between costs of intangible assets and other expenditures that should be charged to expense when incurred under generally accepted accounting principles (GAAP). Examples of such expenses are advertising, research, and development costs. Frequently these expenses are closely related to the development of intangible assets and are sometimes confused with them.

The initial accounting for potential intangible-asset acquisition costs is summarized in Exhibit 13–1.

Exhibit 13–1 shows that separately identifiable intangible assets that have determinable lives should be capitalized in specific intangible-asset accounts, whether they were acquired from another entity, or developed internally. Patents, for example, may be acquired from other enterprises or developed internally. Intangible assets, such as goodwill, that cannot be separately identified but result from transactions with other entities should be established in appropriate intangible-asset accounts. Costs relating to internally developed intangibles that cannot be separately identified should be treated as expenses when incurred, even though they may have many of the characteristics of goodwill. For example, a company may develop an outstanding reputation, much like one that it could acquire through a business merger. Costs incurred to develop this reputation internally should normally be expensed as incurred. Expenditures that are charged to expense when incurred under generally accepted accounting principles, such as research and development or advertising, should not be established as intangible assets, even though they may relate closely to the development, maintenance, or enhancement of certain intangible assets.

Amortization of Intangible Assets

Before the Accounting Principles Board (APB) issued *Opinion No. 17,* companies divided intangible assets into those *with* determinable lives and those *without* determinable lives. Those with determinable lives were amortized, whereas those without determinable lives were not amortized. Under *APB Opinion No. 17,* however, intangible assets must be amortized over the periods benefiting from their use.[2] In establishing this requirement, the APB made the following observation:

---

[2] In requiring the amortization of intangible assets, the APB indicated that companies were not required to amortize intangibles acquired before November 1, 1970, the effective date of *APB Opinion No. 17.* Because some companies began amortizing intangibles that previously had not been amortized whereas others continued to carry these intangibles at their historical cost, intangible assets may still be found on some companies' balance sheets at historical cost.

EXHIBIT 13-1
Initial Accounting for
Potential Intangible-Asset Costs

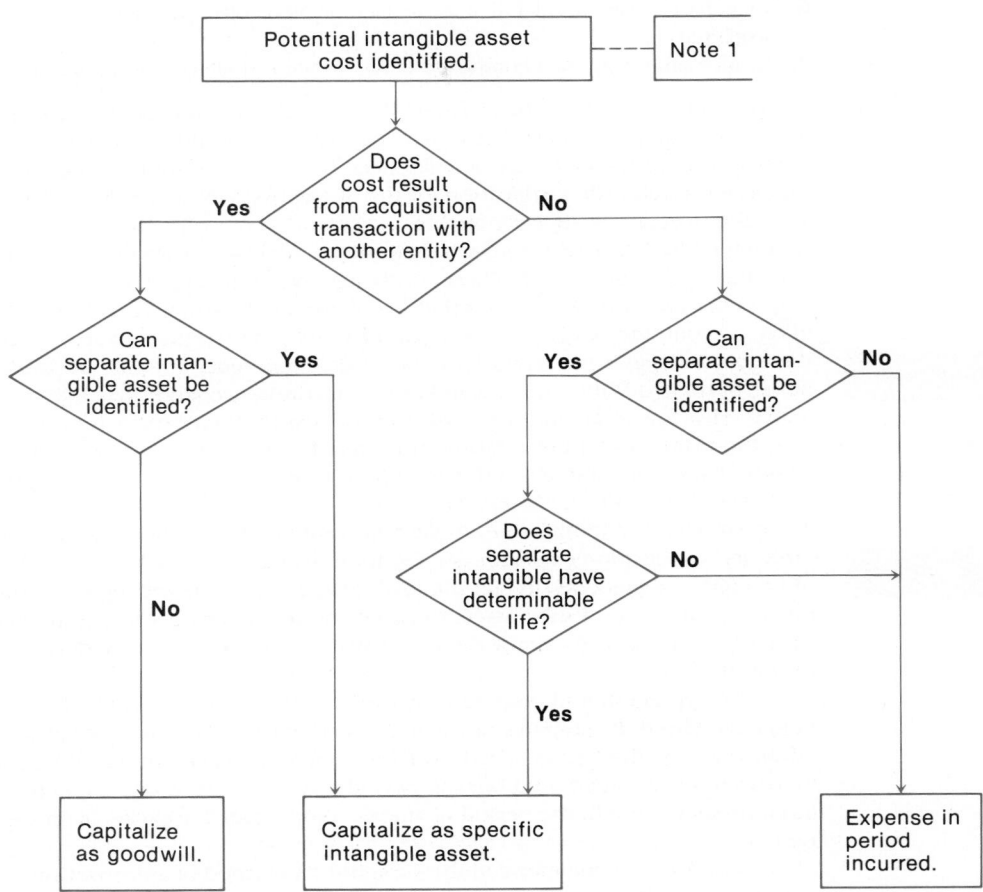

Note 1: If assets are acquired in a group, allocation may be necessary to determine the appropriate cost of each asset.

The value of intangible assets at any one date eventually disappears and . . . the recorded costs of intangible assets should be amortized by systematic charges to income over the periods estimated to be benefited.[3]

A number of pertinent factors must be considered in establishing the periods expected to benefit from the use of intangible assets. These include the following:[4]

[3]*APB Opinion No. 17*, par. 27.
[4]*APB Opinion No. 17*, par. 27.

1. Legal, regulatory, or contractual provisions may limit the maximum useful life.
2. Provisions for renewal or extension may alter a specified limit on useful life.
3. Obsolescence, demand, competition, and other economic factors may affect useful life.
4. Useful life may parallel the service life expectancies of individuals or groups of employees.
5. Present competitive advantage may be restricted by expected actions of competitors or others.
6. An apparent unlimited life may in fact be indefinite and benefits cannot be reasonably projected.
7. An intangible may be a composite of any individual factors with varying effective lives.

As a practical matter the APB established a maximum period of 40 years for the amortization of intangible assets. Thus, an intangible asset should be amortized over the shorter of its economic life (which may be influenced by legal or contractual limitations) or 40 years. The APB offered little justification for the 40-year maximum amortization period; however, several explanations appear possible.

Intangible assets with indeterminate lives, such as goodwill, are frequently amortized over the maximum period. These assets may relate to individual employees or groups of employees and other conditions that are of limited duration. These same conditions are not likely to continue beyond a period of 40 years. Amortization over a 40-year period, even though this is an arbitrary assignment of cost, prevents any one accounting period from being burdened with such a significant amortization charge that income is materially affected. Also, few intangible assets have usefulness to an enterprise for more than 40 years. In fact, the makeup of a corporation in terms of asset structure, personnel, production processes, marketing strategy, and many other aspects will generally be significantly different when viewed in 40-year intervals.

Materiality

Matching

In summary, although the 40-year maximum amortization period appears somewhat arbitrary, justification exists for amortization over a relatively long period. Also, if the value of intangible assets does in fact diminish over time, the matching principle requires some portion of the cost of such assets to enter into the determination of income in the periods benefited. This is true even if the life of the asset is not precisely determinable when it is acquired.

An enterprise should continuously evaluate the period over which intangible assets are being amortized. If estimates of useful lives are changed because of subsequent events and circumstances, the unamortized cost remaining at that point should be allocated to the increased or reduced number of periods in the remaining expected life. Under no circumstances should the period of amortization exceed 40 years from the date of acquisition.

The APB also recommended the straight-line method of amortization unless a company could specifically demonstrate that another method was more appropriate. Accountants typically ignore residual values in applying the straight-line method in the amortization of intangible assets. Policies followed in recognizing amortization for partial years vary, but the alternatives available parallel closely those available for property, plant, and equipment. Amortization may be computed to the nearest full month, half year, or full year in applying the straight-line method in periods during which the intangible asset is disposed of or acquired. Expenditures during the life of the intangible asset that are considered to increase the cost of the asset should be amortized over the remaining life of the related asset.

To illustrate the process of acquiring and amortizing an intangible asset, we shall assume that Howard Company acquired a patent in 1983 from another enterprise for $10,000. Production personnel of Howard Company estimate that the patent will be used for 10 years and will be worthless at the end of that time. The straight-line method of amortization is used by Howard for amortization of intangibles, with a full year's amortization in the first year.

Entries to record the acquisition of the patent and amortization for 1983 are:

Patent	10,000	
Cash		10,000
Amortization Expense	1,000	
Patent		1,000
($10,000/10 years = $1,000)		

Chapters 11 and 12 explain that accumulated depreciation of property, plant, and equipment must be disclosed in the financial statements. No similar requirement exists, however, for intangible assets, so we usually credit amortization directly to the asset account, as illustrated in the Howard example. Although this approach is commonly practiced, an Accumulated Amortization account for intangible assets is certainly acceptable and is sometimes encountered in business. In fact, if a clear record of the relationship of the historical cost of an intangible asset and its related accumulated amortization is particularly important, such an account is preferable. Unless indicated otherwise this text follows the procedure of crediting amortization directly to the intangible-asset account.

Continuing the example of Howard Company, assume that in 1984 the company incurs $2,000 in legal costs for successfully defending the patent when a competitor charges that Howard Company's patent violates a patent held by the competitor. Entries to record the $2,000 additional cost of the patent and amortization expense for 1984 are as follows:

Patent	2,000	
Cash		2,000
Amortization Expense	1,222	
Patent		1,222
[($9,000 + $2,000)/9 years = $1,222]		

The $9,000 book value of the patent and the $2,000 additional cost are added together and amortized over the remaining life of nine years. Amortization of 1984 is thus $1,222, rounded to the nearest dollar.

Disposal of Intangible Assets

Companies may sell separately identified intangible assets in the same way as other assets. When such a transaction occurs the **unamortized cost** of the asset must be removed from the books; the proceeds from the sale or exchange, recorded; and a gain or loss, if any, recognized. The company's amortization policy may require the recording of amortization before the sales transaction is recorded.

The cost of intangible assets should not be written off as a loss in the period of acquisition, as was frequently done before the issuance of *APB Opinion No. 17*. Estimates of value and future benefits of intangible assets may indicate that the unamortized cost should be reduced significantly by a charge against income at some point in the expected useful life. Care must be taken not to record unwarranted losses based on temporary conditions or other circumstances that do not support a diminished value of intangible assets.

Financial-Statement Presentation of Intangible Assets

Financial-statement disclosure should include the method and period of amortization of intangible assets. While balance sheet presentations of intangible assets vary, a typical presentation is a general category designated as "intangible assets," followed by an identification of the various types of intangibles held by the reporting enterprise. In other cases specific intangible assets are included among "other assets" or some other descriptive title.

Exhibit 13–2 presents the disclosure of intangible assets from two annual reports of major corporations. In both examples intangible assets are presented in the balance sheet with a verbal description in related notes. Quaker Oats Company presents a separate classification of intangible assets, including "excess of cost over net assets of acquired businesses" (goodwill) and "patents, trademarks and designs." The related note explains the company's policy concerning amortization.

In the second example in Exhibit 13–2, National Services Industries, Inc., presents the intangible assets, "goodwill and restrictive covenants," in a general asset category called "other assets." The footnote disclosure accompanying the financial statements explains why the goodwill (purchased prior to *APB Opinion No. 17*) is not being amortized.

EXHIBIT 13–2
Example Financial-Statement Disclosures
of Intangible Assets

EXAMPLE NO. 1:   QUAKER OATS COMPANY

Balance Sheet Excerpt	(In millions of dollars)		
	1982	1981	1980
Intangible Assets:			
Excess of cost over net assets of acquired businesses, less amortization	60.5	50.1	46.7
Patents, trademarks and designs, less amortization	5.1	3.0	3.3
	$1,476.7	$1,454.1	$1,334.2

Description in Note
Intangibles. As required by current accounting rules, excess of cost over net assets of acquired businesses resulting from acquisitions after October 31, 1970, is amortized over a maximum of 40 years on a straight-line basis. Costs relating to acquisitions prior to November 1, 1970 (about $22.8 million, principally for Fisher-Price Toys, Inc.), are considered to represent continuing values and are adjusted only if reduction of such values of underlying businesses is indicated.

SOURCE: Quaker Oats Company, 1982 Annual Report.

EXAMPLE NO. 2:   NATIONAL SERVICES INDUSTRIES, INC.

Balance Sheet Excerpt	(In thousands of dollars)	
Other Assets:	1982	1981
Goodwill and restrictive covenants	3,687	3,709
Investment in tax benefits	16,372	—
Miscellaneous	4,546	1,856
	24,605	5,565

Description in Note
Goodwill and Restrictive Covenants
Goodwill of $3,460,000 was recognized in connection with a 1969 acquisition and is not being amortized. Remaining amounts of goodwill and restrictive covenants are being amortized over various periods up to ten years.

SOURCE: National Services Industries, Inc., 1982 Annual Report.

SEPARATELY IDENTIFIABLE INTANGIBLE ASSETS

Companies may acquire separately identifiable intangible assets from other enterprises or governmental entities, or they may develop them internally. Separately identifiable intangibles that are developed internally and have determinable lives or that are acquired from others should be established in separate intangible-asset accounts that describe the nature of the right or privilege involved.

The types of separately identifiable intangible assets encountered in practice are numerous. This section discusses some of the most common types of intangibles: patents, copyrights, trade names, trademarks, franchises, licensing agreements, and leaseholds. It also discusses organization costs and deferred charges, assets that are frequently presented with or close to intangible assets in the balance sheet.

Patents

A **patent** is a document issued by the U.S. Patent Office and grants exclusive rights to the production, use, sale, and profit of an invention without interference by others. **Exclusive right** includes not only the right to use the patent, but also the ability to exclude others from using it. The legal life of a patent is 17 years. A patent is not renewable, but during the legal life of the original patent the holder can sometimes extend its life effectively by obtaining a new patent that includes slight variations.

Many of the consumer products we use every day are manufactured under patents granted to the producing companies. For example, cameras, household appliances, and hair dryers are frequently produced under patents.

Obtaining a patent does not guarantee that the holder has something of value. The value of a patent stems from its potential for creating competitive advantage, which may include the ability to produce and sell a different or superior product, obtain a higher selling price for the product, produce it at a lower cost, and exclude competition from producing a specific product or utilizing a specific process.

Patents acquired from another enterprise are recorded at the fair value of consideration given in the purchasing transaction unless the fair value of the assets received is more readily determinable. The cost of internally developed patents includes legal and registration fees, including the cost of models and drawings that accompany registration applications. Research and development costs incurred in the generation of patents, however, are charged to expense as incurred. (A subsequent section of this chapter covers this topic in greater depth.)

Costs of successful legal defenses of patents are capitalized as part of the patent cost, because such action supports the existence of the inherent value of the patent. Costs of unsuccessful legal defenses of patents, however, are expensed as incurred. In addition, the unsuccessful defense of a patent raises a question concerning the existence of an asset and therefore usually implies that the unamortized patent cost should be written off as a loss. If a new patent is obtained as a result of refinement, improvement, or other modification of an existing patent, the unamortized cost of the existing patent is considered part of the cost of the new patent if the benefits provided by the two patents are essentially the same.

The cost of a patent is amortized over the shorter of the economic or legal life. Numerous factors tend to reduce the useful life of a patent, including:

1. Technical progress resulting in new and more efficient inventions.
2. Substitute products for current products.
3. Changes in customer demands.
4. Developments by competitors that are sufficiently different to qualify for different patents.

Thus, the economic life of a patent is frequently considered to be less than the maximum legal life.

A PUSH TO STRETCH PATENT LIFE

DRUG COMPANIES rely heavily on patents to protect their products because, once formulated, a compound can be analyzed and usually duplicated. So it's not surprising that they are seeking legislation to postpone their patents' death.

The target isn't the Patent Office, but rather that old adversary, the Food & Drug Administration. The big pharmaceutical producers contend that long periods of review, in effect, shorten the patent life—and the profitability—of new drugs.

It works like this: A new chemical that *might* have medical value is discovered. Next, a patent is sought. Two years—the average waiting time for a decision on a patent—pass. Meanwhile, tests on animals begin. These continue, typically, for one to four years. Then, five to six years of human tests may start. Finally, the FDA reviews the tests. Average time for review: two to three years.

Ultimate result: a typical drug patent has run five to 11 years of its 17-year life before it goes on a pharmacist's shelf. Of the 12 new drugs approved by the FDA in 1980, one had no effective patent life remaining and one had less than three years [see table opposite]. The average was about 7½ years.

With the support of the Patent Office, the FDA and the General Accounting Office, the Pharmaceutical Manufacturers Association has been lobbying for a measure that would add up to seven years to the patent life of any drug delayed by regulatory safeguards. The association contends that short patents smother innovation and actually drive up drug costs. "The current downward trend in real R & D [research and development] investment in the pharmaceutical industry can only be halted if the industry perceives that a major change in policy has provided new incentives," argues Peter B. Hutt of the PMA. He notes that a company needs higher profits from each successful drug if its exploitation time is reduced.

SOURCE: "A Push to Stretch Patent Life," *Barron's,* March 8, 1982, pp. 24, 26. Reprinted by permission of *Barron's,* © Dow Jones & Company, Inc., 1982. All rights reserved.

Copyrights

A **copyright** provides the holder with exclusive rights to the publication, production, and sale of the rights for a literary, dramatic, musical, or artistic work. **Exclusive right** means that the holder can use the work and can preclude others from using it. Individuals holding copyrights typically use them to reproduce the work, to sell or otherwise distribute the work, and to perform or record the work.

Prior to January 1978 the Copyright Office (a department of The Library of Congress) granted copyrights good for 28 years with a right to renew for another 28 years. Since January 1978 the Copyright Office has issued copyrights for the length of the author's life plus 50 years.

The cost of acquired copyrights includes the acquisition price and any related expenditure. The cost of internally developed copyrights includes legal and other registration costs. Generally, the cost is amortized over the economic life of the copyright, which is the period over which the copyright is expected to produce revenue. If the economic life exceeds 40 years, a 40-year period should be used for amortization. Due to the limited period of time over which most copyrights are expected to generate revenue, however, the economic life is usually much shorter than the legal life. As a practical matter the cost of copyrights is often amortized over a relatively short period.

DRUG PATENTS: A RACE AGAINST TIME						
Trade Name	Use	Company	Date Patent Filed	Date Patent Issued	Date of FDA Approval	Effective Patent Life
Viroptic	ophthalmic solution	Burroughs-Welcome	9/18/63	8/17/65	4/10/80	2 yrs, 4 mo.
Meclan	acne cream	Johnson & Johnson	12/19/60	5/16/61	5/30/80	none
Cinobac	treatment of urinary infections	Lilly	2/ 4/69	6/13/72	6/13/80	9 yrs.
Meclomen	anti-inflammatory agent	Parke Davis	1/12/61	4/11/67	6/25/80	3 yrs, 10 mo.
Vansil	antiparasitic	Pfizer**	5/29/68 4/19/74	6/28/74 9/ 2/75	7/23/80 7/23/80	10 yrs, 11 mo. 12 yrs, 2 mo.
Calderol	treatment of bone disease associated with kidney failure	Upjohn	3/17/69	9/ 3/74	8/ 5/80	11 yrs, 1 mo.
Yutopar	prevents premature birth	Merrell-National	2/25/65	11/12/68	8/29/80	5 yrs, 3 mo.
Asendin	antidepressant	Lederle**	2/28/64 2/28/64	8/ 1/72 5/16/72	9/22/80 9/22/80	8 yrs, 11 mo. 8 yrs, 8 mo.
Zomax	pain reliever	Johnson & Johnson	7/26/67	8/14/73	10/28/80	9 yrs, 10 mo.
Siseptin	antibiotic*	Schering-Plough**	6/25/73 6/23/73	9/23/75 8/27/74	10/29/80 10/29/80	11 yrs, 11 mo.
Ludiomil	treatment of depression	Ciba-Geigy	11/ 9/61	8/27/68	12/ 1/80	4 yrs, 8 mo.
Spectrobid	oral antibiotic for use against urinary and respiratory infections	Pfizer	9/ 7/71	3/25/75	12/22/80	11 yrs, 3 mo.
Average						**7 years, 8 months**

*Not marketed in the U.S. **Covered by two patents.

SOURCE: Pharmaceutical Manufacturers' Association

Trade Names and Trademarks

A **trade name** or **trademark** is a symbol, design, word, or phrase that is used by an enterprise to distinguish itself or its product from other enterprises. Trademarks frequently consist of designs or other unique symbols to encourage public identification of products or enterprises. Legal protection for trade names and trademarks is granted by registration with the U.S. Patent Office.

We are all familiar with many trade names, such as Coca-Cola, Polaroid, Chevrolet, and Zenith. These, along with many others you can recognize, are trade names that create immediate product identification in our minds.

Registration of trade names and trademarks provides continuous protection, subject to periodic renewal. Capitalizable costs of trade names and trademarks include legal fees, registration costs, design costs, acquisition costs, successful legal defense of a trade name or trademark, and other expenditures directly related to the acquisition of the right to use the trade name or trademark. Although advertising expenditures may enhance the value or extend the life of a trade name or trademark, this association is generally believed to be too indirect to warrant the capitalization of such costs as part of the trade name or trademark.

The cost of a trade name or trademark should be amortized over the shorter of 40 years or the economic life of the asset. Due to the uncertainties inherent in estimating useful life when factors such as consumer demand are particularly important, the cost of trade names and trademarks is typically amortized over a relatively short period of time.

Franchises

A **franchise** is a contractual arrangement in which the holder of the franchise has the right to perform certain functions, to sell certain products or services, to use certain trade names or trademarks, or to do other specific things identified in the franchise agreement. Many of the businesses we encounter daily operate under franchises. Examples are Burger King, McDonald's, and Kentucky Fried Chicken restaurants.

Some enterprises enter into franchise agreements with other enterprises to sell products, use trade names, or engage in other activities in exchange for specific payments and the fulfillment of other obligations. In other cases enterprises enter into franchise agreements with governmental units to use public property or to furnish certain types of services, such as water, gas, electric power, public transportation, and waste disposal.

The initial cost of a franchise is recorded as an intangible asset to be amortized over future periods. The franchise cost is then amortized over the shorter of 40 years or the economic life of the franchise. In computing the economic life of the franchise, the holder must consider the time (if any) specified in the franchise contract. If the franchise can be terminated at the option of the entity granting the franchise, the holder should amortize the cost of the franchise over a relatively short period of time. Periodic payments made under a franchise agreement should generally be charged to expense as incurred.

Licensing Agreements

Some enterprises obtain licensing agreements to engage in certain lines of business or to use properties or rights owned by other entities. For example, radio and television stations obtain licenses from the Federal Communications Commission. The cost of such licenses represents an intangible asset, the accounting for which parallels closely the accounting for franchises. The cost should be amortized over the shorter of the economic life or 40 years.

An interesting example of licensing agreements is found in the trucking industry. Due to deregulation of that industry as a result of the Motor Carrier Act of 1980, the Financial Accounting Standards Board (FASB) issued *Statement of Financial Accounting Standards No. 44,* which requires companies to write off as an expense any unamortized costs of interstate operating rights subject to the provisions of that act. The cost of other licensing agreements, such as *intrastate* operating rights in a state that has not deregulated the industry, may still be carried as intangible assets.[5]

Leaseholds

Leasehold costs are frequently found in balance sheets as either property, plant, and equipment or intangible assets. A **lease** is a contract in which the owner of the property (**lessor**) grants another party (**lessee**) the right to use the property for a specified period of time for fixed or determinable payments. The lease typically states other rights and obligations of both the lessor and lessee.

Substance over Form

In accounting for leases, some are treated as purchases of the property by the lessee. We follow this accounting treatment if the lease contract is very similar to an acquisition of the property by the lessee. This is called the **capitalization of the lease** and is a clear example of substance over form, the modifying convention discussed in Chapter 2. In these cases the

---

[5]*FASB Statement of Financial Accounting Standards No. 44,* "Accounting for Intangible Assets of Motor Carriers," 1980, pars. 3–7.

capitalized cost of the lease, which is usually the present value of the required lease payments, is an asset on the lessee's balance sheet. This is a complex subject, which we treat extensively in Chapter 21 of this text.

When leases are not capitalized, the lessee may have costs that are presented as intangible assets. Lease contracts frequently call for lessees to prepay lease payments. Such payments must be associated with the appropriate periods and therefore represent intangible assets prior to amortization. Some portion of these prepayments may be appropriately classified as current assets.

Lessees frequently make expenditures that improve the quality of service rendered by leased property. Examples of such leasehold improvements include improvements to building space and improvements to land, such as driveways, shrubbery, and parking lots. Although these expenditures are made in anticipation of benefits to be derived by the lessee, the improvements typically become the property of the lessor at the end of the lease term. Leasehold improvements should be capitalized by the lessee in a separate Leasehold Improvement account and amortized over the shorter of the lease term, the life of the property resulting from the improvement, or 40 years.

Organization Costs

Numerous costs are incurred in organizing a business enterprise, particularly a corporation. Such **organization costs** include the following:

1. Legal fees of drafting the corporate charter and bylaws.
2. Legal fees of corporate registration.
3. Compensation to promoters of the enterprise and other promotional costs.
4. Initial stock-issuance costs.
5. Miscellaneous costs of organization.

Theoretically one can argue that all periods in which the enterprise operates benefit from the incurrence of these costs. In practice, however, the life of the enterprise is usually not known or determinable at the inception of the enterprise, when these costs are incurred. On the other hand, support exists for the position that the early years in the enterprise's life benefit most from organization costs and that such costs lose significance once the enterprise becomes an established operating unit.

Organization costs are frequently treated as an intangible asset and amortized over a relatively short period in the early years of the enterprise's life. The fact that such costs may be amortized for income tax purposes over a minimum period of five years has encouraged many enterprises to use the same period of amortization for financial reporting purposes.

Distinguishing between organization costs and costs that relate to normal operations is a difficult determination requiring the accountant to use judgment. Costs of normal operations should not be capitalized as organization costs or any other type of intangible asset. A later section ("Development-Stage Enterprises") of this chapter covers this subject in greater depth.

Deferred Charges

Deferred charges, sometimes called **deferred costs** or **deferred debits,** may be found in balance sheets with or near the intangible assets. As we saw in Chapter 4, deferred charge is a broad term used to identify a number of different items with debit balances that do not fit well in any of the other asset categories of the balance sheet. Organization costs are referred to as deferred charges in some cases. Other costs, such as long-term prepayments, plant rearrangement costs, and deferred income taxes with debit balances, are sometimes referred to as deferred charges.

The presence of deferred charges indicates the problem of attempting to define all costs that have not been amortized in one of the common asset categories. In a sense the

---

EXHIBIT 13–3
United Foods, Inc.
Other-Asset Presentation

| | February 28 | |
	1982	1981
Other		
Option deposit for land purchase	$ 890,137	—
Property and equipment, held for disposal, at lower of depreciated cost or estimated realizable value	481,127	$4,355,329
Receivables, less current maturities	315,216	569,187
Deferred costs	371,900	605,262
Excess of cost over underlying equity in assets purchased	65,415	108,491
Total Other Assets	$2,123,795	$5,638,269

SOURCE: United Foods, Inc., 1982 Annual Report.

---

deferred-charge category is necessary by default, because some debit-balance accounts simply do not fit elsewhere.

Exhibit 13–3 contains the other-asset section of the comparative balance sheet for United Foods, Inc., for 1981 and 1982. United Foods processes and markets frozen vegetables with primary operating units in California and Tennessee. The other-asset category follows the current-asset and property-and-equipment presentations in the balance sheet and includes several items, including both "deferred costs" and "excess of cost over underlying equity in assets purchased" (goodwill). The company's fiscal year ends with the last day of February, as indicated in the columnar heading.

INTANGIBLE ASSETS NOT SEPARATELY IDENTIFIABLE: GOODWILL

Certain transactions give rise to intangible assets that are not separately identifiable in the same way as patents, copyrights, and other intangibles discussed in the previous section. Intangible assets that cannot be separately identified relate to the enterprise as a whole. They frequently exist because of the unique combination of separate assets and personnel of the enterprise, and their synergism explains why the value of an enterprise as a whole—measured in terms of its anticipated earning capacity—may be greater than the sum of the values of the individual parts of the enterprise. While such intangible assets may be identified with a variety of titles, the most common name is goodwill, the term used throughout this text.

Goodwill Concept

Several concepts underlie the existence of goodwill. **Goodwill** is the capability of an enterprise to produce earnings in excess of normal. This unique earning capability results from intangible advantages working for the enterprise in conjunction with the separately identifiable tangible and intangible assets. We apply the excess-earning-capacity concept in the various techniques of estimating the dollar amount of goodwill. Another closely related notion is that the value of an enterprise as a whole may exceed the value of the sum of the individual assets, less the liabilities, of the enterprise. Such situations result from the existence of intangible qualities, such as an outstanding reputation, superior managerial capability, and ability to operate at an above-normal level of efficiency. Any characteristic or combination of characteristics that gives an enterprise a competitive advantage over other enterprises, thereby allowing the enterprise to enjoy a higher level of earnings than would normally be expected, supports the existence of goodwill.

Goodwill has been described as a master valuation account, which indicates that it provides a reconciliation of the difference between the value of an enterprise as a whole and the aggregate value of the individual parts of the enterprise. When viewed in this context, goodwill explains the difference between an enterprise that has above-normal earnings and those enterprises that have normal earnings. The goodwill at work for the former enterprise represents an additional **working asset** that contributes to the enterprise's ability to earn a return on specific individual assets at a level in excess of that normally expected.

Inasmuch as the value of goodwill is identified with an enterprise as a whole, the asset goodwill is inseparable from that enterprise. Thus, goodwill is not exchangeable in the same sense as separately identifiable tangible and intangible assets. In certain circumstances, however, goodwill is exchanged when an entire enterprise is acquired. Therefore, when goodwill is evident in the acquisition of an entire enterprise, an appropriate intangible-asset account should be established. Finally, as reflected in Exhibit 13–1, internally developed goodwill, which has not been acquired from another enterprise, should not be recognized as an asset.

When an enterprise contemplates the acquisition of an entire business, it must determine the value of the business. A starting point is the identification of the current value of all specific assets to be received and liabilities to be assumed. This amount is identified as the fair value of **net assets** received. The seller will desire to include any existing goodwill in determining the exchange price, whether or not the goodwill has previously been recorded as an asset. Once an exchange price is agreed on and a sale takes place, the purchaser acquires the goodwill for the part of the overall purchase price that exceeds the current value of the other net assets received. Goodwill is then recorded by the purchaser. The recorded cost of the goodwill may vary from the valuation of the goodwill estimated to be inherent in the business being acquired, because the goodwill recorded is the amount necessary to reconcile the total purchase price to the current value of the other net assets received.

Conceptually goodwill should be measured by identifying those factors that offer a competitive advantage to an enterprise, such as superior managerial efficiency, an excellent reputation among customers, and ability to operate at a high level of efficiency. By placing a monetary valuation on these features and aggregating these amounts, the value of goodwill could be established.

Realistically, valuing the individual intangible qualities supporting the existence of goodwill involves measurement problems too complex for present accounting practice. Accountants have therefore turned to a somewhat indirect method of valuing goodwill, whereby they estimate the total anticipated excess earning capability rather than the individual elements that support the existence of goodwill. This process involves estimating future periodic earnings from an investment in another enterprise, comparing this estimation with what would normally be expected, and aggregating the excess of anticipated earnings over normal earnings. The estimation of excess earning capacity is made for purposes of determining a price to pay for the enterprise rather than for purposes of financial-statement presentation.

For example, assume that Red Company is considering the acquisition of Blue Company. Red Company will take over all the assets and will assume all the liabilities of Blue Company. Red Company estimates the current value of the net assets (assets less liabilities) of Blue Company at $750,000. In addition, Red Company believes it will be able to achieve a level of earnings substantially in excess of normal on its investment due to Blue Company's outstanding reputation. Specifically, the excess earnings are estimated to total $100,000. Red Company is therefore willing to pay up to $850,000 for the net assets of Blue Company. If an amount greater than $750,000 is paid, the excess is identified as the cost of goodwill resulting from the transaction. Presumably this would not exceed $100,000. It would be less than $100,000, however, if the final bargained exchange price is less than $850,000. For example, if the agreed upon purchase price is $780,000, the amount of goodwill is $30,000 ($780,000 − $750,000). On the other hand if the agreed upon price is $840,000, the amount of goodwill is $90,000 ($840,000 − $750,000).

Accounting for Goodwill

Goodwill is accounted for in much the same way as other intangible assets because the general requirements of *APB Opinion No. 17* apply to goodwill. Exhibit 13–1, presented earlier in this chapter, indicates that goodwill acquired from another enterprises is recorded at cost in an appropriate intangible-asset account. The life of goodwill is not constrained by legal or contractual limitations and therefore may be judged by management to be indeterminate. In such cases we would amortize the goodwill over a 40-year period. In other cases management may decide that the period over which excess earnings can be anticipated is limited to a period shorter than 40 years. In such cases we would amortize the goodwill over the expected period of advantageous operations.

In taking the position that goodwill should be treated as an asset and amortized over its estimated useful life, the APB considered several alternative treatments. These included (1) retaining the cost of goodwill as an asset indefinitely unless a reduction in value becomes evident and (2) deducting the cost of goodwill from stockholders' equity when it is acquired. Supporting the nonamortization approach is the notion that until the future value becomes less than the historical cost, no loss should be recognized. The basis for deducting the cost of goodwill from stockholders' equity at the time of purchase is that the nature of goodwill differs from other assets and warrants special accounting treatment; since goodwill relates to the business as a whole and its value fluctuates widely, estimates of either its value or term of existence are too unreliable for purposes of income determination.[6] These positions were rejected by the APB in favor of the amortization approach we describe in this text.

Many of the same advantages of goodwill that can be acquired externally may be developed internally. For example, a company may develop an excellent reputation, a superior managerial capability, and the other attributes that allow it to earn at an above normal level without acquiring another enterprise. Despite the similarity between these internally developed characteristics and goodwill acquired from another enterprise, only the latter is capitalized in an intangible-asset account. The cost of internally developed attributes that are similar to acquired goodwill should be recognized as expense when incurred.

The reason for not recognizing internally developed goodwill as an asset is primarily the **lack of objective evidence;** in an external acquisition, however, the two enterprises agree on the existence and amount of goodwill. Thus, the difference in accounting for goodwill acquired externally and that developed internally is based on the method of acquisition and not on conceptual differences other than the principle of objectivity. Accordingly, the asset goodwill may be described as the price paid for anticipated excess earning capability over that which is considered normal.

Objectivity

Goodwill Example: Diversified Enterprises/Single Product, Inc.

In the following paragraphs we use a hypothetical example (involving Diversified Enterprises and Single Product, Inc.) to illustrate various computational considerations in accounting for goodwill. Diversified Enterprises is considering the acquisition of Single Product, Inc., a relatively small company that has an excellent reputation. Single Product

---

[6]*APB Opinion No. 17,* pars. 17, 19–20.

EXHIBIT 13–4					
Single Product, Inc.					
BALANCE SHEET					
June 30, 1985					

Assets			Liabilities		
Marketable securities		$ 5,000	Accounts payable		$ 99,000
Accounts receivable		28,000	Bonds payable		112,000
Inventories		140,000			$211,000
Property, plant, and equipment	$ 275,000		**Stockholders' Equity**		
Accumulated depreciation	(125,000)	150,000	Capital stock		$150,000
Patents		85,000	Retained earnings		47,000
					$197,000
			Total liabilities and stockholders'		
Total assets		$408,000	equity		$408,000

deals in a product line into which Diversified wants to move. Diversified Enterprises would acquire all the assets and would assume all the liabilities of Single Product.

The balance sheet of Single Product is presented in Exhibit 13–4. Single Product, Inc., has no cash to be transferred to Diversified Enterprises.

Two important questions must be answered by Diversified Enterprises in determining a reasonable price to pay for the net assets of Single Product, Inc. First, to what extent do the balance sheet figures represent the current value of the individual assets and liabilities? Second, is goodwill evident in the past performance of Single Product, Inc.? The price that Diversified is willing to pay should be based on the current value of Single Product's net identifiable assets (assets less liabilities) plus the value of any excess earning capability included in the acquisition. The total of the two elements establishes an amount around which Diversified should negotiate an acquisition price. The cost of the goodwill acquired equals the difference between the actual price paid and the current value associated with the separately identifiable assets less liabilities.

Because the purchase of Single Product, Inc., by Diversified Enterprises represents an acquisition transaction, the recorded amounts of assets on the books of Single Product are of no particular importance to Diversified except as a possible starting point for the establishment of the current value of the acquired assets. Based on appraisals, current market prices, and the application of specific price indexes to historical cost figures, Diversified Enterprises has established the values presented in Exhibit 13–5 for the assets of Single Product. We shall assume that the amounts of liabilities on Single's books fairly reflect the obligations Diversified is assuming.

Historical Cost

Why are the recorded amounts of assets in the balance sheet of Single Product, Inc., different from the current value estimates in Exhibit 13–5? The recorded amounts of assets are based on generally accepted accounting principles, which do not necessarily reflect the current value of the assets. The basis for recording most assets is historical cost. Adjustments to costs are made to reflect market declines in applying the lower of cost or market method to marketable securities, inventories, and other assets whose realizabilities have been impaired. The balance sheet amounts for these items may be significantly different from the current market values. Also, the accounting method used to account for inventories may cause a difference between recorded amounts and current market values. If the last-in, first-out (LIFO) method is used, for example, the balance sheet amount may be well below the current value, whereas the first-in, first-out (FIFO) method would normally cause the recorded amount and the current value to be closer together. If the inventory to be acquired will be used in a different way by the acquiring enterprise, it may have a greater or lesser

---

EXHIBIT 13–5
Current Value of the Net Assets of Single Product, Inc.

Assets

Marketable securities	$ 6,000	
Accounts receivable	25,000	
Inventories	125,000	
Property, plant, and equipment	182,000	
Patents	100,000	$ 438,000

Liabilities

Accounts payable	99,000	
Bonds payable	112,000	(211,000)
Estimated current value of net assets		$ 227,000

---

value than the amount recorded on the books of the acquired company. Differences in the valuation of receivables most likely reflect differences in the assessment of uncollectible accounts, because the receivables amount reflects the net realizable value of the asset.

Historical Cost

Differences between the recorded amounts and the current values of plant assets or of separately identifiable intangible assets are due primarily to the initial recording of these assets at historical cost and the subsequent amortization of the cost figures. The market price of the assets may remain constant, decline at a different rate from the book value, or increase. The book value as presented in the balance sheet is not designed to reflect current value; it is not unusual for the current market value of the assets to differ from the book value.

The explanation of the differences between balance sheet amounts and estimated current values of assets varies with the specific assets involved, the condition of the assets, current market conditions, and other variables. In any event, when Diversified records the acquisition of Single Product, a starting point for determining the appropriate cost for the assets acquired will be an estimate of the value at the time of that acquisition.

If Diversified pays a price believed fair in light of the earning potential of the enterprise acquired, goodwill will emerge from the acquisition only if that price is in excess of $227,000. For example, if the two enterprises agree on a $250,000 cash purchase price, goodwill will be $23,000, computed as follows:

Purchase price	$ 250,000
Less: Estimated current value	
of net assets received	(227,000)
Cost of goodwill	$ 23,000

In this case the journal entry to record the acquisition of the net assets and the assumption of liabilities of Single Product, Inc., by Diversified Enterprises is as follows:

Marketable Securities	6,000	
Accounts Receivable	25,000	
Inventories	125,000	
Property, Plant, and Equipment	182,000	
Patents	100,000	
Goodwill	23,000	
Accounts Payable		99,000
Bonds Payable		112,000
Cash		250,000

If Diversified pays a higher price, the implied goodwill will be more. For example, if $275,000 is paid, the cost of goodwill will be $48,000, determined by the excess of the $275,000 purchase price over the $227,000 estimated value of the net assets received.

Implicit in this transaction is the belief by Diversified Enterprises that the value of goodwill is at least equal to the cost implied in the transaction. Diversified Enterprises should not pay a price in excess of the estimated current value of the identifiable net assets unless its management believes that the earning potential accruing to it in the transaction equals or exceeds the acquisition price.

In the Diversified illustration we deal with a hypothetical situation. Exhibit 13–6, however, discloses an actual purchase transaction in which goodwill arises. Fairchild Industries, Inc., a company dealing primarily in the aerospace and communications industries, acquired VSI Corporation, a manufacturer of precision metal products during 1980. The cost of $282,541,000 exceeded the fair value of the net assets acquired by $83,382,000 (the value of the goodwill), and that amount is being amortized over 40 years. The company's balance sheet, which is not presented here, includes the asset "costs in excess of net assets acquired, less amortization" of $83,987,000 and $951,000 for 1980 and 1979, respectively. In this particular transaction, the acquisition was made by issuing preferred stock and paying cash.

EXHIBIT 13–6
Fairchild Industries, Inc.
Business Combination Resulting in Goodwill

Note 2. BUSINESS COMBINATION

On November 7, 1980, VSI Corporation (VSI), a company engaged primarily in the manufacture of a wide range of precision metal products, was merged into a subsidiary of the Company. The total acquisition cost, including capitalized expenses, aggregated $282,541,000 of which $161,227,000 represents the issue of new Series A $3.60 cumulative Convertible Preferred Stock at a value of $45.00 per share, and the remainder cash.

The merger has been accounted for by the purchase method of accounting and, accordingly, the results of operations of VSI and its subsidiaries have been included in the consolidated statement of earnings from the date of the merger. The excess of the total acquisition cost over the fair value of net assets acquired of $83,382,000 is being amortized over 40 years.

The following unaudited summary, prepared on a pro-forma basis, presents the summarized results of operations of the Company for the years ended December 31, 1980 and 1979, as though VSI had been acquired as of January 1, 1979 (in thousands, except per-share data):

	1980	1979
Sales	$1,273,926	$1,055,082
Earnings before income taxes	121,398	107,285
Net earnings	67,957	57,535
Earnings per share:		
Primary	3.71	3.21
Fully diluted	3.68	3.14

The above amounts reflect adjustments related to purchase accounting, including amortization of goodwill, and imputed interest costs (at 12 percent) on funds used for the acquisition. Earnings per share calculations assume that convertible preferred shares issued in connection with the acquisition, which represent common stock equivalents, were issued as of January 1, 1979.

SOURCE: Fairchild Industries, Inc., 1980 Annual Report.

Fairchild Industries had a small amount of goodwill in its balance sheet before the acquisition of VSI Corporation, because $951,000 was included in 1979.

Estimating the Value of Goodwill

For goodwill to exist, evidence of a capability to earn amounts in excess of that which would normally be expected must exist. An evaluation of the existence of goodwill therefore requires a comparison of expected earnings with normal earnings. If the anticipated earnings exceed the norm, evidence of goodwill is present.

How is the **normal rate of earnings** for an enterprise determined? The normal rate used for goodwill estimation is typically an approximation of the rate required to attract capital into the company that is acquiring another company. The risk associated with the enterprise is a major variable in determining the cost of capital: The higher the risk associated with the company, the higher the cost of capital. Risk, in turn, is assessed by considering the company's line of business, existing debt-equity relationships, past profitability, and other variables. In determining the normal rate, a common approach is to consult financial services and other sources for an average cost of capital for other companies in the same industry. Of course, care must be taken that industry figures represent companies that are truly comparable.

Projecting expected future earnings for purposes of comparison with normal earnings involves a careful analysis of past earnings and projected changes in future conditions. Although information about the past may be useful in estimating future earnings, unadjusted past earnings would rarely be an appropriate measure of expected future earnings. Trends in the past, however, may be projected into the future and may serve as a solid basis for estimating future profitability. Extraordinary items and other infrequently recurring items included in past earnings are usually excluded when using the past to project the future.

Several methods of estimating the goodwill in an acquisition are discussed in this section. The following four steps are common to all methods:

Step 1. Estimate the periodic earnings that are expected to be achieved on the investment in the current value of the net assets to be received.

Step 2. Estimate the periodic earnings that would normally be expected on the investment in the current value of the net assets to be received.

Step 3. Comparing amounts in Steps 1 and 2, compute the amount of **anticipated periodic excess earnings over normal earnings.**

Step 4. Convert the amount computed in Step 3 from a periodic figure to an aggregate figure that represents an estimate of the **total anticipated excess earnings** (i.e., goodwill).

Several methods are available for making the conversion required in Step 4 of the **periodic** anticipated excess earnings to an **aggregate** figure that represents the total value of future anticipated excess earnings.

Estimating Expected Periodic Earnings

A starting point for **estimating expected future earnings** is past performance. However, our intent is to estimate *future* earnings, and in the future the factors influencing earnings may be different from those in the past. When we base assessments of future earnings on past earnings, we should use several periods in an attempt to eliminate the impact of nonrecurring events and to identify significant trends in earnings or components of earnings.

Continuing the Diversified Enterprises example, we shall assume that earnings information for Single Product for the four years of its existence is as given in Exhibit 13–7.

The average net income for the four years is $50,000 or a 22% return on the current value of the net assets of Single Product, Inc. These amounts are computed as follows:

EXHIBIT 13–7
Single Product, Inc.
Income Data for Years Ending June 30, 1982–1985

	1982	1983	1984	1985
Revenues	$ 255,000	$ 262,000	$ 212,000	$ 238,000
Expenses	(204,000)	(224,000)	(160,000)	(182,000)
Income before extraordinary items		38,000	52,000	
Extraordinary gain (loss)		12,000	(9,000)	
Net income	$ 51,000	$ 50,000	$ 43,000	$ 56,000

$$\frac{\text{Average}}{\text{net income}} = \frac{\$51,000 + \$50,000 + \$43,000 + \$56,000}{4 \text{ years}} = \$50,000$$

$$\frac{\text{\% Return on}}{\text{current value}} = \frac{\$50,000}{\$227,000} = 22\%$$
$$\text{of net assets}$$

Several factors should be considered in deciding on the appropriateness of using $50,000 as an expected level of earnings in the future. The inclusion of the extraordinary items is questionable, because they are by definition not expected to recur frequently. Also, the accounting policies followed by Diversified to determine net income may be different from those used by Single Products. Such a difference could influence the assessment of future earnings. Other factors could also impact the expected future earnings. For example, in the future depreciation and amortization on property, plant, and equipment and patents will be based on the **new cost basis** (i.e., the estimated fair value), and their estimated lives may be extended or reduced.

Furthermore, trends in the components of earnings may reveal that conditions in 1985 are more indicative of the future than the average of several periods. Considerations that are not apparent in the financial statements and that are discernible only through careful consideration of the operating characteristics of the enterprise being acquired may affect the evaluation of expected earnings. For example, the management of Diversified may believe Single Products could be even more profitable with the incorporation of more efficient production processes.

We shall further assume that the average earnings of Single Product during 1982–1985 (after the elimination of extraordinary items and the inclusion of an additional charge of $3,850 per year for expected increases in depreciation and amortization) represent a reasonable estimate of future earnings. This amount is computed as follows:

Average annual income before extraordinary items			
	1982	$ 51,000	
	1983	38,000	
	1984	52,000	
	1985	56,000	
		$197,000 ÷ 4 years =	$49,250
Less: Adjustment for additional depreciation and amortization			(3,850)
Estimated future annual income			$45,400

This estimate reflects a rate of return on the estimated current value of the net assets being acquired of 20% ($45,400/$227,000 = 20%). These amounts are used in the continuation of the Diversified Enterprise illustration.

Estimating Normal Periodic Earnings

The selection of a **normal rate of earnings** should reflect an estimate of the rate necessary to attract capital into the business under existing circumstances. As is the case with determining all interest rates, the risk taken in the investment is an important consideration. A related consideration is the industry in which the enterprise operates.

Published rates that represent averages of a number of similar enterprises can usually be obtained from various financial services (e.g., Dun & Bradstreet or Standard & Poor's) that accumulate such statistics. However, rates obtained in this manner are based on historical figures and may be different from rates based on current values. Also, the unique features of the enterprise under consideration may make the identification of comparable enterprises difficult. Any valid rate must be based on companies that are similar to the one for which goodwill is being computed.

In continuing the example of Diversified Enterprises, 12% is used as a rate that represents a normal cost of attracting capital into enterprises similar to Single Product. Thus, normal annual earnings on the $227,000 investment are $27,240 ($227,000 × 12%).

Computing the Anticipated Annual Excess Earnings

The amounts computed in Steps 1 and 2 are combined to determine the **anticipated annual earnings in excess of normal.** In the case of Single Product, Inc., this computation is made as follows:

Estimated future annual earnings ($227,000 × 20%)	$45,400
Estimated normal annual earnings ($227,000 × 12%)	(27,240)
Estimated excess of expected annual earnings over normal	$18,160

Estimating Total Excess Earnings

Several methods are available to convert the annual amount of anticipated excess earnings to an **estimate of total goodwill.** Three methods are illustrated in the following paragraphs.

Method 1. Years Multiple of Excess Earnings. This method is based on the assumption that the excess earnings will continue for a determinable number of periods. Goodwill is computed by multiplying the excess annual earnings by the number of years the management believes it can sustain the advantages acquired.

For Diversified Enterprises we assume (for this calculation) that management believes it can sustain the anticipated level of excess earnings for six years. In this case goodwill is computed as follows:

$$\text{Goodwill} = 6 \text{ years} \times \$18,160 = \$108,960$$

A deficiency in this method is the failure to recognize the difference between the value of the excess earnings of the first year after the acquisition and that of subsequent years (i.e., the time value of money). The difficulty in accurately estimating the number of years over which the excess earnings can be sustained indicates that this method contains an implementation problem.

Method 2. Present Value of Excess Earnings.   Recognition of the time value of the excess earnings is a major advantage of basing the value of goodwill on the **present value** of excess earnings. In this method, as in Method 1, the period over which the excess earnings can be sustained must be estimated. The amount of annual excess earnings is then discounted to its present value by an appropriate interest rate.

Assuming that Diversified estimates that the excess earnings will continue for six years, we discount at the normal rate (i.e., the estimated cost of capital, which—in this case—is 12%), and goodwill is computed as follows:

$$\text{Goodwill} = 4.11141 \times \$18{,}160 = \$74{,}663$$

Table 6–4 shows that the present value of an annuity factor for six periods at 12% is 4.11141. Therefore, that figure is used in this computation, because the estimated excess earnings of $18,160 per year will accrue to Diversified Enterprises over a six-year period.

The greater risk inherent in the continuation of the excess earnings in the future may encourage the use of a higher interest rate in estimating the total value of goodwill. For example, if the 20% rate is used in estimating the goodwill in the Diversified acquisition of Single Product, goodwill is estimated as follows:

$$\text{Goodwill} = 3.32551 \times \$18{,}160 = \$60{,}391$$

We again use an annuity factor (3.32551 from Table 6–4) to estimate the value of goodwill. In this case, however, the factor is for six periods at *20%*.

Conceptually, the present-value method has merit because explicit recognition is given to the limited life of the excess earnings and the time value of money is considered. Practical problems of implementation are the estimations of the number of years and the interest rate. As seen in the Method 2 examples, judgments about these factors can significantly affect the resulting goodwill figure.

Method 3. Capitalization of Excess Earnings.   The assumption that the excess earnings will continue *indefinitely* leads to estimating goodwill by capitalizing the excess earnings at an appropriate rate. If the normal rate is used in the Diversified example, goodwill is computed as follows:

$$\text{Goodwill} = \frac{\$18{,}160}{12\%} = \$151{,}333$$

Goodwill computed in this manner represents the amount that would have to be invested to yield a return equal to the **excess earnings in perpetuity.** In other words an investment of $151,333 that yields a 12% return will yield $18,160 annually ($151,333 × 12% per year in perpetuity).

The uncertainty concerning the continuity of excess future earnings may encourage the use of a higher interest rate, indicating the higher level of risk. In the Diversified Enterprises case, a 20% rate for capitalizing excess earnings results in the following computation:

$$\text{Goodwill} = \frac{\$18{,}160}{20\%} = \$90{,}800$$

The selection of an appropriate interest rate in applying the capitalization method is a significant factor in the resulting goodwill figure. The primary flaws in this computation are (1) that the computed goodwill figure is based on the assumption that estimated excess earnings will continue indefinitely, and (2) that this perpetual advantage relates entirely to conditions that exist when goodwill is acquired.

In summary, the assumptions underlying the various methods of estimating goodwill and the judgments required in the implementation of the methods present a strong case against the objectivity of the resulting estimates of goodwill. The estimates of goodwill in the Diversified and Single Product illustrations range from $60,391 to $151,333, as indicated in the summary figures in Exhibit 13–8. At best these methods provide a rough approximation of the range in which goodwill falls.[7] An important point to remember is that the amount recorded as goodwill is the actual cost that is implied in the purchase transaction; this cost of goodwill is measured as the excess of the total price paid for the net assets of the enterprise over the sum of the current value of the individual identifiable assets, less liabilities. The estimation procedures previously illustrated are used to quantify the value of goodwill to assist management in determining an appropriate maximum amount for negotiating a purchase price of another enterprise. Once that purchase price has been established, the estimates of goodwill are not used, because goodwill is recorded in the amounts at the actual price paid for it in accordance with the historical cost principle.

Objectivity

Historical Cost

"Negative" Goodwill

In the previous examples we have assumed that the price paid for an enterprise *exceeds* the sum of the current value of the individual identifiable assets, less liabilities. If the sum of the values of the individual assets, less liabilities, is *more* than the price paid, does "negative" goodwill exist? Presumably the answer is no, because this would result in assets being recorded at amounts in excess of the price paid for them, a violation of the historical cost principle.

Historical Cost

If the price paid for an enterprise is *less* than the sum of the values of the individual identifiable assets, less liabilities, the difference should be allocated as a reduction of the recorded cost of those separately identifiable noncurrent assets other than investments. If, in an unusual case, this allocation reduces noncurrent assets (other than investments) to zero, the difference should be recorded as a deferred credit and amortized as an *addition* to

---

[7]Several additional methods have been suggested for estimating the value of goodwill. For example, the amount resulting from the capitalization of expected earnings at the normal rate, reduced by average net assets utilized, may provide an approximation of goodwill. However, methods such as this fail to base goodwill on the estimated excess of expected earnings over normal earnings, and therefore the authors consider such methods deficient.

EXHIBIT 13–8
Single Product, Inc.
Summary of Goodwill Estimates

	Estimated Goodwill
Method 1. Years Multiple of Excess Earnings	$108,960
Method 2. Present Value of Excess Earnings	
12%	74,663
20%	60,391
Method 3. Capitalization of Excess Earnings	
12%	151,333
20%	90,800

future income over a period not to exceed 40 years. Such a deferred credit would be identified as an "excess of book value over cost of purchased subsidiary" or another appropriate title. This item is usually found in the balance sheet among noncurrent liabilities or in a separate deferred credit section between liabilities and stockholders' equity. The process of determining the excess of book value over cost and the subsequent treatment of this item is usually covered in more depth in advanced accounting texts.

BAD WILL

LATER THIS YEAR, if the Federal Reserve Board approves, $2.4 billion (assets) First American Bank Corp., of Kalamazoo, Mich., will finally complete its acquisition of Detroit's $1.4 billion Northern States Bancorporation. If so, it will be a happy day for Northern States and its shareholders: The four-bank holding company lost over $5.1 million in 1980, and badly needs to be bailed out. With a wretched portfolio of low-interest, fixed-rate loans and a loan-loss problem severe enough for an $11 million provision for possible loan losses in 1980, it faces insolvency or further liquidation by the end of this year unless it is infused with some new capital.

Why on earth would profitable First American want to merge with a basket case like Northern States? A quick look at the combined *pro forma* financial statements in the prospectus tells part of the story. Separately, First American reported earnings of $10.7 million in the first nine months of 1980, while Northern States lost $6.7 million. But together the two banks would have reported $11.4 million in net income for that same period. Magically, the whole becomes greater than the sum of the parts.

Accounting is responsible for this mathematical impossibility. Because the deal is structured as a purchase rather than a pooling, Northern States' portfolio is taken in at current, lower market value rather than higher book value. That means First American may be able to buy Northern States for almost nothing. Although the bank holding company has a book value of $53 million, the deal is expected to close at a distress-sale price of around $18.2 million in First American common and preferred stock. That $34.8 million—the difference between the market value and the book value of Northern States' loans and investments—winds up being gradually *added* to the combined banks' earnings.

If that sounds ridiculous, consider this: It's only the mirror image of a situation that comes up all the time. When a company buys another for *more* than the fair value of its assets, the difference is called goodwill and is thrown onto the balance sheet. Then it is gradually depleted by being charged to earnings over some period, often up to 40 years. In this case, however, the "negative goodwill" or bad will—labeled "accretion of discount" in the prospectus—is added to earnings. But there's a slight difference. It's taken into earnings over a far shorter period of time than 40 years—in this case, the terms of the various loan portfolios. Although the bad will wouldn't have been broken out separately on the income statement, it would have added $5.9 million to combined earnings in 1979 and $4.3 million in the first nine months of 1980—38% of total net income.

Was that bad will an incentive to do the deal? "It was definitely part of the consideration in making it work," admits Dean Williams, First American's chief financial officer. "For Northern States, the merger will mean more capital. For us, it means a presence in the Detroit area, and although Northern States will not be in a loss position in the first few years, it will be a slow improvement. That's where the purchase discount comes in, to help out our earnings in the first few years."

First American will take Northern States' loans and investments, throw out the bad ones and write the others down to what it feels they're worth. A $100,000, ten-year loan at 6%, for instance, would be worth only around $75,000 if the market rate of that kind of loan is now 12%. The bank still gets the same payments on these loans, but they will be carried on the books for a lot less than was actually lent out. Over the life of the loan, however, the bank should eventually get back the whole $100,000 in principal—and thus a $25,000 profit.

But are those profits for real? Williams says they are. "They are absolutely earnings, in the sense that it's like buying a Treasury bill for 80 and collecting

100. You've made the difference as income. You bought something for less than its book value, and so it is gain to you." Peat, Marwick, Mitchell partner Mike Moran agrees: "That existing asset is not earning the market rate. The question is, what am I willing to pay for it so that I am getting a market return? The difference is earnings, and it comes in cash, too."

Clearly, it's true that writing down loans makes those loans more profitable. After all, lower assets mean higher return on assets. But the fact is that the same amount of cash is coming into the bank— there's no more money available to meet liabilities and pay for borrowed funds than there was before. That, after all, is why the bank was in trouble in the first place, and improved earnings don't necessarily mean anything has changed.

"This is really phony accounting," claims one bank analyst. "They're paying less than book value for the bank, but they're paying what it's worth." It's rare that a going financial concern gets less than book value for its assets—in fact, there's usually a premium. So the lack of a premium here demonstrates how far underwater Northern States really is. "They're really not earnings," the analyst continues, "they're accounting justifications for prior mistakes, for the fact that book value is a higher number." Jim Hoffman, an analyst with the Federal Reserve's banking division, makes a similar point.

"The earnings are paper earnings, there's no cash behind them. There's one thing that can give you some insight into the quality of the earnings: They're tax-free." Even the IRS won't tax profits where there was no more cash than there was before.

First American's Williams admits those earnings are, to a certain extent, not a sure indicator of better performance. "It is not cash flow earnings improvement. It is a book type of earnings improvement, but it really is earnings, because you are going to collect something eventually." Jerry Lindstrom, a partner with Ernst & Whinney, puts it another way: "They're going to be better off on a consolidated basis than they would be separately. If the acquirer is strong enough to carry that, that's fine."

There's the point: One bank is bailing out another one, and beneath the improved earnings number, cash flow remains the same. Investors who only look at earnings in situations like this won't see the real picture, good or bad. The clues to the performance of these two banks together will lie elsewhere—for example, in their statement of financial position or long-term changes in the bank's return on equity and assets.

Fortunately, such potentially misleading situations don't happen every day. In fact, only one other major bank deal in the past five years has involved a significant discount from book value—when Mercantile Texas Corp. acquired Federated Capital Corp. in 1976, and both of those banks are doing just fine. Then, too, if interest rates take a dive between now and when the First American deal is finally iced, that would boost the value of Northern States' assets considerably—and there goes some of the purchase discount. Of course, First American would then have the option of selling off those loan assets and taking a securities gain. It's more likely, however, the interest rates will continue to torment bank asset portfolios, and that means a lot more potential for situations where acquired losers can look like winners—at least for a little while.

SOURCE: Thomas Baker, "Bad Will," *Forbes,* May 11, 1981, pp. 90, 93. Reprinted by permission of *Forbes* Magazine. © Forbes Inc., 1981.

SPECIAL PROBLEM AREAS

Several problem areas that have not been discussed to this point exist in accounting for intangible assets and related costs. Accounting for research and development costs is closely related to accounting for intangible assets, particularly because some intangible assets are developed internally through research and development. Also, some intangible assets are used in research and development activities. Accounting for development-stage enterprises is another area closely related to accounting for intangible assets. Accounting for costs in the oil and gas industry relates to intangible-asset accounting and represents an area of continuing controversy for the accounting profession. Since some understanding of all these areas is necessary to gain an appreciation of proper accounting for intangible assets, these subjects are discussed in the remaining sections of this chapter.

Research and Development Costs

Research and development (R & D) is an important aspect of business operations for many enterprises. Prior to 1975, R & D costs were frequently capitalized as intangible assets and amortized over several periods. *FASB Statement of Financial Accounting Standards No. 2* was issued in 1974 to establish standards for the accounting and reporting of R & D costs and related tangible and intangible assets.[8] Under this pronouncement many costs that were previously identified as R & D are part of the cost of other tangible and intangible assets. Those costs that are identified as R & D are treated as expenses in the period incurred.

Research and **development** are defined as follows by the FASB:

Research *is planned search or critical investigation aimed at discovery of new knowledge with the hope that such knowledge will be useful in developing a new product or service . . . or a new process or technique . . . or in bringing about a significant improvement to an existing product or process.*

Development *is the translation of research findings or other knowledge into a plan or design for a new product or process whether intended for sale or use.*[9]

The distinction between R & D costs and expenditures that are identified otherwise requires a great deal of judgment on the part of the accountant. Identifying R & D costs is facilitated by understanding the activities from which R & D costs emerge. Such activities typically occur **prior to the beginning of commercial production and distribution of a product or process.** Examples of activities resulting in R & D costs are:[10]

1. Laboratory research aimed at the discovery of new knowledge.
2. Searching for applications of new research findings or other knowledge.
3. Conceptual formulation and design of possible product or process alternatives.
4. Design, construction, and testing of preproduction prototypes and models.
5. Design, construction, and operation of a pilot plant that is not of a scale economically feasible for commercial production.

Activities that relate to commercial production typically do not result in the incurrence of R & D costs, even though many are similar in nature to activities giving rise to R & D costs. Examples of activities that do not result in R & D costs are:[11]

1. Engineering follow-through in an early stage of commercial production.
2. Quality control during commercial production, including routine testing of products.
3. Routine, ongoing efforts to refine, enrich, or otherwise improve on the quality of an existing product.
4. Adaptation of an existing capacity to a particular requirement or customer's need as part of a continuing commercial activity.
5. Seasonal or other periodic design changes to existing products.

In the previous paragraph we defined R & D in terms of activities. Several elements of

---

[8]*FASB Statement of Financial Accounting Standards No. 2,* "Accounting for Research and Development Costs," 1974.
[9]*FASB Statement of Financial Accounting Standards No. 2,* par. 8.
[10]*FASB Statement of Financial Accounting Standards No. 2,* par. 9.
[11]*FASB Statement of Financial Accounting Standards No. 2,* par. 10.

costs identified with R & D activities can be identified: (1) materials, equipment, and facilities; (2) personnel; (3) intangibles purchased from others; (4) contract services; and (5) indirect costs. The R & D expense of an enterprise can potentially include all of the above costs in a given reporting period. If a cost is considered to be R & D, that cost should be charged to expense when incurred, subject to standards discussed in the following paragraphs.

Materials, Equipment, and Facilities

Materials, equipment, and **facilities** acquired for use in R & D activities that have alternative future uses—either in other R & D activities or in non–R & D activities—should be capitalized in appropriate asset categories when acquired. The cost of materials subsequently used in R & D activities and depreciation on equipment and facilities used in R & D activities should be classified as R & D expense when these expenses are recognized. Costs of materials, equipment, and facilities acquired for particular R & D projects that have no alternative use should be expensed as R & D when incurred.

Personnel

Salaries, wages, and other **personnel costs** of employees involved in R & D activities are charged to R & D expense as incurred.

Intangibles Purchased from Others

The costs of **purchased intangible assets** used in R & D activities that have alternative future uses in other R & D activities or non–R & D activities are capitalized in appropriate asset categories. As these intangible assets are amortized, R & D expense is debited rather than amortization expense, as illustrated earlier in this chapter. The amortization of the intangibles used in R & D thus becomes part of R & D expense as they are used. The costs of intangible assets that are purchased for use in present R & D projects only and that have no alternative future use are charged to R & D expense as incurred.

Contract Services

Enterprises frequently engage others to perform R & D activities for them. The costs of such **contract services** are treated as R & D expenses when incurred.

Indirect Costs

A reasonable allocation of **indirect costs** that relate to R & D activities is included in the R & D expense recognized in determining income. Indirect costs include general and administrative expenses not directly related to R & D activity. To be included in R & D expense, however, general and administrative expenses must have some relationship to R & D activity.

R & D expense consists of a combination of the following elements: costs of materials, equipment, facilities, and intangible assets; personnel costs; costs of contract services; and an allocation of general and administrative expenses. Whether the costs of equipment, facilities, and intangible assets represent R & D in the period incurred or in a subsequent period through amortization of costs depends on whether the items have alternative future uses in ongoing R & D activities or in other activities of the enterprise.

To illustrate the identification of R & D costs, we shall assume that Energy-Efficient Company is involved in the production of home heating and air conditioning equipment that is more efficient than similar equipment available from other companies. Energy-Efficient incurs a number of expenditures related to its activities that are listed on the left in Exhibit 13–9. The proper accounting for these activities is described in the analysis on the right.

Numerous examples can be cited to illustrate the distinction between R & D costs and other expenditures. Most of the items in the Energy-Efficient example are obvious from the previous discussion. The capitalization of legal costs (item *e*) and the cost of acquiring a competing patent (item *g*) are appropriately capitalized in the Patent account. Since this patent is related to a product that is being produced for sale, the amortization of the cost

---

EXHIBIT 13–9
Cost Analysis for Energy-Efficient Company

Expenditure	Capitalize as	Expense as
a. Acquisition of equipment and building to be used in ongoing research activity.	Building, equipment	
b. Salaries of research staff responsible for the design of new heating unit.		R & D
c. Material, labor, and overhead of model of new heating unit.		R & D
d. Costs of testing of model of new heating unit.		R & D
e. Legal fees related to patent on new heating unit.	Patent	
f. Costs of research on marketability of new heating unit.		Operating expense
g. Cost of acquiring patent believed to compete with one on new heating unit.	Patent	
h. Salaries of salespersons selling new heating unit.		Operating expense
i. Costs of engineering activity necessary to advance heating unit to point of commercial production.		R & D
j. Costs of quality control in early stages of commercial production.		Manufacturing cost
k. Depreciation of equipment and building acquired in **a.**		R & D
l. Amortization of patent acquired in **e.**		Manufacturing cost
m. Warranty costs on heating units sold.		Operating expense

(item *l*) is treated as a manufacturing cost. If the patent had been used in R & D activities, the amortization would have been classified as R & D expense. The cost of market research (item *f*) on the new product are not included as R & D, because the research relates to the **marketability** of the product, not to its technical development. In summary, those costs incurred prior to the beginning of commercial production are either capitalized in appropriate asset accounts or charged to expense as R & D. Amortization of the cost of assets used in R & D activities are included in R & D expense when recognized.

We indicated earlier that prior to the issuance of *Statement No. 2,* companies frequently capitalized R & D costs and amortized them over future periods. Why did the FASB take the position that R & D costs should be expensed as incurred unless they are for specific assets that have identifiable alternative future uses? The board carefully considered several capitalization alternatives for R & D expenditures: (1) capitalization of all costs when incurred; (2) capitalization of costs when specified conditions are present; and (3) accumulation of all R & D costs in a special category until the existence of future benefits could be determined.

Objectivity

The principle of objectivity was an important consideration, because the future benefits of individual R & D projects involve a high degree of uncertainty and estimates of the rates of success of R & D projects vary considerably. Also, a direct relationship between R & D costs and specific future revenue generally cannot be determined. Even if a relationship between present R & D costs and future revenue can be demonstrated, the problem of measuring the asset still exists. Generally an expenditure is not treated as an asset unless at the time it is made the future economic benefits can be identified and objectively measured.[12] For these reasons, as well as others, the FASB determined that R & D costs will be expensed as

---

[12]*FASB Statement of Financial Accounting Standards No. 2,* pars. 37–44.

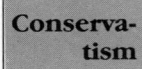

Conservatism

incurred. This position is consistent with the modifying convention of conservatism, which indicates that the least favorable alternative presentation should be followed when doubt exists about the appropriate accounting principle to be applied in a specific situation.

Development-Stage Enterprises

A **development-stage enterprise** is either: (1) an organization that is devoting substantially all of its effort to establishing a new business and that has not begun planned principal operations; or (2) an organization that has begun planned principal operations but that has not generated significant revenue from those operations. Prior to 1976 a variety of accounting and financial reporting practices existed for development-stage enterprises, including the deferral of many costs without regard to their recoverability and the offsetting of revenue against deferred costs. The FASB issued *Statement of Financial Accounting Standards No. 7* in 1975 to standardize accounting and reporting practices by newly developed companies.[13]

Development-stage enterprises typically are devoting a substantial amount of effort to activities like the following:[14]

1. Financial planning.
2. Raising capital.
3. Exploring for natural resources.
4. Developing natural resources.
5. Research and development.
6. Establishing sources of supply.
7. Acquiring property, plant, equipment, and other operating assets.
8. Recruiting and training personnel.
9. Starting up production.

Matching

Development-stage enterprises engaged in these activities incur significant costs but generate little or no revenue against which to match those costs. Thus, development-stage enterprises typically incur operating losses during the development stage.

FASB Statement No. 7 requires development-stage enterprises to account and report on much the same basis as do established operating enterprises in financial statements that purport to present financial position and results of operations. The same generally accepted accounting principles that apply to established enterprises govern the recognition of revenue and expense and the capitalization of costs for development-stage enterprises.

The financial statements issued by a development-stage enterprise should present **financial position, changes in financial position,** and **results of operations** in the same manner as do those issued by established enterprises. Some *additional disclosures* that are necessary because of the unique nature of the development-stage enterprise are summarized in Exhibit 13–10.

The financial statements should clearly indicate that the enterprise is in a development stage and should also include a description of the specific developmental activities in which the enterprise is involved. In the first year that the enterprise is no longer considered to be in the development stage, disclosure should indicate that in previous years it had been a development-stage enterprise.

The reporting requirements of *FASB Statement No. 7* simply apply generally accepted accounting principles of established operating enterprises to development-stage enterprises. Past practices of capitalizing operating losses and nonrecoverable costs as intangible

---

[13]*FASB Statement of Financial Accounting Standards No. 7,* "Accounting and Reporting by Development Stage Enterprises," 1975.
[14]*FASB Statement of Financial Accounting Standards No. 7,* par. 9.

EXHIBIT 13–10
Financial Reporting Requirements of Development-Stage Enterprises

Financial Statements	Special Disclosure Requirements*
Balance sheet	Cumulative net losses reported with a descriptive title, such as "deficit accumulated during the development stage" in stockholders' equity.
Income statement	Cumulative amounts of revenues and expenses from the enterprise's inception.
Statement of changes in financial position	Cumulative amounts of sources and uses of funds since the enterprise's inception.
Statement of stockholders' equity	For each issuance of stock, the date, number of shares of stock, warrants, rights, or other equity securities issued.
	For each issuance, the dollar amounts assigned to the consideration received (per share and in total).
	For each issuance involving noncash consideration, the nature of the transaction and the basis for assigning a dollar amount.

*These special disclosures are required in *addition* to those normally required under generally accepted accounting principles.

---

assets should not be followed. The treatment of a cost should be governed by the nature of the cost rather than the degree of maturity of the company incurring the cost. Under certain circumstances, however, a development-stage company may prepare financial statements on a basis other than generally accepted accounting principles.

In indicating that the enterprise is in a development stage, the financial statements should make the reader aware that the net losses and the deficits relate to incurrence of developmental costs during a period of little or no revenue rather than to the failure to operate profitably as an established enterprise.

Economic Impact

In Chapter 1 we discussed the economic impact of accounting principles and raised the question of whether the FASB should be concerned with the economic impact of the standards it sets. This issue is important with respect to financial reporting by development-stage companies. Some accountants have pointed out that applying generally accepted accounting principles to developing enterprises frequently results in reporting net losses, which may not be fully understood by investors and creditors who could supply capital for these companies. If these reported losses influenced investors and creditors to withhold or delay investments in developing companies, new companies would have an even more difficult time getting started.

In an attempt to consider this issue, the FASB questioned officers of fifteen venture-capital enterprises. The conclusion of this limited research was that the accounting treatment of preoperating losses has little effect, if any, on the amount of capital that would be provided or the terms under which it would be provided to newly developed companies. According to officers, the venture-capital investor typically relies on an assessment of cash flows based on an investigation of the technological, marketing, management, and financial aspects of the enterprise.[15] Other research in this general area tends to support these conclusions.

The FASB concluded that requiring cumulative figures in the financial statements, as described in Figure 13–10, would be useful in understanding the position of the developing

---

[15]*FASB Statement of Financial Accounting Standards No. 7*, par. 49.

company until it reached the position of being fully operative. The FASB determined, in addition, that the special report forms used in the past were less useful than were the financial-statement forms of established operating enterprises, with which investors were already familiar.

Accounting by Oil and Gas Producing Companies

Oil and gas producing companies incur substantial costs in locating and developing oil and gas reserves. Given the current state of technology, exploration activities require many drilling efforts, only some of which locate producible oil and gas reserves. Many drilling efforts result in "dry holes" that provide no producible oil and gas.

Two general methods of accounting for costs incurred in exploration activities are used in the oil and gas industry. The **successful-efforts method** is based on the theory that only the costs of locating producing wells (i.e., those wells from which gas and oil can economically be extracted) should be capitalized and amortized over future periods. In this method costs associated with unsuccessful efforts, or activities not resulting in the location of producible oil and gas reserves, are treated as expenses when they are incurred.

In the alternative method, the **full-cost method,** the costs of *all* efforts are treated as the costs of locating producing wells. Because many unsuccessful efforts are usually necessary to locate reserves that can be successfully exploited, exploration costs that would be treated as expenses when incurred in the successful-efforts method are treated as assets and amortized in the full-cost method.

Both the successful-efforts and the full-cost methods have been widely used in accounting for the numerous costs incurred in oil and gas explorations. In practice, the successful-efforts method has been widely adopted by larger companies, based on the notion that the costs of nonproductive efforts provide no discernible future benefits to the enterprise and therefore should not be capitalized as assets. On the other hand smaller companies have favored the full-cost method because they feel that the costs of unsuccessful efforts are part of the cost of the successful efforts. In addition, they desire to establish a smoother, more predictable earnings pattern over time.

In response to strong encouragement by the Securities and Exchange Commission (SEC), in December 1977 the FASB issued *Statement No. 19.*[16] In this statement, which resulted from a lengthy process of considering many diverse views, the FASB attempted to eliminate the full-cost method and establish successful-efforts as the only acceptable accounting method for oil and gas exploration costs. Costs in oil and gas producing activities fall into several classifications: acquisitions, explorations, development, production, support equipment, and facilities. Under the successful-efforts method, the costs of acquiring oil and gas rights are capitalized when incurred. These costs are amortized as a part of the cost of oil and gas produced. Exploration costs, except for the costs of drilling exploratory wells, are expensed as incurred. The costs of drilling exploratory wells are **temporarily deferred** until a determination is made on whether or not the well is producible. If producible reserves exist, the costs of the exploratory wells are capitalized and amortized as part of the cost of oil and gas produced. If producible reserves do not exist, the costs of the exploratory wells are expensed when this determination is made.

Costs of developing proved reserves are capitalized and depreciated as part of the cost of oil and gas produced. Production costs are treated as part of the cost of oil and gas produced and are expensed as incurred. Costs of support equipment and facilities are capitalized and depreciated as costs of oil and gas produced to the extent that they are used in oil and gas producing activities.

The application of the basic concept underlying the successful-efforts method is appar-

---

[16]*FASB Statement of Financial Accounting Standards No. 19,* "Financial Accounting and Reporting by Oil and Gas Producing Companies," 1977.

ent in the accounting for exploration costs as previously described. All exploration costs, *except* those for drilling exploratory wells that result in producible oil and gas reserves, are treated as expenses as incurred. Thus, costs that are capitalized and amortized over a long period relate only to recoverable oil and gas reserves, the basic concept underlying the successful-efforts method.

Economic Impact

An important issue that emerged in the FASB's consideration of alternative accounting methods used in the oil and gas industry was the potential negative economic impact of requiring companies to expense the costs of unsuccessful explorations. Proponents of the full-cost method argued that the required expensing of the costs of unsuccessful efforts would discourage exploration in the oil and gas industry at a time when exploration was greatly needed. A related argument was that the reduced profitability of companies under the successful-efforts method would discourage investment in oil and gas producing companies. These arguments were stated as being particularly significant for newer, developing companies that had aggressive exploration policies and, therefore, had a greater need for outside capital than established operating enterprises.

Is the accounting method used by a company for exploration activities in the oil and gas industry a significant factor in identifying those companies that are aggressive in exploration? One researcher concluded that full-cost companies are *not* more aggressive in exploration than successful-effort companies, although full-cost companies did make a greater use of outside capital than successful-efforts companies.[17] One interpretation of this research is that the method used to account for oil and gas production costs is not necessarily a factor that encourages or discourages exploration in the oil and gas industry.

Despite the fact that the FASB was cooperating with the SEC in attempting to eliminate the diversity in accounting for oil and gas producing activities, the SEC responded negatively to the position of the FASB. Reacting to numerous pressures, including the strength of the smaller oil and gas producing companies and the fear of discouraging oil and gas exploration activities by the required expensing of exploration costs, the SEC took the position that both full-cost and successful-efforts methods were unsatisfactory methods of accounting by oil and gas producing companies.

The SEC indicated its preference for the development of a method of current-value accounting that would eventually replace both existing methods. It further indicated that it would develop such a method and tentatively referred to it as **reserve-recognition accounting.** In the meantime enterprises reporting to the SEC could continue to use either the full-cost or the successful-efforts method.

In light of these developments, the FASB issued *Statement of Financial Accounting Standards No. 25,* "Suspension of Certain Accounting Requirements for Oil and Gas Producing Companies."[18] As the title implies, this statement suspended the effective date of *Statement No. 19,* thereby allowing companies to continue using either the full-cost or the successful-efforts method. This means that companies that were not required to report to the SEC, as well as those that were required to do so, continued to have the option of reporting under either method. At a later date the SEC abandoned its plan to develop the reserve-recognition accounting method. Its decision was based primarily on the practical problems encountered in attempting to apply a current value approach to oil and gas reserves. Thus, oil and gas producing companies continue to choose either the full-cost method or the successful-efforts method.

This series of events verifies the fact that the SEC has ultimate responsibility for the establishment of standards for reporting by publicly held corporations in the United States.

---

[17]Edward B. Deakin III, "An Analysis of Differences Between Non-Major Oil Firms Using Successful Efforts and Full Cost Methods," *Accounting Review* (October 1979), pp. 722–734.

[18]*FASB Statement of Financial Accounting Standards No. 25,* "Suspension of Certain Accounting Requirements for Oil and Gas Producing Companies," 1979.

Although the positions of the FASB have generally been supported by the SEC, if the two do not agree, the legal position of the SEC is superior. This series of events also indicates that the reporting requirements applicable to those companies that must report to the SEC have a significant influence on those enterprises that do not report to the SEC.

CONCLUDING REMARKS

Historical Cost

Matching

In Chapters 11, 12, and 13 we have studied plant and intangible assets. The problems of determining historical cost for these assets and the importance of matching that cost with revenues throughout the lives of these assets have been emphasized. Variations in the methods that underlie the book value of these assets are due primarily to the different ways accountants compute the amount of depreciation to be recognized in each accounting period.

In studying a company's balance sheet, remember that the principles underlying accounting for different types of assets vary. These differing principles are used in recognition of the fact that the values of various assets are realized in several ways. For example, receivables are shown in the balance sheet at their net realizable value (gross amount less an estimate of the portion that will not be collected). Inventories are shown at the lower of cost

---

THREE WAYS OF LOOKING AT AN OIL COMPANY'S PROFITS

TO ILLUSTRATE how an oil and gas producer's financial statements are affected by various accounting methods, Arthur Andersen made some highly simplified calculations for an imaginary oil company, which might be called Eureka Corp. Eureka is assumed to have begun operations on January 1, 1978, with $10 million in capital. All of it went into drilling ten wells, nine of which were dry holes. Two million barrels of oil reserves were proved in the one productive well. At the outset it was assumed the price would be $12 per barrel, and lifting costs would be $400,000 annually over the well's ten-year life, making the reserves worth $20 million. It was further assumed that Eureka would begin production at the beginning of 1979 and produce 200,000 barrels a year. No other exploration was ever conducted.

In its first year, when Eureka sold not a drop of oil, the company broke even under full-cost accounting—all the $10 million in exploration costs were capitalized and show up as assets on the balance sheet. Under successful-efforts accounting, the $9 million spent on dry holes shows up as a cost— hence the $9-million loss—and only $1 million, the cost of the successful well, as an asset.

Under R.R.A. [Reserve-Recognition Accounting],

the same balance-sheet item is $12.3 million—the present value (discounted at 10 percent) of the $20-million stream of income expected. After subtracting the $10 million in exploration costs, that produces $2.3 million pretax in the first year. (In succeeding years, profits arise primarily from revaluing the expected income stream as the time period in the discount equation diminishes.) The blip in 1982 for R.R.A. profits shows the effect of the price rise indicated on the chart. In 1985, some unanticipated developments—spelled out on the chart—caused profits to rise, on balance, under the two historical-cost-accounting methods because sales went up. But the developments had very little effect under R.R.A. (The dotted lines show how profits would have looked if the price rise and the 1985 changes hadn't occurred.) Pretax income over the entire period added up to precisely $12 million under all three methods—the difference in the annual levels is simply a matter of when revenues and costs are recognized.

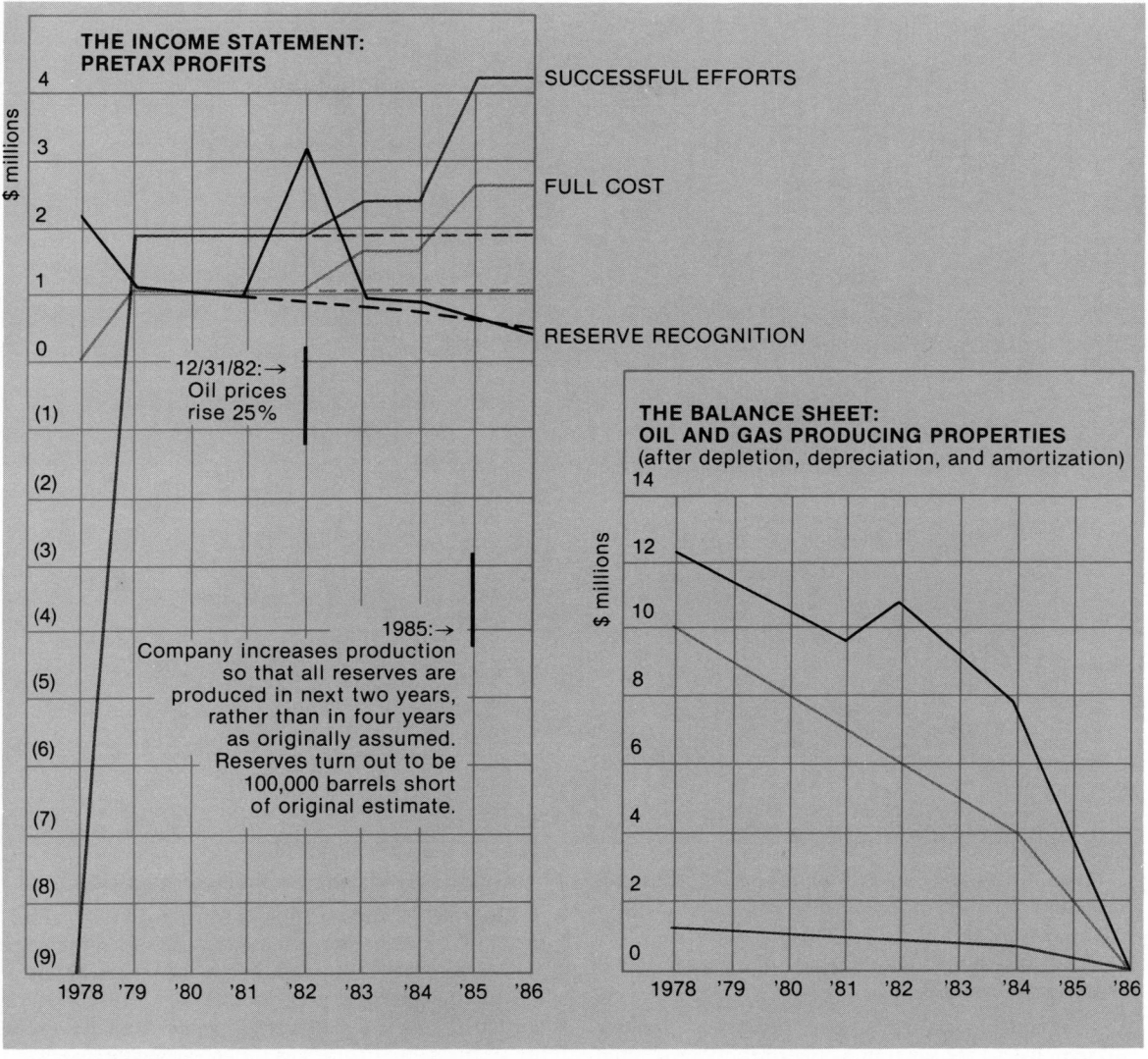

THE INCOME STATEMENT:
PRETAX PROFITS

$ millions

SUCCESSFUL EFFORTS

FULL COST

RESERVE RECOGNITION

12/31/82:→
Oil prices
rise 25%

1985:→
Company increases production
so that all reserves are
produced in next two years,
rather than in four years
as originally assumed.
Reserves turn out to be
100,000 barrels short
of original estimate.

THE BALANCE SHEET:
OIL AND GAS PRODUCING PROPERTIES
(after depletion, depreciation, and amortization)

$ millions

or market. We have seen, however, that cost can be determined by several different flow assumptions and that variations exist in the methods of determining the lower of cost or market once the cost has been determined.

Concerning investments, we learned that a number of different methods are applied. These methods vary, depending on whether the investment is in debt or equity securities and whether it is current or noncurrent.

Now that we have completed our study of the major asset categories, it is useful to review the significance of the dollar amounts to the various types of assets included in a company's balance sheet. A review of the primary valuation techniques included within generally accepted accounting principles is presented in Exhibit 13–11.

EXHIBIT 13–11
Review of Asset Valuation Techniques

Type of Asset	Basis of Valuation Generally Found in Balance Sheet
Current Assets	
Cash	Face amount
Marketable securities	
Debt securities	Cost
Equity securities	Lower of aggregate cost or market
Receivables	Net realizable value
Inventories	Lower of cost or market
Prepaid expenses	Unexpired cost
Investments	
Debt securities	Cost, adjusted for unamortized premium or discount
Equity securities	
Investments lacking significant influence	Lower of aggregate cost or market
Investments providing significant influence	Equity method
Plant and Intangible Assets	
Property, plant, and equipment	Portion of cost not yet recognized as depreciation
Natural resources	Portion of cost not yet recognized as depletion
Intangibles	Portion of cost not yet recognized as amortization
Other Assets	Miscellaneous, depending on nature of specific asset

---

KEY POINTS

1. Intangible assets differ from property, plant, and equipment primarily because the intangibles lack physical substance. Both types of assets have relatively long lives and are used in the production and distribution of goods and services.

2. Some intangible assets (e.g., patents, copyrights, and franchises) are separately identifiable. Some intangibles, usually identified as goodwill, are associated with an enterprise as a whole and cannot be transferred apart from that enterprise.

3. Intangible assets (acquired from other enterprises or developed internally) that can be separately identified and have determinable lives are recorded as assets. Other costs related to internally developed intangibles (including those that have characteristics similar to those of goodwill) are treated as expenses when they are incurred.

4. Intangible assets are initially recorded at historical cost and then amortized over their estimated useful lives. The period of amortization should not exceed 40

years, and the straight-line method is typically used.

5. Goodwill is an intangible asset representing anticipated excess earning capacity. It arises when the price paid for another business exceeds the current value of the identifiable net assets acquired. Goodwill is recorded at cost and amortized over its estimated useful life in the same manner as other intangible assets.

6. The value of goodwill can be estimated by several methods that are based on a comparison between anticipated earnings and normal earnings.

7. Research and development costs are treated as expenses when they are incurred. Some costs related to R & D activities, however, are capitalized in appropriate asset categories and amortized as R & D expense over their estimated useful lives.

8. Development-stage enterprises must apply generally accepted accounting principles in preparing financial statements purporting to present financial position and results of operations in much the same way as do established enterprises. In addition, a development-stage enterprise must disclose in its financial statements certain cumulative figures that relate to the enterprise since its inception.

9. Oil and gas producing companies may account for exploration costs under either the successful-efforts or the full-cost method within current generally accepted accounting principles. This is an area of significant controversy in which the FASB attempted to reduce variation in accounting practice by requiring companies to use only the successful-efforts method. Under pressure from the SEC, however, the FASB suspended this requirement.

QUESTIONS

In questions 13–1 through 13–5, circle the letter of the correct answer.

13–1 The following procedure best depicts the disposition of the cost of intangible assets subsequent to acquisition:

[a] Amortize over the longer of 40 years or the estimated useful life.

[b] Amortize over 40 years.

[c] Amortize over the shorter of the estimated useful life or 40 years.

[d] Amortize over 10 years.

13–2 Assets that should be presented in the intangible-asset category of the balance sheet include all of the following *except:*

[a] Goodwill

[b] Copyrights

[c] Patents

[d] Accounts receivable

13–3 The following characteristic is *not* necessary for an asset to qualify as an intangible asset:

[a] Has a determinable life.

[b] Conveys a right or privilege.

[c] Has a relatively long life.

[d] Is used in the production of other goods or services.

13–4 Capitalizable organization costs include all of the following *except:*

[a] Compensation paid promoters of the corporation.

[b] Initial stock-issuance costs.

[c] Operating expenses incurred prior to beginning full-scale operations.

[d] Legal fees of drafting the corporate charter and bylaws.

13–5 The following statement best describes proper accounting by development-stage companies:

[a] The same as established operating enterprises except for the capitalization of R & D.

[b] The same as established operating enterprises except for the capitalization of operating losses in early years of operations.

[c] The same as established operating enterprises except for the requirement of additional disclosures in the financial statements and related notes.

[d] The same as established operating enterprises except that the statement of changes in financial position is not required.

13–6 Identify in brief phrases the key elements in the definition of the term "intangible asset."

13–7 What basic feature of intangible assets distinguishes them from tangible plant assets?

13–8 Distinguish between intangible assets that can be separately identified and those that cannot be separately identified, indicating the type(s) of transactions in which each typically arises.

13–9 What basic accounting principles are applied in accounting for intangible assets?

13–10 Identify several types of expenditures that are closely related to intangible assets but that should *not* be capitalized and amortized over periods after their incurrence.

13–11 With regard to *APB Opinion No. 17,* what was the basic rationale for requiring the amortization of intangible assets, even in cases in which the life of the intangible is apparently unlimited?

13–12 Identify several factors that should be considered in estimating the useful life of a separately identifiable intangible asset.

13–13 Indicate the current legal life of the following intangible assets: patents, copyrights, and trademarks.

13–14 Cite several examples of intangible assets whose lives may be limited through contractual arrangements between two enterprises or between an enterprise and a governmental unit.

13–15 What types of individual costs are properly included in organization costs?

13–16 How should organization costs be treated subsequent to the beginning of operations?

13–17 Define goodwill. Identify any specific circumstances that must be met for goodwill to be established as an asset in the balance sheet.

13–18 Outline briefly specific procedures that should be followed in accounting for goodwill, incuding the determination of cost and the recognition of periodic amortization.

13–19 Outline briefly the steps that should be followed in placing an estimate on the value of goodwill existing in a potential acquisition.

13–20 Of the various methods of estimating the value of goodwill presented in this chapter, which appears to have the greatest merit on a conceptual basis? Why?

13–21 List the key concepts in the definition of "research" and "development" as defined in *FASB Statement of Financial Accounting Standards No. 2.*

13–22 Research and development costs are classified in five categories: (1) materials, equipment, and facilities; (2) personnel; (3) intangibles purchased from others; (4) contract services; and (5) indirect costs. Describe the items included in each category and provide one or more example(s) of each.

13–23 Distinguish between the full-cost method and the successful-efforts method of accounting by oil and gas producing companies.

13–24 Define the term "development-stage enterprise" and suggest several activities in which such an enterprise would typically be engaged.

13–25 To what extent do the accounting and reporting standards that are applicable to established operating enterprises apply to development-stage enterprises?

CASES

C13–1 Evaluate each of the following statements as true or false in terms of generally accepted accounting principles. Provide explanations for your answers.
[a] Intangible assets are established at historical cost and amortized over their useful lives due to the difficulty in determining the current value of intangibles.
[b] R & D costs are treated as expenses when incurred due to the uncertainty of future benefits of such expenditures.
[c] Estimating the amount of goodwill in a business acquisition is extremely important because the estimate establishes the amount to be amortized over the next 40 years.
[d] Whether an aquisition has an "alternative future use" is important in determining whether a particular expenditure relates to R & D.

C13–2 Accounting practitioners, accounting authors, and the courts have proposed various solutions to the problems of accounting in terms of historical cost for goodwill and similar intangible assets.

Instructions

[a] Compare the problems of accounting for goodwill and similar intangible assets to those for other plant assets.
   [1] What problems are similar? Explain.
   [2] What problems are different? Explain.
[b] [1] Describe the possible accounting treatments for the cost of goodwill and similar intangible assets following acquisition.
   [2] What treatment is consistent with current,

generally accepted accounting principles, and why?

(AICPA adapted)

C13–3 On June 30, 1985, your client, Neth Corporation, was granted two patents for the plastic cartons that it has been producing and marketing profitably for the past three years. One patent covers the manufacturing process and the other covers the related products. Neth executives tell you that these patents represent the most significant breakthrough in the industry in the past 30 years. The products have been marketed under the registered trademarks Safetainer, Duratainer, and Sealrite. Licenses under the patents have already been granted by your client to other manufacturers in the United States and abroad and are producing substantial royalties.

On July 1, Neth commenced patent infringement actions against several companies whose names you recognize as substantial and prominent competitors. Neth's management is optimistic that these suits will result in a permanent injunction against the manufacture and sale of the infringing products and a collection of damages for loss of profits caused by the alleged infringement.

The financial vice-president has suggested that the patents be recorded at the discounted value of expected net royalty receipts.

Instructions

[a] Define an intangible asset.
[b] [1] Explain the meaning of "discounted value of

expected net receipts."

    [2] How would such a value be calculated for net royalty receipts?

[c] What basis of valuation for Neth's patents would be generally accepted in accounting? Give supporting reasons for this basis.

[d] [1] Assuming no practical problems of implementation and ignoring generally accepted accounting principles, describe the preferable basis of valuation for patents.

    [2] What would be the preferable theoretical basis of amortization, and why?

[e] Discuss what recognition, if any, should be made of the infringement litigation in the financial statements for the year ending September 30, 1985.

(AICPA adapted)

C13–4 Thomas Company is in the process of developing a revolutionary new product. A division of the company was formed to develop, manufacture, and market this product. As of year end (December 31, 1985) the new product has not been manufactured for resale; however, a prototype unit is in operation.

Throughout 1985 the new division incurred certain costs. These costs include design and engineering studies, prototype manufacturing costs, administrative expenses (including salaries of administrative personnel), and market research costs. In addition, approximately $500,000 in equipment (estimated useful life, 10 years) was purchased for use in developing and manufacturing the new product. Approximately $200,000 of this equipment was built specifically for the design development of the new product. The remaining $300,000 of equipment was used to manufacture the preproduction prototype and will be used to manufacture the new product once it is in commercial production.

Instructions

[a] What are the definitions of "research" and of "development" as defined in *Statement of Financial Accounting Standards No. 2?*

[b] Briefly indicate the practical and conceptual reasons for the conclusion reached by the FASB on accounting and reporting practices for research and development costs.

[c] In accordance with *Statement of Financial Accounting Standards No. 2,* how should the various costs described above be recorded on the financial statements for the year ended December 31, 1985?

(AICPA adapted)

C13–5 The president of New Company, Thomas P. New, has engaged you to assist in the preparation of financial statements to be used in conjunction with a proposed bank loan. Officials of the bank have requested financial statements which are "based on good accounting."

New Company was organized during 1985. The company has been raising capital, acquiring assets, developing personnel, and developing products which it plans to market in the future. Only insignificant amounts of revenue have been generated to date.

Mr. New has prepared the following balance sheet which he considers adequate for purposes of the proposed bank loan. He also offers the information which accompanies the balance sheet as an explanation of some of the activities of the enterprise to date.

New Company
BALANCE SHEET
October 31, 1985

Assets	
Cash	$ 17,650
Machinery (at cost)	59,350
Land (at cost)	15,000
Intangibles	41,400
	$133,400

Liabilities	
Accrued expenses	$ 11,975
Notes payable (90-day)	21,425
	33,400

Stockholders' Equity	
Common stock	100,000
	$133,400

Notes:

[1] Intangible assets consist of the following:

Research and development	$15,400
Marketing research	3,400
Personnel recruitment and training	12,600
Legal fees relative to organization of corporation	4,750
Operating expenses incurred through October 31, 1985	5,250
	$41,400

[2] Common stock has been issued as follows:

    [a] Thomas P. New, President, acquired 8,000 shares at the $10 par value.

    [b] George M. New, brother of Thomas, received 2,000 shares in exchange for land which he had pur-

chased five years earlier for $15,000.

[c] One thousand shares were issued to John X. New, a cousin of both Thomas and George, for managerial services rendered in operating the enterprise to date. John will become the general manager at some future date when he quits his current position with another company.

Thomas asks you to verify the authenticity of his balance sheet and transfer it to the bank as soon as possible so that he may proceed with his application for the much needed bank loan.

Instructions

[a] Identify deficiencies in Mr. New's balance sheet, considering both his draft of the statement and the additional information which he has provided. Indicate the proper treatment of each item you have listed as a deficiency.

[b] In addition to the changes you propose in [a], what items must be included to provide the bank with financial statements that are prepared in conformity with generally accepted accounting principles?

EXERCISES

E13–1 Determining the amortization period for intangible assets involves a consideration of several important variables.

Instructions

State a general rule for determining the period over which the following intangible assets should be amortized. If an established legal life is involved, indicate that period of time as part of your answer.

[a] Patent
[b] Copyright
[c] Trademark
[d] Franchise
[e] Leasehold improvement

E13–2 On January 2, 1983, Miami Company entered into a franchise agreement to operate a fast food restaurant called Hot Dog Haven. The initial franchise fee was $10,000 and is expected to be revenue-producing as long as the company retains the right to use the designation.

The franchise contract is for a five-year period, at the end of which a new agreement will be negotiated, if desired, by the original parties. The franchise also calls for payment of 5% of gross revenues by Miami Company each year. Revenues for 1983 and 1984 were $72,500 and $103,000, respectively. Straight-line amortization is used on all intangible assets. Miami Company reports on a calendar-year basis.

Instructions

[a] Prepare all journal entries for Miami Company relative to the franchise agreement for 1983 and 1984.
[b] Determine the amounts to be included in the 1984 financial statements relative to the franchise.

E13–3 Distinguishing between R & D costs and other related costs is sometimes difficult.

Instructions

Identify the accounts that should be debited in each of the following transactions or adjustments:

[a] Cost of models of products under development.
[b] Cost of patent usable only in a current R & D project.
[c] Legal fees paid to successfully defend a patent used in ongoing R & D activities.
[d] Amortization of a patent on a product currently being manufactured and sold.
[e] Costs of quality control over the production process.
[f] Amortization of a patent used in ongoing R & D activities.
[g] Warranty costs on products sold.
[h] Costs of R & D contract services expected to be of continuing benefit.
[i] Materials expected to be used only in current R & D projects.

E13–4 Innovative Manufacturing Company acquired three patents in January 1983. The patents have different lives, as indicated in the following schedule:

	Cost	Estimated Useful Life in Years	Remaining Legal Life in Years
Patent X	$10,500	10	17
Patent Y	27,250	5	7
Patent Z	65,620	Indefinite	17

Patent Z is believed to be uniquely useful as long as the company retains the right to use it. In June 1984, the company unsuccessfully attempted to defend its right to Patent Y. Legal fees of $5,735 were incurred in this action.

The company's policy is to amortize intangible assets by the straight-line method to the nearest half year. The company reports on a calendar-year basis.

Instructions

Determine the amount of amortization that should be recognized for 1983, 1984, and 1985.

E13–5 Stone Face Company acquired a patent on June 25, 1982, for $13,000. Management believes that the patent will be useful to the company for its remaining legal life of 13 years.

On January 12, 1984, the company spent $3,000 to successfully defend the patent against a competing company.

During 1985 management determines that the estimated remaining life of the patent should be reduced to five years, including the current year. This decision was made after careful consideration of actions of various competing companies.

Instructions

Prepare all journal entries relating to the patent for 1982 through 1985, assuming the company's year-end is December 31. Company policy is to amortize intangible assets by the straight-line method, computed to the nearest full month.

E13–6 Upstart Manufacturing Company was organized during 1985. In assisting in the preparation of the financial statements for the year ending December 31, you discover that the following items were debited to the Organization Cost account during early January 1985:

Legal fees of corporate registration	$15,250
Compensation of promoters of corporation	12,560
Salaries of employees before the beginning of operations	5,600
Discount on 10-year bonds issued before the beginning of operations	2,770
	$36,180

Plans call for the amortization of organization costs over a five-year period by the straight-line method. The company's accountant does not plan to begin this amortization until 1986, however, due to the large operating loss which the company sustained in 1985.

No amortization of the discount on the bonds has been made. The straight-line method is considered appropriate.

Instructions

Prepare all correcting and adjusting entries that you would propose on December 31, 1985. Closing entries for the year have *not* been made.

E13–7 Statler Enterprises has leased several items of equipment under a lease that does not qualify for capitalization. The lease was entered into on May 1, 1982. Statler paid the $150,000 rental for the first year in advance; a similar payment is made each year on May 1. The lease term is 10 years; the equipment is expected to have a useful life of 25 years.

On May 1, 1984, the company spent $36,000 to make certain improvements on the equipment. These improvements are expected to guarantee the maximum usefulness of the equipment for the duration of the lease term.

Intangible assets are amortized by the straight-line method, computed to the nearest half year.

Instructions

Determine the balance sheet and income statement implications of the equipment lease for the years ending December 31, 1982–1985.

E13–8 Regas Company is considering acquisition of the net assets of Jeremiah Company to expand its operations. The book value and current value of the net assets of Jeremiah Company are $150,000 and $200,000, respectively. The normal rate of return is believed to be 9%, but the management of Regas Company believes it can earn 12% annually on its investment in Jeremiah Company due to the excellent reputation of Jeremiah.

Instructions

Compute the goodwill that results from applying the following methods to the situation described above:
[a] Years multiple of excess earnings (assuming a 10-year period of excess earnings).
[b] Present value of excess earnings at the expected rate (assuming an 8-year period of excess earnings).
[c] Capitalization of excess earnings at the normal rate.
[d] Capitalization of excess earnings at 18%.

E13–9 George Washington Hatchet Company is considering acquisition of the net assets of Dallas Umbrella Company as part of a diversification program. The management of George Washington believes the excellent reputation of Dallas Umbrella provides an opportunity to achieve a level of earnings in excess of the normal rate (10%). In fact, it expects to earn a rate of return of 16% on its investment.

The following information is available on Dallas Umbrella Company:

	Estimated Current Value
Current assets	$ 150,000
Noncurrent assets	280,000
Total reported assets	430,000
Liabilities	(272,000)
Net assets	$ 158,000

In attempting to assess the amount it should bid for Dallas Umbrella Company, the management of George Washington is attempting to estimate a value for goodwill.

Instructions

Compute the goodwill resulting from each of the following methods:
[a] Years multiple of excess earnings (assuming a five-year period).
[b] Present value of excess earnings at the expected rate (assuming a five-year period).
[c] Capitalization of excess earnings at the normal rate.
[d] Capitalization of excess earnings at the expected rate.

E13–10 Denver Diversified acquired Simplified Products Company on January 3, 1985. Conditions of the acquisition include the following:
[1] Denver Diversified issued $1,000,000 of 20-year bonds to finance the transaction. The $1,000,000 received from the issuance of the bonds was transferred to Simplified Products Company to complete the acquisition.
[2] Denver Diversified is to take over all assets (except cash) and all liabilities of Simplified Products Company. Simplified Products is then to liquidate its assets by distributing cash to stockholders in retirement of their shares of stock.
[3] Denver Diversified has established the following current valuations on assets and liabilities to be assumed:

	Book Value on Simplified's Books	Estimated Current Value
Receivables	$ 100,000	$ 80,000
Inventory	550,000	720,000
Property, plant, and equipment	900,000	1,200,000

Current liabilities	(300,000)	(300,000)
Noncurrent liabilities	(1,000,000)	(1,000,000)
Net assets	$ 250,000	$ 700,000

[4] Denver Diversified has determined through various estimation techniques that goodwill inherent in the transaction has a value of at least $400,000. Goodwill is to be amortized over a 10-year period by the straight-line method.

Instructions

Prepare all journal entries on the books of Denver Diversified for the year ended December 31, 1985. Include amortization of goodwill for the full year.

E13–11 An account for a research project identified as AM423 is included on the trial balance of your client, Rochester Company. The account balance of $49,200 consists of the following charges:

Salaries of research staff	$15,850
Patent acquired solely for use in project AM423	12,000
Patent acquired for use in several research projects, including AM423	16,200
Cost of models	5,150
	$49,200

Intangible assets are amortized by the straight-line method over the shorter of the legal life or estimated useful life. The company's patents have generally been found to be useful for approximately 10 years. You determined that both of the patents were acquired in early 1985 and that the cost of models and salaries were incurred throughout 1985.

Instructions

Determine the items that should be presented in the Rochester Company's balance sheet and income statement on December 31, 1985.

E13–12 Jefferson Book Company incorrectly charged the $40,000 cost of a copyright acquired in early 1984 to the retained earnings account. The error was discovered as part of the 1985 audit. The company holds several copyrights and follows the policy of amortizing their cost over the period expected to benefit by the straight-line method, computed to the nearest whole year. This particular copyright was expected to be useful in producing revenue for eight years from the time of acquisition, even though the legal life was 27 years from that date.

Instructions

[a] Prepare the entry necessary in 1985 to correct the error of 1984.

[b] Prepare the entry to record amortization of the copyright for 1985.

E13–13 J. C. Nickel Company acquired three intangible assets during 1985 from other enterprises: patent, $15,270; leasehold improvement, $16,780; and goodwill, $176,000. The patent has a remaining legal life of seven years. The leasehold improvement has an expected life of 25 years. The goodwill is expected to provide benefits in the form of high earnings indefinitely. The leasehold improvement is on property that J. C. Nickel has leased for 15 years; renewal depends on the intent of both parties at that time. No further information on the lives of the various intangible assets is available or determinable.

Instructions

[a] State your recommendation for the useful life to be used for amortization of the three intangible assets.

[b] Assuming that straight-line amortization is used with a full year taken in the year of acquisition, prepare the entry or entries necessary to record the amortization of the intangible assets at the end of 1985, based on your recommendation in [a].

E13–14 For several years South Central Manufacturing Company has accounted for R & D costs in accordance with *Statement of Financial Accounting Standards No. 2.* In 1984 research efforts materialize and three patents are acquired. Patent MP4 will be used in the ongoing R & D activities of the enterprise. Patent MP5 will be used in one specific research project that is currently underway. Patent MP6 will be used in the company's manufacturing process.

Company officials suggest that the cost of the patents be established as follows:

Patent	Legal Costs of Obtaining Patents	Costs Previously Charged to R & D	Total Cost
MP4	$ 5,500	$17,625	$23,125
MP5	2,000	–0–	2,000
MP6	4,250	19,000	23,250
	$11,750	$36,625	$48,375

Because legal costs were charged to the Legal Fees account when they were incurred, the company's accountant recommends the following entry:

Patents	48,375	
Legal Fees		11,750
Retained Earnings		36,625

Instructions

[a] Evaluate the suggested entry to capitalize the patents. Justify your position.

[b] Suggest alternative entries for the capitalization of the patents.

[c] How should the amortization of the patent costs be treated in subsequent years?

E13–15 Greenleaf Company developed a trademark to distinguish its products from those of major competitors. Through advertising and other means, the company is seeking to establish significant product identification to increase future sales.

The similarity between the trademark costs and other intangible and operating costs has caused some confusion over proper accounting. The following items are being treated as part of the cost of the trademark:

Marketing research to study consumer tastes	$15,600
Design costs of trademark	16,270
Legal fees of registering trademark	5,110
Advertising to establish recognition of trademark	18,500
Registration fee with U.S. Patent Office	1,000

Through renewals, the trademark is expected to have an unlimited life.

Instructions

[a] Evaluate each of the costs as appropriate for capitalization in the Trademark account.

[b] Recommend the period of amortization for the cost of the trademark. Justify your recommendation.

E13–16 Oklahoma Company is involved in oil and gas production activities. The following costs were incurred during 1985 relative to these activities:

Acquiring mineral rights	$11,500,000
Exploration	
Drilling exploratory wells resulting in recoverable reserves	5,400,000
Drilling exploratory wells not resulting in recoverable reserves	6,250,000
Other costs	2,750,000
Developing recoverable oil reserves	7,375,000

| Producing oil and gas (after extraction) | 9,550,000 |
| Acquiring equipment for use in oil and gas producing activities | 17,650,000 |

Instructions

For each of the above cost categories, indicate the proper accounting treatment within the successful-efforts method by choosing among the following:

[a] Expense as incurred.

[b] Capitalize and amortize as a cost of oil and gas produced.

[c] Treat as a cost of oil and gas produced as incurred.

PROBLEMS

P13–1 Paper Clip Company has accumulated a number of costs in its Intangibles account. As a new employee in the company's accounting department, you have been asked to analyze the account and recommend any adjustments you think should be made. The Intangibles account for 1985 is presented to you as follows:

Intangibles

Date	Transaction Description	Dr.	Cr.	Balance
Jan. 2	Legal fees related to organization of business	10,500		10,500
Jan. 2	Prepayment of lease on building for one year	12,000		22,500
Feb. 1	Prepayment of insurance for two years	650		23,150
Feb. 20	Advertising expenses (radio, television, and newspaper)	8,000		31,150
Apr. 5	Premium on bonds issued		10,500	20,650
Apr. 30	Interest paid on short-term notes	2,500		23,150
May 12	Legal fees in filing for trade name ("Paper Clip Company")	750		23,900
June 25	Cash discount on merchandise purchased		175	23,725

The company plans to present financial statements as of June 30, 1985, to a local bank to support a request for additional financial support. Company policy is to amortize intangible asset costs over a 10-year period, computed to the nearest full month. The president suggests an amortization on June 30, 1985, of $1,186.25, computed as follows:

$$(\$23,725/10 \text{ years}) \times \frac{1}{2} \text{ year} = \$1,186.25$$

Instructions

[a] Prepare an analysis of the entries in the Intangibles account and indicate adjustments that you would propose in the account.

[b] Prepare the entries to properly record amortization of intangible assets on June 30, 1985. Assume all amounts are material and that straight-line amortization is to be used.

P13–2 Bulldog Publications Company acquired three intangible assets before 1985. The company is involved in the preparation of financial statements on June 30, 1985. Before that date no formal statements were prepared and the cost of intangible assets had been charged to retained earnings when acquired.

The following intangible assets were accounted for in this manner:

Asset	Acquisition Date	Estimated Useful Life in Years	Cost
Copyright No. 1	Jan. 2, 1981	25	$30,000
Copyright No. 2	July 15, 1982	15	33,000
Goodwill	Feb. 28, 1983	Indeterminate	32,000

The decision is made to correct past accounting treatment and to account for the intangibles as if they had been properly capitalized at the time of acquisition and subsequently amortized. The straight-line method of amortization is to be used, computed to the nearest half-year. The company has selected July 1–June 30 for its financial reporting period.

Instructions

[a] Prepare the entries necessary to reclassify the intangible assets and to record amortization for 1985. Provide adequate support for your entries.

[b] Briefly explain in a written paragraph the process you followed in preparing the entry or entries in [a].

P13–3 Nashville Sound Corporation has initiated an extensive research program to develop a more efficient method of recording stereophonic records. Management expects to be able to lease its production facilities, when completely refined, to the many record-producing companies in the area.

You have been asked to assist in the preparation of financial statements for the year ended December 31, 1985. Costs related to the project described above have been accumulated in a master account identified simply as "Recording" since the beginning of the project in early 1985.

Items that have been included in the Recording account as of December 31, 1985, include the following:

Debits

$152,000	Equipment purchased for use in many research projects over a five-year period.
75,000	Salaries of staff working on research project.
15,500	Computer program services purchased through a contract with another enterprise.
32,250	Legal fees related to the patent acquired on the new production process, which is expected to be useful in producing revenue for ten years.

Credits

$ 45,000	Down payments received from other companies that have contracted to use the new production process in the future.

Management has determined that general and administrative expenses of $78,200 were incurred during 1985. Based on the time spent on the various enterprise functions, you estimate that 25% of this amount relates to the research project identified as "recording."

Discussions with corporate officials reveal that all long-lived assets are depreciated with a full year's amortization taken in the year of acquisition and none taken in the year of disposal. You determine that the process began to generate revenue in 1985 and, therefore, the amortization of the patent should begin this year.

Instructions

[a] Prepare all journal entries you would suggest to correct the Recording account and other accounts related to the company's research and development effort.

[b] Prepare all adjusting entries that should be made on December 31, 1985, to reflect amortization and depreciation for the year.

[c] Identify all items that will appear in the financial statements on December 31, 1985, related to intangible assets and research and development.

[d] Describe in a short paragraph your treatment of items that are comprised in the research and development expense in [c].

P13–4 Hiawatha Company acquired two patents, several items of equipment, and a parcel of land for a total of $137,500. Appraisal values of the assets on the date of acquisition are as follows:

Patent A	$30,000
Patent B	40,000
Equipment	19,700
Land	62,000

By acquiring the assets in a group, the company was

able to get a favorable price. The acquisition took place on April 27, 1983. Patent A has a five-year remaining life and Patent B a 12-year remaining life. Amortization on intangible assets is determined on a straight-line basis, computed in whole dollars to the nearest full month.

During 1984 the company became involved in two lawsuits resulting in the successful defense of Patent B but the unsuccessful defense of Patent A. Total legal fees of $17,600 were incurred. Management estimates that approximately equal effort went into defending each patent. The established date of these settlements was March 7, 1984.

No further transactions affecting the patents occurred through October 31, 1985.

Instructions

[a] Prepare journal entries for the years 1983, 1984, and 1985, related to the intangible asset accounts. The company's reporting year ends on October 31.
[b] Briefly explain any difference in your treatment of the legal costs of the defenses of Patents A and B.

P13–5 Franklin Company is negotiating to acquire Jefferson Company. Franklin Company manufactures and sells wood-burning stoves, and Jefferson Company produces parts that are required to manufacture the stoves. Jefferson Company enjoys an exceptional reputation, and the management of Franklin Company believes it can continue the level of income currently experienced by Jefferson Company, as well as satisfy its own need for parts.

Under the contemplated arrangement, Franklin Company will bid on the acquisition of the net assets of Jefferson Company. The following information has been developed to determine the appropriate bid:
[1] Recorded amounts and estimated current values of assets and liabilities of Jefferson Company are as follows:

	Recorded Amounts	Estimated Current Values
Assets to be received	$1,450,000	$1,925,000
Liabilities to be assumed	510,000	510,000
	$ 940,000	$1,415,000

[2] Earnings of Jefferson Company for the past five years averaged $175,000. This is believed to be a reasonable estimate of future income.
[3] The level of income normally experienced by companies similar to Jefferson Company is 9%.

Instructions

[a] Compute the estimated value of goodwill under each of the following methods and assumptions:
   [1] Years multiple of excess earnings, assuming a five-year period of excess earnings.
   [2] Present value of excess earnings, assuming a seven-year period of excess earnings and a 10% interest rate.
   [3] Capitalization of excess earnings at the normal rate.
   [4] Capitalization of excess earnings at twice the normal rate.
[b] If the present-value of excess earnings method is accepted by management as the appropriate value of goodwill for negotiation purposes, what is the maximum price Franklin Company should bid for the net assets of Jefferson Company?

P13–6 McDonald Company is considering the acquisition of Ronald Company. A considerable amount of information about Ronald Company has been accumulated, including the following.
   Net income.   Net income figures are:

1980	$78,500
1981	59,000
1982	67,200
1983	51,500
1984	72,000

Net income for 1980 included a $12,500 extraordinary gain; 1982 net income included a $14,000 extraordinary gain.
   Selected Balance-Sheet Data.   As of the transaction date, recorded amounts and estimated current values of assets are:

	Recorded Amount	Estimated Current Value
Receivables	$125,000	$120,000
Inventories	216,000	415,000
Property, plant, and equipment	300,000	425,000
Patents	10,000	75,000

Liabilities to be assumed are $642,500.

Management of McDonald Company believes the investment in Ronald Company could provide a return in excess of the 10% normal for the industry. Analysis of the components of earnings indicates that average net income for the past five years is a reasonable basis for estimating future income. It is believed, however, that the effect of extraordinary items should be eliminated and that depreciation and amortization can be expected to increase by $12,500 annually.

Instructions

[a] Estimate the amount of goodwill in the Ronald Company acquisition by each of the following methods:

[1] Years multiple of estimated excess earnings, assuming a five-year period of excess earnings.

[2] Present value of estimated excess earnings, discounted at the normal rate over a five-year period.

[3] Capitalization of the estimated excess earnings at a 15% rate.

[b] For each category of assets, indicate the probable reason for the difference between the recorded amount and the estimated current value.

[c] After extended negotiations, a price of $425,000 is finally agreed on by the two companies. Prepare the journal entry to record the acquisition by McDonald Company. You may include all liabilities in a single Liability account. The agreement calls for a cash payment of $200,000 and the issuance of 10,000 shares of $10 par value stock of McDonald Company. The current market price of the stock is 22½.

P13–7 Walters Company has negotiated to acquire the net assets of Robbins Company. The companies have agreed that the purchase price should be established at the fair market value of the assets, less liabilities, plus the value of the goodwill of Robbins Company. The value of the goodwill has been agreed upon as the average of the last three years' excess of income from normal operations over 10% of stockholders' equity, at the beginning of the year, discounted to the present at 10% for a five-year period. The last three years are 1983, 1984, and 1985.

The following figures have been taken from the last four years' financial statements of Robbins Company (December 31 year-end):

You have been engaged as an independent CPA to determine the total purchase price which has apparently been agreed upon by both parties. As part of your investigation you discover the following:

[1] The two companies have agreed on the following estimates of the current value of the assets to be transferred (other than goodwill):

Receivables	$ 150,000
Inventory	400,000
Equipment	500,000
Buildings	1,400,000
Land	1,600,000
Franchise	150,000

[2] Liabilities to be assumed by Walters Company total $1,200,000.

[3] Additional shares of stock were sold in May 1984.

[4] The following questionable items have been recorded by year:

1983. An extraordinary gain of $25,500 was included in net income. This represents the excess of the proceeds over cost of land purchased by the city under condemnation proceedings.

1984. A franchise agreement was entered into in January and $100,000 paid in advance. The period of the franchise is five years. No amortization has been taken. The $100,000 was debited to an intangible asset account.

1985. A sum of $15,000 was received from a customer whose account had been erroneously written off as uncollectible in 1984 by a direct charge to bad debts expense. The arrangement with the customer had explicitly called for repayment in 1985. The $15,000 was credited to Miscellaneous Income when received.

An insurance recovery of $125,000 was received on inventory which was totally destroyed by a flood. The $125,000 was presented as an extraordinary gain

	1982	1983	1984	1985
Net income	$ 225,000	$ 250,000	$ 350,000	$ 550,000
Stockholders' equity				
Common stock	1,000,000	1,000,000	1,200,000	1,200,000
Additional paid-in capital	500,000	500,000	600,000	600,000
Retained earnings	125,000	250,000	400,000	500,000
	$1,625,000	$1,750,000	$2,200,000	$2,300,000

due to the unusual circumstances surrounding the flood. The cost of the inventory, $75,000, was debited to Retained Earnings. The flood was extremely unusual; a similar event has never occurred in the location of the company this century and is not expected to recur.

An additional tax assessment of $97,000 was paid. Of this amount, $25,000 related to 1982, $35,000 to 1983, and $37,000 to 1984. Retained Earnings was debited for the total of $97,000, since this adjustment resulted from an accounting error.

Instructions

[a] Prepare a schedule which includes:
[1] The corrected net income for 1982, 1983, 1984, and 1985.
[2] The amount to be used for computing goodwill for 1983, 1984, and 1985. A conference with officials of the two companies reveals that the phrase "income from normal operations" appears to have meant income before extraordinary items.
[b] Prepare a schedule restating retained earnings for 1982, 1983, 1984, and 1985 at year-end.
[c] Based on information from your schedules in [1] and [2], compute goodwill as agreed upon by the two companies.
[d] Prepare the journal entry to record the net assets of Robbins Company acquired by Walters Company, assuming payment is made by issuing 100,000 shares of Walters Company common stock and the remainder in cash. The common stock has a $20 par value and a $25 market price. The transaction was finalized on January 5, 1986.
[e] Prepare the adjusting entry one year after the acquisition to record amortization on the intangible assets acquired. The franchise is expected to have a three-year life, and the goodwill is to be amortized over a period consistent with the method by which it was computed.

P13–8 Select the best answer.
[1] In January 1981 Idea Company purchased a patent for a new consumer product for $170,000. At the time of purchase, the patent was valid for 17 years. Because the product was competitive, the patent was estimated to have a useful life of 10 years. During 1985 the product was removed from the market under government order because it contained a potential health hazard.

What amount should Idea charge to expense during 1985, assuming amortization is recorded at the end of each year?
[a] $10,000
[b] $17,000
[c] $102,000
[d] $130,000

[2] The general ledger of Flint Corporation as of December 31, 1984, includes the following accounts:

Organization costs	$ 5,000
Deposits with advertising agency (to promote goodwill)	8,000
Discount on bonds payable	15,000
Excess of cost over book value of net assets of acquired subsidiary	70,000
Trademarks	12,000

In the preparation of Flint's balance sheet as of December 31, 1984, what should be reported as total intangible assets?
[a] $87,000
[b] $92,000
[c] $95,000
[d] $110,000

[3] The owners of the Zoot Suit Clothing Store are contemplating selling the business to new interests. The cumulative earnings for the past five years amounted to $450,000, including extraordinary gains of $10,000. The annual earnings based on an average rate of return on investment for this industry would have been $76,000. If excess earnings are to be capitalized at 10%, then implied goodwill should be:
[a] $120,000
[b] $140,000
[c] $440,000
[d] $450,000

[4] Howard Company incurred the following research and development costs in 1985:

Materials	$ 400,000
Equipment that will have alternative uses in future research and development projects	2,000,000
Depreciation for 1985 on equipment	500,000
Personnel costs	1,000,000
Consulting fees	100,000
Indirect costs, reasonably allocable	200,000

The amount of research and development costs charged to Howard's 1985 income statement should be:
[a] $1,500,000
[b] $1,700,000
[c] $2,200,000
[d] $3,500,000

(AICPA adapted)

P13–9 Noelton Company was organized and began operations in 1985. Selected transactions for the first year of operation are listed below:

Jan. 5   Paid $5,000 to the attorneys who assisted in preparing the corporate by-laws, obtaining the corporate charter, and generally advising the company on several legal matters.

Jan. 10   Issued 1,000 shares of the company's common stock to promoters of the corporation. In another recent transaction stock sold at $12 per share. The par value of the stock was $10.

Feb. 5   Paid $10,000 to develop and acquire the exclusive right to use the company's trademark.

Mar. 30   Paid $12,000 to an advertising firm to promote the company and its products, emphasizing the new trademark recently developed. A second installment is to be paid in six months.

Apr. 1   A license to operate a shop in the local airport was obtained for $12,000 from the city on April 1. The license covers a five-year period, at the end of which the company must pay $12,000 for renewal for five years. In addition, the company must pay 5% of gross revenues to the city to cover utilities, maintenance, and other operating expenses. As an estimate of this amount for April 1–December 31, $15,000 was paid on April 15. In subsequent years this payment will be made at the end of the calendar year.

July 19   A marketing research firm was hired to help survey potential customers and assess ways to capitalize more on consumer demand. An initial payment of $2,500 was made to the firm.

Sept. 30   A second payment of $12,000 was made to the advertising firm for promotional services rendered. The advertising is expected to enhance the value of the trademark and to generally benefit the company for several years.

Oct. 5   Another company, Scenic Enterprises, was acquired. In the transaction, $255,000 cash was paid to acquire assets valued as follows: inventory, $92,500; property, plant, and equipment, $175,000; franchise rights, $42,500. Noncurrent liabilities assumed totaled $96,000. Goodwill is estimated to be worth $75,000, based on the present value of excess future earnings over a 10-year period. The franchise has a 5-year remaining life.

Nov. 7   Paid $2,500 in legal fees to successfully defend the trademark against a competitor who had begun using an identical diagram of a different color to market similar products.

Instructions

[a] Prepare general journal entries to record the above transactions.

[b] Prepare any adjusting entries necessary on December 31, 1985, in anticipation of the preparation of financial statements. The following information should be considered:

[1] Revenues for 1985 were $336,000.

[2] Intangible assets are to be amortized by the straight-line method, computed to the nearest full month. Intangibles are to be amortized over the contractual period, if any. Other intangibles are to be amortized over a 10-year period.

[3] Amortization should be rounded to the nearest dollar.

[c] Indicate items and amounts relative to intangible assets that should be presented in the company's balance sheet and income statement on December 31, 1985.

P13–10 On December 31, 1984, certain accounts included in the property, plant, and equipment section of Townsand Company's balance sheet had the following balances:

Land	$100,000
Buildings	800,000
Leasehold improvements	500,000
Machinery and equipment	700,000

During 1985 the following transactions occurred:

[1] Land site number 621 was acquired for $1,000,000. To acquire the land, Townsand paid a $60,000 commission to a real estate agent. Costs of $15,000 were incurred to clear the land. During the course of clearing the land, timber and gravel were recovered and sold for $5,000.

[2] A second tract of land (site number 622) with a building was acquired for $300,000. The closing statement indicated that the land value was $200,000 and the building value was $100,000. Shortly after acquisition, the building was demolished at a cost of $30,000.

A new building was constructed for $150,000 plus the following costs:

Excavation fees	$11,000
Architectural design fees	8,000
Building permit fee	1,000
Interest paid on funds used during construction	6,000

The building was completed and occupied on September 30, 1985.

[3] A third tract of land (site number 623) was acquired for $600,000 and was put on the market for resale.

[4] Extensive work was done to a building occupied by Townsand under a lease agreement that expires on December 31, 1994. The total cost of the work was $125,000, which consisted of the following:

Painting of ceilings	$ 10,000	Estimated useful life, 1 year
Electrical work	35,000	Estimated useful life, 10 years
Construction of extension to current working area	80,000	Estimated useful life, 30 years
	$125,000	

The lessor paid one-half of the costs incurred in connection with the extension to the current working area.

[5] During December 1985, costs of $65,000 were incurred to improve leased office space. The related lease will terminate on December 31, 1987, and is not expected to be renewed.

[6] A group of new machines was purchased under a royalty agreement which provides for payment of royalties based on units of production for the machines. The invoice price of the machines was $75,000, freight costs were $2,000, unloading charges were $1,500, and royalty payments for 1985 were $13,000.

Instructions

[a] Prepare a detailed analysis of the changes in each of the following balance sheet accounts for 1985: land; buildings; leasehold improvements; and machinery and equipment. Disregard the related accumulated depreciation accounts.

[b] List the items in the fact situation which were not used to determine the answer to [a], and indicate *where, or if,* these items should be included in Townsand's financial statements.

(AICPA adapted)

P13–11 Hunley Products is involved in the development, manufacture, and sale of burglar alarm systems, ranging from relatively simple units for private residences to very sophisticated units for large office buildings. The company's operations depend to a large extent on an ongoing research and development program, resulting in the internal development of patents. Also, the company occasionally acquires patents from other companies.

As the accountant for Hunley Products, you are responsible for the proper accounting of many transactions relative to research and operating activities. The following activities have taken place over several years:

1980		
Continuous	Research to develop improved alarm systems	$175,000
May 31	Acquisition of Patent A, with a 12-year remaining legal life, from a competitor	72,000
1981		
Feb. 28	Costs of models of new alarm system	32,250
Oct. 31	Legal fees for acquisition of Patent B on new alarm system	28,000
1982		
Continuous	Development to advance new alarm system to commercial production	38,000
June 30	Initiation of advertising campaign to promote new alarm system, enhancing the value of Patents A and B	42,000

Oct. 25	Legal expenses for the successful defense of Patent B	18,000
1983		
Mar. 19	Legal expenses for the unsuccessful defense of Patent A	8,500
May 24	Acquisition of Patent C, with a six-year remaining legal life, from a competitor in anticipation that it will replace Patent A	43,500
1984		
Continuous	Research on improved alarm system to replace Patent B	87,650

In 1984 it was determined that the remaining life of Patent B was only three years, including the current year. Research was begun in that year to prepare for the replacement of Patent B with a new patent—presumably Patent D—at some future date.

Instructions

Prepare the Patent account for 1980 through December 1984—the end of Hunley Products' current reporting year—following these guidelines:

[a] Amortization is to be made by the straight-line method, with no assumed residual value.

[b] Amortization is to be based on the shorter of the legal life or 10 years, unless indicated otherwise, computed to the nearest half year from acquisition or to disposal.

[c] The book value to be presented in the balance sheet on December 31 of each year should be indicated.

P13–12 Arkansas Diversified Enterprises has been in business for several years. A client-prepared trial balance for December 31, 1985, is presented below:

Arkansas Diversified Enterprises
UNADJUSTED TRIAL BALANCE
December 31, 1985
(in thousands of dollars)

	Dr.	Cr.
Cash	$ 20	
Accounts receivable	50	
Inventory	120	
Equipment	800	
Accumulated depreciation—Equipment		$ 250
Buildings	1,200	
Accumulated depreciation—Buildings		400
Patents	550	
Franchise agreement	95	
Organization costs	102	
Goodwill	345	
Accounts payable		12
Accrued wages payable		5
Accrued taxes payable		60
Bonds payable		500
Premium on bonds payable		35
Preferred stock ($100 par value)		100
Common stock ($25 par value)		1,100
Additional paid-in capital		220
Retained earnings (as of January 1)		400
Sales revenue		900
Cost of goods sold	400	
Selling and administrative expenses	300	
	$3,982	$3,982

Before 1985, Arkansas Diversified Enterprises prepared financial statements internally. The company has not been audited because the ownership is held completely by one family and is not actively sold. As of 1985, however, in anticipation of bank loans and a possible public offering of common stock, the company needs audited financial statements prepared in conformity with generally accepted accounting principles.

As a member of the team of independent auditors responsible for Arkansas Diversified Enterprises, you have been assigned the intangible assets. You have observed that four intangible asset accounts appear on the unadjusted trial balance. Additional investigation reveals the following:

Patents. All patents were purchased from another company when Arkansas Diversified Enterprises began operations on January 2, 1978. These patents are being amortized over an expected useful life of 14 years. Improvements made to equipment covered by the patents costing $75,000 were debited to the account in January 1982. Amortization in 1982–1984 included amortization on the $75,000 for the remaining life of the relevant patent. It is determined that the $75,000 should have been expensed in 1982. It is further determined on December 31, 1985, that one of the patents has a remaining life of only 2 years. This patent was originally assigned a cost of $210,000.

Franchise Agreement.   A franchise agreement was signed on January 1, 1985. A $50,000 fee was paid, covering a 5-year period, at the end of which the company may renew the agreement by paying $50,000. A decision on renewal has not been made as of December 31, 1985. The agreement calls for an annual payment of 5% of revenue. An entry debiting the account for $45,000 was made at the time of the cash payment for 1985.

Organization Costs.   Organization costs include the unamortized portion of amounts paid to promoters for services rendered at the inception of the corporation. These fees have been amortized, since inception, over an estimated 40-year life. The decision is made, as of December 31, 1985, to reduce the total period of amortization of organization costs to 12 years.

Goodwill.   The Goodwill account includes three items:

$ 45,000—Legal expenses relative to incorporation. These were assigned to the account in January 1978.

200,000—Excess of cost over assigned net asset values of an enterprise acquired in early 1983, expected to be of value for an indefinite period.

100,000—Paid to an advertising consulting firm in early 1984 for a major advertising effort expected to be beneficial for an indefinite period.

No amortization has been taken on any amount in the Goodwill account.

Instructions

[a] Prepare an analysis of each intangible asset, indicating (1) the changes needed to restate each intangible account on a corrected basis for determining the amount of amortization for 1985, and (2) the proper amount of amortization for 1985.

[b] Prepare two compound journal entries (1) to correct the intangible asset account balances before the recording of 1985 amortization, and (2) to record 1985 amortization.

Liability and Stockholders' Equity Accounting

4

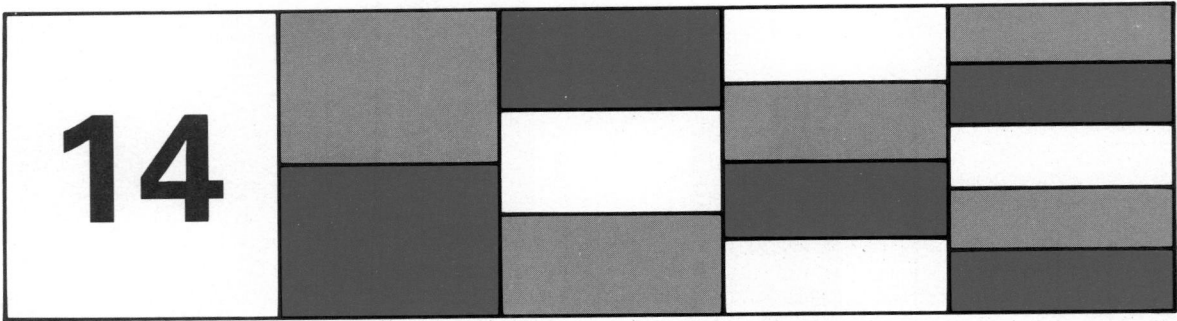

14

CURRENT AND CONTINGENT LIABILITIES

Objectives

To discuss the conceptual characteristics of liabilities of business enterprises.

To present the meaning and nature of current liabilities.

To describe the characteristics distinguishing among determinable, contingent, and estimated liabilities.

To apply acceptable accounting measurement and disclosure practices to a variety of current liabilities.

To describe the various types of obligations arising from payroll transactions.

To classify liabilities between current and long-term, including short-term obligations expected to be refinanced.

To apply acceptable accounting measurement and disclosure practices to a variety of contingent liabilities.

Companies often acquire goods and services that do not require immediate payment of cash. Examples include the purchase of supplies, items of inventory, and other services and assets. The actions of organizations and individuals external to a company can also give rise to various liabilities that eventually must be paid. Examples include obligations to taxing authorities, lawsuits that are initiated against the firm, and claims resulting from warranties and guarantees. Not all potential obligations of a firm are necessarily reportable liabilities, however, since certain criteria must be met before an accounting liability is recognized.

As we discussed in Chapter 3, the Financial Accounting Standards Board (FASB) has defined the elements of financial statements of business enterprises. The term **liability** is defined as:

> *probable future sacrifices of economic benefits arising from present obligations of a particular entity to transfer assets or provide services to other entities in the future as a result of past transactions or events.*[1]

To provide more guidance, the FASB established three characteristics of a liability:

1. *A liability embodies a present duty or responsibility to one or more other entities that entails settlement (of the obligation) by probable future transfer or use of assets at a specified or determinable date, on occurrence of a specified event or on demand.*
2. *The duty or responsibility obligates a particular enterprise, leaving it little or no discretion to avoid the future sacrifice.*
3. *The transaction or other event obligating the enterprise has already happened.*[2]

This chapter discusses a company's obligations that represent accounting liabilities classified as **current.** The first section examines current liabilities that are known to exist and whose amounts are readily determinable. The second section discusses accounting and reporting for liabilities that are contingent. **Contingent liabilities** are uncertain obligations; that is, their existence and, in many cases, their amounts are uncertain. Contingent liabilities include—among other things—lawsuits in progress against the firm, warranties, guarantees, claims, and assessments.

CURRENT LIABILITIES

Our discussion begins with a clear understanding of some of the most important terms. *Accounting Research Bulletin No. 43* provides such a definition for **current liabilities:**

> *The term is used principally to designate obligations whose liquidation is reasonably expected to require the use of existing resources properly classified as current assets, or the creation of other current liabilities.*[3]

Therefore, current liabilities are defined in terms of claims on the working capital of a company rather than in terms of the due date. That is, if the satisfaction of a liability requires the use of existing working capital, then the obligation is considered current regardless of its

---

[1]*FASB Statement of Financial Accounting Concepts No. 3,* "Elements of Financial Statements of Business Enterprises," 1980, par. 28.
[2]*FASB Statement of Financial Accounting Concepts No. 3,* par. 29.
[3]*Accounting Research Bulletin No. 43,* "Restatement and Revision of Accounting Research Bulletins," 1953, Sec. A, Ch. 3, par. 7.

maturity date. Nevertheless, we may logically expect most current liabilities to be paid in the next year or next operating cycle, whichever is longer.

Valuation of Current Liabilities

Materiality

Conservatism

In theory, liabilities should be stated at the present value of the future cash payments necessary to extinguish or satisfy the obligation. We apply present-value techniques to many liabilities in order to present them at their present value. In practice, however, current liabilities are frequently recorded and presented in the financial statements at their full maturity amounts. Even though this practice may result in a slight theoretical overstatement of certain current liabilities, clerical simplicity, immateriality, and conservatism lend support to such a minor overstatement of current liabilities. Generally the time until maturity is short for current liabilities, and the amount of any overstatement inherent in the face amount of the liability is normally relatively small. Furthermore, recording current liabilities at their full amounts results in a larger charge to the goods or services acquired and thereby prevents any overstatement of income. The *Accounting Principles Board (APB),* in its *Opinion No. 21,* requires the presentation of most liabilities at their net present value; then it states:

> *This Opinion is not intended to apply to . . . receivables and payables arising from transactions with customers or suppliers in the normal course of business which are due in customary trade terms not exceeding approximately one year.*[4]

Businesses, therefore, are not required to apply present-value techniques to the valuation of most current liabilities. Current liabilities, however, may be (and, in many cases, are) presented at their net present value because *APB Opinion No. 21* does not prohibit this practice.

Before reading the following discussion on financial accounting and reporting for different types of current liabilities, refer to the balance sheet of Kroger Company presented on the inside front cover of this text. Notice that several types of current liabilities are presented, including the current portion of long-term debt and capital leases, accounts payable, and various accrued expenses. The importance of current liabilities can be seen in this balance sheet, since they make up more than half of the total liabilities of the company and more than a third of the total liabilities and shareholders' equity.

Specific Types of Current Liabilities

Accounts Payable

As previously indicated, there are a great many types of current liabilities; however, probably the most common is represented by trade accounts payable. **Accounts payable** represent those liabilities that arise in the acquisition of goods and services in the normal course of business. Many of the accounting and reporting issues related to accounts payable have counterparts in **accounts receivable,** as discussed in Chapter 7, and many of those problems are reviewed in this section.

Trade accounts payable should be recognized when the acquisition of goods or services results in a liability. For example, if Artesia Company acquires $1,000 worth of supplies on account, the following journal entry should be made at the point of acquisition:

Supplies on Hand	1,000	
Accounts Payable		1,000
(To record the acquisition of supplies.)		

[4] *APB Opinion No. 21,* "Interest on Receivables and Payables," 1971, par. 3.

If the invoice amount is $1,000 and a purchase discount is allowed for early payment, then other problems arise. If Artesia acquired the same supplies on terms of 2/10, n/30, the journal entry would be as follows:[5]

Supplies on Hand	980	
Accounts Payable		980
(To record acquisition of supplies for invoice		
amount of $1,000, terms 2/10, n/30.)		

If the invoice is paid prior to the expiration of the 10-day discount period, the following entry is necessary:

Accounts Payable	980	
Cash		980
(To record payment of invoice within discount period.)		

If the invoice is not paid within the discount period, however, the payment of the invoice should be recorded as follows:

Accounts Payable	980	
Purchase Discounts Lost	20	
Cash		1,000
(To record payment of invoice and lost discount.)		

The Purchase Discounts Lost account is treated as an element of financial or interest expense on the income statement. Furthermore, unpaid invoices existing at the year-end should be evaluated to determine if any discounts have been lost at that time. If, for example, it is determined at year-end that purchase discounts in the amount of $15 have already been lost on unpaid invoices, the following adjusting entry is necessary:

Purchase Discounts Lost	15	
Accounts Payable		15

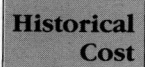

As discussed in Chapter 8 under "Inventories: Basic Valuation Methods," we may expect in practice to encounter a variety of methods of accounting for purchase discounts. Generally, such amounts are immaterial and therefore the issue is relatively unimportant. The differences in these methods may accumulate to a material amount, however, and the following considerations should take precedence:

Historical Cost

1. The good or service acquired should be recorded at its cash-equivalent price at the point of acquisition.
2. Any difference between the cash-equivalent price at acquisition (in 1) and the amount required to be paid to settle the account should be treated as a financial expense.

Current Notes Payable

Items classified as **current notes payable** generally arise from three types of transactions:

1. **Trade notes payable** that result from the acquisition of goods or services (usually equipment or other large items).

---

[5]This entry seems theoretically preferable because $980 represents the cash-equivalent price and present value of the liability at the point of acquisition. Furthermore, the presentation of the liability at the net amount reflects management's intent to take the discount.

2. **Loan notes payable** that result from cash-borrowing activities.
3. **Current maturities** of long-term notes and bonds payable that represent amounts payable from current assets. Such current maturities usually have been previously classified as noncurrent liabilities.

Trade notes payable generally do not present significant accounting and reporting problems. The maturity date, the amount necessary to satisfy the note, and the interest rate are usually available; the major required calculations deal with determining the amount of interest to be accrued at the end of an accounting period.

For example, if we assume that Heyman Company reports on a calendar year and that on November 1, 1983, it acquires machinery with a market value of $1,000 by issuing a $1,000 note bearing interest at 20%, due in six months, the following entries computed to the nearest dollar are necessary:

Nov. 1, 1983	Machinery	1,000	
	Trade Notes Payable		1,000
	(To record the acquisition of machinery by issuing a six-month 20%, $1,000 note.)		
Dec. 31, 1983	Interest Expense	33	
	Interest Payable		33
	(To record accrued interest at year-end. $1,000 × 20% × ⅙ = $33.)		
May 1, 1984	Trade Notes Payable	1,000	
	Interest Payable	33	
	Interest Expense	67	
	Cash		1,100
	(To record payment of note and related interest at maturity.)		

The May 1 entry assumes no reversing entry was made at the beginning of 1984.

Interest-Bearing Notes.   Notes payable that arise from cash-borrowing activities are generally of two types: **interest-bearing notes** and so-called **noninterest-bearing notes.** Accounting and reporting for interest-bearing notes requires the accountant to accrue interest and report a liability in the amount of the accrued interest payable plus the face value of the note. These accounting practices are similar to those previously described for the acquisition of equipment and, therefore, contain no additional accounting complications.

Noninterest-Bearing Notes.   Certain notes do not pay any stated rate of interest in addition to the face amount of the note. We refer to this type as **noninterest-bearing notes.** Interest on such notes, however, is deducted by the lender in advance and the notes are issued at discount; that is, the borrower (the maker of the note) receives an amount that is less than the face value of the note.

To illustrate, assume that on November 1, 1983, Century Company issued a one-year note payable with a face amount of $10,000 to a bank and in return received $8,800 in cash. This note was discounted by the bank at 12% ($10,000 × .12 = $1,200; $10,000 − $1,200 = $8,800). The effective rate of interest in the note exceeds 12%, however, as indicated below:

$$\frac{\text{Interest}}{\text{Amount Received}} = \frac{\$1,200}{\$8,800} = 13.64\% \text{ (For a one-year note)}$$

Therefore, $1,200 of interest was paid for a loan of $8,800 for a one-year period. The journal entry to record the loan, the discount representing future interest, and the amount to be repaid on November 1, 1984, is as follows:

Nov. 1, 1983	Cash	8,800	
	Discount on Notes Payable	1,200	
	Notes Payable		10,000
	(To record issuance of note and receipt of cash.)		

The Notes Payable account could have been credited with the $8,800 instead of the $10,000. In that case no figure would be entered in the Discount on Notes Payable account. If a Discount on Notes payable account is used, it appears on the balance sheet as a **contra account** (reduction) to the Notes Payable account. In any event the note is reported in the balance sheet at its present value ($8,800) at the date of issuance, rather than its maturity value ($10,000).

The adjusting entry at December 31, 1983 appears below:

Dec. 31, 1983	Interest Expense	200	
	Discount on Notes Payable		200
	(To record accrued interest on note payable. $1,200 × $^2/_{12}$ = $200.)		

As a result of this adjusting entry, the note is reported in the balance sheet as a $9,000 ($10,000 − $1,000) current liability at December 31, 1983. We have amortized $200 of the original discount of $1,200 and, therefore, the remaining discount is $1,000.

When the note matures and is paid during 1984, the following entry is necessary:

Nov. 1, 1984	Notes Payable	10,000	
	Interest Expense	1,000	
	Discount on Notes Payable		1,000
	Cash		10,000
	(To record payment of note payable and recognize interest expense.)		

This entry assumes no reversing entry was made January 1, 1984.

Some companies may amortize the discount or premium during the year to facilitate the preparation of interim financial statements. Adjustments at the end of the year are thereby confined to the amount necessary to complete the annual amortization.

Current Maturities. **Current maturities** of long-term notes payable must frequently be reported as current liabilities to the extent they are to be paid from presently existing current assets. A sinking fund may exist to service such liabilities, and, if so, the current maturities of long-term debt should be excluded from current liabilities. Such obligations are classified as noncurrent liabilities in a manner consistent with the sinking fund. Chapter 10 discusses sinking funds in dealing with a variety of investments and funds; consequently, Chapter 14 does not discuss sinking funds any further. Occasionally, a company plans to refinance current debt on a noncurrent basis; such anticipated action produces some additional accounting and reporting problems, which are discussed in the following section.

Short-Term Obligations Expected to Be Refinanced

In certain circumstances a company may desire to **refinance a short-term obligation** on a noncurrent basis. Examples include the current maturity of a previously noncurrent debt or a line of credit with a bank that a company wishes to extend. Furthermore, a short-term obligation may be refinanced on a long-term basis after the date of the balance sheet but before financial statements are issued. Since these debts do not require the use of working capital, questions arise about the proper classification at the balance sheet date.

To provide guidance in regard to these liability classification issues, the FASB issued *Statement of Financial Accounting Standards No. 6,*[6] which called for the following evidence whenever a company excludes a short-term obligation from current liabilities:

1. An indication of the *intent* of the enterprise to refinance the note on a noncurrent basis, and
2. A demonstration of the *ability* of the enterprise to accomplish the long-term refinancing.

Management's **intent** to refinance a short-term obligation is usually evidenced by express representation. The **ability** to refinance a short-term obligation on a long-term basis, however, is more difficult for accountants to establish. *SFAS No. 6* provides two ways in which a company may demonstrate the ability to refinance a short-term obligation:

1. Subsequent to the balance sheet date but prior to the issuance of the balance sheet, the enterprise must issue long-term debt or equity securities to refinance the obligation; *or*
2. Prior to the issuance of the balance sheet, the firm must secure a noncancelable, long-term (the longer of one year or one operating cycle from the balance sheet date) financing agreement that clearly allows the firm to refinance the short-term liability on a long-term basis.

Obviously, if a company actually accomplishes such a refinancing transaction, then both the ability and the intent criteria are met. However, if only the intent condition is met, the accountant should obtain a formal declaration of intent from management and carefully read the details of the refinancing agreement. The accountant must also exercise great care in analyzing the terms of refinancing agreements to assure proper interpretation and application.

If refinancing is accomplished, accountants use information that became available after the balance sheet date to alter accounting measurements and classification on the financial statements of the period already ended. This use of hindsight is appropriate because the newly acquired information relates to a condition that existed at the balance sheet date rather than a new condition.

If both the intent and ability criteria are met, the accountant *must* exclude the short-term obligation from current liabilities. The amount of short-term debt to be excluded from current liabilities should not exceed:

1. The amount available for refinancing under the agreement; *or*
2. A reasonable estimate of the minimum amount expected to be available, if the amount available for refinancing will fluctuate.

The accountant must adjust the amount to be excluded from current liabilities to reflect any financing-agreement limitations or restrictions that indicate that a portion of the amount in the agreement may not be available. For example, a common limitation dealing with working capital may provide "the amounts to be refinanced will not exceed 50% of the company's working capital at the time of refinancing."

Short-term liabilities arising from transactions in the ordinary course of business and due in customary terms are not subject to these reclassification tests. Such short-term liabilities should be routinely classified as current. Examples of these liabilities include accounts payable incurred in the acquisition of raw materials and supplies, collections received in advance of rendering services or providing goods, and other debts resulting from normal operating transactions.

Another question arises when a short-term obligation is repaid after the balance sheet date and the cash used to pay the debt is subsequently replenished through long-term

---

[6]*FASB Statement of Financial Accounting Standards No. 6,* "Classification of Short-Term Obligations Expected To Be Refinanced," 1975.

borrowing. In its *Interpretation No. 8,*[7] the FASB observed that repayment of a short-term obligation before funds are obtained through long-term borrowing requires the use of current assets. Therefore, a short-term obligation repaid after the balance sheet date should be classified as current. This is true even if long-term debt or equity securities are subsequently issued and the proceeds are used to replenish current assets, because working capital, at least temporarily, was employed to retire the short-term debt and therefore the debt is properly considered a current liability.

Disclosure of Short-Term Obligations Classified as Long-Term Liabilities. *SFAS No. 6* requires the total current liabilities to be presented in a classified balance sheet, whether or not a short-term obligation has been excluded from current liabilities. If a short-term obligation is classified as a noncurrent liability, the reasons for the classification should also be disclosed in the notes to the financial statements. Other required disclosures include a general description of any financing agreements, the terms of any new obligations incurred or expected to be incurred, and the terms of any equity securities issued or expected to be issued. These disclosure requirements are illustrated in Exhibit 14–1 for two companies, which we shall call Calico, Inc., and Darnell, Inc.

Disclosure

Dividends Payable

The topics of dividend distributions and related issues are treated more fully in Chapter 17, "Stockholders' Equity: Operations, Earnings, Dividends, and Other Problems." Since many types of dividends result in current liabilities, however, the matter is discussed briefly at this time. When the board of directors of a company declares a cash or property dividend, then the amount to be paid to stockholders becomes a liability of the company. Once declared, dividends are usually paid within a few months. Therefore, dividends payable are usually classified as current liabilities. For example, if on December 26, 1984, Arnold Company declares a $1.50 per share dividend to be paid on January 31, 1985, to shareholders of record as of January 5, 1985, and if 10,000 shares of common stock are outstanding, the accountant should make the following entries:

---

[7]*FASB Interpretation No. 8,* "Classification of a Short-Term Obligation Repaid Prior to Being Replaced by a Long-Term Security: An Interpretation of FASB Statement No. 6," 1976.

EXHIBIT 14–1
Illustrations of Debt Refinancings

Illustration No. 1: Actual Refinancing

Excerpt from Balance Sheet of Calico, Inc.

	Dec. 31, 1983
Current Liabilities	
Accounts payable	$ 2,000,000
Accrued expenses	3,000,000
Income taxes payable	1,000,000
Current maturities of long-term debt	1,000,000
Total current liabilities	$ 7,000,000
Long-Term Debt	
Notes payable refinanced in January 1984 [Note 8]	$ 4,000,000
Other long-term debt	10,000,000
	$14,000,000

Note 8: On January 20, 1984, the Company issued 100,000 shares of common stock and received proceeds totaling $4,500,000 of which $4,000,000 was used to liquidate notes payable that matured on January 31, 1984. Accordingly, such notes payable have been excluded from current liabilities at December 31, 1983.

Illustration No. 2:   Financing Agreement

Excerpt from Balance Sheet of Darnell, Inc.

	Dec. 31, 1983
Current Liabilities	
Accounts payable	$1,000,000
Accrued expenses	1,500,000
Income taxes payable	500,000
Total current liabilities	$3,000,000
Long-Term Debt	
8% Notes payable [Note 9]	$2,000,000

Note 9:   The company has entered into a financing agreement with a bank to borrow up to $3,000,000 at any time through 1985. Amounts borrowed under the agreement mature three years from the date of the loan and bear interest at one percent above the bank's prime interest rate. The agreement requires the Company to maintain working capital of at least $8,000,000 and prohibits the payment of dividends and reacquisition of the Company's common stock without prior approval of the bank. Because the Company intends to borrow $2,000,000 under the agreement to pay its 8% notes payable that mature on April 1, 1984, the notes have been classified as long-term debt.

Dec. 26, 1984	Dividends (or Retained Earnings)	15,000	
	Dividends Payable		15,000
	(To record declaration of cash dividend.)		
Jan. 31, 1985	Dividends Payable	15,000	
	Cash		15,000
	(To record payment of dividend.)		

The accountant should not record a liability for a dividend until it is declared by a company's board of directors, because no liability exists for undeclared dividends, regardless of how profitable the company has been.

Advances from Customers

In many circumstances a company may require its customers to make deposits that are either refundable or applicable to future purchases. Such payments are usually designed to provide security for the company receiving the deposit. For example, a business may require a customer to make a substantial payment before the business will accept and manufacture an order designed specifically for that customer.

Revenue Realization

In transactions such as these, we do not recognize revenue at the time cash is received, because it has not been earned. The recipient company must perform some service or provide some good before the revenue is earned. Therefore, the amount of the deposit should be treated as a liability until the obligation to produce the good or service has been discharged. Liabilities such as these do not require cash repayment but, rather, will be satisfied by providing goods or services. To illustrate, assume that Thin Spread Company, a mill manufacturer of cloth, receives a special order amounting to $500,000 to manufacture a type of cloth with an unusual design. Prior to beginning the mill run, Thin Spread requests a deposit of $50,000 (10% of total order price) from the customer. The entry to record the receipt of the deposit appears as follows:

Cash	50,000	
Advances from Customers		50,000
(To record receipt of deposit.)		

Advances from Customers is a liability to deliver goods or services in the future. When the mill run is complete and shipped, the following entry is necessary:

Accounts Receivable	450,000	
Advances from Customers	50,000	
Sales Revenue		500,000
(To record sale of cloth and		
recognition of revenue.)		

A company may receive advance payments in a variety of other circumstances as well. Examples include magazine subscriptions, construction deposits, gift certificates, airline and other travel tickets, and various promotions, such as ticket-book sales by restaurants or theaters. Deposits such as these will not be refunded in the normal course of business, but they are applied to the total sales price of the goods or services. Such advances should be accounted for as liabilities until the good or service is provided and the revenue earned.

Refundable deposits should also be recorded as liabilities upon receipt. The liability is then reduced when the deposit is refunded. If deposits are forfeited, however, the liability should be removed and the amount recognized as revenue. If the deposit was securing an asset of the company, such as a rental security deposit on equipment that is not returned, then the asset should be written off as a loss and matched with the revenue from the forfeited deposit.

Matching

Tax Liabilities Other Than Income Taxes

Sales Taxes. In many governmental jurisdictions, sales tax laws require merchants to collect and remit sales taxes to a government authority. The tax is usually added to the invoice or sales receipt, and merchants collect the sales tax along with the sales price of the good. To illustrate, if Huntington Company sells $1,000 of merchandise that is subject to a 5% sales tax, the following entry is necessary:

Cash	1,050	
Sales Revenue		1,000
Sales Tax Payable		50
(To record the sale of merchandise.)		

When the sales taxes that have been collected are remitted to the taxing authority, the following entry is made:

Sales Tax Payable	50	
Cash		50
(To record remittance of		
sales taxes collected.)		

Note that sales taxes are expenses of the customer rather than the business collecting the tax. When a company collects sales taxes, the business incurs a liability to the extent of the sales taxes collected. Similarly, when the sales taxes are paid, the liability is merely removed. Neither revenue nor expense should be reported in the financial statements of the tax-collecting enterprise.

In practice, however, many businesses merely record sales taxes collected as additions to revenue and the remittance of the collected taxes as reductions in revenue. In such cases, if financial statements are prepared after sales are made but before the sales taxes are remitted, an adjusting entry is required to report the liability to the taxing authority and the related reduction of revenue. Such a procedure is clerically simple and facilitates recording cash sales. In the previous example, the entries would appear as follows:

Cash	1,050	
Revenue		1,050
(To record sale and related sales tax.)		

Since no liability account is credited, the amount of the sales tax liability is unclear. Therefore, the following calculation is required:

$$X = \text{Taxable sales (cash price of goods alone)}$$
$$X + .05X = \$1,050$$
$$1.05X = \$1,050$$
$$X = \frac{\$1,050}{1.05}$$
$$X = \$1,000 \text{ (cash price of goods alone)}$$

The sales tax payable may then be determined by multiplying the tax rate (5%) times the net sales amount ($1,000). An overpayment of the sales tax occurs if one merely multiplies the tax rate times the unadjusted balance in the sales account ($1,050 × .05 = $52.50). The adjusting entry to reduce revenue and record the liability for sales taxes collected is:

Revenue	50	
Sales Tax Payable		50
(To record sales tax payable.)		

Another problem in accounting for sales taxes arises if the taxing jurisdiction allows collecting merchants a fee to cover the cost of collecting the tax. Continuing with the previous example, we find that if the taxing authority allows merchants a 2% fee for collecting sales taxes, then the $1 fee (.02 × $50) should be reflected as additional revenue at the time the taxes are remitted:

Sales Tax Payable	50	
Cash		49
Miscellaneous Revenue		1
(To record payment of sales-		
tax liability.)		

This illustration of the treatment of sales tax may appear to indicate that sales tax is recorded on each individual sale. In practice, several sales might be combined and sales tax recorded for the group of sales. For example, sales tax might be recorded at one time for all sales occurring in a day or week.

Property Taxes.   Property taxes are usually based on the **assessed value** of various real and personal properties and represent a substantial source of revenue for state and local governments. Such taxes generally become a liability of the paying company at the time they become obligations to the government. This date is usually called the **lien date.** Two accounting questions arise in regard to property taxes:

1. When should the liability be recognized?
2. When should the expense be recognized?

In essence, the liability comes into existence at the lien date, whereas the expense is generally considered to be incurred throughout the period covered by the lien. Property taxes represent expenses associated with the right to use the property subject to the taxes during the fiscal year of the taxing authority. Two accounting methods are commonly encountered in practice and are illustrated in the example that follows.

EXHIBIT 14–2
Property Tax Accounting Methods Compared

Explanation	Immediate Liability-Recognition Method		Accruing Liability-Recognition Method	
Oct. 1, 1984 City levies property tax for coming fiscal year, 10/1/84 to 9/30/85.	Deferred Property Taxes 24,000 Property Taxes Payable	24,000	No entry	

Dec. 31, 1984
Company records adjusted by accruing property-tax expense for financial reporting purposes.
	Property Tax Expense 6,000
	  Deferred Property Taxes
		6,000	Property Tax Expense 6,000
			  Property Tax Payable
				6,000

Feb. 1, 1985
Payment of property tax recorded.
	Property Taxes Payable 24,000
	  Cash
		24,000	Property Tax Payable 6,000
			Deferred Property Taxes 18,000
			  Cash
				24,000

Dec. 31, 1985
Remaining 1984–1985 levied taxes are charged to expense.
	Property Tax Expense 18,000
	  Deferred Property Taxes
		18,000	Property Tax Expense 18,000
			  Deferred Property Taxes
				18,000

Assume that Brauenegg Corporation, which uses a calendar year for financial reporting, owns some real estate which is subject to city property taxes of $24,000 per year. The taxes are levied on October 1, 1984, for the forthcoming fiscal year of the city government and are payable on February 1, 1985. The two methods of accounting for property taxes are illustrated in Exhibit 14–2.

Matching

Under each method the income statement reports the same expense. That is, property taxes are charged to expense during the periods benefited. Because the FASB has stated that the primary purpose of financial reporting is to provide information about an enterprise's earnings, either method seems consistent with the overall goals of financial accounting.[8] The differences between the two methods are confined solely to the balance sheet. The differences, advantages, and disadvantages of each method are summarized below:

	Immediate Liability-Recognition Method	Accruing Liability-Recognition Method
Difference	Liability and deferred charge recognized in total at lien date.	Liability accrued at same amount and time as expense recognized.
Advantage	Liability is recognized in full as legal obligation of company at time it is incurred.	Assets are not overstated as a result of recognizing a deferred charge for unpaid property taxes.
Disadvantage	An "asset" is recognized for unpaid property taxes.	Legal liability of company not recognized at time it is incurred.

The American Institute of Certified Public Accountants (AICPA) has taken the position

---

[8]*FASB Statement of Financial Accounting Concepts No. 1,* "Objectives of Financial Reporting by Business Enterprises," 1978, par. 43.

that the accruing liability-recognition method is preferable,[9] and the authors concur with this position. A liability exists at the time the taxes are levied; however, if the property is sold, the buyer is generally required to pay the seller for property taxes related to the remaining portion of the year. From an economic perspective the liability is thus contingent and not final at the lien date. Furthermore, the accruing liability-recognition method avoids the problem of overstated assets, because it does not recognize an asset for unpaid property taxes.

Liabilities Related to Payroll Taxes.   Another type of tax liability frequently encountered in practice relates to a company's payroll. Employers are required by law to withhold certain amounts from the salaries and wages of employees and to remit these amounts to the appropriate taxing authorities. Furthermore, the law places additional payroll taxes directly on employers. Accountants must be well acquainted with the various types of **payroll taxes** and **payroll withholdings.**

Income tax withholding laws require an employer to withhold an amount from an employee's salary that approximates the federal (and if applicable, state and local) income tax due on those earnings. The withholding requirements pertain only to **employer/ employee relationships.** In essence, if the employer provides the place of work, controls the details and hours of the work, and regularly supervises the subordinate individual, then an employer/employee relationship exists. Payments to independent contractors, such as CPAs or attorneys in public practice who prepare tax returns and render other services to businesses, are not subject to the withholding laws since no employer/employee relationship exists. Care must be taken, therefore, to determine whether a given business arrangement represents an employer/employee situation or an independent-contractor relationship.

The amount to be withheld from employee salaries is determined by the government. Employers use tables or formulas supplied by the government to determine the specific amounts to be withheld from individual employees. Withholding amounts vary according to several factors, such as the amount of earnings, the duration of the pay period, and the employee's marital status and number of dependents. The employer must remit income tax withholdings at regular intervals, the frequency of which is determined by the total amounts withheld. Income tax withholdings are taxes levied on the employee rather than the employer. The employer merely acts as a tax collector for the government in this regard and, therefore, does not recognize an expense when withheld amounts are remitted to the government.

Social Security taxes—also called **Federal Insurance Contribution Act (FICA)** taxes—provide for old-age and survivor benefits for qualified people and hospitalization insurance through the Medicare program. Social Security taxes are levied on both the employer and the employee. Therefore, the employer must withhold amounts from an employee's salary, as in the case of income tax withholding, and also pay an additional amount representing a payroll expense of the employer. Social Security taxes are stated as a percentage rate to be applied to the "base earnings" of each employee (e.g., 8% for earnings up to $30,000 per year). As a result of the rising costs of operating the Social Security system, the rates, base earnings, and employer-contribution amounts have been raised frequently in the past; future upward changes are also assured by law. For purposes of this text, we assume Social Security taxes of 8% for both employer and employee on the first $30,000 per year of the employee's base earnings. The actual rate in effect during 1982 and 1983 was 6.7%. In 1982 this rate was applied to the first $32,400 of earnings and in 1983 to the first $35,700 of earnings. The rates for 1984, 1985, and 1986 are 7%, 7.05% and 7.15%, respectively. The base earnings to which these rates are to be applied is $35,700 plus an amount to be

---

[9]*Accounting Research Bulletin No. 43,* "Restatement and Revision of Accounting Research Bulletins," 1953, Sec. A, Ch. 10, par. 14.

determined at a later date. The increase is determined through the use of a formula that is based primarily on the consumer price index. Employers are required to make periodic remittances of Social Security taxes to the federal government.

The federal unemployment tax (FUTA), instituted by the **Federal Unemployment Tax Act,** is paid by employers to provide for unemployment benefits to individuals who have lost their jobs through no fault of their own. This tax, like Social Security taxes, is expressed as a percentage (e.g., 3.2%) of a base wage (e.g., $4,200) per year. Unlike Social Security taxes, however, FUTA are levied on employers only. A credit of up to 2.7% of the total tax is allowed, however, for contributions made to a qualified state plan. Employers who pay an amount less than 2.7% to a state plan as a reward for low unemployment-compensation claims are, nevertheless, allowed the full 2.7% credit against the total federal tax. As with other employment-related taxes, employers are required to make periodic remittances of FUTA.

A **state unemployment tax (SUTA)** is usually levied only on employers; however, in a few states the tax is levied on employees as well. The most significant distinguishing characteristic of state plans is that most of them allow a merit reduction in the tax rate for favorable employment histories. Under these merit plans enterprises whose former employees have made only a few unemployment claims are rewarded with reduced tax rates for stable employment. Therefore, a company may be paying a rate of only 1% or less while continuing to receive the full 2.7% credit against FUTA.

To illustrate the accounting entries necessary to record various types of payroll taxes, assume that Warder Company payroll for the month ending January 31 is $10,000; Social Security taxes, 8% of the first $30,000 earned by each employee; and unemployment taxes, 3.2% of the first $4,200 of each employee's wages with 2.7% of the total being due to the state and the balance due to the federal government. Federal withholding tax tables reveal that $1,750 is to be withheld for employee income taxes. We should prepare the following entry to record the January payroll:

Jan. 31	Salary Expense	10,000	
	Payroll Tax Expense	1,120	
	Income Tax Withholding Payable		1,750
	FICA (Social Security) Taxes Payable		1,600
	FUTA Payable		50
	SUTA Payable		270
	Cash		7,450
	(To record payment of January payroll.)		

The calculations are as follows:

Taxes Paid by Employer:

FICA $10,000 × .08	= $	800
FUTA $10,000 × .005 =		50
SUTA $10,000 × .027 =		270
(.005 + .027 = .032)		
	$	1,120

Withheld from Employee:

FICA $10,000 × .08	$	800
Federal income tax		
(from tables)		1,750
	$	2,550

Cash Required:

Total payroll	$10,000
Less withholding	2,550
	$ 7,450

Note that FICA taxes are levied on both employer and employee in the same amount ($800) for a total of $1,600. Therefore, $800 of this amount is withheld from employees and the additional $800 represents a payroll tax expense of the employer. FUTA and SUTA are both taxes on the employer in this example and as such represent increases in payroll tax expense. Federal income taxes withheld, however, are not additional payroll tax expenses of employers. They are simply amounts that are withheld from employees' salaries.

As a further example, assume that Warder Company's July 31 payroll also amounts to $10,000. However, only $8,000 of this total amount represents payment to employees who have not earned the FICA maximum of $30,000. Further assume that only $2,000 of the $10,000 is paid to employees who have not earned $4,200, the FUTA maximum. Income tax withholding remains the same as in the previous example. The following entry records the July payroll:

July 31	Salary Expense	10,000	
	Payroll Tax Expense	704	
	Income Tax Withholding Payable		1,750
	FICA Taxes Payable		1,280
	FUTA Payable		10
	SUTA Payable		54
	Cash		7,610
	(To record payment of July payroll.)		

The calculations are as follows:

Taxes Paid by Employer:

FICA $8,000 × .08	= $	640
FUTA $2,000 × .005	=	10
SUTA $2,000 × .027	=	54
	$	704

Withheld from Employee:

FICA $8,000 × .08	= $	640
Federal income tax (from tables)		1,750
		$ 2,390

Cash Required:

Total Payroll	$10,000
Less Withholding	2,390
	$ 7,610

Although the accounts affected are the same, the amounts are different for both FICA and unemployment taxes because some employees have reached the maximum amount limitations. When the various taxes and other amounts withheld are paid to the taxing authorities, Warder credits cash and charges the appropriate liability accounts (i.e., FICA Taxes Payable, FUTA and SUTA Payable, and Income Tax Withholding Payable). In our example no other withholding amounts, such as union dues or insurance premiums are considered.

Although for simplicity we assumed that only taxes were withheld, **other payroll withholdings** would be recorded as liabilities in a similar fashion. To motivate personnel, companies frequently agree to withhold health insurance premiums, union dues, savings-plan deductions, and other amounts from employees' salaries as a convenience to the employee. Such amounts should be accounted for in a fashion similar to any payroll withholding and reported as a liability until remitted to the appropriate agency. Of course, these items are reflected as part of salary expense and do not represent incremental expenses to the employer.

Bonus and Profit-Sharing Plans

To motivate employees, companies often compensate key employees for superior profits made by the enterprise or for those profits attributed to the segment of the enterprise managed by the particular employee. Although there are many variations of such plans, the central theme is to ensure a higher degree of goal congruence between employees and the employing enterprise by directly relating the well-being of the employee to the success of the company. These types of compensation plans give rise to liabilities and expenses that must be measured and reported in the financial statements. To illustrate three commonly employed formulas for computing bonuses, we shall assume that Mark Company reports a net income before deducting income taxes and bonuses of $100,000. Any bonus accrued at the end of the year is deductible for income tax purposes in the year accrued, and the company's income tax rate is 40%.

Example 1. The bonus to be paid is expressed as 5% of net income over $60,000. The computation will be made before bonus and income tax expenses are deducted. Therefore, the following computations and entries are necessary to determine and record the bonus and income taxes:

Bonus:

$$\text{Bonus} = .05(\,\$100,000 - \$60,000\,)$$
$$\text{Bonus} = .05(\,\$40,000\,)$$
$$\text{Bonus} = \$2,000$$

Income taxes:

$$\text{Taxes} = .40(\,\$100,000 - \text{Bonus}\,)$$
$$\text{Taxes} = .40(\,\$100,000 - \$2,000\,)$$
$$\text{Taxes} = .40(\,\$98,000\,)$$
$$\text{Taxes} = \$39,200$$

Entries:

Compensation Expense	2,000	
Bonus Payable		2,000
Income Tax Expense	39,200	
Income Tax Payable		39,200

Example 2. Assume now that the bonus is to be paid in the amount of 5% of net income in excess of $60,000 *after* deducting the bonus but *before* considering income taxes.

Bonus:

$$\text{Bonus} = .05(\,\$100,000 - \$60,000 - \text{Bonus}\,)$$
$$\text{Bonus} = .05(\,\$40,000 - \text{Bonus}\,)$$

$$\text{Bonus} = \$2,000 - .05 \text{ Bonus}$$
$$1.05 \text{ Bonus} = \$2,000$$
$$\text{Bonus} = \$2,000/1.05$$
$$\text{Bonus} = \$1,905$$

Income taxes:

$$\text{Taxes} = .40(\$100,000 - \text{Bonus})$$
$$\text{Taxes} = .40(\$100,000 - \$1,905)$$
$$\text{Taxes} = .40(\$98,095)$$
$$\text{Taxes} = \$39,238$$

The entries are similar to those in Example 1 except for the amounts, which reflect the altered provisions of the bonus plan.

Example 3.   Assume now that the bonus is to be paid in the amount of 5% of net income after deducting *both* bonus and taxes. In this case, the amount of the bonus depends on taxes and the amount of taxes depends on the bonus. Two equations, each containing two unknowns (bonus and income taxes), are required to determine the individual amounts of bonus and income taxes:

$$\text{Bonus} = .05(\$100,000 - \text{Bonus} - \text{Income taxes}) \qquad (14-1)$$
$$\text{Taxes} = .40(\$100,000 - \text{Bonus}) \qquad (14-2)$$

Substitute Equation (14–2) in Equation (14–1):

$$\text{Bonus} = .05[\$100,000 - \text{Bonus} - .40(\$100,000 - \text{Bonus})]$$
$$\text{Bonus} = .05(\$100,000 - \text{Bonus} - \$40,000 + .40 \text{ Bonus})$$
$$\text{Bonus} = \$5,000 - .05 \text{ Bonus} - \$2,000 + .02 \text{ Bonus}$$
$$1.03 \text{ Bonus} = \$3,000$$
$$\text{Bonus} = \frac{\$3,000}{1.03}$$
$$\text{Bonus} = \$2,913$$

$$\text{Taxes} = .4(\$100,000 - \text{Bonus})$$
$$\text{Taxes} = .4(\$100,000 - \$2,913)$$
$$\text{Taxes} = .4(\$97,087)$$
$$\text{Taxes} = \$38,835$$

Proof:

$$\text{Bonus} = .05(\$100,000 - \text{Bonus} - \text{Taxes})$$
$$\$2,913 = .05(\$100,000 - \$2,913 - \$38,835)$$
$$\$2,913 = .05(\$100,000 - \$41,748)$$
$$\$2,913 = .05(\$58,252)$$
$$\$2,913 = \$2,913$$

The journal entries required are again similar to those shown in Example 1 except for the amounts. For the many other types and variations of bonus plans and profit-sharing arrangements accountants are guided by the provisions of those agreements concerning the timing and amount of liabilities and related expenses. Careful study of such agreements is necessary to assure proper comprehension and application.

CONTINGENT LIABILITIES

The term **contingent liability** is used to describe a circumstance in which the existence of a liability is uncertain. In many cases, the amount of a contingent liability, if any, may not be known with precision. A contingent liability is thus distinguishable from an estimated liability. In sum, a contingent liability is uncertain as to its existence and usually its amount. An **estimated liability,** on the other hand, is known to exist but its exact amount is unknown. If an enterprise is almost certain that a contingent liability exists and if the amount can be reasonably estimated, the contingent liability should be recognized in the financial statements. As such, contingent liabilities represent another area in which estimates of future events are necessary to prepare current financial statements.

The FASB considered the issues and problems of accounting and reporting many types of contingencies and issued *SFAS No. 5,* which defines a contingency as:

> *An existing condition, situation, or set of circumstances involving uncertainty as to possible gain or loss to an enterprise that will ultimately be resolved when one or more future events occur or fail to occur.*[10]

An unsettled lawsuit provides an example of both a **gain contingency** and a **loss contingency.** For the plaintiff (the party that brings suit against another), the possibility of gain exists if the suit is won. To the defendent (the party charged by the plaintiff of some wrongdoing), the suit represents a loss contingency because payment must be made if the plaintiff prevails. Uncertainty exists for both parties until the final resolution of the suit in the courts.

Although *SFAS No. 5* recognizes that contingencies may involve either gain or loss, it is concerned exclusively with loss contingencies and carries forward the conclusions of *Accounting Research Bulletin No. 50,* which states that "gain contingencies should not be accrued since to do so might recognize revenue prior to its realization."[11] Revenue realization, including contingent gains, is treated more fully in Chapter 20, which deals with many unusual problems of the timing and amount of revenue to be reported in financial statements. Nevertheless, the role of conservatism is clearly evident in the different accounting treatments accorded gain and loss contingencies. In the following discussion, consider how the modifying convention of conservatism is applied in the specific accounting standards used by our profession in reporting loss contingencies.

| Revenue Realization |

| Conservatism |

Criteria for Accruing Loss Contingencies

| Conservatism |

Loss contingencies, which involve either the impairment of an asset or the incurrence of a liability, require accrual on the basis of less evidence than that required for gain contingencies. This practice, of course, is consistent with the modifying convention of conservatism found throughout the financial accounting process. The FASB set forth three conditions necessary for accrual of a loss contingency:[12]

| Objectivity |

1. The occurrence of the confirming future event or events must be **probable;**
2. The amount of the loss must be **reasonably estimable;** and
3. The event giving rise to the loss must have **taken place** by the balance-sheet date.

Thus, a loss must be *estimable, timely,* and *probable* of being ultimately sustained to require accrual in the financial statements.

---

[10]*FASB Statement of Financial Accounting Standards No. 5,* "Accounting for Contingencies," 1975, par. 1.
[11]*FASB Statement of Financial Accounting Standards No. 5,* par. 17.
[12]*FASB Statement of Financial Accounting Standards No. 5,* par. 8.

Probability of Contingent Losses

To help accountants evaluate the likelihood of the occurrence of the future event confirming a loss, the FASB described three distinct conditions of **probability.** These categories represent a continuum ranging from an extreme of almost complete certainty that a loss has been incurred to an extreme of almost complete certainty that no loss has been incurred. An illustration of such a continuum is presented in Exhibit 14–3.

SFAS No. 5 defines the three categories of probability:[13]

1. **Probable.**   The future event or events are *likely* to occur.
2. **Reasonably possible.**   The chance of the future event or events occurring is *more than remote* but *less than likely.*
3. **Remote.**   The chance of the future event or events occurring is *slight.*

The FASB did not assign probability percentages to these categories but relies on the professional judgment of accountants to assess the category of probability in which a particular set of circumstances should be placed.

Estimability of Contingent Losses

SFAS No. 5 also requires accountants to estimate the amount of contingent losses. An FASB Interpretation[14] provides that when the estimated amount of a loss contingency is a range of amounts, then the condition of reasonable estimability is met. Therefore, if a loss is probable, if the event giving rise to the loss has occurred by the balance sheet date, and if a range of loss can be estimated, then the loss should be accrued. If one particular amount in the range represents a superior estimate of the loss ultimately to be incurred, then *that* amount should

| Conserva-
tism |

be accrued. If no specific amount in the range appears to be a better estimate, however, then the *minimum* amount of the range should be selected. This practice represents the least conservative method of applying a fundamentally conservative procedure. The amount of the range and the nature of the contingency should both be disclosed in such circumstances.

If the estimability, probability, and time conditions are met then the estimated amount of the loss should be charged against income in the current period and the related asset written down or the related liability recognized. Generally disclosures of the nature of the contingency and the amount of the loss accrued are necessary.

Disclosure of Loss Contingencies Not Accrued

| Disclosure |

A loss contingency that is at least reasonably possible, but not probable, must be disclosed even if the loss is not reasonably estimable or if the event giving rise to the loss occurred

---

[13]*FASB Statement of Financial Accounting Standards No. 5,* par. 3.

[14]*FASB Interpretation No. 14,* "Reasonable Estimation of the Amount of a Loss: An Interpretation of FASB Statement No. 5," 1976, par. 3.

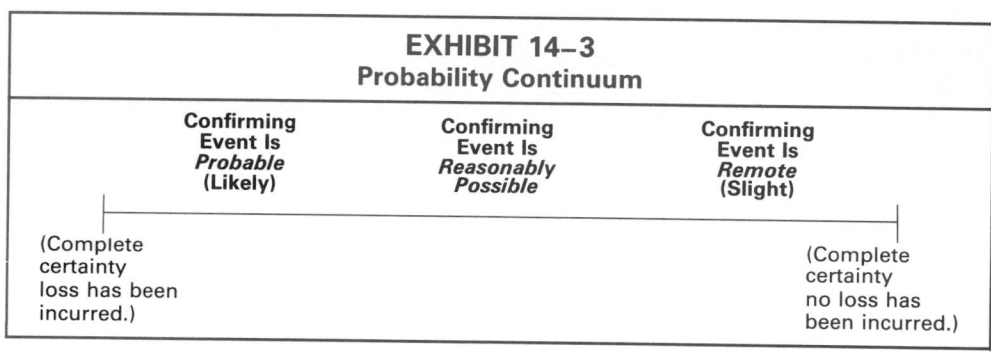

EXHIBIT 14–3
Probability Continuum

Confirming Event Is *Probable* (Likely)	Confirming Event Is *Reasonably* *Possible*	Confirming Event Is *Remote* (Slight)

(Complete certainty loss has been incurred.)   (Complete certainty no loss has been incurred.)

EXHIBIT 14–4
Loss Contingencies

Loss Related To	Usually Should Be Accrued	Should Not Be Accrued	Accrual Depends on Circumstances*
1. Collectibility of receivables.	X		
2. Obligations related to product warranties and product defects.	X		
3. Risk of loss or damage of enterprise property by fire, explosion, or other hazards.		X	
4. General or unspecified business risks.		X	
5. Risk of loss from catastrophes assumed by property and casualty insurance companies, including reinsurance companies.		X	
6. Threat of expropriation of assets.			X
7. Pending or threatened litigation.			X
8. Actual or possible claims and assessments.**			X
9. Guarantees of indebtedness of others.			X
10. Obligations of commercial banks under "standby letters of credit."			X
11. Agreements to repurchase receivables (or the related properties) that have been sold.			X

*Should be accrued when both criteria are met (probable and reasonably estimable).
**Estimated amounts of losses incurred prior to the balance sheet date but settled subsequent thereto should be accrued as of the balance sheet date.

SOURCE: Ernst & Whinney, *Financial Reporting Developments,* "Accounting for Contingencies," August 1975, p. 4.

after the balance sheet date. The disclosure should include the nature of the contingency and an estimate of the loss or a statement that such an estimate is not possible.

Remote Loss Contingencies

The FASB generally does not require the disclosure of remote loss contingencies. Disclosure is not prohibited, however, and if an unusually large potential loss is remotely possible, disclosure of the nature and amount of loss is desirable. Furthermore, certain types of loss contingencies, including the following, must be disclosed even if the probability of loss is remote: (1) guarantees of the indebtedness of others; (2) guarantees to repurchase receivables; and (3) obligations of commercial banks under certain letters of credit.

General or unspecified business risks, such as a practice of self-insurance for fire or other catastrophe, do not meet the criteria for accrual and no disclosure about them is *required* by *SFAS No. 5.* Exhibit 14–4 displays the normal accounting practices for a variety of loss contingencies.

While many of the items in the table are easily understood and applied, the problems of accounting for litigation, claims, and assessments in items 7 and 8 are more complex.

Litigation, Claims, and Assessments

Litigation has become a common problem for many companies in recent years, and when a company is sued certain accounting and reporting implications are evident. If a lawsuit or other claim is lodged against a company and the final outcome is not known at the time that financial statements are issued, then a contingent liability exists and the probability of an unfavorable outcome as well as the amount of the loss, including attorney's fees, must be estimated. Lawyers are usually asked to assist in making these estimates. However, the general criteria for accounting and reporting loss contingencies should be applied and, therefore, accountants must also be well acquainted with the facts of the litigation.

One special type of claim, referred to as an **unasserted claim,** requires additional analysis. An unasserted claim is defined as a situation involving a **potential claim** or assessment in which the **potential claimant** has not evidenced an awareness of a right to proceed with the claim. Examples include violations of tax or customs regulations, pollution of the environment, and a variety of torts (social wrongs) involving possible lawsuits.

In essence, unasserted claims do not require disclosure unless (1) assertion is probable, even if no disclosures are made in the financial statements; and (2) a related loss is at least reasonably possible. The rationale underlying this additional criteria for disclosure of unasserted claims is the idea that a company need not "tell on itself." That is, no disclosure regarding an unasserted claim is required unless the claim will *probably* be asserted even if the disclosures are not made in the financial statements. Unasserted claims that are probable of assertion and meet the other criteria for accruing loss contingencies should be recorded as liabilities.

To illustrate proper accounting and reporting for loss contingencies over a relatively long period of time, a single circumstance covering several years is taken from practice. Exhibit 14–5 is a footnote that appeared in the annual report of Tony Lama Company at the end of its fiscal year on October 31, 1977.

EXHIBIT 14–5
Contingency Disclosure

(10) Contingency
During the year ended July 31, 1976 the U.S. Customs Service instituted an investigation of the duty declarations made by the Company in connection with the importation of footwear parts from Mexico during the period from October 1969 to May 1976. Upon completion of its internal investigation of the customs matter in accordance with guidelines suggested by the Customs Service, the Company, on November 1, 1976, filed with the Service a schedule of applicable costs which reflected unpaid duties aggregating approximately $365,000 and provision was made for this amount in the 1976 consolidated financial statements.

During fiscal 1977 the Customs Service completed its investigation of the Company's duty declarations and the Company was assessed an additional $145,000 for duties lost. This additional deficiency was charged to operations during fiscal 1977 and the aggregate amount of duties lost as determined by the Customs Service was paid by the Company during the year.

In August 1977 the Company pleaded guilty to criminal charges in connection with the duty declarations and subsequently paid a fine of $15,000. In addition, the Customs Service assessed the Company a civil penalty of approximately $36 million, which represents the forfeiture value of the goods imported during the period in question. The Company is preparing its petition for mitigation of the penalty, and normally such penalties are mitigated to a multiple (generally from one to eight) of the alleged loss of revenue ($510,000). The Company has made provision in its 1977 consolidated financial statements for $510,000, the minimum penalty it expects to incur in connection with the customs matter; however, the penalty ultimately assessed may be substantially in excess of this amount. The total ultimate liability to the Company which may result from the customs matter is not presently determinable. Customs penalties normally may be repaid with interest over a period of five years from the date of final adjudication. Such penalties are not deductible for Federal income tax purposes.

EXHIBIT 14–6
Resolution of Contingency

Tony Lama Co. Agrees To Settle Duties Case By Paying $2,549,487

By a WALL STREET JOURNAL *Staff Reporter*

EL PASO, Texas—Tony Lama Co. said it agreed to settle with the U.S. Customs Service for $2,549,487, instead of the $36 million asked in the case involving duties on leather imported from Mexico.

The company had set up an allowance of $510,000 for a possible penalty in the case, so the agreed payment will cause a $2,039,487 charge against earnings for the fourth quarter. This will cause a deficit in the last quarter but won't cause a loss for the year, a spokesman said. For the nine months, the bootmaker earned $1.7 million, or 96 cents a share.

The payment won't be tax deductible. It will be made over three years, in monthly installments of $81,074 at 9% interest, starting in March.

Note that the loss was estimated to be probable, the event giving rise to the loss had occurred, and an estimate of a range of loss was possible. Although the range was extremely large ($510,000–$36,000,000), the company, nevertheless, properly accrued the lower end of the range. In December 1979, Exhibit 14–6 appeared in *The Wall Street Journal*.

The difference between the amount originally accrued ($510,000) and the total liability ($2,549,487) was properly reflected as an expense during the year ended October 31, 1979.

Evidence About Litigation, Claims, and Assessments

Objectivity

Accountants must collect sufficient competent evidence to support accounting entries. In the area of litigation, claims, and assessments, accountants frequently rely on attorneys to study and evaluate the merit and prospects of individual lawsuits. In fact, lengthy written representations from lawyers are usually requested by accountants attempting to apply *SFAS No. 5* to loss contingencies arising from litigation, claims, and assessments. Lawyers are usually requested to analyze each lawsuit and comment on the probability of an unfavorable outcome, amount of possible loss, the defendant's proposed course of action, and any other relevant issues. Accountants typically do not have the requisite legal expertise to make such determinations alone and therefore frequently rely on the knowledge and experience of members of the legal profession.

It is important for us to recognize that the skill and expertise of accountants is limited to the education, training, and experience they have obtained. Therefore, in many cases, including accounting for loss contingencies, accountants rely on the judgment and expertise of specialists to provide the basis for financial reporting practices. The use of specialists is thus quite common as accountants attempt to gather evidence to support the many complex assertions made in the financial statements. Examples of other accounting issues that may be resolved by relying on specialists include the valuation of gems, the assessment of recoverable oil and gas reserves, and estimates of the obsolescence of technologically complex equipment. The key point to remember is that each financial-statement account makes many assertions related to such items as existence, ownership, and value. The accountant must be sure that each assertion made by the financial statements is supported by adequate evidence, and sometimes expert opinions must be obtained.

Warranties and Guarantees

Many companies offer their customers guarantees of product performance or capability that extend well beyond the time of the sale. Reasonable estimates of the selling company's contingent liability for such guarantees are usually possible. The estimated warranty expense and the related liability under the warranty should be recognized at the time of the original sale of the product. If the amount of the liability under the warranty cannot be reasonably estimated, then no expense or liability should be recognized. Revenue from the sale of the item, however, should usually be deferred in such cases until the actual amount of the warranty expense becomes known. In this manner, the matching of revenue and expense is accomplished even if warranty expense is not currently estimable.

To illustrate, assume that Andrews, Inc., a manufacturer of high-quality kitchen appliances, warrants its products to be "oven safe." Engineering estimates and historical analysis, however, indicate that approximately 1% of all products sold will fail within the warranty period and about one-half of those products will be returned. If sales for Andrews, Inc., are $5,000,000 for 1984 and the company's gross margin on sales is 40%, the following entry is necessary to record the estimated warranty expense for 1984:

Dec. 31, 1984	Warranty Expense	15,000
	Estimated Liability	
	for Warranties	15,000

The calculations to arrive at that figure are as follows:

$$\text{Amount originally received for returned products} = \$5,000,000 \times .01 \times .5 = \$25,000$$

$$\text{Sales} - \text{Gross margin} = \text{Cost of goods sold}$$

$$\$25,000 - .4\,(\$25,000) = \text{Cost of goods expected to be returned}$$

Therefore, $15,000 ($25,000 − $10,000) is the amount estimated to be necessary to honor warranties.

If goods costing $2,000 are drawn from inventory on January 15, 1985, to honor warranties, the following entry is appropriate:

Jan. 15, 1985	Estimated Liability for Warranties	2,000
	Inventory	2,000

Even if some of the warranties related to sales made in 1984 were honored during 1984, a similar entry is appropriate. Honoring a warranty simply discharges a liability of the company. The entry to adjust the Warranty Expense account at the end of the year is based on prior experience and estimated remaining warranties to be honored.

Premiums

Premiums often are used to help sell products. Usually a company acquires an inventory of premium items and offers to "give" them away to customers upon proof that the customer has acquired a certain quantity of the primary product. Accounting for premiums of this nature is illustrated in the following example.

Assume that Suds City Soap Company initiated a premium program whereby the company would give customers a kitchen utensil upon presentation of ten box tops from its soap product. During the first year of the program Suds acquired 10,000 kitchen utensils at $1 each and sold 750,000 boxes of the soap product at $2.50 per box. The company estimated that 10% of all sales would result in the return of box tops for the utensil. By the end of the year Suds City had received 50,000 box tops and had sent the kitchen utensils to the customers. The following entries reflect proper accounting for these events.

Inventory of Premiums	10,000	
Cash		10,000
(To record acquisition of		
kitchen utensils.)		
Cash	1,875,000	
Sales		1,875,000
(To record sale of soap. 750,000 × $2.50.)		
Premium Expense	5,000	
Inventory of Premiums		5,000
(To record premiums sent to		
customers based on box tops		
received. 50,000 ÷ 10 =		
5,000 utensils @ $1 each.)		
Premium Expense	2,500	
Estimated Liability Under Premium Plan		2,500
(To record contingent liability		
under premium plan at end of year.)		

Calculations for the fourth entry are as follows:

Total sales (in boxes)	750,000
Percent expected to claim premium	× .10
Total box tops to be received	75,000
Less: Box tops received	− 50,000
Estimated remaining box tops	
to be received	25,000
	÷ 10
Estimated premiums to be sent	2,500
	× $1
Remaining liability and expense	
related to annual sales	$ 2,500

As the 25,000 box tops are subsequently received and utensils shipped, the following entry is necessary:

Estimated Liability Under Premium Plan	2,500	
Inventory of Premiums		2,500

If the original estimate of the liability under the premium plan differs from actual experience, the difference is charged or credited to income in the period in which this fact becomes known.

Compensated Absences

The compensation of employees often exceeds the amount they are immediately paid for services rendered. For example, companies frequently provide retirement benefits, paid vacations, and sick leave for their employees. Sometimes sabbatical leaves are granted to employees such as physicians, college professors, engineers, and other highly skilled individuals. Employees usually earn the right to such **compensated absences** in periods prior to the absence. If certain conditions which are described in the following paragraph are met, compensation expense for each accounting period should include the cost to the employer of future absences earned by employees during that period. Because accounting for pension plans is complex and controversial, Chapter 22 is devoted to that topic. Other types of deferred payments for employee services, however, are clearly in the nature of contingent liabilities, and we discuss some of them in the following paragraph.

FASB Statement of Financial Accounting Standards No. 43[15] addresses financial reporting for various programs of employee benefits. In essence, it indicates that compensated absences represent a type of contingency, and it expands the recognition criteria contained in *SFAS No. 5* to encompass the special aspects of these costs. In accordance with *SFAS No. 43,* employers must accrue a liability for employees' compensation for future absences when four separate conditions exist:

1. The employer's obligation is attributable to services **already rendered** by the balance sheet date;
2. The obligation relates to **vested rights** that are not contingent on continued employment or to rights that accumulate from period to period even if not taken;

---

[15]*FASB Statement of Financial Accounting Standards No. 43,* "Accounting for Compensated Absences," 1980.

OFF-THE-BOOK TIME BOMBS

THE FINANCIAL ACCOUNTING Standards Board has come up with a recent ruling that will force companies to recognize a new set of liabilities. The ruling, number 43, requires all employers to accrue a liability for future vacation benefits and those sick benefits used for extra time off. For firms with a large number of employees, such liabilities can be substantial, not least because employees often bank their benefits just like additional pay.

What's curious is that the FASB—along with the rest of the accounting world—has left the problem unresolved for municipalities. That's where the *real* vacation and sick leave liabilities are stocked away, since city leaders have for years sated employees with sick leave and vacation benefits in lieu of cash.

The origins of the corporate ruling date back to 1973, when the Civil Aeronautics Board ordered domestic airlines to accrue vacation benefits as a liability on their balance sheets instead of paying them out of expenses as they occurred. Eastern Air Lines had problems with the ruling. It was putting out $30 million a year in vacation pay, yet that liability didn't appear anywhere on the books. The CAB backed down in Eastern's case and things were

rosy until March 1977, when the company registered a $50 million debt offering with the SEC. The SEC blew the whistle: Record that liability on your balance sheet, it said, or forget about your debt issue. Eastern needed financing, so it was forced to comply, plopping a $35 million net loss onto its restated 1975 accounts. The result was a record $96 million loss for that year.

Now, with the FASB ruling, *all* companies have been ordered to record vacation and some sick leave benefits as a liability on their balance sheets. Although companies need not have complied with the new rule until this year, some have already chosen to. Alcoa, General Tire & Rubber, Geo. A. Hormel, Holly Sugar and Sherwin-Williams have all booked their vacation benefit liabilities on their 1980 annuals.

Of course, the blow to most companies' earnings will not be nearly as great as it was in the case of Eastern, because the FASB allows companies to assume the liability over previous years and restate earnings. So although Sherwin-Williams' total liabilities are up $16 million, the company earned only $1.2 million less in 1980, on net income of $25 million, than it would have otherwise.

While that's the kind of liability an investor

wants to know about, it's not a matter of life or death, of course, and often is so small it won't even show up as a separate line item. But with cities, these liabilities could be nearly enough to push them over the brink. According to a study of 100 cities published by Ernst & Whinney in 1979, 59% did not provide any information whatsoever on vacation and sick leave liabilities. Often, if they don't disclose the information, they don't have it internally either.

"We're paying vacation benefits with current tax dollars for services that were received in the past when we really didn't recognize their full cost," says Anthony Mottola, head of state and local government services at Coopers & Lybrand. "That means, simply, that governments have mortgaged the future to some extent, and have made a financing decision that they will pay for when they write the checks." That's if there's any money in the bank when they want to write the checks.

Take the case of a Brookline, Mass. assistant superintendent of schools who worked for around 20 years and rarely took a vacation or sick day. A month or so before she retired, the city discovered that she was due nearly $30,000 in accrued benefits. Yet that liability was never on the city's books. The retiring school official settled for somewhat less, and Brookline soon changed its vacation ac-

crual policy. True, cities do not usually pay out 100% of accrued sick benefits when a person retires. Of $100,000 in accrued benefits, a retiring worker might get, say, 40%. Still, multiply that by thousands of workers and you begin to see the problem.

In New York City, vacation and sick leave liabilities were first reported in the annual report in 1978. That year they amounted to $590 million. Last year they hit $670 million, but were still listed as long-term obligations. If they were shown as short-term liabilities, they could conceivably increase New York's $3.2 billion net general fund deficit to nearly $4 billion.

In Dallas, in 1979, the city disclosed vacation liabilities of $8.6 million and a potential $33 million of sick pay liabilities. Contrast that with a mere $3.4 million in the general fund for that year.

Back in 1977, the SEC wouldn't allow Eastern Air Lines to go to the market until it cleaned up its vacation and sick leave liabilities. Why don't Standard & Poor's and Moody's—which have been acting as if they were going to impose good accounting on municipalities—make the same kind of threat?

SOURCE: Alyssa A. Lappen, "Off-the-Book Time Bombs," *Forbes*, May 11, 1981, p. 211. Reprinted by permission of *Forbes* Magazine. © Forbes Inc., 1981.

3. Payment of the compensation is **probable**; and
4. The amount is **reasonably estimable.**

Disclosure

Disclosure of such contingencies is required when the first three conditions exist but the amount is not reasonably estimable. *SFAS No. 5* requires disclosure of loss contingencies when there is at least a reasonable possibility of loss, regardless of whether the amount of the loss is reasonably estimable. Therefore, we should consider the desirability of disclosing unaccrued compensated-absence obligations for which payment is deemed reasonably possible, whether or not the amount is estimable. This logic parallels that of *SFAS No. 5*.

The FASB does not require the accrual of sick leave unless the leave is *vested* in the employee. Unvested but accumulated sick leave is contingent on a future illness; since the illness is not a condition existing at the balance sheet date, accrual is not required. However, the wording of this provision regarding sick leave is "permissive," and the accrual of accumulating nonvesting sick leave is acceptable. The authors of this text recommend disclosure of the particular accounting policy followed for material amounts of accumulating, but nonvesting, sick leave.

Industry Practices

The primary focus of this book is on financial accounting and reporting for business enterprises operated for profit. Standards of financial accounting and reporting, however, also apply to nonbusiness enterprises. The consequences of new pronouncements can be substantial for both profit-seeking and not-for-profit organizations.

1. Financial accounting and reporting for current and contingent liabilities require a good understanding of both the concepts underlying recognition and valuation of liabilities as well as the specific practices required by authoritative bodies.

2. As in other areas of financial reporting, broad and relatively abstract concepts guide accounting practice in the area of liabilities.

3. An obligation must exhibit three characteristics in order to represent a reportable liability: (1) It must entail a probable future economic sacrifice; (2) it must require a transfer of resources; and (3) it must be the result of a past transaction or event. Not all obligations of an enterprise are considered reportable liabilities.

4. A current liability is a liability that will be satisfied with current assets or through the creation of a new current liability.

5. Several major categories of current liabilities exist, including:

[a] Trade accounts payable
[b] Notes payable
[c] Dividends payable
[d] Advances from customers
[e] Various liabilities for taxes (e.g., payroll, property, income)

6. To exclude a short-term obligation from current liabilities an enterprise must *intend* to refinance the obligation on a noncurrent basis and *demonstrate the ability* to accomplish the refinancing.

7. A contingent liability is uncertain as to existence and, usually, as to amount.

8. Examples of contingent liabilities include the following:

[a] litigation
[b] inventory obsolescence
[c] collectibility of receivables
[d] warranties
[e] guarantees
[f] compensated absences

9. For a loss contingency to require accrual it must be probable that a liability has been incurred and the amount of the loss must be reasonably estimable. Also, the event giving rise to the probable loss must have taken place by the date of the balance sheet.

10. Loss contingencies that are at least reasonably possible must be disclosed even if the other conditions for accrual are not met.

11. The concept of conservatism requires that liabilities and loss contingencies be recorded and reflected in the financial statements on the basis of less evidence than is required for receivables and gain contingencies.

_____ **QUESTIONS**

14–1 Define the term "liability" and list its three essential characteristics.

14–2 What characteristics distinguish between a current and a noncurrent liability?

14–3 What are some of the problems that arise in attempting to value current liabilities? Describe what, in your opinion, is the theoretically preferable valuation amount of liabilities. Do not consider implementation problems in your answer.

14–4 How would each of the following be reported on the balance sheet?

[a] Bank overdraft.
[b] Cash dividend declared.
[c] Dividends in arrears on preferred stock.
[d] Estimates of income taxes payable.
[e] Personal-injury claim pending.
[f] Customer accounts with credit balances.
[g] Deposits received by a public utility for meter installations.

[h] Current portion of a serial bond issue.
[i] Interest on note payable that is deducted from the face amount of the note in determining the net proceeds.
[j] Strike settlement calling for retroactive wage payments.

14–5 In what situations should a short-term note payable be reported on the balance sheet at an amount less than face (maturity) value?

14–6 When, if ever, is it proper to report a current obligation as a noncurrent liability?

14–7 If a company pays off a short-term obligation immediately after the balance sheet date and then replenishes the funds used through long-term borrowing, should the short-term debt be classified as a noncurrent liability on the balance sheet? Why?

14–8 Advances from customers are considered to be liabilities, even though they typically will not require a cash payment to customers in the future. Explain how this is consistent with the definition of the term "liability."

14-9 Describe the two methods of accounting for sales tax collection.

14-10 Real estate taxes become a lien on the property owned by Thacker Company on the assessment date in May. Yet the company does not begin to accrue taxes on its books until August, which is the beginning of the city's fiscal year. Comment on this practice.

14-11 What types of liabilities commonly arise in connection with a payroll? Discuss each type briefly, indicating whether the item represents an expense of the employer, the employee, or both.

14-12 The sales manager for Acme Company is entitled to a bonus of "10% of company profits." What problems could arise in interpreting this agreement?

14-13 Define the term "contingent liability."

14-14 A company's working capital position can be affected by the existence and evaluation of contingent claims. Explain this statement.

14-15 Give five examples of contingent liabilities. For each type, discuss the desirability and usual practice of disclosure or accrual accorded it in the current period.

14-16 Discuss the reporting methods and techniques frequently employed to disclose contingent liabilities.

14-17 What are unasserted claims and how should they be presented in the financial statements?

14-18 Warranties and premiums may require the recognition of an estimated liability for services or products to be provided in the future. What basic accounting principle explains these accounting procedures? Discuss briefly.

14-19 Under what conditions should compensated absences be recognized as an expense in the period in which the employee earns the right to the future absence?

14-20 If sick leave does not vest in employees, a company is not required to record a liability at the time the employee earns the right to miss work in the future. Why are compensated absences for sick-pay benefits treated differently from compensated absences for vacations?

CASES

C14-1 The following items are listed under "liabilities" on the balance sheet of Adams Industrial Company on December 31, 1985:

Accounts payable	$ 200,000
Notes payable	300,000
Bonds payable	1,040,000

Accounts payable represent obligations to suppliers which were due in January 1986. Notes payable mature on various dates during 1986. Bonds payable mature on July 1, 1986.

These liabilities must be reported on the balance sheet in accordance with generally accepted accounting principles governing the classification of liabilities as current and noncurrent.

Instructions

[a] What is the general rule for determining whether a liability is classified as current or noncurrent?
[b] Under what conditions may any of Adams Industrial Company's liabilities be classified as noncurrent? Explain your answer.

(CMA adapted)

C14-2 In May 1985 Bow Company became involved in litigation. As a result, Bow will probably have to pay $1,400,000. In July 1985 a competitor commenced a suit against Bow, alleging violation of antitrust laws and seeking damages of $2,200,000. Bow denies the allegations, and the likelihood of Bow paying any damages is remote. In September 1985 Putnam County brought action against Bow for $1,800,000 for polluting Lake Mahapac. It is reasonably possible that Putnam County will be successful in its vigorous suit; however, the amount of damages Bow will have to pay is not reasonably estimable.

Instructions

[a] What amount, if any, should be accrued by a charge to income in 1985?
[b] Prepare any disclosures that Bow Company should make with respect to the pollution suit.

C14-3 O'Malley, Inc., is an entity whose sole operations consist of the manufacture and sale of water skis. Several uncertainties surround certain aspects of O'Malley's operations for the year ended December 31, 1985. As head of O'Malley's accounting department, you are responsible for determining the effect of each of these uncertainties on the company's annual financial statements. Of primary concern are the following situations.

[1] When used in execution of tight turns, the skeg (keel) of the company's top-line slalom ski has a tendency to pop off the ski and skim across the water. In the past year ten people are known to have been hospitalized with head injuries as a result of this defect. Legal counsel believes that while no claims have been made yet, a class action suit will probably be filed soon, and although successful prosecution is unlikely, the company will probably sustain losses of $22,000.

[2] In October 1985 a worker was injured in the manufacturing plant in an accident partially the result of his own negligence. The worker has sued O'Malley for $300,000. Counsel believes it is reasonably possible that the outcome of the action will be unfavorable and that the settlement would cost the company from $50,000 to $250,000.

Instructions

Discuss the appropriate accounting treatment, including any required disclosures in each circumstance. Provide the basis and logic of your conclusions.

C14–4 Emerson Corporation has notes payable of $1,500,000 among its liabilities at December 31, 1984. These notes are due as follows:

Due Date	Amount
May 1, 1985	$250,000
Oct. 1, 1985	650,000
Nov. 1, 1985	600,000

The company is considering the appropriate balance sheet classification of the liabilities at December 31, 1984, and has asked your advice.

Instructions

[a] Discuss briefly the conditions that must be met for short-term obligations to be excluded from the current liabilities in the balance sheet.

[b] Under each of the following independent situations, indicate your recommendation for the proper balance-sheet classification of the notes payable.

[1] At March 15, 1985, before the 1984 financial statements are issued, the company is actively seeking opportunities to refinance the total $1,500,000 on a long-term basis.

[2] On March 1, 1985, before the 1984 financial statements are issued, a bank formally commits to refinance the $250,000 short-term note due on May

1, 1985. The bank has indicated its plans to consider Emerson's request to refinance the remainder of its short-term debt on a long-term basis as those obligations come due. The final decision will depend on the financial situation of Emerson Corporation at the due dates of the short-term obligations.

[3] On February 1, 1985, before the 1984 financial statements are issued, the company issues 500,000 shares of capital stock at $1.25 per share. The funds are to be used to refinance the short-term debt as it comes due during 1985. The company plans another issue of stock before November 1, 1985.

[4] On February 1, 1985, before the 1984 financial statements are issued, the company enters into a long-term agreement with a local bank to refinance its short-term debt on a long-term basis. The agreement provides for refinancing of up to $2,000,000 and requires the company to maintain a $50,000 cash balance with the bank.

[c] Give the definition of a current liability. Why is it logical, in light of this definition, to exclude certain short-term obligations from current liabilities, even though they may come due very soon after the date of the financial statements?

C14–5 Withering Heights Elevator Manufacturing Company has experienced erratic operating performance during the last seven years. In the last two years, substantial operating losses have caused the company to discontinue its line of dumb waiters. The company has defaulted on several debt covenants, and although creditors have waived covenant violations in the past, they are becoming less enthusiastic about future prospects for Withering Heights. In consideration for the waivers, the company has pledged all of its principal assets, except inventory, as security collateral on the loans. Excerpts from Withering's proposed balance sheet and other information are presented below.

Note 1: All assets except inventory have been pledged as security on short- and long-term notes payable. (See Notes 2 and 3.)

Note 2: These notes payable are due in 90 days (Sept. 30, 1985) or on demand. These have been refinanced (due dates extended) three times during the last two years. Each of the previous restructurings was for six months. However, the latest restructuring (June 30, 1985) provided for a 90-day maturity or on demand. Furthermore, the lender has advised the company to seek other sources of financing.

Note 3: Long-term notes payable are due June 30, 1987. They were due June 30, 1985, but were restructured on that date with the new maturity date.

Note 4: Both the short-term and long-term notes

Withering Heights Elevator Manufacturing Company
BALANCE SHEET
June 30, 1985
(in thousands)

Current assets			Current liabilities		
Cash		$ 1,500	Accounts payable		$ 2,500
Accounts receivable			Notes payable [Note 2]		4,500
(net of allowance for uncollect-			Current liabilities		7,000
ible amounts of $1,500)		5,000			
Merchandise inventory		8,000	Long-term debt		
Other current assets		500	Notes payable [Note 3]		9,000
			Bonds payable		
Total current assets		15,000	(due 1994)		15,000
			Total long-term debt		24,000
			Total liabilities [Note 4]		31,000
Plant assets					
(net of accumulated			Stockholders' equity		
depreciation of $20,000)		24,000	Common stock		15,000
			Retained earnings		(7,000)
			Total stockholders' equity		8,000
Total assets [Note 1]		$39,000	Total liabilities and equity		$39,000

payable contain many covenants. Withering violated several of the covenants during the year ended June 30, 1985. However, all covenant defaults have been waived at June 30, 1985. Withering expects to default on several covenants within the next 60 days. Default on any of the debt instruments represents default on all of the others.

Instructions

[a] Should this company's statements be prepared on a going-concern or liquidation basis of accounting? Discuss the reasons for your answer.
[b] Based on the available information, draft any necessary accounting entries or footnote disclosures.

EXERCISES

E14–1 Plex Company purchased equipment on September 5, 1984, with a list price of $15,000 on terms of 2/10, n/30. The company paid the account in full on September 13, 1984.

Instructions

[a] Prepare the general journal entry to record the purchase and the final payment, assuming accounts payable are recorded at their gross amount.
[b] Prepare the general journal entry to record the purchases and the final payment, assuming accounts payable are recorded at an amount net of cash discounts.

E14–2 Albertson Company borrowed $25,000 from the bank in the form of a noninterest-bearing note on August 15, 1985. The note was discounted at 15% and matures in one year. On November 30, 1985, Albertson borrowed $15,000 with interest payable of 12½% per annum, due in six months.

Instructions

Prepare the journal entries to record the above transactions and any December 31, 1985, year-end adjustments.

E14–3 Reed Manufacturing Company is considering a one-year loan from the Central State Bank. Two alternatives are available: (1) a $17,500, 15% note, issued at face value; and (2) a $17,500, noninterest-bearing note, discounted at 15%. Reed plans to borrow the money on November 2. The end of the company's financial reporting year is December 31.

Instructions

For each note, complete the following requirements:
[a] Prepare the general journal entries for the note issued on November 2 and any required adjustment at December 31.
[b] Prepare the financial-statement presentation at December 31.

E14–4 On May 31, 1983, Smithson Company had the following liabilities:

Account	Amount	Description
Accounts Payable	$10,500	Payable in 10–60 days.
Accrued Expenses	7,250	Payable in 10–30 days.
Notes Payable	17,800	$7,800 note payable on July 7, 1983; $10,000 note payable on Aug. 17, 1983.
Bonds Payable	65,000	Payable on May 31, 1990.

On July 7, before the 1983 financial statements were issued, the $7,800 note payable was replaced by an 18-month note for the same amount. The company is considering similar action on the $10,000 note due on August 17, 1983. The 1983 financial statements were issued on July 19, 1983.

Instructions

Prepare the liability presentation for Smithson Company's May 31, 1983, balance sheet, including any required footnotes.

E14–5 Axelson Company has the following capital stock outstanding at October 31, 1984, the end of the company's fiscal year:
[1] 8% preferred stock, $100 par value, 100,000 shares issued and outstanding.
[2] Common stock, $50 par value, 520,000 shares issued and outstanding.
On October 31, 1984, the board of directors declared the specified preferred dividend and a $2.75 dividend per share on the common stock. These dividends were paid on November 30, 1984.

Instructions

[a] Prepare the general journal entries to record the declaration and payment of these dividends. Use separate liability accounts for the two classes of stock.
[b] Describe the presentation of the dividend liabilities in the October 31, 1984, balance sheets.

E14–6 San Diego Printers is willing to produce printed materials to its customers' specifications for orders of $5,000 or more. At the time an order is placed, a 12% advance is required. The balance is due 30 days after delivery of the printed materials.

On May 13, 1983, San Diego Printers received an order totaling $17,850, including the 12% advance. The company delivered the finished products on June 3, 1983, and received final payment, including 4% sales tax, on June 30, 1983.

Instructions

[a] Prepare the general journal entries to record the above events.
[b] Describe briefly the impact of these events on the current liabilities of San Diego Printers.

E14–7 Total amounts received or receivable from sales by Anderson Manufacturing Company in January 1985 were $120,460, including sales tax. Seventy-five percent of the sales are normally on account.

Instructions

Prepare the journal entry to record these data (in whole dollars) for 1985 if the sales tax rate is 4%.

E14–8 Bird Company records sales at amounts which include any state and local sales taxes. During April 1985, Bird recorded sales of $107,100.
[1] Fifty percent of sales were subject to both 7% state sales tax and a 4% city sales tax.
[2] Forty percent of sales were subject to a 4% city sales tax only.
[3] Ten percent of sales were labor and not subject to any tax.

Instructions

Prepare the entry to record the sales for April 1985.

E14–9 The real estate property taxes paid by Basic Company for 1983–1984 were $25,000. The city's fiscal year is July 1–June 30 and the company accrues property taxes quarterly over the fiscal period of the city. Basic makes property improvements during 1984 and the real estate tax bill increases to $30,000. The company protests the increase and pays half of the $30,000 when it receives the tax bill on October 15, 1984. On March 15, 1985, Basic is notified that the assessment has been reduced to $28,500. The balance due is paid on April 1, 1985. Annual financial statements are prepared on June 30, 1985.

Instructions

Prepare any journal entries necessary to record the real estate taxes for July 1, 1984, to June 30, 1985. The company prepares quarterly financial statements and makes property tax accruals only when interim or annual financial statements are prepared.

E14–10 George Braunegg, CPA, has five employees, each paid $300 weekly. The employer is responsible for remitting 16% of the salaries quarterly for Social Security taxes—8% for each of the employee's and employer's contribution. One percent of the base salary, $8,000, is remitted quarterly for federal unemployment insurance. Two and seven-tenths percent of the base salary is remitted quarterly for state unemployment insurance. Weekly federal income tax withholding per person is $70, and weekly state income tax withholding per person is $10.

Instructions

Prepare the entries to record the payment of a weekly salary and the quarterly remittance to the appropriate agencies. Base quarterly computations on 13 weeks, and assume that your computations are for the first ·quarter of a year.

E14–11 Wisper Company provides an incentive compensation plan under which the company president receives a bonus equal to 10% of the company's income in excess of $100,000 before income taxes are deducted but after the bonus is deducted.

Instructions

If income before tax and bonus is $320,000 and the effective tax rate is 40%, what amount should the bonus be?

E14–12 James Company pays a bonus to its branch managers annually. Branch manager A received $5,660. The bonus agreement provided that each branch manager receives a bonus of 10% of the branch's net income after taxes and bonus. The income tax rate is 40%.

Instructions

Determine the amount of Branch A's income before bonus and income tax.

E14–13 Czyzewski Company has an agreement to pay its sales manager a bonus of 6% of the company's earnings. Company income for the year before the bonus and taxes is $110,000. Income taxes are 40% of income after bonus.

Instructions

Compute the bonus in the following independent situations:
[a] Bonus is computed on income before bonus and income tax deductions.
[b] Bonus is computed on income after deduction for bonus but before deduction for income taxes.
[c] Bonus is computed on income before deduction for bonus but after deduction for income taxes.
[d] Bonus is computed on net income after deductions for both bonus and income taxes.

E14–14 Clancy Corporation grants a one-year warranty with each machine it sells. Expenses during the warranty period average $200. Clancy sells a machine for $10,000 cash on July 1, 1985. Assume the Product Warranty Expense account is debited at the time of sale.

Instructions

Prepare the entries to record the sale and subsequent payment of $105 on October 17, 1985, for service covered by the warranty.

E14–15 In 1983 Dubious Corporation began selling a new line of products that carries a two-year warranty against defects. Based on past experience, the estimated warranty costs related to dollar sales are: first year of warranty, 2%; second year of warranty, 5%. Sales and actual warranty expenditures for 1983 and 1984 are presented below.

	1983	1984
Sales	$500,000	$700,000
Actual warranty expenditures	10,000	30,000

Instructions

Determine the estimated warranty liability at the end of 1983 and 1984.

E14–16 Delta Company includes two coupons in each box of corn flakes. Fifteen coupons are needed to receive a free kitchen utensil. In 1985 Delta Company purchased 6,500 kitchen utensils at $1.10 each and sold 115,000 boxes of corn flakes. In 1985, 47,325 coupons were redeemed. Management estimates 65% of the coupons will be sent in for redemption.

Instructions

Prepare the general journal entries to record the premium plan for 1985.

E14-17 Ready-Made Company was named the defendant in a legal action. The plaintiff is asking for $500,000 in damages. The initial judgment called for $220,000 in favor of the plaintiff. Ready-Made attorneys have appealed the case as of December 31, 1984, and believe there is a good chance for reversal because of errors in law and fact in the original judgment.

Instructions

Describe how, if at all, the financial claim resulting from this suit should be recorded on the books and disclosed in the financial statements at the end of 1984.

E14-18 Tackle Company sells football helmets. In 1984 Tackle discovered a defect in the helmets which has led to lawsuits that are reasonably estimated to result in losses of $900,000. Based on its own experience and that of similar enterprises, Tackle believes that additional lawsuits reasonably estimated to result in losses of $1,600,000 will probably occur, even though the parties that will bring suit are not identifiable at this time.

Instructions

Determine the amount of expense, if any, that should be charged to income in 1984 as a result of this situation.

E14-19 The following items represent common liabilities recorded on the books of an ordinary business corporation.
[1] Dividends
[2] Purchase commitments
[3] Purchase of goods on credit
[4] Officers' salaries
[5] Special bonus to employees

Instructions

[a] When should each item be recorded as a liability?
[b] Prepare *pro forma* entries (accounts only) to record these items as liabilities.

E14-20 Blaine Corporation purchased a new home office building on August 1, 1985. To pay for the building, the company secured a $430,000, 12% mortgage. The mortgage is to be repaid over 25 years with monthly payments of $4,528.90, payable on the first of each month. Each payment includes interest for the previous month.

Instructions

Determine how this mortgage should be shown in Blaine's December 31, 1985, balance sheet, assuming the first payment is made on September 1, 1985.

PROBLEMS

P14-1 The following information about Dado Company is available at December 31, 1985:
[1] Employee income taxes withheld, $900.
[2] Cash balance at First Federal Bank, $2,500.
[3] Cash overdraft at Farmers Bank, $1,350.
[4] Accounts receivable with credit balance, $2,850.
[5] Estimated expenses of meeting warranties on merchandise previously sold, $3,200.
[6] Estimated damages as a result of unsatisfactory performance on a contract, $1,250.
[7] Accounts payable, $29,750.
[8] Dividends in arrears on preferred stock, $25,000.
[9] Serial bonds of $500,000, payable in semiannual installments of $50,000, due April 1 and October 1 of each year; the last bond to be paid on October 1, 1992.
[10] Par value of capital stock to be distributed as a result of a stock dividend, $40,000.

Instructions

[a] Prepare the current liability section of the balance sheet for Dado Company on December 31, 1985.
[b] Briefly explain those items that you have *not* included among the current liabilities, citing reasons for their exclusion.

P14-2 The following information is available for Sunshine Company for 1985:

Sales on Account. The total for the year is $201,400 (including sales tax of 6%). Accounts receivable totaling $35,800 remain uncollected at the end of the year. Seventy percent of the sales tax has been remitted by the end of 1985.

Cash Dividend. The sum of $15,000 is declared on December 1, 1985, to be paid in January 1986. Sunshine's accounting period ends on December 31.

Machinery Purchased. A noninterest-bearing, $34,200 note was issued on December 31, 1985, payable in one year to acquire machinery. (An appropriate interest rate for the note is 14%.)

Note Payable. A $7,500, one-year note was discounted at the bank at 10% on November 2, 1985, to provide cash for current operations.

Instructions

[a] Prepare all general journal entries required to record the information presented above.
[b] Prepare the current liability section of the 1985 balance sheet for the Sunshine Company, assuming that additional current liabilities are as follows:

Accounts payable	$15,200
Wages payable	10,600
Payroll taxes payable	2,150

P14–3 Joiner Company, a calendar-year company, was involved in several transactions during 1985 that potentially involved current liabilities. These are described below.
[1] Two purchases of merchandise were made in the last half of December. The first, for $15,500, was made on December 15, subject to terms 2/10, n/30. It has not been paid at year-end. The second, for $18,800, was made on December 28, subject to terms 1/10, n/20. It has not been paid by year-end, but management intends to pay the invoice within the discount period. The company maintains a periodic inventory system and records purchases at the net amount.
[2] On October 16 the company borrowed $10,000 from Second State Bank by issuing a $10,000, 14% note, due one year from the date of issuance.
[3] Accrued wages for the last three days of December totaled $12,500 before the following withholdings:

Income tax	$1,560
FICA tax	875

The company must match the amount withheld from employees for FICA tax.
[4] Dividends declared on December 31, 1985, payable on January 31, 1986, were $1 per share. The company has 54,250 shares of stock outstanding.
[5] On November 8, 1985, a customer signed an agreement for Joiner to produce certain specialty items to the customer's specifications. The items are currently under construction and are expected to be delivered in January 1986. The total amount of the order is $17,500. The customer paid Joiner a 15% advance on November 8, when the agreement was reached.

Instructions

[a] Prepare the general journal entries to record the transactions described in items 1–5 above through the end of 1985. Include any adjustments that would be necessary at December 31, 1985.
[b] Indicate the impact of each item on the current liability section of the December 31, 1985, balance sheet of Joiner Company.

P14–4 Penn, Inc., a publishing company, is preparing its December 31, 1984, financial statements and must determine the proper accounting treatment for each of the following situations:
[1] Penn sells subscriptions to several magazines for a one-year, two-year, or three-year period. Cash receipts from subscribers are credited to Magazine Subscriptions Collected in Advance. This account had a balance of $2,400,000 at December 31, 1984. Outstanding subscriptions at December 31, 1984, expire as follows:

During 1985	$600,000
During 1986	900,000
During 1987	400,000

[2] On January 2, 1984, Penn discontinued collision, fire, and theft coverage on its delivery vehicles and became self-insured for these risks. Actual losses of $45,000 during 1984 were charged to delivery expense. The 1983 premium for the discontinued coverage amounted to $100,000. The controller wants to set up a reserve for self-insurance by a debit to delivery expense of $55,000 and a credit to the reserve for self-insurance of $55,000.
[3] A suit for breach of contract seeking damages of $1,000,000 was filed by an author against Penn on July 1, 1984. The company's legal counsel believes that an unfavorable outcome is probable. A reasonable estimate of the court's award to the plaintiff is between $100,000 and $500,000. No amount within this range is a better estimate of potential damages than any other amount.
[4] During December 1984, a competitor filed suit against Penn for industrial espionage, claiming $2,000,000 in damages. Management and company counsel believe it is reasonably possible that damages will be awarded to the plaintiff, although the amount cannot be reasonably estimated.

Instructions

Prepare the journal entries for 1–4 at December 31, 1984. If you think that no entry is required, explain your reasoning. Show supporting computations in good form.

(AICPA adapted)

P14-5 Lax Corporation, a manufacturer of small tools, provided the following information from its accounting records for the year ended December 31, 1984:

Inventory (based on physical count of goods in Lax's plant at cost on Dec. 31)	$1,750,000
Accounts payable	1,200,000
Net sales (sales less sales returns)	8,500,000

Additional Information

[1] Included in the physical count were tools billed to a customer FOB shipping point on December 31, 1984. These tools had a cost of $28,000 and were billed at $35,000. The shipment was on Lax's loading dock waiting to be picked up.

[2] Goods were in transit from a vendor to Lax on December 31, 1984. The invoice cost was $50,000, and the goods were shipped FOB shipping point on December 29, 1984.

[3] Work-in-process inventory costing $20,000 was sent to an outside processor for plating on December 30, 1984.

[4] Tools returned by customers and held pending inspection in the returned goods area on December 31, 1984, were not included in the physical count. On January 8, 1985, the tools, costing $26,000, were inspected and returned to inventory. Credit memos totaling $40,000 were issued to the customers on the same date.

[5] Tools shipped to a customer FOB destination on December 26, 1984, were in transit at December 31, 1984, and had a cost of $25,000. Upon notification of receipt by the customer on January 2, 1985, Lax issued a sales invoice for $42,000.

[6] Goods, with an invoice cost of $30,000, received from a vendor at 5:00 p.m. on December 31, 1984, were recorded on a receiving report dated January 2, 1985. The goods were not included in the physical count, but the invoice was included in accounts payable at December 31, 1984.

[7] Goods received from a vendor on December 26, 1984, were included in the physical count. However, the related $60,000 vendor invoice was not included in accounts payable at December 31, 1984, because the accounts payable copy of the receiving report was lost.

[8] On January 3, 1985, a monthly freight bill of $4,000 was received. The bill related to merchandise purchased in December 1984, half of which was still in the inventory at December 31, 1984. The freight charges were not included in either inventory or accounts payable at December 31, 1984.

Instructions

Prepare an analysis of the effects of each of the eight situations on inventory, accounts payable, and net sales. Show the amount, if any, by which each would increase or decrease as a result of your adjustment. Briefly explain your conclusion in each situation.

(AICPA adapted)

P14-6 Lewis Company, a manufacturer of heavy machinery, grants a four-year warranty on its products. The Estimated Liability for Product Warranty account shows the following transactions for the year:

Opening balance	$45,000
Provision (made at interim dates)	20,000
	65,000
Cost of servicing claims	12,000
Ending balance (before adjustment)	$53,000

A review of unsettled claims and the company's experience indicates that claims have averaged 2% of net sales per year.

The following additional information is available from the company's records at the end of the current year:

Gross sales	$2,040,000
Sales returns and allowances	40,000
Cost of goods sold	1,350,000

Instructions

[a] Prepare any necessary adjusting journal entries, giving effect to the proper accounting treatment of product warranties. Support any entries with clearly detailed computations. The books have not been closed.

[b] Identify the amount of the expense to be included in the determination of net income and the amount of the liability to be presented in the balance sheet for warranties.

P14-7 Allied Tube Company manufactures television tubes and sells them with a six-month guarantee under which defective tubes are replaced free of charge. On June 30, 1985, the Liability for Product

Warranty account had a balance of $450,000. By December 31, 1985, this amount had been reduced to $45,400 by charges for tubes returned.

Allied has operated for many years and has consistently experienced an 8% return rate. Due to the introduction of new models, the rate increased to 10% on October 1, 1985. It is assumed that no tubes sold during a given month are returned in that month. Each tube is stamped with a date at the time of sale so that the warranty indicates the likely pattern of returns during the six-month period of the warranty, starting with the month following the sale.

Month Following Sale	Percent of Total Returns Expected During That Month
First	20
Second	30
Third	20
Fourth	10
Fifth	10
Sixth	10
Total	100

For example, for January sales, 20% of the returns are expected in February, 30% in March, and so on.

Gross sales of tubes for the second half of 1985 were:

Month	Amount
July	$3,600,000
August	3,300,000
September	4,100,000
October	2,850,000
November	2,000,000
December	1,800,000

The company's warranty also covers the payment of freight cost on defective tubes returned and on new tubes sent as replacements. This freight cost is 10% of the sales price of the tubes returned. The manufacturing cost of the tube is roughly 75% of the sales price, and the salvage value of the returned tubes averages 25% of their sales price.

Instructions

[a] Compute the Product Warranty Liability account balance as of December 31, 1985.
[b] Prepare any adjusting entries necessary.

P14–8 This problem consists of two *independent* parts.

Part 1. The Happy Food Company distributed coupons to consumers which can be presented to grocers for discounts on some of its products. The grocers are reimbursed when they send the coupons to Happy. In Happy's experience, 40% of such coupons are redeemed, and generally, one month elapses between the date a grocer receives a coupon from a consumer and the date Happy receives it. During 1985 Happy issued two separate series of coupons as follows:

Date Issued	Total Value	Amount Disbursed on Redemption as of December 31, 1985
Jan. 1, 1985	$78,000	$22,700
July 1, 1985	93,000	29,900

Instructions

Determine the amount that should appear in the December 31, 1985, balance sheet as a liability for unredeemed coupons. Show all computations.

Part 2. Goldstein Cereals distributes coupons to consumers which can be presented to grocers for discounts on certain cereals, on or before a stated expiration date. The grocers are reimbursed when they send the coupons to Goldstein. In the company's experience, 30% of such coupons are redeemed, and on the average, one month elapses between the date a grocer receives a coupon from the buyer and the date Goldstein receives it. On May 1, 1985, Goldstein issued coupons with a total value of $15,000 and an expiration date of December 31, 1985. As of December 31, 1985, Goldstein has disbursed $3,000 to grocers for these coupons.

Instructions

[a] Prepare the general journal entries to record the above transactions.
[b] Briefly explain the error(s) that would exist in the financial statements if Goldstein recognized the coupon expense only at the time they disbursed cash to grocers.

P14–9 Wheaton Company manufactures a packaged pancake mix. A free spatula is offered to customers who send in three proofs of purchase. The following data have been accumulated:

	1983	1984
Pancake mix sales ($1.25 per box)	$600,000	$500,000
Number of spatula purchases ($.85 per spatula)	17,000	15,000

| Number of spatulas distributed as premiums | 16,500 | 12,750 |
| Spatulas estimated to be distributed in subsequent periods | 4,000 | 2,500 |

Mailing costs are $.30 per spatula.

Instructions

[a] Give the account balances that would appear in the income statements and balance sheet for 1983 and 1984.

[b] Prepare the general journal entries necessary to record sales, premium purchases, redemptions, and year-end adjustments.

P14–10 The Chicago Transit Authority sells tokens good for one bus ride at $.50 each. Sales for 1985 are as follows:

Month	Tokens Sold
January	19,500
February	20,000
March	21,000
April	23,000
May	22,000
June	26,000
July	18,000
August	20,500
September	30,000
October	28,000
November	25,000
December	23,500

Past experience has shown that 70% of the tokens are used in the month of sale, 15% in the following month, and 10% in the next. Five percent of tokens are unused and void after six months.

Instructions

[a] Prepare the entries for 1985, assuming a liability account is credited when the tokens are sold.

[b] Prepare the entries for 1985, assuming a revenue account is credited when the tokens are sold.

P14–11 Kemp, Inc., has been producing quality children's apparel for over 25 years. The company's fiscal year is from April 1 to March 31. The following information relates to the obligations of Kemp as of March 31, 1985:

Bonds Payable. Kemp issued $4,000,000 of 7% bonds on July 1, 1979, at 98, which yielded proceeds of $3,920,000. The bonds will mature on July 1, 1989.

Interest is paid semiannually on July 1 and January 1. Kemp uses the straight-line method to amortize the bond discount.

Notes Payable. Kemp has signed several long-term notes with financial institutions and insurance companies. The maturities of these notes are given in the schedule below. The total unpaid interest for all of these notes amounts to $90,000 on March 31, 1985.

Due Date	Amount Due
Apr. 1, 1985	$ 100,000
July 1, 1985	200,000
Oct. 1, 1985	100,000
Jan. 1, 1986	200,000
Apr. 1, 1986–Mar. 31, 1987	600,000
Apr. 1, 1987–Mar. 31, 1988	400,000
Apr. 1, 1988–Mar. 31, 1989	400,000
Apr. 1, 1989–Mar. 31, 1990	500,000
Apr. 1, 1990–Mar. 31, 1991	500,000
	$3,000,000

Estimated Warranties. Kemp has a one-year product warranty on selected items. The estimated warranty liability on sales made during the 1983–1984 fiscal year and still outstanding as of March 31, 1984, amounted to $55,000. The warranty costs on sales made from April 1, 1984, through March 31, 1985, are estimated at $145,000. The actual warranty costs incurred during the current 1984–1985 fiscal year are as follows:

Warranty claims honored on 1983–1984 sales	$ 55,000
Warranty claims honored on 1984–1985 sales	75,000
	$130,000

Additional Information

[1] **Trade payables.** Accounts payable for supplies, goods, and services purchased on open account amount to $325,000 as of March 31, 1985.

[2] **Payroll related items.** Outstanding obligations related to Kemp's payroll as of March 31, 1985, are:

Accrued salaries and wages	$145,000
FICA taxes	15,000
State and federal income taxes withheld from employees	30,000
Other payroll deductions	3,000

[3] **Taxes.** The following taxes incurred but not due until the next fiscal year are:

State and federal income taxes	$300,000
Property taxes	125,000
Sales and use taxes	185,000

[4] **Miscellaneous accruals.** Other accruals not separately classified amount to $50,000 as of March 31, 1985.

[5] **Dividends.** On March 15, 1985, Kemp's board of directors declared a cash dividend of $.40 per common share and a 10% common stock dividend. Both dividends were to be distributed on April 12, 1985, to the common stockholders of record at the close of business on March 31, 1985. Data regarding Kemp's common stock are as follows:

Par value	$5 per share
Number of shares issued and outstanding	2,500,000 shares
Market value of common stock	
Mar. 15, 1985	$22.00 per share
Mar. 31, 1985	$21.50 per share
Apr. 12, 1985	$22.50 per share

Instructions

[a] Prepare the current liability section of the balance sheet for Kemp, Inc., as of March 31, 1985, as it should appear in the annual report to stockholders.

[b] If you have excluded any items from the presentation of current liabilities, explain why you have done so.

(CMA adapted)

P14–12 Black Derby, Inc., is planning to refinance certain short-term obligations on a long-term basis. The company has a December 31 year-end; 1984 financial statements will be published on March 15, 1985. At December 31, 1984, before the reclassification of short-term debt, the liabilities and stockholders' equity sections of the company's balance sheet appear as follows:

Liabilities and Stockholders' Equity

	1984	1983
Current liabilities		
Accounts payable	$ 7,000,000	$ 5,000,000
Notes payable to banks	12,000,000	4,000,000
Accrued liabilities	4,000,000	4,500,000
Total current liabilities	23,000,000	13,500,000
Long-term debt	4,000,000	3,000,000
Total liabilities	27,000,000	16,500,000

	1984	1983
Stockholders' equity		
Common stock ($1 par value; authorized 4,000,000 shares; issued 2,000,000 shares in 1984 and 1983)	2,000,000	2,000,000
Additional paid-in capital	1,000,000	1,000,000
Retained earnings	6,000,000	5,000,000
Total stockholders' equity	9,000,000	8,000,000
Total liabilities and stockholders' equity	$36,000,000	$24,500,000

The company intends to refinance $9,000,000 of the $12,000,000 notes payable on a long-term basis. Although the entire $12,000,000 is due on June 30, 1985, the bank has informally agreed to extend the maturity date for up to $6,000,000 of this amount to June 30, 1986, if necessary. On January 31, 1985, the company issues 1,000,000 additional shares of the $1 par value common stock for $4,000,000 ($4 per share). After issue costs and underwriting fees, the company's net proceeds from the stock issuance were $3,500,000. On February 15, 1985, the company entered a financing agreement with a financially capable commercial bank, permitting the company to borrow up to $3,000,000 at the bank's prime interest rate. Borrowings, available at the company's options after April 1, 1985, will mature five years after the loan date. The lender can cancel the agreement only if the company's retained earnings drop below $750,000. The company must also maintain compensating balances equal to 10% of the amount borrowed.

Black Derby, Inc., uses the entire proceeds of the sale of the common stock to retire part of the current notes payable and now intends to draw down the entire available commitment of five-year debt on April 1, 1985. The company plans to refinance the rest of the notes before June 30, 1985, and is currently negotiating with various lenders.

Instructions

[a] Prepare the liabilities and stockholders' equity sections of Black Derby's comparative balance sheet as of December 31, 1984 and 1983, after any necessary reclassifications based on the above information. The statements are issued on March 15, 1985.

[b] Describe any financial statement disclosures that would be desirable based on the above information.

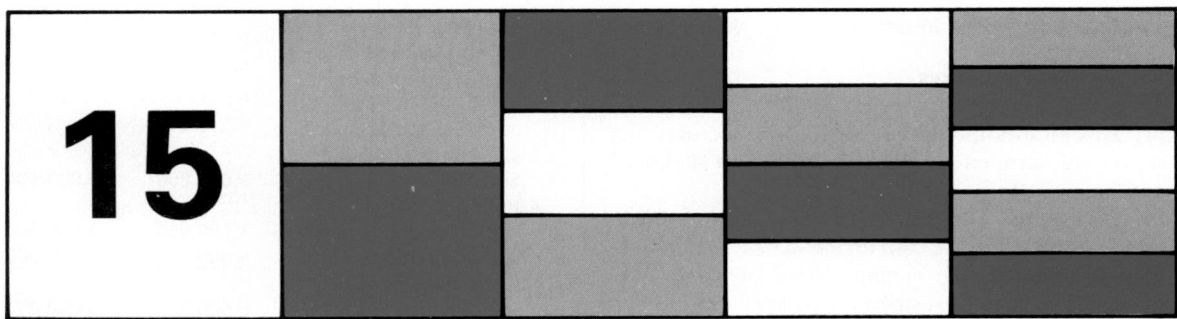

LONG-TERM DEBT

Objectives

To establish the characteristics that distinguish long-term debt from current liabilities.

To describe the nature of bonds and notes payable and distinguish among various types of debt instruments.

To apply acceptable financial accounting and reporting practices to the issuance and reacquisition or retirement of debt.

To discuss why premium and discount frequently arise on long-term debt.

To account for premium and discount on long-term debt, including amortization and balance sheet presentation.

To apply acceptable financial accounting and reporting practices to convertible debt and debt with detachable stock-purchase rights.

M ost companies rely, at least to some extent, on long-term debt as a method of financing operations. Of course, equity investments contributed by owners are also important sources of long-term financing. The decision to support long-term operational needs, such as the acquisition of property, plant, and equipment, by issuing debt rather than raising funds through equity financing is a complex one and receives substantial attention in finance courses. Generally, companies attempt to secure resources at the lowest possible cost. Thus many combinations of debt and equity financing are commonly encountered in practice.

This book, however, focuses primarily on financial accounting and reporting for several types of long-term debt rather than on the decision to incur debt. The following section considers, among other things, the characteristics that distinguish current liabilities from long-term debt and those that separate debt from equity financing.

As we begin our study of long-term debt, turn to the balance sheet of Kroger Company inside the front cover of your text. Notice the large amounts of long-term debt—short-term borrowings to be refinanced, senior debt, and convertible subordinated debt—that are included among the noncurrent liabilities. The details of the individual debt issues making up these total amounts are presented in the notes to the financial statements included in the appendix at the end of this book. Also, briefly review the statement of earnings inside the back cover of your text and notice the relatively large amount of interest expense included in the determination of net income. These items are the end result of the accounting process for long-term debt that is described in detail in Chapter 15.

THE NATURE AND CHARACTERISTICS OF DEBT

Debt/Equity Distinctions

Although the distinction between debt and equity financing is sometimes hazy, certain distinguishing characteristics are evident. Generally, **debt instruments** contain a maturity date that establishes the time at which the face value of the debt must be repaid to the lender. Furthermore, long-term debt usually bears interest that must be paid periodically, regardless of the profitability of the borrowing company.

Equity securities, conversely, usually do not have maturity dates and therefore do not require redemption by the issuing company. Also, dividends are not paid on equity securities except at the discretion of the issuing company's board of directors.

During the last 20 years several "hybrid" securities have been introduced. Corporations have turned to creative financing in order to secure long-term resources at the lowest possible cost. Many of these hybrid securities have characteristics of both debt and equity; examples include convertible bonds that are exchangeable for stock at the option of the bondholder, income bonds requiring the payment of interest only if income is earned, and redeemable stock that may require reacquisition at the discretion of the investor.

Substance over Form

As is the case in other areas of accounting, the determination of whether a given financing instrument represents debt or equity should be based on substance rather than form. In practice most companies account for a security as debt if it (1) requires the periodic payment of interest, (2) contains a fixed maturity date, or (3) allows redemption at the discretion of the investor (lender). Conversely, a security containing none of these characteristics is generally classified as some type of corporate stockholders' equity. Once we have classified a particular security as some type of debt, we must then further classify the item as either current or long-term.

Current and Long-Term Debt

Although Chapter 14 discussed the characteristics that distinguish between **current liabilities** and **long-term debt,** a brief review is useful. The accounting profession has carefully defined the characteristics of current liabilities while all other debt is classified as long-term.

Generally, if the satisfaction of a liability is expected to require presently existing working capital, then a current classification is appropriate. Liabilities not expected to require presently existing working capital are classified as long-term. Thus, even if a liability matures in the near future, we may consider it noncurrent if resources other than current assets are to be used to extinguish the debt. For example, a company may have established a sinking fund to retire a bond issue. You will recall that special funds, such as bond-redemption sinking funds, are classified as noncurrent investments. The bonds that will be redeemed with the assets in the sinking fund are classified in a manner consistent with the sinking fund. Therefore, bonds to be retired with assets in a sinking fund classified as noncurrent are classified as noncurrent liabilities, even if the bonds mature in the very near future. Some noncancelable financing agreements may also cause accountants to classify a liability with a current maturity date as a long-term debt.

Certain types of long-term liabilities are not discussed in this chapter but are considered elsewhere in this book. Specifically, accounting and reporting for lease and pension liabilities are discussed in Chapters 21 and 22, respectively. Contingent liabilities, some of which may be noncurrent, are discussed in Chapter 14. Chapter 15 discusses a variety of long-term bonds and notes payable. Since the accounting and reporting problems associated with bonds and notes are similar, the discussion centers primarily on bonds. You should remember, however, that the underlying ideas apply to both notes and bonds payable.

The Nature of Bonds

Bonds represent contracts of debt whereby one party, an **issuer,** borrows funds from an **investor** or lender. In most cases many bonds, each evidenced by a certificate, are issued and the contractual agreement between the issuer and investors is contained in another document called a **bond indenture.** Companies generally issue bonds to borrow significant amounts while providing a large number of relatively small debt instruments. For example, a company may borrow $10,000,000 by issuing 10,000 separate $1,000 bonds covered by a single bond indenture. In this manner the issuing company obtains a large amount of needed capital while allowing many different investors to provide the funds. This system also allows investors (1) to make smaller investments in a variety of companies, thereby avoiding some risk by diversifying their investments, and (2) to buy or sell additional bonds in the capital market while retaining some or all of their original holdings.

The bond indenture usually requires the appointment of an independent fiscal agent, called a **trustee,** to protect the interests of both the issuer and the investors. Bond indentures also specify other terms, such as the maturity date, bond amounts (e.g., $1,000 and $10,000 denominations), any conversion or call features, sinking-fund requirements, other repayment terms, and any other special provisions or restrictions.

Types of Bonds

Since the goal of an issuing company is to acquire long-term funds at the lowest cost and since investment policies differ from time to time and from company to company, a variety of provisions are found in various bond issues. The following paragraphs discuss some of the most common distinguishing characteristics and types of bonds.

Bonds may be **serial bonds** or **term bonds.** All of the term bonds in a single issue mature on the same date, whereas serial bonds mature at various scheduled times in the future. Serial bonds allow the issuing company to retire an entire bond issue in installments. Term bonds, however, normally require the issuing company to establish a sinking or bond-redemption fund to provide adequate money to retire the entire bond issue at one time. We discuss term bonds throughout this chapter and serial bonds in Appendix B.

Bonds may be **registered bonds** or **coupon bonds.** Interest and principal payments on registered bonds are paid only to the owner of the bonds as recorded in the trustee's records. Interest on coupon bonds, also called **bearer bonds,** is paid to the person submitting a detachable interest coupon. In the case of coupon bonds, the company does not maintain a record of who owns the individual bonds at any point in time.

Senior bonds are those with higher claims on a company's assets; **subordinated bonds** or **second-mortgage bonds** are those whose claim on assets is secondary. **Callable bonds** may be retired (reacquired) prior to maturity if the issuing company opts to pay a call premium to bondholders in addition to accrued interest and the face amount of the bond. **Convertible bonds,** on the other hand, may be exchanged for equity securities of the issuing company at the option of the investor.

State and local governments as well as other nonprofit organizations also frequently issue many types of bonds. For example, **revenue bonds** are those whose interest and principal are payable from resources generated by a particular government operation, such as an airport or a public utility. **General obligation bonds,** conversely, are secured by the full faith and credit of the issuing unit of government.

Corporations issue many types of bonds and other debt instruments and, consequently, the long-term debt section of the balance sheet is frequently complex. Exhibit 15–1 presents a footnote taken from a recent annual report of Oneida Ltd., a diversified company that produces tableware, cookware, industrial wire and cable, and emblematic jewelry. The total long-term debt figures of $38,833,940 and $40,543,593 for 1982 and 1981, respectively, correspond to the long-term debt amounts in the company's balance sheet. The Financial Accounting Standards Board (FASB), in its *Statement of Financial Accounting Standards No. 47,* requires certain disclosures concerning long-term debt in the company's financial statements.[1] This includes the amount of debt maturing in each of the next five years, as presented in the Oneida Ltd. example in Exhibit 15–1.

| **Disclosure** |

ACCOUNTING FOR BONDS PAYABLE

A substantial period of time is required to plan and execute most bond issues, and many of the terms in a bond indenture are established well in advance of the sale of the bonds. Between the time that bond terms are established and the point of sale, many economic and market conditions—as well as the financial status of the issuing company—may change substantially. Such changes in conditions normally affect the desirability of the bonds as investments and cause the market value of the bonds to change.

Investors view the decision to buy a bond as an investment that requires the application of present-value techniques. Basically, a bond may be viewed as a set of future cash flows consisting of (1) the series of interest payments representing an annuity, and (2) a single payment of principal at the maturity date. The cash to be received as interest is determined by multiplying the rate of interest stated on the bond times the face or maturity value of the bonds. Once the aggregate amount of both future cash flows has been determined, an investor then calculates the present value of those flows. The investor selects a discount rate that provides a satisfactory return on an investment with the risk characteristics of the company issuing the bonds. The resulting number, which represents the present value of the two types of cash flows provided by the bond, is the price that the investor is willing to pay to acquire the bond.

If the discount rate employed by the investor differs from the rate of interest stated on the bond, then the present value of the bond determined by the investors' discount rate will differ from the face amount of the bond. Of course, in a normal bond issue, the final price to be received for the bonds is set by the market for all bonds rather than merely a single buyer's appropriate discount rate. The market price for all bonds, however, is based on a consideration of alternative investment opportunities as well as the specific characteristics

---

[1] *FASB Statement of Financial Accounting Standards No. 47,* "Disclosure of Long-Term Obligations," 1981.

EXHIBIT 15-1
Oneida Ltd.
Long-Term Debt Disclosure

8. LONG-TERM DEBT

Long-term debt at January 30, 1982 and January 31, 1981 consisted of the following:

	1982	1981
5¼% senior notes due July 15, 1982	$ 413,000	$ 830,000
6¼% senior notes due January 15, 1983	337,000	670,000
9⅛% senior notes due January 31, 1989, payable $500,000 annually	4,000,000	4,000,000
10% senior notes due July 31, 1991, payable $1,150,000 annually	11,700,000	12,850,000
8¾% subordinated promissory notes due August 1, 1985, payable $2,246,191 annually	8,984,766	11,230,957
Notes payable, prime plus ⅜%, due May 1, 1984, payable $1,250,000 annually	3,750,000	5,000,000
Note payable at the lesser of prime less ½% or average Federal Funds Rate plus 1% due May 15, 1985	5,000,000	6,000,000
Note payable, Eurodollar prime plus ⅝%, due November 24, 1984	4,000,000	
Note payable, prime plus 1% due December 15, 1982	4,117,244	4,096,631
Industrial Revenue Bond, 65% of prime due September 31, 1987, payable $50,000 quarterly	1,000,000	
Other debt at various rates due through 1992	1,717,775	1,431,166
Total	45,019,785	46,108,754
Less amounts due currently	6,185,845	5,565,161
Long-term debt	$38,833,940	$40,543,593

SOURCE: Oneida Ltd., 1982 Annual Report.

The note agreements restrict borrowings, certain business investments, acquisition of the Company's stock and payment of cash dividends. Under these provisions consolidated retained earnings of approximately $40,259,000 were available for the purposes described at January 30, 1982.

On December 21, 1979 the Company called its 5½% Convertible Subordinated Debentures for redemption on January 22, 1980 at 103.57% of their principal amount. The debentures were convertible into common stock of the Company at $18.72 per share, the rate in effect at the time of the call.

The aggregate amounts of long-term maturities due each year to January 1987 and subsequent thereto are as follows:

1983	$ 6,185,845
1984	9,882,493
1985	9,736,115
1986	9,310,567
1987	1,950,103
After	7,954,662
	$45,019,785

Cost of issuing debt is amortized to expense over the term of the related indebtedness.

---

of the issuing company. If the issuer of the bonds receives cash in an amount less than the face amount of the bonds, the bonds are said to be issued at a **discount.** If the issuer receives more than the face amount of the bonds, the bonds are issued at a **premium.** The difference between the selling price and the face amount of the bonds is the premium or discount.

To illustrate a discount, assume the Leverage Corporation decides to issue bonds with terms as described in Exhibit 15–2. If subsequent to printing the bond indenture but prior to issuance, Leverage suffers a serious decline in the demand for its products or if the market interest rate for similar investments rises, then the market value of Leverage bonds will fall as they become a less desirable investment.

We see from the information in Exhibit 15–2 that interest will be paid five times in the amount of $900 each time. If we know what rate of interest is determined by the investors to represent an adequate return for the Leverage bonds, we can then determine the issuance

EXHIBIT 15–2 **Leverage Corporation** **Bond Terms**	
Face amount ($1,000 each)	$10,000
Stated interest rate	9%
Interest payment date	January 1
Date of bonds	January 1, 1985
Date of maturity	December 31, 1989
Issue costs	$500

price. The following present-value formula illustrates how to calculate the issuance price of the bonds in order to yield a 12% rate of interest. Figures are rounded to the nearest dollar.

Present value (PV) of the bonds = (PV of interest payments) + (PV of maturity amount)

= (PV of 5 payments of $900 at an annual rate of 12%) + (1 payment of $10,000 at the end of 5 years at an annual rate of 12%)

= (3.60478 × $900) + (.56743 × $10,000)

= $3,244 + $5,674

= $8,918

In this case the buyers of Leverage bonds are willing to pay $8,918 for the bond issue. At that price the bonds yield 12%, the investor's desired rate, rather than the 9% rate of interest stated on the face of the bonds. The buyers of the bonds for $8,918 will receive repayment of $10,000 on the maturity date in addition to $900 interest per year for the years 1985–1989.

If we assume the interest payment is to be paid semiannually, the conversion is not difficult. In this case the annual rate (12%) must be expressed as a semiannual rate (6%), and the five annual compounding periods are changed to ten semiannual compounding periods. The interest annuity is one-half year's interest, $450, rather than $900. The present value of the bonds (rounded to the nearest dollar) can now be determined by the same technique we illustrated:

PV of bonds = (7.36009 × $450) + (.55839 × $10,000)

= $3,312 + $5,584

= $8,896

In this case interest is assumed to compound more frequently, resulting in a slightly greater amount of interest than in the annual-interest case and, therefore, a slightly smaller present value ($8,896 compared to $8,918).

In this illustration we calculated the price of a bond for which the stated interest rate is less than the rate of return required by investors (market rate), resulting in sales of the bond below its face amount (at a discount). If the stated interest rate had been greater than the rate of interest required by investors (market rate), the bond would sell at a premium rather than a discount. We illustrate this situation later in the chapter.

Once the price at which a particular bond issue will sell has been established, that price is typically stated as a percentage of the par or face value of the bonds, such as 98 or 103. For example, if a $10,000,000 face value bond issue sells for 98, the issuer of the bonds receives $9,800,000 ($10,000,000 × 98%), and the bonds have been sold at a discount of $200,000.

If the \$10,000,000 bonds sell for 103, the issuer of the bonds receives \$10,300,000 (\$10,000,000 × 103%), and the bonds have been sold at a premium of \$300,000.

Issuance of Bonds

Issue Costs

The costs that are usually incurred in preparing and marketing a bond issue include legal and accounting fees, broker commissions, printing and engraving costs, registration fees, and promotional costs. Such issue costs are recorded as deferred charges, reported in the assets section of the balance sheet, and amortized over the life of the related debt. Issue costs are *not* treated as reductions in premium, additions to discount, or direct adjustments to the carrying amount of the bonds. Issue costs are recorded as separate assets, because they are not related to the market rate of interest implicit in the bond issue. As discussed both here and in Chapter 10, a premium or discount results from a difference between the rate of interest stated on the bonds and the effective rate of interest that exists when the bonds are sold. We will also discuss the conceptual and practical accounting issues related to premium and discount more extensively later in this chapter. Accountants usually amortize issue costs by the straight-line method, although other methods are satisfactory and are occasionally encountered in practice.

A Simplified Example

The terms of bond issues generally provide (1) a long period to maturity, (2) an interest rate to be paid, and (3) other terms of payment. The amount of consideration received when the bonds are issued provides the basis for accounting entries. To illustrate accounting for bonds payable, we continue the example of the Leverage Corporation. Assume, however, that interest is payable semiannually on January 1 and July 1.

If Leverage sells the bonds on January 1, 1985, at their face amount, the following entries are necessary during 1985 and at the beginning of 1986.

Jan. 1, 1985	Cash	10,000	
	Bonds Payable		10,000
	(To record sale of bonds at face amount.)		
Jan. 1, 1985	Deferred Bond-Issue Costs	500	
	Cash		500
	(To record issue costs.)		
July 1, 1985	Interest Expense	450	
	Cash		450
	(To record semiannual payment of interest. \$10,000 × .09 × ½ = \$450.)		
Dec. 31, 1985	Interest Expense	450	
	Interest Payable		450
	(To accrue interest for second half of 1984, payable on January 1, 1985.)		
Dec. 31, 1985	Issue Cost Expense	100	
	Deferred Bond-Issue Costs		100
	(To amortize issue costs. \$500 ÷ 5 = \$100.)		
Jan. 1, 1986	Interest Payable	450	
	Cash		450
	(To pay interest accrued on December 31, 1985.)		

In this case the process of recognizing interest expense and the amortization of issue costs continues each year until maturity when the retirement of the bonds is accounted for by the following entry:

Dec. 31, 1989	Bonds Payable	10,000	
	Cash		10,000
	(To account for retirement of bonds.)		

Complicating Factors in Accounting for Bonds

The previous example reflects accounting under simplified conditions. The following section illustrates several more realistic circumstances that complicate financial accounting and reporting for bonds payable. Many of these problems have counterparts discussed in Chapter 10 with respect to investments in the bonds of another corporation. A brief review is provided, however, because there are some differences between accounting for investing in bonds and accounting for issuing bonds. Also certain aspects of accounting for bonds relate exclusively to the liability of issuing companies.

Issuance Between Interest-Payment Dates

Bonds are frequently issued at a point after the date printed on the bonds and between interest-payment dates. If this situation occurs, certain accounting problems arise. For example, assume that the Leverage Corporation issues the bonds described in Exhibit 15–2 on May 1, 1985, at "100" (100% of face amount) plus accrued interest. We continue our assumption that interest is paid semiannually on January 1 and July 1. The following entry and supporting calculations are required:

May 1, 1985	Cash	10,300	
	Interest Expense		300
	Bonds Payable		10,000
	(To record issuance of bonds @ 100 plus accrued interest. $10,000 issuance price of bonds + $300 [$10,000 × .09 × $\frac{4}{12}$ = accrued interest].)		

Interest Expense is credited for the amount of accrued interest *received* by the *issuer*. Although Interest Payable could just as easily have been credited, the entry as made is logical, because on July 1, 1985, when the first semiannual interest payment is made, interest for only two months (May and June) will be reflected as an expense to the Leverage Corporation. The following entry and T-account analysis illustrates this procedure:

July 1, 1985	Interest Expense	450	
	Cash		450
	(To pay semiannual interest. $10,000 × .09 × ½ = $450.)		

Interest Expense

1985			1985		
July 1	Payment of interest	450	May 1	Receipt of accrued interest upon issuance of bonds	300
July 1	Interest expense for six months ended	150			

If the $300 for accrued interest is credited to Interest Payable at the date of issuance, Interest Payable must be debited for $300 and Interest Expense must be debited for $150 when the $450 interest is paid on July 1, 1985.

Recognition of Accrued Interest

Another complication arises if the interest-payment date does not coincide with the company's year-end. Interest payable and interest expense must be accrued in order to apply the matching principle. The entry to record the accrued but unpaid interest expense at December 31, 1985, and related calculation appears below:

Dec. 31, 1985	Interest Expense	450	
	Interest Payable		450
	(To accrue interest		
	expense payable on		
	January 1, 1986.		
	$10,000 × .09 × ½ = $450.)		

Since the interest for the entire six months is payable on the following day (January 1), the entire amount payable at the next interest-payment date is accrued. Lesser amounts are accrued if the payment date is more distant than the following day. For example, if interest is payable on February 1 and August 1, then only five months of interest would be accrued at December 31.

Accounting Subsequent to Issuance

Chapter 10 notes that premium or discount on bonds is treated, respectively, as a direct addition to or subtraction from the face amount of the bonds. In the Leverage Corporation example in which the bonds payable are issued at an effective interest rate of 12%, the issue price drops to $8,918 with a discount of $1,082 ($10,000 − $8,918). This illustration is based on the original assumption of annual interest payments. Thus, immediately following the bond issuance on January 1, 1985, the liability for the bonds is presented in the Leverage balance sheet at $8,918. Since this amount represents the present value of the future cash flows—both interest and principal—on the date of issuance, the requirements of *Accounting Principles Board Opinion No. 21* are satisfied.[2] That pronouncement requires that most receivables and payables be recorded at their present value when issued.

Amortization: The Effective Interest Method.   The discount that emerges as a result of a difference between the rate of interest stated on the bonds (9%) and the market rate of interest (12%) is amortized as an increase of reported interest expense over the life of the bonds. For example, during 1985 the following entries are required:

Dec. 31, 1985	Interest Expense	900	
	Interest Payable		900
	(To accrue annual		
	interest payable at		
	Dec. 31, 1985.)		
Dec. 31, 1985	Interest Expense	170	
	Discount on Bonds Payable		170
	(To record amortization		
	of discount.)		

The discount is computed as follows:

2*APB Opinion No. 21,* "Interest on Receivables and Payables," 1971.

Carrying amount of bonds @	
Jan. 1, 1985	$8,918
Effective rate of interest expense	.12
Total annual interest expense (rounded)	1,070
Less: Interest expense recognized	
with Dec. 31, 1985, interest accrual	900
Amortization—1985	$ 170

The calculation demonstrates the manner in which we can calculate the amount of discount or premium to be amortized. In practice accountants, frequently aided by a computer, usually prepare amortization tables to facilitate recording the amortization of any premium or discount related to the bonds. Such a table is presented in Exhibit 15–3 for the Leverage Corporation.

This process of amortization continues each year until Discount on Bonds is fully amortized at the maturity date of the bonds. If the bonds are issued subsequent to the original date printed on the face of the bonds (as discussed earlier), any premium or discount is amortized over the remaining life of the bonds *beginning at the date of issuance and continuing to the maturity date.* The amortization of premium or discount in such situations does not present any significant additional problems and is treated as in any other circumstance. That is, the premium or discount is amortized over the life of the debt by the use of the **effective interest method** (also called **compound interest method** or simply **interest method**) of amortization.

The total interest expense each year is computed by multiplying the effective rate of interest (12% in the Leverage example) by the carrying amount of the liability at the beginning of each year. The total interest expense computed in this manner is then compared to the interest that has been paid or accrued on the bonds in accordance with the bond indenture. The difference between the amount of interest paid or payable during the year and the total interest expense to be recognized represents the discount or premium to be

---

EXHIBIT 15–3
Leverage Corporation
Amortization of Bond Discount
Effective Interest Method
(amounts rounded to the nearest dollar)

Date	(1) Interest Expense	(2) Cash Paid	(3) Discount Amortization	(4) Par Value Outstanding	(5) Unamortized Discount	(6) Carrying Value
Jan. 1, 1985	—	—	—	$10,000	$1,082	$ 8,918
Dec. 31, 1985	$1,070	$900	$ 170	10,000	912	9,088
Dec. 31, 1986	1,091	900	191	10,000	721	9,279
Dec. 31, 1987	1,113	900	213	10,000	508	9,492
Dec. 31, 1988	1,139	900	239	10,000	269	9,731
Dec. 31, 1989	1,169*	900	269	10,000	—	10,000
	$5,582	$4,500	$1,082			

(1) (Previous year Column 6) × 12%
(2) ($10,000 par value) × 9%
(3) (Column 1) − (Column 2)
(4) $10,000 par value
(5) (Previous year Column 5) − (Current year Column 3)
(6) (Column 4) − (Column 5)

*Adjusted for rounding difference.

amortized. Remaining unamortized discount continues to be classified as a reduction from the par value to determine the carrying amount of the bonds payable in the company's balance sheet.

The carrying amount of the bonds increases each year as the discount is amortized to interest expense until, at the maturity date of the bonds, the discount is fully amortized. At that time the carrying amount of the bonds is their face amount. Therefore, when the bonds are retired at maturity no gain or loss arises, because the cash required to retire the bonds is equal to the carrying amount of the bonds at that time.

Amortization: The Straight-Line Method.   Although the effective interest method of discount amortization is preferable because it recognizes a constant rate of interest on the bonds payable over the life of the bonds, other methods of amortization are often encountered in practice. These alternative procedures are acceptable only if their results do not differ materially from the results of the effective interest method. Since the differences resulting from each method of amortization are frequently immaterial, the **straight-line method** of amortization is commonly encountered in practice.

Materiality

In the Leverage example the straight-line method of amortization results in a charge to interest expense from discount amortization of $216.40 each year. We calculate the amount of amortization by dividing the total discount at the issuance of the bonds ($1,082) by the number of years the bonds are outstanding (5). Total interest expense reported each year is the sum of the cash payment for interest ($900) and the discount amortized ($216, rounded to the nearest whole dollar) or $1,116 each year. When we compare each amount in Column 1 of Exhibit 15–3 with $1,116, the deviations appear to be minor. Entries to record the amortization of discount by the straight-line method and to record the payment of interest each year are as follows:

Dec. 31 (each year)	Interest Expense	900	
	Interest Payable		900
Dec. 31 (each year)	Interest Expense	216	
	Discount on		
	Bonds Payable		216

Under the straight-line method the carrying value of the bonds is computed in the same way as with the effective interest method, by subtracting the unamortized discount from the par value of the bonds. For example, in the December 31, 1985, balance sheet the carrying value of the bonds is $9,134 [$10,000 − ($1,082 − $216)].

Bonds Issued at a Premium.   Companies frequently issue bonds at amounts exceeding the face value of the bonds. We refer to the excess of the price received over the face amount of the bonds as **premium.** Premium, like discount, also represents an adjustment to the stated rate of interest expense on the bonds. In essence, premium exists if the interest rate stated on the bonds is *higher* than the interest rate required by the market for similar securities. Investors are willing to pay more than the face amount of the bonds. Accounting for premium mirrors the procedures we employed in reporting discount.

To illustrate premium, assume that the Leverage bonds sell on January 1, 1985, at an effective interest rate of 6% with interest being paid semiannually at January 1 and July 1 each year. The total amount received for the bonds is $11,280 (rounded to the nearest dollar), determined as follows:

$$PV \text{ of bonds} = (PV \text{ of interest payments}) +$$
$$(PV \text{ of maturity})$$
$$= (\$450 \text{ for 10 six-month periods}$$
$$\text{at 6\% annual interest}) + (\$10,000$$
$$\text{at 6\% annual interest})$$

$$= (\$450 \times 8.53020) + (\$10,000 \times .74409)$$
$$= \$3,839 + \$7,441$$
$$= \$11,280$$

The present-value factor for the interest payments, 8.53020, is the present value of an annuity at *3% for 10 periods,* because interest is paid semiannually. The present-value factor for the maturity value of the bonds, .74409, is the present value of one at 3% for 10 periods. These values are taken from Table 6–4 and Table 6–2, respectively.

The entry to record the issuance follows:

Jan. 1, 1985	Cash	11,280	
	Bonds Payable		10,000
	Premium on Bonds Payable		1,280

The entry to record the first interest payment and amortize six months of premium (rounded to the nearest dollar) by using the effective interest method are presented below:

July 1, 1985	Interest Expense	450	
	Cash		450
	($10,000 × .09 × ½ = $450)		
July 1, 1985	Premium on Bonds Payable	112	
	Interest Expense		112
	($11,280 × .06 × ½ = $338;		
	$450 − $338 = $112)		

The credit to interest expense resulting from amortizing the premium reduces reported interest expense to 6% (the effective rate) of the carrying value of the bonds ($11,280). The carrying value of the bonds during the second six-month period declines from $11,280 by the amount of the premium amortized ($112) to $11,168. Total interest expense for the second six-month period becomes $335 ($11,168 × .06 × ½). The premium amortized during the last half of 1985 is the difference between the cash paid ($450) and the total interest expense to be reported ($335), or $115.

The process of amortization continues each six-month period until the bonds mature and the premium has been fully amortized. An amortization table similar to the one presented for discount in Exhibit 15–3 may be useful in accounting for the premium over the entire life of the bonds. Such a table is presented in Exhibit 15–4. The amortization of the premium *reduces* interest expense below the $450 *cash paid* rather than increasing interest expense, as was true in the discount case.

Materiality

As in the discount case, practitioners frequently use the straight-line method of amortizing premium rather than the more complex, but theoretically superior, effective interest method. As before, if material differences do not result from the straight-line method, there is little objection to its use. Of course, *APB Opinion No. 21* requires the use of the effective interest method if material differences result from other methods. In this case, straight-line amortization would be $128 per six-month period ($1,280/10).

Early Retirements of Bonds. Normally, bonds are retired at maturity, and any premium or discount is amortized over the life of the bonds. Therefore, since the carrying amount of the bonds at their maturity represents the amount of cash required to retire them, no gain or loss on the retirement of bonds at maturity is usually recognized.

If the bonds are retired early, however, recognition of gain or loss is necessary when the carrying amount of the debt, including unamortized premium or discount and issue costs, differs from the amount paid to accomplish the early retirement. The reasons that a company

---

EXHIBIT 15–4
Leverage Corporation
Amortization of Bond Premium
Effective Interest Method
(amounts rounded to the nearest dollar)

Date	(1) Interest Expense	(2) Cash Paid	(3) Premium Amortization	(4) Par Value Outstanding	(5) Unamortized Premium	(6) Carrying Value
Jan. 1, 1985	—	—	—	$10,000	$1,280	$11,280
July 1, 1985	$ 338	450	$ (112)	10,000	1,168	11,168
Dec. 31, 1985	335	450	(115)	10,000	1,053	11,053
July 1, 1986	332	450	(118)	10,000	935	10,935
Dec. 31, 1986	328	450	(122)	10,000	813	10,813
July 1, 1987	324	450	(126)	10,000	687	10,687
Dec. 31, 1987	321	450	(129)	10,000	558	10,558
July 1, 1988	317	450	(133)	10,000	425	10,425
Dec. 31, 1988	313	450	(137)	10,000	288	10,288
July 1, 1989	309	450	(141)	10,000	147	10,147
Dec. 31, 1989	303*	450	(147)	10,000	—	10,000
	$3,220	$4,500	$(1,280)			

(1) (Previous period Column 6) × (6% × ½)
(2) ($10,000 par value) × (9% × ½)
(3) (Column 1) − (Column 2)
(4) $10,000 par value
(5) (Previous period Column 5) − (Current period Column 3)
(6) (Column 4) + (Column 5)

---

*Adjusted for rounding difference.

---

might reacquire its own debt prior to maturity are numerous. For instance, if management thinks interest rates are likely to drop in the near future, the reacquisition of bonds paying a relatively high rate of interest might be prudent. Once the interest rates drop, the market would place a premium on existing instruments bearing higher interest rates and the company would be required to pay the premium to reacquire its own bonds in an open-market purchase.

Occasionally a company reacquires some of its own bonds with an intent to reissue them in the future. Such "treasury bonds" are nevertheless treated as if they are retired, and gains or losses on the reacquisition transaction are recognized. If the bonds are subsequently reissued, accounting follows the same practices discussed earlier for the original issuance of bonds.

The accounting profession has considered the reporting problems associated with extinguishments of debt and issued a series of related pronouncements. The first of these pronouncements, *APB Opinion No. 26,*[3] evaluates how any difference (differential) between the retirement cost of a debt and the carrying amount of the debt at the time of the extinguishment should be treated. Prior to *Opinion No. 26* several methods of accounting for this difference were used. For example, the differential arising from the extinguishment of debt was frequently amortized over the life of the new debt. Some companies amortized the differential over the original life of the debt just extinguished; they maintained that a difference between the carrying amount of the debt and the reacquisition price of the debt was a cost (or benefit) that was incurred to avoid future interest costs. Therefore, those companies contended that the differential should be allocated to the future periods affected by

---

[3]*APB Opinion No. 26,* "Early Extinguishment of Debt," 1972.

the decision to retire the debt. Such alternatives, however, are now unacceptable. Specifically, *Opinion No. 26* states:

> *A difference between the reacquisition price (of the debt) and the net carrying amount of the extinguished debt should be recognized currently in income of the period of the extinguishment as losses or gains.*[4]

Some accountants disagreed strongly with the position of the APB. Others felt that the rule could, in some circumstances, cause the financial statements to appear misleading. An example of a company that decided to depart from the requirements of *APB Opinion No. 26* is presented in Exhibit 15–5. Aeronca, Inc. (manufacturers of aircraft and aerospace structures, jet aircraft, engine components, and environmental and air-control systems), elected to record the difference between the carrying amount of the extinguished bonds and the value of the preferred stock issued to reacquire the bonds as additional paid-in capital rather than as a gain recognized in income. The company contended that reporting a gain in the circumstances described would have caused the financial statements to be misleading.

Materiality

Following the issuance of *APB Opinion No. 26,* gains or losses from the extinguishment of debt were included in income *before* extraordinary items during the period of the extinguishment, because such items generally were not considered both unusual in nature and infrequent in occurrence. The potential materiality of these gains and losses in addition to the ability of a company to control the timing of their recognition caused concern in the professional business community. In essence, company managements could directly, and frequently in an arbitrary fashion, influence reported earnings through debt-retirement activities. In extreme cases (such as described in Exhibit 15–5) the results reported for a debt extinguishment seemed to defy economic realities.

---

[4]*APB Opinion No. 26,* par. 20.

EXHIBIT 15–5
Aeronca, Inc.
Extinguishment of Debt

Notes to Financial Statements
Note 1–Summary of Accounting Policies:

• • • •

Extinguishment of Debt: In October, 1973, the Company issued 50,000 shares of 6% Prior Preferred Shares, par value $100, in exchange for the outstanding $5,000,000 of 6% Senior Subordinated Notes. It also issued 18,040 shares of convertible $6 Serial Preference Shares, Series A, stated value $100 a share, in exchange for $1,300,000 and $504,000 of outstanding 6% convertible subordinated debentures and 5¾% convertible subordinated debentures, respectively. The Company expensed the unamortized balance (approximately $148,000) of the deferred financing costs associated with the issuance of each of the three classes of subordinated debt to the extent that such unamortized balances were allocable to the debt so extinguished.

Opinion No. 26 of the Accounting Principles Board of the American Institute of CPA's states that the excess of the carrying amount of the extinguished debt over the present value of the new securities issued should be recognized as a gain in the statement of operations of the period in which the extinguishment occurred. While it is not practicable to determine the present value of the new equity securities issued, such value is at least $2,000,000 less than the face amount of the debt extinguished. However, the terms and provisions of these new equity securities are substantially similar to those of the debt securities extinguished, both on the basis of the Company's continuing operations and in the event of liquidation. It is the opinion of the management, therefore, that no gain as a result of this exchange has been realized or should be recognized in the financial statements.

SOURCE: Aeronca, Inc., 1973 Annual Report.

Responding to these criticisms, the FASB issued *Statement of Financial Accounting Standards No. 4,* which specified precisely the reporting requirements for such items:

> *Gains and losses from extinguishment of debt that are included in the determination of net income shall be aggregated and, if material, classified as an extraordinary item.*[5]

Thus, while *APB Opinion No. 26* applies only to early extinguishments of debt, *SFAS No. 4* requires gains and losses resulting from *all* extinguishments of debt to be classified as extraordinary items. However, one exception to the SFAS rule relates to cash purchases of debt made within one year of a sinking-fund requirement that an enterprise must meet.[6] For example, a typical bond indenture may specify that at December 31, 1986, a sinking fund to retire an issue of bonds must represent at least 50% of the face amount of the bonds outstanding. If a company retires some of its bonds within one year of December 31, 1986, to comply with this requirement, gains or losses may arise. Since such gains or losses result from well-planned contractual requirements, the FASB concluded that they should *not be classified as extraordinary items.*

Remember that an extraordinary item represents a special type of gain or loss to be reported separately in the income statement. Extraordinary items are presented net of any related tax effects, following income from operations. Financial statement users are thereby put on notice not to expect such unusual and infrequent items of gain or loss to recur in the foreseeable future. While many debt extinguishments may not satisfy both of the criteria for treatment as an extraordinary item (unusual in nature and infrequent in occurrence), *SFAS No. 4* requires that gains or losses from extinguishing debt be treated as extraordinary. The rationale for this treatment, in part, is to avoid some of the problems of management manipulation previously discussed. By excluding gains or losses on debt extinguishments from operating income, financial statement users are made aware of their special nature.

To illustrate accounting for the early extinguishment of debt, we shall again modify the example of the Leverage Corporation. Assume that after amortizing discount for 1985, the company—in anticipation of lower interest rates—reacquires the bonds presented in Exhibit 15–3 for $9,800 on January 4, 1986. The following entry reflects the reacquisition and recognition of the related extraordinary loss:

Loss on Retirement on Bonds—Extraordinary	1,112	
Bonds Payable	10,000	
Cash		9,800
Discount on Bonds Payable		912
Deferred Bond-Issue Costs		400
(To reflect the reacquisition of debt at an		
early date preceding maturity.)		

The remaining discount of $912 at the date of extinguishment is merely the original discount ($1,082) less the amount amortized at December 31, 1985 ($170). The $400 remaining issue costs related to these bonds are also removed from the accounting records, thereby affecting the amount of gain or loss reported.

What would be the proper accounting treatment if only part of the outstanding bonds were reacquired? The percentage of the issue reacquired would be applied to the par value, the unexpired discount or premium, and the deferred bond-issue costs to determine the

---

[5]*FASB Statement of Financial Accounting Standards No. 4,* "Reporting Gains and Losses from the Extinguishment of Debt," 1975, par. 8.
[6]*FASB Statement of Financial Accounting Standards No. 64,* "Extinguishments of Debt Made to Satisfy Sinking-Fund Requirements," 1982, par. 3.

portion of each to be written off. Cash is then credited for the price paid and an extraordinary gain or loss recognized.

To illustrate, we assume the same facts as in the previous illustration except that only 50% of the bond issue is extinguished for $4,900. The entry to record the retirement, including a loss of $556, is presented as follows:

Loss on Retirement of Bonds—Extraordinary	556	
Bonds Payable ($10,000 × 50%)	5,000	
Cash		4,900
Discount on Bonds Payable ($912 × 50%)		456
Defined Bond-Issue Costs ($400 × 50%)		200

As previously discussed, a company may reacquire its own bonds but not retire them. Rather, the company intends to sell the bonds at a later time. Such bonds are called **treasury bonds** and a Treasury Bonds account may be debited when the bonds are acquired rather than the liability account (Bonds Payable). An extraordinary gain or loss should still be recognized on the reacquisition, however, and the Treasury Bonds account should be deducted from the liability Bonds Payable in the balance sheet. Treasury Bonds should not be reported as an asset. Furthermore, interest on treasury bonds should not be paid or recognized in the financial statements.

Companies experiencing financial and operating difficulties occasionally reach agreements with creditors to restructure liabilities or retire debts for less than their maturity amounts. Restructurings of debt occurring because of financial difficulties of the debtor present several interesting accounting issues. A comprehensive discussion of troubled-debt restructurings from the perspective of both creditors and debtors appears in Appendix A of this chapter.

ACCOUNTING FOR DEBT EXTINGUISHMENTS—A CONTROVERSY
PAPER MONEY

THE FIRST FEW LINES of General Host's 1974 income statement sing a mournful song: Pretax income from continuing operations was *down* 25 percent to $4 million. Ah, but General Host's bottom line hums a different tune: Net income for 1974 was *up*—up 300 percent!—to a record of $9.17 per share.

How do you produce higher profits out of lower profits? It's one of the marvels of modern bookkeeping. In this case a nice little gimmick called "gains on extinguishment of debt."

"Extinguishment" is a cute term. It doesn't mean that General Host paid off its debt at less than 100 cents on a dollar and thereby earned a substantial discount. What General Host did was shuffle some pieces of paper and produce a paper profit of nearly $17 million—turning a poor year into a triumphant one. The old paper was "extinguished." New paper was substituted in its place.

It worked like this: Outstanding was $33.9 million in convertible debentures due in 1988, paying 5 percent interest—total annual interest, about $1.7 million. Management offered to swap for it $20.3 million new convertible debentures, paying 11 percent total interest, about $2.2 million. At the same time, the company reduced the conversion price from $27 per common share to $16. The bondholders took the offer. Why not? The holders' current income was enhanced by about 32 percent and conversion terms were improved.

Thus, even though Host's interest expense was increased from $1.7 million to $2.2 million, its books were improved by the wiping out of nearly $13.6 million in debt. And the "profit" came through in 1974, despite the fact that the debt wasn't due.

That is a lot easier way to make money than selling meat and tourism.

For some peculiar reason, the Financial Accounting Standards Board has put its imprimatur on this exercise in funny finance, calling these gains "extraordinary" income—whatever that means. But as Harvard Business School Professor John Shank puts it: "The board didn't raise the basic issue, which is whether this is income at all and in what period."

Boil it down and what you get is this: The company reports a "profit" but incurs a huge increase in interest liability against a very-far-in-the-future reduction in capital liability. Concedes William McHugh, a partner in Coopers & Lybrand: "They've effectively taken a profit this year and will pay it back over the life of the new bonds, through increased charges to future income." Is this what the accounting board calls clearer and more straightforward accounting?

"We're on the horns of a dilemma here," agrees Frank T. Weston, partner of Arthur Young & Co. Weston believes that the only solution to the dilemma is adoption of current value accounting, under which changes in the market value of debt would be recognized as they occur. On the other hand, Philip Defliese, managing partner of Coopers & Lybrand, dissented from the accounting board's ruling in this matter, wanting to see the "profit" amortized over the life of the bonds so that the price paid for the gain would be increased interest in subsequent periods. But he was overruled.

General Host is quick to point out that it didn't invent the gimmick. The ruling is that of the FASB. Nor is General Host the only company to take advantage of this murky provision. Grumman did too last year. Gulf & Western got 19 percent of its reported profits in 1973 that way. Western Union Corp. played the game. In Eli Black's time, United Brands was big on "extinguishment."

Why shouldn't companies be made to amortize the gain, the way Defliese suggested? It seems a mockery to have profit statements—which most investors think reflect the company's health—embellished with "profits" from paper shuffling.

SOURCE: "Paper Money," *Forbes*, July 1, 1975, p. 51. Reprinted by permission of *Forbes* Magazine. © Forbes Inc., 1975.

Hypoed Income: Some companies retire, others swap debt.

Company	Type of Extinguish- ment	Gain (millions)	Pretax Income (millions)	Gain as % of Income	Recent Stock Price	P/E Ratio
Allen Group	Exchange	$ 1.4	$ 5.7	25%	7⅝	9
GAF	Retirement	5.5	56.0	10	10⅝	5
General Host	Exchange	16.9*	20.8	81	7¼	1
Grumman	Exchange	9.3†	49.8	19	17½	6
McCulloch Oil	Exchange	0.8	5.1	16	5⅜	22
Pacific Gas & Elec	Retirement	20.0**	293.5	7	20¼	7
Pan East Pipe	Retirement	4.2**††	103.8	4	29¼	6
Trans World Air	Retirement	2.7**	(22.8)	—	7⅜	—
UAL	Retirement	20.6	224.0	9	18⅝	6

*Includes $751,000 debt retirement. †No income tax paid or gain. **Gain result of sinking fund requirement. ††Gain is being amortized, under Federal Power Commission accounting change January 1, 1974.

LONG-TERM DEBT ACCOUNTING PROBLEMS

Several other types of bonds and long-term debt instruments exist, and the following paragraphs consider several of the unusual accounting issues posed by these liabilities.

Debt Commingled with Equity Rights

Companies have developed many kinds of hybrid debt instruments in their efforts to obtain external financing at the lowest cost. Nowhere is this more obvious than in accounting and reporting for debt instruments containing certain options allowing bondholders the opportunity to become common stockholders under specified conditions. When such obligations are issued, we must resolve several additional accounting and reporting problems.

We may generally classify these debt instruments with equity-acquisition features as either (1) bonds issued with detachable stock-purchase warrants or (2) bonds that may be converted into equity securities. The following discussion describes general accounting theory and reporting practices for each type of debt security.

Accounting Theory and Equity-Acquisition Features

The accounting profession has addressed the issue of accounting for debt with **equity-acquisition features** on several occasions, the most recent of which resulted in the issuance of *APB Opinion No. 14*.[7]

Theoretically, whenever an investor acquires a debt security that in some way facilitates the acquisition of equity securities, some amount of the purchase price is paid for the right to acquire the equity security in an advantageous manner. The remaining amount of the purchase price relates to the liability aspects of the security. Stated alternatively, if the same bond were issued without the equity-acquisition feature, it would normally sell for less. The equity-acquisition feature has a value and serves to enhance the market value of the composite security. Furthermore, to the extent purchasers pay for the equity-conversion right or feature, such payment represents a permanent contribution to equity not requiring repayment. Indeed, only the principal at maturity and related interest when earned must be paid to the investor. Therefore, in theory, some portion of the total consideration received for convertible debt and debt with detachable stock rights should be considered a contribution to equity and the remainder as the incurrence of a liability. The following discussion considers both types of securities, presents the accounting profession's position on each, and illustrates appropriate accounting and reporting techniques.

Accounting for Debt with Detachable Stock-Purchase Rights

When debt is issued with **detachable stock-purchase warrants,** the repayment of the debt at maturity is generally expected, regardless of whether or not the stock-purchase warrants are exercised. Since the stock purchase warrants are detachable and may be exercised separately from the debt, a market for the warrants will normally be established and will provide information on the relative value of the warrants. Furthermore, since a market for the separate debt instrument would also be established, we could easily determine the value of the debt portion of the composite security in an objective manner. Thus, the equity and debt instruments do not represent mutually exclusive investment alternatives, as is the case with bonds that are directly convertible to equity securities.

The debt and equity elements of such securities exist independently and in substance represent separate, distinct securities. Financial accounting and reporting should reflect the dual nature of the composite security; therefore, it is necessary to allocate the total price received for the debt and detachable stock-purchase warrants to the two respective elements.

If active markets for the two securities exist immediately after issuance, the allocation of the total proceeds of the sale is based on the relative fair market values of the two securities. The portion of the total consideration to be allocated to debt is represented by the ratio of the fair market value of the debt alone to the total fair market value of the debt and warrants. The remaining portion of the consideration received is associated with the warrants. To understand this concept consider the following example.

Rosen, Inc., issues 1,000 bonds with a maturity value of $1,000 each. A detachable stock warrant, attached to each bond, may be exchanged for a share of stock with a payment of $25 per share. Rosen, Inc., sells the bonds with the warrants attached at 102. Shortly after

Objectivity

---

[7]*APB Opinion No. 14,* "Accounting for Convertible Debt and Debt Issued with Stock Purchase Warrants," 1969.

issuance the bonds are traded in the market at 103 and the warrants are traded at $5 each. The following calculation presents the basis for an entry to record the issuance:

$$\text{Total consideration to be treated as debt} = \left[\frac{\text{Market value of bonds without warrants}}{\text{Market value of bonds without warrants} + \text{Market value of warrants}} \right] \times \$1,020,000$$

$$= \frac{\$1,030}{\$1,030 + \$5} \times \$1,020,000$$

$$= \frac{\$1,030}{\$1,035} \times \$1,020,000$$

$$= \$1,015,072$$

The remaining proceeds of $4,928 ($1,020,000 − $1,015,072) represent the amount included in the total price that is allocated to the detachable stock-purchase warrants.

The entry to record the issuance of the bonds and warrants, based on the preceding calculation, is:

Cash	1,020,000	
Bonds Payable		1,000,000
Premium on Bonds Payable		15,072
Stock-Purchase Warrants		4,928
(To record issuance of bonds and detachable warrants.)		

For purposes of financial reporting, immediately after issuance the bonds are presented in the balance sheet with the premium added, as follows:

Long-Term Liabilities

Bonds payable	$1,000,000	
Add: Premium on bonds payable	15,072	$1,015,072

The stock warrants appear in the stockholders' equity section of the balance sheet as a separate element of paid-in capital.

From this point forward we account for the bonds in the manner illustrated earlier in this chapter. The premium is amortized over the life of the bonds as a reduction of interest expense. Again, the effective interest method of amortization should be used unless other amortization methods approximate the results of the effective interest method.

If market values of the bonds and attached warrants are not available, other allocation techniques must be used. For example, we may select an estimated interest rate that appears reasonable for the debt security alone. In doing so we should consider the risk class of the issuing company as well as other economic conditions. Factors such as the prime interest rate and government security rates provide useful guides for selecting an appropriate rate. Using the estimated interest rate, we can determine the present value of the liability. The difference between the present value of the debt and the total consideration received may be appropriately attributed to the detachable warrants and reported as contributed capital. This approach should be used only when fair market values of the bonds and the stock warrants are not available. Another possibility is that a market value would be available for either the bonds or the warrants but not both. In this case we would either estimate the unknown value and allocate the total proceeds as before or assign the known value to the one security and allocate the remaining proceeds to the other security.

The amount initially attributed to the warrants is recognized as part of paid-in capital and is classified as such until the warrants are exercised or expire. Accounting for stock-purchase warrants subsequent to issuance is considered in Chapter 16, which deals with a variety of issues involving stockholders' equity.

Accounting for Convertible Debt

Different problems arise if a company issues debt containing a feature allowing conversion into some type of the company's capital stock. In considering the accounting problems of such securities, the APB stated:

> A convertible debt security is a complex hybrid instrument bearing an option, the alternative choices of which cannot exist independently of one another. The holder ordinarily does not sell one right and retain the other. Furthermore, the two choices are mutually exclusive; they cannot both be consummated. Thus the security will either be converted into common stock or will be redeemed for cash. The holder cannot exercise the option to convert unless he foregoes the right to redemption, and vice versa.[8]

Substance over Form

While the APB ultimately selected the logic implicit in this statement for guiding financial accounting and reporting, an alternative argument is based on the idea of substance over form. Specifically the APB acknowledged:

> The contrary view is that convertible debt possesses characteristics of both debt and equity and that separate accounting recognition should be given to the debt characteristics and to the conversion option at the time of issuance. This view is based upon the premise that there is an economic value inherent in the conversion feature or call on the stock and that the nature and value of this feature should be recognized for accounting purposes by the issuer. . . . Similar separate accounting recognition for disparate features of single instruments is reflected in, for example . . . the allocation of the purchase cost in a bulk acquisition between goodwill and other assets.[9]

As indicated, the first position was ultimately adopted and consequently **no portion of the proceeds from the issuance of convertible debt should be attributed to the conversion feature.** In reaching this conclusion, the APB attributed much significance to the inseparability of the debt and conversion option of such instruments. Therefore, all the proceeds from the issuance of convertible debt are attributed to the liability. Stockholders' equity of the issuing company remains unaffected by the issuance of convertible debt. Dis-

Disclosure

closure of the conversion feature in the footnotes is necessary, however, to inform financial statement users of the possible changes in the financial structure of the company.

To illustrate the application of these provisions, consider the previous example of Rosen, Inc., but assume that convertible bonds are issued instead of bonds with detachable warrants. If convertible bonds with a face amount of $1,000,000 are issued for $1,115,000 and if each bond is convertible into 10 shares of common stock, the following entry is necessary:

Cash	1,115,000	
Bonds Payable		1,000,000
Premium on Bonds Payable		115,000
(To record issuance of convertible bonds.)		

The entire amount received is related to the bonds, and no proceeds are considered to be an

---

[8]APB Opinion No. 14, par. 7.

[9]APB Opinion No. 14, par. 9.

A TAXING ISSUE: IS IT DEBT OR EQUITY?

THE TREASURY DEPT.'S latest effort to draw a line between corporate debt and equity will, whatever else, sharpen old arguments between the government and business, from startup ventures to multinationals. Newly proposed regulations for the tax treatment of future issues as either debt (bonds), with tax deductions allowed for the interest paid, or equity (stock), with no deductions permitted for dividend payouts, are likely to be lambasted at a Mar. 10 public hearing, even though they have been liberalized since the trial balloon of a year ago. "Along with others, we'll be submitting comments, you can be sure," says Joseph W. O'Toole, chief tax officer of Phillips Petroleum Co. The regulations, he notes, would exempt "international transactions," but only temporarily. U.S. companies with subsidiaries abroad are concerned with the debt-vs.-equity issue, because the parents typically are sole shareholders of their subsidiaries. When they lend them money, they receive debt or equity instruments, depending on what the Treasury allows. Companies with subsidiaries only in the U.S. generally are not concerned, because their organizations can use consolidated tax returns. The multinationals will likely push for permanent exemption.

'Impossible.' Yet the opposition of small business is apt to be the heaviest. "The regs proposed in December, 1980, were impossible—and these are only a little better for people who want to finance small enterprises and startup companies," complains San Francisco accountant Bruce Fielding, a director of the National Federation of Independent Business.

The Treasury's debt-or-equity campaign reflects its suspicion that many companies of all sizes mislabel equity securities as debt to obtain tax deductions. Consequently, the regulations contain strict debt-to-equity ratios and similar requirements. Some of these rules have been eased in the new version.

For example, a requirement that a business's ratio must be 1-to-1 or more in favor of equity for a borrowing to be interest-deductible has been eased. A company would be able to go as high as $3 in debt outstanding for every $1 of invested capital. Says Fielding: "It ought to be at least 5-to-1 to give a startup business fair treatment."

Wider rate range. The rate of interest permitted on loans between related parties—by a shareholder to a closely held corporation, for example, or a parent to a subsidiary—also has been liberalized. The basic tax rule is that, if the interest rate is too low, the loan is seen as a capital investment and the interest as a nondeductible dividend. The new plan broadens the permissible rate range—now "the prime rate, [up] to 20%"—by lowering the bottom figure to 11%.

Still another rule lets a company borrow without regard to ratio requirements if the loan is repaid

---

addition to stockholders' equity. The liabilities section of the balance sheet at the date of issuance appears as follows:

Long-Term Liabilities		
Convertible bonds payable	$1,000,000	
Premium on bonds payable	115,000	$1,115,000

Chapter 16 discusses the exchange of convertible bonds for common stock and deals with a variety of other issues involving stockholders' equity.

Other Long-Term Liabilities

You may encounter several other types of long-term liabilities. For example, companies frequently issue **serial bonds,** which mature in several scheduled maturity dates rather than at a single maturity date as in the case of term bonds. Although financial accounting and reporting for serial bonds does not differ conceptually from the practices illustrated in this chapter for term bonds, several complicating factors arise. Appendix B of this chapter illustrates the accounting practices unique to serial-bond issues. Furthermore, lease and pension within 120 days of the end of the year in which it is made—an easing that may help small businesses. But Fielding says, "It's of very limited help in most situations."

Preferred stock—in a questionable position under earlier regulations—would be freed from the new debt-equity rules, and muddled rules covering "hybrid instruments" (mainly convertible bonds) are clarified. Here, however, the basic rule remains that if more than 50% of a bond's value is attributable to the conversion feature, the bond will be treated as a stock issue. "The 50% rule is too arbitrary—a simple idea, but maybe not a reliable measure of what a security really is," says Daniel Evans, director of bond research at E. F. Hutton & Co.

The burden falling on closely held and startup companies is stressed by Dean Treptow, president of Brown Deer Bank, near Milwaukee. "Typically," he says, "the person starting a small business relies on borrowing. He borrows $100,000 on his home and other personal property and lends it to the business. It becomes a debt on the company's books, and the business takes the tax deduction for the bank interest." If the deduction is allowed, as in the past, and the interest rate on the $100,000 loan is 17%, the company—assuming a 40% tax bracket—has an aftertax borrowing cost of $10,200, or 10.2%. If the deduction is disallowed to the company and is taken by the owner personally—who would also be reporting the 17% interest as a dividend—there is no benefit and the loan cost is the full $17,000.

Treptow notes that, under the new 3-to-1 debt-equity ratio rule, the enterprise could deduct the

17% cost only if the owner also had invested at least a third of the loan amount, or $33,000, as capital stock. "For many people starting a business, this would mean selling their home or the like to come up with the cash," says Treptow. He and Fielding contend that this demand is punitive.

"Once the new regs go into effect, we [the banks] could adapt and probably change our usual method of financing," Treptow adds. "We might lend the money directly to the business, taking the owner's collateral. The hardest problem now is faced by the thousands and thousands of businesses already set" up under the old lending practice.

Foreign subsidiaries. Multinational companies—as sole shareholders of foreign subsidiaries—face more complex versions of the same debt-equity tax problems. The Treasury, however, has long maintained that some multinationals have reaped unjustified advantages. "A U.S. parent lends money to a subsidiary in Italy, the sub takes the tax deduction on the interest on its Italian tax return, but the U.S. parent treats the interest as a dividend," explains Richard Berkowitz, a Chicago tax partner of Arthur Andersen & Co., an accounting firm. "As a dividend, the income might be offset against taxes paid abroad, so there's a double tax break."

This is the sort of maneuver the Treasury has been tussling with in attempting to write special rules for multinationals, Berkowitz adds. "So far," he says, "they haven't found the answers."

SOURCE: "A Taxing Issue: Is It Debt or Equity?" *Business Week,* February 1, 1982, p. 66. Reprinted by special permission, © 1982 by McGraw-Hill, Inc.

---

obligations are frequently reported as liabilities in the financial statements of business enterprises. Since accounting classification, measurement, and reporting standards for these liabilities are complex, Chapters 21 and 22, respectively, are devoted to each topic. Chapter 18, which deals with financial reporting of income taxes, discusses noncurrent deferred tax credits. Also, certain loss contingencies, discussed in Chapter 14, may represent long-term liabilities of an enterprise. Lawsuits and other claims provide examples of contingent liabilities that may require noncurrent classification.

The present chapter discusses only a limited number of noncurrent liabilities. Although notes and bonds payable frequently represent most of a company's noncurrent liabilities, the other important items mentioned in the preceding paragraph are considered elsewhere in this book.

CONCLUDING REMARKS

Financial accounting and reporting for long-term liabilities, although sometimes considered straightforward, contain several controversial issues. Although the accounting profession has acted to resolve many of the issues, certain controversies still exist. For example, critics observe that a company can issue bonds with a high stated rate of interest, exchange them for previously issued low-interest bonds, and "create" an extraordinary gain on the extinguishment of the previously issued bonds. Furthermore, a greater liability (in terms of future interest and principal payments) might have replaced the liability just extinguished. Thus, even though the company might have executed a generally disadvantageous transaction, an accounting gain may be reported in the financial statements.

The authors recognize that such manipulative practices are occasionally encountered and that such contrivances can cause financial statements to be misunderstood even while conforming to published authoritative literature. Any accepted practice can be abused, however, and the profession attempts to limit such abuses. Authoritative standard-setting organizations frequently act to rectify practices that are suspect. Individual practitioners must also evaluate and select among various accounting and reporting responses to uniquely structured transactions. The ultimate criterion of the acceptability of a particular accounting practice is the accounting treatment that results in the most useful set of financial statements.

KEY POINTS

1. Long-term debts are those reportable obligations of an enterprise that do not require for repayment the use of current assets or the creation of new current liabilities.

2. Long-term debt should usually be recorded at the present value of the future cash obligations.

3. Premium and discount arise when the market rate of interest for an obligation differs from the rate of interest stated on the face of the security.

4. Premium or discount should be amortized over the life of the debt by applying a constant interest rate to the carrying amount of the liability (effective interest method). The straight-line method of amortization is acceptable only if the results do not differ materially from the effective interest method.

5. When debt is extinguished, any difference between its carrying amount and its reacquisition price is treated as an extraordinary gain or loss.

6. When a company sells a debt instrument with detachable stock-purchase warrants, an increase in stockholders' equity is recognized as well as an increase in liabilities. The proceeds from the sale of the hybrid security must be allocated between the debt and equity components based on the relative fair values of the two.

7. When a company sells a convertible debt security, the value that can be attributed to the equity-acquisition feature is not recognized in the accounts. The liability for the debt security is recorded in the accounting records as if the conversion feature did not exist.

APPENDIX A TROUBLED-DEBT RESTRUCTURINGS

When a company experiences financial trouble it may be difficult or impossible to repay its debt on a timely basis. Furthermore, most debt instruments contain covenants requiring a company to maintain certain financial characteristics as evidenced by the financial statements. For example, a debt covenant may require the maintenance of a given debt/equity ratio, current ratio, or working capital amount. A company experiencing operating and financing difficulty may at some time violate some or all of its debt covenants. When such covenant violations occur, a common practice is for creditors and debtors to renegotiate and restructure the troubled debt.

As a result of the variety and complexity of **troubled-debt restructurings,** the FASB issued *Statement of Financial Accounting Standards No. 15,* which discusses the accounting and reporting by both debtors and creditors.[10] Since there is considerable similarity between debtor and creditor accounting, we consider both in this appendix. First, however, we shall explore the steps necessary to *identify* troubled-debt restructurings.

IDENTIFYING TROUBLED-DEBT RESTRUCTURINGS

Not all debt restructurings represent troubled debt; we must therefore exercise care in determining whether a particular debt restructuring is in fact, a *troubled*-debt restructuring. For example, a troubled-debt restructuring is not involved if a creditor, experiencing financial difficulty, makes concessions in debt terms to induce a debtor to pay off the debt at a point *earlier* than the scheduled maturity date. This restructuring to accelerate the creditor's cash flow would relate to problems of the creditor, not the debtor.

To qualify for a troubled-debt restructuring, the *debtor* must be experiencing financial difficulty and the creditor, attempting to make the best of a bad situation and recover at least a portion of the receivable, grants a concession to the debtor that would not be granted in a normal business relationship. Thus, creditors sustain accounting losses on troubled-debt restructurings while debtors realize accounting gains. Examples of restructurings include a modification of debt terms, such as interest-rate reductions or maturity-date extensions, settlement of the debt for less than its face amount, and the granting to creditors of equity interests in the debtor. Once a troubled-debt restructuring has occurred and has been identified as such, appropriate accounting measurements and disclosures must be accorded the restructuring.

ACCOUNTING BY DEBTORS

When a troubled-debt restructuring occurs, a debtor will have been granted some relief by a creditor from the original terms of the debt. Thus, the restructuring generally leaves the debtor in a better financial condition. However, gains on some types of restructuring are not reportable in the financial statements.

Four types of troubled-debt restructurings are recognized for accounting purposes. The first two involve full settlement of the debt as a result of a debtor's (1) transferring assets to the creditor or (2) granting an equity interest to the creditor. The third type involves a modification of debt terms (e.g., extension of maturities, reduction of interest); and the fourth, some combination of the first three types. We shall discuss each of these restructuring possibilities in the following pages.

Transfer of Assets

In a troubled-debt restructuring creditors are sometimes willing to accept various debtor assets in immediate settlement of the debt. In a **transfer of assets** debtors must consider how much of any resulting gain or loss is related to the disposition of the assets and how much is related to the extinguishment of debt.

For example, assume Pomona Company agrees to accept Covina Company's land, which has a fair market value of $40,000, in full settlement of a Covina Company debt. If the land has a book value of $35,000 and the liability is reflected on the books at its maturity value of $50,000, then the following entries are necessary on Covina's books:

Land	5,000	
Gain on Disposal of Land—		
Ordinary		5,000
(To adjust land to its fair market		
value at the time of disposal.)		
Note Payable	50,000	
Land		40,000
Gain from Restructuring of		
Debt—Extraordinary		10,000
(To recognize gain on the		
extinguishment of debt.)		

These illustrative entries demonstrate that two steps may be required when assets are transferred in settlement of a debt. We first adjust the asset transferred from its current carrying amount to its fair market value at the time of transfer with a resulting gain or loss recognized on the disposal of the asset. These gains or losses are *not* extraordinary since gains or losses on asset disposals occur frequently and are not unusual.

After the asset is adjusted to its fair market value, we next recognize any difference between the fair value of the asset and the carrying amount of the extinguished debt as an *extraordinary gain*. We may observe several important points at this time. Losses are

---

[10]*FASB Statement of Financial Accounting Standards No. 15,* "Accounting by Debtors and Creditors for Troubled Debt Restructuring," 1977.

not recognized by debtors on the extinguishment of debt. That is, the fair market value of the asset transferred will never be greater than the carrying amount of the debt in a troubled-debt restructuring. This is consistent with the nature of troubled-debt restructurings wherein creditors grant concessions to debtors so as to provide at least some recovery of a loan. Also, as we learned earlier in this chapter, gains on the extinguishment of debt should be reflected as extraordinary items according to *SFAS No. 4* and *SFAS No. 15*. Finally, the revaluation of assets from their carrying values to fair market values at the time of disposal may give rise to either gains or losses.

Grant of Equity Interest

A second method by which troubled debt may be restructured occurs when a debtor **grants an equity interest** to the creditor in consideration for the debt extinguishment. Debtors should record the fair market value of the equity securities granted and recognize an extraordinary gain for any difference between the carrying amount of the debt extinguished and the fair market value of the equity grant.

To illustrate, assume that instead of transferring land to Pomona Company, the Covina Company grants 1,000 shares of $25 preferred stock to Pomona in consideration for the extinguishment of the $50,000 note. If the preferred stock has a fair market value of $45,000, the following entry is necessary to reflect this transaction:

Note Payable	50,000	
Preferred Stock (1,000 shares @ $25)		25,000
Paid-in Capital in Excess of Par		20,000
Gain from Restructuring of Debt —Extraordinary		5,000
(To record extinguishment of note as a result of equity grant with a fair market value of $45,000.)		

We may observe several additional important points: As before, only gains (not losses) are recognized on this type of troubled-debt restructuring, because the fair market value of the equity grant will not be greater than the carrying amount of the extinguished debt. Also, the gain is treated as extraordinary in accordance with *SFAS No. 15*.

From a practical perspective it is frequently difficult to determine the fair market value of the equity that is granted, because the market value of the securities of a troubled company may be highly volatile or even nonexistent. This is especially true for companies whose securities are not actively traded in a public market. Therefore, we must develop reasonable estimates of fair market value when a debt is extinguished through an equity grant.

Modification of Terms

The third type of restructuring transaction involves a **modification of the terms** of the debt. Although the terms of a debt may be modified in many ways, accounting for all such debt alterations involves the same underlying principles. When the terms of a debt are adjusted in a troubled-debt restructuring, the *total amount* of the future cash payments should be determined. This total should include all payments for both principal and interest required in the future without using present-value techniques. In other words, the gross future cash payments for principal and interest after the modification of terms should be calculated. This number is then compared with the current carrying amount of the debt on the books of the debtor. If the carrying value of the debt is less than the aggregate future cash payments required by the debt, we amortize the difference over the life of the debt as interest expense by using the effective interest method specified in *APB Opinion No. 21* (see footnote 2). No gain is recognized in the period of the extinguishment if the future flows exceed the carrying amount of the debt.

On the other hand, the carrying amount of the debt may be greater than the aggregate total future cash payments required under the modified debt agreement. In this case we adjust the carrying value of the debt to the aggregate total future cash flows and recognize an extraordinary gain for the difference. Furthermore, in these circumstances no interest expense is recognized on the debt following such a write-down. All payments in satisfaction of the debt are considered payments of principal even if some portion of the payments is designated as interest in the revised debt agreement.

To illustrate, assume that the note payable to Pomona Company bears interest at 12% and, as before, is carried as a liability on Covina's books at $50,000. Instead of the previous restructuring examples, however, assume now that Pomona agrees to reduce the principal amount of the note by $10,000 but continues to require interest to be paid at 12% on the remaining $40,000. If the note is due in one year, the following entry is necessary:

Note Payable	5,200	
Gain from Restructuring of		
Debt—Extraordinary		5,200

The calculations are as follows:

$40,000 × .12 =	$ 4,800	Interest to be paid on new principal amount
+	40,000	Remaining principal
	$44,800	Aggregate future cash payments
	$50,000	Current carrying amount of liability
−	44,800	Aggregate payments required after restructuring
	$ 5,200	Gain on restructuring

The carrying value of the liability is now $44,800 as a result of the foregoing entry. Consequently, all cash payments now made in satisfaction of the note are considered payments of principal, even though a portion ($4,800) has been designated in the restructuring agreement as interest. Covina recognizes no interest expense on the note subsequent to this restructuring.

Combination of Methods

The final manner in which a troubled-debt restructuring may occur involves some combination of the first three methods: transfer of assets, grant of equity interest, or modification of terms. In such a **combination restructuring** we apply the following provisions. If an asset is transferred to the creditor in partial settlement of the debt, the asset is adjusted from its carrying value to its fair market value and a gain or loss is recognized on the disposal of the asset. Next, the fair market value of the asset transferred is used to reduce the debt by a similar amount. In a combination restructuring some debt usually remains on the books after this adjustment and therefore no extraordinary gain on the extinguishment is recognized at this point.

An equity interest might also have been granted to the creditor. The debtor should record the fair market value of the equity interest with a corresponding charge to the carrying amount of the debt. If the extinguishment is completed as a result of the asset transfer and equity grant, then an extraordinary gain should normally be recognized. The amount of the gain is the difference between the carrying value of the debt prior to extinguishment and the fair market value of the asset transferred plus the equity grant.

If the debtor still has a residual liability on the restructured debt following a transfer of assets or grant of equity interest, or both, then the provisions governing a modification of terms should be applied. That is, the gross future payments for both interest and principal still required following the asset transfer and/or grant of equity should be compared to the adjusted carrying value of the debt. If the gross future cash payments exceed the adjusted carrying amount of the debt, the difference is recognized as interest expense over the life of the debt. On the other hand, if the gross future cash payments are less than the adjusted amount of the debt, then the debt should be written down to the total of the gross future cash flows with an extraordinary gain recognized to the extent of the difference.

To illustrate accounting for a combination type restructuring, assume that a debtor in a troubled-debt restructuring agrees to the following terms: (1) Debtor will transfer inventory with a carrying value of $15,000 and a fair market value of $12,000 to the creditor; (2) debtor will grant to creditor 100 shares of its $10 par value stock, which has a current fair market value of $6 per share; and (3) in consideration of the asset transfer and equity grant, the creditor will reduce the principal balance of the note from $30,000 to $10,000 and will reduce the interest rate on the note from 12% to 10%, compounded annually. These transactions occur on January 1, 1985, when the note payable has a carrying value of $29,000. Under the restructuring the note matures on December 31, 1986, at which time both accrued interest (compounded annually) and principal are due. Exhibit 15–6 illustrates the necessary calculations and entries to analyze and record this restructuring.

The provisions of *SFAS No. 15* in regard to debtor accounting for troubled-debt restructurings are summarized in Exhibit 15–7. Study this flowchart carefully, reflecting on the previous discussion of the various types of troubled-debt restructurings.

————— ACCOUNTING BY CREDITORS

Creditors' accounting and reporting practices for troubled-debt restructurings parallel those of debtors'; however, certain differences exist. As previously discussed, in a troubled-debt restructuring creditors grant concessions to debtors because of the debtor's impaired ability to fulfill the original terms of the obligation. Since creditors are attempting to recoup as much

---

EXHIBIT 15–6
Comprehensive Illustration of a Combination
Troubled-Debt Restructuring

Journal entries:

Jan. 1, 1985	Loss on Disposal of Inventory	3,000	
	Inventory		3,000
	(To recognize loss on disposal of inventory.)		
Jan. 1, 1985	Note Payable	12,600	
	Discount on Common Stock	400	
	Inventory		12,000
	Common Stock (100 shares @ $10)		1,000
	(To attribute fair market value of inventory transferred and equity granted to an equivalent portion of debt.)		

Calculation for consideration:

Inventory (written down from $15,000 value)	$12,000
Equity grant (par $1,000)	600
Total fair value of consideration	$12,600

On January 1, 1985, the following test is made to determine if further accounting entries are necessary:

Debt carrying value:	
Original carrying amount of debt	$29,000
Less: Write-down from above	12,600
Carrying value of debt	$16,400
Future cash flows:	
Maturity cash requirement	$10,000
Interest	
Dec. 31, 1985	
($10,000 × .10)	1,000
Dec. 31, 1986	
($11,000 × .10)	1,100
Total aggregate future payments required	$12,100

Since the adjusted carrying amount of the debt ($16,400) exceeds the future cash requirements ($12,100), an entry is necessary for the difference ($4,300):

Jan. 1, 1985	Note Payable	4,300	
	Gain from Restructuring of Debt—		
	Extraordinary		4,300
	(To reduce carrying amount of note to aggregate of future cash payments.)		

On December 31, 1985, no entry is required; all payments represent principal following restructuring; thus, no interest should be accrued.

Dec. 31, 1986	Note Payable	12,100	
	Cash		12,100
	(To record retirement of debt at maturity; no interest expense recognized.)		

EXHIBIT 15–7
Troubled-Debt Restructuring—Debtor Accounting

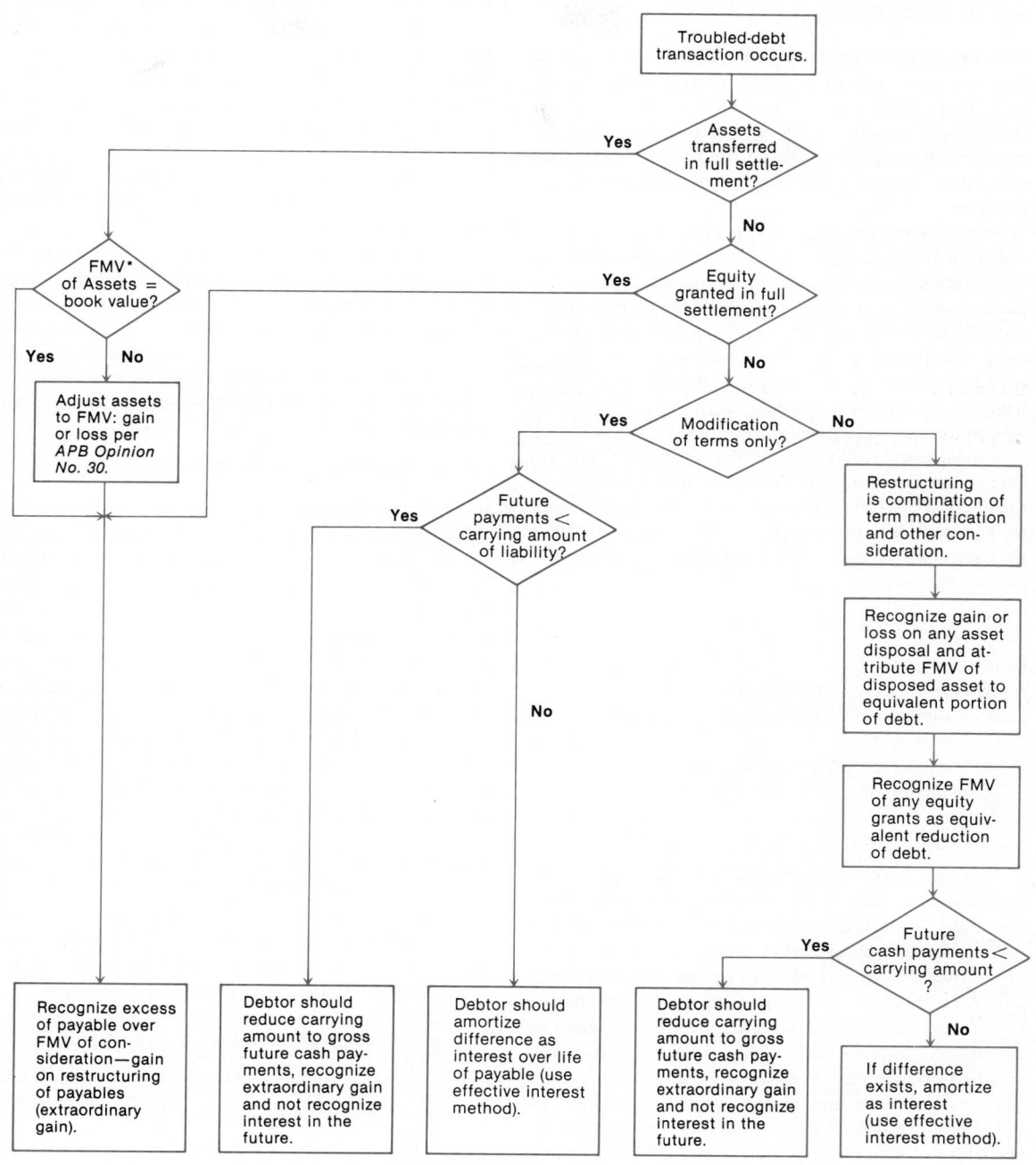

*FMV = fair market value.

of a receivable as possible, losses on the settlement of such receivables are likely to be incurred.

Asset Receipts

A troubled-debt restructuring may take place in several different ways. From the creditor's perspective, however, there is no conceptual difference between the receipt of a debtor's asset such as inventory and the receipt of an equity interest in the debtor. Both types of transfers result in the **receipt of an asset** by the creditor.

When assets are received by a creditor in satisfaction of a receivable in a troubled-debt restructuring, the assets received should be recorded at their fair market value on the date of receipt. If an allowance for uncollectible accounts has been established specifically for the receivable in question, the allowance account as well as the receivable should be removed from the books of the company with a loss recognized for any remaining difference.

To illustrate, if we assume that Pomona Company accepts land with a fair market value of $40,000 in satisfaction of a note receivable with a carrying amount of $50,000, but for which a $6,000 allowance for uncollectible accounts has been established, the following entry is necessary:

Land	40,000	
Allowance for Doubtful Accounts	6,000	
Loss on Settlement of Receivable	4,000	
Note Receivable		50,000
(To record receipt of land in		
satisfaction of note receivable.)		

We can make several important observations in regard to this entry. First, a loss of $10,000 has been sustained in the settlement of this receivable; $6,000 was recognized in an earlier period as a result of the use of the allowance method of recognizing bad debts; and the additional $4,000 loss is recognized in the period of the settlement. Second, these losses are not considered to be extraordinary, because—from the creditor's perspective—they are losses on the collection of receivables and not on the extinguishment of debt. Futhermore, if the assets received are equity securities of the debtor (equity grant), the accounting and reporting techniques are not changed; that is, the equity securities received should be recorded as an

asset at their fair market value on the date received.

Modification of Terms

If the terms of a receivable are changed pursuant to a troubled-debt restructuring, creditors must determine the total amount of cash to be received in the future. This amount is then compared with the carrying amount of the receivable, net of any related allowance account. If the total aggregate cash to be received in the future exceeds the carrying amount of the receivable, the difference should be amortized as interest revenue over the life of the receivable by using the effective interest method.

If the total aggregate payments to be received in the future, however, are less than the carrying amount of the receivable, then an ordinary loss should be recognized for the difference. All remaining collections are then treated as direct reductions of the receivable, and no interest revenue is recognized even if the revised agreement specifies a portion of the amount received as interest.

Combination of Methods

If the restructuring is a combination of a partial settlement by receipt of assets and a modification of terms, the fair market value of the asset received should be used to reduce an equivalent amount of the receivable. If the cash to be received in the future exceeds the net adjusted carrying amount of the receivable, the difference should be amortized as interest revenue over the life of the receivable. Conversely, if the aggregate of the cash to be received in the future is less than the net adjusted carrying amount of the receivable, the receivable should be written down to the total of the aggregate future cash receipts and a loss recognized. Again, no interest revenue should be recognized on future cash receipts in such circumstances. Furthermore, the future cash flows should not be subjected to any present-value calculations.

Exhibit 15–8 summarizes the key decision points and required accounting practices for creditors in a troubled-debt restructuring. Study the flowchart and relate its provisions to the preceding discussion.

COMPARING AND CONTRASTING DEBTOR AND CREDITOR ACCOUNTING

While there are many similarities between debtor and creditor accounting for troubled-debt restructurings, several differences are also apparent. In essence, the

EXHIBIT 15–8
Troubled-Debt Restructuring—Creditor Accounting

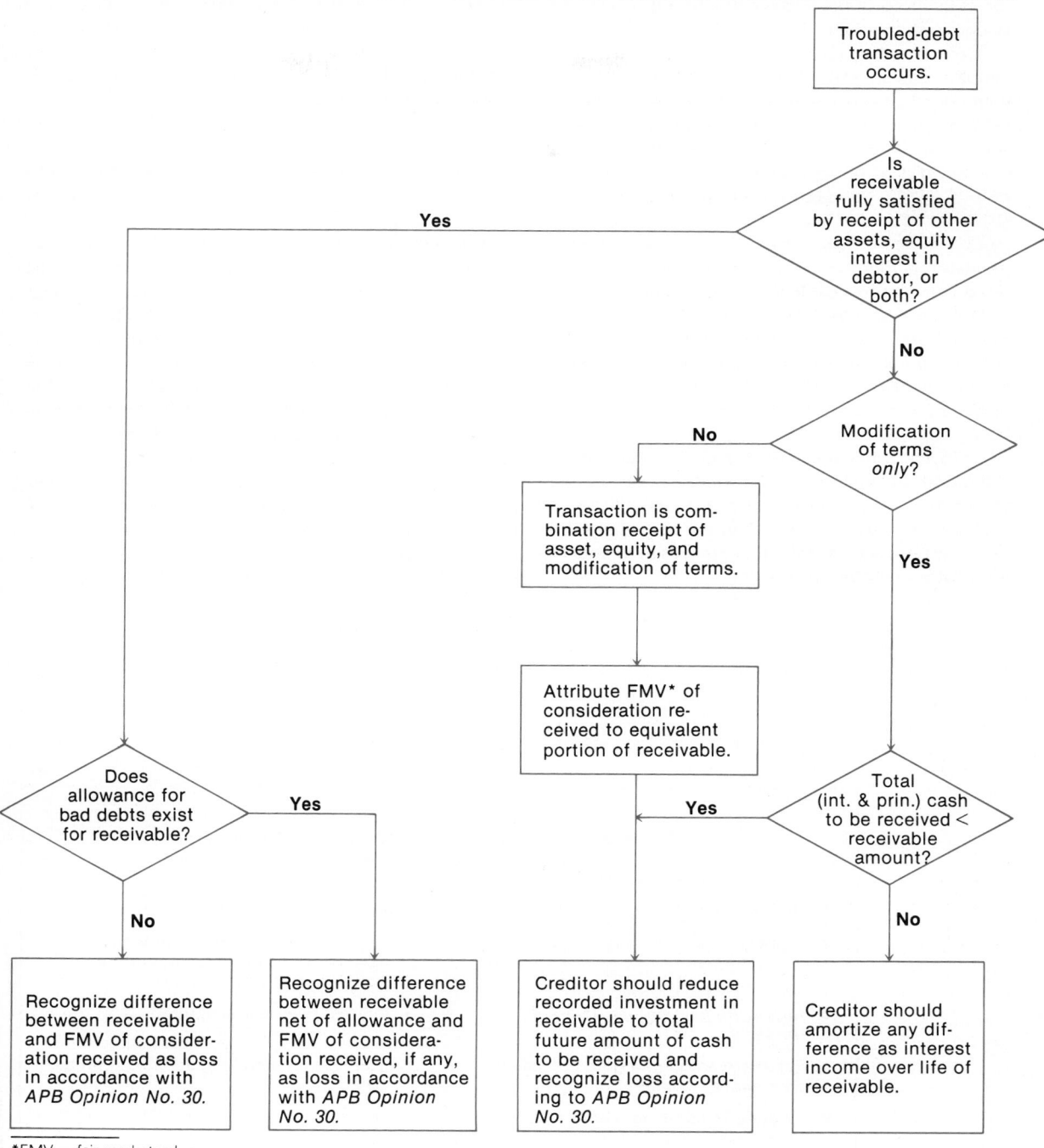

*FMV = fair market value.

differences relate primarily to timing and classification. Gains on the extinguishment of debt should be classified as extraordinary by the debtor, whereas losses on the collections of receivables should not be classified as extraordinary items by the creditor.

Creditors may recognize the impairment of a receivable and a related loss by using the allowance method of bad-debt recognition at an earlier time than debtors recognize gains from the consequences of an actual restructuring. This is consistent with the accrual of loss and gain contingencies discussed in Chapter 14;

Conservatism

that is, gain contingencies should not be accrued prior to realization, because revenue might be recognized prematurely, but loss contingencies should be recognized when it is probable that a loss has been incurred and the amount of the loss is reasonably estimable. Furthermore, these practices are themselves in harmony with the modifying convention of conservatism, which requires that accounting and reporting properly recognize inherent uncertainties in the commercial process.

Different estimates of the fair market value of consideration paid and received can cause other inconsistencies in accounting treatment between debtors and creditors. Existing differences in the recorded values of receivables and payables may also result in nonsymmetrical accounting treatments.

DISCLOSURE OF TROUBLED-DEBT RESTRUCTURINGS

Exhibit 15–9 provides a summary of the disclosure requirements for troubled-debt restructurings. Substantial disclosures are required to assure adequate comprehension of the underlying transactions by the financial statement user.

DEBT EXTINGUISHMENTS: A FINAL NOTE

Although *SFAS No. 15* is specifically limited to *troubled*-debt restructurings, we can reflect upon the accounting practices to be accorded restructurings that are not related to troubled debt. The authors believe that the accounting practices described by *SFAS No. 15* for troubled-debt restructurings, with the exception of certain of the disclosures enumerated in Exhibit 15–9, are desirable and would represent generally accepted accounting principles when applied to any debt restructuring. For a restructuring not related to troubled debt, judgment should be applied in disclosing its nature and extent. Of course, *SFAS No. 4,* "Reporting Gains and Losses from Extinguishment of Debt," stipulates certain disclosures that are necessary for *all* debt extinguishments.

EXHIBIT 15–9
Disclosure of Troubled-Debt Restructurings

Debtor Disclosures	Creditor Disclosures
1. Description of changes in terms.	1. Aggregate recorded investment.
2. Aggregate gain and tax effects of restructuring.	2. Gross interest revenue that *would* have been recognized without the troubled-debt restructuring.
3. Aggregate gain or loss on asset transfers.	3. Interest revenue recognized
4. Per share amount of gain or loss on debt extinguishment	4. Commitments to lend additional funds.
5. Extent of a contingent amount payable in the total liability.	

APPENDIX B ACCOUNTING PROBLEMS OF SERIAL BONDS

Serial bonds provide an issuing company the ability to repay the principal portion of the bonds in a series of installments. Several maturity dates are established for portions of an entire bond issue. When serial bonds are issued, groups of individual bonds within that issue have maturity dates different from those of the other groups. A series of maturity dates allows the issuer to retire the bonds gradually. Serial bonds may eliminate the need for a sinking fund or reduce the financial stress of meeting the maturity requirements of an entire bond issue at a single date.

Serial bonds are also attractive to state and local governments that rely on tax revenues to service debt. For example, if voters approve a bond issue and a related tax to fund a road-building project, the government may choose to issue serial bonds. The governmental unit then constructs the road with the proceeds of the bond issue and, as tax revenues are received, retires the debt in a series of maturities rather than in a single maturity.

Several accounting and reporting problems exist when a company issues serial bonds. Generally, these problems relate to the timing of premium or discount amortization and classification of the liability for the bonds payable. The simplified example in Exhibit 15–10 illustrates these problems.

The entry to record the issuance of the bonds in Exhibit 15–10 is relatively simple and parallels the entries discussed earlier in regard to term bonds. The proceeds of the issue are debited to cash with a credit to bonds payable for the face amount of the entire issue. Any difference is treated as premium or discount on the bonds. As we mentioned earlier, premium or discount represents the difference, if any, between the interest rate stated on the bonds and the effective market rate of interest for those bonds on the date of issuance. The following entry is required to record the issuance of the bonds:

Jan. 1, 1983		
Cash	949,200	
Discount on Bonds Payable	50,800	
Bonds Payable		1,000,000
(To record issuance of serial bonds.)		

We must next determine the effective rate of interest implicit in the bond issue. While this problem is not conceptually different from that encountered for term bonds, there are complicating factors. The several ma-

---

EXHIBIT 15–10
Facts to Illustrate
Accounting for Serial Bonds

Issuing company	Staging
Total bond issue	$1,000,000
Date of bonds and date of issue	Jan. 1, 1983
Maturity dates as shown:	

Group	Amount	Maturity Date
A	$ 250,000	Dec. 31, 1984
B	250,000	Dec. 31, 1985
C	500,000	Dec. 31, 1986
	$1,000,000	

Interest rate stated	10%
Interest payment terms	Annually on Dec. 31
Proceeds of issue	$949,200

Note: Bond issues usually involve much larger amounts and longer periods of time between issuance and maturity. However, for illustrative purposes a smaller amount and shorter period of time are assumed.

turity dates cause uneven cash flows throughout the life of the bonds, not only for principal repayments but for interest payments as well. Cash flow patterns for term-bond interest payments are constant over the life of the bonds, and there is only a single maturity date. While the application of present-value techniques to serial bonds is more difficult, the objective remains the same. Specifically, we are seeking to determine the rate of interest (effective rate) that equates the present value of the liability (cash proceeds of the issue) with the future cash flows (various principal maturities and interest payments) required under the bond indenture. We must make this calculation in order to meet the reporting requirements of *APB Opinion No. 21,* "Interest on Receivables and Payables," which requires the effective interest method for amortizing premium or discount over the life of the debt unless other methods do not cause material differences. Remember that even the simpler straight-line method of premium or discount amortization is not acceptable unless the results are close to those obtained by using the effective interest method. Therefore, we will use only the effective interest method to illustrate accounting for serial bonds.

When a combination of annuity (series of payments) and single amounts of cash flows are involved, we must select a rate of interest that equates the future cash flows with the issue price of the debt. We should select a rate that appears reasonable and test the rate by determining if the future cash flows, discounted at that rate, approximate the present value of the liability (proceeds of the issue).

In the case of Exhibit 15–10, since the bonds sold at a discount we know that the effective or market rate of interest demanded must be higher than the stated interest rate of 10%. In other words, if the stated rate of interest on the bonds provided a rate of return equal to that required by the market, then the bonds would have sold at their par value. Since the bonds were sold at a discount we can conclude that the market required a higher rate of return than was stated on the bonds. Therefore, in attempting to select the appropriate rate we should test a higher rate than the stated rate (10%). We shall select 12%, and the following calculation demonstrates how the effective rate of interest implicit in a serial-bond issue can be determined:

General formula:

$$\text{Proceeds of bond (present value [PV])} = \begin{array}{c} \text{PV of Group-A cash flows} \\ + \\ \text{PV of Group-B cash flows} \\ + \\ \text{PV of Group-C cash flows} \end{array}$$

Application:

Group A
PV of $250,000 due in 2 years +
PV of 2 ordinary annuities of $25,000
+
Group B
PV of $250,000 due in 3 years +
PV of 3 ordinary annuities of $25,000
+
Group C
PV of $500,000 due in 4 years +
PV of 4 ordinary annuities of $50,000

Using a 12% effective interest rate:

Price of Bonds	Present Value at 12%
	Group A
$949,200 = (.79719 × $250,000) + (1.69005 × $25,000)	

$$\text{Group B}$$
$$+ (.71178 \times \$250,000) + (2.40183 \times \$25,000)$$
$$\text{Group C}$$
$$+ (.63552 \times \$500,000) + (3.03735 \times \$50,000)$$

Accumulating:

$$\text{Group A}$$
$$\$949,200 = \$199,298 + \$42,251$$
$$\text{Group B}$$
$$+ \$177,945 + \$60,046$$
$$\text{Group C}$$
$$+ \$317,760 + \$151,868$$

$$\$949,200 \approx \$949,168 \text{ (Approximate equality; therefore the 12\%}$$
$$\text{interest rate is a reasonable approximation.}$$

Note: The annuity amounts are merely the interest payments required under the terms of the bond. $\$250,000 \times .10 = \$25,000$; $\$500,000 \times .10 = \$50,000$.

Since these two amounts are virtually equal, we select 12% as an adequate approximation of the effective rate of interest. If such an approximation does not result from applying the test rate of interest, then another rate is selected for testing. This process continues until a rate is found that satisfactorily equates the present and future values of the cash flows.

In practice, computer routines are used to search for and find the appropriate discount rate. Computers also develop amortization tables assisting further in properly accounting for the bonds payable. Neverthe-

less, you need a firm understanding of the logic and techniques underlying the determination of implicit effective rates in such circumstances.

Once the effective interest rate is established (in this case, 12%), we are prepared to compute and recognize interest expense and amortize the premium or discount on the bonds. The amortization table in Exhibit 15–11 facilitates this process and illustrates how the serial maturities affect interest-expense recognition.

The entries to be made at December 31 of each

EXHIBIT 15–11
Serial Bonds Amortization Table

Date	(1) Interest Expense	(2) Cash Paid	(3) Discount Amortization	(4) Par Value Outstanding	(5) Unamortized Discount	(6) Carrying Value
Jan. 1, 1983	—	—	—	$1,000,000	$50,800	$949,200
Dec. 31, 1983	$113,904	$100,000	$13,904	1,000,000	36,896	963,104
Dec. 31, 1984	115,572	100,000	15,572	750,000	21,324	728,676
Dec. 31, 1985	87,441	75,000	12,441	500,000	8,883	491,117
Dec. 31, 1986	58,883*	50,000	8,883	-0-	-0-	-0-
	$375,800	$325,000	$50,800			

(1) (Previous year column 6) × 12%
(2) (Outstanding par value) × 10%
(3) (Column 1) − (Column 2)
(4) Outstanding par value
(5) (Previous year Column 5) − (Current year Column 3)
(6) (Column 4) − (Column 5)

*Adjusted for rounding difference.

year are based on the table in Exhibit 15–11.

Jan. 1, 1983	Cash	949,200	
	Discount on Bonds Payable	50,800	
	Bonds Payable		1,000,000
	(To record issuance of bonds.)		
Dec. 31, 1983	Interest Expense	113,904	
	Discount on Bonds Payable		13,904
	Cash		100,000
	(To pay interest and amortize discount.)		
Dec. 31, 1984	Interest Expense	115,572	
	Discount on Bonds Payable		15,572
	Cash		100,000
	(To pay interest and amortize discount.)		
	Bonds Payable	250,000	
	Cash		250,000
	(To retire Group-A serial bonds.)		
Dec. 31, 1985	Interest Expense	87,441	
	Discount on Bonds Payable		12,441
	Cash		75,000
	(To pay interest and amortize discount.)		
	Bonds Payable	250,000	
	Cash		250,000
	(To retire Group-B bonds.)		
Dec. 31, 1986	Interest Expense	58,883	
	Discount on Bonds Payable		8,883
	Cash		50,000
	(To pay interest and amortize discount.)		
	Bonds Payable	500,000	
	Cash		500,000
	(To retire Group-C serial bonds.)		

Discount is amortized over the life of the serial bonds in much the same manner as is the case for term bonds. That is, a constant rate of interest (12%) is recognized on the carrying value of the liability.

QUESTIONS

15–1   What are the principal characteristics that distinguish between long-term debt and equity financing?

15–2   Why is it usually desirable for firms to issue large numbers of relatively small long-term debt instruments?

15–3 Define and describe the following types of bonds:
  [a] serial bonds
  [b] term bonds
  [c] registered bonds
  [d] coupon bonds

15–4 What are "issue costs" that are associated with a bond issue? How should such costs be accounted for throughout the term of the bond issue?

15–5 What factors may cause the price of a bond to differ from its face amount at the date of sale?

15–6 If a company has several bond issues outstanding, each with different interest rates, due dates, and other provisions, how might the company disclose this information in the financial statements without burdening the balance sheet with undue detail?

15–7 How should a difference between the carrying amount of debt and the reacquisition price of the debt be recorded when the liability is extinguished at the following times?
  [a] Earlier than its scheduled maturity.
  [b] At the time of its maturity.

15–8 How are discounts and premiums on bonds payable accounted for at the following times?
  [a] At issuance.
  [b] During the term of the debt.
  [c] At the time of the debt retirement.

15–9 How is the amount of the discount or premium computed for a bond issue?

15–10 Describe two methods of amortizing premiums or discounts on bonds payable. Which method is preferable? Why?

15–11 The treasurer of Young Company proposes that treasury bonds be recorded as assets in the investments section of the balance sheet. Do you agree? Why or why not?

15–12 Describe two different types of securities representing a combination of debt and equity instruments. How does financial accounting and reporting differ for each type?

15–13 What is the primary reason for not recognizing a separate value for the equity element in a convertible bond at the time of issuance?

15–14 How is the equity element valued in the case of debt issued with detachable warrants?

15–15 (Appendix A) What characteristics must a debt restructuring possess before it can be considered a troubled-debt restructuring?

15–16 (Appendix A) What are the four types of troubled-debt restructurings?

15–17 (Appendix A) What disclosures should be made in the financial statements about a troubled-debt restructuring?

15–18 (Appendix A) *Statement of Financial Accounting Standards No. 15, "Accounting for Troubled Debt Restructurings,"* should bring accounting for common events by debtors and creditors closer together. Discuss the symmetry of accounting by debtors and creditors for the same transaction and discuss how differences might arise.

15–19 (Appendix B) Briefly describe the accounting procedures employed for serial bonds.

CASES

C15–1 This case consists of two independent parts.

  Part 1. The effective interest method is appropriate for amortizing a premium or discount on issuance of bonds.

Instructions

[a] Describe the effective interest method of amortization and how it compares with the straight-line method of amortization.

[b] How is amortization computed using the effective interest method? How do the results of the effective interest method differ from those computed under the straight-line method, and why?

  Part 2. Gains or losses from the early extinguishment of debt that is refunded can theoretically be accounted for in three ways:
[1] Amortized over remaining life of old debt.
[2] Amortized over the life of the new debt issue.
[3] Recognized in the period of extinguishment.

Instructions

[a] Provide supporting arguments for each of the three methods.

[b] Which method is generally accepted, and how should the appropriate amount of gain or loss be recorded in a company's financial statements?

(AICPA adapted)

C15–2 Norton Company recently issued $1,000,000 face value, 5%, 30-year subordinated debentures at 97. The debentures are redeemable at 103 on demand by the issuer and at any date on 30 days' notice 10 years after the issue. The debentures are convertible into $10 par value common stock of the company at the conversion price of $12.50 per share for each $500 or multiple thereof of the principal amount of the debentures.

Instructions

[a] Explain how the conversion feature of convertible debt is valuable to (1) the issuer and (2) the purchaser.

[b] Management of Norton Company has suggested that in recording the issuance of the debentures, a portion of the proceeds should be assigned to the conversion feature.

　[1] What are the arguments for according separate accounting recognition to the conversion feature of the debentures?

　[2] What are the arguments in favor of accounting for the convertible debentures as a single element?

[c] Assume that no value is assigned to the conversion feature upon issue of the debentures. Assume further that five years after issue, debentures with a face value of $100,000 and book value of $97,500 are tendered for conversion on an interest payment date when the market price of the debentures is 104 and the common stock is selling at $14 per share. The company records the conversion as follows:

Bonds Payable	100,000	
Bond Discount		2,500
Common Stock		80,000
Premium on Common Stock		17,500

Discuss the propriety of the above accounting treatment.

(AICPA adapted)

C15–3 Incurring long-term debt with an arrangement whereby lenders receive an option to buy common stock during all or a portion of the time the debt is outstanding is a frequently used corporate financing practice. In some situations the result is achieved through the issuance of convertible bonds; in others the debt instruments and the warrants to buy stock are separate.

Instructions

[a] Describe the differences that exist in current accounting for original proceeds of the issuance of convertible bonds and of debt instruments with separate warrants to purchase common stock.

[b] Discuss the rationale for the differences described in [a].

[c] Summarize the arguments which have been presented for the alternative accounting treatment.

(AICPA adapted)

C15–4 One way for a corporation to accomplish long-term financing is through the issuance of long-term debt instruments in the form of bonds.

Instructions

[a] Describe how to account for the proceeds from bonds issued with detachable stock-purchase warrants.

[b] Contrast a serial bond with a term (straight) bond.

[c] For a five-year term bond issued at a premium, why would the amortization in the first year of the life of the bond differ using the effective interest method of amortization instead of the straight-line method? Indicate whether the amount of amortization in the first year of the life of the bond would be higher or lower using the effective interest method instead of the straight-line method.

[d] When a bond issue is sold between interest dates at a discount, what journal entry is made and how is the subsequent amortization of the discount affected? Include in your discussion an explanation of how the amounts of each debit and credit are determined.

[e] Describe how to account for and classify the gain or loss from the reacquisition of a long-term bond before its maturity.

(AICPA adapted)

C15–5 The equityholders of a business entity usually include both creditors and owners. These two classes of equityholders share some characteristics, and sometimes it is difficult to make a clear-cut distinction between them. Examples of this problem include (1) convertible debt and (2) debt issued with stock-purchase warrants. While both examples represent debts of a corporation, there is a question as to whether there is an ownership interest in each case which requires accounting recognition.

Instructions

[a] Define convertible debt and debt issued with stock-purchase warrants.

[b] Discuss the similarities and differences of convertible debt and debt issued with stock-purchase warrants.

[c] Describe the alternative accounting treatments for

the proceeds from convertible debt. Explain which treatment is preferable.

[d] Describe the alternative accounting treatments for the proceeds from debt issued with stock-purchase warrants. Explain which treatment is preferable.

(AICPA adapted)

C15–6 Starman Farms, Inc., suffered a crop failure during the summer of 1985. As the end of their reporting year nears, the controller of Starman is searching for ways to increase reported earnings. Among other alternatives, the controller is considering refinancing the company's long-term borrowing. Starman issued $500,000 of 6% notes payable to a bank at 100 several years ago when interest rates were much lower. The bank has since approached Starman with the following proposal. The old note matures at December 31, 2005.

In exchange for the $500,000 note now owed, the bank will allow Starman to issue a new note for only $475,000 maturing in 20 years at the current rate of 20%. Under each alternative, interest is paid annually on the liability.

Instructions

[a] Prepare a *pro forma* journal entry that would be made if Starman accepts the bank's proposal.

[b] Describe the theoretical support for this treatment. Also, comment on any problems you see in this treatment.

[c] Suggest a way to overcome the problem(s) discussed in [b]. Do not limit your discussion to contemporary generally accepted accounting principles.

[d] Comment on the controller's decision. Should Starman refinance the debt? Consider present value concepts in your answer, but do not attempt any present-value calculations.

C15–7 The president of Tiny Tim Toy Company has decided to expand the manufacturing capacity of his company in order to meet increased demand for certain low-cost toys. Bob Kratchit, vice-president for production, has located two similar plant sites on which comparable industrial buildings already exist. Bob has approached the president to decide which site should be selected.

The first site could be purchased for $200,000. The toy company's banker, E. Scrooge, indicates that an 80% loan of $160,000 for 20 years could be arranged at an interest rate of 15% to allow Tiny to buy the facility. Equal annual payments of $25,562 will be made to the bank under the terms of the proposed loan. The second site is available only through a long-term lease which requires a 20-year term with payments of $25,000 at the end of each year.

In evaluating the two alternatives, Mr. Kratchit points out that under the lease, no down payment is required, the annual payments are virtually equal, and best of all, the company will not be required to record any liability for the lease on the financial statements of the company. In this manner the debt to equity and return on assets ratios will be maintained. Under the purchase arrangement, however, both ratios mentioned above will become weaker.

Instructions

[a] If you were president of Tiny Tim Toy Company, would you accept Mr. Kratchit's advice? If not, what additional information would you request?

[b] Discuss the propriety of not recording the lease as a liability. Do not consider current authoritative pronouncements in your answer. Rather, discuss the conceptual meaning and characteristics of liabilities in general.

C15–8 On January 1, 1984, Dover Corporation issued $1,106,775 in 20-year bonds which have a maturity value of $1,000,000 and pay interest semiannually on January 1 and July 1. Bond issue costs were not material in amount. The following three presentations of the long-term liability section of the balance sheet might be used for these bonds at the issue date:

[1] Bonds payable (maturing Jan. 1, 2004)		$1,000,000
Unamortized premium on bonds payable		106,775
Total bond liability		$1,106,775
[2] Bonds payable, principal (face value $1,000,000, maturing Jan. 1, 2004)		$ 252,572*
Bonds payable, interest (semiannual payment $40,000)		854,203**
Total bond liability		$1,106,775
[3] Bonds payable, principal (maturing Jan. 1, 2004)		$1,000,000
Bonds payable, interest ($40,000 per period for 40 periods)		1,600,000
Total bond liability		$2,600,000

*The present value of $1,000,000 due at the end of 40 (six-month) periods at the yield rate of 3½% per period.
**The present value of $40,000 per period for 40 (six-month) periods at the yield rate of 3½% per period.

Instructions

[a] Discuss the conceptual merit(s) of each of the date-of-issue balance sheet presentations shown above

for these bonds.

[b] Explain why investors would pay $1,106,775 for bonds with a maturity value of only $1,000,000.

[c] Assuming that a discount rate is needed to compute the carrying value of the obligations arising from a bond issue at any date during the life of the bonds, discuss the conceptual merit(s) of using for this purpose:

[1] The coupon or nominal rate.

[2] The effective or yield rate at date of issue.

[d] If the obligations arising from these bonds are to be carried at their present value, computed by means of the current market rate of interest, how would the bond valuation at dates subsequent to the date of issue be affected by an increase or a decrease in the market rate of interest?

(AICPA adapted)

C15–9 (Appendix A) While discussing troubled-debt restructurings, a CPA commented: "The determination of whether or not a debt restructuring is a troubled-debt restructuring is simplified because the facts of any restructuring clearly indicate what type of transaction has occurred. Little judgment is required, other than the possible determination of fair market value of assets or equity interests transferred."

Instructions

Describe other areas, if any, requiring interpretation and judgment in identifying and accounting for debt restructurings.

EXERCISES

E15–1 Edwards, Inc., issued $100,000 of 20-year, 10% term bonds on January 1, 1985, at 101. Interest is payable semiannually on June 30 and December 31.

Instructions

Prepare general journal entries to record:

[a] The issuance of the bonds.

[b] The payment of the interest for the first two six-month periods.

[c] The amortization of premium for the year. (For simplicity, use the straight-line method of premium amortization.)

E15–2 Nuttall, Inc., called an outstanding bond issue seven years before its maturity date. At the time the bonds were called, they had a carrying value of $55,000. Furthermore, Nuttall was required to pay $72,000 to reacquire the bonds.

Instructions

[a] What amount of gain or loss, if any, should Nuttall report during the year the call provision was exercised?

[b] How should the gain or loss in [a] be classified?

E15–3 Adled Corporation reports long-term debt of $1,000,000, less unamortized discount of $50,000 at December 31, 1984. While the bonds bear a stated interest rate of 10%, they were issued at an effective yield of 12%. Interest is payable on January 1 of each year. On June 30, 1985, Adled retires the bonds for 103 plus accrued interest. Adled amortizes bond discount by the effective interest method.

Instructions

[a] What gain or loss, if any, should Adled report from the bond retirement on its 1985 income statement?

[b] How should this gain or loss be classified?

E15–4 Alfonzo Company sold 1,000, $100 par value bonds, that had a coupon rate of interest of 14% when the market rate of interest was 16%. The bonds mature 10 years from their date of issuance.

Instructions

[a] Compute the price at which the bonds sold if interest is paid annually, and identify any premium or discount to be recognized.

[b] Compute the price at which the bonds sold if interest is paid semiannually, and identify any premium or discount to be recognized.

E15–5 Toller Company sold 11% bonds at a time when the market rate of interest for comparable securities was 10%. The company sold 10,000, $1,000 par value bonds. The bonds pay interest semiannually and mature 20 years from the date they were issued.

Instructions

[a] Compute the price at which the bonds sold.

[b] Prepare the general journal entry to record the sale of the bonds.

E15–6 Watson Enterprises sold 100, $1,000 par value bonds that bear interest at 12%, at a price to yield an effective 16%. Interest is paid annually on the bonds, which mature eight years from their date of issuance.

Instructions

[a] Compute the issue price of the bonds.

[b] Prepare the general journal entry to record the sale of the bonds.

[c] Determine interest expense and the discount or premium amortization for the first year of the bond issue by the effective interest method.

[d] Determine interest expense and the discount or premium amortization for the first year of the bond issue by the straight-line method.

E15–7 Worthington, Inc., issued 10,000, $100 par value bonds that bear interest at 12% when bonds of comparable quality were paying only 10% interest. Worthington's bonds pay interest semiannually and mature 10 years from their date of issuance.

Instructions

[a] Determine the price at which the bonds sold.

[b] Compute interest expense and the amortization of premium or discount for the first two six-month periods under both the effective interest and straight-line methods.

E15–8 Chatsworth, Inc., issued $1,000,000, 12%, 20-year bonds at 102 plus accrued interest on February 1, 1984. The bonds are dated January 1, 1984, and pay interest semiannually on June 30 and December 31. The premium is to be amortized by the straight-line method over the period during which the bonds are outstanding. Bond issue costs totaled $50,000.

Instructions

Prepare all general journal entries for the bonds for 1984, assuming that amortizations are recorded annually on December 31, the end of the company's financial reporting period.

E15–9 Elliott Manufacturing Company had the following bonds outstanding at December 31, 1984:

Bonds payable	$100,000
Less: Discount	(8,000)
	$ 92,000

The bond discount was being amortized over the 10-year life of the bonds (8 years remaining after December 31, 1984) by the straight-line method.

At June 30, 1985 (a semiannual interest payment date), the company retired $60,000 of the bonds at 101% of par value.

Instructions

[a] Determine the appropriate carrying value of the bonds at June 30, 1985.

[b] Prepare the general journal entry to record the retirement of the bonds at June 30, 1985.

[c] Prepare the balance sheet presentation of the remaining bonds at December 31, 1985.

E15–10 On July 1, 1982, Sanderson Company issued 1000, $1,000 par value bonds at 99. The bonds pay interest annually on June 30, at 13% and mature eight years from their date of issuance. Discount is amortized by the straight-line method.

On June 30, 1985, the company retired the bonds at 102 after interest had been paid.

Instructions

Prepare the entries to record the final interest payment and the retirement of the bonds. Provide computations for each entry.

E15–11 Carlson Company issued $100,000 par value, 12% bonds on January 1, 1985. The bonds mature in 10 years and pay interest semiannually on June 30 and December 31. The bonds were sold for $89,406, which yields an effective annual interest rate of 14%.

Instructions

[a] Determine the amount of interest expense to be recognized in 1985 using the effective interest method of discount amortization.

[b] What amount of the interest expense is represented by the amortization of the discount?

E15–12 On July 1, 1984, Winston Corporation issued $2,000,000 of 7% bonds payable in 10 years. The bonds pay interest semiannually. The bonds include detachable warrants giving the bondholder the right to purchase for $30 one share of $1 par value common stock at any time during the next 10 years. The bonds and warrants were sold for $2,000,000. The value of the warrants at the time of issuance was $100,000. No valuation of the bonds, separate from the warrants, is available.

Instructions

[a] Prepare in general journal form the entry to record the issuance of the bonds.

[b] Explain the basis of your valuation of the warrants.

(AICPA adapted)

E15–13 Haller Corporation issued 100 bonds, each with a $1,000 face amount, on May 31, 1985. The bonds are due in 10 years and pay interest annually at 10%. A detachable stock-purchase warrant was attached to each bond. Each bond with the detachable warrant sold at 102. Immediately after the issuance, the stock-purchase warrants were traded in the market at $40 while the market value of the bonds (without the warrants) was 101.

Instructions

Prepare the entry to record the issuance of the bonds and detachable stock-purchase warrants.

E15–14 Thomas Corporation issued 100, $1,000 par value bonds that pay 12% interest on par value at a price to yield 10%. Each bond is convertible to 10 shares of Thomas Corporation common stock on any interest-payment date. Interest is paid semiannually on January 1 and July 1, and the bonds mature 10 years from the date of issuance.

Instructions

[a] Prepare the general journal entry to record the issuance of the bonds.
[b] Explain briefly your treatment of the equity element included in the bond issue.

E15–15 Sunday Corporation sold a $1,000,000 20-year, 8% bond issue for $1,030,000. Each $1,000 bond has a detachable warrant that permits the purchase of one share of the corporation's common stock for $30. The stock has a par value of $25 per share. Immediately after the sale of the bonds, the corporation's securities had the following market values:

8% bond without warrants	$1,020
Warrants	10
Common stock	28

Instructions

What entry should the corporation make to record the sale of the bonds?

E15–16 Harbor Dredging, Inc., issued $2,000,000 of $1,000 face amount, 7% bonds on January 1, 1985, for $1,920,000. Two detachable stock-purchase warrants were attached to each $1,000 bond. Each warrant conveys the right to purchase one share of $100 par value common stock at $110 per share before July 1, 1985.

When the bonds were issued, Harbor Dredging's common stock was selling exactly at par and the market value of the warrants was $15 each.

Instructions

Prepare the entry that Harbor Dredging should make at the date the bonds were issued.

E15–17 On January 1, 1985, Mary Kay Company issued $100,000 of 10% bonds, due December 31, 2004 (20 years). Interest is to be paid annually on December 31. At the time the bonds were issued, the market rate of interest was 8%.

Instructions

[a] Calculate and record the proceeds of the bond issue.
[b] Prepare a schedule to calculate the interest expense and amortization of the premium or discount for the first four years (through December 31, 1988) using the effective interest method.
[c] Prepare the entry to retire the bonds on January 1, 1989, at 101.

E15–18 Brazos, Inc., reports the following liability on its December 31, 1984, balance sheet:

Bonds payable (9%, due Dec. 31, 1993)	$400,000
Premium on bonds	10,800
	$410,800

The bonds were issued on December 31, 1983, at 103, with interest payable on June 30 and December 31 of each year. On March 1, 1985, Brazos retired $200,000 of the bonds at 98 plus accrued interest.

Instructions

[a] Is Brazos amortizing the premium by the effective interest or the straight-line method?
[b] Prepare the general journal entry to record the retirement of the bonds on March 1, 1985, including the payment of interest for the period January 1 through March 1, 1985.

(AICPA adapted)

E15–19 (Appendix A) Sorry Company is experiencing financial difficulty and is renegotiating debt restructurings with its creditors to relieve its financial stress. Sorry has a $125,000 note payable to First State Bank. The bank is considering two alternatives:

Alternative 1. Acceptance of land owned by Sorry Company, valued at $100,000 and carried on the books of Sorry at its historical cost of $70,000.

Alternative 2. Acceptance of an equity interest in Sorry Company in the form of 11,000 shares of common stock valued at $10 per share. (The common stock has an $8 par value.)

Instructions

Prepare the general journal entry that Sorry Company would make under each alternative. Identify any extraordinary items that would be recognized.

E15–20 (Appendix A) Due to adverse economic circumstances and poor management, Stress, Inc., has negotiated a restructuring of its $85,000 note payable to Normal Bank. Normal Bank has agreed to reduce the face value of the note from $85,000 to $60,000, reduce the interest rate from 14% to 10%, and extend the due date one year from the date of restructuring. The restructuring will occur on August 31, 1984, the last day of Stress, Inc.'s annual reporting period. There is no unpaid interest on the restructured loan at this time.

Instructions

[a] Prepare the general journal entry to record the restructuring on August 31, 1984. Include computations to support your figures.

[b] Prepare the general journal entry one year later to record the final payment of the note, assuming that no interest was paid during the year.

PROBLEMS

P15–1 On January 1, 1981, Wade Company issued $1,000,000 of 7% bonds due to mature in 15 years. Interest was due and payable annually on January 1. The bonds were sold to yield 8%.

Instructions

[a] Calculate the proceeds at the time of issuance.

[b] Prepare the amortization schedule for the years ended December 31, 1981 through 1984 using the effective interest method.

[c] On January 2, 1985, Wade Company purchased $250,000 of the bonds on the open market. At that time the bonds were selling at a price to yield 10%. Prepare a journal entry to record the transaction. Support your entry by computations.

P15–2 Radich Company issued bonds on October 1, 1985. The bonds have a face value of $1,000,000 and are due in 20 years. The bonds were sold to yield 16%, although the stated interest rate was 16½%. Interest is payable semiannually on June 30 and December 31.

Instructions

[a] Determine the issue price of the bonds on July 1, 1985.

[b] Comment on the relative values of each element of the future cash flow.

[c] Determine the amount of interest expense and premium or discount amortization that Radich will recognize at each of the first two interest-payment dates, assuming the effective interest method is used.

P15–3 Mary's Marvelous Melodies, a chain of retail stores that sell musical instruments, issued 12% bonds with a face value of $1,000,000 on January 1, 1985.

Interest is payable quarterly on March 31, June 30, September 30, and December 31 of each year. The bonds mature on December 31, 1994, and were sold to yield a rate of 16% annually. Issue costs of $25,000 were incurred at the time of issuance.

Instructions

[a] Prepare a schedule to determine the net amount received by Mary's from the issuance of the bonds.

[b] Prepare the general journal entries to record the issuance of the bonds, including the payment of the issue costs.

[c] Prepare the long-term liability and any other necessary portions of the balance sheet at the date of issuance to reflect the above information.

P15–4 Blazer Company issued 1,000, $1,000 par value bonds at a price to yield an effective rate of 12%. The bonds are dated May 1, 1984, and pay 11% interest annually on April 30. The bonds mature on April 30, 1989.

Instructions

[a] Prepare an amortization table showing the amount of interest expense and amortization of the discount or premium for each year of the bond issue by the effective interest method.

[b] Prepare an amortization table showing the amount of interest expense and the amortization of the discount or premium for each year of the bond issue by the straight-line method.

[c] Explain why the amortization of the discount or premium by the straight-line method exceeds that by the effective interest method in some years but not in other years.

P15–5 Campball Stereo Company issued 10%, $3,000,000 face value bonds on October 1, 1982. Campball received $3,250,000, plus accrued interest. Interest is payable twice a year on January 1 and July 1. On December 31, 1984, the book value of the bonds, including the unamortized premium, was $3,142,000. On March 1, 1985, Campball purchased the bonds on the open market at 97 plus accrued interest. Campball used the straight-line method of premium amortization since the results did not differ materially from the effective interest method.

Instructions

Prepare general journal entries to record the following:

[a] The issuance of the bonds.
[b] Any adjusting entry necessary at December 31, 1982.
[c] Any entries necessary during 1985.

P15–6 Chapman, Inc., issued $4,000,000 of bonds payable maturing in 20 years and bearing interest at a stated rate of 14%. The interest is payable semiannually and each bond includes a detachable warrant enabling the holder to purchase one share of $50 par

Date	Cash Interest Paid	Interest Expense Recognized	Amortization	Carrying Value of Bonds
July 1, 1983	—	—	—	$846,611
Dec. 31, 1983	$36,000	$33,864	$2,136	844,475
June 30, 1984	36,000	33,779	2,221	842,254
Dec. 31, 1984	36,000	33,690	2,310	839,944

value common stock at par at any time prior to 1990. The bonds were dated and issued on January 1, 1985, for $4,050,000. The total market value of the warrants immediately after issuance was $100,000, and each bond (without the warrant) sold at 99.

Instructions

[a] Prepare the journal entry necessary to record the issuance of these securities at January 1, 1985.
[b] How, if at all, would your answer differ if the bonds were convertible rather than attached to a stock warrant? Assume each bond is convertible into 20 shares of stock with no additional charge for conversion.

P15–7 Watson issued bonds as follows:

Two thousand $1,000 par value bonds.
Ten percent stated annual interest, payable on Feb. 28 (or 29) and Aug. 31 of each year.

Selling price, 103% of par value (plus accrued interest).
Date of bonds, March 1, 1983.
Date of sale, May 1, 1983.
Due date of bonds, Feb. 28, 1993.

The company will amortize (by the straight-line method) any premium or discount at year-end (December 31) for the entire year. (Amortization is rounded to the nearest dollar.) No reversing entries are made on January 1.

Instructions

[a] Prepare all general journal entries required for the years 1983 and 1984.
[b] Prepare the balance sheet and income statement presentations of the bond and interest expense accounts for 1983 and 1984.

P15–8 A company issued $800,000 par value bonds on July 1, 1983. The bonds mature eight years from the date of issuance and pay interest semiannually on December 31 and June 30. Issue costs of the bonds were $12,000 and are amortized by the straight-line method over the life of the bond issue.

The following partial amortization table is used to account for the bonds and the related interest:

The bonds are callable at 110 on any interest payment date after December 31, 1984.

Instructions

[a] Determine the nominal or stated interest rate on the bond issue.
[b] Determine the effective (annual) interest rate on the bond issue.
[c] Prepare all journal entries required for 1983 and 1984 concerning the bond issue.
[d] Prepare the general journal entries to record the June 30, 1985, interest payment and the reacquisition of $400,000 of the bonds at that date.

P15–9 Two comparable companies issued bonds on January 1, 1984, as described below:

Sanders Company. Issued $1,000,000, 10% bonds, at 102. Each $1,000 bond is convertible into

100 shares of the company's $5 par value common stock on any interest payment date after January 1, 1985. Immediately after the sale, the bonds were selling at 102 and the common stock at $11.

Hammer Company. Issued $1,000,000, 10% bonds, at 103. Each $1,000 bond is accompanied by two detachable warrants to purchase one share each of the company's common stock at $100 per share. Immediately after the sale, the bonds were selling at 102, the warrants at $10, and the common stock at $112.

Instructions

For each company, complete the following:
[a] Prepare the general journal entry to record the sale of the bonds.
[b] Explain your treatment of the equity portion of the hybrid security that was recorded in [a].
[c] Prepare the relevant portion(s) of the balance sheet immediately following the sale of the bonds.

P15–10 On July 1, 1984, General Manufacturing Company sold $2,500,000 of bonds dated July 1, 1984, paying interest at 10% and issued to yield 12%. Bond issue costs totaled $28,000.

The bonds mature on June 30, 1994. They pay interest annually at June 30. The company's policy is to amortize bond premium and discount by the effective interest method and bond issue costs by the straight-line method on a monthly basis.

Instructions

[a] Compute the price at which the bonds sold.
[b] Prepare an amortization table for the first four years of the bond issue.
[c] Prepare all general journal entries to record bond-related events for 1984 and 1985. (No reversing entries are made on January 1.)
[d] Prepare the financial-statement presentation of all bond-related items for the company's 1984 and 1985 financial statements. (General's accounting period ends on December 31.)

P15–11 Your client, Wheaton Manufacturing, Inc., is planning to issue new bonds at a lower interest rate in order to extinguish bonds currently outstanding. You have been asked to assist with some calculations regarding these transactions.

After reviewing the data, you realize that the decision to redeem bonds and issue new ones can be viewed as a capital-budgeting decision. When using capital-budgeting techniques, Wheaton has adopted the following cutoff points: maximum payback period

is eight years, and minimum desired rate of return is 16%.

The following data relate to the original (outstanding) bonds and the new bonds to be issued:

	Original Bond Issue	New Bond Issue
Face value	$20,000,000	$20,000,000
Coupon rate	6%	5%
Call premium	4%	4½%
Expired life	5 years	—
Remaining life to maturity	15 years	15 years
Issued at	98½	100
Total issue costs	$120,000	$135,000

The new issue is to be sold, then one month later the original issue is to be redeemed. The overlapping month's interest on the original issue is *not* to be considered a miscellaneous cost of reacquisition.

All discounts and issue cost are amortized on a straight-line basis because that method is not materially different from the effective interest method of amortization. Interest is paid annually. All cash flows are assumed to occur at year-end. The federal income tax rate is 40%.

Instructions

[a] Compute Wheaton's accounting gain or loss on the early extinguishment of the original (outstanding) bonds.
[b] Compute the net cash investment based on the difference between the net cash outflow to redeem the original issue and the amount raised by the new issue.
[c] Compute the net cash benefit per year based on the difference between the annual net cash outlay required on the original issue and that required on the new issue.
[d] Independent of your answers to [b] and [c], assume that the net cash investment was $550,000 and that the net cash benefit per year was $120,000. Evaluate this "investment" by using the following capital-budgeting methods: (1) payback, and (2) present value.

(AICPA adapted)

P15–12 (Appendix A) In connection with a debt restructuring on December 31, 1985, John Blue Corporation, experiencing cash flow problems stemming from poor operating results, transferred real estate to the First International Bank of Hartsville in full settlement of a debt of $1,700,000. However, the real estate was carried on the books of John Blue Corporation at $1,200,000. The current fair market value for similar real estate is $1,350,000.

Instructions

[a] Is the restructuring a troubled-debt restructuring? Why?

[b] Should the debtor recognize a gain or loss on the transfer of the real estate? If your answer is yes, indicate the amount and how it would be presented in the income statement.

[c] Should the debtor recognize a gain or loss in the restructuring? If your answer is yes, indicate the amount and how it would be treated in the income statement.

[d] What is the proper accounting treatment of this debt restructuring by the creditor?

P15–13 (Appendix A) On December 31, 1983, a $100,000 note is restructured by modifying the terms of the debt. The modifications, which are due to debtor financial difficulties, include the following:

[1] Forgiving $10,000 of principal and $6,969 of accrued interest.

[2] Extending the maturity date by five years.

[3] Reducing the interest rate from 10% to 6%.

Interest at 6% is to be paid annually on the new principal amount under the new terms. Therefore, the aggregate future cash payments under the new term total $117,000. This total represents $90,000 of principal and $27,000 of interest (6% × $90,000 × 5).

Instructions

[a] Is the restructuring a troubled-debt restructuring? Why?

[b] Will interest expense be recognized by the debtor in the future? If so, what is the effective interest rate under the new terms?

[c] A partial amortization schedule is provided below.

Complete the schedule for the restructured debt presented in this case.

[d] How should the debtor record the payment made on December 31, 1984?

[e] How should the creditor record the payment made on December 31, 1984?

P15–14 (Appendix B) On December 31, 1977, Rubin Company issued 1,000,000 of 8% serial bonds when the market rate was 10%. The bonds pay interest annually and will be retired according to the following schedule:

12/31/85	$ 400,000
12/31/86	300,000
12/31/87	200,000
12/31/88	100,000
Total	$1,000,000

On December 31, 1985, Rubin Company had excess cash and decided to retire the $100,000 of the bonds due December 31, 1988, on the open market. At that time the market interest rate was 8% per annum. In accordance with generally accepted accounting principles, Rubin uses the effective interest method.

Instructions

Answer the following questions and provide supporting computations. Formal schedules are *not* necessary unless otherwise noted.

[a] Calculate the proceeds from the issuance.

[b] Prepare an amortization schedule for 1978 and 1979.

[c] Show the balance sheet presentation for the bonds at December 31, 1978 and 1979.

[d] How much did it cost to buy back the December 31, 1988, bonds at December 31, 1985?

[e] What was the gain or loss on the retirement of the December 31, 1988, bonds?

Date	(.06 × 90,000) Stated Interest Payment	Principal Payment	Reported Effective Interest Expense	Balance
12/31/83				$106,969
12/31/84	$5,400			
12/31/85	5,400			
12/31/86	5,400			
12/31/87	5,400			
12/31/88	5,400			

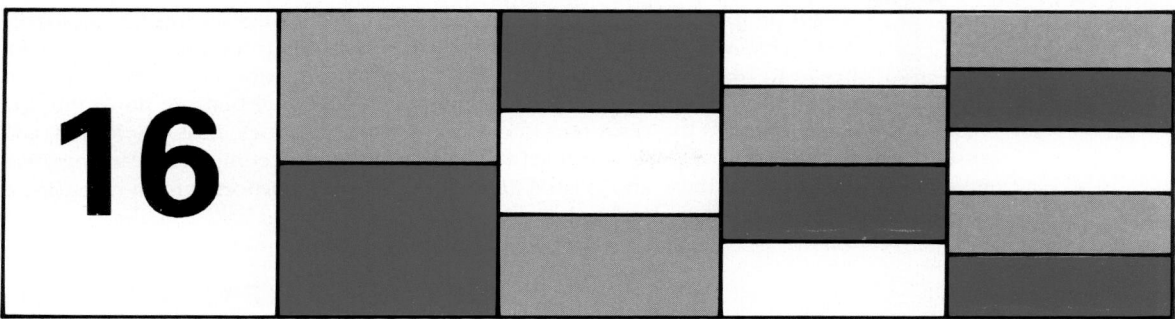

16

STOCKHOLDERS' EQUITY: CORPORATE FORMATION AND CONTRIBUTED CAPITAL

Objectives

To discuss characteristics, advantages, and disadvantages of the corporate form of business.

To explain various stockholders' rights and types of stockholders' equity.

To identify the characteristics of common and preferred stock.

To describe and illustrate acceptable accounting and reporting practices for the issuance of capital stock for both cash and noncash consideration.

To describe and illustrate acceptable accounting and reporting practices for the issuance of capital stock through subscription.

To describe and illustrate the cost and par value methods of accounting for treasury stock.

To describe and illustrate acceptable accounting and reporting practices for the retirement of capital stock and treasury stock.

To describe and illustrate acceptable accounting and reporting practices for property and treasury stock donations.

T he substantial growth in the corporate form of business during the industrial revolution was, in part, a response to the demands of commerce. As capital began to be substituted for labor and as mass production economies replaced individual craft shops, the need for larger accumulations of capital became more intense. Few individuals possessed the resources necessary to build factories, hire employees, and sustain operations until an adequate level of profitability and accumulated earnings was generated. As a result of these and related factors, the modern corporate form of business was developed, expanded, and refined.

THE CORPORATE ENVIRONMENT

Corporations offer several important advantages over other forms of business, such as sole proprietorships and partnerships. For example, the corporate organization: (1) facilitates the accumulation of large amounts of capital; (2) provides for economies of scale in production due to the potential large size of corporate organizations; and (3) contributes to a capital market in which resources are easily allocated to more efficient producers. Other characteristics of corporations that are often viewed as advantages include **limited liability,** in that stockholders have no personal liability for the debts of the corporation and risk only their capital investments; and **unlimited life of the corporation,** in that the death of a stockholder does not cause the termination of the corporation, as in the case of the death of a partner in a partnership.

Unfortunately, the advantages of limited liability and unlimited life do not come without some cost to the stockholder. The cost is in the form of **double taxation.** A corporation, unlike a partnership or a sole proprietorship, is subject to taxation on net income. Furthermore, individual stockholders are subject to taxation on the distributions of net income as dividends. Therefore, income is taxed at the corporate level and again at the individual level.

The stockholders, who own the corporation, often are not involved in the custody and management of corporate assets. Financial accounting and reporting therefore provides valuable communication between the owners and the managers of a corporation. Those with custody of resources report on the efficiency and effectiveness of their performance to the providers of those resources. We classify resource providers of corporations in two categories: (1) owners, or stockholders; and (2) creditors. Chapters 14 and 15 discuss accounting and reporting for the liabilities of the corporation. This chapter and the following one are concerned with financial accounting and reporting for stockholders' investments.

The Corporate Structure

A corporation is established under the authority of state law. In most cases a state official, usually the Secretary of State, responds to a request for a corporate charter. The request is made by **incorporators,** who will become **stockholders** of the corporation. A corporate charter and related **articles of incorporation** describe the nature of business to be conducted, the classes and types of corporate stock to be issued, and other pertinent information. After a corporate charter is granted, the **common stockholders** elect a **board of directors.** In turn, the board of directors appoints members of corporate management, such as the president, several vice-presidents, and other executives. The board of directors also approves the corporate **bylaws** under which the company operates.

Types of Corporations

Corporations are usually considered stock-ownership companies that are organized for profit. There are, however, many other types of corporate organization. For example, **public corporations** may be established and owned by a government unit to meet a social need.

Examples include the Federal Deposit Insurance Corporation, which insures deposits in certain commercial banks, and the Off Track Betting Corporation, which provides revenue to the city of New York from pari-mutuel horse race betting.

Mutual companies are cooperative organizations designed to benefit consumer groups. Shares are distributed to customers of the organization. Many life insurance companies and savings and loan associations are mutual companies. Policyholders of mutual life insurance companies and depositors of savings and loan associations are given the rights and privileges usually afforded owners in a stock company. Corporate profits can be distributed to the customers in the form of lower prices or as dividends. Because mutual companies do not have stockholders, their balance sheets have no owner contributions or stockholders' equity section.

In contrast to public corporations and mutual companies, **private corporations** are owned by individuals or institutions. Private corporations may be publicly held or closely held. **Publicly held corporations** are enterprises whose stock and other securities are actively traded in an organized securities market such as the New York or American Stock Exchange. Ownership of publicly held companies is usually widespread and may include many thousands of shareholders. **Closely held corporations** are those whose stock is held by a limited and well-defined group. Ownership is generally closed to prospective stockholders.

Two types of closely held corporations are the **professional corporation (PC)** and the **subchapter S corporation.** Professional corporations are established by members of a legally recognized profession, such as medicine, law, and accountancy. Ownership shares are available only to members of the profession. The purpose of this limitation is to ensure the integrity of the profession by minimizing conflict of interest and professional compromise. Subchapter S corporations have many advantages of the corporate form, but without the negative element of double taxation. To maintain this favorable tax status, subchapter S corporations can have no more than 35 stockholders.[1]

Exhibit 16–1 summarizes the types of corporations introduced here.

---

[1]This limit may be increased to 70 if spouses are included as shareholders.

EXHIBIT 16–1 Types of Corporations	
Corporation Type	**Nature of Ownership**
Public corporations	Government owned
Mutual companies	Consumer controlled
Private corporations	Stockholder owned
Publicly held corporations	Widely distributed ownership by institutions and/or individuals; shares typically traded on organized exchanges
Closely held corporations	Limited distribution of ownership
Professional corporations	Shares restricted to members of a legally recognized profession
Subchapter S corporations	Designed to avoid double taxation
Other closely held corporations	Limited ownership by institutions and/or individuals; shares not traded on organized exchanges

Tribune Co. Considers Going Public in '83 Or '84, Proposes Rise in Authorized Stock

By a Wall Street Journal *Staff Reporter*

CHICAGO—Closely held Tribune Co. said it is considering a public offering of common stock this year or in 1984 if market conditions and the economic outlook are favorable.

To prepare for the long-rumored move, the newspaper publishing, broadcasting and newsprint concern will seek shareholder approval April 7 to increase authorized common shares to 50 million from 20 million.

A proxy statement said a stock split or distribution would precede a public offering to make the share price more appropriate. As of Dec. 31, there were 7,396¼ shares outstanding held by 378 stockholders of record. The shares were valued at about $73,750 each, according to the proxy statement, which noted that a distribution of 2,949-for-1, for example, would be necessary to produce a value of $25 a share.

In addition, Tribune Co. shareholders will vote on creating a class of preferred stock for possible use in financing or acquisitions. Also proposed is elimination of a requirement for stockholder approval of certain transactions involving the company's two main publishing units, Chicago Tribune Co. and New York News Inc., making it easier to arrange financing related to real estate owned by the two units. But the company said it didn't plan to merge or sell either.

Stanton R. Cook, president and chief executive officer, said in the annual report that the New York Daily News "will show renewed vitality" as it benefits from restructuring, including cuts in employment and relocation of printing operations. The report said that although the operating loss for the Daily News was higher in 1982, operating results for the second half improved compared with 1981. Exact results weren't disclosed.

As previously reported, the 1982 earnings of Tribune Co., which also owns the Chicago Cubs baseball club, plunged to $32.9 million from a record $89.1 million in 1981, though revenue rose 2% to a record $1.43 billion. Earnings were hit by write-offs at the Daily-News, sharply lower profit from newsprint and a leap in interest expense to $37.9 million from $2.6 million in 1981.

Long-term debt of Tribune Co. soared to $415.7 million as of Dec. 31 from $87.6 million four years earlier. The increase reflected financing for a $600 million burst of capital spending during the past three years, more than quadrupling on an annual basis the rate of spending of the previous five years. Much of the spending was for new printing plants in Chicago and Orlando, Fla., and modernization and expansion of a newsprint mill in Thorold, Ontario.

SOURCE: "Tribune Co. Considers Going Public in '83 or '84, Proposes Rise in Authorized Stock," *Wall Street Journal,* March 14, 1983, p. 41. Reprinted by permission of *Wall Street Journal,* © Dow Jones & Company, Inc., 1983. All rights reserved.

Most publicly held and some closely held corporations are subject to filing with the Securities and Exchange Commission (SEC). The last three chapters of this book present certain specialized accounting and reporting practices of publicly held corporations and corporations subject to SEC jurisdiction. The rest of the material in this book is primarily concerned with financial accounting and reporting for all types of private corporations organized for profit, whether publicly held or closely held. Therefore, most of the accounting and reporting standards we discuss apply to all corporations.

STOCKHOLDERS' RIGHTS AND TYPES OF STOCKHOLDERS' EQUITY

Because the rights and risks of the various resource providers differ greatly, accountants must clearly understand stockholders' rights and responsibilities. The basic rights of the shareholder fall into three major categories: (1) rights to management; (2) rights to corporate property; and (3) rights to pass on changes in the original contract.[2] **Rights to management** include the right to elect directors, based on the pro rata ownership share in the firm, and the right to receive financial statements. **Rights to corporate property** include the right to declared dividends and the right to a proportionate share of corporate property at dissolution. **Rights to pass on changes in the original contract** include the right to vote on changes in the corporate bylaws and the right to maintain the pro rata ownership share based on the original investment. The right to maintain the pro rata ownership share is called a **preemptive right,** and it enables a stockholder to purchase additional securities from a new stock offering up to the percentage that he or she owned prior to the new issuance. Accordingly, a stockholder's percentage of ownership cannot be reduced as a result of a corporation issuing additional shares of stock to different investors, unless the stockholder declines the opportunity to acquire additional shares.

Not all stockholders receive all of the rights mentioned above. For example, the preemptive right has often been eliminated in recent elections passing on changes in the corporate bylaws. Furthermore, all stockholders of a corporation may not be entitled to the same rights. Many large corporations issue several classes of stock, with different characteristics and rights (e.g., dividend preferences, dividend amounts, and voting privileges). For example, The New York Times, Inc., publisher of the *New York Times,* has authorized four classes of stock: (1) prior preference stock; (2) serial preferred stock; (3) Class A common stock; and (4) Class B common stock. Exhibit 16–2 is the footnote description of these

---

[2]For more detailed discussion, see Richard A. Scott, "Owners' Equity, the Anachronistic Element," *Accounting Review* (October 1979), pp. 750–763.

EXHIBIT 16–2
The New York Times, Inc.
Footnote Disclosure of Classes of Stock

Note 10—Capital Stock

The 5½% cumulative prior preference stock, which is redeemable on 30 days' notice at par plus accrued dividends, is entitled to an annual dividend of $5.50 payable quarterly.

The serial preferred stock is junior to the 5½% cumulative prior preference stock. The Board of Directors is authorized to set the distinguishing characteristics of each series prior to issuance, including the granting of limited or full voting; however, the consideration received must be at least $100 per share. No such shares have been issued.

The Class A and Class B common stock are entitled to equal participation in the event of liquidation and in dividend declarations. As provided for in the certificate of incorporation, the Class A common stock has the right to elect 30% of the Board of Directors, and the Class A and Class B common stock have the right to vote together on major acquisitions of the stock or assets of other companies, on reservations of company stock for stock options and on the ratification of the selection of independent certified public accountants. Otherwise, except as provided by the laws of the State of New York, all voting power is vested solely and exclusively in the holders of the Class B common stock.

SOURCE: The New York Times, Inc., 1981 Annual Report. © 1981 by The New York Times Company. Reprinted by permission.

classes of stock in the company's annual report. Each class of stock has distinct character-istics and confers certain rights. Class B common stock, for example, provides most of the voting privileges. In this way, control of the corporation can be maintained by a select group of stockholders, while capital can be accumulated from a widespread distribution of Class A common stock. The prior preference (preferred) stock offers preferential dividends over the common shares at a rate of $5.50 per year.

Accountants classify stockholders' equity as either **contributed equity** or **earned equity.** Distinguishing between these types of equity in financial reports is important, because such information enables investors to determine the degree to which a company relies on owner contributions versus profitable operations to sustain its financial base. Earned equity, called **retained earnings,** is discussed in the following chapter. Stockhold-ers' contributed equity, the subject of this chapter, is usually classified for accounting and reporting purposes as **preferred stock** or **common stock.** We will now discuss in greater detail the major characteristics of common stock and preferred stock.

Characteristics of Capital Stock

The term **capital stock** is used to identify shareholder contributions to the enterprise. It can also be used to discuss classes of common stock or preferred stock. Two of the most sig-nificant features of capital stock are the following: (1) capital stock does *not* generally have a maturity date on which the principal portion of the security must be repaid; and (2) divi-dends are *not* required to be paid on capital stock.

These characteristics of capital stock are also the most important factors distinguishing debt financing from stockholders' contributed equity. Most debt instruments require the payment of interest on a regular basis and specify a maturity date. In contrast, equity secu-rities generally require neither dividends nor repayment of the principal amount of the investment.

Minimum Legal Capital

In the event of dissolution of a corporation, creditors receive assets to satisfy their claims before assets are distributed to stockholders. Therefore, the greater the assets contributed to the enterprise by stockholders, the greater the security of creditors. In order to protect creditors from an excessive or unwarranted distribution of assets to stockholders, many states have enacted laws requiring corporations to maintain some minimum level of stock-holders' equity. Through these laws enterprises are prohibited from distributing assets to shareholders to such an extent that the minimum legal capital is impaired. Creditors are thus assured of at least a minimum continuing economic commitment of stockholders in the enterprise.

To assure an adequate measure of minimum legal capital, most state laws require cor-porations to issue stock with a **par value.** Many state laws require corporations: (1) to assign a formal par value to stock; (2) to ensure that the stock not be sold **at discount** (i.e., at an amount less than par); and (3) to maintain a minimum amount of legal capital. Accord-ingly, companies frequently assign a relatively low par value to their stock and issue enough shares to meet the legal requirements. For example, if a company is required to maintain minimum legal capital of $5,000 and issues $10 par value stock, then at least 500 shares should be issued at an amount no less than par to comply with this provision of state law.

In some jurisdictions common stock may be issued at a discount. Under these circumstances the amount of the discount is considered a contingent liability of the owners to the creditors of the corporation. In the event of liquidation of corporate assets, the creditors may recover unsatisfied obligations by assessing the owners for additional contri-butions up to the amount of the original discount. Although most stock is nonassessable, accountants should be alert to the possibility of such a problem, especially if stock has been issued at a discount on par.

A corporation may also issue **no-par stock.** If no-par stock is issued, many states require the company to **assign** or **state a value** for the stock in order to comply with the corporate charter and minimum legal capital requirements. The use of stated or assigned value is usually legally acceptable and poses no significant accounting problems. Some jurisdictions allow the issuance of **true no-par stock,** which has no par, stated, or assigned value. In addition, true no-par stock cannot be issued at a discount and thus involves no contingent liability of the stockholders to corporate creditors.

Par, stated, or assigned value on common stock must not be confused with either market value or book value per share. The **market value per share of stock** is the price at which both buyer and seller would agree to transact a sale. Market values for common stock are quoted for most publicly held companies in publications such as *The Wall Street Journal.* The **book value per share of stock** is the total stockholders' equity divided by the total number of shares outstanding. The book value per share is the dollar amount per share an owner would receive if assets were liquidated and obligations were satisfied at the amounts reported on the financial statements. Both the market value and the book value per share are generally much larger than the par, stated, or assigned value. The par value of a stock is not a measure of the value or worth of a company. Par value is simply a legal device to protect creditors. Many persons would call the concept of par or stated value an anachronism in the context of the modern corporation.

States grant corporate charters to enterprises in their jurisdictions and enforce laws governing corporate conduct. Because there are many differences in these laws, the American Bar Association (ABA) has tried to establish a unified system of law for all states. Specifically, the ABA's Committee on Corporate Laws has suggested a Model Business Corporation Act. However, not all states have adopted the provisions of the model act. Furthermore, the act contains terminology that is unclear and interpreted differently, and certain provisions have become obsolete. Accountants must be aware of the state corporation laws affecting their employers or clients in order to adequately account for the rights and protections of the various resource suppliers.

Classes of Capital Stock

Common Stock

Common stock represents the most fundamental type of equity and generally gives the owner the right to vote, to share in residual profits, and, in the event of dissolution, to share in all assets remaining after creditors' and preferred stockholders' claims have been satisfied. If there is only one class of stock, it is common stock.

Common stockholders have a residual interest in the corporation, because they receive economic benefit *only if* the corporation is successful in meeting its obligations to creditors and preferred stockholders. Therefore, common stockholders are said to assume more risk than other groups associated with the enterprise. Consistent with the relatively high level of risk, however, is the potential for great financial reward. Common stockholders have no upper limit on their economic rewards from profitable operations. Creditors receive only interest and principal repayment, while preferred stockholders, with certain exceptions, receive a fixed or limited return on their investment regardless of profitability. Therefore, if a company is exceptionally profitable in its operation, the common stockholders will become better off as their holdings become more valuable. Conversely, if a company suffers losses, the value of the common stockholders' equity will be reduced as fewer assets are available to satisfy residual claims.

Preferred Stock

Preferred stock represents equity securities that receive a preference over the claims of common stockholders in terms of dividends from earnings and assets in the event of dissolution. Therefore, preferred stock usually represents a somewhat less risky investment than common stock. Although the board of directors of a corporation is not required to declare dividends on either preferred or common stock, any dividend declared must go first to preferred stockholders to the extent of their preference claims. The amount of the dividend to be paid on preferred stock is generally stated as a percentage of the par or stated value of the stock. For example, a holder of $100 par value 12% preferred stock has the right to receive a dividend, if declared, each year of $12 ($100 × .12). Furthermore, in the event of bankruptcy or other dissolution, preferred stockholders receive the par or stated value of their investment before any distribution is made to common stockholders. Occasionally, no-par preferred stock is issued, with the dividend stated as a fixed dollar amount rather than as a percentage of par. An amount to be distributed upon dissolution is also stated in the event of the termination of the business. Preferred stock, which usually conveys no voting rights, often carries other types of preference claims.

Cumulative Preferred Stock.   A **cumulative clause** on preferred stock simply means that all dividends, including dividends that were not declared and paid in prior years, must be brought up to date and paid before any dividends can be paid to common stockholders. Although stockholders cannot directly require the payment of dividends, a cumulative clause protects preferred stockholders from situations in which no dividends are paid on preferred or common shares for several years and then an exceptionally large dividend is declared. If preferred stock is not cumulative, preferred stockholders receive only the dividends attributable to the current year. If, however, preferred is cumulative, the current year's dividend and all **dividends in arrears** must be paid before the common stockholders share in a distribution. The application of the cumulative feature is illustrated in Chapter 17, where we discuss dividends in detail.

Participating Preferred Stock.   Another feature of preferred stock is a **participation right,** which allows preferred stockholders not only to receive the preference dividend but also to share with common stockholders any further dividends that are declared. Participating preferred stock may be either fully or partially participating. If the stock is **fully participating,** the preferred stockholders share dividend distributions with common stockholders without limit. With **partially participating** preferred stock, the stockholders share dividends in excess of the stated rate in only a limited way. The application of participation features is illustrated in Chapter 17 in our general discussion of dividends.

Callable Preferred Stock.   Some preferred stock issues are **callable,** which means the shares may be redeemed at the option of the corporation. Although the individual shareholder cannot demand the exercise of a call provision (as at the maturity date of a bond issue), the corporation can terminate the life of a callable preferred stock issue. When such a feature is present, the stock certificate states a **call price,** which is usually a few percentage points higher than the issuance price. Such a call premium is generally necessary to make the stock attractive to investors.

Corporations may favor a call provision, because it allows them to use the money generated from the stock issue for only as long as needed and then to call the stock and return the money to the stockholders. Excess resources are thus divested, allowing the corporation to retain only needed productive assets. Moreover, the call provision provides an escape mechanism for the corporation in the event of a market decline in the cost of capital. Specifically, if the market cost of capital decreases significantly from the preferred stock's dividend rate, a call provision allows the corporation to redeem the preferred stock and issue a new offering at the lower financing rate. Of course, from the investor's perspective, a call provision is a negative characteristic that may cause the involuntary divestiture of an investment that is generating above-market returns. As a result, investors frequently demand a dividend rate on callable preferred stock above the market rate for similar noncallable preferred stock.

Convertible Preferred Stock.   With this type of stock, stockholders can exchange preferred stock for common stock at a predetermined ratio or price. Convertible preferred stock may be quite attractive to investors, because it provides them with preferred claims on dividends and enables them to become common shareholders and participate without limitation in the earnings of the business.

The outstanding feature of convertible preferred stock is the opportunity for the preferred stock investor to participate in potential gains in the price of common shares. For example, assume the Hydrophonics Corporation (a producer of underwater amplifiers) issues $100 par, 10% preferred stock that is convertible into four common shares. If the market value per common share is $20, the preferred shareholder would not find the conversion feature attractive. Conversion would imply a trade of $100 preferred stock for common stock worth $80. However, if the price of the common stock increased to $35 per share, the conversion feature would accumulate explicit value. A preferred stockholder could trade $100 of preferred stock for common shares worth $140 (4 × $35).

The preferred stockholder could realize this gain not only through conversion but also by selling the preferred stock to someone who would be willing to pay $140 per share. Because of the attractiveness of the convertibility feature to investors, corporate issuers can frequently offer a dividend rate on convertible preferred stock that is less than the rate on similar nonconvertible shares.

Redeemable Preferred Stock.   Corporations have recently found redeemable preferred stock an attractive means of obtaining capital contributions. Redeemable preferred stock has the unique feature of mandatory redemption at a specified date or, less frequently, redemption at the stockholder's discretion. This feature is not to be confused with callability. Callable preferred stock is redeemable at the issuer's discretion, whereas redeemable preferred stock is retired at a specified date according to the provisions of the preferred stock contract.

The question arises whether this type of preferred stock is substantially more consistent with the characteristics of debt than of equity. Redeemable preferred stock is not a form of permanent capitalization and must be retired or refunded at a specified date, much the same as debt. However, redeemable preferred stock does not guarantee a return, as does debt. The omission of a preferred stock dividend payment does not initiate grounds for default, as does the omission of a debt interest payment. Furthermore, redeemable preferred stock is subordinate to debt in the event of final liquidation of assets. Therefore, redeemable preferred stock has the characteristics of *both* debt and equity. If, however, we assume a viable business, the return guarantee and subordination characteristics would not seem critical to the investor. The dominant characteristic would appear to be the mandatory redemption requirement. As a result, many people believe that redeemable preferred stock is in substance a type of psuedo-debt. Indeed, the SEC requires that redeemable preferred stock be disclosed between the long-term debt and preferred stock sections of the balance sheet, and not be included in the total of either.

Exhibit 16–3 illustrates the financial statement disclosure of redeemable preferred stock for the hypothetical company, Suburban Paper Company. The footnote disclosure included in the exhibit presents the details of the redeemable preferred stock which is included in the company's balance sheet.

If redeemable preferred stock is in substance a form of debt, why doesn't the corporate issuer just issue straight debt? This question is especially intriguing because preferred stock dividends are not deductible for tax purposes, whereas debt interest payments are deductible. The answer may lie in the corporate manager's desire to avoid the violation of restrictive bond covenants prohibiting the issuance of further debt. An inspection of corporate lending agreements of publicly held companies reveals the expression of restrictive covenants in terms of generally accepted accounting principles (GAAP).[3] As a result, a corporate

| Substance over Form |

---

[3]See Richard Leftwich, "Evidence of the Impact of Mandatory Charges in Accounting Principles on Corporate Loan Agreements," *Journal of Accounting and Economics* (December 1981), pp. 3–36, for a summary of the types of measurement rules in corporate lending agreements.

EXHIBIT 16-3
Suburban Paper Company
Financial Statement Disclosure of Redeemable Preferred Stock

(in thousands)	1983
Liabilities and Stockholders' Equity	
Current liabilities	
Accounts payable	$ 41,250
Income taxes (Note 3)	13,400
Accrued expenses	82,950
Current portion of long-term debt and redeemable preferred stock (Note 4)	6,790
	$144,390
Long-term debt (Note 5)	217,050
Deferred income taxes (Note 6)	42,700
$10 cumulative preferred stock, $1 par value; stated at $100 redemption value, less $1,500,000 included in current liabilities; 90,000 shares authorized and issued (Note 4)	9,000
Common stock, $5 par value; 5,000,000 shares authorized, 2,700,000 shares issued and outstanding	13,500
Additional paid-in capital	181,000
Retained earnings	195,000
Total liabilities and stockholders' equity	$802,640

Note 4—$10 cumulative preferred stock

The $10 cumulative preferred stock is redeemable at $100 per share. Fifteen thousand shares are required to be redeemed on June 30 annually through 1990. The company has the option of redeeming the stock entirely, or in part, at any time through 1990. Fifteen thousand shares were redeemed in 1983. The cumulative preferred stockholders are not entitled to voting rights.

---

borrower could circumvent a restrictive covenant on the issuance of additional debt by issuing redeemable preferred stock, which has the main characteristics of debt but is not technically debt according to GAAP. In this way the corporate borrower could obtain "near debt" financing without violating existing contracts. Furthermore, if the corporation issues the redeemable preferred stock to other corporations, a below-market dividend rate can be offered. Corporate investors would agree to accept a below-market return, because corporations can exclude 85% of their dividend income from federal income taxation.[4]

---

[4]The **85% exclusion rule** was established to prevent corporate profits distributed to an investor corporation from being taxed more than twice. To illustrate, assume Corporation B has an investment in Corporation A common stock. Without the 85% rule, Corporation A profits that were distributed to Corporation B would be taxed three times: as net income to Corporation A, as dividend income to Corporation B, and as dividend income to individual equity investors in Corporation B. The 85% exclusion rule eliminates most of the second stage of taxation, so that corporate profits are taxed only twice: once at the corporate level, and once at the individual investor level.

ACCOUNTING FOR CAPITAL STOCK

The issuance of capital stock is a fairly infrequent but highly significant event in the operation of a corporation. As an example, in late 1982 CBS, Inc., the second largest broadcaster in the United States, brought a new equity offering to the market for the first time in 45 years. Likewise, RCA, the consumer electronics company, issued new equity shares in 1982 for the first time since the company's inception in 1919.

The issuance of capital stock should not be confused with transactions in the **secondary market,** such as the New York or American Stock Exchange. The secondary market is represented by transactions between owners of previously issued shares of stock. The corporation is not a party to transactions involving its own stock in the secondary market, except in the case of treasury stock transactions, which are discussed later in this chapter. New issues are sold through an intermediary, called an **underwriter.** The underwriter, or more frequently an underwriting syndicate, is responsible for making the new offering available to investors. The underwriter is much like a retail store for new common stock offerings. Exhibit 16–4 is an example of a new issue announcement by an underwriting syndicate. These announcements are called "tombstones" (they look like a tombstone) and are placed in financial publications such as *The Wall Street Journal.*

Issuances of capital stock require the approval of a company's board of directors and also must result in a total number of outstanding shares that is within the number authorized in the corporate charter granted by the state. A great deal of planning and research generally precedes a stock issue in order to make it attractive to investors. Although stock is usually issued for cash, other consideration may be accepted as payment for the shares. Also, subscriptions to acquire stock in the future are frequently sold before the stock is issued.

Stock Issued for Cash

Par or Stated Value Capital Stock

When capital stock is issued for cash, an entry is made to debit Cash, credit either Common Stock or Preferred Stock for the par or stated value, and recognize any Discount on Par or Paid-in Capital in Excess of Par on the issuance. To illustrate, if Haller Company issues 500 shares of $10 par value common stock at $15 per share on October 31, 1984, the following journal entry is necessary:

Oct. 31, 1984	Cash	7,500	
	Common Stock		5,000
	Paid-in Capital in Excess of Par		2,500
	(To record issuance of stock.)		

Note that no gain or loss is recognized on the issuance of stock. Indeed, gains and losses are not recognized on any investment transactions with owners. Such increases and decreases in equity do not result from revenue-generating activities and are therefore excluded from the income statement. Changes in net assets resulting from investment transactions with owners are treated as direct changes in the appropriate contributed stockholders' equity accounts.

Additional paid-in capital in excess of par represents an increase in contributed capital above the par amount, while a discount on par represents owner contributions in an amount less than the total par value. Neither discount on par nor paid-in capital in excess of par affects retained earnings. Again, in many states it is illegal to issue stock at a discount because of laws establishing minimum legal capital. Therefore, the par value of stock is generally set at a low enough level to ensure the stock will sell at an amount above or at least equal to par. Accountants seldom encounter discount on par and we do not discuss discount extensively here.

EXHIBIT 16–4
Molecular Genetics, Inc.
New Issue Announcement

This is neither an offer to sell nor a solicitation of an offer to buy these securities.
The offer is made only by the Prospectus.

NEW ISSUE

March 14, 1983

1,250,000 Shares

Molecular Genetics, Inc.

Common Stock

Price $15.75 per Share

*Copies of the Prospectus may be obtained in any State in which
this announcement is circulated only from such of the under-
writers as may lawfully offer these securities in such State.*

Kidder, Peabody & Co. Incorporated	Donaldson, Lufkin & Jenrette Securities Corporation	Piper, Jaffray & Hopwood Incorporated

Bear, Stearns & Co.   Blyth Eastman Paine Webber   Alex. Brown & Sons   Hambrecht & Quist
                                        Incorporated   *Incorporated*

E. F. Hutton & Company Inc.   Prudential-Bache   L. F. Rothschild, Unterberg, Towbin
                                                    Securities

Warburg Paribas Becker   Dain Bosworth   Montgomery Securities
A. G. Becker   *Incorporated*

A. G. Edwards & Sons, Inc.   Robertson, Colman & Stephens   Thomson McKinnon Securities Inc.

Arnhold and S. Bleichroeder, Inc.   Bateman Eichler, Hill Richards   William Blair & Company   Blunt Ellis & Loewi
                                                Incorporated   *Incorporated*

J. C. Bradford & Co.   Butcher & Singer Inc.   Cowen & Co.   Craig-Hallum, Inc.   Crowell, Weedon & Co.
Incorporated

F. Eberstadt & Co., Inc.   First of Michigan Corporation   Interstate Securities Corporation

Janney Montgomery Scott Inc.   Legg Mason Wood Walker   McDonald & Company
                                        Incorporated

Moseley, Hallgarten, Estabrook & Weeden Inc.   Prescott, Ball & Turben, Inc.   Rotan Mosle Inc.   Rothschild Inc.

Sutro & Co.   Tucker, Anthony & R. L. Day, Inc.   Underwood, Neuhaus & Co.   Wheat, First Securities, Inc.
Incorporated   *Incorporated*

Birr, Wilson & Co. Inc.   Davis, Skaggs & Co., Inc.   R. G. Dickinson & Co.   Eppler, Guerin & Turner, Inc.

First Albany Corporation   First Mid America Inc.   Furman Selz Mager Dietz & Birney   Herzfeld & Stern
                                                            Incorporated

Investment Corporation of Virginia   Johnson, Lane, Space, Smith & Co., Inc.   Johnston, Lemon & Co.
                                                                                    Incorporated

Neuberger & Berman   Parker/Hunter   Reinheimer Nordberg Inc.   Seidler Amdec Securities Inc.   Stephens Inc.
                        Incorporated

Baker, Watts & Co.   Cable, Howse & Ragen   Engler & Budd Company   John G. Kinnard and Company
                                                                        Incorporated

A. E. Masten & Co.   W. H. Newbold's Son & Co., Inc.   Scherck, Stein & Franc, Inc.   Woodman Kirkpatrick & Gilbreath
Incorporated

Paid-in Capital in Excess of Par or Discount on Capital Stock, as an element of contributed capital, remains as an account on the books of the corporation during the entire time the stock is outstanding. Thus, paid-in capital in excess of par or discount on par is reported in the balance sheet from the time the stock is issued until it is reacquired and retired. Nor do the amounts in these accounts vary with changes in the market value of the company's stock. At the time of retirement all accounts related to the issuance of the stock are removed from the contributed stockholders' equity section of the balance sheet.

Costs incurred in issuing stock are appropriately treated as reductions of the related proceeds, and only the net amount of cash received is capitalized. Preferably, such issue costs are charged directly to the Capital Stock or Paid-in Capital in Excess of Par account. Law sometimes prohibits this treatment, however, and Retained Earnings may be charged. There are a limited number of exceptions to these rules, and we discuss them later in this chapter.

True No-Par Capital Stock

On rare occasions a corporation may issue true no-par stock. Accounting for this type of stock issuance poses no special problems. To illustrate, assume that Haller Company issued 500 shares of no-par common stock at $15 per share on October 31, 1984. The following journal entry is appropriate:

Oct. 31, 1984	Cash	7,500	
	Common Stock		7,500
	(To record issuance of no-par stock.)		

In contrast to the journal entry for the par value stock, there is no credit to a Paid-in Capital in Excess of Par account. Indeed, the issuance of true no-par stock never results in the recording of a separate Paid-in Capital in Excess of Par or a Discount on Par account. The total proceeds of the issuance should be credited to the appropriate capital stock account (either common or preferred).

Lump Sum Issuances

A corporation may issue multiple classes of capital stock and/or debt for a lump sum consideration. The accounting problem is to assign the lump sum purchase price to the various classes of securities. The solution to this problem is to allocate to each security in the package an issue price proportional to the fair market value of the security relative to the total fair market value of the package. To illustrate, assume that Haller Company issues the following securities for a lump sum consideration of $800,000:

Security	Number of Shares	Par Value	Market Price per Share	Total Value
Common—Class A	1,000 shares	$ 1.00	$ 30	$ 30,000
Common—Class B	10,000 shares	.50	36	360,000
$10 Preferred	5,000 shares	90.00	102	510,000
				$900,000

The $800,000 issue price is allocated to each security on the basis of relative market values, calculated as follows:

Security	Proportion	× Lump Sum Price	= Security Allocation	= Par Value	+ Paid-in Capital in Excess of Par Value
Common—Class A	$\frac{\$30,000}{\$900,000}$	$800,000	$ 26,667	$ 1,000	$ 25,667

Common—Class B	$\dfrac{\$360,000}{\$900,000}$	800,000	320,000	5,000	315,000
$10 Preferred	$\dfrac{\$510,000}{\$900,000}$	800,000	453,333	450,000	3,333
			$800,000 =	$456,000 +	$344,000

The following journal entry is made by Haller Company for the $800,000 multiple security issuance:

Cash	800,000	
Common Stock—Class A		1,000
Common Stock—Class B		5,000
$10 Preferred Stock		450,000
Paid-in Capital in Excess of Par, Common Stock—Class A		25,667
Paid-in Capital in Excess of Par, Common Stock—Class B		315,000
Paid-in Capital in Excess of Par, $10 Preferred Stock		3,333

Stock Issued for Consideration Other Than Cash

In general, if a company's stock is issued for consideration other than cash, the transaction should be based on the *fair market value of the consideration received or the market value of the stock issued, whichever is more clearly discernible.* To illustrate, assume that Haller Company issues 1,000 shares of its $10 par value common stock for an automobile with a fair market value of $12,500. The following journal entry is required to properly record the transaction:

Equipment—Transportation	12,500	
Common Stock		10,000
(1,000 shares at $10)		
Paid-in Capital in Excess of Par		2,500
(To record acquisition of automobile and issuance of stock.)		

The automobile is subsequently depreciated in normal fashion, but the contributed stockholders' equity accounts are unchanged on successive balance sheets. Retained earnings will, of course, decrease through the recognition of depreciation expense over the life of the asset.

Occasionally, companies issue stock for services received that have no future benefit and do not qualify as assets. To illustrate, assume that an attorney provides legal services to Haller Company and agrees to accept 100 shares of Haller's $10 par value common stock in satisfaction of the legal fee of $1,370. The following entry records these transactions:

Professional Fees Expense	1,370	
Common Stock		1,000
Paid-in Capital in Excess of Par		370
(To record legal fee expense and issuance of common stock.)		

In this case Haller's net assets are unaffected, even though an expense is reported and net income is decreased. The balance sheet effect of this transaction is confined to the stockholders' equity section. Specifically, as retained earnings decrease through the recognition of the expense, contributed stockholders' equity accounts increase. There are no changes in the company's assets or liabilities as a result of this event.

Stock Issued in the Absence of Market Values

A company may issue stock for noncash consideration, and neither the stock nor the consideration has an established market value. This situation most commonly occurs with development-stage companies. Recall from Chapter 13 that a development-stage company devotes substantial effort to establishing a new business, and either planned principal operating activities have not commenced, or, if such activities have begun, no significant revenues have been generated.

Because development-stage corporations frequently lack the resources to acquire the skills or rights necessary to achieve success, they are often willing to issue stock in exchange for noncash considerations. For example, a development-stage high-technology firm may need highly specialized engineering skills and product patent rights in order to begin operations. The cost of these items may be prohibitive, so new stock may have to be offered to the engineers and patent holders in return for their cooperation. An accounting problem **Objectivity** arises if the noncash consideration received in exchange for the stock has no objectively determinable value. The lack of objectively determinable values is not uncommon in the case of legal rights, such as patents or copyrights, or with the acquisition of specialized skills. In addition, the stock may not have an established market value, because the development-stage corporation generally will not have traded stock in an organized market.

How then does the accountant assign a dollar amount to the stock issuance if neither the stock nor the related consideration has an objective market value? The Financial Accounting Standards Board (FASB) has required that a dollar amount be assigned to any noncash consideration received in exchange for equity securities. In the case of a noncash consideration without an objectively determinable market value, the FASB has given the accountant wide latitude in assigning dollar amounts to both the stock and the consideration received. For example, an estimate of the value of the stock issued or consideration received may be made by analyzing other stocks or considerations that are similar to those being exchanged and for which objective determination of market value is possible. In addition, the financial statements of the corporation must disclose the basis for assigning dollar amounts.[5]

Stock Subscriptions

Corporations often sell rights to the shares in an initial stock issue before the stock is actually issued. Such rights are called **stock subscriptions.** Stock subscriptions are a useful way for development-stage corporations to market equity securities to public investors in an orderly manner. Stock subscriptions are generally sold to investors at a fraction of the total cost of the stock. The remaining portion of the stock price is paid by the subscriber at the time the shares are issued. Questions frequently arise about the proper way to record stock subscriptions. Specifically, if cash is received prior to the issuance of stock, how should the transaction be shown in the accounting records? Further, if the subscription down payment is forfeited because the subscription is not exercised and lapses, how should that circumstance be reported?

When a stock subscription contract is initiated, the company records the cash received and a "subscription receivable" for the unpaid balance of the stock price; credits are made to reflect an increase in the par value and the paid-in capital in excess of par value. Although the corporation is required to issue the stock after the subscription receivable has been fully paid, a liability does not exist as a result of the subscription contract. There are no claims on the corporation's assets but rather an obligation to issue capital stock when the subscription

---

[5]*FASB Statement of Financial Accounting Standards No. 7,* "Accounting and Reporting by Development Stage Enterprises," 1975, par. 11. Under SEC rules, a dollar amount may *not* be assigned to noncash consideration lacking objectively determinable market value for issuances by development-stage corporations.

has been fully received. As such, the credit portion of the entry represents a direct increase in the equity of the company.

Another question related to stock subscriptions is whether a subscription receivable is an asset. The unpaid portion of the stock subscription represents a mutual promise of the corporation and the subscriber. The corporation promises to deliver stock in the future, and the subscriber promises to pay the balance of the subscription price. Accountants do not generally consider such *mutual promises* (executory contracts) an accounting event. An accounting event is generally the result of the *partial performance* of a contract by one of the contracting parties. As an example, accounts receivable are recorded when one party to the contract delivers goods or services but remains unpaid. The delivering of goods or services on account is a partial performance of the agreement by the seller to the buyer and is considered a recordable event. The subscription receivable does not have this characteristic, because neither party has partially performed the agreement with respect to the unpaid portion of the subscription.

As a result, some have favored treating the subscription receivable as a reduction in stockholders' equity rather than as an asset. In this way the stockholders' equity section would reflect an increase only for the actual cash consideration. Presently, either an asset or a contra-equity presentation of the subscription receivable is acceptable. The preferred presentation depends, in large part, on the state laws applicable to stock subscriptions. For example, some state laws grant the subscriber all rights of stock ownership, including dividends and voting rights, for the complete subscription; others grant such rights only for the prepaid portion of the subscription. Under the former legal arrangement, the whole subscription should be disclosed as an increase in stockholders' equity; in the latter case a net equity presentation (subscriptions receivable as contra equity) would be more appropriate.

To illustrate the accounting for a subscription contract, assume that Nesor Corporation issues stock subscriptions for 1,000 shares of its $10 par value common stock at a subscribed price of $125. Further assume that investors must make a 50% down payment for all subscribed stock. The following journal entry is appropriate:

Cash	62,500	
Stock Subscriptions Receivable	62,500	
Common Stock Subscribed		10,000
Paid-in Capital in Excess of Par (Subscribed)		115,000
(To record receipt of stock subscriptions.)		

The increase in the stockholders' equity account originates from stock subscriptions rather than the outright sale of stock; the accounts are therefore identified as subscribed accounts. When Nesor receives additional cash that pays the subscription receivable in full, the entries to record the cash receipt and related issuance of stock are as follows:

Cash	62,500	
Stock Subscriptions Receivable		62,500
(To record receipt of cash for full payment of subscribed stock.)		
Common Stock Subscribed	10,000	
Paid-in Capital in Excess of Par (Subscribed)	115,000	
Common Stock		10,000
Paid-in Capital in Excess of Par		115,000
(To record issuance of 1,000 shares of subscribed stock.)		

If the subscription is defaulted because payment is not made in the prescribed time period, the remaining Stock Subscriptions Receivable and Common Stock Subscribed are removed from the books. Questions arise, however, about the proper disposition of down payments on the forfeited shares. Three major alternatives exist:[6]

1. Refund the partial payment on the forfeited shares to the subscriber.
2. Retain the partial payment on the forfeited shares until the subscription is sold to another investor. (Refund the remaining cash to the original subscriber after deducting expenses of the reissue and any reductions in selling price below the subscription price.)
3. Retain the cash advance as a default penalty.

The subscription contract and applicable state laws will guide the contracting parties to the appropriate solution in the event of default.

To illustrate the first alternative, assume that 100 shares of the Nesor Corporation subscription are defaulted after the cash advance is made. The entry necessary to record the default and the refund to the subscriber is as follows:

Common Stock Subscribed ($10 × 100)	1,000	
Paid-in Capital in Excess of Par (Subscribed)	11,500	
Cash ($62.50 × 100)		6,250
Stock Subscriptions Receivable		6,250
(To record defaulted stock subscription and return of cash to subscriber.)		

If Nesor used the third alternative and retained the cash advance, the journal entry would be identical to the one above, except that a paid-in capital in excess of par value account, instead of the Cash account, would be credited for $6,250. Under the second alternative, Nesor's retention of part of the cash down payment would be credited to a paid-in capital account, and the remaining refund would be credited to Cash. As these entries indicate, if the corporation retains any cash advanced under a defaulted stock subscription, the amount should be reflected as an increase in contributed capital. No gain or loss is recognized on such transactions, because their effects are totally associated with contributed equity.

At first glance, retaining the cash advance may appear to be an unreasonably harsh penalty to the defaulting subscriber. However, the purpose of such a provision is to give the subscriber an incentive to purchase shares. Without this incentive the subscriber could treat the stock subscription as a risk-free stock option. To illustrate, if Nesor Corporation already had stock outstanding and trading in an organized market, the investor could subscribe stock at $125 per share and exercise the subscription if the market value of the shares exceeded $125 or default if the market value of the shares was less than $125. If the investor does not stand to lose the down payment, the subscription provides a no-loss investment opportunity. Since this is not the purpose of a stock subscription, provisions for the partial or full forfeiture of the down payment are not unreasonable when previously issued shares are already trading in the secondary market.

TREASURY STOCK

Companies frequently acquire shares of their own stock through market purchases without intending to retire the stock. A company's stock that has been issued and then acquired by the company for some future purpose is referred to as treasury stock. Some of the reasons that a company acquires shares of its own stock include:

---

[6]A fourth alternative requires an amendment to the original contract, such that a pro rata distribution of shares equal to the partial payment is made.

1. Buying out a stockholder or retiring executive.
2. Meeting provisions of stock option plans for employees.
3. Meeting the requirements of a proposed merger in which large amounts of stock are to be exchanged.
4. Preparing to meet the requirements of a stock dividend.
5. Reducing stockholder pressure for an increased dividend rate.

When treasury stock is purchased, the acquisition must be recorded in the accounting records. Some questions persist about the nature of treasury stock. Is it an asset or a reduction of stockholders' equity? On rare occasions, annual reports present small amounts of treasury stock as assets. This practice, however, is generally undesirable and discouraged. A company has equity in its assets and does not have an asset in its own equity. A company cannot own itself via stock purchases. The characteristics of treasury stock are not similar to those of other types of investments, such as plant assets. To illustrate, unlike fixed asset investments, common stock purchases reduce the size (capitalization) of the firm. Furthermore, the retirement of treasury stock cannot be considered the destruction of productive property, as would, for example, the leveling of a corporate plant. Therefore, except in the most unusual circumstances, treasury stock should be presented as a reduction of shareholders' equity and not as an asset.

Two Methods of Accounting for Treasury Stock

There are two acceptable methods of recording the reduction in stockholders' equity that occurs when treasury stock is acquired: (1) the **cost method,** which is more frequently encountered in practice, and (2) the **par value method.** To illustrate, consider the stockholders' equity section of the balance sheet of Bender, Inc., as presented in Exhibit 16–5. Not all of Bender's authorized common stock has been issued. The 50,000 shares which have been authorized but unissued are not presented in the financial statements. A note in the balance sheet discloses the authorization of those shares.

Disclosure

Cost Method

The **cost method** of accounting for treasury stock assumes the eventual reissuance of the stock. Therefore, the cost method is preferred when management intends to hold the treasury shares temporarily for later reissuance, as opposed to later retirement. To illustrate, assume that Bender, Inc., acquires 2,000 shares of its common stock at $145 per share. The company purchases these shares to provide for a stock option plan and intends to reissue the

---

EXHIBIT 16–5
Bender, Inc.
Partial Balance Sheet

Stockholders' Equity [Note 1]	
Preferred stock ($100 par, 7% cumulative; 100,000 shares authorized, issued, and outstanding)	$10,000,000
Common stock ($100 par; 200,000 shares authorized, 150,000 shares issued and outstanding)	15,000,000
Paid-in capital in excess of par (common)	750,000
Contributed equity	25,750,000
Retained earnings	42,500,000
Total stockholders' equity	$68,250,000

Note 1: The 7% cumulative preferred stock was issued at par value and is callable at any time at 103. Fifty thousand common shares were authorized by the board of directors upon approval by the stockholders of record. The authorized shares are intended to be issued to employees as part of a recently introduced employee stock option plan.

shares at a later time. The following entry is necessary to record the transaction using the cost method:

Treasury Stock (2,000 shares × $145)	290,000	
Cash		290,000
(To record acquisition of treasury stock.)		

The Treasury Stock account is classified as a reduction in the contributed equity of the company. Exhibit 16–6 presents the stockholders' equity section of Bender's balance sheet following this transaction.

The Common Stock and Paid-in Capital in Excess of Par accounts are not affected by the treasury stock transaction if the cost method is used. It is also acceptable to reflect the acquired stock as a reduction of Retained Earnings or Total Stockholders' Equity. However, the treatment demonstrated in Exhibit 16–6 is commonly applied in practice and adequately reflects the nature of the item.

When treasury stock is reissued, the cost of the treasury stock is removed from the books. To illustrate, assume that Bender, Inc., sells the treasury stock listed in Exhibit 16–6 for $275,000 cash. The following entry reflects this transaction:

Cash	275,000	
Paid-in Capital in Excess of Par	15,000	
Treasury Stock		290,000
(To record reissuance of treasury stock at $15,000 below cost.)		

In this case the treasury stock was sold below its cost and Paid-in Capital in Excess of Par was reduced by $15,000. State law may require other treatments, such as charging Retained Earnings for the excess, but the entry presented here is acceptable in most circumstances. If the company's stockholders' equity did not include any paid-in capital in excess of par on common stock, the $15,000 difference between the acquisition and resale price of the treasury stock would have been charged to the Retained Earnings account. If the stock was sold for more than its cost, an additional amount of paid-in capital in excess of par would be recognized.[7] In any event, no losses or gains are recognized on treasury stock transactions because they represent transactions in a company's own capital stock. Since the permanent

---

[7]Contributed capital arising from treasury stock transactions may be carried in a separate account, such as Paid-in Capital from Treasury Stock Transactions.

EXHIBIT 16–6
Bender, Inc.
Partial Balance Sheet
with Treasury Stock–Cost Method

Stockholders' Equity	
Preferred stock ($100 par, 7% cumulative; 100,000 shares authorized, issued, and outstanding)	$10,000,000
Common stock ($100 par; 200,000 shares authorized, 150,000 shares issued, 148,000 shares outstanding, 2,000 shares held in treasury)	15,000,000
Paid-in capital in excess of par (common)	750,000
Less: Cost of treasury shares	(290,000)
Contributed equity	25,460,000
Retained earnings	42,500,000
Total stockholders' equity	$67,960,000

contributed capital accounts were not adjusted when the treasury stock was purchased, no further entry is needed to reestablish the status of the stock as outstanding.

An additional complication in the cost method of accounting for treasury stock arises when treasury shares are acquired at different times at different prices. Companies typically follow either a first-in, first-out (FIFO) or a weighted average cost flow assumption, similar to that used in accounting for inventories. As with the case of inventory accounting, consistent application of the method selected is important. To illustrate this problem, assume that a company first acquired 100 shares of treasury stock at $10 per share and then acquired 100 more shares at $12 per share. Later the company sold 50 shares at $13 per share. What is the cost of the treasury shares that have been sold? This is where the cost flow assumption becomes important. If the FIFO method is used, the 50 shares cost $10 per share, the first price paid. If the weighted average method is used, the shares cost $11 per share, because that is the average price paid for the 200 shares of treasury stock the company has when the 50 shares are sold [(100 × $10) + (100 × $12)/200 shares = $11 per share]. The entries to record the sale of the treasury stock under the two methods are as follows:

	FIFO Method	Weighted Average Method
Cash (50 × $13)	650	650
Treasury Stock	500*	550*
Paid-in Capital in Excess of Par	150**	100**

*Cost of treasury shares sold:
  FIFO: 50 × $10 = $500
  Weighted average: 50 × $11 = $550
**Additional Paid-in Capital:
  FIFO: 50 shares ($13 − $10) = $150
  Weighted average: 50 shares ($13 − $11) = $100

Par Value Method

The second acceptable method of accounting for treasury stock is the **par** or **stated value method.** In substance, this method is consistent with the assumption that common stock will be retired. Under this method, treasury stock is recorded at the par (or stated) value of common stock, while the paid-in capital in excess of par from the original common stock issuance is eliminated. As a result, application of this method is preferred if management intends to eventually retire the treasury shares, which rarely occurs.

We illustrate the par value method using Bender, Inc., and the acquisition and reissuance data from the previous example. Recall that Bender acquired 2,000 shares of its $100 par value common stock at $145 per share. The entry to record the acquisition of the treasury stock for $290,000, using the par value method, is presented below:

Treasury Stock	200,000	
Paid-in Capital in Excess of Par	10,000	
Retained Earnings	80,000	
Cash (2,000 × $145)		290,000
(To record purchase of treasury shares.)		

Using this method, the treasury shares are reported at par value (2,000 shares × $100 par). The difference between the cost of the shares ($290,000) and their par value ($200,000) is treated as a reduction in paid-in capital in excess of par on a pro rata basis and next as a reduction in retained earnings. In this case, Bender's stock was originally issued at an average price per share of $105, determined as follows:

Common shares issued and outstanding	150,000
Par value	$15,000,000
Paid-in capital in excess of par	750,000
	$15,750,000

$$\frac{\$15,750,000}{150,000} = \$105 \text{ per share}$$

Therefore, the pro rata portion of paid-in capital in excess of par value on the acquired treasury shares equals 2,000 × ($105 − $100), or $10,000. If the pro rata paid-in capital in excess of par is eliminated, the remainder is treated as a reduction of retained earnings. Since the 2,000 shares were purchased at $145 per share, the excess $40 per share is treated as a direct reduction of retained earnings.

This treatment recognizes the economic notion that the increased value of the stock after its original issuance (from $105 per share to $145 per share) results from earnings which have been retained rather than paid out as dividends. Therefore, when the corporation acquires the stock, it is necessary to recognize that part of the consideration paid for the shares relates to earned equity. Consequently, in such circumstances, we reduce retained earnings. In contrast, if the treasury shares were purchased for less than the total of the par value and paid-in capital in excess of par ($210,000), contributed capital would be increased by a credit to Paid-in Capital in Excess of Par Value for the difference.

Exhibit 16–7 illustrates the stockholders' equity section of Bender's balance sheet after the acquisition of shares for $290,000 under the par value method. Notice that the total stockholders' equity is the same in Exhibits 16–6 and 16–7, but that the disclosure of the treasury stock differs according to the method applied.

If treasury stock is reissued under the par value method, accounting is again different. Continuing the example of Bender, Inc., the reissuance is treated as if the stock were being issued for the first time at par value, except that the credit is to the Treasury Stock account. The entry under the par value method for reissuance of the stock for $275,000 is presented below:

Cash	275,000	
Paid-in Capital in Excess of Par		75,000
Treasury Stock		200,000
(To record reissuance of treasury stock.)		

EXHIBIT 16–7
Bender, Inc.
Partial Balance Sheet
with Treasury Stock–Par Value Method

Stockholders' Equity

Preferred stock ($100 par, 7% cumulative; 100,000 shares authorized, issued, and outstanding)	$10,000,000
Common stock ($100 par; 200,000 shares authorized, 150,000 shares issued, 148,000 shares outstanding, 2,000 shares held in treasury)	14,800,000
Paid-in capital in excess of par (common)	740,000
Contributed equity	25,540,000
Retained earnings	42,420,000
Total stockholders' equity	$67,960,000

The difference between the carrying amount of the Treasury Stock, in this case par value, and the consideration received is treated as an increase in Paid-in Capital in Excess of Par.

Summary of Treasury Stock Accounting

Regardless of whether the cost method or the par value method is used for treasury stock accounting, several points are important:

1. Treasury stock should not be classified as an asset.
2. Dividends are not recorded as paid or received on treasury stock (the company cannot give dividends to itself).
3. Retained earnings are not increased as a result of treasury stock transactions, although decreases in retained earnings are possible when applying the par value method or if shares are sold below cost when applying the cost method.
4. Gains or losses are not recognized on treasury stock transactions.
5. Regardless of which method is used, total stockholders' equity is unchanged, although the individual components may change.
6. Legal minimum capital must be preserved.

RETIREMENT OF STOCK

Common Stock Retirement

If a company acquires stock which is to be retired, accounting is similar to the par value method of accounting for treasury stock. Instead of charging the Treasury Stock account for the par value of the securities, however, the original Capital Stock account is charged. Such an entry effectively removes the stock from the company's accounts, which, of course, is consistent with the nature of the transaction.

To continue the example in the previous section, if Bender, Inc., acquires and retires 2,000 shares of $100 par value stock at $145 per share, the following entry is necessary:

Common Stock	200,000	
Paid-in Capital in Excess of Par	10,000	
Retained Earnings	80,000	
Cash		290,000
(To record acquisition and retirement of 2,000 shares of common stock at $145 per share originally issued at $105 per share.)		

The disclosures of stock authorized, issued, and outstanding are adjusted to reflect the permanent retirement of the acquired stock. The rationale, previously discussed, for the direct charge to Retained Earnings under the par value method of accounting for treasury stock is also valid here. A permanent distribution of $80,000 of earned equity has taken place as a result of the transaction.

If a company acquires and retires stock at a price below the original selling price, additional paid-in capital results from the retirement. To illustrate, assume that Bender, Inc., acquired and retired 2,000 shares of its common stock at $85 per share. In this case the following entry would be appropriate:

Common Stock	200,000	
Cash (2,000 × $85)		170,000
Paid-in Capital in Excess of Par		30,000
(To record acquisition and retirement of		
2,000 shares of common stock at $85 per		
share originally issued at $105 per share.)		

The paid-in capital from the retirement arises because the company was able to retire stock that originally sold for $105 per share for only $85 per share, resulting in a permanent increase in the company's contributed equity of $20 per share ($5 recognized when the stock was sold and $15 when it was retired), even though those shares are no longer outstanding.

Preferred Stock Retirement

Preferred stock can be redeemed through either a call provision or a mandatory redemption provision. Other than this, the principles underlying the redemption of preferred stock are similar to those for the retirement of common stock. When preferred stock is redeemed, the Preferred Stock account and associated Paid-in Capital in Excess of Par on the preferred stock are eliminated. Any difference between the sum of these accounts and the cash redemption price will be either charged to Retained Earnings or credited to the Paid-in Capital in Excess of Par.

To illustrate the accounting, refer to the $10,000,000 preferred stock issue of Bender, Inc., in Exhibit 16–5. Assume that Bender elects to call the preferred stock at 103 according to the provisions of the preferred stock contract (Note 1, Exhibit 16–5). Bender records the following entry for the redemption:

Preferred Stock	10,000,000	
Retained Earnings	300,000	
Cash ($10,000,000 × 1.03)		10,300,000
(To redeem the preferred stock at 103.)		

The Preferred Stock account is eliminated. Because the preferred stock was issued at par, there is no Paid-in Capital in Excess of Par account to eliminate. The $300,000 debit to Retained Earnings represents the distribution of earned equity to the preferred shareholders upon redemption of their shares. If the call provisions specified a call price of 97, the journal entry would appear as follows:

Preferred Stock	10,000,000	
Paid-in Capital in Excess of Par (Common)		300,000
Cash		9,700,000
(To redeem the preferred stock at 97.)		

The credit to the Paid-in Capital in Excess of Par (Common) account represents a contribution to the remaining common stockholders' equity as a result of retiring the preferred stock at an amount less than book value.

Treasury Stock Retirement

A firm may eventually decide to retire treasury stock if there are no plans for reissuance. Retired treasury stock becomes authorized but unissued common stock. Accounting for treasury stock retirement involves removing the Treasury Stock and Common Stock from the accounting records. Since the Treasury Stock is recorded differently under the cost and par value methods, accounting for its retirement also differs under the two approaches.

Recall the Bender situation in which 2,000 shares of $100 par value common stock are purchased for the treasury at $145 a share. Assuming the treasury stock was recorded at cost, the Treasury Stock account balance is $290,000 and the journal entry to retire these shares is as follows:

Common Stock	200,000	
Paid-in Capital in Excess of Par	10,000	
Retained Earnings	80,000	
Treasury Stock		290,000
(To retire treasury stock.)		

The Common Stock, related Paid-in Capital in Excess of Par, and Treasury Stock are eliminated from the accounting records. The $80,000 debit to Retained Earnings can be evaluated in the same manner as discussed previously for the par value method. The Treasury Stock is, of course, eliminated at cost.

Under the par value method, the Paid-in Capital in Excess of Par and the Retained Earnings have already been reduced in the appropriate amounts. The Treasury Stock account has a $200,000 balance, representing the par value of the treasury stock. All that remains is the elimination of the treasury shares and outstanding common stock at their par values. The journal entry is simply:

Common Stock	200,000	
Treasury Stock		200,000
(To retire treasury stock.)		

As expected, both the cost and par value methods produce the same results when the treasury stock purchase and treasury stock retirement transactions are combined.

PROPERTY AND TREASURY STOCK DONATIONS

In this chapter we have discussed obtaining corporate capital through owner contributions. In Chapter 17 we will discuss earnings as a source of corporate capital. The third and less common source of corporate capital is the donation of either property or stock. Such donations are frequently called donated capital. Donated capital should not be confused with contributed capital; the terms "donated" and "contributed" have entirely different meanings in this context. **Donated capital** represents a nonreciprocal transfer of property from an outsider to the company. **Contributed capital** is cash, property, or services received by the company in exchange for ownership shares and attending rights.

Property Donations

Cities and counties often attract new business by donating land or other property to the business. This is not a normal exchange transaction but a unilateral transfer of assets to the corporation. Since the donation is a gift, the firm does not release assets in the acquisition. As a result, strict adherence to the historical cost principle would result in an asset valuation of zero for the donated assets. Clearly, application of the historical cost principle in this situation would not capture the economic realities of the transfer. The firm benefits by receiving a donated asset, and this benefit should be disclosed in the financial statements. The most objective method of disclosing the benefit is to record the donated asset at its fair market value. The offsetting credit is generally to Donated Capital. The use of a separate account, Donated Capital, is preferable to crediting Paid-in Capital in Excess of Par to recognize the nature of the stockholders' equity. Donated assets are not capital contributions by stock-

Historical Cost

Objectivity

holders but capital donations from outsiders. They should therefore be given distinctive disclosure.

To illustrate accounting for asset donations, consider the donation of a warehouse and adjoining land by the city of Ramsey to Valley Electric Company. Valley Electric has the land appraised at $15,000 and the warehouse at $75,000. Valley Electric records the donation as follows:

Land	15,000	
Building	75,000	
Donated Capital		90,000
(To record asset donations.)		

Disclosure Donated capital is disclosed separately in the stockholders' equity section of the balance sheet.

Treasury Stock Donations

Stockholders, or a stockholder's estate, may sometimes donate capital stock back to the company. This transfer is treated somewhat differently from property transfers, because the company should not consider the donated shares as assets. The donated shares are treasury shares to the corporation and are therefore subject to either the cost or the par value method of accounting.

Under the cost method, treasury shares are not formally entered into the records, because the firm incurred no cost in acquiring the treasury stock. The number of shares outstanding is reduced by the donated shares via a memorandum to the accounting records. Subsequent reissue of donated treasury shares requires a credit to Donated Capital for the total reissue price.

Under the par value method, donated treasury shares are recorded at par value with an offsetting credit to Donated Capital. If the donated shares are reissued at a price greater (lesser) than the par value, the difference is disclosed by increasing (decreasing) the Donated Capital account.

Donated treasury stock gives the business an opportunity to issue the same shares twice—first to the initial owner, then as donated treasury stock. The second issuance benefits the firm by generating additional ownership capital. This additional capital results only because the original owner voluntarily forfeited the rights to the shares. Therefore, under both accounting methods, the increase in stockholders' equity from issuance of donated treasury shares is labeled "donated capital."

CONCLUDING REMARKS

In this chapter we have reviewed the basic elements of corporate organization and contributed capital. Corporate ownership capital is provided through the issuance of capital stock to acquiring individuals and institutions (e.g., banks, pension funds, and investment mutual funds). Capital stock offers owners a variety of rights and preferences, as specified by the company's board of directors.

Disclosure The stockholders' equity section of the balance sheet should disclose not only the main classifications of ownership, but also information about the rights and preferences of each class of stock. As an example, the dividend preference rate and provisions should be disclosed for preferred stock. In this way, the various classes of shareholders will understand the basic rights and preferences of an ownership class and in relation to other ownership classes. Furthermore, the shares authorized, issued, and outstanding should be disclosed for each class of stock.

Exhibit 16–8 illustrates the share status relationships. Authorized shares can be either

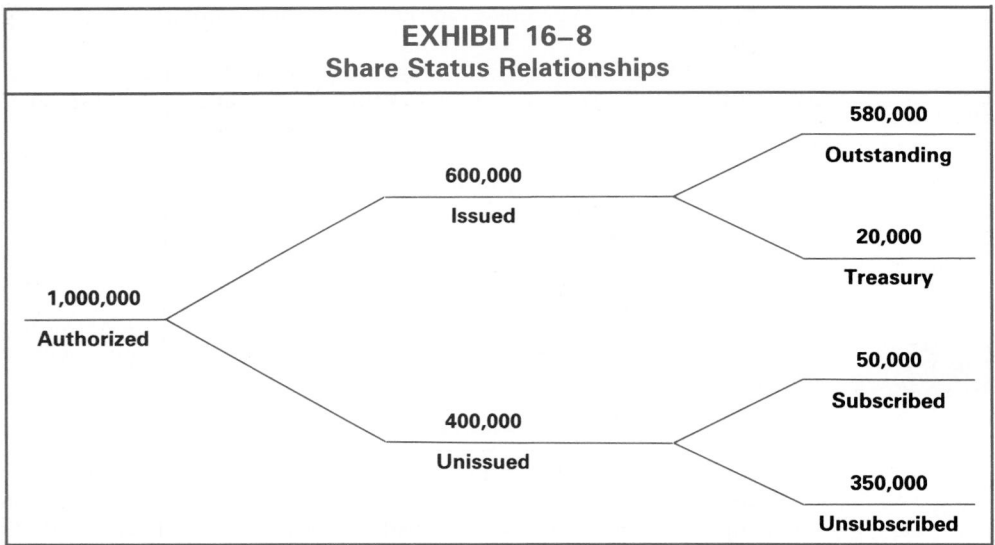

EXHIBIT 16–8
Share Status Relationships

issued or unissued. The unissued shares can be further divided into subscribed and unsubscribed stock. Recall that subscribed stock is authorized but unissued. Issued stock can be classified as issued and outstanding or issued and not outstanding. Shares that are issued but not outstanding result from treasury stock purchases.

Exhibit 16–8 includes hypothetical share amounts to aid in understanding the relationships. To illustrate how the various categories of stockholders' equity change as transactions occur, assume that the 50,000 subscribed shares are issued. In this case the total unissued stock would decrease to 350,000, the total issued stock would increase to 650,000, and the total stock outstanding would increase to 630,000 shares. The unsubscribed and treasury amounts are unchanged by the issuance of the 50,000 shares of subscribed stock. Other adjustments in share status could be evaluated in this way.

To illustrate a simple financial statement presentation of the stockholders' equity section of the balance sheet, refer to the Kroger Company balance sheet, reproduced on the front endpapers of this book. Kroger has two main classes of shareholders, common and preferred. The preferred shareholders have preference rights over common shareholders to dividend distributions and any liquidation of corporate assets. In addition, the financial statements clearly indicate that the preferred shareholders have voting privileges and rights to dividends in arrears through the cumulative clause. The common stock is presented on the financial statement at the stated value, which is an amount greater than the $1 par value. Furthermore, Kroger has no "paid-in capital in excess of par," indicating that the common stock was originally issued at the stated value. The financial statements also disclose treasury stock in the preferred manner, as a contra-stockholders' equity item. The financial statements clearly indicate that Kroger utilized the cost method of accounting for treasury stock. The net unrealized loss on marketable equity securities results from the lowering of the market value relative to the cost of the noncurrent marketable equity investment portfolio, as discussed in greater detail in Chapter 10. The accumulated earnings represent the capital provided by the internal operations of the company. This item is frequently identified as retained earnings. In the next chapter we will discuss in greater detail the accounting issues pertaining to retained earnings and other specialized topics in the context of stockholders' equity.

1. The corporate form of business organization has certain advantages over the sole proprietorship and partnership forms, particularly in terms of allowing the accumulation of large amounts of capital from many diverse owners.

2. Corporations provide limited liability to shareholders, facilitate the generation of additional equity capital, and continue in existence despite the death of one or more shareholders.

3. Preferred stock contains a preference claim over common stock in dividend distributions and in the distribution of assets upon liquidation. Preferred stock may be fully or partially participating, cumulative, or both.

4. A primary disadvantage of the corporate form of business organization is the double taxation of income, first at the corporate level and again as corporate profits are distributed to stockholders.

5. Preferred stock may be callable, convertible, or redeemable.

6. Common stock is considered the residual equity of a corporation because the claims of other investors and creditors must be satisfied before distributions may be made to common stockholders.

7. Common stock may be issued for cash or noncash consideration. In the event of noncash consideration, valuation is based on the market value of the consideration or the stock, whichever is more clearly determinable.

8. Treasury stock is issued stock that has been acquired in the secondary market by the issuing company. Treasury stock is held pending either reissuance or retirement.

9. Treasury stock acquisition and disposition can be accounted for under either the cost or the par value method.

10. Capital stock that is retired should be removed from the stockholders' equity accounts of the corporation.

11. Property or stock donations should be reflected as "donated capital" in the stockholders' equity section of the balance sheet.

16–1 Describe some of the operating and financing advantages of a corporation compared to a partnership and a sole proprietorship.

16–2 What is the difference between publicly held and closely held corporations?

16–3 Why do corporations frequently issue more than one class or type of stock?

16–4 Define cumulative preferred stock and participating preferred stock.

16–5 How should cumulative dividends in arrears on preferred stock be presented (if at all) in a corporation's financial statements?

16–6 Describe redeemable preferred stock. How should redeemable preferred stock be presented on the financial statements?

16–7 Describe the most important distinction between accounting for corporations and accounting for other forms of business organizations.

16–8 In what way is the term "reserve" used, if at all, in financial accounting?

16–9 How does a company account for stock issuances in which there are no established market values for either the stock or the consideration received?

16–10 Explain subscribed common stock. How should common stock subscriptions be presented on the balance sheet?

16–11 What are the various methods of disposing of the cash advance on a defaulted stock subscription?

16–12 How does a company account for the difference between proceeds and cost when the company transacts in its own stock?

16–13 Describe treasury stock. How should treasury stock be presented in the balance sheet?

16–14 Describe the appropriate accounting practice for the acquisition of a company's own shares.

16–15 What is minimum legal capital and why does state law usually require corporations to maintain a certain amount of stockholders' equity?

16–16 If a company issues shares of its own stock in consideration for property or services, at what amount should the transaction be recorded?

16–17 What are the proper accounting considerations and procedures for (1) property donations and (2) donations of the company's stock?

16–18 Why isn't the stockholders' equity of a corporation valued at the aggregate *market* value of the outstanding stock?

CASES

C16-1 Capital stock is an important part of corporate equity. The term "capital stock" generally includes common and preferred stock issued by a corporation.

Instructions

[a] What are the basic rights of ownership of common stock? How are they exercised?
[b] What is preferred stock? Discuss the various preferences afforded preferred stock.

(AICPA adapted)

C16-2 The stockholders' equity section of the balance sheet reports the ownership interest in the corporation. This interest is usually separated into contributed capital and earned capital.

Instructions

[a] Why is the distinction made between these two components of stockholders' equity?
[b] The contributed capital section is frequently divided into legal (or stated) capital and paid-in capital in excess of par. What is the reason for this disclosure method?

C16-3 Lyons Corporation presented its balance sheet to the bank prior to negotiating a loan. The balance sheet included among its current assets $250,000 in stock subscriptions receivable. The bank loan officer took exception to this presentation and suggested that this amount should be reported as a reduction of the stockholders' equity.

Instructions

[a] What arguments could the bank loan officer use for his position?
[b] What arguments are available to Lyons Corporation in support of their presentation method?

C16-4 The right side of Bishop Corporation's balance sheet at December 31, 1984, appears as follows:

Current liabilities	$ 150,000
10% Bond payable (due in 1995)	1,000,000
$5 Redeemable preferred stock ($50 par value; cumulative and nonvoting, to be redeemed in 1995 at par)	1,000,000
Common stock ($5 par value; 600,000 shares authorized, issued, and outstanding)	3,000,000
Total liabilities and stockholders' equity	$5,150,000

Instructions

[a] In what ways is the redeemable preferred stock similar to the 10% bond payable?
[b] In what ways is the redeemable preferred stock similar to the common stock?
[c] Is the redeemable preferred stock more like an equity or a debt?
[d] How should redeemable preferred stock be presented in the financial statements?

C16-5 Preferred stock may be eliminated from a corporation's capital structure in several ways:
[1] The corporation may call the preferred stock.
[2] The corporation may redeem the preferred stock according to a mandatory redemption provision.
[3] The corporation may purchase the preferred stock as treasury stock and retire it at a later date.
[4] The corporation may purchase the preferred stock directly off the market for immediate retirement.
[5] The preferred stockholders may convert the preferred stock to common stock according to a conversion provision.

Instructions

Identify the characteristics of each of the above elimination methods.

EXERCISES

E16-1 Hunt Corporation was organized on January 1, 1983. On that date it issued 100,000 shares of $10 par value common stock at $12 per share (200,000 shares were authorized). During the period January 1, 1983, through December 31, 1985, Hunt earned net income of $400,000 and declared and paid cash dividends of $150,000. On January 10, 1985, Hunt purchased 5,000 shares of its common stock at $10 per share. On December 29, 1985, Hunt subscribed an additional 50,000 shares for 40% down at $14 per share. On December 31, 1985, 3,000 treasury shares were sold at $15 per share. Hunt used the cost method in accounting for treasury stock.

Instructions

Prepare the stockholders' equity section of the Hunt Corporation balance sheet as it should appear on December 31, 1985.

(AICPA adapted)

E16–2 Lassiter Corporation was organized on January 1, 1984, with an authorization of 500,000 shares of common stock with a par value of $5 per share. The company uses the cost method of accounting for treasury stock transactions. During 1984 Lassiter had the following capital transactions:

Jan. 5   Issued 100,000 shares at $5 per share.
Apr. 6   Issued 50,000 shares at $7 per share.
June 8   Issued 15,000 shares at $10 per share.
July 28   Purchased 25,000 shares at $4 per share.
Dec. 31   Sold 25,000 shares held as treasury stock at $8 per share.

Instructions

Provide the appropriate journal entries for each of the above transactions.

(AICPA adapted)

E16–3 Don Juan Corporation incorporated on January 1, 1985, with an authorization of 100,000 shares of no-par common stock and 15,000 shares of $100 par preferred stock. The corporation issued 60,000 shares of common stock and 10,000 shares of preferred stock on January 7, 1985, for a lump sum price of $2,700,000.

Instructions

Provide the appropriate journal entry for the capital stock issuance of January 7, 1985, under each of the following *independent* assumptions:
[a] The common stock and preferred stock traded in the secondary market at $35 and $105 per share, respectively, immediately after the issuance.
[b] The common stock traded immediately in the secondary market at $25 per share. Because the preferred stock was closely held, a market price was not established for the preferred shares.
[c] At the issuance of common stock, the board of directors established a stated value of $25 per share. Both the common and preferred stock issuances became closely held. Therefore, a market price was not established for either issue. (*Hint:* Base the allocation on par and stated values.)

E16–4 Globe Company exchanged 100 shares of treasury stock (its $50 par common stock) for some land to be used in its business. The treasury stock had cost $60 per share, and on the exchange date, it had a fair market value of $65 per share. Globe received $1,200 for scrap when an existing building was immediately removed from this land.

Instructions

Provide the appropriate journal entry to record the acquisition of the land, assuming the treasury shares were originally recorded under:
[a] The cost method
[b] The par value method

(AICPA adapted)

E16–5 In 1984 Springfield, Inc., issued 8,000 shares of $100 par value convertible preferred stock for $105 per share. One share of preferred stock can be converted into three shares of Springfield's $25 par value common stock at the option of the preferred shareholder. In August 1984, all of the preferred stock was converted into common stock. The market value of the common stock at the date of the conversion was $30 per share.

Instructions

[a] What is the appropriate journal entry for the issuance of the preferred stock?
[b] Record the appropriate journal entry for the conversion of preferred shares to common shares.
[c] Why would a company issue convertible preferred stock instead of just placing common stock directly? Why would an investor be willing to accept the conversion feature?

(AICPA adapted)

E16–6 Furr Corporation has 25,000 shares of $5 par value stock authorized, issued, and outstanding. All of these shares were issued at a price of $11 per share. The company had retained earnings of $75,000.

Instructions

Identify the changes in the stockholders' equity section of the balance sheet for each of the following *independent* situations:
[a] Twenty-five hundred shares were acquired at $21 per share (assume the use of the par value method of accounting).
[b] Twenty-five hundred shares were acquired by a stockholder donation (assume the use of the cost method of accounting).
[c] Twenty-five hundred shares were acquired at $21 per share, then reissued at $18 per share (assume the use of the cost method of accounting).

E16–7 On January 1, 1984, Hancock Corporation subscribed 60,000 shares of their $10 par common stock. The subscription contract required a down payment equal to 40% of the total purchase price of the securities, with the remainder due in two months. The contract specified a subscription price of $22 per share. On March 1, 1984, all but 4,000 shares were issued. These shares were not issued because a subscriber defaulted. On March 1, Hancock issued these 4,000 shares to another party for $18 per share.

Instructions

[a] Provide the appropriate January 1, 1984, journal entry to reflect the subscribing of common stock.
[b] Provide the appropriate journal entry on March 1, 1984, to reflect the issuance of common stock.
[c] Provide the appropriate journal entry to record the default on 4,000 shares, assuming each of the following *independent* contract terms:
  [1] The partial payment is refunded.
  [2] The partial payment is refunded, less any expenses or reductions in issue price from the resale of the stock.
  [3] The partial payment is forfeited.
[d] Why would an issuing company insist on provision [c–2] or [c–3] above in a subscription contract?

E16–8   An analysis of the stockholders' equity of Midland Corporation as of January 1, 1984, is as follows:

Common stock ($20 par value; 100,000 shares authorized, 60,000 shares issued and outstanding)	$1,200,000
Paid-in capital in excess of par	140,000
Retained earnings	760,000
Total stockholders' equity	$2,100,000

Midland acquired 1,000 shares of its stock for $35,000, and during 1984 it entered into the following transactions:

Sold 600 treasury shares at $38 per share.
Sold 200 treasury shares at $31 per share.
Retired the remaining treasury shares.

Instructions

[a] Provide the appropriate journal entries to reflect the treasury transactions indicated above. Assume the use of the cost method of accounting.
[b] How should treasury stock be presented on the financial statements? Why?

(AICPA adapted)

E16–9   Fox Corporation acquired 2,000 shares of its

own $5 par value stock at $21 per share on February 10, 1984. Fox sold 1,200 of these shares at $27 per share on May 2, 1984, and an additional 600 shares on August 16, 1984, for $14 per share. Fox Corporation's common stock was originally issued at $16 per share.

Instructions

[a] Provide the journal entries to record the initial purchase of treasury shares under:
  [1] The cost method
  [2] The par value method
[b] Provide the journal entries to record the reissuances of treasury stock under:
  [1] The cost method
  [2] The par value method

E16–10   The stockholders' equity section of Roy Corporation's balance sheet on December 31, 1984, was as follows:

Common stock ($5 par value; 1,200,000 shares authorized, 800,000 shares issued, 700,000 shares outstanding)	$ 4,000,000
Paid-in capital in excess of par	3,250,000
Retained earnings	5,240,000
	12,490,000
Less: Treasury stock, at cost, 100,000 shares	800,000
Total stockholders' equity	$11,690,000

During 1985, Roy reissues 50,000 shares of the treasury stock at $14 per share. No other similar transactions occur during 1985.

Instructions

[a] Provide the appropriate journal entry to record the reissuance of the treasury shares.
[b] Revise the stockholders' equity section of Roy Corporation's balance sheet for December 31, 1985, assuming the par value method was used for all treasury stock transactions. Net income was $300,000. (*Hint:* Restate the December 31, 1984, stockholders' equity, assuming the 100,000 shares of treasury stock had been accounted for by the par value method. Then record the reissue of the 50,000 shares.)

(AICPA adapted)

E16–11   The stockholders' equity section of the balance sheet for Zorba, Inc., appeared as follows on December 31, 1984:

$4 Preferred stock ($40 par value; 5,000
   shares authorized, issued, and
   outstanding, callable at 102%) $ 200,000
Common stock ($5 stated value; 100,000
   shares authorized, 60,000 shares
   issued and outstanding)   300,000
Paid-in capital in excess of par
   (common)   600,000
Retained earnings   1,000,000
Total stockholders' equity $2,100,000

On February 1, 1985, Zorba purchased and retired 5,000 shares of common stock at $18 per share. On March 1, 3,000 shares of common stock were acquired as treasury stock at $14 per share (use the cost method). On April 2 the shares acquired on March 1 were retired. On August 10, Zorba called 3,000 shares of preferred stock.

Instructions

[a] Provide the appropriate journal entries for the transactions indicated in 1985.
[b] How would total stockholders' equity be affected if the par value method was used for the treasury stock acquisition of March 1 and the April 2 retirement?

E16–12 K. D. Moss Corporation was incorporated on January 1, 1984, with an authorization of 150,000 shares of $5 par value common stock and 20,000 shares of 10%, nonparticipating, cumulative, $30 par preferred stock. On February 2, 1984, K. D. Moss issued 100,000 shares of common stock at $24 per share and 15,000 shares of preferred stock at $29 per share. Subscriptions were taken for 40,000 common shares at a contracted price of $25 per share. The subscription contract required a 60% cash advance. The stock will be issued when the subscription price is paid in full on January 31, 1985. In 1984 K. D. Moss received land from the city of Nocksville for future plant expansion at no cost. The land had a cost to Nocksville of $15,000 and a market value on the transfer date of $35,000. In 1984 K. D. Moss purchased 15,000 shares of its own common stock for $30 per share (assume the cost method). K. D. Moss declared

dividends for preferred and common stock only once during 1984. The common stock dividend was $10,000. Net income for 1984 was $65,000.

Instructions

Prepare in good form the stockholders' equity section of the balance sheet on December 31, 1984, for K. D. Moss Corporation.

E16–13 The stockholders' equity section of the balance sheet for Willow Corporation appeared as follows on December 31, 1984:

Preferred stock ($20 par value; 20,000
   shares authorized, issued, and
   outstanding) $ 400,000
Common stock ($2 par value; 100,000
   shares authorized, 60,000 shares
   issued, and 50,000 shares outstanding)   120,000
Paid-in capital in excess of par
   (common)   1,150,000
Paid-in capital from defaulted
   subscriptions   150,000
Retained earnings   70,000
Treasury stock (at par)   (20,000)
Total stockholders' equity $1,870,000

Willow Corporation was formed on January 1, 1984, with the issuance of 20,000 preferred shares and 10,000 common shares. The common shares were issued for $25 per share. Willow issued an additional 50,000 common shares on a subscription basis. The original subscription contract was for 70,000 shares at a subscription price of $25 per share, with a required cash down payment equal to 30% of the purchase price. The subscription contract requires the cash advance on all defaulted shares to be forfeited. Willow earned $100,000 in 1984 but declared no dividends.

Instructions

Provide the journal entries that must have been made in 1984, as determined from the December 31, 1984, stockholders' equity balances and related information.

PROBLEMS

P16–1 The stockholders' equity section of the January 1, 1985, balance sheet for A. G. Betzman Corporation is as follows:

12% Callable preferred stock
   ($100 par value; 1,000 shares
   issued and outstanding) $ 100,000

Common stock ($10 par value;
   40,000 shares authorized, 25,000
   shares issued and outstanding)   250,000
Paid-in capital in excess of par (preferred)   1,000
Paid-in capital in excess of par (common)   1,200,000
Retained earnings   900,000
Total stockholders' equity $2,451,000

The following transactions occurred in 1985:

Jan. 16   Issued 15,000 shares of common stock for $63 per share.

Feb. 18   Purchased 20,000 shares of common stock for the treasury at $54 per share (assume the cost method).

Mar. 10   The city of Maryville donated land with an appraised value of $36,000 for use as a future plant site.

Apr. 1   Retired 10,000 shares of the treasury stock purchased in February. The market price of common shares was $57 per share at the time.

July 29   Called 250 preferred shares at a call price of $103 per share.

Aug. 16   Reissued the remaining treasury shares from February at $66 per share.

Sept. 9   Acquired land and building by issuing 10,000 common shares when the common was selling for $48 per share. Appraised value of the land was $200,000, and the building $350,000. Consider the market value of the stock as the basis for determining the value of the acquired assets.

Oct. 10   A shareholder donated 6,000 common shares to the corporation (assume the cost method).

Dec. 6   Sold the donated shares for $64 per share.

Instructions

Provide the appropriate journal entries for the above transactions.

P16-2 Sentry Corporation began operations on January 1, 1984, by issuing the following shares:

5,000 shares of 12% redeemable preferred stock, $100 par value	$ 500,000
60,000 common shares, $2 par value, 100,000 shares authorized	1,080,000

In addition, the following transactions took place during the year:

Jan. 10   An additional 20,000 shares were subscribed at $20 per share. Subscribers were required to put down 40% of the purchase price, with the remainder due in six months.

Feb. 1   Paid legal fees with respect to the stock offering by issuing 1,000 common shares

when the market price was $21 per common share.

Mar. 19   Purchased 10,000 common shares for the treasury at $16 per share (assume the par value method).

July 1   Purchased and retired 5,000 common shares at $20 per share.

July 10   The remaining amount due on 19,000 shares of the stock subscription was paid. The remaining 1,000 shares were defaulted. The down payment was refunded to the defaulting party. At this time the market price per share was $24.

Aug. 22   Retired 3,000 treasury shares.

Sept. 30   Reissued 7,000 treasury shares at $25 per share.

Nov. 12   The estate of a deceased stockholder donated 1,000 common shares to the company (assume the par value method).

Nov. 23   Sold the donated shares for $26 per share.

Instructions

Provide the appropriate journal entries for each transaction above.

P16-3   Hartford Corporation's stockholders' equity section of the balance sheet appears as follows on January 1, 1984:

11% Callable preferred stock ($100 par value; 60,000 shares authorized, issued, and outstanding)	$ 6,000,000
Common stock ($10 par value; 400,000 shares authorized, issued, and outstanding)	4,000,000
Paid-in capital in excess of par (common)	12,000,000
Retained earnings	15,000,000
Total stockholders' equity	$37,000,000

Common and preferred stock were issued at the corporation's inception. There were no capital stock transactions from the inception of the corporation through January 1, 1984. In 1984 the following transactions took place:

Jan. 16   Purchased 30,000 treasury shares of common stock at $52 per share (assume the cost method).

Feb. 3   Retired 10,000 treasury shares when the market price was $48 per share.

Mar. 6   Called 10,000 preferred shares at $102 per share.

May 22 Received 15,000 shares as a donation from a stockholder when the market price was $41 per share.

Sept. 30 Purchased 10,000 common shares at $38 per share for immediate retirement.

Oct. 16 Reissued 10,000 of the treasury shares purchased in January at $47 per share.

Nov. 17 Reissued 10,000 donated common shares at $51 per share.

Dec. 1 Retired the remaining donated shares.

Net income for 1984 was $1,000,000.

Instructions

[a] Provide the appropriate journal entries for each of the above transactions.

[b] Prepare the stockholders' equity section of the balance sheet for Hartford as it should appear on December 31, 1984.

P16—4 Holston Manufacturing Company initiated operations on January 1, 1984. On December 31, 1984, the company's stockholders' equity section of the balance sheet appeared as follows:

Common stock ($30 par value; 60,000 shares authorized, 50,000 shares issued, and 35,000 shares outstanding)	$1,500,000
Common stock subscribed (5,000 shares)	150,000
Paid-in capital in excess of par value	1,375,000
Retained earnings	800,000
Treasury stock (at cost)	(780,000)
Total stockholders' equity	$3,045,000

During 1985 40% of the remaining purchase price of the subscribed shares was remitted by subscribers. All but 500 of the subscribed shares were issued, because the original subscriber defaulted on the shares. These shares were issued at $50 per share to a new owner, and the remaining cash advance was returned to the original subscriber (less any price loss). The common stock subscriptions were subscribed at the same price as the original issue of 50,000 shares. Furthermore, in 1985 Holston resold 5,000 treasury shares at $56 per share. Later in the year another 5,000 treasury shares were sold at $25 per share after a sharp drop in the company's stock price. Towards the end of the year, 3,000 treasury shares were retired.

Instructions

Provide the appropriate journal entries for Holston

Manufacturing Company for 1985 based on the discussion above.

P16—5 The stockholders' equity section of Speedwell Furniture Company's balance sheet appeared as follows on January 1, 1985:

Common stock ($5 par value; 80,000 shares authorized, issued, and outstanding)	$ 400,000
Paid-in capital in excess of par value	1,000,000
Retained earnings	800,000
Total shareholders' equity	$2,200,000

The following events occurred in sequence during 1985:

[1] Ten thousand common shares were purchased for the treasury at $20 per share.

[2] An additional 10,000 shares were purchased for the treasury at $30 per share.

[3] Twelve thousand treasury shares were resold at a market price of $27 per share.

[4] Five thousand Speedwell common shares were donated to the company by a stockholder's estate.

[5] Eleven thousand treasury shares were reissued at a market price of $23 per share.

[6] The remaining shares were retired.

Instructions

[a] Provide the appropriate journal entries assuming the cost method of accounting for treasury stock, and treasury stock reissuance on a first-in, first-out basis.

[b] Provide the appropriate journal entries assuming the cost method of accounting for treasury stock, and treasury stock reissuance under an average-cost assumption.

[c] Provide the appropriate journal entries assuming the par value method of accounting for treasury stock.

P16—6 The following are comparative stockholders' equity sections of the balance sheets for Hariman Corporation. Some items that require disclosure are not included.

	Dec. 31, 1984	Dec. 31, 1985
10% Preferred stock ($20 par value; 90,000 shares authorized)	$ 100,000	$ 120,000
Common stock ($5 par value; 150,000 shares authorized)	300,000	400,000
Common stock subscribed (10,000 shares)	–0–	50,000

Paid-in capital in excess of par (common)	360,000	410,000
Donated capital (10,000 shares Hariman common)	–0–	50,000
Retained earnings	400,000	660,000
Treasury stock (10,000 shares of common)	–0–	(50,000)
Total stockholders' equity	$1,160,000	$1,640,000

Net income for 1985 was $300,000. The subscribed stock sold at $7.

Instructions

[a] Provide the appropriate journal entries to account for the change in the stockholders' equity account balances for Hariman Corporation.

[b] How many shares were issued and outstanding of the preferred and common stock at December 31, 1984 and 1985?

P16–7   Wall Corporation presented the following balance sheet for December 31, 1984:

Assets

Current assets	$ 30,000
Treasury stock (at market; cost = $15,000)	14,000
Fixed assets	56,000
Total assets	$100,000

Liabilities and Stockholders' Equity

Current liabilities	$ 20,000
Common stock subscribed (500 shares)	10,000
Long-term debt	8,000
Total liabilities	38,000
Stockholders' equity	
Common stock (4,000 shares issued)	18,000
10% Preferred stock (1,000 shares issued)	12,000
Less: Stock subscriptions receivable	(4,000)
Reserve for depreciation	16,000
Earned surplus	20,000
Total liabilities and stockholders' equity	$100,000

Your investigation of Wall Corporation's financial records indicates that all authorized shares have been either issued or subscribed. In addition, the par value for the common and preferred stock was $2 and $10, respectively. The treasury stock was originally purchased when the market price was $20 per share. During 1984, 250 treasury shares were resold for $25 per

share. A "gain on treasury stock transactions" was credited for the difference between the original cost and the selling price. Furthermore, the excess of cost over market of the treasury shares at the end of the period was recognized as an unrealized loss on the 1984 income statement. You also discovered that the city of Kingston donated land with a market value of $9,000 to Wall during 1984.

Instructions

Revise the December 31, 1984, balance sheet for Wall Corporation as it should be presented according to generally accepted accounting principles.

P16–8   Flatt Tire Company is a small, closely held corporation with three stockholders. D. Edwards is planning to retire from the business, leaving M. Adams and K. Strong to manage the business. The owners agreed to alter the capitalization of the firm to reflect this event. Edwards will redeem his capital stock in return for nonvoting preferred stock. Before the agreement, the stockholders' equity section of Flatt's balance sheet appeared as follows:

Common stock ($20 par value; 10,000 shares authorized and issued, 9,000 shares outstanding)	$200,000
Paid-in capital in excess of par	50,000
Retained earnings	140,000
Treasury stock (cost method)	(30,000)
Total stockholders' equity	$360,000

The three owners presently have the following ownership interests: Edwards, 20%; Adams, 40%; and Strong, 40%. The corporation will be reorganized according to the following agreement:

[1] The treasury stock will be canceled.

[2] Two new stock issues will be authorized: $10 par value common stock, and 12% cumulative nonvoting preferred stock ($100 par value).

[3] The stockholders will surrender their shares for cancellation and will receive the newly authorized shares as follows:

[a] Edwards will receive only preferred stock.

[b] Adams will receive 40% of the common stock.

[c] Strong will receive 60% of the common stock and the remainder of the preferred stock.

[4] The total number of shares for the preferred stock and common stock issue is 19,000.

Instructions

[a] Prepare the journal entry to cancel the treasury

stock account on the company's books.

[b] Prepare a schedule computing the amount of each stockholder's equity in the company before the recapitalization.

[c] Compute the number of new common stock and new preferred stock shares to be issued, given that they total 19,000 shares.

[d] Prepare a schedule computing the number of shares of each type of newly issued stock that each stockholder will receive under the agreement described above.

P16–9 Huron, Inc., a manufacturer of restaurant and kitchen equipment, was incorporated in 1950. Its stock is publicly held. The stockholders' equity section of the balance sheet at September 30, 1984, follows.

$2 Cumulative redeemable preferred stock ($15 par value; 500,000 shares authorized, 4,000 shares issued and outstanding)	$ 60,000
Common stock ($10 par value; 1,000,000 shares authorized, 110,000 shares issued and outstanding)	1,100,000
Retained earnings	622,000
Total stockholders' equity	$1,782,000

Huron's capital stock transactions during fiscal 1985 were as follows:

[1] On January 2, 1985, 8,000 preferred shares were issued in exchange for land with an appraised value of $100,000. Six months ago 1,000 shares of Huron preferred were exchanged "over the counter" for $14 per share.

[2] On January 17, 1985, 4,500 shares of common stock were sold to Horace Edwards at $25 per share.

[3] On September 14, 1985, Huron purchased dissident stockholder Edwards' 4,500 shares at $27 per share. The shares are to be held as treasury shares and accounted for at cost. (Edwards violently opposed Huron's business strategy. It was necessary to pay a $2 premium to eliminate his interest.)

[4] On September 28, 1985, Huron contracted with Charles Trenton for the sale of 10,000 previously unissued shares at $25 per share to be issued when the purchase price is fully paid. At September 30, only $195,000 had been paid. Trenton agreed to pay the balance on or before November 3, 1985.

[5] On September 30, 1985, Huron redeemed 4,000 preferred shares according to the issue agreement. The shares were redeemed at $18 per share plus accrued dividends.

[6] A cash dividend of $2 was declared on the preferred shares on March 11, 1985, and paid on March 30, 1985.

[7] A cash dividend of $1.50 per share was declared on September 15, 1985, and payable October 11, 1985.

[8] Huron's net income for fiscal year 1985 was $225,000.

Instructions

Prepare the stockholders' equity section of the balance sheet for the year ended September 30, 1985. This statement should be supported by the following schedules, presented in the order given:

[a] Changes in preferred stock account.

[b] Changes in common stock account.

[c] Calculation of paid-in capital in excess of par.

[d] Changes in retained earnings.

(AICPA adapted)

P16–10 On January 1, 1984, the stockholders' equity section of Universal Electronics Company's balance sheet revealed the following information:

$5 Convertible preferred stock ($40 par value; 50,000 shares authorized, 20,000 shares issued and outstanding)	$ 800,000
Common stock ($5 stated value; 200,000 shares authorized, 120,000 shares issued and outstanding)	600,000
Paid-in capital in excess of par	3,000,000
Retained earnings	4,500,000
Total stockholders' equity	$8,900,000

In addition, the following information is known:

[1] On February 2, 1984, 15,000 common shares were acquired by the company for $33 per share (assume the cost method).

[2] On September 30, 1984, 5,000 preferred shares were converted to common shares. One share of preferred stock is convertible into one share of common stock. At the time of conversion, the common stock had a market value of $42 per share.

[3] On December 21, 1984, Universal placed a stock subscription of 10,000 common shares at a subscription price of $33 per share. The subscription contract required a cash down payment equal to 60% of the subscription price, with the balance due on February 1, 1985.

[4] On February 1, 1985, 8,500 common shares were issued according to the subscription contract. Because of default by a subscriber, 1,500 shares were not issued. The subscription contract requires the subscriber to forfeit all cash advances.

[5] On April 15, 1985, 10,000 shares held in treasury were reissued at $45 per share.

[6] On May 15, 1985, a special dividend of preferred stock was distributed to common stockholders. One hundred shares of common stock entitled a shareholder to one share of preferred stock. The market price of preferred stock was $40 per share at the time. (*Hint:* Record this dividend at the market price of the preferred shares.)

[7] Cash dividends are declared for preferred and common shares on October 31 and April 30 of each year. Semiannual cash dividends for common shares are $0.50 per share.

[8] Net income for 1984 was $760,000, and for 1985, $890,000.

Instructions

Analyze the changes in Universal's stockholders' equity accounts for 1984 and 1985. Create column headings for the stockholders' equity accounts. Enter under each column heading the beginning balances and the changes in the accounts due to transactions in 1984 and 1985. Draw balances for each account for December 31, 1984, and December 31, 1985. Provide in good form a schedule supporting computations for dividend calculations.

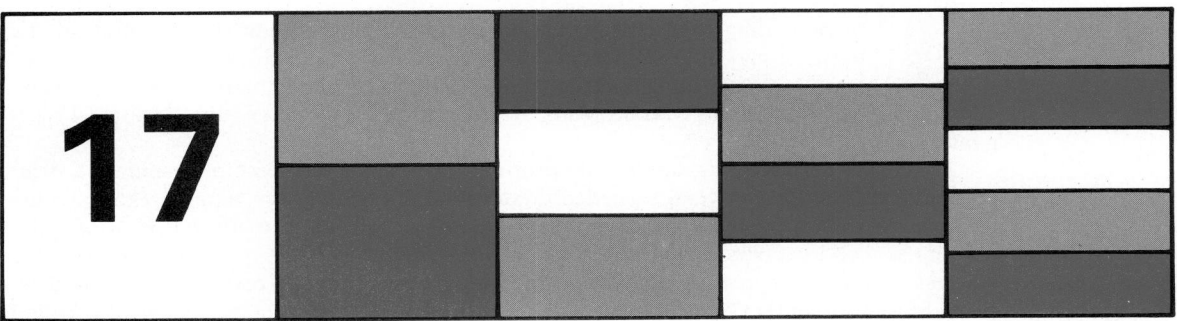

17

STOCKHOLDERS' EQUITY: OPERATIONS, EARNINGS, DIVIDENDS, AND OTHER ISSUES

Objectives

To demonstrate the proper accounting for various types of dividends on certain types of stock.

To distinguish between stock splits and stock dividends.

To describe what an appropriation of retained earnings accomplishes and how it should be reported.

To explain appropriate accounting and reporting standards for a variety of stock option plans and stock warrants.

To describe the circumstances in which a quasi reorganization is appropriate and to demonstrate the accounting procedures that are applied.

The preceding chapter is primarily concerned with the initial incorporation of a business and the issuance and reacquisition of capital stock. In this chapter we consider accounting and reporting problems involving earned equity—specifically, dividends, option and warrant plans, appropriations of earned equity, and quasi reorganizations.

Recall that corporations, unlike sole proprietorships and partnerships, maintain a strict reporting distinction between earned and contributed stockholders' equity. If the owners and managers of a business are different groups of people, as in many corporations, the owners as well as creditors and other financial statement users need to know the relative success of the enterprise in recovering operating costs through revenues generated by providing goods and services. The earned equity portion of total stockholders' equity, called **retained earnings,** provides a cumulative measure of the extent of that success net of dividend distributions. Retained earnings also reveals the extent of reliance on cumulative earnings in financing the enterprise.

In addition to representing a source of financing for a corporation, the Retained Earnings account also reflects equity in assets which are subject to distribution to shareholders as dividends. Dividends are normally paid with resources generated from the earnings of a corporation and therefore represent a distribution of profits (a return *on* invested capital rather than a return *of* invested capital).

Occasionally a company uses the term "earned surplus" in financial statements to describe retained earnings. However, the practice is rare and has been discouraged by the accounting profession for many years. The Committee on Terminology of the American Institute of Certified Public Accountants stated that the term "surplus" connotes excess or unneeded equity and recommended that accountants stop using the term.[1] However, "surplus" is often used in legal instruments and in statutes regulating commerce, and accountants may thus occasionally encounter the term. As used in financial statements, "surplus" connotes "the amount that remains when use or need is satisfied" (Webster)—a definition that is incompatible with the meaning of retained earnings. Accordingly, we emphasize the preferred terminology "retained earnings."

RETAINED EARNINGS

Two financial statements are necessary to broadly reflect results of operations: an income statement and a statement of changes in retained earnings. These two statements are often combined. In some cases, the statement of retained earnings is presented in a statement summarizing changes in all stockholders' equity accounts, including Retained Earnings. Both the income and retained earnings statements present activity for a period of time, in contrast to the balance sheet, which provides information about economic resources and obligations at a point in time. During the closing process, an accountant transfers the amount of a company's net income or loss to retained earnings.

The accounting profession has adopted standards that carefully specify the types of activities and events which affect income and should therefore appear initially on the income statement rather than the statement of retained earnings. Briefly, revenues, expenses, gains, and losses determine income and should always appear on the income statement. It would therefore be improper to directly charge or credit retained earnings for a revenue, expense, gain, or loss.

The statement of retained earnings is affected by a limited and carefully defined set of events. Specifically, the items presented in Exhibit 17–1 are the most common economic events that are charged or credited directly to the Retained Earnings account. As explained

---

[1]*Accounting Terminology Bulletin No. 2,* "Review and Résumé," 1953, par. 65.

EXHIBIT 17-1		
Primary Items Directly Affecting Retained Earnings*		
Nature of Event	Debits to Retained Earnings	Credits to Retained Earnings
Income Summary account closed to Retained Earnings	Net Loss	Net Income
Distributions to stockholders (cash, property, or stock)	Dividends Declared	—
Adoption of certain accounting principles	Retroactive Negative Adjustment (loss, expense)	Retroactive Positive Adjustment (gain, revenue)
Corrections of errors made in prior years	Prior Period Adjustment (loss, expense)	Prior Period Adjustment (gain, revenue)
Reservation of earned equity for a specific purpose (e.g., plant expansion, debt service)	Appropriation	Cancellation of Existing Appropriation
Treasury stock transactions	Negative adjustments from treasury stock transactions	—
Quasi reorganization	Write-down of assets to fair value	Establishment of a zero balance by charging contributed capital

*This list is not intended to be comprehensive. Other items that can affect retained earnings are changes in certain accounting principles and changes in the accounting entity (see Chapter 19).

in Chapter 16, certain treasury stock transactions cause adjustments to retained earnings. In addition, the adoption of certain accounting principles sometimes results in a retroactive adjustment through retained earnings. The Financial Accounting Standards Board (FASB) often requires a retroactive adjustment through retained earnings for the transition to a new accounting standard, as when *FASB Statement of Financial Accounting Standards No. 2,* "Accounting for Research and Development Costs" (1974) became effective. Retroactive adjustment through retained earnings is also appropriate when certain existing standards are adopted, such as the initial application of the equity method by an investor establishing significant influence over an investee (see Chapter 10). Furthermore, when a company is reorganized due to financial difficulty, retained earnings may also be affected. We discuss reorganization more fully later in this chapter. The other items in Exhibit 17-1 are explained in the following sections.

The Income Statement and Retained Earnings

At several points earlier in this text, we have developed various concepts of income. We also discuss income determination and presentation in greater detail in Chapter 20. At the present time the accounting profession supports a modified all-inclusive determination of net income in which most items of revenue, expense, gain, and loss are included in the determination of net income. Thus, in applying the matching principle to determine an enterprise's net income, only selected, well-defined items are excluded and treated as direct charges or credits to the Retained Earnings account.

Matching

Procedurally, all income statement accounts are closed to an Income Summary account, which, in turn, is closed to the Retained Earnings account. Therefore, the net income earned or loss sustained during the period is reflected in a single number on the statement of retained earnings. Individual revenues and expenses comprising net income are displayed on the income statement. Accountants should not bypass the income statement by recording revenues, expenses, gains, and losses directly in the Retained Earnings account.

Prior Period Adjustments

Prior period adjustments are recorded as direct charges or credits to the Retained Earnings account and do not affect net income. **Prior period adjustments** are usually errors made in previous years that have been detected and corrected in the current year. In practice, accounting errors resulting in prior period adjustments are rare. Management has a strong incentive to minimize public disclosure of prior period mistakes in financial reporting. A prior period adjustment informs users of financial information that decisions made in prior years may have been based on flawed information provided by management.

Accounting Principles Board Opinion No. 20 defines errors in financial statements as "mathematical mistakes, mistakes in the application of accounting principles, oversights or misuses of facts that existed at the time the [previous] financial statements were prepared.[2] The Accounting Principles Board (APB) also defined changes from unacceptable accounting principles to generally accepted accounting principles (GAAP) as corrections of errors. Normal recurring changes in accounting estimates, however, do not constitute corrections of errors. For example, the useful lives and salvage values of depreciable assets must be estimated in advance in order to calculate depreciation expense. Revisions in such estimates as a result of new or better information are not considered corrections of errors whose effects are directly recorded in retained earnings. Rather, changes in estimates affect net income of the current and future periods. Other examples of circumstances which require accounting estimates include the recognition of bad debts and the evaluation of loss contingencies.

In sum, if available information is misused or intentional misestimates are made, an error occurs. If new information becomes available to effect a better estimate, a change in estimate results. Accountants must evaluate whether original estimates are wrong as a result of intentional action or honest misestimates. Financial accounting and reporting for each type of event differs greatly. We discuss accounting changes more fully in Chapter 19.

The presentation of prior period adjustments in the retained earnings statement is made net of any related income tax effects. For example, assume that a $3,000 advertising commission which had been incurred and should have been charged to expense in a prior period is paid and charged to expense during the current period. To facilitate proper matching, the correction of this error is properly treated as a prior period adjustment. The advertising expense may also be deductible for federal income taxes. Thus, a tax benefit may be associated with the prior period adjustment, and the effect on retained earnings of the correction of the error should be shown net of the related income taxes. We discuss the techniques for calculating the tax effects of prior period adjustments in Chapter 18.

The presentation of a prior period adjustment in the statement of retained earnings appears as follows, assuming a 40% tax rate and an unadjusted beginning retained earnings balance of $10,000.

Retained earnings, beginning balance	$10,000
Correction of a prior period omission of advertising expense (net of $1,200 income tax effect)	(1,800)
Adjusted retained earnings, beginning balance	$ 8,200

---

[2] *APB Opinion No. 20*, "Accounting Changes," 1971, par. 13.

Matching

Dividends

Dividends involve the unilateral transfer of items of value from a corporation to its stockholders. Corporate assets are usually the items transferred, although, in some cases, additional stock of the corporation is transferred as a stock dividend. In any event, dividends represent a reduction of retained earnings, unless the dividend is a liquidating dividend. Liquidating dividends are presumed to be paid from resources which were originally contributed by stockholders rather than earned by the enterprise. As such, contributed capital accounts are charged when liquidating dividends are declared and paid. The various classes, types, and amounts of dividends and the related accounting and reporting practices are considered next; liquidating dividends are discussed later.

Dividend Distributions of Corporate Assets

The board of directors of a corporation must **declare** a dividend before a liability to pay dividends is incurred by the corporation. The day the board of directors decides that a dividend should be distributed is called the **date of declaration.** Usually, the declaration provides for a **date of record** and a **date of payment.** These three dates are important for accountants, and Exhibit 17–2 summarizes the accounting and reporting implications of each.

The board of directors declares a dividend via a news release to the financial press and shareholders. An example of a typical dividend announcement is provided in Exhibit 17–3 for Comdata Network, a company that provides an electronic funds transfer network.

Although the phrase "dividends are paid out of retained earnings" is frequently used, we should clearly recognize that dividends are paid with cash or other assets. Retained earnings merely represents the funding source or equity for the reduction of assets paying the dividend. For example, a company may have retained earnings far in excess of cash available for supporting operations and dividend payments. Cash generated by operations may be invested in plant assets or used to retire debt and thus not be available for distribution as dividends.

Cash Dividends

When a corporation's board of directors declares a **cash dividend,** the total amount to be disbursed as well as the per share amount of the dividend is usually stated explicitly, and accounting is consistent with that described in Exhibit 17–2. When there is more than one

---

EXHIBIT 17–2
Summary of Dividend Paying Events

Event	Explanation	Accounting Entry		
Date of declaration	Board of directors declares dividend and corporation incurs liability to pay dividend.	Retained Earnings Dividends Payable	XX	XX
Date of record	Declaration specifies that ownership of stock on record date determines the specific dividend recipient.	No journal entry required; however, a memo entry is made to specific stockholder accounts in subsidiary records.		
Date of payment	Cash (or other assets) is disbursed to appropriate stockholders of record.	Dividends Payable Cash	XX	XX

EXHIBIT 17–3
Comdata Network
Dividend Announcement

NEWS RELEASE

Contact: C. W. Harter, Jr.
    President
    (615) 385-0400

FOR IMMEDIATE RELEASE

COMDATA NETWORK DECLARES DIVIDEND

Nashville, Tennessee (January 25, 1983)—It was announced today that the Board of Directors of Comdata Network, Inc. has declared a regular quarterly cash dividend of $.06 per share payable on February 9, 1983 to shareholders of record as of the close of business February 2, 1983.

Comdata Network, Inc. transfers funds throughout the United States and Canada for commercial customers. Comdata also processes an Emergency Cash Service to Master-Card or Visa cardholders providing them with the ability to wire money almost anywhere in the United States by simply calling Comdata directly and charging the transfer to their MasterCard or Visa account. In addition, Comdata offers its Emergency Cash Service in 121 casinos in Las Vegas, Reno, Lake Tahoe, Atlantic City and several overseas locations. Comdata's shares are traded in the over-the-counter market with the NASDAQ [National Association of Securities Dealers Automated Quotations] symbol CASH.

---

class of stock, allocating dividends among the classes of stock can become complex. We discuss several of these complexities in the following pages.

Dividends on Cumulative Preferred Stock. A cumulation clause requires a company to pay all dividends to preferred stockholders, including unpaid dividends from prior years, before any dividends are paid to common stockholders. Unpaid dividends on cumulative preferred stock from prior years, called **dividends in arrears,** are not a liability until a dividend is declared by a corporation's board of directors. Accountants must be aware of such clauses to properly calculate the dividends due each stockholder class.

Exhibit 17–4, the stockholders' equity section of Sundeen Corporation's balance sheet at December 31, 1984, illustrates the difficulties that can arise and the related computations necessary to appropriately distribute dividends. Assume that on December 31, 1984, Sun-

---

EXHIBIT 17–4
Sundeen Corporation
Partial Balance Sheet

December 31, 1984

Stockholders' Equity

Preferred stock ($100 par, 7% cumulative, nonvoting; 10,000 shares authorized, issued, and outstanding)	$1,000,000
Common stock ($25 par; 100,000 shares authorized, 50,000 shares issued and outstanding)	1,250,000
Paid-in capital in excess of par value	750,000
Total paid-in capital	3,000,000
Retained earnings	2,500,000
Total stockholders' equity	$5,500,000

---

deen's board of directors declares a dividend of $600,000 to be paid on January 31, 1985, to stockholders of record at January 15, 1985. Further assume that no dividends have been paid for the previous three years. The following computation demonstrates how the $600,000 dividend will be distributed if Sundeen's preferred stock outstanding was unchanged for the periods in question:

Par value of preferred stock outstanding	$1,000,000
Dividend percentage	× .07
Annual dividend to preferred stockholders	70,000
X number of years in arrears (3) + current year's dividend	× 4
Total dividend to preferred stockholders	$ 280,000

Because the preferred stock is cumulative, the three years' dividends in arrears and the current year's dividend are paid before the common stockholders receive any dividend. Therefore, of the total dividend declared ($600,000), the preferred stockholders receive $280,000 while the common stockholders receive only $320,000. In this case the total dividends declared result in the following dividends per share:

Preferred stock	
In arrears ($210,000/10,000 shares)	$21.00
Current ($70,000/10,000 shares)	7.00
Total dividends per share (preferred)	$28.00
Common stock	
Current ($320,000/50,000 shares)	$ 6.40

The entries to record the declaration and payment of the dividend are:

Dec. 31, 1984	Retained Earnings	600,000	
	Dividends Payable (Preferred)		280,000
	Dividends Payable (Common)		320,000
	(To record declaration of dividend. Preferred 3 years in arrears.)		

Jan. 31, 1985   Dividends Payable
                (Preferred)   280,000
                Dividends Payable
                (Common)   320,000
                    Cash   600,000
                (To record payment of dividends.)

No formal entry is necessary on the date of record, when the stockholders who will receive the dividends are determined.

Dividends on Noncumulative Preferred Stock.   Now assume the same facts as in the previous example, except that the preferred stock is *not* cumulative. The following calculation reflects the distribution of the dividend under this condition:

Par value of preferred stock
   outstanding $1,000,000
Dividend percentage   × .07
Total dividend to preferred
   stockholders $ 70,000

Because the preferred stock is noncumulative, only the current year's dividend is paid to the preferred stockholders. This is the case even though the preferred stockholders have received no dividends for the last three years. The common stockholders will, of course, receive the remaining $530,000. Dividends per share in this case are:

Preferred stock ($70,000/10,000 shares) $ 7.00
Common stock ($530,000/50,000 shares)   10.60

The cumulative feature of preferred stock directly affects the value of common stock and preferred stock. When preferred stock is cumulative, dividends for common shareholders may be reduced if dividends on preferred stock fall in arrears. As a result, common stock investors will likely discount the market value of the common shares. In contrast, preferred stockholders perceive the cumulative feature as an attractive characteristic that provides some protection against omitted dividends. As a result, the market price of the preferred stock will likely be higher than it would be without the cumulation clause.

Dividends on Participating Preferred Stock.   Preferred stock may be fully participating, partially participating, or nonparticipating. Participation features may also be combined with cumulation clauses. (For simplicity we illustrate each separately.) Participating preferred stockholders share additional dividends with common stockholders after each has received an initial dividend. The initial dividend distribution is based on the preference percentage of the preferred stock. The extent of the sharing depends on whether the preferred stock is fully or partially participating.

To illustrate, consider again the stockholders' equity of Sundeen Corporation presented in Exhibit 17–4. For simplicity, however, assume that there are no dividends in arrears and that the preferred stock is fully participating. The following calculation demonstrates the manner in which the $600,000 dividend is distributed:

Step 1.   Preference Distribution to Preferred Stockholders

Total preferred par value $1,000,000
Preference rate   × .07
Initial distribution amount $ 70,000

Step 2. Equivalency Distribution to Common Stockholders

Total common par value	$1,250,000
Equivalency rate (based on preferred rate)	× .07
Initial distribution amount	$ 87,500

Step 3. Participation Distribution

Total dividend declared		$ 600,000
Preference to preferred stockholders	$70,000	
Equivalency to common stockholders	87,500	
Total distributed prior to participation		157,500
Remaining participation dividend		$ 442,500

Step 4. Weighted Average Distribution of Remaining Dividend

Remaining participation dividend (Step 3)		$442,500
Ratio of total par values		
Preferred par	$1,000,000	44.4%
Common par	1,250,000	55.6%
Total combined par values	$2,250,000	100.0%
Portion of remainder to preferred stockholders		
(.444 × $442,500)		$196,470
Portion of remainder to common stockholders		
(.556 × $442,500)		246,030
Total remainder distributed		$442,500

Step 5. Summary of Total Dividend Allocation

Preferred stock		
Preference amount (Step 1)	$ 70,000	
Participation amount (Step 4)	196,470	
Total preferred dividend		$266,470
Common stock		
Preference equivalency amount		
(Step 2)	87,500	
Participation amount (Step 4)	246,030	
Total common dividend		333,530
Total dividend		$600,000

When preferred stock is **fully participating,** both common and preferred shareholders usually receive an equal percentage dividend per share on the par value of their holdings. An exception occurs if the dividend declared is too small to pay common stockholders the preference rate. In the example above, in which the preference rate is 7%, the percentage to be paid is calculated in the following manner:

Preferred stock ($266,470/$1,000,000) 26.7% (rounded)
Common stock ($333,530/$1,250,000) 26.7% (rounded)
Total (dividend/total par value of both classes)
($600,000/$2,250,000) 26.7% (rounded)

The percentage paid to each class, as computed in Step 5 above, is also 26.7%. Since the percentage in our example (26.7%) exceeds the preferred rate (7%), we conclude that each class of stockholder shares the dividend equally on a pro rata basis.

Several other points are significant in the calculations above. First, a participation clause in preferred stock does not apply until the preferred stockholders receive the preference amount and the common stockholders receive dividends equivalent (on a weighted average) to those received by the preferred stockholders. Therefore, if a dividend fails to meet both requirements, the preferred stockholders receive only the preference amount. The participation clause applies only to dividends in excess of the original preference dividend paid on preferred stock and an equivalent dividend on common stock. Of course, if a dividend is too small to meet even the preference amount of the preferred stock, the preferred shareholders receive the entire dividend.

Once a participation clause is in effect, the number of shares outstanding and related par value of each class of stock must be considered on a weighted average to allocate the remaining dividend. The total dividend to be received by each class of stockholder may comprise a base dividend computed on the preference clause in the preferred stock and the participating amount. Finally, if the preferred stock is both cumulative and participating, *any dividends in arrears are paid first and are not considered part of the current distribution to preferred shareholders.*

The example presented above is based on a fully participating clause in the preferred stock issue. In such situations preferred stockholders continue to share dividends with common stockholders regardless of the total dividend declared.

Many participating preferred stock issues are partially rather than fully participating. **Partial participation** means that preferred stockholders may share to a limited extent the dividends declared.

To illustrate, assume that the participation clause of Sundeen Corporation's preferred stock specifies only partial participation. Also assume that preferred stockholders receive a 7% preference dividend and participate with common stockholders up to a maximum of 10%, including the preference amount. In this case the first three steps are those of the previous analysis; the next two steps involve modifications.

Step 1.   Preference Distribution to Preferred Stockholders

Same as fully participating ($70,000 to preferred stockholders).

Step 2.   Equivalency Distribution to Common Stockholders

Same as fully participating ($87,500 to common stockholders).

Step 3.   Participation Distribution

Same as fully participating ($442,500 remaining dividend).

Step 4.   Distribution of Remaining Dividend

Total combined par value of stockholders' equity (preferred and common)	$2,250,000
Partial participation percentage	× .03
Participating dividend	$ 67,500
Preferred share (.03 × $1,000,000)	$ 30,000
Common share (.03 × $1,250,000)	37,500
	$ 67,500

Step 5. Summary of Total Dividend Allocation

Preferred stock		
Preferred amount (Step 1)	$ 70,000	
Participation amount (Step 4)	30,000	
Total preferred dividend		$100,000
Common stock		
Initial common equivalency amount		
(Step 2)	87,500	
Participation amount (Step 4)	37,500	
Remaining dividend		
($600,000 − $225,000)[3]	375,000	
Total common dividend		500,000
Total dividend		$600,000

Again, several important observations are possible. The participation amount of 3% is applied to both common and preferred stock to determine if any nonparticipating additional dividend is available exclusively to common stockholders. In this case, $375,000 of the total dividend is available to common stockholders only. The largest dividend preferred stockholders can ever receive is 10% of the total par value of the outstanding preferred stock, or $100,000 (.10 × $1,000,000), in addition to any dividends in arrears.

If preferred stock is cumulative or participating (or both) accountants must be particularly careful in computing dividends. Note that the overall financial statements are not affected by cumulation or participation clauses. Rather, the total dividend declared is charged to retained earnings regardless of which stockholder class receives a particular amount. The question of which stockholder groups receive what amount of dividends is very important, however, and complicated calculations may be required.

The decision to declare and pay dividends is also highly complex and generally involves careful planning of both the total amount of the dividends as well as the amount to be paid on each share and class of stock. For simplicity we have assumed the total amount of a dividend and illustrated the calculations necessary to allocate the total dividend to various classes of stockholder. In practice, however, most companies attempt to select the per share amount of dividends to be paid to each class of stockholder, then calculate the total dividend necessary. Many companies strive to maintain consistent dividend policies from year to year, because management generally believes that a consistent dividend policy communicates stability and strength to the investment community. If the total dividend is too great, the per share amounts are revised to reduce the total dividend to a more reasonable amount that is consistent with management goals and corporate capabilities.

Property Dividends

While most corporations routinely declare and pay cash dividends, other assets such as marketable securities may be distributed to stockholders as **property dividends.** If a corporation distributes noncash assets as dividends, accounting is based on the fair market value of the property transferred. Such noncash dividends, sometimes referred to as **nonreciprocal transfers of nonmonetary assets,** may require the recognition of a gain or loss on the disposal of the asset.

To illustrate, assume that Drand, Inc., elects to declare a dividend whereby inventory with a recorded book value of $10,000 and a fair market value of $16,000 is to be distributed to stockholders. The entry to record the dividend declaration and distribution appears below:

---

[3]The total dividend is reduced by the preference and participation amounts previously determined: $100,000 + $87,500 + $37,500 = $225,000.

Retained Earnings	16,000	
Inventory		10,000
Gain on Disposal		
of Inventory		6,000
(To record declaration and distribution		
of property dividend.)		

A gain is recognized only on the inventory to be distributed. Remaining amounts of inventory continue to be carried at the lower of cost or market. An exception to the general practice of recognizing gains or losses occurs if the fair value of the asset to be distributed is not determinable. In such cases the dividend declaration and payment should be based on the recorded book values. These practices reflect the provisions of *APB Opinion No. 29,*[4] which is discussed in Chapter 11. In essence, fair market values are used to record most nonmonetary transactions, including nonreciprocal transfers such as the declaration and payment of property dividends. The extent of a property dividend is best represented by the fair market value of the property distributed rather than its historic cost.

An additional accounting and reporting problem arises if a property dividend is declared in one period and is to be paid in the following period. If a property dividend is declared near the end of an accounting period and is to be distributed in the next year, when should any gain or loss on the disposal of the asset be recognized? Further, should changes in the value of the asset between the date of declaration and the date of distribution be recognized and, if so, in what manner?

Although these issues are not explicitly addressed in the authoritative literature, the authors support the recognition of gain or loss when a property dividend is declared. No further adjustments should be made to the asset for later changes in its fair value prior to distribution. In the authors' judgment, the amount of the dividend to be paid is usually established at the declaration date. The board of directors' action to declare a dividend **Disclosure** creates a liability, and the amount of the liability to be recognized should be measured by the fair market value of the consideration to be given. Of course, adequate disclosure of the timing and valuation basis employed is necessary in such circumstances.

As an example, assume that Drand, Inc., declares a property dividend on December 31, 1984, to be paid on January 15, 1985. On December 31, the equipment has a book value of $25,000 and a fair market value of $35,000. The following entries are necessary on December 31, 1984, to record the dividend declaration and the revision in the carrying value of the asset:

Dec. 31, 1984	Retained Earnings	35,000	
	Dividend Payable		35,000
Dec. 31, 1984	Equipment	10,000	
	Gain on Disposition Commitment		
	of Equipment		10,000
	(To record declaration of dividend and to		
	record gain on disposal of property.)		

Note that the liability and related asset to be used in satisfying the liability are now carried on Drand's books at the same amount ($25,000 + $10,000 = $35,000). Net income rises as a result of the recognized gain, which causes a related increase in retained earnings. However, the direct charge to Retained Earnings in the first entry shown above reduces Retained Earnings by an amount equal to the sum of the gain and the carrying amount of the equipment. Thus, the direct effect of the $10,000 *gain* on retained earnings is offset by $10,000 of the $35,000 debit to retained earnings in the first entry.

---

[4]*APB Opinion No. 29,* "Accounting for Nonmonetary Transactions," 1973, par 26.

The entry to record the payment of the dividend on January 15, 1985, is:

Jan. 15, 1985	Dividends Payable	35,000	
	Equipment		35,000
	(To record distribution on property		
	subject to the dividend.)		

If changes in the equipment's fair market value occur following the declaration of the dividend and related revaluation of the property, the authors suggest nonrecognition of the change for the following reasons. First, any change in the value of the asset results in a related change in the liability, because the former is to be used to satisfy the latter. Therefore, any gains or losses on revaluing the asset would be directly offset by losses and gains on revaluing the related liability. Second, once the commitment to the assets disposition has been made and the asset is revalued, no further gain or loss is sustained by the enterprise. This, of course, assumes that no specific event, such as fire or theft, changes the underlying circumstances and requires the dividend to be paid with other assets.

Scrip Dividends

On rare occasions a company may be short of cash and yet still wish to declare a dividend. In such cases a company may issue **scrip dividends** in the form of written promises to pay cash in the future. Such promises are considered similar to notes payable and are accounted for as a liability. Scrip dividends may bear interest and may be traded, sold, or otherwise disposed of by the shareholder or owner of the scrip.

Scrip dividends are usually declared only by companies which are quite profitable but for some reason are temporarily short of cash. For example, a construction company may have generated substantial net income during a period but may have only limited cash available if the other party to a contract retains a large amount of cash pending completion of the project. In such a situation, the company may elect to declare a scrip dividend.

Scrip dividends are rarely encountered in practice. Most companies which are short of cash are unwilling to incur additional claims on cash through their own unilateral action. Further, most companies that have the profitability to declare dividends either have cash available or can arrange short-term financing for such purposes.

Liquidating Dividends

Liquidating dividends represent distributions of corporate assets which are a return of contributed equity rather than a distribution of earned equity resulting from profitable operations. Such dividends are usually encountered in the extractive industries and in situations involving corporate dissolution. If a corporation elects to dissolve, all creditor claims take precedence over the claims of stockholder groups. Even prior to the repayment of all corporate debt, however, it may be possible to pay a liquidating dividend to the extent that creditors are adequately protected and legal minimum stated capital is not impaired.

Accountants recognize liquidating dividends only after retained earnings have been exhausted by prior operating losses or previous dividend distributions. Once retained earnings is completely exhausted, further distributions of assets to stockholders are charged to paid-in capital in excess of par rather than capital stock accounts. Finally, in a complete dissolution, remaining assets distributed to residual equity holders result in the total elimination of both assets and corporate equity, thereby closing corporate records.

Stock Dividends and Splits

Stock dividends and stock splits are two types of stock distributions that are frequently encountered in practice. **Stock dividends** are dividend declarations to be satisfied in the form of additional shares of the declaring company's stock. Since each shareholder receives additional shares based on the extent of present holdings, no problems are encountered in regard to stockholders' preemptive rights.

A **stock split** occurs when a corporation exchanges a different number of shares of stock for the shares currently held by stockholders. Thus, a shareholder owns more shares after the split than before. Conversely, in a **reverse stock split,** a shareholder owns fewer shares after the split.

Stock Dividends

Stock dividends are frequently distributed by companies that, while successful, have operating or financing needs for all available cash. For example, a highly successful company may want to build new factories and expand operations as quickly as possible. Management may therefore wish to retain all available cash. The corporation, however, may also want to distribute dividends to shareholders in recognition of the successful operating results. Stock dividends are a solution to this dilemma.

The nature of stock dividends has been discussed by the accounting profession for a long time, yet the subject remains controversial. The central question about the declaration and distribution of stock dividends is whether a significant accountable event has transpired. According to the current position of the profession, "a stock dividend does not, in fact, give rise to any change whatsoever in either the corporation's assets or its respective shareholders' proportionate interests therein."[5] Further, the declaration of a stock dividend does not give rise to a claim on the assets of a corporation, because *additional* shares of the corporation's own stock are to be issued. The recognition of a liability is thus inappropriate.

When a corporation's board of directors declares a stock dividend, a permanent capitalization of a portion of retained earnings takes place. That is, a stock dividend causes a portion of retained earnings which were previously available for dividends to be permanently capitalized as additional shares of stock.

The amount of retained earnings to be capitalized as contributed equity following a stock dividend depends on the relative size of the dividend. In theory, the declaration of a stock dividend has virtually no effect on the financial position of a company. The company neither disposes of assets nor acquires cash or other assets through the issuance of additional shares. Indeed, the market price of the individual shares may decline in response to a stock dividend in which additional shares are issued but no new assets are received by the company. Under such circumstances each share represents a smaller proportionate interest in the unchanged assets of the company. More shares exist after a stock dividend, while total assets and liabilities remain unchanged.

Small Stock Dividends.   When a stock dividend represents an increase of less than 20% to 25% of the previously outstanding shares of similar stock, it is called a **small stock dividend.** Such dividends are so small that the market value of each outstanding share is not expected to change materially. This perception is best expressed by *Accounting Research Bulletin 43,* which states:

Materiality

> *As has been previously stated, a stock dividend does not, in fact, give rise to any change whatsoever in either the corporation's assets or its respective shareholders' proportionate interests therein. However, it cannot fail to be recognized that, merely as a consequence of the expressed purpose of the transaction and its characterization as a dividend in related notices to shareholders and the public at large, many recipients of stock dividends look upon them as distributions of corporate earnings and usually in an amount equivalent to the fair value of the additional shares received. . . . The committee therefore believes that*

---

[5]*Accounting Research Bulletin No. 43,* "Restatement and Revision of Accounting Research Bulletins," 1953, Ch. 7, Sec. B, par. 10.

where these circumstances exist [small stock dividends] the corporation should in the public interest account for the transaction by transferring from earned surplus [retained earnings] to the category of permanent capitalization . . . an amount equal to the fair value of the additional shares issued. Unless this is done, the amount of earnings which the shareholder may believe to have been distributed to him will be left . . . in earned surplus [retained earnings] subject to possible further similar stock issuances or cash distributions.[6] [Emphasis added.]

Accounting principles require accountants to record the declaration of small stock dividends by transferring from retained earnings to contributed capital an amount equal to the market value of the shares issued. The rationale for this approach is that stockholders believe they are receiving something of value, even when in reality each stockholder's proportionate interest in the company remains unchanged. Accounting policy makers were concerned that unless stock dividends were accounted for in this manner, investors would be mislead into believing the potential for total dividends was greater than was really the case due to the unchanged balance of retained earnings that would remain. Recent research into stock prices indicates that the market prices of securities will fall in proportion to stock dividend distributions and that the resulting market prices will properly reflect the underlying value of the total ownership. As a result, the rationale for recording small stock dividends at market value rests on tenuous, possibly incorrect, assumptions. Regardless, the procedure of transferring an amount equal to the market value of the shares issued from retained earnings to contributed capital remains a part of current accounting practice.

To illustrate the accounting for a small stock dividend, refer to the information about Sundeen Corporation presented in Exhibit 17–4. Sundeen has 50,000 shares of common stock outstanding and declares a 2% stock dividend on December 31, 1984. This declaration will result in the issuance of an additional 1,000 shares of Sundeen common stock (50,000 × .02 = 1,000). If one assumes that the market value of Sundeen's common stock at December 31, 1984, is $30 per share, the following entry is necessary to record this small stock dividend:

Dec. 31, 1984	Retained Earnings	30,000	
	Stock Dividend Distributable		25,000
	Paid-in Capital in Excess of Par Value		5,000
	(To record declaration of a 2% stock dividend. 1,000 shares at $30 per share = $30,000.)		

The fair market value of the stock at the date of declaration ($30,000) is used to prepare the entry. Retained Earnings is charged for the market value of the shares involved (1,000 shares × $30 = $30,000). Stock Dividend Distributable is credited for the par value of the shares to be distributed ($25 × 1,000). The difference between the market value and par value is credited to Paid-in Capital in Excess of Par Value. Stock Dividend Distributable is reported as contributed equity in the stockholders' equity section of the balance sheet. Because the declaration of a stock dividend does not result in a claim on any assets of the corporation, the Stock Dividend Distributable account is not reported as a liability. After the dividend declaration, the stockholders' equity section of Sundeen's balance sheet appears as shown in Exhibit 17–5.

Later, when the stock dividend is distributed, the following entry is necessary to record the issuance of individual shares:

---

[6]*Accounting Research Bulletin No. 43,* Ch. 7, Sec. B, par. 10.

EXHIBIT 17–5
Sundeen Corporation
Partial Balance Sheet
After Stock Dividend Declaration

December 31, 1984

Stockholders' Equity

Preferred stock ($100 par, 7% cumulative, nonvoting; 10,000 shares authorized, issued, and outstanding)	$1,000,000
Common stock ($25 par; 100,000 shares authorized, 50,000 shares issued and outstanding)	1,250,000
Stock dividend distributable (1,000 shares of $25 par common stock)	25,000
Paid-in capital in excess of par value	755,000
Total contributed capital	3,030,000
Retained earnings ($2,500,000–$30,000)	2,470,000
Total stockholders' equity	$5,500,000

Jan. 15, 1985	Stock Dividend Distributable	25,000	
	Common Stock		25,000
	(To record distribution of common stock dividend.)		

As a result of this entry, the stockholders' equity section in Exhibit 17–5 is changed in only one way; the Stock Dividend Distributable is eliminated and Common Stock is increased by the par value of the shares issued in the stock dividend. In sum, the market value of the stock subject to the dividend is permanently capitalized and is no longer treated as part of retained earnings, because the amount is represented by shares of stock. Again, the theory of accounting for small stock dividends is that the issuance of stock is so small that there will be little, if any, effect on the market value of the company's stock. Therefore, the best measure of the earned equity which has been converted to contributed equity through the stock dividend is the market value of the shares issued.

Large Stock Dividends.   When a stock dividend increases the number of outstanding shares by more than 20% to 25%, the value of each share in the market is expected to decline. Such declarations are known as **large stock dividends.** The difference between accounting for a small stock dividend and accounting for a large stock dividend involves the amount of earned equity reclassified as contributed equity. While the fair market value of the stock is used in small stock dividends, the amount to be reclassified in large stock dividends is limited to the par or stated value of the stock. To illustrate, if Sundeen Corporation declares a 30% stock dividend on the 50,000 shares outstanding at December 31, 1984, when the stock is selling for $30 per share, the following entry is required to record the large stock dividend:

Dec. 31, 1984	Retained Earnings	375,000	
	Stock Dividend Distributable		375,000
	(To record declaration of large stock dividends. $25 par value × 15,000 shares = $375,000.)		

Because the dividend is considered large, *par rather than market value* is used to calculate the entry. The following entry is necessary to record the distribution:

Jan. 15, 1985 Stock Dividend
Distributable 375,000
Common Stock 375,000
(To record distribution of
common stock dividend.)

The theory underlying large stock dividends recognizes that if the number of shares of stock outstanding substantially increases and no changes occur in total assets or liabilities, the value of each share of stock declines. As indicated previously, the same case can be made for accounting for small stock dividends, although current accounting practice does not reflect this similarity.

Stock Splits

A **stock split,** sometimes called a **stock split-up,** is a distribution of a company's own capital stock to existing stockholders with the intent of reducing the market price of the stock. For example, in a 2-to-1 stock split, stockholders receive two shares for each share they owned before the split.

The primary purpose of a stock split is to reduce the market price of the stock to a level that will encourage investment in the company. If a company has been operating successfully, the market price of its stock may have risen so high that active trading, particularly by individual investors, is discouraged. For example, the most expensive New York Stock Exchange issue in 1983 was Metromedia, which sold at more than $400 per share. An investor would need $40,000 to purchase a round lot of 100 shares. When the number of shares of a company's stock is increased through a stock split, the price of each share in the market declines. The assets and liabilities of the company remain constant while the number of ownership shares increases. Consequently, each share after the stock split represents a smaller interest in the same total ownership that existed before the stock split. By exchanging a larger number of shares for a smaller number of shares, management may restore the market price of its company's stock to a more desirable level. Most companies try to maintain their stock price in a certain range to encourage trading and wide ownership.

Some believe that the prices of securities will not adjust to the full extent of a stock split but will adjust to a price that reflects a premium after the stock split. To illustrate, they would expect a stock selling at $200 which is split 4 to 1 to sell at more than $50 ($200/4) after the split. The suggestion is that the stock split action increases the value of each shareholder's holdings, even though the theoretical value should remain unchanged. An argument in favor of this position suggests that the stock split (or large stock dividend) significantly increases the potential breadth of ownership. Advocates of this position argue that a decrease in the price of the stock increases the number of individuals able to purchase the stock and thus increases the actual demand (price) for the stock.

Some have also argued that if enough people believe a stock split will increase the total value of stockholder holdings, it will become a self-fulfilling prophecy. Empirical evidence on the adjustment of stock prices to stock splits indicates that stock prices adjust fully for the dilutive effect of stock splits. As A. Wilfred May cogently states, "a pie does not grow through its slicing."[7] The empirical evidence supports the proposition that there is no intrinsic value in stock splits, but that stock prices may reflect a post-split premium because the stock split signals information to market participants about managements' positive expectations for future performance.[8]

---

[7]A. Wilfred May, "Current Popular Delusions About the Stock Split and Stock Dividend," *The Commercial and Financial Chronicle* (November 15, 1956), p. 5.

[8]Eugene Fama, Lawrence Fisher, Michael Jensen, and Richard Roll, "The Adjustment of Stock Prices to New Information," *International Economic Review* (February 1969), pp. 1–21. Also Guy Charest, "Split Information, Stock Returns, and Market Efficiency—I," *Journal of Financial Economics* (June/September 1978), pp. 265–296.

When a stock split is issued, the par or stated value of the stock is adjusted in proportion to the size of the stock split. For example, a $100 par value stock that is split 2:1 will have a $50 par value after the split; a $50 par value stock that is split 5:1 will have a $10 par value after the split.

The accounting procedure for recording a stock split is to simply prepare a memorandum entry that indicates the change in the number of shares and the par value of those shares. No formal general journal entry is required since there is no change in the balance of the capital stock accounts, only a change in the number of shares and the par value of those shares. Recall again the outstanding common stock of Sundeen Corporation presented in Exhibit 17–4 (50,000 shares of $25 par value stock). If the company declared a 2:1 stock split, the company would have 200,000 shares of common stock authorized, 100,000 of which were outstanding at a $12.50 par value. The total amount in the Common Stock account, $1,250,000, is unchanged. No amount of retained earnings is transferred to contributed capital as was done in the case of a stock dividend discussed earlier.

In a **reverse stock split** or **stock split-down,** shareholders own fewer shares after the split. An example of a stock split down is a 1-for-2 split in which a stockholder who holds 50 shares of stock before the split owns only 25 shares after the exchange. The objective of a reverse stock split is the opposite of a stock split. That is, a reverse stock split is designed to increase the price of the stock in the market.

The distinction between a large stock dividend and a stock split is a fine one at best. Basically, a *large stock dividend* is the issuance of stock with the same par (or stated) value as the shares outstanding; hence the increase in legal capital (credit to common stock). A *stock split* is simply the exchange of existing shares for new shares with a different par (or stated) value per share; the total par (or stated) value of the outstanding shares is maintained. The end result of the two approaches is similar: more shares are outstanding, and the total stockholders' equity remains unchanged. With large stock dividends, however, the components of stockholders' equity are altered, since an amount equal to the par (or stated) value of the shares issued has been transferred from retained earnings to contributed capital.

A SPLIT TOO FAR?

CHARLES HURWITZ HAS COME a long way since he was born, 42 years ago, in the east Texas town of Kilgore (pop. 9,495). Before he was 30, the University of Oklahoma graduate was running a Wall Street hedge fund and rating a small mention in a popular book of the time on investment hotshots. Back in Texas, he began building a financial empire that today controls over $700 million in assets. That's big money even in Texas. His financial finesse is much admired, but he has detractors. Some of them think he has cut a few too many corners to get what he wants.

Right now he's involved in a messy battle involving Federated Development, a public company Hurwitz has controlled since 1973 and which is the heart of his corporate domain. Federated started as a real estate and insurance company but has since bought control of such substantial public outfits as McCulloch Oil (now MCO Holdings), Simplicity Pattern and United Financial Group, a large Houston S&L.

Just before 1982 drew to a close, Hurwitz informed Federated's minority shareholders that the company was going forward with a 1-for-600 reverse stock split, reducing the outstanding float from 329,000 shares to 547. Why such a drastic split? Hurwitz says that he wants to reduce the number of shareholders from 260 to fewer than 100 and thus sidestep federal regulations governing public investment companies. Federated might fall under those statutes because it recently sold off its reinsurance business, one of its biggest operating entities, leaving a large percentage of its assets in passive investments.

Hurwitz has another motivation as well. Because Federated stock is very illiquid, the company was approached by a number of shareholders, including one trustee, who wanted to cash in on the company's success in recent years. To those who want it, Hurwitz offers $45 a share.

That sounds helpful. But why through a reverse split? Some Federated shareholders think Hurwitz is trying to squeeze them out at a low price. "The reverse stock split is really a ruse to go private without due compensation," says one investment banker, who calls Hurwitz' attempt "outrageous."

Indeed, Hurwitz himself states in his announcement of the reverse split that most shareholders will probably choose to cash in their old shares with the company rather than "round up" their holdings to one of the new megashares. He is probably right. To own one of the new shares, a holder of 100 old shares will have to lay out $22,500 to "round up."

But the alternative open to minority shareholders is equally unappealing. Hurwitz didn't bother with the customary investment banker's opinion certifying the "fairness" of the $45-a-share buyout offer. Because shareholders have the option of rounding up, he says, "the proposed reverse share split will not result in the forced termination of any shareholder's interest," making an outside appraisal unnecessary.

Hurwitz got that $45 price on recent trades of Federated stock on the over-the-counter market. But Federated stock is so illiquid that in the first half of last year there were no trades at all.

So what's the relationship between $45 and Federated's underlying value? That $45 is less than half book value, and book value is itself understated, it appears. Hurwitz himself says that the market value of Federated's real estate alone is worth $24 a share more than its stated value on the books. The public companies that Federated controls also are carried way under market value. For instance, its interest in MCO Holdings alone is worth $92 a share. "Hurwitz is trying to freeze people out at maybe 20% of what the stock is worth," claims Daniel Cowin, who personally owns 6,000 Federated shares and is a direc-

tor of Drexel, Burnham, Lambert and chairman of United National Corp. . . .

What his critics regard as high-handedness is characteristic of past Hurwitz deals. In 1979 the Federated trustees voted a 1-for-40 reverse share split that wiped out over 200 shareholders. The very next day, the trustees issued a 39-for-1 stock dividend, restoring the number of shares to their prior level. With fewer than 300 shareholders, Federated was soon able to stop reporting its financial results to the SEC.

But just because Hurwitz succeeded with his earlier reverse stock split doesn't mean he will this time around. Among his remaining minority shareholders there are some big names who aren't about to be pushed around so easily. In addition to Cowin, there is Howard Wolf, a top partner at the powerful Houston law firm of Fulbright & Jaworski. A few days after Hurwitz declared his plan, Wolf sued him in federal court for fraud and breach of fiduciary duty. The same day another sophisticated investor, New-York-based Galdi Securities, sued Hurwitz in a state court.

This response may have convinced Hurwitz he was pushing his luck too far. Federated's trustees were supposed to approve the reverse stock split on Jan. 3, but instead they postponed the vote. "This is the first time that I've ever seen Hurwitz back down," says one observer who has followed Hurwitz' career closely.

His litigious shareholders may press for the removal of Federated's trustees and for its liquidation. In that case, Hurwitz would still walk away with a bundle, but he would lose control of the assets he built almost from scratch. Charles Hurwitz, however, is a tough man in a fight and nobody's counting him out.

SOURCE: Pamela Sherrid, "A Split Too Far?" *Forbes*, February 14, 1983, pp. 55, 56. Reprinted by permission of *Forbes* Magazine. © Forbes Inc., 1983.

Treasury Stock and Dividends

Substance over Form

As mentioned previously, cash dividends should not be declared on treasury stock. To do so would imply that the corporation is an owner of itself and is able to earn income from a common stock investment in itself. Clearly, a corporation cannot own itself, and cash dividends on treasury shares are nonsensical. If such dividends were declared, the company would essentially be reducing retained earnings and simultaneously recording dividend income (increasing retained earnings through income) with no corresponding change in resources. Although the economic substance of the corporation remains unchanged, the transfer of retained earnings to dividend income may be misleading to financial statement users. As a result, most states do not allow cash dividends to be declared on treasury shares.

Stock dividends and stock splits on treasury shares are not as potentially misleading, because they involve only a rearrangement within the stockholders' equity accounts and do not affect the income statement. As a result, stock dividends and stock splits may be declared on treasury shares in some states, although a few states prohibit stock dividends on treasury shares. A stock split on treasury shares has the same effect as on outstanding shares. The par value of the treasury shares is adjusted so that the total par value of all treasury shares remains unchanged after the split. Naturally, the total cost of the treasury shares is also unaffected.

Appropriation of Retained Earnings

Occasionally the management of a company decides to commit corporate resources to some project or purpose and wishes to communicate that fact through the financial statements. For example, management may wish to retain resources to expand plant assets or repay debt rather than pay dividends to stockholders. In such situations retained earnings may be appropriated to notify financial statement users about the intended use of the company's resources. To illustrate, if Montclair Company management decides to build a new factory at an estimated cost of $2,500,000, the following appropriation of retained earnings is acceptable:

Retained Earnings	2,500,000	
Retained Earnings Appropriated		
for Plant Expansion		2,500,000
(To appropriate retained earnings		
according to company plans.)		

The account Retained Earnings Appropriated for Plant Expansion is reported as part of stockholders' equity rather than as a liability or a contra asset account. The appropriation provides financial statement users with information on corporate plans and may also help explain a reduction in dividends as resources are held to finance construction.

Appropriating retained earnings does *not* necessarily imply that resources have been set aside for the purpose indicated. The appropriation is simply a reclassification of retained earnings, which signals owners about possible reductions in dividends.

State law occasionally requires an appropriation of retained earnings in the case of treasury stock. Law sometimes requires companies to record an appropriation of retained earnings equal to the cost of any treasury stock. Such regulations are designed to protect the creditors of a company from a substantial reduction of stockholders' equity through treasury stock acquisitions.

Management may also record an appropriation of retained earnings as a reporting response to loss contingencies, as discussed in Chapter 14. An appropriation of retained earnings, however, is not considered an alternative to recording loss contingencies in accordance with *Statement of Financial Accounting Standards No. 5.*[9] Rather, accountants consider an appropriation of retained earnings as a supplement to other practices required by generally accepted accounting principles, such as footnote disclosure.

Disclosure

Finally, when the reason for the appropriation no longer exists, the appropriated retained earnings should be returned directly to unappropriated retained earnings. Losses or gains should be presented in the income statement and never charged or credited to appropriated retained earnings. Similarly, the Appropriated Retained Earnings account should never be

---

[9]*FASB Statement of Financial Accounting Standards No. 5,* "Accounting for Contingencies," 1975, par. 15.

included in the determination of net income. In the example above, after the plant is built and there is no longer a need to communicate the reason for limiting dividend distributions, the following entry is necessary:

Retained Earnings Appropriated		
for Plant Expansion	2,500,000	
Retained Earnings		2,500,000
(To reverse appropriation of		
retained earnings.)		

Statement of Changes in Stockholders' Equity

Disclosure

The foregoing issues complicate the presentation of the statement of retained earnings as well as the disclosure of changes in other stockholders' equity accounts. Although a separate statement of retained earnings is frequently presented in relatively simple equity situations, it is also common to combine the changes in retained earnings with a statement presenting changes in other stockholders' equity accounts. The resulting statement of stockholders' equity reflects the activity that has taken place in all equity accounts during the accounting period. An illustrative comprehensive statement of changes in stockholders' equity and accompanying note is presented in Exhibit 17–6 for Bendix Corporation.

Although not all possible changes in equity accounts are contained in the report of Bendix Corporation (a major defense contractor and automotive supplier), the statement is representative of presentations commonly encountered in practice. The last column of the statement is devoted to events affecting retained earnings. Net income and dividends are, of course, the most prevalent items. Notice that the purchase and retirement of stock in 1980 at $64 per share reduced retained earnings markedly. This implies that the retirement price was much higher than the original issue price. Other events of interest disclosed by this statement include the conversion of preferred stock to common stock, and stock issued to satisfy stock option plans and to acquire a business.

EXHIBIT 17–6
Bendix Corporation
Statement of Changes in Stockholders' Equity

Stockholders' Equity

Each share of the Series A $3 Cumulative Convertible Preferred Stock (Series A Preferred Stock) is convertible into 2.05 shares of Common Stock, subject to adjustment in certain events. The Series A Preferred Stock is entitled to $60 per share in liquidation and is redeemable, at the Corporation's option, at $64 per share at September 30, 1981, decreasing by $1 per share annually at each June 30 through June 30, 1985, and thereafter at $60 per share. Each share of the Series B 9¾% Cumulative Convertible Preferred Stock (Series B Preferred Stock) is convertible into .768 shares of Common Stock, subject to adjustment in certain events. The Series B Preferred Stock is entitled to $41.50 per share in liquidation and will be redeemable, at the Corporation's option, beginning March 31, 1985 at $43.52, decreasing by $.40 annually at each March 31 through March 31, 1990, and thereafter at $41.50 per share.

On February 27, 1981, the Corporation purchased through a tender offer approximately four million shares of its outstanding Common Stock at $64 per share. All such purchased shares have been cancelled and retired.

At September 30, 1981, 5,830,759 shares of Common Stock were reserved for conversion of Series A and Series B Preferred Stock and for the Corporation's Stock Option, Incentive Compensation, Performance Incentive, and Stock Ownership plans, and 380,415 shares of Series B Preferred Stock were reserved for a subsidiary's employee stock option plan.

A summary of Stockholders' Equity is set forth below:

	Series A Preferred Stock		Series B Preferred Stock		Common Stock		Additional Capital	Retained Earnings
	Shares	Amount	Shares	Amount	Shares	Amount		
	(in millions, except number of shares)							
Balance, October 1, 1978	329,739	$2.5			22,305,290	$111.5	$30.2	$ 791.0
Net income								162.6
Cash dividends								
Series A Preferred Stock								(.9)
Common Stock								(57.0)
Conversion of preferred stock	(36,237)	(.3)			74,256	.4	(.1)	
Stock sold under stock option plan and related income tax benefits					31,595	.2	.8	
Other								(1.5)
Balance, September 30, 1979	293,502	2.2			22,411,141	112.1	30.9	894.2
Net income								191.6
Cash dividends								
Series A Preferred Stock								(.7)
Series B Preferred Stock								(8.2)
Common Stock								(64.9)
Stock issued for acquired businesses			3,976,562	$165.0	407,842	2.0	14.3	
Conversion of preferred stock	(42,084)	(.3)	(440)		86,563	.4	(.1)	
Stock sold under stock option plans and related income tax benefits			92,573	3.9	117,415	.6	1.6	
Balance, September 30, 1980	251,418	1.9	4,068,695	168.9	23,022,961	115.1	46.7	1,012.0
Net income								452.8
Cash dividends								
Series A Preferred Stock								(.5)
Series B Preferred Stock								(16.6)
Common Stock								(60.6)
Stock purchase					(4,000,014)	(20.0)	(9.3)	(228.2)
Conversion of preferred stock	(57,258)	(.4)	(11,962)	(.5)	126,463	.6	.3	
Stock sold under stock option plans and related income tax benefits			58,290	2.4	219,570	1.1	5.0	
Balance, September 30, 1981	194,160	$1.5	4,115,023	$170.8	19,368,980	$ 96.8	$42.7	$1,158.9

SOURCE: Bendix Corporation, 1981 Annual Report.

CAPITAL STOCK AND EMPLOYEE COMPENSATION

Stockholders' equity is an area over which corporate management and the board of directors exercise great control. The stock of a company may be used to provide part of the remuneration of employees as well as to provide funds for capital expenditures and to finance ongoing business operations. Stock option plans and stock appreciation rights are frequently used as important incentives for employees. The primary purposes of these plans is to motivate employees, reward high performance, and reduce employee attrition. If employees own stock in their company, the success of the company becomes even more important to them. If the company operates profitably and the value of the stock increases, employees who own stock become better off.

Stock Option Plans

An **employee stock option** is a temporary right granted by the company that permits an employee to purchase a limited amount of corporate stock at a specified price, called the **exercise price.** An employee can exercise the option by purchasing the stock at the exercise price, then resell those shares at the market price to realize a gain or simply hold the shares to sell later. Employee stock options are not transferable, so only the employee can realize the potential benefits. In addition, companies frequently prohibit the exercise of an option until the end of a prespecified **service (holding) period.** This restriction ensures some degree of employee loyalty. The stock option agreement typically establishes an exercise period and an expiration date. Exhibit 17–7 shows a typical stock option plan.

Stock option plans may be compensatory or noncompensatory, depending on whether employee compensation is intended in the specific plan.

Noncompensatory Stock Option Plans

Stock option plans for employees are **noncompensatory** and result in no recognition of salary expense if four characteristics are *all* present. To be noncompensatory, a plan must:[10]

1. Involve substantially all full-time employees (executives may be excluded);
2. Be offered to eligible employees equally or on the basis of a uniform percentage of salary;
3. Limit the time permitted for exercise of an option right to a reasonable period; and
4. Provide for a discount from the market price no greater than would be available to others.

Accounting for noncompensatory stock option plans is relatively simple and straightforward. If an employee exercises an option to acquire shares of stock, the corporation simply records the cash received and the related issuance of the stock. Only the cash received is treated as consideration for the stock issued in a noncompensatory plan. The difference between the market price and the exercise price on the exercise date is a benefit to the employee that is disregarded in the corporate accounting records. The rationale for this treatment is that management does not intend to compensate employees for past or future services but to raise additional capital or to improve loyalty in the workforce.

---

[10]*APB Opinion No. 25,* "Accounting for Stock Issued to Employees," 1972, par. 7.

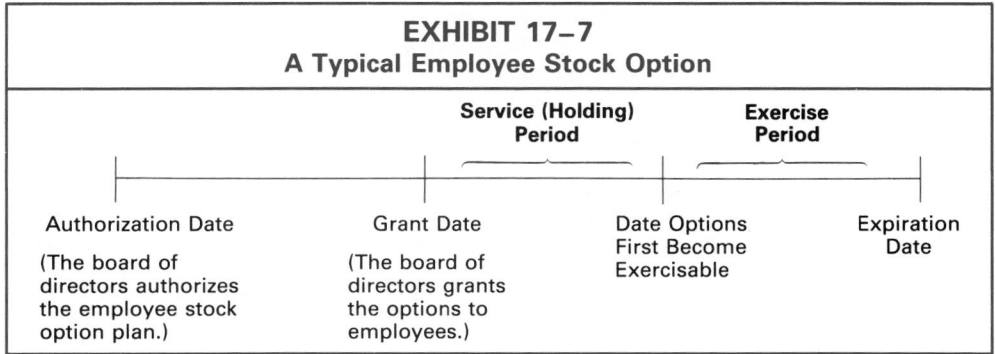

EXHIBIT 17–7
A Typical Employee Stock Option

Compensatory Stock Option Plans

Compensatory stock option plans do not meet all four characteristics of noncompensatory plans. **Compensatory** plans convey a right to selected employees in return for either past or future services to the company. Many large corporations compensate their corporate officers with both salaries and stock options. In compensatory stock option plans, the consideration a corporation receives for stock issued from exercised options consists of the option price and the value of services rendered by employees above their salary levels. A major accounting difficulty is measuring the incremental value of services arising from the stock option plan. These services must be valued in order to correctly assign compensation expense equal to the total value of services rendered by employees.

Objectivity

Accountants objectively measure the compensatory portion of employee stock options as the excess of the market price of the stock over the exercise price. This spread is computed on the date that *both* (1) the number of shares an individual employee is entitled to receive and (2) the option or purchase price of the shares first become known.[11] This date, called the **measurement date,** is used to determine the amount of compensation to be recognized in conjunction with the plan.

As a result of the two criteria for determining the measurement date, the measurement date often coincides with the grant date. Therefore, the compensatory portion of the option is usually determined as the excess of the market value of the stock over the exercise price of the option on the grant date.

Compensation expense is recorded only as the services giving rise to the stock options are rendered. Thus, if an employee must perform services for several periods after the option is granted and before the stock is issued, the employer recognizes salary expense in each period in which services are performed. This principle is applied even though the total amount of compensation may have been known at the grant date. The procedure is simply an application of the matching principle, whereby the compensation expense is allocated to the periods in which services are performed.

Matching

One of the problems with the present method of accounting for compensatory stock options is the measurement of the compensation expense. Many accountants have recognized that compensatory stock options are often granted with the exercise price equal to the market price of the stock. As such, generally accepted accounting principles require no compensation expense to be recorded. This treatment clearly biases financial reporting towards understating compensation expense, because the options have obvious value. An employee who was granted a stock option with the exercise price equal to the market price would not be willing to give the options away. The options are valuable because the employee cannot lose money if the stock price decreases but can realize a substantial gain if the stock price increases.[12]

To illustrate the accounting for compensatory stock options, assume that on January 1, 1981, Value Corporation provides a stock option plan to the president of the corporation whereby 1,000 shares of $50 par value common stock may be purchased for $40 per share after 5 years of employment. The market price on January 1, 1981, is $75. Because both (1) the number of shares that may be acquired (1,000) and (2) the option price ($40) are known, January 1, 1981, is considered the measurement date. The compensation per share

---

[11]*APB Opinion No. 25,* par. 10.

[12]Several methods have been suggested for the valuation of stock options. See, for example, Fischer Black and Myron Scholes, "The Pricing of Options and Corporate Liabilities," *Journal of Political Economy* (May/June 1973), pp. 158–162. The Black and Scholes valuation model was tested for accuracy against a set of publicly traded warrants similar to executive stock options. The valuation model was found to perform admirably. See Eric Noreen and Mark Wolfson, "Equilibrium Warrant Pricing Models and Accounting for Executive Stock Options," *Journal of Accounting Research* (Autumn 1981), pp. 384–398.

to be recognized is the difference between the market price ($75) and the option price ($40) on the measurement date. In this case Value Corporation recognizes compensation expense of $35 per share as the services are rendered over the 5-year period.

At the end of the first year, on December 31, 1981, the following entry is made:

Dec. 31, 1981	Salary Expense	7,000	
	Stock Options Exercisable		7,000
	(To record portion of compensatory stock option plan earned at 12/31/81. 1,000 shares × $35 = $35,000 × ⅕ = $7,000.)		

This entry is repeated each year until the options are exercised.[13] Market price changes in the stock *after* the measurement date are not recognized as additional compensation from the perspective of the employing corporation. The account Stock Options Exercisable is a contributed stockholders' equity account that remains open until the final exercise date on December 31, 1985. When the options are exercised and the employee remits the $40 per share option price, the following entry is necessary:

Dec. 31, 1985	Cash	40,000	
	Stock Options Exercisable	35,000	
	Common Stock		50,000
	Paid-in Capital in Excess of Par Value		25,000
	(To record issuance of stock under compensatory option plan.)		

If the options are not exercised, the Stock Options Exercisable account is reclassified as part of Paid-in Capital in Excess of Par Value. The entry to record the expiration of the options is:

Dec. 31, 1985	Stock Options Exercisable	35,000	
	Paid-in Capital in Excess of Par Value		35,000
	(To record expiration of options.)		

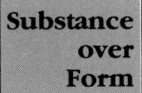

This treatment is acceptable even though the stock option is not exercised. The corporation, as of the grant date, transferred an item of value to the employee. The employee can then choose to exercise the option in order to realize its value or hold the option in an attempt to realize further price appreciation on the security. If the employee allowed the

---

[13]An alternative approach is to record the total future compensation expense on the measurement date as follows:

| Jan. 1, 1981 | Deferred Compensation Expense | 35,000 | |
| | Stock Options Exercisable | | 35,000 |

The Deferred Compensation Expense account is disclosed in stockholders' equity in the balance sheet as a contra account to the Stock Options Exercisable account. The Deferred Compensation Expense account is amortized over the five-year period of intended compensation as follows:

| Dec. 31, 1981 | Compensation Expense | 7,000 | |
| | Deferred Compensation Expense | | 7,000 |

A similar entry is made at the end of each year until the Deferred Compensation Expense account is fully amortized on December 31, 1985.

option to lapse because the price of the stock decreased during the holding period, the speculative behavior should not affect the valuation of the option by the corporation. The paid-in capital in excess of par from nonexercise of the option is theoretically justified as the value of services donated by the employee. In addition, this treatment is similar to that for detachable warrants issued with certain debt instruments which lapse. We discussed this topic in Chapter 15.

Measurement Date Controversy

The choice of the measurement date for determining the total compensation has been an issue of considerable controversy in the accounting profession. As we have already stated, *APB Opinion No. 25* defines the measurement date as the time when (1) the number of shares an employee is entitled to receive *and* (2) the option price (exercise price) are known. As mentioned, these criteria are frequently satisfied on the *grant date*. The grant date is justified as the measurement date on the basis of the opportunity foregone by the corporation. On the grant date the corporation restricts shares of stock that could otherwise be issued on the market at a fair market price. Furthermore, on the grant date the corporation must decide the number of options to grant and the exercise price of each option. These decisions are based on the corporation's estimate of the value of services to be received from the employee. The option compensation is determined as the value of services to be received above the value of salary-compensated services. Advocates of this approach believe that a corporation's intended additional compensation is determined at the grant date and should therefore provide the basis for future expense allocation.

Alternatively, some have supported measuring the total compensation as the excess of the market price of the stock over the exercise price on the *date the option first becomes exercisable*. The rationale for this approach is that the increase in the market value of the stock from the grant date to the exercisable date may be an accurate proxy for the value of services provided by employees who benefit from the stock option plan. In addition, because the employees cannot exercise the option during the service period, some question remains about whether the value of the option to the employee can actually be known until the right to exercise exists. Finally, the date on which options first become exercisable is preferable to subsequent dates because exercise decisions during the exercise period are made by the executives themselves and not by the corporation. Critics contend that such decisions are speculative and should not affect the valuation of services received.

The excess of the market value of the stock over the exercise price has been suggested as the proper measure of the compensation expense on the *exercise date*. Advocates of this position point out that the exercise date is when the true value of the option is realized by the employee. Any valuation prior to exercise is simply an estimate of the final worth of the option contract and, presumably, an estimate of the final value of the incremental employee services associated with these options. The exercise date is the date the employee actually receives an ownership interest and, correspondingly, the date the corporation releases ownership shares at a price below what alternative market sources would provide.

Despite the conceptual merit of these alternatives, *APB Opinion No. 25* requires the recognition of compensation expense based on the difference between the exercise price and the market price at the measurement date. This practice is therefore well established in the accounting literature.

Stock Option Plan Disclosure

Disclosure

The specific characteristics of a stock option plan are typically disclosed in a footnote to the financial statements. The reference should include information about the number of options outstanding, granted, and exercised during the period, as well as the option price. The stock option plan disclosure of Bendix Corporation, presented in Exhibit 17–8, illustrates the type of information normally provided.

EXHIBIT 17–8
Bendix Corporation
Employee Stock Option Plan Disclosure

Stock Option Plans

Under the Corporation's stock option plans, certain employees have been granted options to purchase Common Stock at prices which represented 100% of the fair market value on the dates the options were granted, as adjusted for stock dividends and stock splits. During 1980, the original stock option plan (Original Plan) expired, and during 1981 a new plan (1981 Plan) with the same general provisions as the Original Plan was adopted. Options generally may be exercised over a period of ten years from the date of grant. No option may be exercised earlier than one year from the date on which the option is granted and generally options become exercisable in three equal annual installments beginning with the first anniversary of the date of grant. The 1981 Plan provides that certain option holders have the right to elect alternative settlement methods. Certain information with respect to options granted under the plans is summarized below:

	1981		1980		1979	
	Number of Shares	Option Price Per Share	Number of Shares	Option Price Per Share	Number of Shares	Option Price Per Share
Outstanding at October 1	633,839	$15.30 to $53.95	624,273	$15.30 to $46.10	608,913	$15.30 to $46.10
Granted	361,900	58.90 to 62.95	151,050	49.00 to 53.95	72,500	37.50 to 39.70
Exercised	260,855	15.30 to 53.95	115,679	15.30 to 46.10	29,926	15.30 to 36.40
Terminated or cancelled	39,300	20.81 to 58.90	25,805	25.69 to 53.95	27,214	31.80 to 46.10
Outstanding at September 30	695,584	15.30 to 62.95	633,839	15.30 to 53.95	624,273	15.30 to 46.10
Exercisable at September 30	229,719	15.30 to 53.95	375,645	15.30 to 46.10	379,813	15.30 to 46.10

There were also outstanding at September 30, 1981 and 1980 options for shares of Series B Preferred Stock. These options, certain of which give the option holders the right to elect alternative settlement methods, had been granted by Warner & Swasey prior to its merger. Certain information with respect to such options, all of which are exercisable, is summarized below:

	1981		1980	
	Number of Shares	Option Price Per Share	Number of Shares	Option Price Per Share
Outstanding at October 1 (March 31 for 1980)	232,900	$7.25 to $15.00	362,000	$7.25 to $15.00
Exercised	70,685	7.25 to 15.00	128,900	7.25 to 15.00
Terminated or cancelled	250	13.06	200	10.06
Outstanding at September 30	161,965	7.25 to 15.00	232,900	7.25 to 15.00

SOURCE: Bendix Corporation, 1981 Annual Report.

Stock Appreciation Rights

Compensatory stock options have two major disadvantages to the employee. First, the employee must make a cash outlay equal to the exercise price times the number of shares acquired. The size of the cash outlay could be burdensome to the employee acquiring a large number of optioned shares. Second, optioned shares are taxable for the difference between the market price and the exercise price (on the date of exercise). An employee is thus immediately liable for taxes on optioned shares, even though the employee may want to hold the shares beyond the date of exercise. Therefore, an employee experiences an immediate cash outflow for the exercise price coupled with a tax on the increment of market price over exercise price.

To eliminate these negative characteristics of compensatory stock options, companies may grant **stock appreciation rights (SARs).** An SAR entitles an employee to either cash or corporate stock in an amount equal to the excess of the market value of the company's stock over a predetermined price for a stated number of shares. This right awards the employee participation in price appreciation for a stated number of shares of the company's stock without actually requiring the employee to remit cash, as in the case of stock options.

The FASB has provided guidance in accounting for stock appreciation rights.[14] SARs fall in the category of variable award plans, in which, according to the FASB, the number of shares of stock or the amount of cash that may be awarded to an employee is unspecified on the grant date. As a result, the criteria for determining the measurement data, as discussed earlier, remain unsatisfied on the grant date. The number of shares or amount of cash an employee is entitled to receive becomes known only on the date the employee exercises the SAR. The number of shares of stock or cash awarded is a function of the appreciation of share price over the stated period at the date of exercise. Therefore, the measurement date, used for determining the total compensation, is the exercise date rather than the earlier grant date.

Because the total compensation to be recognized in conjunction with the SAR is unknown until the exercise date, a question remains about how to accrue compensation expense. Total compensation to be allocated is estimated by the excess of the market value over the designated price. This amount is then allocated over the service period (or vesting period). During the period until exercise, subsequent increases or decreases in the market price of the shares require adjustments to the compensation accrued.

To illustrate, consider Pueblo Corporation, which granted an SAR to the chief executive officer (CEO) on January 1, 1982. After the three-year holding period, the SAR entitled the CEO to the appreciation in share price over the market value of the stock, as determined at the grant date. The SAR had the following terms:

> Service (holding) period: Jan. 1, 1982–Dec. 31, 1984
> Number of shares: 1,000
> Exercise date: Jan. 1, 1985
> Form of compensation: Cash or common stock at CEO's discretion

The quoted market prices of Pueblo's shares were as follows:

Jan. 1, 1982	$20
Dec. 31, 1982	28
Dec. 31, 1983	26
Dec. 31, 1984	32

---

[14]*FASB Interpretation No. 28,* "Accounting for Stock Appreciation Rights and Other Variable Stock Option or Award Plans," 1978.

The SAR was exercised on January 1, 1985. Exhibit 17–9 summarizes the accounting for Pueblo Corporation.

The Compensation Expense is adjusted annually to reflect the accrued compensation to date. As of December 31, 1982, the total compensation to be allocated is the difference between the excess of the market price over the options price times the number of shares specified by the SAR. However, only one-third (33%) of this amount was earned by the CEO as of December 31, 1982. The employee must provide services over a three-year period before the right can be exercised. Therefore, the total compensation should be allocated over this period. The total compensation to be allocated is readjusted annually to reflect the new market price of the company's stock. This is an application of a change in accounting estimate as described in *APB Opinion No. 20*. The journal entry would be recorded on December 31, 1982, as follows:

Dec. 31, 1982	Compensation Expense	2,640	
	Compensation Payable		2,640
	(To record accrual of compensation		
	from SAR plan.)		

The credit to Compensation Payable assumes that the appreciation will be paid in cash by the employer. If the plan called for the appreciation to be paid only in the company's common stock, a credit to a stockholders' equity account, such as Stock Appreciation Rights Exercisable, would be appropriate. In this case the employee has the option of receiving either cash or shares of stock, so the liability account is appropriate.

In 1983 the market price of the shares exceeded the option price by $6 per share. This represents a total compensation of $6,000 ($6 × 1,000 shares) to be allocated. Through December 31, 1983, two-thirds (67%) of the service period elapsed; therefore, 67% of the compensation was earned by the CEO. The compensation accrued to date was $4,020 ($6,000 × 67%), of which $2,640 has already been recognized for 1982. The remaining $1,380 is the compensation expense to be recognized in 1983.

Notice that the market price fell between the end of 1982 and 1983. Because the market price fell below the previous period's market price, the total compensation to be allocated decreased. In the example, the total compensation to be allocated fell to $6,000 [($26 − $20) × 1,000 shares] from the previous amount of $8,000. As of the end of 1984 the employee has completely satisfied the service obligation associated with the options, so that the options are now 100% earned. Therefore, $7,980 of Compensation Expense is recognized in 1984, determined in the same manner as in 1983.[15]

On January 1, 1985, the SAR was exercised by the CEO. If the CEO chose to receive cash, the following journal entry would be appropriate:

Jan. 1, 1985	Compensation Payable	12,000	
	Cash		12,000
	(To record exercise of		
	SAR for cash.)		

---

[15]A decline in the market price of the stock could result in a negative Compensation Expense, although this did not occur in the case of Pueblo Corporation. To illustrate, assume that the market price of Pueblo's stock at the end of 1983 was $22 instead of $26. Total compensation to date would be $2,000 ($2 × 1,000 shares). Since $2,640 compensation expense was recognized during 1982, negative compensation of $640 must be recognized in 1983, as follows:

Dec. 31, 1983	Compensation Payable	640	
	Compensation Expense		640

If this occurs, the amount eliminated should never exceed the total amount accrued to date, even though the market price of the stock is less than the exercise price.

EXHIBIT 17-9
Pueblo Corporation
Accrued Compensation Expense Under an SAR Plan

Date	Market Price	Option Price	Compensation to be Allocated	Service Period Allocation	Compensation Accrued to Date	Annual Compensation Expense
1/1/82	$20	$20	–0–	0%	–0–	–0–
12/31/82	28	20	$ 8,000	33%	$ 2,640	$ 2,640
					1,380	1,380
12/31/83	26	20	6,000	67%	4,020	
					7,980	7,980
12/31/84	32	20	12,000	100%	12,000	$12,000

If the CEO chose to receive stock, the following journal entry would be appropriate, assuming the stock has a par value of $20:

Jan. 1, 1985	Compensation Payable	12,000	
	Common Stock (375 shares @ $20)		7,500
	Paid-in Capital in Excess of		
	Par Value		4,500
	(To record exercise of SAR for		
	common stock.)		

Notice in the last entry that the CEO does not receive 1,000 shares of common stock. The 1,000 shares included in the SAR agreement are simply a mechanism for determining the amount that the CEO will receive in either cash or common stock. In this case, if the CEO chooses to receive stock, he or she will receive 375 shares, determined by dividing the stock appreciation on 1,000 shares by the market price of the stock on the exercise date: ($12,000/$32 = 375 shares).

STOCK WARRANTS AND CONVERTIBLE SECURITIES

Stock Warrants

Companies frequently issue **stock warrants** conveying the right to acquire stock in the future. The terms of the warrant specify the price per share of the stock, the number of warrants needed to acquire each share, the expiration date of the warrant, and other relevant information. Stock warrants are usually valuable because they allow a person to acquire stock below the market price.

Warrants are issued for various reasons. For example, if a stock dividend is declared, some stockholders may have the right to receive fractional shares, and warrants may be issued to meet the obligation. Warrants may also be used to protect the preemptive rights of present stockholders if a new stock issue is forthcoming. The warrants allow present stockholders to maintain their existing percentage of ownership. Warrants may also be used as a "sweetener" to improve the market for other securities, such as debt, issued by the company. If debt is issued with detachable stock warrants or options, some of the consideration received for the composite security (debt and equity) is allocated to stockholders' equity. The method usually employed to accomplish the allocation is based on the relative fair market values of bonds and warrants considered individually. We discussed and illustrated accounting for detachable warrants in Chapter 15.

The Stock Warrants Exercisable account appears in the contributed capital section of stockholders' equity until the warrants either are exercised or expire. In the event of exercise, additional consideration is received and the Stock Warrants Exercisable account is removed from the records. The stock issued is recorded at the sum of the carrying amount of the warrants, if any, and the exercise price received.

To illustrate, assume that Harmon Corporation originally issued 1,000 bonds, including one detachable warrant per bond. Also assume that after the proceeds of the issue had been allocated, the Stock Warrants Exercisable account had a credit balance of $15,000 (or $15 per warrant). Each warrant, upon exercise, grants the holder one share of $10 par value common stock at a cash price of $35 per share. Further assume that half of the warrants were exercised when the market price of the common stock was $60 per share. The journal entry to reflect the exercise would be:

Cash ($35 × 500)	17,500	
Stock Warrants Exercisable	7,500	
($15 × 500)		
Common Stock ($10 × 500)		5,000
Paid-in Capital in Excess of Par Value		20,000
(To record exercise of 500		
stock warrants.)		

The $60 market value of the stock when the warrant is issued is not used to record the issuance of the stock. Rather, the stock is recorded at an amount equal to the total of the cash received ($35 per share), plus the amount allocated to the warrant when it was originally issued ($15), for a total per share of $50. Stockholders' equity is thus increased by a total of $25,000 ($50 × 500 shares), $5,000 being the par value of the shares issued and $20,000 being added to Paid-in Capital in Excess of Par Value.

If a warrant is allowed to expire or lapse, the Stock Warrants Exercisable account is reclassified as Paid-in Capital in Excess of Par, unless a portion of the warrant is refunded; in which case the warrant account is removed to the extent of the refund and reclassified as a liability. Any residual balance in the warrant account is then reclassified as Paid-in Capital in Excess of Par Value. To illustrate, if the remaining warrants of Harmon Corporation were allowed to expire, the journal entry would be:

Stock Warrants Exercisable	7,500	
($15 × 500)		
Paid-in Capital in Excess of Par Value		7,500
(To record expiration of 500		
stock warrants.)		

Convertible Securities

If the owner of a convertible security, such as a bond or preferred stock, exercises the conversion feature, certain accounting issues emerge. The carrying amount of the convertible security (par value, plus any premium or less any discount) may differ from the market value of the stock issued at the time the conversion takes place.

To illustrate, assume that Rag Top, Inc., issues convertible bonds which have a maturity value of $1,000,000 and are carried in the corporate books net of a $25,000 discount. Further assume that each $1,000 bond is convertible into 10 shares of $75 par value common stock. The current market value of the common stock is $104 per share. If all 1,000 bonds are converted on January 1, 1985, the following entry is necessary:

Jan. 1, 1985	Bonds Payable	1,000,000	
	Discount on Bonds Payable		25,000
	Common Stock		750,000
	Paid-in Capital in Excess of Par Value		225,000
	(To record the conversion of bonds and issuance of stock.)		

Recording the conversion in this manner results in reporting the stock at the book value of the converted debt ($975,000) rather than the $1,040,000 market value of the stock ($104 per share × 10,000 shares).

Objectivity

The rationale for this position is provided by the treatment accorded the convertible debt when originally issued. Remember that some of the proceeds of convertible debt may be considered a permanent contribution to stockholders' equity. Due to the inseparability of the debt and equity components of a convertible security, however, the proceeds from the issuance of convertible debt are classified as debt. Therefore, when a conversion takes place, an apparent gain or loss on the extinguishing of the debt may result from the accounting treatment at the issuance of the convertible security. The difference between the carrying amount of converted debt and the fair value of the stock issued upon conversion is properly

Substance over Form

treated as an adjustment to stockholders' equity rather than as a gain or loss on the debt retirement. Underlying theory suggests that if the debt is converted to stock, the security represents a permanent increase in stockholders' equity at issuance, and no gain or loss is recognized when the form of the instrument is converted.

MISCELLANEOUS STOCKHOLDERS' EQUITY CONSIDERATIONS

Earnings Per Share

Disclosure

A required disclosure for publicly held corporations is the earnings per share. Basically, the **earnings per share (EPS)** of a corporation results from the division of the accounting net income available to common shareholders for a particular period by the number of *common* shares outstanding during the period. The EPS figure is a measure of the amount of net income attributable to each share of common stock. This measure can be useful to the common stockholder because the market price per share of stock is to some degree dependent upon the EPS of that stock. In addition, with EPS figures the common stock investor can more readily evaluate the dividend policy of the company, because dividends are frequently expressed in per share terms.

Minor complications arise if the corporation changes the number of shares outstanding during the year or has preferred stock outstanding. If the corporation changes the number of shares outstanding during the period, either through new stock issues or purchases of treasury shares, the denominator of the EPS calculation should be adjusted to reflect a weighted average of the number of common shares outstanding during the period. If preferred stock is outstanding during the period, the numerator of the EPS calculation should be adjusted by subtracting all preferred dividends declared during the period or which accumulate under a cumulative feature. In this way the numerator measures the net income available to common shareholders after dividend preferences for preferred stock are satisfied.

To illustrate, assume that Tyler Chemical Company reported a net income of $1,000,000 for 1984. In addition, Tyler declared preferred dividends on their preferred stock of $200,000 for 1984. Tyler had 400,000 common shares outstanding at the beginning of the year and issued an additional 400,000 shares halfway through the year, on June 30, 1984. There were no other stock transactions during the year.

The weighted average number of common shares outstanding during 1984 is calculated as follows:

(1) Outstanding Shares	(2) Period Outstanding	(3) Share-months (Col. 1 × Col. 2)	(4) Weighted Average (Col. 3) ÷ (Col. 2)
400,000	6 mos.	2,400,000	
800,000	6 mos.	4,800,000	
	12 mos.	7,200,000	600,000

The EPS calculation for Tyler Chemical would be:

$$\frac{\$1,000,000 - \$200,000}{600,000 \text{ shares}} = \$1.33 \text{ per share}$$

The common stockholders have $1.33 in earnings for each share of stock.

The EPS calculation is complicated considerably by the introduction of stock dividends and stock splits. Furthermore, securities such as stock warrants, employee stock options, and securities convertible to common stock represent potential common shares (dilution) that must be considered when attempting to determine EPS. These considerations are rather involved and are therefore discussed separately and in greater detail in Chapter 26.

Appraisal Capital

Historical Cost

Conservatism

As discussed in Chapter 2, contemporary accounting theory recognizes the desirability of valuing assets held for exchange, such as inventories or marketable securities, at the lower of cost or market. Plant assets are valued at historical cost less accumulated depreciation and are not revalued upward in the normal course of financial accounting and reporting. The modifying convention of conservatism is powerful and influences financial accounting extensively. At present there is little support for valuing assets at amounts *exceeding* their original cost, because to do so might recognize gains or revenues before they are realized. During the past decade, however, increased professional interest in adjusting the carrying amounts of assets upward has been evident. The theoretical arguments favoring this change usually are based on recognizing the effects of inflation and changing replacement costs.

To illustrate, the FASB requires certain very large companies to disclose supplementary information about the effects of changing price levels and replacement costs. This subject and other topics relating primarily to large publicly held companies are discussed extensively in the final section of this text.

Notwithstanding the controversy of valuing assets above their cost, accountants generally agree that if such asset write-ups occur, a direct increase in a separate section of stockholders' equity is also appropriate. Accountants consider the direct adjustment of stockholders' equity preferable to recognizing gains in the income statement with resultant increases in retained earnings. An account title to recognize such an asset write-up might be "Appreciation Capital" or "Appraisal Capital."

Quasi Reorganization

Occasionally a corporation finds that it simply cannot operate profitably given its operating situation and asset and liability structure. In such circumstances a possible solution is a quasi reorganization. The term "quasi" means "the same as," and accounting for a quasi reorganization is similar to that required in a complete reorganization of a business enterprise. A quasi reorganization, however, costs far less than a complete legal reorganization. In a **quasi reorganization** the assets of a company are generally written down to a point which will provide for profitable operations. For example, a company may have forecasted an expanding demand for their products and invested in major plant expansion. If the forecast is not realized, excess plant assets may result. Idle or partially productive plant assets may cause the company to be unable to operate profitably. Debt repayment may become impossible under original lending terms. In such cases, the plant assets may be written down to an amount approximating their productive value, and debt may be restructured to allow additional time for repayment. In extreme cases creditors may also agree to accept reduced amounts in satisfaction of corporate debts to maximize the partial recovery of loaned funds. Quasi reorganization, which is permitted under many state laws, requires the approval of the corporate board of directors and stockholders, and care must be exercised to ensure the maintenance of minimum legal corporate capital.

In sum, three general conditions usually indicate the desirability of a quasi reorganization:

1. Various assets of the company are overvalued.
2. Retained earnings contains a deficit.
3. The future of the company from an operating perspective appears favorable if adjustments to the assets and liabilities are made.

In most quasi reorganizations, common stockholders sacrifice in terms of reduced equity. Preferred stockholders may sacrifice through a lack of dividends, and creditors may decide to forego some of their legal rights to require payment on a timely basis. The resource providers of the company are thus attempting to make the best of a bad situation and take action to facilitate the survival of the company.

As the carrying value of assets is reduced to a level facilitating future profitable operations, Retained Earnings is charged directly for the amount of the write-down. The Retained Earnings account will have a deficit balance due to operating losses and the asset write-down. Therefore, other entries are frequently necessary to adjust Retained Earnings to a zero balance. To remove a deficit from Retained Earnings, we credit Retained Earnings and charge Paid-in Capital in Excess of Par Value. If insufficient Paid-in Capital in Excess of Par Value is available to absorb the entire deficit in Retained Earnings, the par or stated value of the common stock is usually reduced. A reduction of the par value of the stock gives rise to additional Paid-in Capital in Excess of Par Value, which in turn is credited to the remaining debit balance in Retained Earnings.

Profitable operations following a quasi reorganization may facilitate new stock issues and other financing sources for the troubled enterprise. Dividends may be paid from resources generated by profitable operations after a quasi reorganization.

Following a quasi reorganization, the Retained Earnings account is dated in a manner such as "Retained Earnings from January 1, 1983." In this way financial statement users can assess the degree of operating success attained by a company after a quasi reorganization.

To illustrate accounting for a quasi reorganization, the following example is provided. Exhibit 17–10 presents an abbreviated balance sheet of Waterford Company prior to a quasi reorganization. Note that Waterford's Retained Earnings account contains a deficit even before the quasi reorganization. This condition is typical in that operating losses usually precede the need to reorganize. Because Waterford has been unable to operate profitably and has experienced difficulty servicing its debt, and because profitable operations appear possible in the future if a reorganization is effected, the board of directors authorizes a quasi reorganization.

A review of Waterford's property reveals that various assets should be adjusted to net realizable values as follows:

Assets	Current Carrying Amount	Net Realizable Value
Inventory	$ 30,000	$ 25,000
Machinery	50,000	40,000

EXHIBIT 17–10
Waterford Company
Abbreviated Balance Sheet
Prior to Quasi Reorganization

December 31, 1984

Assets

Current Assets

Cash	$ 1,500	
Accounts receivable (net of allowance for doubtful accounts of 7,000)	10,000	
Inventory at FIFO cost	30,000	
Total current assets		$ 41,500

Property, Plant, and Equipment

Machinery (net of accumulated depreciation of $25,000)	50,000	
Building (net of accumulated depreciation of $75,000)	250,000	
Land	100,000	
Total property, plant, and equipment		400,000
Total assets		$441,500

Liabilities and Stockholders' Equity

Liabilities

Current liabilities	$ 75,000
Long-term bonds payable	250,000
Total liabilities	$325,000

Stockholders' Equity

Common stock ($10 par; 10,000 shares authorized, issued, and outstanding)	100,000
Paid-in capital in excess of par value	75,000
Total contributed equity	175,000
Retained earnings (deficit)	(58,500)
Total stockholders' equity	116,500
Total liabilities and stockholders' equity	$441,500

Building	250,000	250,000
Land	100,000	90,000
	$430,000	$405,000

In this case a total assets write-down of $25,000 takes place, which increases the deficit in Retained Earnings as indicated in the entry below:

Dec. 31, 1984	Retained Earnings	25,000	
	Inventory		5,000
	Machinery		10,000
	Land		10,000
	(To reduce the carrying amounts of various assets to net realizable value in accordance with quasi reorganization.)		

Following this entry, the deficit in retained earnings is $83,500 ($58,500 + $25,000). Because the Paid-in Capital in Excess of Par Value of $75,000 is not sufficient to absorb the $83,500 deficit in retained earnings, the par value of the common stock must be reduced.

We shall assume a reduction in par value to $7.50 per share, which is reflected by the following entry:

Dec. 31, 1984	Common Stock	25,000	
	Paid-in Capital		
	in Excess of Par Value		25,000
	(To reflect change in par value		
	to accomplish quasi reorganization.		
	$2.50 × 10,000 shares.)		

Permission of the stockholders, regulatory agencies, and usually the creditors is necessary before the par value of stock is changed. The final step in completing the quasi reorganization is elimination of the deficit in Retained Earnings of $83,500:

Dec. 31, 1984	Paid-in Capital		
	in Excess of Par Value	83,500	
	Retained Earnings		83,500
	(To eliminate deficit balance in		
	Retained Earnings pursuant to		
	quasi reorganization.)		

Following the quasi reorganization and a year in which operations generate net income of $20,000, the stockholders' equity section of Waterford's balance sheet appears as presented in Exhibit 17–11. Note that retained earnings is dated and that the company reflects a reduced equity structure.

In practice, a quasi reorganization is infrequently encountered, because it is an extreme measure in a company's fight for survival. The "fresh-start" provided by a quasi reorganization does not change the underlying economic difficulties; cash flow and profitability problems usually remain. Therefore, a quasi reorganization is generally not effective unless new management or improved products or conditions tend to support favorable future operating prospects. A quasi reorganization does give a company the opportunity to organize in a way that allows operations to be conducted in a more realistic and orderly fashion. In this way management may be able to generate adequate revenues to sustain the enterprise.

CONCLUDING REMARKS

Transactions affecting stockholders' equity accounts involve a wide range of activities throughout the life of an enterprise. The first economic events affecting a company upon its formation and the final acts of dissolution involve equity accounts. Furthermore, most

---

EXHIBIT 17–11
Waterford Company
Partial Balance Sheet
One Year After Quasi Reorganization

Stockholders' Equity

Common stock ($7.50 par; 10,000 shares authorized, issued, and outstanding	$ 75,000
Paid-in capital in excess of par value	16,500
Total contributed capital	91,500
Retained earnings (since Jan. 1, 1985)	20,000
Total stockholders' equity	111,500

Materiality events directly affecting stockholders' equity are usually material and require careful study to assure acceptable practices.

Creditors and stockholders share many characteristics. For example, both provide resources to the organization, and both accept risk in attempting to make profitable investments. As discussed in Chapter 16, the dividing line between debt and equity is sometimes difficult to discern. This is especially true when dealing with hybrid instruments such as convertible securities and income bonds. The importance of distinguishing between debt and equity, however, is significant. Many restrictive bond covenants, for example, require the maintenance of specified debt/equity ratios, and the classification of hybrid securities may represent the difference between contract compliance and violation.

The equity sections of the balance sheets of most large corporations usually contain many different classes and types of stock which have been issued over a long period of time. Therefore, careful review of each issue is necessary to ensure proper accounting for dividends, new stock issues, and other activities affecting individual stockholders. In summary, the stockholders' equity section of a company's balance sheet must be considered and treated as carefully as any other element of a corporation's financial position.

KEY POINTS

1. The major items affecting retained earnings of a company are earnings and dividends. Less frequent items are corrections of errors, certain treasury stock transactions, initial adoption of certain accounting principles, and quasi reorganizations.

2. Dividends are a liability of a company only when declared by the board of directors.

3. Property dividends, like other dividends, should be accounted for at fair market value, with gains and losses recognized upon disposal of the property.

4. If outstanding preferred stock is cumulative or fully or partially participating, careful analysis is required to properly allocate dividends between common and preferred stockholders.

5. Small stock dividends are accounted for on the basis of fair market value, while large stock dividends are recorded on the basis of par or stated value.

6. Stock splits require no formal accounting treatment, just a memorandum noting the new par or stated value per share and the number of shares authorized, issued, and outstanding.

7. Employee stock options can be considered compensatory or noncompensatory. Compensatory stock options require the recognition of compensation expense. The total compensation is measured as the excess of the market value over the option price on the measurement date, which is usually the grant date.

8. Stock appreciation rights (SARs) entitle certain employees to stock appreciation over some specified price multiplied by a specified number of shares. SARs are compensatory and therefore require compensation recognition in the accounting records. Because the measurement date is the exercise date, accounting recognition is based on estimates until final exercise.

9. Assets should generally not be written up above cost based on appraisals; consequently, the use of appraisal capital is rare.

10. Quasi reorganizations are appropriate only when a company is faced with severe financial or operating problems which appear to be manageable if adjustments to assets, liabilities, and stockholders' equity accounts are made.

QUESTIONS

17–1 What is meant by the term "retained earnings"? Comment on the propriety of using the term "earned surplus."

17–2 Briefly describe some of the items that affect retained earnings.

17–3 Three dates are important in evaluating dividend status: date of declaration, date of record, and date of payment. Describe the accounting implications of each date.

17–4 Preferred stock may have a cumulation clause and/or a participation clause. What does each term imply to the preferred stockholder?

17–5 Can an investor unambiguously state that, for a particular investment, receiving a dividend is preferable to receiving no dividend? Why or why not?

17–6   What is a property dividend, and what are the significant accounting issues related to this kind of dividend?

17–7   What is a scrip dividend, and what are the significant accounting issues related to this kind of dividend?

17–8   What are liquidating dividends, and what are the significant accounting issues related to this kind of dividend?

17–9   What is a stock dividend? What is the economic result of a stock dividend?

17–10   Accounting authoritative pronouncements distinguish between small and large stock dividends. How is this distinction defined, what are the accounting implications, and how is this distinction justified?

17–11   What is the distinction between a large stock dividend and a stock split? What are the accounting implications of this distinction?

17–12   What is the purpose of a large stock dividend or stock split? What is the purpose of a reverse stock split?

17–13   Why aren't cash and property dividends paid on treasury stock?

17–14   Why does a company appropriate retained earnings? What does a retained earnings appropriation communicate to financial statement users?

17–15   What is an employee stock option? What is the distinction between a compensatory and noncompensatory employee stock option?

17–16   What are the significant accounting issues related to compensatory employee stock options?

17–17   What is a stock appreciation right? Why is the measurement date for stock appreciation rights usually different from that for employee stock options? What are the major accounting considerations for stock appreciation rights?

17–18   What is "appraisal capital," and how is it recognized in the accounting records?

17–19   What is a quasi reorganization? What is the economic impact of a quasi reorganization? How is a quasi reorganization effected in the accounting records?

CASES

C17–1 J. F. Hannibal Corporation has been in business for four years. The corporation has never paid a dividend but has accumulated earnings over the past four years of $500,000. The balance sheet on December 31, 1985, appears as follows:

Assets

Current assets	$ 50,000
Land	300,000
Plant assets	500,000
Less: Accumulated depreciation	(100,000)
Patents	300,000
Total assets	$1,050,000

Liabilities and Stockholders' Equity

Current liabilities	$ 50,000
Long-term debt	100,000
Common stock (no par; 10,000 shares authorized, issued, and outstanding)	400,000
Retained earnings	500,000
Total liabilities and stockholders' equity	$1,050,000

Net income for 1985 was $150,000. The statement of retained earnings indicates that $200,000 of retained earnings is appropriated for future plant expansion. Ralph Parker, a stockholder with a 20% holding, is concerned about the lack of dividends over the last four years. Specifically, he notices that retained earnings are $500,000, and he is therefore thinking about pressuring the company to pay some of this amount in dividends. Parker believes 40%, or $200,000 of retained earnings, could be paid in dividends, leaving $200,000 for plant expansion and $100,000 as a cushion against economic downturns.

Instructions

Mr. Parker has come to you for advice on how best to proceed against the company.
[a] What is your advice to Mr. Parker?
[b] How would you alleviate Mr. Parker's concern about the lack of dividends? In other words, show Mr. Parker that the lack of dividends may not be as bad as he thinks.

C17–2 The board of directors of Junetag Appliance Company is considering several strategies for the upcoming annual dividend. Alfred Korn, the treasurer of the company, has been asked to explain to the board of directors the advantages and disadvantages of each strategy. The four strategies are:

[1] Declare the normal cash dividend of $1.00 per share.

[2] Declare a 2% stock dividend on the outstanding common stock.

[3] Declare a 40% stock dividend on the outstanding common stock.

[4] Split the stock, 2 for 1, and declare a $.50 per share dividend on the new outstanding shares.

Junetag has 100,000 shares of $2.50 par value common stock outstanding. The market price of the common stock is $50 per share.

Instructions

[a] Provide the information needed by the board of directors. Be sure to identify the amount to be charged to retained earnings for each method.

[b] The chairman of the board discovers that the amount charged to retained earnings is the same under each alternative and therefore concludes that the methods are identical in terms of economic effect on the firm. Respond to this observation.

C17–3 Miller Company is considering an employee incentive plan for certain key employees. The compensation committee of the board of directors is considering either a stock option plan or a stock appreciation right plan. The compensation committee wants a complete report on the advantages and disadvantages of each type of plan for both employer and employee. In addition, the compensation committee wishes to know the financial statement reporting principles for each method.

Instructions

Provide the information requested by the compensation committee of the board of directors.

C17–4 On December 14, 1982, the board of directors of Plaza Company authorized a grant of nontransferable (restricted) options to company executives for the purchase of 10,000 shares of $50 par value common stock at 52½ any time during 1985 if the executives were still employed by the company. The closing price of Plaza common stock was $55 on December 14, 1982, $52 on January 2, 1985, and 49⅛ on December 31, 1985. None of the options was exercised.

Instructions

[a] Prepare a schedule computing the compensation expense attributable to the stock options that should be recognized by Plaza Company. Prepare any entries for 1982 through 1985.

[b] Assume that the market price of Plaza common stock rose to $57 (instead of declining to $52) on January 2, 1985, and that all options were exercised on that date. What cost would the company incur for executive compensation? Why? Prepare any additional entries necessary in these circumstances.

[c] Discuss the arguments for measuring compensation from executive stock options in terms of the spread between:

[1] Market price and option price when the grant is made.

[2] Market price and option price when the options are first exercisable.

[3] Market price and option price when the options are exercised.

[4] Cash value of the executives' services estimated at the grant date and the amount of their salaries.

(AICPA adapted)

EXERCISES

E17–1 Browning Corporation was organized on January 1, 1983. On that date 10,000 shares of $4 preferred stock ($40 par) were issued. The preferred stock is cumulative and participating up to a maximum amount of 15%, including the preference amount. In addition, 150,000 shares of Browning common ($10 par) were issued. No dividends were declared or paid in 1983. On July 1, 1984, Browning declared a 5% common stock dividend to common stockholders of record on July 20, 1984, distributable on August 1, 1984. The market price of Browning common was $28 a share on July 1, 1984, and $30 a share on August 1, 1984. On December 1, 1984, Browning declared a

$300,000 cash dividend to stockholders of record on December 10, 1984, payable on December 31, 1984.

Instructions

[a] Provide all journal entries relating to dividends by Browning Corporation for 1984. Separately identify the dividends to the common and preferred shares.

[b] Briefly discuss how the cumulation feature on the preferred stock affects the market value of common stock.

E17–2 Calgari Corporation has experienced a highly profitable year, and the board of directors has decided

to bring all dividends in arrears up to date. The preferred stock of the company is fully participating as well as cumulative. The board wishes to accomplish three objectives with the dividend:
[1] Pay all dividends in arrears.
[2] Pay the current year's preference amount.
[3] Pay the maximum possible amount of dividend to the common stockholders without invoking the participation clause of the preferred stock.

The stockholders' equity section of Calgari Corporation's balance sheet is summarized as follows:

Preferred stock ($100 par, 15% cumulative, fully participating; 3 years' dividends in arrears; 10,000 shares authorized, 8,000 shares issued of which 3,000 shares are held in treasury)	$ 500,000
Common stock ($10 par; 500,000 shares authorized, 300,000 shares issued of which 50,000 shares are held in treasury)	2,500,000
Paid-in capital in excess of par value	350,000
Retained earnings	1,150,000
Total stockholders' equity	$4,500,000

The company uses the par value method of accounting for treasury stock.

Instructions

[a] Prepare the calculations necessary to determine the maximum dividend consistent with the three objectives of the board of directors.
[b] If such a dividend was declared, prepare the entry or entries necessary to record the declaration.

E17–3   Naples, Inc., owned 100,000 shares of marketable common stock of Treasure Corporation on December 31, 1984. At that time the Naples account Investment in Marketable Equity Securities had a carrying value of $7 per share, which was the cost of the securities. The market value of the investment on that date was $8 per share. On that same date, Naples' board of directors declared a property dividend in which the shares of Treasure Corporation were to be distributed to Naples stockholders on January 15, 1985. At the time the shares were distributed, the market value of the Treasure Corporation stock had dropped to $6 per share.

Instructions

[a] Prepare the entries necessary to record the declaration and distribution of this property dividend.
[b] What is the proper accounting treatment, if any, of the $2 drop in market value from the declaration to the distribution date?

E17–4   The board of directors of Scott, Inc., wishes to declare a dividend whereby common stockholders are to receive a total per share dividend of $3. Scott's stockholders' equity section appears as follows:

Preferred stock ($100 par, 7%, participating to 10%, noncumulative; 100,000 shares authorized, 25,000 shares issued and outstanding)	$ 2,500,000
Common stock ($25 par; 250,000 shares authorized, issued, and outstanding)	6,250,000
Paid-in capital in excess of par value	1,250,000
Retained earnings	5,000,000
Total stockholders' equity	$15,000,000

Instructions

Determine the total amount of the dividend that must be declared to meet the per share goals of the board of directors.

E17–5   On February 1, 1985, the board of directors of Soskin, Inc., declared a 5% common stock dividend distributable to common stockholders of record on February 15, 1985. Distribution of the dividend took place on February 28, 1985.
Market prices of the stock were as follows:

Feb. 1, 1985	$75 per share
Feb. 15, 1985	80 per share
Feb. 28, 1985	76 per share

There were 100,000 shares of $50 par value stock authorized and 75,000 of the shares were outstanding prior to the stock dividend.

Instructions

[a] Prepare the journal entries to record the stock dividend.
[b] If prior to the stock dividend the retained earnings was $1,000,000, additional paid-in capital was $250,000, and there were no other issues of stock outstanding, prepare the stockholders' equity section of the balance sheet as of:
   [1] February 1, 1985
   [2] February 28, 1985

E17–6   Anthracite Corporation has 20,000 shares of $10 par value common stock and 1,000 shares of $100 par value, 7% preferred stock outstanding. A total dividend of $25,000 is declared by the corporation. No dividends were paid in the prior year.

Instructions

[a] If the preferred stock is neither participating nor cumulative, determine the amount of dividends payable to each class of stock.

[b] Assume that the preferred stock is fully participating but noncumulative. What dividends are payable to each class of stock?

[c] Assume that the preferred stock is cumulative but not participating. What dividends are payable to each class of stock?

[d] Assume that the preferred stock is both cumulative and fully participating. Compute the dividends for each class of stock.

E17–7 As the accountant responsible for preparing the financial statements for Forbes, Inc., you have assembled the following general ledger information related to retained earnings for the year ended December 31, 1985.

Retained Earnings

Date	Item	Dr.	Cr.
1/1/85	Beginning balance		$1,500,000
4/15/85	1st quarterly dividend for 1985 in cash	$12,000	
7/12/85	2nd quarterly dividend for 1985 in cash	10,000	
8/12/85	Small stock dividend	25,000	
10/12/85	3rd quarterly dividend for 1985 in cash	15,000	
11/15/85	Completed litigation— appropriation closed		100,000
11/29/85	Correction of error in inventory pricing of prior year		72,000
12/31/85	Net income for the year		125,000
12/31/85	Ending balance	$62,000	$1,797,000

While reading the minutes of the December 26, 1985, meeting of the board of directors, you learn that a dividend of $13,000 was declared, which is to be paid on January 5, 1986.

Instructions

Prepare a retained earnings statement in good form for Forbes, Inc., for 1985.

E17–8 Cortez, Inc., began operations in January 1981 and had the following reported net income or loss for each of its five years of operations:

1981	$ 150,000 loss
1982	130,000 loss
1983	120,000 loss

1984	250,000 income
1985	1,000,000 income

At December 31, 1985, the Cortez capital accounts were as follows:

Preferred stock, ($100 par value; 8% fully participating, cumulative; 10,000 shares authorized, issued, and outstanding)	$1,000,000
Preferred stock ($100 par value; 4% nonparticipating, noncumulative; 1,000 shares authorized, issued, and outstanding)	100,000
Common stock ($10 par value; 100,000 shares authorized, 50,000 shares issued and outstanding)	500,000

Cortez has never paid a cash or stock dividend. There has been no change in the capital accounts since Cortez began operations. The appropriate state law permits dividends only from retained earnings.

Instructions

Prepare a worksheet showing the *maximum* amount available for cash dividends on December 31, 1985, and how it would be distributable to holders of the common shares and each type of the preferred shares. Show supporting computations in good form.

(AICPA adapted)

E17–9 The balance sheet of Glamor Tone Cosmetics Company appeared as follows on December 31, 1984:

Assets

Cash	$ 10,000
Marketable equity securities	
(market value = $60,000)	50,000
Inventory	70,000
Plant assets	200,000
Less: Accumulated	
depreciation	(50,000)
Total assets	$280,000

Liabilities and Stockholders' Equity

Current liabilities	$ 10,000
Long-term debt	100,000
Common stock ($2 par; 10,000	
shares authorized, issued,	
and outstanding)	20,000
Paid-in capital in excess of par	
value	100,000
Retained earnings	50,000
Total liabilities and	
stockholders' equity	$280,000

The market value of the outstanding common shares on December 31, 1984, was $25 per share.

Instructions

[a] Provide the appropriate journal entries for each of the following *independent* situations:

[1] On January 1, 1985, Glamor Tone declared a property dividend of all holdings of marketable equity securities.

[2] On January 1, 1985, Glamor Tone declared a scrip dividend of $35,000.

[3] On January 1, 1985, Glamor Tone declared a cash dividend of $70,000.

[4] On January 1, 1985, Glamor Tone declared a 10% stock dividend.

[5] On January 1, 1985, Glamor Tone declared a 40% stock dividend.

[b] How do the applications of accounting principles differ for [4] and [5] above? What is the rationale for the difference in procedure?

E17–10 As president of Regan Company, Orlando Oregano received options to buy 100 shares of his employer's $10 par stock on June 30, 1985. The options call for a price of $18 per share and are exercisable for 5 years following the grant date. Oregano exercised his option on August 1, 1985, and sold the shares on November 1, 1985. The market prices of the stock on selected dates were as follows:

June 30, 1985	$18 per share
Aug. 1, 1985	25 per share
Nov. 1, 1985	28 per share

Instructions

[a] Provide the appropriate journal entries for Regan Company with respect to the stock options.

[b] Provide the appropriate journal entries for Regan Company with respect to the stock options, assuming the option prices to Oregano were:

[1] $15 per share

[2] $21 per share

[c] Provide the appropriate journal entry for the exercise of the option on August 1, 1985, under the original assumptions.

[d] What is the distinction between a compensatory and a noncompensatory stock option? How does the accounting for these types of stock options differ?

E17–11 The board of directors of Small, Inc., has decided to embark on substantial plant expansion. In order to demonstrate the need to retain assets in the company, the board agrees on December 31, 1983, to authorize an appropriation of retained earnings in the amount of $1,500,000, the anticipated cost of the plant expansion. The plant was partially constructed on December 31, 1984, and the board decided to reduce the appropriation by $800,000, the cost incurred to date. Finally, in September 1985 the plant was completed and the remaining portion of the appropriation was removed.

Instructions

[a] Prepare the entries to record, reduce, and finally remove the appropriation.

[b] Describe where the Appropriated Retained Earnings account should appear on the 1983 and 1984 financial statements of Small, Inc.

[c] What does the Appropriated Retained Earnings account communicate to the financial statement user?

E17–12 Proctor Company issues a series of bonds along with detachable stock warrants. Each warrant conveys the right to buy one share of $10 par value common stock for $50 per share. One thousand bonds were issued (each with one detachable warrant attached), and $8,000 was correctly recorded as Stock Warrants Exercisable. Eighty percent of the warrants are exercised at a time when the market value of the stock is $65 per share.

Instructions

Record the appropriate journal entry for the exercise of the warrants.

E17–13 On January 1, 1982, Peterson Textile Company offered its top management share appreciation rights with the following terms:

Option price	$50 per share
Number of shares	7,000
Holding period	3 years
Expiration date	Dec. 31, 1985

The share appreciation is to be paid upon exercise in Peterson common stock ($20 stated value). The market value of Peterson common was as follows:

Dec. 31, 1982	$48 per share
Dec. 31, 1983	57 per share
Dec. 31, 1984	55 per share

The stock appreciation rights were exercised on August 16, 1985, when Peterson common had a market value of $56 per share.

Instructions

Provide the correct journal entries to accrue compensation expense for 1982, 1983, and 1984. Record the proper journal entry for the exercise of the stock appreciation rights.

E17–14 Allguard Insurance Company presented the following comparative stockholders' equity sections of the balance sheet:

Allguard Insurance Company
PARTIAL BALANCE SHEET
For the Years Ended December 31

	1984	1985
Stockholders' Equity		
9% Preferred stock ($90 par value; 1,000 shares authorized, issued, and outstanding)	$ 90,000	$ 90,000
Common stock ($5 par; 100,000 shares authorized, 50,000 shares issued and outstanding on December 31, 1984, and 70,000 shares issued and outstanding on December 31, 1985)	250,000	350,000
Paid-in capital in excess of par value	250,000	450,000
Retained earnings	200,000	350,000
Total stockholders' equity	$790,000	$1,240,000

Quarterly common stock dividends of $.25 were declared on March 31, June 30, September 30, and December 31, 1985. Semiannual preferred stock dividends were declared on June 30 and December 31, 1985. On May 1, 1985, and September 1, 1985, 10,000 common shares were issued. The retained earnings of the company were affected by only dividends and earnings for 1985.

Instructions

Compute the earnings per share for Allguard Insurance Company for 1985.

PROBLEMS

P17–1 The following transactions and events of Chee, Inc., occurred during 1985:

[1] A former employee sued Chee for injuries sustained in the company's parking lot. Although legal counsel considered it highly unlikely that the former employee would win the case, Chee's management decided to appropriate retained earnings of $100,000 (10% of the amount sought by the former employee) on January 31, 1985.

[2] A 40% stock dividend was declared on February 10, 1985, when the market price of the stock was $25. On March 1, 1985, 4,000 shares of $10 par value common stock were issued in distributing the stock dividend. The market value of the stock on March 1, 1985 was $18.

[3] On April 15, 1985, a plant expansion fund was created by acquiring certificates of deposit in the amount of $250,000. Retained earnings in the same amount were appropriated.

[4] On June 30, 1985, a second stock dividend of 1,000 shares of $10 par value common stock was declared. The dividend was distributed on July 15, 1985. The market values of a share of common on June 30 and July 15, 1985, were $16.00 and $16.50, respectively.

[5] The lawsuit described in item [1] above was dropped by the former employee on September 1, 1985, with no cost to the company except attorney's fees, which have been paid and properly recorded.

[6] A cash dividend of $.25 per common share was

declared on September 30, 1985, and paid on October 15, 1985.

[7] On December 20, 1985, an expenditure of $45,000 was made from the plant expansion fund using a certificate of deposit which matured earlier that month. The certificate cost $40,000 and matured with interest at $48,000 on December 15, 1985.

Instructions

Prepare necessary entries for the above information. You may assume that adequate additional paid-in capital and retained earnings exist to account for these transactions.

P17–2 Ripka, Inc., has suffered substantial operating losses for several years. The ability of the company to service its debts and pay operating expenses has been impaired. Consequently, Ripka's owners, managers, and creditors have decided to execute a quasi reorganization. An abbreviated balance sheet of Ripka prior to the quasi reorganization is presented below.

Ripka, Inc.
BALANCE SHEET
December 31, 1984

Assets

Current Assets

Cash	$ 10,000
Accounts receivable (less allowance of $5,000)	15,000
Inventory	25,000
Total current assets	50,000

Noncurrent Assets

Plant and equipment (net of accumulated depreciation of $155,000)	340,000
Goodwill	50,000
Total noncurrent assets	390,000
Total assets	$ 440,000

Liabilities and Stockholders' Equity

Current Liabilities

Accounts payable	$ 55,000
Notes payable	25,000
Total current liabilities	80,000

Long-term Liabilities

Mortgage payable	210,000

Stockholders' Equity

Common stock ($10 par value; 25,000 shares authorized, issued, and outstanding)	250,000
Paid-in capital in excess of par value	40,000
Retained earnings	(140,000)
Total stockholders' equity	150,000
Total stockholders' equity and liabilities	$ 440,000

The following information may bear on accounting for the quasi reorganization. The owner of Ripka, Inc., decides to reduce plant assets to a more reasonable level to increase utilization of remaining assets. He has decided to sell certain equipment which originally cost $100,000 and which has been depreciated to $40,000 by the end of 1984. A firm offer for the equipment of $15,000 has been received.

An independent appraisal of the company's inventory reveals goods with a carrying value of $8,000 to be obsolete and worthless. The holder of a $25,000 note agrees to accept the proceeds from the sale of the idle equipment mentioned above in full satisfaction of the note.

The mortgage holder agrees to accept 2,000 shares of new $100 par value preferred stock in satisfaction of the liability. In addition, the par value of the common stock is reduced to $1 per share in order to effect the quasi reorganization.

Instructions

[a] Prepare the necessary entries to record the above events.

[b] Prepare a balance sheet for Ripka as of January 1, 1985, following the quasi reorganization.

P17–3 Rench, Inc., has three classes of stock outstanding at December 31, 1985:

Preferred stock (Class A) ($100 par value, 12%, cumulative and fully participating; 2 years' dividends in arrears; 10,000 shares authorized, issued, and outstanding)	$1,000,000
Preferred stock (Class B) ($100 par value, 10%, noncumulative, participating to 12%; 10,000 shares authorized, 5,000 shares issued and outstanding)	500,000
Common stock ($50 par value; 100,000 shares authorized, 50,000 shares issued, and 40,000 shares outstanding)	2,500,000
Paid-in capital in excess of par value	750,000
Treasury stock (10,000 shares of $50 par value common)	(600,000)
Retained earnings	3,250,000
Total stockholders' equity	$7,400,000

The board of directors of Rench, Inc., is deliberating about the amount of dividend to pay. Because no dividends have been paid for three years, determining how a dividend should be divided is somewhat complex.

Instructions

The chairman of the board of directors of Rench, Inc., has asked you to compute the amount of dividend payable to each class of stock under each of the following assumptions:

[a] The total dividend is $600,000.
[b] The total dividend is $650,000.
[c] The total dividend is $750,000.

P17–4 Adverse financial and operating circumstances warrant that Sligh Company undergo a quasi reorganization at December 31, 1985. The following information may be relevant in accounting for the quasi reorganization.

[1] Inventory with a cost of $215,000 is currently recorded in the accounts at its market value of $200,000.

[2] Plant assets with a fair market value of $700,000 are currently recorded at $875,000 net of accumulated depreciation.

[3] A creditor agrees to extend the maturity date of a loan for five years, although interest as originally stated must continue to be paid.

[4] Individual stockholders contribute $500,000 to create additional paid-in capital to facilitate the reorganization. No new shares of stock are issued.

[5] The par value of the common stock is reduced from $25 to $15.

[6] Immediately before the events described above, the stockholders' equity section appears as follows:

Common stock ($25 par value; 100,000 shares authorized and outstanding)	$2,500,000
Paid-in capital in excess of par value	1,750,000
Retained earnings (deficit)	(750,000)
Total stockholders' equity	$3,500,000

Instructions

Prepare the stockholders' equity section of Sligh Company's balance sheet after the quasi reorganization.

P17–5 On January 2, 1983, the stockholders of Behemoth Company authorized a stock option plan which provided key employees with options to purchase an aggregate of 20,000 shares of the company's $10 par value common stock at $14 per share. The market value of the stock was $16 on this date.

The next day, January 3, 1983, options to purchase 3,000 shares were granted to the president: 1,000 shares for services to be rendered in 1983; 1,000 shares for services to be rendered in 1984; and 1,000 shares for services to be rendered in 1985. The options are exercisable during the six months following the year in which the services were rendered. The market value of the stock was $17 on January 3, 1983.

The president exercised his option for 1,000 shares on April 1, 1984, when the market price was $20 per share. Subsequently he sold the stock on September 1, 1984, at $18 per share.

The president did not exercise his option in 1985. When the option lapsed on June 30, 1985, the market value of the stock was $12 per share.

Instructions

[a] Give the journal entries required in 1983–1985 under the plan, and to record lapsing of the option in 1985 (if necessary).

[b] Explain fully the reasons or principles underlying the entries.

(AICPA adapted)

P17–6 Sicilian, Inc., began operations in 1981 in a state which defines minimum legal capital as $1,000 or the par value of outstanding common stock less 10% to provide for treasury stock transactions, whichever is larger. Stock dividends, once declared, become part of minimum legal capital. The company employs a calendar year for purposes of financial reporting.

Immediately after Sicilian was organized, the stockholders' equity section of its balance sheet appeared as below:

Common stock ($25 par value; 100,000 shares authorized, 25,000 shares issued and outstanding)	$625,000
Paid-in capital in excess of par value	20,000
Retained earnings	–0–
Total stockholders' equity	$645,000

Net income (loss) for the period 1981–1985 appears below:

1981	$ 30,000
1982	40,000
1983	8,000
1984	(10,000)
1985	20,000

Activities related to the various types of dividends are described below:

1981 A cash dividend of $.75 per share was declared on December 31, 1981. The dividend was paid on January 15, 1982.

1982 A 5% stock dividend was declared on December 31, 1982, when the stock was selling for $26 per share. The dividend was distributed on January 20, 1983.

1983 A dividend was declared on December 31, 1983, in the amount of $.60 per share to be paid with marketable equity securities held by Sicilian as a temporary investment. The cost of each share of the marketable equity security held by Sicilian was $45 and the market value at December 31, 1983, was $50. The dividend was paid on January 10, 1984, when the marketable equity security was selling for $56 per share. (The gain on the dividend shares has been included in 1983 net income.)

1984 Despite the loss reported for the current year, Sicilian declared a cash dividend on December 20, 1984, of $.50 per share. The dividend was paid on January 5, 1985.

1985 On June 30, 1985, the company declared a 2-for-1 stock split and changed the par value of the stock to $12.50. On December 26, 1985, the company declared a 2% stock dividend, at which time the company's stock was selling for $17.50 per share.

Instructions

[a] Prepare the entries necessary to record the above events through December 31, 1985.

[b] Prepare an analysis of the changes in stockholders' equity accounts as a result of the above events.

P17–7 Trifilio Company was formed on July 1, 1982. It was authorized to issue 200,000 shares of $5 par value common stock and 50,000 shares of 6%, $10 par value, cumulative and nonparticipating preferred stock. Trifilio has a July 1–June 30 fiscal year.

The following information relates to Trifilio's stockholders' equity accounts.

Common Stock. Prior to the 1984–1985 fiscal year, Trifilio had 105,000 shares of outstanding common stock issued as follows:

[1] On July 1, 1982, 95,000 shares were issued for cash at $20 per share.

[2] On July 24, 1982, 5,000 shares were exchanged for a plot of land which cost the seller $70,000 in 1975 and had an estimated market value of $130,000 on July 24, 1982.

[3] On March 1, 1984, 5,000 shares were issued. The shares had been subscribed for $32 per share on October 31, 1983.

During the 1984–1985 fiscal year, the following transactions involving common stock took place:

Oct. 1, 1984 Subscriptions were received for 10,000 shares at $40 per share. Cash of $80,000 was received in full payment for 2,000 shares and stock certificates were issued. The remaining subscriptions for 8,000 shares were to be paid in full by September 30, 1985, at which time the certificates were to be issued.

Nov. 30, 1984 Trifilio purchased 2,000 shares of its own stock on the open market at $38 per share. Trifilio uses the cost method for treasury stock.

Dec. 15, 1984 Trifilio declared a 2% stock dividend for stockholders of record on January 15, 1985, to be issued on January 31, 1985. Trifilio was having a liquidity problem and could not afford a cash dividend at the time. Trifilio's common stock was selling at $43 per share on December 15, 1984. (The stock dividend was not distributed on treasury shares.)

June 20, 1985 Trifilio sold 500 shares of its own common stock that it had purchased on November 30, 1984, for $21,000.

Preferred Stock. Trifilio issued 30,000 shares of preferred stock at $15 per share on July 1, 1983.

Cash Dividends. Trifilio has followed a schedule of declaring cash dividends in December and June and paying stockholders of record the following month. The cash dividends which have been declared since inception of the company through June 30, 1985, are shown below.

Declaration Date	Common Stock	Preferred Stock
Dec. 15, 1983	$.10 per share	$.30 per share
June 15, 1984	$.10 per share	$.30 per share
Dec. 15, 1984	—	$.30 per share

No cash dividends were declared during June 1985 due to the company's liquidity problems.

Retained Earnings. As of June 30, 1984, Trifilio's Retained Earnings account had a balance of $370,000. For the fiscal year ending June 30, 1985, Trifilio reported net income of $20,000.

In March 1984, Trifilio received a term loan from

Union National Bank. The bank requires Trifilio to establish a sinking fund and restrict retained earnings for an amount equal to the sinking fund deposit. The annual sinking fund payment of $40,000 is due on April 30 each year; the first payment was made on schedule on April 30, 1985.

Instructions

Prepare the stockholders' equity section of the statement of financial position (balance sheet), including appropriate notes, for Trifilio Company as of June 30, 1985, as it should appear in the annual report to shareholders.

(CMA adapted)

P17–8 For the first time, Buena Products, Inc., is including a five-year summary of earnings and dividends per share in its 1985 annual report to stockholders. At January 1, 1981, the corporation had issued 7,000 shares of 4% cumulative, nonparticipating, $100 par value preferred stock and 40,000 shares of $10 par value common stock, of which 108 shares of preferred and 4,000 shares of common stock were held in treasury.

Dividends were declared and paid semiannually on the last day of June and December. Cash dividends paid per share of common stock and net income (loss) for each year were:

	1981	1982	1983	1984	1985
Net income (loss)	$126,568	$(11,812)	$47,148	$115,824	$193,210
Dividend on common					
June 30	.40	.11	.10	.40	.60
December 31	.48	.11	.30	.40	.40

In addition, a 10% stock dividend was declared and distributed on all common stock (including treasury shares) on April 1, 1983, and common stock was split 5 for 1 on October 1, 1985. The corporation has met a sinking fund requirement to purchase and retire 140 shares of its preferred stock on October 1 of each year, beginning in 1984, using any available treasury stock. On July 1, 1982, the corporation purchased 400 shares of its common stock and placed them in the treasury and on April 1, 1984, issued 5,000 shares of common stock to officers, using treasury stock to the extent available.

Instructions

[a] Prepare a schedule showing the computation of preferred stock dividends paid semiannually and annually for the five years. Use the following column headings:

		Number of Shares		Dividends Paid	
Year	Half (1st or 2nd)	Purchased and Retired	Outstanding	Semiannually	Annually

[b] Prepare a schedule which shows for each of the five years the cash dividends paid to common stockholders and the average number of shares of common stock outstanding after adjustment for the stock dividend and split. Use the following format:

	Shares of Common Stock		Dividends Paid		Common Stock Adjusted for	
Dividend Date	In Treasury	Outstanding	Per Share	Total	10% Stock Dividend	5-for-1 Stock Split
6/30/81						
12/31/81				———	———	———
Total for year				═══	═══	═══
Average for year					═══	═══

(Continue this format for the next four years.)

(AICPA adapted)

P17–9   During May 1983, Gilroy, Inc., was organized with 3,000,000 authorized shares of $10 par value common stock, and 300,000 shares of its common stock were issued for $3,300,000. Net income through December 31, 1983, was $125,000.

On July 3, 1984, Gilroy issued 500,000 shares of its common stock for $6,250,000. A 5% stock dividend was declared on October 2, 1984, and issued on November 6, 1984, to stockholders of record on October 23, 1984. The market value of the common stock was $11 per share on the declaration date. Gilroy's net income for the year ended December 31, 1984, was $350,000.

During 1985 Gilroy had the following transactions:

[1] In February Gilroy reacquired 30,000 shares of its common stock for $9 per share. Gilroy uses the cost method to account for treasury stock.

[2] In June Gilroy sold 15,000 shares of its treasury stock for $12 per share.

[3] In September each stockholder was issued (for each share held) one stock right to purchase two additional shares of common stock for $13 per share. The rights expire on December 31, 1985.

[4] In October 250,000 stock rights were exercised when the market value of the common stock was $14 per share.

[5] In November 400,000 stock rights were exercised when the market value of the common stock was $15 per share.

[6] On December 15, Gilroy declared its first cash dividend to stockholders of $.20 per share, payable on January 10, 1986, to stockholders of record on December 31, 1985.

[7] On December 21, in accordance with the applicable state law, Gilroy formally retired 10,000 shares of its treasury stock and had them revert to an unissued basis. The market value of the common stock was $16 per share on this date.

[8] Net income for 1985 was $750,000.

Instructions

Prepare a schedule of all transactions affecting the capital stock (shares and dollar amounts), additional paid-in capital, retained earnings, and the treasury stock (shares and dollar amounts) and the amounts that would be included in Gilroy's balance sheet at December 31, 1983, 1984, 1985, as a result of the above transactions. Show supporting computations in good form.

(AICPA adapted)

P17–10   Arnold Corporation is a publicly owned company whose shares are traded on a national stock exchange. At December 31, 1984, Arnold had 25,000,000 shares of $10 par value common stock authorized, of which 15,000,000 shares were issued and 14,000,000 shares were outstanding.

The stockholders' equity accounts at December 31, 1984, had the following balances:

Common stock	$150,000,000
Additional paid-in capital	80,000,000
Retained earnings	50,000,000
Treasury stock	18,000,000

During 1985, Arnold had the following transactions:

[1] On February 1, a secondary distribution of 2,000,000 shares of $10 par value common stock was completed. The stock was sold to the public at $18 per share, net of offering costs.

[2] On February 15, Arnold issued at $110 per share, 100,000 shares of $100 par value, 8% cumulative preferred stock with 100,000 detachable warrants. Each warrant contained one right which with $20 could be exchanged for one share of $10 par value common stock. On February 15, the market price for one stock right was $1.

[3] On March 1, Arnold reacquired 20,000 shares of its common stock for $18.50 per share. Arnold uses the cost method to account for treasury stock.

[4] On March 15, when the common stock was trading for $21 per share, a major stockholder donated 10,000 shares.

[5] On March 31, Arnold declared a semiannual cash dividend on common stock of $.10 per share, payable on April 10, 1985.

[6] On April 15, when the market price of the stock rights was $2 each and the market price of the common stock was $22 per share, 30,000 stock rights were exercised. Arnold issued new shares to complete the transaction.

[7] On April 30, employees exercised 100,000 options that were granted in 1982 under a noncompensatory stock option plan. When the options were granted, each option had a preemptive right and entitled the employee to purchase one share of common stock for $20 per share. On April 30, the market price of the common stock was $23 per share. Arnold issued new shares to settle the transaction.

[8] On May 31, when the market price of the common stock was $20 per share, Arnold declared a 5% stock dividend distributable on July 1, 1985, to stockholders of record on June 1, 1985. The appropriate state law prohibits stock dividends on treasury shares.

[9] On June 30, Arnold sold the 20,000 treasury shares reacquired on March 1 and an additional 280,000 treasury shares costing $5,600,000 that were on hand at the beginning of the year. The selling price was $25 per share.

[10] On September 30, Arnold declared a semiannual cash dividend on common stock of $.10 per share and the yearly dividend on preferred stock, both payable on October 30, 1985, to stockholders of record on October 10, 1985.

[11] On December 31, the remaining outstanding rights expired.

[12] Net income for 1985 was $25,000,000.

Instructions

Prepare a worksheet to be used to summarize, for each transaction, the changes in Arnold's stockholders' equity accounts for 1985. The columns on this worksheet should have the following headings:

Date of transaction (or beginning date)
Common stock—number of shares
Common stock—amount
Preferred stock—number of shares
Preferred stock—amount
Common stock warrants—number of rights
Common stock warrants—amount
Additional paid-in capital
Retained earnings
Treasury stock—number of shares
Treasury stock—amount

(AICPA adapted)

5

Additional Financial Reporting Issues

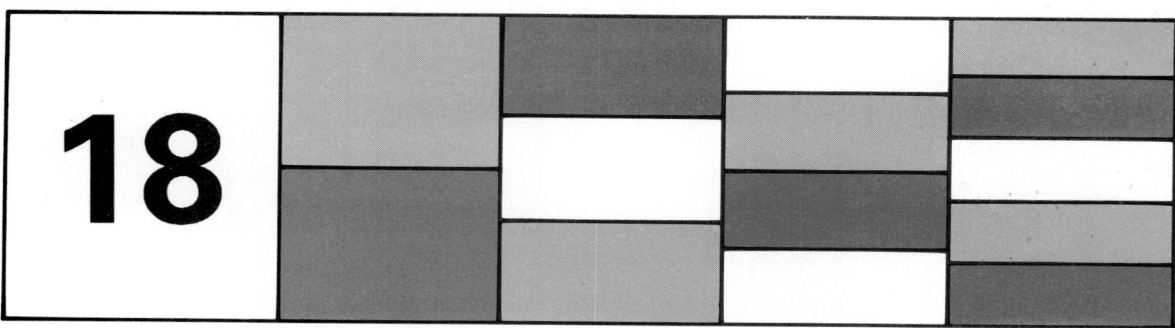

18

FINANCIAL REPORTING OF INCOME TAXES

Objectives

To discuss the major problem areas associated with the financial reporting of income taxes.

To distinguish between interperiod income tax allocation (allocation between accounting periods) and intraperiod income tax allocation (allocation within an accounting period).

To illustrate the differences between accounting methods used for financial reporting and income tax purposes and the corresponding need for interperiod income tax allocation.

To distinguish between permanent and timing differences and to illustrate how to deal with each in accounting for income tax expense.

To determine the income statement and balance sheet elements resulting from applying the deferred method of interperiod income tax allocation.

To illustrate the interaction of the origination and reversal of timing differences and to apply both the net-change and the gross-change methods in accounting for timing differences.

To discuss views on the proper accounting for income taxes other than those currently applied within generally accepted accounting principles.

To explain and illustrate the accounting and disclosure of operating-loss carryforwards and carrybacks.

To explain and illustrate the two accepted methods of accounting for the investment tax credit—the deferred and the flow-through methods—and to discuss the controversy surrounding the current position of the accounting profession whereby both methods are acceptable.

INTRODUCTION TO INCOME TAX REPORTING

Income taxes represent a major expense for many business operations. While income taxes are comparable in many respects to other expenses, there are several unusual and complicating features of accounting for income taxes and the presentation of those taxes in the financial statements. These complications result primarily because the determination of the amount of income taxes to be paid must be in accordance with the Internal Revenue Code. Legal compliance requires complex determinations of the amounts of income taxes to be paid. These amounts then provide the basis for several items that appear in the financial statements and accompanying footnotes of the enterprise.

Although this chapter emphasizes the inclusion of income taxes in financial statements—rather than legal compliance in determining the income taxes—the legal compliance has an undeniable influence on the content of financial statements and accordingly is mentioned frequently as a matter of necessity.

As you begin this chapter, turn to the Kroger Company financial statements on the inside front and back covers of your text. These statements contain several references to income taxes. The income statement includes the expense item "taxes based on income." In the balance sheet, "accrued income taxes" appears among the current liabilities, representing the amounts currently due to the government. Among the noncurrent liabilities, "deferred federal income taxes" represents income taxes that have been deferred (delayed) until future periods. In the statement of changes in financial position, several items relate to income taxes, such as "provision for deferred federal income taxes" and "tax benefit from discontinued operations." At this point you may not understand all of these items, but you will study them in this chapter.

Going Concern

Matching

Several underlying accounting concepts are important in forming specific accounting practices relating to the financial reporting of income taxes. The going-concern assumption is important because we assume that the enterprise will remain in existence in the foreseeable future and, thus, will continue to pay income taxes as profits are earned. The determination of income is heavily influenced by the matching principle in that expenses associated with revenues being recognized are included in the income statement as a part of the determination of the net income figure. While some people view income taxes as a distribution of income of the enterprise, the generally accepted interpretation is that income taxes are appropriately viewed as a **determinant** of income of the enterprise. Thus, **income taxes are an expense** and, within the matching principle, are subject to accrual accounting methods in the same manner as other expenses. Accordingly, income taxes must be recognized as an expense in the income statement in the same period in which the revenues and expenses giving rise to the income are recognized, even if the payment of the income taxes is made in a different accounting period. There is a direct association between the income taxes recognized as an expense in a given accounting period and the revenues and other expenses recognized in determining income of that same period.

Several authoritative pronouncements have been issued dealing with the financial accounting and reporting of income taxes. The primary one is *Accounting Principles Board Opinion No. 11.*[1] Both before and after the issuance of this key pronouncement, the appropriate accounting for various aspects of income taxes was considered by authoritative bodies. References to *Opinion No. 11,* as well as to other relevant pronouncements, are made throughout this chapter.

For purposes of our discussion, this chapter considers the problems of accounting for income taxes in five major sections: (1) "Intraperiod Income Tax Allocation" deals with the division of the income tax to be recognized in an accounting period between the various components of income and retained earnings recognized during that period; (2) "Interpe-

---

[1]*APB Opinion No. 11,* "Accounting for Income Taxes," 1967.

riod Income Tax Allocation," on the other hand, deals with the problem of accounting for differences between the treatment of revenues and expenses in reporting income taxes in the financial statements and the treatment of the same items in determining the enterprise's income tax liability in compliance with appropriate income tax laws; (3) "Operating-Loss Carrybacks and Carryforwards" deals with the financial-statement treatment of the unique feature of the income tax law that allows a loss in one year to be used to reduce previously paid income taxes or taxes that would otherwise have to be paid in the future; (4) "Investment Tax Credit" deals with the financial-statement treatment of the feature of income tax law that allows a reduction of income taxes if certain types of assets are acquired by an enterprise; and (5) "Financial-Statement Disclosure of Income Taxes" considers disclosure requirements related to income taxes.

Accounting standards that govern the presentation of income taxes in the financial statements have been developed over time, giving consideration to the objectives of financial reporting and the basic accounting concepts that underlie financial reporting in general. The basic underlying objective is, thus, to provide useful information to investors, creditors, and other financial statement users for making financial decisions. Income tax laws, on the other hand, have been developed through government action designed to accomplish quite different objectives. While the objectives of tax legislation are numerous, certainly the generation of income for the government, the redistribution of wealth within the economy, and the encouragement of the long-run growth of the economy have been important considerations. Given the different objectives of financial reporting and the income tax laws, we should not be surprised to learn that the treatment of revenue and expense items varies between the two. These differences will become apparent as you study the topics in this chapter.

Corporations are subject to federal income tax rates that vary from time to time as changes are made in the income tax laws. Beginning in 1983, corporate income is taxable at five different rates, which are related to the level of income subject to income taxes, as follows:

Income Tax Rate	Income Subject to This Rate
16%	First $25,000 of taxable income
19%	Next $25,000 of taxable income
30%	Next $25,000 of taxable income
40%	Next $25,000 of taxable income
46%	All taxable income in excess of $100,000

Certain types of transactions are given preferential treatment and are subject to special (lower) income tax rates in determining income taxes that must be paid. In addition, enterprises are frequently subject to state and local income taxes, which in many cases are patterned after federal income tax regulations.

To facilitate the emphasis on the financial-statement reporting of income taxes rather than the intricacies of legal compliance with federal, state, and local income tax laws, reasonable but simplified income tax rates are assumed and used in this chapter. We usually select a single income tax rate, such as 40%, 46%, or 48%, as a basis for the determination of income tax amounts.

INTRAPERIOD INCOME TAX ALLOCATION

Intraperiod income tax allocation refers to the allocation of the total income tax recognized in an accounting period between the various components of income and changes in stockholders' equity recognized during that same period. Earlier chapters explain that certain items are granted special treatment in financial reporting. These include, but are not limited to, the following items:

1. **Extraordinary items.** Presented in a separate income statement category immediately preceding "net income."
2. **Prior period adjustments.** Presented as adjustments to beginning retained earnings of the period in which the correction or other adjustment is made.

For purposes of discussing intraperiod income tax allocation, we refer to these two items as "special items."[2]

Intraperiod income tax allocation is strictly a problem of **financial-statement presentation.** It does not affect the total *amount* of income tax expense recognized; it simply deals with the manner of presentation of income tax expense in the various sections of the income statement or the retained earnings statement.

Intraperiod income tax allocation requires accountants to present special items on a **net-of-tax basis.** The rationale underlying this requirement is that for disclosure of a special item to be complete, the income tax effect of the item must be associated with it. Stated another way, the separate presentation of special items requires that they be presented on a net-of-tax basis in order to maintain the appropriate relationship between the various elements of income and stockholders' equity. This position is described by the Accounting Principles Board (APB) as follows:

> *The Board has concluded that tax allocation within a period should be applied to obtain an appropriate relationship between income tax expense and (a) income before extraordinary items, (b) extraordinary items, (c) adjustments of prior periods (or of the opening balance of retained earnings) and (d) direct entries to other stockholders' equity accounts. The income tax expense attributable to income before extraordinary items is computed by determining the income tax expense related to revenue and expense transactions entering into the determination of such income, without giving effect to the tax consequences of the items excluded from the determination of income before extraordinary items. The income tax expense attributable to other items is determined by the tax consequences of transactions involving these items. If an operating loss exists before extraordinary items, the tax consequences of such loss should be associated with the loss.[3]*

The objective of maintaining the appropriate relationship between income tax expense and other elements of income and changes in stockholders' equity accounts is apparent in the preceding quotation. **The income tax effect of special items should be computed by determining the amount of income tax expense that would be recognized with and without the special item. The difference between these two tax amounts is the tax effect of the special item.**

Several situations involving the application of intraperiod income tax allocation procedures may be encountered. These involve situations of income or loss before income tax, combined with one or both of the special items described earlier. In the following examples, three representative situations are illustrated.

Three companies, Red, White, and Blue, are currently determining the appropriate financial-statement presentation of income tax expense for 1984. During the year the companies reported the following information:

---

[2]In future chapters additional items are covered that also require separate presentation in the financial statements on a net-of-tax basis. These include (1) discontinued operations when a business has disposed of one of its segments, and (2) the cumulative effect of a change in an accounting principle. The application of intraperiod income tax allocation to those items is the same as the application to extraordinary items and prior period adjustments illustrated in this chapter.

[3]*APB Opinion No. 11,* par. 52.

	Income (Loss) Before Income Tax and Special Item	Special Items	Basis for Computing Total Tax
Red Company	$ 20,000	$27,000 extra-ordinary gain	$47,000
White Company	35,000	$(15,000) extra-ordinary loss	20,000
Blue Company	(30,000)	$42,000 posi-tive correction of error	12,000

The appropriate income tax rate on all items is assumed to be 40%.

The total income tax expense to be recognized is based on income before income tax and special items, adjusted upward or downward for the special item. For example, in the case of Red Company, the income before income tax and special item is $20,000; the extraordinary gain is $27,000, resulting in $47,000 as the basis for computing total income tax expense. The income tax expense on this total is separated into two components for presentation in the financial statements: (1) the portion associated with income before the special item and (2) the portion associated with the special item. The income tax expense in the income statement is stated as if the special item did not exist and the special item is then presented on a net-of-tax basis. This process is illustrated for the three companies in Exhibit 18–1.

EXHIBIT 18–1
Examples of Intraperiod Income Tax Allocation

Red Company— Extraordinary Gain

Total income tax to be recognized	
$47,000 × 40%	$18,800
Income tax expense associated with income before extraordinary gain	
$20,000 × 40%	8,000
Additional income tax associated with extraordinary gain	$10,800

Red Company
PARTIAL INCOME STATEMENT
For the Year Ended December 31, 1984

Income before income taxes and extraordinary item	$20,000
Income tax expense	8,000
Income before extraordinary gain	12,000
Extraordinary gain, net of $10,800 income tax expense	16,200
Net income	$28,200

White Company—Extraordinary Loss

Total Income tax to be recognized	
$20,000 × 40%	$ 8,000
Income tax expense associated with income before extraordinary loss	
$35,000 × 40%	14,000
Reduction in income tax associated with extraordinary loss	$(6,000)

White Company
PARTIAL INCOME STATEMENT
For the Year Ended December 31, 1984

Income before income taxes and extraordinary item	$35,000
Income tax expense	14,000
Income before extraordinary loss	21,000
Extraordinary loss, net of $6,000 income tax savings	(9,000)
Net income	$12,000

Blue Company—Prior Period Adjustments

Total income tax to be recognized	
$12,000 × 40%	$ 4,800
Income tax savings associated with loss before considering prior period adjustment	
$30,000 × 40%	12,000
Additional income tax associated with correction of error	$16,800

Blue Company
PARTIAL INCOME STATEMENT
For the Year Ended December 31, 1984

Loss before income taxes	$(30,000)
Income tax savings	12,000
Net loss	$(18,000)

The correction of error will be presented in the retained earnings statement as a positive adjustment to the beginning balance. The amount of this adjustment is $25,200, which represents the $42,000 positive adjustment, net of $16,800 income tax associated with that item.

In all three cases, we see that the income tax effect of the special item is computed by comparing the income tax to be recognized with and without the special item and allocating the difference to the special item. If a single income tax rate applies to all items subject to income tax, this computation is simplified, because the income tax associated with each item can be computed directly, as follows for Red, White, and Blue Companies:

Red Company:	$27,000 × 40% = $10,800	Additional income taxes associated with extraordinary gain.
White Company:	$15,000 × 40% = $ 6,000	Reduction in income taxes associated with extraordinary loss.
Blue Company:	$42,000 × 40% = $16,800	Additional income taxes associated with prior-period adjustment.

This computation becomes more complicated when different levels of income are taxed at different rates, as we see in the following example.

Green Company determines its income to be $20,000 before an extraordinary gain of $16,000 and before income taxes. Appropriate income tax rates are 25% on the first $25,000 of income and 45% on all income in excess of $25,000. The determination of the income tax expense, the income tax associated with the extraordinary gain, and the related income statement presentation at December 31, 1984, are presented in Exhibit 18–2. The direct computation of the income tax associated with the extraordinary gain is more complex in this case, because all income is not taxed at the same rate. We determine the

---

EXHIBIT 18–2
Example of Intraperiod Income Tax Allocation:
Differential Income Tax Rates

Green Company

Total income tax expense

$25,000 × 25%	$6,250	
11,000 × 45%	4,950	$11,200
$36,000		

Income tax expense associated with income before extraordinary item

$20,000 × 25%	5,000

Additional income tax expense associated with extraordinary gain	$ 6,200

Green Company
PARTIAL INCOME STATEMENT
For the Year Ended December 31, 1984

Income before income taxes and extraordinary item	$20,000
Income tax expense	5,000
Income before extraordinary gain	15,000
Extraordinary gain, net of $6,200 income tax expense	9,800
Net income	$24,800

---

income tax effect of the extraordinary item by applying the **marginal tax rate(s).** This simply means that the extraordinary gain is considered to come *after* the income before extraordinary items and, therefore, is subject to the marginal or highest income tax rates applicable. For Green Company the income tax effect of the extraordinary gain is computed by applying the marginal income tax rates as follows:

Taxable at 45%

$36,000 − $25,000 = $11,000	
$11,000 × 45% =	$4,950

Taxable at 25%

$16,000 − $11,000 = $ 5,000	
$5,000 × 25% =	1,250
Income tax applicable to	
special item	$6,200

As we stated earlier and as you can see in the preceding examples, intraperiod income tax allocation deals with the presentation of income tax expense in the financial statements, not the measurement of the total amount of that expense. If distinctively different types of income items (e.g., normal operations, extraordinary items, and prior period adjustments) are presented in the financial statements, the total income tax expense must also be separated into parts for presentation in the financial statements.

Two additional problems may arise in conjunction with intraperiod income tax allocation. First, an item that is given special placement in the financial statements may be subject to income tax at a special rate, such as the capital-gains rate.[4] In the previous cases of Red,

---

[4]The capital-gains rate is applied to certain types of investment transactions. For example, a gain on the sale of investments by a corporation qualifying for long-term capital gains treatment is currently taxed at 28%.

White, and Blue Companies, the extraordinary items and prior period adjustment were taxed at the same rates as other income items. If special items are taxed at different rates, however, the income tax applicable to those items should be based on those special rates. This is exactly the amount of income tax that will result by computing the income tax with and without the item and allocating the difference to the special item.

The second problem involves the existence of more than one special item in the same accounting period. For example, a company might have both an extraordinary item and a prior period adjustment. In this situation the income tax effect of the two or more special items is determined as a single amount by computing the amount of income tax without *any* of the special items and comparing it with the amount of income tax including *all* of the special items. The difference between these two amounts, representing the tax effect of all special items in the aggregate, is then allocated among the individual items. This allocation is based on the ratio of the amount of each special item to the total of all special items.

INTERPERIOD INCOME TAX ALLOCATION

The accrual of most expenses and the related liabilities at the end of an accounting period typically involves a single determination of an amount that is debited to the appropriate expense and credited to the appropriate liability. The recognition of the expense in this manner is part of the process of matching revenues and expenses. The liability side of the entry is included to fairly state the enterprise's liabilities at the end of the accounting period.

Matching

In a simple situation, this description fits the accrual of income tax in the same way as wages, interest, and other expenses and liabilities. For example, we will assume that Howard Company has revenues of $1,500,000 for 1985, has expenses of $965,000, and is subject to a 46% income tax rate. The year-end accrual of income tax might appear as follows if we assume no income tax was paid during the year:

Income Tax Expense	246,100	
Income Tax Payable		246,100
[($1,500,000 − $965,000) × 46% = $246,100]		

This entry incorporates the assumption that the same revenues and expenses recognized in the determination of income for financial-statement purposes (resulting in the debit to income tax expense) are also used to determine the amount of income tax currently payable (resulting in the credit in the entry to income tax payable). If this assumption is not true because some revenues and expenses included in the determination of the expense and the liability are different, we encounter the need for **interperiod income tax allocation.** For example, if a company used one depreciation method for financial reporting and another depreciation method or the Accelerated Cost Recovery System for purposes of determining its income tax liability, the income for financial reporting and the income for determining the taxes to be paid would be different. Situations like this result in the need to allocate income taxes among accounting periods. The recognition of income tax in the financial statements may come either before or after the actual payment of those taxes to appropriate governmental agencies.

For most expense accruals, generally accepted accounting principles govern both the expense and the liability recognized, so the amounts debited and credited are the same. The accrual of income tax is different, however, because the debit to the expense is based on income determined in accordance with generally accepted accounting principles while the credit to the liability is determined by the specific provisions of the Internal Revenue Code applicable to the reporting entity. When two different sets of procedures are used, we should not be surprised if the resulting amounts are different. You can see that we are actually dealing with two types of income (one for financial reporting and one for income tax payment). As a result, we are also dealing with two different income tax amounts (the amount for presentation in the financial statements and the one for income tax payment). To distinguish between these two types of income and income tax, we use the terminology presented in Exhibit 18–3 throughout the remainder of this chapter.

While **interperiod** income tax allocation deals with the allocation of income tax expense among accounting periods, **intraperiod** income tax allocation deals with the allocation of income taxes among the components of income and retained earnings within the same accounting period. Interperiod and intraperiod income tax allocation procedures resolve different problems of financial reporting and, therefore, are not alternatives. Both are required under current generally accepted accounting principles.

The allocation of income tax expense among accounting periods under generally accepted accounting principles is best described as "comprehensive interperiod allocation under the deferred method." The following sections illustrate the process of interperiod income tax allocation under the deferred method and demonstrate its impact on the financial statements.

Permanent and Timing Differences

Differences between pretax-accounting income and taxable income are caused by two phenomena: **permanent differences** and **timing differences.** These are defined as follows:

Permanent differences.   Differences between the statutory definitions of revenues and expenses (for income tax reporting) and definitions of revenues and expenses under current generally accepted accounting principles (for financial-statement reporting). These differences in definitions mean that certain revenues and expenses will affect either pretax-accounting income or taxable income in some accounting period but will *never* affect the other.

Timing differences.   Differences between the methods of reporting revenues and expenses in determining pretax-accounting income and taxable income. These differences in methods mean that certain revenues and expenses will affect pretax-accounting income and taxable income in different accounting periods, even though the total amounts of revenues and expenses recognized are expected to be the same.

Permanent differences may be classified into two categories, as follows:

EXHIBIT 18–3
Income Tax Terminology

For Financial Reporting		For Income Tax Reporting
Pretax-accounting income	**Income**	Taxable income
	×	
	Income Tax Rate	
	=	
Income tax expense	**Related Income Tax**	Income taxes paid or payable

1. Revenues and expenses that affect pretax-accounting income but *never* affect taxable income, such as:

    Interest received by the enterprise on municipal and state securities.

    Premiums paid by the enterprise on life insurance policies on enterprise executives.

    Amortization of goodwill.

2. Revenues and expenses that affect taxable income but *never* affect pretax-accounting income, such as:

    Statutory depletion in excess of the cost of assets subject to depletion.

Since permanent differences relate to the *definitions* of revenues and expenses rather than the *timing* of revenue and expense recognition, pretax-accounting income must be adjusted for permanent differences to determine the amount of pretax-accounting income subject to income tax. This adjustment is made: (1) by adding and/or subtracting revenue and expense items included in pretax-accounting income (for a particular period) that will *never* affect taxable income, and (2) by adding and/or subtracting revenue and expense items included in taxable income (for the same period) that will *never* affect pretax-accounting income. This adjustment process is summarized as follows:

Pretax accounting income	$XXX
± Permanent differences	± XXX
Pretax-accounting income subject to income taxes	$XXX

Pretax-accounting income subject to income taxes is the basis for computing income tax expense. In the absence of any timing differences, it is also the basis for computing income tax payable.

To illustrate, assume that Permo Company reports pretax-accounting income of $120,000. This amount includes $11,500 interest that was earned on municipal securities and is therefore not subject to income taxes. The appropriate income tax rate is 40%. No other differences between pretax-accounting income and taxable income exist. Both income tax expense and income tax payable are based on the pretax-accounting income subject to income taxes and are determined as follows:

Pretax accounting income	$120,000
Less permanent difference: Interest on municipal securities	(11,500)
Pretax-accounting income subject to income tax	$108,500
Income tax expense and income tax liability:	
$108,500 × 40% =	$ 43,400

The following entry is made to reflect the accrual of income taxes at the end of the accounting period:

Income Tax Expense	43,400	
Income Tax Payable		43,400

Matching

Timing differences exist because revenues and expenses may be recognized in different accounting periods for purposes of pretax-accounting income and taxable income. The matching principle requires income tax expense to be based on the revenues and expenses in the pretax-accounting income that are subject to income tax, even if some of these revenues and expenses affect taxable income in a different accounting period.

Timing differences may be classified in four categories, as follows:[5]

1. Revenues (and gains) recognized in pretax-accounting income earlier than in taxable income, such as:

    Profits on installment sales recognized at the time of sale for accounting purposes but delayed until the time of collection for income tax purposes.

2. Expenses (and losses) recognized in pretax-accounting income earlier than in taxable income, such as:

    Estimated costs of guarantees and product warranties in the period of sale for accounting purposes but deferred until actually paid for income tax purposes.

3. Revenues included in taxable income earlier than in pretax-accounting income, such as:

    Rents and royalties that are included in taxable income when received but delayed until they are earned for accounting purposes.

4. Expenses included in taxable income earlier than in pretax-accounting income, such as:

    Rapid write-off of the cost of plant assets (by accelerated depreciation or the Accelerated Cost Recovery System) for income tax purposes and straight-line depreciation for accounting purposes, resulting in a greater write-off in the early years of the asset's life for taxable income than for accounting income.

Comprehensive interperiod income tax allocation requires that the income tax *expense* for an accounting period include the income tax effects of *all* revenues and expenses in the pretax-accounting income that will ultimately be subject to income taxes, even if some or all of the income tax is paid in a different accounting period. The income tax payable will still be based on those revenues and expenses recognized in taxable income, even if they differ from those included in pretax-accounting income. This relationship may be summarized as follows:

Pretax-accounting income subject	
to income tax	$XXX
± Timing differences	± XXX
Taxable income	$XXX

Any difference between the income tax expense (based on pretax-accounting income subject to income tax) and the income tax liability (based on taxable income) is due to timing differences. Timing differences are *temporary* differences between pretax-accounting income subject to income tax and taxable income, because the total revenue or expense to be recognized is expected to be the same eventually. The initial appearance of a timing difference is called the **origin** of the timing difference. The offsetting of that difference in some future accounting period(s) is called the **reversal** of the timing difference.

Between the origin of timing differences and their subsequent reversal, the income tax effects of these differences are included in deferred income tax accounts, which are established to account for the differences between income tax expense and income tax payable. As timing differences originate, deferred income taxes increase; as timing differences reverse, deferred income taxes decrease.

The recognition of timing differences in determining income tax expense and income tax payable is complicated by the fact that income tax rates may change from year to year. This means that the income tax rate in effect when a timing difference originates may be different from the rate in effect when the same timing difference reverses in some future period(s). Under the **deferred method,** the original income tax effects of timing differences are accounted for on the basis of the income tax rate in effect when the timing

---

[5]A more comprehensive list of timing differences is provided in Appendix A of Chapter 18.

differences originate. No consideration is given to expected future changes in income tax rates, and no adjustment is made when income tax rates change, even if the timing difference has not been reversed.

To illustrate the deferred method, assume that Timo Company acquired machinery for $150,000 in January 1980. The machinery was expected to have a five-year life and no salvage value. Timo uses straight-line depreciation for accounting purposes and sum-of-the-years'-digits depreciation for income tax purposes. No other timing differences exist. Timo's income tax rate is 46% throughout the asset's life. Assume further that Timo's income before income taxes and depreciation figures for 1980 through 1984 are as follows:

1980	$ 88,000
1981	97,000
1982	104,000
1983	92,000
1984	107,000

There are no permanent differences between pretax-accounting income and taxable income.

Straight-line depreciation, used in determining pretax-accounting income, is the same for each year and is computed by dividing the cost of the machinery by the estimated life: $150,000/5 = $30,000 per year. Sum-of-the-years'-digits depreciation, used in determining taxable income, is computed by applying the descending fractions of $5/15$, $4/15$, $3/15$, $2/15$, and $1/15$ to the $150,000 cost for years 1980–1984, respectively. A comparison of the depreciation figures is as follows:

	1980	*1981*	*1982*	*1983*	*1984*
Straight-line (SL)	$ 30,000	$ 30,000	$30,000	$30,000	$30,000
Sum-of-the-years'-digits (SYD)	50,000	40,000	30,000	20,000	10,000
(Excess) Deficiency of SYD to SL Depreciation	$(20,000)	$(10,000)	–0–	$10,000	$20,000

The determination of Timo's pretax-accounting income and taxable income are presented in Exhibit 18–4.

What is the nature of the deferred income tax account and where should it appear in the financial statements prepared at the end of each year? In the Timo case, which is typical of many actual business situations, the deferred income tax account is similar to a liability, because the declining depreciation deduction for income tax purposes under the sum-of-the-years'-digits method results in a greater income tax liability in future years (i.e., in 1983 and 1984, when the deferred income tax account is reduced as the amounts currently payable increase). More specifically, Timo's deferred income tax account should be presented in the balance sheet among the noncurrent liabilities, because the underlying asset (property, plant, and equipment) is noncurrent. A later section of this chapter discusses this classification in greater depth.

Based on the Timo example, several observations concerning **comprehensive interperiod income tax allocation** under the deferred method may be made:

1. The difference between pretax-accounting income subject to income tax and taxable income is caused by the *timing difference* resulting from the use of sum-of-the-years'-digits depreciation for tax purposes and straight-line depreciation for accounting purposes.
2. The balance in the deferred income tax account increases as timing differences originate (1980 and 1981) and decreases as timing differences reverse (1983 and 1984).

EXHIBIT 18–4
Timo Company
Example of Interperiod Income Tax Allocation

	1980	1981	1982	1983	1984
Income before depreciation and income tax expense	$ 88,000	$ 97,000	$104,000	$ 92,000	$107,000
Depreciation expense	(30,000)	(30,000)	(30,000)	(30,000)	(30,000)
Pretax-accounting income subject to income tax	58,000	67,000	74,000	62,000	77,000
Timing difference: (Excess) deficiency of SYD depreciation to straight-line depreciation	(20,000)	(10,000)	–0–	10,000	20,000
Taxable income	$ 38,000	$ 57,000	$ 74,000	$ 72,000	$ 97,000
Income tax expense					
46% × $58,000	$ 26,680				
46% × $67,000		$ 30,820			
46% × $74,000			$ 34,040		
46% × $62,000				$ 28,520	
46% × $77,000					$ 35,420
Income tax payable					
46% × $38,000	17,480				
46% × $57,000		26,220			
46% × $74,000			34,040		
46% × $72,000				33,120	
46% × $97,000					44,620
Increase (decrease) in deferred taxes	$ 9,200	$ 4,600	–0–	$ (4,600)	$ (9,200)

Journal Entries to Record Tax Accruals

1980	Income Tax Expense	26,680	
	Income Tax Payable		17,480
	Deferred Income Tax		9,200
1981	Income Tax Expense	30,820	
	Income Tax Payable		26,220
	Deferred Income Tax		4,600
1982	Income Tax Expense	34,040	
	Income Tax Payable		34,040
1983	Income Tax Expense	28,520	
	Deferred Income Tax	4,600	
	Income Tax Payable		33,120
1984	Income Tax Expense	35,420	
	Deferred Income Tax	9,200	
	Income Tax Payable		44,620

3. In a year when pretax-accounting income subject to income and taxable income are the same (1982), no change takes place in deferred income taxes.
4. The deferred income taxes are based on the 46% rate in effect at the origin of the timing differences. For example, the $9,200 credit to deferred income taxes in 1980 may be computed by multiplying the timing difference by the appropriate income tax rate ($20,000 × 46% = $9,200).

Throughout the five-year period covered by the Timo example, a 46% income tax rate was in effect. If the rate had changed while the timing difference was originating, the rate in effect when each timing difference originated would be used. For example, if the 46% income tax rate was in effect in 1980 but the rate increased to 48% in 1981, income taxes on the originating difference in 1980 would be based on 46% and those originating in 1981 would be recognized at 48%. Within the deferred method, in establishing the deferred income tax account, no consideration is given to the income tax rate(s) expected to be in effect in 1983 and 1984 when the timing differences are expected to reverse.

The significance of interperiod income tax allocation on the income statement presentation can be seen by comparing income with and without the application of interperiod income tax allocation procedures. In Exhibit 18–5 the income tax expense in the first column ("With Interperiod Income Tax Allocation") is determined by comprehensive income tax allocation procedures under the deferred method (current generally accepted accounting principles). The income tax expense in the second column ("Without Interperiod Income Tax Allocation") is simply the income tax liability for each year (not currently accepted).

Matching

The first column includes income tax expense that relates to the "income before income tax" that is included in the same income statement. The matching principle is applied and the statement is internally consistent because the income tax expense is based on the same revenues and expenses included in the income statement. The second column simply includes income tax expense equal to the liability for that period. The latter presentation fails to recognize the difference in depreciation methods used for accounting and income tax purposes; therefore, the income tax expense recognized each year does *not* relate to the income-before-income-tax figure, because the two amounts are based on different accounting methods.

EXHIBIT 18–5
Timo Company
Comparison of Income With and Without
Interperiod Income Tax Allocation

	With Interperiod Income Tax Allocation	Without Interperiod Income Tax Allocation
1980		
Income before income tax	$58,000	$58,000
Income tax expense	26,680	17,480
Net income	$31,320	$40,520
1981		
Income before income tax	$67,000	$67,000
Income tax expense	30,820	26,220
Net income	$36,180	$40,780
1982		
Income before income tax	$74,000	$74,000
Income tax expense	34,040	34,040
Net income	$39,960	$39,960
1983		
Income before income tax	$62,000	$62,000
Income tax expense	28,520	33,120
Net income	$33,480	$28,880
1984		
Income before income tax	$77,000	$77,000
Income tax expense	35,420	44,620
Net income	$41,580	$32,380

Interaction of Permanent and Timing Differences

A company may have several permanent and timing differences affecting both the pretax-accounting income subject to income taxes and the taxable income in the same accounting period. The concepts of permanent and timing differences and the related determinations of income tax expense and income tax payable that were developed earlier provide the basis for understanding comprehensive income tax allocation under the deferred method when several permanent and timing differences exist. The relationship of these concepts is summarized as follows:

Pretax-accounting income	$XXX
± Permanent differences	XXX
Pretax-accounting income	
subject to income taxes	XXX
± Timing differences	XXX
Taxable income	$XXX

To illustrate, assume the Johnson Company reports revenues and expenses for financial reporting purposes for 1983 as follows:

Revenues	$ 552,000
Expenses	(365,000)
Pretax-accounting income	$ 187,000

These amounts involve the following permanent and timing differences:

Revenues
Include $32,500 of installment sales not recognized for income
  tax purposes until future periods.
Include $8,100 of interest on municipal securities.
Exclude $10,800 of rents collected in advance and recognized for
  income tax purposes in 1983.

Expenses
Include $10,500 amortization of goodwill.
Include depreciation of $85,000 on the straight-line method.
  (For income tax purposes, double-declining balance depreciation is
  used; the amount for 1983 was $142,500.)
Include estimated warranty costs of $24,000 based on sales recognized
  in 1983. (Actual warranty expenditures made in 1983 and deductible for
  income tax purposes were $18,500.)

Income tax expense is determined by adjusting pretax-accounting income for permanent differences, resulting in pretax-accounting income subject to income tax. The current income tax rate is then applied to this figure to determine income tax expense. Income tax payable is determined by adjusting the pretax income subject to income tax for timing differences, resulting in taxable income, and then applying the current income tax rate.

Pretax-accounting income		$187,000
Permanent differences		
Amortization of goodwill	$ 10,500	
Interest on municipal securities	(8,100)	2,400

Pretax-accounting income subject to income tax		189,400
Timing differences		
Installment sales	(32,500)	
Rents collected in advance	10,800	
Accelerated depreciation		
($142,500 − $85,000)	(57,500)	
Warranty costs ($24,000 − $18,500)	5,500	(73,700)
Taxable income		$115,700

Permanent differences include the amortization of goodwill and interest on municipal securities. Both of these items are included in the determination of pretax-accounting income but will *never* affect taxable income. Accordingly, these items are *excluded* from the determination of *both* pretax-accounting income subject to income taxes and taxable income. Appropriate adjustments are made by adding back the amortization of goodwill (an expense *never* deductible for tax purposes) and deducting the interest on municipal securities (a revenue *never* subject to income tax).

Timing differences include methods such as recognizing installment sales, collection of rent, depreciation, and warranty expense. All these include a difference in the *timing* of recognition rather than the total amount to be recognized. Pretax-accounting income subject to income tax must be further adjusted for these timing differences to determine taxable income, the basis for determining income tax payable. Income must be reduced by the $32,500 for installment sales that are not subject to income tax in 1983. Income must be increased by the $10,800 for rent that is subject to income tax in 1983 but that was not included in pretax-accounting income. Income must be reduced by $57,500, the additional depreciation recognized for tax purposes under accelerated depreciation. Finally, income must be increased by $5,500, the excess of estimated warranty costs over the warranty expenditures that were actually paid in 1983 and that were deductible in determining the income tax payable.

The entry for the income tax accrual at the end of 1983, if we assume a 46% rate, is as follows:

Income Tax Expense ($189,400 × 46%)	87,124	
Income Tax Payable ($115,700 × 46%)		53,222
Deferred Income Tax		33,902

Because the Deferred Income Tax account is established (or increased) by using the income tax rate that is in effect when timing differences originate, we could have determined the credit to Johnson's deferred income tax account by multiplying the net amount of timing differences ($189,400 − $115,700, or $73,700) by the current income tax rate:

Timing differences		Income tax rate		Deferred income taxes
$73,700	×	46%	=	$33,902

In the previous examples, the stated income tax rate for the period of origin was used to compute the income tax effect of timing differences. If the inclusion or exclusion of a timing difference causes the company's income to shift from one income tax bracket to another, the income tax effect of the timing differences is determined by computing income taxes with and without the item and attributing the difference to the timing differences.[6] This procedure is applied in a manner similar to the with-and-without method presented earlier in determining the income tax effect of a special item for purposes of applying intraperiod income tax procedures.

Reversal of Timing Differences

Timing differences are temporary and are expected to reverse at some future time. Those timing differences that originate in one accounting period are expected to be offset by a reversal in later accounting periods. Once interperiod income tax allocation procedures have been applied for several accounting periods, it is likely that in any particular accounting period new timing differences will be originating, while timing differences that arose in past periods will be reversing.

To illustrate, assume Garden Company acquired machines for $10,000 and $12,000 in 1979 and 1980, respectively. Each machine had an expected useful life of four years and a $1,000 salvage value. Straight-line depreciation is used for financial reporting purposes, and double-declining balance depreciation is used for income tax purposes.

A summary depreciation schedule for the two assets is presented in Exhibit 18–6.

For each asset, timing differences originate in the first two years and reverse in the last two years. In 1980, for example, originating differences exist for both machines. In 1981, however, the timing differences of 1979 and 1980 on Machine 1 begin to reverse while an

---

[6]For example, assume that pretax-accounting income for 1984 is $28,000 but taxable income is only $22,000 because of a timing difference that results in the deferral of revenue for income tax purposes. Income tax rates are as follows: 25% of the first $25,000 and 46% of all taxable income over $25,000. The income tax effect of the timing difference in 1984 is as follows:

Income tax on pretax-accounting income ($28,000):
$25,000 × 25% $6,250
$ 3,000 × 46%   1,380 $ 7,630
Income tax on taxable income ($22,000):
$22,000 × 25%   (5,500)
Income tax effect of timing
difference $ 2,130

EXHIBIT 18–6
Garden Company
Originating and Reversing Timing Differences

	Depreciation				
	1979	*1980*	*1981*	*1982*	*1983*
Machine 1 ($10,000)					
Double-declining balance	$5,000	$2,500	$ 1,250	$ 250	—
Straight-line	2,250	2,250	2,250	2,250	—
Difference	$2,750	$ 250	$(1,000)	$(2,000)	—
Nature of difference	Originating	Originating	Reversal	Reversal	—
Machine 2 ($12,000)					
Double-declining balance	—	$6,000	$3,000	$ 1,500	$ 500
Straight-line	—	2,750	2,750	2,750	2,750
Difference	—	$3,250	$ 250	$(1,250)	$(2,250)
Nature of difference	—	Originating	Originating	Reversal	Reversal

additional timing difference originates for Machine 2. A policy of investing in new machinery as old machinery is retired will result in the continuous origination and reversal of timing differences, much like that occurring in 1981 for Garden Company. In this example the timing difference caused by different depreciation methods has been used because it is a frequently encountered timing difference. The same conclusions can be reached, however, concerning other timing differences, such as differences in accounting for marketable securities, revenues received in advance, and warranty costs.

If several timing differences exist, it may be impractical to account for each timing difference and its reversal on an individual basis; in such cases two methods are used to account for the reversal of timing differences: **the net-change method** and the **gross-change method.** The difference between the net-change and gross-change methods is in the treatment of the *reversal* of timing differences rather than the origin of timing differences. Under the net-change method, the reversal of timing differences is treated as a reduction in deferred taxes at the income tax rate in effect when the reversal takes place. Under the gross-change method, however, deferred taxes are reduced by amounts based on income tax rates in effect when the timing differences originated. If income tax rates change between the origination of timing differences and their subsequent reversal, the two methods result in different income tax expense and deferred income tax amounts. If income tax rates remain the same, the two methods result in identical amounts. Either method is acceptable, but the method selected should be applied consistently from period to period.

Consistency

To illustrate these two methods, assume Pickens Company has been using double-declining balance depreciation for income tax purposes and straight-line depreciation for financial reporting purposes for several years. This timing difference has resulted in a deferred tax credit of $62,500 at the beginning of 1984, all of which was accumulated when the income tax rate was 40%. Assume that for 1984, the company reports $165,000 of income before depreciation and income tax, that the income tax rate increases to 46%, and that the following differences between depreciation under the double-declining balance and straight-line methods exist:

	Double-Declining Balance	Straight-Line	Difference
Depreciation for assets where DDB exceeds SL	$75,000	$35,000	$40,000
Depreciation for assets where SL exceeds DDB	18,500	25,000	(6,500)
Total depreciation	$93,500	$60,000	$33,500

Total double-declining balance depreciation is $93,500, and total straight-line depreciation is $60,000, resulting in a $33,500 timing difference. This $33,500 is made up of both originating differences (i.e., depreciation on newer assets for which double-declining balance depreciation *exceeds* straight-line depreciation) and reversing differences (i.e., depreciation on older assets for which double-declining balance depreciation *is less than* straight-line depreciation).

Under the **net-change method,** the income tax expense, the income tax liability, and the net increase in deferred taxes are all based on the current tax rate of 46%. The fact that the deferred taxes were established at a 40% rate in earlier years is not considered. Accordingly, the journal entry to accrue income taxes for 1984 is as follows:

Income Tax Expense [($165,000 − $60,000) × 46%]	48,300	
Income Tax Payable [($165,000 − $93,500) × 46%]		32,890
Deferred Income Taxes ($33,500 × 46%)		15,410

The income tax expense, $48,300, is computed by deducting straight-line depreciation of $60,000 from the $165,000 income before depreciation and taxes and applying the 46% current tax rate to the difference. The income tax payable is computed in the same manner, by using the $93,500 double-declining balance depreciation figure. The increase in deferred income taxes is determined by applying the *current income tax rate* (46%) to the timing difference of $33,500 ($93,500 − $60,000). The increase in deferred income taxes of $15,410 is actually a *net* increase resulting from the excess of originating differences over reversing differences, computed as follows:

Originating differences		
$40,000 × 46%	=	$18,400
Reversing differences		
$(6,500) × 46%	=	(2,990)
Net increase in deferred		
income taxes		$15,410

From the income statement viewpoint, the net-change method seems logical because the resulting expense is based entirely on the current income tax rate of 46%. The resulting balance sheet deferred income tax amount is difficult to explain, however, because the increase is based on the income tax rate in effect when timing differences originate and the decrease is based on the income tax rate in effect when timing differences reverse. In the case of Pickens Company, the reversal of timing differences in 1984 results in a reduction in the Deferred Income Tax account of an amount *greater than* the amount originally established for that timing differences, because the income tax rate increased from 40% to 46% between the origination and reversal of the timing differences. Under the net-change method, the Deferred Income Tax account simply becomes a clearing account through which income tax effects of timing differences are taken. After timing differences have originated and reversed over a long period, the balance in the Deferred Income Tax account becomes difficult, if not impossible, to associate with specific timing differences. The net-change method is sometimes referred to as an **income statement approach** to handling the problem of income taxes on timing differences, because the resulting income tax expense is based solely on the current tax rate.

Under the **gross-change method,** the change in deferred income taxes for Pickens would be determined by accounting for the origination of timing differences in 1984 at the current income tax rate of 46% and the reversal of the timing differences in 1984 at the 40% income tax rate that was in effect when those timing differences originated. This is done as follows:

Deferred income taxes, beginning of 1984		$62,500
Originating timing differences, 1984		
$40,000 × 46% =	$18,400	
Reversing timing differences, 1984		
$(6,500) × 40% =	(2,600)	
Net increase in deferred income taxes		15,800
Deferred income taxes, end of 1984		$78,300

The income tax expense is determined by adding the amounts of the income tax liability and the change in deferred income taxes under the gross-change method. (If the Deferred Income Tax account was debited, the liability and the reduction in deferred income tax would be **netted** to determine the income tax expense.) The entry to record the accrual of income taxes at the end of 1984 is as follows:

Income Tax Expense ($32,890 + $15,800)	48,690	
Income Tax Payable [($165,000 − $93,500) × 46%]		32,890
Deferred Income Taxes		15,800
(See computation above.)		

Under the gross-change method, the balance sheet Deferred Income Tax account is not distorted by changes in income tax rates. The gross-change method also preserves the ability to reconcile the Deferred Income Tax account(s) with specific timing differences that have not yet reversed. Since deferred income taxes are established and reversed based on the same income tax rates, the existing balances can be reconciled to specific timing differences at specific historical income tax rates. A major *disadvantage* of the gross-change method is that it results in an income tax expense figure that is not based entirely on the current income tax rate, because it is partially determined by the reversal of timing differences that are accounted for at income tax rates of past years. The gross-change method is sometimes referred to as the **balance sheet method,** because it seems to favor the balance sheet presentation of deferred income taxes at the cost of distorting the income tax expense presented in the income statement.

Both the net-change and gross-change methods are used in practice, and the method selected should be followed consistently. The methods have no impact on the amount of the current income tax liability recognized. Also, the two methods result in the same income tax expense if income tax rates do not change. If changes in income tax rates are relatively small, the differences in amounts under the two methods would ordinarily not be material. When *APB Opinion No. 11* was published, dramatic changes in income tax rates were not common. In recent years, however, some large income tax rate changes have increased the potential difference between amounts computed by the net-change method and amounts computed by the gross-change method; we can no longer assume that these differences will be immaterial. In the authors' opinions, the net-change method is preferable because it places priority on income presentation. As indicated earlier, the net-change method requires all computations affecting income tax expense to be made at the current income tax rate. We believe this procedure is consistent with other choices in the selection of accounting principles that tend to favor the presentation of income over financial position whenever a choice is necessary.

This section has emphasized the timing differences that arise from the use of accelerated depreciation for income tax purposes and straight-line depreciation for financial reporting purposes. Historically, this has been the most significant timing difference and currently is most frequently encountered in practice. Timing differences do arise, however, from other methods of revenue and expense recognition, as illustrated in the Johnson Company example, which included timing differences resulting from installment sales, rents collected in advance, depreciation, and warranty costs.

Chapter 12 indicates that a new system of asset write-off for income tax purposes—the Accelerated Cost Recovery System (ACRS)—was adopted for assets acquired in 1981 and thereafter. For purposes of interperiod income tax allocation, the ACRS may be viewed as another type of accelerated depreciation that is used for assets acquired after 1980. Assets acquired during or before 1980 continue to be depreciated by methods existing when they were acquired, and they are not switched to ACRS. The procedures illustrated in the present chapter that use the double-declining balance or another accelerated depreciation method are equally applicable when ACRS is used for income tax purposes and straight-line or another method is used for financial reporting. ACRS is reviewed briefly in Appendix B of this chapter, and the relation of ACRS to interperiod income tax allocation is discussed here.

Consis-tency

Materiality

Balance Sheet Presentation of Deferred Income Taxes

Deferred income taxes may exist as a result of numerous timing differences. If the originating timing difference results in an excess of pretax-accounting income over taxable income, the Deferred Income Tax account has a credit balance (i.e., if we assume no balance is carried forward from previous periods). If the originating difference results in an excess of taxable income over pretax-accounting income, the Deferred Income Tax account has a debit balance (if we again assume no balance is carried forward from the previous period).

Deferred income taxes are subject to current and noncurrent classification in much the same way as other assets and liabilities. The distinction between current and noncurrent deferred income taxes is usually based on the nature of the underlying transaction or event giving rise to the deferred income tax.[7] For example, a deferred income tax credit arising from the use of different depreciation methods in determining pretax-accounting income and taxable income would be classified as noncurrent, because it relates to an asset classified as noncurrent. On the other hand, a deferred income tax credit may result from recognizing income at the point of sale on the accrual basis for financial reporting but deferring that revenue for income tax purposes until cash is collected. This procedure is called the **installment sales method,** and the Deferred Income Tax account is classified as current because it relates to receivables classified as current.

Deferred income taxes should be reported in the balance sheet in one or two accounts, depending on the nature of the underlying timing differences: a **net current amount** and a **net noncurrent amount.** All current deferred income taxes are combined and presented in a net current amount. All noncurrent deferred income taxes are combined and presented in a net noncurrent amount. If only current or only noncurrent timing differences exist, then only one deferred income tax item would be presented. Net current deferred income taxes should be presented as either a current asset (debit balance) or a current liability (credit balance). Net noncurrent deferred income taxes with a debit balance should be presented in an "other asset" category. Net noncurrent deferred income taxes with a credit balance should be presented in the long-term liability section of the balance sheet. Alternatively, the noncurrent deferred income tax credit is sometimes presented in a separate deferred credit section placed between liabilities and stockholders' equity.

To illustrate the current/noncurrent classification of deferred income taxes, assume that Numero Uno Company has total deferred income taxes of $117,830 as of the end of 1985. This amount results from four different timing differences:

Timing Difference	Deferred Income Taxes Debit (Credit)
1. Installment sales	$ (72,500)
2. Rents collected in advance	12,600
3. Depreciation	(102,750)
4. Warranty costs	44,820
	$(117,830)

---

[7]In certain situations that are beyond the scope of this text, a timing difference may not be related to recorded assets and liabilities. In these cases the classification related deferred income taxes as current or noncurrent should be based on the expected timing of the reversal of the timing difference in accordance with *Statement of Financial Accounting Standards No. 37,* "Balance Sheet Classification of Deferred Income Taxes," 1980.

EXHIBIT 18–7
Whirlpool Corporation
Example Balance Sheet Presentation of
Deferred Income Taxes

Consolidated Balance Sheet

Assets	December 31	1982	1981
	thousands of dollars		
Current Assets	Cash	$ 23,312	$ 2,533
	Short-term investments	346,236	274,797
	Receivables, less allowances for doubtful accounts (1982—$1,480,000; 1981—$970,000)	166,285	156,169
	Inventories—Note C	228,270	256,546
	Prepaid expenses	7,666	5,743
	Deferred income taxes	12,951	12,708
	Total Current Assets	784,720	708,496
Investments and Other Assets	Appliance Buyers Credit Corporation—Note D .	67,935	60,908
	Affiliated foreign companies—Note E	97,378	78,568
	Other assets	7,707	7,879
		173,020	147,355
Property, Plant and Equipment	Land	8,916	9,162
	Buildings	184,110	182,704
	Machinery, equipment and tools	307,362	275,507
		500,388	467,373
	Less allowances for depreciation and amortization	196,486	189,252
		303,902	278,121
		$1,261,642	$1,133,972
Liabilities and Stockholders' Equity			
Current Liabilities	Accounts payable	$ 108,975	$ 74,824
	Payrolls and other compensation	64,665	64,627
	Taxes and other accrued expenses............	49,043	53,829
	Income taxes	50,924	36,601
	Product warranty	17,381	17,790
	Total Current Liabilities	290,988	247,671
Other Liabilities	Long-term debt—Note G	60,848	60,848
	Product warranty	16,403	17,309
	Deferred income taxes	18,329	16,315
		95,580	94,472
Stockholders' Equity	Capital stock—Notes H and I	36,430	36,265
	Additional paid-in capital	27,489	23,484
	Retained earnings—Notes G and H	811,155	732,080
		875,074	791,829
		$1,261,642	$1,133,972

SOURCE: Whirlpool Corporation, 1982 Annual Report.

The installment sales method is used for income tax purposes but not for financial reporting purposes. Income is deferred until collected for income tax purposes and the related receivables are classified as current. Rents collected in advance are taxed when collected but deferred for financial reporting purposes. The rents will be earned in the next year. Deferred income taxes related to depreciation result from the use of accelerated depreciation for income tax purposes and straight-line depreciation for financial reporting. Estimates of warranty costs are based on actual sales for financial reporting but are included in taxable income only when warranty claims are paid (within one year of the time of the sale).

Deferred income taxes of Numero Uno Company are presented in net current and net noncurrent amounts, determined as follows:

| | Deferred Income Taxes Debit (Credit) | |
Timing Difference	*Current*	*Noncurrent*
1. Installment sales	$(72,500)	
2. Rents collected in advance	12,600	
3. Depreciation		$(102,750)
4. Warranty costs	44,820	
	$(15,080)	$(102,750)

The $15,080 net current deferred credit is presented as a current liability in the balance sheet because it represents the net income tax effect of all timing differences classified as current. The $102,750 net noncurrent deferred credit is presented as a noncurrent liability or in a separate deferred credit category because it represents the income tax effect of the only timing difference considered noncurrent.

To further illustrate the balance sheet presentation of deferred income taxes, we present the comparative balance sheets for 1982 and 1981 of Whirlpool Corporation in Exhibit 18–7. Whirlpool Corporation and its consolidated subsidiaries manufacture home appliances (including automatic washers and dryers, refrigerators, dishwashers, ranges, microwave ovens, and trash compactors) and other products (including central heating and air conditioning systems). "Deferred income taxes" of $12,951,000, listed among the current assets, represents the *net current amount* of deferred (prepaid) income taxes. "Deferred income taxes" of $18,329,000, listed among the other liabilities, represents the *net noncurrent amount* of deferred (payable) income taxes.

The issue of whether or not deferred income taxes should be discounted and reported in the balance sheet at their present value has been raised. Current authoritative pronouncements indicate that deferred income taxes should *not* be discounted, because the amounts are based on historical income tax rates and the pattern of the reversal of timing differences is uncertain.[8]

Are deferred income taxes significant items in corporations' balance sheets? The answer to this question varies from company to company, but overall the response must be positive. Exhibit 18–8 includes the noncurrent deferred income tax credits for selected companies for 1982 in terms of dollars and as a percentage of total assets or equity (liabilities plus stockholders' equity) of the companies.

The dollar amount and relative size of the noncurrent Deferred Income Tax accounts vary, but Exhibit 18–8 indicates that they may be significant balance sheet items. Of these companies, only American Telephone and Telegraph presented a separate item for current

---

[8]*APB Opinion No. 10*, "Omnibus Opinion—1966," 1966, par. 6.

EXHIBIT 18-8
Deferred Income Taxes of Selected Companies for 1982

Company	Noncurrent Deferred Income Tax Credits	
	In Thousands of Dollars	As a % of Total Assets or Equity
American Telephone and Telegraph	17,804,400	12.0
Gulf Oil Corporation	2,258,000	11.0
Consolidated Papers, Inc.	41,397	9.1
The Quaker Oats Company	116,700	7.9
Kellogg Company	82,300	6.3
US Air	56,130	5.3
Abbott Laboratories	107,548	4.2
Inland Steel Company	98,753	3.8
J. P. Stevens & Co.	37,431	3.5
CBS	77,253	2.9
Roadway Services, Inc.	10,435	1.5
Zale Corporation	4,012	.5
A. C. Nielson Company	1,009	.2

deferred income taxes—a credit balance of $263,700,000, or less than 1% of total assets or equity. The large noncurrent deferred tax credit balances are due primarily to the timing differences created by the use of accelerated depreciation or the Accelerated Cost Recovery System for income tax purposes and straight-line depreciation for financial reporting purposes.

Alternative Methods of Accounting for Income Tax

As already mentioned, generally accepted accounting principles require that the income tax expense of the period include the tax effects of *all* timing differences included in pretax-accounting income, even if the impact of these items on taxable income is expected in different accounting periods. Also, Deferred Income Tax accounts necessary to report deferred income taxes are established on the basis of those income tax rates in effect when timing differences originate, and no consideration is given to expected (or actual) changes in the income tax rates after recording the origination of the timing differences. These procedures are described as **comprehensive interperiod income tax allocation** under the **deferred method.** Although these are well established procedures in accounting practice, several proposed alternatives are discussed briefly in the following paragraphs.

One alternative to comprehensive allocation is **partial allocation,** although it is not generally accepted. Partial allocation assumes that for a particular period income tax expense should be the same as income tax payable except for the impact of nonrecurring timing differences. Proponents of partial allocation reason that recurring differences between pretax-accounting income and taxable income, such as those resulting from depreciation, give rise to the *indefinite* postponement of income taxes, and thus the recognition of the tax effects of timing differences in income-tax expense should *not* be required. For example, a company may engage in a continuous investment policy in plant assets, coupled with the use of accelerated depreciation (or ACRS) for income tax purposes, and straight-line depreciation for financial reporting purposes. The reversal of timing differences (when accelerated depreciation falls below straight-line depreciation on older assets) is offset by the origination of timing differences (when accelerated depreciation exceeds straight-line depreciation on newer assets). As a result taxes on timing differences are continuously deferred and effectively never paid in the foreseeable future. Thus, this timing difference takes on many of the characteristics of a permanent difference.

Proponents of partial allocation believe that only **nonrecurring** timing differences between pretax-accounting income and taxable income should give rise to deferred income taxes. Since the reversal of a nonrecurring timing difference is not expected to be offset by the origination of another timing difference (due to the nonrecurring nature of the revenue or expense), income tax expense may be materially misstated if the impact of the timing difference is ignored. Thus, under partial allocation the income tax expense of the period should be increased or decreased by income taxes on nonrecurring timing differences that can reasonably be expected to affect taxable income in the foreseeable future. A five-year period has been suggested as an appropriate time frame for the application of this concept.[9]

Another alternative may be identified as **nonallocation** of income tax. Within this relatively simple method, the income tax paid during the period and that payable at the end of the period constitute the income tax expense, regardless of differences in methods of recognizing revenues and expenses in the financial statements as compared with the tax return. In other words, the income tax amount determined by legal compliance with income tax laws would become the income tax expense figure. Since the concept of interperiod income tax allocation is based on the matching principle, questions can be raised concerning the appropriateness of this approach. On the other hand, historically the methods of determining income for financial reporting and income tax purposes were quite similar. Some feel that the two have gradually drifted so far apart that attempting to link them together via interperiod income tax allocation is no longer appropriate.

Matching

The deferred method emphasizes the tax effects of timing differences on income tax expense, measured in terms of income tax rates in effect when timing differences originate. One alternative that has been proposed is the **liability method,** which accrues currently the income taxes actually expected to be paid as a result of timing differences. If income taxes in the future were expected to be paid at rates different from the current rate, the amounts expected to be paid would be accrued. The components of income tax expense for a period might be computed at different income tax rates, depending on estimates of future income tax rates and the expected pattern of reversal of those timing differences originating in the period. Additionally, under the liability method the initial recognition of income taxes is considered to be tentative, and subject to adjustment as income tax rates change, new taxes are imposed, or the pattern of reversal of timing differences changes significantly.

Another alternative to current practice is the **net-of-tax method.** Under this method the tax effects of timing differences are recognized in the valuation of assets and liabilities and the related revenues and expenses that were factors in the difference between pretax-accounting income and taxable income. Also under this method the income tax effects of timing differences are reflected in the balance sheet as adjustments to the valuation of assets and liabilities that give rise to the timing differences rather than presented as separate assets and liabilities.

Although partial income tax allocation and nonallocation (alternatives to comprehensive allocation) and liability and net-of-tax methods (alternatives to the deferred method) are *not* generally accepted at present, they represent alternatives with some conceptual or practical appeal in attempting to incorporate in financial statements the differences between income tax reporting and financial reporting. Therefore, they may someday be considered for use.

Evaluation of Interperiod Income Tax Allocation

Interperiod income tax allocation has been a controversial subject in the accounting profession for many years. Procedures similar to those followed today were initiated several decades ago when relatively simple timing differences (related primarily to alternative

---

[9]*APB Opinion No. 11,* par. 27.

depreciation methods) emerged.[10] As the concept expanded and was applied to a wide variety of differences between pretax-accounting income and taxable income, numerous questions arose. We have seen several authoritative pronouncements commenting on specific aspects of interperiod income tax allocation since the basic concept was initially developed.

The APB favored comprehensive income tax allocation and based that decision on several general concepts and assumptions relative to the nature of income taxes and their relationship to the determination of income. These concepts and assumptions are summarized as follows:[11]

Going Concern

1. The operations of an entity subject to income taxes are expected to continue on a going-concern basis, in the absence of evidence to the contrary. Accordingly, income taxes are expected to continue to be assessed in the future.

2. Income taxes are an expense of business enterprises earning income subject to income taxes.

Periodicity

3. Accounting for income tax expense requires measurement and identification with the appropriate time period. Accruals, deferrals, and estimations are involved in the same manner as these concepts are applied in the measurement and time-period identification of other expenses.

Matching

4. Matching—one of the basic processes of income determination—involves the association of specific costs with specific revenues or time periods. Expenses of the current period consist of those costs that are identified with revenue of the current period and those costs that are identified with the current period on some basis other than revenues.

The accounting profession's solution to the application of those concepts is comprehensive income tax allocation under the deferred method. Income tax expense should reflect the income tax effect of all differences between pretax-accounting income and taxable income reasonably expected to reverse in some future period. This is true whether the timing differences are recurring differences or nonrecurring differences that result from a single difference between pretax-accounting income and taxable income. Furthermore, under the deferred method income taxes are provided at the income tax rate in effect when the timing difference originates.

At least two major dilemmas arise from this prescribed accounting treatment. First, while the presence of deferred tax credits may imply that the company has a *liability* for future income taxes and the presence of deferred tax debits may imply that the company has an *asset* in the form of reduced future income taxes, these conclusions are true only if the timing differences giving rise to the deferred tax accounts actually reverse in the future.

Empirical research into the behavior of deferred tax credits appear to support the argument that deferred taxes arising from recurring timing differences, namely depreciation, tend to increase over time rather than decrease as timing differences reverse. Davidson, Skelton, and Weil studied 3,108 companies for a 19-year period (1954–1955 through 1972–1973). In their study 18,184 changes in the deferred tax credit accounts were identified, 14,288 (79%) of which were increases and only 3,896 (21%) of which were decreases. Furthermore, the increases amounted to $39.5 billion while the decreases amounted to only $5.9 billion. Stated another way, 87% of the total dollar change in deferred income tax credits studied were increases.[12] Other research generally supports the same conclusions. These studies lend support for the notion that recurring differences between pretax-accounting income and taxable income resulting from depreciation methods give rise to the *indefinite postponement* of income taxes rather than the temporary postponement that will reverse in the foreseeable future.

---

[10]Homer A. Black, *Accounting Research Study No. 9*, "Interperiod Allocation of Corporate Income Taxes" (New York: AICPA, 1966), pp. 12, 64.

[11]*APB Opinion No. 11*, par. 14.

[12]Sidney Davidson, Lisa Skelton, and Roman L. Weil, "A Controversy Over the Expected Behavior of Deferred Tax Credits," *Journal of Accountancy* (April 1977), p. 53.

A related issue is the fact that any liability for future income tax (or any asset in the form of prepaid tax) is based on the assumption that the enterprise will have future taxable income. This fact further explains why many accountants question whether deferred income tax accounts actually represent assets and liabilities that will result in positive or negative future cash flows.

A second dilemma concerns the *amount* of asset or liability that exists for deferred income taxes. Deferred Income Tax accounts reflect the tax effects of timing differences on the basis of income tax rates in effect when timing differences originate. The impact on future income taxes of timing differences will be based on income tax rates in effect when timing differences reverse. The amount of future tax reduction or liability is measured by the deferred method *only* if future tax rates are the same as past tax rates. The requirement that deferred income taxes not be recognized on a discounted basis further confuses the measurement of any future amount of tax liability or tax reduction, because the reversal of timing differences may extend into several future periods.

The requirement of the deferred method appears to be a practical approach to the uncertainty of the pattern of the reversal of timing differences and the uncertainty of the income tax rates that will be in effect when those differences reverse. Deferred Income Tax credits are probably best viewed not as true liabilities but as deferred credit balances that have already been charged to Income Tax Expense, awaiting amortization in future periods. In the same manner, Deferred Income Tax debits should be viewed not as true assets but as deferred debit balances that have not yet been charged to Income Tax Expense, awaiting amortization in future periods when timing differences of past periods reverse in the future. The problem of differences originating in one period but not reversing in the future remains a complexity of financial reporting that will likely be considered again in the future by authoritative accounting bodies.

OPERATING-LOSS CARRYBACKS AND CARRYFORWARDS

Certain provisions of income tax law allow companies to offset losses of one year against income of other years to reduce the total income tax burden of the company. Thus, while the company must report its income periodically for the purpose of paying income taxes, the amount of income taxes ultimately paid is based on the long-run profitability of the enterprise.

The terms **operating-loss carryback** and **operating-loss carryforward** are important in understanding this process. Operating loss carrybacks, or simply **carrybacks,** result when the loss of a particular year is taken back in time and used to reduce income of some past year. The effect of the carryback is that income taxes of that past year are reduced and the enterprise has a right to a refund of income taxes that have already been paid. Operating-loss carryforwards, or simply **carryforwards,** result when the loss of a particular year is taken forward in time and used to reduce income of some future year. The effect of the carryforward is an expected reduction of income taxes that would otherwise have to be paid if operations of future years result in income subject to income taxes. Since carrybacks are based on past income and related income taxes that have already been paid and carryforwards are based on expected future income and related income taxes that *may* have to be paid, carryforwards are more speculative or uncertain than carrybacks. This difference is apparent in the accounting treatment for the two that we discuss in the following paragraphs.

A loss of a particular period can be carried back if the enterprise has reported income and paid income taxes within a specified period.[13] If the enterprise has not had income and

---

[13]At the time of publication, this specified period was three years.

therefore has not paid income taxes within the specified carryback period, the loss of a particular period can be carried forward and offset against income of future periods for a specified period of time.[14] Additionally, if the loss of the current period exceeds the income reported during the carryback period, the portion that cannot be carried back can be carried forward. The enterprise also has the option of carrying the entire loss of a particular period forward instead of back. This election must be made in the loss year and cannot be changed once an option has been selected. However, a company may use one option for one loss year and the other option for another loss year. Once the option is selected, the income of the earliest year possible is reduced by the loss of the year in question. These alternatives are illustrated in Exhibit 18–9.

Under the carryback/carryforward option, the loss of 1983 in Exhibit 18–9 would be used to reduce income and income taxes of 1980, 1981, and 1982, in that order. Income taxes paid in those years would be refundable to the enterprise to the extent that the 1983 loss offset part or all of the incomes reported in those years. If the 1983 loss were so great that it more than offset the incomes of 1980, 1981, and 1982, the remainder would be carried forward to offset income in 1984, 1985, etc., if income were present in those years. The refund of past income taxes for which the company is eligible is determinable and is based on actual income taxes paid in those years. Any reduction in future income taxes is uncertain, however, since it is to be based on future income not yet earned.

Exhibit 18–9, under the option to carry forward only, indicates that the loss of 1983 cannot be carried back but can be carried forward and applied in consecutive order to the carryforward years beginning with 1984. You may wonder why a company would choose only the speculative carryforward option if it could carry back the loss of a particular period and have the certainty of the refund of past income taxes. The answer lies in the *anticipation* of future income to be taxed at *higher* income tax rates than in the past. Since the amount of refund (if the loss is carried back) or the reduction in future income taxes (if the loss is carried forward) are both based on actual taxes paid or to be paid, the income tax rates in effect in the year(s) for which income is reduced by the loss are very important. Income taxes in the future may be greater than in the past because (1) income tax rates may increase or (2) a higher level of future income may place the company in a higher income tax bracket. If either of these is expected to take place, the company that sustains a loss in a given year may select the option of carrying forward the entire loss and forfeiting the

---

[14]At the time of publication, this specified period was 15 years.

EXHIBIT 18–9
Operating-Loss Carrybacks and Carryforwards

Option	Carryback Period (Reduction in Taxes Determinable)			Current Period	Carryforward Period (Reduction in Taxes Speculative)						
	1980	*1981*	*1982*	*1983*	*1984*	*1985*	*1986*	*1987*	*1988*	. . .	*1998*
Carryback and/or carryforward	Carry back 3 years			Loss Reported	Carry forward 15 years						
Carryforward only	Not applicable				Carry forward 15 years						

certainty of the carryback option. The company would be speculating that the future reduction in income taxes would exceed a reduction in income taxes paid in the past.

Another consideration in choosing between the carryback/carryforward option or the carryforward only option is the timing of the receipt of the tax refund. If the loss is carried back, the company can expect to receive the tax refund in the near future, whereas if the loss is carried forward, the company forfeits the right to the funds until some future time—after the company has earned future taxable income.

The previous discussion has centered around the provisions of the income tax law that govern the actual payment of income taxes to the government. A related issue for the reporting enterprise is how the income tax advantages of an operating loss should be reported in its financial statements. We have already discussed the fact that in many cases the recognition of income taxes in financial statements does not equal their recognition in the income tax return. The same is true in reporting the effects of operating-loss carrybacks and carryforwards, although the financial-reporting and income tax treatments tend to parallel closely in most cases.

The income tax effects of loss *carrybacks* should be recognized in the determination of net income (loss) in the loss period. In other words, the loss of the period is reduced by the income taxes of past years that will be refunded because of the carryback of the current year's loss. This conclusion is based on the fact that the refund of past income taxes is measurable and realizable in the loss year and is *not dependent* on the existence of future income. The income tax effects of loss *carryforwards,* however, generally should not be recognized in the loss year, because realization is *dependent on future income* and is thus less certain. Also, estimating the reduction in future taxes is difficult, because the future reduction will be based on income tax rates in effect in future periods. These factors result in a conservative presentation of income, and the reduced income taxes are not recognized until evidence is present to support the recognition of the loss carryforward.

Conserva-tism

To illustrate the way operating-loss carrybacks and carryforwards work, we shall assume that Hanson Company has pretax-accounting income (loss) and income tax rates for 1981 through 1984 as follows:

	1981	*1982*	*1983*	*1984*
Pretax-accounting income (loss)	$75,000	$80,000	$55,000	$(250,000)
Income tax rate	40%	42%	42%	46%

Hanson selects the carryback/carryforward option for purposes of applying the 1984 loss to reduce income taxes. Accordingly, the amount of refund to which they are immediately entitled as a result of the 1984 loss is $86,700, computed as follows:

Year	Income		Income Tax Rate		Refund
1981	$75,000	×	40%	=	$30,000
1982	80,000	×	42%	=	33,600
1983	55,000	×	42%	=	23,100
Total	$210,000				$86,700

The 1981 income tax rate is applied to the 1981 income to determine the refund applicable to that year; the same process is continued for each year. Since the loss of 1984 ($250,000) exceeds the total incomes of 1981–1983 ($210,000), all income taxes previously paid are subject to refund. If the loss of 1984 had been less than $210,000, the amount refundable would be limited to the income tax previously paid on income up to the amount of the 1984 loss.[15]

The journal entry to record income tax for 1984 is as follows:

Receivable for Past Income Taxes	86,700	
Benefit of Net Operating-Loss Carryback		86,700

The receivable of past income taxes is presented in the balance sheet as a current asset because it represents a refund that will be received in the near future. The credit entry, "benefit of net operating-loss carryback," is presented in the income statement in lieu of income tax expense, resulting in the following presentation:

Loss before income tax	$(250,000)
Income tax benefit of net operating-loss carryback	86,700
Net loss	$(163,300)

Hanson chose to use the carryback/carryforward option, and thus the income tax advantage of $210,000 of the $250,000 loss was reflected in the 1984 loss. If the company had elected the option to carry forward *only,* the income tax advantage of the loss would ordinarily not have been recognized in 1984 because of the uncertainty of realization and the difficulty of measuring the amount of the prospective benefit. Therefore, recognition of the tax advantage would have been deferred until it could be realized in future periods when income was reported.

Comparing the income tax consequences on income for 1981 through 1984, the income statement presentations under the two options are summarized in Exhibit 18–10.

If operating losses are carried forward for *any* reason, amounts of such carryforwards and their expiration dates must be disclosed in the financial statements.[16]

Continuing the example of Hanson Company, we shall assume we have data for 1985 and add this information to that presented earlier, as follows:

	1981	1982	1983	1984	1985
Pretax-accounting income (loss)	$75,000	$80,000	$55,000	$(250,000)	$45,000
Income tax rates	40%	42%	42%	46%	44%

The $40,000 of 1984 loss that Hanson could not carry back to 1981–1983 is carried forward to 1985 and used to reduce taxable income of that year to $5,000 ($45,000 − $40,000).

---

[15]For example, if the 1984 loss had been only $165,000, the amount of the refund is computed by starting with the income of the earliest year (1981) and computing the income tax paid on the first $165,000.

Year	Income		Income Tax Rate		Refund
1981	$ 75,000	×	40%	=	$30,000
1982	80,000	×	42%	=	33,600
1983	10,000	×	42%	=	4,200
	$165,000				$67,800

Only $10,000 of 1983 income is included in the refund to reach the level of $165,000 income to offset the 1984 loss of that amount. The remaining $45,000 1983 income ($55,000 − $10,000) may be used as a basis for the refund of income taxes in the future if additional losses in 1985 or 1986 are carried back.

[16]APB Opinion No. 11, par. 63.

EXHIBIT 18–10
Hanson Company 1981–1984
Comparative Income Presentation

Carryback/Carryforward Option	1981	1982	1983	1984
Income (loss) before income tax	$ 75,000	$ 80,000	$ 55,000	$(250,000)
Income tax expense	(30,000)	(33,600)	(23,100)	—
Refund of past income taxes	—	—	—	86,700
Net income (loss)	$ 45,000	$ 46,400	$ 31,900	$(163,300)
Carryforward Only Option				
Income (loss) before income tax	$ 75,000	$ 80,000	$ 55,000	$(250,000)
Income tax expense	(30,000)	(33,600)	(23,100)	—
Net income (loss)	$ 45,000	$ 46,400	$ 31,900	$(250,000)

When a loss carryforward is recognized in a year subsequent to the loss year, the benefit should be presented as an extraordinary gain.[17] The entry to record income tax for 1985 is as follows:

Income Tax Expense ($45,000 × 44%)	19,800	
Income Tax Payable ($5,000 × 44%)		2,200
Extraordinary Item—Benefit of Net Operating-Loss Carryforward ($40,000 × 44%)		17,600

The income tax payable is presented as a current liability in the balance sheet. The income statement presentation incorporates the income tax expense of $19,800 and the extraordinary item of $17,600, as follows:

Income before income tax	$45,000
Income tax expense	19,800
Income before extraordinary item	25,200
Extraordinary gain benefit of net operating-loss carryforward	17,600
Net Income	$42,800

In 1984 if Hanson had selected the option to carry forward *only,* the entire 1985 income of $45,000 would have been offset by the carryforward of the 1984 loss. In this case the income tax expense would still be $19,800, but no income taxes would have been payable for 1985. The extraordinary gain would have also been $19,800, because the entire income of 1985 would be offset by the 1984 loss that was carried forward. The remainder of the 1984 loss, $205,000 ($250,000 − $45,000), is available as a carryforward in 1986 and future years.

---

[17]*APB Opinion No. 11,* par. 61. The classification of the loss carryforward as an extraordinary item is made without regard to the criteria of unusual in nature and infrequent in occurrence that are usually applied in determining the classification of an item as extraordinary.

While the income tax benefits of loss carryforwards are ordinarily not recognized in the loss period, an exception is sometimes made if "realization is assured beyond any reasonable doubt." The special circumstances are described by the APB as follows:

> *Realization of the tax benefit of a loss carryforward would appear to be assured beyond any reasonable doubt [emphasis added] when both of the following conditions exist: (a) the loss results from an identifiable, isolated and non-recurring cause and the company either has been continuously profitable over a long period of time or has suffered occasional losses which were more than offset by taxable income in subsequent years, and (b) future taxable income is virtually certain to be large enough to offset the loss carryforward and will occur soon enough to provide realization during the carryforward period.[18]*

Although the basis for this exception is the high probability of future income, determining the amount of the benefit is still a problem, because future income tax rates are unknown and must be estimated. When a loss carryforward is recognized in the loss period because realization is assured beyond reasonable doubt, however, the benefit is incorporated in the "refund of income taxes" figure and is *not* presented as an extraordinary item.

To illustrate the anticipation of a loss carryforward, assume that American Gold Company had been continuously profitable every year since its inception in 1960 until 1984, a year in which it had a pretax loss of $157,000. The loss resulted from a single catastrophic event that is not expected to recur. The appropriate income tax rate for 1984 is 46%. Management selects the carryforward only option and anticipates the income tax rate for the next several years to be about 48%.

Because the realization of the income tax advantage of the loss carryforward is assured beyond a reasonable doubt, the expected future benefit of the loss carryforward is appropriately included in the determination of 1984 income (loss). The amount of this benefit, which is based on expected future income tax rates of 48%, is $75,360 ($157,000 × 48% = $75,360). The entry to record income taxes for 1984 is as follows:

Receivable—Reduction of Future Income Taxes	75,360	
Estimated Reduction in Future Income Taxes—		
Benefit of Net Operating-Loss Carryforward		75,360

The receivable is an asset in the balance sheet and is subject to current and noncurrent classifications, depending on the expected timing of the future income upon which income taxes will not be paid because of the recognition of the carryforward in 1984. If the carryforward is recognized prior to the time that the income is earned, it seems logical that the receivable would be noncurrent in many cases. In contrast, the receivable is typically current in the case of a carryback, because the claim for past income taxes paid produces a refund that a company normally expects to receive in cash in the near future.

The credit side of the preceding entry reduces the 1984 loss; in the income statement it is presented as follows:

Loss before income taxes	$(157,000)
Estimated reduction in future income taxes—benefit of net operating-loss carryforward	75,360
Net loss	$ (81,640)

[18]*APB Opinion No. 11*, par. 46.

Aetna Scrambles To Replace
Net SEC Disallowed

Big Insurer Will Sell Bonds From Portfolio, May Act To Free Cash in Reserves

By Daniel Hertzberg
Staff Reporter of The Wall Street Journal

NEW YORK—A ruling by the Securities and Exchange Commission on a disputed accounting practice of Aetna Life & Casualty Co. has sent the big insurer scrambling to replace earnings that would be sapped by the decision.

In reaction to the SEC ruling, Aetna said yesterday that it will sell as much as several hundred million dollars of tax-exempt bonds from its investment portfolio this year. At the same time, Aetna also said it probably will transfer a major chunk of insurance business to other insurance companies to free up cash from reserves.

On Tuesday, Aetna disclosed that the SEC ordered it to stop accounting for future tax credits in current earnings, a practice that provided 39% of its 1982 operating profit of $522 million. Aetna, based in Hartford, Conn., is the largest stockholder-owned insurance company in the U.S.

Using Credits Early

Aetna's main problem is its need for additional taxable in-come. Aetna needs this taxable income so it can employ in current earnings tax benefits generated from heavy underwriting losses in its property-casualty insurance operations. Otherwise, it would only be able to employ these tax benefits in future years when it has more taxable income.

To recognize those credits ahead of time, Aetna has been making use of future taxable income that its management said it is sure to earn. But the SEC ruled against Aetna's accounting practice. As a result, Aetna needs a quick infusion of taxable income to prevent its earnings from falling sharply.

Both the prospective bond sales and the reinsurance program would generate additional taxable income, and Charles T. Bell, the company's director of financial relations, who yesterday described plans for the major financial restructuring in the wake of the SEC ruling.

For example, money raised from the sale of tax-exempt municipal bonds would be used to buy taxable bonds, a category that includes corporate and Treasury issues. The tax-exempt bonds would be sold from a $4.9 billion portfolio of tax-exempts in Aetna's property-casualty insurance companies.

In other developments:

—Analysts at several Wall Street securities firms yesterday sharply lowered their estimates of Aetna's 1983 earnings.

—In Washington, SEC officials confirmed that the agency intended in its ruling that there be a full restatement of Aetna's 1982 earnings. Instead, Aetna agreed only to halt its disputed accounting practice starting with the 1982 fourth quarter. One official said that the SEC might consider filing a lawsuit against the big insurance company, but that a course of action hasn't been decided.

—Insurance executives predicted that more property-casualty companies could run into an earnings bind like Aetna's if commercial insurance prices continue to be depressed.

To Avoid Decline in Net

Aetna officials didn't predict how much they expected the financial restructuring of the big insurer to add to 1983 earnings. Aetna's chairman, John H. Filer, said on Tuesday that the big insurer would take steps to avoid a "major" decline in profit. One question is whether Aetna will be able to sell bonds without taking losses. Such trading losses would reduce both shareholder's surplus and net income. Mr. Bell said that Aetna hopes "to minimize" any bond losses.

Under the reinsurance program, Aetna will transfer to other insurers so-called "long tail" property-casualty policies where claims are likely to be paid out 10 years or more in the future. Such policies could cover medical malpractice, liability and workers' compensation, experts said. "In return, we would get immediate cash through a release of reserves" backing those policies, Mr. Bell said.

Wall Street analysts didn't appear impressed by Aetna's restructuring program. Merrill Lynch & Co. analyst Gerald Lewinsohn yesterday cut his per-share estimate of Aetna's 1983 earnings to $4.50 from $5.90 a share. E. Franz of Donaldson, Lufkin & Jenrette Inc. trimmed his estimate to $5 a share from $6.25.

"This is just the latest in a series of negatives" for Aetna, said Mr. Lewinsohn. Like other insurers, Aetna's results have suffered from a price war in the commercial property-casualty business. And Aetna's $638 million acquisition last year of Geosource Inc., an oil service company, was ill-timed. The oil industry ran into trouble, and Geosource had an operating loss in the fourth quarter, which Aetna didn't specify. Some analysts, however, expect Aetna's outlook to brighten in 1984 if the property-casualty business improves.

Investors reacted more cautiously. Aetna common stock closed at $33.375 a share, down 50 cents, in New York Stock Exchange composite trading yesterday on heavy volume of 601,000 shares. Analysts said that the fall of Aetna's per-share price from $44.375 last November, reflected investor fears about an adverse SEC ruling.

In several examples to illustrate the recognition of loss carrybacks and loss carryforwards, we have considered both the carryback/carryforward option and the carryforward only option. We have considered a case in which the realization of a loss carryforward is considered to be assured as well as cases in which it is not assured. The income tax treatment and the financial-statement recognition of loss carrybacks and carryforwards are consistent in most cases. However, when we recognize a loss carryforward in the loss period because realization is assured beyond reasonable doubt, the benefit is recognized in the income statement before it is recognized for income tax purposes.

The reduction in the reported net loss resulting from the recognition of loss carryforwards and carrybacks under the various alternatives is summarized in Exhibit 18–11.

Conservatism

As we stated earlier, a conservative approach in a typical situation requires an operating-loss carryforward not to be recognized in the loss year but to be deferred until future income assures its value. At that time the recognition of the gain from the carryforward is presented in the income statement as an extraordinary item. Any unused loss carryforwards are disclosed in the financial statements, along with their dates of expiration. This type of presentation and disclosure is illustrated in Exhibit 18–12, which includes two excerpts from the 1981 annual report of Digicon Inc. Digicon Inc. is an advanced-technology oil services company that provides geophysical exploration, supplies, and compressor-packaging services to the oil and gas industry. The company also sells and licenses specially designed computing equipment and related software for geophysical data processing.

Although interperiod income tax allocation and operating-loss carrybacks and carryforwards have been treated here as separate subjects, they are interrelated. The eventual payment of deferred income taxes depends on income in the year of the reversal of the timing differences giving rise to the deferred tax. If a loss exists in the period of the reversal of the timing difference, however, an adjustment must be made to reduce the deferred tax and reduce the loss of that period. Similarly, if an operating-loss carryforward exists when the reversal is due, an adjustment may be necessary to account for the anticipated reversal of timing differences.

EXHIBIT 18–11
Basis for Reduction in Reported Net Loss
Resulting from Operating-Loss Carrybacks and/or Carryforwards

	Carryback	Carryforward Not Assured	Carryforward Assured
Current year loss ≤ prior year incomes			
Carryback/carry-forward option selected	Tax on past income	N/A	N/A
Carryforward only option selected	N/A	None	Estimated tax on expected future income
Current year loss > prior year incomes			
Carryback/carry-forward option selected	Tax on past income	None	Estimated tax on expected future income
Carryforward only option selected	N/A	None	Estimated tax on expected future income

Notes: None = No reduction in loss recognized in loss period. Carryforward available for recognition in future period(s). N/A = Not applicable.

EXHIBIT 18–12
Digicon Inc.
Financial Statement Excerpts

Income Statement Excerpt
(in thousands)

	1981	*1980*	*1979*
Income before provision for income taxes and extraordinary item	8,412	3,454	908
Provision for income taxes (Note 3)	3,072	1,114	451
Income before extraordinary item	5,340	2,340	457
Extraordinary item (Note 3)	629		
Net income	$5,969	$2,340	$457

Footnote Excerpt

An extraordinary credit of $629,000 was recorded for the year ended July 31, 1981 to reflect the income tax effect, based on financial statement income, of foreign operating loss carryforwards. Investment tax credit carryforwards for financial statement purposes of $1,065,000 at July 31, 1981, expiring primarily in 1990 through 1996, are available for direct reduction of U.S. income taxes. Foreign operations had operating loss carryforwards of $181,000 at July 31, 1981, which are available indefinitely to reduce future foreign taxable income.

SOURCE: Digicon Inc., 1981 Annual Report.

INVESTMENT TAX CREDIT

Income tax policy is frequently used to accomplish certain economic and social objectives, as well as to serve as a source of governmental revenue and to meet various other objectives. Since 1962, Congress has occasionally attempted to stimulate investment in certain capital assets by allowing a reduction in income taxes equal to a specified percentage of the cost of qualifying assets. Since its inception, the **investment tax credit (ITC)** has been suspended and restored several times in order to accomplish various objectives. The Revenue Act of 1978 permanently established the investment tax credit at 10% of the cost of qualifying assets. Additionally, limitations are placed on the amount of the investment tax credit that can be used in any one year to offset income taxes that would otherwise be paid that year. These limitations change from time to time. Any investment tax credit resulting from the acquisition of assets in one year, but that cannot be used to reduce taxes in that particular year due to these limitations, may be carried forward to future years. This works much like the operating-loss carryforward provisions of the tax law that were covered earlier in this chapter; however, the recognition of an investment tax credit carryforward in a subsequent year is *not* treated as an extraordinary item.[19]

---

[19]*AICPA Accounting Interpretation,* "Accounting for the Investment Tax Credit: An Interpretation of *APB Opinion No. 4*" (New York: AICPA, 1972).

DEFERRED TAX ACCOUNTING SHOULD BE CHANGED

ERTA 1981 CREATES a number of difficult accounting issues. Two issues, in particular, raise questions relating to deferred tax accounting: how the Accelerated Cost Recovery System (ACRS) impacts depreciation recorded for financial reporting purposes and how the longer carryforward period affects net operating losses. These are but the latest in a series of challenges to existing generally accepted accounting principles for accounting for income taxes. It appears that the 1981 Tax Act has been the "straw that broke the camel's back"—the decisive argument for a complete reconsideration of deferred tax accounting.

The Economic Recovery Tax Act of 1981

Two accounting questions created by the 1981 Tax Act seem particularly relevant to a discussion of deferred tax accounting. First is the impact of the Accelerated Cost Recovery System. Under ACRS, the cost of most items of property, plant and equipment will be recovered for tax purposes over a period of three to 15 years—much faster than under previous tax guidelines. In the past, most businesses have used the same depreciation lives for tax and financial reporting purposes. This will no longer be possible for many companies because the ACRS lives are clearly shorter than the economic lives

over which companies must record book depreciation.

Thus, many companies that previously had no book/tax differences will have to provide deferred taxes on depreciation timing differences. Smaller, nonpublic companies are particularly likely to find this objectionable. Some may seek "relief" from this calculation and reporting burden—either by receiving an exception to GAAP in the auditors' report on their financial statements, or by changing to tax-basis reporting. Of course, ACRS also affects companies already providing deferred taxes on depreciation timing differences. The new cost recovery method for tax purposes will cause the deferred taxes account to increase even faster. (See later discussion on "Growing Materiality of Deferred Taxes.")

Another issue under the new Tax Act adds pressure to change APB Opinion No. 11—the question of accounting for the possible future benefits of net operating loss carryovers [NOLs]. The general rule under Opinion 11 emphasizes the concept of matching the tax expense or benefit against the financial reporting income that gave rise to that tax. NOLs are an exception to this general rule. Under paragraph 45 of APB Opinion No. 11, NOLs are not to be recorded as an asset and reduction of current tax expense unless realization is assured beyond a reasonable doubt.

In practice, very few NOLs have been recorded as assets, largely because of the SEC's extremely conservative attitude. Now that the carryover period for NOLs has been extended from seven to 15 years, there undoubtedly will be more pressure to record NOLs in advance of realization in the tax return. Some have argued, in fact, that not recording an NOL refutes the basic "going concern" concept, because it would be difficult, if not impossible, for an entity to stay in business for 15 years without earning a profit.

Growing Materiality of Deferred Taxes

Still another reason for reconsidering deferred tax accounting is the growing materiality of such credits in the balance sheets of corporations. I surveyed the 1980 annual reports of the top 250 *Fortune* industrial companies to see what this impact was. Twenty-seven companies reported deferred taxes in excess of 20 percent of stockholders' equity at that date. The average (unweighted for size of company) for those companies was 26 percent of stockholders' equity, with a range of 20 percent to 39 percent. It is even more remarkable that in 1971 the average for these same companies was less than 10 percent—deferred taxes had increased nearly two and a half times faster than stockholders' equity. See Table 1 for more information on this survey.

SOURCE: Adapted from Dennis R. Beresford, "Deferred Tax Accounting Should Be Changed," *CPA Journal,* June 1982, pp. 16–23. Reprinted by permission of *The CPA Journal.*

TABLE 1
Survey of Growth of Deferred Taxes

Number of Companies	Year	Percent of Stockholders' Equity	
		Average	*Range*
25	1971	9.7%	.5%–36.8%
25	1980	26.7%	20.1%–39.7%
		Percent of Total Assets	
		Average	*Range*
25	1971	4.1%	.3%–12.5%
25	1980	10.3%	6.9–15.7%

Alternative Accounting Methods

Two methods of accounting for the impact of the investment tax credit on the income tax *expense* are used in practice: the **deferred method** and the **flow-through method.** The impact of the investment tax credit on the tax liability is the same, regardless of the method of expense recognition used, because the investment tax credit reduces taxes payable, within specified limitations, in the period in which the qualifying asset is acquired. As our discussion of interperiod income tax allocation indicated, the treatment for income tax purposes does not necessarily dictate the treatment that should be followed in the financial statements.

The deferred method, also called the **cost reduction method,** and the flow-through method, also called the **tax reduction method,** are described in Exhibit 18–13.

To illustrate these two methods, we shall assume that Kapp Company acquires an item of equipment costing $200,000 in 1984. This asset qualifies for the 10% investment tax credit and has an expected useful life of eight years. During 1984 Kapp Company earns $182,000 before income tax, and the appropriate income tax rate is 46%. Entries to account for the investment tax credit under the two alternative methods are illustrated in Exhibit 18–14.

The initial acquisition of the equipment (first entry) and the ultimate payment of income taxes (fourth entry) are identical under the two methods. The difference is found in the

EXHIBIT 18–13
Alternative Methods of Accounting for the Investment Tax Credit (ITC)

Method of Accounting	Description	Accounting Treatment
Deferred (cost reduction)	ITC is a reduction in the cost of the qualifying asset. The benefit of the ITC in the form of reduced income taxes is derived from the *use* of the asset.	ITC is deferred and recognized as a reduction in income tax expense over the periods that benefit from the use of the asset.
Flow-through (tax reduction)	ITC is a reduction in income tax that results from the *investment* in the qualifying asset rather than the use of that asset.	ITC is recognized as a reduction in income tax expense in the period in which the asset is acquired.

EXHIBIT 18–14
Example of Alternative Methods: Investment Tax Credit

Journal Entries: Deferred Method	Transaction Description	Journal Entries: Flow-Through Method

Equipment   200,000
  Cash   200,000
	Acquisition of equipment	Equipment 200,000
		  Cash 200,000

Tax Expense   83,720
  Deferred ITC   20,000
  Tax Payable   63,720
 	
Computation
  Tax on $182,000
    $182,000 × .46 = $83,720
  Deferred ITC
    $200,000 × .10 = $20,000
  Tax payable
    $83,720 − $20,000 = $63,720
	Income tax accrual for 1984	Tax Expense 63,720
		  Tax Payable 63,720
		
		Computation
		  Tax expense
		    $83,720 − $20,000 = $63,720

Deferred ITC   2,500
  Tax Expense   2,500
 	
Computation
  $20,000/8 years = $2,500
	Amortization of ITC	None

Tax Payable   63,720
  Cash   63,720
	Payment of tax liability	Tax Payable 63,720
		  Cash 63,720

treatment of the impact of the investment tax credit on the income tax expense in the second and third entries. The reduced income taxes are treated as a reduction in tax expense of $20,000 in 1984 under the flow-through method but deferred and allocated over the asset's life under the deferred method. Thus, only ⅛ or $2,500 of the benefit is recognized as a reduction in income tax expense in 1984.

Continuing the example of Kapp Company, we find that the income statement and balance sheet amounts for 1984 relative to the investment tax credit would be as follows:

	Deferred Method	Flow-Through Method
Income Statement		
Income tax expense	$81,220	$63,720
Balance Sheet		
Deferred investment tax credit	17,500	NONE

Under the deferred method, the income tax expense of each year in the asset's life is reduced by the allocation of the deferred investment tax credit. For 1984, this results in an income tax expense of $81,220 ($83,720 − $2,500). The declining balance in the Deferred Investment Tax Credit account is presented in the balance sheet as a deferred income tax credit until it is fully amortized. Under the flow-through method, the full impact of the investment tax credit is reflected in 1984, the year of the acquisition of the asset. Thus, no deferred investment tax credit appears in the balance sheet under this method.

Financial-Statement Disclosure

The method used to account for the investment tax credit must be revealed in notes to the financial statements, because the credit represents an area in which more than one accounting method is acceptable. Exhibit 18–15 illustrates the disclosure of the investment tax credit in the 1982 annual reports of two companies. Goodyear uses the flow-through method of accounting for the investment tax credit. General Electric uses the deferred method and amortizes the credits over the lives of the facilities to which the credit applies.

The Investment-Tax-Credit Controversy

The origin of the investment tax credit, the emergence of two methods of accounting for it, and the response of the APB to this new feature of financial reporting resulted in a significant controversy. Both accounting methods that emerged for the investment tax credit—the deferred and the flow-through methods—have merit and thus were attractive to individual accountants. Advocates of the deferred method held that the credit should be considered a

---

EXHIBIT 18–15
Investment Tax Credit Disclosures

Goodyear
United States investment tax credit is recorded using the flow through method as a reduction of the current tax provision. . . . The investment tax credit for 1982, 1981 and 1980 was $14.6 million, $13.7 million and $16.9 million, respectively.

SOURCE: Goodyear Company, 1982 Annual Report.

General Electric
Investment tax credit is deferred and amortized as a reduction of the provision for taxes over the lives of the facilities to which the credit applies. . . . Investment tax credit amounted to $103 million in 1982, compared with $95 million in 1981 and $92 million in 1980. In 1982, $59 million were included in net earnings, compared with $49 million in 1981 and $36 million in 1980. At the end of 1982, the amount deferred to be included in net earnings of future years was $350 million.

SOURCE: General Electric Company, 1982 Annual Report.

reduction in the cost of the asset, because management would be aware of the availability of the credit and would consider the credit in deciding to acquire the asset. Continuing this line of reasoning, they argued that income is generated through the *use,* not the acquisition, of assets. Thus, spreading the credit over the life of the asset was logical and consistent with allocating the asset's cost over its useful life in a systematic and rational manner, much like the method for depreciation. Matching is a major part of the justification for this method. Furthermore, this treatment was consistent with the recapture feature of the income tax law that required the company to repay some or all of the credit if the asset were not held and used for a specified period of time.

Matching

Other accountants advocated the tax reduction or flow-through method primarily on the basis that it represented a selective income tax reduction that was available only to those who met certain specified conditions. They argued that the investment tax credit was a feature of income tax law that did not alter the inherent value of the related asset, but was more like a permanent difference between pretax-accounting income and taxable income than a decline in the depreciation on the asset.

Professional accounting standards for the investment tax credit were originally developed in *APB Opinion No. 2* in 1962 and subsequently modified in *APB Opinion No. 4* in 1964.[20] These opinions were issued when the APB was attempting to establish itself as the major authoritative body responsible for guiding the development of financial accounting standards in the United States. The general acceptance of its pronouncements was an important element in establishing this authority.

Initially the APB advocated the deferred or cost reduction method of accounting for the investment tax credit for the reasons cited earlier. Many practicing CPAs, however, favored the flow-through or tax reduction method for the reasons also cited earlier. The flow-through method has an obvious advantage in terms of the early recognition of income in the financial statements, because the full effect of the reduction in income tax expense is recognized in the initial year.

Two significant developments during this period had a negative impact on the authoritative position of the APB and resulted in the board's subsequent acceptance of *either* method of accounting for the investment tax credit. First, the American Institute of Certified Public Accountants (AICPA) made an urgent plea to members to issue an unqualified audit opinion *only* if clients used the deferred method, because the flow-through method was not consistent with *APB Opinion No. 2.* Despite this plea, many unqualified opinions were issued for financial statements in which the flow-through method was used. Secondly, the Securities and Exchange Commission (SEC) took a position that essentially allowed either the deferred or the flow-through method. In light of these setbacks, the APB issued *Opinion No. 4,* in which it voiced its acceptance of the flow-through method, even though it continued to maintain a *preference* for the deferred method.

In a reconsideration of the two methods in 1971, when Congress reinstated the investment tax credit, the APB again attempted to limit accounting for the credit to the deferred method. At this time a great deal of political pressure emerged as influential businessmen were successful in lobbying Congress to stipulate in the income tax law that no specific method of accounting for the investment tax credit could be required by a standard-setting body such as the APB. This flexibility has led to the diversity in practice that exists today whereby both the deferred and the flow-through methods are used in practice. As in the case of other accounting alternatives, the method followed must be disclosed in the financial statements.

Disclosure

The saga of the diversity in reporting the investment tax credit in the financial statements is of considerable concern to the accounting profession. The lack of general acceptance of the deferred method under *APB Opinion No. 2* and the subsequent changes in *APB Opinion*

---

[20]*APB Opinions Nos. 2 and 4,* "Accounting for the Investment Tax Credit," 1962 and 1964.

No. 4, in which the board adjusted its position to parallel accounting practice, had a detrimental impact on the credibility of the APB. In the opinion of many, this action reduced the ultimate effectiveness of the board on many fronts. The imposition of political pressure and the intervention of Congress in allowing alternative accounting procedures in this one area of accounting have caused considerable concern. Historically, accounting principles have developed within the private sector under the careful observation of the SEC. The precedent set by the situation surrounding the investment tax credit is of concern to those who feel strongly that the future development of financial reporting standards should continue in the private sector to the maximum extent possible.

In reflecting on the events of late 1971, when the second series of episodes concerning the investment tax credit took place, an APB member suggested that the board should perhaps have been renamed the "Accounting Principles–Political Action Board." The following statements summarize his feelings:

> *Will lobbying become the* modus operandi *for generating or blocking the accounting pronouncements of the 1970's? . . . Congress has no monopoly on obtaining "correct" answers. The long-run implications for external financial reporting of the increasing tendencies to contact Congress on every issue are frightening.*
>
> *This may be a sad story but it illustrates why some members of the APB are supersensitive to industry reaction. We live in a democracy, and setting accounting principles is indeed subject to popularity testing. That is why we will continue to see an evolution of accounting principles. A natural resistance to change seems widespread. Radical changes may occur occasionally, but only when there is no widespread hostility among the reporting companies.[21]*

---

[21]Charles T. Horngren, "Accounting Principles: Private or Public Sector?" *Journal of Accountancy* (May 1972), pp. 40–41.

CREDITS WHEN THEY'RE DUE?

ONE OF THE CHRONIC headaches of the makers of accounting rules is again pounding with that familiar dull throb. The pain comes from investment tax credits and the complex question of how companies should report them to shareholders. In the old days, corporations had to spread the credits out over the life of assets, which kept earnings down. Then, in 1971, Congress allowed the credits to be shown on public income statements in the same year they were first taken for tax purposes. But the 1982 tax reforms have complicated matters.

Congress now says that companies claiming the investment credit, usually 10%, must reduce the depreciable value of the asset getting the tax credit by half the credit. Take a $10 credit on a $100 widget, and you must reduce its depreciable value to only $95. Over time, in effect, this means that taxpayers will get only a portion of the full 10% tax credit.

This creates a problem for the accountants. How should they record that reduction in the value of the tax credit? There are two schools of thought. The Financial Accounting Standards Board has recently ruled that companies must show that reduction immediately, along with the tax credit itself. Most of the Big Eight accounting firms and companies like Atlantic Richfield, Monsanto and Scott Paper—which are primarily concerned with the logic of the issue—back up the FASB.

Then there's the opposition. Such industrial giants as Exxon, International Paper, Time Inc. and United Technologies have written strongly worded letters to the FASB arguing that its rule on this seemingly minor question should be changed.

The dollar amount involved here for most companies will only rarely be large. At Exxon, for example, it will probably amount to just a few cents a share. But critics hit the FASB with force in part because any statement that tampers with their ability to flow through immediately the full amount of their investment tax credits touches a raw nerve. Exxon, for example, wrote off $259 million in tax credits last year. Companies don't want anyone fooling with that right, even a little bit.

There is also a broader objection involved. Opponents of the FASB ruling see it as just another example of the board's tendency to issue too many standards involving narrow technical issues. Accountants call the problem "standards overload," and claim they breed only costly paperwork and wasted time. "That's where all the emotions are coming in," says Ronald Wolf, Exxon's assistant controller. "They get all these little nitty-gritty things and they call them standards. But they're not standards. They're just regulations."

Those are the real-world arguments against the new rule. But companies like Exxon can't just argue for or against FASB proposals based on a desire for higher reported earnings and less paperwork. So the formal debate centers on accounting concepts.

Here, Exxon and its allies may find themselves on shaky ground. If there is a strong link between the investment tax credit and the writedown in the depreciable value of the assets, then the FASB's accounting changes make good sense. "The ITC and the writedown are completely intertwined," says Robert Ladig, Scott Paper's vice president for taxes. "The tax credit gives rise to and determines the amount of the reduction."

But, according to Exxon's Wolf, the only connection between the credit and the depreciation is an artificial one, imposed by Congress. That's a bit like saying the only connection between a fire engine and a fire is that they're both brightly colored.

Even though the FASB may be on high ground theoretically, it seems to be backing off. After reading the 114 letters they received over the past few months, board members are now considering demoting this ruling from full-fledged standard to technical bulletin, which carries less weight.

Score one for real-world worries over technical truth.

SOURCE: Christopher Power, "Credits When They're Due?" *Forbes*, April 25, 1983, pp. 84, 86. Reprinted by permission of *Forbes* Magazine. © Forbes Inc, 1983.

FINANCIAL-STATEMENT DISCLOSURE OF INCOME TAXES

Disclosure

A number of disclosures in the body of the financial statements and in related notes were mentioned in the previous discussions of the various topics related to accounting for income taxes. In this section we review and expand these disclosure standards and look at an example of the disclosure of income tax from the published financial statements of a public corporation.

Review of Disclosure Requirements

In addition to amounts of income taxes currently payable, balance sheet accounts related to income taxes are basically of two types:[22]

1. Deferred charges and credits resulting from timing differences.
2. Refunds of past income taxes or offsets to future income taxes arising from the recognition of operating-loss carryforwards and carrybacks.

The deferred charges and credits are presented as net current and net noncurrent amounts based on the nature of the underlying timing differences. Refunds of past income taxes or offsets to future income taxes are classified as current or noncurrent, depending on the timing of expected realization. If only a portion of the receivable is expected to be realized during the current operating cycle or one year, that portion is classified as a current receivable and the remainder as a noncurrent receivable.

Income statement reporting of income taxes centers around the disclosure of the components of the income-tax expense recognized during the period, including the following:[23]

---

[22]*APB Opinion No. 11*, par. 56.
[23]*APB Opinion No. 11*, par. 60.

1. The income taxes estimated to be payable.
2. The income tax effects of timing differences.
3. The income tax effects of operating losses.

This disclosure may be made in the body of the income statement or in accompanying notes. Income tax expense is allocated among income before income tax and before those gains, losses, and other transactions that are separately presented in the financial statements. The income tax effects of these special items is disclosed either in conjunction with the appropriate item or in related notes. When the tax benefit of an operating-loss carryforward is recognized in a year subsequent to the loss year, the tax benefit is presented as an extraordinary item.

Several general disclosures are also required in conjunction with the balance sheet and income statement:[24]

1. Amounts of any operating-loss carryforwards not recognized in the loss period and the expiration dates of those carryforwards.
2. Significant amounts of any other unused deductions or credits, along with expiration dates.
3. Reasons for significant variations in the customary relationships between income tax expense and pretax-accounting income, if they are not otherwise apparent from the financial statements and related disclosures.

An example of the second item is the carryforward of investment tax credits from previous years because of a limitation on the amount that could be recognized in any one year. The third disclosure results from the fact that the income tax expense may vary considerably from the amount that would result from the application of the statutory income tax rate to income before income tax. This difference may be due to a number of circumstances, such as permanent differences, the taxation of certain transactions at special rates, and the reduction in income tax expense because of the recognition of the investment tax credit.

Reporting requirements of the SEC for income tax disclosure go beyond the requirements of *APB Opinion No. 11* and therefore have influenced the content of financial statements included in annual reports. The SEC requires a formal schedule in which the statutory income tax rate is reconciled to the effective income tax rate, including an indication of the impact of each item contributing to the difference between the two. This schedule is frequently used in the annual report to meet the disclosure requirement of an explanation of variations in the customary relationship between income tax expense and pretax-accounting income. In addition, the SEC requires federal and state income taxes to be separately disclosed in the financial statements even though they are not required by authoritative accounting pronouncements.

Example of Income Tax Disclosure

Exhibit 18–16 presents the income tax disclosures from notes of Pennzoil Company's 1982 annual report. Pennzoil Company is a diversified natural resources company with a strong technological base. Pennzoil's 1982 and 1981 balance sheets include "Deferred Income Tax" of $350,134,000 and $299,959,000, respectively, among its noncurrent liabilities, representing 10.7% and 10.0%, respectively, of total liabilities and stockholders' equity. The 1982, 1981, and 1980 income statements include income tax expense of $72,181,000, $123,195,000, and $163,758,000, respectively.

The first table in Pennzoil's financial-statement note (Exhibit 18–16) includes the components of income tax expense, including U.S. and foreign taxes payable currently, deferred taxes, and the reduction in tax expense resulting from the investment tax credit. The second table indicates the tax effects of the timing differences that resulted in deferred taxes each

---

[24]*APB Opinion No. 11,* par. 63.

year. For example, notice in the first table that deferred income taxes arising in 1982 were $50,301,000; this amount is detailed in the second table, which indicates the timing differences that contributed to the $50,301,000. The third table explains why Pennzoil's effective tax rate (i.e., the percentage of tax expense to pretax-accounting income in the income statement) is less than the statutory rate of 46%.

The final two disclosures are that Pennzoil takes investment tax credit into income currently (i.e., it uses the flow-through method) and that a contingency related to an Internal Revenue Service (IRS) examination concerning tax returns of 1971–1978 exists. The company's assessment of this contingency is that it will not have a material impact on the reported results of operations.

EXHIBIT 18–16
Pennzoil Company
Example Income Tax Disclosures

(2) Federal and Foreign Income Tax—

Federal and foreign income tax expense consisted of the following:

| | Year Ended December 31 | | |
	1982	1981	1980
	(Expressed in thousands)		
Current			
United States	$ 25,336	$ 54,062	$106,168
Foreign	22,022	17,410	18,292
Deferred	50,301	70,993	53,286
Investment tax credit	(25,478)	(19,270)	(13,988)
	$ 72,181	$123,195	$163,758

Deferred federal income tax provisions result from timing differences in the recognition of revenue and expense for tax and financial reporting purposes. The sources of these differences and the tax effect of each are as follows:

| | Year Ended December 31 | | |
	1982	1981	1980
	(Expressed in thousands)		
Intangible exploration and development costs deducted for tax purposes over amortization for financial purposes	$ 34,846	$ 45,587	$ 35,595
Interest capitalized for financial purposes, but deducted for tax purposes, over amortization for financial purposes	13,959	12,119	1,125
Depreciation deducted for tax purposes over amount recorded for financial purposes	19,086	8,303	14,724
Mining exploration, development and plant costs deducted for tax purposes over amortization for financial purposes	5,954	2,668	915
Benefit of charitable contribution recognized for financial purposes not currently deductible for tax purposes	(16,623)	—	—
Other, net	(6,921)	2,316	927
	$ 50,301	$ 70,993	$ 53,286

A reconciliation of the statutory federal income tax rate to the effective income tax rate follows:

	Year Ended December 31		
	1982	1981	1980
Statutory rate	46.0 %	46.0 %	46.0 %
Increases (reductions) resulting from			
Percentage depletion			
in excess of cost basis	(5.0)	(5.9)	(9.1)
Investment tax credit	(9.8)	(5.6)	(3.0)
Land contribution	(7.6)	—	—
Other, net	4.1	1.2	.8
Effective rate	27.7 %	35.7 %	34.7 %

Pennzoil follows the practice of taking investment tax credits into income currently.

In connection with the examination of the federal income tax returns for the years 1971 through 1978, the District Director of Internal Revenue has proposed assessments of additional tax. Pennzoil has challenged certain of these proposed adjustments which are now pending before higher administrative levels of the Internal Revenue Service. Pennzoil believes that the final resolution of the issues raised will not have a material effect on reported results of operations.

SOURCE: Pennzoil Company, 1982 Annual Report.

CONCLUDING REMARKS

Income taxes have a significant impact on the financial position and results of operations of business enterprises. Accounting for income taxes represents a unique blend of generally accepted accounting principles and legal compliance.

The amount of income taxes that the enterprise must ultimately pay is determined within the framework of relevant income tax laws. The presentation of income taxes in the financial statements is governed by generally accepted accounting principles. The application of these principles frequently results in the recognition of income taxes in a different manner than they are recognized for purposes of satisfying the enterprise's ongoing responsibility to pay income taxes to governmental bodies. These differences stem primarily from different underlying objectives of legal taxation and financial reporting.

The presentation of income taxes in this chapter has intentionally avoided some complications in order to concentrate on a basic understanding of the major problem areas encountered in accounting for income taxes. Perhaps the major simplification is the treatment of intraperiod income tax allocation, interperiod income tax allocation, operating-loss carrybacks, and carryforwards, and the investment tax credit as separate topics. In reality all of these may exist in a given set of circumstances, thereby complicating the accounting for income taxes considerably. For example, the investment tax credit may be recognized in income tax expense during the same period in which timing differences originate and reverse. Also, the existence of deferred income tax credits when an operating-loss carryback is recognized imposes an additional complication beyond the scope of this text.

The specific standards of accounting for income taxes are continuously developing as new situations concerning the imposition of income taxes emerge. New aspects of income taxation, such as the appearance of the investment tax credit in the early 1960s and the introduction of the ACRS in 1981, pose new and challenging problems for financial reporting. The reporting of income taxes will continue to be significant, and we can predict that financial reporting of income taxes will continue to change as the concepts underlying income taxation and financial reporting grow farther apart.

KEY POINTS

1.   Several major problem areas exist in accounting for income taxes. In this chapter we have considered the following areas: intraperiod income tax allocation, interperiod income tax allocation, operating-loss car-

rybacks and carryforwards, investment tax credit, and financial-statement disclosure.

2.   Certain items are separately presented in the financial statements in order to isolate their impact

more clearly for users of those statements. Extraordinary items and prior period adjustments are examples of these items that are presented on a net-of-tax basis.

3. Amounts of revenues and expenses recognized in an accounting period for financial reporting purposes and for income tax purposes may not be the same because of differences in the underlying objectives of the two systems of accounting. In applying the matching principle, interperiod income tax allocation is necessary so that the income tax expense recognized in the determination of income will relate to the revenues and other expenses recognized in the determination of that income.

4. Permanent differences result from differences in definitions of revenues and expenses between financial reporting and income tax accounting. Timing differences result from differences in the timing or pattern of the recognition of revenues and expenses. Timing differences give rise to deferred income tax accounts that are presented in the balance sheet as assets and liabilities.

5. Whereas timing differences originate in one accounting period, they reverse in other accounting periods. As timing differences originate, deferred income taxes are established under the deferred method at income tax rates in effect at that time. As these differences reverse in future accounting periods, they may be accounted for at their originating rate (gross-change method) or at the rate in effect at the time of their reversal (net-change method).

6. Interperiod income tax allocation results in an amount of income tax expense that is usually not the same as the amount of income tax paid for the same accounting period. The tax effects of the resulting timing differences are presented in the balance sheet as net current and net noncurrent amounts.

7. Comprehensive interperiod income tax allocation under the deferred method is required under current generally accepted accounting principles. Several alternatives exist, however, that have theoretical or practical merit. Alternatives to comprehensive interperiod allocation include partial allocation and nonallocation. Alternatives to the deferred method of applying interperiod income tax allocation include the liability and the net-of-tax methods.

8. Operating-loss carrybacks and carryforwards allow the loss of one accounting period to be used to reduce taxes that have already been paid (carrybacks) or that will otherwise have to be paid in the future (carryforwards). We recognize the benefits of carrybacks in the loss period since they give rise to immediate refund claims from the government. Since carryforwards depend on future taxable income within a specified period, they are speculative in nature and we usually defer their recognition until future periods when that income is actually earned and the uncertainty is eliminated.

9. The investment tax credit provides for a reduction in income tax if investments in qualifying assets are made. The resulting reduction in income tax expense can be recognized by either the deferred method, whereby the reduced income tax expense is spread over the life of the asset, or the flow-through method, whereby income tax expense is reduced in the period in which the qualifying asset is acquired.

10. Accounting for the investment tax credit has resulted in considerable controversy, leaving observers with the clear understanding that the government has the power to dictate accounting principles if Congress or other appropriate bodies determine that it is preferable to do so. Despite the fact that the APB preferred the deferred method of accounting for the investment tax credit, because of governmental intervention both the deferred and flow-through methods are currently acceptable.

11. Several financial-statement disclosure requirements provide users of the statements with information about the impact of income taxes on the enterprise's financial position and on the results of operations.

APPENDIX A EXAMPLES OF TIMING DIFFERENCES

Examples of timing differences are listed in *APB Opinion No. 11*. Selected items from this list are presented below to demonstrate the wide variety of situations that can result in differences between pretax-accounting income subject to income tax and taxable income.

Revenues or gains that are taxed after accrued for accounting purposes:

1. Profits on installment sales are recorded in accounts at date of sale and reported in tax returns later when collected.

2. Revenues on long-term contracts are recorded in accounts on percentage-of-completion basis and reported in tax returns on a completed-contract basis.
3. Revenue from leasing activities as recorded in a lessor's accounts is based on the financing method of accounting, and it exceeds the rent less depreciation that is reported in tax returns in the early years of a lease.

Expenses or losses that are deducted for tax purposes after accrued for accounting purposes:

1. Estimated costs of guarantees and product-warranty contracts are recorded in accounts at date of sale and later deducted in tax returns when paid.
2. Expenses for deferred compensation, profit sharing, bonuses, and vacation and severance pay are recorded in accounts when accrued for the applicable period and later deducted in tax returns when paid.
3. Expenses for pension costs are recorded in accounts when accrued for the applicable period and deducted in tax returns for later periods when contributed to the pension plan.
4. Estimated losses on inventories and purchase commitments are recorded in accounts when reasonably anticipated and later deducted in tax returns when realized.
5. Estimated losses on disposal of facilities and discontinuing or relocating operations are recorded in accounts when anticipated and determinable and later are deducted in tax returns when losses or costs are incurred.
6. Estimated expenses of settling pending lawsuits and claims are recorded in accounts when reasonably ascertainable and deducted in tax returns later when paid.
7. Provisions for major repairs and maintenance are accrued in accounts on a systematic basis and deducted in tax returns later when paid.
8. Organization costs are written off in accounts as incurred and amortized in tax returns.

Revenues or gains that are taxed before accrued for accounting purposes:

1. Rent and royalties are taxed when collected and deferred in accounts to later periods when earned.
2. Fees, dues, and service contracts are taxed when

collected and deferred in accounts to later periods when earned.
3. Profits on intercompany transactions are taxed when reported in separate returns, and those on assets remaining within the group are eliminated in consolidated financial statements.
4. Gains on sales of property leased back are taxed at date of sale and deferred in accounts and amortized during the term of lease.

Expenses or losses that are deducted for tax purposes before accrued for accounting purposes:

1. Interest and taxes during construction are deducted in tax returns when incurred and included in the cost of assets in accounts.

Whether a particular difference between pretax-accounting income and taxable income is a timing difference or a permanent difference may not be readily apparent. Several situations giving rise to this question and the resolution of the question in current accounting pronouncements are summarized below:

Where the equity method is used for non-controlling investments in common stock, accounting income usually exceeds the income from dividends received (the amount included in taxable income). Differences of this type are considered to be timing differences, subject to interperiod tax allocation procedures.[25]

Where a parent-subsidiary relationship exists (i.e., a greater than 50% ownership of stock by the parent), undistributed earnings of the subsidiary should be treated as a timing difference by the parent unless it can be demonstrated that (1) the earnings have been indefinitely invested by the subsidiary in a manner that precludes distribution to the parent or (2) the earnings will be transferred to the parent in a tax-free liquidation.[26]

Special provisions of income tax allow savings and loan associations to reduce taxable income by a specified amount as a reserve for the protection of depositors. This creates a difference between pretax accounting income and taxable income which could possibly reverse in some future period. Due to the fact that this reversal is highly unlikely, however, this difference should generally be treated as a permanent difference and no income taxes provided.[27]

---

[25]*APB Opinion No. 24,* "Accounting for Income Taxes—Investments in Common Stock Accounted for by the Equity Method (Other Than Subsidiaries and Corporate Joint Ventures)," 1971, par. 7.
[26]*APB Opinion No. 23,* "Accounting for Income Taxes—Special Areas," 1971, pars. 10–12.
[27]*APB Opinion No. 23,* par. 23.

IMPACT OF ECONOMIC RECOVERY ACT OF 1981 ON INTERPERIOD INCOME TAX ALLOCATION

APPENDIX B

The Economic Recovery Act of 1981, which became law on August 13, 1981, made many significant changes in income taxes paid by individuals and business enterprises. The Accelerated Cost Recovery System (ACRS), one of the most significant sections of this law, permits accelerated recovery of the cost of assets acquired in 1981 or later over predetermined recovery periods that are generally shorter than the estimated useful lives of the same assets. Under the ACRS, most assets are classified into one of four categories, as follows: 3-year property, 5-year property, 10-year property, and 15-year property. The law indicates the types of property that qualify for each category and also indicates the percentage of the asset's cost that can be deducted each year in determining the enterprise's taxable income.

The cost recovery percentages under ACRS approximate declining-balance depreciation at 150% of the straight-line rate. ACRS uses a half-year convention (one-half year's write-off in the year of acquisition) and disregards salvage value. Taxpayers can elect to use straight-line depreciation rather than the appropriate ACRS percentages. The cost recovery percentages for the 3-year, 5-year and 10-year categories are presented in Exhibit 18–17. The 15-year category applies to real property, and the rates vary, depending on the month

in which the asset was acquired. Assets acquired before 1981 continue to be depreciated by the methods used for those assets before ACRS came into existence.

To illustrate ACRS, assume that a $100,000 asset comes under the 3-year category; it would be written off as a deduction for income tax purposes as follows:

Year 1	25% × $100,000 =	$ 25,000
Year 2	38% × $100,000 =	38,000
Year 3	37% × $100,000 =	37,000
		$100,000

This calculation would be used regardless of the estimated useful life of the property or the residual value expected at the end of that useful life.

A question has been raised concerning the impact of the ACRS provisions in the Economic Recovery Act of 1981 on the presentation of income tax information in financial statements. Specifically, the impact of the ACRS percentages on interperiod income tax allocation has interesting implications.

In the opinion of the authors, the Accelerated Cost Recovery System represents another significant difference between income tax reporting and financial reporting that will require interperiod allocation of income taxes where it was not applied in the past. For a particular asset the length of the cost recovery period and the allowable percentages for each year under the ACRS may bear little relationship to the asset's useful life or the pattern of the decline in usefulness to the reporting enterprise. Before ACRS, differences in depreciation between income tax reporting and financial reporting were sometimes ignored as immaterial, or depreciation for income tax and financial reporting purposes was forced to coincide by the use of tax lives and methods for financial statements. These alternatives appear to be less acceptable under ACRS because of the more significant differences that may arise between the two purposes. The cash flow advantages of rapid cost recovery under ACRS, coupled with the requirements of generally accepted accounting princi-

---

EXHIBIT 18–17
Accelerated Cost Recovery Rates

Recovery Year	Percentage of Cost Recovered		
	3-year	5-year	10-year
1	25	15	8
2	38	22	14
3	37	21	12
4	—	21	10
5	—	21	10
6	—	—	10
7	—	—	9
8	—	—	9
9	—	—	9
10	—	—	9

ples to allocate cost over the useful life in a systematic and rational manner, will likely result in more significant timing differences and, thus, an increase in situations requiring interperiod income tax allocation. Also, as Chapter 12 discusses, as ACRS becomes fully implemented and as assets being depreciated by traditional accounting methods for income tax purposes are replaced, we will likely see a decline in the use of accelerated depreciation methods in the financial statements. The most likely combination of income tax and financial reporting methods will be ACRS and straight-line, respectively.

QUESTIONS

18–1 Explain the significance of the conclusion that income taxes are a determinant of income as opposed to a distribution of income.

18–2 Discuss the significance of the matching principle and going-concern assumption as a basis for accounting for income taxes.

18–3 What is the basic difference between interperiod and intraperiod income tax allocation? Explain why both procedures may be required for the same reporting enterprise.

18–4 How does legal compliance affect the financial-statement presentation of income taxes?

18–5 List five types of transactions and events that give rise to intraperiod income tax allocation.

18–6 What is the basic objective of intraperiod income tax allocation?

18–7 How is it possible for pretax-accounting income and income tax expense to be different from taxable income and income tax payable?

18–8 Distinguish between permanent and timing differences. Which type results in differences between pretax-accounting income and taxable income?

18–9 Give two examples of permanent differences, indicating how they result in a permanent difference between pretax-accounting income and taxable income.

18–10 Give two examples of timing differences, indicating how they result in a temporary difference between pretax-accounting income and taxable income.

18–11 Explain the meaning of the term "comprehensive interperiod income tax allocation under the deferred method."

18–12 Describe the difference in accounting for the reversal of timing differences under the gross-change and net-change methods.

18–13 Describe the difference between an operating-loss carryback and an operating-loss carryforward.

18–14 State briefly the accounting principles that govern the recognition of operating-loss carrybacks and carryforwards in accounting income.

18–15 Explain the difference in concepts underlying the deferred (cost reduction) and the flow-through (tax reduction) methods of accounting for the investment tax credit.

18–16 Describe the accounting procedure that is used in recognizing the investment tax credit under the deferred method. Explain how this procedure differs from the procedure used in the flow-through method of recognizing the investment tax credit.

18–17 How should the deferred income tax account(s) be presented in the balance sheet of a company that applies the concept of interperiod income tax allocation?

18–18 Explain the requirement that the components of the income tax expense must be disclosed in the financial statements or the related notes.

18–19 One of the following requires intraperiod tax allocation. Identify the correct answer.

[a] That portion of dividends reduced by the dividends-received deduction by corporations under existing federal income tax law.

[b] The excess of accelerated depreciation used for tax purposes over straight-line depreciation used for financial reporting purposes.

[c] Extraordinary gains or losses as defined by the APB.

[d] All differences between taxable income and financial-statement earnings.

(AICPA adapted)

18–20 The amount of income tax applicable to an item that must be reported by using intraperiod income tax allocation is computed:

[a] By multiplying the amount of the item by the effective income tax rate.

[b] By obtaining the difference between the tax based on taxable income without including the item and the tax based on taxable income including the item.

[c] By obtaining the difference between the tax that is based on the amount of the item that is used for financial reporting and the tax that is based on the amount of the item that is used in computing taxable income.

[d] By multiplying the amount of the item by the difference between the effective income tax rate and the statutory income tax rate.

(AICPA adapted)

18–21 Interperiod income-tax allocation in corporate financial statements can best be justified by one of the following accounting concepts or principles. Identify the correct answer.

[a] Conservatism
[b] Matching
[c] Realization
[d] Objectivity

(AICPA adapted)

18–22 A company has four Deferred Income Tax accounts arising from timing differences involving: (1) current assets; (2) noncurrent assets; (3) current liabilities; and (4) noncurrent liabilities. The presentation of these four Deferred Income Tax accounts in the statement of financial position should be shown as one of the following. Identify the correct answer.

[a] A single net amount.
[b] A net current and a net noncurrent amount.
[c] Four accounts with no netting permitted.
[d] Valuation adjustments of the related assets and liabilities that gave rise to the deferred tax.

(AICPA adapted)

18–23 One of the following situations would require use of interperiod tax allocation procedures. Identify the correct answer.

[a] Research and development costs are deducted for income tax purposes in the year incurred.
[b] A material gain on a sale-leaseback transaction is taxed in the year of sale.

[c] Unamortized discount and call premium on an early extinguishment of debt are deducted for income tax purposes in the year of extinguishment.
[d] The amount of a material loss on the sale of an asset differs for tax and accounting purposes because of different bases for this asset. The different bases are due to a quasi reorganization recognized for accounting but not for income tax purposes.

(AICPA adapted)

18–24 Both parts of this question are based on the following information:

A company is required to disclose, usually in the footnotes to its financial statements, two main points regarding income taxes. First, it must disclose the factors causing a deferred tax expense, if any. Second, it must disclose the factors causing a difference, if any, between a tax-expense figure computed at the statutory rates and its actual tax expense.

Part 1. One of the following would cause a deferred tax expense. Identify the correct answer.

[a] Amortization of goodwill.
[b] Use of equity method where undistributed earnings of a 30%-owned investee are related to probable future dividends.
[c] Premiums paid on insurance carried by company (beneficiary) on its officers.
[d] Income taxed at capital-gains rates.

Part 2. "Differences between taxable income and pretax-accounting income arising from transactions that, under applicable tax laws and regulations, will not be offset by corresponding differences or turnaround in future periods" is a definition of which one of the following? Identify the correct answer.

[a] Permanent differences
[b] Timing differences
[c] Intraperiod tax allocation
[d] Interperiod tax allocation

(AICPA adapted)

CASES

C18–1 This case consists of two *independent* parts.

Part 1. In preparing financial statements a corporation is expected to follow the practice of comprehensive income tax allocation. At various times three methods of allocation have been used: the deferred method, the liability method, and the net-of-tax method.

Instructions

[a] Discuss the theoretical justification for interperiod income tax allocation. (Do not discuss intraperiod tax allocation.)
[b] Describe briefly each of the above three methods of tax allocation and give reasons why each method is acceptable or unacceptable.

Part 2. The following differences enter into the reconciliation of financial net income and taxable income of A. P. Baxter Corporation for the current year.

[1] Tax depreciation exceeds book depreciation by $30,000.

[2] Estimated warranty costs of $6,000 applicable to the current year's sales have not been paid.

[3] Unearned rent revenue of $25,000 was deferred on the books but appropriately included in taxable income.

[4] A book expense of $2,000 for life insurance premiums on officers' lives is not allowed as a deduction on the tax return.

[5] Gross profit of $80,000 was excluded from taxable income because Baxter had appropriately elected the installment sale method for tax reporting while recognizing all gross profit from installment sales at the time of the sale for financial reporting.

Instructions

Consider each reconciling item independently of all others and explain whether each item would enter into the calculation of income taxes to be allocated. For any which are included in the income tax allocation calculation, explain the effect of the item on the current year's income tax expense and how the amount would be reported on the balance sheet. (Tax allocation calculations are not required.)

(AICPA adapted)

C18–2 Although the Internal Revenue Code requires a taxpayer to use the same accounting method for computing taxable income as that used in keeping the taxpayer's books, there are significant differences in concept and principle between accounting for federal income taxes and accounting for financial reporting.

Instructions

[a] Compare and contrast the doctrine of constructive receipt of income tax accounting with the concept(s) of revenue recognition for financial reporting purposes.

[b] Through the application of income tax allocation, financial accounting seeks to reconcile the differences between tax accounting and financial accounting. Explain the underlying reasons for: (1) interperiod income tax allocation, and (2) intraperiod income tax allocation.

[c] Compare and contrast the accounting treatment of an involuntary conversion (1) in the determination of taxable income and (2) in the determination of income for financial reporting.

(AICPA adapted)

C18–3 Accounting for income taxes is complicated by the fact that a loss of one year may be used to reduce income taxes which have been paid or would otherwise be paid in another year.

Instructions

The following questions address this unique feature of accounting for income taxes:

[a] Describe "operating-loss carryback" and "operating-loss carryforward." Carefully distinguish between the two in your discussion.

[b] Describe the difference in the accounting treatment of loss carrybacks and carryforwards under normal circumstances, justifying the differences in accounting for the two.

[c] Under certain unusual circumstances, the normal accounting treatment for operating-loss carryforwards is not followed. Indicate the circumstances and justification for this departure.

[d] Explain the income statement presentation of operating-loss carrybacks and operating-loss carryforwards in both the usual and the unusual circumstances described in [b] and [c].

EXERCISES

E18–1 In 1984 West Company accrued, for financial statement purposes, estimated losses of $800,000 on the disposal of unused plant facilities. These losses are not deductible for income tax purposes until the assets are sold. The facilities were sold in March 1985. Also, in 1984 West paid $100,000 in premiums on officers' life insurance for which the company is the beneficiary. The effective income tax rate is 40%.

Instructions

Determine the amount of deferred income taxes included in the provision for income taxes in West's income statement for the year ended December 31, 1984.

(AICPA adapted)

E18–2 Raff Company purchased a machine on January 1, 1980, for $5,500,000. The machine has an estimated useful life of 10 years and no salvage value. The machine is being depreciated under the sum-of-the-years'-digits method for income tax reporting and under the straight-line method for financial statement reporting. The income tax rate is 48% for 1980 and 45% for 1981.

Instructions

[a] Compute the amount of deferred taxes which should be charged to Raff's 1980 income statement.
[b] Compute the amount of deferred taxes which should appear in Raff's 1981 balance sheet.

(AICPA adapted)

E18–3 Frazier Manufacturing Company reports $85,000 income before income tax for 1981. This amount includes the following items:
[1] Straight-line depreciation on equipment acquired at the beginning of 1980. The equipment cost $100,000, has an estimated 10-year life, and has an estimated salvage value of 10% of its original cost.
[2] Interest on municipal security investments of $7,500.

Instructions

Determine the income tax expense and income tax liability for 1981. Frazier uses double-declining balance depreciation for tax purposes. The effective income tax rate is 42%.

E18–4 Dugan Enterprises has determined its taxable income for 1985 to be $76,000. This amount includes the following timing differences between taxable and accounting income:
[1] Bad-debt write-offs included in the $76,000 amount to $78,000. The Allowance for Doubtful Accounts account in the company's general ledger reveals the following activity during 1985:

Beginning balance, 1985	$125,000
Write-off of specific uncollectible accounts	(78,000)
	47,000
Estimated uncollectibles, 1985	82,000
Ending balance, 1985	$129,000

Uncollectible accounts are not deducted for income tax purposes until they are written off.
[2] Rent revenue of $120,000 in 1985 has been included in taxable income. Of this amount, $30,000

has been deferred for financial reporting purposes to 1986.

Instructions

Compute the tax expense for 1985 and the tax liability at the end of 1985, assuming a 45% income tax rate.

E18–5 Darnell Company reported the following figures for the years 1983, 1984, and 1985:

	1983	1984	1985
Income (loss) before income tax	$100,000	$130,000	$(170,000)
Income tax rate	42%	44%	46%

The entire loss of 1985 is available to offset income taxes paid or becoming payable. No permanent or timing differences exist in any of the three years.

Instructions

Prepare the income statement for each year, beginning with "income (loss) before income tax." Assume the carryback/carryforward option is employed.

E18–6 Parnell Company reported the following figures for the years 1983 and 1984:

	1983	1984
Income (loss) before income tax	$257,000	$(363,000)
Income tax rate	48%	46%

The entire loss is available to offset income taxes paid or becoming payable. No permanent or timing differences exist in either of the years.

Instructions

[a] Prepare the income statement for each year, beginning with "income (loss) before income tax," applying the carryback/carryforward option.
[b] What amount of 1984 loss is available for carryforward purposes? When can this amount be recognized and at what tax rate? How will the carryforward be classified in the income statement when it is recognized?

E18–7 Income and loss figures, accompanied by income tax rates, for Montana Supply Company for the first four years of operations are as follows:

	1982	1983	1984	1985
Income (loss) before income tax	$175,000	$182,000	$(405,000)	$121,000
Income tax rate	46%	42%	48%	46%

The entire loss in 1984 is available to reduce income taxes paid or that would otherwise be paid. No permanent or timing differences exist in any of the years.

Instructions

Prepare the income statement for each year, beginning with "income (loss) before income tax," applying the carryback/carryforward option.

E18–8   During 1985 McClain Company's taxable income and pretax-accounting income are the same amount except for the following items:

	Pretax Accounting Income	Taxable Income
Rent income	$37,500 earned during 1985	$25,000 (of the $37,500 earned) collected in cash during 1985
Depreciation expense (on assets acquired in 1979 and 1980)	$19,800 under straight-line method during 1985	$30,100 under double-declining balance during 1985
Warranty expense	$18,200 accrued on estimated basis during 1985	$20,900 paid during 1985 ($4,200 for items sold before 1985)

Before considering the above items, income for 1985 is $125,000. The income tax rate was 45% for all years prior to 1985. The rate for 1985 is 48%.

Instructions

Prepare the general journal entry to record the tax accrual for 1985, assuming the net-change method is used in accounting for the reversal of timing differences. Include supporting computations.

E18–9   Harmon Products, Inc., reports $876,000 pretax-accounting income for 1983. Included in this amount are the following items:

[1] Amortization of goodwill, $25,000.
[2] Warranty expense accrued, $70,000. For tax purposes, the cash paid for warranty work is deductible. During 1983 $60,000 was paid, of which $45,000 related to 1983 sales and the remainder to sales of prior years.
[3] Depreciation expense, $88,000, computed by the straight-line method. For tax purposes, the double-declining balance method is used and results in $148,000 depreciation deductible in 1983. No reversal of prior year timing differences took place. (The related assets were acquired in 1980.)

The income tax rate for 1983 is 45%. The rate for all prior years was 42%.

Instructions

Prepare the general journal entry to record the tax accrual for 1983, assuming the gross-change method is used in accounting for the reversal of timing differences. Include supporting computations.

E18–10   Burns Company, an installment seller of furniture, records sales on the accrual basis for financial reporting purposes and on the installment method for tax purposes. As a result, $50,000 of deferred income taxes have been accrued at December 31, 1985. In accordance with trade practice, installment accounts receivable from customers are shown as current assets, although the average collection period is approximately three years.

At December 31, 1985, Burns Company has recorded a $20,000 deferred income tax debit arising from a book accrual of noncurrent deferred compensation expense which is not presently tax deductible. Also at December 31, 1985, Burns has accrued $15,000 of deferred income taxes resulting from the use of accelerated depreciation for tax purposes and straight-line depreciation for financial reporting purposes. The assets giving rise to these deferred income taxes were acquired in 1980.

Instructions

Prepare the appropriate balance sheet presentation of deferred taxes, indicating the specific items and dollar amounts.

(AICPA adapted)

E18–11   Pacter Company, an installment seller, earns a $300 pretax gross profit on each sale. For financial reporting purposes, the entire $300 is recognized at the time of sale, but for income tax purposes the installment method of accounting is used.

Assume Pacter makes one sale in 1984, another sale in 1985, and a third sale in 1986. In each case, one-third of the gross sales price is collected in the year of sale, one-third in the following year, and the final installment in the third year.

Instructions

[a] Assuming an income tax rate of 40%, determine the amount that should be shown on Pacter's December 31, 1986, balance sheet as "deferred income taxes" relative to the three sales.

[b] Independent of your answer to [a], assume that on January 1, 1986, the tax rate increased from 40% to 45%. What is the appropriate amount to report as deferred income taxes under the gross-change method on Pacter's December 31, 1986, balance sheet?

(AICPA adapted)

E18–12 Freeman Manufacturing Company acquired several items of machinery costing a total of $175,000 during 1983. The machinery is expected to be used by the company for 10 years. The machinery qualifies for the 10% investment tax credit, reducing taxes paid in 1983 by $17,500. Income before income tax for 1983 and 1984 is $98,500 and $125,600, respectively. No additional assets qualifying for the investment credit are acquired in 1984. The income tax rate for both years was 48%.

Instructions

Determine the amount of income tax expense to be presented in the income statement in 1983 and 1984 under the following methods of accounting for the investment tax credit:

[a] Tax reduction (flow-through) method.
[b] Cost reduction (deferred) method.

E18–13 Fortune Company acquired a computer for $262,000 in early 1984. The computer is expected to be useful for 20 years. It is subject to a 10% investment tax credit, reducing taxes which would otherwise have been paid in 1984. Income before income taxes in 1984 totaled $192,500, which is subject to a 46% income tax rate. The company intends to depreciate the computer by the straight-line method with no salvage value for both book and tax purposes.

Instructions

Prepare general journal entries under both the deferred and the flow-through methods for all

transactions and events relating to the computer, including the impact of the acquisition on income tax expense.

E18–14 Tucker Instruments, Inc., has properly determined its taxable income for 1985 to be $427,850. There are no permanent or timing differences between taxable and accounting income. Included in taxable income is a gain of $110,000 resulting from a transaction that will be presented as "extraordinary" in the 1985 income statement. The appropriate income tax rate for the extraordinary item is 25%. The appropriate income tax rate for all other items is 48%.

Instructions

[a] Determine the income tax expense to be included in the 1985 income statement.

[b] Describe the disclosure of the extraordinary gain to be included in the 1985 income statement.

E18–15 Rodriguez Company has determined the following items for 1985:

Income before income tax	$158,500
Income (loss) items not included in income before income tax	
Correction of error in 1984 financial statements	7,500
Extraordinary loss	(16,250)
Retained earnings, Jan. 1, 1985, as previously stated	400,000
Dividends declared during 1985	50,000
Appropriate income tax rate	40%

There are no permanent or timing differences between taxable and accounting income. The company's reporting period is January 1–December 31.

Instructions

[a] Prepare the income statement, beginning with "income before income tax," for 1985, giving proper recognition to intraperiod income tax allocation requirements.

[b] Prepare the retained earnings statement for 1985, giving proper recognition to intraperiod income tax allocation requirements.

E18–16 Lexington Company applies the concepts of comprehensive interperiod income tax allocation to timing differences between its taxable income and accounting income. Timing differences arise from two sources:

[1] Differences resulting from the use of accelerated cost recovery for tax purposes and straight-line depre-

ciation for accounting purposes.

[2] Differences resulting from the use of the installment sales method for tax purposes and the accrual method for accounting purposes.

Information related to timing differences at the end of 1985 is as follows:

	Attributable to		
	Periods Prior to 1985	1985	Total
Attributable to installment sales	$120,000	$40,000	$160,000
Attributable to accelerated cost recovery	185,000	50,000	235,000

Taxable income for 1985 was $800,000. The income tax rate applicable to all periods is 46%.

Instructions

[a] Determine the information which should be presented in the balance sheet at the end of 1985 relative to income taxes.

[b] Determine the information which should be presented in the 1985 income statement relative to income taxes.

Note: In applying the concepts of interperiod income tax allocation, the asset write-off under the Accelerated Cost Recovery System (ACRS) may be treated the same as accelerated depreciation when compared to straight-line depreciation to determine the amount of the timing difference.

E18-17 In 1984 Darby Company paid annual premiums of $80,000 on officers' life insurance, for which the company is the beneficiary, and received interest income of $120,000 on municipal obligations. Also in 1984 Darby collected $200,000 in royalties. For income tax purposes the royalties are taxed when collected. For financial reporting purposes, the royalties are recognized as income in the period earned. The unearned portion of the royalties collected in 1984 amounted to $150,000 at December 31, 1984. This amount will be earned in 1985. Darby Company's income tax rate is 46%.

Instructions

[a] Determine the amount of deferred income taxes at the end of 1984, indicating whether the item is current or noncurrent and a debit or credit balance.

[b] Explain your treatment of the insurance premiums, interest on municipal securities, and royalty income in [a].

(AICPA adapted)

E18-18 Osburn Company commenced operations on January 1, 1984. For the year ended December 31, 1984, Osburn had pretax-accounting income of $1,500,000, after accruing estimated warranty expense of $570,000. Osburn's effective income tax rate was 40%, resulting in tax payable of $624,000.

Instructions

Determine the amount of actual warranty payments made in 1984, assuming that these payments are deducted for income tax purposes only when they are paid.

(AICPA adapted)

E18-19 (Appendix B) Las Brazas Company acquired assets at the beginning of 1981 that are subject to cost recovery over a three-year period for income tax purposes under the Accelerated Cost Recovery System. The company expects the $130,000 in assets to be useful for five years with no salvage value. Straight-line depreciation will be used for financial-reporting purposes. The company's income tax rate is 42%.

Instructions

Determine the amount of deferred income taxes to be presented in the balance sheet at the end of each of the five years in the assets' lives.

E18-20 (Appendix B) San Francisco Manufacturing Company acquired an asset for $150,000 in 1983 that is subject to cost recovery over a five-year period for income tax purposes under the Accelerated Cost Recovery System. The company plans to depreciate the asset over its estimated useful life of eight years by the straight-line method, taking a full year's depreciation in 1983. The company's income tax rate is 46%.

Income before depreciation and income tax expense for 1983 and 1984 has been correctly determined as follows:

1983	$125,000
1984	137,500

Instructions

Prepare the income tax accrual for 1983 and 1984, including the recognition of deferred income taxes.

P18–1 Joker Company purchases a machine at the beginning of 1980 for $120,000. The machine is expected to be used for five years and will have no residual value at the end of its life. The effective income tax rate throughout this period is 45%. Joker Company uses sum-of-the-years'-digits depreciation for tax purposes and straight-line depreciation for financial reporting purposes.

Income figures, before depreciation and income taxes, are as follows for the years 1980–1984:

1980	$100,000
1981	125,000
1982	145,000
1983	132,000
1984	119,000

Instructions

[a] Prepare schedules determining the tax expense and the tax liability for each year, 1980–1984.
[b] Prepare general journal entries to record the income tax accrual on December 31, the last day of the fiscal year, for 1980–1984.
[c] Identify the deferred tax amounts to be presented in the balance sheet for 1980–1984.

P18–2 Ingram Production Company has determined its income before income tax for 1985 to be $187,200. Several items included in this amount are subject to different treatment in the company's income tax return. These items are described as follows:
[1] Revenues include interest on municipal securities of $1,950.
[2] Revenues include $22,500 on installment sales which are not to be recognized for tax purposes until collected in 1986.
[3] Revenues exclude $15,500 of rents collected in advance but deferred for income statement purposes until 1986.
[4] Expenses include $2,700 in premiums on key company executives' life insurance policies for which the company is beneficiary.
[5] Expenses include depreciation of $78,000 based on the straight-line method. Depreciation for tax purposes is computed by the Accelerated Cost Recovery System and totals $132,500 for 1985. (The differences between the ACRS write-off and straight-line depreciation should be treated the same as a timing difference resulting from the use of accelerated and straight-line

depreciation.)
[6] Expenses include an accrual of $8,250 for warranties on products sold which have not been paid at the end of 1985.

The appropriate income tax rate is 40%.

Instructions

Determine the income tax expense for 1985 and the income tax liability at the end of 1985, assuming that there are no reversals of timing differences during 1985.

P18–3 Schultz Company is preparing its income and retained earnings statements for 1984 and 1985. The following selected information has been developed to date:

	Fiscal Year 1984	Fiscal Year 1985
Retained earnings, Nov. 1	$575,000	?
Pretax-accounting income	162,000	$135,000
Dividends declared	40,000	42,000
Extraordinary gain	18,700	—
Correction of prior periods— correction of error in 1983 financial statements (loss)	—	(24,000)
Effective income tax rate	48%	46%

There are no permanent or timing differences in 1984 or 1985. Schultz Company's fiscal year-end is October 31. The company had 100,000 shares of common stock outstanding throughout 1984 and 1985. The 1983 income tax rate was 48%. The items in the preceding schedule are included at their total amounts, before income tax consideration.

Instructions

[a] Prepare comparative statements of income and retained earnings for 1984 and 1985.
[b] Briefly explain the rationale for intraperiod income tax allocation.

P18–4 This problem consists of two *independent* parts.

Part 1. Early Manufacturing Company applies interperiod income tax allocation in determining its income tax expense. At the end of 1985, after the recognition of income tax expense, deferred income taxes related to three timing differences exist:

Nature of Timing Differences	Deferred Income Taxes Dr. (Cr.)	Current/ Noncurrent Classification
[1] Recognition of bad debts on estimated basis for financial reporting and by direct write-off method for income taxes	$ 5,420	Current
[2] Use of accelerated depreciation for income tax purposes and straight-line depreciation for financial reporting purposes	(17,580)	Noncurrent
[3] Recognition of income on percentage of completion method on long-term contracts for financial reporting and the completed contracts method for income tax purposes	(25,780)	Current

Instructions

Indicate the appropriate balance sheet disclosure of the deferred income tax accounts in the balance sheet at the end of 1985.

Part 2. Late Manufacturing Company determines its pretax-accounting income to be $755,000 for 1985. The statutory income tax rate is 46%. Additional items must be considered in arriving at the appropriate items to be included in the income statements and related notes:
[1] Interest on municipal securities of $45,000 is included in pretax-accounting income.
[2] A gain included in pretax-accounting income of $100,000 is taxable at 25% rather than the statutory rate.
[3] Accelerated Cost Recovery System (ACRS) write-off (used for income reporting purposes) exceeds straight-line depreciation (used for financial reporting purposes) by $72,500. (The difference between the ACRS write-off and straight-line depreciation should be treated the same as a timing difference resulting from the use of accelerated and straight-line depreciation.)

Instructions

Prepare the income statement presentation and related footnote disclosure of income taxes for 1985.

P18–5 Clinton Products, Inc., has accumulated $18,750 in current deferred taxes at December 31, 1983, the end of the company's fiscal year. This balance results from two timing differences:

Tax Effects of Timing Differences	Dr. (Cr.)
On excess of warranty costs recognized in the income statement over amounts deducted for tax purposes	$ 39,800
On excess of gross profit recognized on installment sales in the income statement over amounts included in taxable income	(21,050)
	$ 18,750

Income tax rates in effect during 1982, 1983, and 1984 were 40%, 45%, and 48%, respectively. Deferred taxes on all timing differences have been established at the tax rates in effect during 1982 and 1983, when the timing differences originated.

During 1984, the following activities concerning warranty costs and installment sales took place:

Warranty Costs

Recognized on estimated basis in 1984 for financial-statement purposes	$245,000
Deducted in 1984 for tax purposes	
Related to 1983 sales	$ 50,000
Related to 1984 sales	160,000
	$210,000

Installment Sales

Recognized in 1984 for financial-statement purposes	$162,000
Recognized in 1984 for tax purpose	
1982 sales	$ 10,000
1983 sales	25,000
1984 sales	80,000
	$115,000

The chief accountant of Clinton Products has properly determined that pretax-accounting income is $165,000 for 1984. This included permanent differences between tax accounting income as follows: (1) $18,200 interest on municipal securities, and (2) $28,800 amortization of goodwill.

Instructions

[a] Determine taxable income and the related income tax liability for 1984.

[b] Prepare the tax accrual at the end of 1984, assuming the *net-change method* is used. At what amount will deferred income taxes be presented in the 1984 balance sheet?

[c] Prepare the tax accrual at the end of 1984, assuming the *gross-change method* is used. Provide a schedule showing the appropriate balance in deferred income taxes at December 31, 1984.

P18–6 Causey Construction Company acquired heavy construction equipment in 1984 for $880,000, which qualified for the investment tax credit. The equipment is expected to be useful for 10 years, and straight-line depreciation will be used. Operating information for 1984 and 1985 is as follows:

	1984	1985
Pretax-accounting income	$982,500	$1,050,000
Income tax rate	48%	46%

Instructions

[a] Prepare all journal entries for 1984 and 1985 to account for equipment, depreciation, and income taxes. The flow-through (tax reduction) method is to be used in accounting for the investment tax credit.

[b] Prepare the journal entries in [a] that would be different if the deferred (cost reduction) method were used in accounting for the investment tax credit instead of the flow-through method.

[c] Compute the amount of net income that would be recognized in 1984 and 1985 under the flow-through method and the deferred method.

P18–7 Danielson Manufacturing Company, which began operations in 1983, continuously invests in equipment for use in its manufacturing process. This equipment qualifies for the investment tax credit (ITC), thereby reducing income taxes paid by 10% of the cost of qualifying assets in the year of acquisition.

Information related to the company during its first three years of operation is shown below:

	1983	1984	1985
Pretax-accounting income	$500,000	$528,000	$617,000
Income tax rate	48%	46%	46%
Equipment acquisitions eligible for ITC	$424,000	$370,000	$360,000
Estimated life of equipment acquisitions	8 years	10 years	9 years

Pretax-accounting income includes $18,000 amortization of goodwill in each year. In addition, 1984 pretax income includes $5,000 of interest received by Danielson on investments in municipal securities.

Instructions

[a] Prepare comparative income statements for each of the three years, assuming the deferred method of accounting for the investment tax credit is used. Include a detailed computation of the income tax expense in each year.

[b] The president of Danielson Manufacturing Company has asked you to determine the impact of the flow-through method on net income by preparing *pro forma* calculations for 1983, 1984, and 1985 under that method.

[1] Prepare *pro forma* calculations showing what net income would have been in 1983, 1984, and 1985 if the flow-through method had been used.

[2] Outline the items you would include in an explanation of the impact of the two alternative methods on the company's financial statements.

P18–8 Jim Myers Mobile Homes is trying to decide whether to exercise the carryback/carryforward option or the carryforward only option in recognizing the income tax refundable as a result of its 1985 loss (before income taxes) of $85,000. The company began operations in 1984 and reported an income before income taxes of $28,000 that year.

An important consideration is the impact of the two options on the income statement and the balance sheet for 1985 and 1986. While the company is optimistic about future operations, income is *not* believed to be assured. The company does expect, however, to report an income of approximately $75,000 in 1986 and anticipates profitable operations in future years.

The appropriate income tax rate for 1984 and 1985 was 42%. It is believed that the rate will increase to 48% in future years. The end of the company's financial reporting period is December 31.

Instructions

[a] Explain the difference between the carryback/carryforward option and the carryforward only option. Indicate why each might be a desirable alternative for Jim Myers Mobile Homes.

[b] Determine the balance sheet and income statement presentation for 1985 (based on actual data) and for 1986 (based on projected data) under each option in [a].

P18–9   Tillis Instrument Company reported net income (loss) before income taxes for 1983, 1984, and 1985 of $525,000, ($675,000), and $850,000, respectively. The income tax rate was 42% for 1983 and 1984 and 46% for 1985.

The potential benefit in terms of future taxes to be paid as a result of the $675,000 net loss in 1984 is *not* believed to be assured beyond a reasonable doubt.

Instructions

[a] Assume that Tillis Instrument Company chooses the carryback/carryforward option:
   [1] Prepare general journal entries to recognize income tax expense or refund in 1984 and 1985.
   [2] Prepare the income statement presentation for 1984 and 1985, beginning with "income (loss) before income tax."

[b] Independent of [a], assume that Tillis Instrument Company chooses the carryforward only option:
   [1] Prepare general journal entries to recognize income tax expense or refund in 1984 and 1985.
   [2] Prepare the income statement presentation for 1984 and 1985, beginning with "income (loss) before income tax."

P18–10 Dapper Dan Company is attempting to determine the appropriate tax amounts for its financial statements. Selected information is presented below.

Excess of revenues over expenses for 1981, before considering depreciation, bad debts, and amortization of goodwill: $185,000.

Year	Income Tax Rates
1981	45%
1980	40%
1979 and all previous years	35%

The following information concerns certain plant assets, accounts receivable, and goodwill:

Plant Asset.   On January 1, 1980, a plant asset was acquired for $600,000 which is being depreciated over its 10-year life by the straight-line method and by the double-declining balance method for tax purposes. Previously all assets had been depreciated by the straight-line method for both tax and financial-reporting purposes.

Accounts Receivable.   The company uses the allowance method of accounting for bad debts in the income statement and the direct write-off method in reporting for tax purposes. Relevant information is as follows:

[1] The $66,000 balance in the allowance at January 1, 1981, was made up of $25,000 of 1979 and prior sales and $41,000 of 1980 sales.

[2] Of $27,000 of specific accounts written off in 1981, $20,000 related to 1979 and prior sales and the remainder to 1980 sales.

[3] The balance in the allowance at December 31, 1981, after adjustment was $77,000.

Goodwill.   Goodwill of $500,000 resulted from a business combination which took place at January 1, 1978. For financial reporting purposes, it is being amortized over its maximum life.

Instructions

[a] Determine the tax liability for 1981, assuming no payments have been made during the year.

[b] Determine tax expense for 1981 using:
   [1] The net-change method of accounting for deferred taxes.
   [2] The gross-change method of accounting for deferred taxes.

[c] Determine the deferred tax figure(s) to be presented in the balance sheet at December 31, 1981, under the gross-change method.

[d] Prepare the income statement presentation for the year ended December 31, 1981, beginning with "income before income tax" under the gross-change method.

P18–11 Purcell Products, Inc., experienced a $750,000 loss before income taxes in 1984, a year in which the effective income tax rate was 46%. The following data pertain to the period 1982–1984:

Year	Income (Loss) Before Income Taxes	Income Tax Rate
1982	$ 192,000	40%
1983	465,000	42%
1984	(750,000)	46%

It is estimated that the income tax rate beyond 1984 will be approximately 48%. The end of Purcell's financial reporting period is December 31.

Instructions

Prepare the 1984 general journal entries to account for income taxes and the income statement presentation of income taxes in each of the following *independent* situations:

[a] Purcell Products intends to carry the entire 1984 loss forward. Future income of $750,000 is believed to be virtually assured in the carryforward period.

[b] Purcell Products intends to carry the entire 1984 loss forward. Future income in the carryforward period is relatively uncertain.

[c] Purcell Products intends to carry the 1984 loss back, to the extent possible. Future income is believed to be virtually assured in the carryforward period in an amount sufficient to offset the total loss of 1984.

[d] Purcell Products intends to carry the 1984 loss back, to the extent possible. Future income in the carryforward period is relatively uncertain.

[e] Briefly explain why under ordinary circumstances, loss carryforwards should not be recognized prior to the year in which income taxes are reduced, whereas loss carrybacks should be recognized in the loss year.

P18–12 (Appendix B) Smiley Company acquired assets in 1983 and 1984 as follows:

Year	Cost	ACRS Category	Depreciation for Financial Reporting
1983	$150,000	3 years	Straight-line over a 5-year life with $12,000 salvage value
1984	$160,000	5 years	Straight-line over an 8-year life with no salvage value

The company's income tax rate is 40% for 1983 and 42% for 1984. Income before income taxes for financial reporting purposes was $180,000 and

$250,000 in 1983 and 1984, respectively, before depreciation. The financial reporting year ends December 31.

Instructions

[a] Prepare the income statement presentation of income tax expense for 1983 and 1984. For each year, identify any deferred portion of that expense.

[b] Prepare the balance sheet presentation of deferred income taxes for 1983 and 1984.

P18–13 (Appendix B) Walsh Company has requested your assistance in determining the proper financial-statement presentation of income taxes at December 31, 1985. You have accumulated the following information.

[1] The company began operations on January 1, 1984 and has kept only marginal accounting records since its inception.

[2] In 1984 the company deducted $25,000 in plant asset costs for income tax purposes under the Accelerated Cost Recovery System (ACRS) ($100,000 cost × 25%). Additional assets acquired in 1985 for $120,000 will also be written off by ACRS. You have prepared the following analysis for determining the income tax liability for 1985:

Year of Asset Acquisitions	Cost	ACRS Percent 1984	ACRS Percent 1985
1984	$100,000	25%	38%
1985	120,000	—	25%

For financial statement purposes, management plans to depreciate these assets over a six-year estimated life with a 10% salvage value. A half-year's depreciation will be taken in the year of acquisition.

[3] Sales for 1984 and 1985 are $1,050,000 and 1,360,000, respectively. You estimate that 0.5% of these will be uncollectible. Specific accounts written off in 1984 and 1985 are as follows:

	1984	*1985*
Write-off of accounts arising in 1984	$1,100	$3,250
Write-off of accounts arising in 1985	—	1,800
	$1,100	$5,050

The company uses the direct write-off method for income tax purposes.

[4] At the end of 1985 the company received a $95,000 advance commission on a contract that will be performed in 1986. Income tax must be paid on this commission in 1985.

An income tax service has correctly determined that the company's taxable income for 1985 is $115,000, based on a 46% income tax rate and the following: (1) ACRS write-off of assets acquired in both 1984 and 1985; (2) recognition of uncollectible ac-counts by the direct write-off method; and (3) inclusion of the $25,000 advance commission.

In consultation with management, you determine that the net change method will be used to account for the reversal of timing differences in determining the income tax expense. The company's income tax rate in 1984 was 42%.

Instructions

[a] Prepare a detailed analysis for determining pretax-accounting income for 1985, beginning with taxable income of $115,000.

[b] Prepare the income tax accrual for 1985, including the recognition of deferred income taxes.

[c] Determine the amount(s) of deferred income taxes to be included in the company's 1985 balance sheet.

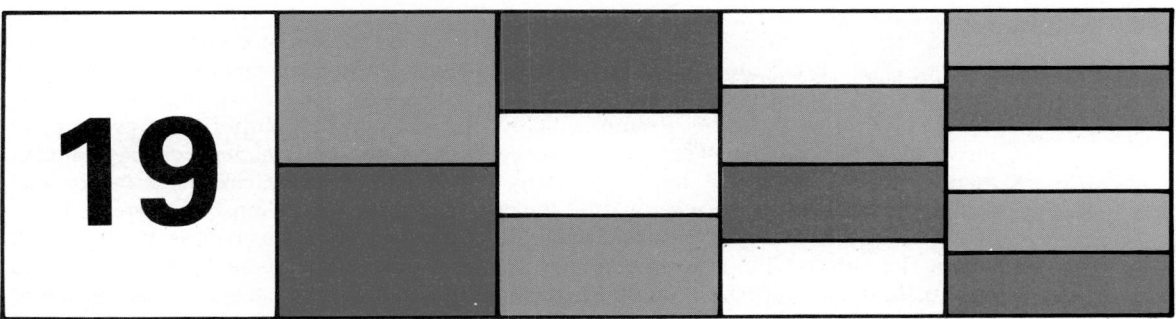

19

ACCOUNTING CHANGES AND CORRECTIONS OF ERRORS

Objectives

To describe the nature of accounting changes and errors and the related financial reporting implications.

To develop the theoretical and practical aspects of financial reporting for accounting changes and errors.

To identify errors and the three basic types of accounting changes.

To discuss the concepts and logic underlying the methods of accounting for each type of change and error.

To demonstrate acceptable financial accounting and reporting practices for each type of change and error.

To discuss the calculations necessary to restate financial statements, including comparative statements of income and retained earnings.

To describe the financial reporting placement of various types of changes in relation to other elements of the financial statements.

To illustrate proper disclosures and summarize the effects of accounting changes.

ill Rogers claimed that the only thing certain about weather was that "it's bound to change." The same might be said for financial accounting and reporting. Indeed, accounting changes may occur frequently and may be caused by a variety of factors. Examples include the effects of new authoritative pronouncements, new business transactions or forms, changes in the environment, changes in estimates, and changes in the reporting entity. Occasionally mistakes are made in financial accounting and reporting; when found, the effects of those errors must be corrected.

The purpose of Chapter 19 is to disclose the nature of accounting changes, to distinguish among the various types of accounting changes, to discuss relevant issues and concepts, and to explain the appropriate accounting practices for each type of change. It also examines various types of errors and describes how corrections to financial statements should be made. Earlier chapters occasionally mention accounting for certain types of changes and errors; for example, Chapter 12, in dealing with depreciation of plant assets, discusses changes in the useful life of a plant asset. Each of these previous illustrations was presented in accordance with the practices to be covered in Chapter 19. Here, however, we consider the topic of accounting changes and corrections of errors in a complete and inclusive fashion. Our discussion begins with a conceptual examination of the various types of changes and possible alternative accounting practices.

ACCOUNTING CHANGES AND CORRECTIONS OF ERRORS: A CONCEPTUAL ANALYSIS

In its *Opinion No. 20,* the Accounting Principles Board (APB) classified the effects of all accounting-related changes in three categories:[1]

1. Changes in accounting principle.
2. Changes in the reporting entity.
3. Changes in accounting estimate.

A similar type of event requiring accounting recognition is the correction of an error. Although not considered an accounting change, recording the correction of an error requires analysis and accounting similar to that accorded the three types of accounting changes. Therefore, this chapter discusses each of the four events.

We must carefully classify all accounting changes into one of the three basic categories, because substantially different accounting and reporting practices are required for each. Before discussing specific accounting practices, however, we shall give a conceptual analysis of each type of accounting change and correction of errors.

Changes in Accounting Principle

A **change in accounting principle** occurs when a company selects a generally accepted accounting principle (GAAP) that is different from the generally accepted accounting principle used in prior reporting periods. Examples of such changes include a change from the specific identification method to the first-in, first-out method of inventory pricing or a change from the sum-of-the-years'-digits to the straight-line method of depreciating plant assets. The term **accounting principle** as used here is broad and includes not only specific practices and procedures, but also the methods of applying the procedure. For example, a company may continue to base its inventory valuation on the lower of cost or market value but change the *application* of method from the inventory as a whole to individual inventory items. Although the lower of cost or market principle is still used, the method of applying the principle has changed. Therefore, such changes are considered to be changes in accounting principle.

---

[1]*APB Opinion No. 20,* "Accounting Changes," 1971, par. 6.

Materiality

**Consis-
tency**

If we initially adopt an accounting principle for items that were previously immaterial or because of new transactions or events, a change in accounting principle does not occur. Furthermore, some changes in accounting methods that are *initially planned* as part of an overall accounting policy do not represent changes in accounting principle. For example, a change from an accelerated depreciation method to the straight-line method at some specific point in an asset's life may be planned at the time the asset is acquired. Consistent application of such an overall policy does not represent a change in accounting principle when the straight-line method is applied.

Changes in the Reporting Entity

A **change in the reporting entity** occurs when the financial statements of the current year are those of a new, or at least substantially different, operating enterprise. Changes of this type arise if the individual companies included in a set of consolidated or combined financial statements are changed or if consolidated statements are presented for a group of companies that previously reported individually. Although this chapter discusses changes in the reporting entity, more extensive treatment of this subject is deferred to advanced accounting courses.[2]

Changes in Accounting Estimates

Changes in accounting estimates frequently arise because the preparation of financial statements requires accountants to estimate the outcome of many future events. Many of those estimates may require accounting adjustments as new information is gained or as different conditions arise. For example, estimates of the useful life and salvage value of plant assets, collectibility of receivables, and the outcome of current or pending litigation represent situations in which management and accountants must forecast the outcome of future events. If differences arise between early estimates by management and the later outcome of the events being estimated, accountants must recognize the effects of those differences in the accounting records.

Although estimates of future events require substantial judgment, most estimates are quite accurate. As more experience is acquired and as new information becomes available, however, substantial revisions of some estimates may be necessary.

Occasionally the effects of a change in estimate are commingled with a change in accounting principle. For example, a company may decide to begin expensing certain costs associated with self-constructed assets when incurred rather than capitalizing and depreciating the costs. Such a change may be made partially in recognition of more doubtful future benefits (change in estimate) of the asset being constructed and partially as a result of a different philosophy about the measurement of periodic earnings and related cost of the asset (change in principle). Accountants consider the effects of such mixed-type changes to be changes in estimate rather than changes in accounting principle.[3] Such changes are frequently caused by the acquisition of new information or changing circumstances and are closely associated with the continuing evolution of existing practices. In effect, changes like the one described above arise in complete or partial recognition of changes in estimated future events.

Corrections of Errors

Errors in financial statements result from mistakes or omissions in the financial accounting process. Examples of errors include "mathematical mistakes, mistakes in the application of

---

[2]The subject of business combinations and changes in the reporting entity are considered extensively in advanced accounting courses. For an excellent discussion of the theoretical issues, concepts, and financial accounting and reporting standards in this area, see Arnold J. Pahler and Joseph E. Mori, *Advanced Accounting: Concepts and Practice* (New York: Harcourt Brace Jovanovich, 1981).

[3]*APB Opinion No. 20,* par. 11.

accounting principles, or oversight or misuse of facts" existing at the time the financial statements were prepared.[4] A change from an accounting principle that is unacceptable to a generally acceptable accounting principle is also considered to be a correction of an error. Thus, a change from the cash basis to the accrual basis of accounting for product warranties is considered a correction of an error rather than a change in accounting principle. Likewise a *misuse* of facts results in an **error,** whereas *newly available* information or the acquisition of *new* facts results in a **change of estimate.** Therefore, for purposes of financial accounting and reporting, intentional distortions or inappropriate estimates create errors rather than mere inaccurate estimates. This distinction is important because substantially different accounting practices are required for each. The next section of this chapter considers several alternatives for accounting for the effects of changes and errors.

REPORTING ALTERNATIVES FOR ACCOUNTING CHANGES

While there are several possible ways to account for the effects of accounting changes and corrections of errors, three fundamental alternatives are quite clear: the restatement method, the cumulative effect method, and the current and prospective method. Only one of the alternatives is acceptable for each type of change. The following sections discuss each method in light of its strengths, problems, and reporting implications. A later section of this chapter identifies the method that should be used for each type of accounting change and for corrections of errors.

Restatement Method

One way to account for the effects of changes involves the retroactive **restatement** of all previous financial statements that are presented with the current financial statements for comparative purposes. When the restatement approach is used, these previously issued financial statements are revised to show the figures that would have appeared in them if the change had been in effect in prior years. For example, if a company changes its method of accounting for inventory from last-in, first-out (LIFO) to first-in, first-out (FIFO), the difference between the figures for beginning inventory as computed under each method is treated as an adjustment to prior years' reported earnings. The effect of the change on past records does not alter the current year's income, at least not directly. The effect of the change at the beginning of the current year is treated as an adjustment of the beginning balance of retained earnings for the current year rather than recorded as a component of income of the current year.

Most published financial statements contain one or more prior year's financial statements for comparative purposes. Indeed, users of financial statements are able to gain better insights and make more informed decisions if comparative statements are presented. Comparative statements may reveal trends and relationships that would not be detected from single-year statements. Although generally accepted accounting principles do not specifically require comparative financial statements, such comparisons are strongly recommended in *Accounting Research Bulletin No. 43:*

> *The presentation of comparative financial statements in annual and other reports enhances the usefulness of such reports and brings out more clearly the nature and trends (of events affecting the enterprise). . . . Such presentation emphasizes the fact that statements for a series of periods are far more significant than those for a single period and that the accounts for one period are but an installment of what is essentially a continuous history.*[5]

---

[4]*APB Opinion No. 20,* par. 13.
[5]*Accounting Research Bulletin No. 43,* "Restatement and Revision of Accounting Research Bulletins," 1953, Ch. 2, Sec. A, par. 1.

Most annual reports of business enterprises contain comparative financial statements. Managements recognize that financial statement users need comparative information. The Securities and Exchange Commission (SEC) also requires comparative financial statements of registrants, and most banks require comparative financial statements as a condition of loan agreements. Consequently, most companies routinely prepare annual reports containing financial statements for two or more periods.

Advantages of the Restatement Method

The restatement alternative possesses several advantages. For example, previously issued financial statements, when reissued after restatement, are "better" than they originally were. Since the prior financial statements are changed for events subsequent to their issuance, more complete or accurate information underlies the reissued statements, thereby resulting in an improved—if somewhat belated—presentation.

Another advantage is that the current financial statements contain no trace of events not actually affecting the current statements. In essence, under the restatement approach a "clean slate" is prepared each time an event occurs which would have caused the previous statements to have been different if the information had been available at the date the original statements were issued. The effects of events relating to a prior period are confined to the prior period only; therefore, the current income statement excludes any of the effects of the past event. Since the restatement method results in the retroactive revision of previously issued financial statements, those statements issued for comparative purposes are presented in conformity with the accounting principle of consistency. In the earlier example of changing from the LIFO method to the FIFO method, if this change were made in 1984 the comparative statements for 1982 and 1983 would be restated and prepared on the FIFO basis, thereby making the three periods that are presented comparable.

Consis-tency

Disadvantages of the Restatement Method

One major problem attributed to the restatement method involves the possibility that items of revenue and expense affecting the enterprise may never be reported as a determinant of *any* year's net income. To illustrate, assume that a company fails to report a material liability and related expense resulting from losing a lawsuit during a period and discovers the error only after financial statements for the period have been issued. Unless comparative financial statements are presented, the loss from the lawsuit is never reported as an expense and related reduction in the net income of any year. The restatement approach causes the loss, in these circumstances, to be reported as an adjustment of the beginning balance of retained earnings. Unscrupulous executives would be able to ignore unfavorable events in the year they arise and instead, report the effects of the events as adjustments to beginning retained earnings in later years. Net income for each year in question is unburdened by the unfavorable event.

A second major problem relates to a possible loss of credibility in published financial statements. If an individual relies on information contained in financial statements while making decisions and then observes the restatement of that information in comparative financial statements in a later year, the reliability and validity of the entire financial accounting and reporting process may become questionable. The possible loss of public confidence in financial reporting is a second strong argument against the extensive use of the restatement method.

Cumulative Effect Method

Another approach of accounting for and reporting the effects of changes involves recording the **cumulative effect** of the event as an adjustment to the current year's income. Under this approach, the cumulative effect of the change is determined as of the beginning of the year of change, and that effect is recorded in the current year's income statement in a special nonoperating category, much like an extraordinary item. The new method of accounting or new information is applied at the beginning of that year in which the event takes place. For example, if a company changes its depreciation method from the straight-line method to an accelerated method, an accountant determines what the accumulated depreciation would have been at the beginning of the year if the company had been using the accelerated method in the past. The accountant then compares the balance in the Accumulated Depreciation account at the beginning of the year with the amount that would have been in Accumulated Depreciation if the new method had been used. The difference between the two balances, stated on a net-of-tax basis, represents the cumulative effect of the change and is reported as a separate component of current net income. Depreciation expense for the year in which the change occurs is based on the new method and reported in normal fashion.

Advantages of the Cumulative Effect Method

Advantages of the cumulative effect method include the fact that the effects of the event are completely accounted for in the year of the change. That is, the accountant prepares entries which adjust the affected accounts and bring them up to date as if the new method had always been used. Future reported earnings and financial position are determined as if the new (and presumably preferable) accounting methods had been consistently employed. Future financial-statement amounts are thus unaffected by changes taking place in prior periods. Advocates of the cumulative effect method also contend that financial statement users are more likely to notice and comprehend the nature and significance of the change if the effects of the change as of the beginning of the current year are included as a special item in the current year's income. Such a treatment spotlights the change and assures that readers of the statements are adequately informed.

Disadvantages of the Cumulative Effect Method

A disadvantage of the cumulative effect method is that financial statements of years prior to the change are presented in their old form for comparative purposes. The old methods or assumptions on which prior financial statements were based have been discontinued or updated in the current year's statements. Thus, the financial position and results of operations reported after the event are not presented on a basis consistent with the information presented for periods prior to the change. Of course, the retroactive restatement method, discussed earlier, avoids this problem.

Consistency

Current and Prospective Method

A third approach to accounting for the effects of accounting changes spreads the cumulative effect of the change over current and future reporting periods. For example, a company may decide that a plant asset will have a longer life than originally estimated. Using the **current and prospective approach,** the company bases depreciation for the *current* and *future* years on the remaining undepreciated cost of the asset and the revised estimate of the asset's life. No attempt is made to apply the new estimate to past statements nor to adjust the existing balances accordingly.

Advantages of the Current and Prospective Method

Supporters of the current and prospective approach observe that many accounting changes are an inevitable part of the accounting process and as such should be reported in a normal fashion without focusing on the effect of the change as do the two previously discussed methods. They also note that immaterial amounts would not require separate presentation through catch-up entries. When changes are due to new or recently available information, one can make a strong case that only the current and future periods are actually affected.

Materiality

The current and prospective approach assures that each event that normally affects net income is included in the income of *some* particular period or periods. Thus, this method also overcomes one of the objections to the restatement method.

Disadvantages of the Current and Prospective Method

Others note that if new information indicates that previous estimates or accounting methods were deficient, the new data should be used to adjust the statements completely, including any cumulative or retroactive effect. Another criticism of the current and prospective method is that the nature and effect of the event may be overlooked by financial statement users because no special financial-statement category or presentation is employed. The items that are normally presented in the financial statements are simply presented in dollar amounts that are different from those that would have been shown had the change not been made. Furthermore, effects of informational deficiencies on past financial statements can affect current and future financial statements if no adjustment is made to bring the statements up to date with regard to the new data.

Comparing and Evaluating the Alternatives

The methods of reporting accounting changes and corrections of errors differ substantially in terms of financial-statement measurement and presentation. Each method also possesses advantages and disadvantages. Exhibit 19–1 summarizes the three methods and specifies the related advantages and disadvantages.

EXHIBIT 19–1
Analysis of Alternatives of
Accounting for Changes and Errors

Issue	Restatement Method	Cumulative Effect Method	Current and Prospective Method
Description of Method	The effect of the change is used to restate any prior period financial statements presented. Any remaining effect is charged or credited to beginning retained earnings of the earliest period presented.	The effect of the change is reported as a component of the current year's income. A special category of gain or loss is used to bring the statements up to date.	The effect of the change is spread over the current and future years' income. No special categories of gain or loss are used in reporting the effect of change, and no catch-up entry is made.
Current Year Nominal Accounts Affected	Direct effect charged or credited to Retained Earnings.	Special nonoperating income statement account charged or credited.	Normal income statement account charged or credited.
Major Advantages	Statements are ultimately presented "correctly." Items affecting prior years are associated individually with those years.	Financial statements are brought up to date, and future amounts are computed as if the new method had been used consistently. Users may easily focus on and understand the effects of the change.	Many changes are normal and recur frequently; such events do not justify catch-up entries or separate presentation. Many changes are due to new information, and only current and future periods should be adjusted.
Major Disadvantages	May erode the credibility of the accounting process. Decisions are made by users of financial statements, and later changes in those statements may cause a lack of faith in financial reporting.	Current and prior financial statements lack comparability. Events affecting prior years are reflected in current income.	The effect of previous "deficiencies" are allowed to affect current and prospective financial position and income. The nature and effects of the changes are obscure because no special category or presentation of the event is required.

The accounting profession carefully considered these accounting treatments and concluded that each is appropriate in certain circumstances. The following sections of this chapter describe the circumstances in which each method is acceptable, illustrate the application of each approach, and provide an example of each method. Our analysis begins by examining financial accounting and reporting for changes in accounting principle.

CHANGES IN ACCOUNTING PRINCIPLE: THE GENERAL RULE

In *Opinion No. 20* ("Accounting Changes") the APB describes two basic types of changes in accounting principle: general and special. **General changes** in accounting principle occur if a company selects and applies an acceptable accounting principle different from a previously used acceptable principle. Examples include alternative depreciation methods, different methods of accounting for the investment tax credit, and changes in inventory policy other than a change away from LIFO.

In *Opinion No. 20* the APB established three distinct **special changes** in accounting principle: (1) a change from the LIFO method of pricing inventory; (2) a change in the method of accounting for long-term construction contracts; and (3) a change to or from the full-cost method of accounting in the extractive industries. Chapter 13, in dealing with intangible assets, briefly discussed accounting practices in the extractive industries. Accounting for long-term construction contracts will be discussed more fully in Chapter 20, which deals with revenue recognition. We must carefully distinguish between general and special changes, because different reporting practices are required for each.

The effect of the *special* changes are reported by restating the financial statements of prior periods. As we explain later, the effects of correcting errors in the financial statements and certain other changes are also reported by the restatement method. Accordingly, we will defer an extensive discussion and illustration of the restatement method until later in this chapter.

General Changes in Accounting Principle

The APB prescribes the cumulative effect method for general changes in accounting principle. The cumulative effect of a general change in accounting principle (which is reported in the income statement of the period of change) is the difference between retained earnings before the change and what retained earnings would have been had the new principle been used in the past. All changes in accounting principle taking place during a particular reporting period are deemed to occur at the beginning of *that* period. In practice accountants calculate the amount of retained earnings that would have been reported at the end of the preceding period if the new accounting principle had been applied in all accounting periods through the beginning of the current year.

Once we calculate the cumulative effect of the change in accounting principle, we must address the issue of financial-statement presentation. *APB Opinion No. 20* requires the cumulative effect of general changes in accounting principle to be reported as a separate element in the determination of net income, following extraordinary items. Thus, the cumulative effects of such changes are excluded from income from operations and are presented net of any related income taxes immediately preceding net income.

Income Tax Effects of Changes in Accounting Principle

You will recall from our discussion of intraperiod income tax allocation in Chapter 18 that extraordinary items and corrections of errors are presented net of their respective income tax effects in financial statements of the period in which the events occur. The same procedure is followed in presenting the cumulative effect of a general change in accounting principle. We determine the amount of income tax expense that would have been reported if the new method had previously been used; then we compare that amount with the income tax expense on accounting income that was recognized by using the original method. The difference between the two tax expense figures is treated as the tax effect of the change in accounting principle.

Exemption for Initial Public Offerings

An exception to presenting the cumulative effect of a general change in accounting principle as a separate component of income in the year of the change arises if a company is using its financial statements for substantially different purposes than it has in the past. For example, a company that is currently closely held may be considering changing certain accounting practices in anticipation of offering shares of its stock to the public for the first time. In this case the potential public investors are probably better served by comparative financial statements that employ the newly adopted accounting principles for all comparative years presented. In such circumstances the cumulative effect of even *general* changes in accounting principle may be applied retroactively by restating all prior period financial statements presented. Specifically, financial statements *may* be restated for the effects of changes in accounting principle when a company first issues financial statements for any of the following purposes:[6]

1. To obtain additional equity capital from investors.
2. To effect a business combination.
3. To register securities, for example, with the SEC.

This exception (i.e., allowing companies to restate financial statements rather than include the cumulative effect of a general change in accounting principle in the income of the period of the change) is available only for changes made at the time a company uses its financial statements for one of the purposes listed above. The exception is not appropriate, however, if a company's securities are already widely held.

Disclosure of Changes in Accounting Principle

Disclosure

Accountants should disclose the nature of and justification for changes in accounting principle, describe the effect of the change on net income and earnings per share, and present the cumulative effect of the change (net of any income tax effect) in the income statement. To aid financial statement users in assessing the significance of the change on previous financial statements, certain *pro-forma* disclosures are also necessary. Specifically, income before extraordinary items and net income computed on a *pro-forma* basis should be presented on the face of income statements for all prior periods presented as if the newly adopted accounting principle had been applied during all periods affected.[7] In this way financial statement users are informed of how a change in accounting principle affects previous statements even though those previous statements are not restated.

Accountants must also demonstrate that the new principle is preferable to the old one in order to justify the change. In other words, the use of the new principle must somehow result in a "fairer" measurement and presentation of financial information. For example, a company may change from the average cost method of inventory valuation to the FIFO method in order to "better" value the ending inventory presented on the balance sheet. The fact that a particular accounting practice results in lower or deferred income taxes is not sufficient to justify a change to that practice for financial reporting purposes. To be "preferable" the new principle must enhance some aspect of the financial statements, such as achieving a superior matching of revenues and expenses or more realistic valuation of balance sheet items.

Matching

---

[6]*APB Opinion No. 20,* par. 29.
[7]*APB Opinion No. 20,* par. 19.

The Financial Accounting Standards Board (FASB) has also provided some additional guidance for accountants attempting to justify changes in accounting principle. *Statement of Financial Accounting Standards No. 32* provides that the burden to justify a change in accounting principle on the basis of preferability is met if a company elects to change *to* the accounting and reporting standards recommended by a variety of American Institute of Certified Public Accountants (AICPA) documents. *SFAS No. 32* has thus enhanced the stature of the AICPA pronouncements it addresses, which include (1) Audit Guides, (2) Accounting Guides, and (3) Statements of Position.[8]

Statement on Auditing Standards No. 43 affirms *SFAS No. 32* by defining the types of documents listed above (as well as AICPA Interpretations and FASB Technical Bulletins) as "established accounting principles."[9] *SAS No. 43* also requires auditors to justify any departures from established accounting principles, thereby further enhancing the preferability of these additional AICPA and FASB documents.

General Change in Accounting Principle Illustrated

To illustrate accounting for a general change in accounting principle, assume that at the end of 1985 Naples Company elects to change its method of computing depreciation. The company changes from the double-declining balance method of depreciation for income tax and financial reporting purposes to the straight-line method for financial reporting purposes only. Income for 1985 before deducting any depreciation or income tax expense is $75,000, and no other income tax timing or permanent differences exist. That is, pretax predepreciation accounting income and predepreciation taxable income are the same for years prior to 1985. The change applies to the company's only asset that was acquired early in 1980, which has a 10-year useful life, an original cost of $200,000, and no salvage value. Exhibit 19–2 summarizes how to determine the cumulative effect of the change in method of depreciating this asset.

The impact of income taxes has been ignored in the following entries to record the cumulative effect of this change and the depreciation expense for 1985. (Remember that changes made at any time during a year are presumed to have taken place at the beginning of the year for purposes of financial reporting.)

Accumulated Depreciation	34,464	
Cumulative Effect of Change in		
Accounting Principle—Depreciation		34,464
Depreciation Expense	20,000	
Accumulated Depreciation		20,000

How would incorporating income taxes into this example affect the journal entry and subsequent financial-statement disclosure? To answer this question we must determine how the accounting principle will be treated for income tax purposes. In this case, we will assume that the company will continue to depreciate the asset by the double-declining balance method for income tax purposes while changing to the straight-line method for financial reporting purposes. To adjust the accounts as though the two methods had been used in the past, we must set up the deferred income taxes that would have been recognized in the previous years on the difference between pretax-accounting income and taxable income. Assuming an effective 30% income tax rate, deferred income taxes at the end of

---

[8]*FASB Statement of Financial Accounting Standards No. 32,* "The Preferability of Accounting Principles and Practices Contained in Certain AICPA Audit Guides, Accounting Guides, and Statements of Position," 1981.

[9]*Statement on Auditing Standards No. 43,* "Omnibus Statement on Auditing Standards—1982," 1982.

EXHIBIT 19–2
Accounting for a Change in Accounting Principle
(Based on Naples Company Illustration)

Year	Straight-Line Depreciation* (New)	200% Declining Balance Depreciation** (Original)	Difference
1980	$ 20,000	$ 40,000	$20,000
1981	20,000	32,000	12,000
1982	20,000	25,600	5,600
1983	20,000	20,480	480
1984	20,000	16,384	(3,616)
	$100,000	$134,464	$34,464
1985	$ 20,000	$ 13,107	$ (6,893)

*Computation for straight-line depreciation:

$$\frac{\$200,000}{10} = \$20,000 \text{ per year}$$

**Computations for 200% declining balance depreciation per year:

1980	$200,000 × .20 = $40,000
1981	$160,000 × .20 = $32,000
1982	$128,000 × .20 = $25,600
1983	$102,400 × .20 = $20,480
1984	$ 81,920 × .20 = $16,384
1985	$ 65,536 × .20 = $13,107

1984 would have been $10,339 ($34,464 × 30%). The cumulative effect of the change in accounting principle on a net-of-tax basis would have been $24,125 [$34,464 × (1 − .30)]. The entry to record the change in accounting principle, including income taxes, is as follows:

Accumulated Depreciation	34,464	
Cumulative Effect of Change in Accounting Principle— Depreciation		24,125
Deferred Income Tax		10,339

The debit to Accumulated Depreciation for $34,464 adjusts that account on the balance sheet and is simply the difference between the balance that is in that account on January 1, 1985 ($134,464) as a result of using double-declining balance depreciation and the balance that would have been in Accumulated Depreciation ($100,000) had the straight-line method been consistently used. The credit to the Cumulative Effect account on the income statement for $24,125 is that same amount, net of the income tax effect of the change. The credit to Deferred Income Tax is the amount that would exist if the double-declining balance method had been used for income tax purposes and the straight-line method had been used for financial reporting purposes since the asset was acquired.

Exhibit 19–3 includes partial comparative income statements for Naples Company for 1984 and 1985, with the assumption that net income was properly reported in 1984 at $35,000. This amount includes depreciation expense determined by the double-declining balance method. The *pro forma* amounts at the bottom of the statement show what net income would have been had the new (straight-line) method been used in both years. The earnings per share are based on 100,000 shares of common stock outstanding and no preferred stock.

EXHIBIT 19–3
Naples Company
Partial Income Statements

	1985	1984
Income before income tax and cumulative effect of change in accounting principle	$55,000*	$50,000
Income tax expense (30%)	16,500	15,000
Income before cumulative effect of change in accounting principle	38,500	35,000
Cumulative effect of change in accounting principle, net of $10,339 income tax	24,125	—
Net income	$62,625	$35,000
Earnings per share		
Income before cumulative effect of change in accounting principle	$.39	$.35
Cumulative effect of change in accounting principle	.24	—
Net income	$.63	$.35
Pro forma restatement of income and earnings per share, applying straight-line depreciation retroactively		
Net income	$38,500**	$32,469†
Earnings per share	$.39	$.32

*Computed as follows:

1985 income before deducting depreciation	$ 75,000	
Straight-line depreciation	(20,000)	
	$ 55,000	

**Same as income before cumulative effect of change in accounting principle.

†Computed as follows:

1984 net income	$ 35,000	
1984 difference between straight-line depreciation and double-declining balance depreciation, net of 30% income tax [$3,616 × (1 − .30)]	(2,531)	
	$32,469	

The 1985 income is determined by using the newly adopted straight-line method. The cumulative effect gain of $24,125 is presented on a net-of-tax basis, and income is presented before and after that item. For 1985 the *pro forma* restated income simply consists of income before the effect of the change in accounting principle. The 1984 *pro forma* restated income is computed by restating the 1984 income for the difference between the two depreciation methods on a net-of-tax basis. In the body of the financial statement the inconsistency resulting from the use of double-declining balance depreciation in 1984 and straight-line depreciation in 1985 remains because the 1984 statement is not restated under the cumulative effect method. However, the effect of restatement is included in the *pro forma* figures.

Cumulative Effect Not Determinable

In some circumstances we may be unable to determine the cumulative effect of certain accounting changes. Perhaps the best example of such a circumstance involves a change *to* the LIFO method of inventory pricing. If we attempt to change from another method of inventory pricing to the LIFO method, we may find it difficult or even impossible to establish what the amount of inventory at the beginning of the year would have been if the LIFO method had previously been used. Remember that the LIFO method treats the cost of the last inventory items acquired as the cost of the first items sold. The cost of the earliest items of inventory acquired are considered to remain in ending inventory. Therefore, LIFO inventory costs may include inventory cost layers that are several decades old. Determining the cost of exceptionally old LIFO cost layers may be difficult or even impossible unless the accounting system was specifically designed to capture that information.

If the cumulative effect of a change in accounting principles is not determinable, we simply apply the new method to the existing account balances and no cumulative effect of the change is reported. In our example of a change from FIFO to LIFO, the ending inventory of the previous year under the FIFO pricing method is treated as if it were the beginning inventory under the LIFO pricing method. Disclosures in the notes to the financial statements should point out that no cumulative effect or *pro forma* amounts are available and explain why the cumulative effect of the change is not determinable.

Disclosure

A Practice Example of a General Change in Accounting Principle

An example of the financial reporting of a change in accounting principle is presented in Exhibit 19–4, which contains a portion of the comparative income statements for 1980–1982 and the footnote disclosure in Du Pont's 1982 annual report. Du Pont is a diversified company that operates in such diverse areas as biomedical products; agricultural and industrial chemicals; petroleum refining, marketing, and transportation; and fibers.

The partial income statement for 1981 in Exhibit 19–4 includes the $320,000,000 cumulative effect of the change in accounting principle related to the change in accounting for the investment tax credit. Also, the *pro forma* retroactive application of the new methods (flow-through) is shown at the bottom of the statement by a restatement of both net

---

EXHIBIT 19–4
E. I. du Pont de Nemours and Company
Example Disclosure of Accounting Change

Partial Consolidated Income Statement
(dollars in millions, except per share)

	1982	1981	1980
Earnings Before Income Taxes...........................	$2,806	$2,155	$1,098
Provision for Income Taxes............................	1,912	1,074	392
Income Before Cumulative Effect of Change in Accounting for Investment Tax Credit	894	1,081	706
Cumulative Effect for Years Prior to 1981 of Change in Accounting for Investment Tax Credit	—	320	—
Net Income..	$ 894	$1,401	$ 706
Earnings Per Share of Common Stock Before Cumulative Effect of Change in Accounting for Investment Tax Credit................................	$ 3.75	$ 5.81	$ 4.49
Cumulative Effect for Years Prior to 1981 of Change in Accounting for Investment Tax Credit	—	1.74	—
Net Income..	$ 3.75	$ 7.55	$ 4.49
Pro Forma—With 1981 Change in Accounting for Investment Tax Credit Applied Retroactively Net Income..	$ 894	$1,081	$ 744
Earnings Per Share of Common Stock	$ 3.75	$ 5.81	$ 4.73

Accounting Changes

Because of the merger with Conoco in 1981 . . . the company was required to conform Conoco's and Du Pont's accounting for investment tax credit (ITC). Conoco used the flow-through method, which recognizes ITC benefits as they are earned for Federal income tax purposes; Du Pont used the deferral method, which amortizes ITC over the expected lives of the related assets. Effective January 1, 1981, Du Pont's accounting was changed to the flow-through method to recognize predominant industry practice. The change resulted in an increase in income before the cumulative effect of the change of $57 ($.31 per share) for 1981. 1980 data were not restated, but pro forma 1980 net income reflecting the retroactive effect of the change is shown on the Consolidated Income Statement. In addition, the cumulative effect of the change, reflecting reversal of ITC deferred in years prior to 1981, resulted in a nonrecurring credit to 1981 net income of $320 ($1.74 per share).

Effective January 1, 1981, the last-in, first-out (LIFO) inventory accounting method, used to value domestic inventories and certain foreign inventories, was extended to include substantially all foreign inventories. This change results in a more realistic statement of international earnings because LIFO accounting more closely matches current costs with current revenues. The effect of this change on 1981 net income was not material.

Also effective January 1, 1981, the company implemented certain pension accounting changes which had the effect of increasing net income for 1981 by $38 ($.20 per share). These changes were based on a comprehensive review of the company's actuarial methods, assumptions and funding objectives and include certain changes necessary to comply with Federal pension regulations.

SOURCE: E. I. du Pont de Nemours and Company, 1982 Annual Report.

income and earnings per share. The 1982 figures in the *pro forma* presentation are the same as those in the income statement, because the new method was applied in 1982. The 1981 and 1980 figures are restated to apply the new method retroactively.

The footnote concerning accounting changes explains the change in accounting for the investment tax credit in the first paragraph. This includes a justification for the change as well as disclosure of the dollar effects of the change on net income and earnings per share. Reference is also made to the *pro forma* restatement at the bottom of the income statement.

Materiality

The second and third paragraphs of the accounting-changes note refer to a 1981 inventory change whose effect on net income was immaterial and a 1981 change in accounting estimate involving pension expense.

DOUBLE STANDARD

ONE OF THE OLD standbys for financial officers when times got tough has always been to try to pick up earnings by slowing depreciation charges.

Last year's Accelerated Cost Recovery System only made that easier by effectively permitting companies to depreciate plant and equipment at different rates for tax and accounting purposes. Says Ronald Murray, Coopers & Lybrand's director of accounting and SEC technical services: "Now you can have a slower book depreciation schedule, which helps financial statements, and yet still stay with fast depreciation for tax purposes, which helps cash flow."

Changing depreciation schedules can make quite a difference for a company. Inland Steel, which recently slowed down its depreciation, will reduce this year's losses by $43 million, or $1.20 per share (Inland made only $57 million last year). In 1980 electrical equipment manufacturer RTE Corp. more than doubled per-share earnings, from 34 cents to 74 cents, by adjusting depreciations.

"We realized that, compared to our competitors, our conservative method of depreciation might have hurt us with investors because of its negative impact on net earnings," comments RTE Controller Douglas Haag. Says Duane Borst, Inland Steel's comptroller: "Why should we put ourselves at a disadvantage by depreciating more conservatively than other steel companies do?"

Up until recently, of course, most corporations were pushing for faster depreciation to escape the ravages of inflation. Now, by dragging out their depreciation schedules, firms may run the risk of repeating the errors of the automobile and steel industries, which found themselves hard pressed to replace assets because of years of underdepreciation.

The easiest way to lower depreciation charges is to switch from accelerated depreciation to straight line, where the same sum gets written off every year.

Those companies who want to lower their depreciation even further in hard times can switch to the units-of-production method, where charges are tied not to time but to production volume. In this way a plant running at 40% of capacity generates 60% lower depreciation charges. Ernst & Whinney's Denny Beresford, partner in charge of accounting standards, expects that more companies will follow the lead of Inland Steel and Asarco by switching to units-of-production depreciation.

For the investor, several questions remain so far unresolved. What about the problem of technological obsolescence, for example? Any slow method of depreciation might well encourage management to keep a piece of machinery in operation long after far superior replacements become available. The risk is great with units of production, especially in slow times.

Beresford raises a related issue: quality of earnings. "Some people would view a company that uses accelerated depreciation as being more conservative in its financial reporting and thus having a higher quality of earnings," he comments. IBM, for example, is still using the so-called sum-of-the-years method, which raises depreciation charges dramatically in the early years of an asset's life and then slows down as time goes on. As Beresford puts it: "A company changing away from accelerated to straight line might be viewed by some people as reporting at that time lower quality earnings."

It's worth watching.

SOURCE: Jill Andresky, "Double Standards," *Forbes*, November 22, 1982, p. 178. Reprinted by permission of *Forbes* Magazine. © Forbes Inc., 1982.

SLOWDOWN

A look at nine companies that switched some or all depreciation schedules and the effect on earnings.

Company	Switch	Year	Addition to net income (per share)	Earnings per share
Asarco	s.l. to u.o.p.	1980	$0.38	$8.02
Bell & Howell	acc. to s.l.	1981	0.04	3.83
Burlington Industries	acc. to s.l.	1981	0.15	3.98
Chrysler	acc. to s.l.	1981	0.52	−7.18
Cone Mills	acc. to s.l.	1981	0.10	5.87
Harsco	acc. to s.l.	1981	0.08	3.15
Inland Steel	s.l. to u.o.p.	1982	1.20	NA
McGraw-Edison	acc. to s.l.	1981	0.13	5.11
JP Stevens	acc. to s.l.	1980	0.06	1.43

Abbreviations: s.l. stands for straight-line; acc. for accelerated; u.o.p. for units-of-production. NA: Not available.

CHANGES IN ACCOUNTING ESTIMATE

Changes in accounting estimate result from uncertainties in forecasting future events and their effects. Many financial-statement elements require current estimates of future events for presentation in financial statements. Examples include the collectibility of receivables, obsolescence of inventory, and useful lives and salvage values of plant and intangible assets. After financial statements are issued, if new or additional evidence indicates previous estimates should be revised, changes affecting the financial statements must be recorded. Changes in accounting estimates should be accounted for in the current period if the changes affect only that period. If they also affect the future, they should be accounted for in the period of change and applicable future periods.[10] As mentioned earlier this treatment is called the **current and prospective method.**

Changes in Estimate Illustrated

To illustrate, assume that Sicilian Company has consistently estimated its bad-debt expense to be 2% of credit sales. During 1984, however, the company recognizes that the estimate for the last two years has been too low and that an additional amount of $100,000 should be recognized to present the accounts receivable at net realizable value. The entry at December 31, 1984, to record the additional provision is as follows:

Bad Debt Expense	100,000	
Allowance for Uncollectible		
Accounts		100,000

The entire amount of the changed estimate is included in income during 1984 because no future periods are affected by the change. If the change in estimate affects future periods, however, the analysis is more complex.

Assume that Sicilian Company also determines during 1984 that one of its buildings will have a useful life greater than originally forecast. The building, acquired in early 1974 at a cost of $300,000, was originally estimated to have a 25-year useful life and a salvage value of $50,000. Sicilian Company, which uses the straight-line depreciation method, now estimates that the building will be used for a total of 40 years and that the original estimate of salvage value still appears reasonable. The depreciation expense to be recorded in 1984 is computed as follows:

Depreciation Recognized on Building Prior to 1984

Original cost	$300,000
Less: Salvage value	50,000
Depreciable cost	250,000
÷ Original estimate of useful life in years	÷ 25
Depreciation expense per year	10,000
× Number of years depreciated (1974–1983)	× 10
Total depreciation expense through 1983 (beginning of 1984)	$100,000

Remaining Depreciable Cost at Beginning of 1984

Original cost	$300,000
Less: Depreciation taken 1974–1983	100,000
Remaining cost	$200,000
Less: Salvage value	50,000
Remaining depreciable cost	$150,000
÷ Number of years of useful life remaining at Jan. 1, 1984	÷ 30
Revised depreciation expense per year (1984–2013)	$ 5,000

---

[10]*APB Opinion No. 20*, par. 31.

In 1984 Sicilian Company records the Depreciation Expense by using the revised estimated life as follows:

Depreciation Expense	5,000	
Accumulated Depreciation		5,000

Each year thereafter Sicilian records depreciation in the amount and manner indicated above. Critics of the current and prospective method observe that the straight-line depreciation of a building with an original depreciable cost of $250,000 ($300,000 − $50,000) and a useful life of 40 years is $6,250 per year ($250,000 ÷ 40). This amount of depreciation expense, however, is never presented on any of the income statements of Sicilian Company. Application of generally accepted accounting principles in accounting for the effects of this change in estimate results in depreciation expense of $10,000 per year for the first 10 years and $5,000 per year for the next 30 years. The arguments discussed earlier in this chapter favoring the current and prospective method were accepted by the APB in formulating the accounting standards of *APB Opinion No. 20* as they relate to changes in accounting estimates.

In contrast to the use of a cumulative effect item in a financial statement to account for a change in an accounting principle, no special financial-statement item exists to account for the effect of a change in an accounting estimate. The accounts affected by the change in an accounting estimate, such as bad-debt expense and depreciation expense, are simply recorded at amounts different from those that would have been used had the change in estimate not been made.

In these examples of changes in accounting estimates, we have ignored income taxes on the assumption that the company uses the same estimates for income tax purposes that it uses for financial reporting purposes. In practice, this will not always be the case, and income taxes may become an issue in the proper reporting of the change. For example, while the company may change to a longer life for depreciation of a plant asset in its financial statements, it may still depreciate that asset as rapidly as possible for income tax purposes. If the two periods were the same before the change in estimate but different after the change, deferred income taxes would need to be recognized as timing differences arise after the change in estimate.

A Practice Example of a Change in Estimate

An interesting example of a change in estimate is provided in a footnote to the 1980 annual report of Sperry and Hutchinson Company, Inc. (Exhibit 19–5). The company operates the S & H Green Stamp program of premiums. Many merchants offer S & H Green Stamps as an inducement for customers to shop at their stores. The stamps can then be redeemed by customers for various premiums or merchandise from Sperry and Hutchinson Company. The stamps are originally sold to the merchants by Sperry and Hutchinson, and stamps are redeemed when submitted to Sperry and Hutchinson by customers of the merchants. In 1979 Sperry and Hutchinson revised the estimate of stamps which would ultimately be redeemed from 95% to 90% of the stamps sold to merchants. Exhibit 19–5 describes the change and indicates the significance of the change to Sperry and Hutchinson Company.

CHANGES AND EVENTS REQUIRING RETROACTIVE RESTATEMENT

The preceding sections discussed two types of accounting changes that are accounted for in substantially different fashions. The cumulative effect of a general change in accounting principle is reported as a separate component of income during the year of the change, whereas the effects of a change in estimate are accounted for currently and, if future periods are affected, prospectively. Several other types of changes and events require retroactive

---

EXHIBIT 19-5
Example of a Change in Estimate

Change in Stamp Redemption Estimate and Inventory Valuation Method

For many years prior to 1979, the company prepared its financial statements and its federal income tax returns on the basis of an estimate that 95% of the trading stamps issued by the company would ultimately be redeemed. The company based its use of this redemption estimate on the actual redemption experience of the company since inception and, in recent years, on statistical evaluations of stamp redemption patterns. However, on the basis of recent special statistical evaluations, the company concluded in 1979 that in recent years there has been a decline in the redemption rate from the historical 95% rate. In order to reflect this decline, the company has prepared its financial statements for 1980 and 1979 on the basis that 90% of the trading stamps issued by the company after 1978 will ultimately be redeemed (see summary of significant accounting policies). As a result of this change in the redemption estimate, net earnings of the company for 1979 were increased by $5,187,000 . . . , after providing for related income taxes of $4,909,000.

SOURCE: Sperry and Hutchinson Company, 1980 Annual Report.

---

restatement, however, rather than current year cumulative treatment or current and prospective treatments. Specifically, the following types of adjustments require retroactive restatement:[11]

1. A change in reporting entity.
2. A special change in accounting principle.
3. The correction of an error.

Since financial accounting for and reporting these items require retroactive restatement, we shall discuss the meaning and nature of each item before we illustrate the general accounting and reporting techniques. Most of the accounting procedures necessary to restate previously issued financial statements are common to each of these items.

Changes in the Reporting Entity

Changes in the reporting entity occur for several reasons. For example, a group of commonly controlled companies may decide to report combined—rather than separate—financial statements, or the group of specific subsidiaries or companies included in consolidated or combined financial statements may change.[12] A business combination accounted for as a pooling of interests also represents a change in the reporting entity, and the financial statements of the companies involved should be restated.[13] Because the subject of accounting for business combinations is beyond the scope of this course, we will not discuss these issues at length. In essence, a change in the reporting entity occurs whenever the current financial statements represent a set of business enterprises different from the previous set. Through restatement the financial information presented in comparative form for prior

---

[11]This does not represent an exhaustive list of those changes that are accounted for by the retroactive restatement method. Certain FASB pronouncements, for example, specify the restatement method when the provisions of those pronouncements are first applied. Certain other situations requiring retroactive restatement are beyond the scope of this text. For example, *FASB Statement of Financial Accounting Standards No. 16* requires the retroactive restatement method when a company recognizes a preacquisition operating-loss carryforward of a purchased subsidiary.

[12]*APB Opinion No. 20,* par. 12.

[13]A pooling of interests is a type of business combination in which the owners of the combining businesses generally continue as owners of the combined enterprise. The subject of business combinations and changes in the reporting entity are considered extensively in advanced accounting courses. For an excellent discussion of the theoretical issues, concepts, and financial accounting and reporting standards in this area, see Pahler and Mori, *Advanced Accounting: Concepts and Practice.*

years becomes comparable to that reported in the current year. Consistent information is thus provided about the *new entity* for all periods presented.

The financial statements for the period in which a change in the reporting entity occurs should describe the reason for the change and the nature of the new entity. The effect of the change on income before extraordinary items and net income should also be disclosed. In contrast, financial statements for periods subsequent to the change need not repeat these disclosures, even if comparative information for periods prior to the change are presented.

Special Changes in Accounting Principle

As mentioned earlier, *APB Opinion No. 20* established three types of changes in accounting principle that are reported by applying the new method retroactively. Rather than requiring the cumulative effect of the change to be reported as a separate component of income in the year of the change, the APB requires the effects of these special changes to be reported, net of any income tax effects, as an adjustment to the beginning balance of retained earnings of the earliest year presented. If only single-year financial statements are presented, the effect of a special change is treated as an adjustment to the beginning balance of retained earnings of the current year.

The three special changes are:

1. A change *from* the LIFO method of inventory pricing to another method.
2. A change in the method of accounting for long-term construction contracts (e.g., from completed contract to percentage-of-completion accounting).
3. A change to or from the full-cost method of accounting in the extractive industries.

The full-cost method of accounting in extractive industries is a technique in which the entire (full) cost of a company's mineral exploration and development activities are capitalized and amortized over the extraction of the aggregate amount of available mineral reserves of the company. Chapter 13, in dealing with intangible assets, briefly discussed these issues, and Chapter 20 extensively discusses accounting for long-term construction contracts.

As in general changes in accounting principle, we must disclose the nature of and justification for these special changes. The effects of the change on net income, on income before extraordinary items, and on the related per share amounts must also be disclosed for all periods presented.

Corrections of Errors in Previously Issued Financial Statements

As mentioned earlier, **errors** in the financial statements include "mathematical mistakes, mistakes in the application of accounting principles, or oversight or misuse of facts that existed at the time the financial statements were prepared."[14] Changes from unacceptable accounting principles to generally acceptable accounting principles are also defined as corrections of errors.

Accountants frequently discover minor errors that occur in the accounting process. Such trivial errors may be quite expensive to correct, however, because of the time necessary to formulate a correcting entry and gain approval to record and post the entry to the company's general ledger. If an error is immaterial and is not expected to have any impact on the decisions made by financial statement users, the error does not necessarily require correction. Several small errors can, nevertheless, amount to a material misstatement of the financial statements. Accountants, therefore, keep track of all the errors they detect in order to determine which, if any, should be corrected. A suggested approach to determining the effects of several errors is described in Appendix A to this chapter. Effects of errors that are

---

[14]*APB Opinion No. 20,* par. 13.

individually material must be accounted for and reported. Errors in the financial statements are corrected by retroactively reporting the effect of the error as a prior period adjustment, net of any income tax effect. Thus, any previously issued financial statements that are presented with the current year's statements for comparative purposes are restated to remove the effects of the error. If only the current year's financial statements are presented, the effects of the error are reported as an adjustment to the beginning retained earnings of the period in which the error is discovered.

Important considerations in the process of correcting errors are the **timing of the error** (when the error took place) and the **timing of the correction** of the error (when the error was discovered and corrected). We refer in this chapter to the correction of errors "in previously issued financial statements." Errors that are made and discovered within an accounting period can ordinarily be corrected easily by adjusting the financial-statement elements affected by the error, including revenue and expense accounts, because they have not been closed to Retained Earnings. Errors in previously issued financial statements, on the other hand, are generally more complex and require an adjustment to Retained Earnings, because the nominal accounts (revenues and expenses) of the period in which the error was made have been closed to Retained Earnings. Care must be taken in analyzing errors to determine the period in which the error was made so that the appropriate accounts can be properly corrected.

Types of Errors in the Financial Statements

Certain errors affect only one financial statement, whereas others affect two or more financial statements. Errors that affect only a single financial statement are frequently called classification errors.

Classification Errors. Classification errors may occur on any financial statement and corrections of this type of error are usually straightforward and relatively simple. For example, a particular note payable in 10 years might have been classified improperly in previously issued financial statements as a current liability. To correct this error, an accountant merely reclassifies the note as a noncurrent liability in both the current year's balance sheet and any previously issued balance sheets that are presented for comparative purposes with the current financial statements.

Since this type of error does not affect income for either the current year or prior years, no adjustments to prior years' income statements or the statement of retained earnings are required. Any classification error affects only a single financial statement.

Self-Correcting Errors. The correction of certain other errors is also fairly straightforward. In fact, many errors are self-correcting over a two-year period. For example, if the ending inventory for 1983 is overstated, cost of goods sold is understated and net income is overstated for 1983. Since 1983's ending inventory becomes 1984's beginning inventory, the error affects 1984 as well. In 1984, however, the beginning inventory is overstated, causing the goods available for sale and the related cost of goods sold to be overstated for 1984. Net income for 1984 is consequently understated. The effect of this self-correcting error is to overstate net income for 1983 and understate net income for 1984 by the same amount. Even if the error is never detected, net income for 1985 and later years will be properly stated, because the effect of the error in 1983 was offset in 1984.

Most errors eventually correct themselves. Consider an extreme example: If an item of equipment is acquired in 1984 and is inadvertently charged to an expense account, net income for 1984 is understated. Net income in later years, however, is overstated, because no depreciation expense on the equipment is recognized. Assuming no salvage value, we find that the effect of the error made in 1984 will be self-corrected over the life of the asset. Eventually the effects of the error are eliminated from the financial statements, even though the financial statements for the intervening years contain the error.

Permanent Errors. Not all errors are self-correcting. For example, if a parcel of land is acquired and inadvertently charged to expense, the effect of this error is not self-correcting.

Since land is not a depreciable asset, the Land and Retained Earnings accounts on the balance sheet will be understated indefinitely.

Accountants must carefully analyze all errors that are identified to ascertain how much, if any, of the effects of the errors remain embedded in the financial statements. Even if the current statements are not affected by the errors, previously issued financial statements presented currently for comparative purposes may require restatement.

Materiality

The Appendix to this chapter presents several techniques that are helpful in identifying errors and isolating their impacts on the financial statements. One of these techniques is a worksheet that is particularly helpful in assessing the materiality of errors where several errors exist at the same time.

An Illustration of Comparative Financial-Statement Restatement

Perhaps the most common event requiring retroactive restatement is the correction of errors. We shall illustrate the general calculations and reporting techniques underlying retroactive restatement through an example involving the correction of an error in comparative financial statements for two years.

Matching

Assume that the controller of Collonade Corporation, a manufacturer of farm implements that began operations in 1981, has overlooked recording the liability for product warranties on tractors sold in the past. Warranty expense has been recognized when the warranty is honored rather than matched with revenue at the time of the sale. The warranties are for a five-year period, and the controller estimates the cost of warranties to approximate 5% of total tractor sales for each year. Tractor sales for the four years (1981–1984) preceding the detection of this error and for the current year (1985), as well as an analysis of estimated warranty expense for each year, are presented in Exhibit 19–6.

Exhibit 19–6 reveals that the liability for warranties at December 31, 1985, is $44,250, and that $37,500 should be reported in 1985 as warranty expense. Since the warranty expense of $48,500 has been recognized during 1985 under the cash basis, warranty expense for 1985 must be reduced by $11,000.

Because we are preparing two-year comparative financial statements, we must also compute the effect of this error on the financial statements of 1984. Warranty expense should have been reported for 1984 as $35,000 (5% of the $700,000 sales). Warranty liability should have been reported on the balance sheet at the end of 1984 as $55,250. The following calculation shows total sales for 1981–1984:

EXHIBIT 19–6
Collonade Corporation
Analysis of Tractor Sales and Estimated Warranty Expense

Year	(1) Tractor Sales	(2) Estimated Warranty Expense (5% of Tractor Sales)	(3) Warranty Costs from Each Year's Sales Paid Through 1984	(4) Warranty Costs from Each Year's Sales Paid in 1985	(5) Estimated Warranty Liability Remaining at Dec. 31, 1985*
1981	$ 650,000	$ 32,500	$25,000	$ 6,000	$ 1,500
1982	675,000	33,750	24,000	7,500	2,250
1983	660,000	33,000	20,000	8,000	5,000
1984	700,000	35,000	10,000	15,000	10,000
1985	750,000	37,500	–0–	12,000	25,500
	$3,435,000	$171,750	$79,000**	$48,500	$44,250

*[Column 2 − (Column 3 + Column 4)]
**Of the $79,000 paid through December 31, 1984, $49,000 was paid in 1981–1983 and $30,000 in 1984.

Year	Sales
1981	$ 650,000
1982	675,000
1983	660,000
1984	700,000
	$2,685,000

If we take 5% of $2,685,000 we have $134,250, the total warranty expense associated with these sales. Since $79,000 of warranties have been honored by the end of 1984, only $55,250 remains as a liability at that date. Ignoring income taxes at this point, the general journal entry at December 31, 1985, to record this correction of an error is as follows:

Retained Earnings	55,250	
Warranty Expense		11,000
Warranty Liability		44,250

The debit to Retained Earnings is equal to the warranty expense (and related unpaid warranty liability) that should have been recognized by the end of 1984 if the accrual method had been used to account for warranties in accordance with generally accepted accounting principles. The credit to Warranty Expense reduces the current year's expense from $48,500 (cash basis) to $37,500 (accrual basis). The credit to Warranty Liability for $44,250 establishes the December 31, 1985, warranty liability that must be recognized within the accrual method.

The introduction of income taxes complicates the accounting for the correction of the error, as we see in the discussion that follows. We shall assume that the company has deducted warranty expense for income tax purposes as payments have been made and will continue to do this in the future after the change to the accrual basis for financial-reporting purposes. If the company had been on the accrual basis in the past, deferred income taxes would have arisen because of the timing differences between taxable and pretax-accounting income. These deferred income taxes would have had debit balances, because pretax-accounting income (and income tax expense) would have been less than taxable income (and income tax payable). Specifically, the entry to recognize deferred income taxes in this situation is as follows, if we assume a 40% income tax rate:

Deferred Income Taxes ($44,250 × 40%)	17,700	
Income Tax Expense ($11,000 × 40%)	4,400	
Retained Earnings ($55,250 × 40%)		22,100

The debit to Deferred Income Taxes for $17,700 establishes the correct balance in that account for the December 31, 1985, liability of $44,250. The debit to Income Tax Expense of $4,400 recognizes the income tax expense on the 1985 timing difference where pretax-accounting income exceeds taxable income by $11,000 ($48,500 − $37,500). The credit to Retained Earnings places the prior period adjustment (correction of error) of $55,250 on a net-of-tax basis.

In practice, the two previous entries would probably be combined into a single entry to record the correction of the error as follows:

Retained Earnings ($55,250 − $22,100)	33,150	
Deferred Income Taxes	17,700	
Income Tax Expense	4,400	
Warranty Expense		11,000
Warranty Liability		44,250

In single-year financial statements, the debit to the Retained Earnings account would appear as an adjustment to the beginning retained earnings of 1985. However, the importance of comparative financial statements and the fact that most financial statements are prepared on a comparative basis compels us to complete our discussion of the presentation of corrections of errors by considering the additional complications that result from the presence of comparative statements.

Let's assume that Collonade Corporation has prepared the following (condensed) retained earnings statements *before the correction of the error* we have been discussing:

	1985	1984
Retained earnings, beginning of year	$ 795,000	$ 705,000
Add: Net income	175,000	190,000
	970,000	895,000
Deduct: Dividends	(100,000)	(100,000)
Retained earnings, end of year	$ 870,000	$ 795,000

We know from the previous journal entry that $33,150 will be presented as an adjustment to the beginning 1985 retained earnings figure and that 1985 net income will be increased by $6,600—the net of an increase in income tax expense of $4,400 and a decrease in warranty expense of $11,000. What about the 1984 comparative statements? We must identify the impact of the change on 1984 income and on the beginning 1984 retained earnings to complete the comparative presentation in the 1984–1985 retained earnings statements.

The impact of the change on 1984 net income is summarized as follows:

Warranty expense on accrual basis	$ 35,000
Warranty payments made	(30,000)
Reduction in income resulting from change from cash to accrual basis	$ 5,000
Reduction in income on net-of-tax basis [$5,000 × (1 − .40)]	$ 3,000

The warranty liability at the beginning of 1984 is computed as follows:

Sales for 1981–1983 ($650,000 + $675,000 + $660,000— operations began in 1981.)	$1,985,000
Estimated warranty percentage	5%
Estimated warranty expense, 1981–1983	99,250
Cash payments for warranties, 1981–1983	(49,000)
Warranty liability at December 31, 1983	$ 50,250
Reduction in beginning 1984 retained earnings, net-of-tax [$50,250 × (1 − .40)]	$ 30,150

The revised retained earnings statements for Collonade Corporation for 1985 and 1984 are presented in Exhibit 19–7.

The comparative income statements for Collonade Corporation for 1984–1985 will present restated net income figures of $187,000 and $181,600, respectively. In those statements, the warranty expense and income tax expense amounts will be restated to reflect the retroactive application of the change from the cash to the accrual method of accounting for warranties. All financial statements will thus be restated to apply the accrual method retroactively and to make the financial statements comparable. The consistency principle has

Consis-tency

EXHIBIT 19–7
Collonade Corporation
Revised Comparative Retained Earnings Statements

	1985	*1984*
Beginning retained earnings as previously reported	$ 795,000	$ 705,000
Correction of error in previously issued financial statements, net of income taxes of $22,100 in 1985 and $20,100 in 1984	(33,150)	(30,150)
Beginning retained earnings restated	761,850	674,850
Net income	181,600*	187,000**
	943,450	861,850
Dividends	(100,000)	(100,000)
Net income	$ 843,450	$ 761,850

*$175,000 + ($11,000 − $4,400) = $181,600
**$190,000 − ($5,000 − $2,000) = $187,000

been followed in this case because of the retroactive restatement of the 1984 comparative information.

In this illustration we have presented the retroactive application of the correction of an error in which the company changed from an unacceptable to an acceptable method of accounting. This same procedure is followed for other types of error corrections, for special changes in accounting principle, and for changes in reporting entity. Because of the similarity of presentations in all of these cases, we do not illustrate the others in this text.

A Practice Example of Correcting an Error

Accountants strive to avoid making errors and, consequently, instances of material errors corrected by restatement are uncommon. Exhibit 19–8 provides an illustration of comparative statements of retained earnings and income and the related footnote taken from actual practice. The name of the company is disguised, but all other information is authentic. The exhibit includes the company's income statement and statement of retained earnings. The beginning retained earnings balance is restated and the explanatory note is referenced. Note 2 contains a detailed explanation of the error.

EXHIBIT 19–8
Example of Correction of an Error
Arben Rother & Company, Inc.
STATEMENTS OF INCOME AND RETAINED EARNINGS
For years ended May 31, 1984 and 1985

	1985	*1984* *[Note 2]*
Net sales	$7,490,868	$7,706,546
Cost of sales	6,338,657	6,377,747
Gross profit	1,152,211	1,328,799
Operating expenses	1,033,091	1,217,956
Operating income	119,120	110,843
Other income (deductions)		
Interest expense		
Short-term bank notes	(42,506)	(140,751)
Long-term debt	(79,247)	(43,776)

Life insurance proceeds of $49,165, net of cash surrender value recorded in prior years	20,731	—
Interest income	17,107	14,485
Furniture rental income, net of depreciation expense	20,446	13,224
Loss on sale of rental furniture	(754)	(5,144)
Miscellaneous	9,708	3,028
Total other income (deductions)	(54,515)	(158,934)
Earnings (loss) before federal and state income taxes (credits)	64,605	(48,091)
Federal and state income taxes (credits) [Note 4]		
Current	40,070	(27,083)
Deferred	(30,364)	5,307
	9,706	(21,776)
Net earnings (loss)	54,899	(26,315)
Retained earnings at beginning of year		
As previously reported	477,556	501,496
Adjustment [Note 2]	(37,517)	(28,110)
As restated	440,039	473,386
	494,938	447,071
Dividends on common stock—$2 per share in 1984	—	7,032
Retained earnings at end of year	$ 494,938	$ 440,039
Earnings (loss) per share of common stock, based on 3,516 shares of common stock outstanding	$15.61	$(7.48)

See accompanying notes to financial statements.

Arben Rother & Company, Inc.
PARTIAL NOTES TO THE FINANCIAL STATEMENT [NOTE 2]
May 31, 1984 and 1985

Prior Year Adjustment—Rebates to Dealers

During the current year and in prior years, the Company has made rebates to dealers based on the volume of their purchases of Acme television and audio equipment from the Company during each of the Company's fiscal years. The rebates are made based upon plans established at the option of the Company. In prior years the aggregate amount of such rebates was included in expenses when distributed. The accompanying financial statements have been restated to include such costs in expenses in the year incurred. As a result of this restatement, retained earnings at May 31, 1983 has been reduced $28,110, net of related deferred Federal and state income taxes of $20,305, and the net loss for 1984 has been increased by $9,407 ($2.67 per share), net of deferred Federal and state income taxes of $7,790.

CONCLUDING REMARKS

Many new pronouncements of the FASB require the implementation of accounting changes. Most of these pronouncements also describe the manner in which such changes should be reported. In many cases the methods of transition contained in a new pronouncement differ from the requirements of *APB Opinion No. 20.* In such circumstances the provisions of the new pronouncement govern and should be followed. If the new pronouncement does not specify how to account for the transition to the new practices, however, then the general provisions of *APB Opinion No. 20* that we have discussed in this chapter should be followed.

Financial accounting and reporting for various types of accounting changes and corrections of errors is complex. While logic and reason underlie the standards of accounting and reporting for changes and errors, many rules must be applied to comply successfully with generally accepted accounting principles. Most knowledgeable accountants refer frequently to the technical literature for guidance if changes or errors are encountered. To help you understand and apply the standards of financial accounting and reporting in this area, Exhibit 19–9 presents a useful summary. Study the summary and refer to the part of the chapter that deals with issues about which you may desire further study.

EXHIBIT 19–9
Accounting Changes and Corrections of Errors

Type of Change or Correction	I. Footnote Disclosure — Explanation and Justification	I. Footnote Disclosure — Impact on Income and EPS	II. Retroactive Application — On *Pro Forma* Basis	II. Retroactive Application — Restatement of Financial Statements	III. Additional Special Accounting Treatment
A. Principle: 1. General	X	X (Current year)	X		—Cumulative effect is presented immediately following extraordinary items
2. Special*	X	X (All years)		X	
B. Estimate: 1. Affecting several periods	X	X (Current year)			
2. Annual	No Special disclosure requirements				
C. Entity:	X	X (All years)		X	
Correction of an error:	X	X (Year of error)		X	—Present as a prior period adjustment

*Special changes: (1) Change from LIFO to another inventory method.
(2) Change in accounting method for long-term construction type contracts.
(3) Change to or from full-cost method of accounting used in extractive industries.
Special exemption: Statements issued in an initial public offering of securities.
SOURCE: Adapted from Jan R. Williams, *FASB/APB Review* (New York: AICPA, 1983), p. 1-2-2.

KEY POINTS

1. Three approaches are available for integrating an accounting change into the financial records: (1) the restatement method; (2) the cumulative effect method; and (3) the current and prospective method.

2. There are three types of accounting changes: (1) changes in accounting principle; (2) changes in accounting estimate; and (3) changes in the reporting entity.

3. Changes in accounting estimate are reported currently if only the current period is affected, or currently and prospectively if both the current and future periods are affected.

4. The cumulative effect of *general* types of changes in accounting principle are reported in a separate special category of the income statement in the year of the change.

5. The cumulative effect of *special* changes in accounting principle are retroactively reported by restating previously issued financial statements.

6. Changes in reporting entity are reported by restating previously issued financial statements.

7. The nature and justification of each accounting change must be disclosed as well as the monetary effects of the change.

8. Errors result from mathematical mistakes, mistakes in the application of accounting principles, oversight or misuse of facts that existed at the time the financial statements were prepared, and using an unaccepted accounting principle.

9. The effects of errors in financial statements are reported by restating previously issued financial statements.

APPENDIX **A** ERROR ANALYSIS

Many types of errors may exist in the accounting records. This chapter briefly discussed several general types of errors. This appendix discusses three specific types of errors that are frequently encountered: (1) errors in recording deferrals and accruals; (2) errors in inventories; and (3) errors in plant assets and depreciation. These discussions are followed by a brief example of a worksheet that may be helpful when several errors exist in the financial statements at the same time.

TYPES OF ERRORS

Failure to Record Deferrals and Accruals

Financial statements prepared in accordance with generally accepted accounting principles apply the accrual concept in accordance with the matching principle. **Accrual accounting** refers to the process whereby revenues are recognized in net income determination when they are earned rather than when cash is received. Likewise, expenses are recognized in the determination of net income when their benefit is received, not necessarily when cash is paid out.

> **Matching**

Four types of **deferrals** and **accruals** are recognized: (1) accrued revenues; (2) unearned revenues; (3) accrued expenses; and (4) prepaid expenses. The purpose of recognizing these items is to adjust the recognition of revenues and expenses from the period in which cash is received or paid to the period in which the item should be recognized in the determination of net income. If the accrual or deferral is not recognized properly, the related revenue or expense will be recognized when the cash is received or paid, but it will be recognized in the wrong accounting period.

The deferrals (unearned revenues and prepaid expenses) and accruals (accrued revenues and accrued expenses) are described as follows:

Accrued revenues. Revenues for which earning is complete but cash has not been received (e.g., interest receivable).

Unearned revenues. Revenues for which cash has been received but earning is not complete (e.g., rent collected in advance).

Accrued expenses. Expenses for which benefit has been received but cash has not been paid (e.g., wages payable).

Prepaid expenses. Expenses for which cash has been paid but benefit has not been received (e.g., prepaid insurance).

Exhibit 19–10 includes a summary of the impact on the financial statements from the *failure* to recognize the four types of deferrals and accruals.

Inventory Errors

Inventory errors usually result from miscounting inventory, incorrectly pricing inventory by the inventory method being applied, or miscalculating the dollar amount of inventory as physical amounts and dollar prices are combined to determine the total inventory figure.

Inventory errors *begin* in the *ending* inventory and, if not corrected, *become errors in the beginning inventory of the next accounting period.* An understanding of inventory errors rests on an understanding of the process by which we determine cost of goods sold within a periodic inventory system. The diagram in Exhibit 19–11 is helpful in recalling the important relationships.

Recall from our earlier discussion of inventory that beginning inventory plus the net cost of purchases equals goods available for sale. At the end of the accounting period these goods have either been sold or they are still in inventory. We see these relationships in the following abbreviated calculation of gross margin, where assumed dollar amounts are used:

Sales		$1,000
Cost of goods sold		
Beginning inventory	$ 150	
Net cost of purchases	700	
Goods available for sale	850	
Ending inventory	(320)	530
Gross margin		$ 470

Notice that the ending inventory is deducted and beginning inventory is added in determining cost of goods sold. Thus, an error in ending inventory has the opposite effect on cost of goods sold as the same error in beginning inventory. This helps explain why an error in inventory that goes uncorrected will be offset in the next accounting period.

Exhibit 19–12 summarizes the impact of inventory errors, beginning with ending inventory errors and continuing to beginning inventory errors.

EXHIBIT 19–10
Analysis of Deferrals and Accruals

Error—Failure to Record	Income Statement Errors*	Balance Sheet Errors*	Journal Entry Needed to Correct Error	
Accrued Revenue				
Example: Accrued interest receivable	− Interest Revenue − Net Income	− Interest Receivable − Retained Earnings	Interest Receivable Interest Revenue	X X
Unearned Revenue**				

Example: Rent received in advance	+ Rent Revenue
	 + Net Income
		− Unearned Rent Revenue
		 + Retained Earnings
			Rent Revenue
			    Unearned Rent
			      Revenue
				X
				
				 X

Accrued Expenses				
Example: Accrued wages payable	− Wages Expense + Net Income	− Wages Payable + Retained Earnings	Wages Expense Wages Payable	X X
Prepaid Expenses†				
Example: Prepaid insurance	+ Insurance Expense − Net Income	− Prepaid Insurance − Retained Earnings	Prepaid Insurance Insurance Expense	X X

*+ = overstatement; − = understatement.

**This analysis assumes that the total unearned rent revenue was credited to Rent Revenue when received. Alternatively, the amount could have been credited to Unearned Rent Revenue, in which case the adjusting entry would be:

Unearned Rent Revenue   X

    Rent Revenue   X

The failure to make this adjustment would cause an understatement of net income, an overstatement of Unearned Rent Revenue, and an understatement of Retained Earnings.

†This analysis assumes that the total expense paid was debited to Insurance Expense. Alternatively, the amount could have been debited to Prepaid Insurance, in which case the adjusting entry would be:

Insurance Expense   X

    Prepaid Insurance   X

The failure to make this adjustment would cause overstatements of net income, Prepaid Insurance, and Retained Earnings.

EXHIBIT 19–11
Relationship of Inventory and Cost of Goods Sold

Inventory (beginning) + Net Cost of Purchases	=	Cost of Goods Sold + Inventory (ending)

Errors in Recording Depreciation

Errors in recording **depreciation** are generally of three types: (1) recording depreciation at an incorrect amount; (2) failing to record depreciation; and (3) expensing plant assets at acquisition. We consider each of these in the following paragraphs.

Recording Depreciation at an Incorrect Amount

When depreciation is recorded at an **incorrect amount,** the financial statement amounts affected are Depreciation Expense and net income in the income statement and Accumulated Depreciation and Retained Earnings in the balance sheet. An understatement of Depreciation Expense results in an overstatement of net income, an understatement of Accumulated Depreciation, and an overstatement of Retained Earnings. An overstatement of Depreciation Expense results in an understatement of net income, an overstatement of Accumulated Depreciation, and an understatement of Retained Earnings.

Failing to Record Depreciation

Failure to record depreciation has the same impact on the financial statements as an understatement of

Depreciation Expense: an overstatement of net income, an understatement of Accumulated Depreciation, and an overstatement of Retained Earnings.

If depreciation is not recorded for a series of accounting periods, the effect of the errors accumulate in the balance sheet while only the amount of depreciation expense omitted each year affects the income statement. For example, if $10,000 of Depreciation Expense is ignored in 1983 and $9,000 in 1984, net income will be overstated by $10,000 and $9,000 in 1983 and 1984. The impact of the errors accumulates in the balance sheet, however, and Accumulated Depreciation will be understated and Retained Earnings will be overstated by $10,000 and $19,000 ($10,000 + $9,000) in 1983 and 1984, respectively.

Expensing Plant Assets at Acquisition

The erroneous **expensing of a plant asset at acquisition** results in an understatement of net income of that period and an offsetting overstatement of net income throughout the asset's life as Depreciation Expense is not recorded.

EXHIBIT 19–12
Analysis of Inventory Errors

Errors	Income Statement Errors*	Balance Sheet Errors*
Ending Inventory		
Overstatement	− Cost of Goods Sold + Net Income	+ Inventory + Retained Earnings
Understatement	+ Cost of Goods Sold − Net Income	− Inventory − Retained Earnings
Beginning Inventory		
Overstatement	+ Cost of Goods Sold − Net Income	None**
Understatement	− Cost of Goods Sold + Net Income	None**

*+ = overstatement; − = understatement.
**This assumes that the error in beginning inventory is the reversal of an error in ending inventory of the previous period.

EXHIBIT 19–13
Example Analysis of Plant-Asset Error

	1980	1981	1982	1983	1984
Overstatement of expense and understatement of income from original error—expensing $10,000 plant asset	$10,000	—	—	—	—
Reversal of error via understatement of depreciation expense ($10,000/5 years)	(2,000)	$(2,000)	$(2,000)	$(2,000)	$(2,000)
Accumulated understatement of net plant assets and retained earnings:					
1980	$ 8,000	8,000			
1981		$ 6,000	6,000		
1982			$ 4,000	4,000	
1983				$ 2,000	2,000
1984					−0−

EXHIBIT 19–14
Andersonville Company
Example Worksheet for Multiple Errors
December 31, 1983

Description of Error	Accounts	Dr.	Cr.	Net Income Inc. (Dec.)	Working Capital Inc. (Dec.)	Non-current Assets Inc. (Dec.)	Non-current Liabilities Inc. (Dec.)	Stock-holders' Equity Inc. (Dec.)
1. Misclassification of note payable	Current Notes Payable	10,000			$10,000			
	Noncurrent Notes Payable		10,000				$10,000	
2. Overstatement of beginning inventory	Retained Earnings	15,000						$(15,000)
	Cost of Goods Sold		15,000	$15,000				
3. Expensing of land acquisition	Land	25,000				$25,000		
	Retained Earnings		25,000					25,000
4. Failure to record accrued interest payable	Interest Expense	2,000		(2,000)				
	Interest Payable		2,000		(2,000)			
5. Failure to adjust for unearned portion of rent received in advance	Rent Revenue	4,000		(4,000)				
	Unearned Rent Revenue		4,000		(4,000)			
				9,000	4,000	25,000	10,000	10,000
Transfer of increase in net income to retained earnings				(9,000)				9,000
				–0–	$ 4,000	$25,000	$10,000	$ 19,000

$29,000 ⌣ $29,000

To illustrate, assume that a $10,000 asset with a five-year life and no salvage value was erroneously treated as an expense when it was acquired. If straight-line depreciation is appropriate and a full year's depreciation would have been taken in 1980, the year of acquisition, the impact of the series of errors on the five years is as presented in Exhibit 19–13.

WORKSHEET ANALYSIS FOR _____ MULTIPLE ERRORS

If many errors have been made, a worksheet may be helpful in accumulating the errors in an organized fashion and making the proper corrections in the financial statements. Appendix A of Chapter 5 illustrated a basic worksheet in which the following columns were included: trial balance, adjustments, adjusted trial balance, income statement, retained earnings statement, and balance sheet. Each of these major headings had both debit and credit columns, resulting in a twelve-column worksheet.

While the worksheet in Chapter 5 was designed to facilitate the adjustment of the accounts at the end of the accounting period, the same sort of worksheet may be used to accumulate and organize the information necessary to correct the accounting records for numerous errors. The worksheet begins with the trial balance columns, which are followed by correction columns (which are used much like the adjustment columns of the Chapter 5 worksheet). Debit and credit corrections are inserted in the correction columns on the appropriate lines of the worksheet, much like adjusting entries were in Chapter 5. A corrected trial balance is computed, and the accounts are then distributed among the income statement, retained earnings statement, and the balance sheet columns in exactly the same way as the worksheet covered earlier. Because of the similarity of this type of analysis to that covered earlier in the text, we do not repeat it here.

One problem frequently encountered by accountants is the necessity of determining whether or not

Materiality adjustments are material in amount. While some mistakes may appear immaterial, others may be individually significant. Material errors obviously require correction. Correcting errors that are individually immaterial, on the other hand, may be quite costly and serve no real benefit. The effects of all errors detected should be summarized to allow the accountant to determine their collective effect on various aspects of the financial statements.

Generally, accountants develop detailed working papers to summarize and analyze the individual and collective effects of all errors detected. An example of such a work paper for Andersonville Company is presented in Exhibit 19–14. This example is prepared as of December 31, 1983, and includes several typical errors at assumed amounts. A brief description of each error follows:

1. **Misclassification of note payable.** A $10,000 note payable due in 1987 was erroneously included among current liabilities. Correction of this error reduces current liabilities (increasing working capital) and increases noncurrent liabilities.

2. **Overstatement of beginning inventory.** Ending inventory of 1982 and beginning inventory of 1983 were overstated by $15,000. Correction of this error reduces Retained Earnings and decreases Cost of Goods Sold for 1983, resulting in an increase in 1983 net income.

3. **Expensing of land acquisition.** Land costing $25,000 was erroneously written off as an expense when it was acquired in 1982. Correction of this error increases both the Land and Retained Earnings accounts.

4. **Failure to record accrued interest payable.** Accrued interest payable of $2,000 was not record-

ed at the end of 1983. Correction of this error results in an increase in Interest Expense (and a related reduction in net income) and an increase in Interest Payable (and resulting reduction in working capital).

5. **Failure to adjust for unearned portion of rent revenue.** Rent of $4,000 received in advance and credited to Rent Revenue was not transferred to an Unearned Rent Revenue account at December 31, 1983. Correction of this error results in a reduction in Rent Revenue (and related reduction in net income) and an increase in a liability for unearned rent (and related reduction in working capital).

In Exhibit 19–14 these errors are accumulated in terms of major financial-statement items (net income, working capital, noncurrent assets, noncurrent liabilities, and stockholders' equity) that are typically used

Materiality to evaluate the materiality of errors. Other categories could be used; these are included only as one example of how this type of analysis can be made.

Inspection of the totals in Exhibit 19–14 reveals that the largest impact of the errors relates to noncurrent assets. While the individual effect of each error may not be material, the aggregate impact of all errors may well be material. A final judgment on the materiality of several errors is facilitated by comparing the columnar totals with the total amounts in the categories they represent. For example, correction of the total errors detected would result in a $4,000 increase in working capital. Comparing this amount with *total* working capital (and perhaps computing a new current ratio with the revised figures) would help in deciding whether the errors should be corrected.

Determining the collective effect of many errors on individual components of the financial statements allows us to assess the materiality of errors from many perspectives. For example, the effect of an error may not be judged material in relation to net income, but it may have a substantial effect on the working capital of the company.

QUESTIONS

19–1   Describe a change in accounting principle and give one example of such a change.

19–2   Describe a change in accounting estimate and give one example of such a change.

19–3   Describe a change in reporting entity and give one example of such a change.

19–4   Identify several situations that result in ac-

counting errors.

19–5   Describe the restatement method of handling accounting changes and corrections of errors.

19–6   What types of accounting changes are incorporated into the financial records by the restatement method in accordance with generally accepted accounting principles?

19–7 Describe the cumulative effect method of handling accounting changes.

19–8 What types of accounting changes are incorporated into the financial records by the cumulative effect method?

19–9 Describe the current and prospective method of handling accounting changes.

19–10 What types of accounting changes are incorporated into the financial records by the current and prospective method?

19–11 In comparative financial statements, which of the three methods of incorporating accounting changes into the financial records is most compatible with the accounting principle of consistency? Justify your answer.

19–12 In applying the cumulative effect method of incorporating an accounting change into the accounting records, how does the accountant determine the cumulative effect and how is this item presented in the income statement?

19–13 What is the purpose of the *pro forma* disclosure that is presented at the bottom of the income statement in the cumulative effect method?

19–14 What procedure is appropriate when the cumulative effect of a change in accounting principle cannot be determined? What financial statement disclosure is appropriate in these circumstances?

19–15 If a company—after depreciating a plant asset for several years—determines that the asset's life should be shortened, how is depreciation expense for each year after the change determined?

19–16 What is meant by "self-correcting" errors? Cite an example of a self-correcting error.

19–17 What is meant by "permanent" errors? Cite an example of a permanent error.

19–18 Assume that an error in previously issued financial statements is detected in 1984, after the books have been closed for 1983. In the comparative statements for 1983 and 1984, how should this item be presented? (Assume that the error correction results in a decrease of net income in both 1984 and 1983 and in the beginning retained earnings of 1983.)

19–19 (Appendix A) Briefly explain the impact that each of the following errors has on the financial statements of the period of the error:

[a] Failure to record accrued wages payable at the end of the year.
[b] Failure to adjust the prepaid insurance account for the portion of the prepaid insurance premiums that have expired.
[c] An overstatement of ending merchandise inventory.
[d] Failure to record depreciation expense for the year.

19–20 (Appendix A) If a company inadvertently expensed the cost of a plant asset that should have been capitalized, what impact will this error have on the financial statements in the year of the error and the next year? (You may assume that the company's policy calls for recording a half-year's depreciation in the year of acquisition.)

CASES

C19–1 *Accounting Principles Board Opinion No. 20* is concerned with accounting changes. You are helping a young accountant to understand this pronouncement.

Instructions

[a] Define, discuss, and illustrate the following terms so clearly that the accountant will be able to distinguish one from the other:
 [1] An accounting change.
 [2] A correction of an error in previously issued financial statements.
[b] Discuss the justification for a change in accounting principle.
[c] Discuss the reporting, as required by *APB Opinion No. 20,* of a change from the LIFO method to another method of inventory pricing.
 (AICPA adapted)

C19–2 Accountants are frequently required to distinguish between various types of accounting changes.

Instructions

[a] If a public company desires to change from the sum-of-the-years'-digits depreciation method to the straight-line method for its fixed assets, what type of accounting change would this be? Discuss the permissibility of this change.
[b] When *pro forma* disclosure is required for an accounting change, how are these *pro forma* amounts determined?
[c] If a public company obtained additional information about the service lives of some of its fixed assets which showed that the service lives previously used should be shortened, what type of accounting change would this be? Include in your discussion how the

change should be reported in the income statement of the year of the change and what disclosures should be made in the financial statements or notes.

[d] Changing specific subsidiaries comprising the group of companies for which consolidated financial statements are presented is an example of what type of accounting change? What effect does it have on the consolidated income statements?

(AICPA adapted)

C19-3 Cowan, Inc., has made two accounting changes during 1983 that affect its 1983 income statement. These changes are described below:

Change in Life of Machinery. During 1983 the decision was made to depreciate all machinery over a 10-year life rather than over the 8-year life used in the past for both book and income tax purposes. The company's bookkeeper correctly determined that accumulated depreciation would have been $37,800 less under the 10-year life than under the 8-year life as of the beginning of 1983. The bookkeeper, therefore, made the following entry during 1983:

Accumulated Depreciation	37,800	
Cumulative Effect of Change in Accounting Estimate		37,800

Depreciation expense of $12,200 (assuming a 10-year life from acquisition) has been recorded during 1983.

Change in Inventory Method. During 1983 a change was made from the FIFO to the weighted average method of costing merchandise inventory. The ending 1982 inventory was $61,750 under FIFO. When management decided to change to the weighted average method in mid-1983, the beginning inventory was recalculated as $67,510, and the bookkeeper made the following entry:

Inventory ($67,510 − $61,750)	5,760	
Retained Earnings		5,760

Instructions

[a] What type of accounting change is the change in the life of the machinery? Do you agree with the bookkeeper's entry? Why? How would you have recorded this accounting change?

[b] What type of accounting change is the change in inventory methods? Do you agree with the bookkeeper's entry? Why? How would you have recorded this accounting change?

C19-4 Below are listed several events that require

accounting recognition as either accounting changes or corrections of errors in previously issued financial statements.

[1] A change from the LIFO to the FIFO method of determining the cost of merchandise inventory.

[2] A change from the cash to the accrual method, resulting in the recognition of deferrals and accruals that have not been recognized in the past.

[3] A change in the subsidiaries making up the group of companies for which consolidated financial statements are prepared.

[4] A change in the percentage of credit sales recognized as doubtful accounts.

[5] A change from the straight-line to the units-of-output method of recognizing depreciation expense on machinery.

[6] A change from the weighted average to the LIFO method of determining the cost of merchandise inventory.

[7] A change in the estimated useful life over which a building is being depreciated.

[8] Correction of an inventory error made in the determination of the previous year's merchandise inventory.

[9] A change from the completed contracts to the percentage-of-completion method of recognizing revenue on long-term construction contracts.

[10] A change from treating all leases as operating leases to an application of *FASB Statement of Financial Accounting Standards No. 13*, in which some leases are treated as capital leases and others as operating leases.

Instructions

For each event identify the following:

[a] The type of event—change in accounting principle, change in accounting estimate, change in accounting entity, or correction of an error.

[b] The proper accounting treatment to adjust or correct for the event—current and prospective, cumulative effect, or retroactive.

C19-5 A change in the method of accounting may be classified as a change in accounting principle, a change in accounting estimate, or a change in reporting entity. Listed below are three independent situations relating to accounting changes:

Situation 1. A company determined that the depreciable lives of its fixed assets were too long to fairly match the cost of the assets with the revenue they generated. The company decided at the beginning of the current year to reduce the depreciable lives of all of its existing fixed assets by five years.

Situation 2. On December 31, 1983, Gary Company owned 70% of Allen Company. At that time Gary used the cost method to report its investment because of political uncertainties in the country in which Allen was located. On January 2, 1984, the management of Gary Company was satisfied that the political uncertainties were resolved and that the assets of the company were no longer in danger of nationalization. Accordingly, Gary plans to prepare consolidated financial statements for Gary and Allen Companies for the year ended December 31, 1984.

Situation 3. A company decides in January 1984 to adopt the straight-line method of depreciation for plant assets. The straight-line method will be used for new acquisitions as well as for previously acquired assets for which depreciation has been recorded on an accelerated basis.

Instructions

For each of those situations provide the information indicated below. Complete [a] through [d] for each situation before going to the next situation.
[a] Type of accounting change.
[b] Manner of reporting the change under current generally accepted accounting principles, including a discussion, where applicable, of how amounts are computed.
[c] Effect of the change on the statement of financial position (balance sheet) and income statement.
[d] Any necessary footnote disclosure.

(AICPA adapted)

EXERCISES

E19–1 Keel Corporation purchased a machine for $150,000 on January 1, 1979, when the machine had an estimated useful life of 10 years with no salvage value. The machine is being depreciated on a straight-line basis. On January 1, 1984, as a result of Keel's experience with the machine, it was decided that the machine had an estimated useful life of 15 years from the date of acquisition.

Instructions

Assuming this change is to be recognized in the company's accounts, compute the amount of depreciation expense on this machine that should be recognized in 1984.

(AICPA adapted)

E19–2 On January 2, 1980, Thacker Corporation acquired machinery at a cost of $150,000. This machinery was being depreciated by the double-declining balance method over an estimated useful life of 10 years, with no residual value. At the beginning of 1982, it was decided to change to the straight-line method of depreciation.

Instructions

[a] Ignoring income tax considerations, compute the amount of the cumulative effect of this accounting change.
[b] Assuming that the income tax rate is 40% and that Thacker will continue to use double-declining balance depreciation for income tax purposes, prepare the general journal entry to record the accounting change.

(AICPA adapted)

E19–3 Brasher Company purchased a machine for $3,000,000 on January 1, 1980, when the machine had an estimated useful life of six years with no salvage value. The machine is being depreciated on a straight-line basis. On January 1, 1983, Brasher determined, as a result of additional information, that the machine had an estimated useful life of eight years from the date of acquisition with no salvage value. An accounting change was made in 1983 to reflect this additional information.

Instructions

[a] Assuming that the direct effects of this change are limited to the effect on depreciation and the related income tax provision and that the income tax rate was 40% throughout 1980–1983, show what should be reported in Brasher's income statement for the year ended December 31, 1983, as the cumulative effect on prior years of changing the estimated useful life of the machine. Explain your answer.
[b] What amount of depreciation expense on this machine should be recognized in Brasher's income statement for the year ended December 31, 1983?

(AICPA adapted)

E19–4 On January 1, 1984, Belmont Company changed its inventory cost-flow method to the FIFO cost method from the LIFO cost method. Belmont can justify the change, which was made for both financial-statement and income tax reporting purposes. Inventories aggregated $4,000,000 on the LIFO basis at December 31, 1983. Supplementary records showed that the inventories would have totaled $4,800,000 at December 31, 1983, on the FIFO basis.

Instructions

[a] Ignoring income taxes, compute the 1984 adjustment for the effect of changing to the FIFO method.
[b] Prepare the journal entry to record this inventory change in January 1984.

(AICPA adapted)

E19-5 During 1984 Howard Company determined, as a result of additional information, that machinery that was previously depreciated over a seven-year life had a total estimated useful life of only five years. An accounting change was made in 1984 to reflect this additional information. If the change had been made in 1983, the allowance for accumulated depreciation would have been $2,600,000 at December 31, 1983, instead of $2,100,000. As a result of this change, 1984 depreciation expense was $200,000 greater than it would have been if the change had not been made. The direct effects of this change are limited to the effect on depreciation and the related income tax expense. The income tax rate in both 1983 and 1984 was 42%.

Instructions

[a] What amount of cumulative effect, if any, should be presented in the 1984 income statement?
[b] Explain briefly how depreciation expense for 1984 should be computed.

(AICPA adapted)

E19-6 Alperi Company acquired machinery on January 1, 1983, for $25,000. For three years the company depreciated the asset over an eight-year life with a $1,000 salvage value. Then Alperi determines that the asset's useful life will be a total of only six years rather than eight years. The salvage value is still expected to be $1,000.

Instructions

Prepare the general journal entry to record depreciation in the fourth year of the asset's life and provide computations to support the depreciation amount.

E19-7 Morley Company estimated uncollectible accounts at 2% of credit sales for several years, including 1983—when credit sales totaled $135,000. During 1984 management decided the percentage estimate should be changed to 3%. Credit sales for 1984 totaled $175,200.

Instructions

[a] The company's accountant recommends a prior period adjustment of $1,350 to apply the new 3% esti-

mate retroactively to 1983 sales, some of which have not been collected by the end of 1984. (The $1,350 was determined by applying an additional 1% to the $135,000 credit sales for 1983.) Do you agree with the accountant's recommendation? Why?
[b] Prepare the journal entry to record uncollectible accounts for 1984.

E19-8 MUB Company sells appliances with a two-year warranty. Historically the company established a liability for product warranties of 2% of sales at the time of the sale to provide for the warranty. (This amount has been debited to an expense and credited to a liability account. Payments have been charged to the liability account.) The company's controller is concerned that 2% of sales does not provide an adequate amount for warranties because of the rapidly increasing warranty costs.

In evaluating the adequacy of this estimate, the following information has been accumulated in early 1984:

Year	Sales	Warranty Payments Through Dec. 31, 1983	Revised Estimated Warranty Payments After Dec. 31, 1983
1980	$185,000	$3,800	—
1981	198,500	4,550	—
1982	251,000	5,000	$1,025
1983	262,800	3,000	3,800

Instructions

[a] Compute to the nearest half percentage of sales the amount of warranty expense you would provide for 1984 sales, which totaled $288,700.
[b] Prepare the journal entry to record the warranty expense and year-end liability for 1984.
[c] What adjustment, if any, would you make for years prior to 1984?

E19-9 The following information represents a comparison of net income computed by the percentage-of-completion and completed contract method for Long Company for the years 1980–1984:

	Net Income	
	Percentage-of-Completion Method	Completed Contract Method
1980	$100,000	$ 80,000
1981	150,000	135,000
1982	195,000	206,000
1983	190,000	175,000
1984	205,000	192,000

At the end of 1984, management decided to change from the completed contracts to the percentage-of-completion method on its long-term contracts because of new engineering estimates of the degree of completion.

Instructions

[a] Ignoring income taxes, show the retroactive adjustments that should be made to beginning retained earnings figures for 1983 and 1984.
[b] The company presented retained earnings for 1983 as follows:

Beginning balance	$500,000
Net income	175,000
	675,000
Dividends	(75,000)
Ending balance	$600,000

Assuming dividends for 1984 were $100,000, prepare comparative retained earnings statements for 1983 and 1984.

E19–10 Afta Company changed its procedure for associating manufacturing overhead with inventory items. The previous procedure for allocating overhead to inventory was based on a percentage of direct labor dollars. The company will now allocate overhead at a predetermined rate based on a fixed amount per direct labor hour.

The change is being implemented in 1984. Comparisons of amounts related to ending inventory for 1981–1984 are as follows:

	Inventory Costs Other Than Overhead	Overhead by Previous Method	Overhead by New Method
1981	$100,000	$ 50,000	$ 45,000
1982	150,000	75,000	80,000
1983	200,000	100,000	125,000
1984	250,000	125,000	130,000

Instructions

[a] What kind of accounting change is the Afta Company making?
[b] Ignoring income taxes, compute the cumulative effect of this change in 1984. Prepare the journal entry to recognize the change.
[c] What amount should be used for the ending inventory in computing the cost of goods sold for the 1984 income statement?

E19–11 On May 1, 1983, Falcon Company prepaid an insurance policy to cover the year beginning on that date. The bookkeeper debited Insurance Expense and

credited Cash for the $2,400 payment. No adjustment was made at October 31, the end of Falcon's fiscal year. For the year ending October 31, the company reported net income of $17,500.

Instructions

Note: You may ignore income taxes in this exercise.
[a] Compute the correct net income for the year ended October 31, 1983.
[b] Assuming the 1983 books have not yet been closed, prepare the entry to adjust the accounts for the correction of the error.
[c] Assuming the 1983 books have been closed, prepare the entry to adjust the accounts for the correction of the error.

E19–12 Public Company included in manufactured inventory only direct materials and direct labor and treated all manufacturing overhead as an expense of the period in which it was incurred. On advice of the company's auditors, the company changed in 1984 to full absorption costing in order to be in conformity with generally accepted accounting principles.

Beginning inventory for 1984 was $152,000, made up of $100,000 of material and $52,000 of labor. Ending inventory was $247,500, made up of $125,000 of material, $70,000 of labor, and $52,500 of overhead. Overhead applied to finished goods is 75% of the direct labor cost. The ending inventory for 1984 was properly determined, but it has not been recorded because adjusting and closing entries have not been made.

Instructions

[a] Ignoring income taxes, prepare the general journal entry to implement this change in accounting policy for determining the cost of manufactured inventory during 1984.
[b] Briefly explain your adjustment to the beginning inventory.

E19–13 While examining the December 31, 1984, financial statements of Handy Company, a new client, you discover the following:
[1] Inventory at January 1, 1984, had been overstated by $3,000.
[2] Inventory at December 31, 1984, was understated by $5,000.
[3] A three-year insurance policy had been purchased on January 2, 1983, for $1,500. The entire amount was charged as an expense in 1983.
[4] During 1984 Handy received a $1,000 cash advance from a customer for merchandise to be manu-

factured and shipped during 1985. The $1,000 was credited to sales revenue. Handy's gross profit on sales is 50%.

[5] Net income reported on the 1984 income statement (before reflecting any adjustments for the above items) is $20,000.

Instructions

Determine the proper net income for 1984 and label any adjustments to the reported net income of $20,000.

(AICPA adapted)

E19–14 Shepherd Corporation began operations on January 1, 1983. Financial statements for the years ended December 31, 1983 and 1984, contained the following errors:

	1983	*1984*
Ending inventory	$16,000 understated	$15,000 overstated
Depreciation expense	$6,000 understated	—
Insurance expense	$10,000 overstated	$10,000 understated
Prepaid insurance	$10,000 understated	—

In addition, on December 31, 1984, fully depreciated machinery was sold for $10,800 cash, but the sale was not recorded until 1985. There were no other errors during 1983 or 1984, and no corrections have been made for any of the errors.

Instructions

Select the correct answer for each of the following questions and provide computations to support your choices:

[a] If you ignore income taxes, what is the total effect of the errors on 1984 net income?
    [1] Net income overstated by $30,200.
    [2] Net income overstated by $11,000.
    [3] Net income overstated by $5,800.
    [4] Net income understated by $1,800.

[b] If you ignore income taxes, what is the total effect of the errors on the amount of working capital at December 31, 1984?
    [1] Working capital overstated by $4,200.
    [2] Working capital understated by $5,800.
    [3] Working capital understated by $6,000.
    [4] Working capital understated by $9,800.

(AICPA adapted)

E19–15 Norris Boat Company received $8,000 of inventory items on the last day of its fiscal year, May 31,

1984. The company employs a periodic inventory system.

Instructions

Determine the impact of the error(s) on the company's 1984 net income in each of the following independent cases:

[a] The items were included in inventory at May 31, but the purchase was not recorded until June 3.
[b] The items were excluded from the May 31 inventory, but the purchase was recorded on May 31.
[c] The items were excluded from the May 31 inventory; the purchase was not recorded until June 3.

E19–16 Morrow, Inc., acquired a machine in 1983 for $100,000 and erroneously charged the cost to an expense account. Correct accounting treatment would have called for the depreciation of the asset over its estimated useful life of five years with a 10% salvage value by the straight-line method. Morrow's policy is to take one-half year's depreciation in the year of acquisition and one-half in the year of disposal.

Instructions

Ignoring income taxes, determine the impact of this error on 1983 and 1984 net income.

E19–17 Dobie Company's bookkeeper is not familiar with accrual accounting concepts. He determined net income for 1984 to be $85,600. In your audit of the company you determine the following:

[1] Accrued, but unpaid, wages at the end of 1984 amounted to $2,550 and have not been recorded.
[2] Insurance premiums paid in 1984 totaled $18,000, only one-third of which relate to coverage for 1984. The other two-thirds relates to coverage in future years. (The complete amount was expensed when paid.)
[3] Accounts receivable of $50,000, which have been properly recorded, are expected to result in specific losses from uncollectibility of $2,000. (No specific accounts have been written off as of the end of the year.)
[4] Cash of $13,500, received in late 1984, was recorded as revenue, although the work to be performed under the related contract will take place in 1985.

Instructions

[a] Prepare a revised net income figure for 1984.
[b] Assuming that the 1984 books have not been closed, prepare separate general journal entries to correct each of the four items.

[c] How will these adjustments affect the 1984 balance sheet?

E19–18 The bookkeeper of Laramie Company, which has an accounting year ending December 31, made the following errors:

[1] A $1,000 collection from a customer on account was received on December 29, 1983, but not recorded until the date of its deposit in the bank, January 4, 1984.

[2] A supplier's $1,600 invoice for inventory items received in December 1983 was not recorded until January 1984. (Inventories at December 31, 1983 and 1984, were based on physical count and stated correctly.)

[3] Depreciation for 1983 was understated by $900.

[4] In September 1983 a $200 invoice for office supplies was charged to the Utilities Expense account. Office supplies are expensed as purchased.

[5] Sales on account of $3,000 for December 31, 1983, were recorded in January 1984.

Instructions

Determine the effect of these errors on each of the following financial statement items and provide your computations.

[a] Net income for 1983.

[b] Working capital at December 31, 1983.

[c] Total assets at December 31, 1983.

(AICPA adapted)

E19–19 South Carolina Supply Company has cash receipts and disbursement records that are summarized as follows for 1984, its first year of operations:

Cash receipts	$ 57,500
Cash disbursements	(36,200)
	$ 21,300

The company wants you to compute its income by accrual accounting principles.

You have identified the following items that may impact your computation:

[1] Depreciation of plant assets for 1984 computed by the straight-line method is $12,500.

[2] Prepaid insurance of $1,800, two-thirds of which relates to 1985, is included in the 1984 cash disbursement figure. This amount was recognized as insurance expense when it was paid.

[3] South Carolina Supply received $12,000 in advance rent for space in its building. The entire amount is included in the cash receipts figure and was recognized as rent revenue when received. However, $7,000 of it was for space that will be provided in 1985.

[4] Employees are due $2,500 at the end of 1984.

[5] Interest amounting to $3,170 from investments is receivable at the end of 1984.

[6] You estimate that your 1984 fee for accounting services that have not been billed will be $300.

Instructions

[a] Compute the correct income before income tax for 1984 by accrual accounting concepts.

[b] Prepare a journal entry to record the items that have not been properly recorded.

E19–20 Your client has prepared a schedule with the following column headings:

Error

1983—Net Income
    Assets
    Liabilities
    Stockholders' Equity

1984—Net Income
    Assets
    Liabilities
    Stockholders' Equity

Instructions

For each of the following errors, indicate whether the item at the head of each column is overstated ($+$), understated ($-$), or not affected (0) by the error:

[a] Omission of wages payable at the end of 1983.

[b] Failure to record depreciation expense for 1983.

[c] Failure to adjust insurance expense recognized in 1983 for amounts representing prepaid insurance for 1984.

[d] Overstatement of ending 1983 inventory.

[e] Understatement of ending 1984 inventory.

[f] Failure to record interest receivable at the end of 1983.

[g] Failure to adjust earned portion of amounts credited to unearned rent in 1983.

[h] Mathematical error in which $10,000 of amortization on an intangible asset was recorded at $1,000.

PROBLEMS

P19–1 Nelson Company reported net income of $140,000 in 1982 and has made a preliminary determination that its 1983 net income is $170,000. Management has now decided, however, to change its method of depreciation on plant assets from the double-declining balance to the straight-line method. (This change is not reflected in the 1983 preliminary income figure.)

All of Nelson's plant assets were acquired before 1981. The company's accountant has correctly determined depreciation for 1980–1983 under the two methods as follows:

	Double-Declining Balance	Straight-Line Method
1980	$100,000	$45,000
1981	90,000	45,000
1982	70,000	35,000
1983	50,000	40,000

Nelson's income tax rate is 46%, and the company had 60,000 shares of common stock outstanding in 1982 and 62,000 shares outstanding in 1983. No preferred stock is in the company's capital structure. The end of the company's accounting period is December 31. Nelson has used double-declining balance depreciation in the past for income tax purposes and will continue that policy in the future.

Instructions

[a] Prepare the general journal entry necessary to record the change from double-declining balance to straight-line depreciation and provide supporting computations.

[b] Prepare comparative income statements for 1982 and 1983 beginning with "income before cumulative effect of accounting change." Include both earnings per share figures and the required *pro forma* disclosures.

[c] Explain the lack of comparability that exists in the body of the income statements prepared in [b]. How does the *pro forma* disclosure resolve this problem?

P19–2   Boyce, Inc., is a calendar-year corporation. Its financial statements for the years 1984 and 1983 contained errors as follows:

	1984	*1983*
Ending inventory	$1,000 understated	$3,000 overstated
Depreciation expense	$800 understated	$2,500 overstated

Instructions

[a] Assume that the proper correcting entries were made at December 31, 1983. Determine the amount that 1984 income will be overstated or understated and provide computations. (Ignore income taxes.)

[b] Assume that no correcting entries were made at December 31, 1983. Ignoring income taxes, compute the amount by which Retained Earnings will be overstated or understated at December 31, 1984. (Provide supporting computations.)

[c] Assume that no correcting entries were made at December 31, 1983, nor at December 31, 1984, and that no additional errors occurred in 1985. Ignoring income taxes, compute the amount by which December 31, 1985, working capital will be overstated or understated and provide supporting computations or explanation.

(AICPA adapted)

P19–3   This problem consists of four *independent* parts, but each company's accounting period ends on December 31. Ignore income taxes except where they are mentioned.

Part 1.   At the beginning of 1980 Orange Company acquired, for $220,000, equipment that is being depreciated over an 8-year life with a salvage value of 10% of historical cost. In 1983 the decision was made to extend the useful life to 12 years with no salvage value.

Instructions

Prepare the general journal entry, if any, to record this change and the 1983 depreciation expense.

Part 2.   Red Company has consistently expensed warranty costs as they were incurred rather than recognize them on an estimated basis in the period in which the products were sold. During 1984 management decided to change to the accrual basis in which estimates of warranty expense are made annually on the basis of sales and past warranty experience. Red Company officials estimate that the liability for warranty at the beginning of 1984 was $35,600. Warranty costs for 1984 are estimated at 2% of sales of $1,500,000. During 1984, $18,000 of warranty costs were paid, $14,500 of which relate to pre-1984 sales. Warranty Expense was debited with $18,000. The company's income tax rate has consistently been 40%. Red will continue to deduct warranty costs for income tax purposes as actual cash payments are made.

Instructions

Prepare the general journal entry, if any, to record this change and warranty expense for 1984.

Part 3.   Blue Company determined in 1983 that repair and maintenance expense of 1981 included the cost of a $25,000 machine that had a five-year estimated useful life with no expected salvage value. If the asset had been properly accounted for in 1981, a half-year's depreciation would have been taken in that year by the straight-line method.

Instructions

Prepare the general journal entry, if any, to correct this oversight and to record depreciation expense in 1983.

Part 4. Purple Company changed inventory methods from FIFO to LIFO in 1984. Inventory figures are as follows:

	FIFO	LIFO
Beginning 1984	$86,500	—
Ending 1984	92,800	$88,700

The beginning 1984 inventory under the LIFO method cannot be determined.

Instructions

Prepare the general journal entry, if any, to record this change and the 1984 ending inventory.

P19–4   John Parris, accountant for Rothchild, Inc., has contacted you concerning a financial reporting situation in a Rothchild subsidiary company. John describes the situation as follows:

The subsidiary company changed from the weighted average to the FIFO method during 1984. Inventory amounts under each method are as follows:

	Weighted Average	FIFO
Beginning 1984 inventory	$88,800	$82,600
Ending 1984 inventory	97,600	84,700

The subsidiary's accountant has recorded the change as follows:

Retained Earnings	6,200	
($88,800 − $82,600)		
Inventory		6,200
(To restate the 1984 beginning inventory.)		

The accountant has then computed the 1984 cost of goods sold as follows:

Beginning FIFO inventory	$ 82,600
Net cost of purchases	200,000
	282,600
Ending FIFO inventory	84,700
Cost of goods sold	$197,900

The subsidiary's income tax rate is 42%. The weighted average method has been used for income tax purposes in the past, and this practice will be continued in the future.

Instructions

[a] Identify the type of accounting change that has taken place and briefly describe the proper accounting treatment for that change (without regard to the approach taken by the subsidiary's accountant).
[b] List the errors you can identify in the accountant's recording of the accounting change.
[c] Prepare a revised entry to record the accounting change in 1984.
[d] Has the accountant properly computed cost of goods sold for 1984? Give reasons for your answer.
[e] How should the effect of this change in inventory method be presented in the company's 1984 income statement?

P19–5   Warm-Glow Company manufactures kerosene heaters for home use. The company's December 31 year-end financial statements contained the following errors:

	Dec. 31, 1983	Dec. 31, 1984
Ending inventory	$2,000 understated	$1,800 overstated
Depreciation expense	$400 understated	—

An insurance premium of $1,500 was prepaid in 1983 to cover 1983, 1984, and 1985. The entire amount was charged to expense in 1983. On December 31, 1984, fully depreciated machinery was sold for $3,200 cash, but the sale was not recorded until 1985. There were no other errors during 1983 or 1984, and no corrections have been made for any of the errors. Ignore income tax considerations.

Before any of the above errors were corrected, the company's 1983 and 1984 net income figures were determined to be $10,500 and $13,600, respectively.

Instructions

[a] Compute revised net income figures for 1983 and 1984 and label any adjustments to the previously determined figures.
[b] What is the effect of these errors on the amount of Warm-Glow's working capital at December 31, 1984?
[c] What is the effect of these errors on the amount of Warm-Glow's retained earnings at December 31, 1984?

(AICPA adapted)

P19–6   APO Corporation is negotiating a loan for expansion. Its books had never been audited and the bank requested an audit. APO then prepared the following comparative financial statements for the years ended December 31, 1983 and 1982:

BALANCE SHEET
As of December 31

	1983	1982
Assets		
Current Assets		
Cash	$ 163,000	$ 82,000
Accounts receivable	392,000	296,000
Allowance for uncollectible accounts	(37,000)	(18,000)
Marketable securities, at cost	78,000	78,000
Merchandise inventory	207,000	202,000
Total current assets	803,000	640,000
Fixed Assets		
Property, plant, and equipment	167,000	169,500
Accumulated depreciation	(121,600)	(106,400)
Total fixed assets	45,400	63,100
Total assets	$ 848,400	$ 703,100

Liabilities and Stockholders' Equity

	1983	1982
Liabilities		
Accounts payable	$ 121,400	$ 196,100
Stockholders' Equity		
Common stock ($10 par value; 50,000 shares authorized, 20,000 shares issued and outstanding)	260,000	260,000
Retained earnings	467,000	247,000
Total stockholders' equity	727,000	507,000
Total liabilities and stockholders' equity	$ 848,400	$ 703,100

STATEMENT OF INCOME
For the Years Ended December 31

	1983	1982
Sales	$1,000,000	$900,000
Cost of sales	430,000	395,000
Gross profit	570,000	505,000
Operating expenses	210,000	205,000
Administrative expenses	140,000	105,000
	350,000	310,000
Net income	$ ·220,000	$195,000

Additional Information

After auditing APO's books and records, the auditor wrote down the following paragraphs:

[1] An analysis of collections and losses on accounts receivable during the past two years indicates a drop in anticipated losses due to bad debts. After consultation with management it was agreed that the loss experience rate on sales should be reduced from the recorded 2% to 1%, beginning with the year ended December 31, 1983.

[2] An analysis of marketable securities revealed that this investment portfolio consisted entirely of short-term investments in marketable equity securities that were acquired in 1982. The total market valuation for these investments as of the end of each year was as follows:

Dec. 31, 1982	$81,000
Dec. 31, 1983	$62,000

[3] The merchandise inventory at December 31, 1982, was overstated by $4,000, and the merchandise inventory at December 31, 1983, was overstated by $6,100.

[4] On January 2, 1982, equipment costing $12,000 (estimated useful life of ten years and residual value of $1,000) was incorrectly charged to operating expenses. APO records depreciation on the straight-line method. In 1982 fully depreciated equipment (with no residual value) that originally cost $17,500 was sold as scrap for $2,500. APO credited the proceeds of $2,500 to property and equipment.

[5] An analysis of 1982 operating expenses revealed that APO charged to expense a three-year insurance premium of $2,700 on January 15, 1982.

Instructions

[a] Prepare the journal entries to correct the books at December 31, 1983. The books for 1983 have not been closed. (Ignore income taxes.)

[b] Assuming that any adjustments will be reported on comparative statements for the two years, prepare a schedule showing the corrected net income for the years ended December 31, 1983 and 1982. The first item on your schedule should be reported income for each year. (Ignore income taxes.)

(AICPA adapted)

P19–7   During 1984, Rolfe, Inc., discovered that a plant asset acquired in 1980 had been erroneously charged to expense rather than capitalized and depreciated over its estimated useful life. The specifics of the asset are as follows:

[1] Machine cost, $75,000.
[2] Estimated residual value, $5,000.
[3] Estimated useful life, 7 years.
[4] Intended method of depreciation, straight-line (full year taken in year of acquisition).

Rolfe's retained earnings statements for 1982–1983 are summarized as follows:

	1982	1983
Retained earnings, beginning	$140,500	$165,500
Net income	40,000	38,500
	180,500	204,000
Dividends declared	(15,000)	(15,000)
Ending balance	$165,500	$189,000

Instructions

[a] Prepare an analysis showing the impact of this error on the retained earnings balance for each year from 1980 through 1983.
[b] Ignoring income taxes, prepare the general journal entry required in 1984 to correct this error.
[c] Prepare comparative retained earnings statements for 1983 and 1984. The company declared dividends of $12,000 in 1984 and has determined that its 1984 income, before correction of the error described above, is $50,000.
[d] How would you respond to [b] and [c] if Rolfe determined that it must file corrected income tax returns for 1980–1983 and its income tax rate was 46%?

P19–8 To save money and keep the nature of its plant assets from being widely known, Coverton Corporation has constructed many of its plant assets. During 1984 the company changed the way it determined the cost of these assets by including in the cost those amounts that were previously treated as expenses when incurred. Both the previous method and the newly adopted method are generally accepted. Management believes the new method more closely approximates the company's investment in the assets, and the depreciation on the new cost method provides a superior matching of revenues and expenses. The previous method had been used since 1982, when the company began operations.

Information for 1982–1984 has been accumulated as follows:

	1984	1983	1982
Income information			
Net income (by old method)	—	$175,000	$180,000
Income before cumulative effect of accounting change (by new method)	$200,000	—	—
Depreciation expense (including depreciation on additional capitalized costs in 1984 figure)	60,000	40,000	35,000
Expenditures incorporated in accounting change			
Expensed in 1982 and 1983	—	45,000	50,000
Capitalized in 1984	40,000	—	—

The plant assets affected by the change in accounting principle are depreciated over a five-year life with no salvage value. A full year's depreciation is taken in the year the assets are constructed. The impact of the change in accounting principle is limited to the capitalization of expenditures and the related impact on depreciation expense. The company had 210,000 shares of common stock outstanding throughout the 1982–1984 period.

The company's effective income tax rate is 46%. The previous method of determining the cost of its assets will continue to be used for purposes of determining the company's income tax liability.

Instructions

[a] Compute the cumulative effect of the change in accounting principle that should be included in 1984 net income.
[b] Prepare comparative income statements, beginning with income before the cumulative effect of the accounting change, for 1983 and 1984. Include earnings-per-share figures and the *pro forma* disclosures required by *APB Opinion No. 20*.
[c] Briefly identify the problems in comparing the information in the body of the comparative income statements you have prepared. Explain how the *pro forma* disclosures remedy these problems.

P19–9 Rho Corporation decided that in the preparation of its 1983 financial statements two changes would be made from the methods used in prior years:

[1] **Depreciation.** Rho always used the declining-balance method for tax and financial reporting purposes but has decided to change during 1983 to the straight-line method for financial reporting only. The effect of this change is as follows:

	Excess of Accelerated Depreciation Over Straight-line Depreciation
Prior to 1982	$1,300,000
1982	101,000
1983	99,000
	$1,500,000

Depreciation is charged to cost of sales and to selling, general, and administrative expenses on the basis of 75% and 25%, respectively.

[2] **Bad-debt expense.** In the past Rho recognized bad-debt expense equal to 1.5% of net sales. After careful review it has been decided that a rate of 2% is more appropriate for 1983. Bad-debt expense is charged to selling, general, and administrative expenses.

The following information is taken from preliminary financial statements, prepared before the two changes were in effect:

Rho Corporation
CONDENSED BALANCE SHEET
December 31, 1983
With Comparative Figures for 1982

	1983	1982
Assets		
Current assets	$ 43,561,000	$ 43,900,000
Fixed assets, at cost	45,792,000	43,974,000
Less: Accumulated depreciation	(23,761,000)	(22,946,000)
	$ 65,592,000	$ 64,928,000
Liabilities and Stockholders' Equity		
Current liabilities	$ 21,124,000	$ 23,650,000
Long-term debt	15,154,000	14,097,000
Capital stock	11,620,000	11,620,000
Retained earnings	17,694,000	15,561,000
	$ 65,592,000	$ 64,928,000

Rho Corporation
INCOME STATEMENT
For the Year Ended December 31, 1983
With Comparative Figures for 1982

	1983	1982
Net sales	$80,520,000	$78,920,000
Cost of sales	54,847,000	53,074,000
	25,673,000	25,846,000

Selling, general, and administrative expenses	19,540,000	18,411,000
	6,133,000	7,435,000
Other income (expense), net	(1,198,000)	(1,079,000)
Income before federal income taxes	4,935,000	6,356,000
Federal income taxes	2,368,800	3,050,880
Net income	$ 2,566,200	$ 3,305,120

There have been no timing differences between book and tax items prior to the above changes. The effective tax rate is 48%.

Instructions

Basing your answer on *APB Opinion No. 20,* "Accounting Changes," compute for the items listed below the amounts which would appear on the comparative (1983 and 1982) financial statements of Rho Corporation after adjustments for the two accounting changes. Show amounts for both 1983 and 1982 and prepare supporting schedules as necessary.
[a] Accumulated depreciation.
[b] Deferred tax liability.
[c] Selling, general, and administrative expenses.
[d] Current portion of federal income tax expense.
[e] Deferred portion of federal income tax expense.
[f] Retained earnings.
[g] *Pro forma* net income.

(AICPA adapted)

P19–10 Centerville Manufacturing Company has an inexperienced bookkeeper who has maintained records on the basis of cash transactions. He recognizes expenses when cash is paid and revenues when cash is received. Operating results, recorded on this basis, are summarized for 1984 as follows:

Revenues		$85,000
Expenses		
Salaries	$18,000	
Equipment	60,000	
Insurance	15,000	93,000
Net loss		$ (8,000)

You have accumulated the following information concerning these revenue and expense items:

Revenues. Of the $85,000 cash received in 1984, $18,500 was related to sales transactions in 1983 and $10,000 was a one-year loan from a bank on December 1, 1984. The interest rate for this loan is 15%. Additional 1984 revenues for which cash has not yet been received amount to $25,000.

Salaries. Of the $18,000 paid in 1984, $1,850 represents salaries for the last four days of 1983. The company owes salaries of $2,200 at the end of 1984 that will be paid in early 1985.

Equipment. The $60,000 cash paid represents the price of a new machine purchased in 1984. This machine should be depreciated over a five-year period with a full year's depreciation taken in 1984 and no salvage value. Pre-1984 acquisitions amounted to $110,000. If the appropriate depreciation policies had been followed, depreciation prior to 1984 would have been $45,000 and 1984 depreciation would have been $22,000 on pre-1984 acquisitions.

Insurance. Of the $15,000 paid in 1984, $10,000 represents prepaid insurance for 1985. Also, $4,000 of $8,000 paid for insurance in 1983 represented prepaid insurance for 1984.

Instructions

[a] Compute a correct income figure for 1984, applying appropriate accrual accounting procedures and ignoring income taxes.
[b] Assuming the 1984 books are not closed, prepare the general journal entries for 1984 to correct the accounts and place them on an accrual basis.

P19–11 You have been engaged to examine the financial statements of Zew Corporation for the year ended December 31, 1984. In the course of your examination you have ascertained the following information:
[1] A check for $1,500 representing the repayment of an employee advance was received on December 29, 1984, but was not recorded until January 2, 1985.
[2] Zew uses the allowance method of accounting for uncollectible trade accounts receivable. The allowance is based on 3% of past due accounts (over 120 days) and 1% of current accounts as of the close of each month. Due to a changing economic climate, the amount of past due accounts has increased significantly, and management has decided to increase the percentage based on past due accounts to 5%. The following balances are available:

	As of Nov. 30, 1984	As of Dec. 31, 1984
	Dr. (Cr.)	Dr. (Cr.)
Accounts receivable	$390,000	$430,000
Past due accounts (included in accounts receivable)	12,000	30,000
Allowance for uncollectible accounts	(28,000)	9,000

[3] The merchandise inventory on December 31, 1983, did *not* include merchandise (having a cost of $7,000) which was stored in a public warehouse. Merchandise having a cost of $3,000 was erroneously counted twice and included twice in the merchandise inventory on December 31, 1984. Zew uses a periodic inventory system.
[4] On January 2, 1984, a new machine was installed in Zew's main factory. The cost of this machine was $97,000, and the machine is being depreciated on the straight-line method over an estimated useful life of 10 years. When the new machine was installed, Zew paid for the following items which were not included in the cost of the machine, but were charged to repairs and maintenance:

Delivery expense	$ 2,500
Installation costs	8,000
Rearrangement of related equipment	4,000
	$14,500

[5] On January 1, 1983, Zew leased a building for 10 years at a monthly rental of $12,000. On that date, Zew paid the landlord the following amounts:

Rent deposit	$ 6,000
First month's rent	12,000
Last month's rent	12,000
Installation of new walls and offices	80,000
	$110,000

The entire amount was charged to rent expense in 1983.
[6] In January 1983 Zew issued $200,000 of 8%, 10-year bonds at 97. The discount was charged to interest expense in 1983. Interest on the bonds is payable on December 31 of each year. Zew has recorded interest expense of $22,000 for 1983 and $16,000 for 1984.
[7] On May 3, 1984, Zew exchanged 500 shares of treasury stock (its $50 par value common stock) for a parcel of land to be used as a site for a new factory. The treasury stock had cost $70 per share when it was acquired, and on May 3, 1984, it had a fair market value of $80 per share. Zew received $2,000 when an existing building on the land was sold for scrap. The land was capitalized at $40,000, and Zew recorded a gain of $5,000 on the sale of its treasury stock.
[8] The Advertising and Promotion account included $75,000, which represented the cost of printing sales catalogs for a special promotional campaign in January 1985.

[9] On January 2, 1984, Zew adopted a pension plan, to be administered by a trustee, for eligible employees. Based on actuarial computations, the annual normal pension cost was $70,000, and the present value of past service cost on that date was $900,000. The company decided to use the maximum provision for pension expense and to fund past service cost. On December 31, 1984, Zew remitted to the trustee $970,000 and charged this amount to the Pension Expense account.

[10] Zew was named as a defendant in a law suit by a former customer. Zew's counsel advised management that Zew has a good defense and that counsel does *not* anticipate that there will be any impairment of Zew's assets or that any significant liabilities will be incurred as a result of this litigation. Management, however, wishes to be conservative and, therefore, has established a loss contingency of $100,000.

Instructions

Prepare a schedule showing the effect of errors upon the financial statements for 1984. The items in the schedule should be presented in the same order as the facts are given, with corresponding numbers 1 through 10. Use the following columnar headings for your schedule:

		Income Statement	Balance Sheet Dec. 31, 1984	
No.	Explanation	Dr. (Cr.)	Dr. (Cr.)	Account

(AICPA adapted)

P19–12 You have been asked to review and prepare any necessary adjustments for the financial statements of Min Electronics, Inc., for the years ended December 31, 1982 and 1983. Min received an unqualified opinion on its December 31, 1981, financial statements. You have extracted the following trial balances from the records:

	Dec. 31, 1982	Dec. 31, 1983
	Dr. (Cr.)	Dr. (Cr.)
Cash	$ 62,300	$ 71,297
Accounts receivable—mini calculators	19,500	6,000
Accounts receivable—other	34,300	45,299
Inventory—mini calculators	7,500	27,500
Inventory—other	89,500	92,019
Work-in-process inventory	7,307	9,409
6.5% note receivable	10,000	10,000
Building	257,220	257,220
Other assets	46,539	47,379
Other liabilities	(128,863)	(143,146)
6.5% construction loan	(168,000)	—
6.5% mortgage payable	—	(156,000)
Common stock	(185,000)	(185,000)
Retained earnings	(65,012)	(52,303)
Sales—mini calculators	(60,000)	—
Sales—other	(293,814)	(323,111)
Service department fees for computer-X	(7,200)	(9,612)
Cost of sales—mini calculators	40,000	—
Cost of sales—other	196,000	206,000
Interest revenue on 6.5% note receivable	—	(650)
Interest on construction loan	11,700	—
Interest on mortgage	—	10,920
Life insurance expense	—	2,500
Other expenses	126,023	84,279
	–0–	–0–

As a result of your investigation you have developed the following information:

[1] On July 1, 1983, Min contracted for a permanent-type, $50,000 mutual life insurance policy on the life of its president. Min designated itself as beneficiary. The annual gross premium of $2,500 is due on the contract date and thereafter on the annual anniversary date. The policy estimates that a dividend of $350 will be due the policyholder on July 1, 1984, and stipulates that the cash surrender value of the policy will be $84 on July 1, 1984. Min has elected to offset policy dividends against future premiums.

[2] In 1982 Min manufactured a new mini calculator. The marketing plan includes shipping the units on consignment to certain retailers. The following facts are available:

	1982	1983
Units produced (at $100 per unit)	475	200
Units shipped on consignment	400	—
Unit sales reported by consignees (at $150 per unit)	300	100

Retailers are entitled to deduct 10% of the sales price as a commission. All consignees' reports of sales were accompanied by full remittances.

[3] An invoice dated December 29, 1982, for a purchase of raw-materials (other) inventory for $4,105 was recorded in January 1983. The material was included in the December 31, 1982, count of physical inventory.

[4] Min services computer-X electronic equipment on

a contractual basis. The service fee is payable one year in advance. Maintenance is generally performed ratably over the life of the contract. Min recorded the following 12-month contracts as revenue when cash was received:

Date of Contracts	Amount
April 1, 1982	$7,200
August 1, 1983	$9,612

[5] The note receivable due December 31, 1985, was issued on January 2, 1982. Interest is due annually on January 2. The prevailing interest rate on similar notes is 6.5%.

[6] An analysis of the building account follows:

Purchase price of land and building	$ 55,000
Unpaid taxes assumed	4,300
Cost of demolition of old building	4,110
Cost of subdividing land	510
Payment to tenants of old building to cancel leases	3,300
Construction of new building	190,000
	$257,220

On January 3, 1982, Min purchased an old building on ten acres of land for $55,000 cash. The company immediately began demolition of the building and subdivision of the land into 10 one-acre lots of equal value. Nine acres were held for speculation and the other acre was used for construction of a new office building, which was begun on January 3, 1982.

To finance the construction, Min obtained $180,000 in proceeds of a one-year, 6.5% construction loan on January 3, 1982. The prevailing interest rate on similar loans was 6.5%. A payment of $12,000 principle plus interest was made on December 29, 1982. The unpaid balance of $168,000 was converted to a 6.5%, 14-year mortgage note on January 3, 1983. Note payments are due in equal installments plus interest annu-

ally on December 31. The note is secured by the building and the one acre of land on which it resides.

Construction of the new building was completed on December 30, 1982. Min occupied the building on January 3, 1983. The building has an estimated life of 40 years and a salvage value of $5,000; depreciation will be computed on a straight-line basis. Depreciation has not been recorded.

[7] Min distributes Super-D AM-FM radios to retailers. The radios are shipped from Min's supplier-manufacturer directly to the retailers. Min does not maintain an inventory of the radios.

In January 1982 Min signed a three-year contract to purchase 2,100 Super-D AM-FM radios each year from Melgren Manufacturing Company at a firm price of $30 per unit.

During January 1983, because of improvements in the production process, all local manufacturers of radios similar to the Super-D lowered their price to $22 per unit. Melgren also reduced its price of the Super-D radio to $22 except to Min. For competitive reasons, comparable reductions in prices to retailers were made by all local distributors, including Min. Because of a long-time business relationship between Melgren and Min and the certainty of future business, Min considers its contract with Melgren binding and will not contest it. Min purchased 2,300 radios in 1982 and 2,100 in 1983 and intends to meet its purchase commitment of 2,100 units in 1984.

Instructions

Prepare a schedule of adjustments which must be made to correct the 1982 and 1983 trial balances. The items on the schedule should be presented in the same order as the facts are given, with corresponding numbers 1 through 7. Include supporting data for item 6. Adjusted trial balances and formal financial statements are not required. Ignore income tax and deferred tax considerations. Use the following columnar headings for your schedule.

		1982			1983		
		Income Statement	Balance Sheet		Income Statement	Balance Sheet	
No.	Explanation	Dr. (Cr.)	Dr. (Cr.)	Account	Dr. (Cr.)	Dr. (Cr.)	Account

(AICPA adapted)

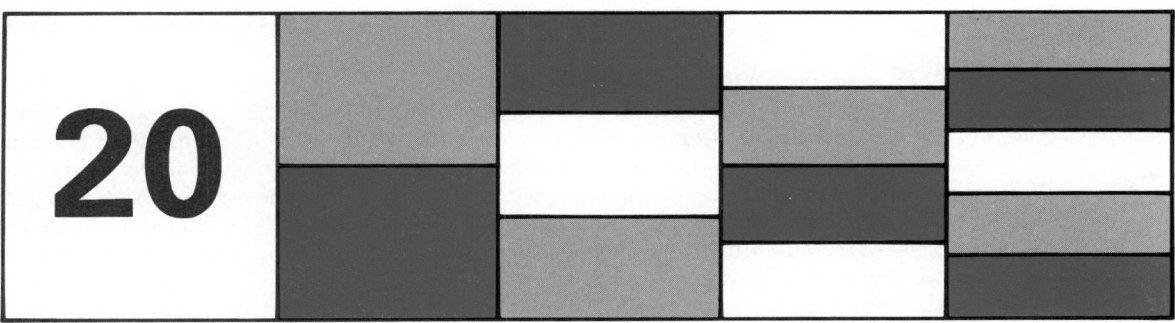

REVENUE MEASUREMENT AND INCOME PRESENTATION

Objectives

To discuss the theory and concepts underlying contemporary revenue-recognition practices.

To describe acceptable accounting practices for several unusual situations involving the recognition of revenue.

To identify and describe acceptable methods of revenue recognition for long-term contracts and to describe the circumstances under which each is appropriate.

To describe circumstances in which the installment sales and cost recovery methods of revenue recognition are acceptable.

To describe the circumstances in which revenue should be recognized when the right of return exists.

To discuss the purposes and objectives of income determination.

To review the proper method of presenting a variety of income statement items.

To discuss the circumstances in which a company has disposed of a segment of a business and to describe the financial reporting requirements for discontinued operations.

To understand how the various components of income come together in a relatively complex income statement.

COMPLEXITIES IN INCOME DETERMINATION

Revenue Realization Matching

The determination and reporting of income is one of the most important and controversial topics in contemporary financial accounting and reporting. A crucial aspect of determining income is the timing of the recognition of revenue and related expenses. In applying the revenue realization principle, accountants must make many decisions concerning the timing and extent to which revenue is recognized. In applying the matching principle, we must also identify the expenses to be included in the determination of income. Finally, we must establish the appropriate form, organization, and content of the income statement.

The appropriate practices governing the recognition of revenue may be complicated in certain situations. Consider, for example, accounting and reporting problems of aerospace companies (such as Boeing, Lockheed, and McDonnell Douglas) which agree—under a variety of long-term contracts—to provide research and development services and to produce aircraft, missiles, space vehicles, and the support systems. Determining when and in what amount to recognize revenue and identifying the related expenses to be matched against the revenue are especially difficult problems.

After accountants make their decisions about revenue recognition and expense identification, they must prepare income statements to reflect the earning performance of their enterprises. In earlier chapters you learned about several alternative methods of income presentation and also about some transactions that complicate the presentation of income. Accountants must exercise seasoned, professional judgment to determine the most appropriate format and the extent of detail to be provided in the presentation of income.

This chapter begins by developing concepts of accounting theory underlying the recognition of revenue and by illustrating their application in several practical situations. Then the chapter looks more closely at theoretical questions underlying the determination and presentation of income and introduces some considerations that complicate the presentation of income. Finally, a comprehensive model income statement summarizes our knowledge of income presentation.

REVENUE RECOGNITION: A CONCEPTUAL ANALYSIS

Revenue Realization

Before beginning an in-depth discussion of the theory of revenue realization and the way accountants recognize revenue in practice, you need to have a good understanding of the term **revenue.** Historically, the word is derived from the French word *revenir,* which means "to return" or "to come again." Thus, "revenue" has its roots in a return-on-investment concept; that is, the business expends resources on a particular project or endeavor in the hope of earning a return on that effort.

More recently, many other attempts have been made to articulate the conceptual meaning of revenue. The Financial Accounting Standards Board (FASB) gives a particularly useful definition in its *Statement of Financial Accounting Concepts No. 3:* "Revenues are inflows or other enhancements of assets of an enterprise, or settlements of its liabilities (or a combination of both) during a period from delivering or producing goods, rendering services, or other activities that constitute the enterprise's ongoing major or central operations."[1] Careful study of this definition reveals several important aspects or characteristics that an event must possess in order to qualify for accounting recognition as an element of revenue.

Revenue Realization

Accountants generally believe that revenue results from productive activity and therefore is earned or realized in a continuous fashion. In order for revenue to qualify for accounting recognition, however, at least three essential criteria must be met. The revenue must be: (1) earned; (2) measurable; and (3) collectible. Revenue should be recognized for

---

[1]*FASB Statement of Financial Accounting Concepts No. 3,* "Elements of Financial Statements of Business Enterprises," 1980, par. 63.

accounting purposes at the earliest point at which all three of these critical tests are met. In many cases, the earliest point is the time of sale.

Chapter 2 states that revenue is typically recognized at the point of sale, because the sale signifies the virtual completion of the earning process and the sale transaction establishes the amount of revenue to be recognized. Only collectibility remains in question, and most sales are not made unless collectibility is reasonably certain. At a minimum, companies can make reasonably accurate estimates of the extent to which credit sales will not be collected, and they establish credit and collection policies that tend to minimize the collectibility problem. Thus, revenue recognition at the point of sale is an established practice that works well in most situations.

To illustrate, consider the revenue-recognition practices appropriate for a company that manufactures and sells television sets to retail customers. From an economic perspective the manufacturing process, wherein raw materials and component parts are combined with labor and overhead to construct a functioning television set, enhances value. Stated simply, the productive process creates wealth and value enhancement. The end product—a functioning television set—is worth more than the sum of the value of its parts. The manufacturing process alone, however, does not provide sufficient evidence of the realization of revenue to support accounting recognition. Specifically, until an external event (sale) takes place, there is inadequate evidence as to how much (measurable) revenue was earned in the manufacturing process and whether the enhancement in value from the manufacturing activity will ever be realized (collected).

Revenue Realization

This position is supported consistently in the accounting literature:

> *Thus it [revenue] represents the accomplishment of the enterprise. Traditionally, revenue is not measured or reported until accepted by the market. The realization test for revenue is based upon the existence of an arm's-length transaction between the selling enterprise and its customers. Until production has passed this test, that is, until it has been sold, traditional accounting refuses to accept it as realized. It is not enough that other transactions by other companies indicate what the product is worth. Until the company itself has been successful in selling the product, no revenue has been realized, in the ordinary accounting sense of the term.[2]*

The actual recognition of revenue must therefore be postponed until additional evidence and information becomes available. In most situations, the point of sale is the time at which the final necessary evidence becomes available. Consider the evidence provided by a sale to an external party:

1. The relative value of the product sold is established by a market transaction between independent parties (measurability).
2. The buying party, who is *deemed* capable of paying the agreed upon price, either pays or promises to pay the contract price (collectibility).
3. Few or no continuing obligations are retained by the seller (earned).

For sales situations in which one or more of the above criteria are not met, the recognition of revenue should be deferred.

Substance over Form

Sometimes sales are made to relatively poor credit risks with a condition for the seller to regain control of the property if the buyer defaults. Such practices are common, for example, in the real estate industry. Repossession of the property pursuant to a loan default is not difficult, because real estate cannot be transported or hidden. Thus, certain types of real estate are frequently sold to relatively poor credit risks. Such sales are similar to short-term leases in terms of their economic substance. In these cases the real estate sale completes the

---

[2]Sidney Davidson, Roman Weil, and R. K. Mautz, "Accounting Concepts and Principles and Auditing Standards and Opinions," *Handbook of Modern Accounting* (New York: McGraw-Hill, 1977), pp. 1–10.

earning process and provides a measure of the profit to be recognized, but the collectibility of that revenue is not deemed adequately predictable. Recognition of revenue is therefore deferred until collectibility is more assured.

Another example is provided by subscription earnings. Magazine, book, and encyclopedia companies frequently sell annual or even longer subscriptions, collecting the full fee in advance. In such circumstances the amount of revenue to be recognized ultimately is both collected and measurable; however, it remains unearned until the materials subject to the subscription agreement have been provided to the customers. Therefore, the recognition of revenue must be deferred until the revenue has been earned. In this situation the earning process follows the point of sale.

TOYING WITH DISCLOSURE—A CHRISTMAS PARABLE

AT CHRISTMAS, the thoughts of children turn to toys marching in. For toy companies, though, the joy is supposed to be from toys marching out and receivables and cash marching in. The last thing a toy company wants to see are those toys marching back in. Topper Toy had that unfortunate experience, and it raises some interesting accounting questions.

In 1970, Topper was the second largest domestic toy manufacturer. Its sales for 1970 were approximately $60 million, and these sales were made on customary toy industry terms. That is, customers had from five to eight months to pay or to return the toys. Despite these liberal terms, Topper recorded the sale at the time of shipment and billing, just as the rest of the toy companies were doing.

In the early 1970s, Topper had caught the fancy of the stock market, and its common shares were selling for $19 a share. Topper sales were growing at a rapid rate, and it had landed a contract with the Children's Television Workshop to produce Sesame Street toys. But, by February 1973, Topper had filed for bankruptcy and shut its doors. Its petition listed assets of $14 million and liabilities of $33 million.

The return of the toys

Basically, the toys had come marching back to Topper. In December 1971, Topper disclosed that approximately $14 million of 1970 sales had been returned by its customers. The effect of this disclosure was disastrous. Topper had been projecting 1971 earnings of about $1.5 million, approximately five times 1970's earnings. The inventory returns, however, showed plainly that '70 and '71 were both significant loss years. To complete the gloomy picture, Topper disclosed that it was sitting on an inventory of 15 million Dawn dolls, 2.8 million Zoomer Boomer cars, and 1.5 million Johnny Lightning cars as of early 1972.

It seems Topper was recording revenue much too early or, the equivalent, failing to establish adequate allowances for returns. However, without the benefit of hindsight, Topper's accounting still sounded disturbingly good. About all the auditors could do was to insist on disclosure of the credit terms and sales and the company's recent experience with returns.

It is tough to confront bad news, such as those sales turning back into unsold inventory. There is an understandable desire to postpone confronting and disclosing bad news. It appears that Topper's management kept the lid on this news for as long as 10 months. Considering the seasonal pattern of toy manufacturer sales and the credit terms, it is likely that the returned sales were initially made in mid '70 with the returns coming in the first few months of '71. Nonetheless, apparently not even Topper's board learned of the returns until December 1971.

As if a disclosure delay of this length was not enough of a problem, on top of the basic bad news Topper issued debentures three months before finally disclosing the returns.

The accounting events presented here are not representative of usual practice and are recounted only for educational purposes. This information is not intended to embarrass or to reflect on anyone.

SOURCE: Earl K. Littrell, "Toying with Disclosure—a Christmas Parable," *Management Accounting,* September 1980, p. 50. Reprinted by permission of *Management Accounting.* Copyright 1980 by National Association of Accountants. All rights reserved.

Objectivity

An accountant must carefully analyze specific transactions to avoid recognizing revenue prematurely. He should accumulate and analyze objective evidence in light of the three critical criteria to assure compliance with generally accepted accounting principles. While many businesses conduct operations in a fashion compatible with recording revenue at the point of sale, many others require unique or unusual revenue-recognition practices.

The following sections of this chapter deal with several unusual circumstances related to the recognition of revenue and discuss each special area in terms of the underlying theoretical framework for revenue recognition.

SPECIAL REVENUE-RECOGNITION PROBLEMS

Industries and businesses in which special revenue-recognition practices are required generally involve complex, lengthy, or unusual earning processes or contractual relationships between buyers and sellers. This section discusses revenue recognition by businesses that deal with long-term construction contracts, installment sales, the right of return, and consignments. The Appendix to this chapter discusses revenue recognition in specialized situations involving real estate transactions, retail land sales, and franchises.

Long-Term Construction Contracts

In many industries, such as shipbuilding, aircraft design and production, and building construction, the earning activities of an enterprise are related to a number of large projects extending through several accounting periods. Accounting and reporting problems posed by such activities are related primarily to the timing and extent of revenue to be recognized and the treatment of costs incurred in the productive process. Because of the variety of circumstances and contractual relationships in construction projects, alternative financial accounting methods have been developed. We now turn our attention to those methods and the circumstances in which each is appropriate.

Accounting and Reporting Issues

While more than one reporting method has been developed to account for long-term contracting activity, the methods should not be viewed as equally acceptable under the same circumstances. Rather, each method is appropriate only when certain conditions are present.

When a large construction project is contemplated, the buyer and the builder usually draw up a contract prior to beginning the construction. When such contracts are signed, a portion of the criteria necessary to recognize revenue is usually met. The construction company usually will not sign the contract if it has significant doubt about the buyer's ability to pay. For example, when an airplane manufacturer signs a contract with the U.S. Department of Defense to develop and produce a new type of aircraft, the collectibility of the contract amount is virtually assured. Although not all long-term contracts involve government buyers, construction companies usually accept only customers with an assured ability to pay the contract amount. The earning process is obviously not complete, however, and the amount of earnings to be ultimately realized in excess of costs incurred may still not be

Revenue Realization

determinable. Therefore, the recognition of revenue must wait until both the earnings and measurability criteria are met. As previously stated, the concept that revenue is realized through the productive process is widely accepted in practice. Therefore, as development and production of the contract item proceed, revenue is said to be "earned." The final criterion of measurability, however, may still remain uncertain, and revenue should not be recognized in the accounting records until all three criteria are met.

Measuring the amount of revenue earned is particularly difficult in the area of long-term construction contracts. Even if the revenue is collectible and earned through production, the amount that has been earned and the related costs associated with the earning process may still not be determinable. The amount of revenue and expenses to be recognized during the production process relate to the **degree of completion** of the project and to the remaining costs and effort to be incurred in finishing the project.

Certain projects are fairly routine and lend themselves to reliable predictions of costs and productive efforts. Other developmental projects may involve many uncertainties. Furthermore, some contracts specify how final sales prices will be determined. For example, a contract may guarantee the contractor with reimbursement of all costs incurred plus some amount of profit. The profit portion may be stated as a certain number of dollars, a percentage above costs incurred, or an amount based on some other variable, such as days or hours of direct labor expended on the project. On the other hand, a contract may specify a total fixed amount to be received regardless of costs incurred. All these factors are considered in determining the appropriate accounting treatment for any specific situation.

Two basic methods are used in accounting for long-term construction contracts: the percentage-of-completion method and the completed-contract method. The **percentage-of-completion method** of accounting for long-term construction contracts provides for the recognition of gross profit as production takes place. The **completed-contract method** defers recognition of gross profit until all production is complete and the customer's acceptance of the project is finalized.

Under the percentage-of-completion method, revenue and expenses are recognized to the extent that production has progressed. Therefore, estimates of costs and effort to complete the project are necessary to determine the amount of profit that should be recognized at interim points during construction. Specifically, *Accounting Research Bulletin No. 45* states:

Disclosure

> *When estimates of costs to complete and extent of progress toward completion of long-term contracts are reasonably dependable, the percentage-of-completion method is preferable. When lack of dependable estimates or inherent hazards cause forecasts to be doubtful, the completed-contract method is preferable. Disclosure of the method followed should be made.[3]*

According to this statement, the selection of the method requires analysis of the *quality* of available evidence, primarily regarding the measurability of revenue earned. When effort has been expended on a long-term construction contract, we generally agree that both the earning process and the collectibility criteria have been satisfactorily met. Therefore, the measurability of the revenue earned is frequently the last critical prerequisite for the recognition of revenue. If the construction company can satisfactorily estimate the amount of revenue earned, it should employ the percentage-of-completion method.

A more recent pronouncement confirms this position. Specifically, *FASB Statement of Financial Accounting Standards No. 56* states, "The percentage-of-completion and completed-contract methods are not intended to be free choice alternatives for the same circumstances."[4] A Statement of Position (SOP) of the American Institute of Certified Public Accountants (AICPA) provides important guidance about the circumstances in which each method should be selected and the manner of applying each method. A company should use the percentage-of-completion method of accounting if estimates are reasonably dependable and three other conditions exist:[5]

1. The contract specifies the enforceable rights of each party, the amount of consideration to be exchanged, and the manner and terms of settlement.

---

[3]*Accounting Research Bulletin No. 45,* "Long-Term Construction-Type Contracts," 1955, par. 15.
[4]*FASB Statement of Financial Accounting Standards No. 56,* "Designation of AICPA Guide and Statement of Position (SOP) 81–1 on Contractor Accounting and SOP 81–2 Concerning Hospital-Related Organizations as Preferable for Purposes of Applying APB Opinion No. 20," 1982, par. 6.
[5]*AICPA Statement of Position 81–1,* "Accounting for Performance of Construction-Type and Certain Production-Type Contracts," 1981, par. 23.

2. The buyer can be expected to honor the obligations of the contract.
3. The contractor can be expected to perform according to the terms of the contract.

According to the SOP, contractors are presumably able to make the necessary reliable estimates and consequently should report most contracting activities under the percentage-of-completion method. The presumption is based on the notion that contractors would refuse contracts if reasonable estimates were impossible. Persuasive evidence is necessary to overcome the presumption that the percentage-of-completion method should be used. Following the issuance of the SOP, even more contractors began using the percentage-of-completion method. However, if the construction company cannot meet the criteria for the percentage-of-completion method, the completed-contract method is appropriate.

Percentage-of-Completion Method

In practice, contractors use two basic methods to measure the progress of the construction:

1. **Input measures** (e.g., ratio of costs incurred to total estimated costs).
2. **Output measures** (e.g., units of delivery).

A common input measure bases the progress on the ratio of the costs *already* incurred to the total *estimated* costs. In using costs incurred as a measure of degree of completion, the accountant must be cautious, because the costs may not be spread evenly over the contract period. For example, if a disproportionate amount of the costs were required in the early part of the contract period, costs incurred might not be a suitable measure of the degree of completion.

Output measures base the progress on the results achieved. One common output measure, the units of delivery approach, recognizes revenue when specific, discrete components of the project are completed and accepted by the buyer. The units of delivery approach to applying the percentage-of-completion method is most useful in contracts which require several large, but individual, components of production. For example, the construction of several condominium units or a group of similar ships or aircraft may be accounted for on a units of delivery basis. Under the units of delivery approach to measuring the percentage of completion, revenue is recognized when a particular discrete component of the entire project is completed and delivered to or accepted by the customer. For example, if a construction company signs a contract to provide ten condominium units and completes four of the units—which are accepted by the buyer—at the end of the first year, then 40% of the total revenue provided under the contract should be recognized. The treatment of costs incurred under the contract, however, is not so obvious. In many contracts, certain costs incurred at the beginning of a contract relate to all the units to be constructed. In the preceding example, the contractor should prorate such costs among the ten units rather than charge them immediately to expense. Costs of planning and design are especially significant in state-of-the-art production, such as the design and construction of defense or scientific projects that have never before been attempted. In the early stages, such projects frequently incur many **learning curve costs** (i.e., expenditures necessary to learn how to do a particular construction project). Once learned, the productive process may be replicated more easily and efficiently. Because the costs are necessary to assure compliance with performance and capability specificiations in the overall contract, they benefit all units produced under the contract. Careful analysis and allocation of learning curve costs to appropriate accounting periods are necessary to ensure a proper matching of revenues and expenses.

| Matching |

Completed-Contract Method

When reasonable estimates of the degree of completion are not possible, the completed-contract method of accounting for long-term contracts is applied. Under completed-contract accounting, no gross profit is recognized on the contract until the contract is complete and the products or services have been accepted by the buyer. At that time all gross profit earned on the contract is recorded. Prior to the recognition of profit, contract costs are presented on the balance sheet as Construction in Progress, an inventory account.

Amounts reflected as assets in the balance sheet for Construction in Progress are subject to net realizable value limitations, regardless of which method of revenue recognition is employed. That is, when costs are incurred under a contract and charged to an inventory account such as Construction in Progress, we must ascertain that the amount reported as an asset does not exceed the net realizable value of the contract. Recall from Chapter 8 that the **net realizable value** of an item of inventory is defined as the sales (contract) value of the item less any costs still to be incurred to complete and sell the product. Thus, even under completed-contract accounting, estimates of the remaining costs are necessary to ensure that the Construction in Progress account is not overvalued.

If we determine that the costs included as an asset under a particular contract exceed the net realizable value of the contract, we should write down the asset to its net realizable value and recognize a loss at that time.

A Long-Term Contract Example

To illustrate the appropriate accounting procedures for the percentage-of-completion and completed-contract methods, we shall consider the following example. Dryden Construction Company agrees to build a large apartment building for Cozy Homes, Inc., for a total contract price of $5,000,000. Cozy Homes will make annual payments to Dryden, but the amounts of these payments cannot exceed the direct costs incurred by Dryden. The contract is signed on October 1, 1983, and Dryden's year-end is December 31. The contract provides Cozy with a final inspection right to ensure compliance with the contract terms prior to accepting the completed project. Exhibit 20–1 provides further information about the contract.

Dryden based its percentage-of-completion method on costs incurred rather than units delivered, because the contract calls for one large project rather than several separate projects. Dryden assumes that costs incurred will accurately measure the progress. Exhibit 20–2 presents the current year's gross profit calculations for the percentage-of-completion

---

EXHIBIT 20–1
Long-Term Contracts—Illustrative Information

Total contract price	$5,000,000		
Total anticipated costs (at 10/1/83)	4,000,000		

Item	1983	1984	1985	Total
Costs incurred each year	$ 500,000	$2,500,000	$1,400,000	$4,400,000
Estimated costs to complete (at year-end)	3,500,000	1,250,000	–0–	–0–
Progress billings each year	400,000	2,000,000	2,600,000	5,000,000
Progress payments received each year	275,000	2,100,000	2,625,000*	5,000,000

*Since the contract was completed and accepted during 1985, the buyer paid the remaining balance of the total contract amount, computed as follows:

Contract amount		$5,000,000
Prior progress payments		
1983	$ 275,000	
1984	2,100,000	2,375,000
Remaining amount		$2,625,000

EXHIBIT 20–2
Revenue Recognized by Percentage-of-Completion Method

	1983	1984	1985
Total contract price	$5,000,000	$5,000,000	$5,000,000
Costs incurred to date	500,000	3,000,000	4,400,000
Anticipated costs to complete	3,500,000	1,250,000	–0–
Total estimated costs	4,000,000	4,250,000	4,400,000
Expected gross profit	$1,000,000	$ 750,000	$ 600,000
Percentage of completion			
$500,000/$4,000,000	12.5%		
$3,000,000/$4,250,000		70.6%	
$4,400,000/$4,400,000			100%
Gross profit earned to date			
$1,000,000 × 12.5%	$ 125,000		
$750,000 × 70.6%		$ 529,500	
$600,000 × 100%			$ 600,000
Less: Gross profit previously recognized	—	(125,000)	(529,500)
Current year gross profit	$ 125,000	$ 404,500	$ 70,500

method. To illustrate the difference in the methods, Exhibit 20–3 shows the accounting entries for each contract year for both the percentage-of-completion and completed-contract methods. The resulting financial-statement presentations for both methods are summarized in Exhibit 20–4.

Careful study of these exhibits reveals that the only difference between the two methods is the timing of the recognition of gross profit on the contract. Both methods ultimately result in the recognition of the same total amount of gross profit ($600,000). The only balance sheet differences between the two methods relate to the carrying value of the Construction in Progress (inventory) account and Retained Earnings. Under the percentage-of-completion method, the amount of gross profit recognized is reflected as an increase in Construction in Progress and as an increase in Retained Earnings after being reported as an increase in net income in the income statement.

Under the percentage-of-completion method, we calculate the amount of revenue to be recognized by determining the gross profit to be recognized during the current year and adding that figure to the actual costs incurred during the year. As Exhibit 20–2 shows, a revised estimate of the cumulative percentage of completion is computed each year. This percentage is applied to the expected gross profit (which will also vary as revised estimates of expected costs to be incurred are made). The difference between the cumulative gross profit and the gross profit recognized in the previous year(s) is the current year's gross profit, which (as mentioned earlier) is added to costs incurred that year to determine the amount of revenue to be recognized. The final entry in Exhibit 20–3 for each year under the percentage-of-completion method records revenues, costs, and the increase in Construction in Progress for the gross profit recognized.

Under the completed-contract method, we defer the recognition of revenue until the project is completed. In the case of Dryden Construction Company, the $5,000,000 of revenue and the $4,400,000 of costs are recognized in 1985 when the contract is complete and the uncertainties that preclude the use of the percentage-of-completion method are resolved. Actual companies may employ different account titles and certain other minor variations, but the procedures illustrated here are representative of the two methods.

Exhibit 20–4 shows the difference between the inventory account, Construction in Progress, and the Contract Billings as a *current* asset. The "current" classification of this item is based on the operating cycle definition. An asset is current if it is expected to be sold,

EXHIBIT 20–3
Comparison of Completed-Contract and Percentage-of-Completion Journal Entries

			Journal Entries			
			Completed-Contract		Percentage-of-Completion	
Date	Event	Accounts	Dr.	Cr.	Dr.	Cr.
1983	Contract signed	(No entry necessary to record contract commitment.)				
	Costs incurred	Construction in Progress	500,000		500,000	
		Cash		500,000		500,000
	Progress billings	Accounts Receivable	400,000		400,000	
		Contract Billings		400,000		400,000
	Billing collections	Cash	275,000		275,000	
		Accounts Receivable		275,000		275,000
	Revenue recognition	Construction in Progress	—		125,000	
		Cost of Earned Revenue	—		500,000	
		Construction Revenue		—		625,000
1984	Costs incurred	Construction in Progress	2,500,000		2,500,000	
		Cash		2,500,000		2,500,000
	Progress billings	Accounts Receivable	2,000,000		2,000,000	
		Contract Billings		2,000,000		2,000,000
	Billing collections	Cash	2,100,000		2,100,000	
		Accounts Receivable		2,100,000		2,100,000
	Revenue recognition	Construction in Progress	—		404,500	
		Cost of Earned Revenue	—		2,500,000	
		Construction Revenue		—		2,904,500
1985	Costs incurred	Construction in Progress	1,400,000		1,400,000	
		Cash		1,400,000		1,400,000
	Progress billings	Accounts Receivable	2,600,000		2,600,000	
		Contract Billings		2,600,000		2,600,000
	Billing collections	Cash	2,625,000		2,625,000	
		Accounts Receivable		2,625,000		2,625,000
	Revenue recognition	Construction in Progress	—		70,500	
		Cost of Earned Revenue	—		1,400,000	
		Construction Revenue		—		1,470,500
	Elimination of inventory	Contract Billings	—		5,000,000	
		Construction in Progress		—		5,000,000
	Recognition of costs and revenues on entire contract	Contract Billings	5,000,000		—	
		Cost of Earned Revenue	4,400,000		—	
		Construction Revenue		5,000,000		—
		Construction in Progress		4,400,000		—

consumed, or converted to cash within the next year (or operating cycle if the cycle exceeds one year). In the case of long-term contracts, the period of the accounting cycle—which frequently exceeds one year—is typically used to identify current assets.

EXHIBIT 20–4
Comparison of Completed-Contract and Percentage-of-Completion
Financial-Statement Presentations

	Dec. 31, 1983		Dec. 31, 1984		Dec. 31, 1985	
Balance Sheet	*Completed Contract*	*Percentage of Completion*	*Completed Contract*	*Percentage of Completion*	*Completed Contract*	*Percentage of Completion*
Current assets						
Accounts receivable	$ 125,000	$ 125,000	$ 25,000	$ 25,000	–0–	–0–
Inventory						
Construction in progress	500,000	625,000	3,000,000	3,529,500	–0–	–0–
Less:						
Contract billings	(400,000)	(400,000)	(2,400,000)	(2,400,000)	–0–	–0–
Construction in progress in excess of billings	100,000	225,000	600,000	1,129,500	–0–	–0–
Income Statement						
Construction revenue	—	$ 625,000	—	$ 2,904,500	$ 5,000,000	$ 1,470,500
Cost of earned revenue	—	(500,000)	—	(2,500,000)	(4,400,000)	(1,400,000)
Gross margin	—	$ 125,000	—	$ 404,500	$ 600,000	$ 70,500

If the contract provided for billings in excess of costs incurred, the Construction in Progress account could be less than the Contract Billings account. In this case, the difference should be presented as a *current liability* labeled "Excess of Contract Billings over Construction in Progress" or another appropriate title.

Although the comparison of the percentage-of-completion and completed-contracts methods in the Dryden example demonstrated the similarities and differences, we must again recognize that *the methods are not equally acceptable in the same circumstances.* We must consider the circumstances and available evidence and select the *appropriate* method. In sum, we should use the completed-contract method only when reliable estimates of effort and resources to complete the project are not available. The percentage-of-completion method is preferable when reasonably dependable estimates of the degree of completion can be made, because it presents the economic substance of the company's transactions and events more clearly and in a more timely fashion than does the completed-contract method. The percentage-of-completion method informs financial statement users of the volume of the economic activity of the company.[6] While the completed-contract method is based on results as finally determined rather than on estimates, it does not reflect current performance when contract periods extend beyond one accounting period and it may result in irregular recognition of income.[7]

Substance over Form

A Hybrid Method

In certain types of contracts (e.g., cost-plus contracts in which the revenue will be the costs incurred plus a specified percentage) the contractor is assured of no loss. If the contractor is protected in this manner but is unable to make reasonable estimates of the percentage of completion, *SOP 81–1* recommends a **hybrid method** described as the percentage-of-completion method based on a **zero profit margin.**[8] Under this method, revenue is recognized in an amount exactly equal to costs incurred until reasonably objective estimates of

Objectivity

---
[6]*AICPA Statement of Position 81–1*, par. 22.
[7]*AICPA Statement of Position 81–1*, par. 30.
[8]*AICPA Statement of Position 81–1*, par. 33.

the percentage of completion can be made. In the earlier example, if Dryden Construction Company had used this method, revenue and costs would be recognized in 1983 and 1984 for $500,000 and $2,500,000 (the amount of costs incurred), respectively:

1983	Cost of Earned Revenue	500,000	
	Construction Revenue		500,000
1984	Cost of Earned Revenue	2,500,000	
	Construction Revenue		2,500,000

In 1985, the year in which the contract was complete, the entire gross profit would have been recognized, much as in the completed-contract method:

1985	Construction in Progress	600,000	
	Cost of Earned Revenue	1,400,000	
	Construction Revenue		2,000,000
	Contract Billings	5,000,000	
	Construction in Progress		5,000,000

The first three entries in Exhibit 20–3 for each year would also be applicable to the hybrid method. The significant difference between the hybrid method and the completed-contract method is that the hybrid method requires the inclusion of both revenues and costs in the income statement for 1983 and 1984. Performance during the period would be included in the income statement, although the method would have no impact on net income since revenue and costs recognized would be equal. The zero profit margin approach gives financial statement users an indication of the volume of the company's business while deferring the recognition of gross profit until more reliable estimates of the degree of completion can be made.

Anticipated Losses on Contracts

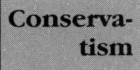

It may become apparent during the contract period that a loss will be incurred on the contract. Under all the methods presented above, a projected loss on a contract must be recognized immediately in conformity with the modifying convention of conservatism.

To illustrate this procedure, assume that Johnson Construction Company is using the completed-contract method on a project. At the end of 1984 the balance in the Construction in Progress account is $2,500,000, representing the costs incurred through the present time. If the company now projects a $350,000 loss on the contract because of unexpected increases in materials, labor, and overhead, the following entry is appropriate:

1984	Loss on Construction Contract	350,000	
	Construction in Progress		350,000

From this point forward, construction costs will be charged to the Construction in Progress account, and the balance in that account at the end of the contract will equal the contract revenue if the loss estimate is accurate. If the loss estimate is not accurate, an adjustment is made when the appropriate amounts are determinable.

How does this procedure vary if the percentage-of-completion method is being used? Assume that on another contract, Johnson is using the percentage-of-completion method. The Construction in Progress account at the end of 1984 has a balance of $6,500,000, made up of the following items:

Construction costs incurred through 1984	$5,700,000
Gross profit recognized in previous years	800,000
Construction in Progress balance	$6,500,000

At the end of 1984 the company expects a $300,000 loss on the contract. The following entry should be made:

1984	Loss on Construction Contract	1,100,000	
	Construction in Progress		1,100,000

The $1,100,000 loss represents a reversal of the $800,000 gross profit recognized earlier plus the $300,000 loss expected on the contract. From this point forward, construction costs will be charged to the Construction in Progress account, and the balance in that account at the end of the contract will equal the contract revenue if the loss estimate is accurate. As in the completed-contract method, if the loss estimate is inaccurate, further adjustment must be made in the future as the appropriate amounts are determinable.

Installment Sales

In most circumstances the collectibility of credit sales is predictable and reasonably assured as a result of credit approval, collection procedures, and historical evidence. However, if a company decides to make a credit sale to a customer of relatively poor credit risk, recognition of revenue at the point of sale is inappropriate. While such revenue may be deemed to have been earned and measurable, collectibility remains uncertain. Therefore, the creditor should defer the recognition of revenue until collecting the amount due. This practice also is supported by the professional literature:

> *There are exceptional cases where receivables are collectible over an extended period of time, and because of the terms of the transactions or other conditions, there is no reasonable basis for estimating the degree of collectibility. When such circumstances exist, and as long as they exist, either the installment method or the cost recovery method of accounting may be used. (Under the cost recovery method, equal amounts of revenue and expense are recognized as collections are made until all costs have been recovered, postponing any recognition of profit until that time.)*[9]

The **installment sales method** recognizes a portion of each cash collection as revenue and the remaining amount of cash collected as a recovery of cost. The **cost recovery method** treats all cash collected as a recovery of cost of the item sold until the full cost of the item sold is collected. Subsequent collections are treated entirely as revenue. The cost recovery method is even more conservative than the installment method, and application of the cost recovery technique is most desirable when the collectibility of receivables is highly uncertain.

Conserva-tism

Under the installment sales method, revenue is recognized on a pro rata basis as each installment is received. To illustrate, assume that EZ Credit Auto Sales Company sells a $6,000 automobile to a customer on November 1, 1985, with the following terms: The customer will pay $600 down and $150 per month for 36 months plus interest at 15%. Since EZ Credit paid $4,500 for the automobile, it will make a gross profit of $1,500 on the sale. For simplicity, we shall ignore the interest revenue, because it is not related to the recognition of profit on the sale.

Because of the significant uncertainty of collection resulting from granting credit to relatively poor credit risks, EZ Credit Company uses the installment sales method of revenue recognition. Exhibit 20–5 presents the entries necessary to record the sale, collection of cash, and recognition of revenue. The gross profit percentage, which indicates the gross profit included in each payment received, is 25%, computed by dividing the gross profit by the sales price [($6,000 − $4,500)/$6,000 = 25%].

The Deferred Gross Profit account established at the point of sale is treated either as a

[9]*APB Opinion No. 10*, "Omnibus Opinion—1966," 1966, par. 12.

EXHIBIT 20–5
Installment Sales Accounting—Illustrative Entries

Date	Accounts	Dr.	Cr.
Nov. 1, 1985	Cash	600	
	Notes Receivable	5,400	
	Inventory		4,500
	Realized Gross Profit* ($600 × 25%)		150
	Deferred Gross Profit ($5,400 × 25%)		1,350
	(To record sale of automobile under installment sales method.)		
Nov. 30, 1985	Cash	150	
	Notes Receivable		150
	(To record receipt of payment.)		
Dec. 31, 1985	Cash	150	
	Notes Receivable		150
	(To record receipt of payment.)		
Dec. 31, 1985	Deferred Gross Profit ($300 × 25%)	75	
	Realized Gross Profit*		75
	(To record revenue for the year based on cash received.)		

*For income statement presentation purposes, the components of Realized Gross Profit may be presented rather than the net amount of $225 ($150 + $75). In this situation, sales of $900 ($600 + $150 + $150) would be included in sales revenue and $675 ($900 × 75%) would be included in Cost of Goods Sold.

contra account to Notes Receivable or as a deferred revenue (liability) account. The entry on December 31, 1985, which reflects the portion of cash collected that is recognized as revenue, may be made as each cash receipt occurs. If this practice is selected, each cash receipt of $150 (ignoring interest) would be recorded in the following manner:

Cash	150.00	
Deferred Gross Profit	37.50	
Notes Receivable		150.00
Realized Gross Profit		37.50
($150 × 25% = $37.50)		

If different sales transactions result in different gross profit percentages, separate gross profit records must be kept for each sale. For example, if installment sales in 1983 result in a gross profit percentage of 32% and installment sales in 1984 result in a gross profit percentage of 34%, the receivables and deferred gross profit amounts related to 1983 sales must be kept separate from the 1984 sales so that a proper accounting may be made of the gross profit recognized as receivables are collected.

When we consider the uncertainty of collection for installment sales, we should not be surprised that sellers typically retain a right of repossession (the right to take the property and resell it) if the buyer defaults. When inventory is acquired in this manner, the installment receivable and any related deferred gross profit on the original sale must be eliminated. If the resale value of the repossessed property is greater or less than the carrying amount of the receivable (face amount, less the related deferred gross profit), a gain or loss is recognized.

To illustrate, assume that Careyville Appliance Company sells a refrigerator to a customer for $500 on an installment contract calling for 25 monthly payments of $20, plus interest. The refrigerator cost Careyville $420, resulting in a gross profit percentage of 16% [($500 − $420)/$500]. After 11 payments the customer discontinued paying and Careyville repossessed the refrigerator. The carrying amount of the receivable is as follows:

Receivable balance [$500 − 11 ($20)]	$280.00
Deferred gross profit balance	
{$80 − [11($20) × 16%]}	(44.80)
Carrying amount of installment receivable	$235.20

If the estimated resale value of the refrigerator is only $200, the entry to record the repossession is as follows:

Repossessed Inventory	200.00	
Deferred Gross Profit	44.80	
Loss on Repossession	35.20	
Installment Receivables		280.00

If the estimated resale value of the refrigerator had been greater than $235.20, a Gain on Repossession would have been recorded.

Revenue Recognition if the Right of Return Exists

A company may sell an item with a provision for the customer to return it under certain circumstances. For example, a manufacturer may sell its products to a retailer with the **right to return** products that are unsatisfactory to the consumer. In such circumstances the manufacturer should not recognize revenue until six conditions are met:

1. *The seller's price to the buyer is substantially fixed or determinable at the date of sale.*
2. *The buyer has paid the seller, or the buyer is obligated to pay the seller and the obligation is not contingent on resale of the product.*
3. *The buyer's obligation to the seller would not be changed in the event of theft or physical destruction or damage of the product.*
4. *The buyer acquiring the product for resale has economic substance apart from that provided by the seller. [That is, a separate, arm's-length relationship between the parties is evident.]*
5. *The seller does not have significant obligations for future performance to directly bring about resale of the product by the buyer.*
6. *The amount of future returns can be reasonably estimated.*[10]

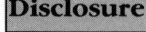

Sales revenue and related expenses which are deferred because at least one of these six conditions does not exist should be recognized as soon as all the conditions are met. If any of these conditions are not met, revenue should not be recognized even when the right of return is not part of a formal contract. Disclosure of the circumstances and the enterprise's accounting policies are, of course, necessary to adequately inform the users of the financial statements.

Consignments

Another type of transaction is the **consignment** of goods by one entity to another. In general, the owner (usually a manufacturer) transfers finished goods to another entity (usually a retailer). However, the receiver does not become liable for payment to the owner until

---

[10]*FASB Statement of Financial Accounting Standards No. 48*, "Revenue Recognition When Right of Return Exists," 1981, par. 6.

Substance over Form

the goods are sold to a third party. The receiver of the consigned goods generally is allowed to return unsold goods to the owner with no payments required. This practice facilitates the sales of a manufacturer's products by allowing a broader retail distribution than would otherwise be possible. Sales with the right of return differ from consignments in that the **consignee** (selling agent) does not own the inventory, and costs of maintaining the inventory—such as storage and insurance—are typically covered by the **consignor** (owner). Accounting and reporting for consignments should, as in other areas, be guided by economic substance.

When the consignor ships goods to the consignee, a sale is not deemed to have taken place, because the consignee has assumed no obligation to the consignor other than to protect the consigned goods. When the consignee sells the goods, then the sales amount, less expenses and a commission, are remitted to the consignor. The consignor should recognize sales of consigned goods only upon notification by the consignee of sale to a third party. Unsold goods shipped on consignment should be included in the inventory of the consignor and excluded from the consignee's inventory. Footnote disclosures of material consignment relationships are necessary for both consignors and consignees.

Disclosure

Other Unusual Revenue-Recognition Circumstances

The timing and magnitude of revenue recognition remain areas of substantial complexity and controversy for the accounting profession. Significant judgments are frequently required in determining when revenue should be recognized and in what amount. These circumstances raise the possibility of manipulation and the "managing" of earnings. Because of the central importance of revenue in the financial statements and the susceptibility to abuse, accountants must remain alert to the possibility of misstatement.

As previously mentioned, many industries (e.g., real estate, franchising, and entertainment) engage in transactions and business relationships that require unusual accounting and reporting practices. The Appendix to this chapter discusses financial accounting and reporting for a variety of these industries.

This chapter has already dealt with the criteria and circumstances influencing the recognition of revenue. While the accounting profession has been active in the development and refinement of such criteria, accounting and reporting standards have also been established in regard to the presentation of various items of revenue and expense on the income statement. The following portion of this chapter considers theories, standards, and practices relevant to the format, organization, and content of the income statement.

INCOME PRESENTATION

A major objective of financial reporting is to provide information to investors and creditors about **financial performance** during the reporting period. Although **performance** may refer to numerous aspects of an enterprise's operations, the FASB has clearly designated **earnings** as the focal point for financial reporting:

> *The primary focus of financial reporting is information about an enterprise's performance provided by measures of* earnings *and its components. Investors, creditors, and others who are concerned with assessing the prospects of net cash flows are especially interested in that information. Their interest in an enterprise's future cash flows and its ability to generate favorable cash flows leads primarily to an interest in information about its* earnings *rather than information about its cash flows.*[11] *[Emphasis added.]*

The emphasis on reporting earnings is so strong in the current authoritative accounting

---

[11]*FASB Statement of Financial Accounting Concepts No. 1,* "Objectives of Financial Reporting by Business Enterprises," 1978, par. 43.

A QUESTION OF JUDGMENT

THERE HAVE BEEN television series on just about every profession known to man except one: the accounting profession. You think something like *The Young Accountants* would bomb in prime time? Don't be so sure. After all, top network executives seem to find accountants absolutely fascinating. See if this real-life adventure in the accounting department at ABC grabs you.

Tucked away in the middle of an ordinary-looking press release mailed out by ABC in December was a line noting that the method of assigning expenses to each showing of prime-time movies was being changed. Trivial? Not to an experienced broadcast accountant. That little change could make quite a difference on the bottom line.

The three networks don't really like to tell how they handle the costs of their programs. It won't do much good looking in their annual reports either.

There's no line that describes the network's annual program expenditures. That number is top secret. When a network buys the rights to show a series or film, that amount goes on the balance sheet under the heading "program rights"—in effect, the network's inventory of shows still to be broadcast. The question is: How much of those costs are charged off on the income statement each time the show is on?

ABC's practice, says Ted James, analyst at Montgomery Securities, had been to charge around 80% of the cost of the show or film the first time it goes on the air. This makes sense. Ad revenues on the first airing are usually higher than later ones, and there's no knowing how long it will run. When the show is broadcast again, that leaves only around 20% of the cost still to be charged off.

What ABC seems to have done is reduce that first-time charge from 80% to around 75% of the show's cost. That doesn't sound like much until you consider the numbers involved. "You're probably looking at around $500 million in first-run programs at ABC during 1980," says James, "so if you start shifting 5% around, you're talking about $25 million, or $12.5 million after taxes. When you realize that it's all being lumped basically into two quarters, it's big."

For ABC, that little switch could well turn a loss into a profit in the first quarter of this year and could also boost earnings thereafter.

Of course, from the auditors' point of view, there is nothing wrong with doing a little shifting like this—as long as it's within reason. Management is supposed to know better than their CPA firm how much revenue can be expected on these later broadcasts, if any. "As long as the judgment doesn't look too unreasonable, it would probably be accepted," says Roger Cason, partner at Main Hurdman & Cranstoun. "It is a judgment—and who am I to say that your judgment is wrong in your business?" The auditing regulations in the area require only that more than 50% of the show's cost be recognized on the first broadcast—and that shows don't stay on the balance sheet long after they're dead and gone.

Deferring the writeoff of bombs was a common route to high profits in the movie industry until 1973, when practices there were tightened up considerably. But the networks may still have a few skeletons in their closets. Reluctant to clobber earnings by writing off bombs in the program rights "inventory," their closets may be bulging. "At a certain point they're just going to have to face the music," complains one broadcast analyst. "In the past, you could do that for a couple of years and then a good year bails you out. Now what if you're facing a few years with not-so-terrific earnings, and you've still got that inventory?"

All three networks, faced with sluggish revenues in 1980 and skyrocketing program costs, have good reason to judge the expected life of its shows more charitably. But ABC may feel especially charitable toward itself. More conservative in writing off shows than the other two, it also has been spending large amounts on first-run films (13 in the fourth quarter of 1980 alone, *vs.* 4 in the same period in 1979). So ABC may only be bringing its program costing in line with industry practice.

The point is, network managements can change their minds conveniently about the prospects of shows anytime they need an earnings boost—and few shareholders would be the wiser for it.

SOURCE: Thomas Baker, "A Question of Judgment," *Forbes,* February 16, 1981, p. 52. Reprinted by permission of *Forbes* Magazine. © Forbes Inc., 1981.

literature that when a choice is necessary between income presentation and some other desirable emphasis (e.g., presentation of financial position), the presentation of earnings usually takes precedence. For example, the use of interperiod income tax allocation emphasizes the determination of income while reporting balance sheet items that differ markedly in nature from other assets and liabilities.

Revenue Realization Matching

Current accounting practice uses a transactions approach to income measurement. Under this approach, positive and negative asset and liability changes are measured and recognized in conformity with accounting principles, such as revenue realization and matching. The combined results of these changes is the determination of net income, perhaps the most prominent figure in financial reporting.

Objectives of Reporting Earnings

We could cite many objectives of reporting earnings. In Chapter 3 we examined the usefulness of accounting income figures and discussed net income as a measure of operating efficiency and a predictor of future cash flows.

The ability of management is a major factor in the success of a business enterprise, and income is the primary measure of business performance. Therefore, one objective of earnings is to provide an evaluation of management efficiency through a comparison of the results of management effort with some standard or goal. The objectives of business activity vary from enterprise to enterprise. A profit-oriented enterprise attempts to achieve some desired level of earnings as the basis for providing a desired level of cash flow to investors and creditors. Net income is a valuable measure of progress toward that goal. Periodic measures of earnings are useful in evaluating how well management has employed the resources at its disposal to achieve the desired level of earnings. The desired level of earnings may be determined in several ways, including management-established goals, industry averages, or individual investor expectations.

The basic objective of financial reporting is to provide useful information for making rational decisions about investment, credit, and other important matters. The primary focus of financial reporting is information about the enterprise's earnings and its components. Information about earnings is generally more useful in predicting and evaluating future cash flow potentials than is information about the enterprise's past cash flows. Therefore, support for the presentation of earnings and its components is based primarily on the need for this information in assessing the enterprise's future activities, particularly those that have cash flow prospects.

Inherent in the presentation of net income is the distinction between investment and income. **Investment** refers to the accumulated resources which the enterprise has as a result of contributions by investors. **Income** is the net result of the inflow of resources resulting from the employment of that investment. Another objective of reporting earnings is to distinguish between the accumulation of investments and the accumulation of additional resources that result from the *employment* of investments. These additional resources are either retained by the enterprise or distributed as dividends to the owners of the enterprise.

Alternative Income Concepts

We shall now look at several concepts regarding what constitutes "income."

Net Income to Stockholders

The current concept of income is founded on the notion that the amount identified as net income is that amount which accrues to *all* stockholders. **Determinants** of income are those revenues, gains, expenses, and losses which are included in the computation of net income, such as sales revenue, cost of goods sold, operating expenses, interest expense, and income tax expense. **Distributions** of income are transfers of assets to owners of all classes.

This concept of income, which is strongly emphasized in traditional accounting thought, is often identified as **net income to stockholders.** All expenses incurred in the generation of revenue are deducted in determining income, but no distributions to owners are deducted. Several alternative approaches to this concept are explained in the following paragraphs.

Value Added Income

Under the value added concept of income, a wide variety of interested parties are identified as the **recipients** of the income of the enterprise. The **value added** is the sales price of the enterprise's products or services minus the cost of the goods and services paid to other enterprises that produced those goods and services. Other groups who receive the advantages of enterprise operations—employees, creditors, government, and owners—are recipients of the income of the enterprise. Whereas the cost of goods sold is a determinant of income, expenditures such as income taxes, interest, and dividends are considered distributions of that income to the various recipients.

Enterprise Net Income

Under the concept of **enterprise net income,** income taxes and interest expense, as well as dividends, are considered distributions of income. Thus, the recipients of the income of the enterprise are the government, creditors, and owners. The income resulting from this concept is much like the operating income figure commonly appearing in income statements today, because taxes and interest are frequently presented after that amount.

Net Income to Investors

Another variation of net income is **net income to investors.** Within this concept all interest payments to creditors and dividend payments to stockholders are considered distributions of the enterprise's income, and all other distributions are considered determinants of income. This interpretation of income varies from current reporting practice only in that interest paid to creditors is treated as a distribution of income rather than a determinant of income.

Net Income to Residual Stockholders

The **residual** (or **common**) **stockholders** are typically thought of as the ultimate owners of the enterprise. Although the claim represented by preferred stock is legally that of an owner, there is some support for income to be regarded as the amount which accrues to the residual stockholders. This concept is reflected in the computation of earnings per share in which the net income (to all stockholders), as reported in the income statement, is reduced by the preferred dividend to derive an income figure accruing to the common stockholders. The resulting amount then becomes the basis for computing earnings per share. This view of income is consistent with the theory that common stockholders are the ultimate risk-bearers and the group to whom the long-run profitability of the enterprise ultimately accrues.

Exhibit 20–6 summarizes these various concepts of income and shows whether wages (return to employees), income taxes (return to government), interest (return to creditors), and preferred dividends (return to preferred stockholders) are treated as determinants or distributions of income under each concept. The concept of income reflected in current income presentation, **net income to stockholders,** is included in the fourth column.

Current Operating Performance Versus All-Inclusive Income

Another controversial question about the presentation of income concerns which specific transactions, if any, should be excluded from income determination because of their unique nature. Accountants today generally agree that sales, cost of goods sold, and other similar revenue and expense items should be *included* in the determination of net income. They

EXHIBIT 20–6
Comparative Income Presentations
(in thousands of dollars)

	(1) Value Added Income	(2) Enterprise Net Income	(3) Net Income to Investors	(4) Net Income to Stockholders	(5) Net Income to Residual Stockholders
Sales	$2,000	$2,000	$2,000	$2,000	$2,000
Determinants of income					
Cost of goods sold	1,000	1,000	1,000	1,000	1,000
Wages	—	400	400	400	400
Income taxes	—	—	150	150	150
Interest	—	—	—	200	200
Preferred dividends	—	—	—	—	50
	1,000	1,400	1,550	1,750	1,800
Income	$1,000	$ 600	$ 450	$ 250	$ 200
Distributions of income					
Wages	$400	—	—	—	—
Income taxes	150	$150	—	—	—
Interest	200	200	$200	—	—
Preferred dividends	50	50	50	$ 50	—
Common dividends	100	100	100	100	$100
Total distributions of income	$900	$500	$350	$150	$100
Groups to whom income accrues					
Employees	X				
Government	X	X			
Creditors	X	X	X		
Preferred stockholders	X	X	X	X	
Common stockholders	X	X	X	X	X

also generally agree that capital transactions, such as dividends and stock transactions, should be *excluded* in determining net income. Opinions differ, however, on the proper treatment of items that differ in nature from normal revenues and expenses, that do not recur in any established pattern, or that represent adjustments of the income of some past accounting period. Suppose, for example, that a company sustains a loss from an earthquake. Such a loss is unusual and will not recur in any predictable pattern. If the primary objective of reporting earnings is to provide information for predicting future events, should the company include this loss in the measurement of income? Assume again that in 1984 the company finds an error in the determination of 1982 net income. Should it include the gain or loss necessary to correct this error in the determination of 1984 net income? Special or irregular events like these are clearly part of the history of the enterprise's earnings, but their unique characteristics have led to disagreement on the most appropriate way to present them in the financial statements. The presentation of items such as those described above has produced two basic and opposing schools of thought: the **current operating performance** view and the **all-inclusive** view.

Proponents of the current operating performance view believe that a company's income should be based on its normal, recurring operations. That is, unusual items, nonrecurring items, and items relating to other accounting periods should be *excluded* from the current year's measurement of income and reported as direct increases or decreases in retained earnings. These types of items would appear in the statement of retained earnings rather than the income statement. Proponents of this view believe that financial statement users rely heavily on reported measurements of *net income* but that they lack the knowledge necessary to understand the detailed components of an income statement. The proponents

also believe that users can make more accurate predictions and more meaningful evaluations of management performance if net income reflects only the normal, recurring activities of the business.

The opposite perspective is the all-inclusive view. Proponents of this position believe
that income for a period should equal the change in owners' equity during the period,
except for dividends and capital stock transactions. They contend that unusual items, events
not recurring frequently, and items related to other accounting periods should be reported
in the current income statement. Advocates of this view assume that financial statement
users will not focus excessively on the bottom-line net income figure and that they will
appropriately consider the components of net income when they interpret the enterprise's
performance. All-inclusive advocates claim that irregular items tend to be unnoticed when
not reported in the income statement. Considerable judgment is required to determine
which items should be included under the current operating performance approach,
which—according to all-inclusive proponents—allows management to manipulate reported income by including or excluding items as desired. This controversy is significant,
because a company could compute substantially different income figures by using each
approach.

A careful analysis of authoritative accounting pronouncements reveals an evolution[12] in
thought from a strong all-inclusive position in 1941 (*Accounting Research Bulletin No. 8*[13])
to an equally strong current operating performance position in 1948 (*Accounting Research
Bulletin No. 35*[14]). By 1953, the pendulum had begun to swing away from the current
operating performance position. A strong step in the direction of the all-inclusive approach
came in 1966 when the Accounting Principles Board, in *Opinion No. 9*, concluded that "net
income should reflect all items of profit and loss recognized during the period with the sole
exception of prior period adjustments."[15] The APB opinion further stated that extraordinary
items should be shown separately from the results of ordinary operations in the income
statement and that prior period adjustments should be reported as adjustments to the beginning balance of retained earnings. Finally, it listed criteria for identifying both extraordinary
items and prior period adjustments. These criteria have subsequently been changed, however, by other authoritative pronouncements.

In 1977, the FASB moved a step closer to an all-inclusive income statement when it
issued *Statement of Financial Accounting Standards No. 16*.[16] Previously, companies were
allowed to treat a variety of items as prior period adjustments. Under *Statement No. 16* the
number of items properly treated as adjustments to retained earnings—rather than included
in income—was reduced considerably. In view of all these events we can conclude that
current accounting practice supports a *modified* all-inclusive view within which all income
items except limited prior period adjustments are included in the determination of net
income.

Contemporary Income Presentation

Contemporary income presentation practices are based on the concept of income to stockholders (see Exhibit 20–6). Emphasis is placed on the all-inclusive concept of income with
limited exceptions. Concern for the presentation of the results of current operations, however, is apparent in the many separate classifications and subtotals required in the statement
if certain types of events have taken place.

Throughout this text, various aspects of income statement presentation have been discussed and illustrated. In the following paragraphs, several of the significant features of

---

[12]For a discussion of the evolutionary process of income presentation, see Jack E. Kiger and Jan R. Williams,
"An Emerging Concept of Income Presentation," *Accounting Historians Journal* (Fall 1977), pp. 63–77.
[13]*ARB No. 8*, "Combined Statement of Income and Earned Surplus," 1941.
[14]*ARB No. 35*, "Presentation of Income and Earned Surplus," 1948.
[15]*APB Opinion No. 9*, "Reporting the Results of Operations," 1966, par. 17.
[16]*FASB Statement of Financial Accounting Standards No. 16*, "Prior Period Adjustments," 1977.

reporting income which have been considered earlier are briefly reviewed. That discussion is followed by a consideration of the circumstances that constitute the disposal of a major segment of an enterprise, and an explanation of how the discontinued operations are reported in the income statement.

Single- and Multiple-Step Income Statements

A **single-step income statement** is a relatively simple presentation in which all revenues and gains included in pretax income are grouped together at the top of the statement. Next, all expenses and losses included in pretax income are grouped together and subtracted from the total of revenues and gains, resulting in the net income figure. In a **multiple-step income statement,** revenues from sales are presented first. From this amount, cost of goods sold is deducted to determine gross margin. Operating expenses, which may be classified into specific categories such as selling and administrative expenses, are deducted from the gross margin to obtain income from operations. Other income and expense items are added to or deducted from the income from operations to obtain net income. Since the resulting net income figure is the same for both statements, the difference between the single-step and multiple-step income statements is in the format and extent of detail. Of course, both types of presentations are acceptable and each is frequently encountered. You may wish to refresh your memory about these two forms of income statement presentation by reviewing Exhibits 4–1 and 4–2.

Individually Identified Gains and Losses

Gains and losses which are unusual in nature *or* infrequent in occurrence should be individually identified in the income statement. Under the multiple-step format, these items are usually displayed among other gains and losses, following income from operations. Examples of this type of item are gains and losses from the sale of plant assets or securities of other companies. Care should be taken not to present these items in a way that implies that they are extraordinary items. They are not presented on a net-of-tax basis, and earnings-per-share figures are not presented on these items.

Intraperiod Income Tax Allocation

Gains and losses presented in the financial statements in separate categories, such as extraordinary items and prior period adjustments, should be presented on a net-of-tax basis. **Intraperiod income tax allocation** procedures require the determination of the income tax effect of these items and the direct association of the tax effect of each item with the related gain or loss. A separately classified gain is reduced by the additional income tax resulting from that gain. A separately classified loss is reduced by the income tax benefit resulting from the reduction in income due to the inclusion of that loss. The income tax expense which relates to all revenues and expenses not separately classified is computed as if any separately classified item(s) did not exist.

Extraordinary Gains and Losses

Gains and losses which are judged to be *both* unusual in nature *and* infrequent in occurrence are defined as **extraordinary** and are presented in a separate income statement category on a net-of-tax basis. This presentation is required in both single- and multiple-step income statements. An income subtotal immediately preceding extraordinary items entitled "income before extraordinary items" must be included in the income statement. This caption is followed by the extraordinary gain or loss presented net of its tax effect and then by the net income amount.

To illustrate the presentation of an extraordinary item, Exhibit 20–7 includes the combined statement of earnings and retained earnings and the related footnote from the Johnson & Johnson 1982 annual report. Johnson & Johnson is engaged in the manufacture and sale of a broad range of health-care products in many countries. The extraordinary loss of $50,000,000 included in the company's 1982 income statement resulted from the highly

EXHIBIT 20–7
Johnson & Johnson
Example Extraordinary Item

Johnson & Johnson and Subsidiaries
Consolidated Statement of Earnings and Retained Earnings

Dollars in Millions Except Per Share Figures (Note 1)	1982	1981*	1980*
Revenues			
Sales to customers	**$5,760.9**	5,399.0	4,837.4
Other revenues			
Interest income	**88.9**	78.8	50.0
Royalties and miscellaneous	**49.3**	28.6	26.4
	138.2	107.4	76.4
Total revenues	**5,899.1**	5,506.4	4,913.8
Costs and expenses			
Cost of products sold	**2,450.9**	2,368.4	2,194.3
Selling, distribution and administrative expenses	**2,248.8**	2,030.6	1,794.2
Research expense	**363.2**	282.9	232.8
Interest expense	**74.4**	60.7	37.0
Interest expense capitalized	**(46.3)**	(43.5)	(32.7)
Other expenses	**20.9**	23.4	12.9
Total costs and expenses	**5,111.9**	4,722.5	4,238.5
Earnings before provision for taxes on income and extraordinary charge	**787.2**	783.9	675.3
Provision for taxes on income (Note 3)	**263.8**	316.3	274.6
Earnings before extraordinary charge	**523.4**	467.6	400.7
Extraordinary charge—withdrawal of TYLENOL capsules (net of $50.0 taxes) (Note 2)	**(50.0)**	—	—
Net earnings	**473.4**	467.6	400.7
Retained earnings at beginning of period	**2,249.1**	1,940.1	1,676.3
Cash dividends paid (per share: 1982, $.97; 1981, $.85; 1980, $.74)	**(182.4)**	(158.6)	(136.9)
Retained earnings at end of period	**$2,540.1**	2,249.1	1,940.1
Per share of common stock			
Earnings before extraordinary charge	**$ 2.79**	2.51	2.17
Extraordinary charge	**(.27)**	—	—
Net earnings per share	**$ 2.52**	2.51	2.17

[*Reclassified to conform to 1982 presentation.]
Note 2. Extraordinary Charge

As a result of the criminal tampering with TYLENOL Extra-Strength Capsules in the Chicago area during the third quarter of 1982, the Company withdrew all TYLENOL capsule products from the market. The withdrawal costs, including disposal, handling, couponing and other associated costs resulted in an extraordinary after-tax charge in 1982 of $50 million or $.27 per share.

SOURCE: Johnson & Johnson, 1982 Annual Report.

publicized criminal tampering with Tylenol, a major Johnson & Johnson product. The loss represents the costs of withdrawing Tylenol capsules from the market.

Previous chapters have discussed two situations that result in extraordinary items without regard to the dual criteria of being unusual in nature and infrequent in occurrence. Chapter 15 indicated that gains and losses from the extinguishment of debt should be presented as extraordinary items in the period of the extinguishment transaction. This conclusion extends to gains of debtors that result from the restructuring of troubled debt. Chapter 18 pointed out that loss carryforwards are usually deferred and recognized in subsequent periods when the company has taxable income. When loss carryforwards are finally recognized in this manner, they are included in the income statement as extraordinary gains.

Cumulative Effect of a Change in Accounting Principle

When an enterprise has changed from one generally accepted accounting principle (or method of applying a principle) to another, the **cumulative effect** of that change on retained earnings at the beginning of the period of change will usually be included in income of the period of the change.[17] The cumulative effect may be a gain or loss, depending on the nature of the specific change. The cumulative effect immediately follows extraordinary items, if any, and is presented on a net-of-tax basis. This is shown in Chapter 19.

Prior Period Adjustments

Corrections of errors in previously issued financial statements and certain other adjustments are *not* included in the determination of net income. Primarily because they do not relate to the period in which they are recorded, these items (presented on a net-of-tax basis) belong in the retained earnings statement as adjustments to the beginning balance of the period— even though they are part of the enterprise's total earnings history.

Several types of events and transactions that are presented as prior period adjustments are discussed in Chapter 19. These include corrections of errors, the recognition of operating loss carryforwards of purchased subsidiaries, and certain retroactive adjustments resulting from the application of authoritative accounting pronouncements.

Earnings Per Share

Earnings-per-share figures must be presented on the income statement of all publicly held companies. Other companies may choose to present earnings-per-share data, and numerous authoritative pronouncements require the presentation of earnings-per-share figures for certain income statement items.

When presented, earnings-per-share figures appear on the face of the income statement and may also be explained in related notes. A common practice is to present an earnings-per-share schedule (which parallels the income statement presentation) at the bottom of the income statement.

Exhibit 20–8 illustrates this method of presentation with Lee Company's 1984–1985 comparative income statement, which includes a typical earnings-per-share presentation at the bottom. The exhibit assumes that 100,000 shares of common stock were outstanding throughout 1984 and 1985.

The computation of earnings per share is complicated by the presence of convertible securities, stock options, warrants and rights, and other arrangements which include the possibility of changing the number of common shares outstanding. Since the presentation of earnings per share is primarily of interest to publicly held companies, an in-depth discussion of the subject is deferred to Chapter 26 of this text.

---

[17]As seen in Chapter 19, the effects of certain special types of changes in an accounting principle are presented by retroactively restating previous financial statements rather than by including the cumulative effect of the change in the income of the period of change.

EXHIBIT 20–8

Lee Company
PARTIAL INCOME STATEMENT
For the Fiscal Years Ended October 31, 1984 and 1985

	1985	*1984*
Income before extraordinary item and cumulative effect of accounting change	$855,000	$ 628,000
Extraordinary loss—Major casualty loss, net of $85,000 income tax benefit	—	(112,000)
Cumulative effect of change in depreciation method, net of $42,500 income taxes	56,300	—
Net income	$911,300	$ 516,000
Earnings per common share		
Income before extraordinary item and cumulative effect of accounting change	$8.55	$ 6.28
Extraordinary loss	—	(1.12)
Cumulative effect of change in accounting principle	.56	—
Net income	$9.11	$ 5.16

Discontinued Operations

When an enterprise has disposed of a major portion of itself, the results of continuing operations should be separated from the operating results of the discontinued portion. Any gain or loss on the disposal of the discontinued part of the business should also be shown separately. Prior to the development of this income statement presentation technique the most frequent extraordinary items in financial reports were gains and losses from the disposal of portions of business enterprises.[18] The frequency of these items, combined with their tendency to represent large amounts of dollars, prompted the APB to establish the reporting standards for discontinued operations as a part of *APB Opinion No. 30.*[19]

Income or loss from the operations of a segment prior to its disposal and any gain or loss on the disposal are *not* extraordinary items under current accounting standards. These items are combined in a section of the income statment identified as **discontinued operations.** This section is *preceded* by an income subtotal, **income from continuing operations.** The income or loss from the operations of the disposed segment and the gain or loss from the actual disposal are presented separately on a net-of-tax basis. This section is followed by "net income" or "income before extraordinary item and/or cumulative effect of change in accounting principles," as appropriate.

Earnings-per-share data for income from continuing operations and net income should be presented on the face of the income statement. In practice, earnings-per-share figures are also frequently presented for the two components of discontinued operations or for the discontinued operations section as a single figure.

What constitutes a *segment* disposal (which, in turn, subjects the company to the discontinued operations presentation described above)? A **segment** is a component (of an enterprise) whose activities represent a separate major line of business or a separate class of customer. A segment may be a subsidiary or other investee, a division, or a department; and the disposal may be accomplished by sale or abandonment. A major criterion distinguishing the disposal of a segment from other transactions requires that the assets and results of

---

[18]Leopold A. Bernstein, "Reporting the Results of Operations—A Reassessment of APB Opinion No. 9," *Journal of Accountancy* (July 1970), pp. 57–58.
[19]*APB Opinion No. 30,* "Reporting the Results of Operations," 1973, par. 13–18.

operations of the discontinued segment can be clearly distinguished physically, operationally, and for financial accounting purposes from other assets, results of operations, and activities of the enterprise. The inability to identify separately the results of operations of the discontinued unit suggests that the transaction is not a disposal of a *segment* of the business.

To illustrate the accounting and reporting for the disposal of a segment, assume that Alexander Company has determined its preliminary aggregate operating figures for 1985 as follows:

Revenue from sales	$8,000,000
Cost of goods sold	3,500,000
Operating expenses	2,000,000
	5,500,000
Income before income tax	$2,500,000

During the year the company disposed of its nuts-and-bolts division, which was operationally separate from the rest of the business. Operating results of this division, which are included in the above aggregate figures, are as follows:

Revenue from sales	$1,500,000
Cost of goods sold	1,400,000
Operating expenses	800,000
	2,200,000
Loss before income tax	$ (700,000)

In addition, the actual disposal of the nuts-and-bolts division resulted in a $450,000 loss before income tax, which is *not* included in the above figures:

Proceeds from the sale of nuts-and-bolts division	$ 6,500,000
Net book value of assets of nuts-and-bolts division	(6,950,000)
Loss on sale before income tax	$ (450,000)

The appropriate income tax rate for all items is 40%.

The presentation of discontinued operations for Alexander Company is illustrated in the income statement in Exhibit 20–9. The revenue and expense amounts for continuing operations are determined by separating the figures for the discontinued division. The earnings-per-share figures are computed on the basis of 1,000,000 shares of common stock outstanding with no preferred stock.

The disposal of a major segment of a business enterprise frequently takes place over an extended period of time. It is not unusual for such a disposal to begin in one accounting period and extend into one or more future accounting periods. In this situation, two dates are particularly important:

> **Measurement Date**—*The date on which the management having the authority to approve the action commits itself to a formal plan to dispose of a segment of the business, whether by sale or abandonment. The plan of disposal should include, as a minimum, identification of the major assets to be disposed of, the expected manner of disposal, the period expected to be required for completion of the disposal, an active program to find a buyer if disposal is to be by sale, the estimated results of operations of the segment from the measurement date to the disposal date, and the estimated proceeds or salvage to be realized by disposal.*

EXHIBIT 20–9

Alexander Company
INCOME STATEMENT
For the Year Ended December 31, 1985

Revenue from sales		$6,500,000
Cost of goods sold	$2,100,000	
Operating expenses	1,200,000	3,300,000
Income from continuing operations before income tax		3,200,000
Income tax expense (at 40%)		1,280,000
Income from continuing operations		1,920,000
Discontinued operations		
Loss from operations of discontinued nuts-and-bolts		
division, less applicable income taxes of $280,000	(420,000)	
Loss on disposal of nuts-and-bolts division, less		
applicable income taxes of $180,000	(270,000)	(690,000)
Net income		$1,230,000
Earnings per share		
Income from continuing operations		$1.92
Discontinued operations		
Loss from operations of nuts-and-bolts division	$(.42)	
Loss on disposal of nuts-and-bolts division	(.27)	(.69)
Net income		$1.23

Disposal Date—The date of closing the sale if the disposal is by sale or the date that operations cease if the disposal is by abandonment.[20]

If the **measurement date** is in one accounting period and the **disposal date** is in a subsequent accounting period, accounting for the disposal of the segment is more complex.

If a loss is expected from the planned disposal of a segment, the estimated loss should be recognized at the measurement date. On the other hand, an anticipated gain should not be recognized until the gain is realized, which is usually the disposal date. This procedure results in a *conservative* approach to income, since an estimated loss is anticipated and recognized at the earlier measurement date, whereas an estimated gain is deferred and recognized at the later disposal date when it is ultimately realized.

Conservatism

Exhibit 20–10 presents the disclosure of discontinued operations in the partial income statement and footnote of Midland-Ross Corporation, a diversified company that deals in newspaper publishing, fuel production, health-care delivery, and a variety of other products and services. As the note in Exhibit 20–10 explains, in 1982 the company sold its Midland Brake Division, resulting in a loss on disposal of $7,580,000. The operating loss of that division has been reclassified as part of the discontinued operations section of the income statement for 1982, 1981, and 1980.

In estimating whether a gain or loss will result from the disposal of the segment, the net amount expected to be received from the disposal should include any estimated costs and expenses directly associated with the disposal. Additionally, if the disposal will take time and if continued operations of the segment are planned for the period of disposal, any estimated income or loss from operations should be included in the estimated gain or loss on the disposal. Amounts of income or loss from operations included in the gain or loss on disposal should be limited to amounts which can be reasonably projected. Normally such projections should not exceed a one-year period.

In addition to the information presented in the discontinued operations section of the

---

[20]*APB Opinion No. 30*, par. 14.

EXHIBIT 20-10
Midland-Ross Corporation
Disclosure of Discontinued Operations

PARTIAL INCOME STATEMENT
(In thousands of dollars except per share amounts)

Year Ended December 31	1982	1981	1980
Net sales	$790,897	$859,030	$866,761
Other income	15,337	18,320	20,164
	806,234	877,350	886,925
Cost and expenses:			
Cost of products sold	591,520	647,655	637,416
Selling and administrative	148,638	144,289	134,810
Depreciation and amortization	28,782	26,399	22,824
Interest expense	20,485	17,057	13,750
Minority interests	983	820	1,563
	790,408	836,220	810,363
Income from continuing operations before income taxes	15,826	41,130	76,562
Income taxes—Note F	6,320	15,486	32,189
Income from continuing operations	9,506	25,644	44,373
Discontinued operation—Note H:			
Operating loss	(676)	(953)	(561)
Loss on sale of assets	(7,580)	—	—
Net Income	$ 1,250	$ 24,691	$ 43,812

Note H—Discontinued Operation

On August 31, 1982, the company sold substantially all the assets of its Midland Brake Division to Echlin Inc. of Branford, Conn. The results of operations of the Midland Brake Division for 1982, 1981, and 1980 and the loss incurred on the sale of assets have been reported in the consolidated statement of income as a discontinued operation, additional detail for which follows:

	(In Thousands of Dollars)		
	1982	1981	1980
Net sales and other income	$29,549	$48,817	$42,554
Cost and expenses	31,014	50,926	43,874
	(1,465)	(2,109)	(1,320)
Income taxes	(789)	(1,156)	(759)
Operating loss	(676)	(953)	(561)
Loss on sale (less applicable income tax benefit of $5,649)	(7,580)	—	—
	$(8,256)	$ (953)	$ (561)

Disclosure income statement, the notes to the financial statements should disclose the following information:[21]

1. The identity of the segment of the business that has been or will be discontinued.
2. The expected disposal date, if known.
3. The expected manner of disposal.

---

[21]*APB Opinion No. 30*, par. 18.

4. A description of the remaining assets and liabilities of the segments at the financial-statement date.
5. The income or loss from operations and any proceeds from disposal of the segment during the period from the measurement date to the financial-statement date.

Objectivity

Many of the items which must be disclosed are also necessary to establish the measurement date. Such information is frequently made available only through management action and estimates. Accountants, therefore, should attempt to gather additional objective evidence to support the assertions and disclosures contained in the financial statements.

Comprehensive Model Income Statement

An example income statement—which incorporates many of the revenue, expense, gain, and loss items discussed in this chapter and in previous chapters—is presented in Exhibit 20–11. The influence of the all-inclusive philosophy can be seen in the inclusion of the discontinued operations, extraordinary gain, cumulative effect of change in depreciation method, and other revenues and expenses not directly related to operations. On the other hand, the influence of the current operating performance philosophy can be seen in the separation of these items from normal, recurring transactions and the resulting subtotals, such as "income from operations," "income from continuing operations," and "income before extraordinary item and cumulative effect of change in accounting principle."

The following aspects of this statement are particularly worthy of attention and provide a review of several concepts covered earlier:

1. The provision for income tax incorporates the income tax effects of all transactions presented above that item in the income statement. All items in the statement below this item are presented on a net-of-tax basis.
2. The major types of irregular items are presented in the following order: discontinued operations, extraordinary item, cumulative effect of a change in accounting principle. Appropriate titles are assigned to the income figures that precede each of these items.
3. The discontinued segment is presented immediately before the extraordinary item and is divided into the results of *operations* of the discontinued segment and the loss on the *disposal* of the discontinued segment. This section is preceded by the caption, "income from continuing operations." All items in this section are presented on a net-of-tax basis.
4. The extraordinary gain is separately disclosed after the discontinued operations section and is also presented on a net-of-tax basis.
5. The cumulative effect of the change in depreciation method follows the extraordinary item and 'is also presented on a net-of-tax basis.
6. The earnings per share and *pro forma* effects of the retroactive application of the newly adopted accounting principle are presented at the bottom of the income statement, following net income.

While it is unlikely that a single income statement would contain all the irregular items in Exhibit 20–11, it is important to understand the relation of each item to the others and to the income statement as a whole. The fictitious Vickory statement is presented to facilitate this understanding.

CONCLUDING REMARKS

The recognition of revenue is one of the most important topics in contemporary financial accounting. It is not enough to know specific technical rules related to when, and in what amount, revenue should be recognized in specific circumstances. Rather, knowledgeable accounting practitioners maintain a firm conceptual understanding of the theories and principles underlying specific procedural practices. The same is true for the proper placement

EXHIBIT 20–11
Vickory Company
INCOME STATEMENTS
For the Years Ended December 31, 1984 and 1985
(in thousands of dollars except earnings-per-share figures)

	1985	1984
Sales	$5,525	$5,108
Cost of goods sold	2,100	1,950
Gross margin	3,425	3,158
Selling and administrative expenses	1,250	1,200
Income from operations	2,175	1,958
Other income		
Gain on sale of plant assets	—	100
Dividend income	75	80
Other expenses		
Interest on long-term debt	(255)	(307)
Unrealized loss on valuations of current marketable equity securities	(92)	—
Income before income tax	1,903	1,831
Provision for income tax	761	732
Income from continuing operations	1,142	1,099
Discontinued operations		
Loss from operations of business segment, net of applicable income tax savings of $44 in 1985 and $48 in 1984	(66)	(72)
Loss on disposal of business segment, net of applicable income tax savings of $80	(120)	—
Income before extraordinary item and cumulative effect of change in accounting principle	956	1,027
Extraordinary item—gain on forced sale of assets to state municipality, net of applicable income taxes of $210	—	525
Cumulative effect of change in method of depreciation, net of applicable income taxes of $68	(102)	—
Net income	$ 854	$1,552
Earnings per common share		
Income from continuing operations	$11.42	$10.99
Discontinued operations	(1.86)	(.72)
Income before extraordinary item and cumulative effect of accounting change	9.56	10.27
Extraordinary gain	—	5.25
Cumulative effect of change in accounting principle	(1.02)	—
Net income	$ 8.54	$15.52
Pro forma amounts assuming retroactive application of new depreciation method		
Income before extraordinary item	$ 956	$ 967
Earnings per common share	$ 9.56	$ 9.67
Net income	$ 956	$1,492
Earnings per common share	$ 9.56	$14.92

and terminology in preparing an income statement when transactions giving rise to irregular items such as discontinued operations and extraordinary items occur. Only through a thorough understanding of accounting theory and the underlying nature of business transactions can we hope to resolve the many complex problems which warrant careful attention and explanation in the financial statements.

1. Revenue should not be recognized until it is earned, measurable, and collectible. In many situations these conditions are met at the point of sale, although departures from revenue recognition at the point of sale are found in certain circumstances.

2. The percentage-of-completion and completed-contract methods of accounting for long-term contracts are acceptable in different circumstances. Within the percentage-of-completion method, revenue is recognized throughout the construction period as objective evidence indicates the proper amount to be recognized. Within the completed-contract method, revenue is deferred and recognized at the completion of the contract.

3. The installment sales method defers the recognition of revenue until cash is collected, and this method is acceptable in financial reporting only when collectibility is highly uncertain.

4. When customers have the right to return products, six conditions must be met before the revenue can be recognized. These conditions relate to the transfer of the risks and rewards of ownership from the seller to the buyer and the ability of the seller to make a reasonably objective estimate of the amount of returns.

5. Consignment transactions appear much like sales. They differ, however, in that ownership and responsibility for the costs of maintaining the products consigned remain with the consignor. Only when the consignee has sold the products to a third party can the consignor recognize revenue.

6. The presentation of income is carefully defined and structured in the authoritative literature. At the present time, income is presented in a manner consistent with a modified all-inclusive concept in that all items of profit and loss, except prior period adjustments, are included in the income statement.

7. Discontinued operations, extraordinary items, and the cumulative effect of a general change in accounting principle are presented in separate income statement categories on a net-of-tax basis.

8. "Discontinued operations"—which follows the caption "income from continuing operations"—is a separate section of the income statement and presents both the gain or loss from the disposal of a discontinued segment of the business and the operating income or loss of that segment. These items are separated from the income or loss from ongoing business activities.

APPENDIX A SPECIAL REVENUE-RECOGNITION PRACTICES

This appendix deals with the unique circumstances and business practices in several industries which require unusual or complex revenue-recognition practices. The general criteria for revenue recognition developed in the body of this chapter apply equally to special industries and routine situations. Therefore, when studying the appendix, consider carefully how each of the practices specified by the accounting profession is consistent with more general or fundamental concepts of revenue recognition.

Although specific practices are discussed, the purpose of this appendix is to develop a conceptual understanding of these special industry circumstances rather than detailed knowledge of the accounting procedures that are applied.

REAL ESTATE TRANSACTIONS

A unique aspect of real estate transactions is that risk of uncollectible receivables is reduced by the nature of the asset sold. Land and other real property is relatively easily repossessed if the purchasing party fails to comply with the terms of the sales agreement. Real property is not readily transportable, does not generally depreciate in value, and is frequently not susceptible to damage and destruction. While the foregoing characteristics are usually associated with land, many structural improvements and buildings possess similar characteristics.

Since sellers of real estate recognize these characteristics of real estate, a greater credit risk may be assumed without creating an unacceptable risk of loss to the selling enterprise. Although the recovery of the investment in real estate may be assured to a greater degree than in other types of sales, the recognition of additional sales revenue should be carefully considered when the buyer is a poor credit risk.

The American Institute of Certified Public Accountants (AICPA) considered these circumstances and issued an Industry Accounting Guide,[22] which subsequently became part of *FASB Statement of Financial Accounting Standards No. 66*. In addition to the issues already mentioned, the guide recognized that many real estate transactions are exceptionally complex and that the legal form of the transaction may often obscure the real economic substance of an event.

Substance over Form

The accounting guide and the subsequent *SFAS No. 66* establish general criteria for the timing of recognition of revenue and provide modifying conventions for use when the conceptual criteria for revenue recognition are not met at the time of the sale.

[Revenue should be recognized] in full when real estate is sold, provided (a) the profit is measurable, that is, the collectibility of the sales price is reasonably assured or the amount that will not be collectible can be estimated, and (b) the earning process is virtually complete, that is, the seller is not obliged to perform significant activities after the sale to earn the profit. Unless both conditions exist, recognition of all or part of the profit shall be postponed.[23]

If the collectibility of the sales price is uncertain, as is the case in many real estate transactions, then the installment sales method of revenue recognition or the even more conservative cost recovery method should be used. In certain circumstances involving the collectibility of the sales price, the seller should use "deposit accounting," wherein no sale is presumed to have occurred and all cash received is treated as deferred revenue (liability) in the balance sheet. Furthermore, if the earning process is incomplete, recognition of revenue moves from the time of sale to the time of the seller's performance of the earning process. Finally, no profit should be recognized until a sale is actually consummated.

Certain requirements must be met in order to recognize revenue when the receivables are material after the sale and completion of the earning process. These criteria relate to: (1) the amount of the down payment; (2) the composition of the down payment; and (3) the terms regarding the receivable portion of the consideration.

In regard to the amount of the initial payment, a range from 5% to 25% of the purchase price, depending on the nature of the property sold, has been established for purposes of profit recognition. Exhibit 20–12, reproduced from *SFAS No. 66*, reflects the appropriate down payment percentages and related types of property.[24]

Even if a down payment is of sufficient size to qualify for the recognition of profit, the composition of the payment and terms of collection must also be considered. Generally, the down payment must consist of cash or notes supported by irrevocable letters of credit from established lending institutions to support the immediate recognition of revenue. Buyers must also maintain a continuing financial commitment in that the payments being made must be sufficient to pay the total indebtedness, including interest, within 20 years for land and within normal first mortgage terms of financial institutions for other real estate.

If a buyer's down payment amount or quality or the buyer's continuing investment is not adequate, then the installment sales method should normally be used to recognize revenue on the sale. However, if there is uncertainty as to whether cost will be recovered if a buyer defaults or if cost has already been recovered through down payment but future collections are uncertain, then the cost recovery method of revenue recognition should be employed.

ACCOUNTING FOR RETAIL LAND SALES

Land developers frequently acquire a large parcel of land, develop a master plan for subdivision and improvement, obtain construction approval, perform necessary improvements, and sell lots. Furthermore, certain characteristics inherent in retail land sales create special problems concerning the recognition of revenue and related expenses. Examples are small down payments, unenforceable sales contracts, and cancellation periods during which buyers can obtain refunds.

---

[22]*AICPA Industry Accounting Guide,* "Accounting for Profit Recognition on Sales of Real Estate," 1973.
[23]*FASB Statement of Financial Accounting Standards No. 66,* "Accounting for Sales of Real Estate," 1982, par. 3.
[24]*FASB Statement of Financial Accounting Standards No. 66,* par. 54.

EXHIBIT 20–12
Real Estate Down Payments

	Minimum Down Payment Expressed as a Percentage of Sales Value
Land:	
Held for commercial, industrial, or residential development to commence within two years after sale	20%[a]
Held for commercial, industrial, or residential development after two years	25%[a]
Commercial and Industrial Property:	
Office and industrial buildings, shopping centers, etc.:	
Properties subject to lease on a long-term lease basis to parties having satisfactory credit rating; cash flow currently sufficient to service all indebtedness	10%
Single tenancy properties sold to a user having a satisfactory credit rating	15%
All other	20%
Other Income-Producing Properties (hotels, motels, marinas, mobile home parks, etc.):	
Cash flow currently sufficient to service all indebtedness	15%
Start-up situations or current deficiencies in cash flow	25%
Multi-Family Residential Property:	
Primary residence:	
Cash flow currently sufficient to service all indebtedness	10%
Start-up situations or current deficiencies in cash flow	15%
Secondary or recreational residence:	
Cash flow currently sufficient to service all indebtedness	15%
Start-up situations or current deficiencies in cash flow	25%
Single Family Residential Property (including condominium or cooperative housing):	
Primary residence of the buyer	5%[b]
Secondary or recreational residence	10%[b]

[a]Not intended to apply to volume retail lot sales by land development companies.
[b]If collectibility of the remaining portion of the sales price cannot be supported by reliable evidence of collection experience, a higher down payment is indicated and should not be less than 60% of the difference between the sales value and the financing available from loans guaranteed by regulatory bodies, such as FHA or VA, or from independent financial institutions.

SOURCE: *FASB Statement of Financial Accounting Standards No. 66,* "Accounting for Sales of Real Estate," 1982, par. 54.

Consideration of the foregoing problems encouraged the AICPA to develop another Industry Accounting Guide; this one pertains to the timing and magnitude of revenue recognition.[25] This guide also became part of *FASB Statement No. 66.* In essence, *SFAS No. 66* contains the following requirements for recording a sale:[26]

1. The buyer must make a down payment and regular subsequent payments throughout the period covered by any cancellation with refund right.

2. The aggregate payments, including interest, must at least equal 10% of the contract sales price.

3. Collection experience on similar sales must indicate that collection of the receivable is reasonably assured.

4. Generally, the receivable from the sale must not be

[25]*AICPA Industry Accounting Guide,* "Accounting for Retail Land Sales," 1973.
[26]*FASB Statement of Financial Accounting Standards No. 66,* par. 45.

subject to subordination to new loans on the property.

5. The seller must not be obligated to complete improvements of lots sold nor to construct facilities applicable to lots sold.

For transactions in which the first four criteria are met and substantial progress has been made toward the completion of improvements and facilities (mentioned in requirement 5), the percentage-of-completion method is applicable.

ACCOUNTING FOR FRANCHISE ACTIVITIES

The growth of franchising as a means of commerce began intense acceleration during the 1960s and continues today. Many contentious accounting and reporting issues are posed by such activities, and these problems are resolved in *FASB Statement of Financial Accounting Standards No. 45.*[27] **Franchises** generally involve the creation or extension of a business in which two parties join together in a continuing contract with a joint public identity. Each party normally contributes resources. The **franchisor** frequently contributes products, processes, equipment, company reputation, and trademarks. The **franchisee** generally provides operating capital and managerial and operational resources. Franchise activities are extremely broad; they cut across industry lines and are radically different in terms of organization, concept, and philosophy. For example, some franchise agreements provide for a relatively passive franchisor role after establishment, while others require extensive participation or the supply of products and skill on a continuing basis. Therefore, precise accounting and reporting standards are not possible. Certain broad guidelines, however, are provided by *FASB Statement No. 45.*

The general bases for accounting and reporting practices are contained in the franchise agreement. Most such agreements require the franchisee to make a substantial initial payment, called a franchise fee, to the franchisor in consideration for the reputation, skill, products, and processes contributed by the franchisor. Financial accounting for the franchise fee in terms of revenue recognition is most controversial, and careful study of the franchise agreement is necessary.

FASB Statement No. 45 notes that the problem of recognizing revenue in regard to franchise fees generally results from two issues: (1) the point at which the fee is to be considered earned, and (2) the assessment of collectibility of any unpaid portion of the fee. Initial fees are generally quite specific and, therefore, the amount of the initial fee is usually known. Most franchise agreements also call for continuing payments related to the level of franchisee business. For example, continuing payments to franchisors are usually based on the sales of products to franchisees or on a percentage of the franchisee's sales or profits.

The three revenue-recognition practices that are used with franchisees are summarized as follows:

1. **Cash basis.** This method calls for recording revenue when cash is received. Proponents cite the simplicity of application, the complexity of franchise agreements, and collection problems as support for this practice.

2. **Spread over life of agreement.** This method treats the initial fee as a prepayment for the privilege of using franchise rights. Accordingly, the prepayment should be recognized ratably over the life of the franchise agreement. Franchisors agree that the franchise fee is payment for a confirmation of initial and continuing services and transfers of rights.

3. **Inception of the franchise agreement.** This method treats the sale of a franchise in a manner similar to the sale of any other commercial property, tangible or intangible. The sale represents the transfer of specified rights in exchange for specified consideration and thus supports the recognition of revenue at the point of sale.

FASB Statement No. 45 finds merit in each argument under certain separate circumstances and indirectly supports each in specific individual situations. In essence, revenue should be recognized when a franchise sale occurs *and* when all material obligations of the franchisor have been substantially performed. Substantial performance may take place at different points in time under different franchise agreements. Even if the franchise agreement requires no further franchisor services, revenue should not be recognized if business conditions or informal policy indicates that substantial voluntary services are likely to be rendered by the franchisor.

Any unpaid franchise fees must also be assessed as to collectibility prior to the recognition of revenue. If collection of the franchise fee is uncertain, the installment method or cost recovery method may be necessary to avoid a premature recognition of revenue.

---

[27]*FASB Statement of Financial Accounting Standards No. 45,* "Accounting for Franchise Fee Revenue," 1981.

20–1 What three conditions must be met for revenue to be recognized?

20–2 Why is the point of sale frequently used as the point of revenue recognition?

20–3 Why do long-term contracts pose a particularly difficult revenue-recognition problem?

20–4 Under what circumstances should the percentage-of-completion method of recognizing revenue on long-term contracts be used?

20–5 Under what circumstances should the completed-contract method of recognizing revenue on long-term contracts be used?

20–6 What is the essential difference in accounting treatment of contract revenues and costs under the percentage-of-completion and completed-contract methods?

20–7 Assuming a contract is started in 1983 and completed in 1985, explain the procedure for estimating the amount of gross profit in each year if the percentage of completion is determined by stating the costs incurred to date as a percentage of total expected costs.

20–8 Under what circumstances is the installment sales method appropriate for financial reporting purposes? How does this method differ from recognizing revenue at the point of sale?

20–9 State briefly the six criteria that must be met for revenue to be recognized if the customer has the right to return the purchased products. If one or more of these conditions are not met, what accounting procedures are appropriate?

20–10 What is a consignment? Why is revenue not recognized by the consignor at the time products are transferred from the consignor to the consignee?

20–11 Explain how the presentation of income contributes to meeting the primary objectives of financial reporting.

20–12 In what way does the presentation of income assist in judging management efficiency?

20–13 Explain the concept of "value added income." How does it differ from the concept of income underlying the income statement as currently prepared?

20–14 What is the difference between "income to stockholders" and "income to residual stockholders"?

20–15 Distinguish between the all-inclusive and current operating performance concepts of income in terms of the meaning of the final income figure resulting from each.

20–16 What determines a "segment" in deciding whether the disposal of a portion of a business qualifies for separate disclosure in a discontinued operations section of the income statement?

20–17 Explain the meaning of the income subtotal "income from continuing operations."

20–18 Distinguish between the "measurement date" and the "disposal date." Explain their significance in reporting discontinued operations in the income statement.

20–19 State a rule for identifying those revenues, expenses, gains, and losses which must be presented on a net-of-tax basis in the income statement.

20–20 Which of the following is an example of an extraordinary item in reporting results of operations?

[a] A loss incurred because of a strike by employees.

[b] The write-off of deferred research and development costs believed to have no future benefit.

[c] A gain resulting from the devaluation of the U.S. dollar.

[d] A gain resulting from the state exercising its right of eminent domain on a piece of land used as a parking lot.

(AICPA adapted)

20–21 Which of the following is not a generally practiced method of presenting the income statement?

[a] Including prior period adjustments in determining net income.

[b] The single-step income statement.

[c] The consolidated statement of income.

[d] Including gains and losses from discontinued operations of a segment of a business in determining net income.

(AICPA adapted)

20–22 Which of the following shows how the gain or loss from an event or transaction that meets the criteria for infrequent occurrence but not unusual nature should be disclosed?

[a] Separately in the earnings statement immediately after earnings from continuing operations.

[b] On a net-of-tax basis in the earnings statement immediately after earnings from continuing operations.

[c] As an extraordinary item and treated accordingly in the earnings statement.

[d] Separately in the earnings statement as a component of earnings from continuing operations.

(AICPA adapted)

20–23 Which of the following is a required disclosure in the earnings statement when the disposal of a segment of the business is reported?

[a] The gain or loss on disposal should be reported as an extraordinary item.

[b] Results of operations of a discontinued segment should be disclosed immediately below extraordinary items.

[c] Earnings per share from both continuing operations and net earnings should be disclosed on the face of the earnings statement.

[d] Revenue and expenses applicable to the discontinued operations should be disclosed in the earnings statement.

(AICPA adapted)

20–24 When a company discontinues an operation and disposes of the discontinued operation (segment), the transaction should be included in the earnings statement as a gain or loss on disposal reported as which of the following?

[a] A prior period adjustment.

[b] An extraordinary item.

[c] An amount after continuing operations and before extraordinary items.

[d] A bulk sale of fixed assets included in earnings from continuing operations.

(AICPA adapted)

CASES

C20–1   The earning of revenue by an enterprise is recognized for accounting purposes when the transaction is recorded. In some situations, revenue is recognized approximately as it is earned in the economic sense. In other situations, however, accountants have developed guidelines for recognizing revenue by other criteria, such as the point of sale.

Instructions

[a] Explain and justify why revenue is often recognized as earned at the point of sale.

[b] Explain in what situations it would be appropriate to recognize revenue as the productive activity takes place.

[c] Other than indicated in [a] and [b], at what times may it be appropriate to recognize revenue? Explain.

(AICPA adapted)

C20–2   In accounting for long-term contracts (those taking longer than one year to complete), the two methods commonly followed are the percentage-of-completion method and the completed-contract method.

Instructions

[a] Discuss how earnings on long-term contracts are recognized and computed under these two methods.

[b] Under what circumstances is it preferable to use one method over the other?

[c] Why is earnings recognition as measured by interim billings not generally accepted for long-term contracts?

[d] How are job costs and interim billings reflected on the balance sheet under the percentage-of-completion method and the completed-contract method?

(AICPA adapted)

C20–3   Income measurement can be divided into different income concepts classified by income recipients. The following income concepts are tailored to the listed categories of income recipients.

Income Concepts	Income Recipients
[1] Net income to residual equity holders.	Common stockholders.
[2] Net income to investors.	Stockholders and long-term debt holders.
[3] Value added income.	All employees, stockholders, governments, and some creditors.

Instructions

For each of the concepts listed above, explain what major categories of revenue, expense, and other items would be included in the determination of income.

(AICPA adapted)

C20–4   Authoritative accounting pronouncements which have appeared over several years have resulted in several categories of items which are given special treatment in the income statement. These items include: (1) extraordinary items; (2) unusual *or* infrequent items; (3) gains or losses on segment disposals;

and (4) cumulative effects of accounting changes.

Instructions

For each of the four categories describe:
[a] The proper placement of the item on the financial statements in terms of the other items.
[b] The manner of presenting the income tax effects of the item.

C20–5 Rabun Company, a publicly held regional manufacturer of western-style clothing, uses a calendar year for financial reporting. During 1983 Rabun purchased a small chain of retail specialty clothing stores which were privately owned and which had been a good customer of Rabun's for a number of years.

Ron Hardy was hired as controller of Rabun Company in May 1984. In preparation for the 1985 budget, he completed a detailed comparison of the 1984 performance with the 1983 figures as reported. Through this analysis he discovered the following items which affected the reported figures for 1983:
[1] The accounts receivable at December 31, 1983, were understated by $63,000. A subsidiary ledger had a balance with a transposed number. The Accounts Receivable control account was reduced by this amount in the adjusting entries of 1983.
[2] In May 1984, $60,000 was received in settlement for a $130,000 claim against a vendor for defective merchandise. The claim was filed in March 1983, but no receivable was recorded by Rabun because the ven-

dor's financial condition was very weak.
[3] In 1983 Rabun paid $48,000 for additional federal income tax that was determined to be due for 1980 by an IRS audit. The additional tax was treated as an extraordinary expense.
[4] Rabun paid $75,000 in August 1984 to settle an employee discrimination suit filed in September 1983 by a Rabun labor union who charged bias in promotion practices. No liability had been recorded in 1983, but the suit had been disclosed in the footnotes to the 1983 financial statements.
[5] The retail chain Rabun acquired in 1983 recorded its bad debts on the direct write-off basis even though the chain had significant credit sales and bad-debt losses. The chain was included in the consolidated earnings of Rabun for 1983. Ron Hardy estimated that the chain would have had an allowance for doubtful accounts of $50,000 if an allowance system had been used.

Instructions

Discuss how Ron Hardy should handle each of the five situations in preparing the 1984 financial statements, paying particular attention to whether the items should be treated as prior period adjustments or as part of 1984 income.

(CMA adapted)

C20–6 The following is the complete set of financial statements prepared by Oberlin Corporation:

Oberlin Corporation
STATEMENT OF EARNINGS AND
RETAINED EARNINGS
For the Fiscal Year Ended August 31, 1983

Sales		$3,500,000
Less: Returns and allowances		35,000
Net sales		3,465,000
Less: Cost of goods sold		1,039,000
Gross margin		2,426,000
Less:		
Selling expenses	$1,000,000	
General and administrative expenses [Note 1]	1,079,000	2,079,000
Operating earnings		347,000
Add other revenue:		
Purchase discounts	10,000	
Gain on increased value of investments in real estate	100,000	
Gain on sale of treasury stock	200,000	
Correction of error in last year's statement	90,000	400,000
Ordinary earnings		747,000

Add extraordinary item—gain on sale of fixed asset	53,000
Earnings before income tax	800,000
Less: Income tax expense	380,000
Net earnings	420,000
Add: Beginning retained earnings	2,750,000
	3,170,000
Less:	
Dividends (12% stock dividend declared but not yet issued)	120,000
Contingent liability [Note 4]	300,000
Ending unappropriated retained earnings	$2,750,000

Oberlin Corporation
STATEMENT OF FINANCIAL POSITION
August 31, 1983

Assets

Current Assets

Cash	$ 80,000	
Accounts receivable, net	110,000	
Inventory	130,000	
Total current assets		$320,000

Other Assets

Land and building, net	4,000,000	
Investments in real estate (current value)	1,508,000	
Investment in Gray, Inc., at cost [Note 2]	160,000	
Goodwill [Note 3]	250,000	
Discount on bonds payable	42,000	
Total other assets		5,960,000
Total assets		$6,280,000

Liabilities and Stockholders' Equity

Current Liabilities

Accounts payable	$ 140,000	
Income taxes payable	320,000	
Stock dividend payable	120,000	
Total current liabilities		$580,000

Other Liabilities

Due to Grant, Inc. [Note 4]	300,000	
Liability under employee pension plan	450,000	
Bonds payable (including portion due within one year)	1,000,000	
Deferred taxes	58,000	
Total other liabilities		1,808,000
Total liabilities		2,388,000

Stockholders' Equity

Common stock	1,000,000	
Paid-in capital in excess of par	142,000	
Unappropriated retained earnings	2,750,000	
Total stockholders' equity		3,892,000
Total liabilities and stockholders' equity		$6,280,000

Footnotes to the Financial Statements

[1] Depreciation expense is included in general and administrative expenses. During the fiscal year, the company changed from the straight-line method of depreciation to the sum-of-the-years'-digits method.

[2] The company owns 40% of the outstanding stock of Gray, Inc. Because the ownership is less than 50%, consolidated financial statements with Gray cannot be presented.

[3] As per federal income tax laws, goodwill is not amortized. The goodwill was "acquired" in 1980.

[4] The amount due to Grant, Inc., is contingent on the outcome of a lawsuit which is currently pending. The amount of loss, if any, is not expected to exceed $300,000.

Instructions

There are *no* arithmetical errors in the statements. Identify and explain the deficiencies in the presentation of Oberlin's financial statements. Organize your answer as follows:

[a] Deficiencies in the statement of earnings and retained earnings.

[b] Deficiencies in the statement of financial position.

[c] General comments.

If an item appears on both statements, identify any deficiency separately for each statement.

(AICPA adapted)

EXERCISES

E20–1 Alvarez Construction Company began work on a contract in 1983 and completed the contract in 1984. The total contract price was $4,000,000.

Information concerning the contract for 1983 and 1984 is as follows:

	1983	1984
Costs incurred during year	$ 600,000	$3,150,000
Estimated costs to complete at end of year	2,400,000	–0–
Billings during year	720,000	3,080,000
Collections during year	400,000	3,000,000

Instructions

[a] Determine the amount of the total contract price to be recognized each year under the completed-contract method.

[b] Determine the amount of the total contract price to be recognized each year under the percentage-of-completion method.

E20–2 Quick-Build Construction Company contracted to construct a building for $400,000. Quick-Build began construction in 1983 and completed the project in 1984. Cost information for the project is as follows:

	1983	1984
Costs incurred	$200,000	$120,000
Estimated costs to complete	100,000	—

Quick-Build uses the percentage-of-completion method for recognizing income on the contract.

Instructions

[a] Determine the amount of income that the company should recognize in 1983 and 1984.

[b] Prove the amount of income you have computed in [a] by computing the total income on the contract and comparing it with the incomes you have computed for 1983 and 1984.

E20–3 Burt Company, which began business on January 1, 1982, uses the installment sales method of recognizing revenue because of the great uncertainty of the collection of its receivables. The following data pertain to 1982 and 1983:

	1982	1983
Installment sales	$350,000	$420,000
Cost of installment sales	280,000	315,000
General and administrative expenses	35,000	42,000
Cash collections on installment sales of:		
1982	150,000	125,000
1983	—	200,000

Instructions

[a] Determine the balance in the Deferred Gross Profit account at December 31, 1983.

[b] A 1982 sale resulted in a default in 1984. At the

date of default, the balance of the installment receivable was $6,000, and the repossessed merchandise had a fair value of $4,100. Assuming the repossessed merchandise is to be recorded at fair value, determine the amount of gain or loss to be recognized on the repossession.

(AICPA adapted)

E20–4 Landi Company sells appliances through installment contracts. Because of the uncertainty of collection and the relatively high potential for repossession, the company recognizes revenue on an installment basis, deferring revenue recognition until cash is collected.

During 1983, Landi determined that its gross profit percentage was 40%; during 1984 this percentage increased to 42%. Of $150,000 sales in 1983, Landi collected $70,000 in 1983 and $50,000 in 1984. Of $170,000 sales in 1984, Landi collected $89,000 by the end of the year.

Instructions

For 1983 and 1984, compute the amounts of gross profit to be recognized and the amounts to be deferred at the end of the year.

E20–5 On August 1, 1983, Robards Company received $240,000 for one year's advance rent on space that it leases to another company. Robards Company's fiscal year ends on October 31.

Instructions

[a] Determine the portion of the $240,000 that should be recognized as revenue for the fiscal year ending October 31, 1983.
[b] Prepare the adjusting journal entry Robards should make on October 31, 1983, if the $240,000 was credited to Unearned Rent Revenue when it was received.
[c] Prepare the adjusting journal entry the company should make on October 31, 1983, if the $240,000 was credited to Rent Revenue when it was received.

E20–6 Parker Company is disposing of a segment of its business. At the measurement date the net loss from the disposal is estimated to be $950,000. Included in this figure are severance pay of $100,000 and employee relocation costs of $50,000 (both of which are directly associated with the decision to dispose of the segment) and estimated net losses from operations of $200,000 from the measurement date to the expected disposal date. Net losses from operations of $150,000

from the beginning of the year to the measurement date are not included in the estimated net loss from the disposal.

Instructions

[a] Determine the loss from discontinued operations that Parker Company should present in its income statement. Identify the components of that loss.
[b] Briefly discuss the placement of the loss from discontinued operations in the income statement.

(AICPA adapted)

E20–7 Hi-Lo Production Company determines its pretax-accounting income for 1985 to be $1,565,000. The appropriate income tax rate for all income items is 46%, and no permanent or timing differences are involved. The company's reporting period ends on December 31. Included in pretax-accounting income are the following items:
[1] A loss of $450,000 on the destruction of a plant facility from a natural disaster. This item is considered both unusual in nature and infrequent in occurrence.
[2] A gain of $16,500 on the sale of stock owned in another company. Although Hi-Lo does not buy and sell stock investments often, this type of transaction is common for companies of this type.

Instructions

Prepare the income statement to the extent possible from the information given, beginning with the caption "income before income tax."

E20–8 Linda Lou Fashions, Inc., has correctly determined the following information related to operations for 1985:

Revenue from sales	$650,000
Expenses	415,000
Income before income tax	$235,000

In receiving the company's records, you discover the following items:
[1] During 1985, the company discovered an error in the amount of depreciation recognized in 1983 and 1984. The correction of this error, which has not been recorded, will result in an increase in depreciation for 1983 of $42,000 and for 1984 of $35,000.
[2] During 1985, an inventory loss of $27,800 was due to a government ban on certain highly flammable fabrics. This loss was considered both unusual and infrequent.

During 1985 dividends of $75,000 were paid on

75,000 shares of common stock, which were outstanding throughout 1985. Income taxes are to be recognized at 40% on all income items.

Instructions

Assuming that retained earnings at January 1, 1985, were previously reported as $505,000, prepare a partial income statement and a retained earnings statement for Linda Lou Fashions, Inc., for calendar year 1985.

E20–9 Chance Company, a holding company, has two operating subsidiaries: one manufacturing wheelbarrows and the other manufacturing toothbrushes. The wheelbarrow subsidiary has been unprofitable, and in late December 1985, Chance contracted to sell that subsidiary to another company for $60,000. The sale will be effective on April 1, 1986. Chance will continue to operate the wheelbarrow subsidiary during the first three months of 1986, even though those operations are expected to result in a $10,000 loss (before income taxes).

At December 31, 1985, the carrying amount of Chance's investment in the wheelbarrow subsidiary is $100,000. Both the $40,000 loss on the sale of the investment and the $10,000 operating loss will be deductible on Chance's 1986 income tax return, resulting in an anticipated tax savings of $20,000 at an assumed 40% tax rate.

Instructions

Determine the amount of the "loss on disposal of wheelbarrow subsidiary, net of applicable income tax benefit" which should be presented in Chance's income statement for the year ended December 31, 1985. Provide computations.

(AICPA adapted)

E20–10 On its December 31, 1985, financial statements Rhur Corporation reported a total of $260,000 under the caption "extraordinary losses." An analysis further revealed that the $260,000 in losses was comprised of the following items:

[1] Rhur recorded a loss of $50,000 in the abandonment of equipment formerly used in the business.

[2] In an unusual and infrequent occurrence, a loss of $75,000 was sustained as a result of hurricane damage to a warehouse.

[3] During 1985 several factories were shut down during a major strike by employees. Shutdown expenses totaled $120,000.

[4] Uncollectible accounts receivable of $15,000 were written off as uncollectible.

Instructions

[a] Ignoring income taxes, compute the amount of loss that Rhur should report as extraordinary on its 1985 statement of income.

[b] Explain the proper disclosure, if any, for any of the four items that should not be reported as extraordinary items.

(AICPA adapted)

E20–11 The following condensed statement of income of Worth Corporation, a diversified company, is presented for the two years ended December 31, 1985 and 1984:

	1985	1984
Net sales	$5,000,000	$4,800,000
Cost of sales	3,100,000	3,000,000
Gross profit	1,900,000	1,800,000
Operating expenses	1,100,000	1,200,000
Operating income	800,000	600,000
Gain on sale of division	450,000	–0–
Income before income taxes	1,250,000	600,000
Provision for income taxes	625,000	300,000
Net income	$ 625,000	$ 300,000

On January 1, 1985, Worth entered into an agreement to sell for $1,600,000 the assets and product line of one of its separate operating divisions. The sale was consummated on December 31, 1985, and resulted in a pretax gain on disposition of $450,000. This division's contribution to Worth's reported operating income before income taxes for each year was as follows:

1985	$(320,000) loss
1984	(250,000) loss

Assume an income tax rate of 50%.

Instructions

[a] In the preparation of a revised comparative statement of income, Worth should report income from continuing operations (after income taxes) for 1985 and 1984, respectively, amounting to:

  [1] $560,000 and $300,000.

  [2] $560,000 and $425,000.

  [3] $625,000 and $300,000.

  [4] $625,000 and $425,000.

[b] In the preparation of a revised comparative statement of income, Worth should report under the cap-

tion "discontinued operations" for 1985 and 1984, respectively:

[1] A loss of $320,000 and a loss of $250,000.
[2] A loss of $160,000 and a loss of $125,000.
[3] Income of $130,000 and a loss of $250,000.
[4] Income of $65,000 and a loss of $125,000.

(AICPA adapted)

E20–12 Swiftline Company reports income before income tax of $952,000 for 1985. This figure *includes* the following items which may require adjustment and/or reclassification before the formal income statement can be prepared:

[1] A change in depreciation method from the straight-line to the accelerated method, resulted in a $40,000 loss that was due to the cumulative effect on previous years. Depreciation for 1985 was computed on the accelerated method.

[2] A gain of $127,500 on the excess of insurance recovery over the book value of a plant destroyed by a hurricane. This was the first hurricane in the county in over a century.

[3] A gain of $18,700 in the sale of noncurrent marketable equity securities.

All items are subject to 46% income tax except the gain on insurance recovery and the gain on the sale of securities. These are subject to 28% income tax. The end of the fiscal year is November 30, 1985.

Instructions

Prepare the income statement, beginning with "income before income tax," and provide computations. You may ignore earnings-per-share figures.

E20–13 Acco Company has accumulated information to be used in the preparation of its income statement for the year ended December 31, 1985. All items are on a pretax basis.

Sales	$5,450,000
Cost of goods sold	2,200,000
Operating expenses	1,200,000
Interest expense	125,000
Extraordinary loss from major casualty	55,000
Cumulative effect (gain) of change in accounting principle	25,700
Number of outstanding shares of common stock throughout 1985	100,000
Income tax rate applicable to all items	45%

Instructions

Prepare a multiple-step income statement for 1985 to conform with generally accepted accounting principles.

E20–14 Sullivan Company has prepared a preliminary income statement for 1984 as follows:

Sullivan Company
INCOME STATEMENT
For the Year Ended December 31, 1984

Sales		$500,000
Cost of goods sold		212,000
Gross profit		288,000
Operating expenses		105,000
Income before special items		183,000
Special items		
Gain on the sale of land	$ 50,000	
Interest expense	(12,500)	
Cumulative effect of change in method of overhead recognition	(35,800)	1,700
Income before income tax		184,700
Income tax expense		66,380
Net income		$118,320

You have been engaged to review this statement and revise it as appropriate. You determine that the gain on the sale of land should be presented as an extraordinary item since it resulted from the forced sale caused by newly enacted legislation. All items are subject to a 40% income tax except this gain, which is subject to a special 25% rate.

Instructions

Prepare a revised income statement based on generally accepted accounting principles. (You may ignore earnings-per-share calculations.)

E20–15 The following classification codes will be used in completing this exercise:

Income Statement Categories/Items
1. Revenue.
2. Cost of goods sold.
3. Operating expenses.
4. Other revenues, expenses, gains, losses.
5. Discontinued operations.
6. Extraordinary items.
7. Cumulative effect of change in accounting principle.

Items Omitted from the Income Statement
8. Included in balance sheet.
9. Included in retained earnings statement.
10. Included in notes to the financial statements.
11. Omitted from the financial statements.

Instructions

Indicate the preferred code number for each of the

following items. If an explanation is necessary, state it briefly. If more than one classification is needed, indicate all appropriate code numbers.

[a] Accumulated depreciation—buildings.
[b] Interest income.
[c] Loss of plant from hurricane.
[d] Revenues and expenses from segment disposed of during current year.
[e] Dividends declared.
[f] Gain on the sale of plant assets.
[g] Loss on expropriation of assets by foreign government.
[h] Annual bonus paid store manager.
[i] Impact on previous years' earnings of changing depreciation method.
[j] Correction of error in inventory that was carried forward from previous year.
[k] Depreciation expense on manufacturing equipment.
[l] Loss on disposal of a segment of the business.
[m] Interest paid on outstanding debt.
[n] Loss on sale of temporary marketable securities.
[o] Accounting policies.
[p] Adjustment for change from unacceptable to acceptable accounting method.
[q] Details of outstanding debt issues.
[r] Revenue received in advance (to be earned in next accounting period).

PROBLEMS

P20–1 Murray Construction Company began operations January 1, 1984. During the year Murray entered into a contract with Rialto Company to construct a manufacturing facility. At that time Murray estimated that it would take five years to complete the facility at a total cost of $4,800,000. The total contract price for construction of the facility is $6,000,000.

During 1984, Murray incurred $1,250,000 in construction costs related to the project. Because of rising material and labor costs, the estimated cost to complete the contract at the end of 1984 is $3,750,000. Rialto was billed for and paid 30% of the contract price in accordance with the contract agreement.

Instructions

Prepare schedules to compute the amount of gross profit to be recognized for the year ended December 31, 1984, and the amount to be shown as "cost of uncompleted contract in excess of related billings" or "billings on uncompleted contracts in excess of related costs" at December 31, 1984, under each of the following methods:
[a] Completed-contract method.
[b] Percentage-of-completion method.
Provide supporting computations in good form.

(AICPA adapted)

P20–2 Maple Corporation sells farm machinery on the installment plan. On July 1, 1984, Maple entered into an installment sale contract with Agriculture, Inc., for an eight-year period. Equal annual payments under the installment sale are $100,000 and are due on July 1. The first payment was made on July 1, 1984.

Additional information is as follows:
[1] The amount that would be realized on an outright sale of similar farm machinery is $556,000.
[2] The cost of the farm machinery sold to Agriculture is $417,000.
[3] The finance charges relating to the installment period are $244,000 based on a stated interest rate of 12%, which is appropriate.
[4] Circumstances show that collection of installments due under the contract is reasonably assured.

Instructions

What income or loss before income taxes should Maple record for the year ended December 31, 1984, as a result of the above transaction? Show supporting computations in good form.

(AICPA adapted)

P20–3 Claiborne Construction Company recognizes income under the percentage-of-completion method on its long-term contracts. During 1982 the company entered into a fixed-price contract to construct a bridge for $15,000,000. Contract costs incurred and estimated costs to complete the bridge were:

	Cumulative Contract Costs Incurred	Estimated Costs to Complete
At Dec. 31, 1982	$ 1,000,000	$8,000,000
At Dec. 31, 1983	5,500,000	5,500,000
At Dec. 31, 1984	10,000,000	2,000,000

Instructions

[a] Prepare a schedule and determine the estimated percentage of completion at the end of each year. (Round percentage to nearest two decimal points.)
[b] Prepare a schedule and determine the amount of

revenue to be recognized each year. (Round dollars to the nearest thousand.)

[c] Prepare a schedule and determine the amount of income to be recognized each year.

(AICPA adapted)

P20–4 Problem 20–4 includes two *independent* parts.

Part 1. Payne Construction Company entered into a firm, fixed-price contract with Axelrod Associates on July 1, 1982, to construct a four-story office building. At that time Payne estimated that it would take between two and three years to complete the project. The total contract price for construction of the building is $4,000,000. Payne appropriately accounts for this contract under the completed-contract method in its financial statements and for income tax reporting. The building was deemed substantially completed on December 31, 1984. Estimated percentage of completion, accumulated contract costs incurred, estimated costs to complete the contract, and accumulated billings to Axelrod under the contract were as follows:

	At Dec. 31, 1982	At Dec. 31, 1983	At Dec. 31, 1984
Percentage of completion	10%	60%	100%
Contract costs incurred	$ 350,000	$2,500,000	$4,250,000
Estimated costs to complete the contract	$3,150,000	$1,700,000	—
Billings to Axelrod	$ 720,000	$2,160,000	$3,600,000

Instructions

[a] Prepare schedules and compute the amount of "cost of uncompleted contract in excess of related billings" or "billings on uncompleted contract in excess of related costs" at December 31, 1982, 1983, and 1984. Ignore income taxes and show supporting computations in good form.

[b] Prepare schedules and compute the profit or loss to be recognized as a result of this contract for the years ended December 31, 1982, 1983, and 1984. Ignore income taxes and show supporting computations in good form.

Part 2. On April 1, 1984, Butler, Inc., entered into a cost-plus-fixed-fee contract to construct an electric generator for Dalton Corporation. At the contract date Butler estimated that it would take two years to complete the project at a cost of $2,000,000. The fixed fee stipulated in the contract is $300,000. Butler appropriately accounts for this contract under the percentage-of-completion method. During 1984 Butler incurred costs of $700,000 related to the project, and the estimated cost at December 31, 1984, to complete the contract is $1,400,000. Dalton was billed $500,000 under the contract.

Instructions

Prepare a schedule and compute the amount of gross profit to be recognized by Butler under the contract for the year ended December 31, 1984. Show supporting computations in good form.

(AICPA adapted)

P20–5 Reed Company sells computers. On January 1, 1985, Reed entered into an installment sale contract with the Banner Company for a seven-year period expiring December 31, 1991. Equal annual payments under the installment sale are $1,000,000 and are due on January 1. The first payment was made on January 1, 1985.

Additional information is as follows:

[1] The cash selling price of the computer (i.e., the amount that would be realized on an outright sale) is $5,355,000.

[2] The cost of sales relating to the computer is $4,284,000.

[3] The finance charges relating to the installment period are $1,645,000—based on a stated interest rate of 10%, which is appropriate. For tax purposes, Reed appropriately uses the accrual basis for recording finance charges.

[4] Circumstances indicate that the collection of the installment sale is reasonably assured.

[5] The installment sale qualifies for the installment method of reporting for tax purposes.

[6] Assume that the income tax rate is 40%.

Instructions

[a] What income (loss) before income taxes should Reed record as a result of this transaction for the year ended December 31, 1985? Show supporting computations in good form.

[b] What provision for deferred income taxes, if any, should Reed record as a result of this transaction for the year ended December 31, 1985? Show supporting computations in good form.

(AICPA adapted)

P20–6 The directors of Lester Construction Company are meeting to determine which method of accounting for long-term construction contracts should be used in the company's financial statements: completed-contract or percentage-of-completion. You have been engaged to assist Lester's controller in preparing a presentation for the meeting.

The controller provides you with the following information:

[1] Lester commenced business on January 1, 1984.

[2] Construction activities for the year ended December 31, 1984 are summarized as follows:

Project	Total Contract Price	Billings Through Dec. 31, 1984	Cash Collections Through Dec. 31, 1984	Contract Costs Incurred Through Dec. 31, 1984	Estimated Additional Costs to Complete Contracts
A	$ 520,000	$ 350,000	$ 310,000	$ 424,000	$106,000
B	670,000	210,000	210,000	126,000	504,000
C	475,000	475,000	395,000	315,000	—
D	200,000	70,000	50,000	112,750	92,250
E	460,000	400,000	400,000	370,000	30,000
	$2,325,000	$1,505,000	$1,365,000	$1,347,750	$732,250

[3] All contracts are with different customers.

[4] Any work remaining to be done on the contracts is expected to be completed in 1985.

Instructions

[a] Prepare a schedule by project to compute the amount of revenue and income (or loss) before selling, and general and administrative expenses for the year ended December 31, 1984, that would be reported under:

[1] The completed-contract method.

[2] The percentage-of-completion method (based on estimated costs).

[b] Following is a balance sheet which compares balances resulting from the use of the two methods of accounting for long-term contracts. For each numbered blank space on the statement, supply the correct balance [indicating Dr. (Cr.) as appropriate]. Disregard income taxes.

Lester Construction Company
BALANCE SHEET
December 31, 1984

Assets	Completed-Contract Method	Percentage-of-Completion Method
Cash	$xxxx	$xxxx
Accounts receivable Due on contracts	(1)	(5)
Cost of uncompleted contracts in excess of billings	(2)	—
Costs and estimated earnings in excess of billings on uncompleted contracts	—	(6)
Property, plant, and equipment, net	xxxx	xxxx
Other assets	xxxx	xxxx
	$xxxx	$xxxx

Liabilities and Stockholders' Equity

Accounts payable and accrued liabilities	$xxxx	$xxxx
Billings on uncompleted contracts in excess of costs	(3)	—
Billings in excess of costs and estimated earnings	—	(7)
Estimated losses on uncompleted contracts	(4)	—
Notes payable	xxxx	xxxx
Common stock	xxxx	xxxx
Retained earnings	xxxx	xxxx
	$xxxx	$xxxx

(AICPA adapted)

P20—7   Babo Company has prepared an income statement for the year ended June 30, 1985. This statement is presented for your evaluation as follows:

Babo Company
INCOME STATEMENT
For the Fiscal Year Ended June 30, 1985

Sales		$765,000
Cost of goods sold	$400,000	
Operating expenses	250,000	
Income tax expense	46,000	696,000
Income before extraordinary item		69,000
Extraordinary loss		24,000
Net income		$ 45,000
Earnings per common share		$.45

In reviewing the statement, you determine the following:
[1] The extraordinary loss resulted from the sale of a division of the company at $24,000 less than its book value. The division had been operating at a loss for several years, including a $15,000 operating loss included in the sales and expense figures in the company's income statement.
[2] The company sold 40,000 shares of common stock on December 31, 1984, resulting in a total of 100,000 shares outstanding. The company has no preferred stock.
[3] All income items are subject to a 40% income tax rate.

Instructions

Prepare a revised income statement beginning with "income before income tax" for the year ended June 30, 1985. Provide computations to support your figures.
   Hint: Note that the income tax benefit of the $15,000 operating loss of the disposed segment is reflected in the $46,000 income tax figure. The $24,000 extraordinary loss, however, is before income tax.

P20—8   Presented below is information concerning the results of operations of Jennings Corporation for the calendar year 1985:

Cost of goods sold	$2,985,000
Administrative expenses	1,300,000
Gain on the sale of marketable securities	15,000

Loss on sale of discontinued segment of business	95,000
Interest expense	65,000
Selling expenses	1,500,000
Sales	8,650,000
Loss on sale of plant assets	25,500
Cumulative effect (gain) resulting from change in depreciation method from double-declining balance to straight-line method	157,000
Correction of error (loss) in previous year's income, due to capitalization of research and development costs	76,000

The following additional information is available:
[1] All income items are subject to a 46% income tax rate except the loss on disposal of a segment of the company's operations, which is subject to a 28% income tax rate.
[2] The company had 1,000,000 shares of common stock outstanding from January 1 to July 31, when an additional 200,000 shares were sold. There was no other stock activity during 1985.
[3] The following amounts related to the disposed segment are included in the appropriate revenue and cost figures:

Sales	$750,000
Cost of goods sold	600,000
Selling expenses	100,000
Administrative expenses	350,000
Interest expense	10,000

Instructions

Prepare an income statement for Jennings Corporation for the year ended December 31, 1985.

P20—9   Dino Company, a diversified manufacturing company, had four separate operating divisions engaged in the manufacture of products in each of the following areas: food products, health aids, textiles, and office equipment.
   Financial data for the two years ended December 31, 1985 and 1984, are presented on the next page.
   On January 1, 1985, Dino adopted a plan to sell the assets and product line of the office equipment division and expected to realize a gain on this disposal. On September 1, 1985, the division's assets and product line were sold for $2,100,000 cash, resulting in a gain of $640,000 (exclusive of operations during the phase-out period).
   The company's textiles division had six manufacturing plants, which produced a variety of textile prod-

	Net Sales		Cost of Sales		Operating Expenses	
	1985	*1984*	*1985*	*1984*	*1985*	*1984*
Food products	$3,500,000	$3,000,000	$2,400,000	$1,800,000	$ 550,000	$ 275,000
Health aids	2,000,000	1,270,000	1,100,000	700,000	300,000	125,000
Textiles	1,580,000	1,400,000	500,000	900,000	200,000	150,000
Office equipment	920,000	1,330,000	800,000	1,000,000	650,000	750,000
	$8,000,000	$7,000,000	$4,800,000	$4,400,000	$1,700,000	$1,300,000

ucts. In April 1985, the company sold one of these plants and realized a gain of $130,000. After the sale, the operations at the plant that was sold were transferred to the remaining five textile plants, which the company continued to operate.

In August 1985, the main warehouse of the food products division, located on the banks of the Bayer River, was flooded when the river overflowed. The resulting damage of $420,000 is not included in the financial data given above. Historical records indicate that the Bayer River normally overflows every four to five years causing flood damage to adjacent property.

For the two years ended December 31, 1985 and 1984, the company had interest revenue of $70,000 and $40,000, respectively, which was earned on investments.

For the two years ended December 31, 1985 and 1984, the company's net income was $960,000 and $670,000, respectively.

The provision for income tax expense for each of the two years should be computed at a rate of 45%.

Instructions

Prepare in proper form a comparative statement of income of Dino Company for the two years ended December 31, 1985 and 1984.

(AICPA adapted)

P20–10 Dalton Company has always prepared its income statement on the current operating performance basis. Since the statements have been used strictly for internal purposes, adherence to generally accepted accounting principles has not been a major consideration.

In early 1985 the company's accountant contacts you for advice in preparing income and retained earnings statements for 1984 in accordance with generally accepted accounting principles for use with a bank loan application. The accountant presents you with the following statements, which had been prepared for internal use:

Dalton Company
INCOME STATEMENT
For the Year Ended December 31, 1984

Sales revenue	$851,000
Cost of goods sold	415,000
Gross profit	436,000
Operating expenses	305,000
Income before income tax	131,000
Income tax expense	55,020
Net income	$ 75,980

Dalton Company
RETAINED EARNINGS STATEMENT
For the Year Ended December 31, 1984

Retained earnings, January 1, 1984		$1,405,000
Additions		
Gain on the sale of investments*	$157,000	
Correction of error— income earned in 1983 but erroneously omitted*	120,000	
Net income for 1984	75,980	352,980
		1,757,980
Deductions		
Extraordinary loss— major casualty*	72,500	
Cumulative effect of change in accounting principle in 1984*	67,000	
Cash dividends, 1984	75,000	
Stock dividends, 1984	50,000	(264,500)
Retained earnings, December 31, 1984		$1,493,480

*Presented on net-of-tax basis.

You determine that all items are appropriately described and that all items subject to income tax appropriately reflect a 42% income tax rate and that the company had 80,000 shares of common stock outstanding throughout 1984.

Instructions

Prepare income and retained earnings statements for 1984 in accordance with generally accepted accounting principles, including all relevant disclosures which can be determined from the given data. Provide computations to support your financial-statement items.

P20—11 Prior to 1982 NewService, Inc., owned and operated successfully several newspapers and television stations in the immediate region. In 1982 NewService, Inc., purchased Rade Corporation, which owned two radio stations in another state. NewService treated Rade as a separate subsidiary. Condensed consolidated statements of income and financial position for the fiscal year 1983 appear below in the schedule of financial statements.

The purchase was consummated on January 1, 1982, when NewService paid $160,000 for Rade's stock. Rade stockholders' equity was valued at $120,000 on the date of purchase. NewService purchased Rade in an attempt to diversify its holdings and to increase earnings. Successful radio stations can be expected to earn approximately 25% on stockholders' equity before taxes, and Rade seemed likely to produce such a return.

The profit performance of Rade has not fulfilled management's expectations. The before-tax earnings of the subsidiary have been one-half of the expected return (see the statements in the schedule). NewService did not believe the earnings pattern could be reversed and decided to sell Rade Corporation.

During November 1984 NewService entered into an agreement to sell Rade to Brady, Inc. The sale was to be completed as of December 31, 1984, with the final price to be agreed upon at the conclusion of business on December 31, 1984, after the financial results for the year had been determined. NewService's 1984 statement of income reflects the income earned by Rade and the amortization of the goodwill arising from the purchase of Rade for the current year. Condensed statements of income and financial position prepared prior to the sale of Rade for both NewService and Rade for the fiscal year 1984 appear in the schedule of financial statements.

Brady agreed to purchase the Rade stock for $125,000. NewService has not recorded the sale of Rade nor prepared final financial statements for 1984, because the company was not sure how *Accounting Principles Board Opinion No. 30,* "Reporting the Results of Operations—Reporting the Effects of Disposal of a Segment of a Business, and Extraordinary, Unusual and Infrequently Occurring Events and Transactions," applied to the reporting of this transaction.

NewService, Inc., treated the acquisition of Rade Corporation as a purchase and has carried the investment on the equity basis. Since the purchase of Rade, NewService has prepared consolidated statements for reporting purposes, although separate tax returns were filed for the parent and subsidiary. The effective tax rates have been 50% for NewService and 30% for Rade; the tax rate for capital gains is 30%. The goodwill arising from the consolidation of Rade is being amortized over a 10-year period by using the straight-line method. Rade has not paid dividends since 1980. NewService, Inc., has not reported any extraordinary or nonrecurring events or transactions on their financial statements for the last four years.

Instructions

[a] NewService's independent auditor has informed management that the sale of Rade Corporation should be treated as a disposal of a segment of a business. Prepare a comparative statement of income for the years ended December 31, 1983 and 1984, for NewService, Inc., which reflects the disposal of Rade under the terms of *APB Opinion No. 30.*
[b] What characteristics must exist for the discontinued operations of a business to be treated as a disposal of a segment of a business under the terms of *APB Opinion No. 30?*

(CMA adapted)

Schedule of Financial Statements
(in thousands)

STATEMENTS OF INCOME
For the Fiscal Years Ended December 31

	NewService, Inc. (Consolidated) 1983	NewService, Inc. (Rade Not Consolidated) 1984	Rade Corp. 1982	Rade Corp. 1983	Rade Corp. 1984
Revenue from operations	$920	$760	$210	$220	$240
Income from Rade Corp.	—	14	—	—	—
Total revenue	920	774	210	220	240

Costs and expenses					
Cost of sales	100	110	—	—	—
Depreciation	52	44	12	12	12
Amortization of goodwill	4	4	—	—	—
Selling expenses	207	155	58	62	68
Administrative expenses	390	275	118	129	140
Total costs and expenses	753	588	188	203	220
Net income before income taxes	167	186	22	17	20
Income taxes	82	88	7	5	6
Net income	$ 85	$ 98	$ 15	$ 12	$ 14

STATEMENTS OF FINANCIAL POSITION
As of December 31

	NewService, Inc. (Consolidated) 1983	NewService, Inc. (Rade Not Consolidated) 1984	Rade Corp. 1984
Assets			
Current assets	$ 667	$ 513	$201
Fixed assets (net)	855	620	195
Investment in Rade Corp.	—	189	—
Goodwill	32	—	—
Other noncurrent assets	100	80	20
Total assets	$1,654	$1,402	$416
Equities			
Current liabilities	$ 335	$ 220	$105
Long-term debt	480	280	150
Common stock	350	350	50
Paid-in capital	260	260	25
Retained earnings	229	292	86
Total equities	$1,654	$1,402	$416

P20–12 Condensed statements of income and retained earnings of Compo Company for the years ended December 31, 1984 and 1983, are presented below:

Compo Company
CONDENSED STATEMENTS OF INCOME AND RETAINED EARNINGS

	Years Ended December 31	
	1984	1983
Sales	$3,000,000	$2,400,000
Cost of goods sold	1,300,000	1,150,000
Gross margin	1,700,000	1,250,000
Selling, general, and administrative expenses	1,200,000	950,000
Income before extraordinary item	500,000	300,000
Extraordinary item	(400,000)	
Net income	100,000	300,000
Retained earnings, Jan. 1	750,000	450,000
Retained earnings, Dec. 31	$ 850,000	$ 750,000

Presented below are four *unrelated* situations involving accounting changes and classification of certain items as ordinary or extraordinary. Each situation is based on the condensed statements of income and retained earnings shown above and requires revisions to these statements.

Situation 1. On January 1, 1982, Compo acquired machinery at a cost of $150,000. The company adopted the double-declining balance method of depreciation for this machinery, and had been recording depreciation over an estimated life of 10 years, with no residual value. At the beginning of 1984 a decision was made to adopt the straight-line method of depreciation for this machinery. Due to an oversight, however, the double-declining balance method was used for 1984. For financial reporting purposes, depreciation is included in selling, general, and administrative expenses.

The extraordinary item in the condensed statement of income and retained earnings for 1984 relates to shutdown expenses incurred by the company during a major strike by its operating employees during 1984.

Situation 2. At the end of 1984, Compo's management decided that the estimated loss rate on uncollectible accounts receivable was too low. The loss rate used for the years 1983 and 1984 was 1% of total sales; because of an increase in the write-off of uncollectible accounts, the rate has been raised to 3% of total sales. The amount recorded in bad-debt expense under the heading of selling, general, and administrative expenses was $30,000 for 1984 and $24,000 for 1983.

The extraordinary item in the condensed statement of income and retained earnings for 1984 relates to a loss incurred in the abandonment of outmoded equipment formerly used in the business.

Situation 3. On December 2, 1984, Compo issued 100,000 shares of its $1 par value common stock in exchange for 100,000 shares of $1 par value (100%) voting common stock of Arco Corporation in a transaction to be properly accounted for as a pooling of interests. The condensed statements of income and retained earnings of Compo shown above do *not* include Arco's operations. A summary of Arco's financial operations for 1984, 1983, and 1982 follows:

	1984	1983	1982
Sales	$600,000	$520,000	$410,000
Cost of goods sold	274,000	238,000	195,000
Gross margin	326,000	282,000	215,000
Selling, general, and administrative expenses	219,000	190,000	165,000
Net income	107,000	92,000	50,000
Retained earnings (deficit), Jan. 1	72,000	(20,000)	(70,000)
Retained earnings (deficit), Dec. 31	$179,000	$ 72,000	$ (20,000)

The extraordinary item in the condensed statement of income and retained earnings for 1984 relates to a loss sustained as a result of damage caused by a tornado to the company's merchandise at its main warehouse in Locust City. This natural disaster was considered to be an unusual and infrequent occurrence for that geographic section of the country.

Situation 4. The extraordinary item appearing in the condensed statement of income and retained earnings for 1984 relates to the correction of an error made by Compo during the years 1979 through 1983. If the item had been properly accounted for, 1983 income would have been reduced by $60,000 and total income for 1979 through 1982 would have been reduced by $340,000. The item in error is included in selling, general, and administrative expenses.

Instructions

For each of the four *unrelated* situations, prepare revised condensed statements of income and retained earnings of Compo Company for the years ended December 31, 1984 and 1983. Each answer should give recognition to the appropriate accounting change and other items outlined in the situation descriptions. Ignore tax considerations, earnings-per-share computations, and *pro forma* presentations.

(*Hint:* In a pooling of interest business combination [Situation 3], financial statements of the companies involved are combined for all years presented.)

(AICPA adapted)

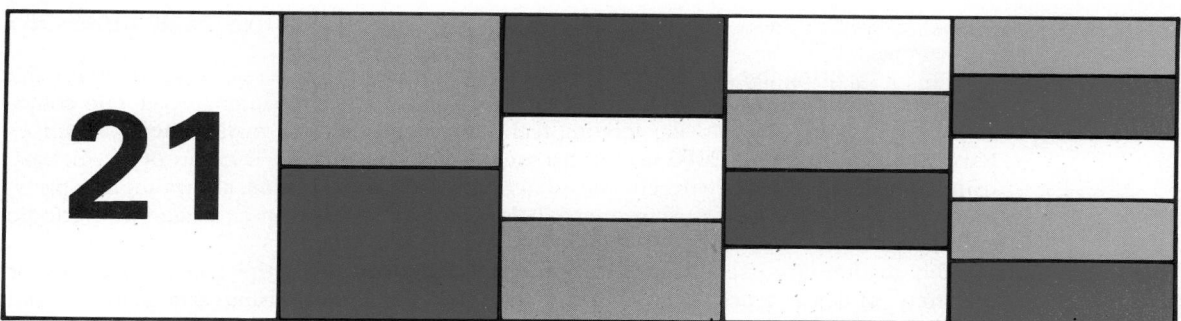

21

ACCOUNTING FOR LEASES

OBJECTIVES

To discuss why many businesses use leasing to acquire service rights to assets.

To describe the financial accounting and reporting issues underlying leases.

To discuss the conditions that cause the economic substance of a lease to change from the rental of property to the presumed sale and purchase of property.

To classify leases for accounting purposes from the perspectives of both lessees and lessors.

To demonstrate the application of appropriate accounting measurement and disclosure principles to various types of leases.

To describe the unique aspects of real estate leases and subleases.

During the last 40 years, business enterprises have increased substantially the extent and complexity of their leasing activities. Changing economic conditions, rapidly accelerating technology, and differing management objectives have stimulated the increased use of this method of acquiring the services of assets. Basically, a **lease** is a contract whereby the owner, identified as the **lessor,** allows another party, identified as the **lessee,** to use property belonging to the lessor in exchange for periodic cash payments.

This chapter discusses financial accounting and reporting by both lessees and lessors for a variety of lease types. It also considers several unusual leasing arrangements and circumstances calling for modifications in normal lease accounting and reporting practices. Furthermore, it examines some of the causes of the increased use and complexity of leasing in our economy. For example, the advanced rate of technological development in the data processing industry has caused many potential buyers to lease rather than purchase equipment in order to avoid possible obsolescence. In this case the potential buyer (lessee) chooses to rent equipment to escape an ownership risk (obsolescence). Some of the rights of ownership, such as the salvage value of this equipment, may be retained by the lessor. Also, the total cost of leasing the equipment may exceed the cost of buying; since many of the risks of ownership remain with the lessor, the rental rates may be high.

Companies have also entered into leases in order to acquire the service rights to assets while avoiding both the disbursement of a large amount of cash and reporting a large liability. In the past a company could lease an asset, rather than buy it, without recording either the asset or a liability on the balance sheet. Such **off-balance-sheet financing** was advantageous, because it allowed companies to acquire the service rights to assets without presenting a less attractive balance sheet. To illustrate, assume that a company buys an asset by incurring a long-term debt. The debt-equity ratio is increased and the rate of return on assets employed declines if net income remains constant. Furthermore, if some of the liability is payable currently, then working capital and the current ratio will be adversely affected. Prior to recent professional pronouncements, leasing allowed companies a method of acquiring the service rights of assets while avoiding these negative financial reporting consequences.

Leasing is attractive to both large and small companies. For example, a small business may be able to acquire the service rights to assets without a large initial commitment of cash by leasing the item. The problems of possible obsolescence may be as great to a small manufacturer as to the largest industrial concern. Leases allow recognition of differences between businesses in terms of size, complexity, and operating and financing objectives. The tax implications of leasing transactions may also be attractive; for example, in some cases lease *payments* are deductible long before the same amount of depreciation could be deducted if the asset had been purchased. All of these reasons help explain the popularity and complexity of lease agreements in our contemporary economy. An example of the significance of leasing is provided in Exhibit 21–1.

The mechanism of leasing allows for much greater flexibility in the process of providing (selling) and acquiring (buying) the service rights of various assets. In other words, some leases are simply executory contracts which transfer the right to use property for a limited time in exchange for future rental payments. The rights and obligations under such contracts are not recognized as assets and liabilities in the financial statements of lessors and lessees under generally accepted accounting principles. Other leases are essentially installment purchases, however, and in these cases the substance of the arrangement, rather than the legal form, determines the accounting treatment. Assets and liabilities for such leased items are established in the accounting records of lessors and lessees as if a legal sale/purchase had taken place.

EXHIBIT 21–1
Example of the Significance of Leasing

Leasing of capital equipment has become a well-accepted financing practice in American business. In 1977, the Department of Commerce estimated that over $100 billion of equipment was under lease, and that the total volume of new leases was growing at the rate of 12 to 15 percent per year. Several potential advantages to leasing, which under the right conditions often make it a more attractive financing option than debt-financed, direct ownership, have contributed to this growth:

• Leasing typically represents 100-percent financing without up-front equity payments, thus freeing capital reserves for investment in other projects.
• Leasing may preserve lines of credit or avoid violating restrictive loan covenants, which prohibit the issuance of additional debt securities.
• Leasing represents a fixed, predictable financing cost over the entire term of a lease, whereas term loans typically fluctuate with market rates.

SOURCE: Michael A. Laros, "Leverage Leasing: Optimizing the Lessee's Decision-Making Process," *Financial Executive*, December 1981, p. 18.

Substance over Form

The primary goal in accounting for all types of leases is to recognize the economic substance of a particular lease rather than its mere legal form if the two differ. When a lease contains provisions to change the transaction from periodic payment of moneys for the use of property (rent) to an installment acquisition of substantial economic rights or benefits (purchase), then the lease should be treated by the lessee as the purchase of an asset and the incurrence of a liability. According to the Financial Accounting Standards Board (FASB),

> *A lease that transfers substantially all of the benefits and risks incident to the ownership of property should be accounted for as the acquisition of an asset and the incurrence of an obligation by the lessee.*[1]

In such leases the lessor should usually record a sale of the property and recognize a receivable for the future rent, again in recognition of the economic substance of the transaction. The concept of substance over form in regard to leases has been long established, well understood, and generally accepted. However, the specific circumstances and criteria under which leases should be treated as sales by lessors and purchases by lessees have also been the subject of debate for many years.

In fact, a long history of problems is associated with accounting for leases. The Accounting Principles Board (APB) issued four separate major opinions dealing with several aspects of the subject. More recently, the FASB issued *Statement of Financial Accounting Standards No. 13*, which superseded all four of the APB Opinions dealing with leases and established comprehensive financial accounting and reporting requirements for both lessees and lessors. However, further demonstrating the complexity of this area of accounting, *SFAS No. 13* has been amended and interpreted many times by the FASB.

Financial reporting for complicated leasing agreements is a technical challenge for most accountants. The ramifications of current authoritative pronouncements and other relevant documents are frequently difficult to apply and contain many subtle provisions and implications. Before accountants can resolve a number of these practical and conceptual leasing problems, they must acquire a detailed and in-depth understanding of many leasing terms employed in the FASB pronouncements. Therefore, before proceeding to a discussion of lease classification, accounting, and disclosure requirements, we shall establish a common ground and understanding in regard to some important leasing terms.

---

[1]*FASB Statement of Financial Accounting Standards No. 13*, "Accounting for Leases," 1976, par. 91.

IMPORTANT LEASING TERMS

The following definitions and related discussions are adapted from *SFAS No. 13* as amended and interpreted by later pronouncements. A firm grasp of the meaning and implications of the terms will enhance considerably your understanding of the remaining topics in this chapter. Other definitions, less central to the overall concepts underlying lease accounting, are introduced when necessary and relevant to the particular issues being discussed.

Lessees

For financial reporting purposes, lessees initially classify every lease as an operating lease or a capital lease.

An **operating lease** is a rental agreement requiring periodic payments for the use of an asset during that period. An operating lease, in substance, does *not* represent the purchase of an asset; consequently, no new assets or liabilities are recorded in the accounting records, nor are they reported on the balance sheet of the lessee. Instead, rent expense is recognized as the leased asset is used by the lessee.

Substance over Form

A **capital lease** is a rental agreement in which the lessee acquires a substantial portion of the rights to an asset and incurs a liability, both of which are recorded in the accounting records and reported on the balance sheet. **A capital lease represents, in substance, the purchase of an asset and incurrence of a liability.** In concept, when most of the rights and risks of ownership of a particular asset are transferred from a lessor to a lessee in a lease transaction, the lease is considered a capital lease. To illustrate, assume that Crater Company enters into a capital lease properly valued at $10,000. At the beginning of the lease term, Crater should record the following entry to reflect the "acquisition" of the asset and "incurrence" of the liability.

Equipment	10,000	
Liability Under Lease		10,000

This asset and liability are subject to accounting requirements in much the same way as are other long-lived assets and liabilities we have studied. The distinction between operating leases and capital leases requires a careful consideration of many circumstances surrounding the lease. Several specific criteria in *SFAS No. 13* are used to make this distinction. These criteria are covered in a later section of this chapter.

Lessors

Lessors are required to classify a lease agreement into one of four possible types: operating, sales-type, direct-financing, and leveraged leases.

An **operating lease** is the direct counterpart of a lessee's operating lease. In essence, an operating lease—from the perspective of the lessor—merely represents an agreement in which rent is received for the use of property owned by the lessor. In substance, **the property subject to the lease is not presumed to have been sold** by the lessor to the lessee. The lessor recognizes rent revenue during the time the leased asset is used by the lessee. Furthermore, the lessor depreciates the leased asset in a normal fashion because the asset has not been sold to the lessee.

The three remaining lease types represent leasing circumstances which, in substance, indicate that the lessor has "sold" the property (or most of the property rights) subject to the lease and obtained a receivable from the lessee. Once a lessor concludes that a particular lease is one of the three types of **capital leases,** rather than an operating lease, further classification as a sales-type, direct-financing, or leveraged lease is necessary.

A **sales-type lease** is a capital lease that gives rise to manufacturer's or dealer's gross profit (or loss) to the lessor. That is, the fair value of the leased property at the inception of the lease is greater (or less) than its cost or carrying value on the books of the lessor. Normally a sales-type lease arises when manufacturers or dealers use leasing as a means of marketing their products. In sales-type leases, the lessor earns profit both from the "sale" of the property and as interest revenue from financing the "sale." Companies that design and manufacture computers frequently employ leasing in their sales activities. In such cases lessee's are shielded from the risk of obsolescence, while lessors are able to stimulate sales by using creative lease agreements. To illustrate, assume that Divert Company enters into a sales-type lease properly valued at $16,000. The cost of the leased asset to Divert was $12,500. The entry to record the lease receivable, remove the leased equipment from the books, and recognize the gross margin on the sale appears below:

Lease Receivable (net)	16,000	
Cost of Goods Sold	12,500	
Equipment		12,500
Sales		16,000

A **direct-financing lease** is a capital lease (other than a leveraged lease) which does *not* give rise to manufacturer's or dealer's gross profit (or loss), on the "sale" of the property to the lessee. In a direct-financing lease, the cost or carrying amount of the property on the lessor's books and the fair value of the leased property at the inception of the lease are not

Materiality

materially different. The revenue to the lessor in a direct-financing lease consists solely of *interest* revenue from the *financing function.* To illustrate, assume that a lessor, Divit Company, enters into a direct-financing lease properly valued at $15,500. The entry to record the lease receivable and remove the leased equipment appears below:

Lease Receivable	15,500	
Equipment		15,500

A **leveraged lease** is a three-party lease agreement involving a lessee, a long-term creditor (such as a bank), and a lessor, in which the long-term creditor provides nonrecourse financing to the lessor. For example, if a shipyard agrees to build a supertanker and lease it to an oil company, construction financing may be needed. In such circumstances, a bank may lend money to the shipbuilder (lessor) but require repayment from the oil company (lessee). The lessor constructs the tanker with a relatively small amount of its own cash and the money provided by the bank. Once the asset is constructed, the oil company operates the ship under a long-term lease, repays the bank, and makes an additional payment to the shipbuilder. If the lessee defaults on the payments to the bank, the lessor does not have to pay the bank, because the money from the bank to the lessor was a nonrecourse loan. Since leveraged leases represent a highly specialized and complex financial arrangement, accounting practices for this type of lease are discussed more fully in Appendix A.

Exhibit 21–2 summarizes the lease categories that are acceptable today for financial accounting and reporting.

While the foregoing discussion relates to the basic issues of lease classification, several other terms are also important from a general perspective. Not all of the technical terms employed in leases are essential to a general understanding of fundamental lease accounting; however, several additional terms are very important.

The **fair value** of the leased property is the price for which the leased property could be sold in an arm's-length transaction. If the lessor is a manufacturer or dealer, the fair value of the property is ordinarily its normal selling price less any applicable volume or trade discounts. If the lessor is not a manufacturer or dealer, the fair value of the property subject to the lease is ordinarily its cost or carrying amount. Fair value should always be determined in light of prevailing market conditions at the inception of the lease.

EXHIBIT 21–2
Lease Classification Summary

General Lease Type	Lessor	Lessee
Noncapitalized (no sale or purchase of asset presumed)	Operating lease	Operating lease
Capitalized (sale and purchase of asset presumed)	Sales-type lease Direct-financing lease Leveraged lease	Capital lease

---

The **inception of a lease** is usually the date the lease agreement is signed. A written and signed commitment to lease property also establishes the inception of a lease; however, if any of the principal provisions of a lease remain to be negotiated, even a written commitment does not establish the inception of a lease. If the asset subject to the lease is still to be constructed or acquired, the inception of the lease may significantly precede the beginning of the lease term. The point in time when a lessee takes control of and begins operating the leased property is the **beginning of the lease term.** The unusual classification and accounting circumstances that must be applied when the inception of a lease precedes the beginning of the lease term are discussed in Appendix B at the end of this chapter. Such circumstances are common only in certain specialized industries, such as construction contracting, and are not frequently encountered in normal leasing transactions.

The **estimated residual value of leased property** is the forecast fair value of the property at the end of the lease term. The estimated residual value, like estimated salvage value for purposes of depreciating plant assets, encompasses consideration of both diminished productivity and obsolescence.

Accountants use several methods of estimating the residual value of a leased asset. For example, appraisals, dealer quotations, engineering estimates, and previous experience in regard to similar assets may prove helpful in formulating residual value estimates. In making such estimates, one should assume a constant price level and not attempt to anticipate increases in value or changes in price level. In other words, one should attempt to assess the value of the leased asset today as if it were in the used condition that it will be at the conclusion of the lease. In this way residual value is useful in allocating the cost of the leased asset over the lease term. Amortization of leased assets, like depreciation of plant assets, is a cost allocation process that is part of applying the matching principle rather than an asset valuation process. Residual value estimates are necessary to determine periodic amortization expense.

Matching

In essence residual value is the amount that will be realized either upon disposal or re-lease of the property at the conclusion of the lease. This residual value may be **guaranteed** to the lessor, in which case the lessee or a third party ensures a particular residual value at the end of the lease term. If the leased asset's value is not as great as the guaranteed residual value at the end of the lease, the guarantor must make up the difference in cash. An **unguaranteed residual value** represents the portion of the residual value that excludes any commitment by the lessee or a third party to ensure a particular residual value.

Accountants usually must determine whether the lessee or the lessor is presumed to possess a claim to the residual value of the asset at the end of the lease term. A clear understanding of the terms and the economic consequences of the lease provides valuable insights regarding proper accounting for residual values. Significant classification and accounting matters are influenced by residual value determinations, and we consider them later in the chapter. Although several other terms will also be defined later, we now turn our attention to lease classification.

LEASE CLASSIFICATION

A lease meeting **any one** of the following four criteria should be treated as a **capital lease** by lessees and tentatively classified as one of the three types of capital leases by lessors:

1. **The lease transfers ownership of the property to the lessee by the end of the lease term.** When a lease contains a transfer of title clause, the lease is presumed to be a sale by the lessor and a purchase by the lessee. Such leases are clearly installment sales of assets.

LEASES *SHOULD* BE CAPITALIZED

THE ASSETS OF an enterprise, as reported in its balance sheet, should reflect all the economic resources of the enterprise. Economic resources are those elements of wealth that possess economic value by reason of their utility, scarcity, and exchangeability. When a long-lived asset is acquired, whether it be a plant building, a machine, an aircraft, or other economic resources, its cost is recognized on the asset side of the balance sheet.

The function of a balance sheet is to report the economic resources of the enterprise. Property that has been leased on a noncancelable basis for any significant period of time is an economic resource of the enterprise. Its value may be less (or more) than if the property were owned outright, but the principal economic benefits possessed by the property unit are under the control of, and available to, the lessee for the full period of the noncancelable lease. This economic resource is an asset that should be reported in the balance sheet. Omission of it results in understatement of economic resources and must be the result of an overemphasis on the lack of ownership of residual-disposal rights.

Looking at the lease arrangement from the liability viewpoint also leads to a conclusion to capitalize noncancelable lease arrangements that cover a significantly long period. Liabilities are the various claims against the existing resources of an enterprise, claims that are legal or substantive (even though not technically legal), claims for services, money, property, goods, or facilities received by an enterprise. The principal question to resolve in connection with lease arrangements is whether the commitment a lessee makes when he enters into a noncancelable lease arrangement is in substance a liability.

Omission from the balance sheet of the substantive claim incurred when a noncancelable lease arrangement is signed creates an understatement of liabilities and must be the result of an overemphasis on legal technicalities. *Fair financial reporting requires that all economic resources and all substantive claims against those resources be reported in the balance sheet. Noncancelable lease arrangements have economic substance that create both an economic resource and a substantive claim that are far more similar to, than different from, other economic resources (assets) and legal and substantive claims (liabilities). Capitalization of noncancelable lease arrangements is both warranted and long overdue.* [Emphasis added.]

Lease arrangements are increasingly important as financing vehicles for the right to obtain the economic services possessed by various types of property. In some noncancelable lease arrangements, the lessee obtains virtually all of the economic services in the property, including (through favorable option clauses) the right to residual values at expiration of the noncancelable lease term. In other noncancelable lease arrangements, the lessee obtains a significant portion of the economic services in the property, while the lessor retains the rights to (and risks in) the services that may materialize in the later years of the life of the property. In still other noncancelable lease arrangements, the lessee obtains a relatively small portion of the economic services in the property. In all three cases, the lessee incurs a substantive obligation in return for the economic services acquired. Conceptually, the lessee should report as an asset the economic benefits associated with a noncancelable lease arrangement and as a liability the substantive obligations incurred.

SOURCE: Adapted from Arthur R. Wyatt, "Leases *Should* Be Capitalized," *CPA Journal,* September 1974, pp. 35–38. Reprinted by permission of *The CPA Journal.*

2. **The lease contains a bargain purchase option.** A bargain purchase option is a lease provision for the lessee to purchase the property at a price substantially lower than the expected fair value of the property at the time the option becomes exercisable. Since determining whether a particular purchase option represents a *bargain* purchase option is important to both lease classification and financial accounting, the economic substance of all purchase clauses must be carefully assessed. If a lease contains a bargain purchase option, accountants consider that the lease is, in substance, a sale of the property by the lessor to the lessee.

3. **The lease term is equal to 75% or more of the remaining estimated economic life of the property at the beginning of the lease term.** When a lessee acquires the use of a leased asset for most of its useful life, accountants conclude that, in substance, a sale has taken place.

4. **The present value of the minimum lease payments at the inception of the lease is 90% or more of the fair market value of the leased asset.** Minimum lease payments should be reduced by any executory costs to be paid by the lessee, whereas fair market value should be reduced for any investment tax credit retained and expected to be realized by the lessor in applying this criterion. **Executory costs** are expenses necessary to operate and maintain the leased property. Examples of such costs are taxes, insurance, and maintenance on the leased property. A lease agreement may require the lessor to retain formal responsibility for paying certain executory costs while the property is being used by the lessee. In such circumstances, lease payments made by the lessee are presumed to include both a lease payment for the use of the property and a reimbursement to the lessor of executory expenses paid by the lessor on the property used by the lessee. The receipt of lease payments by lessors represents both a collection of the receivable and a cost recovery of the executory costs which were originally paid on behalf of the property used by the lessee.

Substance over Form

In the sections which follow, we refer to these four criteria by the following abbreviated titles: (1) The **transfer-of-title** criterion; (2) the **bargain-purchase-option** criterion; (3) the **length-of-lease-term** criterion; and (4) the **amount-of-lease-payment** criterion.

To illustrate these capitalization criteria, we consider the case of San Diego Corporation, a lessor, which enters into a lease with Sacramento Company, a lessee. The 10-year lease is properly valued at $150,000. The lease involves the use of machinery that has a 12-year estimated useful life and is valued at $160,000. The lease contains no transfer of ownership clause and no purchase or renewal options. We draw the following conclusions when we consider each capitalization criterion:

Lease Criteria	Conclusions
1. Transfer of title	This criterion is *not* met because no clause transferring title to the lessee is included in the lease.
2. Bargain purchase option	This criterion is *not* met because no purchase option is included in the lease.
3. Length of lease term	This criterion is *met,* because the lease term of 10 years exceeds 75% of the asset's expected life (75% × 12 years = 9 years).
4. Amount of lease payment	This criterion is *met,* because the amount of the lease, $150,000, exceeds 90% of the value of the leased asset (90% × $160,000 = $144,000).

This is a **capital lease** because at least one capitalization criterion is met.

Now that we have an understanding of some lease terminology and the lease capitalization criteria of *SFAS No. 13,* let us consider the rationale that underlies these concepts. The primary financial reporting problem that the lease capitalization criteria are attempting to

Substance over Form

resolve is that of off-balance-sheet financing by lessees. If lessees enter into leases that are in substance the equivalent of purchases and that obligate lessees in a manner equivalent to that of debt financing, those obligations should be included among the liabilities in the lessee's balance sheet. Of course, if the liabilities are included, then the assets acquired by the incurrence of those liabilities should also be included. The ability under prior accounting standards to incur obligations equivalent to debt and not include those obligations among balance sheet liabilities is what we mean when we refer to "off-balance-sheet financing." Prior to *SFAS No. 13,* this was a prevalent practice and, in fact, was one of the more attractive features of leasing. The four capitalization criteria previously presented attempt to identify those conditions in leases which strongly suggest that the lease is so similar to the purchase of the asset and the incurrence of related debt that the entire transaction should be treated as a purchase rather than as a lease. Of course, if none of the capitalization criteria are met, then the essence of the lease is *not* equivalent to a purchase and the lease should not be treated as a purchase.

Revenue Realization

While we place emphasis here on the lessee and the issue of off-balance-sheet financing, we should not overlook the importance of the lease criteria for the lessor. From the lessor's viewpoint, the criteria are important in resolving important revenue realization issues concerning the timing of lease revenue recognition in the income statement. For the lessor, the lease capitalization criteria govern the pattern of the amounts recognized and whether revenue from leases is recognized at the beginning of the lease or over the life of the lease. For example, in an operating lease, revenue is recognized by the lessor in a straight-line pattern, usually based on the receipt of lease payments from the lessee. In a direct-financing lease, the lessor recognizes no profit from the sale of the property; however, the lessor recognizes interest (based on the investment in the lease and the rate of interest implicit in the lease) over the lease term. In the case of a sales-type lease, the lessor recognizes a gross profit or loss in the period of the inception of the lease and then recognizes interest revenue (based on the investment in the lease and the rate of interest implicit in the lease) over the lease term, in much the same way as in a direct-financing lease. Therefore, *whether* a lease is capitalized, and if it is, *how* it is capitalized, are important factors in the recognition of revenue by the lessor. Later sections of this chapter illustrate the specific accounting procedures for these various kinds of leases.

While some of the terms used in discussing the lease capitalization criteria have been defined, several others have not; their definitions are now presented with the following explanatory and illustrative comments.

Classification-Related Terms

1. The **lease term** is the fixed noncancelable[2] term of the lease plus all of the following periods:
    a. Those covered by bargain renewal options. A **bargain renewal option** allows the lessee to renew the lease for an amount substantially lower than the fair rental of the property at the date the option becomes exercisable. Determining whether a particular renewal option is a bargain renewal option requires substantial judgment and is important because

---

[2]A *noncancelable lease* is a lease that is cancelable only under one or more of the following conditions:

1. Upon the occurrence of some remote contingency.
2. With the permission of the lessor.
3. If the lessee enters into a new lease with the same lessor.
4. Upon payment by the lessee of a large penalty so that continuation of the lease appears reasonably assured.

Even if a lessor has the ability to permit the lease to be canceled, the lease is still considered noncancelable by both the lessee and lessor. This treatment is consistent with accounting practices in other areas, such as convertible debt, and is proper because the lessor can compel the lessee to pay the lease payments and meet the other terms of the lease.

lease classification and related accounting treatments are influenced directly.

b. Periods for which failure to renew the lease imposes a penalty on the lessee in an amount such that renewal appears, at the inception of the lease, to be reasonably assured.

c. Periods covered by ordinary renewal options during which a guarantee by the lessee of the lessor's debt related to the leased property is expected to be in effect.

d. Periods covered by ordinary renewal options preceding the date a bargain purchase option is exercisable.

e. Periods representing renewals or extensions of the lease at the lessor's option.

Accountants always consider the lease term to end at the date a bargain purchase option becomes exercisable.

2. The **estimated economic life** of leased property is the remaining period the property is expected to be economically usable in its intended function without limitation by the lease term.

3. **Minimum lease payments** are the payments that the lessee is obligated to make in connection with the leased property. If the lease contains a bargain purchase option, only the **minimum rental payments** over the lease term preceding that option and the payment called for by the option are minimum lease payments. If the lease does *not* contain a bargain purchase option, *minimum lease payments include* all of the following:

a. The **minimum rental payments** over the lease term.

b. Any **guarantee of the residual value** of the leased property at the expiration of the lease term.

c. Any **payment that the lessee must make** or can be required to make upon failure to renew or extend the lease at the expiration of the lease term.

Although *SFAS No. 13* does not expressly include the payments called for by a bargain renewal option in minimum lease payments, an appendix to the statement provides, "The period covered by a bargain renewal option is included in the lease term . . . and the option rentals [required under a bargain renewal option] are included in the minimum lease payments."[3]

From the standpoint of lessors, minimum lease payments are the same as those described from the standpoint of the lessee, plus any guarantee of residual value or rental payments beyond the lease term by a third party unrelated to either the lessee or the lessor.

Other Lease Classification Issues

An Exclusionary Test.   The transfer-of-title and bargain-purchase-option criteria should be applied to all leases; however, the length-of-lease-term and amount-of-lease-payment criteria should *not* be applied if the lease term begins within the last 25% of the total estimated life of the property. The **exclusionary test** involves a determination of whether or not the lease term begins within the last 25% of the remaining life of the leased asset. In applying this exclusionary test, accountants use the total life of the asset without regard to the beginning or end of the lease term. The *classification* test for the length of lease term, as discussed earlier, uses the estimated *remaining* useful life of the asset at the beginning of the lease term.

The reason we exclude the length-of-lease-term and amount-of-lease-payment criteria from the lease classification process for assets near the end of their useful lives is illustrated by the following example. Assume that a railroad tank car is constructed with a 25-year useful life and that the car is leased for five successive five-year lease terms with no bargain purchase options, no bargain renewal options, and no transfers of title included in any of the five leases. Assume further that the amount of lease payment test is not met in any of the five leases. Therefore, only the length-of-lease-term criterion remains to test for each of the five

---

[3]*FASB Statement of Financial Accounting Standards No. 13*, par. 88.

leases. Remember that if the lease term is equal to 75% or more of the remaining estimated life of the property, the lease is classified as a capitalized lease. This test can be expressed mathematically as

$$\frac{\text{Lease term}}{\text{Remaining asset life}} \geq 75\% = \text{Capital lease}$$

The following graph shows the results of applying the length-of-lease-term classification test.

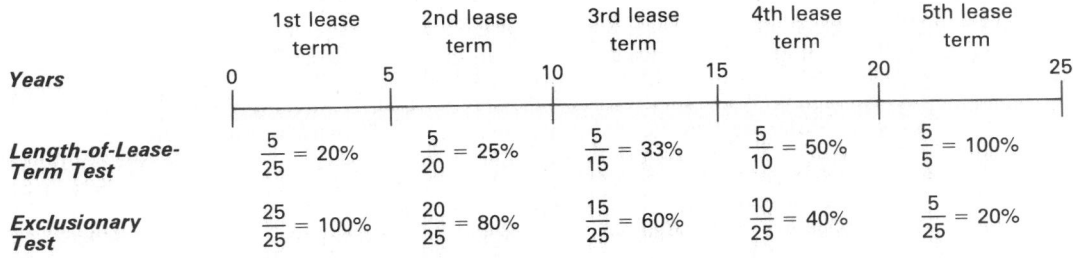

In the first lease term, the length-of-lease-term test is not met, because the lease term of five years is only 20% of the asset's 25-year life. The exclusionary test is applied by dividing the asset's life (25 years) into the period from the beginning of the lease term to the end of the asset's life (also 25 years). The exclusionary test of 100% in the first lease term simply means that the length-of-lease-term test is applicable (although the test is not met during the first lease term).

Note that as the asset becomes older, the percentage obtained from applying the length-of-lease-term test becomes larger until, during the fifth lease term, the test is finally met. However, the beginning of the last lease term occurs during the last 25% of the asset's total life and, therefore, the length-of-lease-term test (and the amount-of-lease-payment test) should not be applied to the fifth lease term. Since neither a transfer of title nor a bargain purchase option are present in any of the leases, all five leases are classified as operating leases. In such circumstances, since the first four leases have been accounted for as operating leases and since the final lease differs in no way from the previous four, logic suggests that all five leases should be accounted for in a similar fashion. In other words, the exclusionary test recognizes that in the later years of an asset's life, the two classification tests using percentages (75% of useful life and 90% of fair market value) are subject to distortion and therefore should not be applied.

Once the four classification criteria have been applied, a lessee will have classified a lease as either a capital or operating lease. However, lessors must apply several other tests before finally completing the classification process.

Additional Lessor Classification Criteria. Lessors must apply two additional criteria to classify a lease as a capitalized lease. These last two tests concern the evidence necessary to record a receivable and the ability to predict any future expenses associated with the leased property. When a lease is classified as a capital lease, lessees record additional assets and liabilities and begin to reflect expenses such as depreciation and interest. When lessors record capital leases, assets are reclassified from plant or inventory to receivables. Interest revenue also begins to be earned and recognized in the income statement.

Consistent with the modifying convention of conservatism, generally acceptable accounting principles require more evidence to record receivables than to record payables,

Conservatism

and the same relationship exists between revenues and expenses. Therefore, lessors are required to assess the **collectibility of rent** *and* future **predictability of costs** prior to recording a capital lease. Unless future rental collections are reasonably assured *and* future costs to be incurred under the lease are reasonably predictable, even a lease meeting one of the initial four criteria, such as containing a transfer of title, will be accounted for as an operating lease by the lessor. In substance, these last two criteria must be met prior to recording a receivable and recognizing gross profit or interest revenue. Remember that conservatism requires the recognition of liabilities when apparent but requires considerably more evidence prior to recording a receivable. The quantity and quality of evidence required to recognize revenue allows little uncertainty as to the receipt of cash or other consideration. Special guidance in the application of conservatism and recognition of revenue is provided by the FASB in the case of leases.

Revenue Realization

If a lease meets *one* of the four initial classification criteria and *both* the rental collectability and cost predictability criteria, then the lease will be classified as a sales-type or direct-financing lease by the lessor. Remember that in applying the four initial classification tests, we consider whether the lease meets one of the following criteria:

1. Transfers title of the property to the lessee.
2. Contains a bargain purchase option.
3. Provides for a minimum lease term equal to 75% or more of the leased asset's remaining life.
4. Calls for lease payments, the present value of which equals or exceeds 90% of the fair market value of the leased asset at the inception of the lease.

Remaining lessor classification criteria in *SFAS No. 13* relate to what type of capital lease a given lease will be, not whether the lease will be an operating or capital lease.

Manufacturer or Dealer Profit. Lessors must next consider whether or not a lease gives rise to a manufacturer's or dealer's profit. If such profit is evident, then a lease should be classified as a **sales-type lease** and gross profit should be recognized at the beginning of the lease term. Of course, interest revenue is also recognized over the term of sales-type leases. To determine whether or not a lease contains an element of dealer's or manufacturer's profit, accountants compare the carrying amount of the leased asset with its fair market value. If the carrying amount of the asset differs from its fair market value, we conclude that the lease contains an element of manufacturer's or dealer's profit. The normal selling price of the asset is usually considered to be its fair market value. It is possible for a sales-type lease to result in the recognition of a loss. If the fair market value of the asset is less than its carrying amount, a loss on the "sale" results from a sales-type lease. Losses on sales-type leases, however, are unusual.

Direct-financing leases are simply those capital leases that do not contain a manufacturer's or dealer's profit. An exception to this rule is provided in the case of leveraged leases. In order for a lease to be treated as a **leveraged lease** instead of a direct-financing lease, it must meet all the criteria for classification as a direct-financing lease plus several additional criteria. A discussion of leveraged lease classification and accounting is provided in Appendix A of this chapter.

Exhibit 21–3 is a learning aid which summarizes the classification provisions for the basic types of leases (excluding leveraged leases) from the perspective of both lessees and lessors. Study the flowchart to ensure your complete understanding of all the criteria and relationships that cause a lease to be classified in a certain manner.

FINANCIAL ACCOUNTING AND REPORTING—LESSEES

We now turn our attention to financial accounting and reporting practices for each lease type. First we consider how lessees account for and report operating and capital leases.

EXHIBIT 21-3
Criteria for Lease Classification

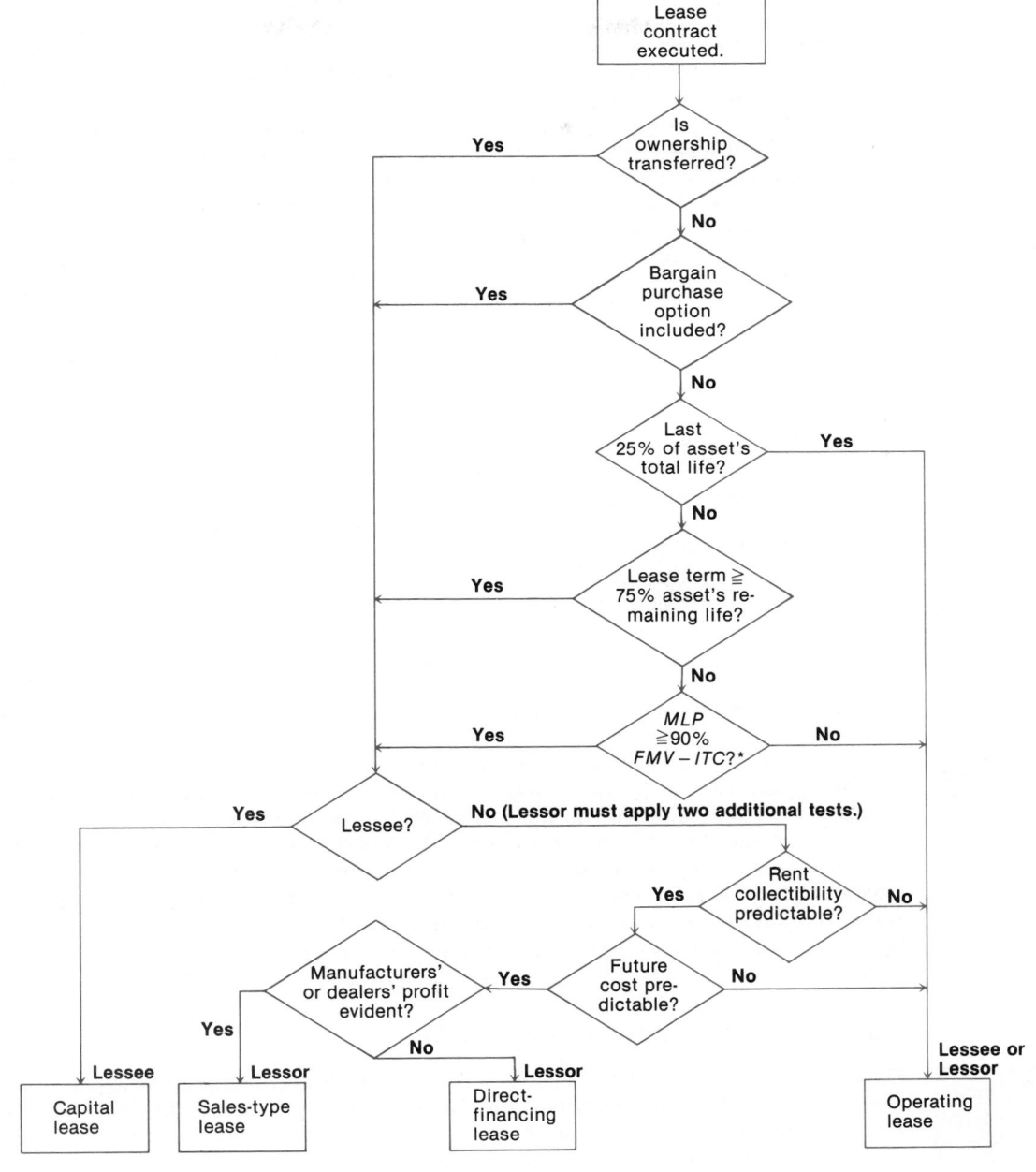

*MLP = present value of minimum lease payments; FMV = fair market value; ITC = investment credit retained by lessor.

SOURCE: Adapted from Raymond J. Clay and William W. Holder, "A Practitioner's Guide to Accounting for Leases," *Journal of Accountancy,* August 1977, p. 63. Copyright © 1977 by the American Institute of Certified Public Accountants, Inc.

Operating Leases—Lessee Accounting

From the perspective of lessees, operating leases are relatively simple to account for and pose few significant problems. Rent expense is recognized on a straight-line basis, usually as lease payments are made. Normally no new assets or liabilities are reflected in the accounting records of the lessee.

When unequal cash payments are required by an operating lease, rent expense should, nevertheless, be recognized on a straight-line basis and determined by the total cash payments to be made over the lease term. For example, if an operating lease has a term of 10 years and requires an initial payment of $15,000 followed by eight annual payments of $10,000 and a final payment of $5,000, the total rent expense to be recognized and cash to be paid over the 10-year period is $100,000 or an average of $10,000 per year. If the lease is executed with the $15,000 payment on January 1, 1984, and the first $10,000 payment is due on January 1, 1985, the following entries to record the first and second cash payments and recognize rent expense are appropriate:

Jan. 1, 1984	Rent Expense	10,000	
	Prepaid Rent	5,000	
	Cash		15,000
Jan. 1, 1985	Rent Expense	10,000	
	Cash		10,000

The prepaid rent arising in the 1984 entry should be classified as a noncurrent asset and remains on the balance sheet until the final payment is due on January 1, 1993. An entry like that of January 1, 1985, is made each year through 1992. The projected final entry on January 1, 1993, would be as follows:

Jan. 1, 1993	Rent Expense	10,000	
	Cash		5,000
	Prepaid Rent		5,000

This approach results in the recognition of an equal $10,000 amount of rent expense each year.

Materiality

If cash payments are deferred at the beginning of the lease, a liability is reflected in the accounting records. Thus, when there is a material difference between the straight-line recognition of rent expense and the individual cash payments required by an operating lease, we recognize the balance sheet implications of the difference as assets or liabilities. Present-value techniques are not required for operating leases. Other expenses, including executory costs, are accounted for in a normal fashion. That is, costs such as insurance or property taxes incurred directly by lessees are accrued and allocated to the periods benefited in accordance with generally acceptable accounting principles.

Capital Leases—Lessee Accounting

Substance over Form

Financial accounting and reporting for capital leases by lessees are more involved. When a lessee signs a capital lease, the transaction is, in substance, a purchase of the asset. The lessee records the asset and a liability at the beginning of the lease term, usually at the present value of the minimum lease payments. However, the amount assigned as the "cost" of the asset should not exceed the fair market value of the asset at that time. Therefore, it is possible for the carrying amounts of the asset and liability to be the fair market value of the asset rather than the present value of the lease payments.

Discount on Lease Liabilities

The discount (interest) rate applied to determine the present value of the future minimum lease payments is the lower of the lessee's incremental borrowing rate or the rate implicit in the lease. The **lessee's incremental borrowing rate** is the rate that the lessee would have incurred if the funds to purchase the asset had been borrowed from a bank or other financial institution. The **interest rate implicit in the lease** is the discount rate that would cause the gross future minimum lease payments to equal the fair value of the leased asset. Any executory costs that are included in the lease payments are subtracted in determining the minimum lease payments. Any residual value that the lessee guarantees to the lessor is included in the minimum lease payments.

The implicit rate may also need to be computed for applying the lease classification test that requires the determination of the present value of the minimum lease payments. Calculation of the implicit rate of interest in the lease is discussed later in this chapter.

Amortization of the Asset

Lessees must address several other issues of significance in accounting for capital leases. For example, the amortization of the asset and discount relating to the lease obligation pose substantial accounting problems. The general principles that govern the systematic depreciation of all assets also apply to leasehold rights recorded as assets under capital leases. Most assets leased under capital leases are considered intangible assets; however, assets acquired through capital leases may be included among plant assets. In fact, if either the transfer of title or bargain purchase option classification tests are met, the lessee has, in substance, acquired all of the property rights—including the residual value of the leased asset at the end of the lease. Under such circumstances the asset is properly classified as a plant asset rather than an intangible asset. Similarly, if the transfer-of-title or bargain-purchase-option tests are not met, and the lease meets either the length-of-lease-term or amount-of-lease-payment test, the lease is still classified as a capital lease. The lessee's capitalized rights to the use of the property during the lease term, however, are properly considered an intangible asset in such circumstances.

> **Substance over Form**

In applying the matching principle, a company depreciates and amortizes leased assets in the same manner that it depreciates and amortizes assets which it owns. However, certain modifications may be necessary in the case of a capitalized leased asset. For example, the useful life of a leased asset depends, to some extent, on the particular lease classification criterion met. If either the transfer-of-title or bargain-purchase-option criterion is met, the leased asset is depreciated over the estimated useful life of the asset without regard to the lease term. The leased asset should not be depreciated below its estimated residual value if either the transfer-of-title or bargain-purchase-option criterion is met. Under such circumstances the entire asset, including the residual value, has been acquired by the lessee. In essence, both tests are considered to transfer ownership; if one of them is met, the lease term is relevant only to accounting for the liability aspects of the lease. On the other hand, if the lease is capitalized because it meets either the length-of-lease-term or amount-of-lease-payment criterion rather than one of the first two tests, then no residual value exists for the lessee, because the asset will be returned to the lessor at the conclusion of the lease. Furthermore, the asset should be amortized over the shorter of the life of the lease or the life of the asset in such leases. While it may seem illogical to enter into a lease for a longer period than the life of the asset, such transactions are common in franchise operations. For example, in fast food and other similar industries, lessees frequently intend to refurbish leased facilities several times during a single, relatively long, lease term.

> **Matching**

Amortization of Discount

Accounting for the liability under a capital lease also presents several accounting issues. Foremost among these is the amortization of the discount on the lease obligation. Recall that we record a liability for capital leases at the **present value of the minimum lease payments.** The difference between the minimum lease payments and their present value is the discount on the lease. Conceptually, the amortization of the discount on a lease obligation does not differ from the amortization of discount on bonds or notes payable or any other long-term liability. The lease obligation is usually recorded at the net present value of the future cash payments. During the term of the lease, discount is amortized as interest expense, and the effective interest method should be used so that a constant rate of interest is recognized each period throughout the lease term. This treatment is consistent with that required by *APB Opinion No. 21*[4] and discussed in Chapters 10 and 15. We shall now illustrate accounting for a capital lease from the perspective of the lessee.

An Illustration of Accounting for a Capital Lease

The following examples illustrate lessee accounting for a capital lease with a series of different assumptions. Sail Company leases a new sail-making machine on January 1, 1984, for six years with an annual rental of $1,000 payable at the beginning of each year. The lease contains neither a transfer of title nor a bargain purchase option. The current fair market value of the asset is $5,000, the life of the asset is nine years, and the residual value is estimated to be $780. The lessee's incremental borrowing rate is 10%, and Sail Company assets are normally depreciated by the straight-line method. Since the transfer-of-title and bargain-purchase-option criteria are not met, we must apply the final two criteria to determine if the lease should be capitalized.

In testing for the length of lease term, we find that the lease term (six years) is less than 75% of the asset's life (nine years). Therefore, this criterion is not met. In determining whether or not the present value (PV) of the minimum lease payments (MLP) is equal to or greater than 90% of the asset's fair market value, we use the computations presented below.

The PV of an annuity due in six payments at 10% is 4.79079. This factor is determined from Table 4 at the end of Chapter 6. Since the annuity is due at the beginning of the year, we add 1.00000 (first payment) to the factor of 3.79079 (second through sixth payments) to arrive at the factor for an annuity due of six payments. Therefore:

$1,000	Annuity
× 4.79079	PV factor
$4,791	PV of MLP

In this lease, we are assuming that the lessee's borrowing rate is less than the rate of interest implicit in the lease. In practice, accountants normally calculate the implicit rate of interest and compare it to the lessee's incremental rate to assure selection of the correct percentage rate for classifying and accounting for capital leases by lessees. Also, in this lease we are assuming that the residual value is not guaranteed by the lessee. If the residual value had been guaranteed, the present value of the residual value would be added to $4,791 to determine the present value of the minimum lease payments.

Remember that if the present value (*PV*) of the minimum lease payments (*MLP*) is 90% or more of the fair market value (*FMV*) of the leased asset, then we can classify the lease as a capitalized lease. Our mathematical test is

$$PV \text{ of } MLP \geqq .9 \times FMV = \text{Capital lease}$$

Since we have determined the present value of the minimum lease payments, the amount-of-lease-payment criterion can now be applied:

---

[4]*APB Opinion No. 21,* "Interest on Receivables and Payables," 1971.

$$\$4,791 \geqq .9 \times \$5,000$$
$$\$4,791 \geqq \$4,500$$

Because the present value of the minimum lease payments exceeds 90% of the fair market value of the asset, the lease is classified as a capital lease.

The following entries (rounded to the nearest whole dollar) are necessary at the beginning of the lease term to record the lease and the first lease payment:

Jan. 1, 1984	Leasehold Rights	4,791	
	Discount on Lease Liability	1,209	
	Liability Under Lease		6,000
	($1,000 × 6)		
	(To record acquisition of leasehold		
	rights and related incurrence		
	of liability.)		
Jan. 1, 1984	Liability Under Lease	1,000	
	Cash		1,000
	(To record first lease payment.)		

At the end of the first year, the leased asset and discount on the liability are amortized as follows:

Dec. 31, 1984	Amortization Expense	799	
	Accumulated Amortization		799
	(To record asset amortization.)		
Dec. 31, 1984	Interest Expense	379	
	Discount on Lease Liability		379
	(To record discount amortization.)		

The asset amortization is computed as follows: $4,791/6 years = $799. The discount amortization is calculated as follows:

$$\begin{array}{ccccc} \text{Carrying amount} & \times & \text{Effective interest} & = & \text{Interest} \\ \text{of liability} & & \text{rate} & & \text{expense} \\ (\$5,000 - \$1,209) & \times & 10\% & = & \$379 \end{array}$$

The entries required during 1985 are as follows:

Jan. 1, 1985	Liability Under Lease	1,000	
	Cash		1,000
	(To record second lease payment.)		
Dec. 31, 1985	Amortization Expense	799	
	Accumulated Amortization		799
	(To record asset amortization.)		
Dec. 31, 1985	Interest Expense	317	
	Discount on Lease Liability		317
	(To record discount amortization.)		

The lease payment and amortization of the asset are the same as presented in the 1984 entries. To arrive at the calculation of the discount amortization, we subtract the previously recorded interest expense ($379) from the discount on the lease liability ($1,209). This leaves $830 of unamortized discount, and the 1985 interest is calculated as follows: ($4,000 − $830) × 10% = $317. Notice that in this calculation the face amount of the liability has been reduced by the $1,000 payment on January 1, 1985 ($5,000 − $1,000 = $4,000).

The series of entries relating to asset and discount amortization continues throughout the lease; however, certain important observations are possible at this point. First, the leased asset is amortized over the *lease term* (six years) rather than the longer life of the asset, because neither the transfer-of-title nor bargain-purchase-option criterion is met. As a result, the leased asset will be returned to the lessor at the conclusion of the lease. If the lease contained a transfer of title or a bargain purchase option, then the machine would be amortized over its useful life of nine years rather than over the lease term.

Second, the amount of discount amortized each year changes in terms of absolute dollars but remains constant as a rate of interest. In practice, accountants usually prepare amortization tables to simplify the process of recognizing interest expense and amortizing discount for the entire lease term. Such a table is presented in Exhibit 21–4 for the above example.

An alternative method of recording a capital lease by the lessee is to combine the Liability Under Lease and the Discount on Lease Liability into a single account equal to the net amount of the two accounts. At December 31 of each year, interest expense is recognized as an increase in the Liability Under Lease; the annual lease payments of $1,000 on each January 1 are recorded as reductions in the Liability Under Lease as in the previous example.

On the opposite page are the entries for the previous example for 1984 and 1985 following this approach. The entries for the amortization of the leased asset are not repeated, because they are the same under both approaches.

EXHIBIT 21–4
Sail Company
Lease Discount Amortization Table

Date	Explanation	(1) Gross Liability	(2) Discount	(3) (Col. 1 − Col. 2) Net Liability During Year	(4) (Col. 3 × .10) Interest Expense
Jan. 1, 1984	Balance	$ 6,000	$1,209		
Jan. 1, 1984	Payment	(1,000)			
1984	Balance	5,000	1,209	$3,791	
1984	Amortization		(379)		$ 379
1985	Payment	(1,000)			
1985	Balance	4,000	830	3,170	
1985	Amortization		(317)		317
1986	Payment	(1,000)			
1986	Balance	3,000	513	2,487	
1986	Amortization		(249)		249
1987	Payment	(1,000)			
1987	Balance	2,000	264	1,736	
1987	Amortization		(174)		174
1988	Payment	(1,000)			
1988	Balance	1,000	90	910	
1988	Amortization		(90)		90*
1989	Payment	(1,000)			
1989	Balance	−0−	−0−	−0−	−0−
Total Interest Expense and Discount Amortized					$1,209

*Rounding adjustment in 1989 to clear Discount account.

Jan. 1, 1984	Leasehold Rights	4,791	
	Liability Under Lease		4,791
Jan. 1, 1984	Liability Under Lease	1,000	
	Cash		1,000
Dec. 31, 1984	Interest Expense	379	
	Liability Under Lease		379
Jan. 1, 1985	Liability Under Lease	1,000	
	Cash		1,000
Dec. 31, 1985	Interest Expense	317	
	Liability Under Lease		317

As in the previous illustration, this process continues until the end of the lease term, and each December 31 the interest expense declines because the liability balance is reduced from that of the previous year-end.

Classification of the Asset

The classification chosen for the asset in the preceding example, leasehold rights, is an intangible asset account. If either of the ownership transfer criteria had been met, the asset would be classified as part of the plant assets. Had this been the case, the amortization expense would more appropriately be identified as Depreciation Expense.

Classification of the Liability

For balance sheet presentation, the liability is divided between **current** and **noncurrent** portions. The gross amount of the next lease payment ($1,000) is a current liability; however, the amount of the discount to be associated with the current portion of the liability is not as clear. Conceptually, the current portion of the liability should be shown at its present value. In our example the portion of the lease obligation classified as a current liability in Sail Company's balance sheet at December 31, 1984, is the $1,000 due January 1, 1985. No discount is associated with this payment because it is due the next day. However, in many situations the next lease payment may be due near the end of the next period; in such cases we must determine the amount of discount to be associated with the current portion of the liability. To illustrate, assume that the next lease payment is due at the end of 1985 rather than at the beginning. Under this new assumption, the portion of the lease obligation classified as a current liability at December 31, 1984, is the present value of $1,000 due in one year, discounted at 10%. Using present-value techniques discussed earlier, we determine that the amount of the discount to be associated with the current liability is $909, computed as follows:

$$PV = \text{Future amount} \times pvf_{\overline{1}|10\%}$$
$$= \$1,000 \times .90909$$
$$= \$909 \text{ (rounded)}$$

The difference between the current portion of the discount and the total discount remaining at the end of each year is considered to be the discount associated with the noncurrent portion of the liability. The current liability will be consistently reported at $909 in each succeeding balance sheet. Under our new assumptions, the "liabilities" section of Sail Company's balance sheet at December 31, 1984, and December 31, 1985, would appear as shown in Exhibit 21–5.

A second method of allocating the total discount between current and noncurrent portions is frequently encountered in practice. In this method the discount associated with the

---

EXHIBIT 21–5

Sail Company
PARTIAL BALANCE SHEET
December 31, 1984

Current Liabilities
Lease obligation	$1,000	
Less: Discount on lease liability	91	
Net current liability		$ 909

Long-Term Liabilities
Lease obligation	4,000	
Less: Discount	1,118	
Net long-term liability		2,882
Total liability under lease		$3,791

Sail Company
PARTIAL BALANCE SHEET
December 31, 1985

Current Liabilities
Lease obligation	$1,000	
Less: Discount on lease liability	91	
Net current liability		$ 909

Long-Term Liabilities
Lease obligation	3,000	
Less: Discount on lease liability	739	
Net long-term liability		2,261
Total liability under lease		$3,170

---

current portion of the liability is the amount of interest expense to be recognized in the next year. If we again assume for Sail Company that the payment is due at the end of 1985 instead of on January 1, the discount of $317 to be amortized to interest expense in 1985 would be treated as a reduction in the current liability at the end of 1984. The remaining discount would then be treated as a reduction in the noncurrent portion of the liability. If the difference between these two methods is material in amount, the issue becomes significant.

The authors prefer the first method because it consistently places the same value on the current liability for each succeeding balance sheet. In other words, the current liability is consistently reported as the present value of the specific $1,000 payment due at the end of the following year. The same type of classification problem also exists for lessors, because receivables resulting from capital leases must also be divided between current and noncurrent portions. In practice, the second method is frequently encountered, because the differences between the methods are usually immaterial.

Materiality

Capital leases result in several types of expenses for lessees. Amortization or depreciation expense is recognized on the purchased asset, as we have seen in the previous example. Interest expense is recognized on the liability resulting from the capitalization of the lease. Executory costs that are paid directly by the lessee, such as taxes and insurance, are recognized as paid or accrued. Executory costs that are included in the lease payments to the lessor are deducted from the total payments in determining the capitalized amount of the asset and liability that are recognized when the capital lease is recorded. As lease payments are made, that portion representing executory costs is recognized as an expense or prepaid expense, as appropriate.

EXHIBIT 21–6
Accounting and Reporting by Lessees

	Capital Lease	Operating Lease
Accounting Treatment	Record at the beginning of the lease term an asset and an obligation at the present value of minimum lease payments over the lease term. That portion of the minimum lease payments representing executory expenses (such as insurance, maintenance, and taxes) to be paid by the lessor should be excluded.	Do not capitalize either the leased asset or obligation. Recognize rent expense on a straight-line basis over the term of the lease even if lease payments are not on a straight-line basis, unless another systematic method is more representative of benefit received.
Balance Sheet Presentation	Assets and obligations recorded in capitalized leases should be separately identified in the balance sheet or in footnotes thereto. Liabilities are subject to the same conditions as other liabilities in distinguishing between current and noncurrent elements.	No direct balance sheet implications.
Disclosure Requirements	1. The gross amount of assets recorded as of the date of each balance sheet presented in the aggregate and by major classes by nature or function. 2. Minimum future payments required as of the date of the latest balance sheet presented, in the aggregate, and for each of the five succeeding fiscal years reduced by executory costs, including profit, and imputed interest. 3. The total of minimum sublease rentals to be received in the future under noncancelable subleases as of the date of the latest balance sheet presented. 4. Total contingent rentals actually incurred for each period for which an income statement is presented. 5. A general description of the leasing arrangements, including (a) the basis on which contingent rentals are determined, (b) the existence and terms of renewal or purchase options and escalation clauses, and (c) restrictions imposed by lease agreements.	For leases with terms in excess of one year: 1. Minimum future payments required as of the date of the latest balance sheet, in the aggregate, and for each of the five succeeding fiscal years. 2. The total of minimum rentals to be received in the future under noncancelable subleases as of the latest balance sheet date. For all leases: 1. Rental expense for each period for which an income statement is presented, with separate amounts for minimum rentals, contingent rentals, and sublease rentals. 2. A general description of the leasing arrangements, including (a) the basis on which contingent rentals are determined, (b) the existence and terms of renewal or purchase options and escalation clauses, and (c) restrictions imposed by lease agreements.

SOURCE: Adapted from Raymond J. Clay and William W. Holder, ''A Practitioner's Guide to Accounting for Leases,'' *Journal of Accountancy,* August 1977, p. 64. Copyright © 1977 by the American Institute of Certified Public Accountants, Inc.

Miscellaneous Lessee Considerations

Exhibit 21–6 provides a summary of the accounting and disclosure requirements for both operating and capital leases from the perspective of the lessee. Use this exhibit to review and test your understanding of lessee accounting and reporting standards before we move to the subject of lessor accounting.

Exhibit 21–7 presents the lease disclosure from the 1982 annual report of Koppers Company, Inc., a diversified manufacturing company with specialized engineering and construction capabilities. Of the present value of net minimum lease payments ($7,534,000), $5,959,000 is included among the company's noncurrent liabilities and the remainder, $1,575,000, among current liabilities. The note also includes information about the company's operating leases (which are not included in the balance sheet).

EXHIBIT 21–7
Koppers Company, Inc.
Lessee Financial Statement Disclosure

4. Leases—The Company, as lessee, has entered into various lease arrangements covering land, buildings, machinery and equipment. The following is an analysis of the property under capital leases:

($ Thousands)	1982	1981
Land and buildings	$ 7,862	$16,813
Machinery and equipment	4,198	6,500
	12,060	23,313
Less accumulated amortization	5,134	10,316
	$ 6,926	$12,997

The following is a schedule by years of future minimum lease payments as of December 31, 1982:

($ Thousands)	Capital Leases	Operating Leases
1983	$ 2,224	$ 4,384
1984	1,046	2,627
1985	845	1,831
1986	721	1,371
1987	732	763
1988 and later	7,287	2,204
Total minimum lease payments	$12,855	$13,180
Less amount representing interest	5,321	
Present value of net minimum lease payments (including $1,575 classified as current obligations under capital leases)	$ 7,534	

SOURCE: Koppers Company, Inc., 1982 Annual Report.

FINANCIAL ACCOUNTING AND REPORTING—LESSORS

Earlier in the chapter, we learned that lessors classify leases into one of four possible categories:

1. Operating
2. Direct financing
3. Sales
4. Leveraged

Although lessors recognize revenue as a result of all successful leasing activity, the nature and timing of the revenue and the related balance sheet treatment differ under each lease type. We begin our discussion with an analysis of operating leases.

Operating Leases—Lessor Accounting

In an operating lease, lessors usually recognize rent revenue on a straight-line basis over the lease term, even if the cash received under the terms of the lease varies from a straight-line pattern. In such cases, a Deferred Revenue account is established on the balance sheet if the cash received exceeds a straight-line recognition of revenue. If the cash received is less than the rent revenue recognized on a straight-line basis, a Rent Receivable asset account is established.

The asset leased to the lessee is classified as part of the "plant assets" section of the balance sheet of the lessor and depreciated in normal fashion. Since an operating lease does not presume that a "sale" has taken place, the asset is normally depreciated over its useful life rather than over the lease term. If the lease agreement contains a transfer of title or a bargain purchase option but the collectibility of rent is not assured and/or future costs under the lease are not predictable, the lease is still classified as an operating lease. In such leases the leased asset is depreciated over the useful life of the asset or the lease term, whichever is shorter, because the asset will *probably* be transferred to the lessee at the conclusion of the lease. Revenue under an operating lease is rent revenue, while expenses incurred under such leases include depreciation expense on the leased asset. Any **initial direct costs** incurred by a lessor should be capitalized and amortized over the term of the operating lease as an expense to be matched against the rental revenue. **Initial direct costs** are those costs incurred by lessors which are directly associated with the *successful* negotiation and consummation of leases. Examples of such costs include commissions, legal fees, costs of credit investigations, and the costs of preparing and processing documents for new leases. In addition, a portion of salespersons' compensation, other than commissions, and the compensation of other employees related to the time spent in the activities described above are also initial direct costs. However, the compensation of employees relating to time spent in discussing leases that are not successfully negotiated and consummated is not part of initial direct costs and should, therefore, be charged to expense when incurred. Furthermore, supervisory and administrative expenses or other indirect expenses, such as rent and facilities costs, are never part of initial direct costs.

| Matching |

Lessors carefully determine initial direct costs because accounting treatments differ among the three lease types. Accountants frequently establish elaborate data-capture mechanisms to estimate and classify initial direct costs properly. For example, the allocation of salespersons' compensation between successfully executed leases and unsuccessful efforts may require time and effort for detailed reports. The accountant should anticipate these data needs and establish systems capable of providing such information on a timely basis.

Direct-Financing Leases—Lessor Accounting

The next type of lease to be considered from the perspective of the lessor is the direct-financing lease. An asset that is subject to a direct-financing lease is presumed to have been sold to the lessee; however, since the lessor is fulfilling only a financing function, no profit or loss is recognized on the sale. Situations involving profit or loss on the "sale" of a leased asset are covered in a later section of this chapter, "Sales-Type Leases." The only type of revenue recognized on direct-financing leases is interest revenue earned in the financing activity. Since the leased asset is presumed to have been sold and is removed from the books of the lessor, no additional depreciation on the asset is recognized by the lessor. The following descriptive entry illustrates and explains how to record a direct-financing lease:

Investment in Lease	(MLP − Executory costs + Residual value)
Equipment	(Cost or carrying amount)
Unearned Income	(Difference between investment and cost or carrying value of asset. Also referred to frequently as discount.)

Terms used in the above journal entry are explained as follows:

MLP = Minimum lease payments.

Executory costs = Executory costs plus any profit thereon.

Residual value (as used in this entry) = Unguaranteed residual value accruing to the lessor. (Transfer-of-title and bargain-purchase-option tests are not met and either the life-of-lease or percent-of-fair-value tests is met.)

Cost or carrying amount = Lessor's cost or carrying amount of the asset at the time of the lease, including any accumulated depreciation.

The investment in the lease is a combination of receivable to be collected and residual value to be reacquired at the expiration of the lease. The Unearned Income, sometimes referred to as a discount on the investment in the lease, is the difference between the gross investment in the leased asset, including residual value, and the present value of the investment. The leased equipment is also removed from the balance sheet.

We described the asset arising from the capital lease as an "Investment in Lease." If the residual value accrued to the lessee rather than the lessor, we would refer to the lessor's asset as a "receivable," because it would be confined to the lease payments that were receivable from the lessee.

You will recall that lessors use the interest rate implicit in the lease to amortize the unearned income over the lease term and that the implicit rate of interest in a lease is the rate necessary to equate the future gross amount of the lease payments with the current fair value (present value) of the leased asset. Subsequent to the preceding entry, the unearned income is recognized as interest revenue over the life of the lease by the effective interest method explained in Chapters 10 and 15. Any initial direct costs incurred in consummating a direct financing lease are charged against the Unearned Income account in the period the lease is recorded. This procedure serves to reduce the amount of the unearned income and alters the interest rate implicit in the lease. A second present-value calculation may be necessary when initial direct costs are material.

Matching

We charge initial direct costs directly to the Unearned Income account in a direct-financing lease to match the revenues and expenses associated with the lease. If initial direct costs related to direct-financing leases are charged to expense when incurred, a loss may appear in that period, because the revenue to be recognized on the lease is in the form of interest and is recognized over the life of the lease rather than at the beginning of the lease term. The interest revenue to be recognized over the life of the lease is therefore reduced by the amount of the initial direct costs to assure proper matching. The following example illustrates accounting for a direct-financing lease.

A Comprehensive Direct-Financing Lease Illustration

Remember from the previous example that Sail Company leased a machine for six years with an annual rental of $1,000 payable at the beginning of each year. The lease was classified as a capital lease because the present value of the minimum rentals exceeded 90% of the $5,000 fair market value. The machine had an estimated residual value of $780. Assume that the cost (carrying amount) of the leased asset to the lessor is $5,000, an amount equal to the fair market value of the asset. For simplicity, ignore initial direct costs.

The first problem is to determine the interest rate implicit in this lease; that is, the discount rate that would cause the future minimum lease payments *(MLP)*, plus any unguaranteed residual value, to equal the fair market value *(FMV)* of the asset at the inception of the lease. In a direct-financing lease the fair market value of the leased asset is also equal to the cost or carrying amount of the asset on the lessor's books. In the Sail Company example we express the equation as follows:

$$FMV = PV \text{ of the } MLP + PV \text{ of the residual}$$
$$\text{value accruing to the lessor at}$$
$$\text{the end of 6 years}$$

Selecting a 12% discount rate to test, we find:

$$FMV = PV \text{ of } MLP + PV \text{ of residual value}$$
$$= (\$1,000 \times 4.60478) + (\$780 \times .50663)$$
$$= \$4,605 + \$395$$
$$= \$5,000$$

The present-value factor of 4.60478 is the appropriate factor for an annuity due for six periods at 12%, including the initial payment at a factor of 1.00000. The present-value factor of .50663 that is applied to the residual value is the present value of one for six periods at 12%. Since the residual value is a single amount to be received at the end of the sixth year, a six-year present-value factor must be used in this calculation.

Because the use of the 12% discount rate results in a present value of the minimum lease payments, plus residual value, that equals the fair value of the asset ($5,000), we conclude that we have found the rate of interest implicit in this lease. If the equation had not been satisfied with the 12% present-value factors, we would have selected a different rate for testing. In practice, computers are normally employed to solve complex leasing problems efficiently and accurately. The *lessee's* incremental borrowing rate was 10%, which is exceeded by the implicit rate that we just determined. Normally both rates would be determined, and the smaller would be used by the lessee. The lessor, of course, uses the interest rate implicit in the lease without regard to the lessee's incremental bargaining rate.

If we use the 12% implicit rate of interest, the present value of the lease payments receivable is $4,605, which exceeds 90% of the fair market value of the asset (.90 × $5,000 = $4,500). In this example, no uncertainties about rent collectibility or cost predictability exist and, consequently, we can conclude that the lease should be classified as a direct-financing lease.

The lessor would make the following entry at the beginning of the lease:

Jan. 1, 1984	Investment in Lease	6,780	
	($6,000 + $780)		
	Equipment		5,000
	Unearned Income		1,780
	(To record execution of		
	the lease.)		

Note that the investment in the leased asset is the sum of the receivable ($6,000) and the unguaranteed residual value accruing to the lessor ($780). Furthermore, the Unearned Income is merely the arithmetical difference between the gross investment ($6,780) and the carrying amount of the asset "sold" ($5,000).

The first lease payment of $1,000 is recorded by the lessee as follows:

Jan. 1, 1984	Cash	1,000	
	Investment in Lease		1,000
	(To record the initial		
	lease payment.)		

Exhibit 21–8 is an amortization table designed to facilitate accounting for this lease. Entries based on this table for the years ending December 31, 1984, and December 31, 1985, to recognize interest revenue and to record the receipt of lease payments are as follows:

Jan. 1, 1984	Cash	1,000	
	Investment in Lease		1,000
	(To record the initial lease payment.)		
Dec. 31, 1984	Unearned Income	480	
	Interest Revenue		480
	(To recognize 1984 interest revenue.)		
Jan. 1, 1985	Cash	1,000	
	Investment in Lease		1,000
	(To record the 1985 lease payment.)		
Dec. 31, 1985	Unearned Income	418	
	Interest Revenue		418
	(To recognize 1985 interest revenue.)		

The process of amortization continues until the entire amount of unearned income is amortized over the lease term and the Investment in Lease account is reduced by collecting the lease payments at $1,000 per year for six years. The balance in the Investment in Lease account at the end of the lease term is $780, which is the amount of the residual value. At the conclusion of the lease, the asset reverts to the lessor, because neither a transfer of title nor a bargain purchase option was in the lease. At this point the lessor should reclassify the $780 balance in the Investment in Lease account to an appropriate plant asset account.

Sales-Type Leases—Lessor Accounting

Sales-type leases are capital leases that result in gross profit (or loss) to the lessor at the beginning of the lease. In lease terminology, such gross profit is referred to as manufacturer's or dealer's profit. In essence, lessors earn two types of revenue from sales-type leases: gross profit or loss on the "sale" of the asset and interest revenue as a result of the financing function fulfilled by the lessor.

EXHIBIT 21–8
Amortization Table for Direct-Financing Lease

Date	Explanation	(1) Gross Investment	(2) Unearned Income	(3) (Col. 1 − Col. 2) Net Investment	(4) (Col. 3 × .12) Interest Revenue
Jan. 1, 1984	Lease inception	$ 6,780	$1,780	$5,000	
Jan. 1, 1984	Payment	(1,000)			
1984	Balance	5,780	1,780	4,000	
1984	Amortization		(480)		$ 480
1985	Payment	(1,000)			
1985	Balance	4,780	1,300	3,480	
1985	Amortization		(418)		418
1986	Payment	(1,000)			
1986	Balance	3,780	882	2,898	
1986	Amortization		(348)		348
1987	Payment	(1,000)			
1987	Balance	2,780	534	2,246	
1987	Amortization		(270)		270
1988	Payment	(1,000)			
1988	Balance	1,780	264	1,516	
1988	Amortization		(182)		182
1989	Payment	(1,000)			
1989	Balance	780	82	698	
1989	Amortization		(82)		82*
Dec. 31, 1989	Balance	$ 780	–0–	$ 780	—
		(Residual value)			

Total Interest Revenue and Unearned Income Amortized $1,780

*Rounding adjustment in 1989 to clear Unearned Income account.

The following descriptive entry illustrates and explains how to record sales-type leases and shows how the elements of the lease entry relate to each other.

Investment in Lease	(*MLP* + Residual value)
Cost of Asset Sold	(Cost of asset − *PV* of residual)
Equipment	(Cost of asset)
Unearned Income	(Investment in lease − *PV* of investment in lease)
Sales Revenue	(*PV* of *MLP*)

Residual value as used here represents the unguaranteed residual value of the asset accruing to the lessor. The fair market value of the leased asset differs from its carrying value on the books of the lessor; therefore, gross profit is recognized because this lease is a sales-type lease. This gross profit is equal to the difference between the sales revenue and the cost of asset sold, as implied in the preceding descriptive entry. If the residual value of the property is to be returned to the lessor at the conclusion of the lease, then the residual has not been sold. Consequently, we do not include the residual value accruing to the lessor in either sales revenue or cost of goods sold. Rather, the residual value accruing to the lessor is recorded as part of the investment in the lease. The cost of the property "sold" is removed from the books of the lessor by the credit to the Equipment account.

A Comprehensive Sales-Type Lease Illustration

We may easily convert the Sail Company example to a sales-type lease by changing only a few assumptions. Assume that the cost (carrying account) of the machine on the lessor's books is $4,000 just prior to the execution of the lease; that initial direct costs are $275; and that all other original information remains constant. That is, the fair market value of the asset is $5,000, the implicit rate of interest in the lease is 12%, and there are no uncertainties about rent collectibility or cost predictability. In these circumstances the lessor would make the following entry:

Jan. 1, 1984	Investment in Lease	6,780	
	Cost of Machine Leased	3,605	
	Equipment		4,000
	Sales Revenue		4,605
	Unearned Income		1,780

The computations are as follows:

Investment in lease	
Minimum lease payments	$ 6,000
Unguaranteed residual value	780
Total	$ 6,780

Present value of residual	
$780 × $pvf_{\overline{6}|12\%}$	
$780 × .50663 =	$ 395

Cost of machine leased	
Carrying amount	$ 4,000
Less: PV of residual accruing	
to lessor	(395)
Expense	$ 3,605

Sales revenue	
$1,000 × $pvadf_{\overline{6}|12\%}$	
$1,000 × 4.60478 =	$ 4,605

Unearned income	
Present value of minimum rentals	$ 4,605
Present value of residual	395
Total present value	$ 5,000
Total investment	$ 6,780
Less: PV of total investment	(5,000)
Unearned Income	$ 1,780

As a result of this entry, gross profit on the lease is recognized in the amount of $1,000, the difference between sales revenue of $4,605 and cost of machine leased, $3,605. A final note is appropriate in regard to the treatment of the residual value, which—in this example—accrues to the lessor: Since the asset returns to the lessor at the end of the lease, the amount of the present value of the residual value is subtracted from the Expense account and is not included in the Sales account. This procedure is necessary because the residual value of the asset was not sold and, in fact, still belongs to the lessor. It is neither an item of revenue nor expense and is therefore added to the asset account, Investment in Lease.

As payments are received on the lease, the investment is reduced. The Unearned Income is amortized over the life of the lease at the 12% rate of interest implicit in the lease. The amortization table presented in Exhibit 21–8 is appropriate for this purpose. Once the profit on a sales-type lease is recognized, the recognition of interest revenue does not differ from a direct-financing lease. The entries for 1984 and 1985, following the entry presented above to record the lease, are as follows:

Jan. 1, 1984	Cash	1,000	
	Investment in Lease		1,000
	(To record the initial lease payment.)		
Dec. 31, 1984	Unearned Income	480	
	Interest Revenue		480
	(To recognize interest revenue for 1984.)		
Jan. 1, 1985	Cash	1,000	
	Investment in Lease		1,000
	(To record the 1985 lease payment.)		
Dec. 31, 1985	Unearned Income	418	
	Interest Revenue		418
	(To recognize interest revenue for 1985.)		

In this example we have assumed that the residual value was *not* guaranteed nor transferred to the lessee at the end of the lease. Accordingly, the asset was labeled Investment in Lease (and included the residual value), and the present value of the residual value was *excluded* from both the Cost of Machine Leased and Sales Revenue accounts. How would these differ if the residual value had been guaranteed by the lessee? First, the Investment in Lease would more appropriately be labeled a receivable. Second, the present value of the residual value would be *included* in both the debit to the Cost of Machine Leased account and the credit to the Sales Revenue account. The entry to record the lease under these changed assumptions is as follows:

Jan. 1, 1984	Lease Receivable	6,780	
	Cost of Machine Leased	4,000	
	Equipment		4,000
	Unearned Income		1,780
	Sales Revenue		5,000

Notice that neither the amount of the asset (Lease Receivable) nor the Unearned Income is changed. Thus, the recognition of interest revenue is the same as in the previous case.

Matching

Initial direct costs related to sales-type leases are charged to expense at the beginning of the lease term and matched with the gross margin on the lease without any effect on the unearned income or amortizing rate of interest. You will recall that for direct-financing leases, the initial direct costs are charged to the Unearned Revenue account and are thereby matched against interest revenue. Direct-financing leases generate no gross profit as do sales-type leases. Consequently, initial direct costs are treated differently in each type of lease. The objective of matching costs and revenue, however, explains each treatment in the light of different circumstances. Recall also that for operating leases, the initial direct costs are deferred as an asset, amortized over the lease term, and matched against rental revenue. In this way initial direct costs are matched appropriately with the revenue generated in each type of lease: sales, direct financing, and operating. The costs of "selling" the asset are thus matched with the gross margin earned from the sale of the asset in a sales-type lease.

To illustrate the recognition of initial direct costs for a sales-type lease, assume Sail incurs legal expenses of $150 and a commission of $125 in negotiating a sales-type lease during January 1984. These expenses would be recognized at the beginning of the lease term as follows:

EXHIBIT 21–9
Accounting and Reporting by Lessors

	Operating Lease	Direct-Financing Lease	Sales-Type Lease
Accounting Treatment, Statement Presentation	**1.** The cost of leased property is included with property, plant, and equipment in the balance sheet and depreciated in normal fashion. **2.** Rent should be reported as income over the lease term on a straight-line basis unless another systematic basis is more representative of the use benefit from the leased property's diminishing value.	**1.** The minimum rentals during the lease term plus the unguaranteed residual value accruing to the benefit of the lessor shall be recorded as receivable. **2.** The difference between the receivable in (1) and the cost of the property shall be recorded as unearned revenue over the term of the lease and amortized in proportion to the remaining balance of the receivable so as to produce a constant rate of return.	**1.** The minimum lease payments during the lease term plus the unguaranteed residual value accruing to the benefit of the lessor shall be recorded as an investment. **2.** The present value of the minimum lease payments in (1) shall be recorded as the sales price; the cost of the property sold less the present value of the residual plus any direct costs of negotiating and closing the lease shall be charged against income in the same period. **3.** The difference between the investment in (1) and the present value of that investment shall be recorded as unearned revenue. This amount should appear as a reduction from the investment and amortized to income over the life of the lease so as to produce a constant rate of return.
Disclosure Requirements	**1.** As of the latest balance sheet, the cost of the property held for leasing by major property category less related accumulated depreciation. **2.** Minimum future rentals on noncancelable leases as of the latest balance sheet presented, in the aggregate and for each of the five succeeding fiscal years. **3.** Total contingent rentals included in income for each period for which an income statement is presented. **4.** A general description of leasing arrangements.	**1.** Minimum rental receivable as of the date of each balance sheet presented, with separate deductions from the total for: (a) amounts representing executory expenses included in the minimum rentals and (b) the accumulated allowance for uncollectible rentals. **2.** Unguaranteed residual values. **3.** Unearned revenue. **4.** A general description of leasing arrangements. **5.** Future minimum lease payments to be received for each of five succeeding fiscal years. **6.** Amount of unearned income included in income to offset initial direct costs charged against income for each period an income statement is presented (direct financing only). **7.** Total contingent rentals.	

SOURCE: Adapted from Raymond J. Clay and William W. Holder, "A Practitioner's Guide to Accounting for Leases," *Journal of Accountancy,* August 1977, p. 64. Copyright © 1977 by the American Institute of Certified Public Accountants, Inc.

Jan. 31, 1984	Commission Expense	125	
	Legal Expense	150	
	Cash		275

(To record initial direct costs.)

Miscellaneous Lessor Considerations

In discussing lessee accounting, we illustrated the separation of the lease payable into current and noncurrent components. The lessor's Investment in Lease or Lease Receivable is subject to the same considerations: The current portion should be presented among current assets and the noncurrent portion among noncurrent assets, usually in an investments category. Because of the similarity of this separation to that of the lessee, we do not repeat that discussion at this time.

Exhibit 21–9 provides a learning aid that summarizes the most significant aspects of lessor accounting for the three major lease types: operating, direct-financing, and sales. The exhibit is a good review tool for assessing your understanding of the accounting and reporting practices required for each type of lease. The exhibit also contains the disclosure requirements for each type of lease.

Exhibit 21–10 presents the disclosure on lessor activities from Xerox Corporation's 1981 annual report. (Xerox Corporation is also involved in other leases as the lessee, although that disclosure is not presented in Exhibit 21–10.) Note that Xerox is a lessor in both operating and sales-type leases. The "revenue recognition" section of the "summary of significant accounting policies" describes the company's involvement in both types of

---

EXHIBIT 21–10
Xerox Corporation
Lessor Disclosures

NOTES TO CONSOLIDATED FINANCIAL STATEMENTS

Summary of Significant Accounting Policies (in part)

Revenue Recognition

Revenues from equipment on lease are accounted for principally by the operating lease method. Rental and service revenues from copiers and duplicators vary each month based on the number of copies produced. Revenues from the sale of equipment under installment contracts and from sales-type leases are recognized at time of sale or at inception of lease.

Leasing Arrangements
  As Lessor

Principal domestic equipment rental plans include maintenance, service and parts, but not supplies such as toner and paper which are sold separately. Different provisions and terms may apply in other countries. Operating lease terms vary, generally from one to thirty-six months. Minimum future rental revenues on operating leases with terms

of one year or longer are (in billions): 1982—$1.5; 1983—$0.5; 1984—$0.1; and in the aggregate—$2.1. Total contingent rentals, principally usage charges in excess of minimum rentals for operating leases, amounted to $1.2 billion in 1981, 1980 and 1979, respectively.

The components of the Company's net investment in sales-type leases as of December 31, 1981 and 1980 were:

(Dollars in millions)	1981	1980
Total minimum lease payments receivable	$338.4	$ 99.8
Less amount representing executory costs	(22.8)	(18.3)
Net minimum lease payments	315.6	81.5
Less: unearned income	(91.2)	(19.5)
Allowance for doubtful receivables	(7.8)	(2.5)
Net investment in sales-type leases	$216.6	$ 59.5

These receivables are collectible as follows (in millions): 1982—$83.7; 1983—$86.0; 1984—$74.2; 1985—$52.9; 1986—$37.9; thereafter—$3.7.

SOURCE: Xerox Corporation, 1981 Annual Report.

leases. The note entitled "leasing arrangements" presents detailed information about both operating and sales-type leases.

SPECIAL LEASING SITUATIONS

Several unusual leasing arrangements and situations require additional or modified procedures. Such problems are usually the result of either the peculiar nature of the leased asset or some unusual circumstances surrounding the lease. This part of the chapter considers several of these unusual areas; some special types of lease problems that are encountered even less frequently are included in Appendix B at the end of the chapter.

Real Estate Leases

The unusual characteristics of the asset land cause most of the differences underlying financial accounting and reporting for real estate leases. Basically, the problem stems from the fact that land is considered to have an unlimited life for purposes of financial accounting. It is not logical, therefore, to consider a lease of land to be a "sale" unless either the transfer-of-title or bargain-purchase-option criterion has been met. In other words, it is impossible for a lease of land to meet the lease term criterion of 75% of useful life, because land is presumed to have an unlimited life. Furthermore, the fact that the present value of the minimum lease payments exceeds 90% of the fair market value of the leased land does not indicate that the lease is in substance a sale of the land. Indeed, the land does not expire; it reverts to the lessor at the end of the lease; and it may be worth a great deal more at the conclusion of a lease than at the beginning. Given a conceptual understanding of the unusual aspects of real estate leases, we now consider the technical requirements of *SFAS No. 13* that are related to a variety of real estate leases.

Leases of Land Only

In order to account for real estate leases, accountants must carefully consider the types of real estate being leased. The first type of real estate lease we consider is a lease of land only. For a lease of land to be considered a capital lease by lessees and lessors, the lease agreement must contain a transfer of title or a bargain purchase option. Furthermore, lessors must also meet the rent collectibility and cost predictability tests to classify the lease as a capital lease. Since real estate lease terms frequently extend for periods of time in excess of 20 years, the assessment of the collectibility of rent is unusually complex. A lease of real estate should not be classified as a sales-type lease with manufacturer's or dealer's profit recognized unless specific criteria are met.[5] The criteria, related to predicting the collectibility of rent, require a certain amount of down payment, which must consist of cash or marketable securities readily convertible to cash. The amount of the required down payment ranges from 5% to 25% of the total purchase price for different types of real estate. Since few leases contain balloon payments, in which large amounts of the total lease payable must be paid at the beginning of the lease term, most real estate leases that otherwise qualify as sales-type leases are properly accounted for as operating leases because of a failure to meet the down-payment quantity and quality criteria.

Leases of Land and Buildings

When a lease represents both land and a building, accountants must assess the magnitude of the portion of the assets represented by the land. If the fair market value of the land portion of the leased assets equals or exceeds 25% of the total fair market value of the leased assets,

---

[5]*FASB Statement of Financial Accounting Standards No. 26,* "Profit Recognition in Sales Type Leases of Real Estate," 1979, states that the criteria for recognizing profit contained in the AICPA *Industry Accounting Guide,* "Accounting for Profit Recognition on Sales of Real Estate," should be applied to leases of real estate.

the land should be considered separately in accordance with the provisions for leases of land only. The building portion of the lease should be classified in the same manner as any other leased asset.

If the fair market value of the land portion of the leased assets is less than 25% of the total fair market value of both the land and building, however, the land portion can be ignored for purposes of lease classification. Therefore, if land represents less than 25% of the fair market value of the package of real estate assets leased and if the lease contains neither a transfer of title nor a bargain purchase option, the lease may still be classified as a capital lease if one of the two remaining classification criteria are met. In that case the land would be considered "sold," and the lessee would amortize the leased assets *(including land)* over the life of the lease or the life of the building, whichever was shorter. However, the asset would not be the land but, rather, a right to *use* the land. The 25% land-portion limitation ensures that the amount of the intangible asset represented by land is relatively small. In such situations lessors remove the leased asset (including land) from the plant assets section of the balance sheet and record an investment in the lease. The residual value, of course, should be added to the investment because the residual value of the leased asset is presumed to revert to the lessor when a transfer of title and a bargain purchase option are absent from the lease.

Leases of Portions of a Building

Another complex issue arises if the leased asset is a *part* of a building. Such situations are common in leases involving shopping centers or high-rise office buildings and occur frequently in practice.

When only a part of a building is leased, the cost and fair market value amounts required to apply the fourth classification test (amount of lease payment) are often difficult to estimate. For example, what is the cost of the fortieth floor of a high-rise office building? Without such estimates, application of the amount-of-lease-payment test, which relies on estimates of fair market value, is impossible. Furthermore, without cost estimates a lessor may have trouble determining whether a given capital lease is a sales-type or direct-financing lease. Because gross profit (or loss) and interest revenue are recognized on sales-type leases whereas only interest revenue is recognized on direct-financing leases, the cost of the property subject to the lease has a direct bearing on the classification of a lease and the nature and timing of the revenue to be recognized.

FASB Interpretation No. 24 provides guidance on how to estimate the cost and fair market value when only a portion of a building is leased.[6] It states that estimates of cost and fair market value are possible in most cases and suggests that appraisals and replacement cost estimates may be appropriate in determining the fair market value and cost of portions of a building. Therefore, although precise figures may be impossible, accountants must attempt to develop reasonable estimates of value and cost.

Related-Party Leases

Substance over Form

SFAS No. 13 states that economic substance, rather than mere form, governs accounting for all leases, including those between related parties. The position of the FASB in regard to related-party leases is, of course, consistent with the theories expressed in this chapter and in earlier chapters of this book. The term **related parties** includes a parent company and its subsidiaries, joint ventures, partnerships and partners, and investors and investees, provided that the parent company, owner, or investor has the ability to exercise **significant influence** over the operating and financial policies of the other party. The test for significant influence is also consistent with the concept of significant influence discussed in Chapter 10 and contained in *APB Opinion No. 18.*[7] Other situations and circumstances may also create related-party conditions. Examples include the extension of credit, guarantees of indebted-

---

[6]*FASB Interpretation No. 24,* "Leases Involving Only a Part of a Building," 1978.
[7]*APB Opinion No. 18,* "The Equity Method of Accounting for Investments in Common Stock," 1971.

HOW LEASEBACKS BEAT THE HIGH COST OF MONEY

THE CORPORATE USE of sale-leasebacks and other real estate leasing schemes traditionally has been confined to hotels and retail and restaurant chains—businesses that need to keep capital fluid rather than tied up in real estate. But now, major industrial companies and utilities also are choosing to lease rather than to own buildings, as high interest rates, volatile capital markets, and surging construction costs raise the cost of capital and restrict its availability.

Late in December, Anheuser-Busch Cos. closed a $25 million lease deal for a new office building in St. Louis. And more companies are following suit. "We've got more negotiations in process than ever before," says Joel M. Pashcow, chairman of American Property Investors, an affiliate of Integrated Resources Inc. and one of the nation's largest packagers of sale-leasebacks.

Rising interest costs provide the main reason for lease financing. "A company can save 200 basis points or more when it finances a property with a sale-leaseback instead of going to the capital markets," says Jay M. Messer, chairman of United Trust Fund, a Miami-based real estate investment firm that specializes in sale-leasebacks. And in some cases, the savings can be even more spectacular: Georgia Power Co. of Atlanta financed its new $70 million headquarters at an effective cost of 8.2%, says Romney E. Scott, vice-president of economic services, while the uitlity's first mortgage bonds sell at a yield of near 15%.

Tax advantages. In a typical sale-leaseback, an office building will be sold to or constructed by a group of investors who can realize tax advantages. Investors are typically near the 70% federal tax ceiling and so "can take better advantage of the depreciation" than can corporations, whose maximum federal tax rate is 46%, explains R. Marty Burns, manager of corporate pension investments at Anheuser-Busch.

Once constructed, the building is leased to the corporation, often at low front-end payments, which provide tax losses for investors and improve short-term earnings for corporations. "During the early years of the lease term, rental expense can be significantly less than would be the sum of interest and depreciation under the ownership alternative,"

says Thomas J. Healey, managing director of the Project Finance Group at Dean Witter Reynolds Inc.

In other leases, payments can be uniform over the life of the lease and then decline if renewal options are taken. Safeway Stores Inc., which has financed about half its stores this way since 1937, recently signed an agreement that called for "rent constant" for 20 years and then declining rent in the seven optional five-year renewal periods. Harry D. Sunderland, Safeway's senior vice-president of finance, explains that rents traditionally have declined after the investment is recovered. But he sees inflation changing all that: "More and more investors are requiring some hedge against inflation," such as tying rents to sales or to the inflation rate.

Calm growth? Leases can also improve a company's balance sheet. The Anheuser-Busch lease does not appear on the balance sheet because it meets strict accounting criteria as an operating lease, according to Burns. A mortgage or bonds sold to finance the building would, on the other hand, be included on the balance sheet. A lease that Owens-Illinois Inc. plans to sign for the $91 million office building investors are constructing in Toledo—reportedly the largest such deal to date—will also qualify as an operating lease and so will not be capitalized, says G. Walton Cottrell, treasurer. By decreasing the amount of mortgage or other debt a company owes, corporations can often "go into the debt markets more easily later on," says Messer.

"As long as the cost of capital stays high and borrowing is difficult," sale-leaseback activity will expand, says Arthur J. Halleran Jr., vice-president of Boston-based Winthrop Financial Co. But sale-leasebacks could continue to grow even after calm returns to the capital markets. Indeed, Stephen E. Roulac, president of Questor Associates, a San Francisco-based real estate and financial consulting firm, sees the growth of sale-leasebacks as part of a larger trend. "They represent a move toward the integration of real estate financing with traditional corporate financial techniques," says Roulac.

SOURCE: "How Leasebacks Beat the High Cost of Money," *Business Week,* January 12, 1981, pp. 26–27. Reprinted by special permission, © 1981 by McGraw-Hill, Inc.

ness, and other relationships and economic dependencies. Accountants should search for the economic and business purpose of related-party leases in order to report properly the substance of those transactions. This is especially true when the form of the agreement is unusual or is not representative of normal business practice.

Sale-Leaseback

A **sale-leaseback transaction** involves property that is simultaneously sold and leased back by the seller. Many times such arrangements are desirable because a large amount of liquid resources are provided to the seller while the *use* of the sold asset is still retained by the seller-lessee. Standards of accounting for sales with leasebacks are established in *FASB Statement of Financial Accounting Standards No. 28.*[8]

Generally a seller-lessee classifies leases arising in sale-leaseback transactions in accordance with the four classification criteria previously discussed. For a capital lease, any profit on the sale is deferred and amortized in proportion to the amortization of the leased asset; for an operating lease, profit on the sale is recognized in proportion to the related gross rent expense recognized over the lease term. If the fair market value of the asset sold is less than its cost or carrying amount, however, a loss on the sale should be recognized in the period of the sale and leaseback. Any other types of losses on the transaction should be deferred and amortized over the lease term. If only a minor portion of the property is leased back, then profit or loss on the sale is generally recognized in a normal fashion at the time of the transaction.

CONCLUDING REMARKS

We have seen that financial accounting and reporting for leases is a highly technical and specialized area. The principal problem in accounting for leases is identifying those that are, in fact, rentals of property and those that represent sales and purchases of the service potential embodied in the leased asset. The FASB has attempted to resolve this classification problem by identifying characteristics in leases which it believes signal the intent of the parties to the lease to enter into a transaction in which significant property rights are transferred from the lessor to the lessee. An important point to remember, however, is that the passage of legal title is *not* a requirement for lease capitalization. Thus, accounting for leases represents a clear application of the modifying convention of substance over form which we introduced in Chapter 2.

> **Substance over Form**

Although we have discussed many of the problems and concepts inherent in the application of authoritative accounting pronouncements, an almost endless variety of specific issues relate to various specialized types of leases. Students are encouraged to review the material in this chapter and to consult the various authoritative pronouncements for additional insights into this difficult area of practice.

---

[8]*FASB Statement of Financial Accounting Standards No. 28,* "Accounting for Sales with Leasebacks," 1979.

KEY POINTS

1. The first step in accounting for leases requires lessees and lessors to classify leases according to the substance of the transaction.

2. Lessees classify leases as either operating leases or capital leases. Operating leases result in the recognition of only rent expense. Capital leases require the recognition of the asset acquired, liability incurred,

amortization or depreciation expense on the asset, and interest expense on the liability.

3. Lessors classify leases as either operating leases or one of three types of capital leases (direct-financing, sale-type, and leveraged leases).

4. A capital lease must meet at least one of four separate tests: (1) It must contain a transfer of title; (2) it must contain a bargain purchase option; (3) the lease term must be equal to or greater than 75% of the asset's remaining life; or (4) the present value of the minimum lease payments must exceed 90% of the leased asset's fair market value.

5. In addition to meeting one of the four initial classification tests, lessors must apply two additional tests to classify a lease as a capital lease: (1) Rent collectibility must be reasonably certain, and (2) future costs must be reasonably predictable.

6. Lessees recognize rent expense on operating leases on a straight-line basis over the lease term.

7. Lessees recognize depreciation or amortization expense, interest expense, and executory costs on capital leases over the lease term. The capitalized lease liability is separated into current and noncurrent components in the balance sheet.

8. Lessors recognize rental revenue on a straight-line basis and continue to depreciate assets subject to operating leases.

9. Lessors recognize only interest revenue on direct-financing and leveraged leases, whereas gross profit and interest revenue are recognized on sales-type leases. Investments in capital leases (or lease receivables) are subject to current and noncurrent balance sheet classifications.

10. Since land has an unlimited life for financial reporting purposes, accounting for real estate leases is more complicated than accounting for other leases.

11. Many other unusual circumstances in regard to leasing activities require careful consideration and analysis in order to properly report such transactions.

APPENDIX A LEVERAGED LEASES

Leveraged leases, a term that applies only to lessors, have been used more and more during the past few years. This increase is a response to the increasing burden of income taxes and to a desire by lessors to avoid reporting the large liabilities that result from the acquisition of property which, in turn, is leased to others under long-term leases. From the standpoint of lessees, leveraged leases are accounted for in the same manner as nonleveraged leases. As a practical matter, leveraged leases are **direct-financing leases** that meet the following four additional criteria:

1. The lease must involve three parties: a lessee, a long-term creditor, and a lessor.
2. The financing provided by the long-term creditor must be nonrecourse as to the general credit of the lessor. (The leased property may, however, be subject to a mortgage.)
3. The lessor's net investment in the lease must decline in the early years of the lease and rise during the later years before final elimination.
4. The lessor's investment tax credit must be deferred and allocated to income over the life of the lease.

If any of these criteria are not met, the lease is considered a direct-financing lease rather than a leveraged lease. Before proceeding to a technical discussion of the financial accounting and reporting aspects of leveraged leases, we need a firm conceptual understanding of the economic sense and meaning of this form of leasing.

We should understand why a leveraged lease is desirable from the lessor's perspective, because an appreciation of the benefits will aid the comprehension of the related accounting and reporting practices. The following list enumerates some of the benefits to the lessor:

1. Most funds necessary to purchase the leased asset are supplied by a long-term creditor.
2. The loan from the long-term creditor provides for no recourse against the lessor.
3. The lessor receives the benefit of the investment tax credit related to the leased asset.
4. During the early years of a leveraged lease arrangement, the tax deductions for depreciation on the leased asset and interest on the nonrecourse long-term debt exceed the annual lease rental revenue. This process provides the lessor with excess deductions to be applied against other taxable income. This advantage relates exclusively to the tax benefits of leveraged leasing.
5. At the conclusion of a leveraged lease agreement, the equipment is returned to the lessor.

We now turn our attention to recording a leveraged lease. The following entry reflects the appropriate financial accounting for a leveraged lease.

Rentals Receivable	XXX
Investment Tax Credit Receivable	XXX
Estimated Residual Value	XXX
Unearned and Deferred Revenue	XXX
Cash	XXX

The Rentals Receivable account is debited with the gross amount of lease rentals *net* of the total amount of the nonrecourse debt. The investment tax credit applicable to the leased asset is recorded as a receivable by the lessor, because the benefit of the investment tax credit for federal income tax purposes is retained by the lessor in a leveraged lease. The estimated residual value is the fair value of the leased property at the end of the lease term. This amount accrues to the benefit of the lessor in a leveraged lease.

The Unearned and Deferred Revenue account consists of: (1) the estimated pretax deferred revenue after deductions for the initial direct costs remaining to be allocated to income over the lease term; and (2) the investment tax credit remaining to be allocated to income over the lease term. The cash amount of the transaction represents the investment made by the lessor in the leased property and is the difference between the cost of the leased property and the non-recourse debt secured from the long-term creditor.

The long-term debt is offset against the lease receivable. From the perspective of the lessor this treatment is desirable, because it improves the debt/equity ratio and rate of return on assets employed. Such an offsetting of receivable and payable is appropriate only because the creditor financing is nonrecourse to the lessor.

Subsequent to this entry the investment tax credit receivable is "collected" in the form of a reduced income tax payment, and the net investment in the lease declines. Furthermore, for income tax purposes the leased asset is depreciated and interest expense on the nonrecourse liability to the creditor is recognized. Rent revenue is recognized as cash is received. From an income tax perspective, therefore, the lease is treated much like an operating lease. As a result, timing differences emerge, because in the early years of the leveraged lease the tax expense computed on the accounting income exceeds the taxes payable, which are based on the tax return. The resulting deferred credits serve to reduce the investment balance. These aspects of leveraged leasing cause a fluctuating investment balance. The *tax effects* of accelerated depreciation, along with interest expense on the third-party creditor loan, contribute to a declining investment account as a result of tax losses and emerging deferred tax credits in the early years of the lease. Later—when depreciation charges and interest expense become less than the gross lease payments being received—taxable income is recognized, thereby causing the deferred tax credits to reverse, and the Investment account rises.

Perhaps the most difficult aspect of leveraged leases to apply involves the calculation of the appropriate rate of interest for use in allocating total cash flow between the recovery of the investment and interest revenue. The amortizing rate represents that rate of interest which, when applied to the investment account balance in the years that the net investment is positive, will fully amortize the unearned revenue as interest revenue over the life of the lease. This process usually involves considerable trial and error, because: (1) the annuity amounts (cash flow after taxes) are uneven; (2) during some years the investment account may be zero or negative (so the annuity series is broken); and (3) the residual value represents a single amount at the conclusion of the lease. In complex situations computers are frequently used to ascertain the appropriate amortizing rate for leveraged leases.

APPENDIX B OTHER SPECIAL LEASING ISSUES

INCEPTION OF A LEASE

In certain cases, notably the construction industry, leases are commonly negotiated and signed before construction of the property. In such cases, the inception of the lease may precede the beginning of the lease term by a long time.

When an asset subject to a lease must be constructed, many of the underlying estimates and decisions related to the lease are made and written into the lease agreement prior to the beginning of the lease term. Financial accounting and reporting for the lease reflects these circumstances. Conversely, many elements of a leasing arrangement may not be known until the construction is completed and the lessee assumes the use of the property. Furthermore, in many leases of this type, escalation and limitation clauses may be present to protect the lessor or the lessee or both.

Exhibit 21–11 reflects the appropriate point in time at which various estimates, costs, and other relevant items should be established for purposes of financial accounting and reporting for the lease in question.[9]

SUBLEASES

The central concept establishing subleases as a special type of lease is that a lessee, now acting as a sublessor, cannot transfer to a sublessee more rights than were obtained in the original lease. (After all, one cannot transfer more rights than one possesses.) For example, if a lessee treats an original lease as an operating lease, then any sublease of that property granted by the orig-

inal lessee (now a lessor) can be considered only as an operating lease.

If the original lease contains either a transfer of ownership or a bargain purchase option, then the original lessee (now a sublessor) is presumed to have acquired all of the rights associated with the property. The original lessee is therefore capable of completely disposing of those rights. In determining the proper classification of a sublease, the lessor should apply all four of the normal classification criteria and the two additional criteria of rent collectibility and cost predictability if either a transfer of ownership or bargain purchase option is in the original lease.

The lease classification criteria are also important for subleases. The transfer-of-title and bargain-

[9]*FASB Statement of Financial Accounting Standards No. 23,* "Inception of the Lease," 1978.

EXHIBIT 21–11
Accounting Issues When Execution of Lease Agreement Precedes Construction/Acquisition

	Item	Lessee	Lessor
Without Escalation Clause*	Fair market value estimate	Before construction	Before construction
	Cost	Before construction (PV of MLPs)	After construction
	Incremental borrowing rate	Before construction	Not applicable
	Implicit rate of return	Before construction	Before construction
	Residual value estimate	Not applicable (if accruing to lessee, included in MLPs)	Before construction
	Estimate of cost uncertainties	Not applicable	After construction
	Receivable collectibility	Not applicable	Before construction
With Escalation Clause*	Fair market value estimate	After construction	Before construction
	Cost	Before construction (PV of MLPs)	After construction
	Incremental borrowing rate	Before construction	Not applicable
	Implicit rate of return	After construction	Before construction
	Residual value estimate	Not applicable (if accruing to lessee, included in MLPs.)	After construction
	Estimate of cost uncertainties	Not applicable	After construction
	Receivable collectibility	Not applicable	Before construction

*An escalation clause allows minimum lease payments to change if certain conditions change. For example, lease payments may vary with price level changes.

purchase-option criteria assume a greater significance than the length-of-lease-term and amount-of-lease-payment criteria. If the original lease does not transfer title to the lessee, a sublease of the property from that lessee cannot contain a transfer of title to a sublessor. If either the length of lease term or the amount of lease payment criterion is met in the original lease but neither a transfer of title nor a bargain purchase option is

provided, then the sublease should be subjected only to new length of lease term and amount of lease payment criteria. Of course, the new rent collectibility and cost predictability tests must also be met.

However, sublessees incur no problems in accounting for subleases that are not encountered in any other leasing arrangements, and, therefore, they apply normal classification procedures.

QUESTIONS

21–1 The issue of "substance versus form" is central in financial accounting and reporting for leases. Discuss the issue of substance and form as it relates to lease accounting.

21–2 Name the usual two parties to a lease and describe their roles.

21–3 What is a capital lease? Under what circumstances do lessees classify leases as capital leases? If a lease fails to meet the requirements for a capital lease, what type of lease is it?

21–4 Under what circumstances are certain leases classified as sales-type leases by lessors?

21–5 How should a lessee account for and report a capital lease?

21–6 How should lessors account for and report sales-type leases?

21–7 What disclosures of capital leases are required in the financial statements of lessees?

21–8 What financial-statement disclosures of operating leases are required of lessees?

21–9 What happens in a sale-leaseback transaction? Discuss the event from the perspective of both parties to the lease.

21–10 Mark Company is a major automobile dealer and is required to lease large parking lots to house its inventory of automobiles. The owner, Mark Williams, has approached you about the accounting problems he faces in regard to these leases. You ascertain that several of the leases contain bargain purchase options while several others do not. Discuss the classification and accounting problems presented by these real estate leases.

21–11 Application of *FASB Statement of Financial Accounting Standards No. 13*, "Accounting for Leases," will generally result in symmetrical treatment of the same lease by both lessee and lessor (i.e., both will treat the same lease as an operating lease or as some form of capital lease). Give two examples of circumstances and situations in which a departure

from this general rule may arise.

21–12 An estimate of residual value is necessary under certain circumstances when applying *SFAS No. 13*. Under what circumstances is it necessary for a lessor and lessee to estimate residual value?

21–13 What are initial direct costs? When is it important to determine initial direct costs under a lease? Explain your answer.

21–14 Indicate whether the following statements are true (T) or false (F) in regard to leases.

[a] The unguaranteed residual value accrues to the lessor only if the lease contains a bargain purchase option.

[b] Changes in residual value estimates should be treated prospectively if gains or losses are indicated by revaluation.

[c] For a capital lease, initial direct costs incurred by lessees should be deferred and allocated over the lease term in proportion to depreciation recognized on the leased asset.

[d] Leveraged leases require third-party creditor involvement unless the lessee guarantees the residual value of the asset.

[e] Salespersons' compensation should never be included in initial direct costs, because it represents a selling expense and is not related to the initial direct costs of executing the lease.

[f] For a sales-type lease, the lessor should use the incremental borrowing rate of the lessee, if known, to alter the present value of the gross investment in the lease.

[g] From the lessor's perspective, minimum lease payments should include the residual value guarantee of the lessee.

[h] Profit or loss indicated by the sale in a sale-leaseback transaction should always be deferred unless the fair value of the property at the time of the transaction is less than its undepreciated cost.

[i] From the lessee's perspective, a lease of land will not result in a capital lease even when the lease

contains a bargain purchase option.

[j] Under direct-financing leases, an amount equal to the initial direct costs shall be transferred from unearned income and recognized as earned in the same period.

21–15 Indicate whether the following statements are true (T) or false (F) in regard to leases.

[a] Under a leasing arrangement, it is possible for lessees to amortize as an expense the full cost of a leased asset, including land and residual values.

[b] If the original lessee enters into a sublease or if the original lease agreement is sold or transferred by the original lessee to a third party, the original lessor must reevaluate his accounting treatment of the lease and make adjustments as required by the sublease arrangement.

[c] If a lease involving real estate also includes equipment, the portion of the minimum lease payments applicable to the equipment element of the lease shall be estimated by whatever means are appropriate in the circumstances.

[d] From the standpoint of the lessee, leveraged leases shall be classified and accounted for in the same manner as nonleveraged leases.

[e] During the term of a capital lease, each minimum lease payment shall be allocated between a reduction of the obligation and interest expense in order to produce a constant periodic rate of interest on the remaining balance of the obligation.

[f] The lessee usually records a capital lease as an asset and an obligation at an amount equal to the current cost of the leased property.

[g] Any profit or loss experienced by the seller-lessee in a sale-leaseback transaction must be included in income at the date of the lease agreement.

[h] A lessor must be a manufacturer or dealer to realize a profit (or loss) at the beginning of a lease that requires application of the sales-type lease accounting.

[i] Under an operating lease, the lessee assigns rent expense to the periods benefiting from the use of the asset and does not record the commitment to make future payments.

[j] When the lessee accounts for a capital lease, the amortization of the asset and the discharge of the lease obligation should be handled in a consistent manner over the same number of accounting periods.

21–16 High Rise Corporation owns a large building complex and leases portions of the complex for offices, retail stores, and a bank. High Rise substantially alters the physical layout of a part of the complex to induce Carolyn's Clothes, a high-fashion retailer, to sign a five-year lease. How should the costs of altering the building be treated if the following conditions are true?

[a] Tenants subsequent to Carolyn's Clothes will probably find the alterations desirable.

[b] Tenants subsequent to Carolyn's Clothes will not be able to use the facility until the modifications are removed.

21–17 Leasing activity has been increasing in our economy for some time. What are three reasons that help explain the popularity of leasing as a means of acquiring the service rights of an asset?

21–18 (Appendix A) *SFAS No. 13* explicitly defines a "leveraged lease" and prescribes the accounting practice for this type of lease. Describe the criteria that must be met for a lease to be classified as a leveraged lease.

21–19 (Appendix B) What is the difference between the beginning of the lease term and the inception of the lease? Why is it important to distinguish between the two?

CASES

C21–1 Kimberly Company, a lessee, leases facilities to use as retail clothing stores. Some of the leases are classified as operating leases and others are considered capital leases. However, Kimberly must alter every site through a series of improvements to the leasehold.

Instructions

Discuss the manner in which these leasehold improvements should be treated for purposes of financial reporting. Discuss each lease classification from the perspective of initial recording and any subsequent entries for leasehold improvements.

C21–2 Moore Company leased equipment from Johns Company. The classification of the lease makes a difference in the amounts reflected on the balance sheet and income statement of both Moore Company and Johns Company.

Instructions

[a] What criteria must be met by the lease in order for Moore Company to classify it as a capital lease?

[b] What criteria must be met by the lease in order for

Johns Company to classify it as a sales-type or direct-financing lease?

[c] Contrast a sales-type lease and a direct-financing lease.

(AICPA adapted)

C21-3 The controller of Kotter Kopper Kettles, in discussing various financing alternatives, made the following statement:

Leasing is consistently the most attractive method of financing. Not only does it normally provide 100% financing with no down payment or compensating balance requirements, it also allows us to acquire only the particular asset rights we want. For example, we may not wish to buy an asset because we have no wish to own it when it becomes obsolete. The lessor is better able to dispose of such an asset at the end of a lease than we would be if we had bought it outright. Furthermore, we avoid tying up our cash unnecessarily. Therefore, the asset we lease, as well as the cash we conserve, can both be used productively. Finally, our balance sheet appears more favorable, because we do not record additional liabilities or lose liquidity when we lease assets.

Instructions

Evaluate the controller's comments.

C21-4 Estes Corporation entered into a lease arrangement with Bayless Leasing Corporation for a certain machine. Bayless's primary business is leasing; it is not a manufacturer or dealer. Estes will lease the machine for three years, which is 50% of the machine's economic life. Bayless will take possession of the machine at the end of the initial three-year lease and lease it to a smaller company that does not need the most current version of the machine. Estes does not guarantee any residual value for the machine and will not purchase the machine at the end of the lease term.

Este's incremental borrowing rate is 10%, and the implicit rate in the lease is 8.5%. Estes has no way of knowing the implicit rate used by Bayless. Using either rate, the present value of the minimum lease payments is between 90% and 100% of the fair value of the machine at the date of the lease agreement.

Estes has agreed to pay all executory costs directly. No allowance for these costs is included in the lease payments.

Bayless is reasonably certain that Estes will meet all lease payments, and because Estes has agreed to pay all executory costs, there are no important uncertainties regarding costs to be incurred by Bayless.

Instructions

[a] With respect to Estes, answer the following:

[1] What type of lease has been entered into? Explain the reason for your answer.

[2] How should Estes compute the appropriate amount to be recorded for the lease or asset acquired?

[3] What accounts will be created or affected by this transaction? How will the lease or asset and other costs related to the transaction be matched with earnings?

[4] What disclosures must Estes make regarding this lease or asset?

[b] With respect to Bayless, answer the following:

[1] What type of lease has been entered into? Explain the reason for your answer.

[2] How should this lease be recorded by Bayless? How are the appropriate amounts determined?

[3] How should Bayless determine the appropriate amount of earnings to be recognized from each lease payment?

[4] What disclosures must Bayless make regarding this lease?

(AICPA adapted)

C21-5 Doss Corporation is a diversified company with nationwide interests in commercial real estate developments, banking, copper mining, and metal fabrication. The company has offices and operating locations in major cities throughout the United States. The corporate headquarters for Doss is located in a metropolitan area of a midwestern state, and executives connected with various phases of company operations travel extensively. Corporate management is presently evaluating the feasibility of acquiring a business aircraft that can be used by company executives to expedite business travel to areas not adequately served by commercial airlines. Proposals for either leasing or purchasing a suitable aircraft have been analyzed, and the leasing proposal was considered to be more desirable.

The proposed lease agreement involves a twin-engine turboprop Viking that has a fair market value of $900,000. This plane would be leased for a period of 10 years beginning January 1, 1984. The lease agreement is cancelable only upon accidental destruction of the plane. An annual lease payment of $127,600 is due on January 1 of each year; the first payment is to be made on January 1, 1984. Maintenance operations are strictly scheduled by the lessor, and Doss Corporation will pay for these services as they are performed. Estimated annual maintenance costs are $6,200. The lessor will pay all insurance premiums and local property taxes, which amount to $3,600 annually and are included in the annual lease payment of $127,600. Upon expiration of the 10-year lease, Doss Corporation can purchase the Viking for $40,000. The estimated useful life of the plane is 15 years, and its salvage value in the used-plane market is estimated to be $100,000 after 10 years. The salvage value probably will never be less than $75,000 if the engines are overhauled and maintained as prescribed by the manufacturer. If the purchase option is not exercised, possession of the plane will revert to the lessor, and there is no provision for renewing the lease agreement beyond its termination on December 31, 1993.

Doss Corporation can borrow $900,000 under a 10-year term loan agreement at an annual interest rate of 12%. The lessor's implicit interest rate is not expressly stated in the lease agreement, but this rate appears to be approximately 8% based on 10 net rental payments of $124,000 per year and the initial market value of $900,000 for the plane. On January 1, 1984, the present value of all net rental payments and the purchase option of $40,000 is $800,000 if the 12% interest rate is used. The present value of all net rental

payments and the $40,000 purchase option on January 1, 1984, is $920,000 if one uses the 8% interest rate implicit in the lease agreement. The financial vice-president of Doss Corporation has established that this lease agreement is a capital lease as defined in *Statement of Financial Accounting Standards No. 13*, "Accounting for Leases."

Instructions

[a] What is the appropriate amount that Doss should recognize for the leased aircraft on its statement of financial position after the lease is signed?
[b] Without prejudice to your answer in [a], assume that the annual lease payment is $127,600 (as stated in the preceding information), that the appropriate capitalized amount for the leased aircraft is $1,000,000 on January 1, 1984, and that the interest rate is 9%. How will the lease be reported in the December 31, 1984, statement of financial position and related income statement? (Ignore income tax implications.)
[c] Explain the four factors which differentiate a capital lease from an operating lease.

(CMA adapted)

EXERCISES

E21–1 Johnson Company agreed to lease a building from Acme Corporation on January 1, 1985, for three years. There is no renewal option, and no purchase option is exercisable. The building, with a book value of $300,000, has a remaining useful life of eight years and no salvage value. Johnson's incremental borrowing rate is 10%, and the company has no knowledge of Acme Corporation's implicit rate. Payments of $85,000 per year are due on December 31 of each year. Johnson and Acme both use straight-line depreciation.

Instructions

Record this transaction for 1985 on Johnson's books and Acme's books.

E21–2 Hodgkins Corporation leased Lewis Corporation's machinery with a sales price of $300,000. Hodgkins's interest rate was 10% and the lease was for eight years with payments due at the end of each year for the life of the lease. Title is transferred to Hodgkins at the end of the lease.

Instructions

Compute the annual payment required by the lease.

E21–3 On July 1, 1985, King Company leased a new

building valued at $4,000,000 to Prince Company for five years. Five equal payments of $250,000 are due on December 31 of each year starting in 1985. Depreciation is calculated on a straight-line basis by both parties, and the building has an expected useful life of 25 years. A full year's depreciation is taken in the year a new asset is acquired.

Instructions

Prepare journal entries to record all aspects of this transaction for 1985 on Prince Company's books and King Company's books.

E21–4 On April 1, 1984, Jackson Corporation leased assets with a book value of $1,000,000 to Long Corporation for three years for an annual lease payment of $150,000 due each March 31. The equipment has a useful life of 17 years left, and at the end of the lease the equipment returns to Jackson. Long Corporation has an incremental interest rate of 10% but has no knowledge of Jackson Corporation's implicit rate. Depreciation is recorded on a straight-line basis.

Instructions

Record this transaction for Jackson for 1984 and 1985. (Round all amounts to the nearest dollar.)

E21–5 On January 1, 1984, Lessee Company signs a six-year lease with Lessor Company for equipment with annual payments $43,263.07 due on December 31 of each year. The fair value of the equipment and the carrying amount on Lessor's books is $200,000. Lessee's incremental borrowing rate is 9%. The lease is a capital lease; Lessor's implicit interest rate is 8%.

Instructions

Record all lease-related transactions on Lessor's books for 1984 and 1985.

E21–6 Expo Corporation leased equipment from Zu Company on January 1, 1985, for four years on a non-cancelable lease. The equipment cost $1,000,000, which is its fair value at the inception of the lease. All maintenance costs are paid by the lessee, and at the end of the lease the equipment reverts to the lessor. The incremental borrowing rate for the lessee is 12%, and the useful life of the equipment is five years. Annual lease payments are $329,234.54.

Instructions

Prepare a schedule showing the amortization of the lease by Expo over its life.

E21–7 Bok Corporation leased equipment costing $150,000 to White Company for an implied profit of $30,000. Bok's implied interest rate is 10% and the lease is for 10 years, which equals the economic life of the equipment. The lease is noncancelable, costs are predictable, and payment is reasonably assured at the end of each lease year.

Instructions

[a] Determine the annual payment Bok will collect from White Company.
[b] Prepare a journal entry to record the lease on Bok's books.

E21–8 On January 1, 1985, O'Hara Company leased a machine to McClure Company. The lease was for 10 years, which approximated the useful life of the machine. O'Hara purchased the machine for $80,000 and expects to earn a 10% return on its investment, based on an annual rental of $11,836 payable in advance each January 1.

Instructions

Assuming this is a direct-financing lease, prepare the entry that should be made on December 31, 1985, to recognize interest revenue.

E21–9 Hinkle Corporation leases from Gray Com-

pany a building with a book value of $250,000. The building has a five-year useful life remaining. The lease calls for annual payments of $75,000, to be paid at the beginning of the year. The lease has a three-year term and is considered an operating lease. Gray Company spends $10,000 a year on maintenance and uses straight-line depreciation.

Instructions

Record journal entries for Gray Company and Hinkle Corporation on January 1 and December 31 of the first year of the lease.

E21–10 Duval Company buys equipment for $100,000 cash and leases it to Quigley Corporation for three years. Lease payments of $25,000 are to be made at the beginning of each year. At the end of the third year, the equipment is to be returned to Duval Company, when its value is estimated to be $46,000.

Instructions

Approximate the interest rate implicit in the Duval Company lease. (Round computations to the nearest dollar.)

E21–11 On Feburary 20, 1985, Booster, Inc., purchased a machine for $1,200,000 for the purpose of leasing it to others. The machine is expected to have a 10-year life and no residual value; it will be depreciated on the straight-line basis. The machine was leased to Rally Company on March 1, 1985, for four years, at a monthly rental of $18,000. There is no provision for the renewal of the lease or purchase of the machine by the lessee upon expiration of the lease. Booster paid $60,000 in commissions associated with negotiating the lease in February 1985.

Instructions

[a] What expense should Rally record for the year ended December 31, 1985? Show supporting computations.
[b] What income or loss before income taxes should Booster record for the year ended December 31, 1985? Show supporting computations.

(AICPA adapted)

E21–12 On January 1, 1985, Float Corporation signed a 10-year noncancelable lease for certain machinery. The terms of the lease call for Float to make annual payments of $30,000 for ten years, with the title to pass to Float at the end of this period. The machinery has an estimated remaining useful life of 15 years and no salvage value. Because Float uses straight-line depreciation for all of its fixed assets, it accounted for this lease transaction as an installment purchase of the machinery. The lease payments have a present value of $201,302 and an effective interest rate of 10%. Payments are made each December 31.

Instructions

With respect to this capitalized lease, what entries should Float make for 1985? (Round all entries to the nearest dollar and record the lease liability in a single account, net of any discount.)

(AICPA adapted)

E21–13 Rath Company leased equipment to Tobe, Inc., on April 1, 1985. The lease is appropriately recorded as a sale by Rath. The lease is for eight years and expires on March 31, 1993. The first of equal annual payments of $500,000 was made on April 1, 1985. Rath had purchased the equipment on January 1, 1985, for $2,800,000. It has an estimated useful life of eight years with no residual value expected. Rath uses straight-line depreciation and takes a full year's depreciation in the year of purchase. The cash selling price of the equipment is $2,934,000.

Instructions

Assuming an implicit interest rate of 10%, what amounts should appear in Rath's 1985 income statement for this lease?

(AICPA adapted)

E21–14 Alderman Company leased equipment from Burnette Company on July 1, 1984, for an eight-year period expiring June 30, 1992. Equal annual payments of $500,000 are due on June 30. The first payment was made on June 30, 1985. The rate of interest contemplated by Alderman and Burnette is 10%. The cash selling price of the equipment is $2,934,000, and the cost of the equipment on Burnette's accounting records was $2,500,000. The lease is properly accounted for as a sale by Burnette Company.

Instructions

Determine the amount of profit on the sale and the interest revenue that Burnette Company should recognize for the year ended December 31, 1984.

(AICPA adapted)

E21–15 Parsons Company leased equipment to Murray, Inc., on January 1, 1984. The lease is for an eight-year period expiring December 31, 1991. The first of eight equal annual payments of $600,000 was made on January 1, 1984. Parsons had purchased the equipment on December 29, 1983, for $3,200,000. The lease is appropriately accounted for as a sales-type lease by Parsons. Assume that the present value at January 1, 1984, of all rent payments over the lease term, discounted at a 10% interest rate, was $3,520,000.

Instructions

Determine the amount of interest revenue that Parsons will record for 1985, the second year of the lease period.

(AICPA adapted)

E21–16 On January 2, 1984, Lafayette Machine Shops, Inc., signed a 10-year noncancelable lease for a heavy-duty drill press. Annual payments of $15,000 are made at the end of each year, with title passing to Lafayette at the expiration of the lease. Lafayette treated this transaction as a capital lease. The drill press has an estimated useful life of 15 years and no salvage value. Lafayette uses straight-line depreciation for all of its fixed assets. Aggregate lease payments were determined to have a present value of $92,170, based on implicit interest of 10%.

Instructions

For 1984 and 1985, determine the amount Lafayette should recognize as interest expense and depreciation expense. (Round all computations to the nearest dollar.)

(AICPA adapted)

PROBLEMS

P21–1 On January 1, 1985, Cowboy Clothes leases a warehouse in which large amounts of clothing inventory are to be stored. Because the warehouse is located in a high crime area, Cowboy Clothes installs bars on windows and an expensive silent alarm system. The improvements acquired on March 1, 1985, which will not be removed when the lease expires, cost $100,000 and have a useful life of 10 years. The lease on the warehouse is for one year, although the lease contains a renewal option for additional one-year periods, up to a maximum of four renewals. The lease payments under each renewal are to be renegotiated but cannot rise more than 20% each year. Consequently, the option is clearly not a *bargain* renewal option. Cowboy Clothes intends to lease the property throughout the renewal periods. The salvage value of the improvements is $90,000 at the end of one year, $20,000 at the end of five years, and $1,000 at the end of 10 years.

Instructions

In your answers to the following, round amounts to the nearest dollar.

[a] Prepare the entry to record the acquisition of the security devices on March 1, 1985.

[b] Prepare the entry at December 31, 1985, if any is necessary, for the security devices.

P21–2 Alabama Equipment Company signed a six-year lease in which it agreed to pay $12,000 per year for the use of a piece of equipment. At the end of the lease term, the equipment becomes the property of Alabama Equipment Company. The equipment is expected to be useful to the company for eight years.

Lease payments are due each May 1, beginning in 1983. The company's fiscal year is from May 1 to April 30. Management estimates that $700 of each lease payment is designated for executory costs that the lessor pays. The lease was executed on May 1, 1983.

Alabama Equipment Company recently acquired financing at 12% for other equipment it was acquiring.

Instructions

In your answers to the following, round amounts to the nearest dollar.

[a] At what amount should Alabama Equipment capitalize this lease in its balance sheet?

[b] Prepare an amortization table for the recognition of interest expense for the six-year lease term.

[c] Prepare the balance sheet presentation of this lease for Alabama Equipment Company as of April 30, 1985.

P21–3 Joe's Trucking Company manufactures diesel trucks for interstate transportation and leases a number of them to All-the-Way Trucking. The trucks have an estimated life of 16 years and the leases are for 14 years. The normal selling price of each truck is $195,000 and the estimated residual value at the end of the lease is $20,000. All-the-Way will pay all maintenance costs, insurance, and taxes in connection with these trucks. Joe's Trucking paid $170,000 to manufacture each truck. Joe's Trucking also requires an implicit rate of 10%, based on the normal selling price. Payments are assumed to be collectible and are paid at the end of each year. The lease is initiated on January 1, 1985.

Instructions

In your answers to the following, round amounts to the nearest dollar.

[a] What type of lease is this from the viewpoint of Joe's Trucking Company and All-the-Way Trucking?

[b] Prepare an entry to record the lease on Joe's books.

[c] Prepare All-the-Way's initial entry for this lease, using separate accounts for the lease liability and the related discount.

P21–4 Tulip Company leased equipment from Rose Company on October 1, 1985. The lease is appropriately accounted for as a purchase by Tulip and as a sale by Rose. The lease is for eight years and expires on September 30, 1993. Equal annual payments under the lease are $600,000, due on October 1. The first payment was made on October 1, 1985. The cost of the equipment on Rose's accounting records was $3,000,000. It has an estimated useful life of eight years with no residual value. A full year's depreciation is taken in the year assets are acquired by Tulip Company. The rate of interest contemplated by Tulip and Rose is 10%.

Instructions

[a] What expenses should Tulip appropriately record for the year ended December 31, 1985? Show supporting computations in good form and round amounts to the nearest dollar.

[b] What income or loss before income taxes should Rose appropriately record for the year ended December 31, 1985? Show supporting computations in good form and round amounts to the nearest dollar.

(AICPA adapted)

P21–5 Lessor Company leases equipment to Lessee Company for four years. The equipment, valued at $1,000 (which is also the cost of the equipment to Lessor Company), is to be transferred to Lessee on January 1, 1984, and lease payments are to be made on December 31, 1984, 1985, 1986, and 1987 in the amount of $295 per year. Salvage value at the end of the four years is negligible and the property may be bought at the end of the lease by Lessee for $1.

Instructions

In your answers to the following, round all amounts to the nearest dollar.

[a] Determine the appropriate interest rate implicit in this lease.

[b] Prepare necessary entries for Lessor's books on January 1, 1984, December 31, 1984, and December 31, 1985.

[c] Prepare the relevant portion of Lessor's balance

sheet and income statement at December 31, 1985 and 1986. Assume that the appropriate amount of interest associated with the current receivable is the interest included in the next year's payment.

[d] Prepare the necessary entries for Lessee's books on January 1, 1984, December 31, 1984, and December 31, 1985. Assume that the lease is treated as an intangible asset. Lessee Company records the lease liability and the related discount in separate accounts.

[e] Prepare the relevant portion of Lessee's balance sheet and income statement on December 31, 1985 and 1986. Assume that the appropriate amount of interest associated with the current payable is the interest included in the next year's payment.

P21–6 On January 1, 1984, Lessor Company leased equipment costing $700 to Lessee Company. The equipment is valued by Lessor Company at $1,000 for purposes of the lease. Annual lease payments of $295 are made on December 31 for the next four years. There is no salvage value and the equipment may be purchased after the four years for $1.

Instructions

[a] Prepare the necessary entries for Lessor's books at January 1, 1984, December 31, 1984, and December 31, 1985.

[b] Prepare the relevant portion of Lessor's balance sheet and income statement at December 31, 1984 and 1985. Assume that the appropriate amount of interest associated with the current receivable is the interest included in the next year's payment.

[c] Discuss any differences in accounting and reporting that the change in circumstances from P21–5 will cause for Lessor Company and Lessee Company.

P21–7 In 1983 Seidel Food Company signed a long-term lease for new warehousing equipment, including conveyors and lifts. The equipment was installed according to Seidel's specifications and was placed in operation on October 1, 1983.

Seidel could have purchased the equipment for $1.5 million but instead decided on a noncancelable lease with the option to purchase the equipment at the end of the lease. The equipment has an estimated useful life of 20 years.

The terms of the lease are as follows:

[1] Lease period 10 years, October 1, 1983, through September 30, 1993.

[2] Rental payments of $300,000 payable to the lessor on October 1 of each of the first five years of the lease.

[3] Rental payments of $120,000 payable to the lessor

on October 1 of each of the last five years of the lease.

[4] All payments for property taxes, insurance, and maintenance are the direct responsibility of the lessee. (Seidel estimates that the total amount will be $30,000 annually.)

[5] Upon termination of the lease, the lessee has the option to purchase the equipment for $41,250.

Seidel's independent auditor has established that the leased equipment and related obligation should be accounted for as an installment purchase. Seidel uses double-declining balance depreciation for plant assets. The lease yields a 12% rate of return to the lessor. Seidel's incremental borrowing rate exceeds 12%.

Use the following present-value factors in making the necessary computations:

Discount Factors for 12% (rounded)

Period	Present Value of $1.00	Present Value of $1.00 per Period Received at End of Period
1	.89	.89
2	.80	1.69
3	.71	2.40
4	.64	3.04
5	.57	3.60
6	.51	4.11
7	.45	4.56
8	.40	4.97
9	.36	5.33
10	.32	5.65

Instructions

[a] Prepare Seidel's balance sheet presentation of this lease on September 30, 1984. Provide supporting computations in good form.

[b] Prepare Seidel's income statement presentation of this lease for the year ended September 30, 1984. Provide supporting computations in good form.

(CMA adapted)

P21–8 Gorin Corporation leases a truck to Rogers Company for petroleum exploration. Such trucks normally last 10 years, but because of the intense use and primitive conditions in oil exploration, the expected useful life is no more than six years. The terms of the lease and other information are as follows:

Beginning of the lease term	May 1, 1985
Lease term	5 years
Lease payments	$4,000/year, beginning May 1, 1985

Cost of truck to Gorin	
Corporation	$14,000
Fair value of truck on	
May 1, 1985	$16,800
Interest rate implicit	
in the lease	12%
Residual value of asset at	
Apr. 30, 1990 (estimated)	$1,000

There is no bargain purchase option or transfer of title in the lease. No significant uncertainties exist about the collectibility of lease payments or any future costs to be incurred by Gorin.

Rogers Company has an incremental borrowing rate of 18%. Rogers can compute the interest rate implicit in the lease and normally depreciates assets on a straight-line basis.

Instructions

[a] From the viewpoint of Gorin Corporation:
  [1] What type of lease is this? Why?
  [2] Prepare the entries to record the lease at May 1, 1985, and December 31, 1985, and any other entries required during 1985. (Round amounts to the nearest dollar.)

[b] From the viewpoint of Rogers Company:
  [1] What type of lease is this? Why?
  [2] Prepare the entries to record the lease at May 1, 1985, and December 31, 1985, and any other entries necessary during 1985. Rogers records the lease liability in a single account, net of any discount. (Round amounts to the nearest dollar.)

P21–9 Stapleton Company leased an asset to Allbright Company on January 1, 1985. Conditions of the lease and other information include the following:

Lease term	6 years
Annual payments made on	
Jan. 1 of each year,	
including $1,000 of	
executory costs	$11,000
Estimated residual value	
at the end of lease term	$5,000
Initial direct costs	$1,500
Estimated life of property	10 years
Selling price of assets	
comparable to the	
asset leased	$53,500
Interest rate implicit in lease	8%
Incremental borrowing rate	
of lessee	10%
Cost of the asset to lessor	$37,500
Fiscal year of lessor	Jan. 1–Dec. 31
Fiscal year of lessee	Oct. 1–Sept. 30

Allbright is aware of the 8% interest rate implicit in the lease.

Instructions

In your answers to the following, round amounts to the nearest dollar.
[a] Stapleton's accounting:
  [1] Prepare all journal entries during 1985, assuming the lessee guarantees the residual value of the leased property.
  [2] Prepare all journal entries during 1985, assuming the residual value is not guaranteed by the lessee or otherwise.
[b] Allbright's accounting:
  [1] Prepare all journal entries during 1985, assuming the lessee guarantees the residual value of the leased asset.
  [2] Prepare the asset and liability presentations for Allbright's September 30, 1985, balance sheet. Assume that the discount related to the current portion of the liability is the amount of interest to be recognized in the next payment.
[c] Discuss briefly how your answer in [b] would differ, if at all, if the lessee's incremental borrowing rate had been 7% instead of 10%.

P21–10 Doright Corporation, a lessor of office machines, purchased a new machine for $500,000 on December 31, 1984. The machine was delivered the same day to Fabian Company, the lessee. The following information relating to the lease transaction is available:
[1] The asset has an estimated useful life of seven years, which coincides with the lease term.
[2] At the end of the lease term, the machine will revert to Doright, at which time it is expected to have a residual value of $60,000 (none of which is guaranteed by Fabian).
[3] The 10% investment tax credit on the asset cost is retained by Doright and is expected to be realized in its 1984 income tax return.
[4] Fabian is aware of the 12% implicit interest rate on Doright's net investment.
[5] Fabian's incremental borrowing rate is 14% at December 31, 1984.
[6] Lease rentals consist of seven equal annual payments, the first of which was paid on December 31, 1984.
[7] The lease is appropriately accounted for as a direct-financing lease by Doright and as a capital lease by Fabian. Both lessor and lessee are calendar-year corporations and depreciate all fixed assets on the straight-line basis.

Instructions

Compute the following to the nearest dollar and show supporting computations in good form.

[a] The annual rental under the lease. (*Hint:* Determine the *net amount* that must be recovered by Doright, then divide by the appropriate present-value factor.)

[b] The amounts of the gross lease rentals receivable and the unearned interest revenue that Doright should disclose on December 31, 1984.

[c] What expense should Fabian record for the year ended December 31, 1985?

(AICPA adapted)

P21–11 On January 1, 1983, Overton Company entered into a five-year lease with Weeter Company. Overton transferred a machine to Weeter on that date, and Weeter agreed to make annual payments on January 1 of $10,000. The first payment was made on January 1, 1983. Approximately $1,000 of each payment is designated for taxes, insurance, and other costs related to the machine that are to be paid by the lessor.

Overton sells as well as leases machines. The following information relates to Overton's operations:

Normal selling price of machine	$39,710
Costs to manufacture machine	$26,000
Initial direct cost-sales commission	$2,000
Interest rate implicit in lease	10%

Weeter expects the machine to be useful for six years. Weeter has an incremental borrowing rate of 12% and is aware that the rate implicit in the lease is 10%. In addition to the annual $10,000 payments, Weeter has guaranteed the residual value at the end of the five-year lease at $3,500. The lease contains no purchase or renewal options.

Instructions

In your answers to the following, round amounts to the nearest dollar. Assume both companies report on a calendar-year basis.

[a] What is the present value of the lease for both the lessor and the lessee?

[b] What is the proper classification of this lease by the lessee? By the lessor?

[c] Prepare an amortization table appropriate for both the lessor and lessee for the five-year lease term.

[d] Prepare the journal entries for the lessee through

January 1, 1984. Weeter records the lease liability, net of discount, in a single account.

[e] Prepare the journal entries for the lessor through January 1, 1984.

P21–12 Bingham Company has two divisions: the Astor Division, which started operating in 1983, and the Tulip Division, which started operating in 1984. The Astor Division leases medical equipment to hospitals. All its leases are appropriately accounted for as operating leases, except for a major lease entered into on January 1, 1985, which is appropriately accounted for as a sale.

Under long-term contracts, Tulip constructs wastewater treatment plants for small communities throughout the United States. All its long-term contracts are appropriately accounted for under the percentage-of-completion method, except for two contracts which are appropriately accounted for under the completed-contract method because of a lack of dependable estimates at the time of entering into these contracts.

For the year ended December 31, 1985, the following information is available:

Astor Division

Operating Leases. Revenues from operating leases were $800,000. The cost of the related leased equipment is $3,700,000, which is being depreciated on a straight-line basis over a five-year period. The estimated residual value of the leased equipment after five years is $200,000. No leased equipment was acquired or constructed in 1985. Maintenance and other related costs and the costs of any other services rendered under the provisions of the leases were $70,000 in 1985.

Lease Recorded as a Sale. The January 1, 1985, lease recorded as a sale is for a six-year period expiring December 31, 1990. The cost of this leased equipment is $3,500,000. The equipment is estimated to have no residual value at the end of the lease. Maintenance and other related costs and the costs of any other services rendered under the provisions of this lease, all of which were paid by the lessee, were $120,000 in 1985. Equal annual payments of $750,000 are due on January 1. The first payment was made on January 1, 1985. The present value of an annuity of $1 in advance at 10% is as follows:

Number of Periods	Present Value
5	4.170
6	4.791
7	5.355

Tulip Division

Long-Term Contracts — Percentage-of-Completion Method. Long-term contracts recorded under the percentage-of-completion method total $6,000,000. Costs incurred on these contracts were $1,500,000 in 1984 and $3,000,000 in 1985. Estimated additional costs of $1,000,000 are required to complete these contracts. Revenues of $1,740,000 were recognized in 1984 and a total of $4,800,000 has been billed, of which $4,600,000 has been collected. No long-term contracts recorded under the percentage-of-completion method were completed in 1985.

The two long-term contracts recorded under the completed-contract method began in 1984. One is a $5,000,000 contract. Costs incurred were $1,400,000 in 1984 and $1,600,000 in 1985. A total of $3,100,000 has been billed and $2,800,000 collected. Although it is difficult to estimate the additional costs required to complete the contract, indications are that the contract will be profitable.

The second contract is for $4,000,000. Costs incurred were $1,200,000 in 1984 and $2,600,000 in 1985. A total of $3,300,000 has been billed and $2,900,000 collected. Although it is difficult to estimate the additional costs required to complete this contract, a $550,000 loss is expected.

Bingham Company

Selling, general, and administrative expenses exclusive of amounts specified above earlier, were $600,000 in 1985.

Other income, exclusive of amounts specified above, was $50,000 in 1985.

Instructions

Prepare an income statement for Bingham Company for the year ended December 31, 1985, stopping at income (loss) before income taxes. Show supporting computations in good form. (Ignore income tax and deferred tax considerations. Footnotes are not required. Use the rounded present-value factors presented in the problem to make necessary computations.)

(AICPA adapted)

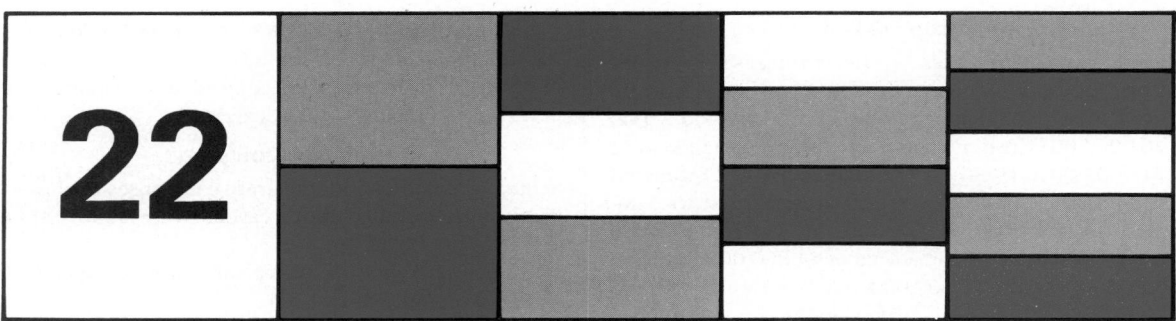

22

ACCOUNTING FOR PENSIONS

Objectives

To describe the essential components of modern pension plans.

To discuss the objectives of financial reporting for pensions by plan sponsors (employers).

To summarize the complicating factors underlying estimates of pension expense and related liabilities.

To describe and illustrate current generally accepted accounting principles (GAAP) for financial reporting of pensions by sponsors.

To illustrate the current disclosure requirements for pensions in the financial statements of sponsors.

To examine likely future trends in financial reporting of pension expenses and liabilities.

THE EVOLUTION AND SIGNIFICANCE OF PENSION PLANS

Pension commitments made by employers to employees are a common characteristic of modern employment agreements. A pension commitment represents an agreement in which an employer promises to make payments to employees after they retire. Pension plans range from relatively simple employer commitments to make specific periodic payments to a retirement fund, to promises to provide a certain level of income to employees after retirement based on a variety of factors. For example, the pension benefits a person receives may be a function of the years of service rendered to the employer, earnings levels prior to retirement, changes in the general price level, and the life span of the retired employee.

Pensions have become increasingly significant in our economy during the last 50 years. Before then the responsibility for one's welfare after retirement was generally considered a function of individual savings and family duty. Events such as the industrial revolution and the great depression, and changing social perceptions of governmental and business responsibilities, increased social awareness of the need to provide relatively comfortable and secure retirement for long-term employees.

Today it is common for an individual's largest asset to be the value of a retirement plan. Employers contribute resources to the plan on behalf of employees. These resources are then available for investment, and investment earnings increase the amounts available for retirement benefits. The assets controlled and invested by retirement plans are enormous, involving billions of dollars. They represent a substantial portion of the available investment capital in our economy. Thus, the activities of pension plans are of interest not only to the businesses and employees directly involved but also to governments and other institutional and individual investors. As a result, much attention is devoted to specific provisions of pension plans, such as eligibility and funding requirements, limitations on investment policies with respect to plan assets, and financial reporting practices.

In this chapter we are concerned with the financial accounting and reporting concepts and standards for several types of pension plans. Specifically, we discuss and illustrate financial accounting and reporting by the business sponsors of various pension plans and the accounting and reporting standards for individual plans.

The relationships and responsibilities of the various parties in a typical employer-sponsored pension plan are illustrated in Exhibit 22–1. The employer has primary responsibility to the employee for the capacity of the pension plan to meet contracted payments. The employer ensures the plan's solvency by making periodic contributions to it. The pension plan is usually administered by a trustee, who is independent of the sponsor and responsible for stewardship of the plan's assets. In addition, the trustee determines actuarially the contributions that are needed to maintain the plan.

THE NATURE OF PENSION PLANS

Pension plans may be broadly classified as either defined contribution plans or defined benefit plans. Financial accounting and reporting is usually much more simple and straightforward for defined contribution plans.

Defined Contribution Plans

Defined contribution plans contain provisions which allow employers to precisely determine the resources that must be contributed to a pension plan each year. Defined contribution plans usually require employers to contribute a percentage of company income or employee salaries to a pension fund. Once the defined contribution is paid, the sponsor has no additional liability to provide pension benefits. An annual contribution (transfer of

---

EXHIBIT 22–1
Relationships and Responsibilities of Parties in a Pension Plan

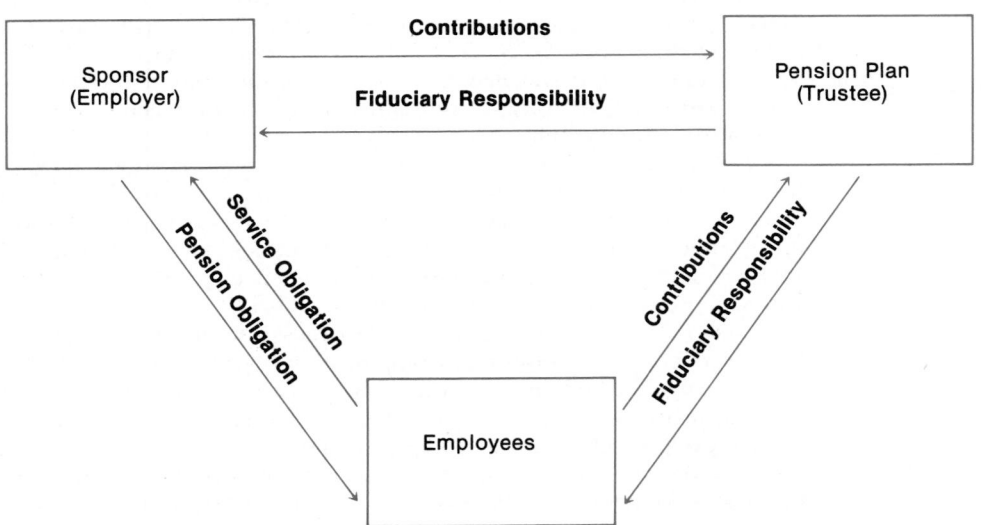

resources) to a plan trustee of the amount computed by the formula is also usually required. Pension expense for the period is measured by the contribution required. Pension benefits are distributed in the future from the assets accumulated in the trust fund, and the employer is not required to provide additional resources. If the defined contribution has not been paid at the balance sheet date, a liability is accrued in that amount. The liability is normally classified as current, because the defined contribution must be paid promptly.

In defined contribution plans the employees accept the risk of the plan's investment performance. In a sense, the accumulated contributions belong to the employees. Therefore, if the plan provides exceptional investment performance, employees share in the gains in the form of increased pension benefits. Likewise, if the plan does poorly, employees share in the losses. The benefits that are ultimately paid to retirees in a defined contribution plan are based on the amounts available, given the defined level of employer contribution and the earnings performance of the plan's portfolio of investments.

Defined Benefit Plans

Most pension plans are referred to as **defined benefit plans** because they specify the benefits to be received by retirees in the future in terms of factors such as employee age, years of service, and salary levels. The benefits are usually expressed in terms of a formula that incorporates the above factors. The formula usually calculates the annual pension cost as a percentage rate times the number of years of service times the final salary (or average of several years' salary) before retirement. As an example, a pension that credited an employee with 1% of final salary for each year worked would grant a pension of 30% of final salary for an employee with 30 years of service.

Defined benefit pension plans describe the benefits employees are to receive, and the related pension expense of the sponsor is based on estimates of benefits to be paid. Employer and employee contributions to the plan plus earnings on investments made with plan assets are designed to provide the benefits promised. Because the liability and related pension expense for defined benefit plans depend on final compensation levels and years of service, the accounting issues become more complex than under a defined contribution plan. Many variables must be estimated to determine the periodic pension contribution required and the pension expense to recognize in the determination of net income. These estimates are commonly referred to as **actuarial assumptions.** They are important considerations in applying **actuarial cost methods** to determine amounts employers must fund and recognize as pension expense in the determination of net income. We discuss actuarial assumptions and actuarial cost methods later in this chapter.

In contrast to defined contribution plans, in defined benefit plans the employer accepts the investment risk of the plan. The employee does not own an accumulated fund, but is promised a contractual pension based on a formula. If the investment performance of the plan is good enough to exceed the actuarially determined pension obligation according to the formula, the employer may reduce further contributions. Likewise, if the plan's investment performance is poor, the employer may have to make additional contributions to ensure that formula benefits are funded. In effect, investment gains and losses accrue to the employer, not the employees.

Other Aspects of Pension Plans

Qualified Plans

If pension plans meet certain criteria contained in the federal income tax laws, substantial tax benefits are available. A **qualified plan** (i.e., one meeting the tax law criteria) has features that allow employees to avoid paying taxes on benefits until they are actually received. Employers are allowed a tax deduction at the time contributions are made to the fund. Earnings on fund assets are also not taxed until distributed to beneficiaries many years in the future. Clearly, our national tax policy encourages well-run pension plans.

Funded and Unfunded Plans

Funded Plans.   Most large pension plans in the United States are either fully or partially funded. A **funded plan** merely means that the resources from which future pension benefits are to be paid have been transferred to a trustee or fiscal agent. If the complete amount that has been recognized as an expense has been transferred to a trustee or fiscal agent, the plan is called **fully funded.** If only part of the expense recognized has been transferred, the plan is considered **partially funded.**

Most private pension plans are subject to the provisions of the **Employee Retirement Income Security Act of 1974 (ERISA).** This law requires companies to establish certain minimum funding, participation, and vesting policies. Employers are required to make annual contributions to pension plans that are sufficient to fully fund the plan in accordance with an acceptable actuarial cost method. If funding in a reasonable fashion does not occur, sponsoring companies are subject to substantial fines and penalties. The sponsoring company usually pays cash to the funding agent, who is then responsible for investing the moneys and paying beneficiaries as retirement or separations occur.

One way of funding a plan is to purchase annuity contracts from an insurance company. The sponsoring company enters into a contract with an insurance company which requires the insurance company to pay the defined benefits as they come due. The sponsoring company pays a premium to the insurance company and, in many cases, effectively transfers the risk of honoring the pension commitments to the insurance company. Such plans are called **insured plans.**

Unfunded Plans.   Pension plans that do not require sponsoring companies to transfer funds to a trustee are considered to be **unfunded.** Unfunded plans are frequently referred to as **pay-as-you-go plans,** because funding takes place when pension benefits are paid to retirees rather than when pension expense was recognized during the period of active employment. Although such plans are rare today, they are still occasionally found in certain industries, such as certain nonbusiness organizations. If the assets set aside to pay the pension plan are retained and controlled by the plan sponsor (employing company), the plan is generally considered *nonfunded*.

Financial Reporting by Employers and by Pension Plans

Issues of financial reporting exist for employers (sponsors) who maintain pension plans and for pension plans themselves. In this chapter we confine our discussion to financial accounting and reporting for pensions by companies that sponsor pension plans. Thus, we emphasize the recognition of pension liabilities, pension expense, and funding procedures for employer-companies. Pension plans, on the other hand, frequently prepare financial statements that are available for employee-participants in the plans and other interested parties. Accounting standards governing the financial reporting of pension plans as separate reporting entities are discussed briefly in Appendix A of this chapter.

BASIC CONCEPTS OF PENSION ACCOUNTING

Financial accounting and reporting for pension plans does not differ conceptually from the accounting practices of similar economic circumstances. As previously observed, a pension plan is merely an arrangement whereby an employer provides a mechanism for employees to receive payments after retirement. In most pension plans the amounts an employee will receive are not precisely known before retirement. Financial accounting and reporting issues, however, are like those for similar circumstances, such as compensated absences for vacation and illness, which we discussed in Chapter 14.

Matching

In essence, an employee renders services for many years prior to retirement, but some of the remuneration for those services is paid only after retirement. However, the cost of those services to the employer should be recognized as an obligation to pay retirement benefits when incurred. In this way, the financial reporting principle of matching is achieved. Stated differently, the cost to a company of an employee's labor should include not only the direct salaries and benefits currently paid but also an amount representing the right to a pension earned by the employee during the year. As an employee works, pension benefits increase each year. The expense and related liability of the company to the employee for these pension benefits requires accounting recognition in the employer's records *at the time the benefits are earned*.

Some controversy remains, however, about the nature of the pension liability. Does the employer's liability extend merely to making adequate contributions to the plan, or does the liability extend to the employee directly? In the former case, a pension liability would arise only for the excess of the actuarially determined contribution over the actual cash contributed to the plan by the employer. In the latter case, the pension liability would remain with the employer until actual cash payments were made to the employee after retirement. Generally accepted accounting principles (GAAP) presently embrace the notion of the liability arising only from contribution shortfalls to the plan. Since many corporations fund their pension plans to avoid contribution shortfalls, many corporate balance sheets do not include pension liabilities. Likewise, the plan assets are not included among the employer's assets. Critics of this approach assert that the employer has an obligation to the employee and not to the plan itself. Therefore, the present value of outstanding pension commitments, as well as the pension assets, should be disclosed on the employer's balance sheet. The pension obligation would then be satisfied only as pension payments from the accumulated pension assets were made to the employees. The Financial Accounting Standards Board (FASB) appears to be moving toward this view in their reevaluation of pension-related accounting issues, which we discuss later in this chapter.

A Conceptual Illustration

As a simple illustration of the concepts underlying a pension plan, consider the pension plan of Burr Corporation. Burr Corporation adopted a pension plan for its single employee, A. Burr. The pension plan was adopted 10 years before A. Burr retires at age 65. When Burr retires, the plan will provide for 10 equal annual payments of $10,000. The first pension payment begins one year after Burr retires. If we assume that the pension plan accumulated interest at 10% compounded annually, the present value (PV) of the pension agreement as of the retirement date is computed as follows:

$$PV = \$10,000 \times [pvoaf_{\overline{10}|\,10\%}]$$
$$= \$10,000\,(6.14457)$$
$$= \$61,446$$

Because A. Burr will receive $10,000 a year, we are dealing with an annuity computation. Because we want to know the value of that annuity at A. Burr's retirement date (after which the payments to him will begin), we need to compute the present value of the annuity. The appropriate present value factor, 6.14457, is taken from the 10% column, 10-period row of Table 6–4.

The amount of $61,446 must be accumulated in the pension plan by the retirement date in order for the plan to be fully funded at the employee's retirement. Burr Corporation has 10 years in which to accumulate this amount. If the corporation wants to make 10 equal annual contributions to the plan, with the first contribution beginning one year from today, the following equation will solve for the amount of the equal contributions (R = required annual contribution):

$$AOA = (R)\,[aoaf_{\overline{n}|\,i}]$$
$$R = \frac{\$61,446}{aoaf_{\overline{10}|\,10\%}}$$
$$R = \frac{\$61,446}{15.93742}$$
$$R = \$3,855.45$$

The amount of an ordinary annuity factor for 10 periods at 10% (15.93742) is taken from Table 6–3.

Burr Corporation can accumulate $61,446 in 10 years by making equal annual contributions of $3,855.45 into a fund that earns interest at 10% compounded annually. Exhibit 22–2 illustrates the accumulation and payment phases of the pension plan. The plan can pay out more than twice the amount of the contributions because of the interest earned.

For financial reporting purposes, the accountant may use the actuarially determined annual contribution as an accurate measure of the pension expense. In this case, pension expense of $3,855.45 would be recognized for each of the 10 remaining years of service. The journal entry each year would simply be:

Pension Expense	3,855.45	
Cash		3,855.45
(To recognize annual		
pension expense.)		

Notice in this example the uncertainties that are assumed away but that would have to be estimated in a real-life situation. We assumed that retirement would begin in 10 years, whereas retirements actually may vary among employees. We assumed an exact payment ($10,000 per year) for an exact period of time (10 years). In reality, pension payments may

EXHIBIT 22–2
Conceptual Illustration of a Pension Plan

$$\$3,855.45 \ [aoaf \ _{\overline{10|}10\%}] = \$61,446 = \$10,000 \ [pvoaf \ _{\overline{10|}10\%}]$$

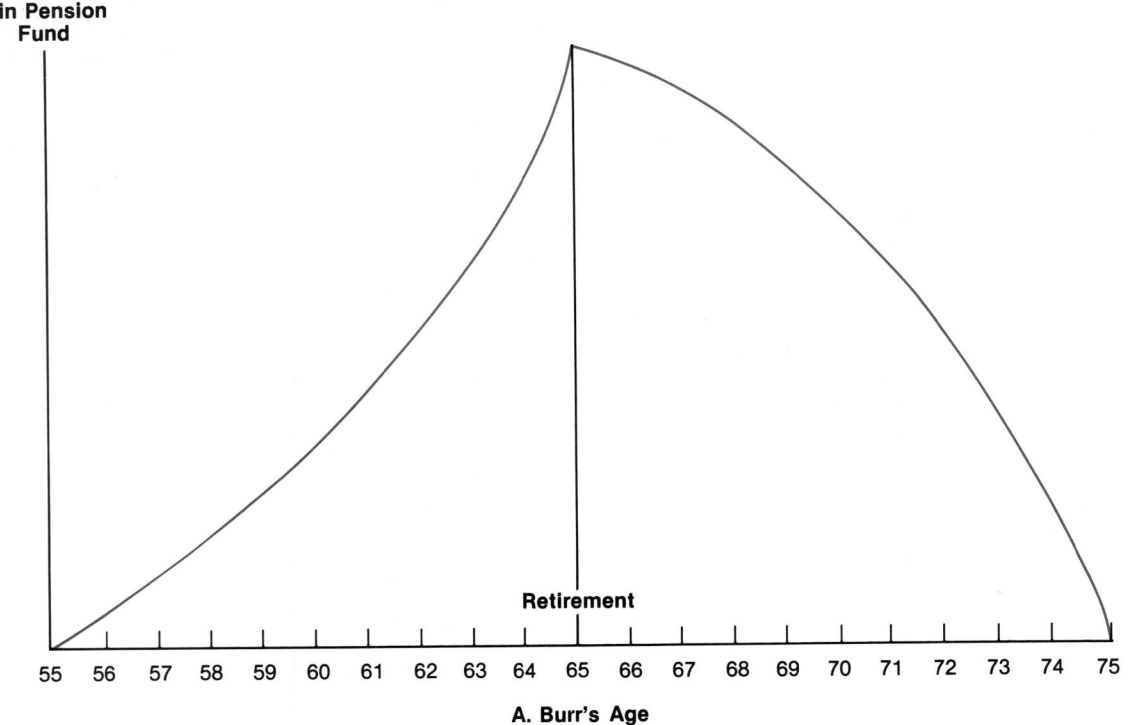

be based on employees' incomes between the time the plan begins and the time of retirement. Also, payments ordinarily continue until the employee's death rather than being limited to a specific number of years. Another uncertainty we assumed away was the interest rate on assets invested in the pension fund (10%). This rate varies, depending on investment policy, economic conditions, and other factors.

Measurement of Pension Expense

Recall from the discussion in Chapter 2 on financial accounting theory and in Chapter 20 on revenue measurement and income presentation that an objective of financial reporting by enterprises is to provide information about earnings and its components. Earnings are composed of revenues, expenses, gains, and losses. The cost incurred by a business each year for its pension commitments represents a type of operating expense. Recall further that **expenses** are defined in *Statement of Financial Accounting Concepts No. 3* as outflows or other using up of assets or *incurrences of liabilities . . . during a period . . .* [and] represent actual or *expected* cash outflows that have occurred or *will eventuate* as a result of the enterprise's . . . operations during the period."[1] (Emphasis added.)

---

[1]*FASB Statement of Financial Accounting Concepts No. 3,* "Elements of Financial Statements of Business Enterprises," 1980, pars. 65–66.

Pension expense certainly meets this definition and is therefore considered a component of income during each accounting period, even though the person earning the pension may not receive benefits for many years. Most accountants agree on these conceptual issues; however, determining the *amount of pension expense* to be recognized during a period in applying the matching principle has created substantial controversy for many years.

<table><tr><td>Matching</td></tr></table>

That an employee earns the right to a pension in the current period but may not receive the payment for many years causes uncertainties. Usually, a formal pension agreement exists setting forth criteria for receiving a pension (e.g., years of service) and the basis on which pension benefits are computed (e.g., salary at date of retirement). Pension plans vary extensively and reflect a "complex array of social concepts and pressures, legal considerations, actuarial techniques, income tax laws and regulations, business philosophies, and accounting concepts and practices."[2] Therefore, many uncertainties exist about the actual cost a business incurs each year in relation to its pension plan. Consequently, many estimates are required to develop the amount used for recording pension expense and the related pension liability. Some of the items which normally must be estimated to properly account for pension commitments include:

1. Employee turnover rates
2. Employee mortality ages
3. Employee compensation levels
4. Employee retirement ages
5. Pension fund earnings

Actuaries are skilled in studying and making such estimates about pension commitments. Accountants commonly rely on actuaries to provide crucial information in estimating pension expense.

---

[2]*APB Opinion No. 8,* "Accounting for the Cost of Pension Plans," 1966, par. 1.

CAN YOU MEASURE THE UNKNOWABLE?

PENSION BENEFITS for white-collar workers are usually based on plan members' pay level for the last few years before retirement. (For union workers, in contrast, the benefits are usually renegotiated with every new contract.) So it follows that if you figure pension benefit liabilities using an estimate of final years' salaries (or final years' contracts), that figure is going to be much higher than if you use current salaries, raising the risk of severely underestimating those liabilities.

This is especially true when you have double-digit inflation. Just keeping up with, say, 10% inflation would double a person's salary in about seven years; that's without merit raises and promotions that would raise the ante even higher.

A 50-year-old executive on the books for $20,000 a year today could, under these circumstances, easily be drawing $50,000 a year on retirement. How inadequate, then, is pension accounting based on his or her present salary.

That's not the only complication. That 50-year-old executive won't start collecting his benefits for 15 years. So, contributions made today will grow to form his annuity. And if interest rates stay in the 13% to 14% range, they will grow quickly. But there's no guarantee of that.

The Financial Accounting Standards Board, the accounting industry's rule-making body, has just stepped into this bucket of worms with a uniform method for pension plan reporting; at present the accounting varies all over the lot.

The FASB has solved the whole salary increase problem by saying that plans cannot take future salary increases into account. In addition, the FASB wants pension plans to use an "accrued benefit" method of accounting. That means, in effect, that in figuring pension expense the company looks only at the pension benefits the worker has accrued so far—it doesn't try to guess the benefits he will earn in the future. Result of these two measures: The company's contribution to the pension fund will generally increase every year as salaries increase and the time remaining to collect interest on the fund decreases.

"Such stupidity!" was the reaction of one respected accountant. He was not alone. Many accountants couldn't believe that, after six years' study and two drafts, this was the best the respected accounting body could do.

The Financial Analysts Federation (FAF), a professional association in New York City, protested to the FASB: "We believe . . . the board has prescribed a uniform method . . . which will substantially, perhaps dangerously, understate pension expenses and reported unfunded pension liabilities."

The FAF's argument boils down to this: If you know that over 20 years a plan needs to accumulate $100 million, isn't it better to show that liability growing at $5 million a year, instead of ignoring the future and funding it at, say, $1 million the first year, $5 million the tenth year and $20 million the last year?

Consider the current situation at Westinghouse. The company's pension plan has been using an accrued-benefit accounting system for the last 20 years. Although the average number of employees declined 15% between 1975 and 1978, to 141,776, the annual pension expense for the company more than doubled, from $66 million to $136 million, over the same years. That was the dirty work of the accrued-benefit system; Westinghouse, like most other companies, *did* take future salary increases into account. Imagine how much worse things would have been if they hadn't.

Right now, unlike Westinghouse, 75% of large companies with pension plan accounting systems look to the future—and do not use an accrued-benefit method—in their calculations. However, many will probably be happy to have their plans seem solid and show higher earnings for now, and run the risk of Westinghouse's problems later.

So, why is the FASB taking this tack? Jules Cassel, FASB's pension plan project manager, explains that the benefits shown under the new system are not intended to reflect the amount that eventually will have to be funded. They will show the status of the plan at that point in time only.

Moreover, Cassel says, these guidlines are for *plans*, not companies. The FASB has a separate project to develop rules for companies' pension reporting.

Robert D. Paul, vice chairman of Martin E. Segal Co., an actuarial firm, makes another point: "The real question being asked here is, 'What are the benefits to date?' There is no commitment to continue a pension plan—no legal commitment. So, the liabilities are only what they are today."

Responds Lee Seidler, an analyst at Bear, Stearns and a member of the FAF committee that studied the FASB proposal: "Fine, but what use is that kind of information? The goal of accounting is to get results which you can use, which means something. The FASB information tells you nothing."

What *do* the FASB's figures show? According to Cassel, they show "a measure of the benefits attributable to service already rendered; like a report card."

As is often the case, the FASB, in its quest for figures that are totally accurate and absolutely irrefutable, winds up showing a world that doesn't really exist.

To be fair, the real world is difficult to describe in accounting terms and even more difficult to predict. Dale Gerboth, an accountant with Arthur Young, argues that salary increases can't be considered because "of the extreme difficulty in projecting inflation rates into the future. Projecting these salary increases would be nearly impossible."

But forecasting is unavoidable. Lee Seidler: "If you're not projecting any inflation, then you're projecting zero inflation. What's the likelihood of that?"

Zero likelihood, obviously. The dilemma of pension plan accounting is a case of damned if you do and damned if you don't. To make statements that do not grossly underestimate liabilities, you have to make subjective predictions that could easily be far off. The aversion to this risk is consistent with the repugnance many historical-cost accountants have for inflationary accounting.

There are never totally acceptable answers to complex questions. But the easiest answer—avoiding the question—is often the least acceptable.

SOURCE: Richard Greene, "Can You Measure the Unknowable?" *Forbes,* March 17, 1980, p. 160. Reprinted by permission of *Forbes* Magazine. © Forbes Inc., 1980.

A distinction must be drawn between the sponsor's accounting recognition of the cost of a pension plan and the funding of a pension plan, both of which require the application of actuarial methods. There is no requirement that the actuarial methods used for recognizing the pension expense and related liability must be identical to the methods used for funding the plan. Although no such requirement exists, many businesses use identical methods and assumptions for accounting and funding purposes. While actuarial cost methods were originally designed to determine the cash contributions required to fund a defined level of pension benefits, these methods may also be appropriate for pension expense recognition if they are systematic, incorporate reasonable actuarial assumptions, and are consistently applied.

Consistency

A Brief History of Pension Accounting

Pension accounting has long been a controversial topic in the accounting profession and among users of accounting information. One of the earliest pronouncements on the subject, *Accounting Research Bulletin No. 47,* stated, in a general way, that pension costs based on current and future services "should be systematically accrued during the expected period of active service of the covered employees, generally upon the basis of actuarial calculations."[3] Little additional guidance was provided to accountants by *ARB No. 47* and, consequently, subsequent accounting practices differed greatly.

In an attempt to clarify accounting principles and narrow the practices applicable to pension plans, the Accounting Principle Board (APB) issued *Opinion No. 8,* which superseded *ARB No. 47* and provided more precise guidance for practitioners. *APB Opinion No. 8,* which we discuss in the following pages, provides for a range of acceptable amounts which may be charged as pension expense. All APB members agreed that "the entire cost of benefit payments ultimately to be made should be charged against income subsequent to the adoption or amendment of a plan and that no portion of such costs should be charged directly against retained earnings."[4] Individual board members differed substantially, however, on how best to measure the annual cost of a given pension plan. Again we observe that there is little controversy over the conceptual aspects of accounting for pensions. The real difficulties lie in putting the concepts into practice. Because of the divergence of views among members, the APB allowed wide latitude in how the cost of a particular pension plan should be measured. At this time many accountants and financial statement users are dissatisfied with the current state of pension accounting and reporting.

A Look to the Future

While *APB Opinion No. 8* remains the current authoritative guide to pension accounting, a search for better practices is currently underway. The FASB is conducting a major project to carefully study the problems of pension accounting and to provide additional accounting guidance to practitioners. In fact, a current preliminary position of the FASB sets forth the tentative conclusions of the FASB about how pension costs should be accounted for and reported. Final issuance of a new accounting standard is anticipated in 1985, although the preparation period may be extended. The problems faced by the FASB are substantial; gaining support and agreement among the business and professional communities is difficult.

Because substantial changes are expected in the foreseeable future, we discuss the provisions of the FASB's preliminary position near the end of this chapter. At that point we will describe the major differences between *APB Opinion No. 8* and the preliminary position and explain the major accounting practices embraced by that position. At this time, we turn to the provisions of *APB Opinion No. 8,* the current guide of accounting practitioners.

FINANCIAL ACCOUNTING AND REPORTING FOR PENSION OBLIGATIONS

As we previously observed, the major issue in accounting for pensions involves estimating the specific amount of pension expense to be recognized by employers during a period in

---

[3]*Accounting Research Bulletin No. 47,* "Accounting for Costs of Pension Plans," 1956, par. 5.
[4]*APB Opinion No. 8,* par. 17.

determining net income. Because of many uncertainties, *APB Opinion No. 8* allows employers to accrue amounts only in a specific range of amounts. Specifically, *APB Opinion No. 8* describes *minimum* and *maximum* amounts that may be properly recorded as a company's pension expense for a particular reporting period.

Both the minimum and maximum amounts are based on the normal cost and past service cost of the pension plan. We define **normal cost** as the annual cost assigned, through an actuarial cost method, to a specific year of service subsequent to the adoption of the plan. **Past service costs** of a pension plan are also determined by actuarial cost methods but relate to the cost of employee service rendered in years prior to the adoption of the plan. When a pension plan is adopted, employers frequently give pension credit to existing employees as a reward for services rendered before adoption of the plan. The costs of granting this credit are referred to as past service costs. In other words, actuarial cost methods are used to determine the total cost of a pension plan for a period of time. This total cost is composed of both past service cost, if any, and the normal cost of the plan. The graph below depicts the relationship between past service cost and normal cost.

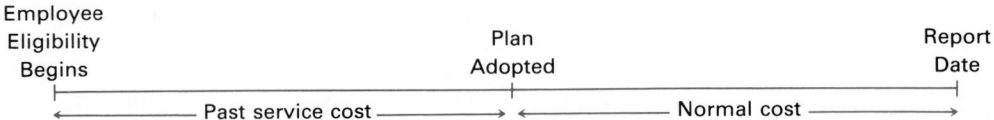

Normal cost is determined periodically (usually annually), beginning with the adoption of the plan. Past service cost is determined once—when the plan is adopted—and relates to the entire past period for which employees are granted credit for services rendered in determining their benefits in the plan.

Past service costs are charged to expense in years subsequent to the adoption of a pension plan even though the costs arise as a result of employee services rendered before the adoption of the plan. Accountants generally agree with this practice because past service costs are incurred to create employee goodwill and reduce turnover in the future by recognizing previous service.

Pension plans frequently undergo **actuarial valuations,** and as more experience is gained about employee turnover, salary levels, and pension fund earnings, some of the previous actuarial estimates may require revision. Changes in the cost of a pension plan related to years prior to a new actuarial valuation or plan amendment are called **prior service costs.** Thus, prior service costs include any remaining unamortized past service costs, as well as the effect of changes in actuarial assumptions for years prior to the new actuarial valuation and the effect of plan amendments. The graph below shows the relationship between past service cost, prior service cost, and normal cost.

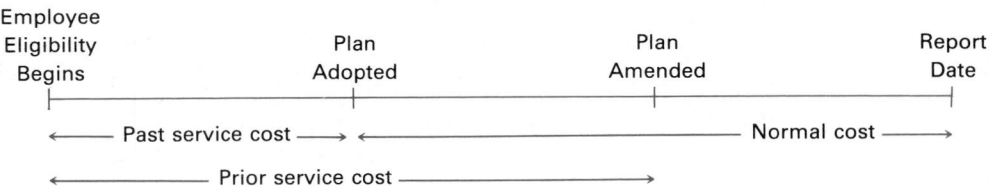

Accountants must also consider the effect of any vested benefits of the plan. **Vested benefits** are pension obligations to employees that are not contingent on the continued employment of the beneficiary. In other words, a vested benefit is a benefit that will be paid to the employee regardless of when or why the employee leaves the company.

We can now summarize the minimum and maximum amounts of pension expense that may be recognized during a period:

The *minimum* (floor) pension cost is the sum of:

1. Normal cost,
2. Interest on any unfunded past or prior service costs, and
3. An allowance for vested benefits in certain cases.

The *maximum* (ceiling) pension cost is the sum of:

1. Normal cost,
2. Ten percent of any past service cost,
3. Ten percent of any increase or decrease in prior service costs resulting from amendment of the plan, and
4. Interest equivalents on the difference between the cumulative pension expense recognized and the amount funded.

The difference between the pension expense recognized in accordance with an acceptable actuarial cost method and the amount funded is reported as a deferred charge or liability in the balance sheet of the sponsoring company. In other words, if a company funds more than the amount of pension expense, prepaid pension expenses arise. Conversely, if a company funds an amount that is less than the pension expense recognized, a liability for unfunded pension expenses is recorded.

Interest equivalents, the fourth item in the computation of maximum pension expense, are required only on the difference between the cumulative pension expense recognized and the amount funded. We stated earlier that companies are not required to recognize pension expense and make funding contributions in exactly the same way. An interest equivalent on the cumulative excess of pension expense recognized over the amount funded (a liability position) increases the maximum pension expense. An interest equivalent on the cumulative excess of amounts funded over pension expense recognized (an asset position) reduces the maximum pension expense.

Illustration of the Minimum and Maximum Provisions

To illustrate the application of minimum and maximum provisions of *APB Opinion No. 8,* consider Blue Max Corporation. Blue Max initiated a pension plan for existing employees on January 1, 1984. On January 1, 1985, Blue Max amended the plan to provide for additional pension benefits. The past service cost related to the plan adoption was $100,000, and the prior service cost related solely to the plan amendment was $80,000. The normal costs for 1984 and 1985 were $10,000 and $15,000, respectively. Past and prior service costs are funded for 12 years, with payments at the end of the year. The recognized pension expense for 1984 was $28,000. None of the pension benefits were vested by the end of 1985. We assume the pension plan earns interest at 10% compounded annually.

Exhibit 22–3 presents the calculations necessary to determine the maximum and minimum amounts for 1985. The minimum includes the interest on the unfunded past and prior service costs. Because the interest on the unfunded past service cost is after one period of funding (1984), the outstanding unfunded balance as of January 1, 1985, must be determined. Footnote "a" of Exhibit 22–3 provides the necessary annuity calculations. The maximum simply includes 10% of the aggregate past and prior service costs, plus interest on the difference between the accumulated pension expense recognized and the amount funded. As of December 31, 1985, the only pension expense recognized is $28,000 from 1984. The amount funded from 1984 is the normal cost of $10,000 plus funding of the past service cost of $14,676. Interest on the difference is $332 as calculated in the exhibit.

Of what relevance are the maximum and minimum amounts? The company must recognize pension expense at one or the other amount, or between the two amounts. If the actuarial cost method produces an amount in this range, the amount is appropriate for determining pension expense for 1985. If the amount is outside that range, either the

---

EXHIBIT 22-3
Blue Max Corporation
Minimum and Maximum Amounts for 1985

	Minimum	Maximum
Normal cost	$15,000	$15,000
Past service cost	9,532[a]	10,000[c]
Prior service cost	8,000[b]	8,000[d]
Interest on the difference between the accumulated pension expense recognized and the amount funded	—	332[e]
	$32,532	$33,332

[a] $100,000 \div [pvoaf_{\overline{12}|10\%}] = \$100,000 \div 6.81369 = \$14,676$ (annual funding of past service cost).

$\$14,676 - (\$100,000 \times 10\%) = \$4,676$ (reduction in unfunded past service cost).

$(\$100,000 - \$4,676) \times 10\% = \$9,532$ (interest on unfunded past service cost for 1985).

[b] $\$80,000 \times 10\% = \$8,000$ (interest on unfunded prior service cost for 1985).

[c] $\$100,000 \times 10\% = \$10,000$.

[d] $\$80,000 \times 10\% = \$8,000$.

[e] $[\$28,000 - (\$14,676 + \$10,000)] \times 10\% = \$332$.

---

maximum or the minimum amount should be used for expense purposes, as appropriate.

Accounting Entries for Pension Expense

A Step-by-Step Process

Accountants must perform several tasks in preparing to make accounting entries for pension cost. These are summarized below:

1. Develop a past service (or prior service) amount. An actuary determines the present value of future benefits expected to be paid as a result of employee services rendered prior to the inception (or amendment) of a pension plan. A complicated actuarial calculation is required.
2. Develop the normal cost amount. An actuary determines the present value of the future benefits expected to be paid as a result of employee services rendered during the current year. This also involves a complicated actuarial computation and must be calculated each year.
3. Establish a policy for amortizing and funding past service costs. (ERISA requires past service costs to be funded over a period not longer than 40 years; the *maximum* amount described in *APB Opinion No. 8* allows amortization of not more than 10% of past service costs per year.)
4. Prepare an amortization schedule based on the policies selected above.
5. Develop accounting entries to report pension costs in the financial statements. (Care must be taken that pension expense falls within the minimum and maximum amounts.)

We will now illustrate the application of these steps in several hypothetical examples. Most of our assumptions remain constant from example to example; some will vary to illustrate different aspects of pension accounting.

Assume that Sayers, Inc., established a pension plan January 1, 1984, 10 years after the company began operations. At the inception of the plan, an actuary determines the present value of the past service costs to be $50,000. The actuary further determines that the normal costs for the two years ended December 31, 1984 and 1985, are $10,000 and $11,000, respectively. We will assume these amounts are funded annually. The actuary also recommends the use of a 6% interest rate. Each of these facts remains constant in the three examples discussed in the following pages. The funding and amortization of past service costs, however, varies in each case.

Funding and Amortization over the Same Period

In this case, assume that Sayers, Inc., decides to amortize (charge to expense) and fund past service costs over a 20-year period, with funding to begin on December 31, 1984. The funding and amortization of past service cost can be visualized as follows:

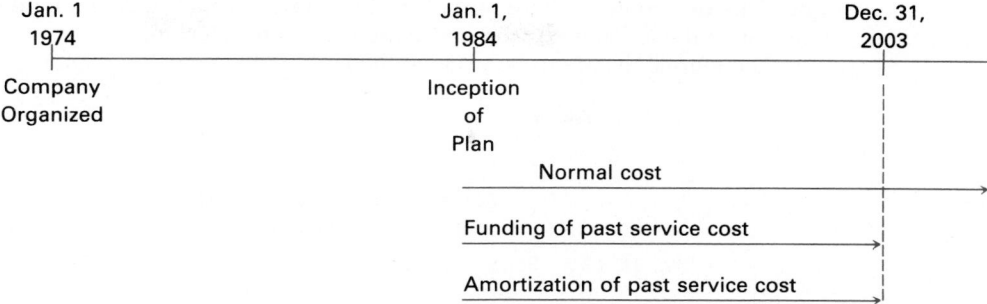

Because funding and amortization of past service cost occur simultaneously, no deferred charges or credits need to be reported on the balance sheet. In order to fund the $50,000 past service cost over a 20-year period, annual payments of $4,359 are required. We determine this amount by using present value techniques. In this case, the present value of an annuity of $1 at 6% for 20 periods is 11.46992 (Table 6–4). By dividing the past service cost ($50,000) by the present value factor (11.46992), we can derive the annuity necessary to execute the funding policy. We will use $4,359 for funding *and* amortizing past service cost because each is accomplished over a 20-year period.

We must verify that the pension expense we have recognized falls between the minimum and maximum amounts established by *APB Opinion No. 8.* Our tentative determination of pension expense for 1984 is $14,359 ($10,000 normal cost, plus $4,359 amortization of past service cost). Recall that the minimum amount to be recorded is the total of normal cost, interest on the unfunded past service cost, and an allowance for vested benefits. In this example, we assume no benefits are vested. The minimum amount for 1984 is computed as follows:

Normal cost		$10,000
Interest on unfunded past service cost:		
Unfunded past service cost at		
the beginning of 1984	$50,000	
Interest rate	6%	3,000
Minimum amount for 1984		$13,000

The maximum amount must also be calculated. Recall that the maximum includes an allocation of past service cost in addition to the normal cost and, in some cases, an interest factor. The following calculation determines the maximum amount for 1984:

Normal cost	$10,000
10% of past service cost	
($50,000 × 10%)	5,000
Interest on any unfunded pension expense recognized	–0–
Maximum amount for 1984	$15,000

The pension expense of $14,359 that we calculated earlier for 1984 falls between the minimum and maximum constraints of $13,000 and $15,000, respectively. Thus, we can record 1984 pension expense at $14,359. Accountants calculate the minimum and maximum amount each year to ensure recording pension expense in accordance with GAAP. We do not calculate these amounts for 1985 at this point. The total of normal cost and amortization of past service cost in 1985 ($11,000 + $4,359 = $15,359) falls within the minimum and maximum amounts, however. In practice, most companies record amounts at or near the maximum because of the impact of ERISA, which specifies funding requirements similar to the amount derived under the maximum calculation.

The journal entries to be made at the end of 1984 and 1985 appear as follows:

Dec. 31, 1984	Pension Expense	14,359	
	Cash		14,359
	(To record pension expense. $10,000 normal cost + $4,359 past service cost amortization.)		
Dec. 31, 1985	Pension Expense	15,359	
	Cash		15,359
	(To record pension expense. $11,000 normal cost + $4,359 past service cost amortization.)		

The credits to cash in the entries above recognize the transfer of cash to the funding agent (trustee). As mentioned previously, under GAAP no assets or liabilities are reported in Sayers's balance sheet at the end of 1984 and 1985 relative to the pension plan. Beginning in the twenty-first year following the adoption of the plan, only the normal cost of each year is reported as an expense and requires transfer to the funding agent. At that time, all past service cost will have been amortized and funded.

Amortizing over a Longer Period than Funding

We will continue to assume the same facts as in the preceding case, except that funding the past service costs will take place over an eight-year period and amortization of the past service cost will take place over a 10-year period.

Because we are using relatively short funding and amortization periods in this illustration, the pension expense we compute does not fall in the minimum–maximum range. Although in practice pension expense must fall in this range, our purpose here is to illustrate the effect of amortization and funding of past service costs over different periods of time. Thus, for purposes of illustration we will overlook the minimum–maximum requirement and deal with shorter time periods.

The funding and amortization of past service cost in this case can be visualized in the following way:

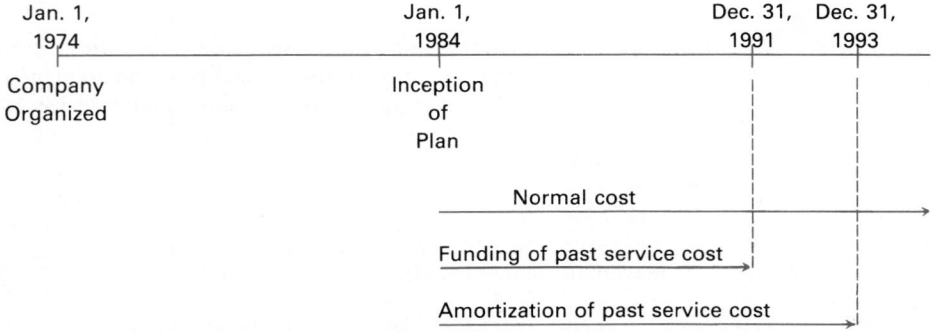

We must first prepare an amortization table to determine the effect of funding past service costs over a shorter period of time than those costs are amortized to expense. We can intuitively observe that a deferred charge (asset) will arise because we are paying cash to the funding agent in amounts *greater than* are being charged to expense. Exhibit 22–4 contains the amortization table which facilitates preparing the necessary accounting entries.

The annual *amortization* amount increases from the amount in the former example because of the shorter amortization period. The specific amount is determined by dividing the present value of the past service cost ($50,000) by the factor for the present value of an annuity of $1 to be paid for 10 years at 6% interest (7.36009 from Table 6–4). The annual amortization thus computed is $6,793.

The annual *funding* requirement also rises due to the shorter funding period of 8 rather than 20 years. We may also calculate the funding amount using similar present value techniques. The required funding amount ($8,052) is calculated by dividing the present value of the past service cost ($50,000) by the present value of an annuity of $1 to be paid for 8 years at 6% interest (6.20979 from Table 6–4).

The following entry should be made at the end of 1984 to record pension expense, report the transfer of cash to the funding agent, and establish the deferred charge resulting from the accelerated funding:

Dec. 31, 1984	Pension Expense ($10,000 + $6,793)	16,793	
	Deferred Charge—Excess of Pension Funding over Pension Expense	1,259	
	Cash ($10,000 + $8,052)		18,052
	(To record 1984 pension expense and funding.)		

The pension expense of $16,793 on the 1984 income statement is the sum of the normal cost ($10,000) and the amortization of past service cost ($6,793). The credit to cash is the sum of the normal cost ($10,000) and the funding requirement ($8,052) for past service cost. The deferred charge appears in the balance sheet among "other assets" or in a separate deferred charge section as a noncurrent asset.

EXHIBIT 22–4
Past Service Cost—Funding over a Shorter Period than Amortization

Year	(1) Annual Amount for Amortization (10 Years)	(2) (Col. 6 x .06) Interest Reduction	(3) (Col. 1–Col. 2) Annual Expense Amount	(4) Funding Amount (8 Years)	(5) Deferred Charge (Col. 4–Col. 3) Current	(6) Deferred Charge Balance
1984	$ 6,793	–0–	$ 6,793	$ 8,052	$ 1,259	$ 1,259
1985	6,793	$ 76	6,717	8,052	1,335	2,594
1986	6,793	156	6,637	8,052	1,415	4,009
1987	6,793	241	6,552	8,052	1,500	5,509
1988	6,793	331	6,462	8,052	1,590	7,099
1989	6,793	426	6,367	8,052	1,685	8,784
1990	6,793	527	6,266	8,052	1,786	10,570
1991	6,793	634	6,159	8,052	1,893	12,463
1992	6,793	748	6,045	–0–	(6,045)	6,418
1993	6,793	375*	6,418	–0–	(6,418)	–0–
	$67,930	$3,514	$64,416	$64,416		

*Rounding adjustment in 1993 to eliminate deferred charge balance.

In 1985 the entry to report pension expense appears as follows:

Dec. 31, 1985	Pension Expense ($11,000 + $6,717)	17,717	
	Deferred Charge—Excess of Pension Funding over		
	Pension Expense	1,335	
	Cash ($11,000 + $8,052)		19,052
	(To record 1985 pension expense and funding.)		

Total pension expense and the transfer of cash each rise because of the increase in normal cost from $10,000 in 1984 to $11,000 in 1985. Notice that the expense reported for the amortization of past service cost is reduced, however, by the interest earned on the assets held by the plan. Pension expense for 1985 is the total of $11,000 normal cost, plus $6,793 amortization of past service cost, less the interest equivalent of $76 (see Exhibit 22–4). This process continues through 1991, when the funding of past service cost is complete. Funding takes place faster than recognition of the expense. Interest revenue is therefore recognized on fund assets resulting from funding greater amounts than are charged to expense. This interest revenue reduces pension expense in the current and future years.

Finally, in 1992 and 1993, years 9 and 10 of the plan, the only cash payment required is for the normal cost of the plan. Past service cost is still being amortized as pension expense in those years, however, and the deferred charge which has been building up in the first eight years is credited in the ninth and tenth years and reduced to zero at the end of 1993. Assuming normal costs of $13,000 and $15,000 for 1992 and 1993, respectively, the pension expense entries for those years are as follows:

Dec. 31, 1992	Pension Expense ($13,000 + $6,045)	19,045	
	Cash		13,000
	Deferred Charge—Excess of Pension Funding over		
	Pension Expense		6,045
	(To record 1992 pension expense and funding.)		
Dec. 31, 1993	Pension expense ($15,000 + $6,418)	21,418	
	Cash		15,000
	Deferred Charge—Excess of Pension Funding over		
	Pension Expense		6,418
	(To record 1993 pension expense and funding.)		

Amortizing over a Shorter Period than Funding

We will continue to assume the same facts as in the previous illustration, except that the funding of past service costs will now occur over a 12-year period, while amortization of those costs will take place over a 10-year period as before. These funding and amortization policies can be visualized as follows:

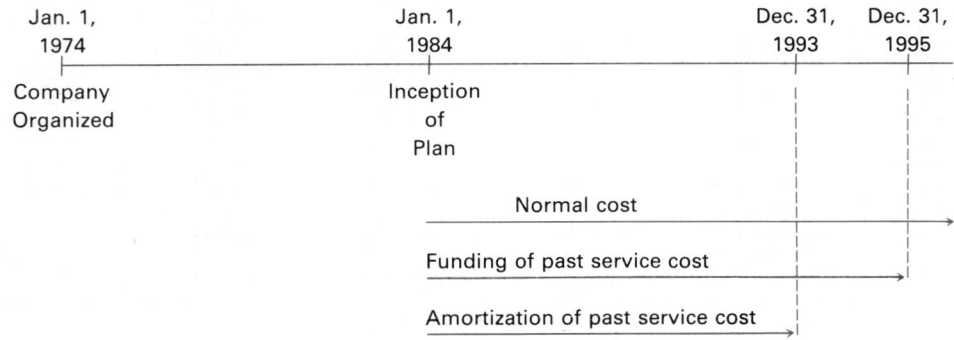

Our assumption of relatively short amortization and funding periods for past service costs again causes the pension expense we calculate to exceed the maximum allowed by *APB Opinion No. 8.* Our purpose, however, is to demonstrate the effect of funding past service costs over a longer period than those costs are amortized. Consequently, for simplicity of illustration, we assume relatively short amortization and funding periods.

Exhibit 22–5 contains an amortization table enabling us to readily compute and record pension expense under our revised assumptions. We can observe that a deferred credit (liability) initially arises because we are recognizing pension expense in larger amounts than we are funding.

The annual amortization of past service cost ($6,793) is determined in the same manner and amount as in the previous illustration. The annual funding amount is determined by dividing the $50,000 present value of the past service cost by the factor for the present value of an annuity of $1 for 12 years at 6% interest (8.38384 from Table 6–4). The resulting amount of $5,964 is the amount that must be paid each year to completely fund the past service cost in 12 years. Notice in Exhibit 22–5 that the interest in Column 2 is in *addition to pension expense* (based on the unfunded liability) rather than a reduction in pension expense (based on the prepaid expense) as in Exhibit 22–4.

Study of Exhibit 22–5 allows us to formulate the entries necessary at the end of each year to record pension expense and funding payments. The entries for 1984 and 1985, assuming normal costs of $10,000 and $11,000, respectively, are as follows:

Dec. 31, 1984	Pension Expense ($10,000 + $6,793)	16,793	
	Cash ($10,000 + $5,964)		15,964
	Deferred Credit—Excess of Pension Expense over		
	Pension Funding		829
	(To record 1984 pension expense and funding.)		

EXHIBIT 22–5
Past Service Cost—Funding Over a Longer Period than Amortization

Year	(1) Annual Amount for Amortization	(2) (Col. 6 × .06) Interest Addition	(3) (Col. 1 + Col. 2) Annual Expense Amount	(4) Funding Amount (12 Years)	(5) Deferred Credit (Col. 3 − Col. 4) Current	(6) Deferred Credit Balance
1984	$ 6,793	—	$ 6,793	$ 5,964	$ 829	$ 829
1985	6,793	$ 50	6,843	5,964	879	1,708
1986	6,793	102	6,895	5,964	931	2,639
1987	6,793	158	6,951	5,964	987	3,626
1988	6,793	218	7,011	5,964	1,047	4,673
1989	6,793	280	7,073	5,964	1,109	5,782
1990	6,793	347	7,140	5,964	1,176	6,958
1991	6,793	417	7,210	5,964	1,246	8,204
1992	6,793	492	7,285	5,964	1,321	9,525
1993	6,793	572	7,365	5,964	1,401	10,926
1994	–0–	656	656	5,964	(5,308)	5,618
1995	–0–	346*	346	5,964	(5,618)	–0–
	$67,930	$3,638	$71,568	$71,568		

*Rounding adjustment in 1995 to eliminate deferred credit balance.

Dec. 31, 1985   Pension Expense ($11,000 + $6,843)   17,843
                     Cash ($11,000 + $5,964)   16,964
                     Deferred Credit—Excess of Pension Expense over
                        Pension Funding   879
                     (To record 1985 pension expense and funding.)

The charge to pension expense in 1984 is the sum of the normal cost and the amortization of past service cost ($10,000 + $6,793). Pension expense increases in 1985 by $1,050, the amount of the increase in normal cost of $1,000 ($11,000 − $10,000) and the interest equivalent of $50 resulting from the deferred credit (liability) recognized at the end of 1984.

The credit to cash includes the normal cost and the funding requirement for past service costs. The amount for 1984 is composed of the $10,000 normal cost and $5,964 past service cost funding amount; for 1985 this increases by $1,000 due to the increase in normal cost.

Entries similar to the ones above are made for each of the first 10 years of the plan. In the eleventh and twelfth years, however, the only expense recognized is the normal cost of each year and interest on the unfunded past service cost. If we assume that normal cost during 1994, the eleventh year of the plan, is $15,000, the following entry is necessary:

Dec. 31, 1994   Pension Expense ($15,000 + $656)   15,656
                     Deferred Credit—Excess of Pension Expense over
                        Pension Funding   5,308
                        Cash ($15,000 + $5,964)   20,964
                     (To record 1994 pension expense and funding.)

The credit to cash is the sum of the normal cost and the funding amount for past service costs. Notice that the deferred credit is reduced in the eleventh year (1994) by $5,308. The deferred credit is again reduced in 1995, after which it is eliminated.

In the two previous examples, in which amortization and funding of past service costs have taken place over different periods of time, we have emphasized the concept of *interest equivalents.* Where funding takes place more quickly than amortization, *a deferred charge (asset)* arises and *interest revenue* is assumed to be earned, *reducing pension expense.* Where funding takes place less quickly than amortization, a *deferred credit (liability)* arises and *interest expense* is assumed to accrue, *increasing pension expense.* Notice that we call these assumed interest amounts "interest equivalents," implying that the computations are appropriate in determining pension expense whether or not interest is actually received or paid in cash. This approach is consistent with the modifying convention of substance over form that we discussed in Chapter 2.

Substance over Form

MISCELLANEOUS PENSION ACCOUNTING ISSUES

In the previous sections we have introduced basic concepts of pension accounting and have explained how an enterprise recognizes pension expense and funds its pension obligation in several relatively simple situations. We now turn our attention to additional considerations, some of which have been mentioned earlier. Specifically, in this section we consider actuarial cost methods, actuarial gains and losses, interest rate assumptions, and the Employee Retirement Income Security Act of 1974.

Actuarial Cost Methods

**Consis-
tency**

The normal cost of a pension plan is a critical determination of both the minimum and maximum amounts as determined by *APB Opinion No. 8*. The normal cost can be determined by a number of actuarial cost methods that assign pension cost in a rational, systematic, and consistent manner. The choice of an actuarial cost method can have a significant effect on the pattern of funding and pension expense recognition through time. The various acceptable actuarial cost methods that we review are presented in Exhibit 22–6.

The major actuarial cost methods can be categorized as either benefit allocation or cost allocation methods. **Benefit allocation methods** assign the incremental present value of the pension benefit to the period of credited service. The computation of pension benefits can be accomplished either by accruing earned pension benefits without projections, or by making projections of estimated compensation levels. In the latter case, the present value of the pension benefit is calculated as a function of the estimated terminal pension (pension at retirement), as opposed to the pension benefit earned to date. Under **cost allocation methods,** the total estimated terminal pension cost is allocated to the years of service under a systematic and rational allocation scheme.

To illustrate each of the actuarial cost methods, we will use a simplified example.[5] Assume the Integrated Electronics Company initiates a defined benefit pension plan on the first day of business, January 1, 1984. The pension plan provides a lump sum pension according to the following formula:

$$\text{Lump sum pension} = \text{Terminal salary} \times \text{Job tenure} \times 5\%$$

Assume further that the salary level of Integrated's only employee is as follows for the end of each year:

1984	$20,000
1985 estimate	$22,000
1986 estimate	$24,200

The employee elects to retire at the end of 1986. With this information, we know that the lump sum pension payable to the employee at the end of 1986 is:

$$\text{Lump sum pension} = \$24,200 \times 3 \text{ years} \times 5\%$$
$$= \$3,630$$

The accounting issues involve allocating the total pension to the three years of service. Recall that the employee theoretically earns the pension as he provides service during his

---

[5]This example is adapted from the FASB Discussion Memorandum on pension issues: *FASB Discussion Memorandum,* "An Analysis of Issues Related to Employer's Accounting for Pensions and Other Post Employment Benefits," 1981.

EXHIBIT 22–6
Actuarial Cost Methods

Benefit Allocation Methods	Cost Allocation Methods
1. Accumulated Benefit	1. Based on Years of Service
2. Projected Benefit/Years of Service	2. Based on Compensation
3. Projected Benefit/Compensation Levels	

EXHIBIT 22-7
Allocation of Total Pension Cost to Periods
Under Various Actuarial Cost Methods
(assumes a 10% interest rate)

Year	Benefit Allocation			Cost Allocation	
		Projected Benefits			
	Accumulated Benefits	Years of Service	Compensation	Years of Service	Compensation
1984	$ 826	$1,000	$ 906	$1,097	$1,000
1985	1,091	1,100	1,097	1,097	1,100
1986	1,430	1,210	1,327	1,097	1,210
Total interest earned	283	320	300	339	320
Total pension cost	$3,630	$3,630	$3,630	$3,630	$3,630

work life. Therefore, some type of allocation must be established in order to properly recognize the total value of services provided. Refer to Exhibit 22–7 for the pension allocations as determined for each of the actuarial cost methods. Our focus here is on the concepts employed for each actuarial cost method and not the specific calculations. However, the calculations underlying the figures in Exhibit 22–7 are provided in Appendix B of this chapter.

Accumulated Benefits

The accumulated benefits approach is the method most consistent with accrual accounting. The pension expense for the period is determined from the change in the present value of the accumulated pension earned since the previous reporting period. The accumulated pension is computed by applying the pension formula to the current compensation levels and years of service. For example, the 1984 pension expense for Integrated Electronics is the present value of $1,000 ($20,000 × 1 × .05), or $826. As a result of ignoring future compensation levels, the pension expense displays a steeper profile than that of any actuarial alternative. In other words, the pension expense is lower in the earlier years and higher in the later years. In addition, the total interest earned from funding the pension is less under the accumulated benefits method than under the alternatives. This conclusion is the result of weighting pension contributions toward the end of the employee's work life, where the dollars do not have as much time to earn interest.

Critics have suggested that the accumulated benefits method understates pension expense in the earlier years by ignoring future compensation. These critics assert that the probability of greater compensation levels is high enough to warrant the incorporation of compensation projections into the pension calculations.

Projected Benefits (Years of Service)

Under this method the years of service pension expense profile is not as steep as that of the accumulated benefits approach. The pension expense for the earlier years is greater because the estimated final salary is incorporated in the calculation. For Integrated Electronics the 1984 pension expense is the present value of $1,210 ($24,200 × 1 × .05), or $1,000. Notice that the accumulated pension is computed using the estimated final salary. As a result, more funds are available at an earlier time for interest accumulation. The total pension expense over the employee's lifetime is less because a greater amount of interest can be earned on the pension funds. Under all of the methods, a total of $3,630 must be accumulated. Naturally, the greater the portion that is earned in interest, the smaller the amount that must be recognized as pension expense in accumulating the total $3,630.

Projected Benefits (Compensation)

Under this method the pension expense for each period is the present value of the total pension cost multiplied by the ratio of the present year's salary to the lifetime salary. As an example, Integrated Electronic's 1984 pension expense is the present value of $1,097 [$3,630 × ($20,000/ $66,200)], or $906. As in the accumulated benefits method, the pension expense increases as the salary increases, but not as dramatically. The reason is that the future salary levels are explicitly considered in the calculation by taking the ratio of the current year's salary to estimated lifetime salary.

Cost Allocation (Years of Service)

This method assumes an equal assignment of pension cost over the employee's estimated work life. The pension expense is the same each year. This method will produce the highest earlier year's pension expense and the lowest later year's pension expense in comparison to other methods. The assumed interest earned would be greatest under this method, because more dollars are available earlier for interest accumulation. The amount of the equal contribution is a straightforward annuity calculation.

Cost Allocation (Compensation)

This method produces a gradual increase in the pension expense as the employee's salary level increases. Generally, this method results in a greater expense in the earlier years than the benefit allocation methods, but less expense in the earlier years than the years-of-service cost allocation method. In the example of Integrated Electronics, the projected benefit (years of service) and the cost allocation (years of service) pension expense profiles are identical. This need not be the case. The similarity between the two methods emerges only because the estimated salary grows at a rate exactly equal to the assumed discount rate (10%).

Both cost allocation methods allocate the total pension cost to the years of service. In essence, these two methods incorporate both the estimated future salary levels and the estimated total years of service into the allocation. As a result, cost allocation methods produce the most conservative funding and pension expense recognition.

Conservatism

At the present time, GAAP support the determination of a pension plan's normal cost by any of the above methods. Most corporations use the accumulated benefits method, because the pension expense is generally lower under this approach. The FASB, in reconsidering the whole area of employer accounting for pensions, has preliminarily specified the projected benefits (years of service) method for determining the normal cost of a pension plan. If this view is eventually adopted, the pension expense recognized by many corporations will increase to reflect the projected benefit assumptions. We discuss the specific proposals of the FASB later in this chapter.

Actuarial Gains and Losses

After a pension plan begins, additional actuarial valuations of the assumptions and estimates of the plan are necessary. Remember that events such as employee attrition, mortality, age, earnings levels, and fund earnings each affect the determination of pension obligations and related expenses. Many pension plans undergo an actuarial valuation annually. Although ERISA requires an actuarial valuation only every three years, most plans are evaluated more frequently. When an actuarial valuation occurs, substantial changes in the estimated pension obligation may arise. For example, if a fund earns at a higher rate than anticipated in an earlier actuarial valuation, the resulting reduction of the pension obligation and expense must be reported. Conversely, if future employee attrition estimates are reduced substantially in a new actuarial valuation, the resulting increase in the pension obligation and expense must be reported.

The APB evaluated several potential ways of reporting the effects of changes in actuarial factors and concluded that two different practices—immediate recognition and deferred recognition—were each acceptable in certain circumstances.

Immediate Recognition

If a single event gives rise to the actuarial gain or loss and the event is not related to the operation of the pension plan and is not in the ordinary course of the employer's business, the effect of the event on pension expense should be recognized **immediately.** This type of actuarial gain or loss should be recognized in the year it occurs or at the time of the actuarial valuation, if later. Examples of such events include a plant closing and the purchase acquisition of a company. An actuarial gain or loss on a pension obligation resulting from a plant closing should be treated as part of the gain or loss on the plant disposal rather than as an adjustment to pension expense.

Deferred Recognition

Actuarial gains and losses other than those described above should be **spread over the current and future years on an average basis.** Such treatment reflects the long-range nature of most pension plans. That is, actuarial gains and losses may be reasonably expected to occur and the effects of such changes are best treated in a systematic fashion reflecting the long-term nature of the pension commitment. The immediate (and perhaps temporary) effect of such gains and losses may never be actually sustained by the company sponsoring the plan. For example, temporary declines in the value of fund assets may be fully recovered before the securities must be sold to honor pension commitments due many years in the future. Many fluctuations in various actuarial assumptions may offset each other in a series of actuarial valuations. For these and other reasons, *most actuarial gains and losses are not recognized immediately.* Some actuarial methods automatically include actuarial gains or losses, while other methods do not. Accountants are careful to avoid unintentionally omitting the effects of actuarial gains and losses or inadvertently double-counting such events.

Two basic methods of charging actuarial gains and losses to current and future years have been developed: **spreading** and **averaging.** A common method of spreading cumulative net actuarial gains and losses is illustrated in this section. In our example, we assume that the actuarial method used does not automatically include spreading actuarial gains and losses and that a separate adjustment is necessary.

Spreading Actuarial Gains and Losses. Assume that Dun Corporation establishes a pension plan on January 2, 1984, arranges to obtain annual actuarial valuations, and elects to spread any actuarial gains or losses over a 10-year period. At the end of the first 10 years of the plan, actuarial gains and losses are as shown in Column 2 of Exhibit 22–8. The exhibit also presents the analysis necessary to spread gains and losses over the 10-year period.

The amount charged to expense each year is based on the cumulative actuarial gains and losses incurred for each of the preceding 10 years. The cumulative net actuarial gain or loss is divided by 10, and the result represents an adjustment to total pension expense. Actuarial gains decrease the amounts an employer must contribute, while actuarial losses cause the employer to increase contributions. To illustrate, if we assume no amortization of past service cost and normal cost of $50,000, pension expense for 1984 would be $51,500 ($50,000 normal cost plus $1,500 actuarial loss). Considering the amounts in Column 4 of Exhibit 22–8, we can see that the spreading of actuarial gains and losses will result in an increase in pension expense in every year except 1986, when the expense will be reduced by $100.

In 1994 the effect of the $15,000 actuarial loss of 1984 will be deleted from the average. To illustrate, if we assume that the actuary reports an actuarial loss of $5,000 in 1994, the cumulative actuarial gain or loss is determined as follows:

EXHIBIT 22–8
Dun Corporation
Illustration of Spreading Actuarial Gains and Losses

(1) Year Ended Dec. 31	(2) Annual Actuarial Gain or (Loss)	(3) Cumulative Actuarial Gain or (Loss)	(4) (Col. 3 ÷ 10) Annual Addition (Reduction) in Income*
1984	$(15,000)	$(15,000)	$(1,500)
1985	10,000	(5,000)	(500)
1986	6,000	1,000	100
1987	(12,000)	(11,000)	(1,100)
1988	(10,000)	(21,000)	(2,100)
1989	8,000	(13,000)	(1,300)
1990	(10,000)	(23,000)	(2,300)
1991	(12,000)	(35,000)	(3,500)
1992	8,000	(27,000)	(2,700)
1993	3,000	(24,000)	(2,400)

*The annual addition (reduction) in income results from the adjustment to pension expense by the amounts in this column. Gains are subtracted from pension expense (1986), and losses are added to pension expense (all other years).

December 31, 1993, cumulative net actuarial loss	$ 24,000
Less: Loss from 1984	(15,000)
Remaining net actuarial loss	9,000
1994 actuarial loss	5,000
December 31, 1994, cumulative net actuarial loss	$ 14,000

The addition to the 1994 pension expense would be $1,400 ($14,000/10).

Averaging Actuarial Gains and Losses. In the following illustration of averaging actuarial gains and losses, we use the same information for Dun Corporation that we used to illustrate spreading. Assume now, however, that Dun's management decides to use a four-year moving average to determine the average actuarial gains and losses for accounting purposes.

Until the end of the plan's fourth year, actual actuarial gains and losses for a complete four-year period are unknown. Therefore, estimates of the total actuarial losses to be incurred during the first four years of the plan are necessary. After consulting with a qualified actuary, the management of Dun Corporation determines that a reasonable estimate for the total actuarial losses for the first four years of the plan is $8,000. Exhibit 22–9 presents the actuarial gains and losses for 1984 through 1989 and the necessary calculation to determine the amount of the actuarial gains and losses to be included in the normal cost each year.

At the end of the fourth year of the plan, Dun Corporation has enough information to use an actual average of four years of actuarial gains and losses. At that time, the company adopts the actual four-year average and drops its use of the $8,000 estimated losses. By the end of 1989, total net actuarial losses of $13,000 have been incurred (total of Column 2); Dun Corporation has recognized total losses of $12,250 (total of Column 4). The amount of the addition (reduction) in income (Column 4) is an adjustment to normal cost in the same manner as was illustrated with the spreading method. The above figures indicate that over a relatively long period of time, we recognize approximately the same amount of losses as are incurred. However, the averaging procedure avoids recognizing the widely fluctuating (and eventually offsetting) annual actuarial gains and losses presented in Column 2.

READING THE TEA LEAVES

IN THE FACE OF disastrous losses for Pan Am and Braniff, Eastern Air Lines looked good in April with a first-quarter profit of $4.1 million. However, had the accountants and actuaries not changed one or two assumptions in Eastern's pension plan it would have been a different story. The airline's pension plan funding in 1981 will be reduced from 1980's $100 million to around $75 million. That's a "saving" of $25 million.

Bet you thought this kind of cookie jar stuff was illegal. Welcome to the rarefied world of actuarial assumptions, where crystal-ball gazing is accepted practice. Simply put, Eastern's squad of actuaries merely penciled in a change in their assumptions of what Eastern's pension fund might earn on its capital in the future. Obviously, if you assume that interest rates will stay high and that you're going to earn more on the money in your fund, then you need to put in less now to meet future obligations. That means you can decrease your annual contribution, as Eastern did.

Is this legitimate? Perfectly. Companies are free to pick any number that feels right to them. "There was a rash of increases in actuarial assumptions in the mid-Seventies, the last bout of high inflation," recalls Ed Davis of Buck Consultants, a New York-based actuarial firm. "People were looking for

places to improve earnings. I have to expect that there is going to be another rash."

That's not going to make things any easier for investors trying to compare two companies' pension expenses, or to keep track of how well the pension is funded. Or, for that matter, to compare earnings figures from year to year.

Here's how the change worked for Eastern. Since 1974 the company had been assuming an interest rate of 7% over the long term. The airline knew, roughly, how much money its plan would have to pay out over the next 20 to 30 years, and assuming that it earned 7% on its portfolio over that time, it knew how much it would have to kick in. But now, Eastern and its actuaries have decided that interest rates are going to stay higher than 7% over the next couple of decades, so it raised its assumed rate to 9%—and cut the contribution.

Eastern's treasurer, Charles Glass, says it was the actuaries' idea: "These were recommendations from them." As it happens, Eastern's assumptions aren't much ahead of current practice: A fall 1980 survey by Greenwich Research Associates showed that the average corporate interest assumption was 6.3%, but since then many funds have been steadily ratcheting their assumptions up to the 7%-to-9% range. Crown Zellerbach, for example, changed its

---

EXHIBIT 22–9
Dun Corporation
Illustration of Averaging Actuarial Gains and Losses

(1) Year Ended Dec. 31	(2) Annual Actuarial Gain or (Loss)	(3) Four- Year Total	(4) (Col. 3 ÷ 4) Annual Addition (Reduction) in Income*
1984	$(15,000)	$ (8,000)[a]	$(2,000)[b]
1985	10,000	(8,000)[a]	(2,000)[b]
1986	6,000	(8,000)[a]	(2,000)[b]
1987	(12,000)	(11,000)[c]	(2,750)[d]
1988	(10,000)	(6,000)[e]	(1,500)[f]
1989	8,000	(8,000)[g]	(2,000)[h]

*The annual addition (reduction) in income results from the adjustment to pension expense by the amounts in this column. In all years presented, losses are added to pension expense.
[a]First 3 years' losses estimated at $8,000.
[b]$(8,000) ÷ 4 = $(2,000).
[c]$(15,000) + $10,000 + $6,000 − $12,000 = $(11,000).
[d]$(11,000) ÷ 4 = $(2,750).
[e]$10,000 + $6,000 − $12,000 − $10,000 = $(6,000).
[f]$(6,000) ÷ 4 = $(1,500).
[g]$6,000 − $12,000 − $10,000 + $8,000 = $(8,000).
[h]$(8,000) ÷ 4 = $(2,000).

rate assumption from 6¼% to 8½% last year for reporting purposes (it used a more conservative 7½% internally). That reduced the present value of CZ's anticipated pension payout from $467 million to $426 million at a time when assets were increasing. That meant the company reported a plan surplus of $85 million. The year before, there was a $77 million shortfall.

Which set of figures is right? It depends on which set of assumptions turns out to be true—if either. What's important to recognize is that company earnings figures can be hoisted up and down by methods and assumptions different for every company.

In an attempt to help, the Financial Accounting Standards Board last year imposed a whole new set of reporting requirements on pension plans (Numbers Game, *Mar. 17, 1980*). The FASB decided that future salary increases shouldn't be taken into consideration when computing how much the plan will have to pay out, and that the interest rate assumption for reporting purposes should be generally higher than many companies use internally.

This FASB ruling only muddied the waters more. One company went so far as to release two sets of figures: one to satisfy the FASB, and then the real numbers—those it uses internally to figure out how to fund the plan. There's a big difference. Under the 10% assumption it thinks the FASB wants, Bethle-

hem Steel's plan looks just fine: assets of $2 billion and liabilities of $2.4 billion. But with Bethlehem Steel's own 7% assumption, benefit liabilities soar to $3 billion. "If we'd used a 10% interest rate assumption and assumed no salary increases, we would have put much less into the fund," explains Bob Gerst, general manager of employment-cost accounting at Bethlehem Steel. As it was, Bethlehem put $309 million in last year—using its own more conservative 7% figure. "This whole thing is a can of worms, if you ask me," moans Bethlehem's Gerst.

Unfortunately, you can't just impose one rate assumption on everyone. Explains Raymond Perry, a partner at Touche Ross & Co.: "A single assumption is apt to be unrealistic because the experience of companies varies with such things as investment performance and employee turnover."

Now the FASB is preparing for July hearings on pension accounting, and the subject is being thought through again. Among the possibilities: One funding method could be imposed on all companies. But, as Perry said, that would not be realistic. So, which do you prefer: a neat fiction, or an anarchic realism?

SOURCE: Thomas Baker, "Reading the Tea Leaves," *Forbes,* June 22, 1981, pp. 77–78. Reprinted by permission of *Forbes* Magazine. © Forbes Inc., 1981.

The rationale for the use of either averaging or spreading is that actuarial gains and losses will probably recur and fluctuate and, because the pension obligation is long-term, such gains and losses may never be realized. Averaging or spreading acknowledges the long-term and uncertain nature of these actuarial gains and losses.

Interest Rate Assumptions

The assumed rate of return on the invested assets of a pension plan has a dramatic effect on the level of pension expense recognized. The higher the assumed rate of return, the lower the required pension contribution; the lower the assumed rate of return, the higher the required pension contribution. Naturally, a high rate assumption will generate a lower pension present value and will therefore reduce the recognized pension expense relative to lower return rate assumptions. Some critics have alleged that allowing managers to select the rate of return assumption reduces the comparability of financial information among companies. In addition, critics have charged that managers can choose interest rate assumptions to "window-dress" the financial statements by artificially reducing the pension expense in a period when the net income is anticipated to be below average. In response, many have argued that interest rate assumptions should be flexible enough to reflect the present rate of return and anticipated return performance. Exhibit 22–10 displays some of the dramatic results that were obtained from increasing rate of return assumptions on pension assets for a selected number of large U.S. corporations.

EXHIBIT 22–10
Pension Fund Obligations: See How They Shrink

A change in accounting rules for reporting pension fund liabilities has slashed obligations for many companies. The biggest reductions result when companies increase their estimated rate of return from the assets.

Company	Liability (millions)		Discount Rate		
	1979	1980	1979	1980	
				For Reporting	For Funding
Armco[1]	$ 186	$ 94	8.5%	8.5%	8.5%
B. F. Goodrich[1]	216	184	7	8	7
Uniroyal[1]	509	509	7	8.3	7.5
Intl. Harvester[1]	910	1,079	7	7	7
Signal Cos.[1]	113	87	6	6	6
Inland Steel[1]	228	50	6	7.5	7.5
Sears[1]	56	68	6	6	6
National Steel[2]	660	104	7	10	7
Republic Steel[2]	526	223	6	9	6
U.S. Steel[2]	1,000	0	7	10	7
Bank America[2]	61	0	7.5	12.2	8.5
Ford Motor[2]	1,920	0	6	7	7
Goodyear Tire[2]	454	0	6	8.5	6
IBM[2]	190	0	4.75	4.75	4.75
Northrop[3]	0	0	6	6	6
American Can[3]	192	139	6	8	6
Bethlehem Steel[3]	1,191	420	7	10	7
LTV[3]	624	62	7	10	N/A
Chrysler[3]	1,200	1,275	7	8.25	7
Deere & Co.[4]	245	77	8.19	8.48	8.48
Firestone Tire[4]	217	0	5.5	10.7	7.5
General Motors[5]	6,100	4,085	6	8.25	6
K mart[6]	0	0	5	7	7
Caterpillar Tractor[7]	445	385	7.5	7.5	7.5

Note: Companies have an option as to the date of their reports. Reporting dates for companies above are (1) January 1 of year; (2) December 31; (3) December 31, 1979 and January 1, 1980; (4) October 31; (5) December 31, 1979 and October 1, 1980; (6) January 28; (7) December 31, 1979 and November 30, 1980. N/A, not available.

SOURCE: Arlene Hershman and G. Bruce Knecht, "Pension Accounting Magic," *Dun's Review,* May 1981, p. 79. Reprinted by special permission of *Dun's Business Month* (formerly *Dun's Review*), May 1981, copyright 1981, Dun & Bradstreet Publications Corporation.

A Brief Look at ERISA

Congress, reacting to pension plan abuses and funding shortfalls, enacted the Employee Retirement Income Security Act of 1974. We have occasionally referred to ERISA throughout this chapter.

The fundamental purpose of ERISA is to protect employee pension rights. Several specific features of the act are designed to accomplish this goal. For example, ERISA establishes strict minimum funding, vesting, and benefit requirements, and requires participation in the plan by employees. Furthermore, certain types and amounts of transactions are prohibited. For example, not more than 10% of a plan's assets can be represented by securities of the sponsoring enterprise.

ERISA also created the Pension Benefit Guaranty Corporation (PBGC) to insure plans and administer terminated plans. If a plan is unfunded or terminates, the PBGC can impose a lien on the employer's assets that takes precedence over virtually all other creditor claims.

In response to ERISA, the FASB issued *Interpretation No. 3.*[6] According to this Interpretation, no changes in pension accounting and financial reporting are necessary as a result of ERISA. The funding requirements of ERISA, however, support the maximum amount of pension cost as defined by *APB Opinion No. 8* and, consequently, the minimum amount loses some of its significance. Most companies subject to ERISA recognize pension expense in amounts approximating the maximum as a result of complying with ERISA. The FASB also concluded that ERISA does not create a reportable liability for unfunded pension costs unless termination of the plan is probable.

Miscellaneous Considerations

Large companies frequently establish several pension plans for various categories of employees or for employees in different locations. All employees who may reasonably be expected to receive pension benefits should be included in the cost computations. Differences in earnings, employee turnover, age, mortality, and other factors among employee groups should, of course, be considered. The Supreme Court of the United States recently held that sex may not be used to determine pension benefits for men and women. Although the life expectancy of a work force may be affected by the relative composition of men and women, employers may not pay benefits in different amounts based on sex. Companies are not required to use the same actuarial cost method for separate pension plans, but the accounting policies used for each plan should conform to the general guidelines for pension accounting in *APB Opinion No. 8.*

DISCLOSURE OF PENSION PLANS IN FINANCIAL STATEMENTS

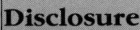

Pension plans are usually one of the most important commitments made by a company. Consequently, extensive disclosures are considered necessary to adequately inform financial statement users of the nature and extent of pension obligations.

The following information about a company's pension plan, commitments, and accounting and funding policies should be disclosed:[7]

1. A statement that pension plans exist, including identification or description of the employee groups covered.
2. A description of the company's accounting and funding policies.
3. The provision for pension cost for the period.
4. The nature and effect of significant matters affecting comparability for all periods presented, such as changes in accounting methods, changes in circumstances, and adoption or amendment of a plan.
5. The actuarial present value of vested accumulated plan benefits.
6. The actuarial present value of nonvested accumulated plan benefits.
7. The pension plans' net assets available for benefits, including any excess of the employer's accrued pension liability over the plans' contributions receivable from the employer.
8. The assumed rates of return used in determining the actuarial present value of vested and nonvested accumulated plan benefits.
9. The date of the last actuarial valuation.

In some cases much of the information for items 5 through 9 may not be available. For example, a company sponsoring a pension may be required to make payments to a multi-employer union-sponsored plan. In such cases, the only information available may relate to

---

[6]*FASB Interpretation No. 3,* "Accounting for the Cost of Pension Plans Subject to the Employee Retirement Income Security Act of 1974," 1974.

[7]*FASB Statement of Financial Accounting Standards No. 36,* "Disclosure of Pension Information," 1980, pars. 7–8. The first four disclosure requirements apply to all pension plans. The last five are applicable to defined benefit pension plans.

the entire pension fund rather than just the amounts for one sponsoring company. If the company sponsoring a plan cannot obtain certain information, the company should disclose the excess, if any, of the actuarially computed value of the vested benefits over the total pension fund and any balance sheet pension accruals, less any pension prepayments or deferred charges. The company should also explain why the information omitted is not available.

Exhibit 22–11 shows how B. F. Goodrich, a major U.S. diversified corporation which manufactures chemical, plastic, and rubber products, presented pension information in its 1982 financial statement notes.

EXHIBIT 22–11
B. F. Goodrich Company
Example Pension Disclosures

Pension expense, including amortization of prior service costs principally over thirty years, amounted to $43.6, $59.3 and $59.5 for the years ended December 31, 1982, 1981 and 1980, respectively. Pension expense of $43.6 for 1982 is exclusive of a $4.0 charge, for unfunded vested benefits arising from the program to restructure operations, which is included in the provision for that program.

In 1982, Goodrich converted a large part of its pension fund from stocks to a dedicated bond portfolio which matches bond maturities and interest to future benefit payments. The bond portfolio assures a fixed return that is significantly higher than the pension fund's historical return and results in all vested benefits becoming fully funded, thus lowering ongoing pension expenses. The effect of this change in 1982 was to reduce pension expense by $21.7 and to decrease the net loss for the year by $11.7.

A summary of accumulated plan benefits, the weighted average rate of return used in determining them, and the net assets available for benefits under Goodrich's domestic defined benefit plans is presented below:

Principally as of January 1,	1982	1981
Actuarial present value of accumulated plan benefits:		
Vested	$442.0	$549.3
Nonvested	63.6	58.3
Total	$505.6	$607.6
Weighted average rate of return assumed	11.5%	9.0%
Net assets available for plan benefits	$465.3	$467.7

The decrease in the actuarial present value of accumulated plan benefits is principally due to the higher weighted average rate of return assumed which reflects the fixed return on the dedicated bond portfolio. For funding of the principal plan, Goodrich will use an assumption of an 8% rate of return, which will result in a higher amount being funded than was accrued.

Goodrich's foreign pension plans are not required to report to certain U.S. governmental agencies under ERISA and do not otherwise determine the actuarial value of accumulated plan benefits or net assets available for benefits as calculated and disclosed above. For these plans, the actuarially computed value of vested benefits exceeded the total of the pension funds and balance sheet accruals by approximately $4.2 as of December 31, 1982.

SOURCE: B. F. Goodrich Company, 1982 Annual Report.

THE FUTURE OF PENSION ACCOUNTING

As we have already seen, GAAP do not require the immediate recognition of a liability for the past and prior service costs associated with a new pension plan or changes in an existing plan. The past and prior service costs are amortized to future periods of employee service. The rationale for this approach is that new plans and favorable plan amendments create employee loyalty and goodwill that will be realized in future higher-productivity returns. **Matching** The cost of this higher productivity should be matched against the revenue it generates by amortizing the costs into future periods as services are rendered. The event obligating the firm to a greater pension commitment is, accordingly, not the plan amendment but the services provided by employees.

Alternatively, some have advocated the immediate recognition of a liability for the unfunded past and prior service costs arising from new pension plans or amendments to existing plans. Under this approach, the establishment of a new plan or the amendment of an existing plan is an accounting event that obligates the company to higher pension commitments. Advocates of this position believe the present value of this pension commitment should be recognized in the accounting records as a liability on the date the plan is adopted or amended. If the past or prior service cost were recognized as a liability, several alternatives would remain for the debit side of the transaction:

1. Recognize an immediate pension expense.
2. Recognize a prior period adjustment.
3. Recognize an intangible asset.

Under the first alternative, past or prior service cost is recognized as a pension expense in the period the plan is initiated or amended. The approval or amendment of the plan is considered the significant accounting event and, as such, the costs associated with that event should be recognized in the period in which the event transpires. Under the second alternative, a debit to retained earnings (as a prior period adjustment) assumes that the past or prior service cost is compensation for unpaid services already rendered. This approach is difficult to justify from an economic perspective because employees provide service benefits equal to compensation, not in excess of compensation. Under the third approach, the credit to the past or prior service cost liability is offset by a debit to an intangible asset. The rationale is that the past or prior service cost gives rise to productivity gains in the future and that these gains can be represented as an intangible asset. The future productivity gains may result from greater worker loyalty, higher morale, reduced turnover, and the like. As **Matching** employee services are provided, the intangible asset is amortized to pension expense in order to properly match the incremental benefits of greater employee productivity with their costs. The liability under all three situations would be eliminated as the past or prior service costs are funded.

The FASB has been considering pension accounting and has issued its preliminary views on the subject. These views are summarized in Exhibit 22–12. Perhaps the most noteworthy proposal is the immediate recognition of the employer's liability for pension benefits resulting from the inception of a new pension plan or a change in an existing plan. The FASB proposal favors the approach whereby an intangible asset is established. This intangible asset would then be amortized over the average remaining service period of active plan participants. In this way the *total obligation of the employer* would appear in the balance sheet as a liability, not simply that portion of the expense already recognized but yet unfunded, as is currently done.

Also worthy of attention is the FASB's favoring the projected benefits (years of service) method of cost determination, believing that this approach best reflects the substance of pension plan provisions. This method is similar to that now used to measure the actuarial

---

EXHIBIT 22–12
Comparison of Current Accounting Practice with FASB's *Preliminary Views*

Issue	Current Accounting	*Preliminary Views*
Recognition of a liability.	A liability recognized equal to accumulated expense based on an acceptable actuarial method less amounts funded.	Recognizes a net pension liability (or asset) based on services rendered by the employees, using an actuarial method the FASB concludes is most appropriate for accounting purposes.
Recognition of plan assets as employer's assets.	Not recognized as employer's assets.	Recognizes plan assets as an offset against the pension obligation. Could result in a net asset.
Measurement of pension liability and expense.	Based on a number of actuarial cost methods that achieve systematic and rational allocation of pension cost.	Proposes the projected-unit-credit method, a form of projected benefit (years of service), as appropriate for most defined benefit pension plans.
Accounting for changes in the plan, including a new one that gives credit for past service.	No immediate recognition of an accounting liability. Pension expense and the related actuarial liabilities are recognized over a number of future periods.	Recognizes the increased pension benefit obligation (liability) and records an intangible asset representing expected future economic benefits. Pension expense would include amortization of the intangible asset over the average remaining service period of active plan participants.
Accounting for actuarial gains or losses (measurement changes).	Included in pension expense in a systematic and rational manner (i.e., spread or averaged over a period of 10 to 20 years).	Establishes a measurement valuation allowance, consisting of realized and unrealized experience gains and losses and effects of changes in actuarial assumptions, which would be a component of the net pension liability.
		Recognizes measurement changes prospectively through amortization of the measurement valuation allowance based on the average remaining service period of active plan participants.

SOURCE: Adapted from Coopers & Lybrand, *Executive Alert,* March 1983, p. 13. Copyright © 1983, Coopers & Lybrand (USA). Reprinted with permission.

---

present value of accumulated plan benefits currently disclosed in notes to the financial statements, with the exception that it involves an estimate of future compensation levels.[8]

CONCLUDING REMARKS

Financial accounting and reporting for pension obligations is highly complex and requires many estimates of distant future events and circumstances. Accountants and actuaries must nevertheless attempt to make those estimates in order to adequately inform financial statement users of the extent of pension commitments made by individual enterprises.

That companies are willing to make commitments to employees for pension benefits strongly supports the contention that reasonable estimates of the nature and extent of such

---

[8]Coopers & Lybrand, *Executive Alert* (March 1983), p. 14.

commitments are possible. However, the political aspects of establishing financial accounting standards play an important role in pension accounting. Some businesses are reluctant to report the magnitude of pension commitments. The failure of *APB Opinion No. 8* to require the recognition of a liability for the full amount of all past and prior service costs is certainly questionable. The FASB has indicated that substantial changes in financial accounting and reporting for pension obligations are quite likely, and its agenda evidences the likelihood of major changes.

The provisions of *SFAS No. 35,* referred to earlier and discussed in Appendix A to this chapter, provide additional valuable insights into the possible direction of future changes. You are encouraged to study Appendix A to gain insights into how pension accounting and reporting may evolve for enterprises sponsoring defined benefit pension plans as well as to understand current requirements for financial reporting of pension plans.

KEY POINTS

1. Pension plans are complex and represent some of the largest commitments made by business enterprises.

2. Financial accounting and reporting for pension plans centers on determining the pension cost incurred by a company during a reporting period.

3. Many estimates of distant future events are necessary to properly account for and report current pension obligations and costs.

4. Some pension plans are classified as defined contribution plans. In these plans, the periodic pension contribution is determined by a formula, and pension benefits paid to retired persons are based on amounts available in the pension fund.

5. Other pension plans are classified as defined benefit plans. In these plans, the benefits to be received by present employees upon retirement are determined by a formula, and amounts estimated to be required to fund those benefits are the basis for pension funding

and pension expense recognition.

6. Enterprises should determine annual pension cost by using an acceptable actuarial cost method.

7. Pension cost reported for a period should be within the minimum and maximum amounts determined in accordance with *APB Opinion No. 8.*

8. Past service costs generally should be amortized over a period not less than 10 years and funded over a period not more than 40 years. (The latter is a result of ERISA.)

9. Actuarial gains and losses generally should be averaged or spread over the current and future years.

10. ERISA, although not changing financial accounting and reporting standards, has had a substantial impact on the way pension plans are administered.

11. Financial accounting and reporting standards for pension commitments will likely change as a result of FASB deliberations.

APPENDIX A FINANCIAL ACCOUNTING AND REPORTING FOR DEFINED BENEFIT PENSION PLANS

Before *SFAS No. 35*[9] was issued, financial accounting and reporting by pension plans as separate entities generally was poorly defined. Most of the attention of the accounting profession had been devoted to reporting pension costs and obligations in the financial statements of companies sponsoring pension plans rather than to the financial reporting of the plans themselves. ERISA requires annual reporting of plans subject to its jurisdiction, and the need for professional guidance has become more intense. *SFAS No. 35* provides that guidance and also sheds light on changes that are likely to be made in the way employers report their pension

[9] *FASB Statement of Financial Accounting Standards No. 35,* "Accounting and Reporting by Defined Benefit Pension Plans," 1980.

EXHIBIT 22–13
Reporting Net Assets Available for Benefits

Term	Definition	Components	Amplification
Net assets available for benefits.	Mathematical difference between plan's assets and liabilities, not including participants' accumulated plan benefits.	Contributions receivable	Amounts due from employers, participants, and others as of the reporting date. Includes formal commitments as well as legal obligations.
		Investments	Valuation should be fair value at the reporting date. Market value, estimates of value, and similar information should be used.
		Operating assets	Valuation should be cost less accumulated depreciation or amortization.

---

obligations. The provisions of *SFAS No. 35* apply to all defined benefit pension plans. Consequently, if a plan is subject to the provisions of ERISA, the plan is also subject to *SFAS No. 35*.

According to the FASB, the primary purpose of financial reporting by defined benefit pension plans is to provide information about the *plan's* financial viability. That is, financial reports for defined benefit plans should provide information about the plan's present and future ability to pay benefits on a timely basis.

To meet this objective, the financial statements of a defined benefit pension plan should include:

1. A statement describing *net assets available for benefits;*
2. A statement revealing *changes during the period in net assets available for benefits;* and
3. Information about (a) the *actuarial present value of accumulated plan benefits* at either the beginning or the end of the year (end-of-year information is encouraged), and (b) factors affecting year-to-year changes in the actuarial present value of accumulated plan benefits.

SFAS No. 35 encourages, but does not require, the presentation of multiple-year comparative financial statements.

Exhibit 22–13 presents the components of the statement of net assets available for benefits. Notice that the term **net assets** refers to the mathematical difference between the plan's total assets and total liabilities. The accumulated benefits that will be paid to beneficiaries in the future are not considered liabilities

of the plan. The benefit obligation to beneficiaries is presented elsewhere in the financial report as a type of plan equity. Financial statements of defined benefit plans view beneficiaries as, in substance, owners or residual equity holders of plan net assets. The net assets of the plan are those that are, in fact, available to pay pension benefits in the future.

Plan assets are classified in three categories:

1. Contributions receivable
2. Investments
3. Operating assets

Of particular significance is the presentation of investments at fair market value rather than the lower of cost or market, as is generally required of business enterprises. While some investments, such as marketable securities, may have a readily determinable market value, other investments, such as real estate holdings, may be much more difficult to value. Estimates of market value and market appraisals may be necessary for some types of investments that do not have a ready market value.

Operating assets should be reported at cost less accumulated depreciation, which, of course, is consistent with business practices. **Operating assets** is the term used in *SFAS No. 35* for such assets as facilities, furniture, and office equipment.

Exhibit 22–14, taken from *SFAS No. 35*, illustrates the presentation of a statement of net assets available for benefits.

The second required financial statement is a statement of changes in net assets available for benefits.

EXHIBIT 22–14
C&H Company Pension Plan
Statement of Net Assets Available for Benefits

	December 31 1981
Assets	
Investments, at fair value	
United States government securities	$ 350,000
Corporate bonds and debentures	3,500,000
Common stock	
C&H Company	690,000
Other	2,250,000
Mortgages	480,000
Real estate	270,000
	7,540,000
Deposit administration contract, at contract value	1,000,000
Total investments	8,540,000
Receivables	
Employees' contributions	40,000
Securities sold	310,000
Accrued interest and dividends	77,000
	427,000
Cash	200,000
Total assets	9,167,000
Liabilities	
Accounts payable	70,000
Accrued expenses	85,000
Total liabilities	155,000
Net assets available for benefits	$9,012,000

The accompanying notes are an integral part of the financial statements.

SOURCE: *Statement of Financial Accounting Standards No. 35*, "Accounting and Reporting by Defined Benefit Pension Plans" (Stamford, Conn.: FASB, 1980), par. 282.

Increases in assets result from holding gains on investments, interest, dividends, and contributions from employers and employees. Decreases in assets result from declines in the market value of investments, administrative expenses, and benefits paid to or on behalf of participants. Exhibit 22–15, also taken from *SFAS No. 35*, illustrates such a statement.

The final item of information, in addition to the usual note disclosures, involves the actuarial present value of accumulated plan benefits. Interestingly, *SFAS No. 35* requires the actuarial information to be determined at the beginning or the end of the year being reported or at another date that year. As we have seen in Chapter 22, actuarial information involves complicated computations that require a great deal of time and effort. Frequently the necessary information as of the end of the reporting period is not available when the financial statements are issued. As an alternative to delaying the issuance of the financial statements, the plan may provide information as of the end of the preceding year (beginning of the current year) and disclose the date to which the information applies. Alternatively, the plan may use a date for actuarial computations that falls in the current reporting period.

Accumulated plan benefits include future payments attributable to employee service rendered to the benefit information date and include obligations to beneficiaries who are retired, terminated, or presently rendering services. The benefit information should separately report vested benefits of participants currently receiving payments, other vested benefits, non-vested benefits, and present employees' accumulated contributions. Financial statement users are thus able to assess the nature, magnitude, and certainty of the benefit obligations of the plan. Actuarial factors which change significantly should also be disclosed.

EXHIBIT 22–15
C&H Company Pension Plan
Statement of Changes in Net Assets Available for Benefits

	Year Ended December 31 1981
Investment income	
Net appreciation in fair value of investments	$ 207,000
Interest	345,000
Dividends	130,000
Rents	55,000
	737,000
Less investment expenses	39,000
	698,000
Contributions	
Employer	780,000
Employees	450,000
	1,230,000
Total additions	1,928,000
Benefits paid directly to participants	740,000
Purchases of annuity contracts	257,000
	997,000
Administrative expenses	65,000
Total deductions	1,062,000
Net increase	866,000
Net assets available for benefits	
Beginning of year	8,146,000
End of year	$9,012,000

The accompanying notes are an integral part of the financial statements.

SOURCE: *Statement of Financial Accounting Standards No. 35,* "Accounting and Reporting by Defined Benefit Pension Plans" (Stamford, Conn.: FASB, 1980), par. 282.

APPENDIX B SUPPORTING CALCULATIONS FOR EXHIBIT 22–7

Accumulated Benefits	Pension Expense	Interest
1984		
$(\$20,000 \times 1 \times .05) \times \left[\dfrac{1}{(1.10)^2}\right]$	$ 826	
1985		
$\$826 \times .10$		$ 83
$(\$22,000 \times 2 \times .05) \times \left[\dfrac{1}{(1.10)}\right]$		
Less: ($826 + $83)	1,091	
1986		
($826 + $83 + $1,091) × .10		200
($24,200 × 3 × .05)		
Less: ($826 + $83 + $1,091 + $200)	1,430	
	$3,347	$283

Projected Benefit (Years of Service)	Pension Expense	Interest
1984		
$(\$24{,}200 \times 1 \times .05) \times \left[\dfrac{1}{(1.10)^2}\right]$	\$1,000	
1985		
$\$1{,}000 \times .10$		\$100
$(\$24{,}200 \times 2 \times .05) \times \left[\dfrac{1}{(1.10)}\right]$		
Less: ($1,000 + $100)	1,100	
1986		
($1,000 + $100 + $1,100) × .10		220
($24,200 × 3 × .05)		
Less: ($1,000 + $100 + $1,100 + $220)	1,210	
	$\underline{\underline{\$3{,}310}}$	$\underline{\underline{\$320}}$

Projected Benefit (Compensation)	Pension Expense	Interest
1984		
$[\$20{,}000/(\$20{,}000 + \$22{,}000 + \$24{,}200)] \times \$3{,}630 \times \left[\dfrac{1}{(1.10)^2}\right]$	\$ 906	
1985		
$\$906 \times .10$		\$ 91
$(\$22{,}000/\$66{,}200) \times \$3{,}630 \times \left[\dfrac{1}{1.10}\right]$	1,097	
1986		
($906 + $91 + $1,097) × .10		209
($24,200/$66,200) × $3,630	1,327	
	$\underline{\underline{\$3{,}330}}$	$\underline{\underline{\$300}}$

Cost Allocation (Years of Service)

The amount charged as interest expense is simply the periodic rent (R) that if invested at the end of each period for 3 periods at 10% equals $3,630:

$$\$3{,}630 = R[aoaf_{\overline{3}|\,10\%}]$$
$$R = \frac{\$3{,}630}{3.31000}$$
$$R = \$1{,}097$$

	Pension Expense	Interest
1984		
$3,630/3.31	\$1,097	
1985		
$1,097 × .10		\$110
$3,630/3.31	1,097	
1986		
($1,097 + $1,097 + $110) × .10		229
$3,630/3.31	1,097	
	$\underline{\underline{\$3{,}291}}$	$\underline{\underline{\$339}}$

	Pension Expense	Interest
Cost Allocation (Compensation)		

Find the terminal value of the salary stream:

$$[\,\$20{,}000 \times (1.10)^2\,] + [\,\$22{,}000 \times (1.10)\,] + \$24{,}200 = \$72{,}600$$

1984

$$\{[\$20{,}000 \times (1.10)^2]/\$72{,}600\} \times \$3{,}630 \times \left[\frac{1}{(1.10)^2}\right] \qquad \$1{,}000$$

1985

$$\$1{,}000 \times .10 \qquad \qquad \$100$$

$$[(\$22{,}000 \times 1.10)/\$72{,}600] \times \$3{,}630 \times \left[\frac{1}{1.10}\right] \qquad 1{,}100$$

1986

$$(\$1{,}000 + \$1{,}100 + \$100) \times .10 \qquad 220$$

$$(\$24{,}200/\$72{,}600) \times \$3{,}630 \qquad \underline{1{,}210} \qquad \underline{}$$

$$\underline{\underline{\$3{,}310}} \qquad \underline{\underline{\$320}}$$

QUESTIONS

22–1 Discuss the nature of the relationship between the employer, employee, and pension plan.

22–2 What is a defined contribution pension plan? What are the major characteristics of such a plan?

22–3 What is a defined benefit pension plan? How do the major characteristics of a defined benefit plan differ from those of a defined contribution plan?

22–4 List and describe some of the uncertainties in estimating future pension commitments.

22–5 Why is accrual accounting appropriate for pension plans?

22–6 What is the "normal cost" of a pension plan?

22–7 For financial reporting purposes under GAAP, when is it appropriate to recognize a pension liability?

22–8 Define past and prior service costs. How do these two types of pension costs differ?

22–9 What is the purpose of the maximum and minimum provisions of *APB Opinion No. 8?*

22–10 How are past or prior service costs accounted for?

22–11 Briefly describe some alternatives to the present method of accounting for past or prior service costs.

22–12 How are past or prior service costs accounted for when the amortization period is different from the funding period?

22–13 Briefly describe the various actuarial cost methods. How do they differ in terms of total contributions and interest earned? Why do these differences exist?

22–14 What effect does the interest rate assumption have on the pension expense recognized for the period?

22–15 What are the two major approaches toward accounting for actuarial gains and losses? How do these approaches differ conceptually?

22–16 What are the two major procedural choices for deferring the recognition of actuarial gains or losses?

22–17 What disclosure is required for pension plans in the footnotes of the sponsor's financial statements?

22–18 (Appendix A) What are the major required financial statements for defined benefit pension plans according to *SFAS No. 35?*

CASES

C22–1 Pension plans have developed in an environment characterized by a complex interaction of social concepts, legal considerations, actuarial techniques, income tax laws, and accounting practices. *APB Opinion No. 8* delineates acceptable accounting practices for the cost of pension plans.

Instructions

[a] The following terms are relevant to accounting for the cost of pension plans. Define or briefly explain each of the following:

[1] Normal cost
[2] Past service cost
[3] Prior service cost
[4] Funded plan
[5] Vested benefits
[6] Actuarial gains and losses
[7] Interest

[b] Identify the disclosures required in financial statements regarding a company's pension plan.

(AICPA adapted)

C22-2 In examining the costs of pension plans, a CPA encounters certain terms. The elements of pension costs which the terms represent must be dealt with appropriately if generally accepted accounting principles are to be reflected in the financial statements of entities with pension plans.

Instructions

[a] [1] Discuss the theoretical justification for accrual recognition of pension costs.
[2] Discuss the relative objectivity of the measurement process of accrual versus cash (pay-as-you-go) accounting for annual pension costs.

[b] Explain the following terms as they apply to accounting for pension plans:

[1] Actuarial valuations
[2] Actuarial cost methods
[3] Vested benefits

(AICPA adapted)

C22-3 Past or prior service costs may give rise to large unfunded amounts that are amortized to pension expense over a specified amortization period. Under GAAP, no liability is recognized when past or prior service costs are identified. Some have suggested that an alternative would be to recognize a liability immediately, as of the plan initiation or amendment date.

Instructions

[a] What is the theoretical support for recognizing a liability for unfunded past or prior service costs?
[b] If a liability is established, what alternatives are available for the offsetting debits? What are the theoretical arguments for each alternative?
[c] What is the theoretical argument for *not* recognizing a liability? What is the difference between this argument and that in [a]?

C22-4 Hampton Power and Light Company has initiated a defined benefit pension plan for all employees. The plan does not grant credit for services before the adoption of the plan. The chief financial officer of Hampton Power and Light is considering various actuarial cost methods for funding the pension and recognizing the periodic pension expense. In addition, the chief financial officer is considering what rate of return assumption would be appropriate for the pension plan. The chief financial officer has asked his assistant to generate a proposal for the proper way to fund and account for the pension plan.

The following is an excerpt from the assistant's recommendations:

The company may fund and account for the periodic contribution to the pension plan by various methods according to present GAAP. The most preferred method is clearly an accumulated benefits approach. In comparison to all the other methods, this approach requires less cash to be invested in the plan during the earlier years of the employees' work lives and more cash later in their work lives. As we all know, present value concepts teach us that cash contributed earlier to the plan is worth more to us than cash invested later. As a result, we should end-weight our contributions as much as possible in order to free more-valuable present dollars. Furthermore, our income statement would benefit in the earlier years by disclosing a lower pension expense figure than under the alternative methods. This should please our shareholders.

In addition, I recommend as high an assumed rate of return on pension fund assets as our independent actuary will allow. The higher our assumed rate of return, the smaller our contribution to the plan and recognized pension expense.

After reading this recommendation, the chief financial officer of Hampton Power and Light released the following memo to his assistant.

I have read your analysis and recommendations. It is obvious to me that you do not understand the concept of pension plans and the nature of our industry. I found your arguments simplistic and naive.

Instructions

[a] How would you have responded to the chief financial officer's original request? Prepare a recommendation.
[b] Why did the chief financial officer find the assistant's recommendations "simplistic and naive"?

C22-5 Ridgewood Bank and Trust Company has provided a pension plan for employees since January 1, 1980. The pension plan has experienced actuarial gains and losses from the market performance of plan assets as follows:

Gain (Loss)

1980	$ 19,000
1981	(26,000)
1982	8,000
1983	33,000
1984	(10,000)
1985	(14,000)

Ridgewood adjusts the normal pension cost for the full effect of actuarial gains and losses in the year incurred. The normal cost of the pension plan for each of the first six years of existence was $40,000.

Instructions

[a] Determine the pension expense according to the method employed by Ridgewood Bank and Trust Company.
[b] Comment on the propriety of Ridgewood's method of accounting for actuarial gains and losses.
[c] What alternative methods of accounting for actuarial gains and losses are available?
[d] Determine the annual pension expense for Ridgewood if actuarial gains and losses are spread over six years. Compare these results with those results in [a].

EXERCISES

E22-1 The actuary of Granger's pension plan determined that the prior service costs of a plan amendment had a present value of $160,382 as of the plan amendment date. Granger decided to amortize and fund the prior service costs over a 12-year period. The normal pension costs for the current year and the following year were $75,000 and $88,000, respectively.

Instructions

[a] Determine the amount necessary to fund the prior service costs, assuming pension plan contributions can earn 10% compounded annually.
[b] Record the pension-related transactions for the first and second year after the plan amendment. Disregard maximum and minimum limits.

E22-2 Westfall Company adopted a pension plan on the first day of operations. The pension plan was designed to provide employees an annual pension based on the following formula:

Annual pension = Years of service × 1½%
× Final annual salary

Westfall estimated that for their 10 employees the average number of years of service will be 25 years, and the average final salary of the work force 25 years from now will be $125,000. Westfall's actuary estimates that the average retirement period for the work force will be 15 years.

Instructions

[a] Westfall wants to contribute an equal annual amount to a pension fund that earns 10% compounded annually in order to completely fund the pension as of the beginning of the retirement period for the average worker. What amount must Westfall contribute annually if the first contribution will be made one year from today, and the first retirement check will be disbursed one year from the retirement date?
[b] Does the method of funding a pension plan have any substantive effect on a company? What actuarial cost method most closely resembles the funding method outlined in [a]?

E22-3 Hollis Corporation provides a group of five employees a pension plan that will pay them (or their beneficiaries) $10,000 per year for 15 years, with the first payment commencing one year after retirement. The group of five employees will retire 12 years from today. The pension plan requires Hollis to deposit an equal amount annually, beginning one year from today, into a fund that will earn interest at 8% compounded annually. The pension plan must be fully funded by the retirement date.

Instructions

[a] Determine the equal contributions that must be made to the pension plan in order to satisfy the plan's requirements.
[b] In addition to the information above, assume that Hollis initiates a change in the plan five years before the retirement date. The change grants each of the five employees a pension of $14,000 for 15 years, as opposed to $10,000. What annual contribution must Hollis make for the remaining five years to fully fund

the plan if the first payment is made one year from the plan amendment date?

E22–4 Helena Roberts Company amended its pension plan on January 1, 1984. The actuarially determined prior service costs were $160,000. The prior service costs are to be funded over four years and amortized over two years. The assumed rate of interest is 6%.

Instructions

[a] Prepare a schedule displaying the amortization and funding of the prior service costs. Ignore minimum and maximum provisions.
[b] Prepare a journal entry for the prior service costs for 1986.

E22–5 Diamond Oil Company adopted a pension plan on January 1, 1983. The past service costs of this pension plan were $780,000 and were to be funded by equal payments over a 4-year period. For financial reporting purposes, the past service costs will be amortized over a 10-year period. The pension fund will earn an estimated rate of return of 8% compounded annually. The normal pension costs for 1984 and 1985 are $100,000 and $160,000, respectively.

Instructions

Provide the appropriate journal entries for 1984 and 1985 for Diamond Oil's pension plan. Ignore minimum and maximum provisions.

E22–6 Garrison Restaurant Corporation initiated a pension plan on January 1, 1984. The past service costs of $610,000 are to be funded over 8 years and amortized over 12 years. Pension fund contributions are made at the end of the year. The normal pension costs for 1984 and 1985 were $90,000 and $115,000, respectively. These amounts were fully funded. An 8% interest rate is assumed.

Instructions

Determine the maximum and minimum amounts for the recognition of pension expense for 1984 and 1985.

E22–7 Olson Company adopted a pension plan on January 1, 1984. The past service costs of this plan were $64,682. Olson elects to fund the past service costs over a five-year period, with the first contribution being made immediately. Olson will amortize the past service costs over a five-year period, with amorti-

zation adjusting entries to be made at the end of the year. The assumed interest rate is 8%.

Instructions

[a] Construct an amortization and funding schedule for 1984–1988.
[b] Provide the journal entries for 1984, assuming normal costs of $120,000 are fully funded at the end of 1984. Disregard minimum and maximum limits.

E22–8 Liberty, Inc., a calendar-year corporation, adopted a company pension plan at the beginning of 1984. This plan is to be funded and noncontributory. Liberty used an appropriate actuarial cost method to determine its normal annual pension cost for 1984 and 1985 as $15,000 and $16,000, respectively, which was paid in the same year.

Liberty's actuarially determined past service costs were funded on December 31, 1984, at an amount properly computed as $106,000. These past service costs are to be amortized at the maximum amount permitted by generally accepted accounting principles. The interest factor assumed by the actuary is 6%.

Instructions

Prepare journal entries to record the funding of past service costs on December 31, 1984, and the pension expenses for 1984 and 1985. Under each journal entry give the reason for your entry. Round to the nearest dollar.

(AICPA adapted)

E22–9 Larson Corporation submits its pension plan for an annual review by its actuarial consultant. The consultant determined the annual actuarial gains and losses of the pension plan from the date of the plan's inception until the present. The schedule below displays the historical experience of the plan.

	Actuarial Gain (Loss)
1973	$ 5,000
1974	9,000
1975	(4,000)
1976	10,000
1977	22,000
1978	(8,000)
1979	(3,000)
1980	7,000
1981	16,000
1982	(60,000)
1983	1,000
1984	10,000

Instructions

[a] Prepare a schedule to spread the actuarial gains and losses over a 10-year period. If the normal cost was $30,000 for each of the years, determine the total pension expense for each year.

[b] If the $10,000 actuarial gain of 1984 was due totally to a plant closing, what would be the 1984 pension expense? Why is your answer different from that in [a]?

E22–10 The Joshua Corporation, which has been in operation for the past 23 years, decided late in 1984 to adopt, beginning on January 1, 1985, a funded pension plan for its employees. The pension plan will be noncontributory and will provide for vesting after 5 years

Date	Amortization	Interest
12/31/84	$17,524	
12/31/85	17,524	$279

of service by each eligible employee. A trust agreement has been entered into whereby a large national insurance company will receive the yearly pension fund contributions and administer the fund.

Management, through extended consultation with the fund trustee, internal accountants, and independent actuaries, arrived at the following conclusions:

[1] The normal pension cost for 1985 will be $30,000.

[2] The present value of the past service cost at date of inception of the pension plan (January 1, 1985) is $200,000.

[3] Because of the large sum of money involved, the past service costs will be funded at $23,365 per year for the next 15 years. The first payment will not be due until January 1, 1986.

[4] In accordance with *APB Opinion No. 8*, the accumulated benefits method of accounting for the pension costs will be followed. Pension costs will be amortized over a 10-year period. The 10-year accrual factor is $29,805 per year. Neither the maximum nor the minimum amortization amount as prescribed by *APB Opinion No. 8* will be violated.

[5] Where applicable, an 8% interest rate was assumed.

Instructions

[a] Define:
　[1] Normal pension costs
　[2] Past service costs

[b] What amounts (use XXX if amount can't be calculated) will be reported in the company's:
　[1] Income statement for 1985?
　[2] Balance sheet as of December 31, 1985?
　[3] Notes to the statements?
Give account titles with the amounts.

[c] What amounts (use XXX if amount can't be calculated) will be reported in the company's:
　[1] Income statement for 1986?
　[2] Balance sheet as of December 31, 1986?
　[3] Notes to the statements?
Give account titles with the amounts.

(CMA adapted)

E22–11 Review the following table.

Pension Expense	Funding	Deferred Current	Deferred Balance
$17,524	$21,011	$3,487	$3,487
17,245	21,011	3,766	7,253

The past service costs associated with the above table are $150,000.

Instructions

[a] Is the December 31, 1985, balance of $7,253 a deferred charge or a deferred credit? How do you know?

[b] What interest rate is assumed in the table?

[c] Is the amortization period greater or less than the funding period? How do you know?

[d] What is the nature or meaning of the "Interest" column?

[e] Determine the amortization period.

[f] Determine the funding period.

E22–12 Dane Enterprises, which started operations in 1979, instituted a pension plan on January 1, 1984. The insurance company which is administering the pension plan has computed the present value of past service costs at $100,000 for the 5 years of operations through December 31, 1983. The pension plan provides for fully vested benefits when employees have completed 10 years of service. Therefore, there will be no vested benefits until December 31, 1988.

The insurance company proposed that Dane Enterprises fund the past service costs in equal installments over 15 years, calculated by the present value method. Using an interest rate of 5% the annual payment for past service cost would be $9,634. The company's treasurer agreed to this payment schedule. In addition, the controller concluded that a 15-year period was reasonable for amortizing the past service costs for book purposes. Consequently, the past service costs will also be amortized at the annual amount of $9,634 for 15 years.

The normal cost for the pension fund is estimated to be $30,000 each year for the next 4 years. The annual payment to the insurance company covering the current year's normal cost and the annual installment on the past service cost is payable on December 31 each year, the end of Dane's fiscal year. The insurance company was paid $39,634 ($30,000 + $9,634) on December 31, 1984, to cover the company's pension obligations for 1984.

Instructions

[a] Calculate and label the components which compose the maximum and minimum 1984 financial statement pension expense limits in accordance with generally accepted accounting principles for Dane Enterprises.

[b] Assume Dane will be unable to remit the full pension payment ($39,634) in 1985 and will only submit $30,000 (the normal cost) to the insurance company. If Dane can recognize $39,634 as pension expense in 1985, show the entry required. If the company cannot recognize the $39,634 as pension expense in 1985, explain why not.

(CMA adapted)

PROBLEMS

P22–1 Bryan Corporation provides a pension plan agreement whereby an employee receives an annual pension of $12,000 for 12 years, with the first payment commencing one year after the retirement date. The retirement plan requires a 60% contribution by the employer and a 40% contribution by the employee in funding the plan. Contributions to the plan accumulate 6% interest compounded annually. The employee will retire 10 years from today, and the first contribution to the pension plan will be made one year from today.

Instructions

Respond to each of the following *independent* situations relating to the pension plan described above.

[a] What equal annual contribution must the employer make to fully fund the plan as of the retirement date? Assume that the last payment is made on the retirement date.

[b] What equal annual contribution must the employer make to fund the pension plan if contributions to the plan are made through the end of the retirement period? Assume that the employer assumes 100% of the pension responsibility as of the employee's retirement date.

[c] Assume that the pension plan is amended 7 years before the employee's retirement such that the employer assumes 100% of the pension responsibility. Assume further that this amendment is applied retroactively such that the employee is given additional matching pension credit equal to his or her previous contributions and accumulated interest thereon. What equal annual contributions must the employer make for the 7 years from the amendment date to the retirement date to fully fund the plan? Assume that the first

revised contribution is made one year from the amendment date and the last contribution is made on the retirement date. What equal pension amount will the employee withdraw for each of the 12 retirement years as a result of the amendment provisions?

P22–2 Webster Corporation adopted a pension plan on January 1, 1984, with retroactive credit for service to date. The past service costs totaled $600,000. On January 1, 1985, the pension plan was retroactively amended to allow for an increase in benefits. The prior service costs on January 1, 1985, were $400,000 in addition to past service costs. Normal costs for 1984 and 1985 were $160,000 and $210,000, respectively. The pension plan is assumed to earn 8% interest compounded annually. Past and prior service costs are funded for 15 years, with contributions made at year-end. None of the pension benefits are vested by the end of 1985. Pension expense of $210,000 was recognized in 1984; none has yet been recognized in 1985.

Instructions

Determine the minimum and maximum amounts for 1984 and 1985.

P22–3 Ingle Corporation initiated a pension plan on January 1, 1984, after being in business for over 25 years. The past service costs associated with the plan initiation were $350,000. Ingle Corporation is going to fund these past service costs over a five-year period. Ingle Corporation is trying to decide the financial reporting effects of amortizing the past service costs over a three-year, five-year, or six-year period. The interest rate is 10%. The projected normal costs for 1984, 1985, and 1988 are as follows:

1984	$26,000
1985	32,000
1988	46,000

Instructions

[a] Provide amortization and funding tables for each of the three amortization alternatives.

[b] Provide the appropriate journal entries for 1984, 1985, and 1988 for each of the three alternatives above. Ignore maximum and minimum amounts.

[c] What are the major reporting effects of each of the three amortization alternatives?

P22–4 Lockman Corporation determines the actuarial gain or loss to be assigned to a particular accounting period under a three-year moving average. The assumed actuarial gain is estimated to be a total of $21,000 for the years 1981 through 1983. Lockman's actual experience was as follows:

Year	Actuarial Gain (Loss)
1981	$ 4,000
1982	16,000
1983	(3,500)
1984	(21,500)
1985	29,000

Instructions

[a] Determine the actuarial gain or loss that should be added or deducted from Lockman's normal cost for the years 1981–1985. In addition, determine the unrecognized accumulated gain or loss to be recognized in future years.

[b] If the normal cost was $100,000 for 1983, 1984, and 1985, provide the appropriate journal entry to record the pension expense.

[c] Why don't we adjust pension expense for the actual gain and loss experience of each year, instead of averaging or spreading?

P22–5 Lynn Rix, controller of Hendrix Corporation, is preparing the 1985 year-end financial statements. Hendrix employs 650 people and adopted a defined benefit pension plan on January 1, 1984. The past service costs at the time of adoption amounted to $2 million, based on a 6% expected rate of earnings on the plan. These past service costs are being amortized over 20 years and funded over 30 years.

The normal pension costs for 1985 amount to $786,900 and are currently being funded. As determined on December 31, 1985, the actuarial present value of the vested accumulated plan benefits of all 650 employees amounted to $3,475,000, and the actuarial present value of nonvested accumulated plan benefits for those employees amounted to $4,978,000. The net assets of the fund available for benefits, according to a report from the trustee, amounted to $1,803,300 on December 31, 1985.

Hendrix calculates an annual provision for pension expense in accordance with *APB Opinion No. 8*.

Instructions

[a] In order to reflect the pension plan properly on the 1985 financial statement of Hendrix:

[1] Calculate the pension expense which would appear on the 1985 statement of income. Disregard minimum and maximum limits.

[2] Calculate the pension liability which would appear on the statement of financial position as of December 31, 1985.

Round all calculations to the nearest $100.

[b] Prepare a note to the 1985 financial statements regarding the pension plan which complies with both *APB Opinion No. 8* and *FASB Statement of Financial Accounting Standards No. 36*.

(CMA adapted)

P22–6 Safenet Insurance Company adopted a pension plan on January 1, 1983. On January 1, 1983, Safenet's accountant treated the $350,000 past service costs as a prior period adjustment by crediting Liability from Unfunded Past Service Costs for the amount. The accountant intends to gradually eliminate the liability as funding contributions are made. At the end of 1983 and 1984, contributions of $65,605 were made. Safenet's accountant debited the liability account for $65,605 for 1983 and 1984. Safenet's accountant figures it will take an additional 3⅓ years to eliminate the liability for service costs under the present funding schedule.

You have just initiated an audit of Safenet Insurance in 1985. In the process of your audit, you discover the above set of transactions relating to the past service costs of the recently adopted pension plan. You conclude that the above treatment is incorrect and requires adjustment to the year-end 1985 financial statements.

Instructions

[a] Provide a schedule with supporting calculations to reconcile the incorrect reporting by Safenet's accountant to the correct reporting required by GAAP. Assume an amortization period of 10 years and a funding

period of 8 years for the past service costs. Disregard minimum and maximum limits.

[b] Provide the appropriate correcting and adjusting entries on December 31, 1985. Assume the books are not closed for 1985.

[c] Provide an explanation to Safenet's controller for the approach you have taken in accounting for the past service costs relative to Safenet's approach.

P22–7 Wilson Hotels Corporation adopted a pension plan on January 1, 1983. The company's actuarial consultant determined that the past service costs associated with the plan adoption were $910,000. Wilson Hotels elected to fund the $910,000 over 14 years and amortize the amount over 20 years. On January 1, 1984, Wilson Hotels amended the plan to increase the level of benefits retroactively. The prior service costs (in addition to the past service costs) associated with this amendment were determined to be $520,000. The $520,000 will be funded over 15 years and amortized over 10 years. All funding contributions are made at the end of the year. The normal costs were:

1983	$57,000
1984	69,000
1985	75,000

The normal costs were fully funded. None of the pension benefits were vested by the end of 1985. Assume an interest rate of 4%.

Instructions

[a] Determine the maximum and minimum limits for 1983–1985.

[b] Provide the appropriate journal entries to recognize pension expense for 1983–1985.

P22–8 (Appendix B) Rising Dough Bakery adopted a pension plan on January 1, 1984, for the bakery's sole employee. The plan provides a lump sum pension benefit beginning one year after retirement according to the following formula:

Lump sum pension = Final salary
$\times$ Years of service
$\times$ 6%

The following actuarial assumptions are provided:

1984 salary	$20,000
1985 salary	$23,000
1990 salary	$47,000
Retirement date	Jan. 1, 1991

Accumulated sum of compensation, 1984–1990	$226,000
Future value of salary stream at 1/1/91	$294,000
Assumed interest rate	8%

The plan provides no credit for service prior to the adoption date.

Instructions

Determine the normal costs for Rising Dough Bakery for 1984 and 1985 under each of the following actuarial cost approaches:

[a] Accumulated benefits

[b] Projected benefits (years of service)

[c] Projected benefits (compensation)

[d] Cost allocation (years of service)

[e] Cost allocation (compensation)

P22–9 Sundown Insurance Company adopted a pension plan on January 1, 1982. The past service costs associated with this adoption were $820,000. Sundown elected to fund the past service costs over 18 years, with the first contribution on December 31, 1982. The past service costs will be amortized over 14 years. On January 1, 1983, Sundown amended the pension plan by increasing benefit levels retroactively. The prior service costs (in addition to the past service costs) associated with this amendment were $240,000. The prior service costs will be funded for 11 years and amortized over 15 years. The first contribution to fund the prior service costs will be made on December 31, 1983. The pension plan is assumed to earn 4% compounded annually. The following information is known about annual normal costs and actuarial gains and losses:

	Normal Cost	Actuarial Gain (Loss)
1982	$ 66,000	$(10,000)
1983	75,000	(7,000)
1984	86,000	22,000
1985	100,000	2,000

Sundown spreads actuarial gains and losses over a 10-year period.

Instructions

[a] Construct funding and amortization tables for the past and prior service costs through 1985.

[b] Construct a table to spread the actuarial gains and losses to the normal pension costs through 1985.

[c] Determine the minimum and maximum limits for

recognition of pension expense for 1984 and 1985. [d] Record the pension expense Sundown would recognize for 1983, 1984, and 1985.

P22–10 Byte-a-Mite Computer Company adopted a formal pension plan on January 1, 1982. The plan is funded through Valley Fidelity Bank, which invests all funds and pays all benefits as they become due. Retirement benefits are provided for employees reaching the age of 65. Full vesting occurs at retirement. The past service costs associated with the plan adoption are $380,000, to be funded over 13 years and amortized over 16 years. The company also funds an amount equal to current normal cost net of actuarial gains and losses, which are spread over 10 years, except in cases where immediate recognition is more appropriate. The plan was amended on January 1, 1984, to provide additional benefits with a present value of $90,000. The amendment costs are amortized for 11 years and funded for 13 years. The first funding contribution is made on December 31, 1984.

The partial report shown below was provided by the independent actuary.

Instructions

Fill in the blanks of the actuary's report. Provide all supporting computations and schedules. Ignore the minimum and maximum limits.

Byte-a-Mite Computer Company
Actuarial Report as of December 31, 1985

Normal cost (before adjustment for actuarial gains and losses)		$59,000
Actuarial gains (losses)		
Investment gains		1,000
Change in employee turnover assumption		(5,000)
Change in mortality assumption		(3,000)
Cumulative actuarial gain for 1982–1984		11,000
Past service costs for 1985		
Funding		40,453
Amortization (after interest)	a) _____	
Amendment costs for 1985		
Funding	b) _____	
Amortization (after interest)	c) _____	
1985 Pension expense	d) _____	
1985 Pension funding	e) _____	
Deferred f)_____ (debit or credit) balance 12/31/85	g) _____	
Assumed interest rate	h) _____	

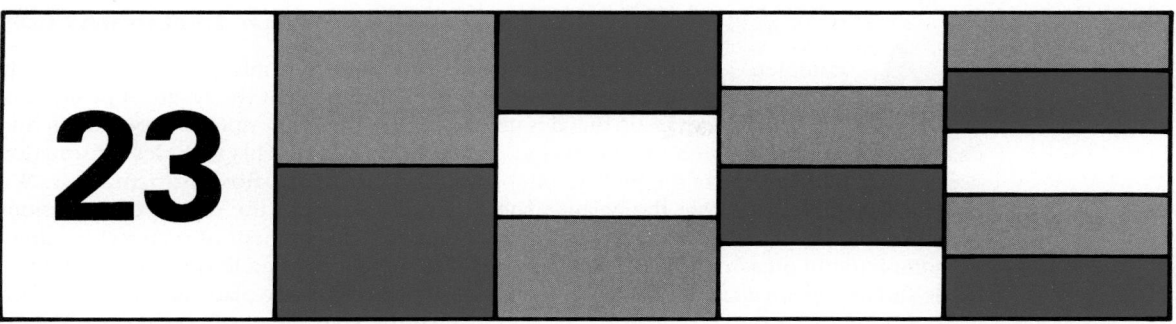

23

REPORTING FUNDS-FLOW INFORMATION AND CHANGES IN FINANCIAL POSITION

Objectives

To identify the relationship of the statement of changes in financial position to the other primary financial statements.

To discuss the importance of funds-flow information to users of financial statements.

To identify the major categories of funds inflows and outflows of business enterprises.

To state the major objectives of the statement of changes in financial position.

To explain the "all financial resources" concept that underlies the statement of changes in financial position.

To explain the three basic steps in preparing a statement of changes in financial position.

To explain various formats for presentation of nonfund transactions in the statement of changes in financial position within the all-financial-resources concept.

To present procedures for preparing a statement of changes in financial position on either a working-capital or cash basis in a relatively complex situation.

NEED FOR FUNDS-FLOW INFORMATION

Acomplete set of financial statements prepared in conformity with generally accepted accounting principles is designed to present the financial position of the enterprise as of the designated date and the results of operations and changes in financial position for the period ending on that date. This includes information concerning the enterprise's liquidity, often described as **funds-flow information.** We present financial position in the balance sheet and the details of the results of operations from profit-directed activities in the income statement and statement of retained earnings. To complete the presentation, a fourth financial statement is needed to describe the flow of funds and to explain all material changes in financial position taking place during the reporting period not reported elsewhere. This statement is the **statement of changes in financial position.**

Accountants generally consider accrual accounting concepts as the most useful in presenting financial position and results of operations. Accrual accounting attempts to relate the benefits received (e.g., revenues) to the efforts expended (e.g., expenses) rather than to emphasize changes in cash or other liquid assets. Many of the accounting principles you have studied in intermediate accounting exist because of our interest in accrual accounting, including adjusting entries, amortization and depreciation of long-lived assets, and the treatment of discounts and premiums on long-term debt obligations. Through accrual accounting

Matching

procedures we attempt to match effort and accomplishment, realizing that the underlying activities may not result in the outflow and inflow of cash in the same period in which the activities are recognized. For example, we include depreciation expense on plant assets in the income statement as we use the assets in generating revenue, whereas the cash outflows to acquire the assets might have been made several accounting periods earlier. On the other hand, we recognize revenues in the income statement as they are realized or "earned," even

Revenue Realization

though cash may not be received until a future accounting period. Although accrual accounting procedures are useful in presenting financial position and results of operations, users of financial statements are also interested in the flow of funds in and out of the enterprise.

There is no single common definition of the term **funds.** The term is frequently used, however, to describe cash or working capital (the excess of current assets over current liabilities). Both are measures of liquidity that are frequently encountered in financial reporting. The interest in funds flow stems primarily from financial statement users' interest in the ability of the enterprise to make cash payments to them in the future. Thus, there is a need for information on a funds basis *in addition to* information on an accrual accounting basis. This information is provided as a part of the statement of changes in financial position.

This chapter deals with the statement of changes in financial position in depth by reviewing the role of the statement in providing useful information to users of financial statements and by considering the detailed procedures that go into the statement's preparation. Two tools that are helpful in accumulating the detailed information necessary for preparing the statement are presented. The worksheet approach is illustrated in the comprehensive example in the latter part of the chapter, and the T-account approach is illustrated in the Appendix to this chapter.

ROLE OF THE STATEMENT OF CHANGES IN FINANCIAL POSITION

In earlier accounting courses and in Chapter 4 of this text you were introduced to the statement of changes in financial position. You learned that a widely used technique for preparing the statement is to present changes in the balance sheet accounts (i.e., changes in financial position) in terms of their impact on working capital. Example A of Exhibit 23–1 repeats the example statement from Chapter 4 (Exhibit 4–8) to refresh your memory on the general format of the statement of changes in financial position. Example B presents another format of the statement. These two statements refer to the same situation, and both focus on changes in working capital as a measure of liquidity for Sunrise Corporation. We discuss the differences between these two examples later in this chapter.

The Primary Financial Statements

How does a statement of changes in financial position relate to the other financial statements? Obviously it includes some information not included in the other financial statements; otherwise it would not be a required part of financial reporting. The relationship of the statement of changes in financial position to the other primary financial statements is depicted in Exhibit 23–2 and described in the following paragraphs.

The balance sheet relates to a *point* in time (e.g., December 31, 1984) and presents the financial position in terms of assets, liabilities, and ownership equity at the date of the statement. The income and retained earnings statements, on the other hand, cover the entire *period* between balance sheet dates; and based on accrual accounting concepts, they disclose how the *profit-directed activities affected the financial position* during the reporting period. However, numerous other financing and investing activities, which are not reported by the income statement or the retained earnings statement, may result in changes in the financial position. Examples are the issuance and retirement of long-term debt and capital stock and the acquisition and disposal of assets. These transactions are not part of the earning history of the company but, nevertheless, may have an important impact on the company's financial position. These activities may also have an important influence—which is not fully described in the other financial statements—on the inflow and outflow of liquid resources (e.g., working capital or cash) of the enterprise. To explain how financial position changes between two balance sheet dates, emphasizing the impact of operations and other financing and investing activities on a company's funds, an accountant presents the statement of changes in financial position.

In other words, the statement of changes in financial position has two important objectives:[1]

1. To summarize the financing and investing activities of the entity, emphasizing the extent to which the enterprise has generated funds (i.e., liquid assets, such as cash or working capital) from operations during the period.

Disclosure   2. To complete the disclosure of changes in financial position during the period not covered elsewhere in the financial statements.

We will refer to the first of these as the **funds-flow objective** and to the second as the **full-disclosure objective** of the statement of changes in financial position.

An important point to keep in mind as we study the statement of changes in financial position is that the statement is designed to report a **process that is continuously taking place** in a business enterprise; that is, changes in financial position continuously taking place through operations and other financing and investing activities. Although we tie the reporting of this process to the working capital or cash balance at a point in time (the end of the reporting period), the major thrust of the statement is to explain the continuous *flow* of transactions within the enterprise. The statement of changes in financial position is thus closely tied to the income statement, which details the flow of revenue and expense transactions for a specified period.

---

[1] *APB Opinion No. 19,* "Reporting Changes in Financial Position," 1971, par. 4.

EXHIBIT 23–1
Example Statements of Changes in Financial Position

EXAMPLE A

Sunrise Corporation
STATEMENT OF CHANGES IN FINANCIAL POSITION
For the Year Ended December 31, 1985

Sources of Working Capital
Operations

Income before extraordinary item	$ 50,400	
Add (Deduct): Items not affecting working capital		
Depreciation expense	7,500	
Amortization	3,200	
Loss on sale of long-term investments	5,100	
Gain on sale of equipment	(6,500)	
Working capital provided by operations, exclusive		
of extraordinary items		$ 59,700
Other sources		
Proceeds from expropriation of land	60,000	
Sale of long-term investments	10,900	
Sale of equipment	16,400	87,300
Total sources of working capital		147,000

Uses of Working Capital

Deposit made in plant expansion fund	7,000	
Payment of long-term note	110,000	
Total uses of working capital		117,000
Subtotal		30,000

Financing and Investing Activities Not Directly Affecting Working Capital

Issuance of common stock for land	55,000
Acquisition of land by issuance of common stock	(55,000)
Increase in working capital	$ 30,000

Schedule of Working Capital Changes

	Working Capital Increase (Decrease)
Current Assets	
Cash	$ 5,500
Marketable securities	(2,000)
Accounts receivable (net)	9,500
Notes receivable	10,000
Merchandise inventory	(5,000)
Prepaid expenses	2,000
Current Liabilities	
Accounts payable	9,400
Notes payable	2,000
Interest payable	500
Salaries payable	1,500
Dividends payable	(1,000)
Income tax payable	(3,000)
Advances from customers	1,800
Unearned rent revenue	(1,200)
Working capital	$30,000

EXAMPLE B

Sunrise Corporation
STATEMENT OF CHANGES IN FINANCIAL POSITION
For the Year Ended December 31, 1985

Financial Resources Provided
Operations

Income before extraordinary item	$ 50,400	
Add (Deduct): Items not affecting working capital		
Depreciation expense	7,500	
Amortization	3,200	
Loss on sale of long-term investments	5,100	
Gain on sale of equipment	(6,500)	
Working capital provided by operations, exclusive of extraordinary items		$ 59,700
Other sources		
Proceeds from expropriation of land	60,000	
Sale of long-term investments	10,900	
Sale of equipment	16,400	
Issuance of common stock for land	55,000	142,300
Total funds provided		202,000
Financial Resources Used		
Deposit made in plant expansion fund	7,000	
Payment of long-term note	110,000	
Acquisition of land by issuance of common stock	55,000	
Total funds applied		172,000
Increase in working capital		$ 30,000

Schedule of Working Capital Changes

	Working Capital Increase (Decrease)
Current Assets	
Cash	$ 5,500
Marketable securities	(2,000)
Accounts receivable (net)	9,500
Notes receivable	10,000
Merchandise inventory	(5,000)
Prepaid expenses	2,000
Current Liabilities	
Accounts payable	9,400
Notes payable	2,000
Interest payable	500
Salaries payable	1,500
Dividends payable	(1,000)
Income tax payable	(3,000)
Advances from customers	1,800
Unearned rent revenue	(1,200)
Working capital	$30,000

EXHIBIT 23–2
Relationship Between Financial Statements

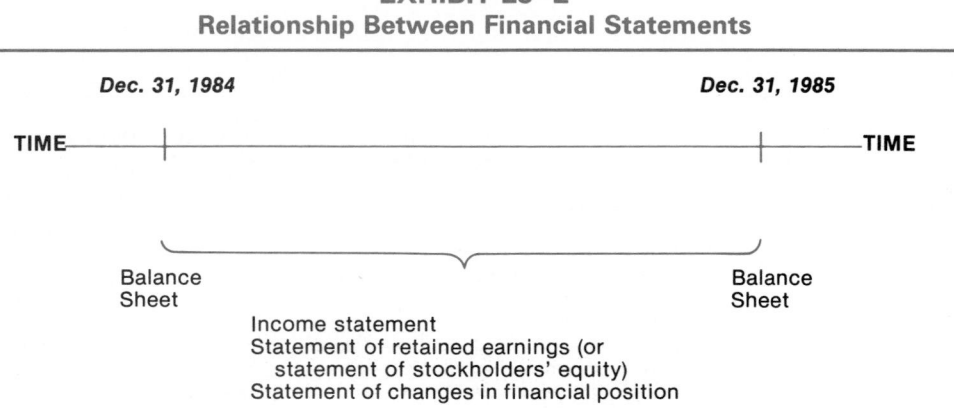

Dec. 31, 1984

Dec. 31, 1985

TIME——TIME

Balance
Sheet

Balance
Sheet

Income statement
Statement of retained earnings (or
   statement of stockholders' equity)
Statement of changes in financial position

Specific Information Included in the Statement

Although the statement of changes in financial position is based on the same underlying accounting information as the other basic financial statements, it includes information that the reader cannot easily obtain, or cannot obtain at all, from the other financial statements. For example, it assists in answering the following types of questions:[2]

1. Where did the profits go?
2. Why were dividends not larger?
3. How was it possible to distribute dividends in excess of current earnings, or in the presence of a net loss for the period?
4. Why did working capital (or cash) go down although the net income was greater than in the previous period?
5. How is it that working capital (or cash) stayed the same even though there was a net loss for the period?
6. Why must money be borrowed to finance purchases of new plant and equipment when the required amount is exceeded by the "cash flow"?
7. How was the expansion in plant and equipment financed?
8. What happened to the proceeds of the sale of plant and equipment resulting from a contraction of operations?
9. How was the retirement of debt accomplished?
10. What became of the assets derived from an increase in outstanding capital stock?
11. What became of the proceeds of the bond issue?
12. How was the increase in working capital (or cash) financed?

In selecting a definition of "funds" for use in the statement of changes in financial position, management should search for the definition that is most useful in answering questions of this type about the enterprise.

Historical Development of the Statement of Changes in Financial Position

For many years the income statement, balance sheet, and retained earnings statement constituted a complete set of financial statements when accompanied by appropriate disclo-

---

[2]Perry Mason, *Accounting Research Study No. 2,* "Cash Flow Analysis and the Funds Statement" (New York: AICPA, 1961), pp. 49–50.

sures in the form of notes and supplementary schedules. Recognizing that all changes in financial position are not disclosed when only these statements are presented, the American Institute of Certified Public Accountants (AICPA) published *Accounting Research Study No. 2* in 1961 (see footnote 2). This was followed in 1963 by *Accounting Principles Board Opinion No. 3,* which discussed the need for a statement to complete the disclosure of changes in financial position and encouraged publication of such a "funds" statement.[3] This voluntary disclosure gained popularity between 1963 and 1971, when the Accounting Principles Board (APB) issued *Opinion No. 19,* which *required* that a statement be presented to fill the disclosure gap existing when only a balance sheet, income statement, and statement of retained earnings are presented.[4] The suggested title of the statement was "Statement of Changes in Financial Position," and such a statement is now found in the annual reports of virtually all business enterprises. *APB Opinion No. 19* provides the basis for much of the material in this chapter.

Disclosure

In the late 1970s and early 1980s a great deal of interest emerged about the statement of changes in financial position. This interest centered on the importance of funds information to users of the financial statements and the concern that attempting to provide funds-flow information *and* describe all changes in financial position in the same financial statement might reduce the clarity and usefulness of the information. We look more closely at these concerns in later sections of this chapter.

REPORTING FUNDS-FLOW INFORMATION

The term "funds" is frequently encountered in financial reporting. **Funds** refers to the liquid resources with which an enterprise operates on a day-to-day basis. In meeting the funds-flow objective of a statement of changes in financial position, the reporting enterprise must select a particular **definition of funds** around which to focus its presentation. Various business activities are then presented in terms of the impact they had on the particular items included in the definition of funds.

Some enterprises focus the statement of changes in financial position on the impact of business activities on cash, the narrowest definition of funds. In this type of presentation, transactions are included as they add to (provide) or take away from (use) cash. Other enterprises focus the statement on the impact of business activities on working capital, a much broader definition of funds. In this type of presentation, transactions are included as they add to (provide) or take away from (use) working capital, the excess of current assets over current liabilities. Others focus on the impact of transactions on cash plus near-cash assets, such as current marketable securities, or on net "quick assets" (cash, current marketable securities, and current receivables less current liabilities). The definition of funds varies among enterprises. Management should select the method of presentation that provides the most useful funds-flow information to the users of its financial statements.

Because financial reporting has historically emphasized reporting business operations on the basis of accrual accounting procedures, revenues are recognized as they are earned and expenses are recognized as they are incurred, even though they may not affect the entity's working capital or cash in the current period. By contrast, a statement based on the concept of **funds flow** is constructed to display the inflows and outflows of a particular definition of funds. The accrual accounting and funds-flow presentations deal with essentially *different aspects of the same business activity.*

Regardless of the definition of funds used to describe changes in financial position, we can generalize on the broad categories of transactions that increase and decrease funds. Exhibit 23-3 demonstrates the major categories of transactions that affect the amount of cash, working capital, or other resources defined as funds.

---

[3]*APB Opinion No. 3,* "The Statement of Sources and Application of Funds," 1963.
[4]*APB Opinion No. 19, par. 7.*

EXHIBIT 23-3
Funds Inflows and Outflows

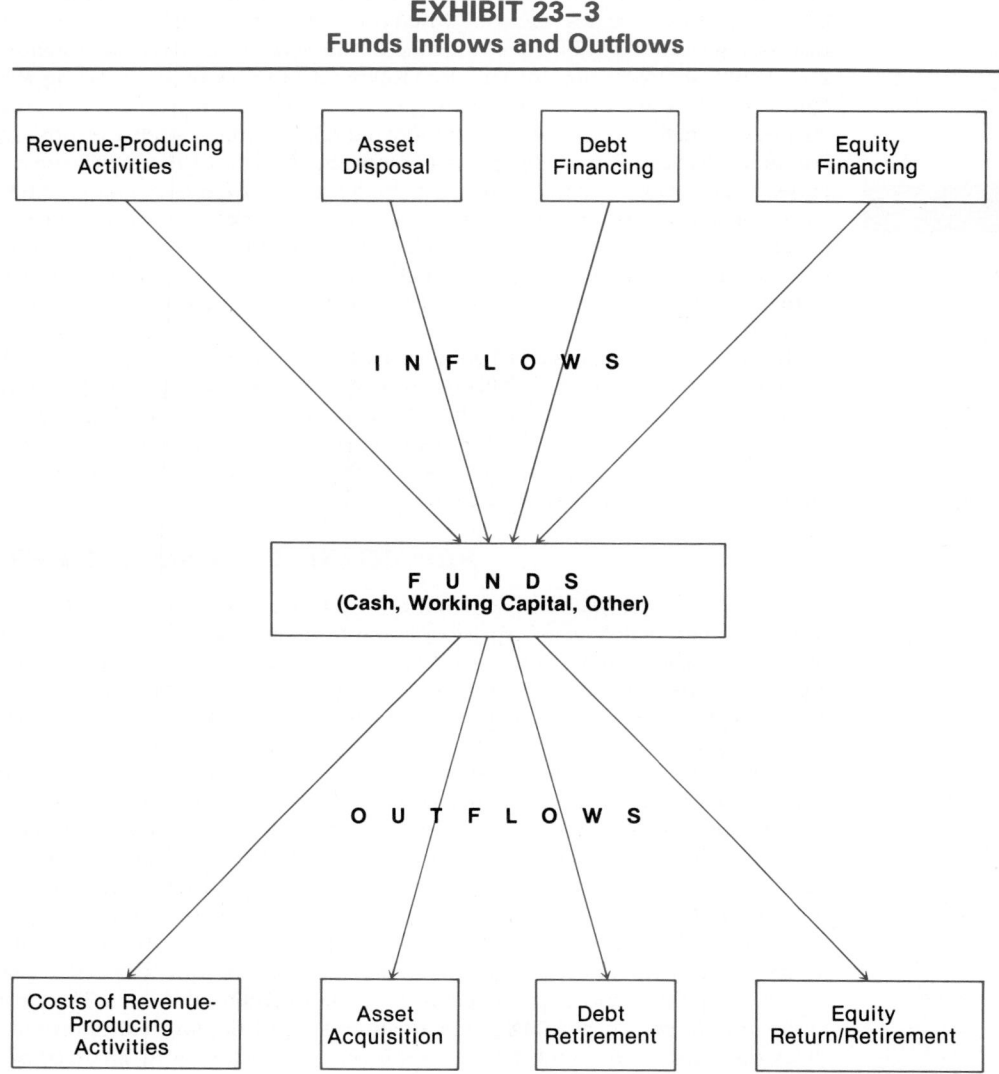

Many decisions are made by business enterprises on the basis of availability of funds. For example, credit policies and dividend distributions are influenced by the availability of funds. Thus, in attempting to judge prospective cash flows, investors and creditors are particularly interested in the impact of financing and investing activities on the flow of funds in and out of the business enterprise.

Businesses continuously convert assets and liabilities into goods and services or into other assets and obligations. In a simplified situation, this conversion process can be viewed as a series of short-term conversions and a series of long-term conversions. In the short-term conversion cycle, cash is converted into inventory that is subsequently converted into receivables and then back into cash. Typically, several of these cycles will take place during a single reporting period. On the other hand, the long-term conversion cycle involves investments of cash into machinery, equipment, furniture, fixtures, buildings, land, and other operating assets. These assets contribute to the operations of the enterprise over several accounting periods, but they subsequently are converted back into cash through successful generation of goods and services that are provided for customers. Both cycles are continuous, and at any point in time the enterprise will be involved in several short- and long-term cycles.

Renewed Interest in Funds Information

The significance of the information concerning funds flows was emphasized by the Financial Accounting Standards Board (FASB) in identifying the objectives of financial reporting. The FASB stressed the importance of information pertaining to liquidity, solvency, and funds flow. Financial reporting should provide information about how an enterprise obtains and spends cash, about its borrowing and repayment of borrowing, about its capital transactions, including cash dividends and other distributions of enterprise resources to owners, and about other factors that may affect the enterprise's liquidity or solvency. Information about funds flow is believed to be useful in understanding the operations of the enterprise, evaluating its financial activities, assessing its liquidity or solvency, and interpreting earnings information.[5]

In a 1980 *Discussion Memorandum* the FASB again emphasized the importance of information concerning funds flows, liquidity, and financial flexibility.[6] The memorandum was prepared to serve as a basis for the discussion of these types of information among accountants in anticipation of changing reporting requirements. As of this writing, these changes have not yet been formalized, but a brief consideration of some of the issues discussed in this document gives us some insight into the future directions of financial reporting.

The 1980 *Discussion Memorandum* identifies six reasons for believing that information about funds flow is useful:[7]

1. It helps directly with the assessment of future cash flows.
2. It helps to identify the relationship between income and net cash flows.
3. It provides feedback about actual cash flows.
4. It provides information about the quality of income.
5. It improves the comparability of information in financial reports.
6. It helps with the assessment of enterprise performance in other ways.

The importance of information on funds flows, liquidity, and financial flexibility is summarized in the following statements from the 1980 *Discussion Memorandum:*

> ### Funds Flows
> *Information about past cash flows or other funds flows may help users of financial statements improve their understanding of the activities of an enterprise, understand the effects on funds flows of income-generating activities, and evaluate the investing and financing activities of an enterprise. In those and other ways the information may be used as a basis for making assessments of future cash flows associated with operating, investing and financing activities.*

> ### Liquidity
> *Liquidity is an indication of the "nearness to cash" of the assets and liabilities of an enterprise. Nearness to cash can be regarded as the time that must elapse before assets and liabilities result in cash receipts and payments through normal operations. Information about liquidity may help to identify the rela-*

---

[5]*FASB Statement of Financial Accounting Concepts No. 1,* "Objectives of Financial Reporting," 1978, par. 49.
[6]*FASB Discussion Memorandum,* "Reporting Funds Flow, Liquidity, and Financial Flexibility," 1980.
[7]*FASB Discussion Memorandum,* p. 23.

*tionship between income-generating activities and the related receipts and pay-
ments of cash. It also may help to identify the pay-back period on investments
in operating assets. A short pay-back period may indicate a high level of financial flexibility.*

Financial Flexibility

*Financial flexibility is the capacity to adapt to favorable and unfavorable
changes in operating conditions. For example, financial flexibility may enable
an enterprise to undertake a new investment or to introduce a new product
line. Equity investors may be particularly interested in this aspect of financial
flexibility. When change has an adverse effect, financial flexibility may be critical to the survival of an enterprise. Declining funds flows from operations and
reduced liquidity may signal an impending cash flow problem. The solvency of
an enterprise may depend on its financial flexibility. . . . Sources of financial
flexibility include the ability to generate additional cash flows by financing, by
liquidating assets, and by modifying operations. Information about past funds
flows and the liquidity of assets and liabilities may be useful in assessing
financial flexibility.*[8]

We see in these statements and in related discussions by the FASB and other important
accounting organizations a renewed emphasis on funds-flow information in financial reporting in the 1980s. In the opinion of the authors, this emphasis represents one of the most
exciting and constructive challenges facing the accounting profession in many decades. In
the past our extreme emphasis on accrual accounting has limited our efforts to improve the
quality of financial reporting, despite the importance of accrual accounting information. We
view the renewed emphasis on funds-flow information *in conjunction with accrual
accounting information* as a positive move that will enhance the presentation of information that is useful to investors, creditors, and other users in making economic decisions.

REPORTING ALL CHANGES IN FINANCIAL POSITION

Disclosure
In addition to the funds-flow objective, we must keep in mind that *APB Opinion No. 19*
includes a full-disclosure objective for the statement of changes in financial position. Specifically, the statement has the responsibility of disclosing all changes in financial position
that are not detailed in the other financial statements.

For many business transactions, a presentation of their funds-flow implications also helps
explain their impact on financial position. For example, if an enterprise issues bonds during
the year and funds are defined as working capital, the addition to working capital provided
by the bond issue also explains the addition to long-term liabilities. For this transaction the
two objectives of the statement are met simultaneously—describing the impact on funds
and describing the impact on financial position.

Some important transactions, however, affect the financial position but do not affect
funds. For example, assume that a company that defines funds as working capital issues
capital stock in exchange for land. Does this transaction affect funds? Does it affect financial
position? The answer to the first question is no, because working capital is not involved in
the transaction. The answer to the second question is yes, however, since both the asset and
liability sections of the company's balance sheet are affected by this nonfund transaction. In
order to meet the full-disclosure objective of the statement of changes in financial position,
this transaction must be disclosed.

Refer to Exhibit 23–1 and notice how Sunrise Corporation reports its nonfund transaction, the issuance of common stock for land. In Example A, the $55,000 transaction is

---

[8]*FASB Discussion Memorandum,* pp. 2, 4.

included in a special section at the bottom of the statement entitled "Financing and investing activities not directly affecting working capital." In Example B, the two sides of the transaction are included along with other sources and uses of working capital: "Issuance of common stock for land" and "Acquisition of land by issuance of common stock." Under either method of presentation, the transaction has no impact on the $30,000 increase in working capital.

APB Opinion No. 19 refers to the "all financial resources" concept and says that the statement must include all significant financing and investing activities, regardless of whether or not they have an impact on funds.[9] Disclosure of nonfund transactions, such as the one previously discussed, in either of the ways presented in Exhibit 23–1 complies with this requirement.

Materiality

The all financial resources concept is consistent with the requirement that all material changes in assets, liabilities, and stockholders' equity be disclosed in the statement of changes in financial position. Within that broad concept, however, the reporting enterprise must select a definition of funds to use in describing those business activities that affect funds. The two most popular definitions of funds in recent years are **working capital** and **cash.** The relationship of these definitions of funds to the all financial resources concept and the resultant statement of changes in financial position are summarized in Exhibit 23–4.

In a statement defining funds as working capital, operations and financing and investing activities are presented in terms of their impact on *working capital* to satisfy the funds-flow objective. Any *nonworking capital transactions* are separately disclosed to satisfy the full-disclosure objective of the statement. If funds are defined as cash, operations and financing

---

[9]*APB Opinion No. 19,* par. 8.

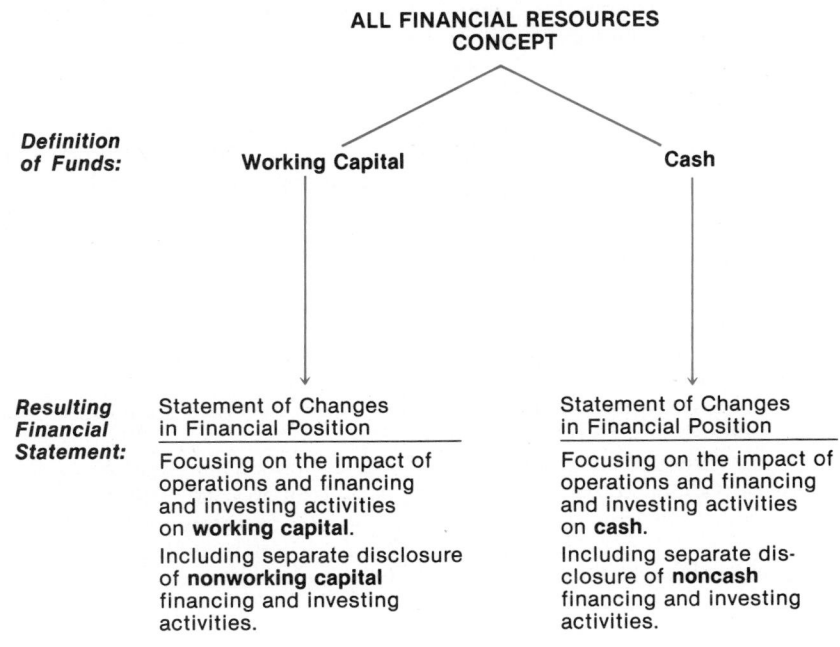

EXHIBIT 23–4
**Alternative Funds Definitions Within
the All Financial Resources Concept**

ALL FINANCIAL RESOURCES
CONCEPT

*Definition
of Funds:*   **Working Capital**   **Cash**

*Resulting   Statement of Changes   Statement of Changes
Financial   in Financial Position   in Financial Position
Statement:*   ――――――――――――――   ――――――――――――――
                  Focusing on the impact of   Focusing on the impact of
                  operations and financing   operations and financing
                  and investing activities   and investing activities
                  on **working capital**.   on **cash**.

                  Including separate disclosure   Including separate dis-
                  of **nonworking capital**   closure of **noncash**
                  financing and investing   financing and investing
                  activities.   activities.

and investing activities are presented in terms of their impact on *cash* to satisfy the funds-flow objective. Any *noncash transactions* are separately disclosed to satisfy the full-disclosure objective of the statement.

SOURCES AND USES OF FUNDS

Exhibit 23–3 illustrates that funds inflows result from: (1) revenue-producing activities; (2) asset disposals; (3) debt financing; and (4) equity financing. Funds flow out of the enterprise as a result of: (1) costs of revenue-producing activities; (2) asset acquisitions; (3) debt retirement; and (4) equity return and retirement. Inflows of funds are typically called **sources of funds,** and outflows of funds are typically called **uses of funds.**

Each category of funds *inflow* is related to an *outflow* category as follows:

Inflow Category	Outflow Category
Revenue-producing activities ⟶	Costs of revenue-producing activities
Asset disposal ⟶	Asset acquisition
Debt financing ⟶	Debt retirement
Equity financing ⟶	Equity return/retirement

Nevertheless, funds flowing into the enterprise in a particular way do not necessarily flow out of the enterprise through the related outflow category. For example, funds inflow by debt financing may be used to finance asset acquisitions rather than to retire debt. Also, funds flowing in as a result of revenue-producing activities may be used to finance the costs of those activities, to acquire assets, to retire debt, to provide a return to equity holders, or some combination of these.

Transactions that fit into one of the inflow or outflow categories do not necessarily produce or use funds. For example, if the definition of funds being applied is that of cash, an asset abandonment (as opposed to sale) does not provide an inflow of cash even though the transaction would be classified as an asset disposal. By the same token the retirement of debt by conversion into common stock reduces debt but does not require an outflow of cash.

The inflow and outflow categories identified as "revenue-producing activities" and "costs of revenue-producing activities" include many of the items incorporated in the determination of net income. In describing changes in financial position, these two categories are combined by treating net income as an inflow and net loss as an outflow of funds. As in the case of the other inflow and outflow categories, however, certain elements in the determination of net income and net loss may not provide or use funds. Depreciation is an example of an element recognized in the determination of net income or net loss that does not require the use of funds. Adjustments are made for such items, as a later section of this chapter explains.

Therefore, as a general rule an enterprise receives funds from some combination of the following sources: (1) operations; (2) disposal of assets; (3) debt financing; and (4) equity financing. Likewise, an enterprise uses funds in some combination of the following ways: (1) operations; (2) asset investment; (3) debt retirement; and (4) stockholders' equity reduction. The reduction in stockholders' equity may take the form of dividends, treasury stock acquisitions, or retirement of stock.

Although an enterprise could not have both a net inflow and a net outflow of funds from operations in the same reporting period, inflows and outflows in any or all categories previously described may take place during a reporting period. Now we shall specify more precisely the circumstances in which the various inflow and outflow categories result in sources and uses of funds within both the cash and working capital definitions.

Funds Defined as Cash

When funds are defined as cash, operations result in a source of funds if net income, plus noncash expenses, less noncash revenues, is positive. If the net result of this computation is negative, operations result in a use of cash. In other words, accrual net income must be adjusted for any items that are included that did not use cash (noncash expenses) or did not provide cash (noncash revenues) to determine the amount of cash provided by operations. Once this net figure is established, one can then determine whether operations resulted in a source or use of cash.

Disposals of assets, debt financing, and equity financing are sources of cash if the result of the transaction is an increase in cash. However, these transactions do not necessarily produce cash. For example, disposal of an asset by abandonment, rather than sale, produces no cash. Issuing debt or equity securities in exchange for plant assets produces no cash. Acquisitions of assets, debt retirement, payments of dividends, and purchases of treasury stock are uses of cash if cash is reduced as a result of the transactions.

Exhibit 23–5 summarizes these concepts by enumerating the circumstances under which general inflow and outflow categories are sources and uses of cash.

Funds Defined as Working Capital

Working capital, defined as the excess of current assets over current liabilities, represents a cushion or buffer between the assets presumed to be available to pay obligations as they come due and those obligations expected to be paid in the near future. Thus, as a measure of liquid resources it is less restrictive than cash alone, because it incorporates not only current cash, but cash expected to become available, less demands on that cash in the near future. Some view working capital as a more useful measure of liquidity than cash alone.

If funds are defined as working capital, operations result in a source of funds when net income, plus nonworking capital expenses, less nonworking capital revenues, is positive. If the net result of this computation is negative, operations result in a use of working capital. Net income, determined by accrual procedures, must be adjusted for any items that did not require the use of working capital (nonworking capital expense) or did not provide working capital (nonworking capital revenues) to determine the working capital provided by or used in operations.

Disposals of assets, debt financing, and equity financing are *sources* of working capital if these transactions result in an increase in working capital; they are *uses* of working capital if

---

EXHIBIT 23–5
Sources and Uses of Cash

	Sources	Uses
Operations	Net income, plus noncash expenses, less noncash revenues, is positive.	Net income, plus noncash expenses, less noncash revenues, is negative.
Asset transactions	Decrease in noncash asset results in an increase in cash.	Increase in noncash asset results in a decrease in cash.
Debt transactions	Increase in debt results in an increase in cash.	Decrease in debt results in a decrease in cash.
Equity transactions	Increase in equity results in an increase in cash.	Decrease in equity results in a decrease in cash.

EXHIBIT 23–6
Sources and Uses of Working Capital

	Sources	Uses
Operations	Net income, plus nonworking capital expenses, less nonworking capital revenues, is positive.	Net income, plus nonworking capital expenses, less nonworking capital revenues, is negative.
Asset transactions	Decrease in noncurrent assets results in an increase in working capital.	Increase in noncurrent assets results in a decrease in working capital.
Debt transactions	Increase in noncurrent debt results in an increase in working capital.	Decrease in noncurrent debt results in a decrease in working capital.
Equity transactions	Increase in equity results in an increase in working capital.	Decrease in equity results in a decrease in working capital.

they result in a reduced level of working capital. Not all transactions that affect working capital accounts are sources or uses of working capital. If two working capital accounts are involved in the same transaction, the amount of working capital remains the same. For example, if inventory is purchased on account, both current assets and current liabilities increase by the same amount and working capital remains the same.

Exhibit 23–6 summarizes these concepts by enumerating the circumstances under which general inflow and outflow categories are sources and uses of working capital.

PREPARING THE STATEMENT OF CHANGES IN FINANCIAL POSITION: WORKING CAPITAL AND CASH DEFINITIONS OF FUNDS

Preparing the statement of changes in financial position involves three basic steps:

1. Determine the change in funds by comparing the beginning and ending amounts of cash or working capital.
2. Identify all transactions that resulted in increases or decreases in funds and all nonfund financing and investing activities.
3. Use the information from steps 1 and 2 to prepare a formal financial statement that conforms with the presentation and disclosure requirements of *APB Opinion No. 19*.

Information to complete these steps is found in the other basic financial statements and in the underlying accounting records of the reporting enterprise. Since this information is accumulated primarily for purposes of preparing balance sheets and income statements on an accrual basis, adjustments may be necessary to prepare the information needed for the statement of changes in financial position. In a sense we begin with the ending balance sheet and work backwards to determine the causes of the changes in financial position during the period. The underlying information used includes explanations of changes in account balances that are not readily apparent from the other financial statements.

Example: Funds Defined as Working Capital

A condensed income statement for 1984 and comparative balance sheets for 1983 and 1984, along with additional information, for Hamilton Company are presented in Exhibit 23–7. The following paragraphs apply the three steps identified earlier to produce the statement of changes in financial position for Hamilton Company for 1984.

Determination of the Change in Working Capital

The change in working capital is determined by computing the amounts of working capital at December 31, 1983, and at December 31, 1984, and comparing the two amounts, as follows:

1983

Current assets:	Cash	$100,000	
	Accounts receivable	400,000	
		500,000	
Current liability:	Accrued expenses	(150,000)	$350,000

1984

Current assets:	Cash	$ 50,000	
	Accounts receivable	300,000	
		350,000	
Current liability:	Accrued expenses	(200,000)	150,000
Decrease in working capital			$200,000

We have determined that the change in working capital is a *decrease* of $200,000 between the end of 1983 and the end of 1984.

Transaction Analysis

Next, we analyze the changes in the noncurrent balance sheet accounts to identify any sources and uses of working capital and any nonworking capital transactions that affected the financial position during the year (see Exhibit 23–8). The decline in working capital of $200,000 provides a check figure for our search. We know that *uses must have exceeded sources by $200,000,* because more working capital was used than was provided.

EXHIBIT 23–7
Financial Information for Hamilton Company

Hamilton Company
COMPARATIVE BALANCE SHEETS
December 31, 1983 and 1984
(in thousands of dollars)

	1983	1984
Assets		
Cash	$ 100	$ 50
Accounts receivable	400	300
Plant assets	1,000	1,700
Accumulated depreciation	(100)	(200)
	$1,400	$1,850
Equities		
Accrued expenses	$ 150	$ 200
Bonds payable	650	800
Capital stock	500	600
Retained earnings	100	250
	$1,400	$1,850

Hamilton Company
INCOME STATEMENT
For the Year Ended December 31, 1984
(in thousands of dollars)

Revenue		$1,500
Expenses		
Depreciation	$ 100	
Other	1,100	1,200
Net income		$ 300

Additional Information

Capital stock was sold at par value during 1984.

Bonds of $100,000 were retired during 1984, and $250,000 of new bonds were issued.

Additional plant assets of $700,000 were acquired during 1984.

Cash dividends of $150,000 were declared and paid during 1984.

EXHIBIT 23–8
Hamilton Company
Sources and Uses of Working Capital
(in thousands of dollars)

	Trial Balance			Working Capital Increase (Decrease)	Financing and Investing Activities	
	1983	1984	Increase (Decrease)		Sources	Uses
Assets						
Cash	$ 100	$ 50	$ (50)	$ (50)		
Accounts receivable	400	300	(100)	(100)		
Plant assets	1,000	1,700	700			$700 (Acquisition of plant assets)
Accumulated depreciation	(100)	(200)	100		$100 (Adjustment to net income)	
	$1,400	$1,850				
Equities						
Accrued expenses	$ 150	$ 200	50	(50)		
Bonds payable	650	800	150		250 (Sale of bonds)	100 (Retirement of bonds)
Capital stock	500	600	100		100 (Sale of stock)	
Retained earnings	100	250	150		300 (Net income)	150 (Cash dividends)
	$1,400	$1,850			750	950
Decrease in working capital				$(200)	200	
					$950	$950

Following the guidelines we studied earlier in this chapter concerning the nature of sources and uses of working capital, we analyze the comparative balance sheet and income statement items, along with the additional information, and identify sources and uses as described in Exhibit 23–6.

We arrive at a figure for the *sources* of working capital for 1984 in the following manner: Net income is reported as $300,000 in the income statement. This includes depreciation of $100,000, a nonworking capital expense, so this amount must be added back to net income to derive the figure for working capital from operations. Capital stock was sold at $100,000, which we determine by computing the change in the Capital Stock account balance from $500,000 to $600,000. The final source is the sale of bonds at $250,000, giving us a total *sources of working capital* of $750,000.

Uses of working capital total $950,000 for 1984, because the retirement of bonds for $100,000, the acquisition of plant assets for $700,000, and the declaration of a cash dividend of $150,000 are the uses of working capital.

Total sources, $750,000, are less than total uses, $950,000, by $200,000, the exact amount of the change in working capital we identified earlier. Further support that we have properly identified sources and uses is the fact that uses *exceed* sources, a finding that is consistent with the fact that working capital declined during the period.

The analysis is more complicated when offsetting transactions affect the change in a noncurrent account. Examples are the Bonds Payable account, which recorded bonds issued and bonds retired during the period, and the Retained Earnings account, which was affected by both net income and the cash dividend. In the statement of changes in financial position, the individual transactions should be shown as separate financing and investing activities, as illustrated in Exhibit 23–8. As a general rule, transactions should not be netted against each other in presenting them in the statement of changes in financial position.

Since we have accounted for all changes in the noncurrent balance sheet accounts and we can reconcile our sources and uses to the change in working capital, we can conclude that no nonworking capital financing and investing transactions occurred during the period. Now we are ready to prepare the statement of changes in financial position.

Preparation of the Statement of Changes in Financial Position

We incorporate the information accumulated in our transactions analysis to prepare a formal statement of changes in financial position, following the guidelines for presentation in *APB Opinion No. 19*. These guidelines, which are followed in the statement that appears in Exhibit 23–9, can be summarized:

1. The statement should begin with net income or loss (before extraordinary items, if any). This figure is adjusted for any nonfund transactions to give a figure described as **funds (cash or working capital) provided by operations.**

EXHIBIT 23–9

Hamilton Company
STATEMENT OF CHANGES IN FINANCIAL POSITION
(Working Capital Focus)
For the Year Ended December 31, 1984
(in thousands of dollars)

Sources of Working Capital		
Operations		
Net income	$300	
Add: Expense not requiring working capital—depreciation	100	
Working capital provided by operations		$400
Other sources		
Sale of capital stock	100	
Sale of bonds	250	350
Total sources of working capital		750
Uses of Working Capital		
Retirement of bonds	100	
Acquisition of plant assets	700	
Declaration of cash dividends	150	950
Decrease in working capital		$200

Schedule of Working Capital Changes

	Working Capital Increase (Decrease)
Current Assets	
Cash	$ (50)
Accounts receivable	(100)
Current Liabilities	
Accrued expenses	(50)
Decrease in working capital	$(200)

2. Other financing and investing activities should be individually presented in broad categories.

3. A summary of the changes in the working capital accounts should be presented as part of the statement.

Example: Funds Defined as Cash

Preparing a statement of changes in financial position focusing on cash as a definition of funds involves the same three steps followed in the previous section: determining the change in funds (cash), identifying sources and uses of funds (cash), and preparing a formal statement of changes in financial position.

Determination of the Change in Cash

We determine the change in cash by comparing the 1984 cash balance of $50,000 with the $100,000 balance for 1983. Cash decreased $50,000 during 1984, so the uses of cash must have exceeded the sources of cash by $50,000.

EXHIBIT 23–10
Hamilton Company
Sources and Uses of Cash
(in thousands of dollars)

| | Trial Balance | | | Cash Increase (Decrease) | Financing and Investing Activities | |
	1983	1984	Increase (Decrease)		Sources	Uses
Assets						
Cash	$ 100	$ 50	$ (50)	$(50)		
Accounts receivable	400	300	(100)		$100 (Adjustment to net income)	
Plant assets	1,000	1,700	700			$700 (Acquisition of plant assets)
Accumulated depreciation	(100)	(200)	100		100 (Adjustment to net income)	
	$1,400	$1,850				
Equities						
Accrued expenses	$ 150	$ 200	50		50 (Adjustment to net income)	
Bonds payable	650	800	150		250 (Sale of bonds)	100 (Retirement of bonds)
Capital stock	500	600	100		100 (Sale of stock)	
Retained earnings	100	250	150		300 (Net income)	150 (Cash dividends)
	$1,400	$1,850			900	950
Decrease in cash				$(50)	50	
					$950	$950

Transaction Analysis

Next we analyze the changes in all balance sheet accounts *other than Cash* to determine the sources and uses of cash. Following the approach we used in Exhibit 23–8 for the working capital focus, we identify the sources and uses of cash as illustrated in Exhibit 23–10. Essentially this analysis is the same as that for working capital except for the treatment of the current assets (other than cash) and the current liabilities. For Hamilton this involves accounts receivable and accrued expenses.

The $100,000 decrease in accounts receivable is shown as a positive adjustment to operations as a source of funds (cash). To understand this treatment, we must look beyond the balance sheet account and consider the income statement implications of that account. Accounts receivable are tied directly to sales when they increase and to cash when they decrease. If accounts receivable decreased during the period ($100,000 in this case), the cash received on account exceeds the amount of sales included in the income statement by that amount. We must add $100,000 to net income in determining cash provided by operations to include the collection of cash on accounts that were recognized from sales in a previous accounting period. Here we see a fundamental difference between information prepared on an accrual basis and a funds-flow basis.

The $50,000 increase in accrued expenses requires a similar analysis. If accrued expenses increased during the period ($50,000 in this case), the cash paid for expenses is less than the amount of expenses recognized in the income statement. Again we see a difference between accrual and funds-flow information. In this case, the increase in accrued expenses requires an addition to net income to determine cash provided by operations.

Preparation of the Statement of Changes in Financial Position

Following the guidelines of *APB Opinion No. 19*, we prepare a statement of changes in financial position as shown in Exhibit 23–11. Because the changes in cash, accounts receiv-

---

EXHIBIT 23–11

Hamilton Company
STATEMENT OF CHANGES IN FINANCIAL POSITION
(Cash Focus)
For the Year Ended December 31, 1984
(in thousands of dollars)

Sources of Cash		
Operations		
Net income	$300	
Accrual to cash adjustments		
Depreciation expense	100	
Decrease in accounts receivable	100	
Increase in accrued expenses	50	
Cash provided by operations		$550
Other sources		
Sale of capital stock	100	
Sale of bonds	250	350
Total sources of cash		900
Uses of Cash		
Retirement of bonds	100	
Acquisition of plant assets	700	
Payment of cash dividends	150	950
Decrease in cash		$ 50

able, and accrued expenses are included in the body of the statement, the analysis of changes in the components of working capital is not necessary in this statement.

COMPREHENSIVE ILLUSTRATION: WORKING CAPITAL DEFINITION OF FUNDS

This section provides a comprehensive illustration of the preparation of the statement of changes in financial position, focusing on changes in working capital. Financial information for Hudson, Inc., for 1984 is presented in Exhibit 23–12, including comparative balance sheets for 1983 and 1984, a partial income statement for 1984, and additional information concerning 1984. This illustration incorporates several complexities that were not included in the simplified examples of Hamilton Company, such as extraordinary items, deferred income taxes, bond discounts and premiums, and gains and losses on the sale of assets.

In some situations the analysis of transactions becomes quite complicated, as you will see in the illustration that follows. Two tools are available to assist in the accumulation of the needed information for preparation of the statement of changes in financial position: the

---

EXHIBIT 23–12
Financial Information for Hudson, Inc.

Hudson, Inc.
COMPARATIVE BALANCE SHEETS
December 31, 1983 and 1984

	1984	1983
Assets		
Cash	$ 65,000	$ 70,000
Accounts receivable, net	60,000	65,000
Inventory	94,600	62,000
Total current assets	219,600	197,000
Property, plant, and equipment	190,000	200,000
Accumulated depreciation	(33,000)	(30,000)
Patents	9,000	10,000
Total noncurrent assets	166,000	180,000
Total assets	$385,600	$377,000
Liabilities		
Dividends payable	$ 17,000	$ 10,000
Accounts payable	35,300	50,000
Income taxes payable	54,200	42,000
Notes payable	–0–	20,000
Total current liabilities	106,500	122,000
Deferred income taxes	8,600	10,000
Convertible bonds payable	60,000	100,000
Unamortized bond discount	(5,300)	(10,000)
Total noncurrent liabilities	63,300	100,000
Stockholders' Equity		
Preferred stock	10,000	10,000
Common stock	75,000	60,000
Additional paid-in capital	18,000	15,000
Retained earnings	112,800	70,000
Total stockholders' equity	215,800	155,000
Total liabilities and stockholders' equity	$385,600	$377,000

Hudson, Inc.
PARTIAL STATEMENT OF INCOME
For the Year Ended December 31, 1984

Income before income tax		$110,000
Income tax expense		
Current	$54,200	
Deferred	(1,400)	52,800
Income before extraordinary item		57,200
Extraordinary gain—retirement of long-term debt, net of $2,400 applicable income tax		2,600
Net income		$ 59,800

Additional Information

[1] Income before income tax includes the following items:

Depreciation expense	$8,000
Amortization of patents	1,000
Amortization of bond discount	800
Loss on sale of plant assets	3,000

[2] Plant assets were purchased for $10,000 during 1984.
[3] Plant assets with a historical cost of $20,000 and a book value of $15,000 were sold at a $3,000 loss during 1984.
[4] Bonds with a $20,000 face value and a book value of $18,100 were retired with a cash outlay of $13,100 during 1984.
[5] Bonds with a $20,000 face value and a book value of $18,000 were converted into 1,500 shares of $10 par value common stock during 1984.
[6] Notes payable represent bank loans of short-term duration.
[7] The dividend liability of $10,000 at December 31, 1983, was paid in early 1984. Dividends of $17,000, which were declared in late 1984, are to be paid in early 1985.

worksheet approach and the T-account approach. Both are helpful in identifying adjustments to net income for nonfund items and sources and uses of funds that may not be evident from simply reviewing the financial statements and related information. The example in this section incorporates the worksheet approach. The same example is included a second time in the Appendix to Chapter 23, illustrating the T-account approach. In preparing a statement of changes in financial position, a careful review of available information may be sufficient to accumulate the specific items that should be presented. If the complexity of the situation warrants a more formalized method of identifying the information needed, the worksheet and T-account approaches are available alternatives.

Determination of Change in Working Capital

The change in working capital for Hudson, Inc., for 1984 is an increase of $38,100. The schedule in Exhibit 23–13 illustrates the determination of this increase. Each current asset and current liability is analyzed to determine the impact that its change during the year had on working capital. Since working capital is the difference between current assets and current liabilities, the following guidelines can be used:

	Impact on working capital if:	
	Balance in Account Increases	Balance in Account Decreases
Current asset	Increase	Decrease
Current liability	Decrease	Increase

EXHIBIT 23–13
Hudson, Inc.
Schedule of Changes in Working Capital

	Dec. 31, 1984	Dec. 31, 1983	Change in Working Capital Increase (Decrease)
Current Assets			
Cash	$ 65,000	$ 70,000	$ (5,000)
Accounts receivable (net)	60,000	65,000	(5,000)
Inventory	94,600	62,000	32,600
	219,600	197,000	
Current Liabilities			
Dividends payable	17,000	10,000	(7,000)
Accounts payable	35,300	50,000	14,700
Income taxes payable	54,200	42,000	(12,200)
Notes payable	–0–	20,000	20,000
	106,500	122,000	
Increase in working capital	$113,100	$ 75,000	$ 38,100

Identification of Sources and Uses of Working Capital

A brief review of the balance sheet, income statement, and additional information in Exhibit 23–12 reveals the following sources and uses of working capital and nonworking capital transactions of Hudson, Inc., during 1984:

Sources of Working Capital

Income before extraordinary items (adjusted for nonworking capital items).

Sale of property, plant, and equipment (loss included in income before extraordinary items).

Uses of Working Capital

Retirement of bonds (extraordinary gain included in net income).

Declaration of cash dividends.

Purchase of plant assets.

Nonworking Capital Transaction

Conversion of bonds into common stock.

Exhibit 23–14 presents a worksheet to assist in the transactions analysis required for preparation of the statement of changes in financial position. The purposes of the worksheet are: (1) to identify the specific amounts of the sources and uses of working capital and the nonworking capital transactions and (2) to ensure that all changes in financial position have been accounted for properly. The worksheet is simply a device to facilitate the preparation of the statement of changes in financial position. Entries made on the worksheet are *not* recorded in the company's formal accounting records. That is, they are neither journalized nor posted to ledger accounts.

EXHIBIT 23–14

Hudson, Inc.
WORKSHEET FOR STATEMENT OF CHANGES IN FINANCIAL POSITION
(Working Capital Focus)

Debits	Dec. 31, 1983	Debit		Credit		Dec. 31, 1984
Working capital	75,000	(k)	38,100			113,100
Property, plant, and equipment	200,000	(i)	10,000	(f)	20,000	190,000
Patents	10,000			(c)	1,000	9,000
Unamortized bond discount	10,000			(e)	800	5,300
				(g)	1,900	
				(j)	2,000	
	295,000					317,400
Credits						
Accumulated depreciation	30,000	(f)	5,000	(b)	8,000	33,000
Deferred income taxes	10,000	(d)	1,400			8,600
Convertible bonds payable	100,000	(g)	20,000			60,000
		(j)	20,000			
Preferred stock	10,000					10,000
Common stock	60,000			(j)	15,000	75,000
Additional paid-in capital	15,000			(j)	3,000	18,000
Retained earnings	70,000	(h)	17,000	(a)	57,200	112,800
				(g)	2,600	
	295,000					317,400

Sources					
Operations					
Income before extraordinary item		(a)	57,200		
Depreciation		(b)	8,000		
Amortization of patents		(c)	1,000		
Reduction in deferred income taxes				(d)	1,400
Amortization of bond discount		(e)	800		
Loss on sale of property, plant, and equipment		(f)	3,000		
Other					
Extraordinary gain		(g)	2,600		
Sale of property, plant, and equipment		(f)	12,000		
Uses					
Book value of bonds retired				(g)	18,100
Dividends on common stock				(h)	17,000
Purchase of property, plant, and equipment				(i)	10,000
Nonworking Capital Transactions					
Retirement of bonds payable				(j)	18,000
Issuance of common stock		(j)	18,000		
Increase in working capital				(k)	38,100
			214,100		214,100

The worksheet is organized as follows:

1. The extreme left and right columns are trial balances of the balance sheet accounts as of the beginning of the period (left) and end of the period (right). The current assets and current liabilities are combined into a single item identified as "working capital" and presented on the first line of the worksheet as if this represented a single asset.

2. Debit and credit columns are placed in the center under "changes" and are used to enter transactions that affected the various account balances during the period.
3. Below the trial balance figures, the basic categories included in the statement of changes in financial position are identified:

> Sources
>   Operations
>   Other
> Uses
> Nonworking capital transactions

4. Mechanical checks provided by the worksheet are:
   a. The trial-balance debit total must equal the trial-balance credit total; this is true for both beginning and ending dates.
   b. In the changes columns the debit total must equal the credit total after all transactions have been identified and entered on the worksheet.
   c. Each account balance must **crossfoot** (i.e., the beginning balance plus and/or minus changes must equal the ending balance) after all transactions have been identified and recorded.

The process by which transactions are analyzed and entered on the worksheet is illustrated below with identifying letters that correspond to those in the change columns of the worksheet.

(a) Income Before Extraordinary Item

Worksheet Entry	Source (Operations)—Income Before		
	Extraordinary Item	57,200	
	Retained Earnings		57,200

Income before extraordinary item of $57,200 is entered as a debit under Source (Operations) for purposes of statement of changes in financial position presentation. The balance sheet account affected by net income is Retained Earnings, which is credited in the worksheet entry.

(b) Depreciation on Property, Plant, and Equipment

Worksheet Entry	Source (Operations)—Depreciation	8,000	
	Accumulated Depreciation		8,000

Depreciation of $8,000 is entered as a debit under Source (Operations) for purposes of statement of changes in financial position presentation. The balance sheet account affected by the recognition of depreciation expense for the period is Accumulated Depreciation, which is credited in the worksheet entry. The entry debiting Depreciation under the Sources caption is not intended to imply that depreciation is a source of working capital. Rather, the debit to Source (Operations) simply indicates the section (of the statement of changes in financial position) in which depreciation will be presented *as an adjustment to net income when the statement is prepared.* This inclusion of depreciation—as well as other nonworking capital items included in the determination of net income—is part of the process of determining the amount of working capital provided by operations. We add depreciation back to net income because it is an expense recognized in the determination of net income that does not require working capital. This type of adjustment is required to convert information prepared on an accrual basis to information presenting funds flow.

(c) Amortization of Patents

Worksheet Entry	Source (Operations)—Amortization of Patents	1,000	
	Patents		1,000

Source (Operations) is debited because it adjusts the net income recognized in (a). The balance sheet account affected by the amortization of patents is the Patents account, which is credited in the worksheet entry.

(d) Reduction in Deferred Income Taxes

Worksheet Entry	Deferred Income Taxes	1,400	
	Source (Operations)—Reduction in Deferred Income Taxes		1,400

As discussed in Chapter 18, interperiod income tax allocation procedures must be followed if timing differences exist between pretax-accounting income and taxable income. In these cases the tax expense recognized in determining net income will not equal the tax to be paid. In the case of Hudson, deferred income taxes are reduced by $1,400, indicating that income tax expense is not as great as the current amount paid or payable. In fact, an analysis of the income statement and balance sheet reveals that the income tax expense is $52,800 while the *current* income tax payable is $54,200. Working capital is therefore reduced by $54,200. Income before extraordinary item as a source of working capital is reduced by $1,400 to adjust for the difference ($54,200 − $52,800 = $1,400). Thus, the worksheet entry is a debit to Deferred Income Taxes, the balance sheet account affected, and Source (Operations) is reduced with a credit of $1,400. In this case Source (Operations) is credited because the working capital used exceeds income tax expense and the amount of working capital provided by operations is reduced.

If deferred income taxes increased during the period—indicating that the amount currently paid or payable was less than the expense recognized—the increase would be treated as a nonworking capital expense, much like depreciation or amortization. The increase would be added to income before extraordinary items. The worksheet entry would appear as follows:

Worksheet Entry	Source (Operations)—Increase in Deferred Income Taxes	XXX	
	Deferred Income Taxes		XXX

In this case, Source (Operations) would be debited, because the working capital used was less than income tax expense, and the amount of working capital provided by operations would be increased.

(e) Amortization of Bond Discount

Worksheet Entry	Source (Operations)—Amortization of Bond Discount	800	
	Unamortized Bond Discount		800

If bonds are sold at a discount or premium, the interest expense for the period is not the same as the amount of working capital change resulting from the payment and accrual of interest expense. The change in working capital resulting from interest payment and accrual is the amount of interest actually paid, adjusted for any increase or decrease in accrued interest payable between the beginning and ending of the accounting period. The interest expense incorporates the amortization of the discount or premium which is a nonworking capital component of that expense.

If a *discount* is being amortized, interest expense exceeds interest paid and accrued, and the worksheet entry must recognize the amortization as an addition to income before extraordinary item as a source of working capital. The preceding worksheet entry therefore includes a debit to Sources (Operations) and an offsetting credit to Unamortized Bond Discount, the appropriate balance sheet account. As in the case of depreciation and amortization recognized in previous entries, the amortization of a bond discount is not a source of working capital, but is rather an adjustment to the amount of working capital provided by income before extraordinary items. The expense recognized on the accrual basis is greater than the amount of funds (working capital) needed to satisfy interest requirements.

If a *premium* is being amortized, the interest expense included in income determination is not as large as the interest paid or becoming payable in the period. In that case, the worksheet entry would effectively reduce the amount of working capital provided by operations. The entry would be:

Worksheet Entry	Unamortized Bond Premium	XXX	
	Source (Operations)—Amortization of Bond Premium		XXX

The credit to Source (Operations) would be deducted from net income in determining working capital provided by operations. The appropriate balance sheet account, Unamortized Bond Premium, would be debited.

(f) Sale of Property, Plant, and Equipment

Worksheet Entry	Source (Operations)—Loss on Sale of Property, Plant, and Equipment	3,000	
	Source (Other)—Sale of Property, Plant, and Equipment	12,000	
	Accumulated Depreciation	5,000	
	Property, Plant, and Equipment		20,000

The sale of noncurrent assets at a gain or loss imposes an additional problem in the determination of the appropriate amounts to be included in the statement of changes in financial position. The increase in working capital is the increase in cash or other current asset or the decrease in current liabilities resulting from the sale transaction. If assets are sold for an amount other than book value, a gain or loss is included in income for the difference between the proceeds from the sale and the book value.

One approach to follow in preparing the statement of changes in financial position is to treat the gain or loss included in income as a nonworking capital transaction. This means that a loss on the sale is added to net income in determining working capital provided by operations, and a gain on the sale is subtracted. This treatment of gains or losses resulting from the sale of assets effectively results in their being treated as "nonoperating" items and eliminates them from the computation of working capital provided by operations.

The worksheet entry identifed as (f) follows this procedure by including a debit to Source (Operations) for $3,000 to eliminate the loss from net income. Source (Other) is then debited for the $12,000 increase in working capital brought about by the sale of the assets. The appropriate balance-sheet accounts affected (Accumulated Depreciation and Property, Plant, and Equipment) are then debited for $5,000 and credited for $20,000, respectively.

Applying this same procedure to a situation in which the asset was sold for a gain, the gain would be deducted from income in determining working capital provided by operations. Otherwise, the amounts would be determined in the same manner as in the sale at a loss. The entry in the case of a gain would be as follows:

Worksheet Entry	Source (Other)—Sale of Property, Plant and Equipment	XXX	
	Accumulated Depreciation	XXX	
	Source (Operations)—Gain on Sale of Property, Plant, and Equipment		XXX
	Property, Plant, and Equipment		XXX

The debit to Source (Other) would be the amount received in the sale. The credit to Source (Operations) would be the gain recognized on the sale.

Some accountants question this treatment of gains and losses on the sale of assets because they are included in income before extraordinary items in the income statement. They argue that to treat these gains and losses as nonoperating items is incorrect because they are by definition not extraordinary items. An alternative procedure for this type of item is not to adjust net income for the gain or loss and simply include the *book value* of the asset sold among other sources of working capital. If this approach is followed, the worksheet entry is as follows:

Worksheet Entry	Source (Other)—Book Value of Property, Plant, and Equipment Sold	XXX	
	Accumulated Depreciation	XXX	
	Property, Plant, and Equipment		XXX

Consis-tency

Either approach for treating gains and losses included in the determination of funds provided by operations is acceptable if followed consistently from period to period. In this text we use the former approach, in which funds from operations are adjusted for any gain or loss and the actual amount of working capital or cash provided by the transaction is presented as a source.

(g) Retirement of Bonds

Worksheet Entries	Source (Other)—Extraordinary Gain	2,600	
	Retained Earnings		2,600
	Convertible Bonds Payable	20,000	
	Unamortized Bond Discount		1,900
	Use—Book Value of Bonds Retired		18,100

Transactions resulting in gains or losses classified as extraordinary and therefore presented on a net-of-tax basis require special treatment in the statement of changes in financial position. The retirement of bonds by Hudson, Inc., provides an example of such a transaction.

The extraordinary gain (or loss) is presented separately, following the caption "Working capital provided by operations, exclusive of extraordinary item" (see Exhibit 23–15). The first worksheet entry under (g) establishes this item by debiting $2,600 to Source (Other) for Extraordinary Gain and crediting Retained Earnings for the same amount. Since the amount recognized in entry (a) is $57,200 (income before extraordinary item), the $2,600 credit in entry (g) completes the adjustments to retained earnings necessary to record net income for the year. The income before extraordinary item is separated from the extraordinary item to establish the former as an "operations" source and the latter as an "other" source. This presentation complies with the following from *APB Opinion No. 19:*

The Statement for the period should begin with income or loss before extraordinary items, if any, and add back (or deduct) items recognized in determining that income or loss which did not use (or provide) working capital or cash during the period . . . the resulting amount of working capital or cash should be appropriately described, e.g., "working capital provided from (used in) operations for the period, exclusive of extraordinary items." This total should be immediately followed by income or loss from extraordinary items, if any.[10]

The second entry is made to establish the *book value* of bonds retired as a use of working capital. Convertible Bonds Payable is debited for $20,000 and the Unamortized Bond Discount is credited for $1,900 in addition to the recognition of the working capital use of $18,100.

The net amount of the source and use recognized in the two entries is $15,500 (use of $18,100 less source of $2,600). This is equal to the actual decrease in working capital resulting from the transaction, computed as follows:

Cash paid to retire bonds	$13,100
Tax currently payable on gain ($5,000 48%)	2,400
	$15,500

Some accountants prefer to present the $15,500 as a single use of working capital on the statement of changes in financial position. However, a literal interpretation of the statement just quoted from *APB Opinion No. 19* appears to favor the presentation of the two separate elements of the transaction.

If the convertible bonds had been retired at a loss that was presented as extraordinary in the income statement, the worksheet entries would be as follows:

Worksheet Entries	Retained Earnings	XXX	
	Source (Other)—Extraordinary Loss		XXX
	Convertible Bonds Payable	XXX	
	Unamortized Bond Discount		XXX
	Use—Book Value of Bonds Retired		XXX

(h) Declaration of Dividends

Worksheet Entry	Retained Earnings	17,000	
	Use—Dividends on Common Stock		17,000

The declaration of a cash dividend represents a use of working capital, because the current liability related to the payment of the dividend is created at the point of declaration. Thus, Use is credited and the appropriate balance sheet account, Retained Earnings, is debited. The subsequent payment of this dividend does not affect working capital, because both current assets and current liabilities decline by the same amount when the current liability is paid.

(i) Purchase of Property, Plant, and Equipment

Worksheet Entry	Property, Plant, and Equipment	10,000	
	Use—Purchase of Property, Plant, and Equipment		10,000

---

[10]*APB Opinion No. 19*, par. 10.

The purchase of noncurrent assets represents a use of working capital. Use is credited in the worksheet entry, and the appropriate asset account is debited.

(j) Conversion of Bonds to Common Stock

Worksheet Entries	Nonworking Capital Transaction—Issuance		
	of Common Stock	18,000	
	Common Stock		15,000
	Additional Paid-In Capital		3,000
	Convertible Bonds Payable	20,000	
	Unamortized Bond Discount		2,000
	Nonworking Capital Transaction—		
	Retirement of Bonds Payable		18,000

The conversion of bonds to common stock is an example of a nonworking capital financing and investing transaction that must be included in the statement of changes in financial position in order to disclose fully all significant changes during the period. In the worksheet entries, the issuance of the common stock is recorded with a debit to Nonworking Capital Transactions, for $18,000 and credits to the appropriate balance sheet accounts, Common Stock and Additional Paid-In Capital for $15,000 and $3,000, respectively.

The bond retirement is recorded as a credit to Nonworking Capital Transactions for $18,000, a debit to Convertible Bonds Payable for $20,000, and a credit to Unamortized Bond Discount for $2,000. Both the retirement of the bonds and the issuance of the common stock are included in the statement of changes in financial position as a part of the full

Disclosure disclosure objective of that statement.

(k) Increase in Working Capital

Worksheet Entry	Working Capital	38,100	
	Increase in Working Capital		38,100

The final entry is a debit to Working Capital and a credit to Increase in Working Capital, the final line on the worksheet. This entry balances the working capital line on the worksheet.

If working capital had *declined* during the year, the entry would be as follows:

Worksheet Entry	Decrease in Working Capital	XXX	
	Working Capital		XXX

Preparation of the Statement of Changes in Financial Position

After preparing all the appropriate transaction entries, the worksheet columns are totaled and lines are crossfooted. The lower section of the worksheet provides the specific information necessary for the preparation of the statement of changes in financial position. The statement for Hudson for 1984 is presented in Exhibit 23–15. *APB Opinion No. 19* requires a schedule that shows the impact of the change in each current asset and current liability on the amount of working capital. This schedule appears at the bottom of Exhibit 23–15. This statement follows the format in Exhibit 23–1 labeled "Example B."

Published Statement of Changes in Financial Position

We stated earlier that the statement of changes in financial position is a required part of the financial statements. Exhibit 23–16 is the statement taken from the 1982 annual report of Federal Express Corporation, a large corporation whose primary line of business is door-

---

EXHIBIT 23–15

Hudson, Inc.
STATEMENT OF CHANGES IN FINANCIAL POSITION
(Working Capital Focus)
For the Year Ended December 31, 1984

Financial Resources Provided

Income before extraordinary item	$57,200	
Adjustments		
Items not using (providing) working capital		
Depreciation	8,000	
Amortization of patents	1,000	
Amortization of bond discount	800	
Loss on sale of property, plant,		
and equipment	3,000	
Reduction in deferred income taxes	(1,400)	
Working capital provided by operations,		
exclusive of extraordinary item		$ 68,600
Extraordinary gain from extinguishment of debt	2,600	
Sale of property, plant, and equipment	12,000	
Issuance of common stock (to retire bonds		
payable)	18,000	32,600
		101,200

Financial Resources Used

Book value of bonds retired	18,100	
Dividends on common stock	17,000	
Purchase of property, plant, and equipment	10,000	
Retirement of bonds payable (by conversion to		
common stock)	18,000	63,100
Increase in working capital		$ 38,100

Schedule of Changes in Elements of Working Capital

	Impact on Working Capital
Current Assets	
Cash	$ (5,000)
Accounts receivable (net)	(5,000)
Inventory	32,600
Current Liabilities	
Dividends payable	(7,000)
Accounts payable	14,700
Income taxes payable	(12,200)
Notes payable	20,000
Increase in working capital	$ 38,100

---

to-door overnight delivery of packages and documents throughout the United States; Federal Express uses an integrated air-ground transportation system. The statement is presented on a comparative basis for three years—1982, 1981, and 1980.

Considering the year 1981, note that sources of funds in the statement are net income (adjusted for nonfund items), new financing by both debt and equity, and asset disposals. Major uses of funds were the acquisition of property and equipment and the reduction of long-term debt. In 1981 the company's working capital increased by $32,003,000, evidenced by a sharp increase in cash and short-term investments. An important item to note is the nonfund transaction in which preferred stock was converted into common stock. This

Disclosure item is included among both sources and uses at $1,499,000 to meet the objective of full disclosure of all changes in financial position for the statement, even though working capital was not affected by the transaction.

EXHIBIT 23–16
Federal Express Corporation
Statement of Changes in Financial Position

Federal Express Corporation and Subsidiary			

Consolidated Statements of Changes in Financial Position
Years ended May 31

	1982	1981	1980
	In thousands		
Funds Provided By:			
Net income	$ 78,385	$ 58,136	$ 37,729
Charges to income not requiring working capital:			
Depreciation and amortization	56,353	39,010	22,012
Deferred income taxes	20,369	6,254	6,215
Other	967	728	441
Working capital provided from operations	156,074	104,128	66,397
Increase in long-term debt	65,479	86,125	206,813
Conversion of preferred stock into common stock	—	1,499	682
Proceeds from issuance of common stock	2,077	43,669	56,620
Disposition of property and equipment	14,512	36,538	92
Decrease in equipment deposits and other assets	—	1,508	—
Total funds provided	238,142	273,467	330,604
Funds Used For:			
Acquisition of property and equipment	155,187	171,096	175,962
Payment of dividends on preferred stock	1,018	1,284	1,343
Mandatory redemption of preferred stock	1,535	1,538	1,531
Conversion of preferred stock into common stock	—	1,499	682
Reduction of long-term debt	4,328	65,885	110,077
Increase in construction funds in escrow	32,855	162	19,568
Increase in equipment deposits and other assets	16,656	—	5,632
Total funds used	211,579	241,464	314,795
Increase in Working Capital	$ 26,563	$ 32,003	$ 15,809
Increase (Decrease) in Working Capital by Component:			
Cash and short-term investments	$ (5,216)	$ 54,291	$ (217)
Receivables	34,021	16,034	17,927
Due from Memphis-Shelby County Airport Authority	(5,191)	4,817	9,281

Spare parts, supplies and fuel	**(2,205)**	5,090	9,298
Prepaid expenses and other	**5,904**	1,266	190
Current portion of long-term debt and redeemable preferred stock	**(885)**	(403)	(2,213)
Accounts payable	**(1,993)**	(6,322)	(11,971)
Income taxes	**16,930**	(21,153)	4,951
Accrued expenses	**(14,802)**	(21,617)	(11,437)
Increase in Working Capital	**$ 26,563**	**$ 32,003**	**$ 15,809**

SOURCE: Federal Express Corporation, 1982 Annual Report.

COMPREHENSIVE ILLUSTRATION: CASH DEFINITION OF FUNDS

We have already mentioned that the statement of changes in financial position may be presented with a focus on changes in working capital, cash, or another definition of funds, and that the most widely used definition of funds has been working capital. The latter conclusion is supported by *Accounting Trends and Techniques,* a summary of corporate reporting practices published by the AICPA, which indicates that more than 75% of the 600 companies included from 1978 to 1981 focused their statements of changes in financial position on working capital."[11]

The current interest of the FASB in cash flows and liquidity, however, provides some evidence that the statement of changes in financial position focusing on cash or cash and short-term marketable securities may be gaining in popularity. In late 1981 the Financial Executives Institute (FEI) urged organization members to focus on cash rather than working capital in their companies' statements of changes in financial position. This apparently has had some impact on corporate reporting practices. The FEI 1982 survey covered about one-third of the Fortune 500 companies' annual reports. Fifty-five of them state changes in financial position in terms of cash or cash and short-term investments. Of these 55 companies, 34 used the cash (or cash and short-term investments) approach in 1982 for the first time, an increase of 160%.[12] Further evidence of this trend is the fact that 93% of the companies included in *Accounting Trends and Techniques* (see footnote 11) focused their statements on working capital in 1978 whereas only 78% did so in 1981. The remaining companies focused on cash or cash and cash equivalents, such as short-term marketable securities.

These facts support the authors' opinion that the cash-based statement of changes in financial position is a relevant topic that deserves our attention. In this section we discuss this type of statement, again using the example of Hudson, Inc., to illustrate the detailed procedures necessary to compile the information to prepare the statement.

An understanding of the working capital approach facilitates an understanding of the cash approach. Much of the material presented earlier is equally appropriate for presenting changes in financial position in terms of either working capital or cash. The preparation of the statement focusing on cash requires the additional consideration of changes in current assets (other than cash) and current liabilities. Increases in the noncash current assets and decreases in current liabilities are usually considered negative adjustments to income as a source of cash. Likewise, decreases in noncash current assets and increases in current liabilities are usually considered positive adjustments to income as a source of cash. The reasoning behind these statements is described in the following paragraphs.

Current-Asset and Current-Liability Adjustments

The relationship of changes in current assets (such as receivables, inventory, and prepaid expenses) and current liabilities (such as accrued expenses and accounts payable) to the

---

[11]*Accounting Trends and Techniques* (New York: AICPA, 1982), p. 344.

[12]Dennis R. Beresford and Robert D. Neary, "Financial Reporting Briefs," *Financial Executive* (June 1982), p. 7.

FEI URGES CASH FLOW FORMAT FOR 1981 FUNDS STATEMENTS

THE FINANCIAL Executives Institute (FEI) has issued an alert which urges members to consider a format for their statement of changes in financial position that emphasizes cash flow instead of working capital. Some excerpts from the alert:

On November 16, 1981 the FASB issued a draft Proposed Concepts Statement on *Reporting Earnings, Cash Flows, and Financial Position of Business Enterprises.* In examining the FASB draft, FEI's Committee on Corporate Reporting reaffirmed its view that the statement of changes in financial position (funds statement) should continue to be required as an integral part of the financial statements.

The Committee believes that for many companies cash and short-term investments represent the primary measure of readily available discretionary resources which best reflects the concept of funds for evaluating operating, financing, and/or investing activities. The Committee also believes that the funds statement will be more meaningful and useful if it focuses on cash flows, rather than on working capital or some other concept. Therefore, FEI urges all members to take a leadership role in encouraging their companies voluntarily to change the format of the funds statement, where applicable, to focus on cash, including short-term investments and the components of cash flow.

APB Opinion No. 19, *Reporting Changes in Financial Position,* permits either the working capital or the cash flow concept. A majority of companies have adopted the working capital format and, until recently, there was little incentive to change the funds statement. Current economic conditions have raised concerns about liquidity and financial

flexibility, and both the FASB and the SEC have addressed these concerns.

The FASB draft recommends the adoption of the cash flow concept for the funds statement and states, among other things, that "the objectives of financial reporting indicate that users need information about cash inflows and outflows to help with assessments of future cash flows and to provide feedback about previous assessments."

Recommended Action

FEI encourages all members to take a leadership role within their companies in developing a more meaningful and informative funds statement that will emphasize cash flows. Members are urged to adopt improvements in the funds statement for their 1981 Annual Reports or, alternatively, to adopt the improvements for the First Quarter of 1982.

In developing a new format for the funds statement, members should seek the most meaningful presentation for their companies, and are encouraged to experiment with alternative formats. Members may want to review the discussion of cash flows and other related topics in the FASB Exposure Draft, the SEC release on management discussion and analysis, and refer to the annual reports of companies that already use the cash flow funds statement format.

Through this effort, FEI members can once again demonstrate that private sector initiative can contribute to more meaningful financial reporting without the need for specific rulemaking.

SOURCE: Deloitte Haskins & Sells, "FEI Urges Cash Flow Format for 1981 Funds Statements," *The Week in Review,* January 8, 1982, pp. 1–2.

---

amount of cash provided by operations is best seen by considering the underlying transactions that affect these balance sheet accounts.

Receivables are directly tied to the recognition of sales. If receivables increase during the period, the portion of sales equal to the receivables increase has not been received in cash. If receivables decline during the period, more cash has been received than is indicated by the sales figure. Inventory is directly linked to cost of goods sold. Assuming accounts payable are constant, if inventory increases during the period, more cash has been paid to purchase inventory than the amount of expense recognized as cost of goods sold. Similarly, if inventory decreases during the period, less cash has been paid to purchase inventory than the amount of expense recognized as cost of goods sold. Prepaid expenses are tied to the recognition of the related expenses in the determination of net income. If prepaid expenses increase during the period, more cash has been paid than is included in the various expense accounts. Likewise, if prepaid expenses decrease during the period, less cash has been paid than is included in the various expenses.

The same type of analysis is important in understanding current liabilities and how their changes impact cash. If accrued expenses increase during the period, less cash was paid than the amount of expenses recognized in determining net income. On the other hand, if accrued expenses decrease during the period, more cash was paid than the amount of expenses recognized. If we assume that accounts payable result from the acquisition of inventory and that the amount of inventory is constant, an increase in accounts payable during the period indicates that the cost of goods sold is greater than the cash paid to purchase inventory. Similarly, if accounts payable decrease during the period, cost of goods sold would be less than the cash paid to fund inventory purchases.

The relationship of these general statements to the determination of cash provided by operations is summarized in Exhibit 23–17.

Marketable securities classified as current assets are short-term investments expected to be reduced when cash is needed and increased when idle cash is available. Since such investments are typically converted directly to and from cash, increases in marketable secu-

---

EXHIBIT 23–17
Adjustments to Net Income to Determine Cash Provided by Operations

	Relationship to Net Income	Accrual to Cash Adjustments to Determine Cash Provided by Operations
Current Assets		
Receivables		
Increase	Sales overstate cash received.	−
Decrease	Sales understate cash received.	+
Inventory*		
Increase	Cost of goods sold understates cash paid.	−
Decrease	Cost of goods sold overstates cash paid.	+
Prepaid expenses		
Increase	Related expenses understate cash paid.	−
Decrease	Related expenses overstate cash paid.	+
Current Liabilities		
Accrued expenses		
Increase	Related expenses overstate cash paid.	+
Decrease	Related expenses understate cash paid.	−
Accounts payable**		
Increase	Cost of goods sold overstates cash paid.	+
Decrease	Cost of goods sold understates cash paid.	−

*Assumes that accounts payable are constant.
**Assumes that inventory is constant.

rities represent uses of cash and decreases in marketable securities represent sources of cash.

Since marketable securities are viewed as a secondary source of cash, any increase in the balance during the period is usually deducted from net income and any decrease is added to net income in determining cash provided by operations. In fact, many companies combine cash and short-term marketable securities for purposes of defining funds in the preparation of a statement of changes in financial position. Gains and losses resulting from sales transactions involving marketable securities are left in net income (rather than deducted out or added back), because the change in the marketable-security balance is an adjustment to net income in arriving at cash provided by operations.

Some notes payable represent short-term bank loans rather than payables related to merchandise acquisitions. As notes payable of this type increase, cash is provided, because the company is borrowing more than it is repaying. As notes payable decrease, cash is used, because the company is repaying more than it is borrowing. If these loans are for purposes of normal operations, the change should be treated as an adjustment to net income in arriving at cash provided by operations. If the notes are for nonoperating purposes, increases should be presented as other sources and decreases as other uses, rather than be presented as adjustments to funds from operations.

Comparison of Cash Focus and Working Capital Focus

Two major differences exist between the statement of changes in financial position focusing on cash changes and a similar statement focusing on working capital changes. For the cash-focus statement:

1. Cash provided by operations includes adjustments for changes in current assets (other than cash) and current liabilities whose increase or decrease relate to revenue and expense items included in the determination of income. (This is not the case in determining working capital provided by operations.)
2. Changes in nontrade notes payable, dividends payable, and other current assets and liabilities not resulting from transactions included in the determination of income are included in the body of the statement of changes in financial position. (These transactions would not appear in the body of a similar statement focusing on changes in working capital.)

As in the previous illustration we continue to use the Hudson example to illustrate the preparation of a statement of changes in financial position, focusing on cash changes; the financial information presented in Exhibit 23–12 provides the basis for this illustration.

Preparing the statement of changes in financial position focusing on changes in cash involves three basic steps, paralleling closely the steps followed in preparing a similar statement focusing on changes in working capital. First, the change in *cash* is determined. Second, transactions that increase cash and decrease cash, as well as noncash financing and investing activities, are identified. Third, the information developed in the first two steps is used to prepare a formal statement that conforms with the disclosure requirements of *APB Opinion No. 19.* The following paragraphs illustrate these steps.

Determination of Change in Cash

We determine the change in cash by comparing the cash balance at the end of the year with the balance at the beginning of the year. For Hudson, the cash balance decreased by $5,000 ($70,000 − $65,000) between December 31, 1983, and December 31, 1984.

Transactions Analysis

Transactions analysis designed to identify all information needed to prepare the statement of changes in financial position focusing on changes in cash may be accomplished by a careful analysis of available information, by preparing a worksheet similar to that presented earlier

EXHIBIT 23–18

Hudson, Inc.
WORKSHEET FOR STATEMENT OF CHANGES IN FINANCIAL POSITION
(Cash Focus)

Debits	Dec. 31, 1983	Changes Debit		Changes Credit		Dec. 31, 1984
Cash	70,000			(k)	5,000	65,000
Accounts receivable, net	65,000			(l)	5,000	60,000
Inventory	62,000	(m)	32,600			94,600
Property, plant, and equipment	200,000	(i)	10,000	(f)	20,000	190,000
Patents	10,000			(c)	1,000	9,000
Unamortized bond discount	10,000			(e)	800	5,300
				(g)	1,900	
				(j)	2,000	
	417,000					423,900
Credits						
Accumulated depreciation	30,000	(f)	5,000	(b)	8,000	33,000
Dividends payable	10,000	(h)	10,000	(h)	17,000	17,000
Accounts payable	50,000	(n)	14,700			35,300
Income taxes payable	42,000			(o)	12,200	54,200
Notes payable	20,000	(p)	20,000			–0–
Deferred income taxes	10,000	(d)	1,400			8,600
Convertible bonds payable	100,000	(g)	20,000			60,000
		(j)	20,000			
Preferred stock	10,000					10,000
Common stock	60,000			(j)	15,000	75,000
Additional paid-in capital	15,000			(j)	3,000	18,000
Retained earnings	70,000	(h)	17,000	(a)	57,200	112,800
				(g)	2,600	
	417,000					423,900

Sources					
Operations					
Income before extraordinary items	(a)	57,200			
Depreciation	(b)	8,000			
Amortization of patents	(c)	1,000			
Amortization of bond discount	(e)	800			
Reduction in deferred income taxes			(d)	1,400	
Loss on sale of property, plant, and equipment	(f)	3,000			
Decrease in accounts receivable	(l)	5,000			
Increase in inventory			(m)	32,600	
Decrease in accounts payable			(n)	14,700	
Increase in income taxes payable	(o)	12,200			
Other					
Extraordinary gain	(g)	2,600			
Sale of property, plant, and equipment	(f)	12,000			
Uses					
Book value of bonds retired			(g)	18,100	
Payment of dividends			(h)	10,000	
Purchases of property, plant, and equipment			(i)	10,000	
Payment of notes payable			(p)	20,000	
Nonworking Capital Transactions					
Retirement of bonds payable			(j)	18,000	
Issuance of common stock	(j)	18,000			
Decrease in cash	(k)	5,000			
		275,500		275,500	

for the working capital approach, or by using a T-account analysis. We illustrate the worksheet approach in this section.

The worksheet (Exhibit 23–18) is similar to the one presented in Exhibit 23–14. The major difference in Exhibit 23–18 is the listing of *all accounts in the trial balance* rather than combining all working capital accounts into a single item as shown in Exhibit 23–14.

Many of the worksheet entries are the same as those presented in the earlier illustration, including entries (a), (b), (c), (d), (e), (f), (g), (i), and (j). The previous explanations of these adjustments apply to the statement focusing on cash as well as to the statement focusing on working capital and are not repeated here.

Entries (h) and (k) are different in the cash statement. Also, several additional entries are included in the cash statement that did not appear in the working capital worksheet: (l), (m), (n), (o), and (p). These are discussed in the following paragraphs.

(h) Payment of Dividends

Worksheet Entries	Dividends Payable	10,000	
	Use—Payment of Dividends		10,000
	Retained Earnings	17,000	
	Dividends Payable		17,000

In a statement of changes in financial position focusing on cash, the *payment* of dividends represents a use of cash. This is different from the working capital approach in which the *declaration* of the dividend represents a use of working capital, because this is the point at which working capital is reduced. For Hudson, dividends payable of $10,000 existing at the end of 1983 were paid in 1984, and represent a use of cash as indicated in the first entry of (h). The declaration of dividends is a reclassification that is necessary in order to balance all accounts on the worksheet but is not a use of cash in 1984. This is reflected in the second (h) entry.

(k) Decrease in Cash

Worksheet Entry	Decrease in Cash	5,000	
	Cash		5,000

The balancing figure in the worksheet focusing on the change in cash is the change in cash itself. Cash is credited for $5,000, representing the decrease during the period, and Decrease in Cash is debited at the bottom of the worksheet.

(l) Decrease in Accounts Receivable

Worksheet Entry	Source (Operations)—Decrease in Accounts Receivable	5,000	
	Accounts Receivable		5,000

The decrease in accounts receivable indicates that more cash was collected than the amount of sales included in net income. Thus, Source (Operations) is debited to increase the amount of cash generated from operations. The credit is to the appropriate balance sheet account, Accounts Receivable.

(m) Increase in Inventory

Worksheet Entry	Inventory	32,600	
	Source (Operations)—Increase in Inventory		32,600

The increase in inventory indicates that cash was paid for the acquisition of inventory in a greater amount than the cost of goods sold included in net income. Cash provided by operations is adjusted downward by a credit to Source (Operations). The appropriate balance sheet account, Inventory, is debited.

(n) Decrease in Accounts Payable

Worksheet Entry	Accounts Payable	14,700	
	Source (Operations)—Decrease		
	in Accounts Payable		14,700

The decrease in accounts payable signifies that the cost of goods sold figure is less than the cash paid out for inventory purchases. (An additional $14,700 was paid to reduce accounts payable.) This step disregards any change in the level of inventory that has been separately accounted for in entry (m). Cash provided by operations is reduced by the credit to Source (Operations), and the appropriate balance sheet account, Accounts Payable, is reduced with a debit of $14,700.

(o) Increase in Income Taxes Payable

Worksheet Entry	Source (Operations)—Increase in		
	Income Taxes Payable	12,200	
	Income Taxes Payable		12,200

The increase in income taxes payable indicates that less cash was paid for income taxes than the income tax expense included in determining income. Thus, cash provided by operations must be increased by a debit to Source (Operations). The appropriate balance sheet account, Income Taxes Payable, is credited for the increase. This adjustment is required in the cash statement in addition to the adjustment for deferred taxes that is included in both the working capital and cash statements.

(p) Payment of Notes Payable

| **Worksheet Entry** | Notes Payable | 20,000 | |
| | Use—Payment of Notes Payable | | 20,000 |

Notes payable of $20,000 are paid during the year, resulting in an equal decrease in cash. Since the notes are for short-term bank loans as contrasted to trade notes payable, the credit is to Use. The appropriate balance sheet account, Notes Payable, is debited.

If the notes payable had been trade notes resulting from inventory purchases, the worksheet entry would have been as follows:

Worksheet Entry	Notes Payable	XXX	
	Source (Operations)—Decrease		
	in Notes Payable		XXX

Preparation of the Statement of Changes in Financial Position

After preparing all the appropriate transaction entries, the worksheet columns are totaled and the lines are crossfooted. The lower section of the worksheet provides the specific information necessary for the preparation of the statement of changes in financial position with a cash focus. Such a statement for Hudson is presented in Exhibit 23–19.

EXHIBIT 23–19

Hudson, Inc.
STATEMENT OF CHANGES IN FINANCIAL POSITION
(Cash Focus)
For the Year Ended December 31, 1984

Financial Resources Provided		
Income before extraordinary item	$ 57,200	
Adjustments		
Items not using (providing) cash		
Depreciation	8,000	
Amortization of patents	1,000	
Amortization of bond discount	800	
Reduction in deferred income taxes	(1,400)	
Loss on sale of property, plant,		
and equipment	3,000	
Decrease in accounts receivable	5,000	
Increase in inventory	(32,600)	
Decrease in accounts payable	(14,700)	
Increase in income taxes payable	12,200	
Cash provided by operations, exclusive of		
extraordinary item		$38,500
Extraordinary gain	2,600	
Sale of property, plant, and equipment	12,000	
Issuance of common stock (to retire bonds		
payable)	18,000	32,600
		71,100
Financial Resources Used		
Book value of bonds retired	18,100	
Payment of dividends	10,000	
Purchase of property, plant, and equipment	10,000	
Payment of notes payable	20,000	
Retirement of bonds payable (by conversion		
to common stock)	18,000	76,100
Decrease in cash		$ 5,000

Published Statement of Changes in Financial Position

Exhibit 23–16 presented the published statement of changes in financial position for Federal Express Corporation, focusing on changes in working capital. The statement of changes in financial position for Kroger Company, presented on the back endpapers of your text, focuses on changes in cash and temporary cash investments. This statement is only a slight variation from the statement of Hudson, Inc., in Exhibit 23–19, because Kroger combines cash and temporary investments in presenting funds-flow information and changes in financial position.

ADDITIONAL STATEMENT PRESENTATION CONSIDERATIONS

Statements of changes in financial position presented throughout this chapter are designed to comply with the requirements of *APB Opinion No. 19*. While the specific disclosure requirements of the statement are somewhat flexible, certain requirements do exist. These are summarized in the following points:

1. The statement should be based on a broad concept embracing all changes in financial position (i.e., the all financial resources concept). The statement title should reflect this broad concept. All important financing and investing activities should be included, regardless of whether cash or other elements of working capital are affected.

Disclosure

2. The statement should prominently disclose working capital or cash provided by or used in operations. Disclosure is thought to be most informative if the effects of extraordinary items are reported separately. The adjustment of net income (or income before extraordinary items, if applicable) for noncash or nonworking capital items results in an amount that should be appropriately labeled as "working capital (or cash) provided by operations (exclusive of extraordinary items, if applicable)." This amount should be followed by working capital or cash provided or used by income or loss from extraordinary items.

3. Whether or not working capital flow is presented in the statement, net changes in each element of working capital should be disclosed at least for the current period. In a statement focusing on working capital changes, this disclosure should be made in a tabulation accompanying the statement. In a statement focusing on cash changes, this disclosure should be included in the body of the statement.

4. The effects of other financing and investing activities should be individually disclosed by major category. Examples of items that should be disclosed are:
   a. Outlays for acquisitions and proceeds from retirements of property.
   b. Long-term borrowing and repayments of long-term debt.
   c. Conversion of long-term debt or preferred stock to common stock.
   d. Issuance, redemption, or purchase of capital stock for cash or for other assets.
   e. Dividends in cash or in kind or other distributions to stockholders.

Provided the above standards are met, flexibility in form, content, and terminology exists. The statement should be prepared in whatever form provides the most useful presentation of the financing and investing activities of the enterprise during the reporting period. Several reporting alternatives and other content and format considerations are presented below.

Balanced Format

Throughout this chapter the total sources of funds or financial resources provided has been reduced by the total uses of funds or financial resources used to determine the increase or decrease in working capital or cash. An alternative format is to treat the decrease in cash or working capital as a source of financial resources and to treat the increase in cash or working capital as a use of financial resources. The statement would then have a **balanced format** in which the total sources figure would equal the total uses figure.

The statement of changes in financial position in Exhibit 23–15 appears in Exhibit 23–20 in a balanced format. However, since the determinants of working capital provided by operations, exclusive of extraordinary item, and the schedule of changes in the elements of working capital are the same as those in Exhibit 23–15, they are not repeated in Exhibit 23–20.

If working capital declined during the period, financial resources provided would be less than financial resources used, excluding the decline in working capital. In that case, the decline in working capital would be presented under financial resources provided, making total sources and uses equal.

Statement Terminology

Other than specifying the title, "working capital (cash) provided or used by operations, exclusive of extraordinary items," *APB Opinion No. 19* does not specify titles to be used in the statement of changes in financial position. In this text, we have used the titles "financial resources provided" and "financial resources used" in some examples and "sources of working capital (or cash)" and "uses of working capital (or cash)" in other examples.

EXHIBIT 23–20

Hudson, Inc.
PARTIAL STATEMENT OF CHANGES IN FINANCIAL POSITION
(Working Capital Focus)
For the Year Ended December 31, 1984

Financial Resources Provided		
Working capital provided by operations,		
exclusive of extraordinary items		$ 68,600
Extraordinary gain	$ 2,600	
Sale of property, plant, and equipment	12,000	
Issuance of common stock (to retire bonds		
payable)	18,000	32,600
Total financial resources provided		$101,200
Financial Resources Used		
Book value of bonds retired	18,100	
Dividends on common stock	17,000	
Purchase of property, plant, and equipment	10,000	
Retirement of bonds payable (by conversion to		
common stock)	18,000	
Working capital	38,100	$101,200

Numerous alternative titles are found in practice. The following are several sets of captions taken from recently published annual reports:

Sources	Uses
Financial resources provided	Financial resources used
Financial resources were provided by	Financial resources were used for
Resources were provided by	Resources were used for
Funds provided	Funds applied
Sources	Disposition
Working capital provided	Working capital used
Funds became available from	These funds were used for

Any of these sets of titles is acceptable under *APB Opinion No. 19.* In preparing the statement, the accountant must decide on the clearest presentation for providing information concerning changes in financial position. One advantage of broad terms (such as financial resources—or simply resources—provided and used) is that they can encompass all changes in financial position, regardless of whether cash or working capital is affected. Terminology incorporating the specific definition of funds (such as working capital or cash provided and used) refers to items that are commonly understood by users of financial statements. They pose some problems, however, when noncash or nonworking capital financing and investing activities are included in the statement, because those transactions do not affect funds as defined in that financial statement. The two approaches presented in Exhibit 23–1 incorporate two sets of terminology that the authors prefer over other terms that might be used.[13] Consistency in applying terminology is particularly important in helping users of financial statements compare changes in financial position between accounting periods.

**Consis-
tency**

---

[13]In CPA examination questions, noncash or nonworking capital transactions are frequently included as both sources and uses. For example, the issuance of common stock for land is included as a source (issuance of common stock) and a use (acquisition of land) as if the two were separate transactions flowing through cash or working capital. This approach is comparable to that taken in Example B of Exhibit 23–1.

Operations as a Use of Funds

Operations are a use of funds (i.e., working capital, cash, or another definition of funds) when net income or loss (or income or loss before extraordinary items, if applicable), *adjusted for nonfund items,* results in a *negative amount.* In such a case the overall level of funds declines during the period as a result of normal business operations. If operations result in a use of funds, the item is presented under the caption "Financial resources used" rather than as a negative amount under "Financial resources provided."

Furthermore, since the statement of changes in financial position always begins with net income (loss) or income (loss) before extraordinary items, all uses should appear before sources in the statement if operations result in a use of funds. The major side captions must be changed so that the "Financial resources used" or "Uses of funds" precedes "Financial resources provided" or "Sources of funds."

Omitted Transactions

Certain transactions affecting financial position are excluded in the preparation of the statement of changes in financial position. For example, the disposal of fully depreciated assets by abandonment is not a factor in explaining changes in financial position, because the total-asset category, net of accumulated depreciation, is not affected. On the worksheet or in T accounts, however, the reclassification must be made in order to account for all changes in the asset and depreciation accounts. Various other reclassifications of this type may be encountered in the preparation of the statement of changes in financial position. A reclassification covered earlier was that of retained earnings to dividends payable, which was required on the worksheet for the statement of Hudson, Inc., focusing on changes in cash.

In *APB Opinion No. 19* two types of transactions are specifically exempted from inclusion in the statement of changes in financial position: stock splits and stock dividends.[14] These transactions represent reassignment of the existing amount of stockholders' equity to a different number of shares of stock and thus do not represent financing and investing activities in the same sense as other transactions included in the statement. Also, they do not represent a change in the relative status of common stockholders in comparison with preferred stockholders or debt holders. Additionally, the statement of changes in financial position is presented in conjunction with other financial statements. A stock split or stock dividend transaction taking place during the period is disclosed in the other statements or in related schedules or notes. The appropriation of retained earnings and the subsequent reversal of retained earnings appropriations are also not presented in the statement of changes in financial position for the same type of reasons.

CONCLUDING REMARKS

The presentation of funds-flow information has progressed from an idea expressed in accounting textbooks in the early 1900s to a required part of financial reporting with the issuance of *APB Opinion No. 19* in 1971. Despite this rise to prominence, the present statement of changes in financial position has been the subject of much criticism recently.

In the 1980 *FASB Discussion Memorandum,* which was described at the beginning of this chapter, criticisms in the accounting literature of the current statement are summarized as follows:[15]

---

[14]*APB Opinion No. 19,* par. 14.

[15]*FASB Discussion Memorandum,* "Reporting Funds Flow, Liquidity, and Financial Flexibility," 1980, p. 10.

1. The statement attempts to present too much information in a single financial statement.
2. The statement does not focus on a single specific definition of funds.

In discussing these criticisms, one writer offered the following analogy:

> *None of the gaps in financial disclosure that the Accounting Principles Board sought to close in Opinion No. 19 have been closed effectively. In practice, statements of changes in financial position are like the miniature cars one sees packed with people in the circus. Those cars are good for entertainment but they are not a good means of transporting large numbers of people.... To get it all in the "car" the APB has had to redefine "funds" so broadly that it has become a meaningless term, and a funds statement that is based on a meaningless concept of funds and that tries to accomplish too much does not communicate information effectively.[16]*

John C. Burton, former chief accountant of the Securities and Exchange Commission, makes the following observations:

> *In December 1980, the FASB ... produced a discussion memorandum entitled* Reporting Funds Flows, Liquidity and Financial Flexibility. *In it the FASB lays out some fundamental issues in regard to what a funds statement should show and just what it should be. It raises such basic problems as whether to retain the old definition of funds as working capital or to redefine funds as liquid assets. It questions whether the funds statement should be segmented in more ways than is the current practice. It asks whether more information should be required about capital expenditures. It suggests that perhaps capital expenditures should be broken into those for maintaining current capacity, those for increasing capacity and those for complying with environmental and other regulations. It is likely that one of the results of this discussion will be the adoption of a radically different funds statement.... At a minimum, information will be presented in a different format, and additional information regarding the areas noted will be included.[17]*

We can conclude that information about funds flow has increased in importance and acceptance in financial reporting. Continuous discussions about the current statement of changes in financial position point toward even greater emphasis on this aspect of financial reporting and toward probable changes in the way accountants present funds-flow information to users of financial statements.

---

[16]Loyd C. Heath, *Accounting Research Monograph No. 3,* "Financial Reporting and the Evaluation of Solvency" (New York: AICPA, 1978), pp. 107–108.

[17]John C. Burton, "Emerging Trends in Financial Reporting," *Journal of Accountancy* (July 1981), p. 60.

THE FUNDS STATEMENT: A DIFFERENT ORIENTATION

*C*ONFUSION CONTINUES *over the purpose of the funds statement and, by implication, over the reporting of cash-significant events. The purpose ... of reporting investment and financing events seems almost completely ignored, and instead the most important issue seems to be what concept of funds should be adopted as the focus of the statement: working capital, net current monetary assets, cash and other short-term investments, or cash. The major emphasis appears to be directed toward how funds from operations should be measured, with the rest of the funds statement being virtually overlooked.*

These views on the funds statement are expressed by Professor George H. Sorter, New York University School of Business, in the current issue of the *Journal of Accounting, Auditing & Finance.* Some highlights:

Why should we be concerned with how funds are defined in terms of a particular balance sheet account or group of accounts? Such concern can be explained only in terms of a narrow concept of the funds statement as an articulating statement describing the changes in certain balance sheet accounts. The implicit conceptual framework of the FASB seems to envision the balance sheet as the linchpin report, with articulating income and funds statements reporting events that produce changes in the balances of particular accounts: retained earnings for the income statement and cash, net liquid assets, or working capital for the funds statement.

A different orientation is suggested in this article. The data base of the accounting system reported in the funds statement is events of a period that produce a significant cash impact (increase or decrease available cash) or have long-run cash consequences (e.g., outflows that will produce future inflows—assets—versus outflows that will not—expenses). The events with future consequences are reported in the balance sheet, while those without future consequences are reported in the income statement. In subsequent periods, past events that no longer have future consequences are removed from the balance sheet and reported in the income statement. This arrangement is illustrated in

the [diagram shown at the bottom of the page].

This view calls for a much broader role for the funds statement as a statement reporting all events with significant cash impact and/or significant long-run cash consequences. The report would have 3 sections to disclose:

- Events with a current cash impact but no future long-run cash consequences (e.g., cash from operations and cash-dividend declarations)
- Investment events—those with favorable long-run cash consequences
- Financing events—events with unfavorable long-run cash consequences.

If this view of the funds statement is accepted, most questions surrounding the statement are more easily answered. "Funds from operations" reports the events producing a significant cash impact without future long-run cash consequences. "Sales less estimated uncollectibility associated with sales" appears to be the critical event determining the positive cash impact from operations, while the acquisition (not payment) of current operating services and the interest expense net of discount and premium amortization (not payment) are the critical events in terms of negative operating cash impacts.

The only problem is posed by the purchase of goods, and the only question here is where—not whether—the event should be reported. Clearly, it is the purchase of goods, not payment or cost of goods sold, that determines cash impact. The question is whether purchases should be shown under

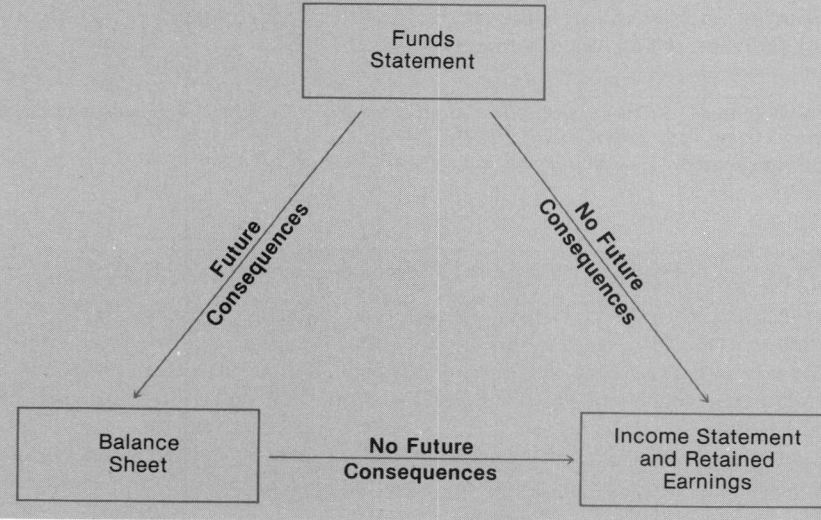

funds from operations as an event with cash impact—but no future long-run cash consequences—or as an investment and, therefore, an event with future long-run consequences. This objective of the funds statement would also answer the somehow vexing question of whether or not to report events such as the acquisition of long-term assets through issuance of stock. Clearly, such events have cash significance and, thus, must be reported as investments and financing events, whether or not their current cash impact cancels out.

Another question that this view of the funds statement would solve once and for all is whether funds from operations should be reported through the add-back or the direct method. If users of financial reporting are interested in predicting cash flows, they are interested in assessing changes that produce a cash impact not in those that do not. The add-back method which focuses on events, such as depreciation, that do not have cash impacts is not useful for this purpose and should not be utilized.

The foregoing notion of the funds statement makes sense in terms of cash-flow emphasis by producing a record of events with cash impact that can be used as feedback for assessing cash-significant investment and financing events of the past, and a record of long-term cash-significant events that can be used to predict the cash impact of the future. If the FASB is serious about adhering to the objectives it proclaims, this is the view of the funds statement that should prevail.

SOURCE: Deloitte Haskins & Sells, "The Funds Statement: A Different Orientation," *The Week in Review*, March 19, 1982, pp. 2–4.

KEY POINTS

1. The statement of changes in financial position is the fourth major financial statement and joins the income statement, retained earnings statement, and balance sheet in presenting the financial position, results of operations, and changes in financial position of business enterprises.

2. Funds-flow information, in conjunction with accrual accounting information, is important in assessing the enterprise's financial position. Specifically, funds-flow information is useful in evaluating the enterprise's liquidity and financial flexibility, important considerations in assessing future cash flow prospects to investors and creditors.

3. Funds flow into business enterprises via operations, the disposal of assets, debt financing, and equity financing. Funds flow out of business enterprises via the costs of operations, asset acquisitions, debt retirement, and reductions in stockholders' equity, such as dividends and the acquisition of treasury stock.

4. The objectives of the statement of changes in financial position are to summarize the financing and investing activities of the enterprise, including the extent to which the enterprise generated funds from operations during the period, and to complete the disclosure of changes in financial position during the period.

5. Within the all financial resources concept, the statement of changes in financial position must include all important financing and investing activities occurring during the period, regardless of whether or not funds were directly affected.

6. Nonfund transactions may be presented in the statement in several ways. One approach is to include the nonfund transactions as both sources and uses of equal amounts. Another approach is to include nonfund transactions in a separate section of the statement, following sources and uses of funds.

7. The three steps in preparing a statement of changes in financial position are: (1) determine the change in funds; (2) analyze transactions to identify all sources of funds, uses of funds, and nonfund transactions; and (3) prepare the statement of changes in financial position.

8. The statement of changes in financial position focusing on changes in cash is prepared in essentially the same way as the statement focusing on changes in working capital, except that on the cash-focus statement, changes in current assets (other than cash) and current liabilities are incorporated into the body of the statement as sources and uses of funds.

9. Two tools are available for analyzing transactions to accumulate the information needed to prepare the statement of changes in financial position: the worksheet and T accounts.

APPENDIX A T-ACCOUNT APPROACH TO TRANSACTIONS ANALYSIS

The T-account approach is an alternative to the worksheet in analyzing transactions for preparation of the statement of changes in financial position. In this approach a T account is established for each balance sheet account. If the working capital definition of funds is applied, all working capital accounts are combined into a single account. Entries are made in these accounts with offsetting entries in master T accounts for the statement of changes in financial position.

This appendix illustrates the T-account approach by considering again the financial information presented earlier for Hudson, Inc., for the years 1983 and 1984 (see Exhibit 23–12). The statement of changes in financial position that is illustrated here focuses on changes in working capital.

Separate T accounts are established for each balance sheet account, with working capital representing a separate account that combines all current assets and current liabilities. For convenience, the change in each T account during the year is identified in parentheses at the top of the account.

Master T accounts are set up for "Summary of sources and uses of working capital" and "Nonworking capital transactions." These accounts are used to identify the basic elements of the statement of changes in financial position. Categories within each of these master accounts are established, paralleling the categories of the statement that will be prepared upon completion of the transaction analysis.

Entries are made between the trial balance T accounts and the master accounts in much the same manner as entries were made in the change columns of the worksheet in Exhibit 23–14. This process is illustrated in Exhibit 23–21.

EXHIBIT 23–21
Hudson, Inc.
T-Account Approach to Transaction Analysis

TRIAL BALANCE T ACCOUNTS

Debits	Credits

Working Capital (+38,100)

(k) 38,100	

Accumulated Depreciation (+3,000)

(f) 5,000	(b) 8,000
	(5,000)
	3,000

Property, Plant, and Equipment (−10,000)

(i) 10,000	(f) 20,000
	(10,000)
	10,000

Deferred Income Taxes (−1,400)

	(d) 1,400

Patents (−1,000)

	(c) 1,000

Convertible Bonds Payable (−40,000)

	(g) 20,000
	(j) 20,000
	40,000

Unamortized Bond Discount (−4,700)

	(e) 800
	(g) 1,900
	(j) 2,000
	4,700

Preferred Stock (−0−)

Common Stock (+15,000)	
	(j) 15,000

Additional Paid-In Capital (+3,000)	
	(j) 3,000

Retained Earnings (+42,800)	
(h) 17,000	(a) 57,200
	(g) 2,600
	59,800
	(17,000)
	42,800

STATEMENT OF CHANGES IN FINANCIAL POSITION T ACCOUNTS
Summary of Sources and Uses of Working Capital

Sources		Uses	
Operations		(g) Book value of bonds retired	18,100
(a) Income before		(h) Cash dividends on common	
extraordinary items	57,200	stock	17,000
(b) Depreciation	8,000	(i) Purchase of property, plant,	
(c) Amortization of		and equipment	10,000
patent	1,000		
(d) Reduction in deferred			
income taxes	(1,400)		
(e) Amortization of bond			
discount	800		
(f) Loss on sale of			
property, plant, and			
equipment	3,000		
Other			
(f) Sale of equipment	12,000		
(g) Extraordinary gain	2,600		
			45,100
		(k) Increase in working capital	38,100
	83,200		83,200

Nonworking Capital Transactions

Equivalent Source		Equivalent Use	
(j) Issuance of common		(j) Retirement of bonds	
stock (in bond		payable (conversion to	
conversion)	18,000	common stock)	18,000

IDENTIFICATION OF T-ACCOUNT ENTRIES

The following items explain each entry in the T-account approach illustrated in Exhibit 23–21:

(a) To establish income before extraordinary items as a source.

(b) To adjust income for nonworking capital expense, depreciation.

(c) To adjust income for nonworking capital expense, amortization of patent.

(d) To adjust income for nonworking capital expense, reduction in deferred income taxes.

(e) To adjust income for nonworking capital expense, amortization of bond discount.

(f) To adjust income for loss on asset sale and to establish sale as a source.

(g) To establish extraordinary gain as a source and

book value of bonds retired as a separate use.

(h) To establish dividend declared on common stock as a use.

(i) To establish acquisition of property, plant, and equipment as a use.

(j) To establish nonworking capital financing and investing transaction—conversion of bonds payable into common stock.

(k) To record change in working capital as the difference between sources and uses of working capital.

We can make several observations on the T-account approach:

1. The net increase or decrease in each trial balance T account is equal to the change indicated above each account. For example, the increase in retained earnings during the year was $42,800. This change is made up of three elements: income before extraordinary item ($57,200), plus the extraordinary gain ($2,600), less the dividends on common stock ($17,000). This change equals the amount presented above the retained earnings account ($57,200 + $2,600 − $17,000 = $42,800).

2. Any entry that reduces income as a source is presented as a negative amount under the Operations section of the master account, "Summary of sources and uses of working capital." An example is entry (d), which records the reduction in deferred income taxes. This entry is made to bring together all amounts to be used in the determination of working capital provided by operations, exclusive of extraordinary items.

3. The master accounts for the summary of sources and uses of working capital and the nonworking capital transactions provide the information for the preparation of the statement of changes in financial position.

The statement presented in Exhibit 23–15 can be developed directly from the summary accounts of Exhibit 23–21.

The T-account approach may be used in analyzing transactions for the preparation of a statement of changes in financial position focusing on changes in cash as well as working capital. A T account must be established for each account in the company's trial balance. Entries are made between those accounts and the master account for the summary of sources and uses of cash and the noncash transactions in much the same way as entries were made in the analysis included in Exhibit 23–18. The master summary sources and uses account, combined with noncash transactions, provides the information for the preparation of the statement of changes in financial position.

QUESTIONS

23–1 The FASB has recently identified several reasons why information concerning funds flow is useful to financial statement users. Discuss these reasons briefly.

23–2 What are the objectives of a statement of changes in financial position?

23–3 What information is included in the statement of changes in financial position that is not available in comparative income statements, balance sheets, and retained earnings statements for the same reporting period?

23–4 Why must adjustments be made to net income to determine "working capital provided by operations"?

23–5 Identify four major categories of transactions that *may* result in increases in working capital, and state a general conclusion about the nature of the transactions that *would* result in a change in working capital.

23–6 Identify four major categories of transactions that *may* result in decreases in working capital, and state a general conclusion about the nature of the transactions that *would* result in a change in working capital.

23–7 Define "nonworking capital transactions." How should they be presented in the statement of changes in financial position?

23–8 What is meant by the "all financial resources concept" in preparing the statement of changes in financial position?

23–9 Explain briefly how net income is a source of working capital and how net loss is a use of working capital.

23–10 Is it possible for a net loss for a period to result in a source of working capital for that same period? Explain.

23–11 A plant asset was sold at a loss during the current year. The loss was included in income before extraordinary item on the enterprise's income statement. Explain the proper presentation of this transaction in the statement of changes in financial position.

23–12 A plant asset was sold in a condemnation proceeding, resulting in a substantial gain. The gain was appropriately presented as an extraordinary item in the enterprise's income statement. Explain the proper presentation of this transaction in the statement of changes in financial position.

23–13 What is the relationship between the change in funds during a period and the total sources and total uses of funds?

23–14 Explain the difference in content of a statement of changes in financial position focusing on working capital changes and a similar statement focusing on changes in cash.

23–15 Explain the difference, if any, in the treatment of the following transactions in a statement of changes in financial position focusing on working capital changes and a similar statement focusing on cash changes:

[a] Declaration of a cash dividend to be paid in the next period.

[b] Declaration and payment of a cash dividend in the current period.

23–16 The controller of Anderson Company, your audit client, argues that the refunding of outstanding 10% debt by issuing 8% debt does not materially affect the company's financial position, because the difference between the net amount of debt outstanding is not great. The controller argues, therefore, that the transaction does not need to be included in the statement of changes in financial position, particularly since working capital was not affected. Do you agree or disagree with the controller? Why?

23–17 Select the correct answer.

The financial statement that has as its primary function the summarization of the financing and investing aspects of all significant transactions affecting financial position is the :

[a] Retained earnings statement.
[b] Earnings statement.
[c] Statement of changes in financial position.
[d] Statement of financial position.

(AICPA adapted)

23–18 Select the correct answer.

In 1983, Darby Company retired convertible bonds for which stock was issued pursuant to a conversion option. The exchange took place on an interest-payment date, and except for the interest payment no money changed hands. In preparing a statement of changes in financial position on a working capital basis, the exchange in securities should be:

[a] Ignored because the "book-value" method was used to record the exchange.

[b] Added to net income to arrive at working capital provided by operations.

[c] Subtracted from net income to arrive at working capital provided by operations.

[d] Reported as both a source (issuance of stock) and an application (retirement of bonds) of working capital.

(AICPA adapted)

23–19 Select the correct answer.

The following item represents a potential use of working capital:

[a] Goodwill amortization.
[b] Sale of plant assets at a loss.
[c] Net loss from operations.
[d] Declaration of a stock dividend.

(AICPA adapted)

23–20 Select the correct answer.

When preparing a statement of changes in financial position by using the cash definition of funds, an increase in ending inventory over beginning inventory will result in an adjustment to reported net income because:

[a] Funds were increased since inventory is a current asset.

[b] The net increase in inventory reduced cost of goods sold but represents an assumed use of cash.

[c] Inventory is not an expense deducted in computing net income, but is *not* a use of funds.

[d] All changes in noncash accounts must be disclosed under the all financial resources concept.

(AICPA adapted)

23–21 A company's income statement includes income tax expense of $100,000, of which $82,500 was paid or is payable at year-end and $17,500 is deferred because of the use of accelerated depreciation for income tax purposes and straight-line depreciation for financial reporting. How will these facts affect the presentation of working capital provided by operations in the statement of changes in financial position?

CASES

C23–1 There have been considerable discussion and research in recent years about the reporting of changes in financial position (sources and application of funds). *APB Opinion No. 19* concluded:

that the statement summarizing changes in financial position should be based on a broad concept embracing all changes in financial position and that the title of the statement should reflect this broad concept. The

Board therefore recommends that the title be State-ment of Changes in Financial Position. (1971, par. 8.)

Instructions

[a] Describe the two common meanings of "funds" as used when preparing the statement of changes in financial position.

[b] Explain what is meant by "a broad concept embracing all changes in financial position" as used by the Accounting Principles Board in its *Opinion No. 19.*

(AICPA adapted)

C23–2 Hall Engineering Company is a young and growing producer of electronic measuring instruments and technical equipment. You have been asked by Hall to help prepare a statement of changes in financial position for the fiscal year ended October 31, 1985. You have obtained the following information concerning certain events and transactions:

[1] The amount of reported earnings for the fiscal year was $800,000, which included a deduction for an extraordinary loss of $93,000 (See item [5]).

[2] Depreciation expense of $240,000 was included in the earnings statement.

[3] Uncollectible accounts receivable of $30,000 were written off against the allowance for uncollectible accounts. Also, $37,000 of bad debts expense was included in determining earnings for the fiscal year, and the same amount was added to the allowance for uncollectible accounts.

[4] A gain of $4,700 was realized on the sale of a machine; it originally cost $75,000, of which $25,000 was undepreciated on the date of sale.

[5] On April 1, 1985, a freak lightning storm caused an uninsured inventory loss of $93,000 ($180,000 loss, less reduction in income taxes of $87,000). This extraordinary loss was included in determining earnings, as indicated in item [1].

[6] On July 3, 1985, building and land were purchased for $600,000. Hall paid $100,000 cash and issued $200,000 market value of its unissued common stock and a $300,000 purchase-money mortgage.

[7] On August 3, 1985, $700,000 face value of Hall's 6% convertible debentures were converted into $140,000 par value of its common stock. The bonds were originally issued at face value.

[8] The board of directors declared a $320,000 cash dividend on October 20, 1985, payable on November 15, 1985, to stockholders of record on November 5, 1985.

Instructions

For each of the eight items above, explain whether the item is a source or use of working capital. Describe how the item should be disclosed in Hall's statement of changes in financial position for the fiscal year ended October 31, 1985. If the item is neither a source nor a use of working capital, explain why, and indicate the disclosure, if any, that should be made in Hall's statement.

(AICPA adapted)

C23–3 The statement of changes in financial position is usually required for each period in which an earnings statement is presented. The reporting entity has flexibility in form, content, and terminology because of different circumstances. For example, the definition of "funds" may be interpreted to mean, among other things, cash or working capital. However, the statement should be prepared according to the "all financial resources" concept.

Instructions

[a] What is the "all financial resources" concept?

[b] What two types of financial transactions would be disclosed under the "all financial resources" concept that would not be disclosed without this concept?

[c] What effect, if any, would each of the following seven items have on a statement of changes in financial position prepared in accordance with generally accepted accounting principles using the cash definition of funds?

[1] Accounts receivable, trade.

[2] Inventory.

[3] Depreciation.

[4] Deferred income tax credit from interperiod allocation.

[5] Issuance of long-term debt in payment for a building.

[6] Payoff of current portion of debt.

[7] Sale of a fixed asset resulting in a loss.

(AICPA adapted)

C23–4 Black and Blue companies operate in the same industry and are similar in size, in terms of investment in assets and sales volume. The ratio of current assets to current liabilities at January 1, 1985, is the same for both companies, approximately 2.4 to 1. This is very close to the average for all companies in the industry.

Selected data from the statements of changes in financial position of the two companies are presented below:

	1982	1983	1984	1985
		(in thousands of dollars)		
Black Company				
Working capital provided				
Operations	$ 100	$ 125	$ 115	$ 128
Long-term debt financing	10	—	—	15
Financing by capital stock	—	25	—	—
Disposition of noncurrent assets	15	12	50	25
	125	162	165	168
Working capital used	(115)	(150)	(170)	(164)
Increase (decrease) in working capital	$ 10	$ 12	$ (5)	$ 4
Blue Company				
Working capital provided				
Operations	$ 50	$ 30	$ (60)	$ 10
Long-term debt financing	75	15	70	—
Financing by capital stock	—	75	100	75
Disposition of noncurrent assets	10	25	50	50
	135	145	160	135
Working capital used	(125)	(133)	(165)	(131)
Increase (decrease) in working capital	$ 10	$ 12	$ (5)	$ 4

Instructions

[a] Identify similarities in the two companies.
[b] Identify differences between the two companies.
[c] Which company appears to be in a stronger position from the viewpoint of potential investors in the company's stock and major creditors? Why?

C23–5 The following financial statement was prepared by Turner Company's accountant:

Turner Company
STATEMENT OF SOURCE AND APPLICATION
OF FUNDS
For the Year Ended September 30, 1985

Source of Funds

Net income	$ 52,000
Depreciation and depletion	59,000
Increase in long-term debt	178,000
Common stock issued under employee option plans	5,000
Changes in current receivables and inventories, less current liabilities (excluding current maturities of long-term debt)	3,000
	$297,000

Application of Funds

Cash dividends	$ 33,000

Expenditures for property, plant, and equipment	202,000
Investments and other uses	9,000
Change in cash	53,000
	$297,000

The following additional information is available for the year ended September 30, 1985:

[1] The balance sheet of Turner Company distinguishes between current and noncurrent assets and liabilities.

[2]

Depreciation expense	$ 58,000
Depletion expense	1,000
	$ 59,000

[3]

Increase in long-term debt	$600,000
Retirement of debt	422,000
Net increase	$178,000

[4] The company received $5,000 in cash from its employees on its employee stock option plans, and wage and salary expense attributable to the plan (which has not been recorded) was an additional $22,000.

[5]

Expenditures for property, plant, and equipment	$212,000
Proceeds from retirements of property, plant, and equipment	10,000
Net expenditures	$202,000

[6] A stock dividend of 10,000 shares of Turner Company's common stock was distributed to common stockholders on April 1, 1985, when the per share market price was $6 and par value was $1.

[7] On July 1, 1985, when its market price was $5 per share, 16,000 shares of Turner Company common

stock were issued in exchange for 4,000 shares of preferred stock.

Instructions

[a] Explain the objectives of a statement of the type shown above.

[b] Identify the weaknesses in the form and format of Turner Company's statement, without reference to the additional information.

[c] For each item of additional information above, indicate the preferable treatment and explain why it is preferable.

(AICPA adapted)

EXERCISES

E23–1 Foster Company reported $100,000 of net income in 1985 with no extraordinary items. Expenses reported in the determination of this income included the following: salaries, $200,000; cost of sales, $400,000; interest, $50,000; depreciation and amortization, $120,000; and income taxes, $400,000 (none of which was deferred).

Instructions

Using only the above information, compute working capital provided by operations for 1985.

E23–2 Alexander Company's income statement for the year ended December 31, 1985, is as follows:

Alexander Company
INCOME STATEMENT
For the Year Ended December 31, 1985

Revenue		
Sales	$100,000	
Services	75,000	$175,000
Expenses		
Cost of goods sold	86,000	
Selling and administrative expenses	45,000	
Depreciation expense	25,000	
Amortization of intangibles	7,000	163,000
Income before income taxes		12,000
Income tax expense		5,760
Net income		$ 6,240
Earnings per common share		$.06

Instructions

Compute the amount of working capital provided by operations for the year, assuming the following:

[a] A sale of $15,000 resulted in the acceptance of a three-year, 8% note receivable.

[b] The $5,760 provision for income taxes is distributed as follows:

Currently payable	$4,500
Deferred	1,260
	$5,760

The deferral relates to the timing difference resulting from the use of accelerated depreciation for tax purposes and straight-line for income statement reporting purposes.

E23–3 Graham Company reports the following summarized income statement data for 1985:

Revenue	$1,700,000
Expenses	1,300,000
Net income	$ 400,000

Accounts receivable resulting from revenue-producing transactions increased by $46,000 from January 1 to December 31, 1985. Depreciation expense amounted to $128,000.

Instructions

Using only the information explicitly given above, compute cash provided by operations for 1985.

E23–4 Net income of the Bell Company for 1985

was reported as $125,000 with no extraordinary items. The following related information is available:

	At Dec. 31, 1984	At Dec. 31, 1985
Accrued interest payable recognized	$10,000	$12,500
Depreciation expense recognized	17,500	16,000
Prepaid expenses recognized	575	1,235

Instructions

Using the above information, determine the cash provided by operations for 1985.

E23–5 Purple Company's income statement for 1984 is presented below with explanatory information on selected items:

Purple Company
INCOME STATEMENT
For the Year Ended December 31, 1984

Revenue from sales [1]		$5,432,000
Cost of goods sold		3,150,000
Gross profit		2,282,000
Expenses		
Selling	$246,000	
Depreciation	235,000	
Amortization of intangibles	52,000	
Salaries and wages [2]	400,000	
Interest [3]	72,000	
Miscellaneous operating	5,000	1,010,000
Income before income taxes		1,272,000
Income tax expense [4]		611,000
Net income		$ 661,000
Earnings per common share		$.66

Additional Information

[1] All sales were on trade account except a $100,000 sale resulting in the acceptance of a three-year, 9% note receivable and a $75,000 sale resulting in the acceptance of a tract of land valued at $75,000.
[2] Accrued salaries and wages at December 31, 1983, and 1984 were $40,000 and $42,500, respectively.
[3] Interest expense includes $3,900 of amortization of bond discount.
[4] Income tax expense includes $110,000 of taxes deferred due to the use of accelerated depreciation for tax purposes and straight-line for reporting purposes.

Instructions

Compute the working capital provided by operations for 1984.

E23–6 Rose Company reported net income of $125,000 for 1985 with no extraordinary items. In addition, the following information is available:
[1] Current assets increased by $27,500 and current liabilities increased by $12,250 during the year.
[2] Dividends of $37,500 were declared and paid to stockholders.
[3] Depreciation expense recognized was $16,900.
[4] Treasury stock was acquired for $10,000.
[5] Long-term debt was retired at $59,150.
[6] New items of property, plant, and equipment were acquired for $20,000.

Instructions

[a] Determine the change in working capital during 1985.
[b] Prepare a statement of changes in financial position, focusing on changes in working capital for 1985. The company's fiscal year ends on December 31.

E23–7 Comparative data taken from the balance sheets of King Company at December 31, 1983 and 1984, are as follows:

	1983	1984
Assets		
Cash	$ 10,000	$ 15,000
Receivables, short-term	35,000	26,700
Inventory	60,000	85,000
Property, plant, and equipment, net	75,000	70,000
Intangibles	12,000	10,000
	$192,000	$206,700
Equities		
Current liabilities	$ 6,500	$ 6,200
Noncurrent liabilities	60,000	40,000
Capital stock	100,000	125,000
Retained earnings	25,500	35,500
	$192,000	$206,700

During 1984 capital stock was sold, noncurrent debt was retired, and dividends of $5,000 were declared and paid. The income statement showed $7,000 of depreciation and amortization combined.

Instructions

[a] Determine the change in working capital during 1984.

[b] Prepare a statement of changes in financial position, focusing on changes in working capital for 1984.

E23–8 Muleshoe Company's balance sheets at December 31, 1983 and 1984, are as follows:

	1983	1984
Assets		
Cash	$ 17,000	$ 2,300
Accounts receivable, net	45,000	42,000
Inventory	23,000	36,200
Property, plant, and equipment, net	165,000	147,000
Intangibles	—	17,500
	$250,000	$245,000
Equities		
Current liabilities	$ 40,000	$ 50,000
Noncurrent liabilities	90,000	90,000
Capital stock	100,000	100,000
Additional paid-in capital	40,000	40,000
Retained earnings	(20,000)	(35,000)
	$250,000	$245,000

The following additional information has been accumulated about 1984 activities:

[1] Patents were acquired during 1984, but no amortization was taken since the acquisition took place at year-end.

[2] The only entries to property, plant, and equipment accounts were for depreciation.

[3] No dividends were declared during 1984.

Instructions

Prepare a statement of changes in financial position, focusing on changes in cash for 1984.

E23–9 Information taken from Elmer Company's balance sheets at December 31, 1983 and 1984 indicate the following:

	Dollar Change Dec. 31, 1983– Dec. 31, 1984
Assets	
Cash	+15,000
Accounts receivable	– 5,000
Inventory	+17,000
Property, plant, and equipment, net	+25,000
	+52,000

	Change
Equities	
Current liabilities	– 7,000
Bonds payable	+16,000
Capital stock	+20,000
Additional paid-in capital	+ 2,000
Retained earnings	+21,000
	+52,000

Depreciation of $7,000 was recognized in the income statement. Additional bonds were sold during the year. Land valued at $22,000 (included in property, plant, and equipment) was acquired by the issuance of stock. No dividends were declared.

Instructions

[a] Prepare a statement of changes in financial position, focusing on changes in working capital, and a schedule of changes in the elements of working capital for the year ended December 31, 1984.

[b] Prepare a statement of changes in financial position, focusing on changes in cash for the year ended December 31, 1984.

E23–10 The following items may appear in the statement of changes in financial position:

[1]   Net income.
[2]   Depreciation expense.
[3]   Acquisition of treasury stock.
[4]   Exchange of common stock for land.
[5]   Declaration of cash dividend.
[6]   Payment of previously declared cash dividend.
[7]   Acquisition of property, plant, and equipment.
[8]   Retirement of long-term debt.
[9]   Conversion of bonds into common stock.
[10] Amortization of intangible assets.
[11] Increase in inventory from previous year-end.
[12] Decrease in accounts receivable from previous year-end.
[13] Sale of property, plant, and equipment.
[14] Sale of capital stock.
[15] Declaration and distribution of stock dividend.

Instructions

[a] For each item indicate the proper classification in a statement of changes in financial position prepared on a working capital basis, using the following code:

	Code
Financial resources provided	
Operations	A
Other	B
Financial resources used	C

		Jan. 1, 1984	Dec. 31, 1984
Schedule of changes in components of working capital — D
Nonworking capital transaction — E
Not disclosed — F

[b] For each item indicate the proper classification in a statement of changes in financial position prepared on a cash basis, using the following code:

	Code
Financial resources provided	
Operations	V
Other	W
Financial resources used	X
Noncash transaction	Y
Not disclosed	Z

E23-11 The beginning and ending balances for Oscar Company for 1983 are as follows:

	Jan. 1, 1983	Dec. 31, 1983
Current assets	$20,000	$25,000
Fixed assets	20,000	20,000
Accumulated depreciation	(4,000)	(5,000)
Investments	10,000	10,000
Intangible assets	5,000	4,000
	$51,000	$54,000
Current liabilities	$10,000	$13,000
Long-term liabilities	13,000	12,000
Capital stock	25,000	25,000
Retained earnings	3,000	4,000
	$51,000	$54,000

The following additional information is available from an analysis of the company's records:
[1] Depreciation and amortization of intangibles included in the determination of net income were $1,000 each.
[2] $1,500 of dividends were declared during the year.
[3] $1,000 of long-term liabilities were retired during the year.

Instructions

Prepare a *worksheet analysis* of the year's transactions as the basis for a statement of changes in financial position, focusing on changes in working capital. (You need not prepare a formal statement of changes in financial position.)

E23-12 (Appendix A) The beginning and ending balances for Oscar Company for 1984 are as follows:

	Jan. 1, 1984	Dec. 31, 1984
Current assets	$25,000	$27,000
Fixed assets	20,000	25,000
Accumulated depreciation	(5,000)	(6,500)
Investments	10,000	10,000
Intangible assets	4,000	3,000
	$54,000	$58,500
Current liabilities	$13,000	$16,000
Long-term liabilities	12,000	8,000
Capital stock	25,000	30,000
Retained earnings	4,000	4,500
	$54,000	$58,500

The following additional information is available from an analysis of the company's records:
[1] Depreciation and amortization of intangibles included in the determination of net income were $1,500 and $1,000, respectively.
[2] $1,500 of dividends were declared during the year.
[3] $5,000 of capital stock was sold, $4,000 of which was subsequently used to retire long-term liabilities.
[4] Fixed assets of $5,000 were acquired.

Instructions

Analyze the transactions for the year by the T-account method to provide the basis for a statement of changes in financial position, focusing on changes in working capital. (A formal statement of changes in financial position is not required.)

E23-13 The net income for Donald Company is $2,500,000 for the year ended December 31, 1984. Additional information is as follows:

Depreciation of fixed assets	$2,900,000
Dividends on preferred stock	200,000
Long-term debt	
Bond discount amortization	50,000
Interest expense	800,000
Provision for doubtful accounts on long-term receivables	250,000
Amortization of goodwill	90,000

Instructions

Determine the amount of working capital provided by operations to be presented in the statement of changes in financial position.

(AICPA adapted)

E23-14 The following information was taken from the accounting records of Phoenix Corporation for 1984:

Proceeds from issuance of preferred stock	$4,000,000
Dividends paid on preferred stock	400,000
Bonds payable converted to common stock	2,000,000
Purchases of treasury stock, common	500,000
Sale of plant building	1,200,000
2% stock dividend on common stock	300,000

Instructions

[a] Select the correct amount of sources and uses of funds to be presented in the company's statement of changes in financial position at December 31, 1984. Provide computations to support your choice:

	Source	Use
[1]	$5,200,000	$1,200,000
[2]	5,500,000	1,200,000
[3]	7,200,000	2,900,000
[4]	7,500,000	3,200,000

[b] Explain any omission of the items in the problem statement from your computations for [a].

(AICPA adapted)

E23–15 The working capital provided by operations in Seago's 1984 statement of changes in financial posi-

tion was $8,000,000. For 1984, depreciation on fixed assets was $3,800,000, amortization of goodwill was $100,000, and dividends on common stock were $2,000,000.

Instructions

Based on the above information, compute Seago's net income for 1984.

(AICPA adapted)

E23–16 Selected information for Baskins Company for 1984 is as follows:

Proceeds from issuance of common stock	$8,000,000
Proceeds from issuance of preferred stock	2,000,000
Dividends on common stock	1,000,000
Dividends on preferred stock	400,000
Purchases of treasury stock	300,000
Sales of stock to officers and employees not included above	200,000

Instructions

Based on the information provided above, and assuming funds are defined as working capital, determine the amount of total sources and total uses of funds that would appear in Baskins Company's 1984 statement of changes in financial position.

(AICPA adapted)

PROBLEMS

P23–1 Information taken from the detailed trial balance sheet of Ross Rental Agency is as follows:

	Dr. (Cr.) Balances	
	At December 31	
	1983	**1984**
Working capital	$ 57,500	$101,000
Investments	15,000	–0–
Property, plant, and equipment	92,600	118,100
Accumulated depreciation	(27,100)	(33,600)
Intangible assets	17,000	16,000
Bonds payable	(25,500)	(25,500)
Common stock, $10 par	(75,000)	(100,000)
Additional paid-in capital	(40,000)	(55,000)
Retained earnings	(14,500)	(21,000)
	–0–	–0–

Other information relating to various financing and investing activities of the company during 1984 is as follows:

[1] Investments were sold at their carrying value.
[2] Items of equipment costing $27,500 and having $18,000 accumulated depreciation were sold at book value. New equipment was acquired to replace the outdated models that were sold.
[3] During the year, 2,500 shares of common stock were sold.
[4] Dividends of $8,500 were declared and paid during the year. No other entries were made to the Retained Earnings account except the recognition of the 1984 net income or net loss.

Instructions

Prepare a statement of changes in financial position, focusing on changes in working capital, for 1984. Your statement should conform to the provisions of *APB Opinion No. 19* to the extent possible from the information given.

P23–2 Gillespie Outdoor Advertising Company is

preparing a statement of changes in financial position for 1984. Information has been accumulated concerning changes in account balances during 1984 as follows:

	Change in Dr. (Cr.) 1984
Cash	$ (5,500)
Accounts receivable, net	12,000
Inventory	60,500
Property, plant, and equipment	17,650
Accumulated depreciation	(7,300)
Intangible assets	10,000
Accrued expenses	(1,600)
Accounts payable	(10,750)
Notes payable, 90-day	(31,150)
Bonds payable	(10,000)
Common stock	(10,000)
Additional paid-in capital	(2,000)
Retained earnings	(21,850)
	–0–

The following explanations of account changes are available:

Property, Plant, and Equipment. Fully depreciated equipment with a cost of $7,500 was discarded. Equipment with a cost of $6,250 and accumulated depreciation of $4,000 was sold for $3,250. Depreciation expense for 1984 was $18,800. Additional items of new equipment were acquired during 1984.

Intangible Assets. A patent was acquired during the year in exchange for 1,000 shares of the company's $10 par value common stock. The market value of the shares on the date of the exchange was $12. Amortization of existing intangible assets was recognized during 1984.

Bonds Payable. $100,000 of 10% bonds payable were retired at book value and $110,000 of 8% bonds were issued.

Retained Earnings. The only entries during 1984 were to recognize net income for the year and dividends declared of $25,000.

Instructions

Prepare a statement of changes in financial position for the fiscal year ended June 30, 1984. The statement should focus on changes in working capital and should follow the provisions of *APB Opinion No. 19*.

P23–3 Four Square Company recorded the items listed below during 1985. The controller believes that some or all of the items may have an impact on the company's statement of changes in financial position, which focuses on changes in working capital.

[1] Net income for the year is $145,000. This amount includes a $15,000 extraordinary loss resulting from the condemnation of land by the city. The company received $165,000 for land carried on the books at $180,000.

[2] Intangible assets increased by $28,000 during the year, representing the acquisition of a patent for $34,000 and amortization of intangibles of $6,000.

[3] During 1985, cash dividends of $12,500 were declared. Payment will be made in early 1986.

[4] Treasury stock with a par value of $17,000 was acquired for $31,000 during 1985 and recorded by the cost method. None of the treasury shares has been resold as of the end of the year.

[5] An analysis of the Accumulated Depreciation account reveals the following:

Balance, end of 1985	$210,000
Balance, beginning of 1985	175,000
Increase in 1985	$ 35,000
Accumulated depreciation on fully depreciated assets retired during 1985	$ 11,250

[6] Convertible bonds issued at $100,000 par value in 1983 were converted into common stock during 1985. The par value of the stock issued was $50,000; additional paid-in capital was increased by $50,000.

[7] The balance of various noncurrent asset accounts changed during 1985 as follows:

Land	decrease	$ 50,000
Equipment	increase	60,000
Building	increase	100,000

[8] An analysis of working capital accounts reveals that working capital increased by $9,750 during 1985.

Instructions

[a] Describe how each of the eight items above should be presented in Four Square Company's statement of changes in financial position for 1985.

[b] Compute the following items, assuming that the change in working capital is presented as the net difference between sources and uses of financial resources. (A formal statement of changes in financial position is not required.)

 [1] Working capital provided by operations, exclusive of extraordinary items.

 [2] Total financial resources provided.

 [3] Total financial resources used.

P23–4 Trial balances at December 31, 1984 and 1985 for Thompson Piano Company are presented below, along with additional information necessary for the preparation of a statement of changes in financial position:

	1984	1985
Debits		
Cash	$ 19,235	$ 25,471
Accounts receivable, net	42,515	41,760
Inventory	55,600	59,255
Prepaid expenses	1,200	1,100
Property, plant, and equipment	125,450	200,450
Intangible assets	57,200	55,000
Treasury stock	–0–	12,000
	$301,200	$395,036
Credits		
Accrued expenses	$ 5,400	$ 6,200
Accounts payable	29,800	27,119
Note payable, 60-day	43,350	23,350
Accumulated depreciation	47,100	44,600
Note payable, 5-year	–0–	10,000
Common stock	125,000	160,000
Additional paid-in capital	10,000	25,000
Retained earnings	40,550	98,767
	$301,200	$395,036

During 1985 a building with a cost of $75,000 and $30,000 of accumulated depreciation was completely destroyed by a fire resulting from an electrical storm. Insurance proceeds of $60,000 were received. The event was considered both unusual in nature and infrequent in occurrence. The building was replaced by a new facility at a cost of $100,000. In addition, 3,500 shares of $10 par value stock were exchanged for equipment during the year. The stock was not actively traded; the equipment had a listed selling price of $50,000.

Dividends of $10,000 were declared and paid during 1985. All notes payable represent bank loans.

Instructions

[a] Prepare a statement of changes in financial position for 1985, focusing on changes in working capital. Include all disclosures required under generally accepted accounting principles.

[b] Prepare a statement of changes in financial position for 1985, focusing on changes in cash. (The 60-day note payable represents a bank loan that the company does not consider part of cash provided by or used in operations.)

[c] Describe briefly the difference between the statements prepared in [a] and [b].

P23–5 The accountant for Cox Enterprises has drafted the following statement of changes in financial position for 1985. The accountant was unaware that the president of the company had decided to present the statement in the format in which changes in cash are emphasized.

Cox Enterprises
WORKING CAPITAL STATEMENT
December 31, 1985

Source of Working Capital		
Net income	$762,750	
Depreciation	19,775	
Issuance of preferred stock	50,000	
Book value of fixed asset sold	35,000	$867,525
Uses of Working Capital		
Acquisition of fixed assets	375,000	
Acquisition of patents	50,000	
Purchase of treasury stock	75,250	
Retirement of bonds	150,000	
Dividends on preferred stock	5,000	
Dividends on common stock	72,000	727,250
Increase in working capital		$140,275

The company's accountant accepted a position as a ski instructor at a Canadian ski resort and left town on short notice. The president of Cox Enterprises has engaged you to evaluate the above statement and to prepare a revision, if necessary, focusing on cash changes. You have found the items included in the above statement to be accurate. Additional information that was apparently not incorporated into this statement, however, includes the following:

[1] In addition to the bonds retired for $150,000, bonds of $350,000 were converted into common stock during 1985.

[2] An analysis of changes in current assets and current liabilities reveals the following:

	Dollar Change in Account Balance During 1985
Cash	–53,650
Marketable securities	+15,750
Accounts receivable, net	+85,623

Inventory	+97,245
Accounts payable	− 4,762
Income taxes payable	+ 9,455

[3] The fixed asset sold during the year resulted in a $15,000 gain that was included in net income. No extraordinary items were recognized during 1985.

[4] The patent account increased $50,000 during 1985. This change included the acquisition of one patent for $37,500, the successful defense of an existing patent for $19,250, and amortization for the year.

Instructions

[a] Identify errors and omissions in the statement prepared by Cox Enterprise's former accountant.

[b] Prepare a statement of changes in financial position, focusing on changes in cash, including all disclosures necessary under generally accepted accounting principles.

P23–6 Select the correct answer and provide computations to support your choice.

[1] The net income for the year ended December 31, 1985, for Kenny Company was $2,100,000. Additional information is as follows:

Capital expenditures	$6,200,000
Depreciation on fixed assets	2,400,000
Dividend paid on common stock	700,000
Net increase in noncurrent deferred income tax liability	200,000
Amortization of goodwill	75,000

Based on the above information, what should be the working capital provided from operations in the statement of changes in financial position for the year ended December 31, 1985?
- [a] $4,075,000
- [b] $4,375,000
- [c] $4,700,000
- [d] $4,775,000

[2] The stockholders' equity of Spain Company at December 31, 1984, was as follows:

Convertible preferred stock, $20 par value; each share convertible into two shares of common stock; authorized 6,000 shares, issued and outstanding 5,000 shares	$100,000
Premium on convertible preferred stock	15,000
Common stock, $10 par value; authorized 30,000 shares, issued and outstanding 20,000 shares	200,000

Additional paid-in capital on common stock	25,000
Retained earnings	650,000
Total stockholders' equity	$990,000

During 1985 a total of 2,000 shares of convertible preferred stock was converted into common stock. Also during 1985, a total of 5,000 shares of common stock was issued at $15 per share. Assuming funds are defined as working capital, how should the above information be shown on Spain's statement of changes in financial position at December 31, 1985?

	Source	Use
[a]	$46,000	$96,000
[b]	$46,000	$121,000
[c]	$121,000	–0–
[d]	$121,000	$46,000

[3] Selected information from the 1984 accounting records of Soccer Company is as follows:

Working capital provided from operations	$ 2,000,000
Collection of short-term receivables	40,000,000
Payments of accounts payable	30,000,000
Capital expenditures	2,800,000
Proceeds from long-term borrowings	1,500,000
Payments on long-term borrowings	500,000
Dividends on common stock	900,000
Purchases of treasury stock	200,000
Sales of stock to officers and employees	100,000
Working capital at December 31, 1983	18,000,000

Assuming funds are defined as working capital, what should be the working capital at December 31, 1984, shown on Soccer's statement of changes in financial position for the year ended December 31, 1984?
- [a] $17,200,000
- [b] $17,300,000
- [c] $18,200,000
- [d] $27,200,000

[4] The following information for 1984 has been provided by Jonathan Company:

Proceeds from short-term borrowings	$ 600,000
Proceeds from long-term borrowings	2,000,000
Purchase of fixed assets	1,600,000
Purchase of inventories	4,000,000
Proceeds from sale of Jonathan's common stock	1,000,000

Assuming funds are defined as working capital, what is the increase in working capital for the year ended

December 31, 1984?

   [a] $400,000

   [b] $1,000,000

   [c] $1,400,000

   [d] $2,000,000

[5] Tallen Company sold some of its fixed assets during 1985. The original cost of the fixed assets was $750,000, and the allowance for accumulated depreciation at the date of sale was $600,000. Proceeds from the sale of the fixed assets were $210,000. Assuming funds are defined as working capital, the sale of the fixed assets should be shown on Tallen's statement of changes in financial position for the year ended December 31, 1985, as:

   [a] A subtraction from net income of $60,000 and a source of $150,000.

   [b] An addition to net income of $60,000 and a source of $150,000.

   [c] A subtraction from net income of $60,000 and a source of $210,000.

   [d] A source of $150,000.

(AICPA adapted)

P23–7 Bennett Company has not yet prepared a formal statement of changes in financial position for the 1985 fiscal year. Comparative statements of financial position as of December 31, 1984 and 1985, and a statement of income and retained earnings for the year ended December 31, 1985, are presented below:

Bennett Company
STATEMENT OF FINANCIAL POSITION
December 31, 1984 and 1985
(in thousands)

	1984	1985
Assets		
Current Assets		
Cash	$ 100	$ 60
U.S. treasury notes	50	–0–
Accounts receivable	500	610
Inventory	600	720
Total current assets	1,250	1,390
Long-Term Assets		
Land	70	80
Buildings and equipment	600	710
Accumulated depreciation	(120)	(180)
Patents (less amortization)	130	105
Total long-term assets	680	715
Total assets	$1,930	$2,105
Liabilities and Ownership		
Current Liabilities		
Accounts payable	$ 300	360
Taxes payable	20	25
Notes payable	400	400
Total current liabilities	720	785
Term notes payable, due 1987	200	200
Total liabilities	920	985
Owners' Equity		
Common stock outstanding	700	830
Retained earnings	310	290
Total owners' equity	1,010	1,120
Total liabilities and equity	$1,930	$2,105

Bennett Company
STATEMENT OF INCOME AND RETAINED EARNINGS
For the Year Ended December 31, 1985
(in thousands)

Sales		$2,408
Less expenses and interest		
Cost of goods sold	$1,100	
Salaries and benefits	850	
Heat, light, and power	75	
Depreciation	60	
Property taxes	18	
Patent amortization	25	
Miscellaneous expense	10	
Interest	55	2,193
Income before income taxes		215
Income taxes		105
Net income		110
Retained earnings, Jan. 1, 1985		310
		420
Stock dividend		130
Retained earnings, Dec. 31, 1985		$ 290

Instructions

Prepare a statement of changes in financial position for 1985, focusing on changes in cash. Treat the sale of U.S. treasury notes as a separate source, not as a part of cash provided by operations.

(CMA adapted)

P23–8 The following information is to be used in developing worksheet entries for the preparation of a statement of changes in financial position. Each item should be treated independently in complying with the problem requirements as stated below. In all cases the year is 1985.

Company 1. Net income for the year is $275,350. This includes the effect of the following transactions involving the sale of fixed assets:

Sales Price	Cost	Accumulated Depreciation	Gain (Loss)
$15,000	$75,000	$70,000	$10,000
42,500	92,000	40,000	(9,500)

Company 2. Income taxes are presented in the income statement as follows:

Income before income taxes		$425,372
Provision for income taxes		
Payable currently	$147,623	
Deferred	56,557	204,180
Net income		$221,192

Company 3. Equipment and the related depreciation accounts for 1985 are as follows:

	Debit	Credit	Balance Dr. (Cr.)
Equipment			
Balance, Jan. 1			$ 472,000
Cost of equipment sold for $72,800		$126,000	346,000
Cost of equipment purchased	$266,000		612,000
Cost of fully depreciated equipment discarded		27,850	584,150
Accumulated Depreciation			
Balance, Jan. 1			(255,000)
Depreciation on equipment sold	102,000		(153,000)
Depreciation on fully depreciated equipment discarded	27,850		(125,150)
Depreciation expense for 1985		86,000	(211,150)

Company 4. Interest expense was recorded during 1985 with the following entry:

Interest Expense	105,000	
Cash		100,000
Unamortized Bond Discount		5,000

Company 5. Interest expense was recorded during 1985 with the following entry:

Interest Expense	388,000	
Unamortized Bond Premium	12,000	
Interest Payable		400,000

Company 6. Income statement data for the company for 1985 are as follows:

Income before extraordinary items	$150,000
Extraordinary loss—retirement of bonds, net of $10,000 tax	15,000
Net income	$135,000

The extraordinary loss resulted from the retirement of

bonds payable with a face value of $300,000 and a related unamortized discount of $2,000 at a cost of $323,000. The tax rate relative to the transaction is 40%.

Company 7. Land was acquired by issuing preferred stock with $100,000 par value. The preferred stock is not actively traded. The land had a current appraisal value of $117,500.

Instructions

Analyze the information given for each company and prepare the entry in general journal form to account for the item on a worksheet designed to assist in the preparation of a statement of changes in financial position. Treat each item independently and provide a brief explanation for each entry. The statement is to focus on changes in working capital.

P23–9 (Appendix A) Lett Construction Company has requested your assistance in the preparation of a statement of changes in financial position for the year ended June 30, 1985. Comparative trial balances as of June 30, 1984 and 1985, are presented below:

	Dr. (Cr.)	
	June 30, 1984	June 30, 1985
Cash	$ 2,825	$ 3,612
Accounts receivable, net	25,600	17,401
Inventory	42,700	33,250
Equipment	126,000	120,750
Accumulated depreciation, equipment	(42,700)	(52,700)
Building	122,000	207,000
Accumulated depreciation, building	(25,000)	(43,500)

Land	90,000	67,500
Patent	–0–	34,500
Accrued expenses	(2,453)	(1,100)
Accounts payable	(12,462)	(11,400)
Notes payable	(50,000)	(40,000)
Deferred income taxes	(5,430)	(6,550)
Bonds payable	(75,000)	(75,000)
Premium on bonds payable	(2,000)	(1,750)
Common stock ($10 par)	(125,000)	(150,000)
Additional paid-in capital	(25,000)	(35,000)
Retained earnings	(44,080)	(67,013)
	–0–	–0–

Other information that pertains to the fiscal year ending June 30, 1985, includes the following:

Income/Dividends. Net income for the year ended June 30, 1985, was $42,933. No extraordinary items were reported in the income statement. Dividends of $20,000 were declared and paid to common stockholders.

Property, Plant, and Equipment. Equipment costing $25,000 with accumulated depreciation of $20,000 was sold at book value. Depreciation of $30,000 was recognized during the year. Additional equipment of $19,750 was acquired.

An addition to the building was made during the year at a cost of $85,000. Depreciation of $18,500 was recognized during the year.

Land with a cost of $57,500 was sold for $97,800. Additional land was acquired by issuing 2,500 shares of common stock that had a total value of $35,000. A recent appraisal value of the land was not available.

Patent. A patent was acquired for $34,500 during the year.

Notes Payable. A series of short-term loans was taken out under a revolving line of credit with a local bank.

Instructions

Prepare a statement of changes in financial position, focusing on changes in working capital, supported by either a worksheet or T-account analysis of transactions.

P23–10 Dove Company's statement of changes in financial position has not yet been prepared for the year ended December 31, 1985. The schedule below compares the net change in the balance sheet accounts at December 31, 1985 and 1984.

	Net Change Increase (Decrease)
Debit Balance Accounts	
Cash	$ (340,000)
Accounts receivable, net	440,000

Inventories	580,000
Property, plant, and equipment	1,800,000
Total	$2,480,000

Credit Balance Accounts

Accumulated depreciation	$ 950,000
Accounts payable	1,250,000
Notes payable, current	(150,000)
Serial bonds payable	(2,000,000)
Common stock, $10 par value	9,000,000
Capital contributed in excess of par value	1,300,000
Retained earnings	(7,870,000)
Total	$ 2,480,000

Additional Information

[1] Dove incurred a net after-tax loss from regular operations of $500,000 for the year ended December 31, 1985. It also had an extraordinary gain from the sale of condemned land in the amount of $1,400,000 net of tax of $600,000. The condemned land had a book value of $2,500,000.

[2] Accounts receivable of $650,000 were written off during 1985, by charging Allowance for Doubtful Accounts. The provision for bad debts during 1985 was $1,250,000.

[3] Machinery acquired in 1980 at a cost of $2,000,000 was sold for $550,000. The machinery had a net book value of $350,000 at the date of sale.

[4] A new parcel of land was purchased during April 1985. The market value of the land was $6,300,000. Cash of $1,500,000 and 400,000 shares of Dove's common stock were given in exchange for the land.

[5] The serial bonds mature at a rate of $2,000,000 each year. The bonds were sold at par value.

[6] A 5% stock dividend was declared January 15, 1985, on 10,000,000 shares of Dove's common stock. The stock dividend was issued on February 10, 1985, to all stockholders of record as of January 31, 1985. The market value of the stock at these three dates was as follows:

Jan. 15, 1985	$11.00 per share
Jan. 31, 1985	$10.45 per share
Feb. 10, 1985	$10.60 per share

[7] A cash dividend of $.30 per share of common stock was declared on June 30, 1985, to all stockholders of record as of July 15, 1985. The dividend was paid on July 31, 1985.

[8] The notes payable resulted from extended terms granted by one of Dove Company's major suppliers of inventory.

Instructions

Prepare a statement of changes in financial position for the year ended December 31, 1985. Dove Company defines funds as cash for purposes of this statement.

(CMA adapted)

P23–11 Presented below are comparative statements of financial position of Moore Corporation at December 31, 1984 and 1983:

	December 31 1984	December 31 1983	Increase (Decrease)
Assets			
Current assets			
Cash	$ 450,000	$ 287,000	$163,000
Notes receivable	45,000	50,000	(5,000)
Accounts receivable (net of allowance for uncollectible accounts of $17,100 and $24,700, respectively)	479,200	380,000	99,200
Inventories	460,000	298,000	162,000
Total current assets	1,434,200	1,015,000	419,200
Investment in common stock of Reading Company	—	39,000	(39,000)
Investment in common stock of Zip Corporation	246,300	—	246,300
Total	246,300	39,000	207,300
Machinery and equipment	455,000	381,000	74,000
Less: accumulated depreciation	(193,000)	(144,000)	49,000
Total	262,000	237,000	25,000
Patents (less accumulated amortization)	26,000	19,000	7,000
Total assets	$1,968,500	$1,310,000	$658,500
Liabilities and Shareholders' Equity			
Liabilities			
Dividends payable	$ 181,000	—	$181,000
Accounts payable	156,000	40,800	115,200
Accrued expenses	92,000	84,000	8,000
Total liabilities	429,000	124,800	304,200
Shareholders' equity			
Preferred stock, par value $2; authorized 50,000 shares; issued and outstanding, 30,000 shares and 26,500 shares, respectively	60,000	53,000	7,000
Capital contributed in excess of par, preferred stock	6,000	2,500	3,500
Common stock, par value $10; authorized 100,000 shares; issued and outstanding, 75,200 shares and 70,000 shares, respectively	752,000	700,000	52,000
Capital contributed in excess of par, common stock	20,000	9,600	10,400
Earnings appropriated for contingencies	85,000	—	85,000

Retained earnings	616,500	420,100	196,400
Total shareholders' equity	1,539,500	1,185,200	354,300
Total liabilities and share-holders' equity	$1,968,500	$1,310,000	$658,500

Additional Information

[1] For the year ended December 31, 1984, Moore Corporation reported net income of $496,000.

[2] Uncollectible accounts receivable of $4,000 were written off against the allowance for uncollectible accounts.

[3] Moore's investment in the common stock of Reading Company was made in 1980 and represented a 3% interest in the outstanding common stock of Reading. During 1984 Moore sold this investment for $26,000.

[4] Amortization of patents charged to operations during 1984 was $3,000.

[5] On January 1, 1984, Moore acquired 90% of the outstanding common stock of Zip Corporation (45,000 shares, par value $10) in a transaction appropriately accounted for as a purchase. To consummate this transaction, Moore paid $72,000 cash and issued 3,500 shares of its preferred stock and 2,400 shares of its common stock. The consideration paid was equal to the underlying book value of the assets acquired. The fair market value of Moore's stock on the date of the transaction was as follows:

Preferred	$ 3
Common	12

Zip Corporation is considered to be an unrelated business and not compatible with the operations of Moore Corporation. Therefore, consolidation of the two companies is not required. For the year ended December 31, 1984, Zip Corporation reported net income of $150,000.

[6] During 1984, machinery and equipment acquired in 1977 at a cost of $22,000 was sold as scrap for $3,200. At the date of the sale, this machinery had an undepreciated cost of $4,400. Moore also acquired new machinery and equipment for $81,000. The remaining increase in machinery and equipment resulted from major repairs that were accounted for as capital expenditures.

[7] On January 1, 1984, Moore declared and issued a 4% stock dividend on its common stock, The market value of the shares on that date was $12 a share. The market value of the shares was not affected by the dividend distribution. On December 31, 1984, cash dividends were declared on both the common and preferred stock as follows:

Common	$145,000
Preferred	36,000

[8] In December 1984 a reserve for a contingent loss of $85,000 arising from a lawsuit was established by a charge against retained earnings.

Instructions

Prepare a statement of changes in financial position for Moore Corporation for the year ended December 31, 1984. Use a working capital format.

(AICPA adapted)

P23–12 Webster Company has prepared its financial statements for the year ended December 31, 1984, and for the three months ended March 31, 1985. The company's balance sheet at December 31, 1984, and March 31, 1985, and its income statement data for the three months ended March 31 are presented below. You are satisfied that the amounts presented are correct.

BALANCE SHEET

	Dec. 31, 1984	Mar. 31, 1985
Cash	$ 25,300	$ 87,400
Marketable investments	16,500	7,300
Accounts receivable, net	24,320	49,320
Inventory	31,090	48,590
Total current assets	97,210	192,610
Land	40,000	18,700
Building	250,000	250,000
Equipment	—	81,500
Accumulated depreciation	(15,000)	(16,250)
Investment in 30%-owned company	61,220	67,100
Other assets	15,100	15,100
Total	$448,530	$608,760
Accounts payable	$ 21,220	$ 17,330
Dividend payable	—	8,000
Income taxes payable	—	34,616
Total current liabilities	21,220	59,946
Other liabilities	186,000	186,000
Bonds payable	50,000	115,000

Discount on bonds payable	(2,300)	(2,150)
Deferred income taxes	510	846
Preferred stock	30,000	—
Common stock	80,000	110,000
Dividends declared	—	(8,000)
Retained earnings	83,100	147,118
Total	$448,530	$608,760

INCOME STATEMENT DATA

	For the Three Months Ended Mar. 31, 1985
Sales	$242,807
Gain on sale of marketable investments	2,400
Equity in earnings of 30%-owned company	5,880
Gain on condemnation of land	10,700
	261,787
Cost of sales	138,407
General and administrative expenses	22,010
Depreciation	1,250
Interest expense	1,150
Income taxes	34,952
	197,769
Net income	$ 64,018

Your discussion with the company's controller and a review of the financial records have revealed the following information:

[1] On January 8, 1985, the company sold marketable securities for cash. These securities had been held for more than six months.

[2] The company's preferred stock is convertible into common stock at a rate of one share of preferred for two shares of common. The preferred stock and common stock have par values of $2 and $1, respectively.

[3] On January 17, 1985, three acres of land were condemned. An award of $32,000 in cash was received on March 22, 1985. Purchase of additional land as a replacement is not anticipated.

[4] On March 25, 1985, the company purchased equipment for cash.

[5] On March 29, 1985, bonds payable were issued by the company at par for cash.

[6] The investment in 30%-owned company included $3,220 attributable to goodwill at December 31, 1984. Goodwill is being amortized at an annual rate of $480.

[7] The company's tax rate is 40% for regular income and 20% for capital gains.

Instructions

[a] Prepare a statement of changes in financial position, focusing on changes in working capital, for Webster Company for the three months ended March 31, 1985.

[b] Prepare a statement of changes in financial position, focusing on changes in cash, for Webster Company for the same period. The marketable investments were sold at carrying value.

[c] Comment on the difference between funds provided by operations in [a] and [b].

(AICPA adapted)

P23–13 Presented below are the comparative statements of position of Kelson Corporation as of December 31, 1984 and 1983:

Kelson Corporation
STATEMENTS OF FINANCIAL POSITION

	December 31		Increase
	1984	1983	(Decrease)
Assets			
Current assets			
Cash	$ 100,000	$ 90,000	$ 10,000
Accounts receivable (net of allowance for uncollectible accounts of $10,000 and $8,000, respectively)	210,000	140,000	70,000
Inventories	260,000	220,000	40,000
Total current assets	570,000	450,000	120,000
Land	325,000	200,000	125,000
Plant and equipment	580,000	633,000	(53,000)
Less: Accumulated depreciation	(90,000)	(100,000)	10,000

| Patents | 30,000 | 33,000 | (3,000) |
| Total assets | $1,415,000 | $1,216,000 | $199,000 |

Liabilities and Shareholders' Equity

Liabilities			
Current liabilities			
Accounts payable	$ 260,000	$ 200,000	$ 60,000
Accrued expenses	200,000	210,000	(10,000)
Total current liabilities	460,000	410,000	50,000
Deferred income taxes	140,000	100,000	40,000
Long-term bonds (due			
Dec. 15, 1990)	130,000	180,000	(50,000)
Total liabilities	730,000	690,000	40,000
Shareholders' equity			
Common stock, par value $5;			
authorized 100,000 shares;			
issued and outstanding 50,000			
and 42,000 shares, respectively	250,000	210,000	40,000
Additional paid-in capital	233,000	170,000	63,000
Retained earnings	202,000	146,000	56,000
Total shareholders' equity	685,000	526,000	159,000
Total liabilities and share-			
holders' equity	$1,415,000	$1,216,000	$199,000

Presented below is the income statement of Kelson Corporation for the year ended December 31, 1984:

Kelson Corporation
INCOME STATEMENT
For the Year Ended December 31, 1984

Sales		$1,000,000
Expenses		
Cost of sales	560,000	
Salary and wages	190,000	
Depreciation	20,000	
Amortization	3,000	
Loss on sale of equipment	4,000	
Interest	16,000	
Miscellaneous	8,000	
Total expenses		801,000
Income before income taxes		
and extraordinary item		199,000
Income taxes		
Current	50,000	
Deferred	40,000	
Provision for income taxes		90,000
Income before extraordinary item		109,000
Extraordinary item—gain		
on repurchase of long-term		
bonds (net of $10,000 income tax)		12,000
Net income		$ 121,000
Earnings per share		
Income before extraordinary item		$2.21
Extraordinary item		.24
Net income		$2.45

Additional Information

[1] On February 2, 1984, Kelson issued a 10% stock dividend to shareholders of record on January 15, 1984. The market price per share of the common stock on February 2, 1984 was $15.

[2] On March 1, 1984, Kelson issued 3,800 shares of common stock for land. The common stock and land had current market values of approximately $40,000 on March 1, 1984.

[3] On April 15, 1984, Kelson repurchased long-term bonds with a face value of $50,000. The gain of $22,000 was reported as an extraordinary item on the income statement.

[4] On June 30, 1984, Kelson sold equipment costing $53,000, with a book value of $23,000, for $19,000 cash.

[5] On September 30, 1984, Kelson declared and paid a $.04 per share cash dividend to shareholders of record August 1, 1984.

[6] On October 10, 1984, Kelson purchased land for $85,000 cash.

[7] Deferred income taxes represent timing differences relating to the use of accelerated depreciation for income tax reporting and straight-line depreciation for financial reporting.

Instructions

[a] Analyze Kelson's transactions and prepare a worksheet for use in preparing a statement of changes in

financial position, focusing on changes in working capital for the year 1984.

[b] Prepare a statement of changes in financial position for Kelson Corporation for 1984, focusing on changes in working capital. (You are not required to prepare the accompanying schedule of changes in working capital accounts.)

(AICPA adapted)

P23–14 The management of Harmon Company, concerned over a decrease in working capital, has provided you with the following comparative analysis of changes in account balances at December 31, 1983 and 1984:

	December 31 1984	December 31 1983	Increase (Decrease)
Debit Balances			
Cash	$ 145,000	$ 186,000	$ (41,000)
Accounts receivable	253,000	273,000	(20,000)
Inventories	483,000	538,000	(55,000)
Securities held for plant expansion purposes	150,000	—	150,000
Machinery and equipment	927,000	647,000	280,000
Leasehold improvements	87,000	87,000	—
Patents	27,800	30,000	(2,200)
Totals	$2,072,800	$1,761,000	$311,800
Credit Balances			
Allowance for uncollectible accounts receivable	$ 14,000	$ 17,000	$ (3,000)
Accumulated depreciation of machinery and equipment	416,000	372,000	44,000
Allowance for amortization of leasehold improvements	58,000	49,000	9,000
Accounts payable	232,800	105,000	127,800
Cash dividends payable	40,000	—	40,000
Current portion of 6% serial bonds payable	50,000	50,000	—
6% serial bonds payable	250,000	300,000	(50,000)
Preferred stock	90,000	100,000	(10,000)
Common stock	500,000	500,000	—
Retained earnings	422,000	268,000	154,000
Totals	$2,072,800	$1,761,000	$311,800

Additional Information

During 1984 the following transactions occurred:

[1] New machinery was purchased for $386,000, and obsolete machinery, with a book value of $61,000, was sold for $48,000. No other entries were recorded in Machinery and Equipment or related accounts other than provisions for depreciation.

[2] Harmon paid $2,000 legal costs in the successful defense of a new patent. Amortization of patents amounting to $4,200 was recorded.

[3] Preferred stock, par value $100, was purchased at 110 and subsequently canceled. The premium was charged to retained earnings.

[4] On December 10, 1984, the board of directors declared a cash dividend of $.20 per share payable to holders of common stock on January 10, 1985.

[5] A comparative analysis of retained earnings as of December 31, 1984 and 1983, is presented below:

	December 31 1984	1983
Balance, Jan. 1	$268,000	$131,000
Net income	195,000	172,000
	463,000	303,000
Dividends declared	(40,000)	(35,000)
Premium on preferred stock repurchased	(1,000)	—
	$422,000	$268,000

Instructions

[a] Prepare a statement of changes in financial position for Harmon Company for the year ended December 31, 1984, focusing on changes in working capital.

[b] Prepare a schedule of changes in working capital to accompany your statement in [a].

(AICPA adapted)

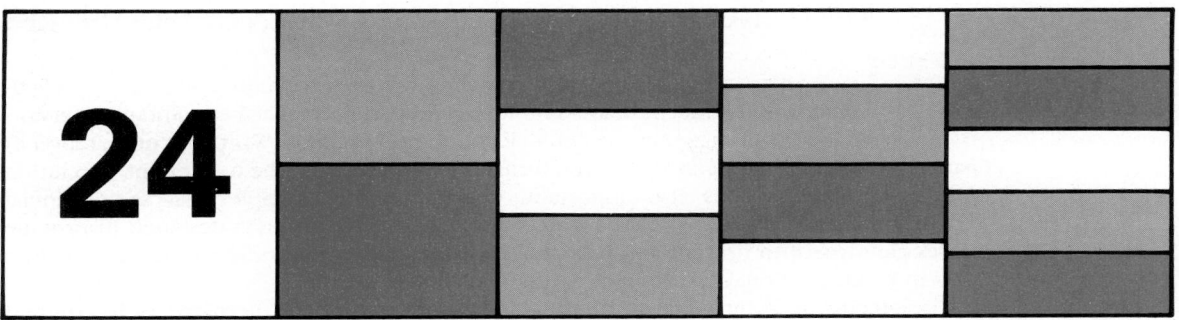

24

FINANCIAL-STATEMENT DISCLOSURE AND ANALYSIS

Objectives

To discuss the role and purposes of financial-statement disclosures.

To consider the meaning of "adequate disclosure" in relation to financial statements.

To present an acceptable summary of significant accounting policies.

To describe the nature of items requiring disclosure.

To discuss the need to use financial-statement-disclosure checklists.

To describe comprehensive financial-statement analysis.

To assess the present and near future liquidity of a business enterprise.

To evaluate the long-term profitability and capital-maintenance prospects of a business enterprise.

To evaluate the financial structure and viability of a business enterprise.

To assess the efficiency of asset utilization in the generation of revenue and earnings.

To interpret financial statements at a relatively sophisticated level.

NEED FOR FINANCIAL-STATEMENT DISCLOSURES

The primary focus of this book concerns the theories, concepts, standards, and practices that accountants employ in preparing financial statements in accordance with generally accepted accounting principles. While the preparation of financial statements has been the central thrust of our discussion, the use and interpretation of financial statements is also important. Remember, for example, that the Financial Accounting Standards Board (FASB) stated that financial reporting is designed to provide information useful to present and potential investors and creditors and other information users in making rational investment, credit, and similar decisions.[1]

The success of the financial accounting and reporting process, therefore, is determined by the *usefulness* of the information provided rather than the process itself. As accountants, we strive to ensure that financial statements are clear, consise, complete, and adequately informative in all significant matters. Financial statement users should not be burdened with an overload of information, nor should they be deprived of data relevant to their decisions. The balancing of these competing objectives and purposes requires substantial professional judgment. We attempt to anticipate the needs of financial statement users and how the information provided will be employed in their decision-making processes. Based on our determination of the way information will be used and in accordance with many authoritative pronouncements, great amounts of financial-statement disclosures are necessary to ensure that the statements are adequately informative.

Research evidence tends to support the position that the value of a company's securities in the market is affected by all available pertinent information. Stated more broadly, a large body of capital-market research reveals that footnotes (and all other disclosures) are considered by the aggregate marketplace and the resulting value placed on each company's securities is a function of all available information. This research evidence further emphasizes the importance of adequate disclosure in the functioning of capital markets such as national stock exchanges.

The first part of this chapter considers the nature and extent of disclosures necessary to prepare financial statements in accordance with generally accepted accounting principles. Many specific disclosure requirements related to such areas as leases, pensions, and investments have been considered in earlier chapters in which these topics were discussed. Many other types of disclosure, however, are more general and do not relate to any single topic or specific chapter. Our primary focus here is on the latter type of issues. We discuss several items of financial-statement disclosure that are pervasive and frequently of compelling significance.

The second part of this chapter deals with the analysis of financial statements. It develops and discusses many ratios, trends, and other relationships that provide insight into the financial health and prospects of a particular enterprise. It also considers the limitations of financial analysis and some possible pitfalls that confront analysts attempting to interpret financial statements.

THE ROLE OF DISCLOSURE IN COMMUNICATING FINANCIAL INFORMATION

Disclosure

While generally acceptable accounting principles require substantial disclosures in the form of parenthetical information in the financial statements or as footnotes to the financial statements, the issue of the role of disclosure is not without controversy. For example, the executive vice-president of International Telephone and Telegraph, Inc., writes:

---

[1] *FASB Statement of Financial Accounting Concepts No. 1,* "Objectives of Financial Reporting by Business Enterprises," 1978, par. 34.

> *The credibility of the financial statements is being undermined by the process of attempted improvement. The failure to dispose of basic differences in concept, logical inconsistencies within the legislative framework, reports which inadequately present their primary data, and the attempt to substitute disclosure for sound principles has eroded the public's faith in the accounting discipline.*[2]

A past president of the American Institute of Certified Public Accountants (AICPA) echos this concern:

> *We are in the midst of a period of proliferating disclosure requirements and have reached a point where the footnotes in many cases overshadow the financial statements. There is widespread concern that an overload of disclosure may be counterproductive to understanding and that the benefits may not be worth the costs involved.*[3]

Others, however, think differently. A former commissioner of the Securities and Exchange Commission (SEC) points out:

> *It [the SEC] is not engaged in an effort to embarrass industry by mandating awkward disclosures, bestow advantages upon competitors, or hamper development. It is concerned with carrying out conscientiously the Congressional mandate given to it 40 years ago to protect investors by requiring disclosures that are useful, meaningful, complete, and accurate so that the investment process may be rational and informed.*[4]

The role of disclosure in financial statements continues to be as controversial today as it has ever been. Some feel that financial statements are merely "propped up" by massive disclosures, while others view disclosure as an absolutely necessary corollary to the basic statements. Regardless of these philosophical arguments, however, many items of disclosure are currently required. Perhaps the most fundamental and comprehensive pronouncement on disclosure requires the presentation of a summary of significant accounting policies.

Summary of Significant Accounting Policies

We have seen in previous chapters that several equally acceptable alternative accounting practices exist in certain areas of financial reporting. For example, first-in, first-out (FIFO), last-in, first-out (LIFO), and weighted-average methods of inventory valuation are each acceptable, as are several depreciation methods. Furthermore, many industries employ unusual or unique accounting practices that are not widely used or understood outside that industry. In recognition of these circumstances, the Accounting Principles Board (APB) issued *Opinion No. 22*.[5] Among other requirements, *Opinion No. 22* requires companies to provide as the first footnote, or as a separate section preceding the footnotes to the financial statements, a summary of significant accounting policies. This summary describes the specific accounting practices employed, discusses unusual or unique accounting practices, and provides other information about the company's operations and accounting decisions not apparent elsewhere in the financial statements. While the disclosure provided in the summary of significant accounting policies does not duplicate information presented elsewhere, references from the summary to details presented in other notes is acceptable.

The "Summary of Significant Accounting Policies" of Federal Express Corporation, an air-ground transportation company that provides overnight door-to-door delivery of packages and messages throughout the United States, is reproduced in Exhibit 24–1. The exhibit

---

[2]H. C. Knortz, "The New Financial Environment," *Management Accounting* (March 1975), p. 15.
[3]Wallace B. Olson, quoted in *The Week in Review* (April 2, 1976), p. 1.
[4]A. A. Sommers, Jr., "Financial Reporting: Who is Liable?" *Financial Executive* (March 1974), p. 29.
[5]*APB Opinion No. 22*, "Disclosure of Accounting Policies," 1972.

EXHIBIT 24–1
Example Summary of Significant Accounting Policies
Federal Express Corporation

Federal Express Corporation and Subsidiary	**Notes to Consolidated Financial Statements**

**Note 1
Summary of Significant
Accounting Policies**

Principles of consolidation. The consolidated financial statements include the accounts of Federal Express Corporation and Federal Express Leasing Corporation, a wholly-owned subsidiary whose operations consist primarily of the acquisition and leasing of equipment to the Company. All significant intercompany accounts and transactions have been eliminated.

Property and equipment. Expenditures for major additions, improvements, flight equipment modifications and certain overhaul costs are capitalized. Maintenance and repairs are charged to expense as incurred. The cost and accumulated depreciation of property and equipment disposed of are removed from the related accounts and any gain or loss reflected in income.

For financial reporting purposes, depreciation and amortization of property and equipment is provided on a straight-line basis over the asset's estimated service life or related lease term as follows:

Flight equipment	7 to 12 years
Package handling and ground support equipment	5 to 28 years
Buildings and leasehold improvements	5 to 31 years
Other property and equipment	5 to 8 years

For income tax purposes, depreciation is generally computed utilizing accelerated methods.

Capitalized interest. Interest on funds used to finance the acquisition of aircraft and construction of certain facilities is capitalized as an additional cost of the asset up to the date the asset is placed in service. For income tax purposes, interest capitalized is deducted currently.

Short-term investments. Short-term investments are carried at cost, which approximates market and consist of commercial paper, repurchase agreements, certificates of deposit and other money-market instruments.

Construction expenditures under bond issues. In accordance with the provisions of several bond issues of the Memphis-Shelby County Airport Authority, the Company makes construction expenditures and is reimbursed from bond proceeds held by a trustee upon compliance with the terms of the construction contracts and presentation of proof of payment.

Spare parts, supplies and fuel. Spare parts, supplies and fuel are stated principally at standard cost (approximates actual cost on a first-in, first-out basis) which is not in excess of current replacement cost.

Deferred charges. Significant costs associated with the introduction of new types of aircraft are deferred and amortized over periods of up to five years. Expenses applicable to the issuance of long-term debt are deferred and amortized over the term of the related debt.

Income taxes. Deferred income taxes are provided for the tax effect of timing differences which occur in the recognition of certain expenses (principally depreciation of property and equipment) for tax and financial reporting purposes. Investment tax credit is accounted for using the flow-through method as a reduction of Federal income taxes in the year in which the credit is utilized.

Earnings per share. Earnings per share are computed by dividing net income (adjusted for dividend requirements on the $9.50 Cumulative Preferred Stock) by the weighted average number of common and common equivalent shares outstanding during the year. Common equivalent shares are the number of shares of common stock that would be issued upon the exercise of all outstanding stock options and warrants.

Earnings per share assuming full dilution are substantially the same as earnings per share as stated and, accordingly, are not shown separately.

Reclassifications. Certain amounts for 1981 and 1980 have been reclassified to conform to the 1982 presentation.

SOURCE: Federal Express Corporation, 1982 Annual Report.

illustrates the types of disclosures commonly made in such summaries, although many variations of these disclosures are encountered in practice.

Several other items are frequently discussed in the summary of significant accounting policies. Exhibit 24–2 presents most of the commonly encountered items in a summary of significant accounting policies. Of course, new types of business forms and transactions are almost constantly emerging, and important accounting issues related to such practices should be disclosed.

Some of the disclosures in a summary of significant accounting policies represent the selection of a particular accounting practice from among several equally acceptable practices. Examples of such alternatives include inventory-flow assumptions (e.g., LIFO, FIFO, and average cost) and depreciation policies (e.g., straight line, sum-of-the-years'-digits, and percentage declining-balance).

Other disclosures in the summary of significant accounting policies represent the application of a specific practice that is required because of the circumstances surrounding the reporting entity. Although alternative practices may exist in these situations, not every alternative is acceptable in all circumstances. For example, both the percentage-of-completion and completed-contract methods of accounting for long-term contracts represent acceptable practice in certain circumstances. When the collection of a contract fee or estimates of costs required to complete the contract are uncertain, however, gross profit should not be recognized on the percentage-of-completion basis. Rather, when such uncertainties exist, the completed-contract method should be used.

Thus, even though only a single accounting policy may be acceptable in a given set of circumstances, disclosure of the method applied is still necessary to adequately inform users of the circumstances and appropriate accounting policies for the reporting entity. Since

---

EXHIBIT 24–2
Items Usually Included in a Summary of Significant Accounting Policies

Business

Ownership

Definition of fiscal year

Principles of consolidation

Format and classification comparability among years

Investments in affiliated companies

Inventories

Intangibles

Depreciation

Income taxes: Deferred items
            Investment tax credits
            Tax sharing agreements

Pension plans

Capitalization of costs (deferred charges)

Deferred income

Long-term contracts

Property

Foreign currency

Unusual industry practices (e.g., fund accounting in nonbusiness entities)

Classification and information aggregation levels

SOURCE: Reproduced by permission of Satin, Tennenbaum, Eichler, and Zimmerman, CPAs, Los Angeles, California.

several practices are available, selection of the particular appropriate policy in a given circumstance is necessary. Revenue recognition and long-term contracting were discussed in Chapter 20, so they are not explained completely again at this time. If necessary, refer back to Chapter 20 for a more comprehensive discussion of accounting for long-term contracts.

Another example, also related to revenue realization, is the use of the installment sales method of profit recognition. *APB Opinion No. 10* states:

> There are exceptional [emphasis added] cases where receivables are collectible over an extended period of time and, because of the terms of the transaction or other conditions, there is no reasonable basis for estimating the degree of collectibility. When such circumstances exist, and as long as they exist, either the installment method or the cost recovery method of accounting may be used.[6]

Users of financial statements usually assume that revenue is recognized at the point of sale unless there is disclosure to the contrary. Thus, the use of installment sales, cost recovery, or any other exceptional revenue-recognition practice should be disclosed in the summary of significant accounting policies. Again refer to Chapter 20 for a description of these methods of accounting and the circumstances in which their use is acceptable.

In a curious provision in *Opinion No. 22,* the APB stated that unaudited interim financial statements need not contain a summary of significant accounting policies if the reporting entity has not changed its accounting policies since the end of the last annual reporting period.[7] The rationale offered is that most, if not all, users of interim financial statements have access to the most recent annual report. However, distinguishing between audited and unaudited interim financial statements in requirements for disclosure seems questionable at best. Financial statements should normally be presented in accordance with generally accepted accounting principles, including adequate disclosure, regardless of any auditor association. Nevertheless, the provisions of *APB Opinion No. 22* represent accepted practice in spite of this unusual provision distinguishing between audited and unaudited interim financial statements. The entire subject of interim financial reporting is discussed more extensively in Chapter 25, since the topic is of major significance to publicly held companies.

Other General Disclosures

Disclosure

As previously mentioned, disclosures related to individual or specific areas of accounting, such as leases or pensions, are discussed in chapters of this text devoted to those topics. Certain disclosures, however, are more general or are not necessarily related to any single type of transaction. Therefore, we now examine several types of disclosures not discussed extensively elsewhere in this book.

Related-Party Transactions

Materiality

Many companies engage extensively in transactions with related parties; such transactions, if material, must be disclosed. Related parties include "affiliates of the enterprise; entities for which investments are accounted for by the equity method by the enterprise; trusts for the benefit of employees, such as pension and profit-sharing trusts that are managed by or under the trusteeship of management; principal owners of the enterprise; its management; members of the immediate families of principal owners of the enterprise and its management; and other parties . . . which control or can significantly influence the management or operating policies of the other."[8]

---

[6]*APB Opinion No. 10,* "Omnibus Opinion—1966," 1966, par. 12, footnote 8.
[7]*APB Opinion No. 22,* par. 10.
[8]*FASB Statement of Financial Accounting Standards No. 57,* "Related Party Disclosures," 1982, par. 24.

Of course, all entities have some related parties; however, not all entities engage in related-party transactions. The management of a company must establish procedures to identify related parties and enumerate any material related-party transactions, because disclosures of such transactions is necessary.

Although types of related-party transactions are almost limitless, several examples occur frequently in practice: Related parties commonly lend money to and borrow money from each other; they may sell products to and buy products from each other; and services may be provided by one related party to another without charge. When such related-party transactions are material, several accounting issues arise.

Substance over Form

As a general rule, accountants attempt to recognize the substance of a related-party transaction (as in all other transactions) rather than its mere form. Many accounting pronouncements deal with the modifying convention of substance over form. Examples of situations in which substance is recognized over form include accounting for leases, equity-method investments, and pensions. Many transactions between related parties differ in substance and purpose from normal transactions, however, merely because the participants in the transaction are related. Accountants must gain an understanding of the business purposes of such transactions in order to account for and disclose the events properly.

For example, one party may lend money to a related second party without specifying timing and amount of repayment. In such a case the proper classification (current or noncurrent) and valuation (imputation of interest) are uncertain and pose problems for accountants. To gain an understanding of the underlying purpose of the event, an accountant may need to have extensive discussions with the related parties.

Substance over Form

Another common related-party transaction arises when an asset is sold at an amount that differs substantially from its market value. When such transactions occur, accountants emphasize the substance of the event; however, in some cases the *substance* of the transaction is highly unusual. For example, a major shareholder may sell an automobile to a closely held corporation at a price substantially lower than the market value of the vehicle. The shareholder may be providing assistance to a financially troubled business; if so, that fact may need to be disclosed. At any rate, the accountant must attempt to understand the underlying business purpose of the unusual transaction.

Once a related-party transaction is identified and an understanding of the transaction is gained, the accountant should disclose the following aspects of the event:[9]

1. The nature of the relationship between the transacting parties.
2. The nature and description of the transaction.
3. The dollar volume of the transaction and any changes in terms and effects from the preceding period.
4. Any amounts due from or to the related parties.

In addition, the disclosure of common control may be necessary even if no related-party transactions occur, because common control of several entities can itself cause the operating results and financial position of each controlled entity to differ. For example, assume that Rhonda Rich owns two clothing stores that operate as separate corporate entities. Rhonda also has a contract to provide all uniforms to a city's hospital, street maintenance, police, and fire departments. Some years she decides one of the clothing stores will fulfill the contract whereas in other years the other store fulfills the contract. The contract is large enough and profitable enough to materially affect the financial statements of either company. Thus, even though neither company transacts business with the other, the existence of common control clearly affects each of them. Disclosure of the common control and other details of these circumstances, therefore, is necessary to fully inform financial statement users of this condition.

---

[9]*FASB Statement of Financial Accounting Standards No. 57,* par. 2.

Economic dependency may create a higher level of risk if one enterprise relies on another for a material amount of financing or operational support. *Statement on Auditing Standards No. 6,* points out that although economic dependence does not give rise to related parties, "disclosure of economic dependence may . . . be necessary."[10] For example, if much of the output of a small factory is purchased by a large retail department-store chain, the chain can probably exert significant influence over the management and operating policies of the small factory. Even if significant influence is not exerted, disclosure of economic dependency may be necessary to adequately inform financial statement users of the risk of relying on a limited number of customers or suppliers.

Information about material related-party transactions is sometimes quite sensitive; however, such information is also vital to an intelligent use of the financial statements. An accountant's responsibility to external users of financial statements cannot be subordinated to management's desire for privacy. Indeed, in extreme cases the lack of adequate disclosure of related-party transactions and their effects have harmed independent CPAs in later litigation.[11] An example of a disclosure of a related-party transaction is presented in Exhibit 24–3; although the names, amounts, and dates are fictitious, the disclosure is based on an actual financial statement.

Disclosure of Illegal Acts

Disclosure   Information indicating that a company or its personnel might have committed an illegal act occasionally comes to the attention of accountants. Watergate-related inquiries revealed that several major U.S. corporations had engaged in bribes, kickbacks, and other questionable practices. Consequently Congress enacted the Foreign Corrupt Practices Act of 1977,

---

[10]*Statement on Auditing Standards No. 6,* "Related Party Transactions" (New York: AICPA, 1975), par. 5.
[11]For example, in the case of Continental Vending Company, Inc., independent CPAs were held guilty of criminal fraud. Material loans made by a company to another commonly controlled company were never repaid. The court held that disclosure of more facts and circumstances regarding the loan and its questionable collectibility was necessary, and the findings of the court contributed to the issuance of *Statement on Auditing Standards No. 6,* "Related Party Transactions."

EXHIBIT 24–3
Related-Party Disclosures

Longworth, Arvel, & Jones*
A Legal Corporation
ANNUAL REPORT
December 31, 1984

Note 4—Related-Party Transactions

Notes receivable from related parties consist of:	
L, A, & J Partnership, due on demand, with annual interest of 6%	$37,000
L, A, & J Investment Partnership, due on demand, with annual interest of 6%	7,900
Total	$44,900

Management does not anticipate payment to be received on these notes during 1985. Included in notes payable is a $50,000 noninterest-bearing note to a stockholder that is payable on demand.
Notes receivable from stockholders of $42,500 are due on demand at interest rates from 17% to 19%.

*Although the identity of the corporation has been disguised, this exhibit is based on an actual case.

which has had a substantial impact on the responsibilities of practicing accountants. In essence, if a company engages in transactions within the purview of the Foreign Corrupt Practices Act, heavy penalties may be sustained by the company and the personnel involved. Financial-statement disclosures are also usually necessary in such circumstances. For example, if a company generates material revenue as a result of engaging in an illegal act, such as a bribe of a foreign official, that information should be disclosed. In this manner readers of the financial statements are made aware of the unusual risks of a company that generates revenue illegally. Although the problem of reporting illegal activity is of exceptional importance, the incidence of such acts is infrequent. Nevertheless, the required disclosure of illegal acts remains a controversial issue and holds many unanswered implications for all business enterprises. Exhibit 24–4 presents a portion of the disclosure from the annual report of Tony Lama Company, presented in Chapter 14. The company produces boots and other leather footwear.

Subsequent-Events Disclosure

A relatively long period is usually required to prepare the financial statements of a company following the end of the year. The period of time between the balance sheet date and the day the financial statements are issued is called the **subsequent period.** Exhibit 24–5 illustrates the subsequent period in relation to annual financial statements. In this example the income statement, statement of retained earnings, and statement of changes in financial position report activity for the year ended December 31, 1984, and the balance sheet presents the financial position on December 31, 1984. The subsequent period is January 1, 1985 through February 28, 1985—the time required to prepare and issue the financial statements for the year ended December 31, 1984.

Disclosure

Thus, although the subsequent period is not an integral part of the reporting period, accountants must disclose certain material events taking place during the subsequent period. Indeed, in some cases the amount of an asset or liability at the end of the reporting year may be changed as a result of information becoming available during the subsequent period.

Accountants must be concerned with two types of subsequent events. A **type-one subsequent event** consists of those events providing "additional evidence with respect to conditions that existed at the date of the balance sheet and affect the estimates inherent in

---

EXHIBIT 24–4
Illustrative Disclosure

Tony Lama Company
ANNUAL REPORT
December 31, 1977

(10) Contingency
   In August 1977 the Company pleaded guilty to criminal charges in connection with the duty declarations and subsequently paid a fine of $15,000. In addition, the Customs Service assessed the Company a civil penalty of approximately $36 million, which represents the forfeiture value of the goods imported during the period in question. The Company is preparing its petition for mitigation of the penalty, and normally such penalties are mitigated to a multiple (generally from one to eight) of the alleged loss of revenue ($510,000). The Company has made provision in its 1977 consolidated financial statements for $510,000, the minimum penalty it expects to incur in connection with the customs matter; however, the penalty ultimately assessed may be substantially in excess of this amount. The total ultimate liability to the Company which may result from the customs matter is not presently determinable. Customs penalties normally may be repaid with interest over a period of five years from the date of final adjudication. Such penalties are not deductible for Federal income tax purposes.

EXHIBIT 24–5
The Subsequent Period

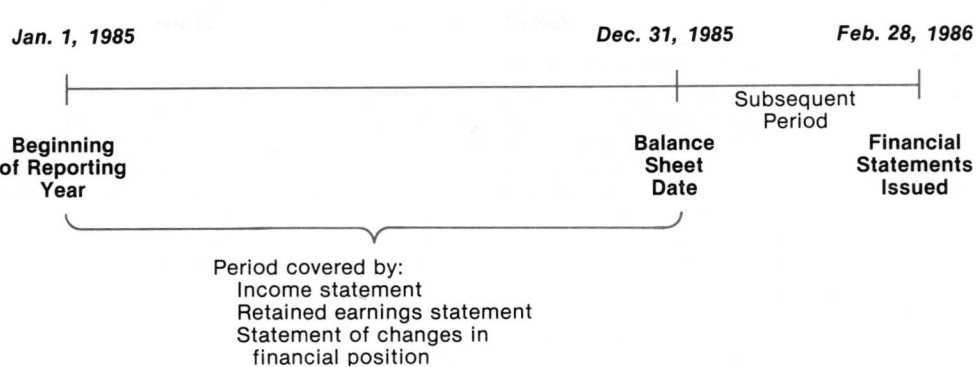

the process of preparing financial statements."[12] Since the evidence provided by a type-one subsequent event relates to a condition existing at the balance sheet date, the financial statements should be adjusted for any changes in estimates resulting from the new evidence. For example, if a company is a defendant in a lawsuit at December 31, 1985, and the suit is subsequently settled out of court for $100,000 on January 25, 1986, the company should use the subsequently acquired information to accrue a liability and a loss in the amount of $100,000 for the year ended December 31, 1985. In sum, the ultimate resolution of the suit during **the subsequent period provided additional information about a condition existing at the balance sheet date.**

A **type-two subsequent event** consists of "those events that provide evidence with respect to conditions that did not exist at the date of the balance sheet . . . but arose subsequent to that date."[13] Accountants should not adjust the financial statements for the year just ended for type-two subsequent events; however, disclosure of such events is necessary. Indeed, if a type-two subsequent event is sufficiently material, the historical unadjusted financial statements should be *supplemented* with *pro forma* financial information treating the event as if it had occurred on the balance sheet date. Examples of type-two subsequent events requiring disclosure but not resulting in adjustments include:

1. Sale of a bond or capital-stock issue.
2. Purchase of a business.
3. Loss of plant or inventories as a result of fire or flood.
4. Litigation loss if the event giving rise to the lawsuit took place subsequent to the balance sheet date.

A type-two subsequent event represents **a new event or new condition,** not merely new information about an existing condition, as in the case of a type-one subsequent event.

Exhibit 24–6 contains a disclosure of a type-two subsequent event from the annual report of Du Pont, a diversified international company that produces and sells fuels and other energy products and a broad range of high-technology products. The disclosure

---

[12]*Statement on Auditing Standards No. 1,* "Codification of Auditing Standards and Procedures" (New York: AICPA, 1972), Sec. 560, par. 3.
[13]*Statement on Auditing Standards No. 1,* Sec. 560, par. 5.

EXHIBIT 24–6
Subsequent-Event Disclosure

E. I. du Pont de Nemours and Company
BALANCE SHEET
December 31, 1980

Note 13—Subsequent Event

   In January 1981, Du Pont and New England Nuclear Corporation executed an agreement whereby New England Nuclear will be acquired by Du Pont. Under the agreement, which is subject to the approval of New England Nuclear's stockholders, Du Pont will issue 1.3 shares of its common stock for each outstanding share of New England Nuclear common stock, or a total of approximately 8.7 million shares. The transaction will be accounted for as a pooling of interests. If the transaction had been consummated prior to December 31, 1980, consolidated Du Pont sales, net income, and earnings per share of common stock for 1980 (unaudited) would have been as follows [dollars in millions except earnings per share]:

Sales	$13,744
Net income	727
Earnings per share of common stock	4.63

SOURCE: E. I. du Pont de Nemours and Company, 1980 Annual Report.

---

describes the nature and economic aspects of the event. Again, the standard of adequate disclosure relates to informing an external financial statement user of all material facts relevant to understanding the economic, operational, and financial aspects of a business enterprise.

   Substantial judgment is necessary to strike the appropriate balance between adequately informing financial statement users and burdening them with trivia irrelevant to the decisions being made. Furthermore, if disclosures of insignificant matters are included in the financial statements, those immaterial events may assume an importance beyond their original significance, because financial statement users ascribe a high level of importance to items selected for disclosure in the financial statements. Accountants constantly strive to provide an optimal level of disclosure, avoiding overdisclosure as well as underdisclosure. Of course, conservatism usually results in disclosing items that are of marginal importance rather than omitting them. Nevertheless, financial statements should not be cluttered with irrelevant or immaterial disclosures.

Conservatism

Disclosure of Pervasive Uncertainties

Chapter 14 ("Current and Contingent Liabilities") discussed financial accounting and reporting for loss contingencies. Most of the issues examined in Chapter 14 were concerned with specific types of events, such as lawsuits, uncollectible receivables, and liabilities under warranties or guarantees. We now consider the accounting measurement and disclosure problems associated with pervasive uncertainties (i.e., those loss contingencies that, if ultimately sustained, may require many assets and liabilities to be revalued or reclassified). Perhaps the most commonly encountered type of pervasive uncertainty involves questions about the appropriateness of the going-concern assumption.

Going Concern

   In the absence of evidence to the contrary, we assume that a business enterprise will continue operating indefinitely. As long as a company can meet its obligations on a timely basis and generate resources in a sufficient amount to pay all costs of operation, the life of the business is considered unlimited. *APB Statement No. 4* considers the going-concern assumption a basic feature of financial accounting. Continuation of entity operations is usually assumed in financial accounting in the absence of evidence to the contrary:

> *Because of the relative permanence of enterprises, financial accounting is formulated basically for going concerns. Past experience indicates that continuation of operations is highly probable for most enterprises although continuation cannot be known with certainty. An enterprise is not viewed as a going concern if liquidation appears imminent.[14]*

Circumstances may change, however, and evidence may negate the appropriateness of the going-concern assumption. If it is necessary to abandon the going-concern assumption, assets and liabilities should be valued and classified on a liquidation basis. Under the liquidation basis, all assets are presumed to be held for sale rather than to support operations. Furthermore, all liabilities are normally considered current, because a cessation of operations and dissolution of the business is imminent. Perhaps *Statement on Auditing Standards No. 34* expresses these problems best: "When the continued existence of an entity is imperiled, there is heightened concern about the recoverability and classification of recorded asset amounts and the amounts and classification of liabilities."[15] Of course, if we are certain that an enterprise will dissolve and cease operations, then we know not to apply the going-concern assumption. In such cases, the liquidation basis of accounting should be directly applied.

In such circumstances, however, we are frequently uncertain as to whether or not a business enterprise will continue to exist and operate. If a company is experiencing severe operating and cash flow difficulties, then the possibility of insolvency and bankruptcy must be considered. We are unsure as to whether the company can resolve its problems and continue to operate or whether it faces liquidation and bankruptcy. Accountants gather all available evidence to assess carefully the prospects of a company in such situations.

Statement on Auditing Standards No. 34 provides several examples of information that tend to raise questions about the appropriateness of the going-concern assumption. The factors we should consider include:

A. *Information that may indicate solvency problems:*
- *Negative trends (for example, recurring operating losses, working capital deficiencies, negative cash flow from operations, and adverse key financial ratios).*

- *Other indications (for example, default on loan or similar agreements, arrearages in dividends, denial of usual trade credit from suppliers, noncompliance with statutory capital requirements, and necessity of seeking new sources or methods of financing).*

B. *Information that may raise a question about continued existence without necessarily indicating potential solvency problems:*
- *Internal matters (for example, loss of key management or operations personnel, work stoppages or other labor difficulties, substantial dependence on the success of a particular project, and uneconomic long-term commitments).*

- *External matters (for example, legal proceedings, legislation, or similar matters that might jeopardize an entity's ability to operate; loss of a key franchise, license, or patent; loss of a principal customer or supplier; and uninsured catastrophes such as drought, earthquake, or flood).[16]*

---

[14]*APB Statement No. 4,* "Basic Concepts and Accounting Principles Underlying Financial Statements of Business Enterprises," 1970, par. 117.
[15]*Statement on Auditing Standards No. 34,* "The Auditor's Considerations When a Question Arises About an Entity's Continued Existence" (New York: AICPA, 1981), par. 1.
[16]*Statement on Auditing Standards No. 34,* par. 4.

EXHIBIT 24–7
Illustration of Loan Covenant Violations

As losses mounted, Continental failed to maintain the financial ratios required in its credit pacts. Lenders took mortgages on all unsecured planes. In February, to get a $25 million seasonal working capital loan for Continental without being forced to sell some real estate, Lorenzo put up a $10 million guarantee from Texas Air. Continental has made all interest and principal payments on its bank loans. But because it is still in violation of its covenants, which the lenders thus far have waived each month, most of its long-term debt has been reclassified as a current obligation.

SOURCE: "A New Management Tries to Reroute Continental," *Business Week,* June 7, 1982, p. 72. Reprinted from *Business Week* by special permission, © 1982 by McGraw-Hill, Inc.

Exhibit 24–7 illustrates problems created for a company if it violates loan covenants with its lenders. This exhibit relates to Continental Airlines, a major air carrier that operates primarily in the southwest United States. After the time of this disclosure, Continental combined with Texas Air Corporation.

Factors that should be considered may vary in importance and may not be individually significant. Collectively or in partial combination with each other, however, they may tell a great deal about the future prospects of a business. Furthermore, factors may exist that tend to mitigate the seriousness or significance of the negative information. For example, a company may have several alternative methods of maintaining adequate cash flow during a period of reduced or declining revenues and financial stress. Excess plant capacity may be sold or needed operating assets may be refinanced, for example, in a sale-leaseback arrangement. Management may also factor receivables, extend debt, or raise additional equity capital.

Going Concern

Considerable judgment is required to assess properly the significance and implications of information contrary to the going-concern assumption. Similar expertise is necessary to evaluate information that tends to mitigate the contrary information. Nevertheless, when we conclude that there is a reasonable possibility that a company may be forced into liquidation or bankruptcy, extensive disclosures are usually necessary.

Disclosure

In addition to a general discussion of the operating and financial problems of the company, many specific items of disclosures may also be necessary. For example, if a company has defaulted on a loan covenant, such as an agreement to maintain a certain working capital ratio, that fact should be disclosed. The disclosure should also include a discussion of management's proposed course of action to overcome the company's problems. Finally, the position of creditors and future financing possibilities should also be discussed. For example, if a creditor has waived the condition of loan default, that fact should also be disclosed.

Although it is relatively common to encounter a company in financial or operating distress, no two sets of difficulties are ever the same. Consequently, disclosure of such problems should describe the exact situation in question. Exhibit 24–8 contains a footnote disclosure from the 1980 annual report of Chrysler Motor Corporation, the third largest producer of passenger cars and trucks in the United States and Canada. The exhibit illustrates the type of wording and expression that is common to troubled companies; however, most of the issues discussed are peculiar to the circumstances of Chrysler Motor Corporation.

The Nature of Adequate Disclosure Summarized

APB Statement No. 4 observes that "information about economic resources and obligations of a business enterprise is needed to form judgments about the ability of the enterprise to survive, to adapt, to grow, and to prosper amid changing economic conditions."[17] The

---

[17]*APB Statement No. 4,* par. 77.

EXHIBIT 24–8
Going-Concern Uncertainty Disclosure

Note 2. 1980 Developments and Future Risk and Uncertainties

Chrysler incurred losses of $1,097.3 million in 1979 and $1,709.7 million in 1980. Chrysler's 1980 loss significantly exceeded the loss projected in the December 17, 1979 Operating Plan submitted to the United States government, primarily due to the depressed conditions that existed in the automotive industry during 1980. Although certain of the financing risks that existed at December 31, 1979 were resolved as Chrysler restructured most of its institutional debt (see Note 3) and obtained a commitment from the United States government for loan guarantees of up to a maximum of $1.5 billion, providing certain conditions are met, significant financing and other risk and uncertainties still exist.

Through December 31, 1980, the Chrysler Corporation Loan Guarantee Board ("the Board") had authorized guarantees totaling $800.0 million and Chrysler issued notes for that amount which are due in 1990 unless certain prepayment options are exercised (see Note 3). On February 27, 1981, the Board authorized an additional $400.0 million of guarantees and additional long-term debt was incurred by the issuance of notes due in 1990 with basically the same prepayment options as those in the earlier notes. Therefore, the total amount of federally guaranteed debt now outstanding is $1.2 billion. In accordance with the Chrysler Corporation Loan Guarantee Act ("the Act"), the Board is required to make periodic determinations as to Chrysler's present and future viability and the Board has the power to accelerate the maturity of outstanding guaranteed loans and terminate the commitment to guarantee future loans, under certain circumstances if such determinations cannot be made.

In conjunction with the authorization of the additional $400.0 million of guarantees, the Board required that certain concessions be finalized between Chrysler and its lenders, suppliers, and employees. The agreed to concessions include the conversion of approximately $686 million of long-term debt to preferred stock, the option to liquidate approximately $623 million of long-term debt at 30 cents per dollar, price concession objectives from suppliers totaling $72 million, and wage and other benefits concessions from employees totaling $783 million through September, 1982. The effects of these concessions were reflected in revised (January 14, 1981) Operating and Financing Plans ("the Plans") submitted to the Board. The Board made the determination that the Plans meet the requirements of the Act. In addition, the Board has received satisfactory assurances that the Plans are realistic and feasible.

The Plans project a significant improvement in operating results for 1981 over 1980, and profits for the subsequent years. The 1981 projection assumes a U.S. car industry of 9.6 million units and Chrysler achieving 9.1% penetration. The 1981 projection also assumes U.S. truck retail sales of 2.5 million units and Chrysler achieving 9.0% penetration. Capital expenditures for 1981 have been projected to be substantially below 1980 levels and the Plans indicate an ability to finance these expenditures without any additional federally guaranteed loans.

The Corporation's long-term viability is predicated on a return to sustained profitable operations. The Plans project that improvement in earnings will be achieved through increased automotive industry sales; improvements in vehicle profit margins; reduced fixed costs; and reduced advertising and dealer incentives from 1980 levels. Achievement of the objectives in the Plans is dependent on other basic assumptions, including improved general economic conditions and consumer acceptance of Chrysler's vehicle offerings. If the current economic recession continues, this and other factors beyond the Corporation's control could have a substantial effect on the ability of Chrysler to achieve the objectives outlined in the Plans.

SOURCE: Chrysler Motor Corporation, 1980 Annual Report.

Disclosure numbers and account descriptions in the basic financial statements provide a great deal of this information. A large volume of additional disclosure, usually in the form of footnotes to the financial statements, is also necessary to adequately inform users of the practices, assumptions, and characteristics of the data in the financial statements. Disclosures also provide information about the environment of a business enterprise and enhance comparability between the reporting company and other business enterprises.

Since the volume and nature of required disclosures are so extensive, most accountants employ financial-statement-disclosure checklists to ensure that no important elements of disclosure are omitted. An excerpt from such a checklist is contained in Appendix A of this chapter. You are urged to review the checklist to gain an appreciation of the scope and magnitude of issues that must be addressed and disclosed in a set of financial statements.

Several elements of disclosure are required only of publicly held companies. Examples include information about earnings per share, industry segments, and interim results. Financial accounting and reporting problems peculiar to publicly held companies, including incremental and supplemental disclosures, are discussed in the last three chapters of this book.

Disclosure

Adequate disclosure simply means that the financial statements inform a user of all material, relevant data with respect to a reporting enterprise. Financial statements, including related disclosures, are a *means to an end, not* an end in themselves. The ultimate goal of financial reporting is improved decision making; to the extent that an item of information can contribute to that goal, disclosure is desirable.

Several of the disclosures we have just discussed are required by the authoritative auditing, rather than accounting, literature. **Statements on Auditing Standards (SASs)** primarily guide independent CPAs performing audits of companies. Occasionally, however, an SAS requires some type of disclosure, and in such cases the authors believe those disclosures become a part of generally accepted accounting principles. Disclosures required by the auditing literature represent substantial authoritative support for the practices recommended, and consequently CPAs are careful to comply with the accounting disclosure provisions of SASs.

Auditors issue reports on the financial statements they audit. There are many reasons why a CPA might issue a qualified audit report or, in extreme cases, disclaim an opinion or express an adverse opinion. Most audits conducted by CPAs, however, resulted in unqualified or "clean" opinions. Exhibit 24–9 illustrates an unqualified opinion that relates to the financial statements of General Motors and its subsidiaries.

The first paragraph of the auditor's report is commonly referred to as the **scope paragraph,** which describes what the CPA did. In Exhibit 24–9, the accounting firm of Deloitte Haskins & Sells audited the financial statements for each year in the three-year period ending December 31, 1982. In the financial statements that accompany this audit report, balance sheets are presented for the most recent two years and the other financial statements are presented for the most recent three years.

Consis-tency

The second paragraph, commonly referred to as the **opinion paragraph,** describes what the CPA found as a result of the audit. In Exhibit 24–9, Deloitte Haskins & Sells concluded that the financial statements were fairly presented in conformity with generally accepted accounting principles applied on a consistent basis.

If the CPAs had not performed their audit in accordance with generally accepted auditing standards or if the financial statements had departed from generally accepted accounting principles, the audit report would have been qualified to call attention to the deficiencies. There are other reasons, which are not discussed here, that would also require the auditor to modify an audit report.

Investors rely on the auditor's report to provide reasonable assurance that the financial statements are presented fairly (i.e., free from material error, either unintentional or deliberate). Therefore, the auditor's report on a set of financial statements also provides useful information about the reliability and condition of the accounting records of the company.

The next section of this chapter discusses how to analyze the financial statements of a business for better decision making. While much of the analysis illustrated deals primarily with the numbers contained in the statements, the notes and other disclosures also provide valuable information for interpreting those numbers.

EXHIBIT 24–9
General Motors
Illustrative Auditor's Report

ACCOUNTANTS' REPORT

Deloitte
Haskins + Sells
CERTIFIED PUBLIC ACCOUNTANTS

1114 Avenue of the Americas
New York, New York 10036

General Motors Corporation, its Directors and Stockholders: February 7, 1983

We have examined the Consolidated Balance Sheet of General Motors Corporation and consolidated subsidiaries as of December 31, 1982 and 1981 and the related Statements of Consolidated Income and Changes in Consolidated Financial Position for each of the three years in the period ended December 31, 1982. Our examinations were made in accordance with generally accepted auditing standards and, accordingly, included such tests of the accounting records and such other auditing procedures as we considered necessary in the circumstances.

In our opinion, these financial statements present fairly the financial position of the companies at December 31, 1982 and 1981 and the results of their operations and the changes in their financial position for each of the three years in the period ended December 31, 1982, in conformity with generally accepted accounting principles applied on a consistent basis.

Deloitte Haskins & Sells

SOURCE: General Motors, 1982 Annual Report.

SOME IMPLICATIONS OF EFFICIENT MARKET RESEARCH

THE BEHAVIOR of security prices with respect to financial statement data is a widely discussed and hotly debated topic. . . . The prevailing opinion in the accounting profession is that the market reacts naively to financial statement information. This view is reinforced by . . . the obvious fact that the market is populated by several million uninformed, naive investors, whose knowledge or concern with the subtleties of accounting matters is nil. However, in spite of this obvious fact, the formal research in this area is remarkably consistent in finding that the market, at least as manifested in the way in which security prices react, is quite sophisticated in dealing with financial statement data. One rationale for the observed sophistication of security prices is that the professional investors "make the market" and the competitive bidding among one another for securities effectively makes the prices behave in such a manner that they reflect a considerable amount of sophistication. . . . In the terminology of this literature, the securities market is said to be "efficient" with respect to financial statement data.

A market is said to be efficient if security prices act as if they "fully reflect" publicly available information, including financial statement data. . . . Specifically, this means no investor can expect to use published information in such a way as to earn abnormal returns on his securities. Each investor can expect to earn a return on a security commensurate with its risk. All securities of the same degree of riskiness will offer the same expected return, regardless of what accounting methods are used and no matter how much time is spent gleaning the secrets of the financial statements hidden in the footnotes. Hence, no amount of security analysis, based on published financial statement data, will lead to abnormal returns. . . .

What are the implications (of efficient market research) for the FASB?

1. Many reporting issues are trivial and do not warrant an expenditure of FASB resources. The

properties of such issues are twofold: (1) There is essentially no difference in cost to the firm of reporting either method. (2) There is essentially no cost to statement users in adjusting from one method to the other. In such situations, there is a simple solution. Report one method, with sufficient footnote disclosure to permit adjustment to the other, and let the market interpret implications of the data for security prices.

2. The role of financial statement data is essentially a preemptive one—that is, to prevent abnormal returns accruing to individuals by trading upon inside information. This purpose leads to the following disclosure policy: If there is no additional costs of disclosure to the firm, there is *prima facie* evidence that the item in question ought to be disclosed.

3. The FASB must reconsider the nature of its traditional concern for the naive investor. If the investor, no matter how naive, is in effect facing a fair game, can he still get harmed? If so, how? . . . The harm is more likely to occur because firms are following policies of less than full disclosure and insiders are potentially earning monopoly returns from access to inside information. Harm is also likely to occur when investors assume speculative positions with excessive transactions costs, improper diversification and improper risk levels in the erroneous belief that they will be able to "beat the market" with published accounting information.

4. Accountants must stop acting as if they are the only suppliers of information about the firm. Instead, the FASB should strive to minimize the total cost of providing information to investors. In an efficient market, security prices may be essentially the same under a variety of financial accounting standards, because, if an item is not reported in the financial statements, it may be provided by alternative sources. Under this view . . . the market uses a broad set of information set, and the accountant is one—and only one—supplier of information.

The implications of market efficiency for accounting are frequently misunderstood. There are at least two common misinterpretations. The first belief is that, in an efficient market world, there are no reporting issues of substance because of the "all-knowing" efficient market. Taken to its extreme, this error takes the form of asserting that accounting data have no value and hence the certification process is of no value. The efficient market in no way leads to such implications. It may well be that the publishing of financial statement data is precisely what makes the market as efficient as it is. . . . Disclosure is a substantive issue. A second erroneous implication is, simply find out what method is most highly associated with security prices and report that method in the financial statements. . . . One major reason (that this is incorrect) is that such a simplified decision rule fails to consider the costs of providing information.

Financial statement information is inherently a social commodity. However, it is clear that decisions regarding its generation and dissemination are of a much different nature than we have traditionally thought them to be.

SOURCE: Adapted from William H. Beaver, "What Should Be the FASB's Objectives?" *Journal of Accountancy,* August 1973, pp. 49–56. Copyright © 1973 by the American Institute of Certified Public Accountants, Inc.

ANALYSIS OF FINANCIAL STATEMENTS

"The next several years will see unparalleled opportunities for accountants to expand their analytical and advisory roles, for both the private and public sectors," said Leland S. Prussia, chairman of the board of Bank of America, at an AICPA National Conference on Banking.[18] Prussia also noted that, because of the ever-increasing complexity of America's economic system, the accounting profession will be called on more frequently to help decision makers cope. He added that the accounting profession in particular will be called on "to devise ever-better financial analysis and 'early warning' systems to correctly assess the 'going concern' value of institutions."

Individuals use financial statements as an aid in making a great many decisions. Present and prospective stockholders are interested primarily in future earnings, cash flow, and

---

[18]Leland S. Prussia, speech before AICPA National Conference on Banking, Chicago, Nov. 16, 1981.

dividend prospects. Short-term creditors, such as banks and other lenders, are concerned about the ability of a company to repay debt in the immediate future. Bondholders usually have a primary concern, however, with the longer-term ability of the company to repay debt on a timely basis. Of course, a company's management and employees also use accounting information in their relationships with the enterprise. Employees are interested in the entity's long-term stability and ability to pay wages. Management uses accounting information to revise and set operating policies sensitive to the current and future environment.

One common characteristic among all of these uses of accounting information is that each user analyzes current and past information in an attempt to anticipate and forecast the future. Nowhere does the old adage—"those who are ignorant of the past are condemned to repeat it"—seem more appropriate than in the interpretation and analysis of financial statements.

Knowledgeable and intelligent analysis of financial statements requires not only a firm understanding of analytical tools, but also comprehension of the major concepts, assumptions, and standards underlying contemporary financial accounting. Furthermore, the interpretation of financial statements is not the exclusive domain of financial analysts. Accountants are frequently called on not only to prepare financial statements, but also to study and interpret the meaning and implications of those statements. Indeed, as preparers and communicators of financial information, accountants must understand the concepts and techniques of sophisticated financial-statement analysis. This section of the chapter discusses many common analytical tools that are frequently used to glean inferences and messages that, although contained in the financial statements, may remain hidden until placed under the "microscope" of the skillful analyst.

Fundamental Analysis of Financial Statements

Analysis of financial statements is designed to focus on and clarify relationships among financial information and to facilitate an understanding of the significance of various factors. Furthermore, the objectives of applying analytical procedures may vary from case to case. For example, an auditor attempting to determine if financial statements are free from material errors or irregularities may apply procedures similar to those applied by a creditor attempting to assess the ability of a company to repay a loan. Therefore, regardless of the reason for applying the procedure, a basic premise of financial-statement analysis is that "relationships among data may be expected . . . to exist and continue in the absence of known conditions to the contrary."[19]

Thus, an investor may know that the gross margin percentage for companies in a given industry averages 40%. Furthermore, if the individual company in question has reported a gross margin of 42% for the last three years and that margin suddenly drops to 25% in the current period, the change in the customary relationship concerns the investor. Perhaps a careful reading of the footnotes will reveal that a material amount of obsolete inventory was charged to expense in the current year and that normal profit is anticipated in the future. Unusual relationships, therefore, represent "red flags" that we should evaluate in attempting to understand the underlying causes. In many cases, footnote disclosures can provide much useful explanatory information.

Financial-statement analysis can also take many forms. For example, financial-statement analysis includes all of the following:[20]

1. Comparison of the financial information with information for comparable prior periods.
2. Comparison of the financial information with anticipated results, such as budgets and forecasts.

---

[19]*Statement on Auditing Standards No. 23,* "Analytical Review Procedures" (New York: AICPA, 1978), par. 3.
[20]*Statement on Auditing Standards No. 23,* par. 6.

3. Study of the relationships of elements of financial information (e.g., working capital) that are expected to conform to a predictable pattern.
4. Comparison of the financial information with similar information from the entity's industry.
5. Study of the relationships of the financial information with relevant nonfinancial information.

Actual analysis may take the form of ratios, trends, percentages, and other tests and measures. The objectives of our analysis and the magnitude of the decisions we are to make help determine the nature and extent of the analytical tools we will apply.

One useful way to view financial-statement analysis is from the information objectives of the analyst. In this regard, four basic areas of inquiry serve as a logical starting point:

1. **Liquidity analysis** evaluates the ability of the enterprise to pay its short-term obligations on a timely basis.
2. **Profitability/capital-maintenance analysis** evaluates the earnings capability, performance, and preservation of equity with a long-term time horizon.
3. **Activity analysis** evaluates how efficiently and effectively enterprise assets are being productively employed.
4. **Financial structure and viability analysis** evaluates the long-term ability of an enterprise to pay its obligation on a timely basis and the degree of protection afforded creditors and investors.

Obviously these aspects of financial analysis are interrelated, and a comprehensive evaluation is necessary to gain a complete understanding of the financial and operational health of a business. Nevertheless, classification strategies such as the one presented here are useful to focus on each of the several areas of concern.

We shall illustrate the use of basic analytical techniques by using a comprehensive case selected from practice. The financial statements of an actual company are presented in Exhibit 24–10. However, we have changed the dates and the name of the company, omitted

---

EXHIBIT 24–10
Concomp, Inc.
BALANCE SHEET
December 31, 1985 and 1984
(in thousands)

Assets

	1985	1984
Current Assets		
Cash (including interest-bearing time deposits of $51 and $67)	$ 687	$ 1,761
Short-term investments at cost (which approximates market)	406	1,867
Trade receivables, less allowances of $205 and $178	4,916	4,295
Inventories (at cost or market, whichever is lower)	3,435	3,413
Other current assets (materials, supplies, prepaid expenses)	1,564	1,620
Total current assets	11,008	12,956
Noncurrent Assets		
Investment in real estate	2,202	2,014
Investment in bonds	1,442	223
Plant assets, less accumulated depreciation of $19,174 and $17,838	30,970	28,066
Construction in progress	6,414	6,083
Deferred charges (financing and other)	344	270
Total assets	$52,380	$49,612

Liabilities and Stockholders' Equity

Current Liabilities

Accounts payable	$ 2,230	$ 1,805
Notes payable	26	77
Current maturities of long-term debt	298	320
Current maturities of capital leases	109	100
Current income taxes	166	1,267
Other liabilities (accrued wages, taxes, interest, vacation, and retirement)	3,346	2,970
Total current liabilities	6,175	6,539

Long-Term Liabilities

Long-term debt	12,694	11,849
Capital lease obligations	1,472	1,575
Pension and other liabilities	1,865	1,557
Deferred income tax credits	1,519	575
Total long-term liabilities	17,550	15,556
Total liabilities	23,725	22,095

Stockholders' Equity

Preferred shares (4,100 shares authorized, issued, and outstanding, $10 par)	41	41
Common shares (600,000 shares authorized, issued and outstanding, $10 par)	6,000	6,000
Paid-in capital in excess of par	2,877	2,921
Retained earnings	19,737	18,555
Total stockholders' equity	28,655	27,517
Total liabilities and stockholders' equity	$52,380	$49,612

Concomp, Inc.
INCOME STATEMENT
For the Years Ended December 31, 1985 and 1984
(in thousands)

	1985	*1984*
Revenue		
Sales of retail clothing	$45,358	$44,226
Real estate rental revenue	511	570
Other revenue [Note 1]	333	370
Total revenue	46,202	45,166
Expenses		
Cost of goods sold	31,838	29,932
Selling, general, and administrative costs	3,364	3,035
Depreciation and amortization	4,107	3,325
Advertising and development costs	522	449
Interest expense	1,077	1,046
Total	40,908	37,787
Earnings before taxes and extraordinary item	5,294	7,379
Income taxes	2,080	2,261
Earnings before extraordinary item	3,214	5,118
Extraordinary casualty loss—net of tax effect [Note 2]	(435)	—
Net earnings	$ 2,779	$ 5,118
Earnings per share (not in thousands)		
Earnings before extraordinary item	$5.36	$8.53
Extraordinary item	(.73)	
Net earnings	$4.63	$8.53

Note 1: Principally commissions and consignment profits.
Note 2: Uninsured loss of large warehouse and inventory from natural disaster.

some disclosures, and presented only two of the basic financial statements for brevity and ease of understanding. We begin our analysis by using techniques to evaluate the liquidity of Concomp, Inc., a major clothing retailer.

Liquidity Analysis

Short-term creditors and suppliers are primarily interested in the ability of a business to repay current borrowings on a timely basis. Such financial statement users are less interested, for example, in the long-term profitability of the enterprise or the ability of the business to pay off bonds maturing in 20 years. Although Concomp has total liabilities of $23,725,000, only $6,175,000 of those mature during the coming period. Will Concomp be able to pay off these current debts as they mature? The following analysis attempts to provide insight to the answer to this question.

Working Capital.   You will recall that **working capital** is the excess of current assets over current liabilities and that current assets are those resources that are available or will become available in the current period to support operations and pay off existing current liabilities. Not all amounts that must be paid in the next period, however, are recorded as current liabilities. For example, salaries that Concomp employees will earn in the next period and which must be paid are not included in liabilities at the end of the year. Thus, most companies maintain an excess of current assets over current liabilities to assure the ability to meet all arising obligations on a timely basis. Current assets, however, are normally not considered productive assets, and excess current assets may reduce the earnings capability of the firm. In such cases long-term investors may become disillusioned and choose not to extend credit and equity capital to the company. A deficiency of current assets may impair the ability of a firm to meet its debts and, therefore, cause financial and operational difficulties. An excess of current assets may cause the firm to perform in a sluggish fashion. The appropriate level of working capital varies from industry to industry and even among businesses in the same industry. For every enterprise, however, some optimal level of current assets, current liabilities, and working capital exists. Thus, the amount of working capital (and a comparison of that amount with similar amounts of previous periods) is a useful measure of liquidity. Concomp's working capital for 1985 and 1984 are computed as shown in Exhibit 24–11.

Observe that Concomp's working capital has dropped since the end of 1984. While the information about the current year is useful, the implications of current conditions take on greater significance when compared to past conditions. The usefulness of most information takes on added significance when trends can be studied and analyzed. Furthermore, no single ratio or measure can provide adequate insight to answer all the questions we may have about a company.

Current Ratio.   We compute the current ratio by dividing current assets by current liabilities. Although working capital is an absolute amount, the **current ratio** provides a **relative measure of liquidity.** Concomp's current ratio is computed in Exhibit 24–12.

EXHIBIT 24–11 Concomp, Inc. Working Capital (in thousands)		
	1985	*1984*
Current assets	$11,008	$12,956
Less: Current liabilities	(6,175)	(6,539)
Working capital	$ 4,833	$ 6,417

EXHIBIT 24–12		
Concomp, Inc.		
Current Ratio		
(amounts in thousands)		
	1985	*1984*
Current assets	$11,008	$12,956
÷ Current liabilities	÷ $ 6,175	÷ $ 6,539
Current ratio	1.78	1.98

Concomp's current ratio, although still reflecting current assets in excess of current liabilities, declined during 1985.[21] While the downward trend is somewhat disturbing, we can see that substantial financial strength remains. A more conservative measure of liquidity is the quick ratio, and even more insights are possible when that number is computed.

Quick Ratio. The **quick ratio,** also referred to as the **acid-test ratio,** recognizes that some assets (such as prepaid expenses or supplies) that benefit current operations will not be converted directly into cash. Since inventory may contain slow-moving items and since a company must await a willing and capable buyer, inventory is also excluded from the quick ratio. Only cash, temporary investments, and current receivables are considered "quick" assets (those closest to cash) and included in this ratio. The quick ratio for Concomp is presented in Exhibit 24–13.

The quick ratio also shows a material decline from 1984; however, the 1985 ratio of .97 still seems adequate, especially when compared with the comparable average industry ratio of .9 obtained from Robert Morris Associates.[22] While we are beginning to gain valuable insights into liquidity, several other tests can be applied to Concomp's financial statements.

---

[21]The use and interpretation of ratios in financial analysis, while somewhat subjective, nevertheless yield valuable insights into the financial status of enterprises. We may consider how well the enterprise being evaluated operates relative to other enterprises in the same industry and of similar size. In this case, Robert Morris Associates' *Financial Statement Studies* (1982) indicates that the normal current ratio for companies in the same industry as Concomp, and of similar size, is about 2.1 to 1. The use of industry comparisons with companies of similar size is recommended.

[22]Robert Morris Associates, *Financial Statement Studies.*

EXHIBIT 24–13		
Concomp, Inc.		
Quick Ratio		
(amounts in thousands)		
	1985	*1984*
Quick assets*	$6,009	$7,923
÷ Current liabilities	÷ $6,175	÷ $6,539
Quick ratio	.97	1.21
*Quick assets include:		
Cash	$ 687	$1,761
Current marketable securities	406	1,867
Current receivables	4,916	4,295
Totals	$6,009	$7,923

Up to this point we have evaluated liquidity by analyzing elements of the balance sheet exclusively. Other valuable information can be gained by relating aspects of the income statement to certain balance sheet amounts.

Ratio of Working Capital Provided by Operations to Current Liabilities. If we add the expenses not requiring the expenditure of cash in the current period back to net earnings, we arrive at the amount of cash (or near cash) resources that were generated by operations. In 1985, however, Concomp reported an extraordinary loss, net of tax, of $435,000. Because extraordinary items are unusual in nature and infrequent in occurrence, we do not expect this type of loss to recur in the foreseeable future. Therefore, we add depreciation and amortization expenses of $4,107,000 (for 1985) back to *earnings before extraordinary item* rather than to the net earnings.

Of course, other nonrecurring items (such as the effects of discontinued operations, the cumulative effects of changes in accounting principles, and the effects of correcting errors) are also normally excluded from an analysis that attempts to foresee likely future events. In the Concomp example we consistently exclude the extraordinary item from our ratio analysis; however, the effects of the item and the underlying causes of the item should not be completely forgotten.

Depreciation and amortization is added back to earnings because cash was not currently required to pay these expenses and, therefore, operations (earnings) provided cash (or at least working capital) in an amount greater than the amount of earnings reported. This amount may be expressed as a ratio to current liabilities as shown in Exhibit 24–14.

Industry ratios for comparative purposes are generally unavailable for unusual or unique ratios. Nevertheless, insight may be obtained by focusing on specific aspects of different companies through the use of nonstandard analytical techniques. The ratios computed in Exhibit 24–14 confirm the trend of reduced liquidity and ability to service current debts; this level of liquidity is not overly troublesome, however, because the company appears to possess adequate strength to service current debt. The company still appears to have the ability to pay all operating expenses that require cash and to pay existing liabilities within one operating cycle.

We could analyze many other ratios, trends, and relationships associated with liquidity. Indeed, we are limited only by our own imagination and creativity in developing relevant analytical techniques. The ratios we have illustrated here are intended to be suggestive of the type of analysis possible rather than an exhaustive coverage of the subject. The next category of analysis we consider relates primarily to the level of profitability and maintenance of capital.

EXHIBIT 24–14
Concomp, Inc.
Ratio of Working Capital Provided by
Operations to Current Liabilities
(amounts in thousands)

	1985	1984
Earnings before extraordinary item	$3,214	$5,118
Add: Depreciation and amortization	$4,107	$3,325
Working capital provided by operations	$7,321	$8,443
÷ Current liabilities	÷ $6,175	÷ $6,539
Ratio of working capital provided by operations to current liabilities	1.19	1.29

Profitability and Capital-Maintenance Analysis

The evaluation of profitability and maintenance of equity is directed toward assessing the ability of the company to generate revenues adequate to pay all costs of operations and provide a return to owners while maintaining or enhancing the equity investment position of the stockholders. Profitability ratios are concerned primarily with relating earnings to various measures of investment. The first ratio we consider is called the rate of return on assets employed.

Rate of Return on Assets Employed. This ratio attempts to relate the level of return achieved to the assets employed in the earnings process. For Concomp this ratio is demonstrated in Exhibit 24–15. The amount of contruction in progress is subtracted from total assets in arriving at the assets actually used or usable in the generation of revenue. Earnings before extraordinary items is also used, as before, because the extraordinary item is, by definition, not expected to recur. In this illustration we have used the average assets employed rather than the assets present at the end of the accounting period in order to get a more realistic measure of the investment of assets that were used to produce the income for the period. If the level of productive assets does not vary significantly from the beginning to the ending of the period, the ending level of productive assets may be used in the computation. In some cases only the ending balance will be available (for example, in the comparative year), and the ratio must be based on that figure rather than on an average. If the assets available at the beginning and end of the year are close to the same amounts, little difference results from using the average rather than the year-end figures.

The effects of inflation are especially troublesome in evaluating profitability. For example, assets may be understated in terms of constant price level or replacement cost dollars. Expenses, likewise, may also be understated during an inflationary period, because the depreciation of assets is based on historical cost. Nevertheless, substantial insights may be obtained by applying this or a similar procedure. Concomp's profitability declined substantially from 1984, and assets did not generate earnings at the same level.

Earnings per Share of Common Stock. One measure of return on stockholders' investment is provided on the face of Concomp's income statement. Earnings per share on income before extraordinary item and on net income represent the earnings associated with

Historical Cost

EXHIBIT 24–15
Concomp, Inc.
Rate of Return on Assets Employed
(amounts in thousands)

	1985	1984
Total assets	$52,380	$49,612
Less: Construction in progress	(6,414)	(6,083)
Productive assets employed	$45,966	$43,529
Average productive assets employed 1985 = ($45,966 + $43,529)/2 1984 = ($43,529 + $40,000*)/2	$44,748	$41,765
Earnings before extraordinary item	$ 3,214	$ 5,118
÷ Average productive assets employed	÷ $44,748	÷ $41,765
Rate of return on assets employed	7.2%	12.3%

*Assumed for purposes of this exhibit.

each share of stock. For purposes of these calculations, the appropriate earnings figures are divided by the 600,000 shares of common stock outstanding. We assume that no preferred dividends were declared and that preferred dividends do not accumulate. The calculations and assumptions related to earnings per share are discussed extensively in Chapter 26; however, the importance of this statistic must not be overlooked by analysts.

Price/Earnings Ratio.   Another measure frequently employed by stock market analysts expresses the market price of a share of stock as the multiple of the earnings per share of the stock. This ratio, as well as certain others, is based on external information (stock market prices). Such measures should be approached with caution because of the many variables that influence external information. If this ratio becomes higher, it is an indication that investors think the company will grow fast. Conversely, a lower price/earnings ratio indicates investors think that the company will grow at a relatively slower rate. Assuming the market prices of a share of Concomp stock at December 31, 1985 and 1984, are $58 and $77, respectively, Exhibit 24–16 presents the price/earnings ratio for the two years.

The price/earnings ratios for Concomp (12.5 and 9.0 for 1985 and 1984, respectively) indicate that the marketplace attributes a reasonable growth potential for the company. The 9.0 ratio in 1984 may reflect the expectations by investors of the company's downturn in 1985. We computed the 1985 price/earnings ratio by using earnings per share *after* the extraordinary loss. As discussed earlier, we may conclude that it is more appropriate to use earnings per share *before* the extraordinary loss, in which case the 1985 price/earnings ratio is 10.8 ($58/$5.36).

Rate of Return on Stockholders' Investment.   A third measure of return to investors, the rate of return on stockholders' equity, is presented in Exhibit 24–17.

EXHIBIT 24–16
Concomp, Inc
Price/Earnings Ratio

	1985	1984
Market price per common share of Concomp	$58.00*	$77.00*
÷ Earnings per share	÷ $ 4.63	÷ $ 8.53
Price/earnings ratio	12.5	9.0

*Assumed for purposes of this exhibit; usually available from national securities exchange quotations.

EXHIBIT 24–17
Concomp, Inc.
Rate of Return on Stockholders' Investment
(amounts in thousands)

	1985	1984
Average stockholders' equity		
1985 = ($28,655 + $27,517)/2	$28,086	
1984 = ($27,517 + $25,000*)/2		$26,259
Earnings before extraordinary item	$ 3,214	$ 5,118
÷ Average stockholders' equity	÷ $28,086	÷ $26,259
Rate of return on stockholders' investment	11.4%	19.5%

*Assumed for purposes of this exhibit.

EXHIBIT 24–18
Concomp, Inc.
Return on Revenue
(amounts in thousands)

	1985	1984
Earnings before extraordinary item	$ 3,214	$ 5,118
÷ Total revenue	÷ $46,202	÷ $45,166
Return on revenue	7.0%	11.3%

We can see that the reduction in the rate of return on stockholders' equity is substantially more than the reduction in the rate of return on total productive assets (compare Exhibit 24–17 with Exhibit 24–15). These computations differ (e.g., construction in progress is excluded in Exhibit 24–15), and so do the objectives and implications of the two tests. The rate of return on productive assets evaluates management's ability to productively employ all of the assets of the enterprise. The rate of return on stockholders' equity, however, measures the productivity and desirability of the equity *investment* made by stockholders. Although the two ratios are similar, differences in perspective make both of them important.

Return on Revenue. Another common and useful measure of profitability is the amount of each revenue dollar retained as net income. The profit margin on revenue is found by dividing earnings before extraordinary items by total revenue. Exhibit 24–18 presents this statistic for 1985 and 1984. If segment information on the industry or product line is available, more detailed analysis may be possible. In the Concomp example, most revenue is generated by clothing sales. When significant revenue is produced by various activities, the return on each type of revenue-generating activity is an important element of information; however, it is frequently difficult to determine this information from published financial statements.

In Exhibit 24–18 a marked decline in profitability is again obvious. To gain further insights we may wish to express each element of the income statement as a percentage of sales and compare the percentages. Although we do not compute these percentages here, reading the income statement reveals that cost of goods sold has become a larger percentage of sales revenue. Whether this is due to inventory obsolescence, theft, or damage, or to reduced sales prices is not evident from our analysis. Furthermore, little information is available as to whether the condition is temporary or of longer duration. We should carefully read the notes to the financial statements to gain additional insights into issues such as these.

Book Value per Share. If we divide the stockholders' equity attributable to common stockholders by the number of shares of common stock outstanding, the book value of each common share is determined. We calculate common stockholders' equity by subtracting the claims of preferred stockholders from the total stockholders' equity. Although there are several limitations on the meaning of this ratio, some important insights are possible. By computing the book value per share for a number of years, we may isolate trends relative to maintaining common stockholders' equity. Exhibit 24–19 presents the book value per share at December 31, 1985 and 1984, for Concomp, Inc.

Dividend Payout Ratio. The dividend payout ratio is computed by dividing the declared dividend by the earnings before extraordinary items. This measure of capital maintenance reveals the extent to which a company distributes assets in the form of dividends. Investors find information of this type especially useful in evaluating alternative investment opportunities. For example, some investors may desire sustained capital growth while others prefer a relatively constant stream of cash earnings on their investments. A high dividend

---

EXHIBIT 24–19
Concomp, Inc.
Book Value per Share
(amounts in thousands)

	1985	1984
Total stockholders' equity	$28,655	$27,517
Less: Par value of preferred stock outstanding	(41)	(41)
Common stockholders' equity	$28,614	$27,476
÷ Number of common shares outstanding (also in thousands)	÷ 600	÷ 600
Book value per common share (not in thousands)	$ 47.69	$ 45.79

---

payout ratio may identify a desirable investment to an individual wishing a consistent stream of cash dividends. On the other hand, investors interested primarily in capital growth may prefer investing in companies that retain most of their earnings to finance continued growth and expansion. Exhibit 24–20 presents the dividend payout ratio for Concomp, Inc.

Concomp's dividend payout ratio indicates that the company retains most of the assets generated by earnings, because in both years it paid out only 15% of its income before extraordinary items.

As in liquidity analysis, we have analyzed only a few of the many possible relationships that may provide valuable information. Creative analysts can develop special analyses focusing on unusual or unique areas of interest in the financial statements.

Activity Analysis

Management is charged with a responsibility, among others, to use the assets of the enterprise in as productive a fashion as possible. Investors and others are interested in the degree to which management is able to generate revenues and earnings by productively employing the resources of the entity. Several analytical techniques are useful in assessing the activity and intensity of asset utilization of an enterprise. Productivity, of course, implies efficiency and effectiveness of resource utilization. For example, inventory should be quickly sold, receivables collected, and cash expended to acquire new inventory. Other assets, such as plant assets, are used to manufacture inventory or otherwise support sales activities. Each of these classes of assets can be analyzed to determine the relative intensity of utilization or degree to which revenue is generated by their use.

Turnover of Receivables and Days' Sales in Accounts Receivable.   If we divide total annual credit sales by the average outstanding accounts receivable, we obtain an esti-

---

EXHIBIT 24–20
Concomp, Inc.
Dividend Payout Ratio
(amounts in thousands)

	1985	1984
Dividend declared	$ 482*	$ 768*
÷ Earnings before extraordinary item	÷ $3,214	÷ $5,118
Dividend payout ratio	15%	15%

*Assumed for purposes of this exhibit.

EXHIBIT 24–21
Concomp, Inc.
Turnover of Receivables and
Days' Sales in Accounts Receivable
(amounts in thousands)

	1985	1984
Turnover of Receivables		
Sales of clothing	$45,358	$44,226
÷ Average trade receivables 1985 = ($4,916 + $4,295)/2 1984 = ($4,295 + $3,800*)/2	÷ $4,606	÷ $4,048
Turnover of accounts receivable	9.8	10.9
Days' Sales in Accounts Receivable		
Sales of clothing	$45,358	$44,226
÷ Number of days in year	÷ 365	÷ 366**
Sales per day	$124.27	$120.84
Accounts receivable	$4,916	$4,295
÷ Sales per day	÷ $124.27	÷ $120.84
Days' sales in accounts receivable	39.6	35.5

*Assumed for purposes of this exhibit.
**366 days in 1984, a leap year.

mate of the number of times a year the receivables are collected. In the Concomp example, we have only the beginning and ending balances of accounts receivable for computing the average accounts receivable. Frequently only *total* sales (rather than credit sales) information is available in external financial statements. As long as we are consistent in the use of total sales, however, and no material changes in the mix of cash and credit sales occur, our analysis is still useful. For Concomp the receivable turnover ratio and days' sales in accounts receivable are computed in Exhibit 24–21.

We can see that collections slowed somewhat in 1985, because the number of days of uncollected revenue has risen by four. Reduced collection speed can be due to many factors, some of which may be beyond the control of management. Examples include credit problems of customers, downturns in production and other economic activities, and higher rates of interest. Such factors may cause customers to buy less and wait longer to pay for the goods they do acquire. Management, however, can exercise some influence through credit granting, discount policy, and other collection procedures.

In computing the Days' Sales in Accounts Receivable, we used calendar days. This ratio (and others that rely on a number of days) are sometimes based on the number of *business* days. For example, a business operating six days a week and closed on holidays may base the Days' Sales in Accounts Receivable on approximately 300 days. Consistency in calculating comparative figures is particularly important in situations such as these. In this text we will use 365 days in ratios requiring a number of days unless specifically stated otherwise.

Turnover of Inventory and Days' Sales in Inventory. The ability of a company to sell its inventory quickly is another measure of the efficient use of assets. This relationship and the number of days' sales in inventory are presented in Exhibit 24–22 for Concomp. Inventory turnover is calculated by dividing the cost of goods sold annually by the average inventory. The Days' Sales in Inventory is calculated by dividing the inventory by the cost of goods sold per day.

EXHIBIT 24–22
Concomp, Inc.
Turnover of Inventory and Days' Sales in Inventory
(amounts in thousands)

	1985	*1984*
Turnover of Inventory		
Cost of goods sold	$31,838	$29,932
÷ Average inventory 1985 = ($3,435 + $3,413)/2 1984 = ($3,413 + $3,300*)/2	÷ $3,424	÷ $3,357
Turnover of inventory	9.3	8.9
Days' Sales in Inventory		
Cost of goods sold	$31,838	$29,932
÷ Number of days in year	÷ 365	÷ 366**
Cost of goods sold per day	$87.23	$81.78
Inventory	$3,435	$3,413
÷ Cost of goods sold per day	÷ $87.23	÷ $81.78
Days' sales in inventory	39.4	41.7

*Assumed for purposes of this exhibit.
**366 days in 1984, a leap year.

The turnover of inventory reveals that Concomp is selling its average inventory somewhat more quickly in 1985 than in 1984. This trend is perceived as positive only to the extent that out-of-stock items, ordering costs, and shortened production runs do not create additional costs.

Of course, inventory cost-flow assumptions affect this ratio directly. If changes in inventory methods occur (such as a change from FIFO to LIFO) analysts must consider the effects of the change and use only ratios that are comparable. Note that the numerator is the *cost* of goods sold, not the amount of sales, because inventory is carried at *cost*.

Turnover of Assets.   Management uses assets to generate revenues. The extent to which assets are used to contribute to or generate revenue may be measured as illustrated in Exhibit 24–23. The turnover of assets is computed by dividing the annual revenue by the average assets.

The management of Concomp has generated about $.91 in revenue for each dollar of asset invested during 1985. We have used total revenue in this measure because management uses all assets to generate all types of revenue. A variation of this ratio is computed by using only sales from the company's primary line of business in the numerator. Also nonproductive assets, such as Construction in Progress, may be excluded from the total asset figure.

Like other ratios, the turnover of assets is most useful when compared over a long period and among several other companies in the same industry. The number alone does little to reveal the adequacy of operations or profitability. Furthermore, the age of a company's assets, the nature of its business, and other factors may cause this ratio to change without necessarily reflecting a real change in operating or financial status.

Financial Structure and Viability Analysis

Business enterprises typically obtain their assets and support their operations through a

---

EXHIBIT 24–23
Concomp, Inc.
Turnover of Assets
(amounts in thousands)

	1985	1984
Total revenue	$46,202	$45,166
÷ Average total assets		
1985 = ($52,380 + $49,612)/2	÷ $50,996	
1984 = ($49,612 + $45,000*)/2		÷ $47,306
Turnover of assets	.91	.95

*Assumed for purposes of this exhibit.

---

combination of debt financing and equity capital. Although debt financing allows a company to leverage upward the return to the equity holders, as additional debt is incurred the risks of insolvency and bankruptcy rise, because interest and principal payments on debt must be paid. Of course, dividends on equity securities are not legally required and capital stock does not mature; therefore, principal repayment is not required on equity financing.

A company relying exclusively on equity financing has less risk of insolvency but may perform sluggishly because the company does not benefit from a return on the borrowed funds. If the company earns a return on the borrowed funds in excess of the cost of borrowing, then the excess earnings accrue to equity holders. This phenomenon is called **financial leverage** or **trading on the equity.** A prudent amount of debt financing is normally desirable to provide equity holders an acceptable rate of return. Indeed, if a company relies exclusively on equity financing, the returns to equity holders may be significantly less than those available when a reasonable amount of debt is incurred to finance the company. Similarly, overreliance on debt financing raises the relative riskiness of a company to an unacceptable level. A balance between debt and equity financing is, therefore, generally desirable.

Debt/Equity Ratio.   Certain ratios have been developed to assist in evaluating a company's relative reliance on debt and equity financing. One of those measures, termed the **debt/equity ratio,** is presented in Exhibit 24–24 for Concomp. As the term implies, the debt/equity ratio is computed by dividing the debt by the stockholders' equity.

Concomp, Inc., relied to a slightly greater extent on debt financing in 1985 than in 1984. All other things being equal, this change represents a modest increase in the risk that cash flow problems may arise as a result of increased debt service requirements. In response equity holders may demand a higher rate of return on equity investments to maintain the

---

EXHIBIT 24–24
Concomp, Inc.
Debt/Equity Ratio
(amounts in thousands)

	1985	1984
Total debt	$23,725	$22,095
÷ Total stockholders' equity	÷ $28,655	÷ $27,517
Debt/equity ratio	82.8%	80.3%

EXHIBIT 24–25
Concomp, Inc.
Debt/Total Assets Ratio
(amounts in thousands)

	1985	1984
Total debt	$23,725	$22,095
÷ Total assets	÷ $52,380	÷ $49,612
Debt/total assets ratio	45.3%	44.5%

---

value of the capital stock in the marketplace. However, if earnings remain constant, the value of Concomp's stock may decline because of the greater risk associated with the investment.

Debt/Total Assets Ratio.   Another measure of a company's relative reliance on debt financing expresses debt as a percentage of total assets. In this manner another perspective on financing leverage is obtained. Exhibit 24–25 presents this ratio for Concomp.

Over half of the total assets of Concomp are financed from equity capital. Although the percent of debt financing increased slightly during 1985, the company maintains a comfortable equity cushion. The ability of the company to service the debt structure is also important, and several other ratios are useful in assessing Concomp's debt service capability.

The ratios of debt to equity and debt to total assets are sometimes computed by using only long-term liabilities rather than total liabilities. Since many such variations exist, particular care must be exercised when comparing ratios between periods or among companies to be certain that the ratios are comparable.

Times Interest Earned.   Interest charges are fixed and must be paid each year, regardless of the level of activity or profitability. The ability of the business to pay interest from resources generated by operations is, therefore, of great significance. Exhibit 24–26 calculates the number of times annual interest expense is earned through operations at Concomp.

This calculation uses earnings before interest expense, taxes, and extraordinary items for the following reasons: (1) If interest expense were deducted from earnings before the times interest earned was calculated, the result would be distorted, because the interest expense equals *one* times the interest; (2) interest expense is tax deductible and income tax is *based*

EXHIBIT 24–26
Concomp, Inc.
Times Interest Earned
(amounts in thousands)

	1985	1984
Earnings before interest expense, taxes, and extraordinary items*	$6,371	$8,425
÷ Interest expense	÷ $1,077	÷ $1,046
Times interest earned	5.92	8.05

*This figure is calculated by adding interest expense to earnings before taxes and extraordinary items.

on earnings; therefore, the ability to pay interest is not dependent on the amount of income tax that must be paid; and (3) extraordinary and other similarly treated items are not expected to recur and, hence, are not expected to retard the company's ability to pay interest in the future.

Concomp's ability to service the interest charges on its debt appears reasonable, even though some decline in this ability is evident. Again remember that a balance between debt and equity financing is usually desirable in establishing the financial structure of the business. The times-interest-earned calculation provides information about the entity's ability to service its debt on a timely basis and, thus, assist in selecting a desirable level of reliance on debt financing.

Basic Defensive Interval.   Although interest is one charge that must be paid to operate a business, many other expenses are also unavoidable. For the basic defensive interval, a measure based on future projections, we use past information in the denominator only if we think the data are representative of future expenditures. The defensive interval is a highly conservative measure that evaluates the ability of the company to pay operating expenses from available current assets without reliance on revenues generated from operations. It estimates the number of days that the company could operate without spending revenues from operations. This relationship also provides insights about the liquidity of Concomp and about its financial structure and viability. Exhibit 24–27 calculates the basic defensive interval for Concomp and explains the way the figure is computed.

Consistent with the other analyses, the basic defensive interval indicates a deterioration of the ability of Concomp to continue operations in the face of a reduction in revenue. This relationship tends to confirm other indicators of a decrease in ability to service short-term debt and of a reduction in the profitability of the enterprise.

Margin note: Conservatism

Comparative Information

We have confined our analysis to a comparison of data for two years and certain limited industry comparisons. Access to additional years of information would clearly enhance our ability to detect and evaluate trends and other conditions that are of major significance.

Many companies publish multiyear summaries of key items in addition to the basic financial statements. Exhibit 24–28 presents an example of such a summary, drawn from the 1982 annual report of Justin Industries, which produces building materials (such as brick

---

EXHIBIT 24–27
Concomp, Inc.
Basic Defensive Interval
(amounts in thousands)

	1985	*1984*
Defensive interval assets*	$6,009	$7,923
÷ Daily expenditures**	÷ $100.82	÷ $94.16
Basic defensive interval	60 days	84 days

*Cash, temporary investments, and current receivables:
  1985: $687 + $406 + $4,916 = $6,009
  1984: $1,761 + $1,867 + $4,295 = $7,923
**Expenses minus nonworking capital charges (depreciation) divided by number of days in year (366 in 1984, a leap year):
  1985: ($40,908 − $4,107) ÷ 365 = $36,801 ÷ 365 = $100.82
  1984: ($37,787 − $3,325) ÷ 366 = $34,462 ÷ 366 = $94.16

EXHIBIT 24-28
Example Multiyear Summary

Justin Industries, Inc.
ANNUAL REPORT

ELEVEN-YEAR FINANCIAL SUMMARY

Years Ending on December 31	1982	1981	1980	1979
Summary of operations:				
(in thousands of dollars)				
Net sales:				
Building Materials	132,229	122,614	121,926	131,060
Western and Outdoor	94,326	94,074	60,633	39,033
Industrial Equipment	13,315	15,472	15,303	14,403
	239,870	232,160	197,862	184,496
Operating profit (loss): (see note)				
Building Materials	14,456	13,023	16,722	23,464
Western and Outdoor	(8,926)	9,465	7,601	3,994
Industrial Equipment	1,319	2,326	2,392	1,105
	6,849	24,814	26,715	28,563
Selected costs and expenses:				
Cost of goods sold	191,758	170,405	140,620	128,382
Selling, general, and				
administrative	50,702	43,479	36,864	33,531
Interest	13,630	10,771	7,624	5,610
Depreciation	9,420	8,816	7,921	7,269
Income taxes	(8,292)	2,075	4,875	6,220
Net income (loss)	(6,345)	5,430	7,879	10,753
Net income (loss) per share	(1.57)	1.38	2.09	2.83
Dividends declared per share	.30	.60	.60	.50
Capital expenditures	7,736	17,017	8,273	14,851
Year-end statistics:				
(in thousands of dollars)				
Working capital	68,405	77,950	59,225	45,957
Net property, plant, and equipment	71,462	73,636	63,789	64,343
Total assets	197,929	208,423	157,926	142,458
Long-term debt	67,104	71,342	55,655	48,763
Shareholders' equity	67,851	76,358	64,283	59,164
Key financial ratios:				
Pre-tax profit margin (%)	(6.10)	3.23	6.45	9.20
Net income—return on sales (%)	(2.65)	2.34	3.98	5.83
Return on shareholders' equity (%)	(8.80)	7.72	12.76	19.66
Return on assets (%)	(3.12)	2.96	5.25	8.20
Effective income tax rate (%)	(56.7)	27.6	38.2	36.7
Ratio of long-term debt to				
shareholders' equity (%)	.99:1	.93:1	.87:1	.82:1
Ratio of total debt to shareholders'				
equity (%)	1.46:1	1.31:1	1.03:1	.99:1
Ratio of current assets to current				
liabilities (%)	2.3:1	2.5:1	2.9:1	2.6:1
Shareholders' statistics:				
Number of shareholders of record	4,005	4,338	3,990	2,930
Average number of shares				
outstanding (in thousands)	4,049	3,935	3,768	3,795
Book value per share	16.93	18.68	17.30	15.76
Dividends as a percent of net				
income	—	44.2	28.4	17.5
Market price (bid price) of common				
stock:				
High	19½	28¼	22¼	21¾
Low	9¾	16	10¾	14

Note: Operating profit is before unallocated corporate general and interest expenses. Net income per share has been computed on the average number of common and common equivalent shares outstanding during each year and includes preferred stock as common share equivalents. Book value per

SOURCE: Justin Industries, Inc., 1982 Annual Report.

1978	1977	1976	1975	1974	1973	1972
127,543	105,610	64,268	39,987	41,156	34,026	36.075
27,714	27,589	26,160	22,412	21,050	16,919	13,605
15,693	11,197	8,660	6,994	8,400	3,984	5,823
170,950	144,396	99,088	69,393	70,606	54,929	55,503
25,548	15,087	9,068	5,138	4,484	4,914	6,039
1,338	1,217	1,813	2,589	1,926	1,317	1,255
(1,272)	(7)	1,244	1,131	1,410	298	984
25,614	16,297	12,125	8,858	7,820	6,529	8,278
119,957	105,123	71,055	49,059	52,385	39,586	38,604
30,431	26,311	18,622	13,492	12,025	10,398	10,019
3,673	2,796	1,490	1,353	1,284	401	293
5,581	4,992	3,480	2,929	2,580	1,886	1,598
6,600	4,040	3,350	2,413	1,906	1,823	2,969
10,289	6,211	4,533	3,076	3,006	2,721	3,618
2.72	1.67	1.35	.91	.89	.79	1.04
.39	.31	.25	.18	.15	.09	.07
22,105	16,476	5,184	2,028	5,474	4,422	3,217
33,675	32,778	31,374	20,740	15,762	13,552	12,079
59,566	43,263	32,497	21,603	22,808	17,511	15,093
119,735	97,033	80,347	52,057	51,125	38,775	33,647
40,569	32,428	24,624	11,563	10,511	5,540	4,088
50,221	41,311	33,137	29,389	27,111	24,865	22,630
9.88	7.04	7.99	7.91	6.96	8.27	11.87
6.02	4.30	4.57	4.43	4.26	4.95	6.52
22.48	16.69	14.50	10.89	11.57	11.46	17.23
9.49	7.00	6.84	5.96	6.69	7.51	11.31
39.1	39.7	42.3	44.0	38.8	40.1	45.1
.81:1	.79:1	.74:1	.39:1	.39:1	.22:1	.18:1
.91:1	.91:1	.88:1	.48:1	.66:1	.32:1	.42:1
2.4:1	2.7:1	3.0:1	3.3:1	2.4:1	3.0:1	3.2:1
2,229	2,112	1,396	1,283	962	958	885
3,782	3,720	3,360	3,366	3,387	3,456	3,488
13.44	11.10	9.92	8.83	8.05	7.27	6.56
14.1	18.6	18.0	19.4	15.4	10.0	5.7
17⅞	9½	8⅞	4¾	5½	8½	8¾
8¾	7½	4½	2½	2¼	2½	4¾

equivalent share of common stock has been computed on the number of common shares outstanding at December 31. All per share information has been adjusted for the 2-for-1 stock split in 1972 and the 3-for-2 stock splits in both 1978 and 1979.

and clay), footwear, and industrial equipment. The "key financial ratios" section of the summary includes several of the ratios discussed in this chapter.

Comments and other communications by management, such as the president's letter, also afford valuable insights, especially when related to comprehensive financial-statement analysis. Many valuable insights not presently available about Concomp would also be possible if a longer-term summary were available. For example, such a summary would allow us to determine if the current year's downturn is a continuation of a long-term trend, is due primarily to a single event such as the ripple effect of the extraordinary item, or perhaps represents the moderation of a previous favorable trend. Many important insights about the direction and status of companies are possible by careful study of such trends.

Exhibit 24–29 summarizes all of the ratios discussed in the Concomp example. Although each of the measures focuses on a somewhat different phenomenon, many are interrelated and a well-defined understanding of the financial and operational status of the company requires careful study.

Exhibit 24–29 refers to net income in several computations. As already indicated, most ratios are more meaningful if income before extraordinary items or income from continuing operations is used when nonrecurring events such as extraordinary items and disposals of segments of a business are included in net income. The term "net income" in Exhibit 24–29 assumes that these types of unusual transactions are not present.

Footnote Disclosure

Knowledgeable financial analysts recognize the crucial importance of carefully reading the footnotes. Much valuable information about accounting assumptions and policies, commitments, contingencies, subsequent events, related-party transactions, and many other significant items are discussed in the footnotes.

The financial statements on which we based the Concomp example discuss the extraordinary item in the footnotes. The peripheral effects and long-range impact of the event are significant to users of the financial statements. Reading and understanding footnotes add great substance, because they explain and complement the trends and relationships gleaned from a basic analysis of the financial statements.

Limitations of Financial-Statement Analysis

Financial analysis should be based on a deep understanding of the enterprise, the industry in which it operates, and the implications of the general economic environment. As a result, inexperienced analysts frequently fail to detect subtle trends and meanings in the information being analyzed. Furthermore, ratios, percentages, and trend analysis reduce complex activities and interrelationships to simple indexes and measures of performance and status. However, such measures are only as valid as the data on which they are based.

For example, one of the primary concerns about the validity of traditional financial-statement analysis is the effect of inflation on the underlying accounting information. Although accounting for inflation is treated extensively in Chapter 27, a brief discussion is useful at this point. Basically the problem arises because assets are acquired in different periods and, therefore, at different price levels. The same is true for liabilities. Depreciation

Matching

and other expenses are mixed in terms of the relative purchasing power of the dollars used to acquire the service rights. As such, current dollars of revenue are matched with expense dollars incurred at different price levels. As inflation rates change, the impact on the financial statements also changes. Thus, the accounting information on which much analysis is based becomes distorted, and comparability of relationships, both over several years and among several business enterprises, is reduced. Analysts should be aware of the general effects of inflation and its specific impact on the company being analyzed.

The management of a company is frequently able to influence ratios. For example, unusual end-of-period activities and transactions can cause ratios to change in a manner

EXHIBIT 24–29
Summary of Analytical Procedures

ANALYTICAL PROCEDURES		COMPUTATION
Liquidity Analysis		
1. Working capital	=	Current assets − Current liabilities
2. Current ratio	=	Current assets ÷ Current liabilities
3. Quick ratio	=	(Cash + Marketable securities + Current receivables) ÷ Current liabilities
4. Ratio of working capital provided by operations to current liabilities	=	(Net income + Expenses not using working capital) ÷ Current liabilities
Profitability and Capital-Maintenance Analysis		
5. Rate of return on assets employed	=	Net income ÷ Average assets employed
6. Earnings per common share	=	Net income ÷ Number of common shares outstanding
7. Price/earnings ratio	=	Market price per common share ÷ Earnings per share
8. Rate of return on stockholders' investment	=	Net income ÷ Average stockholders' equity
9. Return on revenue	=	Net income ÷ Total revenue
10. Book value per share	=	Common stockholders' equity ÷ Number of common shares outstanding
11. Dividend payout ratio	=	Dividends declared ÷ Net income
Activity Analysis		
12. Turnover of receivables	=	Credit sales ÷ Average accounts receivable
13. Days' sales in accounts receivable	=	Accounts receivable ÷ Credit sales per day
14. Turnover of inventory	=	Cost of goods sold ÷ Average inventory
15. Days' sales in inventory	=	Inventory ÷ Cost of goods sold per day
16. Turnover of assets	=	Total revenue ÷ Average total assets
Financial Structure and Viability Analysis		
17. Debt/equity ratio	=	Total debt ÷ Total stockholders' equity
18. Debt/total assets ratio	=	Total debt ÷ Total assets
19. Times interest earned	=	Income before interest and taxes ÷ Interest expense
20. Basic defensive interval	=	(Cash + Temporary investments + Current receivables) ÷ Daily expenditures

DISCLOSURE IMPLEMENTATION CONSIDERATIONS

ONCE AN ACCOUNTANT determines that a particular item of information should be disclosed, the question of where the data should be placed remains unanswered. For example, the amount of accumulated depreciation on plant assets must be disclosed somewhere in the financial statements. Common placement practices for accumulated depreciation include presenting the number directly in the balance sheet as a reduction of the assets' original cost, showing accumulated depreciation parenthetically on the face of the balance sheet, or disclosing the amount of accumulated depreciation in the footnotes to the financial statements. This general problem is especially troublesome because of the large quantity of information that must be disclosed somewhere.

While, for the most part, no fixed rules exist regarding the placement of individual disclosures, several "rules of thumb" have been developed in practice. No priority or significance should be attached to the order of the considerations discussed here; rather, individual, seasoned judgment should be applied to ensure an intelligible, easy-to-understand set of financial statements.

In general, the more significant or critical an item is, the more prominently it should be presented. For example, if a substantial merger took place during the year, the discussion of the merger and its effects should be presented as one of the first footnotes, thereby calling the item to the attention of a reader early in the analytical process.

Items which can be presented in a brief or abbreviated fashion may be placed directly on the face of the financial statements; however, care should be exercised to ensure that the statements not become too cluttered, complex, or intimidating to the reader. Again, the skill levels and specific needs of financial statement users should be anticipated to the extent possible. For example, the allowance for doubtful accounts and accumulated depreciation on plant assets is frequently disclosed parenthetically next to the account title on the balance sheet. This practice reduces the individual numbers actually presented in the statement and thereby simplifies the presentation. The reader of the statement, however, is still provided with the information without referring to a note on another page of the report.

Finally, footnotes should be written in clear, unequivocal, simple language to ensure comprehension. Many public accounting firms require a partner who is not involved with the particular engagement to read the financial statements just prior to issuance. This practice assures compliance with technical accounting and reporting standards and allows accountants not closely involved with the enterprise to assess how easily the statements could be understood by an unrelated reader.

Many other practices are employed by skilled accountants to ensure the overall quality and usefulness of their work. Accounting students should constantly strive to become better able to express their thoughts in a clear, concise fashion and to develop creativity of expression and presentation. Such skills will contribute substantially to their long-term success in virtually any business endeavor.

---

desired by management. Paying current liabilities with current assets, while not affecting working capital, changes the current ratio and acid-test ratios. The ability of management to influence arbitrarily various ratios and relationships may represent another limitation on the usefulness of such an analysis.

The use of alternative accounting principles may also reduce comparability between two companies. For instance, if one company employs the LIFO method of pricing inventory while a second company uses FIFO, material differences in working capital positions will likely result. Yet such differences do not necessarily relate to substantial or fundamental economic differences between companies; they may be due *exclusively* to differences in accounting methods. Again the crucial role of financial-statement disclosure is apparent. Knowledgeable analysts rely extensively on footnote disclosures to enhance and qualify financial-statement interpretation.

CONCLUDING REMARKS

Disclosure Financial statement disclosure and analysis, while distinct from each other in concept, are fundamentally related in practice. The accountant, attempting to provide adequate disclosure, anticipates the information needs of a broad range of financial statement users. Similarly, the analyst, attempting to interpret and evaluate a business enterprise, looks to footnote and other disclosures to gain an understanding of the assumptions, practices, and unusual events underlying the financial statements and also for certain significant environmental information.

Disclosure standards are many, varied, and frequently quite complex. Accountants normally employ financial-statement-disclosure checklists to assure adherence to the standards of adequate disclosure. The omission or misstatement of a material fact or circumstance increases considerably the accountant's exposure to legal liability. Generally accepted accounting principles require that the statements contain adequate disclosure in addition to proper measurements.

Analysts must recognize the limits and weaknesses of accounting information as well as its strengths. The problem of changing price levels, acceptable alternative accounting practices for similar events, and unusual or unique industry practices all tend to complicate the analyst's work and limit the usefulness of accounting information. Nevertheless, the information produced by the financial accounting and reporting function is extremely useful to decision makers and is available only at a great cost to the reporting enterprise. The allocation of resources within our economy is based on knowledgeable analysis of available information. Financial reporting in accordance with generally accepted accounting principles provides decision makers with much of the raw material used in these decisions.

KEY POINTS

1. The purpose of financial-statement disclosure is to adequately inform readers of all pertinent, material facts not otherwise obvious from reading the statements.

2. Research indicates that the market price of various securities reflects all available information about the financial and operational activities of companies.

3. A summary of significant accounting policies is required to disclose the reporting entity's selection of a particular accounting practice from among several acceptable alternatives, to describe accounting principles and methods peculiar to the industry, and to discuss any unusual or innovative applications of generally accepted accounting principles.

4. Many significant items should be disclosed even in the absence of a specific authoritative pronouncement requiring such disclosure.

5. Financial-statement analysis requires a comprehensive understanding of the reporting entity's business, accounting practices, industry, and economic conditions.

6. The report of the independent auditor provides additional useful information about the quality and reliability of the financial statements examined.

7. Financial analysis usually centers around assessing an entity's liquidity, profitability, activity, and financial structure and viability.

8. Liquidity analysis centers around a company's ability to repay current obligations on a timely basis. Analytical techniques center around a company's current assets and current liabilities.

9. Profitability analysis deals with a company's ability to generate revenues adequate to cover its costs of operations and provide a return to owners. Accordingly, profitability analysis centers on the relationship of various factors to elements of stockholders' equity.

10. Activity analysis considers the manner in which management has used the assets of the enterprise in a productive fashion.

11. Financial structure and viability analysis centers on the extent to which the enterprise has appropriately combined debt and equity financing in providing for the long-run financial stability of the enterprise.

12. The usefulness of financial-statement analysis, while significant, is limited by certain financial accounting assumptions and concepts and, frequently, by a lack of comparability that is due to equally acceptable alternative accounting practices.

APPENDIX A EXAMPLE DISCLOSURE CHECKLIST

An excerpt from the disclosure checklist of the AICPA's *Audit and Accounting Manual* is included in Exhibit 24–30. Only the sections on the balance sheet—general, cash, and marketable securities—are included to illustrate the content of such a checklist. Following each item are relevant references; the abbreviation "TB" in these references stands for "Technical Bulletin."

EXHIBIT 24–30
Excerpt from Financial Statement Disclosure Checklist

	Yes	No	N/A
.05 Balance Sheet			
A. General			
1. For classified balance sheets are assets and liabilities segregated into current and noncurrent classifications with totals presented for current assets and current liabilities? (ARB 43, Ch. 3A: SFAS 6, par. 15; FASBI 8, par. 3; TB 79–3.)	_____	_____	_____
2. Are assets not expected to be realized during the current operating cycle classified as noncurrent? (ARB 43, Ch. 3A, pars. 5–6.)	_____	_____	_____
3. Are valuation allowances contra to such assets as receivables and investments shown as deductions from their related assets with appropriate disclosure? (APB 12, par. 3.)	_____	_____	_____
B. Cash			
1. Is restricted cash appropriately segregated from cash available for current operations? (ARB 43, Ch. 3A, par. 6.)	_____	_____	_____
2. Are restrictions on cash appropriately disclosed? (SFAS 5, pars. 18–19.)	_____	_____	_____
C. Marketable Securities			
1. For entities in industries not having certain specialized practices for marketable securities (and also personal financial statements per FASBI 10):			
a. Are the carrying amounts of the marketable equity securities portfolios (current and noncurrent) each at the lower of aggregate cost or market? (SFAS 12, pars. 8 & 15.)	_____	_____	_____
b. Is the amount by which aggregate cost exceeds aggregate market value of a portfolio accounted for as a valuation allowance? (SFAS 12, par. 8; FASBI 12; FASBI 13.)	_____	_____	_____
c. Are changes in the valuation allowances appropriately accounted for? (SFAS 12, par. 11.)	_____	_____	_____

   d. Are realized gains and losses included in net
income of the period in which they occur?
(SFAS 12, par. 11.)   _____   _____   _____

2. Are marketable equity securities portfolios of
consolidated affiliates appropriately treated in
consolidation?
(SFAS 12, par. 9, 15 & 18–20; FASBI 13.)   _____   _____   _____

3. Are marketable equity securities portfolios of
nonconsolidated subsidiaries accounted for by the
equity method appropriately treated?
(SFAS 12, pars. 9 & 18–20; TB 79–19, par. 6.)   _____   _____   _____

4. If particular marketable securities for which changes
in carrying amounts are included in stockholders'
equity have declines in market value below cost, and
the declines are "judged to be other than
temporary," is the cost basis written down and the
write down accounted for as a loss?
(SFAS 12, par. 21; FASBI 11.)   _____   _____   _____

5. Are income tax effects for unrealized gains or losses
on marketable securities:
   a. Recognized in conformity with APB No. 11?   _____   _____   _____
   b. For unrealized capital losses are tax benefits
recognized only when there is "assurance beyond
a reasonable doubt" that the benefit will be
realized by an offset of loss against capital gains?
(SFAS 12, par. 22.)   _____   _____   _____

6. For marketable equity securities do disclosures
include:
   a. For each balance sheet presented, aggregate cost
and market value (each segregated between
current and noncurrent portfolios when
applicable) with identification of which is the
carrying amount?
(SFAS 12, par. 12a.)   _____   _____   _____
   b. For the latest balance sheet presented, gross
unrealized gains and gross unrealized losses
(each segregated between current and noncurrent
portfolios when applicable)?
(SFAS 12, par. 12b & 16a.)   _____   _____   _____
   c. The following information for each period for
which an income statement is presented:
     (1) Net realized gain or loss included in
determination of net income?
(SFAS 12, par. 12c.)   _____   _____   _____
     (2) For entities with certain specialized
accounting practices, the change in net
unrealized gain or loss?
(SFAS 12, par. 16b.)   _____   _____   _____
     (3) Basis on which cost was determined in
computing realized gain or loss (e.g. average
cost, FIFO)?
(SFAS 12, par. 12c.)   _____   _____   _____
     (4) The change in valuation allowance(s) included
in the equity section of the balance sheet
during the period and when a classified
balance sheet is presented, the amount of
such change included in determination of net
income?
(SFAS 12, par. 12c.)   _____   _____   _____

7. Are significant net realized and net unrealized gains and losses that arose after the latest balance sheet date but before issuance of the financial statements disclosed in the notes? (SFAS 12, pars. 13 & 17; FASBI 11; FASBI 13.)

_____   _____   _____

8. Are valuation allowances shown as deductions from their related portfolios with appropriate disclosure? (APB 12, par. 3.)

_____   _____   _____

SOURCE: *Audit and Accounting Manual* (New York: AICPA, 1982), pp. 8412–8415.

QUESTIONS

24–1   Financial statements should provide "adequate disclosure." What is meant by the term "adequate disclosure" in the context of financial reporting?

24–2   A complete set of financial statements must include at least statements of financial position, income, retained earnings, changes in financial position, and certain disclosures. Is there any prescribed form that the disclosures must take?

24–3   A "Summary of Significant Accounting Policies," which is required to accompany the basic financial statements, normally includes what types of items?

24–4   The summary of significant accounting policies for Ball Corporation includes the following items:

[a] The method used for inventory valuation.
[b] The depreciation method used.
[c] *Pro forma* information related to an accounting change.
[d] Disclosure of the principal business activity of the company.
[e] Description of an unusual manner of recognizing revenue.

Which of the above items, if any, should be excluded from the summary of significant accounting policies?

24–5   Name three ratios that would be useful primarily in evaluating a company's liquidity. Describe how they are calculated.

24–6   What are three of the factors that can limit the comparability of one company's current ratio with that of another business operating in the same industry?

24–7   Winn Corporation has a current ratio of 2 to 1 and enters into a transaction that reduces this ratio. What effect does this event have on the working capital of Winn Corporation?

24–8   Pros, Inc., writes off an uncollectible account receivable against the allowance account. What effect does this entry have on the current ratio, the quick ratios, and the working capital?

24–9   Diane Company declared a cash dividend and one month later paid the dividend. What effect does each of these events have on working capital and the current ratio?

24–10 Cathy Corporation, earning a profit during 1985 from its own operations, owns a 25% (significant influence) investment in the common voting stock of Lovin Company. If Lovin earns a net income for the year but pays no dividends, what effect will this event have on the following ratios, trends, or percentages of Cathy Corporation?

[a] Current ratio.
[b] Earnings per share.
[c] Return on assets employed.
[d] Basic defensive interval.
[e] Return on average stockholder's investment.
[f] Debt/equity ratio.
[g] Debt/total assets ratio.

24–11 The controller of Bard Corporation remarked, "Because of a high level of operating leverage, only a small degree of financing leverage is acceptable to this company." Explain the statement.

24–12 What does the ratio "book value per share" indicate? Would you expect a company's book value and the current market value of its stock to be the same? Why?

24–13 What does the dividend payout ratio measure? As an investor, would you prefer the company in which you owned stock to have a high or a low dividend payout ratio?

24–14 Many of the ratios computed in this chapter were based on average figures, which had been based on the year's beginning and ending figures. Why were averages (rather than year-end figures) used? When would year-end figures give you approximately the same ratios as average figures?

24–15 What does the ratio "turnover of assets" represent? After you had computed this ratio for a company, how would you use it?

24–16 What is the relationship between the debt/ equity ratio and the debt/total assets ratio? Do these ratios measure the same thing or different things?

24–17 The basic defensive interval ratio has been characterized as a very conservative measure of a company's financial structure and one that is not necessarily consistent with the going-concern assumption. Discuss these comments and indicate whether you agree or disagree.

24–18 State briefly several of the most significant limitations of financial-statement analysis.

CASES

C24–1 The following comments were made by a financial analyst:

Financial-statement analysis involves ratios to test past performance of a company. Past performance is compared to a predetermined standard, and the company is evaluated accordingly. One such ratio is the current ratio, which is computed by dividing current assets by current liabilities or by dividing monetary assets by monetary liabilities. A current ratio of 2 to 1 is considered good for companies; but the higher the ratio, the better the company's financial position is assumed to be. The current ratio is dynamic because it helps to measure fund flows.

Instructions

Discuss the appropriateness of each of these comments. Be sure to include in your analysis positive observations as well as criticisms.

(AICPA adapted)

C24–2 Below are six *independent* situations involving financial-statement disclosure and analysis. Respond briefly to each.

[a] Cossey Company sells a material amount of its output to a commonly controlled company. The management of Cossey Company wishes to avoid disclosing this fact and maintains that the transactions are accomplished on a basis no less and no more favorable than would be the case if the buyer were an independent customer. Should these transactions be disclosed? If so, what information should be included?

[b] Oberst Corporation is facing severe financial difficulties. In fact, suppliers have informed Oberst that purchases must be paid for in cash at the time of delivery. Other creditors have advised the company to seek other sources of financing. The financial statements of Oberst reflect clearly the extent of the company's poor performance. Specifically, Oberst has reported a net loss for each of the past three years, working capital is very low, and the debt/equity ratio has increased significantly. Should Oberst also include a footnote that discusses the company's poor results of operations, its financial position, and the actions of its creditors? Why?

[c] On January 15 a fire at Ham's Fireworks destroyed one warehouse and a material amount of inventory. Since Ham's followed a practice of self-insurance, a material loss was sustained. The independent auditor suggested recognizing the loss in the income statement for the year just ended and writing off the inventory and warehouse from the balance sheet. The company president stated, "We will not write off our assets nor even disclose the fire, because the entire event took place after the end of the year. Your responsibility as an auditor relates exclusively to the financial statements under audit." Who is right? Why?

[d] During your audit of Sleep Well, Inc., you determine that the company has been violating customs regulations through their import practices for mattress covers. Upon learning of the problem, the president of Sleep Well terminates the employee who was perpetrating the fraud, notifies the customs department to arrange for a settlement, and adopts a formal policy to avoid such practices in the future. The president then tells you that in view of the company's conduct in correcting the situation, no disclosure of the events is necessary. Evaluate the president's position.

[e] The president of Rhonda's Framework states, "Our inventory turnover continues to rise, as has been the case during the previous four years. I view this trend as positive, because the higher our turnover, the more efficiently we are using our resources. Obsolete inventory is virtually nonexistent." Comment on the president's assertions.

[f] Lindy Idywild, an inexperienced bond analyst, stated, "My job is easy, because I am exclusively concerned with the long-term profitability and structure of the firms I evaluate. I am not concerned about liquidity, because my investment advice relates to securities that will not come due for many years." Evaluate Lindy's comments.

C24-3 As the CPA responsible for the audit engagement of a small client, you are requested by the client to provide him at the earliest possible date with some key ratios based on the final audited figures appearing on the comparative financial statements. The information is to be used to convince creditors that the client's business is solvent and to justify a request for continued financial support. The client wishes to save time by concentrating on only these key data.

The requested data and the computations taken from the financial statements follow:

	Last Year	This Year
Current ratio	2.0:1	2.5:1
Quick (acid-test) ratio	1.2:1	.7:1
Ratio of property, plant, and equipment to owners' equity	2.3:1	2.6:1
Ratio of sales to owners' equity	2.8:1	2.5:1
Net income	Down 10%	Up 30%
Earnings per common share	$2.40	$3.12
Book value per common share	Up 8%	Up 5%

Instructions

[a] The client asks that you prepare a list of brief comments stating how each of these items supports the solvency and going-concern potential of his business. He wishes to use these comments to support his presentation of data to his creditors. Prepare the requested comments by listing the implications and the limitations of each item separately. Then explain the collective inference that one may draw from them about the client's solvency and going-concern potential.

[b] Prepare a brief list of additional ratio-analysis-type data that you think this client's creditors will request to supplement the data provided in [a]. Explain why the additional data will be helpful to these creditors in evaluating this client's solvency.

[c] What warnings should you offer these creditors about the limitations of ratio analysis for the purpose stated here?

(AICPA adapted)

C24-4 Ratio analysis often is employed to gain insight into the financial character of a firm. The calculation of ratios can often lead to a better understanding of a firm's financial position and performance. A specific ratio or a number of selected ratios can be calculated and used to measure or evaluate a specific financial or operating characteristic of a firm.

Instructions

[a] Identify and explain what financial characteristic of a firm would be measured by an analysis in which the following four ratios were calculated:
[1] Current
[2] Quick (or acid test)
[3] Accounts receivable turnover
[4] Inventory turnover
Do these ratios provide adequate information to measure this characteristic or are additional data needed? If other data are needed, list two types.

[b] Identify and explain what specific characteristic regarding a firm's operations would be measured by an analysis in which the following three ratios were calculated:
[1] Gross margin rate (gross margin ÷ sales)
[2] Operating income rate (operating income ÷ sales)
[3] Return on revenue (net income ÷ sales)
Do these ratios provide adequate information to measure this characteristic or are additional data needed? If other data are needed, list two types.

(CMA adapted)

C24-5 Dell Company is listed on the New York Stock Exchange. The market value of its common stock was quoted at $18 per share at both December 31, 1984, and December 31, 1983. Dell's balance sheets at December 31, 1984, and December 31, 1983, and its statements of income and retained earnings for the years ended on those dates are presented on the following two pages.

Additional Information

[1] "Selling, general, and administrative expenses" for 1984 included a usual but infrequently occurring charge of $9,000,000.
[2] "Other, net" for 1984 included an extraordinary item (charge) of $10,000,000. If the extraordinary

Dell Company
BALANCE SHEETS
December 31, 1984 and 1983
(in thousands)

Assets

Current Assets	1984	1983
Cash	$ 3,500	$ 3,600
Marketable securities, at cost which approximates market	13,000	11,000
Accounts receivable, net of allowance for doubtful accounts	105,000	95,000
Inventories at lower of cost or market	126,000	154,000
Prepaid expenses	2,500	2,400
Total current assets	250,000	266,000
Noncurrent Assets		
Property, plant, and equipment, net of accumulated depreciation	311,000	308,000
Other assets	29,000	34,000
Total assets	$590,000	$608,000

Liabilities and Stockholders' Equity

Current Liabilities		
Notes payable	$ 5,000	$ 15,000
Accounts payable and accrued expenses	62,500	74,500
Income taxes payable	1,000	1,000
Payments due within one year on long-term debt	6,500	7,500
Total current liabilities	75,000	98,000
Noncurrent Liabilities		
Long-term debt	169,000	180,000
Deferred income taxes	74,000	67,000
Other liabilities	9,000	8,000
Total liabilities	327,000	353,000
Stockholders' Equity		
Common stock, par value $1.00 per share; authorized 20,000,000 shares; issued and outstanding 10,000,000 shares	10,000	10,000
Additional paid-in capital	111,000	111,000
Retained earnings	142,000	134,000
Total stockholders' equity	263,000	255,000
Total liabilities and stockholders' equity	$590,000	$608,000

Dell Company
STATEMENTS OF INCOME AND RETAINED EARNINGS
For the Years Ended December 31, 1984 and 1983
(in thousands)

	1984	1983
Net sales	$600,000	$500,000
Costs and expenses		
Cost of goods sold	480,000	400,000
Selling, general, and administrative expenses	66,000	60,000
Other, net	17,000	6,000
Total costs and expenses	563,000	466,000

Income before income taxes	37,000	34,000
Income taxes	16,800	15,800
Net income	20,200	18,200
Retained earnings at beginning of period, as previously reported	141,000	132,000
Adjustment required for correction of an error	(7,000)	(6,000)
Retained earnings at beginning of period, as restated	134,000	126,000
Dividends on common stock	12,200	10,200
Retained earnings at end of period	$142,000	$134,000

item (charge) had not occurred, income taxes for 1984 would have been $21,800,000 instead of $16,800,000.

[3] "Adjustment required for correction of an error" was a result of a change from an accounting principle that is not generally accepted to one that is generally accepted.

[4] Dell Company has a simple capital structure and has disclosed earnings per common share for net income in the Notes to the financial statements.

Instructions

[a] Determine from the additional facts whether or not the presentation of those facts in the Dell statements of income and retained earnings is appropriate. If the presentation is appropriate, discuss the theoretical rationale for the presentation. If the presentation is not appropriate, describe the appropriate presentation and discuss its theoretical rationale.

Do not discuss disclosure requirements for the notes to the financial statements.

[b] Describe the general significance of the following financial analysis tools:

[1] Quick (acid-test) ratio
[2] Inventory turnover
[3] Return on stockholders' equity

[c] Basing your response on the Dell balance sheets, statements of income and retained earnings, and additional facts, describe how to determine each analysis tool listed in [b].

(AICPA adapted)

C24–6 Majors Corporation was formed in 1980 through a public subscription of common stock. Lucinda Street, who owns 15% of the common stock, was one of the organizers of Majors and is its current president. The company has been successful, but currently it is experiencing a shortage of funds. On June 10, 1985, Street asked First National Bank for a 24-month extension of two $30,000 notes, which were due on June 30, 1985, and September 30, 1985. Another note

of $7,000 is due on December 31, 1985, but she expects no difficulty in meeting that due date. Street explained that Majors' cash flow problems are due primarily to the company's desire to finance a $300,000 plant expansion over the next two fiscal years through internally generated funds.

The commercial loan officer of First National requested financial reports for the last two years. These reports were provided, as follows:

Majors Corporation
STATEMENT OF FINANCIAL POSITION
For the Fiscal Years Ended March 31, 1984 and 1985

Assets	1984	1985
Cash	$ 12,500	$ 16,400
Notes receivable	104,000	112,000
Accounts receivable (net)	68,500	81,600
Inventories (at cost)	50,000	80,000
Plant and equipment (net of depreciation)	646,000	680,000
Total assets	$881,000	$970,000

Liabilities and Owners' Equity	1984	1985
Accounts payable	$ 72,000	$ 69,000
Notes payable	54,500	67,000
Accrued liabilities	6,000	9,000
Common stock (60,000 shares, $10 par)	600,000	600,000
Retained earnings*	148,500	225,000
Total liabilities and owners' equity	$881,000	$970,000

*Cash dividends were paid at the rate of $1.00 per share in fiscal year 1984 and $1.25 per share in fiscal year 1985.

Majors Corporation
INCOME STATEMENT
For the Fiscal Years Ended March 31, 1984 and 1985

	1984	1985
Sales	$2,700,000	$3,000,000
Costs of goods sold**	1,720,000	1,902,500
Gross margin	980,000	1,097,500
Operating expenses	780,000	845,000

Net income before taxes	200,000	252,500
Income taxes (40%)	80,000	101,000
Income after taxes	$ 120,000	$ 151,500

**Depreciation charges of $100,000 and $102,500 on the plant and equipment for fiscal years ended March 31, 1984 and 1985, respectively, are included in cost of goods sold.

Instructions

[a] Calculate the following items for Majors Corporation:

[1] Current ratio for fiscal years 1984 and 1985.

[2] Acid test (quick) ratio for fiscal years 1984 and 1985.

[3] Inventory turnover for fiscal year 1985.

[4] Return on assets for fiscal years 1984 and 1985.

[5] Percentage change in sales, cost of goods sold, gross margin, and net income after taxes from fiscal year 1984 to 1985.

[b] Identify and explain what other financial reports and/or financial analyses might be helpful to the commercial loan officer of First National Bank in evaluating Street's request for a time extension on Majors' notes.

[c] Assume that the percentage changes (when comparing fiscal year 1985 with fiscal year 1984) for sales, cost of goods sold, gross margin, and net income after taxes will be repeated in each of the next two years. Is Majors' desire to finance the plant expansion from internally generated funds realistic? Explain your answer.

[d] Should First National Bank grant the extension on Majors' notes, in light of Street's statement about financing the plant expansion through internally generated funds? Explain your answer.

(CMA adapted)

C24–7 Konrath Company is considering extending credit to Hawk Company. It is estimated that sales to Hawk would amount to $2,000,000 annually. Konrath wholesales throughout the midwest, and Hawk (a retail chain) has a number of stores in the midwest. Kon-

rath has had a gross margin of approximately 60% in recent years and expects to have a similar gross margin on the Hawk order, which would be approximately 15% of Konrath Company's present sales.

Information derived from Hawk's financial statements for the years 1983–1985 is as follows:

	1983	1984	1985
Rate of return on total assets	1.96%	1.12%	(.87)%
Return to sales	1.69%	.99%	(.69)%
Acid test ratio	1.73/1	1.36/1	1.19/1
Current ratio	2.39/1	1.92/1	1.67/1
Inventory turnover (times)	4.41	4.32	4.52
Equity relationships			
Current liabilities	36.0%	43.0%	48.0%
Long-term liabilities	16.0	10.5	5.0
Shareholders	48.0	46.5	47.0
	100.0%	100.0%	100.0%
Asset relationships			
Current assets	77.0%	72.5%	69.5%
Property, plant, and equipment	23.0%	27.5%	30.5%
	100.0%	100.0%	100.0%

Instructions

[a] For each of the first five items of information given above, indicate whether it is favorable, unfavorable, or a neutral statistic in the decision to grant credit to Hawk.

[b] Based on the information provided, would you grant credit to Hawk? Support your answer with facts given for the case.

[c] What additional information, if any, would you want before making a final decision?

(CMA adapted)

C24–8 You have been assigned by the acquisitions committee of Roberts Company to examine a potential acquisition of Arber, Inc., a merchandising company that is available because of the death of its founder and principal shareholder. The following are Arber's financial statements for the past few years.

Arber, Inc.
BALANCE SHEET
January 31, 1982, 1983, and 1984

	1982	1983	1984
Cash	$ 100,000	$ 120,000	$ 130,000
Accounts receivable	300,000	370,000	430,000
Inventory	200,000	400,000	400,000
Fixed assets	700,000	800,000	900,000

Less: Accumulated depreciation	(200,000)	(250,000)	(325,000)
Total assets	$1,100,000	$1,440,000	$1,535,000
Accounts payable	$ 220,000	$ 260,000	$ 300,000
8% Notes payable due Jan. 31, 1992	–0–	280,000	280,000
Common stock outstanding	690,000	690,000	690,000
Retained earnings	190,000	210,000	265,000
Total equity	$1,100,000	$1,440,000	$1,535,000

Arber, Inc.
INCOME STATEMENTS
For the Fiscal Years Ended January 31, 1983 and 1984

	1983	1984
Sales	$2,629,000	$2,943,000
Expenses		
Cost of goods sold	2,000,000	2,200,000
Wages	300,000	350,000
Supplies	36,600	42,600
Depreciation	75,000	100,000
Interest charges	22,400	22,400
Loss on sale of fixed assets	105,000	75,000
Total expenses	2,539,000	2,790,000
Net income before taxes	90,000	153,000
Income taxes	40,000	68,000
Net income	$ 50,000	$ 85,000

Arber, Inc.
CHANGES IN FINANCIAL POSITION
For the Fiscal Years Ended January 31, 1983 and 1984

	1983	1984
Sources		
Net income	$ 50,000	$ 85,000
Add back: Depreciation	75,000	100,000
Loss	105,000	75,000
Notes payable	280,000	–0–

	1983	1984
Total sources	510,000	260,000
Uses		
Net fixed assets purchased	230,000	200,000
Dividends paid	30,000	30,000
Total uses	260,000	230,000
Increase in net working capital	$250,000	$ 30,000

Instructions

[a] Calculate the inventory turnover for 1983 and for 1984. Is it better or worse in 1984 than in 1983?
[b] Calculate the current ratio for 1984.
[c] Calculate a rate of return on the stockholders' equity for 1984.
[d] Describe the cash flow for 1984 by redrawing the Statement of changes in financial position to explain the changes in cash position instead of net working capital.
[e] Does the amount shown for "net fixed assets purchased" equal the funds spent for newly acquired assets? Explain your answer.
[f] The statement of changes in financial position is required in published financial reports. What reasons are given to support the requirement that this statement be included along with the other primary financial statements?

(CMA adapted)

EXERCISES

E24–1 Information for Connecticut Manufacturing Company for 1984 and 1983 is as follows:

	1983	1984
Current assets at Dec. 31	$2,000,000	$2,100,000
Current liabilities at Dec. 31	1,000,000	900,000
Stockholders' equity at Dec. 31	2,500,000	2,700,000
Net sales for year	8,300,000	8,800,000
Cost of goods sold for year	6,200,000	6,400,000
Operating income for year	500,000	550,000

Instructions

Compute the current ratio as of the end of each year.

(AICPA adapted)

E24–2 Information taken from the 1984 balance sheet of Maxwell Company is as follows:

Current Assets	
Cash	$ 4,000,000
Marketable securities	12,500,000
Accounts receivable	96,000,000
Inventories	110,500,000
Prepaid expenses	2,000,000
Total current assets	$225,000,000
Current Liabilities	
Notes payable	$ 3,000,000
Accounts payable	39,000,000
Accrued expenses	25,000,000

Income taxes payable	1,000,000
Payments due within one year on long-term debt	7,000,000
Total current liabilities	$ 75,000,000

Instructions

[a] Compute the current and acid-test ratios.

[b] Discuss briefly what each represents and explain the difference between the two.

(AICPA adapted)

E24–3 Rogers Company's inventory on January 1, 1985, was $250,000. During 1985 Rogers acquired $1,300,000 more in inventory. At the end of 1985 inventory of $380,000 remained unsold.

Instructions

Determine the inventory turnover ratio for Rogers Company for 1985.

E24–4 Selected data for Marlboro Company are as follows:

Balance Sheet Data

	December 31	
	1985	1984
Accounts receivable	$500,000	$470,000
Allowance for doubtful accounts	(25,000)	(20,000)
Net accounts receivable	475,000	450,000
Inventories, lower of cost or market	600,000	550,000

Income Statement Data

	Year Ended December 31	
	1985	1984
Net credit sales	$2,500,000	$2,200,000
Net cash sales	500,000	400,000
Net sales	$3,000,000	$2,600,000
Cost of goods sold	$2,000,000	$1,800,000
Selling, general, and administrative expenses	300,000	270,000
Other	50,000	30,000
Total operating expenses	$2,350,000	$2,100,000

Instructions

[a] What is the accounts receivable turnover for 1985?

[b] What is the inventory turnover for 1985?

(AICPA adapted)

E24–5 Financial information for McPherson Company for 1984 and 1983 is given as follows:

	December 31	
	1984	1983
Cash	$ 10,000	$ 80,000
Accounts receivable (net)	50,000	150,000
Merchandise inventory	90,000	150,000
Short-term marketable securities	30,000	10,000
Land and buildings (net)	340,000	360,000
Mortgage payable (no current portion)	270,000	280,000
Accounts payable (trade)	70,000	110,000
Short-term notes payable	20,000	40,000

	Year ended December 31	
	1984	1983
Cash sales	$1,800,000	$1,600,000
Credit sales	500,000	800,000
Cost of goods sold	1,000,000	1,400,000

Instructions

Compute the following ratios for 1984 from the information given:

[a] Acid test

[b] Receivables turnover

[c] Inventory turnover

[d] Current

(AICPA adapted)

E24–6 The controller of Mix, Inc., is analyzing her company's inventory accounting policy and requests you to perform certain calculations. She is particularly concerned with the effects a proposed change to LIFO may have on certain key ratios. The following information is available to you.

	December 31	
	1985	1984
Inventory using present FIFO method	$ 500,000	$ 450,000
Inventory using proposed LIFO method	400,000	375,000
Current assets (using FIFO)	1,000,000	800,000
Current liabilities	500,000	425,000
Cost of goods sold (using FIFO)	2,100,000	1,900,000

Instructions

[a] Compute the following items for the year ended December 31, 1985, by using the current inventory method and the proposed method:

[1] Current ratio

[2] Working capital

[3] Inventory turnover

[b] Comment on the analysis you have performed.

E24–7   Cassidy Corporation's accounts receivable, net of the allowance for doubtful accounts, were $700,000 at December 31, 1984, and $900,000 at December 31, 1985. Total sales during 1985 were $4,400,000, of which $400,000 were cash sales.

Instructions

[a] What was the accounts receivable turnover ratio for Cassidy Corporation during 1985?
[b] How many days of revenue are outstanding at the end of 1985?

E24–8   Venetia Company had a debt/equity ratio for 1985 of $3,879,000 to $10,000,000, or .3879.

Instructions

Based on this information alone, what were Venetia's equity/total assets ratio and its debt/total assets ratio for 1985?

E24–9   The net income of Beaver Corporation during 1985 was $250,000, which resulted in an earnings per share of $.625. The company's stock was $10 par value, but it had originally sold for $11 at the beginning of 1985, when the corporation commenced operations.

Instructions

Assuming that only one class of stock was issued and that earnings accrued evenly during the year, determine the rate of return on the average stockholders' equity.

E24–10   The following is information from the financial records of the Rolaver Company:

Net accounts receivable at Dec. 31, 1984	$1,500,000
Net accounts receivable at Dec. 31, 1985	1,800,000
Inventories at Dec. 31, 1984	2,200,000
Inventories at Dec. 31, 1985	2,500,000
Accounts receivable turnover	10
Inventory turnover	4

Instructions

[a] How much were sales during 1985? (Assume all sales were on credit.)
[b] How much was cost of goods sold for 1985?
[c] Assuming a 300-day year, compute the number of days' sales in average receivables for 1985.
[d] Assuming a 300-day year, compute the number of days' sales in average inventory for 1985.

E24–11   Selected information from the accounting records of California Electronics Company, all of whose sales are on credit, is as follows:

Net accounts receivable at Dec. 31, 1984	$ 900,000
Net accounts receivable at Dec. 31, 1985	1,000,000
Inventories at Dec. 31, 1984	1,100,000
Inventories at Dec. 31, 1985	1,200,000
Accounts receivable turnover	5
Inventory turnover	4

Instructions

[a] What was the company's gross margin for 1985?
[b] Assuming a business year consisting of 300 days, compute the number of days' sales in average receivables for 1985 and the number of days' sales in average inventories for 1985, respectively.

(AICPA adapted)

E24–12   Mitchell Corporation's condensed financial statements provide the following information:

BALANCE SHEET
December 31, 1984 and 1983

Assets	1984	1983
Cash	$ 60,000	$ 50,000
Accounts receivable (net)	220,000	200,000
Inventories	260,000	230,000
Property, plant, and equipment	730,000	650,000
Accumulated depreciation	(330,000)	(260,000)
Total assets	$940,000	$870,000

Liabilities and Stockholders' Equity		
Current liabilities	$270,000	$330,000
Stockholders' equity	670,000	540,000
Total liabilities and stockholders' equity	$940,000	$870,000

STATEMENT OF INCOME
For the Year Ended December 31, 1984

Net sales	$1,200,000
Cost of goods sold	780,000
Gross profit	420,000
Operating expenses	240,000
Net income	$ 180,000

Instructions

[a] Assuming all sales are credit sales, compute Mitchell's accounts receivable turnover for 1984.

[b] What is Mitchell's rate of return on average assets for 1984?

(AICPA adapted)

E24–13 Reading the financial records of the Autrey Company revealed the following at the end of 1985.

Sales revenue	$4,000,000
Cost of goods sold	1,500,000
Bond interest expense	135,000
Income tax expense	550,000
Net income	800,000

Instructions

Determine how many times interest expense was protected (covered) by earnings in 1985.

E24–14 At December 31, 1984, Furrough Company had 100,000 shares of $10 par-value common stock issued and outstanding. There was no change in the number of shares outstanding during 1985. Total stockholders' equity at December 31, 1985, was $2,800,000. The net income for the year ended December 31, 1985, was $800,000. During 1985 Furrough paid $3 per share in dividends on its common stock. The quoted market price of the common stock on a national stock exchange was $24 on December 31, 1985.

Instructions

Compute the price/earnings ratio on common stock for 1985.

(AICPA adapted)

E24–15 Information on the Fantacy Company's operations and common stock on a per-share basis, as of the end of 1984, is as follows:

	Per Share
Book value at Dec. 31, 1984	$12.00
Quoted market value on New York Stock Exchange on Dec. 31, 1984	9.00
Earnings for 1984	3.00
Par value	2.00
Dividend for 1984	1.00

Instructions

Compute the price/earnings ratio on common stock for 1984.

(AICPA adapted)

E24–16 Flying Tiger, Inc., reports the following figures in its 1985 and 1984 income statements:

	1985	1984
Income before extraordinary item	$505,000	$463,500
Extraordinary gain	42,700	—
Net income	$547,700	$463,500

In 1985 the company had 100,000 shares of $10 par-value common stock outstanding, and a $1 per-share dividend was paid. In 1984, 95,000 shares were outstanding and a $.70 per-share dividend was paid.

Instructions

[a] Calculate the dividend payout ratio each year.
[b] As an investor, discuss briefly whether you would prefer the dividend payout to be high or low.

E24–17 For 1984 Wimberly Manufacturing Company reported the following condensed financial information, in thousands of dollars:

BALANCE SHEET

Assets

Cash	$ 100
Short-term marketable securities	50
Current receivables, net	212
Inventories	319
Plant assets, net	850
Intangibles, net	75
	$1,606

Liabilities

Current	$ 151
Noncurrent	675

Stockholders' Equity

Capital stock	422
Retained earnings	358
	$1,606

INCOME STATEMENT

Revenues	$2,010
Expenses (including $100 depreciation and $12 amortization)	1,850
Net Income	$ 160

Instructions

[a] Compute the basic defensive interval ratio.
[b] Comment briefly on the meaning of this ratio.

E24–18 The December 31, 1985, balance sheet of Irvine Company is presented below. These are the only accounts in the company's balance sheet. Amounts indicated by a question mark (?) can be calculated from the additional information given.

Assets

Cash	$ 25,000
Accounts receivable (net)	?
Inventory	?
Property, plant, and equipment (net)	294,000
	$432,000

Liabilities and Stockholders' Equity

Accounts payable (trade)	$?
Income taxes payable (current)	25,000
Long-term debt	?
Common stock	300,000
Retained earnings	?
	$?

Additional Information

Current ratio (at year end)	1.5 to 1
Total liabilities divided by total stockholders' equity	.8
Inventory turnover based on sales and ending inventory	15 times
Inventory turnover based on cost of goods sold and ending inventory	10.5 times
Gross margin for 1985	$315,000

Instructions

Compute the following items for Irvine Company:
[a] Balance in trade accounts payable.
[b] Balance in retained earnings.
[c] Balance in inventory.

(AICPA adapted)

E24–19 Danube Company had interest-bearing debt of $1,000,000 on its balance sheet at December 31, 1985, which represented an increase of $500,000 over interest-bearing debt at December 31, 1984. The company had interest expense of $50,000 for the year ended December 31, 1985. The market rate of interest during the year was 12%.

Instructions

[a] Comment on the reasonableness of Danube's interest expense to debt ratio. Give possible explanations for any unreasonable relationships that exist.
[b] Assume the same information except that the market rate of interest was 10% and the $500,000 additional debt represented an interest-free loan from Seine Company, a major customer of Danube. The two-year Seine loan was granted on January 1, 1984, in exchange for Danube's agreement to sell its special production equipment to Seine at a 5% discount during 1984 and 1985. Seine is expected to purchase from Danube equipment with a fair value of $2,000,000 over the two-year period.
Prepare the entry that Danube should have made at the end of 1984.
[c] Prepare any footnote disclosure that should be included in Danube's financial statements as a result of the situation in [b].

E24–20 Ryder, Inc., generated sales revenue of $5,000,000 during 1985. Ryder's statistical summary indicates the following ratios for the year ended December 31, 1985.

Rate of return on stockholders' equity	15%
Rate of return on assets employed	10%
Net income/sales	8%
Debt/equity	50%

Instructions

Based on this information, compute the following:
[a] Total assets
[b] Stockholders' equity
[c] Net income
[d] Total debt
[e] Total expenses

PROBLEMS

P24–1 Gibson Sales Company reports the following selected financial information:

	December 31	
	1985	**1984**
Cash	$ 37,000	$ 24,000
Accounts receivable (net)	40,000	110,000
Merchandise inventory	55,000	70,000
Short-term investments	42,000	15,000
Prepaid expenses	10,000	8,000
Plant assets (net)	295,000	310,000
Long-term liabilities	265,000	270,000
Accounts payable	60,000	95,000
Short-term note payable	32,000	44,000

	Year Ended December 31	
	1985	**1984**
Total revenue	$2,450,000	$2,100,000
Cash sales	1,850,000	1,580,000
Cost of goods sold	1,200,000	1,050,000

Instructions

[a] Compute the quick ratio at December 31, 1985.

[b] Compute the current ratio at December 31, 1985.

[c] Determine the dollar amount of working capital at December 31, 1985.

[d] Compute the accounts receivable turnover during 1985.

[e] Compute the inventory turnover during 1985.

P24–2 Executer Company includes the following information as a footnote to its December 31, 1983, annual report:

Subsequent Event:
One of the company's major warehouses and its contents were totally destroyed by fire on January 20, 1984. The cost of the contents was approximately $150,000, and the warehouse had a book value of $750,000. The company carries insurance in the amount of 80% of the market value of assets destroyed. The replacement costs of the inventory and warehouse on the date they were destroyed were $200,000 and $1,000,000, respectively. Furthermore, uninsured losses resulting from business interruption are estimated at $250,000.

Instructions

[a] Assume the fire had occurred on December 20, 1983, rather than in January 1984. Prepare any accounting entries necessary to record these events.

[b] Comment on the entries and on whether any additional disclosures would be necessary. Be sure to discuss any conflicting indication between the accounting entries and the economic circumstances.

P24–3 The Petroleum, Inc., annual report dated December 31, 1985, contained the following consolidated statements of changes in stockholders' equity along with a footnote on related-party transactions:

Petroleum, Inc.
CONSOLIDATED STATEMENTS OF CHANGES IN STOCKHOLDERS' EQUITY

	Preferred Stock		Common Stock		Paid-in Capital	Retained Earnings	Total
	Shares	Value	Shares	Value			
Balances at Jan. 1, 1985	29,058	$290,580	63,660	$318,300	$92,410	$740,457	$1,441,747
Issuance of common stock for services	—	—	—	—	—	—	—
Redemption of preferred stock in exchange for property	(29,058)	(290,580)	—	—	—	(67,400)	(357,980)
Issuance of common stock	—	—	—	—	—	—	—
Net earnings	—	—	—	—	—	1,179,742	1,179,742
Balances at Dec. 31, 1985	—	—	63,660	$318,300	$92,410	$1,852,799	$2,263,509

Related-Party Transactions
In August 1983 the company issued 1,518 shares of common stock to an officer in exchange for a proven oil and gas property valued at $100,000, the property's approximate cost. The company incurred costs of approximately $61,000 to further develop the oil and gas property. In April 1984 the company entered into an agreement with the officer whereby the company exchanged the proven oil and gas property (which then had an estimated fair market value of $300,000) for a drilling rig and related equipment. The transaction resulted in a gain for the company of approximately $139,000 and is included in gain on sale of property and equipment in the consolidated statements of earnings.

In February 1984 the company issued 29,058 shares of preferred stock to an officer and forgave him for an indebtedness of an $88,000 note receivable in exchange for a drilling rig and related equipment having a fair market value of $378,580. In January 1985 the company redeemed all of the outstanding preferred stock for $11 per share and paid accrued dividends aggregating $38,342 in exchange for certain proven oil and gas properties carried on the books at $105,140, their approximate current value. This transaction resulted in a gain of approximately $253,000 and is included as a gain on the sale of property and equipment in the consolidated statements of earnings.

Instructions

[a] Prepare the entries to record the transactions that are described in the footnote.

[b] Discuss the propriety of the treatment accorded these events. Be sure to include a discussion of the basic theoretical issues involved.

P24–4   DD Sales Corporation's management is concerned over the corporation's current financial position and return on investment. They request your assistance in analyzing their financial statements.

DD Sales Corporation
STATEMENT OF WORKING CAPITAL DEFICIT
December 31, 1985

Current liabilities		$223,050
Less current assets:		
Cash	$ 5,973	
Accounts receivable, net	70,952	
Inventory	113,125	190,050
Working capital deficit		$ 33,000

DD Sales Corporation
INCOME STATEMENT
For the Year Ended December 31, 1985

Sales	$760,200
Costs of goods sold	452,500
Gross profit	307,700
Selling and general expenses, including	
$22,980 depreciation	155,660
Income before taxes	152,040
Income taxes	76,020
Net income	$ 76,020

Assets other than current assets consist of land, building, and equipment with a book value of $352,950 on December 31, 1985.

Instructions

Assuming DD Sales Corporation operates 300 days per year, compute the following ratios and show your computations:

[a] Number of days' sales uncollected.
[b] Inventory turnover.
[c] Number of days' operations required to cover the working capital deficit.
[d] Return on total assets as a product of asset turnover and the return on revenue (net income to sales) ratio.

(AICPA adapted)

P24–5   The market value of Arnold Company's common stock, which is listed on the American Stock Exchange, was $10 per share at December 31 in both 1984 and 1985. Arnold's balance sheet at December 31, 1985 and 1984, and statement of income and retained earnings for the years then ended are as follows:

Arnold Company
BALANCE SHEET
December 31, 1985 and 1984

Assets	1985	1984
Current Assets		
Cash	$ 3,500,000	$ 3,600,000
Marketable securities, at cost which		
approximates market	13,000,000	11,000,000
Accounts receivable, net of allowance		
for doubtful accounts	105,000,000	95,000,000
Inventories, lower of cost or market	126,000,000	154,000,000
Prepaid expenses	2,500,000	2,400,000
Total current assets	250,000,000	266,000,000
Noncurrent Assets		
Property, plant, and equipment, net of		
accumulated depreciation	311,000,000	308,000,000
Investments, at equity	2,000,000	3,000,000
Long-term receivables	14,000,000	16,000,000
Goodwill and patents, net of accumulated		
amortization	6,000,000	6,500,000
Other assets	7,000,000	8,500,000
Total assets	$590,000,000	$608,000,000

Liabilities and Stockholders' Equity

	1985	1984
Current Liabilities		
Notes payable	$ 5,000,000	$ 15,000,000
Accounts payable	38,000,000	48,000,000

Accrued expenses	24,500,000	27,000,000
Income taxes payable	1,000,000	1,000,000
Payments due within one year on		
long-term debt	6,500,000	7,000,000
Total current liabilities	75,000,000	98,000,000

Noncurrent Liabilities

Long-term debt	169,000,000	180,000,000
Deferred income taxes	74,000,000	67,000,000
Other liabilities	9,000,000	8,000,000
Total liabilities	327,000,000	353,000,000

Stockholders' Equity

Common stock, par value $1 per share;		
authorized 20,000,000 shares; issued		
and outstanding 10,000,000 shares	10,000,000	10,000,000
5% cumulative preferred stock, par value		
$100 per share; $100 liquidating		
value; authorized 50,000 shares; issued		
and outstanding 40,000 shares	4,000,000	4,000,000
Additional paid-in capital	107,000,000	107,000,000
Retained earnings	142,000,000	134,000,000
Total stockholders' equity	263,000,000	255,000,000
Total liabilities and stockholders'		
equity	$590,000,000	$608,000,000

Arnold Company
STATEMENT OF INCOME AND RETAINED EARNINGS
For the Years Ended December 31, 1985 and 1984

	1985	*1984*
Net sales	$600,000,000	$500,000,000
Cost and expenses		
Cost of goods sold	490,000,000	400,000,000
Selling, general, and administrative		
expenses	66,000,000	60,000,000
Other, net	7,000,000	6,000,000
Total costs and expenses	563,000,000	466,000,000
Income before income taxes	37,000,000	34,000,000
Income taxes	16,800,000	15,800,000
Net income	20,200,000	18,200,000
Retained earnings at beginning of period	134,000,000	126,000,000
Dividends on common stock	12,000,000	10,000,000
Dividends on preferred stock	200,000	200,000
Retained earnings at the end of period	$142,000,000	$134,000,000

Instructions

Compute the following for 1985 and show supporting computations in good form:

[a] Current (working capital) ratio.
[b] Quick (acid-test) ratio.
[c] Number of days' sales in average receivables, assuming a business year of 300 days and all sales on account.
[d] Inventory turnover.
[e] Book value per share of common stock.
[f] Earnings per share on common stock.
[g] Price/earnings ratio on common stock.
[h] Dividend payout ratio on common stock.

(AICPA adapted)

P24–6 Hozel Corporation, a cosmetics producer, has been supplying Hi Ya Corporation, a broker, with merchandise for the past ten years. Hi Ya carries exclusively Hozel products. In the past two years Hi Ya has not been doing a satisfactory job marketing Hozel Products, and consequently Hozel's board of directors decided to acquire Hi Ya Corporation. The following financial information has been gathered on the Hi Ya Corporation.

Hi Ya Corporation
BALANCE SHEET
October 1, 1985

Assets

Current Assets

Cash	$ 135,000	
Receivables	165,000	
Inventory	2,350,000	
Total current assets		$2,650,000

Noncurrent Assets

Equipment	70,000	
Trucks (book value)	295,000	
Building (book value)	900,000	
Total noncurrent assets		1,265,000
Total assets		$3,915,000

Liabilities and Owners' Equity

Current Liabilities

Accounts payable (Hozel)	$ 685,000	

Noncurrent Liabilities

Notes payable	890,000	
Total liabilities		$1,575,000

Owners' Equity

Retained earnings	1,060,000	
Capital stock	1,280,000	
Total owners' equity		2,340,000
Total liabilities and owners' equity		$3,915,000

Additional Information

[1] The company is currently involved in a lawsuit in which former employees are charging the company with unfair employment practices. The outcome of this suit is not determinable at this time. Legal counsel for the company estimates that the maximum liability that could be incurred from the suit is $50,000.

[2] The current values of the company's assets are as follows:

Receivables	$ 146,000
Inventory	1,965,000
Trucks	460,000
Equipment	65,000
Building	1,634,000

[3] The inventory, which includes no obsolete inventory, was appraised on a long-term sales basis. Hi Ya acquired all of its inventory from Hozel at 30% above Hozel's cost of goods sold as it appears on Hozel's books plus 5% shipping costs.

[4] Hozel agrees to pay Hi Ya Corporation $1,000,000 cash, a $3,000,000 note at 12% (the current interest rate) due in two years, and to forgive the payable that Hi Ya currently has to Hozel. In exchange, Hozel will receive all of Hi Ya's assets and will assume the note payable on Hi Ya's balance sheet.

Instructions

[a] Prepare the journal entry or entries to record the acquisition of Hi Ya by Hozel and provide a brief explanation.

[b] Draft a suitable footnote that describes the acquisition of Hi Ya for inclusion in the Hozel financial statements immediately following the acquisition.

[c] What disclosure, if any, should Hozel make in its financial statements for the contingent liability of Hi Ya concerning the pending suit by former employees? If you believe a footnote is required, draft that footnote.

P24-7 Tot Company manufactures and sells children's plastic toys. The company has experienced continued growth over the past three years and has forecast sales of $3,000,000 for 1985. Tot applied to Anderson State Bank for a short-term loan of $50,000 to cover expanding working capital needs. This is the first loan application Anderson State Bank has ever received from Tot, and the bank is anxious to develop a lasting relationship.

The following financial and other information has been supplied by Tot at the bank's request or developed by bank personnel.

Tot Company
STATEMENT OF FINANCIAL POSITION
December 31, 1983 and 1984
(in thousands)
(unaudited)

Assets	1983	1984
Current assets		
Cash	$ 85	$ 60
Marketable securities (cost)	20	20
Accounts receivable (net)	520	600
Inventories	365	475
Prepaid items	40	45
Total current assets	1,030	1,200

			Days Past Due	Amount	Industry Collection Experience
Investments (cost)	80	80			
Property, plant, and equipment (net)	590	520	Not due	$340,000	99% collected
Total assets	$1,700	$1,800	1–60	120,000	97% collected
			61–120	40,000	90% collected
Equities			121–180	70,000	80% collected
Current liabilities			Over 181	70,000	50% collected
Notes payable (trade)	$ 90	$ 80		$640,000	
Notes payable (officers)	100	100			
Accounts payable	190	280			
Accrued expenses and taxes	50	40			
Total current liabilities	$ 430	$ 500			
Long-term debt, 7%	420	400			
Total liabilities	$ 850	$ 900			
Stockholders' equity	850	900			
Total equities	$1,700	$1,800			

[2] **Inventory.**

	1983	1984
Raw materials (LIFO)	$100,000	$100,000
Work in process (FIFO)	50,000	300,000
Finished goods (FIFO)	215,000	75,000

Tot Company
INCOME STATEMENT
For the Year Ended December 31, 1983 and 1984
(in thousands)
(unaudited)

	1983	*1984*
Net sales	$2,500	$2,800
Cost of goods sold	1,750	2,100
Gross margin	750	700
Operating expenses		
Advertising	145	155
Bad debts estimate	25	28
Depreciation	70	70
Insurance	35	36
Lease payment	—	8
Salaries	185	190
Supplies	13	8
Taxes (nonincome)	25	25
Interest	42	40
Total operating expenses	540	560
Earnings before income taxes	210	140
Income taxes	105	70
Net income	$ 105	$ 70

Additional Information

[1] **Accounts receivable.** Sales are highly seasonal, with most sales occurring in the summer and fall for the upcoming Christmas season. Tot allows many customers to wait until January or February to settle their accounts (a common practice in the industry).

The allowance for uncollectible accounts had a balance of $30,000 on December 31, 1983, and $40,000 on December 31, 1984.

The aged accounts receivable balance on December 31, 1984, is shown as follows:

The raw materials consist primarily of plastic. Plastic prices rose approximately 10% in 1983 and by the same amount in 1984. Tot began its LIFO program on January 1, 1983.

[3] **Employment contract.** The company president has a five-year contract at $45,000 per year with three years remaining.

[4] **Insurance.** The company has purchased ordinary life insurance on its key officers. The policies have accrued a total of $5,000 cash surrender value.

[5] **Marketable securities.** The marketable securities were worth $21,000 at December 31, 1984.

[6] **Investments.** The investments of $80,000 consist of 800 shares of Fisher Company, which is owned in part by several of Tot's directors. Fisher discontinued one of its major products as a result of a legal suit concerning product safety standards. The stock declined to $60 per share following this action.

[7] **Property, plant, and equipment.** The company uses the same depreciation methods for book and tax purposes. The straight-line method is used on the plant, and the double-declining balance method is used on all equipment.

A purchase agreement for a parcel of land was signed in September 1984. Payment was to be made on January 10, 1985. The check for $10,000 was written on December 27, 1984, and delivered to the seller. The transaction was not recorded in December.

In January 1984 a noncancellable lease for equipment was signed by Tot. The lease calls for Tot to make annual payments of $8,000 for five years. The equipment can be purchased at the end of the lease for $10,000. The purchase price of the equipment was $40,000. At the date the lease was signed the value of the lease payments and option price was $40,000 (using a 10% rate), and the present value of the remaining lease payments and option price at December 31, 1984 is $35,000.

[8] **Notes payable (officers).** The officers loaned the company $100,000 early in 1982. The notes have been renewed each year, and it is expected they will be renewed annually for the next three years. The notes are subordinated to other notes outstanding.

[9] **Dividends.** The company paid dividends of $20,000 to its stockholders during 1984.

Instructions

[a] Calculate the following ratios for 1984 by using the preceding financial information:
  [1] Return on total assets.
  [2] Acid-test ratio.
  [3] Average collection period for receivables.
  [4] Inventory turnover.
  [5] Times interest earned.

[b] Revise the statement of financial position on a *pro forma* basis as of December 31, 1984, to make it more useful for the bank's needs.

[c] Prepare an estimated cash flow statement for the year ending December 31, 1984.

(CMA adapted)

P24-8 Ratio analysis is often applied to test the reasonableness of the relationships among current financial data against those of prior financial data. Given prior financial relationships and a few key amounts, an accountant can prepare estimates of current financial data to test the reasonableness of current financial information.

Manning Company, Inc., has in recent years maintained the following relationships among the data in its financial statements:

Gross profit rate on net sales	40%
Net profit rate on net sales	10%
Rate of selling expenses to net sales	20%
Accounts receivable turnover	8 per year
Inventory turnover	6 per year
Acid-test ratio	2 to 1
Current ratio	3 to 1
Quick-asset composition:	
8% cash	
32% marketable securities	
60% accounts receivable	
Asset turnover	2 per year
Ratio of total assets to intangible assets	20 to 1

Ratio of accumulated depreciation to cost of fixed assets	1 to 3
Ratio of accounts receivable to accounts payable	1.5 to 1
Ratio of working capital to stockholders' equity	1 to 1.6
Ratio of total debt to stockholders' equity	1 to 2

The corporation had a net income of $120,000 for 1984, which resulted in earnings of $5.20 per share of common stock.

Additional Information

[1] Capital stock authorized, issued (all in 1976), and outstanding: common, $10 per share par value, issued at 10% premium; preferred, 6% nonparticipating, $100 per share par value, issued at 10% premium.

[2] Market value per share of common stock at December 31, 1984: $78.

[3] Preferred dividends paid in 1984: $3,000.

[4] Times interest earned in 1984: 33.

[5] The amounts of the following were the same at December 31, 1984, as at January 1, 1984: inventory, accounts receivable, 5% bonds payable—due in 1986—and total stockholders' equity.

[6] All purchases and sales were "on account."

Instructions

[a] Prepare in good form the condensed balance sheet and income statement for the year ended December 31, 1984, presenting the amounts you would expect to find in Manning's financial statements based on the ratios and other information provided.

Major captions appearing on Manning's balance sheet are: Current Assets, Fixed Assets, Intangible Assets, Current Liabilities, Long-Term Liabilities, and Stockholders' Equity. In addition to the accounts divulged in the problem, you should include accounts for Prepaid Expenses, Accrued Expenses, and Administrative Expenses. Supporting calculations should be in good form. You may ignore income taxes.

[b] Compute the following ratios for 1984 and show your computations:
  [1] Rate of return on stockholders' equity.
  [2] Price/earnings ratio for common stock.
  [3] Dividends paid per share of common stock.
  [4] Dividends paid per share of preferred stock.
  [5] Yield on common stock.

(AICPA adapted)

6

Financial Reporting by Publicly Held Companies

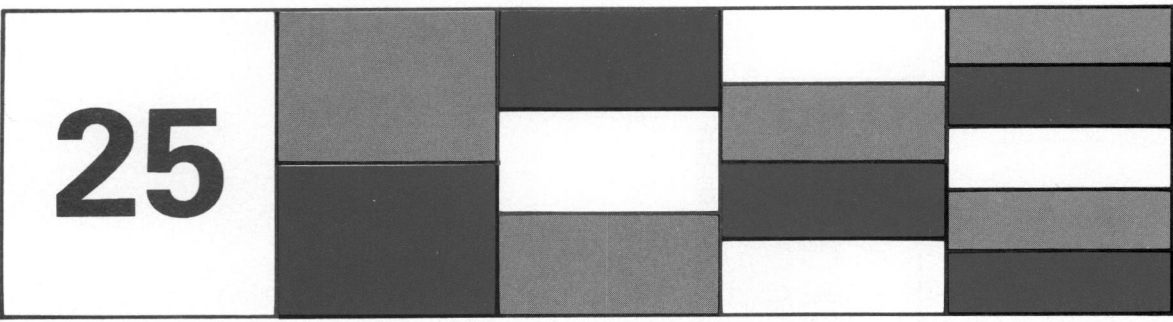

25

PUBLICLY HELD COMPANIES: SELECTED FINANCIAL REPORTING TOPICS

Objectives

To introduce the problem of standards overload, a situation that many accountants believe exists in current financial reporting whereby small and privately held companies are burdened with complex financial reporting requirements designed primarily for large public companies.

To consider factors underlying the standards overload problem: dimensions of the problem, possible differences in the financial reporting environment of different companies, and possible directions for change.

To introduce the concept of interim reporting and to discuss some of the accounting complexities of reporting for periods of time less than one year.

To illustrate the interim reporting process with the disclosure of a publicly held company.

To introduce the need for presenting disaggregated information concerning enterprise operations for purposes of making investment and credit decisions.

To discuss and illustrate the major areas of segment disclosure required by the Financial Accounting Standards Board (FASB): industry information, information by geographic area, and major customer information.

Should generally accepted accounting principles (GAAP) apply equally to all companies without regard to their size or the distribution of their capital stock? Should small or closely held companies be subject to simplified accounting requirements or reduced disclosure requirements? These and other similar questions are currently being widely discussed within the accounting profession as we attempt to resolve a problem that some have termed the "standards overload" problem.

Standards overload is a name that has been given to the financial reporting burden that companies have under current accounting standards. As a general rule these standards apply to all companies with no distinction being made between small and large companies or publicly held and closely held companies. This chapter discusses the background and current status of the standards overload problem and some possible solutions to this problem. While authoritative accounting pronouncements generally apply to all companies, in a few instances the Financial Accounting Standards Board (FASB) has limited the applicability of pronouncements to publicly held companies. This chapter discusses two of those areas: interim reporting and segment reporting. Chapters 26 and 27 consider two other areas (earnings per share and constant dollar/current cost disclosures) in which the FASB has limited the applicability of current authoritative pronouncements to companies that are publicly held.

Certain publicly held companies are required to report directly to the Securities and Exchange Commission (SEC) in addition to presenting financial statements to investors and creditors through their annual reports. Reporting to the SEC is a complex subject that is covered in depth in more advanced texts, including some specifically on that subject. The appendix to this chapter is included to give a brief introduction to SEC reporting and to develop an appreciation of the SEC in the environment of financial reporting.

THE STANDARDS OVERLOAD PROBLEM

In recent years wide segments of the business community and the accounting profession have become both concerned about and critical of the increased number and complexity of authoritative accounting pronouncements. This concern is summarized as follows:

> *The rising crescendo of complaints rings a loud echo in the inner chambers of the American Institute of CPAs and the Financial Accounting Standards Board. The mounting frustrations with complicated measurement rules such as the standards on lease accounting, interperiod income tax allocation, business combinations and interest capitalization indicates that many accounting standards users now believe that the situation has reached the point of accounting standards overload.*
>
> *The accounting standards overload syndrome is apparent in businesses of all sizes, but the brunt of the burden falls on small businesses because they are the least able to bear its cost. It is fully understandable that a deep-seated longing for relief should spring up and that incentives for action should focus on the plight of those most affected—the owners of small businesses and their accountants.[1]*

The primary objective of financial reporting is to provide present and potential investors, creditors, and other users with information that is useful in making investment, credit, and other decisions. Financial statements are important sources of information flow between an enterprise and interested parties. Owners and creditors—both present and prospective— are generally the primary user groups, and the form and content of financial statements have

---

[1]Gerald W. Hepp and Thomas W. McRae, "Accounting Standards Overload: Relief Is Needed," *Journal of Accountancy* (May 1982), p. 52.

THE DOMINANT PUBLIC INTEREST—THE PUBLIC CORPORATION

PUBLIC CORPORATIONS—the giant multinational and national companies and the lesser ones—have had a major impact on our economic way of life. Though far fewer in number than the private companies, their public importance is immeasurably greater.

The public interest arises not only from their economic dominance but to the fact that they are financed by millions of individual stockholders and by other investors (e.g., banks, insurance companies, mutual funds, etc.) who in turn are financed by millions of individuals.

Decisions to buy, sell, and hold equity and debt securities of these corporations are made daily. The money involved runs into many billions. These decisions are made, in large part, on the financial statements of the public corporations.

For obvious reasons, it has been increasingly necessary to improve the quality of the profession's auditing and reporting expertise as the size, complexity, and place of the operations and financing methods evolved. More and better disclosure has been demanded. The medium for the development of the improved standards was the AICPA. The job has been so big, and so difficult, that it necessarily dominated much of the organization's effort.

The pressure on the profession has grown substantially in recent years because of criticisms of the independent auditor's role in financial reporting and a rash of notorious cases involving accountants and enormous suits for damages arising from them. This stepped up the Institute's activities in respect to public corporation accounting, increasing the apparent "discriminatory" direction.

Since a very small number of accounting firms, perhaps about twelve, dominates 90 percent or more of all public corporation accounting services, it would appear that our national professional society, in concentrating on public corporation practice, was, in effect, working primarily for the handful of affected accounting firms.

However, it must be understood that all that has been done to further better auditing and reporting for public corporations is also applicable, with some exception, to private companies. And, many of the smaller accounting firms observe the quality standards conscientiously. But, the accounting standards should not have been made mandatory to public and private companies without exception. In some instances, later exemplified, they should have been made *optional* to private companies.

SOURCE: Max Block, "Duality in the Accounting Profession," *CPA Journal*, July 1974, p. 30. Reprinted by permission of *The CPA Journal*.

---

been heavily influenced by the perceived needs of these groups. While we recognize that different user groups may have need for different types of information, **general purpose financial statements** prepared in conformity with generally accepted accounting principles are believed to include information that is relevant to virtually all user groups.

In addition to our insistence that financial-statement information be useful for decision-making purposes, in recent years more interest has been expressed in the relationship between the costs and benefits of accounting information. We have mentioned at various points in this text that the FASB has paid particular attention to the cost-benefit question in identifying the qualitative characteristics of accounting information. Specifically, the FASB has indicated that in addition to useful information being relevant and reliable, the benefits to be derived from it must exceed the costs associated with it before the information should be required to be presented.

Relevance Reliability

Historically, promulgated standards of financial reporting have applied to all enterprises without regard to size or the distribution of the enterprise's ownership interests. Considerable concern has been expressed that many accounting standards were developed with the very large, publicly held corporations in mind. The argument continues that applying these same standards to all enterprises imposes an unreasonable burden on smaller companies whose ownership is not widely distributed. Certain reporting requirements are said to be inappropriate for these companies. Compliance with all measurement and disclosure standards requires small companies to incur significant costs that are due, in part, to reliance

THE SAGA OF SAM'S DELICATESSEN*

I MET WITH MY old friend Sam Applemeister last week and was delighted to learn that his business, Sam's Delicatessen, Inc. was doing well. So well, in fact, that Sam had been stricken with a bad case of "compliance syndrome."

"I've been doing my own accounting," he told me, "but now I can afford to hire you and I want my financial statements to be really professional."

"That's a good idea," I told him. "I'm sure you'll find the information in your financial statements will be valuable. For instance, you'll have a 'Statement of Changes in Financial Position.'"

"What's that?" Sam inquired.

"Well, in its simplest terms," I replied, "it tells you where your cash came from and where it went. It's all spelled out in Accounting Principles Board Opinion no. 19."

"I already know where it came from and where it went," exclaimed Sam. "All I care about is what's left at the end of the year."

"Sorry Sam," I said, "it's required if you want full financial statements."

"O.K.," he responded, "but if it weren't for my catering business there wouldn't be that much to account for."

"The catering business, Sam?" I asked.

"Sure," he said. "In addition to the retail trade, my take-out business has really grown and a big part of my income is from catering parties."

"Oops," I replied, "you may be subject to Statement of Financial Accounting Standards no. 14, *Financial Reporting for Segments of a Business Enterprise,* in which case you'll have to segregate the revenues, profitability and identifiable assets of the retail and catering lines. You must also provide information about your major customers."

"But I don't have those figures," complained Sam. "We do all of our business out of the store, and I don't keep records about how much business we do with each customer."

"That's all right," I told him. "We can help you set up a management information system."

"I don't know how that information can be of value to anyone except my competitors, but if I can

afford to own the building that the store is in, I guess I can afford such a system."

"Do you own the building personally?"

"Yes," he replied. "I made a small down payment and there is a long-term lease from the corporation that provides for the mortgage payments and all other expenses."

"Well, it looks like this comes under Statement of Financial Accounting Standards no. 13, *Accounting for Leases.* Ordinarily we would have to consider the fair value of the property, any bargain purchase options, the estimated economic life of the property, estimated residual value, the lessee's incremental borrowing rate and some other factors. In your case, because of the relationship of the lessee and lessor, we'll have to make the accounting match the economic substance rather than the legal form."

"It sure sounds complicated," said Sam, scratching his head. "But as long as my earnings are there I still want to go ahead."

"Don't worry about your earnings. Under Accounting Principles Board Opinion no. 15, your earnings per share will be clearly stated."

"What do you mean, 'earnings per share'?" cried Sam. "There are only 100 shares issued and I own them all."

"Don't panic, Sam," I told him. "You said you wanted proper financial statements."

"I do, I do," he said, wiping away his tears, "but how much will all of this cost?"

Taking out my pencil, I figured it out. "Here's good news, Sam," I said. "It looks as though you won't have to worry about earnings per share after all."

---

*As we shall see later in this chapter, shortly after this article was first published some relief was granted to small businesses with regard to per-share and segment information. However, the general problems discussed in the article still exist.

SOURCE: Charles Chazen and Benjamin Benson, "Fitting GAAP to Smaller Businesses," *Journal of Accountancy,* February 1978, pp. 46–47. Copyright © 1978 by the American Institute of Certified Public Accountants, Inc.

---

on external CPAs to provide services that larger enterprises obtain from their own personnel. In short, excessive costs are said to be incurred with little or no benefit being derived in terms of providing information that is useful to those people interested in the company.

The idea that current accounting standards seem primarily to address the needs of large companies is emphasized in the following quotation:

> *I have come to the conclusion that there is a standards overload. I think the emphasis of present standard setting is to identify the needs of the users of financial statements, and yet present standards seem to be basically addressed to institutional investors and security analysts—essentially, the sophisticated investor. The needs of sophisticated investors, who are not intimately acquainted with a company, who are not part of management and who have no direct involvement with the management of the company, are different from the needs of users of the financial statements of a small, closely held company. Management and the owners are intimately acquainted with its operations. The banker, if he's worth his salt and has a sizable credit extended to the company, knows the operations. Therefore, the types of disclosures and, I am beginning to conclude, perhaps even the measurement principles that are appropriate for a publicly held company may not be appropriate for that smaller, closely held entity.[2]*

Dimensions of the Problem

The American Institute of Certified Public Accountants (AICPA) and the FASB have been actively involved in considering the standards overload problem. These organizations have identified the following dimensions that must be examined in considering the need to ease the financial reporting burden of selected companies:[3]

1. In what circumstances do smaller companies need to prepare GAAP financial statements? What other kinds of financial statements might be adequate for those companies and in what circumstances?
2. What measurements and disclosures are appropriate in GAAP financial statements of small companies as compared with GAAP financial statements of other companies?
3. What degree of responsibility should external CPAs have for the financial statements of small companies? How should they report on those financial statements?

One difficult aspect of the standards overload problem is the identification of those companies for which some relief from existing financial reporting requirements should be made. For purposes of gathering input on the three dimensions of the standards overload problem listed above, the FASB tentatively defined a **small company** as follows:

> *A company whose operations are relatively small, usually with total revenues of less than $5 million. It typically (a) is owner-managed, (b) has few other owners, if any, (c) has all owners actively involved in the conduct of enterprise affairs except possibly for certain family members, (d) has infrequent transfer of ownership interests, and (e) has a simple capital structure.[4]*

A **large company** is any company other than the above-defined "small company" and is usually a company whose securities trade in a public market.

The FASB has defined a **public company** as follows:

> *A company (a) whose securities trade in a public market on a stock exchange or in the over-the-counter market or (b) that is required to file finan-*

[2]"Accounting and Auditing: The Technical Challenges Ahead," *Journal of Accountancy* (November 1980), pp. 62–63. This statement was made by Thomas P. Kelley, Vice President–Technical of the AICPA.
[3]Glendon R. Hildebrand, "Let's Look at Financial Reporting by Smaller Businesses," *Management Accounting* (April 1982), p. 43.
[4]Financial Accounting Standards Board, *Financial Reporting by Private and Small Public Companies* (Stamford, Conn.: FASB, 1981), pp. 3–4.

cial statements with the Securities and Exchange Commission. A company is also considered a public company if its financial statements are issued in preparation for the sale of any class of securities in a public market.[5]

A **private company** is any company that is not a public company.

If a standards overload problem exists, should relief be provided for small companies, for private companies, or for private and small public companies? This is an important part of the current study by the AICPA and the FASB.

Possible Differences Among Companies

Several reasons have been suggested as to why the informational needs of financial statement users might differ between small or private companies and large public companies. These include the following:[6]

1. A small or private company has fewer or simpler transactions that may be easier to understand without complicated disclosures.
2. The external financial statement users are different and may make different decisions. For example, a private company may have only a bank lender making short-term lending decisions, whereas a public company usually has numerous investors and creditors making various types of decisions.
3. The users' methods of making decisions may differ. For example, the financial statement users of a private company may already know more about the company or may have the ability to obtain information apart from the financial statements and, thus, rely less on those statements.

Another difference between small or private companies and large public companies is the difference in their abilities to absorb the costs of providing the information required by current GAAP. Many CPAs feel that the cost burden is relatively greater for small or private companies, particularly when viewed in comparison with the benefits derived from the information.

Possible Direction of Change

Several possible alternative outcomes have been suggested as solutions to the standards overload problem if, indeed, the problem is judged by the FASB to be so significant that corrective action must be taken. This section briefly discusses the following alternatives: (1) simplify GAAP for all companies; (2) provide additional disclosure relief for small or private companies; (3) provide accounting measurement relief for small or private companies; and (4) develop an alternative basis of accounting (other than GAAP) for use by small or private companies.

Simplify GAAP for All Companies

Some CPAs feel that a standards overload exists for *all* companies, not just small or private companies. Their solution depends on a revision of GAAP for all companies, eliminating many of the overly complex financial reporting requirements. Some have observed that the FASB's conceptual framework will assist in the effort to simplify financial reporting and eliminate current inconsistencies.

Additional Disclosure Relief

As stated earlier, the FASB has limited a few requirements—primarily in the disclosure area—to public companies. One resolution to the standards overload problem is to continue this emphasis and exempt small or private companies from additional disclosure requirements of current GAAP. One view is that disclosures should be divided into two

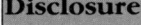

Disclosure

---

[5]FASB, *Financial Reporting,* p. 4.
[6]FASB, *Financial Reporting,* p. 30.

groups: (1) a core group that would apply to *all* companies, and (2) a group that would apply only to specifically defined companies, primarily large public companies.

Accounting Measurement Relief

Materiality

Some CPAs have proposed that selected accounting measurement requirements be eliminated for small or private companies. Variations of this proposal include the view that different (higher) materiality standards might be applicable for small or private companies, thereby screening out some FASB measurement standards. Others indicate that cost-benefit considerations should be used to screen out certain accounting requirements for small or private companies that would otherwise be required.[7] Accounting areas often cited as a burden for small or private companies and from which relief should be considered include:

1. The equity method of accounting for investments.
2. Capitalization of interest.
3. Imputed interest on receivables and payables.
4. Lease accounting.
5. Interperiod income tax allocation.
6. Accounting for marketable securities.

Alternative Basis of Accounting

For companies that have few or no external financial statement users, simplified financial statements prepared on a basis other than GAAP may be sufficient. Possible alternatives that have been suggested include cash basis, modified cash basis, and income tax basis.

Disclosure

Perhaps the alternative basis that has attracted the greatest amount of attention is the income tax basis. An AICPA special committee has encouraged small private companies to prepare financial statements on the income tax basis as an experiment in situations in which GAAP financial statements do not seem reasonable in light of the needs of known financial statement users and the costs of preparing those statements. Financial statements prepared on an income tax basis reflect transactions that determine taxable income as reported on federal income tax returns. The statements also include revenue and expense items that are not taxable or deductible under income tax rules. Minimum disclosure requirements have been outlined by the AICPA for financial statements prepared on an income tax basis.[8]

What Does the Future Hold?

The stage is set for major change in the area of financial reporting by small or private companies. As indicated earlier, the AICPA and the FASB have been actively considering the standards overload problem. In 1983, the Special Committee on Accounting Standards Overload of the AICPA concluded that the problem requires immediate action:

> *The increasing specificity and the complexity of mandated accounting standards have led to growing concern and mounting frustration, especially among small and closely held businesses and the CPAs who serve them. We find the following factors have contributed to accounting standards overload:*
> 1. *Too many standards.*
> 2. *Standards that are too detailed.*
> 3. *An inability to be selective in the application of standards.*
> 4. *Failure to provide sufficiently for differences between public and nonpublic entities, annual and interim financial statements, and large and small enterprises.*
> 5. *Requirements for excessive disclosures and complex measurements.*[9]

---

[7]FASB, *Financial Reporting,* p. 38.
[8]Hildebrand, p. 46.
[9]*Report of the Special Committee on Accounting Standards Overload* (New York: AICPA, 1983), p. 1.

The report of the AICPA committee makes several specific suggestions. First, the report states, the FASB should promptly reconsider certain accounting standards that are widely perceived to be unnecessarily burdensome and costly, particularly for small nonpublic entities. Second, the FASB should attempt to simplify financial reporting standards for all enterprises by avoiding complex and detailed rules to the extent possible. Finally, where simplicity and flexibility are not possible, the FASB should explicitly and specifically consider the information needs of the users of the financial statements of small nonpublic entities and the costs and benefits of providing differential disclosure alternatives as well as differential measurement alternatives for such entities.[10]

Disclosure

Final action by the FASB will require a great deal of study. In addition to determining the nature (i.e., small or large, public or private), of those companies which require relief, the FASB must find answers to other questions.

> *The FASB . . . is taking steps to learn more about the financial reporting environment of smaller businesses. Although in recent years this matter has received attention within the public accounting profession, few specifics are available about what kinds of decisions are made on the basis of financial statements of small businesses, what kinds of information are needed to make those decisions, and, most critically, how and why those decisions and that information differ from the decisions and information needed for large companies. Findings about those aspects must be related to costs and other burdens that accounting requirements place on small companies.[11]*

Disclosure

The remainder of this text considers several subjects wherein the FASB has allowed differential disclosure by private and public companies. We cover the subjects of interim reporting and segment reporting in the following sections of this chapter; Chapter 26 considers earnings per share; and Chapter 27 considers the disclosure requirements related to constant dollar and current cost information. These are areas for which the FASB has limited the applicability of current accounting pronouncements to publicly held or very large companies. Some private companies also present this type of information, even though it is not required. If a company that is not required to report certain information chooses to do so, it must follow the standards of reporting that are set for that type of information.

INTERIM REPORTING

Historically, generally accepted accounting principles have been established in the context of the annual period. Prior to the early 1970s the accounting profession paid little attention to the form and content of financial information for periods of time shorter than a year. Most Accounting Principles Board (APB) Opinions and Accounting Research Bulletins (ARBs) make few references to the applicability of GAAP to financial statements or summarized financial information that is presented monthly, quarterly, or otherwise more frequently than once a year.

In the 1960s and early 1970s **interim reports** emerged as a significant source of information for investors and creditors in assessing the financial position and results of company operations. **Interim reporting** refers to the presentation of financial information for a period of less than one year. As the significance of interim information increased, the need for standards to guide the measurement and presentation of information on an interim basis became apparent. In 1973 the APB issued *Opinion No. 28* to clarify the applicability of accounting principles and reporting practices in interim financial reports. In addition, the

---

[10]*Report of the Special Committee on Accounting Standards Overload,* pp. 3–4.
[11]Hildebrand, p. 47.

pronouncement included a listing of minimum information to be disclosed in interim reports of publicly held companies.[12] Authoritative pronouncements issued after *APB Opinion No. 28* have made more frequent references to the applicability of pronouncements to interim period reporting. Thus, over time, a set of principles establishing standards for interim reporting has begun to emerge.

Basic Interim Period Positions

Attempting to determine the results of business operations for intervals of less than a year has some inherent difficulties. Wide fluctuations in revenue that are due to seasonal business patterns, for example, or substantial fixed costs incurred in a single interim period for the benefit of several periods complicate the determination of earnings on a short-term basis. Although the same problems may exist in annual reporting, the longer period allows the business cycle to more nearly complete its course, thereby offsetting some of the fluctuations.

The unique features of interim reporting have resulted in two basic positions concerning the nature of interim financial statements. These positions are the **discrete** or **independent view** and the **integral** or **dependent view.** Advocates of the discrete view of interim reporting regard each interim period as a basic accounting period, regardless of the length of time involved. The results of operations for each interim period are therefore determined in essentially the same way as for an annual period. In the determination of income, those accruals, deferrals, and estimations that would normally be applied for annual periods are also applied for interim periods.

Advocates of the integral view see each interim period as an important part of the annual period and emphasize this feature in reporting results of operations. Accruals, deferrals, and estimates required at the end of each interim period are applied in the context of expected annual results of operations. Allocations between interim periods are sometimes made to reflect the relationship of the interim period to the annual period, whereas the same allocation between annual periods would not be appropriate.

To illustrate the difference between the discrete and integral views, assume that a company launches a major advertising campaign in January. Although the costs are incurred entirely in the first quarter, the company expects results throughout the year. Within the discrete view of interim reporting, the entire cost of the advertising campaign should be included as an expense in the first quarter because advertising would ordinarily not be carried forward as a prepaid expense at the end of an annual period. Within the integral view of interim reporting, however, an expense such as advertising might be allocated among four quarters in order to more clearly reflect the relationship of each quarter's results of operations to the annual period.

The APB took the position that interim financial information is important to investors, creditors, and other financial statement users in assessing the progress of the enterprise. In fact, this need by financial statement users appears to be the primary reason for the APB's interest in interim reporting and for their issuance of *APB Opinion No. 28.* The APB further concluded that the usefulness of this information depends on the **relationship that it has to annual results of operations.** Therefore, the board decided that each interim period should be viewed as an **integral part** of the corresponding annual period. In general, financial information presented in interim reports should be based on the accounting principles used by the enterprise in its annual reporting unless an accounting change has occurred. However, because of the unique nature of the interim period as a part of a longer period, certain modifications in accounting principles may be necessary for the interim information to relate better to annual results of operations.

---

[12]*APB Opinion No. 28,* "Interim Financial Reporting," 1973.

Basic Accounting Principles for Interim Reporting

Revenues from products sold or services rendered are generally recognized for interim periods on the same basis as for the annual period. Methods of revenue recognition that are used in annual reporting, such as the percentage-of-completion method on long-term contracts, should be followed in interim reports as well.

The recognition of costs and expenses in interim periods poses the most significant problem in interim reporting. Costs and expenses for interim reporting purposes are classified in two categories: (1) costs associated directly with revenue, and (2) all other costs and expenses.

> **Matching**

Costs associated directly with revenue are matched against revenue in those interim periods in which the related revenue is recognized. Examples of costs associated directly with revenue are material costs; wages, salaries, and related fringe benefits; manufacturing overhead; and warranties.

The application of traditional inventory methods in determining the inventory and cost of goods sold at the end of interim periods raises some interesting questions. The practical problem of applying complete inventory procedures at the end of each interim period is significant. Also, the application of annual inventory procedures for interim periods may produce interim figures that would not, when added together, equal the annual figures. As a result, practices vary in determining the cost of inventory at the end of interim periods. While essentially the same procedures used for annual reporting should also be used at interim dates, several exceptions are appropriate at interim dates:[13]

1. Some companies use estimated gross margin rates to determine the cost of goods sold during interim periods or use other methods different from those used at annual inventory dates. (We discussed this method of inventory estimation in Chapter 9.) These companies should disclose the method used at the interim date and any significant adjustments that result from reconciliations with the annual physical inventory.

2. Companies that use the LIFO method may encounter a liquidation of base period inventories at an interim date that is expected to be replaced by the end of the annual period. In such cases the inventory at the interim reporting date should not give effect to the LIFO liquidation, and cost of sales for the interim reporting period should include the expected cost of replacement of the liquidated LIFO base.

3. Inventory losses from market declines should not be deferred beyond the interim period in which the decline occurs. Recoveries of such losses on the same inventory in later interim periods of the same fiscal year through market price recoveries should be recognized as gains in the later interim period. Such gains should not exceed losses recognized in previous interim periods. Some market declines at interim dates, however, can reasonably be expected to be restored in the fiscal year. Such *temporary* market declines need not be recognized at the interim date since no loss is expected to be incurred in the fiscal year.

4. Companies that use standard cost accounting systems for determining inventory and product costs should generally follow the same procedures in reporting purchase price, wage rate, usage or efficiency variances from standard cost at the end of an interim period as followed at the end of a fiscal year. Purchase price variances or volume or capacity cost variances that are planned and expected to be absorbed by the end of the annual period, should ordinarily be deferred at interim reporting dates. The effect of unplanned or unanticipated purchase price or volume variances, however, should be reported at the end of an interim period following the same procedures used at the end of a fiscal year.

The influence of the integral view of financial reporting is evident in these procedures. For example, in the case of the last-in, first-out (LIFO) liquidation the procedure to be

---

[13]*APB Opinion No. 28,* par. 14.

followed in the interim period is based on the desire to apply LIFO on an annual basis. Therefore, any LIFO liquidation that takes place in an interim period but which is expected to be replaced by the end of the annual period is not treated as a LIFO liquidation in the interim period. Similarly, if market declines in inventory at interim dates are temporary and are expected to be recovered by the end of the annual period, no loss is recognized in the interim period. In these cases the interim report should present figures that are most indicative of annual results expected rather than those obtained by strictly applying GAAP in each interim period as they would be applied in an annual period.

All other expenses (i.e., those not directly associated with revenue) should be recognized in interim periods as incurred or be allocated among interim periods on the basis of an estimate of time expired, benefit received, or activity associated with the period. The objective of recognizing costs and expenses is to achieve a fair measure of **results of operations for the annual period** and to present fairly the **financial position at the end of the annual period.** To meet this objective, procedures may be followed at the end of an interim period that would normally not be followed at the end of an annual period. Assume, for example, that a cost (such as repair and maintenance) usually expensed for annual reporting purposes is incurred in one interim period but clearly benefits two or more interim periods. Accruals or deferrals should then be used to charge an appropriate portion of the annual cost to each interim period. However, if no discernible benefits exist, arbitrary amounts should not be allocated among interim periods.

The amount of certain expenses that can be reasonably estimated at interim dates are subject to year-end adjustments. Examples of such items are inventory shrinkage, uncollectible receivables, and discretionary year-end bonuses. As the year progresses, more reliable estimates of annual amounts are usually possible. Estimates of such costs and expenses should be made at interim dates, with consideration given to all available information that is expected to influence the amount of cost or expense to be recognized for annual reporting purposes. To the extent possible, estimated costs and expenses should be assigned to interim periods so that the interim periods bear a reasonable portion of the anticipated annual amount.

At this point you may want to refer to Appendix A of Chapter 5, where we discussed using a worksheet to prepare interim financial statements.

Special Principles of Interim Reporting

The general principles described above apply to the recognition of a wide range of revenues and expenses in interim reports, but a number of unique problems are encountered in applying to interim reports specific accounting principles that were originally designed for annual reporting. Several of these problem areas are discussed below.

Seasonal Revenues and Expenses

Revenues and expenses of certain businesses are subject to material **seasonal variations.** In these circumstances, to avoid the possible misinterpretation that interim results are indicative of estimated annual results, companies should disclose the seasonal nature of their business activities.

To further emphasize the relationship of interim information to information relating to the annual period, *APB Opinion No. 28* requires that companies present information either for year to date or for the last twelve months to date along with quarterly information. We discuss and illustrate these specific disclosure requirements, as well as others, later in this chapter.

Income Taxes

Interim period income tax expense should reflect the concepts of interperiod and intraperiod income tax allocation applicable in annual reporting. At the end of each interim period an estimate is made of the effective income tax rate expected to be applicable for the annual period. This rate is then applied to income earned to date for that year. Any income tax recognized in previous interim periods is subtracted from the amount resulting from the above computation, and the difference is recognized as income tax expense in the current interim period. The estimate of the annual effective income tax rate should reflect anticipated investment tax credits, capital gains rates, and other information available from tax planning techniques. In arriving at this rate, no effect should be included for the income tax related to extraordinary or other items that will be reported on a net-of-tax basis when they are recognized.

For example, assume that during the first quarter of 1984 Atkins Company estimated its effective annual income tax rate to be 44%. Income before income tax for the first quarter was $485,000. During the second quarter of 1984, the estimate of the effective annual income tax rate was reduced to 42% because of revised plans to take advantage of certain income tax credits. Pretax-accounting income for the second quarter of 1984 was $650,000. The income tax expense for the first two quarters is determined in the schedule below:

First Quarter

Pretax-accounting income for first quarter of 1984	$485,000
Estimated annual income tax expense rate	44%
Income tax expense for first quarter	$213,400

Second Quarter

Pretax-accounting income for first quarter of 1984	$485,000	
Pretax-accounting income for second quarter of 1984	650,000	$1,135,000
Estimated annual income tax expense rate		42%
Income tax for first and second quarters of 1984		$ 476,700
Income tax expense recognized in first quarter		(213,400)
Income tax expense for second quarter		$ 263,300

The same process is followed for subsequent quarters of the year as additional information on pretax-accounting income and the annual effective income tax rate becomes available.

Losses recognized in interim periods should be carried back or forward by following the same procedures as those appropriate for annual reporting. (These procedures were covered in detail in Chapter 18.) Operating losses that cannot be carried back should be recognized as carryforwards only if realization within the carryforward period is assured beyond reasonable doubt. An established pattern of losses in early interim periods offset by income in later interim periods may constitute this evidence if there is no apparent reason that this pattern will not prevail in the current year. When the loss carryforward from an early interim period is recognized in a subsequent interim period of the same year, income tax expense of the subsequent interim period should be reduced, and recognition of carryforward should not be treated as an extraordinary item, as is done in annual reporting.

Disclosure of Irregular Income Items

Materiality

Extraordinary items should be separately disclosed in the interim period in which they occur. The materiality of extraordinary items should be judged in relation to estimated income for the entire year. Gains and losses on disposals of a segment of a business and unusual or infrequently occurring transactions that are material with respect to the operating results of the interim period should be separately disclosed. Extraordinary items, gains and losses from segment disposals, and unusual or infrequently occurring items should *not* be allocated over several interim periods of the year in which they occur. Irregular income items that would be presented on a net-of-tax basis in annual financial statements are presented in the same manner in interim financial statements.

Accounting Changes

The Accounting Principles Board recommended that accounting changes be made in the first interim period of a fiscal year. This recommendation is supported by the APB's belief that changes in accounting principles and methods made in later interim periods of a fiscal year tend to obscure operating results and complicate disclosure in interim periods. Accounting changes in interim periods should generally be accounted for in the same way as those same changes would be in annual reporting. Chapter 19 discussed the proper procedures for accounting changes.

An exception to this general conclusion is found in the case of a change in accounting principle for which there is a cumulative effect that must be recognized in income in the period of change. If the change is made in the first interim period, accounting for the change is the same as in annual reporting, because the cumulative effect to the beginning of the first interim period is the same as the cumulative effect to the beginning of the annual period in which the change is made. However, a problem arises if a change in accounting principle is made in a subsequent interim period, because the cumulative effect to the beginning of the interim period of change is not the same as the cumulative effect to the beginning of the annual period. This difference is due to the additional time encompassed by the interim periods prior to the interim period of change. *FASB Statement of Financial Accounting Standards No. 3* gives special consideration to this problem and concludes that a cumulative effect type accounting change made in other than the first interim period should be accounted for **as if the change had been made in the first interim period.**[14] Income of previous interim periods of the fiscal year in which such a change is made should be restated, with consideration given to the impact of the change in the first interim period. This procedure is consistent with the integral view of interim reporting, because it makes the amount of the cumulative effect included in interim income the same as the amount to be included in the determination of annual income.

Adjustments of Previous Interim Periods

An item of profit or loss that occurs in an interim period may relate to previous annual periods or previous interim periods of the same year or both. Examples are settlements of litigation and adjustments of income taxes. If this type of event is recorded in an interim period other than the first interim period, the following guidelines should be followed:[15]

1. The portion of the item that is directly related to business activities of the current interim period should be included in the determination of net income for that period.
2. The portion of the item that relates to previous interim periods of the same annual period should be included in the restated income of those periods.
3. The portion of the item that relates to previous annual periods should be included in the determination of net income of the first interim period of the fiscal year.

Disclosure Requirements for Interim Reports

Many companies present interim financial information in considerably less detail than that provided in annual financial statements. When publicly traded companies report summarized financial information to security holders at interim dates, at least the following data should be presented:[16]

---

[14]*FASB Statement of Financial Accounting Standards No. 3,* "Reporting Accounting Changes in Interim Financial Statements," 1974, par. 10.
[15]*FASB Statement of Financial Accounting Standards No. 16,* "Prior Period Adjustments," 1977, par. 14.
[16]*APB Opinion No. 28,* par. 30.

1. Selected income statement items, as applicable:
    a. Sales or gross revenues.
    b. Provision for income taxes.
    c. Unusual or infrequently occurring items.
    d. Disposal of a segment of a business.
    e. Extraordinary items, including related income tax effects.
    f. Cumulative effect of accounting change.
    g. Net income.
    h. Earnings per share.
2. Seasonal revenues, costs, or expenses.
3. Contingent items.
4. Changes in accounting principles or estimates, including significant changes in estimates or provision for income taxes.
5. Significant changes in financial position.

When summarized financial information is regularly reported on a quarterly basis, information for the current quarter and the current year to date or last twelve months to date should be presented. In addition, similar information for the preceding year should be presented on a comparative basis. These disclosures are designed to facilitate comparison of the current quarter with a longer period of time (year to date or last twelve months) and with the comparable quarter of the previous year.

Many companies that report on a quarterly basis do not provide a separate fourth quarter statement, since the end of the fourth quarter coincides with the end of the annual reporting period. Where a separate fourth quarter report is not issued, significant events occurring in the fourth quarter should be separately disclosed in the notes to the annual financial statements.

EXHIBIT 25–1
Allright Auto Parks Inc.
Interim Reporting Example

Allright Auto Parks Inc. and Subsidiaries
Consolidated Statement of Income

	Three Months Ended March 31 1982 | 1981 (000's omitted)		Nine Months Ended March 31 1982 | 1981 (000's omitted)	
PARKING SERVICES REVENUES	$23,447	$19,994	$67,506	$60,011
COSTS AND EXPENSES:				
Cost of parking services, exclusive of depreciation and amortization	18,583	15,942	54,058	48,965
Depreciation and amortization	856	755	2,437	2,237
General and administrative expenses	1,514	1,040	3,698	2,989
Interest and debt expense, net of interest income.	595	307	1,271	892
Provision for federal and state income taxes . .	931	981	2,957	2,447
	22,479	19,025	64,421	57,530
PROFIT FROM PARKING OPERATIONS	968	969	3,085	2,481
GAIN ON SALES OF PROPERTY, principally land, net of income taxes	106	741	2,823	1,886
NET INCOME	$ 1,074	$ 1,710	$ 5,908	$ 4,367
EARNINGS PER COMMON SHARE:				
Profit from parking operations	$ .22	$ .23	$ .70	$ .58
Gain on sales of property	.03	.17	.65	.43
Net income.	$ .25	$ .40	$ 1.35	$ 1.01

Consolidated Balance Sheet

ASSETS	March 31 1982 (000's omitted)	June 30 1981	LIABILITIES AND STOCKHOLDERS' EQUITY	March 31 1982 (000's omitted)	June 30 1981
			CURRENT LIABILITIES:		
			Notes payable to banks .	$11,800	$ —
CURRENT ASSETS			Accounts payable and		
Cash and certificates of			accrued liabilities	7,307	6,861
deposit	$ 4,731	$ 1,934	Federal income tax	1,214	462
Receivables and prepaid			Dividend payable	522	464
expenses	1,749	1,346	Current maturities on		
Total current			long-term debt	1,551	1,554
assets	6,480	3,280	Total current		
			liabilities	22,394	9,341
PROPERTY AND					
EQUIPMENT, at cost:			**LONG-TERM DEBT,** less		
Land	40,911	31,097	current maturities	8,805	8,770
Parking garages,					
equipment and			**DEFERRED INCOME TAX**	845	907
leasehold					
improvements	29,336	28,834	**STOCKHOLDERS' EQUITY:**		
	70,247	59,931	Common stock—$75 par		
			value, 10,000,000		
Less accumulated			shares authorized,		
depreciation and			4,497,373 issued, less		
amortization	12,029	14,958	148,038 treasury		
	58,218	44,973	shares	3,262	3,261
			Capital in excess of par		
LEASEHOLDS, at cost less			value	15,484	15,478
amortization	4,147	3,983	Retained earnings	21,220	16,886
			Total stockholders'		
OTHER ASSETS	3,165	2,407	equity	39,966	35,625
	$72,010	$54,643		$72,010	$54,643

The financial statements reflect all adjustments which are, in the opinion of management, necessary to a fair presentation for the interim periods. The statements are prepared from the books without audit, and are not necessarily indicative of fiscal year results due to seasonal and other factors.

SOURCE: Allright Auto Parks Inc., 1982 Third Quarter Report.

The listing presented above represents the *minimum* information to be provided by publicly traded companies that report quarterly information on a regular basis. The APB encouraged such companies to publish condensed balance sheet and funds-flow information at interim dates because such information is often helpful to users of interim financial information in understanding and interpreting the income data that are reported.

Example Financial-Statement Disclosure

The interim report for Allright Auto Parks, Inc., for the third quarter of fiscal 1982 is presented in Exhibit 25–1. Allright Auto Parks, Inc., operates more parking facilities than any other company in the world. The majority of these facilities are leased from or managed for others, but the company also owns a large number of parking facilities. Allright's fiscal year ends on June 30 and the third quarter report for 1982 covers the period January 1 through March 31, 1982.

Comparative income statement figures are presented for the current quarter and the comparative quarter of 1981, as well as the year-to-date (nine-month) figures for each year. Condensed balance sheets are also presented. This goes somewhat beyond the requirement of disclosing significant changes in financial position. The comparative balance sheet items reveal that significant changes, such as in cash and notes payable to banks, have occurred since June 30, 1981 (the end of the previous fiscal year). The company's interim report also includes consolidated statements of changes in financial position for the nine months ended March 31, 1982 and 1981, but they are not presented in Exhibit 25–1. While this information is not required by *APB Opinion No. 28,* management apparently believes that this information is of particular interest to users of Allright's interim reports.

Exhibit 25–1 demonstrates the usefulness of an interim report in assessing the progress of the enterprise toward its annual results. This is the stated objective of interim reporting, and the development of standards for the presentation of this information continues as new areas of financial reporting emerge.

SEGMENT REPORTING

In financial analysis, an important consideration is the industry in which the enterprise operates. The markets in which an enterprise buys and sells vary by industry. The risks and potential rewards of business operation vary considerably by industry. If an enterprise operates in a single industry, consideration of industry factors is relatively straightforward; if an enterprise operates in more than one industry, the consideration of industry factors in financial analysis becomes complicated.

During the 1960s a significant trend toward diversification developed. Many companies that previously operated in a single industry moved into additional industries as a result of natural growth or by acquiring other companies. These companies diversified their operations for several reasons, including the desire of corporate managements to spread the risks of investment over a number of industries and product lines to reduce dependence on any one set of suppliers and customers. This trend became very pronounced, and many **conglomerate companies** (i.e., companies operating in several industries simultaneously) emerged.

For over a decade the APB, and then the FASB, considered whether special information relative to operations in different industries should be required. The name given to this type of disclosure was **segment reporting.** Many advantages and disadvantages of segment reporting were identified, and the problems of separating aggregate financial information into components were carefully considered by the authoritative bodies.

In 1976 the FASB issued *Statement of Financial Accounting Standards No. 14.* While the major consideration centered around information along industry lines, the separation of information on other bases was also considered. *SFAS No. 14* resulted in disclosure requirements in three different areas:[17]

1. The enterprise's operations in different industries.
2. The enterprise's foreign operations and export sales.
3. The enterprise's dependence on major customers.

In subsequent pronouncements, the applicability of these requirements has been limited in several ways. A major limitation was the suspension of segment reporting requirements for nonpublic enterprises, as indicated in *SFAS No. 21.*[18] As a result of this pronouncement, the disclosure requirements discussed here were limited to publicly held companies. Another limitation states that segment disclosures are not required in interim financial presentations.[19]

---

[17]*FASB Statement of Financial Accounting Standards No. 14,* "Financial Reporting for Segments of a Business Enterprise," 1976, par. 3.

[18]*FASB Statement of Financial Accounting Standards No. 21,* "Suspension of the Reporting of Earnings per Share and Segment Information by Nonpublic Companies," 1978, par. 12.

[19]*FASB Statement of Financial Accounting Standards No. 18,* "Financial Reporting for Segments of a Business Enterprise—Interim Financial Statements," 1977, par. 7.

In deciding to require segment reporting for selected companies, the FASB was aware of the fact that the evaluation of risk and return is the central element of investment and lending decisions. Generally, the greater the perceived degree of risk associated with an investment or lending alternative, the greater the required rate of return to the investor or lender. Information presented in an enterprise's financial statements is important in assessing conditions, trends, and ratios that assist in predicting cash flows. Many financial statement users indicate that consolidated information is more useful if supplemented by disaggregated information that assists them in assessing differences in risk resulting from operations under different circumstances.[20] The FASB ultimately determined that disaggregated information along industry lines, by geographic area, and by major customers is most useful for purposes of assessing the risk and return inherent in investment and credit decisions. Therefore, these are the three areas of disclosure specified in *SFAS No. 14* that are discussed in the following sections of this chapter. While specific disclosure requirements are identified by the FASB, considerable flexibility exists in the manner of accumulating the necessary information that underlies this disclosure. This fact, coupled with the fact that each enterprise has unique operating characteristics, led the FASB to conclude that segment information may be of limited usefulness in attempting to compare the information of one enterprise with similar information of other enterprises.

Disclosure

Information About Different Industries

Information about industry segments is required if the enterprise has significant operations in more than one industry. An **industry segment** is defined as a component of an enterprise that tries to earn a profit by providing a product or service or a group of related products or services primarily to customers outside the enterprise. Industry segments are determined by identifying the products and services of an enterprise and grouping those products and services by industry lines. Those industry segments that meet certain materiality guidelines which are described below are then identified as **reportable segments.**

Materiality

Several standardized systems exist for classifying business activities. These include the **Standard Industrial Classification (SIC)** and the **Enterprise Standard Industrial Classification (ESIC),** both of which are used by the U.S. Government. The SIC is a system of classifying business enterprises by the type of economic activity in which they are engaged. The ESIC system is based on the form of business organization. The FASB has indicated that these systems may help an enterprise to identify its industry segments and reportable segments. Since no single system of classification is universally applicable for determining the industry segments of all enterprises, identification of an enterprise's industry segments depends largely on managerial judgment. In determining whether products and services are related or unrelated for purposes of identifying reportable segments, factors such as the following should be considered: the nature of the products and services, the nature of the production process, and markets and marketing methods for the distribution of the products and services.

Management's primary responsibility in identifying industry segments is to separate the enterprise's operations into those components that will be most meaningful to the readers of the financial statements. To provide some indication of the diversity of industry segments included in financial statements, Exhibit 25–2 identifies the segments presented in the financial statements of seven publicly held U.S. corporations.

Each of the companies identified in Exhibit 25–2 also includes a "miscellaneous" or "other" category in which all less significant lines of business are combined.

In identifying reportable segments and preparing the information to be presented, the terms **revenue, operating profit or loss,** and **identifiable assets** are significant:

1. Revenue. The revenue of an industry segment includes both sales to unaffiliated customers

---

[20]*FASB Statement of Financial Accounting Standards No. 14,* pars. 57–60.

EXHIBIT 25–2
Identification of Industry Segments

Corporation	Major Lines of Business
Arcata	Printing Forest products Molded containers
Bendix Corporation	Automotive Aerospace-electronics Industrial
Georgia-Pacific	Building products Pulp, paper, and paperboard products Chemicals
Koppers Company, Inc.	Organic materials Road materials Forest products Engineering metal products Engineering and construction
Pitney Bowes	Business equipment Retail systems Business supplies and services
Teleflex Incorporated	Commercial products Technical products and services
Texaco, Inc.	Gasolines Middle distillates Avjet fuels Residual fuel oils Lubricating oils

---

and intersegment sales or transfers of products or services similar to those sold to unaffiliated customers.

2. **Operating profit or loss.** The operating profit or loss of an industry segment is its revenue less all operating expenses. Operating expenses include expenses that relate to revenues as defined above. Operating expenses which are not directly traceable to an industry segment are allocated on a reasonable basis among the segments benefiting from the expense. Revenues and expenses of a general corporate nature and not associated with the operations of specific industry segments are not included in the determination of operating profit or loss of industry segments.

3. **Identifiable assets.** The identifiable assets of an industry segment are the assets used by the segment, including those assets used exclusively by the segment and an allocated portion of assets used jointly by two or more industry segments. Assets used for general corporate purposes and not used in the operation of any industry segment are not allocated to industry segments.

The criteria for translating **industry segments** into **reportable segments** are based on the revenues, operating profits or losses and identifiable assets of the industry segments. An industry segment constitutes a reportable segment (i.e., a segment which must be disclosed separately) if *any one* of the following criteria is met:

1. Revenue of the segment is 10% or more of the combined revenue of all industry segments.
2. The absolute amount of the operating profit or loss of the segment is 10% or more of the greater (in absolute amount) of the following:

a. The combined operating profit of all industry segments with an operating profit.

b. The combined operating loss of all industry segments with an operating loss.

3. The identifiable assets of the segment are 10% or more of the combined identifiable assets of all industry segments.

Let's consider an example in which we apply these criteria to identify reportable segments. Assume that Conglomerate, Inc., has identified five industry segments in which it operates. Revenue, operating profit (loss), and identifiable assets in millions of dollars for each industry are as follows:

Industry	Revenue	Operating Profit (Loss)	Identifiable Assets
Food products	$150	$ 17	$250
Publishing	125	5	108
Metal products	62	(10)	38
Lumber	30	2	18
Electrical machinery	18	(1)	40
	$385	$ 13	$454

We have seen that any one of the three criteria of 10% revenue, operating profit or loss, and identifiable assets is sufficient for an industry segment to qualify as a reportable segment. In this example all three criteria will be applied to illustrate the entire process of identifying reportable segments.

Based on revenue alone, food products, publishing, and metal products are reportable segments, because revenue associated with each of these exceeds $38.5 million ($385 million × 10%). Based on identifiable assets, food products and publishing are reportable segments, because identifiable assets associated with each of these exceed $45.4 million ($454 million × 10%).

Applying the criterion of 10% of operating profit or loss is somewhat more complicated, because some segments have an operating profit and others have an operating loss. The operating profits must be combined and the operating losses must be combined to determine which is greater (based on the absolute amounts of the two). For Conglomerate, total operating profits are $24 million and total operating losses are $11 million, determined as follows (in millions of dollars):

Industry Segment	Absolute Amount of Operating Profit	Loss
Food products	$17	
Publishing	5	
Metal products		$10
Lumber	2	
Electrical machinery		1
	$24	$11

Since the total profit figure exceeds the total loss figure, $24 million provides the basis for the identification of the reportable segment. Any industry with an **operating profit or loss** of $2.4 millon or greater ($24 million × 10%) qualifies as a reportable segment. Food products, publishing, and metal products are industry segments under this criterion.

Summarizing for Conglomerate, Inc., we have identified the industry segments of food products, publishing, and metal products as reportable segments. The other two industries (lumber and electrical machinery) may be combined, because they do not meet any one of the materiality criteria for identification as reportable segments.

Materiality

Judgment must be applied in identifying reportable segments. Comparability between periods is important. Accordingly, an industry segment that does not meet any of the above criteria in a particular year but that has been significant in the past and is expected to be significant in the future might be considered a reportable segment. Also, an industry that is significant by these criteria in one year but has not been significant in the past and is not expected to be significant in the future may be excluded as a reportable segment. Here we can see the elusive nature of the materiality decision and the significance of applying judgment in making important materiality decisions.

SFAS No. 14 requires that reportable segments account for 75% or more of the combined revenue from sales to unaffiliated customers of all industry segments. If this criterion is not met, industry segments should be redefined to include additional industries as reportable segments so that the amount of revenue from sales to unaffiliated customers accounted for by reportable segments does equal at least 75% of the combined total. This requirement exists to ensure that the reportable segments account for the major portion of business activity of the enterprise as a whole.

For example, assume that Newton Company has identified three reportable segments by applying the criteria of 10% of revenue, operating profit or loss, and identifiable assets. These segments are tobacco, chemicals, and rubber. ("Miscellaneous other" includes amounts from several smaller segments.) Revenue information (in millions of dollars) for these segments is as follows:

Segment	Sales to Unaffiliated Companies	Intersegment Sales	Total Revenue
Tobacco	$ 812	$ 38	$ 850
Chemicals	311	114	425
Rubber	128	125	253
Miscellaneous other	140	8	148
	$1,391	$285	$1,676

To determine if the reportable segments represent a sufficient portion of enterprise operations, 75% of the sales to unaffiliated companies must be accounted for by the reportable segments. This criterion is met in the case of the Newton Company, because sales to unaffiliated companies of the reportable segments total $1,251 ($812 + $311 + $128) and this exceeds 75% of the total of all sales to unaffiliated companies ($1,251/$1,391 = 89.9%). If this condition had not been met, some industry segments included in "miscellaneous other" would need to be combined with each other or with the previously identified reportable segments until the reportable segments accounted for 75% or more of sales to unaffiliated companies.

Once the reportable segments have been identified, the following information must be presented for each reportable segment and for other segments in the aggregate:

1. Revenue.
2. Operating profit or loss.
3. Identifiable assets.
4. Depreciation, depletion, and amortization expense.
5. Expenditures for property, plant, and equipment.
6. Equity in the net income and net assets of vertically integrated investees that are either unconsolidated subsidiaries or accounted for by the equity method.
7. Effects of changes in accounting principle.

Companies may present this information in the body of the primary financial statements, in accompanying notes, or in separate supplemental schedules. If the latter approaches are used, the information should be related to consolidated information in the primary financial statements.

As a practical matter the number of industry segments presented should not be so great that information becomes overly detailed. The FASB indicates a preference for no more than *10* segments. If the number of industry segments exceeds 10, closely related segments should be combined to reduce the number of reportable segments. This requirement is consistent with the FASB's objective of providing useful information to users of financial statements and avoiding information overload in which overly detailed information obscures the important information.

A company that operates in several industries may be dominated by operations in a single industry. A single industry segment is considered dominant if it accounts for more than 90% of revenue, operating profit or loss, and identifiable assets and if no other industry segment meets any of the 10% tests discussed earlier. When an enterprise operates predominantly in a single industry, this industry should be identified in the financial statements.

Information on Foreign Operations and Export Sales

Many companies derive much of their revenue from operations in foreign countries and from exporting goods and services from the United States to foreign countries. **Foreign operations** refers to the presence of production and distribution facilities in countries other than the United States. **Export sales** refers to the operation of facilities in the United States from which goods and services are distributed to foreign countries.

Due to differences in the economic and political environment in foreign countries, significant uncertainty may be associated with foreign operations and export sales. For example, companies with operations in Iran and several South American countries have found **Disclosure** their operations in jeopardy because of political unrest. *SFAS No. 14* establishes disclosure requirements in these areas when certain conditions are met. These requirements apply even if the industry segment disclosures and major customer disclosures do not apply to a particular enterprise. A publicly held company is required to present information concerning foreign operations if *either* of the following conditions is met:[21]

1. Revenue generated by foreign operations from sales to unaffiliated customers is 10% or more of consolidated revenue as reported in the enterprise's income statement.
2. Identifiable assets of the enterprise's foreign operations are 10% or more of consolidated total assets as reported in the enterprise's balance sheet.

If a significant portion of foreign operations is conducted in two or more geographic areas, information should be presented for each area separately. A particular geographic area is considered significant if its revenue from sales to unaffiliated customers or its identifiable assets are 10% or more of related consolidated amounts. The determination of what constitutes a **geographic area** is a management decision and should reflect such factors as proximity, economic relationship, similarity of business environment, and the nature and interrelationship of business activities in various foreign locations.

Information concerning foreign operations that should be presented (by geographic area, if appropriate) includes: (1) revenues; (2) operating profit or loss or some other measure of profitability; and (3) identifiable assets.

If products and services exported from a company's domestic operations to foreign countries make up 10% or more of the total revenue from sales to unaffiliated customers, that amount of revenue must be separately disclosed. If significant exports are made into different geographic areas, separate disclosure by geographic area should be made as considered appropriate in the circumstances.

For example, assume that Proffitt Company is a publicly held U.S. company with significant foreign operations and export sales. The total revenue of $230,000,000 for 1983, all of

---

[21]*FASB Statement of Financial Accounting Standards No. 14,* par. 32.

which is to unaffiliated customers, is distributed over various components of the company's operations as follows:

	Revenue (in millions of dollars)
Domestic operations	
Sales in United States	$105
Export sales	45
	$150
Foreign operations	
France	25
Germany	30
Miscellaneous other countries	25
	80
Total revenue	$230

Assume further that the $45 million of export sales is made in a single geographic area and that the $25 million of revenues from "miscellaneous other countries" represents sales in five countries, none of which exceed $7 million. In addition, none of the foreign operations from which these sales are derived represent an investment in 10% or more of identifiable assets.

Separate disclosure that the Proffitt Company should make is summarized as follows:

Segment	Information Disclosed	Justification
Export portion of domestic operations	Revenue	Exports make up more than 10% of total revenue ($45/$230 = 19.6%)
Foreign operations in France and Germany	Revenue Operating profit Identifiable assets	Revenues in France and Germany exceed 10% of total revenues (France: $25/$230 = 10.9%; Germany: $30/$230 = 13.0%)

Since all exports sales are made to a single geographic area, no further separation of this revenue amount is necessary. Since foreign operations in countries other than France and Germany do not meet the significance tests of 10% of revenues or identifiable assets, no further separation of the amounts attributable to operations in these countries is necessary.

As in the case of industry segment disclosure, information on foreign operations and export sales may be presented in the body of the primary financial statements, in notes to the financial statements, or in supplementary schedules to the financial statements.

Major Customer Information

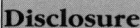

If an enterprise derives 10% or more of its revenue from sales to a single customer, that fact and the amount of revenue from each customer meeting this criterion must be disclosed. The purpose of this disclosure is to make the users of the financial statements aware of the extent of reliance of the enterprise on a small number of customers. The identity of the customer is not required.

To illustrate, suppose a company produces automobile seat belts, which it sells to a major automobile manufacturer as well as to independent automobile-parts suppliers throughout the United States. If a major portion of its sales is to the manufacturer, this fact may be important to readers of the company's financial statements, because future sales are linked to the success of the automobile manufacturer.

EXHIBIT 25–3
Segment Disclosure Example

14. Business Segment Information

By Industry—The Company operates in three industry segments: Industrial; Aviation/Space/Marine; and Automotive. The Industrial operations include a broad line of fluid system components used in virtually every major agricultural, manufacturing and processing operation. Aviation/Space/Marine operations design and produce fluid system equipment for hydraulic, pneumatic, fuel and cryogenic applications in military aircraft, spacecraft, commercial airliners, general aviation aircraft and marine operations. Automotive operations include a broad line of safety products, cooling systems products, specialty tools and equipment sold primarily in the automotive aftermarket and air conditioning components sold primarily to original equipment manufacturers.

Table I contains a summary of the net sales, operating profits, identifiable assets, property additions and depreciation of each business segment for 1982, 1981 and 1980. Corporate assets are principally Headquarters facilities.

Intersegment sales are recorded at fair market value. There was no cutomer to whom sales were 3 percent or more of consolidated sales.

By Geographic Area—The operations of the Company are located primarily in the United States and Europe.

Table II contains a summary of the net sales, operating profits and identifiable assets of each area for 1982, 1981 and 1980. Interarea sales are recorded at fair market value.

Table I—Business Segment Information by Industry

	1982	1981	1980
Net sales, including intersegment sales—			
Industrial:			
Fluid Connectors	$ 332,569	$ 293,379	$ 257,140
Fluidpower	186,153	205,711	209,273
Seal	112,231	116,160	115,731
Refrigeration Components	37,595	35,260	30,406
Identifiable assets:			
Industrial	$ 492,935	$ 473,451	$ 386,351
Aviation/Space/Marine	165,495	170,066	155,387
Automotive	127,370	109,467	107,961
	785,800	752,984	649,699
Corporate assets	12,750	13,905	10,007
	$ 798,550	$ 766,889	$ 659,706
Property additions:			
Industrial	$ 44,779	$ 75,587	$ 37,412
Aviation/Space/Marine	10,022	9,849	10,420
Automotive	4,324	4,387	4,185
Corporate	912	1,006	2,995
	$ 60,037	$ 90,829	$ 55,012
Depreciation:			
Industrial	$ 22,609	$ 19,543	$ 15,235
Aviation/Space/Marine	5,020	4,481	3,958
Automotive	3,931	3,836	3,447
Corporate	521	483	852
	$ 32,081	$ 28,343	$ 23,492

Table II—Business Segment Information by Geographic Area

	1982	1981	1980
Net sales, including interarea sales:			
United States	$ 943,941	$ 917,284	$ 857,181
Europe	179,325	161,247	141,188
All Other	47,271	53,067	48,495
Interarea	(22,456)	(25,707)	(24,488)

Total	668,548	650,510	612,550
Aviation/Space/Marine	257,696	247,322	223,705
Automotive	223,459	209,532	187,635
Intersegment sales	(1,622)	(1,473)	(1,514)
	$1,148,081	$1,105,891	$1,022,376

Income from operations before corporate general and administrative expenses—

Industrial:			
Fluid Connectors	$ 46,298	$ 47,779	$ 43,006
Fluidpower	9,574	17,879	19,753
Seal	10,744	15,866	17,513
Refrigeration Components	2,066	3,893	2,760
Total	68,682	85,417	83,032
Aviation/Space/Marine	31,761	30,893	28,202
Automotive	17,902	18,581	14,718
	118,345	134,891	125,952
Corporate general and administrative expenses	(16,647)	(17,416)	(13,890)
Income from operations	101,698	117,475	112,062
Other income (deductions):			
Interest expense	(20,102)	(22,818)	(20,408)
Interest and other income, net	2,926	1,665	1,722
Gain on disposal of assets	7,993	6,745	—
Income before income taxes	$ 92,515	$ 103,067	$ 93,376

	$1,148,081	$1,105,891	$1,022,376
Income from operations before corporate general and administrative expenses:			
United States	$ 98,722	$ 110,836	$ 103,258
Europe	15,292	15,580	16,431
All Other	4,331	8,475	6,263
	118,345	134,891	125,952
Corporate general and administrative expenses	(16,647)	(17,416)	(13,890)
Income from operations	101,698	117,475	112,062
Other income (deductions):			
Interest expense	(20,102)	(22,818)	(20,408)
Interest and other income, net	2,926	1,665	1,722
Gain on disposal of assets	7,993	6,745	—
Income before income taxes	$ 92,515	$ 103,067	$ 93,376
Identifiable assets:			
United States	$ 573,838	$ 555,353	$ 497,022
Europe	176,617	160,896	118,544
All Other	35,345	36,735	34,133
	785,800	752,984	649,699
Corporate assets	12,750	13,905	10,007
	$ 798,550	$ 766,889	$ 659,706

SOURCE: Parker Hannifin Corporation, 1982 Annual Report.

The disclosure of reliance on **major customers** is required even if the other segment reporting requirements do not apply. If industry segment information is presented and major customer disclosure is also required, the industry segment making the sales should be disclosed.

For purposes of applying the major customer disclosure, a group of entities under common control is considered a single customer. In dealings with domestic governments, the federal government, an individual state government, or an individual local government is considered a single customer. The governments of individual foreign countries are considered single customers.

The major customer disclosure usually appears in the footnotes to the financial statements.

Example Financial-Statement Disclosures

The segment disclosure of Parker Hannifin Corporation for 1982 with the comparative years 1981 and 1980 is presented in Exhibit 25–3. Table I includes industry segment information; Table II includes segment information by geographic area.

As shown in Table I, the company operates in three industries: industrial, aviation/space/marine, and automotive. Revenue figures for these industries are presented with intersegment sales deducted to obtain the net sales figure. Income from operations before corporate expenses is presented by industry segment; then corporate expenses and interest expense are deducted and miscellaneous income amounts are added to obtain income before income taxes. Identifiable assets are presented by industry segment, and corporate assets are added to obtain total assets. The following figures in this schedule reconcile with the same items in the company's financial statements: net sales, income before income taxes, and total assets. Property additions and depreciation are the final items presented in Table I.

Table II presents sales by geographic area and combines all areas not meeting the 10% significance criterion in the caption "all other." Interarea sales are deducted to obtain net sales. The presentation of income before income taxes and identifiable assets is similar to the industry disclosure in Table I except the information is presented by geographic area.

The note introducing the segment disclosure indicates that there was no customer to whom sales were 10% or more of consolidated sales. This note also includes a brief explanation of the industry segments and geographic areas in which the company operates.

In Exhibit 25–4 you will find the major customer disclosure from Bendix Corporation's 1981 annual report. In the annual report from which this disclosure was drawn, total revenues for 1981, 1980, and 1979 were $4,425.4 million, $3,864.1 million, and $3,412.7 million, respectively.

CONCLUDING REMARKS

Do current financial reporting requirements pose an unreasonable burden on small or private companies? This is a topic of much conversation in the business community and in the

---

EXHIBIT 25–4
Major Customer Disclosure Example

Sales to a large automotive customer amounted to $394.9 million in 1981, $344.8 million in 1980, and $448.1 million in 1979; sales to the U.S. government and its agencies, virtually all from the aerospace-electronics segment, amounted to $866.2 million in 1981, $749.9 million in 1980 and $618.0 million in 1979.

SOURCE: Bendix Corporation, 1981 Annual Report.

accounting profession in the 1980s. As the FASB and other professional organizations continue to study this significant question, we should watch for changes that may significantly impact the financial reporting of small or private companies.

The FASB has already recognized this problem by relieving companies that are not publicly held from complex disclosure requirements in selected areas. In Chapter 25, we have considered two of those areas: interim reporting and segment reporting. We consider two additional areas in the next two chapters: earnings per share and constant dollar/current cost disclosures.

One rationale for this developing trend is that most publicly held enterprises must report to the Securities and Exchange Commission. Information reported to the SEC is publicly available to current and prospective investors. Since information provided by these enterprises is already available, their reporting requirements should not unduly influence standards of reporting under GAAP applicable to all enterprises. In the Appendix to this chapter we briefly introduce the process of reporting to the SEC.

KEY POINTS

1. Standards overload refers to the burden on small or private companies that is due to the requirement that GAAP be followed by all companies (with limited disclosure exceptions).

2. Some accountants believe that many of the accounting and disclosure requirements of GAAP were developed with large public companies in mind. They feel that the reporting environment of small or private companies is sufficiently different to warrant different financial reporting requirements. Several alternatives have been proposed to simplify financial reporting for small or private companies.

3. The FASB has recognized the standards overload problem in the past by limiting the applicability of authoritative pronouncements in certain areas to publicly held companies. These areas include interim reporting, segment reporting, earnings per share, and constant dollar/current cost disclosures.

4. Interim reporting refers to reporting for periods of less than a year. In developing standards of interim reporting, the APB adopted the integral view, in which

the interim period is viewed as an important part of the annual period. Accounting and disclosure requirements are specified that assist the user of the interim information in assessing progress of the enterprise toward the annual results.

5. The FASB has specified requirements that publicly held companies provide disaggregated information concerning several important aspects of their operations: operations in different industry segments, operations in different geographic areas, and reliance on major customers.

6. Industry segment information must be presented if a material portion of the company's operations extends over more than one industry segment or product line.

7. Geographic area information must be presented if a material portion of the company's operations is carried out in more than one geographic area.

8. Major customer disclosure is required if the company generates a substantial portion of its sales revenue from a single customer.

APPENDIX A REPORTING TO THE SECURITIES AND EXCHANGE COMMISSION

The Securities and Exchange Commission, frequently referred to as the SEC, was established by Congress in 1934 to assist in the regulation of securities markets in the United States. The SEC plays an important role in

the initial sale of securities in the public markets and in the subsequent exchange of securities between buyers and sellers.

The SEC is a complex governmental organization

which operates under the authority of several federal laws. SEC reporting is frequently covered in advanced accounting courses, often at the graduate level. Our objective in this appendix is to give you a brief overview of some aspects of the SEC to help you understand its significance in the overall environment of financial reporting. To accomplish this objective, we look briefly at the objectives of the SEC, the organizational structure of the SEC, the primary legal acts under which the SEC operates, and the process of registration with the SEC. A detailed coverage of these and other aspects of SEC reporting is left to advanced accounting texts and texts specifically designed to cover SEC reporting in depth.

OBJECTIVES OF THE SEC

The need for the SEC is closely tied to the growth of the corporate form of business organization. One advantage of the corporation is the widespread distribution of financial interests accomplished by issuing debt and equity securities. The separation of ownership and management that is characteristic of the corporate form of organization created the need for reliable financial information on which investors could base their financial decisions. Abuses in the capital markets during the period preceding the formation of the SEC in 1934 prompted governmental action to protect the interests of investors.

The primary objective of the SEC is to ensure the full and fair disclosure of all material facts concerning securities offered to the public. As mentioned in a later section of this discussion, the authority to meet this objective comes primarily from the Securities Act of 1933 and the Securities Exchange Act of 1934. These acts, in conjunction with others, give the SEC the authority to protect the public interest by requiring the availability of adequate information when securities are sold or exchanged. The SEC's activities, therefore, center around publicly held companies that are initially offering securities to the public or whose securities trade between security holders in the secondary markets.

ORGANIZATIONAL STRUCTURE

The SEC consists of five members appointed by the president of the United States. The commissioners have five-year terms, and the term of one commissioner expires each year. One commissioner is appointed by the president to serve as chairman. The commission has a large professional staff consisting primarily of accountants, lawyers, and financial personnel. The commission has headquarters in Washington, D.C., with regional and branch offices throughout the United States.

The SEC is organized in five divisions: Division of Corporation Finance, Division of Corporate Regulation, Division of Market Regulation, Division of Investment Management, and Division of Enforcement.

The **Division of Corporation Finance** is particularly important for accountants. This division is responsible for establishing financial accounting and disclosure standards for companies under SEC jurisdiction. In addition, the division is responsible for reviewing registration statements and reports that companies file with the SEC to determine whether the information is prepared in accordance with the rules and regulations of the SEC. The SEC does not audit a company's financial statements. Rather, reliance is placed on the audit report of independent CPAs. Thus, the work of accountants is very important in reporting to the SEC in terms of both the preparation of the financial information that is reported and the audit of this information.

There are many offices within the SEC. The office of the Chief Accountant is particularly important to accountants, because the Chief Accountant is the primary accounting officer of the SEC and has responsibility for all accounting and auditing matters. The Chief Accountant is responsible for all rules and regulations governing the form and content of financial statements that must be filed with the SEC.

LEGAL ACTS UNDERLYING SEC ACTIVITIES

The SEC receives its authority from several securities laws. The first law was the Securities Act of 1933. The purpose of this act is to regulate the initial sale of securities rather than the exchange of securities after their initial sale. Specifically, the Securities Act of 1933 intends to provide investors with financial and other information concerning securities offered for public sale and to prohibit fraudulent acts in the sale of securities.

The Securities Exchange Act of 1934 is designed to regulate the trading of securities on secondary markets through stock exchanges and other brokers. The SEC was created under the Securities Exchange Act of 1934. This act and subsequent amendments gives the SEC broad powers to regulate the trading of securities on stock exchanges and in over-the-counter markets. The Securities Act of 1934 establishes extensive re-

---

EXHIBIT 25–5
Selected Acts Affecting SEC Operations

Act	Purpose
Public Utility Holding Company Act of 1935	To correct abuses in the financing and operation of electric and gas public utility holding company systems.
Trust Indenture Act of 1939	To require that debt securities offered for public sale be issued under a trust indenture approved by the SEC.
Investment Company Act of 1940	To govern the issuance of securities of companies engaged in the business of investing, reinvesting, and trading securities.
Investment Advisers Act of 1940	To govern the conduct of brokers and dealers in securities.
Securities Investor Protection Act of 1970	To provide a fund through the Securities Investor Protection Corporation for the protection of investors.
Foreign Corrupt Practices Act of 1977	To govern questionable or illegal payments by U.S. corporations to foreign political officials and to require accurate and fair record-keeping and internal control systems by all public companies.

---

porting requirements for companies having over $3,000,000 in assets and 500 or more stockholders. Most of the information required by the SEC is made publicly available and is thus available to investors.

The responsibility of the SEC has been broadened and strengthened through the passage of a number of additional laws since the original acts in 1933 and 1934. Several of these acts are listed in Exhibit 25–5, along with a brief description of their purposes.

The SEC has statutory authority to prescribe the accounting principles to be used by companies under its jurisdiction. What is the relationship, then, between the SEC and the FASB? In the past the SEC has relied heavily on the accounting profession to set accounting standards. Currently the SEC monitors the activities of the FASB, and the two bodies work closely to establish accounting principles acceptable to both bodies. From time to time, the SEC exhibited its legal strength by moving the FASB in a particular direction. This has taken the form of encouraging the FASB to consider a particular subject or to adopt a particular position on a subject. In a few extreme cases, the SEC adopted a position different from the FASB and prohibited the use of certain practices. In other cases the SEC established more extensive disclosure requirements for its registrants than were required for all companies under authoritative accounting pronouncements. At various places in this text we have discussed areas of disagreement between the SEC and the FASB, pointing out the reliance of the SEC on the FASB but also noting the ultimate legal authority of the SEC.

SEC REGISTRATION

Regulation S-X specifies the form and content of the financial statements and related schedules and notes required under all of the acts administered by the SEC. *Regulation S-K* specifies certain nonfinancial information which must be included. The SEC has issued a large number of *Accounting Series Releases,* which deal with amendments or revisions of *Regulation S-X* and policy statements concerning certain accounting problems, as well as other items.

Registration of the initial sale of securities under the Securities Act of 1933 begins by filing with the SEC the required information on the proper *form.* While many different forms are available for filing under the Securities Act of 1933, **Form S-1** is widely used because it is applicable for all issues for which one of the specialized forms is not appropriate. The forms on which companies file with the SEC are very specific in terms of the financial and nonfinancial information that must be provided. Information provided on the appropriate form is called a **registration statement.**

The registration statement is examined by the SEC when it is initially submitted. If deficiencies are noted by the SEC, they issue a letter in which the specific deficiencies in the registration statement are outlined. At this point changes are usually made, resulting in an amended registration statement. Assuming that this amended registration statement is acceptable to the SEC, the statement becomes effective and the company is permitted to proceed with the sale of the securities covered by the registration statement.

The Securities Exchange Act of 1934 deals with the exchange of securities after the initial sale. An important aspect of this act is the continuous flow of information which companies whose securities are traded must provide. Many forms are used to provide this information. The most widely used forms are the 8-K, the 10-K, and the 10-Q, which are described in the following paragraphs.

Form 8-K is used to provide information on a current basis when certain specified events occur. For example, if a company goes into bankruptcy or receivership, Form 8-K must be filed. Likewise, if a company changes the CPA serving as its external auditor, Form 8-K must be filed. The 8-K must be filed within 15 days of the event being reported in most cases.

Form 10-K is an annual form which must be filed within 90 days of the end of the company's fiscal year. While this form includes much of the information in the company's annual report, it also includes additional information required only by the SEC. Form 10-K requirements include the basic financial statements and related notes as well as a great deal of additional information.

Within 45 days of the end of each quarter a company must file **Form 10-Q.** The Form 10-Q requirements are similar to the Form 10-K requirements except that the financial statement information may be condensed. Form 10-Q requires a narrative analysis by management of the results of the quarter covered by the report with appropriate explanation of the quarterly results compared to the previous quarter and the same quarter of the previous year.

CONCLUDING REMARKS

The SEC has broad legal authority to establish accounting and disclosure requirements for companies that are required to report to it. To date the SEC has exercised this authority through a cooperative effort with the accounting profession to advance the quality of financial reporting in the United States. The SEC does not protect investors from sustaining losses on securities. Rather, its purpose is to ensure that companies provide investors with adequate information on which to base their investment decisions. In some cases, reporting to the SEC imposes significant requirements on companies in addition to those required by generally accepted accounting principles.

QUESTIONS

25–1 Briefly explain "standards overload."

25–2 Briefly stated, what are the three major dimensions to the standards overload problem?

25–3 What is the distinction between a small and large company? What is the distinction between a public and private company?

25–4 Describe briefly possible differences between small or private companies and large public companies that might lead to the conclusion that different financial reporting standards are appropriate for the two.

25–5 What possible directions of change may take place in the future to alleviate the standards overload problem?

25–6 What is meant by "interim reporting"?

25–7 Explain the difference between the discrete (independent) and integral (dependent) views of interim financial reporting periods.

25–8 Which of the two concepts of interim reporting—the discrete or the integral—appears to be supported by the authoritative accounting pronouncements? Support your position by references to specific interim reporting practices.

25–9 Describe the process by which income tax expense should be determined in interim periods.

25–10 Should separately classified income statement items, such as extraordinary items, be prorated over several interim periods or recognized in a single interim period? Explain.

25–11 *APB Opinion No. 28* identifies several items of information that must be presented when publicly traded companies provide interim information to security holders on a regular basis. In addition to current-quarter information, for what additional time periods must information be presented? What is the purpose of this additional information?

25–12 In considering interim financial reporting, the APB concluded that such reporting should be viewed in which of the following ways?

[a] As a special type of reporting that need *not* follow generally accepted accounting principles.

[b] As useful only *if* activity is evenly spread throughout the year so that estimates are unnecessary.

[c] As reporting for a basic accounting period.

[d] As reporting for an integral part of an annual period.

(AICPA adapted)

25–13 Which of the following is an inherent difficulty in the determination of the results of operations on an interim basis?

[a] Cost of sales reflects only the amount of product expense allocable to revenue recognized as of the interim date.

[b] Depreciation on an interim basis is a partial estimate of the actual annual amount.

[c] Costs expensed in one interim period may benefit other periods.

[d] Revenues from long-term construction contracts accounted for by the percentage-of-completion method are based on annual completion, and interim estimates may be incorrect.

(AICPA adapted)

25–14 Minimum disclosure requirements for companies issuing interim financial information would include which of the following?

[a] An interim statement of financial position and statement of changes in financial position data.

[b] Primary and fully diluted earnings-per-share data for each period presented.

[c] Sales and cost of goods sold for the current quarter and the current year to date.

[d] The contribution margin by product line for the current quarter and the current year to date.

(AICPA adapted)

25–15 Which of the following reporting practices is permissible for interim financial reporting?

[a] Use of the gross-profit method for interim inventory pricing.

[b] Use of the direct-costing method for determining manufacturing inventories.

[c] Deferral of unplanned variances under a standard-cost system until year-end.

[d] Deferral of inventory market declines until the end of the year.

(AICPA adapted)

25–16 Discuss the basic rationale behind the need of financial statement users for information by industry for an enterprise that operates in several industries at the same time.

25–17 The FASB outlines disclosure requirements in three different areas: industry operations, foreign operations and export sales, and major customers. Are these requirements independent of each other?

25–18 Which of the following is the primary purpose of segment reporting information?

[a] Interperiod comparisons of the particular enterprise.

[b] Comparisons between different enterprises.

25–19 What is the distinction between the terms "industry segment" and "reportable segment"? How is each determined?

25–20 What guidelines exist to ensure that industry segment information conforms with each of the following:

[a] It incorporates the majority of total enterprise operations.

[b] It does not become overly detailed by the presentation of an excessive number of industries?

25–21 What is the basic rationale underlying the requirement for disclosure of foreign operations and export sales?

25–22 Define major customer. What is the purpose of major customer disclosure?

CASES

C25–1 Timely financial information is important to users of financial statements. As a result, many companies produce financial information more frequently than annually.

Instructions

[a] How are revenues, costs, and expenses recognized for interim reporting related to those recognized for year-end reporting?

[b] How are income taxes recognized at interim dates?

(AICPA adapted)

C25–2 Interim financial reporting has become an

important topic in accounting. There has been considerable discussion as to the proper method of reflecting results of operations at interim dates. Accordingly, the APB issued an opinion clarifying some aspects of interim financial reporting.

Instructions

[a] Discuss generally how revenue should be recognized at interim dates. Discuss specifically how revenue should be recognized for industries subject to large seasonal fluctuations in revenue and for industries that are involved in long-term contracts and that use the percentage-of-completion method at annual reporting dates.

[b] Discuss generally how product and period costs should be recognized at interim dates. Also discuss how inventory and cost of goods sold may be afforded special accounting treatment at interim dates.

[c] Discuss how the provision for income taxes is computed and reflected in interim financial statements.

(AICPA adapted)

C25–3 The following statement is an excerpt from Paragraphs 9 and 10 of *APB Opinion No. 28*, "Interim Financial Reporting":

Interim financial information is essential to provide investors and others with timely information as to the progress of the enterprise. The usefulness of such information rests on the relationship that it has to the annual results of operations. Accordingly, the [APB] concluded that each interim period should be viewed primarily as an integral part of an annual period.

In general, the results for each interim period should be based on the accounting principles and practices used by an enterprise in the preparation of its latest annual financial statements unless a change in an accounting practice or policy has been adopted in the current year. However, the [APB] concluded that certain accounting principles and practices followed for annual reporting purposes may require modification at interim reporting dates so that the reported results for the interim period may better relate to the results of operations for the annual period.

Instructions

Listed below are six independent cases on how accounting facts might be reported on an individual company's interim financial reports. For *any four* of the six cases, state whether the method proposed to be used

for interim reporting would be acceptable under generally accepted accounting principles applicable to interim financial data. Support each answer with a brief explanation.

[a] Coe Company was reasonably certain it would have an employee strike in the third quarter. As a result, it shipped heavily during the second quarter but management plans to defer the recognition of the sales in excess of the normal sales. The deferred sales will be recognized as sales in the third quarter, when the strike is in progress. The Coe management thinks this is more nearly representative of normal second and third quarter operations.

[b] Day Company takes a physical inventory at year-end for annual financial-statement purposes. Inventory and cost of sales reported in the interim quarterly statements are based on estimated gross profit rates, because a physical inventory would result in a cessation of operations. Day Company has reliable perpetual inventory records.

[c] Ball Company is planning to report one-fourth of its annual pension expense each quarter.

[d] Fragle Company wrote inventory down to reflect lower of cost or market in the first quarter of 1985. At year-end the market exceeds the original acquisition cost of this inventory. Consequently, management plans to write the inventory back up to its original cost as a year-end adjustment.

[e] Good Company realized a large gain on the sale of investments at the beginning of the second quarter. The company wants to report one-third of the gain in each of the remaining quarters.

[f] Jay Company has estimated its annual audit fee. The Jay management plans to prorate this expense equally over the four quarters.

(CMA adapted)

C25–4 Allen Manufacturing Company, a California corporation listed on the Pacific Coast Stock Exchange budgeted activities for 1985 as follows:

	Amount	Units
Net sales	$6,000,000	1,000,000
Cost of goods sold	3,600,000	1,000,000
Gross margin	2,400,000	
Selling, general, and administrative expenses	1,400,000	
Operating earnings	1,000,000	
Nonoperating revenues and expenses	–0–	
Earnings before income taxes	1,000,000	

Estimated income taxes (current and deferred)	550,000	
Net earnings	$ 450,000	
Earnings per share of common stock	$4.50	

Allen has operated profitably for many years and has experienced a seasonal pattern of sales volume and production similar to the following amounts forecasted for 1985. Sales volume is expected to follow a quarterly pattern of 10%, 20%, 35%, and 35%, respectively, because of the seasonality of the industry. Because of production and storage limitations, production is expected to follow a pattern of 20%, 25%, 30%, and 25%, per quarter, respectively.

At the conclusion of the first quarter of 1985, the controller of Allen prepared and issued the following interim report for public release:

	Amount	Units
Net sales	$ 600,000	100,000
Cost of goods sold	360,000	100,000
Gross margin	240,000	
Selling, general and administrative expenses	275,000	
Operating loss	(35,000)	
Loss from warehouse fire	(175,000)	
Loss before income taxes	(210,000)	
Estimated income taxes	–0–	
Net loss	$(210,000)	
Loss per share of common stock	$(2.10)	

The following additional information is available for the first quarter just completed, but was not included in the public information released:

[1] The company uses a standard cost system in which standards are set at currently attainable levels on an annual basis. At the end of the first quarter there was underapplied fixed factory overhead (volume variance) of $50,000 that was treated as an asset at the end of the quarter. Production during the quarter was 200,000 units, of which 100,000 were sold.

[2] The selling, general, and administrative expenses were budgeted on a basis of $900,000 fixed expenses for the year plus $.50 variable expenses per unit of sales.

[3] Assume that the warehouse fire loss met the conditions of an extraordinary loss. The warehouse had an undepreciated cost of $320,000; $145,000 was recovered from insurance on the warehouse. No other gains or losses are anticipated this year from similar events or transactions, nor has Allen had any similar losses in

preceding years; thus, the full loss will be deductible as an ordinary loss for income tax purposes.

[4] The effective income tax rate, for federal and state taxes combined, is expected to average 55% of earnings before income taxes during 1985. There are no permanent differences between pretax-accounting earnings and taxable income.

[5] Earnings per share were computed on the basis of 100,000 shares of capital stock outstanding. Allen has only one class of stock issued, no long-term debt outstanding, and no stock option plan.

Instructions

[a] Without reference to the specific situation described above, what are the standards of disclosure for interim financial data (published interim financial reports) for publicly traded companies? Explain.

[b] Identify the weakness in form and content of Allen's interim report without reference to the additional information.

[c] For each of the five items of additional information, indicate the preferable treatment for each item for interim reporting purposes and explain why that treatment is preferable.

(AICPA adapted)

C25–5 Multipro, Inc., manufactures a wide variety of pharmaceuticals, medical instruments, and other related medical supplies. Eighteen months ago the company developed and began to market a new product line of antihistamine drugs under various trade names. Sales and profitability of this product line during the current fiscal year greatly exceeded management's expectations. The new product line will account for 10% of the company's total sales and 12% of the company's operating income for the fiscal year ending June 30, 1984. Management believes sales and profits will be significant for several years.

Multipro fears that disclosure in its annual financial statements about the volume and profitability of its new product line will adversely affect its market position in relation to its competitors. Management is not sure how *FASB Statement of Financial Accounting Standards No. 14,* "Financial Reporting for Segments of a Business Enterprise," applies in this case.

Instructions

[a] What is the purpose of requiring that segment information be disclosed in financial statements?

[b] Explain the factors which should be considered when attempting to decide how products should be grouped to determine a single business segment.

[c] What options, if any, does Multipro, Inc., have regarding the disclosure of its new antihistamine product line? Explain your answer.

(CMA adapted)

C25–6 The following case consists of two *independent* parts.

Part 1. In order to properly understand current generally accepted accounting principles with respect to accounting for and reporting on segments of a business enterprise, as stated by the FASB in its *SFAS No. 14,* it is necessary to be familiar with certain unique terminology.

Instructions

With respect to segments of a business enterprise, explain the following terms:

[a] Industry segment
[b] Revenue
[c] Operating profit and loss
[d] Identifiable assets

Part 2. A central issue in reporting on industry segments of a business enterprise is the determination of which segments are reportable.

Instructions

[a] What are the tests to determine whether or not an industry segment is reportable?
[b] What is the test to determine if enough industry segments have been separately reported? What is the guideline on the maximum number of industry segments to be shown?

(AICPA adapted)

EXERCISES

E25–1 In January 1985 Hunter, Inc., estimated that its year-end bonus to executives would be $240,000 for 1985. The amount paid for the year-end bonus for 1984 was $224,000. The estimate for 1985 is subject to year-end adjustment.

Instructions

Select the amount of bonus expense that should be reflected in Hunter's quarterly income statement for the three months ended March 31, 1985, and justify your choice.
[a] $0
[b] $56,000
[c] $60,000
[d] $240,000

(AICPA adapted)

E25–2 In August 1985 Ella Company spent $150,000 on an advertising campaign for subscriptions to its magazine on preparing for the skiing season. There are only two issues: one in October and one in November. The magazine is sold only on a subscription

basis, and the subscriptions started in October 1985. Ella's fiscal year ends on March 31, 1986.

Instructions

Select the amount of expense that should be included in Ella's quarterly income statement for the three months ended December 31, 1985, as a result of this expenditure, and justify your choice.
[a] $37,000
[b] $50,000
[c] $75,000
[d] $150,000

(AICPA adapted)

E25–3 In May 1985 an inventory loss of $600,000 occurred from a market decline. Kup Company recorded this loss in May 1985 after its March 31, 1985, quarterly report was issued. None of this loss was recovered by the end of the year.

Instructions

Explain the general treatment of market declines in

		Three Months Ended		
	Mar. 31, 1985	*June 30, 1985*	*Sept. 30, 1985*	*Dec. 31, 1985*
[a]	–0–	–0–	–0–	$600,000
[b]	–0–	$200,000	$200,000	200,000
[c]	–0–	600,000	–0–	–0–
[d]	$150,000	150,000	150,000	150,000

inventory in interim reports. How does this treatment apply to Kup's circumstances? Select the answer from the bottom of page 1172 that shows how Kup's loss should be reflected in its quarterly income statements.

(AICPA adapted)

E25–4 In May 1985 Roy Company spent $200,000 on an advertising campaign for subscriptions to the school magazine it sells. The subscriptions do not start until September 1985, and the magazine is sold only on a yearly subscription basis.

Instructions

How would you recognize the $200,000 advertising expense in the interim periods of 1985? Select the amount of the advertising expense which should be included in Roy's quarterly income statement for the three months ended June 30, 1985, and justify your choice.
[a] $0
[b] $50,000
[c] $66,667
[d] $200,000

(AICPA adapted)

E25–5 Texas Products Company reported income before income tax of $85,000 and $128,000 for the first two quarters of 1984. The company's estimate of the annual effective income tax rate was 46% at the end of the first quarter and 42% at the end of the second quarter.

Instructions

Determine the income tax expense for the first two quarters of 1984.

E25–6 McKee Manufacturing's revenue, standard cost of goods sold, and variance information for the four quarters of 1985 are as follows:

Instructions

Determine the amount of gross profit to be recognized in each quarter's income statement.

E25–7 Bell Company made sales in 1984 to customers as follows:

Blue Company	$ 8,000,000
White Company	4,200,000
Brown Company	2,500,000
Red Company	1,850,000
Domestic governments	9,500,000
Foreign governments	7,260,000
Other	20,190,000
	$53,500,000

The following additional information is available:
[1] "Other" sales include sales to many customers, none of which exceed $1,000,000.
[2] Red and White Companies are both subsidiaries of Purple Company. Sales made to Purple Company amounted to $850,000 and are included in the "other" amount.
[3] Sales to domestic governments include $6,000,000 to federal governmental agencies, $2,250,000 to state governmental agencies, and $1,250,000 to local governmental agencies.
[4] Sales to foreign governments consisted of $4,800,000 to the government of Country Yellow and $2,460,000 to the government of Country Maroon.

Instructions

Identify the customers for which major customer disclosure must be made, justifying each one.

E25–8 Sherman Production Company operates in three industries. Information on industry operations is as follows:

	Quarter Ending			
	Mar. 31, 1985	**June 30, 1985**	**Sept. 30, 1985**	**Dec. 31, 1985**
Revenue	$450,000	$480,000	$510,000	$502,000
Standard cost of goods sold	200,000	220,000	240,000	250,000
Variance from standard*				
Planned	10,000	(15,000)	20,000	—
Unplanned	12,000	(7,000)	5,000	8,000

*Amounts in parentheses represent favorable variances or cost reductions. Other amounts represent unfavorable variances or additions to cost.

	Identifiable Assets	Revenue	Operating Profit
Industry 1	$600,000	$695,000	$43,500
Industry 2	50,000	55,000	2,750
Industry 3	12,000	15,000	975
	$662,000	$765,000	$47,225

Instructions

Identify the reporting requirements for the company in terms of industry segments in accordance with *SFAS No. 14.*

E25–9 Magic Manufacturing Company operates in four basic industries. Operating statistics (in millions of dollars) for the four industries are as follows for 1985:

Industry	Revenue	Operating Profit	Identifiable Assets
Plastics	$100	$27	$120
Metals	75	24	67
Tobacco	18	4	20
Glass	7	1	10

There were no sales between segments in 1985.

Instructions

Determine the reportable industry segments for Magic Manufacturing for 1985, applying all relevant criteria from *SFAS No. 14.* Present figures to support your conclusions.

E25–10 Extra Special, Inc., is a publicly held company with domestic (U.S.) operations as well as several operating units in foreign countries. Information (in millions of dollars) concerning these operations is summarized below:

	Revenue	Operating Profit	Identifiable Assets
Domestic operations	$545	$ 60	$508
Foreign operations			
Country A	160	20	250
Country B	80	8	106
Country C	45	24	50
Country D	30	(5)	71
Consolidated totals	$860	$107	$985

Instructions

[a] Identify the separate disclosures related to foreign operations which must be presented in accordance with *SFAS No. 14,* justifying each item requiring disclosure.

[b] Prepare the disclosure of information concerning foreign operations for Extra Special, Inc., based on the limited information given, in a format of your choice.

E25–11 In its U.S. production facility Weatherly Manufacturing Company produces a single product, which it sells in a number of domestic and foreign markets. In 1985 sales totaled $12,000,000, of which $5,500,000 were export sales in the following geographic areas:

European Common Market countries	$3,000,000
South American countries	2,000,000
Miscellaneous other countries	500,000
	$5,500,000

Instructions

Determine the specific information concerning domestic and export sales which must be presented with the 1985 financial statements to comply with the reporting requirements of *SFAS No. 14.*

E25–12 Farley Fabrications, Inc., is subject to industry segment reporting requirements. Operating figures for 1984 are as follows:

Industry	Revenue	Operating Profit	Identifiable Assets
Metal containers	$ 850,000	$177,000	$ 628,000
Recording	700,000	5,000	919,000
Stereophonic equipment	200,000	22,000	275,000
Lawn equipment	172,000	32,000	250,000
Household appliances	658,000	90,000	400,000
Electronic calculators	230,000	11,000	198,000
	$2,810,000	$337,000	$2,670,000

Interindustry sales are as follows: metal containers to household appliances, $82,000; recording to stereophonic equipment, $17,000.

Instructions

Determine the industries which require separate disclosure in the 1984 financial statements. Present computations to support your conclusions.

E25–13 Operating profit and loss figures for the seven

industries in which the Dexter Company operates are as follows:

	1985 Operating Profit (Loss)
Industry 1	$1,100,000
Industry 2	100,000
Industry 3	650,000
Industry 4	(208,000)

Industry 5	(14,000)
Industry 6	5,000
Industry 7	(2,000)
	$1,631,000

Instructions

Identify those industries which meet the criterion of 10% or more of operating profit or loss for Dexter Company for 1985.

PROBLEMS

P25–1 Campbell Company reports quarterly to its stockholders. Condensed financial information is presented, emphasizing quarterly results of operations. The company reports on a calendar-year basis with quarterly reports provided on March 31, June 30, September 30, and December 31.

Selected information for the four quarters of 1985 is shown below. All "other costs and expenses" are to be recognized in the period incurred except the following:

[1] $80,000 of machinery repairs incurred in the first quarter are expected to benefit each quarter equally.

[2] Advertising costs are allocated among the remaining quarters of the annual period, including the quarter in which the costs are incurred, on the basis of the historical pattern of sales: 20%, 30%, 15%, and 35% in the first through fourth quarters, respectively. Advertising expense amounted to $100,000 of the other costs and expenses incurred in the second quarter.

other methods of reducing income taxes which had not previously been anticipated.

Figures for the four quarters of 1985 are:

End of Quarter	Anticipated Annual Income Tax Rate at This Date	Income for Quarter Ending on This Date
Mar. 31, 1985	46%	$150,000
June 30, 1985	44	185,000
Sept. 30, 1985	42	127,000
Dec. 31, 1985	40	168,000

Instructions

Determine the amount of income tax expense which should be recognized in determining net income for each quarter of 1985.

P25–3 Fisher Corporation is preparing information for its 1985 second quarter interim report that is provided to stockholders. The company is on a calendar-

	Quarter			
	1	*2*	*3*	*4*
Revenue	$550,000	$675,000	$352,000	$890,000
Costs associated directly with revenue	265,000	308,000	176,000	490,000
Other costs and expenses (indicated in the period incurred)	110,000	165,000	45,000	162,000

Instructions

Determine income before income taxes for each quarter of 1985.

P25–2 Ross Company makes a quarterly estimate of the annual income tax rate and recognizes income tax expense on a cumulative year-to-date basis in the interim reports at the end of each quarter. For 1985, the expected income tax rate gradually declined as the company took advantage of certain tax credits and

year basis. Information which has been accumulated to date includes the following:

[1] Revenue for the second quarter totaled $2,785,000, including a reduction for a loss on the sale of securities of $28,000, which is considered infrequent but not unusual.

[2] Expenses directly related to revenues are $1,600,000. During the first quarter of 1985, a loss of $125,000 on inventory declines below cost was recognized. During the second quarter inventory market val-

ues increased to a level in excess of cost. This increase in market is not reflected in the revenue or expense figures described above.

[3] Other costs and expenses incurred during the second quarter totaled $285,000. None of these are allocable to other quarters. In the first quarter, however, other costs and expenses of $40,000 were allocated to the second quarter.

[4] Income tax expense of $86,250 was recognized in the first quarter report. This was determined in the following way:

Income before income tax to Mar. 31, 1985	$187,500
Estimated annual income tax rate	46%
	$ 86,250

At June 30, 1985, the estimate of the annual effective income tax rate was revised to 42%.

Instructions

Determine net income for the quarter ended June 30, 1985.

P25–4 Carter Construction Company is publicly held and provides stockholders with quarterly financial information prepared in accordance with generally accepted accounting principles.

Selected data for the four quarters of 1985 are presented in the following schedule:

which are expected to benefit all periods equally.

[3] Estimates of the annual effective income tax rate made at the end of each quarter are as follows: March 31, 46%; June 30, 40%; September 30, 44%; December 31, 42%.

[4] 100,000 shares of common stock were outstanding throughout 1985. The company has no preferred stock.

[5] Sales and costs directly associated with sales in 1985 followed a relatively normal seasonal pattern based on the past performance of Carter Construction Company.

Instructions

[a] Prepare condensed income statements for each quarter of 1985, including schedules to support your figures.

[b] Based on the limited information given in this problem, prepare a schedule for the quarter ending September 30, 1985, which includes the minimum disclosures required to be presented to stockholders.

P25–5 Brown Company is a publicly held corporation which is subject to the reporting requirements of *SFAS No. 14*. The company's controller has asked your assistance in determining whether industry segment information is necessary in the 1985 financial statements. The controller presents you with the following information:

	Quarter Ended			
	Mar. 31	**June 30**	**Sept. 30**	**Dec. 31**
Revenue	$1,150,000	$1,068,000	$875,000	$1,245,000
Expenses				
Directly associated with revenue	$655,000	$548,000	$389,000	$625,000
Other	50,000	180,000	125,000	258,000
Income before tax	$705,000	$728,000	$514,000	$883,000

You determine the following information concerning this data and other items of importance to Carter's interim reporting.

[1] Included in third quarter revenue is an extraordinary gain of $212,000 (before income tax) which resulted from the involuntary conversion of a plant asset. The gain is subject to a 25% income tax rate.

[2] Included among other expenses of the second quarter are annual machinery repair costs of $120,000,

Industry	Identifiable Assets	Revenues	Expenses Directly Allocable to Industry
Wholesale	$ 9,500,000	$8,300,000	$6,850,000
Retail trade	400,000	265,000	180,000
Manufacturing	300,000	420,000	263,800
Construction	300,000	197,000	125,200
	$10,500,000	$9,182,000	$7,419,000

General expenses are as follows:

Operating expenses associated with all industry segments	$ 762,000
General corporate expenses associated with corporate office	1,225,000
	$1,987,000

Further investigation reveals that all figures are accurate and that the additional operating expenses are allocable to industry segments as follows: 70% to wholesale trade and 10% to each of the other industries.

Instructions

[a] Prepare a recommendation concerning the need to present industry segment information. Provide computations to support your opinion.

[b] Identify the financial-statement disclosures, if any, which are needed in relation to the company's operations in different industries.

P25–6 Cross Corporation is attempting to determine the operating profit (loss) of each of its industry segments. The following information (in millions of dollars) relative to industry segments for 1984 has been accumulated:

Industry Segment	Revenue	Expense Directly Associated with Industry
Transportation equipment	$108	$ 67
Rubber products	80	60
Apparel	22	17
Lumber and wood products	7	5
Paper products	13	12
	$230	$161

The following additional revenue and expense information has been accumulated:

Revenue earned at the corporate level	$10,500,000
General corporate expenses	7,850,000
Operating expenses allocable to industry segments	22,000,000

The operating expenses allocable to industry segments relate to the rubber products, lumber and wood products, and paper products industries. Allocation is to be based on the relative amounts of revenue generated by each industry.

Instructions

[a] Determine the operating profit or loss of each segment for purposes of segment reporting requirements.

[b] Apply the 10% of revenue and operating profit tests to determine the reportable segments for Cross Corporation for 1984. (For purposes of this problem, ignore the 10% of identifiable assets test.)

[c] Assuming that no intersegment sales were made, does your identification of reportable segments in [b] comply with the requirements of *SFAS No. 14?* You may assume that there are no comparability problems with previous years.

P25–7 Parker Corporation has significant domestic and foreign operations. Revenues from the domestic operations result from sales within the United States and export sales.

You have been asked to help identify disclosure requirements in conformity with generally accepted accounting principles. As a part of your work you determine the following:

[1] Parker Corporation is a publicly held company whose stock is traded in the over-the-counter market.

[2] Revenue from sales for the year 1985 (the year under consideration) totaled $138,000,000 ($85,000,000 from domestic operations and $53,000,000 from foreign operations).

[3] Seventy percent of the domestic revenues were derived from sales within the United States. The remaining 30% resulted from export sales distributed as follows:

England	$15,000,000
Sweden	2,800,000
Canada	4,600,000
Mexico	3,100,000
	$25,500,000

[4] Activities from foreign operations are summarized in the following schedule:

	Revenue	Operating Profit	Identifiable Assets
South American operations	$44,000,000	$7,000,000	$52,000,000
African operations	5,000,000	100,000	4,000,000
Australian operations	4,000,000	(500,000)	4,500,000
	$53,000,000	$6,600,000	$60,500,000

[5] Summary figures from Parker's 1985 consolidated income statement and other company records are as follows:

Revenues (including $2,000,000 general corporate revenues)		$140,000,000
Expenses		
Operating expenses— Domestic operations	$70,000,000	
Operating expenses— Foreign operations	46,400,000	
General corporate expenses	8,600,000	125,000,000
Income before income tax		$ 15,000,000

Assets are as follows:

Identified with domestic operations	$ 78,000,000
Identified with foreign operations	60,500,000
Identified with corporate headquarters	10,500,000
	$149,000,000

Instructions

[a] Identify the information, if any, which must be presented concerning export sales.

[b] Identify the information, if any, which must be presented concerning foreign operations.

[c] Prepare a supplementary schedule incorporating the information you have identified in [a] and [b]. Design the schedule so that the disclosure of export sales and foreign operations relate to aggregate amounts taken from the company's financial statements.

P25–8 In the early 1970s Halpern Industries, Inc. (a publicly held company), entered a diversification program which resulted in its involvement in six different industries. In attempting to apply appropriate accounting and disclosure requirements in the 1985 financial statements, accountants have accumulated the data (in millions of dollars) on Halpern's industries as shown in the following list.

Additional operating expenses allocable to industry operations total $45,000,000. It is determined that these expenses should be allocated as follows: 40% to agriculture, 20% each to mining and construction, 10% to transportation, and 5% each to wholesale trade and retail trade.

General corporate expenses total $12,500,000. Interest income at the corporate level was $1,780,000.

Industry	Total Revenue	Expenses Directly Incurred by Industry	Assets Used Directly by Industry
Agriculture	$110	$ 60	$120
Mining	80	55	140
Construction	70	60	80
Transportation	20	21	17
Wholesale trade	5	2	4
Retail trade	3	2	2
	$288	$200	$363

Equity in earnings of an investment in an affiliated company was $2,450,000.

An analysis of Halpern's assets reveals that $38,500,000 of assets are used at the corporate level. This includes the $18,000,000 equity accounting basis in the affiliated company. Also, assets of $27,000,000 are used jointly by three industries and are allocable to them as follows: agriculture, 60%; mining, 30%; and wholesale trade, 10%.

Interindustry sales during 1985 are as follows: mining industry to construction industry, $7,000,000; transportation industry to agriculture industry, $15,500,000.

Instructions

[a] Identify the reportable segments for 1985 for Halpern Industries, applying all relevant tests of significance included in *SFAS No. 14.*

[b] Prepare a supplementary schedule, based on the information presented in the problem and your response in [a], to be used to present industry segment information in the 1985 financial statements. Use the general format of the Parker Hannifin 1982 annual report included in this chapter.

[c] What additional information, not available in this problem, would be required to complete the industry segment disclosure requirements of *SFAS No. 14?*

P25–9 Locke Company is a publicly held manufacturing company whose fiscal year ends March 31. On December 1, 1984, after several months of discussion and analysis, Locke's management decided for financial reporting purposes to change from accelerated depreciation to straight-line depreciation and to increase the warranty expense accrual. These revisions were to be effective immediately, but they would not affect tax accounting procedures.

The table below presents the accelerated depreciation for the past two quarters and the estimated amount for the third quarter of the current fiscal year as reported for financial-statement purposes. The table also presents the recalculated figures for the same periods under the straight-line method. The accumulated depreciation as of April 1, 1984, amounted to $980,000 under the accelerated depreciation method but would only have been $700,000 if straight-line depreciation had been used.

Fiscal Quarter	Accelerated Depreciation*	Straight-Line Depreciation**
Fiscal year ending Mar. 31, 1985		
First (Apr. 1–June 30, 1984)	$62,000	$50,000
Second (July 1–Sept. 30, 1984)	58,000	50,000
Third (Oct. 1–Dec. 31, 1984, estimated)	55,000	50,000

*Actual amount used for financial reporting purposes.
**Recalculated amounts.

Locke Company has a one-year warranty on its products. Management has been accruing warranty expense at the rate of 1% of net sales. The balance of the Accrued Warranty account as of April 1, 1984, was $47,000. The following table shows the warranty accruals and expenditures for the past six quarters and the estimates for the current third quarter. Actual warranty expenditures have exceeded the accrual for the past three quarters and are expected to exceed the accrual for future quarters if a 1% accrual rate continues to be used. Consequently, management has decided to increase the accrual rate to 1.25% of net sales, effective with the third quarter of the current year.

Fiscal Quarter	Accrued Warranty Expenses @ 1%	Actual Warranty Expenditures
Fiscal year ending Mar. 31, 1984		
First (Apr. 1–June 30, 1983)	$40,000	$32,000
Second (July 1–Sept. 30, 1983)	42,000	35,000
Third (Oct. 1–Dec. 31, 1983)	45,000	42,000
Fourth (Jan. 1–Mar. 31, 1984)	35,000	44,000
Fiscal year ending Mar. 31, 1985		
First (Apr. 1–June 30, 1984)	43,000	47,000
Second (July 1–Sept. 30, 1984)	46,000	55,000
Third (Oct. 1–Dec. 31, 1984, estimated)	50,000	58,000

The estimated financial results and related earnings per share for the third quarter and for the nine months ending December 31 for the current fiscal year are shown below. The third-quarter and nine-month data presented for the current fiscal year were compiled before the two accounting revisions were implemented. One million shares of common stock have been outstanding for the past two years. Locke Company is subject to a 40% income tax rate.

	Fiscal Year Ending 3/31/85	
	Third Quarter (10/1/84– 12/31/84)	Nine Months (4/1/84– 12/31/84)
Income before extraordinary items	$ 600,000	$ 1,500,000
Extraordinary loss, net of related income tax effect	(400,000)	(1,000,000)
Net income	$ 200,000	$ 500,000
Earnings per share		
Earnings before extraordinary loss	$ .60	$ 1.50
Extraordinary loss	(.40)	(1.00)
Net earnings	$ .20	$ .50

Instructions

[a] Discuss the disclosure requirements for current and prior year data which Locke Company would need to make in its interim financial statements as a consequence of the change in depreciation method and increase in warranty expense accrual.

[b] Locke Company will prepare and distribute to its stockholders interim financial statements at the end of the third quarter of the current fiscal year. These statements will present third quarter and year-to-date data following generally accepted accounting procedures. Present the financial results and related earnings-per-share data as they would appear in the interim financial statements issued at the end of the third quarter reflecting the change in depreciation method and increase in warranty expense accrual. Explain your presentation completely, showing supporting calculations. (Where information is not available to complete specific dollar amounts, prepare *pro forma* disclosures using $XXX.)

(CMA adapted)

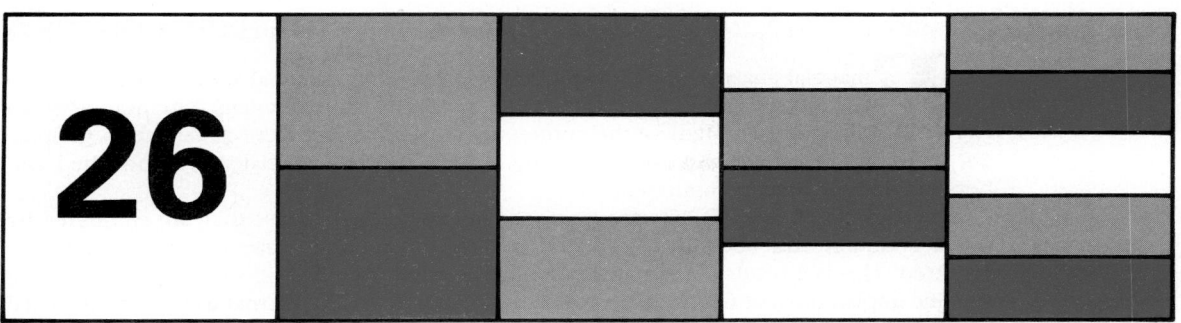

26

PUBLICLY HELD COMPANIES: EARNINGS PER SHARE

Objectives

To explain the significance of earnings per share (EPS) figures, particularly for publicly held companies.

To explain the various situations that present the potential for dilution (reduction) in earnings per share.

To distinguish between companies with simple capital structures and complex capital structures and to identify the EPS requirements of each.

To demonstrate the computation of EPS for companies with simple capital structures and primary and fully diluted EPS for companies with complex capital structures.

To prepare the appropriate financial statement presentation of EPS, based on the specific circumstances of a company.

To discuss how certain modifying conventions explain the need to incorporate potential dilution in EPS calculations.

Financial analysts, individual investors, and other financial statement users often use indexes, ratios, and percentages to relate various financial statement items to one another. Many of the commonly used measures were discussed in Chapter 24. Although these measures are not usually included in the financial statements, the numbers needed for their computation are.

Earnings-per-share (EPS) figures represent an exception, because they are computed by the accountant and become an integral part of the income statement when they are required. This is a result of the many complexities that may exist in the computations, the specific implications of which are generally not available to an external user of the financial statements.

In its simplest form, EPS is computed by dividing the net income by the number of shares of common stock outstanding:

$$\text{EPS} = \frac{\text{Net income}}{\text{Number of shares of common stock outstanding}}$$

The concept of EPS relates only to an enterprise's common stock and is best thought of as "earnings per *common* share." The concept of EPS does not apply to preferred stock, because preferred stock typically receives a fixed return and is not the ownership interest to which residual earnings accrue.

Historical Development of EPS

The development of the concept of EPS over the last several decades demonstrates an interesting reversal of position by the authoritative accounting organizations in reaction to the ways financial statements are used and the needs of their users. Before 1966 the computation of EPS was a matter of management discretion, and many years ago accountants were actually *discouraged* from using the concept.

In 1966 the Accounting Principles Board (APB), in *APB Opinion No. 9,* "Reporting the Results of Operations," strongly *encouraged* companies to disclose EPS. This was followed in 1969 by *APB Opinion No. 15,* which *required* the disclosure of EPS and set up the relatively complicated structure of computation and presentation that now exists.[1] This pronouncement provides the basis for most of the material in this chapter.

Another development in the presentation of EPS came in 1978, when the Financial Accounting Standards Board (FASB) concluded in *Statement of Financial Accounting Standard No. 21*[2] that EPS figures should *not* be required in the financial statements of **nonpublic enterprises.**[3] At the present time, therefore, EPS figures are *required* only in the financial statements of public enterprises. EPS figures may nevertheless be presented in the financial statements of nonpublic companies on a voluntary basis.

In no longer requiring nonpublic companies to present EPS in their income statements, the FASB apparently gave careful consideration to both the cost burden of preparing and presenting EPS figures and the usefulness of the information to financial statement users. As we discussed in Chapter 25, a growing concern is the excessive burden placed on small or nonpublic companies when they are subject to the same financial reporting requirements as large, publicly held companies. The FASB lightened this burden somewhat by excluding the

---

[1]*APB Opinion No. 15,* "Earnings Per Share," 1968.

[2]*FASB Statement of Financial Accounting Standards No. 21,* "Suspension of the Reporting of Earnings Per Share and Segment Information by Nonpublic Enterprises," 1978.

[3]A **nonpublic enterprise** is one whose debt or equity securities do not trade in a public market on a foreign or domestic stock exchange or in the over-the-counter market, or that is not required to file financial statements with the Securities and Exchange Commission.

EPS requirement for nonpublic companies. As we shall see in the following section, the significance of EPS is frequently interpreted in relation to stock market prices. The lack of active trading of stock in the case of nonpublic companies supports the position that EPS figures are generally not of great usefulness to users of financial statements of nonpublic companies. Thus, limiting the requirement of EPS to public companies appears reasonable. Even though nonpublic companies are not required to present EPS figures in their income statements, if management decides to present the figures, the reporting standards for public companies presented in this chapter must be followed.

Significance of EPS Figures

EPS is regarded by many as the most important single number in the financial statements. EPS figures are frequently cited in corporate annual reports, press releases, investment service publications, financial periodicals, and elsewhere as measures of an enterprise's success in achieving its profit objective. Many financial statement users believe EPS figures are useful indicators of an enterprise's management effectiveness, earnings potential, and future dividends.

The usefulness of EPS figures in financial analysis is supported by several studies. For example, one researcher gathered data from Chartered Financial Analysts (CFAs) concerning the importance of items in the financial statements. He concluded:

> *Security analysts are more interested in information items that concern the income statement and affect the amount of income earned by a corporation than in balance sheet information items.* Earnings per share continues to lead the list as the most important item.[4] *[Emphasis added.]*

Net income is an **aggregate earnings concept,** based on the use of all of the enterprise's resources derived from many sources, such as creditors, preferred stockholders, and common stockholders. However, the extent to which creditors and investors other than common stockholders share in earnings is normally fixed in amount due to their contractual arrangements with the enterprise. For example, preferred stocks and bonds have stated dividend and interest rates that establish the return that investors in those securities may expect to receive. Common stock, on the other hand, represents the **residual equity** that is the first to lose if earnings decrease and is in a position to benefit if earnings increase. Thus, the concept of EPS may have relevance as income increases and decreases, if the return to creditors and preferred stockholders is recognized first.

Since EPS is actually a measure of **earnings per common share,** we must deduct the required return to any senior security, such as bonds and preferred stock, to derive the earnings attributable to common stock. Interest to debt holders has already been deducted (as an expense) in determining net income. One of the first adjustments we must make in computing EPS is to subtract the dividend on preferred stock from net income to determine the amount of income that should be associated with common stock. We can now modify our general notion of EPS as follows:

$$\text{EPS} = \frac{\text{Net income} - \text{Preferred dividend}}{\text{Number of shares of common stock outstanding}}$$

Comparing the relative desirability of common stock of different companies is particularly difficult if the analysis is based on net income and dollars invested in the company's common stock, as is the case in computing such ratios as return on stockholders' equity. Because of differences in asset structure, dollars invested by various classes of creditors and

---

[4]Gyan Chandra, "Information Needs of Security Analysts," *Journal of Accountancy* (December 1975), p. 70.

EARNINGS PER SHARE AND THE INSENSITIVE DENOMINATOR

EARNINGS PER SHARE is a device used by managements to relate aggregate earnings performance to shareholders of the business in terms of the evidence of ownership held by the latter, i.e., the common share. Appearances to the contrary, there is no valid correlation implicit in this concept between reported earnings applicable to each share and the respective total common stockholders' capital employed incidental to such earnings. . . .

Retention of earnings for use in the continuing business operations triggers an automatic though spurious increase in the reported earnings per share of subsequent periods. Indeed, reporting apparent improvement in performance, when in fact regression has occurred, is another inherent, though little publicized, defect of the concept and use of earnings per share data. . . .

This phenomenon is demonstrated by a simple but fundamentally sound analogy. For example, assume that a company earns $100,000 during a twelve-month period when its stockholders' equity averaged $1,000,000 and included 100,000 shares of outstanding common shares. A return of 10% on stockholders' equity is thus indicated ($100,000/ $1,000,000 = 10%). The company then distributes cash dividends equal to $60,000 of the $100,000 earned and retains the balance. The following year the company again earns 10% of its average stockholders' equity ($104,000 on $1,040,000). Between the two years, therefore, management has maintained the same earnings rate in relation to its equity capital, 10%. . . .

Using the earnings per share device, however, management will not report maintenance of the status quo to stockholders. Rather, the company's press release as well as audited earnings report will announce to the world an *increase in earnings per share* over the amount reported per share for the prior period. The conclusions are verified by the computations below. . . .

Note in the example that the amount earned per dollar of common stockholders' equity did not change. Reported earnings per share, however, indicates an improvement in the second year over the first of 4% since earnings per share increased from $1.00 to $1.04. . . .

The explanation for this phenomenon is simply that the denominator of the earnings per share fraction—the outstanding common shares—is insensitive to changes in all stockholders' equity accounts except common stock. Hence, as the capital investment base grows year after year, reflecting a policy of consistent earnings reinvestment, a rising earnings per share trend should be anticipated. . . .

Disclosure of the type now required has made the earnings report even more confusing—i.e., from forest to jungle in the name of progress. Incorporating earnings per share data into audited earnings reports not only extends the auditor's responsibilities to that of a quasi-securities analyst but also finds him embracing and highlighting as the ultimate measure of a firm's performance, a device of limited scope and of equally inconclusive stature.

SOURCE: Adapted from John J. Mahoney, "Earnings Per Share and the Insensitive Denominator," *Management Accounting,* July 1970, pp. 15–20. Reprinted by permission of *Management Accounting.* Copyright 1970, National Association of Accountants. All rights reserved.

SIGNIFICANCE OF RETAINED EARNINGS	XYZ Company	First year		Next year	
	Net earnings (a)		$100,000		$104,000
	Average shares outstanding	100,000		100,000	
	Earnings per share	$1.00		$1.04	
	Net earnings (a)		$100,000		$104,000
	Common stockholders' equity		$1,000,000		$1,040,000
	Earnings on common stockholders' equity	10% (b)		10% (b)	

(a) After deducting dividend requirements applicable to preferred stock, if any.
(b) This is the equivalent of 10 cents earned on each dollar of stockholders' equity.

investors, rates of change in these variables over time, and other considerations, comparing companies on an aggregate basis is difficult for certain types of investment decisions. Since market prices of common stock are quoted per share, users of financial statements want a per share measure of income to facilitate comparisons among companies. This desire has resulted in the emphasis on EPS in addition to net income.

EPS figures are frequently quoted in direct comparisons between companies. For example, one company may report EPS of $1.75 ($175,000 net income divided by 100,000 common shares outstanding), and another company may report EPS of $1.25 ($10,625,000 net income divided by 8,500,000 common shares outstanding). Because a number of differences in the enterprises might explain such a difference in EPS, a reader of financial statements should not necessarily conclude that the first company is more profitable or a more desirable investment than the second company. One important difference may be the number of shares of common stock in the common stockholders' equities and the relative number of dollars representing those equities. Also, differences in accounting principles used in determining net income can cause significant differences in EPS.

EPS figures are frequently used in conjunction with other per share measures of an enterprise. The price/earnings ratio, for example, is computed by dividing the market price of the stock (which is stated on a per share basis) by EPS. To illustrate, assume that a company has common stock with a market price of $25 and has EPS of $4.50. The related price/earnings ratio is 5.6 ($25.00/$4.50), indicating that the stock is selling at 5.6 times EPS. Care must be taken in interpreting the price/earnings ratio. If the price/earnings ratio is judged to be low relative to other stocks, at least two alternative explanations exist. The stock may be considered an excellent investment opportunity because of the low price at which it can be acquired in relation to earnings. Alternatively, a declining trend in the price/earnings ratio may reflect a negative attitude on the part of the investors in the enterprise's growth potential.

Another frequently cited measure is dividend payout, in which the dividend paid on a per share basis is divided by the EPS for the same time period. For example, if a company with EPS of $4.50 pays $2.00 in dividends, the dividend payout is 44% ($2.00/$4.50), indicating that cash in an amount equal to 44% of net income was paid out as dividends to common stockholders. As a general rule, if the investor's primary objective is the periodic cash return that can be expected on the dollars invested, a company with a high dividend payout may be considered a superior stock investment compared with a company that retains a higher portion of earnings and thus has a lower dividend payout. Of course, many factors affect the relationship between a company's net income and its cash dividends paid to stockholders for the same period of time. We would normally expect dividends paid to be less than net income as companies usually retain assets generated by income activities for other uses. In fact, too high a dividend payout ratio may raise significant questions about the future of the enterprise.

The purpose of these illustrations is to indicate the desire for per share measures that enhance the value of comparisons among enterprises. Although the examples are not comprehensive, they show how EPS figures may be used in comparing enterprises. A word of caution is in order. Care should be taken when attempting to simplify the results of complex events and transactions into a single figure that is then used as a comparative tool. Many transactions and events influence the determination of net income and other items that appear in the financial statements of a business enterprise. Many judgments and estimates must be made when reporting these transactions and events. Finally, differences in business enterprises and the economic circumstances surrounding them must also be considered.

In summary, while figures may provide important input into an investment or other decision about an enterprise, they should be interpreted in light of the circumstances of the enterprise and the decision maker. This is true for EPS as well as many other measures that are commonly used to evaluate and compare business enterprises.

ARE EARNINGS-PER-SHARE FIGURES REALLY IMPORTANT?

A NUMBER OF studies indicate that EPS figures are among the most important items of information in financial statements. The following excerpt from *The Wall Street Journal* indicates a possible declining interest in EPS.

Study Finds Per-Share Profit Less Noted By Executives Than Other Reported Data

NEW YORK—A new survey shows that business and financial executives pay a lot less attention to earnings per share than to other factors such as cash flow.

The survey of 415 corporate, government and accounting industry executives and others conducted for the Financial Accounting Foundation, concludes there are signs of "an important shift away from the traditional importance given the bottom line earnings per share measurement" in financial reporting.

Cash flow, rated by 67% of the executives as highly important, was at the top of the executives' list. Other elements of financial reporting that were ranked highly included return on investment, changes in a company's financial position, components of earnings, such as operating earnings or income from continuing operations, and the effects of inflation.

By contrast, only 49% of the executives gave earnings per share a top-importance rating.

The findings of the survey, which was carried out by Louis Harris & Associates Inc., support critics who say many company chief executives and investors place too much emphasis on earnings in judging corporate financial performance.

The survey reported that close to a three-to-one majority of the executives believe return on investment "is a better and more desirable measure than earnings per share." By four to one, they believe it would be a "positive development" if there were less emphasis on earnings per share and more on such earnings components as revenue and operating income. However, relatively few expect such a change to happen quickly.

The Financial Accounting Foundation, which commissioned the survey, raises funds for and names the members of the Financial Accounting Standards Board, the rule-making body of the accounting profession.

But the survey gave only a lukewarm endorsement to the work of the FASB. In assessing the total output of the FASB to date, 55% of people surveyed said it had been "somewhat effective." Of the rest, 24% rated the board "highly effective" and 12% "not very effective" or "not effective at all."

Potential Dilution in EPS

The concept of allocating income to the number of shares of common stock is relatively simple. In certain situations, however, the existence of convertible securities, rights to acquire stock, and obligations to distribute shares of stock under various arrangements may complicate the calculation of EPS. These situations create the potential for a decline in EPS if certain actions are taken. This possible decline in EPS is referred to as **potential dilution** and is of particular concern because it may result from actions over which the enterprise has no control. For example, if outstanding stock options allow the option holders to acquire shares of common stock at a fixed or determinable price, the potential for reduced EPS exists because the number of shares of common stock outstanding may increase if the options are exercised. Arrangements such as stock options and convertible bonds are identified as **potentially dilutive securities,** or simply **potential diluters,** for purposes of computing EPS.

The capital structures of some corporations include potential diluters, while others do not. For purposes of computing EPS, a distinction is made between simple and complex capital structures. A **simple capital structure** is one that includes no potential diluters; a **complex capital structure** includes one or more potential diluters. The capital structures of large corporations often include several types of potential diluters. Some large corporations, however, have no potential diluters. It is important to keep in mind, therefore, that the distinction between a simple and a complex capital structure is based not on the size of the enterprise but on whether or not the capital structure includes arrangements that may potentially dilute EPS.

The computation of EPS for companies with simple capital structures requires understanding the treatment of the claim on income of those securities that are senior to common stock, such as preferred stock, and understanding the number of shares of common stock that should be used to compute EPS. These concepts are equally important for computing EPS figures for companies with complex capital structures. EPS of companies with complex capital structures are further complicated by potential diluters. These considerations are the subjects of the following sections. In all illustrations in the text and in the cases, exercises, and problems at the end of the chapter, the enterprises for which information is presented are assumed to be public companies that are required to present EPS figures in their financial statements.

EPS COMPUTATIONS FOR SIMPLE CAPITAL STRUCTURES

The computation of EPS in a simple capital structure is not complicated by potential diluters. Two factors, however, may complicate the determination of EPS in a simple capital structure. First, the number of shares of common stock outstanding during the reporting period may change as a result of the sale of stock, treasury stock transactions, stock splits, stock dividends, and other stock transactions. The EPS computation must be based on the **weighted average number of common shares outstanding during the period.** Second, the existence of preferred stock with a prior claim on income must be considered in determining the income allocable to common stock.

Weighted Average Number of Common Shares

The **weighted average number of common shares,** as used in computing EPS, is defined as the number of shares of common stock outstanding during the accounting period, giving consideration to the length of time that specific numbers of shares were actually outstanding. The most frequently encountered activities that change the number of shares of common stock outstanding are the sale of additional shares of common stock and treasury stock transactions. The sale of new shares of stock increases the number of outstanding shares; the acquisition of treasury stock decreases the number of outstanding shares; and the resale of treasury stock increases the number of outstanding shares.

To illustrate the determination of a weighted average, assume that Wallace Company reports a net income of $170,000 and has the following common stock activity during 1984:

	Stock Activity	Number of Shares
Jan. 1	Common stock outstanding	100,000
Mar. 1	Sale of common stock	20,000
		120,000
July 1	Purchase of treasury stock	(5,000)
		115,000
Nov. 1	Sale of treasury stock	3,000
Dec. 31	Common stock outstanding	118,000

The weighted average number of common shares outstanding is computed by developing a schedule in which the number of months is multiplied by the number of shares outstanding.[5] The "months X shares" figures are totaled and divided by 12 to determine the weighted average, as follows:

Period	Months	×	Shares Outstanding	=	Months × Shares
Jan. 1–Feb. 28	2		100,000		200,000
Mar. 1–June 30	4		120,000		480,000
July 1–Oct. 31	4		115,000		460,000
Nov. 1–Dec. 31	2		118,000		236,000
	12				1,376,000

1,376,000/12 = 114,667

EPS for 1984 is then computed as follows:

$$\text{EPS} = \frac{\$170,000}{114,667} = \$1.48$$

When the enterprise has issued a stock dividend or a stock split during the accounting period, the number of shares of stock outstanding during the different parts of the period must be restated to retroactively apply to the stock dividend or stock split. Remember that stock splits and stock dividends do not increase the total stockholders' investment in the corporation. They simply represent a *reallocation of the common stock investment over a larger number of shares of common stock*. Treating the stock dividend or stock split retroactively restates the common stock activity during the year in terms of the stock at the end of the year, *after* the stock dividend or stock split.

Continuing the example of Wallace Company above, assume that in 1985 a net income of $225,000 is reported and the following common stock activity took place:

	Stock Activity	Number of Shares
Jan. 1	Common stock outstanding	118,000
Mar. 1	Sale of common stock	10,000
		128,000
July 1	Purchase of treasury stock	(5,000)
		123,000
Oct. 1	Distribution of 2:1 stock split	123,000
		246,000
Nov. 1	Purchase of treasury stock	(6,000)
Dec. 31	Common stock outstanding	240,000

[5]An alternative method may be used that weights the various numbers of shares outstanding by multiplying each number by the length of time outstanding, with 12 months as the denominator of the fraction. For Wallace Company in 1984, this computation is as follows:

Number of Shares	Fraction of Year Outstanding	Weighted Average
100,000	$^{12}/_{12}$	100,000
20,000	$^{10}/_{12}$	16,667
(5,000)	$^{6}/_{12}$	(2,500)
3,000	$^{2}/_{12}$	500
		114,667

The weighted average number of common shares outstanding is computed in a manner similar to that in the previous example, except that the number of shares outstanding prior to the 2:1 stock split must be converted to the basis of the shares at the end of the year. This is done by multiplying the number of shares by 2, as illustrated below:

| | | | | | Months × Shares | | |
| | | | | | | Stock Split | |
Period	Months	×	Shares Outstanding	=	Original	× Conversion	= Restated
Jan. 1–Feb. 28	2		118,000		236,000	2	472,000
Mar. 1–June 30	4		128,000		512,000	2	1,024,000
July 1–Sept. 30	3		123,000		369,000	2	738,000
Oct. 1–Oct. 31	1		246,000				246,000
Nov. 1–Dec. 31	2		240,000				480,000
	12						2,960,000

2,960,000/12 = 246,667

EPS for 1985 is then computed as follows:

$$\text{EPS} = \frac{\$225,000}{246,667} = \$.91$$

In this illustration, the stock conversion factor, 2, is used because the increase in shares in a 2:1 split results in twice as many shares outstanding after the split as before. This factor must be determined, based on the specific distribution made. For example, if a 3:1 split is distributed, the factor would be 3; if a 10% stock dividend is distributed, the factor would be 1.10. It is important to notice that this adjustment is made only to those shares outstanding prior to the stock split or stock dividend.

Preferred Stock

Certain securities have claims that must be satisfied before dividends may be paid on common stock. These securities are called **senior securities,** indicating their preferential rights over common stock.

Debt instruments are an example of senior securities, and the return to debt holders is deducted in determining net income. Preferred stock is also a senior security, but since net income is the income accruing to *all* owners (stockholders) of the enterprise, the dividends on preferred stock are *not* deducted in determining net income. Because EPS is a concept relating only to common stock, however, the income figure in the computation must be reduced by the return on all senior securities. Accordingly, net income as reported in the income statement must be reduced by the dividends on preferred stock to obtain a "residual" income figure that represents the amount allocable only to common stockholders. This deduction, in effect, simply treats the dividend on preferred stock as an expense from the viewpoint of the common stockholders, much like interest on debt has already been treated in computing net income.

To illustrate, Estes Company reports net income of $2,500,000 for 1984 and has 2,200,000 weighted average number of shares of common stock outstanding for the year. In addition, the company has preferred stock outstanding throughout 1984 as follows: 1,000,000 shares, $10 par, 7% dividend rate. The preferred dividend of $700,000 (1,000,000 × $10 × 7%) must be deducted from the reported net income in determining EPS, as follows:

$$EPS = \frac{\$2,500,000 - \$700,000}{2,200,000} = \$.82$$

How is the preferred dividend treated if the company reports a net loss rather than a net income? The preferred dividend is subtracted from the net loss in computing a loss per share on common stock. To illustrate, Estes Company reports a net loss of $1,700,000 in 1985 and still has 2,200,000 outstanding shares of common stock and a $700,000 preferred dividend requirement. The 1985 *loss per share* is computed as follows:

$$\begin{aligned} \text{Loss per share} &= \frac{\$(1,700,000) - \$700,000}{2,200,000} \\ &= \frac{\$(2,400,000)}{2,200,000} \\ &= \$(1.09) \end{aligned}$$

In adjusting the reported net income for preferred dividends, the following guidelines should be observed. If the preferred stock is cumulative, the dividends are deducted from net income or net loss whether or not they were declared. If preferred dividends are not cumulative, only dividends actually declared are deducted from net income or net loss in computing EPS. Any dividends in arrears on cumulative preferred stock are not subtracted in determining the income that accrues to the common stockholders.

Financial Statement Presentation

Investors attach a great deal of importance to EPS figures and frequently evaluate them in conjunction with other information contained in the financial statements. Accordingly, EPS figures should be prominently presented on the face of the income statement, and the presentation should be consistent with the income statement presentation in which the EPS figures are included.

To illustrate the financial presentation of EPS, consider Calumet Company, which had 110,000 shares of common stock outstanding throughout 1985 and 95,000 shares throughout 1984. Dividends on the company's cumulative preferred stock amounted to $50,000 each year. The company's income statement shows net income of $230,500 in 1985 and $208,000 in 1984, with a $44,500 gain (net of $40,000 income tax) on the refunding of long-term debt in 1985. The income and EPS figures are presented in Exhibit 26–1.

EXHIBIT 26–1
Calumet Company
Partial Income Statement

	1985	1984
Income before extraordinary items	$186,000	$208,000
Extraordinary item—Gain on refunding of long-term debt, net of $40,000 income tax	44,500	—
Net income	$230,500	$208,000
Earnings per common share:		
Income before extraordinary items	$1.24[a]	$1.66[d]
Extraordinary item	.40[b]	—
Net income	$1.64[c]	$1.66

[a]($186,000 − $50,000)/110,000 shares = $1.24.
[b]$44,500/$110,000 = $.40.
[c]($230,500 − $50,000)/110,000 shares = $1.64.
[d]($208,000 − $50,000)/95,000 shares = $1.66.

EXHIBIT 26–2
Texaco Inc.
Net Income and Statement of Consolidated Retained Earnings

Texaco Inc. and Subsidiary Companies

	Millions of dollars		
For the years ended December 31,	**1982**	1981	1980
Net Income:			
Net income before extraordinary credit	$ 1,281	$ 2,310	$ 2,240
Extraordinary credit—Gain on sale of interest in Belridge Oil Company less applicable income taxes of $186 million	—	—	402
Net income	$ 1,281	$ 2,310	$ 2,642
Per share data (dollars):			
Net income per share before extraordinary credit	**$4.92**	$8.75	$8.31
Extraordinary credit per share	—	—	1.48
Net income per share	**$4.92**	$8.75	$9.79
(Based on average number of shares outstanding: 1982—260,101,000; 1981—264,028,000; and 1980—269,791,000)			
Retained Earnings:			
Balance at beginning of year	**$11,915**	$10,345	$ 8,364
Add: Net income for the year	**1,281**	2,310	2,642
Deduct: Cash dividends—$3.00 per share in 1982, $2.80 per share in 1981, and $2.45 per share in 1980	**780**	740	661
Balance at end of year	**$12,416**	$11,915	$10,345

SOURCE: Texaco Inc., 1982 Annual Report.

EPS figures must be presented for each of the following income figures if they appear in the income statement: income from continuing operations; income before extraordinary items; and net income. In addition to requiring EPS figures for these three income figures, various authoritative accounting pronouncements require disclosure of EPS either in the body of the income statement or in related notes for specific types of items. For example, EPS must be presented for the cumulative effect of a change in accounting principle and for an extraordinary gain or loss that results from extinguishment of debt.

Exhibit 26–2 is an example of the EPS presentation of Texaco Inc. for 1982 and the comparative years 1981 and 1980. The exhibit includes only the lower portion of the income statement, beginning with income before extraordinary credit. Notice that the EPS data, presented below the income figures, follow the structure of the income figures; EPS is presented for income before the extraordinary credit, and net income. Also presented are the numbers of shares of common stock on which the EPS figures are based.

EPS COMPUTATIONS FOR COMPLEX CAPITAL STRUCTURES

In complex capital structures, EPS may be reduced because of one or more potential diluters. Although the arrangements that could result in the dilution of EPS are numerous, the following three classifications of potential diluters are commonly encountered:

1. **Stock options, warrants, and rights.** Arrangements whereby the holder has the right to purchase common stock in accordance with the terms of the agreement or instrument upon payment of a specified amount.
2. **Convertible securities.** Senior securities that, by their terms, allow the holders to receive shares of common stock in exchange for the senior securities. Convertible preferred stock and

convertible bonds are examples of convertible securities.

3. **Contingent issuances.**   Potential future issuances of common stock that may depend on the satisfaction of certain future conditions. For example, shares of common stock that a company may be required to issue in the future as a result of a past transaction or contractual agreement are contingent issuances.

In all of these cases, the potential exists for additional shares of common stock to be issued and EPS to be reduced as the net income is distributed over a larger number of common shares.

Dual EPS Presentation

For companies with complex capital structures, a dual presentation of EPS is necessary, incorporating the potentially dilutive impact of securities and arrangements such as stock options, warrants and rights, convertible securities, and contingent issuances. The first EPS figure, commonly referred to as **primary EPS,** is based on the outstanding common stock and securities that are substantially equivalent to common stock, known as **common stock equivalents.** The second presentation, commonly called **fully diluted EPS,** reflects the dilution of EPS that would have taken place if the common stock represented by *all* potential diluters had been issued. Common stock equivalents and other potential diluters are included in the dual presentation of EPS only if they reduce EPS (i.e., their effect is **dilutive**). If the effect of the assumed issuance of a potential diluter is **antidilutive** (i.e., results in an increase in EPS or a reduction in loss per share) in a particular accounting period, the shares are not included in the EPS computations of that period.

We can see from the above discussion that potential diluters are of two types: common stock equivalents and others. The relationship of this distinction to the dual presentation of EPS is depicted in Exhibit 26–3. The distinction between potential diluters that are common stock equivalents and those that are not is extremely important, because it determines which securities should be treated like common stock when computing primary EPS.

At this point, we can define more precisely several terms introduced in the above discussion.

1. **Potential diluters.**   Arrangements under which an enterprise *may be* required to issue shares of common stock in certain circumstances.
2. **Common stock equivalents.**   Potential diluters which, because of the terms of their issuance, are treated substantially *the same as* common stock. Although a common stock equivalent is not common stock in form, it derives a large portion of its value from its common stock characteristics.
3. **Primary EPS.**   The amount of income attributable to each share of common stock outstanding and common stock equivalent.
4. **Fully diluted EPS.**   The amount of income per common share, reflecting the maximum dilution that would result from conversions, exercises, and other contingent issuances of common stock that would have individually decreased earnings per share.

EXHIBIT 26–3
Relationship of Potential Diluters to EPS Figures

Potential Diluters		Resulting EPS Figures
Common stock equivalents $\longrightarrow$	Combined with outstanding common stock $\longrightarrow$	Primary EPS
All potential diluters (including common stock equivalents) $\longrightarrow$	Combined with outstanding common stock $\longrightarrow$	Fully diluted EPS

Substance
over
Form

Conserva-
tism

In Chapter 2 we discussed the modifying convention of substance over form. We stated that when an apparent difference exists between the economic substance of an item and its legal form, accountants emphasize the economic substance. The application of this concept is evident in computing EPS where potential dilution is included. In legal form, potential diluters are not outstanding common stock. They are convertible bonds, stock options, and other arrangements which *may* result in additional shares of outstanding common stock in the future. In substance, however, management in such cases usually expects to eventually increase the number of shares of common stock outstanding. Assuming certain conditions are met, we anticipate that increase in outstanding shares by conservatively stating EPS at the lower figure that would have resulted if the outstanding shares had already been increased.

The treatment of the potential diluters and the resulting dual EPS presentation are summarized in Exhibit 26–4.[6]

Two major decisions must be made about each potential diluter. First, we must decide whether the potential diluter is a common stock equivalent. This decision, which is discussed in greater detail below, determines whether the potential diluter will be considered in computing both primary and fully diluted EPS or only in fully diluted EPS. Second, we must decide whether the potential diluter is, in fact, dilutive. This decision, which is also discussed below, must be made periodically (i.e., each time a company computes EPS), in the context of the income or loss and the outstanding shares for that accounting period. A potential diluter may be dilutive in one period but not in another. The outcome of this second decision determines whether the potential diluter will be used in the EPS computations for the accounting period under consideration.

Basic EPS Computations

The treatment of preferred dividends and the computation of the weighted average number of common shares presented earlier in the section on computing EPS for simple capital structures also apply to the determination of primary and fully diluted EPS in the dual presentation. Because the primary and fully diluted EPS computations include activities that have not actually occurred, additional adjustments must be made in the numbers reported. The EPS calculations in a complex capital structure are referred to as *pro forma* because they incorporate dilution that *might* take place.

The potential diluters identified earlier are discussed individually below. In this section we will limit our discussion to basic computations, ignoring certain complications which are explained later in the chapter and in the Appendix.

Stock Options, Warrants, Rights

Stock options, warrants, and rights are, by definition, *always* identified as common stock equivalents. They usually have no cash yield, and they derive their value from the right to obtain common stock at specified prices for a specified period of time. Because such arrangements are always considered common stock equivalents, they are elements in the computation of both primary and fully diluted EPS if they are dilutive.

The **treasury stock method** is used to determine the dilutive effect of stock options, warrants, and rights. The treasury stock method involves the following three steps:

Step 1. Shares of stock are assumed to be sold according to the stock option, warrant, or right agreement. The amount to be received from these sales is identified as the **proceeds.**

Step 2. The proceeds from the sale of the stock (Step 1) are assumed to be used to acquire common stock at the existing market price.

---

[6]The model in Exhibit 26–4 presents an overview of the decision-making process required to develop the primary and fully diluted EPS figures. In certain circumstances exceptions to this general process exist. Several of these exceptions are covered later in this chapter.

EXHIBIT 26–4
EPS Decision Diagram

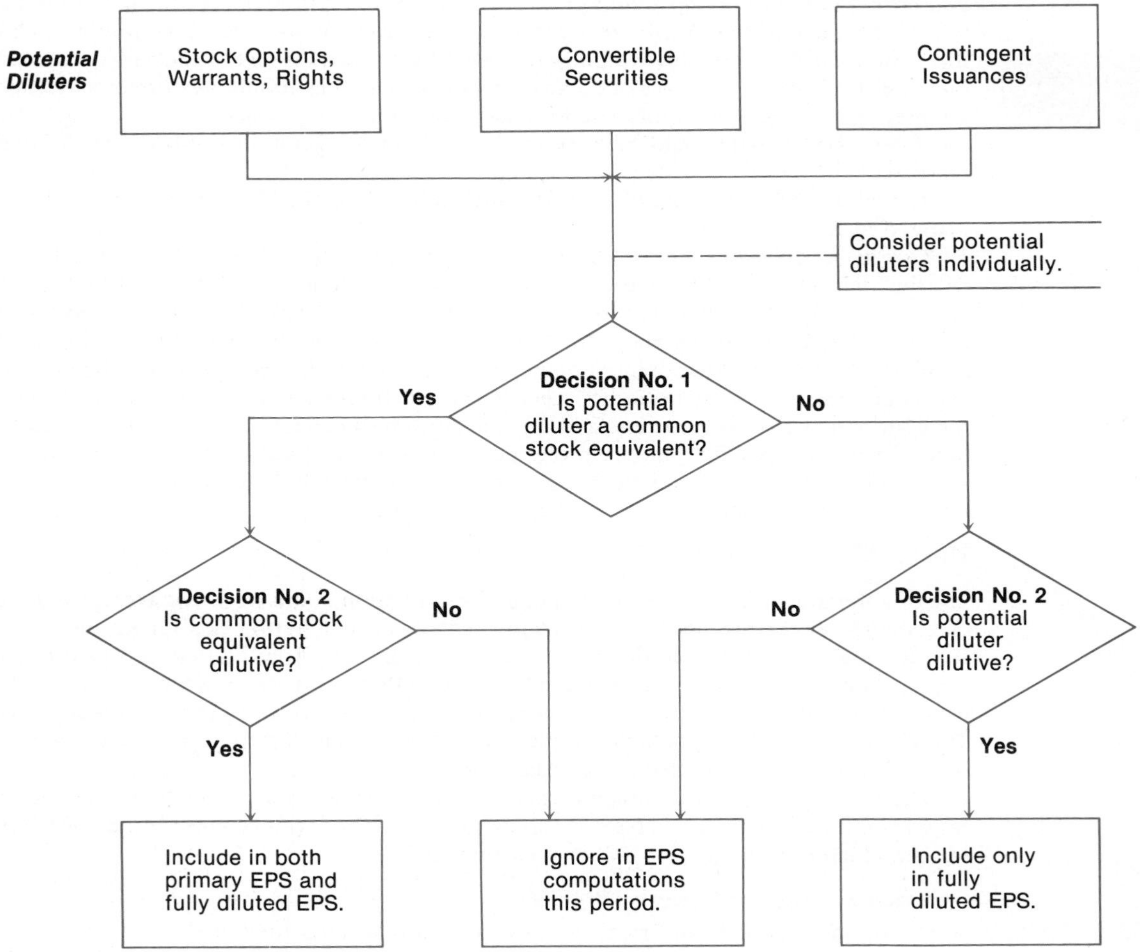

Potential Diluters

| Stock Options, Warrants, Rights | Convertible Securities | Contingent Issuances |

Consider potential diluters individually.

Decision No. 1
Is potential diluter a common stock equivalent?

Yes   No

Decision No. 2
Is common stock equivalent dilutive?

No

Decision No. 2
Is potential diluter dilutive?

No

Yes   Yes

| Include in both primary EPS and fully diluted EPS. | Ignore in EPS computations this period. | Include only in fully diluted EPS. |

Step 3. The net increase in the number of shares is determined by deducting the shares reacquired (Step 2) from the shares sold (Step 1). The *net increase* in the number of shares is added to the outstanding common shares.

This series of computations deals with **hypothetical** (assumed) transactions. The sale-of-stock assumption in Step 1 is followed by an assumption about the way the company uses the proceeds from the sale. In Step 2 we assume that shares of stock were reacquired from the market. The assumed *net* increase, computed in Step 3, is then used in the EPS computations. The treasury stock method gets its name from the basic assumption that underlies the method, namely, that the company will acquire relatively small numbers of shares of common stock to meet stock option requirements by acquiring treasury stock.

The number of shares outstanding will increase only if the market price used in Step 2 exceeds the price in Step 1 at which the holders of options, warrants, or rights can acquire stock (i.e., the exercise price). In this case, the number of shares sold will be greater than the number repurchased. If the opposite were true (i.e., the market price were *less than* the exercise price), the assumed exercise would be illogical, because the holder of the option, warrant, or right could purchase the stock at a lower price from the market. Moreover, it would also be antidilutive, because the number of shares sold would be fewer than the number reacquired. In this case, the outstanding shares would be reduced, resulting in an increased EPS.

To illustrate the treasury stock method, assume that Diane Doll Company has 500,000 shares of common stock outstanding through 1984 and reported a net income of $356,500 for the year. In 1983 the company issued 100,000 options to acquire common stock in the company at the par value of $50. No options have been exercised by the end of 1984. The market price of the stock throughout 1984 was $65. No other potential diluters exist.

Remember that the stock options are common stock equivalents by definition. Also note that the options are dilutive because the market price of $65 exceeds the exercise price of $50. Thus, when the treasury stock method is applied, more shares will be sold (at $50) than can be repurchased (at $65). In addition, since options are the only potential diluter and they are common stock equivalents, primary and fully diluted EPS will be the same.

The application of the treasury stock method in this situation indicates a net increase of 23,077 in the number of common shares:[7]

Step 1. One hundred thousand shares assumed sold at $50 = $5,000,000.

Step 2. Five million dollars used to buy stock at $65, resulting in the reacquisition of 76,923 shares ($5,000,000/$65).

Step 3. Number of shares sold (100,000) exceeds the number of shares repurchased (76,923) by 23,077.

Primary and fully diluted EPS are computed as follows:

$$\text{Primary and fully diluted EPS} = \frac{\$356,500}{500,000 + 23,077} = \$.68$$

If options, warrants, and rights are outstanding for only part of the financial reporting period, the incremental number of shares identified by the treasury stock method must be weighted for the length of time they were outstanding. For example, in the above illustration, if the options had been issued on May 1, 1984, and Diane Doll Company reported on a

---

[7]A short-cut method for computing the number of shares that results from the application of the treasury stock method uses the following formula:

$$I = \left[\frac{M - E}{M}\right] N$$

where I = incremental number of shares
M = market price per share
E = exercise price per share
N = number of shares obtainable

Applying this formula to the information presented for Diane Doll Company, the incremental number of shares obtained from the treasury stock method is computed as follows:

$$I = \left[\frac{\$65 - \$50}{\$65}\right] 100,000$$
$$I = 23,077$$

calendar-year basis, the equivalent number of shares would be 15,385, because the common stock equivalents were outstanding for only $^8/_{12}$ of the year:

$$\text{Common equivalent shares} = 23,077 \times {}^8/_{12} = 15,385$$

What market price should be used in applying the treasury stock method where the price changes during the financial reporting period? In the previous illustration, we assumed a single market price of $65. Now we will assume that $65 is the average market price for the year 1984 but that the ending market price is a different figure. In computing primary EPS, we use the average market price in applying the treasury stock method to determine the dilutive effect of stock options, warrants, and rights. If the market price at the end of the accounting period is higher than the average, however, we use the higher (ending) figure for computing fully diluted EPS.

To understand the impact of this difference, we must recall the assumptions that underlie the treasury stock method. First, we assume that shares are sold to holders of stock options, warrants, and rights at the prices established by those agreements. Next, we assume that the company used the proceeds from the sale of these shares to acquire treasury stock. Keep in mind that the higher the market price, the fewer shares we would be able to obtain with the fixed amount of money we have received from the sale of shares. Finally, we determine the net increase in the number of shares of common stock outstanding that results from the sale of shares and the subsequent reacquisition of treasury shares. The higher the market price used to determine the number of shares that can be reacquired, the fewer shares will be bought. Likewise, the fewer shares bought, the greater the net increase in the number of outstanding shares and the greater the dilution in EPS when those shares are incorporated into the EPS calculations.

For example, in the illustration of Diane Doll Company above, we will assume that the average market price was $65 but the market price at the end of the accounting period was $85. Also, we will assume again that the options were issued in 1983 and were therefore outstanding throughout 1984. Primary EPS is $.68, as computed earlier. Fully diluted EPS is $.66, however, because the use of the $85 ending market price results in a greater assumed dilution:

Step 1. One hundred thousand shares assumed sold at $50 = $5,000,000.

Step 2. Five million dollars used to buy stock at $85, resulting in the reacquisition of 58,824 shares ($5,000,000/$85).

Step 3. Number of shares sold (100,000) exceeds the number of shares repurchased (58,824) by 41,176.

$$\text{Fully diluted EPS} = \frac{\$356,500}{500,000 + 41,176} = \$.66$$

Conservatism

If the ending market price of the stock is equal to or less than the average for the period, the average price is used to compute both primary and fully diluted EPS. In this procedure we see the strong emphasis on conservatism in computing EPS figures, because EPS will always be the lowest possible figure.

In the illustrations of the treasury stock method above, we used the average market price in computing EPS, except where the higher ending market price was used in computing fully diluted EPS. The possibility exists that the average market price might exceed the exercise price of stock options, warrants, or rights, but the market price *at the end of the period* might be below the exercise price. In this situation, the assumption that the options, warrants, and rights are exercised is not logical, because the holders could acquire shares at a lower price by acquiring them without the option, warrant, and right. To cover this situation, the APB determined that the assumption that stock options, warrants, and rights have been exercised should not be reflected in EPS calculations until the market price of the stock has been above the exercise price for substantially all of the last three months of the period for which EPS is being computed.[8]

The application of the treasury stock method, as we have used it here, is limited to situations where no more than 20% of the outstanding common stock can be reacquired with the assumed proceeds of the exercise of stock options, warrants, and rights. Where the proceeds are so great that more than 20% of the outstanding stock could be acquired, a modification must be made in the application of the method. This procedure is covered in the Appendix to this chapter.

Convertible Securities

Convertible securities are considered common stock equivalents if the return to the holder at the time of issuance is significantly less than the return on a comparable security without the conversion privilege. As we discussed in Chapter 15, convertible securities are complex hybrid securities that incorporate elements of more than one type of debt or ownership interest. The logic behind the treatment of convertible securities as common stock equivalents when there is a significant reduction in return is that investors' willingness to accept the reduced return to obtain the conversion privilege signifies that the conversion privilege has substantial value and, therefore, the value of the convertible security depends to a large extent on the value of common stock.

How could we determine that an investor was sacrificing a significant amount of return in order to acquire a security with a conversion feature? Ideally, we would like to compare the return on the convertible security with the return on an identical security in all respects except that it was not convertible. This is impractical, however, since the convertible security would not also be available without the conversion feature.

In its *Opinion No. 15,* the APB sought to achieve a degree of uniformity in making this important decision by stating that a convertible security was a common stock equivalent if its **cash yield**[9] at the date of issuance was **less than two-thirds of the bank prime interest rate at that date.** If this test is met, the convertible security is treated as if conversion had already taken place for purposes of computing both primary and fully diluted EPS. If this test is not met, the convertible security is treated as if conversion had taken place only in computing fully diluted EPS. The rationale behind this rule is that an investor who would accept a return substantially below other investment alternatives in order to acquire a convertible security has placed a great deal of emphasis and value on conversion. An important feature of this test is that the classification of a convertible security is made only once—when the security is issued. This classification remains with the convertible security as long as it is outstanding and is not changed as market conditions change that might affect the desirability of the conversion feature.

Several aspects of this classification method were criticized by accountants, especially the use of the bank prime interest rate (a measure of the short-term borrowing cost of financially strong companies) for classifying long-term securities for purposes of computing EPS. In 1982 the FASB issued its *Statement of Financial Accounting Standards No. 55,*[10] which changed the standard for this evaluation from the bank prime interest rate to the average Aa corporate bond yield. The FASB noted that since *APB Opinion No. 15* was issued in 1968, the bank prime interest rate had become more volatile and the high degree of

---

[8]*APB Opinion No. 15,* par. 36. If stock options, warrants, and rights are issued during the last three months of the accounting period, this stipulation is usually interpreted to mean the last three months of the period or the length of time outstanding, if shorter.

[9]The **cash yield** on a convertible bond is the effective interest rate, determined by adjusting the nominal interest rate for any premium or discount resulting from sale of the bond. This is computed by dividing the annual interest by the market price of the bond at the date of issuance. The cash yield on a preferred stock is the effective return, determined by dividing the stated dividend amount by the selling price of the stock.

[10]*FASB Statement of Financial Accounting Standards No. 55,* "Determining Whether a Convertible Security Is a Common Stock Equivalent," 1982.

EXHIBIT 26–5
Aa Corporate Bond Yield Rule

Aa corporate bond yield	12%	↑	Convertible securities with a cash yield in this range *are not common stock equivalents.*
⅔ × 12%	8%		
Less than 8%		↓	Convertible securities with a cash yield in this range *are common stock equivalents.*

---

correlation between the bank prime interest rate and the rates of return on long-term debt and preferred stock no longer existed.

Exhibit 26–5 depicts the two-thirds of the average Aa corporate bond yield rule, using a 12% yield rate as an example.

In selecting the average Aa corporate bond yield over the bank prime interest rate for purposes of applying this test, the FASB was influenced by the relationship of the bank prime interest rate to short-term securities and the Aa corporate bond yield to long-term securities. For example, the board cites the fact that in recent years the United States and some other countries have experienced an inverted yield curve in which short-term interest rates have exceeded long-term rates.[11] In applying the two-thirds test, the FASB intends Aa to refer to bonds of equal quality to those rated Aa by either Moody's or Standard & Poor's. Aa bonds are defined by those organizations as bonds of high quality, issued by companies with a strong capacity to pay interest and repay principal. The average Aa bond yield should be based on bond yields for a brief period of time, such as one week preceding the date of issuance of the security being tested.

The change in the two-thirds rule as a result of *FASB Statement No. 55* does not change any other aspect of the procedure. The classification is still made at the date of issuance and is not changed thereafter. In applying the two-thirds test in this text, including the cases, exercises, and problems at the end of the chapter, we use figures for the Aa corporate bond yield that do not necessarily reflect actual yield rates for the year specified.

Convertible Bonds.   To incorporate convertible securities into the EPS computations, the **"if converted" method** is applied. Under this method, convertible securities are assumed to have been converted at the beginning of the accounting period or at their date of issuance, if later. The interest (after income taxes) or the preferred dividend that would not have been paid if the security had been converted must be taken into consideration in addition to the increased number of shares of common stock that would have been outstanding. This procedure recognizes that the holders of senior securities cannot share in distributions of earnings that apply to common stock without first relinquishing their rights to the senior securities.

Because the "if converted" method results in an adjustment to both the numerator and the denominator of the EPS computation, it may not be immediately obvious whether the assumed conversion is dilutive. In such cases, EPS must be computed with and without the assumed conversion to determine whether the conversion will reduce EPS. This procedure is illustrated in the following example.

Roberts Manufacturing Company calculates EPS for 1985, without considering any potential dilution, as $2.50. This was correctly determined by dividing the $10,000,000 net income for 1985 by the weighted average number of common shares outstanding, 4,000,000. In addition, however, the company has $5,000,000 par value of convertible bonds that were sold in 1984 at par and yield an 8% interest rate. The bonds are convertible

---

[11] *FASB Statement of Financial Accounting Standards No. 55*, par. 5.

into 50 shares of common stock per $1,000 bond. The Aa corporate bond yield when the bonds were issued was 11%; the company's income tax rate is 48%.

The first step is to determine whether the potential diluter is a common stock equivalent. Because the cash yield (8%) is greater than two-thirds of the Aa corporate bond yield at the date of issuance (11% × ⅔ = 7.3%), we conclude that the security is *not a common stock equivalent.* Therefore, the assumed dilution will be incorporated only into the fully diluted EPS computation.

Next, the numbers to incorporate the effect of the conversion into the EPS figures are accumulated as follows:

Numerator Adjustment

Reduction in interest expense ($5,000,000 × 8%)	$ 400,000
Increase in income tax expense ($400,000 × 48%)	(192,000)
Increase in net income	$ 208,000

Denominator Adjustment

Number of shares of common stock (5,000 bonds × 50 shares of common stock per bond)	250,000

The bonds are convertible into 250,000 shares of common stock. If converted, Roberts would incur $400,000 less interest expense, but because the interest is tax deductible, it would incur $192,000 in additional income taxes. The *net* savings is $208,000. This can be computed directly by multiplying the interest savings by one minus the income tax rate:

$$\begin{aligned}\text{Increase in income} &= (\text{Interest savings}) \times (1 - \text{Income tax rate})\\ &= (\$5,000,000 \times 8\%) \times (1 - .48)\\ &= (\$400,000) \times (.52)\\ &= \$208,000\end{aligned}$$

Because the convertible bond is not a common stock equivalent, the EPS as originally computed by the company represents primary EPS:

$$\text{Primary EPS} = \frac{\$10,000,000}{4,000,000} = \$2.50$$

Fully diluted EPS is computed by incorporating the assumed conversion of the convertible bond into the above computation:

$$\text{Fully diluted EPS} = \frac{\$10,000,000 + \$208,000}{4,000,000 + 250,000} = \$2.40$$

The assumed conversion of the bond is dilutive in this case, because it reduces EPS from $2.50 to $2.40.

A useful shortcut for testing dilution is to compute a **dilution index** by dividing the adjustment to the numerator by the adjustment to the denominator. In this case the dilution index is $.83 ($208,000/250,000). If this index is *less than EPS without considering dilution,* the potential diluter is dilutive, because its inclusion will reduce EPS. The dilution index is compared with EPS assuming no dilution each time EPS is computed, because the numbers representing both the net income and the weighted average number of common shares outstanding may change from period to period. The dilution index may be used in all cases in which potential diluters result in adjustments to both the numerator and the denominator in EPS calculations. In the above case the dilution index tells us that the convertible bond is dilutive, because the index ($.83) is less than EPS assuming no dilution ($2.50).

Preferred Stock. Preferred stock plays a dual role in EPS computations when it is a potential diluter. On the one hand, preferred stock is a senior security for purposes of computing EPS. On the other hand, preferred stock that is convertible into common stock is a potential diluter that must be treated like a convertible security in computing primary EPS and fully diluted EPS.

In computing EPS without dilution, net income is reduced by the dividend on preferred stock, as described earlier. If the preferred stock is convertible, however, the dividend must be added back to net income, and the equivalent number of common shares must be added to the weighted average number of common shares outstanding. This procedure is identical to the way we treated convertible bonds, with one exception. Interest on the bonds is tax deductible, and the exclusion of interest expense results in increased income taxes. This is why we adjusted net income for the reduced interest expense, net of the income tax effects. Dividends that a company pays on its preferred stock are not tax deductible. Therefore, when the numerator in the EPS computation is adjusted for preferred dividends, the adjustment is for the full amount of those dividends and is not reduced by an income tax adjustment.

To illustrate the application of the "if converted" method to convertible preferred stock, we will use the case of Holden Manufacturing Company, which reports a $5,000,000 net income for 1985 and has 500,000 shares of common stock outstanding the entire year. In addition, 100,000 shares of $100 par value, 9%, cumulative preferred stock are outstanding. Each share of preferred stock may be converted into two shares of common stock. The preferred stock was sold in 1980 at par value when the Aa corporate bond yield was 10%.

In this situation the preferred stock is *not* a common stock equivalent, because the cash yield of 9% (the same as the nominal interest rate since the stock sold at par) is greater than two-thirds of the Aa corporate bond yield at issuance ($10\% \times \frac{2}{3} = 6.7\%$). EPS without assuming dilution, also primary EPS in this case, is computed by subtracting the preferred dividend in the numerator and dividing by the 500,000 shares of common stock outstanding:

$$\begin{matrix} \text{Primary EPS} \\ \text{(also EPS without} \\ \text{dilution)} \end{matrix} = \frac{\$5,000,000 - (9\% \times \$100 \times 100,000)}{500,000} = \$8.20$$

Fully diluted EPS is computed by adding back the preferred dividend in the numerator and adding the increased number of common shares to the figures in the primary EPS computation. Since the preferred dividend is the $900,000 subtracted above (9% × $100 × 100,000), we are simply returning to the $5,000,000 net income figure. The preferred dividend is *not* added back net-of-tax, because it is not tax deductible. The increased number of common shares that would result from the conversion of the preferred is 200,000 (100,000 shares of preferred × 2). Fully diluted EPS is computed as follows:

$$\text{Fully diluted EPS} = \frac{\$5,000,000}{500,000 + 200,000} = \$7.14$$

As in the case of convertible bonds, the dilution index can be computed to determine if the conversion is dilutive. Here the index is $4.50 ($900,000/200,000). Since this is less than EPS without considering dilution ($8.20), the conversion is dilutive.

If convertible securities are issued during the period for which EPS is being computed, the adjustments to both the numerator and the denominator must be weighted for the length of time the securities are actually outstanding.

Contingent Issuances

Contingent issuances represent potential future distributions of common stock that may or may not depend on the satisfaction of certain future conditions. If the shares to be issued depend on merely the passage of time, they are treated as common stock equivalents and included in the computation of both primary and fully diluted EPS. If shares are issuable upon the attainment of certain conditions and those conditions are met, the shares are included in computing both primary and fully diluted EPS. Shares awaiting issuance in a stock dividend are an example of a contingent issuance that would be included in both primary and fully diluted EPS because the distribution would depend on only the passage of time, and the distribution would be dilutive because the number of outstanding shares would increase with no adjustment to net income.

Other contingent issuances occur only when certain future conditions are met, such as attaining a specified level of income. Such issuances are frequently encountered in business combinations. If attaining a stated level of income is a condition for issuance and that condition is not being met, the contingent shares are included only in fully diluted EPS. For this computation, earnings should be adjusted to include the higher level of income specified in the agreement. As in the case of all potential diluters, shares in a contingent issuance should not be included in fully diluted EPS unless their effect is dilutive. Also, if the contingent issuance arose during the accounting period for which EPS is being computed, the figures should be weighted for the appropriate length of time.

To illustrate, Crystal Company had 1,000,000 shares of common stock outstanding throughout 1985, a year in which the company reported a net income of $3,250,000. Dividends of $72,500 on noncumulative preferred stock were declared and paid during the year. Under the terms of a business combination of a previous year, the company is required to issue 500,000 additional shares of common stock if the net income reaches $4,000,000 and is maintained at that level between the year of the business combination and the end of 1989. This condition has not been met through 1985.

Primary EPS is computed without considering the contingent issuance resulting from the business combination, because the condition for issuance has not been met. Primary EPS is thus computed by reducing net income by the preferred dividend and dividing by the number of shares of common stock:

$$\text{Primary EPS} = \frac{\$3,250,000 - \$72,500}{1,000,000} = \$3.18$$

The computation of fully diluted EPS must consider the impact of the contingent issuance, taking into consideration the increase in income that must be achieved, if the contingent issuance is dilutive. In this case dilution would result, because the increase in the numerator and the increase in the denominator result in an index below $3.18:

Increase in Income

Required income for distribution	$4,000,000
1985 income	3,250,000
Incremental Income	$ 750,000
Increased number of shares	500,000
Dilution index ($750,000/500,000)	$1.50

Fully diluted EPS is computed as follows:

$$\text{Fully diluted EPS} = \frac{\$3,250,000 - \$72,500 + \$750,000}{1,000,000 + 500,000} = \$2.62$$

Three Percent Minimum Dilution Presented

As noted earlier, companies with complex capital structures must make the dual presentation of primary and fully diluted EPS in their income statements. As a practical matter, the dual presentation must be made only if the aggregate dilution of all potential diluters is at least 3%. To assess whether aggregate dilution is 3% or greater, *EPS assuming no dilution* is compared with *EPS assuming full dilution.* If the latter is 97% or less of the former, the aggregate dilution meets the 3% minimum dilution test.

To illustrate this test, EPS assuming no dilution for American Pipe Company is $1.85 for 1985. To report dual EPS, fully diluted EPS must be $1.79 (97% × $1.85) or less. For example, if the company's fully diluted EPS is $1.50, the dual presentation is required. On the other hand, if fully diluted EPS is computed to be $1.82, the 3% test is not met and the dual presentation need not be made. In the latter case EPS might be presented as follows:

Earnings per common share (no material potential dilution) $1.85

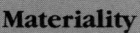

The 3% minimum dilution test is a practical application of the modifying convention of materiality. We do not further complicate the financial statements with the dual EPS figures unless the dollar impact is significant. The 3% materiality standard used here is solely for purposes of presenting EPS. A similar standard for materiality in other situations is not implied by the use of 3% in the case of EPS.

Financial Statement Presentation

Primary and fully diluted EPS are terms used for computational purposes to determine the numbers to be presented in the income statement. The APB did not specify titles to identify EPS figures in the income statement. As you review financial statements, you will find that some companies use these terms and other companies use terms such as the following:

	Primary EPS Concept	Fully Diluted EPS Concept
No common stock equivalents	Earnings per common share—assuming no dilution	Earnings per common share—assuming full dilution
With common stock equivalents	Earnings per common and common equivalent share	Earnings per common share—assuming full dilution

Note that the designations above vary, depending on whether or not the capital structure of the company includes common stock equivalents.

Disclosure   In addition to disclosure in the income statement, disclosure in the notes to the financial statements should be made to explain the rights and privileges of the holders of potentially dilutive securities, the bases on which primary and fully diluted EPS are computed, and other information necessary for an understanding of the EPS figures. Such information includes dividend and liquidation preferences, participating rights, call prices and dates, conversion or exercise prices or rates and dates, sinking fund requirements, and unusual voting rights.

In discussing the financial statement presentation of EPS for companies with simple capital structures, we stated that EPS figures must be presented on income from continuing operations, income before extraordinary items, and net income, if these figures appear in the income statement. For complex capital structures, potential diluters should be included in the EPS computations on all of these income figures if they are dilutive in any one of the income figures. This is true even if they are antidilutive in one or both of the other income figures.

To illustrate this possibility, we will assume that Sterling Manufacturing Company reports the following items in its 1985 income statement:

Income before extraordinary item	$ 28,500,000
Extraordinary loss	(37,900,000)
Net loss	$ (9,400,000)

The company has 10,000,000 shares of common stock outstanding and no preferred stock. Applying the treasury stock method to outstanding stock options results in 1,000,000 common stock equivalent shares. This situation is dilutive for purposes of computing EPS on income before extraordinary items but antidilutive for purposes of computing EPS on net loss, as we see below:

	EPS Without Dilution	EPS With Dilution
Income before extraordinary items		
$28,500,000/10,000,000 shares	$2.85	
$28,500,000/11,000,000 shares		$2.59
Net loss		
$(9,400,000)/10,000,000 shares	$(.94)	
$(9,400,000)/11,000,000 shares		$(.85)

The assumed exercise of the options is **antidilutive** in the net loss situation because it spreads the loss over a larger number of shares, thereby resulting in a smaller loss per share. In this case, the exercise of the stock options would still be incorporated in all computations, even though it results in an antidilutive effect for one of the income figures.

Exhibit 26–6 presents a portion of the income statement of B. F. Goodrich Company for 1982 with the comparative years of 1981 and 1980. B. F. Goodrich is a major producer of chemical, plastic, and rubber products with operations throughout the world. The primary and fully diluted EPS figures are presented at the bottom of the income statement. The portion of the company's accounting policy statement that relates to EPS is also presented as part of Exhibit 26–6. That note includes information underlying the computation of both primary and fully diluted EPS.

Summary of EPS Computations for Complex Capital Structures

The circumstances in which the alternative EPS treatments are appropriate are summarized in Exhibit 26–7.

The computations to determine primary and fully diluted EPS in the case of dual presentation are summarized below:

$$\text{Primary EPS} = \frac{(\text{Net income}) - (\text{Preferred dividends}) + (\text{Adjustments})}{(\text{Weighted average common shares}) + (\text{Common stock equivalents})}$$

$$\text{Fully diluted EPS} = \frac{(\text{Net income}) - (\text{Preferred dividends}) + (\text{Adjustments})}{(\text{Weighted average common shares}) + (\text{All potential diluters})}$$

EXHIBIT 26–6
B. F. Goodrich Company
Income Statement Excerpt and Related Note

The B. F. Goodrich Company and Subsidiaries

Consolidated Statement Of Income

(Dollars in millions, except per share amounts) Year ended December 31,	1982	1981	1980
Income (loss) before extraordinary gain	(32.8)	91.5	61.7
Extraordinary gain from exchange of preferred stock for debentures	—	18.0	—
Net income (loss)	$(32.8)	$109.5	$61.7
Earnings (loss) per share: Primary:			
Income (loss) before extraordinary gain	$(2.43)	$4.71	$3.57
Extraordinary gain	—	1.04	—
Net income (loss)	$(2.43)	$5.75	$3.57
Fully Diluted: Income (loss) before extraordinary gain	$(2.43)	$4.62	$3.56
Extraordinary gain	—	.93	—
Net income (loss)	$(2.43)	$5.55	$3.56

See Notes to Consolidated Financial Statements

Excerpt from Accounting Policy Statement:

Earnings (Loss) Per Share: Primary earnings (loss) per share of common stock are computed by dividing the earnings (loss) applicable to common stock by the weighted average number of common and, when dilutive, common equivalent shares outstanding each year. Common equivalent shares are shares contingently issuable from exercises of stock options and warrants. The number of common equivalent shares is determined by the treasury stock method, using the average market price. To determine the earnings (loss) applicable to common stock for purpose of this computation, the net income for the year is reduced or the net loss is increased by the amount of the dividend requirements ($9.9 in 1982; $8.9 in 1981; and $2.1 in 1980) on all series of preferred stock. The earnings (loss) applicable to common stock and the weighted average number of shares entering into the primary computation are as follows:

	Earnings (Loss) Applicable to Common Stock	Weighted Average Number of Shares
1982	$ (42.7)	17,609,636
1981	100.6	17,484,380
1980	59.6	16,735,480

Fully diluted earnings per share in 1981 assume that the Series C Cumulative Convertible Preferred Stock was converted into common stock at the date of issuance and that the $7.0 dividend paid on it in 1981 was restored to the earnings applicable to common stock. The additional dilutive effects of stock options using the year-end market price is also reflected in the 1981 and 1980 computations. In 1982, the conversion of the Series C Cumulative Convertible Preferred Stock is not assumed since its effect would be anti-dilutive. The earnings (loss) applicable to common stock and the weighted average number of shares entering into the fully diluted computation are as follows:

	Earnings (Loss) Applicable to Common Stock	Weighted Average Number of Shares
1982	$ (42.7)	17,609,636
1981	107.6	19,379,911
1980	59.6	16,744,424

SOURCE: B. F. Goodrich Company, 1982 Annual Report.

EXHIBIT 26–7
Alternative EPS Presentations

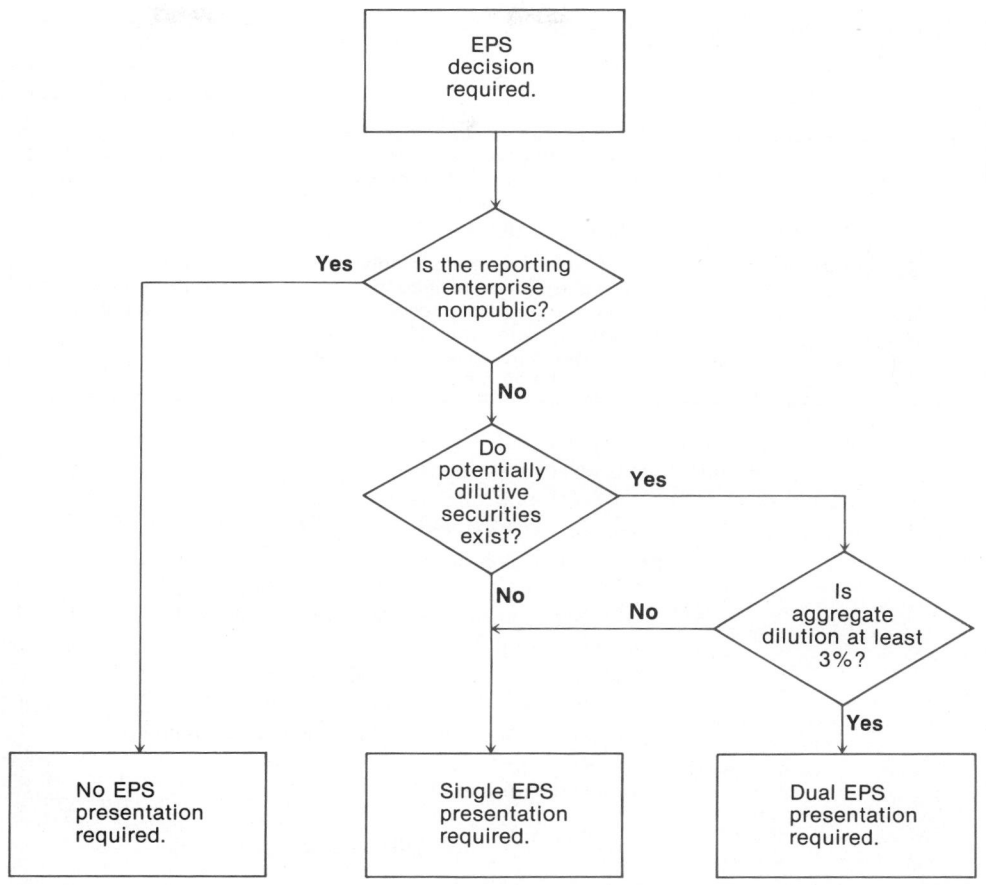

Adjustments in the numerator of each computation are necessary when the potential diluters affect the income that is attributed to the residual (common) stockholders. Potential diluters are included in EPS computations only when they are individually dilutive. Each potential diluter must be evaluated in terms of its common stock equivalency status and its dilutive impact. The decision process that must be followed in making these decisions is summarized in Exhibit 26–8.

EXAMPLE EPS COMPUTATIONS

This section presents a step-by-step approach to the computation of EPS for a company with a complex capital structure. We illustrate this approach by preparing the EPS presentation for West Company for 1984. Excerpts from the financial statements of West Company for

---

EXHIBIT 26–8
Summary of EPS Decisions

Potential Diluters	*Decision No. 1:* Is Potential Diluter a Common Stock Equivalent (CSE)?	*Decision No. 2:* Does Potential Diluter Reduce EPS?
Stock options, warrants, rights	Always CSE.	Application of the treasury stock method results in dilution if the market price of the stock exceeds the exercise price.
Convertible securities	CSE if the cash yield is less than two-thirds of the Aa corporate bond yield at the date of issuance. If cash yield is equal to or exceeds this level, not CSE.	Must be tested by computing EPS with and without assumed conversion.
Contingent issuances	CSE if issuance depends only on passage of time or if conditions necessary for issuance are currently being met. Not CSE if conditions necessary for issuance are not being met.	Must be tested by computing EPS with and without assumed issuance of stock.

1984 and other relevant information are presented below.

Partial Balance Sheet at December 31, 1984

Stockholders' Equity

Preferred stock ($50 par, 7% cumulative; 100,000 shares authorized, 65,000 shares issued and outstanding)	$ 3,250,000
Common stock ($10 par; 4,000,000 shares authorized, 1,700,000 shares issued)	17,000,000
Paid-in capital in excess of par value on common stock	4,685,000
Retained earnings	12,755,000
	$37,690,000
Less: Treasury stock (75,000 shares of common at $17 cost)	(1,275,000)
	$36,415,000

Common Stock Activity in 1984

			Number of Common Shares
Jan. 1	Number of shares outstanding		1,100,000
Apr. 1	Distribution of 10% stock dividend		110,000
May 1	Sale of previously unissued stock		490,000
Oct. 1	Acquisition of treasury stock		(300,000)
Dec. 1	Sale of treasury stock		225,000
Dec. 31	Number of shares outstanding		1,625,000

Other Data

1. West Company had 300,000 stock options outstanding throughout 1984; each option allowed

the acquisition of one share of common stock at $15. The market price of the common averaged $24 during 1984. The market price at the end of 1984 was $30.

2. West Company had 275,000 stock purchase warrants outstanding throughout 1984; each warrant allowed the acquisition of one share of common stock at $32.

3. As the result of a business combination in 1982, West Company is required to issue 1,000,000 shares of common stock if income reaches the $5,000,000 level in any year through 1985. This level of income has not been reached before 1984.

4. West Company has outstanding $10,000,000 of convertible bonds that were issued at par in 1980 and yield 7%. Each $1,000 bond may be converted into 40 shares of common stock. The Aa corporate bond yields since the year of issuance have been as follows:

1980	12%
1981	11%
1982	11½%
1983	10½%
1984	9%

5. Net income reported by West Company for 1984 is $4,750,000.
6. The income tax rate for West Company is 48%.

Step 1. Determine Weighted Average Number of Common Shares Outstanding

The weighted average number of common shares outstanding is determined by considering the amount of time various numbers of shares of common stock were outstanding during the year. The 10% stock dividend of March 31, 1984, is applied retroactively.

			Months × Shares		
Period	Number of Months ×	Number of Shares Outstanding =	Original ×	Stock Dividend Conversion =	Restated
Jan. 1–Mar. 31	3	1,100,000	3,300,000	1.10	3,630,000
Apr. 1–Apr. 30	1	1,210,000			1,210,000
May 1–Sept. 30	5	1,700,000			8,500,000
Oct. 1–Nov. 30	2	1,400,000			2,800,000
Dec. 1–Dec. 31	1	1,625,000			1,625,000
	12				17,765,000

Weighted average = 17,765,000/12 = 1,480,417

Step 2. Compute Base EPS (EPS assuming no dilution)

Base EPS is computed by reducing the net income of $4,750,000 by the preferred dividend and dividing by the weighted average common shares. The preferred dividend is $227,500 (65,000 shares × $50 par × 7%).

$$\text{Base EPS} = \frac{\$4,750,000 - \$227,500}{1,480,417} = \$3.05$$

Base EPS provides the basis for comparing potential diluters to determine whether they dilute EPS if included in the computations.

Step 3. Evaluate Potential Diluters for Common Stock Equivalency Status

Each potential diluter must be evaluated to determine if it is a common stock equivalent and therefore included in primary EPS (if dilutive). The four potential diluters of West Company are evaluated as follows:

Potential Diluter	Evaluation
Stock options	Common stock equivalent (by definition).
Stock purchase warrants	Common stock equivalent (by definition).
Contingent issuance resulting from business combination	Not a common stock equivalent since the conditions required for the stock to be issued have not been met (i.e., the $5,000,000 level of income has not been attained).
Convertible debt	Common stock equivalent since the cash yield (7%) is less than two-thirds of the Aa corporate bond yield when the bonds were issued ($\frac{2}{3} \times 12\% = 8\%$).

Step 4. Determine Whether Potential Diluters Are Dilutive in This Accounting Period

Because potential diluters are included in EPS computations only when they are individually dilutive, each must be evaluated to determine if it will be included in the EPS computations in the current period. This evaluation is made as follows:

Potential Diluter	Evaluation
Stock options	Dilutive—Both the average and ending market prices ($24 and $30) exceed the exercise price ($15).
Stock purchase warrants	Antidilutive—Both the average and ending market prices ($24 and $30) are less than the exercise price ($32).
Contingent issuance resulting from business combination	Dilutive—The dilution index resulting from the addition to income and the addition to outstanding shares is less than base EPS:

Addition to income	$250,000	
Addition to shares	1,000,000	
Dilution index ($250,000/1,000,000)		.25

Potential Diluter	Evaluation
Convertible debt	Dilutive—The dilution index resulting from the addition to income and the addition to outstanding shares is less than base EPS:

Addition to income ($10,000,000 × 7%) (1 − .48)		$364,000
Addition to shares (10,000 × 40)		400,000
Dilution index ($364,000/400,000)		.91

Step 5. Summarize Potential Diluters

The potential diluters must be summarized to determine how they will affect the computation of primary and fully diluted EPS. This is done for West Company as follows:

| | Use in Computing | |
Potential Diluter	Primary EPS	Fully Diluted EPS
Stock options (common stock equivalent, dilutive)	Yes	Yes
Stock purchase warrants (common stock equivalent, antidilutive)	No	No
Contingent issuance (not common stock equivalent, dilutive)	No	Yes
Convertible debt (common stock equivalent, dilutive)	Yes	Yes

From this summary we see that the primary EPS will include the elements of base EPS, plus the dilutive effect of the *stock options* and the *convertible debt.* Fully diluted EPS will include the dilutive effect of these same items plus the contingent issuance. Also, the dilutive effect of the options will be greater in fully diluted EPS than in primary EPS, because the year-end market price of the stock exceeds the average price for the year.

Step 6. Compute Primary and Fully Diluted EPS and Apply 3% Test

The elements for computing primary and fully diluted EPS are calculated as follows:

Numerator

Net income	$4,750,000
Less: Preferred dividend (see Step 2)	(227,500)
Plus: Interest (after tax) on convertible debt (see Step 4)	364,000
For primary EPS	4,886,500
Plus: Income increase for contingent issuance (see Step 4)	250,000
For fully diluted EPS	$5,136,500

Denominator

Weighted average common shares outstanding (see Step 1)	1,480,417
Plus: Application of treasury stock method to stock options (at the average market prices)	
Proceeds from sale: 300,000 × $15 = $4,500,000	
Shares acquired: $4,500,000/$24 = 187,500	
Net increase: 300,000 − 187,500 =	112,500
Plus: Equivalent shares for convertible debt (see Step 4)	400,000
For primary EPS	1,992,917
Plus: Shares increase from contingent issuance (see Step 4)	1,000,000
Application of treasury stock method to stock options (at the ending market price)	
Proceeds from sale: 300,000 × $15 = $4,500,000	
Shares acquired: $4,500,000/$30 = 150,000	
Net increase: 300,000 − 150,000 = 150,000	
Excess of increase for fully diluted over primary: 150,000 − 112,500 =	37,500
For fully diluted EPS	3,030,417

Primary and fully diluted EPS are then computed using the appropriate numbers from the schedule above:

$$\text{Primary EPS} = \$4,886,500/1,992,917 = \$2.45$$
$$\text{Fully diluted EPS} = \$5,136,500/3,030,417 = \$1.69$$

For the dual presentation of EPS to be required, fully diluted EPS must be 97% or less of base EPS as computed in Step 2 above. Because base EPS is $3.05, the dual presentation is required if fully diluted EPS is $2.96 or less ($3.05 × 97%). This condition is clearly met in this case since fully diluted EPS is $1.69.

Step 7.   Prepare the Income Statement Presentation of EPS

The dual presentation of EPS is reported after the net income figure at the bottom of the income statement. Appropriate wording depends on the circumstances of the presentation. The presentation for West Company for 1984 might appear as follows:

Net income	$4,750,000
Earnings per share	
Earnings per common and common equivalent share	$2.45
Earnings per common share, assuming full dilution	$1.69

CONCLUDING REMARKS

Earnings per share is an area of accounting where many types of situations may be encountered. Several aspects of EPS that are beyond the scope of this text have been omitted in an attempt to focus our attention on basic concepts and methods of computation. Several additional considerations in the computation of EPS are covered in the Appendix to this chapter.

Substance over Form

The requirements of *APB Opinion No. 15* regarding EPS computations represent an interesting combination of the modifying conventions of substance over form and conservatism. Substance over form refers to emphasizing in financial reporting the economic implications of events rather than the legal form when the two are different. This concept is applied in an attempt to provide information in financial statements that better reflects the economic impact of activities being presented. Securities other than common stock and agreements to issue common stock under certain circumstances are treated as common stock outstanding in computing both primary and fully diluted EPS, thus applying the concept of substance over form. Presenting the substance of various potential diluters in EPS computations is thought to provide more useful information than presenting the legal form.

Applying substance over form in computing EPS requires that we incorporate events and activities that have not actually occurred. This is different from traditional accounting. The adjustments to net income and to the number of shares of common stock outstanding are only for the purposes of computing diluted EPS figures. These adjustments are not entered in the accounting records except as a memorandum in conjunction with the documentation of EPS calculations.

Conservatism

Conservatism refers to the financial reporting practice of using the accounting alternative that results in the least favorable impact on net income when reporting in a context of significant uncertainty. Uncertainties about EPS computations center primarily on the ultimate issuance of additional shares of common stock that may reduce EPS (i.e., potential dilution). Procedures for computing EPS are designed to state EPS on a diluted basis, thereby reflecting the potential decline expected from these potential increases in the number of common shares outstanding.

1.   EPS is frequently cited by users of financial statements as one of the most important figures on which they base financial decisions.

2.   The term dilution refers to a reduction in EPS resulting from the issuance of additional shares of common stock. Potential dilution refers to possible future reductions in EPS.

3.   The potential for dilution of EPS exists in situations such as stock options, warrants, and rights; convertible securities; and contingent issuances of common stock.

4.   A company with a simple capital structure has no potential diluters. A company with a complex capital structure has one or more potential diluters.

5.   A publicly held company with a simple capital structure must present EPS in the income statement, based on the outstanding common stock for that period.

6.   A publicly held company with a complex capital structure must present EPS in the income statement based on both the outstanding common stock for that period and the potential diluters in its capital structure. (If the potential dilution is not material, however, the potential dilution is not required to be presented.)

7.   EPS figures are based on the weighted average number of shares of common stock outstanding. Securities whose claim on income precedes the claim of the common stockholders, such as preferred stock, must be deducted before computing EPS.

8.   Primary EPS is based on the outstanding common stock, plus potential diluters identified as *common stock equivalents*. Fully diluted EPS is based on the outstanding common stock plus *all potential diluters*.

9.   In preparing the EPS figures for complex capital structures, events that have not actually taken place are incorporated, resulting in *pro forma* figures. Methods used to incorporate these assumed events include the treasury stock method for stock options, rights, and warrants, and the "if converted" method for convertible securities.

10.   EPS figures are presented on the face of the income statement. The precise wording and disclosure varies, depending on the circumstances of each company.

11.   The modifying conventions of substance over form and conservatism explain the incorporation of potential dilution in EPS figures. We attempt to reflect the economic substance of events rather than simply their legal form. We incorporate only those events that reduce EPS.

APPENDIX A ADDITIONAL EPS CONSIDERATIONS

In practice, many variations are encountered in computing EPS, particularly in the case of companies with complex capital structures. The model for computing EPS presented in this chapter is designed to cover major problem areas.

This appendix discusses several additional considerations in computing EPS. Some relate to circumstances that were intentionally avoided in the previous discussion. Others concern points that must be understood for a more complete knowledge of EPS but that the authors consider less important than material covered earlier.

Throughout our discussion of these additional considerations, we use Pioneer Company as an example.

Selected data for Pioneer Company are presented for 1985, the accounting period for which EPS is being computed, at the top of the next page.

Data presented in each of the following sections are designed to supplement this information and apply only to the specific EPS refinement discussed in that section.

DILUTIVE SECURITIES OUTSTANDING PART OF THE YEAR

In some cases potentially dilutive securities are outstanding only part of the accounting period for which EPS figures are being computed. When this occurs, the

Pioneer Company
SELECTED INCOME STATEMENT INFORMATION
For the Year Ended December 31, 1985

Net income	$350,000
Income tax rate	46%

Pioneer Company
SELECTED BALANCE SHEET INFORMATION
December 31, 1985

Common stock outstanding at December 31, 1985	200,000 shares
Number of shares issued in 2:1 stock split during 1985 (no other stock activity during year)	100,000 shares

number of common shares represented by the poten-

convertible securities outstanding for only a portion of the accounting period. For example, assume that Pioneer Company had convertible bonds outstanding throughout 1985 that had been issued in a previous year. The bonds were issued at par and carry a 10% interest rate. Each $1,000 bond is convertible into 50 shares of common stock (after adjustment for the stock split). On January 1, 1985, $1,000,000 par value bonds were outstanding; at March 31, 1985, $200,000 of the bonds were converted to common stock, and at September 30, 1985, another $100,000 were converted.

To incorporate the potential dilution from the bonds into EPS, consideration is given to the length of time various amounts of debt were outstanding during the year. A schedule such as the following assists in the preparation of the needed information:

Period	Number of Months	Equivalent Number of Common Shares	Interest for Portion of Year Outstanding
Jan. 1–Mar. 31	3	$1,000 \times 50 \times \frac{3}{12} = 12,500$	$\$1,000,000 \times 10\% \times \frac{3}{12} = \$25,000$
Apr. 1–Sept. 30	6	$800 \times 50 \times \frac{6}{12} = 20,000$	$800,000 \times 10\% \times \frac{6}{12} = 40,000$
Oct. 1–Dec. 31	3	$700 \times 50 \times \frac{3}{12} = 8,750$	$700,000 \times 10\% \times \frac{3}{12} = 17,500$
	12	41,250	$82,500

tial diluters must be stated on a weighted average basis, taking into consideration the length of time the potential diluters were outstanding.

For example, Pioneer Company issued stock options on February 28, 1985, that provided for the acquisition of 20,000 shares of common stock at $20 a share after adjustment for the 2:1 split. The price of the stock was $37 throughout 1985 (also adjusted for the stock split). In this case, the treasury stock method is applied as usual, but the resulting net increase in the number of shares is weighted for the part of the year the options were outstanding. This is done as follows:

Proceeds from issuance: 20,000 × $20 = $400,000
Shares reacquired: $400,000/$37 = 10,811
Net increase: 20,000 − 10,811 = 9,189
Weighting for portion of year outstanding:

$$9,189 \times \frac{10 \text{ months}}{12 \text{ months}} = 7,658$$

Primary EPS is then computed as follows:

$$\text{Primary EPS} = \frac{\$350,000}{200,000 + 7,658} = \$1.69$$

The same general approach is applied in the case of

The numerator of the EPS computation should be increased by $44,550 [$82,500 × (1 − .46)], and the denominator should be increased by 41,250 shares of stock. Of course, the weighted average number of common shares outstanding will also be affected by the conversion of the bonds, because the issuance of common stock at the intermediate dates during the period increases the number of shares actually outstanding.

MODIFICATION OF THE TREASURY STOCK METHOD

The treasury stock method is used to determine the dilutive effect of stock options, warrants, and rights. With this method, we assume that a company acquires treasury stock with the proceeds from the sale of shares of common stock with stock options, warrants, and rights. In developing the methods for computation of EPS figures, the Accounting Principles Board concluded that companies would rarely acquire treasury stock in excess of 20% of their outstanding stock. Thus, the treasury stock method is modified when the proceeds from the assumed sale of common stock by stock options, warrants, and rights provides proceeds in excess of the amount needed to reacquire 20% of the shares of common stock that are actually outstanding at the end of the accounting period.

When this situation exists, the assumed use of the proceeds should be distributed as follows:

1. As if the funds were first applied to the repurchase of common stock, up to 20% of the shares outstanding at the end of the period.
2. As if the remaining funds were used to reduce short-term or long-term borrowing and any remaining funds were invested in U.S. government securities or commercial paper.

If the net effect is dilutive, the results of these two steps should be combined and included in EPS computations.

To illustrate, assume that Pioneer Company has options outstanding throughout 1985 that allow the acquisition of 100,000 shares of common stock (after adjustment for the 2:1 split) at $20. The average market price for the year (and the year-end price) is $37. The modification in the treasury stock method is appropriate because the number of shares which can be repurchased, 54,054 [(100,000 × $20)/$37], exceeds 40,000 (20% of the 200,000 shares outstanding at December 31, 1985). Assuming that the company has at least $520,000 of debt carrying a 15% interest rate, we determine the dilutive effect of the options as follows:

Proceeds from assumed exercise of options (100,000 × $20)	$2,000,000
20% limitation, 20% × 200,000 = 40,000	
Reacquisition of treasury shares (40,000 × $37)	1,480,000
Proceeds available for debt reduction	$ 520,000
Interest savings, after tax ($520,000 × 15%)(1 − .46)	$42,120
Increase in outstanding shares	

Shares sold	100,000	
Shares repurchased	40,000	60,000

Primary EPS, incorporating the dilution caused by the assumed exercise of the options, is computed as follows:

$$\text{Primary EPS} = \frac{\$350,000 + \$42,120}{200,000 + 60,000} = \$1.51$$

APB Opinion No. 15 does not indicate the order in which the company's debt should be assumed to have been retired. Also, if the proceeds available for debt reduction ($520,000 in the above example) exceed the amount of outstanding debt, the remaining amounts should be assumed to have been invested in U.S. government securities or commercial paper. This has a similar impact on income as debt reduction, because the interest, after income tax, would be added to income.

RETROACTIVE APPLICATION OF STOCK SPLITS AND STOCK DIVIDENDS

In computing the weighted average number of common shares outstanding, stock splits and stock dividends are applied retroactively to restate stock outstanding prior to the split or dividend on the basis of the stock at the end of the accounting period. Financial statements are typically presented on a comparative basis, with the current period set in the context of one or more additional (historical) accounting periods.

If a stock split or stock dividend takes place in the current year, the split or dividend is applied retroactively to the comparative year figures, as well as within the current period, as we studied earlier.

To illustrate this point, assume that EPS for Pioneer Company for 1984, presented as comparative data in the 1985 financial statements, was originally reported as $3.26. This figure was based on a net income of $326,000 and 100,000 shares of outstanding common stock. For comparative purposes in 1985, the 1984 EPS must be restated to apply the 2:1 stock split of 1985 retroactively. The restated EPS figure for 1984 is $1.63 ($326,000/200,000 shares). The comparative figures of $1.63 for 1984 and $1.75 for 1985 ($350,000/ 200,000 shares), presented in adjoining columns, are comparable on the basis of the stock outstanding at the end of 1985.

Exhibit 26–9 illustrates the retroactive application of stock splits and stock dividends for Overseas Shipholding Group, Inc., which is among the largest bulk shipping companies in the world. The company has experienced stock splits in 1981 and 1980 and a stock dividend in 1979, all of which have been applied retroactively for purposes of presenting comparative EPS figures.

ADDITIONAL ANTIDILUTION CONSIDERATIONS

Potential diluters must be tested to determine if they actually reduce EPS in each period for which EPS is computed. If they do not reduce EPS, they are not used in the EPS computations in that period, but they must

---

EXHIBIT 26–9
Overseas Shipholding Group, Inc.
EPS Presentation

	For the Year Ended December 31,		
	1981	1980	1979
Number of shares used in computing per share amounts—Note M	25,815,000	25,815,000	25,775,000
Net income per share	$3.43	$3.06	$2.56

Note M—Common Stock and Per Share Amounts:

A summary of changes in Common Stock and Paid-in Additional Capital follows:

	Common Stock		Paid-in Additional Capital
	Shares	Amount	
Balance December 31, 1978	10,966,151	$10,966,000	$35,678,000
Issuance of 4% stock dividend	439,505	440,000	9,174,000
Stock options exercised	59,389	59,000	656,000
Balance December 31, 1979	11,465,045	11,465,000	45,508,000
3-for-2 stock split (distributed March 1980)	5,736,527	5,736,000	(5,745,000)
Stock options exercised	8,773	9,000	93,000
Balance December 31, 1980	17,210,345	17,210,000	39,856,000
3-for-2 stock split (distributed June 1981)	8,604,769	8,605,000	(8,616,000)
Balance December 31, 1981	25,815,114	$25,815,000	$31,240,000

In May 1981 the stockholders approved an increase in the authorized common stock from 30,000,000 to 60,000,000 shares.

Amounts per share of Common Stock are based on the weighted average number of shares outstanding after giving retroactive effect to the stock splits declared in 1981 and 1980 and the 4% stock dividend declared in 1979.

SOURCE: Overseas Shipholding Group, Inc., 1982 Annual Report.

---

be used in future periods if their impact in those periods is dilutive.

Potentially dilutive securities may actually be antidilutive. For example, the adjustment to the numerator and denominator from a convertible security may actually combine to *increase* rather than decrease EPS. For this reason, computing the actual impact of the assumed conversion is important. We have illustrated this several times in the chapter, using the dilution index approach, where the dilutive impact of the potential diluter is compared to base EPS.

Particular care must be taken where operations result in a net loss, because increases in outstanding stock that distribute a net loss over a larger number of shares result in a *reduced loss per share* and are thus *antidilutive.*

DELAYED EFFECTIVENESS AND CHANGING RATES OR PRICES

Some convertible securities are not convertible until a future date, and in some cases conversion rates vary over time. Similarly, some options or warrants are not exercisable until a future date, and in some cases exercise prices vary over time. Conversion rates on convertible securities and exercise prices on stock options and warrants are important in applying the "if converted" and treasury stock methods to compute primary and fully diluted EPS.

In computing primary EPS, the conversion rate or price in effect for the period of computation should be used. If the conversion or exercise privilege is delayed, the earliest rate or price in the *next five years* should be used. If conversion or exercise is not available within the five-year period, the potential diluter should not be used to compute primary EPS.

In computing fully diluted EPS, the most advantageous conversion rate or exercise price to the holder that becomes effective in the *next ten years* should be used. If conversion or exercise is not available within the 10-year period, the potential diluter should not be used in computing fully diluted EPS.

26–1   What is meant by the term "dilution" as it relates to EPS?

26–2   Describe three types of potential diluters and indicate how each may reduce EPS.

26–3   What is meant by the term "senior security" when computing EPS? How does the existence of senior securities affect EPS?

26–4   Describe the difference between companies with simple and those with complex capital structures, and indicate the type of EPS presentation that each must make.

26–5   In computing EPS, a weighted average number of common shares outstanding should be used. Indicate the impact, if any, of each of the following common stock transactions on the weighted average computation:
[a] Sale of additional shares.
[b] Acquisition of treasury stock.
[c] Distribution of a stock dividend.
[d] Resale of treasury stock.
[e] Distribution of a cash dividend.
[f] Distribution of a stock split.

26–6   In what circumstances should the dividend on preferred stock be subtracted from net income in computing EPS? In what circumstances should this subtraction not be made?

26–7   Describe the difference between the two EPS figures in each pair below and indicate when the two might be the same:
[a] Base EPS and primary EPS.
[b] Primary EPS and fully diluted EPS.

26–8   Distinguish between common stock equivalents and other potentially dilutive securities in general. Explain when each of the following would be considered common stock equivalents:
[a] Convertible securities.
[b] Stock options, warrants, and rights.
[c] Contingent issuances.

26–9   How could a common stock equivalent be included in the determination of EPS in one year but not in another year, even though it was outstanding throughout both years?

26–10 When incorporating the dilutive impact of some potential diluters on EPS, the numerator in the computation is adjusted. In other cases, the numerator is not adjusted. Explain the reason for this difference and indicate when an adjustment is necessary.

26–11 Explain the distinction between companies that are publicly held and those that are not publicly held and the importance of this distinction in determining the appropriateness of presenting EPS.

26–12 The treasury stock method is used to determine the dilutive effect of the exercise of stock options, warrants, and rights. Explain how it is possible to determine whether the application of the method will result in a reduction in EPS prior to actually making the computations to determine the amount of the dilution.

26–13 The presentation of EPS is best described as:
[a] Required in the financial statements of all companies.
[b] Required in the financial statements of companies whose stock is publicly held.
[c] Required in the financial statements of companies whose stock is not publicly held.
[d] Not required in the financial statements of any company.

26–14 When EPS figures are presented, they should be located:
[a] In the income statement following net income.
[b] In the stockholders' equity section of the balance sheet.
[c] In the notes to the financial statements.
[d] In any of the three places suggested in [a], [b], and [c].

26–15 Potential diluters of EPS include all of the following except:
[a] Stock options, warrants, and rights to acquire common stock.
[b] Contingent issuances of common stock.
[c] Debt that is convertible into common stock.
[d] Preferred stock that is cumulative and nonconvertible.

26–16 Primary EPS is based on the shares of common stock described as:
[a] The number outstanding at the end of the accounting period.
[b] The weighted average number of shares outstanding plus common stock equivalents.
[c] The weighted average number of shares outstanding plus all potential diluters.
[d] The simple average of common shares outstanding.

26–17 Fully diluted EPS is best described as:
[a] EPS assuming the dilutive effect of events judged most likely to occur.

[b] EPS based on historical income and outstanding shares.

[c] EPS incorporating the negative effect of all possible extraordinary losses that could occur in the future.

[d] EPS based on the assumption of full dilution of all potential diluters.

26–18 (Appendix A) To what extent is treasury stock assumed to be acquired by a corporation applying the treasury stock method in EPS calculations?

[a] To the maximum extent possible.

[b] Up to 20% of earnings for the period being reported on.

[c] None until all long-term debt has been retired, then to the maximum extent possible.

[d] Up to 20% of outstanding common stock.

(AICPA adapted)

26–19 Which of the following statements best describes the effect of cash yield at issuance of convertible securities on calculating EPS?

[a] If less than two-thirds of the then current Aa corporate bond yield, these securities are used to calculate primary EPS but not fully diluted EPS.

[b] If less than two-thirds of the then current Aa corporate bond yield, these securities are used to calculate fully diluted EPS but not primary EPS.

[c] If greater than two-thirds of the then current Aa corporate bond yield, these securities are used to calculate primary EPS and fully diluted EPS.

[d] If greater than two-thirds of the then current Aa corporate bond yield, these securities are used to calculate fully diluted EPS but not primary EPS.

(AICPA adapted)

26–20 In computing EPS, the equivalent number of shares of convertible preferred stock is added as an adjustment to the denominator (number of shares outstanding). If the preferred stock is preferred as to dividends, which amount should be added as an adjustment to the numerator (net earnings)?

[a] Annual preferred dividend.

[b] Annual preferred dividend $\times$ (1 − income tax rate).

[c] Annual preferred dividend $\times$ income tax rate.

[d] Annual preferred dividend $\div$ income tax rate.

(AICPA adapted)

26–21 A company issued a new class of convertible preferred stock during the year. At the date of issuance, the cash yield on the stock was 60% of the Aa corporate bond yield; by the end of the year, the cash yield was 90% of the Aa corporate bond yield. At the end of the year, what type of classification should this security receive for computation of EPS?

[a] Long-term debt equivalent.

[b] Other potentially dilutive security.

[c] Convertible preferred stock.

[d] Common stock equivalent security.

(AICPA adapted)

26–22 The computation of EPS in accordance with generally accepted accounting principles may involve the consideration of securities deemed common stock equivalents. Common stock equivalents are an example of:

[a] Form over substance.

[b] Substance over form.

[c] Form over accounting principle.

[d] Substance over accounting principle.

(AICPA adapted)

CASES

C26–1 Financial accounting usually emphasizes the economic substance of events, even though the legal form may differ and suggest different treatment. For example, under accrual accounting, expenses are recognized when they are incurred (substance) rather than when cash is disbursed (form).

Although substance over form dominates most generally accepted accounting principles and practices, form sometimes prevails over substance.

Instructions

Discuss EPS for a complex capital structure, identifying specific instances where substance or form prevails.

(AICPA adapted)

C26–2 (Appendix A)   Barron Company had the following account titles on its December 31, 1985, trial balance:

6% cumulative convertible preferred stock, $100 par value
Premium on preferred stock
Common stock, $1 stated value
Premium on common stock
Retained earnings

The following additional information about Barron Company is available for the year ended December 31, 1985:

[1] Two million shares of preferred stock were authorized, of which 1,000,000 were outstanding. All shares outstanding were issued on January 2, 1982, for $120 a share. The Aa corporate bond yield was 8.5% on January 2, 1982, and 10% on December 31, 1985. The preferred stock is convertible into common stock on a one-for-one basis until December 31, 1991, after which the preferred stock ceases to be convertible and is callable at par value by the company. No preferred stock has been converted into common stock, and there were no dividends in arrears at December 31, 1985.

[2] The common stock has been issued at amounts above stated value per share since Barron's incorporation in 1967. Of the 5,000,000 shares authorized, 3,500,000 shares were outstanding at January 1, 1985. The market price of the outstanding common stock has increased slowly, but consistently, for the last five years.

[3] The company has an employee stock option plan whereby certain key employees and officers may purchase shares of common stock at 100% of the market price at the date of the option grant. All options are exercisable in installments of one-third each year, beginning one year after the date of the grant, and expire if not exercised within four years of the grant date. On January 1, 1985, options for 70,000 shares were outstanding at prices ranging from $47 to $83 a share. Options for 20,000 shares were exercised at $47 to $79 a share during 1985. No options expired during 1985 and additional options for 15,000 shares were granted at $86 a share during the year. The 65,000 options outstanding at December 31, 1985, were exercisable at $54 to $86 a share; of these, 30,000 were exercisable at that date at prices ranging from $54 to $79 a share.

[4] The company also has an employee stock purchase plan whereby the company pays one half and the employee pays the other half of the market price of the stock at the date of the subscription. During 1985, employees subscribed to 60,000 shares at an average price of $87 a share. All 60,000 shares were paid for and issued late in September 1985.

[5] On December 31, 1985, a total of 355,000 shares of common stock was set aside for the granting of future stock options and for future purchases under the employee stock purchase plan. The only changes in the stockholders' equity for 1985 were those de-scribed above, 1985 net income, and cash dividends paid.

Instructions

[a] Prepare the stockholders' equity section of Barron Company's balance sheet at December 31, 1985. Substitute Xs, where appropriate, for unknown dollar amounts. Use good form and provide full disclosure. Write appropriate footnotes as they should appear in the published financial statements.

[b] Explain how the denominator should be determined to compute *primary* EPS for presentation in the financial statements. Be specific about the handling of each item. If additional information is needed to determine whether an item should be included and to what extent, identify the information needed and how the item would be handled if the information were known. Assume Barron Company had substantial net income for the year ended December 31, 1985.

(AICPA adapted)

C26–3 (Appendix A) EPS is one of the most frequently featured financial statistics of modern corporations. Daily quotations of stock prices have recently been expanded to include a "times earnings" figure for many securities which is based on EPS. Analysts often focus their discussions on the EPS of corporations in which they are interested.

Instructions

[a] Explain how dividends or dividend requirements on any class of preferred stock that may be outstanding affect the computation of EPS.

[b] One of the technical procedures used in computing EPS is the treasury stock method.

[1] Briefly describe the circumstances in which the treasury stock method should be applied.

[2] There is a limit to the applicability of the treasury stock method. Identify this limit and briefly indicate the procedures that should be followed beyond the limit of the treasury stock method.

[c] Under some circumstances convertible debentures are considered common stock equivalents.

[1] When should convertible debentures be treated as common stock equivalents? In such cases what is the effect on the computation of EPS?

[2] When convertible debentures are not considered common stock equivalents, how are they handled in EPS computations?

(AICPA adapted)

E26–1 Blue Sky Company had 135,000 shares of common stock outstanding throughout 1985. The income statement for the year includes the following:

Income before extraordinary item	$175,000
Extraordinary loss	27,500
Net income	$147,500

The company had 50,000 shares of $10 par value, 6% cumulative preferred stock outstanding throughout 1985.

Instructions

Prepare the EPS presentation for the company's income statement for 1985.

E26–2 Black Cloud Company had 100,000 shares of common stock outstanding on January 1, 1984. During the year the company sold and subsequently repurchased stock as follows:

July 1, 1984   Sold 70,000 shares of common stock.
Dec. 1, 1984   Purchased 15,000 shares of common treasury stock.

The company reported a net income for 1984 of $601,875.

Instructions

Compute EPS for the company for 1984.

E26–3 Alfred Company had 100,000 shares of common stock outstanding throughout 1985, a year in which the company reported a $150,000 net income. In addition to common stock, the company had the following securities in its capital structure:

Cumulative preferred stock—10,000 shares, 7%, $100 par value.
Long-term debt—$1,000,000, 6%, convertible into 50 shares of common stock per $1,000 bond. These bonds were issued when the average Aa corporate bond yield was 8%.

The company's income tax rate is 48%.

Instructions

Compute primary and fully diluted EPS for 1985.

E26–4 Rosie Company had 157,000 shares of common stock outstanding at December 31, 1985. There were 150,000 shares outstanding at January 1, 1985, and 7,000 shares were sold on August 1, 1985. Net income for the year was reported as $325,000.

Outstanding throughout the year were stock options allowing the holders to acquire 30,000 shares of common stock at $25 per share. The market price of the stock averaged $35 in 1985, was $41 at December 31, 1985, and did not fall below $25 during the year.

Instructions

Compute primary and fully diluted EPS for 1985.

E26–5 Oppenheimer Company has two classes of capital stock:

Cumulative preferred stock—1,000,000 shares authorized, $10 par value, 500,000 shares outstanding, 7% dividend rate, each share convertible into 3 shares of common stock.
Common stock—10,000,000 shares authorized, $5 par value, 7,000,000 shares outstanding.

In 1985, a net income of $10,000,000 was reported. No capital stock activity took place during 1985. The company's income tax rate is 48%.

The preferred stock was issued in 1983 at par value when the average Aa corporate bond yield was 10%.

Instructions

Compute primary and fully diluted EPS for 1985.

E26–6 Dolphin Company had 745,000 shares of common stock outstanding at the beginning of 1985. During the year the company had the following common stock activity:

Feb. 28   Sold 100,000 additional shares.
May 31   Acquired 10,000 shares of treasury stock.
Aug. 31   Resold 1,000 shares of treasury stock.
Nov. 30   Resold 5,000 shares of treasury stock.

Instructions

Compute the weighted average common shares outstanding for 1985 to be used in computing EPS.

E26–7 Falcon Company had 1,475,000 shares outstanding at December 31, 1985, the end of the company's fiscal year. On March 31, 1985, the company had sold 150,000 additional shares of stock; a 2:1 stock split was declared on August 1, 1985, and distributed on September 1, 1985.

Instructions

Compute the weighted average common shares outstanding for 1985 to be used in computing EPS.

E26–8 At December 31, 1984, Welsch, Inc., had 500,000 shares of common stock outstanding. On October 1, 1985, an additional 120,000 shares of common stock were issued for cash. Welsch also had $4,000,000 of 8% convertible bonds outstanding at December 31, 1985, which are convertible into 100,000 shares of common stock. The bonds were considered common stock equivalents at the time of issuance and are dilutive in the 1985 EPS computations. No bonds were issued or converted into common stock during 1985.

Instructions

Determine the number of shares that should be used in computing primary EPS for the year ended December 31, 1985.

(AICPA adapted)

E26–9 Osborn Company has asked you to help compute EPS figures for its 1984 income statement. Net income for the year is $10,000,000 and the company had 2,500,000 shares of common stock outstanding the entire year. The company has no preferred stock in its capital structure.

Osborn officials are attempting to determine whether the following securities will have a dilutive effect on EPS if they are assumed to have been converted or exercised:

Convertible bonds—$10,000,000 par value, 12%, each 1,000 bond convertible into 20 shares of common stock.

Stock options—1,000,000 options to acquire one share each at $15.

Osborn's income tax rate is 46% and its common stock sold for $12 throughout 1984. Both the convertible bonds and the stock options were issued in 1982.

Instructions

Test the convertible bonds and the stock options for dilution and indicate your results.

E26–10 Clyde Corporation has 100,000 shares of common stock outstanding throughout 1984. The reported net income for the year is $125,000, after an income tax rate of 48%.

Instructions

Determine whether the potential diluters below are dilutive in 1984. Treat each item *independently*.
[a] Convertible bonds are outstanding as follows: $100,000 par value, 6%, convertible into 50 shares of common stock per $1,000 bond.
[b] Convertible bonds are outstanding as follows: $200,000 par value, 7%, convertible into 10 shares of common stock per $1,000 bond.
[c] Fifty thousand stock options are outstanding that allow the holders to purchase one share per option for $10. The stock sold for $12 throughout the year.
[d] Preferred stock (10,000 shares with a par value of $10) is outstanding. The preferred has a 7% dividend rate and is convertible into one share of common per preferred share.

E26–11 Boot Hill Company had stock options outstanding throughout 1984 that allow the acquisition of 75,000 shares of common stock from the company at $10 per share. There are 1,000,000 shares of common stock outstanding in the current capital structure.

Instructions

Determine the number of common shares which should be used in computing both primary and fully diluted EPS resulting from the options in each of the following *independent* situations:
[a] The average market price of the common stock was $15, and the year-end price was $15.
[b] The average market price of the common stock was $16, and the year-end price was $17.
[c] The average market price of the common stock was $14, and the year-end price was $13.
[d] The average market price of the common stock was $9, and the year-end price was $12.

E26–12 (Appendix A) New Dawn Company had stock options outstanding throughout 1985, allowing the holders to acquire 100,000 shares of common stock from the company at the $50 par value per share. The market price of the stock was $75 throughout the year and at year-end.

The company has a 48% income tax rate and pays 8% interest on its $5,000,000 debt. Net income for 1985 was $268,500.

Instructions

Compute primary and fully diluted EPS for 1985 in each of the following *independent* situations:
[a] The weighted average number of outstanding shares of common stock was 600,000 during 1985, with 610,000 outstanding at December 31.
[b] The weighted average number of outstanding shares of common stock was 300,000 during 1985, with 325,000 outstanding at December 31.

E26–13 Thompson Manufacturing Company began

operation in 1983 and in that year issued the following securities:

Preferred stock—175,000 shares, $100 par value, 7½%, issued at $110, convertible into 5 shares of common stock per preferred share.

Bonds—$10,000,000 par value, 6½%, issued at par value and convertible into 4 shares per $100 bond.

In 1984 the preferred stock and bonds described above are still outstanding, none having been converted or retired. Thompson Manufacturing Company's income tax rate is 46%.

Instructions

For both the preferred stock and the bonds, determine the adjustments that would have to be made to the 1984 EPS calculations, assuming each has a dilutive effect.

E26–14 Public Company has two potentially dilutive securities, as follows:

Cumulative preferred stock (8%)—50,000 shares authorized and outstanding, $100 par value, issued at $140 in 1982, convertible into two shares of common per preferred share.

Convertible debt (6%)—$2,000,000 par value, issued at par in 1981, convertible into 15 shares of common stock per $1,000 bond.

Public Company is attempting to compute EPS for 1985 and has correctly determined that EPS, without considering potential dilution, is $3.25. The Aa corporate bond yield from 1981 to 1983 was 10½% and in 1984 and 1985 was 9%. The company's income tax rate is 48%.

Instructions

[a] Determine whether the potential diluters are common stock equivalents.
[b] Determine whether the potential diluters are dilutive in 1985.

E26–15 Denver Company is attempting to determine whether the potential dilution in its capital structure is sufficient to warrant a dual EPS presentation in 1985. The company has not had to present primary and fully diluted EPS in the past.

In 1985 the company reported a $500,000 net income and has 300,000 shares of common stock outstanding. The company's income tax rate is 48%. The following potentially dilutive securities exist:

Stock options—50,000 outstanding, allowing the purchase of one share each of common stock at

$100. The market price of common stock throughout 1985 was $103.

Convertible debt—$500,000 par value, 6%, convertible to 20 shares of common stock per $1,000 bond.

Instructions

[a] Determine whether the company must make a dual presentation of EPS by applying the 3% guideline.
[b] Would your answer to [a] be different if the bonds were convertible into 60 shares per $1,000 bond?

E26–16 (Appendix A) The fiscal year of Coffee Cup Company ends June 30. On September 30, 1984, the company issued 50,000 stock options to its employees, allowing them to acquire one share of common stock for each option at the $10 par value of the stock.

During fiscal year 1985, Coffee Cup Company had a weighted average of 386,500 shares outstanding and reported a net income of $576,200. The stock of the company sold at $17 throughout the year.

Instructions

Compute primary EPS for 1985.

E26–17 (Appendix A) On May 31 of the last calendar year, Candy Company issued $1,000,000 of 7% bonds at par value. Each $1,000 bond may be converted into 50 shares of common stock.

Candy Company reports $92,900 of net income for the year ended December 31. The weighted average number of shares of common stock outstanding was 100,000 and the company's income tax rate is 48%.

Instructions

Assuming that the convertible debt is not a common stock equivalent, compute primary and fully diluted EPS for Candy Company for the last calendar year.

E26–18 (Appendix A) The 1984 income statement of Martin, Inc., a calendar-year company, included earnings per share of $2.00. This figure was determined as follows:

1984 net income	$1,500,000
Less: Preferred dividend	(100,000)
	1,400,000
Divided by: Number of common shares outstanding entire year	700,000
Earnings per share	$2.00

During 1985 the company issued a 2:1 stock split on March 1, reported a net income of $2,250,000, and had no other capital transactions. A $100,000 preferred dividend was paid on December 31, 1985.

Instructions

[a] Determine EPS for 1985.
[b] Apply the stock split of 1985 retroactively to 1984 and restate the EPS for that year.

E26–19 (Appendix A) Pahler, Inc., a company with a simple capital structure, reported EPS of $1.57 for the calendar year 1983, computed as follows:

Net income	$18,800,000
Divided by: Weighted average common shares outstanding	12,000,000
Earnings per share	$1.57

At January 1, 1984, the company declared a 10% stock dividend on the 12,500,000 shares of common stock outstanding at that time. The dividend shares were issued on February 28, 1984.

Instructions

[a] Determine EPS for 1984, assuming that the company reports a $25,000,000 net income.
[b] Determine EPS for 1983 that should be presented for comparative purposes in the 1983–1984 comparative income statement.

E26–20 (Appendix A) Appleton Company has 150,000 options outstanding to acquire one share of common stock each. These options can be exercised at any time after December 31, 1990, at $50 per share.

During 1984 Appleton Company reports a net income of $8,500,000; has 1,000,000 shares of common stock outstanding; and has 500,000 shares of 8%, $100 par value, cumulative preferred stock outstanding. The average and year-end market price of the company's common stock was $72 during 1984.

Instructions

Compute primary and fully diluted EPS for 1984.

PROBLEMS

P26–1 Knox Company had the following common stock activity in 1985:

	Number of Shares
Outstanding, Jan. 1	150,000
New shares issued, May 1	25,000
Treasury shares acquired, July 1	10,000
Treasury shares resold, Dec. 1	7,500
Outstanding, Dec. 31	172,500

The company had 100,000 shares of cumulative preferred stock outstanding during 1985. The preferred stock has a $10 par value and a 6% dividend rate.

Instructions

[a] Prepare the EPS presentation for 1985, assuming income before extraordinary items is $600,000 and net income is $675,000. There is one extraordinary item in 1985.
[b] Independent of [a], prepare the earnings (loss) per share presentations for 1985, assuming the company sustained a $572,000 net loss for 1985.

P26–2 Oak Ridge Company had the following common stock activity in 1984:

	Number of Shares
Outstanding, Jan. 1	500,000
New shares issued, Mar. 1	50,000
Stock issued in 2:1 split, June 1	550,000
Treasury shares acquired, Nov. 1	40,000
Outstanding, Dec. 31	1,060,000

Oak Ridge had 200,000 shares of $25 par value cumulative preferred stock outstanding throughout 1984. The dividend rate of this stock is 7%. The company reports a net income of $1,750,000 for 1984 with no extraordinary items.

The accountant for Oak Ridge indicates that EPS should be reported as $1.65, determined by dividing the reported net income by 1,060,000 shares of common stock.

Instructions

[a] Do you agree with the accountant's computation? What specific items have not been considered by the accountant?
[b] Recompute EPS for Oak Ridge Company for 1984. Provide supporting schedules for the amounts used in your computation.

P26–3 Canary Company had 175,000 shares of common stock outstanding at July 1, 1983, the beginning of its fiscal year. On September 30, 1983, the company sold an additional 25,000 shares. On May 31, 1984, 15,000 shares of treasury stock were acquired off the market.

The company had 57,000 shares of preferred stock outstanding throughout the year ended June 30, 1984. The preferred stock has a $10 par value and a 7½% dividend rate and is cumulative and nonconvertible.

In addition to the common and preferred stock, the company has the following securities outstanding:

[1] Ten percent short-term notes payable of $25,000 due in varying amounts in 30, 60, and 90 days.

[2] Stock options which allow employees to purchase 35,000 shares of common stock at $25 per share. The stock sold for $32.50 throughout the 1984 fiscal year. The options were originally issued in 1980.

[3] Convertible bonds, issued at the par amount of $500,000 in 1981. The bonds yield 10% interest, payable semiannually, and each $100 bond is convertible into 10 shares of common stock on any interest payment date (December 31 and June 30).

For the year ended June 30, 1984, the following items have been determined to be appropriate for inclusion in the company's income statement:

Income before tax	$320,000
Income tax expense	128,000
Net income	$192,000

The Aa corporate bond yield was 8% in 1980 and increased 1% each year from 1981–1984.

Instructions

Following the seven-step process outlined in the chapter, prepare the financial statement presentation of EPS for Canary Company for the year ended June 30, 1984.

P26–4 Tanya Corporation is considering several methods of increasing its long-term capitalization to provide funds for an expansion of facilities. One consideration is the impact of the method on EPS.

Tanya Corporation reported an EPS of $2.25 for the most recent fiscal year, determined on the basis of $1,687,500 net income and 750,000 shares of common stock outstanding.

The plans under consideration for obtaining approximately $1,000,000 include the following alternatives:

[1] Sell 200,000 additional shares of common stock at approximately $5 per share.

[2] Sell $1,000,000 of 9% bonds approximately at par value.

[3] Sell 100,000 shares of 8% preferred stock approximately at $10 par value, each share convertible into 2 shares of common stock.

[4] Sell $1,000,000 of 7½% convertible bonds approximately at par value, each $1,000 bond convertible into 50 shares of common stock.

The company expects to earn 15% (before income tax) on the increased funds available. The 48% income tax rate for the company is expected to continue. The Aa corporate bond yield throughout the period is expected to be 11%.

Instructions

[a] Determine the EPS which the company may be expected to present in the income statement under each of the four alternative plans.

[b] Identify factors which the company should consider in addition to the specific figures in [a] above.

[c] From the viewpoint of a current common stockholder, which alternative method of financing the $1,000,000 is preferable? Why?

P26–5 For each item below, select the correct answer and provide computations to support your choice.

[1] The 1985 net income of Mack Company was $100,000, and 100,000 shares of its common stock were outstanding during the entire year. In addition, there were outstanding options to purchase 10,000 shares of common stock at $10 per share. These options were granted in 1981 and none had been exercised by December 31, 1985. Market prices of Mack's common stock during 1985 were:

Jan. 1	$20 per share
Dec. 31	40 per share
Average price	25 per share

The amount which should be shown as Mack's fully diluted EPS for 1985 is (rounded to the nearest cent):

[a] $\dfrac{\$100,000}{110,000 \text{ shares}} = \$.91$

[b] $\dfrac{\$100,000}{105,000 \text{ shares}} = \$.95$

[c] $\dfrac{\$100,000}{106,000 \text{ shares}} = \$.94$

[d] $\dfrac{\$100,000}{107,500 \text{ shares}} = \$.93$

[2] At December 31, 1984, Back Company had 350,000 shares of common stock outstanding. On Sep-

tember 1, 1985, an additional 150,000 shares of common stock were issued. In addition, Back had $10,000,000 of 8% convertible bonds outstanding at December 31, 1984, which are convertible into 200,000 shares of common stock. The bonds were not considered common stock equivalents at the time of their issuance and no bonds were converted into common stock in 1985. The net income for the year ended December 31, 1985, was $3,000,000. Assuming the income tax rate was 50%, what should be the fully diluted EPS for the year ended December 31, 1985?

[a] $4.33
[b] $5.00
[c] $5.67
[d] $7.50

Items [3] and [4] are based on the following information.

Information about the capital structure of Petrock Corporation is as follows:

	Dec. 31, 1984	Dec. 31, 1985
Common stock	90,000 shares	90,000 shares
Convertible preferred stock	10,000 shares	10,000 shares
8% convertible bonds	$1,000,000	$1,000,000

During 1985, Petrock paid dividends of $1.00 per share on its common stock and $2.40 per share on its preferred stock. The preferred stock is convertible to 20,000 shares of common stock but it is not consid-

ered a common stock equivalent. The 8% convertible bonds are convertible into 30,000 shares of common stock and are considered common stock equivalents. The net income for the year ended Dec. 31, 1985, was $285,000. Assume that the income tax rate was 50%.

[3] What should be the primary EPS for the year ended December 31, 1985, rounded to the nearest cent?

[a] $2.38
[b] $2.51
[c] $2.84
[d] $3.13

[4] What should be the fully diluted EPS for the year

ended December 31, 1985, rounded to the nearest cent?

[a] $2.15
[b] $2.32
[c] $2.61
[d] $2.74

[5] Fountain, Inc., has 5,000,000 shares of common stock outstanding on December 31, 1983. An additional 1,000,000 shares of common stock were issued on April 1, 1984, and 500,000 more on July 1, 1984. On April 1, 1983, Fountain issued 10,000, $1,000 face value, 7% convertible bonds. Each bond is convertible into 40 shares of common stock. The bonds were not considered common stock equivalents at the time of their issuance and no bonds were converted into common stock in 1983 or 1984. What is the number of shares to be used in computing primary and fully diluted EPS, respectively, for 1984?

[a] 5,750,000 and 5,950,000
[b] 5,750,000 and 6,150,000
[c] 6,000,000 and 6,100,000
[d] 6,000,000 and 6,400,000

(AICPA adapted)

P26–6 Cowboy Boot Manufacturing Company is attempting to determine its primary and fully diluted EPS for 1984. The controller believes that it may be necessary to consider some or all of the following securities, all of which were issued prior to 1984:

Security	Number or Par Value (in dollars)	Interest/Dividend Rate	Aa Corporate Bond Yield at Issuance	Convertibility (in total) or Purchase Option
Bonds A	$100,000	10%	12%	10,000 shares
Bonds B	$200,000	9%	9½%	None
Bonds C	$500,000	7%	11%	15,000 shares
Preferred stock	$500,000	7½%	10%	50,000 shares
Options	45,000	—	12½%	1 share per option at $30

The controller has correctly determined that the net income for 1984 is $550,000 and the weighted average number of outstanding shares is 460,000. The company's income tax rate is 48% and the Aa corporate bond yield in 1984 was 11½%. The common stock sold for $47 throughout 1984. The preferred stock is cumulative.

Instructions

[a] Prepare a schedule indicating the common stock equivalency status of each security listed and whether each security is dilutive in 1984.

[b] Compute primary and fully diluted EPS for 1984.

P26–7 Elliott Corporation's capital structure is as follows:

	Dec. 31, 1985	Dec. 31, 1984
Outstanding shares of:		
Common stock	336,000	300,000
Nonconvertible		
preferred stock	10,000	10,000
8% convertible bonds	$1,000,000	$1,000,000

Additional Information

[1] On September 1, 1985, Elliott sold 36,000 additional shares of common stock.

[2] Net income for the year ended December 31, 1985, was $750,000.

[3] During 1985 Elliott paid dividends of $3 per share on its nonconvertible preferred stock.

[4] The 8% convertible bonds are convertible into 40 shares of common stock for each $1,000 bond and were not considered common stock equivalents at the date of issuance.

[5] Unexercised stock options to purchase 30,000 shares of common stock at $22.50 per share were outstanding throughout 1985. The average market price of Elliott's common stock was $36 per share during 1985. The market price was $33 per share at December 31, 1985.

[6] Warrants to purchase 20,000 shares of common stock at $38 per share were attached to the preferred stock at the time of issuance. The warrants, which expire on December 31, 1990, were outstanding at December 31, 1985.

[7] Elliott's effective income tax rate was 40% for 1984 and 1985.

Instructions

[a] Determine the number of shares that should be used to compute primary EPS for the year ended December 31, 1985.

[b] Compute the primary EPS for the year ended December 31, 1985.

[c] Determine the number of shares that should be used to compute fully diluted EPS for the year ended December 31, 1985.

[d] Compute the fully diluted EPS for the year ended December 31, 1985.

(AICPA adapted)

P26–8 The statement of income and the stockholders' equity section of the statement of financial position for the fiscal year ended September 30, 1984, are presented below for Hanks Company.

Hanks Company
STATEMENT OF INCOME
For the Fiscal Year Ended September 30, 1984
(in thousands)

Sales		$1,000,000
Cost of goods sold		750,000
Gross profit		250,000
Operating expenses (including		
interest expense of $6,000)		50,000
Income before income taxes		200,000
Income taxes (40%)		
Current	$60,000	
Deferred	20,000	80,000
Income before extraordinary		
item		120,000
Extraordinary gain, net of		
income taxes of $20,000		30,000
Net income		$ 150,000

Hanks Company
Stockholders' Equity Section of the
Statement of Financial Position
September 30, 1984
(in thousands)

Preferred stock ($50 par value, 6%; 10,000,000 shares authorized, 5,000,000 shares issued and outstanding)	$250,000
Common stock ($1 par value; 100,000,000 shares authorized with 54,250,000 issued and 53,250,000 shares outstanding)	54,250
Paid-in capital in excess of par value	275,000
Retained earnings	200,000
Total equity	$779,250
Less: Treasury stock—at cost (1,000,000 shares)	40,000
Total stockholders' equity	$739,250

Additional Information

[1] Hanks issued 6% convertible debentures during the 1980–1981 fiscal year at par value of $1,000 each. Each debenture is convertible into 30 shares of common stock. No conversions were made during the fiscal year ended September 30, 1984, and the value of the outstanding debentures is $100,000,000.

[2] A 5% common stock dividend was declared in January 1984 and issued during February 1984 to all stockholders of record; 2,250,000 shares were issued.

[3] Hanks' management has the following options to purchase shares of the company's common stock, adjusted for all dividends declared to date:

Option	Number of Shares	Option Price	Expiration Date
A	2,000,000	$25	Sept. 30, 1986
B	3,000,000	45	Sept. 30, 1988

[4] Market price information for Hanks Company common stock and data on the Aa corporate bond yield are as follows:

	For the Year Ended Sept. 30			
	1981	1982	1983	1984
Average price of common stock	$28	$35	$38	$40
Year-end market price of common stock	$25	$38	$35	$40
Average Aa corporate bond yield	8%	9%	10%	10%

[5] Changes in the number of common shares outstanding during the current fiscal year are summarized below:

Date	Shares Outstanding	Explanation
Oct. 1, 1983	45,000,000	Shares outstanding at the beginning of the year.
Feb. 1, 1984	47,250,000	Shares after a 5% stock dividend was issued.
June 1, 1984	53,250,000	Shares after 6,000,000 new shares were issued for $42.

[6] The outstanding preferred stock is noncumulative and no preferred dividend was declared or paid during 1984.

Instructions

[a] Calculate the weighted average number of common shares outstanding for Hanks Company for the fiscal year ended September 30, 1984.

[b] Prepare an analysis of the potentially dilutive securities included in Hanks Company's capital structure. Indicate whether they are included in only primary EPS or in both primary and fully diluted EPS, or excluded from EPS computations.

[c] Compute primary and fully diluted EPS for the year ended September 30, 1984.

Hint: When a stock dividend is distributed, the number of shares into which the convertible debentures may be converted should be adjusted to an after-dividend basis.

(CMA adapted)

P26–9 The controller of Lafayette Corporation has asked you to help to determine both primary and fully diluted EPS for presentation in the company's income statement for the year ended September 30, 1985.

Your working papers disclose the following opening balances and transactions in the company's capital stock accounts during the year:

[1] Common stock (at October 1, 1984, stated value $10, authorized 300,000 shares; effective December 1, 1984, stated value $5, authorized 600,000 shares):

Balance, Oct. 1, 1984—issued and outstanding 60,000 shares.

Dec. 1, 1984—60,000 shares issued in a 2-for-1 stock split.

Dec. 1, 1984—280,000 shares (stated value $5) issued at $39 per share.

[2] Treasury stock—common:

Mar. 1, 1985—purchased 40,000 shares at $38 per share.

Apr. 1, 1985—sold 40,000 shares at $40 per share.

[3] Stock purchase warrants, Series A (initially each warrant was exchangeable with $60 for one common share; effective December 1, 1984, each warrant became exchangeable for two common shares at $30 per share):

Oct. 1, 1984—25,000 warrants issued at $6 each.

[4] Stock purchase warrants, Series B (each warrant is exchangeable with $45 for one common share):

Apr. 1, 1985—20,000 warrants authorized and issued at $10 each.

[5] First mortgage bonds, 5½%, due 2000 (nonconvertible; priced to yield 5% when issued):

Balance, Oct. 1, 1984—authorized, issued, and outstanding at $1,400,000 face value.

[6] Convertible debentures, 7%, due 2004 (initially each $1,000 bond was convertible at any time until maturity into 12½ common shares; effective December 1, 1984, the conversion rate became 25 shares for each bond):

Oct. 1, 1984—authorized and issued at their face value (no premium or discount) of $2,400,000.

The table on the following page shows market prices for the company's securities and the assumed Aa corporate bond yield during 1984–1985.

Instructions

Assuming that net income for the year was $620,000 and that the income tax rate was 48%, prepare computations of primary and fully diluted EPS. Provide

	Price (or Rate)			Average for Year Ended Sept. 30, 1985
	Oct. 1, 1984	Apr. 1, 1985	Sept. 30, 1985	
Common stock	66	40*	42*	37½*
First mortgage bonds	88½	87	86	87
Convertible debentures	100	120	119	115
Series A warrants	6	22	19½	15
Series B warrants	—	10	9	9½
Aa corporate bond yield	8%	7¾%	7½%	7¾%

*Adjusted for stock split.

schedules and analyses which support your conclusions on each of the following:

[a] Common stock equivalency status of all potential diluters.

[b] Dilutive status of all potential diluters.

[c] Consideration of the minimum materiality standard for a dual presentation of EPS.

(AICPA adapted)

P26–10 (Appendix A) Willie Company reported net income of $475,000 for the 1984 calendar year. The weighted average number of common shares outstanding for the year was 95,000, with 100,000 outstanding at December 31, 1984. The company's income tax rate is 48%.

Instructions

For each of the following *independent* cases (except as indicated):

[a] Determine the EPS for the income statement for the year ended December 31, 1984.

[b] Prepare the appropriate income statement captions to be used for the presentation of EPS in each case.

Case 1. Willie Company has no potentially dilutive securities.

Case 2. Willie Company has one bond issue outstanding in the face amount of $100,000. The bonds sold at par value, carry an 8% interest rate, and are convertible into 50 shares of common stock per $1,000 bond. The Aa corporate bond yield at December 31, 1984, is 12%; at the date of issuance of the bonds the yield was 8½%.

Case 3. Same as Case 2, except that each $1,000 bond is convertible into 5 shares of common stock.

Case 4. Same as Case 2, except that the interest rate on the bonds is 5½%.

Case 5. Willie Company has options outstanding which allow the holders to purchase 18,000 shares of common stock at $50 per share. The average market

price of the stock for the year (as well as the year-end price) is $62.50.

Case 6. Same as Case 5, except the year-end stock price is $78. The average for the year remains $62.50.

Case 7. Same as Case 5, except the year-end stock price is $59. The average for the year remains $62.50.

Case 8. Same as Case 5, except options are outstanding for the purchase of 30,000 shares of common stock. The company currently pays 9% interest on debt outstanding.

Case 9. Willie Company has 10,000 shares of nonconvertible, cumulative preferred stock outstanding, 7% dividend rate, $10 par value. The market price at the date of issuance of the preferred (in 1983) was $12 and the December 31, 1984, market price is $15.

Case 10. Same as Case 9, except the preferred is convertible into two shares of common stock per share of preferred. The Aa corporate bond yield at the date the preferred was issued was 9%. At December 31, 1984, the yield is 7%.

Case 11. Same as Case 10, except the Aa corporate bond yield at the date of the issuance of the preferred stock was 7%. At December 31, 1984, the yield is 9%.

P26–11 (Appendix A) Albuquerque Construction Company has accumulated the following data concerning the current year (1985) and the comparative year (1984) to be presented in its current financial statements.

	1984	1985
Net income	$500,000	$600,000
Dividend on cumulative preferred stock	(50,000)	(50,000)
Numerator for primary EPS calculation	450,000	550,000
Interest (after income tax) on convertible debt, not common stock equivalent	75,000	75,000
Numerator for fully diluted EPS	$525,000	$625,000

Albuquerque Construction Company had the following common stock in 1984 and 1985:

	Number of Shares Issued	Number of Shares Outstanding
Outstanding, Jan. 1, 1984	—	120,000
Oct. 1, 1984—10% stock dividend	12,000	132,000
Mar. 1, 1985—sold 25,000 shares	25,000	157,000
Dec. 31, 1985—2:1 stock split	157,000	314,000

The convertible bonds, issued on January 1, 1984, were originally convertible into 50,000 shares of common stock. This rate has been adjusted for the stock dividend in 1984 and the stock split in 1985.

Instructions

[a] Compute primary and fully diluted EPS as they would have been presented in the 1984 income statement at December 31, 1984.

[b] Compute primary and fully diluted EPS as they would appear in the 1985 income statement at December 31, 1985.

[c] Compute 1984 primary and fully diluted EPS as they would be presented for comparative purposes in the 1985 financial statements.

[d] Discuss briefly why stock splits and stock dividends are applied retroactively, including the comparative year(s) presented, for purposes of EPS calculations.

P26–12 (Appendix A) The stockholders' equity section of Franklin Company's balance sheet as of December 31, 1985, contains the following:

$1 cumulative convertible preferred stock (par value $25; 1,600,000 shares authorized, 1,400,000 shares issued, 750,000 shares converted to common, and 650,000 shares outstanding; involuntary liquidation value, $30 a share, aggregating $19,500,000)	$16,250,000
Common stock (par value $.25; 15,000,000 shares authorized, 8,800,000 shares issued and outstanding)	2,200,000
Additional paid-in capital	32,750,000
Retained earnings	40,595,000
Total stockholders' equity	$91,795,000

On April 1, 1985, Franklin Company acquired the business and assets and assumed the liabilities of Diane Corporation in a transaction accounted for as a pooling of interests. For each of Diane Corporation's 2,400,000 shares of $.25 par value common stock outstanding, the owner received one share of common stock of Franklin Company.

Included in the liabilities of Franklin Company are 5½% convertible subordinated debentures issued at their face value of $20,000,000 in 1984. The debentures are due in 2004 and until then are convertible into the common stock of Franklin Company at the rate of five shares of common stock for each $100 debenture. To date none of these have been converted.

On April 2, 1985, Franklin Company issued 1,400,000 shares of convertible preferred stock at $40 per share. Quarterly dividends to December 31, 1985, have been paid on these shares. The preferred stock is convertible into common stock at the rate of two shares of common for each share of preferred. On October 1, 1985, 150,000 shares and on November 1, 1985, 60,000 shares of the preferred stock were converted into common stock.

During July 1984, Franklin Company granted options to its officers and key employees to purchase 500,000 shares of the company's common stock at $20 a share. The options do not become exercisable until 1986.

During 1985 dividend payments and average market prices of the Franklin common stock were as follows:

	Dividend per Share	Average Market Price per Share
First quarter	$.10	$20
Second quarter	.15	25
Third quarter	.10	30
Fourth quarter	.15	25
Average for the year		25

The December 31, 1985, closing price of the common stock was $25 a share.

Assume that the Aa corporate bond yield was 7% throughout 1984 and 1985. Franklin Company's consolidated net income for the year ended December 31, 1985, was $9,200,000. The company's income tax rate is 48%.

Instructions

[a] Prepare a schedule evaluating the common stock equivalency status of:

[1] Convertible debentures.

[2] Convertible preferred stock.

[3] Employee stock options.

[b] Prepare a schedule which shows for 1985 the computation of:

[1] The weighted average number of shares for computing primary EPS.

[2] The weighted average number of shares for computing fully diluted EPS.

[c] Prepare a schedule which shows for 1985 the computation (to the nearest cent) of:

[1] Primary EPS.

[2] Fully diluted EPS.

Hint: In computing the weighted average number of shares outstanding, shares issued in a pooling of interest, as was done on April 1, 1985, by Franklin Company, should be treated as if they were outstanding from the beginning of the accounting period.

(AICPA adapted)

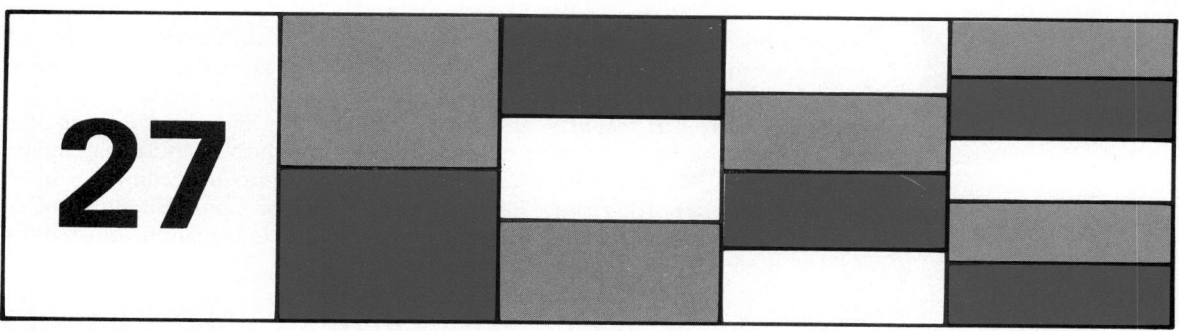

27

PUBLICLY HELD COMPANIES: FINANCIAL REPORTING AND CHANGING PRICES

Objectives

To discuss the nature and measurement of price changes.

To explain the difference between a general price-level change and a specific price change.

To discuss and illustrate constant dollar accounting.

To explain the major forms of current value accounting.

To discuss and illustrate current cost accounting.

To discuss and illustrate current cost/constant dollar accounting.

To present an overview of the requirements of the Financial Accounting Standards Board's *Statement of Financial Accounting Standards No. 33,* "Financial Reporting and Changing Prices."

C onventional financial statements often are criticized because they do not reflect current values and are not reported in dollars of the same purchasing power. These criticisms are particularly strong because of the magnitudes of price changes that have occurred in recent years in the United States and elsewhere. In this chapter we shall discuss the nature of price changes and illustrate how financial statements can be adjusted for them. We shall also discuss *Statement of Financial Accounting Standards No. 33,* "Financial Reporting and Changing Prices." This pronouncement requires large public companies to report selected items of supplementary information adjusted for changing prices in their published annual reports.

NATURE AND MEASUREMENT OF PRICE CHANGES

A **price change** is an increase or decrease in the price of a good or service that occurs in a given market, such as a wholesale market or a retail market. Two major types of price changes are general price-level changes and specific price changes. Some of the concepts relating to these types of price changes were initially explained in Chapter 3.

General Price-Level Changes

A **general price-level change** is an increase or decrease in the overall level of prices of goods and services throughout the economy. An increase in the general price-level means that money's **purchasing power** (its ability to buy goods and services) has decreased; this is known as **inflation.** A decrease in the general price-level, known as **deflation** (sometimes called **disinflation**), means that money's purchasing power has increased. During most of the twentieth century, inflation has occurred much more frequently than deflation in the United States and in most other countries. For this reason most of the illustrations and problem assignments in this chapter assume the existence of inflation. Recognize, however, that the same general principles apply when deflation occurs.

General price-level changes are measured by using a **general price-level index** constructed by the federal government. Such an index is designed to show how much the overall level of prices in the economy has changed over time. Theoretically, a general price-level index should be constructed by monitoring changes in the prices of *all* goods and services in the economy. For practical reasons, however, the federal government derives a general price-level index by considering price changes in only a sample of goods and services in the economy. The government derives several different indexes, and each one is calculated in relation to a predetermined subset or "market basket" of goods and services.

In the construction of an index, a base period is selected and assigned an index number of 100. All other periods in the index are then assigned index numbers that relate to the base. Suppose, for example, that 1980 is selected as the base period of a particular index and that prices in the "market basket" comprising the index rise by an average of 25% during 1981. Under these circumstances, 1980 and 1981 would be assigned index numbers of 100 and 125, respectively. Dividing 125 by 100 indicates that prices have risen by 25% during 1981 ($125 \div 100 = 1.25$). The reciprocal of this ratio ($100 \div 125 = .80$) indicates that a dollar in 1981 could buy only 80% of what a dollar in 1980 could buy. General price-level indexes in use today provide only rough approximates of general price-level changes, because they are not based on all prices in the economy. Furthermore, these indexes do not accurately reflect changes in the quality of products over time.

The most comprehensive general price-level index in the United States is the **Gross National Product Implicit Price Deflator (GNP Deflator),** which is published quarterly by the U.S. Department of Commerce. Perhaps the most widely publicized index of general prices is the **Consumer Price Index for all Urban Consumers (CPI-U),** published monthly by the U.S. Department of Labor. Generally, the inflation rates measured by the GNP

EXHIBIT 27–1				
Average Consumer Price Index for All Urban Consumers				
1960	88.7		1971	121.3
1961	89.6		1972	125.3
1962	90.6		1973	133.1
1963	91.7		1974	147.7
1964	92.9		1975	161.2
1965	94.5		1976	170.5
1966	97.2		1977	181.5
1967	100.0 (base year)		1978	195.4
1968	104.2		1979	217.4
1969	109.8		1980	246.8
1970	116.3		1981	272.4
			1982	289.1

SOURCE: U.S. Department of Labor.

Deflator and the CPI-U are similar over the long run. For this reason and because the CPI-U is calculated more frequently and is more widely publicized than the GNP Deflator, the FASB currently requires companies to use the CPI-U when disclosing information under *SFAS No. 33.* Exhibit 27–1 shows the average annual level of the CPI-U during each year since 1960. Observe that 1967 is the base year of the CPI-U and is accordingly assigned an index number of 100. To simplify the calculations involved, we shall merely assume certain values of the CPI-U in the illustrations and assignment material in this chapter.

Specific Price Changes

A second type of price change is known as a **specific price change.** A specific price change is an increase or decrease in the price of a specific good or service, such as food or entertainment. Specific price changes occur primarily because of changes in the demand for or supply of particular goods or services. An increase in the demand for Buick Skylarks, for example, tends to increase the automobile's price. On the other hand, an increase in the supply of Buick Skylarks tends to decrease the price. Forces of supply and demand interact to determine the specific price of each good and service in the economy.

Distinguishing clearly between a general price-level change and a specific price change is important. The price of a specific good or service may change at a different rate and even in the opposite direction from the overall level of prices in the economy. In a particular year, for example, the general price-level might increase by 10% while the price of medical care rises by 16%, the price of new cars rises by 7%, the price of fuel oil remains stable, and the price of home video games falls by 20%. To assume that the price of a particular product will increase by 10% during a given year merely because the inflation rate is 10% in that year is incorrect.

Specific price changes may be measured by using the following methods of determining an asset's current cost:

1. **Direct pricing.** This method requires the use of current market prices to calculate the current cost of an asset. Current market prices may be obtained by referring to current invoice prices, vendors' price lists, current standard manufacturing costs, and appraisals. Suppose, for example, that a company acquired an inventory item for $100 at the beginning of the current year and that a seller's price list shows that the same item would cost $130 if purchased at year-end. Under these circumstances, the specific price increase associated with the inventory item is $30 ($130 − $100).

2. **Indexing.** This method requires the use of an appropriate specific price index to restate the historical cost of an asset to a current cost basis. A company may obtain the index internally or

externally. Specific price indexes for many different kinds of assets are available from a variety of government and industry sources. Unlike a general price-level index which measures changes in the overall level of prices in the economy, a specific price index applies only to a particular good or service. To illustrate, suppose that a company purchased a building at the beginning of a year for $100,000 and that an appropriate specific price index indicates that the cost of similar buildings increased by 20% during the year. Under these circumstances, a specific price increase of $20,000 [($100,000 × 1.20) − $100,000] has occurred.

FOUR BASES OF ACCOUNTING

Attribute Measured and Measuring Unit

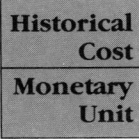
Historical Cost
Monetary Unit

Financial statements prepared in accordance with generally accepted accounting principles (GAAP) are based on the historical cost and monetary unit principles. Because of the historical cost principle, the historical cost of an asset is generally retained in the accounting records until the asset is sold. Because of the monetary unit principle, the measuring unit used for financial reporting purposes is the **nominal dollar** (a dollar that has not been adjusted for inflation). The combined effect of the historical cost and monetary unit principles is that neither specific price changes nor general price-level changes are recognized separately in conventional financial statements. Critics of the conventional accounting model contend that financial statements would be more useful for decision-making purposes if the statements were adapted to reflect specific price changes, general price-level changes, or both types of price changes.

The various approaches that have been suggested for accounting under conditions of changing prices are shown in Exhibit 27–2.[1] The exhibit shows that either the historical cost attribute or the current value attribute of the elements of financial statements may be measured and reported. The exhibit also indicates that either nominal dollars or **constant dollars** (dollars that have been adjusted for inflation) may be used as the measuring unit in financial statements.

Cell 1 of the matrix shown in Exhibit 27–2 represents the intersection of historical cost and nominal dollars (HC/ND). HC/ND financial statements are the type that accountants presently produce under GAAP. These financial statements are not adjusted for either specific price changes or general price-level changes. HC/ND financial statements were discussed in previous chapters of this textbook and are therefore not covered extensively in this chapter.

---

[1]Paul Rosenfield, "The Confusion Between General Price-Level Restatement and Current Value Accounting," *Journal of Accountancy* (October 1972), pp. 63–68.

EXHIBIT 27–2
Four Bases of Accounting

Measuring Unit Used in Financial Statements	Attribute Measured in Financial Statements	
	Historical Cost (HC)	Current Value (CV)
Nominal Dollars (ND)	1	2
Constant Dollars (CD)	3	4

Cell 2 of the matrix depicts current value/nominal dollar (CV/ND) accounting. CV/ND financial statements are adjusted to reflect specific price changes, because current values are used instead of historical costs. Because nominal dollars are the measuring unit, however, CV/ND financial statements are not adjusted for general price-level changes.

Cell 3 presents the intersection of historical cost and constant dollars (HC/CD). HC/CD financial statements are adjusted for general price-level changes, because constant dollars are used. But these statements are not adjusted for specific price changes, because the attribute measured is historical cost, not current value.

Cell 4 of the matrix shows the current value/constant dollar (CV/CD) basis of accounting. CV/CD financial statements include adjustments for both specific price changes (because current values are used) *and* general price-level changes (because constant dollars are used).

A Simplified Example[2]

To illustrate the income statement results that would occur under each of the four bases of accounting shown in Exhibit 27–2, we shall assume the following facts about Carter Company:

1. The company was organized on January 1, 1984. On that date the company sold common stock for $10,000 and immediately invested the proceeds in land costing $10,000.
2. On December 31, 1984, the land held by Carter Company was estimated to have a market value of $12,000.
3. On December 31, 1985, Carter Company sold the land for $15,000 and used the proceeds to retire all the common stock. The company terminated its operations at that time.
4. The inflation rate was zero in 1984 and 10% in 1985.

Based on these facts, the income statement results that Carter Company would report in 1984 and 1985 under each of the four bases of accounting are shown in Exhibit 27–3. Under HC/ND accounting (the conventional accounting model), Carter Company reports no gain

---

[2]The idea for this example is based on Rosenfield, pp. 67–68.

EXHIBIT 27–3
Carter Company
Income Statement Results
Under Four Bases of Accounting

(1) Results Under HC/ND Accounting		(2) Results Under CV/ND Accounting	
1984	–0–	1984	$2,000 gain
1985	$5,000 gain	1985	$3,000 gain
Total	$5,000 gain	Total	$5,000 gain

(3) Results Under HC/CD Accounting, Measured in 1985 Constant Dollars		(4) Results Under CV/CD Accounting, Measured in 1985 Constant Dollars	
1984	–0–	1984	$2,200 gain
1985	$4,000 gain	1985	$1,800 gain
Total	$4,000 gain	Total	$4,000 gain

or loss in 1984, because the company did not sell the land in that year. In 1985 the company reports a $5,000 gain ($15,000 − $10,000), because it sold the land.

Under CV/ND accounting, Carter Company reports a $2,000 gain in 1984. This amount equals the $12,000 market price at the end of 1984 minus the historical cost of $10,000. In 1985 the company reports a $3,000 gain, because it sold the land for $15,000, which is $3,000 more than the land's market price at the beginning of 1985. Observe carefully that when we sum Carter Company's income statement results for *both* 1984 and 1985 under either HC/ND accounting or CV/ND accounting, we derive a *total gain* of $5,000.

The key to understanding the results under HC/CD accounting and CV/CD accounting is to recognize that these results are not measured in nominal dollars but in *1985 constant dollars*. Under HC/CD accounting, Carter Company reports no gain or loss in 1984, because no sale occurred in that year. In 1985, when the land is sold, the company reports a $4,000 gain. This amount equals the $15,000 selling price minus the $10,000 historical cost adjusted for the 10% inflation that has occurred since the land was acquired [$15,000 − ($10,000 × 1.10) = $4,000].

Under CV/CD accounting, Carter Company reports a $2,200 gain for 1984. This amount equals the $12,000 market price at the end of 1984 minus the historical cost of $10,000, adjusted for the 10% inflation that occurred during *1985* [($12,000 − $10,000) × 1.10 = $2,200]. It is important to remember at this point that we are measuring the 1984 results in *1985 constant dollars;* of course we can do this only at the end of 1985, after we know the 1985 inflation rate. In 1985 Carter Company reports a gain of $1,800 under the CV/CD approach. This amount equals the selling price of $15,000 minus the market price at the beginning of 1985 adjusted for the 1985 inflation of 10% [$15,000 − ($12,000 × 1.10) = $1,800]. Observe carefully that when we sum Carter Company's income statement results for *both* 1984 and 1985 under either HC/CD accounting or CV/CD accounting, we calculate a $4,000 *total gain*.

The Carter Company example is highly simplified, but it allows us to see more clearly the following major differences between the four bases of accounting:

1. Changing from historical cost accounting to current value accounting changes the *timing* but not the total amount of income recognized over the life of a firm. When the measuring unit is nominal dollars, Carter Company's *total gain* is $5,000, but it is allocated differently between 1984 and 1985, depending on whether historical cost (HC/ND) or current value (CV/ND) measurement is used. Measured in constant dollars, Carter Company's total gain is $4,000, but once again the manner in which the total gain is allocated between years depends on whether historical cost (HC/CD) or current value (CV/CD) measurement is used. The reason that current value accounting produces a timing change is because under historical cost accounting, we generally recognize income only when a sale occurs, whereas under current value accounting, we recognize income when specific prices change. The timing of income recognition can make a big difference to investors and creditors when they evaluate the amount, timing, and uncertainty of the cash flows they expect to receive from their investments in the future.

2. Changing from nominal dollar measurement to constant dollar measurement changes the total amount of income recognized over the life of a firm. Carter Company's total gain is $5,000 when expressed in nominal dollars (HC/ND and CV/ND) and $4,000 when measured in 1985 constant dollars (HC/CD and CV/CD). The reason for the difference is that the measuring unit itself has changed.

In later sections of this chapter, we shall illustrate complete financial statements prepared under the HC/CD, CV/ND, and CV/CD bases of accounting. In practice, these statements may be prepared by using the conventional HC/ND financial statements and certain additional information. Journal entries to record adjustments for general price-level changes or specific price changes are unnecessary.

AUTHORITATIVE PRONOUNCEMENT ON ACCOUNTING FOR CHANGING PRICES

Accounting for changing prices has probably been the most widely discussed topic in financial accounting during the twentieth century. Numerous individuals and organizations, including the Committee on Accounting Procedure (CAP), the Accounting Principles Board (APB), the Financial Accounting Standards Board (FASB), and the Securities and Exchange Commission (SEC), have actively participated in the discussion at one time or another. Studying the many books, monographs, articles, and other publications in this area can be a very interesting experience in an accounting theory or accounting history course.

Spurred on by the SEC, the FASB in 1979 issued *SFAS No. 33,* "Financial Reporting and Changing Prices." *SFAS No. 33* applies only to certain large companies, specifically "to public enterprises that have either (1) inventories and property, plant, and equipment (before deducting accumulated depreciation) amounting to more than $125 million or (2) total assets amounting to more than $1 billion (after deducting accumulated depreciation)."[3] *SFAS No. 33* does *not* change the primary financial statements, which are based on historical cost/nominal dollar accounting. Instead, the pronouncement requires the disclosure of selected items of **supplementary information** in published annual reports. Most of these supplementary items are prepared in accordance with the historical cost/constant dollar basis, the current value/nominal dollar basis, or the current value/constant dollar basis of accounting.

When *SFAS No. 33* was issued, the FASB stated that the supplementary information required was experimental and that the pronouncement would be reviewed extensively within five years. The idea behind *SFAS No. 33* is to require certain companies to report the supplementary information adjusted for changing prices and then assess the usefulness of the information from the perspectives of preparers and users of financial statements. Only large companies are affected because many people regularly use these companies' financial statements and because these companies are more capable than smaller companies of bearing the costs of producing the information. Currently the FASB and many individual researchers are studying the costs and benefits associated with information required by *SFAS No. 33.* As a result of these studies, the FASB's requirements for the disclosure of information adjusted for changing prices may change.

In a later section of this chapter, we shall present the specific disclosures required by *SFAS No. 33.* In the meantime, however, we shall discuss and illustrate the preparation of comprehensive financial statements adjusted for changing prices. The FASB encourages but does not presently require the presentation of comprehensive statements such as those we are about to discuss. Nevertheless, in order to adequately understand the topic of accounting for changing prices as well as the specific disclosures required by *SFAS No. 33,* a person should understand the complete process of adjusting financial statements for changing prices. With this understanding, a person will be able to quickly grasp not only the present disclosure requirements of *SFAS No. 33* but also the requirements of professional pronouncements that may replace *SFAS No. 33.*

CONSTANT DOLLAR ACCOUNTING

Nature and Objective

Historical cost/constant dollar accounting, represented by Cell 3 of the matrix in Exhibit 27–2, is commonly called **constant dollar accounting.** It is sometimes referred to as **general price-level accounting** or **general purchasing-power accounting.** Under con-

---

[3]*FASB Statement of Financial Accounting Standards No. 33,* "Financial Reporting and Changing Prices," 1979, Summary.

stant dollar accounting, the attribute measured in financial statements is historical cost, and the measuring unit is the constant dollar.

The objective of constant dollar accounting is to report the elements of financial statements in dollars that have the same purchasing power. To accomplish this objective, the amounts reported in the conventional historical cost/nominal dollar financial statements are restated in constant dollars by using a general price-level index, such as the CPI-U. The financial statement amounts are converted to constant dollars by using the following general formula:

$$\begin{aligned}\text{Constant dollar amount} \atop \text{(HC/CD amount)} = {}& {\text{Nominal dollar amount} \atop \text{(HC/ND amount)}} \\ & \times \frac{\text{General price-level index adjusting to}}{\text{General price-level index adjusting from}}\end{aligned}$$

The quotient obtained by dividing the general price-level index we are adjusting *to* by the one we are adjusting *from* is called a **conversion factor** because it is used to convert nominal-dollar amounts to constant-dollar amounts. The general price-level index to adjust *from* is the one that existed at the time of origination of the financial statement amount being converted. The general price-level index to adjust *to* could be an index as of any date, although the dates most commonly suggested are the base year of the CPI-U (1967), the average CPI-U for the current accounting period, and the ending CPI-U for the current period. In an effort to focus on the underlying concepts and avoid needless confusion, we shall convert to the year-end CPI-U in the examples and problem assignments in this chapter. Use of the year-end CPI-U is acceptable under *SFAS No. 33* if a company prepares comprehensive constant dollar financial statements such as those we shall illustrate shortly.

To briefly illustrate the basic idea behind constant dollar conversion, suppose that Rupp Company acquired a parcel of land on January 1, 1985, for $10,000. On that date the CPI-U was 100. Here is how Rupp Company would express the acquisition price of the land in year-end constant dollars, assuming that the CPI-U is 115 on December 31, 1985:

$$\$10,000 \times \frac{115}{100} = \$11,500$$

Historical Cost

Rupp Company would report the land at $10,000 on a conventional (HC/ND) balance sheet dated December 31, 1985, and at $11,500 on a constant dollar balance sheet with the same date. Be careful to interpret the $11,500 correctly. This amount represents the land's historical cost expressed in 1985 year-end constant dollars. In effect, we are saying that because the inflation rate during 1985 was 15% (115 ÷ 100 = 1.15), $11,500 would be needed at the end of 1985 to buy the same quantity of goods and services that $10,000 could buy at the beginning of the year.

How much would Rupp Company have to pay at the end of 1985 if the company had to replace the land? How much could Rupp Company sell the land for on December 31, 1985? What is the present value on December 31, 1985, of the net cash receipts that the land will generate for Rupp Company in the future? These are interesting questions that cannot be answered by constant-dollar information, because the answers depend on what has happened to the specific price of Rupp Company's land during the year. Remember that constant dollar accounting adjusts for general price-level changes but not for specific price changes. Constant dollar accounting is not a departure from historical cost accounting but merely a system for reporting historical cost financial statements in units that have the same purchasing power.

Monetary and Nonmonetary Items

When preparing constant dollar financial statements, monetary and nonmonetary items must be distinguished. A **monetary item** is cash, assets that represent a fixed number of dollars to be received, or obligations that represent a fixed number of dollars to be paid. Examples of monetary assets include cash, accounts receivable, and notes receivable; examples of monetary liabilities include accounts payable, notes payable, and bonds payable.

Simply stated, a **nonmonetary item** is any financial statement item that is not monetary in nature. Examples of nonmonetary assets include inventories, plant assets, and intangible assets; examples of nonmonetary equities include obligations under product warranties and common stock. Although they are liabilities, obligations under product warranties are nonmonetary because they do not require settlement in a fixed number of dollars but rather in goods and services (or a price that reflects the value of the goods or services).

The distinction between monetary and nonmonetary assets and liabilities is *not* the same as the distinction between current assets and current liabilities. Inventories, for example, are nonmonetary assets even though classified as current. As another example, a 10-year note payable is monetary even though classified as a long-term liability.

Monetary items are automatically stated in current purchasing power and therefore do not require restatement when preparing constant dollar financial statements. Cash, for example, is always stated in current dollars. Consequently, if an enterprise has cash of $5,000 on December 31, 1985, the amount represents $5,000 of general purchasing power at that time, and the correct amount of cash to report on a constant dollar balance sheet dated December 31, 1985, is $5,000. The same rationale applies to other monetary items.

In contrast with monetary items, nonmonetary items are not automatically stated in current purchasing power and therefore must be restated when preparing constant dollar financial statements. Each nonmonetary item is restated to reflect the total change in the general price-level that has occurred since the time of origin of the item being restated. The restatement of nonmonetary items does not produce any gains or losses. Instead, the restatement merely alters the measuring unit from nominal dollars to constant dollars.

Purchasing Power Gains and Losses

Purchasing power gains and losses occur as a result of holding monetary items during periods of inflation or deflation. These gains and losses occur because monetary items are receivable or payable in a *fixed number of dollars* whose *purchasing power* changes when inflation or deflation occurs. Purchasing power gains and losses are measured and reported in the income statement when the measuring unit is constant dollars, but not when it is nominal dollars.

To illustrate, suppose that Brown Company keeps its cash of $10,000 in a checking account throughout a year in which the CPI-U increases from 105 to 210. The actual number of dollars of cash remains constant at 10,000, while the prices of goods and services steadily rise. Clearly, the company has lost purchasing power by holding the cash during the period. Under these circumstances, in which the inflation rate was 100%, Brown Company would need $20,000 at the end of the year to be able to buy the same quantity of goods and services that the company could buy with $10,000 at the beginning of the year. Because the company has only $10,000 at year-end, the purchasing power *loss* expressed in terms of the year-end price level is $10,000 [($10,000 × 210/105) − $10,000].

To generalize, maintaining a positive monetary position (a position in which monetary assets exceed monetary liabilities) results in a purchasing power loss during periods of inflation and a purchasing power gain during periods of deflation. On the other hand, maintaining a negative monetary position (a position in which monetary liabilities exceed monetary assets) results in a purchasing power gain when inflation occurs and a purchasing power loss when deflation occurs. These outcomes are shown in Exhibit 27–4.

EXHIBIT 27–4
Purchasing Power Gains and Losses Under
Different Circumstances

	Economic Condition	
Monetary Position	Inflation	Deflation
Positive (monetary assets > monetary liabilities)	Loss	Gain
Negative (monetary liabilities > monetary assets)	Gain	Loss

Preparation of Constant Dollar Financial Statements

Now that the general principles underlying constant dollar accounting have been explained, the process of preparing a set of comprehensive constant dollar financial statements will be illustrated. The information shown in Exhibits 27–5, 27–6, and 27–7 pertains to Craig Company and is used for the illustration.

EXHIBIT 27–5
Basic Information About Craig Company

1. Craig Company was organized and began operations on January 1, 1985.
2. The company's comparative balance sheets on January 1 and December 31, 1985, are shown in Exhibit 27–6.
3. The company's combined statement of income and retained earnings for 1985 is shown in Exhibit 27–7.
4. Selected values of the CPI-U during 1985 are shown below:

Jan. 1	130.0
Average for 1985	143.0
Dec. 31	157.3

5. Conversion factors required to restate financial statement amounts to year-end constant dollars are computed below:

   Conversion factors to restate from
Jan. 1 index	157.3/130.0 = 1.21
Average index for 1985	157.3/143.0 = 1.10
Dec. 31 index	157.3/157.3 = 1.00

6. Sales and purchases were made evenly throughout 1985.
7. Operating expenses and income tax expense were incurred evenly throughout 1985.
8. The company declared and paid dividends on December 31, 1985.
9. The company acquired the beginning inventory, land, and equipment on January 1, 1985.
10. The company uses the first-in, first-out (FIFO) method of determining inventory cost. The ending inventory was acquired when the CPI-U was 143.
11. The company uses the straight-line method to depreciate the equipment. A 10-year useful life and no salvage value are assumed.

EXHIBIT 27–6

Craig Company
COMPARATIVE BALANCE SHEETS
Historical Cost/Nominal Dollar Basis
January 1 and December 31, 1985

Assets

	Jan. 1	Dec. 31
Cash	$10,000	$40,000
Accounts receivable	–0–	67,000
Inventory	100,000	90,000
Land	70,000	70,000
Equipment	120,000	120,000
Less: Accumulated depreciation	–0–	(12,000)
Total assets	$300,000	$375,000

Liabilities and Stockholders' Equity

	Jan. 1	Dec. 31
Accounts payable	–0–	$35,000
Long-term note payable	$ 90,000	90,000
Total liabilities	90,000	125,000
Common stock	210,000	210,000
Retained earnings	–0–	40,000
Total stockholders' equity	210,000	250,000
Total liabilities and stockholders' equity	$300,000	$375,000

EXHIBIT 27–7

Craig Company
COMBINED STATEMENT OF INCOME AND RETAINED EARNINGS
Historical Cost/Nominal Dollar Basis
For 1985

Sales		$400,000
Cost of goods sold		
Beginning inventory	$100,000	
Purchases	210,000	
Goods available	310,000	
Ending inventory	90,000	220,000
Gross margin on sales		180,000
Operating expenses	68,000	
Depreciation expense	12,000	80,000
Income before taxes		100,000
Income tax expense		40,000
Net income		60,000
Retained earnings, Jan. 1		–0–
Less: Dividends		20,000
Retained earnings, Dec. 31		$ 40,000

A Constant Dollar Combined Statement of Income and Retained Earnings
Based on the facts presented for Craig Company, a combined statement of income and
retained earnings restated in 1985 year-end constant dollars would be reported as shown in

---

EXHIBIT 27–8

Craig Company

COMBINED STATEMENT OF INCOME AND RETAINED EARNINGS

Historical Cost/Constant Dollar Basis

For 1985

Sales ($400,000 × 1.10)		$440,000
Cost of goods sold		
Beginning inventory ($100,000 × 1.21)	$121,000	
Purchases ($210,000 × 1.10)	231,000	
Goods available	352,000	
Ending inventory ($90,000 × 1.10)	99,000	253,000
Gross margin on sales		187,000
Operating expenses ($68,000 × 1.10)	74,800	
Depreciation expense ($12,000 × 1.21)	14,520	89,320
Income before taxes		97,680
Income tax expense ($40,000 × 1.10)		44,000
Income before purchasing power gain		53,680
Purchasing power gain (see Exhibit 27–9)		8,600
Net income		62,280
Retained earnings, Jan. 1		–0–
Less: Dividends ($20,000 × 1.00)		20,000
Retained earnings, Dec. 31		$ 42,280

Exhibit 27–8. The following sections explain the calculation of each constant-dollar amount shown in the exhibit.

Sales. As indicated in Exhibit 27–5, Craig Company's sales were made evenly throughout 1985. The nominal dollar sales of $400,000 are therefore stated in terms of the average price index for 1985. To restate the nominal-dollar amount of sales in year-end constant dollars, we must multiply by the conversion factor 1.10. This conversion factor restates sales from the average index (143) to the December 31 index (157.3).

In reality, of course, sales are generally made on each business day of the year. To be technically precise, each day's sales should be restated separately in year-end constant dollars. But general price-level indexes are not published daily, and even if they were, the benefits of using daily indexes would probably not outweigh the costs. Therefore, companies usually assume that sales are made evenly throughout the year when preparing their constant dollar financial statements. This assumption, which is also typically made in regard to costs incurred throughout the year (such as purchases, salaries, and taxes), simplifies the constant dollar restatement process by permitting a conversion from the average price index for the year.

Cost of Goods Sold. The beginning inventory was acquired on January 1, 1985, when the CPI-U was 130. Therefore, to restate the nominal-dollar amount of the beginning inventory in year-end constant dollars, we multiply by the conversion factor 1.21. This conversion factor equals the December 31 index of 157.3 divided by the January 1 index of 130.

In the preparation of constant dollar financial statements, purchases are generally assumed to have occurred evenly thoughout the year. Because Craig Company's purchases were made evenly, the company would restate its purchases by multiplying by the conversion factor of 1.10 (the December 31 index of 157.3 divided by the average index of 143).

Craig Company uses the first-in, first-out (FIFO) inventory costing method, and the company's ending inventory was acquired when the CPI-U was 143. Therefore, to restate the ending inventory in year-end constant dollars, we multiply by the conversion factor 1.10 (the December 31 index of 157.3 divided by the average index of 143).

The calculation of cost of goods sold and ending inventory on a constant-dollar basis is affected by the inventory costing method that a comapny uses. If, for example, Craig Company had used last-in, first-out (LIFO) instead of FIFO, the company would restate its ending inventory of $90,000 by using the conversion factor 1.21 (the December 31 index of 157.3 divided by the January 1 index of 130), instead of 1.10. Under the LIFO assumption, the ending inventory of $90,000 would be assumed to be part of the $100,000 of inventory that was on hand on January 1.

Operating Expenses.   Operating expenses were incurred evenly throughout 1985 and are therefore restated by multiplying by the 1.10 conversion factor used to restate from the average index for the year.

Depreciation Expense.   The historical cost/nominal dollar depreciation expense of $12,000 represents an allocation of a cost ($120,000) incurred on January 1, 1985. To restate the nominal dollar amount in year-end constant dollars, we multiply by the 1.21 conversion factor used to restate from the January 1 index.

Observe that to restate depreciation expense, we use a conversion factor that adjusts from the acquisition date of the asset being depreciated. Most businesses have many depreciable assets acquired at various dates. Under these circumstances, we must multiply the historical cost/nominal dollar depreciation expense for each asset by a conversion factor that adjusts from the price index in existence when the asset was purchased. This process results in several layers of constant-dollar depreciation amounts that must be summed to derive the total constant-dollar amount of depreciation expense.

Income Tax Expense.   Income tax expense was incurred evenly throughout the year and is restated by multiplying by the 1.10 conversion factor used to restate from the average index. Observe that income tax expense in constant dollar financial statements is derived in relation to the amount shown in the conventional historical cost/nominal dollar income statement. It is not based directly on the amount of the pretax constant-dollar income, because general price-level adjustments are not allowed for income tax purposes.

Purchasing Power Gain.   Earlier in the chapter we explained the nature of purchasing power gains and losses and gave a simple example of a purchasing power loss sustained by a company that held cash during a period of inflation. In reality, all monetary assets, monetary liabilities, and the changes in them that occur during an accounting period must be considered when calculating purchasing power gains and losses. To facilitate the calculation, an accountant prepares a separate schedule or working paper that is not usually published. This schedule is similar to a funds flow statement in which funds are defined as **net monetary items** (monetary assets minus monetary liabilities).

A schedule showing the computation of Craig Company's purchasing power gain is shown in Exhibit 27–9. The preparation of a schedule showing the calculation of purchasing power gains and losses requires three major steps that are explained below.

1. On a conventional nominal-dollar basis, start with the net monetary items on hand at the beginning of the period; then add the sources and deduct the uses of net monetary items during the period to derive the net monetary items actually on hand at the end of the period.

    As shown in Exhibit 27–9, Craig Company's monetary liabilities exceed its monetary assets by $80,000 on January 1. The company's only source of net monetary items during the period was sales. When sales occur, either cash or accounts receivable increases; thus an increase in net monetary items occurs. Other frequently encountered sources of net monetary items are the sale of nonmonetary assets, such as land or equipment, and the issuance of capital stock.

    Craig Company's uses of net monetary items during the period consisted of purchases, operating expenses, income tax expense, and dividends. Notice that each of these uses represents either a decrease in monetary assets or an increase in monetary liabilities (and therefore a decrease in *net* monetary items). A purchase, for example, either decreases cash (a monetary asset) or increases accounts payable (a monetary liability); in either case a decrease

---

EXHIBIT 27-9

Craig Company

SCHEDULE SHOWING COMPUTATION OF PURCHASING POWER GAIN

For 1985

	Nominal-Dollar Basis	Conversion Factor	Constant-Dollar Basis
Net monetary items, Jan. 1	$ (80,000)*	1.21	$ (96,800)
Add: Sources of net monetary items			
Sales	400,000	1.10	440,000
Deduct: Uses of net monetary items			
Purchases	(210,000)	1.10	(231,000)
Operating expenses	(68,000)	1.10	(74,800)
Income tax expense	(40,000)	1.10	(44,000)
Dividends	(20,000)	1.00	(20,000)
Net monetary items, Dec. 31, actually on hand	$ (18,000)**		
Net monetary items, Dec. 31, that should be on hand if no purchasing power gain or loss exists			$ (26,600)
Purchasing power gain ($26,600 − $18,000)			$ 8,600

*Net monetary items, Jan. 1 (amounts obtained from Exhibit 27-6):

Cash	$ 10,000
Long-term note payable	(90,000)
Net monetary items, Jan. 1	$(80,000)

**Net monetary items, Dec. 31 (amounts obtained from Exhibit 27-6):

Cash	$ 40,000
Accounts receivable	67,000
Accounts payable	(35,000)
Long-term note payable	(90,000)
Net monetary items, Dec. 31	$(18,000)

---

in net monetary items occurs. In addition to the uses listed by Craig Company, other frequently encountered uses of net monetary items are the acquisition of nonmonetary assets and the purchase of treasury stock. Depreciation expense does not represent a use of net monetary items, because the credit side of the depreciation entry (i.e., accumulated depreciation) does not affect either monetary assets or monetary liabilities.

After adding the sources and deducting the uses of Craig Company's net monetary items, we find that the company's monetary liabilities exceed its monetary assets by $18,000 on December 31. The accuracy of this amount should be verified by determining the net monetary items that appear on the historical cost/nominal dollar balance sheet dated December 31; this verification is shown in the second footnote to Exhibit 27-9. If the two amounts are not equal, an error must have been made in preparing the schedule.

2. Restated in terms of year-end constant dollars, start with the net monetary items on hand at the beginning of the period; then add the sources and deduct the uses of net monetary items during the period to derive the net monetary items that should be on hand at the end of the period if no purchasing power gain or loss has occurred. To comply with this step, we multiply each of the nominal-dollar amounts listed in Step 1 by a conversion factor that adjusts from the time that the measurement of the amount was made.

For Craig Company, net monetary assets on January 1 are multiplied by 1.21 (the December 31 index of 157.3 divided by the January 1 index of 130). Sales, purchases, operating expenses, and income tax expense are each multiplied by 1.10 because this is the conversion factor that adjusts from the average price index for the year. Finally, the dividends are multiplied by 1.00 (157.3 ÷ 157.3) because they were declared and paid on December 31 and therefore are already stated in terms of year-end constant dollars. After making the appropriate conversions to year-end constant dollars, then adding the sources and deducting the uses of Craig Company's net monetary items, we find that Craig Company's monetary liabilities *would exceed* its monetary assets by $26,600 on December 31 *if no purchasing power gain or loss occurred during the year.*

3. The final step is to compare (1) the net monetary items actually on hand at the end of the period with (2) the net monetary items that should be on hand if no purchasing power gain or loss exists. If (1) exceeds (2), a purchasing power gain has occurred; if (2) exceeds (1), a purchasing power loss has occurred.

In the case of Craig Company, (1) exceeds (2), because a negative $18,000 is larger than a negative $26,600. A purchasing power gain of $8,600 therefore exists, as shown in Exhibit 27–9. An important factor contributing to this gain was Craig Company's indebtedness (the long-term note payable of $90,000) throughout a period of inflation. The company can now pay the debt with dollars that have less purchasing power than the dollars received when the debt was incurred.

Including the $8,600 purchasing power gain in the constant-dollar income statement results in a constant-dollar net income of $62,280 for Craig Company. In this example, the purchasing power gain is the major reason that the constant-dollar net income ($62,280) exceeds the conventional nominal-dollar net income ($60,000).

Dividends. In this example, the nominal-dollar dividends of $20,000 are also stated in terms of year-end constant dollars, because the dividends were declared on December 31. Consequently, we simply multiply the nominal-dollar amount by the conversion factor 1.00 (157.3 ÷ 157.3) to obtain the year-end constant-dollar amount shown in Exhibit 27–8. Dividends are always restated in constant dollars by using a conversion factor that adjusts from the date on which they were declared. Thus, if Craig Company had declared dividends on a date other than December 31, we would have used a conversion factor that adjusts from the date of declaration.

Craig Company's constant-dollar retained earnings balance on December 31, 1985, may now be computed by adding the constant-dollar net income to the constant-dollar retained earnings balance on January 1 and deducting the constant-dollar dividends. As shown in Exhibit 27–8, the December 31 balance is $42,280. This is the correct amount of retained earnings to report in a constant dollar balance sheet dated December 31, 1985.

In our example, Craig Company had no retained earnings on January 1, 1985, because the company began operations on that date. If the company had been operating for several years and had retained earnings on January 1, the constant-dollar retained earnings balance on January 1 to include in Exhibit 27–8 would be the December 31, *1984,* constant-dollar retained earnings balance multiplied by 1.21 (157.3 ÷ 130).

A Constant Dollar Balance Sheet

A constant dollar balance sheet for Craig Company on December 31, 1985, is shown in Exhibit 27–10. The following sections explain the calculation of each balance sheet amount.

Monetary Items. The monetary items (cash, accounts receivable, accounts payable, and long-term note payable) are already stated in terms of year-end constant dollars and therefore do not require restatement for the constant dollar balance sheet. The amounts reported for these items on a constant dollar balance sheet (Exhibit 27–10) are the same as on a nominal dollar balance sheet (Exhibit 27–6).

Inventory. Craig Company uses the FIFO costing method, and the ending inventory was acquired when the CPI-U was 143. The nominal-dollar amount of $90,000 is therefore restated in terms of year-end constant dollars by multiplying by 1.10 (157.3 ÷ 143). As we

---

EXHIBIT 27–10
Craig Company
BALANCE SHEET
Historical Cost/Constant Dollar Basis
December 31, 1985

Assets

Cash		$ 40,000
Accounts receivable		67,000
Inventory ($90,000 × 1.10)		99,000
Land ($70,000 × 1.21)		84,700
Equipment ($120,000 × 1.21)	$145,200	
Less: Accumulated depreciation ($12,000 × 1.21)	(14,520)	130,680
Total assets		$421,380

Liabilities and Stockholders' Equity

Accounts payable	$ 35,000
Long-term note payable	90,000
Total liabilities	125,000
Common stock ($210,000 × 1.21)	254,100
Retained earnings (see Exhibit 27–8)	42,280
Total stockholders' equity	296,380
Total liabilities and stockholders' equity	$421,380

---

pointed out earlier when discussing the calculation of cost of goods sold, we would restate Craig Company's inventory using the conversion factor of 1.21 instead of 1.10 if the company had used LIFO instead of FIFO.

Land.   Craig Company acquired the land on January 1, 1985. The constant-dollar amount to report for the land therefore equals the nominal-dollar amount of $70,000 multiplied by the conversion factor 1.21 (157.3 ÷ 130) that adjusts from the price index on January 1.

Equipment and Accumulated Depreciation.   The equipment costing $120,000 was acquired on January 1, 1985, and the $12,000 of accumulated depreciation has resulted from charging one-tenth of the equipment's cost to expense during 1985. Accordingly, both amounts are restated to constant dollars by multiplying by the 1.21 (157.3 ÷ 130) conversion factor that adjusts from the price index on January 1.

Common Stock.   The common stock of $210,000 was issued on January 1 and is therefore multiplied by 1.21 (157.3 ÷ 130) to convert the nominal-dollar measurement to year-end constant dollars. Once again we use a conversion factor that adjusts from the price index on January 1, because this is the date on which Craig Company issued the common stock.

Retained Earnings.   The ending balance of retained earnings is obtained directly from the constant dollar statement of income and retained earnings shown in Exhibit 27–8. Recall that in Chapter 5 we used the same general approach to derive the ending retained earnings balance in a conventional nominal dollar balance sheet (i.e., we added net income to the beginning retained earnings balance and deducted dividends). The ending balance of retained earnings shown on the combined statement of income and retained earnings should cause total assets to equal total liabilities and stockholders' equity; if this equality does not exist, an error must have been made.

Subsequent Years
When preparing constant dollar financial statements in subsequent years, Craig Company should follow the same general approach illustrated thus far. If the company prepares *com-*

parative financial statements at the end of 1986, the individual amounts shown in the constant dollar financial statements prepared at the end of 1985 would simply be **rolled forward** (adjusted) for comparative purposes to the price index that exists at the end of 1986. This would be done to permit a meaningful comparison of the 1985 and 1986 financial statements expressed in terms of the same 1986 constant dollar measuring unit. To roll forward the 1985 constant dollar financial statements to 1986 year-end constant dollars, each amount shown in Exhibits 27–8 and 27–10 (including the monetary items) would simply be multiplied by a conversion factor, the numerator of which is the price index at the end of 1986 and denominator of which is the price index at the end of 1985 (157.3).

Arguments For and Against Constant Dollar Accounting

Accountants have actively debated for the pros and cons of constant dollar accounting during most of the twentieth century. Here are the major arguments that have been cited in favor of constant dollar accounting:

1. Constant dollar accounting provides measurements that can be added and subtracted logically, because a uniform measuring unit is used. In contrast, nominal dollar measurements reflect dollars of mixed purchasing power; adding and subtracting nominal dollars in financial statements is similar to adding and subtracting apples and oranges.
2. Constant dollar accounting enables users of financial statements to make more meaningful comparisons between different companies. Under constant dollar accounting, each company would report a set of financial statements expressed in terms of the same measuring unit.
3. Constant dollar accounting permits users to make more meaningful comparisons of a given company's performance over time, because each year's financial statements are expressed in terms of the same measuring unit.
4. Constant dollar accounting does not depart from historical cost accounting. Historical cost information has been used for many years, is widely understood in the financial community, and is generally perceived as highly reliable.

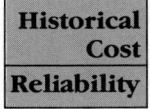

On the other hand, many people oppose constant dollar accounting. These are the major arguments used against it:

1. Constant dollar accounting does not reflect adjustments for specific price changes. The general price-level index used in constant dollar accounting may bear little relation to the changes in the specific prices of the goods and services that a particular company actually purchases or manufactures.
2. Constant dollar accounting may confuse users of financial statements. These users may erroneously believe that constant dollar financial statements present current values instead of historical costs.
3. Purchasing power gains and losses, which are included in constant-dollar net income, are never received or paid in cash. Unlike purchasing power gains and losses, other income statement elements are associated with past, present, or expected future cash receipts or disbursements.
4. Inflation in the United States has not been severe enough to warrant constant dollar accounting. Nominal dollar financial statements are not materially distorted unless the inflation rate is sufficiently high over a sustained period.

CURRENT VALUE ACCOUNTING

Nature and Objective

Suppose that a company buys some land for $50,000 at the beginning of a year and sells it 10 years later for $150,000. Assume further that the land's market value increased by $10,000 during each of the 10 years it was held. Under these circumstances, the land would be reported on a conventional historical cost balance sheet at $50,000 during the entire time it was held, and a $100,000 gain ($150,000 − $50,000) would be reported on the income statement prepared at the end of the tenth year. The reason for reporting these amounts is that historical cost accounting is based on completed transactions. Increases that occur in the market values of a company's assets are ignored until the time the assets are sold.

Proponents of current value accounting believe that ignoring changes in market values when they occur is misleading. In the example cited in the previous paragraph, current value proponents would argue that the company is actually *better off* by $10,000 each year the land is held. Consequently, the usefulness of year-end balance sheets would be enhanced by increasing the carrying value of the land by $10,000 each year it is held. Moreover, periodic income statements would be more useful if they reflected $10,000 of income each year. Why postpone the recognition of all the income until the tenth year merely because the land was sold at that time? Although current value accounting may be somewhat less reliable than historical cost accounting, advocates argue that it is much more relevant, and more useful, to users of financial statements.

> **Usefulness**
> **Relevance**
> **Reliability**

Current value/nominal dollar accounting is represented by Cell 2 of the matrix presented earlier in Exhibit 27–2. Under this system of accounting, the attribute measured in financial statements is current value; the measuring unit is the nominal dollar. Because the nominal dollar is the conventional measuring unit used in financial statements, current value/nominal dollar accounting is often referred to simply as **current value accounting.**

The objective of current value accounting is to report financial statements that reflect the effects of specific price changes. In a set of current value financial statements, assets and liabilities are reported at their current values (instead of their historical costs) on the balance sheet date, and holding gains and losses (discussed below) are reported as the specific prices of a company's assets and liabilities change.[4] As explained earlier in the chapter, specific price changes are commonly measured by direct pricing or indexing methods.

Fundamentally, the current value of an item refers to the item's value at the present time. But the term "value" can have many different meanings, and the term "current value accounting" therefore can mean different things to different people. In the accounting literature, "current value accounting" refers to three major forms or types of accounting: (1) present value accounting, (2) exit value accounting, and (3) current cost accounting. Just as historical cost accounting is based primarily (but not exclusively) on the historical cost attribute, each form of current value accounting is based primarily (but not exclusively) on an attribute other than historical cost.

Present Value Accounting

In **present value accounting,** an asset is measured at the present discounted amount of the net cash inflows that the asset is expected to generate in the future. Income consists of three components: (1) an amount determined when an asset is acquired by subtracting the asset's cost from its present value; (2) interest revenue that is earned on the asset over time; and (3) holding gains and losses that are based on changes that occur in the asset's present value while it is held.

Determining an asset's present value requires that we discount all the net cash inflows that the asset is expected to generate in the future. The discounting process requires estimates of the amount of the net cash inflows, the timing of those flows, and the discount rate to use in computing the present value.

> **Relevance**

A strong theoretical case can be made that present value accounting information would be extremely relevant to users of financial statements. The existence of expected future economic benefits is the essence of an asset, and the asset's present value is a measure of

---

[4]In this chapter we cover current value accounting primarily from the standpoint of assets. Current value accounting for liabilities has not been widely discussed in the accounting literature and is not required by *SFAS No. 33.*

Reliability

how much those benefits currently are worth. A major weakness of present value accounting is that the information generally lacks reliability. Because of uncertainty about the future and because it is usually impossible to determine exactly how much cash inflows are associated with each one of a company's many interacting assets, accountants cannot reliably measure present values for most types of nonmonetary assets, such as equipment, buildings, and patents.

Exit Value Accounting

Under **exit value accounting,** an asset is measured at the amount of cash it could be sold for in an orderly liquidation. Income consists of two components: (1) an amount determined when an asset is acquired by subtracting the asset's cost from its exit value, and (2) holding gains and losses that are based on changes that occur in the asset's exit value while it is held.

Relevance

Reliability

The exit value of an asset indicates the opportunity cost that a company incurs by holding rather than selling the asset. Proponents argue that exit values are relevant because they indicate the ability of a company to adapt to its changing environment by selling assets and investing the money elsewhere. Exit values are also considered more objective and reliable than present values.

Opponents of exit value accounting believe that exit values lack relevance for assets, such as equipment, that a company intends to use rather than sell. Opponents also point out that many assets, such as goodwill, work-in-process inventory, and specialized plant assets, do not usually have readily determinable exit values.

Current Cost Accounting

In **current cost accounting,** an asset is measured at the amount of cash (or cash equivalent) that a company would currently have to pay to acquire the same asset in its existing condition. Income consists of two components: (1) holding gains and losses based on changes that occur in the asset's current cost while it is held, and (2) an amount determined when an asset is sold by subtracting the asset's current cost on the date of sale from its selling price.

Relevance
Reliability

Proponents argue that current cost information is relevant because it helps users to make more accurate predictions of future cash flows and more meaningful evaluations of a company's financial position and performance. Opponents tend to question the reliability of current cost measurements in relation to those based on historical costs.

Reliability

Although all forms of current value accounting are highly controversial and still in the early stages of their development, current cost accounting appears to be the most widely supported form of current value accounting today. The FASB opted for current cost measurements in *SFAS No. 33.* Many people prefer current cost accounting because they regard current costs as more reliable than the other types of current value measurements. Moreover, although current costs are used instead of historical costs, current cost accounting still represents an approach based on costs rather than selling prices. Conventional historical cost accounting is also, of course, a cost-based approach. Finally, present value accounting and exit value accounting systems allow income to be recognized when goods are purchased or manufactured. Thus, under these systems, all of the income associated with an asset such as inventory may be recognized before the time of sale. In contrast, when current cost accounting is used, holding gains and losses are recognized before the time of sale, but additional income is also recognized when a sale occurs based on the difference between the selling price and the current cost of the asset sold. The current cost approach therefore requires a less radical departure from the age-old general rule in accounting that income should be recognized only at the time of sale.

We shall emphasize current cost accounting in the rest of this chapter because of the support it has received and because it may be even more widely accepted in the future.

Holding Gains and Losses Under Current Cost Accounting

Holding gains and losses in current cost accounting result from changes in the current cost of an asset while it is held over time. Suppose, for example, that a company invests in land costing $10,000 on January 1, 1983. Assume further that the company holds the land on December 31, 1983, when the land's current cost is $14,000, and on December 31, 1984, when the land's current cost is $19,000. On December 31, 1985, the land is determined to have a current cost of $25,000, and the company sells it for that amount. Under current cost accounting, the company would report a holding gain of $4,000 in 1983 ($14,000 − $10,000), $5,000 in 1984 ($19,000 − $14,000), and $6,000 in 1985 ($25,000 − $19,000). The rationale for reporting these amounts as gains is that the company's management has been smart enough or lucky enough to achieve a cost saving by purchasing the land before its price increased. Holding gains sometimes are called **cost savings.** The *total* holding gain reported during the three-year period would be $15,000 ($4,000 + $5,000 + $6,000). In conventional historical cost accounting, all of the $15,000 gain would be reported in 1985, the year in which the land was sold. The amount of the gain, of course, would be determined in 1985 by subtracting the land's cost of $10,000 from its selling price of $25,000.

Holding gains and losses may be either unrealized or realized. **Unrealized holding gains and losses** pertain to assets still on hand at the end of a period. The adjective "unrealized" is appropriate because the assets have not yet been sold or used in operations. The *total* unrealized holding gain or loss equals the difference between the current cost and the historical cost of the asset on hand. However, the amount of unrealized holding gain or loss to recognize in a current cost income statement in any year is the *increase or decrease* in the *total* unrealized holding gain or loss during the year. This increase or decrease is computed by subtracting the total unrealized holding gain or loss at the beginning of the period from the total unrealized holding gain or loss at the end of the period.

To illustrate, suppose that a company buys an inventory item costing $100 on January 1, 1983, and that the company continues to hold the item on December 31, 1983, when the current cost is $120 and on December 31, 1984, when the current cost is $150. Under these circumstances, the *total* unrealized holding gain is $0 on January 1, 1983 ($100 − $100), $20 on December 31, 1983 ($120 − $100), and $50 on December 31, 1984 ($150 − $100). The correct amount of unrealized holding gain to report in a current cost income statement is $20 for 1983 ($20 − $0) and $30 for 1984 ($50 − $20). Notice carefully that $50 is *not* the correct amount of unrealized holding gain to report in 1984, because $20 of that amount pertains to an increase in current cost during 1983.

Realized holding gains and losses pertain to assets sold or consumed in operations during a period. The adjective "realized" applies because the assets to which the gains or losses pertain have been sold or consumed. The amount of realized holding gain or loss to report in a current cost income statement is the difference between the current cost and the historical cost of the asset sold or consumed. If the inventory item described in the previous paragraph is sold in 1985 for $200 at a time when the current cost is $170, the realized holding gain to report in 1985 will be $70 (the current cost on the date of sale of $170 minus the historical cost of $100).

Current Cost Versus Historical Cost Income Statements

An example will now be presented to illustrate the major elements of a current cost income statement and to compare the statement with a historical cost income statement. Suppose that Miles Company acquires an inventory item on January 1, 1984, for $300. The item has a current cost of $500 on December 31, 1984; Miles Company sells the item for $1,000 on December 31, 1985, at which time the item's current cost is $900. A comparison of the income statement results under historical cost accounting and current cost accounting is shown in Exhibit 27−11. For the sake of simplicity, we shall assume that cost of goods sold is the only expense.

EXHIBIT 27–11
Miles Company
Historical Cost and Current Cost Income Statements

Historical Cost Basis

	For 1984	For 1985
Sales	–0–	$1,000
Cost of goods sold	–0–	300
Net income	–0–	$ 700

Current Cost Basis

	For 1984	For 1985
Sales	–0–	$1,000
Cost of goods sold	–0–	900
Current operating income	–0–	100
Realized holding gain	–0–	600
Conventional income	–0–	700
Unrealized holding gain (loss)	$200	(200)
Net income	$200	$ 500

Under historical cost accounting, Miles Company reports no income in 1984 because the company did not sell the inventory in that year. In 1985 the company sells the inventory and reports net income of $700, which equals the inventory's selling price of $1,000 minus the historical cost of $300.

Observe carefully the major components of the current cost income statement in Exhibit 27–11. Under current cost accounting, cost of goods sold is measured at the current cost on the date of sale and is deducted from sales revenue to derive **current operating income.** Realized holding gains and losses are then added and subtracted to derive **conventional income** (often called **realized income**). Note that Miles Company had a realized holding gain of $600 in 1985. This amount was calculated by subtracting the historical cost of the inventory item ($300) from its current cost ($900) on the date of sale. Unrealized holding gains and losses are then added and subtracted to derive **current cost net income.** Miles Company reported an unrealized holding gain of $200 in 1984; this amount equals the total unrealized holding gain of $200 at the end of 1984 minus the total unrealized holding gain of $0 at the beginning of 1984. In 1985 the company reported an unrealized holding loss of $200. This amount was calculated by subtracting the total unrealized holding gain of $200 at the end of 1984 from the total unrealized holding gain of $0 at the end of 1985. (The total unrealized holding gain was $0 at the end of 1985 because the inventory was sold in 1985 and is therefore not on hand at year-end.)

Several important observations about current cost income statements can now be made.

1. Current operating income is measured by matching current costs (not historical costs) with current revenues. Proponents of current cost accounting believe that requests from labor organizations for higher wages, from governments for additional taxes, and from stockholders for greater dividends should be based on current operating income and not on historical cost net income. In our example, $600 of Miles Company's historical cost net income resulted from specific price changes; only $100 was due to operations. If Miles Company were to distribute the $700 of historical cost income to employees, governments, and stockholders, the company could not replace the inventory item that was sold. The company's physical capacity would therefore contract. In a broader sense, any company that pays out cash equal to its historical cost net income during periods in which the current costs of inventories and plant assets increase will not be able to maintain its physical capacity without obtaining outside financing.

Proponents of current cost accounting also believe that current operating income is a better measure for predictive purposes than is historical cost net income. They believe that current operating income more accurately reflects an amount that the company can expect to earn from future operations.

2. Conventional income in a current cost income statement always equals historical cost net income. Observe in Exhibit 27–11 that these amounts equal $0 in 1984 and $700 in 1985. The equality exists because historical cost net income actually consists of income from operations and realized holding gains. But these two components are not separately identified in a historical cost income statement, which means that users of the statement cannot determine how much of the historical cost net income was due to operations and how much was due to specific price changes.

3. Realized and unrealized holding gains and losses are reported separately on a current cost income statement. Current cost advocates believe this is desirable because holding gains and losses are generally less predictable than current operating income and are not caused by the same factors.

4. Unrealized holding gains and losses are included in the calculation of current cost net income, but not historical cost net income. Proponents believe that current cost net income provides a better measure than historical cost net income of how much better or worse off a company is each period.

5. The total amount of net income reported over the life of a company is the same under current cost accounting as under historical cost accounting, but the timing differs. Note in Exhibit 27–11 that if we add Miles Company's net incomes for 1984 and 1985, we obtain the same total under either historical cost accounting or current cost accounting ($0 + $700 = $700; $200 + $500 = $700).

Preparation of Current Cost Financial Statements

We shall now illustrate the process of preparing a set of comprehensive current cost financial statements. The illustration is based on the information presented earlier in the chapter for Craig Company (see Exhibits 27–5, 27–6, and 27–7) and on the *current cost* amounts in Exhibit 27–12.

We shall assume that the current cost amounts of financial statement items not shown in Exhibit 27–12 are the same as their historical cost amounts. The methods used to obtain current cost measurements such as the ones shown in Exhibit 27–12 were explained earlier in the chapter. When solving the assignment materials at the end of this chapter, you will be given current cost amounts on which to rely.

A Current Cost Combined Statement of Income and Retained Earnings

A combined statement of income and retained earnings presented on a current cost basis for Craig Company is shown in Exhibit 27–13. In the following sections we explain the current cost amounts shown in the exhibit.

EXHIBIT 27–12
Craig Company
Current Cost Information

	Current Cost
Cost of goods sold for 1985	$260,000
Inventory, Dec. 31, 1985	102,000
Land, Dec. 31, 1985	160,000
Equipment (gross), Dec. 31, 1985	140,000

EXHIBIT 27-13

Craig Company
COMBINED STATEMENT OF INCOME AND RETAINED EARNINGS
Current Cost/Nominal Dollar Basis
For 1985

Sales		$400,000
Cost of goods sold		260,000
Gross margin on sales		140,000
Operating expenses	$68,000	
Depreciation expense	13,000	81,000
Income before taxes		59,000
Income tax expense		40,000
Current operating income		19,000
Realized holding gain*		41,000
Conventional income		60,000
Unrealized holding gain**		120,000
Net income		180,000
Retained earnings, Jan. 1		-0-
Less: Dividends		20,000
Retained earnings, Dec. 31		$160,000

*Realized holding gain for 1985:

Inventory sold ($260,000 − $220,000)	$40,000
Equipment used ($13,000 − $12,000)	1,000
Total	$41,000

**Unrealized holding gain for 1985:

Inventory on hand ($102,000 − $90,000)	$ 12,000
Land on hand ($160,000 − $70,000)	90,000
Equipment on hand—net ($126,000 − $108,000)	18,000
Total on Dec. 31	120,000
Less: Unrealized holding gain, Jan. 1	-0-
Amount to recognize in 1985	$120,000

Sales. Sales are made at current selling prices throughout the period. Craig Company's historical cost/nominal dollar sales of $400,000 are therefore not restated when preparing a current cost income statement.

Cost of Goods Sold. In current cost accounting, cost of goods sold equals the current costs of the units sold at the time of sale. In practice, cost of goods sold is usually based on the average current costs of the units sold during the period. An average is considered appropriate because sales generally are made fairly evenly throughout a period. Craig Company's current cost of goods sold, as given earlier, is $260,000.

Operating Expenses. The historical cost/nominal dollar operating expenses of $68,000 are measured at current costs when incurred. Accordingly, these expenses are already stated on a current cost basis.

Matching

Depreciation Expense. Recall that depreciation expense is recorded because of the matching principle. Because sales are made at current selling prices throughout the period, we measure depreciation expense based on the average current cost of the service potential of the assets used during the period. For Craig Company, the 1985 current cost depreciation expense is calculated as follows:

$$\frac{\$120,000 + \$140,000}{2} = \$130,000 \text{ average current cost of equipment during 1985}$$

$130,000 ÷ 10 years = $13,000 current cost depreciation expense for 1985

Income Tax Expense.   Income tax expense on a current cost basis is computed in relation to pretax historical cost/nominal dollar income. Accordingly, Craig Company's income tax expense is shown at $40,000 in Exhibit 27–13.

Realized Holding Gain.   As explained earlier, realized holding gains and losses pertain to assets sold or consumed during a period and equal the difference between the current cost and the historical cost of the assets sold or consumed. As shown in the first footnote of Exhibit 27–13, Craig Company has a realized holding gain of $40,000 on the inventory sold (the current cost of goods sold of $260,000 minus the historical cost of goods sold of $220,000) and a realized holding gain of $1,000 on the equipment used in operations (the current cost depreciation expense of $13,000 minus the historical cost depreciation expense of $12,000). The total realized holding gain is $41,000.

Unrealized Holding Gain.   Earlier we explained that unrealized holding gains and losses pertain to assets still on hand at the end of a period and that the correct amount to report in a given year equals the increase or decrease in the total unrealized holding gain or loss during the year. As shown in the second footnote of Exhibit 27–13, Craig Company's unrealized holding gain for 1985 is attributable to the inventory, land, and equipment on hand at year-end. The unexpired historical cost of each asset on December 31, 1985, is subtracted from the unexpired current cost on that date in order to derive the total unrealized holding gain for each asset. These totals are then summed to derive the total unrealized holding gain of $120,000 on December 31, 1985. Because no unrealized holding gains or losses existed on January 1, 1985 (when the company began operations), $120,000 is the correct amount of unrealized holding gain to report for 1985.

The calculation of the unrealized holding gain of $18,000 on the equipment deserves additional explanation. Note that we derived the $18,000 amount by subtracting the historical cost book value of $108,000 from the current cost book value of $126,000 on December 31, 1985. But remember that the current cost of the equipment before accumulated depreciation is $140,000 and the current cost depreciation expense is $13,000. Why then is the current cost book value $126,000 instead of $127,000 ($140,000 − $13,000 = $127,000)? The answer is because the depreciation expense of $13,000 is based on an *average* of beginning and ending current cost amounts, while the accumulated depreciation to report at year-end is based only on the *ending* current cost amount and equals $14,000 ($140,000 × 10% = $14,000). The year-end accumulated depreciation ($14,000) must be based on the year-end current cost ($140,000) so that the ending balance sheet will correctly show the current cost of the asset's remaining service potential of $126,000 ($140,000 − $14,000 = $126,000; $140,000 × 90% = $126,000).

Dividends.   The historical cost/nominal dollar dividends of $20,000 were declared at year-end and are already stated in terms of year-end current costs.

A Current Cost Balance Sheet

A current cost balance sheet for Craig Company on December 31, 1985, is shown in Exhibit 27–14. The amounts are explained in the following sections.

Cash and Accounts Receivable.   These items are normally reported on a current value basis in conventional financial statements and are therefore not restated when preparing a current cost balance sheet.

Inventory and Land.   These items are reported at their respective current cost amounts determined at year-end.

Equipment and Accumulated Depreciation.   The equipment is shown at the current cost amount of $140,000 determined at year-end. Accumulated depreciation of $14,000 ($140,000 ÷ 10 years = $14,000) is subtracted so that the equipment's remaining service potential is reported at a current cost book value of $126,000 on December 31, 1985.

Accounts Payable and Long-Term Note Payable.   Accounts payable are conventionally reported on a current value basis and therefore do not require restatement in a

---

EXHIBIT 27–14
Craig Company
BALANCE SHEET
Current Cost/Nominal Dollar Basis
December 31, 1985

Assets

Cash		$ 40,000
Accounts receivable		67,000
Inventory		102,000
Land		160,000
Equipment	$140,000	
Less: Accumulated depreciation	(14,000)	126,000
Total assets		$495,000

Liabilities and Stockholders' Equity

Accounts payable	$ 35,000
Long-term note payable	90,000
Total liabilities	125,000
Common stock	210,000
Retained earnings (see Exhibit 27–13)	160,000
Total stockholders' equity	370,000
Total liabilities and stockholders' equity	$495,000

---

current cost balance sheet. We shall assume that the market rate of interest on the long-term note payable has not changed during the year; therefore, the current cost amount to report for the note is the same as the amount shown in a historical cost/nominal dollar balance sheet. Current cost accounting for liabilities has not been widely discussed in the accounting literature and is not required by *SFAS No. 33*. We therefore do not discuss this topic in detail in this chapter.

Common Stock.   This item is reported on a current cost balance sheet at the amount originally paid in by the stockholders. This is the same amount reported on a historical cost/nominal dollar balance sheet.

Retained Earnings.   The amount of this item is obtained directly from the current cost combined statement of income and retained earnings shown in Exhibit 27–13. For Craig Company, the amount is determined as follows:

Current cost retained earnings, Jan. 1	–0–
Add: Current cost net income	$180,000
Subtotal	180,000
Less: Current cost dividends	20,000
Current cost retained earnings, Dec. 31	$160,000

The ending balance of retained earnings shown on the combined statement of income and retained earnings should be the amount that causes total assets to equal total liabilities and stockholders' equity on the current cost balance sheet. If these totals are not equal after including retained earnings, we know that an error has been made.

Arguments For and Against Current Cost Accounting

Current cost accounting has been one of the most widely discussed topics in the financial community in recent years. The major arguments in favor of current cost accounting are:

Usefulness

1. Current cost accounting leads to income statements that are useful for predictive purposes. Current operating income is more predictable than holding gains and losses; these two kinds of income are reported separately on a current cost income statement.

Usefulness

2. Current cost accounting leads to income statements that are useful for evaluating management's performance. The separation of current operating income from holding gains and losses allows users of financial statements to evaluate management's **operating activities** (activities directly related to producing and selling products) separate from **holding activities** (holding assets while specific prices change).

3. Current cost accounting can help a company to maintain its physical capacity. During periods of rising costs, current operating income indicates the maximum amount that a company can distribute and still maintain its capacity to produce and sell products without obtaining new debt or equity capital.

Relevance

4. Current cost balance sheets are relevant because they reflect current valuations of a company's resources and equities.

Here are the major arguments against current cost accounting:

Reliability

1. Current cost measurements are too subjective and unreliable. This argument is particularly strong in the case of specialized assets that do not have a ready market.

2. Current cost financial statements are denominated in dollars of mixed purchasing power. Holding gains and losses are therefore not adjusted for inflation, and purchasing power gains and losses are not even reported. Suppose that a company buys land for $10,000 on January 1, 1985, and holds the land on December 31, 1985, when the current cost is $11,000. The company is better off by $1,000 on December 31 only if no inflation occurred during the year. If, in fact, the inflation rate for the year was 20%, the company is actually $1,000 *worse off* at year-end [$11,000 - ($10,000 × 1.20) = ($1,000)].

CURRENT COST/CONSTANT DOLLAR ACCOUNTING

Nature and Objective

We have discussed constant dollar accounting, in which the attribute measured is historical cost and the measuring unit is the constant dollar. We have also discussed current cost accounting, in which the attribute measured is current cost and the measuring unit is the nominal dollar. In this section we shall see that it is possible to combine current cost and constant dollar accounting in a single set of financial statements. Current cost accounting and constant dollar accounting are not mutually exclusive but are highly compatible with one another.

Current cost/constant dollar accounting is represented by Cell 4 of the matrix presented earlier in Exhibit 27–2. The objective of this system of accounting is to measure the current cost attribute of the elements of financial statements using dollars that have the same purchasing power. Current cost/constant dollar financial statements reflect adjustments for general price-level changes as well as for specific price changes. These statements therefore contain complete adjustments for the effects of changing prices and are regarded as theoretically sound.

Purchasing Power Gains and Losses and Holding Gains and Losses Adjusted for Inflation

Purchasing power gains and losses are measured and reported under constant dollar accounting, and holding gains and losses are measured and reported under current cost accounting. Both types of gains and losses are measured and reported under current cost/constant dollar accounting. Purchasing power gains and losses are measured in the same manner as in constant dollar accounting. Holding gains and losses in current cost/constant dollar accounting are reported net of inflation. To illustrate, suppose that a company buys an inventory item for $100 on January 1, 1985. Assume further that the 1985 inflation rate is 8% and that the company holds the inventory item on December 31, 1985, when the item's current cost is $120. In current cost accounting, a holding gain of $20 ($120 − $100) would be reported for 1985. But in current cost/constant dollar accounting, the holding gain would be adjusted for inflation and reported at $12 [$120 − ($100 × 1.08)]. Under current cost/constant dollar accounting, we say that only $12 of the $20 nominal dollar holding gain is a *real holding gain*. The other $8 is merely a *fictional holding gain* due to inflation.

Preparation of Current Cost/Constant Dollar Financial Statements

Using the same information given earlier for Craig Company (see Exhibits 27−5, 27−6, 27−7, and 27−12), we shall now illustrate how to prepare a set of current cost/constant dollar financial statements.

A Current Cost/Constant Dollar Combined Statement of Income and Retained Earnings

A combined statement of income and retained earnings reported on a current cost/constant dollar basis for Craig Company is shown in Exhibit 27−15. The amounts shown in the exhibit are explained below.

Sales. Craig Company's sales of $400,000 were made at current selling prices throughout the year and are adjusted to year-end constant dollars by multiplying by 1.10. Recall that 1.10 (157.3 ÷ 143) is the conversion factor used to restate amounts *from* the average price-level index of 143 *to* the December 31 index of 157.3.

Cost of Goods Sold. Cost of goods sold expense was incurred throughout the year. Therefore, the current cost amount of $260,000 is adjusted to year-end constant dollars by multiplying by 1.10.

Operating Expenses. The operating expenses were incurred throughout the year; the current cost amount is restated in year-end constant dollars by multiplying by 1.10.

Depreciation Expense. The current cost depreciation expense is based on the average current cost of the equipment during the year. Accordingly, this amount is multiplied by 1.10 in order to adjust to year-end constant dollars.

Income Tax Expense. Income tax expense is incurred throughout the year. Therefore, the current cost amount of $40,000 is restated in year-end constant dollars by multiplying by 1.10.

Purchasing Power Gain. As indicated earlier, purchasing power gains and losses under current cost/constant dollar accounting are calculated in the same manner as they are under constant dollar accounting. The $8,600 amount shown in Exhibit 27−15 is calculated exactly as shown in Exhibit 27−9.

Realized Holding Gain, Adjusted for Inflation. Recall from our earlier discussion that realized holding gains and losses pertain to assets sold or consumed during a period. In a current cost/constant dollar system, these gains and losses are reported net of inflation.

As shown in the first footnote of Exhibit 27−15, Craig Company has a realized holding gain, adjusted for inflation, of $33,000 on the inventory sold. The $33,000 amount equals the current cost/constant dollar cost of goods sold of $286,000 (as shown in Exhibit 27−15) minus the historical cost/constant dollar cost of goods sold of $253,000 (as shown in Exhibit 27−8). Observe that both cost of goods sold amounts are expressed in *constant dollars*; therefore, the difference between them equals a realized holding gain *adjusted for inflation*. Craig Company also has a realized holding loss, adjusted for inflation, of $220 on the equipment used in operations. The $220 amount equals the current cost/constant dollar depreciation expense of $14,300 (as shown in Exhibit 27−15) minus the historical cost/constant dollar depreciation expense of $14,520 (as shown in Exhibit 27−8). The difference

---

EXHIBIT 27–15

Craig Company
COMBINED STATEMENT OF INCOME AND RETAINED EARNINGS
Current Cost/Constant Dollar Basis
For 1985

Sales ($400,000 × 1.10)		$440,000
Cost of goods sold ($260,000 × 1.10)		286,000
Gross margin on sales		154,000
Operating expenses ($68,000 × 1.10)	$74,800	
Depreciation expense ($13,000 × 1.10)	14,300	89,100
Income before taxes		64,900
Income tax expense ($40,000 × 1.10)		44,000
Current operating income		20,900
Purchasing power gain (see Exhibit 27–9)		8,600
Current operating income after purchasing power gain		29,500
Realized holding gain, adjusted for inflation*		32,780
Conventional income, adjusted for inflation		62,280
Unrealized holding gain, adjusted for inflation**		73,620
Net income		135,900
Retained earnings, Jan. 1		–0–
Less: Dividends ($20,000 × 1.00)		20,000
Retained earnings, Dec. 31		$115,900

*Realized holding gain, adjusted for inflation, for 1985:

	CC/CD	HC/CD	Difference
Inventory sold	$286,000	$253,000	$33,000
Equipment used	14,300	14,520	(220)
Total			$32,780

**Unrealized holding gain, adjusted for inflation, for 1985:

	CC/CD	HC/CD	Difference
Inventory on hand	$102,000	$ 99,000	$ 3,000
Land on hand	160,000	84,700	75,300
Equipment on hand—net	126,000	130,680	(4,680)
Total on Dec. 31			73,620
Less: Unrealized holding gain, adjusted for inflation, Jan. 1			–0–
Amount to recognize in 1985			$73,620

---

between the two depreciation amounts represents a realized holding loss *adjusted for inflation,* because both amounts are expressed in *constant dollars.* The total realized holding gain, adjusted for inflation, is $32,780.

Notice that after including the $32,780 amount in the combined statement of income and retained earnings, we derive a conventional income adjusted for inflation of $62,280. Through no coincidence, this amount equals the net income shown in Craig Company's constant dollar combined statement of income and retained earnings (as shown in Exhibit 27–8).

Unrealized Holding Gain, Adjusted for Inflation. Unrealized holding gains and losses are also reported net of inflation in current cost/constant dollar financial statements. Remember that unrealized holding gains and losses pertain to assets still on hand at the end of a period.

As shown in the second footnote of Exhibit 27–15, Craig Company has a total unrealized holding gain, adjusted for inflation, of $73,620 at the end of 1985. This amount is associated with the inventory, land, and equipment on hand at year-end. Notice that for each asset, we

---

EXHIBIT 27–16
Craig Company
BALANCE SHEET
Current Cost/Constant Dollar Basis
December 31, 1985

Assets

Cash		$ 40,000
Accounts receivable		67,000
Inventory		102,000
Land		160,000
Equipment	$140,000	
Less: Accumulated depreciation	(14,000)	126,000
Total assets		$495,000

Liabilities and Stockholders' Equity

Accounts payable	$ 35,000
Long-term note payable	90,000
Total liabilities	125,000
Common stock ($210,000 × 1.21)	254,100
Retained earnings (see Exhibit 27–15)	115,900
Total stockholders' equity	370,000
Total liabilities and stockholders' equity	$495,000

---

subtracted the historical cost/constant dollar amount (as shown in Exhibit 27–10) from the current cost/constant dollar amount (as shown in Exhibit 27–16). Because the two amounts for each asset are expressed in *constant dollars,* the differences between them represent holding gains (or losses) *adjusted for inflation.* The total holding gain, adjusted for inflation, of $73,620 is also the correct amount to report for 1985, because Craig Company began operations on January 1, 1985, and no unrealized holding gains or losses adjusted for inflation existed at that time.

Dividends. Craig Company's dividends were declared at year-end and are already stated in terms of year-end constant dollars. We therefore simply multiply by a conversion factor of 1.00 (157.3 ÷ 157.3), as shown in Exhibit 27–15.

A Current Cost/Constant Dollar Balance Sheet

A current cost/constant dollar balance sheet for Craig Company is shown in Exhibit 27–16. Notice the similarity between this balance sheet and the current cost balance sheet shown in Exhibit 27–14. Each of the assets and liabilities is reported at the same amount on a current cost/constant dollar balance sheet as on a current cost balance sheet. The reason for this is because the current cost measurements of the assets and liabilities are obtained *at year-end* and are therefore automatically expressed in terms of year-end constant dollars.

The differences between a current cost balance sheet and a current cost/constant dollar balance sheet are in the stockholders' equity section. As shown in Exhibit 27–16, Craig Company's common stock balance of $210,000 is adjusted to year-end constant dollars by multiplying by 1.21. Recall that this conversion factor is the one used to restate amounts *from* the January 1 price-level index of 130 *to* the December 31 price-level index of 157.3 (157.3/130 = 1.21). The 1.21 conversion factor is appropriate to use because the common stock balance originated on January 1.

The ending balance of retained earnings for a current cost/constant dollar balance sheet is obtained, as usual, directly from the combined statement of income and retained earnings. The amount for Craig Company is calculated as follows:

Current cost/constant dollar retained earnings, Jan. 1	–0–
Add: Current cost/constant dollar net income	$135,900
Subtotal	135,900
Less: Current cost/constant dollar dividends	20,000
Current cost/constant dollar retained earnings, Dec. 31	$115,900

Arguments For and Against Current Cost/Constant Dollar Accounting

The major argument in favor of current cost/constant dollar accounting is that it combines the most desirable features of the current cost and constant dollar approaches. The use of current costs enhances the relevance of financial statements; the use of constant dollars provides a stable measuring unit that helps users make better comparisons over time and between companies.

Relevance

Opponents of current cost/constant dollar accounting argue that the measurements are unreliable, relatively costly to derive, and likely to confuse most users.

Reliability

STATEMENT OF FINANCIAL ACCOUNTING STANDARDS NO. 33

Earlier in the chapter we explained that *SFAS No. 33* applies only to certain large companies, does not change the primary financial statements, and requires the disclosure of selected items of supplementary information in published annual reports. We also indicated that the FASB encourages but does not presently require the reporting of comprehensive statements such as those we have discussed and illustrated in this chapter. Although comprehensive statements are not required at this time, the FASB may decide to require them in the future. But even if comprehensive statements are never required, an understanding of them helps a person to appreciate the issues involved in accounting for changing prices. Moreover, a knowledge of comprehensive statements can help a person to more easily grasp the disclosure requirements of *SFAS No. 33*.

Disclosure Requirements

SFAS No. 33 requires the following major items of supplementary information:[5]

1. Income from continuing operations for the current fiscal year on a historical cost/constant dollar basis.
2. The purchasing power gain or loss on net monetary items for the current fiscal year.
3. Income from continuing operations for the current fiscal year on a current cost basis.
4. The current cost amounts of inventory and property, plant, and equipment at the end of the current fiscal year.
5. Increases or decreases for the current fiscal year in the current cost amounts of inventory and property, plant, and equipment, net of inflation. (These are essentially the total holding gains or losses adjusted for inflation, as measured in a current cost/constant dollar system. Realized and unrealized amounts are simply combined and reported as a single amount.)
6. A summary for each of the five most recent years of:
   a. Net sales and other operating revenues.
   b. Income from continuing operations on a historical cost/constant dollar basis.
   c. Income per share from continuing operations on a historical cost/constant dollar basis.
   d. Net assets at fiscal year-end on a historical cost/constant dollar basis.
   e. Income from continuing operations on a current cost basis.
   f. Income per common share from continuing operations on a current cost basis.

---

[5]*FASB Statement of Financial Accounting Standards No. 33*, pars. 29, 30, and 35.

g. Net assets at fiscal year-end on a current cost basis.

h. Increases or decreases in the current cost amounts of inventory and property, plant, and equipment, net of inflation (the total of the realized and unrealized holding gains or losses adjusted for inflation, as mentioned under current cost/constant dollar accounting).

i. Purchasing power gain or loss on net monetary items.

j. Cash dividends declared per common share.

k. Market price per common share at fiscal year-end.

Under *SFAS No. 33,* purchasing power gains and losses are not included in the calculation of income from continuing operations on a historical cost/constant dollar basis. Moreover, the increases or decreases in the current cost amounts of inventory and property, plant, and equipment (net of inflation) are not included when calculating income from continuing operations on a current cost basis. These two kinds of gains and losses are controversial; some people believe that one or both of them should be debited or credited directly to stockholders' equity rather than included as a part of income. The FASB has avoided this controversy by merely requiring the disclosure of these kinds of gains and losses.

THE CLOSEST LOOK YET AT INFLATION'S CORPORATE TOLL

IN HIS NEW BOOK, *Managing in Turbulent Times,* Peter Drucker admonishes that during inflation, "the figures lie." Drucker argues that the illusion of record profits "leads to the wrong actions, the wrong decisions, the wrong analysis of the business"—in short, "gross mismanagement."

Now, thanks to the Financial Accounting Standards Board's new pronouncement on inflation accounting, investors and managers can begin to measure how sharply inflation has sliced into the seemingly handsome but deceptive record sales and earnings for some 1,300 of the nation's largest publicly owned corporations. A new study, released on June 5 by Price Waterhouse & Co., one of the nation's largest CPA firms, analyzes that impact on 157 giant industrial companies in 14 key industries plus 58 other companies in finance, retailing, transportation, and utilities.

The broad conclusions:

• Inflation-adjusted earnings of most of these broad business groupings are 40% to 70% lower than the traditional profits reported under historical-cost accounting.

• Effective tax rates typically are 15 to 25 percentage points higher with inflation adjustments—often far exceeding the U.S. statutory maximum rate of 46% on corporate income.

• Return on assets in real terms is only one-third to one-half that under more familiar historical-cost measures.

• Many industries are paying out twice as much in dividends as commonly thought; for retailers and utilities, dividends exceed inflation-adjusted income, which amounts to paying dividends out of capital.

• Sales growth during the past four years, after adjusting for inflation, has been less than half as strong as initially calculated. And dividend growth for most groups after adjustment shows even a more pronounced lag.

"I don't accept the view that everybody knew it was this bad," says Joseph E. Connor, Price Waterhouse's chairman. "While there's been some recognition in the stock market, the actual effect really had not been measured before."

Under the new FASB rules, companies have to compute inflation's effect on profits in two different ways. The first, known as the constant-dollar method, adjusts inventory costs and depreciation for changes in the consumer price index (CPI) since the related assets were purchased. A second method, known as current-cost accounting, adjusts these key items for price changes of specific assets that a company actually holds. While all big companies will have to show both figures when they report 1980 results next spring, for 1979 operations they had the option of presenting only constant-dollar inflation data. Even though only some 40% of the 215 companies in the Price Waterhouse study disclosed both constant-dollar and current-cost profit numbers, the sample still was broad enough to draw valid conclusions for most industries.

Real profits. Among the industrial group, the

HOW INFLATION CUTS REPORTED CORPORATE PROFITS

inflation-adjusted income as percent of 1979 historical-cost income

Industry	Using constant-dollar method	Using current-cost method
Aerospace	78%	70%
Automotive	51	28
Chemicals	62	60
Electrical & appliances	59	68
Food & beverage	53	29
Glass & containers	58	70
Machinery & equipment	67	61
Metal mfg.	55	51
Office machinery	42	102
Paper & forest products	56	63
Petroleum	62	43
Pharmaceuticals	63	81
Publishing	77	79
Tobacco	55	73
All-industrial average	60	63
Financial	95	NR
Retailing	42	NR
Transportation	56	30
Utilities	31	17

NR = not reported
Data: Price Waterhouse & Co.

overall inflation-adjusted performance measures showed surprisingly similar results whether computed in current costs or constant dollars. "Real" profits came only to about 60% of those reported under historical cost. Return on net assets tumbled from 17% to 8%. Dividend payout came to about 65% of earnings, compared with a 33% average payout with traditional accounting. And the effective tax rate climbed from 39% to 53%.

Among the 14 individual industrial groups, however, the two inflation measures did produce some contrasting results. In general, profits of industries with relatively newer plant and equipment, such as electronics, tobacco, and pharmaceuticals, showed better results under the current-cost measure than under constant-dollar accounting with its more general consumer-inflation index. Connor suggests that such industries may be "reflecting increasing efficiency of productive plant and effective cost containment in the manufacture of products."

Indeed, current-cost income for the average company in the high-technology office-equipment industry was even higher than its reported historical-cost earnings. In contrast, for the less modern automotive industry, profits adjusted for the rate of consumer inflation came to only half of historical earnings. And when computed on the current cost of replacing productive assets, profits tumbled more than 70%.

Closely related. Compared with measures for the industrial sector, inflation-adjusted data for other broad business segments show a somewhat different pattern. Because financial companies have no inventories as such and fixed assets are a relatively small part of total assets, inflation-adjusted income for that group of companies closely tracks reported profits. Most financial corporations did not make a current-cost calculation because the results were not materially different than under constant-dollar accounting using the consumer price index.

The picture of other areas, however, is even more sobering than that of the nation's industrial sector. For the transportation group, constant-dollar income amounts to only 56% of traditionally calculated profits; for retailers it is 42%, and for utilities 31%. And measured at current replacement cost, "real" earnings in all three groups are even lower. What is more, dividend payout for utilities and retailers exceeds their inflation-adjusted profits several fold. That factor has been reflected in the stock price for both groups over the past five years. Adjusted for consumer inflation, the average price of retailers' shares fell 21% from 1975 to 1979, while that of the average utility in the study tumbled 32%.

Dealing with debt. Skeptics argue that such calculations fail to take into consideration a company's overall debt position. They contend that companies that hold more debt than cash and other such monetary assets gain purchasing power during inflation because their liabilities can be paid off in cheaper dollars.

If such gains were added to inflation-adjusted income, earnings for retailers would be 18% higher than historical profits, while income would double for utilities. Even so, Price Waterhouse concludes that the high dividend payout ratios for these two groups still exceed "real" profits.

Similarly, inflation-adjusted profits for both the industrial and transportation areas also would be boosted sharply if gains on debt holdings were included. Only financial companies would show a drastic drop in profits—to 43% of historical earnings—because they hold more monetary assets than liabilities, and net cash positions lose purchasing power during inflation. But banks and related finance companies argue that, in turn, they are able to adjust loan rates and other fees to offset such an apparent drop in purchasing power—and profits.

Such inflation gains or losses on debt are only on paper, however. They may or may not be realized at some point in the future when repayment transactions actually are made. As Connor notes, those paper gains "do not necessarily represent hard dollars" with which to pay dividends or make new capital investments. "Informed opinion differs sharply on whether such gains are sometimes, always, or never a component of inflation-adjusted earnings," Connor says, "but, in any event, those companies appear to have shifted a portion of the inflationary burden from owners to creditors."

The notion that there may be gains or losses on net debt positions during inflation "is a concept we all recognize, but don't know quite how to deal with," Connor concludes. For the moment, the FASB requires only that such paper gains or losses be disclosed on a separate line from inflation-adjusted earnings and lets investors make their own calculations of their possible effect.

Connor says that he is disturbed by the sobering combination of high inflation-adjusted dividend payout percentages and draining effective tax rates. "A tremendous amount of income is being distributed, but what is being distributed impedes the ability to plow funds back into operations and to grow," he explains. "You can't have it both ways."

Little comfort. Even though 1979 earnings did

INFLATION'S IMPACT ON KEY MEASURES OF FINANCIAL PERFORMANCE

Category	Effective tax rate	Return on net assets	Dividend payout ratio	1975–79 growth in: Sales	Dividends	Stock price
						Percent
Industrial						
Historical-cost	39%	17%	33%	76%	90%	74%
Constant-dollar	53	8	65	33	41	24
Current-cost	53	8	66	NA	NA	NA
Financial						
Historical-cost	28%	14%	32%	86%	46%	69%
Constant-dollar	28	13	35	38	12	22
Current-cost	NR	NR	NR	NA	NA	NA
Retailing						
Historical-cost	42%	16%	31%	112%	104%	12%
Constant-dollar	68	5	299	57	51	−21
Current-cost	NR	NR	NR	NA	NA	NA
Transportation						
Historical-cost	30%	16%	29%	99%	81%	99%
Constant-dollar	44	5	42	49	33	42
Current-cost	50	2	72	NA	NA	NA
Utilities						
Historical-cost	34%	10%	76%	64%	18%	−4%
Constant-dollar	62	4	543	22	−9	−32
Current-cost	78	2	521	NA	NA	NA

NR = not reported   NA = not applicable
Data: Price Waterhouse & Co.

not keep pace with inflation, the Price Waterhouse study indicates that growth in sales, dividends, and stock prices over the past four years for most industries did manage at least to offset the ravages of inflation. Only among utilities did dividend growth lag behind the inflation rate, more confirmation of the very real but not readily apparent drag on earnings that rapid inflation brings. And growth in stock prices for chemicals, food and beverage companies, paper, glass products and containers, pharmaceuticals, retailers, and utilities declined in inflation-adjusted terms.

But investors can take little comfort from knowing that most of their number managed to hold their own during the five inflation-ridden years. "Many investors haven't," Connor asserts, "and none did as well as they thought they were doing."

In Connor's view, much of the problem springs from considering financial figures as being etched in stone. Traditional accounting assumes that "once a dollar, always a dollar, whether invested in the business a century ago or booked as sales a week ago," he explains.

Inflation demolishes the stable-unit assumption, Connor continues. As U.S. purchasing power erodes, "financial statements that mix dollars of 1965, 1972, 1976, and 1979 are, in effect, commingling four different currencies" to measure costs, and those costs are "not recovered by a dollar of 1979 revenue." Failure to recover costs overstates earnings—both as reported and as taxed, Connor concludes. "The results are the famous 'obscene' profits—and the infamous unseen taxation of shareholders' capital."

SOURCE: "The Closest Look Yet at Inflation's Corporate Toll," *Business Week*, June 16, 1980, pp. 148–149. Reprinted from *Business Week* by special permission, © 1980 by McGraw-Hill, Inc.

To present the supplementary information required by *SFAS No. 33*, a company "needs to measure the effects of changing prices on inventory, property, plant, and equipment, cost of goods sold, and depreciation, depletion and amortization expense. No adjustments are required to other revenues, expenses, gains, and losses."[6] Thus, the other revenues, expenses, gains, and losses are assumed to be the same amounts for constant dollar and current cost reporting as they are for historical cost/nominal dollar reporting. In essence, *SFAS No. 33* requires a restatement of only those financial statement items that are likely to be affected the most by changing prices. Although financial statements that reflect comprehensive adjustments for the effects of changing prices may be more useful to users (and are encouraged under *SFAS No. 33*), the FASB has concluded that the costs of requiring comprehensive adjustments would likely exceed the benefits derived from the information at this time.

Meaning of Current Cost

Under *SFAS No. 33*, the current cost of inventory is the current cost of purchasing or producing the goods owned by the company. The current cost of property, plant, and equipment is the current cost of acquiring the same service potential as embodied in the asset owned.[7]

Measurement of Current-Cost Amounts

As stated earlier in the chapter, the current cost of an asset is the amount a company would have to pay currently to acquire the same asset *in its existing condition*. A company may measure the current cost of a used asset that it owns by:

> *1. Measuring the current cost of a new asset that has the same service potential as the used asset had when it was new and deducting an allowance for depreciation.*

---

[6]*FASB Statement of Financial Accounting Standards No. 33*, Summary.

[7]*FASB Statement of Financial Accounting Standards No. 33*, pars. 57 and 58.

> **2.** *Measuring the current cost of a used asset of similar age and condition as the used asset owned.*
>
> **3.** *Measuring the current cost of a new asset with a different service potential and adjusting that cost for the value of the differences in service potential due to differences in life, output capacity, nature of service, and operating costs.*[8]

SFAS No. 33 specifies that a company may measure current costs by using the direct pricing method or the indexing method (or both). These methods were explained earlier in the chapter.

Measurement of Constant-Dollar Amounts

As explained earlier, *SFAS No. 33* requires companies to use the CPI-U when calculating constant-dollar amounts. Companies that choose to report comprehensive constant dollar financial statements or comprehensive current cost/constant dollar financial statements may measure the elements of those statements in either average-for-the-year constant dollars or year-end constant dollars. Companies that report only the minimum disclosures for the current year must calculate constant-dollar amounts in average-for-the-year constant dollars. The use of average-for-the-year constant dollars simplifies the constant dollar restatement process by eliminating the need to restate revenues and expenses that are spread evenly throughout a year. In the five-year summary of selected financial information, companies may report the constant-dollar amounts in average-for-the-year constant dollars (or year-end constant dollars if used in comprehensive statements) or in constant dollars of the base period of the CPI-U (1967). The use of base-period constant dollars is permitted because it eliminates the need to "roll forward" constant dollar information that relates to previous years in the five-year summary. The flexibility that *SFAS No. 33* offers when measuring constant-dollar amounts is evidence not only of the experimental nature of the pronouncement but also of the FASB's concern with minimizing the costs and confusion associated with the information.

Recoverable Amounts

SFAS No. 33 provides that assets and related expenses should be measured at recoverable amounts under certain circumstances that do not occur very often. Specifically, if the recoverable amount of an asset is judged to be *significantly and permanently* lower than the constant-dollar or current-cost amount, the recoverable amount is used for reporting purposes under *SFAS No. 33*. **Recoverable amounts** are measured at the net realizable value (the expected selling price less costs to complete and sell) of assets expected to be sold in the near future (such as inventory) and at value in use (the present value of the expected future net cash inflows) of assets not expected to be sold in the near future (such as most plant assets). The use of recoverable amounts is considered desirable under the circumstances described above in order to avoid material overstatements of a company's assets. A rational manager would not acquire an asset at a price higher than the asset's net realizable value or value in use.

Materiality

Disclosure Format

SFAS No. 33 states that income from continuing operations on a constant-dollar basis and on a current-cost basis may be presented in a **statement format** or a **reconciliation format.** A statement format discloses the company's revenues, expenses, gains, and losses on the constant-dollar basis and on the current-cost basis. A reconciliation format discloses the adjustments necessary to reconcile income from continuing operations, as reported in the primary financial statements, with income from continuing operations on a constant-dollar basis and on a current-cost basis.

---

[8]*FASB Statement of Financial Accounting Standards No. 33,* par. 58.

Exhibit 27–17 presents the *SFAS No. 33* disclosures recently made by General Instrument Corporation, a company that manufactures a variety of electronic products, such as TV tuners and automotive radio tuners. General Instrument used the statement format to present income adjusted for changing prices for fiscal year 1982. Exhibit 27–18 shows the information that Sears, Roebuck and Co. recently disclosed in accordance with *SFAS No. 33*. Sears used the reconciliation format to disclose selected data for 1982, adjusted for the effects of changing prices. Income from continuing operations was the same as net income for General Instrument and for Sears. That is why each company reported the net income amount (instead of income from continuing operations).

EXHIBIT 27–17
General Instrument Corporation
SFAS No. 33 Disclosures

Note 12—Accounting for the Effects of Inflation (Unaudited)

The accompanying statements adjusted for changing prices have been prepared in accordance with the requirements of FAS No. 33 as an experimental attempt to reflect the impact of inflation on the results of operations and financial position of the Company. In accordance with these requirements, this supplementary information attempts to show the impacts of inflation on those areas that are most affected by continuing inflation: inventories and property, plant and equipment, and related expenses. The impact of inflation has been computed by restating traditional historical financial data under two methods.

The first, constant dollar, provides financial statement information adjusted for general inflation based on changes in the Consumer Price Index for all Urban Consumers ("CPI"). The CPI is a broad-based measure of the general inflation rate, and adjustment under this method is made by restating historical financial information to dollars having equal purchasing power in terms of the average CPI for the current year.

The second method, current cost, provides for the different effects of inflation on individual assets through adjustment for changes in specific prices of each major category of the Company's inventories and property, plant and equipment and related expenses. In adjusting historical financial data for changes in specific prices, the Company generally applies specific indices to the historical cost components of property, plant and equipment and related depreciation. The specific indices are based on the nature and geographic location of the asset. Certain items, principally land and assets manufactured by the Company for its own use, for which specific price change indicators are not available, were adjusted for valuations obtained from various sources. Inventories and cost of sales were adjusted to average 1982 material, labor and overhead costs.

The adjustment of historical amounts to current cost values increases the net assets, or stockholders' equity, of the Company as most assets cost more today than they did when originally purchased. At February 28, 1982, the current cost of inventories and net property, plant and equipment was $172,628,000 and $299,098,000, respectively.

The portion of the increase in current cost amounts over historical cost amounts which arose in the current year is set forth in the accompanying statements as the increase in inventories and property, plant and equipment due to the increase in specific prices. As the impact of inflation on the specific assets of the Company has been less than the general inflation rate, principally due to the high technology nature of the Company's assets, the current cost holding gain is less than the constant dollar gain. This relationship is also evident in inflation-adjusted results of operations, as current cost of sales and services and depreciation expense is less than the constant dollar amount, as set forth below:

	Historical Cost	Current Cost	Constant Dollar
Cost of sales, services and research and development exclusive of depreciation	$688,288,000	$694,083,000	$699,921,000
Depreciation expense	48,159,000	56,800,000	61,402,000

Although current cost and constant dollar adjustments affect income before income taxes, current tax-laws do not recognize the increased costs required to replace existing assets at current prices; therefore, the provision for income taxes has not been adjusted. If the inflation adjustments were deductible for tax purposes, the provision for income taxes would be reduced and the resultant net income would be greater than presented herein.

During 1982 the Company experienced a loss in purchasing power on its net monetary asset position. This loss is an estimate of the decrease in purchasing power of cash and obligations to receive cash net of obligations to pay cash. This loss, however, was more than offset by interest earned on invested funds.

The five-year summary, setting forth certain financial data adjusted for general inflation, shows that, in dollars of equal purchasing power, the inflation-adjusted year-end market value of the Company's common stock has appreciated approximately 270% from 1978 to 1982, while dividends increased from an inflation adjusted $.15 in 1978 to $.40 in 1982.

Consolidated Statement of Income Adjusted for Changing Prices for the Year Ended February 28, 1982

In thousands except per share amounts

	Historical Cost	Current Cost	Constant Dollar
Revenue	$957,059	$957,059	$957,059
Costs and expenses:			
Cost of sales, services and research and development	731,632	745,203	755,183
Selling, general and administrative expenses	81,022	81,886	82,346
Interest income	(20,469)	(20,469)	(20,469)
Interest expense	4,245	4,245	4,245
	796,430	810,865	821,305
Income before income taxes	160,629	146,194	135,754
Provision for income taxes	70,600	70,600	70,600
Net income	90,029	75,594	65,154
Dividends on preferred stock	15	15	15
Earnings on common stock	$ 90,014	$ 75,579	$ 65,139

Earnings per common share-primary	$3.01	$2.53	$2.18
Stockholders' equity	$509,896	$574,823	$556,205
Loss in purchasing power of net monetary assets		$ (6,159)	$ (6,159)
Increase in inventories and net property, plant and equipment due to general inflation		$ 32,107	
Less effect of increase in specific prices		26,592	
Effect of increase in general inflation over specific prices		$ 5,515	

Five Year Summary*	Feb. 28, 1982	Feb. 28, 1981	Feb. 29, 1980	Feb. 28, 1979	Feb. 28, 1978
Revenue	$957,059	$905,841	$891,651	$765,745	$756,053
Market price per common share at year-end	35.36	27.47	18.62	12.49	9.58
Cash dividends per common share	.40	.35	.31	.25	.15
Constant dollar information:					
Net income	65,154	50,295	36,647		
Primary earnings per share	2.18	1.82	1.38		
Stockholders' equity at year-end	556,205	505,928	401,800		
Current cost information:					
Net income	75,594	59,538	48,179		
Primary earnings per share	2.53	2.16	1.83		
Stockholders' equity at year-end	574,823	526,621	424,413		
Excess of increase in general inflation over specific prices	5,515	8,214	8,797		
Gain (loss) in purchasing power of net monetary assets	(6,159)	(160)	4,065		
Average consumer price index	275.9	251.3	222.2	198.4	183.5

*In average 1982 dollars, except consumer price index.
SOURCE: General Instrument Corporation, 1982 Annual Report.

Instead of specifying a precise format for companies to use in reporting *SFAS No. 33* information, the FASB "encourages enterprises to experiment with the use of different forms of presentation."[9] The examples shown in Exhibits 27–17 and 27–18 are presented in this textbook for illustrative purposes only.

[9]*FASB Statement of Financial Accounting Standards No. 33,* par. 70

EXHIBIT 27–18
Sears, Roebuck and Co.
SFAS No. 33 Disclosures

Sears, Roebuck and Co. Supplemental Financial Information Regarding Inflation (Unaudited)

In accordance with Financial Accounting Standards Board (FASB) Statement No. 33 "Financial Reporting and Changing Prices", the company is providing the following supplementary information which is an experimental effort to quantify the effects of changing price levels. Required disclosures include selected financial information computed on the Constant Dollar Method (general inflation using the Consumer Price Index for all Urban Consumers) and on a Current Cost basis (reflecting specific price changes).

The following data is experimental and involves the use of numerous assumptions and estimates. It must be interpreted with care in assessing the effect of inflation on the company. Statement No. 33 prohibits any adjustment of historical income tax expense. As a result, the effective income tax rate that results under the inflation adjusted data varies significantly from the company's 1982 historical effective income tax rate.

Selected Data for 1982 Adjusted for Effects of Changing Prices

millions in average 1982 dollars

Net income as reported		$861
Adjustments to restate costs for the effect of changes in current costs		
Cost of goods sold	$136	
Depreciation expense	205	
Gain on sale of property	56	397
Net income adjusted for changes in current costs		464
Adjustments for the difference between changes in current costs and general inflation		
Cost of goods sold	55	
Depreciation expense	(24)	
Gain on sale of property	(3)	28
Net income adjusted for general inflation		436
Gain from decline in purchasing power of net amounts owed		11
Increase in current costs of assets held during the year		
Inventories	69	
Property and equipment	411	480

Effect of increase in general price level		
Inventories	141	
Property and equipment	250	391

Excess of increase in general price level over increase in current costs		89

The adjustments to cost of sales decreased earnings by $136 million and $191 million under the current cost and constant dollar methods, respectively. Constant dollar adjustment based on a general inflation rate of 3.9 percent is greater than the current cost adjustment based on changes in specific prices of inventory averaging 2.6 per cent (according to the Bureau of Labor Statistics Department Store Price Index).

During periods of rising prices, the holding of monetary assets results in a loss of general purchasing power. Similarly, holding monetary liabilities results in a gain of general purchasing power because the amount of money required to settle liabilities represents dollars of diminished purchasing power. The insurance operations of Sears, Roebuck and Co. employ large amounts of monetary assets which in prior years caused a loss in purchasing power. In 1982, due to a lower inflation rate and the inclusion of the monetary liabilities of the new real estate and financial services operations, a small gain in purchasing power resulted.

At Dec. 31, 1982, the current cost of inventories was $3.6 billion and the current cost of net property and equipment, including rental properties, was $7.3 billion. The historical net costs are $3.1 and $4.0 billion, respectively.

The current cost of inventory, net property and equipment, and cost of goods sold has been estimated based upon various methods including indexation and direct pricing.

The current cost of depreciation has been estimated based upon the above restatements of property and equipment using the same useful lives and depreciation methods utilized in preparing the historical cost financial statements.

Five-Year Comparison of Selected Financial Data Adjusted for Effects of Changing Prices

millions, except per share data

(Data adjusted to average 1982 dollars, except for as reported amounts)	1982	1981	1980	1979	1978
Operating revenues as reported	$30,020	$27,357	$25,161	$24,528	$24,475
Adjusted for general inflation	30,020	29,034	29,473	32,616	36,211
Net income as reported	$861	$650	$610	$830	
Adjusted for changes in current costs	464	334	507	918	
Adjusted for general inflation	436	224	279	599	

Net income per common share as reported	$2.46	$2.06	$1.93	$2.60
Adjusted for changes in current costs	1.32	1.06	1.60	2.87
Adjusted for general inflation	1.24	.71	.88	1.88
Net assets at year-end as reported	$ 8,812	$ 8,269	$ 7,665	$ 7,446
Adjusted for changes in current costs	12,595	12,214	11,841	12,204
Adjusted for general inflation	11,855	11,809	11,923	12,267
Excess of increase in general price level over increase in current costs	89	58	281	1,057
Gain (loss) from decline in purchasing power of net monetary items	11	(101)	(168)	(232)

Cash dividends declared per common share					
As reported	$1.36	$1.36	$1.36	$1.28	$1.27
Adjusted	1.36	1.44	1.59	1.70	1.88
Book value per common share at year-end					
As reported	$25.08	$23.77	$24.32	$23.44	$21.84
Adjusted year-end 1982 dollars	25.08	24.69	27.52	29.81	31.47
Closing market price per common share at year-end					
As reported	$30.125	$16.125	$15.38	$18.00	19.75
Adjusted to year end 1982 dollars	30.125	16.75	17.40	22.89	28.46
CPI-U (1967=100)					
Year average	289.1	272.4	246.8	217.4	195.4
End of calendar year	292.4	281.5	258.4	229.9	202.9

SOURCE: Sears, Roebuck and Co., 1982 Annual Report.

CONCLUDING REMARKS

Accounting for changing prices has been one of the most widely debated financial accounting topics during the twentieth century. The topic deals with fundamental issues of accounting measurement and has far-reaching implications concerning the types of information that companies may be required to report in the future. Should the FASB require companies to report comprehensive financial statements adjusted for changing prices? If so, should these statements replace or merely supplement the conventional financial statements? Also, should the financial statements reflect adjustments for general price-level changes, specific price changes, or both? Ultimately, the answers to these and similar questions will depend

Relevance
Reliability

on the relevance and reliability of the information and on whether the benefits of information exceed the costs of providing it.

SFAS No. 33 is a milestone in the long and interesting history of accounting for changing prices. But *SFAS No. 33* is experimental and will likely be modified as the FASB learns more about the uses, limitations, and costs of the information presently required. Many research projects that will help the FASB to acquire this knowledge are currently in progress. Readers of this textbook should be prepared to actively participate in the debate about accounting for changing prices and to understand the changes that likely will occur in this area.

KEY POINTS

1. A price change is an increase or decrease in the price of a good or service that occurs in a given market.

2. A general price-level change is an increase or decrease in the overall level of prices of goods and services throughout the economy. It is measured by using a general price-level index, such as the CPI-U, constructed by the federal government.

3. A specific price change is an increase or decrease in the price of a good or service. It may be measured by applying direct pricing or indexing methods.

4. Constant dollar accounting calls for historical cost measurements in dollars having the same purchasing power. Adjustments are made for general price-level changes, but not for specific price changes.

5. Purchasing power gains and losses are measured and reported when constant dollars are used as the measuring unit in financial statements. They occur as a result of holding monetary items during periods of inflation or deflation.

6. Current value accounting calls for current value measurements in dollars that are not adjusted for inflation or deflation. Adjustments are made for specific price changes, but not for general price-level changes.

7. The three major forms of current value accounting are:

  [a] Present value accounting, in which an asset is measured at the present discounted amount of the net cash inflows that the asset is expected to generate in the future.

  [b] Exit value accounting, in which an asset is measured at the amount of cash it could be sold for in an orderly liquidation.

  [c] Current cost accounting, in which an asset is measured at the amount of cash that a company would currently have to pay to acquire the same asset in its existing condition.

8. The disclosure requirements of *SFAS No. 33* reflect the current cost version of current value accounting.

9. Holding gains and losses are measured and reported when current costs are used in financial statements. They occur as a result of changes in the current cost of an asset held over time.

10. Unrealized holding gains and losses pertain to assets still on hand at the end of a period; realized holding gains and losses pertain to assets sold or consumed in operations during a period.

11. Current cost/constant dollar accounting calls for current cost measurements in dollars having the same purchasing power. Adjustments are made for general price-level changes and specific price changes.

12. Current cost/constant dollar accounting requires the reporting of purchasing power gains or losses *and* holding gains or losses adjusted for inflation.

13. *SFAS No. 33* applies only to large public companies, does not change the primary financial statements, and requires certain supplemental disclosures.

14. The supplemental disclosures required by *SFAS No. 33* reflect the constant-dollar basis, the current-cost basis, and the current cost/constant dollar basis of accounting.

15. *SFAS No. 33* is experimental and may be modified in the future.

QUESTIONS

27–1 Distinguish between a general price-level change and a specific price change.

27–2 What is the basic nature of a general price-level index?

27–3 Explain the methods that may be used to determine an asset's current cost.

27–4 What is constant dollar accounting?

27–5 Explain the difference between a monetary

item and a nonmonetary item. Include four examples of each type of item in your explanation.

27–6 What are purchasing power gains and losses?

27–7 Discuss the major arguments for and against constant dollar accounting.

27–8 What is current value accounting?

27–9 Explain current cost accounting.

27–10 What are holding gains and losses in current cost accounting?

27–11 Distinguish between realized and unrealized holding gains and losses in current cost accounting.

27–12 Why does conventional income for any given year under current cost accounting always equal net income for that year under historical cost accounting?

27–13 Discuss the major arguments for and against current cost accounting.

27–14 What is current cost/constant dollar accounting?

27–15 What are holding gains and losses, adjusted for inflation, in current cost/constant dollar accounting?

27–16 Discuss the major arguments for and against current cost/constant dollar accounting.

27–17 What is the nature and purpose of *SFAS No. 33?*

27–18 Summarize the major disclosure requirements of *SFAS No. 33.*

CASES

C27–1 This case consists of two *independent* parts.

Part 1. Constant dollar financial statements are prepared in an effort to eliminate the effects of inflation or deflation. An integral part of determining restated amounts and applicable gain or loss from restatement is the segregation of all assets and liabilities into monetary and nonmonetary classifications. One reason for this classification is that purchasing power gains and losses for monetary items are currently matched against earnings.

Instructions

What factors determine whether an asset or a liability is classified as monetary or nonmonetary? Include in your response the justification for recognizing gains and losses from monetary items and *not* for nonmonetary items.

Part 2. Proponents of price-level restatement maintain that a basic weakness of financial statements not adjusted for price-level changes is that they are made up of "mixed dollars."

Instructions

[a] What is meant by the term "mixed dollars" and why is this a weakness of unadjusted financial statements?

[b] Explain how financial statements restated for price-level changes eliminate this weakness. Use property, plant, and equipment as your example in this discussion.

(AICPA adapted)

C27–2 Published financial statements of U.S. companies are currently prepared on a stable-dollar assumption, even though the general purchasing power of the dollar has declined considerably because of inflation in recent years. To account for this changing value of the dollar, many accountants suggest that financial statements should be adjusted for general price-level changes. Three *independent* statements about general price-level adjusted financial statements follow. Each statement contains some fallacious reasoning.

Statement 1. The accounting profession has not seriously considered price-level adjusted financial statements before because the rate of inflation usually has been so low from year to year that the adjustments would have been immaterial in amount. Price-level adjusted financial statements represent a departure from historical cost accounting. Financial statements should be prepared from facts, not estimates.

Statement 2. If financial statements were adjusted for general price-level changes, depreciation charges in the earnings statement would permit the recovery of dollars of current purchasing power and thereby equal the cost of new assets to replace the old ones. General price-level adjusted data would yield statement-of-financial-position amounts closely approximating current values. Furthermore, management can make better decisions if general price-level adjusted financial statements are published.

Statement 3. When adjusting financial data for general price-level changes, a distinction must be made between monetary and nonmonetary assets and liabilities, which, under historical cost accounting, have been identified as "current" and "noncurrent." When using historical cost accounting, no purchasing power gain or loss is recognized in the accounting process, but when financial statements are adjusted for general price-level changes, a purchasing power gain or loss will be recognized on monetary and nonmonetary items.

Instructions

Evaluate each of the independent statements. Identify the areas of fallacious reasoning in each, and explain why the reasoning is incorrect. Complete your discussion of each statement before proceeding to the next statement.

(AICPA adapted)

C27–3 Barden Corporation, a manufacturer with large investments in plant and equipment, began operations in 1950. The company's history has been one of expansion in sales, production, and physical facilities. Recently, some concern has been expressed that the conventional financial statements do not provide sufficient information for decisions by investors. After consideration of proposals for various types of supplementary financial statements to be included in the 1985 annual report, management has decided to present a balance sheet as of December 31, 1985, and a statement of income and retained earnings for 1985, both restated for changes in the general price level.

Instructions

[a] On what basis can it be contended that Barden's conventional statements should be restated for changes in the general price level?
[b] Distinguish between financial statements restated for general price-level changes and current value financial statements.
[c] Distinguish between monetary and nonmonetary assets and liabilities, as the terms are used in general price-level accounting. Give examples of each.
[d] Outline the procedures Barden should follow in preparing the proposed supplementary statements.
[e] Indicate the major similarities and differences between the proposed supplementary statements and the corresponding conventional statements.
[f] Assuming that in the future Barden will want to present comparative supplementary statements, can the 1985 supplementary statements be presented in 1986 without adjustment? Explain.

(AICPA adapted)

C27–4 This case consists of two *independent* parts.

Part 1. Advocates of current value accounting propose several methods for determining the valuation of assets to approximate current values. Two of the methods proposed are replacement cost and present value of future cash flows.

Instructions

Describe each method cited above and discuss the pros and cons of the various procedures used to arrive at the valuation of each method.

Part 2. The financial statements of a business entity could be prepared on the basis of historical cost or current value. In addition, the basis could be stated in terms of unadjusted dollars or dollars restated for changes in purchasing power. The variations of these two distinct areas are shown in the following matrix:

	Unadjusted Dollars	Dollars Restated for Changes in Purchasing Power
Historical cost	1	2
Current value	3	4

Cell 1 of the matrix represents the traditional method of accounting for transactions; the absolute (unadjusted) amount of dollars given up or received is recorded for the asset or liability obtained (**relationship between resources**). Amounts recorded in the method represented by Cell 1 reflect the original cost of the asset or liability and do not give effect to any change in value of the unit of measure (**standard of comparison**). This method assumes the validity of the accounting concepts of going concern and stable monetary unit. Any gain or loss (including holding and purchasing power gains or losses) resulting from the sale or satisfaction of amounts recorded under this method is deferred in its entirety until sale or satisfaction.

Instructions

For each of the remaining cells (2, 3, and 4), respond to the following questions. *Limit your discussion to nonmonetary assets only.* Complete your discussion of *each cell* before proceeding to the next one.
[a] How will this method of recording assets affect the relationship between resources and the standard of comparison?
[b] What is the theoretical justification for using this method?
[c] How will this method of asset valuation affect the recognition of gain or loss during the life of the asset and ultimately from the sale or abandonment of the asset? Your response should include a discussion of the timing and magnitude of the gain or loss and conceptual reasons for any difference from the gain or loss computed using the traditional method.

(AICPA adapted)

C27–5 In September 1979, *Statement of Financial*

Accounting Standards No. 33, "Financial Reporting and Changing Prices," was released. This statement applies to public enterprises that have either (1) inventories and property, plant, and equipment (before deducting accumulated depreciation) of more than $125 million or (2) total assets of more than $1 billion (after deducting accumulated depreciation). No changes are required in the basic financial statements, but information required by *SFAS No. 33* is to be presented in supplementary statements, schedules, or notes in the financial reports.

Instructions

[a] A number of terms are defined and used in *SFAS No. 33.*

[1] Differentiate between the terms "constant dollar" and "current cost."

[2] Explain what is meant by "current cost/constant dollar accounting" and how it differs from "historical cost/nominal dollar accounting."

[b] Identify the accounts for which an enterprise must measure the effects of changing prices in order to present the supplementary information required by *SFAS No. 33.*

[c] *SFAS No. 33* is based upon FASB *Concepts Statement No. 1,* "Objectives of Financial Reporting by Business Enterprises," which concludes that financial reporting should provide information to help investors, creditors, and other financial statement users assess the amounts, timing, and uncertainty of prospective net cash inflows to the enterprise.

[1] Explain how *SFAS No. 33* may help in attaining this objective.

[2] Discuss two ways in which the information required by *SFAS No. 33* may be useful for internal management decisions.

(CMA adapted)

EXERCISES

E27–1 Listed below are selected accounts that pertain to Dove Company on December 31, 1985.

[1] Land acquired on July 31, 1968.

[2] Purchases made evenly throughout 1985.

[3] Common stock issued on April 30, 1965.

[4] Accounts receivable resulting from credit sales made on November 30, 1985.

[5] Bonus expense incurred on March 31, 1985.

[6] Twenty-year bonds payable issued on August 31, 1981.

[7] Interest expense applicable to the 20-year bonds payable issued on August 31, 1981.

[8] Cash in bank.

[9] Depreciation expense applicable to equipment purchased on January 31, 1978.

[10] Investment in common stock acquired on May 31, 1983.

[11] Sales made evenly throughout 1985.

[12] Income tax expense for 1985.

[13] Cash dividends declared on June 30, 1985.

[14] Inventory acquired evenly throughout 1985.

[15] Note receivable acquired on October 31, 1984.

Selected values of the CPI-U are given below.

Apr. 30, 1965	61	Mar. 31, 1985	192
July 31, 1968	78	June 30, 1985	194
Jan. 31, 1978	112	Nov. 30, 1985	199
Aug. 31, 1981	147	Dec. 31, 1985	200
May 31, 1983	165	Average	
Oct. 31, 1984	187	for 1985	195

Instructions

Indicate the numerator and the denominator of the conversion factor that should be used to restate each of the accounts listed above to 1985 year-end constant dollars.

E27–2 Hyatt Company acquired land on April 30, 1978, for $120,000. The CPI-U was 110 on April 30, 1978, and 176 on December 31, 1985.

Instructions

[a] At what amount would the land be reported in a December 31, 1985, balance sheet prepared in constant end-of-year dollars?

[b] Explain the meaning of your answer to [a].

[c] Based only on the information presented above, can you calculate how much Hyatt Company could sell the land for on December 31, 1985? Explain your answer.

E27–3 Stark Company began operations on January 1, 1985. Information about the company's inventory during 1985 appears below.

	Number of Units	Unit Cost
Inventory, Jan. 1, 1985	300	$5
Purchases made evenly during 1985	900	6
Sales made evenly during 1985	800	
Inventory, Dec. 31, 1985	400	

The CPI-U during 1985 was as follows:

Jan. 1, 1985	90
Average for 1985	120
Dec. 31, 1985	135

Instructions

Compute the ending inventory and cost of goods sold for Stark Company in 1985 year-end constant dollars, assuming the company uses the FIFO method of inventory pricing.

E27–4 Refer to the information presented for Stark Company in Exercise 27–3.

Instructions

Compute the ending inventory and cost of goods sold for Stark Company in 1985 year-end constant dollars, assuming the company uses the LIFO method of inventory pricing.

E27–5 Brown Company wants to prepare constant dollar financial statements on December 31, 1985. An analysis of the company's Equipment and related Accumulated Depreciation accounts on December 31, 1985, after adjusting entries have been made, reveals the following information:

	Equipment		Accumulated Depreciation
Item	**Cost**	**When Acquired**	
A	$100,000	Dec. 1978	$ 80,000
B	50,000	Dec. 1980	30,000
C	175,000	Dec. 1981	87,500
	$325,000		$197,500

Selected values of the CPI-U at the end of the years appear below:

Year	CPI-U
1978	100
1979	106
1980	110
1981	132
1982	141
1983	149
1984	156
1985	165

Instructions

Compute the 1985 year-end constant-dollar amount to report for (1) equipment and (2) accumulated depreciation.

E27–6 The following information pertains to Bradford Company for 1985:

[1] The company had net monetary items of $50,000 on January 1.

[2] Sales of $300,000 and purchases of $120,000 were made evenly throughout the year.

[3] Operating expenses of $90,000 and income tax expense of $60,000 were incurred evenly throughout the year.

[4] Cash dividends of $10,000 were declared on December 31. Selected values of the CPI-U during 1985 appear below:

Jan. 1	110.0
Average for year	121.0
Dec. 31	133.1

Instructions

Prepare a schedule showing the computation of Bradford Company's purchasing power gain or loss for 1985 expressed in constant end-of-year dollars.

E27–7 Reed Company's financial position, shown below, did not change during January 1985. The CPI-U was 90 on January 1, 1985, and 99 on January 31, 1985.

Reed Company
BALANCE SHEET
January 1 and January 31, 1985

Assets

Cash	$ 5,000
Accounts receivable	10,000
Short-term investment in common stock	8,000
Inventory	50,000
Land	27,000
Total assets	$100,000

Equities

Accounts payable	$ 40,000
Common stock	50,000
Retained earnings	10,000
Total equities	$100,000

Instructions

[a] Compute the purchasing power gain or loss in constant January 31 dollars.

[b] Explain why Reed Company had a purchasing power gain (or loss) during January.

E27–8 At the end of its first year in business, Jones Company prepared the combined statement of income and retained earnings shown below.

Jones Company
COMBINED STATEMENT OF INCOME AND RETAINED
EARNINGS
Historical Cost/Nominal Dollar Basis
For 1985

Sales		$160,000
Cost of goods sold		
Beginning inventory	$10,000	
Purchases	88,000	
Goods available	98,000	
Ending inventory	8,000	90,000
Gross margin on sales		70,000
Operating expenses	15,000	
Depreciation expense	25,000	40,000
Income before taxes		30,000
Income tax expense		12,000
Net income		18,000
Retained earnings, Jan. 1		–0–
Less: Dividends		6,000
Retained earnings, Dec. 31		$ 12,000

Additional Information

[1] Sales, purchases, operating expenses, and income tax expense occurred evenly throughout 1985.
[2] Jones Company uses the LIFO method of inventory pricing. The company acquired the beginning inventory on January 1, 1985.
[3] Depreciation expense relates to machinery acquired on March 1, 1985.
[4] Dividends were declared on November 1, 1985.
[5] Jones Company had a purchasing power gain of $1,500 during 1985.
[6] The CPI-U on various dates during 1985 appears below.

Jan. 1	100
Mar. 1	150
Nov. 1	250
Dec. 31	300
Average for year	200

Instructions

Prepare a combined statement of income and retained earnings in constant end-of-year dollars for 1985.

E27–9 Carver Company prepared the balance sheet shown below in accordance with GAAP.

Carver Company
BALANCE SHEET
December 31, 1985

Assets

Cash	$ 16,000
Receivables	28,000
Inventory	34,000
Plant assets (net)	67,000
Total assets	$145,000

Equities

Payables	$ 50,000
Common stock	60,000
Retained earnings	35,000
Total equities	$145,000

Additional Information

[1] The cash, receivables, and payables originated when the CPI-U was 105.
[2] The inventory and plant assets were acquired when the CPI-U was 99.
[3] The common stock was issued when the CPI-U was 90.
[4] The average CPI-U for 1985 was 100, and the ending CPI-U was 108.9.

Instructions

Prepare a balance sheet on December 31, 1985, in constant end-of-year dollars.

E27–10 Wyatt Company has prepared constant dollar financial statements for five years and is currently preparing the statements for 1985. The company's balance sheet prepared at the end of 1984, and expressed in 1984 year-end constant dollars, appears below.

Wyatt Company
CONSTANT DOLLAR BALANCE SHEET
December 31, 1984

Assets

Cash	$ 12,000
Accounts receivable	28,000
Temporary investments	15,000
Inventory	40,000
Equipment (net)	55,000
Total assets	$150,000

Equities

Accounts payable	$ 25,000
Bonds payable	50,000

Common stock	60,000
Retained earnings	15,000
Total equities	$150,000

The CPI-U increased from 100 on December 31, 1984, to 200 on December 31, 1985.

Instructions

[a] Prepare a balance sheet, dated December 31, 1984, expressed in terms of 1985 year-end constant dollars.

[b] Assuming that Wyatt Company prepares a constant dollar balance sheet as of December 31, 1985, why would the balance sheet you prepared in [a] be useful to the company at the end of 1985?

E27–11 Bailey Company purchased land costing $10,000 on January 1, 1983. The current cost of the land was $15,000 on December 31, 1983, and $25,000 on December 31, 1984. The company sold the land on December 31, 1985, for $40,000, an amount equal to the land's current cost on that date.

Instructions

Compute the unrealized and realized holding gains or losses to report for 1983, 1984, and 1985.

E27–12 Borne Company purchased inventory costing $5,000 on January 1, 1983. The company sold the inventory for $12,000 on December 31, 1985. By examining the prices quoted in suppliers' catalogs, Borne Company determined that the current cost of the inventory was $6,000 on December 31, 1983, $8,000 on December 31, 1984, and $11,000 on December 31, 1985.

Instructions

Prepare income statements for 1983, 1984, and 1985 under the accounting bases listed below. You may assume that cost of goods sold is Borne Company's only expense.

[a] Historical cost/nominal dollar basis.

[b] Current cost/nominal dollar basis.

E27–13 Thomas Company acquired land costing $50,000 on January 1, 1985. The company continued to hold the land on December 31, 1985, and on that date an independent appraisal indicated that the land's current cost was $60,000. The CPI-U was 110 on January 1, 1985, and 121 on December 31, 1985.

Instructions

[a] Compute the amount of holding gain or loss for 1985 under current cost accounting.

[b] Compute the amount of holding gain or loss, adjusted for inflation, for 1985 under current cost/constant dollar accounting.

[c] Explain your answers to [a] and [b].

E27–14 The Aker and Baker Partnership was formed on January 1, 1984. On that date, Aker and Baker each contributed $20,000 to their partnership, and the partnership immediately invested the $40,000 in a parcel of land. The partnership continued to hold the land on December 31, 1984, at which time the land was appraised at $50,000. On December 31, 1985, the partnership sold the land for $65,000, distributed the proceeds to the partners, and ended operations.

Instructions

Compute the gain or loss attributable to the land for 1984 and for 1985 under (1) historical cost accounting and (2) current cost accounting.

E27–15 Refer to the information presented in Exercise 27–14 for the Aker and Baker Partnership. Assume that the CPI-U was as follows:

Jan. 1, 1984	100
Dec. 31, 1984	100
Dec. 31, 1985	132

Instructions

Expressed in terms of December 31, 1985, constant dollars, compute the gain or loss attributable to the land for 1984 and for 1985 under (1) constant dollar and (2) current cost/constant dollar accounting.

E27–16 On January 1, 1985, Pena Company acquired inventory for $20,000. The inventory consisted of 10,000 identical units. The current cost of the inventory was $30,000 on July 1, 1985; on that date Pena Company sold three-fourths of the inventory for $29,000. On December 31, 1985, the current cost of the inventory on hand was $7,500.

Instructions

Prepare a current cost income statement for 1985. Assume that cost of goods sold is Pena Company's only expense.

E27–17 Refer to the information presented for Pena Company in E27–16. The CPI-U on various dates is:

Jan. 1, 1985	110.0
July 1, 1985	121.0
Dec. 31, 1985	133.1

Instructions

Prepare a current cost/constant dollar income statement for 1985. Assume that cost of goods sold is Pena Company's only expense and that no purchasing power gain or loss exists.

E27–18 Weimer Company acquired a machine on January 1, 1985, for $50,000. Depreciation will be computed using the straight-line method, assuming a five-year useful life and no salvage value. A specific price index applicable to the machine was 150 on Jan-

uary 1, 1985, and 225 on December 31, 1985. The CPI-U was 100 on January 1, 1985, and 121 on December 31, 1985. The average CPI-U for 1985 was 110.

Instructions

Compute the amount of depreciation expense for 1985 under each basis of accounting listed below.
[a] Historical cost/nominal dollar basis.
[b] Historical cost/constant dollar basis.
[c] Current cost/nominal dollar basis.
[d] Current cost/constant dollar basis.

PROBLEMS

P27–1 The following information pertains to Hamlen Company:

Sales (all on account) made evenly throughout 1985	$200,000
Equipment purchased for cash on May 1, 1985	50,000
Purchases (all on account) made evenly throughout 1985	80,000
Cash received evenly throughout 1985 from customers on account	190,000
Cash dividends declared on Sept. 1, 1985, and paid on Oct. 1, 1985	20,000
Land acquired for cash on June 1, 1985	30,000
Depreciation expense for 1985	10,000
Common stock issued for cash on Mar. 1, 1985	60,000
Operating expenses paid evenly throughout 1985	40,000
Income tax expense paid evenly throughout 1985	25,000
Purchase of treasury stock for cash on Nov. 1, 1985	15,000
Sale of investment in Gant Company's common stock on Aug. 1, 1985, for cash (cost = $5,000; selling price = $8,000)	8,000
Cash paid evenly throughout 1985 on accounts payable	60,000
Monetary assets	
Jan. 1, 1985	20,000
Dec. 31, 1985	48,000
Monetary liabilities	
Jan. 1, 1985	10,000
Dec. 31, 1985	30,000

The following values of the CPI-U for 1985 are available:

1/1	100	8/1	114
2/1	102	9/1	116
3/1	104	10/1	118
4/1	106	11/1	120
5/1	108	12/1	122
6/1	110	12/31	124
7/1	112	Average for year	112

Instructions

Prepare a schedule showing the computation of Hamlen Company's purchasing power gain or loss for 1985 in end-of-year dollars.

P27–2 Ashton Company was formed on January 1, 1985. Financial statements pertaining to the company's first year of operations are shown below:

Ashton Company
COMPARATIVE BALANCE SHEETS
Historical Cost/Nominal Dollar Basis
January 1 and December 31, 1985

	Jan. 1	Dec. 31
Assets		
Cash	$ 22,000	$ 88,000
Accounts receivable	–0–	147,400
Inventory	220,000	198,000
Land	154,000	154,000
Equipment	264,000	264,000

Less:

Accumulated depreciation	–0–	(26,400)
Total assets	$660,000	$825,000

Liabilities and Stockholders' Equity

Accounts payable	–0–	$ 77,000
Note payable	$198,000	198,000
Total liabilities	198,000	275,000
Common stock	462,000	462,000
Retained earnings	–0–	88,000
Total stockholders' equity	462,000	550,000
Total liabilities and stockholders' equity	$660,000	$825,000

Ashton Company
COMBINED STATEMENT OF INCOME AND
RETAINED EARNINGS
Historical Cost/Nominal Dollar Basis
For 1985

Sales		$880,000
Cost of goods sold		
Beginning inventory	$220,000	
Purchases	462,000	
Goods available	682,000	
Ending inventory	198,000	484,000
Gross margin on sales		396,000
Operating expenses	149,600	
Depreciation expense	26,400	176,000
Income before taxes		220,000
Income tax expense		88,000
Net income		132,000
Retained earnings, Jan. 1		–0–
Less: Dividends		44,000
Retained earnings, Dec. 31		$ 88,000

The following current cost information pertains to Ashton Company:

[1] The current cost of the equipment (before deducting accumulated depreciation) on December 31, 1985, was $308,000.

[2] The current cost of the land on December 31, 1985, was $352,000.

[3] The current cost of the inventory on December 31, 1985, was $224,400.

[4] Cost of goods sold on a current-cost basis at the time of sale for 1985 was $572,000.

Additional information pertaining to Ashton Company is as follows:

[1] Sales, purchases, operating expenses, and income

tax expense occurred evenly throughout 1985.

[2] The beginning inventory, land, and equipment were purchased on January 1, 1985.

[3] The LIFO method of inventory pricing is used.

[4] The equipment is being depreciated over a 10-year life using the straight-line method. No salvage value is assumed.

[5] Dividends were declared when the CPI-U was 132. Selected values of the CPI-U during 1985 are shown below:

Jan. 1	110.0
Average for 1985	132.0
Dec. 31, 1985	158.4

Instructions

[a] Prepare a combined statement of income and retained earnings for 1985 under the current cost/nominal dollar basis of accounting.

[b] Prepare a balance sheet as of December 31, 1985, under the current cost/nominal dollar basis of accounting.

P27–3   Refer to the information presented in P27–2 for Ashton Company.

Instructions

[a] Prepare a schedule showing the computation of Ashton Company's purchasing power gain or loss for 1985. The gain or loss should be expressed in constant end-of-year dollars.

[b] Prepare a constant dollar combined statement of income and retained earnings for 1985 in end-of-year dollars.

[c] Prepare a constant dollar balance sheet as of December 31, 1985, in end-of-year dollars.

P27–4   Refer to the information presented in P27–2 for Ashton Company.

Instructions

[a] Prepare a current cost/constant dollar combined statement of income and retained earnings for 1985 in end-of-year dollars.

[b] Prepare a current cost/constant dollar balance sheet as of December 31, 1985, in end-of-year dollars.

P27–5   Rose Company began operations on January 1, 1985. A balance sheet prepared on the opening day of business appears below.

Rose Company
BALANCE SHEET
Historical Cost/Nominal Dollar Basis
January 1, 1985

Assets

Cash	$ 10,000
Inventory	30,000
Land	50,000
Equipment	80,000
Total assets	$170,000

Equities

Common stock	$170,000

Additional information pertaining to Rose Company is as follows:

[1] Sales (all on account) of $300,000 were made evenly throughout 1985. Seventy-five percent of the credit sales were collected during 1985; the remaining 25% is expected to be collected in 1986.

[2] Purchases (all on account) of $150,000 were made evenly throughout 1985. Eighty percent of the credit purchases were paid during 1985; the remaining 20% will be paid in 1986.

[3] Operating expenses of $40,000 and income tax expense at a rate of 40% of pretax income were incurred and paid in cash evenly throughout 1985.

[4] Cash dividends of $12,000 were declared and paid on December 31, 1985.

[5] The company uses the FIFO method of inventory pricing. The 1985 ending inventory of $20,000 was acquired when the CPI-U was 210.

[6] The company uses the straight-line method of depreciation for the equipment. An eight-year useful life and no salvage value are assumed.

The following *current-cost* information pertains to Rose Company:

Cost of goods sold for 1985	$190,000
Inventory, Dec. 31, 1985	24,000
Land, Dec. 31, 1985	65,000
Equipment (before deducting accumulated depreciation), Dec. 31, 1985	96,000

Selected values of the CPI-U during 1985 appear below:

Jan. 1	200.0
Average for year	210.0
Dec. 31	220.5

Instructions

[a] Prepare a combined statement of income and retained earnings for 1985 under the historical cost/nominal dollar basis of accounting.

[b] Prepare a balance sheet on December 31, 1985, under the historical cost/nominal dollar basis of accounting.

[c] Prepare a combined statement of income and retained earnings for 1985 under the current cost/nominal dollar basis of accounting.

[d] Prepare a balance sheet on December 31, 1985, under the current cost/nominal dollar basis of accounting.

P27-6 Refer to the information presented for Rose Company in P27-5.

Instructions

[a] Prepare a schedule showing the computation of Rose Company's purchasing power gain or loss for 1985 in end-of-year dollars.

[b] Prepare a historical cost/constant dollar combined statement of income and retained earnings for 1985 in end-of-year dollars.

[c] Prepare a historical cost/constant dollar balance sheet on December 31, 1985, in end-of-year dollars.

P27-7 Refer to the information presented for Rose Company in P27-5.

Instructions

[a] Prepare a current cost/constant dollar combined statement of income and retained earnings for 1985 in end-of-year dollars.

[b] Prepare a current cost/constant dollar balance sheet on December 31, 1985, in end-of-year dollars.

P27-8 Several transactions concerning one asset of a calendar-year company are summarized as follows:

1983	Purchased land for $40,000 cash on Dec. 31. Current cost at year-end was $40,000.
1984	Held the land all year. Current cost at year-end was $52,000.
1985	Dec. 31—sold the land for $68,000.

Selected values of the CPI-U appear below:

Dec. 31, 1983	100
Dec. 31, 1984	110
Dec. 31, 1985	120

Instructions

[a] Determine the balance sheet valuation that should be assigned to the land *at the end of 1983, 1984, and 1985* under (1) the historical cost basis, (2) the constant-dollar basis, (3) the current-cost basis, and (4) the current cost/constant dollar basis of accounting.

[b] Determine the amount of net income that should be reported *at the end of 1983, 1984, and 1985* under (1) the historical cost basis, (2) the constant-dollar basis, (3) the current-cost basis, and (4) the current cost/constant dollar basis of accounting.

[c] Why is the timing of income recognition associated with the land different under current cost accounting than under constant dollar accounting?

(AICPA adapted)

P27–9 Retail Showcase Mart was organized on December 15, 1984. The company's initial statement of financial position is presented below.

Retail Showcase Mart
STATEMENT OF FINANCIAL POSITION
December 31, 1984

Assets

Cash	$200,000
Inventory (at historical cost, which equals market value; FIFO; periodic)	400,000
Furniture and fixtures	200,000
Land (held for future store site)	100,000
Total assets	$900,000

Liabilities and Stockholders' Equity

Accounts payable	$300,000
Capital stock ($5 par, 200,000 shares authorized; 120,000 issued and outstanding)	600,000
Total liabilities and stockholders' equity	$900,000

The statement of income and the statement of financial position prepared at the close of business on December 31, 1985, are presented below.

Retail Showcase Mart
STATEMENT OF INCOME
For the Year Ended December 31, 1985

Sales		$1,100,000
Cost of goods sold		
Inventory 1/1/85	$ 400,000	
Purchases	1,000,000	
Goods available	1,400,000	
Inventory 12/31/85	600,000	800,000
Gross profit		300,000
Operating expenses		
Rent	36,000	
Depreciation	20,000	
Other (all required cash expenditures)	44,000	100,000
Income before taxes		200,000
Income tax expense		80,000
Net income		$ 120,000
Earnings per share		$1.00

Retail Showcase Mart
STATEMENT OF FINANCIAL POSITION
December 31, 1985

Assets

Cash	$ 240,000
Accounts receivable	400,000
Inventory (at historical cost; FIFO; periodic)	600,000
Furniture and fixtures (net)	180,000
Land (held for future store site)	100,000
Total assets	$1,520,000

Liabilities and Stockholders' Equity

Accounts payable	$ 800,000
Capital stock ($5 par, 200,000 shares authorized; 120,000 issued and outstanding)	600,000
Retained earnings	120,000
Total liabilities and stockholders' equity	$1,520,000

Retail Showcase Mart rents its showroom facilities on an operating lease basis at a cost of $3,000 per month. The rent would be $5,000 per month if it were based on the current cost of the facility. All sales and cash outlays for costs and expenses occur uniformly throughout the year.

The following information is indicative of the changing prices since Retail Showcase Mart began its operations.

[1] The CPI-U for the following times is:

Dec. 31, 1984	200
Oct. 1, 1985	216
Dec. 31, 1985	220
Average for 1985	212

[2] The ending inventory was acquired on October 1, 1985.

[3] Inventory at current cost on December 31, 1985, is $700,000.

[4] Cost of goods sold at current cost as of date of sale is $875,000.

[5] Current cost of the land on December 31, 1985, is $150,000.

[6] The sales and purchases occurred uniformly throughout 1985.

[7] The "net recoverable amounts" for inventories and fixed assets have been determined by management to be in excess of the net current costs.

The accounting manager of Retail Showcase Mart has decided to comply voluntarily with the reporting requirements presented in *Statement of Financial Accounting Standards No. 33*, "Financial Reporting and Changing Prices."

Instructions

[a] Calculate Retail Showcase Mart's purchasing power gain or loss for 1985 in terms of December 31, 1985, dollars. Round all computations to the nearest $100.

[b] Prepare a constant dollar income statement for 1985 for Retail Showcase Mart in terms of December 31, 1985, dollars. Round all computations to the nearest $100.

[c] Identify and explain the advantages and disadvantages of constant dollar financial statements.

(CMA adapted)

P27–10 Hyatt, Inc., a retailer, was organized during 1982. Hyatt's management has decided to supplement its December 31, 1985, nominal dollar financial statements with constant dollar financial statements. The following general ledger trial balance (nominal dollar) and additional information have been furnished:

Hyatt, Inc.
TRIAL BALANCE
December 31, 1985

	Dr.	Cr.
Cash and receivables (net)	$ 540,000	
Marketable securities (common stock)	400,000	
Inventory	440,000	
Equipment	650,000	
Equipment—Accumulated depreciation		$ 164,000
Accounts payable		300,000
6% First mortgage bonds, due 2003		500,000
Common stock, $10 par		1,000,000
Retained earnings, Dec. 31, 1984	46,000	
Sales		1,900,000

Cost of sales	1,508,000	
Depreciation	65,000	
Other operating expenses and interest	215,000	
	$3,864,000	$3,864,000

[1] Monetary assets (cash and receivables) exceeded monetary liabilities (accounts payable and bonds payable) by $445,000 at December 31, 1984. The amounts of monetary items are fixed in terms of numbers of dollars, regardless of changes in specific prices or in the general price level.

[2] Purchases ($1,840,000 in 1985) and sales are made uniformly throughout the year.

[3] Depreciation is computed on a straight-line basis, with a full year's depreciation being taken in the year of acquisition and none in the year of retirement. The depreciation rate is 10% and no salvage value is anticipated. Acquisitions and retirements have been made fairly evenly over each year, and the retirements in 1985 consisted of assets purchased during 1983 that were scrapped. An analysis of the equipment account reveals the following:

Year	Beginning Balance	Additions	Retirements	Ending Balance
1983	—	$550,000	—	$550,000
1984	$550,000	10,000	—	560,000
1985	560,000	150,000	$60,000	650,000

[4] The bonds were issued in 1983 and the marketable securities were purchased fairly evenly over 1985. Other operating expenses and interest are assumed to be incurred evenly throughout the year.

[5] Assume that values of the CPI-U were as follows:

Annual Averages	Index	Conversion Factors (1985 4th Qtr. = 1.000)
1982	113.9	1.128
1983	116.8	1.100
1984	121.8	1.055
1985	126.7	1.014

End-of-Quarter		
1984 4th	123.5	1.040
1985 1st	124.9	1.029
2nd	126.1	1.019
3rd	127.3	1.009
4th	128.5	1.000

Instructions

[a] Prepare a schedule to convert the Equipment ac-

count balance at December 31, 1985, from nominal dollars to 1985 year-end constant dollars.

[b] Prepare a schedule to analyze in nominal dollars the Equipment—Accumulated Depreciation account for 1985.

[c] Prepare a schedule to analyze in 1985 year-end constant dollars the Equipment—Accumulated Depreciation account for 1985.

[d] Prepare a schedule to compute Hyatt's purchasing power gain or loss on its net holdings of monetary assets for 1985 (ignore income tax implications). The schedule should consider appropriate items on or related to the balance sheet and the income statement.

(AICPA adapted)

P27–11 To obtain a more realistic appraisal of her investment, Susan Watts, your client, has asked you to adjust certain financial data of Archer Company for price-level changes. On January 1, 1983, she invested $50,000 in Archer Company in return for 10,000 shares of common stock. Immediately after her investment, the trial balance appeared as follows:

	Dr.	Cr.
Cash and receivables	$ 65,200	
Merchandise inventory	4,000	
Building	50,000	
Accumulated depreciation—building		$ 8,000
Equipment	36,000	
Accumulated depreciation—equipment		7,200
Land	10,000	
Current liabilities		50,000
Capital stock, $5 par		100,000
	$165,200	$165,200

Balances in certain selected accounts as of December 31 of each of the next three years were as follows:

	1983	1984	1985
Sales	$39,650	$39,000	$42,350
Inventory	4,500	5,600	5,347
Purchases	14,475	16,350	18,150
Operating expenses (excluding depreciation)	10,050	9,050	9,075

Assume the 1983 price level as the base year and that all changes in the price level take place at the beginning of each year. Further assume that the 1984 price level is 10% above the 1983 price level and that the 1985 price level is 10% above the 1984 level.

The building was constructed in 1979 at a cost of $50,000, with an estimated life of 25 years. The price level at that time was 80% of the 1983 price level.

The equipment was purchased in 1981 at a cost of $36,000, with an estimated life of 10 years. The price level at that time was 90% of the 1983 price level.

The LIFO method of inventory valuation is used. The original inventory was acquired in the same year the building was constructed and was maintained at a constant $4,000 until 1983. In 1983 a gradual buildup of the inventory was begun in anticipation of an increase in the volume of business.

Watts considers the return on her investment as the dividend she actually receives. In 1983 and again in 1985, Archer Company paid cash dividends in the amount of $8,000.

On July 1, 1984, there was a reverse stock split-up of the company's stock in the ratio of one-for-ten.

Instructions

[a] Compute the 1985 earnings per share of common stock in terms of 1983 dollars.

[b] Compute the percentage return on investment for 1983 and 1985 in terms of 1983 dollars.

(AICPA adapted)

P27–12 Melgar Company purchased a tract of land as an investment in 1982 for $100,000. Late that year the company decided to construct a shopping center on the site. Construction began in 1983 and was completed in 1985; one-third of the construction was completed each year. Melgar originally estimated the costs of the project would be $1,200,000 for materials, $750,000 for labor, $150,000 for variable overhead, and $600,000 for depreciation.

Actual costs (excluding depreciation) incurred for construction were:

	1983	1984	1985
Materials	$418,950	$434,560	$462,000
Labor	236,250	274,400	282,000
Variable overhead	47,250	54,208	61,200

Shortly after construction began, Melgar sold the shopping center for $3,000,000, with payment to be made in full on completion in December 1985. One hundred and fifty thousand dollars of the sales price was allocated for the land.

The transaction was completed as scheduled and now a controversy has developed between the two major stockholders of the company. One thinks that the company should have invested in land, because a high rate of return was earned on the land. The other believes that the original decision was sound and that unanticipated changes in the price level affected the original cost estimates.

You were engaged to furnish guidance to these stockholders in resolving their controversy. As an aid, you obtained the following information:

[1] Using 1982 as the base year, price-level indexes for relevant years are:

1979	90
1980	93
1981	96
1982	100
1983	105
1984	112
1985	120

[2] The company allocated $200,000 per year for depreciation of fixed assets allocated to this construction project. Of that amount, $25,000 was for a building purchased in 1979 and $175,000 was for equipment purchased in 1981.

Instructions

[a] Prepare a schedule to restate in base-year (1982) costs the actual costs, including depreciation, incurred each year. Disregard income taxes and assume that each price-level index was valid for the entire year.

[b] Prepare a schedule comparing the originally estimated costs of the project with the total actual costs for each element of cost (materials, labor, variable overhead, and depreciation) adjusted to the 1982 price level.

[c] Prepare a schedule to restate the amount received on the sale in terms of base year (1982) purchasing power. The gain or loss should be determined separately for the land and the building in terms of base-year purchasing power and should exclude depreciation.

(AICPA adapted)

AUTHORITATIVE ACCOUNTING PRONOUNCEMENTS

Generally accepted accounting principles (GAAP) are determined in a variety of ways, including the promulgation of standards by authoritative accounting bodies. Certified public accountants are required to understand and apply GAAP as a result of *Rule 203* of the Code of Professional Ethics of the American Institute of Certified Public Accountants (AICPA). *Rule 203* states the following:

> Accounting Principles. *A member shall not express an opinion that financial statements are presented in conformity with generally accepted accounting principles if such statements contain any departure from an accounting principle promulgated by the body designated by Council to establish such principles which has a material effect on the statements taken as a whole, unless the member can demonstrate that due to unusual circumstances the financial statements would otherwise have been misleading. In such cases his report must describe the departure, the approximate effects thereof, if practicable, and the reasons why compliance with the principle would result in a misleading statement.*

Rule 203 requires an understanding of GAAP as promulgated by the body designated by the AICPA council to establish such principles. The rule is based on the presumption that compliance with promulgated accounting principles will result in financial statements that are not misleading. From 1939 to 1959, the body responsible for promulgating accounting principles was the Committee on Accounting Procedure (CAP) of the AICPA. From 1959 to 1973, the responsible body was the Accounting Principles Board (APB), also a committee of the AICPA. Since 1973, the responsible organization has been the Financial Accounting Standards Board (FASB), an independent body supported by several organizations with a strong commitment to quality and integrity in financial reporting.

The following list presents the authoritative accounting pronouncements that have been issued by these three organizations and that are encompassed by *Rule 203*. Many of these pronouncements have been cited in the text in the explanation of current accounting practices and alternatives to those practices. Others deal with subjects that are not ordinarily covered in intermediate accounting courses. Many pronouncements have been amended, partially or completely superseded, or interpreted by more recent pronouncements and therefore no longer apply.

The authoritative accounting bodies have issued other types of pronouncements that apply only indirectly to current accounting practices and thus do not come under *Rule 203*. These include such publications as APB Statements and FASB Statements of Financial Accounting Concepts. These publications are not listed here, but they are also important considerations in determining the appropriate form and content of financial statements.

The development of GAAP is a continuous process. Existing pronouncements are subject to reconsideration and new pronouncements are pending. A list such as the following one is therefore tentative and illustrates not only the extensive body of knowledge of financial accounting but also the evolutionary nature of generally accepted accounting principles.

Accounting Research Bulletins

Date Issued	Number	Title
1953	No. 43	Restatement and Revision of Accounting Research Bulletins Nos. 1–42 (originally issued 1939–1953)

Chapter 1 Prior Opinions
    A. Rules Adopted by Membership (amended)
    B. Opinion Issued by Predecessor Committee (amended, superseded)
Chapter 2 Form of Statements
    A. Comparative Financial Statements (amended)
    B. Combined Statement of Income and Earned Surplus (superseded)
Chapter 3 Working Capital
    A. Current Assets and Current Liabilities (amended, partially superseded)
    B. Application of United States Government Securities Against Liabilities for Federal Taxes on Income (superseded)
Chapter 4 Inventory Pricing
Chapter 5 Intangible Assets (amended, partially superseded)
Chapter 6 Contingency Reserves (superseded)
Chapter 7 Capital Accounts
    A. Quasi-Reorganization or Corporate Readjustment
    B. Stock Dividends and Stock Split-Ups (amended)
    C. Business Combinations (superseded)
Chapter 8 Income and Earned Surplus (superseded)
Chapter 9 Depreciation
    A. Depreciation and High Costs (amended)
    B. Depreciation on Appreciation (superseded)
    C. Emergency Facilities—Depreciation, Amortization and Income Taxes (amended)
Chapter 10 Taxes
    A. Real and Personal Property Taxes (amended)
    B. Income Taxes (amended, superseded)
Chapter 11 Government Contracts
    A. Cost-Plus-Fixed-Fee Contracts
    B. Renegotiation (amended)
    C. Terminated War and Defense Contracts
Chapter 12 Foreign Operations and Foreign Exchange (amended, partially superseded)
Chapter 13 Compensation
    A. Pension Plans—Annuity Costs Based on Past Service (superseded)
    B. Compensation Involved in Stock Option and Stock Purchase Plans (amended)
Chapter 14 Disclosure of Long-Term Leases in Financial Statements of Lessees (superseded)
Chapter 15 Unamortized Discount, Issue Cost, and Redemption Premium on Bonds Refunded (amended, partially superseded)

Date Issued	Number	Title
1954	No. 44	Declining-Balance Depreciation (revised 1958)
1955	No. 45	Long-Term Construction-Type Contracts
1956	No. 46	Discontinuance of Dating Earned Surplus
1956	No. 47	Accounting for Costs of Pension Plans (superseded)
1957	No. 48	Business Combinations (amended, superseded)
1958	No. 49	Earnings per Share (superseded)
1958	No. 50	Contingencies (superseded)
1959	No. 51	Consolidated Financial Statements (amended, partially superseded)

APB Opinions

Date Issued	Number	Title
1962	No. 1	New Depreciation Guidelines and Rules (amended, partially superseded)
1962	No. 2	Accounting for the "Investment Credit" (amended, partially superseded, interpreted)
1963	No. 3	The Statement of Source and Application of Funds (superseded)
1964	No. 4	Accounting for the "Investment Credit" (Amending No. 2) (interpreted)
1964	No. 5	Reporting of Leases in Financial Statements of Lessee (amended, superseded)
1965	No. 6	Status of Accounting Research Bulletins (partially superseded)
1966	No. 7	Accounting for Leases in Financial Statements of Lessors (amended, superseded)

Date Issued	Number	Title
1966	No. 8	Accounting for the Cost of Pension Plans (amended, partially superseded, interpreted)
1966	No. 9	Reporting the Results of Operations (amended, partially superseded)
1966	No. 10	Omnibus Opinion—1966 (amended, partially superseded)
1967	No. 11	Accounting for Income Taxes (amended, partially superseded, interpreted)
1967	No. 12	Omnibus Opinion—1967 (partially superseded)
1969	No. 13	Amending Paragraph 6 of APB Opinion No. 9, Application to Commercial Banks
1969	No. 14	Accounting for Convertible Debt and Debt Issued with Stock Purchase Warrants
1969	No. 15	Earnings per Share (amended, interpreted)
1970	No. 16	Business Combinations (amended, partially superseded, interpreted)
1970	No. 17	Intangible Assets (amended, partially superseded, interpreted)
1971	No. 18	The Equity Method of Accounting for Investments in Common Stock (amended, partially superseded, interpreted)
1971	No. 19	Reporting Changes in Financial Position (amended)
1971	No. 20	Accounting Changes (amended, partially superseded, interpreted)
1971	No. 21	Interest on Receivables and Payables (amended, interpreted)
1972	No. 22	Disclosure of Accounting Policies (amended)
1972	No. 23	Accounting for Income Taxes—Special Areas (amended, partially superseded, interpreted)
1972	No. 24	Accounting for Income Taxes—Investments in Common Stock Accounted for by the Equity Method (Other than Subsidiaries and Corporate Joint Ventures) (partially superseded, interpreted)
1972	No. 25	Accounting for Stock Issued to Employees (interpreted)
1972	No. 26	Early Extinguishment of Debt (amended, partially superseded)
1972	No. 27	Accounting for Lease Transactions by Manufacturer or Dealer Lessors (superseded)
1973	No. 28	Interim Financial Reporting (amended, partially superseded, interpreted)
1973	No. 29	Accounting for Nonmonetary Transactions (amended, interpreted)
1973	No. 30	Reporting the Results of Operations—Reporting the Effects of Disposal of a Segment of a Business, and Extraordinary, Unusual and Infrequently Occurring Events and Transactions (amended, interpreted)
1973	No. 31	Disclosure of Lease Commitments by Lessees (superseded)

FASB Statements of Financial Accounting Standards

1973	No. 1	Disclosure of Foreign Currency Translation Information (superseded)
1974	No. 2	Accounting for Research and Development Costs (partially superseded, interpreted)
1974	No. 3	Reporting Accounting Changes in Interim Financial Statements (amendment of APB Opinion No. 28)
1975	No. 4	Reporting Gains and Losses from Extinguishment of Debt (amendment of APB Opinion No. 30) (amended, partially superseded)
1975	No. 5	Accounting for Contingencies (amended, partially superseded, interpreted)
1975	No. 6	Classification of Short-Term Obligations Expected to Be Refinanced (amendment of ARB No. 43, Chapter 3A) (interpreted)
1975	No. 7	Accounting and Reporting by Development Stage Enterprises (amended, interpreted)
1975	No. 8	Accounting for the Translation of Foreign Currency Transactions and Foreign Currency Financial Statements (amended, interpreted, superseded)
1975	No. 9	Accounting for Income Taxes—Oil and Gas Producing Companies (amendment of APB Opinions Nos. 11 and 23) (superseded)
1975	No. 10	Extension of "Grandfather" Provisions for Business Combinations (amendment of APB Opinion No. 16)
1975	No. 11	Accounting for Contingencies—Transition method (amendment of FASB Statement No. 5)
1975	No. 12	Accounting for Certain Marketable Securities (interpreted)
1976	No. 13	Accounting for Leases (amended, partially superseded, interpreted)

Date Issued	Number	Title
1976	No. 14	Financial Reporting for Segments of a Business Enterprise (amended, partially superseded)
1977	No. 15	Accounting by Debtors and Creditors for Troubled Debt Restructurings (partially superseded)
1977	No. 16	Prior Period Adjustments (partially superseded)
1977	No. 17	Accounting for Leases—Initial Direct Costs (amendment of FASB Statement No. 13)
1977	No. 18	Financial Reporting for Segments of a Business Enterprise—Interim Financial Statements (amendment of FASB Statement No. 14)
1977	No. 19	Financial Accounting and Reporting by Oil and Gas Producing Companies (amended, partially superseded, interpreted)
1977	No. 20	Accounting for Forward Exchange Contracts (amendment of FASB Statement No. 8) (superseded)
1978	No. 21	Suspension of the Reporting of Earnings per Share and Segment Information by Nonpublic Enterprises (amendment of APB Opinion No. 15 and FASB Statement No. 14)
1978	No. 22	Accounting for Leases—Changes in the Provisions of Lease Agreements Resulting from Refundings of Tax-Exempt Debt (amendment of FASB Statement No. 13) (partially superseded)
1978	No. 23	Inception of the Lease (amendment of FASB Statement No. 13)
1978	No. 24	Reporting Segment Information in Financial Statements That Are Presented in Another Enterprise's Financial Report (amendment of FASB Statement No. 14)
1979	No. 25	Suspension of Certain Accounting Requirements for Oil and Gas Producing Companies (amendment of FASB Statement No. 19) (partially superseded)
1979	No. 26	Profit Recognition on Sales-Type Leases of Real Estate (amendment of FASB Statement No. 13) (amended)
1979	No. 27	Classification of Renewals or Extensions of Existing Sales-Type or Direct Financing Leases (amendment of FASB Statement No. 13)
1979	No. 28	Accounting for Sales with Leasebacks (amendment of FASB Statement No. 13) (amended)
1979	No. 29	Determining Contingent Rentals (amendment of FASB Statement No. 13)
1979	No. 30	Disclosure of Information About Major Customers (amendment of FASB Statement No. 14)
1979	No. 31	Accounting for Tax Benefits Related to U.K. Tax Legislation Concerning Stock Relief
1979	No. 32	Specialized Accounting and Reporting Principles and Practices in AICPA Statements of Position and Guides on Accounting and Auditing Matters (amendment of APB Opinion No. 20) (amended, partially superseded)
1979	No. 33	Financial Reporting and Changing Prices (amended, partially superseded)
1979	No. 34	Capitalization of Interest Cost (amended, partially superseded, interpreted)
1980	No. 35	Accounting and Reporting by Defined Benefit Pension Plans (amended)
1980	No. 36	Disclosure of Pension Information (amendment of APB Opinion No. 8)
1980	No. 37	Balance Sheet Classification of Deferred Income Taxes (amendment of APB Opinion No. 11)
1980	No. 38	Accounting for Preacquisition Contingencies of Purchased Enterprises (amendment of APB Opinion No. 16)
1980	No. 39	Financial Reporting and Changing Prices: Specialized Assets—Mining and Oil and Gas (supplement to FASB Statement No. 33)
1980	No. 40	Financial Reporting and Changing Prices: Specialized Assets—Timberlands and Growing Timber (supplement to FASB Statement No. 33)
1980	No. 41	Financial Reporting and Changing Prices: Specialized Assets—Income-Producing Real Estate (supplement to FASB Statement No. 33)
1980	No. 42	Determining Materiality for Capitalization of Interest Cost (amendment of FASB Statement No. 34)
1980	No. 43	Accounting for Compensated Absences (partially superseded)
1980	No. 44	Accounting for Intangible Assets of Motor Carriers (amendment of Chapter 5 of ARB No. 43 and interpretation of APB Opinions Nos. 17 and 30)

Date Issued	Number	Title
1981	No. 45	Accounting for Franchise Fee Revenue
1981	No. 46	Financial Reporting and Changing Prices: Motion Picture Films (supplement to FASB Statement No. 33)
1981	No. 47	Disclosure of Long-Term Obligations
1981	No. 48	Revenue Recognition When Right of Return Exists
1981	No. 49	Accounting for Product Financing Arrangements (partially superseded)
1981	No. 50	Financial Reporting in the Record and Music Industry
1981	No. 51	Financial Reporting by Cable Television Companies (partially superseded)
1981	No. 52	Foreign Currency Translation (interpreted)
1981	No. 53	Financial Reporting by Producers and Distributors of Motion Picture Films
1982	No. 54	Financial Reporting and Changing Prices: Investment Companies (amendment of FASB Statement No. 33)
1982	No. 55	Determining Whether a Convertible Security Is a Common Stock Equivalent (amendment of APB Opinion No. 15)
1982	No. 56	Designation of AICPA Guide and Statement of Position (SOP) 81-1 on Contractor Accounting and SOP 81-2 Concerning Hospital-Related Organizations as Preferable for Purposes of Applying APB Opinion No. 20 (amendment of FASB Statement No. 32)
1982	No. 57	Related Party Disclosures
1982	No. 58	Capitalization of Interest Cost in Financial Statements That Include Investments Accounted for by the Equity Method (amendment of FASB Statement No. 34)
1982	No. 59	Deferral of the Effective Date of Certain Accounting Requirements for Pension Plans of State and Local Governmental Units (amendment of FASB Statement No. 35)
1982	No. 60	Accounting and Reporting by Insurance Enterprises
1982	No. 61	Accounting for Title Plant
1982	No. 62	Capitalization of Interest Cost in Situations Involving Certain Tax-Exempt Borrowings and Certain Gifts and Grants
1982	No. 63	Financial Reporting by Broadcasters
1982	No. 64	Extinguishment of Debt Made to Satisfy Sinking-Fund Requirements (amendment of FASB Statement No. 4)
1982	No. 65	Accounting for Certain Mortgage Banking Activities
1982	No. 66	Accounting for Sales of Real Estate
1982	No. 67	Accounting for Costs and Initial Rental Operations of Real Estate Projects
1982	No. 68	Research and Development Arrangements
1982	No. 69	Disclosures About Oil and Gas Producing Activities (amendment of FASB Statements Nos. 19, 25, 33, and 39)
1982	No. 70	Financial Reporting and Changing Prices: Foreign Currency Translation (amendment of FASB Statment No. 33)
1982	No. 71	Accounting for the Effects of Certain Types of Regulation
1983	No. 72	Accounting for Certain Acquisitions of Banking or Thrift Institutions (amendment of APB Opinion No. 17 and FASB Interpretation No. 9, interpretation of APB Opinions Nos. 16 and 17)
1983	No. 73	Reporting a Change in Accounting for Railroad Track Structures (amendment of APB Opinion No. 20)
1983	No. 74	Accounting for Special Termination Benefits Paid to Employees
1983	No. 75	Deferral of the Effective Date of Certain Accounting Requirements for Pension Plans of State and Local Government Units (amendment of FASB Statement No. 35)
1983	No.76	Extinguishment of Debt (amendment of APB Opinion No. 26)
1983	No. 77	Reporting by Transferors for Transfers of Receivables with Recourse
1983	No. 78	Classification of Obligations That Are Callable by the Creditor (amendment of ARB No. 43, Chapter 3A)

FASB Interpretations

Date Issued	Number	Title
1974	No. 1	Accounting Changes Related to the Cost of Inventory (interpretation of APB Opinion No. 20)
1974	No. 2	Inputing Interest on Debt Arrangements Made Under the Federal Bankruptcy Act (interpretation of APB Opinion No. 21)
1974	No. 3	Accounting for the Cost of Pension Plans Subject to the Employee Retirement Income Security Act of 1974 (interpretation of APB Opinion No. 8)
1975	No. 4	Applicability of FASB Statement No. 2 to Business Combinations Accounted for by the Purchase Method (interpretation of FASB Statement No. 2)
1975	No. 5	Applicability of FASB Statement No. 2 to Development Stage Enterprises (interpretation of FASB Statement No. 2)
1975	No. 6	Applicability of FASB Statement No. 2 to Computer Software (interpretation of FASB Statement No. 2)
1975	No. 7	Applying FASB Statement No. 7 in Financial Statements of Established Operating Enterprises (interpretation of FASB Statement No. 7)
1976	No. 8	Classification of a Short-Term Obligation Repaid Prior to Being Replaced by a Long-Term Security (interpretation of FASB Statement No. 6)
1976	No. 9	Applying APB Opinions Nos. 16 and 17 When a Savings and Loan Association or a Similar Institution is Acquired in a Business Combination Accounted for by the Purchase Method (interpretation of APB Opinions Nos. 16 and 17)
1976	No. 10	Application of FASB Statement No. 12 to Personal Financial Statements (interpretation of FASB Statement No. 12)
1976	No. 11	Changes in Market Value After the Balance Sheet Date (interpretation of FASB Statement No. 12)
1976	No. 12	Accounting for Previously Established Allowance Accounts (interpretation of FASB Statement No. 12)
1976	No. 13	Consolidation of a Parent and Its Subsidiaries Having Different Balance Sheet Dates (interpretation of FASB Statement No. 12)
1976	No. 14	Reasonable Estimation of the Amount of a Loss (interpretation of FASB Statement No. 5)
1976	No. 15	Translation of Unamortized Policy Acquisition Costs by a Stock Life Insurance Company (interpretation of FASB Statement No. 8)
1977	No. 16	Clarification of Definitions and Accounting for Marketable Equity Securities That Become Nonmarketable (interpretation of FASB Statement No. 12)
1977	No. 17	Applying the Lower of Cost or Market Rule in Translated Financial Statements (interpretation of FASB Statement No. 8)
1977	No. 18	Accounting for Income Taxes in Interim Periods (interpretation of APB Opinion No. 28)
1977	No. 19	Lessee Guarantee of the Residual Value of Leased Property (interpretation of FASB Statement No. 13)
1977	No. 20	Reporting Accounting Changes under AICPA Statements of Position (interpretation of APB Opinion No. 20)
1978	No. 21	Accounting for Leases in a Business Combination (interpretation of FASB Statement No. 13)
1978	No. 22	Applicability of Indefinite Reversal Criteria to Timing Differences (interpretation of APB Opinions Nos. 11 and 23)
1978	No. 23	Lease of Certain Property Owned by a Governmental Unit or Authority (interpretation of FASB Statement No. 13)
1978	No. 24	Leases Involving Only Part of a Building (interpretation of FASB Statement No. 13)
1978	No. 25	Accounting for an Unused Investment Tax Credit (interpretation of APB Opinions Nos. 2, 4, 11, and 16)
1978	No. 26	Accounting for Purchase of a Leased Asset by the Lessee During the Term of the Lease (interpretation of FASB Statement No. 13)

Date Issued	Number	Title
1978	No. 27	Accounting for a Loss on a Sublease (interpretation of FASB Statement No. 13 and APB Opinion No. 30)
1978	No. 28	Accounting for Stock Appreciation Rights and Other Variable Stock Option or Award Plans (interpretation of APB Opinions Nos. 15 and 25)
1979	No. 29	Reporting Tax Benefits Realized on Disposition of Investments in Certain Subsidiaries and Other Investees (interpretation of APB Opinions Nos. 23 and 24)
1979	No. 30	Accounting for Involuntary Conversions of Nonmonetary Assets to Monetary Assets (interpretation of APB Opinion No. 29)
1980	No. 31	Treatment of Stock Compensation Plans in EPS Computations (interpretation of APB Opinion No. 15 and modification of FASB Interpretation No. 28)
1980	No. 32	Application of Percentage Limitations in Recognizing Investment Tax Credit (interpretation of APB Opinions Nos. 2, 4, and 11)
1980	No. 33	Applying FASB Statement No. 34 to Oil and Gas Producing Operations Accounted for by the Full Cost Method (interpretation of FASB Statement No. 34)
1981	No. 34	Disclosure of Indirect Guarantees of Indebtedness of Others (interpretation of FASB Statement No. 5)
1981	No. 35	Criteria for Applying the Equity Method of Accounting for Investments in Common Stock (interpretation of APB Opinion No. 18)
1981	No. 36	Accounting for Exploratory Wells in Progress at the End of a Period (interpretation of FASB Statement No. 19)
1983	No. 37	Accounting for Translation Adjustments upon Sale of an Investment in a Foreign Entity (interpretation of FASB Statement No. 52)

APPENDIX
KROGER COMPANY
FINANCIAL REPORT 1982

MANAGEMENT'S DISCUSSION AND ANALYSIS OF
FINANCIAL CONDITION AND RESULTS OF OPERATION

The analysis of Company operations encompassing the years 1980, 1981 and 1982 should be considered in conjunction with the Consolidated Financial Statements and the Ten Year Summary.

Liquidity and Capital Resources

Cash provided from current operations over the past three years accounted for $810.6 million of the $1.026 billion required during that period for capital expenditures and dividends. Long-term financing arrangements were the primary source for the balance of cash requirements, and 1982 arrangements included the issuance of $142.4 million in industrial revenue bonds. Short-term borrowings increased by $75.8 million and averaged $36.3 million during 1982 compared to $16.4 million in 1981. It is the intention of the Company to refinance the $75.8 million of short-term debt on a long-term basis during 1983. Cash and temporary cash investments decreased by $128.0 million to $153.3 million at January 1, 1983.

Capital expenditures during 1982 totaled $388.6 million, an increase of $128.4 million over 1981 and $149.4 million higher than 1980. In 1983 capital spending is expected to approximate $410 million. Plans include approximately 75 new food stores, 18 convenience stores and more than 60 new SupeRx stores, plus the remodel of 107 food stores and 20 drug stores and continued expansion in manufacturing and distribution facilities.

Summary of Retail Expansion

	1982	1981	1980
Food Stores:			
Opened	101	111	118
Remodeled	85	57	49
Closed or Sold	160	98	107
Stores—End of Year	1,199	1,258	1,245
Total Area*	37,142	36,985	34,529
Drug Stores:			
Opened or Acquired	77	57	42
Remodeled	25	15	27
Closed or Sold	21	64	32
Stores—End of Year	563	507	514
Total Area*	6,261	5,715	5,841

* In thousands of square feet.

At January 1, 1983, the Company had available a revolving credit aggregating $250.0 million against which it may obtain interim loans until March, 1988. At the Company's request, the interim loans may be converted into a term loan payable over six years. In addition, the Company had commitments for financing of real estate and equipment totaling $59.0 million.

$50.0 million of convertible debt was called in the third quarter 1982, resulting in 100% conversion and a corresponding increase in equity. Although long-term debt and capitalized lease obligations continued to increase as a percent of long-term capitalization (Long-Term Debt + Capitalized Lease Obligations + Share-owners' Equity) due to increasing store ownership versus leasing, the pretax earnings coverage of interest and rents has remained stable.

	Percent Of Long-Term Capitalization		
	1982	*1981*	*1980*
Short-term Borrowings to be Refinanced	4.9%	—	—
Senior Debt	29.7	27.3%	25.4%
Subordinated Debt	—	3.7	—
Capitalized Lease Obligations	9.4	9.8	11.1
Total	44.0%	40.8%	36.5%
Pre-Tax Coverage of Interest and Rent (times)	1.92	2.02	1.98

Average (FIFO) inventory turns in 1982 declined to 9.0 compared to 9.5 in both 1981 and 1980 due primarily to higher inventory levels in the increasing number of combination stores.

Results of Operations

Consolidated sales in 1982 of $11.9 billion increased 5.6% over 1981 including sales for both years in the Company's 65 Market Basket stores, which were disposed of during the third quarter 1982. The increase would have been 8.1% excluding sales for the southern California stores from both years. Food business sales of $11.2 billion in 1982 increased 5.7% over 1981 and drug store sales of $716 million were 5.0% over the previous year.

ward trend to 76.0% compared to 76.7% in 1981 and 77.7% in 1980. Approximately 71% of 1982 inventories and 72% of 1981 inventories were valued using the last-in, first-out (LIFO) method. The LIFO charge to inventories for 1982 was $18.5 million compared to $30.5 million in 1981, the reduction reflecting the lower level of food inflation.

LIFO Effect on Merchandise Costs as a Percent of Sales (in millions)

	1982		*1981*		*1980*	
	Amt.	*% Sales*	*Amt.*	*% Sales*	*Amt.*	*% Sales*
Mdse. Costs (FIFO)	$9,029	75.9	$8,615	76.4	$7,962	77.2
LIFO Charge	19	.1	30	.3	50	.5
Mdse. Costs (LIFO)	$9,048	76.0	$8,645	76.7	$8,012	77.7

1982 food business merchandise costs, including warehousing and transportation, were 76.4% of sales compared to 77.1% in 1981 and 78.2% in 1980. A change in product mix resulting from a greater number of stores with specialty and non-foods/general merchandise departments was a significant cause of the decline. Drug store merchandise costs, including warehousing and transportation, were 69.9% of sales in 1982 compared to 70.9% in 1981 and 69.4% in 1980.

Consolidated Sales (in millions)

	1982		*1981*		*1980*	
	Amt.	*Chg.*	*Amt.*	*Chg.*	*Amt.*	*Chg.*
Food Business	$11,186	+5.7%	$10,584	+9.3%	$ 9,682	+14.4%
Drug Stores	716	+5.0%	683	+7.5%	635	+12.0%
Total	$11,902	+5.6%	$11,267	+9.2%	$10,317	+14.3%

Factors influencing food business sales in 1982 compared to 1981:

	Including Market Basket	*Excluding Market Basket*
Food Prices	+2.1%	+2.2%
Food Tonnage	+2.9%	+5.4%
Food Store Square Footage	+3.7%	+7.2%
Customer Transactions	− .3%	+2.9%

1982 drug store sales were affected by an approximate 8% price increase and a 3.6% increase in average store square footage.

Merchandise costs, including warehousing and transportation, as a percent of sales continued a down-

Operating, general and administrative expenses continued to increase and were 8.0% higher than 1981. On a percent of sales basis, the 1982 costs were 19.5%, compared to 19.1% in 1981 and 18.4% in 1980. Major contributing factors for the increase over 1981 were higher employee related costs, which were up 7.9% over 1981 and utility costs which reflected a 14.3% rise over the prior year.

Food business operating profit (before taxes based on income and unallocated expenses) was $263.0 million in 1982 compared to $244.6 million in 1981 and $198.4 million in 1980. 1982 included a $14.2 million gain resulting from the store closing program.

Operating profit (before taxes based on income and unallocated expenses) for drug stores increased to

$15.2 million from $6.5 million in 1981 and $9.8 million in 1980. A gain of $4.3 million resulting from the sale of real estate is included in 1981 results. The continued revitalization of drug store facilities and refinement of operations and merchandising strategies have produced improved results.

Net Earnings

Earnings from continuing operations in 1982 were $143.8 million compared to $129.5 million in 1981 and $102.8 million in 1980. A lower effective tax rate primarily resulting from investment tax credits and capital gains favorably impacted 1982 earnings. The Company's store closing program increased 1982 earnings by $14.2 million. This was the result of the gain realized from the disposal of certain stores and other properties offset in part by operating losses and closing costs associated with these properties.

The Company's reported sales, earnings, shareowners' equity and other pertinent financial data have been affected by the high rates of inflation in recent years. An estimation and evaluation of the effect of inflation, as defined by Statement of Financial Accounting Standards No. 33, Financial Reporting and Changing Prices, follows on pages [1312–1315].

Management's Responsibility for Financial Reporting

The consolidated financial statements of The Kroger Co. and Consolidated Subsidiary Companies and other financial information contained in this report were prepared by management, which is responsible for their integrity and completeness. These statements were prepared in conformity with generally accepted accounting principles and necessarily include some amounts that are based on management's best estimates and judgments.

The Company has, over the years, maintained a system of internal accounting controls to provide reasonable assurance that Company assets are adequately protected, and that transactions are executed in accordance with management's authorizations and are reflected accurately in the Company's books and records as a basis for the reliable preparation of the financial statements. The system of controls includes careful selection and training of financial management personnel, clearly defined limits of authority and division of responsibility, the dissemination of detailed formal accounting and business policies and procedures, and an extensive program of internal audit examinations to monitor the effectiveness of the system. The Company has distributed to key employees its policy requiring high moral, ethical and legal standards in the conduct of its business.

Coopers & Lybrand, certified public accountants, has examined the consolidated financial statements in accordance with generally accepted auditing standards. Its report on the consolidated financial statements appears on page [1311].

The Board of Directors, acting through its Audit Committee comprised entirely of outside directors, oversees the fulfillment by management of its responsibilities in the preparation of financial statements and for financial control. The Committee recommends the selection of the Company's certified public accountants, reviews the scope and cost of the internal and external audit programs and meets formally at least three times per year with the internal and external auditors, providing them direct free access at these and other times.

CONSOLIDATED BALANCE SHEET (In thousands of dollars)

ASSETS	January 1, 1983	January 2, 1982
Current Assets		
Cash and temporary cash investments	$ 153,307	$ 281,257
Receivables	112,858	96,935
Inventories:		
FIFO cost	1,085,916	928,489
Less LIFO reserve	(136,072)	(117,543)
	949,844	810,946
Property held for resale	65,758	25,275
Prepaid and other current assets	83,635	63,928
Total current assets	1,365,402	1,278,341
Notes receivable	25,834	15,059
Investments		
Marketable investment securities	8,903	15,772
Other investments	35,742	25,177
Total investments	44,645	40,949
Property, Plant and Equipment		
Land	46,163	40,468
Buildings and land improvements	255,281	207,563
Equipment	1,089,657	901,842
Leaseholds and leasehold improvements	316,882	275,233
Leased property under capital leases	189,631	173,480
	1,897,614	1,598,586
Allowance for depreciation and amortization	(609,796)	(545,822)
Property, plant and equipment, net	1,287,818	1,052,764
Excess of cost of investments in consolidated subsidiaries over equities in net assets	5,860	18,177
Total Assets	$ 2,729,559	$ 2,405,290

The accompanying notes are an integral part of the consolidated financial statements.

LIABILITIES	January 1, 1983	January 2, 1982
Current Liabilities		
Current portion of long-term debt	$ 41,577	$ 3,281
Current portion of obligations under capital leases	4,355	4,193
Accounts payable	608,385	589,100
Accrued expenses:		
Salaries and wages	128,988	122,704
Taxes, other than income taxes	78,586	69,310
Other	120,823	79,542
Accrued income taxes	20,078	13,966
Total current liabilities	1,002,792	882,096
Other Liabilities		
Long-term debt:		
Short-term borrowings to be refinanced	75,755	
Senior debt	462,662	372,816
Convertible subordinated debt		50,000
Obligations under capital leases	146,788	134,523
Deferred federal income taxes	148,699	135,253
Employees' benefit fund	21,810	23,131
Total other liabilities	855,714	715,723
Total Liabilities	1,858,506	1,597,819
SHAREOWNERS' EQUITY		
Convertible preferred capital stock,		
Cumulative, voting, par $100		
Authorized: 5,000,000 shares		
Issued: 1982—500,000, 9% Series B shares		
1981—500,000, 9% Series B shares	50,000	50,000
Common capital stock, par $1, at stated value		
Authorized: 50,000,000 shares		
Issued: 1982—30,634,966 shares		
1981—28,280,429 shares	164,778	100,083
Accumulated earnings	763,199	673,740
	977,977	823,823
Common stock in treasury, at cost		
1982—2,635,824 shares		
1981— 287,873 shares	(98,749)	(4,509)
Net unrealized loss on marketable equity securities	(8,175)	(11,843)
Total Shareowners' Equity	871,053	807,471
Total Liabilities and Shareowners' Equity	$ 2,729,559	$ 2,405,290

CONSOLIDATED STATEMENT OF EARNINGS

(In thousands of dollars, except per share amounts) Years Ended January 1, 1983, January 2, 1982 and January 3, 1981

	1982 (52 Weeks)	1981 (52 Weeks)	1980 (53 Weeks)
Sales	$ 11,901,892	$ 11,266,520	$ 10,316,741
Costs and Expenses:			
Merchandise costs, including warehousing and transportation	9,048,038	8,645,000	8,011,872
Operating, general and administrative expenses	2,323,996	2,152,155	1,901,178
Rent	168,050	144,002	130,632
Depreciation and amortization	120,874	103,816	86,166
Dividend and interest income	(25,744)	(18,520)	(11,403)
Interest expense, including interest on obligations under capital leases	58,720	45,778	35,736
Total	11,693,934	11,072,231	10,154,181
Earnings from continuing operations before taxes based on income	207,958	194,289	162,560
Taxes based on income	64,200	64,805	59,774
Earnings from continuing operations	143,758	129,484	102,786
Loss from discontinued operations		(1,439)	(8,400)
Net earnings	$ 143,758	$ 128,045	$ 94,386
Earnings (loss) per share:			
Primary:			
From continuing operations	$4.84	$4.56	$3.71
From discontinued operations		(.05)	(.30)
Net earnings	$4.84	$4.51	$3.41
Fully diluted:			
From continuing operations	$4.64	$4.43	$3.71
From discontinued operations		(.05)	(.30)
Net earnings	$4.64	$4.38	$3.41

The accompanying notes are an integral part of the consolidated financial statements.

CONSOLIDATED STATEMENT OF CHANGES IN FINANCIAL POSITION

(In thousands of dollars) Years Ended January 1, 1983, January 2, 1982 and January 3, 1981

	1982 (52 Weeks)	1981 (52 Weeks)	1980 (53 Weeks)
Cash Provided (Used) Through Current Operations:			
Net earnings	$ 143,758	$ 128,045	$ 94,386
Loss from discontinued operations		1,439	8,400
Earnings from continuing operations	143,748	129,484	102,786
Charges not involving cash:			
Depreciation and amortization	120,874	103,816	86,166
Provision for deferred federal income taxes	13,446	20,578	13,091
Tax benefit from discontinued operations			18,000
Loss on marketable investment securities	405		94
Write-off of excess of cost of investment over equity in net assets	12,294		
Earnings and non-cash expenses	290,777	253,878	220,137
Increase in current cost of inventory	(157,427)	(66,148)	(44,986)
LIFO charge	18,529	30,470	50,416
Decrease (increase) in other current assets	(35,630)	13,402	(58,788)
Decrease in notes payable		(14,700)	(2,325)
Increase in other current liabilities	120,696	96,295	95,954
Cash provided from current operations	236,945	313,197	260,408
Cash Provided (Used) Through Financing Activities:			
Cash dividends paid	(54,299)	(44,734)	(38,768)
Preferred stock issued		50,000	
Common stock issued	62,793	1,937	1,227
Short-term borrowings to be refinanced	75,755		
Additions to long-term debt and obligations under capital leases	159,025	194,303	77,946
Reductions of long-term debt and obligations under capital leases	(106,914)	(22,929)	(31,973)
Net book value of fixed asset disposals	46,943	11,126	9,981
Increase in properties held for resale	(40,483)	(25,275)	
Capital expenditures	(388,575)	(260,218)	(239,130)
Treasury shares exchanged for assets	(95,882)		
Increase in leased property under capital leases	(16,600)	(21,893)	(15,596)
Other changes, net	(6,658)	(7,129)	(6,457)
Cash used through financing activities	(364,895)	(124,812)	(242,770)
Increase (Decrease) In Cash And Temporary Cash Investments	(127,950)	188,385	17,638
Cash and temporary cash investments:			
Beginning of year	281,257	92,872	75,234
End of year	$ 153,307	$ 281,257	$ 92,872

The accompanying notes are an integral part of the consolidated financial statements.

CONSOLIDATED STATEMENT OF SHAREOWNERS' EQUITY

(In thousands of dollars) Years Ended January 1, 1983, January 2, 1982
and January 3, 1981

| | Preferred Stock | |
| | Issued | |
	Shares	Amount
Balance, December 29, 1979		
Net earnings for the year		
Dividends on common stock, $1.40 per share		
Exercise of stock options		
Decrease in net unrealized loss on marketable equity securities		
Stock contributed to employee stock ownership plan		
Tax benefit from exercise of non-qualified stock options		
Dividends reinvested under stock purchase plan		
Balance, January 3, 1981		
Net earnings for the year		
Issuance of preferred capital stock	500,000	$50,000
Dividends on preferred stock		
Dividends on common stock, $1.57 per share		
Exercise of stock options		
Increase in net unrealized loss on marketable equity securities		
Stock contributed to employee stock ownership plan and others		
Tax benefit from exercise of non-qualified stock options		
Dividends reinvested under stock purchase plan		
Balance, January 2, 1982	500,000	50,000
Net earnings for the year		
Dividends on preferred stock		
Dividends on common stock, $1.76 per share		
Exercise of stock options		
Stock issued in exchange for debt		
Stock issued for conversion of debentures		
Treasury shares exchanged for assets		
Decrease in net unrealized loss on marketable equity securities		
Stock contributed to employee stock ownership plan and others		
Tax benefit from exercise of non-qualified stock options		
Dividends reinvested under stock purchase plan		
Balance, January 1, 1983	500,000	$50,000

The accompanying notes are an integral part of the consolidated financial statements.

| Common Stock | | | | Accumulated Earnings | Valuation Allowance | Total Shareowners' Equity |
| Issued | | In Treasury | | | | |
Shares	Amount	Shares	Amount			
28,038,187	$ 94,749	(426,660)	$ (6,534)	$534,811	$(11,698)	$611,328
				94,386		94,386
				(38,768)		(38,768)
89,680	903					903
					1,559	1,559
	417	56,259	862			1,279
	355					355
15,005	324					324
28,142,872	96,748	(370,401)	(5,672)	590,429	(10,139)	671,366
				128,045		128,045
						50,000
				(963)		(963)
				(43,771)		(43,771)
103,154	1,116	(15,474)	(371)			745
					(1,704)	(1,704)
	629	98,002	1,534			2,163
	769					769
34,403	821					821
28,280,429	100,083	(287,873)	(4,509)	673,740	(11,843)	807,471
				143,758		143,758
				(4,500)		(4,500)
				(49,799)		(49,799)
415,246	5,592	(31,202)	(995)			4,597
205,966	5,939					5,939
1,710,000	50,498					50,498
		(2,398,702)	(95,882)			(95,882)
					3,668	3,668
58	404	81,953	2,637			3,041
	1,498					1,498
23,267	764					764
30,634,966	$164,778	(2,635,824)	$(98,749)	$763,199	$ (8,175)	$871,053

	1982 (52 Weeks)	1981 (52 Weeks)	1980 (53 Weeks)
	(In millions of dollars)		
Sales:			
Food Business	$ 11,186	$ 10,584	$ 9,682
Drug Stores	716	683	635
Total	$ 11,902	$ 11,267	$ 10,317
Operating Profit:			
Food Business	$ 263.0(a)	$ 244.6	$ 198.4
Drug Stores	15.2	6.5(b)	9.8
Total	278.2	251.1	208.2
Unallocated Expenses:			
Corporate expenses, net	11.5	11.0	9.9
Interest expense	58.7	45.8	35.7
Total	70.2	56.8	45.6
Earnings from continuing operations before taxes based on income	208.0	194.3	162.6
Taxes based on income	64.2	64.8	59.8
Earnings from continuing operations	$ 143.8	$ 129.5	$ 102.8
Identifiable Assets:			
Food Business	$2,124.5	$1,921.4	$1,634.8
Drug Stores	239.6	203.0	208.6
Other unallocated	365.5	280.9	155.1
	$2,729.6	$2,405.3	$1,998.5
Capital Expenditures:			
Food Business	$ 347.6	$ 234.0	$ 224.5
Drug Stores	$ 20.9	$ 15.8	$ 13.2
Depreciation and Amortization:			
Food Business	$ 112.2	$ 96.6	$ 80.0
Drug Stores	$ 5.8	$ 5.2	$ 4.3

(a) Food Business Operating Profit includes a gain of $14.2 million resulting from the store closing program.

(b) Drug Stores Operating Profit includes a gain of $4.3 million resulting from the sale of 21 stores.

QUARTERLY DATA (Unaudited) Quarterly sales, merchandise costs (including warehouse and transportation), net earnings and fully diluted net earnings per share for 1982 and 1981 were:

Quarter	Sales In Millions		Merchandise Costs In Millions		Net Earnings In Millions		Net Earnings Per Share	
	1982	1981	1982	1981	1982	1981	1982	1981
1st (12 Weeks)	$ 2,689	$ 2,483	$2,057	$1,917	$ 20.3	$ 16.3	$ .66	$ .59
2nd (12 Weeks)	2,810	2,589	2,138	1,991	35.9	28.6	1.15	.98
3rd (16 Weeks)	3,611	3,453	2,743	2,658	37.8	30.5	1.24	1.05
4th (12 Weeks)	2,792	2,742	2,110	2,079	49.8	52.6	1.64	1.70
Total	$11,902	$11,267	$9,048	$8,645	$143.8	$128.0	$4.64	$4.38

—Earnings per share for the year is not equal to the sum of each quarter's earnings per share. See earnings per share note.

—1982 net earnings were increased $6,500,000 in the third quarter (21¢ per share) and $7,100,000 in the fourth quarter (23¢ per share) due to the disposal of certain stores and other properties.

—1981 net earnings were reduced $786,000 in the third quarter (3¢ per share) and $653,000 in the fourth quarter (2¢ per share) for losses resulting from the disposal of the Company's investments in the amusement park business.

The LIFO method of valuing inventories reduced net earnings as follows:

(In thousands of dollars except per share figures)

	1982		1981	
	Net Earnings	Net Earnings Per Share	Net Earnings	Net Earnings Per Share
1st Quarter	$ 4,114	$ .13	$ 6,072	$ .22
2nd Quarter	4,442	.14	5,764	.20
3rd Quarter	2,953	.10	7,532	.25
4th Quarter	(1,504)	(.05)	(2,914)	(.09)
	$10,005	$ .32	$16,454	$ .56

	Common Stock Price Range				Dividends Paid Per Share of Common Stock		
	1982		1981				
	High	Low	High	Low	Date Paid	1982	1981
1st Quarter	29½	23⅜	27¼	19¼	March 1	$ .43	$ .38
2nd Quarter	32⅝	28½	27⅞	23	June 1	.43	.38
3rd Quarter	47¼	31⅛	25⅛	19¼	September 1	.43	.38
4th Quarter	47⅛	36⅛	27⅛	21¼	December 1	.47	.43
						$1.76	$1.57

Main trading market—New York Stock Exchange
  (Symbol KR)
Number of shareowners at year end
  1982—36,198
  1981—37,549

Accounting Policies

The following is a summary of the significant accounting policies followed in preparing the financial statements which are not presented elsewhere in the notes. These policies conform to generally accepted accounting principles and have been consistently applied.

Principles of Consolidation

The consolidated financial statements include the Company and all of its subsidiaries except a wholly-owned life insurance subsidiary formed in 1982, which is included on the equity basis. Partially-owned affiliated companies are included in the financial statements on the equity basis. Certain amounts in the financial statements for prior years have been reclassified to conform to the 1982 presentation.

Marketable Investment Securities

Marketable investment securities consist of bonds, notes, and common and preferred stocks held for investment. Dividend and interest income are accrued as earned. The cost of marketable investment securities sold is determined on the specific identification method.

Marketable equity securities (common and preferred stocks) are carried at the lower of cost or market. A valuation allowance, representing the excess of cost over market of these equity securities, is included in shareowners' equity. Other marketable investment securities (bonds and notes) are carried at cost unless there is a permanent impairment of value, at which time the securities are valued at market. In management's opinion there is no indication of a permanent loss in value of the portfolio and there is no present intention to liquidate the securities at less than cost.

Property, Plant and Equipment

Property, plant and equipment are stated at cost. Depreciation and amortization, which include the amortization of assets recorded under capital leases, are computed principally on the straight-line basis. Buildings and land improvements are depreciated based on lives varying from twenty to forty years and equipment based on lives varying from three to fifteen years. Leasehold improvements are being amortized over their useful lives, which generally approximate twelve and one-half years.

Excess of Cost of Investments in Consolidated Subsidiaries Over Equities in Net Assets

The excess of cost of investments in consolidated subsidiaries over equities in net assets at dates of acquisition originating prior to November, 1970, is not being amortized because, in the opinion of management, there has been no decrease in value. Amounts arising after October, 1970, are not significant and are being amortized on the straight-line basis over forty years.

Capitalization of Interest

Interest attributed to funds used to finance major capital expenditures is capitalized as an additional cost of the related assets. Capitalization of interest ceases when the related assets are substantially complete and ready for their intended use.

Deferred Federal Income Taxes and Investment Tax Credits

Deferred federal income taxes consist primarily of the amount of tax applicable to the excess of depreciation for tax purposes over depreciation used for financial reporting purposes less the amount of tax applicable to the unfunded pension liability.

Investment tax credits are included as reductions of income tax expense in the years in which the credits arise.

The cost of tax benefits purchased as a result of the Company's participation in safe harbor leases is included in Other Investments and is subsequently reduced for the amount of these tax benefits utilized by the Company. Tax benefits purchased had no material effect on income tax expense or net earnings.

Property Held for Resale

Property held for resale represents the cost of certain land and buildings committed by the Company for sale and leaseback during the next year and on which title has not transferred to a purchaser.

Discontinued Operations

In 1980, the Company decided to dispose of its investments in the amusement park business. The Company and Taft Broadcasting Company (Taft) had been 50% joint-owners of Family Leisure Centers, Inc. (FLC), which operated the Carowinds and Kings Dominion amusement parks, and the Hanna-Barbera's Marineland amusement park. A reorganization of FLC during 1980 resulted in the Company increasing its ownership to 81% from 50% and Taft becoming the sole owner of Carowinds. Under a subsequent agreement, the Company sold the Kings Dominion assets to Taft for one million shares of Taft Series B preferred stock (Series B Stock) with a par value of $20 per share with an estimated value of $17,800. The Series B Stock, which is included in Other Investments at January 1, 1983, receives an annual dividend of $1.38 per share. Beginning in 1982, Taft is redeeming the Series B Stock in varying amounts, with all shares to be redeemed by 1993. The sale of the Kings Dominion assets provided approximately $18,000 in tax benefits. The loss on discontinued operations, after deducting anticipated tax benefits, was provided at January 3, 1981, to reflect the estimated net realizable value of the Company's investments in amusement parks.

During 1981, the Company sold its interest in the Hanna-Barbera's Marineland amusement park. The amount of loss on discontinued operations in 1981 represents the excess of the actual loss on discontinued operations over the amount estimated at January 3, 1981.

Inventories

Inventories are stated at the lower of cost (principally LIFO) or market. Approximately 71% of inventories for 1982 and 72% of inventories for 1981 were valued using the LIFO method. Cost for the balance of the inventories was determined by the FIFO method of inventory valuation.

The Company uses the LIFO method of valuing certain of its grocery inventories to minimize inflation-induced inventory profits and to achieve a better matching of current costs with current revenues. Supplemental FIFO information (net earnings plus the after-tax effect of the LIFO change) is presented to permit a more complete comparison to various other companies. Earnings and earnings per share on a FIFO basis for the three fiscal years ended January 1, 1983 were:

	From Continuing Operations		Net Earnings	Net Earnings Per Share
	Earnings	Per Share		
		(fully diluted)		(fully diluted)
1982	$153,763	$4.96	$153,763	$4.96
1981	$145,938	$4.99	$144,498	$4.93
1980	$130,011	$4.70	$121,611	$4.39

Marketable Investment Securities

Marketable investment securities consist of:

	1982	1981
Equity securities, at cost	$ 15,015	$ 26,762
Less valuation allowance charged against shareowners' equity	(6,541)	(11,843)
Equity securities, at market	8,474	14,919
Bonds and notes, at cost	429	853
	$ 8,903	$ 15,772

The valuation allowance included in shareowners' equity includes the excess of cost over market, amounting to $1,634, of the marketable equity securities owned by a subsidiary accounted for on the equity basis.

Debt Obligations

Long-term debt as of January 1, 1983 and January 2, 1982 consists of:

	1982	1981
Short-term borrowings to be refinanced:	$ 75,755	
Senior debt:		
14⅜% notes maturing in 1991	50,000	$ 50,000
12⅜% sinking fund debentures maturing in 2005, with annual payments of $2,500 required from 1988 through 2004	50,000	50,000
9⅞% notes maturing in 1983	32,224	33,284
9% sinking fund debentures maturing in 1995, with annual payments of $2,500 required from 1985 through 1995	26,325	27,248
8.7% sinking fund debentures maturing in 1998, with annual payments of $3,000 required from 1985 through 1998	41,145	45,189
8½% sinking fund debentures maturing in 2001, with annual payments of $2,500 required from 1986 through 2001	38,717	42,217
6⅜% to 14¼% industrial revenue bonds, with annual payments due in varying amounts through 2022	239,185	100,685
4½% to 9½% secured notes, with annual payments due in varying amounts through 2004	26,643	27,474
	504,239	376,097
Less amount due within one year	(41,577)	(3,281)
Total senior debt	462,662	372,816
Subordinated debt:		
10¼% convertible subordinated sinking fund debentures		50,000
Total long-term debt	$538,417	$422,816

The aggregate annual maturities and required payments of long-term debt for the five years subsequent to 1982 are:

1983	$41,577
1984	$ 4,165
1985	$ 8,882
1986	$18,312
1987	$29,292

Under certain of the loan agreements, payments of cash dividends are limited. Under the most limiting agreement, accumulated earnings were unrestricted in the amount of $234,000 at January 1, 1983.

The 10¼% convertible subordinated sinking fund debentures were called for redemption during 1982. These debentures were converted into 1,710,000 shares of common stock at a conversion price of $29.24 per share.

The Company periodically engages in short-term borrowing. Short-term borrowing for the three years ended January 1, 1983 was:

	1982	1981	1980
Weighted average for the year	$ 36,331	$16,412	$ 8,907
Highest level outstanding during the year	$188,351	$73,265	$31,779
Weighted average interest rate	9.50%	16.0%	13.9%

The Company intends to refinance on a long-term basis during 1983, the $75,755 of short-term borrowings outstanding at January 1, 1983.

At January 1, 1983, the Company had available a revolving credit aggregating $250,000 against which it may obtain interim loans until March, 1988. The interest rate on the interim loans would vary between The First National Bank of Chicago corporate base rate, and 100¾% of this rate. The interim loans may be converted into term loans payable over six years. No amounts have been borrowed under this agreement.

Interest costs capitalized in 1982, 1981 and 1980 amounted to $7,655, $4,351 and $1,327, respectively.

Leases

The Company operates principally in leased premises. Lease terms generally range from ten to twenty-five years with options of renewal for additional periods.

Options provide in some cases for reduced rentals and/or the right to purchase. Certain of the leases provide for contingent payments based upon a percent of sales.

Rent expense (under operating leases) consists of:

	1982	1981	1980
Minimum rentals, net of minor sublease rentals	$154,128	$130,838	$118,404
Contingent payments	13,922	13,164	12,228
Total	$168,050	$144,002	$130,632

Assets recorded under capital leases consist of:

	1982	1981
Distribution and manufacturing facilities	$102,966	$ 97,216
Store facilities	86,665	76,264
Less accumulated amortization	(51,985)	(46,412)
	$137,646	$127,068

Minimum annual rentals, net of sublease rentals under operating leases of $237,661, for the five years subsequent to 1982 and in the aggregate are:

	Capital Leases	Operating Leases
1983	$ 20,500	$ 162,060
1984	20,098	156,124
1985	19,560	150,094
1986	18,806	145,815
1987	18,691	143,264
1988 and thereafter	281,089	1,564,386
	378,744	$2,321,743
Less estimated executory costs included in capital leases	(23,603)	
Net minimum lease payments under capital leases	355,141	
Less amount representing interest	(203,998)	
Present value of net minimum lease payments under capital leases	$151,143	

Convertible Preferred Stock

In 1981, the Company entered into a financing arrangement with an investor company to own jointly a subsidiary, Kroco, Inc. (Kroco), which was formed in 1981. The Company contributed $50,000 of plant, inventories and cash to Kroco in exchange for 100% of Kroco's common stock with a 20% voting interest, $20,000 of Kroco non-voting 7% preferred stock and a $20,000 Kroco 9% convertible debenture. The investor company invested $50,000 in cash in exchange for the 9% cumulative voting preferred stock of Kroco with an 80% voting interest. In January, 1982, Kroco invested $50,000 in 500,000 shares of the Company's cumulative convertible preferred stock with a 9% dividend rate, the holders of which are entitled to one vote per share. The voting preferred stock of Kroco may be exchanged for the Company's 9% cumulative convertible preferred stock held by Kroco which is convertible into the Company's common stock at a price of $38.26 per share declining to $33.15 per share in January, 1985. The convertible debenture held by the Company can be converted after October 31, 1986, or prior thereto upon the occurrence of certain events, into Kroco common shares which would result in the Company having two-thirds voting control of Kroco.

The Company and Kroco formed a partnership BHK, Ltd. (BHK) as part of the financing arrangement. Kroco contributed the plant, inventories and cash received from the Company for a 90% limited partnership interest. The Company contributed $11,000 of plant and inventories for a 10% general partnership interest.

As the general partner, the Company accounts for its interest in BHK using the consolidation method of accounting. The investment in Kroco is accounted for using the equity basis. The Company's equity in the earnings of Kroco, $51,817 in 1982 and $8,932 in 1981, is reported on a pre-tax basis and is offset by $53,210 in 1982 and $7,758 in 1981, which represents the minority interest in the earnings of BHK. The Kroco earnings include $1,393 of net interest expense in 1982 and $1,174 of net interest income in 1981. Also, the minority interest in the net assets of BHK, $99,666 at January 1, 1983, has been netted against the Company's investment in Kroco, $99,447 at January 1, 1983, in the Company's consolidated balance sheet so that the consolidated balance sheet reflects the Company's interest in the various assets owned by BHK. As the investor company owns 80% of the voting control of Kroco and includes the taxable income of Kroco in its consolidated tax return, the tax expense of Kroco included in the Company's financial statements represents amounts payable to the investor company under a tax allocation agreement. The net effect of this financing arrangement was to generate cash and increase equity by $50,000.

A Director of the Company is President and a Director of the investor company and another Director of the Company is also a Director of the investor company.

Stock Option Plans

At January 1, 1983, options were outstanding to purchase 1,129,029 shares of common stock under the 1969, 1976, and 1981 Stock Option Plans (of which options on 627,569 shares were exercisable at that date) at prices ranging from $7.78 to $42.44 a share. Each option outstanding was granted at an option price equal to the fair market value of the stock at the date of grant. No further options may be granted under the 1969 Plan. Options may be granted under the 1976 and 1981 Plans until 1986 and 1991, respectively. At January 1, 1983, shares of common stock available for future options under the 1976 and 1981 Plans amounted to 5,713 and 487,200 shares, respectively.

Changes in options outstanding under the Stock Option Plans of the Company were:

	Shares Subject To Option	Option Price Range Per Share
Outstanding, December 29, 1979	964,323	$ 7.78–$25.06
Granted	249,000	$16.63–$22.00
Exercised	(89,680)	$ 7.78–$17.94
Cancelled or expired	(7,505)	$12.85–$19.75
Outstanding, January 3, 1981	1,116,138	$ 7.78–$25.06
Granted	342,600	$20.31–$25.44
Exercised	(103,154)	$ 7.78–$19.75
Cancelled or expired	(25,889)	$ 7.91–$21.25
Outstanding, January 2, 1982	1,329,695	$ 7.78–$25.44
Granted	227,000	$25.19–$42.44
Exercised	(415,246)	$ 7.78–$26.81
Cancelled or expired	(12,420)	$ 7.78–$25.44
Outstanding, January 1, 1983	1,129,029	$ 7.78–$42.44

The stock option plans provide for the exercise of options by exchanging issued shares of stock of the Company in lieu of cash payments.

The Company has a Stock Appreciation Rights Plan available to certain officers. In general, the eligible optionees are permitted to surrender the related option and receive cash and shares of the Company's common stock having a value equal to the appreciation on the shares subject to the option. The appreciation of Stock Appreciation Rights is charged to earnings based upon the market values of common stock. At January 1, 1983, no Stock Appreciation Rights were outstanding.

Under the Company's dividend reinvestment plan, shareowners of record may purchase additional shares of common stock by reinvesting dividends and/or making optional cash investments.

Taxes Based on Income

The provision for taxes based on income consists of:

	1982	1981	1980
Federal			
Current	$11,688	$25,987	$31,796
Deferred	13,446	20,578	13,091
	25,134	46,565	44,887
State and Local			
Current	15,200	14,243	14,887
Payments in lieu of federal income taxes	23,866	3,997	
Total	$64,200	$64,805	$59,774

Investment and other tax credits reduced the tax provision by $27,007 in 1982, $27,652 in 1981 and $18,217 in 1980.

Payments in lieu of federal income taxes represent the estimated amounts payable to Baldwin-United Corporation under a tax allocation agreement. See Convertible Preferred Stock note.

A reconciliation of the statutory federal rate and the effective rate is as follows:

	1982	1981	1980
Statutory rate	46.0%	46.0%	46.0%
State income taxes, net of federal tax benefit	3.9	4.0	4.9
Investment and other tax credits	(13.0)	(14.2)	(11.2)
Write-off of excess of cost of investment over equity in net assets	2.7		
Capital gains	(6.0)		
Other, net	(2.7)	(2.4)	(2.9)
Effective rate	30.9%	33.4%	36.8%

Deferred federal income taxes included in the Consolidated Statement of Earnings consist of:

	1982	1981	1980
The tax effect of amounts expensed (included in earnings) for tax purposes in excess of amounts used for financial reporting:			
Depreciation	$26,419	$19,831	$11,785
Excess pension contribution	(4,911)	(410)	475
Other	(8,062)	1,157	831
	$13,446	$20,578	$13,091

Pension Plans

The Company has three non-contributory retirement plans for eligible employees, two of which have historically been funded. The third retirement plan, which was previously unfunded, is being funded over a period of forty years beginning in 1976. The Company also contributes to multi-employer plans jointly administered by management and union representatives. The total pension expense for 1982, 1981 and 1980 was $98,143, $94,658, and $85,587, respectively. Past service costs of the Company's plans are amortized over periods ranging from thirty to forty years.

As a result of changes in actual plan experience, several actuarial assumptions used in calculating pension expense were changed in 1982. The most significant change was to increase the assumed rate of return on investments from 6½% to 7½%. The net effect of these changes was to reduce 1982 pension expense by $5,725.

Accumulated plan benefits and plan net assets for the Company administered plans were:

	January 1, 1982	January 1, 1981
Actuarial present value of accumulated plan benefits:		
Vested	$203,581	$198,181
Nonvested	19,366	19,395
	$222,947	$217,576
Net assets available for benefits	$242,382	$208,241

The weighted average assumed rate of return used in determining the actuarial present value of accumulated plan benefits was increased effective January 1, 1982 from 6½% to 7½%, resulting in a decrease in the actuarial present value of accumulated plan benefits of $28,423.

Information with respect to the actuarial present value of accumulated plan benefits and net assets available for benefits relating to the multi-employer plans was not available.

Earnings Per Share

Primary earnings per share for 1982 and 1981 equal net earnings divided by the weighted average number of common and dilutive common equivalent shares outstanding during the year. Common stock equivalents include shares issuable upon exercise of outstanding stock options and conversion of the Company's cumulative convertible preferred stock. Fully diluted earnings per share equals net earnings, after the elimination of interest expense, net of income tax effect, applicable to the Company's convertible debentures, divided by the weighted average number of common shares, dilutive common equivalent shares and shares issuable upon conversion of the Company's convertible debentures. The weighted average number of shares of common stock outstanding for 1980 does not include common equivalent shares because the resulting dilution of earnings per share of common stock was not material.

The average number of shares used to compute earnings per share was:

	Primary	Fully Diluted
1982	29,687	31,392
1981	28,369	29,726
1980	27,681	27,681

Earnings per share for a quarter is based on the average number of primary and fully diluted shares outstanding or assumed to be outstanding during the quarter. Earnings per share for a year is based on an average of each quarter's average of shares outstanding or assumed to be outstanding for primary earnings per share and on an average for the year of shares outstanding or assumed to be outstanding for fully diluted earnings per share. The sum of each quarter's earnings per share may not equal earnings per share for the year.

Store Closing Program

During 1982, the Company adopted a plan to close approximately 140 stores by the end of 1983, including all Market Basket stores located in southern California, as part of the Company's continuing review of underproductive assets. Net earnings for 1982 included a gain of $14,200 or $.45 per share resulting from the actual and anticipated proceeds from the disposal of these properties offset by the net book value of assets sold or written-off and the known and anticipated operating losses and closing costs associated with the properties included in the plan. At January 1, 1983, 101 stores had been disposed of and a $13,000 allowance was established to provide for estimated future costs to be incurred in connection with the disposal of the remaining properties. These costs include operating costs to the date of closing, loss on investment, and post closing costs such as rental payments, property taxes and maintenance.

Proceeds received in connection with the disposal of certain of the Market Basket stores included 1,656,309 shares of the Company's outstanding common stock valued at $66,599. An additional 742,393 shares of common stock were purchased by the Company out of additional proceeds from the store closing program.

Litigation

There are pending against the Company various claims and lawsuits arising in the normal course of business, including suits charging violations of certain antitrust and civil rights laws. Some of these suits purport or have been determined to be class actions and/or seek substantial damages. Any damages that may be awarded in antitrust cases will be automatically trebled.

Seventeen antitrust suits alleging, among other things, price fixing in the purchase and sale of meat have been consolidated for pretrial and discovery purposes in the United States District Court in Dallas. The Company is named as a defendant in sixteen of these suits. The Court has entered orders dismissing all damage claims in all seventeen suits. In July and August 1982, the orders and judgments of the Court dismissing such damage claims were appealed by the plaintiffs to the Fifth Circuit Court of Appeals.

Although the amount of liability with respect to all claims and lawsuits cannot be ascertained, the Company is of the opinion that any resulting liability will not have a material effect on the Company's financial position.

Business Combination

On January 25, 1983, Dillon Companies, Inc. (Dillon) became a wholly-owned subsidiary of the Company.

Dillon is a multi-regional operator of supermarkets and convenience stores. Under the terms of the Agreement and Plan of Merger, the shareowners of Dillon received an aggregate 16.6 million shares of the Company's common stock. The merger will be accounted for as a pooling of interests in 1983, and the consolidated financial statements for prior years will be restated to reflect the combined companies.

The following tables summarize on an unaudited pro forma basis the combined financial position and results of operations of the combined companies for the periods indicated:

Pro Forma Combined Condensed Balance Sheet

	January 1, 1983	January 2, 1982
Assets		
Current assets		
Cash and short-term investments	$ 178,156	$ 325,557
Inventories	1,108,787	951,773
Other current assets	289,720	213,036
Total current assets	1,576,663	1,490,366
Notes receivable	25,834	15,059
Investments	44,645	40,949
Property, plant and equipment, net	1,610,693	1,339,626
Other assets	35,826	45,837
Total Assets	$3,293,661	$2,931,837
Liabilities		
Current liabilities		
Accounts payable and accrued expenses	$1,142,658	$1,057,965
Other current liabilities	60,202	20,469
Total current liabilities	1,202,860	1,078,434
Long-term debt	604,007	477,501
Obligations under capital leases	194,195	187,516
Other liabilities	206,255	188,337
Total Liabilities	2,207,317	1,931,788
Shareowners' Equity		
Convertible preferred capital stock, 9% Series B	50,000	50,000
Common stock, par $1, at stated value	350,627	264,407
Accumulated earnings	792,641	701,994
Common stock in treasury	(98,749)	(4,509)
Net unrealized loss on marketable equity securities	(8,175)	(11,843)
Total Shareowners' Equity	1,086,344	1,000,049
Total Liabilities and Shareowners' Equity	$3,293,661	$2,931,837

Pro Forma Statement of Earnings
(Combined on a Recast Basis)

	1982 (52 Weeks)	1981 (52 Weeks)	1980 (53 Weeks)
Sales	$14,761,764	$13,957,554	$12,616,082
Costs and expenses:			
Merchandise costs, including warehousing and transportation	11,264,943	10,743,133	9,815,389
Operating, general and administrative expenses	3,019,306	2,777,868	2,448,780
Depreciation and amortization	149,754	130,689	110,202
Dividend, interest and other income	(33,277)	(30,327)	(18,467)
Interest expense including interest on obligations under capital leases	69,818	55,583	44,662
Total	14,470,544	13,676,946	12,400,566
Earnings from continuing operations before taxes based on income	291,220	280,608	215,516
Taxes based on income	99,096	103,300	81,626
Earnings from continuing operations	192,124	177,308	133,890
Loss from discontinued operations		(1,439)	(8,400)
Net earnings	$ 192,124	$ 175,869	$ 125,490
Earnings per share:			
Primary:			
From continuing operations	$4.15	$3.95	$3.03
Net earnings	$4.15	$3.91	$2.84
Fully diluted			
From continuing operations	$4.05	$3.87	$3.03
Net earnings	$4.05	$3.84	$2.84

Dillon's fiscal year is based on a 52–53 week year ending the Saturday nearest to June 30. However, the preceding pro forma data of the combined companies includes the results of operations of Dillon recast to coincide with the Company's fiscal year. If the pro forma data was prepared using the fiscal year of Dillon combined with the fiscal year of Kroger, the results, which are not significantly different, would have been:

Pro Forma Combined Summary of Earnings
(Combined on a Fiscal Year Basis)

	1982	1981	1980
	(52 Weeks)	(52 Weeks)	(53 Weeks)
Sales	$14,725,566	$13,761,097	$12,394,006
Net earnings	$ 194,339	$ 168,398	$ 120,496
Net earnings per share (fully diluted)	$4.09	$3.68	$2.72

The pro forma per share computations are based on the exchange ratio of .8539 of a share of the Company's common stock for each share of Dillon common stock. The pro forma information is not necessarily indicative of results which would have occurred if the companies had actually been combined for the periods presented.

On January 25, 1983, shareowners also approved an amendment to the Company's Amended Articles of Incorporation increasing the number of authorized shares of Common Stock from 50 million to 125 million shares.

Segments of Business

The Company's segments of business information for 1982, 1981 and 1980 is included on page [1300].

Changing Prices (Unaudited)

The Company's information regarding the impact of changing prices on a constant dollar and current cost basis is presented on pages [1312–1315].

REPORT OF INDEPENDENT CERTIFIED PUBLIC ACCOUNTANTS

To the Shareowners and Board of Directors
The Kroger Co.

We have examined the consolidated balance sheets of The Kroger Co. and Consolidated Subsidiary Companies as of January 1, 1983 and January 2, 1982, and the related consolidated statements of earnings, shareowners' equity, and changes in financial position for the years ended January 1, 1983, January 2, 1982 and January 3, 1981. Our examinations were made in accordance with generally accepted auditing standards and, accordingly, included such tests of the accounting records and such other auditing procedures as we considered necessary in the circumstances.

In our opinion, the financial statements referred to above present fairly the consolidated financial position of The Kroger Co. and Consolidated Subsidiary Companies at January 1, 1983 and January 2, 1982, and the consolidated results of their operations and changes in their financial position for the years ended January 1, 1983, January 2, 1982 and January 3, 1981, in conformity with generally accepted accounting principles applied on a consistent basis.

Coopers & Lybrand

Coopers & Lybrand
Cincinnati, Ohio
February 18, 1983

In an effort to produce financial information that discloses the effects of inflation, the Financial Accounting Standards Board (FASB) issued Statement No. 33, Financial Reporting and Changing Prices, which requires companies to explain the effect of inflationary factors on their operations by adjusting historical financial information using two different methods. This information includes disclosures about the effects of changes in both general inflation (constant dollars) and specific prices (current cost).

The constant dollar method measures the effect of the general rate of inflation on the Company's earnings, by expressing certain historical cost amounts in units of the same purchasing power as measured by the Consumer Price Index for All Urban Consumers (CPI-U). This measure of general inflation encompasses a wide range of commodities and is not necessarily representative of the inflation effect upon our business. The current cost method attempts to reflect the changes in prices of the resources employed specifically in our operations. These methods involve the use of assumptions, approximations and estimates. The results should not be viewed as precise measurements of the effects of inflation.

Earnings derived under these methods include adjustments to merchandise costs and depreciation and amortization expense for these inflationary factors. The effects of inflation, on merchandise costs, have been recognized in the historical financial statements, to some extent, due to the use of the LIFO method of inventory valuation.

The accompanying statement of earnings and five-year summary of selected financial data were prepared to reflect those inflationary factors due to increases in the historical costs of merchandise and depreciation and amortization and their related assets. Amounts prior to 1982, have been adjusted to average 1982 dollars by use of the CPI-U.

The restated net assets result in an indicated increase in shareowners' equity which was greater on a general inflation basis than on a specific price basis. The gain from decline in purchasing power of net amounts owed is primarily attributable to the debt which has been used to finance inventories and capital expenditures. During a period of inflation, holders of monetary assets suffer an unrealized loss of general purchasing power, while holders of monetary liabilities experience an unrealized gain.

Both the constant dollar method and the current cost method result in lower net income than reported in the primary financial statements. Taxation of earnings under present tax law reduces the amount of earnings available to support future business growth because these changing prices adjustments are not deductible for income tax purposes. The effects of the higher taxation of earnings are demonstrated in the effective tax rates shown on the supplementary income statement.

CONSOLIDATED STATEMENT OF EARNINGS FROM CONTINUING OPERATIONS ADJUSTED FOR CHANGING PRICES

For the Year Ended January 1, 1983 (52 Weeks) (In thousands of dollars)

	As Reported In The Primary Statements (Historical Costs)	Adjusted For General Inflation (Average 1982 Constant Dollars)	Adjusted For Changes In Specific Prices (1982 Current Costs)
Sales	$11,902,000	$11,902,000	$11,902,000
Cost and Expenses:			
Merchandise costs, including warehousing and transportation	9,048,000	9,058,000	9,060,000
Operating, general and administrative expenses	2,324,000	2,324,000	2,324,000
Rent	168,000	168,000	168,000
Depreciation and amortization	121,000	146,000	158,000
Dividend and interest income	(26,000)	(26,000)	(26,000)
Interest expense, including interest on obligations under capital leases	59,000	59,000	59,000
Total	11,694,000	11,729,000	11,743,000
Earnings from continuing operations before taxes based on income	208,000	173,000	159,000
Taxes based on income	64,000	64,000	64,000
Earnings from continuing operations	$ 144,000	$ 109,000	$ 95,000
Effective tax rate—taxes based on income	30.9%	37.0%	40.3%
Gain from decline in purchasing power of net amounts owed		$ 51,000	$ 51,000
Decrease in specific prices of inventories and property, plant and equipment			$ (30,000)
Less effect of increase in general prices			102,000
Excess of decrease in specific prices over increase in general prices			$ (132,000)

At January 1, 1983 specific prices of inventories totaled $1,089,000 and specific prices of property, plant and equipment, net of accumulated depreciation totaled $1,731,000.

The adjustment to merchandise costs, including warehousing and transportation, in the supplemental income statements is less than one percent, which reflects the Company's use of the LIFO method of accounting for approximately 71% of its inventories. The difference results primarily from restating the remaining inventories to a current cost equivalent.

FIVE-YEAR COMPARISON OF SELECTED FINANCIAL DATA ADJUSTED FOR EFFECTS OF CHANGING PRICES

(In thousands of average 1982 dollars, except per share amounts)

	1982	1981	1980(a)	1979	1978
Sales	$11,902,000	11,958,000	12,085,000	12,008,000	11,582,000
Constant Dollar Data:					
Earnings from continuing operations	$ 109,000	93,000	49,000	46,000	16,000
Primary earnings per share from continuing operations	$ 3.68	3.28	1.76	1.65	.59
Net assets at year-end	$ 1,593,000	1,456,000	1,374,000	1,269,000	1,141,000
Current Cost Data:					
Earnings from continuing operations	$ 95,000	81,000	40,000	32,000	
Primary earnings per share from continuing operations	$ 3.21	2.87	1.46	1.17	
Net assets at year-end	$ 1,437,000	1,586,000	1,504,000	1,349,000	
Excess of increase or decrease in specific prices over increase in general prices	$ (132,000)	(90,000)	44,000	(12,000)	
General Information:					
Gain from decline in purchasing power of net amounts owed	$ 51,000	105,000	134,000	144,000	99,000
Dividends per share	$ 1.76	1.67	1.63	1.68	1.32
Market price per share at year-end	$ 38⅝	26⅝	24¼	23⅞	25⅜
Average consumer price index	289.1	272.4	246.8	217.4	195.4

(a) Fifty-three weeks

NOTES TO SUPPLEMENTARY DATA ON CHANGING PRICES

Accounting Policies

The supplementary data on changing prices is based upon the historical financial information as reported in the primary financial statements adjusted for (1) general inflationary factors relating to property, plant, and equipment and inventories and (2) the changes in specific prices relating to these items.

Depreciation expense was calculated using the same methods and rates of depreciation as used in the historical financial statements.

Income tax expense has not been modified for any timing differences, allocations or adjustments that may result from applying the different methods in preparing the supplementary data.

No attempt has been made to calculate the benefit derived from additional realization of selling price increases necessitated by a higher level of cost of oper-

ations resulting from the application of the constant dollar or current cost adjustments to the original historical cost of property, plant, and equipment and inventories.

Constant Dollars

The supplementary data on a constant dollar basis is expressed in average for the year dollars and reflects adjustments that have occurred in the purchasing power of the dollar as measured by the CPI-U published by the Bureau of Labor Statistics. These amounts do not purport to represent appraised values or any other measure of current value.

Current Cost

The current cost of inventories, and merchandise costs, represents the cost of purchasing the goods at year-end prices for inventory and prices in effect at date of sale for merchandise costs. They are estimated based upon the latest prices and information of merchandise costs available as of January 1, 1983.

The current cost of property, plant, and equipment and the related depreciation expense are estimates of what the Company's existing assets would cost at the respective balance sheet dates. The amounts for 1979, 1980 and 1981 have been adjusted to average 1982 dollars based on the CPI-U. Several methods, including indexation, direct pricing and application of square footage building and equipment costs based upon current merchandising and facility concepts, were used in estimating these amounts. These values represent the estimated current costs of existing assets and do not consider technological improvements and efficiencies associated with the normal replacement of productive capacity.

	1982	1981	1980
Operations (In thousands of dollars, except per share amounts)			
Sales	$11,901,892	11,266,520	10,316,741
Costs and Expenses	$11,693,934	11,072,231	10,154,181
Earnings from Continuing Operations before Taxes Based on Income	$ 207,958	194,289	162,560
Taxes Based on Income	$ 64,200	64,805	59,774
Earnings from Continuing Operations	$ 143,758	129,484	102,786
Discontinued Operations	$	(1,439)	(8,400)
Net Earnings	$ 143,758	128,045	94,386
Dividends on Common Stock	$ 49,799	43,771	38,768
Per Share			
Earnings From Continuing Operations	$ 4.64	4.43	3.71
Discontinued Operations	$	(.05)	(.30)
Net Earnings	$ 4.64	4.38	3.41
Dividends on Common Stock	$ 1.76	1.57	1.40
Balance Sheet Statistics (In thousands of dollars, except per share amounts)			
Inventories	$ 949,844	810,946	775,268
Working Capital	$ 362,610	396,245	241,904
Property, Plant and Equipment, net	$ 1,287,818	1,052,764	884,617
Total Assets	$ 2,729,559	2,405,290	1,998,494
Long-Term Debt	$ 538,417	422,816	268,146
Obligations under Capital Leases	$ 146,788	134,523	117,819
Shareowners' Equity	$ 871,053	807,471	671,366
Per Share of Common	$ 29.32	27.06	24.17
Other Statistics (In thousands of dollars, except stock prices)			
Cash Provided from Operations	$ 236,945	313,197	260,408
Capital Expenditures	$ 388,575	260,218	239,130
Rent	$ 168,050	144,002	130,632
Interest Expense	$ 58,720	45,778	35,736
Common Stock Price Range	$ 23⅜–47¼	19¼–27⅞	14–23¾
Retail Facilities (Areas in thousands of square feet)			
Food Stores			
Opened	101	111	118
Remodeled	85	57	49
Closed	160	98	107
Stores—End of Year	1,199	1,258	1,245
Total Area	37,142	36,985	34,529
Drug Stores			
Opened and Acquired	77	57	42
Closed	21	64	32
Stores—End of Year	563	507	514
Total Area	6,261	5,715	5,841

(a) In 1979, the Company changed from the First-In, First-Out (FIFO) method of valuing certain of its grocery inventories to the Last-In, First-Out (LIFO) method. (b) 1976 and 1980 were fifty-three-week years. (c) Amounts for 1973 were not restated for a change in accounting for leases and for the consolidation of previously unconsolidated subsidiaries. Restatement would not have a material effect on the amounts reported.

1979	1978	1977	1976	1975	1974	1973
9,029,315	7,828,071	6,747,553	6,182,991	5,421,296	4,893,384	4,319,960
8,882,807	7,674,815	6,640,881	6,097,816	5,362,417	4,811,772	4,266,267
146,508	153,256	106,672	85,175	58,879	81,612	53,693
60,787	68,660	46,649	37,250	24,822	36,729	23,777
85,721	84,596	60,023	47,925	34,057	44,883	29,916
85,721	84,596	60,023	47,925	34,057	44,883	29,916
34,524	24,218	20,551	18,577	18,298	18,088	17,461
3.13	3.11	2.22	1.78	1.26	1.66	1.11
3.13	3.11	2.22	1.78	1.26	1.66	1.11
1.26	.89	.76	.69	.68	.67	.65
780,698	697,327	623,645	558,347	500,110	490,640	438,219
264,537	308,677	294,157	298,528	216,524	158,418	229,095
725,220	621,292	570,989	544,472	534,979	526,439	344,088
1,786,691	1,653,029	1,528,721	1,445,302	1,302,049	1,269,045	1,077,517
233,937	223,736	238,892	259,561	213,085	164,498	151,471
106,055	105,131	96,077	94,343	85,110	80,998	
611,328	554,507	489,972	455,273	423,721	418,477	392,852
22.14	20.34	18.06	16.85	15.71	15.51	14.57
156,673	162,733	115,872	106,441	65,673	154,150	36,620
176,933	114,504	96,417	81,906	70,161	116,720	70,244
112,527	99,785	88,363	82,611	74,632	67,341	71,925
29,385	29,983	30,626	27,713	25,438	23,384	12,199
17½−27	12¾−18½	11⅝−14⅜	8⅞−12⅝	7⅞−12⅛	7⅛−12½	7½−12¼
88	104	98	90	71	83	80
91	58	35	33	40	84	68
56	90	83	137	92	127	160
1,234	1,202	1,188	1,173	1,220	1,241	1,285
32,460	30,673	28,642	26,850	26,415	25,594	24,706
38	7	11	20	56	64	36
21	48	41	13	27	35	19
504	487	528	558	551	522	493
5,657	5,591	6,108	6,399	6,234	5,633	4,883

INDEX

AAA (American Accounting Association), 19
AAERs (Accounting and Auditing Enforcement Releases), 18
Absorption costing, 295
Accelerated depreciation methods, 491– 494
Account balance, 158
Accounting: accrual basis, 37, 48, 82– 87, 163; cash versus accrual basis, 82– 84; constant dollar, 1235– 1245; controls, 245– 246; current cost, 1247– 1254; current cost/constant dollar, 1254– 1258; current value, 1245– 1254; cycle, 156– 157; defined, 3; exit value, 1247; financial, 3; present value, 1246– 1247; process, 156– 157; theory, 32
Accounting and Auditing Enforcement Releases (AAERs), 18
Accounting changes: entity, 825; estimates, 118– 119, 264, 514, 825, 837– 839; principle, 112– 113, 824– 825, 830– 837. *See also* Cumulative effect method; Current and prospective method; Restatement method
Accounting Interpretations of APB Opinions, 13; *Accounting Interpretation of APB Opinions Nos. 2 and 4*, 797; *Accounting Interpretation of APB Opinion No. 30*, 111
Accounting principles: broad, 43– 50; detailed, 50– 51. *See also* Generally accepted accounting principles
Accounting Principles Board (APB), 12– 14
Accounting Principles Board (APB) Opinions, 12. See under *APB Opinion No.* for specific opinions
Accounting Principles Board Statements. *See* APB Statements
Accounting Research Bulletins (ARBs), 12. See under *ARB No.* for specific bulletins
Accounting Research Study No. 1, 13
Accounting Research Study No. 2, 1018
Accounting Research Study No. 3, 13
Accounting Research Study No. 9, 787
Accounting Research Study No. 13, 311
Accounting Review, 19
Accounting Series Releases (ASRs), 17; *ASR No. 150*, 18

Accounting Standards Executive Committee (AcSEC), 16
Accounting Terminology Bulletins, 12; *Accounting Terminology Bulletin No. 1*, 12, 135– 136; *Accounting Terminology Bulletin No. 2*, 712
Accounting theory: assumptions, 39– 41; broad principles, 43– 50; concepts and elements, 41– 43; defined, 32; detailed principles, 50– 51; model, 34– 35; modifying conventions, 51– 54; objectives, 35– 37; qualitative characteristics, 37– 39
Accounts, 158
Accounts payable, 594– 595
Accounts receivable, 256– 270
Accounts receivable used to generate cash, 266– 270
Accrual basis of accounting, 37, 48, 82– 87, 163
Accruals, 165– 166
Accruals and deferrals compared, 167
Accrued expenses, 165– 166
Accrued revenues, 165
Acid test ratio. *See* Quick ratio
AcSEC (Accounting Standards Executive Committee), 16
Actuarial cost methods: accumulated benefits, 988; projected benefits (compensation), 989; projected benefits (years of service), 988; cost allocation (compensation), 989; cost allocation (years of service), 989
Actuarial gains and losses, 989– 993
Actuarial valuations, 978
Additional markup, 352
Additional paid-in capital, 128, 680– 681
Additions, 451
Adjunct account, 161
Adjusted trial balance, 170– 172
Adjusting entries: accumulating adjusting data, 164; classification of, 165; preparation of, 163– 170; purpose of, 164
Adjustments, 163
Administrative controls, 245– 246
Advances from customers, 600– 601
Adverse audit opinion, 9

AICPA (American Institute of Certified Public Accountants), 11

AICPA Code of Professional Ethics, 13

AICPA Industry Accounting Guides: "Accounting for Profit Recognition on Sales of Real Estate," 900, 950; "Accounting for Retail Land Sales," 901

All financial resources concept, 1023–1024

All-inclusive income, 887–889

Allocation problem, 509–511

Allowance method: applied to uncollectible accounts, 259–260; other applications, 264–265

American Accounting Association (AAA), 19

American Institute of Certified Public Accountants (AICPA), 11

Amount of a lump sum, 205–208

Amount of an annuity due, 215–217

Amount of an annuity due factor, 216

Amount of an ordinary annuity, 211–215

Amount of an ordinary annuity factor, 212

Amount of an ordinary annuity of 1 table, 236–237

Amount of 1 table, 232–233

Analysis of financial statements: activity, 1108–1110; financial structure and viability, 1111–1113; limitations, 1116–1118; liquidity, 1099–1104; profitability and capital maintenance, 1105–1108

Annuity, 211

Annuity due, 211

Annuity problems, 211–224

Antidilution, 1192, 1213–1214

APB (Accounting Principles Board), 12–14

APB Opinion No. 2, 801

APB Opinion No. 3, 1019

APB Opinion No. 4, 801

APB Opinion No. 6, 469

APB Opinion No. 8, 975, 977

APB Opinion No. 9, 889

APB Opinion No. 10, 784, 881, 1087

APB Opinion No. 11, 763, 765, 786, 787, 791, 792, 793, 803, 804

APB Opinion No. 12, 119, 168, 511

APB Opinion No. 14, 647, 649

APB Opinion No. 15, 1182, 1197

APB Opinion No. 16, 840

APB Opinion No. 17, 408, 541, 543, 554

APB Opinion No. 18, 405, 411, 951

APB Opinion No. 19, 129, 136, 1015, 1019, 1040, 1054

APB Opinion No. 20, 49, 113, 119, 514, 714, 824, 825, 826, 831, 838, 840, 841

APB Opinion No. 21, 73–74, 76, 272, 392, 393, 594, 638, 934

APB Opinion No. 22, 133, 1083, 1087

APB Opinion No. 23, 808

APB Opinion No. 24, 808

APB Opinion No. 25, 733, 734

APB Opinion No. 26, 642, 643

APB Opinion No. 28, 362–363, 1148, 1149, 1152

APB Opinion No. 29, 460, 461, 467, 722

APB Opinion No. 30, 110–112, 459, 893, 895, 896

APB Opinions, 12

APB Statements, 12; *APB Statement No. 4*, 3, 6, 10, 11, 12, 13, 33, 35, 46, 48, 310, 486, 1093, 1094

Appraisal capital, 743

ARB No. 43: Ch. 1 of, 318; Ch. 2 of, 826; Ch. 3 of, 124, 126, 256, 376, 386, 593; Ch. 4 of, 310, 312, 313, 318; Ch. 7 of, 724, 725; Ch. 10 of, 604

ARB No. 45, 874

ARB No. 47, 977

ARBs, 12

Arm's-length exchange transactions, 44

Articles of incorporation, 676

Articulation, 6, 87, 108, 130, 263

ASB (Auditing Standards Board), 16

ASRs (Accounting Series Releases), 17; *ASR No. 150*, 18

Assets: defined, 42, 69, 121; financial attributes of, 70–75; measurement of, 70–75; nature of, 69–70

Asset/liability view, 87

Assignee, 267

Assigning accounts receivable, 267–68

Assignor, 267

Assumptions, 39–41

Audit, 9

Auditing, 8

Auditing Standards Board (ASB), 16

Auditors, competency and independence of, 10

Audit report, 9, 136, 1096–1097

Audit trail, 157

Average cost method, 303–305

Bad-debt loss, 259

Balance sheet, 5, 120–129; account form, 122; classifications, 121–124; elements of, 121; financial position form, 122–123; report form, 122–123

Bank charges, 248

Bank collections, 248

Bank reconciliation, 248–250

Bank statement, 248

Base stock (inventory) method, 324–325

Basic defensive interval, 1113

Basket purchase, 449–450

Big GAAP/Little GAAP issue, 25, 1141–1147

Body of financial statements, 135

Bond types: bearer, 633; callable, 633; convertible, 633; coupon, 632; general obligation, 633; registered, 632; revenue, 633; second-mortgage, 633; serial, 632; subordinated, 633; term, 632

Bonus and profit-sharing plans, 607–608

Book of original entry, 159

Book value, 126, 168, 681, 1107
Broad accounting principles, 43– 50
Buildings, 438– 439
Business paper, 157

Callable preferred stock, 682
CAP (Committee on Accounting Procedure),
    11– 12
Capitalization of interest, 446– 448
Capital lease, 922, 925– 927, 928– 930, 932– 939,
    941– 949
Capital stock, 128; accounting for, 685– 691;
    classes, 681– 684; discount on, 680; minimum
    legal capital, 680– 681
Capital structure, 120
Cash: composition of, 243– 245; control, 245;
    planning, 245; valuation of, 243
Cash basis accounting versus accrual basis
    accounting, 82– 84
Cash basis of accounting, 48, 82, 163
Cash discounts, 257– 258, 299, 440– 441
Cash flow prospects, 36– 37
Cash in bank, 247– 255
Cash payments journal, 160, 184– 185
Cash receipts journal, 160, 182– 183
Cash short and over account, 247
Cash surrender value of life insurance, 414– 415
Casualty insurance, 519– 522
CDs (Certificates of deposit), 244
Certificate in Management Accounting (CMA), 8
Certificates of deposit (CDs), 244
Certified Public Accountant (CPA), 8
CFA (Chartered Financial Analyst), 20
Changes in accounting estimates, 118– 119, 264,
    514, 825, 837– 839
Changes in accounting principle, 112– 113,
    824– 825, 830– 837
Changes in financial position, 42– 43
Changes in reporting entity, 825
Characteristics and limitations of financial
    statements, 6– 7
Chartered Financial Analyst (CFA), 20
Chart of accounts, 161
Check register, 185
Closing entries, 174– 176
CMA (Certificate in Management Accounting), 8
Coinsurance, 519– 520
Code of Professional Ethics, AICPA, 13
Combined statement of income and retained
    earnings, 119– 120
Commercial bank loan officers, 20
Committee on Accounting Procedure (CAP),
    11– 12
Common stock, 681
Common stock equivalents, 1192– 1205
Compensated absences, 615– 617

Compensating balances, 245
Competency of auditors, defined, 10
Completed contract method, 875– 879
Complex capital structures (EPS), 1191– 1205,
    1211– 1214
Components of accounting theory, 35
Compound interest, 203
Compound interest equations, 225
Compound journal entry, 159
Concepts and elements, 41– 43
Conceptual framework issue, 21– 22
Conceptual Framework Project, 16, 21– 22
Conservatism, 53– 54, 301, 307, 317, 323, 325, 354,
    378, 461, 463, 466, 568, 594, 609, 610, 743, 790,
    795, 880, 881, 895, 929, 989, 1092, 1113, 1193,
    1196
Consignee, 298
Consignment, 298, 883– 884
Consignor, 298
Consistency principle, 48– 49, 299, 300, 301, 312,
    314, 319, 456, 498, 500, 694, 779, 781, 825, 827,
    828, 841, 845, 977, 987, 1053, 1096
Constant dollar, 44, 67, 1232
Constant dollar accounting, 1235– 1245
Consumer Price Index for All Urban Consumers
    (CPI-U), 67, 1230– 1231
Contingent issuances (EPS), 1201– 1202
Contingent liabilities, 609– 617
Contra account, 161
Control account, 162
Control influence investments, 397
Conventional retail method, 352– 354
Convertible preferred stock, 682– 683
Convertible securities, 649– 650, 741– 742
Corporate environment, 676– 679
Corporation types: closely held, 677; mutual, 677;
    private, 677; professional, 677; public, 676– 677;
    publicly held, 677; subchapter S, 677
Correcting entries, 164
Corrections of errors, 118, 515– 516, 825– 826
Cost method (treasury stock), 692– 694
Cost of goods manufactured, 294– 295
Cost of goods sold adjustment, 169– 170
Cost of goods sold calculation, 294
Costs, 109
CPA (Certified Public Accountant), 8
CPI-U (Consumer Price Index for All Urban
    Consumers), 67, 1230– 1231
Credit, 158
Credit sales, 256– 259
Cumulative effect method (accounting changes),
    113, 827– 828, 892– 893
Cumulative preferred stock, 682
Current and prospective method (accounting
    changes), 828– 829, 837– 839
Current assets, 124– 125
Current cost, 71– 72, 85

Current cost accounting, 1247–1254
Current cost/constant dollar accounting, 1254–1258
Current cost/constant dollar financial statements, 1255–1258
Current cost financial statements, 1250–1253
Current exit value in orderly liquidation, 72–78, 85
Current liabilities: defined, 126, 127, 593–594; specific types, 594–608; valuation, 594
Current operating performance income, 887–889
Current proceeds, 77
Current ratio, 1102–1103
Current value accounting, 1245–1254

Days' sales in accounts receivable, 1108–1109
Days' sales in inventory, 1109–1110
Debit, 158
Debt/equity ratio, 1111–1112
Debt/total assets ratio, 1112
Debt with detachable stock-purchase rights, 647–649
Declining-balance depreciation method, 492–494
Deferral period, 222
Deferrals, 166–168
Deferred annuities, 222–224
Deferred charges, 126, 551–552
Deferred credits, 127
Deferred expenses, 167–168
Deferred income taxes, 782–785
Deferred payment plans, 441–444
Deferred revenues, 166
Defined benefit pension plans, 970–971
Defined contribution pension plans, 969–970
Deflation, 67, 1230
Depletion, 506–509
Depositor errors, 248
Deposits in transit, 248
Depreciation: alternative methods, 516–518; defined, 486–489; estimates required, 488–489; fractional-year problems, 498–500; group systems, 500–506; methods (individual assets), 489–497; selecting an appropriate method, 497–498
Detailed accounting principles, 50–51
Development-stage companies, 568–570
Direct costing, 295
Direct-financing lease, 923, 941–944
Direct labor, 293
Direct matching, 47
Direct materials, 293
Direct pricing, 1231
Disclaimer of opinion, 9
Disclosure amount, 135
Disclosure checklist, 1120–1122
Disclosure methods, 50, 135

Disclosure of illegal acts, 1089–1090
Disclosure of major customer, 1161–1164
Disclosure of pervasive uncertainties, 1092–1094
Disclosure principle, 49–50, 132, 135, 301, 310, 312, 316, 319, 383, 393, 399, 411, 599, 610, 617, 633, 649, 692, 699, 722, 730, 731, 736, 742, 801, 803, 831, 835, 841, 874, 883, 884, 896, 995, 1014, 1019, 1022, 1041, 1043, 1052, 1082, 1087, 1089, 1090, 1091, 1094, 1095, 1096, 1145, 1146, 1147, 1156, 1160, 1161, 1202
Disclosure system, integrated, 17
Discontinued operations, 893–897; disposal date, 895; measurement date, 894–895
Discount, 274
Discounting, 208
Discount on capital stock, 680
Discount rate, 274
Discovery value, 468–469
Discrete view of interim reporting, 1148
Discussion Memorandum, 15
Disposal date (discontinued operations), 895
Disposal of a business segment, 112, 893–897
Dividend payout ratio, 1107–1108
Dividends, 119, 175, 599–600, 715–730
Dollar value LIFO: application procedures, 346–348; description of, 344–347; double extension method, 346; illustration, 348–350; internal index, 346; reasons for use, 347
Donated assets, 467
Donations of property and treasury stock, 698–699
Double-entry system, 157–158
Drawing, 175

Earnings per share (EPS), 116, 742–743, 1181–1214. *See also* Complex capital structures; Contingent issuances; Fully diluted EPS; "If converted" method; Primary EPS; Simple capital structure; Treasury stock method
Economic entity assumption, 39–40
Economic impact issue, 22, 569, 571–572
Economic Recovery Act of 1981, 809–810
Effective interest method, 392–397, 638–642, 933–937, 943–945
Efficient capital markets, 24, 1097–1098
Employee Retirement Income Security Act of 1974 (ERISA), 994–995
Enterprise resources, claims and changes, 37
EPS. *See* Earnings per share
Equity method, 402–411
Equity securities (investment), 377
ERISA (Employee Retirement Income Security Act of 1974), 994–995
Error analysis, 849–853
Estimated economic life of leased property, 928
Estimated residual value of leased property, 924
Ethics, AICPA Professional Code of, 13

Exit value accounting, 1247

Expected exit value in due course of business, 72– 73, 76– 77, 85– 86

Expense advances, 244

Expenses, 42, 87, 109

Exploration, development, and restoratior costs, 507– 508

Exposure draft, 16

External accountants, 8– 10

External users, 3

Extraordinary gains and losses, 110– 111, 890– 892

Factor, 268

Factoring of accounts receivable, 268– 270

Factory supplies, 293

FAF (Financial Analysts Federation), 20

Fair value of leased property, 923

FASB (Financial Accounting Standards Board), 14– 17

FASB Interpretations, 14

FASB Interpretation No. 3, 995

FASB Interpretation No. 8, 599

FASB Interpretation No. 11, 401

FASB Interpretation No. 14, 610

FASB Interpretation No. 24, 951

FASB Interpretation No. 28, 738

FASB Interpretation No. 35, 405

Federal Insurance Contribution Act (FICA), 604– 605

Feedback value, 38

FEI (Financial Executives Institute), 19– 20

FICA (Federal Insurance Contribution Act), 604– 605

FIFO. *See* First-in, first-out inventory method

Financial accounting defined, 3

Financial Accounting Foundation, 16

Financial Accounting Standards Advisory Council, 16

Financial Accounting Standards Boards (FASB), 14– 17

Financial Analysts Federation (FAF), 20

Financial Analysts Journal, 20

Financial Executive, 20

Financial Executives Institute (FEI), 19– 20

Financial flexibility, 1022

Financial forecasts: benefits of public disclosure, 94– 95; costs of public disclosure, 95; defined, 91

Financial position, 41

Financial reporting, 6

Financial Reporting Releases (FRRs), 18

Financial statements, 4, 50, 108; basic, 108– 132; characteristics and limitations of, 6– 7; comparative, 134; constant dollar, 1238– 1245; current cost, 1250– 1253; current cost/constant dollar, 1255– 1258; income statement, 897– 898; other topics, 132– 136; preparation of, 172– 174; relationship between, 130– 132; statement of

changes in financial position, 1041– 1044, 1050– 1051; statement of stockholders' equity, 731– 732

Financing activities, 42, 129

Finished goods, 293

First-in, first-out (FIFO) inventory method, 302– 303

FOB destination, 297– 298

FOB shipping point, 297

Foreign operations and export sales disclosure, 1160– 1161

Franchises, 550, 902

FRRs (Financial Reporting Releases), 18

Fully diluted EPS, 1192– 1205

Funds definitions, 129, 1025– 1026

Funds flow, 1014, 1019– 1022, 1024– 1026

Future value, 204

Future value factor, 206

GAAP. *See* Generally accepted accounting principles

Gains, 42, 87, 109

General and administrative expenses, 113

General journal, 159

General ledger, 160

Generally accepted accounting principles (GAAP): defined, 10– 11; development, 11– 20; future developments, 21– 25; other influences, 18– 20; sources, 20– 21, *See also* Big GAAP/Little GAAP issue.

General price-level change, 1230– 1231

General price-level index, 67

General purchasing power, 43

GNP Deflator (Gross National Product Implicit Price Deflator Index), 67, 1230

Going-concern assumption, 40– 41, 763, 787

Goodwill, 552– 562

Gross-change method of interperiod tax allocation, 779– 781

Gross margin inventory method: applied to classes of goods, 363; described, 360– 361; uses, 362– 363

Gross margin on cost percentage, 362

Gross margin on sales, 113

Gross margin on sales percentage, 361– 362

Gross method of recording credit purchases, 299– 300

Gross method of recording credit sales, 258

Gross National Product Implicit Price Deflator Index (GNP Deflator), 67, 1230

Group and composite depreciation systems, 504– 506

Historical cost, 71, 85

Historical cost principle, 44– 46, 109, 294, 295, 298, 299, 300, 301, 312, 319, 350, 360, 363, 436, 441, 444, 446, 449, 461, 466, 467, 486, 488, 504,

506, 508, 509, 514, 541, 555, 556, 562, 572, 595, 698, 743, 1105, 1232, 1236, 1245
Historical market rate, 76
Historical proceeds, 77
Holding gain, 71
Holding gains and losses, 1248; adjusted for inflation, 1254– 1255

"If converted" method (EPS), 1198– 1201
Illegal acts, disclosure of, 1089– 1090
Imprest cash fund, 246
Inception of a lease, 924, 955– 956
Income, 42, 79– 91, 884– 887
Income from operations, 113
Income statement, 5, 108– 116, 889– 898; comprehensive illustration, 889– 898; elements of, 109– 113; format, 113– 117; multiple-step, 113– 116; multiple-step versus single-step form, 116; single-step, 116; uses, 108– 109
Income summary, 174
Income taxes: deferred, 782– 785; interim reporting, 1150– 1151; interperiod tax allocation, 769– 788; intraperiod tax allocation, 115, 764– 769, 890; withholding, 604
Income tax law, 18– 19; withholding, 604
Incorporators, 676
Independence of auditors, defined, 10
Indexing, 1231– 1232
Indirect matching, 48
Indirect materials, 293
Industry practices, 52– 53, 318, 323, 617
Industry segment disclosure, 1156– 1160
Inflation, 67, 1230
Input market, 70– 71
Input value, 71
Installment sales, 881– 883
Intangible assets: accounting standards, 541– 546; defined, 126, 541; goodwill, 552– 564; separately identifiable intangible assets, 547– 552; special problem areas, 564– 573
Integral view of interim reporting, 1148
Integrated disclosure system, 17
Intercompany comparisons, 48
Interest, 73
Interest rate, 204
Interim reporting, 180– 181, 1147– 1155
Internal accountants, 7– 8
Internal audit staff, 8
Internal control system, 245
Internally constructed assets, 444– 445
Internal users, 3
Interperiod comparisons, 48
Interperiod income tax allocation, 769– 788
Interpolation, 214– 215
Interpretations, 14
Intraperiod income tax allocation, 115, 764– 769, 890

Inventory: average cost method, 303– 305; base stock method, 324– 325; classification of, 293; conceptual considerations, 319, 322– 323; consigned goods, 298; cost flow methods, 301– 312; costs to include, 299– 301; defined, 293; depreciation system, 500– 503; determination of quantities, 296– 298; effects of errors, 318– 319; FIFO method, 302– 303; flow of costs, 294– 296; goods in transit, 298; goods to include, 297– 298; gross margin method, 360– 363; invoice cost, 299– 300; LIFO method, 305– 310; manufacturing business, 293; merchandising business, 293; moving average method, 304; nature of valuation problem, 296; periodic system, 296– 297; perpetual system, 296– 297; profits, 307; retail method, 350– 360; selection of a cost flow method, 310– 312; specific identification method, 301; subsidiary ledger, 296; transportation costs, 300– 301; valuation above cost, 317– 318; valuation at cost, 298– 312; valuation at LCM, 312– 317. *See also* Lower of cost or market rule (inventory)
Inventory depreciation system, 500– 503
Investing activities, 43, 129
Investments. *See* Lower of cost or market rule (investments)
Investments and funds, 125; funds, 415– 416; noncurrent investments, 391– 415; temporary investments, 376– 391
Investment tax credit, 797– 806

Journal defined, 159
Journalizing, 159
Journal of Accountancy, 11
Journal of Commercial Bank Lending, 20

Land, 438
Last-in, first-out (LIFO) inventory method, 305– 310; arguments against, 307– 309; arguments for, 306– 307; conformity requirements, 307; dollar value method, 344– 350; retail method, 354– 360; specific goods method, 306, 343; specific goods pooling method, 343– 345
LCM rule (inventory). *See* Lower of cost or market rule (inventory)
Leases: intangible asset, 550– 551; lease classification, 925– 930; lease terms, 922– 924; lessee acounting, 930– 940; lessor accounting, 941– 950; other special leasing issues, 955– 957; reasons for leasing, 920– 921; special leasing situation, 950– 953
Leased property: estimated economic life of, 928; estimated residual value of, 924; fair value of, 923
Lease term, 927
Ledger, 161
Leveraged lease, 923

Liabilities: contingent, 609–617; current, 593–608; defined, 42, 74, 121, 593; financial attributes of, 75–79; long-term, 127, 631–651; long-term debt, 630–651; measurement of, 75–79; nature of, 74–75

Licensing agreements, 550

LIFO inventory method. *See* Last-in, first-out inventory method

Liquidating dividends, 509, 723

Liquidity, 120, 243, 1021–1022, 1099–1104

Litigation, claims and assessments, 611–613

Little GAAP. *See* Big GAAP/Little GAAP issue

Long-term contracts: accounting and reporting issues, 873–875; anticipated losses, 880–881; completed-contract method, 875–879; hybrid method, 879–880; percentage-of-completion method, 875–879

Long-term debt: bonds payable, 633–647; equity acquisition features, 647–650; nature and characterstics, 631–633

Long-term liabilities, 127, 631–651

Losses, 42, 87, 109

Lower of cost or market (LCM) rule (inventory), 312; ceiling, 313; current replacement cost, 313; floor, 313; meaning of market, 312–314; methods of applying, 314–315; pros and cons, 316–317; recording in accounts, 315–316

Lower of cost or market (LCM) rule (investments): current, 377–384; noncurrent, 378–402

Lump sum issuance of capital stock, 687–688

Lump sum problems, 205–211

Machinery, equipment, furniture, and fixtures, 439

Major customer disclosure, 1161–1164

Maker of promissory note, 270

Management Accounting, 20

Managerial accounting defined, 3

Manufacturing costs, 293

Manufacturing overhead, 293

Markdown, 352

Markdown cancellation, 352

Marketable equity securities, 377

Marketable securities, 377

Markup cancellation, 352

Matching principle, 47–48, 87, 88, 109, 163, 164, 166, 167, 168, 169, 219, 259, 260, 263, 264, 294, 300, 303, 306, 308, 319, 324, 354, 436, 437, 438, 440, 450, 453, 456, 467, 486, 487, 489, 494, 497, 506, 509, 514, 541, 544, 568, 572, 601, 603, 610, 638, 713, 714, 734, 763, 769, 771, 775, 786, 787, 801, 831, 843, 849, 870, 875, 886, 924, 933, 941, 942, 947, 972, 975, 997, 1014, 1116, 1149, 1251

Materiality, 51–52, 77, 110, 111, 124, 128, 133, 134, 135, 174, 247, 256, 259, 265, 266, 272, 274, 276, 297, 298, 299, 300, 301, 316, 386, 395, 408, 440, 441, 446, 450, 453, 454, 459, 544, 594, 595, 640, 641, 643, 644, 724, 781, 825, 828, 836, 841, 843, 853, 923, 932, 938, 1022, 1087, 1091, 1146, 1151, 1156, 1158, 1202, 1245, 1263

Maturity value of a note, 274

Maximum pension expense, 979–980

Measurement, 66

Measurement date (discontinued operations), 894–895

Measuring unit, 67–69

Merchandise, 293

Minimum lease payments, 928

Minimum pension expense, 979–980

Mixed accounts, 161

Modifying conventions, 51–54

Monetary item, 1237

Monetary unit principle, 43–44, 66, 1232

Moving average inventory method, 304

NAA (National Association of Accountants), 20

National Association of Accountants (NAA), 20

Natural resources, 439, 506–509

Negative goodwill, 562–564

Net change method of interperiod tax allocation, 779–781

Net income: as a measure of past performance, 89–90; as a predictor of cash flows, 90–91; components of, 87–88, 116; lifetime, 80–81; measurement of periodic, 82–87; nature of, 80, 110; periodic, 81–82; permanent component, 90; transitory component, 90; usefulness, 88–91

Net markdown, 352

Net markup, 352

Net method of recording credit purchases, 299–300

Net method of recording credit sales, 258

Net of tax basis, 115

Net realizable value, 72, 124, 256, 313, 318

Neutrality, 38

Nominal accounts, 161

Nominal dollar, 43, 67, 1232

Noncurrent investments: debt securities, 391–397; equity securities, 397–415

Nonmonetary item, 1237

Nonmonetary transactions, 461–466

Nonnotification basis, 267

No-par value stock, 681

Nontrade receivables, 256

Normal balance, 158

Normal (pension) cost, 978

Notes payable, 595–597

Notes receivable, 270–276

Notes receivable discounted: contra account approach, 274–275; footnote approach, 274–275

Notes receivable, discounting, 273–276

Notes receivable dishonored, 275–276

Notes to financial statements, 50, 132–133, 135, 1087–1095, 1116

Notification basis, 267
Not sufficient funds (NSF) checks, 244
NSF (not sufficient funds) checks, 244

Objectives of financial reporting, 7, 35– 37
Objectivity principle, 44, 86, 157, 325, 448, 463,
554, 562, 567, 609, 610, 647, 689, 698, 733, 742,
873, 879, 897
Offset account, 161
Offsetting, 135, 322
Oil and gas accounting, 570– 573
Operating cycle, 124
Operating expenses, 113
Operating leases, 922, 932, 941
Operating loss carrybacks and carryforwards,
788– 796
Opinion paragraph, 9
Ordinary annuity, 211
Organization costs, 551
Original retail price, 352
Other assets, 126
Other expenses, 113
Other revenues, 113
Output market, 70– 71
Output value, 71
Outstanding checks, 248
Overdraft, 245
Owners' equity, 42, 78, 79, 121, 127– 129

Paid-in capital, 128, 680– 691
Parenthetical disclosures, 135
Par value method (treasury stock), 694– 696
Par value stock, 680
Participating preferred stock, 682, 718– 721
Passive investments, 397, 398– 402
Past service (pension) cost, 978
Patents, 547– 548
Pay-as-you-go (pension) plan, 971– 972
Payee of promissory note, 270
Payroll register, 185
Payroll taxes, 604– 607
Pension accounting: basic pension concepts,
972– 977; defined benefit pension plans,
999– 1002; financial accounting and reporting,
977– 996; future of pension accounting,
997– 998; nature of pension plans, 969
Pension plan types: defined benefit, 970– 971;
defined contribution, 969– 970; funded, 971;
qualified, 971; unfunded, 971– 972
Percentage-of-completion method (long-term
contracts), 875– 879
Period costs, 299
Periodic inventory system, 296– 297
Periodicity assumption, 40, 787, 1092, 1094
Permanent accounts, 161
Permanent differences, 770– 771, 776– 778
Permanent impairment in value, 467– 468

Perpetual inventory system, 296– 297
Pervasive uncertainties, disclosure of, 1092– 1094
Petty cash, 246– 247
Plant assets, 125, 433– 470
Pledging accounts receivable, 267
Postage stamps, 244
Post-closing trial balance, 176
Postdated checks, 244
Posting, 160
Post to ledger accounts, 160– 162
Potential diluters, 1192– 1205
Predictive value, 38
Preemptive right, 679
Preferred stock, 681– 684, 1189– 1190
Premiums, 614– 615
Prepaid expenses, 167– 168
Present value, 204
Present value accounting, 1246– 1247
Present value factor, 209
Present value of a lump sum, 208– 211
Present value of an annuity due, 219– 222
Present value of an annuity due factor, 220
Present value of an ordinary annuity, 217– 219
Present value of an ordinary annuity factor, 218
Present value of an ordinary annuity of 1 table,
238– 239
Present value of expected cash flows, 73– 74, 76, 86
Present value of 1 table, 234– 235
Price/earnings ratio, 1106
Primary EPS, 1192– 1205
Prior period adjustments, 117– 118, 714
Prior service (pension) cost, 978
Proceeds of a discounted note, 274
Product costs, 299
Productive-output depreciation method, 494– 495
Profitability, 4
Promissory note, 270
Proof of cash, 250– 255
Property dividends, 721– 723
Property, plant, and equipment, 125– 126;
acquisitions and disposals by exchange,
460– 466; application of cost principle,
437– 450; departures from historical cost,
466– 469; disposals, 458– 459; postacquisition
expenditures, 451– 458
Property taxes, 602– 604
Protest fee, 275
Public versus private sector issue, 22– 23
Purchase discount, 258
Purchases journal, 160, 183– 184
Purchases returns and allowances journal, 185
Purchasing power, 1230
Purchasing power gains and losses, 68– 69,
1237– 1238, 1241– 1243, 1254– 1255

Qualified audit opinion, 9
Qualitative characteristics of accounting

information, 37–39
Quality of earnings, 307
Quasi reorganization, 468, 743–746
Quick ratio, 1103–1104

Rate of return on assets employed, 1105–1106
Rate of return on stockholders' investment, 1106–1107
Ratio of working capital provided by operations to current liabilities, 1104–1105
Raw materials, 293
R & D (research and development) costs, 565–568
Real accounts, 161
Real estate leases, 950–951
Real estate transactions, 899–902
Realized gains and losses, 381, 383
Realized holding gain, adjusted for inflation, 1255–1256
Realized holding gains and losses, 1248, 1252
Rearrangements and relocations, 453
Receivables, 255–276
Reclassification entries, 164
Recourse, 268, 270, 273
Redeemable preferred stock, 683–684
Registration statement, 17, 1167–1168
Regulation S-K, 1167
Regulation S-X, 17, 1167
Related party leases, 951–953
Related party transactions, 135, 1087–1089
Relevance, 38, 1142, 1246, 1247, 1254, 1258, 1270
Reliability, 38, 1142, 1245, 1246, 1247, 1254, 1258, 1270
Rents, 211
Repair and maintenance, 453–458
Replacements and betterments, 451–453
Representational faithfulness, 38–39
Research and development (R & D) costs, 565–568
Restatement method (accounting changes), 826–827, 839–847
Retail inventory method: conventional, 352–354; cost percentage, 350; LIFO, 354–360; terminology, 352; uses, 351
Retail LIFO method: application procedures, 356–357; description of, 354–356; illustration, 357–360
Retained earnings, 128–129, 712–732
Retained earnings appropriations, 128, 730–731
Retirement and replacement depreciation systems, 503–504
Retirement of capital stock, 696–698
Return on revenue, 1107
Revenue/expense view, 87
Revenue realization principle, 46–47, 85, 109, 163, 164, 165, 166, 256, 318, 319, 398, 402, 407, 461, 600, 609, 870, 871, 873, 886, 929, 930, 1014

Revenues, 42, 87, 109
Reversing entries, 176–177
Right of return, 265–266, 883
RMA (Robert Morris Associates), 20
Robert Morris Associates (RMA), 20
Rounding of amounts, 134
Rule 203 (AICPA Code of Professional Ethics), 13
Rule 204 (AICPA Code of Professional Ethics), 13

SABs (Staff Accounting Bulletins), 17–18
Sale and leaseback, 953
Sales discount, 258
Sales journal, 160, 181–182
Sales returns and allowances journal, 185
Sales taxes, 601–602
Sales-type lease, 922–923, 944–949
SARs (stock appreciation rights), 738–740
SASs (Statements on Auditing Standards), 1096. See under *Statement on Auditing Standards No.* for specific statements
Schedule of working capital changes, 130, 1030
Schedules, 50, 135
Scope paragraph, 9
Scrip dividends, 723
SEC (Securities and Exchange Commission), 17–18, 1165–1168; reporting to, 1165–1168
SEC 8-K report, 17, 1168
SEC 10-K report, 17, 1168
SEC 10-Q report, 17, 1168
Securities Act of 1933, 17
Securities and Exchange Commission (SEC), 17–18, 1165–1168; reporting to, 1165–1168
Securities Exchange Act of 1934, 17
Selling expenses, 113
Serial bonds, 632, 650, 661–664
Service-quantity depreciation method, 495–497
SFAC No. 1, 4, 5, 6, 7, 35–37, 603, 884, 1021, 1082
SFAC No. 2, 38–39, 51–52
SFAC No. 3, 41–42, 69, 74, 78, 109, 121, 593, 870, 974
SFACs (Statements of Financial Accounting Concepts), 14
SFAS No. 2, 565, 567
SFAS No. 3, 1152
SFAS No. 4, 644
SFAS No. 5, 259, 273, 609, 610, 730
SFAS No. 6, 598
SFAS No. 7, 568, 569, 689
SFAS No. 12, 377, 378, 381, 383, 398, 400
SFAS No. 13, 921, 928
SFAS No. 14, 1155, 1156, 1160
SFAS No. 15, 653
SFAS No. 16, 117–118, 515, 889, 1152
SFAS No. 18, 1155
SFAS No. 19, 570
SFAS No. 21, 1155, 1182
SFAS No. 25, 571

SFAS No. 26, 950
SFAS No. 28, 953
SFAS No. 32, 832
SFAS No. 33, 69, 72, 1235; disclosure format, 1263–1269; disclosure requirements, 1258–1259, 1262; meaning of constant dollar amounts, 1263; meaning of current cost, 1262; measurement of current cost amounts, 1262–1263; recoverable amounts, 1263
SFAS No. 34, 299, 446
SFAS No. 35, 999
SFAS No. 36, 995
SFAS No. 37, 782
SFAS No. 43, 616
SFAS No. 44, 550
SFAS No. 45, 902
SFAS No. 47, 633
SFAS No. 48, 266, 883
SFAS No. 55, 1197, 1198
SFAS No. 56, 874
SFAS No. 57, 1087, 1088
SFAS No. 64, 644
SFAS No. 66, 900, 901
SFASs (Statements of Financial Accounting Standards), 14
Short-term obligations expected to be refinanced, 597–599
Significant influence investments, 397, 402–411
Simple capital structure (EPS), 1187–1191
Simple interest, 203
Simple journal entry, 159
Social security taxes (FICA), 604–605
Solvency, 4
SOPs. *See* Statements of Position
Source document, 157
Special items, 168–170
Special journals, 160, 181-185
Specific identification (inventory) method, 301
Specific price change, 1231, 1232
Specific price index, 67
Staff Accounting Bulletins (SABs), 17–18
Standard costing, 295–296
Standard-setting process, 15–16
Standards overload, 25, 1141–1147
Stated value stock, 681
Statement of changes in financial position, 5, 129–131, 1014–1019, 1022–1054
Statement of Position No. 81–1, 874, 879
Statement of retained earnings, 5, 116–119
Statement of stockholders' equity, 5, 119–121, 731–732
Statement on Auditing Standards No. 1, Sec. 560, 1091
Statement on Auditing Standards No. 6, 1089
Statement on Auditing Standards No. 23, 1099
Statement on Auditing Standards No. 34, 1093
Statement on Auditing Standards No. 43, 832

Statements of Financial Accounting Concepts (SFACs), 14. See under *SFAC No.* for specific statements
Statements of Financial Accounting Standards (SFASs), 14. See under *SFAS No.* for specific statements
Statements of Position (SOPs), 16; *Statement of Position No. 81–1*, 874, 879
Statements on Auditing Standards (SASs), 1096. See under *Statement on Auditing Standards No.* for specific statements
Stock appreciation rights (SARs), 738–740
Stock dividends, 391, 724–727
Stockholder rights, 679–680
Stockholders' equity, 128. *See also* Owners' equity
Stock option plans: compensatory, 733–737; noncompensatory, 733
Stock-purchase warrants, 389–390, 740–741
Stock rights, 390–391
Stock splits, 391, 727–729
Stock subscriptions, 689–691
Straight-line depreciation method, 490
Subleases, 956–957
Subsequent events, 133–134, 1090–1092
Subsidiary ledgers, 161–162
Substance over form, 54, 272, 392, 397, 411, 467, 550, 631, 649, 683, 729, 735, 742, 821, 879, 884, 900, 921, 922, 926, 927, 932, 933, 951, 953, 1088, 1193
Summary of accounting policies, 133, 1083–1087
Sum-of-the-years'-digits depreciation method, 491–492
Supplementary statements, 50, 135

T account, 158, 1058–1060
Taxes: as current liabilities, 601–608; federal unemployment (FUTA), 605; income, 18–19, 604; payroll, 604–607; property, 602–604; sales, 601–602; social security (FICA), 604–605; state unemployment (SUTA), 605. *See also* Interperiod income tax allocation; Intraperiod income tax allocation
Technical Bulletins, 15
Temporary accounts, 161
Temporary investments: debt securities, 386–391; equity securities, 377–385
Terminology, 135–136
Time diagram (compound interest), 205
Timeliness, 38
Time periods, 204–205
Times interest earned, 1112–1113
Timing differences, 770–782, 807–808
Trade discounts, 257, 299
Trade names and trademarks, 549–550
Trade-off between relevance and reliability, 39
Trade receivables, 256
Transaction, defined, 157

Transactions: analysis of, 157–159; external, 157; identification of, 157; internal, 157; recording in journals, 159–160
Treasury stock, 128–129, 691–696, 729–730
Treasury stock method (EPS), 1193–1197, 1212–1213
Trial balance, 162
Troubled-debt restructuring: creditor accounting, 655–658; debtor accounting, 653–655; defined, 653
Trueblood Report, 35
Turnover of assets, 1110
Turnover of inventory, 1109–1110
Turnover of receivables, 1108–1109

Unadjusted trial balance, 162–163
Uncollectible accounts: accounting for, 259–264; aging of accounts receivable, 262–263; allowance method, 259–260; balance sheet approach, 261–262; collection of accounts written off, 264; direct write-off method, 259; income statement approach, 260–261; percentage of accounts receivable, 261–262; writing off, 264
Undelivered checks, 245
Unearned revenues, 166, 600–601
Unemployment tax: federal (FUTA), 605; state (SUTA), 605

Uniformity versus flexibility issue, 23–24, 310
Unqualified audit opinion, 9, 1096–1097
Unrealized holding gains and losses, 1248, 1252
Unrealized holding gains, adjusted for inflation, 1256–1257
Unrealized loss, 378
Unrealized loss recovery, 379
Unusual or infrequently occurring items, 111–112, 890
Usefulness, 36, 1246, 1254

Valuation, 66
Valuation of marketable equity securities, 378
Variable costing, 295
Verifiability, 38
Voucher, 185
Voucher register, 185

Warranties and guarantees, 614
Weighted average number of common shares, 1187–1189
Withholding, payroll, 604–607
Working capital, 127, 1025–1030, 1032–1044, 1103
Work-in-process, 293
Worksheet: annual statements, 177–180; interim statements, 180–181

CONSOLIDATED STATEMENT OF EARNINGS

(In thousands of dollars, except per share amounts) Years Ended January 1, 1983, January 2, 1982 and January 3, 1981

	1982 (52 Weeks)	1981 (52 Weeks)	1980 (53 Weeks)
Sales	$ 11,901,892	$ 11,266,520	$ 10,316,741
Costs and Expenses:			
Merchandise costs, including warehousing and transportation	9,048,038	8,645,000	8,011,872
Operating, general and administrative expenses	2,323,996	2,152,155	1,901,178
Rent	168,050	144,002	130,632
Depreciation and amortization	120,874	103,816	86,166
Dividend and interest income	(25,744)	(18,520)	(11,403)
Interest expense, including interest on obligations under capital leases	58,720	45,778	35,736
Total	11,693,934	11,072,231	10,154,181
Earnings from continuing operations before taxes based on income	207,958	194,289	162,560
Taxes based on income	64,200	64,805	59,774
Earnings from continuing operations	143,758	129,484	102,786
Loss from discontinued operations		(1,439)	(8,400)
Net earnings	$ 143,758	$ 128,045	$ 94,386
Earnings (loss) per share:			
Primary:			
From continuing operations	$4.84	$4.56	$3.71
From discontinued operations		(.05)	(.30)
Net earnings	$4.84	$4.51	$3.41
Fully diluted:			
From continuing operations	$4.64	$4.43	$3.71
From discontinued operations		(.05)	(.30)
Net earnings	$4.64	4.38	$3.41

The accompanying notes are an integral part of the consolidated financial statements.

Source: Kroger Company, *Financial Report*, 1982.